# ACM Press Database and Electronic Products

EDWARD A. FOX, EDITOR-IN-CHIEF

# RESOURCES IN COMPUTING

**OTHER VOLUMES IN THE RESOURCES IN COMPUTING SERIES:**

Resources in Ada
Resources in Parallel and Concurrent Programming Systems
Resources in Distributed Systems and Networks

# RESOURCES IN Human-Computer Interaction

with an introduction by
Wendy E. Mackay

ACM Press, New York, NY

Library of Congress Cataloging-in-Publication Data

Resources in human-computer interaction / with an introduction by
   Wendy E. Mackay.
      p.     cm. -- (Resources in computing)
   Includes bibliographical references and indexes.
   ISBN 0-89791-373-6
   1. Human-computer interaction.   I. ACM Press.   II. Series.
QA76.9.H85R47   1990
004'.01'--dc20                                                            90-1108
                                                                             CIP

*Computing Reviews* Categories:

   D.2.2 Software—Software Engineering—Tools and Techniques—User Interfaces

   D.2.6 Software—Software Engineering—Programming Environments—Interactive

   D.4.7 Software—Operating Systems—Organization and Design—Interactive Systems

   H.1.2 Information Systems—User/Machine Systems—Human Factors, Human Information Processing

   I.2.1 Computing Methodologies—Artificial Intelligence—Applications and Expert Systems—Natural Language Interfaces

   I.3.6 Computing Methodologies—Computer Graphics—Methodology and Techniques—Ergonomics, Interaction Techniques

   I.5.5 Computing Methodologies—Pattern Recognition—Implementation—Interactive Systems

ISBN 0-89791-373-6

ACM Order Number 219901

Copyright © 1990 by the ACM Press, a division of the Association for Computing Machinery, Inc. (ACM), 11 West 42nd Street, New York, NY 10036.

All rights reserved. No part of this publication may be reproduced, stored in a retrieval system, or transmitted, in any form or by any means, electronic, mechanical, photocopying, or otherwise, without the prior written permission of the publisher. Printed in the United States of America.

# Contents

| | | |
|---|---|---|
| **Introduction** | | **vii** |
| **1** | **Reviews** | |
| | Books and Proceedings | **1** |
| | Comparative Book Review | **88** |
| | Nonbook Literature | **108** |
| **2** | **Bibliography** | |
| | Books | **347** |
| | Journals | **377** |
| | Proceedings | **469** |
| | Doctoral Theses | **516** |
| **3** | **Indexes** | |
| | Author Index | **519** |
| | Keyword Index | **697** |
| | Subject Index | |
| |     ACM Computing Reviews Classification System | **929** |
| |     Category Index | **947** |
| | Proper Noun Index | **1160** |
| | Reviewer Index | **1172** |
| | Periodicals Cited | **1186** |

# INTRODUCTION

## BY WENDY E. MACKAY, Ph.D.

**Resources in Human-Computer Interaction** is a collection of reviews, bibliography, and indexes designed to provide an important reference to the recent literature on Human-computer interaction. It is one of the first books in the ACM Press Database and Electronic Products series derived from ACM's reference database of computer and information science literature. *Computing Reviews* and *ACM Guide to Computing Literature* are periodical print publications that feed this growing resource.

ACM was founded in 1947 as the society for the then young computing community. It was dedicated to the development of information processing as a discipline, and to the responsible use of computers in diverse applications. The publication of information about the sciences and arts of information processing remains one of the main purposes of the society.

In 1960, ACM established *Computing Reviews*, a review journal, to provide the community with synoptic coverage of the relevant world's literature. With the explosive growth of the field and its publications over the next two decades, it became apparent that comprehensive review coverage was impractical and possibly undesirable. *Computing Reviews* took on a new winnowing function. Its task became the publication of critical reviews of the most important literature. The *ACM Guide to Computing Literature* was split off as a distinct publication aimed at providing a comprehensive indexed bibliography.

From this growing reference database, ACM has launched a series of selective bibliographic and review publications. This book is among the first in the series.

These resource books group information on a discrete topic from several sources to ease the search time for a researcher or student with a particular interest. The bibliographic collection covers literature from 1986 to the present; reviews are of items generally published since 1982.

The reference nature of this collection makes it appropriate for a wide variety of readers: the student, the computing professional, the professor or the researcher needing a guide to the published literature, and the technical librarian.

Computers are everywhere—and most of them are not particularly easy to use. Since a major part of the cost of computing is people's time, software designers are finding it increasingly important to make software easier to use. This has lead to a new research area, the field human-computer interaction. The goal is to understand and improve the ways in which people interact with computer technology. The problems are complex and the issues continue to evolve as computers, users, and our understanding of them change. This book provides an important reference to the initial work in the field, with both critical reviews and references to over 1200 publications.

The recent growth of the field is perhaps not surprising when viewed within the historical context of computing. Computers have become smaller, cheaper, faster—and ubiquitous. We take for granted that hardware will decrease in size and increase in speed by orders of magnitude. Today, the term "computer" includes mainframes, minicomputers, workstations, personal computers and laptops. Software languages have evolved as well. No longer a strict reflection of the operation of the hardware, they represent a variety of designs that reflect the kinds of tasks being performed. Models of computing have changed and include time-sharing, personal computing, parallel processing and distributed-processing networks. Computers are no longer valued solely for their ability to "crunch numbers"; they are found in almost every aspect of work as well as entertainment, education, and communication. While some computers continue to require special rooms and a staff to support them, others are small and portable and still others are practically invisible, integrated into other products.

As computers have changed, so have computer users. Early computer users were highly-trained specialists who tended expensive machines and worked in the way that was most convenient for the computer. Now the emphasis has shifted and computers are valued for their ability to help *people* accomplish work. The term "user" encompasses a wide variety of people, ranging from novices to experts, who use computers for many different kinds of tasks. Scientists use computers to collect, analyze and visualize complex sets of data. White collar professionals use word-processing and spreadsheets as an integral part of their daily work. Teachers use computers to help students learn and explore new domains. Engineers use them to design and build new products. Even people who don't think of themselves as computer users use automated bank tellers and computer-controlled devices in cars. Electronic mail and other communication media help people communicate with each other and exchange information.

As both the technology and users have changed, so has user interface research and development. A few computer pioneers have been interested in user interfaces from the very beginning. Some envisioned sophisticated uses for computers long before the technology became available. In the 1950's, Vannevar Bush proposed hypertext and hypermedia, which are only now becoming widely available. Alan Kay proposed the "dynabook," a portable personal computer that still does not exist. Other pioneers witnessed faster progress. Ivan Sutherland, who created Sketchpad, one of the first tools for creating computer graphics, has seen the development of highly sophisticated computer graphics workstations and software.

Early input devices were extremely limited; the most popular was probably the teletype which has since evolved into the "QWERTY" keyboard. However, some people, such as Douglas Englebart, who created the mouse, were interested in expanding the range of possible interactions with computers. Input devices now include pointing devices, such as joysticks, light pens and touch-sensitive screens, voice recognition, and more recently data gloves. Researchers at Xerox PARC in the late 1960's and 1970's revolutionized ideas about computing. They created distributed networks of workstations, object-oriented programming, graphical user interfaces and many other innovations that have become the basis for many commercial products. The Apple Macintosh created a different kind of revolution. By providing users with an inexpensive computer with an easy-to-learn graphical interface, they showed that making computers easy to use sells computers.

# INTRODUCTION

Widespread interest in user interfaces is still very recent, really within the past decade. In the early 1980's, much of the research was limited by the technology then available. Researchers studied the use of menus, measured reaction times and examined the effects of different screen layouts. The complexity of the technology has increased and with it, the variety of research strategies and approaches. Human-computer interaction research now includes the software development process, the tools for creating user interfaces, designs for new user interfaces and investigations of how individuals and groups use computers. Even so, developing effective user interfaces is still as much an art as a science.

## Different dimensions of user interface research

This book provides a reference to the first articles and books written by the early researchers in the field of human-computer interaction. The topics are organized according to the categories identified in the ACM *Computing Reviews* classification system. More than ten categories are represented, illustrating both the diversity of the field and the relevance of this work to all of computer science. Because of the recent growth of the field, the *CR* classification system is being updated to include human-computer interaction as an area in its own right. This will make it even easier to find topics of interest in subsequent issues.

The multi-disciplinary nature of human-computer interaction research often makes it difficult to compare results among articles. As with any new field, this is due partly to a lack of a shared paradigm upon which everything builds. However, it is also due to the range of goals, values and interests of people within the field. In order to compare work, it is helpful to understand the perspective of the author who wrote the article. Human-computer interaction research can be divided along three dimensions: the topic or subject being studied, the discipline of the author, and the work orientation of the author.

The subject dimension matches *CR* categories and includes:

1. User interface design: What kinds of interfaces are most effective under what circumstances, e.g. natural language, direct manipulation? Which characteristics are important, e.g. screen layout or level of user control? How can we accommodate different input and output devices and integrate different media? How do different interface designs affect how quickly or efficiently people use the computer to perform different tasks?
2. Software development process: How does taking the user's needs into account affect the process of designing, developing and testing software? How can we take advantage of iterative design, rapid prototyping, and participatory design to improve the resulting user interfaces?
3. User interface design tools: How can we design software (e.g. user interface management systems or user interface toolkits) to help designers create effective user interfaces?
4. Analysis methods: What theories and methods can we apply to better understand the interaction between users and software?
5. Empirical studies of users: How can we understand, model and predict what users do? How are users affected by the software they use and how do they modify the software they use?

6. Domain specific designs: How can we provide useful tools and methods for particular domains, such as aids for the handicapped, CAD/CAM, scientific visualization, education, and information systems?
7. Group work: How can groups of people work more productively together, through the use of the computer? What does the use of computers to communicate teach us about human communication in general? What kinds of software help to support cooperative work?

The authors of these books and articles are generally trained in a particular discipline. Computer scientists are trained to think about the technology and are more likely to be interested in developing tools for creating better user interfaces or examples of new kinds of user interfaces. Experimental psychologists are trained to examine the individual user and are more likely to run experiments that examine user behavior or develop models of individual users. Anthropologists, sociologists and other social scientists are trained to look at users as part of a community and often study the use of computers in the field. Graphic designers are trained to think about effective presentation of information and are interested in improving the aesthetic and information content of objects on the screen. People from these and other disciplines bring different sets of assumptions, methods, tools and perspectives to the study of user interfaces.

In order to really understand the perspective of the author, it is also important to know the author's orientation. Academic researchers are interested in publishing research articles that contribute to our understanding or present creative new ideas. Software developers want to produce effective products that meet the needs of their customers. Managers are rewarded for establishing processes that result in cheaper, better, faster or more effective user interfaces. Lawyers and policy makers have a different perspective, as do the actual users of the products and prototypes that are created. The orientation of the author affects the way in which he or she applies knowledge from one or more disciplines to the study of a particular subject area.

Taken together, it is possible to place authors within this three-dimensional space and compare their findings with those of others in related areas. The research articles described in this volume include the full range of perspectives, and it may be helpful to keep these perspectives in mind when evaluating the work.

## ACM SIGCHI

Although SIGCHI, ACM's Special Interest Group on Computers and Human Interaction, is less than ten years old, it is at this writing the fastest growing special interest group in the ACM, with over 4600 members. In 1982, the founders of SIGCHI put on a small conference in Gaithersburg, Maryland. The conference was a success, with more than twice as many attendees as expected. The following year, the first CHI conference was held in Boston. Attendance was more than double that of the previous conference and SIGCHI, the organization, was launched. Subsequent CHI conferences have grown both in size and scope and they are considered the flagship conference in the field of human-computer interaction. The most recent conference, held in Seattle, Washington, was attended by over 2300 people. Each conference consists of parallel technical tracks with daily plenary addresses, refereed technical papers and panels (with an acceptance rate of less than 25%), as well as videos, exhibits, demonstrations, poster sessions,

# INTRODUCTION

special interest group meetings, SIGCHI business meetings and social functions. In addition, workshops, tutorials and a doctoral consortium are held in conjunction with the conference.

In addition to the annual CHI Conference, SIGCHI sponsors or co-sponsors conferences and workshops in related fields. We have recently sponsored: CSCW '88 (Conference on Computer-Supported Cooperative Work), DOCPROC '88 (Conference on Document Processing), Hypertext '89, UIST (User Interface Software Technology), as well as workshops on "Video as a Research and Design Tool" and "Mixed Modes of Interaction."

SIGCHI has a strong commitment to education. The Curriculum Development Group is responsible for making recommendations for curricula in human-computer interaction for each of our constituent disciplines. Our doctoral consortium brings top graduate students to the CHI conferences each year, and gives them an opportunity to meet established researchers in the field and receive constructive criticism about their doctoral dissertations. The Education Survey identifies institutions that offfer graduate degrees in human-computer interaction and serves as an important reference guide to educational opportunities in HCI.

The Publication Committee oversees SIGCHI's publications and relationships to academic journals. The SIGCHI Bulletin is published quarterly and contains research articles, reports on conferences, workshops and standards activities, ACM and SIGCHI news, announcements, abstracts of books and articles, a calendar of upcoming conferences and calls for papers. In addition to the four regular issues, subscribers also receive the annual CHI conference proceedings and a SIGCHI membership directory.

SIGCHI is also working to raise awareness of human-computer interaction issues within ACM, through self-assessment, curriculum studies, academic surveys; and in the larger community, by contributing to standards committees and creating public support for good user interface practices.

The field of human-computer interaction is still very young and can be considered a multi-disciplinary, as opposed to inter-disciplinary, field. We draw our strength from the many different views we have of users and their interactions with technology. Members of the CHI community come from many different academic disciplines, are interested in many different subject areas, and approach the problem from different orientations. However, they all share the goal of identifying and supporting the needs of users.

# How to use this book

This book is divided into three major sections: Reviews, Bibliography, and Indexes. Each section contains a short organizational description. The work can be used in several ways. The student or computing professional may want to skim through the reviews. The expert researcher will want to make use of the extensive indexing by author, keyword subject, and proper noun.

The reviews are written by qualified reviewers and were originally published in *Computing Reviews*. They are arranged by subject as categorized by the *Computing Reviews* Classification Scheme. The classification scheme is reprinted in full on page 929 as part of the Category Index. Reviews are printed under their primary category. Reviews are numbered consecutively starting with HCI-0001. The reviews are divided into two parts: the books section contains monographs and reports and descriptions of collections of papers; the non-books section includes the individual papers from conferences, journals, and book collections.

The bibliography is organized by the type of literature: books, journals, proceedings, and doctoral theses. Each item is given an accession number and contains the author, full title and source information. All bibliographic citations and reviews are indexed in section three. The indexes include the full title for ease of retrieval. They also contain the HCI review number or the bibliographic accession number. Look up these numbers in the appropriate section (review or bibliography) to get full source information or a review of the item. All items are indexed by all authors, by keywords from the title, by the *ACM Computing Reviews* classification system, and by proper nouns. In addition, a journal listing contains the full title of each journal cited, and the name and address of its publisher.

# PART 1

# REVIEWS

Books and Proceedings ................................................... 1
Comparative Book Review .................................................. 88
Nonbook Literature ....................................................... 108

# Books and Proceedings

The Review Section is divided into two parts: reviews of books and proceedings, followed by reviews of individual papers. These reviews of books on Human-Computer Interaction are arranged by subject according to ACM's *Computing Reviews* Classification Scheme. The complete classification system is printed beginning on page 929. The scheme is hierarchical, and each review appears under the heading or headings of its primary subject. Under each subject heading the reviews will tend to be in chronological order. Each review also contains a review number starting with "HCI" and a complete citation including the authors' names and affiliations, title, publisher, and other bibliographic information. Please note that all prices are the original publication price, and should be used a general guide only.

## A. GENERAL LITERATURE

### A.1 Introductory and Survey

BISHOP, PETER (Peter Bishop Associates, Richmond, Surrey, UK)  HCI-0001
**Fifth generation computers: concepts, implementations and uses.**
Halsted Press, New York, NY, 1986, 166 pp., $29.95, ISBN 0-470-20269-6. [Ellis Horwood Series: Computers and the Applications.]

I was excited by the title and table of contents of this book. They promised a concise (166 pages!) overview of fifth generation computing. Members of the information technology community who are not directly involved in fifth generation computing are the intended audience.

The book's strength is its emphasis on concepts. It has value as a reference to what fifth generation computing is. But, although thoughtful, the author's treatment is less than masterful. Important ideas and their interconnection are explained, but the explanations lack clarity. Diagrams would have succeeded in many cases far better than words (e.g., a Turing machine or Robinson's proof by resolution). In addition, the book contains several vague and unsubstantiated generalizations, and I was rarely persuaded by the force of an argument. For example, the author never demonstrates the main thesis of the book, namely, that a von Neumann machine cannot cope with fifth generation computing tasks, and that a radically different architecture is necessary.

The first chapter summarizes (in 10 pages) the evolution of computer concepts and technology from the time of Babbage to the 1980s. More space is given to the British scientific collaboration in World War II than to the ideas of Turing or Church or to the invention of the transistor. This is an example of a slight but discernible British bias throughout the book. (And the

American reader needs to understand that in British English a *valve* is a vacuum tube.) This chapter needs to be longer; it is somewhat superficial as an intellectual overview.

Chapter 2 is about artificial intelligence. In section 2.1 the author points out that the notion of intelligence is poorly understood as is the philosophical status of what we know or how knowledge has evolved. In section 2.2 he notes that Turing's test of machine intelligence is a method for recognizing intelligent behavior without attempting to define intelligence. Section 2.3 differentiates between information and knowledge and very informally discusses first order predicate calculus as a method for representing knowledge and drawing inferences. Different strategies and problems of inference processing are discussed (fuzzily) in general terms. The remaining chapter sections deal with game-playing, reasoning, natural language recognition, image recognition, and expert systems. Newell's contribution to artificial intelligence and his definition of intelligence are not mentioned; the combinatorial explosion problem is not sharply defined or illustrated.

Chapter 3 discusses and assesses the fifth generation programs in Japan, the United States, the European Economic Community, and the United Kingdom.

Chapter 4 deals with the overall structure of fifth generation computers whose function is not traditional information processing but rather drawing inferences from knowledge bases. There is a good schematic of the basic configuration image of a fifth generation computer. The author discusses hardware and software aspects of this configuration image's components: the knowledge base management system, the inference processor, and the intelligent user interface.

Chapter 5 is about fifth generation hardware. The main idea is that chip design should more closely reflect the structure of algorithms. The most interesting part of the book is found in the sections of this chapter dealing with dataflow architecture, graph reduction architecture, and the Inmos transputer. Each architecture is well illustrated by example and diagram, and the author shows the close connection between the architecture and algorithmic processing.

Chapter 6 discusses software engineering. There are sections about program structure, program design, program correctness, and software development environments. The discussion does not seem particularly relevant to fifth generation computing.

In Chapter 7, the author discusses fifth generation programming languages: LISP; new developments in procedural languages (Ada, Occam); declarative languages (PROLOG); and applicative languages (HOPE). The author suggests that more than one language might be used for the software controlling the different components of the basic configuration image.

Chapter 8 is about intelligent knowledge-based systems. The author notes that there is at present no theory of knowledge on which to build an intelligent knowledge-based system. Successive chapter sections deal with knowledge representation (semantic networks, frames, and production systems); knowledge processing; searching a knowledge base; evidential reasoning; and procedural reasoning.

Chapter 9 deals with intelligent user interfaces. In fifth generation computing, the computer has to learn to think like a user instead of vice versa. The author reviews some fourth generation interface techniques (windows, icons, and mouse), and then discusses fifth generation techniques (speech synthesis and voice recognition, natural language recognition, and image processing). The last section is an interesting discussion about the psychology of human-computer interaction.

Chapter 10 reviews some applications of fifth generation computers. Chapter 11 looks at the fifth generation in perspective. A worrisome military implication of intelligent knowledge-based systems is the transfer of tactical and strategic decision making to computer-assisted or even fully automated systems. The author concludes by emphasizing Japan's decisive contribution in defining the fifth generation initiative and by summarizing the main hurdles to attaining the goals of the initiative.

The book has some (not enough) good diagrams. A glossary of terms and an index are included. References are given at the end of each chapter. The list is not comprehensive and is British-oriented. Since it is not a textbook, there are no exercises or chapter summaries. There are some backward reference errors—for example, in discussing fifth generation programming languages (chap. 7), the author refers to a discussion of the transputer in section 5.6; the discussion is in section 5.7. In general, the frequent backward references are not very helpful—they yield little information that is not repeated in the forward reference.

—*Nicholas Ourusoff*, Flagstaff, AZ

# B. HARDWARE

## B.4 Input/Output and Data Communications

### B.4.2 Input/Output Devices

**Voice**

PROCHNOW, DAVE      HCI-0002
**Chip talk: projects in speech synthesis.**
TAB Books, Blue Ridge Summit, PA, 1987, 209 pp., $14.95, ISBN 0-8306-2812-6.

This should not be considered as a book. Rather, it is a sort of catalog of various simple speech synthesizers. However, it does not cover any of the chips in depth. It could be useful for those who do not know what is available in the synthesizer market. There is no other such catalog available, so it may be said to fill a niche. I believe National's Digitalker is no longer in production. If so, some of the information in this work might be considered outdated. The index is adequate. This cannot be used as a textbook for any class, but it can be used as a reference or catalog.

—*Young Hwan Oh*, Dallas, TX

# C. COMPUTER SYSTEMS ORGANIZATION

## C.2 Computer-Communication Networks

### C.2.1 Network Architecture and Design

MALAMUD, CARL     HCI-0003
**DEC networks and architectures.**
Intertext Pubs./McGraw-Hill Book Co., New York, NY, 1989, 472 pp., $39.95, ISBN 0-07-039822-4.

The Digital Equipment Corporation Network Architecture (DNA) can be fairly complex. In this book, an attempt is made to describe DNA by grouping the major products into two categories: architectures and networks. The book also touches on several other topics, such as internetworks, OSI, and user interface standards. Since the book includes no problems or worked examples, it should not be used as a textbook. It could be handy as a basic guide to DEC networking products, however.

In the sections on architectures and networks, Carl Malamud presents a very general overview of the DNA product suite. He gives some discussion of the various protocols, such as MOP, DDCMP, Ethernet, CTERM, DFS, and DNS. An important note is that the DECnet protocols are not described or diagrammed; these sections of the book only describe the function of each protocol. Malamud does give an interesting overview of VAX clusters in the architecture section, however. Again, only a minimal amount of technical detail is given.

The section on OSI and internetworking would only be helpful to readers who know almost nothing about the subjects. The book covers most of the topics related to TCP/IP and OSI, but gives no hint on how to implement them on DEC systems. Again, the protocols are not described. Since only the function of each protocol layer is presented, this book is suitable as a starting point for learning about the role of OSI within DECnet.

The last section of the book, "User Interface Standards," is puzzling. The transition from internets and OSI to this section is not straightforward. After reading about the X.400 system in the previous section, the reader then starts in on the very basic concepts of X-Windows. Finally, the section concludes with a discussion of Postscript. Although these are important topics, these sections seem to be outside the scope of this book.

For the most part, this book is quite comprehensive. The flow from subject to subject is not obvious, though. A central theme is also not evident. The book could have been improved by focusing on DEC's networking philosophy. As it is, *DEC networks and architectures* is only suitable as a very first look at DEC networking.

—*J. W. Kyle,* Eagan, MN

# D. SOFTWARE

## D.2 Software Engineering

### D.2.1 Requirements/Specifications

MARTIN, CHARLES F. (Charles F. Martin Associates)     HCI-0004
**User-centered requirements analysis.**
Prentice-Hall, Inc., Englewood Cliffs, NJ, 1988, 305 pp., $37.60, ISBN 0-13-940578-X.

This book describes the process necessary to define detailed requirements for new custom computer software applications. It was developed based on the author's experiences with training a business staff of systems analysts. The requirements are defined in terms of the user of the system rather than the designer.

The book contains eighteen chapters and three appendices. The chapters are grouped into six parts.

Part 1, "Introduction," establishes the reasons for performing user-centered requirements analysis, identifies the software development cycles, states the objectives of requirements analysis, and defines the top-down process for preparing agreed-upon requirement specifications.

Part 2, "Getting Started," describes how to use objective analysis to obtain information about the application concept in order to perform a feasibility study. Three approaches are discussed in the chapter: organizational data flow analysis, critical success factor interviews, and application concept components. The information obtained is then used to determine "whether the automation application appears to be implementable in a practical manner."

Part 3, "Functional Analysis," describes how to generate a graphical user concept diagram of the top-level system flow, defining verifiable functional requirements, mapping the functional requirements to the user diagram, and defining the output reports and the user interactive screens.

Part 4, "Data Analysis," contains more information than any other part. It discusses database organization methods, data relationships and diagramming notations, the creation of a data dictionary, and methods for checking the conceptual data model.

Part 5, "Performance Analysis," discusses the techniques for determining and improving the performance of the proposed system. Performance is defined in the requirements as how fast the application must perform under expected operational workloads. The author suggests that the analyst use Delphi analysis to obtain user performance requirements. Performance is evaluated in terms of the number of users of the systems, the database size, the function processing rates, and the expected interactive user response times. The final chapter of this part discusses implementation risk assessment.

Part 6, "Planning the Requirements Analysis," discusses the tools, documentation, and user participation in the definition of the requirements. Tools are used to assist in the generation of the requirements specifications and to assist in the transition of the requirements in the design and development phases. A small number of tools are mentioned in the text. The Ada programming language is briefly mentioned as a possibility for matching requirements against a library of reusable software. User-oriented documentation formats are listed. A DoD-STD-7935, "Automated Data Processing Systems Documentation," format is also mentioned. The final chapter discusses project schedule and staff planning.

Appendix A contains a table of commercial computer-aided software engineering environments. Appendix B contains a limited list of some common application development environments. Appendix C contains a glossary of terms.

This book is intended for business systems analysts who are not familiar with requirements analysis. It does not talk about the implementation, testing, or maintenance of the proposed system. I found that this book, like all of Martin's books, presents material in a well-organized manner. The charts, tables, and diagrams are clear and supportive of the text without being cute. The tone of the text is professional and businesslike.

The only flaw I could find in the book is that it lacks a comprehensive case study carried throughout the entire text. Each technique is illustrated by a new example.

I would recommend this text for use in a business systems analysis class. The examples and exercises are all relevant to the material presented. If the instructor is willing to supplement the text with related material, the text could also be used in a software engineering course.

—*John Cupak, Jr.*, Boalsburg, PA

ANDRIOLE, STEPHEN J. (George Mason Univ., Fairfax, VA; and International Information Systems)
**Storyboard prototyping: a new approach to user requirements analysis.**
Q.E.D. Information Sciences, Inc., Wellesley, MA, 1989, 280 pp., ISBN 0-89435-246-6.

This book introduces the idea of storyboard prototyping: developing a series of sample screen displays as a way of presenting the possible behavior of a system to users. Its chapters give a rough overview of conventional software design processes, draw a useful distinction between *user requirements* and *software requirements*, and present the idea of storyboarding. About three-quarters of the book consists of appendices that give weakly explained examples of storyboards for four different systems, one of which is discussed in the main text.

In my view, the only contribution of this book is the interesting idea of storyboarding. The author mentions several methods to use during requirements analysis, but not in enough detail for the reader to learn how to apply them. The prose tends to skip around among several different topics; I found it rather disorganized, despite the reasonable chapter layout. The presentation of storyboard prototyping is surprisingly weak. I am reasonably glad I read this book but also glad I did not have to pay for it.

—*David Alex Lamb,* Kingston, Ont., Canada

### D.2.2 Tools and Techniques

*User interfaces*

SHNEIDERMAN, BEN (Univ. of Maryland)
**Designing the user interface: strategies for effective human-computer interaction.**
Addison-Wesley Publ. Co., Inc., Reading, MA, 1986, 448 pp., $29.95, ISBN 0-201-16505-8.

This book is a welcome addition to the literature on human-computer interaction, pulling together material that the author has previously used effectively in tutorials and courses. It is intended as a practical aid for user interfaces. In addition, there is a broad treatment of the research literature on the issues discussed, to justify the pragmatic suggestions and to motivate further research. While the book is explicitly addressed to designers and researchers, it would also be a useful text for students of user interface design.

The good news about this book is that the author has documented our knowledge about many areas of user interfaces, while still conveying his characteristic infectious enthusiasm. Researchers will feel it contains no surprises, but will find the book a handy reference to the literature in the following areas:

- ☐ dialogue styles,
- ☐ interaction devices,
- ☐ response times, and
- ☐ system messages.

These topics take up about three-quarters of the book, and despite a few shortcomings (e.g., color plates which seem to include bad examples as well as good ones, and mundane graphic design for the book as a whole) the material is presented well. Whether user interface designers can be convinced to read all about the empirical studies remains an open question; the author has done his best to lure them along with practical summaries. These checklists can provide immediate benefit for designers, but without the background research, they would be left without the skills and perspectives for complex tradeoffs and for future techniques. The author is to be commended for the balance achieved in the book.

The not-so-good news about this book is that some topics are not treated with the same thoroughness as the main areas listed above. These are contained in the chapter preceding the main topics, entitled Theories, Principles and Guidelines, and in the chapter covering the process of design and evaluation which follows the main sections.

Theories, Principles and Guidelines suggests some discussion of the different kinds of knowledge which might be applicable to design. This epistemology does not in fact appear. One theoretical model is presented: a semantic/syntactic differentiation of knowledge; however, it is unclear whether this is intended as a psychological model of the user based on experimental evidence or as a convenient device for designers. Other cognitive models are mentioned briefly but not compared, and the semantic/syntactic distinction rarely appears in the rest of the book. The principles and guidelines appear to be valid enough, but there is no sense of an integrated framework that justifies these particular suggestions. I felt there was a distinct cut-and-paste flavor about this material.

Similarly, the chapter on design processes and evaluation seems strangely foreign to the main topic areas. There are no summaries of experiments, no reference to the literature on questionnaires, and little discussion of practical difficulties in the design cycle. The impression left with the reader is that this material is of minor importance, that if we understood the design of specific features and interaction styles then the process of design would be smooth and evaluation almost unnecessary. We don't for a moment think that the author holds that position, but the contrast in care given to the various topics is unmistakable.

There is one additional subject that we would like to have seen given substantial coverage: the components of user tasks and how they affect the design of a user interface. This would build on the discussion of semantic knowledge, and it would illustrate how a designer conducts a task analysis to construct appropriate functions and a conceptual model for the user. There are glimmers of this in the book (e.g., pp. 200–203), but they get lost in the enthusiasm about direct manipulation (such as DMDOS, the author's own design, which is a good example of the technique but needs to illustrate how the semantics of the task drive the design process). (Presenting a translation of an existing product has pedagogical advantages, but leaves the impression that interaction style is *the* critical factor in a user interface, and testing is an afterthought.) Design "strategies" as promised in the book's subtitle will not materialize without more concern for getting the function right. Also, despite the extensive discussion of studies on interface features, there is little comment on the need for testing in real task settings.

If this is not the ultimate book on user interface design, it is certainly at the top of the current literature. Given the rate of change in the field, anyone who devoted enough time to cover all the necessary areas would probably find it impossible to keep sufficiently current to produce a quality text. The comments above focus on the missing pieces, but the parts that are done well set something of a standard for user interface design topics.

This book can be recommended as a text for courses on user interface design. A designer who wants to avoid learning about the empirical studies can choose instead a useful practicum like [1], and a researcher wanting a more philosophical discussion can choose a collection of papers like [2]. Neither of these tries for the balance of research and practice as in Shneiderman's book, and neither conveys the same, well, passion about "fighting for the user."

—*T. Carey,* Guelph, Ont., Canada; and *L. Nadeau,* Guelph, Ont., Canada

**REFERENCES**

[1] RUBINSTEIN, R.; AND HERSH, H. *The human factor: designing computer systems for people,* Digital Press, Burlington, MA, 1984.

[2] NORMAN, D. A.; AND DRAPER, S. W. (ED.) *User centred system design: new perspectives on human-computer interaction,* Lawrence Erlbaum Associates, Hillsdale, NJ, 1986.

O'BRIEN, BILL     HCI-0007
**Opening Windows.**
Scott, Foresman & Co., Glenview, IL, 1987, 387 pp., $19.95, ISBN 0-673-18581-8.

This book describes Microsoft Windows Version 1.0. In effect it is an alternate manual for that product. The book covers the installation and use of Windows and its associated components: Calc (a calculator), Calendar, Cardfile, Clipboard, Clock, Control (a control panel), Notepad, Paint (a monochrome paint program), Spooler (a print spooler), and Write (a simple word processing program). Appendices describe setting up an AUTOEXEC.BAT file, using memory for a RAM disk, PIF files (program information files for integration with standard window products), running DOS programs under Windows, the use of the special EGA driver that has been provided by Microsoft, and the use of Windows in countries other than the United States.

The book is softbound; the copy I was given had already begun to fall apart. Although the covers are printed in color and feature pictures of various MS-Window screens, the interior illustrations are uniformly black-and-white and are produced as direct reductions of bit-mapped screens. There are about two pictures for every four to five pages. The typography is readable, and good use is made of boldface to highlight points.

The organization of the book is clear and straightforward. After guiding the user through the installation process, the author discusses each feature of a window in detail. He then proceeds with each screen by moving through menus from left to right across the screen and item by item within each menu, top to bottom. He proceeds to do this for each application in rough alphabetical order. For each item, he discusses the use of commands generated by keystrokes or mouse clicks. This spatial organization permits easy use of the book as a reference manual. For those items that are described as hints or that are out of spatial order, an excellent index permits rapid retrieval.

I suspect that the principal and best use of this book would be to determine whether or not you would like to buy Microsoft Windows. If you do buy it, you will discover that MS-Windows comes with an excellent manual covering the same material. Alternatively, if you do not like the style or the presentation of the manual, you may prefer this book.

—*E. A. Feustel,* Framingham, MA

MYERS, BRAD A. (Carnegie-Mellon Univ., Pittsburgh, PA)
**Creating user interfaces by demonstration.**
Academic Press, Inc., San Diego, CA, 1988, 276 pp., $29.95, ISBN 0-12-512305-1.
[Perspectives in computing, vol. 22.]

Peridot is a new experimental tool for creating visual user interfaces without programming. The interface designer draws the screen that the user will see, performs sample user actions, and gives examples of typical values. Peridot infers how the constructed parts will interact, checks these inferences with the designer to be sure they are valid, and produces parametrized procedures that can be called from application programs. The program is implemented in Interlisp-D on a Xerox 1109, and Myers has used it to duplicate many of the interaction techniques found in the Macintosh Toolbox. The work, as documented in this outstanding book, makes major research contributions to the evolving area of user interface management systems (UIMSs).

Though based on doctoral work done over several years at the University of Toronto, this book provides depth of insight, quality of design, and explanatory value far beyond what you might expect to find in a typical thesis. Peridot integrates techniques of visual programming, programming by example, constraints, and plausible inference in a masterful demonstration of skilled design tradeoffs. The book will be useful to a wide variety of people. The cross-references throughout the book and the detailed index will be helpful to both casual and intensive readers, and the comprehensive illustrations provide an essential visual perspective.

As a reviewer I have prior familiarity with UIMS work, but I have not constructed a UIMS. Thus, I can interpret and appreciate the contribution of the work, but I cannot provide a point-by-point critique of details. One of the merits of this book is that Myers himself is refreshingly candid and thorough throughout the book in stating explicitly the limits of what he has accomplished and in making cogent suggestions for extensions needed.

Chapter 1 provides a valuable and well-written tutorial by defining terms, outlining the motivation for a UIMS, listing problems with existing UIMS designs, and setting out the goals and design principles for Peridot. The specific contributions of the Peridot work are listed here (and repeated in chapter 15 as a conclusion). Chapter 2 gives a 23-page, critical, in-depth review of related work and indicates the specific problems addressed by Peridot. These two chapters alone will be worth the price of the book to a reader who wants to gain a compact, insightful, and comprehensive review of the field with pointers to sources for more detail.

Chapter 3 provides an overview of the scope of Peridot through the use of an extended example. Chapters 4 through 9, written in an easy-to-read modular form, discuss the author's accomplishments in addressing a range of difficult problems:

- Establishing graphical constraints between objects (e.g., string centering within a rectangle even though the rectangle changes shape) and simple though effective inferencing (to guess what these constraints should be),
- Visual editing of graphic objects (e.g., erasing, copying, and changing dependencies),
- Specifying iterations (e.g., formatting menu items after the first two in a list have been laid out on the screen),
- Using conditionals (e.g., to control visibility or shading of constructed objects when they are shown on the screen to users),
- Using active values as an efficient, easy-to-understand way of controlling displayed objects at run time (e.g., object position can be set by the mouse or by an application procedure), and
- Handling the mouse (e.g., design decisions that allow the mouse interactions to be programmed by demonstration).

Only the mouse, a clock, and a custom-built slider box are currently supported as input devices at run time. Myers indicates in chapter 10 how other input devices could be integrated to allow additional multiple, concurrent user-device interactions.

After the interface is designed, the system can write out procedures to be called by an Interlisp application at run time. As chapter 11 points out, some environment-specific constraints are present, and an extension to Peridot is needed in order to read procedures back in for further editing. Such a detail would be of most interest to Interlisp users, but the author, as he does throughout the book, states the problem in such a way that the issues become general for the implementer of a UIMS in other environments.

The closing chapters compare the Peridot results in visual programming and example-based programming with the challenges outlined in chapter 2, describing future work that could extend the Peridot ideas. Myers makes important points about the value of iterative design techniques that include the user as part of the design cycle. In one informal experiment he compared the time it took him and a novice Peridot user to construct example menus with the time it took others using tools familiar to them. What took Myers and the novice 4 and 15 minutes, respectively, took five expert programmers from $1\frac{1}{2}$ to 8 hours to accomplish. While Myers recognizes that these results are hardly conclusive, he is justified in citing them as evidence of the productivity gains that may be available with the use of the techniques embodied in Peridot.

In another small test, five experienced programmers and five nonprogrammers who had some computer experience used the system for about $1\frac{1}{2}$ hours one-on-one with Myers so that he could guide the learning process (no user's manual or online help is available). This helped him to understand what it would be like for other people to construct simple menus of their own design with the system.

I applaud Myers's reports of empirical testing and his acknowledgment of the design refinements he made to the Peridot user interface as a result of this experience. But the after-the-fact small trials were done too late to have any real influence on the design—a situation all too common in computer science practice. This reader wonders, however, if Myers might not have had some major design insights if he had involved users as an essential part of the design process rather than as an apparent afterthought. Tools such as Peridot that are now becoming available make such user-in-the-loop design procedures increasingly feasible in computer science.

## BOOKS & PROCEEDINGS

I recommend this as a milestone book by a knowledgeable author in a field important for rapid evolution toward more usable computer applications.

—*J. Bennett,* San Jose, CA

KEARSLEY, GREG
**Online help systems: design and implementation.**
Ablex Publishing Corp., Norwood, NJ, 1988, 115 pp., $27.50, ISBN 0-89391-472-X.

This short book has two parts. The first 60 pages are a useful summary of online help systems, and the last 40 pages are an overview of user interface design concepts as applied to these systems. Despite its cursory treatment of the material, this book fills a useful niche in the human-computer interaction literature. Its major contribution is that it outlines the design options open to designers and implementors of help systems and indicates the other sources available to guide their decisions.

The coverage of online help begins with a chapter that describes the decisions to be made during the design of a help system. The following chapter illustrates how existing systems provide help, and the final chapter in this part outlines empirical research results that are applicable to help systems.

In principle, one might want to reorder the material so that form follows function: that is, first discuss when and why people need online help, then show how these needs can be met. In practice, the author's arrangement works well: the audience for this book probably needs to see the variety of design choices first, in order to be convinced that there is a lot worth learning about online help. The book does this job commendably.

I was not satisfied with the author's coverage of the different functions required of a help system. The promised "what works and what doesn't" was probably the wrong target, but more of "what works when" would have been useful. A summary of Rasmussen's malfunction analysis [1], for example, would have helped to explain the different situations to which a help system must respond (and to provide a context within which to evaluate the different forms in the previous chapters).

The user sees a help system in the context of an application. Many of the design decisions discussed in the early chapters could not be made in isolation from the application. For example, decisions on screen format, access methods, and extensibility should be integrated with the design decisions in the application system. Kearsley does not adequately address this relationship between the application system and the help system, nor does he question the appropriateness of our frequent practice of treating help as a separate add-on function. How is the design process (or this book) affected if we consider help as an integral requirement of every application, rather than as something to be designed separately?

The second part of the book gives an overview of user interface design. The risk here is that a little knowledge could become dangerous. I would like to have seen more disclaimers about the cursory nature of the discussion, as well as some more explicit recommendations about the additional knowledge the readers need before engaging in the design steps. For example, the author does not mention work to validate user satisfaction questionnaires [2] or to analyze effective methods of collecting verbal protocols [3].

Flaws in the graphs and the glossary detract from the book's utility. The captions of some graphs, such as Figure 4.2, are incomplete, so the diagrams make no sense without the accompanying text. In the case of Figure 5.3, a graph that depicts improvements in a proposed help system, I was not sure whether the author thought a designer should construct such a table, or whether it was meant only to illustrate the analysis that should be conducted informally. In the glossary of 34 terms, I found 8 of the definitions misleading, in some cases because the author implicitly restricts their scope to commonly available help systems. For example, "bullet proofing" is not finding all the errors in a program, but rather protecting the user and the program from each other's unanticipated actions. A menu is not just a "list of program options"—it could be a list of file names, for example.

This book would be a useful introduction for someone unfamiliar with the literature on human-computer interaction, such as a technical writer who is now being asked to produce an online help system. The book's brevity, despite its disadvantages, may be an asset in attracting readers who do not yet recognize the scope of the knowledge required for systematic design. If this work encourages them to read further in this area, it will have played a valuable role.

—*T. Carey*, Guelph, Ont., Canada

**REFERENCES**

[1] RASMUSSEN, J. *Information processing and human-machine interaction: an approach to cognitive engineering.* Elsevier-North Holland, Amsterdam, 1986.

[2] COLEMAN, W. D.; WILLIGES, R. C.; AND WIXON, D. R. Collecting detailed user evaluation of software interfaces. *Proc. Human Factors Soc.* (1985), 240–244.

[3] ERICSSON, K. A. AND SIMON, H. A. *Protocol analysis: verbal reports as data.* MIT Press, Cambridge, MA, 1984.

DUMAS, JOSEPH S. (American Institutes for Research)     HCI-0010
**Designing user interfaces for software.**
Prentice-Hall, Inc., Englewood Cliffs, NJ, 1988, 174 pp., $31, ISBN 0-13-201971-X.

Corporations such as Apple and IBM have issued specific guidelines [1,2] as one step in achieving a particular "look and feel." This small book (8 cartoons and 146 pages of text in a 5 × 9 format) complements similar publications such as Heckel [3] and Rubenstein and Hersh [4] and seems oriented toward small projects and organizations with few existing user interface design procedures. It aims to provide practical advice to "professionals who create software, managers who guide development, and students."

Dumas writes from the perspective of a consultant who has evaluated software and worked with groups developing personal computer software. His book is organized around 7 principles and offers 21 guidelines for controlling transactions, 25 for displaying information, 16 for entering data, and 30 for online documentation. Dumas notes that the scientific foundations for user interface design and evaluation are still being developed, and so he feels free to base his recommendations for "taking the user's point of view" as much on his own experience as on experimental data. The book's 56 references represent a mix of both old and new literature from the fields of human factors and computer science.

The book contains good advice, has useful examples, and reads well. Dumas makes many perceptive and useful observations, and some groups producing personal computer software may find his succinct distillation valuable. I am troubled, though, perhaps more by what the author omits than by what he includes.

Development groups are finding usability engineering practices (and also software engineering practices) increasingly necessary in order to meet requirements (see, for example, Whiteside et al. [5] and Gilb [6]), but Dumas does not mention them. He seems instead to focus on *one* usability test (p. 26) and characterizes as a first stage "all of those activities that lead up to the test" and as the second stage "the usability test and the changes that will have to be made as a result." Although it acknowledges the need for changes, his approach fails to emphasize sufficiently the importance of iterative design based on frequent and specific interaction with users (see, e.g., Gould et al. [7]).

Another troubling example is Dumas's suggestion that developers create a handbook for their group that "should contain all of the information needed to design the user interface." He further suggests that they keep this handbook up to date with information from publications such as *Ergonomics, The International Journal of Man-Machine Studies,* and *Human Factors.* Developers who need to be reminded of these sources, however, probably do not have the background to interpret them, and those who can interpret them do not need to be reminded. In any event, no handbook can contain "all of the information needed."

But these are small points. Guidelines are, after all, "a convenient way to communicate the accumulated experience that . . . professionals have obtained from their work," and this can't hurt—or can it? As the industry increasingly emphasizes consumer products, developers of personal computer software struggle to cope effectively with user demands. This book, and similar collections of guidelines, *can* hurt if they give management a false sense of security and conceal the need for more effective engineering practices, though Dumas does point out examples where the appropriate interpretation of guidelines is context-sensitive.

This little book is useful. The danger is that the casual reader (or, more perniciously, the inexperienced software development manager) will pick it up and reinforce an erroneous impression that "this is all there is to it." Can developers who do not have appropriate concrete experience successfully make the necessary interpretations and trade-offs implied by generic guidelines? Does a forum exist that developers who follow the advice in this book and other similar guideline collections could use to share their results?

—*J. Bennett,* San Jose, CA

### REFERENCES

[1] APPLE COMPUTER, INC. *Human interface guidelines: the Apple desktop interface.* Addison-Wesley, Reading, MA, 1987.

[2] IBM CORP. *Systems application architecture, common user access, panel design and user interaction.* IBM, Armonk, NY, 1987.

[3] HECKEL, P. *The elements of friendly software design.* Warner Books, New York, 1984.

[4] RUBENSTEIN, R. AND HERSH, H. *The human factor.* Digital Press, Burlington, MA, 1984.

[5] WHITESIDE, J.; BENNETT, J.; AND HOLTZBLATT, K. Usability engineering. In *Handbook of Human-Computer Interaction*. M. Helander (Ed.), North Holland, Amsterdam, 1988.

[6] GILB, T. *Principles of software engineering management*. Addison-Wesley, Reading, MA, 1987.

[7] GOULD, J. D. ET AL. The 1984 Olympic Message System. *Commun. ACM* **30**, 9 (Sept. 1987), 758–769. See Review HCI-0125.

BROWN, C. M. (Xerox Corporation, Sunnyvale, CA)   **HCI-0011**
**Human-computer interface design guidelines.**
Ablex Publishing Corp., Norwood, NJ, 1988, 236 pp., $32.50, ISBN 0-89391-332-4.

While software engineers frequently design the human-computer interfaces (HCIs) of the systems they build, they are rarely trained to do this job well, and most programmers have neither the time nor the inclination to survey the relevant research literature. The value of this book is that it provides such individuals with a complete and accessible catalog of principles and rules of thumb for interface design.

The book begins with a short introduction to general principles that govern HCI design. The chapters that follow list guidelines grouped by topics such as designing display formats, effective wording, proper use of color, effective use of graphics, dialogue design, data entry conventions, use of control and display devices, and provision of error messages and online help. Each guideline is discussed in detail, and examples and illustrations accompany many of these discussions. The author references papers and books in cases where research or experience supports the use of a guideline. The final chapter gives general advice and strategy for using HCI guidelines in system design and analysis, and the end matter includes the references, author and subject indices, and a guideline checklist.

The book's discussion of graphics is its weakest section; readers would do better to consult Tufte [1] or Cleveland [2]. The bibliography is extensive but not exhaustive. The page format is surprisingly poor for a book about human factors: chapter titles appear in running footers at the bottom of the pages, rather than in running headers at the top of the pages, and the page numbers appear in the middle of the outside margins. This format violates strong conventions about the placement of headers and page numbers and is especially annoying when one is hunting for a particular page.

This book should provide students and software engineers with effective guidance on most HCI design issues. It would be a valuable reference during interface design and a good model when formulating design guidelines for development projects. I recommend it to any programmer who wishes to learn the basics of HCI design as quickly and painlessly as possible.

—*Christopher Fox,* Lincroft, NJ

**REFERENCES**

[1] TUFTE, E. R. *The visual display of quantitative information.* Graphics Press, Cheshire, CT, 1983. See *Computing Reviews,* Rev. 8901-0017.

[2] CLEVELAND, W. S. *The elements of graphing data.* Wadsworth, Monterey, CA, 1985. See Review HCI-0035.

BOOKS & PROCEEDINGS                                              [HCI-0014]

BULLINGER, H.-J. (Fraunhofer Institute for Industrial Engineering, Stuttgart, W.          **HCI-0012**
Germany) (ATH.)GUNZENHÄUSER, R. (Univ. of Stuttgart, W. Germany) (ED.)
**Software ergonomics: advances and applications.**
Halsted Press, New York, NY, 1988, 138 pp., $39.95, ISBN 0-470-21177-6. [Ellis Horwood series in computers and their applications.]

This book is a translation of the 1986 German edition; its contents are based upon a course taught at the Technical Academy of Esslingen in 1984 and again in 1985. Nearly all the references (which include both US and German items) are from 1985 or earlier. The eight chapters all have German authors, and one has a US coauthor. Topics covered include dialogues (chapters 1 and 2), screen design (chapter 3), knowledge-based interfaces (chapters 5 and 6), interaction devices (chapter 7), and computer-assisted instruction and interfaces for the handicapped (chapter 8). The material is a broad, high-level survey of aspects of computer-user interaction that contains few specific details and no example system. The text could serve as a guide to topics in user interaction, but a course that used it would require supplementary reference items that covered specific languages, interface systems, and software tools. The book contains no program or homework assignments, no "worked examples," and no coverage of any formal models or formal specifications of user interaction.

—*W. Hankley,* Manhattan, KS

### Windows

QUEDENS, GUY; AND BEASON, PAMELA S.                                    **HCI-0013**
**Introduction to Windows programming.**
Scott, Foresman & Co., Glenview, IL, 1989, 370 pp., $21.95, ISBN 0-673-38058-0.

This book is as much an example of how to write a good introduction to a technical topic as it is a book on Windows programming. It is exceptionally clear; the examples are graduated and right on the mark. The subject is limited to Microsoft Windows, Windows/286, and Windows/386. Code examples are in C, though Pascal and Assembler are also usable with Windows.

The authors stress the device independence of windows and show how they can be integrated into a range of applications. The advice is very low level: it even describes how to set up directories for development using the Windows functions and explains the use of Make. The later chapters also deal with advanced topics such as memory management and painting and graphics in a window. The book includes a complete glossary.

In general, for someone who wants a clear introduction to Windows and how it can be used in applications, this is the book. Knowledge of programming using C is highly recommended.

—*J. E. Tomayko,* Wichita, KS

### D.2.5  Testing and Debugging

SPENCER, RICHARD H. (IBM Corp., Information Systems and Communication Group,    **HCI-0014**
Boca Raton, FL)
**Computer usability testing & evaluation.**
Prentice-Hall, Inc., Englewood Cliffs, NJ, 1985, 224 pp., $27.50, ISBN 0-13-164088-7.

In recent years, the discipline of testing and evaluation of computer systems has come to the forefront. It has been recognized that early detection and correction of system problems is cost-effective, and that testing needs to extend over the entire product life cycle. However, too often testing and evaluation efforts place a great deal of emphasis on system design, performance, and production issues at the expense of evaluating whether the system is suitable for use by humans.

This book is intended to provide usability test guidelines to producers and evaluators of computer systems. *Usability* is defined in the book as ". . . convenient and practicable for use. . . ." Usability testing is different from other specialized test areas, such as design testing or software testing. *Usability*, as the book points out, "refers to the relationship between people and things and/or process designed to enable people to achieve results." Often used in conjunction with product usability are terms such as human factors, ergonomics, ease of use, productivity, and, last but not least, the familiar user-friendliness.

The book has 8 chapters and 4 appendices, as follows:

Chapter 1  Introduction.
Chapter 2  Usability Mission.
Chapter 3  Product, User, and Evaluator.
Chapter 4  Product and Evaluation Planning Cycles.
Chapter 5  Usability Documentation.
Chapter 6  Criteria—Qualitative and Quantitative.
Chapter 7  Evaluating Usability.
Chapter 8  Data and Reporting.
Appendix A  Checklist of Usability Considerations for Computer Design Evaluations.
Appendix B  Usability Test Plan—Example.
Appendix C  Human Factors Considerations—Examples.
Appendix D  Standards.

This book is useful, educational, and easy to read. Indeed, in writing this book, the author practices what he preaches. If one considers this book as a product, which it surely is, then it is clearly user-friendly and reader-friendly. Without boring the reader, the author uses many familiar examples from everyday situations to make his point. This reviewer found the Checklist of Usability Considerations, appearing in Appendix A, of value in testing and evaluation of diverse systems. Likewise, the example of the well laid-out usability test plan found in Appendix B may be readily applied to other systems.

The book should be read not only by people whose primary convern is testing and evaluation of computer systems, but also by system designers and producers. It can do much good in sensitizing the designers and producers to the factors that are necessary to the success of any computer system. In the final analysis, the system must be usable. Indeed, even the best-designed system is "useless" if it is not "usable."

—*H. Gabrieli*, Margate, NJ

### D.2.6 Programming Environments

LYONS, T. G. (Software Sciences Ltd., UK); AND NISSEN, J. C. (GEC Software Ltd., UK)
**Selecting an Ada environment.**
Cambridge University Press, New York, NY, 1986, 239 pp., $29.95, ISBN 0-521-32594-3. [The Ada companion series.]

The objectives of this book are set forth in the Introduction. It is a book on software engineering, particularly on software engineering environments. The authors assert that this book should provide

(1) help in specifying an environment to be implemented,
(2) help in implementing an environment,
(3) help in selecting an environment (from a number of existing ones),
(4) help in using an environment,
(5) help in understanding the issues,
(6) help for organizations attempting to produce standards for environments, and
(7) help for those considering environments for languages other than Ada. The book certainly can provide the help that the objectives listed in the Introduction suggest. While concentrating on the software engineering environments issue, the book surveys most of the other issues and categories in software engineering. However, some things, such as software reusability (except in conjunction with the book's ideas on configuration management) and formal technical reviews, are lightly touched upon. The book points to the tools and techniques of the coming automated environments, and the reader can come away with the idea that the primary emphasis in the book is on the computer system aspects of environments.

A fine Table of Contents, Index, Glossary, and Table of Acronyms are provided; however, the authors' concepts of software must be gleaned from the book. The reviewer feels the authors' point of view is that of a broad characterization of software. However, more attention could be paid in the book to other aspects than those of the coding phase of software engineering. This is particularly the opinion when reviewing the emphasis on code testing and debugging aspects of verification and validation. The issue of quality assurance teams versus everyone participating and being responsible for quality assurance in software engineering is covered very slightly in the discussion of software engineering environments.

The book is a useful guide to practitioners, as well as a source for research for students and other researchers in software engineering. Many areas requiring further research are cited in the book, while the attentive reader will be able to discern many more. The book supplies five pages of useful references. It provides a good supplement to standards that have been developed over the last ten years and that are currently being developed. The book presents a nice matrix that brings face to face the activities within the phases of a model development life cycle. It is not a classroom book, but it could be in a library for use as a reference and source. It is a compact book, yet it offers much material for discussion. The typography is good (there are very few typographical errors), and is quite readable (it is easy to go back and reread sections in response to discussions). The book leaves some things out, but it provides a concise tablet from which people working in, responsible for, or teaching about software engineering environments can work.

—*J. Fendrich,* Peoria, IL

### D.2.7 Distribution and Maintenance

*Documentation*

FOEHR, THERESA (Foehr Incorporated, Boulder, CO); AND CROSS, THOMAS B. (Cross Information Company, Boulder, CO)
**The soft side of software: a management approach to computer documentation.**
Wiley-Interscience, New York, NY, 1986, 160 pp., $22.95, ISBN 0-471-81527-6.

This is a short, softcover book that attempts to present a comprehensive view of the role of documentation in computer systems. This includes design, development, and production of documentation. Many peripheral issues that impinge upon documentation are also discussed.

Chapter 1 contains an overview of computer system documentation: what it is and what it should be in the context of a computer system. Chapter 2 contains a brief synopsis of organizational behavior and organizational dynamics techniques. The authors base their discussion on the premise that poor documentation results in part from poor integration of the documenters with the system developers. The chapter is ended with an outline of how to manage a software project: particular attention is paid to the scheduling of documentation development.

Chapter 3 discusses how to determine the content of technical documentation. Many of the processes and techniques used in classical task analysis and system analysis are included. Several subsections in the chapter have checklists of things one should be looking for, or at, in a system. A nine-step model of the documentation development process, which includes cost accounting after the project is completed, is provided. Cost accounting should be done, but it is often omitted.

Chapter 4 contains a discussion of the human-computer interface and a section on how to write. Chapter 5 presents the thesis that documentation with integrated graphics will be better accepted by users. The authors argue strongly that careful attention should be paid to the visual characteristics of documentation.

Two appendices are provided. The first contains a discussion of a research project on information storage and retrieval. The second is a compendium of references on documentation.

This book is a model of good documentation; the authors have thoughtfully applied most of the principles they have discussed. Topics are discussed in short paragraphs and sections, and illustrations are used generously. The book is an excellent road map for a manager who wishes to guarantee that documentation is produced on time and that it is of high quality. The book suffers, though, when it begins to wander off the topic of documentation. Chapter 4 meanders through a discussion of the human-computer interface at the "gee-whiz" level, illustrating the text with a hodgepodge of mouse, icon, and future interface technologies. It is not clear whether this is meant to imply that systems will become harder or easier to document.

Appendix A also seems out of place. It presents some research on information storage and retrieval that is being performed by one of the authors, and seems more like technical advertising copy than useful information.

Finally, the authors have ignored one crucial point: the process of choosing good technical writers, noting merely that the typical document author lacks a good technical background. Why not instead try to hire writers with a technical background, or train them by sending them to school?

In summary, the book has brought together, in a concise way, many diverse elements of the documentation process. It would be an excellent starting point for anyone faced with the responsibility of managing software documentation. It may be most useful, though, in evaluating documentation. The frequent checklists in the text offer an easy way of determining what documentation has or lacks.

—*A. Cohill,* Newport, VA

KATZIN, EMANUEL
**How to write a really good user's manual.**
Van Nostrand Reinhold Co., New York, NY, 1986, 249 pp., $32.95, ISBN 0-442-24758-3.

Writing good manuals for computer systems is a sadly underrated art. I approached this book, therefore, with enthusiasm and the hope of learning some useful skills.

The first 30 pages are encouraging. They contain sensible advice on identifying the needs and characteristics of the reader and on the use of good writing techniques. There are excellent short sections on readability and clarity, together with helpful lists of frequently misused words and of words and phrases to avoid. At this point, my expectations were high.

Unfortunately, I then suffered an increasing sense of disappointment and frustration as I read on. The book contains plenty of good advice and copious examples, but it does not cover user manuals for general-purpose computer systems, for workstations, or for personal computers. Instead it concentrates almost entirely on data collection for payroll, inventory, and other data processing systems. It should, indeed, have a prominent subtitle proclaiming "—Or How to Instruct Users to Fill Forms with Data Which May Subsequently Be Entered onto Punched Cards."

The bulk of the book deals with form filling or procedural matters. Two typical extracts taken from an example inventory system are:

EMPLOYEE NUMBER—This is the employee number of the person who reports the information on this form and whose name appears to the left. Enter the number in format 99999. Use leading zeros if necessary. For example, if the employee number is 5642, enter 05642.

This form is completed each month, at the end of the month, by authorized personnel and mailed to the Transportation department in Houston on the first day of the succeeding month.

The last few sections of the book discuss terminal use for data entry and interactive systems. The interactive systems are divided into *batch-type* ("The input screen on which the User enters the data typically resembles, as closely as possible, the source document. It usually contains the same fields and columns that the old punch card contained when the data was punched into it") and *conversation-type* ("When dealing with interactive processing, you must recognize that every entry on the screen immediately affects the computer and its files, and is, therefore, more potentially critical. Compare this with filling out the traditional paper form and its subsequent data entry processing, then computer processing.").

In many ways, the book is an interesting commentary on the unfriendly nature of the user interface for data processing applications. The examples tell you how to instruct the user to enter the six-character device name "2A113V" left-justified into an eight-character field, and how to help him or her decipher poorly designed and poorly printed financial reports. Slightly more friendly material comes towards the end of the book when simple screen menus are covered, but you would search in vain for any advice on the use of windows, pointing devices, online help systems, or online documentation of any description.

In summary, the book contains a few sections of general interest. But do not try this book unless your primary interests are in data collection and data processing.

—*H. Brown,* Kent, UK

## D.3 Programming Languages

### D.3.2 Language Classifications

HOROWITZ, ELLIS (Univ. of Southern California) (ED.)  **HCI-0018**
**Programming languages: a grand tour (2nd ed.).**
Computer Science Press, Inc., Rockville, MD, 1985, 758 pp., $39.95, ISBN 0-88175-073-5. [Computer software engineering series.]

In examining the second edition of this book, I had hoped that some of the aspects I viewed as defects would be corrected. Unfortunately, this is not true. The only difference between the second edition and the first (which was reviewed in *Computing Reviews* **24**, 7 (July 1983), Rev. 40,450) is the replacement of the full *ADA 1980 Reference Manual* by the approved standard (ANSI/MIL-STD-1815A-1983). This increases the size of the book by 100 pages.

The other comments—both favorable and critical—made in the review of the first edition remain valid in my opinion. In particular, I continue to regret that 44 percent of this book is comprised of the ADA reference manual which is available free.

—*Jean E. Sammet,* Bethesda, MD

KLERER, MELVIN (Polytechnic Univ., Brooklyn, NY)  **HCI-0019**
**User-oriented computer languages: analysis and design.**
Macmillan Publishing Co., Inc., New York, NY, 1987, 208 pp., $34.95, ISBN 0-02-949911-9. [Macmillan database/data communications series.]

Transforming a problem specification into a working program is very difficult. One of the major impediments to this process is the difficulty of translating the language the programmer typically uses, such as English or mathematics of some sort, into the language required by the machine. The past forty years have seen the evolution of higher and higher level languages that attempt to allow a programmer to express problems more naturally. In this book, the author examines the design of higher-level languages for specific domains. The domain used for examples throughout the book is engineering mathematics.

The author states that the intended audience includes both professionals who want insight into friendly language design and students who want a supplement to programming language texts. Since the book is clearly written, either of these groups should find it accessible.

The book, however, fails to deliver in several ways. The major problem is that the book does not spend enough time on the major topic, while far too much time is spent on reviewing standard material that can be found in many programming language texts. Many of these are cited in the book's bibliography. Given the intended audience, much of the elementary material could have been assumed or referenced.

The chapter titles reflect the book's coverage:

(1) The Nature of the Computer-Language Problem
(2) Methods of Language Definition
(3) The Assignment Statement
(4) Basic Control Structures
(5) Input and Output
(6) Declarations, Types, and Scopes
(7) Procedures and Parameters: Iteration and Recursion
(8) The Language Design of a System for Scientific/Engineering/Mathematical Application Programming
(9) Additional User-Oriented Concepts.

Another problem with the book is that the only examples given are from mathematics. Since mathematics is highly formalized, with a precise notation, syntax, and semantics, developing a domain-specific computer language for mathematics is much easier than it would be for less formal domains. Some discussion of attempts at other user-oriented computer languages, such as AI languages and declarative languages, would be expected in a book with this title, but is lacking.

—*William B. Frakes,* Holmdel, NJ

## *AWK*

AHO, ALFRED V.; KERNIGHAN, BRIAN W., AND WEINBERGER, PETER J. (AT&T Bell Laboratories, Murray Hill, NJ)
**The AWK programming language.**
Addison-Wesley Publ. Co., Inc., Reading, MA, 1987, 210 pp., $21.95, ISBN 0-201-07981-X. [Addison-Wesley series in computer science.]

When I first saw the title of this book, I said to myself Are they kidding? AWK is just one of those handy Unix tools for making simple data filters. I suppose its notation can be considered a language, but is it not a gross overstatement to call it a programming language?

Well, no. Actually, AWK has every right to be called a programming language. It has such things as variables, including arrays; floating-point arithmetic, including transcendental functions; all the control constructs of the C language; and formatted output. The most recent version even allows users to define their own functions. If a programmer uses all of these features, an AWK program looks almost like a C program. AWK's greatest strength, though, is still that it is easy to write very small and concise programs for data manipulation—reading input lines, breaking them into fields or classifying them by pattern-matching, performing simple transformations, and writing corresponding output lines. It is ideally suited for producing quick-and-dirty implementations that can be used once and discarded or that can be used as prototypes for larger-scale, more efficient implementations.

The book is quite clear and pleasant to read. Chapter 1 is a tutorial, chapter 2 is the reference manual, and the remaining chapters illustrate the use of AWK in various applications. Titles of these chapters are "Data Processing," "Reports and Databases," "Processing Words," "Little Languages," and "Experiments with Algorithms." The examples demonstrate the wide applicability of AWK and illustrate a variety of programming techniques.

A possible criticism of the book might be that to explain a language as simple as AWK, you do not need a 210-page book. Indeed, the first two chapters occupy only 66 pages. But it would be a shame to do without the examples. Besides being quite clever in places, they give you a ready-made collection of lots of useful programs that you can adapt to your own needs. Chapters 3 through 7 are almost completely independent of each other, and you may browse through them according to your interests and needs.

I enjoyed the book, and I recommend it.

—A. M. Stavely, Socorro, NM

## CSP

ALEXANDER, HEATHER (STC Technology Ltd., Newcastle-under-Lyme, UK)
**Formally-based tools and techniques for human-computer dialogues.**
Halsted Press, New York, NY, 1987, 161 pp., $41.95, ISBN 0-470-20996-8. [Ellis Horwood series in computers and their applications.]

This book describes a restricted implementation of theoretical CSP in which events are associated with attributes in much the way that Backus-Naur Form (BNF) rules have actions in YACC. It is used for the specification and prototyping of a human-computer interface at the syntactic level, where a parsing metaphor is used:

> The semantic layer is defined by the application designer in the course of designing the objects and operations of the application. . . . Next, the syntactic layer, which defines the sequence of inputs and outputs in the dialogue. . . . Finally, the lexical layer defines the layout of the screen, windows, colour, internal representation for user input and so on. (p. 28)

The project is worthwhile, and the author has interesting ideas in concurrent semantics, interface specification, and prototype development. Also, there is a pressing need for books that apply formal methods of program design to significant problems, since the best way to convince the computing community that such approaches have merit is by presenting examples of

# BOOKS & PROCEEDINGS

(1) a clear and understandable specification;
(2) a list of design issues and decisions, together with reasons governing the choices made;
(3) a portable and efficient solution; and
(4) a proof that the solution satisfies the specification.

Unfortunately this is not quite the case here.

The problem is that this book appears to be a severely edited version of a Ph.D. thesis, with the virtues and vices that this entails. On the plus side, it is based on a newly developed, working system that is virtually state-of-the-art. The prose is clear, there are very few typographical errors, and the references are wide ranging. On the minus side, this is the rough structure:

(1) Introduction, related work, and blind alleys (45 pages). These are necessary in a thesis, but are better left to an appendix in a book. The false trails are supposed to reflect the iterative approach used in prototyping, but the goal is to provide an environment that supports prototyping, and that environment is not used in the early parts of the book. They only distract the reader.
(2) Description of the final notations using examples (26 pages). This section is very concise; it requires considerable background knowledge of CSP on the part of the reader. The language **me too** (an executable specification language) is referred to extensively throughout the book, as one would expect from a research student of Peter Henderson; but since it is actually used only for the implementation, and is invisible at the top level, it seems to be another red herring.
(3) Implementation details (20 pages). This is a sketchy overview of the approaches and data structures used. With the appendices and either **me too** or C, it might be sufficient to generate an implementation; as the necessary code is not gathered in one place, it is not immediately obvious how easy it would be. Nor is it clear how much work would be needed to modify the underlying assumptions about human-computer dialogue, for instance, to allow two users to access a common database, since the user interface seems to be treated as a special case in terms of communications that affect the program state.

The intended audience is postgraduate students and practicing software designers; the purpose of the book seems to be that of an advertising brochure, to encourage readers to send off for copies of the system. In this sense the book is successful; those who are seeking a base for a research project will find it appealing. Unfortunately, it will probably fail to convince less specialized readers that an attribute CSP is a practical way to solve their problems.

—*C. M. Holt,* Newcastle upon Tyne, UK

## *INTERLISP*

KAISLER, STEPHEN H. (Defense Advanced Research Projects Agency)
**INTERLISP: the language and its usage.**
Wiley-Interscience, New York, NY, 1986, 1144 pp., $49.95, ISBN 0-471-81644-2.

This book describes INTERLISP, a dialect of the LISP programming language that was developed by researchers with the Xerox Corporation's Palo Alto Research Center. INTERLISP used to be one of the two main dialects of LISP in wide use within the research community, but the introduction of Common LISP as an industry standard in 1983 has reduced its role to an essentially historical one.

In view of these considerations, a book on INTERLISP is a difficult one to write. The language it describes is moving out of active duty, and therefore the major strength of such a book could have been the description of the historical role played by INTERLISP in the development of the LISP philosophy and its influence on other languages and programming environments. The last point is especially relevant since in the late 1970s INTERLISP was one of the most advanced interactive programming environments in existence. However, I was disappointed to find out that the author has taken an entirely different direction. Rather than a historical perspective on the most interesting features of the language, the book is essentially an overly detailed language reference manual. It presents no historical perspective whatsoever, and it would be difficult to extract from the book alone any notion of what the really important features of INTERLISP are.

Since it is essentially a language reference manual, such a book would have been most useful had it been published ten years ago when it would have filled an important documentation gap. From several references in the text, I have the impression that most of the book was written in late 1983; the actual publication date, however, is 1986. That date forces me to look severely upon some of the statements the author makes. The preface, for instance, states flatly that "there is no standard for LISP, and it is unlikely that we will see one in the near future." Such a statement would have been at best questionable in late 1983, and is inconceivable in a book published in 1986 when an ANSI committee had already been proposed for turning Common LISP into an international standard. The preface of the book does not even mention Common LISP, which first appears as an incidental reference on p. 5. The short section on Common LISP, on p. 7, totally fails to describe the real role of that language.

The overall organization of the book is also disappointing. The author does not present or highlight the main features of INTERLISP, but simply lists a huge number of low-level facts and details about the language. Even the most significant features of the programming environment are simply listed as a set of functions, without any attempt to bring out the motivations behind them and their true importance. For a book of well over one thousand pages, this is an inexcusable omission.

Figures are almost absent. A few CONS-cell diagrams are presented without any real explanation of their meaning; the diagrams themselves are of the teletype graphics variety and are not even formatted properly (see pp. 50–51). Extensive listings of the internal implementation of many system functions clutter every chapter of the book. Such listings serve no real purpose; a few well-designed and well-commented examples would have been more useful than a myriad of function listings. Furthermore, the listings have few comments, are poorly formatted, and almost exclusively use primitive control structures like PROG and GO. This problem is compounded by the over-abundance of such listings. Chapter 6, for instance, contains 30 pages of listings, and of the remaining 54 pages, easily half are taken by short examples. The rest of the chapter consists of detailed function descriptions. Several function listings in the book take five or more pages.

The first few chapters of the book (Chapters 3 through 13) introduce the reader to the basic features of the language, with great emphasis on list manipulation. Such chapters are among the weakest of the book; they assume that the reader is already completely familiar with the ideas and the material. It is often unclear exactly what features are part of the language and what are user-extensions to it. The function listings are especially annoying since the user cannot be expected to understand them at this point.

Chapters 14 through 18 present more advanced features of the language, but the general tone is pretty much the same: lots of function definitions, extensive program listings, a myriad of facts, and few ideas. Chapter 19 presents the INTERLISP Editor, a teletype-oriented structure editor that sounds pretty dated. Chapters 20 through 28 present the more interesting material: the DWIM (Do What I Mean) facility, which provides interactive or automatic correction of typos and a few simple programming mistakes; the Programmer's Assistant, which provides for comprehensive undoing facilities; Masterscope; and the History Package. Unfortunately, the presentation is once again cluttered with low-level details, and it is hard to gather what the important contributions really are. There is no indication of how often the advanced features are used, what type of users prefer them, or how effective they are in improving programmer productivity.

The best feature of the book is that it does indeed describe the language, as it existed sometime in 1983, in minute detail. Such a description, however, is no longer useful to today's readers, and thus the book reminds me of those out-of-date reference manuals that gather dust on a bookshelf. In addition, the presentation is cluttered with program listings and generally speaking contains little original material.

The book contains an extensive list of references, but there is not much in the text or in the bibliography that would give the reader any idea about their relative importance. The index is fairly good and contains references to all the functions defined in the book and several important topics. The text contains some spelling errors, and the listings of computer output are not always exempt from mistakes, but in general the typography is adequate. I found the choice of type fonts sometimes confusing and not always well balanced.

In conclusion, my overall reaction to the book is one of disappointment. With over 1,100 pages, the book drags on and on in an endless sequence of function definitions and program listings. I was hoping to find a clear presentation of the strengths and weaknesses of INTERLISP and its many contributions to the LISP language and the AI research community, but I did not. The book does a poor job of historically placing the language and offers the reader no idea about what has happened in the field since 1982. Judging by this book alone, I would think that the LISP world was still in the sorry state of confusion it was in back then. Fortunately, this is no longer true.

—*Dario Giuse*, Pittsburgh, PA

## LISP

WILENSKY, ROBERT (Univ. of California, Berkeley)
**LISPcraft.**
W. W. Norton & Co., Inc., New York, NY, 1984, 385 pp., $19.95, ISBN 0-393-95442-0.

"This tutorial is designed to give the reader a working knowledge of Franz LISP. No formal description of the language is attempted. . . .Instead, certain useful programming styles are suggested to the reader for consideration." These three sentences from the Preface describe the book adequately. The book is about Franz LISP, but it would be useful to someone using any of the other MacLISP-like dialects, though in this case careful reading of the dialect reference would be necessary, since by no means are all nonstandard features of Franz identified. The book concentrates on simplicity at the expense of precise definitions or descriptions, and essentially could not be used as a reference manual (it points the user to [1] instead). This is a great pity, since a short but precise glossary would be a great help to the reader—as it is, he is left with oversimplifications, which are hard to correct from the manual.

The order of topics in the book is unusual—for example, splicing reader macros are treated before the representation of lists in terms of pairs. The book appears to be more a collection of useful LISP features than any real attempt to teach the reader about the essence of LISP. Indeed, while the reviewer could recommend it to an application programmer who had been told that the next program was to be written in Franz LISP, the reviewer is unable to recommend it for university use. Winston & Horn [2] seems substantially better for that purpose, and the 2nd edition (1984) is even better.

Some examples of specific problems in the text are given below; there are 21 other errors or major omissions that space does not permit us to list:

p. 3   "The LISP evaluation rule" is a gross over-simplification. LISP does not use purely applicative-order evaluation, but a mixed order depending on the presence of fexprs and macros. While it is not possible to give the full rule at this stage, it would be less misleading if the author had explained that this was a simplification.

p. 7   The use (which is the nearest the author comes to definition) of "binding" here is, at best, confusing. The author says "Binding is just another name for assigning a value, as far as we are concerned," and "LISP has a special function which binds the value of one of its arguments to the other argument. This function goes under the rather peculiar name of SETQ." This is certainly not the standard LISP terminology, in which SETQ is referred to as *assignment*, leaving *binding* as the description of what LAMBDA and associated forms do.

p. 10  The author asserts that (SETQ PLUS 17) has "absolutely no effect whatsoever on PLUS's role as a function name." This is true in Franz LISP, and in all other LISPs that employ separate functions cells, but it is not universally true, as we see from Cambridge LISP [3] and LISP/VM [4]. Since this is a major difference in programming possibilities, it is a pity that the author did not live up to his Preface, in which he claims to "[specify] those points at which other LISPs are likely to differ from the one described herein." Now is not the right place to argue the relative merits of the two styles (especially since the two inventors of the function cell disagree as to whether it was a good idea [5, 6], but it does seem a pity to exclude one view totally. This one-sided view is apparent throughout the treatment of functional values (e.g., on p. 95).

p. 30  The author repeats the old criticism that CONS is extremely expensive, saying that "the effective cost of a single CONS, when garbage collection is considered, might be a millisecond" (while CAR is a microsecond). While the reviewer has been unable to use Franz LISP to measure this, the measurements he has made on other LISPs give a relative time CONS/CAR of anywhere from 8.6 (checked CAR; excluding garbage collection) to 34.5 (unchecked CAR, including garbage collection). Specialized hardware can reduce this ratio even further [7]. What is expensive is not the consing—it is the total amount of data structure that counts. Interestingly, as we shall see later, the author rarely gives a space-efficient solution to the problems he poses. There is also no mention of the efficiency that can come from sharing data structures rather than copying them.

p. 121  The author says "Lambda is useful, but most LISP programs would work just as well if lambda did not exist as a separate abstraction." This is unclear to me—how could lambda be defined in terms of the other LISP abstractions that the author has introduced? Perhaps the author means that most casual LISP programmers do not need to know about lambda, which is certainly true. But this is not the same as saying that LISP programmers do not use lambda, though it may be packaged up in DEFUN or similar functions.

—*J. H. Davenport*, Bath, UK

**REFERENCES**

[1] FODERADO, J. K. *The Franz LISP manual*, Univ. of California at Berkeley, 1979.
[2] WINSTON, P. H.; AND HORN, B. K. H. *LISP*, Addison-Wesley, 1981. See *Computing Reviews* **22**, 8 (Aug. 1981), Rev. 38,264.
[3] FITCH, J. P.; AND NORMAN, A. C. Implementing LISP in a high-level language, *Softw. Pract. Exper.* **7** (1977), 713–725. See *Computing Reviews* **19**, 11 (Nov. 1978), Rev. 33,698.
[4] IBM *LISP/VM reference manual*, SH20-6477-0, IBM, 1984.
[5] DEUTSCH, P. Function cells, *LISP Forum* **23** (Aug. 1983).
[6] BOBROW, D. Function cells, *LISP Forum* **30** (Aug. 1983).
[7] MOON, D. A. Garbage collection in a large LISP system, *Proc. 1984 ACM symp. on LISP and functional programming* (Austin, TX, Aug. 6–8, 1984), ACM, New York, 1984, 235–246.

## D.3.4 Processors

### Translator writing systems and compiler generators

REPS, THOMAS W. (Univ. of Wisconsin, Madison); AND TEITELBAUM, TIM (Cornell Univ., Ithaca, NY)    **HCI-0024**
**The synthesizer generator: a system for constructing language-based editors.**
Springer-Verlag New York, Inc., New York, NY, 1989, 317 pp., $39.20, ISBN 0-387-96857-1.
[Texts and monographs in computer science series.]

REPS, THOMAS W. (Univ. of Wisconsin, Madison); AND TEITELBAUM, TIM (Cornell Univ., Ithaca, NY)    **HCI-0024**
**The synthesizer generator reference manual (3rd ed.).**
Springer-Verlag New York, Inc., New York, NY, 1989, 171 pp., $20, ISBN 0-387-96910-1.
[Texts and monographs in computer science series.]

The Synthesizer Generator is a software tool for the creation of language-specific editors, such as editors for programming languages, document preparation systems, and program verification tools. It uses the spreadsheet paradigm of immediate computation, in which any edit operation causes immediate error reporting, analysis, and translation of affected text. The specification language for the Synthesizer Generator is based on attribute grammars and allows the user to write modular specifications for abstract syntax, concrete input syntax, display format, context-sensitive relationships, and transformation rules. *The synthesizer generator: a system for constructing language-based editors* is an in-depth account of this system, including its design philosophy, a tutorial introduction, a more detailed treatment, several examples of its use, and technical material on its implementation; the authors also provide algorithms for incremental attribute evaluation. The book is well organized and well written. It sustains the reader's interest by careful presentation of topics and the use of illuminating examples, and it contains several pointers to other work in the area.

Although the book is about a specific tool, it will interest anyone doing research or development on interactive programming environments, compilers and language translation systems, or software tools. The authors assume little background, but some familiarity with attribute grammars and language specifications would be helpful: even with this background, the reader has to assimilate a great deal of material. The tutorial introduction is essential for a prospective user of the Synthesizer Generator. The chapter on "Practical Advice" makes excellent reading for anyone designing an editor, whether he or she intends to build it by hand or to use either this particular system or any other editor-generator. The book may also be useful supplementary reading for an advanced course on compilers.

This book is a very interesting account of a major piece of research in interactive programming environments. This research has developed into a powerful software tool for generating customized editors which is available commercially and for research.

The authors intend the reference manual to be the defining document for the Synthesizer Generator; it contains the technical documentation for the user of the system. As a specification, it would also be of interest to anyone designing an editor-generator. It gives a shorter account than the other book and omits the tutorial material and the discussion of design philosophy and implementation technicalities.

—*Julia Dain*, Warwick, UK

## D.4  Operating Systems

### D.4.0  General

FINKEL, RAPHAEL A. (Univ. of Wisconsin, Madison)  HCI-0025
**An operating systems vade mecum: 2nd edition.**
Prentice-Hall, Inc., Englewood Cliffs, NJ, 1988, 385 pp., $42, ISBN 0-13-637950-8.

This book is a text for a first course in operating systems. It differs from other such books in that the design of an operating system is developed from two principles, resource management and beautification (hiding the details of the hardware from the user). For example, the chapters on job control and memory management discuss the algorithms involved as exemplifying the principle of managing resources (time and space, respectively), and the chapters on input/output, file structures, the user interface, and concurrency control constructs emphasize aspects of the beautification principle. This organization unifies the seemingly disparate aspects of an operating system into a coherent whole. Other texts approach the topics in similar fashion, but none so directly.

This is perhaps the greatest strength of the book: the presentation is clear, direct, and in most cases deep. The treatment of several topics exemplifies this. The job scheduling algorithms are described with examples, and for many of them results from queueing theory are used to discuss their properties (although the formulae are not derived, which is not surprising since this is not a book on that theory). Eleven different language-based and hardware-based concurrency control mechanisms are described, each with an example; the higher-level constructs are used to solve either the readers-writers problem or the bounded-buffer problem, to show how they work; this makes comparisons of the constructs fairly simple. The discussion on the lowest levels of device drivers is superb.

Unfortunately, the book suffers from two weaknesses, one minor and one major. The minor one is that the author at times eschews conventional terminology and supplies his own. As he writes in the introduction, "I have striven to use a consistent nomenclature throughout the book" (p. xiii). Nonetheless, I wish he had also indicated the generally accepted terms.

The major failing is that certain topics are skimmed or omitted entirely. In some cases, these topics could be used to exemplify the thematic principles of the book; for example, although the discussion on interprocess communication is quite good, the author never mentions the higher-level interface provided by remote procedure calls that can be used to hide the details of the more primitive interprocess communication constructs from the user (the beautification principle). The discussion of networks is cursory and at a high level; no coverage of network layering or any of the standard network models is presented, again missing a chance to explore another application of both principles and provide a firmer basis for the discussion of distributed computing. These shortcomings are offset by the reference sections at the end of each chapter, and by the ability of a teacher to supplement the text with additional explanations and materials in class. The exercises reinforce the text very well, and in some cases entice the student to explore matters only hinted at or omitted entirely—something the best texts do.

Compared to other textbooks, it is more compact and incisive, but somewhat lacking in comprehensiveness. In the next edition I hope the author expands his coverage of networking and distributed systems somewhat; this will make the text much better than any I have seen yet. As it stands now, supplemented with additional reading, it would be an excellent general text on operating systems for a class.

—*Matt Bishop,* Hanover, NH

ELLZEY, ROY S.
**Computer systems software: the programmer/machine interface.**
Science Research Associates, Inc., Chicago, IL, 1986, 274 pp., $27, ISBN 0-574-21965-X.

This 1987 update of a book originally published in 1974 appears to retain most of its 1974 organization and emphasis. Using a subset of IBM 370 assembly language as a grounding to reality, the 274-page text manages to hit high points of sample architectures for (1) von Neumann computers, (2) assemblers, (3) loaders and linkers, (4) compilers and interpreters, and (5) operating systems. Each has one chapter. Of course, at this pace there is little hope of any reasonable level of detail to give these architectures some flesh. For example, the concept of cache memory gets one paragraph.

I would not use this text in my computer architecture course because it lacks many important contemporary architectural concepts. For example, object-oriented architectures are completely absent, as are fourth-generation languages, parallel architectures, the C language, any integration of microcomputer examples, and mentions of modern architectural standards. Instead, there are references to the Motorola 6502, IBM's OS/MVT, and absolute loaders. Where the text has been updated, it often adds a sentence or two noting new concepts but fails to integrate them. I also suspect that a typical undergraduate would find a blizzard of concepts (understandable when trying to cover this much ground in one book) without finding strong threads of continuity other than the sporadic assembly language examples.

Each chapter has a few questions at the end. The first questions test understanding of the technical terms introduced in the chapter; the last ones ask the student to extrapolate to one additional level of detail.

I wonder whether any text that attempts to cover so much disparate material could do so in a satisfying way. But in any case, I would rather see one that emphasizes contemporary concepts in proportion to our present-day understanding of their importance.

—*Glenn Ricart,* College Park, MD

## UNIX

BACH, MAURICE J. (AT&T Bell Laboratories, Murray Hill, NJ)
**The design of the UNIX operating system.**
Prentice-Hall, Inc., Englewood Cliffs, NJ, 1986, 471 pp., $31.95, ISBN 0-13-201799-7.
[Prentice-Hall software series.]

Advertised as the *"first ever* to document the sophisticated workings of the UNIX kernel," this book provides a readable introduction to UNIX system internals. In the Preface, the author states that the book originated in a course that he taught at AT&T Bell Laboratories; it is, therefore, no surprise that the book is ideally structured for use in a classroom environment.

Chapters 1 and 2 present an overview of the UNIX operating system and a short discussion of the internal structure. The rest of the book divides into three parts: Chapters 3–5—The File System; Chapters 6–9—Process Control; and Chapters 10–13—Advanced Topics. Each part is broken down into discussions on the logical flow of the various algorithms used in the system, with a description of how they interact with each other. The algorithms are presented in a C-like pseudocode that I found easy to read and understand. Small C programs are also provided as examples of how various system calls are used. Finally, each chapter ends with a collection of exercises, including some that are "exploratory in nature, designed for investigation as a research problem."

It is the discussion of interactions between different parts of the operating system that I found to be the most interesting. Without getting into hardware-specific issues, or "exposing" AT&T's copyrighted source to the non-licensed public, the author shows how different algorithms have been used and modified to support context switching, scheduling of priorities, interrupt handling, etc., and warns of potentially wrong assumptions about these interactions.

Because of its structured format, large bibliography, and complete index, this book will also be a valuable addition to any reference library. Below is a chapter-by-chapter outline of the contents.

(1) *General Overview of the System*—History, System Structure, User Perspective, Operating System Services, Assumptions about Hardware, Summary.

(2) *Introduction to the Kernel*—Architecture of the UNIX Operating System, Introduction to System Concepts, Kernel Data Structures, System Administration, Summary and Preview, Exercises.

(3) *The Buffer Cache*—Buffer Headers, Structure of the Buffer Pool, Scenarios for Retrieval of a Buffer, Reading and Writing Disk Blocks, Advantages and Disadvantages of the Buffer Cache, Summary, Exercises.

(4) *Internal Representation of Files*—Inodes, Structure of a Regular File, Directories, Conversion of a Path Name to an Inode, Super Block, Inode Assignment to a New File, Allocation of Disk Blocks, Other File Types, Summary, Exercises.

(5) *System Calls for the File System*—Open, Read, Write, File and Record Locking, Adjusting the Position of File I/O—LSEEK, Close, File Creation, Creation of Special Files, Change Directory and Change Root, Change Owner and Change Mode, Stat and Fstat, Pipes, DUP, Mounting and Unmounting File Systems, Link, Unlink, File System Abstractions, File System Maintenance, Summary, Exercises.

(6) *The Structure of Processes*—Process States and Transitions, Layout of System Memory, The Context of a Process, Saving the Context of a Process, Manipulation of the Process Address Space, Sleep, Summary, Exercises.

(7) *Process Control*—Process Creation, Signals, Process Termination, Awaiting Process Termination, Invoking Other Programs, The User ID of a Process, The Shell, System Boot and the Init Process, Summary, Exercises.

(8) *Process Scheduling and Time*—Process Scheduling, Systems Calls for Time, Clock, Summary, Exercises.

(9) *Memory Management Policies*—Swapping, Demand Paging, A Hybrid System with Swapping and Demand Paging, Summary, Exercises.

(10) *The I/O System*—Driver Interfaces, Disk Drivers, Terminal Drivers, Streams, Summary, Exercises.

(11) *Interprocess Communication*—Process Tracing, System V IPC, Network Communications, Sockets, Summary, Exercises.

(12) *Multiprocessor Systems*—Problem of Multiprocessor Systems, Solution with Master and Slave Processors, Solution with Semaphores, The Tunis System, Performance Limitations, Exercises.

(13) *Distributed UNIX Systems*—Satellite Processors, The Newcastle Connection, Transparent Distributed File Systems, A Transparent Distributed Model without Stub Processes, Summary, Exercises.

Also included is an appendix on System Calls, a Bibliography, and an Index.

—*R. E. Van Cleef*, Campbell, CA


ARTHUR, LOWELL J.
**UNIX shell programming.**
Wiley-Interscience, New York, NY, 1986, 261 pp., $22.95, ISBN 0-471-83900-0; Hardcover, $29.95, ISBN: 0-471-84932-4.

The author states in the preface that "this book is not designed for the novice UNIX user; I would recommend reading any of the excellent introduction-to-UNIX books before tackling this one. Anyone with some experience, however, should find the material easy to read, with sufficient examples to get hooked on the UNIX shell. I wrote this book for people who want to get the most out of their UNIX system. . . . "

The book contains the following chapters:

(1) Introduction to the UNIX Shell
(2) Shell Commands
(3) Shell Control Structures
(4) Interactive Shell Usage
(5) Shell Programming
(6) Microcomputer Shell Programming
(7) User Friendly Interfaces
(8) Advanced Shell Programming
(9) Handling Documents
(10) The Shell and C-Language Programming
(11) Working with Numbers
(12) UNIX System Administration

Even though I am not an experienced UNIX user, I found the book easy to read and follow. It has a good summary at the end of each chapter. Even though the book is not advertised as a text, it has exercises at the end of each chapter. The author has made good use of examples and illustrations. The book has a chapter on Microcomputer Shell Programming that is rather shallow and useless. Outside of that, I found the book useful and easy to understand.

—*Santosh Chokani*, Arlington, VA

## VM/CMS

CHASE, PAUL (Univ. of California, Berkeley)
**VM/CMS: a user's guide.**
John Wiley & Sons, Inc., New York, NY, 1989, 466 pp., $29.95, ISBN 0-471-50170-0.

VM/CMS is an interactive, screen-oriented, multiuser operating system available for a range of IBM computers from minis to the 3090 supercomputer. A quote from the preface of this user's guide describes the target audience: "This book presents the material that anyone learning VM/CMS needs for a comprehensive understanding of how to accomplish tasks with VM/CMS and how the system works." The scope of the book is restricted to the VM/CMS operating system, which includes the XEDIT screen editor and the commands for managing disk files, communicating with other users, and using virtual devices. The book describes VM/CMS up through Release 5, but it does not cover application software, such as database management with SQL/DS or programming with languages such as FORTRAN or COBOL.

A list of the chapter titles further reveals the contents of the book:

(1) A Conceptual Overview of VM/CMS
(2) Accessing and Leaving VM/CMS
(3) Becoming Acquainted with VM/CMS
(4) CMS Disks and CMS Disk Files
(5) Becoming Acquainted with XEDIT
(6) Performing Common Editing Tasks with XEDIT
(7) Special Topics in XEDIT
(8) Customizing the XEDIT Environment
(9) Working with Disk Files
(10) Managing Disk Files
(11) Communicating with Other Computer Users
(12) Managing Your Virtual Machine
(13) Virtual Devices and Spooling
(14) Customizing the CP/CMS Environment
(15) Diagnosing and Correcting Problems

A number of features enhance the value of the book. The first chapter provides a concise overview of the functions of an operating system and the distinction between a virtual and a real machine. Every chapter begins with a one-page introduction that summarizes the contents of the chapter (in lieu of a review at the end of the chapter). Every page of the text is labeled either *First Reading* (at least 80 percent of the pages) or *Second Reading*, which indicates whether the material is essential for a basic understanding of the system. The exercises interspersed throughout the text make it valuable as a VM/CMS tutorial. I found that the book's diagrams of the various screens made for a smoother transition to using the system at a terminal. The varying type fonts and ample use of white space make the text visually appealing.

The book includes neither a glossary of terms nor a command summary, but the author provides an extensive index. This index appears to be fairly comprehensive, although I could not find an entry for the FILEDEF command referred to on page 370. Most of the few typographical errors I found appeared in the last third of the text. The preface includes an annotated list of the system documentation available from IBM that is most relevant to this book.

The author accomplishes his purpose of providing a gentle and comprehensive introduction to the VM/CMS system. I am familiar with a variety of operating systems, but I had never used VM/CMS before. By systematically working through the book I was able to use the system effectively—by creating and editing files with XEDIT, managing disk files, and using the electronic mail facility. It is often difficult to evaluate a book like this without also evaluating the system it describes; in this case, however, I give a much higher recommendation to the book than to the system.

—*S. K. Andrianoff*, St. Bonaventure, NY

## XINU

COMER, DOUGLAS (Purdue Univ., West Lafayette, IN; and AT&T Bell Labs, Murray Hill, NJ); AND FOSSUM, TIMOTHY V. (Univ. of Wisconsin-Parkside, Kenosha)
**Operating system design. Vol. 1: the XINU approach (PC edition).**
Prentice-Hall, Inc., Englewood Cliffs, NJ, 1988, 504 pp., $48, ISBN 0-13-638180-4.

Starting from the idea that operating systems should be taught in a practical way that attempts to get students actively involved in the concrete design and implementation of a complete system, the authors present a basic pattern for the development of a real operating system. This pattern includes a description of the main concepts and a guideline for the systematic realization of the components together with their interaction in a final configuration. The authors illustrate the development by means of PC-XINU, a UNIX-like operating system that was originally written for an LSI-11 and later ported to an Intel 8088 in an improved and extended version. (The folklore includes versions of XINU, written by students, for other processors.) PC-XINU has about 8K lines of code (mostly C with some assembler) and can be obtained from the authors for a moderate price ($79.95). The authors assume that most students have ready access to an MS-DOS PC on which to run the system for exercises. The book is aimed at advanced undergraduates or graduate students.

As in the first edition (published in 1983), the first part of the text (chapters 1–13) describes a minimal system on which simple applications can be run. The components include storage and processor management, synchronization and communication primitives, terminal I/O, and clock management. The PC is not well suited for multitasking; for compatibility reasons, the authors have chosen to use the usual PC Basic I/O System instead of handling hardware I/O in a direct and more efficient way. Chapters 14–18 are more specifically tuned to the PC in providing, for example, simple window and XINU file management, including an interface to MS-DOS files. Chapters 19 and 20 discuss further system utilities and support for putting PC-XINU on differently configured systems. The authors intend to provide a discussion of networks and the integration of protocol software in volume 2.

## BOOKS & PROCEEDINGS

The presentation of subjects is rather detailed and straightforward, and the idea of a coherent system development dominates. In several programs, comments would have been helpful. The authors rarely discuss alternatives and options in the design process; they relegate some options to the exercises. More positively, the chapters conclude not only with exercises, most of them practical, but also with some suggestions for further reading. The layout shows great care and experience. The structure of the PC-XINU programmer's manual follows that of "real UNIX," as does the denotation of system calls.

This text will be very valuable for an introductory, project-oriented operating systems course. It could also be a good companion text even for more research-oriented instructors.

—*A. B. Cremers,* Dortmund, W. Germany

### D.4.7 Organization and Design

*Interactive systems*

BIGGERSTAFF, TED J. (Microelectronics and Computer Technology Corporation, Austin, TX)                    HCI-0030
**Systems software tools.**
Prentice-Hall, Inc., Englewood Cliffs, NJ, 1986, 317 pp., $28.95, ISBN 0-13-881772-3.

This is a fine book for a hacker who wants to learn more about his IBM PC. It describes two sophisticated example programs: the smart terminal emulator and the virtual terminal window package, the first being preparatory to the second. After a short introductory chapter, there is an outline of the language C. Its purpose is unclear; this may be due to the presentation of some (though not all) C declarations translated into pidgin English. The reader who knows standard C will not learn the particulars of C86. Common programming language constructs (if, block, etc.) are described instead of C library support. Fluency with C is required anyway.

Similarly, Chapter 3 lists OS calls and gives an assembly routine to access them, with examples of keyboard and screen handling. A huge background knowledge (including 8086 chip, 8086 assembler, IBM PC internals, and MS DOS principles) is required.

In the following chapter, 8259A PIC and 8250 UART chips are described extensively, together with the RS-232C interface. This is the only self-contained material, enclosing even more information than is needed by following chapters. It was certainly added later (many remarks in Chapter 5 should have been changed afterwards). It is relatively straightforward then to complete the program in Chapter 5.

The remaining four chapters describe the second example. It lacks a diagram of overall data and control flow and call hierarchy. With over 70 subroutines (also assembly and never returning ones), it is far too complex for a reader to intuit.

The ten pages of Chapter 6 are too much for a reminder of OS concepts, but too little for the reader to learn them.

The boundary between Chapters 7 (Overview) and 8 (Multitasking Package) is somewhat artificial (there are not even any exercises at the end of Chapter 7). The author buries himself in details of loading a program, particular to MS DOS. Finally, Chapter 9 presents the window management module.

There are exercises in almost every chapter (a total of over two dozen) complementing the programs. In the first part, they have time estimates (5 to 10 months together). The reader needs to have much extra knowledge to solve some of the exercises.

Two Appendices collect almost all the "#include" files used in the second example. Hardly any names of variables are listed in the index, although subroutines are. There's no bibliography, only footnotes (referring mostly to IBM materials) scattered within the book.

The programs presented were not rewritten for publication, but left as they were written for the first time by the author: many variables are declared but not used; there is inconsistency in the use of "ext" declarations; clumsy C code; defined macros are not used; function headers are not unified; index and appendices are inconsistent; and so on. Only in the later chapters has the author decided to edit out trace statements, which are not discussed in the text.

The author avows that he didn't check the particulars of MS DOS, on top of which his programs are built. The code is not written in a structural manner; sometimes it is strange, ineffective, or not in perspective.

Was the material tested with real students? There are bugs in what appear to be printouts of programs: misprints, inappropriate constants and procedure calls, and disagreement with documentation. I have not had the opportunity to test the accompanying diskette; I hope the programs are runable there.

Another annoyance is the editorial side of the book. I don't mean the dozen or so typos, but, for example, the variations in font size in listings: the larger (and more important) a procedure, the smaller the letters. On (very frequent) multipage figures, you have to turn a page over to read the titles or to find that it continues overleaf. The index is impossible to search through: multicolumn and multipage subtopics are listed under general terms with indentation only (without any kind of marker in front of them) in a way that successfully confuses the reader. Most entrants are listed also under their proper names (the index is therefore twice as long as it need be). The definitions are not emphasized among usage occurrences.

The order of presentation should be changed, as related concepts are not presented in successive paragraphs, but throughout the text, as the need arises. Several chapters should be coalesced. A dozen topics are used heavily before actual definitions are given (if any). Assembly language procedures are not commented on as thoroughly as C ones.

The word "system," without a qualifying adjective, means completely nothing; this book is only about virtual terminals. I expected base-building blocks creating an envelope environment to conduct various experiments or write production software. Instead, only two rudimentary programs are presented, without a variety of examples illustrating every basic principle. It can't even run under itself; I prefer to read the C code of a more ambitious book [1].

The author states that "people learn best by doing." What am I supposed to build with these tools? Am I supposed to add remaining code (solving exercises)? Or to buy the accompanying $50 diskette with a program far inferior to GEM (I expect the exercises are solved on diskettes)? As a "lab book" it lacks both exercises extending the material and a bibliography for further study.

The book presents no sharp, polished image. Instead, it appears to be "in transit."

Nevertheless, this book presents a large amount of algorithmic details about multiprocessing, communications, and display management. The programs are written without "clever use of tricks," step-by-step, moreover, in an HLL language; so the reader has no difficulty in following its logic. Is it suitable for use in everyday programming? I regret to think that probably the inclusion of windows into OSs for modern PCs will exempt programmers from the necessity of doing it all again themselves.

—*J. Klaczak,* Katowice, Poland

**REFERENCES**

[1] GAMMIL, R.; AND PRITHVI, R. VT—virtual terminal window package for UNIX, *ACM SIGPC Newsletter* (May 1984), p. 21.

KEARSLEY, GREG (Park Row Software)     **HCI-0031**
**Authoring: a guide to the design of instructional software.**
Addison-Wesley Publ. Co., Inc., Reading, MA, 1986, 100 pp., $10.95, ISBN 0-201-11731-2.

The author states in the Preface: "This is not a how-to book. It does not tell you the steps to follow in order to create good instructional programs. It is a style guide that tells you what principles to follow and what to avoid."

In the reviewer's opinion, the book is indeed a style guide on user interfaces. However, the problem of a good interface is common to all applications programs, and it is hard to distinguish, at least in this book, what makes instructional programs different from other programs. In fact, a conceptual model of an instructional program is never presented, except for a simple example of lesson synopsis on p. 25. Another example shown on p. 17 is misleading because it associates a flow diagram with a throttle and a dial, leaving the reader with the impression that it is straightforward to transform numbers into stickshift and dial positions.

An expert on instructional programs might catch some ideas on how to improve the quality of his or her work by glancing quickly through the 100 pages of this book.

—*D. P. Bovet,* Rome, Italy

### D.4.9 Systems Programs and Utilities

*Command and control languages*

BEECH, DAVID (Hewlett-Packard Laboratories, Palo Alto, CA) (ED.)     **HCI-0032**
**Concepts in user interfaces: a reference model for command and response languages.**
Springer-Verlag New York, Inc., New York, NY, 1986, 116 pp., $14.30, ISBN 0-387-16791-9; By members of IFIP Working Group 2.7. [Lecture notes in computer science; no. 234.]

The art of designing command languages for interactive systems lags by at least a decade behind the state-of-the-art in programming languages. As no widely accepted concepts are existing, today's command languages tend to give the appearance of ad hoc collections of individual commands, rather than of structures designed according to general principles. Thus, all efforts toward a more systematic approach regarding the design and implementation of interactive systems are important and highly welcome. The editor's intention goes in this direction: In the Preface, he states "The present document attempts to identify and describe some appropriate concepts, and put them together in the form of an abstract model which should serve as a useful reference for anyone interested in obtaining a better understanding or bringing about improvements in this area." The book is thus quite relevant. We only have to assess whether this goal has been achieved.

The present document has been constructed by IFIP Working Group 2.7 (founded in 1975). The report is structured into 13 chapters; two appendices define the metalanguage of the document. Being active in the field of interactive systems for many years, I was eager to compare the proposed model with a couple of interactive systems implemented in my environment. After reading the Introduction (Chapter 1), I agreed with the outline of the next two chapters: first provide an overview of the Reference Model (Chapter 2) and then illustrate how a designer might apply the model (Chapter 3). Indeed, Chapter 2 presents a framework; however, to my surprise, it is a framework for the implementation part. Access Points, Transmitter, CRLProcessor, UserManager, Protector, etc., are entities useful to explain the main structure of an interactive system from the implementation point of view. As "the model is offered as an aid to anyone studying or comparing existing command and response languages" (p. 1), I expected to read more about commands ("a form of input which may cause the generation of one or more macros, a change in the state of the system, or both" (p. 2)), response, macros, etc. So I put all my hope on Chapters 6 to 8. The examples in Chapter 3 were a little bit disappointing: Is the login command this important in today's powerful work stations? In the Copy $(A,B)$ example, if $A$ is not existing I don't want to type in $B$ as suggested in the second example. The next two chapters (4 and 5) and Chapters 9 through 13 concentrate on problems typically found in multiuser timesharing systems. Finally, Chapters 6 to 8 refer to the parts with the most direct influence to the user of a system. "The Customizer performs the transformations of user generated input into sequences of commands" (p. 42). The list of functional requirements is interesting and outlines the importance of such a component. However, the model remains rather vague in defining two operations. (DeriveCommand, CustomizeResponse). The same holds for Helper and History. For instance, on p. 47, the author states, "Normal completion of help dialogue returns to the state in which help was thought." I would like to see formal definitions here. However, these chapters remain rather informal.

Let me conclude here. The document reflects the fact that the committee started work in the 1970s, a time when large multiuser timesharing environments had been dominant. The document clearly aids in the implementation of new multiuser systems. On the other hand, certain key elements, such as Customization, Help, and History, need more refinement in order to be useful for a designer of a modern command language. I liked the Functional Requirements spread all over the document; they once more clearly outline the complexity of this topic. I am sure the committee has, by this document, stimulated further work in this direction. As the Reference Model was discussed at a recent conference, I recommend that the potential reader study the proceedings [1].

—*H. Burkhart,* Basel, Switzerland

**REFERENCES**

[1] HOPPER, K.; AND NEWMAN, I. A. (EDS.) *Foundation for human-computer communication*, Proc. of the IFIP working conference (Rome, Italy, 1985), Elsevier North-Holland, New York, 1986.

# E. DATA

## E.4 Coding and Information Theory

WELSH, DOMINIC (Merton College and the Mathematical Institute, Oxford Univ., Oxford, UK)     **HCI-0033**
**Codes and cryptography.**
Clarendon, New York, NY, 1988, 257 pp., $32.50, ISBN 0-19-853287-3.

This delightful introduction to coding theory and cryptography does an admirable job of reporting on the frontiers of current research in cryptography and related areas while remaining at the mathematical level of an undergraduate textbook. Despite the absence of elaborate mathematical machinery, the book manages to be precise and concise and at the same time provide insight into and motivation for the material it presents. The writing is lucid and stimulating. The book is suitable for a wide range of audiences, from advanced undergraduate and graduate students of mathematics, computer science, and electrical and computer engineering, to researchers in areas related to coding theory and cryptography, to professionals who simply want an easy-to-understand and readable, yet correct and precise, overview of and introduction to these fields. I recommend it without reservation.

    The book is organized into 13 chapters. The first five are devoted to coding theory proper, and the last seven cover the more important aspects of cryptography. Chapter 6, on the structure of natural languages, serves as a link between the two parts. More specifically, the first chapter sets the stage by introducing the key concepts of entropy, uncertainty, and information. The second chapter presents the noiseless coding theorem for memoryless sources and introduces various codes. The third chapter introduces the problem of communicating via a noisy channel, and the fourth chapter provides one solution by introducing error-correcting codes. The fifth chapter outlines a theory of general sources, including entropy and ergodicity. The sixth chapter discusses entropy and redundancy as applied to natural languages and leads to the second part of the book. Chapter 7 introduces classical (symmetric) encryption methods along with some general foundations of cryptography, and chapter 8 discusses Vernam's one-time pad, linear shift-register sequences, and cyclic codes. Since the book aims to be self-contained except for some background in rather elementary mathematics and probability theory, chapter 9 gives a very readable sketch of computational complexity (but omits many proofs). Chapter 10 introduces one-way functions and discusses several approaches to obtaining them, including DES, discrete logarithms, and factoring. Chapter 11 introduces asymmetric or public-key cryptography and discusses the RSA implementation and Rabin's approach (both based on factoring) and systems based on the discrete logarithm and on error-correcting codes; this discussion is reasonably precise but emphasizes intuition. This chapter also gives a post mortem on knapsack-based systems (without proofs). Chapter 12 covers authentication schemes and digital signatures, while the last chapter introduces current work on randomized encryption (again without proofs).

My only quibble is that the book was edited rather carelessly; while none of them are serious, I encountered ten misprints or errors without looking for them specifically. Also, there is no reference to Kraft's inequality (see pp. 17–18), and the reference 'Oxford, 1986' on page 25 is missing from the bibliography. Finally, I found the numbering of theorems very confusing: the same theorem is referenced differently within a section, in a different section of the same chapter, and in different chapters. The numbering of the exercises and the corresponding answers and hints suffers from the same problem. I hope the publisher will take advantage of a reprinting or second edition (which I expect) to eliminate these small imperfections in an otherwise very impressive and highly recommendable book.

—*E. Leiss*, Houston, TX

# F. THEORY OF COMPUTATION

## F.1 Computation by Abstract Devices

### F.1.1 Models of Computation

ARBIB, MICHAEL A. (Univ. of Southern California, Los Angeles)
**Brains, machines, and mathematics (2nd ed.).**
Springer-Verlag New York, Inc., New York, NY, 1987, 202 pp., $27, ISBN 0-387-96539-4.

The second edition of *Brains, machines, and mathematics* follows the first edition by 23 years. This has been a complex time in the areas addressed by this book; paradigms have come and gone or changed substantially. Although the purpose of this latest monograph is not to be a chronicle of those events, some of the shifts of direction are inextricably linked to the topics of the book, and several of them are discussed explicitly. The purpose of the book is to provide an update on the topics of the first edition and to discuss salient and common features of brains, machines, and mathematics. There are few who could undertake a project of this nature and bring more experience and competence to the task than Michael Arbib. Original references that he has written or coauthored are cited at the end of each chapter.

This book is most accessible to those having a reasonable knowledge of set theory, predicate calculus, and partial differential equations. Set theory is accorded a brief appendix, and predicate calculus is given a brief review, but there is no similar aid for the encounter with partial differential equations in the chapter on learning networks. For those without a background in these areas, some details will remain obscure; but some of the discussions and general ideas will nonetheless be understandable without major difficulty.

Changes from the first edition include a diminution of the space directly devoted to cybernetics, although its dissolution to other areas is discussed briefly. The material on the correction of errors in communication and computation, including Shannon's communication theory and his fundamental theorem for a discrete noisy channel, has been eliminated. In the second edition a short chapter on historical perspective has been added, there is a briefer version of the material on neural nets and finite automata in chapter 2, and the material on feedback and pattern recognition has been reorganized. There are also entire new chapters on learning networks (chapter 5), Turing machines and effective computations (chapter 6), and automata that construct (and can self-reproduce) as well as compute (chapter 7). Both editions end with a chapter on Gödel's incompleteness theorem (chapter 5 in the first edition, and chapter 8 in the second edition). These chapters end with a persuasive discussion of the mind-machine controversy, in which Arbib espouses his philosophy that Gödel's work is as limiting for brains (minds) as it is for machines. Scriven's contributions are quoted and acknowledged in the first edition, but are not mentioned in the second (although Arbib's philosophy, which is described in considerable detail, seems to be the same as his).

Some specific comments about the second edition follow. Chapter 2, which covers neural nets and finite automata, and chapter 3, which covers feedback and realization, are quite brief and omit much relevant material that could have been included. Nevertheless, the material selected is definitional, with just enough suggestion as to its applicability for later use. Chapter 4, on pattern recognition, is somewhat more inclusive, although the topics are severely restricted to the direct goals of the monograph, as expected. The discussion of perceptrons includes the work of Minsky and Papert [1], which Arbib puts in proper perspective. The work of Winograd [2], Spira [3], and Spira and Arbib [4] on computation times is also discussed, providing insights not available in other monographs known to me. The discussion on connectionism in chapter 5 begins with a suitable motivation from biological systems and some simple examples from the recent literature (cf. [5,6]). Current topics discussed (albeit very briefly) include synaptic matrices, which provide for distributed, associative memory, and autoassociative nets, which have a continuous output, with the output fed back to the input. Hopfield nets and Boltzmann machines are also discussed, and the concepts of hidden units and energy are introduced. Learning is introduced using the Hebb rule and Francis Crick's suggestion to prevent saturation of synaptic weights. Back-propagation is also introduced as a paradigm for learning, with an associated convergence theorem. The descriptions of connectionist models are extremely brief but are sufficient to impart some of the major concepts. Chapters 6 and 7 cover topics that are more foundational than current (Turing machines and automata, respectively), but that nevertheless contribute to the overall objectives of the monograph by providing support for the discussion of Gödel's work and the brain-machine controversy in chapter 8. For those desiring more detailed expositions of the material in this monograph, Arbib has authored or coauthored five other recent and relevant books (for example, see [7]). Relationships between this monograph and those books are discussed briefly in the preface to the second edition.

In summary, this monograph is a brief but wide-reaching exposition of some important issues in brain theory (and of artificial intelligence, in a fundamental sense) and the association between brain theory and machines. Its scope is surprising in light of its brevity. It provides suitable introductions to several areas important to the modeling of brains, and it delineates some of the research issues involved.

—*D.W. Dearholt*, Las Cruces, NM

**REFERENCES**

[1] MINSKY, M. L., AND PAPERT, S. *Perceptrons: An Essay in Computational Geometry.* The MIT Press, Cambridge, MA, 1969.

[2] WINOGRAD, S. On the time required to perform multiplication. *J. ACM* **14**, 4 (1967), 798–802. See *Computing Reviews* **9**, 5 (May 1968), Rev. 14,376.

[3] SPIRA, P. M. The time required for group multiplication. *J. ACM* **16** (1969), 235–243. See *Computing Reviews* **10**, 11 (Nov. 1969), Rev. 17,920.

[4] SPIRA, P. M. AND ARBIB, M. A. Computation times for finite groups, semigroups and automata. In *Proceedings of the IEEE 8th Annual Symposium on Switching and Automata Theory.* (1967) 291–295.

[5] RUMELHART, D., AND MCCLELLAND, J. (Eds.) *Parallel distributed processing: explorations in the microstructure of cognition.* The MIT Press/Bradford Books, Cambridge, MA, 1986.

[6] MCCLELLAND, J. L., AND RUMELHART, D. E. An interactive activation model of context effects in letter perception: Part 1. An account of basic findings. *Psych. Rev.* **88**, (1981), 375–407.

[7] ARBIB, M. A. *Computers and the cybernetic society.* Academic Press, Orlando, FL, 1984.

## *Statistical computing*

CLEVELAND, WILLIAM S. (AT&T Bell Laboratories)
**The elements of graphing data.**
Wadsworth Publ. Co., Inc., Belmont, CA, 1985, 323 pp., $18.95, ISBN 0-534-03730-5.

Good science depends upon clear communication. For that reason, many computer scientists keep works such as Fowler's *Modern English Usage* and Strunk and White's *The Elements of Style* close at hand. *The Elements of Graphing Data* belongs on the same shelf, for the same reason.

Although Cleveland's book has essentially nothing to do with computer graphics *per se*, computer scientists should be interested in graphing data for three reasons. First, using graphical displays to convey quantitative information is one of the dominant applications of computer graphics. Second, the ways in which information can be effectively encoded and conveyed graphically is fundamental to the development of modern computing environments. Third, the graphical presentation of research results or of computations is an important element in clear communication.

The author effectively demonstrates the appallingly low quality of graphical displays in prestigious scientific publications. "Low quality" here does not mean aesthetically unattractive. Rather, it means that fundamental information contained in the graph either cannot be extracted or cannot be perceived accurately. What distinguishes the author's work from that of others who criticize graphical practice is that he systematically shows how each graph can be improved. In the process, he often makes it simpler, clearer, and more clearly to the point.

After an introductory first chapter, the author devotes his second chapter to enunciating and illustrating a series of principles for constructing graphs. This chapter could be read with profit by anyone whose work involves writing about quantitative information. These principles provide a context in which it is possible to focus on the primary message of a graph and to assess whether aspects of the display are interfering with that message. The chapter makes it clear that constructing a good graph is at least as much work as constructing a good paragraph, and the rewards for doing so are commensurate.

Chapter 3 deals with graphical methods, that is, about kinds of graphs and their relative strengths in making assessment of the information they encode more accurate. For example, a new kind of graph, the dot chart, is described; the dot chart can effectively replace such tired and ineffective displays as bar charts and pie charts. A major theme is the question of how graphs can be used to highlight comparisons of a set of measurements to either a standard or to another set of measurements. Many of the recommendations in this chapter are simply the author's opinion. Nonetheless, his opinions are strikingly good ones, and they have the virtue of stemming from a theoretical framework which is coherent, if imperfect.

Of what use might this material be? Among his many examples, the author considers graphing the results of an experiment concerning a bin-packing algorithm whose asymptotic average-case behavior is known [1]. At what point does asymptopia set in? How well do the asymptotics describe the behavior for small problems? How much variability is there about the average-case behavior? Good graphs help to display these things clearly, and, consequently, they lead to better understanding of the algorithm and its applicability.

The author's final chapter on a theory (or paradigm) for graphical perception is the most ambitious of the four, yet it is the least successful. Although the conclusions are plausible, the distinctions on which they are based (between perception and cognition, for example) are not clearly made, and important elements of the paradigm are defined only by example. The theory takes little account of multiple perceptions, of possible reinforcement or interaction between elements of a graph, and of the representation of multivariate information. As the author himself correctly claims, however, his paradigm represents an initial context which can serve as a framework within which predictions can be made, hypotheses tested, and theories revised.

This is an admirable book. It is clearly written and intellectually engaging. Reading it can only make the eye more critical and scientific communication more effective.

—*R. A. Thisted,* Chicago, IL

**REFERENCES**

[1] BENTLEY, J. C.; JOHNSON, D.; LEIGHTON, F.; MCGEOCH, C.; AND MCGEOCH, L. Some unexpected behavior results for bin packing, in *Proc. 16th annual symposium on theory of computing* (Washington, D.C., April 30–May 2, 1984), ACM, New York, 1984, 279–288.

# H. INFORMATION SYSTEMS

## H.1 Models and Principles

### H.1.1 Systems and Information Theory

MACHLUP, FRITZ; AND MANSFIELD, UNA (Princeton Univ., Princeton, NJ) (EDS.)     **HCI-0036**
**The study of information: interdisciplinary messages.**
John Wiley & Sons, Inc., New York, NY, 1983, 743 pp., $44.95, ISBN 0-471-88717-X.

[Papers in this volume have been individually reviewed; each paper is cross-referenced to this main entry to provide complete source and citation data. In this book see Reviews HCI-0185; HCI-0186.]

[The] vast communication industries that have sprung up in this century now bathe every willing citizen in a continuous and unprecedented flow of written, spoken, musical and pictorial messages. . . . Social and economic changes that have accompanied this effusion of communication . . . do clearly signal a New Industrial Revolution.

The Viennese intellectual and economist Fritz Machlup was among those who first recognized and tried to characterize the economic consequences of this revolution. . . . Machlup decided that what he came to call the Knowledge Industry deserved comprehensive description and analysis.

In 1959 and 1960 the economic role of knowledge became the subject of a series of five invited lectures, the first at Cornell, the next four at Fordham. Encouraged by their reception, Machlup expanded the lectures into a book that was published in 1962 by the Princeton University Press: *The Production and Distribution of Knowledge in the United States.* The two longest chapters were IV, entitled Education, and V, Research and Development.

In 1971, when he retired as Walker Professor of Economics and International Finance at Princeton, Machlup decided that he had a moral obligation to update his statistical analysis. . . . [He] undertook an eightfold expansion of the 1962 book: the initial plan was for a series of eight volumes, roughly one volume for each chapter of the earlier book, the whole to be entitled *Knowledge: Its Creation, Distribution, and Economic Significance,* with the Princeton University Press as publisher.

Volume IV was to deal with the information sciences, the remaining part of the originally planned second volume. In preparation, Machlup persuaded 39 information scientists to write a total of 56 essays on their various specialties so that he, in his role as an editor, could go to school under the experts—could "see the stir of the great Babel, and not feel the crowd." The result is the present book, prepared in collaboration with Una Mansfield. It is not Volume IV, of course, but some indications of Machlup's reactions to this heroic exercise can be gathered from the co-authored Prologue and his own Epilogue.

—*From the Foreword by George A. Miller*

## H.1.2  User/Machine Systems

THOMAS, JOHN C. (IBM T. J. Watson Research Center, Yorktown Heights, NY); AND SCHNEIDER, MICHAEL L. (ITT Advanced Technology Center, Shelton, CT) (EDS.)
**Human factors in computer systems.**
Ablex Publishing Corp., Norwood, NJ, 1984, 276 pp., $34.50, ISBN 0-89391-146-1.

It is becoming obvious to more and more people that the tremendous advances in the computer industry in the past decades are heralding a revolution at least as profound as the industrial revolution. Hardware costs have plummeted and now, at least to many of us, the major challenge facing the computer industry is making comuters that are easy to learn and easy to use. In other words, the question is, how can we make computer systems with good human factors?

BOOKS & PROCEEDINGS [HCI-0038]

While much is know about the physical aspects of human factors. . ., relatively little is known about how to write software to maximize its usability. Certainly, given our current state of knowledge, it would be premature to claim that we even know "the" best way to study the problem of software human factors. In this book, therefore, a number of different approaches to various related problems are discussed. . . .

By the intelligent use of graphics and the proper selection of pictures from data banks of video images, entire arrays of data could be presented to people much more quickly than is possible by writing and speaking. We stand on the threshold of a new age brought about by new technology. The extent to which that new age represents progress in human productivity and enjoyment or merely a change of fashion without real progress depends heavily upon the work of investigators such as the ones who contributed to this volume.

—From the Introduction

VASSILIOU, YANNIS (New York Univ., New York) (ED.) **HCI-0038**
**Human factors and interactive computer systems.**
Proc. of the NYU symposium on user interfaces, (New York, May 26-28, 1982), Ablex Publishing Corp., Norwood, NJ,1984, 287 pp., $34.50, ISBN 0-89391-182-8. [Human/computer interaction series.]

[Papers in this volume have been individually reviewed; each paper is cross-referenced to this main entry to provide complete source and citation data. In this book see Reviews HCI-0107; HCI-0133; HCI-0136; HCI-0186; HCI-0230; HCI-0233; HCI-0254; HCI-0255; HCI-0286; HCI-0305.]

In his introductory article to a special issue of *ACM Computing Surveys* [1], Moran made a simplified, yet effective, anaphora to the three distinctly different ways a technologist, a designer, and a cognitive psychologist view the interaction of a user with a computer system. Make no mistake—they all care about the user. Only their approaches to helping the user differ.

Generally, the attitude of the technologist is that system power is the key to successful user-machine interaction. All problems can be handled through sheer system power and flexibility. The system designer,. . .without undermining system power, places more emphasis on the qualitative aspects of the interaction. Often using intuition and common sense, a designer develops a system that appears to meet the user's needs and expectations. Some graphics, elegant menus, helpful system messages—all the obvious things. The system is then termed: "user-friendly." It is only the methodology employed for the determination of user behavior that differentiates the attitude of the designer from that of the cognitive psychologist. As opposed to the designer's use of intuition and common sense (often termed "armchair psychology"), the psychologist employs scientific methods to understand the complexities of user behavior during the interaction with a computer system.

Let us step back for a moment and consider the result of these differing points of view. At first, the problem seems to be that the technologist is not also a psychologist and a designer, or, that the psychologist does not have expertise in building computer systems. However, these are not realistic expectations. Therefore, the key problem is to find a way to do exactly that. A practical solution lies not in creating the "super-developer," but in creating more communication lines between the different disciplines, so that all can benefit from the information exchange and learn from each other. This may imply, for example, that the technologist does not perform a human factors study for the evaluation of a computer system, but works with a psychologist for such a study—the latter has the formal education and expertise.

Such considerations led to the New York University Symposium on User Interfaces. . . . Under the same roof, scientists from three disciplines (in academia and industry), with potential users of computer systems as the audience, had the opportunity to describe their research. The common goal of all the work described was the development of interactive computer systems, which employ advanced technology to meet the needs of an expanding user population, while they remain sensitive to human requirements.

Contributions from leading professionals in such diverse areas as state-of-the-art user interface technology, controlled experimental evaluations of systems, and human factors principles are included in this volume. Topics include recommendations for dialogue design, views of organizations on human factors, graphical and multimedia human-computer interaction, perspectives for the future of interactive systems, and the design of languages for applications in teleconferencing, videotex systems and office automation.

—From the Overview

**REFERENCES**

[1] MORAN, T. P. An applied psychology of the user, *ACM Comput. Surv.* (Special issue: The psychology of human-computer interaction), **13**, 1 (March 1981), 1–11.

VAN DER VEER, G. C. (Vrije Univ. Amsterdam, The Netherlands); TAUBER, MICHAEL J. (IBM Science Center, Heidelberg, West Germany); GREEN, THOMAS R. (MRC Applied Psychology Unit, Cambridge, UK); AND GORNY, PETER (Univ. Oldenburg, Oldenburg, West Germany) (EDS.)
**Readings on cognitive ergonomics - mind and computers.**
Proc. of the 2nd European conference, (Gmunden, Austria, Sept. 10-14, 1984), Springer-Verlag New York, Inc., New York, NY,1984, 269 pp., ISBN 0-387-13394-1. [Lecture notes in computer science 178.]

[Papers in this volume are reviewed individually. In this book see Reviews HCI-0097; HCI-0108; HCI-0164; HCI-0182; HCI-0188; HCI-0241; HCI-0379.]
This book is comprised of papers from the Second European Conference on Cognitive Engineering, held in Gmunden, Austria. Cognitive ergonomics is a hybrid field combining concepts from both computer science and psychology.

This field is an emerging and interesting research area. The proceedings are representative of the issues and methods. The editors examine Models and Methodology, Cognitive Aspects, Software Environments, Novices and Learning, Interfaces in the Field, and Organizations and Systems. Many of the papers describe ongoing research and are closer to working papers documenting accomplishments to date.

Students of cognitive ergonomics and related fields will find the contributions rich in references with very complete bibliographies. Though this reading is classified as part of computer science, it has merit in the disciplines of psychology, decision science, and philosophy.
—*H. N. Dreifus,* Rosemont, PA

SUCHMAN, LUCY A. (Xerox Palo Alto Research Center, Palo Alto, CA)
**Plans and situated actions: the problem of human-machine communication.**
Cambridge University Press, New York, NY, 1987, 203 pp., $34.50, ISBN 0-521-33137-4; ISBN 0-521-33739-9 Paperback $11.95.

This book explains the *situated action model* of purposeful human activity and illustrates its importance in the design of *interactive artifacts*—intelligent machines that interact with people. The situated action model and related theories of purposeful human activity have only recently been gaining widespread attention in the artificial intelligence (AI) and cognitive science communities (see [1]). The situated action model questions the standard AI view, which emphasizes that purposeful actions are largely guided by plans (internal mental models of behaviors used to achieve goals). Instead, the situated action model tries to show that purposeful actions emerge out of essentially ad hoc situated actions (actions taken in the context of particular, concrete circumstances). In the planning model, a plan is the principal basis for actions, but in the situated action model a circumstance is the main resource giving rise to actions. For instance, when a mother is teaching her son to cook a particular dish, compare the relative importance of the recipe (plan) and the moment-to-moment kitchen context (situation) in determining what actions are being performed. Neither model completely denies the importance of the other (preconditions, opportunism, and execution monitoring are context-sensitive aspects of the planning model, while plans and hypotheses about other agents' internal mental states are resources in the situated action model), but where the emphasis is placed is diametrically opposed in the two models.

The book consists of the following eight chapters:

(1) Introduction
(2) Interactive Artifacts
(3) Plans
(4) Situated Actions
(5) Communicative Resources
(6) Case and Methods
(7) Human-machine Communication
(8) Conclusion

Before providing a detailed explanation of the alternative notions of plans and situated actions, Suchman illustrates the practical importance of theories of human action in the context of designing interactive artifacts. As machines become more sophisticated, the need for machines to be able to explain themselves to potential users, to monitor whether users are successfully accomplishing their tasks, and to provide interactive help to users who have problems becomes more and more important. A survey of relevant research on human-human communications in chapter 5 sets the stage for chapters 6 and 7, in which human-machine interactions are discussed. Human-machine interactions are discussed in the context of designing and evaluating an expert help system: a computer-based help system for a large, complex photocopier. Instead of providing the users with lists of instructions (plans) as is commonly done with machines today, an alternative approach was undertaken. In the new approach, the machine was equipped with a video display and sensors of its own internal state, thereby allowing it to become an active, responsive participant in accomplishing a photocopying task.

This book is important for the theoretical perspective it presents as well as for the practical and methodological recommendations it offers for designing and evaluating interactive artifacts. This book should appeal to a wide range of readers, including artificial intelligence researchers, cognitive scientists, linguists, philosophers, and social scientists. System designers grappling with the issues of designing intelligent machines have the most to gain from this work. I was least convinced by the author's arguments about the limitations "in principle" of the existing AI approach in chapters 2 and 3. I most enjoyed her detailed and insightful analysis of the user-machine protocol data in chapter 7.

—*J. Spohrer,* New Haven, CT

**REFERENCES**

[1] WINOGRAD, T., AND FLORES, F. *Understanding computers and cognition: A new foundation for design.* Ablex Publishing Corporation, Norwood, NJ, 1986. See Review HCI-0054.

JONES, MARK S. (Utah State Univ., Logan)
**Human-computer interaction: a design guide.**
Educational Technology Publications, Englewood Cliffs, NJ, 1989, 150 pp., $21.95, ISBN 0-87778-207-5.

Designing computer systems that work with users and are "easy to learn and exciting to use" (from the back cover of the book) is a subtle and challenging task. As the author points out, interface design is essentially a creative act—as much an art as a science—and tends to begin from scratch with each new system. Can the art and the science be distilled and made accessible to designers so that they can make principled, rather than ad hoc, design decisions? Jones intends to do just that:

> My audience is the professional designer of human-computer interfaces. . . . My goal is to bring as much of the knowledge and as many of the exciting ideas in this area together in one accessible volume, with enough detail to provide a basis for selecting which information is relevant to a particular design decision, but not so much as to deter its being used on a regular basis. (p. vii)

Thus, the book is intended to provide both breadth and depth of coverage rather than just a set of guidelines or principles. Given the diversity of the field, this is a difficult task. The author has made it even more challenging by limiting himself to under 100 pages of substantive text, including 22 figures. Unfortunately, the effort is not a complete success. The book is simply too short to accommodate both adequate breadth and supporting details.

The book is organized into an introduction and three main chapters: "The User's Model of the System," "Display Design," and "Dialog Design." The chapters are subdivided into 22 topic sections, including "Visual Momentum," "Closure," "Screen Layout," "Text and Graphics," "Modelling the User," "Human Memory," and "Icons." At the end of each chapter the author provides a summary of the recommendations and guidelines discussed in that chapter. These summaries are among the best features of the book, as they succinctly present the design principles discussed in the text and distill more general discussions into maxims (e.g., "Support browsing as a secondary means of access to the data"). Jones provides a glossary of terms, a list of references, and a topic index but no author index. The glossary is eclectic; definitions range from the useful to the obscure. Unfortunately the text provides no clues to what is available in the glossary, and the glossary entries do not refer back to examples in the text; these omissions limit the glossary's usefulness to the reader.

The central theme of the book is "user-centered design," i.e., taking the user's needs and characteristics as the starting point for designing an interface. The author presents a strong case for this approach. Many designers might find this discussion enlightening. A second theme concerns the richness of the human perceptual and cognitive apparatus and its implications for improving human-machine interaction. The author invokes concepts such as visual momentum, browsing, and closure to illustrate techniques through which interfaces might provide a richer, more satisfying medium in which to work. These sections should be thought-provoking for the interested reader. Finally, the author covers some topics, such as display design, quite well, presenting design principles, research findings, user characteristics, and application considerations. This material should prove useful in appropriate design contexts. Overall, the book has considerable practical value.

On the other hand, one of the salient characteristics of this volume is its unevenness. It covers some topics quite well while treating others (such as graphics, human memory, and help) quite shallowly. Certain topics, such as the usability of a design, are not discussed at all. The author generally presents opinions, assertions, and recommendations without attempting to evaluate them for the reader or to draw attention to alternative positions. In some cases, he covers a topic entirely by paraphrasing from a single source. A reader unfamiliar with the literature might think that these issues are pretty much cut-and-dried. While the author draws references from a wide range of relevant literature, including psychology, environmental design, information science, computer science, and human-machine interaction, he seems out of touch with the mainstream literature in human-computer interaction. Many important basic sources are missing from the bibliography. Finally, the book has not been carefully edited. I identified a couple of major errors (e.g., "Novice users are not confused by the display of too many [menu] options" (p. 102); "not" should be omitted) and many minor ones.

In the final analysis, I cannot unequivocally recommend or dismiss this volume. If you seek a handful of design guidelines, a number of interesting insights and maxims, or a concise introduction to a practical philosophy of user-centered interface design, then you may find this volume useful. On the other hand, if you seek a guide to the literature in the field, an understanding of the data underlying the author's recommendations, or an evaluative discussion of the many issues outlined in the book, then you should look elsewhere. I would like to see a serious revision of this book that capitalized on the strengths and corrected the weaknesses. Professional interface designers are sorely in need of a practical guide to design principles and a practical philosophy of design. A brief volume that provided those features would be a significant contribution to the field.

—*Robert Root,* Morristown, NJ

BAILEY, ROBERT W.
**Human performance engineering: using human factors/ergonomics to achieve computer system usability (2nd ed.).**
Prentice-Hall, Inc., Englewood Cliffs, NJ, 1989, 563 pp., $60, ISBN 0-13-445180-5.

This well-known textbook on human factors, produced at the recommendation of the Advisory Committee for Applied Behavioral Sciences at Bell Labs, was first published in 1982. The second edition is greatly revised; it is nearly 100 pages shorter than the first edition, and improved typesetting enhances its readability. Bailey has also added references to the latest human factors research, student exercises at the end of each chapter, and a computer disk that contains three human factors tools.

The disk's limited functionality demonstration software on the disk (which requires an IBM PC, XT, AT, or compatible system with 256K and DOS 2.0 or later) allows the user to conduct cost-benefit analyses, prototype alphanumeric displays, and evaluate the usability of a display via an expert system. The author provides the reader with the names and addresses of sources from which she or he can purchase the complete versions of these tools.

The book is suited for use as an introductory text in undergraduate courses or corporate in-house training programs, or for an introductory graduate-level course in conjunction with supplemental reading material and projects. The first two chapters (Part 1) present an introduction to basic human factors concepts and give a historical overview of human factors.

Part 2 focuses on topics that are essential to understanding human cognitive capabilities. Chapter 3 explores human sensory response and cognitive processing limitations and considers individual differences with regard to these limits. Chapter 4 covers the process of sensing. Chapter 5 presents anthropometric considerations in the design of system workstations and the workplace. Chapters 6–8 focus on basic topics in cognitive psychology, such as human information processing, skill development, perception, problem solving, decision making, and human learning and memory. Chapter 9 discusses motivation.

Part 3 explores issues in the design of human/human and human/machine interfaces, the role of human factors in the system development process, and the development of documentation and training. Chapters 10 and 11 focus on the activities of the human factors engineer in the early stages of system development, including functional allocation, setting performance requirements, and task analysis. The human/machine interface discussion in chapter 12 covers the layout of displays, controls, and the workplace. Chapter 13 presents human-to-human communication issues. Chapters 14–16 cover the design of the human/computer interface. Specifically, these chapters discuss input and output devices, input language and dialogue design, screen design, help facilities, messages, and computer response time considerations. Noticeably omitted are discussions of the use of graphic displays in the human/computer interface, the design of graphic displays, and the use of color in screen design. Chapters 17–21 focus on developing selection criteria for users and on developing documentation and end user training. Chapter 22 presents techniques for evaluating the human/computer interface design.

Part 4 (chapter 23) discusses the impact of the physical and social environment within which the system is to be used on human performance with that system. Part 5 (chapter 24) presents several statistical techniques with step-by-step procedures.

Appendix A presents standard statistical tables for the tests discussed in chapter 24. Appendix B lists sources of human factors information, including professional societies, journals, abstracts, and newsletters. Appendix C gives tables for use in code design. Appendix D presents guidelines for developing questionnaires and Appendix E provides guidelines for forms development. Appendix F discusses the software tools included with the book and gives instructions for using them (to start the program that analyzes displays the user should type "display filename.extension," not "design filename.extension" as stated here).

The book is well written and easy to read. Bailey explains human factors and cognitive psychology concepts clearly and provides examples to support the explanation. The inclusion of the computer disk with demonstration software is an innovative and effective means of demonstrating how the computer itself can be used as a tool by human factors professionals to address human/computer interface issues. The student exercises focus on the important concepts in each chapter and require the student to analyze a problem and provide a rationale for his or her conclusions. Most of the exercises require a written report, which will help the student to develop the written communication skills needed by human factors engineering professionals.

Overall, this book provides a balanced introduction to human factors engineering and covers the role of human factors in the system development process, human/computer interface design issues, and basic cognitive psychology. It would not be helpful to an experienced human factors professional who was already knowledgeable about the subject. It would, however, be informative to human factors students and to system engineers, programmers, and project managers seeking to learn more about human factors engineering techniques and human cognitive limitations.
—*M. P. Tarka,* Gaithersburg, MD

SUTCLIFFE, A. (City Univ., London, UK)
**Human-computer interface design.**
Springer-Verlag New York, Inc., New York, NY, 1989, 205 pp., $29.95, ISBN 0-387-91339-4.

Human-computer interface (HCI) design has become more important with the advance of technology, new strategies of software development, and the appearance of a number of diverse applications. This book describes general guidelines so that software with good HCI can be developed. The author claims that this topic is vast and ill-defined. Hence, such subjects are taught in very few computer science courses. The initial five chapters describe concepts from psychology that are relevant to HCI. General concepts, theory, and interpretations are useful to a systems analyst for developing better designs. There is an attempt to use a structured approach to HCI, similar to the structured systems analysis and design with which a number of readers are familiar. Attempts have been made to describe qualitative characteristics in a way which can be followed easily while designing good HCI. The chapter on different types of interface design is particularly useful.

Systems analysts will benefit from this book. It can be a good reference for topics in HCI in computer science teaching. It should also help researchers in understanding the complexity of HCI. The author has succeeded admirably in the philosophy of software development: "A bad interface ruins excellent systems and a good interface saves poor software."

—*V. Kaujalgi,* Bangalore, India

## *Human information processing*

KEANE, MARK T. (The Open Univ., Milton Keynes, UK)
**Analogical problem solving.**
John Wiley & Sons, Inc., New York, NY, 1988, 151 pp., $41.95, ISBN 0-470-21057-5. [Ellis Horwood series in cognitive science.]

Mark Keane's slim volume on analogical problem solving presents the work done for his Ph.D. at Trinity College, Dublin. This work concerns the way people use analogy to learn from what they have observed in one situation and apply it to another. In an experimental psychology paradigm, he used situations in which subjects were presented with a technical problem (such as "how to use radiation to destroy a tumour without killing the patient") and a set of stories that illustrate, as in a parable, a strategy for its solution. The interest in these experiments is in Keane's exploration of analogical retrieval and mapping: how we detect an analogy and subsequently apply it to the solution of a problem. In the course of constructing a theory of analogy, Keane draws on the work of several cognitive scientists associated with artificial intelligence, including Wilensky and Schank.

Keane uses the work of Deirdre Gentner [1,2] and K. J. Holyoak [3,4] as a starting point. Gentner's "structure mapping" theory (first stated in 1983) sets out to explain how analogies are used to understand new concepts in terms of conceptual structures that are already known. The classic example is that of the analogy between the atom and the solar system with which we have been taught atomic structure. However, this theory has been the starting point for much discussion of the mechanism of analogical thinking. Gentner does not successfully approach either the question of how a conceptual structure is recognized or retrieved, or that of determining whether an analogy is successful or valid. Keane's analysis of Gentner's and Holyoak's work leads him to seek further afield for useful notions that will help to answer some of the questions that have been raised.

In his consideration of analogy retrieval, Keane uses Schank's notion of "thematic organization points" for understanding the structure of stories, especially in the notion of *indices* or features that can be matched up between analogous stories. These indices are used in both retrieval and validation of an analogy. Keane tries to show how and why some indices are valuable aids in understanding a problem, while others match but are useless or misleading. Keane's discussion of analogical mapping concentrates on this point and extends it by considering what constitutes an object and its *functionally relevant attributes* (FRAs). This is the basis for Keane's own analogical theory, which is tested in the final set of experiments.

Keane's "solution generation" theory is one of process rather than structure, as its name implies, and it deals not just with the FRAs themselves but necessarily with the relations between them. Human problem solvers are shown to deal not only with matching feature for feature in an analogy, but also with an abstract analogy between purposes. Thus, when constructing an analogy about destruction of an inimical object, there is a powerful functional analogy between fighting a tumor and fighting a human enemy.

Keane's contribution is well thought-out and coherent, if not revolutionary in concept. It should be considered as a university-level reference of some interest to those engaged in psychological research on problem solving or creativity, and is highly recommended to those computer scientists researching in artificial intelligence who want to get a firm grip on the existing work on analogy. The book has a minor flaw: Keane suffers from a mild case of psych-speak. (I offer as an example the phrase "task-specific retrieval strategies of dubious ecological validity").

—*V. S. Begg*, Cambridge, MA

**REFERENCES**

[1] GENTNER, D. AND STEVENS, A. L. *Mental models.* Erlbaum, Hillsdale, NJ, 1983.
[2] GENTNER, D. AND TOUPIN, C. Systematicity and surface similarity in the development of analogy. *Cognitive Sci.* **10** (1986), 227–300.
[3] HOLYOAK, K. J. The pragmatics of analogical transfer. *Psychol. Learn. Motiv.* **19** (1985), 59–87.
[4] HOLYOAK, K. J. AND THAGARD, P. R. A computational model of analogical problem solving. 1986. Based on paper to appear in *Similarity and Analogy*, A. Ortony and S. Vosniadou (Eds.).

## H.2 Database Management

### H.2.1 Logical Design

BLOKDIJK, ANDRÉ (IBM European Systems Research Institute); AND BLOKDIJK, PAUL (IBM Information Systems Management Institute, La Hulpe, Belgium)
**Planning and design of information systems.**
Academic Press, Inc., San Diego, CA, 1987, 578 pp., $65, ISBN 0-12-107070-0.

Blokdijk and Blokdijk have written a book that was long overdue in the world of data processing literature. Information systems planning and design is an ambitious subject that can always benefit from increased discussion.

It is significant that they have limited the title of their book to "Planning and Design" when they have included several good sections on project management and systems implementation. A more appropriate name might be *How to implement information systems*.

The book is divided into the following parts:

(1) Planning and Design: Methodology
(2) Users and Information Systems
(3) Information Systems Planning
(4) Application Planning
(5) Logical Design of the Application.

Several facets of the book are worth noting for their excellence:

☐ The structure is well thought-out and makes for a book that is easy to read and, more important, easy to reference. The well-organized table of contents and index enable one to use the book as a reference tool to be consulted on an as-needed basis.

☐ The content of the book is unusual in that it not only identifies *what* should be done but also provides the reader with excellent sections on *how* to do it. The authors have also provided, when appropriate, guidelines and suggestions on "Quality Metrics." Very often authors only discuss what should be done and never provide the reader with the guidance and methodologies for performing the tasks. I found this added dimension to be of significant benefit.

The book is written in a style and format that assume the reader has a university education and understands the formalizations of data processing. To me, this trend is long overdue. I am personally tired of reading data processing books that reduce every concept to the lowest common denominator. There is a difference between data processors (i.e., coders) and computer science/information professionals. This book is written for the information professional, not the journeyman coder or dilettante data processor.

I did take exception to several of the authors' choices of methodologies and approach. Two of the most notable are described below.

They use Nassi-Schneiderman charts for the definition of application logic. I have found Nassi-Schneiderman charts to be difficult to use during the design process due to the difficulty of revising and drawing new charts. They are, however, more popular in Europe than in the United States and this may account for the authors' use of them. According to the Blokdijks, European CASE tools support their use. I have not seen an American CASE tool set that does.

Their definition of the difference between a *DO WHILE* and a *DO UNTIL* (page 114) is that they both use the same logic structure: "test" then "perform." There is a difference between the two. This may seem like a trivial point to the uninitiated, but it is in fact very important to those who are familiar with the underlying mathematical foundations of structured programming. The orthodox definition of a DO WHILE is check the condition, then perform the action; that of a DO UNTIL is perform the action, then check the condition. Only DO WHILEs are to be used in structured programming. The confusion is understandable since IBM chose to implement the COBOL "Perform Until" as a DO WHILE.

In summary, I recommend *Planning and design of information systems* to the serious computer professional. It would be helpful if all data programming books were as well written and structured.

—*Phil Teplitzky*, New York, NY

## H.3 Information Storage and Retrieval

### H.3.3 Information Search and Retrieval

HARTER, STEPHEN P. (Indiana Univ., Bloomington)                HCI-0046
**Online information retrieval: concepts, principles, and techniques.**
Academic Press, Inc., San Diego, CA, 1986, 259 pp., $19.95, ISBN 0-12-328456-2. [Library and information science series.]

While there exist numerous books on the techniques of information retrieval, most draw heavily on a particular computer system or command language. Only a few stress the general concepts and lead the reader to comprehend not only the steps of a retrieval session but also the very nature of searching, including an appreciation of its potentials as well as its inherent limitations. It is this deeper understanding that is striven for and achieved by the author.

Let us start with some highlights of the nine chapters. The Introduction explains some basic ideas and gives examples of databases and search services. The next chapter presents different types of command languages, including menu-driven and command-driven languages, controlled and free vocabularies, natural languages with their pitfalls, and citation indexing (searching for publications that cite a known one).

Chapter 3 acquaints the reader with technical concepts, like bits and bytes, fields and records, field codes, inverted indexes, Boolean logic, truncation, and word proximity searching. As throughout the book, carefully chosen, small examples illuminate the ideas.

The emphasis clearly lies on reference databases (in particular, bibliographic and referral databases) characterized in Chapter 4. Chapter 8 adds the peculiarities of source databases containing numerical data or full texts (actually, long texts, since they still may be only excerpts of the full texts) or combinations thereof.

Equipped with the basics of the first half of the book, the reader is led in Chapters 5 to 7 through the constituent parts of an online search: understanding the user's information need, evaluating the results, desirable personal characteristics of the searcher, important components of the communication between the searcher and end-user, and search strategies and heuristics. It is stressed that the online dialogue itself is only a small and primarily technical part of the whole process.

Chapter 9 finally promises "trends, problems, and issues" but is mainly restricted to expected technical innovations in computer memories and telecommunications, with a sketch of some legal issues. There is no debate on promises of expert systems that would be expected here, although the existing products that call themselves expert systems do hardly more than choosing an appropriate database, connecting to it, or translating one search language into another.

Many users still expect an information system to exactly retrieve all relevant documents. A main concern of the author is to show that this is inherently impossible. Already in Chapter 1, and again at various other places, attention is drawn to the "noise" that inevitably accompanies and distorts the mappings (1) from the client's information need, to the meaning of question, to the spoken or written question, to the received question, to the understood meaning of the question, to the searcher's action, and (2) from the information source, to its summary, to its translation into the indexing languages; it could be added that even the information source is a noisy and, therefore, incorrect representation of what the author intended to put down.

Another aspect is the distinction between four levels of questions: the visceral (underlying), conscious, formalized, and compromised information needs. While the last one is posed to the retrieval system, it is actually the first one (only vaguely defined, constantly changing with incoming new information, and hardly expressible in words) that the client wants to be met. It is no surprise then that the author questions, though only briefly in Section 6.6, the widespread naive notion of relevance (or of pertinence, the former one intending a more objective measure and the latter one reflecting the subjective satisfaction). Although essential for all evaluations of retrieval strategies or systems, the relevance of a particular document with respect to a particular information need cannot reliably be measured, even in principle.

The author concentrates on retrieval strategies that are generally available; thus, some techniques that have been shown to improve the search results but are lacking in most systems have not been mentioned, such as ranking and computer-assisted relevance feedback.

There are numerous problems at the end of each chapter that aim at understanding the material by laying hands on, for instance, by looking into thesauruses or by performing certain searches.

There are well over 200 references that go into 1984, with occasional contributions from 1985. Papers in languages other than English are virtually missing. The reviewer dislikes the habit of scattering the references over the ends of all the chapters, particularly in the absence of a name index. The book ends with a sizeable glossary and a subject index. The reviewer found a single typographical error, a misspelling of the German word "Weltanschauung," on p. 163.

The book is written for, and provides valuable reading for, the end-user who wants to understand the underlying ideas, benefits, and limits of information retrieval. It therefore requires no specific background and avoids any mathematical formulas. Needless to say, the expert will also find some thought-provoking ideas.

—*F. Gebhardt,* St. Augustin, West Germany

JONASSEN, DAVID H. (Univ. of Colorado, Denver)
**Hypertext/hypermedia.**
Educational Technology Publications, Englewood Cliffs, NJ, 1989, 91 pp., $24.95, ISBN 0-87778-217-2.

*Hypertext/hypermedia* is not a typical book: it is an ink-on-paper hypertext about hypertext and hypermedia. The nodes of the hypertext are short sections, each one or two pages long. These sections are divided in turn into small subsections that follow a standard pattern. Each node begins with a description or introduction of its topic. Some elaboration of the topic, a discussion of collateral or related material, or an example may follow. Next, a labeled graph shows links from the current node to related nodes. Finally, links to other documents are presented as citations.

Besides the links shown graphically in each node, node text often contains boxed, boldface words or phrases followed by page numbers referring the reader to related nodes. Nodes are arranged into chapters and organized linearly to fit the conventions of a book. A hypermap (a labeled graph) at the beginning of the book shows links between chapters, and each chapter begins with a brief description of its contents and a hypermap of the nodes in the chapter. The book also includes a traditional table of contents and an index.

In his introduction, Jonassen encourages his readers to use the links to explore the book nonlinearly, directing their own learning and absorbing the material as they like. In following this advice, I found it neither difficult nor distracting to flip through pages following links, and I never felt lost or confused as so often happens when navigating hypertext on a computer. On the other hand, I did not find following links especially useful or interesting. At one point I simply read backwards through the book for a while, and found this no better or worse than following the links. I ended up reading forward page by page to ensure that I did not miss any nodes.

The book surveys hypertext and hypermedia. It contains chapters on characteristics of hypertext and hypermedia, arguments for their use, candidate applications, problems in creating and using hypertext, approaches to designing hypertext and hypermedia systems, the historical roots of the idea, popular hypertext and hypermedia systems, and storage media. The book is short (87 pages of nodes, with lots of white space and graphics) and covers much the same material as Conklin's oft-cited survey [1], though it is somewhat broader in scope. The capsule discussions in the nodes are very short, but pithy, clear, and honest. The many graphics are well done; the screen dumps illustrating popular hypertext and hypermedia systems are especially helpful.

The weakest aspect of the book is its lack of a collected bibliography; citations are scattered through the nodes where they may be hard to find if needed later. I also noticed many obviously missing links.

This book adds little to the information given by Conklin, but its attempt to make an ink-on-paper hypertext is interesting. Certainly someone completely unfamiliar with hypertext can get a better idea of it by both seeing it and reading about it in Jonassen's book than they could from just reading about it in Conklin's paper. Some may even find that they prefer a hypertext book to a traditional book.

—*Christopher Fox,* Lincroft, NJ

**REFERENCES**
[1] CONKLIN, J. Hypertext: an introduction and survey. *IEEE Comput.* **20,** 9 (Sept. 1987), 17–41.

## H.4 Information Systems Applications

### H.4.1 Office Automation

HIRSCHHEIM, R. A. (Oxford Univ., Oxford, UK)  [HCI-0048]
**Office automation: a social and organizational perspective.**
John Wiley & Sons, Inc., New York, NY, 1986, 327 pp., $29.95, ISBN 0-471-90909-2.

I probably should not admit it, but I usually read very little of the research-based papers in our most scholarly journals. I skim quickly over the data collection and methodology sections and aim directly for the discussion and conclusions. Only if I disagree with or question the authors' results do I go back and study the methods or data.

Hirschheim, however, has accomplished, for me at least, something rare; he has written a practical and informative book while still retaining the scholarship befitting a member of the Oxford University faculty. As stated in the title, he examines the technology of office automation from a social and organizational perspective. But he does more: he examines that unique artifact of industrial society, the office, from what I consider to be a cultural anthropological viewpoint.

This is not a book for someone who wants to know more about word processors or graphics software. In fact, the technical aspects of office automation are mentioned only in Chapter 2, A Background to Office Automation. This chapter does include an illustration which describes all the various office automation technologies in a complex set of concentric circles and circle-segments, but practical advice on hardware and software is not the purpose of this text. This chapter does mention some benefits of office automation, but, again, a reader seeking to justify the technology would do better studying [1].

But for those of us who want to *think* about the office, its work, its effect on people, this is the book. It is full of "structures" into which ideas can be organized. For example, Hirschheim quotes one study which shows that an office contains three basic elements—people, paper, and files—and that these elements are involved in five processes: people to people communication, people to paper communication, paper to paper transfer, paper to file transfer, and files to people transfer. The word "paper" may need liberal interpretation in these days of cathode ray tubes and magnetic media, but the ideas hold.

Hirschheim describes social and ethical issues and presents models and methodologies for studying these and other topics within the office. He describes and critiques some of the models used by other researchers and finally offers suggestions of his own.

My favorite chapter is Chapter 5, which describes the social implications of office automation implementation. The problems he describes are faced daily by everyone involved in the installation and support of information systems, and his insights are meaningful even to a scarred veteran like me.

Ever the academic, however, Hirschheim follows each chapter with lengthy lists of references so that every subject mentioned in the chapter can be studied further. And, in his last chapter, he offers suggestions where further research would be appropriate.

As I implied above, this book offers much for both the academic and the practitioner. The academic will enjoy the broad scope of the materials and the linking of the office technologies to more basic sciences. The practitioner will find many models into which specific proposals can fit. I can see many of them as bullets on transparencies, used as background in presentations requesting additional office automation resources. Hirschheim also offers some very pragmatic checklists, the best of which, in Appendix B, lists Key Questions for Office Automation Implementation.

BOOKS & PROCEEDINGS [HCI-0049]

A book like this makes me even less patient with the usual journal paper, in which the value, if any, is hidden in a forest of statistics. Hirschheim shows that it is possible to communicate well and still remain academically sound. Other researchers, please take note.

—*J. L. Podolsky,* Palo Alto, CA

**REFERENCES**

[1] STRASSMAN, P. *Information payoff*, The Free Press, New York, 1985.

## H.4.2 Types of Systems

### *Decision support*

ROCKART, JOHN F. (CISR and Massachusetts Institute of Technology, Cambridge); AND DE LONG, DAVID W. (CISR, Cambridge, MA)
**Executive support systems: the emergence of top management computer use.**
Dow Jones-Irwin, Homewood, IL, 1988, 280 pp., $29.95, ISBN 0-87094-955-1.

HCI-0049

Corporate information systems have evolved through three distinct levels of technology and functionality: transaction-oriented systems, management information systems (MIS), and decision support systems (DSS). These three levels correspond, through some amazing coincidence, to the three levels of information in an organization: operational, tactical, and strategic. The hypothesis is that each stage of information systems evolution supports a different level of management. This characterization has been both popular and useful. It has been popular because the model is easy to understand and successfully describes the situation on a superficial level. It has been useful because it helps organize the sometimes overwhelming complexity of organizational computing and evolving technologies.

This perspective, however, has been losing ground in the last few years because technological evolution has outpaced the fidelity of the concept. Where do expert systems, for example, fit into the pyramid of management systems? What about office automation and robotics? Perhaps even more to the point, why didn't decision support systems catch on in a big way as expected?

This book is an attempt to resurrect the management view of computing by handing decision support systems over to quantitative analysts and replacing them in the pyramid with a new concept called executive support systems (ESS); these systems are more closely aligned with the unstructured adaptive organizational behavior of top executives. In many ways it appears that ESS is really an overhaul of DSS without the discipline of quantitative models and structured data.

The book is smoothly written and well documented. It represents a lot of legwork and literature reviews by the authors. In their attempt to determine how top executives use computers and ultimately to define the emerging concept of executive support systems, they visited over 30 companies throughout the US, Canada, and Great Britain. The results of those interviews, combined with comments from experts in both management and information systems and with the authors' own analysis and opinions, make up the body of this book.

I have three main problems with this book. First, it essentially defines executive support systems as those systems that support executives. Thus, once an executive uses a technology, it becomes part of the executive support system. Second, the executive support system is a loosely bound collection of functions with few defining themes. Thus the boundaries between DSS and ESS, for example, are not really clear. Third, each new concept, whether it be MIS, DSS, or now ESS, takes credit for the accomplishments of its predecessors; much of this book is only a thorough editing away from a book describing DSS.

The audience for this book, although the authors never really state it, is clearly nontechnical managers or management-oriented information systems professionals. These people can easily read the book in a couple of evenings and quickly decide, within the first two chapters, whether it interests them. As to whether the authors have truly identified an emerging concept in information systems, I suspect that six readers might give six different answers.

—*J. M. Artz*, Rockville, MD

### H.4.3 Communications Applications

HOLLIGAN, PATRICK J. (Primary Communications Research Center, Univ. of Leicester, Leicester, UK)
**Access to academic networks.**
Taylor Graham Publishers, London, UK, 1986, 91 pp., $26.50, ISBN 0-947568-08-5.

The Joint Academic Network (JANET) was established in April 1984 to provide network links to universities and research centers within the United Kingdom. It achieved a major national policy objective by simplifying the procedures necessary for using computer systems linked together by transmission lines. Holligan presents the results of an investigation conducted early in JANET's history concerning the existing and potential uses of networks for computer-mediated communication within the academic communities of the UK.

The report begins with three prefatory chapters that define the objectives, methodology, and finds of the investigation. Chapter 1 explains the elements of a computer network and provides historical background on the academic networking community. Chapter 2 addresses the different forms of computer-mediated communication, such as computer conferencing and electronic mail, and the ways in which UK academicians perceive the uses of these new modes of communication. Chapter 3 describes the users of the networks, the contents of the transmissions, and the costs involved.

Chapter 4 summarizes eight case studies of network usage at different university centers. Chapter 5 lists the following conclusions about the applications of networking to areas other than computation and data processing: (1) Academic staff must become computer-literate. (2) National policies and institutional policies must build up a viable community of users. (3) Networks must be monitored to meet the needs of new categories of users. (4) Greater accessibility and user-friendly interfaces are needed for the less computer-literate. (5) Economic factors of national and international networking need to be resolved. (6) More cooperation between libraries and computer centers will be necessary. (7) Other issues remain, including: new users, existing users, and adequate financial resources.

Holligan stresses the age-old cyclical problem of funding vs. usage. At the present time, many university people in the humanities and the arts have not yet defined the activities they hope to perform on the networked system. Because they are not currently heavy users, these fields are not allocated much in the way of terminals, training, and other resources. Because their resources are skimpy, little effort has been made to explore the ways in which academic network usage could enhance their work.

Computer networks are becoming more numerous and more diverse. This monograph, published in 1986, is highly recommended as an introduction to academic networking within and between university communities. It is well organized and well written. The book conveys a great deal of useful information about physical aspects of networking, as well as about forms of human communication to be transmitted electronically.

For a broader and somewhat more technical perspective, a concurrently published paper by Quarterman and Hoskins [1] makes an excellent companion piece that reinforces and extends the UK findings.

—*G. W. Abramson,* New York, NY

**REFERENCES**
[1] QUARTERMAN, J. S.; AND HOSKINS, J. C. Notable computer networks, *Commun. ACM* **29**, 10 (Oct. 1986), 932–971.

## *Teleconferencing*

HILTZ, STARR R. (Upsala College, East Orange, NJ)     **HCI-0051**
**Online communities.**
Ablex Publishing Corp., Norwood, NJ, 1984, 261 pp., $32.50, ISBN 0-89391-145-3. [Human/computer interaction series.]

This book attempts to assess the impacts of a comuterized conferencing system on communication patterns and productivity in scientific research communities. The author studied usage of EIES, a message/conferencing/text composition system, over a two year period (roughly 1979-80). EIES provides delivery of messages to individual or groups, conferences (time-sequenced transcripts of group discussions), notebooks (text composition and word processing functions), and a membership directory.

Some 220 users (80 percent of them in academic insitutions) were studied via their responses to both pre- and post-use questionnaires. EIES features, participant characteristics, and survey methodology, are described. The bulk of the book is taken up with statistical analyses of the survey results. (This reviewer found the analyses somewhat lengthy and often inconclusive, with the more anecdotal end-of-chapter summaries being easier reading.)

Among the findings are these: (1) The best predictor of acceptance by a new user of such a system is that person's expectation about how useful the system will be, and how many coworkers will be online. This is much more important than skills such as prior computer experience or typing ability. (2) A substantial learning period is required — about five hours of online time to learn the basics and about 50 hours before it becomes second nature. (3) For those who make it through the learning period (many dropped out), such a system does indeed expand their professional network and leads to perceived increases in quality of work.

An update of this work would be interesting. Most of the users studied had less than 50 hours of online time; more expert users might behave much differently (as the author points out). Also, the typical interface to the system was a 30 CPS TTY-style terminal connected via a phone line. The vastly improved communication now afforded by local area networks, bitmapped displays, pointing devices, and menu-oriented multiple window interfaces makes such systems far easier to learn and use.

This book should be of interest to sociologists interested in the impact of computer-assisted communications, to designers of such systems, and to those contemplating doing a usage study of a computer-based communication system.

—*R. W. Sauvain*, Rochester, NY

# I. COMPUTING METHODOLOGIES

## I.2 Artificial Intelligence

### I.2.0 General

ELITHORN, ALICK; AND BANERJI, RANAN (EDS.)  HCI-0052
**Artificial and human intelligence.**
Proc. of the international NATO symposium, (Lyon, France, Oct. 1981), Elsevier North-Holland, Inc., New York, NY, 1984, 344 pp., $40, ISBN 0-444-86545-4.

[Papers in this volume have been individually reviewed; each paper is cross-referenced to this main entry to provide complete source and citation data. In this book see Reviews HCI-0239; HCI-0240, HCI-0322; HCI-0353]

> The literature on Artificial Intelligence is already becoming unmanageable. As the proceedings of a conference organized at the behest of the NATO Scientific Committee . . . this volume presents a distillation of stimulating and productive intellectual exhanges covering a wide range of disciplines. Consequently the contributions include several which will be compulsory reading for many years.
>
> Artificial Intelligence is a relatively new field of scientific exploration which already has a chequered history. It is one of great promise but like nuclear research, genetic engineering and indeed like all scientific endeavor, it has potential for both good and evil and stirs deep feelings.
>
> Artificial Intelligence research is not the concern only of computer scientists and psychologists. The breadth of coverage and the quality of the contributions means that Artificial and Human Intelligence will for some time be a vade-mecum for research scientists, teachers and students from many disciplines.
>
> —*From the Preface by A. Elithorn*

SHAFTO, MICHAEL (Office of Naval Research, Arlington, VA): (ED.)
**How we know.**
Harper & Row, Publishers, Inc., New York, NY, 1985, 171 pp., $14.95, ISBN 0-06-250777-X.

There are two branches of metaphysics, *ontology* and *epistemology*. Ontology is concerned with what actually exists out there in the world, and epistemology is concerned with how we know. The pursuit of epistemological truth goes all the way back to Socrates and includes such household names as Rene Descartes, John Locke, and Immanuel Kant. The philosophical debate on the nature of knowledge raged at full fury about 2½ centuries ago. It then went into remission until it was reanimated in the second half of this century under the name of cognitive science. The interdisciplinary subfields of cognitive science each attack the age-old problem of how we know from a slightly different perspective, ranging from clinical research to conceptual modeling. This book provides six essays from pioneers in this fledgling field. Neuroscience, psychology, artificial intelligence, and philosophy are all represented from various perspectives in the six papers. The three of most interest to *Computing Reviews* readers are the papers by R. Schank and C. Seifert, H. Simon, and D. Dennett.

The paper by Schank and Seifert, entitled "Modeling Memory and Learning," discusses the difficulties encountered in interpreting natural language, especially considering the knowledge and background needed to interpret subtle differences in very similar statements. It offers a very sobering perspective on the practicality of computers attempting to interpret and/or process natural language.

Certainly, it is difficult to get a computer to behave in the same unpredictable, inconsistent, and undisciplined fashion that a person behaves, especially with regard to language. What is not clear from the paper is why one would want to do this. Is the role of a technology to automate processes in their raw undisciplined state, or to first bring order and then to automate? After all, is language any more "natural" than, for example, accounting?

Simon offers a much more optimistic outlook on machine intelligence in "Some Computer Models of Human Learning." He discusses the physical symbol system hypothesis which underlies the metaphor of the brain as a computer. This hypothesis states that the ability of a system to process symbols is equivalent to the capacity for intelligent behavior. A corollary of this hypothesis is that computers can be made to behave intelligently. This is a hotly debated issue, but it seems to skirt the subject of intelligence by defining equivalence between intelligence and a physical symbol system. The paper does not address intelligence directly, and it leaves the reader with an empty feeling of optimism.

Dennett discusses variations on the Turing test for determining machine intelligence in a fascinating paper called "Can Machines Think?" He makes the salient point that expert systems are "cleverly constructed facades. . . . And even if all the reasonable, cost-effective steps are taken to minimize the superficiality of expert systems, they will still be facades, just somewhat thicker or wider facades." Good point! Given this perspective, all the Turing text does is examine the quality of the facade.

I wish I could say that this book is a must for everyone. Certainly, an introduction to the philosophical problems of epistemology is relevant for anyone in artificial intelligence or for anyone involved in computer systems which model or supplement human problem solving behavior. Unfortunately, this book is a rather loosely knit collection of essays which briefly describes the research interests of each of the contributors. I found three of the papers to be excellent—Dennett's, Schank and Seifert's, and Simon's, in that order. I suspect that someone with a slightly different background might choose the winners differently.

The editor states, "the issues in the debate are not accessible to common sense." In this spirit, the papers have not been written for the average reader. Thus, I would not recommend this book as an introduction to these concepts. Instead, I would describe it as a collection of scholarly position papers for a more educated audience.

—*J. M. Artz,* Rockville, MD

WINOGRAD, TERRY (Stanford Univ., Stanford, CA); AND FLORES, FERNANDO (Action Technologies Inc., San Francisco, CA) (EDS.)
**Understanding computers and cognition.**
Ablex Publishing Corp., Norwood, NJ, 1985, 207 pp., $24.95, ISBN 0-89391-050-3.

This is a fascinating and thought-provoking book with a rather disappointing punchline. It is yet another sojourn into the philosophical bedrock underlying artificial intelligence (AI) but is not a simple rehash of existing arguments. The tenets of the authors' position are fresh, clearly relevant, and thought-provoking, if not entirely convincing. The authors assert that much of artificial intelligence is based on a philosophical perspective called rationalism. Rationalism, which provides a philosophical basis for logic and mathematics and much of formal science, provides the metaphysical justification for formalism and abstraction. Many of the fundamental assumptions in AI, such as a representational level, rest on this foundation.

The claim made in this book is that rationalism is not an appropriate orientation for artificial intelligence and thus much of today's research is unproductive. Do we hear the hoofbeats of the British empirical cavalry coming over the hill? Not at all!

The authors introduce hermeneutics (a theory of interpretive reasoning) and the phenomenology of Heidegger and others to challenge the assumptions of rationalism and hence the current assumptions in AI research. They provide a startling counterpoint to the current rationalistic orientation. The net result is a reduced emphasis on objectivity and a greater emphasis on subjectivity. Some representative quotes convey the flavor of this perspective: "Our implicit beliefs and assumptions cannot all be made explicit," and "Practical understanding is more fundamental than detached theoretical understanding." It would be unfair to present these insights out of context without mentioning that the arguments behind them are well developed and convincing.

Ultimately, the authors carry their arguments through to design objectives for computer systems, and this, I believe, is their downfall. While bridging this gap is an important step, the final results are much less appealing than the intermediate arguments.

Indeed, I expected the conclusions to be much more startling. There is more work to be done in this area, and this book is really just the beginning. I think this is a good text for a class or seminar in the philosophical foundations of artificial intelligence. It is useful reading for researchers and really for anyone who enjoys the intellectual challenge of opposing viewpoints. Though I did not come away from this book convinced, I did come away with some things to think about.

—*J. M. Artz,* Rockville, MD

WALDROP, M. M.
**Man-made minds: the promise of artificial intelligence.**
Walker & Co., New York, NY, 1987, 280 pp., $22.95, ISBN 0-8027-0899-4.

Here is an easy-to-read book that covers a great deal of ground in 280 pages, 30 of which are taken by references, suggested readings, and an index. The book deals with the following: the history of Artificial Intelligence (AI); the technology of expert systems, natural-language processing, machine vision, and parallel computing; the Japanese fifth-generation computing initiative and the American and European responses to it; and, finally, the impact of computers and AI on people and society.

Well, that's a lot of interesting and important stuff, and, as I said, the book is easy to read. Now, let's see, there should be someone I can recommend this book to—someone willing to spend more than one afternoon reading in a style and at a level he or she might find in a Sunday newspaper magazine; someone who might be satisfied with a broad picture of the topic, where major features are described but never fully explained; someone who might want to know what people who have thought about it have to say about what computers are doing and might do to the mental and social fabric of society; yet someone willing to accept an outline of a debate rather than a reasoned justification of any one position; someone, perhaps, who can decide that this book does not provide the educated layperson with sufficient material to truly understand AI and is willing to search other sources before deciding whether to await the maturation of this stupendous technology with anticipation or with apprehension.

All this said, if a young adult or a mature teenager tells me that he or she wants to find out what AI is all about, I think I will recommend this book with the proviso that he or she must first read at least two others: McCorduck's *Machines who think* [1] and Johnson's *Machinery of the mind* [2]. McCorduck's book will bring up close the excitement, the players, and the superb intellectual adventure of AI; and Johnson's book will provide a clear, thorough description of the technology and its applications. Thus informed, my friend may be eager to learn more and to become a knowledgeable participant in a fascinating forum: What does it mean to be intelligent? What will people do with artificial intelligence? What will—or might—artificial intelligence do to people? Waldrop's book could then provide my friend with a current, nearly comprehensive outline for further research.

—*Edgar R. Chavez,* West Chester, PA

**REFERENCES**

[1] MCCORDUCK, P. *Machines who think: a personal inquiry into the history and prospects of artificial intelligence,* W. H. Freeman and Co., San Francisco, CA, 1979. See *Computing Reviews* **21**, 4 (April 1980), Rev. 36,014.

[2] JOHNSON, G. *Machinery of the mind: inside the new science of artificial intelligence,* Times Books, New York, NY, 1986.

GREGORY, RICHARD L. (Univ. of Bristol, Bristol, UK); AND MARSTRAND, PAULINE K. (Huddersfield Polytechnic, UK) (EDS.)
**Creative intelligences.**
Ablex Publishing Corp., Norwood, NJ, 1987, 143 pp., $29.50, ISBN 0-89391-440-1.

This book consists of ten papers about intelligence presented at the 1986 meeting of the British Association for the Advancement of Science (BAAS). The introduction provides a light-hearted overview of the activities of BAAS and states that "the chapters of the book represent the lifelong cogitations of authorities in the broad field of intelligence." The contents of the book are as follows:

(1) Intelligence Based on Knowledge—Knowledge Based on Intelligence by Richard Gregory.
(2) Intelligence and Children's Development by Peter Bryant.
(3) Designing Intelligence by Daniel C. Dennett.
(4) Intelligent Machines for Process Control by Janet Efstathiou.
(5) Expert Systems and Evidential Reasoning by James Baldwin.
(6) Intelligence and the Man-machine Interface by Terry Walton.
(7) Turing's Conception of Intelligence by Andrew Hodges.
(8) The Advent of Intelligent Robots by Michael Brady.
(9) 'This is a Very Unpredictable Machine': on Computers and Human Cognition by Janni Nielsen.
(10) Creativity, Intelligence, and Evolution by Euan MacPhail.

Chapters 1 and 3 derive from a philosophical perspective, chapters 2, 9, and 10 are from a psychological perspective, chapters 4, 5, and 8 are from an artificial intelligence perspective, chapter 6 is from a technological perspective, and chapter 7 is from a historical/biographical perspective. The main point of each paper is briefly described below.

Gregory is concerned with the problems of measuring intelligence (IQ) when two quite different types of intelligence are seen to exist: skilled use of domain specific knowledge and creative reasoning involving little or no domain specific knowledge. Bryant points out that children may have the ability to reason about certain types of logical operations but fail to solve tasks requiring those operations for a number of reasons, including memory limitations. Dennett is concerned with showing that human reflective consciousness can be understood as the solution to a design problem that both evolution and unconscious self-design have been partners in solving. Efstathiou describes the design of an intelligent knowledge-based system (IKBS) for automating process control in factories. Baldwin's Prolog-based SLOP system allows for heuristic reasoning when confronted with uncertain data. Walton describes the evolution of the telephone system and shows how technological advances have lead to improved human-machine interfaces. Hodges explores the factors in Turing's life that led to the development of precise mathematical theories of computational intelligence. Brady provides an overview of the present state of the field of robotics and speculates about where the field may be heading. Nielsen has studied the problems novices have learning to use computers and concludes that novices are not simply learning about symbolic formal systems but are also attempting to acquire sensory motor and emotive knowledge for dealing with machines. Finally, MacPhail proposes a controversial theory that all nonhuman vertebrates are of roughly equal intelligence, as demonstrated by experiments in which pigeons solve problems comparable to problems solved by monkeys and dolphins.

For readers desiring a wide-ranging view of current research on intelligence, this book may partially serve that purpose. The book contains adequate references and an index to facilitate browsing. The major shortcoming of the book is that it does not provide a satisfactory overview of the topic area. The ten papers are like single points in a vast space that leave the reader very much at a loss for an overall organization. A topic area as wide ranging as intelligence can not be satisfactorily addressed without such an overview.

—*J. Spohrer,* New Haven, CT

SOWA, J. F. (IBM Systems Research Institute)
**Conceptual structures: information processing in mind and machine.**
Addison-Wesley Publ. Co., Inc., Reading, MA, 1984, 481 pp., $32.95, ISBN 0-201-14472-7. [Addison-Wesley systems programming series.]

This is a very odd—but good—book. Its scope is almost as broad as that of any general text on Artificial Intelligence (AI), but it is not an overview of issues and research in AI. Instead, the author applies a particular formal notation, conceptual graphs, to a wide range of problems. These conceptual graphs are part of the large family of graphical notations used in AI, primarily for knowledge representation and grammatical structures.

Unlike most authors, Sowa is most concerned with demonstrating the logical adequacy of his graphs, extending and defining them to include not only first-order logic, but modal logics as well. He even uses them to represent computation *a la* dataflow. This is the strength of the book. Even if Sowa fails to convince you that conceptual graphs are preferable to linear notations, he definitely makes them a serious contender. At the same time, he raises most of the important representational problems that have to be handled by any other notation.

The book begins and ends with its weakest material. Chapters 1 and 2 cover the philosophical and psychological motivational background. This coverage, despite its brevity, raises more issues than the rest of the book can hope to deal with. The core of the book rests in Chapters 3, 4, and 5. Chapter 3 defines most of the essential features of conceptual graphs. Two notations are given, one using two-dimensional networks, and the other using a bracketed linear notation. For example, the conceptual graph (in linear notation) "[CAT] − ½(STAT) − ½[SIT] − ½(LOC) − ½[MAT]" connects the concepts "[CAT]," "[SIT]," and "[MAT]" with the relationships "(STAT)" and "(LOC)" to represent the description, "a cat that is in the state of sitting on a mat." Conceptual graphs are used to represent propositions. Concepts and conceptual relationships fit into type hierarchies, e.g., "[CAT]" has the type "[ANIMAL]" as a higher type, so this graph could be generalized into (among others) "[ANIMAL] − ½(STAT) − ½[SIT] − ½(LOC) − ½[PHYSOBJ]."

Topics covered include individual names, canonical graphs, generalization, specialization, abstraction, and definitions. Much of what is presented is standard semantic network material, but it is fleshed out and formalized with great care and clarity. Chapter 4 continues this development to include schemata, quantification, deduction, model semantics, modal logic, and dataflow.

Chapter 5 links this material to language, including case frames, augmented phrase structure grammar, generation, and parsing.

Chapter 5 ends with an informal discussion of some of the hardest issues in natural language processing, i.e., context, conversational implication, and metaphor. From this point on, the book becomes much less technical. Chapter 6 is a reasonable survey of issues in applied AI, including expert systems, natural language interfaces, conceptually based systems analysis, and knowledge acquisition. The final chapter is a surprisingly strong criticism of what has gone before, stressing the significant limitations of discrete conceptual representation systems. Appendix A gives mathematical underpinnings of conceptual graph theory. The coverage is much too brief to learn from, but is probably adequate as a minirefresher course. Appendix B is a catalog of the concepts and conceptual relationships used in the text.

Appendix B isolates what I think is a major weakness of the book. Appendix B begins by noting the difference between a theory of form and a theory of content. The book has been concerned with the former, but evaluating the theory's worth rests on just how well the forms work when applied to particular domains. The catalog of concepts and relationships listed is much too incomplete and scattered to allow any evaluation based on content. It covers no coherent subset of meaning in any way. For example, it presents a few communication concepts, such as "[COMMAND]," "[COMMUNICATE]," "[MESSAGE]," "[TEACH]," and "[ORDER]," but does not relate them to others presented in the text, such as "[WRITE]" and "[ASK]." To some of us in AI, what is of most interest is working out what the relationships are between concepts of communication, knowledge, action, and so on. Sowa understands this, and points it out in several places; but by following linguistic tradition and using a wide variety of unrelated examples to illustrate different points, he has missed an opportunity to make a contribution to any particular theory of content.

Still and all, the breadth of material covered, and (in the central chapters) the depth to which the material is treated, is amazing. There are many surveys of AI in print, and a handful of volumes on programming techniques, but very few theoretically rich textbooks. Sowa has managed to produce one. I recommend it to all students interested in knowledge representation.

—*C. Riesbeck,* Evanston, IL

### I.2.1 Applications and Expert Systems

LEVINE, ROBERT I. (Sperry Corp.); DRANG, DIANE E. (New York City Jewish Board of Family and Children Services, New York, NY); AND EDELSON, BARRY
**A comprehensive guide to AI and expert systems.**
McGraw-Hill, Inc., New York, NY, 1986, 245 pp., $19.95, ISBN 0-07-037470-8.

This short (245 pages, 6" × 9" format) paperback is aimed at "advanced high school students, college students, corporate presidents" and attempts to present AI and expert systems in a "greatly simplified" manner. There are 18 chapters divided into six sections: human and machine intelligence, inference mechanisms, expert systems, advanced programming techniques, advanced knowledge representation, and languages used in AI. The book has an adequate index.

Although each chapter is supposed to be self-contained and has related program listings written in BASIC, several chapters depend strongly on the contents of previous chapters (e.g., Chapters 12 and 11). This dependency is also found in at least one program. Typographically, several figures contain errors, and at least one sample program cannot execute because of a missing DIMENSION statement.

In an effort to simplify concepts, the authors create confusion. For example, the cases presented do not clearly differentiate forward chaining from backward chaining, especially since almost all of the backward chaining is done in the conditional portion of individual production rules, rather than through the rules themselves. Object-oriented programming is discussed using a useful object structure definition; the chapter's program listing, however, does not use this definition in an appropriate way. To add to the confusion, this same definition is used in the chapter on semantic nets. The program listings are a good feature of this book and can be obtained on an IBM PC-compatible floppy disk.

The best feature of this book is the toy expert systems developed in individual chapters. They are varied in type and interesting. But even here the authors fall short. Several different knowledge representation schemes are used, but without any attempt to relate them to a particular type of problem to be solved. Compared to other texts of similar intent, this book is about 300 pages too short. The authors made a mistake in trying to write a comprehensive guide. They should have discussed fewer concepts in much greater detail.

—*A. D. Vanker*, Tampa, FL

BOOSE, JOHN H. (Boeing Artificial Intelligence Center, Seattle, WA)
**Expertise transfer for expert system design.**
Elsevier Sci. Pub. B. V., Amsterdam, The Netherlands, 1986, 312 pp., $72.25, ISBN 0-444-42634-5. [Advances in human factors/ergonomics; no. 3.]

Since the inception of expert system technology about a decade ago, one major goal has been to eliminate knowledge engineers from the loop—allowing domain experts to build expert systems on their own. This book describes the Expertise Transfer System (ETS), which does not achieve this goal but constitutes an important step in that direction. ETS is a program, developed at the Boeing Artificial Intelligence Support Center, that interviews experts and helps them build expert systems. The interviewing technique employed by ETS is drawn from *Personal Construct Theory* in psychology and is well known in knowledge engineering circles as the *Repertory Grid Technique*. The first chapter of this book provides a well-referenced introduction to expert systems, knowledge engineering, and personal construct theory.

The second, third, and sixth chapters detail how ETS is used by domain experts to develop example applications. The examples illustrate that the repertory grid technique is especially effective for eliciting knowledge required for classification tasks. ETS has been used to build over 300 prototype systems, including the following:

☐ AI Market Analysis Advisor
☐ Aircraft Identifier

- ☐ Bank Examiner
- ☐ Crime Avoidance Advisor
- ☐ Expert Systems Tool Advisor
- ☐ Halloween Costume Consultant
- ☐ Negotiation Advisor—Joint Gain
- ☐ Program Bug Advisor (FORTRAN)
- ☐ Statistics Package Use Advisor
- ☐ Vacation City Advisor

The knowledge that ETS elicits from experts is represented in the form of *rating grids*, which can be transformed into rules with associated certainty factors for many different target languages, including OPS5, Prolog, KEE, ART, LOOPS, and MRS.

Chapter 4 covers the strengths and limitations of ETS; Chapter 5 describes work in progress to address these limitations. The greatest strength of the system is that, for many applications, knowledge engineers and experts can rapidly develop prototype expert systems in literally hours as opposed to months. Another important strength of the system is that by letting several experts build grids independently, and then combining the grids, the process of extending and tuning knowledge bases can be substantially shortened. Some limitations of ETS are summarized below:

- ☐ Many expert tasks (such as configuration, planning, control, and repair) do not fit well into a diagnosis/classification framework.
- ☐ Rating grids are an impoverished representation unable to capture various causal knowledge and different levels of abstraction. The grid's bipolar constructs impose an artificial constraint on variable values.

Future work will be directed towards extending the types of knowledge that can be represented and improving the system's ability to interact intelligently with domain experts, thereby improving the system's ability to handle complex and diverse problem domains.

This book should be of interest to knowledge engineers and students of artificial intelligence, as well as others interested in eliciting and representing knowledge from domain experts. The technical, theoretical, and even the economic repercussions of the work presented in this book make it well worth reading. However, this reviewer found the writing very uneven and, on the whole, far too dense. Some sections read like a barely fleshed-out outline that might accompany slides for an oral presentation—too dense for the average reader. With this warning in mind, this reviewer recommends the book because of its state-of-the-art technical content.

—*J. Spohrer,* New Haven, CT

CLEAL, D. M. (PA Computers and Telecommunications, London, UK); AND HEATON, N. O. (Loughborough Univ. of Technology)
**Knowledge-based systems: implications for human-computer interfaces.**
Halsted Press, New York, NY, 1988, 253 pp., $49.95, ISBN 0-470-21082-6. [Series in expert systems.]

Knowledge-based systems typically support decision making in complex or unstructured situations. Users of these systems are often computer novices. If such systems are to be used safely and effectively, their user interfaces must be designed for understandability and ease of operation. Knowledge engineers and programmers also require special tools to facilitate system development. These include tools for knowledge acquisition, system tracing and debugging, and maintenance of the knowledge base. This book discusses a potpourri of topics related to human-computer interaction and the development of knowledge-based systems.

Chapter 1 describes the relationship between research in interface design and the development of knowledge-based systems, then leaps to a discussion of conversational interactions between users and computers. Chapter 2 assesses the practical advantages and limitations of various data-input devices, including keyboards and pointing and speech-recognition devices. Chapter 3 discusses how the system's implicit or explicit model of the user, and the user's implicit model of the system, affect human-computer interactions. Chapter 4 briefly summarizes approaches to natural language understanding and reviews several application areas, and chapter 5 provides examples of intelligent front ends to software systems such as databases, statistical packages, and simulation programs. Chapter 6 discusses explanations in rule-based systems, while chapter 7 describes the capture of knowledge through analysis of textual information, observation of human experts, and machine learning. Chapter 8 describes the design and development of three knowledge-based systems and assesses the strengths and weaknesses of the systems' interfaces. Chapter 9 surveys specific commercial tools for building knowledge-based systems, focusing on their programmer and user interfaces. Chapter 10 recounts the rapid prototyping approach to the development of knowledge-based systems, stressing the importance of involving domain experts and users at every step of the process. References are provided at the end of every chapter, and subject and author indices are included at the end of the book.

Although the book contains material appropriate to a discussion of human-computer interfaces and knowledge-based systems, it is poorly organized and fails to construct the coherent framework needed to tie the various topics together. In particular, it lacks robust discussions of users' needs and the desirable features of interfaces. Without an adequate understanding of the problems to be solved, a reader would find it difficult to evaluate the solutions discussed in the text. At the chapter level, the important points are difficult to extract from the discussions, and too much of the narrative is unfocused, unclear, and imprecise. In addition, the entire book is plagued by typographical errors and misspellings.

The book's intended audience comprises all people who have "an active interest in information technology," including technical specialists, managers, researchers, and students. The text is too disorganized and vague, however, to provide a comprehensive overview of the field, and it lacks sufficient depth to be valuable to those who are already familiar with issues of human-computer communication. Both of these shortcomings are aggravated by the book's failure to discuss or reference fundamental research related to the design of both user interfaces and knowledge-based systems. In sum, this book is more likely to confuse than to enlighten.

—*L. E. Perreault,* Stanford, CA

## Law

GARDNER, ANNE V.D.L.  **HCI-0061**
**An artificial intelligence approach to legal reasoning.**
MIT Press, Cambridge, MA, 1987, 240 pp., $22.50, ISBN 0-262-07104-5. [Artificial intelligence and legal reasoning.]

Gardner feels that the majority of existing legal expert systems are inadequate because these systems do not distinguish between the solutions experts agree upon and the solutions they disagree upon. She believes that such ambiguities arise from the open texture of legal predicates. To overcome this problem, a distinction between "clear" and "hard" cases is implemented in an AI program. This program identifies the issues raised in a fact situation dealing with the offer and acceptance problem (contract law). The program distinguishes those situations in which there is enough information to solve the problem from those in which there is not. She states that her system has produced a description of legal reasoning that is applicable to appropriate subproblems.

The author's program reasons from given facts and distinguishes between those cases it can solve and those it cannot. To distinguish clear and hard cases, she devises sophisticated heuristics. She correctly argues that the problem arises not so much from ambiguous rules as from the difficulty of applying rules to particular situations.

Whether or not the author's heuristics distinguishing clear and hard cases would contribute to an understanding of legal reasoning is uncertain. While she has successfully solved the computational problem, it is questionable whether she is entitled to claim success in solving a problem that is the subject of debate by leading authorities on jurisprudence.

Gardner has made a courageous attempt to solve a significant problem basic to understanding the legal reasoning process. However, her main finding has limited application to other AI research in law because it lacks theoretical validity.

The human interface becomes the central issue here. Gardner is skeptical of user input. "The user may not know, and may wrongly assume that he or she does know" (p. 189).

An alternative approach to the clear and hard case distinction would shift the problem's solution from the program to the user. Such an approach assumes that legal expert systems are designed for use only by lawyers (experts) and not by technicians. The human decision maker would specify the relationship between facts and rules through an interface. Although two experts could specify different fact-rule relationships and reach opposite results, this should cause no concern: the legal system itself is adversarial.

—*W. F. Grunbaum*, St. Louis, MO

### I.2.4  Knowledge Representation Formalisms and Methods

ARBIB, MICHAEL A. (Univ. of Massachusetts, Amherst)  **HCI-0062**
**In search of the person: philosophical explorations in cognitive science.**
University of Massachusetts Press, Amherst, MA, 1985, 156 pp., $20, ISBN 0-87023-499-4.

The aim of this book is to explore some philosophical questions on the basis of recent work in the fields of cognitive science, brain theory, and artificial intelligence. More specifically, the wider questions discussed relate to natural language, to some notions of Freud, and to some issues of human society and freedom. Throughout, the style of the discussion is non-technical and aimed at a wide readership.

I found the book unsatisfactory both in its overall argument and in many details. The overall argument starts with a discussion of what are called schemas (or the schema theory). Persons or some aspects of persons are supposed to be made up of schemas. This is not made clear. Somewhere it is suggested that at any stage in a person's development, his or her mental situation consists of a large number of schemas—hundreds of thousands—in a subtle interplay. Elsewhere it is said that schemas are what can be programmed in computers. However, surely nobody has any idea how to program anything even remotely similar to many thousands of partially independent units in any kind of subtle interplay. Thus the relation to computing claimed in the book is an empty postulate.

In later chapters this problematic notion of schemas is compared with certain views of language and society and with some ideas of Freud. Many of these ideas are themselves highly problematic and controversial, particularly those of Freud. I find the discussion of this comparison as tenuous and doubtful as the schemas themselves.

In addition to my misgivings about the overall argument of the book, I also have concerns about certain details. There is just too much throwing about of phrases such as "reality of physical matter," "reality of the person," "realities that transcend space and time," and "models of cognition and intelligence." I find these phrases too mythical and their use in context too vague to be worth pursuing in detail. The main questions posed by Arbib are "To what extent can cognitive science give a theory of the person? And to what extent, if any, does the reality of the person transcend what cognitive science can hope to explain?" I cannot imagine any kind of answers to these questions that might make sense.

To judge from this book, I have grave doubts about the validity of what is here called cognitive science.

—*P. Naur,* Copenhagen, Denmark

## *Representations (procedural and rule-based)*

JOHNSON-LAIRD, P. N. (Medical Research Council Applied Psychology Unit, Cambridge, UK)
**Mental models: towards a cognitive science of language, inference, and consciousness.**
Harvard University Press, Cambridge, MA, 1983, 513 pp., $12.95, ISBN 0-674-56882-6. [Cognitive Science Series, 6.]

The book presents a unified theory of the major properties of mind: reasoning, comprehension, natural language processing, and consciousness. It is devoted to the development of a scientific theory of cognition, bringing together ideas and methods of experimental psychology, linguistics, and artificial intelligence, and synthesizing them in a nontrivial way. Although the theory of mental models as a functional description of the background of basic mental processes is, first of all, a psychological theory, it may also provide a significant contribution to various branches of artificial intelligence, such as reasoning schemes, knowledge representation, or natural language understanding.

The exposition of the theory of mental models is based on the doctrine of functionalism, i.e., on the development of a functionally adequate model of mental processes, and on the consideration of mental processes as effective (computable) procedures. The central idea of the book is that human beings construct mental models of the world. It is argued that the mind is essentially a model-building device that can itself be modeled on a computer. The book provides a blueprint for building such a model as well as a lot of experimental data to support the framework.

In 16 chapters, the book provides a treatment of the concepts of thought, meaning, grammar, and consciousness. Chapter 1 exposes the methodological background of psychological theory expressed as an effective procedure, presents fundamental criteria for explanations, and outlines the basics of the theory of computability. The second chapter presents an outline of the doctrine of mental logic, which constitutes an orthodox view of the mechanism for making deductions, and describes problems connected with this approach. Chapter 3 introduces propositional reasoning, together with the properties appropriate to a psychological theory of reasoning. Chapter 4 presents the goals of a psychological theory of reasoning, experimental data concerning syllogistic reasoning, and fundamental theories of syllogistic reasoning. Shortcomings of the theories are demonstrated and all of the theories are shown to be inadequate in the face of the experiments. Chapter 5, How to Reason Syllogistically, describes the theory of syllogistic inference, based on the concept of mental models. The author demonstrates this theory to be a remedy for the experimental problems of the classical theories, and presents experimental results that thoroughly demonstrate the descriptional adequacy of the theory.

The subsequent ten chapters refine various aspects of the properties of mind from the viewpoint of the proposed theory. Chapter 6 outlines a general theory of inference based on mental models. Chapter 7 discusses various types of mental representation and argues that at least three types of mental representation—viz., propositional representations, mental models, and images—are necessary for a plausible explanation of the experimental data. Chapter 8, which presents an exposition of various conceptions of meaning in model-theoretic semantics of natural language, introduces the concept of possible worlds and Montague's intensional logic [1]. Chapters 9 and 10 discuss psychological aspects of meaning and meaning representation. Chapter 11 outlines a procedural theory of semantics together with a description of a computer realization of this theory for simple spatial knowledge representation and inference. Mental models play the role of representative samples from the set of models satisfying an assertion, and they provide a mentally-representable counterpart to the model-theoretic concept of possible worlds. Chapter 12 deals with the relation of grammar and psychology. It presents an outline of the recent work of Peters [2], Gazdar [3], and Chomsky [4] on grammatical structures for natural language description. Chapter 13 presents a detailed overview of possible parsing techniques, discusses their performance, and derives requirements for the mental parser architecture. Mental parsing is demonstrated to be performed in parallel with semantic analysis, and computer implementation of a semantic transition network yielding the meaning of a sentence directly in terms of mental models is described. Chapter 14 discusses coherence of discourse, argues against the theory of story grammars, and explains related problems within the theory of mental models. Chapter 15 presents an account of the basic principles along which mental models are constructed. Methods of world representation are described, a set of forms of mental models for various roles and purposes is presented, processes constructing and interpreting mental models are summarized, basic sets of primitive concepts and conceptual primitives for mental models are discussed, and a typology of mental models is given. A powerful feature is the possibility of the embedding of mental models and the forming of nested mental models that allow a sound treatment of propositional attitudes within the theory. Eventually, the ways of representing a large or infinite number of entities with the help of small mental models is described. The last chapter of the book presents a discussion of the relationship between consciousness and computation. The essential role of parallelism in the mind's "operating system" is stressed; a treatment of consciousness, unconsciousness, and self-awareness within the functional theory, based exclusively on effective/computable processes, is provided; and arguments strongly defending the treatment of the mind as an automaton within a scientific theory are given. The book is accompanied by suggestions for further reading in computational theory, syntactic theory, logic, and model-theoretic semantics, in a bibliography containing more than 450 titles, and by name and subject indexes.

The book is lively and lucid. Although it explores material from several disciplines, it is accessible to the expert and non-expert alike. There are few, if any, points one could criticize. One of them might be the implicit treatment of syllogisms, which, according to Aristotle, suppose the existence of *A*s in judgments of the form all *A* are *B*. This is not explicitly mentioned until p. 90, although the judgment following an example of a difficult syllogism on p. 68 heavily depends on this supposition. This may confuse a reader who has only had a basic course in mathematical logic. In Chapter 8, although the exposition of Montague's intensional logic is made as clear and concise as possible, involvement of an alternative intensional logic (cf., e.g., [5]) could, in my opinion, suit the author's purposes even better. Moreover, an adequate treatment of propositional attitudes within that logic has been presented in [6] that somewhat weakens the case in Chapter 15 against model-theoretic treatment of propositional attitudes. Finally, in Chapter 12, I would also be interested in the author's possible treatment of the findings of [7], which may also contribute to a theory of language acquisition.

All in all, this is an exciting and authoritative book that provides a deep insight into how the mind works. The author succeeds in bringing together important results from psychology, computer science, linguistics, and logic, and in synthesizing them into an original scientific treatment of mental functioning.

—*J. Zlatuška*, Brno, Czechoslovakia

### REFERENCES

[1] MONTAGUE, R. *Formal philosophy: selected papers*, Yale University Press, New Haven, CT, 1974.

[2] PETERS, P. S.; AND RITCHIE, R. W. On restricting the base component of transformational grammars, *Inf. Control* **18** (1971), 483–501.

[3] GAZDAR, G. Unbounded dependencies and coordinate structure, *Linguist. Inquiry* **12** (1981), 155–184.

[4] CHOMSKY, N. *Aspect of the theory of syntax*, MIT Press, Cambridge, MA, 1965.

[5] TICHY, P. Two kinds of intensional logic, *Epistemologia* **1** (1978), 143–164.

[6] MATERNA, P. Kritische ausainander setzung mit der fregeschen kategorie des sinnes, II, in *Frege Konferenz Schwerin*, 1984.

[7] BICKERTON, D. *Roots of language*, Karoma Publishers, Ann Arbor, MI, 1981.

### I.2.6 Learning

*Induction*

HOLLAND, JOHN H.; HOLYOAK, KEITH J.; NISBETT, RICHARD E.; AND THAGARD, PAUL R. (Univ. of Michigan, Ann Arbor)
**Induction: processes of inference, learning, and discovery.**
MIT Press, Cambridge, MA, 1986, 385 pp., $24.95, ISBN 0-26208160-1. [Computational models of cognition and perception.]

The authors take induction to encompass "all inferential processes that expand knowledge in the face of uncertainty." The purpose of this book is to present their "framework for understanding induction," which is centered around the if-then rule, but also includes such notions as category, hierarchy, default, prediction, message, search, support, competition, and variation.

Chapter 1 is a reasonable introduction to the problem of induction. The authors lay out the important issues, argue against naive syntactic approaches, and lay out their framework. Chapter 2 explains how rules can model the environment. Chapter 3 is perhaps the key chapter. The first topic is rule modification, with the focus on modifying rule strengths and the credit-assignment problem. A partial solution, the bucket-brigade algorithm, is presented poorly, with confusing analogies and suggestive examples. Discussion of the second topic, learning new rules, is vague, unfortunately. Chapter 4 is on computational models. The account of Holland's genetically inspired classifier systems (also hard to read) is at a much lower level than the rest of the book. The discussion of PI, a program under development, serves to situate learning in the context of problem solving.

One of the authors' main points is that rules compete among themselves for the right to analyze the environment (both for categorization and prediction) and for the right to suggest behavior. Chapter 5 illustrates this by showing how some data on the conditioning of rats are best explained in these terms. Chapter 6, on category formation, reviews the important ideas on categories and some unimportant new experiments. Chapter 7 sketches the findings on naive physics and on models of personality, including the fundamental attribution error. Chapter 8 discusses the role of knowledge of variability in generalization—how knowledge of the typical variability of categories (among members of a species, or among inhabitants of a region) affects the propensity to generalize from a small number of examples. Chapter 9 relates learning to education. Statistics courses help people reason about uncertainty, whereas logic courses do not help people reason formally very much. Experiments show the cause: naive people are sensitive to variability, but do not think logically. For example, "If A then B" is often thought of in terms of a "pragmatic schema" of permission. Chapter 10 surveys research in analogy. Chapter 11 discusses the process of scientific discovery and stresses the importance of mental models to scientists.

The book has its flaws: It is annoyingly repetitive. The authors digress frequently for no reason. Some sections have no reason to be here. The authors' framework is too loose to lead them to say anything new about most of the fields they survey. The book casts no new light on the traditional problem of induction.

The book is directed toward cognitive scientists in general. As such, it reports a large number of psychology experiments and presents a broad range of ideas on learning at a fairly accessible level. It's very sensible and never simplistic. People interested in Machine Learning, Computer-Aided Instruction, and Learning in general should find this book interesting.

—*Nigel Ward,* Berkeley, CA

### I.2.7 Natural Language Processing

HARRIS, MARY D. (Loyola Univ., New Orleans)
**Introduction to natural language processing.**
Reston Publishing Co., Reston, VA, 1985, 368 pp., $27.95, ISBN 0-8359-3253-2.

HCI-0065

The Preface states, "This book has been designed for two primary audiences: undergraduate Computer Science students and programmers interested in adding natural language interfaces to their software products." In the present state of development of the software arts, the book's appearance is very timely. The need for good input handling software interposed between user and application has never been greater than it is now.

The design of Natural Language Systems (NLS) is developed by modeling humans as information processing systems where written (rather than spoken) text is used as the medium of communication. The author attempts to examine language understanding and language processing from a number of different perspectives with a pronounced practical orientation. The Preface continues, "Anyone who works through this book will have a good grasp of major problems of computer understanding of language and should be able to apply these ideas to a restricted version of the English language. He will be able to read and understand the current literature describing research in Natural Language Understanding and Cognitive Science."

Part 1 of the book reviews some basic material of the science of language and linguistics, and defines some terminology. Highlights of various theories due to Bloomfield [1] and others are presented, and some detail of Chomsky's theory of syntax [2] and Filmor's case grammar [3] is developed.

Part II is concerned with low-level input and output of natural language including machine representation, Huffman coding, and the like. A number of programs are presented using PASCAL, along with some fairly obvious extensions closely modeled on the UCSD implementation which will permit the user to perform basic string processing operations. Lexical considerations, such as dictionary structure, data structures, and hashing, round out this section.

The largest and most important part of the book is found in Part III, which deals with the structures and algorithms of natural language. Transformational generative grammars are dealt with in one chapter and various types of transition networks in the next. The latter starts out with finite state networks and proceeds to recursive and augmented transition networks. In all cases, implementation details are given (in PASCAL) and many program fragments are listed to aid the practitioner. An entire chapter is devoted to case grammars and another one to procedural, partitioned, and extended semantic networks. The conceptual dependency theory of Schank [4] is discussed at some length in the final three chapters.

Part IV is on the design of natural language understanding systems. Its purpose is to give the program designer a scheme of a complete system for manipulating natural language.

As is evident from its title, the book is meant to be an introduction to the field. It does not treat any of its constituents in great depth, although it does an admirable job within its stated limits. Students of computer science will likely find that the material of Part II is already well known to them. The use of PASCAL as an implementation vehicle will appeal to many programmers, although this will appear very awkward to those used to programming in a more appropriate language such as LISP. Apart from this, a good balance has been struck between theory and practice and between depth and breadth. This book is recommended as a good introduction to the subject.

—*G. M. White,* Ottawa, Ont., Canada

**REFERENCES**

[1] BLOOMFIELD, L. *Language,* Henry Holt & Co., New York, 1933.
[2] CHOMSKY, N. *Syntactic structures,* Mouton, Hawthorne, NY, 1957.
[3] FILMOR, C. A case for case, in *Universals in linguistic theory,* Holt, Rinehart and Winston, New York, 1968.
[4] SCHANK, R. Conceptual dependency: a theory of natural language, in *Computer models of thought and language,* R. Schank and K. Colby (Eds.), W. H. Freeman & Co., San Francisco, CA, 1973.

BOLC, L.; AND JARKE, M. (EDS.)
**Cooperative interfaces to information systems.**
Springer-Verlag New York, Inc., New York, NY, 1986, 328 pp., $39, ISBN 0-387-16599-1.
[Topics in information systems.]

The book presents a collection of eight papers that provide detailed descriptions and empirical investigations of natural language systems that have made a substantial contribution to the idea of cooperative interfaces to information systems. The editors call an interface *cooperative* "if it does not just accept user requests passively or answer them literally, but actively attempts to understand the users' intentions and to help them solve their application problems." This notion covers the aspects of the formulation and acceptance of user requests, the presentation of the answer, the reaction to exceptional situations, the navigation through complex dialogs, and the adaptability of the interface to new applications or even languages.

The book is divided into three parts. Part 1 addresses general application-independent issues in natural language comprehension and (graphical) output presentation. Chapter 1 describes a large and complex augmented phrase-structure grammar for interpreting English language dialogs. In chapter 2, a system is presented that constructs graphic displays according to incomplete declarations of their content, structure, and appearance.

Part 2 introduces three natural language interfaces that were or still are considered for commercial product development. Chapter 3 discusses considerations for the development of natural-language interfaces to database management systems and concludes with a comprehensive checklist of necessary functional capabilities of such systems. In chapter 4, the need for a formal empirical evaluation of information systems interfaces is emphasized, the framework for such studies is designed, and its application to a domain-independent natural language query system is described. In chapter 5, an interactive customization program is introduced, allowing end users to define their own vocabulary and grammar rules to be used when querying a relational database. These users need not be linguists but should be familiar with the database to be accessed.

Part 3 describes three major projects in knowledge-based natural language processing. Chapter 6 concentrates on a semantics-based approach to the analysis of natural language queries over a relational database. A thorough treatment is given to problems of ambiguity, conjunction, and ellipsis. The contribution demonstrates that an approach ignoring most of the syntactic features of the query can yield nontrivial results. A particular result of language-oriented research in the field of artificial intelligence is described in chapter 7. It is a broadly based cooperative natural language dialog system, HAM-ANS, which can provide access to a wide variety of information systems—a database, an image processing system, and an expert system. Detailed examples of these applications are given. This chapter emphasizes the need for explicit user modeling and presents suggestions for the representation and application of user models. The final chapter 8 describes an expert interface to an information retrieval system. Starting from the natural language query by the user, the rule-based system selects and executes an appropriate strategy to evaluate the query.

The book gives a clear idea of the rapidly evolving field of cooperative interfaces to information systems and introduces the goals of the research, the problems, and the important solutions. Its best feature is that it presents the wealth of problems that still remain to be solved before truly cooperative interfaces are achieved—this area of research is still in its early phase. Some results, however, are rather outdated. Chapter 3 is based on experience with a system whose development ended in 1981, and the examples in chapter 7 quote the system version of 1983.

The book is aimed at AI researchers and students; only a general background in AI is required. References from all the contributions are collected at the end of the book, and a sufficiently detailed subject index is provided.

—*T. Chrz,* Prague, Czechoslovakia

GROSZ, BARBARA J. (SRI International, Menlo Park, CA); SPARCK-JONES, KAREN (Univ. of Cambridge, Cambridge, UK); AND WEBBER, BONNIE L. (Univ. of Pennsylvania, Philadelphia) (EDS.)
**Readings in natural language processing.**
Morgan-Kaufmann, Palo Alto, CA, 1986, 664 pp., $28.95, ISBN 0-934613-11-7.

This book is a collection of 38 articles published during the past 25 years in the literature on the subject of natural language processing (NLP). The editors have organized the papers into six chapters. The first chapter, on Syntactic Models, and associated papers primarily deal with parsers for context-free grammars. The editors also provide a brief summary of each of the nine papers in this chapter. The second chapter, on Semantic Interpretation, contains nine papers dealing with general subject-matter issues as well as with how some of the systems solve specific problems. The third chapter, on Discourse Interpretation, contains five papers on determining pronoun and noun phrase referents. The fourth chapter, on Language Action and Intention, contains four papers that examine the ways in which the belief and intentions of the natural language communicator can assist in the interpretation. Chapter 5, on Generation, has three papers dealing with issues of content determination, text planning, and realization/generation. Finally,

Chapter 6, on Systems, contains eight papers on NLP systems. The editors identify several systems-level issues in NLP systems: modularity, integration, problem factorization, transportability, habitability, extensibility, speed, and cognitive veracity. The editors go on to define these issues. Most of the definitions are self-evident from the terms and the context (NLP systems). The editors define habitability as a system's ability to react adequately to utterances outside its coverage. The editors go on to provide a brief description of each of the eight systems and how they deal with the aforementioned systems-level issues.

The editors have put together an impressive and a comprehensive set of papers, but it is not complete; Sowa's work on Conceptual Graphs and Sager's work on Linguistic String Processing come to mind as missing concepts. In the introduction of the book, the editors state "there are some conspicuous absences: for example, the treatment of ill-formed input, and tasks, such as translation . . . grammatical formalisms . . . speech processing. . . ."

The editors have done an excellent job of organizing the material in six chapters. I found the historical perspective for each of the chapters very useful. The editors' definition of key issues in each of the chapters is excellent. The editors do not relate these issues to the papers selected in all cases. While the summary for each paper in the chapter is good and useful, a more provocative and comparative analysis of the different approaches used to address the issues would have been a much-needed contribution to the field. The editors could have looked at how different research ideas are similar, complement each other, or can be combined.

In the introduction to the book, the editors state "The aim of these readings is to bring together key papers in the field of automatic natural language processing (NLP) to provide an introduction and reference collection for students and researchers . . . it puts in their hands many articles that have heretofore only appeared in technical journals, conference proceedings, and other books with limited availability." The book definitely meets this objective.

The editors' comments on the state of the art in NLP should give a feeling of déjà vu to both AI and NLP researchers. They state "Bringing principled theoretical approaches to bear effectively on practical, and hence usually idiosyncratic, applications remains a challenge." The editors feel that the research in syntactic parsing has matured; some semantic techniques have proven useful in specific cases; some valuable initial work has been done in discourse interpretation; a beginning has been made on generation. The editors conclude by stating "those aspects of natural language understanding research ready for development primarily consist of being able to deal with literal meaning and direct function in a limited and well-defined task and domain context." Haven't we heard this before?

—*Santosh Chokani,* Arlington, VA

## I.2.9 Robotics

### *Manipulators*

COIFFET, PHILIPPE (Automation Laboratory, Montpellier, France)
**Modelling and control.**
Prentice-Hall, Inc., Englewood Cliffs, NJ, 1983, 160 pp., $53.33, ISBN 0-13-782094-1. [Robot technology, vol. 1.]

COIFFET, PHILIPPE (Automation Laboratory, Montpellier, France)
**Interaction with the environment.**
Prentice-Hall, Inc., Englewood Cliffs, NJ, 1983, 240 pp., $53.33, ISBN 0-13-782128-X. [Robot technology, vol. 2.]

VERTUT, JEAN; AND COIFFET, PHILIPPE (Automation Laboratory, Montpelier, France)
**Teleoperations and robotics: evolution and development.**
Prentice-Hall, Inc., Englewood Cliffs, NJ, 1986, 332 pp., $53.33, ISBN 0-13-782194-8. [Robot technology, vol. 3A.]

VERTUT, JEAN; AND COIFFET, PHILIPPE (Automation Laboratory, Montpellier, France)
**Teleoperations and robotics: applications and technology.**
Prentice-Hall, Inc., Englewood Cliffs, NJ, 1986, 256 pp., $42.95, ISBN 0-13-782202-2. [Robot technology, vol. 3B.]

L'HOTE, FRANCOIS; KAUFFMANN, JEAN-MARIE; ANDRÉ, PIERRE; AND TAILLARD, JEAN-PIERRE
**Robot components and systems.**
Prentice-Hall, Inc., Englewood Cliffs, NJ, 1983, 346 pp., $53.33, ISBN 0-13-782160-3. [Robot technology, vol. 4.]

PARENT, MICHEL; AND LAURGEAU, CLAUDE
**Logic and programming.**
Prentice-Hall, Inc., Englewood Cliffs, NJ, 1985, 190 pp., $53.33, ISBN 0-13-782178-6. [Robot technology, vol. 5.]

ALEKSANDER, IGOR; FARRENY, HENRI; AND GHALLAB, MILIK
**Decision and intelligence.**
Prentice-Hall, Inc., Englewood Cliffs, NJ, 1987, 203 pp., $45.67, ISBN 0-13-782079-8. [Robot technology, vol. 6.]

LIÉGEOIS, ALAIN
**Performance and computer-aided design.**
Prentice-Hall, Inc., Englewood Cliffs, NJ, 1985, 268 pp., $53.33, ISBN 0-13-782210-3. [Robot technology, vol. 7.]

COIFFET, PHILIPPE (Automation Laboratory, Montpellier, France)
**Indexes and bibliography.**
Prentice-Hall, Inc., Englewood Cliffs, NJ, 1987, 105 pp., $33, ISBN 0-13-782046-1. [Robot technology, vol. 8.]

Overall, this series of books is impressive, although not all the books have the same value. The books were written in French between 1981 and 1986 and later translated into English. Some are more outdated, or better written, than others. The authors vary, but some wrote or co-wrote more than one book in the series.

The series attempts to cover all aspects of robotics while devoting enough attention to both basic foundations and research problems. A volume of indices and bibliographies helps to unite the series; this is especially useful since some topics are covered in two or more books written by different authors at different times. The books are not designed to be textbooks, though some of them could be used for specialized courses. Since they form a series, it is unclear why there are a lot of repetitions (most of the books begin by defining a robot) and why no attempt was made to use a consistent and unified notation.

The books cover most of the relevant topics, but not always in sufficient depth. The balance between depth and breadth of coverage is not easy to maintain, and the authors often prefer breadth. I have the impression that when the series was planned, the size of the material was not clear. For instance, the original plan included only one book on telemanipulation; the two thick books that now exist make it one of the best-covered topics.

Writing about robotics is difficult because people working in the field often have quite different backgrounds. One problem with this series is that it makes no attempt to specify the intended audience for the books or the background needed to understand them. Throughout the series, the authors present an unusual combination of fundamental principles and specific technology, which sometimes looks odd. References to specific technologies and research projects are often outdated, but this is to be expected from a collection of this size that was written over a number of years.

**Volume 1: Modelling and Control**

This book was one of the first two volumes in the series (it was originally published in 1981). It is quite short and disappointing.

The book covers the kinematics and dynamics of stationary articulated robots and includes a short description of robot programming. It contains the following chapters:

(1) Definitions and Objectives
(2) Structure and Specification of Articulated Robots
(3) Articulated Mechanical Systems: Determination of Kinematic Elements
(4) Calculation of Robot Articulation Variables
(5) Positional Control of Articulated Robots
(6) Speed Control of Articulated Robots
(7) Articulated Mechanical Systems: The Dynamic Model
(8) Dynamics and Control of Articulated Robots
(9) Learning and Trajectory Generation
(10) Task and Performance of Articulated Robots

The book also contains conclusions, references, and an index.

The notation is nonstandard and unnecessarily complicated. The author uses many abbreviations, such as S1 for $\sin \tau_1$, which he defines within the text. These definitions are hard to find, which makes it difficult to use this book as a reference. The problem is especially critical since the notation is very complex—most symbols have a subscript, a superscript, or both, and many have additional appendages such as underscores and stars. The descriptions are very formal in the mathematical sense, so the reader needs a clear understanding of the meaning of the notation.

Chapter 2 presents several systems for giving a formal description of a robot. These systems are not consistent, yet they are sufficiently complicated to require detailed study. It appears that the notation used in the rest of the book is not based directly on any of these descriptions, though it does use the graphical elements in Figure 11.

It is often hard to see what point the author is trying to make. For example, in Table B on page 110, many of the "methods to reduce the time" are generic to any problem in any scientific or computational domain. The author discusses a few of the remaining methods, but they do not seem to accomplish much. For example, the conclusion to chapter 7 (p. 105) says only that it is difficult to produce a dynamic model of a robot. This does not speak very highly of all the mathematics developed in that chapter.

Some of the statements in the book are less than helpful. For example, chapter 1 opens with a "definition" of robotics: "the theory and practice of automation of tasks which, because of their nature, were previously thought to be reserved for man alone." Since the author does not define "tasks" until four pages later, this definition does not even specify the domain about which robotics is concerned. Every advanced monograph in computer science talks about some development that was previously "thought to be reserved for man alone," so this phrase conveys no meaning.

The mathematical descriptions are hard to follow, not only because of the complex notation but also because of confusion in the text. For example, the author states that the underdetermined linear system (6-63) has $m - n + 1$ linearly independent solutions. The following page states that, for the specific example being discussed on pages 86–87, the three solutions listed on page 87 are independent and hence "form a basis for the solution of equation (6-17)." Since the generalized inverse is a basic concept of linear algebra that the reader is likely to have seen, it would be useful to use terms that are consistent with linear algebra terms. The use of the terms "linearly independent" and "basis" seems to imply that the solution space (6-53) is a linear subspace, which it is not; rather, it can be expressed as a constant vector (particular solution) plus any vector in the nullspace of $G$.

## Volume 2: Interaction with the environment

This book, originally published in 1981, shows its age. The overall quality is disappointing. The artificial vision part, which takes up more than half the book, is often confusing and incomplete. A footnote (p. 103) tells the reader that the area of vision has changed a lot since the book was published, but my main problem with the book is the lack of material that was known when it was originally written.

The first chapter is a short introduction to what a robot is and how it can be used. This chapter is fine, but some of the material has already been covered in the first book.

The second chapter covers interaction with gravity and load. The author mentions underwater applications when he describes the interaction of a robot with its medium, but he says very little. The material is an extension of what was covered in the first book and could have been placed there.

The three chapters on stress, tactile sensing, and proximity sensing are aged but still valid even though they are somewhat short. The chapter on proximity sensing is disappointing because it is so short that it contains little useful information.

The remaining four chapters are devoted to computer vision with an emphasis on industrial applications. Overall this is the most disappointing part of the book, perhaps because so many better books on the subject are available. The discussion of methods for depth reconstitution in chapter 6 does not even mention stereo vision and vision from motion. Range finding is mentioned only in passing; the most important topic seems to be where to position the camera. Chapter 7 covers filtering, coding, and extraction of features, but unfortunately does not even mention zero-crossings, Gaussian filtering, convolutions, or "Mexican hat." The feature extraction portion is modeled after industrial vision systems suited to 2D processing of isolated objects. Chapter 8 covers various template matching and pattern recognition approaches to classification that are clearly applicable only to 2D objects and to images where objects are not occluding each other or overlapping. This is the case in most industrial vision systems, but a separate chapter covers vision systems for industrial robots. Assuming that all the problems in using vision for robotics can be solved with the simple approaches taken by early industrial vision systems is a disservice to the robotics community.

Strangely, the chapter on industrial applications includes the Waltz labeling methods for line drawings and a little bit of stereo vision. I do not know of any industrial application of the contour labeling methods. The chapter describes various vision experiments, most of which were performed by research groups and not used in production. There are notable omissions, such as GM's CONSIGHT system. Clearly missing is a discussion on the importance of controlling the environment (light conditions, reflectance, and colors).

**Volume 3A: Teleoperations and robotics: evolution and development**
This volume is subtitled "Part I—Introduction" and consists of the following chapters:

(1.1) Background
(1.2) Classification of Teleoperation Systems
(1.3) Mechanized Master-Slave Telemanipulators for Radioactive Materials
(1.4) Motorized Telemanipulators with Open-Loop Control
(1.5) Bilateral Servo Manipulators
(1.6) Transporters and Vehicles
(1.7) The State of the Art in Teleoperation at the Time of the Introduction of Computer Science

It also contains references and an index.

**Volume 3B: Teleoperations and robotics: applications and technology**
Part II, "The Contribution of Computer Science," contains three chapters:

(2.1) A Description of Teleoperation Systems
(2.2) The Operator Substitution Function by Computer
(2.3) The Use of Computer Feedback to the Operator

Part III, "Performance and Man-machine Interface," is divided into two chapters:

(3.1) Performance Evaluation of Teleoperation Systems
(3.2) The Human Operator in the Teleoperation System

Part IV, "Applications of Teleoperation," covers the following:

(4.1) Nuclear Applications
(4.2) Underwater Applications
(4.3) Space Applications of Teleoperation
(4.4) Medical Applications of Teleoperation
(4.5) Industrial Applications of Teleoperation
(4.6) Applications in Security and Civil Protection
(4.7) Conclusion

This volume also contains a bibliography and an index.

The two books are comparatively recent (the first was originally written in 1984, the second in 1985). They are long and detailed and provide excellent coverage of the history of manipulators and teleoperators. An incredible collection of pictures and drawings completes the books, which are a pleasure to read.

**Volume 4: Robot components and systems**
This book was written in 1983. It is relatively long and contains a good collection of material on robot components.

The book consists of nine chapters:

(1) Introduction
(2) Arm Structures
(3) Direct Current Motors
(4) Stepping Motors
(5) Pneumatic and Hydraulic Actuators
(6) Transmission Systems
(7) Robot Control
(8) End Effectors
(9) Energy Sources, Effects of Gravity and Vibration, and Operational Peripherals

The authors provide references and an index.

Chapters 2 and 7 contain material already covered in the first book of the series. The other chapters are long and will certainly appeal to anybody interested in designing robots.

**Volume 5: Logic and programming**
This short book starts (again) with some definitions about robots. It was written in 1983, after most of the interesting robot programming languages were designed.

The book is divided into five chapters and three appendices:

Chapter 1  Introduction
   Appendix 1  Definitions for Mechanics, Geometry, Control and Programming
   Appendix 2  Designation of Geometrical Axes and Movements
Chapter 2  Maximal Effort Manipulators
   Appendix  Concepts and Rules for the Development of GRAFCET
Chapter 3  Servocontrolled Robots
Chapter 4  Programming Languages
Chapter 5  CAD Robot Programming

As usual, the book contains references and an index.

Chapter 2 covers maximal effort manipulators (pick-and-place robots) with bang-bang control and describes GRAFCET, a method for describing the operation of robots that is popular in France. Chapter 3 includes a short description of motors and robot components even though more detailed similar material appears in volume 4.

Chapter 4 covers programming languages. The authors say very little about the fundamental issues in robot programming: what makes programming robots difficult, why no standard programming languages for robots exist, and areas of future development. Most of the material is a review and comparison of various of the most popular programming languages. This choice tends to provide the reader with unimportant details. Nice tables compare the features of different robot programming languages, but the authors do not provide examples of complete programs written in different languages. The chapter on CAD robot programming covers important issues of geometric modeling.

The index is very short and too many items are missing. For instance, the robot programming languages described in the book do not appear in the index.

**Volume 6: Decision and intelligence**
This volume covers the following topics:

(1) Prospects for Knowledge-Based Robots
(2) Robots and AI: Parallel Developments
(3) Expert Systems and Knowledge-Based Languages
(4) Production-Rule Expert Systems
(5) Introduction to Search Techniques
(6) Heuristic Graph Searching
(7) AND/OR Graphs
(8) First Order Predicate Logic
(9) Future Prospects for Knowledge-Based Robots

It also contains a bibliography and an index.

Most of the 202 pages of the book discuss artificial intelligence (AI) theory that has nothing to do with robotics. Readers will be better served by real AI books, which are more accurate and up to date. Most of the parts of AI relevant to robotics are missing, including intelligent scheduling, planning, qualitative physics, truth-maintenance systems, blackboard-based architectures, frame-based systems, reasoning about space, reasoning about time, and reasoning about processes.

Even though the book is recent (1986), it does not mention recent applications of expert systems in manufacturing. The two chapters on expert systems are sketchy, yet they contain redundant material. The authors devote less than two pages to certainty factors in expert systems even though almost every expert system shell includes them. Some of the material is imprecise (for instance, the use of variables in MYCIN is more limited than is described here) or obsolete (many of the expert systems described are no longer in use).

Three chapters discuss search (65 pages) and one covers logic (30 pages). The chapters on search are very formal, with proofs of many of the properties of the algorithms described. The notation is confusing and unnecessarily cumbersome. These chapters include many mistakes, some of which result from poor proofreading, some from missing definitions, and some from incorrect steps in algorithms. In addition, the authors use some terms incorrectly. The names *depth-first* and *breadth-first search* are always used to describe uninformed search, rather than as the authors use them here. What the book calls depth-first search is known everywhere else as a form of best-first search.

The authors devote too many pages to AND/OR graphs, a topic of little practical importance in AI. They give lots of details of uninteresting algorithms. Some material is referenced but not really described. For instance, where does the book introduce the STRIPS type of operators? The authors mention them on page 124 but it is hard for the reader to figure out what they are.

In conclusion, I cannot recommend this poor book to anyone interested in AI, much less to anyone interested in learning what AI could do for robotics.

**Volume 7: Performance and computer-aided design**
This book covers the following topics:

(1) The Rigid Body: Configuration and Motion
(2) Definition and Measurement of Precision: Operation-Performance Relationship
(3) Introduction to Dynamics
(4) Structure of Robots: Geometrical and Mechanical Constraints
(5) 3D Models of Static Performances
(6) Analysis, Generation, and Optimization of Movements
(7) The Dynamic Behaviour of Robots: Characterization and Use of Models

The author has provided references and an index.

The book is concerned with mathematical modeling and graphic representation of robot performance. It considers three aspects of performance: geometrical and kinematic, static, and dynamic aspects.

The book is well written, well illustrated, and detailed. It compensates for some of the material missing or poorly described in the first book. Chapters 1 and 3 discuss material covered in volume 1, but handle it much more crisply and clearly. Chapter 6 gives some material on legged locomotion, a nice addition to a series that is primarily on articulated arms and not on navigation.

**Volume 8: Indexes and Bibliography**
This volume contains the subject bibliography, subject index, and author index for the entire series. It has some errors, such as missing references and incorrect pages, but overall it is a useful book that helps in finding topics spread across more than one volume of the series.

The subject bibliography is divided into many groups (such as active sensors, AND/OR graphs, and artificial intelligence), which appear in alphabetical order. The author index contains references to papers cited in the text or listed in the bibliography of all the books in the series. This is a very good idea, but many references are missing and some page numbers are wrong.

—*M. Gini*, Minneapolis, MN

**I.3  Computer Graphics**

**I.3.0  General**

# COMPARATIVE BOOK REVIEW

ROGERS, DAVID F. (United States Naval Academy, Annapolis, MD)
**Procedural elements for computer graphics.**
McGraw-Hill, Inc., New York, NY, 1985, 433 pp., $27.95, ISBN 0-07-053534-5.

FOLEY, JAMES D. (George Washington Univ., Washington, DC); AND VAN DAM, ANDRIES (Brown Univ., Providence, RI)
**Fundamentals of interactive computer graphics.**
Addison-Wesley Publ. Co., Inc., Reading, MA, 1982, 664 pp., $43.95, ISBN 0-201-14468-9.

SPROULL, ROBERT F. (Carnegie-Mellon Univ., Pittsburgh, PA) (ATH.) NEWMAN, WILLIAM M. (Xerox Corporation) (ED.)
**Principles of interactive computer graphics (2nd ed.).**
McGraw-Hill, Inc., New York, NY, 1979, 541 pp., $47.95, ISBN 0-07-046338-7.

HEARN, DONALD (Univ. of Illinois); AND BAKER, M. P. (Western Illinois Univ., Macomb)
**Computer graphics.**
Prentice-Hall, Inc., Englewood Cliffs, NJ, 1986, 592 pp., $48, ISBN 0-13-165382-2.

Whereas the human retina communicates to the brain via the optic nerve at a rate of about 1M baud, humans can only read text at about 1K baud. Computer graphics is the art of drawing pictures with a computer for better communication with a human user and trying to capitalize on this three-orders-of-magnitude discrepancy. Computer graphics is demanding of all computer resources, but as computer power has become cheaper, it is economic to use some of that power in order to provide the better user interaction that pictorial computer output provides. The data structures and algorithms employed in the process have a large impact on the cost and viability of the graphical interface. Thus, university courses on these techniques are a common part of computer science syllabi.

There are approximately two dozen different books on computer graphics. Many are aimed at the home hobbyists, some at the users of personal computers; some are aimed at artists, some at engineers and mathematicians. A few are appropriate for a tertiary-level course on computer graphics within a computer science course. Four examples of this last type of book are reviewed below.

All four books have abundant diagrams, photographs, coded program segments, sample questions, and a bibliography. All are excellent for both tutorial and reference purposes. The major topics covered by texts such as these include the following:

- introduction (e.g., history, applications),
- output devices (e.g., hardcopy, raster architecture),
- input devices,
- data structures (e.g., segments, polyhedra),
- interactive techniques,
- geometric algorithms,
- transformations (2D and 3D),
- hidden line and surface removal, and
- shading (including color, ray tracing).

An important factor is whether a particular book defines its own graphics primitives, or whether it uses those of the ISO standard: the Graphical Kernel System (GKS). This is becoming increasingly important as more hardware and software suppliers offer the GKS interface to their systems.

### *Newman and Sproull*

This is the oldest book, which is a second and greatly revised edition of a book first published in 1973. Readers in the offshore colonies can obtain a paperback International Student Edition of the book at a markedly reduced price ($8.25), but it is not available on mainland North America. Newman and Sproull is the only one of the four books to include a movie (a rotating skeleton of a molecule homologous with 3,4 di-para-ethyl-phenyl-n-hexane, printed on the corners of pp. 293–409). The age of the book is betrayed by its early chapter on line drawing displays and the code in the procedure "Transmit Coords" on p. 89, which produces graphic commands for the Tektronic 4010 series of displays. Nevertheless, five out of the 28 chapters are on raster graphics, and point plotting is introduced before line plotting. It covers well all the topics described above. However, its publication date (1979) puts limits on the utility of the references, and no mention is made of GKS.

*Foley and Van Dam*

The largest book, it is competitively priced compared with the hardcover Newman and Sproull, covering much the same material, but in greater depth. This book mentions the GKS standard (six times), but it does not include even such key items as "bundles" or "polylines" in the index. Nevertheless, it has excellent explanations of the use of hierarchical graphic data structures, and also the design of user computer-graphic conversations. A feature of the book is the continuous interweaving of the various topics listed above, giving students an integrated development of computer graphics. The lack of orthogonality between chapters makes it a disconcerting book to teach from, but the student maintains a useful, coherent understanding of the whole field at every stage. One small point is the use of capitals for procedure names in the code segments. This may be comforting to old FORTRAN programmers (like the reviewer), but it makes the code harder for the eye to run over.

*Rogers*

This is a newer book, devoted mainly to geometric software. It has only five chapters: (1) Introduction, (2) raster scan graphics (including line and circle drawing, various filling algorithms, and antialiasing), (3) clipping (2D and 3D), (4) hidden line and surface removal (in particular, Roberts, Warnock, and Weiler-Atherton), and (5) rendering (shading, transparency, shadows, and texture). Unlike the other books, it assumes familiarity with vectors, matrices, and perspective. However, it has nearly a page on fractals, whereas Foley and Van Dam has only a paragraph, and Newman and Sproull has no mention of them. While the other two books have their code segments in Pascal, Rogers uses a pseudocode (which is like Pascal).

*Hearn and Baker*

The most recent book uses GKS throughout. Indeed, it even has a second index specifically on GKS keywords. It covers all the topics listed above in a straightforward manner. It also includes some more modern material, such as 3D displays, octrees, constructive solid geometry, and eight

Table 1—Approximate Statistics

|  | Newman and Sproull | Foley and Van Dam | Rogers | Hearn and Baker |
|---|---|---|---|---|
| **Length (in pages)** | 540 | 660 | 430 | 352 |
| **Number of index entries** | 650 | 880 | 910 | 930 + 86 |
| **Number of bibliography entries** | 530 | 480 | 170 | 240 |
| **Number of lines of code (including comments)** | 1700 | 4140 | 1910 | 1350 |
| **Number of diagrams** | 310 | 370 | 240 | 340 |
| **Number of monochrome photographs** | 21 | 41 | 25 | 47 |
| **Number of color images** | 2 | 48 | 10 | 91 |
| **Number of questions** | 240 | 230 | 40 | 260 |

BOOKS & PROCEEDINGS                                                     [HCI-0070]

pages on fractals. The book uses color a great deal not only in the photographs, but also in the diagrams, giving them extra clarity. A curious exception is the set of pages on 295 to 308, in the chapter on Shading and Color Models, where color in the diagrams and photographs would have been very beneficial.

*Conclusions*
There are a number of limitations to all the books. They all have a very similar style of writing. While the style is not overly academic, it is not particularly exciting. There is room for more distinction in each between a reference book and a tutorial text. There are also a number of topics which are of importance but are barely treated, if at all, in these four books: e.g., electroluminescent displays, memory contention, animation, quaternions. The books are good, and are excellent texts, but coupling the omissions with the rapid pace of computer graphics research, there is clearly room for improvement.

—*D. Herbison-Evans,* Sydney, Australia


### I.3.6  Methodology and Techniques

*Device independence*

SPROULL, ROBERT F.; SUTHERLAND, W. R.; AND ULLNER, MICHAEL K. (Sutherland,         **HCI-0070**
Sproull, and Associates, Pittsburgh, PA)
**Device-independent graphics: with examples from IBM personal computers.**
McGraw-Hill, Inc., New York, NY, 1985, 546 pp., $35.95, ISBN 0-07-060504-1.

According to the Preface, this text is particularly aimed at scientists and engineers wishing to apply computer graphics without an in-depth knowledge of the field. It does not cater to an audience which is only willing to use computer graphics as long as it does not get any more involved than business graphics. In other words, the potential clientele of this book should be willing to write, and in fact should already have considerable experience in writing, computer programs at a reasonably advanced level. To these people, the authors offer an extension of their knowledge in the graphics area.

Fortunately, the acquisition of this knowledge does not have to be supported by very expensive graphics hardware. To many people's surprise, IBM has not only established itself as a PC leader, but the company maintains a very advanced level in that area. In this philosophy, IBM also decided to extend the PC with powerful graphics capabilities, properly named the Professional Graphics (PG) option.

This text, on almost every page, refers to what by some is now the IBM/PG. The title is therefore somewhat of a misnomer. It is not that there isn't a lot of discussion on device-independent graphics in the book, but this goal is continually compared and illustrated with what the PG has to offer. In fact, a sizeable portion of the text is devoted to device-dependent graphics.

Nevertheless, this book gives a lucid exposition of the ISO GKS standard, in particular as it has been implemented on the PG. It consists of four major parts in which practically everything a programmer of graphics applications might want to know is dealt with. In addition to GKS, there is a not too deep, but fairly complete, discussion of geometry, including viewing and modeling transformations, 3D graphics, hidden-surface problems, and shading. There is also a full-length chapter (device-dependent) on raster graphics.

Initially, the book not only promises a presentation of GKS but also of the Virtual Device Interface standard, VDI. There are some vague statements, such as "VDI offers less functionality than GKS but more control at a smaller size," but a description akin to the level of detail of GKS is unfortunately missing.

The book is particularly strong on full-length, ready-to-use programs, illustrating almost every topic being discussed in the text. It is rather annoying that the authors chose to use FORTRAN as their notational programming language. Although it is FORTRAN-77, the authors religiously adhere to six-letter variables. They also seem to think that variables must never start with a capital, resulting in such user-friendly names as "kbdTxt" and "xKbdMnu." Also, variables are only declared when necessary. In this spirit, variables are forced to type integer by prefixing them with the letter "i." Practically every program would have been much more readable if a language such as, for example, PASCAL had been used.

In spite of these critical remarks, this book is a very valuable asset to practitioners of computer graphics; they can learn a lot from the discussions and the numerous examples and utilities. The usefulness of this text will be even greater when the graphics is practiced on an IBM/PG. In the light of this, it is an unforgivable mistake that the publishers chose to market the book not only in soft cover, but also with a coil rather than proper binding, causing the book to almost come apart as a result of the reviewing process alone.

—*J. van den Bos,* Leiden, The Netherlands

### I.3.7 Three-Dimensional Graphics and Realism

ADAMS, LEE

**High performance interactive graphics: modeling, rendering and animating for IBM PCs and compatibles.**
TAB Books, Blue Ridge Summit, PA, 1987, 403 pp., $22.95, ISBN 0-8306-2879-7.

This book, while not fulfilling the promise of its title, does provide readers with sample BASIC code and instructions for generating an impressive level of graphics on personal computers. These programs cannot be called high performance nor can they be termed interactive. However, the author's advice to experiment with changing specific variables and with re-executing the program may be more pedagogically useful than running a truly interactive program would be. Hobbyists and others will find the introduction to many topics in graphics useful.

The book moves from simple to more complex arrangements of solid models. It includes topics such as the approximation of spheres by faceting, methods for shading and for hiding lines, the design of the packaging, animation, and simulation. It is assumed that the readers use a variety of different computers (e.g., PC, PC Jr., PC/XT and PC/AT) and different graphical displays. The code and the explanation provide for the alternatives, sometimes in clever ways. The dictionary of variables and the commentary prepare the reader for more extensive graphics programming.

The book can be criticized for coming too close to claiming that everything possible on more complex and expensive hardware and software is attainable on personal computers. As a result, the reader may be confused if and when she or he reaches the next stage. For example, in many cases the modeling and graphics terms used are not standard. Also, though the approach used in organizing the BASIC code could be termed modular, in more sophisticated languages one can actually access libraries of modules, so code does not have to be rewritten. No hint is given that there are programming environments with graphics subroutine packages that are accessible and distinct from the manipulation of models. More generally, no references of any kind (graphics, geometry, programming) are given. In spite of these drawbacks, the book provides many lessons in programming practice and in geometry in an entertaining way.

As is now common, a diskette containing the routines described in the text can be obtained from the publisher. Since most of these programs are quite long, this seems a worthwhile investment. However, the reader should note that I did not actually enter and run any of the code!

—*Jeanine Meyer,* White Plains, NY

## 1.5 Pattern Recognition

### 1.5.0 General

WATANABE, SATOSI (Univ. of Hawaii)     **HCI-0072**
**Pattern recognition: human and mechanical.**
John Wiley & Sons, Inc., New York, NY, 1985, 570 pp., $44.95, ISBN 0-471-80815-6.

This is an interesting introduction to pattern recognition, emphasizing primarily the human cognition capabilities ranging from concrete object perception to abstract theory building. The title originally considered for this work was: "Form, Figure, Feature," implying that the general concept (Form) is presented in terms of class characteristics (Feature) derived from the intuitive image (Figure) of a class, which is typical of the way the material is presented in the book. The text also includes, besides the mathematical modeling and analysis, non-mathematical, historical descriptions (Chapter 1-4). Chapter 6 (pattern recognition as entropy minimization), is especially important since the overall presentation of known pattern recognition algorithms can, according to the manuscript, be derived from the heuristic principle of minimum entropy. Chapters 7-10 deal with pattern recognition as covariance diagonalization, statistical decision making, discrimination process, and structure analysis, respectively.

Among the challenging aspects of the text are its emphasis on the philosophical, psychological, and neurophysiological bearings of pattern recognition and a repudiation of the deductive, logical, statistical, and linguistic tendencies among researchers in the field and its establishment as an inductive empirical science. Watanabe criticizes the widespread aftereffect of the logical empiricism and introduces the concept of "paradigmatic symbol" as the tool to establish a parallel between pattern analysis and new findings in brain neurophysiology.

With a few exceptions, like sample 18 of the so-called "mon," or family crests (Figure 10.2.4, p. 401) (which I was surprised to find in a book written by Watanabe and published with the inspiration of Bea Shube of the Wiley-Interscience Division), I really liked the book.

This book is the first interesting attempt to provide a unified presentation of pattern recognition, which should interest the non-mathematical audience, as well as those specialized students of science who have been exposed to the many mathematical theories on pattern recognition.

—*Abraham Kandel,* Tallahassee, FL

## I.6 Simulation and Modeling

### I.6.3 Applications

STEINHAUER, GENE D.     **HCI-0073**
**Artificial behavior: computer simulation of psychological processes.**
Prentice-Hall, Inc., Englewood Cliffs, NJ, 1986, 150 pp., $25.67, ISBN 0-13-048844-5.
[Prentice-Hall personal computing series.]

This text contains interactive programs for animated graphics and computer simulation of the psychological behavior of living organisms. The user can construct the behaviors through interactions with the computer program, and the intent of this text is to present simulation techniques that address behavior problems.

    The programs discussed in the text simulate various aspects of psychological behavior. One program addresses the expectation of rewards. The relationship between rewards and behavior is studied by giving food to a laboratory rat at the end of a raceway and observing the changes in the rat's speed as rules of expectation are changed. This experiment is simulated, and the user can interact to change various parameters and observe the results through the graphics output.

    Other programs describe frustration, courage, spontaneity, choice, freedom, discrimination, and superstition. All the programs which are included in the text are written in Applesoft BASIC and will run on the Apple II. They are also available from the author on a tape at a nominal charge.

    This is an interesting application of computer simulation and could be a useful approach in an educational environment where an animal laboratory is not available.

—*G. W. Zobrist,* St. Louis, MO

## I.7 Text Processing

### I.7.2 Document Preparation

RUBINSTEIN, RICHARD (Digital Equipment Corporation)     **HCI-0074**
**Digital typography: an introduction to type and composition for computer system design.**
Addison-Wesley Publ. Co., Inc., Reading, MA, 1988, 340 pp., $32.25, ISBN 0-201-17633-5.

Good typography is (to quote Beatrice Warde) invisible; it allows the reader to focus on the content of the text without distraction, while at the same time giving the document a feel that complements, perhaps even enhances, that of the text. As a result of this invisibility, the skills of the typographer and typographical designer are also invisible—and unappreciated.

Consequently, there are too many people with no aesthetic sense who think that because they can write systems programs, they can also write text formatters or design fonts for computer systems. The resulting formatters, unfortunately, rarely make it easy to produce well-designed documents, and the fonts are often ugly and hard to read. Moreover, the font editors that come with many systems allow users to make changes, generally for the worse. The desktop publishing revolution has given us a lot of bad typography and general bad design (which finds its apotheosis in the gratuitous and inappropriate use of Gothic all-caps text, an abomination previously committed only by unlicensed users of Letraset). Even systems such as TeX, Metafont, the Computer Modern fonts, and L<sup>a</sup>TeX, which were designed by people who knew what they were doing and expended much effort to do it well, are at best only partially successful.

It is therefore a delight to see Rubinstein's fine book, *Digital typography,* which lays out for the computer professional exactly what is involved in typography as an art and what the problems and issues in computer typography are. The book is divided into two parts, each about 140 pages long. The first part covers individual letters: the design of fonts, readability issues, the various characteristics of output devices, and systems for digital font design. The second part covers the problems of composing text from the letters: hyphenation and line breaking, page layout, and WYSIWYG (what you see is what you get) previewing devices.

Rubinstein is careful to distinguish computer issues from artistic issues. He does not try to teach font design, for example; rather, he teaches an appreciation of what is involved in this task, and what the computer systems designer needs to know in order to tell a good font from a bad font for a particular purpose. There is an appropriately heavy emphasis on human factors, and a discussion of how the characteristics of output devices affect what is needed in a font. This part of the book will also interest the typographic designer who needs to understand just how fonts are used in computer systems.

In the second part, on laying out text, there is considerable discussion of the many issues that are involved in designing layout systems. Human factors are again emphasized, centering on the problem of ensuring that the system does what the user expects. For Rubinstein, the issue is not WYSIWYG per se, but rather what he calls WYGINS, "what you get is no surprise."

The book would be a good text for a course in digital typography, and may indeed inspire the creation of more such courses.

—*G. Hirst,* Toronto, Ont., Canada

## J. COMPUTER APPLICATIONS

### J.3 Life and Medical Sciences

FLYNN, GEORGE J.
**Medicine in the age of the computer.**
Prentice-Hall, Inc., Englewood Cliffs, NJ, 1986, 166 pp., $21.95, ISBN 0-13-572975-0.

This short book begins with a broad, *Readers' Digest* style, view of medicine and its limitations in the 1980's, and of the potential role of computers in medicine. Specific chapters are introduced with a "cute" (and often marginally relevant) lead-in about a patient with a problem that describe recent applications of computers in medicine. The subjects covered include computerized analysis of ECGs; medical diagnosis; artificial intelligence techniques applied to medicine; Myers and Pople's CADEUCEUS; Rutgers work on glaucoma; AI work at Stanford; etc. The few references that are included are largely out of date; few are from later than 1981, despite this being a rapidly moving field.

It is hard to know who would find this book interesting. There is an interesting survey of the field for someone wanting an easy-to-read overview of computer applications in medicine. Many of the widely described systems are included in the survey. At the same time, the style seems aimed at Sunday suppement readers and most people with any sophistication will find it hard to dig much meat out of this book. Doctors will find the book simplistic and computer scientists interested in medical applications will find the details lacking.

—*E. P. Hoffer,* Boston, MA

## J.6 Computer-Aided Engineering

### Computer-aided design (CAD)

SCHAEFER, A. T.; AND BRITTAIN, JAMES L. (Applied Technical Support, Tulsa, OK)
**The AutoCAD productivity book: tapping the hidden power of AutoCAD.**
Ventana Press, Inc., Chapel Hill, NC, 1986, 314 pp., $39.95, ISBN 0-940087-00-6.

This book has two distinct parts. The first, which constitutes just less than 60 percent of the length, is a tutorial by the first author; the second is a catalogue of 70 command macros or programs for use with AutoCAD, written by the second author.

AutoCAD is widely used, generally by self-taught computer amateurs who have acquired a haphazard, unsystematic patch of knowledge. It is certain that they mostly underutilize the potential of the system. With software and hardware getting more powerful and cheaper, this phenomenon will increase in all fields. The task of expanding existing users' knowledge, which Schaefer and Brittain tackle for AutoCAD users, has a tremendous potential payoff. However, it is impossible to fix a standard baseline of knowledge from which to begin explaining new concepts, and the tutorial part of the book is affected by this (unavoidable) uncertainty. Its seven chapters include sections on elementary MS-DOS, and a good deal of time is spent explaining how to use EDLIN. You certainly can't assume that AutoCAD users know this already, but nevertheless they seem out of place here. In general, the tutorials are patiently explained and yet cover a lot of ground. They should achieve their primary objective of giving confidence for users to venture out of their patch of knowledge; when they do so, they will have to progress to additional reference documentation. The "productivity" theme in the book's title is relentlessly reiterated—every new pill of information is sugared with promises of time and dollars that will be saved.

The main topics covered are: custom menus, menu-invoked macros with and without AutoLISP, AutoLISP routines, and custom tablets. AutoLISP, an implementation of LISP that is fully integrated with AutoCAD, is one of the most significant features of the AutoCAD software.

The tutorial does not cover basic AutoCAD drafting commands—the reader is assumed to know them already—but most users are sure to pick up other useful information about AutoCAD along the way.

The catalog part of the book contains examples that vary from the very simple—bundling up a few keystrokes into one menu-invoked macro—up to a 56-line AutoLISP routine. They are well explained and variants are suggested, extending the scope of the examples. Of course, their ultimate value is to stimulate completely new examples written by users. The great majority of the examples streamline quite generalized graphic operations, but a few are more application-oriented; for example, creating door openings on architectural plans, or setting out baseplate drawings for steel fabrication. The examples are complete and can be copied directly into an AutoCAD system. The publisher also offers a diskette with all the examples and some additional material. This would be worthwhile if a user intended to copy more than a few items from the book.

The book does not set out to offer any theoretical insights, but its intention of raising the understanding of AutoCAD users is admirably served. The paucity of illustrations is surprising, but generally the material is well presented. As a piece of book production the price is high, but no doubt it is intended to be set against the productivity claimed in the title.

—*William Hugh Fawcett,* Cambridge, UK

BETHUNE, JAMES D. (Boston Univ., Boston, MA); AND KEE, BONNIE A. (Martin Marietta Missile Systems)
**Modern drafting: an introduction to CAD.**
Prentice-Hall, Inc., Englewood Cliffs, NJ, 1989, 413 pp., $30, ISBN 0-13-591058-7.

In this book the "D" in CAD stands unambiguously for "drafting." The first author is an experienced writer of drafting textbooks and the second author is presumably a computer specialist. In the preface they maintain that "the principles and techniques developed over the years to create correct, easy-to-understand drawings are directly applicable to computer-aided drafting." Do not expect any revolutionary propositions; the role of conventional engineering drawings is not questioned and the book does not, for example, describe CAD/CAM.

The book begins with two introductory chapters on computers and graphics. The first is a rather feeble review of computer technology. The photo of a typical computer graphics system shows an Apple II-based setup; we are told that "a high resolution screen might have 640 × 400 pixels." Two pages on the binary system appear for no obvious reason, and an unillustrated glossary includes such unenlightening definitions as "Clipping: erasure of all or part of an element." The second chapter, "Mathematical Concepts," discusses drafting units, screen units, and coordinate units. It does not refer specifically to mapping between coordinate systems or viewports.

Ten chapters on drafting follow. "Basic Two-Dimensional Constructions" deals with lines, circles, arcs, fillets, and splines. "Geometric Constructions" offers parallel descriptions of traditional techniques based on striking arcs on paper and the use of exactly the same techniques with circles on a screen; the built-in commands of CAD packages make much of this discussion obsolete. The chapter on dimensioning reiterates traditional drafting practice. The chapters on orthographic views, sectional views, and auxiliary views of engineering objects ignore solid modeling techniques and treat the creation of views purely as a drafting task. Chapters on tolerancing and on threads and fasteners have no computer-specific content. The chapter on production drawings aims to help the reader create computer drawings that are interchangeable with, and probably indistinguishable from, traditionally drafted drawings. The final chapter, "Three-Dimensional Drawings: Pictorials," refers to three-dimensional coordinates and Boolean operations on shapes, but it also describes the creation of three-dimensional views using drafting techniques. Appendices list thread sizes, metal gages, and so on. Each chapter includes a set of exercises.

Drafters who never use CAD would find the greater part of the book equally relevant, as it gives information about basic drafting conventions. The computer-related material is not specific to any particular CAD system: this choice is understandable, but it means that the book does not acknowledge the range of abilities that most CAD drafters will actually have at their disposal. Students will spend more time reading the system manual than this book.

The real question is whether computers have made traditional drafting an obsolete skill. Engineering schools are reluctant to abandon traditional drafting because it teaches students geometry; will giving up drafting leave gaps in students' geometric skills? One possible response is computer-aided learning packages for geometry.

The production of this book does not reflect the graphic standards we have come to expect in the best CAD publications. The text is not a worthwhile introduction to CAD but may serve a purpose where traditional drafting tasks are being carried out in a CAD environment.

—*William Hugh Fawcett,* Cambridge, UK

## J.7 Computers in Other Systems

*Consumer products*

PHILIPS INTERNATIONAL, INC. (ED.)
**Compact disc-interactive: a designer's overview.**
McGraw-Hill, Inc., New York, NY, 1988, 239 pp., $39.95, ISBN 0-07-049816-4.

Compact disc-interactive (CD-I) is intended to be the next generation medium after the familiar digital audio compact disc (CD-DA). The physical CD-I disc is mechanically identical to the CD-DA disc, but rather than storing 72 minutes of digitized stereo sound, it stores combinations of video, sound, executable programs, and program data. For audio, there are three encoding schemes, which trade off data rate against sound quality. For video, several screen resolutions and image encoding techniques trade off data rate against picture quality and smoothness of motion. A disc has room for only 4.5 minutes of continuous TV-quality video (with nothing else on the disc), so the CD designer needs considerable ingenuity to produce CDs with interesting moving images.

A CD-I player is a fairly powerful computer. It contains a 68000 microprocessor with a megabyte of RAM, a pointing device such as a joystick, a fairly complicated video generator, and some other computer paraphernalia. (A major question is whether a CD-I player can be made cheaply enough to appeal to the mass market.) It runs an extended version of the OS-9 operating system, rechristened CD-RTOS, which provides the environment in which CD applications run. For all but the very simplest discs, software on the disc is loaded into the CD-RTOS environment, which controls the display of material and interaction with the user.

So much for the technology, now on to the book. As suggested by the subtitle, the book is aimed at people who might want to design CD-I discs or at least understand what is involved in doing so. It describes some proposed CD-I software the authors expect to be typical. One example is a golf video game, with TV-quality images of golf courses and high-fidelity sound effects. Others include an interactive multimedia encyclopedia, various sorts of music videos, and animated, interactive foreign language lessons.

The first three chapters give an overview of CD-I, with a taste of some of the applications, and promise to finish explaining them later. Chapters 4 and 5 describe the CD-I design process, give a confusing and incomplete description of the technical details of CD-I, and promise to finish explaining them later too. Chapter 6 then finishes describing the sample applications. Chapter 7, by far the longest in the book, goes into the details of disc formats, image, data, and sound encoding techniques, and the resources of the player's computer system, and explains a little bit about CD-RTOS. The authors intend chapter 7 to be optional, but I found that chapter 5 is so sketchy that I needed the later material to make sense of it. The organization and style of the book clearly suffer from it having been assembled from materials written by a great number of people.

The appendices include a 45-page glossary, which reiterates almost the entire book, and the rest of the discussion about CD-RTOS.

It appears that producing successful CD-I software will be extremely difficult. Since full-motion TV takes up so much disc space, authors will have to come up with clever combinations of cartoon animation, still video images, and snippets of partial-screen full motion. The player arm seeks very slowly, so ugly pauses in the program will occur unless the software somehow disguises seek time. Limits on the player's data rate and the computer's RAM will force compromises in the program; for example, it takes about $\frac{1}{2}$ second to read in a full-screen TV image, so smooth motion is possible only if 15 percent or less of the screen changes from frame to frame. The book admits all of this, but encourages the reader to think of it as an entertaining little puzzle rather than a major technical hurdle.

The writing style varies wildly, from dry technical prose to chatty first-person narrative. Some of it reads as though it were translated from the Dutch, quite possibly because it was. For all of its flaws and its unashamed enthusiasm for its topic, though, the book does give the reader a feeling for the possibilities of the technology and the effort required to create software for it. I can't say I'm ready to rush out and buy a CD-I player, but now I understand why I might or might not want to do so.

—*J. R. Levine,* Cambridge, MA

# K. COMPUTING MILIEUX

## K.3 Computers and Education

### K.3.1 Computer Uses in Education

*Computer-assisted instruction (CAI)*

HUDSON, KEITH  HCI-0079
**Introducing CAL: a practical guide to writing computer-assisted learning programs.**
Chapman & Hall, Ltd., London, UK, 1984, 171 pp., $19.95, ISBN 0-412-26240-1; Distributed in US by Methuen, 733 Third Ave., New York, NY 10017. [Chapman and Hall computing.]

After several years of media hype about the educational benefits of microcomputers, it seems inevitable that someone would create a guide for writing Computer-Assisted Learning programs (CAL). The guide which Hudson has written is entertaining and informative.

Hudson's emphasis is on providing practical information about CAL to CAL writers. He ostensibly places some emphasis upon microcomputer-based CAL, but the concepts presented in this book are not constrained by any machine independency. An underlying aspect of Hudson's approach to CAL is to regard the computer as a medium that should be exploited in its own right for the presentation of educational material. In this respect, Hudson rejects the practice of converting lecture notes or textbook materials into a CAL unit.

The writing style of the author is pleasant and does not have the ponderous characteristics that could easily be found in a book of this type. It is difficult to say what audience the author was addressing in writing this book. It appears that the brevity of the text, the content of the illustrations, and the underlying intent of the author, which is to provide practical information about CAL, makes this book attractive to a group ranging from undergraduate students to university professors.

—*W. E. Mihalo,* Whiting, IN

WENGER, ETIENNE (Univ. of California, Irvine)  HCI-0080
**Artificial intelligence and tutoring systems: computational and cognitive approaches to the communication of knowledge.**
Morgan-Kaufmann, Palo Alto, CA, 1987, 486 pp., $32.95, ISBN 0-934613-26-5.

Intelligent tutoring systems (ITS) is the current name of the field that is concerned with employing ideas and techniques from artificial intelligence in order to develop instructional computing systems. During the past two decades there has been much research activity pertaining to the design, expectations, performance, and requirements of such systems. Information about this research has mostly been published in the form of technical reports, conference proceedings, and journal papers. Attempts to compare or to present an overview of such systems have been infrequent and often limited in scope. Wenger's book is a welcome contribution in this regard; it offers an extensive and comprehensive view of intelligent tutoring systems.

The book is divided into three sections. The first section is an introduction to intelligent tutoring systems. This part contains historical information and a discussion of the issues that are basic to intelligent systems. The second section includes eleven chapters and comprises a survey of individual systems. Systems are grouped according to the contributions that they have made toward the explication or resolution of specific issues of interest for intelligent tutoring systems. Over 50 tutoring systems are mentioned in this section and many are described in some detail. The third section provides a conceptual perspective for intelligent tutoring systems; this is based upon the accumulated knowledge about these systems and can serve as a foundation for future work.

Throughout the book the author stresses that the notions of knowledge and communication are central to the understanding of intelligent tutoring systems. The term *knowledge communication* is introduced to emphasize the significance for intelligent tutoring systems of the interrelationship between the study of communication processes and the nature of knowledge. Knowledge communication provides the unifying theme of Wenger's work.

The purpose of this work is to serve as a reference volume on intelligent tutoring systems. Wenger attempts to present a comprehensive survey of research activity in intelligent tutoring systems, an assessment of this activity, and those directions for further study that can be identified. This purpose is certainly achieved: the survey of research work is extensive, historical and personal assessments are provided, and open questions are regularly indicated.

The most notable feature of this book is the manner in which breadth and depth have been achieved simultaneously. It is truly a comprehensive reference work. All major tutoring systems are included and appropriately discussed. This is not done in catalog format, however; the discussion of tutoring systems is always from the perspective of knowledge communication. Unifying conceptual and theoretical views pervade the consideration of individual systems.

One weakness of Wenger's book appears in the development of the knowledge communication theme. There is a noticeable absence of references to potential contributions from learning theorists and educational psychologists. Much is known about teaching and learning that does not appear in this volume. While this work focuses primarily on contributions from artificial intelligence, the interdisciplinary nature of the subject matter suggests that a more visible presence of other sources would be desirable.

Overall, Wenger's book is a valuable contribution to the literature of artificial intelligence and intelligent tutoring systems. The extensive and comprehensive treatment of the field, and the movement toward a theoretical perspective centered about a unifying theme, make this work an important addition to the literature.

This book is an excellent reference tool. A sophisticated reader will find it very useful. A naive reader will benefit from the book by receiving a synopsis, some discussion, and bibliographic pointers for the further study of a specific system of interest. This volume is not intended to be a primary textbook and would best be used as a supplementary resource.

The physical format of the book is very good. Figures and narrative are nicely arranged and support the use of this volume. There is a subject and author index that is very complete and helpful. Each chapter contains a discussion of the primary sources for its subject matter. The reference list is extensive and current.

—*J. Ritschdorff*, Poughkeepsie, NY

EDUCATIONAL TECHNOLOGY PUBLICATIONS
**Interactive video: vol. 1.**
Educational Technology Publications, Englewood Cliffs, NJ, 1989, 200 pp., $24.95, ISBN 0-87778-211-3. [The educational technology anthology series.]

This book is the first volume in a series of anthologies of articles that have appeared over the last several years in *Educational Technology Magazine*. As many as 20 more volumes are planned for this series—treating topics which range from distance education to testing and evaluation—and the publisher plans to have the remaining volumes in this series available by the fall of 1989.

*Interactive Video* contains 30 reprints of articles that appeared between April 1984 and July 1988. One of the reprints is itself an annotated bibliography of 51 articles that appeared in a number of journals and magazines between 1982 and 1985. While the reader will find much valuable information and guidance in this anthology, one frequently encounters views about the nature of the instructional process which need to be questioned. Here is a statement typical of many found in this anthology:

> Today the communicator is challenged with design tasks requiring the use of a variety of powerful and sophisticated electronic tools to attract and hold the attention of the viewer and to present complex systems of information.

The explicit message in the above statement is both wholly justified and crucial to the success of the instructional enterprise: the quality of interactive video instruction is judged—like it or not—by the same standards which prevail in other forms of video, such as entertainment or advertising. Interactive video materials which stray too far from those prevailing standards will fail to attract and hold the attention of their viewers. Many of the articles in this anthology contain sound advice from experts in television, film, graphics, and video, advice which instructional designers ignore at their peril.

However, the above quotation also carries an implicit message, which defines the instructional designer's task in terms of attracting and holding attention and presenting information. It evokes a model of the instructional transaction in which it is the teacher's job to present, and it is the student's job to learn, a model which I thought had long ago been discredited. With what is known about the instructional interaction, it should not be necessary to argue that to instruct is to do more than attract and hold the student's attention, or that to instruct is to do more than present systems of information (whether complex or not). The problem with the above-quoted formulation is that it leaves out any mention of those design challenges which are related to the results of instruction, described in terms of what the students can do after they have been instructed that they could not do before the instruction occurred.

Having pointed to these issues around models of instruction, I must also point the reader to two of the papers in this volume that deserve special notice: "Project Management Guidelines to Instructional Interactive Videodisc Production" and "Design Factors for Successful Video-Based Instruction." The first of these papers—written by Tarrant, Kelly, and Walkley (pp. 57–68)—is notable because it includes an 80-event PERT chart, supplemented by 4½ pages of material describing the 80 events. Despite the authors' disclaimer that the chart is "virtually untried and unvalidated as a unit apart from the project for which it was derived . . . ," the mere fact that 80 distinctly separate events have been identified, and related to each other in a "logical" (if not temporal) sequence, should be very helpful to anyone faced with producing an instructional videodisc.

The second paper—written by Kearsley and Frost (pp. 79–85)—is notable for summing up experience in many different areas of the instructional application of videodiscs and for relating to each other many disparate parts of the instructional process. Their treatment of "interactivity," for example, is refreshingly straightforward, cutting through a lot of the fog found in other discussions of this crucial concept.

—*James Rogers,* Amherst, NH

## K.4 Computers and Society

### K.4.0 General

TURKLE, SHERRY
**The second self: computers and the human spirit.**
Simon & Schuster, Inc., New York, NY, 1984, 352 pp., $17.95, ISBN 0-671-46848-0.

Sherry Turkle is a sociologist concerned with how ideas move out from "a sophisticated technical world" into the general culture. The present study treats an instance of this topic: the way in which individual contact with computers "affects the way that we think, especially the way we think about ourselves" (p. 13). With excellent connections to the "sophisticated technical world" of the computer (she is a member of MIT's Program for Science, Technology, and Culture), Turkle was well placed to explore this question. Starting at MIT and Harvard, and moving outward to nodes of various computer subcultures, she conducted hundreds of taped interviews over a period of six years. Her book consists of detailed recapitulations and analyses of a selection of these interviews, interspersed with generalizations derived from them.

Each chapter (except for two final, speculative ones) examines a particular group of computer users, from small children through researchers in artificial intelligence. The first several chapters—which comprise the freshest and most interesting material in the book—treat groups of young people, from preschoolers responding to computerized toys to adolescent programmers and video-game players. The unifying concern of these chapters is the ways in which computers contribute to the child's developing sense of the world and himself. For very young children, the "intelligent" responses of computerized toys tend to complicate and sophisticate the crucial early process of distinguishing what is alive—and human—from what is not. For older children, the computer's main role is often in consolidating or extending the child's sense of his or her identity (thus, "the second self"). Virtuosity as a LOGO programmer gives some children a sense of self-worth and a certain standing among their peers; others project their personalities onto the computer, and thus learn to know themselves through examining their reflection in it. For other, lonely children, the computer becomes their only friend.

For younger children, Turkle views these relationships as generally healthy: the computer powerfully facilitates the processes of self-definition and self-expression, and reinforces the child's sense of the importance of *feelings* as a defining element in the "human." With some children, though, and especially with adolescents and some adults, the seductions of the machine are dangerous. For the addicted video-game player or the hacker (the subject of a later chapter), the price of the sense of power provided by the computer can be increasing isolation and arrested development. For others, the tendency to understand human mental functioning in terms of computer analogues can reinforce a cynical and desponding view of men as "meat machines."

Concentration on the disturbing, fascinating, and thought-provoking nature of computers gives this book a singular and somewhat disturbing appeal. It is not that some of the aspects of the "computer culture" addressed here have not been addressed before. For example, Weizenbaum gave passionate descriptions of the hacker phenomenon and of the tendency to see ourselves as machines [1], and Kidder's tale of a specific project was almost too realistic in its portrayal of the potentially addictive nature of technology [2]. But Turkle's book focuses solely on what she calls the "evocative" aspects of the technology. Further, it is not based on a few anecdotes, but on an extended social-scientific study. In particular, the material dealing with children's reactions to computers seems based on enough cases to be representative of real phenomena. At the same time, the book could have been stronger, though less popularly attractive, if it had included an even more careful assessment of evidence; a determination of how widespread some of these phenomena are; and what factors, other than mere exposure to the technology, bear on them. Nonetheless, this is an intriguing and important book, which should significantly affect future studies of the social impact of computers. It can profitably be read by most of us who use and determine the use of computers.

—*D. T. Barnard,* Kingston, Ont., Canada; and *G. M. Logan,* Kingston, Ont., Canada

**REFERENCES**

[1] WEIZENBAUM, J. *Computer power and human reason: from judgement to calculation*, W. H. Freeman & Co., San Francisco, 1976. See *Computing Reviews* **17**, 7 (July 1976), Revs. 30,001 and 30,002.

[2] KIDDER, T. *The soul of a new machine*, Little, Brown, Boston, MA, 1981. See *Computing Reviews* **23**, 7 (July 1982), Rev. 39,498.

### K.4.2 Social Issues

ZUBOFF, SHOSHANA (Harvard Business School, Cambridge, MA)
**In the age of the smart machine: the future of work and power.**
Basic Books, Inc., New York, NY, 1988, 457 pp., $19.95, ISBN 0-465-03212-5.

During her research and consultancy on organizational change and workplace innovation, Zuboff realized that the course of automation in the past ten years represented the beginning of an important historical event, a transformation of such immense proportions as the creation of the factory system in the 19th century. She saw that for the workers who were suffering automation, "a world of sensibilities and expectations was being irretrievably displaced by a new world." She determined to try to learn enough about the process and its potentialities to frame the choices that would be laid open and suggest how we might seize new opportunities and avoid the worst mistakes of the past, rather than simply repeat old patterns. This book is the result.

Zuboff tells about her five-year research program of face-to-face interviews with and observations of dozens of workers from eight disparate but anonymous firms (ranging from pulp and paper mills to banks) that were, to some extent, applying computer-based information technology to their operations. The author reports, often in the stilted style of Harvard Business School case studies, that her subjects generally did not like what was happening to them and their jobs, an opinion with which she is in total sympathy. The book jacket blurb gives the tone, saying a "wrenching sense of disorientation ... follows in the wake of the 'smart machine'" and "computers may merely further automate blue- and white-collar jobs, achieving unprecedented speed and consistency, robbing workers of whatever skill and gratification they may retain, and increasing the impersonality and remoteness of management." The author takes it for granted that this is wrong.

Then she goes beyond the mere facts and, in a style characteristic of a professor and a social scientist, she prescribes how it should be done to get it right. Unfortunately, she found it necessary to coin new words like "textualization," "intellective," and the most pervasive "informate," which seems to mean 'to collect and furnish a lot of information': "Activities, events, and objects are translated into and made visible by information when a technology informates as well as automates." She says little about the technology of automation or computer-based information handling, and not much about the results unless they are clearly bad, but she has a lot to say about organization, interpersonal relations, hierarchy, authority, and (especially) power. Her prescription is again previewed on the book jacket: "that same technology, however, may 'informate,' empowering ordinary working people with overall knowledge of the productive process, making them capable of critical and collaborative judgments about production and distribution." The author clearly hopes for a more egalitarian and democratic organization of work in the future and sees computer technology, properly applied, as a means to this dreamy end.

As Robert Howard wrote in the *New York Times*, the book is imaginatively conceived and closely argued with scholarly seriousness. I might add that it is full of references to social science, historical, and literary writings and totally devoid of technical references. In short, it is the kind of book that social scientists will like and that technologists and managers who have fought real automation battles will dislike and feel uncomfortable about.

The author is naive about the nature of industrial work. She has watched it, but she has not done it for wages or for very long. Her discussions of how pulp plants operated before automation and how splendid it was for the worker to squeeze the sulfite stuff between his fingers reminded me of Gilbert and Sullivan's phrase, "To lay aloft in a howling gale, may tickle the landsman free ... ," Similar criticisms apply to her vignettes of how bank and investment department paper shufflers worked before they had keyboards. Those of us who have seen sailing ships, hand-stoked locomotives, hand-mined coal, and hand-dug ditches replaced by mechanization and the early forms of automation are skeptical about the romantic aspects of the sweaty and dangerous old crafts. Machines make things better, not worse, and they make work easier and faster.

The author is on sounder ground when she deals with organizational theory and practice. Several of her sketched case studies reveal the consequences of stupid management and skimped training, but her dream of a democratic workplace is about as visionary as a dream of a democratic Harvard Business School and for the same reasons.

Like the history of the industrial revolution, the popular and academically accepted history of the information revolution will be written by historians and social scientists. They will explain it in terms they understand, that is, in terms of organizations, people, power, psychology, and politics. They will make little intelligent reference to the prime moving cause of the revolution, the remarkable and compelling technology. Indeed, they will denigrate technology by saying it was of little importance. This book is an early contribution to that history. In spite of Zuboff's excellent qualities of observation and an analysis of some important situations, it suffers severely from the author's perhaps deliberate downplaying of the technology involved.

Joseph Weizenbaum says this book is "an important scholarly masterpiece that will soon find its place in the libraries of everyone at all interested in what difference the computer makes to how business, industry and management work." Uncharacteristically, Weizenbaum's accolade is too strong.

—*Eric A. Weiss,* Honolulu, HI

### K.4.3 Organizational Impacts

DONNELLY, DENIS P. (Siena College, Loudonville, NY) (ED.)
**The computer culture.**
Proc. of a symposium to explore the computer's impact on society, (Loudonville, NY, 1981), Associated University Presses, Cranbury, NJ, 1985, 176 pp., $24.50, ISBN 0-8386-3220-3.

Every significant technological development invariably alters the culture that adopts it. Those choosing to make use of a new development have at their disposal power and control to a different degree than they had previously. These transforming capabilities often result from a change in rate, that is, the speed with which a process can be carried out, and when the increased speed—or rate—is large enough or distinctive enough, its influence can be extraordinary. Such changes range from those directly within our experience . . . to those outside our experience but sufficiently dramatic to gain attention from the media . . . to the subtle technological change that remains unnoticed by the layman until it becomes "worthy" of popular coverage. . . .

Such changes involve more than minor perturbations of the status quo. When changes effect quantitative displacements, they also become agents of qualitative change in a given environment whether one is logging in a forest or waging war on a battlefield, for example. If adopting the new process changes the fundamental rates of existing dynamic patterns of a society, the social infrastructure of the culture is altered.

. . . The Computer Culture Symposium (1981), . . . was organized to consider the computer's present role in our culture. The program was divided into two categories: artificial intelligence (AI) and computer influences in the sociopolitical realm. This collection consists of six essays and three question-and-answer sessions—edited versions of the lectures and discussions that took place at the symposium—with the addition of a postscript.

—*From the Preface*

## K.6 Management of Computing and Information Systems

### K.6.1 Project and People Management

*Systems development*

WOOD-HARPER, A. T. (Georgia State Univ., Atlanta; and Univ. of East Anglia, Norwich, UK); ANTILL, LYN (Polytechnic of the South Bank, London, UK); AND AVISON, D. E. (Aston Univ., Birmingham, UK)
**Information systems definition: the Multiview approach.**
Blackwell Scientific Publications, Ltd., Oxford, UK, 1985, 167 pp., ISBN 0-632-01216-8.
[Blackwell Scientific Publications computer science text.]

The authors describe an approach to analysis and design of information systems that they call "Multiview." They divide the process into five phases, or views: (1) analysis of human activities in the existing system; (2) information modeling, or definition of dataflow in the new system; (3) design of the sociotechnical system, meaning the intended interaction of people and computers in the new system; (4) design of the human-computer interface; and (5) design of the data system (data structures and programs). It is suggested that common approaches to information system design concentrate on the last phase, often to the exclusion of the first four that, in the opinion of the authors, are just as important. The emphasis throughout is on the interactions among the analyst, people, and organizations, and on the effects of organizational phenomena such as politics and jurisdictional disputes on systems design.

The book consists of 12 chapters grouped into seven sections: an introduction, one section for each view, and a summary. A single case study (an actual system designed by the authors) is integrated into all the sections. Each chapter has a short bibliography.

The device of treating one case study exhaustively is potentially effective; however, the amount of detail on the case was inadequate. Often, interesting problems in the case are identified, and the reader is then left wondering how they were handled. Nevertheless, this small book contains much useful advice for the beginning analyst.

—*J. J. Hirschfelder,* Seattle, WA

# Nonbook Literature

Nonbook literature includes papers from proceedings, journals and book collections. These reviews are arranged by the *Computing Reviews* Classification Scheme (reprinted on page 929) in the same manner as the Books Section. Each review appears under its main subject and contains a review number and complete citation. Complete source information is provided for papers from books and proceedings. Journal papers are identified by the abbreviation for the journal name. A complete list of journals for the reviews and citations in this volume appears on page 1186.

## A. GENERAL LITERATURE

### A.m  Miscellaneous

GORN, SAUL (Univ. of Pennsylvania, Philadelphia) (ED.)  **HCI-0086**
**Informatics (computer and information science): its ideology, methodology, and sociology.**
[in *The study of information: interdisciplinary messages*, F. Machlup; and U. Mansfield (Eds.), John Wiley & Sons, Inc., New York, NY, 1983, 121-183.]

[The book in which this paper appears is also reviewed here. See HCI-0036.]

In this section, Gorn sets forth his opinions on the way in which such topics as cybernetics, information theory, librarianship, and pedagogy fit into the framework which he calls "informatics." His presentation is diffuse, full of jargon, and seems to have little substance.
 Next comes a commentary by C. Pearson and V. Slamecka, which draws on the authors' experience with the information science program at Georgia Institute of Technology. Again verbiage abounds. A. J. Perlis next offers comments in a paper entitled The Role of Information in Computer Science. In general, he agrees with Gorn, but he thinks that the word "informatics" is too weak. V. Zwass, J. Moses, and P. Wegener each contribute a paper, but the theme is the same: What constitutes informatics?
 The section ends with a reply from Gorn entitled, A Pragmatist Replies. To the reviewer, the pragmatism was not obvious! There is little of substance in these pages. It is worth adding to the numerous quotations provided by the authors: "What can be said simply" (Wittengenstein).
—*A. D. Booth*, Sooke, B.C., Canada

NONBOOKS

# B. HARDWARE

## B.4 Input/Output and Data Communications

### B.4.2 Input/Output Devices

*Data terminals and printers*

PICKERING, J. A.     **HCI-0087**
**Touch-sensitive screens: the technologies and their application.**
*Int. J. Man-Mach. Stud.* **25,** 3 (Sept. 1986), 249–269.

This paper covers various methods that use touch to enter information into a computer. Acoustic, touch-sensitive diaphragms and various speculative methods are described, and an attempt is made to evaluate and rank them.

User response and satisfaction from these devices is compared with that from keyboards and "mice." It is concluded that the latter are more popular for relatively coarse input from, for example, bins, but that track balls are preferred for precision applications such as air traffic control.

—*A. D. Booth,* Sooke, B.C., Canada

*Image display*

MILLS, CAROL B. (Univ. of Maryland, College Park and Goucher College, Towson,     **HCI-0088**
MD); AND WELDON, LINDA J. (Univ. of Maryland, College Park and Essex Community College, Baltimore, MD)
**Reading text from computer screens.**
*ACM Comput. Surv.* **19,** 4 (Dec. 1987), 329–357.

The purpose of this up-to-date and well-documented paper is to review empirical studies on the factors that affect the readability of computer screens. It concentrates on research into presentation factors that influence the reading of complex, realistic displays of text. The authors focus on the readability, rather than the legibility, of text on computer screens. (They use "legibility" to refer to the identification of individual characters, and "readability" for the reading of words and sentences.)

This paper is divided into five sections. The first section describes research that has compared the readability of computer screens and paper. The next four sections discuss research on features of the screen that may affect the readability of text: the character set, the formatting of the screen, the contrast and color of the characters and background, and the dynamic aspects of the text.

This review of research results will help practitioners evaluate the guidelines they are currently using and determine the limitations of the available evidence. By concentrating on what has been found in experimental investigations of readability, areas for further research can be established.

The difficulty of writing such a paper is considerable, due to both the large number of references and the synthetic effort required from the authors. The comparative study of paper versus screen readability at the end of the paper must therefore be highly appreciated.

—E. Grecu, Bucharest, Romania

## Voice

DAMPER, ROBERT I. (Univ. of Southampton, UK)
**Voice-input aids for the physically disabled.**
Int. J. Man-Mach. Stud. **21,** 6 (Dec. 1984), 541–553.

HCI-0089

The author reviews Automatic Speech Recognition (ASR) devices as they seem appropriate in the aid of the physically handicapped. Any ASR device attached to any level of computing device was considered. Damper highlights five areas: environmental control, wheelchair control, editing, manipulators, and computers (as computers rather than as one of the previous four). He then focuses on a single area, environmental control.

An environmental control system is described for which an ASR was designed. He discusses the principles of systems design for this hardware, software, and man-machine interaction. The author states that "evaluation of the system has demonstrated the feasibility of employing (ASR) in environmental control." He makes comments about training and adaptation and concludes the article with the belief that ASR devices bode well for the future.

The references comprise excellent coverage of some of the proceedings and conference literature. The speech recognition electronics literature is not searched or referenced. ASR devices have been discussed in the literature relating to the deaf (*Volta Review, American Annals of the Deaf*, etc.). This literature was not cited.

The work suffers from a basic flaw: it was all "drylabbed." The author did not try any part of any system on even *one* patient! There is no evidence of having ever worked with patients in any capacity. If one has never worked with handicapped patients, even the best intentions will wind up paving a road well known to us all. Application of computers to the physically handicapped is neither science nor art: it is the interaction of science, technology, medicine, and *experience* which gives us judgment to accompany our wishes to improve the life of the handicapped. Many of the ideas and concepts are reasonable, but nearly every comment is juxtaposed with a comment which indicates the author is writing *tabula rasa* with respect to patients.

References to James Martin's book [1] fail to take into account that none of the data or any of the concepts refer to quadraplegics. The error rates of most ASR devices cause most quads to experience intense frustration, followed immediately by fatigue. This may take as little as ten minutes. The control of an environment, in which some of the elements are televisions, windows, moving beds, and telephones, involves a large component of noise. The user wants to be entertained and use his telephone, not look at a color screen. A few tries at an ASR device that does not work "right" or shuts all noise sources (including windows) while recognizing one simple command will drive users crazy and drive a commercial producer of such a device out of business.

NONBOOKS [HCI-0090]

The admission that they have not considered the factors of "stress, fatigue, emotion and change of voice quality" is a grave problem. Patients are already stressed. The addition of error-prone "help" may be counterproductive.

In summary, this article presents an adequate theoretical overview of general principles of ASR devices which he hopes, without evidence or data, to apply to the handicapped. This is good reading for a general overview, but has neither depth nor the wisdom of experience.

—*R. W. Lambert*, Chicago, IL

**REFERENCES**

[1] MARTIN, J. *Design of man-computer dialogues*, Prentice-Hall, Englewood Cliffs, NJ, 1973. See *Computing Reviews* **14**, 8 (Aug. 1973), Rev. 25,475.

## B.7  Integrated Circuits

### B.7.2  Design Aids

#### Layout

LLOYD, ERROL L.; AND RAVI, S. S. (Univ. of Pittsburgh, Pittsburgh, PA)  **HCI-0090**
**One-layer routing without component constraints.**
*J. Comput. Syst. Sci.* **28**, 3 (June 1984), 420–438.

This well-written paper considers the problem of wiring together, in one layer, $n$ corresponding pairs of terminals that are located in two parallel rows on opposite sides of a channel. The channel width may either be fixed or variable. The variable width case is solved by finding the fixed width case for each possible width. The wiring models used are the river routing model and its generalizations. The *internal* wiring model is one in which each wire is completely inside the channel. This is identical to the river routing model, which is studied independently by a number of researchers (see [1]). The *internal-external* wiring model is one in which each wire is either completely inside or completely outside the channel area. The main objective is to minimize the wiring area and the number of tracks used. The paper gives polynomial time algorithms for each of these problems. Furthermore, it shows that more compact wiring (i.e., less area) may be obtained by using the internal-external model instead of the internal model. More specifically, a savings factor of $O(n^{1/2})$ in area is achievable. Finally, it is shown how the solution to the one layer internal-external problem can be used to obtain a wiring according to the two layer internal model.

—*A. Mirzaian*, Toronto, Ont., Canada

**REFERENCES**

[1] DOLEV, D.; KARPLUS, K.; SIEGEL, A.; STRONG, A.; AND ULLMAN, J. D. Optimal wiring between rectangles, *Proc. 13th annual ACM symposium on theory of computing* (Milwaukee, WI, May 11-13, 1981), ACM, New York, 1981, pp. 312-317.

# C. COMPUTER SYSTEMS ORGANIZATION

## C.0 General

### Andrew

MORRIS, JAMES H.; SATYANARAYANAN, MAHADEV; CONNER, MICHAEL H.; HOWARD, JOHN H.; ROSENTHAL, DAVID S.; AND SMITH, F. D. (Carnegie-Mellon Univ., Pittsburgh, PA)
**Andrew: a distributed personal computing environment.**
*Commun. ACM* **29,** 3 (March 1986), 184–201.

**HCI-0091**

Andrew is a project for personal computing in universities. Individual workstations communicate with shared processing elements. The system provides computer-aided instruction, computer-based tools, personal computer-mediated communication, and database retrieval services for its users. The paper outlines the history of Andrew, a joint project of Carnegie-Mellon University and IBM. Three major companies—the shared file system, the user interface, and the backbone network—are described at length in a tutorial style.

The 3–M machines (containing a million-instruction-per-second processor, a million display pixels, and a megabyte of memory) represent a significant landmark in personal computing power, and Andrew is a significant use of these machines. This paper will be a valuable historical reference and also a useful text for people designing networks of personal computers.

—*Bob Hofkin,* Fairfax, VA

### Hardware/software interfaces

CARROLL, JOHN M.; AND MAZUR, SANDRA A. (IBM T. J. Watson Research Center, Yorktown Heights, NY)
**LisaLearning.**
*Computer* **19,** 11 (Nov. 1986), 35–49.

**HCI-0092**

When Apple released the Lisa computer in 1983, the computer industry regarded it as an innovative landmark in interface design. Lisa introduced interface features that allegedly made it easy to learn and use, such as a mouse-driven pointer, extensive use of icons, an online tutor, and a metaphor to a desktop. Among the dozens of claims about Lisa's miraculous prowess was the claim that users could be working productively on the Lisa after 30 minutes. Unfortunately, Lisa fell substantially short of the expectations. Carroll and Mazur have provided a very readable, captivating, and expert analysis of the problems with Lisa's interface. They also reflect on some lessons that the computer industry can learn from Lisa's success and failures.

Carroll and Mazur conducted a study that uncovered many of the design problems with Lisa. Six professionals learned how to use the system and to master one of its applications (LisaProject). The professionals worked on their own, providing "think-aloud" protocols as they worked. As a growing number of studies have shown, the think-aloud protocols furnish an extremely rich and important source of data about a system; the protocols expose many of the users' perceptions, cognitions, misperceptions, strategies, and emotions during their interactions with the system.

Indeed, this single empirical study by Carroll and Mazur provided the most extensive and informative catalogue of interface problems with Lisa that I have seen. The study also illustrated the general strategies that typical users adopt when they learn any new system. Perhaps new systems and software products should routinely be submitted to an empirical evaluation that collects verbal protocols. A single empirical study may be more informative than the impressions of a hundred critics, enthusiasts, designers, and reviewers.

—*Arthur Graesser,* Memphis, TN

## C.1  Processor Architectures

### C.1.3  Other Architecture Styles

HERTZBERGER, L. O. (Univ. of Amsterdam, Amsterdam, The Netherlands)  **HCI-0093**
**The architecture of fifth generation inference computers.**
*Future Gener. Comput. Syst.* **1,** 1 (July 1984), 19–21.

This paper reports on the work of the Fifth Generation Computer System (FGCS). The project started in 1982 under the auspices of the Institution of New Generation Computer Technology (ICOT). ICOT was organized with the support from the Ministry of International Trade and Industry (MITI) and eight leading electronics manufacturers in Japan.

This paper first summarizes the goals, research, and development targets, and the FGCS case for basing its work on PROLOG rather than LISP. It describes, in some detail, the architecture of the Personal Sequential Inference machine (PSI). The purpose of the PSI is to provide FGCS researchers with a programming environment for developing software for the project. The design of the PSI is based on Kernel Language Zero (KL0), a new programming language for logic programming. Next, the paper describes models for parallel inference machines that are under study. The various models mentioned are: multiprocessing, dataflow, functional, and logic. The paper also discusses a possible architecture for a parallel inference engine. The author summarizes the FGCS work by stating that "with more than half a year in the first period of the FGCS project to go, it could be said that the research goals of the first three year period are fulfilled."

This paper is a clear, concise summary of the work done to date by the Fifth Generation Computer System project. It is accessible to anyone with a basic knowledge of the computer field. It will be interesting reading for anyone who is curious about what the highly publicized FGCS project is actually accomplishing.

—*G. T. Boswell,* Lewisville, TX

## C.2  Computer-Communication Networks

### C.2.4  Distributed Systems

*Distributed applications*

FALCONE, JOSEPH R. (Digital Equipment Corporation, Shrewsbury, MA)  **HCI-0094**
**A programmable interface language for heterogeneous distributed systems.**
*ACM Trans. Comput. Syst.* **5,** 4 (Nov. 1987), 330–351.

Since distributed systems are becoming a promising alternative for high performance computer architecture, this paper is welcome. From the user's point of view, a distributed system is usually seen as a distributed file system. Services are accessible via an operating system type of interface. The author's approach is different. The key idea is to provide an architecture in which communication follows a programming paradigm. The remote access to system services by clients and the communication between clients and servers occur by programming in a programming language developed for this purpose.

The first two sections of the paper briefly survey the topic and discuss current approaches to service interface design in Ethernet-like distributed systems. The conceptual foundation for the network command language (NCL) is also provided.

Section 3 outlines the NCL specifications by providing NCL expressions, classes, and element types.

The last two sections are devoted to short descriptions of the standard functions library and to implementation considerations.

To provide a high-level language interface like NCL for access to remote services instead of using explicit remote procedure calls is like using powerful macrodefinitions instead of simple machine code instructions. Even if the use of an object-oriented language seems more natural in such environments, the author's approach in developing a LISP-like, function-oriented language is interesting and valuable. It provides an efficient way for remote function evaluation and communication through the exchange of compact NCL expressions.

The text is both well structured and highly readable. The presentation is mainly informal. The reader should have a basic knowledge of distributed systems. Some LISP experience is also desirable.

—*T. Moisa,* Bucharest, Romania

# D. SOFTWARE

## D.2 Software Engineering

### D.2.0 General

HALL, WENDY (Univ. of Southampton, Southampton, UK)  **HCI-0095**
**The art of programming.**
[in *Information technology in the humanities: tools, techniques and applications,* S. Rahtz (Ed.), Halsted Press, New York, NY, 1987, 80-91.]

This is a well-written and very readable exposé concerning the value of teaching programming to undergraduate humanities students. As such, the title *The art of programming* is somewhat misleading.

This chapter does a very nice job of offering a brief history of programming languages and the major distinctions between these languages. A good analysis is offered regarding the currently popular idea of "computer literacy" and the different interpretations that surround this phenomenon. A comparison is made between compiled and interactive languages and their utility as teaching tools. A good bit of attention is given to Prolog.

The issue of the virtue of teaching programming as a method of teaching logic and analytical thinking skills is addressed. The author's conclusion, based on research citations, is that programming skills are not correlated with improved analytical thinking.

—*Charlene Dykman,* Houston, TX

PERKINS, JACK; AND ISAACS, RON I. (National Institute for Medical Research, London, UK) **HCI-0096**
**Design of computer programs for the physically handicapped.**
*Microprocess. Microprogram.* **13,** 1 (Feb. 1989), 55–61.

The paper describes several ways that the human-to-computer interface can be improved to enable the severely handicapped to use microcomputers. The general assumption is that most handicapped persons can master the task of turning one or two switches on and off. Such on/off devices could then be adapted to the disability and used as input devices to microcomputers that perform a variety of functions.

The authors have visited centers for the disabled and identified certain areas of need. They have developed programs, in BASIC, that address those needs (communications, education, interest, rehabilitation, assessment, and therapy). They identify the greatest need as communications. The paper only indirectly addresses the other areas, though the proposed tools would be usable in those as well. The authors only address the problems of the visually impaired to a limited extent. Similar techniques might be used to develop programs to allow them to interface with computers in a related way using oral menus rather than visual menus.

The approach seems very sensible. The paper is well written and easy to understand. Any group dealing with the severely handicapped should request copies of these programs and stay abreast of the authors' activities. Their program development has been for very inexpensive desktop microcomputers that would be considered outdated technology (64K RAM, 100KB floppy) but are nonetheless inexpensive to acquire.

—*Don B. Mitchell,* Topeka, KS

### D.2.1 Requirements/Specifications

*Methodologies*

TRAUNMULLER, ROLAND (Johannes Kepler Univ. Linz-Auhof, Austria) **HCI-0097**
**Information systems design methodologies and their compliance with cognitive ergonomy.**
[in *Readings on cognitive ergonomics - mind and computers.* Proc. of the 2nd European conference (Gmunden, Austria, Sept. 10-14, 1984), G. van der Veer; M. Tauber; T. Green; and P. Gorny (Eds.), Springer-Verlag New York, Inc., New York, NY, 1984, 44–61.]

[The whole proceedings volume is reviewed here. See Review HCI-0039.]

This paper has all the virtues and faults that one might expect from an excerpt from a conference on an emerging discipline. The paper attempts to place some order into the profusion of methodologies—and of uses of the word "methodology"—in information systems development. Using important modern examples of methodologies for systems design, the author begins by articulating the need for formal methodological approaches, shows differences between some state-of-the-art systems, and discusses in more general terms the role of information modeling as part of the design process.

The audience for this paper is surely limited, probably to those researchers who will read the conference proceedings in its entirety. Managers of information systems development projects might find it worth a brief reading because the way that the author arranges ideas and topics relating to systems design is thought provoking. (For example: "The success of early systems analysts was largely based on their intuitive feeling in juxtaposing technology and organization. This is no longer the case in computer-aided methods, where the intuition has to be replaced by new ways of socio-technical engineering.") On the other hand, the paper seems to be little more than a collection of statements, such as the preceding, collated into categories, but not connected well by narrative or example.

—*Dennis P. Geller,* Needham Heights, MA

BRUNO, G.; AND BALSAMO, A. (Politecnico di Torino, Turin, Italy)
**Ada-based executable modelling of distributed systems.**
[in *Ada-components: libraries and tools.* Proceedings of the Ada-Europe International Conference (Stockholm, Sweden, May 26–28, 1987), S. Tafvelin (Ed.), Cambridge University Press, New York, NY, 1987, 279–292.]

This work presents a methodology for systems modeling based on PROT nets (a form of Petri nets), which exploits the formal properties of the PROT graphical notation in a way that makes it suitable for use with automated techniques. Specifications created from a combination of PROT diagrams and textual input using Ada syntax are shown to be executable in the sense that compilable Ada source code can be produced from them. The methodology and associated software tools are intended to facilitate a rapid prototyping approach to systems analysis. This approach has been shaped to a large extent by methodological considerations that have developed within the Ada community, and exploits "advanced tasking and structuring" mechanisms of Ada. Emphasis is placed on object-oriented analysis and software reuse.

Following an introduction to the context and motivation for this work, the bulk of the paper is divided into two sections. The first of these gives a conceptual overview of the methodology, while the second illustrates the ways in which the representations employed may be transformed into Ada code. A simple example is presented which shows a partial specification of a computer integrated manufacturing system.

The methodology proceeds in three steps. The first is concerned with specifying the control flow and inner behavior of classes of objects identified within the problem domain. The second introduces data types into these objects, and the third specifies the makeup of a system in terms of instantiated objects and the communications between them. The description of the conventions for transformation of the system specification into Ada provides the most valuable aspects of the paper, and involves some interesting uses of generics.

While the paper is timely in a number of respects, and suggests some powerful techniques that can be automated, its presentation is rather sketchy. In several places, a lack of clarity and detail makes it difficult to determine how the translation to Ada takes place and to what extent it is susceptible to automation (that is, how much Ada code is derived from the graphical notation, and how much must be hand-coded). The potential benefits of techniques such as these are readily apparent, however, and the concepts employed here are well worth considering. Familiarity with Petri nets is assumed.

—*David Martin,* Encino, CA; and *Herman Fischer,* Los Angeles, CA

### D.2.2  Tools and Techniques

HANSON, STEPHEN J. (Bell Communications Research, Murray Hill, NJ); AND
ROSINSKI, RICHARD R. (AT&T Information Systems Laboratories, Lincroft, NJ)
**Programmer perceptions of productivity and programming tools.**
*Commun. ACM* **28,** 2 (Feb. 1985), 180–189.

HCI-0099

The authors describe three ways to measure tool use: (1) controlled experiments, (2) measure programmers to determine which tools they naturally use, and (3) survey their preferences. This paper describes an experiment based upon this third method. From this reviewer's experience, the first technique is quite expensive and the second technique does not clearly identify contributory factors. However, the third technique depends heavily on the knowledge of those being surveyed.

The authors reduced the 400 tools in the National Bureau of Standards database into 20 classes and gave 25 expert COBOL programmers pairwise choices of tools which they had to rate. The results must be read with two restrictions: (1) Tools—even by the 20 classes—vary greatly (e.g., only one testing tool mentioned was a test coverage analyzer, and there are various versions of these) (2) More importantly, the background of the programmer influences these. Even though definitions are given, that is no substitute for use. So while most programmers have used a screen editor and know its value, few have used testing tools. It is hard to anticipate the value of a tool you have never used (e.g., try to explain the value of a computer to a prehistoric individual who can barely count).

The results of this paper can be used as a first approximation of useful tools for a programming environment. It is necessary to use programmers well versed in these tools to better refine these results.

—*M. Zelkowitz,* College Park, MD

BRINTZENHOFF, ALTON L. (SYSCON Corporation, San Diego, CA)
**SKETCHER, an interactive, graphical Ada software tool—its development and use.**
[in *Ada-components: libraries and tools.* Proceedings of the Ada-Europe International Conference (Stockholm, Sweden, May 26–28, 1987), S. Tafvelin (Ed.), Cambridge University Press, New York, NY, 1987, 209–222.]

HCI-0100

Ada's expressiveness, as well as the maturity of Ada-related methods and their potential for a high degree of standardization, affords special opportunities for the development of computer-aided software engineering (CASE) tools. Tools that provide automated uses of graphics in software development form one of the most important categories of CASE. This paper is structured around the presentation of such a tool and portrays various aspects of the tool's motivation, conceptual foundations, and operation. A discussion of a CASE tool's capabilities must be additionally concerned with the methodology supported by the tool and the graphical notations associated with that methodology. The methodology supported by SKETCHER is object-oriented, and its graphics are based on the notational schemes of Booch and Buhr. (Although these topics are touched upon in the paper, they are not explored in depth.)

A paper of this nature may be of interest on several counts. For example, in order of increasing generality, it can portray the underlying rationale for and capabilities of a particular tool; it can reflect software development practices in widespread use within the Ada community; it can reveal general problems related to software methodology, graphics, and automation; and it can point the way to some useful solutions to these problems.

This paper begins by providing some useful background remarks regarding the use of Ada-specific graphics in software design and the ways in which use of an automated graphical tool can be of value. The major sections are concerned with the design criteria that shaped SKETCHER's development, some aspects of the tool's architecture and user interface, and, most of all, the tool's method of operation. These sections provide a fair amount of detail and include a simple design example with illustrations. A section on "Lessons Learned" and a summary section give some insights into the nature of the benefits that have been gained from the tool's use.

The content of this paper is weighted toward the more particular rather than the more general. It gives a clear description of the tool under discussion. A readable exposure to some of the mainstream issues involved in the use of Ada-specific methodologies and graphics, and an explanation of some of the benefits that can be realized by their automation, are also provided. The paper tends to present only the positive aspects of the tool's use, however, and fails to address the more difficult issues, such as integration of the tool with other tools of the environment; integration of the methodology employed with those of other life cycle phases; and maintenance of consistency between the graphical representations produced by SKETCHER and textual (PDL or Ada source) representations as they evolve through later stages of the design process.
—*David Martin,* Encino, CA; and *Herman Fischer,* Los Angeles, CA

LEWERENTZ, CLAUS (Aachen Univ. of Technology, Aachen, W. Germany)  HCI-0101
**Extended programming in the large in a software development environment.**
*SIGPLAN Notices* **24**, 2 (February 1989), 173–182. [Special issue: Proceedings of the ACM SIGSOFT/SIGPLAN software engineering symposium on practical software development environments.]

One way in which programming in the small differs from programming in the large is that many tasks that can be left to the programmer's own discipline in the former have to be formalized in the latter. For effective use, both programming in the large and programming in the small tools should be unified. One such unified system is the incremental software project support environment (IPSEN), which provides a set of integrated tools for programming in the large. This paper provides a user's view of the documentation and management support tools in IPSEN.

Lewerentz discusses five tool areas. The *editor for software architecture* provides both textual and graphical views of the relationship between software components and provides checks for consistency. Each individual component may be available in differing revisions or variants. The *variant editor* provides the means for mapping the logical software components to their current realizations. The *implementation support* derives from the software architecture the initial textual implementation frame for the development of the module using programming in the small tools. The frame has to be dynamically linked to the software architecture description so that changes can be automatically propagated. *The integrated documentation editor* is a syntax-oriented text editor with the ability to relate portions of the text with other documents in the system. The *responsibility and access control* module provides a user with only those commands that she or he is entitled to use. The paper is a good introduction for someone interested in the "user feel" of a support system for programming in the large.

—*M. Whitelaw*, Wagga Wagga, Australia

## Sassafras

HILL, RALPH D. (Univ. of Toronto, Toronto, Ont., Canada)     **HCI-0102**
**Supporting concurrency, communication, and synchronization in human-computer interaction—the Sassafras UIMS.**
*ACM Trans. Graph.* **5,** 3 (July 1986), 179–210.

Sassafras is a prototype User Interface Management System (UIMS) developed by Hill as part of a doctoral thesis at the University of Toronto [1]. This paper is a well-written and important summary of current issues, technical progress, and significant results from this UIMS research work.

Hill points out that it is not possible to build a good user interface on the first attempt. Therefore, an iterative approach must be used, and this requires new tools that are suited to the demands of high-function displays and operating systems (high resolution color graphics, multiple simultaneous inputs from the user, and multitasking). Sassafras extends the range of user interfaces beyond those supported by current UIMS. The new contributions are (1) an event-response technique that can be used to specify concurrent dialogues and (2) a local event broadcast method that supports a run-time structure, allowing the multiple components of the user interface to communicate and to synchronize.

As would be expected in thesis work, Hill acknowledges that the current implementation of Sassafras is optimized for flexibility. This initial system was developed in the INTERLISP-D programming language, and it makes heavy use of the tools available in that environment. Hill recommends reimplementation with an improved editor for the dialogue specification phase, run-time data collection, and support for more detailed follow-up analysis of that data. He asserts that study is needed of both (1) the effectiveness of support at initial specification (and for the needed design iterations) and (2) the efficiency of computer and user run-time performance.

Hill has done an outstanding job of encapsulating his work in an informative and insightful style. Rather than attempting to summarize it further, I recommend that you read the paper if you are at all interested in the technical challenges and opportunities in the important, emerging topic of user interface management systems.

—*J. Bennett,* San Jose, CA

**REFERENCES**

[1] HILL, R. D. Supporting concurrency, communication and synchronization in human-computer interaction, PhD dissertation, Dept. of Computer Science, University of Toronto, Toronto, Ont., Canada.

## *Structured programming*

RATCLIFF, BRYAN (Aston Univ., Birmingham, UK); AND SIDDIQI, JAWED I.  **HCI-0103**
(Wolverham Polytechnic, Wolverhampton, UK)
**An empirical investigation into problem decomposition strategies used in program design.**
*Int. J. Man-Mach. Stud.* **22,** 1 (Jan. 1985), 77–90.

This paper is recommended to individuals concerned with human factors aspects of program specification and design. The authors report on an interesting series of experiments involving a program specification and its associated input sequences. They discovered that two major decomposition paradigms were used by the subjects, and that one of those paradigms was dominant. The paradigms chosen were seemingly motivated by the specification and the order of the inputs.

The first part of the paper consists of descriptions of the experiments and presentations of the subsequent statistical results; the latter part discusses possible underlying psychological bases for the paradigm selection. While the study is limited in scope, the accompanying discussion provides a more general interpretation of the results.

—*N. S. Coulter,* Boca Raton, FL

## *User interfaces*

STOTT, JACK W.; AND KOTTEMANN, JEFFREY E. (Univ. of Hawaii, Honolulu)  **HCI-0104**
**Anatomy of a compact user interface development tool.**
*Commun. ACM* **31,** 1 (Jan. 1988), 56–66.

The authors describe a tool that provides a forms capability for field operations within a windowing environment. The user interface development tool, called PANES, is designed to allow the moderately-skilled programmer to develop modeless application software by means of standard capabilities as well as to allow the creation of sophisticated interfaces by experienced programmers.

PANES supports field level editing, text displays, and function key responses within specified windows. While the tool is accessible to variously skilled programmers, it appears to be somewhat dated compared to graphical iconic user interfaces such as Microsoft's Windows Presentation Manager and Apple's Macintosh interface.

—*Michael L. Gordon,* Dobbs Ferry, NY

NONBOOKS [HCI-0105]

SMITH, SCOTT R.; BARNARD, DAVID T.; AND MACLEOD, IAN A. (Queen's Univ., Ontario, Canada) **HCI-0105**
**Holophrasted displays in an interactive environment.**
*Int. J. Man-Mach. Stud.* **20,** 4 (April 1984), 343–355.

This paper concentrates mainly on a new general display algorithm which decides which segment of concrete text (referred to as the focus of attention) should appear near the center of the screen, while the top and bottom portions of the screen are being used to display contextual information (more important to the user than arbitrary concrete text) surrounding the focus.

The authors state, "this algorithm fills the screen after a user interaction by placing the focus of attention and a few surrounding lines near the center of the screen and then attempts to include as many frames (matching pairs of symbols in an application grammar which define a meaningful context, for example, BEGIN...END in PASCAL) as possible surrounding the focus." Ellipses are substituted in place of text, elided from a concrete display representation.

As the authors point out, two distinct approaches to holophrasting (preparing text for a user in the manner specified above) exist: using an automatic algorithm [1], and a manual selective) approach, as developed for COPE [2]. The suggested algorithm is described in detail in this paper with emphasis on two of this holophrasting realization's characteristics: generality of use, and avoiding manual interaction.

Generality of use has been achieved through the introduction of externality to the holophrasting program data structures, the contents of which govern the holophrasting process. Such data structures, the authors continue, reflecting someone's aesthetic views, can be created, matching the structure of each type of text that should be viewed interactively. Thus, the holophrasting program need not be changed when used in viewing different textual objects.

Apart from their useful work on holophrasting, the authors have gone too far in praising the fully automatic nature of their algorithm more than to the selective technique, employed in COPE. The automatic-manual argument could remain in the realms of pure philosophy (as the authors evidently wish) if only it did not concern a most real area of vital importance — that of interactive computer systems.

Examples of the negative and harming consequences of the fully automatic approach one of them being the discontinuity of the text presentation are easy to construct and cannot be overlooked. Probably, for that reason, there has admittedly been some user involvement in the holophrasting process, but with evident disapproval, only as "special cases."

While it is true that contexts help clarify the focus of interest, the authors refuse to recognize any other type of context except the syntactic one. At the same time, the really useful contexts that matter most to the interactive user are problem specific an as dynamic in nature as the problems, changing and constantly arising throughout a session. Such contexts can be defined only (and therefore used in holophrasting) dynamically; the advocated automatic approach is most self-limited in this area.

A basic principle in interactive computer systems has always been that the user should have explicit control over the computing proccess. Any attempts to neglect it, e.g., by exaggerating automatization, are bound to have grave consequences. Leaving those considerations aside, it can be concluded that this paper's main contribution lies in the detailed presentation of a new holophrasting algorithm.

**REFERENCES**

[1] MIKELSON, R. J. Prettyprinting in an interactive programming environment, *SIGPLAN NOTICES* **6**, 6 (1981), 108-116.

[2] ARCHER, J. Jr.; and CONWAY, R. Display condensation of program text, *IEEE Trans. Softw. Eng.*; **SE-8** (Sept. 1982), 526-529. See *Computing Reviews* **24**, 10 (Oct. 1983), Rev. 40,777.

—*D. D. Novatchev,* Sofia, Bulgaria

---

BENBASAT, IZAK; AND WAND, YAIR (The Univ. of British Columbia, British Columbia, Canada)     **HCI-0106**
**A structured approach to designing human-computer dialogues.**
*Int. J. Man-Mach. Stud.* **21,** 2 (Aug. 1984), 105-126.

This article would be most interesting to a practicing designer of interactive interfaces who is faced with the following problem. A large command language interface is to be designed with economy and consistent structure. The economy arises in this methodology from the table-like description of the interactions, which could be implemented more quickly than by brute-force programming. The structural consistency arises from the notation for prompt, input, action, flow control, escape, help, and input editing for each interaction. The principal human factors benefit would be this consistency, which is only one of many issues that need to be considered in designing a good interface.

—*John M. Hammer,* Norcross, GA

---

OTTE, FRED H. (IBM Corporation, Poughkeepsie, NY)     **HCI-0107**
**Consistent user interface.**
[in *Human factors and interactive computer systems.* Proc. of the NYU symposium on user interfaces (New York, May 26-28, 1982), Y. Vassiliou (Ed.), Ablex Publishing Corp., Norwood, NJ, 1984, 261-275.]

[See main entry Review HCI-0038.]

The Consistent User Interface (CUI) is a set of internal guidelines used at IBM. They were developed to provide applications programmers at the company with a standard set of features to consider when designing a system-user interface. There is nothing that is either innovative or new in the list. The article also leaves out some information that would have been helpful to anyone who reads the article. For example:

☐ There is no mention of any attempt to measure the effectiveness of systems developed using the guidelines, as compared to previous or competing products.
☐ There is no indication of how users reacted to systems designed with CUI. Even anecdotal information would have been interesting.

NONBOOKS [HCI-0109]

- There is no indication as to how widely the guidelines have been used by IBM. Are 50 percent of new applications being developed with CUI, or is it only one percent?
- There is no mention of how or why individual guidelines were chosen.
- If some particular model of system-user interaction was used, it would have been nice to know what the model was and if any attempt at validation was made.

—*A. Cohill,* Newport, VA

FISCHER, GERHARD; LEMKE, ANDREAS; AND SCHWAB, THOMAS (Univ. of Stuttgart, West Germany) **HCI-0108**
**Active help systems.**
[in *Readings on cognitive ergonomics - mind and computers.* Proc. of the 2nd European conference (Gmunden, Austria, Sept. 10-14, 1984), G. van der Veer; M. Tauber; T. Green; and P. Gorny (Eds.), Springer-Verlag New York, Inc., New York, NY, 1984, 116–131.]

[See main entry, Review HCI-0039.]

HELP systems have been a long neglected part of the computing environment. Two different HELP systems are discussed in this paper.

The first system incorporates "passive" HELP, which is implemented with a fixed set of information and rules. The HELP responses are similar to the CAI (Computer-Aided Instruction) programs found on some systems; i.e., the system is interactive but always responds in a predetermined way.

The second system is "active." Written in Franz LISP, it attempts to understand what the user is trying to do, evaluate how the user tries to accomplish tasks, and construct a model of the user based on the information gained from the first two items. Finally, the HELP system tries to decide when to interrupt the user and offer information.

The authors do not have any empirical study results, so it is difficult to know the effectiveness of their systems. However, they have clearly stated their objectives. The paper is worth reading for anyone interested in HELP systems and automated assistants.

—*A. Cohill,* Newport, VA

CROFT, W. B. (Univ. of Massachusetts, Amherst) **HCI-0109**
**The role of context and adaptation in user interfaces.**
*Int. J. Man-Mach. Stud.* **21,** 4 (Oct. 1984), 283–292.

This paper clearly argues the case for *context* and *adaptation* in building user interfaces. These factors are in contrast to the issues of presentation and the mechanics of interaction, such as windows, icons, and pop-up menus. A user interface is viewed as a means by which a user maps his task onto the available set of tools. Context defines the features of the environment which are important in determining the flow of the interaction. Adaptation is the ability of the system to act appropriately in a given context. An office system and a document retrieval system are used to illustrate the use of context and adaptation.

In the office system, the context is used to adapt the user interface and the system to the user in several ways. For example, planning can be used to automate certain tasks which can be anticipated because of the context. The system can propose possible actions to the user based on what has already transpired. The context can be used to recognize and correct local and global errors of the user. This last feature is one which I think is quite important. For example, I can certainly see its utility in a database management system environment. The mechanics of forming a query are now so much simpler (e.g., with QBE) than with earlier interfaces (e.g., DL-I) that most users would have little difficulty in forming a *syntactically* correct query. But the query may not be semantically accurate and the naive user may not realize this since the magnitude of the data involved will usually be large enough to preclude hand checking. Many people also view any results which come from a computer as being unchallenged gospel.

The paper includes a formalism for task definition, which may be helpful in defining adaptive user interfaces. In the document retrieval example, the types of documents retrieved are adjusted based upon the user satisfaction with previous retrievals. Every designer of a user interface should consider the principles of context and adaptation described in this paper. Their use will certainly lead to more powerful and easier to use computer interfaces.

—*A. L. Tharp,* Raleigh, NC

YAGER, RONALD R. (Iona College, New Rochelle, NY)  HCI-0110
**General multiple-objective decision functions and linguistically quantified statements.**
*Int. J. Man-Mach. Stud.* **21,** 5 (Nov. 1984), 389–400.

Propositions using linguistic quantifiers (such as most, at least, several) are studied in this paper and used to present a variety of forms for multiple-objective decision functions. Two approaches to propositions using linguistic quantifier have been considered: a summerization type aggregation and a competitive type aggregation based on substitution. This paper deals with the later statements in the context of multiple objective decision makings such as: "most objectives are satisfied by x."

A secondary classification can be considered as an enhancement in which the collection of objectives which are of concern are associated with a measure of how important that objective is to the decision maker. Within this formulaton, two kinds of quantifiers—absolute (all, at least one, . . .) and proportional or relative quantifier (most, at least half, . . .)—are considered. Thus, the paper deals with the formulation of approaches for determining the truth of four possible cases of quantified propositions as described above. The formulations of each case are developed based on t-norms and a final result shows the general relationship between quantified statements with and without importance measures.

—*F. Petry,* New Orleans, LA

BRIDGER, R. S. (U.C.T. Medical School, Cape Town, South Africa); AND LONG, J.  HCI-0111
(Univ. College, London, UK)
**Some cognitive aspects of interface design in a two-variable optimization task.**
*Int. J. Man-Mach. Stud.* **21,** 6 (Dec. 1984), 521–539.

The authors describe the results of three experiments in which subjects were asked to locate the minimum value of a function on a two-dimensional lattice. The functions used were inverted ellipsoidal pyramids. The subjects entered coordinates of points on the keyboard of a display terminal and the corresponding function value was displayed.

The authors conclude that performance is aided when the subject is provided with a record of the results of his previous interrogations, but not by prior knowledge of the minimum function value being sought. It is suggested that this result has applications to design of user interfaces, but none are given.

Data were analyzed using analysis of variance methods, and values of the resulting F-statistics are presented. The data are not included.

—*J. J. Hirschfelder,* Seattle, WA

BASS, LEONARD J. (Univ. of Rhode Island, Kingston)
**A generalized user interface for applications programs (II).**
*Commun. ACM* **28**, 6 (June 1985), 617–627.

The programmer implementing a display manager intends to provide mechanisms by which a user (or an application-oriented person in contrast with a programming-oriented person) "can modify the user interface without having to tamper with the underlying application program." The "Karlsruhe Screen-Based Application Support System" has been designed to meet this need. This system has been used with a character-oriented VT100 terminal attached to a computer running the VAX/VMS operating system.

The Karlsruhe system allows use of a simple programming language interface to specify operations on the application data as it is formatted for display on the screen in accord with a display template. The system also uses the simple programming language interface to interpret the logic of user actions for sending data to the application. A full-screen editor is used to modify the display template when the user wants to change the geometry of the screen-layout. The approach of using logic and templates separate from the application avoids making the display system dependent upon any particular application programming language environment. The disk file describing the template is read in by the application program without requiring linking or compiling.

The paper contains a detailed example showing: (1) steps taken to separate the screen management from the application program, (2) use of input data verification at the level of the screen management, (3) logic within a display, (4) a list of valid user commands, and (5) error messages.

The design described by this practitioner (the author indicates a separate theoretical description is in preparation) will be of interest to other practitioners. It may also be of interest to those working on the theory of display managers and those who find it stimulating to consider worked examples. For instance, some kinds of scrolling are addressed, but I suspect the cases of fields partially displayed (because of horizontal scrolling) are not handled. Other interesting fundamental questions arise when one considers adding graphics to such a display manager. An important theoretical issue is how far one can go, and under what conditions, in successfully insulating the screen manager from application knowledge.

On another dimension, the goal of the system design is to make the system "simple enough so that the end user controls the dialog" and, at the same time, "powerful enough to provide for user specification of screen geometry, input constraints, computation facilities, and display logic quite independently of the application system." This is an empirical goal, and the author gives no indication of any testing that would show how well this goal has been met in practice.

—*J. Bennett,* San Jose, CA

GOULD, JOHN D.; LEWIS, CLAYTON; AND BARNES, VINCENT (IBM Thomas J. Watson Research Center, Yorktown Heights, NY)
**Cursor movement during text editing.**
*ACM Trans. Office Inf. Syst.* **3,** 1 (Jan. 1985), 22–34.

Gould, Lewis, and Barnes have attempted to measure the role and result of cursor movement speed in text editing. Their basic findings are as follows: (1) between 9 and 14 percent of editing task time is spent moving and controlling the cursor; (2) the speed of cursor movement does not affect the overall time required to complete an editing task; and (3) the speed of cursor movement does have an effect on users' attitudes toward the editing task. Specifically, they found that the slower the cursor movement, the lower the user satisfaction.

The study does have some potentially valuable ramifications, but there are some significant shortfalls in the methods used to determine the outcome. The most striking problem is that there were only nine subjects in the study, and that they were all experienced users of IBM XEDIT (the text editor used in the study). This seems to be both a very small and a biased sample. In fact, some of the XEDIT users had already manipulated their own word processors to change cursor speed to a preferred level, and all had evolved methods of "getting around" use of the cursor, by employing other commands available through XEDIT. This sample may be too small and restictive to measure the real effect of cursor speed on an average user.

Another possible problem in the study is that attitude of users toward cursor speed was measured in discrete rankings ("really like, like, am neutral about, dislike, really dislike"), rather than a continuous measure such as a dot scale. Thus, it is impossible to know whether user attitude really follows a smooth curve continuum or is more accurately a step function. This is a critical factor if we wish to use this information to build a product that is more attractive to users. Is there an ultimate plateau? Or are all small increases in cursor speed perceived as improvements to users?

The authors have admitted that the method used to measure the amount of time spent moving the cursor needs improvement, and I must agree. Ultimately, all I can really tell from these study methods is that some percentage, ranging from 9 to 30, is spent moving the cursor during an editing task. This obviously needs to be refined.

The subjects only experienced the different cursor speed for a short length of time. It was noted that during faster-than-normal cursor speed, more cursor movements occurred, and editing time was not significantly improved. The authors posit that the additional cursor movements resulted from the users' overshooting their goal, and having to move the cursor back.

That seems to be a very reasonable conclusion. What the authors do not address is that it is possible that there could be a positive practice effect with the fast-moving cursor: that is, an individual might become accustomed to the faster speed if given enough time to learn the new, quicker response of the cursor control keys. This seems to be a possibility that should be explored.

The most significant result of this study is that users felt better about their task when the cursor was not moving at low speed. This supports the finding of other studies which show that users do feel better about fast cursor response time. The implication, though an untested one, is that slow cursor movement causes negative feelings toward a text editing task, and that those negative feelings psychologically influence the user to perform more slowly.

The authors have raised more questions than they have answered in this paper, but they are important questions. Considerably more research needs to be done in this area, and methods need to be improved also. As word processing becomes common in every office, subtle influences such as speed of cursor movement may may result in significant changes in office productivity. The human and economic ramifications of this concept are very important. As an answer to any of the questions that the authors of this study posed, the study fails, since little definitive information is generated. As a springboard for further research, this study provides an important beginning.
—*Myril Clement Shaw,* Tampa, FL; and *Susan Soltis Shaw,* Tampa, FL

COUTAZ, JÖLLE (Centre de Recherche Bull-IMAG, Grenoble, France)
**Abstractions for user interface design.**
*Computer* **18,** 9 (Sept. 1985), 21–34.

Recent tools for design and development of interactive software generally separate aspects of the user interface from the programs providing application function. The aspects include sharing a terminal screen among several processes, generating menus and forms, and various programs to hide details of physical devices. These kinds of tools can increase consistency across applications and provide customized interfaces, as well as reducing development effort.

This paper outlines several ways in which a user interface toolkit might provide applications with a standard virtual interface built around abstractions of the "real" interface seen by the user. The levels proposed are:

- ☐ A virtual device level (logical devices) to hide device dependent details.
- ☐ A virtual terminal level, to allow applications sharing a terminal screen to act as if they each had a unique terminal.
- ☐ A virtual input/output level (external views) to map between application objects and their representation to the user.
- ☐ A virtual dialogue level (dialogue sockets and dialogue handlers) to hide lexical and syntactic details from applications.

The most important contribution of this paper is the attempt to synthesize a number of approaches in these last two areas. The abstraction proposed for input and output objects, external views, is a description of structural and representational relationships among objects of the application. Views are provided to the toolkit by the application, which is then freed from managing the details of appearance and position. Dialogue sockets are proposed as an abstraction for the conversational protocol with the user. They provide an interface between the application, which sees a high level dialogue of function calls and raw feedback, and dialogue handlers which implement particular lexical, syntactic, and format conventions.

The paper is replete with small examples, but the reader might be better served by a single, in-depth example. For instance, the dialogue socket example (Fig. 12) shows how an actual implementation might work through an 11 step sequence. But there are steps missing which the reader has to fill in, and we are never shown the dialogue style actually seen by the user. One suspects an overzealous editor at work.

The paper is a valuable contribution to the development of an understanding of how user interfaces should be decomposed into modules. The positions taken in the paper are presented as tentative and many issues could not be considered. For instance, modular interaction styles may require a closer integration of object input/output with dialogue rules. Some styles will require the virtual dialogue component to have a representation of the activity sequence inherent to applications, or external views of the dialogue rules themselves with the same conventions as the views of objects provided by the application.

—*T. Carey,* Guelph, Ont., Canada

EKLUNDH, KERSTIN S. (Royal Institute of Technology, Stockholm, Sweden);
MARMOLIN, HANS; AND HEDIN, CARL-ERIC (National Defense Research Institute, Linköping, Sweden)
**Experimental evaluation of dialogue types for data entry.**
*Int. J. Man-Mach. Stud.* **22,** 6 (June 1985), 651–661.

This paper reports the result of an experiment whose purpose is to provide a quantitative evaluation of different methods of entering numeric data. The experimental design can be described as follows.

Four different types of dialogue designed for data entry were used. The types were

(1) question-answer, one question presented at a time;
(2) form-based, with the form displayed on the screen;
(3) command, with the command schema and the currently entered values shown on the screen; and
(4) extended command, permitting sequences of values to be entered by specifying the name of the first parameter in the sequence.

Data consisted of records of random, three-digit numbers. Records were of two distinct sizes, and were either ordered or unordered. Ten subjects were used. The results showed that unordered data could be entered faster using command dialogues, that strict command dialogues perform badly for large data records, and that the extended command dialogue performed relatively well for all data types. Results were obtained using analysis of variance on performance times. There was no significant statistical difference in error-rates among the four dialogue types.

Results were obtained using analysis of variance on performance times. There was no significant statistical difference in error-rates among the four dialogue types.

This experiment is probably not generalizable because of:

(1) the small, atypical sample of subjects (two secretaries, five researchers, and three programmers),
(2) the atypical experimental environment, characteized, for example, by requiring the subjects to read input data from a separate display placed on top of the input display, and
(3) the randomness of the input data (real data may be likely to have some correlation between and within records).

Presentation of the experiment could have been improved by stating the null hypothesis that was being tested.

—*David M. Weiss,* Silver Spring, MD

BARKER, P. G.; AND NAJAH, M. (Teesside Polytechnic, County Cleveland, UK)    **HCI-0116**
**Pictorial interfaces to data bases.**
*Int. J. Man-Mach. Stud.* **23,** 4 (Oct. 1985), 423–442.

This paper describes a relatively simple system that allows a user to associate pictures on paper with objects in a database. To use the system, the user first registers a page on a digitizing surface, then identifies the page by pointing to two prepositioned boxes which identify the page being used. The user may then select an object by pointing to it, or to a related "peck" box.

There is a brief discussion of the database requirements for supporting two similar components sharing common data but existing in different environments (e.g., two identical spark plugs used in different engines). This discussion is not very sophisticated and does not mention the master/instance type of relationship used in most CAD databases.

The authors conclude from questioning and observing users of this system that "pictorial interfaces provide an extremely useful mechanism for supporting end-user interaction with databases." While I believe this to be true, I am not convinced by this paper and I was not convinced that the system or the techniques described would be very useful.

—*J. A. Meads,* Portland, OR

NEWMAN, A. (Loughborough Univ., Leicestershire, UK); AND SETHI, J. (Derbyshire    **HCI-0117**
College of Higher Education, Derby, UK)
**Some observations on user interface design and user performance.**
[in *Proceedings of the fourth British national conference on databases (BNCOD 4).* (Univ. of Keele, UK, July 10-12, 1985), A. Grundy (Ed.), Cambridge University Press, New York, NY, 1985, 199–213.]

Newman and Sethi describe the results of an iterative development process of a user interface for a simple relational database management system. Their work is based on the proposition that a satisfactory user interface is specific to a particular type of use and group of users, and can only be derived through an iterative development process. Logs of user behavior and interviews with the users led to: modified interfaces which allowed for easier access to commonly used actions; new capabilities, not apparent before use of the interface by users; and less ambiguity in selecting help or default actions. It was observed that the users did not read the manual, but instead guessed or experimented with the interface.

One complete cycle of the interface development process is reported. The actual interfaces are described, together with the observations, comments, and analysis. The consequent changes are reported and the revised results are noted.

—*Michael L. Gordon,* Dobbs Ferry, NY

AKIN, OMER; AND RAO, D. R. (Carnegie-Mellon Univ., Pittsburgh, PA)
**Efficient computer-user interface in electronic mail systems.**
*Int. J. Man-Mach. Stud.* **22,** 6 (June 1985), 589–611.

Computer-human interaction is an area of computer, cognitive, and information sciences that transcends traditional disciplines. Successful integration of diverse technologies is challenging, and depends on the development of system design and measurement techniques, such as those described in this paper.

The authors provide a "general purpose method for encoding and measuring efficiency of use in computer systems." The method is used to examine the user interface of RdMail, an electronic mail system used at the Carnegie-Mellon University Computer Science Department.

Major strengths of the paper are the thorough discussions of the study context, previous research in this area, and definition of terms. Especially useful are the definition of efficiency, the definition of an efficient interface system, how these terms are used to determine measurements, and the research method.

The application of the method to RdMail includes discussions of task goals, codification of user behavior, a comparison of expert and regular users, and implications for system design. These discussions include hypotheses and experimental results that should be useful to researchers and practitioners of computer-human interaction design. The collected data also provided the raw material for error analysis and recommendations for error avoidance and recovery.

Most of the tables in the paper are well organized and communicate statistical information clearly. I noted one inconsistency in Table 2, which shows an RdMail command error rate for regular users at 0.054 instead of 0.084 (regular user total errors divided by RdMail commands). Tables showing RdMail commands will be more understandable to a reader with electronic mail experience.

The paper succeeds in presenting the general purpose technique and demonstrating its use with RdMail. It would be interesting to see the technique applied to other computer-human interaction systems.

—*S. C. Tarr,* Seattle, WA

## NONBOOKS

PLAMONDON, R.; AND BARON, R. (Ecole Polytechnique de Montreal, Montreal, Que., Canada) **HCI-0119**
**A dedicated microcomputer for handwritten interaction with a software tool: system prototyping.**
*J. Microcomput. Appl.* **9,** 1 (Jan. 1986), 51–61.

This paper describes a microcomputer-based system dedicated to online character recognition for handwriting communication with a software tool.

*Online character recognition*—The method used for characters/symbols recognition was kept as simple as possible. All entries to the system are made via a squared grid fixed to the digitizer. The rules for character recognition are based on preferred pathways for the formation of block letters according to the ANSI-3.45 standard (1974).

*Software tool*—Its primary task is to assist software engineers in the development, the documentation of the control flow, and the coding of source programs which can be compiled and executed. The system is fully interactive. The user is asked to write his piece of program in a sketchy, very efficient way; for instance, a program loop is simply defined by a double vertical line on the side of the concerned statements. Then, the system produces a properly drawn diagram and, when approved, generates the corresponding piece of FORTRAN code.

The general scheme seems very promising inasmuch as it works smoothly. It would be interesting to hear about the reliability of the online character recognition, the practicality of the sketchy program description, and the performance of the generated code. Unfortunately, the system is not assessed.

—*W. Rey,* Eindhoven, The Netherlands

RAMBALLY, GERARD K. (Univ. of Regina, Saskatchewan, Canada) **HCI-0120**
**The influence of color on program readability and comprehensibility.**
[in *Computer science education.* Papers of the seventeenth SIGCSE technical symposium (Cincinnati, Ohio, Feb. 6-7, 1986), J. Little; and L. Cassel (Eds.), Association for Computing Machinery, New York, NY, 1986, 173–181.]

This paper investigates the readability and comprehensibility of traditional (i.e., black and white) versus color-coded (colored statements, structures) programs. The most readable programs were those color-coded by statement type (e.g., blue procedure calls, red functions).

Although the research topic has a small scope, there are implications for improving programmer productivity (using colored CRTs and printout). The research is well executed and given a good presentation.

—*L. G. Herberts,* Richmond, B.C., Canada

DISESSA, A. A. (Univ. of California, Berkeley); AND ABELSON, H. (MIT, Cambridge, MA) **HCI-0121**
**Boxer: a reconstructible computational medium.**
*Commun. ACM* **29,** 9 (Sept. 1986), 859–868.

Boxer, a research tool for educational studies, is under development in the Laboratory for Computer Science at MIT, and the School of Education at the University of California, Berkeley. Prototypes have been implemented on Symbolics and Texas Instruments' LISP machines. The project explores what a programming language intended for laypeople might be like. Just as writing on paper is a widely available skill for both the everyday notes of people and the highly skilled creation of expert writers, could a medium be provided that would enable programming by a wide variety of people?

The term "reconstructable" refers to using the computer screen itself as an expressive medium. Images on the screen originally produced by experts (e.g., in a dynamic book) might be modified by people who are not experts but who know how to program "a little." The authors acknowledge a similarity to Logo [1]. Their intended innovation begins by addressing the display screen as a medium that encompasses written language, hierarchical structures, databases, and interactive graphical tools.

The box structure notion of containment is related to object-oriented programming [2]. Displayed boxes have computational semantics, and users have access to organization beneath the image on the screen. The boxes package local data and procedures, and computations are organized by sending messages to boxed procedures. The notion of "porting" provides an escape from the hierarchical structure by allowing a view on a box at some other place in the system to enable cross-referencing and sharing.

Boxer makes use of a *spatial metaphor* by representing computational objects in boxes as regions of the screen that contain text, graphics, or boxes-within-boxes representing hierarchical structure. The language makes use of *naive realism* by showing the computational world in its entirety on the screen. The user sees computational objects, not just interfaces to them. Anything that appears on the screen should be available for the user to "run" or modify.

The ultimate success of approaches such as that of Boxer will be dependent on the way in which the basic box structure is elaborated. Careful reading will reveal the tension between simplicity and triviality of function. What will be an effective way to support naive debugging? What styles of use should be taught to enable the less capable student to grow in effective use of a language such as Boxer? Will programs scale up from the examples shown in the text? Since the user can modify everything, what kind of recovery mechanism needs to be provided?

Problems of scale and details aside, this is a well-written, thought-provoking challenge to provide a programming language usable "for personal construction by people at all levels of competence." The authors appeal for research directed to the day when "programming will be a part of the everyday lives of many people who do not have expert programming skills."

—*J. Bennett,* San Jose, CA

**REFERENCES**

[1] PAPERT, S. *Mindstorms: children, computers, and powerful ideas,* Basic Books, New York, 1980. See *Computing Reviews* **23**, 2 (Feb. 1982), Rev. 38,960.

[2] GOLDBERG, A.; AND ROBSON, D. *Smalltalk-80: the language and its implementation,* Addison-Wesley, Reading, MA, 1983. See *Computing Reviews* Rev. 8501-0004.

NONBOOKS [HCI-0123]

NORMAN, KENT L.; WELDON, LINDA J.; AND SHNEIDERMAN, BEN (Univ. of Maryland,   **HCI-0122**
College Park)
**Cognitive layouts of windows and multiple screens for user interfaces.**
*Int. J. Man-Mach. Stud.* **25**, 2 (Aug. 1986), 229–248.

This paper describes a variety of ways that information might be distributed among multiple displays. It initially claims to also deal with similar issues involving multiple windows on a single display, but this idea is abandoned after a few pages. The authors begin with a nice distinction between three different layout modes. There is the *surface layout*, the physical arrangement of information on the screens; the *machine layout*, the internal representation of the surface layout; and the *cognitive layout*, the user's mental model of the surface layout. They clearly describe and justify the need for designers to consider all three modes.

They then go on to discuss seven types of surface layouts and seven (not necessarily parallel) cognitive layouts. No particular justification for their choices is given, though in the case of surface layouts they seem to have pretty well covered all the possibilities. The cognitive layouts are derived from analogy to a variety of cognitive phenomena. In many cases the analogies are stretched to the breaking point. A typical example is the cognitive layout they call "selective attention," where the user attends to primary information on one screen while less important, secondary information scrolls by on a second screen. By analogy to a well-known auditory effect called the "cocktail party phenomenon," where people will process information of personal importance to them (such as their name) in conversations they are otherwise ignoring, the authors claim that users will notice relevant information on the second screen. This effect, like all of the layouts they describe, has not been tested, so most experts in perceptual psychology would probably dispute this.

This paper would be useful to designers of applications that use multiple screens; it will suggest several ways of laying out information that they might not otherwise think of. However, one should take the psychological claims cautiously. The authors provide no evidence that the cognitive layouts they propose will induce the indicated mental processing, and in several cases there is reason to doubt that they will.

—*Robin Jeffries,* Palo Alto, CA

JACOB, ROBERT J.K. (Naval Research Laboratory, Washington, DC)   **HCI-0123**
**A specification language for direct-manipulation user interfaces.**
*ACM Trans. Graph.* **5**, 4 (Oct. 1986), 283–317. [Special issue on user interface software.]

Many of us use and benefit daily from computers equipped with direct-manipulation interfaces (such as an Apple Macintosh or an MS-DOS machine equipped with Microsoft Windows). I, for one, have never stopped to think how I would specify the flow of logic of an application being developed for such an environment. The problem, of course, is that with a mouse or the equivalent and a number of windows and pull-down menus, the user can cause a wide variety of actions to take place, far more than the relatively few that exist in a traditional command-oriented application. This research is important and should be of interest to those who select a documentation method for what users refer to as window applications.

A system for specifying the user interface is presented. It focuses upon the flow of logic. The language defined is based upon characteristics of direct-manipulation interfaces:

- ☐ They are usually made up of a number of simple dialogues.
- ☐ The dialogues are related to each other as a set of coroutines.
- ☐ The layout details can be dealt with separately.
- ☐ They seem to have nodes and states (despite appearances).

The specification language has been implemented and tested, with some success, for some relatively simple applications. The development of these concepts to the point of generating an applications development environment, perhaps even a standard environment, would be useful.

—*W. S. Hoffman,* Wilmington, DE

OLSEN, DAN R., JR. (Brigham Young Univ., Provo, UT)     **HCI-0124**
**MIKE: the menu interaction kontrol environment.**
*ACM Trans. Graph.* **5,** 4 (Oct. 1986), 36–62. [Special issue on user interface software.]

In general, a user interface management system permits the implementer to define an interaction dialogue between the user and the application by writing a formal syntax or a state-transition diagram describing the dialogue. In contrast, the MIKE system examines the set of procedures and functions that describe the semantic commands supported by the application; it uses the strong typing information provided by the formal parameters of the subprogram specifications to generate a default user interface. Editing facilities provided by MIKE then permit the implementer (or a human factors expert) to refine the generated presentation interface to improve its usability. The approach permits the designer to concentrate on the functionality of the human interface prior to serious work on its exact form; this, in turn, allows the specialization and separation of effort between the application developer and the human factors expert.

The work described in the paper is innovative and should be of particular interest to those desiring to emphasize application prototyping as a key portion of the software development cycle. The paper is well written and provides ample links to related work by the author and by others.

—*J. Moore,* Potomac, MD

GOULD, JOHN D.; BOIES, STEPHEN J.; LEVY, STEPHEN; RICHARDS, JOHN T.; AND     **HCI-0125**
SCHOONARD, JIM (IBM Research Center, Yorktown Heights, NY)
**The 1984 Olympic Message System: a test of behavioral principles of system design.**
*Commun. ACM* **30,** 9 (Sept. 1987), 758–769.

This paper describes the application of a computer system design methodology to the design and development of the Olympic Message System (OMS), a voice mail system. The design methodology emphasizes an early focus on the user and the tasks that would be performed by the user, the use of empirical measurements, and iterative design. The paper details 15 behavioral techniques (e.g., demonstrations, field tests, and interviews with representatives from the user community) that were used to design the OMS. The authors conclude that using the methodology leads to a system that is easy to use.

This paper is well written, and sufficient detail is provided to understand the methodology. It should be read by human factors engineers and systems designers who are designing interactive systems for two reasons. First, it documents the successful application of a design methodology that focuses on the user of the design and the development of a system. Second, it discusses the application of this methodology from the system's initial conception to its final prototype test and provides the reader with a wide range of valuable experiential data.

—*M. P. Tarka,* Gaithersburg, MD

EFE, KEMAL (Univ. of Missouri, Columbia)  **HCI-0126**
**A proposed solution to the problem of levels in error-message generation.**
*Commun. ACM* **30,** 11 (Nov. 1987), 948–955.

This paper describes a method of dealing with errors detected by the lower level routines and processes of a software package. Rather than having a print spooler present a cryptic message such as "file creation error" and terminate, the user is able to engage the system in a question-and-answer dialogue to discover what went wrong and (if possible) how to correct the problem. The author presents a model of software that explains the approach and then, using a desk calculator program, shows an implementation and some possible dialogues between the user and the program.

The author attempts to describe how the results of earlier work suggesting the dialogue approach (called LTAI or "Let's Talk About It") can be implemented. He succeeds in this but should have gone into more depth about prior work. (Were there any other experiments to validate the approach? What other approaches have been tried, and how did they fare?) This lack of depth may be a result of the author's aiming at the general audience, but it makes reading the paper unsatisfying. One other major flaw is that the dialogue approach only works on time-sharing systems; when using a batch computer, the approach presented is useless. The modifications needed to make the method work in that environment are not obvious (clearly, the error messages need to be written out, but how many and precisely which ones is another question). This issue should have been dealt with.

Other than these problems, the paper is clearly written and discusses the method both in terms of a theoretical model and an experiment, so the reader understands the basis of the work as well as exactly what was done. It is a good paper for someone who wants a quick tour of an implementation of the LTAI approach but is quite unsatisfying for those interested in a deeper exploration of the subject.

—*Matt Bishop,* Hanover, NH

MANTEI, MARILYN M. (Electronic Data System Corporation, Ann Arbor, MI); AND  **HCI-0127**
TEOREY, TOBY J. (Univ. of Michigan, Ann Arbor)
**Cost/benefit analysis for incorporating human factors in the software lifecycle.**
*Commun. ACM* **31,** 4 (April 1988), 428–439.

This paper adds specific human factors engineering steps to the software development life cycle. The authors call for a market analysis, using focus groups, prior to the feasibility study; production of a videotape mock-up of the product interface and analysis of user reactions to it, followed by task analysis done by a human factors specialist; a prototype, which they define as screen layouts and screen transitions; user testing and evaluation of the prototype; user testing of the product just prior to release; and a post-release user survey. They provide fairly detailed descriptions and cost estimates for each of their recommended human factors design steps, using a hypothetical system taken from one of the examples in Boehm's COCOMO model. Their decomposition and detailed cost breakdowns, especially of the focus-group and user-survey steps, may be useful to practicing project planners and managers.

The tangible benefits of human factors design mentioned are reduced training costs, reduced error costs, and avoidance of design changes. The intangible benefits of human factors designed software derive from the fine tuning with respect to the user that these additional steps produce. The paper ends with an abbreviated cost/benefit analysis of the example system. The analysis seems to conclude that the recommended human factors approach is justifiable only on projects of 32,000 delivered source lines or more, which is a medium-sized or large development project.

The authors state that their intent was to "fill the current gap that exists between the human-computer interaction research papers and the pragmatic needs of the software developer." The paper is clearly between research and practice, but the gap is still large.

—*J. D. Naumann,* Minneapolis, MN

TELLO, ERNEST R. **HCI-0128**
**Between man and machine.**
*BYTE* **13,** 9 (Sept. 1988), 288–293.

Ernest Tello briefly describes some of the novel user interface techniques currently being investigated by the government and by private companies. These techniques include new hardware devices such as three-dimensional "joystrings" and combination hardware/software interfaces that obtain data primarily by scanning eye movements.

The paper is written clearly, in a nontechnical style, and the diagrams and photos are appropriately matched with the text. The reader will not need any specific background in order to understand the material. No references are given.

This paper is descriptive rather than exploratory and does not provide a technical explanation of the underlying principles of these new techniques. It is a light overview of the direction of recent research in this area.

—*B. W. O'Connor,* Sydney, Australia

ROSSON, MARY B.; KELLOGG, WENDY (IBM T. J. Watson Research Center, Yorktown **HCI-0129**
Heights, NY); AND MAASS, SUSANNE (Univ. Hamburg, Hamburg, W. Germany)
**The designer as user: building requirements for design tools from design practice.**
*Commun. ACM* **31,** 11 (Nov. 1988), 1288–1298.

This paper reports on a set of interviews with user interface designers. The purpose of these interviews was to uncover the current practices of successful user interface designers and to gather guidelines for user interface design tools.

The study describes interviews with 22 designers, all of whom had been involved in the design of iterative systems for unsophisticated users. The interviews consisted of four sections that covered the designer's background, the general design process used, the user interface produced, and the designer's thoughts on the topic of idea generation.

The authors' primary conclusion is that user interface designers are very different from one another. The authors also make some observations about tools for designing interfaces. A design tool for a business environment should provide controls needed to meet outside business requirements; a design tool for multiperson design teams must assist cooperation; and a prototyping tool should maximize development speed since the prototype is often discarded later.

I found this paper well written and readable, but somewhat shallow in content. It does serve as an early pilot study. I commend the authors for obtaining opinions from experienced practitioners rather than merely theorizing about these pragmatic design concerns. The paper's title led me to expect more, however; the observations presented are speculations rather than requirements.

—*J. Kiper,* Oxford, OH

SENA, JAMES A.; AND SMITH, L. M. (Texas A & M Univ., College Station)   **HCI-0130**
**Applying software engineering principles to the user application interface.**
[in *Human factors in management information systems,* J. Carey (Ed.), Ablex Publishing Corp., Norwood, NJ, 1988, 103-115.]

This chapter is concerned primarily with the use of database packages such as dBASE to fashion applications such as order entry for IBM PC–compatible microcomputers. The authors address "software engineering principles" to some extent with respect to developing the user interface for applications. Given the state of the art in this area, the content is both timeless and obsolete (except possibly for do-it-yourself managers who want to build their own database applications and need help getting organized). The references are old (1971–1980), and most computing professionals would do better looking elsewhere.

—*M. G. Murphy,* Houston, TX

LINTON, MARK A.; VISSIDES, JOHN M.; AND CALDER, PAUL R. (Stanford Univ.,   **HCI-0131**
Stanford, CA)
**Composing user interfaces with InterViews.**
*Computer* **22,** 2 (Feb. 1989), 8–22.

This paper describes the role of object-oriented techniques and structural composition in graphical user interfaces. After a clear introduction to the topic and its impact on application programs, the authors present a user interface toolkit named InterViews, which demonstrates the role of composition as a user interface structuring mechanism.

The authors give a good perspective on current trends in the field and clearly expose the main problems that face user interface builders. The central concepts include the object-oriented approach, effective support for non-graphical interaction, and the distinction between user interface objects and composition mechanisms.

InterViews objects are combined through a model similar to the boxes and glues in Knuth's T<sub>E</sub>X, which allows interface objects to be combined with little concern for undesired interactions. Another key concept is the distinction between interactive objects and application-dependent objects. InterViews is implemented in C++ and the X toolkit, and it provides a user interface system independent of the window system.

This paper gives an excellent introduction to important themes of current user interface research, and it presents the InterViews toolkit in a thoroughly understandable way. The authors present system details carefully and with attention to the important concepts. The discussion of the text-based component is an interesting introduction to a topic that is often treated too lightly in graphical user interfaces. Without presupposing a detailed knowledge of the field, the authors give a good introductory view and at the same time provide an interesting technical description of InterViews.

—*Dario Giuse,* Pittsburgh, PA

MALONE, THOMAS W.
**Heuristics for designing enjoyable user interfaces: lessons from computer games.**
[in *Human factors in computer systems,* J. Thomas; and M. Schneider (Eds.), Ablex Publishing Corp., Norwood, NJ, 1984, 1-12.]

[See main entry, Review HCI-0037]

This paper applies some data acquired from a study of computer games to system-user interfaces. The computer game studies are summarized briefly, and the results are used to justify a set of guidelines for designing "enjoyable" user interfaces.

The author identifies three characteristics of an enjoyable interface: challenge, fantasy, and curiosity. For an activity to be challenging, it should have clearly defined goals and an uncertain outcome. In a computer system, the uncertain outcome can be achieved by presenting a variable level of difficulty. Feedback, in the form of score-keeping, is also important. Fantasy can play a part in a system by providing an analogy that makes it easier for the user to understand how the system works. Finally, the system can be more stimulating, or curiosity-provoking, by introducing a carefully controlled amount of randomness and humor.

The author's main point is a set of heuristics for designing "enjoyable" user interfaces. The information is useful for system designers, and helps to explain why many computer systems are so boring. There seems to be an unwritten rule, particularly in the commerical world, that software must be properly serious. Perhaps this paper will promote the design of a system that does not take itself so seriously.

In the course of the discussion, the author gives the definition of a tool and the definition of a game (or toy). These two ideas offer an interesting insight into the design of systems. A good game is easy to learn, but difficult to master. A good tool is easy to learn and easy to master. Given these distinctions, one begins to see that many computer systems (which should be tools) have more in common with the games (hard to master); obscure syntax and myriad options make it difficult to master, but pleasing, perhaps, to the games-playing nature of its designer.

—*A. Cohill,* Newport, VA

NONBOOKS [HCI-0134]

HEROT, CHRISTOPHER F. (Computer Corp. of America, Cambridge, MA) **HCI-0133**
**Graphical user interfaces.**
[in *Human factors and interactive computer systems*. Proc. of the NYU symposium on user interfaces (New York, May 26-28, 1982), Y. Vassiliou (Ed.), Ablex Publishing Corp., Norwood, NJ, 1984, 83–103.]

[See main entry, Review HCI-0038.]

This paper describes graphical user interfaces for two systems: a database system (illustrated with databases for ships and for oilwells) and a software design and management system (with simulated user screens). Both systems have been previously described [1,2], but the concept is worth repeating. Both systems provide a user with concrete graphic representations of data organization together with direct physical manipulation for traversing the data. The author notes that visitors were able to learn to use the databases within seconds—much like video games! The paper does not present information about size and performance, nor about how to design an effective graphic representation for other kinds of data objects.

—*W. Hankley*, Manhattan, KS

**REFERENCES**

[1] FRIEDELL, M.; BARNETT, J.; AND KRAMLICH, D. Context-sensitive, graphic presentation of information, *ACM SIGGRAPH* (July 1982), 181–188.

[2] HEROT, C. ET AL. An integrated environment for program visualization, in *Automated tools for systems design*, Proc. IFIP WG 8.1 working conference (New Orleans, LA, Jan. 26-28, 1982), H.-J. Schneider and A. I. Wasserman (Eds.), Elsevier North-Holland, New York, 1982, 237–259.

BOURNIQUE, RICHARD (AT&T Bell Laboratories, Holmdell, NJ); AND TREU, **HCI-0134**
SIEGFRIED (Univ. of Pittsburgh, Pittsburgh, PA)
**Specification and generation of variable, personalized graphical interfaces.**
*Int. J. Man-Mach. Stud.* **22**, 6 (June 1985), 663–684.

This paper seems to be a summary of the author's dissertation results [1]. It consists of a literature review, a discussion of a BNF-based representation language for graphics, a description of a tool for graphical interface specifications, and a brief summary of a small evaluation study of the tool.

It is the author's view that "a theory of user-computer interaction . . . must necessarily be based on an effective interdisciplinary combination of at least computer science and psychology." Unfortunately, the connection between psychological theory and experimentation and system development is often tenuous. This is reflected in the paper by the lack of a clear connection between the literature the author reviews and the system he builds.

A BNF-based language for interface specifications is an interesting idea if only because it would allow unambiguous requirements for this portion of a system. The tool the author describes based on such a representation would allow considerable freedom in system prototyping and development. It should be of great interest to designers of interactive systems.

The experiment used to evaluate this system is only briefly described. The reader is referred to the author's dissertation [1] for details. The experiment employed only four subjects and two interfaces. It would thus seem to be exploratory at best. The conclusions drawn from the study seem to be obvious; for example, (1) the syntax of the interaction language will be important to a user, or (2) consistent system response will be better than inconsistent response.

—*William B. Frakes,* Holmdel, NJ

**REFERENCES**

[1] BOURNIQUE, R. User-oriented features and language-based agents: a study of graphical interaction language specification, PhD dissertation, Dept. of Computer Science, Univ. of Pittsburgh, Pittsburgh, 1981.

---

KIGER, JOHN I. (American Bell, Holmdel, NJ)     HCI-0135
**The depth/breadth trade-off in the design of menu-driven user interfaces.**
*Int. J. Man-Mach. Stud.* **20,** 2 (Feb. 1984), 201–213.

This paper reports on an experiment which investigates breadth/depth tradeoffs for menus and tree structures in user interfaces for information retrieval systems. Retrieval time and accuracy are used as the basic measures of performance. Data on performance is supplemented by subjective ratings of preference and ease of use across different tree structures.

The experiment used a videotex-style interactive retrieval service. The database of information sources and services was designed so that several different tree structures could be used to provide a range of breadth and depth values. Sixteen goals were developed to serve as instructions for the database searches. The goals described a situation in which the subject was to use a particular service to perform a task or find a piece of information. Subjects in the experiment used each of the five tree structures once with each of the 16 goals for a total of 80 trials per subject. The subjective rating task was presented at the conclusion of the last trial.

The results of the experiment show that broad, shallow tree structures yielded significantly better performance than narrow, deep tree structures with respect to total task time and accuracy. The results obtained from the subjective rating task suggest that preference, as well as performance, may be more sensitive to the depth of tree structures than the breadth. Shallow, broad trees had a higher subjective rating by the subjects than narrow, deep tree structures.

This study, as well as others in this area, refer to the short-term memory capacity estimation of Miller [1] as a possible explanation for shallow, broad tree structures showing the best performance. These comments must be viewed with caution since the nature of short-term memory is still unclear. Studies conducted by Simon [2] and Glanzer [3] suggest that the complexity of the information unit (chunk) has an effect on the number of these units stored in short-term memory (i.e., increasing complexity results in a lower number of chunks being stored). Miller's estimate is neither magical nor an absolute.

The paper provides a good synopsis of relevant material. The experiment itself was well designed. The menus were designed to minimize differences in the amount of information present in the different tree structures. This tended to lengthen menu items as the depth of the trees was reduced. This study provides support for the findings of other studies conducted in this area, as well as subject preference for broad, shallow tree structures.

—*T. Carey,* Guelph, Ont., Canada; and *H. Smith,* Guelph, Ont., Canada

## REFERENCES

[1] MILLER, G. A. The magical number seven plus or minus two: some limits on our capacity for processing information, *Psychol. Rev.* **63** (1956), 81–87.

[2] SIMON, H. A. How big is a chunk?, *Science* **183** (1974), 482–488.

[3] GLANZER, M.; AND RAZEL, M. The size of the unit in short-term storage, *J. of Verbal Learn. and Verbal Behav.* **13** (1974), 114–131.

REITMAN-OLSON, JUDITH S.; WHITTEN, WILLIAM B., II; AND GRUENENFELDER, **HCI-0136**
THOMAS M. (Bell Laboratories, Holmdel, NJ)
**A general user interface for creating and displaying tree-structures, hierarchies, decision trees, and nested menus.**
[in *Human factors and interactive computer systems.* Proc. of the NYU symposium on user interfaces (New York, May 26-28, 1982), Y. Vassiliou (Ed.), Ablex Publishing Corp., Norwood, NJ, 1984, 223–241.]

[See main entry in this book, Review HCI-0038]

It is often necessary to process a tree structure within a computer system. A Menu system is the most common form, but instructions for operation, and/or correction of operation, are other forms. This article discusses the display format of how to present this to a user. The title suggests that this is a complete effort, but the reviewer believes this is more of a proposal for discussion. The concepts presented are well thought out and should be considered. The proposed implementation seems a bit awkward to this reviewer, but probably would need to be seen in a running version before such an evaluation could be correctly made. This reviewer believes that the human factor problems in computer systems are often forgotten, and recommends that more people consider these ideas.

—*Charles W. Bash*, Midland, MI

BASS, LEONARD J. (Univ. of Rhode Island, Kingston) **HCI-0137**
**An approach to user specification of interactive display interfaces.**
*IEEE Trans. Softw. Eng.* **SE-11,** 8 (Aug. 1985), 686–698.

This paper presents a theory to explain the nature and relationships among data displayed on interactive terminals. The theory allows for independence from a particular data source, so the data to be formatted and displayed could be from a database, a program, or some other mechanism. Thus, the forms generated by a system based upon this model could be application independent.

One of the aims of the research was to implement a system based upon the model, and to provide a way for end users to modify forms-based data entry screens without affecting the underlying application. This was accomplished by not binding the screen specifications to the application program until execution time. Thus, the user can change the appearance of the screens and immediately reexecute the application to see the effect. However, it is not clear from the description just how easily this can be done.

Although the user does not need to understand how the application program works, there is an underlying assumption made that the user understands the relationships among the data. An elegant system may not necessarily be easy to use. However, the development of a formal model to describe the relationships among screen data represents an important step towards developing systems that can exchange data and formats easily and flexibly.

—*A. Cohill,* Newport, VA

SANTAELLA, EDUARDO M.; AND SLAMECKA, VLADIMIR (Georgia Institute of Technology, Atlanta, GA)
**Toward native language software for information management.**
*Inf. Process. Manage.* **20,** 4 (1984), 527–534.

HCI-0138

This article turns out to be about modifying software so that it is usable in languages other than English. The authors first take about two pages to say that people who do not speak English will find it easier to use software that deals with their native language, rather than software that works only in English.

They then take a page to say that making such modifications is easier if you have the source code and the cooperation of the software vendor. This is a topic they later return to, explaining that changing software is easier with source code. The alternative is "filters," pre- and post-processors that translate between the English phrases understood by the programs and the native language of the user.

Next, they make a somewhat useful division of programs into *token dependent, communications intensive,* and *language dependent* types. The first describes programs which are driven by commands that resemble English words, since such words would have to be translated. The second describes programs that produce a lot of messages in English. The third describes programs, such as text formatters, that have to know something about linguistic or typographical conventions of the language being processed.

The authors finish up with some examples of trying to modify office software for Spanish speakers. They end up with the unsurprising conclusion that if software is written so that the language-specific parts are separated out, it is easier to adapt.

I suppose that this article might be of some use to people who had never thought about issues involved in modifying office software for international markets. A more useful reference is a pamphlet entitled *Software without Borders,* distributed by IBM United Kingdom, which better addresses issues such as message length (messages in English always seem to be shorter than those in other languages), character sets, collating sequences, and keyboard layouts.

—*J. R. Levine,* Cambridge, MA

MASON, M. V.; AND THOMAS, R. C. (Univ. of Leeds, Leeds, UK)
**Experimental adaptive interface.**
*Inf. Tech. Res. Dev. Appl.* **3,** 3 (Aug. 1984), 162–167.

HCI-0139

Mason and Thomas have constructed an enhanced version of the UNIX *man* command which prints, on the user's terminal, information about UNIX commands. Those familiar with the command know that it is, at best, clumsy to use and only occasionally informative.

The authors, after examining some of the features often found in hardcopy manuals, have tried to incorporate some of them in their online version. These include the ability to move backward and forward, windows, indexes, a glossary, cross-referencing, and an adaptive HELP system. Four levels of information are available, and an uncomplicated and sensible set of heuristics are used to decide what to show the user. Online monitoring is used to provide feedback to the design process.

The design of this system is refreshing both in its simplicity and its sensibility. There has been much interest in adaptive information/HELP systems recently, but many of them appear to be more complicated than the systems they are intended to support. Mason and Thomas are interested in providing something useful to users, rather than to designers, a novel approach.

—*A. Cohill,* Newport, VA

## D.2.3 Coding

### Program editors

HAMMER, JOHN M. (Georgia Institute of Technology, Atlanta)     HCI-0140
**A display editor with random access and continuous control.**
*Int. J. Man-Mach. Stud.* **21,** 3 (Sept. 1984), 203–212.

This paper considers aspects of man-machine interaction to enhance the use of a text editing system. Two features were seen to be of major significance: random access to pages of text by names; and the ability of the user to dynamically control the performance of editor commands, called in the text "continuous control."

Random access to text is not new; however, the use of names as opposed to numbers is uncommon and was found to improve the utility of the editor. Continuous control offers the advantage of feedback to the user—he is always aware of what the editor is doing on his behalf, and he may exercise control at any time, even when a command is in progress. The authors found that additional values of the continuous control design were the simplification of the editor's code design and the reduced severity of actions caused by human error in issuing commands.

I found the paper interesting since one seldom encounters investigations into editing. Although editing is one of the most common activities in interactive computing, editors are usually taken for granted. I do have two criticisms of this work:

(1) I would have preferred a discussion of the intended use of the editor. The design of a word processing editor is radically different from that of a programming language editor. Do the concepts presented here (e.g., continuous control) have relevance in both environments? This sort of question should be addressed.
(2) The computing environment was minicomputer based. Since microcomputers offer the superior terminal interface to the user, more mention of work done on microcomputers is in

order. For example, some of the design ideas mentioned in the paper have been implemented in current products commercially available on microcomputing equipment.

Overall, I found the paper worthwhile, although these flaws detracted from it somewhat.

—*G. R. Mayforth,* Houston, TX

MEYER, BERTRAND (Univ. of California, Santa Barbara); NERSON, JEAN-MARC (CIMSA, Velizy, France); AND KO, SOON H. (Univ. of California, Santa Barbara) **HCI-0141**
**Showing programs on a screen.**
*Sci. Comput. Program.* **5,** 2 (June 1985), 111–142.

This paper describes a way of displaying a structured text, such as a computer program, on a video screen. The authors state the problem well: given a structured document and a screen of finite size, find a representation of the document that will fit on the screen and, at the same time, give the user a clear view of the document's structure. Usually what is wanted is not the whole document but rather some part of it called the *focus*. To solve the problem, you need a strategy both for indentation and for deciding when a chunk of text should be replaced by a brief description of that text. Ordinarily that brief description is just the syntactic category of the text.

The display program is aware of, and uses, the structure of the text (more precisely, its abstract syntax). This approach was pioneered by Teitelbaum and Reps [1], and applied specifically to the display problem by Mikelsons [2]; both of these references are cited in the paper. Each node of the syntax tree is associated with a rectangular window of text. The paper develops a calculus of windows and then presents a display algorithm based on that calculus.

This paper should be useful to anyone writing or studying structured editors. It is clearly written and its approach has been used in practice (for a language called Cèpage). However, it does not solve the problem completely; a notable omission is how comments are handled—a difficult problem since comments are not generally part of the abstract syntax of a programming language.

—*P. Abrahams,* Deerfield, MA

**REFERENCES**

[1] TEITELBAUM, T.; AND REPS, T. The Cornell program synthesizer: a syntax-directed programming environment, *Commun. ACM* **24** (1981), 563–573.
[2] MIKELSONS, M. Prettyprinting in an interactive programming environment, *SIGPLAN Not.* **16** (1981), 108–116.

## D.2.5 Testing and Debugging

### CBUG

GAIT, JASON (Tektronix, Inc., Beaverton, OR) **HCI-0142**
**A debugger for concurrent programs.**
*Softw. Pract. Exper.* **15,** 6 (June 1985), 539–554.

This paper describes a source level debugger (CBUG) for concurrent programs written in C. Although C does not directly support concurrent processes, it is traditionally augmented by the standard UNIX system calls (fork, etc.). The basic object to CBUG is a process. Support exists for monitoring, tracing, and single stepping at message and synchronization granularity. A multiwindow user environment supports windows for processes, I/O (pipes, files, etc.), and menus. The paper is oriented towards C and UNIX experts, although the references are extensive.

CBUG uses hooks in the C source, compiling a modified version with the debugger. A concurrent program is monitored by a supervisory routine that starts each process, waits for it to finish, and cleans up after it. Processes are invoked with embedded copies of CBUG which communicate with one another to support interactive breaks, deadlock recovery, single stepping, and redirection of output to the windows.

The paper includes a nice discussion of how program behavior is altered when timing delays are introduced. (Probe Effect) CBUG is actually powerful enough to determine how much overhead can be tolerated without introducing the probe effect. In another example, CBUG demonstrates exactly how correct answers can be obtained from incorrectly synchronized processes.

—*Roger D. H. Warburton,* Middletown, RI

### D.2.6 Programming Environments

GILNERT, EPHRAIM P.; AND TANIMOTO, STEVEN L. (Univ. of Washington)
**PICT: an interactive graphical programming environment.**
*Computer* **17**, 11 (Nov. 1984), 7–25.

This paper describes a limited graphical programming system. Programs in the PICT environment use, for example, at most four different numerical variables in each program or subprogram. The authors describe the system as follows: "PICT provides all tools users need to compose, edit, and run their programs integrated within a simple, consistent command structure. Users communicate with the PICT system throughout all phases of their work by pointing to icons in a menu tree; PICT responds by altering its display in an appropriate manner or, if the user has erred, by presenting a Help message."

As admitted by the authors, the limited scope/capabilities of the PICT system restrict its use to research and beginners. They experimented with over 60 volunteer student users of PICT at the University of Washington. In a nonrigorous, but informative, manner they report on that experimentation.

This 19-page article is approximately one-third background, one-third a description of PICT, and the rest an analysis and projection of future work. The authors do a good job of laying the foundation for research in graphical programming environments, as several similar and dissimilar efforts are mentioned. It could be a very useful reference for someone starting to explore graphical programming environments, especially since it includes 42 references to other relevant articles and books.

—*Lyle Smith,* Naperville, IL

### Interactive

YANG, YIYA (Heriot-Watt Univ., Edinburgh, Scotland, UK)  **HCI-0144**
**Undo support models.**
*Int. J. Man-Mach. Stud.* **28,** 5 (May 1988), 457–481.

It is difficult for users to be comfortable with an interactive computer system when they feel that their actions are irreversible. User interface management systems (UIMSs) therefore generally support one or more varieties of *undo* command. Primitive undo, the simplest of these, consists of a single undo command whose effect is to undo previous commands in stack-like fashion (LIFO). The undo command itself can be undone. Meta undo, a more powerful model, provides a redo command that cancels the effect of an undo. This model also specifies that undo itself only undoes commands other than undo.

This paper discusses the primitive and meta undo models and presents their formal descriptions in terms of abstract data types and a set of four adequacy criteria. It then goes on to argue that neither model is adequate and presents its own model, the *triadic undo*. This model consists of three commands: undo, redo, and rotate. All three are $n$-step commands—that is, they accept an additional parameter that specifies how many commands are to be undone, redone, or rotated.

Although the paper presents informal descriptions of one-step undo and redo, its lack of such descriptions for the commands in the triadic undo model is a notable shortcoming. The triadic undo model is undoubtedly more powerful, but the author fails to demonstrate that users can understand and use it. While the $n$-step generalization adds power, it also introduces another difficulty: in practice, how does the user specify the value of $n$? A user will rarely know how many commands actually need to be undone, redone, or rotated, especially in a system that collects consecutive cursor movements into a single command or provides macros.

The paper includes proofs of various properties of the different models and a Prolog program that implements the triadic undo model. Despite the difficulties with the author's proposal, the formal analyses this paper contains will be useful to specialists.

—*P. Abrahams*, Deerfield, MA

### PECAN

REISS, STEVEN P. (Brown Univ., Providence, RI)  **HCI-0145**
**PECAN: program development systems that support multiple views.**
*IEEE Trans. Softw. Eng.* **SE-11,** 3 (March 1985), 276–285.

This paper is a report on development in progress on the PECAN programmer support environment. PECAN, a programmer development environment which supports multiple views of the user's program, is designed to make use of the new generation of high-resolution personal computers now available, such as the Apollo and Sun 68000-based workstations.

PECAN is a collection of features, some original, and some derived from earlier work. Most of the features currently implemented are already available on high-end systems such as Symbolics LISP machines. These features are interactive syntactic error feedback, unlimited undo in the editor, various menu types, incremental compiling, and multiple window display. The PECAN design is meant to support all programming languages; however, the paper gives no indication that sophisticated program and data abstractions have been used. It seems that the system will support only linear, algebraic languages.

While the overall project goals are ambitious, this report seems premature. The only language supported is PASCAL. Only two program views are implemented: a syntax-directed editor, and a Nassi-Schneiderman flow-chart view (read-only). Thus, editing must be done in the text editor. Even this editor will only reformat based on internal representation for program units which fit on one line of the editor. Algorithmic templates are provided, but no indication of their scope is given in the paper.

In sum, while this project may be valuable to PASCAL developers using an Apollo system at Brown, there appears to be no real contribution to the theory of program development environments. Also, there is little of value here which could not be found in earlier work.
—*Keith Sawyer,* Cambridge, MA

## PegaSys

MORICONI, MARK; AND HARE, DWIGHT F. (SRI International, Menlo Park, CA)     **HCI-0146**
**The PegaSys System: pictures as formal documentation of large programs.**
*ACM Trans. Program. Lang. Syst.* **8**, 4 (Oct. 1986), 524–546.

The authors declare that data and control dependencies play an important role in programming in the large. (Examples of typical dependencies are "calls" dependencies between subprograms and "dataflow" dependencies between processes.) To address this problem, they've developed a software system called PegaSys. In PegaSys, the user supplies a pictorial description, called a Formal Dependency Diagram (FDD), of all the relevant dependencies of a program written in Ada. The PegaSys system will establish whether an FDD hierarchy is logically consistent with the program it is intended to describe. The pictures are meant to be a somehwat easier method for stating dependencies than the logical formulas which they denote. Indeed, the user is given the illusion that logical formulas do not exist. A major component of the PegaSys is its "program verifier," which could be changed to support a different programming language. (The verifier is not intended to establish that a program satisfies its output requirement; instead it is a method for establishing that a program is consistent with its FDD hierarchy.)

The authors provide a convincing and rigorous argument for why and how the PegaSys and all its major components work. This kind of comprehensive (and domain-specific) programming environment could prove to be an invaluable tool to the practicing software engineer. Overall, the paper is very well written, clear, and informative.
—*S. Javey,* North York, Ont., Canada

## SLCSE

STRELICH, TOM (General Research Corp., Santa Barbara, CA)     **HCI-0147**
**The Software Life Cycle Support Environment (SLCSE): a computer based framework for developing software systems.**
*SIGPLAN Notices* **24,** 2 (February 1989), 35–44. [Special issue: Proceedings of the ACM SIGSOFT/SIGPLAN software engineering symposium on practical software development environments.]

Tom Strelich gives an overview and technical description of "The Software Life Cycle Support Environment" (SLCSE), a software development environment that includes integrated tools, a project information database, and a uniform user interface. This environment is not especially innovative, but seems to be an industrial-strength implementation of existing ideas in software development environments. The intended audiences for this product are DoD industries, particularly the Air Force.

Strelich describes three primary components of SLCSE: the user interface, the integrated tool set, and the project information repository. The user interface is a windowed, menuing environment which is built with two tools: Winnie, to support windows, and MOO (Menu Operations Organizer). SLCSE does not yet support X-windows or a mouse since these are not generally available among the primary user groups. User roles that give access to role-specific tools are defined.

Strelich describes the extensive tool set component-by-component. The tools supported range from management-oriented to programming support tools. He describes the support for integrating new and existing tools. The languages SLCSE supports are those used by DoD: Ada, Jovial J73, FORTRAN, and COBOL.

The project information database is designed to contain project management information as well as the software itself. An entity/relationship model has been developed to meet the DoD-STD-2167A Life Cycle. (The paper includes a portion of an E/R diagram. Its meaning is obscured by the many acronyms and by its incompleteness. It must have been included to prove that the database has an underlying E/R model.)

Strelich seems to have done an adequate job of describing the components of SLCSE. After reading this paper, I have a good understanding of the purpose of the system and an overview of the implementation techniques used. The motivations for various design decisions are described well. The primary shortcoming of this paper is that it reads like an advertisement. The paper is by no means a critical review of SLCSE. It contains no comparisons to other direct competitors in this market. Given Strelich's position as an employee of General Research Corporation, the developer of SLCSE, this perspective is understandable.

*—J. Kiper,* Oxford, OH

### D.2.7 Distribution and Maintenance

*Documentation*

KNUTH, DONALD E. (Stanford Univ., Stanford, CA)     **HCI-0148**
**Literate programming.**
*Comput. J.* **27,** 2 (May 1984), 97–111.

Any paper authored by Knuth is worth reading, and often entertaining, even when somewhat irritating. This one is exactly in that mood, as exemplified by its provocative title. The paper describes and assesses, mainly by way a long example, a programming language and documentation system called WEB. Input text contains both a complete program and its documentation in a disciplined and systematic form. Depending upon the system component into which this text is fed, the output is a source PASCAL program, ready to be compiled into an executable program, or a source $T_EX$ text, ready to be compiled into a phototypesetter script.

The sections are as follows: introduction, the WEB system, a complete example, how the example was specified, the tangled output (the PASCAL text), the woven output (the $T_EX$ text), additional bells and whistles, Occam's razor (WEB macros), portability, programs as webs, stylistic issues, economic issues, related work, and retrospect and prospects.

The paper is phototypeset using the WEB system (of course). It is very well presented, although somewhat too sumptuous in its use of various fonts, as is generally the case in texts typeset by programmers instead of typographers. Using at least ten different fonts in a 15 page text is really too much. However, the paper is very easy and pleasant to read, and almost free of typos.

On the positive aide, I found the whole idea extremely interesting and fruitful. Since the program is hidden in its documentation, it becomes impossible to modify it without changing the documentation at the same time. (In fact, the program is a byproduct of the documentation.) More importantly, in my opinion the order in which the program is designed and written no longer needs to be related to the order in which it will be compiled. What is good for a compiler is not necessarily good for a programmer, and vice versa. It is time to consider as obvious that the text by the compiler is the result of come preprocessing (collecting scattered pieces, reordering them, macroprocessing, etc.) Another very important point is that the WEB idea is entirely independent of the supporting languages: $T_EX$ and PASCAL in this case, but TROFF/NROFF and C in another experiment.

On the negative side, most offensive is the lack of readability and writeability of the input text: to be forced to write character sequences like "ef[{$]]$" is really unbearable. The blame mainly lies with $T_EX$, but TROFF/NROFF would not be better. As demonstrated by Knuth's unfortunate choice of MIX in his opus magnum, he is not really interested in the cosmetics of the support languages of his work. Here the difficulty is increased by the extreme dissimilarity between input and output. In order to modify the output result, users must modify something unreadable and very far from the result they see. This is a customary problem in most text processing systems, although there exist at least three possibilities: the input text is the reference text, upon which all modifications are made; (2) the output text is the reference text, and modifications are made in terms of pages, columns, sections, paragraphs, sentences, words, etc.; and (3) input and output are very similar, the visible structure of the input text being the natural way to describe the final appearance of the output text. Solution 3 is extremely infrequent, although the easiest to use. Solution 2, equally infrequent, has at least the immense merit of uniformity. Solution 1 is presently the rule in text processing systems, simply because it is easier to implement and does not necessitate a specialized text editor; but this is really unfortunate.

Another important shortcoming of WEB, which is in fact inherent in the idea, is that the graph structure of the program and of its documentation is hardly visible, although this structure would be the best tool for mastering program complexity. Maybe this is the major point where an improvement would be needed.

Finally, it is regrettable that phototypeset output is so slow and expensive that the user normally does not work on an up-to-date version of the output text, or uses the unreadable input as the support of modifications. This inconvenience is strongly related to the criticism I made about the distance between input and output forms. Here too, much progress has to be done in text processing. It is time that designers take interest in less primitive input languages, and find idea other than interspersing unreadable code sequences among the material to be typeset.

—*O. Lecarme,* Nice, France

SOMMERVILLE, I.; WELLAND, R.; BENNETT, I.; AND THOMPSON, R. (Univ. of Strathclyde, Glasgow, UK)
**SOFTLIB—A documentation management system.**
*Softw. Pract. Exper.* **16,** 2 (Feb. 1986), 131–143.

This is an excellent paper. It not only describes an exceptional tool (SOFTLIB), but it is also a well-written description of the tool, its development, and application. I found it thoroughly interesting. The paper should be read by all software developers. The authors are to be commended. Their tool is a definite contribution to the progress of software development. It is amazing that they got the support and funding to develop such a tool. This type of tool would normally be developed by industry. This reviewer intends to contact to the authors to determine their interest in tailoring their tool to the discipline of configuration management, particularly software configuration management.

Documentation is always a "thorn in the project's back." By that, I mean most programmers don't like to document and if they do document at all, it is generally done poorly and after the fact, rather than properly before the fact. A tool such as SOFTLIB could significantly contribute to more proper documentation, a better software project, and more than likely at a lower cost than what it presently costs.

This tool should have wide application. It seems very cost effective and very useful over the software life cycle. This reviewer feels it is very applicable in a software quality assurance program.

—*L. G. Egan,* Santa Maria, CA

HASELKORN, MARK P. (Univ. of Washington, Seattle)
**The future of "writing" for the computer industry.**
[in *Text, context, and hypertext: writing with and for the computer,* E. Barrett (Ed.), MIT Press, Cambridge, MA, 1988, 3-13.]

This paper presents the opinion that the role of documentation writers in the computer industry is expanding beyond its traditional boundaries. It argues that in the quest to provide better products to the end user, writers are an underutilized resource capable of providing additional valuable input to product design and development. The author suggests that this potential can be realized first by having writers involved earlier in the development process, and second by having writers test prototypes for usability, not only to adjust documentation but also to feed the results back into design and development, as part of their emerging role as user advocates.

The arguments for this position are well developed. The author first examines trends and developments that are driving the change in the status of writers and then projects how writers' tasks will change in the future. He gives examples of the fine line between documentation and design. For instance, it might be easier to incorporate a help function into the interface design of a product than to write and deliver text.

The paper is fairly well written and organized. It contains many seeds for healthy discussion, and further research and development, in the realms of both academia and business.

—*G. A. Caruso,* Etobicoke, Ont., Canada

LEVINE, LAWRENCE B. (Harvard Business School, Boston, MA)     **HCI-0151**
**Corporate culture, technical documentation, and organization diagnosis.**
[in *Text, context, and hypertext: writing with and for the computer,* E. Barrett (Ed.), MIT Press, Cambridge, MA, 1988, 149-174.]

Levine believes in the corporate culture model, and he says that documentation managers ought to believe in it too. The purpose of his chapter (originally a workshop given in 1987 at the Fourth Annual Conference on Writing for the Computer Industry at MIT) is to give document writers a lever with which to move their organizations. In many companies, Levine says, writers have low status and high frustration levels. Writers can change this situation if they start to focus on processes and people instead of products and tasks.

He lists six points of cultural analysis:

(1) Do the writers sit near the developers, programmers, and engineers? (Physical proximity can be a key to successful interaction.)
(2) Are writers integrated into development groups, or are they segregated into documentation groups?
(3) What is the history of the relationship between the documentation and development departments? (In other words, if there are conflicts, when and why did they start?)
(4) Who writes product specifications? (Does anyone?) Can the professional writers help the developers by clarifying the specification process as well as the specifications themselves?
(5) What is the writer/developer ratio—a reasonable 1 writer to 5–10 programmers or engineers, or an unreasonable 1 to 35? and
(6) What are the backgrounds of the writers and the developers? Is there any crossover (and therefore sympathy) between the two groups?

The point of his analysis is this: How do corporations see themselves, and how can smart documentation managers change or take advantage of these self-images? If it is true, as Levine says, that managing information is as important as making and selling products—that the glue that allows most companies to make and sell products *is* information—then writers are in a good position to raise their status. After all, what is writing but visible thinking and portable information?

—*S. L. Fowler,* New York, NY

RUBENS, PHILIP; AND KRULL, ROBERT (Rensselaer Polytechnic Institute, Troy, NY)   HCI-0152
**Designing online information.**
[in *Text, context, and hypertext: writing with and for the computer,* E. Barrett (Ed.), MIT Press, Cambridge, MA, 1988, 291-309.]

Widespread availability of graphical interfaces will finally liberate users from inconsistent, hard-to-learn, and hard-to-use applications, from those shelves of manuals, and from training classes that take valuable time from work. The commercial success of the Apple Macintosh is clear evidence, and this is only the beginning. This chapter explores a vital aspect of online environments: information (or documentation). Unless this documentation is also consistent and easy to learn and use, some of the benefits will be lost.

The authors present an outline of key online documentation tasks and issues. The major topics include types of online information (e.g., reference material, tutors, prompts, demonstrations, and messages), design teams, authoring tools, and processes (e.g., information gathering, screen design, and storyboarding). The authors have some doubt about the vitality of graphical interfaces. I would strongly disagree with this: humans evolved as signal processors, not as text processors. Newer technologies that will be useful are listed (e.g., sound, voice, and motion). Artificial intelligence techniques to search for information are mentioned briefly. Each of the topics outlined here could be the subject of a chapter in a how-to book.

—*W. S. Hoffman,* Wilmington, DE


SHIRK, HENRIETTA N. (Northeastern Univ., Boston, MA)   HCI-0153
**Technical writers as computer scientists: the challenges of online documentation.**
[in *Text, context, and hypertext: writing with and for the computer,* E. Barrett (Ed.), MIT Press, Cambridge, MA, 1988, 311-327.]

The author asserts that techniques used to develop paper documents are not adequate for creating online documentation, and proposes that technical writers should become "a special type of computer scientist, with skills drawn from many fields." This chapter describes a hierarchy of types of online documentation, compares paper and online documentation tasks, defines a structure for online documentation standards, and explores cross-disciplinary knowledge requirements.

The author, as befits someone affiliated with a department of English, approaches the question of preparing online documentation from the viewpoint of the documentation specialist. It may develop, however, that computer scientists (or application developers) will acquire presentation skills to supplement their knowledge of user requirements and how an application will fulfill them. As applications become more integrated with work processes, developers will need to acquire skills drawn from social sciences such as psychology. To achieve the required level of consistency and integration, documentation must be viewed as one part of the total application, rather than as a component to be added after development.

—*W. S. Hoffman,* Wilmington, DE

NONBOOKS

PRICE, JONATHAN (Wordplay, Oakland, CA)  **HCI-0154**
**Creating a style for online help.**
[in *Text, context, and hypertext: writing with and for the computer,* E. Barrett (Ed.), MIT Press, Cambridge, MA, 1988, 329-341.]

There is a real need for applications that combine the right functionality with a consistent and easy to learn and use "look and feel" so users see the application as a natural extension of their own capabilities (like a hammer is to a carpenter). As discussed in the review of the Rubens and Krull paper [1], the style of online documentation, including help, should not be different from that of the application itself, lest the benefits cited above be partially lost.

The author lists thirteen 'dilemmas', the answers to which "will shape the style and atmosphere of your online world." Again, the 'world' cannot be defined only by help. The dilemmas include the scope of help (in the sense of extending beyond the application itself), mobility, variety, and blending of images, text considerations, organization and paths through the material, user control and modifiability, and friendliness. At the end, the author quotes Shaw in asking "does the style do the job?" An equally good question would be "does the style undo the job?"

—*W. S. Hoffman,* Wilmington, DE

**REFERENCES**

[1] RUBENS, P. AND KRULL, R. Designing online information. In *Text, Context, and Hypertext: writing with and for the computer.* E. Barrett, Ed. MIT Press, Cambridge, MA, 1988, 291–309. See *Computing Reviews* Rev. 8911-0809.


### D.2.8  Metrics

#### *Software science*

KORSON, TIMOTHY D. (Southern College of Seventh Day Adventists, Collegedale, TN);  **HCI-0155**
AND VAISHNAVI, VIJAY K. (Georgia State Univ., Atlanta)
**An empirical study of the effects of modularity on program modifiability.**
[in *Empirical studies of programmers.* Papers presented at the first workshop on empirical studies of programmers (Washington, DC, June 5-6, 1986), E. Soloway; and S. Iyengar (Eds.), Ablex Publishing Corp., Norwood, NJ, 1986, 168–186.]

An empirical study of the effects of modularity on adaptive program maintenance (enhancing, adding, or changing existing features) is reported by the authors. The study provides evidence that a modular program can be modified faster than a nonmodular version of the program when one of the following conditions holds: (1) modularity has been used to implement information hiding; (2) existing modules in a program perform generic operations, some of which can be used in a modification; or (3) a significant understanding of, and changes to, the existing code are required for performing a modification. The study provides evidence that modifications other than those described above are unaided by modularity. The work also indicates that modularity offers no benefit when a modification requires additions that are spread throughout the source code.

The authors' research utilizes experienced professional programmers or advanced computer science students; the same subject is tested with modular and monolithic material in different experiments. They propose further research examining the levels of modularity, the effect of modularity on program development time, and the likelihood of errors.

—*Michael L. Gordon,* Dobbs Ferry, NY

### D.2.9 Management

COOK, PETER; ELLIS, CLARENCE; GRAF, MIKE; REIN, GAIL; AND SMITH, TOM    **HCI-0156**
(MCC Technology Corporation, Austin, TX)
**Project Nick: meetings augmentation and analysis.**
*ACM Trans. Office Inf. Syst.* **5,** 2 (April 1987), 132–146.

The paper discusses a research project carried out by the authors at MCC to provide an environment and facilities that enable systems designers to conduct better face-to-face meetings.

The authors provide a classification of different types of meetings, though for the purpose of the early phase of their research they focus on face-to-face meetings. They develop a model of such meetings as an underpinning for their developmental and experimental work. They briefly review other projects in the United States that attempt to facilitate the process of meetings with the use of automated facilities. Readers with an interest in the topic might like to note some work on meeting environments and supporting software carried out in the United Kingdom [1,2,3].

The authors present an interesting model of *meeting progressions* including the notion of *pots*. A pot is a repository of knowledge and understanding, filtered by some process. Each participant at a meeting has a *notional pot*, and there is also a *public pot*. The quality of a meeting can be judged by the extent to which there is congruence between the contents of individual pots and the public pot. As described in the paper, an impression (unintentional I believe) is given that participants enter the meeting with empty pots (see fig. 1 in the paper). I would have preferred the model to lay more stress on the processes by which the contents of the pots are changed from before the meeting starts to the end of the meeting. Perhaps more should be said about the premeeting knowledge, understanding, ideological positions and biases, ambitions, and coalition formation of participants.

The authors stress the importance of evaluation, but hardly evaluate their experimental work or discuss how such evaluations can be carried out. If the notion of pots has any value in the theory, it must be possible to examine the contents of pots. But, as workers in the theory of knowledge and knowledge acquisition have shown, that subject presents considerable and possibly insuperable difficulties.

Nevertheless, I welcome this paper. A great deal of attention is being paid to the topic of software engineering. Much of the effort is devoted to the development of formal methods, to CASE tools, and to notions of software factories. This paper focuses on aspects of the software engineering process that are equally important. More research into ways of enhancing the knowledge and understanding of the processes that are used can only have a beneficial impact on the effectiveness of software engineering. But the type of research conducted by the authors also has relevance for the much larger topic of systems to support office activities.

—*Frank Land,* London, UK

NONBOOKS [HCI-0158]

**REFERENCES**

[1] AUSTIN, N. C. A management support environment. *ICL Tech. J.* **5**, 2 (1986).
[2] PHILLIPS, L. Group D.S.S. for senior managers achieving consensus. *Datamation* **32**, 20 (1986).
[3] PREEDY, D. K., AND BITTLESTONE, R. G. A. O. R. and the boardroom of the 90s. *J. Oper. Res. Soc.* **36**, 9 (1985).

### D.2.m Miscellaneous

LAUGHERY, K. R., JR.; AND LAUGHERY, KENNETH R., SR. (Micro Analysis and Design, Boulder, CO)     **HCI-0157**
**Human factors in software engineering: a review of the literature.**
*J. Syst. Softw.* **5**, 1 (Feb. 1985), 3–14.

This paper reviews the literature on human factors in software engineering. The authors organize the literature into eight topics: (1) psychology of programmer behavior, (2) individual differences among programmers, (3) programmer training, (4) effectiveness of various language/coding practices, (5) human errors in computer programming, (6) program debugging, (7) estimating programmer performance and software cost, and (8) evaluation of software quality. Within this framework, the authors summarize the research that has been conducted and identify issues that need to be addressed. The main conclusion of the review is that a general theory of programmer behavior is needed to guide future research.

    The authors stated three purposes for this paper: (1) provide a framework for studying human factors in software engineering, (2) summarize the literature, and (3) identify some research issues. In this reviewer's opinion, this paper fulfills these three purposes, with one reservation. There is an ample number of references for a review paper, but most (approximately two-thirds) of them are older than six years. In such a rapidly changing area, a more up-to-date reference list would have been valuable and might have led to further insights by the authors as to issues that need to be researched. This paper should be of value to software, system, and human factors engineers interested in a well-written, though perhaps outdated, review of the literature in human factors in software engineering.

—*M. P. Tarka,* Gaithersburg, MD

## D.3 Programming Languages

### D.3.2 Language Classifications

MONTANARI, UGO (Univ. of Pisa, Pisa, Italy)     **HCI-0158**
**Towards an integration between language and software development environment.**
[in *Theory and practice of software technology.* Proc. international seminars on software engineering (Capri, Italy, 1980 & 1982), D. Ferrari; M. Bolognani; and J. Goguen (Eds.), Elsevier North-Holland, Inc., New York, NY, 1983, 195–202.]

In this paper, it is proposed that the various languages which are used in the software life cycle, the command language, and the tools should be embedded in one orthogonal, extensible language. Furthermore, distributed programming requires means for communication and synchronization, access to physical resources, and network configuration. An implementation of such a functionally distributed system is presented in a short manner.

Surely, orthogonality is a useful and powerful language feature but, from the viewpoint of the reviewer, the author should have balanced it against other features like simplicity of efficiency. Furthermore, there is no reference to other approaches to this problem (e.g., program transformations or program synthesis). Since there are no new arguments or insights into language design, the paper should be seen as a short project report.

—*F. Stetter,* Mannheim, West Germany

## Ada

MYERS, WARE  **HCI-0159**
**Ada: first users—pleased; prospective users—still hesitant.**
*Computer* **20,** 3 (March 1987), 68–73.

This nontechnical paper dealing with first impressions on the use of the Ada programming language is well worth reading. It reports statements from early users on three main areas where the language is expected to play a major role: productivity of software development and the reliability and performance of the resulting products. The discussion of productivity issues—including the reported assessment by Lawrence H. Putnam [1]—is particularly interesting.

The most suprising fact emerging from this paper is that existing Ada applications fall outside the area for which the language was especially designed. No large embedded systems have yet been completed in Ada. Most initial applications have been in building tools for Ada or in small research projects. However, the author ends with an optimistic comment. "Now that adequate compilers and environments are available, Ada usage is likely to reach critical mass within the time it takes to do the projects now getting under way—projects that should definitely establish the value of Ada. Thereafter its use should expand rapidly."

—*C. Ghezzi,* Milan, Italy

**REFERENCES**

[1] PUTNAM, L. H. *Software cost estimating and life-cycle control: getting the software numbers.* Computer Society Press, Los Alamitos, CA, 1980.

## DIAG2

BROWN, A. D. (Univ. of Southampton, Hampshire, UK)  **HCI-0160**
**Computer-aided hierarchical diagrams.**
*Comput. Aided Des.* **16,** 5 (Sept. 1984), 249–252.

This article discusses a diagram drawing language called DIAG2. There are three basic constructs: the straight line, the segment of a circle, and text blocks. These constructs can be linked together to form groups, and these groups can also be linked together. A recursion facility is embedded in the language for the production of diagrams that have self-similarity. A nonlinear transformation is also provided for "rubber sheet' transformations of groups. The program has been used for drawing production and as a teaching aid to demonstrate the advantages of hierarchical descriptions.

—*G. W. Zobrist,* St. Louis, MO

NONBOOKS

## Very high-level languages

CHANG, SHI-KUO (Univ. of Pittsburgh, Pittsburgh, PA)  **HCI-0161**
**Icon semantics—a formal approach to icon system design.**
*Int. J. Pattern Recogn. Artif. Intell.* **1,** 1 (April 1987), 103–120.

Icons are normally defined as symbolic objects used in computer systems to communicate possible actions nonverbally. This paper describes the author's approach to a general theory of an iconic algebra. He constructs the algebra from a number of iconic operators that operate on generalized, dual-representation icons. This approach differs from the familiar icon system used, for example, in the Macintosh. The author has made an important step toward a more general iconic language and should be rewarded for advancing beyond the average level.

Chang defines a general icon as a dual representation of an object, with a logical part (representing the meaning of the icon), and a physical part (representing its image). General icons are used to describe formal icon systems as five-tuples that consist of a set of logical objects, a set of physical objects, and a finite set of icon names along with their root icon name. The tuple also includes a set of rules that define the icons in terms of the logical and physical objects. The icon system is hierarchical and the algebra based upon it has a fairly large number of useful operators. The paper is rich with illustrations, which makes it easy to read and understand.

My overall view of this research paper, which takes an original approach, is positive. It might, however, be difficult for an end user to understand the general hierarchical structure of a single icon system unless its structure is visually displayed. Also, I question whether some of the illustrations (e.g., example 1, the image database) really correspond to icons.

—*Erland Jungert,* Linköping, Sweden


## D.3.3  Language Constructs

### Abstract data types

FORD, RAY (Univ. of Iowa, Iowa City); AND MILLER, KEITH (The College of William  **HCI-0162**
and Mary, Williamsburg, VA)
**Abstract data type development and implementation: an example.**
*IEEE Trans. Softw. Eng.* **SE-11,** 10 (Oct. 1985), 1033–1037.

This paper describes an application of the ADT methodology to the design and implementation of a Vision Research Programming System. As expected, the authors show that the principles of ADT are well suited to an ADA-like implementation. However, they also give some substantial evidence that these principles may be implemented also in older languages like standard FORTRAN IV, through the imposition of some programming methodologies. Nevertheless, they reckon that the FORTRAN implementation is less than the corresponding ADA implementation. The paper should be of interest for those working in the field of computer vision and those interested in new programming methodologies.

—*R. Nicolescu,* Bucharest, Romania

### D.3.4 Processors

#### Compilers

BURKE, MICHAEL G.; AND FISHER, GERALD A. (Thomas J. Watson Research Center, Yorktown Heights, NY)  **HCI-0163**
**A practical method for LR and LL syntactic error diagnosis and recovery.**
*ACM Trans. Program. Lang. Syst.* **9,** 2 (April 1987), 164–197.

The authors of this paper build a strong and well-organized case for the use of the adjective *practical* in their title. The paper has been very carefully written and effectively presents a method for detection, diagnosis, recovery, and repair of syntax errors. The method is applicable within the frameworks of LR and LL parsing and is for the most part language-independent, but it does allow for fine-tuning via language-specific parameters. The primary innovation, parse action deferral, coupled with heuristic repair criteria leads to high quality diagnosis and recovery without substantial space or time overhead for correct programs. Space and time trade-offs are carefully presented and discussed with respect to justifying the inclusion of this method in a production compiler. Helpful examples in Pascal and Ada are given to illustrate the effect of the method, and selected metrics are reported to illustrate the general effectiveness of the method. Overall, the paper represents a valuable step in the transition of syntax error-handling from art to science.

—*M. G. Murphy,* Houston, TX

#### Preprocessors

DU BOULAY, BENEDICT (Univ. of Sussex, UK); AND MATTHEW, IAN (Univ. of Aberdeen, UK)  **HCI-0164**
**Fatal error in pass zero: how not to confuse novices.**
[in *Readings on cognitive ergonomics - mind and computers.* Proc. of the 2nd European conference (Gmunden, Austria, Sept. 10-14, 1984), G. van der Veer; M. Tauber; T. Green; and P. Gorny (Eds.), Springer-Verlag New York, Inc., New York, NY, 1984, 132–141.]

[See main entry in this book, Review HCI-0039]

It is nice to know that well into the era of 4th and 5th generation languages, application generators, software engineering, and the like, someone is still worrying about novice programmers. Pity the poor programmer whose innocent error results in "Fatal Error in Pass 0" from the less-than-friendly PASCAL compiler, or worse. I wish I had a collection of similar messages, including a gem from a UNIVAC FORTRAN compiler which said, "SIMPLIFY THIS STATEMENT," and meant it!

The authors' point is that many messages are not nearly so clear. They feel compiler writers have placed emphasis on producing efficient code, and not on helping the programmer determine what is wrong, especially when a simple error (e.g., fori:=1 to 10 do) results in a cascade of error messages. Perhaps the worst case—omitted data definitions (which can produce pages of messages describing illegal use of data)—is not discussed. Debugging in modern environments, where procedural language code is generated, is also not discussed. At a minimum, new programmers are now or will soon use tools which aid even traditional coding by providing prompts for statements, a check of logic levels, and ending of iteration loops, etc., thereby avoiding most errors of the types described.

The authors report on their work to develop a prototype checker for PASCAL, "... not as a model of how this task should be carried out but to underline our argument that the task should be done." It is doubtful many need convincing that it would be nice. Ten or 15 years ago such work would have been of real value. Whether the effort is justified today in light of the clear trend towards much higher level languages for general use is questionable. The paper also includes a survey of work on program error detection and correction efforts.

—*W. S. Hoffman*, Wilmington, DE

## D.4 Operating Systems

### UNIX

QUARTERMAN, JOHN S.; SILBERSCHATZ, ABRAHAM; AND PETERSON, JAMES L. (Univ. of Texas, Austin)  **HCI-0165**
**4.2BSD and 4.3BSD as examples of the UNIX system.**
*ACM Comput. Surv.* **17,** 4 (Dec. 1985), 379–418.

The paper is an excellent overview of UNIX from a historical and modern perspective. The paper describes the historical development of UNIX as an operating system and shows why some features are being included in the newest Berkeley release. The authors also discuss topics such as memory mapping, control block structure, and I/O system in straightforward language that both the advanced and novice programmer can understand and appreciate.

This is a worthwhile paper for those who are encountering UNIX for the first time, in order to understand the philosophy and operation of this wonderful operating system. These gentlemen have done a superb job of bringing together, in one paper, information that is scattered over many other UNIX manuals and that is critical for the new UNIX user to appreciate.

—*Linda McInnis*, Albany, VT

### D.4.4 Communications Management

#### Network communication

LINTON, A.; AND PANZIERI, F. (Univ. of Newcastle upon Tyne, Newcastle upon Tyne, UK)  **HCI-0166**
**A communication system supporting large datagrams on a local area network.**
*Softw. Pract. Exper.* **16,** 3 (March 1986), 278–289.

The paper describes a plausible UNIX implementation of a simple network communication scheme. The main characteristics of the method are that: (1) it tries to optimize the transfer of large quantities of data by allowing up to 2 Gbytes to be transferred with a single call on i/o primitives; (2) it provides for a simple network addressing scheme where each destination and source is identified by a single pair; and (3) it provides for an interesting "scatter-gather" facility that lets the user copy data from and into noncontiguous areas of memory. The rationale for this scatter-gather facility is that it may speed up data transfers by restricting the number of context switches required between user and system code.

Interfaces for this "Uniform Datagram Service" (UDS) were implemented for various flavors of local area networks, ranging from the Cambridge Ring to an ad hoc network built from RS-232 interfaces. The interface provides users with six standard i/o primitives for sending and receiving data and for obtaining information about the mapping between logical and real network addresses. The work may be a useful guideline for similar efforts to implement datagram services. The performance measurements reported are not too remarkable. As expected, they confirm that it is efficient to minimize the number of context switches in a UNIX environment, and similarly beneficial to transfer data in large chunks rather than in small ones. The data transfer rates achieved with the UDS on the Cambridge Ring are between 4 and 5 Kbytes/s.

—*G. Holzmann,* Murray Hill, NJ

## D.4.6 Security and Protection

### Access controls

BARTON, BEN F.; AND BARTON, MARTHALEE S. (Univ. of Michigan, Ann Arbor) **HCI-0167**
**User-friendly password methods for computer-mediated information systems.**
*Comput. Secur.* **3,** 3 (Aug. 1984), 186–195.

Existing literature concerning password methods stresses the technical aspects of the security issue while ignoring the human element. This paper proposes that memorability, as well as security of passwords, should be a critical issue in establishing appropriate password methods. Several models for user-friendly password selection and recreation are presented. The models are rooted in cognitive psychology and are adaptable to expert and inexpert users. Simple methods of selecting passwords that are easily recalled, but not easily discovered, are recommended.

The paper identifies shortcomings in the existing literature concerning passwords and password security, and offers practical solutions to overcome these shortcomings. The paper is rich in ideas and well worth reading.

—*G. A. Caruso,* Etobicoke, Ont., Canada

## D.4.7 Organization and Design

### Interactive systems

RUNCIMAN, COLIN; AND THIMBLEBY, HAROLD (Univ. of York, York, UK) **HCI-0168**
**Equal opportunity interactive systems.**
*Int. J. Man-Mach. Stud.* **25,** 4 (Oct. 1986), 439–451.

This paper discusses the concept of equal opportunity computer systems. According to the authors, computer systems have been viewed as requiring the users to supply information that is known about a given problem while the computer outputs the answer to the problem. In equal opportunity systems, all information that can be provided or demanded by the system can be provided or demanded by the user. The purpose of this paper is to show that the concept of equal opportunity can be applied to the design of interactive computer systems. It does this in a clear and fairly concise manner that will be readily understandable by the target population for this paper: system designers. Although the paper contains several examples in which the concept of equal opportunity has been successfully applied to interactive systems, it would have been a more valuable paper had the authors provided the system designer with criteria for judging when the equal opportunity concept should or should not be employed in an interactive system.

The authors conclude that it is not known whether users have the capability to fully utilize equal opportunity in complex tasks and that the costs of implementing equal opportunity systems may be prohibitive. Whether the equal opportunity concept will eventually be valuable (in cost/benefit terms) for the design of interactive systems where complex tasks are being performed (e.g., air traffic control or ground control systems for spacecraft) depends on whether systems designers receive concrete answers to the issues raised by the authors in their conclusions.

—*M. P. Tarka,* Gaithersburg, MD

## D.4.8 Performance

### Monitors

JOYCE, JEFFREY (Univ. of Cambridge, Cambridge, UK); LOMOW, GREG; SLIND, KONRAD; AND UNGER, BRIAN (Univ. of Calgary, Calgary, Alberta, Canada)
**Monitoring distributed systems.**
*ACM Trans. Comput. Syst.* **5,** 2 (May 1987), 121–150.

Monitoring involves the collection, analysis, and presentation of dynamic information concerning a computational process. A distributed system presents difficulties in all three areas.

This paper outlines several approaches to the analysis and presentation tasks, and it discusses software supporting these approaches. Collection consists of gathering information on nine fixed events or their failures, e.g., entering the system, sending a message, or creating a process. Analysis consists of filtering events, calculating statistics, checking for cycles of blocked processes, checking event streams against a protocol specification, and computing abstract events from sequences of primitive events. The data can be presented textually, graphically, or as a collection of time lines. Finally, the paper discusses how monitoring can be coupled with software, such as a debugger that controls the monitored system.

The strength of this paper is that it carefully separates the three tasks, both conceptually and in the implementation. This partitioning permits several options for each task and simplifies the implementation of the monitoring software. The primary disadvantages are that the software is less efficient and exhibits a much larger monitoring artifact. The reason for this is that since information on the desired analysis and presentation is not available for earlier tasks, all data that might be useful must be collected, stored, and analyzed. While the advantages of the approach are enumerated clearly in the paper, no details on the system's efficiency or monitoring artifact are provided.

—*R. Snodgrass,* Tucson, AZ

## D.4.9 Systems Programs and Utilities

### Command and control languages

SAVAGE, RICKY E.; AND HABINEK, JAMES K.     **HCI-0170**
**A Multilevel menu-driven user interface: Design and evaluation through simulation.**
[in *Human factors in computer systems*, J. Thomas; and M. Schneider (Eds.), Ablex Publishing Corp., Norwood, NJ, 1984, 165-186.]

The authors propose that operating systems driven either by command languages alone or rigid tree-structured menu prompting alone are either too hostile for novice users, or too inflexible for experienced users. They propose a combination of both extremes. Menus prompt inexperienced users and keyword input is available for those more familiar with the underlying operating system's command language. Examples of their interface technique are said to be superior to a vendor-supplied product, according to the authors' criteria.

The authors' conclusions are certainly relevant for the operating system discussed, but they may have set up a "straw man" to criticize. Menu-driven systems that allow keyword inputs are not uncommon e.g., IBM's Professional Office Systems (PROFS). Thus, their basic thesis has been shown to be valid by being usurped commercially.

A more conceptual objection concerns their premise that natural language systems are neither "currently feasible," nor "really desirable." There is sufficient evidence (from the marketplace) that natural language systems such as Artificial Intelligence Corp.'s INTELLECT product are well-regarded. When coupled with knowledge-based systems, they will go a long way to provide suitable interfaces for all levels of computer users.

I do not fault the authors for their failure to foretell the future, but I feel that their work is dated and outmoded by the rapid progress in man-machine interface and AI. This paper does not make a useful contribution to the literature.

—*Ross Jay Bettinger,* Silver Spring, MD

## D.m Miscellaneous

### Software psychology

KLERER, MELVIN (Polytechnic Institute of New York, Brooklyn, NY)     **HCI-0171**
**Experimental study of a two-dimensional language vs. FORTRAN for first-course progammers.**
*Int. J. Man-Mach. Stud.* **20,** 5 (May 1984), 445–467.

This paper uses computer science graduate students to determine possible differences in time-to-problem solution as a surrogate for the ease and rapidity of becoming minimally proficient in solving numerically oriented problems using FORTRAN vs. the Klerer-May 2-D language. Although it is not stated, this reviewer is led to assume that the reported work was performed several years ago: i.e., (1) the textbook was a 1972 edition; (2) the computer science graduate students had no previous programming experience; (3) FORTRAN was used; (4) keypunches were used to prepare the input; (5) all of the references are dated 1972 or earlier with one exception (1977), despite fairly extensive recent work in the area of human factors.

In the opinion of this reviewer, the data reported in this paper do not constitute valid evidence bearing on the question posed in the title. The experimental methods were so seriously flawed that conclusions are both inappropriate and misleading. The initial error was in the choice of experimental subjects with which to assess the K-M 2-D language, in that they were not "pure beginners" but were "contaminated" by a minimal programming background making the basic comparison invalid in the sense of comparing apples and oranges.

Although the mean time to problem solution was uniformly smaller for the student groups employing the K-M 2-D language, the variation within groups was so large as to prevent meaningful conclusions. Additionally, there is reason to question the normality of the data and therefore the appropriateness of drawing conclusions using the statistical method employed. This reviewer does not believe that any statement can be made about the probabilities of the differences in the means not being due to chance. Note from the following table derived from the reported data that only two out of eight means were larger than their standard deviations.

It is the opinion of this reviewer that the flaws in the data on which this paper is based are not only fatal but most unfortunate. It is very possible that with the use of currently available input technologies two-dimensional special-purpose languages such as the Klerer-May 2-D language could constitute an important advance towards user-friendly systems for noncomputer specialists. Statistically valid data bearing on this question would constitute a valuable contribution. Unfortunately, this paper does not furnish such data.

—*G. W. Gorsline,* Blacksburg, VA

WEIDENBECK, SUSAN (Univ. of Nebraska, Lincoln)  **HCI-0172**
**Processes in computer program comprehension.**
[in *Empirical studies of programmers.* Papers presented at the first workshop on empirical studies of programmers (Washington, DC, June 5-6, 1986), E. Soloway; and S. Iyengar (Eds.), Ablex Publishing Corp., Norwood, NJ, 1986, 48–57.]

This work reports on a modest experiment that tries to confirm that certain details of program texts, called *beacons,* are especially important for program comprehension. In the experiment, programmers were each given the same short program for brief study, and their recall of its lines was recorded. It was confirmed that experienced programmers have better recall of the expected beacon lines relative to novices. The remarks made on the significance of this result for our understanding of program comprehension are cautious. However, the caution does not extend so far as to the questioning of the notion of the program comprehension process; it seems that the author is committed to regarding the human mind as an information processor.

—*P. Naur,* Copenhagen, Denmark

LITTMAN, DAVID C.; PINTO, JEANNINE; LETOVSKY, STANLEY; AND SOLOWAY, **HCI-0173**
ELLIOT (Yale Univ., New Haven, CT)
**Mental models and software maintenance.**
[in *Empirical studies of programmers*. Papers presented at the first workshop on empirical studies of programmers (Washington, DC, June 5-6, 1986), E. Soloway; and S. Iyengar (Eds.), Ablex Publishing Corp., Norwood, NJ, 1986, 80–98.]

This paper discusses a study that attempted to discover how professional programmers approach program maintenance. They found two distinct modes of behavior: the systematic strategy and the as-needed strategy. Programmers using the first approach are much more successful at making enhancements to programs they had not seen before. Systematic strategy users try to understand a program globally before making changes. As-needed programmers attempt to make changes without trying to understand the data and control flow of the program.

The study is well thought out and executed, and the results are of interest to anyone involved with program maintenance. However, the conclusions are disappointing. The authors call for yet another "automated" tool for constructing program models. This may be of some help to those stuck with fixing other people's programs but the real significance is for computer science education. This study shows what many of us have always known intuitively: good documentation is a must, and good documentation includes not only word descriptions but pictures too. These should be pictures of global data and control flow that show the links between subroutines and pictures of data structures. The call for automated, after-the-fact programs to do this kind of documentation suggests that the as-needed approach to programming will continue for a long time. The fact that these programs can be written avoids a more basic issue—should they be written, or should documentation be part of a programmer's job?

—*A. Cohill,* Newport, VA

ONORATO, LISA A.; AND SCHVANEVELDT, ROGER W. (New Mexico State Univ., Las **HCI-0174**
Cruces)
**Programmer/nonprogrammer differences in specifying procedures to people and computers.**
[in *Empirical studies of programmers*. Papers presented at the first workshop on empirical studies of programmers (Washington, DC, June 5-6, 1986), E. Soloway; and S. Iyengar (Eds.), Ablex Publishing Corp., Norwood, NJ, 1986, 128–137.]

This paper purports to investigate to what degree written English is influenced by a writer's computer proficiency. To make this determination, writing assignments were given to test subjects classified as having a naive, beginner, or expert skill level in programming. Results are presented in terms of the different "writing strategies" employed by the skill groups. However, the astute reader will note that essentially the same results are obtained for all three groups. To be sure, some small variations are noted, but these may not have resulted from the varying degrees of computer programming proficiency; rather, they may be indicative of the different personality types contained in the various groups. In fact, no differences could be found in the writing skills of the beginners before and after they took a computer course; this would seem to be the most direct measure undertaken in the study.

The paper also attempts to stretch the findings to draw unwarranted inferences about computer systems that understand natural language. However, the reader will note the heavy use of such phrases as "It might be the case that" and "may have" in these discussions. The inferences are actually speculations.

Next, the paper defines several categories of English statements. For example, one category consists of statements analogous to a programmer's loop; another category consists of action verbs. The writing assignments are then analyzed to determine how frequently the statement categories appear in the assignments. Again, computer training does not affect the results obtained from the beginner group, although the computer experts tend to make greater use of programming constructs in their writing. From this, the authors come to the rather surprising conclusion that programmers—not generally noted for their outstanding communications skills—"have an edge in both conciseness and preciseness" of their writing. (The quality of the writing was not assessed by these, or any other criteria, in the study.)

Even though many excellent software psychology studies have been carried out over the years, and much further research is needed, many software professionals do not consider software psychology to be a serious discipline. Unfortunately, this paper will not help to overcome such perceptions.

—*A. E. Salwin*, Rockville, MD

THOMAS, MARK; AND ZWEBEN, STUART (Ohio State Univ., Columbus) **HCI-0175**
**The effects of program-dependent and program-independent deletions on software cloze tests.**
[in *Empirical studies of programmers.* Papers presented at the first workshop on empirical studies of programmers (Washington, DC, June 5-6, 1986), E. Soloway; and S. Iyengar (Eds.), Ablex Publishing Corp., Norwood, NJ, 1986, 138–152.]

Understanding what makes software more or less comprehensible is important because comprehensible software is easier and less costly to maintain. Software cloze tests attempt to measure software comprehensibility in the following way: A program has tokens deleted from it and then a subject attempts to "fill in the blanks"—the subject's accuracy indicates how well the subject understood the program and thereby reflects, to some degree, program comprehensibility. This paper by Thomas and Zweben presents a clear introduction to software cloze testing, and, more importantly, it provides empirical support for a methodological refinement in the use of software cloze tests. The refinement is based on the observation that not all tokens are created equal, and therefore some deleted tokens are easy to fill in (program-independent) while others are difficult to fill in (program-dependent). Research by Hall [1] established criteria for distinguishing between the two types of deleted tokens. When the authors replicated an earlier study that had not controlled for deleted token complexity, they were able to explain the earlier result based on the fact that the study had not controlled for the relative proportion of program-independent and program-dependent deletions.

—*J. Spohrer*, New Haven, CT

**REFERENCES**
[1] HALL, W. E. *The cloze procedure and software comprehension*, Ph.D. thesis, The Ohio State Univ., Columbus, 1984.

HAROLD, FRED G. (Florida Atlantic Univ., Boca Raton)     **HCI-0176**
**Experimental evaluation of program quality using external metrics.**
[in *Empirical studies of programmers*. Papers presented at the first workshop on empirical studies of programmers (Washington, DC, June 5-6, 1986), E. Soloway; and S. Iyengar (Eds.), Ablex Publishing Corp., Norwood, NJ, 1986, 153–167.]

This paper provides a comparison of the quality of code produced by COBOL programmers who have been exposed to structured programming concepts and by those who have not. The author carried out this project by having independent evaluators measure the quality of COBOL programs written by two groups of students (each group consisted of 18 subjects).

The quality of the code was measured by the assignment of subjective scores indicating the degree to which a program displays almost a dozen characteristics that are thought to affect the readability, modifiability, and/or verifiability of a program.

The results of the study are as one might expect. The quality of the code written by students who were exposed to structured programming is significantly superior to the quality of code written by students who were not exposed to structured programming.

I found the paper to be well written and well organized. Unfortunately, the content seems to add little to our knowledge of computer programming. Structured programming, whether supported by empirical studies or not, is widely accepted as being a good thing and has been for at least the last ten years. Had the results not supported structured programming, they would perhaps be of more interest.

Perhaps the most interesting aspect of the paper is the description of how the author encouraged the evaluators to sit through the tedious task of evaluating a number of COBOL programs. As related in the paper, the author hosted a social hour and dinner at a local restaurant for the 21 evaluators, after which the evaluation process took place. I wonder if this means we shall soon see funding proposals with line items for entertainment expenses?

—*W. Harrison,* Portland, OR

PERKINS, D. N.; AND MARTIN, FAY (Harvard Graduate School of Education,     **HCI-0177**
Cambridge, MA)
**Fragile knowledge and neglected strategies in novice programmers.**
[in *Empirical studies of programmers*. Papers presented at the first workshop on empirical studies of programmers (Washington, DC, June 5-6, 1986), E. Soloway; and S. Iyengar (Eds.), Ablex Publishing Corp., Norwood, NJ, 1986, 213–229.]

This paper describes a small clinical study involving 20 high school students carrying out a sequence of increasingly difficult short programming assignments in BASIC. The authors define the concept of *fragile knowledge*, which they subdivide into *missing, inert, misplaced,* and *conglomerated* knowledge. Assistance provided to the students is characterized as *prompts, hints,* or *provides*. The paper includes sample interactions between the student and the instructor.

The authors conclude, not surprisingly, that one characteristic of novices' difficulties with programming is "fragile knowledge exacerbated by a shortfall in elementary problem-solving strategies." They recommend, among other things, teaching programming so as to reduce the impact of fragile knowledge; for example, each command should be defined precisely.

I recommend this paper to anyone teaching or writing materials for elementary programming classes.

—*Tom Kurtz,* Hanover, NH

SPOHRER, JAMES G.; AND SOLOWAY, ELLIOT (Yale Univ., New Haven, CT)    **HCI-0178**
**Analyzing the high frequency bugs in novice programs.**
[in *Empirical studies of programmers.* Papers presented at the first workshop on empirical studies of programmers (Washington, DC, June 5-6, 1986), E. Soloway; and S. Iyengar (Eds.), Ablex Publishing Corp., Norwood, NJ, 1986, 230–251.]

This paper reports on research in the analysis of Pascal programs written by novice programmers. The results show that certain classes of bugs occur more often in novice programs than others, and that the cause of nonsyntactic bugs is not misconception of language semantics but rather errors in design.

The authors' purpose is to provide readers with results that might improve their understanding of the nature of bugs in novice programs and perhaps direct them away from semantic-based solutions. Accordingly, the intended audience is educators of novice programmers.

The paper's length is suitable for the material covered. The paper is well written in a clear, easy-to-comprehend style, and it makes copious use of program examples and tables.

There are some negative features of the paper. The examples of correct programs that are used for comparison against novice programs exhibit poor style and design. The authors use phrases that have simpler and more commonly understood counterparts: for example, *programming goals* instead of program specifications and *programming plans* instead of program design. Their claim that it is a common belief that nonsyntactic bugs arise because of a misunderstanding of program semantics is debatable. Indeed, a dysfunctional program often arises because the design is wrong—the program is often the correct construction of an incorrect design. This is brought out by their research but not developed by them. The section where the authors attempt to guess the reasoning processes behind novice misconceptions is dubious and quite possibly untestable.

The tabulated quantitative results of the frequency and types of bugs found in novice programs are useful.

Overall, the paper meets its objectives and highlights the need for further research on design-related bugs.

—*B. W. O'Connor,* Sydney, Australia

LETOVSKY, STANLEY (Yale Univ., New Haven, CT)    **HCI-0179**
**Cognitive processes in program comprehension.**
[in *Empirical studies of programmers.* Papers presented at the first workshop on empirical studies of programmers (Washington, DC, June 5-6, 1986), E. Soloway; and S. Iyengar (Eds.), Ablex Publishing Corp., Norwood, NJ, 1986, 58–79.]

This paper reports on a protocol analysis study designed to investigate cognitive processes that relate to program understanding. The study attempts to examine cognitive processes that occur over seconds and minutes in order to investigate the understanding of specific lines of code. Six programmers (four experts and two junior-level programmers) with between 3 and 30 years of professional programming experience were asked to "think out loud" as they modified a 250-line FORTRAN program. The verbal transcripts of the protocols were analyzed for their content so that a cognitive model of program understanding could be developed. Based on the protocol analysis, questions, conjectures, and searches are grouped into a higher-order structure called an *inquiry*. Further, a cognitive model of program understanding is presented based on three major components: a knowledge base, a mental model, and an assimilation process. Discussion of these aspects of programming performance is aimed at developing a *computational mechanism* to generate the observed programming performance.

The paper represents a standard technique used to analyze the thought processes of an individual programmer and provides interesting theoretical information on the development of a cognitive model for program understanding. In future studies to explore specific aspects of the model presented, however, empirical techniques should be used. Other measures of performance, such as program comprehension for specific tasks, should also be employed to allow a broader understanding of the richness of programming performance.

—*Woodrow Barfield,* Seattle, WA

# F. THEORY OF COMPUTATION

## F.2 Analysis of Algorithms and Problem Complexity

### F.2.2 Nonnumerical Algorithms and Problems

*Pattern matching*

UKKONEN, ESKO (Univ. of Helsinki, Helsinki, Finland)
**Algorithms for approximate string matching.**
*Inf. Control* **64,** 1-3 (Jan./Feb./March 1985), 100–118.

The main result of this paper is an algorithm to find the minimal sequence of editing steps required to transform one string into another and the associated cost, which is called the edit distance. Typical editing steps are insertion, deletion, and character change, all of which may have different costs. Asymptotically, this algorithm is no better than the naive tabulation method. However, if $s$ is the edit distance and $m$ and $n$ are the lengths of the two strings, this algorithm runs in time and space $O(s \cdot \min(m,n))$ which is significantly better than the naive algorithm when $s$ is small, i.e., when the two strings are "similar." Algorithms requiring less space are presented for the special cases where all editing steps have the same cost and where only the edit distance is required. Some other special cases are considered and an application to finding the longest common subsequence is also presented.

All algorithms are based on careful observations of the table in the naive algorithm and have a very pictorial flavor. Since very few diagrams are actually provided, the long arguments, though inherently simple, become very hard to follow.

—*Richard J. Lorentz,* Northridge, CA

## F.4 Mathematical Logic and Formal Languages

### F.4.3 Formal Languages

RESTIVO, ANTONIO (Universita di Palermo, Palermo, Italy); AND REUTENAUER, CHRISTOPHE (CNRS, Paris, France)
**Some applications of a theorem of Shirshov to language theory.**
*Inf. Control* 57, 2/3 (May/June 1983), 205–213.

Let $A$ be a totally ordered finite alphabet. If $w \in A^*$, then an *n-division* of $w$ is a factorization $w = ux_1 \cdots x_n v$ such that for any non-identity permutation $s$ of $\{1, \ldots\}$, $w\ ux_{s(1)} \cdots x_{s(n)} v$.

We say that $w$ is *n-divided* if it admits at least one *n*-derivation. Moreover, $w$ contains a $p$th power of a word $x$ if $x$ is nonempty and if $w$ may be written $w = ux^p v v$ for some words $u$ and $v$.

The paper draws attention to a nice result by Shirshov:

> **Theorem:** For any integers $k,p,n$
> W 1 such that $p$
> W $2n$, there exists an integer $N(k,p,n)$ such that each word of length at least $N(k,p,n)$ on an alphabet of cardinality $k$ either is *n*-divided or contains a $p$th power of a word of length at most $n$ 5E 1.

The authors derive several nice results based on the theorem. It is shown that a set is bounded (i.e., contained in $u_1^* \cdots u_q^*$ for some words $u_1, \ldots, u_q$) if and only if for some integer $n$ it contains no *n*-divided word. From this, two nice corollaries follow:

> **Corollary 1:** Let $L$ be a regular language. The following two conditions are equivalent: (1) For some $p$, $L$ contains arbitrarily long words without $p$th power. (2) For each $n$, $L$ contains an *n*-divided word.

The context free case is quite neat also:

> **Corollary 2:** Let $L$ be a context-free language. The following conditions are equivalent: (1) For some $p$, there are arbitrarily long words without $p$th power which are factors of words of $L$ (2) For each $n$, $L$ contains an *n*-divided word.

To summarize, this is a very nice paper which should be of interest to those involved in formal language theory.

—*M. A. Harrison,* Berkeley, CA

# H. INFORMATION SYSTEMS

## H.1 Models and Principles

### H.1.0 General

OBERQUELLE, HORST (Univ. Hamburg, Hamburg, West Germany)      **HCI-0182**
**On models and modelling in human-computer co-operation.**
[in *Readings on cognitive ergonomics - mind and computers.* Proc. of the 2nd European conference (Gmunden, Austria, Sept. 10-14, 1984), G. van der Veer; M. Tauber; T. Green; and P. Gorny (Eds.), Springer-Verlag New York, Inc., New York, NY, 1984, 26–43.]

[See main entry, Review HCI-0039.]

Present advancements in the design of computer systems work towards making them "user friendly"; this paper tries to model Human-Computer Communication (HCC) using hardware and cognitive ergonomics. Earlier models, such as the state transition model, sites/modes/traits model, human processor model, and abstract model, are proposed in the literature.

The paper initially defines terms like models, modeling procedures, and modeling tools. The modeling procedure proposed by the author is based on the Channel and Agencies network (CA-net) and the Means/Activity network (MA-net). This approach is a graphic representation of the HCC. Based on these representations, a meta-model of HCC is proposed, consisting of user, designer, and dialogue system. According to the author, users of interactive systems cannot easily model them because of various reasons.

Based on the meta-model, various known models in the literature are discussed: finite state mechanics model; IFIP model of interactive systems; the human processor model; the TOTE model of users based on cognitive processes inside the user; sites/modes/traits model; and the desk-top model.

Until now, generally, the user was left in a passive role when HCCs have been designed. In this paper, a co-operative model between user and designer using the proposed meta-model is suggested. Self-explaining dialogue systems are not produced by the system, but instead by the designer. Such explanations may be inadequate for the user because there is no feedback to the system about the user's understanding of such messages.

As a first step, the user must learn the semiformal model using CA-net and MA-net. Then, as a next step, the users and designers can develop an acceptable net showing static amd dynamic characteristics. A prototype should be the following step. Efficient implementation is the final step, along with the training of users.

The present model is still an approach. It has to be tested before it can be accepted as a standard approach in designing HCCs. Hence, this paper may prove to be interesting to the designers of human-computer communication systems. The paper concludes with some future directions of research and a good list of references.

—*V. Kaujalgi*, Bangalore, India

BLACK, JOHN B. (Columbia Univ., New York, NY); KAY, DANA S.; AND SOLOWAY, ELLIOT M. (Yale Univ., New Haven, CT)
**Goal and plan knowledge representations: from stories to text editors and programs.**
[in *Interfacing thought: cognitive aspects of human-computer interaction*, J. Carroll (Ed.), MIT Press, Cambridge, MA, 1987, 36-60.]

"Almost all of human behavior can be characterized in terms of goals and plans," write Black, Kay, and Soloway. This view informs their entire treatment of three different domains: stories, text editors, and programs.

That readers use the goal-plan approach in reading and understanding stories is supported by the following evidence: (1) Different goal-plan episodes show independence in memory recall. To give just one example, the length of an episode affects the recall of actions within that episode, but is unrelated to recall of actions in other episodes. (2) Incomplete plans for a story's goal are filled in by the reader—who will later claim to have read the entire plan! Also, readers remember plan actions in the order needed to reach the goal, not in the order presented by the story. (3) Two stories with analogous plans and goals will cause the reader to generalize and apply the same type of plan to any similar goal.

Text editor users also organize their thoughts using plans and goals, as shown by the following evidence: (1) At the close of each subgoal in editing a text, there is a pause, presumably so that the plan for the next subgoal can be formulated. (2) As users become more familiar with the text editor, plans often found together (e.g., locate error and delete error) are chunked together, forming larger plans. The authors then go into considerable detail discussing the users' experience level and how it affects their use of the text editor.

The third domain the paper reviews is programming. Programming differs from the other domains in that the programmer must keep track of several plans at once. Perhaps, the authors suggest, the number of active plans will turn out to be a good metric of program complexity. Evidence supporting the goal-plan approach to understanding programs includes the following: (1) Statements in sub-plans are less likely to be remembered than statements in plans higher in the hierarchy, both after insertion (recall) and before insertion (namely, a bug). (2) Programmers seeing typical constructs (plans) can fill them in. (To give one example, "total:=total+new" requires the previous statement "total:=0," etc.) (3) Changing the order of certain statements to conform to plan paradigms improves programmer performance.

The section concludes with an interesting discussion of the transfer of planning knowledge across domains.

The paper concludes with an interesting speculation on why programming is "hell" and "torture," while stories are fun. I leave this discussion for the reader to discover.

The paper as a whole is very interesting, carries its point successfully, is supported by well-chosen examples, and should be of interest to a large segment of the computing community.

—*Joseph Fulda*, New York, NY

## H.1.1 Systems and Information Theory

ROUSE, WILLIAM B.; AND ROUSE, SANDRA H. (Georgia Institute of Technology, Atlanta, GA)  **HCI-0184**
**Human information seeking and design of information systems.**
*Inf. Process. Manage.* **20**, 1-2 (1984), 129–138. [Special issue: Empirical foundations of information and software sciences..]

This is a short think piece with six pages of text and 84 references. Because it is short and covers several topics, none of the topics are well developed. Rather, there is a set of statements identifying ideas and referencing research on the topic. The paper is an overview of three topics: the nature of information seeking, human information seeking, and dsign of information systems. There is an attempt to integrate literature across several fields; there is perhaps some bias toward library science issues and literature.

The focus of the paper is on information seeking (rather than information processing or information use). Information seeking is described as a process in which information needs and information vary in time. The central theoretical issue discussed is the need for defining and measuring the value of information, and the difficulties in doing so.

—*Gordon B. Davis,* Minneapolis, MN


PYLYSHYN, ZENON W. (The Univ. of Western Ontario, London, Ont., Canada)  **HCI-0185**
**Information science: its roots and relation as viewed from the perspective of cognitive science.**
[in *The study of information: interdisciplinary messages,* F. Machlup; and U. Mansfield (Eds.), John Wiley & Sons, Inc., New York, NY, 1983, 63-118.]

[See main entry, Review HCI-0036.]

Pylyshyn's paper provides a broad perspective on the topic of information science from the perspective of cognitive science. It is a wide ranging "Philosophy of Science" discussion of the recent historical developments in information and control theory, cognitive science, and artificial intelligence.

His paper consists of essentially two parts. One part provides a general overview of the role and relationships of cognitive science. The other part provides an argument for the existence of a distinct discipline of cognitive science. The paper is then followed by comments by five researchers (Michale Arbib, Michael Gazzaniga, Saul Gorn, Allen Newell, and George Miller) with different perspectives. Not all of the commentators view the history of cognitive science in the same light as Pylyshyn. Nor do they all subscribe to the value of an independent disciple of cognitive science.

All parts of the paper are interesting and well presented. However, I believe that the largest audience will be interested in the first section; those who have a direct interest in cognitive science as a distinct discipline will be interested in the later sections.

—*David R. Harris,* Fairfax, VA

# REVIEWS

### H.1.2 User/Machine Systems

SHNEIDERMAN, BEN (Univ. of Maryland)     HCI-0186
**The future of interactive systems and the emergence of direct manipulation.**
[in *Human factors and interactive computer systems*. Proc. of the NYU symposium on user interfaces (New York, May 26-28, 1982), Y. Vassiliou (Ed.), Ablex Publishing Corp., Norwood, NJ, 1984, 1–28.]

[See main entry, Review HCI-0038.]

This paper begins with an examination of the reasons for the computer industry's current interest in human factors. The author then briefly reviews several human factors issues that have arisen in his use and studies of various interactive systems. The tradeoffs between command language and menu dialogs are discussed and guidelines are presented for response time, display rates, and the wording of system messages. He concludes the section with a discussion of some factors that need to be considered when providing online tutorials and HELP, and when selecting hardware devices. The paper's attention is then focused on methods and tools for facilitating user involvement in the system design process.

The final section of the chapter presents a detailed analysis of a user interface dialog which the author calls "direct manipulation." The central principles of direct manipulation are:

- ☐ the visibility of the object of interest.
- ☐ rapidly reversible actions whose impact on the objects are immediately apparent, and
- ☐ the use of physical actions, rather than command syntax, to directly manipulate the objects of interest.

The author cites several examples of interactive systems that incorporate these principles, including Visicalc, Macintosh, video games, and computer-aided design tools. Several beneficial attributes of systems designed using the direct manipulation principles are then presented as goals for future system design. The author describes a cognitive model of user behavior that was developed to further his understanding of how direct manipulation supports these goals. Finally, potential applications of direct manipulation to personal address listing, checkbook maintenance, bibliographic searching, and airline reservations systems are described.

To this reviewer, this chapter actually represents two substantive papers. The first paper, which consists of the first three sections, presents a clear, concise discussion of the need for human factors input in the design of interactive systems, as well as a set of issues and tools that human factors specialists should be aware of in designing a user interface. This part of the paper would serve as an excellent introduction to current human factors work in system design for those who are not human factors practitioners.

Three key points are made by the author in the first three sections of the paper:

- ☐ Controlled experimentation is needed in investigating human factors issues.
- ☐ Testing of user interface designs is needed to provide data for making design decisions and modifications.
- ☐ Users of interactive systems need to be involved in the design of the system.

This reviewer concurs that design decisions and resolutions of human factors issues should be based on data and not on expert judgement or guidelines, when possible. In order to support the testing of interfaces with end users, time must be set aside in the system design lifecycle and rapid prototyping tools must be available.

The second paper, the last section of this chapter, introduces the reader to the concept of direct manipulation and its applicability to interactive system design. This section should be of interest to the experienced system designer looking for innovative approaches to interface design for interactive systems. Research into the concept of direct manipulation will clarify whether and how the benefits stated by the author can be realized in large-scale systems for record keeping and retrieval, reservation tracking, and command and control.

—*M. P. Tarka,* Gaithersburg, MD

MONK, ANDREW F. (Univ. of York, UK) **HCI-0187**
**Reading continuous text from a one-line visual display.**
*Int. J. Man-Mach. Stud.* **21**, 3 (Sept. 1984), 269–277.

Continuous text may be presented via a one-line visual display by dividing it into "frames," each of which is displayed for some specified time. Two different approaches to determine the contents of these frames can be distinguished: character-stepped display and word-stepped display. In the former the start of each frame is "stepped" some number of characters through the text for each frame presented. Viewed in this way the text appears to be moving jerkily behind a slot. In a word-stepped display the contents of each frame depend on word boundaries (e.g., having a separate word in each frame).

Experiments are described which compare different ways of displaying text. Readers can cope with character- and word-stepped displays at high rates of presentation. The parameter which was identified as having most influence on performance was the expected proportion of words occurring whole on some frame.

—*Author's Abstract*
—Abstract recommended by *J. Major,* Eau Claire, WI

ROHR, GABRIELE; AND TAUBER, MICHAEL J. (IBM Germany Heidelberg Scientific **HCI-0188**
Center, West Germany)
**Representational frameworks and models for human-computer interfaces.**
[in *Readings on cognitive ergonomics - mind and computers.* Proc. of the 2nd European conference (Gmunden, Austria, Sept. 10-14, 1984), G. van der Veer; M. Tauber; T. Green; and P. Gorny (Eds.), Springer-Verlag New York, Inc., New York, NY, 1984, 8–25.]

[See main entry, Review HCI-0039]

The authors, a psychologist and a computer scientist, describe various approaches to modeling human-computer interaction. They use the term "user interface architecture" to represent a complete and formal description of the surface of a system as seen by the user. By commenting on a variety of models that have been used, the authors give an overview of what has to be done in

# REVIEWS

constructing various abstracted representations of the user, the system, and the flow of data between them. Modeling requires that the designer abstract from the presentation details of a particular interface in order to identify the basic form underlying the details of an implementation. The stated goal of the paper is to clarify the knowledge and methods required to construct an adequate model of interaction.

A key point developed throughout this paper is the creative role of the modeler in choosing which components to model and in establishing the level of detail appropriate to the particular purpose of the model. Models may be characterized by the distinctions made by the modeler and the set of parameters used to describe or predict the behavior and performance in the modeled situation.

This short chapter is an important review of current approaches to modeling the user interface. However, because of multiple typographical and spelling errors and many awkward sentence structures, the text requires study, not just reading. These difficulties are probably related to problems in translating from the native German of the authors. The chapter will be stimulating to a person who is already familiar with the ideas of models, has thought about applications, and is seeking references to important current work. Unfortunately the text is lacking in the examples and in the detailed development of the various approaches described that would probably be needed by a reader seeking an introductory understanding. Their reference to Norman (1983) would be a better place to begin for that purpose. The bibliography is especially useful to European work in modeling.

—*J. Bennett,* San Jose, CA

**REFERENCES**

[1] NORMAN, D. A. Some observations on mental models, in *Mental models*, D. Gentner and A. Stevens (Eds.), Erlbaum Assoc., Hillsdale, NJ, 1983.

NORMAN, DONALD A. (Univ. of California, San Diego, La Jolla)
**Stages and levels in human-machine interaction.**
*Int. J. Man-Mach. Stud.* **21,** 4 (Oct. 1984), 365–375.

This paper is an overview of the author's approach to describing "the overall process of interaction with the computer." The author, in an easily understandable first-person style, says he wants "to avoid an emphasis on detailed aspects of that interaction and ask about the nature of the interaction."

In the author's view, four stages of a user interaction are considered:

(1) the intention by the operator to perform an operation,
(2) the selection by the operator of a (set of) action(s) that will accomplish the operation,
(3) the execution of the selected actions, and
(4) evaluation, comparing the outcome of the actions to what was originally intended.

Each of these four stages is considered in some detail, followed by a discussion of how a computer system could be programmed to help its users as much as possible at each stage. It is this part of the paper that is of most interest to the computing community: how can the systems we build be most (sorry) "user-friendly"? Using menus as an example, the author shows the ways a user interface medium can be used at each of his four stages. He also discusses tradeoffs between the use of the medium at each stage and the overall design of the system's interaction scenario.

The reasoning done in the paper is not the kind that many system designers today are used to doing. It is, however, something that we need to be doing if our systems are to gain truly global acceptance. The paper is worth reading for several reasons, but it mainly serves to show those of us whose specialty is not human engineering how the work in that area can be of real benefit to us.

—*Tom Davis,* Dripping Springs, TX

CUMMING, GEOFF (La Trobe Univ.) **HCI-0190**
**QWERTY and keyboard reform: the soft keyboard option.**
*Int. J. Man-Mach. Stud.* **21,** 5 (Nov. 1984), 445–450.

This is essentially a position paper recommended for those who are very involved in human factors and relevant issues of typewriter/computer keyboard design. The main message is: we should not be willing to accept a manufacturer-determined keyboard layout (specifically the QWERTY) as an unalterable or irreplaceable standard merely because it has become so widely used. We should instead pursue performance studies of alternative layouts and configurations, especially the "soft keyboard" which is flexibly modifiable under software control. A dual layout keyboard (i.e., with one of each of the above types) might then become a feasible option.

—*S. Treu,* Pittsburgh, PA

WASSERMAN, ANTHONY I. (Univ. of California, San Francisco) **HCI-0191**
**Extending state transition diagrams for the specification of human-computer interaction.**
*IEEE Trans. Softw. Eng.* **SE-11,** 8 (Aug. 1985), 699–713.

This paper reports on one phase of the author's work in developing the User Software Engineering (USE) methodology and tool set for designing and executing user interfaces. The USE methodology stresses user participation at early stages in the development process, as well as the capability to rapidly create system prototypes based on the user-computer interface design.

In this paper, the author describes a notation for specifying the design of user-computer interfaces in the USE methodology. The notation, which is based on extensions to state transition diagrams, allows the designer to specify the input and output syntax of the interface. The author also describes a textual representation of the diagrams that facilitates their encoding into a machine-processable form. This feature of the notation permits the designer to create a formal, executable version of the interface for user evaluation and testing. The author reports that various types of user interfaces have been handled with the diagrammatic notation, including menu driven, command language, and natural language interfaces. In addition, the author mentions that the notation can be used to define multiple interfaces to the same action (e.g., command language and menu driven). The paper concludes with a description of the automated tool set that supports the execution of the interface specified in the notation.

To this reviewer, the flexibility and executability of the notation are the most important characteristics for designers of interactive systems. The USE notation and tool kit would seem to support the needs of these designers to quickly design, execute, and evaluate alternative interfaces for interactive systems.

This paper should be of value to those readers interested in rapid prototyping and methods for specifying the design of a user interface. The author provides sufficient description of the USE methodology and tool kit to provide the reader with ample context for understanding how the notation fits into the overall methodology. A strong point of the paper is the use of several small examples that show how the notation can be used to specify different features (e.g., windows) of user-computer interfaces. This approach helps the reader understand the more in-depth example presented at the end of the paper.

—*M. P. Tarka,* Gaithersburg, MD

BEAUMONT, J. G. (Leicester Univ., Leicester, UK)                          **HCI-0192**
**Speed of response using keyboard and screen-based microcomputer response media.**
*Int. J. Man-Mach. Stud.* **23,** 1 (July 1985), 61–70.

This paper describes an experiment observing response times for different response media, including a standard QWERTY keyboard, numeric keypad, light-pen, and touch-screen. Beaumont concludes that the touch-screen allowed fastest response, while the light-pen provided the slowest. This study is interesting as it gives us new experimental evidence. System designers are no longer entirely dependent upon their intuition for these decisions. Now it is easier to know what specific devices help or hinder the operator using a computer.

Omitted from the study was the use of a mouse pointing device. This would be helpful since so many microcomputers are equipped with an electronic mouse. Also, the paper was difficult to read. The wording and language used was somewhat cumbersome for an American audience. Nevertheless, I recommend this paper as a reference resource for designing microcomputer systems which demand high productivity.

—*Linda McInnis,* Albany, VT

FULTON, MARGARET A. (Utah State Univ., Logan)                         **HCI-0193**
**A research model for studying the gender/power aspects of human-computer communication.**
*Int. J. Man-Mach. Stud.* **23,** 4 (Oct. 1985), 369–382.

User interface designers know that the wording of error messages, prompts, instructions, and help screens can influence the perceptions and performance of novice and expert computer users. Specificity, clarity, positive tone, constructive guidance, and user centeredness have been empirically studied in the past. This paper reports on four innovative experiments with gender and power aspects of human-computer communication. Message changes included the addition of the word "please" and five writing style differences, identified from previous research, that were linked to male or female styles.

After working with the computer in one of these styles, the subjects used semantic differential scales to rate potency and other attributes. The outcomes indicated significant differences as a function of the subject's sex and computer experience.

The research methodology is of interest to researchers and the results are intriguing for designers. However, performance measures, such as speed of error rates, as well as subjective measures should be used in future studies to determine the overall impact and provide guidance to designers.

—*B. Shneiderman,* College Park, MD

LINDQUIST, T. E.; FAINTER, R. G.; AND HAKKINEN, M. T. (Arizona State Univ., Tempe)     **HCI-0194**
**GENIE: a modifiable computer-based task for experiments in human-computer interaction.**
*Int. J. Man-Mach. Stud.* **23,** 4 (Oct. 1985), 391–406.

The authors have constructed a software system which can serve as a testbed for conducting experiments, and to which a variety of test equipment can be attached. The version of GENIE (Generic ENvironment for Interactive Experiments) described here is implemented on a Digital Equipment Corporation's GGI graphics keyboard, with two BARCO GD33 color monitors serving as workstation displays, and runs on a VAX/VMS system. The hardware and software was originally developed at the University of Virginia under the direction of Ehrich and Williges.

The example application described in some detail is designed to study a person acting as a simulated air traffic controller who is giving directions to a pilot landing at an airport. However, most of the paper is devoted to a description of the software "designed to allow the syntactic characteristics of its interface to be altered." One example describes changes to allow multiple commands to be entered on the same line. A second example shows how the grammar can be altered to allow the parser to react to individual words of the user command input as it is typed by the user. Readers interested in the experimental results derived through use of the system will find them described in another referenced paper [1].

—*J. Bennett,* San Jose, CA

**REFERENCES**
[1] FAINTER, R. G.; GUY, S. R.; MAYNARD, J. F.; AND LINDQUIST, T. E. Generic environment for interactive experiments, Tech. Rep. CS830009, Virginia Tech. Dept. of Computer Science, Blacksburg, 1983.

CHAPANIS, ALPHONSE (Communications Research Laboratory, Baltimore, MD)     **HCI-0195**
**Taming and civilizing computers.**
[in *Computer culture: the scientific, intellectual, and social impact of the computer.* Proc. of a symposium (New York, April 5-8, 1983), H. Pagels (Ed.), New York Academy of Sciences, New York, NY, 1984, 202–219.]

The author, an expert in the field of man-machine communications, presents a very readable account of how computers can be better designed to aid people who use them (an ever-growing proportion of the population). He cites some difficulties people have in using computers and then discusses factors which should be considered in integrating computers into the workplace. A skillful combination of cartoons and photographs helps to underline his major points.

The author's comparison of the computer with the automobile is not new, but his approach is definitely unique. His point about how society has learned to accommodate the automobile, as well as how to use and live with it, is especially enlightening. Certainly one of the biggest problems we face today is how to integrate the computer into society so as to best serve the whole of society and not just the technologically elite. The bottom line in this, as well as in several other papers in these proceedings, is that in the final analysis computers should serve people and be controlled by people—not the other way around.

—*R. M. Aiken,* Philadelphia, PA

BENBASAT, IZAK; DEXTER, ALBERT S.; AND TODD, PETER (Univ. of British Columbia, Vancouver, B.C., Canada)
**An experimental program investigating color-enhanced and graphical information presentation: an integration of the findings.**
*Commun. ACM* **29,** 11 (Nov. 1986), 1094–1105.

This paper studies the results of three experiments using tabular, graphical, monocolor, and multicolor output presentations in support of decision making tasks. The experiments measure the influences of color and information presentation on (1) decision making quality and individuals of differing personality styles; (2) decision making behavior and report use; and (3) decision making quality under varying time constraints.

The results of the experiments are encapsulated and presented clearly in several tables accompanying the text. The paper draws two propositions:

(1) "The influence of presentation format on decision making effectiveness depends on how well the format supports the solution to the task."
(2) "Color has a positive influence on decision making effectiveness; however, the benefits of color are more evident for graphical reports, under time constraints, during the learning period, and for field-dependent individuals." The authors' use of scientific method and the isolation of the key variables used in the experiments is very good. The text of the document, however, assumes that the reader is well versed in the current literature on this topic. Extensive references are provided.

—*D. McQuilken,* Windsor, CT

SCHMIDT, ALBERT L. (Southern Illinois Univ , Edwardsville)
**Effects of experience and comprehension on reading time and memory for computer programs.**
*Int. J. Man-Mach. Stud.* **25,** 4 (Oct. 1986), 399–409.

Schmidt's paper is a minor contribution to the literature on the comprehension of computer programs. The hypothesis that he explores is that people skilled in interpreting programs (or bridge, music, electronics, etc.) both understand protocols in the notation they use more quickly than novices and remember more of what they have read. He fails to reproduce the finding of McKeithen et al. [1] that meaningful groups of symbols are recalled more readily than random groups, but admits that if the material that the subjects memorized had been more complex, the effect would probably have been seen. Altogether, this is a clearly presented piece of work but is of slight interest, offering no new insight into the relation between cognitive skill and the recall of protocols.

—*V. S. Begg,* Cambridge, MA

**REFERENCES**

[1] MCKEITHEN, K. B.; REITMAN, J. S.; REUTER, H. H.; AND HIRTLE, S. C. Knowledge organization and skill differences in computer programmers, *Cogn. Psychol.* **13** (1981), 307–325.

POLSON, PETER G. (Univ. of Colorado, Boulder)     **HCI-0198**
**A quantitative theory of human-computer interaction.**
[in *Interfacing thought: cognitive aspects of human-computer interaction,* J. Carroll (Ed.), MIT Press, Cambridge, MA, 1987, 184-235.]

This chapter presents recent results in a continuing line of research involving human-computer interaction. Polson states that the goals of the research program are "to develop and verify a comprehensive, quantitative theory of human-computer interaction and to explore the applied implications of the theory."

Polson presents a theory describing ways of modeling the learning and productivity of certain tasks; he formalizes those tasks through production systems. He emphasizes ways of quantifying learning time and the transfer of learned rules from one task to another. The experiments involve using a word processor and other aspects of operating a computer.

The chapter is well written and has good graphic support. It succeeds in proposing a model and demonstrating empirical support for the theory behind it. The chapter should be interesting to researchers investigating the cognitive aspects of computer science.

—*N. S. Coulter,* Boca Raton, FL

OLSON, JUDITH R.     **HCI-0199**
**Cognitive analysis of people's use of software.**
[in *Interfacing thought: cognitive aspects of human-computer interaction,* J. Carroll (Ed.), MIT Press, Cambridge, MA, 1987, 260-293.]

Olson provides a concise review of the cognitive issues and existing aids in the field of computer systems user interface design. She analyzes both the functionality and the usability of information systems from three perspectives: the system's behavior, the user's cognitive processing, and the user's cognitive limitations.

Olson begins her discussion by presenting alternate methods for representing and analyzing office tasks that involve information. She evaluates these methods according to their effectiveness in redesigning the work flow and automating tasks that computers perform better than people do. Next, the author reviews formal grammar and generalized transition networks for representing interactive dialogues. She examines variants of production system methods for representing the goal structure of human-computer dialogues, evaluating them according to how well they account for cognitive limitations in the design of interactive dialogues. Then she reviews three ways to translate the user's goals into system requirements. Olson concludes that production systems are currently the most effective way to represent important cognitive attributes of human-computer interactions, but that they are weak in representing the perceptual aspects of displays.

This chapter does not attempt to be a comprehensive review of all representational formats or methods for designing interactive dialogues. Rather, it presents a useful summary of the analyses that should be performed and of some of the better-known methods available for performing them. It is a well-organized, readable overview of the state-of-the-art methods for designing user dialogues.

—*Bill Curtis,* Austin, TX

NORMAN, DONALD A. (Univ. of California, San Diego)      **HCI-0200**
**Cognitive engineering—cognitive science.**
[in *Interfacing thought: cognitive aspects of human-computer interaction,* J. Carroll (Ed.), MIT Press, Cambridge, MA, 1987, 325-336.]

This chapter discusses aspects of the interesting interplay between cognitive science and "cognitive engineering." The new term "cognitive engineering" emphasizes the common interests and goals of ergonomics, human factors, and engineering psychology; alternate terms would include "software psychology" and "cognitive ergonomics." Problems in this area are inherently interdisciplinary; an example is given of how a person with a drama background helped to illuminate a problem. Norman also describes how systems design tasks have often led to the development of new cognitive theory. For example, a theory of action is needed to describe how people deal with computer interfaces and why such interfaces vary with respect to ease of use. This short chapter does not attempt a systematic overview of developments in this area, and the basic points it makes are, presented in summary, relatively prosaic. What it does achieve, however, is to give a sense of how workers in the field are reaching out to find the tools to understand better and perhaps even solve some of the many problems clustered around the human-computer interface.

—*R. L. Stout,* Providence, RI

GOULD, JOHN D.; AND SALAUN, JOSIANE (IBM Thomas J. Watson Research Center,      **HCI-0201**
Yorktown Heights, NY)
**Behavioral experiments on handmarkings.**
*ACM Trans. Office Inf. Syst.* **5,** 4 (Oct. 1987), 358-377.

Handmarkings or handwritten editing marks can be used as direct editing commands to an interactive computer system. Five exploratory experiments studied the potential value of handmarkings for editing text and pictures, as well as for some specific results. Circles are the most frequently used scoping mark, and arrows are the most frequently used operator and target indicators. Experimental comparisons showed that handmarkings have the potential to be faster than keyboards and mice for editing tasks. Their ultimate value will, however, depend on the style and details of their user-interface implementation.

—*Authors' Abstract*

This paper reports on some basic research comparing a "non-existent" new technology to existing forms of technology. In the first four experiments, people were asked to produce handwritten symbols to indicate various editing functions on either pictures or text. A fifth experiment examined the ways in which people make modifications to other systems (toys and maps). The authors use the data collected to make some suggestions as to "natural" methods for accomplishing modification (or editing) tasks.

The research is a good example of the kind of work that can be done in this area. It integrates several approaches to the same problem and lays out some limitations of the work. The authors appear to have made certain assumptions about how a handmarking recognition system might work, however, which lead them to raise issues that might not be that important. For example, the authors seem to assume that an editing system will require all users to enter the same handmarking for a given function. They also seem to assume that symbols (such as circles) must be reproduced perfectly in order to be recognized by a system. A system with which I am familiar (produced by Linus Technologies Inc.) does not have these requirements. Finally, it would be nice if the paper included a direct comparison of a handmarking recognition system to other existing technologies. The paper does, however, provide benchmark times against which other systems can be evaluated. The paper is well worth the time needed to read it.

—*D. A. Boehm-Davis*, Fairfax, VA

SCHMELL, RICHARD W. (Univ. of Houston, Houston, TX); AND UMANATH, NARAYAN S. (Pennsylvania State Univ., University Park)
**An experimental evaluation of the impact of data display format on recall performance.**
*Commun. ACM* **31**, 5 (May 1988), 562–570.

This paper reports two experiments on how information displays influence one's memory of the information displayed. The experiments are based on the idea that managers often rely upon their memory of information initially presented by computer. The two experiments reported here compare alphanumeric tables and graphical presentation, where bar charts should be better for showing trends and tabular presentation should be preferable for detailed facts. The measure is recall accuracy. In experiment 1 immediate recall of pattern information was better with graphs, but memory for detailed facts was not significantly better. Memory after two days showed no differences. In the second experiment the recall tests were derived using part of the data to improve sensitivity. Yet again graphical presentation was significantly better for patterned data. There was no effect for detail.

The basic question posed is important: are graphics worthwhile? The results do not add much to our knowledge, with meager hypotheses and overanalyzed data. Furthermore, the results suggest a memory benefit only for general trends, which contrasts with our intuitions about the expressive power of graphics. Perhaps memory is an inappropriate measure if the benefit from graphics lies more in its ability to support immediate perception of relationships. Simple presentation techniques like bar charts may well be prevalent in managers' reports, but it need not follow that the relationship with what serves as the basis of those managers' memories is based directly upon the data and the presentation. What should be considered is the possibility that recall is based on a mental representation and that the quality of this *is* determined by the presentation technique, but that further performance is dependent upon other factors that were not differentiated in this study.

—*P. Hudson,* Leiden, The Netherlands

Foss, Donald J.; and DeRidder, Mitchell
**Technology transfer: a new computer-based system.**
[in *Interfacing thought: cognitive aspects of human-computer interaction,* J. Carroll (Ed.), MIT Press, Cambridge, MA, 1987, 159-183.]

Foss and DeRidder propose an evaluation metric intended to help designers choose between two different interfaces. The metric described in this paper is derived from the classic field of transfer of training. That is, the authors assume that one can measure the effectiveness of a new interface by looking at the level of transfer between the old and new interfaces. The similarity between two human-computer interactions is further described in terms of similarities that occur at the subgoal level.

In order to test their metric, the authors conducted an experiment in which three groups of subjects were asked to learn two text editors. The similarities between the text editors varied between each of the three groups. It was hypothesized that the group that had the two most similar text editors would perform the evaluation tasks in the shortest time. Unfortunately, there were no "real" significant differences between the three groups.

The authors conclude that their theory is worth further exploration. There appear, however, to be several problems with this approach. It seems evident from this experiment that the initial learning condition (i.e., an initial model of text processing) is so pervasive that people have little difficulty learning a second editor. Also, transfer is a flawed metric for selecting a second interface. Ease of learning is merely one aspect of interface selection. A second interface may be more difficult to learn, but easier to use once learned. It is obvious that the task of deciding between two different interfaces remains both difficult and complicated and that the authors have merely discovered the complexity of the task.

—*K. M. Swigger,* Denton, TX

Hansen, Wilfred J.; and Haas, Christina (Carnegie-Mellon Univ., Pittsburgh, PA)
**Reading and writing with computers: a framework for explaining differences in performance.**
*Commun. ACM* **31,** 9 (Sept. 1988), 1080–1089.

Understanding the factors that influence human performance in writing and reading tasks becomes increasingly important as we spend more and more of our time writing and reading with computer screens instead of with paper. The authors present a list of seven factors that they use to explain performance differences when people write and read with paper, personal computers, and workstations. They identify four primary factors—page size, legibility, responsiveness, and tangibility—and three secondary factors—sense of text, sense of direction, and sense of engagement. These seven factors can be varied to influence the quality and speed of reading and writing performance.

The authors explain the results of four experimental tasks—spatial recall, retrieval, reordering lines, and writing letters—in terms of their seven factors. All experiments showed that for reading tasks, paper was superior, followed by workstations and finally by personal computers. For writing tasks, working on paper produced the highest quality letters, while those letters composed on workstations were longer. The authors have used the results of these experiments to improve the user interface of their computer-based system for reading and writing documents.

This paper will interest both researchers studying human-computer interface issues and designers of computer-based systems for reading and writing documents. It is quite concise but still manages to relate the authors' research to other work in the field. The framework that the authors present also serves as a useful introduction to the factors that influence the behavior of those who write and read with computers.

—*J. Spohrer,* New Haven, CT


BEARD, JON W.; AND PETERSON, TIM O. (Texas A & M Univ., College Station)  HCI-0205
**A taxonomy for the study of human factors in management information systems.**
[in *Human factors in management information systems,* J. Carey (Ed.), Ablex Publishing Corp., Norwood, NJ, 1988, 7-25.]

The most important job of the first chapter in any book is to hook the readers so that they will willingly, and even anxiously, read more. This chapter does its job well. The major point is succinctly made: in human-machine systems the human part is at least as important as the machine part, and the interface between them is crucial.

The authors provide a historical framework, showing that Taylor's and Gilbreth's early industrial engineering studies focused (perhaps for the wrong reasons) on how humans work. Until the recent past, human interaction with MIS was limited. Technical "priests" used arcane language and methods inside air-conditioned, secure temples adequately buffering the business laypeople from interface gibberish. In fact, the technicians usually relished and perpetuated the complexities as justification for their positions in the organization.

Now, however, computer systems have burst the boundaries of the computer room and present blinking temptation on every desk in the organization. We no longer can or should tolerate either the unnecessary jargon of operating systems or the cute, trivial icons of windowing environments. We want, deserve, and must insist upon well-designed, professionally engineered structures that facilitate the work of the enterprise; these interfaces will meet our business needs rather than jam us into the channels of technological limitations. Toward this end, the authors suggest that there are really two types of humans with whom systems must interact—the analysts who build and maintain the system, and the users for whom the system works.

Next, the authors offer a small taxonomy to help us focus our search for further information. They include an extensive bibliography grouped into these categories:

# REVIEWS

- ☐ Human-Machine Interaction;
- ☐ Interface Specification Tools;
- ☐ Information Presentation;
- ☐ System-User Documentation; and
- ☐ End-User Documentation.

This brief chapter does more than lead us into the rest of its book. It persuades us that human-machine factors are important, even crucial, and offers us a structure through which we can further explore the subject. Beard and Peterson provide a lot of value in these few pages.

—*J. L. Podolsky,* Palo Alto, CA

LAI, KUM-YEW (Mssachusetts Institute of Technology, Cambridge); MALONE, THOMAS W.; AND YU, KEH-CHIANG (Massachusetts Institute of Technology, Cambridge)
**Object lens: a "spreadsheet" for cooperative work.**
*ACM Trans. Office Inf. Syst.* **6,** 4 (Oct. 1988), 332–353.

The use of objects has become the latest fad in software engineering, picking up where artificial intelligence left off. The description of the Object Lens in this paper is useful, however, because it provides some specific examples of how objects might work in a real-world environment and offers the notion of semiautomated, semiautonomous software behavior.

The Object Lens is a user interface that integrates hypertext, object-oriented databases, electronic messaging, and rule-based intelligent agents. Still in the prototype stage, this system succeeds the earlier, less capable Information Lens and is designed to be a knowledge-based environment for developing applications in a cooperative fashion, where the work is distributed among several people, teams, or geographic locations.

The authors try to relate their system to commercially successful spreadsheet packages by offering a very general definition of spreadsheet software. The success of products like Lotus 1-2-3, however, was largely due to a factor they do not mention—the target market's familiarity with the paper spreadsheet. Although the Object Lens does incorporate elements that have analogies in nonautomated processes, the authors do not state these analogies explicitly, and the system has no single manual metaphor. It does, however, resemble a meeting where project team members exchange various finished pieces of programs and documentation that other team members then use.

The authors call their system "semiformal," that is, one that represents and automatically processes certain information in formally specified ways, represents and facilitates the human processing of the same or different information in ways that are not formally specified, and allows the boundary between formal processing by the system and informal processing by humans to be changed easily and frequently. Their system can also represent and manipulate "semistructured" objects; fields can be structured or not, and the data in them can be restricted or flexible in type or content. The Object Lens uses "template-based" user interfaces, and displays may be defined by the user. As in other object-oriented software, all elements of the software can be treated as objects to be called by or embedded into other objects. New objects can inherit some or all of the characteristics of the old objects, and objects can be collected into folders and linked into tables or tree structures.

Semiautonomous agents can process information. These agents can take a series of actions without human intervention; the processing rules, however, are easily visible to human users, who can change them. The agents may also refer objects to a human user for action. Agents are also objects, of course, that can be called by or embedded in other objects with full or partial inheritance.

Frankly, this paper did not add much to my knowledge of objects, but the notion of human/computer interaction that the various "semi-" functions offer did impress me. I know too much about computers and software to trust them very much, and I like the idea that the power of this system is visible to and under the convenient and explicit control of the human user.

The Object Lens is currently a prototype implemented in Interlisp-D on Xerox 1100 workstations. The authors claim that all the features they describe are actually implemented, although some are not fully tested. This good work in progress may eventually result in a powerful family of products, but even if the Object Lens should fail in the marketplace, the ideas in this paper are valuable and will further research in the area by ratcheting our expectations a few notches higher.

—*J. L. Podolsky,* Palo Alto, CA

DIAPER, DAN, DR. (Univ. of Liverpool, Liverpool, UK) (ED.)
**Interacting with Computers**
(*Interact. Comput.*)
Vol. 1, No. 1 (April 1989). Published three times a year for the British Computer Society by Butterworth Scientific Ltd., P.O. Box 63, Westbury House, Bury Street, Guildford, Surrey GU2 5BH, UK. Annual subscription—£92 (UK); £105 (outside the UK). North American orders should be sent to Journals Fulfillment Dept., Butterworths, 80 Montvale Avenue, Stoneham, MA 02180. ISSN 0953-5438.

. . . Human-Computer Interaction (HCI) is an endeavour that involves many disciplines. It is debatable whether HCI is a discipline. What should not be debatable is that the 'I' in 'HCI' stands for 'interaction' and not for 'interface.' The latter assumes that solutions to problems in HCI always involve the interface between a computer and its operator. However, unless 'interface' is defined too broadly to be useful, there are solutions in HCI that do not involve changing the interface at all. For example, some problems may be solved by providing training, or by changing the operators' tasks or the practices of their organisation. . . .

If HCI is a discipline then it should possess at least a set of common goals, if not common axioms. This editorial proposes that the goals of HCI are: 'to develop or improve the safety, utility, effectiveness, efficiency, and usability of systems that include computers' . . . HCI safety issues, for example, need to encompass not only the computer system and its individual users, but also colleagues who do not use the computer, the organisation that owns the computer, and also those less immediately involved including households, other organisations, classes within society and society itself, both national and global. A concern with systems of this breadth clearly requires an eclectic approach involving many disciplines. . . .

HCI needs to be a church of broad foundations if it is to achieve real success. The engineering discipline of HCI may be relatively constrained exclusively to involve systems that include both people and computers, but there are probably few disciplines that could not make some contribution. The editorial board of *Interacting with Computers* aims to produce a journal of intellectual quality but also one that can be understood and used by a diverse audience with different needs, interests and knowledge.

*—From the Editorial*

## Human factors

CARROLL, JOHN M. (IBM Thomas Watson Res. Cntr., Yorktown Heights, NY); AND CARRITHERS, CAROLINE (Columbia Univ., New York, NY)
**Training wheels in a user interface.**
*Commun. ACM* **27,** 8 (August 1984), 800–806.

A word processing interface was modified to limit the functions available to novice users. These functions, which were unnecessary for basic word processing, had been previously observed to be error states that novices had difficulty recovering from. When evaluated against the original system, the modified system was superior for novices in terms of time to finish a task, successful completion rate, time spent correcting errors, etc. This paper is useful because it provides a design approach. In contrast, a great deal of literature in this area produces empirical facts of limited generality.

*—John M. Hammer,* Norcross, GA

ROBERTS, TERESA L.; AND MORAN, THOMAS P. (Xerox Research Center, Palo Alto, CA)
**The evaluation of text editors: methodology and empirical results.**
*Commun. ACM* **26,** 4 (April 1983), 265–283.

This paper proposes a methodology, based on the Keystroke-Level Model, with which to evaluate text editors on interactive computeing systems. The authors claim that this methodology can also be applied to word processing. The authors believe that their evaluation technique is standadized, in that it measures the significant dynamics associated with using several different text editors of varying complexity and hardware implementation. They further claim that their measurement techniques is objective, through, and easy to use. This methodology is intended for use by text editor designers, word processing center managers, and other nonpsychologists who need to evaluate text editors, but who have limited time and equipment.

It is this writer's opinion that, while the authors' methodology is objective and thorough, the requirements for trained personnel to (1) teach novice users, (2) perform accuate data collection, and (3) interpret the results of the study believe the authors' claim that the measurement techniques described in this paper would be human factors engineers and industrial psychologists, precisely the opposite audience for which the paper was intended.

—*Ross Jay Bettinger,* Silver Spring, MD

SMITH, MICHAEL J. (Univ. of Wisconsin-Madison, Madison) **HCI-0210**
**Human factors issues in VDT use: environmental and workstation design considerations.**
*IEEE Comput. Graph. Appl.* **4,** 11 (Nov. 1984), 56–63.

Smith's paper provides a summary of human factors issues which relate to the design and use of VDTs. Smith summarizes the results from a number of field studies on the health problems associated with the use of VDTs. Topics such as screen glare, improper illumination, screen flicker, and temperature and humidity problems associated with workstation design are discussed. The paper is recommended reading as an introductory source on the topic of human factors in VDT use.

—*Woodrow Barfield,* Seattle, WA

GALOTTI, KATHLEEN M. (Univ. of Pennsylvania, Philadelphia); AND GANGON, **HCI-0211**
WILLIAM F., III (Kurzweil Applied Intelligence Inc., Waltham, MA)
**What non-programmers know about programming: natural language procedure specification.**
*Int. J. Man-Mach. Stud.* **22,** 1 (Jan. 1985), 1–10.

This paper reports on a simple experiment the authors performed to determine how frequently nonprogrammers use control statements. Because the authors addressed basic issues and carefully tried to eliminate additional variables, they were able to demonstrate believable results. This is in contrast to the large number of papers on human factors and computing that I have read over the past several years, where the authors are apparently blind to additional variables which may affect their studies. In fact, the authors of this paper clearly address that issue:

> The basic idea here is that performance on tasks designed to measure an underlying ability might be sensitive to other abilities or factors unrelated to the one of interest.

Thirty-two undergraduates with no programming backgrounds were asked to provide written instructions for the game of War and for a file-checking task. Half were told the recipient of the instructions was "an English-speaking Martian with no common sense." The other half were told the recipient was "a person like yourself." The instructions were graded according to the number of control statements used.

The results of the study indicate that nonprogrammers spontaneously use control statements and do so in proportion to novice programmers writing FORTRAN programs. But this is only so when they perceive that the instrument receiving the instructions is unable to make inferences about the instructions. Fewer control statements were used in the instructions provided to "persons like yourself" than to "Martians." The authors make no claims regarding the correctness of the instructions given.

—*J. A. Meads,* Portland, OR

KIDD, ALISON L.; AND COOPER, MARTIN B. (British Telecom Research Laboratories, Ipswich, UK)
**Man-machine interface issues in the construction and use of an expert system.**
*Int. J. Man-Mach. Stud.* **22,** 1 (Jan. 1985), 91–102.

HCI-0212

Although this paper is billed as an investigation of [hu]man-machine interface issues, it is actually a very good introduction to the whole realm of training expert systems. In other words, the authors don't so much cover human-machine interfaces in detail (graphics, menus, etc.), but rather they take a more general approach, getting into issues like "How do you get knowledge out of an expert's head and into a system?"

The authors cite three central issues upon which their evaluation of expert system interfaces is based: knowledge acquisition, knowledge representation, and communications interface. A specific expert system shell is described—Edinburgh University's AL/X, which embodies an expert system as a network of logical inferences. Then, using the AL/X shell, the paper studies the specific case of building an expert system to locate faults in a piece of radio equipment.

The human-machine interface aspects of the training of the system are considered in some detail. The main problem, it turned out, was not how to get knowledge into the system, but rather how to get *usable* knowledge out of the expert.

The major conclusion of the study is that effective knowledge acquisition is going to take much better human-machine interfaces than we have now: natural-language interfaces; graphics (for both operator presentation and knowledge input); and a new interface philosophy, in which the expert system itself is used to assist with knowledge input, based on knowledge obtained up to that point.

Even if you don't know much about expert systems, you should read this paper. It is quite informative and a good introduction to a field that is soon going to become much more important.
—*Tom Davis,* Dripping Springs, TX

GAIT, JASON (Tektronix, Inc., Beaverton, OR)
**An aspect of aesthetics in human-computer communications: pretty windows.**
*IEEE Trans. Softw. Eng.* **SE-11,** 8 (Aug. 1985), 714–717.

HCI-0213

The essence of this paper is to propose that the windows presented to users by the high-resolution interfaces of workstations (e.g., Xerox 1100, Sun 2) be dimensioned in more aesthetically appealing ways. Instead of doing so arbitrarily, most windows should be proportioned according to the "golden ratio," resulting in rectangles whose length/width relationships are determined using the sequence of ratios of successive Fibonacci numbers. Such windows are called pretty. Certain inconspicuous windows (e.g., clock windows) are exceptions that need/should not be prettied up. An algorithm for carrying out the required conversion, expected to be callable as a library procedure, is presented and an example of the results is displayed.

This paper represents an interesting and useful step in the right direction toward improved interface design. However, it is only one step. This reviewer would contend that other relevant design objectives, such as controlling the numbers and relative locations of windows on the display screen, should take precedence over considerations of aesthetics. While the latter do ultimately become important, the user must first learn to cope with the potentially confusing multiwindow interface situation. This means that characteristics of human memory/learning (including spatial location, ordering, information volume, etc.) must be taken into account.

It is delightful to see increasing attention being paid, especially by computer scientists, to the design of user interfaces based on user psychology. The author will hopefully continue along that vein. This short paper is recommended as easy reading for any researcher in the area of user-computer interaction.

—*S. Treu*, Pittsburgh, PA

LINDE, LENA (National Defence Research Institute, Stockholm, Sweden); AND WAERN, YVONNE (Univ. of Stockholm, Stockholm, Sweden)
**On search in an incomplete database.**
*Int. J. Man-Mach. Stud.* **22,** 5 (May 1985), 563–579.

HCI-0214

This paper clearly presents preliminary research results on how people interact with an incomplete database. An incomplete database is one in which the answer to a question cannot be located directly (in a single query to the database). Examples of such searching include making a medical diagnosis or solving a crime. The study described in this paper is actually on how to *solve problems* with the aid of a database management system. Since the task is more problem solving than database related, more references could have been made to the problem solving literature.

Since this study was limited in scope, its primary contribution is in introducing an important topic. The symbiotic relationship between a person and a computer (in the form of a DBMS) is certainly one which deserves attention. In particular, questions about the distribution of intelligence in such a system come to mind.

—*A. L. Tharp*, Raleigh, NC

DICKSON, GARY W.; DESANCTIS, GERARDINE; AND MCBRIDE, D. J. (Univ. of Minnesota, Minneapolis)
**Understanding the effectiveness of computer graphics for decision support: a cumulative experimental approach.**
*Commun. ACM* **29,** 1 (Jan. 1986), 40–47.

HCI-0215

Under what conditions should information be presented in graphs rather than tables? Answers to this question are of key importance to the designers and users of decision support systems. Experimental work has, as yet, provided little in the way of clear answers. This paper contributes to the debate by reporting three experiments that examined the effectiveness of graphs and tables as aids to decision making.

In these experiments, the authors vary the nature of the decision making tasks. With a simple task, graphical and tabular formats for presenting information resulted in similar levels of user performance. With a more complex task, graphical presentation proved superior. For tasks of even greater complexity, users of graphs marginally outperformed users of tables, but only under conditions of high information load.

# REVIEWS

In highlighting the importance of task conditions, this research makes a valuable contribution. The effectiveness of alternative formats for information presentation clearly depends upon what the information is being used for. However, in order to understand how information is being used, it is necessary to relate the precise structure and content of tables and graphs to the nature of the decisions being made. Without a penetrating analysis of this sort, it is difficult to assess whether or not the most appropriate form of graphical presentation was being compared with the most appropriate type of table. Until such analyses are forthcoming, robust answers to the essential question are not going to emerge, and guidelines based upon this sort of evidence should be viewed with caution.

—*Philip Barnard,* Cambridge, UK

LEHMAN, JOHN; VAN WETERING, JAY; AND VOGEL, DOUG (Univ. of Minnesota, Minneapolis) **HCI-0216**
**Mainframe and microcomputer-based business graphics: What satisfies users?**
*Inf. Manage.* **10,** 3 (March 1986), 133–140.

If one can stay alert through the essentially uniform dullness of presentation and writing style in this report, there may actually be a gem or two of information hiding in it. As a statistical analysis of the results of a questionnaire (with a 25 percent return rate), the paper tries to let us know how and why business people use computer graphics on mainframes and microcomputers.

One of the observations that sort of leans out at you is that there is really a difference between business mainframe and microcomputer graphics use: The fact that mainframe graphics use is still way ahead of microcomputer graphics use, both in numbers of people using them and in the time that each type has been in use.

The authors list the "determinants of satisfaction" that they deduce from their data, in both the hardware and the software area for both micro and mainframe users. (Exception: They find *no* significant software satisfaction correlations for graphics users on micros.) Their three major results are:

(1) "empirical confirmation of the importance of information centers,"
(2) "the existence of a relationship between hardware configuration strategy and user satisfaction," and
(3) "the existence of organizational strategies to maximize user satisfaction with each hardware strategy."

—*Tom Davis,* Dripping Springs, TX

MCQUARRIE, EDWARD F. (Santa Clara Univ., Santa Clara, CA) **HCI-0217**
**The computer imperative among owners of home computers: explanation by social factors.**
*Comput. Soc. Sci.* **1,** 3/4 (July-Dec. 1985), 155–161. [A special double issue on the social impact of computers.]

The computer imperative is the belief that involvement with computers is both good and necessary. The strength of this belief was studied among 950 owners of home computers who completed a mail questionnaire. Demographics, group membership, and social interaction were able to explain some of the variance in this belief with the latter being most powerful. Total variance explained was low, leaving open the possibility that macro-social factors might be superior in explaining adherence to the computer imperative.

*—Author's Abstract*

This paper explores an interesting topic: the belief that computers have become as much a part of everyone's everyday life as automobiles. The mode of inquiry is through the reaction of owners of personal computers to two statements: (1) "Everyone should at least consider buying a computer," and (2) "People who do not understand computers will soon have trouble succeeding in life." According to the author, the responses to these two questions were "only weakly associated" and, hence, they (the responses) were analyzed separately.

As a novice in the methodologies of public opinion surveys, but a lifelong avid reader of the information the surveys contain, it appears to me that the paper could and should have avoided this dichotomy. At the level of understandability, the tables refer to two themes: the micro imperative and the computer imperative. The text does not specifically identify or define the first of these two, and the reader is left wondering. This is not a good place to be while shrouded in the trappings of the methodology.

Couldn't a small market test have identified that the two questions address different attitudes? The first certainly is influenced by personal economics; the second, not obviously so. Perhaps some other question or questions might have been more illuminating; for example, the questions could involve the goodness or intrinsic worth of a personal computer or, possibly, the actual need for and utility of a PC.

The paper is also an example of another of my pet peeves, which has to do with the assertion of "significance." In discussing the results included in Table 2, the author states, "Immediately clear is that demographic and membership variables are much less powerful than the measure of social interaction." Table 2 contains the means of responses on scales of 1 to 5 to the demographic, membership, and social interaction questions. The figures in the table do not appear to support the author's assertion—not immediately or clearly anyway.

There was a good idea here, but for me it got lost. We need to know more about the impact, current and pending, of computers on our lives. Particularly in America, where pride of place is frequently accorded to the technological guru, we need to establish the attitudinal underpinnings which will enable us not to be overawed. The impact of computing in general, and personal computing in particular, is far-reaching; there is very little question about that. The technological geniuses out there who are "putting it all into one small box" are intellectually awesome.

Technology, however, is only one aspect of our lives. Despite its swiftly mounting complexity, it remains easier to do something about than the social aspects. We do need to be enlightened about the place of personal computers in our lives so that we don't forsake the struggle for peace with justice while we wrestle with the latest versions of MS-DOS.

*—Jim Hammerton,* Pittsford, NY

REVIEWS

PILGRIM, JÜRGEN (Academy of Sciences of the GDR, Berlin, E. Germany)    HCI-0218
**On the purpose and analysis of EDP user systems.**
*Int. J. Man-Mach. Stud.* **24,** 5 (May 1986), 435–452.

As the title implies, the author describes a method of analyzing user needs based on user characteristics and their interaction with computer systems. Interaction with computer systems is defined as a set of user characteristics, such as EDP qualifications, user attitudes, the EDP task, etc. The author computes a metric called "complicatedness" based on the responses to each of the questions on user characteristics. These scores are then compared to a measure of "complicatedness" derived from software designers or the computer center director. The author validated his method by questioning a group of computer users at a biomedical research center. Results of this study indicate that the method was and is useful in identifying computational requirements of a particular group. More specifically, the system determined that the software designer and the computer center director had anticipated a much more "complicated" system than was actually needed by this user community. This specific user community did not need or access some of the more sophisticated software packages that resided on the system.

The author argues effectively for his methodology, claiming that the information from the system can help in the planning and use of EDP performance. More than anything else, the paper points out the need to question users about what they need, how they want to use the system, and how they perceive the "complicatedness" of the system.

—*K. M. Swigger,* Denton, TX

CRAWFORD, R. G.; AND BECKER, H. S. (Queen's Univ., Kingston, Ont., Canada)    HCI-0219
**A novice user's interface to information retrieval systems.**
*Inf. Process. Manage.* **22,** 4 (Aug. 1986), 287–298.

The paper describes the design of a user interface for information retrieval systems (specifically for bibliographic retrieval) with the goal of providing an interface that can be used without training, external help, or documentation. The paper is well written, easy to read, and well organized. The user interface design captures many desirable features, such as menus, form-filling, windowing, online help, and error-feedback. The emphasis of the paper is on initial design and implementation. The authors do not support their assumptions with experimental data.

Conducting experiments with various classes of users can help in many ways: developing practical guidelines for "do's" and "don'ts" for designing user interfaces; finding differences in user interfaces for various levels of user experience; creating user interfaces that can detect and adapt to user experience levels; and finding distributed user interfaces (i.e., downloading appropriate interface software to user workstations based on user experience level).

—*Santosh Chokani,* Arlington, VA

ROUSE, WILLIAM B. (Search Technology, Inc., Norcross, GA)    HCI-0220
**A note on the nature of creativity in engineering: implications for supporting system design.**
*Inf. Process. Manage.* **22,** 4 (Aug. 1986), 279–285.

The author uses an uncritical review of the psychology literature on creativity to motivate a few rather dubious ideas on computer-based support systems for designers. These include providing access to information across disciplines, giving access to information across individuals, supporting multiple modes of thinking, supporting the pursuit of multiple solutions, and providing a sense of ownership. However, the paper contains no discussion beyond the level of what appears here. For example, it does not even allude to the fact that there are significant technical issues in accessing different forms of knowledge in distinct databases or manipulating different modalities such as geometry and semantic networks. In the same way, simplistic statements are made about the sociology of the environment and the individual (e.g., that the organization is demonstrably supportive and that acceptance of managerial roles not be excessive), without mention of the hybrid role of most CAD/CAM/CAE systems as aids to the design process *and* as instruments for the official checking of designs and releasing products to manufacturing. The paper is clearly written and does fulfill its stated purpose, but it does not demonstrate any creativity or technical depth.

—*Jeanine Meyer,* White Plains, NY

RUSHINEK, AVI; AND RUSHINEK, SARA F. (Univ. of Miami, Coral Gables, FL)   **HCI-0221**
**The effects of communication monitors on user satisfaction.**
*Inf. Process. Manage.* **22,** 4 (Aug. 1986), 345–351.

The authors attempted to analyze the influence of Communications Monitors (CMs) on the user satisfaction of an overall computer system. While CMs may be an important contributor to computer user satisfaction, a computer system has many other dimensions—e.g., processing speed, number of users supported, etc.—that can affect user satisfaction. The authors do not give any indication regarding how heavily user satisfaction relies on CMs alone.

The authors conclude that variables such as "Manufacturers of CM," "Vendors of CM," "Home grown CM," etc., have the greatest impact on user satisfaction. It is not clear how these variables can relate to such factors as technical support from CM manufacturers and CM performance. This reviewer believes that the latter are more important in determining the levels of user satisfaction.

—*W. S. Lai,* Holmdel, NJ

LEMAY, MOIRA (Montclair State College, Upper Montclair, NJ); AND HIRD, ERIC   **HCI-0222**
(California Institute of Technology, Pasadena)
**Operator work load: when is enough enough?.**
*Commun. ACM* **29,** 7 (July 1986), 638–642.

A small field experiment was conducted to test the effect of increased operator workload at NASA's Goldstone Deep Space Communications Complex. The experiment was designed in anticipation of a system upgrade at the station. The authors hypothesized that the pending workload increase could lead to an increase in the number of operator errors at the installation.

Nine operators served as subjects for the simulation experiment. They were asked to perform a series of tasks within low, medium, and high workload situations. Three measures of their performance were collected: (1) operator ratings of workload on sequential subtasks; (2) ratio of time required to time available to complete a particular subtask; and (3) starting time, or time taken to initiate the physical portion of a subtask. The first two were thought to be significant.

The experiment used a very small sample, and it is not surprising that two of the three measures were not statistically significant. The paper suggests that there were large differences among the operators. These differences would seem to have a large effect on the findings given the small sample size.

Overall, this is an interesting case study. However, no general conclusions can be drawn from it, due to the small sample size and the unique setting of the study.

—*J. Fedorowicz,* Boston, MA

HATIVA, NIRA (Tel Aviv Univ., Tel Aviv, Israel)
**The microcomputer as a classroom audio visual device: the concept, and prospects.**
*Comput. Educ. (Elmsford, NY)* **10**, 3 (1986), 359–367.

Hativa's paper discusses some reasons for using a microcomputer as a classroom audiovisual device. Hativa notes that many schools in the United States are not likely to achieve a student-to-microcomputer ratio that will provide pupils with extensive hands-on experience. Due to the expenses that are associated with microcomputers, the author suggests it would be more expedient to regard a microcomputer as an audiovisual device comparable to a slide projector.

Citing the results of a questionnaire that was given to 53 educators, Hativa identifies the following as the most important attributes that make microcomputers adoptable for use as an audiovisual device: reliability, conservation of teacher time, simplicity and comfort of use, control by teachers, low noise level, presentation of pictures or graphics, flexibility, and versatility.

The observation that microcomputers are regarded as reliable audiovisual devices may surprise many computer professionals. Hativa notes that a microcomputer that is permanently installed in a classroom facilitates fast integration with a lesson. However, permanently installed microcomputers are more likely to be subjected to abuse and may have problems with mechanical components, such as disk drive alignment or keyboard operations. Some of Hativa's other observations can also be questioned. For example, comparing a microcomputer with an overhead projector can result in a favorable perception of the microcomputer. Yet, a microcomputer and the equipment that is needed to effectively display its output to a class is far more expensive than an overhead or slide projector. Costs associated with large display devices for microcomputers are dropping but it will be years before overhead or slide projectors are completely removed from classrooms.

Finally, Hativa has not provided a background discussion for explaining why microcomputers will be successful as audiovisual devices in a classroom without analyzing other technologies. For example, television had the opportunity of providing students with comparable information. Yet television has not been successfully integrated into many educational curricula. The revolution that was predicted with the development of television decades ago has not sparked a strong educational revolution. The same situation may occur with the development of microcomputer technology over a decade ago.

—*W. E. Mihalo,* Whiting, IN

FURNAS, G. W.; LANDAUER, T. K.; GOMEZ, L. M.; AND DUMAIS, S. T. (Bell Communications Research, Inc., Morristown, NJ)
**The vocabulary problem in human-system communication.**
*Commun. ACM* **30,** 11 (Nov. 1987), 964–971.

> In almost all computer applications, users must enter correct words for the desired objects or actions. For success without extensive training, or in first-tries for new targets, the system must recognize terms that will be chosen spontaneously. We studied spontaneous word choice for objects in five application-related domains, and found the variability suprisingly large. In every case two people favored the same term with probability < 0.20. Simulations show how this fundamental property of language limits the success of various design methodologies for vocabulary-driven interaction. For example the popular approach in which access is via one designer's favorite single word will result in 80–90 percent failure rates in many common situations. An optimal strategy, unlimited aliasing, is derived and shown to be capable of several-fold improvements.
>
> —*Authors' Abstract*

This is an excellent paper for anyone interested in interface design where users' choice of words is involved, especially those who believe that vocabulary is not a problem. The authors show that a few aliases (synonymous terms) can improve the success of spontaneous selection markedly, and they suggest that unlimited aliasing is the optimum solution. Three approaches to identify good alternate terms are suggested: (1) having a few users supply a "fair number" of terms apiece (say, 3–6); (2) extracting words from the text of descriptions of objects (a la full-text indexing of documents); and (3) adaptively, by noting what new terms users attempt to apply in operation of the system.

The authors recognize that there is an *imprecision* problem, in that one term can be selected by different users to mean different objects. However, they point out that many aliases may be more precise terms than the common terms for which they substitute and thus may actually improve precision. In any case, the authors point out that there are techniques for managing the ambiguities. Their preferred method is interactively to display choices, ordered by frequency of occurence, for the user in order to enable disambiguation. The authors note that effective disambiguation may require good system explanations, which is a problem in itself. The authors also note other possible disambiguation methods (multiterm Boolean expressions, formal query languages, and natural language understanding) but turn away from these as being difficult to implement and not very successful. While I recognize the cogent analysis of much of this paper, I might question the strong emphasis on spontaneous selection. Perhaps some pre-selection mediation by the system (e.g., via menus) could avoid much post-selection disambiguation. More generally, the authors' apparent aversion to considering a combination of methods in approaching this problem is questionable, although I recognize that any one of those denigrated by the authors may be inferior to unlimited aliasing as a single solution.

—*R. S. Marcus,* Cambridge, MA

REVIEWS

HOWARTH, IAN (Univ. of Nottingham, Nottingham, UK)     **HCI-0225**
**Psychology and information technology.**
[in *Information technology & people: designing for the future,* F. Blackler; and D. Oborne, MIT Press, Cambridge, MA, 1987, 1-22.]

Howarth has written an overview of the role of psychologists in the United Kingdom who might be involved in the information technology field. At the end of the chapter, he highlights the contributions psychologists can make in systems design and development. A strong point in the chapter is a good summary of the virtues of well-designed technology. Probably the weakest feature is the effect of poor proofreading.

In one section, the author refers to a government-supported research program but offers no bibliographic references for further information. Later, in commenting upon expert systems, he suggests that they are intended to replace expertise. The predominant view in the field is that such systems will be useful as an adjunct to the decision-making process, but will never be given the power Howarth suggests. However, the author is aware of the inherent problems in knowledge engineering and of size limitations for expert systems.

—*J. N. Rose,* Delhi, NY

LONG, JOHN (Univ. College London, London, UK)     **HCI-0226**
**Information technology and home-based services: improving the usability of teleshopping.**
[in *Information technology & people: designing for the future,* F. Blackler; and D. Oborne, MIT Press, Cambridge, MA, 1987, 211-230.]

This chapter deals with methods for modeling interactive systems and frameworks for applying scientific knowledge (in this case, psychology) to nonscientific areas. The author introduces two approaches, the *applications model* and the *theory approach,* which lead to the *combined approach.* The application of the combined approach is as follows: Define the scope, including the variables; generate an empirical database of user difficulties by videotaping users of a simulated system; analyze the difficulties encountered; generalize and make a *block interaction model*; experiement with that model; and tell the system designers what is found.

The author says "this chapter describes a home-based teleshopping service, and describes three possible ways in which psychology can be used to make the system easier to use." Although the chapter describes features of a home shopping system and uses that system as an example and frame of reference, the emphasis is on methodology, not on "improving the usability of teleshopping."

Characteristics of the example system that lead to diminished usability include very poor quality graphics, which might be too expensive to fix directly. Psychological theory indicates that different views of the merchandise, using the same graphics system, might ameliorate the problem. That possibility is held out in a discussion of the various approaches, but neither the results of implementing system design changes, specific design recommendations, nor simulation results are presented. Similarly, the display describing the merchandise is severely limited, but the reader never knows how the author recommended that the problem be addressed. The same applies to the ambiguous user instructions in the initial system.

It is curious that a paper dealing with usability analysis and psychological factors nowhere mentions issues of response time.

—*T. C. Lowe,* Washington, DC

SCHMALHOFER, FRANZ (McGill Univ., Montreal, P.Q., Canada)  **HCI-0227**
**Expert systems as cognitive tools for human decision making.**
[in *Expert judgment and expert systems,* J. Mumpower; O. Renn; L. Phillips; and V. Uppuluri (Eds.), Springer-Verlag, Berlin, West Germany, 1987, 269-288.]

Schmalhofer begins "Expert Systems as Cognitive Tools for Human Decision Making" by distinguishing between descriptive theories of decision making (i.e., models of human decision making) and prescriptive theories (i.e., formal operations research (OR) procedures to obtain an optimal decision under specified conditions). He notes that empirical research has shown that prescriptive theories are not generally employed by experts; i.e., they are not descriptive theories also.

A substantial mathematical treatment follows, with the object of relating computational effort to decision quality. It is shown that, if done right, a substantial reduction in effort may result in only a slight degradation of quality. Although clearly written, this section is dense and requires a significant background in OR or a significant degree of mathematical sophistication to be fully appreciated.

The implication of this work for expert systems follows in the final section. Experts often violate apparently optimal decision making (as given by prescriptive theories) by both ignoring relevant information and considering irrelevant information. This, however, may well be adaptive. Simplifying the problem by not considering all relevant inputs may decrease the decision quality only slightly, as noted above, and it also makes the decision easier for the expert to explain and justify. Considerations of irrelevant information may simply be the expert's foresight as to its future relevance. (The paper gives an example of this.)

Other papers in *Expert judgment and expert systems* treat these subjects better—more clearly, more comprehensively (the paper surely does not cover much of what its title—no abstract is provided—suggests it might), and with a more uniform degree of technical content. Nevertheless, the paper is useful for its thorough, technical treatment of the quality-effort tradeoff.

—*Joseph Fulda,* New York, NY

GUYNES, JAN L. (Univ. of Texas at Arlington, Arlington)  **HCI-0228**
**Impact of system response time on state anxiety.**
*Commun. ACM* **31**, 3 (March 1988), 342-347.

This paper reports on a study conducted to test the effect of system response time on the state anxiety of the end user. The author predicts that type A personalities, those "composed primarily of competitiveness, excessive drive, and an enhanced sense of time urgency" (p. 342) would exhibit greater state anxiety when encountering long or inconsistent system response times.

Eighty-six subjects participated in the experiments. Three treatment groups completed tasks with good, variable, or poor response times. (The good response times were defined as less than 5 seconds, which, with today's technology, might be less than acceptable.)

Analysis of the data shows that there was a significant positive relationship between response time and state anxiety, but personality type was not a contributing factor toward this relationship. That is, type A personalities did not exhibit a larger increase in state anxiety than type B personalities. In addition, those subjects in the poor treatment group exhibited the largest increase in state anxiety overall.

This study was designed and conducted well. The findings, although not tremendously surprising, demonstrate that response time is a major concern for all system users. It should therefore be a major issue for designers as well.

—*J. Fedorowicz*, Boston, MA

CARROLL, JOHN (IBM T. J. Watson Research Center, Yorktown Heights, NY); AND  **HCI-0229**
AARONSON, AMY (IBM US Marketing and Services Group, Franklin Lakes, NJ)
**Learning by doing with simulated intelligent help.**
*Commun. ACM* **31,** 9 (Sept. 1988), 1064–1079.

This paper reports the results of a study on the usability of an on-line intelligent help facility. This facility was simulated in an environment in which users learned to use an interactive application by performing tasks with it. The authors state that their research had two goals: to define usability issues for on-line intelligent help and to investigate interface simulation as a technique for research into the use of on-line intelligent help. Notes, videotapes, and think-aloud commentaries from the study are the principal sources of data discussed in the paper. The authors conclude that although potential problems exist, intelligent on-line help can support users in a task completion scenario. The paper discusses these problems, citing portions of the think-aloud commentaries to support the discussion, and concludes with an extensive discussion of directions for future research.

The paper is well written and organized and provides a thoughtful analysis of the data. The authors provide sufficient detail for the reader to understand the methodology. This paper should be read by user interface designers and researchers interested in applying artificial intelligence to on-line help or to training materials for computer systems.

—*M. P. Tarka*, Gaithersburg, MD

THOMAS, JOHN C. (IBM Thomas J. Watson Research Center, NY)  **HCI-0230**
**Organizing for human factors.**
[in *Human factors and interactive computer systems.* Proc. of the NYU symposium on user interfaces (New York, May 26-28, 1982), Y. Vassiliou (Ed.), Ablex Publishing Corp., Norwood, NJ, 1984, 29–46.]

[See main entry, Review HCI-0038.]

This paper is concerned with the problem of "How can an organization that develops computer products ensure good human factors in those products?" Thomas provides his definition of "human factors" and outlines reasons for concern. He points out that there are tradeoffs associated with good human factors, and that the tradeoff with cost today is often based on last year's costs. This frequently means that systems are less friendly than they might be in order to save a few dollars, a few bytes, or a few machine cycles. The author stresses the need to develop systems for the way people are, rather than the way system designers wish them to be. The author suggests that good human factors will cost an organization less in the long run and will aid it in turning out a better product. Good human factors design will probably increase the design time and cost, but will also increase the value of the product and reduce redesign. When the primary user of the system is computer naive, good human factors may mean the difference between successfully using the system and abandoning it. This is important because many nonDP professional users can make discretionary use of a computer system. Thomas emphasizes the need to test a new system on representative users before submitting the system to general use.

Thomas' comments and ideas are pragmatic and could be of use to those who design or modify computer systems. The paper provides good background reading on the problem. Tighter editing and fewer repetitive examples would have been better. The paper is a bit too much of a sales pitch for human factors, and the author is too evangelical in his presentation style.

—*David R. Harris,* Fairfax, VA

GOULD, JOHN D. (IBM Thomas J. Watson Research Center, Yorktown Heights, NY); AND LEWIS, CLAYTON (ECOT 7-7 Engineering Center, Boulder, CO)
**Designing for usability: key principles and what designers think.**
*Commun. ACM* **28**, 3 (March 1985), 300–311.

This article covers three design principles which the authors believe are both important and frequently neglected: (1) Early focus on users and tasks, (2) Empirical measurement, and (3) Iterative design. Gould and Lewis spend more than half of the article discussing why these "common sense" principles are not well understood and why they are undervalued. They then elaborate the principles and explain how they are applied in an initial design phase, followed by an iterative development phase. They complete their discussion by presenting a case study in which they applied these principles to the design of a computer-based audio message system.

It is certainly difficult to argue with the importance of these principles. Nevertheless, while the authors go to great lengths to justify them, they do so primarily from the perspective of human factors experts. They, for example, quote Brooks [1] on prototypes, but ignore him on the principle he claims is most important: conceptual integrity. They mention iterative design but do not cite Basili and Turner's seminal article [2] on this topic. While the externally visible aspects of a system are clearly important in satisfying user needs, systems need to possess other attributes to ensure they are buildable and maintainable, and the final design may have to be a compromise as a result. Furthermore, even in the case of externally visible aspects, designers need to ensure that expressed user needs are extrapolated to a complete design which performs in a consistent manner when faced with unexpected inputs. (The reviewer has experience with the system covered in the authors' case study and believes it could be improved in this area.) Thus, while you should read this article to add to your store of knowledge about what needs to be done to satisfy user needs, you should not assume that these principles are the only ones to apply.

—*F. T. Baker,* Bethesda, MD

**REFERENCES**

[1] BROOKS, F. P., JR. *The mythical man-month: essays in software engineering,* Addison-Wesley, Reading, MA, 1975. See *Computing Reviews* **16,** 10 (Oct. 1975), Rev. 28,944.

[2] BASILI, V. R.; AND TURNER, A. J. Iterative enhancement: a practical technique for software development, in *Proc. of the first national conference on software engineering,* IEEE, New York, 1975, 56–62.

HOWARD, GEOFFRY S.; AND SMITH, ROBERT D. (Kent State Univ., Kent, OH)   **HCI-0232**
**Computer anxiety in management: myth or reality?.**
*Commun. ACM* **29,** 7 (July 1986), 611–615.

This work presents some significant conclusions on a topic of importance to anyone faced with implementing computer technology in organizations. The effort builds on past research, uses sound methodology, and its presentation is understandable and well organized.

The authors respond to three major questions:

(1) Is computer anxiety a real or imagined problem? (Their conclusion is that it is less real than once thought.)
(2) What is the nature of computer anxiety? (They respond to ten common beliefs. Especially important were results that showed neither age nor sex correlated significantly with computer anxiety, that high levels of math anxiety accompanied high levels of computer anxiety, and the relationship of computer anxiety with computer knowledge was not significant. This latter finding led to the conclusion that actual hands-on experience is what is needed.)
(3) Can computer anxiety be treated? (They conclude yes, and explain how this might happen when the anxiety has either psychological, educational, or operational roots.)

—*E. A. Kallman,* S. Lyndeboro, NH

LOCKHOVSKY, FRED H.; AND TSICHRITZIS, DIONYSIOS C. (Univ. of Toronto,   **HCI-0233**
Toronto, Ont., Canada)
**Querying external databases.**
[in *Human factors and interactive computer systems.* Proc. of the NYU symposium on user interfaces (New York, May 26-28, 1982), Y. Vassiliou (Ed.), Ablex Publishing Corp., Norwood, NJ, 1984, 117–140.]

[See main entry, Review HCI-0038.]

As the number of people accessing an increasing number of commercial databases grows, so too do the problems inherent in that access. Not the least of these problems is what we might call the "language barrier." Each database, and/or each access service, has its own language; Babel quickly results. Lochovsky and Tsichritzis propose, in this very readable article, a language structure for accessing such "external" databases.

Their design for a query language begins with an analysis of the functions to be performed when accessing an external database. The analysis proceeds—quite effectively—from an analogy with space travel. While their design stops short of the syntax required for such a query language, it does outline the requirements for: (1) "pointing" to the desired object in the information space; (2) "positioning" one's self in the data space; (3) noting information about the current state of the query; and (4) specifying the manner in which requests are made.

While realizing that "naive" users must be guided through their interactions with such systems, the authors recognize (as too little of the human factors literature seems to) that complex queries will require complex solutions. All in all, this is a good article.

—*M. C. Harris,* Houston, TX

KERBER, KENNETH W. (College of the Holy Cross, Worcester, MA)     HCI-0234
**Attitudes towards specific uses of the computers quantitative, decision-making and record-keeping applications.**
*Behav. Inf. Tech.* **2,** 2 (April-June 1982), 197–209.

Somewhere, some time, psychology was defined as the study of college freshman. Although the population has been expanded to include all college students, this observation is still valid. This article examines the attitudes of the college students available to the authors toward specific applications. It also attempts to determine the attitude based on the students' perceptions.

The authors present an extensive and very representative sample of computer applications for testing. A questionnaire was used as the test mechanism for 203 samples. Most of the students had some familiarity with computers, and almost half had written at least a small program.

The analysis characterized the students as to major, age, sex, and computer background. The responses were assessed with the semantic differential method developed by Zoltan and Chapanis [1], providing a pair of adjectives about their beliefs and opinions concerning computers.

The one objection I have about the testing was the author's instructions for the applications study using Likert-type scales. "In the instructions for these items, it was suggested that the use of human beings to accomplish these identical tasks would be reduced because of the use of computers. This suggestion was made because it provided a common reference point for responses to the items." This could produce a reaction that prejudices the response. Four areas of investigation were examined: relationships with previous research, perceptions of the computer, computers and dehumanization, and decisions regarding computer applications.

—*B. F. Cohen,* Aurora, CO

**REFERENCES**

[1] ZOLTAN, E.; AND CHAPANIS, A. What do professional persons think about computers?, *Behav. Inf. Tech.* **1** (1982), 55–68.

SEWELL, WINIFRED (Univ. of Maryland, College Park); AND TEITELBAUM, SANDRA     HCI-0235
(Welch Medical Library, Baltimore, MD)
**Observations of end-user online searching behavior over eleven years.**
*J. Am. Soc. Inf. Sci.* **37,** 4 (July 1986), 234–245.

REVIEWS [HCI-0236]

This paper is of interest to anybody concerned with end-user searching of online databases. It reports preliminary broad results of investigations conducted in the School of Pharmacy and the Department of Pathology at the University of Maryland from 1974 to 1984. The studies accompanied a program of end-user searching put in place by the authors: terminals in work areas with access to MEDLINE and other NLM databases, one-to-one instruction on a need-to-know basis, consultation, and a search manual were provided. Data were collected through computer monitoring (8,000 search sessions of 150 users, 70 of which are identifiable in at least some of their sessions), through a survey, and through observations of the authors in their interactions with the users.

Search logs were analyzed for content. Here is one sample result: While OR is seldom used explicitly, it is often used implicitly when a user enters two search statements such as "PHENELZINE AND AGORAPHOBIA" followed by "PHENIPRAZINE AND AGORAPHOBIA." Increasing sophistication of users and the effects of the search manual could be observed. While content analysis of search logs goes further than merely computing transition probabilities from one operation to the next, as well as other crude measures, it may not go far enough. Content analysis allows one to gauge the internal consistency of the search and its sophistication, but it can tell us little about other important questions: How adequate is the search with respect to the information needed? What is the searcher's rationale for the steps that he or she took? To answer these questions requires observation of the searchers (having them think aloud) with a follow-up interview. However, this method is much more expensive and could have been used only for a small sample of the search sessions.

The survey covered a whole range of topics regarding users' need for and satisfaction with online searching—both delegated and their own—and user attitudes to various methods of training. Many insights come from the author's interactions with the user. For example, it transpired that a user entering a search term expects to find material on all narrow terms as well, but no widely used search system delivers this kind of response as the default, and very few allow the user to achieve it through a special command, provided he knows it.

In summary, the paper describes a rich mine of data and gives some preliminary results of analysis. More detailed results are promised. Designers of online systems and administrators of libraries and information centers should look forward to gaining more insights from them.

—*D. Soergel,* College Park, MD

POWERS, MATTHEW; LASHLEY, CONDA; SANCHEZ, PAMELA; AND SHNEIDERMAN, BEN (Univ. of Maryland, College Park, MD)  HCI-0236
**An experimental comparison of tabular and graphic data presentation.**
*Int. J. Man-Mach. Stud.* **20,** 6 (June 1984), 545–566.

For presenting quantitative information, is it better to use graphics, tables, or a combination of display formats? What form of data presentation is easier to understand and remember?

To answer these questions, one needs to conduct a controlled study to help sort out the effects of factors like memory and display format on comprehension. Powers et al. have designed such an experiment to test the hypothesis that more usable information can be conveyed using a combination of graphic and tabular data than by using either format alone. In their study, data in graphic, tabular, and graphic + tabular formats were presented to subjects, who were later given a multiple-choice questionnaire to test their understanding of the material. The study was structured as a two-by-three experimental design: the independent variables were *memory* (two levels, recall vs. non-recall) and *format* (three levels, graphic vs. tabular vs. graphic + tabular). Material for the study consisted of hypothetical test scores and letter grades, which were arrayed in the formats described above and presented to 74 subjects (undergraduates in computer science courses). Performance of these subjects on the questionnaire was measured by a weighted method that took account of number of items attempted, number answered correctly, and complexity of each item.

Overall, the accuracy of performance (percentage correct) was highest when data were presented in the graphic + tabular format *and* subjects were not required to recall the materials from memory. From this finding, the authors go on to generalize to data users who wish to present quantitative information in business settings: viz., they should use both graphs and tables and review details prior to presenting the information at meetings. This recommendation is of course straightforward and useful as general advice, but does not follow directly from the work reported in the article. The experimental design has two major problems which stand in the way of making the generalization work:

(1) The variables of MEMORY and COMPREHENSION are defined ambiguously between data users ("managers") and data understanders ("audience"); but performance is measured solely by looking at how well the "audience" (subject pool) does on questionnaires.
(2) The graphic displays used in the study differ with respect to inherent complexity.

According to recent work of Cleveland and McGill [1], the line plots, pie charts, and bar graphs which comprise the "graphics" treatment in the experiment would each present different levels of perceptual difficulty to subjects.

In the opinion of this reviewer, future work should be focused on simplifying the experimental design and taking more care to control for materials effects, instead of increasing the complexity and volume of data to be presented to subjects (as the authors suggest). Advice on how to present data to the board of directors should wait for more conclusive findings!

—*J. R. Kornfeld,* Burlington, MA

**REFERENCES**

[1] CLEVELAND, W. S.; AND MCGILL, R. Graphical perception: theory, experimentation & applications to the development of graphical methods, *J. Am. Stat. Assoc.* **79** (1984), 531–554.

LEGGETT, JOHN; AND WILLIAMS, GLEN (Texas A & M Univ., College Station)     **HCI-0237**
**An empirical investigation of voice as an input modality for computer programming.**
*Int. J. Man-Mach. Stud.* **21,** 6 (Dec. 1984), 493–520.

The experiment discussed in this paper compared voice input with keyboard input in the use of a syntax-directed editor. The subjects were generally faster when using the keyboard than with using voice input. In the task of entering a program, however, the error rate for voice input was significantly less than that for keyboard; the difference was much smaller in the task of modifying a program.

The authors seem a little disappointed in their results, perhaps because the gee-whiz, hi-tech speech recognition approach was not shown to be unequivocably superior to plain old keyboards. However, the reminder that newer is not always better is what makes this work valuable. One wishes the authors would not keep using the expression "controlled experiment"; in this sort of research, anything that's not controlled shouldn't be called an experiment.

—*G. Hirst,* Toronto, Ont., Canada

## *Human information processing*

WOODS, DAVID D. (Westinghouse Research and Development Center, Pittsburgh, PA)    **HCI-0238**
**Visual momentum: a concept to improve the cognitive coupling of person and computer.**
*Int. J. Man-Mach. Stud.* **21,** 3 (Sept. 1984), 229–244.

The author proposes that the concept of "visual momentum," based upon knowledge about human perception, be used as a heuristic. So used, this concept is said to contribute to improved display design, so that users will be better able to cognitively process successive displays, thus maximizing the amount of information they obtain from the display system. "Visual momentum" is defined as "a measure of the user's ability to extract and integrate information across displays...a measure of the distribution of attention."

Looking at a CRT is a subset of the psychological perceptual processes involved in looking at the world. Certain general propositions from the psychological literature are referenced: i.e., perception is an active, selective process; the form of problem representation influences problem solving performance; and "cognitive maps" can be constructed by users. The principle of "visual momentum" consolidates several human performance problems with visual displays, in order to better inspire solutions. Techniques that provide information about the location of one view with respect to another increase the "visual momentum" within a display system. These include providing an outline or menu, landmarks, overlapping displays, or maps.

The strong feature of the paper is a carefully documented excursion into the relevant literature. The consolidation of ideas about computer display system use led to a worthwhile theoretical statement.

—*J. N. Rose,* Delhi, NY

STERNBERG, ROBERT J.; AND LASAGA, MARIA I. (Yale Univ., New Haven, CT)    **HCI-0239**
**Approaches to human reasoning: an analytic framework.**
[in *Artificial and human intelligence.* Proc. of the international NATO symposium (Lyon, France, Oct. 1981), A. Elithorn, and R. Banerji (Eds.), Elsevier North-Holland, Inc., New York, NY, 1984, 213–227.]

[See main entry, Review HCI-0052]

This paper compares and contrasts different approaches to the study of human reasoning. The authors classify the approaches in four broad categories: psychometric, stimulus-response, Gestalt, and information processing. The latter category is further divided into response-time-based, computer-based, and rule-based approaches.

The psychometric approach uses individual differences to isolate reasoning from other abilities. The focus of this research has been the role of reasoning in understanding intelligence. In contrast, the stimulus-response method emphasizes the role of past learning in present learning. Here again the primary focus has not been on reasoning per se. With its concern for perception, the Gestalt approach emphasizes the role of restructuring in the solution of problems. Rather than reasoning, this research studies individual behaviors that stand in the way of effective problem solving.

The response-time-based information processing approach assumes that a problem can be decomposed as a sequence of processes. The duration of each process can be determined by subtracting the time taken to complete a problem with one less element from the time to complete with the one element included. The rule-based approach assumes that reasoning can be characterized by the rules or ministrategies that individuals use in solving problems. A person's description of their problem solving is used to infer the rules that they are operating under. Finally, in the computer-based approach, a computer program is written to *functionally* simulate how human subjects solve problems.

To compare the approaches for research potential, three sets of criteria are used. The first set of criteria specifies what one learns about human reasoning from the approach. The second set states the form of input needed to test a theory and the form of output that is generated by the theory. Finally, the third set specifies the depth of analysis that could be obtained (competence) and that actually is attained (performance). Using 12 criteria, the authors conclude that the computer-based approach has the greatest research potential for understanding human reasoning. However, they assert that research will be served best by using converging operations. Even though they have their favorite method, they encourage the use of other productive approaches.

The authors claim to have been surprised with the results since their own previous work had been with the response-time and rule-based approaches. There is a sense, though, in which the analysis is a foregone conclusion given the selection of features of each approach and the criteria to evaluate these features. Using other features to characterize and other criteria for evaluation, the reader might come to a different conclusion about the relative value of the approaches. The reader with a general interest in the variety of theories about the nature of human reasoning will find Hampden-Turner's book [1] good reading. One- to three-page summaries are provided for 60 theories.

—*William Taggart,* Miami, FL

**REFERENCES**

[1] HAMPDEN-TURNER, C. *Maps of the mind*, Macmillan Publ. Co., New York, 1981.

LAVOREL, P. M. (CNRS; INSERM, Bron, France)
**The distributed processing of knowledge and belief in the human brain.**
[in *Artificial and human intelligence.* Proc. of the international NATO symposium (Lyon, France, Oct. 1981), A. Elithorn; and R. Banerji (Eds.), Elsevier North-Holland, Inc., New York, NY, 1984, 229–238.]

[See main entry, Review HCI-0052.]

# REVIEWS

The stated aim of this paper is to demonstrate that the "brain sciences" have much to offer to cognitive psychologists and computer system analysts. I can only applaud another attempt to break down the formal mathematical barriers with which present-day computer theoreticians seem determined to surround themselves. Unfortunately, it seems that the author has been let down in a variety of ways.

Most importantly, in terms of the contents: the editors, whose names are blazoned on the front of my reprint, have clearly not edited. The paper displays all the well-meaning disconnectedness of a first draft of a master's thesis. The author provides a pseudostructure of numbered paragraphs; however, this structure is not obvious in the written material. He announces the later treatment of subjects which are not heard of again. Lavorel throws pieces of jargon from several different fields into a mishmash of incomprehensibility. The paper ends in the middle of announcing an intriguing topic not mentioned in the summary: that, in any case, humans don't act in a logical way, which seems to destroy rather effectively the stated aim of the paper, i.e., to show that brain modeling "will have to find . . . its theory in the general tenets of computation and informatics."

Another problem concerns language. Certain statements may have read well in some other language, but more help should have been made available during translation. In spite of all this, some of the points raised are much too important in the future development of computing theory to be ignored.

The author adduces evidence from brain analyses to suggest:

- *Breakdown of hierarchical control concepts*—Information processing is often *duplicated* locally, and local results are propogated slowly to neighboring areas. At the same time, data is propogated quickly to selected distant locations by fibre bundles.
- *Inputs from different senses processed together*—Tissue specialized to the processing of visual, auditory, and somato-sensory inputs is closely associated with more generalized material.
- *Top-down and bottom-up processes co-existing*—The eye movements during reading show a mixture of detailed observation of some parts of a scene, and the ignoring of other parts in a deliberate way. Sometimes, processing is unsuccessful and the scanning process is modified and repeated.

A range of modeling principles is presented with which I concur heartily. They include:

- *Representation of knowledge as a database*—The relative importance of different experiences are weighted with respect to expected frequency of occurrence, and these weightings are modified as experience is obtained.
- *Provision of alternative processing strategies for analyzing inputs*—There will be no single consistent method of processing at a fixed level of detail as in present models. Alternative strategies will be tried when a selected one fails; it is always possible that all will fail, just as when a human "can't make sense" of something.
- *The need to tolerate inconsistent inputs*—This is clearly essential to have any hope of making sense of real-world inputs.

☐ *The need to 'forget'*—Forgetting is an essential part of a system which is taking on board new information all the time; otherwise the processing speed will tend to zero. Weights can be assigned to data depending on its frequency of use.

☐ *The need for some belief system to drive the processing*—Learning is essentially a setting up of biases or expectations about the world which enable the system to use its previous experience to avoid processing repeatedly the same information. Simple examples of expectations are such as: *A* is always followed by *B*, or *A* and *B* always occur together. These expectations cannot be modeled as simple tree structures because further experience must be allowed to "make connections" between previously "distant" nodes.

Finally the author speculates on what he sees as a threat: that dynamic adaptive systems such as he proposes may display human qualities which he considers unfortunate, such as paranoia.

The reviewer must now declare a personal interest, and probably a bias, in selecting out these important ideas from others presented in the paper. This is because he first supported them in 1973 [1] and has continued to present them, most recently in a popular UK microcomputing journal [2,3].

Let me applaud once again the attempt to juxtapose brain studies and computing theory, and encourage the author to continue to develop his ideas. However, we will require well-organized minds to tackle this interdiscipline, and even better organized reports if we are to communicate effectively with those from a wide range of backgrounds.

—*E. James,* London, UK

**REFERENCES**

[1] JAMES, E. B.; AND PARTRIDGE, D. P. Adaptive corrections of program statements, *Commun. ACM* **16** (1973), 27–37.

[2] JAMES, E. B. Teaching a computer to learn from your mistakes, *Pract. Comput.* **4** (1981), 70–72.

[3] JAMES, E. B. Beyond reasonable doubt, *Pract. Comput.* **5** (1982), 110–114.

---

SCHNEIDER, WERNER; LIND, MATS; ALLARD, ROBERT; AND SANDBLAD, BENGT (Uppsala Univ., Sweden)
**Human cognition and human computer interaction.**
[in *Readings on cognitive ergonomics - mind and computers.* Proc. of the 2nd European conference (Gmunden, Austria, Sept. 10-14, 1984), G. van der Veer; M. Tauber; T. Green; and P. Gorny (Eds.), Springer-Verlag New York, Inc., New York, NY, 1984, 76–80.]

[See main entry, Review HCI-0039]

The authors announce their intention to present an alternative approach to human-computer interaction—presumably an alternative to verbal communication via keyboard and screen. They proceed from the assumption that in order to use a program effectively, the user must understand how it works. This assumption is based on their statement "Not too long ago the programmer and. . .user were. . .the same," although this has been true to a limited extent in scientific computation and has never been true in data processing.

REVIEWS [HCI-0243]

The authors propose that human-computer interfaces should be so designed that the user will think of the program as a set of operators operating on a data structure which is perceived as a three-dimensional geometrical construct. However, they do not suggest how this can be done.

—*J. J. Hirschfelder,* Seattle, WA

Murphy, Elizabeth D.; and Mitchell, Christine M. (Computer Technology Associates, McLean, VA; and Georgia Institute of Technology, Atlanta)     **HCI-0242**
**Cognitive attributes: implications for display design in supervisory control systems.**
*Int. J. Man-Mach. Stud.* **25,** 4 (Oct. 1986), 411–438.

Using a combination of relevant perspectives from the literature in cognitive psychology, the authors identify 18 attributes of human cognition and provide a critique of display design implications for each one. Their intent is to delineate a background for empirical research on alternative human-computer interface design. Some of their suggestions might also be implemented in existing supervisory control system modifications, that is, to alter displays to enhance operator functions.

The best features of the paper are the thoughtful suggestions for improvement upon traditional design approaches, as well as the examples from command and control environments. Three typographical errors detract somewhat from the presentation, and the overview of the cognitive system is a bit confusing concerning how components are counted.

In spite of these limitations, I would recommend this document to persons involved in the design or modification of supervisory control systems because of the numerous practical ideas and suggestions. Overall, I was impressed with the way the paper neatly combines theory and practice.

—*J. N. Rose,* Delhi, NY

Kawai, Hideo; Tamura, Shinichi (Osaka Univ., Osaka, Japan); Kani, Kazutaka     **HCI-0243**
(Hyogo College of Medicine, Hyogo, Japan); and Kariya, Kmoyo (Ritsumeikan Univ., Kyoto, Japan)
**Eye movement analysis system using fundus images.**
*Pattern Recogn.* **19,** 1 (Jan./Feb. 1986), 77–84.

The authors report a small computer system that performs analysis of eye movements. The system might be useful in helping with a few ophthalmic procedures. It is difficult to see how the system could be of general use in human-machine studies. It is too narrow in scope and too slow in processing time. There is some evidence that the authors can detect foveation. They say that other systems cannot detect rotational movement and that they plan to. They do not claim that they can yet detect rotational movement. It is unclear whether this system is any better than other systems for detecting eye movements. The reported system is slow; they hope to speed it up. This has a familiar ring of hope. We need evidence of operating results. This seems to be a preliminary report. It would have been better if the authors had waited until they had completed further studies and refined the system before reporting. It appears that the paper is a translation from Japanese into English, with several awkward phrases. It is suggested that any interested readers contact the authors for more complete information.

—*G. Carlson,* Provo, UT

[HCI-0244]  NONBOOKS

LANDAUER, THOMAS K. (Bell Communications Research, Morristown, NJ)   HCI-0244
**Relations between cognitive psychology and computer system design.**
[in *Interfacing thought: cognitive aspects of human-computer interaction,* J. Carroll (Ed.), MIT Press, Cambridge, MA, 1987, 1-25.]

As the title implies, this paper shows how cognitive psychology can be used by computer systems designers. The author organizes the paper around four major themes that relate the benefits of cognitive psychology to systems design work. These four themes are (1) the application of existing knowledge and principles, (2) the application of theoretical machinery, (3) the application of investigative methods, and (4) applied knowledge as a source of research for cognitive psychology. Simply stated, the author argues that designers of computer systems can benefit greatly from those psychological studies that show how people process and organize information.

Along with praising his colleagues, Landauer is critical of some of the present studies done by cognitive psychologists. For example, he notes the field's "fascination with the act" rather than an effort to discover a realistic approach to the problem of what makes a system effective or ineffective. The author also recognizes the need to translate the experimental world into the world of design. Further, he cautions his colleagues to use statistics properly by discussing the difference between comparing two systems and comparing a single feature shared by two systems.

This chapter is useful for computer system designers who are interested in integrating cognitive psychology into their work. Although he promotes the field of cognitive psychology, the author presents a realistic view of how systems designers can use this science. One can only hope that a similar paper is being written by the system designers to be shared with the cognitive psychologists.

—*K. M. Swigger,* Denton, TX

SIMON, TONY (ARC Applied Psychology Unit., UK)   HCI-0245
**Analysing the scope of cognitive models in human-computer interaction: a trade-off approach.**
[in *People and computers IV.* Proceedings of the Fourth Conference of the British Computer Society (Univ. of Manchester, UK, Sept. 5–6, 1988), D. Jones; and R. Winder (Eds.), Cambridge University Press, New York, NY, 1988, 79–93.]

Simon attempts to provide a taxonomy of cognitive models of human-computer interaction. I agree with his belief that referring to the taxonomy will help would-be users of such models to select the best model for the pariticular job they have in mind.

On can learn some interesting things about human-computer interaction models by reading this paper carefully. I am not convinced, however, that the comparative diagrammatic representation the author presents is at all necessary. A simple checklist of criteria for each model discussed might have been a reasonable alternative. In particular, I found that eight acronyms in the diagram confusing, as they are not identified in a legend. Aside from this flaw in the presentation, I believe the suggested audience would appreciate the statements about the different applications and the limitations of each of the models discussed.

—*J. N. Rose,* Delhi, NY

# REVIEWS

## ZOG

McCracken, Donald L.; and Akscyn, Robert M. (Carnegie-Mellon Univ., Pittsburgh, PA)
**Experience with the ZOG human-computer interface system.**
*Int. J. Man-Mach. Stud.* **21**, 4 (Oct. 1984), 293–310.

HCI-0246

This article is primarily a reflection on more than 8 years of research with the ZOG human-computer interface system. During that time we have experienced extensive use of ZOG. We begin this article with a short description of the current ZOG implementation; then we proceed to a higher plane to describe a general ZOG philosophy that has evolved from our experience. Following the philosophy, we briefly describe the applications we have explored with ZOG, including a major application project for the Navy. Then we provide a critique of the current ZOG implementation by elucidating its strong and weak points. We end the paper with a brief glimpse at our plans for ZOG in the future.

—*Authors' Abstract*

This paper provides a status report on the ZOG human-computer interaction research project, which continues at Carnegie-Mellon University. That system is based primarily on the concept of menu selection. The paper is recommended to anyone with an interest in user interfaces. It is informative and supplies guidelines to others constructing similar systems.

—*N. S. Coulter,* Boca Raton, FL

### H.1.m Miscellaneous

Yager, Ronald R. (Iona College, New Rochelle, NY)
**Measuring the quality of linguistic forecasts.**
*Int. J. Man-Mach. Stud.* **21**, 3 (Sept. 1984), 253–257.

HCI-0247

This is an interesting and well-written short paper presenting a possible approach to representing linguistic forecasts by the use of fuzzy set theory. Forecasts such as weather predictions of a low temperature "around 20 " is what is meant here by a linguistic forecast. The quality criteria in such forecasts should involve specificity as well as validity of the forecast. The use of fuzzy sets is introduced as a natural mechanism for dealing with this imprecision in linguistic forecasts. Validity is represented by a truth measure of Bellman and Zadeh [1] which is basically the membership grade of the actual value occurring in the fuzzy subset corresponding to the linguistic forecast (in general, the actual *value* itself may be a fuzzy subset). Yager then proposes, as a specificity measure, a summation of the inverse of the cardinality of alpha-level sets of the fuzzy forecast set. This measure is similar to ordinary entropy and is combined with the truthfulness criteria by a Nash type "anding" to provide an overall quality of forecast measure.

—*F. Petry,* New Orleans, LA

**REFERENCES**

[1] Bellman, R. E.; and Zaden, L. A. Logical and fuzzy logics, in *Modern uses of multivalued logic*, J. M. Dunn and G. Epstein (Eds.), D. Reidel Publ. Co., Hinghams, MA, 1977, 103–165.

## H.2  Database Management

### H.2.0  General

**ARES**

ICHIKAWA, TADAO; AND HIRAKAWA, MASAHITO (Hiroshima Univ., Higashi-Hiroshima, Japan)  **HCI-0248**
**ARES: a relational database with the capability of performing flexible interpretation of queries.**
*IEEE Trans. Softw. Eng.* **SE-12,** 5 (May 1986), 624–634.

This paper describes a system called ARES which extends the usual relational comparators "=", "<", etc. to include "@", which means "approximately equal to." This extension is meaningful only for read-only operations.

ARES includes a two-dimensional formatted screen (QBE-style) user interface for queries, as well as interactive tools to allow the user to quantify "approximately" for pairs of values in domains from which selections are to be made.

The motivation for this work is to make databases easier to use for nonprofessionals, according to the authors. However, I feel there is a basic contradiction in this approach. If the measure of similarity between domain element pairs is to be assigned by the user, that user must do considerable work with fairly unwieldy machinery. If the assignment (which is based on the semantics of the data) is performed by a professional, it would seem quite fortuitous if the professional's quantitative estimates matched the user's.

This work is interesting in what it tries to accomplish. Whether this approach is the most promising way to attack the problem must be decided by the reader.

—*C. R. Attanasio,* Yorktown Heights, NY

### H.2.1  Logical Design

COBB, RICHARD E.; FRY, JAMES P.; AND TEOREY, TOBY J. (Univ. of Michigan, Ann Arbor)  **HCI-0249**
**The database designer's workbench.**
*Inf. Sci. (New York)* **32,** 1 (Feb. 1984), 33–45.

This paper discusses an experimental tool for database design. The tool is implemented on a Multics-based system using an IBM PC as a graphics generator. In addition to providing better access to the data dictionary and a preliminary data manipulation language design, the system also includes a logical record access evaluator to judge actual read requirements and a usage dependency model to indicate where physical joins on the database may be necessary.

This paper is too short for a discussion of anything except the basic concept. Tools of this nature will be necessary if data administration and database administration are to beome more than the black arts they are currently based on. Combining a graphics workstation based on a PC is also likely to take place in the future, but that development will require a better defined graphic interface architecture than currently exists.

—*Charles W. Bash,* Midland, MI

# REVIEWS

## Data models

HUDSON, SCOTT E.; AND KING, ROGER (Univ. of Colorado, Boulder)     **HCI-0250**
**A generator of direct manipulation office systems.**
*ACM Trans. Office Inf. Syst.* **4,** 2 (April 1986), 132–163.

This paper describes a generator of Direct Manipulation Office Systems (DMOS). According to the authors, in a DMOS, "... the user directly manipulates graphical representations of office entities instead of dealing with these entities abstractly through a command language or menu system." The HIGGENS system (Human Interface Graphical Generation System) does not seem to be restricted to the domain of office systems, as it is used in the paper. HIGGENS is composed of three parts: *active data*, which encapsulates not only data but a description of its semantics in a nonprocedural specification through the use of attribute grammars; *semantic restructuring view generators*, which filter the underlying active data and construct useful "views" into the stored information; and a *picture planning* system, which generates the actual graphical objects that reflect the constructed views. This separation of active data, filtering processes, and rendering processes allows the implementor to focus his attention on each area in turn and generate very modular systems. Constraint propagation using Boolean attributes, coupled with a lazy evaluation scheme in a dataflow architecture, makes the system both efficient and responsive. Simple undo and macro capabilities are also provided.

The paper is wordy and could have been shortened through the judicious use of extra diagrams. The concepts behind the system are simple and the theory behind the implementation straightforward. Uninteresting details, like the section on display primitives, could have been considerably shortened with no loss of information. An example is used effectively in the paper to illustrate the DMOS generation process.

The paper is aimed at the technical reader who has little knowledge of User Interface Management Systems (UIMS) and Direct Manipulation Office Systems (DMOS). A general computer science background is assumed, but no knowledge of advanced (graduate-level) concepts is required.

—*W. Lee*, Sunnyvale, CA


FIADEIRO, JOSE; AND SERNADAS, AMILCAR (Instituto Superior Técnico, Portugal)     **HCI-0251**
**Specification and verification of database dynamics.**
*Acta Inf.* **25,** 6 (Aug. 1988), 625–661.

This paper introduces a language for the structured specification and verification of databases; this language is based on an extended many-sorted first-order linear tense logic. The authors apply research in object-oriented modeling to the algebraic semantics of conceptual modeling of dynamic databases.

An event-triggering formalism provides the conceptual modeling framework that allows the authors to assume an integrated and structured approach to the specification and verification of the behavioral aspects of databases. The authors use these events to model atomic database operations and communication actions; causal relationships between events thus model behavioral aspects of the database. Logical formulas that state the validity conditions of events and triggers are used to specify processes; processes are then considered in terms of trigger/reaction patterns of behavior. The authors outline an axiomatic approach to computational semantics of events and processes and illustrate some concepts for data integrity and verification of the safety and liveness of properties of processes.

The paper is very long and based on examples. The reader will, however, need some knowledge of the theoretical fundamentals of algebraic semantics and object-oriented modeling, and of solutions for concurrency problems in databases, to understand and evaluate it.

—*B. Thalheim,* Kuwait and Rostock

### H.2.3 Languages

#### GQBR

PATNAIK, L. M. (Indian Institute of Science, Bangalore, India); AND CHOWDHARY, D. M. (Reactor Research Centre, Kalpakkam, India)
**Generalized query-by-rule: a heterogeneous database query language.**
*Comput. Lang. (Elmsford, NY)* **10,** 3/4 (1985), 165–178.

The authors identify the "need for an interface between the user and non-integrated (heterogeneous distributed database) environment." After listing seven general problems which such an interface should solve, all of which are valid, the paper goes on to limit itself to a treatment of one of the problems. The general problem discussed is that of "transforming a query expressed in the user's language into a set of subqueries expressed in the languages supported by local database management systems." The paper further limits itself to a specific facet of the general problem: the "development of a user-friendly interface by which one can issue queries."

There seems to be a conflict inherent in these two statements. The general problem states that the user's language will be transformed into subqueries, and the specific problem addressed is the development of a (new) user-friendly interface by which one can issue queries.

The (new) user-friendly interface, Generalized Query-by-Rule (GQBR), is based on "a recently developed formalism called database logic," and the illustrations are contrasted with GCALC (Generalized Calculus Data Manipulation Language). The "syntax of GQBR has been obtained by simplifying the syntax of GCALC."

Although the interface constructs are well developed and adequately explained, the paper suffers from a number of deficiencies. The major one is that although it claims to describe an interface which "is capable of specifying complex queries for network, hierarchical, and relational databases," the examples and illustrations are all network oriented, and it is unclear as to how it would work in either the relational or hierarchical modes. There is an Appendix which illustrates the definition of all three modes using Database Logic "views." Since GQBR is based on database views defined in Database Logic form, this would seem to imply the need for the additional step of defining all of the user heterogeneous databases using the constructs of Database Logic. The databases could then be interrogated by the GQBR compiler. It also seems to be the authors' intention to replace the DML of the subject DBMS with the GQBR language.

REVIEWS [HCI-0253]

The second major deficiency is with the illustrations themselves. There are a number of typos within the illustrative text, the illustrations are not consistent and the mixture of type fonts used in the illustrations makes those that are presented very difficult to cross-reference to either themselves or to the database views. Additionally, data element names are referenced in the query examples which do not appear within the defined schema, and the illustrative database definitions and queries do not seem to match the schematic diagrams which accompany them.

Although billed as a simplified query language, GQBR is complex and confusing. It would seem to need further simplification to be truly useful.

—*M. E. Modell,* Cambridge, MA

## HERCULES

CUFF, R. N. (IBM United Kingdom Laboratories Ltd., Winchester, Hampshire, UK)  HCI-0253
**HERCULES: database query using natural language fragments.**
[in *Proc. of the third British national conference on databases (BNCOD3).* (Leeds, UK, July 11-13, 1984), J. Longstaff (Ed.), Cambridge University Press, New York, NY, 1984, 133–149.]

Great strides have been made toward ease-of-use in today's relational database systems. The query syntax and navigational requirements have been simplified. However, they still pose serious problems for the casual user who may not know important details such as available tables and their system names, or who may be seriously disadvantaged trying to formulate a complex query. Natural language, on the other hand, is often ambiguous. It does not automatically allow for system specific naming conventions, and it creates unrealistic expectations of the system's power.

In this paper, the author introduces a database interface called HERCULES (HEuristic Retrieval: a Casual User LanguagE System) which integrates the formalism of relational query languages with the flexibility of natural languages. A natural language interface uses predefined information about the database to help the user interactively formulate a query. Once the proper query is constructed, it can be submitted to the database to be satisfied. The author developed a prototype in ULISP to demonstrate the feasibility and compared it favorably in several examples with Query Be Examples (QBE).

The author presents a lot of good ideas through this prototype; consequently, this paper should be of great interest to anyone interested in database query languages or the integration of database theory with artificial intelligence. There are two potential problems. First, it is no major conquest for a tailored, well-targeted prototype such as HERCULES to outperform a full-blown implementation such as QBE in certain specific instances. Second, the prototype, if implemented, would place a heavy, if not impossible, burden on the DBA to define the database fully to HERCULES since the data it requires is far beyond the data normally captured in the data dictionary.

—*J. M. Artz,* Rockville, MD

## Query languages

VASSILIOU, YANNIS; AND JARKE, MATTHIAS (New York Univ., New York)  **HCI-0254**
**Query languages—a taxonomy.**
[in *Human factors and interactive computer systems*. Proc. of the NYU symposium on user interfaces (New York, May 26-28, 1982), Y. Vassiliou (Ed.), Ablex Publishing Corp., Norwood, NJ, 1984, 47–81.]

[See main entry, Review HCI-0038.]

> The taxonomies developed in this paper are based on a new interpretation of the development of database query languages as being influenced by the areas of programming languages, database management, and human factors engineering. This observation led to a two-level classification of query languages: by the user senses employed, and by the language methods used. The language types were illustrated by examples and characterized using a uniform two-level evaluation scheme. In addition, [they] developed a comprehensive classification scheme of query language users from which most existing user categorizations can be derived.
>
> —*From the Authors' Conclusion*

Forty-nine query languages were examined in the study, in varying degree of detail. The tables of language comparisons would be interesting to anyone involved in the design or use of query languages. An encouraging result of the study is summarized in the closing remarks:

> Each single language type will have problems accommodating the variety of user types discussed in this paper. [The authors] envision future query languages employing multiple interaction modes in order to have a broader coverage and usability. In addition, [they] believe that new languages will provide facilities allowing users to customize the interaction to their own needs and preferences.

—*J. Fedorowicz*, Boston, MA


TURNER, JONN A.; JARKE, MATTHIAS; STOHR, EDWARD A.; AND VASSILIOU, YANNIS  **HCI-0255**
(New York Univ., New York, NY)
**Using restricted natural language for data retrieval: a plan for field evaluation.**
[in *Human factors and interactive computer systems*. Proc. of the NYU symposium on user interfaces (New York, May 26-28, 1982), Y. Vassiliou (Ed.), Ablex Publishing Corp., Norwood, NJ, 1984, 163–190.]

[See main entry, Review HCI-0038.]

The first results of this study-in-progress indicate that people querying databases perform at about the same level whether they are using an artificial or a natural language. Eight subjects were trained to access an alumni database. Some used a restricted natural language query system known as the User Specialty Language; others used the formal language SQL, a predecessor of SEQUEL. A detailed experimental design is given, with lengthy statistical analyses of results of the first part of the study. The report concludes with a set of general observations that are of general interest to those involved in database query languages. As the authors point out, not much of statistical significance can be concluded from a sample of eight users, but the research plan for the study might be of interest to those designing similar experiments.

—*R. W. Sauvain*, Rochester, NY

WILLIAMS, MICHAEL D. (IntelliGenetics, Menlo Park, CA)
**What makes RABBIT run?.**
*Int. J. Man-Mach. Stud.* **21,** 4 (Oct. 1984), 333–352.

A novel database query facility was implemented using three main windows and pop-up windows. The user views a presentation of entity and attribute names and values which can be refined by six critiques: require, prohibit, alternatives, describe, specialize, and predicate. As critiques are applied by mouse pointing and clicking, the searcher gets closer to the intended query and result.

This is an intriguing alternative to the usual query language, with some similarity to Query-by-Example. Entity-by-Example-and-Instance might be a descriptive name. Since retrieval is the goal, neither insert/delete/update nor database definition appear to be supported.

I am attracted to the idea underlying the design and would like to see further refinement and enhancement. The current report does not deal adequately with the question of the expressiveness of RABBIT. A more precise discussion about whether relational completeness was attained would have been appropriate; even a comparison with SQL or QBE would have helped to convey the power of RABBIT. Also, there is no empirical trial or even a description of whether any community of users successfully employed RABBIT. By now the proliferation of query facilities demands that researchers provide more than personal testimonial.

Authors of papers on user interface design have a special responsibility in showing exemplars of excellence. Careful review and testing should have eliminated such distractions as a misspelled menu title, meaningless font or case changes for words, a mixture of centered and left-justified menus, and the inadequate visual presentation of embedded queries ({QUERY}.A0055' is not comprehensible to me). Considering the concern for screen space limitations, I also could not understand why the RABBIT window set appears to have an unused L-shaped area surrounding the Query window. Finally, would an entity-relationship diagram have been preferred to the indented textual presentation?

—*B. Shneiderman*, College Park, MD

DE, SURANJAN; PAN, SHUH-SHEN; AND WHINSTON, ANDREW B. (Purdue Univ., West Lafayette, IN)
**Natural language query processing in a temporal database.**
*Data Knowl. Eng.* **1,** 1 (June 1985), 3–15.

This paper starts off by outlining a number of interesting goals. Choosing equational logic as their vehicle, the authors address a number of issues on representations and querying of temporal information in a database setting. In addition, in order to provide a natural language interface to the temporal database, they aim at dealing with natural language sentences including those with a temporal reference.

Knowledge representation is done by using a scheme that is based on points and intervals. They consider all the possible relationships between points and intervals, such as "point 1 is before point 2" or "interval 1 overlaps interval 2." However, this scheme is hardly used in the subsequent sections. (A reference, though, is made to a previous internal report that discusses how the temporal system can be incorporated into the equational logic framework [1].)

The most interesting section of the paper is the one dealing with natural language processing. The authors have developed algorithms for translating queries written in a natural language into executable expressions. After discussing the classification of the rules of grammar, they present (through a number of examples) how natural language queries are dealt with.

Overall, the project is interesting and seems to have good potential. As a followup, it would be appropriate to work out a formal semantics for the extension to equational logic of temporal framework.

—*F. Golshani,* Tempe, AZ

**REFERENCES**

[1] DE, S.; PAN, S.-S.; WHINSTON, A. B. Temporal semantics and natural language processing in decision support systems, Working Paper, Krannert School of Management, Purdue Univ., May 1984.

LARSON, JAMES A. (Honeywell Computer Science Center)
**A visual approach to browsing in a database environment.**
*Computer* **19,** 6 (June 1986), 62–71. [Computer science education in the US.]

Database management systems are large, complex pieces of software, and their query languages are equally large and complex. SQL, for example, was originally put forward as a language which would enable the nonprogramming end-user to retrieve data easily from large databases. It is now generally agreed, however, that SQL is totally unsuited for this task. On the other hand, the graphical approach proposed in this paper is aimed specifically and, perhaps, exclusively, at the end-user.

Such graphical interface systems are commonly found in database packages for microcomputers but are difficult to provide in a sufficiently flexible and efficient form for large databases on mainframe computers. The author's method can be regarded as an up-to-date version of one of the earliest and most successful graphical interfaces to databases, namely Query-by-Example. Rather than the flat two-dimensional approach of Query-by-Example, he makes extensive use of templates and windows to provide a powerful method of retrieving information from general databases.

The author identifies four operations which he feels form the basis of database browsing for the user who has only a vague notion of the information he is seeking, but will probably recognize it when he sees it. These operations are *structuring*, which is equivalent to the selection of a database subschema; *filtering*, selecting particular instances of the objects identified as being of interest; *panning*, examining neighboring instances of those objects; and *zooming*, determining the level of detail for examining object instances. Experience with micro-based software and fourth generation languages has shown that graphical interfaces are much easier for end-users than command-driven interfaces. In the corporate database environment, however, these systems will have to run alongside conventional "heavy-duty" computing (accounts, payroll, etc.), and performance is likely to be an important factor.

—*J. B. Grimson,* Dublin, Ireland

ZEMANKOVA, MARIA (Univ. of Tennessee, Knoxville); AND KANDEL, ABRAHAM  **HCI-0259**
(Florida State Univ., Tallahassee)
**Implementing imprecision in information systems.**
*Inf. Sci. (New York)* **37,** 1/2/3 (Dec. 1985), 107–141. [Special issue on expert systems.]

Will the ability to process "fuzzy" queries like "Select city from USA where summer-temperature is not much greater than winter-temperature" become one of the key factors determining the (commercial) success of the next generation DBMS? Are the potential users of such DBMSs interested in tailoring the comparison operators (e.g., "greater than") to their individual perception of data? If so, this paper would be of particular value to any professional in the DBMS field. In any case, it describes an interesting application of a fuzzy set theory.

The paper starts with an introduction to the fuzzy sets and relational databases. It proceeds with the Fuzzy Relational Data Base (FRDB) model and query language description. Finally, some hints about the implementation are given. All of this is presented in a clear manner with a lot of useful examples.

Somewhat surprisingly, the DB schema has not been considered to be a part of the FRDB architecture. Also, it would be interesting to have at least a fuzzy evaluation of the cost for "F" in the FRDB, both in terms of the preparatory work to be done by the user and in terms of the complexity of the query processing algorithms.

—*J. Tepandi,* Tallinn, USSR

BROSDA, VOLKERT (Institut für Informatik, TU Clausthal, W. Germany); AND VOSSEN,  **HCI-0260**
GOTTFRIED (Lehrstuhl für Angewandte Mathematik, RWTH Aachen, W. Germany)
**Update and retrieval in a relational database through a universal schema interface.**
*ACM Trans. Database Syst.* **13,** 4 (Dec. 1988), 449–485.

The authors attempt to lay the theoretical foundations for a universal schema interface. They claim that the user of a database based on a universal relation (UR) model is freed of the burden of knowing its logical structure when he or she is either querying the database (a situation for which theoretical support already existed) or updating it. To restrict updates to "meaningful" ones, however, the user has to know which "objects" (combinations of attributes) were specified during the design phase of the database. In my opinion this necessity just makes implicit what would otherwise be explicit knowledge about functional constraints. Of course, it is important that users need not know where some attributes are found.

Brosda and Vossen define two types of update transactions: insertion and deletion. They propose a new notion of "insertability" for a database scheme with no necessarily unique relation schemes and derive several new results on objects and their "uniqueness regions."

The authors state definitions and theorems clearly in the context of previous work in the field, give comprehensive proofs, and supply a large body of examples. It might have been useful to relate newer concepts and conditions to classical ideas in relational database theory, such as the various normal forms.

Only a general knowledge of relational database theory is necessary to understand this paper fully. I recommend it to everyone interested in database design.

—*Edward Sava-Segal,* Bucharest, Romania

### VIADUCT

SCHACH, STEPHEN R. (Vanderbilt Univ., Nashville, TN); AND WOOD, PETER T. (Univ. of Toronto, Toronto, Ont., Canada)
**An almost path-free very high-level interactive data manipulation language for a microcomputer-based database system.**
*Softw. Pract. Exper.* **16,** 3 (March 1986), 243–268.

The work described in this paper has its origins in the MDBS database management system developed by Micro Data Base Systems, Inc., of Lafayette, Indiana. MDBS uses the CODASYL network data model, which is unusual for a microcomputer-based database management system.

Micro Data Base Systems also provides a stand-alone query/report language, QRS, for querying MDBS databases. QRS requires explicit path specification, which the authors of this paper feel is not compatible with ease-of-use. Also, QRS is a retrieve-only language.

To overcome these limitations, the authors developed the VIADUCT language. VIADUCT provides commands and menus for creating, maintaining, and listing MDBS databases. The language allows reference only to records and items (for example, "LIST TEACHER.NAME, SECTION.TITLE, STUDENT.NAME"). Reference to sets is not provided. (The terms "record," "item," and "set" are CODASYL terms.) If there is a single primary entry path to a specified record, it is used. (A primary entry path is one that is unique, or, that consists only of *automatic* and *fixed* or *mandatory* sets.) If multiple primary entry paths exist, VIADUCT will automatically choose the one that minimizes the number of record accesses. If no primary entry path exists, the user will be asked to choose one. It is in this sense that VIADUCT is "almost path-free."

The bulk of the paper is devoted to a detailed description of the VIADUCT user interface and path-finding algorithms. The descriptions are clearly written and should be of value to persons developing end-user interfaces to CODASYL-type databases.

Although VIADUCT is characterized as a "very high-level" DML, it is actually at the same logical level as the CODASYL data model. It appears to be at a higher logical level because the CODASYL set construct is (normally) not visible to the end-user. The down-side of this strategy is that it prevents the user from using his or her knowledge of the relationships that exist in a database in order to make queries more precise or more efficient. The use of relationship information in queries is not, in the reviewer's opinion, inconsistent with ease-of-use objectives, and need not (as is commonly assumed) expose the implementation or "structure" of the database to the user.

—*W. C. McGee,* Los Altos, CA

## H.2.4 Systems

AMANO, KANAME; AND MOCHIDA, AKENO (Hokkaido Univ. Computing Center, Sapporo, Japan)  **HCI-0262**
**A supporting system for effective construction and sharing of scientific databases by general researchers.**
Inf. Process. Manage. **21,** 6 (Dec. 1985), 535–544.

A supporting system is presented for effective construction and sharing of scientific databases in a research environment, where various databases are constructed by general users who are often not familiar with the information retrieval system ORION and the database management system ADABAS. The Hokkaido University Computing Center adopted ORION and ADABAS as basic software and implemented a supporting system called COMDBS (Controlling Monitor of DataBase Systems). COMDBS consists of a database called DBAT (DataBase Administration Table), which stores dictionary information on the individual databases, and a set of commands for their effective construction and utilization. Users can construct and share their databases easily by themselves with full functions of ORION and ADABAS. About 30 databases have been constructed by general users.

The paper is simply written and illustrated with a number of figures. Here is the authors' list of subjects: Classification of databases; Main commands of COMDBS; General organization of COMDBS; General flow of works for ORION database construction; COMDBS commands for ORION database construction; Flow of works for ORION database construction with COMDBS commands; Example of an ORION database construction; ORION data structures and user interface; and ADABAS data structure and user interface.

—*P. Vondracek,* Prague, Czechoslovakia

## DAVID

LAENDER, A. H.F.; AND STOCKER, P. M. (Univ. of East Anglia, Norwich, UK)  **HCI-0263**
**An interactive database end user facility for the definition and manipulation of forms.**
[in *Research and development in information retrieval.* Proc. of the third joint BCS and ACM symposium (King's College, Cambridge, July 2–6, 1984), C. van Rijsbergen (Ed.), Cambridge University Press, New York, NY, 1984, 41–54.]

A system named DAVID has been proposed and partially implemented which is designed to help the user in defining and manipulating his own view on a (relational) database of hierarchically related data items. DAVID resolves any incomplete or ambiguous requests by a sequence of questions to the user which have to be answered by "yes" or "no" confirming or denying the conjectures of DAVID. The text of these questions is based on simple statements by the database administrator on the semantic relations between entity types and their data items. The system is able, for example, to find the correct field among a number of equally named fields related to different entity types. Once the user's view is set up, queries to the database can be issued by specifying the permitted values or ranges of some variables. It seems that the user has to know the correct field names but not the structure of the database.

—*F. Gebhardt,* St. Augustin, West Germany

## H.3 Information Storage and Retrieval

### H.3.0 General

VICKERY, A. (Univ. of London, London, UK)
**An intelligent interface for online interaction.**
*J. Inf. Sci. Princ. Pract.* **9,** 1 (Aug. 1984), 7–18.

The need to incorporate some form of "intelligence" into information retrieval systems has been recognized by many researchers, many of whom (e.g., Clarke and Cronin [1], Hjerppe [2], and Smith [3]) have tentatively looked towards the use of techniques that are now emerging from the area of artificial intelligence. In her paper, Vickery concentrates on AI techniques likely to be of value in the human-computer interface, roughly corresponding to the query formulation stage.

Vickery provides a good review, along with nearly 80 references, of recent research into the interface by both the AI and information retrieval communities. She sees the goal of both communities as the construction of an automated intermediary. Vickery gives a comprehensive list of user requirements for an intelligent interface, including a learning mechanism, knowledge of the user, and assistance in the selection of search strategies. Each of these poses its own particular challenges; for example, it is not obvious how an effective learning mechanism could be developed in the face of a multitude of different queries from a large, heterogeneous user population. Vickery discusses our limited understanding of the nature of human-computer interaction through a useful classification of the problem areas into: (1) personal knowledge structures, (2) the nature of questions, (3) interaction in question-answering, and (4) the structure of subject domains. In the first of these, she mentions semantic networks, scripts, and the influences on information-seeking behavior as being potentially valuable tools. In the third, she commendably emphasizes the social nature and value judgements of any interaction, whether that interaction is human-human or human-computer.

From the field of AI, Vickery selects the following techniques as being particularly relevant to information retrieval: natural language interfaces, knowledge elicitation techniques, and problem solving modes. Natural language interfaces are high on the list of desiderata for any computer-based system, but her proposal to use knowledge elicitation techniques to determine the users' requirements is an interesting idea, as is her analogy between searching for documents and expert system problem solving. In the latter case, she sees backward-chaining, forward-chaining, and heuristic problem solving as being, in theory at least, transferable to information retrieval.

Where the user is interacting with an information system in a problem solving task, such as information retrieval (and decision support systems), the interface is obviously of considerable importance and the best available tools should be utilized to make such interaction easier and more effective. However, in the case of information retrieval, two reservations come to mind. The first applies to the underlying system, to which the intelligent interface is but a (crucial) gateway. Unlike structured databases, information retrieval databases are severely lacking in semantic information. Searches are usually based on content with documents represented by a string of index terms. These terms may be related to each other through a thesaurus showing "broader term," "narrower term," or "related term," but there is a significant loss of semantic information with such a crude representation. The richness of ideas, the way the terms are related within the document, and the objectives and conclusions of the document are lost. The ultimate challenge to AI techniques in information retrieval would seem to be in this area of document representation and the associated matching of those representations with queries. Documents have been the basic receptacles of knowledge, especially scientific knowledge, since the introduction of writing and so the issue becomes one of knowledge representation in the broadest possible sense. As it is, an intelligent interface hooked up to a system relying on the Boolean matching of bare index terms is liable to be seriously constrained.

This point leads directly to the second concern. The "internal" problems of document representation and matching have been the subject of considerable research by the information retrieval community through experiments in automatic indexing, the weighting of terms in queries and documents, and the clustering of similar documents together through statistical techniques. However, the common factor in most of this research is that, despite the apparent success of many of the experimental evaluations of these techniques, very few have been adopted in practice by the large database vendors. Whether this is just a temporary delay, or results from more profound problems of commercial feasibility or machine efficiency, is debatable. Vickery appears to assume that such improved internal processes will be available; while this may be true in research environments, it is less likely in commercial practice. Alternatively, the arrival of intelligent interfaces may prove to be the catalyst to an overhaul of the internal workings of large textual databases.

In conclusion, Vickery's paper is a further advance in laying the foundations for the application of AI techniques in information retrieval. It should be widely read.

—*S. Smithson,* London, UK

**REFERENCES**

[1] CLARKE, A.; AND CRONIN, B. Expert systems in library information work, *J. Libr.* **15** (1983), 277–292.

[2] HJERPPE, R. What artificial intelligence can, could and can't do for libraries and information sources, in *Proc. 7th int. online inf. mtg.* (London, Dec. 1983), Learned Inf., Oxford, 1984.

[3] SMITH L. C. Implications of artificial intelligence for end user use of online systems, *Online Rev.* **4** (1980), 383–391. See *Computing Reviews* **22**, 3 (March 1981), Rev. 37,605.

CHRISTODOULAKIS, STAVROS (Univ. of Waterloo, Waterloo, Ont., Canada); AND
FALOUTSOS, CHRISTOS (Univ. of Maryland, College Park)
**Design and performance considerations for an optical disk-based, multimedia object server.**
*Computer* **19,** 12 (Dec. 1986), 45–56.

The low cost per bit and high storage capacity of optical disks, together with the user's desire to store information in unformatted forms such as voice, make new demands on information system designers. The authors present such a system, composed of a multimedia (voice, text, visual) object server connected to a large number of user workstations. Users submit requests about the contents of objects through a query specification interface. A retrieval browsing interface then allows the user to browse through relevant objects. Upon selecting an object, the multimedia object presentation manager presents the object's information. The bulk of this paper describes browsing and object presentation, mostly from the functional viewpoint: what capabilities are desirable and how to provide them in a consistent, systematic manner for the widely different information forms. (However, *why* this is the best approach, given the significant differences among text, voice, and visual data, is not discussed.)

Performance is considered in the last two pages, though limited to issues in searching text data based on content. The brief description concentrates on signature methods. While the description is technically accurate, it is too short to add enough understanding to the paper to warrant its inclusion.

Although the authors do a good job of presenting functional and user interface issues for a multimedia information system, they cover performance issues in only a limited manner and system design issues hardly at all. Nor do the authors really show how optical disks affect the issues considered, other than by providing the necessary cheap, plentiful storage.

—*Andrew R. Huber,* Research Triangle Park, NC

### H.3.1 Content Analysis and Indexing

PEJTERSEN, ANNELISE M. (Royal School of Librarianship, Copenhagen, Denmark); OLSEN, SVEND E. (Risø National Laboratory, Roskilde, Denmark); AND ZUNDE, PRANAS (Georgia Institute of Technology, Atlanta)

**Development of a term association interface for browsing bibliographic data bases based on end users' word associations.**

[in *Knowledge engineering: expert systems and information retrieval,* I. Wormell (Ed.), Taylor Graham Publishers, London, UK, 1987, 92-112.]

HCI-0266

Conventional thesauri and other word classification schemes used in information retrieval systems typically reflect the formal meanings of words. The central thesis of this paper is that associative meanings may be more relevant to nonspecific search strategies such as browsing.

The authors define the associative meaning of a word to be the distribution of response words to the given word in a word association experiment. Thus two words are similar with respect to their associative meanings if they have quantifiably similar distributions. Techniques for empirically determining these distributions, and quantifying word associations, are well established. The authors conducted such a study and built what they call a "term association thesaurus." They then conducted a series of carefully controlled experiments to evaluate the thesaurus.

The study is well designed and the results should accurately reflect their underlying subject database and population. The research methods are appropriate, well documented, and generalizable. The results are interesting but inconclusive, since data from the experiments had not yet been analyzed.

The thesaurus is necessarily specific to the authors' subject database and population and therefore will need to be updated as the database, population, and population needs change. The authors suggest that the information retrieval interface might elicit users' associations during the query formulation process and thus constantly update the word association measures.

The paper is clear, direct, and well organized. It will be of interest to both practitioners and researchers concerned with the user interface to information retrieval systems.

—*L. Swanson,* Princeton, NJ

REVIEWS                                                                                              [HCI-0269]

*Abstracting methods*

HAHN, UDO; AND REIMER, ULRICH (Univ. Konstanz, Constance, West Germany)         **HCI-0267**
**Computing text constituency: an algorithmic approach to the generation of text graphs.**
[in *Research and development in information retrieval.* Proc. of the third joint BCS and ACM symposium (King's College, Cambridge, July 2-6, 1984), C. van Rijsbergen (Ed.), Cambridge University Press, New York, NY, 1984, 343–368.]

The authors describe their algorithm for automatic abstracting and indexing, which forms the basis of the TOPIC system under development at the University of Konstanz. A detailed example from a computer text fragment is presented with adequate detail to show how the system works in practice. The method is a good example of an expert system. It will be interesting to see how effective it is when tested on a large body of data.
—*K. Booth,* Sooke, B.C., Canada

## H.3.2  Information Storage

*File organization*

JONES, WILLIAM P.; AND DUMAIS, SUSAN T. (Bell Communications Research,          **HCI-0268**
Morristown, NJ)
**The spatial metaphor for user interfaces: experimental tests of reference by location versus name.**
*ACM Trans. Office Inf. Syst.* **4,** 1 (Jan. 1986), 42–63.

I found this paper to be thorough, educational, and informative. The authors have conducted several experiments to assess the role of spatial information on the system and man-machine interfaces design. The methodology presented is clear, easy to follow, and could be used in other experiments.
   The paper would have been better if the authors had used footnotes instead of references to define certain terms. A minor case in point is "proactive" and "retroactive" inhibitions. In summary, it is a good paper to read for the man-machine interfaces designers. Unfortunately, the research results do not point towards ways to exploit spatial metaphor in designing user interfaces. In that sense, we have not heard the last word on this issue.
—*Santosh Chokani,* Arlington, VA

## H.3.3  Information Search and Retrieval

*Query formulation*

FISCHHOFF, BARUCH; AND MACGREGOR, DONALD (Decision Research, Eugene, OR)       **HCI-0269**
**Calibrating databases.**
*J. Am. Soc. Inf. Sci.* **37,** 4 (July 1986), 222–233.

In this paper, the authors take a behavioral decision theoretic approach to the problem of optimizing interfaces to information retrieval systems. They propose certain measures of user performance for comparing alternative retrieval designs, and they report on two empirical studies of those measures.

The paper is well referenced and well researched. The experimental design is sound, its findings are consistent with other studies of similar cognitive tasks, and its conclusions are reasonable. The paper makes some contribution to theory, injecting behavioral aspects of decision making into the issue of system design. Its major contributions are methodological, and it seems to me that the proposed methods could be applied beyond the information retrieval context to the more general issue of human-machine interactions.

Unfortunately, the authors spend too much time on the results of their particular study, which is interesting only as an exemplar of the methodology; and not enough time on the methodology itself, for which they have only scratched the surface. In other respects, the paper is clear and well organized. The suggestions for further research are brief. This paper will be of interest to database designers and those concerned with human-machine interactions.

—*L. Swanson*, Princeton, NJ

*Retrieval models*

DANILOWICZ, CZESLAW (Wroclaw Technical Univ., Wroclaw, Poland)
**Users and experts in the document retrieval system model.**
*Int. J. Man-Mach. Stud.* **21,** 3 (Sept. 1984), 245–252.

This paper addresses the problem of using expert system concepts in a document retrieval system. The basic premise of the paper is that any attempt to apply an ordering to the documents retrieved will be unsatisfactory unless some allowance is made for the preferences of the users. A procedure is presented that incorporates expert profiles into the ordering scheme so that the user can use the expert knowledge in ordering the documents. The procedure also allows the user to estimate the competence of the experts.

The paper begins with an Introduction tracing the history and nature of document retrieval from antiquity to the modern work place. It is Danilowicz's contention that the fundamental problem with retrieval systems is the volume of data retrieved. In particular, the system should be sensitive to the user's expectations about the system's response to a query. In ordering the documents by their perceived value, the volume of information is restricted implicitly as the user need only consider the first $N$ documents, having confidence that no document further down the list will be judged as more valuable. The Introduction states the hypothesis that the incorporation of expert profiles can produce the desired ordering and that any ordering not based upon preferences "cannot produce good results."

The second section of the paper presents a formal model for an expert system. Formulas are presented to define concepts such as selectivity and similarity of profiles.

Section three develops the equations used to order the retrieved documents. Additional equations are given to estimate the competence of experts. Competence measure allows the user to select the experts that provide the results of his queries. The section concludes with an example.

Section four provides a review and summary of the issues presented in the Introduction. The author also offers some observations about how lists of experts may be defined.

While the author discusses a very interesting application of expert system concepts, this is not an introductory paper intended for the novice. Danilowicz assumes that the reader is familiar with other of his works. There is no explanation about how to obtain profiles, nor are any proofs or derivations of the various formulas given. The paper's main value lies in extending the author's previous work on document retrieval models and in stimulating thought on the subject of artificial intelligence in these types of systems.

—*M. J. Wallach*, Staten Island, NY

JONES, WILLIAM P. (Microelectronics and Computer Technology Corporation, Austin, TX)    **HCI-0271**
**On the applied use of human memory models: the memory extender personal filing system.**
*Int. J. Man-Mach. Stud.* **25,** 2 (Aug. 1986), 191–228.

In the Abstract, the author states, "The Memory Extender (ME) system improves the user interface to a personal database by actively modeling the user's own memory for files and for the context in which these files are used." However, it is later stated, "We are much less interested in the psychological validity of the ME system components than we are in their psychological utility (i.e., how do these components help users get what they need?)."

The system described is designed for personal databases. The author states that "text objects" (like documents or files) in a public-domain system are better suited for automatic (context-based) indexing than other classes of object, and he describes several schemes for retrieval that utilize indexing and query history. This forms the basis for characterizing contexts and objects.

As operations progress, the representations of context and file objects are modified to reflect new successful events; a decay mechanism is also present. "Spreading activation" introduces a transitive relationship, not unlike relevance feedback. The system contains several different options that may or may not be activated at any given time. It is implemented in Zetalisp and "can run on any 3600 series Symbolics Lisp Machine."

Because there is little experience with the system, which can be used to quantify performance, its utility is described in statements relating the anticipated performance of its components to the characteristics of standard techniques. Operation is illustrated by display screens.

The paper describes an existing system that has a multiplicity of storage and retrieval features, has some intuitive attractiveness, and has no recommendation based on systematic testing.

—*T. C. Lowe*, Washington, DC

SPARCK JONES, KAREN (Univ. of Cambridge, Cambridge, UK)    **HCI-0272**
**Architecture problems in the construction of expert systems for document retrieval.**
[in *Knowledge engineering: expert systems and information retrieval,* I. Wormell (Ed.), Taylor Graham Publishers, London, UK, 1987, 7-33.]

The idea of an expert system front end offering the user direct access to a document retrieval system is an attractive one. The paper considers two specific approaches to the construction of such an expert interface.

—*From the Author's Abstract*

Both projects are directed toward automating the operations of the trained intermediary in determining the user's need, expressing that need in the indexing language, and forming a query geared to the collection being searched. Brooks has laid out the requirements such an automated intermediary should meet and proposed a general system design [1]. Pollitt's CANSEARCH [2] shows that some automation is possible and that a specific implementation of the type of system Brooks suggested is feasible.

The author believes that major problems exist with the proposed architecture, and she describes them under four headings: control, blackboards, messages, and the expert's communication language. In particular, she argues that the nature of the language used for communication between the contributing experts requires more attention than it has received. This paper is interesting and persuasive; anyone involved with the expert system approach to document retrieval systems or interfaces should read it.

—*R. Crawford,* Kingston, Ont., Canada

**REFERENCES**

[1] BROOKS, H. M. *An intelligent interface to document retrieval systems: developing the problem description and retrieval strategy components.* Ph.D. Thesis, City University of New York, New York, 1986.

[2] POLLITT, A. S. A rule-based system as an intermediary for searching cancer therapy literature on Medline. In *Intelligent information systems: progress and prospects.* R. Davies (Ed.), Wiley, New York, 1986.

INGWERSEN, PETER (Royal School of Librarianship, Copenhagen, Denmark)   **HCI-0273**
**Towards a new research paradigm in information retrieval.**
[in *Knowledge engineering: expert systems and information retrieval,* I. Wormell (Ed.), Taylor Graham Publishers, London, UK, 1987, 150-168.]

This paper discusses the development of three approaches to information retrieval (IR) research. The author considers the system-driven approach to be the traditional one. He describes the user-modeling approach as having emerged in the 1970s, and considers the cognitive paradigm the most recent and encompassing.

Initially, I found myself disagreeing with the author about the distinctions and features of the models. For example, he refers to the user-modeling paradigm as the "opposite approach to IR research," when compared to the system-driven paradigm. I would view these approaches as more complementary than opposite. However, I feel that the particular characterizations are not very important. Rather, it is useful to see how looking at a problem in a variety of ways may affect the direction of research. Finally, the author's vision of the direction of information retrieval research is interesting and helpful.

—*R. Crawford,* Kingston, Ont., Canada

## Search process

FAIRHALL, DONALD (Ballarat College of Advanced Education, Ballarat, Vic., Australia)   **HCI-0274**
**In search of searching skills.**
*J. Inf. Sci. Princ. Pract.* **10**, 3 (1985), 111–123.

The author of this paper attempts to identify skills (or tactics) which contribute to success in searching an index. An extensive list of skills has been compiled, and an experiment was conducted to identify critical skills. The experiment and subsequent statistical analysis are exhaustively described, but no statistically significant results were obtained. Given the importance of search formulation in overall system performance, this is clearly a problem that merits continued research.

—*R. W. Elliott,* Austin, TX

PRATT, G. E. C. (Mirach Consultants, Surrey, UK)     **HCI-0275**
**Using the micro-computer to simplify database access: designing interfaces to complex files.**
*J. Inf. Sci. Princ. Pract.* **10,** 3 (1985), 131–138.

This paper presents a technique for developing a user-friendly interface to complex databases (e.g., World Patent Index, Chemical Abstracts) using a microcomputer and any proprietary relational database system. The aim is to enable the user consulting such large databases on a regular basis to produce an inexpensive, convenient, and simple interface to those databases. The ideas presented in the paper are not new and the application chosen, namely, The World Patent Index, is of only specialized interest. Nevertheless, the author has shown how easy it is, given a microcomputer, to adopt existing, cheaply available software to produce a really useful system tailored to one's own needs.

—*J. B. Grimson,* Dublin, Ireland

WILLIAMS, MARTHA E. (Univ. of Illinois at Urbana-Champaign, Urbana)     **HCI-0276**
**Transparent information systems through gateways, front ends, intermediaries, and interfaces.**
*J. Am. Soc. Inf. Sci.* **37,** 4 (July 1986), 204–214.

This paper is a summary of the author's research on design requirements for "transparent" information retrieval systems. The author defines a transparent information retrieval system as one that allows the user to query for data without worrying about where or in what format the data is stored. The author has done extensive work in this area since 1976, and has authored or co-authored 14 of the 27 articles included in the bibliographic references.

    The emphasis of the paper is on public databases where the number of computer readable databases has grown ten-fold in the past ten years. The paper begins by describing the perceived need for, and history of, transparent information retrieval systems. The author then outlines the taxonomy of terms and functions that must be packaged together to make such a system workable. This is followed by a discussion of the major issues, such as centralization versus decentralization, privacy, value added by database vendors, and new technological breakthroughs that could be useful. The paper concludes that by 1990, 85 percent of the functions listed in the taxonomy would be automated and available to the general public.

    The paper is well written and serves as a good ten-page overview of the subject. Its best features are its readability and its development of the case for transparent information retrieval systems. However, the paper fails to mention technical and political roadblocks to implementing such systems. For instance, transparent information retrieval may never occur across multiple database vendors. The data in public databases form an expensive resource, and access to this data is very carefully guarded for political reasons. Unless this changes, we will continue to see only a very limited number of narrowly scoped transparent information retrieval systems.

The concept of transparent information retrieval systems is ten years old, and much of the paper's content has been presented in at least 14 conferences between 1977 and 1983. However, I would still recommend the paper to those researching the concept and to those looking at better man-machine interface techniques.

—*R. J. Tufts,* Washington, DC

SMITH, PHILIP J.; SHUTE, STEVEN J.; GALDES, BEB (Ohio State Univ., Columbus); AND CHIGNELL, MARK H. (Univ. of Southern California, Los Angeles)  **HCI-0277**
**Knowledge-based search tactics for an intelligent intermediary system.**
*ACM Trans. Inf. Syst.* **7**, 3 (July 1989), 246–270.

This paper summarizes past and current work on knowledge-based systems for bibliographic information retrieval. It discusses thesaurus systems; partial-match systems, including rule-based systems and associative semantic networks; frame-based semantic networks; knowledge representation in semantically based search; and tactics for suggesting new retrieval terms. The authors briefly report on an empirical study of how human intermediaries use domain knowledge to suggest search strategies and propose related search terms. They characterize the knowledge that such intermediaries bring to bear, draw conclusions about differences in the ways alternative approaches use knowledge, suggest possibilities for computerized intermediaries, and recommend areas for further research.

The paper is clear, well-written, thorough in its treatment of past and current work in this field, and extensively referenced. However, it should have included less discussion of conventional retrieval methods and more consideration of certain aspects of the use of knowledge. For example, the distinction between knowledge contained in the system (i.e., the knowledge base) and that contained in the document base is an important one and warrants further discussion.

The authors have made an important contribution in bringing together several methods, particularly thesaurus and frame-based approaches, in their own system. They have also strengthened the body of objective evidence about how human intermediaries perform their task. This paper will be of interest to developers of bibliographic information retrieval systems and researchers in knowledge-based systems.

—*L. Swanson,* Princeton, NJ

### H.3.4  Systems and Software

WEYER, STEPHEN A. (Atari Sunnyvale Research Laboratory); AND BORNING, ALAN H.  **HCI-0278**
(Univ. of Washington, Seattle)
**A prototype electronic encyclopedia.**
*ACM Trans. Office Inf. Syst.* **3**, 1 (Jan. 1985), 63–88.

Weyer and Borning describe a prototype electronic encyclopedia which combines extensive full text browsing and retrieval capabilities with graphics and simulation features to create a powerful, user-responsive, interactive information system. Well thought out, the prototype brings together a variety of information processing techniques to create an environment which supports the multiple access and analysis approaches which an intelligent user might employ. The tour-filter-guide-model methaphor which they develop for navigation and presentation of the system is imaginative, but useful. The system is written in the object-oriented language ZETALISP. Future plans called for implementation on a VAX 11/780 using RTI's INGRES, but premature termination of the project interrupted this effort. Hopefully, the work can be resumed in the future. There is a good review of earlier, as well as current, related work and an extensive list of references.

—*H. Burton,* Livermore, CA

## *ASK*

THOMPSON, BOZENA H.; AND THOMPSON, FREDERICK B. (California Institute of Technology, Pasadena)
**ASK is transportable in half a dozen ways.**
*ACM Trans. Office Inf. Syst.* **3,** 2 (April 1985), 185–203.

According to the authors, "ASK, A Simple Knowledge System, is a total system for structuring, manipulating, and communicating information. The primary ASK user interface is a simple dialect of English." The rather odd title of this paper is somewhat of a misnomer in that the most commonly used definition of transportability is from machine domain to machine domain. In this instance the authors treat the verb "to 'transport' as a subcase of to 'extend.' " That is, they present six ways in which the ASK system can be extended to include new capabilities.

The six ways in which ASK is extendible and thus transportable are:

- ☐ to a new domain,
- ☐ to a new object type,
- ☐ to access data from a foreign database,
- ☐ to a new natural language,
- ☐ to a new programming language, and
- ☐ to a new computer family.

Each of the six proposed areas of extension is discussed in some detail, including the steps and methodology employed. The authors' actual experiences are described, both pro and con, along with helpful hints. Comparisons are made with similar implementations using other systems.

The authors employ extensive query/response examples to illustrate the proposed methods of extension. Their style is easy to read, and the material is presented in a highly undertandable manner. Some of the authors' statements are of an editorial nature; however, this does not detract in any way from their presentation. On the contrary, their comments seem right on the mark. For example:

- ☐ It would be nice if there were a "universal" database structure, but there is not. The "epistemological" levels . . . of current database theories leave little room for linguistic subtleties.

☐   Ninety-nine percent of ASK is written in standard PASCAL. The machine-dependent parts of ASK are few in number, well isolated and well defined. It would seem that ASK should be easily transportable. Sadly, writing in standard PASCAL does not make that true. . . . Truly transportable PASCAL is not by any means documented, and it is doubtful that it exists.

One does not need a preexistent knowledge of ASK, or any natural language or expert system to appreciate the content of this paper. The liberal use of illustrations from the authors' own work indicates extensive work with, and deep understanding of both the specific subject matter of ASK itself, and the wider topic of designing and implementing user-friendly, and thus user-effective, systems. Much of the reference literature originates at the California Institute of Technology, Pasadena, CA, and includes other papers from the same authors. If this paper is any indication, the other papers should be well worth reading.

—*M. E. Modell,* Cambridge, MA

## Information networks

RAGAN, RICHARD R. (Control Data Corporation, Sunnyvale, CA)
**CONTEXT: an on-line documentation system.**
*Softw. Pract. Exper.* **16,** 3 (March 1986), 217–224.

This paper describes CONTEXT, an online documentation system that runs on CDC CYBER mainframes. A tree-structured database is used to store screens of information. In addition to vertical links between the screens, horizontal links are also permitted. This gives the HELP screen authors the ability to reduce the search time needed to find topics. Screens can be accessed by traversing menus, or by keyword. The HELP screens can be created with any standard editor or word processor, so authors do not have to learn a new system of text generation. Six simple commands are all that are needed to link screens and put them in the database. Screens can also be indexed, and the index is available to users for browsing purposes. The user can enter index terms, and several algorithms are used to try to match the user pattern with stored index patterns. User commands are simple, and screen output is terminal independent.

CONTEXT offers several innovative features that should improve the quality of online HELP. For some reason, the designers found that document authors indexed online CONTEXT documents better than the hard-copy counterparts, making it easier to find things online than in the paper manuals.

—*A. Cohill,* Newport, VA

## Question-answering (fact retrieval) systems

BOLC, LEONARD (Warsaw Univ., Warsaw, Poland); KOWALSKI, ADAM (Polish Academy of Sciences, Warsaw, Poland); KOZLOWSKA, MALGORZATA (Warsaw Univ., Warsaw, Poland); AND STRZALKOWSKI, TOMASZ (Simon Fraser Univ., B.C., Canada)
**A natural language information retrieval system with extentions towards fuzzy reasoning.**
*Int. J. Man-Mach. Stud.* **23,** 4 (Oct. 1985), 335–367.

This paper describes an experimental version of a conversational, natural language, information retrieval system. The system under discussion deals with gastroenterology, a branch of internal medicine. One interesting point is that this system has been implemented on that venerable tool of AI research, the IBM 370/148, using a local dialect (UWLISP) of LISP 1.5.

The introduction presents a fine review of some expert systems for medicine. Then we see a lengthy discussion of the components of the system. First, there is the Transformation Expert System (TESS) that translates Polish (precisely what one expects natural language to be at the Institute for Informatics of Warsaw University) sentences into a formal representation that expresses their meaning. This is used to process the text of documents such as medical descriptions. The first component of TESS is the Analytical Stage (AS), which uncovers the syntactic structure of an input sentence. This stage uses five ATN nets to handle the complexities of Polish grammar, which is briefly discussed. The second component of TESS is the Interpretational Stage (IS), which provides the semantics in terms of pattern-concept pairs. Some discussion of rule construction is provided. Again, ATN nets are used, as is a semantic dictionary.

The next component is the deduction module to assist in query processing. It is based upon the theory of fuzzy sets and was written in the FUZZY programming language. (Modified to run on the IBM machine, it can be considered an extension of PLANNER.) This allows the system to be extended to cover such notions as "frequently," "possibly," "often," "rarely," and "predominately." Deduction is used to find an assertion that has precisely the same form or contains the same description as the query, has a slightly different form, or can be traced through a reason-to-effect chain. The final component is a natural language answer generator. Again, one is confronted with the issue of Polish grammar. An example scenario for a query and response is given in the paper as:

Q: What is the reason [sic] acute pancreatitis?
A: The predominant reason of [sic] acute pancreatitis is cholelithiasis. Alcoholism is often a reason of acute pancreatitis. Hypertension is pancreatic ducts perhaps causes acute pancreatitis.

This paper is a must read for afficionados of information retrieval. The combination of natural language and retrieval can obviously yield much fruit. In addition, the incorporation of fuzzy logic demonstrates how imprecision can and should be handled.

—*Donald H. Kraft,* Baton Rouge, LA

### H.3.5 On-line Information Services

YANKELOVICH, NICOLE; MEYROWITZ, NORMAN; AND VAN DAM, ANDRIES (Brown Univ., Providence, RI)
**Reading and writing the electronic book.**
*Computer* **18**, 10 (Oct. 1985), 15–30.

It was during the mid-1400s that Gutenberg invented the type mold which made printing from movable metal type practical. This lead to the development of the printing and book publishing industries. Over 500 years have passed and many improvements have been made, but the essential printing concepts of today are similar to those used by Gutenberg and his associates in producing their magnificent 42-line Bible. Now, as we enter the information age, entirely new technologies have been invented for use in the creation of electronic books and electronic document systems. Many of these new technologies have been developed at the Institute for Research in Information and Scholarship (IRIS) at Brown University. It is these developments that are described by the authors of this paper.

After a brief introduction, the advantages and disadvantages of hard-copy print media are listed and briefly discussed. Books are portable, accessible, easy to read, and aesthetically appealing. However, they are limited to presenting information in a two-dimensional format composed of static text and graphics which readers cannot customize. Nor can they be easily updated to provide the most current information. Electronic document systems have been designed to overcome the disadvantages of print and to create "connectivity," i.e., webs of elated information within a single document and among related documents, as well as links among scholars working together in "online communities." Four such electronic document systems have been developed at Brown University:

(1) FRESS (File Retrieval and Editing System),
(2) The Electronic Document System (completed in 1982 and "far more modern than FRESS"),
(3) BALSA (Brown Algorithm Simulator and Animator, "an environment designed to facilitate the creation of computer science and educational software"), and
(4) Intermedia ("a multimedia system that will ideally provide most of the major capabilities desirable for a good electronic document system" and which is currently under development).

This reviewer, unfortunately, has not used any of these systems and so cannot add any personal observations to the information provided by the authors. However, the concept is exciting and the implications for the future are many.

—*H. Borko,* Los Angeles, CA

OJALA, MARYDEE (Bank of America, San Francisco, CA)
**Views on end-user searching.**
*J. Am. Soc. Inf. Sci.* **37,** 4 (July 1986), 197–203.

This paper is aimed primarily at librarians and vendors of online databases; users of those databases may find the paper interesting as well. In this overview of the use of online databases, the author attempts to define who constitutes an end user, what types of searches they make and why, and what the future of online database searching holds.

The paper nearly bogs down in its attempt to define an "end user," but fortunately the pace picks up by mid-paper. Basically, end users are defined as those who search an online database for information that fills their own needs, rather than the needs of others. Ojala makes a special point of the quandary of librarians who are not yet comfortable with computers and yet must either act as expert searchers for their patrons or risk seeing their role usurped by the combination of computer system and end user.

As the author explores the trends and probable future of end-user searching, she draws conclusions that make the librarian feel that there is still hope. While some people will do their own searches, many will need or prefer to leave that effort to a specialist, just as in the past when the searches were through printed material. The librarian's job and tools will change, but the need for their special capabilities and their role in research are not likely to disappear.

—*David A. Studebaker,* Glen Ellyn, IL

YANG, YIYA (Heriot-Watt Univ., Edinburgh, Scotland, UK)
**A user oriented design process for user recovery and command reuse support.**
[in *People and computers IV*. Proceedings of the Fourth Conference of the British Computer Society (Univ. of Manchester, UK, Sept. 5–6, 1988), D. Jones; and R. Winder (Eds.), Cambridge University Press, New York, NY, 1988, 179–198.]

This paper addresses a problem of growing concern to online, interactive users—the ability to change one's mind in case an entered command does not provide the desired result. The user will need at least three online capabilities to do this: *undo, redo,* and *reuse*. Undo reverses the effects of a previous command or set of commands, redo reverses the effects of an undo, and reuse allows the application of previously saved commands.

The purpose of this paper was to survey existing systems to see how well they satisfy the need for an undo, redo, and reuse capability. Yang surveyed Janet's News Network and received 25 responses covering six systems (UNIX, *vi* text editor, Macintosh, SunView, Smalltalk-80, and EMACS). None of these systems has the full capabilities called for, but most have two of the three.

As the author mentions, analyses of the limited survey results would have "serious limitations" because of the sample set and evaluation method. That did not, however, deter the author from giving these results and spicing them with respondent comments that showed practical insights into what users need from on-line systems. The paper concludes with a description of how systems should be designed to provide undo, redo, and reuse capabilities from their inception.

The paper seems a bit long for the amount of data received in the survey. The author frequently expounds on self-explanatory comments from survey respondents. He also draws a number of conclusions that he applies to all types of systems although the respondents were primarily describing text editing applications. In short, the paper's worst feature is its limited data from which to draw accurate conclusions. Graphics, scientific, real-time, and data processing applications should all have been included.

The best part of the paper is its clear description of what is really needed for online users to back out of previous commands. Its coverage of the human-machine interaction aspects of such commands and controls is weak, however. The references are good but sparse, reflecting the relative newness of this subject.

I would recommend this paper as an introduction to the subject for designers of online systems. It is easy to read and presents some thought-provoking problems that people who sit at a CRT all day long are facing.

—*R. J. Tufts,* Washington, DC

### H.3.6 Library Automation

CRAWFORD, WALT (Research Libraries Group)  **HCI-0285**
**Testing bibliographic displays for online catalogs.**
*Inf. Technol. Libr.* **6,** 1 (March 1987), 20–33.

Many university libraries and some public libraries have closed their card catalogs and now provide public access to the library holdings by means of an online bibliographic catalog. A very important aspect of this catalog is the information displayed on the CRT screen. This information needs to be informative, understandable, and attractively organized. The design of an online catalog is complex, involving hundreds of elements and a multitude of design decisions. Most of these decisions, according to the author, are made in a vacuum, without the benefit of experimental evidence as to which design will work best. Consequently, research focused on specific aspects of catalog design is needed to provide a context for design decisions; this paper describes one such experimental study.

The Research Library Group (RLG), a consortium of universities and independent research institutions, sponsored the project to study the effectiveness of different bibliographic displays. The initial tests included a range of different screen designs, a range of display options, and the use of labeled and unlabeled data formats. Eventually the tests focused on the use of a single overall screen format, a single set of data elements that included a full bibliographic description, and two display alternatives—one similar to the traditional library catalog and the other with each element labeled.

The paper contains illustrations of both the labeled and card-like displays. The results indicate that "Labeled displays are more legible, but do take up more room than card-like displays; the study shows how much more room and explores some variations on card-like and labeled displays." In discussing these results, the author concludes "The tests do not prove that a particular bibliographic display is ideal but do provide some interesting comparisons and examples."

—*H. Borko,* Los Angeles, CA

## H.4 Information Systems Applications

### H.4.1 Office Automation

GREIF, IRENE (Massachusetts Institute of Technology, Cambridge)  **HCI-0286**
**The user interface of a personal calendar program.**
[in *Human factors and interactive computer systems.* Proc. of the NYU symposium on user interfaces (New York, May 26-28, 1982), Y. Vassiliou (Ed.), Ablex Publishing Corp., Norwood, NJ, 1984, 207–222.]

[See main entry, Review HCI-0038.]

This article describes user interface aspects of PCAL, a calendar program for the DEC 2060, accessed through terminals of the VT100 class (character displays, no pointing device). Users can make or change items in their personal calendars, and can read (but not write) calendars of others.

Sample screen layouts and a list of commands are included. While the idea (cooperative calendar management among a group on online users) is interesting, this particular user interface is unremarkable compared to the calendar programs now available on large bitmapped displays with pointing devices.

—*R. W. Sauvain,* Rochester, NY

KINCAID, CHRISTINE M.; DUPONT, PIERRE B. (Gandalf Systems Group, Ottawa, Ont., **HCI-0287**
Canada); AND KAYE, A. R. (Carleton Univ., Ottawa, Ont., Canada)
**Electronic calendars in the office: an assessment of user needs and current technology.**
*ACM Trans. Office Inf. Syst.* **3,** 1 (Jan. 1985), 89–102.

This paper presents some results of a survey of office workers to assess their attitudes toward and usage of electronic calendars. The conclusions presented are drawn from the 30 respondents, who were each interviewed and each a daily user of an office system containing an electronic calendar system. These conclusions are quite similar to previous ones [1]. They infer that current electronic calendar systems are mostly not used, and that most users prefer paper calendars. An exception to this is the use of the electronic system to schedule and reserve conference rooms and other shared resources.

Many have stated that until the electronic calendar is as portable as the paper-based calendar book, it will simply not serve the majority of people. This critical point is totally missing from the authors' list (Section 5) of Recommendations for Electronic Calendaring Systems.

The paper does present and explain many conferencing system functions and features. One potential problem with an assessment of this type is that it may measure users' perceived needs rather than actual needs. Finally, it appears that part of this assessment (Group One) suffers from the "threshold effect" in which the system's user interface is so bad that it is below the threshold of comfortable usage by anyone except a computer jock. This has occurred before with office systems, and it explains why Group One respondents were all negative. This can have the effect of totally overshadowing all other factors; perhaps the authors should repeat this experiment some time later when electronic calendars are in common use in integrated systems with high resolution displays, fast interaction, voice activation, and portability. Then it will be possible to measure calendar functionality rather than user interface interference level.:

—*C. Ellis,* Austin, TX

**REFERENCES**
[1] KELLEY, J. F., AND CHAPANIS, A. How professional persons keep their calendars: implications for computerization, *J. Occup. Psychol.* **55** (1982), 241–256.

POWER, DANIEL J.; AND HEVNER, ALAN R. (Univ. of Maryland, College Park) **HCI-0288**
**Executive workstations: issues and requirements.**
*Inf. Manage.* **8,** 4 (April 1985), 213–220.

Future executive workstations are the subject of this well-written and easy-to-read paper. An executive workstation is defined by the authors as "an integrated hardware/software system that can provide business executives with powerful capabilities for making and implementing decisions."

Current management reluctance to use the existing workstations is dealt with summarily by the authors through the use of Nolan's model of information system development [1]. The authors indicate that the current lack of acceptance of workstations by managers is the result of the fact that these people are not far enough along the development curve. This allows the authors to immediately jump to an analysis of workstation requirements. At the same time, however, they avoid a thorough analysis of the human factors involved.

The technological requirements for a workstation are presented using the scenario method. The underlying assumption is that the executive who is further along developmentally on Nolan's curve will, to a large extent, gather, store, manipulate, and retrieve data in order to execute his or her job functions. The scenario also assumes a device with a keyboard, a "mouse," voice input, a windowed environment, and some teleconferencing capabilities. Simplistic alternative scenario modifications are mentioned, including use of support staff for some function execution, keyboard base environment, and no video capability.

The paper is an interesting introduction to current executive workstations with a limited perspective on future enhancements. The capability required in a workstation for management decision implementation is the focus of much of the paper; this makes the paper interesting reading. The paper is, however, somewhat shallow in making predictions. For instance, it glosses over completely the whole issue of the fundamental functions needed for making management decisions (DSS). The paper is recommended for new students of office automation and management, and for end users of such systems.

—*E. A. Unger,* Manhattan, KS

**REFERENCES**

[1] NOLAN, R. Managing the crisis in data processing, *Harvard Bus. Rev.* **57** (1979), 115–126.

DONAHUE, JAMES (Xerox Palo Alto Research Center, Palo Alto, CA); AND WIDOM, JENNIFER (Cornell Univ., Ithaca, NY)
**Whiteboards: a graphical database tool.**
*ACM Trans. Office Inf. Syst.* **4,** 1 (Jan. 1986), 24–41.

The Cedar Whiteboards program is essentially a menu package, providing a way of organizing text and programs as a network that a user browses by pointing. The Whiteboard screen can contain a lot of text, and the program lets the screen designer arrange the text (and the small bitmap images representing programs) to his or her liking. The paper is an interesting case study in developing an application program for a powerful workstation with a rich software environment.

Documentation for the Cedar system has been organized using a network of 18 interconnected Whiteboards. This is, no doubt, a fine technique for introducing new users to the system, but it does not take the place of a well-constructed index.

Calling Whiteboards a "database tool" is stretching things a bit; a Whiteboard is represented as a database, but the Whiteboard program can only browse databases that it has created.

—*M. R. Brown,* Palo Alto, CA

MALONE, THOMAS W.; GRANT, KENNETH R.; LAI, KUM-YEW; RAO, RAMANA; AND
ROSENBLITT, DAVID (Massachusetts Institute of Technology, Cambridge)
**Semistructured messages are surprisingly useful for computer-supported coordination.**
*ACM Trans. Office Inf. Syst.* **5,** 2 (April 1987), 115–131.

This paper describes aspects of the Information Lens, "an intelligent system for information sharing in organizations." Older members of the computing community will recognize the Information Lens as a development of SDI (Selective Dissemination of Information) systems [1], implemented in modern (object-oriented) programming methodology. The argument advanced in the paper is that much of the information passing through an organization can be at least partially formatted and that doing this allows one to build a flexible information dissemination system. Moreover, these partially-structured messages can serve as the data structures for secondary systems such as calendar management.

The paper is well written and clearly describes the implemented system. At the time of writing, no experience outside the development group had yet been accumulated. Consequently, it was not possible to judge how well the constructs provided could be utilized by someone unfamiliar with the implementation. The paper is certainly worth reading by anyone who is concerned with computer-mediated communication systems.

—*Fred J. Damerau,* Yorktown Heights, NY

**REFERENCES**

[1] SALTON, G. *Automatic information organization and retrieval,* McGraw-Hill, New York, 1968, pp. 381–383. See *Computing Reviews* **10,** 6 (June 1969), Rev. 16,841.

CHRISTIE, BRUCE (City of London Polytechnic, London, UK); AND GARDINER,
MARGARET M. (Communi Con Ltd., London, UK)
**Office systems.**
[in *Information technology & people: designing for the future,* F. Blackler; and D. Oborne, MIT Press, Cambridge, MA, 1987, 85-102.]

This is a chapter from the book *Information technology and people: designing for the future.* I mention that because after reading the work, one has the feeling that there must be something more. It covers three topics in the development of office systems: the analysis of functional requirements, the development of models of human behavior, and the design and evaluation of new products.

This chapter was apparently intended as an overview, because the material is covered very briefly and at a high level. By itself, the chapter would be appropriate for a manager or software programmer who has little knowledge of human factors techniques and methods. It offers little for the human factors practitioner.

The paper does make one interesting comment on using cognitive psychologists (or human factors experts) as part of a software development team. The authors note that the human factors personnel must be willing to recognize the exigencies of the business world and act, from time to time, on their best judgment of the situation, rather than stopping a project dead in its tracks "until data can be collected."

—*A. Cohill,* Newport, VA

## Word processing

CARROLL, JOHN M.; AND MACK, ROBERT L.
**Learning to use a word processor: by doing, by thinking, and by knowing.**
[in *Human factors in computer systems,* J. Thomas; and M. Schneider (Eds.), Ablex Publishing Corp., Norwood, NJ, 1984, 13-51.]

[See main entry, Review HCI-0037.]

This paper takes an educational psychologist's approach to learning how to use word processing software. The authors suggest that most designers of software and its training materials assume that persons will learn to use these software products in a "passive" or laboratory-like atmosphere. However, the authors suggest that this learning will actually take place in an "active" or real world environment. Rather than reading manuals or studying "help" screens, people learning to use software products will tend to strike out on their own and learn by doing.

This learning approach is probably used by many data processing professionals today when they learn to use a new package of microcomputer software. However, the authors devote considerable space to interviews with persons in a laboratory attempting to learn a word processing package. Much of this is of little interest to the data processing professional; it takes the form of:

Instructor: You're in control.
Learner: Let's see what happens. If I were alone that's what I would do.
Instructor: Yup! You're all alone.

While the authors spend considerable time with these transcriptions of rather mindless laboratory conversations, they do have a point. It is that learners of word processing packages and software packages do not generally take a structured approach of reading manuals and then following the step by step tutorial instructions. Rather, they plunge into the problems with a take charge manner. While manuals and system user interfaces attempt to put these users in a passive role, users will generally ignore this system-dictated role.

The paper provides some other interesting observations about the design of software in a manner that will promote user learning. For example, they observe that learners have little use for a help screen that says, "Parameter omitted or not valid." Rather, they want to find out what is the problem with their immediate input problem. The user thinks of his needs in a problem oriented sense, while the software tends to be more problem neutral.

It is suggested that a task analysis driven approach might be better for designing useful user interfaces. Such an approach would require building some form of intelligence into systems. The authors also suggest that such system interfaces should attempt to be consistent with prior user knowledge. For example, users might learn a word processing system faster and better if it were presented as a super typewriter.

The authors present some interesting and worthwhile observations on the design of user interfaces in software products in order to allow persons to learn and use them more effectively. It is only unfortunate that the authors elected to include the rather long laboratory transcriptions instead of developing further their theories about learning software systems.

—*R. R. Moeller,* Chicago, IL

REVIEWS  [HCI-0294]

### H.4.2 Types of Systems

HALASZ, FRANK G. (Microelectronics and Computer Technology Corp., Austin, TX)  HCI-0293
**Reflections on NoteCards: seven issues for the next generation of hypermedia systems.**
*Commun. ACM* **31**, 7 (July 1988), 836–852.

Halasz's paper is an important step in the emergence of hypertext and hypermedia systems within the computer science community. While both the idea and the implementation of hypertext systems have been around for over two decades, the past few years have seen a resurgence of research and development activity, perhaps due to the increasing availability of powerful personal computing workstations.

The author, who made substantial contributions to the development of the NoteCards hypermedia environment for Xerox, provides a first-hand look at the development, use, and evolution of these systems. Drawing from experiences, at Xerox PARC and elsewhere, with NoteCards and similar hypertext environments, he identifies for researchers and developers of these environments a core of central issues for further investigation: search and query-based access to information, composite node/link types, virtual structures for creating temporary views of logically related information, computation attached within and/or across nodes, versioning of link and node contents, group-work support, and extensibility and personalization facilities. These seven issues lie at the intersection of information retrieval, cooperative information sharing ("groupware"), object-oriented databases, artificial intelligence, and computer-aided (software) engineering.

This paper is informative because these issues are common to a diverse set of professional interests and communities; they therefore represent a statement of the matters that not only concern large segments of the computer science community during the late 1980s but will probably be important into the early 1990s. In that regard the paper is a milestone in the field.

Rather than recapitulating the technical discussions of each issue, it is probably sufficient to say here that researchers who know about and understand these issues have almost certainly begun to investigate or prototype systems that address some of them. For these people, Halasz's discussion may represent more a point of departure, or a set of requirements that will be (or can already be) demonstrated in laboratory prototypes. Those whose interests are more peripheral to these concerns will perhaps find the paper informative, but probably not controversial. Nonetheless, the paper is a solid statement that locates the state of the art in hypermedia environments during the late 1980s. I recommend it.

—*Walt Scacchi,* Los Angeles, CA

### *Decision support*

SANDERS, G. L. (State University of New York at Buffalo, Buffalo); COURTNEY, JAMES  HCI-0294
F.; AND LOY, STEPHEN L. (Texas Tech University, Lubbock, TX)
**The impact of DSS on organizational communication.**
*Inf. Manage.* **7**, 3 (June 1984), 141–148.

SAKAWA, MASATOSHI (Kobe Univ., Kobe, Japan); AND YANO, HITOSHI (Kagawa Univ., Kagawa, Japan)  **HCI-0295**
**Interactive fuzzy decision-making for multi-objective nonlinear programming using reference membership intervals.**
*Int. J. Man-Mach. Stud.* **23,** 4 (Oct. 1985), 407–421.

The authors present an interactive approach to solving ill-specified decision problems involving utilities that are nonlinear, but separable, functions of the objective functions in a linear programming problem. The problems of eliciting usable utility functions from human decision makers have been extensively studied by psychologists and economists [1]. Sakawa and Yano's approach to estimating differential weights for attributes by eliciting "reference membership intervals" seems ad hoc and offers no advantages over standard methods. The technique that the authors present addresses only a few of the main difficulties encountered in complex multiattribute decision problems. It is likely to be of interest only to specialists.

—*R. L. Stout,* Providence, RI

**REFERENCES**

[1] KEENEY, R. L.; AND RAIFFA, H. *Decisions with multiple objectives: preferences and value tradeoffs,* John Wiley & Sons, New York, 1976.

BARKI, HENRI (McGill Univ., Montreal, Que., Canada); AND HUFF, SID L. (Univ. of Western Ontario, London, Ont., Canada)  **HCI-0296**
**Change, attitude to change, and decision support system success.**
*Inf. Manage.* **9,** 5 (Dec. 1985), 261–268.

User attitudes are the usual criteria for measuring successful implementation of information systems. The authors investigated 32 Decision Support Systems (DSS) and sought to demonstrate that significant relationships exist between the extent of changes caused by a DSS and its success; between individual user attitudes towards work related changes and the perceived degree of success their DSS enjoys; and between individual user attitudes toward work related changes and the extent of perceived DSS induced changes. Using questionnaires for each DSS they were using, six measures were obtained (User Information Satisfaction, System Use, Realization of Expectations, User Satisfaction, Extent of Changes Caused, and Attitude Toward Change). Correlational methods (N = 42) were employed and 15 pairwise correlations were tested, with 11 of them significant (0.05 level). The authors concluded that a DSS brings change to the decision maker/users' work environments. Decision maker/users expect a DSS to bring change, and a DSS that causes change is perceived to be more useful and, therefore, more widely used.

This is a solid research paper which should be of special interest to those decision/behavioral scientists who study change, attitudes to change, and their relationships to a DSS's success. The strength of the research lies in the authors' careful attention to the review of literature and their concern with classical psychometric validity and reliability details of the variables. On the other hand, this reviewer felt that the data analytic section might have been improved by additional analyses. Instead of relying on testing simple correlational coefficients, the authors might employ

Canonical Analysis (CA), in which the first four of the six measures listed above serve as the set of criterion variables and the last two variables be used as the set of independent variables. I believe that CA might have strengthened the discussion of the structure of the inter- and intra-relationships among the variables. In addition, the authors might consider the use of Canonical Judgment Analysis (C-JAN) procedures as an alternative way of capturing the policies of experts and decision scientists about their concepts of the possible linkage between the two sets of variables.

—*Sam Houston,* Greeley, CO

BUI, TUNG X. (Naval Postgraduate School, Monterey, CA); AND JARKE, MATTHIAS (New York Univ., New York, NY)
**Communications design for Co-oP: a group decision support system.**
ACM Trans. Office Inf. Syst. **4,** 2 (April 1986), 81–103.

Bui and Jarke define the problem of group decision making and show how a computer system can be used to support the process. Their paper, which is clearly written, describes many aspects of office dynamics—both of the group itself and of an individual relating to the group. From this basis, the paper describes the communications manager of Co-oP, a Group Decision Support System (GDSS). The communications manager of Co-oP controls the flow of information to individuals and between individuals.

The paper has a strong description of the problems to be solved with a GDSS, but fails to adequately describe the architecture of the communications manager and how it fits into the GDSS. It is written for a general audience, with the assumption that the reader is familiar with preference aggregation techniques for creating a group norm. There is a rich set of references (54 in number) which would have been improved by an indication of the more important contributors to the GDSS problem. Overall, I found this paper informative and valuable in its definition of the role of a GDSS and of the needs for communications within it.

—*D. A. Kirkman,* McLean, VA

SMITHIN, TIM; AND EDEN, COLIN (Univ. of Bath, Bath, UK)
**Computer decision support for senior managers: encouraging exploration.**
Int. J. Man-Mach. Stud. **25,** 2 (Aug. 1986), 139–152.

This is a paper on decision support systems from a slightly unusual perspective. Instead of offering technological solutions to decision making problems, it examines the psychological and political environment in which decisions are made. The authors present a collection of significant issues and suggest that avoidance of addressing these issues has hampered the acceptance of decision support systems. One of the issues they raise, for example, is the need to differentiate between machine intelligence and human intelligence, and to define the roles of each and the relationship between them. While this may appear to many as a philosophical question, it is both concrete and relevant to anyone designing a system that is intended to provide cognitive leverage.

Within the political environment of the organization they emphasize the need to view the decision maker as a "purposive and political actor" using the decision support system in the pursuit of personal and organizational objectives.

The authors of this paper are to be commended for writing about what they learned in the process of building a decision support system, rather than simply presenting the end result as an overwhelming success. I would strongly recommend this paper for anyone interested in information systems design, not just decision support systems. Though it raises more problems than it solves, it heightens the reader's awareness of important human factors issues beyond screen design and work flow analysis.

—*J. M. Artz,* Rockville, MD

LEE, DANIEL T. (Pan American Univ., Edinburg, TX) **HCI-0299**
**Personal computing for decision support.**
[in *Oxford surveys in information technology; vol. 2, 1985,* P. Zorkoczy (Ed.), Oxford University Press, Inc., New York, NY, 1985, 149-163.]

The author of this paper identifies three stages of evolution in computing over the past four decades: Electronic Data Processing, Management Information Systems, and Decision Support Systems. The last of these is seen to address the evident deficiencies of the previous stage through the provision of mechanisms that allow an executive user to browse through both individual files and corporate databases. This is accomplished by integration of computer and data management technologies, communications networking, decision models, and organizational management concepts.

Languages for end-users are discussed briefly, with specific reference to several common fourth generation languages. Operating systems for personal computers are also mentioned, with emphasis on MS-DOS (through its widespread acceptance) and UNIX (for the portability of applications implemented thereunder).

Under the heading Personal Computing and Data Communications, the author discusses local area networks (for information/resource sharing within the corporate environment) and digital communications networks (for accessing news, bulletin boards, and other external information sources). Satellite communications systems are also mentioned.

Overall, the paper suffers from the broad extent of its coverage. Also, the level of detail belies the promise of its title. Moreover, the extraordinary speed of progress in the field has left this paper (published in 1985) looking somewhat dated.

—*G. K. Jenkins,* Ashwood, Australia

CONKLIN, JEFF; AND BEGEMAN, MICHAEL L. (MCC, Austin, TX) **HCI-0300**
**gIBIS: a hypertext tool for exploratory policy discussion.**
*ACM Trans. Office Inf. Syst.* **6,** 4 (Oct. 1988), 303–331.

Computers have been most successfully employed to deal with well-structured problems in which inputs and outputs can be clearly specified and related. Over the years, however, interest has increased regarding the application of computers to unstructured problems such as complex decision making, collaboration among groups, and even conflict. This excellent paper describes a fascinating project that implemented a design process, *Issue Based Information Systems,* within a graphics system, gIBIS. The system records a design discussion by using nine kinds of links to connect issues, positions, and arguments. The graphic display of fragments enables users to recognize the current state of the discussion and make useful contributions.

This paper described the concepts behind gIBIS, the implementation of the specialized hypertext system, and user interface issues such as the browser, node indexes, color, and search and query facilities. The system was used by 33 issue groups; these groups produces 2094 nodes and 2214 links in the first year of use. The authors are careful with their enthusiasm and open enough to provide thoughtful criticism of their efforts, but gIBIS was clearly a successful prototype and we should expect to see more of it. In summary, this fine paper starts with an interesting concept, describes a real implementation, reports on actual usage, and makes thoughtful suggestions for the future.

—*B. Shneiderman,* College Park, MD

KASPER, GEORGE M. (Texas Tech Univ., Lubbock); AND CERVENY, ROBERT P. (State Univ. of New York at Buffalo, Buffalo)  **HCI-0301**
**A laboratory study of user characteristics and decision-making performance in end-user computing.**
*Inf. Manage.* **9,** 2 (Sept. 1985), 87–96.

Ninety-six students enrolled in a second year MBA class chose whether to use a command-language decision support tool or an end-user programming model as part of an eight-week class exercise. Students made weekly allocation of resources affecting the performance of a firm modeled in the computer. At some time during the eight weeks, 47 of the 96 students chose to develop an application as end user programmers. Prior use of a computer was observed to be a predictor for programming early in the period, but this became less important in the later weeks as students became more experienced with the computer tools available to them. Students who programmed and used their own applications consistently outperformed the students who only used the command-level preprogrammed facilities. The end-user programmers appeared to develop successful performance strategies in allocating resources that the command language users did not discover.

The authors acknowledge uncertainties in extrapolating observations made in an academic laboratory to field performance. They do discuss a correlation of questionnaire responses with management experience as a preliminary calibration. This work may be continued in later studies. This paper, appearing in the management literature, will be of peripheral interest to most computer scientists.

—*J. Bennett,* San Jose, CA

DOLK, DANIEL R. (Naval Postgraduate School, Monterey, CA)  **HCI-0302**
**A generalized model management system for mathematical programming.**
*ACM Trans. Math. Softw.* **12,** 2 (June 1986), 92–126.

This clearly written paper first proposes a conceptual framework, called a Model Management System (MMS), for the description, storage, manipulation, display, and solution of models, especially mathematical models, of real world systems. It then describes a prototype MMS called GXMP (Generalized eXperimental Math Programming system). GXMP has been implemented to handle some of the MMS functions for some mathematical programming models, particularly those solvable using Linear Programming (LP) techniques.

The author argues persuasively that an MMS should satisfy the following objectives:

(1) it should handle models and their conceptual components as database management systems (DBMS) handle data;
(2) it should be independent of particular solution algorithms;
(3) it should support multiple user views of models (from manager to model-builder);
(4) it should provide (expert system) support for building, integrating, and understanding models.

To support these objectives, the author proposes the representation of a model by a *model abstraction* consisting of objects, procedures, and rules. This is another generalization of the abstract data type. To facilitate processing related to objective (4), all three components of the model abstraction would be described in the first-order predicate calculus.

GXMP, which the author describes as "a first pass" at building an MMS, is described in terms of the following six components:

(1) *databases* of model parameters, equations, procedures, and abstractions, plus a *metadatabase* covering these four types of model object;
(2) a *modeling language* for expressing LP constraints and objective functions;
(3) a *model translator* to translate LP equations into sparse matrix form;
(4) a *model solver* to generate subroutine calls appropriate to the model;
(5) a *solution reporter* to control user-friendly display of the model solution; and
(6) a *menu dialog*.

Although GXMP is, as the author points out, in many respects far from achieving a full MMS, it does nevertheless provide support for the view that the comprehensive approach provided by an MMS is valuable in practice. In particular, there is evidence that the use of the model abstraction, the DBMS, and the modeling language could yield immediate, positive benefits. What is not so clear is the extent to which GXMP, the prototype, can feasibly be extended to satisfy objectives (1)–(4); nor does the author provide specific information about the processing overheads required for GXMP.

The author lists a number of areas for further research and development of GXMP, and he points out that in many cases, the appropriate course to follow is simply unknown. Developments such as the extension from LP to the mathematical programming techniques, or the introduction of a graphical rather than equational view of the model, or the introduction of inference mechanisms would raise questions for which there are at present simply no answers. The author perhaps places more faith in AI and systems technology than is really justified [1,2], and does not perhaps place enough emphasis on the enormous processing overheads that would result from extensions of GXMP.

All in all, I would have been more comfortable if the adverb "potentially" had been inserted in the paper's conclusion that "the model abstraction concept is a valuable tool for generalizing model management." It does not seem likely that an MMS much beyond the existing prototype in complexity can be achieved without the introduction of significant new techniques, such as massive parallelism [3].

—*W. F. Smyth,* Hamilton, Ontario, Canada

**REFERENCES**

[1] DREYFUS, H. L. *What computers can't do* (rev. ed.), Harper & Row, New York, 1979.

[2] VAN DE RIET, P. Expert systems in trouble?, in *Information Processing 86* (participants edition). Proc. IFIP 10th World Computer Congress, Dublin, 1986, 545–548.

[3] DENNING, P. J. Parallel computing and its evolution, *Commun. ACM* **29** (1986), 1163–1167.

MAHMOOD, MO A.; AND MEDEWITZ, JEANETTE N. (Univ. of Missouri, St. Louis)     **HCI-0303**
**Impact of design methods on decision support systems success: an empirical assessment.**
*Inf. Manage.* **9,** 3 (Oct. 1985), 137–151.

The purpose of the paper is to investigate the relationship between the choice of design method for a Decision Support System (DSS) and its ultimate success as measured by usage, user satisfaction, and user attitudes. Each of 16 teams of graduate students designed a DSS using one of three design methods: representation-based, evolutive, and adaptive. Each team consisted of three students with assigned roles of manager, designer, and intermediary. All participants rated the completed DSS according to eight criteria in each of the three categories mentioned above. In terms of usage and user satisfaction, participants in all three roles found the evolutive design method superior to the other two. The results were mixed in terms of user attitudes and perceptions.

The paper does give some insight into the relationship between the success and design method of a DSS. This is a first step that needs to be verified by further research. It is conceivable that some bias was introduced when the students learned the design methods. The categorization of each of the 24 criteria as to usage, user satisfaction, or user attitude was not entirely clear.

—*D. C. Haddad,* Oxford, OH

### H.4.3 Communications Applications

CULNAN, MARY J. (University of California)     **HCI-0304**
**The dimensions of accessibility to online information: implications for implementing office information systems.**
*ACM Trans. Office Inf. Syst.* **2,** 2 (April 1984), 141–150.

This paper is for the research and not recommended to the general reader. The article is tentative and based on a small student sample. The scale used to measure terminal accessibility may be of use to a research.

—*F. Newpeck,* Chicago, IL

TUROFF, MURRAY (New Jersey Institute of Technology)            **HCI-0305**
**Interface design in computerized conferencing systems: a personal view.**
[in *Human factors and interactive computer systems.* Proc. of the NYU symposium on user interfaces (New York, May 26-28, 1982), Y. Vassiliou (Ed.), Ablex Publishing Corp., Norwood, NJ, 1984, 243–259.]

[See main entry, Review HCI-0038.]

This paper puts forward four related propositions:

(1) That the design and evaluation of interactive information systems is, with our present knowledge of human behavior, an art rather than a science.
(2) That the use of interactive systems results in the evolution of new cognitive styles and new ways of working.
(3) That appropriate empirical research into the impact of information systems are difficult to organize and are probably best carried out by means of longitudinal studies.
(4) That two very important but sometimes neglected characteristics of certain classes of interactive systems are what Turoff calls "comprehension" and "sense of community."

    The author uses as an example to illustrate these propositions the interface design of the Electronic Information Exchange System (EIES) located at the New Jersey Institute of Technology. EIES is a multifeature system including conferencing, electronic mailing, and notebook facilities for use by a varying community of users, ranging from the most naive to the most highly sophisticated. The design of the system is flexible and evolving. The author stresses the importance of learning—both learning by the user and by the designer. This is facilitated by means of selected members of the user community called "user consultants" who advise on design, experiment with evolving features, and assist new users to become familiar with the system. The conclusion reached by Turoff seems, to this reviewer, to be valid and useful. The description of elements of the design of EIES should be interesting to designers of interactive systems.

                                                                                      —*Frank Land,* London, UK

KAYE, A. R. (Carleton Univ., Ottawa, Canada); AND MCDOWELL, RUSSELL      **HCI-0306**
(Bell-Northern Research, Ottawa, Canada)
**A user agent for multiple computer-based message services.**
[in *Computer-based message services.* Proc. of the IFIP WG 6.5 working conference (Nottingham, UK, May 1-4, 1984), H. Smith (Ed.), Elsevier North-Holland, Inc., New York, NY, 1984, 127–136.]

This paper is outdated by at least four years. It is aimed at the users of simple personal computers lacking refined software. The construction of an "umbrella environment" for accessing diverse nonstandardized CBMSs is documented here.

    A very useful functional specification, followed by adequate design and implementation considerations, is given together with the discussion of difficulties encountered. Unfortunately, inappropriate tools were used. It is surprising that the authors fail to ever mention the concepts of macros or pattern matching. As a result, a dumb agent was created, which does not understand the responses of a peer system but instead mechanically replays predetermined command sequences. No results of field-test experiments, if there were any, are provided.

The reviewer would suggest that the interested reader should become acquainted with such early works as [1], or selected papers presented at the ICS'81 conference in London [2,3].

—*J. Klaczak,* Katowice, Poland

**REFERENCES**

[1] ASH, W. L. MXEC reference manual, Report # 4372, BBN, Inc., July, 1979 (revised Feb. 1980), 136 pp.
[2] SOMMERVILLE, I. Providing the user with a tailor-made interface, in *System architecture,* Proc. of the sixth ACM European regional conference (London, UK, March 30–April 1, 1981), Westbury House, Surrey, UK, 1981, 321–329.
[3] EFE, K.; AND HOPPER, K. The KIWINET/NICOLA approach: matching OS responses to users, in *System architecture,* Proc. of the sixth ACM European regional conference (London, UK, March 30–April 1, 1981), Westbury House, Surrey, UK, 1981, 393–402.

EHRLICH, SUSAN F. (Wang Laboratories, Lowell, MA)                   HCI-0307
**Strategies for encouraging successful adoption of office communication systems.**
*ACM Trans. Office Inf. Syst.* **5,** 4 (Oct. 1987), 340–357.

The adoption of new computer communication systems into organizations requires behavioral change. Planning for successful adoption requires knowledge of individual organizational communication patterns and the relationship between those patterns and particular communication system solutions. This paper documents a sequence of studies of organizational communication. . . .

—*From the Summary*

The studies in question were (1) a series of studies done at three Wang customer sites on the adoption and use of Wang's centralized voice messaging system; (2) a generic evaluation of communication problems found in a manufacturing facility of an electronics firm; (3) a series of studies on the use of electronic calendars and electronic mail done internally at Wang; and (4) an internal study at Wang to explore social and psychological issues affecting the use of answering machines.

The first series included (1) the executive and sales network of an office furniture manufacturer, (2) the international department of a cigarette manufacturer, and (3) an internal "pilot" in an oil company.

There is an interesting emphasis in this paper on how people react to new technology. Is it a toy? Does my manager use it? Will it give me better access to people in power? How difficult is it to use? Is it reliable? Can I depend on it? Is it easy to master?

Computer folks have long been absorbed in the technical complexities of their trade to the exclusion of worrying about human interfaces, customer acceptance, and the like. This reluctance to tangle with a user's perceived problems is probably behind us at this point. However, it is useful to be reminded that it is not only a legitimate concern but also a swamp into which the best developed technical system can sink without a trace.

Can people learn to leave content-rich messages for unavailable people rather than simply a name and number to call back? Can meetings be rescheduled simply by altering the electronic calendars of the intended participants? Technically it can be done, but what rules govern the change? Who can make the change based on what criteria? How close to meeting time can a change be made and by whom? How much "jerking around" is OK? Does the ready ability to forward messages to others lead to the proliferation of junk mail? How soon must the system be combined with a security system to avoid the dissemination of confidential or private information? The paper contains some interesting observations and conclusions about these issues.

It will, however, occur to the information systems person that much of the subject matter focuses on how to use new technologies to support old ways of doing business. Why, in the furniture company where sales are dependent on the availability of inventory information on specific one-of-a-kind items, are messages still being routed around the company to ascertain availability?

The basis of information systems is that they attempt to represent what is going on in the real world—the physical world; it is possible to consult the information system for information rather than having to go out there and see if we have one. So, rather than improving the person-to-person message transfer system, should not the company bite the bullet and install a centralized inventory system—one that never sleeps, never takes an afternoon off to play golf, never is in a meeting? Of course it has to be right or, more precisely, it has to be accurate—both correct and up to date. If information about the situation right now is what is required, then a real-time system is needed. But do not be alarmed; this is 1988; these things have been done and are being done—affordably.

So I suppose I am left with the thought that the author's energies and skills might have been better employed telling us about strategies for encouraging the successful adoption of new office communication systems rather than old ones.

—*Jim Hammerton*, Pittsford, NY

## *Electronic mail*

SAKATA, SHIRO; AND UEDA, TETSUO (NEC Corporation, Kawasaki, Kanagawa, Japan) **HCI-0308**
**A distributed interoffice mail system.**
*Computer* **18,** 10 (Oct. 1985), 106–116.

A look inside an established NEC Corporation office support prototype, which integrates text and graphics into a distributed mail system, is given in this paper. The strength of the system appears to be the use of a NEC corporate standard for computer messaging systems: Information Interchange Architecture (IIA) and Information Content Architecture (ICA). These standards are used for the transmission of documents through a CMSA/CD LAN similar to Ethernet.

The authors explain the implementation of fundamental mail functions and the software structure that supports the system's text and graphics capabilities, in terms of document manipulation and user interface.

A previous version of this paper was presented at Compcon Fall '84 [1]. Because the system has been operating since February 1984, the current paper benefits from a good historical record

REVIEWS

that is being used to plan changes and additions to the system. For example, early system users had problems working with the large number of characters in kana (170) and kanji (2000) word processors. The authors report that later enhancements have shown that their system works effectively in the Japanese office environment.

While the references are oriented towards the internal system structure, this paper appears in a special issue of *IEEE Computer* devoted to multimedia communications. That issue is a good source of other efforts in this area.

Appropriate limits on implementation details and good use of figures, tables, and reproductions of workstation images are largely responsible for the success of the paper. There are some awkward passages that are difficult to comprehend, but a reader with basic knowledge of LANs, office automation, or human factors will be able to benefit from reading the paper.

—*S. C. Tarr,* Seattle, WA

**REFERENCES**

[1] SAKATA, S.; AND UEDA, T. Distributed interoffice mail system based on integrated document interchange protocols, *Proc. Compcon Fall '84*, Sept. 1984, 429–436.

---

POSTEL, JONATHAN B.; FINN, GREGORY G.; KATZ, ALAN R.; AND REYNOLDS, JOYCE K. (Univ. of Southern California, Marina del Rey)
**An experimental multimedia mail system.**
*ACM Trans. Office Inf. Syst.* **6**, 1 (Jan. 1988), 63–81.

> A computer-based experimental multimedia mail system that allows the user to read, create, edit, send, and receive messages containing text, images, and voice is discussed.

—*Authors' Abstract*

The world of interactive computers is not nearly as rich as the world we all live in every day. While many interactions between people actively combine sounds, motions, pictures, text, colors, and music, the terminal or workstation is limited to text, graphs, crude pictures, and poor sound and cannot really deal with rich combinations of elements. The system described in this paper explores ways to provide a much richer environment involving multiple media—text, pictures, and sound—as part of a next-generation electronic mail system.

Adding pictures and sound to mail systems requires the resolution of a surprisingly large number of design issues because no such system exists today. First, what should multimedia mail look like. Should all the elements of a message be delivered serially? Perhaps it makes sense to allow the sound to be delivered in parallel with the visual display to allow voice annotation or musical backgrounds. Should the display model be a fixed-size page? Perhaps a richer structure should be developed so the recipient of a message can choose to see certain support elements and ignore others.

Once we have developed a model for the appearance of our system, a host of human interface issues arise, such as getting images into the system, entering sounds, and editing images and soundtracks. When these issues have finally been dealt with, a new level of implementation considerations arises, including the encoding, storage, and reliable transmission of complex messages.

This paper is written at just the right level to be an excellent introduction to this fascinating topic. It provides a kind of design travelogue, which makes it easy for the reader to begin to understand how a multimedia mail system might be built. The authors supply enough technical details to allow an insight into the possible trade-offs, but the paper stays at a high enough level to be quite readable.

The authors begin with some background about the evolution of the system and its environment. Sponsored by DARPA, the research is intended to yield a real testbed that can be used to understand what having a multimedia mail system (MMMS) is like. The background includes a light introduction to the ARPANET and its support for the transmission of complex data streams, but it is hard to determine which aspects of the ARPA delivery system were developed as part of this project and which parts are standard.

Next, the paper describes a system model that divides the world in two:

(1) *message processing modules* move complex packages from user to user, and
(2) *user interface programs* help people create, send, receive, and read these messages.

All the issues about dealing with the richness of multiple media surface in the third section of the paper, which develops the presentation model. The authors experimented with several ways of providing the user with data, including parallel versus sequential presentation and fixed two-dimensional placement versus richer structures. This part of the paper is in many ways the most interesting and thought-provoking.

Next, the authors describe the actual program for creating and apprehending (reading/hearing/seeing?) messages. Most of the design comprises variations of concepts from other systems, such as multi-window editing, hierarchical linking, graphical editing, and raster scanning. They use a novel method for editing voice and sound—the user manipulates energy level graphs—which apparently works pretty well.

Finally, the authors briefly explore the future of MMMS. Some basic design issues remain unresolved—is multimedia mail just a richer form of traditional mail, or is it something completely new? The authors discuss the ramifications of each attitude.

This fascinating and well-written paper should be required reading for anyone thinking about the future of computer support for people who work together. Dealing with new kinds of data raises fundamental questions about our basic model of how computers support people. Approaching these questions by experimenting with actual design trade-offs allows the reader to learn a lot quickly, and the level of the description is exactly right for a reader who does not work with such a system every day.

Perhaps the only area where the authors should have spent more time is the future of multimedia mail. Given the amount of valuable information in the paper and the expressed goal of describing the actual experimental system, however, the paper is well done, well written, and worth reading.

—*D. Vaskevitch*, Bellevue, WA

REVIEWS

MACKAY, WENDY E. (Massachusetts Institute of Technology, Cambridge) **HCI-0310**
**Diversity in the use of electronic mail: a preliminary inquiry.**
*ACM Trans. Office Inf. Syst.* **6,** 4 (Oct. 1988), 380–397.

This tantalizing paper presents the results of preliminary surveys of electronic mail users taken just before the MIT Information Lens was introduced into their environment. The questions it raises are interesting enough to make the reader want to hear more, but no answers are available yet.

The Lens organizes and filters mail messages both before and after the user reads them; it uses rules and semistructured templates designed by and for the user to help people deal with a previously unstructured electronic world. To determine the effects of this software on a group of professional office workers, Mackay conducted a series of interviews measuring their pre-Lens states. The results, as reported in this paper, are inconclusive but suggest future research directions.

Mackay acknowledges repeatedly that the survey results do not answer any questions. Instead, she notes, they generate hypotheses for future testing. The data seem to suggest that electronic mail has diverse uses, though the diversity is constrained. People vary widely in their feelings of control over the environment, ranging from those who feel "in control," through those who are "on the edge," to some who freely admit that their electronic mail is completely out of control. I found this paper worthwhile despite preliminary nature and look forward to seeing the end results of the study.

—*Alan Wexelblat*, Austin, TX

NICHOLSON, ROBERT T. (Sydis Inc., San Jose, CA) **HCI-0311**
**Usage patterns in an integrated voice and data communications system.**
*ACM Trans. Office Inf. Syst.* **3,** 3 (July 1985), 307–314.

Many electronic mail users already sing the praises of this fast and efficient communication system. But what if you could also send a voice message on a sort of online tape recorder that enabled you to file, throw away, or mail voice messages, even in duplicate, to other system users? Using the Sydis Information Manager (SIM), developed by Sydis in San Jose, California, two offices, one in-house and the other located at a customer site, tested this communications system for more than a year. The findings were that both groups used voice messages and electronic mail. However, voice was preferred for short messages. Voice messages were primarily used for notes, to "add a personal touch," "convey nuances," or "replace face-to-face explanations." It took less time for users to compose voice messages than handwritten messages. Who knows? This could sound the death knell for yellow stickies.

—*Lenore Weiss*, Oakland, CA

## Teleconferencing

STEFIK, MARK (Xerox Palo Alto Research Center, Palo Alto, CA); FOSTER, GREGG (Univ. of California, Berkeley); BOBROW, DANIEL G.; KAHN, KENNETH; LANNING, STAN; AND SUCHMAN, LUCY (Xerox Palo Alto Research Center, Palo Alto, CA)
**Beyond the chalkboard: computer support for collaboration and problem solving in meetings.**
*Commun. ACM* **30,** 1 (Jan. 1987), 32-47.

HCI-0312

In one class of meetings, a small group works together (preferably face-to-face) to produce a report, a design, or a decision. At Xerox PARC, an experimental facility (Colab) has been set up to determine whether computer support can improve this class of meeting. This thorough paper describes Colab and its distributed computer system. It also describes initial experimental results in (a) collaborative writing and (b) proposal evaluation. Each person in the room has a workstation on which to "draw" or "type" inputs to the group activity. The displays are easy to read; all screens show the same windows. All the data can be retained, retrieved, reorganized, extended, evaluated, and changed by anyone at any time. It is easy to store everything and resume the meeting at a later date. Eventually, tie-ins to text processing and host information systems would let the group publish their results in a form ready for distribution. On the negative side, the use of a workstation requires some skill and probably takes something away from face-to-face interaction. The local network must be fast, transparent, and reliable. When all desired functions are installed in Colab, these performance objectives may be hard to meet. The authors plan to address these issues in future research. By analyzing both "meetings" and "meetings with computer support," they should be able to place a value on the Colab type of facility.

—*J. D. Aron,* Vienna, VA

## Videotex

NOLL, A. M. (Univ. of Southern California, University Park, CA)
**Videotex: anatomy of a failure.**
*Inf. Manage.* **9,** 2 (Sept. 1985), 99–109.

HCI-0313

Noll has previously worked at AT&T Consumer Products in the identification of opportunities for new products and services. He is thus eminently qualified to analyze the apparent failure, thus far, of videotex in the residential marketplace.

The slow penetration of Prestel in the UK is examined, and some reasons for this are offered. Among these are overenthusiasm on the part of the service provider and the information providers, a serious shortage of appropriate receivers, and a high usage cost. Some less tangible possibilities (e.g., frustration associated with tree searches of large databases) are also advanced, and the evident success of (broadcast) teletext in the UK is highlighted in support of these possibilities.

It is pointed out that the UK experience has been replicated in Germany, Sweden, France (with some differences in service emphasis), Canada, and the US. In light of this, some videotex characteristics are presented in a most valuable table, showing positive and negative attributes associated with each characteristic. Thus, the "color and graphics" characteristic is seen to be "pleasing" and to have "education and entertainment value"; at the same time, it results in "costly frame creation" and is "not needed for many services."

Some characteristics which are absent or underdeveloped in existing videotex implementations are also examined. Among these are interpersonal messaging and bulletin boards (e.g., for classified advertisement application). The usage of special (e.g., NAPLPS) character sets, rather than the universally available ASCII character set, is also presented as a significant disadvantage.

The paper concludes with a caution concerning the overenthusiasm of consultants and computer vendors. A comprehensive list of reference material is included. Overall, the paper is eminently readable, and is recommended for anyone with any degree of involvement in the videotex or public information system areas.

—*G. K. Jenkins,* Ashwood, Australia

# I. COMPUTING METHODOLOGIES

## I.2 Artificial Intelligence

### I.2.0 General

FELDMAN, JEROME A. (Univ. of Rochester, Rochester, NY); FANTY, MARK A. (International Computer Science Institute, Berkeley, CA); GODDARD, NIGEL H. (Hughes Aircraft Company, Calabasas, CA); AND LYNNE, KENTON J. (Univ. of Rochester, Rochester, NY)
**Computing with structured connectionist networks.**
*Commun. ACM* **31,** 2 (Feb. 1988), 170–187.

HCI-0314

This fascinating paper describes a research project to discover the algorithms that allow the brain to carry out vision, locomotion, and language understanding. The study of neural computation reveals that the brain can solve difficult problems in vision and language in a few hundred milliseconds or about 100 time steps. Today's MIMD/SIMD programs for such tasks are less general and require millions of computational time steps. The authors take the 100-step rule as a constraint in their algorithmic and computational research with connectionist networks. Their structural connectionist models could lead to advances in our ability to automate complex AI tasks. They propose research merging the neural network tradition with the computer science (algorithms plus data structures) tradition: the former is based on relaxation and adaption, and the latter on inference and representation.

—*P. C. Patton,* Minneapolis, MN

### I.2.1 Applications and Expert Systems

JACKSON, PETER (Univ. of Edinburgh, Edinburgh, Scotland); AND LEFRERE, PAUL (Open Univ., Milton Keynes, UK)

**On the application of rule-based techniques to the design of advice giving systems.**

*Int. J. Man-Mach. Stud.* **20,** 1 (Jan. 1984), 63–86. [Special issue: Developments in expert systems, part 2.]

Even the first-generation computer was able, if not to give advice, then at least to signal abnormal occurrences like overflow, low voltage, etc. A second-generation computer, developed in the 1960s with much more "intelligence" embodied in its software, gave a user with two clocks, one broken and the other losing four minutes per day, the advice to use the broken one; for it indicated the exact time two times a day, as opposed to two times a year for the retarder. The computers of the third-generation, using operating and virtual memory systems, oriented the user in the construction and debugging of programs via many-choice menus and progressive explanations. With the actual fourth-generation, a sophisticated planning system like PANDORA can deal with requests such as, "How can I save this file temporarily if I have no space left and can't contact the system manager?" The answer is: mail it to yourself.

The problem is now to improve the operating, planning, and expert systems in the light of the engineering knowledge principles, in order to give the next generation computers that dreamed-of capacity of entertaining long and substantial dialogues with users, analyzing situations, and offering valuable advice, so that even Turing would not be able to distinguish between natural and artificial minds. Is that possible? The present article and its 69 references seem to point in the affirmative direction. But the problem is not simple, for the natural languages were constructed during millions of years (see Hockett [1]). Hockett cites Edward Sapir, who wrote in 1921, "the lowliest South African Bushman speaks in the forms of a rich symbolic system that is in essence perfectly comparable to the speech of the cultivated Frenchman." Such a level is far from being attained by the most sophisticated artificial languages of the 20th century.

The authors, after reviewing current approaches to the provision of on-line advisory interaction with users (including Coombs and Alty; Naiman's WordStar; Stallman's EMACS; the "help key" of Foderaro's Franz LISP; Klemperer's MELVYL; Cullingford's CADHELP; Schrager's DCL-VMS; Faletti's PANDORA; Davis' TEIREISIAS; and Clancey's GUIDON), enunciate the principal problems facing an advisor for open-ended tasks. These include: establishing what a user is trying to do, helping him to plan ways to reach his goals, allowing for a two-way commentary, giving feedback on the progress or side-effects of commands, and deciding when to volunteer advice or to question the user. (All this seems to be good common sense, but the common sense is not so universally distributed as Descartes had thought.)

The man-machine dialogue, considered as a manifestation of a physical symbol system, is then analyzed in terms of speech acts, plans, and meta-level inference (interpreting user inputs, supporting planful behavior, and reasoning about control). The analysis of context-dependent interpretation of questions ("$p$?" = "how do I make $p$ true?" or "how do I do $p$?") and commands ("$p$" = "make $p$ true!" or "do $p$!") entails aspects of plan formation, plan revision, plan recognition, and plan generalization. An advice-giving program would have to be capable of a good deal of introspection. It would need access to a representation of its own theory of representation of the user's model of itself. But this goes beyond reasoning about control, for it bears the very creation of an artificial conscience.

The proposed application of rule-based systems to the interface between user and advice-giving program asks for "metahelp," needs continuous global representation, entails increasing system complexity, and gives rise to a lot of difficult questions (e.g., what constitutes a good mental model of a system?). Nevertheless, the approach can bring some valuable contribution through the very kind of analysis carried out and required by the codification of expertise, through the use of meta-rules allowing such program to reason about the way in which they are being used, and through the modularization of rule-like representations, lending extensions to principled systems.

—*T. Oniga,* Rio de Janeiro, Brazil

**REFERENCES**

[1] HOCKETT, C. F. The origin of speech, in *Human communication-language and its psychobiological base: readings from Scientific American* (reprinted from the Sept. 1960 issue), W. H. Freeman and Co., San Francisco, CA, 1982, 5–12.

ZIMMER, ALF C. (Westfalische Wilhelms Univ., Münster, West Germany)     **HCI-0316**
**A model for the interpretation of verbal predictions.**
*Int. J. Man-Mach. Stud.* **20,** 1 (Jan. 1984), 121–134.

The author proposes a model that makes use of an expert's qualitative predictions. This model "accounts for the verbal judgements in situations where predictions are made or knowledge is updated in the light of new information." The author argues that in many cases people are unable to make accurate predictions because numerical estimates require "more mental effort." The author ties this problem to fuzzy set theory. The results from one experiment indicate that the numerical predictions from the model are in good agreement with the judgements and behavior of subjects. The model was validated in a second experiment where bank clerks predicted exchange rates: "The analysis of qualitative judgements according to this model provided significantly more information than numerical predictions."

This article will not be of great interest to most computer scientists because of the "soft" nature of the variables being studied. AI researchers dealing with natural language, decisionmaking, or expert systems may find the material useful. Some very interesting ideas and figures are presented. However, little information of practical use is presented.

—*David R. Harris,* Fairfax, VA

CHIGNELL, MARK H.; AND PETERSON, JAMES G. (Univ. of Southern California, Los     **HCI-0317**
Angeles)
**Strategic issues in knowledge engineering.**
*Hum. Factors* **30,** 4 (Aug. 1988), 381–394.

This paper surveys potential interactions between knowledge engineering and human factors techniques from a human factors perspective. Its purpose is to introduce five aspects of knowledge engineering that may benefit from human factors techniques: selecting tasks, describing objects, identifying rules, validating expertise, and extending the paradigm. The authors briefly illustrate results and methods from the field of human factors that would pertain to each of these areas. They succinctly describe human factors methods such as repertory grid analysis, ranking, scaling, and verbal protocol analyses and also provide an extensive list of references.

This excellent introduction is intended to stimulate discussion between these two disciplines. Interaction with human experts and the efficient extraction of knowledge are vital, yet poorly understood, aspects of expert system construction. Good user interfaces are important not only for sales, but also for proficient use of the finished product. Since most knowledge engineers are more computer-oriented than people-oriented, this cross-fertilization should prove particularly beneficial.

—*Randy Garrett,* Alexandria, VA

TAYLOR, JOHN
**Expert systems—where do we go from here?.**
[in *Advanced information technology in the new industrial society: the Kingston seminars,* A. Cotterell, Oxford University Press, Inc., New York, NY, 1988, 73-82.]

This good paper would be excellent if the author had generalized his conclusions and related them to his opening remarks. Taylor begins by pointing out that AI research has moved from "trying to build machines with some aspect of general human intelligence" to "building increasingly powerful knowledge-based tools . . . to . . . solve quite specific types of problems in quite specific domains." These tools are expert systems.

Taylor believes that three advances will characterize the field over the next decade. (1) He expects a movement from "small, hand-crafted special-purpose knowledge bases to large assemblages of knowledge which can be used by a wide variety of different application systems for many different purposes." (2) Knowledge-based consultants will "cooperate with the user in a flexible dialogue where either side may have the initiative according to the needs of the problem"; they will also "co-operate with each other" to help the user solve more general problems. (3) The use of networks will proliferate and "islands of AI" will be connected by bridges of all sorts, making possible the kind of general problem solving no single system and its associated knowledge base could support.

What is missing from this discussion is that these three developments in concert bring us back to trying to build machines (or networks of machines) with general intelligence. The author hints at this by mentioning the possibility of obtaining an "engineering science" out of future expert systems. I cannot be sure whether progress in expert systems will lead the AI community back, in some respects, to its original goals, but Taylor makes a plausible case and his paper is interesting reading.

—*Joseph Fulda,* New York, NY

# REVIEWS

BOYLE, C. D. (Univ. of London, UK)  **HCI-0319**
**Acquisition of control and domain knowledge by watching in a blackboard environment.**
[in *Expert systems 85*. Proc. of the fifth technical conference of the British Computer Society Specialist Group on Expert Systems (Univ. of Warwick, Warwick, UK, Dec. 17-19, 1985), M. Merry (Ed.), Cambridge University Press, New York, NY, 1986, 273–286.]

This paper addresses the problem of acquiring control information for expert systems. Specifically, the author considers the desirability of attaining such information by observing experts solve problems. The discussion is in the context of a system using a blackboard environment, JOBBES, which provides career advice. The basic approach is to make use of multiple levels of abstraction and to have experts solve problems and provide reasons for their actions. Then the program compares the experts' actions with its own rules and appropriately modifies the rule base.

The problem with which this paper deals is an important one, and the approach seems interesting. However, there is not really enough detail to fully understand the method. Further, there is not much description of how this work relates to other research; thus it is hard to get a handle on the major contributions. In addition, reading the paper is rather tough sledding in a few places. A substantial example is provided, but it is not easy to determine the key points. Since the approach seems promising, the interested reader—researchers concerned with the future of expert systems should be interested—should look for a fuller treatment of the author's work.

—*M. Lebowitz*, New York, NY

## Industrial automation

BROWN, DAVID C. (Worcester Polytechnic Institute, MA); AND CHANDRASEKARAN, B.  **HCI-0320**
(Ohio State Univ.)
**Knowledge and control for a mechanical design expert system.**
*Computer* **19**, 7 (July 1986), 92–100. [Special issue on expert systems in engineering.]

Knowledge engineering in design is an immature field. The authors say that existing design expert systems (mostly rule-based) have been ad hoc responses to particular design domains, and post the objective of treating design as a "generic task in knowledge-based reasoning" with appropriate "families of high-level languages." This paper deals with "routine design," argued to be a significant subclass of design, where design alternatives and selection methods are known for each design decision. A language for routine design (DSPL), written in LISP, is applied to air-cylinder design; it is put forward as a generalized language, not specific to this domain, but no other applications are mentioned. An informal description of the language is supplemented by fairly full examples. The actual performance of the air-cylinder test case, with 15 parts to be specified, is not made clear.

Unlike a rule-based system where actions are taken by matching independent rules against the state of the system, here design actions ("steps") are grouped into definite plans, so behavior is tightly controlled. A design domain is broken down into subproblems ("specialists"), each with a number of alternative plans. Specialists call subspecialists in a top-down hierarchy. The language includes explicit failure-recovery strategies.

Apart from some repetition, the paper is clearly organized. However, it uses a number of familiar words in context-specific ways that should have been more carefully defined. The tone is optimistic rather than rigorous.

This does not add up to a generalized model of design, but there is one key idea, that "specialists" can capture task-level design knowledge. The paper's contribution lies in putting a little flesh around this idea.

—*William Hugh Fawcett,* Cambridge, UK

FAUGHT, WILLIAM S. (IntelliCorp, Mountain View, CA)
**Applications of AI in engineering.**
*Computer* **19,** 7 (July 1986), 17–27. [Special issue on expert systems in engineering.]

This paper is an advertisement for IntelliCorp's Knowledge Engineering Environment (KEE), ActiveImages, SIMKIT, and KEEPictures. That is one part of the bad news.

One of the stated goals of this paper is to describe typical engineering applications, presumably of AI, in the areas of fault diagnosis, simulation, and configuration. These applications are as follows:

- ☐ A NASA prototype of a fault diagnostic expert system for Space Station.
- ☐ A system, being developed by Ford Aerospace and Communications Corp., to diagnose faults in satellite subsystems.
- ☐ Northrop's simulation of a sheet metal factory to evaluate methods to reduce setup and throughput time.
- ☐ Electric Power Research Institute's prototype expert program to determine fuel shuffling strategies in a nuclear power plant.

The rest of the bad news is that the Northrop example is a simulation application, not an Artificial Intelligence application. The applications are prototypes or demonstration projects. Hopefully, these are not *typical* engineering applications of AI. If these were typical applications, then there should have been a discussion of the problems of scaling the applications up from their current toy size. Maybe the title should have been "Applications of IntelliCorp's Software to Some Toy Engineering Problems."

Now here is the good news. Most of the paper is devoted to a top-level description of each application from a knowledge engineer's point of view. These descriptions are clear and complete. The paper is worth reading for the descriptions. Also, the rules of thumb, called in the paper the "methodology" of developing systems, offer an insight into the analysis of the applications.

—*F. S. Shipman,* Newport News, VA

# REVIEWS

## Natural language interfaces

COLOMBETTI, MARCO; GUIDA, GIOVANNI; PERNICI, BARBARA; AND SOMALVICO,     **HCI-0322**
MARCO (Politecnico di Milano, Milan, Italy)
**Reasoning in natural language for designing a data base.**
[in *Artificial and human intelligence*. Proc. of the international NATO symposium (Lyon, France, Oct. 1981), A. Elithorn; and R. Banerji (Eds.), Elsevier North-Holland, Inc., New York, NY, 1984, 297–314.]

[See main entry, Review HCI-0052.]

This paper is devoted to the problem of interactive design of a database schema using a natural language interface. It relies on the observation that the knowledge representations used for natural language processing and for computer-aided design must have a significant intersection. The research reported is preliminary: an architecture for a CAD system with a natural language component is suggested. The architecture is sound; the theoretical foundations for the project are proper.

—*S. Nirenburg,* Hamilton, NY


DEFUDE, B. (Laboratoire Genie Informatique (IMAG), St Martin D'Heres Cedex,     **HCI-0323**
France)
**Knowledge based systems versus thesaurus : an architecture problem about expert systems design.**
[in *Research and development in information retrieval*. Proc. of the third joint BCS and ACM symposium (King's College, Cambridge, July 2-6, 1984), C. van Rijsbergen (Ed.), Cambridge University Press, New York, NY, 1984, 267–280.]

This paper presents the argument that a language thesaurus should play a central role in natural language interfaces to information retrieval systems. The thesaurus will include terms related to the application area and the semantic relations connecting them (e.g., synonymy, semantic proximity, generic/specific relations). The natural language interface will support both interrogation and reformulation of queries, and will be sensitive to the user's level of expertise (thus identifying him as a specialist user if his queries are accurately and precisely formulated).

The "architecture problem" referred to in the title is the question of whether the thesaurus is integrated into the knowledge-based system or stands alone as a separate module which is queried by it. The practical impact of this distinction remains somewhat unclear to this reviewer. The author concludes that "an integrated thesaurus is relatively complex but it has many interesting deduction aspects; on the other hand, an independent thesaurus may be more complete but is more difficult to use in deduction processes."

—*Ian H. Witten,* Calgary, Alta., Canada

MAAS, ROBERT E.; AND SUPPES, PATRICK (Stanford Univ., Stanford, CA)
**Natural-language interface for an instructable robot.**
*Int. J. Man-Mach. Stud.* **22**, 2 (Feb. 1985), 215–240.

The problem of instructing a robot is similar to that of instructing a child, but much more difficult, because the robot has no linguistic background to understand declarations and interpret instructions for specific actions. Some 30 years ago, Giuglio Pasqualigo, in a communication sent to the Brazilian Academy of Science, made a very curious inquiry: Could a population of intelligent robots (or "cybes," according to his designation) exhibit or simulate the behavior of a human society? The answer was negative because an artificial brain lacks at least 20 basic thinking principles, such as the notion of number (and the very possibility to elaborate general concepts starting from perceptions), that of infinity, the basic axioms of arithmetic (according to Peano) and geometry (due to Hilbert), the logical mechanisms of deduction, and those, much more complex, of induction; besides, an artificial brain lacks the capacity to feel emotions and to manifest will or intention. Nevertheless, analyzing the problems related with the instruction of an artificial mind (robot), one can identify the necessary steps to progressively create and enlarge the missing background for intelligent and concise communication through natural language.

In preceding work (e.g., Winograd's SHRDLU program [1], the HEARSAY-II [2], HARPY [3], and Miller and Johnson-Laird [4]), the principal objective was the understanding of the speech uttered in natural language. The present work aims at the general and more ambitious question of designing systems capable of building new procedures out of already known ones. This is approached by using interactive features somehow similar to the interactive theorem provers and much more flexible and elaborate than simple "macro" instructions. The basic experimental system is comprised of the following:

- a grammar and a parser (consisting of a preparser, a main parser, and a postparser);
- the translation from parsed English to operator language, providing a semantic interpretation for the new primitive LISP-atoms that can occur: operators (e.g., ADD), actors (e.g., DEFAULT-NUMBER), and data (e.g., TOP);
- the execution of procedures, including an interpretation and full analysis of the execution, with references to past steps; and
- a learning procedure, enabling the change in behavior, without any restriction imposed on the English as source language; hence, it allows ambiguities, which are resolved by asking questions.

The last aspect seems of fundamental importance because, in the traditional programming of computers, the source language must be completely free of ambiguities: the computer cannot have doubts. The compilation of the English to formulate new procedures in LISP S-expressions involves three parts: (1) the translation of the English into operator language, containing some ambiguities; (2) the interaction of that translation with the problem context, which resolves some of the ambiguities; and (3) the interaction with the user (as a teacher) to resolve the remaining ambiguities.

The first program was limited to the teaching of addition and subtraction by columns. Various improvements appeared necessary before extending the system to other forms of knowledge representation; but the results seem valid and encouraging, notwithstanding the limitation to a very restricted domain of the procedures involved.

Further developments the authors hope to accomplish in the future will certainly entail (1) the necessity to use a very large memory, (2) the adoption of specialized techniques for classification and retrieval of abstract concepts, and (3) intensive use of parallel programming; then they may be able to imitate the extraordinary capacity of the human brain.

—*T. Oniga,* Rio de Janeiro, Brazil

**REFERENCES**

[1] WINOGRAD, T. *Understanding natural language,* Academic Press, New York, 1972. See *Computing Reviews* **13**, 11 (Nov. 1972), Rev. 24,047.

[2] ERMAN, L. D.; HAYES-ROTH, F.; LESSER, V. R.; AND REDDY, D. R. The Hearsay-II speech understanding system: integrating knowledge to resolve uncertainty, *ACM Comput. Surv.* **12** (1980), 213–253. See *Computing Reviews* **22**, 8 (Aug. 1981), Rev. 38,292.

[3] LOWERRE, B. T.; AND REDDY, R. The HARPY speech understanding system, in *Trends in speech recognition,* W. A. Lea (Ed.), Prentice-Hall, Englewood Cliffs, NJ, 1980.

[4] MILLER, G. A.; AND JOHNSON-LAIRD, P. N. *Language and perception,* Harvard University Press, Cambridge, MA, 1976.

SLEEMAN, D. (Stanford Univ., Stanford, CA)
**UMFE: a user modelling front-end subsystem.**
*Int. J. Man-Mach. Stud.* **23,** 1 (July 1985), 71–88.

HCI-0325

Most interactive computer systems respond to users as if each possessed an identical and high expertise, which is an obviously incorrect assumption. The present paper describes a system which can act as a sympathetic interpreter between the user and the output of a package which is providing, as an example, the explanation for a particular medical diagnosis. Two very important ideas are introduced: that this protective interface should be able to learn discreetly of its user's strengths and weaknesses; and that it should also be able to interpret and explain the responses from other system facilities in a special way appropriate to the particular user.

As so often happens in AI work, the practical results seem rather trivial compared with the expertise so clearly deployed, and I am not convinced that simple mathematical logic is a suitable basis for describing the user. I also believe that systems which are not able to ignore inconsistencies and still produce usable results by some sort of "rough" reasoning will end up in a complexity explosion, which I think of as a wall of porridge (you don't know you are in it until you have gone too far to stop). But then, AI programs are always written in "logical" languages which have the approximate aspects of natural language carefully expunged. Perhaps that is where we should start the search for user-friendliness.

—*E. James,* London, UK

KIDD, A. L. (British Telecom Research Laboratories, Ipswich, UK)  **HCI-0326**
**What do users ask? Some thoughts on diagnostic advice.**
[in *Expert systems 85*. Proc. of the fifth technical conference of the British Computer Society Specialist Group on Expert Systems (Univ. of Warwick, Warwick, UK, Dec. 17-19, 1985), M. Merry (Ed.), Cambridge University Press, New York, NY, 1986, 9–19.]

The paper is concerned with the requirements of expert systems for providing advice to persons (so-called users) who are faced with acute problems of practical, everyday life. The main contribution of the study is a review of observations made of actual conversations between users and expert advisors.

The main conclusions are that users seeking practical advice are primarily concerned with remedies, not with identifications of faults, and that the proper remedy can only be found by the expert who is guided by the user's specific intentions, expectations, and constraints, as brought up in the conversations. What is not noted is that these conclusions are obvious as soon as it is realized that the very notion of a problem implies a person in a problem situation, and that any problem must include, as an inherent aspect, that person's situation, attitudes, experience, etc.; in other words, items that are infinitely varied and can be brought out only by the person himself or herself. It is realized in the paper that artificial response systems that take these aspects into account in full generality "will not be achieved for some time yet." Meanwhile, the authors are engaged in experiments on less ambitious formulations of the advice-giving problem.

—*P. Naur,* Copenhagen, Denmark

DIEDERICH, JOACHIM; RUHMANN, INGO; AND MAY, MARK (German Research  **HCI-0327**
Institute for Mathematics and Data Processing, Sankt Augustin, W. Germany)
**KRITON: a knowledge-acquisition tool for expert systems.**
*Int. J. Man-Mach. Stud.* **26**, 1 (Jan. 1987), 29–40. [Knowledge acquisition for knowledge-based systems, part 1. Based on an AAAI workshop.]

The goal of the research described here is to develop a system, called KRITON, that can acquire domain-specific problem-solving knowledge by interviewing experts, analyzing protocols, and understanding documents.

KRITON interviews the expert using the *repertory grid approach*, that is, it presents triples of semantically similar concepts and asks the expert to distinguish two of the concepts from the third. If this proves difficult, the system tries *laddering*, that is, it asks the expert for important concepts supported by examples, supertypes, and subtypes.

KRITON analyzes transcribed protocols of problem-solving sessions in five steps: using the expert's pauses to segment the session into chunks, extracting propositions in the form of operations and arguments from the text, evaluating the appropriateness of each proposition, resolving pronominal references, and ordering propositions according to their appearance in the protocol.

KRITON analyzes relevant documents by interacting with an expert. The expert, based on keyword statistics on articles, selects portions of texts for propositional analysis using the same tools used in protocol analysis. Since documents are normally not as problem oriented as protocols, the expert adds goal information to the results of the analysis.

This paper raises some major questions. First and foremost, how does KRITON understand protocols and documents when unrestricted text understanding is one of the great unsolved problems in AI? Second, when KRITON interviews experts using the repertory grid and laddering approaches, how does it avoid sounding like a lunatic hopping from concept to concept? Does KRITON also solve the hard problem of designing conversational human-machine interfaces? Although a prototype has been implemented in InterLisp, no examples of output are given, so it is impossible to see how the system behaves or how it answers the concerns just raised. Either this paper is more promise than practice, or KRITON is a true breakthrough in artificial intelligence applications.

—*C. Riesbeck,* Evanston, IL

DE MORI, RENATO (Concordia Univ., Montreal, Canada); GIORDANA, ATTILIO (Università di Torino, Torino, Italy); LAFACE, PIETRO (Politecnico de Torino, Torino, Italy); AND SAITTA, LORENZA (Università di Torino, Torino, Italy)
**An expert system for mapping acoustic cues into phonetic features.**
*Inf. Sci. (New York)* **33,** 1/2 (July/Aug. 1984), 115–155.

This paper describes the concepts of sublexical levels of speech understanding system. This paper is easy to read, understand, and it is well footnoted. The authors address the areas of "speaker independence" and the "acquisition of new knowledge." Readers involved in speech understanding systems will find it interesting. A summary of the paper follows.

The concepts introduced in this paper will serve as the basis for two future papers which the authors indicate will be developed. One future paper will be on the different approaches to slot fitting (knowledge acquisition). The second will be an architectural design for a real-time implementation of the system described in this paper.

The authors start the paper with a short introduction to the structure of expert systems. Following the introduction, there is a brief definition of how the tasks of speech understanding are broken down. This breakdown is based on existing knowledge and experiences with speech understanding systems. Using sets of algorithms and/or knowledge performed in parallel, communications between tasks is performed.

A procedural language known as frame is introduced. This procedural language is an effort to formalize a method of speech perception. This frame language allows the integration between structural and procedural knowledge. Structural knowledge deals with relationships between facts, like acoustic-cue descriptions, and phonetic-feature hypotheses. Procedural knowledge deals with rules ofr the use of relations, for the generation fo contextual constraints for relation application, and for the extraction of new cues in specified contexts.

Finally, some experimental results on the proposed system are discussed in the paper. The experimental results indicate good performance for an unconstrained set of English, French, and Italian sentences, spoken by both males and females.

—*G. Paseika,* New York, NY

### I.2.3 Deduction and Theorem Proving

RENC, ZDENĚK (Charles Univ., Prague, Czechoslovakia); AND SETIKOVSKA, LENKA     **HCI-0329**
(Computing Technics Enterprise, Liberec, Czechoslovakia)
**Decision trees: a contribution to automatic interpretation of GUHA results.**
*Int. J. Man-Mach. Stud.* **22,** 2 (Feb. 1985), 193–207.

The GUHA method is a class of methods for the mechanized construction of interesting hypotheses justifiable on the basis of given data. In this paper, the results are represented by elementary implications which are verifiable on some model (experimental data). However, the set of elementary implications can be very large, and the process of finding subsets of implications which are interesting requires an efficient data structure for implementation. The data structure used for this purpose is a decision tree which is defined within the context of the GUHA method.

This paper gives the necessary background on the GUHA method with implicational quantifiers and investigates the following problem: to decide whether, for a set of elementary implications based on some model, there exists a decision tree for this model. If such a decision tree exists, the paper describes a labeling scheme for the decision tree such that an ordering of decision trees can be defined and consequently the best decision tree determined. Furthermore, the algorithms for the generation of these decision trees and the finding of the best decision tree are detailed in the paper, along with examples which motivate the methods under discussion.

—*R. W. Wilkerson,* Rolla, MO

### I.2.4 Knowledge Representation Formalisms and Methods

MAIDA, ANTHONY S. (Pennsylvania State Univ., University Park)     **HCI-0330**
**Selecting a humanly understandable knowledge representation for reasoning about knowledge.**
*Int. J. Man-Mach. Stud.* **22,** 2 (Feb. 1985), 151–161.

Knowledge representation for objects and concepts that serve in multiple roles is the topic of this paper. This problem arises primarily in natural language processing. An example is representing the equivalence of the Morning Star, the Evening Star, and the planet Venus. Agent X may know their equivalence, and agent Y may not. Further, X may know that Y does not know their equivalence. Both logic and semantic network approaches are discussed. While the paper gives a good overview of the problem, the interested reader will most likely have to consult its references for more details.

—*John M. Hammer,* Norcross, GA

HOLLNAGEL, ERIK (Computer Resources International, Copenhagen)     **HCI-0331**
**Cognitive models, cognitive tasks, and information retrieval.**
[in *Knowledge engineering: expert systems and information retrieval,* I. Wormell (Ed.), Taylor Graham Publishers, London, UK, 1987, 34-52.]

Cognitive systems engineering emphasizes the cognitive functions and characteristics that are essential in interactions between two cognitive systems. This paper focuses on two considerations:

cognitive task analysis and transparency. Hollnagel discusses both of these aspects of cognitive systems in the context of human-machine systems. The paper is not explicitly related to information retrieval, as the title and abstract claim.

—*R. Crawford,* Kingston, Ont., Canada

## I.2.6 Learning

HINTON, GEOFFREY E. (Carnegie-Mellon Univ., Pittsburgh, PA)  HCI-0332
**Learning in parallel networks: simulating learning in a probabilistic system.**
*BYTE* **10,** 4 (April 1985), 265–273.

This is a short, popular account of some current work in machine learning, introduced with a description of convergence in perceptron-like networks. The author discusses Hopfield nets, which seek "minimum energy" patterns such that active units have maximal interfacilitation, and his own Boltzmann Machines, in which unit activation is probabilistic and the network settles to a "thermal equilibrium" in the presence of such background noise. The reference list contains a couple of more substantial papers.

—*J. R. Sampson,* Edmonton, Alberta, Canada

SHRAGER, JEFF; AND KLAHR, DAVID (Carnegie-Mellon Univ., Pittsburgh, PA)  HCI-0333
**Instructionless learning about a complex device: the paradigm and observations.**
*Int. J. Man-Mach. Stud.* **25,** 2 (Aug. 1986), 153–189.

This paper deals with the analysis of protocols. The data are taken from seven college students at Carnegie-Mellon University as they attempt to learn how to operate a programmable tank-like toy called BigTrak (manufactured by Milton Bradley Corporation), without having been given instructions. The authors are concerned with the interaction of such cognitive processes as concept formation, rule induction, learning by analogy, and design of experiments, as they contribute to a comprehensive model called Instructionless Learning. They focus on several aspects of the knowledge-acquisition process and provide quantitative and qualitative analysis of protocol data.

While the basic purpose of this research was fulfilled, the paper could probably have been shortened a bit. Overall, it does read well and provides a clear statement of the need for this kind of study. The intended audience is anyone involved in cognitive theory construction. Compared with other research involving analysis of human protocols, this document is admirable. One does not easily become lost in cryptic notation. The references are reasonable and the example raw protocol in the Appendix enhances the presentation. A larger number of subjects, having a more diverse age range, would have added considerably to the generalizability of statistical results. For someone interested in this area of research, this document is definitely worthwhile.

—*J. N. Rose,* Delhi, NY

ENGELBART, DOUGLAS C.; AND ENGLISH, WILLIAM K. (SRI International, Menlo Park, CA)  **HCI-0334**
**A research center for augmenting human intellect.**
[in *Computer-supported cooperative work: a book of readings,* I. Greif (Ed.), Morgan-Kaufmann, Palo Alto, CA, 1988, 81-105.]

This paper describes a research project at Stanford Research Institute that is intended to increase human intellectual capabilities. The authors claim that the research emphasizes the development of principles and techniques that will allow researchers to understand the process of augmenting these capabilities. This includes concern not only for providing an interactive computing environment, but also for making it easier to conceptualize, visualize, and organize working materials. They also discuss the hardware, software, and user interface of the center's computing facility. What they fail to mention is exactly how this augmentation of human intellectual capabilities will take place. In other words, how are this research group and its environment different from any other research group? How will this work augment, rather than merely support, human intellectual capabilities? Augmentation of human intellectual capabilities is a strong phrase that needs to be supported by proper documentation. The presence of state-of-the-art hardware, software, and user interfaces is necessary but not sufficient for this purpose.

An interesting aspect of the research project is that the researchers themselves will be used as subjects in the experiment. This should provide them with first-hand information about the difficulties encountered in designing complex computer-based information systems. The flaw in this approach is that the sample is biased toward the environment the subjects are working in. In other words, it will not replicate the real-world problem in the real-world setting.

—*M. Mahmood,* El Paso, TX

YASDI, R. (Univ. of Windsor, Windsor, Ont., Canada); AND ZIARKO, W. (Univ. of Regina, Regina, Sask., Canada)  **HCI-0335**
**An expert system for conceptual schema design: a machine learning approach.**
*Int. J. Man-Mach. Stud.* **29,** 4 (Oct. 1988), 351–376.

In this paper, we report the design specifications and design principles of EXIS, an expert system for conceptual schema design for an information system currently under development. We focus on machine learning aspects applicable to schema design. The main idea can be highlighted better if integrated with a complete framework of the design environment. Therefore, we first describe a conceptual database model consisting of a semantic model and an event model. Hereafter, we present our approach to design knowledge acquisition and representation which is based on inducing schema design rules from examples. We also present relevant aspects of the theory of Rough Sets and the learning method used in our system. Throughout the paper we discuss several concepts and techniques for expert system design which proved very useful and can be adapted to any other application. Here we tend to avoid being ambiguous by using first order logic to express our ideas.

—*Authors' Abstract*

NONBOOKS [HCI-0337]

## Knowledge acquisition

BOOSE, JOHN H.; AND BRADSHAW, JEFFREY M. (Boeing Computer Services, Seattle, WA) **HCI-0336**
**Expertise transfer and complex problems: using AQUINAS as a knowledge-acquisition workbench for knowledge-based systems.**
*Int. J. Man-Mach. Stud.* **26,** 1 (Jan. 1987), 3–28. [Knowledge acquisition for knowledge-based systems, part 1. Based on an AAAI workshop.]

Aquinas is a tool for creating knowledge bases for several different expert system shells. In this system, knowledge is represented by a set of *rating grids*. A rating grid consists of a number of problem solutions, which are differentiated by assigning weighted ranking values to their properties. Rating grids provide the basic data for performing "reasoning." They are structured hierarchically within the knowledge base, grouping together problem solutions at equivalent levels of abstraction. The hierarchical structure also permits subgrouping of expert knowledge sources within problem-solving contexts. A knowledge base may therefore be assembled from modules created by a number of experts.

In the construction phase, a dialogue manager provides guidance to the expert. Each module can be tested and checked for inconsistencies before inclusion. Despite the interactive dialogue manager, Aquinas requires mastery of many advanced conceptual skills, and it would seem unlikely that a subject expert would be able to use Aquinas without assistance from a knowledge engineer. This is obviously important because both ease of use and time spent are directly related to the cost of knowledge base production.

The rating grid principle itself is not new. It can successfully cope with problems whose solutions can be enumerated in a satisfactory way, but I would suggest that only essentially trivial problems are amenable to this approach, not those that would demand consultation with an expert.

No reference is made to the appearance of the system to an end-user making inquiries of the knowledge base. If the system is to be used in environments outside the laboratory, it must be simple to understand and use. It must also be able to present sufficient background information to an inquirer, in a variety of formats, to allow reasoned judgments to be made.

—*R. P. Lister,* London, UK

STEVENSON, R. J. (Univ. of Durham, Durham, UK); MANKTELOW, K. I. (Sunderland Polytechnic, Sunderland, UK); AND HOWARD, M. J. (Univ. of Durham, Durham, UK) **HCI-0337**
**Knowledge elicitation: dissociating conscious reflections from automatic processes.**
[in *People and computers IV.* Proceedings of the Fourth Conference of the British Computer Society (Univ. of Manchester, UK, Sept. 5–6, 1988), D. Jones; and R. Winder (Eds.), Cambridge University Press, New York, NY, 1988, 565–579.]

The authors discuss a well-known phenomenon: a skill that is at first performed laboriously becomes internalized and automatic. Drawing from the work of Fitts and Posner [1] and, more recently, Anderson [2], the authors suggest that "proceduralization" is the process by which a skill becomes automatic: the knowledge that underlies the skill is at first declarative but becomes procedural. They attribute the difficulty of verbalizing automatic skills to this proceduralization. In my opinion, this theoretical argument needs far more supporting evidence than the authors give here.

The authors go on to describe a small empirical study that contrasted three methods of knowledge acquisition: traditional verbalization, statistical methods, and a new approach—verbalization during the replay of a videotape made of the task. They conclude that the last technique is the most successful, and they attribute its success to the dissociation of automatic actions from conscious reflections. This dissociation allows for the construction of production rules after the fact, mirroring what occurs during the task. For this reason, the authors suggest that their technique—which they term an *evaluation task*—is the best approach to use in knowledge elicitation situations where much of the knowledge is automatic.

While I am in sympathy with this final suggestion for a variety of *other* reasons, neither the bibliographic nor the empirical research in this paper convinces me that the technique's success is due to the reasons given or is limited to the situations the authors consider. Knowledge engineers should read this paper because it poses an interesting question and raises some alternatives as potential answers.

—*Joseph Fulda*, New York, NY

**REFERENCES**

[1] FITTS, P. M. AND POSNER, M. I. *Human performance*. Brooks/Cole, Belmont, CA, 1967.
[2] ANDERSON, J. R. The acquisition of cognitive skill. *Psychol. Rev.* **18** (1982), 396–406.

### I.2.7 Natural Language Processing

BOGURAEV, B. K.; AND SPARCK JONES, K. (Univ. of Cambridge, Cambridge, UK)
**A natural language front end to databases with evaluative feedback.**
[in *New applications of data bases*. Proc. of the ICOD-2 workshop (Cambridge, UK, Sept. 2-3, 1983), G. Gardarin; and E. Gelenbe (Eds.), Academic Press, Inc., San Diego, CA, 1984, 159–182.]

The problem of interpreting a question formulated in Natural Language (NL), in order to derive a search query in the domain-dependent and administrative knowledge language of a database, has acquired a high priority in the last ten and, mainly, in the last five years. It is, in fact, a particular case of the construction of a natural language translator, conceived as an interface between exigent users and intelligent computers, which is (or will be) a very large and memory-consuming program, for it must include a vocabulary of up to 100,000 words and a cumbersome semantics, besides some hundreds or thousands of syntactic rules and exceptions. Nevertheless, the authors adopted a very general system, designed to promote transportability and to facilitate interactive natural language feedback with the user, in the subconscious (because not explicit) assumption that a complete syntax and a limited (because specialized) vocabulary will not create unmanageable difficulties. As this limited-in-vocabulary-but-syntactically-complete translation system has not yet been given a baptism name, one could suggest NLFED (from Natural Language Front End to Databases).

The structure of the proposed NLFED, according to the given description, can be summarized by the following scheme:
The modularity (Analyser, Translator, Converter, etc.) and the strong connection established between the real and domain worlds, by examining their semantic descriptions with the same representation language, seem to open promising perspectives for the NLFED.

In spite of all the interest in the subject, one can nevertheless formulate a more fundamental question: is it worthwhile to surcharge the artificial memory of a computer with such a large translation program from a very slow, complicated, mediocre, redundant and inadequate natural language? Instead, can't one teach the user a very restricted and efficient language, which is that of the DBMS? The scientific community could perhaps concentrate more efforts on the fundamental improvement of the NL, in order to create a truly efficient programming language for the largest computer existing in the universe, which is the human brain.

—*T. Oniga,* Rio de Janeiro, Brazil

JOHNSON-LAIRD, PHILIP N. (MRC Applied Psychology Unit, Cambridge, UK)     **HCI-0339**
**Semantic primitives or meaning postulates: mental models or propositional representation?.**
[in *Computational models of natural language processing,* B. Bara; and G. Guida (Eds.), Elsevier North-Holland, Inc., New York, NY, 1984, 227-246.]

This chapter is a well-researched, novel attempt at resolving two theoretical controversies in the area of cognitive psychology/artificial intelligence. One general issue that is dealt with is that vague grammatical references are often not conducive to the formation of mental images; however, no mention is made of fuzzy measure theory. In another section, it seemed I had found an interesting treatment of the mind-body controversy couched in computer science lexicon. The last two sections of the chapter concisely present the main thesis—a statement of a natural phenomenon that unifies two controversies: (1) Are images isomorphic to sets of propositions, and (2) are words really semantic primitives or sets of meaning postulates?

—*J. N. Rose,* Delhi, NY

## DATALOG

HAFNER, CAROLE D.; AND GODDEN, KURT (General Motors Research Laboratories, Warren, MI)     **HCI-0340**
**Portability of syntax and semantics in DATALOG.**
*ACM Trans. Office Inf. Syst.* **3,** 2 (April 1985), 141–164.

DATALOG is a natural language database query system which is under development at GM Research Laboratories. The objective is to produce a "portable" system, i.e., one which may be easily adapted for use with a variety of databases.

After a brief review of existing work in the field, the authors discuss (with examples) the implementation of syntactic analysis and semantic interpretation in DATALOG. They then describe the Application Lexicon, this being the place where the concepts, attributes, and values specific to a particular database are defined. In general, this lexicon will be redefined whenever DATALOG is to be used in a new application. Examples are given of the creation of two application lexicons. Finally, some areas for improvement of the system are discussed.

This is a well-written description of an interesting system. It is made much more comprehensible by the inclusion of well-chosen examples.

—*K. Booth,* Sooke, B.C., Canada

*Language generation*

MCKEOWN, KATHLEEN R. (Columbia Univ., New York, NY)  HCI-0341
**Using focus to constrain language generation.**
[in *Computational models of natural language processing,* B. Bara; and G. Guida (Eds.), Elsevier North-Holland, Inc., New York, NY, 1984, 261-274.]

This paper deals with the use of discourse focus in an automatic language generation system. The proper use of focus is important in language generation and language understanding; it provides coherence to the discourse and helps in eliminating many potential linguistic ambiguities. In determining how to say what one wants to say, the writer distinguishes between immediate and global focus, and gives the order of preference used in the TEXT systems in determining the immediate focus. The order given is:

(1) shift focus to item mentioned in previous proposition,
(2) maintain focus,
(3) return to topic of previous discussion, and
(4) select a proposition with the greatest number of implicit links to previous propositions.

The author also shows how the text generation system chooses between active and passive construction, and uses "there" insertions.

This reader would have wished to see a more complete explanation of the TEXT system. This paper is, however, a useful addition to the literature on the role of focus in text generation and understanding.

—*Gerard Salton,* Ithaca, NY

HOVY, EDUARD H.; AND SCHANK, ROGER C. (Yale Univ., New Haven, CT)  HCI-0342
**Language generation by computer.**
[in *Computational models of natural language processing,* B. Bara; and G. Guida (Eds.), Elsevier North-Holland, Inc., New York, NY, 1984, 165-195.]

This paper describes a prototype system capable of generating text tailored to a particular listener's interests or sympathies. The system requires information about each potential listener's social status, interests, sympathies, antipathies, and emotional state as part of its knowledge base. A story representation is then given as input to the system which generates different text for different hearers. The text can be focused on either a particular listener's interests or sympathies.

The paper includes a good example of the system in use. The example story, one used elsewhere in conceptual dependency-oriented research, is about an act of terrorism carried out by the IRA, in which a British soldier and a female bystander are shot and killed, and a 12-year-old girl is injured. The system then generates text for the IRA terrorist, the terrorist's wife, a British soldier, and a neutral American by first focusing on each listener's interests and then on his or her sympathies.

The system selects words which will best play on the emotions of a particular listener. In the example, the IRA man is referred to as a terrorist in the British version, a freedom fighter in the IRA version, and a gunman for the neutral American. The system orders the sentences of the text in such a way that the particular listener's interests and/or sympathies are presented first. In addition to word selection and sentence order, the system may decide to expand on or omit certain information depending on a particular listener's interests or sympathies. For example, the text generated for the British soldier describes the gun used in great detail since the soldier has an interest in guns. The other versions do not describe the gun in detail, reflecting the lack of interest on the part of the other listeners.

One problem associated with this system, which is not addressed by the authors, is the collecting of the required data on each listener's interests, sympathies, antipathies, and emotional state. This data is different not only for each listener but for each listener in each situation. In the example, the emotional state of the American is considered neutral and relaxed. However, if the woman shot and killed in the story happened to be the American's vacationing wife, his emotional state would be anything but relaxed and neutral. This situation-dependent analysis is required for each text generation problem and may be difficult to automate. This leads to a second problem, namely: How does one go about objectively assigning the interests of particular listeners? The interest of an IRA terrorist may be "British losses" from a neutral American's point of view, but from an IRA terrorist's viewpoint IRA interests are "freeing Ireland from English oppression." A British observer may offer a third viewpoint by assigning IRA interests to "the destabilization of British-Irish relations." The problem occurs when trying to assign objective values in subjective situations.

The paper raises many questions in the area of custom tailored text generation and is a good introductory study of the subject. It is recommended reading, but keep in mind the unaddressed problems in such a system.

—*Arthur J. Riel,* Boston, MA

JACOBS, PAUL S. (GE Corporate Research and Development, Schenectady, NY)
**Knowledge-intensive natural language generation.**
*Artif. Intell.* **33,** 3 (Nov. 1987), 325–378.

Jacobs's paper is not for neophytes of natural language generation or knowledge representation. It is written for an audience that can appreciate the difficulties of providing a plausible mechanism for a knowledge representation that can be easily and straightforwardly extended into generation applications. Herein lies the crux of the paper: is the plausibility of a mechanism enough to attack a problem as significant as that of language generation? Jacobs makes it clear that conceptual and linguistic knowledge should be separated, yet linked as needed. Through a series of processing steps, he then aims at a reduction of the problem of language generation to a problem of search. The paper describes a smart way of generating language, at least on the practical (software) level. There is little theoretical contribution to the problem of language generation in particular and language processing in general. However, Jacobs's methodology will contribute to theories in the long run.

—*Klaus K. Obermeier,* Columbus, OH

## Language models

REICHMAN-ADAR, RACHEL (Univ. of California, La Jolla)  HCI-0344
**Extended person-machine interface.**
*Artif. Intell.* **22,** 1 (March 1984), 157–218.

ARBIB, MICHAEL A. (Univ. of Massachusetts, Amherst)  HCI-0345
**From schema theory to computational (neuro-)linguistics.**
[in *From models to modules: studies in cognitive science from the McGill workshops,* I. Gopnik; and M. Gopnik (Eds.), Ablex Publishing Corp., Norwood, NJ, 1986, 240-253.]

The author seeks "to understand the brain mechanisms of language within a wider analysis of brain mechanisms subserving action and perception." Arbib rejects Chomsky's "language faculty" and embraces Piaget's constructivist theory of cognitive development, but with a computational perspective, instead of being purely descriptive.

Arbib argues that schema theory—structured representations for real-world knowledge—provides a bridge between specific implementations (either computational or neurological), and actual observed behaviors, such as speech or vision.

Arbib supports his view with results from three recent dissertations from the University of Massachusetts at Amherst. Helen Gigley modeled sentence understanding as affected by brain lesions; Jane Hill simulated language acquisition of a two-year-old child; and Jeffrey Conklin developed a program to provide natural language descriptions of visual scenes.

This work represents solid contributions to the field of cognitive science.

—*S. Slade,* New Haven, CT

FRAZIER, LYN (Univ. of Massachusetts, Amherst)  HCI-0346
**The mapping between grammar and processor.**
[in *From models to modules: studies in cognitive science from the McGill workshops,* I. Gopnik; and M. Gopnik (Eds.), Ablex Publishing Corp., Norwood, NJ, 1986, 117-134.]

This paper deals with the field of psycholinguistics, where proofs are normally not possible, but where only evidences can be shown and degrees of probability can be discussed. Regarding the human brain as a linguistic processor offers the author the possibility of handling these fuzzy facts as clearly as possible.

The paper discusses the problem of how linguistic performance is directed by the internally stored linguistic competence; it studies how many translation functions affect the performance as governed by the competence, giving preference to the possibility that only one translation function exists for each module of the grammar.

Giving an overview of psycholinguistic experiments, the author can suppose as rather evident that, e.g., humans use online phrase structure rules while processing a sentence, and only if this directly accessible set of rules doesn't suffice, then more complex sets of PS-rules are activated. This seems to be true for the strategy of the linguistic processor, which, on first trial, adds constituent structure nodes as minimal attachments. The PS-rules seem to be stored as a series of rules or definitions.

As for the processing of filler-gap-dependencies, perceivers evidently assign to the first gap encountered the most recent potential filler, thus following not a grammatical rule but a heuristic one.

On the fields of morphology, results of experiments are presented for inflection and for derivation.

As a consequence of the evidences shown, the Consistent Realization Hypothesis is formulated: "Any two rules of the same formal type will receive a consistent interpretation in any given performance system (production, comprehension, acquisition)" (p. 126). For the explanation of this hypothesis, facts about the acquisition of language are discussed and interpreted; the author tends toward the opinion that some LAD exists.

The paper gives a condensed summary of some experimental research in the field of linguistic processing, offering the Consistent Realization Hypothesis as a suitable approach to the understanding of the interaction between linguistic competence and performance. Two other hypotheses of the same phenomena presented at the beginning of the paper are shown not to be so explanatory.

The rules of human processing of linguistic data, as presented in this paper, can give hints for the judgment of grammar models as well as for the automatic processing of language.

—*G. Willee,* Bonn, West Germany

ZOEPPRITZ, MAGDALENA
**A framework for investigating language-mediated interaction with machines.**
*Int. J. Man-Mach. Stud.* **25,** 3 (Sept. 1986), 295–315.

The models of language that underlie most programming and query language experimentation are generally too weak to deal adequately with the linguistic processes involved. A more powerful model can be derived from linguistic theory, that supplements the formal description of languages by describing their communicative aspects as well. Such a model is outlined in the paper and its components are exemplified by corresponding phenomena in natural languages and programming languages.

—*Author's Abstract*

The model contains no new insights on language, nor does its designer claim that it does, but it does extend the descriptive apparatus of linguistics to programming and query languages. Linguistic theory is introduced, and its terminology is explained quite well.

The model is presented as having several components: a linguistic system, a cognitive system, processes, pragmatics, and some derived categories. Most components of the model are exemplified by crosswise confronting two natural languages (English and either French or German) and two formal languages (PL/I and either APL or SQL).

The author concludes, "The problem of designing user-friendly languages may not necessarily be solved by keeping the syntax simple and the number of keywords low, rather, the model suggests to reduce the distance between the conceptualizations of the prospective users and the concepts underlying the structure and the keywords of the language to be used."

The paper includes a rather thorough review of the literature with over 30 citations. It serves, indeed, as a framework for investigating language-mediated interaction with machines.

—*J. Major,* Eau Claire, WI

### Language parsing and understanding

HOCKENOS, WARREN (Skidmore College, Saratoga Springs, NY)
**Postscript: computers and the modeling of mind.**
[in *The computer culture.* Proc. of a symposium to explore the computer's impact on society (Loudonville, NY, 1981), D. Donnelly (Ed.), Associated University Presses, Cranbury, NJ, 1985, 153–166.]

[See main entry, Review HCI-0084.]

This paper contains a discussion about the work of Roger Schank in the area of cognitive modeling at a philosophical level, specifically his paper in this volume [1]. The author presents Schank's theory of cognitive modeling and evaluates this theory as a semantic theory. In the discussion, the author poses general questions about semantics and then answers the questions according to Schank's semantic theory. Some of the issues discussed, such as truth conditions, word references, and intentionality, are used to exhibit the various aspects of Schank's complete theory. Also included is a comparison of Schank's work to other semanticists and philosophers such as Locke, Carnap, and Searle.

The paper is a good, high-level overview of the different components of Schank's semantic theory. This paper is not useful as a detailed discussion of his cognitive theory from a computational viewpoint.

—*H. Smith,* East Hartford, CT

**REFERENCES**

[1] SCHANK, R. C. The problem of natural language, in *The Computer Culture.* Proc. of a symposium to explore the computer's impact on society, Denis P. Donnelly (Ed.), Associated University Presses, Cranbury, NJ, 1985, 44–69. See *Computing Reviews* Rev. 8607-0641.

SLATOR, BRIAN M.; ANDERSON, MATTHEW P.; AND CONLEY, WALT (New Mexico State Univ., Las Cruces)
**Pygmalion at the interface.**
*Commun. ACM* **29,** 7 (July 1986), 599–604.

The problem of man-machine communication is extremely difficult, as all researchers and developers of interactive systems are well aware. Despite the development of command languages, menus, and pointing devices, many users still find communication with computer systems difficult and frustrating. Natural Language (NL)-based interfaces attempt to solve this problem by translating a user's NL input into the formal language required by the system. Unfortunately, current NL systems can handle only a subset of natural language input. One major problem current NL parsers have is handling ambiguous expressions.

In this paper, the authors discuss a method of educating system users so that the number of ambiguous user inputs is reduced. This method consists of feeding back to a user the formal language translation of his natural language input. For example, if a user of a graphics system types

Make the graph name red

the user will be fed back the system command

TITLE COLOR RED

The authors report that while 22.4 percent of the inputs entered by an experimental group not receiving feedback were ambiguous, only 7.9 percent of the statements entered by a group receiving feedback were ambiguous. This difference was statistically significant.

The authors explain this effect in terms of the native linguistic abilities of human beings to acquire pidgin languages. While this hypothesis is appealing, no real evidence is offered to support it. Experimental work along these lines would be quite interesting.

In summary, the authors have identified a promising technique for improving man-machine communication involving NL interfaces. They have further proposed an interesting theoretical basis to explain their findings. This paper should be of interest to anyone interested in natural language interfaces.

—*William B. Frakes,* Holmdel, NJ

SEIDENBERG, MARK S. (McGill Univ., Montreal, Que., Canada); AND TANENHAUS, MICHAEL K. (Univ. of Rochester, Rochester, NY)
**Modularity and lexical access.**
[in *From models to modules: studies in cognitive science from the McGill workshops,* I. Gopnik; and M. Gopnik (Eds.), Ablex Publishing Corp., Norwood, NJ, 1986, 135-157.]

The authors provide an almost comprehensive survey of the literature of lexical processing that supports the modularity-of-mind hypothesis commonly associated with MIT's cognitive intelligentsia (e.g., Chomsky, Fodor, Marr). Citing numerous psycholinguistic experiments, Seidenberg and Tanenhaus argue for an autonomy of a lexical processing module, separate and *a priori* independent from syntactic, semantic, and pragmatic modules. Counterevidence to their theory that lexical access is independent of other aspects of the comprehension process is refuted by postulating pre- and postlexical contextual effects that should account for the differences in reaction times in word recognition tasks.

The authors of this chapter try to promote a particular brand of lexical processing research. Anyone not well versed in the psycholinguistic literature will find the disputes fascinating, yet frustrating when it comes to evaluating their significance. Modular or not, research into lexical processing is in its infancy at best.

—*Klaus K. Obermeier,* Columbus, OH

GROSZ, BARBARA J.; APPELT, DOUGLAS E.; MARTIN, PAUL A.; AND PEREIRA, **HCI-0351**
FERNANDO C.N. (SRI International, Menlo Park, CA)
**TEAM: an experiment in the design of transportable natural-language interfaces.**
*Artif. Intell.* **32,** 2 (May 1987), 173–243.

For someone concerned with writing natural-language interfaces (NLI), any step forward in making such interfaces transportable should be of great interest. This research paper's section comparing TEAM (transportable English database access medium) with other attempts to create transportable systems makes clear some of the achievements of this project. The major point is that, when adapting TEAM to a new database, the level of expertise need not include any special knowledge about linguistics, n-1 processing, or NLI in particular. During the menu-driven acquisition process, the so-called database expert (DBE) only provides information about the database structure and its subject domain. TEAM is supposed to extract any special linguistic information it requires from answers the DBE gives about sample sentences.

Transportability, keeping the system as context-sensitive as possible, has made necessary the sequential processing of queries (i.e., completing syntactic structures before semantic analysis). This approach is without a doubt justified, but I think problems will arise upon extending TEAM's use of discourse. Persons are using anaphora in querying a database as much as they do in any other situation.

In the third section, the authors discuss major issues addressed in building TEAM, such as verb acquisition, feature fields, quantifiers, scoping, lexical ambiguity, noun-noun modification, and transforming logical representations of a query's meaning into an efficient database query. Even if these problems must be solved in building any NLI, many of them are more difficult than usual to handle because of the circumstances in which TEAM is supposed to work. Special methods have been designed so that solutions depend only on information that can be acquired from a DBE.

It is a pity that the paper does not contain more examples of TEAM's ability to adapt to the various databases and the various individuals querying it. I am sure that further testing will prove the TEAM project's success. A linguistic background may be needed to fully understand this well-written paper, which should interest anyone concerned with understanding natural language.

—*Edward Sava-Segal,* Bucharest, Romania

## LSP

MARSH, ELAINE (Navy Center for Applied Research in Artificial Intelligence, **HCI-0352**
Washington, DC); AND FRIEDMAN, CAROL (Courant Institute of Mathematical Sciences,
New York, NY)
**Transporting the linguistic string project system from a medical to a Navy domain.**
*ACM Trans. Office Inf. Syst.* **3,** 2 (April 1985), 121–140.

LSP (Linguistic String Project) is a natural language processing system that was originally developed for a medical domain. This paper describes LSP in the context of applying the system to a new domain, namely, Navy messages about shipboard equipment failures. LSP reads messages and produces detailed categorizations of the meaning of the texts.

The same initial syntactic analysis was applied in both cases. The messages in each domain exhibited sentence fragments and deleted articles. The syntactic analysis is followed by a production rule system for extracting the meaning from the regularized parse tree.

The content of the messages "can be viewed as sister nodes in a generalization/specialization hierarchy of discourse domains. The parent node represents the general *domain of system failures*." Thus, the authors constructed the semantic categories for the equipment failure domain in a way that reflected their previous work in the medical problem domain.

The authors report that the equipment failure version of LSP took ten months to build, at a cost of three man-years. The system was developed using the Restriction Language programming language. Little is said about this language except that it is itself implemented in FORTRAN-77. This is quite an unusual choice for a natural language program, especially one named so suggestively.

—*S. Slade,* New Haven, CT

## Machine translation

NAGAO, MAKOTO (Kyoto Univ., Kyoto, Japan) **HCI-0353**
**A framework of a mechanical translation between Japanese and English by analogy principle.**
[in *Artificial and human intelligence.* Proc. of the international NATO symposium (Lyon, France, Oct. 1981), A. Elithorn; and R. Banerji (Eds.), Elsevier North-Holland, Inc., New York, NY, 1984, 173–180.]

[See main entry, Review HCI-0052]

This is a short paper about a mechanical translation system that translates between Japanese and English. The author's premise is that since word order is very different in Japanese than in European languages, it is difficult to translate from one to the other. A solution is presented which is based on the analogy principle, whereby positive instances of sentences and their translation are given. During this learning phase, the system stores frequencies and sample phrases. The system reasons, by analogy, to determine the necessary rules to translate between the languages. The system is then capable of translating fragments, such as case frame units, individually, and then putting the fragments together. This method mimics a human approach to translation which looks for analogies to base the translation, without using a thorough linguistic analysis. An additional feature of the system includes "thesauri" which are a grouping of words of similar nature.

The approach seems very time consuming, which the author realizes, and he has broken the process down into substages. But still, from the evidence in this paper, the approach has yet to be implemented and tested on any reasonably sized body of text. It is unclear how viable this method will prove to be. The major interest in this paper would be for people interested in translation between Japanese-type languages and European languages. It would not be useful in translating between two European languages.

—*H. Smith,* East Hartford, CT

## Speech recognition and understanding

SPINE, THOMAS M.; WILLIGES, BEVERLY H.; AND MAYNARD, JOSEPH F. (Virginia Polytechnic Institute and State Univ., Blacksburg, VA)
**An economical approach to modeling speech recognition accuracy.**
*Int. J. Man-Mach. Stud.* **21**, 3 (Sept. 1984), 191–202.

What determines operator acceptance of an Automatic Speech Recognizer (ASR)? (For the purposes of this study, the typical ASR available commercially is assumed to be speaker-dependent and capable of recognizing only isolated word utterances.) A large number of factors that affect ASR performance, ranging from task-specific features (e.g., throughput rate) to algorithmic characteristics (e.g., type of pattern-matching strategy used) certainly influence operator acceptance. However, the four measurable performance factors that appear to have the most direct effects on operator acceptance include:

- Recognition accuracy—the frequency that a valid audio input (user utterance) is correctly recognized.
- Discrimination accuracy—the frequency that an invalid audio input gets rejected.
- Response time—the lapsed time from the end of user utterance to the user's perception that the ASR has "reacted" appropriately.
- Vocabulary size—the number of unique utterances that the ASR can recognize correctly.

This study focuses on *recognition accuracy*, and addresses two major concerns of system designers:

(1) How does recognition accuracy vary as a function of factors such as number of training passes, reject threshold, vocabulary size, speaker sex, and language material?
(2) How can knowledge about recognition accuracy variance and its determinants be used to build a design tool that will help dialogue authors predict the optimal operating conditions for voice input?

To investigate these issues, the authors used a "four-factor, within-subjects, second-order response surface methodology central-composite design," described in [1]. The experimental procedure involved the following steps:

[1] *Training* subjects for vocabulary items, which required prompting repetition of words to create reference pattern sets (templates) for the recognizer.
[2] *Testing* recognition accuracy of the ASR, which involved random prompting of each vocabulary item.
[3] *Development of empirical models*, based on second-order regression equations for the data sets analyzed in the study. These equations predicted the proportion of words correctly recognized.
[4] *Validation* of the models by a second experiment, using additional subjects and a larger sample size (vocabulary items tested).
[5] *Development of a "dialogue design tool,"* an interactive PASCAL program that incorporated the empirical models from number [3] above (to predict the proportion of correct recognitions) and additional prediction models to specify other measures of recognizer performance.

The design tool works by finding the optimal operating conditions for voice input; e.g., for a specified vocabulary size, the program performs a search to find the combination of other variables used in the study (number of training passes, reject threshold level, difference score threshold between the top two word choices used in the recognition algorithm).

The paper merits reading for several reasons: (1) it presents a validated empirical method for building a tool to aid users of ASRs, (2) the methodology illustrates the practical use of quantitative modeling of human/machine performance; and (3) it sets a precedent for developing standardized procedures that can be used to evaluate speech recognition system.

—*J. R. Kornfeld,* Burlington, MA

**REFERENCES**

[1] COCHRAN, W. G.; AND COX, G. M. *Experimental designs (2nd ed.),* John Wiley & Sons, New York, 1957.

BIERMANN, ALAN W.; RODMAN, ROBERT D.; RUBIN, DAVID C.; AND **HCI-0355**
HEIDLAGE, J. F.
**Natural language with discrete speech as a mode for human-to-machine.**
*Commun. ACM* **28,** 6 (June 1985), 628–636.

This paper reports the results of tests on a speech recognizer used in conjunction with a natural language processing system. The speech recognizer drives an error-correcting parser that sends output to a language semantics processing system. A domain-simulation module then executes the desired action. The authors conclude that the system is relatively easy to learn and use, and that subjects gave a generally positive report of their experience. All four test criteria—learnability, correctness, timing, and user response—were passed.

This paper is well written and easy to follow. To their credit, the authors maintain objectivity by pointing out that while the 100-word vocabulary size used in their tests was satisfactory for a controlled experiment, it is in general not adequate for typical applications. One may also question whether the reported 77 percent success rate for processing sentences is even close to adequate for real-world environments. In the reviewer's opinion, this paper is one of many over the past decade indicating that, while voice recognition offers tremendous potential, the current state-of-the-art has not yet achieved it.

—*A. E. Salwin,* Rockville, MD

LONGUET-HIGGINS, CHRISTOPHER (Univ. of Sussex, Sussex, UK) **HCI-0356**
**Tones of voice: the role of intonation in computer speech understanding.**
[In *Computer speech processing,* F. Fallside; and W. Woods (Eds.), Prentice-Hall International, Englewood Cliffs, NJ, 1985, 293-304.]

The stress patterns, intonation, pauses, and timing structures in speech are known as the "suprasegmental" parameters. Lately, they have come to be recognized as important determinants for speech understanding, especially for the recognition of the longer stretches of continuous speech. Sentences, when spoken, are much more than mere sequences of vowels and consonants. Their meaning can be altered drastically by the careful manipulation of the pitch contour (intonation), by the strategic placement of the pauses, by the stress patterns of the syllables, and by the tempo (or the rate of speech).

The chapter under review is an overview of the role of intonation in speech understanding by machines. It is written in an interesting way. After reading it, however, one is left with the feeling that the author could have dealt with some of the experimental observations on the role played by intonation and stress in speech perceived by listeners.

—*A. K. Menon,* Cochin, India

HEWITT, JILL (Hatfield Polytechnic, Hatfield, UK); AND FURNER, STEPHEN (British Telecom Research Laboratories, UK)    **HCI-0357**
**Text processing by speech: dialogue design and usability issues in the provision of a system for disabled users.**
[in *People and computers IV.* Proceedings of the Fourth Conference of the British Computer Society (Univ. of Manchester, UK, Sept. 5–6, 1988), D. Jones; and R. Winder (Eds.), Cambridge University Press, New York, NY, 1988, 529–544.]

The authors interfaced a commercial speech recognition system to a text processor in order to allow a disabled student, who was unable to type by hand, to 'type' by speaking the names of the keys or of common editor commands. They found that the resulting system was less efficient for text entry than typing with a mouthstick and that many kinds of editing operations, especially those that require repeated use of a cursor 'key,' were difficult to perform. Misrecognition and the need to recover from it were major limits on the speed of the system. Nevertheless, the student found the system useful for taking notes while reading, because he was unable to have both the book and a keyboard for mouthstick manipulation in front of him at the same time.

—*G. Hirst,* Toronto, Ont., Canada

LADEFOGED, PETER (UCLA, Los Angeles, CA)    **HCI-0358**
**The phonetic basis for computer speech processing.**
[in *Computer speech processing,* F. Fallside; and W. Woods (Eds.), Prentice-Hall International, Englewood Cliffs, NJ, 1985, 3-27.]

This little paper is an excellent, if all too abbreviated, account of the elements of acoustic phonetics by one of the world's foremost authorities on the subject. It covers the definition of phonemes and allophones, respectively the logical and acoustical units of speech; the basic facts about position and manner of articulation; and the notion of formants. It describes the acoustic parameters of speech, based on the series-formant model of Fant [1], and the use of sound spectrograms for speech analysis (with several examples). It is a skillful summary of some of the highlights of Ladefoged's excellent book, *A course in phonetics* [2], first published 12 years ago. But rather than study this paper, readers interested in learning about phonetics would do better to give themselves a treat and spend an evening with the book itself, which is a delightful introduction to phonetics and highly relevant to computer speech processing.

—*Ian H. Witten,* Calgary, Alta., Canada

**REFERENCES**
[1] FANT, C. G. M. *Acoustic theory of speech production,* Mouton, The Hague, 1960.
[2] LADEFOGED, PETER *A course in phonetics,* Harcourt Brace Jovanovich, Orlando, FL, 1975 (2nd ed. published in 1982).

## I.2.8 Problem Solving, Control Methods, and Search

HUNT, RUSTON M.; AND ROUSE, WILLIAM B.
**A fuzzy rule-based model of human problem solving.**
*IEEE Trans. Syst. Man Cybern.* **SMC-14**, 1 (Jan./Feb. 1984), 112–120.

In this paper, the authors set out "...to present a robust and yet testable (i.e., computerizable) model of human problem solving." The problem domain (for both model-building and model-validating) is *fault diagnosis*, troubleshooting for failed components in automotive and aircraft systems, in particular. The proposed model assumes a production system format, employing rules that search the problem space in two different modes: "Symptomatic (S)-rules," which look for familiar patterns (of malfunction); and "Topographic (t)-rules," which select an action based on the functional layout or topography of the malfunctioning system as a whole.

Four factors are said to determine *which* rules are applied—recall, applicability, expected usefulness, and simplicity. These factors figure as fuzzy sets, whose members are S- and T-rules. A set of *choosable rules* can be defined as the (fuzzy) intersection of the four (fuzzy) sets. The model works by selecting the rule with the highest membership in the choosability set.

How well does the model work compared to human performance? Disregarding individual differences among 34 subjects who were each asked to solve 85 problems, the authors report a model-to-subject performance match of 50 percent. Comparisons of rule-usage between the model and subjects showed a 70 percent convergence, and cost estimate scores (for solving each problem) were approximately equal.

The work reported by Hunt and Rouse is ambitious and serves to demonstrate the application of methods Rouse has described elsewhere [1] for modeling human-machine system performance. The article is in fact too ambitious as a standalone piece. Although the proposed model and *model*-performance data are presented in sufficient detail, less care is taken to explain *human* performance and data collection methods that were used on the studies run to validate the model. It is only by a thorough reading of the preceding article [2] that we learn the range of actions subjects could perform in locating a failed component in a graphically displayed network; viz., reading gauges, testing continuity between parts, and carrying out bench testing of individual parts. The emphasis in this earlier article is admittedly on the psychological perspective, but this background is critical for appreciating the relevance of the model and how it is derived.

Other problems can be found with internal constructs of the model itself, and its empirical validation. The attributes of recall, applicability, usefulness, and simplicity are "... meant to be independent." Yet the behavioral implications of applying these factors in real-world settings suggest otherwise. Intuitively, recall, applicability, and simplicity would seem to be *dependent* attributes; the authors themselves state that "...T-rules might be recalled longer because of their more general, widely applicable nature." And, "It is reasonable to assume that the perceived simplicity of a rule will increase as it is used more frequently."

Estimating the model's free parameters would also appear to present difficulties in the validation phase. For example, the function defining membership in the set of "recalled rules" contains the parameter "r," the "...rate at which rules are forgotten." Though one can juggle parameter values such as "r" until the model performance closely matches system performance, it is certainly an open question how "rate of forgetting" can be measured in real-life contexts.

Aside from these objections, the work reported by Hunt and Rouse does deserve serious attention. The model indeed provides an explanation for two modes of human search strategies (symptomatic and topographic). It can be used to design further experiments and it can be made to produce quantitative predictions that might be used in the future to design improved system. The process of deriving set membership expressions is itself constructive—even if one finds that certain parameters are difficult or impractical to measure empirically.

**REFERENCES**

[1] ROUSE, W. B. *Systems engineering models of human-machine interaction*, Elsevier North-Holland, New York, 1980.

[2] HENNEMAN, R. L.; and ROUSE, W. B. Measures of human problem solving performance in fault diagnosis tasks, *IEEE Trans. Syst. Man. Cybern*, **SMC-14**, 1 (Jan./Feb. 1984), 99-111.

—*J. R. Kornfeld,* Burlington, MA

KANT, E.; AND NEWELL, A. (Carnegie-Mellon Univ., Pittsburgh, PA)
**Naive algorithm design techniques—a case study.**
[in *Progress in artificial intelligence*. Selected and updated papers from the proceedings of the 1982 European conference (Orsay, France, 1982), L. Steels; and J. Campbell (Eds.), John Wiley & Sons, Inc., New York, NY, 1985, 41–51.]

The authors describe this paper as an attempt to understand more about the process of human design and to discover what lessons can be carried over to building systems that automatically derive algorithms or assist human designers. To this end, they present their analysis and interpretation of one subject's recorded comments as a first attempt is made to design an algorithm to construct a convex hull. The algorithm is designed, given a set of points, to find a subset of the points which, when suitably joined together, will form a polygon enclosing all the other points.

The interpretation of the subject's comments is claimed to be based on theories of Newell and Simon [1], which model problem solving as a progress through a problem space from some initial state (the problem) to a final (solution) state under the control of a collection of search rules; these search rules include refinement, means-end analysis, and symbolic execution. The concept of a dataflow problem space is introduced, and an attempt is made to describe the gradual refinement of the algorithm in terms of dataflow concepts.

Conclusions from a final discussion are as follows:

(1) Algorithm representations must necessarily be ambiguous initially.
(2) A variety of search rules must allow for naive and expert problem solving styles.
(3) Means-end analysis must be involved in searching, as well as trying a succession of predetermined operators.

I believe that work of the type described must be persevered, however vague and unsatisfactory it may appear in the reporting, particularly by those accustomed to achieving results by applying formal methods to comparatively trivial problems.

Using a subject's recorded comments as a guide to his or her thought processes of course begs the question of a relationship. The need to actually provide comments would, I think, be certain to modify how the work progresses. However, I have no better method to suggest.

I have two overall comments. First, it seems so often to me that the attempt to formalize a human process mathematically is prone to lose exactly those parts of the process that are significant in some human sense. Second, it seems that there is widespread confusion over what is meant by analysis. I see analysis not as getting to "what is really there," but as a creative process of constructing a necessarily limited model of an event; the model would inevitably reflect both the skill and the personal biases of the analyst. Building models of human performance clearly depends on the depth and the width of experience of the builder in the particular area concerned. I am not confident that computer science provides the ideal background for this daunting task, but I suppose that we must continue humbly to do our best from wherever we are.

Finally, I am delighted to support the authors' insistence on the essential need of copying human methods of problem solving because they can be continually augmented and adapted, and because they are flexible and robust; current formally designed "computing systems" are sadly lacking, as they say, in these areas.

—*E. James,* London, UK

**REFERENCES**

[1] NEWELL, A.; AND SIMON, H. *Human problem solving*, Prentice-Hall, Englewood Cliffs, NJ, 1972.

## *Graph and tree search strategies*

MACKWORTH, ALAN K. (Univ. of British Columbia, Vancouver, B.C., Canada); AND FREUDER, EUGENE C. (Univ. of New Hampshire, Durham)
**The complexity of some polynomial network consistency algorithms for constraint satisfaction problems.**
*Artif. Intell.* **25,** 1 (Jan. 1985), 65–74.

This paper is concerned with properties of *filtering algorithms for Constraint Satisfaction Problems* (*CSP*). Problems in this class have the following form: Given a finite set of variables, each with an associated finite domain of values, and a set of constraining relations, each involving a subset of the variables, find all possible assignments of values to variables that satisfy the given constraints. There are variants of this formulation where the goal is to find a single assignment.

The problem of assigning interpretations to features of visual images (e.g., the edge labeling problem) was recognized in the early 1970s as being a CSP, and so were various types of cryptoarithmetic problems. By now, there is a wide range of other AI tasks that can be seen as CSPs; for example, problems of circuit design and of truth maintenance. As pointed out by Simon and Lea [1] in their analysis of CSPs, these processes involve simultaneous work in two spaces—the space of solution structures (sets of unique assignments of values to variables), and the space of problem conditions (specified by the relational constraints between variables). The key design problem is how to coordinate the work in these two spaces.

Working on vision tasks, Waltz [2] developed a *filtering algorithm* for reducing the space of possible solutions of a CSP via an analysis of its problem conditions. The algorithm focuses on the binary constraints between variables, and it eliminates all values in the domains of variables that are inconsistent with the binary constraints. Montanari [3] developed another filtering algorithm which is based on the elimination of value pairs from domains of variables that are inconsistent with the structure of binary constraints of a problem. Mackworth [4] further generalized and clarified the nature of filtering algorithms for CSPs.

This paper takes additional steps towards the clarification and analysis of filtering algorithms for CSPs, which are also called *Network Consistency Algorithms*. Four algorithms are presented and analyzed; two of them are general versions of Waltz's and Montanari's algorithms.

A significant result obtained in the paper is that the time complexity of a Waltz-like filtering algorithm is at most $O(a^3 e)$ where $a$ is the domain size of a variable and $e$ is the number of binary constraints in a problem; i.e., it is linear in the number of binary constraints. For highly connected constraint graphs, this leads to a time complexity of $O(a^3 n^2)$, where $n$ is the number of variables in the problem. For sparse constraint graphs, the time complexity is $O(a^3 n)$; since planar graphs are sparse, then their associated time complexity is linear in the number of variables. This analysis provides a clear illustration of how the complexity of problem solving depends on the degree of interaction between problem conditions (the constraints).

The authors argue that since the constraint graphs of edge labeling problems in vision are planar, then application of the Waltz filtering algorithm to these problems produces behavior which has linear time complexity. This is a significant theoretical result because it shows that the (empirically observed) linear behavior of this algorithm is not due to special peculiarities of the vision problem, but derives from more general characteristics of the problem, i.e., the structure of its constraint graph. Another interesting result is that when the constraint graph of a problem is a strict tree, a solution to the CSP can be found in linear time. It is unfortunate that this result cannot be extended to produce better complexity bounds for the Waltz algorithm for edge labeling, as the constraint graphs in this domain are not strict trees in general. In any event, the result for trees is interesting, and it may be used in a variety of special applications (including vision), either directly or as a heuristic guide for the solution of "similar" problems.

The paper presents an analysis of Montanari-like filtering algorithms for which an upper bound time complexity of $O(a^5 n^5)$ is obtained, and an analysis of a second algorithm that eliminates value pairs from domains of variables in a manner analogous to Waltz-like filtering algorithms, which results in a time complexity of $O(a^5 n^3)$. These are interesting results that show the growth in polynomial complexity of filtering algorithms as they proceed to narrow down the space of solutions by analyzing interactions between problem conditions that are increasingly global.

The paper does not deal directly with ways of using filtering algorithms in systems for obtaining complete solutions to CSPs; it offers, however, several suggestions. This is a fertile area for further work. There is much more to be done in understanding the appropriate balance between the polynomial complexity of processes for eliminating solution options and the exponential complexity of processes for generating and testing solution candidates. This well-written paper should be of interest to workers in vision, to researchers having a more general interest in the design of algorithms for CSPs, and to those who are concerned with the development of a theory of problem solving in AI.

—*S. Amarel*, New Brunswick, NJ

## REFERENCES

[1] SIMON, H. A.; AND LEA, G. Problem solving and rule induction: a unified view, in *Knowledge and cognition*, L. Gregg (Ed.), Halstead Press, New York, 1974, 105–127. See *Computing Reviews* **16**, 3 (March 1975), Rev. 27,945.

[2] WALTZ, D. Understanding line drawings of scenes with shadows, in *The psychology of computer vision*, Winston (Ed.), McGraw-Hill, New York, 1975.

[3] MONTANARI, U. Networks of constraints: fundamental properties, and applications to picture processing, *Inf. Sci.* **7** (1974).

[4] MACKWORTH, A. K. Consistency of networks of relations, *Artif. Intell.* **8** (1977), 99–118. See *Computing Reviews* **20**, 4 (April 1979), Rev. 34,360.

### Plan execution, formation, generation

CURRIE, KEN; AND TATE, AUSTIN (Univ. of Edinburgh, Edinburgh, Scotland)  **HCI-0362**
**O-Plan: control in the open planning architecture.**
[in *Expert systems 85*. Proc. of the fifth technical conference of the British Computer Society Specialist Group on Expert Systems (Univ. of Warwick, Warwick, UK, Dec. 17-19, 1985), M. Merry (Ed.), Cambridge University Press, New York, NY, 1986, 225–240.]

This paper describes O-Plan, an architecture for a planning system. The O-Plan strategy seems to be intended for development of large planning systems that may include experimental components representing ongoing research. The architecture therefore focuses on the capability for clear communication between diverse components via a set of general planning and control algorithms.

The paper offers a fairly clear discussion of the design of O-Plan, its representations, and algorithms. Of particular interest is the discussion of some real-world issues, such as user interaction with the planner and the possibility of the planner invoking problem solvers (or knowledge sources) that may fail. These issues are treated well, with an interesting extension to the planning architecture paradigm that allows the handling of these problems in a domain-independent fashion. This will be an interesting paper to read if you are embarking upon or currently building systems that do planning in the practical environment.

—*C. Apte,* Yorktown Heights, NY

### I.2.10 Vision and Scene Understanding

FELDMAN, JEROME A. (Univ. of Rochester, Rochester, NY)  **HCI-0363**
**Connectionist models and parallelism in high level vision.**
*Comput. Vision Graph. Image Process.* **31**, 2 (Aug. 1985), 178–200.

Like a Phoenix rising from the ashes, the descendants of the perceptron are again marching across the computer science stage. *Connectionism*, its new name, is the idea that the computations performed by a processing system should be controlled by the connections among a large number of simple processing units, with long-term knowledge stored as the strengths of the connections among the elements. The conventional computer mechanism of passing complex structures is not used; instead, the burden of computation lies in the connection structures of the network.

Connectionism is interesting because it takes the point of view that many cognitive activities cannot be partitioned into elementary, understandable steps of an algorithmic nature. This shift of paradigm, from the conventional approach that believes that problems are decomposable, may lead to interesting results.

Feldman, the author of this survey of connectionist models for high-level vision, is one of the leading gurus of this movement. He is the leader of the *localist* school that uses elementary units that each represent an item of interest, such as a concept or a line segment. This is in contrast to the *distributed* approach that uses a simple threshold device as the basic element, as in the original perceptron approach. (The rejuvenation of the distributed approach is due to the development of new algorithms that can design, or "train," multilayered threshold networks; see, e.g., [1].)

The units used in the localist approach have a large number of incoming and outgoing connections and communicate with the rest of the network by transmitting a simple value. A unit transmits the same value to all units to which it is connected. All inputs to a unit are weighted and combined at one or more *sites*, with each site having an associated site-function. These functions carry out local computations based on the input values at the site, and the result of this affects the overall unit processing. A separate unit is devoted to each possible value of each parameter.

The author first discusses the model of vision that supports parallel vision, and briefly reviews relaxation techniques and Hough transform approaches. He then reviews the connectionist computational model giving the biological motivation, the basic units used, and how these units can be used as the basis of memory. The third part of the paper describes recent results in parallel algorithms for high-level visual recognition. Much of this part of the paper is taken from [2], in which Feldman describes four representational frames that capture information:

(1) retintopic—the view of the world that changes with each eye movement;
(2) head-based—the illusion of a stable visual world;
(3) symbolic—the observer's general knowledge of the world; and
(4) allocentric—modeling the animal's representation of the space around it at a given moment.

The last part of this paper is a discussion of the limitations of parallelism. In particular, the problems of *crosstalk* and of expressing relationships seem to require a sequential approach. Crosstalk is the vulnerability to confusion that arises when indexing from feature values into world knowledge. The relationship problem arises because relational information among features is lost in the parallel indexing process.

There are two motivations for this type of paper: (1) to relate physiological processes to computational concepts so as to motivate investigations in psychology and physiology; and (2) to inspire work in computational vision. The peer commentary of psychologists, neurophysiologists, and computer scientists at the end of [2], and the author's responses, deal extensively with these two topics and are well worth reading.

This connectionist point of view, given in general, broad strokes, is interesting to the computer scientist because it is an attempt to pull together, in a unified system, the various connectionist algorithms relating to vision. However, to really understand the basis for the generalities, the reader will have to go back to the original papers cited, since the descriptions of the techniques are somewhat terse. Understanding of the paper is not made easier by the fact that a figure pertaining to the discussion on p. 186 is missing (it is in [2]), and that there are several errors in citations. (The Winter 1985 issue of *Cognitive Science* cited is actually the Jan.-March 1985 issue, and Ref. 16 should be to the DARPA IU Workshop, June 1983, not CVPR.)

—*O. Firschein*, Menlo Park, CA

**REFERENCES**

[1] ACKLEY, D. H.; HINTON, G. E.; AND SEJNOWSKI, T. J. A learning algorithm for Bolzmann machines, *Cognitive Sci.* **9** (1985), 147–169.

[2] FELDMAN, J. A. Four frames suffice: a provisional model of vision and space, *Behav. Brain Sci.* **8** (1985), 265–289.

SMITH, BEVERLY J. (Interact Research & Development Corporation, Victoria, Canada)     **HCI-0364**
**Perception of organization in a random stimulus.**
*Comput. Vision Graph. Image Process.* **31**, 2 (Aug. 1985), 242–247.

This paper describes an experimental test involving human perception. It claims to test a hypothesis that concerns the processing operations of the visual system. The research does indeed provide a test and confirmation of the hypothesis that successive reproductions of a visual stimulus would show an increase in perceptual organization. I do, however, have two general criticisms. First, while those involved in the area of computer vision, graphics, and image processing might find this study interesting and possibly of some use, it lacks any direct statement of utility or application for this audience. Second, and perhaps more importantly, the operational definitions and construction of relevant variables were questionable. A "random stimulus" was determined by a "quasi-random process." This stimulus was then presented to the subjects, who were asked to create systematic reproductions from visual memory.

I appreciate the fact that the study was clearly described. My greatest difficulty with the study concerns the interpretation of a phenomenon akin to identifying constellations in random star patterns, as being attributed to purely perceptual organization. Possible alternative explanations of the observed results, such as the subjects' cognitive organization or aesthetic needs, were simply not mentioned.

—*J. N. Rose*, Delhi, NY

## *Modeling and recovery of physical attributes*

POGGIO, TOMASO (Massachusetts Institute of Technology, Cambridge)     **HCI-0365**
**Early vision: from computational structure to algorithms and parallel hardware.**
*Comput. Vision Graph. Image Process.* **31**, 2 (Aug. 1985), 139–155.

This paper presents a theoretical synthesis of early computational vision based on variational principles, describes implementations using analog networks, and then states the limitations on the work presented. The paper first discusses a theoretical framework that covers a number of the variational methods previously developed independently for early vision problems. It is shown that many such methods (including computation of motion, shape from shading, surface interpolation, and stereo matching) are special cases of rigorous regularization theories for solving ill-posed (in the sense used by Hadamard in 1923) mathematical problems [1]. An example shows that the framework includes previous variational approaches to the computation of motion. Another example applies the variational approach to edge detection, providing results that are similar to those of commonly used edge detection filters.

The second part of the paper discusses how analog networks, which can directly solve variational problems, offer a computational model of early vision that is quite different from the digital computer model. An example using resistor networks to solve the optical flow computation is presented. Appropriate sets of chemical reactions can, in principle, simulate the electrical currents. The author believes that the style of computation represented by analog circuits is a very useful model for neural computations as well as a challenge for future VLSI circuit designs.

The conclusion discusses the limitations on variational solutions proposed so far. The current theory offers little help for the problem of integrating different sources of information or computing with symbolic representations. The integration of ideas in this paper is carefully documented by 70 references.

—*Michael D. Kelly*, Reston, VA

**REFERENCES**

[1] HADAMARD, J. *Lectures on the Cauchy problem in linear partial differential equations.* Yale University Press, New Haven, CT, 1923.

TREISMAN, ANNE (Univ. of British Columbia, B.C., Canada)　　　　　　　　　　　　　　　　　　　　HCI-0366
**Preattentive processing in vision.**
*Comput. Vision Graph. Image Process.* **31,** 2 (Aug. 1985), 156–177.

Information processing models of visual perception attempt to relate the elements of vision to each other via structural theory and confirmative behavioral tests. This paper reviews studies of the major dichotomy of preattentive versus attentive vision and the attributes of each. For example, visual search for objects with a single characteristic can be done preattentively, but a conjunction of characteristics requires attentive search. Use of a visual attention distractor degrades the search for a conjunction. New work is reported on the perception of the absence of a feature, showing it to belong to the attentive phase.

—*Albert L. Zobrist,* Westlake Village, CA

*Perceptual reasoning*

BECK, JACOB (Univ. of Oregon, Eugene)　　　　　　　　　　　　　　　　　　　　　　　　　　HCI-0367
**Perception of transparency in man and machine.**
*Comput. Vision Graph. Image Process.* **31,** 2 (Aug. 1985), 127–138.

This research paper compares the reasoning used by man to judge transparency with that of a machine programmed to estimate true transparency. Two types of transparency, additive and subtractive color mixture, are considered. The first is caused when either a mesh, whose detail cannot be resolved, or a fast-moving object blurs and partially obscures the target. Beck develops earlier work by Metelli [1] using an episcotister, a device which revolves, partially obscuring the target object. Beck's model establishes boundary constraints which must not be violated for true transparency. The second is caused when a transparent filter obscures an object. Here, an alternative model's boundary constraints are related to the first case.

Beck demonstrates by example that the human visual system is not sensitive to certain violations of these constraints. He suggests a partial explanation, in terms of a revision of Metelli's work, to take account of lightness rather than reflectance. He further considers the degree of transparency perceived, the effect of figural clues, such as shape, and covers a number of cases where humans inaccurately judge transparency.

This paper is not very readable, in particular when it is defining terms, such as the causes of perception of transparency. However, the author does introduce some important ideas. When applied, they will help designers identify areas of potential misunderstanding, such as when shape cues mislead a human into the belief that what is in fact a separate object behind a transparent object is part of an opaque object. This paper is worth study by any researcher working on the generation or evaluation of computer-generated scenes containing transparent objects.

—*M. A. Evans,* Cambridge, UK

**REFERENCES**

[1] METELLI, F. The perception of transparency, *Sci. Am.* **230**, 4 (1974), 90–98.

## I.2.m Miscellaneous

STEVENS, JOHN K. (Univ. of Toronto, Toronto, Ont., Canada)
**Reverse engineering the brain.**
*BYTE* **10**, 4 (April 1985), 287–299.

Artificial Intelligence has two sides: mimicking human intelligence by performing similar tasks, and modeling the natural structures and functions. This article appears under a banner of "Artificial Intelligence," probably because it describes nerve cells and some analogs, and perhaps because it leaps to speculation about a computer structure based on components with similarities to nerve cells. As a technical article, it should be dismissed out of hand on the evidence of the title alone. But in BYTE it is most likely to reach a number of technical neophytes whose imaginations will be stirred by this speculative, popularized article.

Most of the article describes the major electrical, chemical, and geometrical processes of two classes of nerve cells: transmitting or "output cells," and processing "interneuron" cells. Elementary but clear descriptions are interspersed with appeals to analogies in electronics which may not always be illuminating to the naive reader. But if you don't mind your kidney being compared to a battery charger, then the descriptions of actions of "Active Axons," "Driven Dendrites," and supporting structures will be easy to accept. Although I am not qualified to rule on the accuracy, I found the descriptions generally consistent. When Stevens says an output neuron's output is a "fixed waveform" I assume he means a nearly constant pulse shape. When he says, "...interneurons have graded analog inputs but also have graded analog outputs," it seems he refers to variable-amplitude pulses.

A major part of the article lays the basis for the premise in the title. This part describes an electrical-circuit model for the electrodynamics of the passive components of a single cell. The dendrite is said to be modeled by a battery-powered resistor-capacitor ladder circuit. The action of a synapse input is said to be modeled by a "gate" consisting of a changing conductance in series with one battery. Although this section contains one of the highlights of the paper (a diagram of an axon, not a dendrite, constructed from a sequence of scanning electron micrographs of thin sections), the section lacks a clear comparison of the pulses produced by the model with some of real nerves. The results of some simulation calculations are shown, but in the graph it seemed quite unclear just what was being plotted.

Stevens goes on to discuss nerve circuits as if there are just two significantly different behaviors to model. He then sketches part of an electrical-circuit analog, and presents as examples only cells from the retina. Yet in the last part of the paper, he leaps to the statement that one can, by etching shapes of cells into silicon, "quite easily" create silly-sounding "silicrons" which "could simulate brain circuits." There is no intervening discussion of any variety in brain neurons or of a role which might be played by major modular structures. Since the gross functions of circuits with large numbers of nerve cells (i.e., optic bundles or brains) and "how the brain modifies its own circuits" are not well understood, the time at which one could build a computer "using circuitry copied directly from the brain. . .continues to be 'Probably not right away.'" What Stevens leaves unaddressed is why we would want to, except for the understanding gained by modeling. He compares the complexity of structure of an integrated circuit as much lower than that of a retina and confuses that with "performance." He implies that because simulating the actions of the respective nerves would require an enormous amount of processing, a computer built on the basis of a neurological model is a candidate for a "sixth-generation."

Despite the omissions of fact and logic, here is one vote to encourage such imaginative pieces. The article is likely to stimulate any reader: it contains some significant illustrations, should please the dilettante, and contains material for some good fun.

—*V. Michael Powers,* Beaverton, OR

## I.3 Computer Graphics

### I.3.1 Hardware architecture

*Raster display devices*

WESTMORE, RICHARD J. (National Semiconductor, Santa Clara, CA)
**A window-based graphics frame store architecture.**
*ACM Trans. Graph.* **7,** 4 (Oct. 1988), 227–242.

In order to cope with the real-time demands of a window-based graphics environment, one would ideally have a distributed architecture with one processor with local memory for each window, provided that the image data could be read at a speed sufficient to sustain the video scanning rate. Although this scheme may be realized in the future, when multi-megabit memory chips will supposedly be dirt-cheap, at the present time such an approach seems out of the question.

This paper proposes something similar in terms of window panes. Actually, it introduces the term *microframe* for what I would call an intelligent (but small) bitmap. Thousands of these microframes are envisaged; at least eight are needed in order to define a colored pane. The microframe stores are pipelined on the pixel clock. For each pixel the store determines whether it should play a role, depending on position and pane priority. If so, it copies a pixel bit to the color bus, together with its priority.

Such an architecture would still need massive amounts of image memory. In addition, the high bandwidth required for image memory update, which can only be done by propagating the corresponding data through the pipeline, would make this a rather costly proposition as well. To this cost must also be added the expense of the fast-switching logic for the various local controllers of each microframe. I question whether this architecture could be implemented at a reasonable expense for the high pixel rate (60 megapixels/sec) envisaged by the author.

It is somewhat annoying that the author does not define his terms except in vague figures. For instance, why are viewports (i.e., the visible areas in a window) needed? What is the exact difference, in hardware, between tiles and panes? The author seems uncertain whether to tie the microframes to one or the other. These and other inconsistencies (the abstract reads " . . . pixel rates of up to 400 MHz . . . ," but the text only mentions "[p]ixel rates well in excess of 100 MHz . . . ") should not have been missed in the editorial process. It is a poor show for the journal that three years transpired between the submission and publication of this paper.

—*J. van den Bos,* Leiden, The Netherlands

### I.3.2  Graphics Systems

#### Distributed/network graphics

SCHEIFLER, ROBERT W. (Massachusetts Institute of Technology, Cambridge); AND
GETTYS, JIM (Digital Equipment Corporation; and Massachusetts Institute of
Technology, Cambridge)
**The X window system.**
*ACM Trans. Graph.* **5,** 2 (April 1986), 79–109.

This is the first major publication on the X window system, and as such is required reading for anyone working in the field. The system was developed at MIT and provides virtual terminal interfaces to users. It is written in C and has been ported to a great variety of machines and systems. It seems most popular, however, under UNIX operating systems. One of the strongest points of the system is the focus on device independence. Display windows can be opened and maintained transparently across a local area network. The base system is defined by an asynchronous byte-stream network protocol. The paper describes the underlying network model and the high-level primitives for manipulating a hierarchy of window structures in a device-independent manner. Some of the design criteria that are mentioned are as follows:

- ☐ The system should be implementable on a variety of displays; it must be network transparent; it should support text, 2-D graphics, and imaging; and it must be extensible. It should support a hierarchy of resizable, overlapping windows, and must be capable of supporting different application and management interfaces.
- ☐ Applications for the system must be device-independent. Multiple applications must be able to maintain their displays concurrently, and any single application must be able to use many windows at once.

The paper is quite long, and it is not easy to discover an overall structure. It describes the design of X in four main areas: system software, the programming interface, the output structure, and the input structure. The system model is a conventional client-server model. For each physical display there is a server process that communicates with the client (application) process over a reliable duplex byte stream. The output structure is a hierarchy of windows. Windows are meant to be cheap enough to be used even to build, for instance, menu lists or individual items in forms and spreadsheet programs. The section on input structure deals with the keyboard, the mouse, and the inevitable race conditions that can happen if concurrently active multiple windows must share the usage of these.

The X system is an important piece of software. The paper describes it well.

—*G. Holzmann*, Murray Hill, NJ

### I.3.3 Picture/Image Generation

ROBERTSON, PHILIP K. (Australian National Univ.; and CSIRO Division of Information Technology, Canberra, Australia); AND O'CALLAGHAN, JOHN F. (CSIRO Division of Information Technology, Canberra, Australia) **HCI-0371**
**The application of scene synthesis techniques to the display of multidimensional image data.** *ACM Trans. Graph.* **4,** 4 (Oct. 1985), 247–274.

This paper presents a technique for interpreting multidimensional data by viewing the spatial superposition of one data set upon the other. The authors suggest that when the two data sets have different underlying spatial structures, then a two-color display (say red and green) may not result in a representation which is easy for the viewer to understand.

In the technique presented here, the authors model one of the two data sets as a surface, using shaded-relief techniques to display the topography with a single color. The other data set is represented in one of two ways, either by coloring the surface representing the first data set, or by overlaying a colored transparency upon the surface representing the first data set. Color illustrations depict the differences in the results which are derived from the two-color technique, as well as those proposed by the authors. For a contour map of an area and a map of magnetic field strength, the authors present color photographs depicting the various techniques of data representation. Their approach does indeed present the two data sets such that the magnetic field strength data appear to be overlaid upon a contour map. To this reviewer, a geologist could find more information in the resulting image than in a traditional two-color representation.

The great difficulty of the technique, however, is that it is extremely complex. Models of surface reflection and pigmentation are computationally complex, as well as difficult for persons untrained in computer graphics to comprehend. It will be quite difficult for, say, a geologist unfamiliar with computer graphics and color theory to implement these techniques without reference to a number of other texts and papers (or perhaps a colleague who works in the area). Nevertheless, when a simple two-color display of data from two data sets does not yield useful information, this approach may be of great value.

—*Robert Cannon*, Columbia, SC

## Display algorithms

SALESIN, DAVID; AND BARZEL, RONEN (California Institute of Technology, Pasadena)  **HCI-0372**
**Two-bit graphics.**
*IEEE Comput. Graph. Appl.* **6,** 6 (June 1986), 36–42.

This paper describes an extension to bit-mapped graphics operations to allow more flexibility in combinatorial manipulations. The basic method described supplements the standard graphic bitmap with a separate bitmap which indicates coverage, and which operates on the pair as a unit. This method allows transparency and selective overlay techniques while using the same basic techniques as standard bitmaps.

The paper is clear and well organized in its presentation. It presents a notational and mathematical basis for the methods used, and then develops several examples of application. Performance comparisons are given to standard bitmap (bitblt) techniques. The integration of the method into existing software systems and the usage of existing hardware support, is not considered.

With the increasing use of bitmap graphics in interactive and printing applications, and the availability of specialized support hardware for these, this paper is relevant and informative. I recommend the paper to anyone involved in implementation or study of interactive graphics systems.

—*G. R. Guthrie,* Fairfield, IA

MEYER, GARY W.; RUSHMEIER, HOLLY E.; COHEN, MICHAEL F.; GREENBERG,  **HCI-0373**
DONALD P.; AND TORRANCE, KENNETH E. (Cornell Univ., Ithaca, NY)
**An experimental evaluation of computer graphics imagery.**
*ACM Trans. Graph.* **5,** 1 (Jan. 1986), 30–50.

Two experiments are presented in which comparisons are made between computer generated images of computer models and the physical environments that the models represent. The authors' objective is to test the accuracy, both measured and perceptual, of their synthesis of realistic scenes. They are dealing with diffuse environments, a class of scenes for which standard image synthesis techniques are particularly deficient.

The first experiment compares, for three different environments, radiometric measurements made of the radiant energy flux densities with the computed predictions based on the radiosity method. The model of light propagation takes into account the measured spectral reflectance of materials in the scene and the spectral and directional characteristics of the light source. The results show agreement to within ±7 percent.

The second experiment compares the *perception* of the real and synthesized scenes by subjects in a controlled setting. The setup consisted of placing a view camera pointing at the real scene next to another similar camera pointing at a color monitor displaying the synthesized image. It is worth noting that the computer image is compared with light emitted from a real scene, not with a televised image of the scene. The results are that 45 percent of the subjects selected the wrong answer, about the same as they would have by guessing.

While the radiosity method copes with diffuse and interbody illumination allowing a computation of "bleeding," the spectral accuracy of the method was not demonstrated by these experiments due to the type of radiometer used. (The authors do concede in the Conclusion that this is an area for further research.) This paper does demonstrate that realism of image synthesis can be experimentally validated. It is a start of what may evolve into more routine techniques for obtaining benchmarks of realism among competing image synthesis methods.

—*P. Sabella,* St. Laurent, Quebec, Canada

### I.3.4 Graphics Utilities

*Graphics packages*

BROYAYE, P.; PUDET, T.; AND VICARD, J. (Centre Mondial Informatique et Ressource Humaine, Paris, France)     **HCI-0374**
**Managing the semantic content of graphical data.**
[in *New applications of data bases.* Proc. of the ICOD-2 workshop (Cambridge, UK, Sept. 2-3, 1983), G. Gardarin; and E. Gelenbe (Eds.), Academic Press, Inc., San Diego, CA, 1984, 63–84.]

It seems like a good idea: the separation of the semantic aspect of a graphical entity from its physical implementation on a CRT or some other device. This paper discusses an experimental interactive system that can be used to define, draw, and modify an electrical network or a queueing network. The word "experimental" is not used in the paper; however from my reading, it is clear that the ultimate potential that the paper suggests has not yet been realized. To read the paper it helps if the reader is familiar with production grammars, LISP syntax, and terms such as "graphical instantiation function" and "abstract syntax tree."

The authors allude to possible memory savings that might accrue from the use of a semantic representation of a graphical system (e.g., network). That is, by storing the semantic information for user interaction and leaving physical display to the "system," they say implementation on microcomputers may be feasible.

The paper is *not* a convincing "New Application of Data Bases," as implied in the title of the book in which it appears. However, it *is* a useful discussion of managing the semantic content of graphical data.

—*Lyle Smith,* Naperville, IL

*Software support*

ENGLAND, DAVID (Univ. of Lancaster, Lancaster, UK)     **HCI-0375**
**Graphical prototyping of graphical tools.**
[in *People and computers IV.* Proceedings of the Fourth Conference of the British Computer Society (Univ. of Manchester, UK, Sept. 5–6, 1988), D. Jones; and R. Winder (Eds.), Cambridge University Press, New York, NY, 1988, 407–420.]

This short paper describes a tool set for the interactive specification and construction of graphical user interfaces. The tool set was at the partial prototype stage when the paper was written. The author mentions four specification techniques for comparison: functional specification notation, based on the Vienna development method; a notation based on Hoare's communicating sequential processes (CSP), which describes the user interface in terms of input events and processes; an object-oriented user interface management system for graphical interfaces, in which the interactive system is decomposed into representational, interaction, and application object classes; and the specification language Z.

England uses augmented transition nets (ATNs), which augment the object model with a private ATN (Object-ATN) for each class of interaction object, as the paper's tool set. He gives two examples of their use: a disk icon and its ATN and a pie menu with its ATN. Programmers can use Object-ATNs to prototype user interfaces using a layout/painting tool, an ATN diagram editor, and an ATN executive to execute the interface. The tool kit proposed in this paper is part of the ECLIPSE project.

—*Lyle Smith,* Naperville, IL

### I.3.6 Methodology and Techniques

MARCUS, AARON (Aaron Marcus Associates, Berkeley, CA)
**Graphic design for computer graphics.**
*Comput. Ind.* **5,** 1 (March 1984), 51–63.

HCI-0376

This article discusses how graphics design can improve the three different modes of computer graphics. The three modes of computer graphics are: outerfaces, interfaces, and innerfaces. Outerfaces are the final computation displays — texts, graphs, tables, and charts. Interfaces are the command/control and documentation that users encounter, such as menus and table input. Innerfaces are the programming languages and operating systems, i.e., the commond/control and documentation that computer experts encounter. Examples are given of undesigned and designed graphics for the "faces" and how the graphics representation can be improved through design. The improvements come from sophisticated type fonts, three-dimensional structures, color relationships, spatial organization, and temporal sequencing.

—*G. W. Zobrist,* St. Louis, MO

### Ergonomics

FOLEY, JAMES D. (The George Washington Univ., Washington, DC); WALLACE, VICTOR L. (The Univ. of Kansas, Lawrence); AND CHAN, PEGGY (Arthur Young & Co., and The George Washington Univ., Washington, DC)
**The human factors of computer graphics interaction techniques.**
*IEEE Comput. Graph. Appl.* **4,** 11 (Nov. 1984), 13–48.

HCI-0377

The design of man-machine interfaces utilizing interactive computer graphics is still largely an art. This paper attempts to provide a foundation for some aspects of this design process. The early part of the paper provides an overview of the ergonomic aspects of interactive graphics. The main subject matter of the paper concerns "interaction tasks." These are similar to the "logical input devices" found in several device independent graphics packages (e.g., SIGGRAPH Core, GKS). Six interaction tasks are defined:

☐ Select—Choose one from a finite set of alternatives.
☐ Position—Define a position in $n$-dimensional space ($n$ depends upon the application).
☐ Orient—Define an orientation in $n$-dimensional space.
☐ Path—Define a path through $n$-dimensional space.
☐ Quantify—Specify a value.
☐ Text—Define a text string.

The factors affecting the choice of implementation technique for the interaction tasks are described. A large number of implementation options are presented, together with relevant ergonomic factors and results of comparative experiments. Tables are presented summarizing the relative merits of various techniques.

The paper makes reference to much ergonomic and human factors literature which is, as yet, little known by the computer graphics fraternity. A bibliography provides a wealth of background reading.

Papers about the design of interactive graphic interfaces are generally disappointing to the person who expects to find out from the literature how to design the best interface for his application. This is not a criticism of the papers themselves, but a comment on the state-of-the-art. The present paper makes a significant contribution; not by providing answers, but by making designers aware of more options, and of the many ergonomic considerations which should be taken into account.

—*Rick Rolph,* Cambridge, UK

MURCH, GERALD M. (Tektronix, Inc., Beaverton, OR)
**Physiological principles for the effective use of color.**
*IEEE Comput. Graph. Appl.* **4,** 11 (Nov. 1984), 49–54.

This paper is required reading for anyone designing visual information displays, whether or not the displays incorporate color. It contains the sorts of principles too often ignored by those who construct computer displays to convey information, principles which rest on the physical characteristics of the human information processing machine.

Unlike many papers in this genre, it is *not* a compendium of personal opinions or empty platitudes. Instead, it is a clearly written collection of facts which are not generally known or widely appreciated, together with a closely argued list of their implications for the design of effective color displays. The density of directly useful information in this paper is very high.

The first of two sections in the paper deals with the physiology of color, including the lens, retina, and optic nerve. It describes the basic signal processing characteristics of the human eye, and it includes a discussion of color deficiencies ("color blindness"). The second section, on using color effectively, contains ten principles which show how this information can be applied. Some important and non-obvious conclusions drawn from this section are that thin blue lines should be avoided, that red and green should not be used on the periphery of a display, and that a gray-level encoded monochrome display may actually be *harder* for a color-blind individual to deal with than an appropriately encoded color display.

—*R. A. Thisted,* Chicago, IL

PERUCH, PATRICK; CAVALLO, VIOLA (Laboratoire de Psychologie de l'Apprentissage, **HCI-0379**
Marseille, France); DEUTSCH, CHRISTIAN (Société Opeform, Malakoff, France); AND
PAILHOUS, JEAN (Laboratoire de Psychologie de l'Apprentissage, Marseille, France)
**Real time graphic simulation of visual effects of egomotion.**
[in *Readings on cognitive ergonomics - mind and computers.* Proc. of the 2nd European conference (Gmunden, Austria, Sept. 10-14, 1984), G. van der Veer; M. Tauber; T. Green; and P. Gorny (Eds.), Springer-Verlag New York, Inc., New York, NY, 1984, 192–199.]

[See main entry, Review HCI-0039]

In the Abstract of this paper, the authors promise to present results on (1) multidisciplineary team work on the project, (2) a cognitive model, and (3) real-time simulation by means of graphic images. But, in fact, they only report on the last item. The computer simulation has to do with maneuvering a ship through a harbor using the following data: ship speed; rate; heading and helm; and positional parameters, such as distance from mid-channel, drift angle, and distance to the next buoys, all of which are supplied by a port radio system. The ship has to stay within the channel while it is subjected to the effects of the current. The operator is aided by two forms of display; either by a perspective view, or by a local map. The simulation is carried out based on data from Le Havre's oil terminal. Bridge constructions (speed and helm) are entered into the system by a keyboard operator.

Results on two sets of subjects are reported (the subjects do not operate the keyboard themselves). One category comprises naive users, the other professional pilots. Not surprisingly, the latter category performed consistently better using fewer course adjustments. Another objective was to find out which display is more suited to human use; the perspective (as seen from the bridge), or the map. Both pictures carry the digital data in overlay. Again, it came as no surprise to me that the perspective picture turned out to be the superior output form.

All things considered, this paper presents few, if any, new results in ergonomics that could not have been obtained by intuition. In my opinion, it would have been worthwhile to study the effects of more comprehensive graphics, including the role of color. The pictures the authors used in the experiment are mere skeletons of the scene to be shown. They are not really shown in real-time, but at a rate of one new picture every three seconds. Higher rates of more complex pictures could have easily been produced with today's graphics hardware. Considering the purpose of the simulation, steering a ship through a harbor under poor external circumstances (by night, in fog, etc.), it should be a worthwhile investment to use more expensive powerful computer gear.
—*J. van den Bos,* Leiden, The Netherlands

FARHOOSH, HAMID (Univ. of California, San Diego); AND SCHRACK, GUNTHER (Univ. **HCI-0380**
of British Columbia, Vancouver, B.C., Canada)
**CNS-HLS mapping using fuzzy sets.**
*IEEE Comput. Graph. Appl.* **6,** 6 (June 1986), 28–35.

Traditional color specification systems, such as the RGB (Red/Green/Blue) and HLS (Hue/Lightness/Saturation) systems, use a triple of numbers to describe a color. The CNS (Color

Naming System) is a variant of the HLS system, where English words instead of numbers are used to describe the lightness, saturation, and hue (for example: very dark, strong, greenish blue). The authors describe a method for translating color descriptions from CNS to HLS, using elementary fuzzy set concepts, and a particular implementation for the Tektronix 4027 color display terminal.

The paper is self-contained and easily readable. In fact, it presents only simple and straightforward ideas. Its audience thus consists mainly of people who have to deal with practical implementations of color specification systems.

—*Christian Ronse,* Brussels, Belgium

SCHWARZ, MICHAEL W. (Bell Northern Research, Ottawa, Ont., Canada); COWAN, WILLIAM B. (National Research Council of Canada, Ottawa, Ont., Canada); AND BEATTY, JOHN C. (Univ. of Waterloo, Waterloo, Ont., Canada) **HCI-0381**
**An experimental comparison of RGB, YIQ, LAB, HSV, and opponent color models.**
*ACM Trans. Graph.* **6,** 2 (April 1987), 123–158.

The authors describe a color matching experiment in which subjects interactively matched target colors displayed on a CRT display. The five color models selected were RGB, YIQ, LAB, HSV, and opponent colors. Twelve groups of subjects were formed by combining two tablet-based input techniques with the five color models.

While the data are presented with enough statistical detail to be credible, a casual browser can also grasp the conclusions. The surprising result is the vindication of the RGB model, which, as the authors indicate, has traditionally been regarded as user hostile. Users of the RGB model are among the fastest to make a match, although they are not the most accurate. Users of the HSV model are the slowest; however, they are more accurate.

Since an independent factor is investigated, the inclusion of different input techniques complicates the results. The conclusion here is that techniques using two axes of the tablet are faster but less accurate than those that only use one axis.

This study provides a basis for comparing color spaces used for interactive input. New color models can be tested by these means. For example, the opponent color model is shown to be relatively fast in achieving a match. Although the starting condition for HSV space may be questioned, the fact that a controlled experiment does exist is a great aid for graphics programmers in choosing the right form for color interaction.

—*P. Sabella,* St. Laurent, Quebec, Canada

*Interaction techniques*

OLSEN, DAN R., JR. (Arizona State Univ., Tempe) **HCI-0382**
**Pushdown automata for user interface management.**
*ACM Trans. Graph.* **3,** 3 (July 1984), 177–203.

A modification of pushdown automata is suggested as the principal structure of user interfaces. This paper applies techniques from automata theory and compiler design to software engineering. The method is only concerned with the sequence of the interactions between man and machine; it is not concerned with any of the spatial aspects of the interface. The relevance of this method to graphics derives from its attention to device independence, a subject of much concern in the standards business.

—*S. L. Tanimoto,* Seattle, WA

LAKIN, FRED (Stanford Univ., Stanford, CA; and Palo Alto Veterans Hospital, Palo Alto, CA)  **HCI-0383**
**A performing medium for working group graphics.**
[in *Computer-supported cooperative work: a book of readings,* I. Greif (Ed.), Morgan-Kaufmann, Palo Alto, CA, 1988, 367-396.]

Members of a designing group might communicate easily by using a common display such as a blackboard or a large sheet of paper. These media contain elements of graphics and text, which must be drawn and manipulated by one or more operators. In the first part of this research paper, the author uses a stepwise approach to discuss the features required of an efficient performing medium for working group graphics. He briefly describes three examples of non-computer media (although his third example, "manipulable card paper graphics," is unclear) and gives a systematic list of the required features.

In the second part of the paper, Lakin presents **vmacs,** a computer medium for working group graphics that is a powerful graphics editor (**vmacs** is the author's trademark). He shows how **vmacs** works and evaluates its performance based on generality, speed, quality, and dynamics.

The reader or even the user will find very interesting ideas in this paper. The text is short but clear. Some of the figures are too small, though, and the hand sketches are too crude.

—*Claudiu Popescu,* Bucharest, Romania

FRENKEL, KAREN A. (ACM Headquarters, New York, NY)  **HCI-0384**
**The next generation of interactive technologies.**
*Commun. ACM* **32,** 7 (July 1989), 872–881.

This paper is an interesting introduction to an exciting special section about the power and potential of the new interactive technologies. The author gives a competent overview of the current, commercially available systems. She reviews current trends in videodisc technology, compact disc systems (CD-ROM), and digital video interactive (DVI). One of the best sections is a comparison between the characteristics of DVI and CD-I, which even a novice can understand. But, most important, Frenkel captures both the excitement and the confusion over the new media and multimedia computer technologies. The excitement is obviously due to the knowledge that they can have dramatic effects in the areas of education and entertainment. The confusion is over which standards will prevail. The key issue may be the selection of a standard platform that can deliver this exciting new technology. The age-old struggle between innovation and standards continues into the "new generation of interactive technologies."

—*K. M. Swigger,* Denton, TX

## Languages

REYNOLDS, C. F. (Brunel Univ., Uxbridge, Middlesex, UK)  HCI-0385
**The use of colour in language syntax analysis.**
*Softw. Pract. Exper.* **17,** 8 (Aug. 1987), 513–519.

The author has devised a scheme for using color in output displays to highlight the parsing of user input. He demonstrates this scheme in the context of the MicroCODIL windowed input language as used for teletext applications on the Acorn BBC microcomputer. The basic idea is that each category of typed input (e.g., item name, qualifier, value) is displayed in a distinctive color as the computer parses. Thus, an unexpected color pattern alerts the user to an input error.

This seems like a reasonable way to take advantage of color as a medium through which the computer can communicate with the user. The paper would be more useful if it gave some indication of how effective this approach proved to be in actual use, e.g., by comparing its effectiveness with that of the use of audible tones or messages in error windows (in fact, the author describes both of these techniques as also included in his MicroCODIL implementation). It would also have been interesting to compare this approach to others involving color graphics.
—*R. S. Marcus,* Cambridge, MA

### I.3.7 Three-Dimensional Graphics and Realism

*Color, shading, shadowing, and texture*

OLSON, JUDY M. (Michigan State Univ., East Lansing)  HCI-0386
**Color and the computer in cartography.**
[in *Color and the computer,* H. Durrett (Ed.), Academic Press, Inc., San Diego, CA, 1987, 205-219.]

Judy Olson, whose research on the effectiveness of cartographic symbols includes several widely cited studies of color schemes for bivariate maps, provides a concise overview of the decorative and functional uses of color on maps. One of eight visual variables, color is often employed improperly or ineffectively by mapmakers unaware of conventional associations, proven strategies, and the cartographic theory of its use. Olson reviews the appropriate use and relative effectiveness of several color strategies for statistical maps, including qualitative, single-sequence, double-ended (that is, with a light color in the center and darker colors at the ends), shading, and two- and three-variable schemes. She also examines the graphic quality of various display devices, including CRTs, slide generators, large-format filmwriters, pen plotters, ink-jet plotters, scribing and photohead plotters, and laser platemakers.

Given the wide use and misuse of color in computer-generated maps, this short but lucid chapter is an appropriate addition to a book on color and the computer. The references are few but well chosen, and the supporting illustrations included in the tipped-in color-plate insert are visually effective and carefully related to the discussion. The chapter's principal deficiency is the brevity inherent in an attempt to treat color maps in one of a diverse collection of chapters. Yet the pragmatic focus on a set of guidelines allows Olson to address most of the major blunders perpetrated by amateur or impromptu mapmakers and untrained developers of cartographic software.

—*Mark S. Monmonier,* De Witt, NY

## I.4  Image Processing

### I.4.0  General

#### IPL

CHANG, SHI-KUO (Illinois Institute of Technology, Chicago); JUNGERT, ERLAND (National Defense Research Institute, Linköping, Sweden); LEVIALDI, S. (Univ. of Rome, Rome, Italy); TORTORA, G. (Univ. of Salerno, Salerno, Italy); AND ICHIKAWA, TADAO (Hiroshima Univ., Hiroshima, Japan)
**An image processing language with ICON-assisted navigation.**
*IEEE Trans. Softw. Eng.* **SE-11,** 8 (Aug. 1985), 811–819.

HCI-0387

A pre-prototype image processing language, IPL, and a supporting programming environment are described. The proposed generic language is introduced in order to investigate aspects lacking in the existing image processing languages, which are abundant.

The primary notion of IPL is that it allows the user to navigate through the image database, which is a complex hierarchical structure of picture objects and relational objects (both are sets of attribute triples). The navigation is via the creation and manipulation of icons, windows, region-frames, and ports. Icons are symbols with graphical representation referring to an entity (an object, a window, or a command) or to a set of entities. A window and region-frame are facilities for visualizing portions of the image, for constructing large image databases, and for designing high-level user interfaces. A port is simply a logical channel to parts of the database or to an external device.

IPL maintains a metadatabase user workspace containing all the application-dependent data and the current entities of interest (a currency concept related to that of CODASYL). IPL also allows the direct application of PROLOG-like rules in image processing and the association of such rules with icons.

IPL consists of three subsets: a logical IPL, which is used to retrieve/manipulate logical images stored in the database; a physical IPL to process/manipulate physical images; and an interactive IPL to interact with the image information system.

—*A. Kaufman,* Stony Brook, NY

### I.4.7  Feature Measurement

#### Size and shape

NACCACHE, NABIL J. (Concordia Univ., Montreal, Que., Canada); AND SHINGHAL, RAJJAN (Concordia Univ., Montreal, Queb., Canada)
**An investigation into the skeletonization approach of Hilditch.**
*Pattern Recogn.* **17,** 3 (1984), 279–284.

HCI-0388

The authors present some historical research into early methods of skeletonization. The background to their work may be summarized as follows. Let **I** be the set of points $(i, j)$ with $i, j$ integral and let **P** be a finite subset of **I**. Then a set **S** is a *skeleton* for **P** if (1) **S** is thin, (2) **S** and **P** have the same connectivity, and (3) **S** reflects the shape of **P**. **S** is said to be *thin* if every point of **S** has a *neighbor* in the complement **Š**; for *connectivity* see Rosenfeld and Kak [1]. Condition 3 is the most difficult to define; perhaps the most attractive definition is that of Pfaltz and Rosenfeld [2] for whom it is equivalent to 3'. However, a connected set **P** may be "represented" by a disconnected skeleton **S** which is somewhat disconcerting. Davis and Plummer [3] devised a more elaborate approach and proved that their method generates a skeleton **S** satisfying conditions 1, 2 and 3'.

Research on skeletonization is not over; for a given set **P** one may define very different sets **S** all of which satisfy criteria 1, 2 and 3'; thus, if **P** is a rectangle, the sets
are equally valid skeletons. Should one be preferred to the other and if so why?

Skeletons often have *spurs*, i.e., limbs of length one, which add little to an understanding of the shape of the figure. Should these spurs be removed while the skeleton is being produced—as suggested by Beun [4]—or should their removal wait till a later stage, as argued by Davies and Plummer?

Most important of all, the pattern on which skeletonization is to operate is often not just a binary pattern, but a grey-valued one; i.e., not just a set **P** but a set **P** together with a density function $f$ defined on the set **P**. It is interesting to note that Hilditch [5] devised an algorithm to deal with this grey-weighted case, although most later authors deal only with the simpler binary version of the problem.

The authors' contribution may be briefly summarized as follows. They define two algorithms for skeletonization, $H$, which they assert "truly reflects Hilditch's approach" and $S$, which they assert "is the Stefanelli-Rosenfeld version of the . . . approach of Hilditch." The authors exhibit two binary patterns for which $H$ preserves and $S$ fails to preserve the shape of the pattern.

The authors believe that in simplifying the Hilditch algorithm, Stefanelli and Rosenfeld [6] left out an important criterion with the result that the "simplified" procedure produces inferior skeletons. Your reviewer agrees with them, but to make this belief into a paper it is necessary to examine both sets of criteria and relate the different behavior of the algorithms to differences between the criteria. If the authors had done this they would have made a contribution to research in the history of skeletonization; however they go no further than the observation "thus algorithm $H$ was able to prevent excessive erosion along slanting strokes of width 2, which algorithm $S$ failed to do," a statement which does not offer any explanation of the behavior.

They go on to show "that for a certain restrictive kind of data, alg $H$ may be heuristically modified to achieve a marginal speed-up." To put it another way, they can go 5 percent faster by abandoning one of the tests and with it the guarantee that the skeleton will have the correct properties.

Since $H$ works correctly and $S$ was superceded by the Davis and Plummer method the paper offers little that is new. The interested reader will find discussion of recent developments in

Hilditch [7] and Davies and Plummer [3]; Rosenfeld and Kak ([1], p. 400) trace the history of the subject.

—*K. Paton,* Montreal, Que., Canada

**REFERENCES**

[1] ROSENFELD, A.; AND KAK, A. C. *Digital picture processing,* Academic Press, New York, 1976.
[2] PFALTZ, J. L.; AND ROSENFELD, A. Computer representation of planar regions by their skeletons, *Commun. ACM* **10** (1967), 119–122. See *Computing Reviews* **8**, 3 (May-June 1967), Rev. 12,090.
[3] DAVIES, E. R.; AND PLUMMER, A. P. N. Thinning algorithms: a critique and a new methodology, *Pattern Recogn.* **14** (1981), 53–63.
[4] BEUN, M. A flexible method for automatic reading of handwritten numerals, *Philips Tech. Rev.* **33** (1973), 130–137.
[5] HILDITCH, C. J. Linear skeletons from square cupboards, in *Machine intelligence,* B. Meltzer and D. Michie (Eds.), Edinburgh Univ. Press, Edinburgh, UK, 1969, 403–420. See *Computing Reviews* **10**, 12 (Dec. 1969), Rev. 17,968.
[6] STEFANELLI, R.; AND ROSENFELD, A. Some parallel thinning algorithms for digital pictures, *J. ACM* **18** (1971), 255–264. See *Computing Reviews* **12**, 9 (Sept. 1971), Rev. 21,858.
[7] HILDITCH, C. J. Comparison of thinning algorithms on a parallel processor, *Image and Vision Comput.* **1** (1984), 116–131.

## I.5 PATTERN RECOGNITION

### I.5.0 General

ROSENFELD, AZRIEL (Univ. of Maryland, College Park)
**Recognizing unexpected objects: a proposed approach.**
*Int. J. Pattern Recogn. Artif. Intell.* **1**, 1 (April 1987), 71–84.

HCI-0389

This paper proposes a parallel technique for quickly recognizing many different objects. The proposal is based on five approaches for recognition: use a set of two-dimensional characteristic views, describe objects in terms of primitive parts, use simple local properties, use relations defined in terms of relative values of properties, and specify classes using simple constraints on property values. These approaches are not directly supported in the paper with references to relevant psychological research but are presented as reasonable properties of human vision. Based on the approaches, Rosenfeld gives a proposal for a three-stage technique for a parallel system: input the image, find primitive parts, and compute property values; broadcast these properties to object processors; and in each object processor, compare the input description with its stored description, in order to recognize the input. This is simply a proposal designed to encourage researchers to think about parallel techniques and to develop techniques that may fit in the proposed framework.

—*Keith Price,* Los Angeles, CA

### I.5.2 Design Methodology

*Classifier design and evaluation*

REEKE, GEORGE N., JR.; AND EDELMAN, GERALD M. (The Rockefeller Univ., New York, NY)
**Selective networks and recognition automata.**
[in *Computer culture: the scientific, intellectual, and social impact of the computer.* Proc. of a symposium (New York, April 5-8, 1983), H. Pagels (Ed.), New York Academy of Sciences, New York, NY, 1984, 181–201.]

**HCI-0390**

This paper describes a biological approach to automaton theory. It presents a qualitative set of concepts that are checked by simulation studies. The paper differentiates between the biological and computer system approach by the need for the problem to be defined in the case of computer models. (Categories are formulated and stimuli categorized.) Pattern recognizers are based on selection processes in biological models using two procedures, viz, comparison with exemplars and probabilistic feature matching.

Taking analogues with the brain, the authors argue that the basis of neuronal group selection theory is based on the three criteria set out below:

(1) a collection of variant entities (repertoire) capable of responding to the environment,
(2) sufficient opportunities for the entities to encounter the environment, and
(3) a mechanism to enhance/amplify differentially the numbers/strengths of those entities whose responses to the environment are in some sense adaptive.

There must be a balance of the specificity of the recognition. This is covered in neural nets by the concept of degeneracy that gives some redundancy in recognition.

The authors set up a simulation model of two recognizers, corresponding to the exemplar and probabilistic categorization. In the first case, the recognizer responds to local features and another transforms the features into an abstract transform. In the second approach, the trace is developed and virtual groups are formed and resolved by the abstracting network. The second level recognizers are corrected and resolved.

The results of the simulation give good correlation with expected results and show the useful analogy with the human system.

—*A. J. Payne*, UK

*Pattern analysis*

FUKUSHIMA, KUNIHIKO (NHK Science and Technical Research Laboratories, Tokyo, Japan)
**A neural network for visual pattern recognition.**
*Computer* **21,** 3 (March 1988), 65–75.

**HCI-0391**

This paper proposes a neural network model that has the following properties and abilities: pattern recognition, selective attention, segmentation, and associative recall. This network of neuron-like analog cells has a hierarchical multilayered structure composed of a chain of cell layers. It supports forward connections between cells for pattern recognition and backward connections for selective attention, pattern segmentation, and associative recall.

The author discusses forward and backward paths in the network and network self-organization. He describes interaction between forward and backward signals, the threshold control for extraction of incomplete features, and the mechanism that switches attention when a composite stimulus consisting of two or more patterns is presented to the model that has finished learning.

This new model can be considered a model of associative memory; it has perfect associative recall and can repair imperfect patterns. The paper presents the model well and also offers principles for new information processor designs. Its length is just right for this subject, and it provides good recent references.

—*G. Albeanu*, Bucharest, Romania

## I.5.4 Applications

### Computer vision

SEDGWICK, H. A.; AND LEVY, S. (State College of Optometry, New York, NY)　　　HCI-0392
**Environment-centered and viewer-centered perception of surface orientation.**
*Comput. Vision Graph. Image Process.* **31,** 2 (Aug. 1985), 248–260.

There are two competing models for the appropriate representation of spatial data collected in early visual processing: Viewer-Centered (VC), where data is referenced to the viewer's line-of-sight; and Environment-Centered (EC), where data is related to the fixed framework of the environment. Marr was the leading proponent of the VC representation [1], and Sedgwick has been the champion of EC representations (see, for example, [2]). This paper reports on a simple experiment to decide which representation is used by humans. Subjects were asked to rotate slanted planes to have the same angle with respect to their line-of-sight, or with respect to the environment. The experiment did not reveal a difference in the accuracy of the rotations chosen by the subjects, but there was a clear difference in the variability. The VC results were more variable than the EC results, indicating that observers find EC matches easier to make. The authors cautiously conclude that the results are at least consistent with the hypothesis that the EC representation is primary in humans.

—*Joseph O'Rourke*, Northampton, MA

**REFERENCES**

[1] MARR, D. *Vision: a computational investigation into the human representation and processing of visual information*, W.H. Freeman & Co., San Francisco, CA, 1982.

[2] SEDGWICK, H. A. Environment-centered representation of spatial layout: available visual information from texture and perspective, in *Human and machine vision*, J. Beck, B. Hope, and A. Rosenfeld (Eds.), Academic Press, New York, 1983.

KROTKOV, ERIC P. (Univ. of Pennsylvania, Philadelphia)  **HCI-0393**
**Visual hyperacuity: representation and computation of high precision position information.**
*Comput. Vision Graph. Image Process.* **33,** 1 (Jan. 1986), 99–115.

The term "hyperacuity" emphasizes the difference of an order of magnitude between the threshold limits of resolution (1min arc) and localization (2s arc). Localization is much finer than the sampling mosaic of the retina, where the cones in the fovea are separated by at least 20s arc.

In this paper, two computational hypotheses about hyperacuity are presented and then developed for machine vision: the gaps between discrete photoreceptors are filled either by an averaging process of luminance features (the centroid computation) or by an interpolating process. One alternative for the interpolation is to reconstruct some important features (edge features represented as zero-crossings in the difference of two filtered images, i.e., filtered difference computation) of the image.

The centroid computation has an accuracy on the order of 1s arc (1/30 pixel); the filtered difference, although more expansive than the centroid, has a higher accuracy, on the order of 0.1s arc (1/300 pixel).

The paper is presented at an undergraduate level of accessibility. It contains well-informed research with useful information for computer vision scientists and psychologists. The practical value of the computational methods is questionable.

—*I. Garbacea,* Brasov, Rumania

### I.5.5  Implementation

#### Interactive systems

HONDA, NAKAJI (Univ. of Electro-Communications, Tokyo, Japan); AND SUGIMOTO,  **HCI-0394**
FUTOSHI (Toyo Univ., Saitama, Japan)
**Multivariate data representation and analysis by face pattern using facial expression characteristics.**
*Pattern Recogn.* **19,** 1 (Jan./Feb. 1986), 85–94.

The paper describes a method for representing multidimensional data by mapping onto a representation of a human face. Various data groups are associated with specific facial expressions based on various compositions of facial features. The goal is to facilitate human interpretation of complicated multidimensional data. Unfortunately, the mappings are too subjective to be of much general use, and other representation schemes (color coding or textual displays with detailed explanations of the data) are more suitable. It does not seem possible to provide any sound framework for such techniques.

—*T. Henderson,* Salt Lake City, UT

## I.6  SIMULATION AND MODELING

### I.6.3  Applications

LAURENT, DANIEL; AND MOTET, SERGE (Université de Paris, Paris, France)  HCI-0395
**Geomatic: a 3-D graphic relief simulation system.**
*Computer* **17,** 12 (Dec. 1984), 25–30.

The Relief Simulation System (RSS) is a menu-driven system running on an Intergraph, VAX 11-780 machine. The RSS is in a state of flux, but the basic approach to the 3D and 2D Digital Terrain Model and Contour Drawing is established. The paper presents a flexible user oriented system, based on matrix oriented terrain models and stacked files for contour drawing. The issues related to shading and viewer positioning are addressed, together with their approach to the hidden line question. There are indications that the contouring algorithms lack smoothing capabilities. The user interface has a menu-driven hierarchical structure.
—*K. Bulow,* Houston, TX

HOLMES, J. N. (Joint Speech Research Unit, Cheltenham, Gloucestershire, UK)  HCI-0396
**A parallel formant synthesizer for machine voice output.**
[in *Computer speech processing,* F. Fallside; and W. Woods (Eds.), Prentice-Hall International, Englewood Cliffs, NJ, 1985, 163-187.]

This is *almost* a tutorial paper on a type of speech synthesizer. The author covers a parallel-formant synthesizer in depth, and he fulfills this basic purpose in an appropriate length.

The comparison of the parallel-formant synthesizer with the cascade-form synthesizer is good, i.e., the author points out that there are a few significant disadvantages in the cascade-form synthesizer. However, he does not explain why he only modeled from the glottis to the lips. This in turn means that it is difficult to use the cascade form for generating nasalized vowels, nasal consonants, and any consonants that have their main excitation point above the glottis. Or is it impossible to model these three with the cascade form? On the other hand, the author is successful at approximating as closely as possible those features of speech signals that are perceptually significant.

I am sure readers would love to see a more detailed comparison between the cascade and the parallel form. This paper should be of interest to speech scientists, graduate-level signal processing students, and industrial researchers. The references are comprehensive.
— *Young Hwan Oh,* Dallas, TX

## I.7  TEXT PROCESSING

### I.7.1  Text Editing

MORRISON, D. L. (UWIST, Cardiff, Wales); GREEN, T. R. (The University, Sheffield,  HCI-0397
U.K.); SHAW, A. C. (SYSTIME Ltd, Leeds, U.K.); AND PAYNE, S. J. (The University, Sheffield, U.K.)
**Speech-controlled text-editing: effects of input modality and of command structure.**
*Int. J. Man-Mach. Stud.* **21,** 1 (July 1984), 49–63.

NIX, ROBERT P. (Yale Univ., New Haven, CT)  **HCI-0398**
**Editing by example.**
*ACM Trans. Program. Lang. Syst.* **7,** 4 (Oct. 1985), 600–621.

An editing by example system is an automatic program synthesis facility, embedded in a text editor, that can be used to solve repetitive text editing problems. The system analyzes a few examples the user provides it with and generalizes them into a program transforming the rest of the text. In order to get a running system, the author focused his attention on gap pattern replacement. A gap pattern is a sequence of strings separated by gaps, i.e., formal parameters. This approach has the advantage that a program can be synthesized after the user has provided two or three examples.

After presenting some typical text transformations, the author outlines the theoretical background of his algorithm without proofs and discusses its performance. Finally, he mentions some heuristics used to improve the realized system. A weakness of the gap pattern approach is that many text processing problems can't be expressed in this way and decision problems are NP-hard.

This is a well-written paper. Its primary contribution is in demonstrating the feasibility of program synthesis in text processing without hiding the limits of the approach. The paper is worth reading by anyone interested in augmenting editor facilities.

—*H. J. Schneider,* Erlangen, West Germany

## Spelling

PETERSON, JAMES L. (Microelectronics and Computer Technology Corporation,  **HCI-0399**
Austin, TX)
**A note on undetected typing errors.**
*Commun. ACM* **29,** 7 (July 1986), 633–637.

It is often easy to tell a document whose author has substituted the use of a spelling checker for careful human proofreading. Each word in the document is a perfectly spelled English word, but not all are exactly the words the author intended; rather, they are typos that just happen to be legal words. A common example is "form" where "from" was intended. A less common example is "wold" where "world" was intended. But as online dictionaries get larger in order to be sure that correctly spelled uncommon words are not rejected, the chances increase that a typo will be missed because it forms a correct, albeit rare, word. Peterson's paper is a first attempt at quantifying the probabilities involved.

Peterson's method is to create a very large online dictionary, create all possible "common" typos of the words in it, and see how many of these are legal words. "Common" typos are those in which a letter is added, omitted, or mistyped, or two letters are transposed. On a dictionary of 369,546 words, using 158,583.0 seconds of CPU time on a VAX 11/780, it was found that 215,882 words can be mistyped as one or more legal words. (Peterson loves numbers!) But the proportion of typos that were legal words was less than half a percent.

This sounds reassuring, but unfortunately reality isn't so neat. The high-frequency words of the language tend to be the ones that are short and easy to mistype as another word. When Peterson added a weighting for word frequency to his statistics, he found that the probability of an undetected typo was 0.13 for a dictionary of 100,000 words, much less favorable than the unweighted result of 0.005. Peterson ends by cautioning against spelling checker word lists that are too long or contain terms unnecessary for the particular user's topic. He calls for spelling checkers that are more intelligent, using syntax and semantics instead of just a dictionary lookup, and reminds us that human proofreading still remains necessary.

Peterson's study does not take into account the possibility that typing slips are biased towards legal words by the unconscious mind [1], nor such factors as keyboard layout (an incorrect letter is much more likely to be an adjacent or mirror-image key) or the relative frequency of the four kinds of typos. Extensive data is available on error patterns in skilled and novice typing [2], and could be used in follow-up studies. Nevertheless, the study is a useful reminder of the importance of careful human proofreading. For example, careful human proofreading would have noticed that Figures 2 and 3 of the paper are interchanged.

—*G. Hirst,* Toronto, Ont., Canada

**REFERENCES**

[1] RUMELHART, D. E.; AND NORMAN, D. A. Simulating a skilled typist: a study of skilled cognitive-motor performance. *Cogn. Sci.* **6** (1982),1–36.

[2] GRUDIN, J. T. Error patterns in novice and skilled transcription typing, in *Cognitive aspects of skilled typewriting,* W. E. Cooper (Ed.), Springer-Verlag, New York, 1983, 121–143.

### I.7.2  Document Preparation

WITTEN, IAN H.; AND BRAMWELL, BOB (The Univ. of Calgary, Calgary, Alberta, Canada)

**A system for interactive viewing of structured documents.**
*Commun. ACM* **28,** 3 (March 1985), 280–288.

The authors define the subject of this paper below:

> The system described in this paper interfaces to an existing interactive page-presentation program to achieve the effect of dual-purpose, hard-copy, and interactively browsable documents. The bridging software . . . is quite simple and has proved extremely useful in practice. It has allowed existing documents to be integrated into existing test databases and new documents to be proofread for both content and format before being printed.

With a few caveats as to known shortcomings, and a "wish list" of possible enhancements, the authors describe an existing UNIX-based system which looks very useful. (This is a system which will hide print composition information from an online browser and control information, e.g. menus, from the print composition hardware. You can very nearly have your cake and eat it too.

The paper is a good, short presentation of the system's capabilities and high level design. There is sufficient detail to understand what the system does, how it does it, and what software and hardware is required to bring it all about.

—*C. A. Wolfe,* Sylmar, CA

TRIGG, RANDALL H.; AND WEISER, MARK (Univ. of Maryland)     HCI-0401
**TEXTNET: a network-based approach to text handling.**
*ACM Trans. Office Inf. Syst.* **4**, 1 (Jan. 1986), 1–23.

Since scholarly texts contain footnotes that refer to other texts, is it possible that a collection of text should not be recorded on paper, but should be an amorphous, online corpus with a rich and growing network of links? The TEXTNET system described in this paper is one of several attempts to implement a system which will make possible experiments with this thesis. In TEXTNET, text is in *chunk* nodes connected together with *links*, each having a type: example, proof, refutation, etc. The paper makes the usual claims that readers and authors can join together in collective enrichment of the corpus.

Unique to this effort is the notion that chunk nodes are linked only to *toc* nodes, which have links but no text. Thus, structural information is disjoint from the text itself and users can comment upon the connectivity as well as on the text. An important tool of the system is the *path*, an ordered list of nodes which constitutes a linear rendering of the text for perusal. This may have been taken too far, however: it is reported that users complained that digressory nodes had to be spliced into the current path in order to be read.

A brief study was made of users working with TEXTNET. Half made no contribution to the corpus and the rest either wrote new material or made links between existing material. The authors noted with surprise that none of the 16 subjects both wrote chunks and made links, though this may not be surprising since the average usage time was little more than an hour and a half. It is a tribute to the interface design that users could contribute at all with such little exposure to the system. The illustrations reveal that the user is restricted by hardware to a painfully small viewing area.

It appears as though the paper itself was written in "chunks": paragraphs are short, choppy, and somewhat disconnected; and there are too many sets of bulleted paragraphs comprising lists of marginally related items. If this writing style resulted from use of TEXTNET, I would have to recommend against its use for publication quality material. It may be that creating a text as a collection of separate chunks impedes development of a feeling of narrative flow or sustained argument. Writing readable, linear text is difficult enough without having to write individual chunks so they are sensible when read in random sequence.

—*W. J. Hansen,* Pittsburgh, PA

DOOIJES, E. H. (Univ. of Amsterdam, Amsterdam, The Netherlands)     HCI-0402
**Synthesis of print-quality cursive script based on a model of the human handwriting mechanism.**
[in *Document manipulation and typography.* Proceedings of the International Conference on Electronic Publishing (Nice, France, April 20–22, 1988), J. van Vliet (Ed.), Cambridge University Press, New York, NY, 1988, 261–273.]

This paper describes a method for the generation of the paths of cursive script characters on high-resolution output devices. The method is based on the author's work on modeling the human handwriting system; indeed, the sample output has many of the characteristics of calligraphy, not least that of being innately unreadable. The author justifies overlooking this not unexpected problem by maintaining that the project's real goal is an analogous system for Arabic script, although Dooijes mentions this more understandable target only once.

In addressing the problem of generating a continuous sequence of letter shapes (a single brush path for an entire word), Dooijes examines a conventional mechanism based on polygon-guided cubic B-splines, but discards this because of problems with the specification and calculation of inter-letter regions. Dooijes describes a novel alternative approach that consists of projecting a continuous helical curve, imposed on the surface of several circular cylinders whose axes lie parallel to the viewing surface, onto that surface. The system specifies the curve as a one-dimensional B-spline that governs the pitch of the helix and applies inter-letter segments as patches between the functions that govern the connected letters. The paper does not address the problems of 'fleshing out' the path so generated in terms of the emulation of brush pressure variations or of character outline generation, but Dooijes has discussed them elsewhere.

—*Ian Utting,* Kent, UK

MORRIS, ROBERT A. (Univ. of Massachusetts, Boston; and Interleaf, Inc.)    **HCI-0403**
**Image processing aspects of type.**
[in *Document manipulation and typography.* Proceedings of the International Conference on Electronic Publishing (Nice, France, April 20–22, 1988), J. van Vliet (Ed.), Cambridge University Press, New York, NY, 1988, 139–155.]

This paper discusses the spatial frequencies present in typed text and their relation to the frequency response of the human visual system. One-dimensional Fourier transforms illustrate the peaks at high frequency, which are due to letter strokes, as well as the lower-frequency peaks due to word spacing. The author also shows two-dimensional Fourier transforms of six individual characters, illustrating frequency-domain features such as those that arise from the serif. He briefly discusses the reconstruction of amplitude information from phase data, and he concludes by discussing how the spectral aspects of type fit with models of the frequency channels in the human visual system.

This well-written paper has a broad scope. It assumes virtually no mathematical background; the author relies on informal discussions rather than on statements of mathematical results. Readers will find the specific spectral plots informative, and the comments on human vision are interesting, although preliminary.

—*D. Blostein,* Kingston, Ont., Canada

SOUTHALL, RICHARD (Xerox PARC/Rank Xerox Cambridge EuroPARC)    **HCI-0404**
**Visual structure and the transmission of meaning.**
[in *Document manipulation and typography.* Proceedings of the International Conference on Electronic Publishing (Nice, France, April 20–22, 1988), J. van Vliet (Ed.), Cambridge University Press, New York, NY, 1988, 35–45.]

In this paper the author works toward a formalization of the relationship between actual documents and the messages they carry. He treats documents as graphic objects that are interpreted visually. The paper consists primarily of definitions and associated discussions. Terms defined include *actual document, virtual document, graphic object, graphic structure, visual structure,* and *content structure*. A document, for example, carries a message via a graphic encoding of the content and content structure of the message. This encoding operates at four levels: verbal content, semantic attribute encoding, syntactic structure encoding, and content structure encoding. Finally, Southall discusses the problem of interchanging documents between incompatible document-production systems.

The author's considerations in the paper are rather preliminary and are restricted to text. He does not mention figures or tables. Although his extensive terminology draws useful distinctions, the definitions should have been more concise and, if possible, more formal. Southall claims that any immediate practical application of these ideas would be in the field of document interchange. The informality of his definitions, however, limits this applicability. Because it lacks formal definitions of message content and structure, the author's terminology can be used to state requirements but will offer little in the way of solutions. The ideas in this paper are worth pursuing and formalizing.

—*D. Blostein,* Kingston, Ont., Canada

## Format and notation

CHAMBERLIN, DONALD D. (IBM Almaden Research Center, San Jose, CA)
**Document convergence in an interactive formatting system.**
*IBM J. Res. Dev.* **31,** 1 (Jan. 1987), 58–72.

The second part of the title of this paper is somewhat misleading as the underlying formatting system, GML (Generalized Markup Language), is a batch system. ICEF2 (Interactive Composition and Editing System), the formatting system alluded to in the title, bundles GML with an interactive user interface that provides a WYSIWYG type (print) preview to the GML source text. Since screen and paper modes of convergence are not typically identical (the paper mode must always be complete whereas the screen mode need be only as complete as required) this point could have been made more explicit (perhaps by way of an association between the PERFECT command and the paper mode). In any case, since the problems of document convergence are to a large extent shared between Markup and WYSIWYG systems, this paper will be of interest to advocates/developers of either system.

After a brief history in which some of the distinctions between WYSIWYG, Direct Manipulation, and Markup are touched upon, the author introduces the concept of and some of the associated problems of document convergence. Complex documents that maintain markup tags having forward references to other markup tags require at least two passes to properly resolve all the references. A realistic example is given of a situation where a document can "oscillate" between odd and even formatting passes without ever converging. (In practice though, this situation can be prevented by the imposition of some additional straightforward checking.) Another interesting example of the necessity for more than one formatting pass over a document is given by those markup tags that reference their *own* page number. This example is amply explained.

A unique feature (and one that holds great promise in answering some of the outstanding problems of document convergence) of ICEF2 is the dynamic Data Store that ICEF2 maintains during an edit/view session. The dynamic Data Store is essentially a simplified relational database system (the author was the developer of the SQL language) that captures structural changes in a document not as they are applied to the GML source but rather on invocation of commands that provide screen formatting. This underlying data structure effectively provides ICEF2 with most of the internal information processing capability it requires for its screen formatting.

In closing the paper, Chamberlin points to a promising area of further research: minimization of processing to converge a document after editing. The answer most likely lies in further refinement of the persistent data store concept used by ICEF2.

—*Mel Goldberg,* Toronto, Ont., Canada

## J. COMPUTER APPLICATIONS

### J.2 PHYSICAL SCIENCES AND ENGINEERING

*Engineering*

LAGODIMOS, A. G. (HAF Technology Research Centre, Athens, Greece); AND SCARR, A. J. (Cranfield Institute of Technology, Beds, UK)
**Interactive computer program for the selection of interference fits.**
*Comput. Aided Des.* **16,** 5 (Sept. 1984), 272–278.

The article presents a good example of minicomputer application to the solution of everyday engineering design problems. The problem is essentially that of evaluating fit joint stress/deformation effects and load transmission capacity. (A fit joint is basically an oversized shaft mated to an undersized hole.) The designer is particularly interested in finding the dimensions that result in an acceptable fit. In solving this simple problem, however, numerous shaft/hub physical dimensions and material structural properties interplay. An interative computational process is involved. The authors, after describing the problem and the shortcomings of the present solution methods, provide the flow diagram of a computer program that they have developed for the solution of this problem.

From a few cases that the authors have analyzed, they conclude that the computer program saves a great deal of tedious work. But more importantly, it eliminates calculation errors that are inherent with existing fit joint selection methods.

—*T. J. Mirsepassi,* Claremont, CA

## J.3 LIFE AND MEDICAL SCIENCES

MANDELL, STEVEN F. (South Baltimore General Hospital, Baltimore, MD)     **HCI-0407**
**Resistance to computerization: an examination of the relationship between resistance and the cognitive style of the clinician.**
*J. Med. Syst.* **11**, 4 (Aug. 1987), 311–318. [1987 Hawaii International Conference on Systems Sciences.]

This paper discusses the results of a survey designed to investigate the relationship between the cognitive style of the clinician and the introduction of computer technology in the health care field. The author states, "The relationship between the cognitive style of the clinician and resistance to computerization has been given scant attention in the literature." This assertion may be true for the health care field; however, resistance to the implementation of computer-based technology in the workplace has been actively investigated for the past 20 years, and much of that literature is pertinent to this study. One difficulty of the present study is methodological. The sample is 35 nurses and clinical social workers. Thus, the sample size is too small to support a valid and meaningful interpretation of the results. Another problem lies with the selection of subjects to participate in the study, which was not based on randomization procedures. With these deficiencies in mind, the strength of the paper lies in the discussion of the cognitive style of the clinician versus that of the computer. The author states that the clinician uses intuitive problem-solving processes while the computer operates to force qualitative data into quantitative niches. Further, borrowing from cognitive consistency theory, this difference in approach creates "unpleasant cognitions" and thus resistance to computers in the health care field. Finally, the results of the survey are inconclusive and provide little empirical evidence to support the author's assertions.

*—Woodrow Barfield*, Seattle, WA

### Health

FRITTER, MICHAEL J. (Univ. of Sheffield, Sheffield, UK)     **HCI-0408**
**The development and use of information technology in health care.**
[in *Information technology & people: designing for the future*, F. Blackler; and D. Oborne, MIT Press, Cambridge, MA, 1987, 105-127.]

The author summarizes research done in the United Kingdom on attempts to bring information technology into health care settings. The primary focus of the paper is on the role of social, organizational, and to some extent psychological factors in the adoption of proposed innovations. Fitter argues for the primacy of such factors, rather than technological ones, in determining the fate of computerization in medical settings. American students of health care information systems will easily recognize the attitudes and responses shown by British patients, physicians, and administrators, despite important differences in the way health care is administered in the two countries. The commonalities and differences between the countries are useful for putting one's local experience into perspective. Despite the author's emphasis on the importance of the social and organizational context, however, there is no discussion of how these contexts are changing.

In most of the studies cited, an isolated computer application such as medical history-taking is introduced into a setting as the first piece of computer technology any of the staff has ever seen. The strategic choice Fritter discusses between patient-centered treatment and a disjointed, specialized approach will remain an important one, but choices about how information systems can be integrated into the health care delivery system now range beyond those discussed in this chapter.

—*R. L. Stout,* Providence, RI

## Medical information systems

BROWNBRIDGE, GARRY; FITTER, MIKE; AND SIME, MAX (The University, Sheffield, UK)
**The doctor's use of a computer in the consulting room: an analysis.**
*Int. J. Man-Mach. Stud.* **21,** 1 (July 1984), 65–90.

HCI-0409

A report is made of a computerized medical consultation system that prompts the physician user for symtoms related to a particular class of ailment. The paper focuses on an assessment of human factors issues in the use of the system. Two distinct patterns were noted during videotaped consultations: minimal computer use during the consultation, and conversational use of the terminal. Possible problems with response time, length of consultation sessions, coverage of symptom topics, errors in categorization of symptoms, and sequence of topic discussion are evaluated. A significant conclusion was that computer-aided consultations followed a similar pattern to that of precomputer consultations.

—*J. Fedorowicz,* Boston, MA

## RECONSIDER

NELSON, STUART J.; BLOIS, MARSDEN S.; TUTTLE, MARK S.; ERLBAUM, MARK; HARRISON, PETER; KIM, HYO; WINKELMANN, BERNHARD; AND YAMASHITA, DALE
**Evaluating RECONSIDER: a computer program for diagnostic prompting.**
*J. Med. Syst.* **9,** 5/6 (Dec. 1985), 379–388.

HCI-0410

RECONSIDER is a computer program that is designed to be a diagnostic aid in general internal medicine. The paper begins with an easily understandable explanation of the medical diagnosis process and describes how the capabilities of RECONSIDER fit into this process. An experiment designed to show how well RECONSIDER meets its objective of suggesting diagnoses to the physician is described in detail. The criterion was whether or not the ultimate correct diagnosis was among the possibilities suggested by the program. The authors candidly discuss both the benefits and shortcomings of the program and of the experiment, so the paper should be very helpful to researchers in medical decision making.

—*K. A. Duncan,* Los Altos, CA

## J.4  SOCIAL AND BEHAVIORAL SCIENCES

### IDECAP

VAN DEN BOS, J.; VAN NAELTEN, M.; AND TEUNISSEN, W. (University of Nijmegen, Nijmwegen, The Netherlands)
**IDECAP: interactive pictorial information system for demographic and environmental planning applications.**
*Comput. Graph. Forum* **3,** 1 (March 1984), 91–102.

HCI-0411

IDECAP is an interactive system for displaying maps of the Dutch 1971 census and 1978 land use data. The system is implemented on a PDP-11/45 in augmented C, and on a VAX11/780 in augmented PASCAL. In each case the augmentation is "input/output tools," which are "interaction modules" implementing rules for the system's response to user stimuli. The displays show values taken from a small (<10 Mbytes) database that has been preprocessed into 500m × 500m cells, overlaid on a topographic/cadastral outline base, resembling grid cell social atlases such as [1]. Through menus, the user can select the region to be displayed, map scale, variables(s), class intervals, symbols, and colors. With a color monitor two variables can be shown simultaneously, one represented by the size and the other by the color of the symbol. The authors cite seven (not very recent) similar systems and discuss possible extensions, but they suggest possible enhancement difficulties resulting from the hierarchical database structure. The original data and the grid cell transformation are not discussed.

The paper stresses the graphics and user interface, which are described by example rather than formally. The point of departure is that analog displays (such as maps) allow the viewer to use his or her pattern-recognition faculties; this also limits the system development problem to obtaining user requests and displaying data. IDECAP is a display system, and the human does the interpretation — this is a reasonable division of labor, although not a geographic information system.

—*J. R. Geissman,* Van Nuys, CA

**REFERENCES**

[1] POULSEN, M.; and SPEARRITT, P. *Sydney: A social and political atlas,* Allen and Unwin, New York, 1981.


## J.5  ARTS AND HUMANITIES

### Music

PENNYCOOK, BRUCE W. (Queen's Univ., Kingston, Ont., Canada)
**Computer-music interfaces: a survey.**
*ACM Comput. Surv.* **17,** 2 (June 1985), 267–289.

HCI-0412

Mathematics can be useful to composers. Sound samples can be identified and stored in many languages in any of the following ways:

(1) more or less traditional printed notations;
(2) tape recorded performance;
(3) a list of data which describe (for each note) amplitude, pitch, starting time and duration, timber, and more complex coded concepts; and
(4) graphics displays of functions (or other informative images) describing relations between subsets of previously mentioned attributes.

Computers, in particular, can be helpful to composers. Interactive manipulations are made easy and comfortable by input tools which avoid typing. In addition, realtime translations of sound information from any language to any other language produce immediate auditory tests.

Music theory notions, from tonal to modern, can be coded in algorithms. Computers can furnish a realtime theoretical analysis of sets of notes; they can point out those which wouldn't follow style requirements stated by the composer and tested by automatic composition.

Pennycook's paper is an extensive, organized, critical survey of recent studies involving the identification and storing of sound samples.

—*E. Gagliardo,* Pavia, Italy

## J.6 COMPUTER-AIDED ENGINEERING

WILFERT, H. G.; AND SEELAND, HORST (Daimler-Benz AG, Stuttgart, W. Germany)     **HCI-0413**
**CAD/CAM: integration in the automobile industry.**
[in *Product data interfaces in CAD/CAM applications: design, implementation and experiences.* Proc. of a seminar of the ZGDV (Technical Univ. of Darmstadt, Darmstadt, W. Germany, Dec. 1984-Feb. 1985), J. Encarnação; R. Schuster; and E. Vöge (Eds.), Springer-Verlag New York, Inc., New York, NY, 1986, 34–62.]

This paper covers the following topics: demands and requirements of an integrated concept of CAD/CAM in the automobile industry; information and communication in the process chain; application to production planning and engineering; applications to quality control; and possible hardware, network, and software architecture. The chapter is quite informative. It is based on the authors' local experiences in the German automobile industry. The basic purpose of the material is to survey the area of CAD/CAM application in industry. The nature of the presentation is introductory; no specific background knowledge is required from the reader.

—*R. G. Fenton,* Toronto, Ont., Canada

### *Computer-aided design (CAD)*

STRELNIKOV, Y. N. (The Ulyanov (Lenin) Electrical Engineering Institute, Leningrad,     **HCI-0414**
USSR); PULKKIS, G. (Helsinki Univ. of Technology); AND DMITREVICH, G. D. (The Ulyanov (Lenin) Electrical Engineering Institute, Leningrad, USSR)
**An approach to CAD system performance evaluation.**
*Int. J. Man-Mach. Stud.* **21,** 5 (Nov. 1984), 429–444.

The development of a general model of a CAD process, so that performance of a proposed system can be evaluated, is presented. Initially, the problem is defined and candidate performance measures are chosen. Next, the problem representation is proposed with discussion of inputs, outputs, transfer function, and how the performance measures are affected by the system variables. The problem representation results in a CAD system, CAD process formalization, and a CAD process simulation.

An example to illustrate these ideas is presented. The example chosen is the routing process in a printed circuit board layout. A Pro-Net description is used for the representation of the CAD system which corresponds to the performance model. Pro-Net is an interpreted modified Petri net and is useful in hierarchical modeling of structural and behavioral properties of systems [1,2].

This paper presents a methodology for the analysis and evaluation of the CAD process. The authors also suggest simulation techniques that can be used for solving the problem of evaluating the performance of CAD system architectures.

—*G. W. Zobrist*, St. Louis, MO

**REFERENCES**

[1] NOE, J. D. Abstraction levels with Pro-Nets: an algorithm and examples. Tech. Report no. 77-03-01, Dept. of Computer Science, Univ. of Washington, Seattle, 1977.

[2] NOE, J. D. Pro-Nets: For modeling processes and processors. Tech. Report no. 75-07-15, Dept. of Computer Science, Univ. of Washington, Seattle, 1977.


SAGIE, IKE (IBM Israel Scientific Center, Haifa, Israel)
**Computer-aided modeling and planning (CAMP).**
*ACM Trans. Math. Softw.* **12**, 3 (Sept. 1986), 225–248.

Computer-Aided Modeling and Planning (CAMP) was developed and designed for its first application: regional rural planning for developing countries. The planning models and the planning methodology, according to the author, are based on the widely known Rehovot approach to integrated rural development, developed by Weitz [1]. The methodology has been applied in the last 20 years in over a dozen countries in Africa, Asia, and Latin America. A region in Kenya was replanned, and Andalucia, Spain has a third planning project under way. The overall experience with CAMP is said to be satisfactory.

Architecture, design, and implementation of CAMP are introduced in this paper. A plan developed via CAMP is composed of four constituents: models, data banks, pictures, and text. A model file contains the definition of a mathematical model, e.g., linear programming with constraints, written in a Model Definition Language as macros. Data banks are written in a Data Definition Language (DDL). The main components of DDL are scalars, sets, and arrays. Pictures, which range in complexity from a simple list of variables or graphics to elaborate artwork, are created by the Picture Definition Language. The values for the pictures are automatically retrieved from the data banks and formatted according to definition. Text with directives is written in a Text Definition Language. Using a man-machine interface and command language on interactive panels, economic planning can be controlled and analyzed by statistical software. The system is reportedly being implemented on an IBM 4341.

The possibility of merging a picture file with a text file shows advances in word processing. With wise use of feedback data, the controlling of the said model could be meaningful.

NONBOOKS [HCI-0417]

The paper under review is fairly edited, with a few typing mistakes and some minor confusion about operations on arrays. Otherwise it is lucidly written, and it contains 13 references. CAMP is said to have possible applications in urban planning, water resources management, and other disciplines. The software system is worth recommendation and attention.
—*T. C. Huang,* New York, NY

**REFERENCES**
[1] WEITZ, R. Integrated rural development—the Rehovot approach, Settlement Study Center, Rehovot, Israel, 1979.

VOGE, ERNST (BMW AG, Munich, W. Germany) **HCI-0416**
**Goals in the application of CAD interfaces.**
[in *Product data interfaces in CAD/CAM applications: design, implementation and experiences.* Proc. of a seminar of the ZGDV (Technical Univ. of Darmstadt, Darmstadt, W. Germany, Dec. 1984-Feb. 1985), J. Encarnação; R. Schuster; and E. Vöge (Eds.), Springer-Verlag New York, Inc., New York, NY, 1986, 1–12.]

This paper begins with a historical overview of the application of computers to engineering design and manufacture. Following this is an outline of the conventional design process. The remainder of the paper presents strong arguments regarding simple and smooth interfaces for passing data between different stages of design. Many well-chosen, specific examples are included.
—*C. R. Crawford,* Toronto, Ont., Canada

ENDERLE, GÜNTER (Standard Elektrik Lorenz AG, Stuttgart, W. Germany) **HCI-0417**
**Graphical standards.**
[in *Product data interfaces in CAD/CAM applications: design, implementation and experiences.* Proc. of a seminar of the ZGDV (Technical Univ. of Darmstadt, Darmstadt, W. Germany, Dec. 1984-Feb. 1985), J. Encarnação; R. Schuster; and E. Vöge (Eds.), Springer-Verlag New York, Inc., New York, NY, 1986, 74–82.]

This paper is a chapter from a book that is devoted to an overall consideration of computer graphics. This particular chapter addresses the current status of standards in computer graphics technology.
The introduction states that "much activity in the last ten years has concentrated on the development of standard interfaces. Now the first project has attained the status of an International Standard: the Graphical Kernel System, GKS. . . . The goal is to create a family of compatible and consistent standard interfaces that covers the whole area of computer graphics."
The paper describes not only GKS but also other standards under development (3D-GKS, PHIGS, CGM, CGI, and WSI) and their interrelationships. The objective of all this activity is to ensure the portability of graphics application software between computers and computer environments.
The GKS standard in particular provides the following: standard functionality, device independence, application independence, language independence, a reference model, a sound basis for education in computer graphics, and a standard terminology.

Functionally, the GKS standard requires extension to include three-dimensional graphical functions (3D-GKS) and a standard for processing fast real-time 3D-transformations (PHIGS—Programmer's Hierarchical Interactive Graphical System). Interface standards are also required with devices and work stations (CGI and WSI) and with the storing and transfer of graphics (CGM—M for Metafile).

The development of these interlocking standards is timely, particularly for the further evolution of computer-aided design systems. These have as their functional endpoint the storing of design data in electronic form rather than as blueprints and the retrieval of these "master prints" electronically and remotely. Much of this is happening today and the further evolution of related technologies needs the security of guaranteed nonobsolescence of developed applications.

Standardization efforts in graphical systems face the same twin threats that exist in other areas of standardization. On the one hand, too early and too rigid standards throttle the development of newer, improved technologies; and on the other hand, developing standards too late abandons the field to unrestrained genius and freewheeling anarchy.

—*Jim Hammerton,* Pittsford, NY

PASEMANN, KLAUS (Volkswagen AG, Wolfsburg, Germany)
**Interfaces for CAD applications.**
[in *Product data interfaces in CAD/CAM applications: design, implementation and experiences.* Proc. of a seminar of the ZGDV (Technical Univ. of Darmstadt, Darmstadt, W. Germany, Dec. 1984-Feb. 1985), J. Encarnação; R. Schuster; and E. Vöge (Eds.), Springer-Verlag New York, Inc., New York, NY, 1986, 63–71.]

This paper is a tutorial on the need and availability of interfaces for mechanical computer-aided design (MCAD) data structures. The author is with Volkswagen AG and he emphasizes products currently in use within the company.

Interfaces briefly discussed include GKS, IGES, and VDAFS. The role of these interfaces within the ISO-OSI seven-layer model is mentioned. IGES limitations and a brief history of VDAFS are presented. A table of VDAFS/IGES entities implemented in selected systems is given. These systems include EUCLID, DDM, CADDS, ICEM (CD2000 and DUCT), CASS, OGSURF E, OGSURF P, and PATRAN. A concise test for IGES systems is proposed.

The paper seems well suited for the seminar for which it was developed. It appears to be targeted at readers with little or no knowledge of CAD interfaces. It is not a research paper but provides a practical view of the need for and current status of MCAD data structure interfaces. The major contribution seems to be the table of implemented VDAFS/IGES entities. The presentation suffers slightly from poor English composition. There are no references.

—*Roy Rathja,* Corvallis, OR

NONBOOKS                                                                [HCI-0420]

ENCARNAÇAO, JOSE                                                        **HCI-0419**
**Interfaces and data transfer formats in computer graphics systems.**
[in *Product data interfaces in CAD/CAM applications: design, implementation and experiences.* Proc. of a seminar of the ZGDV (Technical Univ. of Darmstadt, Darmstadt, W. Germany, Dec. 1984-Feb. 1985), J. Encarnação; R. Schuster; and E. Vöge (Eds.), Springer-Verlag New York, Inc., New York, NY, 1986, 13–33.]

The paper is a concise, easy-to-understand presentation of the most important documents used to standardize the functional interfaces in a graphics system. The presentation includes standards for graphics programming (GKS, 3D-GKS, GKS output level 3, GSPC Core, PHIGS), graphics metafiles (GKSM, VDM), device interfaces (VDI), videotext files (NAPLPS), and product data transfer formats (IGES). The main features of these standards and their interrelationships are emphasized by means of 18 self-explanatory figures, which complete this concise presentation.

This paper is useful for getting a glimpse of the general problems connected with computer graphics systems. However, I found the coverage of CGM and CGI standards, in the section on graphics metafiles and device interfaces, inadequate. Deeper insight into these standards is provided by Bono [1].

—*Marius Cosma,* Bucharest, Romania

**REFERENCES**

[1] BONO, P. R. A survey of graphics standards and their role in information interchange. *Computer,* **8,** 10 (Oct. 1985), 63–75.

### Computer-aided manufacturing (CAM)

RENZ, W. (Daimler-Benz AG, Sindelfingen, W. Germany)                    **HCI-0420**
**VDAFS—a pragmatic interface for the exchange of sculptured surface data.**
[in *Product data interfaces in CAD/CAM applications: design, implementation and experiences.* Proc. of a seminar of the ZGDV (Technical Univ. of Darmstadt, Darmstadt, W. Germany, Dec. 1984-Feb. 1985), J. Encarnação; R. Schuster; and E. Vöge (Eds.), Springer-Verlag New York, Inc., New York, NY, 1986, 144–149.]

This paper introduces a set of interesting papers dealing with the structural, functional, methodological, and pragmatic framework of the surface interface (VDAFS) developed by the German Association of the Automobile Industry. It constitutes a concise introduction to VDAFS.

This paper is only a short overview of the problems presented by the definition and implementation of this standard. It begins with a brief history of the efforts to define the goals and the realm of VDAFS. The main goal of VDAFS is to provide a data format for exchanging sculptured surface data between automotive manufacturers and their suppliers. This pragmatic goal is achieved by using a small number of geometrical elements and simple syntax rules (similar to APT). These geometrical elements and general rules are presented in a concise manner in the paper. A short, self-explanatory example is given to complete the picture of this interface. Some comparative results about VDAFS and IGES are given, together with information about the state of the art and further developments of VDAFS. The author declares that VDAFS is not a subset of

IGES and is not intended to be, but that relations exist between these two standards. I think that it would be useful to define these relations in order to realize, if possible, specifications for translators from IGES into VDAFS and vice versa.

—*Gabriel Barzescu,* Brasov, Romania

NOWACKI, HORST (Technische Univ. Berlin, Berlin, W. Germany); AND DANNENBERG, LOTHAR (EDS Electronic Data Systems GmbH, Rüsselsheim, W. Germany) **HCI-0421**
**Approximation methods used in the exchange of geometric information via the VDA/VDMA surface interface.**
[in *Product data interfaces in CAD/CAM applications: design, implementation and experiences.* Proc. of a seminar of the ZGDV (Technical Univ. of Darmstadt, Darmstadt, W. Germany, Dec. 1984-Feb. 1985), J. Encarnação; R. Schuster; and E. Vöge (Eds.), Springer-Verlag New York, Inc., New York, NY, 1986, 150–159.]

This paper summarizes some important theoretical and practical results obtained by the authors in VDAFS-related research sponsored by the VDA (Association of Automobile Industry). The intended reader of this paper is one with a special interest in geometric modeling, interpolation, and approximation methods. A background in these fields is assumed.

A brief introduction reveals the main aspects of the VDAFS framework. Then the practical problem of converting curve and surface geometric information, embedded in parametric polynomial representations between CAD/CAM systems supporting different maximum polynomial degrees, is presented. In order to maintain a high degree of accuracy in these approximate conversions, the authors decided to develop a method and an algorithm based on a combination of Hermite interpolation and least squares approximation.

After a short description of the curve and surface entities of the VDAFS neutral file, the authors focus on the approximation methods, with an emphasis on the goals of the methods, the distinct cases to be considered, and the relevant error types analyzed to meet tolerances. Both cases of degree reduction and degree elevation are discussed, and solution procedures are presented, together with numerical results obtained with test data. Although the work on this project is still in progress, the results are important and seem to confirm the authors' decision. I look forward to further development of the method and comparisons with other approximate conversion methods.

—*Gabriel Barzescu,* Brasov, Romania

HOPERT, D.; AND WEISSBARTH, T. (Control Data GmbH, Hanover, W. Germany) **HCI-0422**
**A tentative implementation of VDAFS.**
[in *Product data interfaces in CAD/CAM applications: design, implementation and experiences.* Proc. of a seminar of the ZGDV (Technical Univ. of Darmstadt, Darmstadt, W. Germany, Dec. 1984-Feb. 1985), J. Encarnação; R. Schuster; and E. Vöge (Eds.), Springer-Verlag New York, Inc., New York, NY, 1986, 160–166.]

This third paper of Section 4 (VDAFS—Functionalities, Approximation Methods, Implementation, Experience) deals with some implementational aspects of VDAFS. After a short description

of VDAFS, the authors present a tentative implementation and the usage of a program called TVDA (Transform VDA files), whose main purpose is to transform a VDA file into a neutral file format and vice versa. The neutral file format is provided by some CAD/CAM systems as an interface with other systems. The TVDA program was successfully used to exchange data between ICEM DDN and DUCT, PATRAN/G, VWSURF, EUCLID, CATIA, and SYSTRID systems. Two types of problems that arise when implementing and using VDAFS are stated: the problem of approximate conversion between systems supporting different maximal degrees of polynomial representations (see the previous paper [1]) and the problem of explicit information on connectivity at the segment boundaries needed for some representations but not contained in the VDAFS definition. Unfortunately, the paper does not clarify if and how the TVDA program copes with these problems. In my opinion the paper itself is of real interest for people directly involved in VDA activities, but it provides scarce general information about the implementation of VDAFS.
—*Gabriel Barzescu*, Brasov, Romania

**REFERENCES**

[1] NOWACKI, H.; AND DANNENBERG, L. Approximation methods used in the exchange of geometric information via the VDA/VDMA surface interface, in *Product data interfaces in CAD/CAM applications: design, implementation and experiences*, J. Encarnação, R. Schuster, and E. Vöge (Eds.), Springer-Verlag, New York, 1986. See Review HCI-0421.

GRABOWSKI, HANS; AND GLATZ, RAINER (Univ. Karlsruhe/TH, Karlsruhe, W. Germany)
**Testing and validation of IGES processors.**
[in *Product data interfaces in CAD/CAM applications: design, implementation and experiences*. Proc. of a seminar of the ZGDV (Technical Univ. of Darmstadt, Darmstadt, W. Germany, Dec. 1984-Feb. 1985), J. Encarnação; R. Schuster; and E. Vöge (Eds.), Springer-Verlag New York, Inc., New York, NY, 1986, 221–235.]

The International Graphics Exchange Specification (IGES) was developed to provide a general and useful solution to the problem of exchanging product definition data between different CAD/CAM systems. The use of IGES to actually exchange data involves pre- and post-processors that map the source data into the IGES model and then map from IGES into the target system. This 15-page paper examines the problems associated with the use and validation of IGES and mentions partial testing/validation tools that have been implemented. Testing an arbitrary implementation of IGES' transferring of data is essentially an impossible job as the pre- and post-processors can be so different.

Some of the general test criteria that are discussed in the paper are entity set (how much of IGES is implemented), exchangeability of entities between systems (e.g., are definitions different?), functionality, graphical representation, accuracy, syntactical correctness, and software quality. Testing IGES processors by cycle-tests, inter-system-tests, library-tests and file-analysis-tests is discussed. A library of tests that has taken a lot of time to develop tests only 19 of 46 entities in IGES.

The validation of test results involves comparing pictures, comparing databases, comparing operations, and hand checking. Some software tools for validating IGES files are mentioned.

[HCI-0424]

However, there are many aspects of the validation that make it very difficult and costly to fully automate testing and validation.

The paper is a useful summary of IGES and the validation efforts that had been made as of its publication.

—*Lyle Smith,* Naperville, IL

## J.7 COMPUTERS IN OTHER SYSTEMS

*Command and control*

MULDER, MICHAEL C. (ED.)
**Computer**
IEEE Press, New York, NY 10017, 20, 2 (Feb. 1987), ISSN 0018-9162.

HCI-0424

The Federal Aviation Administration's Advanced Automation Program is intended to modernize the nation's air-traffic control system, believed by some to be the world's largest and most complex command and control system. It is a system consisting of 1 million lines of application software source code and more than 0.5 million lines of support program source code. The investment in time and money needed to design, develop, test, and install such a sophisticated system is estimated to exceed $3 billion. The first phase of the program, in which antiquated computer systems at 20 en route control centers are to be replaced, is now nearing its successful completion. In the second phase, increased levels of automation and improved human-computer interface methods are to be introduced as part of the future system called the Advanced Automation System.

The February 1987 issue of *Computer* is entirely devoted to the Advanced Automation System. This special issue, coedited by the former program manager, contains seven papers covering a spectrum of issues related to the design and development of this system.

In addition to a high-level review of the program in general and a well written discussion on the elements of the current and the future air-traffic control system, the reader is also introduced to methods for evaluating alternative architectures of a complex distributed system. Two papers address the formulation of human-computer interface requirements. A detailed analysis of operational requirements is performed, followed by the formation of a system requirement validation team and the subsequent application of human factors methods. The function of the team is to verify the requirements from the user's point of view.

Another paper discusses the elements of managing the capacity of such a vast system, in order to insure that the system can meet its performance goals. Capacity management includes such challenges as the specification of performance requirements, workload projections, system modeling, and performance prediction.

Finally, the last of six papers on the subject of air-traffic control development is devoted to the familiar issue of ensuring that the reliability, maintainability, and availability of the Advanced Automation System are attained.

NONBOOKS [HCI-0425]

Although the papers specifically address methods that have been employed in the Advanced Automation System, many of these methods can be directly applied or used as a model in developing other complex large-scale systems. This collection of well-thought-out, well-written technical papers will therefore be of interest to those looking for an introduction to the current air-traffic control system and the basic features of its future concepts. It will also interest practitioners involved in designing, managing, and ensuring the quality of large critical command and control systems.

—*H. Gabrieli,* Margate, NJ

*Consumer products*

FRUDE, NEIL (University College, Cardiff, Wales)     **HCI-0425**
**Information technology in the home: promises as yet unrealized.**
[in *Information technology & people: designing for the future,* F. Blackler; and D. Oborne, MIT Press, Cambridge, MA, 1987, 231-249.]

In this chapter, Neil Frude attempts to assess the future of information technology and of the demand for it by domestic consumers, including no doubt the avant-garde who purchased talking teddy bears for their children last Christmas.

He begins by classifying users of information technology (IT) into two groups. First, there are those who welcome an involvement with IT. These include experts, who benefit directly from their involvement through intellectual, professional, and financial gains; workers, whose jobs involve the use of word processors, robots, or accounting systems; and hobbyists, who gain their thrills from developing systems via IT whether or not there is any gain in efficiency at the end. "Most people," who may not understand the technology and who see it as offering few benefits beyond temporary satisfactions such as playing games, make up the second group.

Frude notes that "at this point the costs for the ordinary user outweigh the benefits." He then develops his ideas as to how these conclusions may change in the not-so-distant future because of the progress being made in research and development. His futurist gaze encompasses technical, functional, and product changes, and he predicts in some detail how the commercial potential will accelerate changes in computers, robots, and the like. These, together with growing demand by consumers, should cause progress to be made in several areas, such as intelligent systems. Not only will a robot wash dishes, it will also put the crockery and cutlery away. Not only will the robot animal repeat tape recorded words, but, when the technical problems of speech synthesis have been solved, it will be able to say *anything.*

The author investigates the psychological and social effects of IT, taken together with the rapidly changing social scene. Thus, he comments

> Systems with 'artificial personality' could be expected to exert a powerful influence on their users. There is a basic psychological tendency to treat certain kinds of objects anthropomorphically . . . it is clear that many of the ways in which artificial systems will in future be enhanced will render them highly susceptible to such a response.

The author sees the future in terms of product and of serving the consumer market. IT will speed up the life cycle of many products by shortening the development process and will make it simpler and cheaper to incorporate enhanced features into many products. Whether, as Frude suggests, customers will be delighted with real toy animals and thinking domestic robots will no doubt shortly become apparent. However, the ideas of futurists often are adopted. W. H. Preece, in a lecture delivered to young persons in London one hundred years ago, said,

> There is a friend of mine, Sir Francis Truscott, who has his house fitted with electricity. He used to employ two men every day in raising water from a depth of 150 feet to fill his tanks, but when he had secured the use of electricity for lighting the house, I suggested to him that he might just as well use it for raising his water. It was no sooner suggested than acted upon. [1]

We still depend on electricity; IT certainly does.

—*Walter R. Crowe,* Thunder Bay, Ont., Canada

**REFERENCES**

[1] PREECE, W. H. From the Journal of 1888. *J. Royal Soc. Arts* **126** (5378) (Jan. 1988), 152.

## Publishing

JAMES, GEOFFREY

**The ethics of automated publishing systems (a response to Dr. Brockmann).**
[in *Text, context, and hypertext: writing with and for the computer,* E. Barrett (Ed.), MIT Press, Cambridge, MA, 1988, 50-54.]

The title of this chapter is slightly misleading; I think the author is addressing professional practices in desktop publishing, not the ethics of the documenter. Nevertheless, the chapter is short, well written, and direct.

This chapter is a response to the previous chapter of the book [1]. The author clarifies the five ethical implications of the document database methodology: reusability, quality, user friendliness, standardization, and job security. Distinguishing between computerization and automation, he contends that automation lessens the requirement for clerical labor but not for professional labor. According to the author, a professional writer is "someone who can synthesize ideas and then express them with clarity." The intellectual skill of writing can never be automated.

—*John Cupak, Jr.,* Boalsburg, PA

**REFERENCES**

[1] BROCKMAN, R. J. Exploring the connections between improved technology—workstation and desktop publishing and improved methodology—document databases. In *Text, Context, and Hypertext: Writing with and for the Computer,* MIT Press, Cambridge, MA, 1988. See *Computing Reviews,* Rev. 8803-0166.

# K. COMPUTING MILIEUX

## K.1 THE COMPUTER INDUSTRY

### Markets

MORIK, KATHARINA (Univ. Hamburg, Hamburg, West Germany)
**Customers' requirements for natural language systems: results of an inquiry.**
*Int. J. Man-Mach. Stud.* **21,** 5 (Nov. 1984), 401–414.

HCI-0426

This article presents the results of a market inquiry concerning the value of natural language-based application. The market research was done in West Germany. The article is straightforward and presents conclusions reached by the author based on the data obtained. The sample was from the population of West German business executives.

One of the problems with this study is that to date no natural language systems are available on the German market. As a consequence, only hypothetical inquiries about product type could be made. The study was performed by using a questionnaire consisting of 50 items to provide broad coverage, and by structured in-depth interviews. Random samples were taken from throughout industry, although the computer industry was included as a separate category to avoid skewing the results by the possibly greater receptivity of computer firms towards new data processing techniques.

The return quota for the 927 questionnaires was 22.6 percent. This was considered a high return rate since a response required about 40 minutes of a high-level manager's time. Natural language systems were viewed positively by the surveyed managers. The in-depth interviews revealed that these managers viewed natural language systems as a way to gain direct access to the firm's data and regain control from the computer department. They also recognized that such use would increase their workload. Although the respondents recognized that the cost-benefit relationship would be negative in the short run, 71 percent would invest in natural language systems now if they were available.

The survey also investigated the preference for typed *vs.* spoken input or output, and the importance of graphic output and response time. The study also examined the difference in preferences of users whose interaction with the system would be a part of their job and users whose use was casual. The paper reports three applications examples stemming from the in-depth interviews to illustrate that typical application of a natural language system is anticipated by those interviewed.

According to the author, the study revealed that there is a large demand for natural language systems by high-level managers in West Germany, and that the chief advantage seen is as an improvement and extension of the user's decision making capabilities.

The article is an interesting one, but disappointing in that it does not provide much of the raw data that was gathered. The reader is dependent on the author's interpretation of the results. Still, it must be recommended to those who are developing natural language systems.

—*G. T. Boswell,* Lewisville, TX

RUSHINEK, AVI; AND RUSHINEK, SARA F. (Univ. of Miami, Coral Gables, FL)    HCI-0427
**What makes users happy?.**
*Commun. ACM* **29,** 7 (July 1986), 594–598.

This paper reports on a controlled survey which asked the question "What makes users happy?" The responses are based on a mailing sent to subscribers of *Computerworld* magazine. The question is answered by relating 17 independent variables (satisfaction with response time, the extent to which systems are meeting users' expectations, etc.) to one dependent variable—overall user satisfaction.

Some results are not surprising: users like short response time, for example. Some are puzzling. The authors ask, for example, "Why, for instance, do mainframes have a relatively large negative effect on the dependent variable?"

Certainly, the paper serves to remind us that the old criteria of what is *good, better,* or *worse* should be reviewed. However, it is not always possible to agree with the authors' reasoning. For example, it appears from Table I that about 7.5 percent of the users are reporting on microcomputers, and it is reasonable to conclude that very few of these are portables. If Figure 1 gives a clear picture of the survey instrument(s), then one of the questions requires that the subject provide a numerical percentage of the time the following is a correct statement: "System is power/energy efficient." The analysis provides a single relative satisfaction provided by the "power/energy" factor for all categories of systems, from microcomputers to mainframes. The authors then attribute the importance of that factor to arguments relating to power supply, including both portables with their own sources and large computers with their own generators. It is a far reach from a small positive influence of the "power/energy" factor on overall satisfaction, to the reasoning explaining that correlation. This reasoning includes the statement that "Computers with their own power supply can be safer and more easily protected from instable sources of energy, and are likely to be more economical since they will not overheat, and go down very frequently."

—*T. C. Lowe,* Washington, DC

### Standards

ABERNETHY, C. N.; AND AKAGI, K. (Digital Equipment Corp., Hudson, MA)    HCI-0428
**Experimental results do not support some ergonomic standards for computer video terminal design.**
*Comput. Stand.* **3,** 3/4 (Dec. 1984), 133–141.

It is amazing to see how little work some people can get away with, and still publish a paper on it. This paper is an example. It deals with the ergonomic factors of video terminals, particularly in light of emerging and existing regulations for ergonomic standards (yes, indeed, 11 of them from Germany). Here, keyboard height and inclination, as well as user posture and distance of the terminal user from the screen, are investigated. The authors report results on two experimental studies they conducted, and compare the findings with the outcome of similar studies. (I am always intrigued to see that studies on 20 subjects can give a mean and a standard deviation with up to four significant digits.) The main conclusion of the authors hardly comes as a surprise: regulations for standards in the area should be updatable.

—*J. van den Bos,* Leiden, The Netherlands

## Suppliers

BELADY, LASZLO A. (Microelectronics and Computer Technology Corporation) **HCI-0429**
**The Japanese and software: is it a good match?.**
*Computer* **19,** 6 (June 1986), 57–61. [Computer science education in the US.]

This paper, condensed from the plenary address at Compcon Spring 1986, is the author's personal account based on 18 months in a research organization in Tokyo. It starts with a brief overview of the Japanese software industry and contrasts the links between the industry and universities with that in the United States, and also relates it to Japanese education in general. The paper continues with a discussion of Japanese distinction and separation between planning and implementation phases in solving problems. These activities are further related to Japanese attitudes where the author is impressed by their problem orientation, motivation, and willingness to cooperate, characteristics considered to have particular relevance to producing good software. However, the paper concludes with the view that the characteristics are less useful in handling exception cases and coping with technological and other changes and that flexibility is the best counter-strategy for Japan's competitors.

—*A. J. Powell,* Wolverhampton, UK

## K.3  COMPUTERS AND EDUCATION

### K.3.0  General

HUMPHRIES, CHRIS **HCI-0430**
**Implications for education and training.**
[in *Advanced information technology in the new industrial society: the Kingston seminars,* A. Cotterell, Oxford University Press, Inc., New York, NY, 1988, 28-41.]

Few people today feel that explanations, predictions, and analyses are necessary for us to understand the impact on society of the steam engine, the telephone, or the knife and fork. This is not true of advanced information technology (AIT); Humphries's paper discusses the impact of AIT on education and training.

Education itself is not well understood. The author comments, "all I can say is I do not know how people learn." In this context, he expects AIT to offer a "two-way flow of information" that may eventually tell us how people learn. Expert systems will apparently play a prominent role in this understanding.

Unfortunately, Humphries describes none of these developments in any detail. All he tells us is that "Kingston College . . . has pioneered the application of Expert Systems to practical problems in education and training." He also informs us that similar efforts in the United States, Canada, and Japan can be described as "disasterous," straight talk from an author who confesses not to know how people learn.

—*Antony Stevens,* Brasilia, Brazil

## K.3.1 Computer Uses in Education

*Computer-assisted instruction (CAI)*

ANDERSON, JOHN R.; AND REISER, BRIAN J. (Carnegie-Mellon Univ., Pittsburgh, PA)
**The LISP tutor: it approaches the effectiveness of a human tutor.**
*BYTE* 10, 4 (April 1985), 159–175.

HCI-0431

The authors describe an Intelligent Computer-Aided Instruction (ICAI) program for teaching LISP programming to novices. The program, GREATERP (Goal-Restricted Environment for Tutoring and Educational Research on Programming), is itself written in LISP as a rule-based expert system running on a VAX 725. The authors, both psychologists at Carnegie-Mellon University, have done extensive testing of the program and compared those results with the results of students taught by individual human tutors and by classroom instruction. "Ninety-eight percent of the tutored students did better on performance tests than the average classroom student did. Interestingly, the major benefit occurred with the poorer students. There was relatively little advantage of private tutoring for the best students." The authors have also developed ICAI programs for algebra and geometry, and plan "to create tutors for calculus and other programming languages such as PASCAL and PROLOG."

The program's knowledge base is in three parts:

- ☐ A domain expert, which knows how to solve the problems presented to the student.
- ☐ A bug catalog, which comprises the possible mistakes that a student can make.
- ☐ A tutoring module, which has general knowledge about methods of instruction.

The program presents a programming problem to the student and effectively looks over his shoulder while the student composes a program. When the student makes a mistake while coding, the program points out the error and presents the student with alternatives, one of which is right. Ineluctably, the student arrives at a correct program, which he or she can then run.

The program assumes an *ideal model* of the programming knowledge of the student. That is, the authors have developed a theory of how people learn to program, based on Anderson's more general ACT* theory for acquisition of cognitive skills [1]. This theory suggests that problem solving is organized hierarchically with goals and sub-goals. This approach then imposes a top-down programming methodology which is followed throughout GREATERP. One can view the program as leading the student through a structured search space of possible programs.

The trial results presented by the authors suggest that this approach is an effective way for teaching programming. One drawback, however, is that this method of leading the student to the correct solution does not allow the student to detect and correct errors on his or her own. It does not appear that the student learns how to debug programs. One could argue, though, that the best way to debug is not to make mistakes in the first place.

—*S. Slade*, New Haven, CT

**REFERENCES**

[1] ANDERSON, J. R.; FARRELL, R.; AND SAUERS, R. Learning to program in LISP, *Cogn. Sci.* **8**, 2 (April–June 1984), 87–129.

SQUIRES, DAVID (Univ. of London, London, UK); AND DOUGALL, ANNE (Monash Univ., Melbourne, Australia)
**Computer-based microworlds—a definition to aid design.**
*Comput. Educ. (Elmsford, NY)* **10**, 3 (1986), 375–378.

This very short paper suggests a definition of a microworld and speculates on the construction of a variety of them. It continues to promote a most dangerous myth, most ably propagated by Papert [1], that the turtles of Logo should be a fundamental factor in childrens' learning. I believe that the use of Logo can be valuable in providing a logically consistent environment where the idealized "truths" of mathematics and physics can be explored without unpleasant intrusion from the real, alogical world. In spite of Karl Popper's crystal-clear statements of 50 years ago about not confusing the world of ideas with the real world, it seems that many workers in computing do not yet appreciate the difference.

—*E. James*, London, UK

**REFERENCES**

[1] PAPERT, S. *Mindstorms: children, computers, and powerful ideas*, Basic Books, New York, 1980. See *Computing Reviews* **23**, 2 (Feb. 1982), Rev. 38,960.

### K.3.2 Computer and Information Science Education

KNELLER, GEORGE R. (Univ. of Southwestern Louisiana, Lafayette)
**Adult learners: away with computerphobia.**
[in *Computer science education.* Papers of the seventeenth SIGCSE technical symposium (Cincinnati, Ohio, Feb. 6-7, 1986), J. Little; and L. Cassel (Eds.), Association for Computing Machinery, New York, NY, 1986, 34–37.]

Kneller's paper contends that computer anxiety ("computerphobia") and public speaking anxiety (stage fright) are closely related phenomena, and that techniques that have proven successful in helping to overcome stage fright can be adapted to computerphobia. Kneller cites research [1] which has determined that the Jungian Extroverted-Perceptive personality type is usually unsuccessful at computing. He criticizes this and other related research because it ignores the fear factor, noting that his stage fright approach is superior because it directly addresses fear, which for many adults is the primary barrier to computer use.

His specific proposals for easing internalized fear are to (1) relabel computerphobia as "Computer Apprehension," (2) encourage adult computer novices to share their fears in groups, (3) start newcomers off with video games, (4) assign beginning computer programs that are relevant to learners' lives, (5) stress the need for considerable exposure to the machine, and (6) liberally praise adult students' progress.

Although the paper does not objectively support the connection between computerphobia and stage fright, the concept has sufficient face validity to warrant further investigation.

—*Geoffry S. Howard*, Kent, OH

**REFERENCES**

[1] HOFFMAN, J. L.; AND WATERS, K. Some effects of student personality on success with computer-assisted instruction, *Educ. Technol.* **22** (1982), 20–21.

CARROLL, JOHN M.; AND ROSSON, MARY B. (IBM T. J. Watson Research Center, Yorktown Heights, NY)
**Paradox of the active user.**
[in *Interfacing thought: cognitive aspects of human-computer interaction,* J. Carroll (Ed.), MIT Press, Cambridge, MA, 1987, 80-111.]

HCI-0434

The paper explores two issues in the design of training materials for computer users. These are the *production paradox,* in which learners often bypass training examples in favor of directly applying the object of study to their real work, and the *assimilation paradox,* in which learners tend to apply prior and often incorrect knowledge to new learning contexts.

Attempting to design training materials that address these issues results in conflicting design goals. For example, bypassing conceptual material in favor of "how to do it" may address the production paradox but make assimilation more difficult.

Following a description and discussion of the effects of and general approaches to these paradoxes, the authors present their own approach to effective learning. Using a training document called the "minimal manual," they attempt to balance the production and assimilation problems by doing the following:

☐ Basing curriculum designs on the real-life needs of the learners;
☐ Analyzing secondary skills needed for success in using the computer software, and addressing these in the training document;
☐ Avoiding conceptual material in favor of concrete action steps, but using concepts as needed to steer the learner away from incorrect assumptions; and
☐ Including sections in the material suggesting ways to creatively explore more advanced areas important to the learner.

To verify the concepts, the authors conducted user training using commercial training manuals and their minimal manual. Results indicated an order-of-magnitude increase in effectiveness of the learners who used the minimal manual.

This paper is worthwhile reading for those involved in the preparation of training materials for users of computer systems. The authors' contention that most people learn and use computers at relatively low skill levels is readily verifiable by observation. Any method that successfully addresses this area of productivity deserves further exploration, given the current number of computer users and the continuing expansion of computer use. Ample references are provided.
—*G. R. Mayforth,* Houston, TX

*Computer science education*

NOWACZYK, RONALD H. (Clemson Univ., Clemson, South Carolina)
**The relationship of problem-solving ability and course performance among novice programmers.**
*Int. J. Man-Mach. Stud.* **21,** 2 (Aug. 1984), 149–160.

HCI-0435

The purpose of the paper is an attempt to identify problem-solving skills and other factors that predict success for a college student enrolled in computer science courses. Approximately 300 students enrolled in introductory programming, elementary COBOL, or advanced level computer science courses were given a test at the beginning of the course. The test contained seven problems to be solved, and requested information on the student's previous academic performance in mathematics and language courses, previous computer programming experience, attitude toward computer science, and personal locus of control. (The term "personal locus of control" refers to the view that either one is in control of his or her actions or is responding to primarily outside influences.)

The problems tested the student's ability to understand and represent the problem in a solvable form (e.g., algebraic form) and his or her ability to approach this representation with a solution procedure. The problems were of several types: representation of word problems in algebraic form, identification of problems that had similar solution strategies, state-space problems (e.g., missionary-cannibal problem or Tower of Hanoi problem), and problems involving inductive and deductive logic.

The paper uses statistical analyses to conclude that performance on the test is related to the performance in the course indicated by the final grade in the course. The study found significant differences in problem solving performance between students in elementary classes and those in advanced classes. Significant differences in problem solving performance were also found between students receiving a grade of "A" and those receiving a grade of "D" or "F" in the elementary courses. No such differences were found for students in the advanced courses. Some problems were better at predicting course grade than others. Other factors that were related to differences in grades include previous computer programming experience and previous academic performance in math and English courses.

The paper extends the findings of Cheney [1] and those of Kurtz [2]. Although the paper presents no startling conclusions, it is interesting and informative. The author does provide a nice list of references for the reader interested in this or related subjects.

—*D. C. Haddad*, Oxford, OH

**REFERENCES**

[1] CHENEY, P. Cognitive style and student programming ability: an investigation, *AEDS J.* **13** (1980), 285–291. See *Computing Reviews* **22**, 1 (Jan. 1981), Rev. 37,261.

[2] KURTZ, B. L. Investigating the relationship between the development of abstract reasoning and performance in an introductory programming class, *SIGSCE Bull.* **12** (1980), 110–117.

VAN DAM, ANDRIES (Brown Univ., Providence, RI)
**The electronic classroom: workstations for teaching.**
*Int. J. Man-Mach. Stud.* **21**, 4 (Oct. 1984), 353–363.

Personal workstations are increasingly becoming a fixture at major universities. In particular, some private universities are requiring every student to purchase a personal computer for use during their collegiate studies. According to the author, Brown University is implementing such a program with workstations that use graphics-based software developed at that institution. The installation of workstations began with a network of personal computers for use in two computer science courses; this paper reports on the results of this experiment.

The workstations were installed in a special classroom that was used in both an introductory class and a data structures/algorithms course. Sample programs could be executed in class. As a visual aid, these programs were executed in BALSA, ". . .a software environment that provides multiple concurrent views of PASCAL or C programs. . .System-provided views include code highlighted one course statement at a time and various standard diagrams of common data structures such as arrays, linked lists, and graphs." According to the author, this "electronic blackboard" was responsible for an increase in student comprehension, although no statistics were presented. The paper describes the user interface in detail.

There are two major questions left unanswered by the author. First, the workstations are shown only performing CAI functions; is this their sole purpose for the proposed university-wide implementation? Second, it was never made clear whether BALSA was only a demo environment, or whether students could also write programs using this system.

—*D. J. Bagert, Jr.,* Lubbock, TX

SHERMAN, MARK; AND MARKS, ANN (Dartmouth College, Hanover, NH)     **HCI-0437**
**Using low-cost workstations to investigate computer networks and distributed systems.**
*Computer* **19,** 6 (June 1986), 32–41. [Computer science education in the US.]

This paper is a short description of a networking course taught at the authors' university. The course is oriented towards engineering and math students. The main emphasis of the paper is in the justification of the use of microcomputers (the title's workstation) in the lab associated with the course. The authors start with their philosophy of upper division computer science courses. They present the course syllabus together with the lab assignments that were developed for the course. Finally, the largest body of the paper is devoted to a rationalization for the use of networked microcomputers as the ideal lab setup for a course of this nature.

The extended narratives in developing the justification, emphasizing microcomputers vs. mainframes, seem unnaturally forced—like justifying the acceptance of a lower level species into a privileged circle. The arguments are straightforward and, for the most part, obvious. Still, what the authors achieved, with the course material and student motivation, is no small achievement. The authors might consider using microcomputers of different brands/operating systems/ protocols, etc., in their lab. Nowadays, these types of hybrid distributed systems that talk to each other are quite common.

—*J. Babilonia,* Rió Piedras, PR

ANDERSON, J. R.; AND SKWARECKI, E. (Carnegie-Mellon Univ., Pittsburgh, PA)     **HCI-0438**
**The automated tutoring of introductory computer programming.**
*Commun. ACM* **29,** 9 (Sept. 1986), 842–849.

This paper, part of a special issue devoted to the challenges of teaching programming, describes an Intelligent Tutor for LISP. The tutor is one of the products of a project aimed at developing a theory of skill acquisition. The authors' goal seems to be to expose the tutor to a larger audience of computer professionals and educators. The paper is a readable, relatively nontechnical overview. It focuses on the workings of the tutor, with only cursory mention of attempts to evaluate its effectiveness. The authors describe the limitations of the current system and their plans to extend it.

The authors have applied state-of-the-art technology in cognitive psychology and artificial intelligence to the construction of a practical tutoring system. The result is an innovative blend of standard Computer Assisted Instruction (CAI) and Intelligent Computer Assisted Instruction (ICAI). The final product is a large, complex decision tree, quite comparable to the more ambitious CAI systems developed over the last few decades. However, the decision tree is not laboriously handcrafted; rather, for the most part, it is automatically generated via an expert-system-like program that instantiates the authors' theory of tutoring. The resulting instruction can be much more fine-grained and complete than is typically achieved with conventional CAI, and it can be generated at a much lower cost per instructional hour. Furthermore, while a high-powered workstation is needed to develop the tutoring material, it can be delivered to students with low-cost personal computers.

This paper ought to be read by anyone involved in computer-based instruction. It should give developers from both the ICAI and traditional CAI camps ideas that are potentially relevant to their own work.

—*Robin Jeffries*, Palo Alto, CA

### K.3.m Miscellaneous

MAYER, RICHARD E. (Univ. of California, Santa Barbara)  
**Cognitive aspects of learning and using a programming language.**  
[in *Interfacing thought: cognitive aspects of human-computer interaction,* J. Carroll (Ed.), MIT Press, Cambridge, MA, 1987, 61-79.]

"Cognitive Aspects of Learning and Using a Programming Language" opens by listing the three kinds of knowledge involved in learning to use a computer language: syntactic knowledge, conceptual knowledge, and the mapping between these.

Mayer provides the reader with several examples of short BASIC programs together with what he terms "transactional analysis"—a method of breaking down program statements into primitive steps involving actions, objects, and locations. (I am reminded of assembly language here yet, curiously, assembly language is usually found difficult by students whereas transactional analysis eases the learning task.) Thus the BASIC program

```
10  INPUT A
20  LET B=A+1
30  PRINT B
```

involves 23 individual transactions. In addition to primitives, here and elsewhere Mayer discusses *chunks*, "with each chunk accomplishing a specific goal." (This is very similar to the "plans" described by Black et al. [1].)

Mayer and his colleagues devised a series of tests which showed that conceptual knowledge is indeed correlated to the successful mastery of BASIC programming. The importance of conceptual knowledge is underscored by the relative ease of learning a second programming language, where gaining merely syntactic knowledge is the primary task. Furthermore, tests showed that the ability to respond quickly to a particular BASIC statement was dependent on the number of transactions in the statement and the number of other statements in the program (this is a factor because of the chunks). Mayer contends that the same is true of procedures in English, but that the qualitative difficulty of the transactions is also a factor. This last point seems not well taken, since the example he uses to demonstrate this could and probably should be rewritten as several statements' worth of transactions. There is also a discussion of the conceptual models of BASIC—correct and incorrect—that students initially possess or subsequently acquire.

By focusing on transactional analysis, rather than syntactic knowledge, low-ability students (chosen based on their SAT quantitative scores) did much better, although high-ability students gained nothing.

The paper's main thesis regarding the importance of conceptual knowledge may be obvious, but the transactional analysis approach is not. We have here, then, a proven technique that can help nonscience students taking a computer literacy course to learn. This material is therefore worthwhile reading for educators with the task of teaching these students. The paper contains one printing error ("students" for "studies") and one incorrectly cited reference.

—*Joseph Fulda,* New York, NY

**REFERENCES**

[1] BLACK, J.; KAY, D.; AND SOLOWAY, E. M. Goal and plan knowledge representation: from stories to text editors and programs. In *Interfacing Thought: Cognitive Aspects of Human-Computer Interaction,* J. M. Carroll (Ed.), MIT Press, Cambridge, MA, 1987. See Review HCI-0183.

## K.4 COMPUTERS AND SOCIETY

### K.4.2 Social Issues

*Employment*

TURNER, JON A. (New York Univ., New York)
**Computer mediated work: the interplay between technology and structured jobs.**
*Commun. ACM* **27,** 12 (Dec. 1984), 1210–1217. [Special section on management of information systems.]

This paper presents the results of a study undertaken to determine the effects of application system interface on the operator's perceived task environment and well-being. The study doesn't try to determine *if* computer-aided work affects the operator, but rather attempts to determine how different types of computer interfaces affect the operator.

The author presents the results of a study of 620 Claims Representatives in 48 offices of the Social Security Administration in New York and New Jersey. Although there is one computerized system which is used to maintain claimant records, two different front-ends provide access to the system. One of these is a serial processing interface that uses a teletype telecommunications network. The other is an online parallel system interface with CRTs for data entry and response.

A questionnaire was "designed to measure the psychosocial factors that are potential stressors or stress moderators. These included task characteristics, work load, interface type and usage, as well as various outcomes including job satisfaction, strain symptoms, absenteeism and performance."

> [There were significant differences] in task demands and problems between subjects using the two interfaces, but not in job discretion or interdependence. Unexpectedly, workers using the faster, online system appear to have the greater task demands and number of problems. Consistent with this finding, workers using the online system show significantly higher levels of mental strain symptoms, lower job satisfaction, and higher absenteeism. On the basis of this analysis, online system operators appear to face greater stress and uncertainty as a result of an increased number of interviews. (This is made possible by the faster response time of the system in use, and thus faster claim turn-around.) This, in turn, results in poorer perceived task environment and poorer perceived working life quality.

The author concludes that the adverse impact on the operators of the online system

> is attributed to the fact that these workers perform a greater number of interviews per day and consequently interact with more clients. . . . The more clients served, the greater the operator stress. It appears that involvement with clients, with their various problems, brings about an expenditure of emotional energy. This expenditure is more detrimental to operator well-being than the frustration associated with a poor performing system interface, even though total client-contact time is the same.

The current trend toward online systems stresses improved worker productivity (a topic the author touches on in his conclusions). The results of this study seem to indicate that although worker speed in processing tasks increases, so, too, does worker stress. Although the author concludes that this increase in stress is due to the increased number of clients handled and the resultant increase in the variety of problems (an uncertainty) which the worker must deal with, there would seem to be a variety of other potential explanations for the results observed. For instance:

(1) The online system pushes the operator to greater accuracy of data entry, provides faster feedback, and these factors may provide a greater perception of machine-oversight of operator work.
(2) The decreased time between activities (in this case claimant interviews) leaves less time for the operator to "unwind."
(3) The operators may perceive that they are expected to work harder (faster) because the new system is faster.
(4) The increased functionality of the online system (greater editing of data, benefit calculation, etc.) may present the operator with a perception of decreased involvement in the work itself.

This study seems to only touch the surface of the effects of "productivity improvement" assisted by technology. It has been estimated that within ten years, every office worker will be interfacing with an automated system of some sort, either mainframe or micro. As the man-machine interface increases, this study would seem to imply that the quality of worker life will decrease rather than increase. Much study is needed to determine if there are limits to productivity improvement, and if there are ways in which productivity may be improved without adverse impact on the worker.

—*M. E. Modell,* Cambridge, MA

KRAUT, ROBERT E.; DUMAIS, SUSAN T. (Bellcore, Morristown, NJ); AND KOCH, SUSAN (U.S. Congress, Office of Technology Assessment, Washington, DC)
**Computerization, productivity, and quality of work-life.**
*Commun. ACM* **32,** 2 (Feb. 1989), 220–238.

Anyone who has tried to evaluate the impact of a newly installed computerized information system on an organization and on the work experiences of the employees who use the system has become aware of the many difficulties that such a study involves. This paper describes research that examined the effects of introducing a computerized record system into the customer service department of a large public utility. It contains more than just a record of the results obtained, even though these results are of general interest; "an overarching goal is to illustrate via this case study the methodological and conceptual complexities involved in assessing technological effects."

The reported study is based on an analysis of 169 employees (40 percent of the service representatives attending work on a typical day) who completed both a pre-computerization questionnaire and at least one of two post-computerization questionnaires. The questionnaires elicited responses on productivity, quality of training, job satisfaction, job pressure, anxiety, and attitudes toward computers. In addition to the questionnaire data, the researchers conducted 60 open-ended interviews with service representatives and their managers two to four weeks after the automated record system was introduced. They used multiple regression analysis to control the differential effects of the system on such variables as gender, age, offices of different sizes, and offices run by managers of different quality.

The bulk of the report consists of a detailed analysis using statistical t-tests, that shows the extent to which changes between the pre-computer and post-computer systems are greater than would be expected by chance. For example, the new system increased productivity significantly, but the results were not all positive; high-frequency tasks were made easier, but uncommon tasks were made more difficult. Also, while the new technology had generally positive effects on the service representatives, it had negative effects on their supervisors.

The study clearly indicates that while office automation and computerization can have profound effects on job effectiveness and employment quality, these effects do not conform to simple models. The authors conclude their analysis by presenting a revised model of technological impact which "extends the simple impact model in three ways: by expanding what one considers the technology to be; by identifying individual and organizational contingencies that moderate the impact of technology; and by recognizing the bi-directional nature of technological change."

—*H. Borko,* Los Angeles, CA

NONBOOKS [HCI-0443]

## K.4.3 Organizational Impacts

OAKLEY, BRAIN **HCI-0442**
**An overview of research and co-operation in advanced information technology.**
[in *Advanced information technology in the new industrial society: the Kingston seminars,* A. Cotterell, Oxford University Press, Inc., New York, NY, 1988, 1-27.]

Oakley reviews the state of information technology and discusses the competitive problems the computer industry faces in the UK. The technological challenge is to catch up with other nations in parallel computing, inference computing, speech recognition, and natural language. The author sees Britain's lack of experience with artificial intelligence and expert systems as a major handicap to progress in these important fields. The biggest threat is the UK's lack of large computer companies: only one of the world's top twenty firms is British. The author encourages increased joint research between the academic and industrial communities. This insightful essay is written in a light and witty style.

—*J. L. McKenney,* Boston, MA

## K.5 LEGAL ASPECTS OF COMPUTING

### K.5.m Miscellaneous

STRAUS, DONALD B. (Moderator) **HCI-0443**
**Computer-assisted negotiations: a case history from the law of the sea negotiations and speculation regarding future uses.**
[in *Computer culture: the scientific, intellectual, and social impact of the computer.* Proc. of a symposium (New York, April 5-8, 1983), H. Pagels (Ed.), New York Academy of Sciences, New York, NY, 1984, 234–265.]

This transcript of a panel discussion on the law of the sea negotiations describes the use of a computer model to help negotiators with a complex issue. The panelists, none of whom are computer scientists, are all eminent in their fields.

Although little is mentioned about the software, and nothing is said about the magnitude of the software, the underlying need for the model and how it is used are described well. Other than the fact that the software has been licensed to the EEC by MIT, its potential use in other applications is not clearly defined. Some important points are made. Management factors in decision making are welded into the model for this very sizable project. The author alludes to other uses for the model. The point of user participation in model design is well supported, as is increased user-friendliness. This paper may have great relevance for designers and users of large-scale models.

—*R. A. Bassler,* Washington, DC

## K.6 MANAGEMENT OF COMPUTING AND INFORMATION SYSTEMS

### K.6.1 Project and People Management

HARTSON, H. R.; AND HIX, DEBORAH (Virginia Polytechnic Institute and State Univ., Blacksburg) **HCI-0444**
**Human-computer interface development: concepts and systems for its management.**
*ACM Comput. Surv.* **21,** 1 (March 1989), 5–92.

As the title implies, this survey paper discusses the important issues concerning human-computer interface management systems. The authors' major point is that designers of interface management systems ought to create design tools that allow for "dialogue independence," a feature that enables the interface portion of the program to be independent of the computational component of the application. Such a feature also means that the interface can be easily modified without disturbing any other portion of the application. Such a concept is not new to the software engineering world, which has been responsible for promoting ideas such as modularization, data hiding, and many other design principles. Indeed, dialogue independence has been achieved by some of the current dialogue management systems described in the paper, especially those that support sequential dialogue processing. However, the problem occurs whenever designers need to construct what the authors call a multi-thread dialogue, which refers to a type of human-computer dialogue associated with direct manipulation devices that allow the user to pursue any number of different task paths at any given instant. Although multi-thread dialogues tend to be highly usable, they are also difficult to specify and document. Thus, there is a great need to create a tool that allows designers to specify, document, and prototype multi-thread dialogues.

The authors also discuss current interactive tools for interface development, systems for rapid prototyping, and methodologies for interface design. What is obviously missing in this paper, as well as in many of the systems cited by the authors, is a discussion of the "science" of human interface development. Perhaps this is because there is no science of human interface development and, as authors argue, "because development of quality interfaces involves an interactive cycle of design and evaluation. . . ." (p. 12). Thus, the human interface developer is more like the architect or creative designer who uses experience and knowledge of basic design to create a useful and usable system. The challenge is to create an environment that allows the "artist" to create.

—*K. M. Swigger,* Denton, TX

### Management techniques

BARBER, T. J.; MARSHALL, G.; AND BOARDMAN, J. T. (Brighton Polytechnic, Brighton, UK) **HCI-0445**
**Interactive critical path analysis (ICPA)—microcomputer implementation of a project management and knowledge engineering tool.**
*J. Microcomput. Appl.* **9,** 1 (Jan. 1986), 1–13.

The authors state in the Introduction that an "... objective of the research was to establish and implement a simple to use, highly graphical experimentation tool on which project networks could be constructed, analysed and interactively modified and updated." Their second, and perhaps more interesting, objective was "... [to] investigate the application of artificial intelligent computer systems to the project management domain." The paper does not fully meet these stated objectives:

(1) The choice of the BBC computer, which has only 41 KB of usable memory, resulted in reduced capability and functionality (e.g., limiting the size of the network to only 100 nodes). There are several portable computers currently available that would have significantly increased the capability of the system; for example, the Macintosh or Amiga both offer excellent graphics with significantly increased memory and storage capabilities.
(2) Discussion of the application of artificial intelligence to project management was not thorough. Seven of the nine pages of text are spent describing the microcomputer-based project management tool that the authors developed; only one part of one page was devoted to artificial intelligence.

In summary, the ideas and concepts put forth in the paper are interesting. The choice made regarding the physical implementation is, however, somewhat puzzling.

—*Phil Teplitzky,* New York, NY

## Systems analysis and design

PADDOCK, CHARLES E. (Arizona State Univ., Tempe); AND SWANSON, NEIL E. (Southwest Missouri State Univ., Springfield)
**Open versus closed minds: the effect of dogmatism on an analyst's problem-solving behavior.**
*J. Manage. Inf. Syst.* **3,** 3 (Winter 1986-87), 111–122.

The study investigated "whether dogmatism, the degree to which an individual's belief-disbelief system is open or closed can be related to systems analysts' problem-solving approach (flexible vs. inflexible) and problem-solving attitude (positive vs. negative)."

Seventy-four college seniors and graduate students who were enrolled in a systems analysis and design course responded to the 40 questions of a Rokeach Dogmatism Scale test by answering "agree" or "disagree" on a six point scale. Higher scores were assumed by the authors to correlate with "stronger dogmatism." The students were then asked how they would respond to being told "management is considering scrapping your recently implemented system." Three information systems professors then evaluated the responses on the basis of their own understanding of problem-solving approaches and attitudes. The results showed "that dogmatism is not significantly related to an individual's problem-solving approach or attitude."

For most readers of *Computing Reviews,* I would expect that the central issue in such a study is how to connect abstract concepts such as "time-perspective—beliefs about past, present, and future" to concrete design or development issues. That is, how can labels such as "closed-mindedness" be connected to observable behavior? The next step would be to make some plausible link from student responses in a hypothetical situation to analyst responses in a real situation. Finally, how could such a connection become a basis for effective action that makes a difference in systems development results? This paper, which appears in the management literature, will be of peripheral interest to most computer scientists.

—*J. Bennett,* San Jose, CA

## Training

POLLOCK, CLARE (Univ. College London, London, UK)  HCI-0447
**Training for optimising transfer between word processors.**
[in *People and computers IV.* Proceedings of the Fourth Conference of the British Computer Society (Univ. of Manchester, UK, Sept. 5–6, 1988), D. Jones; and R. Winder (Eds.), Cambridge University Press, New York, NY, 1988, 309–328.]

The aim of this study was to determine a preferred approach to the design of word processor training programs. It examined individuals' ability to transfer skills from one word processor to another, with the object of achieving the greatest transfer with the least retraining. Minsky's concept of *frames* [1] provided the research context; this concept represents knowledge as 'packets' that can relate to different levels of comprehension. While lower-level knowledge tends to employ more specific detail, higher-level knowledge performs an organizing function by permitting associative recall and thus providing a generalized model.

The subjects were initially trained on WordStar and then retrained on WordPerfect. The researchers found that providing low-level information about WordPerfect and relating it to previously acquired knowledge of WordStar was the most efficient method of retraining, although this effect was not consistent over all tested functions.

The study was well constructed and invites further inquiry into whether the findings hold for retraining in other applications and for other computer skills in general. Pollock's description of the model, however, does not sufficiently define the concepts of low and high levels of knowledge.

—*D. Miller,* Hattiesburg, MS

**REFERENCES**

[1] MINSKY, M. *The psychology of computer vision.* McGraw-Hill, New York, 1975.

### K.6.3  Software Management

## Software development

BAROUDI, JACK J.; OLSON, MARGRETHE H. (New York Univ., New York, NY); AND  HCI-0448
IVES, BLAKE (Dartmouth College, Hanover, NH)
**An empirical study of the impact of user involvement on system usage and information satisfaction.**
*Commun. ACM* **29,** 3 (March 1986), 232–238.

User involvement during system design could conceivably cause improved user satisfaction, system utilization, or both. In addition, satisfaction could cause improved utilization, or vice versa. The causal connection between these three is examined via a survey. It was found that involvement caused increased satisfaction and utilization, and in addition that satisfaction caused increased usage.

—*John M. Hammer,* Norcross, GA

### Software selection

KOPP, EILEEN F.; AND TIMMER, H. J. (IBM Corporation)     **HCI-0449**
**A plan for evaluating usability of software products.**
[in *Human factors in management information systems,* J. Carey (Ed.), Ablex Publishing Corp., Norwood, NJ, 1988, 207-219.]

This paper describes IBM's methodology for evaluating the user friendliness of software. It explains the purpose and overview of the evaluation, describes the location and layout of the evaluation facilities, and discusses the composition of the evaluation team. The paper ends with a summary followed by references and appendices. The appendices contain scenarios of evaluations, subject characteristics, and sample questionnaires.

IBM's recommended methodology requires a "usability lab," which consists of two rooms divided by a one-way mirror. One room, where the subject sits, is a studio that contains video cameras and audio equipment. The other room, where the observers sit, is a control room with video and audio monitors. The subject sits in the studio alone and tries to use the software package while the observers watch through the mirror and make notes.

Although this methodology is very effective, it is obviously only applicable to companies that have the money and resources to develop and maintain these facilities. While the paper does make some interesting points, it has little relevance for most readers.

—*L. Ferguson,* New Westminster, B.C., Canada

## K.6.m Miscellaneous

### Security

CHAMOUX, J. P. (Droit et Informatique, Paris, France)     **HCI-0450**
**Data security and confidentiality in Europe.**
*Comput. Secur.* **4,** 3 (Sept. 1985), 207–210.

This brief paper is presumably a critical review of the findings of a European Economic Community study of data security and confidentiality. However, the author does not cite any report or document containing the findings. According to the author, "The main findings demonstrate that the spreading of computers with versatile facilities made obsolete some of the established control systems; a better level of security is required."

—*A. Mowshowitz,* Croton on Hudson, NY

## K.7 THE COMPUTING PROFESSION

### K.7.m Miscellaneous

IVANCEVICH, JOHN M. (Univ. of Houston, Houston, TX); NAPIER, H. A. (Rice Univ., Houston, TX); AND WETHERBE, JAMES C. (Univ. of Minnesota, Minneapolis)  **HCI-0451**
**An empirical study of occupational stress, attitudes and health among information systems personnel.**
*Inf. Manage.* **9,** 2 (Sept. 1985), 77–85.

This excellent paper is a significant initial step in the research of stress and the behavior of information systems personnel. Empirical findings indicate that Type A (behavior pattern) personnel reported significantly higher levels of stress in terms of time pressure/work overload and work relationship patterns than did Type B counterparts. Similar significant differences in findings occur with respect to job-related tensions, tension discharge, and health disorders and severity; no significant differences were found with respect to job satisfaction and organization commitment.

Research of this nature assists the manager in understanding stress factors and associated attitudes and behavior of information system personnel. The paper raises further interesting research questions, such as: Are Type A personnel better performers than their Type B counterparts?

The paper has a good introduction with background references. It also gives comparisons of research results of other employment groups.

—*T. Carey,* Guelph, Ont., Canada


CARO, DENIS H.; AND SETHI, AMARJIT S. (Univ. of Ottawa, Ottawa, Ont., Canada)  **HCI-0452**
**Strategic management of technostress: The chaining of Prometheus.**
*J. Med. Syst.* **9,** 5/6 (Dec. 1985), 291–304.

This is a review paper which presents in a well-organized manner the results found in many research projects dealing with stress. The Bibliography contains 65 items. The particular kind of stress dealt with in the paper is that "brought about by the introduction of computer technologies in organizations, which we call technostress." The authors present a list of factors that cause stress (stressors), classified into five categories. They present a list of factors that tend to mitigate or amplify the effect of the stressors (moderators), classified into four categories. They also list positive and negative manifestations of stress. Then they offer suggestions to management that are designed to control the stressors and the moderators so as to minimize the negative manifestations and maximize the positive manifestations.

The paper should be read by industrial psychologists and human resources personnel. It could also be read by managers of small businesses who are planning to introduce computers into the business.

—*M. Snyder,* Ramat-Gan, Israel

# PART 2

# BIBLIOGRAPHY

| | |
|---|---|
| Books .................................................................. | 347 |
| Journals ............................................................... | 377 |
| Proceedings ......................................................... | 469 |
| Doctoral Theses ................................................... | 516 |

# BIBLIOGRAPHY

The following citations include works published on Human-Computer Interaction from 1986 to the present. The bibliography is divided into several sections: books, journals, proceedings and doctoral theses. Each citation has been assigned a consecutive identification number. Items reviewed at the front of the book have an identification number preceded by "HCI." Use this number to find a critical evaluation of the work. (Reviews begin on page 1.) Locate the full citation of non-reviewed items by searching the Bibliography on the identification number retrieved from the Author, Reviewer, Keyword, Category, or Proper Noun Index. You can also browse the Bibliography a section at a time. Each section has its own internal sort criteria.

## BOOKS

The Books Section is arranged alphabetically by the first author's last name. Papers in anthologies are listed under the main entry for the whole book. All prices are original amounts and should be used only as a guide.

0001 Human foundations of advanced computing technology: the guide to the select literature. The Report Store, Lawrence, KS, 1986, 300 pp., $75, ISBN 0-916313-09-3.

0002 Second IEEE Conference on Computer Workstations: proceedings. IEEE Computer Society, Washington, DC, 1988, 188 pp., $50.00, ISBN 0-8186-0810-2.

0003 ABU-MOSTAFA, Y. (Ed.) Complexity in information theory. Springer-Verlag New York, Inc., New York, NY, 1988, 131 pp., ISBN 0-387-96600-5.

0004 HOPFIELD, J. Collective computation, content-addressable memory, and optimization problems. See 0003. 99–114.

HCI-0071 ADAMS, L. High performance interactive graphics: modeling, rendering and animating for IBM PCs and compatibles. TAB Books, Blue Ridge Summit, PA, 1987, 403 pp., $22.95, ISBN 0-8306-2879-7.

0005 AHITUV, N.; AND NEUMANN, S. Principles of information systems for management (2nd ed.). William C. Brown Publ. Co., Dubuque, IA, 1986, 606 pp., ISBN 0-697-08267-9.

HCI-0020 AHO, A.; KERNIGHAN, B.; AND WEINBERGER, P. The AWK programming language. [Addison-Wesley series in computer science] Addison-Wesley Publ. Co., Inc., Reading, MA, 1987, 210 pp., $21.95, ISBN 0-201-07981-X.

0006 AKMAN, V.; TEN HAGEN, P.; AND VEERKAMP, P. (Eds.) Intelligent CAD systems II: implementational issues. [Tutorials and perspectives in computer graphics] Springer-Verlag New York, Inc., New York, NY, 1989, 324 pp., ISBN 0-378-50914-3.

0007 RUTTKAY, Z. Multi-media presentation in CAD systems. See 0006. 77–92.

0008 BEYNON, M.; AND CARTWRIGHT, A. A definitive programming approach to the implementation of CAD software. See 0006. 126–145.

0009 BEN-ARIEH, D. Product and process design in intelligent CAD workstations. See 0006. 209–216.

0010 MACCALLUM, K.; AND GREEN, S. THESYS—implementation of a knowledge-based design system with multiple viewpoints. See 0006. 228–244.

HCI-0068  ALEKSANDER, I.; FARRENY, H.; AND GHALLAB, M. Decision and intelligence. [Robot technology, vol. 6] Prentice-Hall, Inc., Englewood Cliffs, NJ, 1987, 203 pp., $45.67, ISBN 0-13-782079-8.
HCI-0021  ALEXANDER, H. Formally-based tools and techniques for human-computer dialogues. [Ellis Horwood series in computers and their applications] Halsted Press, New York, NY, 1987, 161 pp., $41.95, ISBN 0-470-20996-8.
    0011  AMBRON, S.; HOOPER, K.; AND SCULLEY, J. Interactive multimedia. Microsoft Press, Redmond, WA, 1988, 350 pp., $24.95, ISBN 1-55615-124-1.
    0012  AMMERAAL, L. Interactive 3D computer graphics. John Wiley & Sons, Inc., New York, NY, 1988, 249 pp., $24.95, ISBN 0-471-92014-2.
    0013  AMMERAAL, L. Graphics programming in Turbo C. John Wiley & Sons, Inc., New York, NY, 1989, 199 pp., $27.95, ISBN 0-471-92439-3.
HCI-0005  ANDRIOLE, S. Storyboard prototyping: a new approach to user requirements analysis. Q.E.D. Information Sciences, Inc., Wellesley, MA, 1989, 280 pp., ISBN 0-89435-246-6.
HCI-0062  ARBIB, M. In search of the person: philosophical explorations in cognitive science. University of Massachusetts Press, Amherst, MA, 1985, 156 pp., $20, ISBN 0-87023-499-4.
    0014  ARBIB, M.; AND HANSON, A. (Eds.) Vision, brain, and cooperative computation. MIT Press, Cambridge, MA, 1987, 730 pp., 65.00, ISBN 0-262-01094-1.
    0015  ARBIB, M.; AND HANSON, A. Vision, brain, and cooperative computation: an overview. See 0014. 1–83.
    0016  ROBINSON, D. Why visuomotor systems don't like negative feedback and how they avoid it. See 0014. 89–107.
    0017  SPARKS, D.; AND JAY, M. The role of the primate superior colliculus in sensorimotor integration. See 0014. 109–128.
    0018  ARBIB, M.; AND HOUSE, D. Depth and detours: an essay on visually guided behavior. See 0014. 129–163.
    0019  SPINELLI, D. A trace of memory: an evolutionary perspective on the visual system. See 0014. 165–182.
    0020  BURR, D.; AND ROSS, J. Visual analysis during motion. See 0014. 187–207.
    0021  WEISSTEIN, N.; AND WONG, E. Figure-ground organization affects the early visual processing. See 0014. 209–230.
    0022  ZUCKER, S. The diversity of perceptual grouping. See 0014. 231–261.
    0023  BURT, P. The interdependence of temporal and spatial information in early vision. See 0014. 263–277.
    0024  BRADY, M.; AND YUILLE, A. An extremum principle for shape from contour. See 0014. 329–260.
    0025  LAWTON, D.; RIEGER, J.; AND STEENSTRUP, M. Computational techniques in motion processing. See 0014. 419–488.
    0026  ARBIB, M.; IBERALL, T.; AND LYONS, D. Schemas that integrate vision and touch for hand control. See 0014. 489–510.
    0027  FELDMAN, J. A functional model of vision and space. See 0014. 531–562.
    0028  BALLARD, D. Cortical connections and parallel processing: structure and function. See 0014. 563–621.
    0029  TREHUB, A. Visual-cognitive neuronal networks. See 0014. 623–664.
    0030  BARTO, A. An approach to learning control surfaces by connectionist systems. See 0014. 665–701.
HCI-0034  ARBIB, M. Brains, machines, and mathematics (2nd ed.). Springer-Verlag New York, Inc., New York, NY, 1987, 202 pp., $27, ISBN 0-387-96539-4.
HCI-0027  ARTHUR, L. UNIX shell programming. Wiley-Interscience, New York, NY, 1986, 261 pp., $22.95, ISBN 0-471-83900-0.
    0031  AT&T, C. UNIX system V: release 3.0 Intel 80286/80386 computer version: system administrator's guide. Prentice-Hall, Inc., Englewood Cliffs, NJ, 1988, 250 pp., ISBN 0-13-940891-6.
    0032  ATHALE (Ed.) Neural network models for optical computing. SPIE, Bellingham, WA, 1988, $43, ISBN 0-89252-917-2.
    0033  ATKINSON, M.; BUNEMAN, P.; AND MORRISON, R. (Eds.) Data types and persistence. Springer-Verlag, Berlin, West Germany, 1988, 292 pp., ISBN 3-540-18785-5.
    0034  NIKHIL, R. Functional databases, functional languages. See 0033. 51–67.
    0035  AZEVEDO, J. ISPF: the strategic dailog manager. Intertext Pubs./McGraw-Hill Book Co., New York, NY, 1989, 334 pp., $39.95, ISBN 0-07-002673-4.

## BOOKS

**HCI-0026**  BACH, M. The design of the UNIX operating system. [Prentice-Hall software series] Prentice-Hall, Inc., Englewood Cliffs, NJ, 1986, 471 pp., $31.95, ISBN 0-13-201799-7.

**036**  BUXTON, W. (Ath.) BAECKER, R. (Ed.) Human-computer interaction. [A multidisciplinary approach] Morgan-Kaufmann, Palo Alto, CA, 1987, 738 pp., ISBN 0-934613-24-9.

**0037**  GOULD, J.; AND BOIES, S. Speech filing—An office system for principals. See 0036. 8–24.

**0038**  GOULD, J.; AND BOIS, S. Human factors challenges in creating a principal support office system—The speh filing system approach. See 0036. 25–37.

**0039**  A historical and intellectual perspective of the context of human computer interaction. See 0036. 41–54.

**0040**  The Socio/Political Environment. See 0036. 55–60.

**0041**  BODDY, D.; AND BUCHANAN, D. Information technology and the experience of work. See 0036. 61–67.

**0042**  MARKUS, M. Power, politics, and MIS implementation. See 0036. 68–82.

**0043**  KLEIN, H.; AND HIRSCHHEIM, R. Issues and approaches to appraising technological change in the office: A consequentialist perspective. See 0036. 83–92.

**0044**  SCHWEDER, H.; WESTIN, A.; BAKER, M.; AND LEHMAN, S. The changing workplace: A guide to managing the people, organizational, and regulatory aspects of office technology (book excerpt). See 0036. 93–102.

**0045**  The physical environment. See 0036. 103–108.

**0046**  SMITH, M. Human factors issues in VDT use: Environmental and workstation design considerations. See 0036. 109–116.

**0047**  SAUTER, S.; CHAPMAN, L.; AND KNUTSON, S. Preventing back strain. See 0036. 117–127.

**0048**  Guide to the Draft American National Standard for Human Factors Engineering of Visual Display Terminal Workstations. See 0036. 127–128.

**0049**  SPRINGER, T. The statutes and standards movement. See 0036. 129–130.

**0050**  MONK, A. How and when to collect behavioural data. See 0036. 138–142.

**0051**  MONK, A. Statistical evaluation of behavioural data. See 0036. 143–146.

**0052**  CURTIS, B.; SOLOWAY, E.; BROOKS, R.; BLACK, J.; EHRLICH, K.; AND RAMSEY, H. Software psychology: the need for an interdisciplinary program. See 0036. 150–164.

**0053**  SHEIL, B. The psychological study of programming. See 0036. 165–174.

**0054**  CARD, S. Human limits and the VDT computer interface (excerpt). See 0036. 180–191.

**0055**  CARD, S.; MORAN, T.; AND NEWELL, A. The keystroke-level model for user performance time with interactive systems. See 0036. 192–206.

**0056**  CARD, S.; MORAN, T.; AND NEWELL, A. Computer text-editing: an information-processing analysis of a routine cognitive skill. See 0036. 219–240.

**0057**  NORMAN, D. Some observations on mental models. See 0036. 241–244.

**0058**  ROBERTS, T.; AND MORAN, T. The evaluation of text editors: Methodology and empirical results. See 0036. 250–268.

**0059**  MACK, R.; LEWIS, C.; AND CARROLL, J. Learning to use word processors: problems and prospects. See 0036. 269–277.

**0060**  CARROLL, J.; AND MACK, R. Learning to use a word processor: by doing, by thinking, and by knowing. See 0036. 278–298.

**0061**  MURCH, G. Colour graphics—Blessing or Ballyhoo? See 0036. 333–341.

**0062**  BUXTON, W. There's more to interaction than meets the eye: Some issues in manual. See 0036. 366–375.

**0063**  BUXTON, W.; HILL, R.; AND ROWLEY, P. Issues and techniques in touch-sensitive tablet input. See 0036. 376–385.

**0064**  CARD, S.; ENGLISH, W.; AND BURR, B. Evaluation of mouse, rate-controlled isometric joystick, step keys, and text keys, for text selection on a CRT. See 0036. 386–392.

**0065**  SIMPSON, C.; MCCAULEY, M.; ROLAND, E.; RUTH, J.; AND WILLIGES, B. System design for speech recognition and generation. See 0036. 400–413.

**0066**  KAPLAN, G.; AND LERNER, E. Realism in synthetic speech. See 0036. 414–419.

**0067**  BUXTON, W.; BLY, S.; FRYSINGER, L.; LUNNEY, D.; MANSUR, D.; MEZRICH, J.; AND MORRISON, R. Communicating with sound. See 0036. 420–425.

0068   NIEVERGELT, J.; AND WEYDERT, J. Sites, modes, and trails: Telling the user of an interactive system where he is, what he can do, and how to get to places (excerpt). See 0036. 438–441.
0069   RICH, E. Natural-language interfaces. See 0036. 442–450.
0070   PERLMAN, G. Making the right choices with menus. See 0036. 451–455.
0071   CARD, S.; PAVEL, M.; AND FARRELL, J. Window-based computer dialogues. See 0036. 456–460.
0072   SHNEIDERMAN, B. Direct manipulation: A step beyond programming languages. See 0036. 461–467.
0073   HUTCHINS, E.; HOLLAN, J.; AND NORMAN, D. Direct manipulation interfaces (excerpt). See 0036. 468–470.
0074   BAECKER, R. Towards a characterization of graphical interaction. See 0036. 471–482.
0075   NORMAN, D. Design principles for human-computer interfaces. See 0036. 492–501.
0076   RUBINSTEIN, R.; AND HERSH, H. The human factor: Designing computer systems for people. See 0036. 502–509.
0077   WASSERMAN, A.; PIRCHER, P.; SHEWMAKE, D.; AND KERSTEN, M. Developing interactive information systems with the user software engineering methodology. See 0036. 508–527.
0078   GOULD, J.; AND LEWIS, C. Designing for usability: Key principles and what designers think. See 0036. 528–539.
0079   ANDERSON, N.; AND OLSON, J. Methods for designing software to fit human needs and capabilities (excerpt). See 0036. 540–554.
0080   WASSERMAN, A. Extending state transition diagrams for the specification of human-computer interaction. See 0036. 561–575.
0081   BUXTON, W.; LAMB, M.; SHERMAN, D.; AND SMITH, K. Towards a comprehensive user interface management system. See 0036. 576–583.
0082   HENDERSON JR., D. The Trillium user interface design environment. See 0036. 584–590.
0083   SCHMUCKER, K. MacApp: An application framework. See 0036. 591–594.
0084   MYERS, B.; AND BUXTON, W. Creating highly-interactive and graphical user interfaces by demonstration. See 0036. 595–604.
0085   WRIGHT, P. Manual Dexterity: A user-oriented approach to creating computer documentation. See 0036. 613–620.
0086   CARROLL, J. Minimalist design for active users. See 0036. 621–626.
0087   LEWIS, C.; AND NORMAN, D. Designing for error. See 0036. 627–638.
0088   CARROLL, J. The adventure of getting to know a computer. See 0036. 639–648.
0089   SMITH, D.; IRBY, C.; KIMBALL, R.; VERPLANK, W.; AND HARSLEM, E. Designing the star user interface. See 0036. 653–661.
0090   BEWLEY, W.; ROBERTS, T.; SCHROIT, D.; AND VERPLANK, W. Human factors testing in the design of Xerox's 8010 "Star" office workstation. See 0036. 662–668.
0091   NICKERSON, R. On conversational interaction with computers. See 0036. 681–693.
0092   BOLT, R. Conversing and computers. See 0036. 694–702.
0093   RISSLAND, E. Ingredients of intelligent user interfaces. See 0036. 703–708.
0094   BOWE, F. Making computers accessible to disabled people. See 0036. 709–714.
HCI-0042   BAILEY, R. Human performance engineering: using human factors/ergonomics to achieve computer system usability (2nd ed.). Prentice-Hall, Inc., Englewood Cliffs, NJ, 1989, 563 pp., $60, ISBN 0-13-445180-5.
0095   BARA, B.; AND GUIDA, G. (Eds.) Computational models of natural language processing. [Fundamental studies in computer science, No. 9] Elsevier North-Holland, Inc., New York, NY, 1984, 327 pp., $52.00, ISBN 0-444-87598-0.
0096   CASTELFRANCHI, C.; PARISI, D.; AND STOCK, O. Knowledge representation and natural language: extending the expressive power of proposition nodes. See 0095. 59–89.
0097   FUM, D.; GUIDA, G.; AND TASSO, C. A propositional language for text representation. See 0095. 121–150.
HCI-0342   HOVY, E.; AND SCHANK, R. Language generation by computer. See 0095. 165–195.
HCI-0339   JOHNSON-LAIRD, P. Semantic primitives or meaning postulates: mental models or propositional representation? See 0095. 227–246.
HCI-0341   MCKEOWN, K. Using focus to constrain language generation. See 0095. 261–274.

BOOKS

0098 BARRETT, E. (Ed.) Text, context, and hypertext: writing with and for the computer. [MIT Press series in information systems] MIT Press, Cambridge, MA, 1988, 368 pp., $35, ISBN 0-262-02275-3.
HCI-0150 HASELKORN, M. The future of "writing" for the computer industry. See 0098. 3–13.
0099 BARRETT, E. Introduction: a new paradigm for writing with and for the computer. See 0098. 13–34.
HCI-425A JAMES, G. The ethics of automated publishing systems (a response to Dr. Brockmann). See 0098. 50–54.
0100 KATZ, B. Text processing with the START natural language system. See 0098. 55–76.
0101 YOUNGGREN, G. Using an object-oriented programming language to create audience-driven hypermedia environments. See 0098. 77–92.
0102 CARLSON, P. Hypertext: a way of incorporating user feedback into online documentation. See 0098. 93–110.
0103 GRICE, R. Information development is part of product development—not an afterthought. See 0098. 133–148.
HCI-0151 LEVINE, L. Corporate culture, technical documentation, and organization diagnosis. See 0098. 149–174.
0104 WEISS, E. Usability: stereotypes and traps. See 0098. 175–185.
0105 KIRSCH, J. Investment in computer-product documentation: causes and effects. See 0098. 187–209.
0106 BARRETT, E.; AND PARADIS, J. The on-line environment and in-house training. See 0098. 227–249.
0107 KEYES, E.; SYKES, D.; AND LEWIS, E. Technology + design + research = information design. See 0098. 251–264.
0108 SULLIVAN, P. Writers as total desktop publishers: developing a conceptual approach to training. See 0098. 265–278.
0109 ZIMMERMAN, M. Are writers obsolete in the computer industry? See 0098. 279–288.
HCI-0152 RUBENS, P.; AND KRULL, R. Designing online information. See 0098. 291–309.
HCI-0153 SHIRK, H. Technical writers as computer scientists: the challenges of online documentation. See 0098. 311–327.
HCI-0154 PRICE, J. Creating a style for online help. See 0098. 329–341.
0110 KIRKMAN, J. How "friendly" is your writing for readers around the world? See 0098. 343–364.
0111 BARRETT, E. (Ed.) The society of text: hypertext, hypermedia, and the social construction of information. [Information systems] MIT Press, Cambridge, MA, 1989, 459 pp., $37.50, ISBN 0-262-02291-5.
0112 RUBENS, P. Online information, hypermedia, and the idea of literacy. See 0111. 3–21.
0113 GRICE, R. Online information: what do people want? What do people need? See 0111. 22–44.
0114 HERRSTROM, D.; AND MASSEY, D. Hypertext in context. See 0111. 45–58.
0115 CARLSON, P. Hypertext and intelligent interfaces for text retrieval. See 0111. 59–76.
0116 HODGES, M.; DAVIS, M.; AND SASNETT, R. Investigations in multimedia design documentation. See 0111. 79–89.
0117 IRISH, P.; AND TRIGG, R. Supporting collaboration in hypermedia: issues and experiences. See 0111. 90–106.
0118 MEYROWITZ, N. The missing link: why we're all doing hypertext wrong. See 0111. 107–114.
0119 SHNEIDERMAN, B. Reflections on authoring, editing, and managing hypertext. See 0111. 115–131.
0120 WALKER, J. Authoring tools for complex document sets. See 0111. 132–147.
0121 JAYNES, J. Limited freedom: linear reflections on nonlinear texts. See 0111. 148–161.
0122 BROCKMANN, R.; HORTON, W.; AND BROCK, K. From database to hypertext via electronic publishing: an information odyssey. See 0111. 162–205.
0123 KIRSCH, J. Trends in the emerging profession of technical communication. See 0111. 209–234.
0124 LEVINE, L. Consulting skills for technical writers. See 0111. 265–283.
0125 STEWART, J. How to manage educational computing initiatives-lessons from the first five years of Project Athena at MIT. See 0111. 284–304.
0126 BARRETT, E. Textual intervention, collaboration, and the online environment. See 0111. 305–321.
0127 NEUWIRTH, C. Techniques of user message design: developing a user message system to support cooperative work. See 0111. 325–342.
0128 ALSCHULER, L. Hand-crafted hypertext-lessons from the ACM experiment. See 0111. 343–361.
0129 DUFFY, T.; MEHLENBACHER, B.; AND PALMER, J. The evaluation of online help systems: a conceptual model. See 0111. 362–387.

**0130** RAMEY, J. Escher effects in online text. See 0111. 388–402.
**0131** GAULDING, J.; AND KATZ, B. Using "word-knowledge" reasoning for question answering. See 0111. 403–422.
**0132** CARROLL, J.; AND AARONSON, A. Learning by doing with simulated intelligent help. See 0111. 423–452.
**0133** BARTEE, T. Expert systems and artificial intelligence. [Applications and Management] Howard W. Sams & Co., Inc., Indianapolis, IN, 1988, 307 pp., ISBN 0-672-22471-2.
**0134** LAFFERTY, E. Space. See 0133. 3–31.
**0135** LEIWEBER, D. Finance. See 0133. 33–59.
**0136** HARRIS, L. Natural languages. See 0133. 131–146.
**0137** WOODS, W. Knowledge representation. See 0133. 147–176.
**0138** BONASSO, R. Military systems. See 0133. 177–209.
**0139** KAHN, R. Later years at IPTO. See 0133. 245–253.
**0140** DENICOFF, M. AI development and the Office of Naval Research. See 0133. 271–289.
**HCI-0032** BEECH, D. (Ed.) Concepts in user interfaces: a reference model for command and response languages. [Lecture notes in computer science; no. 234] Springer-Verlag New York, Inc., New York, NY, 1986, 116 pp., $14.30, ISBN 0-387-16791-9.
**0141** BERGERUD, M.; AND KELLER, T. Computers for managing information. John Wiley & Sons, Inc., New York, NY, 1988, 480 pp., $27.95, ISBN 0-471-84441-1.
**0142** BERNOLD, T. User interfaces: gateway or bottleneck. Elsevier Sci. Publ. Co., New York, NY, 1988, 234 pp., $79, ISBN 0-444-70424-8.
**0143** BERRY, R.; AND MEEKINGS, B. A book on C. 1984.
**HCI-0077** BETHUNE, J.; AND KEE, B. Modern drafting: an introduction to CAD. Prentice-Hall, Inc., Englewood Cliffs, NJ, 1989, 413 pp., $30, ISBN 0-13-591058-7.
**HCI-0030** BIGGERSTAFF, T. Systems software tools. Prentice-Hall, Inc., Englewood Cliffs, NJ, 1986, 317 pp., $28.95, ISBN 0-13-881772-3.
**HCI-0001** BISHOP, P. Fifth generation computers: concepts, implementations and uses. [Ellis Horwood Series: Computers and the Applications] Halsted Press, New York, NY, 1986, 166 pp., $29.95, ISBN 0-470-20269-6.
**0144** BLACKLER, F.; AND OBORNE, D. Information technology & people: designing for the future. MIT Press, Cambridge, MA, 1987, 262 pp., $30, ISBN 0-262-02260-5.
**HCI-0225** HOWARTH, I. Psychology and information technology. See 0144. 1–22.
**0145** BLACKLER, F.; AND BROWN, C. Management, organizations and the new technologies. See 0144. 23–43.
**0146** CLEGG, C.; AND WALL, T. Managing factory automation. See 0144. 45–64.
**0147** OBORNE, D. Ergonomics and the new technologies. See 0144. 65–83.
**HCI-0291** CHRISTIE, B.; AND GARDINER, M. Office systems. See 0144. 85–102.
**HCI-0408** FRITTER, M. The development and use of information technology in health care. See 0144. 105–127.
**0148** HALES, G. The disabled. See 0144. 149–166.
**0149** UNDERWOOD, G.; AND UNDERWOOD, J. The computer in the classroom: a force for change? See 0144. 167–190.
**0150** KEMP, N. Attitudes to information technology. See 0144. 193–210.
**HCI-0226** LONG, J. Information technology and home-based services: improving the usability of teleshopping. See 0144. 211–230.
**HCI-0425** FRUDE, N. Information technology in the home: promises as yet unrealized. See 0144. 231–249.
**HCI-0045** BLOKDIJK, A.; AND BLOKDIJK, P. Planning and design of information systems. Academic Press, Inc., San Diego, CA, 1987, 578 pp., $65, ISBN 0-12-107070-0.
**0151** BÖSSER, T. Learning in man-computer interaction: a review of the literature. [Research reports ESPRIT. Project 385, HUFIT; Vol. 1] Springer-Verlag New York, Inc., New York, NY, 1987, ISBN 0-387-18391-4.
**0152** BODEN, M. Computer models of mind: computational approaches in theoretical psychology. Cambridge University Press, New York, NY, 1988, 310 pp., $42.50, ISBN 0-521-24868-X.
**0153** BOLAND JR., R.; AND HIRSCHHEIM, R. (Eds.) Critical issues in information systems research. [Wiley series in information systems] John Wiley & Sons, Inc., New York, NY, 1987, 394 pp., ISBN 0-471-91281-6.

# BOOKS

**0154** STAMPER, R. Semantics. See 0153. 43–78.
**0155** BANBURY, J. Towards a framework for systems analysis practice. See 0153. 79–96.
**0156** TURNER, J. Understanding the elements of system design. See 0153. 97–111.
**0157** MUMFORD, E. Managerial expert systems and organizational change: some critical research issues. See 0153. 135–155.
**0158** FRANZ, C.; AND ROBEY, D. Strategies for research on information systems in organizations. A critical analysis of research purpose and time frame. See 0153. 205–225.
**0159** BOLAND JR., R. The in-formation of information systems. See 0153. 363–394.
**0160** BOLC, L.; AND JARKE, M. (Eds.) Cooperative interfaces to information systems. [Topics in information systems] Springer-Verlag New York, Inc., New York, NY, 1986, ISBN 09387-16599-1.
**HCI-0066** BOLC, L.; AND JARKE, M. (Eds.) Cooperative interfaces to information systems. [Topics in information systems] Springer-Verlag New York, Inc., New York, NY, 1986, 328 pp., $39, ISBN 0-387-16599-1.
**0161** TEMPLETON, M.; AND BURGER, J. Considerations for the development of natural-language interfaces to database management systems. See HCI-0066. 67–99.
**0162** JARKE, M.; KRAUSE, J.; AND VASSILIOU, Y. Studies in the evaluation of a domain-independent natural language query system. See HCI-0066. 101–130.
**0163** DAMERAU, F. An interactive customization program for a natural language database query system. See HCI-0066. 131–139.
**0164** JANAS, J. The semantics-based natural language interface to relational databases. See HCI-0066. 143–188.
**0165** HOEPPNER, W.; MORIK, K.; AND MARBURGER, H. Talking it over: the natural language dialog system HAM-ANS. See HCI-0066. 189–258.
**0166** BRAJNIK, G.; GUIDA, G.; AND TASSO, C. An expert interface for effective man-machine interaction. See HCI-0066. 259–308.
**0167** BOLOCAN, D. Q & A simplified. TAB Books, Blue Ridge Summit, PA, 1987, 353 pp., $18.95, ISBN 0-8306-2828-2.
**0168** BOND, A.; AND GASSER, L. (Eds.) Distributed Artificial Intelligence. Morgan-Kaufmann, Palo Alto, CA, 1988, 649 pp., ISBN 0-934613-63-X.
**0169** GENESERETH, M.; GINSBERG, M.; AND ROSENSCHEIN, J. Cooperation without communication. See 0168. 220–226.
**0170** ROSENSCHEIN, J.; AND GENESERETH, M. Deals among rational agents. See 0168. 227–234.
**0171** CROFT, W.; AND LEFKOWITZ, L. Knowledge-based support of cooperative activities. See 0168. 599–605.
**HCI-0059** BOOSE, J. Expertise transfer for expert system design. [Advances in human factors/ergonomics; no. 3] Elsevier Sci. Pub. B. V., Amsterdam, The Netherlands, 1986, 312 pp., $72.25, ISBN 0-444-42634-5.
**0172** BRERETON, P. (Ed.) Software engineering environments. [Ellis Horwood books in information technology] Halsted Press, New York, NY, 1988, 233 pp., $59.95, ISBN 0-470-21022-2.
**0173** PULFORD, K.; CARTMELL, J.; HALL, A.; HIGGS, M.; MAIR, P.; PICKETT, M.; AND WHITNEY, D. The evaluation of project support environments for the STARTS user guide. See 0172. 6–12.
**0174** BRISTOW, G. (Ed.) Electronic speech recognition: techniques, technology, and applications. McGraw-Hill, Inc., New York, NY, 1986, 395 pp., $48.50, ISBN 0-07-007913-7.
**0175** NOLAN, F. The nature of speech. See 0174. 18–48.
**0176** LEA, W. The elements of speech recognition. See 0174. 49–129.
**0177** PECKHAM, J. Human factors in speech recognition. See 0174. 172–190.
**0178** TECOSKY, J. Interfacing standards for recognisers. See 0174. 244–255.
**0179** TAYLOR, M. Voice input applications in aerospace. See 0174. 322–337.
**0180** BRODIE, M.; AND MYLOPOULOS, J. (Eds.) On knowledge base management systems: integrating artificial intelligence and d atabase technologies. [Topics in information systems] Springer-Verlag New York, Inc., New York, NY, 1986, 660 pp., $38, ISBN 0-387-96382-0.
**0181** WEBBER, B. Natural language processing: a survey. See 0180. 353–363.
**0182** WEBBER, B. Questions, answers, and responses: interacting with knowledge base systems. See 0180. 365–402.
**0183** HILLIS, W. Parallel computers for AI databases. See 0180. 551–563.

0184 BROWN, C. Human-computer interface design guidelines. [Human/computer interaction] Ablex Publishing Corp., Norwood, NJ, 1988, ISBN 0-893-91332-4.
HCI-0011 BROWN, C. Human-computer interface design guidelines. Ablex Publishing Corp., Norwood, NJ, 1988, 236 pp., $32.50, ISBN 0-89391-332-4.
0185 BROWN, J.; AND CUNNINGHAM, S. Programming the user interface principles and examples. John Wiley & Sons, Inc., New York, NY, 1989, 371 pp., ISBN 0-471-63843-9.
0186 BROWN, M. Algorithm animation. [ACM Distinguished Dissertation 1987] MIT Press, Cambridge, MA, 1988, 186 pp., $30, ISBN 0-262-02278-8.
0187 BUCKLAND, J. Supporting the microcomputer end user. Chantico Publishing Co., Dallas, TX, 1986, 101 pp., $35, ISBN 1-557-11034-4.
HCI-0012 BULLINGER, H. (Ath.) GUNZENHÄUSER, R. (Ed.) Software ergonomics: advances and applications. [Ellis Horwood series in computers and their applications] Halsted Press, New York, NY, 1988, 138 pp., $39.95, ISBN 0-470-21177-6.
0188 BULLINGER, H. Principles and illustrations of dialogue design. See HCI-0012. 13–26.
0189 FÄHNRICH, K. How to design dialogue systems for large computer applications. See HCI-0012. 27–51.
0190 VON BENDA, H. Practical experience in designing software ergonomic projects for large application systems. See HCI-0012. 65–72.
0191 GUNZENHÄUSER, R.; AND KNOPIK, T. Knowledge-based human-computer interfaces and software ergonomics. See HCI-0012. 73–88.
0192 FISCHER, G.; AND HERCZEG, M. Knowledge-based systems and communication between computers and human beings. See HCI-0012. 89–101.
0193 BULLINGER, H. (Ed.) Software ergonomics: advocations & applications for the human computer interface. John Wiley & Sons, Inc., New York, NY, 1988, $39.95, ISBN 0-470-21177-6.
0194 BYSOUTH, P. (Ed.) The economics of online. [The foundations of information science, vol. 2] Taylor Graham Publishers, London, UK, 1987, 229 pp., £20, ISBN 0-947568-14-X.
0195 BUNTROCK, R. Cost effectiveness of on-line searching of chemical information: an industrial viewpoint. See 0194. 116–118.
0196 CAMERON, K. Computer assisted language learning: program structure and principles. Ablex Publishing Corp., Norwood, NJ, 1989, 115 pp., $22.50, ISBN 0-89391-560-2.
0197 DURRANI, O. Designer labyrinths: text mazes for language learners. See 0196. 38–48.
0198 CAMPBELL, J. (Ath.) CUENA, J. (Ed.) Perspectives in artificial intelligence vol. 2: machine translation, NLP, databases and computer-aided instruction. [Ellis Horwood series in artificial intelligence] Halsted Press, New York, NY, 1989, 211 pp., ISBN 0-470-21435-X.
0199 YOSHINO, T.; IZUMIDA, Y.; AND MAKINOUCHI, A. A practical natural language interface to databases. See 0198. 110–121.
0200 CAREY, J. (Ed.) Human factors in management information systems. [Human/computer interaction: a series of monographs] Ablex Publishing Corp., Norwood, NJ, 1988, 289 pp., $42.50, ISBN 0-89391-448-7.
HCI-0205 BEARD, J.; AND PETERSON, T. A taxonomy for the study of human factors in management information systems. See 0200. 7–25.
0201 KOPPA, R. User computer interface guidelines research for keyboards and function keys. See 0200. 43–62.
0202 MARTIN, M. Adaptive general audience models: a research framework. See 0200. 65–81.
0203 PARADICE, D.; AND COURTNEY, J. SmartSLIM: a DSS for controlling biases during problem formulation. See 0200. 83–100.
HCI-0130 SENA, J.; AND SMITH, L. Applying software engineering principles to the user application interface. See 0200. 103–115.
0204 CHOOBINEH, J. Formflex: a user interface tool for forms definition and management. See 0200. 117–133.
HCI-0449 KOPP, E.; AND TIMMER, H. A plan for evaluating usability of software products. See 0200. 207–219.
0205 TAGGART, W. A human information processing model of the managerial mind: some MIS implications. See 0200. 253–268.
0206 CARROLL, J. (Ed.) Interfacing thought: cognitive aspects of human-computer interaction. MIT Press, Cambridge, MA, 1986, ISBN 0-262-03125-6.

# BOOKS [0223]

0207   CARROLL, J. (Ed.) Interfacing thought: cognitive aspects of human-computer interaction. MIT Press, Cambridge, MA, 1987, 370 pp., $30, ISBN 0-262-03125-6.
HCI-0244   LANDAUER, T. Relations between cognitive psychology and computer system design. See 0207. 1–25.
0208   LEWIS, C. Learning about computers and learning about mathematics. See 0207. 26–35.
HCI-0183   BLACK, J.; KAY, D.; AND SOLOWAY, E. Goal and plan knowledge representations: from stories to text editors and programs. See 0207. 36–60.
HCI-0439   MAYER, R. Cognitive aspects of learning and using a programming language. See 0207. 61–79.
HCI-0434   CARROLL, J.; AND ROSSON, M. Paradox of the active user. See 0207. 80–111.
0209   BARNARD, P. Cognitive resources and the learning of human-computer dialogs. See 0207. 112–158.
HCI-0203   FOSS, D.; AND DERIDDER, M. Technology transfer: a new computer-based system. See 0207. 159–183.
HCI-0198   POLSON, P. A quantitative theory of human-computer interaction. See 0207. 184–235.
0210   MCKENDREE, J.; AND ANDERSON, J. Effect of practice on knowledge and use of basic Lisp. See 0207. 236–259.
HCI-0199   OLSON, J. Cognitive analysis of people's use of software. See 0207. 260–293.
0211   MALONE, T. Computer support for organizations: toward an organizational science. See 0207. 294–324.
HCI-0200   NORMAN, D. Cognitive engineering—cognitive science. See 0207. 325–336.
0212   REISNER, P. HCI, what is it and what research is needed? See 0207. 337–352.
0213   WHITESIDE, J.; AND WIXON, D. Improving human-computer interaction—a quest for cognitive science. See 0207. 353–365.
0214   CARROLL, J.; AND OLSON, J. (Eds.) Mental models in human-computer interaction: research issues about what the user of software knows. National Academy Press, Washington, DC, 1987, 39 pp.
0215   CERCONE, N. Computational linguistics. Pergamon Press, Inc., Elmsford, NY, 1986, 245 pp., $37.50, ISBN 0-08-030253-X.
HCI-0028   CHASE, P. VM/CMS: a user's guide. John Wiley & Sons, Inc., New York, NY, 1989, 466 pp., $29.95, ISBN 0-471-50170-0.
0216   CHORAFAS, D. Interactive workstations. Petrocelli Books, Inc., Princeton, NJ, 1986, 196 pp., ISBN 0-894-33258-9.
0217   CHU, W. (Ed.) Distributed systems, Vol. II: distributed data base systems. Artech House, Inc., Dedham, MA, 1986, 519 pp., ISBN 0-89006-213-7.
0218   BERTINO, E.; HAAS, L.; AND LINDSAY, B. View management in distributed data base systems. See 0217. 103–105.
0219   CHURCHLAND, P. Neurophilosophy: toward a unified science of the mind-brain. [Computational models of cognition and perception] MIT Press, Cambridge, MA, 1986, 546 pp., ISBN 0-262-03116-7.
HCI-0060   CLEAL, D.; AND HEATON, N. Knowledge-based systems: implications for human-computer interfaces. [Series in expert systems] Halsted Press, New York, NY, 1988, 253 pp., $49.95, ISBN 0-470-21082-6.
HCI-0035   CLEVELAND, W. The elements of graphing data. Wadsworth Publ. Co., Inc., Belmont, CA, 1985, 323 pp., $18.95, ISBN 0-534-03730-5.
0220   COATS, R.; AND VLAEMINKE, I. Man-computer interfaces: an introduction to software design and implementation. Blackwell Scientific Publications, Inc., Palo Alto, CA, 1987, ISBN 0-632-01771-6.
0221   COHN, A.; AND THOMAS, J. (Eds.) Artificial intelligence and its applications. John Wiley & Sons, Inc., New York, NY, 1986, 291 pp., $49.95, ISBN 0-471-91175-5.
0222   SCHUSTER, E.; AND FININ, T. VP$^2$: the role of user modelling in correcting errors in second language learning. See 0221. 197–209.
HCI-0068   COIFFET, P. Modelling and control. [Robot technology, vol. 1] Prentice-Hall, Inc., Englewood Cliffs, NJ, 1983, 160 pp., $53.33, ISBN 0-13-782094-1.
HCI-0068   COIFFET, P. Interaction with the environment. [Robot technology, vol. 2] Prentice-Hall, Inc., Englewood Cliffs, NJ, 1983, 240 pp., $53.33, ISBN 0-13-782128-X.
HCI-0068   COIFFET, P. Indexes and bibliography. [Robot technology, vol. 8] Prentice-Hall, Inc., Englewood Cliffs, NJ, 1987, 105 pp., $33, ISBN 0-13-782046-1.
0223   COLLINS, A. (Ed.) Readings in cognitive science: a perspective from psychology & artificial intelligence. Morgan-Kaufmann, Palo Alto, CA, 1988, 630 pp., $28.95.

**HCI-0029** COMER, D.; AND FOSSUM, T. Operating system design. Vol. 1: the XINU approach (PC edition). Prentice-Hall, Inc., Englewood Cliffs, NJ, 1988, 504 pp., $48, ISBN 0-13-638180-4.
**0224** COOLING, J. Real-time interfacing: engineering aspects of microprocessor peripheral systems. Van Nostrand Reinhold Co., New York, NY, 1986, 222 pp., ISBN 0442317557.
**0225** COTTERELL, A. Advanced information technology in the new industrial society: the Kingston seminars. Oxford University Press, Inc., New York, NY, 1988, 113 pp., $18.95, ISBN 0-19-853290-3.
**HCI-0442** OAKLEY, B. An overview of research and co-operation in advanced information technology. See 0225. 1–27.
**HCI-0430** HUMPHRIES, C. Implications for education and training. See 0225. 28–41.
**HCI-0318** TAYLOR, J. Expert systems—where do we go from here? See 0225. 73–82.
**0226** ALEKSANDER, I. The management of advanced information technology. See 0225. 96–105.
**0227** COULBECK, B.; AND ORR, C. (Eds.) Computer applications in water supply: vol. 1—systems analysis and simulation. Research Studies Press Ltd., Taunton, UK, 1988, 445 pp., ISBN 0-471-91783-4.
**0228** ORR, C.; AND COULBECK, B. A systems approach to extended GINAS applications. See 0227. 175–195.
**0229** CULICOVER, P.; AND COOPER, L. (Eds.) Neural connections, mental computation. [Computational models of cognition & perception] MIT Press, Cambridge, MA, 1988, 320 pp., $35.
**0230** CURTH, M.; AND EDELMANN, H. APL: a problem-oriented introduction. [Ellis Horwood computers and their applications] Halsted Press, New York, NY, 1989, 180 pp., $49.95, ISBN 0-470-21395-7.
**0231** DE RUITER, M. (Ed.) Advances in Computer Graphics III. [Tutorials and Perspectives in Computer Graphics] Springer-Verlag New York, Inc., New York, NY, 1988, 322 pp., ISBN 0-387-18788-X.
**0232** THOMAS, A. VLSI for solid modelling. See 0231. 1–97.
**0233** ERO, J.; AND VAN LIERE, R. User interface management systems. See 0231. 99–131.
**0234** WISSKIRCHEN, P. Object-oriented graphics. See 0231. 133–146.
**0235** LANSDOWN, J. Computer graphics: A tool for the artist, designer and amateur. See 0231. 147–175.
**0236** BRONSVOORT, W.; AND POST, F. Geometric modelling. See 0231. 207–239.
**0237** MITTELSTAEDT, K.; AND TRIPPNER, D. CAD data exchange. See 0231. 241–292.
**0238** TUCKER, H. Desktop publishing. See 0231. 293–322.
**0239** DEBUS, G.; AND SCHROIFF, H. (Eds.) The psychology of work and organization: current trends and issues. North-Holland Publishing Co., Amsterdam, The Netherlands, 1986, 407 pp., ISBN 0-444-70029-3.
**0240** SANDERS, A. Contexts and conflicts between ergonomics and industrial psychology. See 0239. 7–13.
**0241** HACKER, W. Complete vs. incomplete working tasks—a concept and its verification. See 0239. 23–36.
**0242** GOGUELIN, P. Ergonomics and organizational consulting: accentuation or neglect of psychology. See 0239. 37–42.
**0243** SCHARDT, L. Integrated software-design: a work-oriented approach to the humanization of computerized clerical tasks. See 0239. 63–71.
**0244** ZIMOLONG, B. Evaluation of expert systems for decision support. See 0239. 73–81.
**0245** STREITZ, N. Cognitive ergonomics and human computer interaction. See 0239. 83–90.
**0246** TEN HORN, L.; AND ROE, R. Automation in public libraries: effects on the organization, quality of working life, and quality of services. See 0239. 91–98.
**0247** DE CORTE, W. The algorithmic approach in ergonomics: the case of optimal colours and ambients for display work. See 0239. 99–106.
**0248** BAECK, K.; AND BOSTYN, Y. The SIMONA project: the introduction of information processing in labour market administration. See 0239. 149–154.
**0249** KREUZIG, A.; AND BORRETTY, R. Methodological problems of field-research on workplaces in offices. See 0239. 199–206.
**0250** ROSSEEL, E. The impact of changes in work ethics upon organizational life. See 0239. 291–299.
**0251** SCHROIFF, H.; AND MÖHLER, W. Visual information pick-up in a simulated driving situation. See 0239. 343–350.
**0252** DOUKIDIS, G.; LAND, F.; AND MILLER, G. (Eds.) Knowledge based management support systems. [Ellis Horwood books in information technology] Halsted Press, New York, NY, 1989, 356 pp., $39.95, ISBN 0-470-21218-7.

# BOOKS [0282]

**0253** ARINZE, B. Develping decision support systems from a model of the DSS/user interface. See 0252. 166–182.
**HCI-0010** DUMAS, J. Designing user interfaces for software. Prentice-Hall, Inc., Englewood Cliffs, NJ, 1988, 174 pp., $31, ISBN 0-13-201971-X.
**0254** DURRETT, H. (Ed.) Color and the computer. Academic Press, Inc., San Diego, CA, 1987, 299 pp., ISBN 0-12-225210-1.
**0255** MURCH, G. Color displays and color science. See 0254. 1–25.
**0256** SILVERSTEIN, L. Human factors for color display systems: concepts, methods, and research. See 0254. 27–61.
**0257** MERRIFIELD, R. Visual parameters for color CRTs. See 0254. 63–81.
**0258** MEYER, G.; AND GREENBERG, D. Perceptual color spaces for computer graphics. See 0254. 83–100.
**0259** SMITH, W. Ergonomic vision. See 0254. 101–113.
**0260** WIGERT-JOHNSTON, M. Color graphic displays for network planning and design. See 0254. 139–149.
**0261** REISING, J.; AND ARETZ, A. Color computer graphics in military cockpits. See 0254. 151–169.
**0262** MCSHAN, D.; AND GLICKMAN, A. Color displays for medical imaging. See 0254. 189–203.
**HCI-0386** OLSON, J. Color and the computer in cartography. See 0254. 205–219.
**0263** DURRETT, H.; AND STIMMEL, D. Color and the instructional use of the computer. See 0254. 241–253.
**0264** EARNSHAW, R. (Ed.) Workstations and publication systems. Springer-Verlag New York, Inc., New York, NY, 1987, 229 pp., $29.50, ISBN 0-387-96527-0.
**0265** NANARD, J.; NANARD, M.; AND COTTIN, G. PLEIADE: A system for interactive manipulation of structured documents. See 0264. 73–86.
**0266** HARKE, U.; BURGER, M.; AND GALL, D. Embedding graphics into documents by using a graphic-editor. See 0264. 87–101.
**0267** BROWN, P. Presenting documents on workstation screens. See 0264. 122–128.
**0268** ANGELL, I.; LOW, Y.; AND WARMAN, A. GENIE-M: A generator for multimedia information environments. See 0264. 129–143.
**0269** PREECE, J.; DAVIES, G.; WOODMAN, M.; AND INCE, D. A coherent specification method for the human interface to documentation systems. See 0264. 144–159.
**0270** BUTCHER, M. A graded interface for novice/expert interaction. See 0264. 160–168.
**0271** CLARKE, M. Back to basics: Simple but high-quality text pagination systems. See 0264. 203–211.
**HCI-0081** EDUCATIONAL TECHNOLOGY PUBLICATIONS Interactive video: vol. 1. [The educational technology anthology series] Educational Technology Publications, Englewood Cliffs, NJ, 1989, 200 pp., $24.95, ISBN 0-87778-211-3.
**0272** HOSIE, P. Adopting interactive videodisc technology for education. See HCI-0081. 10–18.
**0273** JONASSEN, D. Interactive lesson designs: a taxonomy. See HCI-0081. 19–29.
**0274** HARPER-MARINICK, M.; AND GERLACH, V. Designing interactive, responsive instruction: a set of procedures. See HCI-0081. 39–41.
**0275** WELLER, H. Interactivity in microcomputer-based instruction: its essential elements and how it can be enhanced. See HCI-0081. 42–46.
**0276** DAVIDOVE, E. Design and production of videodisc programming. See HCI-0081. 49–56.
**0277** KEARSELY, G.; AND FROST, J. Design factors for successful videodisc-based instruction. See HCI-0081. 79–85.
**0278** DALTON, D. How effective is interactive video in improving performance and attitude? See HCI-0081. 149–151.
**0279** ROSEN, D. History in the making: a report from Microsoft's First International Conference on CD ROM. See HCI-0081. 163–169.
**0280** DEBLOOIS, M. Anticipating compact disc-interactive (CD-I): ten guidelines for prospective authors. See HCI-0081. 177–179.
**0281** MILLER, D. CD ROM joins the new media homesteaders. See HCI-0081. 180–182.
**HCI-0361** ELLZEY, R. Computer systems software: the programmer/machine interface. Science Research Associates, Inc., Chicago, IL, 1986, 274 pp., $27, ISBN 0-574-21965-X.
**0282** ENNALS, R.; GWYN, R.; AND ZDRAVCHEV, L. (Eds.) Information technology and education: the changing school. [Ellis Horwood series in information technology and education] Halsted Press, New York, NY, 1986, 235 pp., $29.95, ISBN 0-470-20757-4.

0283 NICHOL, J.; AND DEAN, J. Computers and children's historical thinking and understanding. See 0282. 160–176.
0284 HANNA, J. Logic for learning. See 0282. 177–196.
0285 HANNA, J. Learning environment criteria. See 0282. 197–230.
0286 EZZELL, B. Programming the IBM User Interface: Using Turbo Pascal. Addison-Wesley Publ. Co., Inc., Reading, MA, 1988, $22.95, ISBN 0-201-15009-3.
0287 FALLSIDE, F.; AND WOODS, W. (Eds.) Computer speech processing. Prentice-Hall International, Englewood Cliffs, NJ, 1985, 506 pp., $48.33, ISBN 0-13-163841-6.
HCI-0358 LADEFOGED, P. The phonetic basis for computer speech processing. See 0287. 3–27.
0288 BLADON, A. Acoustic phonetics, auditory phonetics, speaker sex and speech recognition: a thread. See 0287. 29–38.
0289 ATAL, B. Linear predictive coding of speech. See 0287. 81–124.
HCI-0396 HOLMES, J. A parallel formant synthesizer for machine voice output. See 0287. 163–187.
HCI-0356 LONGUET-HIGGINS, C. Tones of voice: the role of intonation in computer speech understanding. See 0287. 293–304.
0290 MARSLEN-WILSON, W. Aspects of human speech understanding. See 0287. 383–404.
0291 TYLER, L. The sequential organization of spoken word recognition. See 0287. 405–417.
0292 FERRATÉ, G.; PAVLIDIS, T.; SANFELIU, A.; AND BUNKE, H. (Eds.) Syntactic and structural pattern recognition. [NATO ASI series] Springer-Verlag New York, Inc., New York, NY, 1988, 467 pp., ISBN 0-387-19209-3.
0293 TANAKA, E. A string correction method based on the context-dependent similarity. See 0292. 3–17.
0294 PAVLIDIS, T. Problems in recognition of drawings. See 0292. 103–113.
0295 KAYSER, K. Application of structural pattern recognition in histopathology. See 0292. 115–135.
HCI-0025 FINKEL, R. An operating systems vade mecum: 2nd edition. Prentice-Hall, Inc., Englewood Cliffs, NJ, 1988, 385 pp., $42, ISBN 0-13-637950-8.
0296 FISCHLER, M.; AND FIRSCHEIN, O. (Eds.) Readings in computer vision: issues, problems, principles, and paradigms. [Morgan Kaufmann Readings Series] Morgan-Kaufmann, Palo Alto, CA, 1987, 800 pp., ISBN 0-934613-33-8.
0297 JULESZ, B.; AND BERGEN, J. Textons, the fundamental elements in preattentive vision and perception of textures. See 0296. 243–256.
0298 MALONEY, L.; AND WANDELL, B. Color constancy: a method for recovering surface spectral reflectance. See 0296. 293–297.
0299 EVANS, T. A heuristic program to solve geometric-analogy problems. See 0296. 444–455.
0300 MARR, D.; AND NISHIHARA, H. Visual information processing: artificial intelligence and the sensorium of sight. See 0296. 616–637.
0301 POGGIO, T.; TORRE, V.; AND KOCH, C. Computational vision and regularization theory. See 0296. 638–643.
0302 PENTLAND, A. Perceptual organization and the representation of natural form. See 0296. 680–699.
HCI-0075 FLYNN, G. Medicine in the age of the computer. Prentice-Hall, Inc., Englewood Cliffs, NJ, 1986, 166 pp., $21.95, ISBN 0-13-572975-0.
HCI-0016 FOEHR, T.; AND CROSS, T. The soft side of software: a management approach to computer documentation. Wiley-Interscience, New York, NY, 1986, 160 pp., $22.95, ISBN 0-471-81527-6.
HCI-0069 FOLEY, J.; AND VAN DAM, A. Fundamentals of interactive computer graphics. Addison-Wesley Publ. Co., Inc., Reading, MA, 1982, 664 pp., $43.95, ISBN 0-201-14468-9.
0303 FOLEY, J. James D. Foley, Oct. 12: user interface strategies '88. University of Maryland, College Park, MD, 1988, 112 pp.
0304 FOSDICK, H. Using IBM's ISPF dialog manager: under MSV, VM, and VSE. [Van Nostrand Reinhold data processing series] Van Nostrand Reinhold Co., New York, NY, 1986, 272 pp., ISBN 0-442-22626-8.
0305 FRESE, M.; ULICH, E.; AND DZIDA, W. (Eds.) Psychological issues of human-computer interaction in the work place. North-Holland Publishing Co., Amsterdam, The Netherlands, 1987, 451 pp., ISBN 0-444-70318-7.
0306 LANDY, F.; RASTEGARY, H.; AND MOTOWIDLO, S. Human—computer interactions in the workplace: psychosocial aspects of VDT use. See 0305. 3–22.

BOOKS [0337]

0307 NULLMEIER, E.; AND ROEDIGER, K. The limitations of task complexity through information technologies: results of a field study. See 0305. 41–57.
0308 HACKER, W. Computerization versus computer aided mental. See 0305. 115–130.
0309 ACKERMANN, D.; AND ULICH, E. The chances of individualization in human-computer interaction and its consequences. See 0305. 131–145.
0310 SPINAS, P. VDU—work and user—friendly human—computer interaction: analysis of dialogue structures. See 0305. 147–162.
0311 BOUCSEIN, W. Psychophysiological investigation of stress induced by temporal factors in human-computer interaction. See 0305. 163–181.
0312 ÇAKIR, A. Ergonomic features of interactive systems—the interdependency of software and hardware. See 0305. 185–201.
0313 ARNOLD, B.; AND ROE, R. User errors in human—computer interaction. See 0305. 203–220.
0314 CARROLL, J. Five gambits for the advisory interface dilemma. See 0305. 257–274.
0315 FRESE, M. A theory of control and complexity: implications for software design and integration of computer systems into the work place. See 0305. 313–337.
0316 DZIDA, W. On tools and interfaces. See 0305. 339–355.
0317 GREIF, S.; AND GEDIGA, G. A critique and empirical investigation of the "One-Best-Way-Models" in human-computer interaction. See 0305. 357–377.
0318 BRIGGS, P. Usability assessment for the office: methodological choices and their implications. See 0305. 381–401.
0319 MOLL, T. On methods of analysis of mental models and the evaluation of interactive computer systems. See 0305. 403–417.
0320 LONG, J.; AND BUCKLEY, P. Cognitive optimisation of Videotex dialogues: a formal—empirical approach. See 0305. 419–436.
0321 GALE, A. (Ed.) Artificial intelligence and statistics. Addison-Wesley Publ. Co., Inc., Reading, MA, 1986, 418 pp., $39.95, ISBN 0-201-11569-7.
0322 HUBER, P. Environments for supporting statistical strategy. See 0321. 285–294.
0323 BUTLER, K.; AND CORTER, J. Use of psychometric tools for knowledge acquistion: a case study. See 0321. 295–319.
0324 BROOKING, A. The analysis phase in development of knowledge based systems. See 0321. 321–334.
0325 GARDINER, M.; AND CHRISTIE, B. Applying cognitive psychology to user-interface design. [Wiley series in information processing] John Wiley & Sons, Inc., New York, NY, 1987, 372 pp., ISBN 0-471-91184-4.
0326 GARDINER, M.; AND CHRISTIE, B. Introduction. See 0325. 3–12.
0327 HAMMOND, N.; GARDINER, M.; AND CHRISTIE, B. The role of cognitive psychology in user-interface design. See 0325. 13–52.
0328 SCANE, R. Key areas of cognitive psychology: a historical perspective. See 0325. 57–82.
0329 MANKTELOW, K.; AND JONES, J. Principles from the psychology of thinking and mental models. See 0325. 83–117.
0330 HITCH, G. Principles from the psychology of memory: Part I Working memory. See 0325. 119–134.
0331 GARDINER, M. Principles from the psychology of memory: Part II-Episodic and semantic memory. See 0325. 135–161.
0332 HAMMOND, N. Principles from the psychology of skill acquisition. See 0325. 163–187.
0333 HAMPTON, J. Principles from the psychology of language. See 0325. 189:8N216.
0334 MARSHALL, C.; NELSON, C.; AND GARDINER, M. Design guidelines. See 0325. 221–278.
0335 MARSHALL, C.; CHRISTIE, B.; AND GARDINER, M. Assessment of trends in the technology and techniques of human-computer interaction. See 0325. 279–312.
0336 CHRISTIE, B.; AND GARDINER, M. Future directions. See 0325. 315–334.
HCI-0061 GARDNER, A. An artificial intelligence approach to legal reasoning. [Artificial intelligence and legal reasoning] MIT Press, Cambridge, MA, 1987, 240 pp., $22.50, ISBN 0-262-07104-5.
0337 GARRETT, P. Computer interface engineering with model-based analysis. Prentice-Hall, Inc., Englewood Cliffs, NJ, 1987, ISBN 0131630237.

**0338** GAUL, W.; AND SCHADER, M. (Eds.) Data, expert knowledge and decisions. Springer-Verlag, Berlin, West Germany, 1988, 380 pp., ISBN 3-540-19038-4.
**0339** DADUNA, J. A decision support system for vehicle scheduling in public transport. See 0338. 93–102.
**0340** GAYESKI, D. Interactive Toolkit. Omnicon Institute, Vienna, VA, 1988, 140 pp., $95, ISBN 0-944650-01-5.
**0341** GERTMAN, D.; AND BLACKMAN, H. The user-computer interface in process control: a human factors engineering handbook. Academic Press, Inc., San Diego, CA, 1989, 365 pp., $49.95, ISBN 0-12-283965-X.
**0342** GÖRANZON, B.; AND JOSEFSON, I. (Eds.) Knowledge, skill and artificial intelligence. [Springer series on foundations and applications of artificial intelligence] Springer-Verlag New York, Inc., New York, NY, 1988, 193 pp., ISBN 0-387-19519-X.
**0343** GÖRANZON, B. The practice of the use of computers. A paradoxical encounter between different traditions of knowledge. See 0342. 9–18.
**0344** PERBY, M. Computerization and skill in local weather forecasting. See 0342. 39–52.
**0345** JANIK, A. Tacit knowledge, working life and scientific method. See 0342. 53–63.
**0346** COOLEY, M. Creativity, skill and human-centered systems. See 0342. 127–137.
**0347** GOLDBERG, A. (Ed.) A history of personal workstations. [ACM Press history series] Association for Computing Machinery, New York, NY, 1988, 537 pp., $51.75, ISBN 0-201-11259-0.
**0348** LICKLIDER, J. Some reflections on early history. See 0347. 115–140.
**0349** SHCULTZ, J. A history of the promis technology: an effective human interface. See 0347. 439–488.
**0350** CARD, S.; AND MORAN, T. User technology: from pointing to pondering. See 0347. 489–526.
**0351** GOODWIN, M. User interfaces in C: programmer's guide to state-of-the-art interfaces. Mis Press, Mis Press, 1989, 344 pp., $24.95, ISBN 1-55828-002-2.
**0352** GOPNIK, I.; AND GOPNIK, M. (Eds.) From models to modules: studies in cognitive science from the McGill workshops. [Theoretical issues in cognitive science] Ablex Publishing Corp., Norwood, NJ, 1986, 295 pp., $39.95, ISBN 0-89391-255-3.
**0353** MACWHINNEY, B.; AND ANDERSON, J. The acquisition of grammar. See 0352. 3–23.
**0354** HALL, W.; AND NAGY, W. Theoretical issues in the investigation of words of internal report. See 0352. 26–65.
**0355** GRIMES, J. An interaction between morphology and discourse. See 0352. 85–96.
**HCI-0346** FRAZIER, L. The mapping between grammar and processor. See 0352. 117–134.
**HCI-0350** SEIDENBERG, M.; AND TANENHAUS, M. Modularity and lexical access. See 0352. 135–157.
**0356** PARADIS, M. The optimal level of abstraction for models of cerebral representation of language processes: the state of the question. See 0352. 191–195.
**0357** BUCKINGHAM, H. Language, the mind, and psychophysical parallelism. See 0352. 209–228.
**HCI-0345** ARBIB, M. From schema theory to computational (neuro-)linguistics. See 0352. 240–253.
**0358** GOSLING, J.; ROSENTHAL, D.; AND ARDEN, M. The NeWS book: an introduction to the network/extensible window system. Springer-Verlag New York, Inc., New York, NY, 1989, 235 pp., ISBN 0-387-96915-2.
**HCI-0056** GREGORY, R.; AND MARSTRAND, P. (Eds.) Creative intelligences. Ablex Publishing Corp., Norwood, NJ, 1987, 143 pp., $29.50, ISBN 0-89391-440-1.
**0359** GREGORY, R. Intelligence based on knowledge—knowledge based on intelligence. See HCI-0056. 1–8.
**0360** BRYANT, P. Intelligence and children's development. See HCI-0056. 9–18.
**0361** DENNETT, D. Designing intelligence. See HCI-0056. 19–30.
**0362** EFSTATHIOU, J. Intelligent machines for process control. See HCI-0056. 31–55.
**0363** WALTON, T. Intelligence and the man-machine interface. See HCI-0056. 68–80.
**0364** NIELSEN, J. 'This is a very unpredictable machine': on computers and human cognition. See HCI-0056. 110–128.
**0365** MACPHAIL, E. Creativity, intelligence and evolution. See HCI-0056. 129:8N137.
**0366** GREIF, I. (Ed.) Computer-supported cooperative work: a book of readings. Morgan-Kaufmann, Palo Alto, CA, 1988, 781 pp., $36.95, ISBN 0-934613-57-5.
**0367** BUSH, V. As we may think (Reprint). See 0366. 17–34.
**0368** ENGELBART, D. A conceptual framework for the augmentation of man's intellect (Reprint). See 0366. 35–65.

BOOKS [0398]

**0369** ENGELBART, D. Toward high-performance knowledge workers (Reprint). See 0366. 67–78.
**HCI-0334** ENGELBART, D.; AND ENGLISH, W. A research center for augmenting human intellect. See 0366. 81–105.
**0370** ENGELBART, D. Authorship provisions in AUGMENT (Reprint). See 0366. 107–126.
**0371** CHAPANIS, A. Interactive human communication (Reprint). See 0366. 127–140.
**0372** JOHANSEN, R.; AND BULLEN, C. Thinking ahead: what to expect from teleconferencing (Reprint). See 0366. 185–198.
**0373** ELLIS, C.; AND NUTT, G. Office information systems and computer science (Reprint). See 0366. 199–247.
**0374** KEDZIERSKI, B. Communication and management support in system development environments (Reprint). See 0366. 253–268.
**0375** SATHI, A.; MORTON, T.; AND ROTH, S. Callisto: an intelligent project management system (Reprint). See 0366. 269–309.
**0376** STEFIK, M.; FOSTER, G.; BOBROW, D.; KAHN, K.; LANNING, S.; AND SUCHMAN, L. Beyond the chalkboard: computer support for collaboration and problem solving in meetings (Reprint). See 0366. 335–366.
**HCI-0383** LAKIN, F. A performing medium for working group graphics. See 0366. 367–396.
**0377** SARIN, S.; AND GREIF, I. Computer-based real-time conferencing systems (Reprint). See 0366. 397–422.
**0378** CONKLIN, J. Hypertext: an introduction and survey (Reprint). See 0366. 423–475.
**0379** GREIF, I.; AND SARIN, S. Data sharing in group work (Reprint). See 0366. 477–508.
**0380** THOMAS, R.; FORSDICK, H.; CROWLEY, T.; SCHAAF, R.; TOMLINSON, R.; TRAVERS, V.; AND ROBERTSON, G. Diamond: a multimedia message system built on a distributed architecture (Reprint). See 0366. 509–532.
**0381** LANTZ, K. An experiment in integrated multimedia conferencing. See 0366. 533–556.
**0382** CLEMENT, A.; AND GOTLIEB, C. Evolution of an organizational interface: the new business department at a large insurance firm (Reprint). See 0366. 609–621.
**0383** WINOGRAD, T. A language/action perspective on the design of cooperative work (Reprint). See 0366. 623–653.
**0384** KIESLER, S.; SIEGEL, J.; AND MCGUIRE, T. Social psychological aspects of computer-mediated communication (Reprint). See 0366. 657–682.
**0385** SPROULL, L.; AND KIESLER, S. Reducing social context cues: electronic mail in organizational communication (Reprint). See 0366. 683–712.
**0386** CROWSTON, K.; MALONE, T.; AND LIN, F. Cognitive science and organizational design: a case study of computer conferencing (Reprint). See 0366. 713–740.
**0387** KRAUT, R.; GALEGHER, J.; AND EGIDO, C. Relationships and tasks in scientific research collaborations (Reprint). See 0366. 741–769.
**0388** BLOMBERG, J. The variable impact of computer technologies on the organization of work activities. See 0366. 771–789.
**HCI-0067** GROSZ, B.; SPARCK-JONES, K.; AND WEBBER, B. (Eds.) Readings in natural language processing. Morgan-Kaufmann, Palo Alto, CA, 1986, 664 pp., $28.95, ISBN 0-934613-11-7.
**0389** BRUCE, B. Generation as a social action. See HCI-0067. 419–422.
**0390** COHEN, P.; AND PERRAULT, C. Elements of a plan-based theory of speech acts. See HCI-0067. 423–440.
**0391** ALLEN, J.; AND PERRAULT, C. Analyzing intention in utterances. See HCI-0067. 441–458.
**0392** WILENSKY, R. Points: a theory of the structure of stories in memory. See HCI-0067. 459–473.
**0393** HENDRIX, G.; SACERDOTI, E.; SAGALOWICZ, D.; AND SLOCUM, J. Developing a natural language interface to complex data. See HCI-0067. 563–584.
**0394** MARTIN, P.; APPELT, D.; AND PEREIRA, F. Transportability and generality in a natural-language interface system. See HCI-0067. 585–593.
**0395** BOBROW, D. GUS, a frame driven dialog system. See HCI-0067. 595–604.
**0396** GUZAITIS, J.; BYRD, J.; AND BALMA, P. The world of GEM. Prentice-Hall, Inc., Englewood Cliffs, NJ, 1987, 229 pp., $20, ISBN 0-13-967696-1.
**0397** HANCOCK, P. Human Factors Psychology. [Advances in Psychology] North-Holland Publishing Co., Amsterdam, The Netherlands, 1987, 433 pp., ISBN 0-444-70319-5.
**0398** KLAPP, S. Short-term memory limits in human performance. See 0397. 1–27.

**0399** WICKENS, C. Attention. See 0397. 29–80.
**0400** KANTOWITZ, B. Mental workload. See 0397. 81–121.
**0401** KLEINMUNTZ, D. Human decision processes: Heuristics and task structure. See 0397. 123–157.
**0402** FISK, A.; ACKERMAN, P.; AND SCHNEIDER, W. Automatic and controlled processing theory and its applications to human factors problems. See 0397. 159–197.
**0403** JAGACINSKI, R.; PLAMONDON, B.; AND MILLER, R. Describing movement control at two levels of abstraction. See 0397. 199–247.
**0404** EBERTS, R. Human computer interaction. See 0397. 249–304.
**0405** HANCOCK, P.; AND CHIGNELL, M. Adaptive control in human-machine systems. See 0397. 305–345.
**0406** HENDRICK, H. Human factors in organizational design and management. See 0397. 347–398.
**HCI-0065** HARRIS, M. Introduction to natural language processing. Reston Publishing Co., Reston, VA, 1985, 368 pp., $27.95, ISBN 0-8359-3253-2.
**HCI-0046** HARTER, S. Online information retrieval: concepts, principles, and techniques. [Library and information science series] Academic Press, Inc., San Diego, CA, 1986, 259 pp., $19.95, ISBN 0-12-328456-2.
**0407** HARTSON, H.; AND HIX, D. (Eds.) Advances in human-computer interaction. Ablex Publishing Corp., Norwood, NJ, 1988, 380 pp., $47.50, ISBN 0-89391-428-2.
**0408** THOMAS, J. Human factors and artificial intelligence. See 0407. 1–44.
**0409** NADIN, M. Interface design and evaluation—Semiotic implications. See 0407. 45–100.
**0410** EFE, K. The problem of levels and automatic response generation in a "Let's Talk AboutIt" strategy. See 0407. 101–127.
**0411** CAREY, T. The gift of good design tools. See 0407. 159–174.
**0412** SIBERT, J.; HURLEY, W.; AND BLESER, T. Design and implementation of an object-oriented user interface management system. See 0407. 175–213.
**0413** TULLIS, T. A system for evaluating screen formats: Research and application. See 0407. 214–286.
**0414** WHITESIDE, J.; WIXON, D.; AND JONES, S. User performance with command, menu, and iconic interfaces. See 0407. 287–315.
**0415** SHLECHTER, T. An examination of the research evidence for computer-based instruction. See 0407. 316–367.
**0416** HATON, J. (Ed.) Fundamentals in computer understanding: speech and vision. Cambridge University Press, New York, NY, 1987, 276 pp., ISBN 0-521-30983-2.
**0417** SPERANDIO, J.; AND SCAPIN, D. Ergonomic aspects of man-machine communications. See 0416. 79–90.
**0418** CHRISMENT, C.; AND ZURFLUH, G. Advanced databases multi-media interface. See 0416. 91–112.
**0419** DE MORI, R.; LAM, L.; AND PROBST, D. Rule-based detection of speech features for automatic speech recognition. See 0416. 155–179.
**0420** HAWLEY, R. (Ed.) Artificial intelligence programming environments. [Ellis Horwood books in computing science] John Wiley & Sons, Inc., New York, NY, 1987, 214 pp., $39.95, ISBN 0-470-20989-5.
**0421** PAIN, H.; AND BUNDY, A. What stories should we tell novice PROLOG programmers? See 0420. 119–130.
**HCI-0069** HEARN, D.; AND BAKER, M. Computer graphics. Prentice-Hall, Inc., Englewood Cliffs, NJ, 1986, 592 pp., $48, ISBN 0-13-165382-2.
**0422** HEATON, N. (Ed.) Designing end-user interfaces: state of the art report 15.8. Pergamon Press, Inc., Elmsford, NY, 1988, 300 pp., ISBN 0-08-034120-9.
**0423** HEID, J. Power windows: maximizing the speed and performance of Windows 2.0 & Windows 386. Microsoft Press, Redmond, WA, 1988, 289 pp., $19.95, ISBN 1-55615-008-3.
**0424** HEINES, J. Screen design strategies for computer-assisted instruction. Digital Press/Digital Equipment Corp., Bedford, MA, 1984, 159 pp., ISBN 0-932376-28-2.
**0425** HENDLER, J. (Ed.) Expert systems: the user interface. [Human/Computer Interaction] Ablex Publishing Corp., Norwood, NJ, 1987, 324 pp., ISBN 0-89391-429-0.
**0426** HENDLER, J.; AND LEWIS, C. Introduction: designing interfaces for expert systems. See 0425. 1–13.
**0427** MUSEN, M.; FAGAN, L.; AND SHORTLIFFE, E. Graphical specification of procedural knowledge for an expert system. See 0425. 15–35.
**0428** MITTAL, S.; BOBROW, D.; AND DE KLEER, J. DARN: Toward a community memory for diagnosis and repair tasks. See 0425. 57–79.

# BOOKS

0429 BAROFF, J.; SIMON, R.; GILMAN, F.; AND SHNEIDERMAN, B. Direct manipulation user interfaces for expert systems. See 0425. 99–125.

0430 HAYES, P. Using a knowledge base to drive an expert system interface with a natural language component. See 0425. 153–182.

0431 STELZNER, M.; AND WILLIAMS, M. The evolution of interface requirements for expert systems. See 0425. 285–306.

0432 LEHNER, P.; AND KRALJ, M. Cognitive impacts of the user interface. See 0425. 307–318.

0433 HENDLER, J. (Ed.) Expert systems: the user interface. Ablex Publishing Corp., Norwood, NJ, 1988, 324 pp., ISBN 0-89-391429-0.

HCI-0051 HILTZ, S. Online communities. [Human/computer interaction series] Ablex Publishing Corp., Norwood, NJ, 1984, 261 pp., $32.50, ISBN 0-89391-145-3.

0434 HINTON, G. (Ed.) Neural network architectures for artificial intelligence. Amer. Assn. for Artificial Intelligence, Menlo Park, CA, 1988, 75 pp., $5, ISBN 0-929280-15-6.

HCI-0048 HIRSCHHEIM, R. Office automation: a social and organizational perspective. John Wiley & Sons, Inc., New York, NY, 1986, 327 pp., $29.95, ISBN 0-471-90909-2.

0435 HOC, J. Cognitive psychology of planning. Academic Press, Inc., San Diego, CA, 1988, 200 pp., ISBN 0-12-350770-7.

HCI-0064 HOLLAND, J.; HOLYOAK, K.; NISBETT, R.; AND THAGARD, P. Induction: processes of inference, learning, and discovery. [Computational models of cognition and perception] MIT Press, Cambridge, MA, 1986, 385 pp., $24.95, ISBN 0-26208160-1.

HCI-0050 HOLLIGAN, P. Access to academic networks. Taylor Graham Publishers, London, UK, 1986, 91 pp., $26.50, ISBN 0-947568-08-5.

0436 HOLLNAGEL, E.; MANCINI, G.; AND WOODS, D. Cognitive engineering in complex dynamic worlds. Academic Press, Inc., San Diego, CA, 1988, 300 pp., ISBN 0-12-352655-8.

0437 HOPGOOD, F.; HUBBOLD, R.; AND DUCE, D. (Eds.) Advances in computer graphics II. Springer-Verlag New York, Inc., New York, NY, 1986, 186 pp., ISBN 3-540-16910-5.

0438 MURCH, G. Human factors of color displays. See 0437. 1–27.

HCI-0018 HOROWITZ, E. (Ed.) Programming languages: a grand tour (2nd ed.). [Computer software engineering series] Computer Science Press, Inc., Rockville, MD, 1985, 758 pp., $39.95, ISBN 0-88175-073-5.

0439 HU, D. C/C++ for expert systems: "unleashes the power of a artificial intelligence". Mis Press, Mis Press, 1989, 1,989 pp., $24.95, ISBN 0-943518-86-5.

HCI-0079 HUDSON, K. Introducing CAL: a practical guide to writing computer-assisted learning programs. [Chapman and Hall computing] Chapman & Hall, Ltd., London, UK, 1984, 171 pp., $19.95, ISBN 0-412-26240-1.

0440 HUSBAND, T. (Ed.) Education and training in robotics. [International trends in manufacturing technology] Springer-Verlag New York, Inc., New York, NY, 1986, 315 pp., ISBN 0-948507-04-7.

0441 SENKER, P. Coping with new technology: the need for training. See 0440. 3–11.

0442 BELL, D. Employment skills for the robot age. See 0440. 13–17.

0443 ARGOTE, L.; GOODMAN, P.; AND SCHKADE, D. The human side of robotics: how workers react to a robot. See 0440. 19–32.

0444 MULLIN, A. Preparing for new technology. See 0440. 33–41.

0445 CURE, K. Man is not a robot. See 0440. 43–48.

0446 HYMAN, M. Microsoft windows 2.0 program development. Management Information Source, Portland, OR, 1987, $23, ISBN 0-943-51834-2.

0447 INGWERSEN, P.; KAJBERG, L.; AND PEJTERSEN, A. (Eds.) Information technology and information use: towards a unified view of information and information technology. Taylor Graham Publishers, London, UK, 1986, 194 pp., $37.00, ISBN 0-947568-06-9.

0448 ANDERSEN, P. Semiotics and informatics: computers as media. See 0447. 64–97.

0449 SMITH, L. Knowledge-based systems, artificial intelligence and human factors. See 0447. 98–110.

0450 INGWERSEN, P.; AND PEJTERSEN, A. User requirements—empirical research and information systems design. See 0447. 111–124.

0451 PEJTERSEN, A. Design and test of a database for fiction, based on an analysis of children's search behavior. See 0447. 125–146.
0452 LANCASTER, F. The evaluation of information services: a typology. See 0447. 147–155.
0453 IRVING, A. Preparing new generations for the information age. See 0447. 156–164.
0454 JAGODZINSKI, P.; AND CLARKE, D. User systems analysis: a user oriented approach to computer systems analysis, design, and implementation. Abacus Press, Bedford, MA, 1988, $36, ISBN 085626430X.
0455 JARKE, M. Managers, micros and mainframes: integrating systems for end-users. [John Wiley information systems series] John Wiley & Sons, Inc., New York, NY, 1986, 302 pp., $29.95, ISBN 0-471-90988-2.
0456 JARKE, M. Managers, micros and mainframes: an introduction. See 0455. 1–7.
0457 WOHL, A. Designing advanced workstations. See 0455. 21–28.
0458 RIES, D. Distributed databases and distributed processing between personal computers and mainframes. See 0455. 45–52.
0459 PORTER, L. Managing the diffusion of end-user computing technologies: a fifties mindset with eighties tools. See 0455. 55–72.
0460 BULLEN, C. Company experiences with end-user computing. See 0455. 73–85.
0461 ALAVI, M. User-developed DSS: steps toward quality control. See 0455. 119–131.
HCI-0063 JOHNSON-LAIRD, P. Mental models: towards a cognitive science of language, inference, and consciousness. [Cognitive Science Series, 6] Harvard University Press, Cambridge, MA, 1983, 513 pp., $12.95, ISBN 0-674-56882-6.
0462 JOHNSON-LAIRD, P. The computer and the mind. Harvard University Press, Cambridge, MA, 1988, 448 pp., $29.50, ISBN 6-674-15615-3.
0463 JOHNSON-LAIRD, P. The computer and the mind: an introduction to cognitive science. Q.E.D. Information Sciences, Inc., Wellesley, MA, 1988, 444 pp., ISBN 0-674-15615-3.
0464 JONASSEN, D. (Ed.) Instructional designs for microcomputer courseware. Lawrence Erlbaum Associates, Inc., Hillsdale, NJ, 1988, ISBN 0-89-859813-3.
HCI-0047 JONASSEN, D. Hypertext/hypermedia. Educational Technology Publications, Englewood Cliffs, NJ, 1989, 91 pp., $24.95, ISBN 0-87778-217-2.
HCI-0041 JONES, M. Human-computer interaction: a design guide. Educational Technology Publications, Englewood Cliffs, NJ, 1989, 150 pp., $21.95, ISBN 0-87778-207-5.
HCI-0022 KAISLER, S. INTERLISP: the language and its usage. Wiley-Interscience, New York, NY, 1986, 1,144 pp., $49.95, ISBN 0-471-81644-2.
0465 KALAY, Y. (Ed.) Principles of computer-aided design: computability of design. [Principles of computer-aided design] Wiley-Interscience, New York, NY, 1987, 363 pp., $59.95, ISBN 0-471-85387-9.
0466 WOODBURY, R. Strategies for interactive design systems. See 0465. 11–36.
0467 GROSS, M.; ERVIN, S.; ANDERSON, J.; AND FLEISHER, A. Designing with constraints. See 0465. 53–83.
HCI-0017 KATZIN, E. How to write a really good user's manual. Van Nostrand Reinhold Co., New York, NY, 1986, 249 pp., $32.95, ISBN 0-442-24758-3.
HCI-0044 KEANE, M. Analogical problem solving. [Ellis Horwood series in cognitive science] John Wiley & Sons, Inc., New York, NY, 1988, 151 pp., $41.95, ISBN 0-470-21057-5.
HCI-0031 KEARSLEY, G. Authoring: a guide to the design of instructional software. Addison-Wesley Publ. Co., Inc., Reading, MA, 1986, 100 pp., $10.95, ISBN 0-201-11731-2.
HCI-0009 KEARSLEY, G. Online help systems: design and implementation. Ablex Publishing Corp., Norwood, NJ, 1988, 115 pp., $27.50, ISBN 0-89391-472-X.
0468 KEARSLEY, G. (Ed.) Artificial intelligence and instruction: Applications and methods. Addison-Wesley Publ. Co., Inc., Reading, MA, 1987, 351 pp., ISBN 0-201-11654-5.
0469 BEGG, I.; AND HOGG, I. Authoring systems for ICAI. See 0468. 323–346.
0470 KENT, W.; AND LEWIS, R. (Eds.) Computer assisted learning in the humanities and social sciences. Blackwell Scientific Publications, Ltd., Oxford, UK, 1987, 213 pp., $46.00, ISBN 0-632-01555-1.
0471 LIGHT, P.; AND COLBOURN, C. The role of social processes in children's microcomputer use. See 0470. 109–114.

# BOOKS [0498]

**0472** SCHRETTENBRUNNER, H. Evaluation of a program on "distance". See 0470. 115–123.
**0473** WILTON, J. User behaviour in computer networked groups. See 0470. 124–131.
**0474** FORER, P. Symbiotic software: development and usage issues on stand-alone and networked systems. See 0470. 135–145.
**0475** KIM, W. (Ath.) LOCHOVSKY, F. (Ed.) Object-oriented concepts, databases, and applications. [ACM Press frontier series] Association for Computing Machinery, New York, NY, 1989, 602 pp., $43.25, ISBN 0-201-14410-7.
**0476** TARLTON, M.; AND TARLTON, P. Pogo: a declarative representation system for graphics. See 0475. 151–176.
**0477** TSICHRITZIS, D.; AND NIERSTRASZ, O. Directions in object-oriented research. See 0475. 523–536.
**0478** KLAHR, D.; LANGLEY, P.; AND NECHES, R. (Eds.) Production system models of learning and development. [Computational models of cognition and perception] MIT Press, Cambridge, MA, 1987, 466 pp., $35, ISBN 0-262-11114-4.
**0479** NECHES, R.; LANGLEY, P.; AND KLAHR, D. Learning, development, and production systems. See 0478. 1–53.
**0480** ANZAI, Y. Doing, understanding, and learning in problem solving. See 0478. 55–97.
**0481** LANGLEY, P. A general theory of discrimination learning. See 0478. 99–161.
**0482** NECHES, R. Learning through incremental refinement of procedures. See 0478. 163–219.
**0483** ROSENBLOOM, P.; AND NEWELL, A. Learning by chunking: a production system model of practice. See 0478. 221–286.
**0484** OHLSSON, S. Truth versus appropriateness: relating declarative to procedural knowledge. See 0478. 287–327.
**0485** LEWIS, C. Composition of production. See 0478. 329–358.
**0486** WALLACE, I.; KLAHR, D.; AND BLUFF, K. Self-modifying production system model of cognitive development. See 0478. 359–435.
**0487** ANDERSON, J. Production systems, learning, and tutoring. See 0478. 437–458.
**HCI-0019** KLERER, M. User-oriented computer languages: analysis and design. [Macmillan database/data communications series] Macmillan Publishing Co., Inc., New York, NY, 1987, 208 pp., $34.95, ISBN 0-02-949911-9.
**0488** KOWALIK, J. (Ed.) Parallel computation and computers for artificial intelligence. [Kluwer International series in engineering and compter science] Kluwer Academic Publishers, Norwell, MA, 1988, 291 pp., $58.5, ISBN 0-89838-227-0.
**0489** ALLEN, D.; AND SRIDHARAN, N. Application of the butterfly parallel processor in artificial intelligence. See 0488. 153–164.
**0490** KOWALIK, S. (Ed.) Knowledge based problem solving. Prentice-Hall, Inc., Englewood Cliffs, NJ, 1986, 336 pp., ISBN 0-13-516576-8.
**0491** BOOSE, J. ETS—a system for the transfer of human expertise. See 0490. 112–165.
**0492** KRETCHMAN, L. Keyboarding for personal computer use. John Wiley & Sons, Inc., New York, NY, 1988, 172 pp., $19.95, ISBN 0-471-79752-9.
**0493** KUIJK, A.; AND STRASSER, W. (Eds.) Advances in computer graphics hardware II. [Eurographic Seminares: tutorials and perspectives in computer graphics] Springer-Verlag New York, Inc., New York, NY, 1988, 258 pp., ISBN 0-387-50109-6.
**0494** KAUFMAN, A. A two-dimensional frame buffer processor. See 0493. 93–109.
**0495** EYLES, J.; AUSTIN, J.; FUCHS, H.; CREER, T.; AND PAULTON, J. Pixel-planes 4: a summary. See 0493. 183–207.
**0496** JANSEN, F. A multi-processor workstation with a logic-enhanced distributed frame buffer. See 0493. 229–238.
**HCI-0068** L'HOTE, F.; KAUFFMANN, J.; ANDRÉ, P.; AND TAILLARD, J. Robot components and systems. [Robot technology, vol. 4] Prentice-Hall, Inc., Englewood Cliffs, NJ, 1983, 346 pp., $53.33, ISBN 0-13-782160-3.
**0497** ROSENBLOOM, P.; AND NEWELL, A. Universal subgoaling and chunking: the automatic generation and learning of goal hierarchies. [The Kluwer International Series in Engineering and Computer Science] Kluwer Academic Publishers, Norwell, MA, 1986, 313 pp., $39.95, ISBN 0-89838-213-0.
**0498** LANGEFORS, B.; VERRIJN-STUART, A.; AND BRACCHI, G. (Eds.) Trends in information systems. [An anthology of papers from conferences of the IFIP technical committee 8 'inf] North-Holland Publishing Co., Amsterdam, The Netherlands, 1986, 450 pp., $50.00, ISBN 0-444-87949-8.

0499 MUMFORD, E. Participation–from Aristotle to today. See 0498. 303–312.
0500 LAST, R. Artificial intelligence techniques in language learning. [Ellis Horwood computers and their applications] Halsted Press, New York, NY, 1989, 173 pp., $64.95, ISBN 0-470-21503-8.
0501 LAURILLARD, D. (Ed.) Interactive media: working methods and practical applications. Halsted Press, New York, NY, 1987, 241 pp., $49.95, ISBN 0470-20885-6.
0502 FULLER, R. Setting up an interactive videodisc project. See 0501. 15–27.
0503 BORK, A. Lessons from computer-based learning. See 0501. 28–43.
0504 BUTCHER, P. Computer-assisted learning and interactive video. See 0501. 44–59.
0505 LAURILLARD, D. Pedagogical design for interactive video. See 0501. 74–90.
0506 BOYD, G.; AND PASK, G. Why do instructional designers need conversation theory? See 0501. 91–96.
0507 PASK, G.; AND BOYD, G. Conversation theory as a basis for instructional design. See 0501. 97–115.
0508 RUSHBY, N. From trigger video to videodisc: a case study in interpersonal skills. See 0501. 116–131.
0509 SMITH, R. The creation of an integrated IVD curriculum. See 0501. 132–142.
0510 DOWLING, R.; AND CAMSTRA, B. A question of delivery—an outline classification of interactive video delivery systems. See 0501. 145–159.
0511 WRIGHT, M.; AND NELSON, D. Interactive video—a producer's medium. See 0501. 160–170.
0512 HART, A. The political economy of interactive video in British higher education. See 0501. 171–189.
0513 MABLY, C. Interactive video as a school resource: Rolls-Royce or Model T Ford? See 0501. 190–204.
0514 ARMSTRONG, P. Producing resource discs—the Domesday project experience. See 0501. 205–210.
0515 JACKSON, C. Videodisc and videotex: love-match or passing acquaintance? See 0501. 211–221.
0516 LAWLER, R.; AND YAZDANI, M. (Eds.) Artificial intelligence and education; vol. 1: learning environments and tutoring systems. Ablex Publishing Corp., Norwood, NJ, 1987, 439 pp., ISBN 0-89391-439-8.
0517 FEURZEIG, W. Algebra slaves and agents in a Logo-based mathematics curriculum. See 0516. 27–54.
0518 DISESSA, A. Artificial worlds and real experience. See 0516. 55–77.
0519 RIEL, M.; LEVIN, J.; AND MILLER-SOUVINEY, B. Learning with interactive media: dynamic support for students and teachers. See 0516. 117–134.
0520 LIEBERMAN, H. An example-base environment for beginning programmers. See 0516. 135–151.
0521 LEBERT, J.; AND MASSONI, J. Advanced interactive cobol for micros: a practical approach. Prentice-Hall, Inc., Englewood Cliffs, NJ, 1988, 352 pp., $24, ISBN 0-13-011479-0.
0522 LEBERT, J. Advanced interactive COBOL for micros: a practical approach. Prentice-Hall, Inc., Englewood Cliffs, NJ, 1988, $24, ISBN 0-13-011479-0.
HCI-0058 LEVINE, R.; DRANG, D.; AND EDELSON, B. A comprehensive guide to AI and expert systems. McGraw-Hill, Inc., New York, NY, 1986, 245 pp., $19.95, ISBN 0-07-037470-8.
0523 LEVITAN, K. (Ed.) Government infostructures: a guide to the networks of information resources and technologies at federal, state, and local levels. Greenwood Press, Westport, CT, 1987, 320 pp., ISBN 0-313-24864-8.
0524 DUTTON, W.; AND MEADOW, R. A tolerance for surveillance: American public opinion concerning privacy and civil liberties. See 0523. 147–170.
0525 ORIOL, W. Information and the "Aging Network". See 0523. 173–185.
0526 LEVY, D. (Ed.) Computer chess compendium. Springer-Verlag New York, Inc., New York, NY, 1988, 440 pp., ISBN 0-387-91331-9.
0527 GREENBLATT, R.; EASTLAKE, D.; AND CROCKER, S. The Greenblatt chess program. See 0526. 56–66.
0528 WILKINS, D. Using patterns and plans in chess. See 0526. 233–257.
HCI-0068 LIÉGEOIS, A. Performance and computer-aided design. [Robot technology, vol. 7] Prentice-Hall, Inc., Englewood Cliffs, NJ, 1985, 268 pp., $53.33, ISBN 0-13-782210-3.
0529 LOVELESS, R. (Ed.) The computer revolution and the arts. University of South Florida, Tampa, FL, 1989, 99 pp., $19.95, ISBN 0-8130-0912-X.
0530 YOUNGBLOOD, G. The new renaissance: art, science and universal machine. See 0529. 8–20.
0531 LUZADDER, W. Fundamentals of engineering drawing: with an introduction to interactive computer graphics for design and production, (9th ed.). Prentice-Hall, Inc., Englewood Cliffs, NJ, 1986, 642 pp., ISBN 0-13-338427-6.

BOOKS [0552]

HCI-0015    LYONS, T.; AND NISSEN, J. Selecting an Ada environment. [The Ada companion series] Cambridge University Press, New York, NY, 1986, 239 pp., $29.95, ISBN 0-521-32594-3.

HCI-0036    MACHLUP, F.; AND MANSFIELD, U. (Eds.) The study of information: interdisciplinary messages. John Wiley & Sons, Inc., New York, NY, 1983, 743 pp., $44.95, ISBN 0-471-88717-X.

HCI-0185    PYLYSHYN, Z. Information science: its roots and relation as viewed from the perspective of cognitive science. See HCI-0036. 63–118.

HCI-0086    GORN, S. (Ed.) Informatics (computer and information science): its ideology, methodology, and sociology. See HCI-0036. 121–183.

HCI-0003    MALAMUD, C. DEC networks and architectures. Intertext Pubs./McGraw-Hill Book Co., New York, NY, 1989, 472 pp., $39.95, ISBN 0-07-039822-4.

0532    MALONE, T. Thomas W. Malone, Oct. 5: user interface strategies '88. University of Maryland, College Park, MD, 1988, 41 pp.

0533    MANCUSO, J. Cognition & personal structure. Praeger Publishers, New York, NY, 1988, 352 pp., $32.50, ISBN 0-89859-884-2.

0534    MANDL, H.; AND LESGOLD, A. (Eds.) Learning Issues for Intelligent Tutoring Systems. Springer-Verlag New York, Inc., New York, NY, 1988, 307 pp., ISBN 0-387-96616-1.

0535    COLLINS, A.; AND BROWN, J. The computer as a tool for learning through reflection. See 0534. 1–18.

0536    VANLEHN, K. Toward a theory of impasse-driven learning. See 0534. 19–41.

0537    OHLSSON, S.; AND LANGLEY, P. Psychological evaluation of path hypotheses in cognitive diagnosis. See 0534. 42–62.

0538    FISCHER, G. Enhancing incremental learning processes with knowledge-based systems. See 0534. 138–163.

0539    STREITZ, N. Mental models and metaphors: implications for the design of adaptive user-system interfaces. See 0534. 164–186.

0540    FISCHER, P.; AND MANDL, H. Improvement of the acquisition of knowledge by informing feedback. See 0534. 187–241.

0541    LEPPER, M.; AND CHABAY, R. Socializing the intelligent tutor: bringing empathy to computer tutors. See 0534. 242–257.

0542    SCANLON, E.; AND O'SHEA, T. Cognitive economy in physics reasoning: implications for designing instructional materials. See 0534. 258–277.

0543    CAUZINILLE-MARMÈCHE, E.; AND MATHIEU, J. Experimental data for the design of a microworld-based system for algebra. See 0534. 278–286.

0544    WEDEKIND, J. Computer-aided model building. See 0534. 287:8N294.

0545    MANDL, H.; AND LESGOLD, A. (Eds.) Learning issues for intelligent tutoring systems. Springer-Verlag New York, Inc., New York, NY, 1988, $40, ISBN 0-38-796587-4.

0546    MANNINEN, M. Task-oriented approach to interactive control of heavy-duty manipulators based on coarse scene description. [ACTA Polytecnica Scandinavica; Ma 42] ACTP Polytechnica Scandinavica, Helsinki, Finland, 1986, 81 pp., ISBN 951-666-193-9.

HCI-0004    MARTIN, C. User-centered requirements analysis. Prentice-Hall, Inc., Englewood Cliffs, NJ, 1988, 305 pp., $37.60, ISBN 0-13-940578-X.

0547    MARTIN, J.; LEBEN, J.; AND THE ARBEN GROUP INC. Principles of data communication. Prentice-Hall, Inc., Englewood Cliffs, NJ, 1988, 346 pp., $33, ISBN 0-13-709891-X.

0548    MOORE, R. (Ed.) Reliability in computing: the role of interval methods in scientific computing. [Perspectives in Computing, vol. 19] Academic Press, Inc., San Diego, CA, 1988, 428 pp., ISBN 0-12-505630-3.

0549    RUMP, S. Algorithms for verified inclusions—theory and practice. See 0548. 109–126.

0550    MORONE, J.; AND HILBUSH, M. Experiencing artificial intelligence: an interactive approach to the IBM PC. TAB Books, Blue Ridge Summit, PA, 1987, 179 pp., $29.95, ISBN 0-8306-2830-4.

0551    MORONE, J.; AND HILBUSH, M. Experiencing artificial intelligence: an interactive approach for the APPLE. TAB Books, Blue Ridge Summit, PA, 1987, 197 pp., $36.95, ISBN 0-8306-2860-6.

0552    MUMPOWER, J.; RENN, O.; PHILLIPS, L.; AND UPPULURI, V. (Eds.) Expert judgment and expert systems. [NATO ASI Series F] Springer-Verlag, Berlin, West Germany, 1987, 361 pp., $59.50, ISBN 0-387-17986-0.

0553   MACCRIMMON, K.; AND WAGNER, C. Expert systems and creativity. See 0552. 173–193.
HCI-0227   SCHMALHOFER, F. Expert systems as cognitive tools for human decision making. See 0552. 269–288.
HCI-0008   MYERS, B. Creating user interfaces by demonstration. [Perspectives in computing, vol. 22] Academic Press, Inc., San Diego, CA, 1988, 276 pp., $29.95, ISBN 0-12-512305-1.
0554   NEMES, L. Information control problems in manufacturing. World Scientific Publishing Co., Inc., Teaneck, NJ, 1988, 500 pp., $60, ISBN 9971-50-100-7.
0555   NEWCOMER, L. Schaum's outline of theories and problems of programming with advanced structured COBOL with file processing structured systems deveolpment and interactive cons. [Schaum's outline series] McGraw-Hill, Inc., New York, NY, 1986, 350 pp., ISBN 0-070-37999-8.
0556   NEWHOUSE, V. (Ed.) Progress in medical imaging. Springer-Verlag New York, Inc., New York, NY, 1988, 301 pp., $86, ISBN 0-387-96713-3.
0557   HERMAN, G.; TRIVEDI, S.; AND UDUPA, J. Manipulation of 3D imagery. See 0556. 123–157.
HCI-0069   SPROULL, R. (Ath.) NEWMAN, W. (Ed.) Principles of interactive computer graphics (2nd ed.). McGraw-Hill, Inc., New York, NY, 1979, 541 pp., $47.95, ISBN 0-07-046338-7.
0558   NOF, S. (Ed.) Robotics and Material Flow. Elsevier Sci. Pub. B. V., Amsterdam, The Netherlands, 1987, 205 pp., ISBN 0444-42621-3.
0559   HELANDER, M.; AND DOMAS, K. Task allocation between humans and robots in manufacturing. See 0558. 175–185.
0560   NORMAN, D. Donald A. Norman, Oct. 12: user interface strategies '88. University of Maryland, College Park, MD, 1988, 432 pp.
0561   NYE, A. Xlib programming manual for version 11: Vol. 1. O'Reilly & Associates, Inc., Newton, MA, 1988, 611 pp., ISBN 0-937175-26-9.
HCI-0007   O'BRIEN, B. Opening Windows. Scott, Foresman & Co., Glenview, IL, 1987, 387 pp., $19.95, ISBN 0-673-18581-8.
0562   O'REILLY, T.; QUERCIA, V.; AND LAMB, L. X window system user's guide for version 11: vol. 3. O'Reilly & Associates, Inc., Newton, MA, 1988, 344 pp., ISBN 0-937175-29-3.
0563   OFFEN, R. (Ed.) VLSI image processing. McGraw-Hill, Inc., New York, NY, 1986, 326 pp., $36.95, ISBN 0-07-047771-X.
0564   BUXTON, H.; AND WIEJAK, J. Towards computer vision. See 0563. 188–236.
0565   OLSON, G.; SHEPPARD, S.; AND SOLOWAY, E. (Eds.) Empirical studies of programmers: second workshop. [A series of monographs, edited volumes, and texts] Ablex Publishing Corp., Norwood, NJ, 1987, 263 pp., $37.50, ISBN 0-89391-461-4.
0566   CUNNIFF, N.; AND TAYLOR, R. Graphical vs. textual representation: an empirical study of novices' program comprehension. See 0565. 114–131.
0567   OWEN, T.; AND EDWARDS, P. Information processing today, with applications. Burgess International Group, Inc., Edina, MN, 1986, 599 pp., ISBN 0-808-76409-8.
0568   OWENS, T.; AND EDWARD, P. Information processing today, with applications. Macmillan Publishing Co., Inc., New York, NY, 1986, ISBN 0-023-90260-4.
0569   OWENS, T.; AND EDWARDS, P. Information processing today, with applications and BASIC. Burgess International Group, Inc., Edina, MN, 1986, 599 pp., ISBN 0-808-76410-1.
0570   OWENS, T.; AND EDWARDS, P. Information processing today, with applications and BASIC: updat 87/88. Macmillan Publishing Co., Inc., New York, NY, 1986, ISBN 0-023-90270-1.
0571   OWENS, T.; AND EDWARDS, P. Principles of information processing. Burgess International Group, Inc., Edina, MN, 1986, 311 pp., ISBN 0-808-76412-8.
0572   OWENS, T.; AND EDWARDS, P. Principles of information processing with applications and BASIC. Burgess International Group, Inc., Edina, MN, 1986, ISBN 0-808-77126-4.
HCI-0068   PARENT, M.; AND LAURGEAU, C. Logic and programming. [Robot technology, vol. 5] Prentice-Hall, Inc., Englewood Cliffs, NJ, 1985, 190 pp., $53.33, ISBN 0-13-782178-6.
0573   PARTRIDGE, C. Innovations in Internetworking. Artech House, Inc., Dedham, MA, 1988, 532 pp., ISBN 0-89006-337-0.

0574   THOMAS, R.; FORSDICK, H.; CROWLEY, T.; SCHAAF, R.; TOMLINSON, R.; TRAVERS, V.; AND ROBERTSON, G. Diamond: A multimedia message system built on a distributed architecture. See 0573. 434–447.

0575   PEA, R.; AND SHEINGOLD, K. (Eds.) Mirrors of minds: patterns of experience in educational computing. Ablex Publishing Corp., Norwood, NJ, 1987, 329 pp., $42.50, ISBN 0-89391-422-3.

0576   HAWKINS, J. The interpretation of Logo in practice. See 0575. 3–34.

0577   MARTIN, L. Teachers' adoption of multimedia technologies for science and mathematics instruction. See 0575. 35–56.

0578   NEWMAN, D. Functional environments for microcomputers in education. See 0575. 57–66.

0579   KURLAND, D.; CLEMENT, C.; MAWBY, R.; AND PEA, R. Mapping the cognitive demands of learning to program. See 0575. 103–127.

0580   PEA, R. Integrated human and computer intelligence. See 0575. 128–146.

0581   PEA, R.; AND KURLAND, D. On the cognitive effects of learning computer programming. See 0575. 147–177.

0582   PEA, R.; KURLAND, D.; AND HAWKINS, J. Logo and development of thinking skills. See 0575. 178–197.

0583   SHEINGOLD, K. The microcomputer as a symbolic medium. See 0575. 198–208.

0584   HAWKINS, J.; AND KURLAND, D. Informing the design of software through context-based research. See 0575. 258–272.

0585   HAWKINS, J.; MAWBY, R.; AND GHITMAN, J. Practices of novices and experts in critical inquiry. See 0575. 273–298.

0586   PENZIAS, A. Ideas and information: managing in a high-tech world. W. W. Norton & Co., Inc., New York, NY, 1989, 224 pp., $17.95, ISBN 0-393-02649-3.

0587   PETZOLD, C. Programming the OS/2 presentation manager. Microsoft Press, Redmond, WA, 1989, 845 pp., $29.95, ISBN 1-55615-170-5.

HCI-0078   PHILIPS INTERNATIONAL, I. (Ed.) Compact disc-interactive: a designer's overview. McGraw-Hill, Inc., New York, NY, 1988, 239 pp., $39.95, ISBN 0-07-049816-4.

0588   PINKER, S.; AND MEHLER, J. (Eds.) Connections and symbols. MIT Press, Cambridge, MA, 1988, 255 pp., $17.50, ISBN 0-262-66064-4.

0589   FODOR, J.; AND PYLYSHYN, Z. Connectionism and cognitive architecture: a critical analysis. See 0588. 3–71.

0590   PINKER, S. On language and connectionism: analysis of a parallel distributed processing model of language acquisition. See 0588. 73–193.

0591   LACHTER, J.; AND BEVER, T. The relation between linguistic structure and associative theories of language learning models: constructive critique of some connectionist learning models. See 0588. 195–247.

0592   POLSON, M.; AND RICHARDSON, J. (Eds.) Foundations of intelligent tutoring systems. Lawrence Erlbaum Associates, Inc., Hillsdale, NJ, 1988, ISBN 0-805-80053-0.

HCI-0002   PROCHNOW, D. Chip talk: projects in speech synthesis. TAB Books, Blue Ridge Summit, PA, 1987, 209 pp., $14.95, ISBN 0-8306-2812-6.

0593   PYLYSHYN, Z. Computation and cognition: toward a foundation for cognitive science. Massachusetts Institute of Technology, Cambridge, MA, 1984, 292 pp., $25.00, ISBN 0-262-16098-6.

0594   QED INFORMATION SCIENCES, I. Critical issues in information processing management and technology: vol. 6. Q.E.D. Information Sciences, Inc., Wellesley, MA, 1989, 459 pp., ISBN 0-89435-296-6.

HCI-0013   QUEDENS, G.; AND BEASON, P. Introduction to Windows programming. Scott, Foresman & Co., Glenview, IL, 1989, 370 pp., $21.95, ISBN 0-673-38058-0.

0595   RAHTZ, S. (Ed.) Information technology in the humanities: tools, techniques and applications. [Ellis Horwood series in computers and their applications] Halsted Press, New York, NY, 1987, 188 pp., $39.95, ISBN 0-470-20852-X.

HCI-0095   HALL, W. The art of programming. See 0595. 80–91.

0596   RAMSOWER, R. Telecommuting the organizational and behavioral effects of working at home. University Microfilms, Ann Arbor, MI, 1986, 195 pp., $39.95, ISBN 0-8357-1628-7.

0597   RAVANI, B. (Ed.) CAD Based Programming for Sensory Robots. Springer-Verlag New York, Inc., New York, NY, 1988, 565 pp., ISBN 0-387-50415-X.

0598   JAYARAMAN, R.; AND LEVAS, A. A workcell application design environment (WADE). See 0597. 91–120.

**0599** IMAM, I.; AND DAVIS, J. Robot simulation and off-line programming—an integrated CAE-CAD approach. See 0597. 189–201.
**0600** DE SCHUTTER, J.; AND SIMKENS, P. CAD Based verification and refinement of high level compliant motion primitives. See 0597. 203–222.
**0601** WECK, M.; AND CLEMENS, R. Experiences with off-line robot programming via standardized interfaces. See 0597. 223–234.
**0602** YOUNG, K.; AND BENNATON, J. Off-line programming of robots using 3D graphical simulation system. See 0597. 235–252.
**0603** CRANE, C.; DUFFY, J.; AND LOCKE, M. Off-line programming and path generation for robot manipulators. See 0597. 425–432.
**0604** HOFFMANN, C.; AND HOPCROFT, J. Model generation and modification for dynamic systems from geometric data. See 0597. 481–492.
**0605** COTSAFTIS, M.; AND VIBET, C. Modeling of robot system dynamics for CAD based robot programming. See 0597. 493–509.
**0606** SPUR, G.; KIRCHHOFF, U.; BERNHARDT, R.; AND HELD, J. Computer aided application program synthesis for industrial robots. See 0597. 527–548.
**0607** LUMIA, R. CAD-based off-line programming applied to a cleaning and deburring workstation. See 0597. 549–565.
**0608** RAVDEN, S.; AND JOHNSON, G. Evaluating usability of human-computer interfaces: a practical method. [Ellis Horwood books in information technology] Halsted Press, New York, NY, 1989, 126 pp., $37.95, ISBN 0-470-21496-1.
**0609** RAYNER, K. (Ed.) Eye movements in reading: perceptual and language processes. [Perspectives in Neurolinguistics, Neuropsychology, and Psycholingusitics] Academic Press, Inc., San Diego, CA, 1986, 526 pp., $60.50, ISBN 0-12-583680-5.
**0610** RCOK-EVANS, R. An introduction to data and activity analysis. Q.E.D. Information Sciences, Inc., Wellesley, MA, 1989, 254 pp., ISBN 0-89435-309-8.
**0611** REILLY, R. (Ed.) Communication failure in dialogue and discourse: detection and repair processes. Elsevier North-Holland, Inc., New York, NY, 1986, ISBN 0-444-70112-5.
**HCI-0024** REPS, T.; AND TEITELBAUM, T. The synthesizer generator: a system for constructing language-based editors. [Texts and monographs in computer science series] Springer-Verlag New York, Inc., New York, NY, 1989, 317 pp., $39.20, ISBN 0-387-96857-1.
**HCI-0024** REPS, T.; AND TEITELBAUM, T. The synthesizer generator reference manual (3rd ed.). [Texts and monographs in computer science series] Springer-Verlag New York, Inc., New York, NY, 1989, 171 pp., $20, ISBN 0-387-96910-1.
**0612** RICH, C.; AND WATERS, R. (Eds.) Readings in artificial intelligence and software engineering. Morgan-Kaufmann, Palo Alto, CA, 1986, 602 pp., $26.95, ISBN 0-934613-12-5.
**0613** BARSTOW, D. An experiment in knowledge-based automatic programming. See 0612. 133–156.
**0614** FLOYD, R. Toward interactive design of correct programs. See 0612. 331–334.
**0615** RICHARDS, W.; AND ULLMAN, S. (Eds.) Image understanding 1985-86. Ablex Publishing Corp., Norwood, NJ, 1987, 356 pp., $45, ISBN 0-89391-311-1.
**0616** ULLMAN, S. Visual routines. See 0615. 286–344.
**0617** RICHARDS, W. (Ed.) Natural computation: selected readings. MIT Press, Cambridge, MA, 1988, 480 pp., $50, ISBN 0-262-18132-0.
**HCI-0049** ROCKART, J.; AND DE LONG, D. Executive support systems: the emergence of top management computer use. Dow Jones-Irwin, Homewood, IL, 1988, 280 pp., $29.95, ISBN 0-87094-955-1.
**HCI-0069** ROGERS, D. Procedural elements for computer graphics. McGraw-Hill, Inc., New York, NY, 1985, 433 pp., $27.95, ISBN 0-07-053534-5.
**0618** ROLSTADAS, A. (Ed.) Computer-aided production management IFIP. [State of the arts reports] Springer-Verlag New York, Inc., New York, NY, 1988, 404 pp., ISBN 0-387-18748-0.
**0619** ROLSTADÅS, A. Production management systems. See 0618. 3–19.
**0620** HARHEN, J. MRP/MRP II. See 0618. 23–35.

## BOOKS

**0621** ELORANTA, E. User interface. See 0618. 181–199.
**0622** DOUMEINGTS, G. Systems analysis techniques. See 0618. 201–224.
**0623** THUROW, W. Production control in car industry. See 0618. 355–361.
**0624** HIRSCH, B.; AND HUMBERT, G. Production control in the aircraft industry. See 0618. 363–373.
**0625** BURBIDGE, J. A drafted PM glossary. See 0618. 399–402.
**0626** ROSS, S.; LUND, P.; LARSEN, S.; AND HAYDEN, B. Understanding & using application software. West Publishing Co., St. Paul, MN, 1988, 464 pp., $30, ISBN 0-314-34740-2.
**0627** RUBEL, M. Programming the dBASE III Plus user interface. [The Business productivity library] Bantam Books, Inc., New York, NY, 1987, 304 pp., $21.95, ISBN 0-553-34408-0.
**0628** RUBIN, T. User interface design for computer systems. [Ellis Horwood series in computers and their applications] Halsted Press, New York, NY, 1988, 195 pp., ISBN 0-470-21172-5.
**HCI-0074** RUBINSTEIN, R. Digital typography: an introduction to type and composition for computer system design. Addison-Wesley Publ. Co., Inc., Reading, MA, 1988, 340 pp., $32.25, ISBN 0-201-17633-5.
**0629** RUMELHART, D.; MCCLELLAND, J.; AND PDP RESEARCH GROUP Parallel distributed processing: explorations in the microstructures of cognition; Vol. 2: Psychological and biological models. [Computational models of cognition and perception] MIT Press, Cambridge, MA, 1986, 611 pp., $27.50, ISBN 0-262-13218-4.
**0630** RUMELHART, D.; SMOLENSKY, P.; MCCLELLAND, J.; AND HINTON, G. Schemata and sequential thought processes in PDP models. See 0629. 7–57.
**0631** MCCLELLAND, J.; AND ELMAN, J. Interactive processes in speech perception: the TRACE model. See 0629. 58–121.
**0632** MCCLELLAND, J. The programmable blackboard model of reading. See 0629. 122–169.
**0633** MCCLELLAND, J.; AND RUMELHART, D. A distributed model of human learning and memory. See 0629. 170–215.
**0634** RUMELHART, D.; AND MCCLELLAND, J. On learning the past tenses of English verbs. See 0629. 216–271.
**0635** MCCLELLAND, J.; AND KAWAMOTO, A. Mechanisms of sentence processing: assigning roles to constituents. See 0629. 272–325.
**0636** CRICK, F.; AND ASANUMA, C. Certain aspects of the anatomy and physiology of the cerebral cortex. See 0629. 333–371.
**0637** SEJNOWSKI, T. Open questions about computation in cerebral cortex. See 0629. 372–389.
**0638** SMOLENSKY, P. Neural and conceptual interpretation of PDP models. See 0629. 390–431.
**0639** ZIPSER, D. Biologically plausible models of place recognition and goal location. See 0629. 432–470.
**0640** MUNRO, P. State-dependent factors influencing neural plasticity: a partial account of the. See 0629. 471–502.
**0641** MCCLELLAND, J.; AND RUMELHART, D. Amnesia and distrubuted memory. See 0629. 503–527.
**0642** NORMAN, D. Reflections on cognition and parallel distributed. See 0629. 531–546.
**0643** RUTKOWSKA, J.; AND COOK, C. (Eds.) Computers, cognition, and development: issues for psychology and education. [Wiley series in developmental psychology and its applications] John Wiley & Sons, Inc., New York, NY, 1987, 311 pp., $48, ISBN 0-471-91583-1.
**0644** SAGE, A. (Ed.) System design for human interaction. [IEEE Press selected reprint series] IEEE Press, New York, NY, 1987, 488 pp., ISBN 0-879-42218 1.
**0645** SAGE, A. (Ed.) System design for human interaction. IEEE Press, New York, NY, 1987, 488 pp., ISBN 0-87942-218-1.
**0646** SAGE, A. An overview of system design for human interaction. See 0645. 3–14.
**0647** JOHNSON-LAIRD, P. Mental models in cognitive science. See 0645. 17–39.
**0648** PITZ, G.; AND SACHS, N. Judgement and decision: theory and application. See 0645. 94–106.
**0649** FREELING, A. A philosophical basis for decision aiding. See 0645. 109–122.
**0650** WATSON, S.; WEISS, J.; AND DONNELL, M. Fuzzy decision analysis. See 0645. 123–131.
**0651** FREELING, A. Fuzzy sets and decision analysis. See 0645. 132–145.
**0652** GARDENFORS, P.; AND SAHLIN, N. Decision making with unreliable probabilities. See 0645. 146–157.
**0653** ROUSE, W. Models of human problem solving: detection, diagnosis, and compensation for system failures. See 0645. 278–290.

**0654** RASMUSSEN, J. Skills, rules, and knowledge; signals, signs, and symbols, and other distinctions in human performance models. See 0645. 291–300.

**0655** HENNEMAN, R.; AND ROUSE, W. Measures of human problem solving performance in fault diagnosis tasks. See 0645. 311–324.

**0656** HUNT, R.; AND ROUSE, W. A fuzzy rule-based model of human problem solving. See 0645. 325–333.

**0657** MORRIS, N.; AND ROUSE, W. The effects of type of knowledge upon human problem solving in a process control task. See 0645. 334–343.

**0658** MINCH, R.; AND BURNS, J. Conceptual design of decision support systems utilizing management science models. See 0645. 377–385.

**0659** WANG, M.; AND COURTNEY, J. A conceptual architecture for generalized decision support system software. See 0645. 386–396.

**0660** BUEDE, D.; YATES, G.; AND WEAVER, C. Concept design of a program manager's decision support system. See 0645. 397–408.

**0661** SAGE, A.; AND WHITE III, C. ARIADNE: A knowledge-based interactive system for planning and decision support. See 0645. 415–427.

**0662** TAYLOR, J.; AND FREDERICK, D. An expert system architecture for computer-aided control engineering. See 0645. 431–441.

**0663** WALKER, R.; SHAH, S.; AND GUPTA, N. Computer-aided engineering (CAE) for system analysis. See 0645. 442–455.

**0664** SALMAD, T. A natural language interface for computer-aided design. Kluwer Academic Publishers, Norwell, MA, 1986, 188 pp., ISBN 0-89838-222-X.

**0665** SAVORY, S. (Ed.) Artificial intelligence and expert systems. John Wiley & Sons, Inc., New York, NY, 1988, 278 pp., $39.95, ISBN 0-470-21038-9.

**0666** ROESNER, H. Expert systems for commercial use. See 0665. 35–59.

**HCI-0076** SCHAEFER, A.; AND BRITTAIN, J. The AutoCAD productivity book: tapping the hidden power of AutoCAD. Ventana Press, Inc., Chapel Hill, NC, 1986, 314 pp., $39.95, ISBN 0-940087-00-6.

**0667** SCHAEFER, R. Thinking: information processing, mathematical models and computer simulation. Springer-Verlag New York, Inc., New York, NY, 1985, 272 pp., ISBN 0387157247.

**0668** SCHAEFER, T.; AND BRITTAIN, J. The AutoCAD productivity book: tapping the hidden power of AutoCAD: 2nd edition. Ventana Press, Inc., Chapel Hill, NC, 1988, 362 pp., $39.95, ISBN 0-940087-10-3.

**0669** SCHEIFLER, R. X Protocol reference manual for version II: vol. 0. [The X Window system] O'Reilly & Associates, Inc., Newton, MA, 1989, 398 pp., $30, ISBN 0-937175-40-4.

**0670** SCHILDT, H. OS/2 programming: an introduction. Osborne/McGraw-Hill, Berkeley, CA, 1988, 389 pp., $21.95, ISBN 0-07-881427-8.

**0671** SELF, J. (Ed.) Artificial intelligence & human learning: intelligent computer-aided instruction. Routledge, Chapman & Hall, Inc., New York, NY, 1988, 456 pp., $85.00, ISBN 0-412-30130-X.

**0672** SELKIRK, E. Phonology and syntax: the relationship between sound and structure. MIT Press, Cambridge, MA, 1986, 476 pp., ISBN 0-262-69098-5.

**0673** SENN, J. Information systems in management: 3rd edition. Wadsworth Publ. Co., Inc., Belmont, CA, 1987, 800 pp., ISBN 0-534-07482-0.

**HCI-0053** SHAFTO, M. (Ed.) How we know. Harper & Row, Publishers, Inc., New York, NY, 1985, 171 pp., $14.95, ISBN 0-06-250777-X.

**0674** SHAPIRO, E. Concurrent Prolog: collected papers. MIT Press, Cambridge, MA, 1988, 653 pp., ISBN 0-262-19267-5.

**0675** SILVERMAN, W.; HIRSCH, M.; HOURI, A.; AND SHAPIRO, E. The Logix system user manual version 1.21. See 0674. 46–77.

**0676** KATZENELLENBOGEN, D.; COHEN, S.; AND SHAPIRO, E. An architecture of a distributed window system and its FCP implementation. See 0674. 101–139.

**0677** SHAPIRO, E.; AND TAKEUCHI, A. Object oriented programming in Concurrent Prolog. See 0674. 251–273.

**0678** SHERMAN, C. The CD ROM handbook. Intertext Pubs./McGraw-Hill Book Co., New York, NY, 1988, 510 pp., $59.95, ISBN 0-07-056578-3.

BOOKS                                                                    [HCI-0014]

0679   TRAUB, D. An historical perspective of CD ROM. See 0678. 17–49.
0680   BRUNO, R. Compact disc–interactive. See 0678. 131–185.
0681   LUTHER, A. Digital video interactive. See 0678. 187–207.
0682   WATSON, B.; NOREAULT, T.; AND TURTLE, H. Designing a CD ROM information structure. See 0678. 243–267.
0683   PINCUS, M.; PINCUS, K.; AND GOLDEN, J. Artificial intelligence systems. See 0678. 329–340.
HCI-0006 SHNEIDERMAN, B. Designing the user interface: strategies for effective human-computer interaction. Addison-Wesley Publ. Co., Inc., Reading, MA, 1986, 448 pp., $29.95, ISBN 0-201-16505-8.
0684   SHNEIDERMAN, B.; MALONE, T.; NORMAN, D.; AND FOLEY, J. User interface strategies '88 (Videotape). University of Maryland, College Park, MD, 1988, $1,800.
0685   SHNEIDERMAN, B. Ben Shneiderman, Oct. 5,12: user interface strategies '88. University of Maryland, College Park, MD, 1988, 110 pp.
0686   SHNEIDERMAN, B.; AND KEARSLEY, G. Hypertext hands-on!: an introduction to a new way of organizing and accessing information. Addison-Wesley Publ. Co., Inc., Reading, MA, 1989, 165 pp., $26.95, ISBN 0-201-15171-5.
0687   SHNEIDERMAN, B. Designing the user interface (Videotape). University of Maryland, College Park, MD, 1987, $1,200.
0688   SHNEIDERMAN, B. Designing the user interface: professional development courses from the Univ. of Maryland. University of Maryland, College Park, MD, 1987, 89 pp.
0689   SHNEIDERMAN, B. Designing the user interface: supplemental materials. University of Maryland, College Park, MD, 1987, 86 pp.
0690   WEGNER, P. (Ath.) SHRIVER, B. (Ed.) Research directions in object-oriented programming. [MIT Press series in computer systems] MIT Press, Cambridge, MA, 1987, 585 pp., ISBN 0-262-19264-0.
0691   SMITH, R.; BARTH, P.; AND YOUNG, R. A substrate for object-oriented interface design. See 0690. 253–316.
0692   SHROBE, H. (Ed.) Exploring artificial intelligence. Morgan-Kaufmann, Palo Alto, CA, 1988, 693 pp., ISBN 0-934613-67-2.
0693   PERRAULT, C.; AND GROSZ, B. Natural-language interfaces. See 0692. 133–172.
0694   SHU, N. (Ed.) Visual programming. Van Nostrand Reinhold Co., New York, NY, 1988, $29.95, ISBN 0-442-28014-9.
0695   SILVERMAN, B. (Ed.) Expert systems for business. Addison-Wesley Publ. Co., Inc., Reading, MA, 1987, 446 pp., $22.95, ISBN 0-201-07179-7.
0696   FORDYCE, K. Looking at worksheet modeling through expert system eyes. See 0695. 246–285.
0697   SIMONS, G. Is man a robot? John Wiley & Sons, Inc., New York, NY, 1986, 316 pp., $15.00, ISBN 0471911062.
0698   SIMPSON, H. Programming the Macintosh User Interface. McGraw-Hill, Inc., New York, NY, 1986, 224 pp., $19.95, ISBN 0-07-057320-4.
0699   SIMPSON, H. Developing effective user documentation: a human factors approach. McGraw-Hill, Inc., New York, NY, 1988, $39.95, ISBN 0-07-057336-0.
0700   SLATTER, P. Building expert systems; cognitive emulation. [Ellis Horwood books in information technology] Halsted Press, New York, NY, 1987, 147 pp., ISBN 0-470-2.891-0.
0701   SNODGRASS, R. (Ed.) Automating interfaces in a software system. W. H. Freeman & Co., New York, NY, 1988, 420 pp., $44.95, ISBN 0-7167-8198-0.
0702   SOUCEK, B. (Ed.) Nueral & massively parallel computers: the sixth generation. John Wiley & Sons, Inc., New York, NY, 1988, $49.95, ISBN 0-471-63533-2.
0703   SOUTER, G. (Ed.) The disconnection: how to interface computers and video. Knowledge Industry Publications, White Plains, NY, 1988, 200 pp., $45.00, ISBN 0-86729-219-9.
HCI-0057 SOWA, J. Conceptual structures: information processing in mind and machine. [Addison-Wesley systems programming series] Addison-Wesley Publ. Co., Inc., Reading, MA, 1984, 481 pp., $32.95, ISBN 0-201-14472-7.
HCI-0014 SPENCER, R. Computer usability testing & evaluation. Prentice-Hall, Inc., Englewood Cliffs, NJ, 1985, 224 pp., $27.50, ISBN 0-13-164088-7.

0704 SPERBER, D.; AND WILSON, D. Relevance: communication and cognition. Harvard University Press, Cambridge, MA, 1986, 279 pp., $8.95, ISBN 0-674-75476-1.

HCI-0070 SPROULL, R.; SUTHERLAND, W.; AND ULLNER, M. Device-independent graphics: with examples from IBM personal computers. McGraw-Hill, Inc., New York, NY, 1985, 546 pp., $35.95, ISBN 0-07-060504-1.

0705 STALLINGS, W.; HUTCHISON, S.; AND SAWYER, S. (Eds.) Computers : the user perspective. Times Mirror/Mosby, London, UK, 1988, ISBN 0-801-64752-5.

HCI-0073 STEINHAUER, G. Artificial behavior: computer simulation of psychological processes. [Prentice-Hall personal computing series] Prentice-Hall, Inc., Englewood Cliffs, NJ, 1986, 150 pp., $25.67, ISBN 0-13-048844-5.

0706 STONEBRAKER, M. (Ed.) The INGRES papers: anatomy of a relational database system. [Addison-Wesley series in computer science] Addison-Wesley Publ. Co., Inc., Reading, MA, 1986, 452 pp., $33.95, ISBN 0-201-07185-1.

0707 STONEBRAKER, M.; AND ROWE, L. Database portals: a new application program interface. See 0706. 261–277.

0708 STONEBRAKER, M. Readings in database systems. Morgan-Kaufmann, Palo Alto, CA, 1988, 644 pp., $29.95, ISBN 0-934613-65-6.

0709 ASTRAHAN, M.; BLASGEN, M.; CHAMBERLIN, D.; ESWARAN, K.; GRAY, J.; GRIFFITHS, P.; KING, W.; LORIE, R.; MCJONES, P.; MEHL, J.; PUTZOLU, G.; TRAIGER, I.; WADE, B.; AND WATSON, V. System R: a relational approach to database management. See 0708. 16–36.

0710 ROWE, L. "Fill-in-Form" programming. See 0708. 348–358.

0711 ROGERS, T.; AND CATTELL, R. Entity-relationship database user interfaces. See 0708. 359–368.

0712 BANERJEE, J.; CHOU, H.; GARZA, J.; KIM, W.; WOELK, D.; BALLOU, N.; AND KIM, H. Data model issues for object-oriented applications. See 0708. 445–456.

0713 STONIER, T.; AND CONLIN, C. The three c's: children, computers, and communication. John Wiley & Sons, Inc., New York, NY, 1985, 218 pp., $14.95, ISBN 0-471-90828-2.

0714 STUART, A. (Ed.) Screen input/output programming techniques using Turbo Pascal. Management Information Source, Portland, OR, 1987, 457 pp., $24.95, ISBN 0-943-51828-8.

HCI-0040 SUCHMAN, L. Plans and situated actions: the problem of human-machine communication. Cambridge University Press, New York, NY, 1987, 203 pp., $34.50, ISBN 0-521-33137-4.

HCI-0043 SUTCLIFFE, A. Human-computer interface design. Springer-Verlag New York, Inc., New York, NY, 1989, 205 pp., $29.95, ISBN 0-387-91339-4.

0715 TEN HAGEN, P.; AND TOMIYAMA, T. (Eds.) Intelligent CAD systems I: theoretical and methodological aspects. [Tutorials and perspectives in computer graphics] Springer-Verlag New York, Inc., New York, NY, 1987, 360 pp., ISBN 0-387-18281-0.

0716 RUTTKAY, Z.; ALLEN, R.; AND LACZIK, B. A multiparadigm user interface for intelligent CAD systems. See 0715. 242–255.

0717 VETH, B. An integrated data description language for coding design knowledge. See 0715. 295–313.

0718 THOMAS, J.; AND SCHNEIDER, M. (Eds.) Human factors in computer systems. Ablex Publishing Corp., Norwood, NJ, 1984, 276 pp., ISBN 0-89391-146-1.

HCI-0132 MALONE, T. Heuristics for designing enjoyable user interfaces: lessons from computer games. See 0718. 1–12.

HCI-0292 CARROLL, J.; AND MACK, R. Learning to use a word processor: by doing, by thinking, and by knowing. See 0718. 13–51.

HCI-0170 SAVAGE, R.; AND HABINEK, J. A Multilevel menu-driven user interface: Design and evaluation through simulation. See 0718. 165–186.

HCI-0037 THOMAS, J.; AND SCHNEIDER, M. (Eds.) Human factors in computer systems. 1984, 276 pp., $34.50, ISBN 0-89391-146-1.

0719 TRAUB, J.; GROSZ, B.; LAMPSON, B.; AND NILSSON, N. (Eds.) Annual review of computer science vol. 1, 1986. [Annual reviews of computer science] Annual Reviews Inc., Palo Alto, CA, 1986, 459 pp., $39, ISBN 0-8243-3201-6.

0720 PERRAULT, C.; AND GROSZ, B. Natural-language interfaces. See 0719. 47–82.

0721 CLANCEY, W. Qualitative student models. See 0719. 381–450.

BOOKS

HCI-0082   TURKLE, S. The second self: computers and the human spirit. Simon & Schuster, Inc., New York, NY, 1984, 352 pp., $17.95, ISBN 0-671-46848-0.
0722   VANCE, M. Computer crime. Vance Bibliographies, Monticello, IL, 1988, $8.75, ISBN 1-55590-675-3.
HCI-0068   VERTUT, J.; AND COIFFET, P. Teleoperations and robotics: applications and technology. [Robot technology, vol. 3B] Prentice-Hall, Inc., Englewood Cliffs, NJ, 1986, 256 pp., $42.95, ISBN 0-13-782202-2.
HCI-0068   VERTUT, J.; AND COIFFET, P. Teleoperations and robotics: evolution and development. [Robot technology, vol. 3A] Prentice-Hall, Inc., Englewood Cliffs, NJ, 1986, 332 pp., $53.33, ISBN 0-13-782194-8.
HCI-0055   WALDROP, M. Man-made minds: the promise of artificial intelligence. Walker & Co., New York, NY, 1987, 280 pp., $22.95, ISBN 0-8027-0899-4.
HCI-0072   WATANABE, S. Pattern recognition: human and mechanical. John Wiley & Sons, Inc., New York, NY, 1985, 570 pp., $44.95, ISBN 0-471-80815-6.
0723   WATERWORTH (Ed.) Speech & language based interaction with machines. John Wiley & Sons, Inc., New York, NY, 1988, 170 pp., $44.95, ISBN 0-470-21033-8.
0724   WATERWORTH, J.; AND TALBOT, M. Speech and language-based interaction with machines: towards the conversational computer. Halsted Press, New York, NY, 1987, ISBN 0-74-580146-3.
0725   WEINMAN, D.; AND KURSHAN, B. VAX-BASIC with structured problem solving: 2nd edition. Prentice-Hall, Inc., Englewood Cliffs, NJ, 1988, 389 pp., ISBN 0-13-940990-4.
0726   WEISKAMP, K. Advanced Turbo C programming. Academic Press, Inc., San Diego, CA, 1988, 559 pp., $45.95, ISBN 0-12-742689-2.
HCI-0033   WELSH, D. Codes and cryptography. Clarendon, New York, NY, 1988, 257 pp., $32.50, ISBN 0-19-853287-3.
HCI-0080   WENGER, E. Artificial intelligence and tutoring systems: computational and cognitive approaches to the communication of knowledge. Morgan-Kaufmann, Palo Alto, CA, 1987, 486 pp., $32.95, ISBN 0-934613-26-5.
HCI-0023   WILENSKY, R. LISPcraft. W. W. Norton & Co., Inc., New York, NY, 1984, 385 pp., $19.95, ISBN 0-393-95442-0.
0727   WILHELMSON, R. (Ed.) High-speed computing: scientific applications and algorithm design. University of Illinois Press, Urbana, IL, 1988, 228 pp., $29.95, ISBN 0-252-01440-5.
0728   SMARR, L. The computational science revolution: technology, methodology, and sociology. See 0727. 12–33.
0729   ZABUSKY, N. Coherent and chaotic structures in 2D vortex dynamics: progress and problems. See 0727. 51–69.
0730   KLEMP, J. Computing needs in thunderstorm modeling: supercomputers and interactive graphics. See 0727. 70–71.
HCI-0054   WINOGRAD, T.; AND FLORES, F. (Eds.) Understanding computers and cognition. Ablex Publishing Corp., Norwood, NJ, 1985, 207 pp., $24.95, ISBN 0-89391-050-3.
0731   WOLF, D. Working with Lotus HAL: a 1-2-3 user's guide. TAB Books, Blue Ridge Summit, PA, 1988, 176 pp., $15.95, ISBN 0-8306-2973-4.
HCI-0085   WOOD-HARPER, A.; ANTILL, L.; AND AVISON, D. Information systems definition: the Multiview approach. [Blackwell Scientific Publications computer science text] Blackwell Scientific Publications, Ltd., Oxford, UK, 1985, 167 pp., ISBN 0-632-01216-8.
0732   WOOD, M. (Ed.) The development of a postmodern self: a computer-assisted comparative analysis of personal documents. [Contributions in society, vol. 70] Greenwood Press, Westport, CT, 1988, 192 pp., $37.95, ISBN 0-313-25458-3.
0733   WOODSON, W. Human factors reference guide for electronics and computer professionals. [McGraw-Hill engineering reference guide series] McGraw-Hill, Inc., New York, NY, 1987, 204 pp., $32.50, ISBN 0-07-071766-9.
0734   WOODSON, W. Human factors reference guide for electronics and computer professionals. [McGraw-Hill engineering reference guide series] McGraw-Hill, Inc., New York, NY, 1987, $32.50, ISBN 0070717664.
0735   WORMELL, I. (Ed.) Knowledge engineering: expert systems and information retrieval. Taylor Graham Publishers, London, UK, 1987, 182 pp., $39, ISBN 0-947-56830-1.

HCI-0272  SPARCK JONES, K. Architecture problems in the construction of expert systems for document retrieval. See 0735. 7–33.
HCI-0331  HOLLNAGEL, E. Cognitive models, cognitive tasks, and information retrieval. See 0735. 34–52.
0736  MAYOH, B. Are machines as good as people in drawing conclusions from knowledge represented in catalogues, data bases and expert systems? See 0735. 53–58.
0737  SORMUNEN, E. A knowledge-based intermediary system for information retrieval. See 0735. 59–73.
0738  JENSEN-BJØRN, R. Intelligent interfaces to Nordic data bases. See 0735. 74–91.
HCI-0266  PEJTERSEN, A.; OLSEN, S.; AND ZUNDE, P. Development of a term association interface for browsing bibliographic data bases based on end users' word associations. See 0735. 92–112.
0739  LARSEN, H. KIWI: knowledge-based user-friendly system for the utilization of information bases. See 0735. 113–126.
0740  SANDAHL, K. The migration of expert systems into the production environment. See 0735. 127–149.
HCI-0273  INGWERSEN, P. Towards a new research paradigm in information retrieval. See 0735. 150–168.
0741  YAZDANI, M. (Ed.) New horizons in educational computing. [Ellis Horwood series in artificial intelligence] Halsted Press, New York, NY, 1984, 314 pp., ISBN 0-470-20022-7.
0742  LAWLER, B. Designing computer-based microworlds. See 0741. 40–53.
0743  HASEMER, T. A very friendly software environment for SOLO. See 0741. 84–100.
0744  KAHNEY, H. Modelling novice programmer behaviour. See 0741. 101–118.
0745  KAHN, K. A grammar kit in PROLOG. See 0741. 178–189.
0746  NICHOL, J.; AND DEAN, J. Pupils, computers and history teaching. See 0741. 190–204.
0747  SLOMAN, A. Beginners need powerful systems. See 0741. 220–234.
0748  GIBSON, J. POP-11: an AI programming language. See 0741. 235–251.
0749  GRAY, M. POP-11 for everyone. See 0741. 252–271.
0750  YAZDANI, M. (Ed.) New horizons in educational computing. Wiley-Interscience, New York, NY, 1987, 314 pp., $29.95, ISBN 0470-20792-2.
0751  KAHNEY, H. Modelling novice programmer behaviour. See 0750. 101–118.
0752  GRAY, M. UNIX and the naive user: children meet a grown-up operating system. See 0750. 272–281.
0753  ZORKOCZY, P. (Ed.) Oxford Surveys in Information Technology. Oxford University Press, Inc., New York, NY, 1987, 318 pp., ISBN 0-19-859019-9.
0754  DUTTON, W.; ROGERS, E.; AND JUN, S. The diffusion and impacts of information technology in households. See 0753. 133–193.
0755  ZORKOCZY, P. (Ed.) Oxford surveys in information technology; vol. 2, 1985. Oxford University Press, Inc., New York, NY, 1985, 231 pp., $59, ISBN 0-19-859004-0.
0756  WITTEN, I.; AND GREENBERG, S. User interfaces for office systems. See 0755. 69–104.
HCI-0299  LEE, D. Personal computing for decision support. See 0755. 149–163.
HCI-0083  ZUBOFF, S. In the age of the smart machine: the future of work and power. Basic Books, Inc., New York, NY, 1988, 457 pp., $19.95, ISBN 0-465-03212-5.

# Journals

Journals are sorted alphabetically by journal name, then by volume and issue number. Within each issue, the articles are listed in page number order. A guide to journal abbreviations and their full addresses appears on page 1186.

## Abacus

**0758** Misconception in human factors. LEDGARD, H. *Abacus* **3**, 2, (Winter 1986) 21–27.

**0759** Improving human/computer interactions. BURKHARDT, H.; COUPLAND, J.; FRASER, R.; PHILLIPS, R.; AND RIDGWAY, J. *Abacus* **5**, 3, (Spring 1988) 34–48.

## ACM Computing Surveys

**0760** Response time and display rate in human performance with computers. SHNEIDERMAN, B. *ACM Comput. Surv.* **16**, 3, (Sept. 1984).

**HCI-0412** Computer-music interfaces: a survey. PENNYCOOK, B. *ACM Comput. Surv.* **17**, 2, (June 1985) 267–289.

**0761** A framework for choosing a database query language. JARKE, M.; AND VASSILIOU, Y. *ACM Comput. Surv.* **17**, 3, (Sept. 1985) 313–340.

**HCI-0165** 4.2BSD and 4.3BSD as examples of the UNIX system. QUARTERMAN, J.; SILBERSCHATZ, A.; AND PETERSON, J. *ACM Comput. Surv.* **17**, 4, (Dec. 1985) 379–418.

**HCI-0088** Reading text from computer screens. MILLS, C.; AND WELDON, L. *ACM Comput. Surv.* **19**, 4, (Dec. 1987) 329–357.

**HCI-0444** Human-computer interface development: concepts and systems for its management. HARTSON, H.; AND HIX, D. *ACM Comput. Surv.* **21**, 1, (March 1989) 5–92.

## ACM SIGADA Ada Letters

**0762** Interfacing Ada and relational databases. MCCOY, L. *Ada Lett.* **7**, 3, (May/June 1987) 50–59.

**0763** Ada-embedded SQL: the options. DONAHO, J.; AND DAVIS, G. *Ada Lett.* **7**, 3, (May/June 1987) 60–72.

**0764** Using representation clauses as an operating system interface. NYBERG, K. *Ada Lett.* **8**, 4, (July, Aug. 1987) 98–101.

## ACM SIGAPL APL Quote Quad

**0765** Bringing graphic dialogues to APL. SOOP, K. *APL Quote Quad* **16**, 1, (1986) 96–102.

**0766** Open fullscreen systems. GFELLER, M.; AND STENGL, M. *APL Quote Quad* **16**, 4, (1986) 197–201.

**0767** Increasing productivity with ISPF/APL2. MAYHEW, L. *APL Quote Quad* **16**, 4, (1986) 243–251.

**0768** Is the unified keyboard better? EISENBERG, M. *APL Quote Quad* **18**, 4, (June 1988) 13–14.

## ACM SIGARCH Computer Architecture News

**0769** An introduction to computing with neural nets. LIPPMANN, R. *Comput. Archit. News.* **16**, 1, (March, 1988) 7–25.

**0770** Software for neural networks. ANDERSON, J.; WISNIEWSKI, E.; AND VISCUSO, S. *Comput. Archit. News.* **16**, 1, (March, 1988) 26–36.

0771 An integrated system for neural network simulations. GARTH, S.; AND PIKE, D. *Comput. Archit. News.* **16,** 1, (March, 1988) 37–44.

0772 Conference report: IEEE 1'st Int'l conference on neural networks. MAREN, A. *Comput. Archit. News.* **16,** 1, (March, 1988) 45–46.

## ACM SIGART Newsletter

0773 Idea for a mind. JACKSON, J. *SIGART Newsl.* 101, (July 1987) 23–26.

0774 Automatic menu generation. COUSINS, S. *SIGART Newsl.* 102, (October 1, 1987) 21–23.

0775 The effects of restricted syntax on menu-based interaction. HEDEEN, A. *SIGART Newsl.* 103, (Jan., 1988) 35–37.

0776 Interactive learning: a multiexpert paradigm for acquiring new knowledge. LECLAIR, S. *SIGART Newsl.* **108,** (April 1989) 34–44.

0777 Hypertext as a means for knowledge acquisition. WELLS, T. *SIGART Newsl.* **108,** (April 1989) 136–138.

## ACM SIGBDP Data Base

0778 Educating the CBIS user: a case analysis. NELSON, R.; AND CHENEY, P. *Data Base* **18,** 2, (Dec. 1987) 11–16.

0779 Assessment of an effort to integrate computer functions in an engineering design firm. MORELL, J.; AND LEEMON, J. *Data Base* **18,** 2, (Dec. 1987) 17–21.

0780 End-user computing by top executives. HACKATHORN, R. *Data Base* **19,** 1, (Fall/Winter 1987/88) 1–9.

0781 ICE: information center expert: a consultation system for resource allocation. HELTNE, M.; VINZE, A.; KONSYNSKI, B.; AND NUNAMAKER JR., J. *Data Base* **19,** 2, (Summer 1988) 1–15.

## ACM SIGCAPH Newsletter

0782 The MAGNEX text editor for the Comodore Amiga personal computer. VENER, A.; AND GLINERT, E. *SIGCAPH Newsl.* 39, (Spring 1988) 17–20.

0783 Communication methods of the vocally disabled: a review. CONDIE, L. *SIGCAPH Newsl.* **41,** (January 1989) 7–15.

0784 An overview of $T^3$-PBE. YORK, B.; AND KARSHMER, A. *SIGCAPH Newsl.* **41,** (January 1989) 17–20.

## ACM SIGCAS Computers and Society

0785 The interactionist perspective on computer implementation. KOCH, S. *SIGCAS Comput. Soc.* **15,** 4, (Winter 1986) 18–26.

0786 The rational, the pragmatic and the inquiry process: The social study of information- communication systems. TUROFF, M. *SIGCAS Comput. Soc.* **15,** 4, (Winter 1986) 27–31.

0787 Applying the human relations perspective to the study of new media. RICE, R. *SIGCAS Comput. Soc.* **15,** 4, (Winter 1986) 32–37.

0788 Action research on systems development: case study of changing actor roles. FRIIS, S. *SIGCAS Comput. Soc.* **18,** 1, (January 1988) 22–31.

0789 Computer literacy: the pigeonhole principle. MAGRASS, Y.; AND UPCHURCH, R. *SIGCAS Comput. Soc.* **18,** 3, (July 1988) 1–9.

0790 Professional and expert systems: a meeting of minds. NEWMAN, M. *SIGCAS Comput. Soc.* **18,** 3, (July 1988) 14–27.

0791 Computer ethics: an antidote to despair. BLOOMBECKER, J. *SIGCAS Comput. Soc.* **16,17,** 4,1, (Oct./Feb. 1987) 3–11.

0792 The uneasy eighties: the transition to an information society. CORDELL, A. *SIGCAS Comput. Soc.* **16,17**, 4,1, (Oct./Feb. 1987) 12–18.

0793 The effects of computer use in early childhood socialization. BARAKETT, J.; AND PROCHNER, L. *SIGCAS Comput. Soc.* **16,17**, 4,1, (Oct./Feb. 1987) 19–27.

## ACM SIGCHI Bulletin

0794 A user interface for deaf-blind people (preliminary report). LADNER, R.; DAY, R.; GENTRY, D.; MEYER, K.; AND ROSE, S. *SIGCHI Bull.* (May 1987).

0795 Designing optimum CRT text blinking video image presentation. KITAKAZE, S.; AND KASAHARA, Y. *SIGCHI Bull.* (May 1987) 1–6.

0796 Generalization, consistency, and control. LEWIS, C.; HAIR, D.; AND SCHOENBERG, V. *SIGCHI Bull.* (March 1989) 1–5.

0797 Why reading was slower from CRT displays than from paper. GOULD, J.; ALFARO, L.; FINN, R.; HAUPT, B.; AND MINUTO, A. *SIGCHI Bull.* (May 1987) 7–11.

0798 Artifact as theory-nexus: hermeneutics meets theory-based design. CARROLL, J.; AND KELLOGG, W. *SIGCHI Bull.* (March 1989) 7–14.

0799 On the parameters of human visual performance: an investigation of the benefits of antialiasing. BOOTH, K.; BRYDEN, M.; COWAN, W.; MORGAN, M.; AND PLANTE, B. *SIGCHI Bull.* (May 1987) 13–19.

0800 Programmable user models for predictive evaluation of interface designs. YOUNG, R.; GREEN, T.; AND SIMON, T. *SIGCHI Bull.* (March 1989) 15–19.

0801 Approximate modelling of cognitive activity: towards an expert system design aid. BARNARD, P.; WILSON, M.; AND MACLEAN, A. *SIGCHI Bull.* (May 1987) 21–26.

0802 Experience with contextual field research. GOOD, M.; CAMPBELL, R.; LYNCH, G.; AND WRIGHT, P. *SIGCHI Bull.* (March 1989) 21–24.

0803 Color in user interface design: functionally and aesthetics. MARCUS, A.; COWAN, W.; AND SMITH, W. *SIGCHI Bull.* (March 1989) 25–27.

0804 Transfer between text editors. POLSON, P.; BOVAIR, S.; AND KIERAS, D. *SIGCHI Bull.* (May 1987) 27–32.

0805 LIZA: an extensible groupware toolkit. GIBBS, S. *SIGCHI Bull.* (March 1989) 29–35.

0806 Predicting the time to recall computer command abbreviations. JOHN, B.; AND NEWELL, A. *SIGCHI Bull.* (May 1987) 33–40.

0807 Collaboration in KMS, a shared hypermedia system. YODER, E.; AKSCYN, R.; AND MCCRACKEN, D. *SIGCHI Bull.* (March 1989) 37–42.

0808 Voice: technology searching for communication needs. AUCELLA, A.; KINKEAD, R.; WICHANSKY, A.; AND SHMANDT, C. *SIGCHI Bull.* (May 1987) 41–44.

0809 The effects of bargaining orientation and communication medium on negotiations in the bilateral monopoly task: a comparison of decision room and computer conferencing communication media. SHEFFIELD, J. *SIGCHI Bull.* (March 1989) 43–48.

0810 Notecards in a nutshell. HALASZ, F.; MORAN, T.; AND TRIGG, R. *SIGCHI Bull.* (May 1987) 45–52.

0811 University of Colorado at Boulder, Institute of cognitive science. FISCHER, G.; AND DOANE, S. *SIGCHI Bull.* (March 1989) 49–50.

0812 What is EuroParc? MORAN, T. *SIGCHI Bull.* (March 1989) 51–52.

0813 A multiple, virtual-workspace interface to support user task switching. CARD, S.; AND HENDERSON JR., A. *SIGCHI Bull.* (May 1987) 53–59.

0814 NYNEX intelligent systems group. ATWOOD, M. *SIGCHI Bull.* (March 1989) 53–54.

0815 NASA Johnson Space Center, Human-Computer Interaction. RUDISILL, M.; AND GILLAN, D. *SIGCHI Bull.* (March 1989) 55–56.

0816 Inducing programs in a direct-manipulation environment. MAULSBY, D.; AND WITTEN, I. *SIGCHI Bull.* (March 1989) 57–62.

0817 Experiences with the alternate reality kit: an example of the tension between literalism and magic. SMITH, R. *SIGCHI Bull.* (May 1987) 61–67.

0818 A system for example-based programming. NEAL, L. *SIGCHI Bull.* (March 1989) 63–68.
0819 A case example of human factors in product definition: needs finding for a voice output workstation for the blind. KANE, R.; AND YUSCHIK, M. *SIGCHI Bull.* (May 1987) 69–73.
0820 Some strategies of reuse in an object-oriented programming environment. LANGE, B.; AND MOHER, T. *SIGCHI Bull.* (March 1989) 69–73.
0821 Towards universality of access: interfacing physically disabled students to the Icon educational microcomputer. VERBURG, G.; FIELD, D.; ST. PIERRE, F.; AND NAUMANN, S. *SIGCHI Bull.* (May 1987) 75–80.
0822 A spreadsheet interface for logic programming. SPENKE, M.; AND BEILKEN, C. *SIGCHI Bull.* (March 1989) 75–80.
0823 On-line tutorials: What kind of inference leads to the most effective learning? BLACK, J.; BECHTOLD, J.; MITRANI, M.; AND CARROLL, J. *SIGCHI Bull.* (March 1989) 81–83.
0824 How some advice fails. HILL, W. *SIGCHI Bull.* (March 1989) 85–90.
0825 Responding to "HUH?": answering vaguely articulated follow-up questions. MOORE, J. *SIGCHI Bull.* (March 1989) 91–96.
0826 Interface design: a neglected issue in educational software. FRYE, D.; AND SOLOWAY, E. *SIGCHI Bull.* (May 1987) 93–97.
0827 Protecting user interfaces through copyright: the debate. SAMUELSON, P. *SIGCHI Bull.* (March 1989) 97–104.
0828 Cognition-sensitive design and user modeling for syntax-directed editors. NEAL, L. *SIGCHI Bull.* (May 1987) 99–102.
0829 A self-regulating adaptive system. TREVELLYAN, R.; AND BROWNE, D. *SIGCHI Bull.* (May 1987) 103–107.
0830 Drama and personality in user interface design. MOUNTFORD, S.; BUXTON, B.; KRUEGER, M.; LAUREL, B.; AND VERTELNEY, L. *SIGCHI Bull.* (March 1989) 105–108.
0831 Cumulating the science of HCI: from s-R compatibility to transcription typing. JOHN, B.; AND NEWELL, A. *SIGCHI Bull.* (March 1989) 109–114.
0832 Learning and transfer of measurement tasks. LEE, A.; POLSON, P.; AND BAILEY, W. *SIGCHI Bull.* (March 1989) 115–120.
0833 Social science and system design: interdisciplinary collaborations. SUCHMAN, L.; BEEMAN, W.; PEAR, M.; FOX, B.; AND SMOLENSKY, P. *SIGCHI Bull.* (May 1987) 121–123.
0834 Skilled financial planning: the cost of translating ideas into action. LERCH, F.; MANTEI, M.; AND OLSON, J. *SIGCHI Bull.* (March 1989) 121–126.
0835 Positioning human factors in the user interface development chain. GRUDIN, J.; EHRLICH, S.; AND SHRINER, R. *SIGCHI Bull.* (May 1987) 125–131.
0836 A case study of user interface management system development and application. MANHEIMER, J.; BURNETT, R.; AND WALLERS, J. *SIGCHI Bull.* (March 1989) 127–132.
0837 The interface is often not the problem. GORANSSON, B.; LIND, M.; PETTERSSON, E.; SANDBLAD, B.; AND SCHWALBE, P. *SIGCHI Bull.* (May 1987) 133–136.
0838 A high-level user interface management system. SINGH, G.; AND GREEN, M. *SIGCHI Bull.* (March 1989) 133–138.
0839 Designing for designers: an analysis of design practice in the real world. ROSSON, M.; MAASS, S.; AND KELLOGG, W. *SIGCHI Bull.* (May 1987) 137–142.
0840 Graphical specification of user interfaces with behavior abstraction. DESOI, J.; LIVELY, W.; AND SHEPPARD, S. *SIGCHI Bull.* (March 1989) 139–144.
0841 Center for coordination science, MIT. MALONE, T. *SIGCHI Bull.* (March 1989) 145–146.
0842 CHI research at MCC. HOLLAN, J.; AND CURTIS, B. *SIGCHI Bull.* (March 1989) 147–149.
0843 Cognitive science and machine intelligence laboratory, University of Michigan. OLSON, G. *SIGCHI Bull.* (March 1989) 151–152.
0844 The ergonomics psychology project at Inria. BISSERET, A. *SIGCHI Bull.* (March 1989) 153–154.
0845 Issues limiting the acceptance of user interfaces using gesture input and handwriting character recognition. SIBERT, J.; BUFFA, M.; CRANE, H.; DOSTER, W.; AND RHYNE, J. *SIGCHI Bull.* (May 1987) 155–158.
0846 Bat brushes: on the uses of six position and orientation parameters in a paint program. WARE, C.; AND BAXTER, C. *SIGCHI Bull.* (March 1989) 155–160.

0847 Circling: a method of mouse-based selection without button presses. JACKSON, J.; AND ROSKE-HOFSTRAND, R. *SIGCHI Bull.* (March 1989) 161-166.

0848 Systemic implications of leap and an improved two-part cursor. RASKIN, J. *SIGCHI Bull.* (March 1989) 167-170.

0849 A programming language basis for user interface. OLSEN, D. *SIGCHI Bull.* (March 1989) 171-176.

0850 Statemaster: A UIMS based on statechart for prototyping and target implementation. WELLNER, P. *SIGCHI Bull.* (March 1989) 177-182.

0851 Task-oriented representation of asynchronous user interfaces. SIOCHI, A.; AND HARTSON, H. *SIGCHI Bull.* (March 1989) 183-188.

0852 Innovation in user interface development: obstacles and opportunities. POLTROCK, S. *SIGCHI Bull.* (March 1989) 191-195.

0853 User interface design in large corporations: coordination and communication across disciplines. GRUDIN, J.; AND POLTROCK, S. *SIGCHI Bull.* (March 1989) 197-203.

0854 How do experienced information lens users use rules? MACKAY, W.; MALONE, T.; CROWSTON, K.; RAO, R.; ROSENBLITT, D.; AND CARD, S. *SIGCHI Bull.* (March 1989) 211-216.

0855 Performance, preference, and visual scan patterns on a menu-based system: implications for interface design. HENDRICKSON, J. *SIGCHI Bull.* (March 1989) 217-222.

0856 "My user interface is the best because...". FARRAND, A.; ERICKSON, T.; HOEBER, T.; PARKHURST, B.; AND WILSON, T. *SIGCHI Bull.* (March 1989) 223-225.

0857 Synergistic use of direct manipulation and natural language. COHEN, P.; DALRYMPLE, M.; MORAN, D.; PEREIRA, F.; AND SULLIVAN, J. *SIGCHI Bull.* (March 1989) 227-233.

0858 A synthetic visual environment with hand gesturing and voice input. WEIMER, D.; AND GANAPATHY, S. *SIGCHI Bull.* (March 1989) 235-240.

0859 Speech and gestures for graphic image manipulation. HAUPTMANN, A. *SIGCHI Bull.* (March 1989) 241-245.

0860 Design rationale: the argument behind the artifact. MACLEAN, A.; YOUNG, R.; AND MORAN, T. *SIGCHI Bull.* (March 1989) 247-252.

0861 Conversational resources for situated action. FROHLICH, D.; AND LUFF, P. *SIGCHI Bull.* (March 1989) 253-258.

0862 Prototyping techniques for different problem contexts. GUTIERREZ, O. *SIGCHI Bull.* (March 1989) 259-264.

0863 The role of laboratory experiments in HCI: help, hindrance, or ho-hum? WOLF, C.; CARROLL, J.; LANDAUER, T.; JOHN, B.; WHITESIDE, J.; AND WOLF, C. *SIGCHI Bull.* (March 1989) 265-268.

0864 Design environments for constructive and argumentative design. FISCHER, G.; MCCALL, R.; AND MORCH, A. *SIGCHI Bull.* (March 1989) 269-275.

0865 Generating highly interactive user interfaces. WIECHA, C.; BENNETT, W.; BOIES, S.; AND GOULD, J. *SIGCHI Bull.* (March 1989) 277-282.

0866 Directed dialogue protocols: verbal data for user interface design. KNOX, S.; BAILEY, W.; AND LYNCH, E. *SIGCHI Bull.* (March 1989) 283-287.

0867 Conversational hypertext: information access through natural language dialogues with computers. WHALEN, T.; AND PATRICK, A. *SIGCHI Bull.* (March 1989) 289-292.

0868 The tourist artificial reality. FAIRCHILD, K.; MEREDITH, G.; AND WEXELBLAT, A. *SIGCHI Bull.* (March 1989) 299-304.

0869 Human-computer interaction department, Hewlett-Packard Laboratories. KENDZIERSKI, N. *SIGCHI Bull.* (March 1989) 305-306.

0870 Cognitive user interface laboratory, GMD-IPSI. HOPPE, H.; KING, R.; AND TISSEN, A. *SIGCHI Bull.* (March 1989) 307-308.

0871 Human-computer interaction lab, University of Maryland. SHNEIDERMAN, B. *SIGCHI Bull.* (March 1989) 309-310.

0872 Search technology, Inc. HUNT, R. *SIGCHI Bull.* (March 1989) 311-312.

0873 Planar maps: an interaction paradigm for graphic design. BAUDELAIRE, P.; AND GANGNET, M. *SIGCHI Bull.* (March 1989) 313-318.

0874 Encapsulating interactive behaviors. MYERS, B. *SIGCHI Bull.* (March 1989) 319-324.

0875 Constraint grammars–a new model for specifying graphical applications. ZANDEN, B. *SIGCHI Bull.* (March 1989) 325–330.
0876 The effects of device technology on the usability of advanced telephone functions. ROBERTS, T.; AND ENGELBECK, G. *SIGCHI Bull.* (March 1989) 331–337.
0877 An experiment into the use of auditory cues to reduce visual workload. BROWN, M.; NEWSOME, S.; AND GLINERT, E. *SIGCHI Bull.* (March 1989) 339–346.
0878 The design of phone-based interfaces for consumers. HALSTEAD-NUSSLOCH, R. *SIGCHI Bull.* (March 1989) 347–352.
0879 Tools for supporting cooperative work near and far: highlights from the CSCW conference. EHRLICH, S.; BIKSON, T.; MACKAY, W.; AND TANG, J. *SIGCHI Bull.* (March 1989) 353–356.
0880 Helgon: extending the retrieval by reformulation paradigm. FISCHER, G.; AND NIEPER-LEMKE, H. *SIGCHI Bull.* (March 1989) 357–362.
0881 User-interface design for a clinical neurophysiological intensive monitoring system. COLLURA, T.; JACOBS, E.; BURGESS, R.; AND KLEM, G. *SIGCHI Bull.* (March 1989) 363–368.
0882 A document layout system using automatic document architecture extraction. IWAI, I.; DOI, M.; YAMAGUCHI, K.; FUKUI, M.; AND TAKEBAYASHI, Y. *SIGCHI Bull.* (March 1989) 369–374.
0883 Models of user interactions with graphical interfaces: 1. statistical. GILLAN, D.; LEWIS, R.; AND RUDISILL, M. *SIGCHI Bull.* (March 1989) 375–380.
0884 Understanding Bayesian reasoning via graphical displays. COLE, W. *SIGCHI Bull.* (March 1989) 381–386.
0885 Mathematical formula editor for CAI. NAKAYAMA, Y. *SIGCHI Bull.* (March 1989) 387–392.
0886 User interface design: Are human factors principles used? GRIMES, J.; EHRLICH, K.; AND VASKE, J. *SIGCHI Bull.* **17**, 3, (Jan. 1986) 22–26.
0887 Human-computer interaction research at the university of Maryland. SHNEIDERMAN, B. *SIGCHI Bull.* **17**, 3, (Jan. 1986) 27–32.
0888 The role of menu titles as a navigational aid in hierarchical menus. GRAY, J. *SIGCHI Bull.* **17**, 3, (Jan. 1986) 33–40.
0889 Learning disabled students' difficulties in learning to use a word processor: implications for design. MACARTHUR, C.; AND SHNEIDERMAN, B. *SIGCHI Bull.* **17**, 3, (Jan. 1986) 41–46.
0890 Bibliography: Individual differences and computer-human interaction. BUIE, E. *SIGCHI Bull.* **17**, 3, (Jan. 1986) 47–47.
0891 The information lens: an intelligent system for information sharing in organizations. MALONE, T.; GRANT, K.; AND TURBAK, F. *SIGCHI Bull.* **17**, 4, (April 1986) 1–8.
0892 Graphic interfaces for knowledge-based system development. POLTROCK, S.; STEINER, D.; AND TARLTON, P. *SIGCHI Bull.* **17**, 4, (April 1986) 9–15.
0893 Generalized fisheye views. FURNAS, G. *SIGCHI Bull.* **17**, 4, (April 1986) 16–23.
0894 User modeling in UC, the UNIX consultant. CHIN, D. *SIGCHI Bull.* **17**, 4, (April 1986) 24–28.
0895 TNT: a talking tutor 'n' trainer for teaching use of interactive computer systems. NAKATANI, L.; EGAN, D.; RUEDISUELI, L.; HAWLEY, P.; AND LEWART, D. *SIGCHI Bull.* **17**, 4, (April 1986) 29–34.
0896 Advising roles of a computer consultant. MCKENDREE, J.; AND CARROLL, J. *SIGCHI Bull.* **17**, 4, (April 1986) 35–40.
0897 The computer as musical accompanist. BUXTON, W.; AND DANNENBERG, R. *SIGCHI Bull.* **17**, 4, (April 1986) 41–43.
0898 The enhancement of understanding through visual representations. BOCKER, H.; FISCHER, G.; AND NIEPER, H. *SIGCHI Bull.* **17**, 4, (April 1986) 44–50.
0899 Transfer between word processing systems. KARAT, J.; BOYES, L.; WEISGERBER, S.; AND SCHAFER, C. *SIGCHI Bull.* **17**, 4, (April 1986) 67–71.
0900 Learning and transfer for text and graphics editing with a direct manipulation interface. ZIEGLER, J.; HOPPE, H.; AND FAHNRICH, K. *SIGCHI Bull.* **17**, 4, (April 1986) 72–77.
0901 A test of a common elements theory of transfer. POLSON, P.; MUNCHER, E.; AND ENGELBECK, G. *SIGCHI Bull.* **17**, 4, (April 1986) 78–83.
0902 Classifying users: a hard look at some controversial issues. POTOSNAK, K.; HAYES, P.; ROSSON, M.; SCHNEIDER, M.; AND WHITESIDE, J. *SIGCHI Bull.* **17**, 4, (April 1986) 84–88.

**0903** How are windows used? Some notes on creating an empirically-based windowing benchmark task. GAYLIN, K. *SIGCHI Bull.* **17**, 4, (April 1986) 96–100.
**0904** A comparison of tiled and overlapping windows. BLY, S.; AND ROSENBERG, J. *SIGCHI Bull.* **17**, 4, (April 1986) 101–106.
**0905** A cognitive model of database querying: a tool for novice instruction. SCHLAGER, M.; AND OGDEN, W. *SIGCHI Bull.* **17**, 4, (April 1986) 107–113.
**0906** DOMAIN/DELPHI: retrieving documents online. ORWICK, P.; JAYNES, J.; BARSTOW, T.; AND BOHN, L. *SIGCHI Bull.* **17**, 4, (April 1986) 114–121.
**0907** The effects of structured, multi-level documentation. HOLT, R.; BOEHM-DAVIS, D.; AND SCHULTZ, A. *SIGCHI Bull.* **17**, 4, (April 1986) 122–128.
**0908** Socio-tech: what is it (and why should we care)? PEW, R.; ASSUNTO, K.; BAKER, W.; DRAY, S.; AND TAYLOR, J. *SIGCHI Bull.* **17**, 4, (April 1986) 129–130.
**0909** Animated graphical interfaces using temporal constraints. DUISBERG, R. *SIGCHI Bull.* **17**, 4, (April 1986) 131–136.
**0910** Defining constraints graphically. BORNING, A. *SIGCHI Bull.* **17**, 4, (April 1986) 137–143.
**0911** A user interface for multiple-process, turnkey systems targeted for the novice user. KIMERER, B. *SIGCHI Bull.* **17**, 4, (April 1986) 137–143.
**0912** Learning modes and subsequent use of computer-mediated communication systems. HILTZ, S. *SIGCHI Bull.* **17**, 4, (April 1986) 149–155.
**0913** Voice messaging enhancing the user interface design based on field performance. AUCELLA, A.; AND EHRLICH, S. *SIGCHI Bull.* **17**, 4, (April 1986) 156–161.
**0914** Designing a quality voice: an analysis of listeners' reactions to synthetic voices. ROSSON, M.; AND CECALA, A. *SIGCHI Bull.* **17**, 4, (April 1986) 192–197.
**0915** Speech recognition enhancement by lip information. NISHIDA, S. *SIGCHI Bull.* **17**, 4, (April 1986) 198–204.
**0916** Comparison of elderly and younger users on keyboard and voice input computer-based composition tasks. OGOZALEK, V.; AND VAN PRAAG, J. *SIGCHI Bull.* **17**, 4, (April 1986) 205–211.
**0917** Usability testing in the real world. MILLS, C.; BURY, K.; ROBERTS, T.; TOGNAZZINI, B.; WICHANSKY, A.; AND REED, P. *SIGCHI Bull.* **17**, 4, (April 1986) 212–215.
**0918** Rapid prototyping and system development: examination of an interface toolkit for voice and telephony applications. RICHARDS, J.; BOIES, S.; AND GOULD, J. *SIGCHI Bull.* **17**, 4, (April 1986) 216–220.
**0919** The Trillium user interface design environment. HENDERSON JR., D. *SIGCHI Bull.* **17**, 4, (April 1986) 221–227.
**0920** An interactive environment for dialogue development: its design, use and evaluation; or, is aide useful? HIX, D.; AND HARTSON, H. *SIGCHI Bull.* **17**, 4, (April 1986) 228–234.
**0921** The elicitation of system knowledge by picture probes. BARNARD, P.; WILSON, M.; AND MACLEAN, A. *SIGCHI Bull.* **17**, 4, (April 1986) 235–240.
**0922** User-derived impact analysis as a tool for usability engineering. GOOD, M.; SPINE, T.; WHITESIDE, J.; AND GEORGE, P. *SIGCHI Bull.* **17**, 4, (April 1986) 241–246.
**0923** On designing for usability: an application of four key principles. HEWETT, T.; AND MEADOW, C. *SIGCHI Bull.* **17**, 4, (April 1986) 247–252.
**0924** Human computer interaction in the year 2000. THOMAS, J.; BROWN, J.; BUXTON, W.; CURTIS, B.; AND LANDAUER, T. *SIGCHI Bull.* **17**, 4, (April 1986) 253–255.
**0925** The formal specification of adaptive user interfaces using command language grammar. BROWNE, D.; SHARRATT, B.; AND NORMAN, M. *SIGCHI Bull.* **17**, 4, (April 1986) 256–260.
**0926** An input-output model of interactive systems. SHAW, M. *SIGCHI Bull.* **17**, 4, (April 1986) 261–273.
**0927** Formatting space-related displays to optimize expert and nonexpert user performance. BURNS, M.; WARREN, D.; AND RUDISILL, M. *SIGCHI Bull.* **17**, 4, (April 1986) 274–280.
**0928** Designing in the dark: logics that compete with the user. GRUDIN, J. *SIGCHI Bull.* **17**, 4, (April 1986) 281–284.
**0929** A formal interface design methodology based on user knowledge. McDONALD, J.; DEARHOLT, D.; PAAP, K.; AND SCHVANEVELDT, R. *SIGCHI Bull.* **17**, 4, (April 1986) 285–290.
**0930** The memory extender personal filing system. JONES, W. *SIGCHI Bull.* **17**, 4, (April 1986) 298–305.

0931 A model of mental model construction. LEWIS, C. *SIGCHI Bull.* **17**, 4, (April 1986) 306–313.
0932 Intelligent interfaces: user models and planners. QUINN, L.; AND RUSSELL, D. *SIGCHI Bull.* **17**, 4, (April 1986) 314–320.
0933 A study in two-handed input. BUXTON, W.; AND MYERS, B. *SIGCHI Bull.* **17**, 4, (April 1986) 321–326.
0934 Autocompletion in full text transaction entry: a method for humanized input. JAKOBSSON, M. *SIGCHI Bull.* **17**, 4, (April 1986) 327–332.
0935 Of moles and men: the design of foot controls for workstations. PEARSON, G.; AND WEISER, M. *SIGCHI Bull.* **17**, 4, (April 1986) 333–339.
0936 Managing the design of user-computer interfaces. FOLEY, J.; BOIES, S.; AND ZIMMER, W. *SIGCHI Bull.* **17**, 4, (April 1986) 340–342.
0937 Seven plus or minus two central issues in human-computer interaction. SHNEIDERMAN, B. *SIGCHI Bull.* **17**, 4, (April 1986) 343–349.
0938 The standards factor. MEADS, J. *SIGCHI Bull.* **18**, 1, (July 1986) 33–34.
0939 Legal liability for malfunction and misuse of expert systems. LUCASH, R. *SIGCHI Bull.* **18**, 1, (July 1986) 35–43.
0940 Interactive recognition of handprinted characters for computer input. WARD, J.; AND BLESSER, B. *SIGCHI Bull.* **18**, 1, (July 1986) 44–57.
0941 A directory of sources for interactive technologies. BUXTON, W. *SIGCHI Bull.* **18**, 1, (July 1986) 58–63.
0942 Developing computer aided design technology in China. GALLAGHER, R. *SIGCHI Bull.* **18**, 2, (Oct. 1986) 9–13.
0943 No members, no officers, no dues: A ten year history of the software psychology society. SHNEIDERMAN, B. *SIGCHI Bull.* **18**, 2, (Oct. 1986) 14–16.
0944 In search of a user interface reference model. LYNCH, G.; AND MEADS, J. *SIGCHI Bull.* **18**, 2, (Oct. 1986) 25–33.
0945 Dialogue management reference model. SISSON, N. *SIGCHI Bull.* **18**, 2, (Oct. 1986) 34–35.
0946 On user interface reference models. LANTZ, K. *SIGCHI Bull.* **18**, 2, (Oct. 1986) 36–42.
0947 Pictorial representations of abstract concepts relating to human-computer interaction. ROGERS, Y. *SIGCHI Bull.* **18**, 2, (Oct. 1986) 43–44.
0948 Separating the user interface from the functionality of application programs. SZEKELY, P. *SIGCHI Bull.* **18**, 2, (Oct. 1986) 45–46.
0949 Dialog management in interactive systems: a comparative survey. BRITTS, S. *SIGCHI Bull.* **18**, 3, (Jan. 1987) 30–42.
0950 Graphic invention for user interfaces: an experimental course in user-interface design. VERPLANK, B.; AND KIM, S. *SIGCHI Bull.* **18**, 3, (Jan. 1987) 50–66.
0951 Usability testing in the real world. MILLS, C. *SIGCHI Bull.* **18**, 3, (Jan. 1987) 67–70.
0952 The standards factor. MEADS, J. *SIGCHI Bull.* **19**, 1, (July 1987) 34–35.
0953 Usability testing in the real world. MILLS, C. *SIGCHI Bull.* **19**, 1, (July 1987) 43–46.
0954 A comparison of textual information retention from CRT terminals and paper. WYLE, M. *SIGCHI Bull.* **19**, 1, (July 1987) 47–50.
0955 CSCW '86 Conference summary report. KRASNER, H. *SIGCHI Bull.* **19**, 1, (July 1987) 51–53.
0956 Computer-support cooperative work. NIELSEN, J. *SIGCHI Bull.* **19**, 1, (July 1987) 54–61.
0957 Human factors in computer systems: some useful readings. GREEN, P. *SIGCHI Bull.* **19**, 2, (October 1, 1987) 15–20.
0958 How faithfully should the electronic office simulate real one? JOHNSON, J. *SIGCHI Bull.* **19**, 2, (October 1, 1987) 21–25.
0959 Software development snapshots: A preliminary investigation. LEVENTHAL, L. *SIGCHI Bull.* **19**, 2, (October 1, 1987) 26–29.
0960 Classification of dialog techniques. NIELSEN, J. *SIGCHI Bull.* **19**, 2, (October 1, 1987) 30–35.
0961 A change of mind or the story of Fuzzies in Purgatory. LUEBKING, S. *SIGCHI Bull.* **19**, 3, (January 1988) 28–36.
0962 Videotex information packagers: a field study aimed at tomorrow's videotex authoring interface. KELLEY, J. *SIGCHI Bull.* **19**, 3, (January 1988) 37–47.

## JOURNALS

0963 Modes survey. JOHNSON, J.; AND ENGELBECK, G. *SIGCHI Bull.* **19**, 4, (April, 1988) 6–10.
0964 Interact '87. NIELSEN, J. *SIGCHI Bull.* **19**, 4, (April, 1988) 36–42.
0965 The standards factor. GRUDIN, J. *SIGCHI Bull.* **20**, 1, (July 1988) 16–19.
0966 History, state and future of user interface management systems. LÖWGREN, J. *SIGCHI Bull.* **20**, 1, (July 1988) 32–44.
0967 Once more, with meaning. LUEBKING, S. *SIGCHI Bull.* **20**, 1, (July 1988) 54–58.
0968 Designing conceptual models of dialog: a case for dialog charts. ARIAV, G.; AND CALLOWAY, L. *SIGCHI Bull.* **20**, 2, (Oct. 1988) 23–27.
0969 The effectiveness of a keystroke line in interactive tutorials. CAMPBELL, G. *SIGCHI Bull.:A* **20**, 2, (Oct. 1988) 27–29.
0970 Navigational aids and learning styles: structural optimal training for computer users. COHAN, L.; AND NEWSOME, S. *SIGCHI Bull.* **20**, 2, (Oct. 1988) 30–32.
0971 Preferences for power in expert systems by novice users. COOVERT, M.; MCNELIS, K.; RAMAKRISHNA, K.; AND SALA, E. *SIGCHI Bull.* **20**, 2, (Oct. 1988) 32–33.
0972 Evaluation of mental models and meta models through interactions between users and helpers about software usage problems. DEHDASHTI, P. *SIGCHI Bull.* **20**, 2, (Oct. 1988) 33–33.
0973 Dialing a name: alphabetic entry through a telephone keypad. FAST, L.; AND BALLANTINE, R. *SIGCHI Bull.* **20**, 2, (Oct. 1988) 34–34.
0974 An authoring system for the creation of interfaces for disabled users. FERRIER, L.; AND FELL, H. *SIGCHI Bull.* **20**, 2, (Oct. 1988) 35–38.
0975 Fine tuning selection semantics in a structure editor based programming environment: some experimental results. GOLDENSON, D.; AND LEWIS, M. *SIGCHI Bull.* **20**, 2, (Oct. 1988) 38–43.
0976 Computer aids for vision and employment (CAVE). GRIFFITH, D.; DOSS, H.; AND WINFREE, D. *SIGCHI Bull.* **20**, 2, (Oct. 1988) 43–45.
0977 Articulating the experience of transparency: an example of field research techniques. HOLTZBLATT, K.; JONES, S.; AND GOOD, M. *SIGCHI Bull.* **20**, 2, (Oct. 1988) 45–47.
0978 Problem solving performance and display preference for information displays depicting numerical functions. LALOMIA, M.; COOVERT, M.; AND SALAS, E. *SIGCHI Bull.* **20**, 2, (Oct. 1988) 47–51.
0979 User interface primitives to allow full functional use of computers by physically disabled persons. MCDOUGALL, J.; FELS, D.; MILNER, M.; AND MACMILLAN, H. *SIGCHI Bull.* **20**, 2, (Oct. 1988) 51–52.
0980 Development of a three-dimensional auditory display system. WENZEL, E.; WIGHTMAN, F.; AND FOSTER, S. *SIGCHI Bull.* **20**, 2, (Oct. 1988) 52–57.
0981 CHI '88 trip report. NIELSEN, J. *SIGCHI Bull.* **20**, 2, (Oct. 1988) 58–66.
0982 Designing real-time, decision support computer-human interaction. HEFLEY, W. *SIGCHI Bull.* **20**, 2, (Oct. 1988) 67–69.
0983 Designing menu display format to match input device format. PERLMAN, G.; AND SHERWIN, L. *SIGCHI Bull.* **20**, 2, (Oct. 1988) 78–82.
0984 Word processing techniques and user learning preferences. RABAN, A. *SIGCHI Bull.* **20**, 2, (Oct. 1988) 83–87.
0985 A vision of education in user-centered system and interface design. BAECKER, R. *SIGCHI Bull.* **20**, 3, (Jan. 1989) 10–13.
0986 The standards factor. MEADS, J. *SIGCHI Bull.* **20**, 3, (Jan. 1989) 22–23.
0987 The development of ergonomic standards. DZIDA, W. *SIGCHI Bull.* **20**, 3, (Jan. 1989) 35–42.
0988 Posture and VDU operator satisfaction. OMAN, P.; GOMES, C.; RAINS, K.; AND MORANDI, M. *SIGCHI Bull.* **20**, 3, (Jan. 1989) 52–57.
0989 Human factors in teaching. SHARPE, D.; AND WILLSHIRE, M. *SIGCHI Bull.* **20**, 3, (Jan. 1989) 58–62.
0990 Coordinating user interfaces for consistency. NIELSEN, J. *SIGCHI Bull.* **20**, 3, (Jan. 1989) 63–65.
0991 CHI '88 Workshop on Real Time, decision support computer-human interaction. JACOBS, S. *SIGCHI Bull.* **20**, 3, (Jan. 1989) 66–70.
0992 CHI '88 poster session papers and abstracts. EVANS, S. *SIGCHI Bull.* **20**, 3, (Jan. 1989).
0993 Development and evaluation of direct manipulation lists (poster session). BECK, D.; AND ELKERTON, J. *SIGCHI Bull.* **20**, 3, (Jan. 1989) 72–78.

0994 Report on the Collaborative Technology Developers' Workshop. ABEL, M.; AND REIN, G. *SIGCHI Bull.* **20**, 3, (Jan. 1989) 86–89.

0995 Visual system browser. HUDLICKA, E. *SIGCHI Bull.* **20**, 4, (April 1989) 18–24.

0996 Seven experiences with contextual field research. GOOD, M. *SIGCHI Bull.* **20**, 4, (April 1989) 25–32.

0997 Dynamic versus static menus: an exploratory comparison. MITCHELL, J.; AND SHNEIDERMAN, B. *SIGCHI Bull.* **20**, 4, (April 1989) 33–37.

0998 Modes survey results. JOHNSON, J.; AND ENGELBECK, G. *SIGCHI Bull.* **20**, 4, (April 1989) 38–50.

0999 How would your favourite user model cope with these scenarios? YOUNG, R.; BARNARD, P.; SIMON, T.; AND WHITTINGTON, J. *SIGCHI Bull.* **20**, 4, (April 1989) 51–55.

01000 Including a user interface management system (UIMS) in the performance relationship model. TRUMBLY, J.; AND ARNETT, K. *SIGCHI Bull.* **20**, 4, (April 1989) 56–62.

01001 Report on the workshop on analytical models. BUTLER, K.; BENNETT, J.; POLSON, P.; AND KARRAT, J. *SIGCHI Bull.* **20**, 4, (April 1989) 63–79.

01002 CSCW'88: report on the conference & review of the proceedings. GRUDIN, J. *SIGCHI Bull.* **20**, 4, (April 1989) 80–84.

01003 The standard factor. BILLINGSLEY, P. *SIGCHI Bull.* **21**, 1, (July 1989) 14–16.

01004 An annotated bibliography on user interface design. FRASER, P.; AND LAMB, D. *SIGCHI Bull.* **21**, 1, (July 1989) 17–28.

01005 Methodology for comparative selection of interactive database interface types. CRISTIANO, L. *SIGCHI Bull.* **21**, 1, (July 1989) 29–36.

01006 Stimulating change through usability testing. DUMAS, J. *SIGCHI Bull.* **21**, 1, (July 1989) 37–44.

01007 Teaching user interface design based on usability engineering. NIELSEN, J.; AND MOLICH, R. *SIGCHI Bull.* **21**, 1, (July 1989) 45–48.

01008 The 1988 CSCW: trip report. GREENBERG, S. *SIGCHI Bull.* **21**, 1, (July 1989) 49–55.

01009 Interfaces for cooperative work: an eclectic look at CSCW '88. ERICKSON, T. *SIGCHI Bull.* **21**, 1, (July 1989) 55–64.

01010 Information detective: a workstation for exploring three dimensional information space. KOJIMA, K. *SIGCHI Bull.* **21**, 1, (July 1989) 78–79.

01011 Item selection from menus: the influence of menu organization, query interpretation, and programming experience on selection strategies. ARNOLD, L. *SIGCHI Bull.* **21**, 1, (July 1989) 81–85.

01012 Creating consistency in the user interface: opinions and procedures of software developments experts. HAPP, A.; AND COHEN, K. *SIGCHI Bull.* **21**, 1, (July 1989) 85–87.

01013 An empirical approach to the evaluation of icons. WEBB, J.; SORENSON, P.; AND LYONS, N. *SIGCHI Bull.* **21**, 1, (July 1989) 87–90.

01014 Beacons an initial program comprehension. WIEDENBECK, S.; AND SCHOLTZ, J. *SIGCHI Bull.* **21**, 1, (July 1989) 90–91.

01015 A transfer of skill between programming languages. SCHOLTZ, J. *SIGCHI Bull.* **21**, 1, (July 1989).

01016 Designing the "cockpit": the application of a human-centered design philosophy to make optimization systems accessible. COLGAN, L.; SPENCE, R.; RANKIN, P.; AND APPLERLEY, M. *SIGCHI Bull.* **21**, 1, (July 1989) 92–95.

01017 FINGER—Formalizing Interaction for Gesture Recognition. WEBER, G.; AND WETZEL, P. *SIGCHI Bull.* **21**, 1, (July 1989) 96–97.

## ACM SIGCOMM Computer Communication Review

01018 Resource management scheme in distributed environments. NAKAMURA, O.; AND SAITO, N. *Comput. Commun. Rev.* **17**, 5, (August 1987) 328–334.

## ACM SIGCPR Computer Personnel

01019 Key factors in knowledge acquisition. FELLERS, J. *Comput. Pers.* **11**, 1, (May 1987) 10–24.

## JOURNALS

**01020** PLEXACT: an architecture & design of a knowledge-based system for information systems development. CHEN, M.; NUNAMAKER JR., J.; AND KONSYNSKI, B. *Comput. Pers.* **11**, 2, (Sept. 1987) 2–10.

**01021** Job histories as predictors of career success in management information systems. MORGAN, M. *Comput. Pers.* **11**, 2, (Sept. 1987) 11–15.

**01022** Validation of a Jungian instrument for MIS research. MAWHINNEY, C.; AND LEDERER, A. *Comput. Pers.* **11**, 3, (Jan., 1988) 2–9.

**01023** People and organizations in software production: a review of the literature. NASH, S.; AND REDWINE, S. *Comput. Pers.* **11**, 3, (Jan., 1988) 10–21.

**01024** Behavioural and organisational factors involved in the turnover of high tech professionals. GARDEN, A. *Comput. Pers.* **11**, 4, (Sept. 1988) 6–9.

**01025** Maintaining the spirit of excitement in growing companies. GARDEN, A. *Comput. Pers.* **11**, 4, (Sept. 1988) 10–12.

**01026** Environments: Austria compared to the United States. COUGER, J.; AND ADELSBERGER, H. *Comput. Pers.* **11**, 4, (Sept. 1988) 13–17.

## ACM SIGCSE Bulletin

**01027** An evaluation of a realistic approach to MIS. YAVERBAUM, G. *SIGCSE Bull.* **19**, 1, (Feb. 1987) 36–39.

**01028** Issuing each undergraduate student a personal computer: living with it for three years. MEIN, B. *SIGCSE Bull.* **19**, 1, (Feb. 1987) 76–78.

**01029** Leadership style vs. succssus in student chief programmer teams. TENNY, T. *SIGCSE Bull.* **19**, 1, (Feb. 1987) 103–114.

**01030** Retraining high school teachers to teach computer science—observations on the first course. EPSTEIN, R.; AIKEN, R.; SNELBECKER, G.; AND POTOSKY, J. *SIGCSE Bull.* **19**, 1, (Feb. 1987) 136–140.

**01031** Dealing with disparate audiences in computer science courses using a project group within a traditional class. ROTH, R.; AND WHITE, A. *SIGCSE Bull.* **19**, 1, (Feb. 1987) 148–154.

**01032** Data-structures students may prefer to learn algorithms using graphical methods. SCANLAN, D. *SIGCSE Bull.* **19**, 1, (Feb. 1987) 302–307.

**01033** A historical perspective for teaching. SHIFLET, A. *SIGCSE Bull.* **19**, 1, (Feb. 1987) 413–414.

**01034** Let's motivate! THARP, A. *SIGCSE Bull.* **19**, 1, (Feb. 1987) 415–422.

**01035** Profile of undergraduate software engineering courses: results from a survey. MYNATT, B.; AND LEVENTHAL, L. *SIGCSE Bull.* **19**, 1, (Feb. 1987) 523–528.

**01036** Student-oriented features of an interactive programming environment. FISHER, G. *SIGCSE Bull.* **19**, 1, (Feb. 1987) 532–537.

**01037** Integrating software engineering into an intermediate programming class. WERTH, L. *SIGCSE Bull.* **20**, 1, (Feb. 1988) 54–58.

**01038** Interactive graphics: a tool for beginning programming students in discovering solutions to novel problems. HAYS, H. *SIGCSE Bull.* **20**, 1, (Feb. 1988) 137–141.

**01039** Application frameworks: experience with MacApp. PUGH, J.; AND LEUNG, C. *SIGCSE Bull.* **20**, 1, (Feb. 1988) 142–147.

**01040** IBM 3270 full screen interactive programming without CICS. CHEN, H.; AND SUMMERS, W. *SIGCSE Bull.* **20**, 1, (Feb. 1988) 219–222.

**01041** The impact of menus and command-level feedback on learners' acquisition of data base language skills. SUMNER, M.; AND BENJAMIN, J. *SIGCSE Bull.* **20**, 1, (Feb. 1988) 230–234.

**01042** A study of an advance organizer as a technique for teaching computer programming concepts. MACFARLANE, K.; AND MYNATT, B. *SIGCSE Bull.* **20**, 1, (Feb. 1988) 240–243.

**01043** The small computer assisted lecturing system. PIOTROWSKI, J. *SIGCSE Bull.* **20**, 2, (June, 1988) 8–12.

**01044** Binary jargon: the metaphoric language of computing. VAN DYKE, C. *SIGCSE Bull.* **20**, 3, (Sept. 1988) 34–41.

**01045** A comparison of male and female computer science students' attitudes toward computers. OGOZALEK, V. *SIGCSE Bull.* **21**, 2, (June 1989) 8–14.

## ACM SIGCUE Outlook

01046 The study of user behavior on information retrieval systems. BORGMAN, C. *Outlook* **19**, 3/4, (Spring/Summer 1987) 35–48.

## ACM SIGDOC Asterisk*

01047 Help texts vs. help mechanisms: A new mandate for documentation writers. BORENSTEIN, N. *Asterisk\** **12**, 2, (Aug. 1986) 8–10.
01048 The effect of windows on man-machine interfaces. HOLCOMB, R.; AND THARP, A. *Asterisk\** **12**, 3, (Oct. 1986) 9–20.
01049 Documentation for user-developed applications with high documentation requirements. PIERSON, J.; FORCHT, K.; AND MOSER, J. *Asterisk\** **14**, 1, (March, 1988) 3–10.
01050 A help system for command driven applications. COYNE, M.; AND KONSTAM, A. *Asterisk\** **14**, 1, (March, 1988) 18–31.
01051 Breaking the grip of user manuals. WEISS, P. *Asterisk\** **14**, 2, (Summer 1988) 4–11.

## ACM SIGGRAPH Computer Graphics

01052 Snap-dragging. BIER, E.; AND STONE, M. *Comput. Graph.* **20**, 4, (Aug. 1986) 233–240.
01053 A multitasking switchboard approach to user interface management. TANNER, P.; MACKAY, S.; STEWART, D.; AND WEIN, M. *Comput. Graph.* **20**, 4, (Aug. 1986) 241–248.
01054 Creating highly-interactive and graphical user interfaces by demonstration. MYERS, B.; AND BUXTON, W. *Comput. Graph.* **20**, 4, (Aug. 1986) 249–258.
01055 An object-oriented user interface management system. SIBERT, J.; HURLEY, W.; AND BLESER, T. *Comput. Graph.* **20**, 4, (Aug. 1986) 259–268.
01056 Goals and objectives for user interface software. BETTS, B.; BURLINGAME, D.; FISCHER, G.; FOLEY, J.; GREEN, M.; KASIK, D.; KERR, S.; OLSEN, D.; AND THOMAS, J. *Comput. Graph.* **21**, 2, (April 1987) 73–78.
01057 Tools and methodology for user interface development. RHYNE, J.; EHRICH, R.; BENNETT, J.; HEWETT, T.; SIBERT, J.; AND BLESER, T. *Comput. Graph.* **21**, 2, (April 1987) 78–87.
01058 Reference models, window systems, and concurrency. LANTZ, K.; TANNER, P.; BINDING, C.; HUANG, K.; AND DWELLY, A. *Comput. Graph.* **21**, 2, (April 1987) 87–97.
01059 The run-time structure of UIMS-supported applications. DANCE, J.; GRANOR, T.; HILL, R.; HUDSON, S.; MEADS, J.; MYERS, B.; AND SCHULERT, A. *Comput. Graph.* **21**, 2, (April 1987) 97–101.
01060 Collaboration of UIMS designers and human factors specialists. BENNETT, J. *Comput. Graph.* **21**, 2, (April 1987) 102–105.
01061 An object-oriented construction and tool kit for human-computer communication. FISCHER, G. *Comput. Graph.* **21**, 2, (April 1987) 105–109.
01062 Transformations on a formal specification of user-computer interfaces. FOLEY, J. *Comput. Graph.* **21**, 2, (April 1987) 109–113.
01063 Directions for user interface management systems research. GREEN, M. *Comput. Graph.* **21**, 2, (April 1987) 113–116.
01064 Some important features and issues in user interface management systems. HILL, R. *Comput. Graph.* **21**, 2, (April 1987) 116–120.
01065 UIMS support for direct manipulation interfaces. HUDSON, S. *Comput. Graph.* **21**, 2, (April 1987) 120–124.
01066 Multi-process structuring of user interface software. LANTZ, K. *Comput. Graph.* **21**, 2, (April 1987) 124–130.
01067 Gaining general acceptance for UIMSs. MYERS, B. *Comput. Graph.* **21**, 2, (April 1987) 130–134.
01068 Larger issues in user interface management. OLSEN JR., D. *Comput. Graph.* **21**, 2, (April 1987) 134–137.
01069 Dialogue management for gestural interfaces. RHYNE, J. *Comput. Graph.* **21**, 2, (April 1987) 137–142.

JOURNALS

01070 Multi-thread input. TANNER, P. *Comput. Graph.* **21**, 2, (April 1987) 142–145.
01071 Bibliography of software tools for user interface development. *Comput. Graph.* **21**, 2, (April 1987) 145–147.
01072 Principles of traditional animation applied to 3D computer animation. LASSETER, J. *Comput. Graph.* **21**, 4, (July 1987) 35–44.

## ACM SIGIR Forum

01073 Writing to be searched: A workshop on document creation principles. *SIGIR Forum* **19**, 1-4, (Winter 1986) 9–14.
01074 Comment on some recent comments on information retrieval. MEADOW, C. *SIGIR Forum* **22**, 1-2, (Fall 87/Winter 88) 5–8.
01075 Toward hypertext publishing. HANSON, R. *SIGIR Forum* **22**, 1-2, (Fall 87/Winter 88) 9–26.
01076 IRX: an information retrieval system for experimentation and user applications. HARMAN, D.; BENSON, D.; FITZPATRICK, L.; HUNTZINGER, R.; AND GOLDSTEIN, C. *SIGIR Forum* **22**, 3-4, (Spring/Summer 1988) 2–10.
01077 An information retrieval system for software components. WOOD, M.; AND SOMMERVILLE, I. *SIGIR Forum* **22**, 3-4, (Spring/Summer 1988) 11–28.

## ACM SIGMICRO/IEEE CSTC-MICRO Newsletter

01078 The design of an interactive compiler for optimizing microprograms. VEGDAHL, S. *SIGMICRO TC-MICRO Newsl.* **16**, 4, (Dec. 1985) 129–136.
01079 A development environment for horizontal microcode programs. AIKEN, A.; AND NICOLAU, A. *SIGMICRO TC-MICRO Newsl.* **17**, 4, (Dec. 1986) 23–31.

## ACM SIGMOD Record

01080 Principles of an icons-based language. FRASSON, C.; AND ER-RADI, M. *SIGMOD Rec.* **15**, 2, (June 1986) 144–152.
01081 Rule base management using meta knowledge. HARANDI, M.; SCHANG, T.; AND COHEN, S. *SIGMOD Rec.* **15**, 2, (June 1986) 261–267.
01082 Panel: user interfaces and database management systems. ANDERSON, T.; AND ARIAV, G. *SIGMOD Rec.* **15**, 2, (June 1986) 293–294.
01083 The multimedia object presentation manager of MINOS: a symmetric approach. CHRISTODOULAKIS, S.; HO, F.; AND THEODORIDOU, M. *SIGMOD Rec.* **15**, 2, (June 1986) 295–310.
01084 An object-oriented approach to multimedia databases. WOELK, D.; KIM, W.; AND LUTHER, W. *SIGMOD Rec.* **15**, 2, (June 1986) 311–325.
01085 The proteus bibliography: Representation and interactive display in databases. LOUGENIA ANDERSON, T.; ECKLUND, E.; AND MAIER, D. *SIGMOD Rec.* **15**, 3, (Sept. 1986) 46–55.
01086 Reference model for DBMS user facility. GERSTING, J.; KINSLEY, K.; MCDONALD, N.; NORTH, J.; SASTRY, M.; AND STULL, E. *SIGMOD Rec.* **17**, 2, (June 1988) 23–52.
01087 Implementation of a Prolog-INGRES interface. GHOSH, S.; LIN, C.; AND SELLIS, T. *SIGMOD Rec.* **17**, 2, (June 1988) 77–88.
01088 The problem of identification. SCHIEL, U. *SIGMOD Rec.* **17**, 4, (Dec. 1988) 31–36.
01089 Extending a relational database with deferred referential integrity checking and intelligent joins. CAMMARATA, S.; RAMACHANDRA, P.; AND SHANE, D. *SIGMOD Rec.* **18**, 2, (June 1989) 88–97.
01090 Concurrency control in groupware systems. ELLIS, C.; AND GIBBS, S. *SIGMOD Rec.* **18**, 2, (June 1989) 399–407.

## ACM SIGOIS Bulletin

**01091** Adaptive interface design: a symmetric model and a knowledge-based implementation. TYLER, S.; AND TREU, S. *SIGOIS Bull.* **7**, 2-3, (Summer-Fall 1986) 53–60.

**01092** Efficiency vs. effectiveness. MEYER, N. *SIGOIS Bull.* **8**, 1, (Winter 1987) 7–8.

**01093** Some design guidelines for an information center to support office information systems. LEDERER, A.; AND SETHI, V. *SIGOIS Bull.* **8**, 2, (March 1987) 2–6.

**01094** A natural language interface to a multiple databased office information system. DESAI, B.; POLLOCK, R.; AND VINCENT, P. *SIGOIS Bull.* **9**, 4, (Oct. 1988) 19–33.

## ACM SIGOPS Operating Systems Review

**01095** A UNIX clone with source code for operating systems courses. TANENBAUM, A. *Oper. Syst. Rev.* **21**, 1, (Jan. 1987) 20–29.

## ACM SIGPLAN Notices

**01096** Polylith: an environment to support management of tool interfaces. PURTILO, J. *SIGPLAN Notices* **20**, 7, (July 1985) 12–18.

**01097** Dialogues: a basis for constructing programming environments. O'DONNELL, J. *SIGPLAN Notices* **20**, 7, (July 1985) 19–27.

**01098** The PSG—programming system generator. BAHLKE, R.; AND SNELTING, G. *SIGPLAN Notices* **20**, 7, (July 1985) 28–33.

**01099** Maintained and constructor attributes. BESHERS, G.; AND CAMPBELL, R. *SIGPLAN Notices* **20**, 7, (July 1985) 34–42.

**01100** Attribute propagation by message passing. DEMERS, A.; ROGERS, A.; AND ZADECK, F. *SIGPLAN Notices* **20**, 7, (July 1985) 43–59.

**01101** A semantic editor. DYBVIG, R.; AND SMITH, B. *SIGPLAN Notices* **20**, 7, (July 1985) 74–82.

**01102** Libraries as programs preserved within compiler continuations. WELLS, M.; HUG, M.; AND SILVER, R. *SIGPLAN Notices* **20**, 7, (July 1985) 83–92.

**01103** Relations and attributes. HORWITZ, S.; AND TEITELBAUM, T. *SIGPLAN Notices* **20**, 7, (July 1985) 93–106.

**01104** A new notion of encapsulation. GRIES, D.; AND PRINS, J. *SIGPLAN Notices* **20**, 7, (July 1985) 131–139.

**01105** Structured editor support for modularity and data abstraction. CAPLINGER, M. *SIGPLAN Notices* **20**, 7, (July 1985) 140–147.

**01106** An environment for logic programming. FRANCEZ, N.; GOLDENBERG, S.; PINTER, R.; TIOMKIN, M.; AND TSUR, S. *SIGPLAN Notices* **20**, 7, (July 1985) 179–190.

**01107** A model and an implementation of a logic programming environment. KOMOROWSKI, H.; AND OMORI, S. *SIGPLAN Notices* **20**, 7, (July 1985) 191–198.

**01108** The Mesa programming environment. SWEET, R. *SIGPLAN Notices* **20**, 7, (July 1985) 216–229.

**01109** The structure of Cedar. SWINEHEART, D.; ZELLWEGER, P.; AND HAGMANN, R. *SIGPLAN Notices* **20**, 7, (July 1985) 230–244.

**01110** Integration mechanisms in Cedar. DONAHUE, J. *SIGPLAN Notices* **20**, 7, (July 1985) 245–251.

**01111** A notation for specifying menus. HEKMATPOUR, S. *SIGPLAN Notices* **22**, 4, (April 1987) 59–62.

**01112** Use of object-oriented programming in a time series analysis system. KERR, R.; AND PERCIVAL, D. *SIGPLAN Notices* **22**, 12, (Dec. 1987) 1–10.

**01113** Teaching object-oriented programming with the KEE system. KEMPF, R.; AND STELZNER, M. *SIGPLAN Notices* **22**, 12, (Dec. 1987) 11–25.

**01114** Constraint hierarchies. BORNING, A.; DUISBERG, R.; FREEMAN-BENSON, B.; KRAMER, A.; AND WOOLF, M. *SIGPLAN Notices* **22**, 12, (Dec. 1987) 48–60.

01115  An object-oriented framework for interactive data graphics. YOUNG, R. *SIGPLAN Notices* **22**, 12, (Dec. 1987) 78–90.

01116  An information system based on distributed objects. CAPLINGER, M. *SIGPLAN Notices* **22**, 12, (Dec. 1987) 126–137.

01117  CLAM- an open system for graphical user interfaces. CALL, L.; COHRS, D.; AND MILLER, B. *SIGPLAN Notices* **22**, 12, (Dec. 1987) 277–286.

01118  Painless panes for Smalltalk windows. ALEXANDER, J. *SIGPLAN Notices* **22**, 12, (Dec. 1987) 287–294.

01119  INSIST: Interactive Simulation in Smalltalk. VAN DER MEULEN, P. *SIGPLAN Notices* **22**, 12, (Dec. 1987) 366–376.

01120  RAPID: Prototyping control panel interfaces. FREBURGER, K. *SIGPLAN Notices* **22**, 12, (Dec. 1987) 416–422.

01121  Common LISP object system specification X3J13 Document 88-002R. BOBROW, D.; DEMICHIEL, L.; GABRIEL, R.; KEENE, S.; KICSALES, G.; AND MOON, D. *SIGPLAN Notices* **23**, (Sept. 1988) 1–143.

01122  Clarify function! ANAND, N. *SIGPLAN Notices* **23**, 6, (June, 1988) 69–79.

01123  Non-intrusive and interactive profiling in parasight. ARAL, Z.; AND GERTNER, I. *SIGPLAN Notices* **23**, 9, (Sept. 1988) 21–30.

01124  Tenuring policies for generation-based storage reclamation. UNGAR, D.; AND JACKSON, F. *SIGPLAN Notices* **23**, 11, (Nov. 1988) 1–17.

01125  A user interface toolkit based on graphical objects and constraints. SZEKELY, P.; AND MYERS, B. *SIGPLAN Notices* **23**, 11, (Nov. 1988) 36–45.

01126  Transportable applications environment (TAE) plus experiences in "Object"-ively modernizing a user interface environment. SZCZUR, M.; AND MILLER, P. *SIGPLAN Notices* **23**, 11, (Nov. 1988) 58–70.

01127  An integrated color smalltalk-80 system. WIRFS-BROCK, R. *SIGPLAN Notices* **23**, 11, (Nov. 1988) 71–82.

01128  A smalltalk window system based on constraints. EPSTEIN, D.; AND LALONDE, W. *SIGPLAN Notices* **23**, 11, (Nov. 1988) 83–94.

01129  Configuring stand-alone smalltalk-80 applications. SRIDHAR, S. *SIGPLAN Notices* **23**, 11, (Nov. 1988) 95–104.

01130  Fabrik: a visual programming environment. INGALLS, D.; WALLACE, S.; CHOW, Y.; LUDOLPH, F.; AND DOYLE, K. *SIGPLAN Notices* **23**, 11, (Nov. 1988) 176–190.

01131  An interactive environment for object-oriented music composition and sound synthesis. SCALETTI, C.; AND JOHNSON, R. *SIGPLAN Notices* **23**, 11, (Nov. 1988) 222–233.

01132  A smalltalk implementation of an intelligent operator's associate. RUBIN, K.; JONES, P.; MITCHELL, C.; AND GOLDSTEIN, T. *SIGPLAN Notices* **23**, 11, (Nov. 1988) 234–247.

01133  An object-oriented framework of pattern recognition systems. YOSHIDA, N.; AND HINO, K. *SIGPLAN Notices* **23**, 11, (Nov. 1988) 259–267.

01134  Interactive blackbox debugging for concurrent languages. GOLDSZMIDT, G.; KATZ, S.; AND YEMINI, S. *SIGPLAN Notices* **24**, 1, (Jan. 1989) 271–282.

01135  Foundations for the Arcadia environment architecture. TALYOR, R.; BELZ, F.; CLARKE, L.; OSTERWEIL, L.; SELBY, R.; WILEDEN, J.; WOLF, A.; AND YOUND, M. *SIGPLAN Notices* **24**, 2, (February 1989) 1–13.

01136  Centaur: the system. BORRAS, P.; CLEMENT, D.; DESPEYROUX, T.; INCERPI, J.; LANG, B.; AND PASCUAL, V. *SIGPLAN Notices* **24**, 2, (February 1989) 14–24.

HCI-0147  The Software Life Cycle Support Environment (SLCSE): a computer based framework for developing software systems. STRELICH, T. *SIGPLAN Notices* **24**, 2, (February 1989) 35–44.

01137  Interacting with an active, integrated environment. RODDEN, T.; SAWYER, P.; AND SOMMERVILLE, I. *SIGPLAN Notices* **24**, 2, (February 1989) 76–84.

01138  Graph attribution as a specification paradigm. ALPERN, B.; CARLE, A.; ROSEN, B.; SWEENEY, P.; AND ZADECK, K. *SIGPLAN Notices* **24**, 2, (February 1989) 121–129.

01139  User interface support for the integration of software tools: an iconic model of interaction. BEAUDOUIN-LAFON, M. *SIGPLAN Notices* **24**, 2, (February 1989) 143–152.

**01140** Transformational derivation of programs using the focus system. REDDY, U. *SIGPLAN Notices* **24**, 2, (February 1989) 163–172.

**HCI-0101** Extended programming in the large in a software development environment. LEWERENTZ, C. *SIGPLAN Notices* **24**, 2, (February 1989) 173–182.

## ACM SIGSIM SIMULETTER

**01141** A prolog simulation for a Delphi-based problem solver. ELMAGHRABY, A. *SIMULETTER* **19**, 4, (Winter 1988/1989) 36–43.

## ACM SIGSMALL/PC Notes

**01142** Attitudes toward unauthorized software copying: general public vs. business faculty member. LIN, J. *SIGSMALL/PC Notes* **15**, 2, (May 1989) 3–6.

## ACM SIGSOFT Software Engineering Notes

**01143** Applying direct manipulation concepts. ISEKU, O.; AND SHNEIDERMAN, B. *Softw. Eng. Notes* **11**, 2, (April 1986) 22–26.

**01144** Requirements checklist for a system development workstation. WINTER, E. *Softw. Eng. Notes* **11**, 5, (Oct. 1986) 57–62.

**01145** Characteristics and functions of software environments: an overview. HOUGHTON, R.; AND WALLACE, D. *Softw. Eng. Notes* **12**, 1, (Jan. 1987) 64–84.

**01146** A graphical tool for the design and prototyping of distributed systems. DÄHLER, J.; GERBER, P.; GISIGER, H.; AND KÜNDIG, A. *Softw. Eng. Notes* **12**, 3, (July 1987) 25–36.

## ACM SIGUCCS Newsletter

**01147** Staying afloat—a collective enterprise. SLATER, J. *SIGUCCS Newsl.* **19**, 1, (April 1, 1989) 18–22.

**01148** From arcane ASCII to the printed page - computer basics. LEE, G.; AND SUTER, V. *SIGUCCS Newsl.* **19**, 1, (April 1, 1989) 28–29.

## ACM Transactions on Computer Systems

**HCI-0169** Monitoring distributed systems. JOYCE, J.; LOMOW, G.; SLIND, K.; AND UNGER, B. *ACM Trans. Comput. Syst.* **5**, 2, (May 1987) 121–150.

**HCI-0094** A programmable interface language for heterogeneous distributed systems. FALCONE, J. *ACM Trans. Comput. Syst.* **5**, 4, (Nov. 1987) 330–351.

**01149** The profile naming service. PETERSON, L. *ACM Trans. Comput. Syst.* **6**, 4, (Nov. 1988) 341–365.

## ACM Transactions on Database Systems

**HCI-0260** Update and retrieval in a relational database through a universal schema interface. BROSDA, V.; AND VOSSEN, G. *ACM Trans. Database Syst.* **13**, 4, (Dec. 1988) 449–485.

## ACM Transactions on Graphics

- HCI-0382   Pushdown automata for user interface management. OLSEN, D. *ACM Trans. Graph.* **3**, 3, (July 1984) 177–203.
- HCI-0371   The application of scene synthesis techniques to the display of multidimensional image data. ROBERTSON, P.; AND O'CALLAGHAN, J. *ACM Trans. Graph.* **4**, 4, (Oct. 1985) 247–274.
- HCI-0373   An experimental evaluation of computer graphics imagery. MEYER, G.; RUSHMEIER, H.; COHEN, M.; GREENBERG, D.; AND TORRANCE, K. *ACM Trans. Graph.* **5**, 1, (Jan. 1986) 30–50.
- HCI-0370   The X window system. SCHEIFLER, R.; AND GETTYS, J. *ACM Trans. Graph.* **5**, 2, (April 1986) 79–109.
- 01150   Automating the design of graphical presentations of relational information. MACKINLAY, J. *ACM Trans. Graph.* **5**, 2, (April 1986) 110–141.
- HCI-0102   Supporting concurrency, communication, and synchronization in human-computer interaction—the Sassafras UIMS. HILL, R. *ACM Trans. Graph.* **5**, 3, (July 1986) 179–210.
- 01151   Rooms: the use of multiple virtual workspaces to reduce space contention in a window-based graphical user interface. HENDERSON, D.; AND CARD, S. *ACM Trans. Graph.* **5**, 3, (July 1986) 211–243.
- 01152   A survey of three dialogue models. GREEN, M. *ACM Trans. Graph.* **5**, 3, (July 1986) 244–275.
- HCI-0124   MIKE: the menu interaction kontrol environment. OLSEN, D. *ACM Trans. Graph.* **5**, 4, (Oct. 1986) 36–62.
- HCI-0123   A specification language for direct-manipulation user interfaces. JACOB, R. *ACM Trans. Graph.* **5**, 4, (Oct. 1986) 283–317.
- 01153   Constraint-based tools for building user interfaces. BORNING, A.; AND DUISBERG, R. *ACM Trans. Graph.* **5**, 4, (Oct. 1986) 345–374.
- HCI-0381   An experimental comparison of RGB, YIQ, LAB, HSV, and opponent color models. SCHWARZ, M.; COWAN, W.; AND BEATTY, J. *ACM Trans. Graph.* **6**, 2, (April 1987) 123–158.
- HCI-0369   A window-based graphics frame store architecture. WESTMORE, R. *ACM Trans. Graph.* **7**, 4, (Oct. 1988) 227–242.

## ACM Transactions on Information Systems

- 01154   Formative design evaluation of superbook. EGAN, D.; REMDE, J.; GOMEZ, L.; LANDAUER, T.; EBERHARDT, J.; AND LOCHBAUM, C. *ACM Trans. Inf. Syst.* **7**, 1, (Jan. 1989) 30–57.
- HCI-0277   Knowledge-based search tactics for an intelligent intermediary system. SMITH, P.; SHUTE, S.; GALDES, B.; AND CHIGNELL, M. *ACM Trans. Inf. Syst.* **7**, 3, (July 1989) 246–270.
- 01155   Information retrieval using a hypertext-based help system. CAMPAGNONI, F.; AND EHRLICH, K. *ACM Trans. Inf. Syst.* **7**, 3, (July 1989) 271–291.

## ACM Transactions on Mathematical Software

- HCI-0302   A generalized model management system for mathematical programming. DOLK, D. *ACM Trans. Math. Softw.* **12**, 2, (June 1986) 92–126.
- HCI-0415   Computer-aided modeling and planning (CAMP). SAGIE, I. *ACM Trans. Math. Softw.* **12**, 3, (Sept. 1986) 225–248.

## ACM Transactions on Office Information Systems

- HCI-0304   The dimensions of accessibility to online information: implications for implementing office information systems. CULNAN, M. *ACM Trans. Office Inf. Syst.* **2**, 2, (April 1984) 141–150.
- HCI-0113   Cursor movement during text editing. GOULD, J.; LEWIS, C.; AND BARNES, V. *ACM Trans. Office Inf. Syst.* **3**, 1, (Jan. 1985) 22–34.

HCI-0278  A prototype electronic encyclopedia. WEYER, S.; AND BORNING, A. *ACM Trans. Office Inf. Syst.* **3**, 1, (Jan. 1985) 63–88.

HCI-0287  Electronic calendars in the office: an assessment of user needs and current technology. KINCAID, C.; DUPONT, P.; AND KAYE, A. *ACM Trans. Office Inf. Syst.* **3**, 1, (Jan. 1985) 89–102.

HCI-0352  Transporting the linguistic string project system from a medical to a Navy domain. MARSH, E.; AND FRIEDMAN, C. *ACM Trans. Office Inf. Syst.* **3**, 2, (April 1985) 121–140.

HCI-0340  Portability of syntax and semantics in DATALOG. HAFNER, C.; AND GODDEN, K. *ACM Trans. Office Inf. Syst.* **3**, 2, (April 1985) 141–164.

HCI-0279  ASK is transportable in half a dozen ways. THOMPSON, B.; AND THOMPSON, F. *ACM Trans. Office Inf. Syst.* **3**, 2, (April 1985) 185–203.

HCI-0311  Usage patterns in an integrated voice and data communications system. NICHOLSON, R. *ACM Trans. Office Inf. Syst.* **3**, 3, (July 1985) 307–314.

HCI-0401  TEXTNET: a network-based approach to text handling. TRIGG, R.; AND WEISER, M. *ACM Trans. Office Inf. Syst.* **4**, 1, (Jan. 1986) 1–23.

HCI-0289  Whiteboards: a graphical database tool. DONAHUE, J.; AND WIDOM, J. *ACM Trans. Office Inf. Syst.* **4**, 1, (Jan. 1986) 24–41.

HCI-0268  The spatial metaphor for user interfaces: experimental tests of reference by location versus name. JONES, W.; AND DUMAIS, S. *ACM Trans. Office Inf. Syst.* **4**, 1, (Jan. 1986) 42–63.

HCI-0297  Communications design for Co-oP: a group decision support system. BUI, T.; AND JARKE, M. *ACM Trans. Office Inf. Syst.* **4**, 2, (April 1986) 81–103.

HCI-0250  A generator of direct manipulation office systems. HUDSON, S.; AND KING, R. *ACM Trans. Office Inf. Syst.* **4**, 2, (April 1986) 132–163.

01156  Understanding the office: A social-analytic perspective. *ACM Trans. Office Inf. Syst.* **4**, 4, (Oct. 1986) 331–344.

01157  Data model issues for object-oriented applications. BANERJEE, J.; CHOU, H.; GARZA, J.; KIM, W.; WOELK, D.; BALLOU, N.; AND KIM, H. *ACM Trans. Office Inf. Syst.* **5**, 1, (Jan. 1987) 3–26.

HCI-0290  Semistructured messages are surprisingly useful for computer-supported coordination. MALONE, T.; GRANT, K.; LAI, K.; RAO, R.; AND ROSENBLITT, D. *ACM Trans. Office Inf. Syst.* **5**, 2, (April 1987) 115–131.

HCI-0156  Project Nick: meetings augmentation and analysis. COOK, P.; ELLIS, C.; GRAF, M.; REIN, G.; AND SMITH, T. *ACM Trans. Office Inf. Syst.* **5**, 2, (April 1987) 132–146.

01158  WYSIWIS revised: early experiences with multiuser interfaces. STEFIK, M.; BOBROW, D.; FOSTER, G.; LANNING, S.; AND TATAR, D. *ACM Trans. Office Inf. Syst.* **5**, 2, (April 1987) 147–167.

HCI-0307  Strategies for encouraging successful adoption of office communication systems. EHRLICH, S. *ACM Trans. Office Inf. Syst.* **5**, 4, (Oct. 1987) 340–357.

HCI-0201  Behavioral experiments on handmarkings. GOULD, J.; AND SALAUN, J. *ACM Trans. Office Inf. Syst.* **5**, 4, (Oct. 1987) 358–377.

01159  Office-by-example: an integrated office system and database manager. WHANG, K.; AMMANN, A.; BOLMARCICH, A.; HANRAHAN, M.; HOCHGESANG, G.; HUANG, K.; KHORASANI, A.; KRISHNAMURTHY, R.; SOCKUT, G.; SWEENEY, P.; WADDLE, V.; AND ZLOOF, M. *ACM Trans. Office Inf. Syst.* **5**, 4, (Oct. 1987) 393–427.

HCI-0309  An experimental multimedia mail system. POSTEL, J.; FINN, G.; KATZ, A.; AND REYNOLDS, J. *ACM Trans. Office Inf. Syst.* **6**, 1, (Jan. 1988) 63–81.

01160  Knowledge-based tools to promote shared goals and terminology between interface designers. NECHES, R. *ACM Trans. Office Inf. Syst.* **6**, 3, (July 1988) 215–231.

HCI-0300  gIBIS: a hypertext tool for exploratory policy discussion. CONKLIN, J.; AND BEGEMAN, M. *ACM Trans. Office Inf. Syst.* **6**, 4, (Oct. 1988) 303–331.

HCI-0206  Object lens: a "spreadsheet" for cooperative work. LAI, K.; MALONE, T.; AND YU, K. *ACM Trans. Office Inf. Syst.* **6**, 4, (Oct. 1988) 332–353.

HCI-0310  Diversity in the use of electronic mail: a preliminary inquiry. MACKAY, W. *ACM Trans. Office Inf. Syst.* **6**, 4, (Oct. 1988) 380–397.

01161  Guided tours and tabletops: tools for communicating in a hypertext environment. TRIGG, R. *ACM Trans. Office Inf. Syst.* **6**, 4, (Oct. 1988) 398–414.

# JOURNALS

## ACM Transactions on Programming Languages and Systems

HCI-0398  Editing by example. NIX, R. *ACM Trans. Program. Lang. Syst.* **7**, 4, (Oct. 1985) 600–621.
HCI-0146  The PegaSys System: pictures as formal documentation of large programs. MORICONI, M.; AND HARE, D. *ACM Trans. Program. Lang. Syst.* **8**, 4, (Oct. 1986) 524–546.
HCI-0163  A practical method for LR and LL syntactic error diagnosis and recovery. BURKE, M.; AND FISHER, G. *ACM Trans. Program. Lang. Syst.* **9**, 2, (April 1987) 164–197.
01162  Abstract interaction tools: a language for user interface management systems. VAN DEN BOS, J. *ACM Trans. Program. Lang. Syst.* **10**, 2, (April 1988) 215–247.

## Acta Informatica

HCI-0251  Specification and verification of database dynamics. FIADEIRO, J.; AND SERNADAS, A. *Acta Inf.* **25**, 6, (Aug. 1988) 625–661.

## Advances in Applied Mathematics

01163  A Computational model for interfaces. GLIMM, J.; AND MCBRYAN, O. *Adv. Appl. Math.* **6**, 4, (December 1985) 422–435.
01164  A model of the neocortex. MYCIELSKI, J.; AND SWIERCZKOWSKI, S. *Adv. Appl. Math.* **9**, 4, (Dec. 1988) 465–480.

## Advances in Engineering Software

01165  Interactive microcomputer programs for linear and non-linear static analysis of frameworks. KEARNS, C.; AND MCCONNELL, G. *Adv. Eng. Softw.* **8**, 4, (Oct. 1986) 190–193.
01166  SMART: Scientific database management and engineering analysis routines and tools. ARORA, J.; LEE, H.; AND JAO, S. *Adv. Eng. Softw.* **8**, 4, (Oct. 1986) 194–199.
01167  A user-friendly program of human judgments in engineering decision analysis. QUADDUA, M.; AND POH, K. *Adv. Eng. Softw.* **10**, 2, (April, 1988) 83–89.
01168  A human-computer interactive design program for a multisolution nonlinear problem. KUZNETSOV, H. *Adv. Eng. Softw.* **10**, 2, (April, 1988) 106–108.

## AI Expert

01169  Concurrency in intelligent systems. HEWITT, C. *AI Expert* **1**, 1, (1986) 44–59.
01170  Apollo domain series 3000. PERKINS, B. *AI Expert* **1**, 2, (Oct. 1986) 83–86.
01171  Catching knowledge in neural nets. JORGENSEN, C.; AND MATHEUS, C. *AI Expert* **1**, 4, (Dec. 1986) 30–41.
01172  Understanding natural languages. BRITTAIN, S. *AI Expert* **2**, 5, (May 1987) 30–38.
01173  Mathematical building blocks. JOHNSON, S. *AI Expert* **2**, 5, (May 1987) 42–50.
01174  Designing a practical interface. BATES, M.; MELTZER, D.; AND SHEA, S. *AI Expert* **2**, 5, (May 1987) 60–66.
01175  Why artificial intelligence isn't (yet). ANDERSON, H. *AI Expert* **2**, 7, (July 1987) 36–44.
01176  Selecting a shell. CITRENBAUM, R.; GEISSMAN, J.; AND SCHULTZ, R. *AI Expert* **2**, 9, (Sept. 1987) 30–39.
01177  Diagramming objects. CUNNINGHAM, W.; AND BECK, K. *AI Expert* **2**, 10, (Nov. 1987) 52–58.
01178  Neural networks primer, part I. CAUDILL, M. *AI Expert* **2**, 12, (Dec. 1987) 46–52.
01179  The human factor in expert systems. GORDON, S. *AI Expert* **3**, 1, (Jan. 1988) 55–59.
01180  How to talk to an expert. EVANSON, S. *AI Expert* **3**, 2, (Feb. 1988) 36–42.
01181  Neural networks primer, Part II. CAUDILL, M. *AI Expert* **3**, 2, (Feb. 1988) 55–61.
01182  Neural networks primer, part III. CAUDILL, M. *AI Expert* **3**, 6, (June, 1988) 53–59.

01183 How to choose natural language software. RETTIG, M.; AND BATES, M. *AI Expert* **3**, 7, (July 1988) 40–49.
01184 Wall Street speaks English. KEYES, J. *AI Expert* :0B3, 7, (July 1988) 50–55.
01185 Connectionism, cybernetics, and the cerebellum. TRELEASE, R. *AI Expert* **3**, 8, (August 1988) 30–36.
01186 Twelve neural network cliches. ROBERTS, M. *AI Expert* **3**, 8, (August 1988) 40–46.
01187 Integrating neural networks with robots. JOSIN, G. *AI Expert* **3**, 8, (August 1988) 50–58.
01188 Neural networks primer, part IV. CAUDILL, M. *AI Expert* **3**, 8, (August 1988) 61–67.
01189 Twelve-product wrap-up: neural networks. SCHWARTZ, T. *AI Expert* **3**, 8, (August 1988) 73–85.
01190 Graphic objects. GRAHAM, P. *AI Expert* **3**, 10, (Oct. 1988) 17–21.
01191 Direct manipulation interfaces. POTTER, A. *AI Expert* **3**, 10, (Oct. 1988) 28–35.
01192 Neural networks primer, Part VII. CAUDILL, M. *AI Expert* **4**, 5, (May 1989) 51–58.

## AI Magazine

01193 Cognitive technologies: The design of joint human-machine cognitive systems. WOODS, D. *AI Mag.* **6**, 4, (Winter 1986) 86–92.
01194 YANLI: a powerful natural language front-end tool. GLASGOW III, J. *AI Mag.* **8**, 1, (Spring 1987) 40–48.
01195 The problem of extracting the knowledge of experts. HOFFMAN, R. *AI Mag.* **8**, 2, (Summer 1987) 53–67.
01196 Various views on spatial prepositions. RETZ-SCHMIDT, G. *AI Mag.* **9**, 2, (July/August 1988) 95–105.
01197 What AI practitioners should know about the law, part 2. FRANK, S. *AI Mag.* **9**, 2, (July/August 1988) 109–114.
01198 On interface requirements for expert systems. WEXELBLAT, R. *AI Mag.* **10**, 3, (Fall 1989) 66–78.

## ALLC Journal

01199 Lexical organisation from three different angles. MEIJS, W. *ALLC J.* **6**, 1, (Jan. 1985) 1–10.

## Angewandte Informatik

01200 Some principles of perceptual and cognitive psychology applied to the design of help menus. ROSEMANN, H. *Angew. Inf.* (Feb. 1987) 65–74.
01201 Help systems-assisting the user. MEINHARD, A.; AND LORENZ, V. *Angew. Inf.* **28**, 11, (Nov. 1986) 475–479.
01202 A method framework for the statistical package SPSS/PC+ to support occasional users. BODENDORF, F.; AND OSIANDER, U. *Angew. Inf.* **30**, 1, (Jan. 1988) 3–8.
01203 Teachware for power engineering education. SCHWAB, A.; AND SCHAUB, B. *Angew. Inf.* **30**, 3, (March 1988) 125–131.
01204 Determination of work contexts—an important aspect of future user interfaces. ZOLLER, P. *Angew. Inf.* **31**, 2, (February 1989) 57–62.

## Annals of Operations Research

01205 A supervisory control paradigm for real-time control of flexible manufacturing systems. AMMONS, J.; GOVINDARAJ, T.; AND MITCHELL, C. *Ann. Oper. Res.* **15**, 1-4, (October 1988) 313–335.

## Applied Artificial Intelligence

01206 Choice of words in the generation process of a natural language interface. HORACEK, H. *Appl. Artif. Intell.* **1**, 2, (Oct. 1987) 117–132.
01207 Knowledge and experience. JOSEFSON, I. *Appl. Artif. Intell.* **1**, 2, (Oct. 1987) 173–180.

**01208** DATENBANK-DIALOG: a German language interface for relational databases. TROST, H.; BUCHBERGER, E.; HEINZ, W.; HÖRTNAGEL, C.; AND MATIASEK, J. *Appl. Artif. Intell.* **1,** 2, (Oct. 1987) 181–203.

## Applied Mathematics Letters

**01209** Curve tailoring with interactive computer. DENNIS, J.; AND WOODS, D. *Appl. Math. Lett.* **1,** 1, (1988) 41–43.
**01210** Speculating on the future of mathematics. SAATY, T. *Appl. Math. Lett.* **1,** 1, (1988) 79–82.

## Artificial Intelligence

**HCI-0344** Extended person-machine interface. REICHMAN-ADAR, R. *Artif. Intell.* **22,** 1, (March 1984) 157–218.
**HCI-0351** TEAM: an experiment in the design of transportable natural-language interfaces. GROSZ, B.; APPELT, D.; MARTIN, P.; AND PEREIRA, F. *Artif. Intell.* **32,** 2, (May 1987) 173–243.
**HCI-0343** Knowledge-intensive natural language generation. JACOBS, P. *Artif. Intell.* **33,** 3, (Nov. 1987) 325–378.
**01211** Motivation analysis, abductive unification, and nonmonotonic equality. CHARNIAK, E. *Artif. Intell.* **34,** 3, (April 1988) 275–295.
**01212** Towards a computational theory of cognitive maps. YEAP, W. *Artif. Intell.* **34,** 3, (April 1988) 297–360.
**01213** Reasoning about action II: the qualification problem. GINSBERG, M.; AND SMITH, D. *Artif. Intell.* **35,** 3, (July 1988) 311–342.
**01214** On the relation between default and autoepistemic logic. KONOLIGE, K. *Artif. Intell.* **35,** 3, (July 1988) 343–382.

## ASLIB Proceedings

**01215** Starting end-users. NORTON, R.; AND WESTWATER, J. *ASLIB Proc.* **38,** 11/12, (Nov. 1986) 381–388.
**01216** Online use and end-users in media and advertising: an overview. HARRIS, K.; NICHOLAS, D.; AND ERBACH, G. *ASLIB Proc.* **38,** 11/12, (Nov. 1986) 389–397.
**01217** Introducing information technology: experiences of a large industrial unit. DUTTON, B. *ASLIB Proc.* **38,** 11/12, (Nov. 1986) 399–410.
**01218** The value of downloading for database users and database producers. WINDER, J. *ASLIB Proc.* **38,** 11/12, (Nov. 1986) 411–416.
**01219** Do VDU's make you sick? MACMORROW, N. *ASLIB Proc.* **39,** 3, (March 1987) 65–74.
**01220** Are you sitting comfortably? MACMORROW, N. *ASLIB Proc.* **39,** 4, (April 1987) 97–105.
**01221** End-users: threat, challenge or myth? NICHOLAS, D.; ERBACH, G.; AND HARRIS, K. *ASLIB Proc.* **39,** 11/12, (Nov./Dec. 1987) 337–344.
**01222** A folklore view of information. HANNABUSS, S. *ASLIB Proc.* **41,** 2, (February 1989) 57–64.
**01223** Dialogue and the search for information. HANNABUSS, S. *ASLIB Proc.* **41,** 3, (March 1989) 85–98.
**01224** End-user searching—What are the implications? DUTTON, B. *ASLIB Proc.* **41,** 4, (April 1989) 149–156.
**01225** Information retrieval using micros. WOODWARD, T. *ASLIB Proc.* **41,** 4, (April 1989) 157–162.

## AT&T Technical Journal

**01226** The AT&T soft touch-sensitive screen. SCHWARTZ, T. *AT&T Tech. J.* **65,** 1, (Jan. 1986) 62–67.

## Australian Computer Journal

**01227** A FORTRAN input program generator. SMITH, G. *Aust. Comput. J.* **18,** 3, (Aug. 1986) 106–114.

**01228** Planning for hospital information systems using the Lancaster Soft Systems methodology. LeFevre, A.; and Pattison, E. *Aust. Comput. J.* **18**, 4, (Nov. 1986) 180–185.

**01229** Graphical data presentation for decision support systems. Edmundson, R.; and Terry, J. *Aust. Comput. J.* **18**, 4, (Nov. 1986) 191–195.

**01230** Instrumenting systems to measure components of interactive response times. Penny, J.; Ashton, P.; and Tripp, D. *Aust. Comput. J.* **20**, 2, (May 1988) 79–84.

**01231** Representation of dynamic features in a conceptual schema. Prabhakaran, N.; and Falkenberg, E. *Aust. Comput. J.* **20**, 3, (August 1988) 98–104.

## Australian Journal of Physics

**01232** Profile data acquisition for the JCPDS-ICDD database s. Jenkins, R. *Aust. J. Phys.* **41**, 2, (June 1988) 145–154.

## Automatic Control and Computer Sciences

**01233** The selection of a servicing discipline in a multiterminal conversational information retrieval system. Kavalerchik, B. *Autom. Control Comput. Sci.* **20**, 4, (March 1986) 54–59.

## Automatica (Journal of IFAC)

**01234** Automation, work organization and skills: the case of numerical control. Cavestro, W. *Automatica (Journal of IFAC)* **22**, 6, (Nov. 1986) 739–744.

**01235** Conceptual design of a human error tolerant interface for complex engineering systems. Rouse, W.; and Morris, N. *Automatica (Journal of IFAC)* **23**, 2, (March 1987) 231–235.

**01236** On the design of man-machine systems: principles, practices and prospects. Rouse, W.; and Cody, W. *Automatica (Journal of IFAC)* **24**, 2, (March 1987) 227–238.

**01237** A man-machine interface for computer-aided and simulation of control systems. Barker, H.; Chen, M.; Grant, P.; Jobling, C.; and Townsend, P. *Automatica (Journal of IFAC)* **25**, 2, (March 1989) 311–316.

## Behaviour & Information Technology

**HCI-0234** Attitudes towards specific uses of the computers quantitative, decision-making and record-keeping applications. Kerber, K. *Behav. Inf. Tech.* **2**, 2, (April-June 1982) 197–209.

**01238** Technology adaptation: a typology for strategic human resource management. Gattiker, U. *Behav. Inf. Tech.* **7**, 4, (Oct.–Dec. 1988) 345–359.

**01239** An empirical investigation of two electronic mail systems. Safayeni, F.; Lee, E.; and MacGregor, J. *Behav. Inf. Tech.* **7**, 4, (Oct.–Dec. 1988) 361–372.

**01240** A cognitively based methodology for evaluating human performance in the computer-aided design task domain. Sharit, J.; and Cuomo, D. *Behav. Inf. Tech.* **7**, 4, (Oct.–Dec. 1988) 373–397.

**01241** Problems associated with the off-line programming of robots. Humrich, A.; and Wilson, I. *Behav. Inf. Tech.* **7**, 4, (Oct.–Dec. 1988) 399–416.

**01242** Human intelligence models and their implications for expert system structure and research. Cook, J.; Whittaker, A.; Thieme, R.; Smith, O.; and Salvendy, G. *Behav. Inf. Tech.* **7**, 4, (Oct.–Dec. 1988) 417–430.

**01243** What we know and what we need to know: the user model versus the user's model in human-computer interaction. Briggs, P. *Behav. Inf. Tech.* **7**, 4, (Oct.–Dec. 1988) 431–442.

**01244** The concept of an information management system and its use within design studies. Tainsh, M. *Behav. Inf. Tech.* **7**, 4, (Oct.–Dec. 1988) 443–455.

01245 A feature matching approach to the retrieval of graphical information. MACGREGOR, J.; AND LEE, E. *Behav. Inf. Tech.* **7**, 4, (Oct.–Dec. 1988) 457–465.

01246 Efforts of display format on proof-reading with VDUs. CREED, A.; DENNIS, I.; AND NEWSTEAD, S. *Behav. Inf. Tech.* **7**, 4, (Oct.–Dec. 1988) 467–478.

## Biological Cybernetics

01247 Statistical inference on spontaneous neuronal discharge patterns. I. Single neuron. LÁNSKÝ, P.; AND RADIL, T. *Biol. Cybern.* **55**, 5, (Feb. 1987) 299–311.

01248 A self-organizing neural network sharing features of the mammalian visual system. FROHN, H.; GEIGER, H.; AND SINGER, W. *Biol. Cybern.* **55**, 5, (Feb. 1987) 333–343.

01249 Representation of local geometry in the visual system. KOENDERINK, J.; AND VAN DOOM, A. *Biol. Cybern.* **55**, 6, (March 1987) 367–375.

01250 Modeling of control and learning in a stepping motion. FLASHNER, H.; BEUTER, A.; AND ARABYAN, A. *Biol. Cybern.* **55**, 6, (March 1987) 387–396.

01251 Muscle models: what is gained and what is lost by varying model complexity. WINTERS, J.; AND STARK, L. *Biol. Cybern.* **55**, 6, (March 1987) 403–420.

01252 A multivariate solution for cyclic data, applied in modelling locomotor forces. HINES, W.; O'HARA-HINES, R.; AND BROOKE, J. *Biol. Cybern.* **56**, 1, (April 1987) 1–9.

01253 Information compression in biological systems. HAKEN, H. *Biol. Cybern.* **56**, 1, (April 1987) 11–17.

01254 Diffusion approximation of the neuronal model with synaptic reversal potentials. LÁNSKÝ, P.; AND LÁNSKÁ, V. *Biol. Cybern.* **56**, 1, (April 1987) 19–26.

01255 Characteristics of neuronal systems in the visual cortex. VON SEELEN, W.; MALLOT, H.; AND GIANNAKOPOULOS, F. *Biol. Cybern.* **56**, 1, (April 1987) 37–49.

01256 Vertical disparity nulling in random-dot stereograms. PRAZDNY, K. *Biol. Cybern.* **56**, 1, (April 1987) 61–67.

01257 Facts on optic flow. KOENDERINK, J.; AND VAN DOOM, A. *Biol. Cybern.* **56**, 4, (June 1987) 247–254.

01258 A study of stability of electrocortical rhythm generators. MITRASZEWSKI, P.; BLINOWSKA, K.; FRANASZCZUK, P.; AND KOWALCZYK, M. *Biol. Cybern.* **56**, 4, (June 1987) 255–260.

01259 Identification of MGB cells by Volterra kernels. III. A glance into the black box. YESHURUN, Y.; DYN, N.; AND WOLLBERG, Z. *Biol. Cybern.* **56**, 4, (June 1987) 261–268.

01260 On the identification of neural responses. OĞUZTÖRELI, M.; STEIL, G.; AND CAELLI, T. *Biol. Cybern.* **56**, 2/3, (May 1987) 97–106.

01261 Single sweep analysis of visual evoked potentials through a model of parametric identification. CERUTTI, S.; BASELLI, G.; LIBERATI, D.; AND PAVESI, G. *Biol. Cybern.* **56**, 2/3, (May 1987) 111–120.

01262 Disjunctive models of boolean category learning. HAMPSON, S.; AND VOLPER, D. *Biol. Cybern.* **56**, 2/3, (May 1987) 121–137.

01263 Simulation of chaotic EEG patterns with a dynamic model of the olfactory system. FREEMAN, W. *Biol. Cybern.* **56**, 2/3, (May 1987) 139–150.

01264 A scaling model for dichotomous branching processes. NONNENMACHER, T. *Biol. Cybern.* **56**, 2/3, (May 1987) 155–157.

01265 Projected free fall trajectories. I. Theory and simulation. SAXBERG, B. *Biol. Cybern.* **56**, 2/3, (May 1987) 159–175.

01266 Projected free fall trajectories. II. Human experiments. SAXBERG, B. *Biol. Cybern.* **56**, 2/3, (May 1987) 177–184.

01267 A method for computing spectral reflectance. YUILLE, A. *Biol. Cybern.* **56**, 2/3, (May 1987) 195–201.

01268 Quantitative determination of orientational and directional components in the response of visual cortical cells to moving stimuli. WÖRGÖTTER, F.; AND EYSEL, U. *Biol. Cybern.* **57**, 6, (1987) 349–355.

01269 A model-based monitor of human sleep stages. KEMP, B.; GRÖNEVELD, E.; JANSSEN, A.; AND FRANZEN, J. *Biol. Cybern.* **57**, 6, (1987) 365–378.

01270 Uncertainty analysis of human EEG spectra: A multivariate information theoretical method for the analysis of

brain activity. REINKE, W.; AND DIEKMANN, V. *Biol. Cybern.* **57**, 6, (1987) 379–387.
01271 Interpolation coding: A representation for numbers in neural models. BALLARD, D. *Biol. Cybern.* **57**, 6, (1987) 389–402.
01272 Comparison of color sensation in dichoptic and in normal vision. WEHRHAHN, C. *Biol. Cybern.* **57**, 4/5, (1987) 213–215.
01273 A model of the motor servo: Incorporating nonlinear spindle receptor and muscle mechanical properties. GIELEN, C.; AND HOUK, J. *Biol. Cybern.* **57**, 4/5, (1987) 217–231.
01274 Visual pattern recognition in humans: I. Evidence for adaptive filtering. CAELLI, T.; RENTSCHLER, I.; AND SCHEIDLER, W. *Biol. Cybern.* **57**, 4/5, (1987) 233–240.
01275 The control of hand equilibrium trajectories in multi-joint arm movements. FLASH, T. *Biol. Cybern.* **57**, 4/5, (1987) 257–274.
01276 Electric and magnetic fields of the brain computed by way of a discrete systems analytical approach: Theory and validation. VAN ROTTERDAM, A. *Biol. Cybern.* **57**, 4/5, (1987) 301–311.
01277 Physiology based simulation model of triangle shape recognition. PIZLO, Z. *Biol. Cybern.* **58**, 1, (January 1988) 51–62.
01278 Shape from texture. ALOIMONOS, J. *Biol. Cybern.* **58**, 5, (April 1988) 345–360.
01279 Self-organizing system obtaining communication ability primitive model for language generation. NAKANO, K.; SAKAGUCHI, Y.; ISOTANI, R.; AND OHMORI, T. *Biol. Cybern.* **58**, 6, (Feb. 1988) 417–425.

## BIT

01280 On formalisms. MAYOH, B. *BIT* **28**, 3, (1988) 412–426.

## Bulletin of the American Society for Information Science

01281 Information science and the PSI phenomenon. LEVINE, E. *Bull. Am. Soc. Inf. Sci.* **11**, 5, (June/July 1985) 6–7.
01282 The moving target: future trends in networking. JACOB, M. *Bull. Am. Soc. Inf. Sci.* **11**, 6, (Aug./Sept. 1985) 12–14.
01283 Human factors for design and evaluation of software. MORARIU, J. *Bull. Am. Soc. Inf. Sci.* **12**, 1, (Oct./Nov. 1985) 18–19.
01284 Perception and acceptance of a local area network and electronic mail. TALLY, R.; AND PEDERSEN, G. *Bull. Am. Soc. Inf. Sci.* **12**, 1, (Oct./Nov. 1985) 20–21.
01285 A science of information for the information age. BROWN, J. *Bull. Am. Soc. Inf. Sci.* **12**, 4, (April/May 1986) 15–16.

## BYTE

HCI-0431 The LISP tutor: it approaches the effectiveness of a human tutor. ANDERSON, J.; AND REISER, B. *BYTE* **10**, 4, (April 1985) 159–175.
HCI-0332 Learning in parallel networks: simulating learning in a probabilistic system. HINTON, G. *BYTE* **10**, 4, (April 1985) 265–273.
HCI-0368 Reverse engineering the brain. STEVENS, J. *BYTE* **10**, 4, (April 1985) 287–299.
01286 A simple windowing system, part 1: basic principles. WEBSTER, B. *BYTE* **11**, 3, (March 1986) 129–133.
01287 Computing for the blind user. ARDITI, A.; AND GILLMAN, A. *BYTE* **11**, 3, (March 1986) 199–208.
01288 Enhanced console driver. ZACKIN, A. *BYTE* **11**, 10, (Oct. 1986) 183–192.
01289 Constructing an associative memory. KOSKO, B. *BYTE* **12**, 10, (Sept. 1987) 137–144.
01290 Spying on windows. GEARY, M. *BYTE* **12**, 12, (Oct. 1987) 97–110.
01291 Application input drivers. SAGAN, J. *BYTE* **12**, 12, (Oct. 1987) 143–154.
01292 Windows for BASIC. ROSS, J. *BYTE* **12**, 12, (Oct. 1987) 201–212.

# JOURNALS

01293 Comparison of Windowing Systems. STERN, H. *BYTE* **12,** 13, (Nov. 1987) 265–272.
01294 A C Interface. RIDGWAY, D. *BYTE* **12,** 13, (Nov. 1987) 363–368.
01295 The BCC180 multitasking controller part 3: memory management and windowing. CIARCIA, S. *BYTE* **13,** 3, (March 1988) 243–248.
01296 Computers on the brain, part 1. CIARCIA, S. *BYTE* **13,** 6, (June 1988) 273–285.
01297 Error-free fractions. CIARCIA, S. *BYTE* **13,** 6, (June 1988) 289–298.
01298 Computers on the brain, part 2. CIARCIA, S. *BYTE* **13,** 7, (July 1988) 289–296.
HCI-0128 Between man and machine. TELLO, E. *BYTE* **13,** 9, (Sept. 1988) 288–293.
01299 DOS 4.0. MALLOY, R. *BYTE* **13,** 11, (Fall 1988) 75–78.
01300 Working together. ENGELBART, D.; AND LEHTMAN, H. *BYTE* **13,** 13, (Dec. 1988) 245–252.
01301 Where the action is. WINOGRAD, T. *BYTE* **13,** 13, (Dec. 1988) 256–258.
01302 Perils and pitfalls. GRUDIN, J. *BYTE* **13,** 13, (Dec. 1988) 261–264.
01303 Intelligent software agents. CROWSTON, K.; AND MALONE, T. *BYTE* **13,** 13, (Dec. 1988) 267–272.
01304 A groupware toolbox. OPPER, S. *BYTE* **13,** 13, (Dec. 1988) 275–282.
01305 Face to face with Open Look. HOEBER, T. *BYTE* **13,** 13, (Dec. 1988) 286–296.
01306 Turbo pascal windowing system. BUTLER, C. *BYTE* **14,** 2, (February 1989) 283–291.
01307 Hard disk interfaces. GLASS, B. *BYTE* **14,** 2, (February 1989) 293–297.
01308 Digital video interactive. GLASS, L. *BYTE* **14,** 5, (May 1989) 283–289.
01309 Domesticating microsoft windows. LANE, A. *BYTE* **14,** 6, (June 1989) 205–207.
01310 Claris CAD. TUTEN, P. *BYTE* **14,** 6, (June 1989) 209–210.
01311 The Mac interface: showing its age. CRABB, D. *BYTE* **14,** 6, (June 1989) 235–237.

## CAD/CAM Digest

01312 The economics of UNIX workstations. FERRINGTON, L. *CAD/CAM Dig.* **6,** 9/10, (June/July 1985) 6–8.

## Canadian Journal of Information Science

01313 Technological development and the integrated workstation. FORGIE, D. *Can. J. Inf. Sci.* **9,** (June 1986) 105–113.
01314 Online searching: a five star review of research. FOSTER, J. *Can. J. Inf. Sci.* **11,** 1, (1986) 1–17.

## CD-ROM Review

01315 The look and feel . . . and sound of the user interface. BREWER, B. *CD-ROM Rev.* **2,** 3, (Aug. 1987) 26–30.
01316 Putting Texas on disc. KERR, D.; AND FERRIS, J. *CD-ROM Rev.* **2,** 5, (Dec., 1987) 40–42.

## CIM Review

01317 Bringing image processing into focus. MOODY, G. *CIM Rev.* **2,** 4, (June 1986) 26–28.
01318 MADEMA: an approach to intelligent manufacturing systems. CHRYSSOLOURIS, G. *CIM Rev.* **3,** 3, (March 1987) 11–17.

## Collegiate Microcomputer

01319 Communication barriers in microcomputer—based courses. GOLEN, S.; AND KELLER, T. *Collegiate Microcomput.* **5,** 1, (April/May 1988) 77–79.

## Communications of the ACM

HCI-0209  The evaluation of text editors: methodology and empirical results. ROBERTS, T.; AND MORAN, T. *Commun. ACM* **26**, 4, (April 1983) 265–283.

HCI-0208  Training wheels in a user interface. CARROLL, J.; AND CARRITHERS, C. *Commun. ACM* **27**, 8, (August 1984) 800–806.

HCI-0440  Computer mediated work: the interplay between technology and structured jobs. TURNER, J. *Commun. ACM* **27**, 12, (Dec. 1984) 1210–1217.

HCI-0099  Programmer perceptions of productivity and programming tools. HANSON, S.; AND ROSINSKI, R. *Commun. ACM* **28**, 2, (Feb. 1985) 180–189.

HCI-0400  A system for interactive viewing of structured documents. WITTEN, I.; AND BRAMWELL, B. *Commun. ACM* **28**, 3, (March 1985) 280–288.

HCI-0231  Designing for usability: key principles and what designers think. GOULD, J.; AND LEWIS, C. *Commun. ACM* **28**, 3, (March 1985) 300–311.

HCI-0112  A generalized user interface for applications programs (II). BASS, L. *Commun. ACM* **28**, 6, (June 1985) 617–627.

HCI-0355  Natural language with discrete speech as a mode for human-to-machine. BIERMANN, A.; RODMAN, R.; RUBIN, D.; AND HEIDLAGE, J. *Commun. ACM* **28**, 6, (June 1985) 628–636.

HCI-0215  Understanding the effectiveness of computer graphics for decision support: a cumulative experimental approach. DICKSON, G.; DESANCTIS, G.; AND MCBRIDE, D. *Commun. ACM* **29**, 1, (Jan. 1986) 40–47.

HCI-0091  Andrew: a distributed personal computing environment. MORRIS, J.; SATYANARAYANAN, M.; CONNER, M.; HOWARD, J.; ROSENTHAL, D.; AND SMITH, F. *Commun. ACM* **29**, 3, (March 1986) 184–201.

HCI-0448  An empirical study of the impact of user involvement on system usage and information satisfaction. BAROUDI, J.; OLSON, M.; AND IVES, B. *Commun. ACM* **29**, 3, (March 1986) 232–238.

01320  Embedded menus: selecting items in context. KOVED, L.; AND SCNEIDERMAN, B. *Commun. ACM* **29**, 4, (April 1986) 312–318.

HCI-0427  What makes users happy? RUSHINEK, A.; AND RUSHINEK, S. *Commun. ACM* **29**, 7, (July 1986) 594–598.

HCI-0349  Pygmalion at the interface. SLATOR, B.; ANDERSON, M.; AND CONLEY, W. *Commun. ACM* **29**, 7, (July 1986) 599–604.

HCI-0232  Computer anxiety in management: myth or reality? HOWARD, G.; AND SMITH, R. *Commun. ACM* **29**, 7, (July 1986) 611–615.

HCI-0399  A note on undetected typing errors. PETERSON, J. *Commun. ACM* **29**, 7, (July 1986) 633–637.

HCI-0222  Operator work load: when is enough enough? LEMAY, M.; AND HIRD, E. *Commun. ACM* **29**, 7, (July 1986) 638–642.

HCI-0438  The automated tutoring of introductory computer programming. ANDERSON, J.; AND SKWARECKI, E. *Commun. ACM* **29**, 9, (Sept. 1986) 842–849.

HCI-0121  Boxer: a reconstructible computational medium. DISESSA, A.; AND ABELSON, H. *Commun. ACM* **29**, 9, (Sept. 1986) 859–868.

HCI-0196  An experimental program investigating color-enhanced and graphical information presentation: an integration of the findings. BENBASAT, I.; DEXTER, A.; AND TODD, P. *Commun. ACM* **29**, 11, (Nov. 1986) 1094–1105.

01321  Interface design issues for advice-giving expert systems. CARROLL, J.; AND MCKENDREE, J. *Commun. ACM* **30**, 1, (Jan. 1987) 14–32.

HCI-0312  Beyond the chalkboard: computer support for collaboration and problem solving in meetings. STEFIK, M.; FOSTER, G.; BOBROW, D.; KAHN, K.; LANNING, S.; AND SUCHMAN, L. *Commun. ACM* **30**, 1, (Jan. 1987) 32–47.

01322  Intelligent information-sharing systems. MALONE, T.; GRANT, K.; TURBAK, F.; BROBST, S.; AND COHEN, M. *Commun. ACM* **30**, 5, (May 1987) 390–402.

HCI-0125  The 1984 Olympic Message System: a test of behavioral principles of system design. GOULD, J.; BOIES, S.; LEVY, S.; RICHARDS, J.; AND SCHOONARD, J. *Commun. ACM* **30**, 9, (Sept. 1987) 758–769.

HCI-0126  A proposed solution to the problem of levels in error-message generation. EFE, K. *Commun. ACM* **30**, 11, (Nov. 1987) 948–955.

## JOURNALS

HCI-0224    The vocabulary problem in human-system communication. FURNAS, G.; LANDAUER, T.; GOMEZ, L.; AND DUMAIS, S. *Commun. ACM* **30,** 11, (Nov. 1987) 964–971.

HCI-0104    Anatomy of a compact user interface development tool. STOTT, J.; AND KOTTEMANN, J. *Commun. ACM* **31,** 1, (Jan. 1988) 56–66.

HCI-0314    Computing with structured connectionist networks. FELDMAN, J.; FANTY, M.; GODDARD, N.; AND LYNNE, K. *Commun. ACM* **31,** 2, (Feb. 1988) 170–187.

HCI-0228    Impact of system response time on state anxiety. GUYNES, J. *Commun. ACM* **31,** 3, (March 1988) 342–347.

HCI-0127    Cost/benefit analysis for incorporating human factors in the software lifecycle. MANTEI, M.; AND TEOREY, T. *Commun. ACM* **31,** 4, (April 1988) 428–439.

HCI-0202    An experimental evaluation of the impact of data display format on recall performance. SCHMELL, R.; AND UMANATH, N. *Commun. ACM* **31,** 5, (May 1988) 562–570.

HCI-0293    Reflections on NoteCards: seven issues for the next generation of hypermedia systems. HALASZ, F. *Commun. ACM* **31,** 7, (July 1988) 836–852.

HCI-0229    Learning by doing with simulated intelligent help. CARROLL, J.; AND AARONSON, A. *Commun. ACM* **31,** 9, (Sept. 1988) 1064–1079.

HCI-0204    Reading and writing with computers: a framework for explaining differences in performance. HANSEN, W.; AND HAAS, C. *Commun. ACM* **31,** 9, (Sept. 1988) 1080–1089.

HCI-0129    The designer as user: building requirements for design tools from design practice. ROSSON, M.; KELLOGG, W.; AND MAASS, S. *Commun. ACM* **31,** 11, (Nov. 1988) 1288–1298.

01323    User interface design from a real time perspective. KUO, F.; AND KARIMI, J. *Commun. ACM* **31,** 12, (Dec. 1988) 1456–1466.

HCI-0441    Computerization, productivity, and quality of work-life. KRAUT, R.; DUMAIS, S.; AND KOCH, S. *Commun. ACM* **32,** 2, (Feb. 1989) 220–238.

01324    Why the look and feel of software user interfaces should not be protected by copyright law. SAMUELSON, P. *Commun. ACM* **32,** 5, (May 1989) 563–572.

01325    The coming revolution in interactive digital video. FOX, E. *Commun. ACM* **32,** 7, (July 1989) 794–801.

01326    Virtual video editing in interactive multimedia applications. MACKAY, W.; AND DAVENPORT, G. *Commun. ACM* **32,** 7, (July 1989) 802–810.

01327    DVI—a digital multimedia technology. RIPLEY, G. *Commun. ACM* **32,** 7, (July 1989) 811–822.

01328    Life before the chips: simulating digital video interactive technology. DIXON, D. *Commun. ACM* **32,** 7, (July 1989) 824–831.

01329    Intelligent interactive video simulation of a code inspection. STEVENS, S. *Commun. ACM* **32,** 7, (July 1989) 832–843.

01330    Coding image sequences for interactive retrieval. LIPPMAN, A.; AND BUTERA, W. *Commun. ACM* **32,** 7, (July 1989) 852–860.

HCI-0384    The next generation of interactive technologies. FRENKEL, K. *Commun. ACM* **32,** 7, (July 1989) 872–881.

01331    ER model clustering as an aid for user communication and documentation in database design. TEOREY, T.; WEI, G.; BOLTON, D.; AND KOENIG, J. *Commun. ACM* **32,** 8, (Aug. 1989) 975–987.

01332    A graphics interface for linear programming. MA, P.; MURPHY, F.; AND STOHR, E. *Commun. ACM* **32,** 8, (Aug. 1989) 996–1012.

01333    The case against user interface consistency. GRUDIN, J. *Commun. ACM* **32,** 10, (Oct. 1989) 1164–1173.

01334    Impact of a restricted natural language interface on ease of learning and productivity. NAPIER, H.; BATSELL, R.; GUADANGO, N.; AND LANE, D. *Commun. ACM* **32,** 10, (Oct. 1989) 1190–1198.

01335    User cube: a taxonomy of end users. COTTERMAN, W.; AND KUMAR, K. *Commun. ACM* **32,** 11, (Nov. 1989) 1313–1320.

01336    Information technologies for the 1990's: an orgnizational impact perspective. STRAUB, D.; AND WETHERBE, J. *Commun. ACM* **32,** 11, (Nov. 1989) 1328–1339.

01337    The adaptable user interface. KANTOROWITZ, E.; AND SUDARSKY, O. *Commun. ACM* **32,** 11, (Nov. 1989) 1352–1358.

## Complex Systems

01338 Scaling relationships in back-propagation learning. TESAURO, G.; AND JANSSENS, B. *Complex Syst.* **2**, 1, (Feb, 1988) 39–44.

01339 Neural networks and NP-complete optimization problems; a performance study on the graph bisection problem. PETERSON, C.; AND ANDERSON, J. *Complex Syst.* **2**, 1, (Feb, 1988) 59–89.

01340 Basins of attraction in a perceptron-like neural network. KRAUTH, W.; MEZARD, M.; AND NADAL, J. *Complex Syst.* **2**, 4, (Aug. 1988) 387–408.

01341 Competitive dynamics in a dual-route connectionist model of print-to-sound transformation. REGGIA, J.; MARSLAND, P.; AND BERNDT, R. *Complex Syst.* **2**, 5, (Oct. 1988) 509–547.

## Computational Linguistics

01342 Integrated processing produces robust understanding. SELFRIDGE, M. *Comput. Linguist.* **12**, 2, (April/June 1986) 89–106.

01343 Summarizing natural language database responses. KALITA, J.; JONES, M.; AND MCCALLA, G. *Comput. Linguist.* **12**, 2, (April/June 1986) 107–124.

01344 Attention, intention, and the structure of discourse. GROSZ, B.; AND SIDNER, C. *Comput. Linguist.* **12**, 3, (July/Sept. 1986) 175–204.

01345 Reference identification and reference identification failures. GOODMAN, B. *Comput. Linguist.* **12**, 4, (Oct/Dec. 1986) 273–305.

01346 Tense, qualifiers, and contexts. HINRICHS, E. *Comput. Linguist.* **14**, 2, (June 1988) 3–14.

01347 Temporal ontology and temporal reference. MOENS, M.; AND STEEDMAN, M. *Comput. Linguist.* **14**, 2, (June 1988) 15–28.

01348 Modeling the user in natural language systems. KASS, R.; AND FININ, T. *Comput. Linguist.* **14**, 3, (Sept. 1988) 5–22.

01349 Modeling the user's plans and goals. CARBERRY, S. *Comput. Linguist.* **14**, 3, (Sept. 1988) 23–37.

01350 Recognizing and responding to plan-oriented misconceptions. QUILICI, A.; DYER, M.; AND FLOWERS, M. *Comput. Linguist.* **14**, 3, (Sept. 1988) 38–51.

01351 Reasoning on a highlighted user model to respond to misconceptions. MCCOY, K. *Comput. Linguist.* **14**, 3, (Sept. 1988) 52–63.

01352 Tailoring object descriptions to a user's level of expertise. PARIS, C. *Comput. Linguist.* **14**, 3, (Sept. 1988) 64–78.

01353 The relationship between user models and discourse models. SCHUSTER, E.; CHIN, D.; COHEN, R.; KOBSA, A.; MORIK, K.; JONES, K.; AND WAHLSTER, W. *Comput. Linguist.* **14**, 3, (Sept. 1988) 79–103.

01354 Natural language querying of historical data bases. CLIFFORD, J. *Comput. Linguist.* **14**, 4, (December 1988) 10–34.

01355 The Berkeley UNIX consultant project. WILENSKY, R.; CHIN, D.; LURIA, M.; MARTIN, J.; AND MAYFIELD, J. *Comput. Linguist.* **14**, 4, (December 1988) 35–84.

## Computer

HCI-0143 PICT: an interactive graphical programming environment. GILNERT, E.; AND TANIMOTO, S. *Computer* **17**, 11, (Nov. 1984) 7–25.

HCI-0395 Geomatic: a 3-D graphic relief simulation system. LAURENT, D.; AND MOTET, S. *Computer* **17**, 12, (Dec. 1984) 25–30.

HCI-0114 Abstractions for user interface design. COUTAZ, J. *Computer* **18**, 9, (Sept. 1985) 21–34.

HCI-0282 Reading and writing the electronic book. YANKELOVICH, N.; MEYROWITZ, N.; AND VAN DAM, A. *Computer* **18**, 10, (Oct. 1985) 15–30.

## JOURNALS

HCI-0308  A distributed interoffice mail system. SAKATA, S.; AND UEDA, T. *Computer* **18**, 10, (Oct. 1985) 106–116.
HCI-0437  Using low-cost workstations to investigate computer networks and distributed systems. SHERMAN, M.; AND MARKS, A. *Computer* **19**, 6, (June 1986) 32–41.
HCI-0429  The Japanese and software: is it a good match? BELADY, L. *Computer* **19**, 6, (June 1986) 57–61.
HCI-0258  A visual approach to browsing in a database environment. LARSON, J. *Computer* **19**, 6, (June 1986) 62–71.
01356  The workstation: the interpress page and document description language. BHUSHAN, A.; AND PLASS, M. *Computer* **19**, 6, (June 1986) 72–77.
HCI-0321  Applications of AI in engineering. FAUGHT, W. *Computer* **19**, 7, (July 1986) 17–27.
HCI-0320  Knowledge and control for a mechanical design expert system. BROWN, D.; AND CHANDRASEKARAN, B. *Computer* **19**, 7, (July 1986) 92–100.
HCI-0092  LisaLearning. CARROLL, J.; AND MAZUR, S. *Computer* **19**, 11, (Nov. 1986) 35–49.
HCI-0265  Design and performance considerations for an optical disk-based, multimedia object server. CHRISTODOULAKIS, S.; AND FALOUTSOS, C. *Computer* **19**, 12, (Dec. 1986) 45–56.
01357  The FAA's Advanced Automation System: strategies for future air traffic control systems. HUNT, V.; AND ZELLWEGER, A. *Computer* **20**, 2, (Feb. 1987) 19–32.
01358  Engineering the man-machine interface for air traffic control. KLOSTER, G.; AND ZELLWEGER, A. *Computer* **20**, 2, (Feb. 1987) 47–62.
01359  The quantification of operational suitability. PHILLIPS, M. *Computer* **20**, 2, (Feb. 1987) 63–71.
HCI-0159  Ada: first users—pleased; prospective users—still hesitant. MYERS, W. *Computer* **20**, 3, (March 1987) 68–73.
01360  Hypertext: an introduction and survey. CONKLIN, J. *Computer* **20**, 9, (Sept. 1987) 17–41.
01361  The "neural" phonetic typewriter. KOHONEN, T. *Computer:A* **21**, 3, (March 1988) 11–22.
01362  Neural nets for adaptive filtering and adaptive pattern recognition. WIDROW, B.; AND WINTER, R. *Computer* **21**, 3, (March 1988) 25–39.
01363  VLSI implementation of a neural network model. GRAF, H.; JACKEL, L.; AND HUBBARD, W. *Computer* **21**, 3, (March 1988) 41–49.
HCI-0391  A neural network for visual pattern recognition. FUKUSHIMA, K. *Computer* **21**, 3, (March 1988) 65–75.
01364  The ART of adaptive pattern recognition by a self-organizing neural network. CARPENTER, G.; AND GROSSBERG, S. *Computer* **21**, 3, (March 1988) 77–88.
01365  Computing with structured neural networks. FELDMAN, J.; FANTY, M.; AND GODDARD, N. *Computer* **21**, 3, (March 1988) 91–103.
01366  Self-organization in a perceptual network. LINSKER, R. *Computer* **21**, 3, (March 1988) 105–116.
01367  Exploring algorithms using Balsa-II. BROWN, M. *Computer* **21**, 5, (May, 1988) 14–36.
01368  The programmer's apprentices: a research overview. RICH, C.; AND WATERS, R. *Computer* **21**, 11, (Nov. 1988) 10–25.
01369  Segue: support for distributed graphical interfaces. SCHAFFNER, S.; AND BORKAN, M. *Computer* **21**, 12, (Dec. 1988) 42–55.
HCI-0131  Composing user interfaces with InterViews. LINTON, M.; VISSIDES, J.; AND CALDER, P. *Computer* **22**, 2, (Feb. 1989) 8–22.
01370  Prototypes from standard user interface management systems. LEWIS, T.; HANDLOSER, F.; BOSE, S.; AND YANG, S. *Computer* **22**, 5, (May 1989) 51–60.

## Computer Bulletin

01371  Cognitive aspects of HCI. GREEN, T. *Comput. Bull.* **2**, 3, (Sept. 1986) 7–9.
01372  Human factors in the IT specification process. MACAULAY, L.; FOWLER, C.; AND HUTT, A. *Comput. Bull.* **2**, 3, (Sept. 1986) 10–12.
01373  User interface design and formal methods. THIMBLEBY, H. *Comput. Bull.* **2**, 3, (Sept. 1986) 13–15.
01374  Human factors in computer based message systems. RUBIN, T. *Comput. Bull.* **2**, 3, (Sept. 1986) 16–18.
01375  The use and misuse of VDU'S. WALMISLEY, P. *Comput. Bull.* **2**, 3, (Sept. 1986) 34–36.
01376  OA: bridging the language gap. BLAAZER, C. *Comput. Bull.* **3**, 1, (March 1987) 8–10.

01377 Information management—the realities. BALES, V. *Comput. Bull.* **3**, 1, (March 1987) 15–16.
01378 ...from the end user angle. TAGG, R. *Comput. Bull.* **3**, 4, (Dec., 1987) 12–13.
01379 Neural computing: ideas from the brain. ALEKSANDER, I. *Comput. Bull.* **4**, 1, (March, 1988) 14–15.
01380 Interactive video in language learning. ROBERTSON, I.; AND PICCIOTTO, M. *Comput. Bull.* **4**, 1, (March, 1988) 16–17.
01381 Live-Net in education. FARMER, M. *Comput. Bull.* **4**, 3, (Sept. 1988) 30–32.
01382 The many faces of HMI. INNOCENT, P. *Comput. Bull.* **4**, 3, (Sept. 1988) 33–35.

## Computer Communications

01383 Office automation—can it be justified? PICKERING, T. *Comput. Commun.* **10**, 3, (June 1987) 140–146.
01384 User-network interfaces. DAVIES, D.; AND RUMSEY, D. *Comput. Commun.* **11**, 4, (August 1988) 197–202.
01385 ISPBXs and terminals. DAVIES, I.; AND MCBAIN, A. *Comput. Commun.* **11**, 4, (August 1988) 203–207.
01386 User system interaction standards. HOLDAWAY, K.; AND BEVAN, N. *Comput. Commun.* **12**, 2, (April 1989) 97–101.

## Computer Design

01387 Advanced computers. WILLIAMS, T. *Comput. Des.* **26**, 5, (March 1, 1987) 47–62.
01388 Windowlike user interfaces link systems and applications. WILLIAMS, T. *Comput. Des.* **27**, 7, (April 1, 1988) 34–43.

## Computer Graphics Forum

01389 Managing multiple context-frames through GKS. HERMAN, I. *Comput. Graph. Forum* **3**, 1, (March 1984) 79–82.
HCI-0411 IDECAP: interactive pictorial information system for demographic and environmental planning applications. VAN DEN BOS, J.; VAN NAELTEN, M.; AND TEUNISSEN, W. *Comput. Graph. Forum* **3**, 1, (March 1984) 91–102.
01390 Graphical interaction management. BARN, B.; AND WILLIS, P. *Comput. Graph. Forum* **6**, 2, (May 1987) 119–124.
01391 A user-interface toolkit in object-oriented PostScript. DENSMORE, O.; AND ROSENTHAL, D. *Comput. Graph. Forum* **6**, 3, (Sept. 1987) 171–179.
01392 Making drawings talk: pictures in minds and machines. BIJL, A. *Comput. Graph. Forum* **6**, 4, (Dec., 1987) 289–298.
01393 Logical input devices and interaction. VAN LIERE, R.; AND TEN HAGEN, P. *Comput. Graph. Forum* **6**, 4, (Dec., 1987) 349–357.
01394 An editor for constructing graphics with $T_EX$. WALDSCHMIDT, H. *Comput. Graph. Forum* **6**, 4, (Dec., 1987) 359–364.
01395 Architectures of graphic processors for interactive 2D graphics. FONTENIER, G.; AND GROS, P. *Comput. Graph. Forum* **7**, 2, (June 1988) 79–89.
01396 GRAFLOG: understanding drawings through natural language. PINEDA, L.; KLEIN, E.; AND LEE, J. *Comput. Graph. Forum* **7**, 2, (June 1988) 97–103.
01397 Experience with chisl, a configurable hierarchical interface specification language. WOOD, C.; GRAY, P.; AND KILGOUR, A. *Comput. Graph. Forum* **7**, 2, (June 1988) 117–127.
01398 Construction of interactive programs in computer graphics. DUFOURD, J. *Comput. Graph. Forum* **7**, 3, (September 1988) 161–176.
01399 Continuous processing of images through user sketched functional blocks. KAYA, A.; AND ÖZGÜÇ, B. *Comput. Graph. Forum* **7**, 4, (November 1988) 273–280.

01400 Dialogue cell resource model and basic dialogue cells. SCHOUTEN, H.; AND TEN HAGEN, P. *Comput. Graph. Forum* **7**, 4, (November 1988) 311–322.

01401 A top down method for interactive drawing. SLATER, M. *Comput. Graph. Forum* **7**, 4, (November 1988) 323–329.

01402 The controller animation system. JOHN, N.; AND WILLIS, P. *Comput. Graph. Forum* **8**, 2, (June 1989) 133–138.

## Computer Journal

HCI-0148 Literate programming. KNUTH, D. *Comput. J.* **27**, 2, (May 1984) 97–111.

01403 Implementing neural network models on parallel computers. FORREST, B.; ROWETH, D.; STROUD, N.; WALLACE, D.; AND WILSON, G. *Comput. J.* **30**, 5, (Oct. 1987) 413–419.

01404 A flexible synonym interface with application examples in CAL and help environments. GWEI, G.; AND FOXLEY, E. *Comput. J.* **30**, 56, (Dec. 1987) 551–557.

01405 The 'window' terminal. PARKER, J.; AND KENNARD, A. *Comput. J.* **30**, 56, (Dec. 1987) 558–564.

01406 A formal specification of the QMS message system: the underlying abstract model. ROBERTS, W. *Comput. J.* **31**, 4, (August 1988) 313–324.

01407 Are 'human factors' human? BJORN-ANDERSON, N. *Comput. J.* **31**, 5, (Oct. 1988) 386–390.

01408 Individual and organizational factors and the design of IPSEs. LEQUESNE, P. *Comput. J.* **31**, 5, (Oct. 1988) 391–397.

01409 Information systems and user resistance: theory and practice. HIRSCHHEIM, R.; AND NEWMAN, M. *Comput. J.* **31**, 5, (Oct. 1988) 398–408.

01410 A multidimensional approach to the measurement of human-computer performance. JAGODZINSKI, A.; AND CLARKE, D. *Comput. J.* **31**, 5, (Oct. 1988) 409–419.

01411 The use of prototyping and simulation in the development of large-scale applications. HARKER, S. *Comput. J.* **31**, 5, (Oct. 1988) 420–425.

01412 The supplier's role in the design of products for organisations. EASON, K.; AND HARKER, S. *Comput. J.* **31**, 5, (Oct. 1988) 426–430.

01413 Employing usability engineering in the development of office products. TYLDESLEY, D. *Comput. J.* **31**, 5, (Oct. 1988) 431–436.

01414 Human-computer interface recording. MORRIS, D.; THEAKER, C.; PHILLIPS, R.; AND LOVE, W. *Comput. J.* **31**, 5, (Oct. 1988) 437–444.

01415 Approximate modelling of cognitive activity with an expert system: a theory-based strategy for developing an interactive design tool. BARNARD, P.; WILSON, M.; AND MACLEAN, A. *Comput. J.* **31**, 5, (Oct. 1988) 445–456.

01416 Reading from paper versus reading from screen. DILLON, A.; MCKNIGHT, C.; AND RICHARDSON, J. *Comput. J.* **31**, 5, (Oct. 1988) 457–464.

01417 Experience with adaptive interfaces. BENYON, D.; AND MURRAY, D. *Comput. J.* **31**, 5, (Oct. 1988) 465–473.

01418 Non-strict languages-programming and implementation. WRAY, S.; AND FAIRBAIRN, J. *Comput. J.* **32**, 2, (April 1989) 142–151.

## Computer Language

01419 Build your own user interface. MEACHAM, W. *Comput. Lang. (San Francisco, CA)* **4**, 10, (Oct. 1987) 57–62.

01420 Jeff Garbers and the ergonomics of software. GETTS, J. *Comput. Lang. (San Francisco, CA)* **4**, 10, (Oct. 1987) 79–86.

01421 Turbo windows. KERR, J. *Comput. Lang. (San Francisco, CA)* **5**, 6, (June, 1988) 55–59.

01422 HIC: the human interface column. KELLY-BOOTLE, S. *Comput. Lang. (San Francisco, CA)* **5**, 7, (July 1988) 75–82.

01423 Orthodox dialectical interfaces. KELLY-BOOTLE, S. *Comput. Lang. (San Francisco, CA)* **5**, 8, (August 1988) 79–85.

**01424** Building a self-modifying user interface. TYLUTKI, G. *Comput. Lang. (San Francisco, CA)* **6**, 5, (May 1989) 1–47.
**01425** Designing with databases. RAPAPORT, M. *Comput. Lang. (San Francisco, CA)* **6**, 5, (May 1989) 87–94.
**01426** Tools for buidling interfaces. PARKER, T.; AND POWELL, J. *Comput. Lang. (San Francisco, CA)* :0B6, 5, (May 1989) 105–115.

## Computer Languages

**HCI-0252** Generalized query-by-rule: a heterogeneous database query language. PATNAIK, L.; AND CHOWDHARY, D. *Comput. Lang. (Elmsford, NY)* **10**, 3/4, (1985) 165–178.
**01427** Design of a graphics interface for computer-based biomedical applications. ZAKI, M. *Comput. Lang. (Elmsford, NY)* **13**, 3/4, (1988) 125–141.

## Computer Networks and ISDN Systems

**01428** MH: a multifarious user agent. ROSE, M.; STEFFERUD, E.; AND SWEET, J. *Comput. Networks ISDN Syst.* **10**, 2, (Sept. 1985) 65–80.
**01429** Attacking a complex distributed algorithm from different sides: an experience wih complementary validation tools. GROZ, R.; JARD, C.; AND LASSUDRIE, C. *Comput. Networks ISDN Syst.* **10**, 5, (Dec. 1985) 245–257.
**01430** Evaluation and intergration of specification languages. BRUIJNING, J. *Comput. Networks ISDN Syst.* **13**, 2, (March 1, 1987) 75–89.
**01431** Session on the requirements of international user groups. BAUERFELD, W. *Comput. Networks ISDN Syst.* **13**, 3, (Dec. 1987) 227–227.
**01432** A user view of virtual terminal standardisation. GILMORE, B. *Comput. Networks ISDN Syst.* **13**, 3, (Dec. 1987) 229–233.
**01433** Some remarks on videotex interaction. How to write for a new reader. BASEVI, E. *Comput. Networks ISDN Syst.* **14**, 2-5, (February 1988) 179–185.
**01434** Presentation of a description language for office tasks. MARITORENA, C. *Comput. Networks ISDN Syst.* **14**, 2-5, (February 1988) 187–197.
**01435** Communication analysis in the company. KAIVERS, R. *Comput. Networks ISDN Syst.* **14**, 2-5, (February 1988) 199–205.
**01436** The telephone in question: questions on communication. CLAISSE, G.; AND ROWE, F. *Comput. Networks ISDN Syst.* **14**, 2-5, (February 1988) 207–219.
**01437** The silent force of the screen. A research note on the impact of microelectronics on work autonomy among clerical workers in public administration. BAERT, P.; CUYPERS, C.; AND DE SCHAMPHELEIRE, J. *Comput. Networks ISDN Syst.* **14**, 2-5, (February 1988) 267–270.
**01438** Successful implementation of an office system. TAMINE, J. *Comput. Networks ISDN Syst.* **14**, 2-5, (February 1988) 279–282.
**01439** Socio-technical aspects of electronic mail implementation. LATRILLE, J. *Comput. Networks ISDN Syst.* **14**, 2-5, (February 1988) 283–290.
**01440** An interdisciplinary approach to human factors in telematic systems. A review of the problems and possible solutions by a COST-11 ter working group. VAN DER VEER, G.; GUEST, S.; HASELAGER, P.; INNOCENT, P.; AND MCDAID, E. *Comput. Networks ISDN Syst.* **15**, 1, (January 1988) 73–80.
**01441** A communication mechanism supporting actions. ROTHERMEL, K. *Comput. Networks ISDN Syst.* **15**, 2, (Feb. 1988) 97–108.
**01442** Traffic study on primary rate ISDN user-network interface. MIYAKE, K. *Comput. Networks ISDN Syst.* **15**, 5, (October 1988) 359–367.
**01443** What users want. MOUNT, R. *Comput. Networks ISDN Syst.* **16**, 1 & 2, (September 1988) 146–149.

## Computer Newsletter

01444 Supporting end users in the office. *Comput. Newsl.* 12, (Jan./Feb. 1986) 2–3.
01445 Helping the disabled. TAIT, A. *Comput. Newsl.* 34, (April, 1988) 9–10.
01446 VDUs can ruin your health. *Comput. Newsl.* 34, (April, 1988) 16–16.

## Computer Science in Economics and Management

01447 A user-friendly interface to Kendrick's DUAL code. GRISCHOW, C.; AND UEBE, G. *Comput. Sci. Econ. Manage.* **1**, 2, (June 1988) 153–161.

## Computer Speech and Language

01448 Improving speaker consistency in an automatic speech recognition framework. ROBERTS, L.; WILPON, J.; EGAN, D.; AND BAKK, J. *Comput. Speech Lang.* **1**, 1, (March 1986) 61–93.

## Computer Standards and Interfaces

01449 Ergonomic guidelines for computerized user interfaces. FOOTE-LENOX, T. *Comput. Stand. Interfaces* **5**, 3, (March 1986) 195–199.
01450 Lessons from the MOSI project. MOONEY, J. *Comput. Stand. Interfaces* **5**, 3, (March 1986) 201–210.
01451 On the interface between the high level languages and Chinese character information. WANG, M. *Comput. Stand. Interfaces* **6**, 2, (1987) 181–186.
01452 The architecture of an inexpensive and portable talking-tactile terminal to aid the visually handicapped. KARSHMER, A.; MYLER, H.; AND DAVIS, R. *Comput. Stand. Interfaces* **6**, 2, (1987) 207–220.
01453 A map of the world of software-related standards, guidelines, and recommended practices. NASH, S.; AND REDWINE, S. *Comput. Stand. Interfaces* **6**, 2, (1987) 245–265.
01454 The use of the IBM personal computer in the man-machine interface to a nuclear research accelerator. LETTS, S. *Comput. Stand. Interfaces* **6**, 3, (September 1, 1987) 331–340.
01455 ISDN and the move to integrated communications—an introduction. SZPAK, M. *Comput. Stand. Interfaces* **7**, 4, (April 1988) 349–362.
01456 Necessary functions of institutions for test and certification from the viewpoint of users in IT. STEINBRINCK, T. *Comput. Stand. Interfaces* **7**, 1/2, (January, 1988) 53–55.
01457 Why users must co-operate internationally on standardization. WALKER, R. *Comput. Stand. Interfaces* **7**, 1/2, (January, 1988) 57–62.
01458 User investigation into practical systems. GREAVES, W. *Comput. Stand. Interfaces* **7**, 1/2, (January, 1988) 73–76.
01459 Artificial intelligence techniques in man–machine communication. HATON, J.; AND HATON, M. *Comput. Stand. Interfaces* **8**, 1, (1988) 37–40.
01460 The committee support system. HAHN, J. *Comput. Stand. Interfaces* **8**, 1, (1988) 57–66.

## Computer Vision, Graphics, and Image Processing

HCI-0367 Perception of transparency in man and machine. BECK, J. *Comput. Vision Graph. Image Process.* **31**, 2, (Aug. 1985) 127–138.
HCI-0365 Early vision: from computational structure to algorithms and parallel hardware. POGGIO, T. *Comput. Vision Graph. Image Process.* **31**, 2, (Aug. 1985) 139–155.

HCI-0366  Preattentive processing in vision. TREISMAN, A. *Comput. Vision Graph. Image Process.* **31**, 2, (Aug. 1985) 156–177.
HCI-0363  Connectionist models and parallelism in high level vision. FELDMAN, J. *Comput. Vision Graph. Image Process.* **31**, 2, (Aug. 1985) 178–200.
01461  Generative systems of analyzers. LEYTON, M. *Comput. Vision Graph. Image Process.* **31**, 2, (Aug. 1985) 201–241.
HCI-0364  Perception of organization in a random stimulus. SMITH, B. *Comput. Vision Graph. Image Process.* **31**, 2, (Aug. 1985) 242–247.
HCI-0392  Environment-centered and viewer-centered perception of surface orientation. SEDGWICK, H.; AND LEVY, S. *Comput. Vision Graph. Image Process.* **31**, 2, (Aug. 1985) 248–260.
HCI-0393  Visual hyperacuity: representation and computation of high precision position information. KROTKOV, E. *Comput. Vision Graph. Image Process.* **33**, 1, (Jan. 1986) 99–115.
01462  Anything you can do, I can do better (no you can't). PRICE, K. *Comput. Vision Graph. Image Process.* **36**, 2/3, (Nov/Dec. 1986) 387–391.
01463  Contingent aftereffects and isoluminance: psychophysical evidence for separation of color, orientation, and motion. SAVOY, R. *Comput. Vision Graph. Image Process.* **37**, 1, (Jan. 1987) 3–19.
01464  Nested structures of control: an intuitive view. LEYTON, M. *Comput. Vision Graph. Image Process.* **37**, 1, (Jan. 1987) 20–53.
01465  Machines should not see as people do, but must know how people see. HOCHBERG, J. *Comput. Vision Graph. Image Process.* **37**, 2, (Feb. 1987) 221–237.
01466  Detecting structure by symbolic constructions on tokens. STEVENS, K.; AND BROOKES, A. *Comput. Vision Graph. Image Process.* **37**, 2, (Feb. 1987) 238–260.
01467  Selection of image primitives for general-purpose visual processing. WALTERS, D. *Comput. Vision Graph. Image Process.* **37**, 2, (Feb. 1987) 261–298.
01468  Line connectivity algorithms for an asynchronous pyramid computer. EDELMAN, S. *Comput. Vision Graph. Image Process.* **40**, 2, (November 1, 1987) 169–187.
01469  A new algorithm for extracting the interior of bounded regions based on chain coding. ALI, S.; AND BURGE, R. *Comput. Vision Graph. Image Process.* **43**, 2, (August, 1988) 256–264.
01470  Automating knowledge acquisition for aerial image interpretation. MCKEOWN JR., D.; HARVEY, W.; AND WIXSON, L. *Comput. Vision Graph. Image Process.* **46**, 1, (April 1989) 37–81.

### Computer-Aided Design

HCI-0160  Computer-aided hierarchical diagrams. BROWN, A. *Comput. Aided Des.* **16**, 5, (Sept. 1984) 249–252.
HCI-0406  Interactive computer program for the selection of interference fits. LAGODIMOS, A.; AND SCARR, A. *Comput. Aided Des.* **16**, 5, (Sept. 1984) 272–278.
01471  SML: a solid modelling language. VAN WIJK, J. *Comput. Aided Des.* **18**, 8, (Oct. 1986) 443–449.
01472  Unified interactive geometric modeller for simulating highly complex environments. BROCK, P.; POLINSKY, A.; SLIVKA, R.; AND GREENBERG, D. *Comput. Aided Des.* **18**, 10, (Dec. 1986) 539–545.
01473  Computer graphics language bindings: programmer interface standards. SPARKS, M.; AND GALLOP, J. *Comput. Aided Des.* **19**, 8, (Oct. 1987) 418–424.
01474  Automatic construction of surfaces with prescribed shape. ANDERSSON, E.; ANDERSSON, R.; BOMAN, M.; ELMROTH, T.; DAHLBERG, B.; AND JOHANSSON, B. *Comput. Aided Des.* **20**, 6, (July/Aug. 1988) 317–324.
01475  Exchange of solid models: current state and future trends. BRÄDLI, N.; AND MITTELSTAEDT, M. *Comput. Aided Des.* **21**, 2, (March 1989) 87–96.
01476  Initial work on a system-independent computer model of a 3D anthropomorphic dummy. OKEY, R.; SUFFELL, C.; AND BLOUNT, G. *Comput. Aided Des.* **21**, 6, (July/Aug. 1989) 393–403.

## Computer/Law Journal

01477  Broderbund Software, Inc. v. Unison World, Inc. 648 F. Supp. 1127 (1986). TITO, C. *Comput./Law J.* **7**, 4, (Fall 1987) 535–542.

## Computers and Artificial Intelligence

01478  Natural language interface to the question-answering system for physicians. BOLC, L.; AND STRZALKOWSKI, T. *Comput. Artif. Intell.* **3**, 1, (1984) 31–46.
01479  Two notes concerning the society theory of thinking. KELEMEN, J. *Comput. Artif. Intell.* **5**, 1, (Jan. 1986) 43–52.
01480  How can cognitive psychology help solve an artificial intelligence problem? FARKASH, A. *Comput. Artif. Intell.* **5**, 4, (Sept. 1986) 315–320.
01481  An alternative approach to the conceptual database design using fragments of nat. KREJČÍ, F.; AND ZLATUŠKA, J. *Comput. Artif. Intell.* **5**, 6, (1986) 543–560.
01482  Real time speech synthesis—development and employment. OTT, A.; AND SIIL, I. *Comput. Artif. Intell.* **6**, 2, (April 1987) 173–180.
01483  The ring machine. MONIEN, B.; AND VORNBERGER, O. *Comput. Artif. Intell.* **6**, 3, (July 1987) 195–208.
01484  Processor for man-machine natural-language-like communication. BABKA, O. *Comput. Artif. Intell.* **6**, 4, (1987) 311–320.
01485  Functional modelling in the execution of actions. AIRENTI, G.; AND COLOMBETTI, M. *Comput. Artif. Intell.* **6**, 5, (August 1, 1987) 469–480.
01486  Evaluating user utterances in natural language interfaces to databases. SCHRÖDER, M. *Comput. Artif. Intell.* **7**, 4, (1988) 317–337.
01487  The contemporary psychology of thinking and expert systems. STRÍŽENEC, M. *Comput. Artif. Intell.* **7**, 4, (1988) 339–346.
01488  Algebraic approach to the problem of addressation. ANANIASHVILI, G. *Comput. Artif. Intell.* **7**, 6, (Dec. 1988) 531–541.
01489  The direct memory access paradigm and its applications to natural language processing. TOMABECHI, H.; AND TOMITA, M. *Comput. Artif. Intell.* **8**, 5, (Sept. 1989) 443–478.

## Computers and Biomedical Research

01490  An investigation of data entry methods with a personal computer. CROMBIE, I.; AND IRVING, J. *Comput. Biomed. Res.* **19**, 6, (Dec. 1986) 543–550.
01491  Computer quantification of delta activity in sleep EEG. HOFFMAN, R.; AND JEAKINS, D. *Comput. Biomed. Res.* **20**, 4, (Aug. 1987) 366–372.
01492  Interactive graphic editor for analysis and enhancement of medical images. RUSINEK, H.; AND MOURINO, M. *Comput. Biomed. Res.* **22**, 4, (Aug 1989) 328–338.

## Computers and Education

HCI-0223  The microcomputer as a classroom audio visual device: the concept, and prospects. HATIVA, N. *Comput. Educ.* (Elmsford, NY) **10**, 3, (1986) 359–367.
HCI-0432  Computer-based microworlds—a definition to aid design. SQUIRES, D.; AND DOUGALL, A. *Comput. Educ.* (Elmsford, NY) **10**, 3, (1986) 375–378.
01493  Computer text access. DUCHASTEL, P. *Comput. Educ.* (Elmsford, NY) **10**, 4, (1986) 403–409.
01494  Human factors in CAI design. RAMBALLY, G.; AND RAMBALLY, R. *Comput. Educ.* (Elmsford, NY) **11**, 2, (April 1987) 149–153.

01495　Computer literacy in secondary education: the performance and engagement of girls. VOOGT, J. *Comput. Educ. (Elmsford, NY)* **11**, 4, (December 1, 1987) 305–312.

01496　Learning from a plan-based interface. WEIR, G. *Comput. Educ. (Elmsford, NY)* **12**, 1, (January 1988) 247–251.

01497　Some issues related to the design and development of an interactive video disc. MCCORMICK, S.; AND BRATT, P. *Comput. Educ. (Elmsford, NY)* **12**, 1, (January 1988) 257–260.

01498　Variations in user involvement with educational software. WISHART, J.; AND CANTER, D. *Comput. Educ. (Elmsford, NY)* **12**, 3, (1988) 365–380.

01499　PC networks: usage and graphics tutorials. HOYLE, B. *Comput. Educ. (Elmsford, NY)* **12**, 3, (1988) 407–414.

01500　Automated construction of interactive learning programs in Modula-2. POLACSEK-VANCSO, K.; AND FISCHLIN, A. *Comput. Educ. (Elmsford, NY)* **12**, 4, (1988) 507–512.

01501　Interactive timetabling in universities. WHITE, G.; AND WONG, S. *Comput. Educ. (Elmsford, NY)* **12**, 4, (1988) 521–529.

01502　Development of the wedding planner—extensions to reach a young audience. KLINE, J.; AND WIGGINS, E. *Comput. Educ. (Elmsford, NY)* **12**, 4, (1988) 531–534.

## Computers and Electrical Engineering

01503　A similarity-based reasoning model for intelligent interfaces. NAKAMURA, K.; SAGE, A.; AND IWAI, S. *Comput. Electr. Eng.* **12**, 3/4, (1986) 175–186.

## Computers and Geosciences

01504　A PC-interactives stereonet plotting program. PILANT, W. *Comput. Geosci.* **15**, 1, (Jan. 1989) 43–58.

01505　MINID—a BASIC program to assist in the optical identification of minerals in thin section. REEVES, M. *Comput. Geosci.* **15**, 1, (Jan. 1989) 121–133.

## Computers and Industrial Engineering

01506　Computerized design and analysis of sitting workplace. ABDEL-MOTY, E.; AND KHALIL, T. *Comput. Ind. Eng.* **11**, 1-4, (June 1986) 22–26.

01507　The design of a user friendly engineering economy analysis package for a microcomputer. ZWAHLEN, H.; AND PUETZ, G. *Comput. Ind. Eng.* **11**, 1-4, (June 1986) 141–145.

01508　Interactive multiple objective linear programming system implemented on a microcomputer. GEN, M.; AND IDA, K. *Comput. Ind. Eng.* **11**, 1-4, (June 1986) 220–224.

01509　User friendly micro computer program for solving fractional and linear programming problems. WOLFE, O.; HAWALESHKA, O.; AND MOHAMED, A. *Comput. Ind. Eng.* **11**, 1-4, (June 1986) 225–231.

01510　A comprehensive data base for the design of manual materials handling. BIENKOWSKI, T.; ASFOUR, S.; WALY, S.; AND GENAIDY, A. *Comput. Ind. Eng.* **11**, 1-4, (June 1986) 351–354.

01511　A graphical database interface. BURGESS, C.; LEIGH, W.; AND ALI, D. *Comput. Ind. Eng.* **11**, 1-4, (June 1986) 355–359.

01512　User facilities for engineering support stations. LEIGH, W.; BURGESS, C.; HUFFMAN, G.; AND PAZ, N. *Comput. Ind. Eng.* **11**, 1-4, (June 1986) 495–498.

01513　Human aspects of factory modernization. LARSEN, J.; AND SYLVESTER, W. *Comput. Ind. Eng.* **11**, 1-4, (June 1986) 507–511.

01514　A structure for enhancing user participation in model development. VAN EPPS, T. *Comput. Ind. Eng.* **11**, 1-4, (June 1986) 512–515.

01515　Needs and perceived needs of electronic workstations by engineering project managers. MORSE, L. *Comput. Ind. Eng.* **11**, 1-4, (June 1986) 521–524.

## JOURNALS

01516 Knowledge-based system for task analysis and reliability enhancement. HOSNI, Y.; LEE, C.; AND WITHROW, R. *Comput. Ind. Eng.* **11**, 1-4, (June 1986) 536–541.

01517 An interactive programming system for the IBM 7545 robot. JAYARAMAN, R.; AND DEISENROTH, M. *Comput. Ind. Eng.* **12**, 4, (1987) 275–282.

01518 Modelling the human factors aspects of a computer-based text-graphics layout system. SYLLA, C.; AND BABU, A. *Comput. Ind. Eng.* **13**, 1-4, (1987) 180–184.

01519 A knowledge-based system for assessment of human physiological abilities in manual lifting tasks. ASFOUR, S.; AND GENAIDY, A. *Comput. Ind. Eng.* **13**, 1-4, (1987) 319–322.

01520 A graphics interface to an engineering economy program. MEYER, B. *Comput. Ind. Eng.* **13**, 1-4, (1987) 351–355.

01521 The design of a user friendly interactive personal computer package for quality control charts, project management, and linear programming applications. ZWAHLEN, H.; AND EVRENOL, M. *Comput. Ind. Eng.* **13**, 1-4, (1987) 397–401.

01522 Human-computer interaction in manufacturing. ELSHENNAWY, A.; AND LEE, C. *Comput. Ind. Eng.* **13**, 1-4, (1987) 402–405.

01523 Job characteristic perceptions of manual drafting and CADD: A field study of the effects of computerization on drafting & design personnel. MANDEVILLE, D. *Comput. Ind. Eng.* **13**, 1-4, (1987) 406–410.

01524 Biomechanical evaluation of lifting tasks: a microcomputer-based model. KHALIL, T.; AND RAMADAN, M. *Comput. Ind. Eng.* **14**, 2, (July, 1988) 153–160.

01525 Evaluating formatted alphanumeric displays. SARIN, S.; AND RAM, B. *Comput. Ind. Eng.* **14**, 2, (July, 1988) 219–226.

01526 Effects of graphic boundaries in tabular displays: a human factors evaluation. THACKER, P.; AND BABU, A. *Comput. Ind. Eng.* **14**, 3, (June, 1988) 307–314.

01527 Assessing the impact of human factors on data processing inspection errors. J.; AND T. *Comput. Ind. Eng.* **14**, 4, (September 1988) 503–512.

01528 Smart help for operator performance. KNIGHT, D.; AND WALL, M. *Comput. Ind. Eng.* **15**, 1, (December 1988) 67–71.

01529 Helping users use UNIX. BURGESS, C. *Comput. Ind. Eng.* **15**, 1, (December 1988) 244–248.

01530 Touchscreen usage in plant computer systems: a case study. PAUL, R. *Comput. Ind. Eng.* **15**, 1, (December 1988) 410–417.

01531 Designing screens for people to use easily. HALTON, T.; AND WIGINTON, J. *Comput. Ind. Eng.* **15**, 1, (December 1988) 428–436.

01532 Ergonomic job design in frequent manual lifting tasks: a microcomputer-based model. GENAIDY, A.; DUGGAL, J.; AND AYOUB, M. *Comput. Ind. Eng.* **15**, 1, (December 1988) 437–442.

01533 An industrial chemical hazards database with a natural language interface: an application of artificial intelligence. PARKER, S.; ASFAHL, C.; AND JOHNSEN, S. *Comput. Ind. Eng.* **15**, 1, (December 1988) 443–445.

01534 Optimal allocation of a work force in a toxic substance environment. VILLEDA, R.; AND DEAN, B. *Comput. Ind. Eng.* **15**, 1, (December 1988) 446–449.

01535 System user/system implementer: a joint responsibility for success. HYDER, D.; AND COX, J. *Comput. Ind. Eng.* **15**, 1, (December 1988) 450–455.

## Computers and Operations Research

01536 Network generation using the Prufer code. MURPHY, C.; AND HUNG, M. *Comput. Oper. Res.* **13**, 6, (1986) 693–705.

01537 Implementation issues for operations research software. LIEBMAN, J. *Comput. Oper. Res.* **13**, 2/3, 347–358.

01538 An interactive simulation description interpreter. O'KEEFE, R. *Comput. Oper. Res.* **14**, 4, (Oct. 1987) 273–283.

01539 An interactive outranking system for multi-attribute decision making. VETSCHERA, R. *Comput. Oper. Res.* **15**, 4, (July 1988) 311–322.

## Computers and People

01540  Questions, intelligence, and intelligent behavior. FISCHLER, M.; AND FIRSCHEIN, O. *Comput. People* **36**, 3-4, (March-April 1987) 18–21.
01541  Artificial intelligence and natural language systems. SCOWN, S. *Comput. People* **36**, 3-4, (March-April 1987) 22–24.
01542  Questions, intelligence and intelligent behavior. FISCHLER, M.; AND FIRSCHEIN, O. *Comput. People* **36**, 5-6, (May-June 1987) 9–12.

## Computers and Security

HCI-0167  User-friendly password methods for computer-mediated information systems. BARTON, B.; AND BARTON, M. *Comput. Secur.* **3**, 3, (Aug. 1984) 186–195.
01543  A human approach to the technological challenges in data security. ALAGAR, V. *Comput. Secur.* **5**, 4, (Dec. 1986) 328–335.
01544  The hackers' comfort. HERSCHBERG, I. *Comput. Secur.* **6**, 2, (April 1987) 133–138.
01545  Networks without user observability. PFITZMANN, A.; AND WAIDNER, M. *Comput. Secur.* **6**, 2, (April 1987) 158–166.
01546  The moral cracker? BARID, B.; BAIRD JR., L.; AND RANAURO, R. *Comput. Secur.* **6**, 6, (December 1, 1987) 471–478.
01547  The human immune system as an information systems security reference model. WOOD, C. *Comput. Secur.* **6**, 6, (December 1, 1987) 511–516.
01548  The case of the "Gerbil Virus" that wasn't. GLATH, R. *Comput. Secur.* **7**, 5, (October 1988) 451–453.

## Computers and Standards

HCI-0428  Experimental results do not support some ergonomic standards for computer video terminal design. ABERNETHY, C.; AND AKAGI, K. *Comput. Stand.* **3**, 3/4, (Dec. 1984) 133–141.
01549  Guide to the draft American national standard for human factors engineering of visual display terminal workstations. CBEMA *Comput. Stand.* **4**, 2, (1985) 113–116.

## Computers and the Humanities

01550  Human language and computers. LEHMANN, W.; AND BENNETT, W. *Comput. Hum.* **19**, 2, (April-June 1985) 77–83.

## Computers and the Social Sciences

01551  Keyboarding as a social form. ALTHEIDE, D. *Comput. Soc. Sci.* **1**, 2, (April-June 1985) 97–106.
01552  The inept and the computer revolution: some clues from other innovations. FEINBERG, W. *Comput. Soc. Sci.* **1**, 3/4, (July-Dec. 1985) 149–154.
HCI-0217  The computer imperative among owners of home computers: explanation by social factors. McQUARRIE, E. *Comput. Soc. Sci.* **1**, 3/4, (July-Dec. 1985) 155–161.
01553  The effects of a computerized information system on a hospital. SALLOWAY, J.; COUNTE, M.; AND KJERULFF, K. *Comput. Soc. Sci.* **1**, 3/4, (July-Dec. 1985) 167–172.

## Computers and Translation

01554  Language, sublanguage, and the promise of machine translation. BARON, N. *Comput. Transl.* **1**, 1, (Jan. 1986) 3–19.

JOURNALS

01555 The engineering of a translator workstation. TONG, L. *Comput. Transl.* **1**, 4, (October - December 1987) 263–273.
01556 Two-level data banks for translators. VAUMORON, J. *Comput. Transl.* **1**, 4, (October - December 1987) 275–280.
01557 A user perspective on computer-assisted translation for Minority languages. BARNES, J. *Comput. Transl.* **2**, 3, (July - Sept. 1987) 131–134.
01558 Left-associative grammar: an informal outline. HAUSSER, R. *Comput. Transl.* **3**, 1, (Jan., 1988) 23–67.

## Computers in Human Services

01559 Computer work skills training for persons with developmental disabilities. SAKA, T. *Comput. Hum. Serv.* **1**, 4, (Winter 1985) 39–51.
01560 Issues in research on clinical computer applications for mental health. MATHISEN, K. *Comput. Hum. Serv.* **2**, 3/4, (Fall/Winter 1987) 87–108.

## Computers in Industry

HCI-0376 Graphic design for computer graphics. MARCUS, A. *Comput. Ind.* **5**, 1, (March 1984) 51–63.
01561 Real-time failure detection on complex mechanical structures via parallel data processing. BARSCHDORFF, D.; DRESSLER, T.; AND NITSCHE, W. *Comput. Ind.* **7**, 1, (Feb. 1986) 23–30.
01562 Barriers to plant transparency, barriers to plant rigidity—A sketch of the problems posed by the radical changes in work forms in the machine-building industry. DÖRR, G. *Comput. Ind.* **7**, 2, (April 1986) 115–130.
01563 A first order theory of common sense object positioning. DI MANZO, M.; AND GUINCHIGLIA, F. *Comput. Ind.* **7**, 3, (June 1986) 257–262.
01564 The design of distributed transport systems as a major standard interface in computer integrated manufacturing. BIEMANS, F. *Comput. Ind.* **7**, 4, (August 1986) 319–331.
01565 Standardization aspects on software for CAD of control systems. HENSEL, H. *Comput. Ind.* **7**, 6, (Dec. 1986) 543–545.
01566 Interface concepts for plug-compatible production management systems. MCLEAN, C. *Comput. Ind.* **9**, 4, (Dec. 1987) 307–318.
01567 Software development approach in FMS. DMITROV, D.; AND TODOROV, N. *Comput. Ind.* **10**, 3, (July 1988) 171–175.
01568 Simulation of CNC controller features in graphics-based programming. KOLLURI, S.; AND TSENG, A. *Comput. Ind.* **11**, 2, (January 1989) 135–146.
01569 Successful use of CADCAM—a combination of technology, organization, and people. STARK, J. *Comput. Ind.* **11**, 2, (January 1989) 181–193.
01570 CAD system GISK for interactive graphical modelling of planar mechanisms. LUCK, K.; AND REBER, J. *Comput. Ind.* **11**, 3, (Jan. 1989) 219–222.
01571 Interactive CAD/CAM in engineering industry. DODONOV, S.; AND VISIKIRSKY, V. *Comput. Ind.* **11**, 3, (Jan. 1989) 223–227.
01572 Application of decision support system on sandwich beams, verified by experiments. JÁRMAI, K. *Comput. Ind.* **11**, 3, (Jan. 1989) 267–274.
01573 ORGPLAN an information-decisive aid system to resolving organizing problems. KRUZYDLOWSKA, A.; AND PIASECKI, S. *Comput. Ind.* **11**, 3, (Jan. 1989) 275–285.

## Computers in Physics

01574 Retinex: physics and the theory of color vision. LA BRECQUE, M. *Comput. Phys.* **2**, 6, (Nov./Dec. 1988) 16–21.
01575 Brain research: theory and experiment. COOPER, L. *Comput. Phys.* **2**, 6, (Nov./Dec. 1988) 29–38.

01576 Optical systems that imitate human memory. ANDERSON, D. *Comput. Phys.* **3**, 2, (Mar/Apr 1989) 18–25.
01577 Supercomputers in the classroom. DECYK, V.; AND SLOTTOW, J. *Comput. Phys.* **3**, 2, (Mar/Apr 1989) 50–54.
01578 Digital waveform sampling rate converter. FEIBIG, P.; BROWN, L.; AND ETTER, D. *Comput. Phys.* **3**, 3, (May/Jun 1989) 38–41.

## Computers in the Schools

01579 A scale for assessing student attitudes toward computers preliminary findings. RICHARDS, P.; JOHNSON, D.; AND JOHNSON, R. *Comput. Sch.* **3**, 2, (June 1986) 31–38.
01580 The effects of microcomputers on children's attention to reading. ZUK, D. *Comput. Sch.* **3**, 2, (June 1986) 39–52.
01581 A brief review of developments in problem solving. SHERMAN, T. *Comput. Sch.* **4**, 3/4, (Fall/Winter 1987/1988) 7–16.
01582 Problem solving: a behavioral interpretation. PALUMBO, D.; AND VARGAS, E. *Comput. Sch.* **4**, 3/4, (Fall/Winter 1987/1988) 17–27.
01583 The erotetic logic of problem-solving inquiry. GARRISON, J.; AND MACMILLAN, C. *Comput. Sch.* **4**, 3/4, (Fall/Winter 1987/1988) 29–45.
01584 Creative computer problem solving. ARMISTEAD, L.; AND BURTON, J. *Comput. Sch.* **4**, 3/4, (Fall/Winter 1987/1988) 47–53.
01585 Computer programming and generalized problem-solving skills: in search of direction. BURTON, J.; AND MAGLIARO, S. *Comput. Sch.* **4**, 3/4, (Fall/Winter 1987/1988) 63–90.
01586 Adolescents' chunking of computer programs. MAGLIARO, S.; AND BURTIN, J. *Comput. Sch.* **4**, 3/4, (Fall/Winter 1987/1988) 129–138.
01587 Computer programming and general problem solving by secondary students. MCCOY, L.; AND OREY III, M. *Comput. Sch.* **4**, 3/4, (Fall/Winter 1987/1988) 151–157.
01588 The relationship of computer programming and mathematics in secondary students. MCCOY, L.; AND BURTON, J. *Comput. Sch.* **4**, 3/4, (Fall/Winter 1987/1988) 159–166.
01589 Problem solving and software design. NELSON, W. *Comput. Sch.* **4**, 3/4, (Fall/Winter 1987/1988) 207–217.
01590 Self-efficacy expectations as a predictor of computer use: a look at early childhood administrators. JORDE-BLOOM, P. *Comput. Sch.* **5**, 1/2, (1988) 45–63.
01591 Assessing gender bias in computer software. ROSENTHAL, N.; AND DEMETRULIAS, D. *Comput. Sch.* **5**, 1/2, (1988) 153–163.
01592 Personality characteristics of junior high school students successful with computers. LUTZ, J.; DURHAM, T.; AND COBLE, C. *Comput. Sch.* **5**, 1/2, (1988) 257–269.

## Cybernetica

01593 Computer, quantized time and human duration. OLSON, A.; AND SAWADA, D. *Cybernetica* **16**, 2, (1988) 65–76.
01594 Fundamentals of psychosomatic transduction. PETREL, J. *Cybernetica* **16**, 2, (1988) 77–80.
01595 Model of the neuro-muscular recruitment example of the extensor digitorum communis muscle in man: I—identification of motoneurons and of muscular fibers. VALENTINI, F.; AND NELSON, P. *Cybernetica* **16**, 2, (1988) 81–95.
01596 The cybernetic principle: its transdisciplinarity to science and religion and the challenging task. CHAR, M. *Cybernetica* **16**, 2, (1988) 97–98.
01597 Principles of information. ZELEZNIKAR, A. *Cybernetica* **16**, 2, (1988) 99–122.
01598 Recursive complementarity in the cybernetics of education. SAWADA, D.; AND CALEY, M. *Cybernetica* **29**, 2, (April 1986) 93–104.
01599 The cybernetic mechanisms of stress. RESTIAN, A. *Cybernetica* **29**, 2, (April 1986) 105–125.
01600 The informational substrata of psychic illnesses. RESTIAN, A. *Cybernetica* **29**, 3, (Aug. 1986) 211–248.

## JOURNALS

01601 The effects of sources of applications programs on user satisfaction: an empirical study of micro, mini & mainframe computers using an interactive artificial intelligence expert-system. RUSHINEK, S.; AND RUSHINEK, A. *Cybernetica* **30**, 1, (Jan. 1987) 75–96.

01602 The memory channel machine: part of a proposed learning machine. READER, A. *Cybernetica* **30**, 2, (1987) 25–42.

01603 Some historical currents concerning the 'societal learning' approach to policy and planning. WATTS, T. *Cybernetica* **30**, 2, (1987) 43–57.

01604 Morphologic machines and conservative networks. CARON, A. *Cybernetica* **30**, 3, (Dec. 1987) 5–30.

01605 Cybernetic consciousness. HEATHER, M. *Cybernetica* **31**, 1, (Jan, 1988) 7–24.

01606 A survey on systems informational paradigm to the psychic. PRIMOV, G. *Cybernetica* **31**, 1, (Jan, 1988) 25–42.

01607 A holography-based computer-aided translation system-conceptual analysis. PRIMOV, G. *Cybernetica* **31**, 1, (Jan, 1988) 43–55.

01608 Time, structure and levels of consciousness. FATMI, H. *Cybernetica* **31**, 1, (Jan, 1988) 57–58.

### Cybernetics and Systems

01609 Organizational humanity and architecture: Duality and complementarity of papa-logic and mama-logic in managerial conceptualizations of change. BROEKSTRA, G. *Cybern. Syst.* **17**, 1, (Jan. 1986) 13–41.

01610 Self-authorization: A characteristic of some elements in certain self-organizing systems. UMPLEBY, S. *Cybern. Syst.* **17**, 1, (Jan. 1986) 79–87.

01611 Short-term memory as a metastable state.III. Diffusion approximation. KIRILLOV, A.; BORISYUK, G.; BORISYUK, R.; KOVALENKO, Y.; AND KRYUKOV, V. *Cybern. Syst.* **17**, 2-3, (April 1986) 169–182.

01612 Design of a control room for the air force logistics command (AFLC) command, control, and communication and intelligence ($C^3I$) system. TRIPP, R.; AND RAINEY, L. *Cybern. Syst.* **17**, 2-3, (April 1986) 211–235.

01613 Kinetic theory of "hot" neural systems. VENTRIGLIA, F. *Cybern. Syst.* **18**, 2, (March 1987) 147–155.

01614 The way you look determines what you see (or self-organization in management and society). BEN-ELI, M.; AND PROBST, G. *Cybern. Syst.* **18**, 4, (Aug. 1987) 275–284.

01615 A logical model of co-operative processes in cerebral dynamics. MIRA, J.; AND DELGADO, A. *Cybern. Syst.* **18**, 4, (Aug. 1987) 319–349.

01616 A cognitive approach for graph drawing. SUGIYAMA, K. *Cybern. Syst.* **18**, 6, (Dec. 1987) 447–488.

01617 Cybernetics and organization theory: a critical review. FLOOD, R.; AND JACKSON, M. *Cybern. Syst.* **19**, 1, (Jan., 1988) 13–33.

01618 Evolution of interactional human behavior with age: a theoretical/experimental approach. SILVESTRI, A.; LEFONS, E.; AND DE GIACOMO, P. *Cybern. Syst.* **19**, 1, (Jan., 1988) 35–59.

01619 Self-organizing systems and transformational-generative (TG) grammar. BENNETT, T. *Cybern. Syst.* **19**, 1, (Jan., 1988) 61–81.

01620 Ordinals and the hemispheres of the brain. FIDELMAN, U. *Cybern. Syst.* **19**, 2, (March/April 1988) 109–122.

01621 An approach to a mathematics of phenomena: canonical aspects of reentrant form eigenbehavior in the extended calculus of indications. BERKOWITZ, G.; GREENBERG, D.; AND WHITE, C. *Cybern. Syst.* **19**, 2, (March/April 1988) 123–167.

01622 The magical number three—plus or minus zero. WARFIELD, J. *Cybern. Syst.* **19**, 4, (July-Aug. 1988) 339–358.

### Data & Knowledge Engineering

HCI-0257 Natural language query processing in a temporal database. DE, S.; PAN, S.; AND WHINSTON, A. *Data Knowl. Eng.* **1**, 1, (June 1985) 3–15.

### Data Engineering

01623 Algebras for nested relations. ROTH, M.; AND KIRKPATRICK, J. *Data Eng.* **11**, 3, (September 1988) 39–47.

## Data Processing

01624 Trends in printer technology. HENNY, C. *Data Process.* **28,** 1, (Jan./Feb. 1986) 21–23.
01625 Patterned systems design. SHORROCK, B. *Data Process.* **28,** 3, (April 1986) 142–145.
01626 Artificial intelligence in the man/machine interface. LAWRENCE, K. *Data Process.* **28,** 5, (June 1986) 244–246.
01627 Machine assisted translation with a human face. BEESLEY, K. *Data Process.* **28,** 5, (June 1986) 251–257.
01628 Uniforms: an automatic forms facility. HULL, M.; AND WILSON, T. *Data Process.* **28,** 5, (June 1986) 258–264.
01629 Standards and system development. BHABUTA, L. *Data Process.* **28,** 7, (Sept. 1986) 344–350.
01630 Demanding higher productivity. VERYARD, R. *Data Process.* **28,** 7, (Sept. 1986) 351–355.

## Database

01631 Beta tests and end-user surveys: are they valid? SWEETLAND, J. *Database* **11,** 1, (Feb., 1988) 27–32.
01632 Who's behind the help desk? KLEIN, R. *Database* **11,** 4, (August 1988) 15–19.
01633 What the help desk needs from you. WINIARSKI, M. *Database* **11,** 4, (August 1988) 20–20.
01634 The linear file—restrictions on online information use: a searcher's perspective. FEIDER, M. *Database* **11,** 6, (Dec. 1988) 7–9.
01635 Designing a user manual to support an in-house database. KRAFT, M.; AND PUGH, W. *Database* **11,** 6, (Dec. 1988) 62–64.
01636 End-user prototyping: sophisticated users supporting system development. PLISKIN, N.; AND SHOVAL, P. *Database* **18,** 4, (Summer 1987) 7–17.
01637 Information systems strategy and end-user application development. SUMNER, M.; AND KLEPPER, R. *Database* **18,** 4, (Summer 1987) 19–30.
01638 Organizational issues of end-user computing. AMOROSO, D. *Database* **19,** 3/4, (Fall/Winter 1988) 49–58.

## DataBased Advisor

01639 Magic PC- the "UN-LANGUAGE" approach. PHILLIPS, R. *DataBased Advis.* **5,** 6, (June 1987) 49–54.
01640 dANALYST attempts to do it all. FREELAND, R. *DataBased Advis.* **5,** 6, (June 1987) 55–57.
01641 dBUG III offers source level solutions. FREELAND, R. *DataBased Advis.* **6,** 2, (February 1988) 86–91.
01642 More on the mouse. SPENCE, R. *DataBased Advis.* **6,** 12, (Dec. 1988) 58–64.

## Datamation

01643 Managing the PC revolution. VOGT, E. *Datamation* **30,** 19, (Nov. 15, 1984) 113–114.
01644 Shucking Dp. SOJKA, D. *Datamation* **30,** 21, (Dec. 15, 1984) 32–36.
01645 The importance of good relations. PERCY, T. *Datamation* **30,** 21, (Dec. 15, 1984) 86–92.
01646 Dp and the disabled. BURNETT, N.; AND NEIMARK, J. *Datamation* **31,** 1, (Jan. 1, 1985) 22–30.
01647 The real cost of OA. STRASSMANN, P. *Datamation* **31,** 3, (Feb. 1, 1985) 82–94.
01648 In search of the perfect programmer. BUSH, C.; AND SCHKADE, L. *Datamation* **31,** 6, (March 15, 1985) 128–132.
01649 Steel yields in Pa. LANSNER, J. *Datamation* **31,** 7, (March 15, 1985) 1–22.
01650 Friendly or frivolous? MEADS, J. *Datamation* **31,** 7, (March 15, 1985) 96–100.
01651 Stress. WARRICK, D.; GARDNER, D.; COUGER, J.; AND ZAWACKI, R. *Datamation* **31,** 8, (April 15, 1986) 88–92.
01652 High tech, high stress? MARKS, S. *Datamation* **31,** 8, (April 15, 1986) 97–100.
01653 Users are people too. KING, L. *Datamation* **31,** 8, (April 15, 1986) 104–108.
01654 Oil and water? CASWELL, S. *Datamation* **31,** 8, (April 15, 1986) 112–118.
01655 The psychological costs of master computer. WAGENAAR, W. *Datamation* **31,** 13, (July 1, 1985) 157–159.
01656 Information politics. KLEIN, M. *Datamation* **31,** 15, (Aug. 1, 1985) 86–92.
01657 Power and credibility in office automation. MEYER, D. *Datamation* **31,** 15, (Aug. 1, 1985) 97–100.

**01658** Getting straight again. HOWE, C. *Datamation* **31,** 16, (Aug. 15, 1985) 32–38.
**01659** The system understands. EDWARDS, P. *Datamation* **31,** 16, (Aug. 15, 1985) 88–92.
**01660** A PC policy primer. MICHIELSEN, K. *Datamation* **31,** 16, (Aug. 15, 1985) 96–98.
**01661** The designing mind. EDWARDS, P. *Datamation* **31,** 18, (Sept. 15, 1985) 105–110.
**01662** The trouble with application generators. STAHL, B. *Datamation* **32,** 7, (April 1, 1986) 93–94.
**01663** Grow your own programmers. DIGHT, J. *Datamation* **32,** 13, (July 1, 1986) 75–78.
**01664** Battling for new roles. WINKLER, C. *Datamation* **32,** 20, (Oct. 15, 1986) 82–88.

## Decision Support Systems

**01665** A general purpose computer aid to judgemental forecasting: Rationale and procedure. WRIGHT, G.; AYTON, P.; AND WHALLEY, P. *Decis. Support Syst.* **1,** 4, (Dec. 1985) 333–340.
**01666** Understanding and validating results in model-based decision support systems. BRENNAN, J.; AND ELAM, J. *Decis. Support Syst.* **2,** 1, (March 1986) 49–54.
**01667** Propaedeutics of decision-making: supporting managerial learning and innovation. HUNT, R.; AND SANDERS, L. *Decis. Support Syst.* **2,** 2, (June 1986) 125–134.
**01668** Providing effective decision support: modeling users and their requirements. DE, S. *Decis. Support Syst.* **2,** 4, (Dec. 1986) 309–319.
**01669** A modular user-oriented decision support for physical database design. MAIO, D.; SARTORI, C.; AND SCALAS, M. *Decis. Support Syst.* **3,** 2, (June 1987) 155–163.
**01670** The metaphor machine: a database method for creativity support. YOUNG, L. *Decis. Support Syst.* **3,** 4, (Dec. 1987) 309–317.
**01671** A natural language discourse model to explain linear programming models and solutions. GREENBERG, H. *Decis. Support Syst.* **3,** 4, (Dec. 1987) 333–342.
**01672** A framework for designing adaptive DSS Interfaces. DOS SANTOS, B.; AND HOLSAPPLE, C. *Decis. Support Syst.* **5,** 1, (March 1989) 1–11.

## Discrete Applied Mathematics

**01673** Interactive L systems with a fast local growth. RAZ, Y. *Discrete Appl. Math.* **22,** 2, (February 1989) 163–179.

## EDP Performance Review

**01677** Measuring user satisfaction. *EDP Perform. Rev.* **14,** 6, (JUNE 1987) 6–6.
**01678** User satisfaction: A vital management issue. STANTON, J. *EDP Perform. Rev.* **15,** 11, (Nov. 1987) 7–9.

## Educational Technology

**01679** Authoring considerations for hypertext. KEARLSEY, G. *Educ. Technol.* **28,** 11, (Nov. 1988) 21–24.
**01680** The Perseus project: an interactive curriculum on classical greek civilization. CRANE, G.; AND MYLONAS, E. *Educ. Technol.* **28,** 11, (Nov. 1988) 25–32.

## Electrical Communication

**01681** Human factors support for product development. BRIGHAM, F. *Electr. Commun.* **60,** 3/4, (July 1986) 286–293.

01682   Design of user-system interfaces using a cognitive design aid. BYERLEY, P.; LEISER, R.; AND SAFFIN, R. *Electr. Commun.* **60**, 3/4, (July 1986) 294-302.

01683   Computer assisted video analysis system. DE ALBERDI, M. *Electr. Commun.* **60**, 3/4, (July 1986) 303-307.

## Finite Elements in Analysis and Design

01684   Interactive color graphical postprocessing as a unifying influence in numerical analysis research. ABEL, J.; INGRAFFEA, A.; MCGUIRE, W.; AND GREENBERG, D. *Finite Elem. Anal. Des.* **2**, 1 & 2, (April 1986) 1-17.

01685   An interactive approach to local remeshing around a propagating crack. WAWRZYNEK, P.; AND INGRAFFEA, A. *Finite Elem. Anal. Des.* **5**, 1, (April 1989) 87-96.

## Future Generations Computer Systems

HCI-0093   The architecture of fifth generation inference computers. HERTZBERGER, L. *Future Gener. Comput. Syst.* **1**, 1, (July 1984) 19-21.

01686   Visual terminals and user interfaces. KAMAE, T. *Future Gener. Comput. Syst.* **1**, 5, (Sept. 1985) 257-278.

01687   Problems of machine translation system - effect of cultural differences on sentence structure. NITTA, Y. *Future Gener. Comput. Syst.* **2**, 2, (June 1986) 101-115.

01688   Language and artificial intelligence conference report. *Future Gener. Comput. Syst.* **2**, 2, (June 1986) 141-143.

01689   Expert systems in management science. COOPER, P. *Future Gener. Comput. Syst.* **2**, 4, (Dec. 1986) 217-223.

01690   Developing and running expert systems with PESYS. DOUKIDIS, G.; AND WHITKEY, E. *Future Gener. Comput. Syst.* **3**, 3, (Sept., 1988) 189-199.

01691   Neurocomputing—neurons as microcomputers. MATSUMOTO, G. *Future Gener. Comput. Syst.* **4**, 1, (August 1988) 39-51.

## Fuzzy Sets and Systems

01692   Towards the development of human work-performance standards in futuristic man-machine systems: a fuzzy modeling approach. MITAL, A.; AND KARWOWSKI, W. *Fuzzy Sets Syst.* **19**, 2, (June 1986) 133-147.

01693   A fuzzy knowledge base of an expert system for analysis of manual lifting tasks. KARWOWSKI, W.; MULHOLLAND, N.; AND JAGANNATHAN, V. *Fuzzy Sets Syst.* **21**, 3, (March 1, 1987) 363-374.

01694   Usage of linguistic variable concept for human operator modelling. SVAROVSKI, S. *Fuzzy Sets Syst.* **22**, 1/2, (April 1, 1987) 107-114.

01695   Fuzzy reasoning in pseudo-physical logics. POSPELOV, D. *Fuzzy Sets Syst.* **22**, 1/2, (April 1, 1987) 115-120.

01696   Human specifics fuzzy categories and counteraction in decision making problems. SHAPIRO, D. *Fuzzy Sets Syst.* **22**, 1/2, (April 1, 1987) 155-170.

01697   The fuzzy approach to facilities layout problems. GROBELNY, J. *Fuzzy Sets Syst.* **23**, 2, (Aug. 1987) 175-190.

01698   Simplicial differential geometric theory for language cortical dynamics. BURSTEIN, G.; NICU, M.; AND BALACEANU, C. *Fuzzy Sets Syst.* **23**, 3, (Sept. 1987) 303-313.

01699   The fuzzy paradigm for knowledge representation in cerebral dynamics. MIRA, J.; DELGADO, A.; AND MORENO-DÍAZ, R. *Fuzzy Sets Syst.* **23**, 3, (Sept. 1987) 315-330.

01700   The fuzzy decodings of educative texts. THEOTO, M.; SANTOS, M.; AND UCHIYAMA, N. *Fuzzy Sets Syst.* **23**, 3, (Sept. 1987) 331-345.

01701   The fuzzy logic of text understanding. GRECO, G.; AND ROCHA, A. *Fuzzy Sets Syst.* **23**, 3, (Sept. 1987) 347-360.

01702   An approach to human reliability on man-machine systems using error possibility. ONISAWA, T. *Fuzzy Sets Syst.* **27**, 2, (August 1988) 87-103.

JOURNALS

## Harvard Business Review

01703 Your office is where you are. STONE, P.; AND LUCHETTI, R. *Harvard Bus. Rev.* **63,** 2, (March/April 1985) 102–117.
01704 Putting expert systems to work. LEONARD-BARTON, D.; AND SVIOKLA, J. *Harvard Bus. Rev.* **66,** 2, (March/April 1988) 91–98.
01705 How technology brings blind people into the workplace. ANDERSON, J. *Harvard Bus. Rev.* **67,** 2, (March-April 1989) 36–40.
01706 The human costs of manufacturing reform. KLEIN, J. *Harvard Bus. Rev.* **67,** 2, (March-April 1989) 60–66.
01707 How executives can shape their company's information systems. DAVENPORT, T.; HAMMER, M.; AND METSISTO, T. *Harvard Bus. Rev.* **67,** 2, (March-April 1989) 130–134.

## Hong Kong Comput. J.

01674 A computing service using linked minis. SAMET, P. *Hong Kong Comput. J.* **2,** 4, (April 1986) 34–41.
01675 The pick of the crop. *Hong Kong Comput. J.* **2,** 9, (Sept. 1986) 16–19.
01676 The age of the end-user and the shift from corporate MIS to corporate DSS. BRAUN, T. *Hong Kong Comput. J.* **4,** 5, (May 1988) 28-35.

## Human Factors

01708 The effects of syntactic complexity on the human-computer interaction. CHECHILE, R.; FLEISCHMAN, R.; AND SADOSKI, D. *Hum. Factors* **28,** 1, (Feb. 1986) 11–22.
01709 Multimodal detection and recognition performance of sonar operators. KOBUS, D.; RUSSOTTI, J.; SCHLICHTING, C.; HASKELL, G.; CARPENTER, S.; AND WOJTOWICZ, J. *Hum. Factors* **28,** 1, (Feb. 1986) 23–29.
01710 Optimal colors, phosphors, and illuminant characteristics of CRT displays: the algorithmic approach. DE CORTE, W. *Hum. Factors* **28,** 1, (Feb. 1986) 39–47.
01711 The effects of set size on color matching using CRT displays. LURIA, S.; NERI, D.; AND JACOBSEN, A. *Hum. Factors* **28,** 1, (Feb. 1986) 49–61.
01712 Reading from microfiche, a VDT, and the printed page: subjective fatigue and performance. CUSHMAN, W. *Hum. Factors* **28,** 1, (Feb. 1986) 63–73.
01713 Intermittent illumination from visual display units and fluorescent lighting affects movements of the eyes across text. WILKINS, A. *Hum. Factors* **28,** 1, (Feb. 1986) 75–81.
01714 An integrated display for vertical and translational flight: eight factors affecting pilot performance. TATRO, J.; AND ROSCOE, S. *Hum. Factors* **28,** 1, (Feb. 1986) 101–120.
01715 The optimal number of menu options per panel. PAAP, K.; AND ROSKE-HOFSTRAND, R. *Hum. Factors* **28,** 4, (Aug. 1986) 377–385.
01716 Optimizing the structure of database menu indexes: a decision model of menu search. MACGREGOR, J; LEE, E.; AND LAM, N. *Hum. Factors* **28,** 4, (Aug. 1986) 387–399.
01717 The effect of number ordering and orientation on marking speed and errors for mark-sensed labels. MADDOX, M.; AND TURPIN, J. *Hum. Factors* **28,** 4, (Aug. 1986) 401–405.
01718 On the selection and evaluation of visual display symbology: factors influencing search and identification times. REMINGTON, R.; AND WILLIAMS, D. *Hum. Factors* **28,** 4, (Aug. 1986) 407–420.
01719 Statistical dependency in visual scanning. ELLIS, S.; AND STARK, L. *Hum. Factors* **28,** 4, (Aug. 1986) 421–438.
01720 The effect of perspective geometry on judged direction in spatial information instruments. MCGREEVY, M.; AND ELLIS, S. *Hum. Factors* **28,** 4, (Aug. 1986) 439–456.
01721 Visual fatigue and spatial frequency adaptation to video displays of text. LUNN, R.; AND BANKS, W. *Hum. Factors* **28,** 4, (Aug. 1986) 457–464.
01722 Maintenance training simulator fidelity and individual differences in transfer of training. ALLEN, J.; HAYS, R.; AND BUFFARDI, L. *Hum. Factors* **28,** 5, (Oct. 1986) 497–509.

01723 Processing demands, training, and the vigilance decrement. WILLIAMS, P. *Hum. Factors* **28**, 5, (Oct. 1986) 567–579.
01724 No effect of noise on vigilance performance? KOELEGA, H.; BRINKMAN, J.; AND BERGMAN, H. *Hum. Factors* **28**, 5, (Oct. 1986) 581–593.
01725 The influence of visual workload history on visual performance. MATTHEWS, M. *Hum. Factors* **28**, 6, (Dec. 1986) 623–632.
01726 A simultaneous regression model for double stimulation tasks. AYKIN, N.; CZAJA, S.; AND DRURY, C. *Hum. Factors* **28**, 6, (Dec. 1986) 633–643.
01727 Beware the reliability of slope scores for individuals. CARTER, R.; KRAUSE, M.; AND HARBESON, M. *Hum. Factors* **28**, 6, (Dec. 1986) 673–683.
01728 Estimating reliability with small samples: increased precision with averaged correlations. DUNLAP, W.; SILVER, N.; AND BITTNER, A. *Hum. Factors* **28**, 6, (Dec. 1986) 685–690.
01729 Modeling fault diagnosis as the activation and use of a frame system. SMITH, P.; GIFFIN, W.; ROCKWELL, T.; AND THOMAS, M. *Hum. Factors* **28**, 6, (Dec. 1986) 703–716.
01730 Optimizing the touch tablet: the effects of control display gain and method of cursor control. ARNAUT, L.; AND GREENSTEIN, J. *Hum. Factors* **28**, 6, (Dec. 1986) 717–726.
01731 Comparison of speech and pictorial displays in a cockpit environment. ROBINSON, C.; AND EBERTS, R. *Hum. Factors* **29**, 1, (Feb. 1987) 31–44.
01732 Radiation detection by ear and by eye. TZELGOV, J.; SREBRO, R.; HENIK, A.; AND KUSHELEVSKY, A. *Hum. Factors* **29**, 1, (Feb. 1987) 87–95.
01733 Cognitive factors in user/expert-system interaction. LEHNER, P.; AND ZIRK, D. *Hum. Factors* **29**, 1, (Feb. 1987) 97–109.
01734 Changes in electromyographic activity associated with occupational stress and poor performance in the workplace. GOMER, F.; SILVERSTEIN, L.; BERG, W.; AND LASSITER, D. *Hum. Factors* **29**, 2, (April 1987) 131–143.
01735 A psychophysiological assessment of operator workload during simulated flight missions. KRAMER, A.; SIREVAAG, E.; AND BRAUNE, R. *Hum. Factors* **29**, 2, (April 1987) 145–160.
01736 Operator effort and the measurement of heart-rate variability. AASMAN, J.; MULDER, G.; AND MULDER, L. *Hum. Factors* **29**, 2, (April 1987) 161–170.
01737 Spectral analysis of sinus arrhythmia: a measure of mental effort. VICENTE, K.; THORNTON, D.; AND MORAY, N. *Hum. Factors* **29**, 2, (April 1987) 171–182.
01738 Beyond heart rate in the cardiac psychophysiological assessment of mental effort: the T-wave amplitude component of the electrocardiogram. FUREDY, J. *Hum. Factors* **29**, 2, (April 1987) 183–194.
01739 The spatial allocation of visual attention as indexed by event-related brain potentials. MANGUN, G.; AND HILLYARD, S. *Hum. Factors* **29**, 2, (April 1987) 195–211.
01740 Effects of information-processing demands on physiological response patterns. BAUER, L.; GOLDSTEIN, R.; AND STERN, J. *Hum. Factors* **29**, 2, (April 1987) 213–234.
01741 Part-task training strategies in simulated carrier landing final-approach training. WIGHTMAN, D.; AND SISTRUNK, F. *Hum. Factors* **29**, 3, (June 1987) 245–254.
01742 Training consistent task components: application of automatic and controlled processing theory to industrial task training. MYERS, G.; AND FISK, A. *Hum. Factors* **29**, 3, (June 1987) 255–268.
01743 Reading is slower from CRT displays than from paper: attempts to isolate a single-variable explanation. GOULD, J.; ALFARO, L.; BARNES, V.; FINN, R.; GRISCHKOWSKY, N.; AND MINUTO, A. *Hum. Factors* **29**, 3, (June 1987) 269–299.
01744 Improving visual performance through volitional focus control. ROSCOE, S.; AND COUCHMAN, D. *Hum. Factors* **29**, 3, (June 1987) 311–325.
01745 Hesitations in continuous tracking induced by a concurrent discrete task. KLAPP, S.; KELLY, P.; AND NETICK, A. *Hum. Factors* **29**, 3, (June 1987) 327–337.
01746 A closed-loop causal model of workload based on a comparison of fuzzy and crisp measurement techniques. MORAY, N.; KING, B.; TURKSEN, B.; AND WATERTON, K. *Hum. Factors* **29**, 3, (June 1987) 339–348.

01747 Assaying and isolating individual differences in searching a hierarchical file system. VICENTE, K.; HAYES, B.; AND WILLIGES, R. Hum. Factors **29**, 3, (June 1987) 349–359.

01748 Perspective traffic display format and airline pilot traffic avoidance. ELLIS, S.; MCGREEVY, M.; AND HITCHCOCK, R. Hum. Factors **29**, 4, (Aug. 1987) 371–382.

01749 Effects of functionally or topographically presented process schemes on operator performance. VERMEULEN, J. Hum. Factors **29**, 4, (Aug. 1987) 383–394.

01750 Display formatting in information integration and nonintegration tasks. BOLES, D.; AND WICKENS, C. Hum. Factors **29**, 4, (Aug. 1987) 395–406.

01751 Internal models, tracking strategies and dual-task performance. EBERTS, R. Hum. Factors **29**, 4, (Aug. 1987) 407–419.

01752 Models of procedural control for human performance simulation. STICHA, P. Hum. Factors **29**, 4, (Aug. 1987) 421–432.

01753 Effect of pixel height, display height, and vertical resolution on the detection of a simple vertical line signal in visual noise. MOULDEN, B.; AND KINGDOM, F. Hum. Factors **29**, 4, (Aug. 1987) 433–445.

01754 Temporal resolution: an insight into the video display terminal (VDT) "problem". HARWOOD, K.; AND FOLEY, P. Hum. Factors **29**, 4, (Aug. 1987) 447–452.

01755 Alternative option selection methods in menu-driven computer programs. SHINAR, D.; AND STERN, H. Hum. Factors **29**, 4, (Aug. 1987) 453–459.

01756 Slot versus insertion magnetic stripe readers: user performance and preference. LEWIS, J. Hum. Factors **29**, 4, (Aug. 1987) 461–464.

01757 Review and evaluation of physiological cost prediction models for manual materials handling. GENAIDY, A.; AND ASFOUR, S. Hum. Factors **29**, 4, (Aug. 1987) 465–476.

01758 Reading from CRT displays can be as fast as reading from paper. GOULD, J.; ALFARO, L.; FINN, R.; HAUPT, B.; AND MINUTO, A. Hum. Factors **29**, 5, (Oct. 1987) 497–517.

01759 The effects of panel arrangements and locus of attention on performance. DOWNING, J.; AND SANDERS, M. Hum. Factors **29**, 5, (Oct. 1987) 551–562.

01760 Measurement of seat pressure distribution. TREASTER, D.; AND MARRAS, W. Hum. Factors **29**, 5, (Oct. 1987) 563–575.

01761 Menu organization and user expertise in information search tasks. HOLLANDS, J.; AND MERIKLE, P. Hum. Factors **29**, 5, (Oct. 1987) 577–586.

01762 The effects of target wavelength on dynamic visual acuity under photopic and scotopic viewing. LONG, G.; AND GARVEY, P. Hum. Factors **30**, 1, (Feb., 1988) 3–13.

01763 Display proximity in multicue information integration: the benefits of boxes. BARNETT, B.; AND WICKENS, C. Hum. Factors **30**, 1, (Feb., 1988) 15–24.

01764 Factors affecting the readability of moving text on a computer display. CHEN, H.; AND TSOI, K. Hum. Factors **30**, 1, (Feb., 1988) 25–33.

01765 The role of stimulus-to-rule consistency in learning rapid application of spatial rules. FISK, A.; AND LLOYD, S. Hum. Factors **30**, 1, (Feb., 1988) 35–49.

01766 Using color dimensions to display data dimensions. WARE, C.; AND BEATTY, J. Hum. Factors **30**, 2, (April, 1988) 127–142.

01767 Variability in brightness matching of colored lights. POLYNTER, D. Hum. Factors **30**, 2, (April, 1988) 143–151.

01768 Spatial requirements for visual simulation of aircraft at real-world distances. KENNEDY, R.; COLLYER, S.; MAY, J.; AND DUNLAP, W. Hum. Factors **30**, 2, (April, 1988) 153–161.

01769 Operator performance as a function of type of display: conventional versus perspective. BEMIS, S.; LEEDS, J.; AND WINER, E. Hum. Factors **30**, 2, (April, 1988) 163–169.

01770 Information transfer rate with serial and simultaneous visual display formats. MATIN, E.; AND BOFF, K. Hum. Factors **30**, 2, (April, 1988) 171–180.

01771 Counting, computing, and the representation of numbers. NICKERSON, R. Hum. Factors **30**, 2, (April, 1988) 181–199.

01772 Effects of visual display and motion system delays on operator performance and ueasiness in a driving simulator. FRANK, L.; CASALI, J.; AND WIERWILLE, W. *Hum. Factors* **30**, 2, (April, 1988) 201–217.

01773 Effects of vehicle handling characteristics on driving strategy. GODHELP, H.; AND KAPPLER, W. *Hum. Factors* **30**, 2, (April, 1988) 219–229.

01774 Human performance evaluation of digitizer pucks for computer input of spatial information. ROSENBERG, D.; AND MARTIN, G. *Hum. Factors* **30**, 2, (April, 1988) 231–235.

01775 Some generalizations about generalization. CHAPANIS, A. *Hum. Factors* **30**, 3, (June 1988) 253–267.

01776 Conceptualizing in assembly tasks. BAGGETT, P.; AND EHRENFEUCHT, A. *Hum. Factors* **30**, 3, (June 1988) 269–284.

01777 Reading self-paced moving text on a computer display. CHEN, H.; CHAN, K.; AND TSOI, K. *Hum. Factors* **30**, 3, (June 1988) 285–291.

01778 Long workdays versus restdays: assessing fatigue and alertness with a portable performance. ROSA, R.; AND COLLIGAN, M. *Hum. Factors* **30**, 3, (June 1988) 305–317.

01779 A human factors design investigation of a computerized layout system of text-graphic technical materials. SYLLA, C.; DRURY, C.; AND BABU, A. *Hum. Factors* **30**, 3, (June 1988) 347–358.

HCI-0317 Strategic issues in knowledge engineering. CHIGNELL, M.; AND PETERSON, J. *Hum. Factors* **30**, 4, (Aug. 1988) 381–394.

01780 The role of human factors in expert systems design and acceptance. MADNI, A. *Hum. Factors* **30**, 4, (Aug. 1988) 395–414.

01781 Cognitive engineering: human problem solving with tools. WOODS, D.; AND ROTH, E. *Hum. Factors* **30**, 4, (Aug. 1988) 415–430.

01782 Adaptive aiding for human/computer control. ROUSE, W. *Hum. Factors* **30**, 4, (Aug. 1988) 431–443.

01783 Likelihood alarm displays. SORKIN, R.; KANTOWITZ, B.; AND KANTOWITZ, S. *Hum. Factors* **30**, 4, (Aug. 1988) 445–459.

01784 An experimental study of Chinese information displays on VDTs. HWANG, S.; WANG, M.; AND HER, C. *Hum. Factors* **30**, 4, (Aug. 1988) 461–471.

01785 Reader-controlled computerized presentation of text. MUTER, P.; KRUK, R.; BUTTIGIEG, M.; AND KANG, T. *Hum. Factors* **30**, 4, (Aug. 1988) 473–486.

01786 Magnification effects with imaging displays depend on scene content and viewing condition. MEEHAN, J.; AND TRIGGS, T. *Hum. Factors* **30**, 4, (Aug. 1988) 487–494.

01787 Performance measurement during simulated air-to-air combat. KELLY, M. *Hum. Factors* **30**, 4, (Aug. 1988) 495–506.

01788 The effect of adding symbols to written warning labels on user behavior and recall. FRIEDMANN, K. *Hum. Factors* **30**, 4, (Aug. 1988) 507–515.

01789 Speech responses and dual-task performance: better time-sharing or asymmetric transfer? VIDULICH, M. *Hum. Factors* **30**, 4, (Aug. 1988) 517–529.

01790 The role of practice in dual-task performance: toward workload modeling in a connectionist/control architecture. SCHNEIDER, W.; AND DETWEILER, M. *Hum. Factors* **30**, 5, (Oct. 1988) 539–566.

01791 Examination of the role of "higher order" consistency in skill development. FISK, A.; ORANSKY, N.; AND SKEDSVOLD, P. *Hum. Factors* **30**, 5, (Oct. 1988) 567–581.

01792 Automaticity, resources, and memory: theoretical controversies and practical implications. LOGAN, G. *Hum. Factors* **30**, 5, (Oct. 1988) 583–598.

01793 Codes and modalities in multiple resources: a success and a qualification. WICKENS, C.; AND LIU, Y. *Hum. Factors* **30**, 5, (Oct. 1988) 599–616.

01794 Multiple resources for processing and storage in short-term working memory. KLAPP, S.; AND NETICK, A. *Hum. Factors* **30**, 5, (Oct. 1988) 617–632.

01795 Task-sharing within and between hemispheres: a multiple-resources approach. POLSON, M.; AND FRIEDMAN, A. *Hum. Factors* **30**, 5, (Oct. 1988) 633–643.

01796 Capacity equivalence curves: a double trade-off curve method for equating task performance. COLLE, H.; AMELL, J.; EWRY, M.; AND JENKINS, M. *Hum. Factors* **30**, 5, (Oct. 1988) 645–656.

## JOURNALS

01797 Visual control of displacement at slow speeds. MESTRE, D. *Hum. Factors* **30,** 6, (Dec. 1988) 663–675.
01798 Comprehensino aids for on-line reading of expository text. LACHMAN, R. *Hum. Factors* **31,** 1, (Feb. 1989) 1–15.
01799 Visual Displays: the highlighting Paradox. FISHER, D.; AND TAN, K. *Hum. Factors* **31,** 1, (Feb. 1989) 17–30.
01800 Modeling the Cognitive content of displays. CHECHILE, R.; EGGLESTON, R.; FLEISCHMAN, R.; AND SASSEVILLE, A. *Hum. Factors* **31,** 1, (Feb. 1989) 31–43.
01801 Processing demands, effort, and individual differences in four different vigilance tasks. KOELEGA, H.; BRINKMAN, J.; HENDRIKS, L.; AND VERBATEN, M. *Hum. Factors* **31,** 1, (Feb. 1989) 45–62.
01802 Visual accommodation and target detection in the vicinity of a window post. CHONG, J.; AND TRIGGS, T. *Hum. Factors* **31,** 1, (Feb. 1989) 63–75.
01803 Simultaneous adaptation to size, distance, and curvature underwater. VERNOY, M. *Hum. Factors* **31,** 1, (Feb. 1989) 77–85.
01804 Simulator design and instructional features for air-to-ground attack: a transfer study. LINTERN, G.; SHEPPARD, D.; PARKER, D.; YATES, K.; AND NOLAN, M. *Hum. Factors* **31,** 1, (Feb. 1989) 87–99.

## Hypermedia

01805 Hyperwelcome. NELSON, T. *Hypermedia* **1,** 1, (Spring 1989) 3–5.
01806 Hypermedia as an interpretive act. DOLAND, V. *Hypermedia* **1,** 1, (Spring 1989) 6–19.
01807 Structuring knowledge bases for designers of learning materials. DUNCAN, E. *Hypermedia* **1,** 1, (Spring 1989) 20–33.
01808 Evaluating the usability of the Glasgow online. HARDMAN, L. *Hypermedia* **1,** 1, (Spring 1989) 34–63.

## IBM Journal of Research and Development

01809 OS/2 query manager overview and prompted interface. WATSON, S. *IBM J. Res. Dev.* **27,** 2, (June 1988) 119–133.
01810 Interfaces for knowledge-base builders' control knowledge and application-specific procedures. HIRSCH, P.; KATKE, W.; MEIER, M.; SNYDER, S.; AND STILLMAN, R. *IBM J. Res. Dev.* **30,** 1, (Jan. 1986) 29–38.
01811 A theory for the representation of knowledge. GUENTHNER, F.; LEHMANN, H.; AND SCHÖNFELD, W. *IBM J. Res. Dev.* **30,** 1, (Jan. 1986) 39–56.
01812 Implementing a semantic interpreter using conceptual graphs. SOWA, J.; AND WAY, E. *IBM J. Res. Dev.* **30,** 1, (Jan. 1986) 57–69.
HCI-0405 Document convergence in an interactive formatting system. CHAMBERLIN, D. *IBM J. Res. Dev.* **31,** 1, (Jan. 1987) 58–72.
01813 An experiment in computational discrimination of English word senses. BLACK, E. *IBM J. Res. Dev.* **32,** 3, (March 1988) 185–194.

## IBM Systems Journal

01814 An incidence-matrix-driven panel system for the IBM PC. HALPERN, P.; ROBERTS, S.; AND LOPEZ, L. *IBM Syst. J.* **26,** 2, (1987) 201–214.
01815 Advanced interactive executive (AIX) operating system overview. LOUCKS, L.; AND SAUER, C. *IBM Syst. J.* **26,** 4, (Dec. 1987) 326–345.
01816 Advanced interactive executive program development environment. CORDELL II, R.; MISRA, M.; AND WOLFE, R. *IBM Syst. J.* **26,** 4, (Dec. 1987) 361–382.
01817 AIX usability enhancements and human factors. WATERS, F.; BIAS, R.; AND SMITH-KERKER, P. *IBM Syst. J.* **26,** 4, (Dec. 1987) 383–394.

01818 An architecture for a business and information system. DEVLIN, B.; AND MURPHY, P. *IBM Syst. J.* **27**, 1, (January, 1988) 60–80.
01819 Common user access—a consistent and usable human-computer interface for the SAA environments. BERRY, R. *IBM Syst. J.* **27**, 3, (1988) 281–300.
01820 Enabling the user interface. UHLIR, S. *IBM Syst. J.* **27**, 3, (1988) 306–314.
01821 Designing SAA applications and user interfaces. DUNFEE, W.; MCGEHE, J.; RAUF, R.; AND SHIPP, K. *IBM Syst. J.* **27**, 3, (1988) 325–347.

## IEEE Computer Graphics and Applications

HCI-0377 The human factors of computer graphics interaction techniques. FOLEY, J.; WALLACE, V.; AND CHAN, P. *IEEE Comput. Graph. Appl.* **4**, 11, (Nov. 1984) 13–48.
HCI-0378 Physiological principles for the effective use of color. MURCH, G. *IEEE Comput. Graph. Appl.* **4**, 11, (Nov. 1984) 49–54.
HCI-0210 Human factors issues in VDT use: environmental and workstation design considerations. SMITH, M. *IEEE Comput. Graph. Appl.* **4**, 11, (Nov. 1984) 56–63.
01822 A graphics system architecture for interactive application-specific display functions. ENGLAND, N. *IEEE Comput. Graph. Appl.* **6**, 1, (Jan.1986) 60–70.
01823 An interactive procedure for constructing line and circle tangencies. FREUND, D. *IEEE Comput. Graph. Appl.* **6**, 4, (April 1986) 59–63.
01824 A theory of productivity in the creative process. BRADY, J. *IEEE Comput. Graph. Appl.* **6**, 5, (May 1986) 25–34.
01825 whim, the window handler and input manager. GOODFELLOW, M. *IEEE Comput. Graph. Appl.* **6**, 5, (May 1986) 46–52.
HCI-0380 CNS-HLS mapping using fuzzy sets. FARHOOSH, H.; AND SCHRACK, G. *IEEE Comput. Graph. Appl.* **6**, 6, (June 1986) 28–35.
HCI-0372 Two-bit graphics. SALESIN, D.; AND BARZEL, R. *IEEE Comput. Graph. Appl.* **6**, 6, (June 1986) 36–42.
01826 PHIGS: a standard, dynamic, interactive graphics interface. SHUEY, D.; BAILEY, D.; AND MORRISSEY, T. *IEEE Comput. Graph. Appl.* **6**, 8, (Aug. 1986) 50–57.
01827 Editing templates: a user interface generation tool. OLSEN, J. *IEEE Comput. Graph. Appl.* **6**, 11, (November 1986) 40–45.
01828 Interactive design of 3D computer-animated legged animal motion. GIRARD, M. *IEEE Comput. Graph. Appl.* **7**, 6, (June 1987) 39–51.
01829 Near-real-time control of human figure models. ARMSTRONG, W.; GREEN, M.; AND LAKE, R. *IEEE Comput. Graph. Appl.* **7**, 6, (June 1987) 52–61.
01830 HutWindows: an improved architecture for a user interface management system. KOIVUNEN, M.; AND MANATYLA, M. *IEEE Comput. Graph. Appl.* **8**, 1, (Jan. 1988) 43–52.
01831 Marcosby example in a graphical UIMS. OLSEN, J.; AND DANCE, J. *IEEE Comput. Graph. Appl.* **8**, 1, (Jan. 1988) 68–78.

## IEEE Micro

01832 An intelligent braille display device. GROSSNER, C.; RADHAKRISHNAN, T.; AND SCHENA, A. *IEEE Micro* **6**, 3, (June 1986) 43–51.

## IEEE Spectrum

01833 The lure of molecular computing. CONRAD, M. *IEEE Spectrum* **23**,:0R 10, (Oct. 1986) 55–60.
01834 Instrumentation. VOELCKER, J. *IEEE Spectrum* **24**, 1, (Jan. 1987) 48–49.
01835 The specialties. JURGEN, R. *IEEE Spectrum* **24**, 1, (Jan. 1987) 69–70.

JOURNALS

01836 Neurocomputing. HECHT-NIELSEN, R. *IEEE Spectrum* **25**, 3, (March 1988) 36–41.
01837 Of mice and menus: designing the user-friendly interface. PERRY, T.; AND VOELCKER, J. *IEEE Spectrum* **26**, 9, (September 1989) 46–51.

## IEEE Transactions on Pattern Analysis and Machine Intelligence

01838 Perceptual organization and curve partitioning. FISCHLER, M.; AND BOLLES, R. *IEEE Trans. Pattern Anal. Mach. Intell.* **8**, 1, (Jan. 1986) 100–105.
01839 On kineopsis and cimputation of structure and motion. MITICHE, A. *IEEE Trans. Pattern Anal. Mach. Intell.* **8**, 1, (Jan. 1986) 109–112.
01840 An automatic wafer inspection system using pipelined image processing techniques. YODA, H.; OHUCHI, Y.; TANIGUCHI, Y.; AND EJIRI, M. *IEEE Trans. Pattern Anal. Mach. Intell.* **10**, 1, (Jan. 1988) 4–6.
01841 Automated concept acquisition in noisy environments. BERGADANO, F.; GIORDANA, A.; AND SAITTA, L. *IEEE Trans. Pattern Anal. Mach. Intell.* **10**, 4, (July 1988) 555–578.
01842 Using perceptual organization to extract 3-D structures. MOHAN, R.; AND NEVATIA, R. *IEEE Trans. Pattern Anal. Mach. Intell.* **11**, 11, (Nov. 1989) 1121–1139.
01843 Digital parallelism, perpendicularity, and rectangles. KRISHNASWAMY, R.; AND KIM, C. *IEEE Trans. Pattern Anal. Mach. Intell.* **PAMI-9**, 2, (March 1987) 316–321.
01844 New methods for matching 3-D objects with single perspective views. HORAUD, R. *IEEE Trans. Pattern Anal. Mach. Intell.* **PAMI-9**, 3, (May 1987) 401–412.
01845 A new sense for depth of field. PENTLAND, A. *IEEE Trans. Pattern Anal. Mach. Intell.* **PAMI-9**, 4, (July 1987) 523–531.
01846 Extension of conditional probability and measures of belief and disbelief in a hypothesis based on uncertain evidence. IHARA, J. *IEEE Trans. Pattern Anal. Mach. Intell.* **PAMI-9**, 4, (July 1987) 561–568.

## IEEE Transactions on Software Engineering

01847 Comments on "formal specification of user interfaces: a comparison and evaluation of four axiomatic approaches". ALEXANDER, H. *IEEE Trans. Softw. Eng.* **14**, 4, (April 1988) 438–439.
01848 Providing quality responses with natural language interfaces: the null value problem. KAO, M.; CERCONE, N.; AND LUK, W. *IEEE Trans. Softw. Eng.* **14**, 7, (July 1988) 959–984.
01849 A system for specification and rapid prototyping of application command languages. STELOVSKY, J.; AND SUGAYA, H. *IEEE Trans. Softw. Eng.* **14**, 7, (July 1988) 1023–1032.
01850 The tinkertoy graphical programming environment. EDEL, M. *IEEE Trans. Softw. Eng.* **14**, 8, (August 1988) 1110–1115.
01851 Semantic feedback in the Higgens UIMS. HUDSON, S.; AND KING, R. *IEEE Trans. Softw. Eng.* **14**, 8, (August 1988) 1188–1206.
01852 User validation of information systems requirements: some empirical results. NOSEK, J.; AND SCHWARTZ, R. *IEEE Trans. Softw. Eng.* **14**, 9, (Sept. 1988) 1372–1375.
01853 Design of knowledge-based systems with a knowledge-based assistant. SCHOEN, E.; SMITH, R.; AND BUCHANAN, B. *IEEE Trans. Softw. Eng.* **14**, 12, (Dec. 1988) 1771–1791.
01854 Software engineering for user interfaces. DRAPER, S.; AND NORMAN, D. *IEEE Trans. Softw. Eng.* **SE-11**, 3, (March 1985) 252–258.
HCI-0145 PECAN: program development systems that support multiple views. REISS, S. *IEEE Trans. Softw. Eng.* **SE-11**, 3, (March 1985) 276–285.
HCI-0137 An approach to user specification of interactive display interfaces. BASS, L. *IEEE Trans. Softw. Eng.* **SE-11**, 8, (Aug. 1985) 686–698.
HCI-0191 Extending state transition diagrams for the specification of human-computer interaction. WASSERMAN, A. *IEEE Trans. Softw. Eng.* **SE-11**, 8, (Aug. 1985) 699–713.

**HCI-0213** An aspect of aesthetics in human-computer communications: pretty windows. GAIT, J. *IEEE Trans. Softw. Eng.* **SE-11**, 8, (Aug. 1985) 714–717.

**HCI-0387** An image processing language with ICON-assisted navigation. CHANG, S.; JUNGERT, E.; LEVIALDI, S.; TORTORA, G.; AND ICHIKAWA, T. *IEEE Trans. Softw. Eng.* **SE-11**, 8, (Aug. 1985) 811–819.

**HCI-0162** Abstract data type development and implementation: an example. FORD, R.; AND MILLER, K. *IEEE Trans. Softw. Eng.* **SE-11**, 10, (Oct. 1985) 1033–1037.

**01855** A high level language-based computing enviornment to support production and execution of reliable programs. TSUBOTANI, H.; MONDEN, N.; TANAKA, M.; AND ICHIKAWA, T. *IEEE Trans. Softw. Eng.* **SE-12**, 1, (Jan. 1986) 134–146.

**01856** Developing interactive information systems with the user software engineering methodology. WASSERMAN, A.; PIRCHER, P.; SHEWMAKE, D.; AND KERSTEN, M. *IEEE Trans. Softw. Eng.* **SE-12**, 2, (Feb. 1986) 326–345.

**HCI-0248** ARES: a relational database with the capability of performing flexible interpretation of queries. ICHIKAWA, T.; AND HIRAKAWA, M. *IEEE Trans. Softw. Eng.* **SE-12**, 5, (May 1986) 624–634.

**01857** Edmas: an object-oriented, locally distributed mail system. ALMES, G.; AND HOLMAN, C. *IEEE Trans. Softw. Eng.* **SE-13**, 9, (September 1, 1987) 1001–1009.

## IEEE Transactions on Systems, Man and Cybernetics

**01858** Aiding the operator during novel fault diagnosis. YOON, W.; AND HAMMER, J. *IEEE Trans. Syst. Man Cybern.* **18**, 1, (January/February 1988) 142–148.

**01859** Modeling of task-dependent characteristics of human operator dynamics during pursuit manual tracking. ABDEL-MALEK, A.; AND MARMARELIS, V. *IEEE Trans. Syst. Man Cybern.* **18**, 1, (January/February 1988) 163–172.

**01860** ARIADNE: a knowledge-based interactive system for planning and decision support. SAGE, A.; AND WHITE, C. *IEEE Trans. Syst. Man Cybern.* **SMC-14**, 1, (Jan./Feb. 1984) 35–47.

**HCI-0359** A fuzzy rule-based model of human problem solving. HUNT, R.; AND ROUSE, W. *IEEE Trans. Syst. Man Cybern.* **SMC-14**, 1, (Jan./Feb. 1984) 112–120.

**01861** Interpretation of natural language database queries using optimization methods. LEIGH, W.; AND EVANS, J. *IEEE Trans. Syst. Man Cybern.* **SMC-16**, 1, (Jan./Feb. 1986) 40–52.

**01862** Directed graph representations of association structures: A systematic approach. MIYAMOTO, S.; OI, K.; ABE, O.; KATSUYA, A.; AND NAKAYAMA, K. *IEEE Trans. Syst. Man Cybern.* **SMC-16**, 1, (Jan./Feb. 1986) 53–61.

**01863** Stochastic dynamics of neural networks. PERETTO, P. *IEEE Trans. Syst. Man Cybern.* **SMC-16**, 1, (Jan./Feb. 1986) 73–83.

**01864** A model for the fading of stabilized images in a visual system. SALEH, B.; AND TULUNAY-KEESEY, U. *IEEE Trans. Syst. Man Cybern.* **SMC-16**, 1, (Jan./Feb. 1986) 84–92.

**01865** Automation effects in a multiloop manual control system. HESS, R.; AND MCNALLY, B. *IEEE Trans. Syst. Man Cybern.* **SMC-16**, 1, (Jan./Feb. 1986) 111–121.

**01866** Application of a mathematical model of human decisionmaking for human-computer communication. REVESMAN, M.; AND GREENSTEIN, J. *IEEE Trans. Syst. Man Cybern.* **SMC-16**, 1, (Jan./Feb. 1986) 142–147.

**01867** Significance testing of rules in rule-based models of human problem solving. LEWIS, C.; AND HAMMER, J. *IEEE Trans. Syst. Man Cybern.* **SMC-16**, 1, (Jan./Feb. 1986) 154–158.

**01868** Goodness of fit in the user-computer interface: A hierarchical control framework related to "friendless". THESEN, A.; AND BERINGER, D. *IEEE Trans. Syst. Man Cybern.* **SMC-16**, 1, (Jan./Feb. 1986) 158–162.

**01869** The influence of troubleshooting, education, and documentation on computer user satisfaction. RUSHINEK, A.; AND RUSHINEK, S. *IEEE Trans. Syst. Man Cybern.* **SMC-16**, 1, (Jan./Feb. 1986) 165–168.

**01870** Open-loop experiments for modeling the human eye movement system. BAHILL, A.; AND HARVEY, D. *IEEE Trans. Syst. Man Cybern.* **SMC-16**, 2, (March/April 196) 240–250.

**01871** GISMO: A visual problem-structuring and knowledge-organization tool. PRACHT, W. *IEEE Trans. Syst. Man Cybern.* **SMC-16**, 2, (March/April 196) 265–270.

## JOURNALS

01872 A user preference guided approach to conflict resolution in rule-based expert systems. WHITE, C.; AND SYKES, E. *IEEE Trans. Syst. Man Cybern.* **SMC-16**, 2, (March/April 196) 276–278.
01873 A knowledge-based human-computer cooperative system for ill-structured management domains. NIWA, K. *IEEE Trans. Syst. Man Cybern.* **SMC-16**, 3, (May/June 1986) 335–342.
01874 A discrete control model of operator function: A methodology for information dislay design. MITCHELL, C.; AND MILLER, R. *IEEE Trans. Syst. Man Cybern.* **SMC-16**, 3, (May/June 1986) 343–357.
01875 The emergence of Zipf's law: Spontaneous encoding optimization by users of a command language. ELLIS, S.; AND HITCHCOCK, R. *IEEE Trans. Syst. Man Cybern.* **SMC-16**, 3, (May/June 1986) 423–427.
01876 Two views of generality. MILLER, T. *IEEE Trans. Syst. Man Cybern.* **SMC-16**, 3, (May/June 1986) 450–453.
01877 A rule-based model for the human operator in a time-constrained competing-task environment. GOVINDARAJ, T. *IEEE Trans. Syst. Man Cybern.* **SMC-16**, 3, (May/June 1986) 470–473.
01878 Acquisition of process control skills. MORAY, N.; LOOTSTEEN, P.; AND PAJAK, J. *IEEE Trans. Syst. Man Cybern.* **SMC-16**, 4, (July/Aug. 1986) 497–504.
01879 Analysis of user procedural compliance in controlling a simulated process. MANN, T.; AND HAMMER, J. *IEEE Trans. Syst. Man Cybern.* **SMC-16**, 4, (July/Aug. 1986) 505–510.
01880 Aiding the human decisionmaker through the knowledge-based sciences. SAGE, A.; AND ROUSE, W. *IEEE Trans. Syst. Man Cybern.* **SMC-16**, 4, (July/Aug. 1986) 511–521.
01881 Neural network model with rhythm-assimilation capacity. TORRAS I GENIS, C. *IEEE Trans. Syst. Man Cybern.* **SMC-16**, 5, (Sept./Oct. 1986) 680–693.
01882 Two simulation studies investigating means of human-computer communication for dynamic task allocation. GREENSTEIN, J.; AND REVESMAN, M. *IEEE Trans. Syst. Man Cybern.* **SMC-16**, 5, (Sept./Oct. 1986) 726–730.
01883 Capturing expertise: Some approaches to modeling command decisionmaking in combat analysis. FARRELL, R.; BONDER, S.; PROEGER, L.; MILLER, G.; AND THOMPSON, D. *IEEE Trans. Syst. Man Cybern.* **SMC-16**, 6, (Dec. 1986) 766–773.
01884 A framework for task cooperation within systems containing intelligent components. SCHWARTZ, J.; KULLBACK, J.; AND SHRIER, S. *IEEE Trans. Syst. Man Cybern.* **SMC-16**, 6, (Dec. 1986) 788–793.
01885 Distributed tactical decisionmaking: conceptual framework and empirical results. ADELMAN, L.; ZIRK, D.; LEHNER, P.; MOFFETT, R.; AND HALL, R. *IEEE Trans. Syst. Man Cybern.* **SMC-16**, 6, (Dec. 1986) 794–805.
01886 Distributed decisionmaking with constrained decisionmakers: a case study. BOETTCHER, K.; AND TENNEY, R. *IEEE Trans. Syst. Man Cybern.* **SMC-16**, 6, (Dec. 1986) 813–823.
01887 Adaptive user interfaces for planning and decision aids in $C^3I$ systems. NOAH, W.; AND HALPIN, S. *IEEE Trans. Syst. Man Cybern.* **SMC-16**, 6, (Dec. 1986) 909–918.
01888 Graphic equivalence, graphic explanations, and embedded process modeling for enhanced user-system interaction. ANDRIOLE, S. *IEEE Trans. Syst. Man Cybern.* **SMC-16**, 6, (Dec. 1986) 919–926.
01889 Understanding and enhancing user acceptance of computer. ROUSE, W.; AND MORRIS, N. *IEEE Trans. Syst. Man Cybern.* **SMC-16**, 6, (Dec. 1986) 965–973.
01890 Building and understanding adaptive systems: a statistical/numerical approach to factory automation and brain research. WERBOS, P. *IEEE Trans. Syst. Man Cybern.* **SMC-17**, 1, (Jan./Feb. 1987) 7–20.
01891 A qualitative model of human interaction with complex dynamic systems. HESS, R. *IEEE Trans. Syst. Man Cybern.* **SMC-17**, 1, (Jan./Feb. 1987) 33–51.
01892 Representations of perceived relations among the properties and variables of a complex system. HOPKINS, R.; CAMPBELL, D.; AND PETERSON, N. *IEEE Trans. Syst. Man Cybern.* **SMC-17**, 1, (Jan./Feb. 1987) 52–60.
01893 The information capacity of the human fingertip. KOKJER, K. *IEEE Trans. Syst. Man Cybern.* **SMC-17**, 1, (Jan./Feb. 1987) 100–102.
01894 Prediction of the smallest channel in early human vision. NGUYEN, D. *IEEE Trans. Syst. Man Cybern.* **SMC-17**, 1, (Jan./Feb. 1987) 106–108.
01895 Electronic implementation of associative memory based on neural network models. MOOPENN, A.; LAMBE, J.; AND THAKOOR, A. *IEEE Trans. Syst. Man Cybern.* **SMC-17**, 2, (March/April 1987) 325–331.
01896 Direct comparison of the relative efficiency on intuitive and analytical cognition. HAMMOND, K.; HAMM, R.; GRASSIA, J.; AND PEARSON, T. *IEEE Trans. Syst. Man Cybern.* **SMC-17**, 5, (Sept./Oct. 1987) 753–770.

**01897** The use of measures of entropy in evaluating human supervisory control of a manufacturing system. SHARIT, J. *IEEE Trans. Syst. Man Cybern.* **SMC-17,** 5, (Sept./Oct. 1987) 815–820.

**01898** An empirical investigation as to the need for multicomponent decision models. ADELMAN, L.; PLISKE, R.; AND LEHNER, P. *IEEE Trans. Syst. Man Cybern.* **SMC-17,** 6, (Nov./Dec. 1987) 913–919.

**01899** Information systems engineering for distributed decisionmaking. SAGE, A. *IEEE Trans. Syst. Man Cybern.* **SMC-17,** 6, (Nov./Dec. 1987) 920–936.

**01900** Qualitative approximation methodology for modeling and simulation of large dynamic systems: Applications to a Marine power plant. GOVINDARAJ, T. *IEEE Trans. Syst. Man Cybern.* **SMC-17,** 6, (Nov./Dec. 1987) 937–955.

**01901** Rule-based reasoning as Boolean transformations. LOONEY, C.; AND ALFIZE, A. *IEEE Trans. Syst. Man Cybern.* **SMC-17,** 6, (Nov./Dec. 1987) 1077–1082.

## IMC Journal

**01902** The dubious dangers of VDT radiation. *IMC J.* **22,** 3, (May/June 1986) 37–38.

## Industrial Engineering

**01903** The IE's future role in improving knowledge. HARRIS, M.; AND VINING, G. *Ind. Eng.* **19,** 7, (July 1987) 28–32.

**01904** Ergonomic improvements boost AS/RS performance. WINSHIP, W.; AND MUSTAFA PULAT, B. *Ind. Eng.* **19,** 7, (July 1987) 38–41.

**01905** Process control and people at General Motors' Delta Engine Plant. BLACHE, K.; STEWART, K.; ZIMMERMAN, R.; SHAULL, J.; AND BENNER, R. *Ind. Eng.* **20,** 3, (March 1988) 24–30.

**01906** Barriers to factory automation. SNYDER, K.; AND ELLIOTT, C. *Ind. Eng.* **20,** 4, (April, 1988) 44–51.

**01907** Tennessee Eastman employee teamwork raises quality, customer service. DINGUS, V. *Ind. Eng.* **20,** 8, (August 1988) 28–35.

**01908** Dow Chemical makes continuous improvement part of everyone's job. BOWMAN, J.; AND BRADY, L. *Ind. Eng.* **20,** 8, (August 1988) 40–45.

**01909** Methods improvement kit uses IE technique to simplify work. COPP, E. *Ind. Eng.* **20,** 8, (August 1988) 46–50.

## Information Age

**01910** 'Remember to lock the door': MMI and the hacker. ROBERTS, W. *Inf. Age* **10,** 3, (July 1988) 146–150.

**01911** Access-control software. FRIEDMAN, M. *Inf. Age* **10,** 3, (July 1988) 157–161.

## Information and Computation

**01912** Relativized Arthur-Merlin versus Merlin-Arthur games. SANTHA, M. *Inf. Comput.* **80,** 1, (January 1, 1989) 44–49.

## Information and Management

**HCI-0294** The impact of DSS on organizational communication. SANDERS, G.; COURTNEY, J.; AND LOY, S. *Inf. Manage.* **7,** 3, (June 1984) 141–148.

**HCI-0288** Executive workstations: issues and requirements. POWER, D.; AND HEVNER, A. *Inf. Manage.* **8,** 4, (April 1985) 213–220.

## JOURNALS

HCI-0451  An empirical study of occupational stress, attitudes and health among information systems personnel. IVANCEVICH, J.; NAPIER, H.; AND WETHERBE, J. *Inf. Manage.* **9**, 2, (Sept. 1985) 77–85.

HCI-0301  A laboratory study of user characteristics and decision-making performance in end-user computing. KASPER, G.; AND CERVENY, R. *Inf. Manage.* **9**, 2, (Sept. 1985) 87–96.

HCI-0313  Videotex: anatomy of a failure. NOLL, A. *Inf. Manage.* **9**, 2, (Sept. 1985) 99–109.

HCI-0303  Impact of design methods on decision support systems success: an empirical assessment. MAHMOOD, M.; AND MEDEWITZ, J. *Inf. Manage.* **9**, 3, (Oct. 1985) 137–151.

HCI-0296  Change, attitude to change, and decision support system success. BARKI, H.; AND HUFF, S. *Inf. Manage.* **9**, 5, (Dec. 1985) 261–268.

01913  The feature chart: A tool for communicating the analysis for a decision support system. SEAGLE, J.; AND BELARDO, S. *Inf. Manage.* **10**, 1, (Jan. 1986) 11–19.

01914  A critical view of factors affecting successful application of normative and socio-technical systems development approaches. PADDOCK, C. *Inf. Manage.* **10**, 1, (Jan. 1986) 49–57.

HCI-0216  Mainframe and microcomputer-based business graphics: What satisfies users? LEHMAN, J.; VAN WETERING, J.; AND VOGEL, D. *Inf. Manage.* **10**, 3, (March 1986) 133–140.

01915  Applying a pilot system and prototyping approach to systems development and implementation. JANSON, M. *Inf. Manage.* **10**, 4, (April 1986) 209–216.

01916  A survey of information technology in the U.K. service sector. YAP, C.; AND WALSHAM, G. *Inf. Manage.* **10**, 5, (May 1986) 267–274.

01917  Insights on the implementation of a computer-based message system. KAYE, A.; AND BYRNE, K. *Inf. Manage.* **10**, 5, (May 1986) 277–284.

01918  CHI '86 - human factors in computing systems. *Inf. Manage.* **10**, 5, (May 1986) 285–298.

01919  An exploratory contingency model of user participation and MIS use. KIM, E.; AND LEE, J. *Inf. Manage.* **11**, 2, (Sept. 1986) 87–97.

01920  Establishing user-centered criteria for information systems: a software ergonomics perspective. KNITTLE, D.; RUTH, S.; AND GARDNER, E. *Inf. Manage.* **11**, 4, (Nov. 1986) 163–172.

01921  One view of the future of industrial control. WILLIAMS, T. *Inf. Manage.* **11**, 5, (Dec. 1986) 217–227.

01922  BCS human—computer interaction conference. *Inf. Manage.* **11**, 5, (Dec. 1986) 245–249.

01923  Strategies for managing user developed systems. BEHESHTIAN, M.; AND VAN WERT, P. *Inf. Manage.* **12**, 1, (Jan. 1987) 1–7.

01924  The quality of user documentation. DOLL, W.; AND TORKZADEH, G. *Inf. Manage.* **12**, 2, (Feb. 1987) 73–78.

01925  ACM SIGUCCS User Services Conference XIV. *Inf. Manage.* **12**, 2, (Feb. 1987) 87–100.

01926  Encouraging user management participation in systems design. DOLL, W. *Inf. Manage.* **13**, 1, (August 1, 1987) 25–32.

01927  End-user computing environments—finding a balance between productivity and control. O'DONNELL, D.; AND MARCH, S. *Inf. Manage.* **13**, 2, (September 1, 1987) 77–84.

01928  A systems architecture for supporting senior managers' messy tasks. YOUNG, L. *Inf. Manage.* **13**, 2, (September 1, 1987) 85–94.

01929  The information center approach for developing computer-based information systems. NECCO, C.; GORDON, C.; AND TSAI, N. *Inf. Manage.* **13**, 2, (September 1, 1987) 95–101.

01930  A preliminary specification of an on-line expert help system. MOILY, J.; MURRAY, T.; AND AGARWAL, R. *Inf. Manage.* **13**, 4, (November, 1987) 191–196.

01931  Implementing computer-mediated communication technologies: a technoacceptance approach to critical mass utilization. WHITE, K.; AND MASSELLO, J. *Inf. Manage.* **13**, 4, (November, 1987) 197–208.

01932  Managing information systems for effectiveness and humanity: applying research of organizational behavior. BRANCHEAU, J.; AND HOFFMANN, T. *Inf. Manage.* **13**, 5, (December, 1987) 233–243.

01933  Measuring implementation outcome: beyond success and failure. CALE JR., E.; AND CURLEY, K. *Inf. Manage.* **13**, 5, (December, 1987) 245–253.

01934  An empirical investigation of DSS usage and the user's perception of DSS training. MYKYTYN JR., P. *Inf. Manage.* **14**, 1, (Jan., 1988) 9–17.

**01935** Differences in analyst's attitudes towards information systems development: evidence and implications. DOS SANTOS, B.; AND HAWK, S. *Inf. Manage.* **14,** 1, (Jan., 1988) 31–41.

**01936** End user—IS design professional interaction—information exchange for firm profit or end user satisfaction? MARSDEN, J.; AND PINGRY, D. *Inf. Manage.* **14,** 2, (Feb. 1988) 75–80.

**01937** The management of the end-user environment: an empirical investigation. BERGERON, F.; AND BÉRUBÉ, C. *Inf. Manage.* **14,** 3, (March 1988) 107–113.

**01938** Information systems user–designer communication problems. VERRIJN-STUART, A.; AND ANZENHOFER, K. *Inf. Manage.* **14,** 3, (March 1988) 133–142.

**01939** Key human resource issues in IS in the 1990s: Views of IS executives versus human resource executives. COUGER, J. *Inf. Manage.* **14,** 4, (April 1988) 161–174.

**01940** Informatics and municipalities: the Greek approach. SIDERIDIS, A. *Inf. Manage.* **14,** 4, (April 1988) 183–188.

**01941** Competition and cooperation in information systems innovation. CLEMONS, E.; AND KNEZ, M. *Inf. Manage.* **15,** 1, (Aug. 1988) 25–35.

**01942** The dual role of information centers: an assessment of end user computing management strategies. SA'AKSJÄRVI, M.; HEIKKILÁ, J.; AND SAARINEN, T. *Inf. Manage.* **15,** 1, (Aug. 1988) 69–78.

**01943** An entity-relationship framework for information resource management. BLANNING, R. *Inf. Manage.* **15,** 2, (September 1988) 113–119.

**01944** An object-oriented approach to the design of a mail system for a heterogeneous environment. KUO, F. *Inf. Manage.* **15,** 3, (March 1, 1988) 173–182.

**01945** Business graphics trends, two years later. LEHMAN, J.; AND MURTHY, V. *Inf. Manage.* **16,** 2, (Feb. 1989) 57–69.

**01946** Definitional distinctions and implications for managing end user computing. SIPIOR, J.; AND SANDERS, G. *Inf. Manage.* **16,** 3, (March 1989) 115–123.

**01947** Decision support systems for workers: a bridge to advancing productivity. YOUNG, L. *Inf. Manage.* **16,** 3, (March 1989) 131–140.

**01948** The implementation of information systems for workers: a structural equation model. ANDERSON, E. *Inf. Manage.* **16,** 4, (April 1989) 171–186.

**01949** Microcomputer applications: an empirical look at usage. IGBARIA, M.; PAVRI, F.; AND HUFF, S. *Inf. Manage.* **16,** 4, (April 1989) 187–196.

**01950** Automatic information processing activities and operational decision making: a case study of consequence. VAN DER VLIST, R. *Inf. Manage.* **16,** 4, (April 1989) 219–225.

**01951** An analysis of human and computer decision-making capabilities. JACOB, V.; MOORE, J.; AND WHINSTON, A. *Inf. Manage.* **16,** 5, (May 1989) 247–255.

**01952** Successful application of communication techniques to improve the systems development process. BOSTROM, R. *Inf. Manage.* **16,** 5, (May 1989) 279–275.

**01953** Examining the duality role of I.S. executives: a study of I.S. issues. AMOROSO, D.; THOMPSON, R.; AND CHENEY, P. *Inf. Manage.* **17,** 1, (August 1989) 1–12.

**01954** Utilizing high technology: computer-aided-design and user performance. GUEUTAL, H. *Inf. Manage.* **17,** 1, (August 1989) 13–21.

**01955** Impact of prototyping on user information satisfaction during the IS specification phase. IIVARI, J.; AND KARJALAINEN, M. *Inf. Manage.* **17,** 1, (August 1989) 31–45.

**01956** Methodology for end user computing in development administration. SANWAL, M. *Inf. Manage.* :0B17, 2, (Sept. 1989) 117–126.

### Information and Software Technology

**01957** Ill-formedness and miscommunication in person-machine dialogue. REILLY, R. *Inf. Softw. Technol.* **29,** 2, (March/April 1987) 69–74.

**01958** Advanced diagnostics: a PASCAL interactive system. WHITE, N.; AND HAYLETT, G. *Inf. Softw. Technol.* **29,** 2, (March/April 1987) 75–80.

**01959** Intelligent help systems. ERLANDSEN, J.; AND HOLM, J. *Inf. Softw. Technol.* **29,** 3, (April 1987) 115–121.

## JOURNALS

**01960** MAJIC—an integrated program support environment. SUTCLIFFE, A.; AND DAVIES, C. *Inf. Softw. Technol.* **29**, 3, (April 1987) 122–136.
**01961** Theory and practice in user interface management systems. KILGOUR, A. *Inf. Softw. Technol.* **29**, 4, (May 1987) 171–175.
**01962** Interaction ergonomics, control and separation: open problems in user interface management. COCKTON, G. *Inf. Softw. Technol.* **29**, 4, (May 1987) 176–191.
**01963** Human factors and the design of user interface management systems: EASIE as a case study. MACLEAN, A. *Inf. Softw. Technol.* **29**, 4, (May 1987) 192–201.
**01964** User interface management and graphics standards. GALLOP, J. *Inf. Softw. Technol.* **29**, 4, (May 1987) 202–206.
**01965** Trillium: an interface design prototyping tool. EASTERBY, R. *Inf. Softw. Technol.* **29**, 4, (May 1987) 207–213.
**01966** The user is always right. LARKIN, I. *Inf. Softw. Technol.* **29**, 4, (May 1987) 214–218.
**01967** GRAPE programming environment. PALMER, T. *Inf. Softw. Technol.* **29**, 4, (May 1987) 219–225.
**01968** Teaching software engineering at university. GARRATT, P.; AND EDMUNDS, G. *Inf. Softw. Technol.* **30**, 1, (January/February) 5–11.
**01969** An input/output primitive for object-oriented systems. POWELL, M. *Inf. Softw. Technol.* **30**, 1, (January/February) 44–56.
**01970** Emeraude portable common tool environment. CAMPBELL, I. *Inf. Softw. Technol.* **30**, 4, (May 1988) 210–217.
**01971** Mental gymnastics of sequential programming. MIDDLETON, A. *Inf. Softw. Technol.* **30**, 4, (May 1988) 250–255.
**01972** Communicating with users during systems development. MORRISON, W. *Inf. Softw. Technol.* **30**, 5, (June 1988) 295–298.
**01973** WIMP interface for Unix. BEZ, H. *Inf. Softw. Technol.* **30**, 8, (Oct. 1988) 477–483.
**01974** A new approach to cursor movements in user interfaces of integrated programming environments. MADHAVJI, N.; PINSONNEAULT, L.; TOUBACHE, K.; AND DESHARNAIS, J. *Inf. Softw. Technol.* **30**, 9, (Nov. 1988) 535–546.
**01975** Effect of computer knowledge on user performance over time. MARTIN, M.; AND FUERST, W. *Inf. Softw. Technol.* **30**, 9, (Nov. 1988) 561–566.
**01976** Experiences in use of SSADM: series of case studies. Part 1: first time users. EDWARDS, H.; THOMPSON, J.; AND SMITH, P. *Inf. Softw. Technol.* **31**, 8, (Oct. 1989) 411–419.
**01977** Experiences in use of SSADM: series of case studies. Part 2: experienced users. EDWARDS, H.; THOMPSON, J.; AND SMITH, P. *Inf. Softw. Technol.* **31**, 8, (Oct. 1989) 420–428.
**01978** Responsibility sharing between sophisticated users and professionals in structured prototyping. PLISKIN, N.; AND SHOVAL, P. *Inf. Softw. Technol.* **31**, 8, (Oct. 1989) 438–448.

### Information Display

**01979** Spatial misorientation exacerbated by collimated virtual flight display. ROSCOE, S. *Information Display* **2**, 9, (September 1986) 27–28.
**01980** Are video displays a health hazard? CORPORATE *Information Display* **2**, 11, (Nov. 1986) 21–24.
**01981** From vision science to HDTV: bridging the gap. GLENN, K.; AND GLENN, W. *Information Display* **3**, 2, (Feb. 1987) 22–25.
**01982** Human factors and flat panels challenge the CRT. MURCH, G. *Information Display* **3**, 3, (March 1987) 8–11.
**01983** Display legibility guidelines: a design aid. SAWYER, D.; AND TALLEY, W. *Information Display* **3**, 11, (Dec. 1987) 13–16.
**01984** Understanding and evaluating a computer graphics display. VIRGIN, L. *Information Display* **3**, 11, (Dec. 1987) 17–19.
**01985** CRTs—present and future. INFANTE, C. *Information Display* **4**, 12, (Dec. 1988) 8–11.
**01986** Interactive data visualization. ALEXANDER, J.; AND WINARSKY, N. *Information Display* **5**, 4, (April 1989) 14–15.

**01987** CRT picture vibration caused by low-frequency magnetic field and its reduction method. NITTA, S.; MAEHANA, Y.; AND ITO, T. *Information Display* **29**, 1, (Jan. 1988) 7–11.

## Information Economics and Policy

**01988** Private copying, reproduction costs, and the supply of intellectual property. BESEN, S. *Inf. Econ. Policy* **2**, 1, (March 1986) 5–22.

## Information Processing and Management

**HCI-0138** Toward native language software for information management. SANTAELLA, E.; AND SLAMECKA, V. *Inf. Process. Manage.* **20**, 4, (1984) 527–534.

**HCI-0184** Human information seeking and design of information systems. ROUSE, W.; AND ROUSE, S. *Inf. Process. Manage.* **20**, 1-2, (1984) 129–138.

**01989** The value of information and computer-aided information seeking: problem formulation and application to fiction retrieval. MOREHEAD, D.; PEJTERSEN, A.; AND ROUSE, W. *Inf. Process. Manage.* **20**, 5/6, (1984) 583–601.

**01990** A common interface for accessing document retrieval systems and dbms for retrieval of bibliographic data. SHEPHERD, M.; AND WATTERS, C. *Inf. Process. Manage.* **21**, 2, (1985) 127–138.

**HCI-0262** A supporting system for effective construction and sharing of scientific databases by general researchers. AMANO, K.; AND MOCHIDA, A. *Inf. Process. Manage.* **21**, 6, (Dec. 1985) 535–544.

**01991** *Library*—An electronic ordering system. WALDSTEIN, R. *Inf. Process. Manage.* **22**, 1, (1986) 39–44.

**01992** Processes and problems in information consolidation. SARACEVIC, T. *Inf. Process. Manage.* **22**, 1, (1986) 45–60.

**01993** Indeterminacy in the subject access to documents. BLAIR, D. *Inf. Process. Manage.* **22**, 3, (1986) 229–241.

**HCI-0220** A note on the nature of creativity in engineering: implications for supporting system design. ROUSE, W. *Inf. Process. Manage.* **22**, 4, (Aug. 1986) 279–285.

**HCI-0219** A novice user's interface to information retrieval systems. CRAWFORD, R.; AND BECKER, H. *Inf. Process. Manage.* **22**, 4, (Aug. 1986) 287–298.

**HCI-0221** The effects of communication monitors on user satisfaction. RUSHINEK, A.; AND RUSHINEK, S. *Inf. Process. Manage.* **22**, 4, (Aug. 1986) 345–351.

**01994** User modeling in intelligent information retrieval. BRAJNIK, G.; GUIDA, G.; AND TASSO, C. *Inf. Process. Manage.* **23**, 4, (July 1987) 305–320.

**01995** Search success and expectations with a computer interface. MACGREGOR, D.; FISCHHOFF, B.; AND BLACKSHAW, L. *Inf. Process. Manage.* **23**, 5, (Sept. 1987) 419–432.

**01996** The convergence of Moore's/Mooers' laws. KOENIG, M. *Inf. Process. Manage.* **23**, 6, (July 1, 1987) 583–592.

**01997** On meanings menus for measurement: disentangling evaluative issues in system design. ROUSE, W. *Inf. Process. Manage.* **23**, 6, (July 1, 1987) 593–604.

**01998** On two roles decision support systems can play in negotiations. KERSTEN, G. *Inf. Process. Manage.* **23**, 6, (July 1, 1987) 605–614.

**01999** Online text retrieval via browsing. COVE, J.; AND WALSH, B. *Inf. Process. Manage.* **24**, 1, (January 1988) 31–37.

**02000** A tool for measuring analysis end user computing. CHENEY, P.; AND NELSON, R. *Inf. Process. Manage.* **24**, 2, (March 1988) 199–203.

**02001** A logic assistant for the database searcher. HEINE, M. *Inf. Process. Manage.* **24**, 3, (May 1988) 323–329.

**02002** Perceptions of the information search process in libraries: a study of changes from high school through college. KUHLTHAU, C. *Inf. Process. Manage.* **24**, 4, (May 1988) 419–427.

**02003** OAKDEC, a program for studying the effects on users of a procedural expert system for database searching. MEADOW, C. *Inf. Process. Manage.* **24**, 4, (May 1988) 449–457.

**02004** Correlation of term usage and term indexing frequencies. NELSON, M. *Inf. Process. Manage.* **24**, 5, (1988) 541–547.

02005 Information requirements specification II: Brainstorming collective decision-making technique. TELEM, M. *Inf. Process. Manage.* **24,** 5, (1988) 559–566.

02006 A priori analysis of natural language queries. SPIEGLER, I.; AND ELATA, S. *Inf. Process. Manage.* **24,** 6, (November 1988) 619–631.

02007 Querying the French *Yellow Pages*: natural language access to the directory. CLEMENSIN, G. *Inf. Process. Manage.* **24,** 6, (November 1988) 633–649.

02008 Prospects for knowledge-based customization of natural languages query systems. DAMERAU, F. *Inf. Process. Manage.* **24,** 6, (November 1988) 651–664.

02009 Selection devices for users of an electronic encyclopedia: an empirical comparison of four possibilities. OSTROFF, D.; AND SHNEIDERMAN, B. *Inf. Process. Manage.* **24,** 6, (November 1988) 665–680.

02010 A comparative survey of the friendliness of online 'help' in interactive information. TRENNER, L. *Inf. Process. Manage.* **25,** 2, (1989) 119–136.

02011 All users of information retrieval systems are not created equal: an exploration into individual differences. BORGMAN, C. *Inf. Process. Manage.* **25,** 3, (May 1989) 237–251.

02012 Evaluation of the user interface in an information retrieval system: a model. TAGUE, J.; AND SCHULTZ, R. *Inf. Process. Manage.* **25,** 4, (1989) 377–389.

02013 Online searching using speech as a man/machine interface. PETERS, B.; PHILIP, G.; SMITH, F.; AND CROOKES, D. *Inf. Process. Manage.* **25,** 4, (1989) 391–406.

02014 Tools for reading and browsing hypertext. FOSS, C. *Inf. Process. Manage.* **25,** 4, (1989) 407–418.

## Information Processing Letters

02015 The automated solution of logic puzzles. VALENTINE, M.; AND DAVIS, R. *Inf. Process. Lett.* **24,** 5, (16 March 1987) 317–324.

02016 Synchronizing the I/O behavior of functional programs with feedback. DWELLY, A. *Inf. Process. Lett.* **28,** 1, (May 30, 1988) 45–51.

## Information Sciences

HCI-0249 The database designer's workbench. COBB, R.; FRY, J.; AND TEOREY, T. *Inf. Sci. (New York)* **32,** 1, (Feb. 1984) 33–45.

HCI-0328 An expert system for mapping acoustic cues into phonetic features. DE MORI, R.; GIORDANA, A.; LAFACE, P.; AND SAITTA, L. *Inf. Sci. (New York)* **33,** 1/2, (July/Aug. 1984) 115–155.

02017 Modeling rule-based systems by stochastic programmed production systems. TSATSOULIS, C.; AND FU, K. *Inf. Sci. (New York)* **36,** 3, (Sept. 1985) 207–230.

02018 Reasoning with imprecise knowledge in expert systems. DUTTA, A. *Inf. Sci. (New York)* **37,** 1/2/3, (Dec. 1985) 3–24.

HCI-0259 Implementing imprecision in information systems. ZEMANKOVA, M.; AND KANDEL, A. *Inf. Sci. (New York)* **37,** 1/2/3, (Dec. 1985) 107–141.

02019 Principles of information structure common to six levels of the human cognitive system. LEYTON, M. *Inf. Sci. (New York)* **38,** 1, (March 1986) 1–120.

02020 Computing human oriented descriptions. AVIAD, Z.; AND LOZINSKII, E. *Inf. Sci. (New York)* **38,** 2, (April 1986) 181–191.

02021 Arithmetic codes resembling neural encoding. FUHRMANN, G. *Inf. Sci. (New York)* **39,** 2, (Sept. 1986) 197–203.

02022 A practical approach to transforming extended ER diagrams into the relational model. YANG, D.; TEOREY, T.; AND FRY, J. *Inf. Sci. (New York)* **42,** 2, (July 1987) 167–186.

02023 A multiprocessor system for real-time robotic control. KAZANIDES, P.; WASTI, H.; AND WOLOVICH, W. *Inf. Sci. (New York)* **44,** 3, (April, 1988) 225–247.

02024 A representation of human reliability using fuzzy concepts. ONISAWA, T. *Inf. Sci. (New York)* **45,** 2, (July, 1988) 153–173.

02025 Fuzzy control of a mobile robot for obstacle avoidance. TAKEUCHI, T.; NAGAI, Y.; AND ENOMOTO, N. *Inf. Sci. (New York)* **45,** 2, (July, 1988) 231–248.

02026 Manual control of an intrinsically unstable system and its modeling by fuzzy logic. TERANO, T.; MASUI, S.; TANAKA, K.; AND MURAYAMA, Y. *Inf. Sci. (New York)* **45,** 2, (July, 1988) 249–273.

02027 Convexly combined fuzzy relational equations and several aspects of their application to fuzzy information processing. OHSATO, A.; AND SEKIGUCHI, T. *Inf. Sci. (New York)* **45,** 2, (July, 1988) 275–313.

02028 A design for a fuzzy logic controller. MAEDA, M.; AND MURAKAMI, S. *Inf. Sci. (New York)* **45,** 2, (July, 1988) 315–330.

02029 A fuzzy decision-making method and its application to a company choice problem. MAEDA, H.; AND MURAKAMI, S. *Inf. Sci. (New York)* **45,** 2, (July, 1988) 331–346.

02030 Knowledge representation and use in pattern analysis. BERGADANO, F.; GIORDANA, A.; AND SAITTA, L. *Inf. Sci. (New York)* **47,** 1, (February 1989) 1–16.

## Information Services and Use

02031 Integrated communications and work efficiency: impacts on organizational structure and power. WIGAND, R. *Inf. Serv. Use* **5,** 5, (Oct. 1985) 241–258.

02032 Design of personal information retrieval systems. AGOSTI, M.; AND SPILOTRO, F. *Inf. Serv. Use* **6,** 4, (1986) 161–168.

02033 The contribution of cognitive engineering to the effective design and use of information systems. GARG-JANARDAN, C.; AND SALVENDY, G. *Inf. Serv. Use* **6,** 5/6, (1986) 235–252.

02034 A menu interface to formulate boolean logic-can it be done? DE STRICKER, U. *Inf. Serv. Use* **8,** 1, (January 1988) 39–46.

02035 Enhancing search results by editing, analysis and packaging. MCPHERSON, M.; HARRAP, C.; AND O'REILLY, J. *Inf. Serv. Use* **9,** 1/2, (Sept. 1989) 101–106.

## Information Systems

02036 A semantic data model as the basis for an automated database design tool. BERMAN, S. *Inf. Syst.* **11,** 2, (1986) 149–165.

02037 Action based model of information system. LEHTINEN, E.; AND LYYTINEN, K. *Inf. Syst.* **11,** 4, (Oct. 1986) 299–317.

02038 Temporal semantics and natural language processing in a decision support system. DE, S.; PAN, S.; AND WHINSTON, A. *Inf. Syst.* **12,** 1, (Jan. 1987) 29–47.

02039 Non-first normal form universal relations: an application to information retrieval systems. DESAI, B.; GOYAL, P.; AND SADRI, F. *Inf. Syst.* **12,** 1, (Jan. 1987) 49–55.

02040 Linkage versus integration for binding database and interactive graphics systems. ZAKI, M.; AND SALAMA, R. *Inf. Syst.* **12,** 3, (1987) 271–280.

02041 Cooperative behaviour in the FIDO system. DI EUGENIO, B. *Inf. Syst.* **12,** 3, (1987) 295–316.

02042 GISD: a graphical interactive system for conceptual database design. SHOVAL, P.; GUDES, E.; AND GOLDSTEIN, M. *Inf. Syst.* **13,** 1, (Jan., 1988) 81–95.

02043 How to recognize interesting topics to provide cooperative answering. CUPPENS, F.; AND DEMOLOMBE, R. *Inf. Syst.* **14,** 2, (March 1989) 163–173.

## Information Technology and Libraries

02044 Microcomputer-based user interface. CHENG, C. *Inf. Technol. Libr.* **4,** 4, (Dec. 1985) 346–351.

02045 Library processing systems and the man/machine interface. HIGHSMITH, A. *Inf. Technol. Libr.* **5,** 4, (Dec. 1986) 267–279.

**HCI-0285** Testing bibliographic displays for online catalogs. CRAWFORD, W. *Inf. Technol. Libr.* **6**, 1, (March 1987) 20–33.
**02046** The engineering information system: a guided tour. DEERWESTER, S. *Inf. Technol. Libr.* **6**, 2, (June 1987) 126–132.
**02047** Investigating computer anxiety in an academic library. SIEVERT, M.; ALBRITTON, R.; ROPER, P.; AND CLAYTON, N. *Inf. Technol. Libr.* **7**, 3, (September 1988) 243–252.
**02048** The effects of entry arrangement in search times: a cross-generational study. WILKINSON, M.; BURT, P.; AND KINNUCAN, M. *Inf. Technol. Libr.* **7**, 3, (September 1988) 253–262.
**02049** User interaction with the authority structure of the online catalog: results of a survey. NYE, J. *Inf. Technol. Libr.* **7**, 3, (September 1988) 313–317.
**02050** A comparative study of subject searching in an OPAC among branch libraries of a university library system. KASKE, N. *Inf. Technol. Libr.* **7**, 4, (Dec. 1988) 359–372.
**02051** Improved browsable displays for online subject access. MASSICOTE, M. *Inf. Technol. Libr.* **7**, 4, (Dec. 1988) 373–380.

## Information Technology Research Development Applications

**HCI-0139** Experimental adaptive interface. MASON, M.; AND THOMAS, R. *Inf. Tech. Res. Dev. Appl.* **3**, 3, (Aug. 1984) 162–167.

## Infosystems

**02052** User-developers: the new software resource. SHEER, R. *Infosystems* **33**, 7, (July 1986) 69–70.

## Instruction Delivery Systems

**02053** A powerful solution meets an overwhelming problem. GOLD, P. *Instr. Deliv. Syst.* **3**, 5, (Sep. 1989) 6–7.

## InTech

**02054** Local work station concepts in a small distributed system. MARSH, C.; AND TUCKER, T. *InTech* **33**, 5, (May 1986) 41–45.
**02055** Will you be replaced by a knowledge base? HOGLEY, J.; AND KORNCOFF, A. *InTech* **33**, 9, (Sept. 1986) 41–45.
**02056** Adapting expert systems to simulation training of process operators. KOSAR, R.; AND BLAHUT, N. *InTech* **33**, 9, (Sept. 1986) 79–81.
**02057** Power plant simulation using a distributed control system. STULLER, P. *InTech* **34**, 4, (April 1987) 43–46.

## Interacting with Computers

**02058** Task analysis, systems analysis and design: symbiosis or synthesis? SUTCLIFFE, A. *Interact. Comput.* **1**, 1, (April 1989) 6–12.
**02059** Embedded user model-where next? RIVERS, R. *Interact. Comput.* **1**, 1, (April 1989) 13–30.
**02060** People interact through computers not with them. BENCH-CAPON, T.; AND McENERY, A. *Interact. Comput.* **1**, 1, (April 1989) 31–38.
**02061** Interacting with computers. BARLOW, J.; RADA, R.; AND DIAPER, D. *Interact. Comput.* **1**, 1, (April 1989) 39–42.
**02062** Lean cuisine: a low fat notation for menus. APPERLEY, M.; AND SPENCE, R. *Interact. Comput.* **1**, 1, (April 1989) 43–68.

**02063** Expanatory dialogues. CAWSEY, A. *Interact. Comput.* **1**, 1, (April 1989) 69–92.
**02064** Moral judgements in designing better systems. PULLINGER, D. *Interact. Comput.* **1**, 1, (April 1989) 93–104.
**02065** Icons at the interface: their usefulness. ROGERS, Y. *Interact. Comput.* **1**, 1, (April 1989) 105–117.
**02066** Who's joking? The information system at play. ORD, J. *Interact. Comput.* **1**, 1, (April 1989) 118–128.

## Interacting with computers: the interdisciplinary journal of human-computer interaction

**02067** Shaping user input: a strategy for natural language dialogue design. RINGLE, M.; AND HALSTEAD-NUSSLOCH, R. *Interacting Comput.* **1**, 3, (Dec. 1989) 227–244.
**02068** A knowledge-based system with audio-visual aids. TABATA, K.; AND SUGIMOTO, S. *Interacting Comput.* **1**, 3, (Dec. 1989) 245–258.
**02069** Interacting with electronic mail can be a dream or a night: a user's point of view. PLISKIN, N. *Interacting Comput.* **1**, 3, (Dec. 1989) 259–272.
**02070** The application of metaphor, analogy, and conceptual models in computer systems. WOZNY, L. *Interacting Comput.* **1**, 3, (Dec. 1989) 273–283.
**02071** Exploiting convergence to improve natural language understanding. LEISER, R. *Interacting Comput.* **1**, 3, (Dec. 1989) 284–298.
**02072** The user interface in a hypertext, multiwindow program browser. SEABROOK, R.; AND SHNEIDERMAN, B. *Interacting Comput.* **1**, 3, (Dec. 1989) 299–337.

## International Journal of Approximate Reasoning

**02073** Hidden patterns in combined and adaptive knowledge networks. KOSKO, B. *Int. J. Approx. Reasoning* **2**, 4, (Oct. 1988) 377–393.
**02074** On the applicability of maximum entropy to inexact reasoning. PARIS, J.; AND VENCOVSKÁ, A. *Int. J. Approx. Reasoning* **3**, 1, (Jan. 1989) 1–34.
**02075** Epistemic necessity, possibility, and truth. Tools for dealing with imprecision and uncertainty in fuzzy knowledge-based systems. MAGREZ, P.; AND SMETS, P. *Int. J. Approx. Reasoning* **3**, 1, (Jan. 1989) 35–57.
**02076** Causality and maximum entropy updating. HUNTER, D. *Int. J. Approx. Reasoning* **3**, 1, (Jan. 1989) 87–114.

## International Journal of Expert Systems

**02077** Linguistic knowledge as expertise. MANASTER-RAMER, A.; AND LINDSAY, R. *Int. J. Expert Syst.* **1**, 4, (Oct. 1988) 329–343.

## International Journal of Man-Machine Studies

**02078** Cognitive systems engineering: new wine in new bottles. HOLLNAGEL, E.; AND WOODS, D. *Int. J. Man-Mach. Stud.* **18**, 6, (June 1983) 583–600.
**HCI-0315** On the application of rule-based techniques to the design of advice giving systems. JACKSON, P.; AND LEFRERE, P. *Int. J. Man-Mach. Stud.* **20**, 1, (Jan. 1984) 63–86. [Special Issue: Developments in expert systems, Part 2.]
**HCI-0316** A model for the interpretation of verbal predictions. ZIMMER, A. *Int. J. Man-Mach. Stud.* **20**, 1, (Jan. 1984) 121–134. [Special Issue: Developments in expert systems, Part 2.]
**02079** The application of human factors to the needs of the novice computer user. PAXTON, A.; AND TURNER, E. *Int. J. Man-Mach. Stud.* **20**, 2, (Feb. 1984) 137–156.
**02080** A methodology for interactive evaluation of user reactions to software packages:an empirical analysis of system performance, interaction, and run time. RUSHINEK, A.; RUSHINEK, S.; AND STUTZ, J. *Int. J. Man-Mach. Stud.* **20**, 2, (Feb. 1984) 169–188.

## JOURNALS

HCI-0135    The depth/breadth trade-off in the design of menu-driven user interfaces. KIGER, J. *Int. J. Man-Mach. Stud.* **20**, 2, (Feb. 1984) 201–213.

02081    The influence of rule-generated stress on computer-synthesized speech. MCPETERS, D.; AND THARP, A. *Int. J. Man-Mach. Stud.* **20**, 2, (Feb. 1984) 215–226.

HCI-0105    Holophrasted displays in an interactive environment. SMITH, S.; BARNARD, D.; AND MACLEOD, I. *Int. J. Man-Mach. Stud.* **20**, 4, (April 1984) 343–355.

02082    Natural artificial languages: low level processes. PERLMAN, G. *Int. J. Man-Mach. Stud.* **20**, 4, (April 1984) 373–419.

02083    Modelling degrees of item interest for a general database query system. ROWE, N. *Int. J. Man-Mach. Stud.* **20**, 5, (May 1984) 421–443.

HCI-0171    Experimental study of a two-dimensional language vs. FORTRAN for first-course progammers. KLERER, M. *Int. J. Man-Mach. Stud.* **20**, 5, (May 1984) 445–467.

02084    Preserving the integrity of the medium: a method of measuring visual and auditory comprehension of electronic media. WHITE, M.; SANDBERG, B.; BEHAR, E.; MOCKLER, J.; PEREZ, E.; POLLACK, J.; AND ROSENBLAD, K. *Int. J. Man-Mach. Stud.* **20**, 5, (May 1984) 511–517.

HCI-0236    An experimental comparison of tabular and graphic data presentation. POWERS, M.; LASHLEY, C.; SANCHEZ, P.; AND SHNEIDERMAN, B. *Int. J. Man-Mach. Stud.* **20**, 6, (June 1984) 545–566.

02085    Organization and learnability in computer languages. GREEN, T.; AND PAYNE, S. *Int. J. Man-Mach. Stud.* **21**, 1, (July 1984) 7–18.

02086    Perceptual structure cueing in a simple command language. PAYNE, S.; SIME, M.; AND GREEN, T. *Int. J. Man-Mach. Stud.* **21**, 1, (July 1984) 19–29.

02087    Comprehension and recall of miniature programs. GILMORE, D.; AND GREEN, T. *Int. J. Man-Mach. Stud.* **21**, 1, (July 1984) 31–48.

HCI-0397    Speech-controlled text-editing: effects of input modality and of command structure. MORRISON, D.; GREEN, T.; SHAW, A.; AND PAYNE, S. *Int. J. Man-Mach. Stud.* **21**, 1, (July 1984) 49–63.

HCI-0409    The doctor's use of a computer in the consulting room: an analysis. BROWNBRIDGE, G.; FITTER, M.; AND SIME, M. *Int. J. Man-Mach. Stud.* **21**, 1, (July 1984) 65–90.

HCI-0106    A structured approach to designing human-computer dialogues. BENBASAT, I.; AND WAND, Y. *Int. J. Man-Mach. Stud.* **21**, 2, (Aug. 1984) 105–126.

HCI-0435    The relationship of problem-solving ability and course performance among novice programmers. NOWACZYK, R. *Int. J. Man-Mach. Stud.* **21**, 2, (Aug. 1984) 149–160.

HCI-0354    An economical approach to modeling speech recognition accuracy. SPINE, T.; WILLIGES, B.; AND MAYNARD, J. *Int. J. Man-Mach. Stud.* **21**, 3, (Sept. 1984) 191–202.

HCI-0140    A display editor with random access and continuous control. HAMMER, J. *Int. J. Man-Mach. Stud.* **21**, 3, (Sept. 1984) 203–212.

HCI-0238    Visual momentum: a concept to improve the cognitive coupling of person and computer. WOODS, D. *Int. J. Man-Mach. Stud.* **21**, 3, (Sept. 1984) 229–244.

HCI-0270    Users and experts in the document retrieval system model. DANILOWICZ, C. *Int. J. Man-Mach. Stud.* **21**, 3, (Sept. 1984) 245–252.

HCI-0247    Measuring the quality of linguistic forecasts. YAGER, R. *Int. J. Man-Mach. Stud.* **21**, 3, (Sept. 1984) 253–257.

HCI-0187    Reading continuous text from a one-line visual display. MONK, A. *Int. J. Man-Mach. Stud.* **21**, 3, (Sept. 1984) 269–277.

HCI-0109    The role of context and adaptation in user interfaces. CROFT, W. *Int. J. Man-Mach. Stud.* **21**, 4, (Oct. 1984) 283–292.

HCI-0246    Experience with the ZOG human-computer interface system. MCCRACKEN, D.; AND AKSCYN, R. *Int. J. Man-Mach. Stud.* **21**, 4, (Oct. 1984) 293–310.

HCI-0256    What makes RABBIT run? WILLIAMS, M. *Int. J. Man-Mach. Stud.* **21**, 4, (Oct. 1984) 333–352.

HCI-0436    The electronic classroom: workstations for teaching. VAN DAM, A. *Int. J. Man-Mach. Stud.* **21**, 4, (Oct. 1984) 353–363.

HCI-0189  Stages and levels in human-machine interaction. NORMAN, D. *Int. J. Man-Mach. Stud.* **21**, 4, (Oct. 1984) 365–375.

02088  Ingredients of intelligent user interfaces. RISSLAND, E. *Int. J. Man-Mach. Stud.* **21**, 4, (Oct. 1984) 377–388.

HCI-0110  General multiple-objective decision functions and linguistically quantified statements. YAGER, R. *Int. J. Man-Mach. Stud.* **21**, 5, (Nov. 1984) 389–400.

HCI-0426  Customers' requirements for natural language systems: results of an inquiry. MORIK, K. *Int. J. Man-Mach. Stud.* **21**, 5, (Nov. 1984) 401–414.

HCI-0414  An approach to CAD system performance evaluation. STRELNIKOV, Y.; PULKKIS, G.; AND DMITREVICH, G. *Int. J. Man-Mach. Stud.* **21**, 5, (Nov. 1984) 429–444.

HCI-0190  QWERTY and keyboard reform: the soft keyboard option. CUMMING, G. *Int. J. Man-Mach. Stud.* **21**, 5, (Nov. 1984) 445–450.

02089  An icon-driven end-user interface to UNIX. GITTINS, D.; WINDER, R.; AND BEZ, H. *Int. J. Man-Mach. Stud.* **21**, 5, (Nov. 1984) 451–461.

HCI-0237  An empirical investigation of voice as an input modality for computer programming. LEGGETT, J.; AND WILLIAMS, G. *Int. J. Man-Mach. Stud.* **21**, 6, (Dec. 1984) 493–520.

HCI-0111  Some cognitive aspects of interface design in a two-variable optimization task. BRIDGER, R.; AND LONG, J. *Int. J. Man-Mach. Stud.* **21**, 6, (Dec. 1984) 521–539.

HCI-0089  Voice-input aids for the physically disabled. DAMPER, R. *Int. J. Man-Mach. Stud.* **21**, 6, (Dec. 1984) 541–553.

HCI-0211  What non-programmers know about programming: natural language procedure specification. GALOTTI, K.; AND GANGON, W. *Int. J. Man-Mach. Stud.* **22**, 1, (Jan. 1985) 1–10.

02090  The effect of microcomputer presentation and response medium on digit span. BEAUMONT, J. *Int. J. Man-Mach. Stud.* **22**, 1, (Jan. 1985) 11–18.

02091  Metaphor, computing systems, and active learning. CARROLL, J.; AND MACK, R. *Int. J. Man-Mach. Stud.* **22**, 1, (Jan. 1985) 39–57.

02092  Combining functions for certainty degrees in consulting systems. HAJEK, P. *Int. J. Man-Mach. Stud.* **22**, 1, (Jan. 1985) 59–76.

HCI-0103  An empirical investigation into problem decomposition strategies used in program design. RATCLIFF, B.; AND SIDDIQI, J. *Int. J. Man-Mach. Stud.* **22**, 1, (Jan. 1985) 77–90.

HCI-0212  Man-machine interface issues in the construction and use of an expert system. KIDD, A.; AND COOPER, M. *Int. J. Man-Mach. Stud.* **22**, 1, (Jan. 1985) 91–102.

02093  A workstation assessor for crew operations-WOSTAS. PULAT, B.; AND PULAT, P. *Int. J. Man-Mach. Stud.* **22**, 1, (Jan. 1985) 103–114.

HCI-0330  Selecting a humanly understandable knowledge representation for reasoning about knowledge. MAIDA, A. *Int. J. Man-Mach. Stud.* **22**, 2, (Feb. 1985) 151–161.

HCI-0329  Decision trees: a contribution to automatic interpretation of GUHA results. RENC, Z.; AND SETÍKOVSKÁ, L. *Int. J. Man-Mach. Stud.* **22**, 2, (Feb. 1985) 193–207.

HCI-0324  Natural-language interface for an instructable robot. MAAS, R.; AND SUPPES, P. *Int. J. Man-Mach. Stud.* **22**, 2, (Feb. 1985) 215–240.

02094  On the interaction of man and EDP use as work activity. PILGRIM, J. *Int. J. Man-Mach. Stud.* **22**, 5, (May 1985) 493–505.

02095  The use of modal default reasoning in information systems. RYCHLIK, P. *Int. J. Man-Mach. Stud.* **22**, 5, (May 1985) 507–522.

02096  How to tell people where to go: comparing navigational aids. STREETER, L.; VITELLO, D.; AND WONSIEWICZ, S. *Int. J. Man-Mach. Stud.* **22**, 5, (May 1985) 549–562.

HCI-0214  On search in an incomplete database. LINDE, L.; AND WAERN, Y. *Int. J. Man-Mach. Stud.* **22**, 5, (May 1985) 563–579.

HCI-0118  Efficient computer-user interface in electronic mail systems. AKIN, O.; AND RAO, D. *Int. J. Man-Mach. Stud.* **22**, 6, (June 1985) 589–611.

HCI-0115  Experimental evaluation of dialogue types for data entry. EKLUNDH, K.; MARMOLIN, H.; AND HEDIN, C. *Int. J. Man-Mach. Stud.* **22**, 6, (June 1985) 651–661.

## JOURNALS

**HCI-0134** Specification and generation of variable, personalized graphical interfaces. BOURNIQUE, R.; AND TREU, S. *Int. J. Man-Mach. Stud.* **22**, 6, (June 1985) 663–684.

**HCI-0192** Speed of response using keyboard and screen-based microcomputer response media. BEAUMONT, J. *Int. J. Man-Mach. Stud.* **23**, 1, (July 1985) 61–70.

**HCI-0325** UMFE: a user modelling front-end subsystem. SLEEMAN, D. *Int. J. Man-Mach. Stud.* **23**, 1, (July 1985) 71–88.

**HCI-0281** A natural language information retrieval system with extentions towards fuzzy reasoning. BOLC, L.; KOWALSKI, A.; KOZLOWSKA, M.; AND STRZALKOWSKI, T. *Int. J. Man-Mach. Stud.* **23**, 4, (Oct. 1985) 335–367.

**HCI-0193** A research model for studying the gender/power aspects of human-computer communication. FULTON, M. *Int. J. Man-Mach. Stud.* **23**, 4, (Oct. 1985) 369–382.

**HCI-0194** GENIE: a modifiable computer-based task for experiments in human-computer interaction. LINDQUIST, T.; FAINTER, R.; AND HAKKINEN, M. *Int. J. Man-Mach. Stud.* **23**, 4, (Oct. 1985) 391–406.

**HCI-0295** Interactive fuzzy decision-making for multi-objective nonlinear programming using reference membership intervals. SAKAWA, M.; AND YANO, H. *Int. J. Man-Mach. Stud.* **23**, 4, (Oct. 1985) 407–421.

**HCI-0116** Pictorial interfaces to data bases. BARKER, P.; AND NAJAH, M. *Int. J. Man-Mach. Stud.* **23**, 4, (Oct. 1985) 423–442.

**02097** From timesharing to the sixth generation: the development of human-computer interaction. Part I. GAINES, B.; AND SHAW, M. *Int. J. Man-Mach. Stud.* **24**, 1, (Jan. 1986) 1–27.

**02098** An experimental comparison of a mouse and arrow-jump keys for an interactive encyclopedia. EWING, J.; MEHRABANZAD, S.; SHECK, S.; OSTROFF, D.; AND SHNEIDERMAN, B. *Int. J. Man-Mach. Stud.* **24**, 1, (Jan. 1986) 29–45.

**02099** The user's mental model of an information retrieval system: an experiment on a prototype online catalog. BORGMAN, C. *Int. J. Man-Mach. Stud.* **24**, 1, (Jan. 1986) 47–64.

**02100** Foundations of dialog engineering: the development of human-computer interaction. Part II. GAINES, B.; AND SHAW, M. *Int. J. Man-Mach. Stud.* **24**, 2, (Feb. 1986) 101–123.

**02101** Comparison of decision support strategies in expert consultation systems. SHOVAL, P. *Int. J. Man-Mach. Stud.* **24**, 2, (Feb. 1986) 125–139.

**02102** ADDS-a dialogue development system for the Ada programming language. BURNS, A.; AND ROBINSON, J. *Int. J. Man-Mach. Stud.* **24**, 2, (Feb. 1986) 153–170.

**02103** Training by exploration: facilitating the transfer of procedural knowledge through analogical reasoning. KAMOURI, A.; KAMOURI, J.; AND SMITH, K. *Int. J. Man-Mach. Stud.* **24**, 2, (Feb. 1986) 171–192.

**02104** A taxonomy of user-oriented functions. CARTER, J. *Int. J. Man-Mach. Stud.* **24**, 3, (March 1986) 195–292.

**02105** Star, maximal rectangles, lattices: a new perspective on Q-analysis. JOHNSON, J. *Int. J. Man-Mach. Stud.* **24**, 3, (March 1986) 293–299.

**02106** A virtual protocol model for computer-human interaction. NIELSEN, J. *Int. J. Man-Mach. Stud.* **24**, 3, (March 1986) 301–312.

**02107** Mode errors: a user-centered analysis and some preventative measures using keying-contingent sound. MONK, A. *Int. J. Man-Mach. Stud.* **24**, 4, (April 1986) 313–327.

**02108** A review and synthesis of recent research in intelligent computer-assisted instruction. DEDE, C. *Int. J. Man-Mach. Stud.* **24**, 4, (April 1986) 329–353.

**02109** An empirical comparison of model-based and explicit communication for dynamic human-computer task allocation. GREENSTEIN, J.; ARNAUT, L.; AND REVESMAN, M. *Int. J. Man-Mach. Stud.* **24**, 4, (April 1986) 355–363.

**02110** An experimental evaluation of prefix and postfix notation in command language sytax. CHERRY, J. *Int. J. Man-Mach. Stud.* **24**, 4, (April 1986) 365–374.

**02111** On-line recognition of Pitman's hand-written shorthand—an evaluation of potential. LEEDHAM, C.; AND DOWNTON, A. *Int. J. Man-Mach. Stud.* **24**, 4, (April 1986) 375–393.

**HCI-0218** On the purpose and analysis of EDP user systems. PILGRIM, J. *Int. J. Man-Mach. Stud.* **24**, 5, (May 1986) 435–452.

**02112** A three-level human-computer interface model. CLARKE, A. *Int. J. Man-Mach. Stud.* **24**, 6, (June 1986) 503–517.

02113 Icon-based human-computer interaction. GITTINS, D. *Int. J. Man-Mach. Stud.* **24**, 6, (June 1986) 519–543.

02114 On methods for interface specification and design. RICHARDS, J.; BEZ, H.; GITTINS, D.; AND COOKE, D. *Int. J. Man-Mach. Stud.* **24**, 6, (June 1986) 545–568.

02115 Negative knowledge towards a strategy for asking in logic programming. EDMONDS, E. *Int. J. Man-Mach. Stud.* **24**, 6, (June 1986) 597–600.

02116 Support for tentative design: incorporating the screen image, as a graphical object, into PROLOG. SCHAPPO, A.; AND EDMONDS, E. *Int. J. Man-Mach. Stud.* **24**, 6, (June 1986) 601–609.

02117 Studying depth cues in a three-dimensional computer graphics workstation. WALDERN, J.; HUMRICH, A.; AND COCHRANE, L. *Int. J. Man-Mach. Stud.* **24**, 6, (June 1986) 645–657.

02118 A multi-purpose system for alpha-numeric input to computers via a reduced keyboard. ROBERTS, M.; AND RAHBARI, H. *Int. J. Man-Mach. Stud.* **24**, 6, (June 1986) 659–667.

02119 Dealing with a database query language in a new situation. KATZEFF, C. *Int. J. Man-Mach. Stud.* **25**, 1, (July 1986) 1–17.

02120 A descriptive/prescriptive model for menu-based interaction. ARTHUR, J. *Int. J. Man-Mach. Stud.* **25**, 1, (July 1986) 19–32.

02121 Adaptive command prompting in an on-line documentation. MASON, M. *Int. J. Man-Mach. Stud.* **25**, 1, (July 1986) 33–51.

02122 A comparison of menu selection techniques: touch panel, mouse and keyboard. KARAT, J.; MCDONALD, J.; AND ANDERSON, M. *Int. J. Man-Mach. Stud.* **25**, 1, (July 1986) 73–88.

HCI-0298 Computer decision support for senior managers: encouraging exploration. SMITHIN, T.; AND EDEN, C. *Int. J. Man-Mach. Stud.* **25**, 2, (Aug. 1986) 139–152.

HCI-0333 Instructionless learning about a complex device: the paradigm and observations. SHRAGER, J.; AND KLAHR, D. *Int. J. Man-Mach. Stud.* **25**, 2, (Aug. 1986) 153–189.

HCI-0271 On the applied use of human memory models: the memory extender personal filing system. JONES, W. *Int. J. Man-Mach. Stud.* **25**, 2, (Aug. 1986) 191–228.

HCI-0122 Cognitive layouts of windows and multiple screens for user interfaces. NORMAN, K.; WELDON, L.; AND SHNEIDERMAN, B. *Int. J. Man-Mach. Stud.* **25**, 2, (Aug. 1986) 229–248.

HCI-0087 Touch-sensitive screens: the technologies and their application. PICKERING, J. *Int. J. Man-Mach. Stud.* **25**, 3, (Sept. 1986) 249–269.

HCI-0347 A framework for investigating language-mediated interaction with machines. ZOEPPRITZ, M. *Int. J. Man-Mach. Stud.* **25**, 3, (Sept. 1986) 295–315.

HCI-0197 Effects of experience and comprehension on reading time and memory for computer programs. SCHMIDT, A. *Int. J. Man-Mach. Stud.* **25**, 4, (Oct. 1986) 399–409.

HCI-0242 Cognitive attributes: implications for display design in supervisory control systems. MURPHY, E.; AND MITCHELL, C. *Int. J. Man-Mach. Stud.* **25**, 4, (Oct. 1986) 411–438.

HCI-0168 Equal opportunity interactive systems. RUNCIMAN, C.; AND THIMBLEBY, H. *Int. J. Man-Mach. Stud.* **25**, 4, (Oct. 1986) 439–451.

02123 Is top-down natural? Some experimental results from non-procedural languages. FINNIE, G. *Int. J. Man-Mach. Stud.* **25**, 5, (Nov. 1987) 469–478.

02124 Considerations of menu structure and communication rate for the design of computer menu displays. SISSON, N.; PARKINSON, S.; AND SNOWBERRY, K. *Int. J. Man-Mach. Stud.* **25**, 5, (Nov. 1987) 479–489.

02125 An experiment in graphical perception. CLEVELAND, W.; AND MCGILL, R. *Int. J. Man-Mach. Stud.* **25**, 5, (Nov. 1987) 491–500.

02126 A perceptual study of the Flury-Riedwyl faces for graphically displaying multivariate data. DE SOETE, G. *Int. J. Man-Mach. Stud.* **25**, 5, (Nov. 1987) 549–555.

02127 Which way to computer literacy, programming or applications experience? MYNATT, B.; SMITH, K.; KAMOURI, A.; AND TYKODI, T. *Int. J. Man-Mach. Stud.* **25**, 5, (Nov. 1987) 557–572.

02128 Online library catalog systems: an analysis of user errors. JANOSKY, B.; SMITH, P.; AND HILDRETH, C. *Int. J. Man-Mach. Stud.* **25**, 5, (Nov. 1987) 573–592.

02129 Novices on the computer: a review of the literature. ALLWOOD, C. *Int. J. Man-Mach. Stud.* **25**, 6, (Dec. 1986) 633–658.

02130 What "question-asking protocols" can say about the user interface. KATO, T. *Int. J. Man-Mach. Stud.* **25,** 6, (Dec. 1986) 659–673.

02131 An experiment to test user validation of requirements: data-flow diagrams vs task-oriented menus. NOSEK, J.; AND AHRENS, J. *Int. J. Man-Mach. Stud.* **25,** 6, (Dec. 1986) 675–684.

02132 Beacons in computer program comprehension. WIEDENBECK, S. *Int. J. Man-Mach. Stud.* **25,** 6, (Dec. 1986) 697–709.

02133 Computer anxiety: sex, race and age. GILROY, F.; AND DESAI, H. *Int. J. Man-Mach. Stud.* **25,** 6, (Dec. 1986) 711–719.

HCI-0336 Expertise transfer and complex problems: using AQUINAS as a knowledge-acquisition workbench for knowledge-based systems. BOOSE, J.; AND BRADSHAW, J. *Int. J. Man-Mach. Stud.* **26,** 1, (Jan. 1987) 3–28.

HCI-0327 KRITON: a knowledge-acquisition tool for expert systems. DIEDERICH, J.; RUHMANN, I.; AND MAY, M. *Int. J. Man-Mach. Stud.* **26,** 1, (Jan. 1987) 29–40.

02134 Modelling human expertise in knowledge engineering: some preliminary observations. LITTMAN, D. *Int. J. Man-Mach. Stud.* **26,** 1, (Jan. 1987) 81–92.

02135 On comprehending a computer manual: analysis of variables affecting performance. FOSS, D.; SMITH-KERKER, P.; AND ROSSON, M. *Int. J. Man-Mach. Stud.* **26,** 3, (March 1987) 277–300.

02136 Representing and using metacommunication to control speakers' relationships in natural-language dialogue. SANFORD, D.; AND ROACH, J. *Int. J. Man-Mach. Stud.* **26,** 3, (March 1987) 301–319.

02137 Using computer knowledge in the design of interactive systems. MARTIN, M.; AND FUERST, W. *Int. J. Man-Mach. Stud.* **26,** 3, (March 1987) 333–342.

02138 Structure of a directory space: a case study with a UNIX operating system. AKIN, O.; BAYKAN, C.; AND RAO, D. *Int. J. Man-Mach. Stud.* **26,** 3, (March 1987) 361–382.

02139 The application of psychological scaling techniques to knowledge elicitation for knowledge-based systems. COOKE, N.; AND MCDONALD, J. *Int. J. Man-Mach. Stud.* **26,** 4, (April 1987) 533–550.

02140 Formatting alphanumeric crt displays. PULAT, B.; AND NWANKWO, H. *Int. J. Man-Mach. Stud.* **26,** 5, (May 1, 1987) 567–580.

02141 An interactive environment for tool selection, specification and composition. ARTHUR, J.; AND COMER, D. *Int. J. Man-Mach. Stud.* **26,** 5, (May 1, 1987) 581–595.

02142 Multi-window displays for readers of lengthy texts. TOMBAUGH, J.; LICKORISH, A.; AND WRIGHT, P. *Int. J. Man-Mach. Stud.* **26,** 5, (May 1, 1987) 597–615.

02143 An error correcting protocol for medical expert systems. LANDAU, J.; NORWICH, K.; EVANS, S.; AND PICH, B. *Int. J. Man-Mach. Stud.* **26,** 5, (May 1, 1987) 617–625.

02144 Menu search: random or systematic? MACGREGOR, J.; AND LEE, E. *Int. J. Man-Mach. Stud.* **26,** 5, (May 1, 1987) 627–631.

02145 Cognitive processing differences between novice and expert computer programmers. BATESON, A.; ALEXANDER, R.; AND MURPHY, M. *Int. J. Man-Mach. Stud.* **26,** 6, (June 1, 1987) 649–660.

02146 Procedural and non-procedural query languages revisited: a comparison of relational algebra and relational calculus. HANSEN, G.; AND HANSEN, J. *Int. J. Man-Mach. Stud.* **26,** 6, (June 1, 1987) 683–694.

02147 Predicting end-user acceptance of microcomputers in the workplace. HATCHER, M.; AND DIEBERT, T. *Int. J. Man-Mach. Stud.* **26,** 6, (June 1, 1987) 695–705.

02148 Analogy and other sources of difficulty in novices' very first text-editing. ALLWOOD, C.; AND ELIASSON, M. *Int. J. Man-Mach. Stud.* **27,** 1, (July 1, 1987) 1–22.

02149 Creating categories for databases. FISCHHOFF, B. *Int. J. Man-Mach. Stud.* **27,** 1, (July 1, 1987) 33–63.

02150 On matching programmers' chunks with program structures: an empirical investigation. VESSEY, I. *Int. J. Man-Mach. Stud.* **27,** 1, (July 1, 1987) 65–89.

02151 The use of hand-drawn gestures for text editing. WOLF, C.; AND MORREL-SAMUELS, P. *Int. J. Man-Mach. Stud.* **27,** 1, (July 1, 1987) 91–102.

02152 Knowledge elicitation using discourse analysis. BELKIN, N.; BROOKS, H.; AND DANIELS, P. *Int. J. Man-Mach. Stud.* **27,** 2, (August 1987) 127–144.

02153 Cognitive biases and corrective techniques: proposals for improving elicitation procedures for knowledge-based systems. CLEAVES, D. *Int. J. Man-Mach. Stud.* **27,** 2, (August 1987) 155–166.

02154 A mixed-initiative workbench for knowledge acquisition. KAHN, G.; BREAUX, E.; DEKLERK, P.; AND JOSEPH, R. *Int. J. Man-Mach. Stud.* **27**, 2, (August 1987) 167–179.

02155 Generalization and noise. KODRATOFF, Y.; MANAGO, M.; AND BLYTHE, J. *Int. J. Man-Mach. Stud.* **27**, 2, (August 1987) 181–204.

02156 Analysis of the performance of a genetic algorithm-based system for message classification in noisy environments. PETIT, E.; AND PETIT, M. *Int. J. Man-Mach. Stud.* **27**, 2, (August 1987) 205–220.

02157 Simplifying decision trees. QUINLAN, J. *Int. J. Man-Mach. Stud.* **27**, 3, (September 1987) 221–234.

02158 Creating the domain of discourse: ontology and inventory. REGOCZEI, S.; AND PLANTINGA, E. *Int. J. Man-Mach. Stud.* **27**, 3, (September 1987) 235–250.

02159 KITTEN: knowledge initiation and transfer tools for experts and novices. SHAW, M.; AND GAINES, B. *Int. J. Man-Mach. Stud.* **27**, 3, (September 1987) 251–280.

02160 Knowledge base refinement by monitoring abstract control knowledge. WILKINS, D.; CLANCEY, W.; AND BUCHANAN, B. *Int. J. Man-Mach. Stud.* **27**, 3, (September 1987) 281–293.

02161 Cognitive aids in process environments: prostheses or tools? REASON, J. *Int. J. Man-Mach. Stud.* **27**, 5&6, (Nov/Dec 1987) 463–470.

02162 How can computer-based visual displays aid operators? DE KEYSER, V. *Int. J. Man-Mach. Stud.* **27**, 5&6, (Nov/Dec 1987) 471–478.

02163 Human interaction with an "intelligent" machine. ROTH, E.; BENNETT, K.; AND WOODS, D. *Int. J. Man-Mach. Stud.* **27**, 5&6, (Nov/Dec 1987) 479–525.

02164 Trust between humans and machines, and the design of decision aids. MUIR, B. *Int. J. Man-Mach. Stud.* **27**, 5&6, (Nov/Dec 1987) 527–539.

02165 Operator assistant systems. BOY, G. *Int. J. Man-Mach. Stud.* **27**, 5&6, (Nov/Dec 1987) 541–554.

02166 Human error detection processes. RIZZO, A.; BAGNARA, S.; AND VISCIOLA, M. *Int. J. Man-Mach. Stud.* **27**, 5&6, (Nov/Dec 1987) 555–570.

02167 Cognitive engineering in complex dynamic worlds. WOODS, D. *Int. J. Man-Mach. Stud.* **27**, 5&6, (Nov/Dec 1987) 571–585.

02168 Accidents at sea: multiple causes and impossible consequences. WAGENAAR, W.; AND GROENEWEG, J. *Int. J. Man-Mach. Stud.* **27**, 5&6, (Nov/Dec 1987) 587–598.

02169 Modelling operators in accident conditions: advances and perspectives on a cognitive model. AMENDOLA, A.; BERSINI, U.; CACCIABUE, P.; AND MANCINI, G. *Int. J. Man-Mach. Stud.* **27**, 5&6, (Nov/Dec 1987) 599–612.

02170 Human supervisor modelling: some new developments. STASSEN, H. *Int. J. Man-Mach. Stud.* **27**, 5&6, (Nov/Dec 1987) 613–618.

02171 Intelligent aids, mental models, and the theory of machines. MORAY, N. *Int. J. Man-Mach. Stud.* **27**, 5&6, (Nov/Dec 1987) 619–629.

02172 Models of the decision maker in unforeseen accidents. MANCINI, G. *Int. J. Man-Mach. Stud.* **27**, 5&6, (Nov/Dec 1987) 631–639.

02173 Information and reasoning in intelligent decision support systems. HOLLNAGEL, E. *Int. J. Man-Mach. Stud.* **27**, 5&6, (Nov/Dec 1987) 665–678.

02174 The MDR algorithm and its application to the generation of explanations for novel events. COOMBS, M.; AND HARTLEY, R. *Int. J. Man-Mach. Stud.* **27**, 5&6, (Nov/Dec 1987) 679–708.

02175 Reading from screen versus paper: there is no difference. OBORNE, D.; AND HOLTON, D. *Int. J. Man-Mach. Stud.* **28**, 1, (January 1988) 1–9.

02176 Prompting, feedback and error correction in the design of a scenario machine. CARROLL, J.; AND KAY, D. *Int. J. Man-Mach. Stud.* **28**, 1, (January 1988) 11–27.

02177 Conditional statements, looping constructs, and program comprehension: an experiments study. ISELIN, E. *Int. J. Man-Mach. Stud.* **28**, 1, (January 1988) 45–66.

02178 Verifying identity via keystroke characteristics. LEGGETT, J.; AND WILLIAMS, G. *Int. J. Man-Mach. Stud.* **28**, 1, (January 1988) 67–76.

02179 Analysis of competition-based spreading activation in connectionist models. WANG, P.; SEIDMAN, S.; AND REGGIA, J. *Int. J. Man-Mach. Stud.* **28**, 1, (January 1988) 77–97.

02180 Four different perspectives on human-computer interaction. KAMMERSGAARD, J. *Int. J. Man-Mach. Stud.* **28**, 4, (April 1988) 343–362.

02181 Representing the structure of jobs in job analysis. DOWNS, C. *Int. J. Man-Mach. Stud.* **28**, 4, (April 1988) 363–390.

02182 Adapting menu layout to tasks. MCDONALD, J.; DAYTON, T.; AND MCDONALD, D. *Int. J. Man-Mach. Stud.* **28**, 4, (April 1988) 417–435.

02183 Extending Petri nets for specifying man-machine dialogues. VAN BILJON, W. *Int. J. Man-Mach. Stud.* **28**, 4, (April 1988) 437–455.

HCI-0144 Undo support models. YANG, Y. :CInt. J. Man-Mach. Stud. **28**, 5, (May 1988) 457–481.

02184 Experience of programming beauty: some patterns of programming aesthetics. LEVENTHAL, L. *Int. J. Man-Mach. Stud.* **28**, 5, (May 1988) 525–550.

02185 Optimization of string length for spoken digit input with error correction. AINSWORTH, W. *Int. J. Man-Mach. Stud.* **28**, 6, (June 1988) 573–581.

02186 Talking to computers: an empirical investigation. HAUPTMANN, A.; AND RUDNICKY, A. *Int. J. Man-Mach. Stud.* **28**, 6, (June 1988) 583–604.

02187 Enhancing PIXIE's tutoring capabilities. MOORE, J.; AND SLEEMAN, D. *Int. J. Man-Mach. Stud.* **28**, 6, (June 1988) 605–623.

02188 Structural displays as learning aids. PATRICK, J.; AND FITZGIBBON, L. *Int. J. Man-Mach. Stud.* **28**, 6, (June 1988) 625–635.

02189 Changes in contrast sensitivity function produced by VDT use. MIKEALAIN, H. *Int. J. Man-Mach. Stud.* **28**, 6, (June 1988) 637–642.

02190 $DM^2$: an algorithm for diagnostic reasoning that combines analytical models and experiential knowledge. LEE, N. *Int. J. Man-Mach. Stud.* **28**, 6, (June 1988) 643–670.

02191 A hybrid approach to deductive uncertain inference. LIU, X.; AND GAMMERMAN, A. *Int. J. Man-Mach. Stud.* **28**, 6, (June 1988) 671–681.

02192 Effects of breadth, depth and number responses on computer menu search performance. PARKINSON, S.; HILL, M.; SISSON, N.; AND VIERA, C. *Int. J. Man-Mach. Stud.* **28**, 6, (June 1988) 683–692.

02193 ISIS: the interactive spatial information system. MCCANN, C.; TAYLOR, M.; AND TUORI, M. *Int. J. Man-Mach. Stud.* **28**, 2&3, (Feb/Mar 1988) 101–138.

02194 Evaluating the intelligence in dialogue systems. EDWARDS, J.; AND MASON, J. *Int. J. Man-Mach. Stud.* **28**, 2&3, (Feb/Mar 1988) 139–173.

02195 Layered protocols for computer-human dialogue. 1: principles. TAYLOR, M. *Int. J. Man-Mach. Stud.* **28**, 2&3, (Feb/Mar 1988) 175–218.

02196 Layered protocols for computer-human dialogue. 11: some practical issues. TAYLOR, M. *Int. J. Man-Mach. Stud.* **28**, 2&3, (Feb/Mar 1988) 219–257.

02197 Surveying projects on intelligent dialogue. MASON, J.; AND EDWARDS, J. *Int. J. Man-Mach. Stud.* **28**, 2&3, (Feb/Mar 1988) 259–307.

02198 Toward intelligent dialogue with ISIS. EDWARDS, J.; AND MASON, J. *Int. J. Man-Mach. Stud.* **28**, 2&3, (Feb/Mar 1988) 309–342.

02199 A model of fault diagnosis performance of expert marine engineers. GOVINDARAJ, T; AND SU, Y. *Int. J. Man-Mach. Stud.* **29**, 1, (July 1988) 1–20.

02200 An application of computerized fuzzy graphics rating scale to the psychological measurement of individual differences. HESKETH, T.; PRYOR, R.; AND HESKETH, B. *Int. J. Man-Mach. Stud.* **29**, 1, (July 1988) 21–35.

02201 The effect of different conceptual models using reasoning in a database query writing task. KATZEFF, C. *Int. J. Man-Mach. Stud.* **29**, 1, (July 1988) 37–62.

02202 Question asking when learning a text-editing system. ALLWOOD, C.; AND ELIASSON, M. *Int. J. Man-Mach. Stud.* **29**, 1, (July 1988) 63–79.

02203 Validation in a knowledge support system: construing and consistency with multiple experts. SHAW, M.; AND WOODWARD, B. *Int. J. Man-Mach. Stud.* **29**, 3, (September 1988) 329–350.

HCI-0335 An expert system for conceptual schema design: a machine learning approach. YASDI, R.; AND ZIARKO, W. *Int. J. Man-Mach. Stud.* **29**, 4, (Oct. 1988) 351–376.

02204 Effects of computer programming experience on network representations of abstract programming concepts. COOKE, N.; AND SCHVANEVELD, W. *Int. J. Man-Mach. Stud.* **29**, 4, (Oct. 1988) 407–427.

02205 Refining problem-solving knowledge in repertory grids using a consultation mechanism. SHEMA, D.; AND BOOSE, J. *Int. J. Man-Mach. Stud.* **29**, 4, (Oct. 1988) 447–460.

02206 Design goals for sloppy modeling systems. WROBEL, S. *Int. J. Man-Mach. Stud.* **29**, 4, (Oct. 1988) 461–477.

02207 A survey of formal tools and models for developing user interfaces. FAROOQ, M.; AND DOMINICK, W. *Int. J. Man-Mach. Stud.* **29**, 5, (November 1988) 479–496.

02208 Human performance in relational algebra, tuple calculus, and domain calculus. HANSEN, G.; AND HANSEN, J. *Int. J. Man-Mach. Stud.* **29**, 5, (November 1988) 503–516.

02209 User-adaptive computer graphics. HOLYNSKI, M. *Int. J. Man-Mach. Stud.* **29**, 5, (November 1988) 539–548.

02210 Protos: an examplar-based learning apprentice. BAREISS, E.; PORTER, B.; AND WIER, C. *Int. J. Man-Mach. Stud.* **29**, 5, (November 1988) 549–561.

02211 On the representation and the impact of reliability on expert system weights. O'LEARY, D. *Int. J. Man-Mach. Stud.* **29**, 6, (Dec. 1988) 637–646.

02212 Accommodating individual differences in searching a hierarchical file system. VICENTE, K.; AND WILLIGES, R. *Int. J. Man-Mach. Stud.* **29**, 6, (Dec. 1988) 647–668.

02213 The mental rotation and perceived realism of computer-generated three-dimensional images. BARFIELD, W.; SANDFORD, J.; AND FOLEY, J. *Int. J. Man-Mach. Stud.* **29**, 6, (Dec. 1988) 669–684.

02214 Cognitive primitives. RAPPAPORT, A. *Int. J. Man-Mach. Stud.* **29**, 6, (Dec. 1988) 733–747.

02215 Learning iteration recursion from examples. WIEDENBECK, S. *Int. J. Man-Mach. Stud.* **30**, 1, (January 1989) 1–22.

02216 Toward a theory of computer program bugs: an empirical test. VESSEY, I. *Int. J. Man-Mach. Stud.* **30**, 1, (January 1989) 23–46.

02217 Strategies in controlling a continuous process with long response latencies: needs for computer support to diagnosis. HOC, J. *Int. J. Man-Mach. Stud.* **30**, 1, (January 1989) 47–67.

02218 Combining stochastic uncertainty and linguistic inexactness: theory and experimental evaluation of four fuzzy probability models. ZWICK, R. *Int. J. Man-Mach. Stud.* **30**, 1, (January 1989) 69–111.

02219 Patterns of inductive reasoning in a parallel expert system. SILER, W.; AND TUCKER, D. *Int. J. Man-Mach. Stud.* **30**, 1, (January 1989) 113–120.

02220 Interactive communication of sentential structure and content: an alternative approach to man-machine communication. CHANDRASEKAR, R.; AND RAMANI, S. *Int. J. Man-Mach. Stud.* **30**, 2, (February 1989) 121–148.

02221 DYNABOARD: user animated display of deductive proofs in mathematics. KALTENBACH, M.; AND FRASSON, C. *Int. J. Man-Mach. Stud.* **30**, 2, (February 1989) 149–170.

02222 Cognitive issues in the process of software development: review and reappraisal. KOUBEK, R.; SALVENDY, G.; DUNSMORE, H.; AND LEBOLD, W. *Int. J. Man-Mach. Stud.* **30**, 2, (February 1989) 171–191.

02223 Study of combination of belief intevals in lattice-structured networks. CHANG, L.; AND KASHYAP, R. *Int. J. Man-Mach. Stud.* **30**, 2, (February 1989) 193–211.

02224 The structure of command languages: an experiment on task-action grammar. PAYNE, S.; AND GREEN, T. *Int. J. Man-Mach. Stud.* **30**, 2, (February 1989) 213–234.

02225 Underlying dimensions of human problem solving and learning: implications for personnel selection, training tasks design and expert system. ENKAWA, T.; AND SALVENDY, G. *Int. J. Man-Mach. Stud.* **30**, 3, (March 1989) 235–254.

02226 Issues in the verification of knowledge in rule-based systems. NAZARETH, D. *Int. J. Man-Mach. Stud.* **30**, 3, (March 1989) 255–271.

02227 Heuristic graph displayer for G-BASE. WATANABE, H. *Int. J. Man-Mach. Stud.* **30**, 3, (March 1989) 287–302.

02228 An interface architecture to provide adaptive task-specific context for the user. TYLER, S.; AND TREU, S. *Int. J. Man-Mach. Stud.* **30**, 3, (March 1989) 303–327.

02229 Concept learning from examples and counter examples. RALESCU, A.; AND BALDWIN, J. *Int. J. Man-Mach. Stud.* **30**, 3, (March 1989) 329–354.

02230 The utility of speech input in user-computer interfaces. MARTIN, G. *Int. J. Man-Mach. Stud.* **30**, 4, (April 1989) 355–375.

02231 Rough sets and dependency analysis among attributes in computer implementations of expert's inference models. MRÓZEK, A. *Int. J. Man-Mach. Stud.* **30**, 4, (April 1989) 457–473.

02232 Visual information chunking in spreadsheet calculation. SAARILUOMA, P.; AND SAJANIEMI, J. *Int. J. Man-Mach. Stud.* **30**, 5, (May 1989) 475–488.

02233 Are there individual concepts? Proper names and individual concepts in SI-Nets. FRIXONE, M.; GAGLIO, S.; AND SPINELLI, G. *Int. J. Man-Mach. Stud.* **30**, 5, (May 1989) 489–503.

02234 The electronic book Ebook3. SAVOY, J. *Int. J. Man-Mach. Stud.* **30**, 5, (May 1989) 505–523.

02235 Absolute dates and relative dates in an inferential system on temporal dependencies between events. HAJNICZ, E. *Int. J. Man-Mach. Stud.* **30**, 5, (May 1989) 537–549.

02236 Development and validation of a reader-based documentation measure. GUILLEMETTE, R. *Int. J. Man-Mach. Stud.* **30**, 5, (May 1989) 551–574.

02237 Modelling blind users' interactions with an auditory computer interface. EDWARDS, A. *Int. J. Man-Mach. Stud.* **30**, 5, (May 1989) 575–589.

02238 Making the transition from print to electronic encyclopaedias: adapation of mental models. MARCHIONINI, G. *Int. J. Man-Mach. Stud.* **30**, 6, (June 1989) 591–618.

02239 Theoretical training and problem detection in a computerized database retrieval task. DAYTON, T.; GETTYS, C.; AND UNREIN, J. *Int. J. Man-Mach. Stud.* **30**, 6, (June 1989) 619–637.

02240 Support for browsing in an intelligent text retrieval system. THOMPSON, R.; AND CROFT, W. *Int. J. Man-Mach. Stud.* **30**, 6, (June 1989) 639–668.

02241 A formal representation system for the human-computer interaction process. KITAJIMA, M. *Int. J. Man-Mach. Stud.* **30**, 6, (June 1989) 669–696.

02242 Measuring change in the programming process. REDMOND, R.; AND GASEN, J. *Int. J. Man-Mach. Stud.* **30**, 6, (June 1989) 697–711.

02243 A graphical thesaurus-based information retrieval system. MCMATH, C.; TAMARU, R.; AND RADA, R. *Int. J. Man-Mach. Stud.* **31**, 2, (Aug. 1989) 121–147.

02244 XTRA: a natural-language access system to expert systems. ALLGAYER, J.; HARBUSCH, K.; KOBSA, A.; REDDIG, C.; AND REITHINGER, N. *Int. J. Man-Mach. Stud.* **31**, 2, (Aug. 1989) 161–195.

02245 The influence of programmers' cognitive complexity on program comprehension and modification. KHALIL, O.; AND CLARK, J. *Int. J. Man-Mach. Stud.* **31**, 2, (Aug. 1989) 219–236.

02246 Measuring the effectiveness of personal database structures. RAYMOND, D.; CAÑAS, A.; TOMPA, F.; AND SAFAYENI, F. *Int. J. Man-Mach. Stud.* **31**, 3, (Sept. 1989) 237–256.

02247 The effects of relational and entity-relationship data models on query performance of end users. JIH, W.; BRADBARD, D.; SNYDER, C.; AND THOMPSON, N. *Int. J. Man-Mach. Stud.* **31**, 3, (Sept. 1989) 257–267.

02248 An attempt to incorporate expertise about users into an intelligent interface for Unix. JERRAMS-SMITH, J. *Int. J. Man-Mach. Stud.* **31**, 3, (Sept. 1989) 269–292.

02249 Comparison of student performance in artithmetic exercises TOAM us paper-and-pencial testing. OSIN, L.; AND NESHER, P. *Int. J. Man-Mach. Stud.* **31**, 3, (Sept. 1989) 293–313.

02250 Programmer variations in software debugging approaches. CARVER, D. *Int. J. Man-Mach. Stud.* **31**, 3, (Sept. 1989) 315–322.

02251 Pictorial dialogue methods. BARKER, P.; AND MANJI, K. *Int. J. Man-Mach. Stud.* **31**, 3, (Sept. 1989) 323–347.

02252 Some effects of cognitive style on learning UNIX. COVENTRY, L. *Int. J. Man-Mach. Stud.* **31**, 3, (Sept. 1989) 349–365.

02253 Integration issues in knowledge support system. GAINES, B. *Int. J. Man-Mach. Stud.* **31**, 5, (Nov. 1989) 495–515.

02254 Coping with human errors through system design: implications for ecological interface design. RASMUSSEN, J.; AND VICENTE, K. *Int. J. Man-Mach. Stud.* **31**, 5, (Nov. 1989) 517–534.

02255 The flexibility of case grammar representations: a porting procedure for naturallanguage interfaces. HAAS, S.; AND METZLER, D. *Int. J. Man-Mach. Stud.* **31**, 5, (Nov. 1989) 535–556.

02256 A cognitive study of the decision-making process in a business context: implications for design of expert systems. PREKUMAR, G. *Int. J. Man-Mach. Stud.* **31**, 5, (Nov. 1989) 556–572.

## International Journal of Pattern Recognition and Artificial Intelligence

HCI-0389 Recognizing unexpected objects: a proposed approach. ROSENFELD, A. *Int. J. Pattern Recogn. Artif. Intell.* **1**, 1, (April 1987) 71–84.

HCI-0161 Icon semantics—a formal approach to icon system design. CHANG, S. *Int. J. Pattern Recogn. Artif. Intell.* **1**, 1, (April 1987) 103–120.

## International Journal of Robotics Research

02257 Mapping the manipulator workspace using interactive computer graphics. KUMAR, A.; AND PATEL, M. *Int. J. Rob. Res.* **5**, 2, (Summer, 1986) 122–130.

02258 Task compatibility of manipulator postures. CHIU, S. *Int. J. Rob. Res.* **7**, 5, (Oct. 1988) 13–21.

02259 A survey of general-purpose manipulation. GRUPEN, R.; HENDERSON, T.; AND MCCAMMON, I. *Int. J. Rob. Res.* **8**, 1, (February 1989) 38–62.

## Journal a

02260 Critical review of visual inspection. SUETENS, P.; AND OOSTERLINCK, A. *J. a* **26**, 4, (Oct. 1985) 197–207.

02261 Introduction to expert systems. EFSTATHIOU, J. *J. a* **27**, 2, (April 1986) 57–61.

02262 Personal computer training software for adaptive control. DE KEYSER, R. *J. a* **27**, 3, (July 1986) 155–161.

## Journal of Automated Reasoning

02263 Model minimization—an alternative to circumscription. HINTIKKA, J. *J. Autom. Reasoning* **4**, 1, (March 1988) 1–13.

## Journal of Chemical Information & Computer Sciences

02264 Primary journals today and tomorrow. BOWEN, D. *J. Chem. Inf. Comput. Sci.* **26**, 2, (May 1986) 45–47.

02265 Comparison of manual and online searches of chemical abstracts. AKAHO, E.; BANDAI, A.; AND FUJII, M. *J. Chem. Inf. Comput. Sci.* **26**, 2, (May 1986) 59–63.

02266 Microcomputer software. 2. Scientific and technical word processing on a personal computer: has the time come? MARSHALL, J. *J. Chem. Inf. Comput. Sci.* **26**, 3, (Aug. 1986) 87–92.

02267 Simps: Secondary ion mass image processing system. LING, Y.; BERNIUS, M.; AND MORRISON, G. *J. Chem. Inf. Comput. Sci.* **27**, 2, (May 1, 1987) 86–94.

02268 "Structure—reaction type" paradigm in the conventional methods of describing organic reactions and the concept of imaginary transitions structures overcoming this paradigm. FUJITA, S. *J. Chem. Inf. Comput. Sci.* **27**, 3, (August 1, 1987) 120–126.

02269 End-user searching of CAS ONLINE. Results of a cooperative experiment between Imperial Chemical Industries and Chemical Abstracts Services. WARR, W.; AND JACKSON, A. *J. Chem. Inf. Comput. Sci.* **28**, 2, (May 1988) 68–72.

## Journal of Complexity

02270 Dynamics and architecture for neural computation. PINEDA, F. *J. Complexity* **4**, 3, (Sept. 1988) 216–245.

## Journal of Computer and System Sciences

02271 Equivalence of views by query capacity. CONNORS, T. *J. Comput. Syst. Sci.* **33**, 2, (Oct. 1986) 234–274.

JOURNALS

## Journal of Computer Science and Technology

02272   An interactive system SDI on microcomputer. RENBAO, Z.; LIN, X.; AND ZHAOYANG, R. *J. Comput. Sci. Technol.* **2**, 1, (Jan, 1987) 64–71.

## Journal of Computer-Based Instruction

02273   Computer analysis of students' procedural "bugs" in an arithmetic domain. TATSUOKA, K.; AND EDDINS, J. *J. Comput.-Based Instruct.* **12**, 2, (Spring 1985) 34–38.
02274   Student evaluation of motivational and learning attributes of microcomputer soft. PEREZ, E.; AND WHITE, M. *J. Comput.-Based Instruct.* **12**, 2, (Spring 1985) 39–43.
02275   Systematic evaluation strategies for computer-based music instruction systems. WOOD, R.; AND CLEMENTS, P. *J. Comput.-Based Instruct.* **13**, 1, (Winter 1986) 17–24.
02276   Developing the technology for intelligent maintenance advisors. RICHARDSON, J.; AND JACKSON, T. *J. Comput.-Based Instruct.* **13**, 2, (Spring 1986) 47–51.
02277   Psychologically based techniques for improving learning within computerized tutorials. MACLACHLAN, J. *J. Comput.-Based Instruct.* **13**, 3, (Summer 1986) 65–70.
02278   Efficacy of higher cognitive and factual questions in computer assisted instruction modules. SCHLOSS, P.; SINDELAR, P.; CARTWRIGHT, G.; AND SCHLOSS, C. *J. Comput.-Based Instruct.* **13**, 3, (Summer 1986) 75–79.
02279   The accuracy of approximate string matching algorithms. NESBIT, J. *J. Comput.-Based Instruct.* **13**, 3, (Summer 1986) 80–83.
02280   A comparison of children's reading comprehension and reading rates at three text presentation speeds on a CRT. BLANK, D.; MURPHY, P.; AND SHNEIDERMAN, B. *J. Comput.-Based Instruct.* **13**, 3, (Summer 1986) 84–87.
02281   The accuracy of cognitive monitoring during computer-based instruction. GARHART, C.; AND HANNAFIN, M. *J. Comput.-Based Instruct.* **13**, 3, (Summer 1986) 88–93.
02282   Computer-assisted instruction in academic libraries. AKEN, R.; AND OLSON, L. *J. Comput.-Based Instruct.* **13**, 3, (Summer 1986) 94–97.
02283   Research and evaluation models for the study of interactive video. REEVES, T. *J. Comput.-Based Instruct.* **13**, 4, (Autumn 1986) 102–106.
02284   A theoretical framework for interactivating linear video. ALLEN, B. *J. Comput.-Based Instruct.* **13**, 4, (Autumn 1986) 107–112.
02285   An interactive videodisc drama: The case of Frank hall. HARLESS, W. *J. Comput.-Based Instruct.* **13**, 4, (Autumn 1986) 113–116.
02286   The efficacy of computer-assisted video instruction on rule learning and attitudes. DALTON, D. *J. Comput.-Based Instruct.* **13**, 4, (Autumn 1986) 122–125.
02287   The effects of orienting objectives and review on learning from interactive video. HO, C.; SAVENYE, W.; AND HAAS, N. *J. Comput.-Based Instruct.* **13**, 4, (Autumn 1986) 126–129.
02288   Using interactive videotaped-based instruction to teach on-the-job social skills to handicapped adolescents. MALOUF, D.; MACARTHUR, C.; AND RADIN, S. *J. Comput.-Based Instruct.* **13**, 4, (Autumn 1986) 130–133.
02289   The effects of orienting, processing, and practicing activities on learning from interactive video. HANNAFIN, M.; PHILLIPS, T.; AND TRIPP, S. *J. Comput.-Based Instruct.* **13**, 4, (Autumn 1986) 134–139.
02290   Citation patterns in the computer-based instruction literature. WEDMAN, J. *J. Comput.-Based Instruct.* **14**, 3, (Summer) 91–95.
02291   The influence of personality on self-paced instruction. KERN, G.; AND MATTA, K. *J. Comput.-Based Instruct.* **15**, 3, (Summer 1988) 104–108.
02292   Formative evaluation of pre-Logo programming environments: a collaborative effort of researchers, teachers, and children. COHEN, R. *J. Comput.-Based Instruct.* **15**, 4, (Autumn 1988) 112–122.
02293   Expert systems and interactive video tutorials: separating strategies from subject matter. ALLEN, B.; AND CATERS, C. *J. Comput.-Based Instruct.* **15**, 4, (Autumn 1988) 123–130.
02294   Color, graphics, and animation in a computer-assisted learning tutorial lesson. BAEK, Y.; AND LAYNE, B. *J. Comput.-Based Instruct.* **15**, 4, (Autumn 1988) 131–135.

02295 A comparison of a microcomputer progressive state drill and flashcards for learning paired associates. SALISBURY, D.; AND KLEIN, J. *J. Comput.-Based Instruct.* **15**, 4, (Autumn 1988) 136–143.

02296 Computers as composition tools: a case study of student attitudes. BAER, V. *J. Comput.-Based Instruct.* **15**, 4, (Autumn 1988) 144–148.

## Journal of Documentation

02297 Improved design of graphic displays in thesauri—through technology and ergonomics. BERTRAND-GASTALDY, S.; AND DAVIDSON, C. *J. Doc.* **42**, 4, (Dec. 1986) 225–251.

02298 Cognitive models in information retrieval—an evaluative review. DANIELS, P. *J. Doc.* **42**, 4, (Dec. 1986) 272–304.

02299 How well do we acknowledge intellectual debts? KOCHEN, M. *J. Doc.* **43**, 1, (March 1987) 54–64.

02300 Interactive document display and its use in information retrieval. BOVEY, J.; AND BROWN, P. *J. Doc.* **43**, 2, (June 1987) 125–137.

02301 Readability formulas: An overview. TEKFI, C. *J. Doc.* **43**, 3, (Sept. 1987) 257–269.

02302 Subject searching behaviour at the library catalogue and at the shelves: implications for online interactive catalogues. HANCOCK, M. *J. Doc.* **43**, 4, (Dec. 1987) 303–321.

02303 Subjective probability and information retrieval: a review of the psychological literature. THOMPSON, P. *J. Doc.* **44**, 2, (June 1988) 119–143.

02304 A behavioral approach to information retrieval system design. ELLIS, D. *J. Doc.* **45**, 3, (Sept. 1989) 171–212.

## Journal of FORTH Application and Research

02305 Interactive videodiscs control and computer-based training on the Apple Macintosh. FRANCESCO, N. *J. FORTH Appl. Res.* **3**, 2, (1986) 145–148.

02306 User-oriented suggestions for floating-point and complex-arithmetic Forth standard extensions. MACINTYRE, F.; AND DOWLING, T. *J. FORTH Appl. Res.* **3**, 4, (1986) 65–84.

02307 REPTIL-promoting dialog between humanoid and computer. URIELI, I. *J. FORTH Appl. Res.* **4**, 2, (June 1986) 231–234.

02308 A single-board Forth computer with versatile analog I/O circuitry. VOLD, T. *J. FORTH Appl. Res.* **4**, 2, (June 1986) 295–296.

02309 Compiling Forth for performance. ALMY, T. *J. FORTH Appl. Res.* **4**, 3, (April 1987) 379–388.

02310 A stand-alone Forth system. BRUMM, D.; AND KULKARNI, U. *J. FORTH Appl. Res.* **4**, 3, (April 1987) 389–404.

02311 Biological aspects of neural nets. BROWNING, I. *J. FORTH Appl. Res.* **5**, 1, (August 1988) 9–10.

02312 Pride-II physical layout program of modifying Forth for "non-believers". ALMY, T. *J. FORTH Appl. Res.* **5**, 1, (August 1988) 75–78.

02313 High performance neural networks. DRESS, W. *J. FORTH Appl. Res.* **5**, 1, (August 1988) 137–140.

02314 A unification of software and hardware; a new tool for human thought. HAYDON, G. *J. FORTH Appl. Res.* **5**, 1, (August 1988) 149–152.

## Journal of Information Processing

02315 A natural language interface processor based on the hierarchical-tree structure model of relation tables. KINUKAWA, H. *J. Inf. Process.* **11**, 2, (1988) 83–91.

02316 The man-machine interface aspect of an automatic classification numbering system in a computerized library system. ISHIKAWA, T. *J. Inf. Process.* **11**, 3, (Sept. 1988) 199–205.

# JOURNALS

## Journal of Information Science: Principles & Practice

- **HCI-0264** An intelligent interface for online interaction. VICKERY, A. *J. Inf. Sci. Princ. Pract.* **9**, 1, (Aug. 1984) 7–18.
- **02317** Using a cognitive model of dialogue for reference retrieval. OFORI-DWUMFUO, G. *J. Inf. Sci. Princ. Pract.* **9**, 1, (Aug. 1984) 19–28.
- **02318** An analysis of humanists' requests received by an information service for the humanities. MÉNDEZ, A. *J. Inf. Sci. Princ. Pract.* **9**, 3, (1984) 97–105.
- **HCI-0274** In search of searching skills. FAIRHALL, D. *J. Inf. Sci. Princ. Pract.* **10**, 3, (1985) 111–123.
- **HCI-0275** Using the micro-computer to simplify database access: designing interfaces to complex files. PRATT, G. *J. Inf. Sci. Princ. Pract.* **10**, 3, (1985) 131–138.
- **02319** Notions and dynamics of information. LIGOMENIDES, P. *J. Inf. Sci. Princ. Pract.* **10**, 4, (1985) 149–158.
- **02320** Emerging communications technology paradigms. MORE, E.; AND LAIRD, R. *J. Inf. Sci. Princ. Pract.* **11**, 2, (1985) 63–75.
- **02321** Moral issues in information science. CAPURRO, R. *J. Inf. Sci. Princ. Pract.* **11**, 3, (March 1986) 113–123.
- **02322** The real information society: present situation and some forecasts. CAWKELL, A. *J. Inf. Sci. Princ. Pract.* **12**, 3, (March 1986) 87–95.
- **02323** Electronic information systems analysis. Present and future information systems use by academics involved in development studies. BELL, S. *J. Inf. Sci. Princ. Pract.* **12**, 3, (March 1986) 119–127.
- **02324** Can finding information be easy, fun and successful? NOERR, K. *J. Inf. Sci. Princ. Pract.* **12**, 3, (March 1986) 139–141.
- **02325** Time-life, world reporter and the secretary: experiments with end-users. NICHOLAS, D.; HARRIS, K.; AND ERBACH, G. *J. Inf. Sci. Princ. Pract.* **12**, 4, (Sept. 1986) 167–175.
- **02326** An assessment of the major computerised databases relating to disabled people in the UK and Scandinavia. MEADOWS, S. *J. Inf. Sci. Princ. Pract.* **12**, 4, (Sept. 1986) 185–191.
- **02327** Information systems and the stimulation of creativity. BAWDEN, D. *J. Inf. Sci. Princ. Pract.* **12**, 5, (Sept. 1986) 203–216.
- **02328** Research on information interaction and intelligent information provision mechanisms. BROOKS, H.; DANIELS, P.; AND BELKIN, N. *J. Inf. Sci. Princ. Pract.* **12**, 1,2, (Jan. 1986) 37–44.
- **02329** Weighting, ranking and relevance feedback in a front-end system. ROBERTSON, S.; THOMPSON, C.; MACASKILL, M.; AND BOVEY, J. *J. Inf. Sci. Princ. Pract.* **12**, 1,2, (Jan. 1986) 71–75.
- **02330** Education and training in office technology. YATES-MERCER, P.; AND ROUCOUX, J. *J. Inf. Sci. Princ. Pract.* **12**, 1,2, (Jan. 1986) 77–84.
- **02331** Man—machine interaction by voice: developments in speech technology. Part I: The state-of-the-art. PHILIP, G.; AND YOUNG, E. *J. Inf. Sci. Princ. Pract.* **13**, 1, (Feb. 1987) 3–14.
- **02332** Man—machine interaction by voice: developments in speech technology. Part 2: general applications and potential applications in libraries and information services. PHILIP, G.; AND YOUNG, E. *J. Inf. Sci. Princ. Pract.* **13**, 1, (Feb. 1987) 15–23.
- **02333** The foreign language barrier: a study among pharmaceutical research workers. THORP, R.; SCHUR, H.; BAWDEN, D.; AND JOICE, J. *J. Inf. Sci. Princ. Pract.* **14**, 1, (January 1988) 17–24.
- **02334** Viewdata in the office—user-friendly page identification. AMADI, A. *J. Inf. Sci. Princ. Pract.* **14**, 1, (January 1988) 59–61.
- **02335** Voice input/output interface for online searching: some design and human factor onsiderations. PHILIP, G.; SMITH, F.; AND CROOKES, D. *J. Inf. Sci. Princ. Pract.* **14**, 2, (1988) 93–98.
- **02336** Professional education and subsequent careers in library/information work: a follow-up study of former students on the MA/MSc information studies course at the University of Sheffield. HULME, A.; AND WILSON, T. *J. Inf. Sci. Princ. Pract.* **14**, 2, (1988) 109–117.
- **02337** The computer as mask: a problem of inadequate human interaction examined with particular regard to online public access catalogues. AZUBUIKE, A. *J. Inf. Sci. Princ. Pract.* **14**, 5, (June 1988) 275–283.
- **02338** Personal transferable skills for the modern information professional: a discussion paper. GASH, S.; AND REARDON, D. *J. Inf. Sci. Princ. Pract.* **14**, 5, (June 1988) 285–292.

02339 Managers' reading habits in the electronics industry. GENT, A.; BOTTLE, R.; AND CRAWSHAW, H. *J. Inf. Sci. Princ. Pract.* **14**, 5, (June 1988) 301–304.
02340 Reading, culture and modern mass media. VAN PEER, W. *J. Inf. Sci. Princ. Pract.* **14**, 5, (June 1988) 305–309.
02341 The seacher/information interface project—final report. ROWLEY, J.; AND BUTCHER, D. *J. Inf. Sci. Princ. Pract.* **14**, 6, (July 1988) 355–363.

## Journal of Logic Programming

02342 An approach to natural-language semantics in logic programming. SAINT-DIZIER, P. *J. Logic Program.* **3**, 4, (Dec. 1986) 329–356.

## Journal of Management Information Systems

02343 Controlling bias in user assertions in expert decision support systems for problem formulation. PARADICE, D.; AND COURTNEY, J. *J. Manage. Inf. Syst.* **3**, 1, (Summer 1986) 52–64.
02344 Organizational factors affecting the success of end-user computing. CHENEY, P.; MANN, R.; AND AMOROSO, D. *J. Manage. Inf. Syst.* **3**, 1, (Summer 1986) 65–80.
02345 Adaptive information systems control: A reliability-based approach. DE, P.; AND HSU, C. *J. Manage. Inf. Syst.* **3**, 2, (Fall 1986) 33–51.
02346 Effects of decision support training and cognitive style on decision process attributes. GREEN, G.; AND HUGHES, C. *J. Manage. Inf. Syst.* **3**, 2, (Fall 1986) 83–93.
HCI-0446 Open versus closed minds: the effect of dogmatism on an analyst's problem-solving behavior. PADDOCK, C.; AND SWANSON, N. *J. Manage. Inf. Syst.* **3**, 3, (Winter 1986-87) 111–122.
02347 Expansion and control of end-user computing. MUNRO, M.; HUFF, S.; AND MOORE, G. *J. Manage. Inf. Syst.* **4**, 3, (Winter 1987-1987) 5–27.
02348 Strategies for end-user computing: An integrative framework. ALAVI, M.; NELSON, R.; AND WEISS, I. *J. Manage. Inf. Syst.* **4**, 3, (Winter 1987-1987) 28–49.
02349 Motivation norms of knowledge engineers compared to those of software engineers. COUGER, J.; AND MCINTYRE, S. *J. Manage. Inf. Syst.* **4**, 3, (Winter 1987-1987) 82–93.
02350 The effect of presentation media on recipient performance in text-based information systems. KASPER, G.; AND MORRIS, A. *J. Manage. Inf. Syst.* **4**, 4, (April 1988) 25–43.
02351 A short-form measure of user information satisfaction: a psychometric evaluation and notes on use. BAROUDI, J.; AND ORLIKOWSKI, W. *J. Manage. Inf. Syst.* **4**, 4, (April 1988) 44–59.
02352 An investigation of the effects of age, size, and hardware option on the critical success factors applicable to information centers. MAGAL, S.; AND CARR, H. *J. Manage. Inf. Syst.* **4**, 4, (April 1988) 60–76.
02353 User perceptions of decision support system restrictiveness: an experiment. SILVER, M. *J. Manage. Inf. Syst.* **5**, 1, (July 1988) 51–65.
02354 A longitudinal study of spreadsheet program use. CARLSSON, S. *J. Manage. Inf. Syst.* **5**, 1, (July 1988) 82–100.
02355 Current and future uses of the group decision support system technology: report on a recent empirical study. STRAUB JR., D.; AND BEAUCLAIR, R. *J. Manage. Inf. Syst.* **5**, 1, (July 1988) 101–116.
02356 The quality of user documentation: an instrument validation. TORKZADEH, G. *J. Manage. Inf. Syst.* **5**, 2, (Fall 1988) 99–108.
02357 The effects of display formats on information systems design. LIBERATORE, M.; TITUS, G.; AND DIXON, P. *J. Manage. Inf. Syst.* **5**, 3, (Winter 1988-89) 85–99.
02358 The effects of modes of information presentation on decision-making: a review and meta-analysis. MONTAZEMI, A.; AND WANG, S. *J. Manage. Inf. Syst.* **5**, 3, (Winter 1988-89) 101–127.
02359 The effects of task differences on the work satisfaction, job characteristics, and role perceptions of programmer/analysts. GOLDSTEIN, D. *J. Manage. Inf. Syst.* **6**, 1, (Summer 1989) 41–57.

## Journal of Mathematical Psychology

**02360** Induction of categories: The problem of multiple equilibria. MOLANDER, P. *J. Math. Psychol.* **30**, 1, (March 1986) 42–54.

**02361** A theory of information structure. I. General principles. LEYTON, M. *J. Math. Psychol.* **30**, 2, (June 1986) 103–160.

**02362** A theory of information structure. II. A theory of perceptual organization. LEYTON, M. *J. Math. Psychol.* **30**, 3, (Sept. 1986) 257–305.

**02363** Mathematical modeling of fatigue in physically demanding jobs. GUASTELLO, S.; AND MCGEE, D. *J. Math. Psychol.* **31**, 3, (Sept. 1987) 248–269.

**02364** Non-Reimannian approach to geometry of visual space: An application of affinely connected geometry to visual alleys and horopter. YAMAZAKI, T. *J. Math. Psychol.* **31**, 3, (Sept. 1987) 270–298.

**02365** A limitation theorem for the differentiable prototypification of shape. LEYTON, M. *J. Math. Psychol.* **31**, 4, (Dec. 1987) 307–320.

**02366** A group model of form recognition under plane similarity transformations. CHEN, M.; AND CHEN, K. *J. Math. Psychol.* **31**, 4, (Dec. 1987) 321–337.

**02367** Grid analysis: continuing the search for a metric of shape. GREENE, E.; AND WAKSMAN, P. *J. Math. Psychol.* **31**, 4, (Dec. 1987) 338–365.

**02368** Counting and timing models in psychophysics and the conjoint Weber's law. ASHBY, F. *J. Math. Psychol.* **31**, 4, (Dec. 1987) 419–428.

**02369** Expectation and variance of item resemblance distributions in a convolution-correction model of distributed memory. WEBER, E. *J. Math. Psychol.* **32**, 1, (March 1988) 1–43.

**02370** Psychological models of deferred decision making. BUSEMEYER, J.; AND RAPOPORT, A. *J. Math. Psychol.* **32**, 2, (June 1988) 91–134.

**02371** The accumulator model of two-choice discrimination. SMITH, P.; AND VICKERS, D. *J. Math. Psychol.* **32**, 2, (June 1988) 135–168.

**02372** A probabilistic dominance measure for binary choices: analytic aspects of a multi-attribute random weights model. SCHOEMAKER, P.; AND WAID, C. *J. Math. Psychol.* **32**, 2, (June 1988) 169–191.

**02373** A note on mimicking additive reaction time models. RATCLIFF, R. *J. Math. Psychol.* **32**, 2, (June 1988) 192–204.

**02374** Alleys on an apparent frontoparallel plane. INDOW, T. *J. Math. Psychol.* **32**, 3, (Sept. 1988) 259–284.

**02375** The psychophysical function of binocular space perception. DRÖSLER, J. *J. Math. Psychol.* **32**, 3, (Sept. 1988) 285–297.

## Journal of Medical Systems

**HCI-0452** Strategic management of technostress: The chaining of Prometheus. CARO, D.; AND SETHI, A. *J. Med. Syst.* **9**, 5/6, (Dec. 1985) 291–304.

**HCI-0410** Evaluating RECONSIDER: a computer program for diagnostic prompting. NELSON, S.; BLOIS, M.; TUTTLE, M.; ERLBAUM, M.; HARRISON, P.; KIM, H.; WINKELMANN, B.; AND YAMASHITA, D. *J. Med. Syst.* **9**, 5/6, (Dec. 1985) 379–388.

**02376** A regression model to identify successful learner traits with CAI. PAULANKA, B. *J. Med. Syst.* **10**, 2, (April 1986) 121–138.

**02377** An inexpensive and portable talking-tactile terminal for the visually handicapped. KARSHMER, A.; MYLER, H.; AND DAVIS, R. *J. Med. Syst.* **10**, 3, (June 1986) 229–244.

**02378** Design of an integral computer-based wheelchair controller/linear synchronous motor system. KELLY, G.; ROSS, D.; BASS, R.; AND DAVEY, K. *J. Med. Syst.* **10**, 3, (June 1986) 245–254.

**02379** Human factors design of a video monitor emulator and display (VMED) for visuallyimpaired computer users. KELLY, G.; ROSS, D.; AND MOODY, L. *J. Med. Syst.* **10**, 3, (June 1986) 255–264.

HCI-0407 Resistance to computerization: an examination of the relationship between resistance and the cognitive style of the clinician. MANDELL, S. *J. Med. Syst.* **11**, 4, (Aug. 1987) 311–318.

02380 Implementation of a multirule, multistage quality control program in a clinical laboratory computer system. EGGERT, A.; WESTGARD, J.; BARRY, P.; AND EMMERICH, K. *J. Med. Syst.* **11**, 6, (December 1987) 391–411.

02381 AI/learn: an interactive videodisk system for teaching medical concepts and reasoning. MITCHELL, J.; LEE, A.; TENBRINK, T.; CUTTS, J.; AND CLARK, D. *J. Med. Syst.* **11**, 6, (Dec. 1987) 421–429.

## Journal of Microcomputer Applications

02382 Microtechnology and user friendly systems—the CONNECT dialogue executor. ALTY, J.; AND BROOKS, A. *J. Microcomput. Appl.* **8**, 4, (Oct. 1985) 333–346.

02383 A serial interface for process control. RANDALL, E.; AND FLACH, L. *J. Microcomput. Appl.* **8**, 4, (Oct. 1985) 359–368.

HCI-0445 Interactive critical path analysis (ICPA)—microcomputer implementation of a project management and knowledge engineering tool. BARBER, T.; MARSHALL, G.; AND BOARDMAN, J. *J. Microcomput. Appl.* **9**, 1, (Jan. 1986) 1–13.

HCI-0119 A dedicated microcomputer for handwritten interaction with a software tool: system prototyping. PLAMONDON, R.; AND BARON, R. *J. Microcomput. Appl.* **9**, 1, (Jan. 1986) 51–61.

02384 Microcomputing in motion analysis. BURNIE, J.; TAYLOR, M.; AND YUEN, P. *J. Microcomput. Appl.* **10**, 2, (April 1, 1987) 113–117.

## Journal of Molecular Graphics

02385 An interactive modeling program for DNA. TREGER, M.; AND WESTOF, E. *J. Mol. Graph.* **5**, 4, (December 1987) 178–183.

02386 An interactive biomolecule graphics system. WU, J.; GUAN, Y.; AND ZHENG, Q. *J. Mol. Graph.* **5**, 4, (December 1987) 190–192.

02387 The MIDAS database system. FERRIN, T.; HUANG, C.; JARVIS, L.; AND LANGRIDGE, R. *J. Mol. Graph.* **6**, 1, (March 1988) 2–12.

02388 The MIDAS display system. FERRIN, T.; HUANG, C.; JARVIS, L.; AND LANGRIDGE, R. *J. Mol. Graph.* **6**, 1, (March 1988) 13–27.

02389 MOL3D, a modular and interactive program for molecular modeling and conformational analysis: I—basic modules. PATTOU, D.; AND MAIGRET, B. *J. Mol. Graph.* **6**, 2, (June 1988) 112–121.

## Journal of Object-Oriented Programming

02390 A cookbook for using the model-view controller user interface paradigm in Smalltalk-80. KRASNER, G.; AND POPE, S. *J. Object-Oriented Program.* **1**, 3, (Aug./Sept. 1988) 26–49.

02391 Graphics through the looking glass. LALONDE, W.; AND PUGH, J. *J. Object-Oriented Program.* **1**, 3, (Aug./Sept. 1988) 52–58.

## Journal of Pascal, Ada & Modula-2

02392 EM2—a Modula-2 programming environment. BUCHS, D.; HARMS, J.; AND LIGIER, Y. *J. Pascal Ada Modula-2* **7**, 6, (Nov./Dec. 1988) 22–29.

02393 Programming the mouse in Turbo Pascal 4.0. RIGHTER, D. *J. Pascal Ada Modula-2* **7**, 6, (Nov./Dec. 1988) 62–67.

## JOURNALS

**02394** Mac programming tools: prototyper version 2.0 eases interface design. SHAFER, D. *J. Pascal Ada Modula-2* **8**, 2, (March/April 1989) 33–39.

**02395** Ada info: apologies to TEXT_10. JONES, D. *J. Pascal Ada Modula-2* **8**, 2, (March/April 1989) 51–52.

## Journal of Quality Technology

**02396** Classifying sensory inspectors with heterogeneous inspection-error probabilities. BENSON, G.; AND OHTA, H. *J. Qual. Technol.* **18**, 2, (April 1986) 79–90.

## Journal of Symbolic Computation

**02397** GI/S: A graphical user interface for symbolic computation systems. YOUNG, D.; AND WANG, P. *J. Symbolic Comput.* **4**, 3, (Dec. 1988) 365–380.

**02398** A deductive database based on Aristotelian logic. MOZES, E. *J. Symbolic Comput.* **7**, 5, (May 1989) 487–507.

## Journal of Systems and Software

**HCI-0157** Human factors in software engineering: a review of the literature. LAUGHERY, K.; AND LAUGHERY, K. *J. Syst. Softw.* **5**, 1, (Feb. 1985) 3–14.

**02399** Automated interactive simulation modeling system: AISIM. MERRIMAN, M. *J. Syst. Softw.* **7**, 1, (March 1, 1987) 61–72.

**02400** Toward a formal specification of menu-based systems. ARTHUR, J. *J. Syst. Softw.* **7**, 1, (March 1, 1987) 73–82.

**02401** DRAT: A program for maintaining listings. LAMB, D.; DURHAM, I.; AND NEWCOMER, J. *J. Syst. Softw.* **7**, 2, (June 1, 1987) 163–170.

**02402** Experience with a functional layered multicomputer architecture for interactive processing. AMBLER, A. *J. Syst. Softw.* **7**, 4, (December 1, 1987) 267–277.

**02403** Cognitive processes in program comprehension. LETOVSKY, S. *J. Syst. Softw.* **7**, 4, (December 1, 1987) 325–339.

**02404** Mental models and software maintenance. LITTMAN, D.; PINTO, J.; LETOVSKY, S.; AND SOLOWAY, E. *J. Syst. Softw.* **7**, 4, (December 1, 1987) 341–355.

**02405** Programmer-nonprogrammer differences in specifying procedures to people and computers. ONORATO, L.; AND SCHVANEVELDT, R. *J. Syst. Softw.* **7**, 4, (December 1, 1987) 357–369.

**02406** Linkage versus integration for binding database and interactive graphics systems. ZAKI, M.; AND SALAMA, R. *J. Syst. Softw.* **8**, 5, (Dec. 1988) 361–372.

**02407** Problems, problems, problems... WETZEL, G.; AND BULGREN, W. *J. Syst. Softw.* **9**, 4, (May 1989) 297–303.

## Journal of Systems Management

**02408** Selection systems for sales representatives. NYKODYM, N.; WILKINS, P.; AND RUUD, W. *J. Syst. Manage.* **37**, 8, (Aug. 1986) 11–17.

**02409** Education requirements for the entry level business systems analyst. JENKINS, G. *J. Syst. Manage.* **37**, 8, (Aug. 1986) 30–33.

**02410** The human connection in systems design. MARTIN, M. *J. Syst. Manage.* **37**, 10, (Oct. 1986) 6–29.

**02411** Designing information systems for people. BURCH, J. *J. Syst. Manage.* **37**, 10, (Oct. 1986) 30–33.

**02412** Qualities of a good forms designer. MYERS, G. *J. Syst. Manage.* **37**, 11, (Nov. 1986) 38–39.

**02413** A database primer on natural language. BARBARY, C. *J. Syst. Manage.* **38**, 4, (April 1987) 20–25.

**02414** TA: Can it improve worker satisfaction with organizational decision-making? KYKODYM, N.; RUUD, W.; AND LIVERPOOL, P. *J. Syst. Manage.* **38**, 5, (May 1, 1987) 18–21.

**02415** User programmer and costs of the misinformed user. GIBSON, M.; AND CORMAN, L. *J. Syst. Manage.* **38,** 5, (May 1, 1987) 23–29.
**02416** User's complaints: Information system problems from the user's perspective. HOWARD, G.; AND WEINROTH, G. *J. Syst. Manage.* **38,** 5, (May 1, 1987) 30–34.
**02417** Change and the systems person. HOKANSSON, N. *J. Syst. Manage.* **38,** 5, (May 1, 1987) 35–36.
**02418** Application software documentation. GUILLEMETTE, R. *J. Syst. Manage.* **38,** 5, (May 1, 1987) 36–39.
**02419** Human factors principles. MARTIN, M. *J. Syst. Manage.* **38,** 7, (July 1, 1987) 6–13.
**02420** Designing systems for change. MARTIN, M. *J. Syst. Manage.* **38,** 7, (July 1, 1987) 14–18.
**02421** Prototypes for user training. MARTIN, M. *J. Syst. Manage.* **38,** 7, (July 1, 1987) 19–22.
**02422** Importance of the human factor in the information system life cycle. SEILHEIMER, S. *J. Syst. Manage.* **38,** 7, (July 1, 1987) 24–27.
**02423** The impact of information systems strategy on end user computing. SUMNER, M.; AND KLEPPER, R. *J. Syst. Manage.* **38,** 10, (October 1, 1987) 12–17.
**02424** The end user attack: Will the real computer professionals stand up and fight. CORBIN, D. *J. Syst. Manage.* **38,** 10, (October 1, 1987) 24–25.
**02425** Managing end user computing when the only constant is change. KARTEN, N. *J. Syst. Manage.* **38,** 10, (October 1, 1987) 26–29.
**02426** Structuring informal information. BARLOW, J. *J. Syst. Manage.* **39,** 1, (January 1988) 28–32.
**02427** Components of user work stations. GIBSON, M. *J. Syst. Manage.* **39,** 2, (February 1988) 6–14.
**02428** End user computing—the human interface. SPENCE, J. *J. Syst. Manage.* **39,** 2, (February 1988) 15–21.
**02429** Documentation in a user work station environment. RICHARDS, R.; AND WINDSOR, J. *J. Syst. Manage.* **39,** 2, (February 1988) 23–29.
**02430** Managing the work station environment. HUGHES, G. *J. Syst. Manage.* **39,** 2, (February 1988) 30–35.
**02431** The user designer/developer and the user work station. GIBSON, M.; AND HUGHES, G. *J. Syst. Manage.* **39,** 2, (February 1988) 36–41.
**02432** Strategic IRM plan: user involvement spells success. CORBIN, D. *J. Syst. Manage.* **39,** 5, (May 1988) 12–16.
**02433** Motivators vs. demotivators in the IS environment. COUGER, J. *J. Syst. Manage.* **39,** 6, (June 1988) 36–41.
**02434** End user software selection. ARCHER, N. *J. Syst. Manage.* **39,** 7, (July 1988) 32–39.
**02435** Use of fourth generation languages: application development and documentation problems. NECCO, C.; AND TSAI, N. *J. Syst. Manage.* **39,** 8, (August 1988) 26–33.
**02436** Strategies for managing end user computing. SAARINEN, T.; HEIKKILA, J.; AND SAAKSJARVI, M. *J. Syst. Manage.* **39,** 8, (August 1988) 34–39.
**02437** A practical guide to the first time user/systems developer. PODOROWSKY, G. *J. Syst. Manage.* **39,** 9, (September 1988) 24–27.
**02438** The case of the rejected applicants. STEVENS, R. *J. Syst. Manage.* **39,** 9, (September 1988) 38–39.
**02439** The VDTs are here: health hazard and all. TRINKAUS, J.; AND GREENBERG, M. *J. Syst. Manage.* **39,** 10, (Oct. 1988) 6–14.
**02440** Expert systems as human resource management decision tools. EXTEJT, M.; AND LYNN, M. *J. Syst. Manage.* **39,** 11, (Nov. 1988) 10–15.
**02441** An expert system for system design. HEINRICH, S.; AND CHRYSLER, E. *J. Syst. Manage.* **39,** 11, (Nov. 1988) 17–25.
**02442** How well do you write user documentation? KLINNER, P.; AND FRIDAY, K. *J. Syst. Manage.* **39,** 12, (Dec. 1988) 27–30.
**02443** Quality control of personal computing. FRANK, J. *J. Syst. Manage.* **39,** 12, (Dec. 1988) 32–39.
**02444** Utilizing the trend of end user development. LIU, J. *J. Syst. Manage.* **40,** 1, (January 1989) 38–40.

## Journal of the American Society for Information Science

**02445** Person-to-person communication in an applied research/service delivery setting. SALASIN, J.; AND CEDAR, T. *J. Am. Soc. Inf. Sci.* **36,** 2, (March 1986) 103–115.

## JOURNALS

02446   Electronic publishing: The predicament of occasional users in the editorial proc. STANDERA, O. *J. Am. Soc. Inf. Sci.* **36**, 4, (July 1985) 230–240.

02447   An investigation of online searcher traits and their relationship to search outcomes. BELLARDO, T. *J. Am. Soc. Inf. Sci.* **36**, 4, (July 1985) 241–250.

02448   The dimensions of perceived accessibility to information: Implications for the delivery if information systems and services. CULNAN, M. *J. Am. Soc. Inf. Sci.* **36**, 5, (Sept. 1986) 302–308.

02449   Inference control mechanism for statistical database frequency-imposed data distortions. LIEW, C.; CHOI, U.; AND LIEW, C. *J. Am. Soc. Inf. Sci.* **36**, 5, (Sept. 1986) 322–329.

02450   The effects of gender and age on preschool children's choice of the computer as a child-selected activity. BEESON SPILLERS, B.; AND WILLIAMS, A. *J. Am. Soc. Inf. Sci.* **36**, 5, (Sept. 1986) 339–341.

HCI-0283   Views on end-user searching. OJALA, M. *J. Am. Soc. Inf. Sci.* **37**, 4, (July 1986) 197–203.

HCI-0276   Transparent information systems through gateways, front ends, intermediaries, and interfaces. WILLIAMS, M. *J. Am. Soc. Inf. Sci.* **37**, 4, (July 1986) 204–214.

HCI-0269   Calibrating databases. FISCHHOFF, B.; AND MACGREGOR, D. *J. Am. Soc. Inf. Sci.* **37**, 4, (July 1986) 222–233.

HCI-0235   Observations of end-user online searching behavior over eleven years. SEWELL, W.; AND TEITELBAUM, S. *J. Am. Soc. Inf. Sci.* **37**, 4, (July 1986) 234–245.

02451   Forecasting consumer adoption of information technology and services—lessons from home video forecasting. KLOPFENSTEIN, B. *J. Am. Soc. Inf. Sci.* **40**, 1, (January 1989) 17–26.

02452   Information-seeking strategies of novices using a full-text electronic encyclopedia. MARCHIONINI, G. *J. Am. Soc. Inf. Sci.* **40**, 1, (January 1989) 54–66.

02453   The design and evaluation of a front-end user interface for energy researchers. BORGMAN, C.; CASE, D.; AND MEADOW, C. *J. Am. Soc. Inf. Sci.* **40**, 2, (March 1989) 99–109.

02454   Supporting collaboration in Hypermedia: issues and experiences. IRISH, P.; AND TRIGG, R. *J. Am. Soc. Inf. Sci.* **40**, 3, (May 1989) 192–199.

## Journal of the Chinese Institute of Engineers

02455   A computer aided design system for artistic chinese fonts. CHEN, K.; YANG, C.; AND WU, W. *J. Chin. Inst. Eng.* **9**, 4, (July 1986) 431–436.

02456   Human supervisory control in flexible manufacturing systems: Allocation of functions and system size. HWANG, S. *J. Chin. Inst. Eng.* **10**, 3, (May 1, 1987) 251–261.

## Knowledge Acquisition

02457   Conceptual models of interacitve knowledge acquisition tools. MUSEN, M. *Knowl. Acquis.* **1**, 1, (March 1989) 73–88.

## LASIE: Bulletin of LASIE Australia Company Ltd.

02458   Implementation of the Geac circulation system within the CLANN network. O'MARA, R. *LASIE Bull.* **16**, 2, (Sept./Oct. 1985) 8–20.

02459   Assessing the impacts of new technology on library employees. WATERS, D. *LASIE Bull.* **17**, 1, (July 1986) 20–27.

02460   The design and construction of a vital database. PARER, D. *LASIE Bull.* **17**, 2, (Sept. 1986) 30–38.

02461   Microcomputer availability to public library clients. WILLARD, P. *LASIE Bull.* **17**, 2, (Sept. 1986) 39–46.

02462   The user at the online catalogue. HENTY, M. *LASIE Bull.* **17**, 2, (Sept. 1986) 47–52.

## Library Hi Tech

02463 Effects of the adoption of an integrated online system on a technical services department. RHINE, L. *Libr. Hi Tech* **4**, 4, (Dec. 1986) 89–92.

02464 Technology's impact on library interior planning. MICHAELS, D. *Libr. Hi Tech* **5**, 4, (Winter 1987) 59–63.

02465 Common sense and user interfaces: issues beyond the keyboard. CRAWFORD, W. *Libr. Hi Tech* **6**, 2, (May 1988) 7–17.

02466 User interfaces for CD'ROM PACs. BILLS, L.; AND HELGERSON, L. *Libr. Hi Tech* **6**, 2, (May 1988) 73–115.

02467 The emerging role of workstations in the library environment. BAUER, M. *Libr. Hi Tech* **6**, 4, (1988) 37–46.

## Machine-Mediated Learning

02468 Development of a hand-held computerized vocabulary tutor. BRIDGEMAN, B.; AND WISHER, R. *Mach.-Mediat. Learn.* **1**, 3, (1985) 255–277.

02469 Error analysis and tutor design. GITOMER, D.; AND VAN SLYKE, D. *Mach.-Mediat. Learn.* **2**, 4, (1987/1988) 333–350.

## Macintosh Hands On

02470 Hyperbiorhythms. LAIRD, A. *Macintosh Hands On* **4**, 3, (March 1989) 30–32.

## Management Science

02471 A study of organizational effectiveness and its predictors. CAMERON, K. *Manage. Sci.* **32**, 1, (Jan. 1986) 87–112.

02472 Chief executive personality and corporate strategy and structure in small firms. MILLER, D.; AND TOULOUSE, J. *Manage. Sci.* **32**, 11, (Nov. 1986) 1389–1409.

02473 Reducing social context cues: electronic mail in organizational communication. SPROULL, L.; AND KIESLER, S. *Manage. Sci.* **32**, 11, (Nov. 1986) 1492–1512.

02474 The accuracy of combining judgemental and statistical forecasts. LAWRENCE, M.; EDMUNDSON, R.; AND O'CONNOR, M. *Manage. Sci.* **32**, 12, (Dec. 1986) 1521–1532.

02475 Adaptive coordination of a learning team. LOUNAMAA, P.; AND MARCH, J. *Manage. Sci.* **33**, 1, (Jan. 1987) 107–123.

02476 Cognitive process as a basis for MIS and DSS design. RAMAPRASAD, A. *Manage. Sci.* **33**, 2, (Feb. 1987) 139–148.

02477 Combining overlapping information. CLEMEN, R. *Manage. Sci.* **33**, 3, (March 1987) 373–380.

02478 Frames of mind in intertemporal choice. LOEWENSTEIN, G. *Manage. Sci.* **34**, 2, (Feb. 1988) 200–214.

02479 A study of user interface aids for model-oriented decision support systems. DOS SANTOS, B.; AND BARIFF, M. *Manage. Sci.* **34**, 4, (April 1988) 461–468.

02480 Decision analysis: practice and promise. HOWARD, R. *Manage. Sci.* **34**, 6, (June 1988) 679–695.

02481 Managerial influence in the implementation of new technology. LEONARD-BARTON, D.; AND DESCHAMPS, I. *Manage. Sci.* **34**, 10, (October 1988) 1252–1265.

02482 The effect of task demands and graphical format on information processing strategies. JARVENPAA, S. *Manage. Sci.* **35**, 3, (March 1989) 285–303.

02483 Modeling managerial behavior: misperceptions of feedback in a dynamic decision making experiment. STERMAN, J. *Manage. Sci.* **35**, 3, (March 1989) 321–339.

02484 Forgetting and the learning curve: a laboratory study. BAILEY, C. *Manage. Sci.* **35**, 3, (March 1989) 340–352.

02485 Firm strategies for costly engineering learning. MODY, A. *Manage. Sci.* **35**, 4, (April 1989) 496–512.

## Mathematics and Computers in Simulation

02486  The role of computer graphics in validating simulation models. GIPPS, P. *Math. Comput. Simul.* **28**, 4, (August 1986) 285–289.

02487  A model of the controller responses of the human temperature regulating system to changes in water temperature. RINGUEST, J.; GULLEDGE JR., T.; AND NEGHABAT, M. *Math. Comput. Simul.* **29**, 5, (Oct. 1987) 385–397.

## Microprocessing & Microprogramming

HCI-0096  Design of computer programs for the physically handicapped. PERKINS, J.; AND ISAACS, R. *Microprocess. Microprogram.* **13**, 1, (Feb. 1989) 55–61.

02488  Microcomputer hardware education at a Czechoslovakian Technical University. BLAZEK, Z.; AND JANES, V. *Microprocess. Microprogram.* **17**, 2, (Feb. 1986) 77–78.

02489  A Unix distributed application support suitable for mini and microcomputer based systems. MARTINS, J.; AND NOGUEZ, G. *Microprocess. Microprogram.* **21**, 1-5, (Aug. 1987) 205–210.

02490  An abstract description generator for the reliability analysis in the design of real time systems. BINAGHI, E.; LISCA, L.; PROSERPIO, A.; AND SECHI, G. *Microprocess. Microprogram.* **23**, 1-5, (March 1988) 157–166.

02491  A model for assessing the performance of a local area network employing technical office protocol (TOP) as part of MAP/TOP network in a computer integrated manufacturing (CIM) research project, for the transmission of real time interactive speech. LINES, B. *Microprocess. Microprogram.* **23**, 1-5, (March 1988) 199–202.

02492  A portable query language for small scale systems. PAPAZOGLOU, M. *Microprocess. Microprogram.* **23**, 1-5, (March 1988) 299–304.

02493  A personal computer based graphic workstation. BRUCK, K.; KIRILOV, A.; KRUSHINSKY, D.; PRIKHODKO, V.; AND VOIGT, K. *Microprocess. Microprogram.* **23**, 1-5, (March 1988) 357–358.

02494  Graphics fundamentals for a PCB-CAD PC system. BERCE, J. *Microprocess. Microprogram.* **23**, 1-5, (March 1988) 359–364.

02495  An external data structure tool for Pascal. BISSETT, A.; AND FORREST, J. *Microprocess. Microprogram.* **25**, 1-5, (Jan. 1989) 387–390.

## Microprocessors & Microsystems

02496  Graphbug - a microprocessor software debugging tool. DAVIES, A.; AND GOUSSOUS, A. *Microprocess. Microsyst.* **10**, 4, (May 1986) 195–201.

02497  :10Transparent:10 interfacing of speech recognizers to microcomputers. DABBAGH, H.; DAMPER, R.; AND GUY, D. *Microprocess. Microsyst.* **10**, 7, (Sept. 1986) 371–376.

02498  Natural language interface based on keyword extraction using AWK. PRASAD, K.; AND LAMBA, T. *Microprocess. Microsyst.* **11**, 3, (April 1, 1987) 157–160.

02499  Modelling 8-bit microprocessors for a general-purpose simulator. WINDER, R. *Microprocess. Microsyst.* **12**, 8, (Oct. 1988) 443–453.

## Mini-Micro Software

02500  Headstart—a lifeline for the disabled. *Mini-Micro Softw.* **11**, 4, (1986) 4–5.

## MIS Quarterly

02501  Information systems development success: Perspectives from project team participants. WHITE, K.; AND LEIFER, R. *MIS Q.* **10**, 3, (Sept. 1986) 215–223.

02502 The effects of 3D imagery on managerial data interpretation. LEE, J.; MACLACHLAN, J.; AND WALLACE, W. *MIS Q.* **10**, 3, (Sept. 1986) 257–269.
02503 Service support levels: An organizational approach to end-user computing. LEITHEISER, R.; AND WETHERBE, J. *MIS Q.* **10**, 4, (Dec. 1986) 337–351.
02504 System development methods—a comparative investigation. MAHMOOD, M. *MIS Q.* **11**, 3, (Sept. 1987) 293–311.
02505 Message equivocality, media selection and manager performance: implications for information systems. DAFT, R.; LENGEL, R.; AND TREVINO, L. *MIS Q.* **11**, 3, (Sept. 1987) 355–366.
02506 Training end users: an exploratory study. NELSON, R.; AND CHENEY, P. *MIS Q.* **11**, 4, (Dec. 1987) 547–559.
02507 Critical factors in the user environment: an experimental study of users, organizations and tasks. YAVERBAUM, G. *MIS Q.* **12**, 1, (March 1988) 75–88.
02508 The effect of user involvement on system success: a contingency approach. TAIT, P.; AND VESSEY, I. *MIS Q.* **12**, 1, (March 1988) 91–108.
02509 Restoring a sense of control during implementation: how user involvement leads to system acceptance. BARONAS, A.; AND LOUIS, M. *MIS Q.* **12**, 1, (March 1988) 111–124.
02510 The measurement of end-user computing satisfaction. DOLL, W.; AND TORKZADEH, G. *MIS Q.* **12**, 2, (June 1988) 259–274.
02511 Are information systems people different? An investigation of how they are and should be managed. FERRATT, T.; AND SHORT, L. *MIS Q.* **12**, 3, (Sept. 1988) 427–443.
02512 Dialogue management: support for dialogue independence. KUO, F.; AND KONSYNSKI, B. *MIS Q.* **12**, 3, (Sept. 1988) 481–499.

## Multilingua

02513 LSP-automatic translation and information technology. PENNING, L. *Multilingua* **5**, 2, (1986) 110–111.
02514 Environments for Eurota. KING, M. *Multilingua* **5**, 3, (1986) 170–174.

## New Generation Computing

02515 Spreadsheets with incremental queries as a user interface for logic programming. VAN EMDEN, M.; OHKI, M.; AND TAKEUCHI, A. *New Gen. Comput.* **4**, 3, (1986) 287–304.

## Office Technology and People

02516 Systems design and social responsibility: the political implications of "computer-supported cooperative work". A commentary. HOWARD, R. *Off. Technol. People* **3**, 2, (August 1, 1987) 175–187.

## Online

02517 History offers clues to the future: user control returns. CUADRA, C. *Online* **11**, 1, (January 2, 1987) 46–48.
02518 Choreography for technology and humans. EDDISON, E. *Online* **11**, 1, (January 2, 1987) 49–50.
02519 End-users: Dreams or dollars. ARNOLD, S. *Online* **11**, 1, (January 2, 1987) 71–81.
02520 Putting on a show: using computer graphics to train end-users. BATISTA, E.; AND EINHORN, D. *Online* **11**, 3, (May 1987) 88–92.
02521 How good an Online searcher are you? Twenty questions about BIOSIS previews. VAN CAMP, A. *Online* **11**, 6, (Nov. 1987) 41–42.
02522 What is the role of the intermediary in end-user training? WITIAK, J. *Online* **12**, 5, (September 1988) 50–52.
02523 IBM DOS 4.0: a bridge to OS/2. PHILLIPS, B. *Online* **13**, 4, (July 1989) 28–32.

02524 An online interface within a hypertext system: project Jefferson's electronic notebook. KINNELL, S.; AND RICHARDS, T. *Online* **13,** 4, (July 1989) 33–38.

02525 Datastream: numeric data—all you can use at a fixed price. HALPERIN, M. *Online* **13,** 4, (July 1989) 78–80.

## Operations Research

02526 An empirical formula for visual search. KOOPMAN, B. *Oper. Res.* **34,** 3, (May-June 1986) 377–383.

02527 Descriptive analysis for computer-based decision support. SILVER, M. *Oper. Res.* **36,** 6, (Nov./Dec. 1988) 904–916.

02528 Design and implementation of an interactive optimization system for network design in the motor carrier industry. POWELL, W.; AND SHEFFI, Y. *Oper. Res.* **37,** 1, (Jan.-Feb. 1989) 12–29.

## Pattern Recognition

02529 Handprinted chinese character recognition via neural networks. YONG, Y. *Pattern Recogn.* **7,** 1, (January 1988) 19–25.

02530 Multidimensional attribute analyhsis and pattern recognition for seismic interpretation. JUSTICE, J.; HAWKINS, D.; AND WONG, G. *Pattern Recogn.* **18,** 6, (1985) 391–407.

HCI-0243 Eye movement analysis system using fundus images. KAWAI, H.; TAMURA, S.; KANI, K.; AND KARIYA, K. *Pattern Recogn.* **19,** 1, (Jan./Feb. 1986) 77–84.

HCI-0394 Multivariate data representation and analysis by face pattern using facial expression characteristics. HONDA, N.; AND SUGIMOTO, F. *Pattern Recogn.* **19,** 1, (Jan./Feb. 1986) 85–94.

02531 On the minimum number of templates required for shift, rotation and size invariant pattern recognition. CAELLI, T.; AND LIU, Z. *Pattern Recogn.* **21,** 3, (1988) 205–216.

02532 A high accuracy algorithm for recognition of handwritten numerals. BAPTISTA, G.; AND KULKARNI, K. *Pattern Recogn.* **21,** 4, (1988) 287–291.

02533 Image compression using polylines. PHAM, D.; AND ABDOLLAHI, M. *Pattern Recogn.* **21,** 6, (1988) 631–637.

02534 Structural aspects of semantic-directed clusters. SHEKAR, B.; MURTY, M.; AND KRISHNA, G. *Pattern Recogn.* **22,** 1, (January 1989) 65–74.

## Pattern Recognition Letters

02535 Interactive curve drawing by segmented Bezier approximation with a control parameter. CHAUDHURI, B.; AND DUTTA, S. *Pattern Recogn. Lett.* **4,** 3, (July 1986) 171–176.

02536 Algorithm for interactive forming matrix data representation and estimation of its efficiency. VERIN, L.; AND GRISHIN, V. *Pattern Recogn. Lett.* **4,** 3, (July 1986) 193–200.

02537 Pattern storage and associative memory in quasi-neural network. FORSHAW, M. *Pattern Recogn. Lett.* **4,** 6, (Dec. 1986) 427–431.

02538 Thresholding for edge detection using human psychovisual phenomena. KUNDU, M.; AND PAL, S. *Pattern Recogn. Lett.* **4,** 6, (Dec. 1986) 433–441.

02539 Effect of fuzzy membership on recognition of gray level images. CHEN, N.; AND BEFROSIAN, S. *Pattern Recogn. Lett.* **4,** 6, (Dec. 1986) 443–447.

02540 A system for the representation of human body movement from dance scores. HACHIMURA, K.; AND OHNO, Y. *Pattern Recogn. Lett.* **5,** 1, (January 2, 1987) 1–9.

02541 An outline of the primal sketch in human vision. WATT, R. *Pattern Recogn. Lett.* **5,** 2, (February 1, 1987) 139–150.

02542 An appropriate representation for early vision. MOWFORTH, P.; JELINEK, J.; AND JIN, Z. *Pattern Recogn. Lett.* **5,** 2, (February 1, 1987) 175–182.

02543 Segmentation using contrast and homogeneity measures. PAL, S.; AND PAL, N. *Pattern Recogn. Lett.* **5**, 4, (April 1, 1987) 293–304.

## PC/Computing

02544 User interface wars: the next wave. BONNER, P. *PC/Comput.* **1**, 4, (Nov. 1988) 72–82.
02545 Videotex redux. MARGULIUS, D. *PC/Comput.* **2**, 1, (January 1989) 190–202.
02546 NEXT. BRODY, H. *PC/Comput.* **2**, 2, (February 1989) 263–268.
02547 KIDS. SUMMER, T. *PC/Comput.* **2**, 2, (February 1989) 271–274.
02548 The body in question: how to stay healthy at the PC. BRODY, H. *PC/Comput.* **2**, 3, (March 1989) 140–145.
02549 VDTs: are they safe? ROSS, R. *PC/Comput.* **2**, 3, (March 1989) 146–147.
02550 Building a great windows system. BONNER, P. *PC/Comput.* **2**, 5, (May 1989) 104–113.
02551 Portfolio: kaleidoscopic visions. ELLIDON, C. *PC/Comput.* **2**, 5, (May 1989) 116–121.
02552 Mondo media. BRAND, S. *PC/Comput.* **2**, 5, (May 1989) 140–147.

## Personal Computing

02553 Breaking away. CARUSO, D. *Pers. Comput.* **10**, 7, (July 1986) 90–97.
02554 Graphics. LOCKWOOD, R. *Pers. Comput.* **11**, 10, (Oct. 1987) 138–143.
02555 Unix: tomorrow's operating system? O'MALLEY, C. *Pers. Comput.* **12**, 6, (June, 1988) 100–108.
02556 What's new in personal information managers. O'MALLEY, C. *Pers. Comput.* **12**, 7, (July 1988) 123–128.

## Perspectives on Technology

02557 Peopleware. BISBERG, C. *Perspec. Technol.* **1**, 1, (Fall 1987) 15–16.

## Physica D

02558 Nonlinear dynamics of pattern formation and pattern recognition in the rabbit olfactory bulb. BAIRD, B. *Physica D* **2D**, 1-3, (Oct.-Nov. 1986) 150–175.
02559 The immune system, adaptation, and machine learning. FARMER, J.; PACKARD, N.; AND PERELSON, A. *Physica D* **2D**, 1-3, (Oct.-Nov. 1986) 187–204.
02560 Neural network models of learning and adaptation. DENKER, J. *Physica D* **2D**, 1-3, (Oct.-Nov. 1986) 216–232.
02561 A teachable neural network based on an unorthodox neuron. HOFFMANN, G.; BENSON, M.; BREE, G.; AND KINAHAN, P. *Physica D* **2D**, 1-3, (Oct.-Nov. 1986) 233–246.
02562 A self-optimizing, nonsymmetrical neural net for content addressable memory and pattern recognition. LAPEDES, A.; AND FARBER, R. *Physica D* **2D**, 1-3, (Oct.-Nov. 1986) 247–259.
02563 Machine learning using a higher order correlation network. LEE, Y.; DOOLEN, G.; CHEN, H.; SUN, G.; MAXWELL, T.; LEE, H.; AND GILES, C. *Physica D* **2D**, 1-3, (Oct.-Nov. 1986) 276–306.
02564 Psychological concepts in a parallel system. ANDERSON, J.; AND MURPHY, G. *Physica D* **2D**, 1-3, (Oct.-Nov. 1986) 318–336.
02565 Can mathematics explain natural intelligence? MYCIELSKI, J. *Physica D* **2D**, 1-3, (Oct.-Nov. 1986) 366–375.

## Production and Inventory Management

02566 Using worker's survey to improve production. CHONG, P.; AND MUCCI, M. *Prod. Inventory Manage.* **6**, 10, (Oct. 1986) 68–76.

02567  Produciton and inventory management software packages related to user reactions. RUSHINEK, A.; AND RUSHINEK, S. *Prod. Inventory Manage.* **27**, 1, (Jan. 1986) 75–84.

## Program

02568  OST— a training package for end-users of online systems. ARMSTRONG, C.; AND LARGE, J. *Program* **21**, 4, (Oct. 1987) 333–349.

02569  STATUS with IQ—escaping from the Boolean straitjacket. PAPE, D.; AND JONES, R. *Program* **22**, 1, (January 1988) 32–43.

## Programmed Learning and Educational Technology

02570  Natural language processing and the language-impaired. WARD, R. *Program. Learn. Educ. Technol.* **23**, 2, (May 1986) 144–149.

02571  Inactive video at work. GRIFFITHS, M. *Program. Learn. Educ. Technol.* **23**, 3, (August 1986) 212–218.

02572  Learning in British Airways-A case of putting people first. BRUCE, M. *Program. Learn. Educ. Technol.* **23**, 3, (August 1986) 236–241.

## Resource Sharing and Information Networks

02573  Barriers to cooperative computerized circulation systems in public libraries. HEISE, G. *Resour. Shar. Inf. Networks* **3**, 1, (Fall/Winter 1985-86) 83–99.

## Scholarly Publishing

02574  Technology and the author's labour. LUEY, B. *Sch. Publ.* **20**, 2, (January 1989) 72–83.

## Science Digest

02575  A boy and his brain machine. CRYPTON *Sci. Dig.* **94**, 8, (Aug. 1986) 36–39.

02576  Gossip as creativity. TOMPKINS, J. *Sci. Dig.* **94**, 8, (Aug. 1986) 58–63.

## Science of Computer Programming

HCI-0141  Showing programs on a screen. MEYER, B.; NERSON, J.; AND KO, S. *Sci. Comput. Program.* **5**, 2, (June 1985) 111–142.

## Scientific American

02577  Features and objects in visual processing. TREISMAN, A. *Sci. Am.* **255**, 5, (Nov. 1986) 114–125.

02578  Interfaces for advanced computing. FOLEY, J. *Sci. Am.* **257**, 4, (Oct. 1987) 126–135.

## SIAM Journal on Control and Optimization

02579  Relative information capacity of simple relational database schemata. HULL, R. *SIAM J. Control Optim.* **15**, 3, (August 1986) 856–886.

## Signal Processing

02580 Joint spatial/spatial-frequency representation. JACOBSON, L.; AND WECHSLER, H. *Signal Process.* **14**, 1, (January 1988) 37-68.

02581 Image processing with personal computers. GROEN, F.; EKKERS, R.; AND DE VRIES, R. *Signal Process.* **15**, 3, (Oct. 1988) 279-291.

## Simulation

02582 One hundred differential equations execute directly on the IBM PC. KORN, G. *Simulation* **47**, 6, (Dec. 1986) 230-232.

02583 An interactive simulator for the designing of woven fabric structures second place. SHYONG, S. *Simulation* **48**, 2, (February 1, 1987) 62-62.

02584 An expert manufacturing simulation system. FORD, D.; AND SCHROER, B. *Simulation* **48**, 5, (May 1, 1987) 193-200.

02585 Visual interactive simulation - history, recent developments, and major issues. BELL, P.; AND O'KEEFE, R. *Simulation* **49**, 3, (September 1, 1987) 109-116.

02586 Interactive graphics in GPSS/PC. COX, S. *Simulation* **49**, 3, (September 1, 1987) 117-122.

02587 Expanding the domain of systems analysis. BRANNEN, J.; AND HEIBERT-DODD, K. *Simulation* **49**, 4, (October 1, 1987) 141-149.

02588 Hierarchical, modular discrete-event modelling in an object-oriented environment. ZEIGLER, B. *Simulation* **49**, 5, (November 1, 1987) 219-230.

## Simulation and Games

02589 Student perceptions of skill acquisition through cases and a general management simulation. MILES, J.; BIGGS, W.; AND SCHUBERT, J. *Simul. Games* **17**, 1, (March 1986) 7-24.

02590 But what will the workers do? simulating what the workers do to us when we do what we do to them. ESTES, J. *Simul. Games* **17**, 2, (June 1986) 245-262.

02591 Simulations of behavior in competitive situations. NAUMIENKO, E.; AND NAUMIENKO, B. *Simul. Games* **17**, 3, (Sept. 1986) 301-319.

02592 Simulations and anxiety related to public speaking. JONES, K. *Simul. Games* **17**, 3, (Sept. 1986) 327-344.

02593 Human and computer involvement in simulation. CROOKALL, D.; MARTIN, A.; SAUNDERS, D.; AND COOTE, A. *Simul. Games* **17**, 3, (Sept. 1986) 345-375.

02594 Comparison of video game and conventional test performance. JONES, M.; DUNLAP, W.; AND BILODEAU, I. *Simul. Games* **17**, 4, (Dec. 1986) 435-446.

02595 The marble company: The design and implementation of a simulation board game. LEDERMAN, L.; AND STEWART, L. *Simul. Games* **18**, 1, (March 1, 1987) 57-81.

02596 Community design and gaming/simulation: Comparison of communications techniques in participatory design sessions. HASELL, M. *Simul. Games* **18**, 1, (March 1, 1987) 82-115.

02597 Team cohesion effects on business game performance. WOLFE, J.; AND BOX, T. *Simul. Games* **19**, 1, (March 1988) 82-98.

02598 Using simulation to study complex problem solving: a review of studies in the FRG. FUNKE, J. *Simul. Games* **19**, 3, (Sept. 1988) 277-303.

## Small Computers in Libraries

02599 Front end games. ALBERICO, R. *Small Comput. Libr.* **6**, 2, (Feb. 1986) 10-15.

02600 Real librarians don't program...do they? BEISER, K. *Small Comput. Libr.* **6**, 2, (Feb. 1986) 16-19.

02601 Where person meets machine. ALBERICO, R. *Small Comput. Libr.* **7**, 4, (April 1, 1987) 12-15.

JOURNALS

02602 User-supported artificial intelligence. ALBERICO, R. *Small Comput. Libr.* **8**, 2, (Feb. 1988) 4–9.
02603 A user-unfriendly WELCOME. GIMPEL, M. *Small Comput. Libr.* **8**, 2, (Feb. 1988) 27–28.
02604 Directories, DOS, and hard disks: impact on the user. PETERSON, D. *Small Comput. Libr.* **8**, 10, (November 1988) 4–9.
02605 User orientation for the electronic encyclopedia. PURCELL, R. *Small Comput. Libr.* **9**, 2, (February 1989) 16–18.

## Social Science Computer Review

02606 Communication issues among psychologists working with computers: a view from the top. MRUK, C. *Soc. Sci. Comput. Rev.* **6**, 4, (December 1988) 527–535.

## Software Engineering Journal

02607 Towards the formal specification of a simple programming support environment. SUFRIN, B.; AND WOODCOCK, J. *Softw. Eng. J.* **2**, 4, (July 1987) 86–94.
02608 Direct manipulation of an object store. SAWYER, P.; AND SOMMERVILLE, I. *Softw. Eng. J.* **3**, 6, (Nov. 1988) 214–222.
02609 Dynamic reconfigurability for fast prototyping of user interfaces. GRAY, P.; KILGOUR, A.; AND WOOD, C. *Softw. Eng. J.* **3**, 6, (Nov. 1988) 257–262.
02610 A model for graphical interaction. ROBINSON, P. *Softw. Eng. J.* **3**, 6, (Nov. 1988) 263–268.

## Software-Practice & Experience

HCI-0142 A debugger for concurrent programs. GAIT, J. *Softw. Pract. Exper.* **15**, 6, (June 1985) 539–554.
02611 A VLSI interactive layout editor (VILE). ALLEN, G.; AND PERRY, S. *Softw. Pract. Exper.* **15**, 8, (Aug. 1985) 795–806.
HCI-0149 SOFTLIB—A documentation management system. SOMMERVILLE, I.; WELLAND, R.; BENNETT, I.; AND THOMPSON, R. *Softw. Pract. Exper.* **16**, 2, (Feb. 1986) 131–143.
HCI-0280 CONTEXT: an on-line documentation system. RAGAN, R. *Softw. Pract. Exper.* **16**, 3, (March 1986) 217–224.
HCI-0261 An almost path-free very high-level interactive data manipulation language for a microcomputer-based database system. SCHACH, S.; AND WOOD, P. *Softw. Pract. Exper.* **16**, 3, (March 1986) 243–268.
HCI-0166 A communication system supporting large datagrams on a local area network. LINTON, A.; AND PANZIERI, F. *Softw. Pract. Exper.* **16**, 3, (March 1986) 278–289.
02612 Interactive documentation. BROWN, P. (Ed.) *Softw. Pract. Exper.* **16**, 3, (March 1986) 292–299.
02613 The construction of information management system prototypes in Ada. BURNS, A.; AND KIRKHAM, J. *Softw. Pract. Exper.* **16**, 4, (April. 1986) 341–350.
02614 Dbxtool: A window-based symbolic debugger for sun workstations. ADAMS, E.; AND MUCHNICK, S. *Softw. Pract. Exper.* **16**, 7, (July. 1986) 653–669.
02615 Icecream, transportable software for creating friendly human interfaces. LINNAINMAA, S. *Softw. Pract. Exper.* **16**, 8, (Aug. 1986) 739–750.
02616 A practical approach to data modelling in spatial applications. NORRIS-SHERBORN, A.; AND MILNE, W. *Softw. Pract. Exper.* **16**, 10, (October 1986) 893–913.
02617 Computing advice at a distance: the 'remote advisory' concept. ANSTEY, P. *Softw. Pract. Exper.* **16**, 11, (November 1986) 1045–1052.
02618 Strongly typed user interfaces in an abstract data store. POWELL, M. *Softw. Pract. Exper.* **17**, 4, (April 1987) 241–266.
02619 The design of a terminal independent package. THIMBLEBY, H. *Softw. Pract. Exper.* **17**, 5, (May 1987) 351–367.
02620 Generating reversible programs. BRIGGS, J. *Softw. Pract. Exper.* **17**, 7, (July 1987) 439–454.

02621 Dynamic compilation in the Unix environment. CROWE, M. *Softw. Pract. Exper.* **17,** 7, (July 1987) 455–467.
02622 Music—a language for typesetting music scores. FOXLEY, E. *Softw. Pract. Exper.* **17,** 8, (Aug. 1987) 485–502.
HCI-0385 The use of colour in language syntax analysis. REYNOLDS, C. *Softw. Pract. Exper.* **17,** 8, (Aug. 1987) 513–519.
02623 A debugger for a graphical workstation. BOVEY, J. *Softw. Pract. Exper.* **17,** 9, (September 1, 1987) 647–662.
02624 fsh—a functional UNIX command interpreter. MCDONALD, C. *Softw. Pract. Exper.* **17,** 10, (October 1, 1987) 685–700.
02625 GCI—a tool for developing interactive CAD user interfaces. GUDES, E.; AND BRACHA, G. *Softw. Pract. Exper.* **17,** 11, (November 1, 1987) 783–799.
02626 A programmer-friendly LL(1) parser generator. GRUNE, D.; AND JACOBS, C. *Softw. Pract. Exper.* **18,** 1, (Jan., 1988) 29–38.
02627 An architectural approach to improved program maintainability. EINBU, J. *Softw. Pract. Exper.* **18,** 1, (Jan., 1988) 51–62.
02628 JDB: an adaptable interface for debugging. WINDER, R.; AND NICOLSON, J. *Softw. Pract. Exper.* **18,** 3, (March, 1988) 221–238.
02629 VIS: a virtual image system for image-understanding research. VERNON, D.; AND SANDINI, G. *Softw. Pract. Exper.* **18,** 5, (May, 1988) 395–414.
02630 Dragonmail: an exercise in distributed computing. PETERSON, L. *Softw. Pract. Exper.* **18,** 8, (August 1988) 791–803.
02631 GPROC—an integrated system for the processing of numerical scientific data. O'NEIL, M. *Softw. Pract. Exper.* **18,** 9, (September 1988) 841–857.
02632 A LISP implementation of the model for 'communicating sequential processes'. FIDGE, C. *Softw. Pract. Exper.* **18,** 10, (October 1988) 923–943.
02633 Support for graphs of processes in a command interpreter. MCDONALD, C.; AND DIX, T. *Softw. Pract. Exper.* **18,** 10, (October 1988) 1011–1016.
02634 Program generation for Ada—a case study. ALLEN, P.; AND BURNS, A. *Softw. Pract. Exper.* **18,** 12, (Dec. 1988) 1125–1138.
02635 Q'Nial: a portable interpreter for the nested interactive array language, Nial. JENKINS, M. *Softw. Pract. Exper.* **19,** 2, (February 1989) 111–126.
02636 GMB: a tool for manipulating and animating graph data structures. JABLONOWSKI, D.; AND GUARNA, V. *Softw. Pract. Exper.* **19,** 3, (March 1989) 283–301.
02637 A session editor with incremental execution functions. HOLSTI, N. *Softw. Pract. Exper.* **19,** 4, (April 1989) 329–350.
02638 The ECLIPSE user interface. SOMMERVILLE, I.; WELLAND, R.; POTTER, S.; AND SMART, J. *Softw. Pract. Exper.* **19,** 4, (April 1989) 371–391.
02639 Generation of file processing programs based on JSP. ENGMANN, R.; AND VAN HOEVE, F. *Softw. Pract. Exper.* **19,** 4, (April 1989) 393–409.
02640 A visual shell interface to a database. ROWE, L.; DANZIG, P.; AND CHOI, W. *Softw. Pract. Exper.* **19,** 6, (June 1989) 515–528.

## Speech Communication

02641 X-ray microbeam method for measurement of articulatory dynamics-techniques and results. KIRITANI, S. *Speech Commun.* **5,** 2, (June 1986) 119–140.
02642 Influence of palate shape on lingual articulation. HIKI, S.; AND ITOH, H. *Speech Commun.* **5,** 2, (June 1986) 141–158.
02643 Estimating articulatory motion from speech wave. SHIRAI, K.; AND KOBAYASHI, T. *Speech Commun.* :0B5, 2, (June 1986) 159–170.
02644 An acoustic of pathological voice and its application to the evaluation of laryngeal pathology. KASUYA, H.; OGAWA, S.; KIKUCHI, Y.; AND EBIHARA, S. *Speech Commun.* **5,** 2, (June 1986) 171–191.
02645 Research on individuality features in speech waves and automatic speaker recognition techniques. FURUI, S. *Speech Commun.* **5,** 2, (June 1986) 183–197.

02646 Speech analysis and synthesis methods developed at ECL in NTT-From LPC to LSP-. SUGAMURA, N.; AND ITAKURA, F. *Speech Commun.* **5,** 2, (June 1986) 199–215.

02647 Composite phoneme units for the speech synthesis of Japanese. SAGISAKA, Y.; AND SATO, H. *Speech Commun.* **5,** 2, (June 1986) 217–223.

02648 Recognition of phonemes using time-spectrum pattern. MAKINO, S.; AND KIDO, K. *Speech Commun.* **5,** 2, (June 1986) 225–237.

02649 Vowel normalization by frequency warped spectral matching. MATSUMOTO, H.; AND WAKITA, H. *Speech Commun.* **5,** 2, (June 1986) 239–251.

02650 A computer model of peripheral auditory processing incorporating phase-locking, suppression and adaptation effects. COOKE, M. *Speech Commun.* **5,** 3,4, (December 1986) 261–281.

02651 Changes in prosodic features of speech due to environmental factors. VILKMAN, E.; AND MANNINEN, O. *Speech Commun.* **5,** 3,4, (December 1986) 331–345.

02652 Structure of German syllable initial and final consonant clusters based on articulatory features. SECK, R.; AND RUSKE, R. *Speech Commun.* **5,** 3,4, (December 1986) 347–354.

02653 The effect of varying voice and noise parameters on the perception of voicing in Dutch two-obstruent sequences. VAN DEN BERG, R. *Speech Commun.* **5,** 3,4, (December 1986) 355–367.

02654 The measurement of the signal-to-noise ratio (SNR) in continuous speech. KLINGHOLZ, F. *Speech Commun.* **6,** 1, (March 1, 1987) 15–26.

02655 Speech motor control and stuttering: a computational model of adaptive sensory-motor processing. NEILSON, M.; AND NEILSON, P. *Speech Commun.* **6,** 4, (December 1, 1987) 325–333.

02656 Perceptual normalization of the vowels of a man and a child in various contexts. VAN BERGEM, D.; POLS, L.; AND KOOPMANS-VAN BEINUM, F. *Speech Commun.* **7,** 1, (March, 1988) 1–20.

02657 Higher pole correction in vocal tract models and terminal analogs. LAINE, U. *Speech Commun.* **7,** 1, (March, 1988) 21–40.

02658 An evaluation of auditory performances in patients with Cochlear implants. BERGER-VACHON, C.; AND MORGON, A. *Speech Commun.* **7,** 1, (March, 1988) 87–95.

02659 Distinctive regions and modes: a new theory of speech production. MRAYATI, M.; CARRÉ, R.; AND GUERIN, B. *Speech Commun.* **7,** 3, (Oct. 1988) 257–286.

02660 Coproduction: evidence from EPG data. MARCHAL, A. *Speech Commun.* **7,** 3, (Oct. 1988) 287–295.

02661 An acoustic-phonetic oriented system for synthesizing Chinese. YANG, S.; AND XU, Y. *Speech Commun.* **7,** 3, (Oct. 1988) 317–325.

## System Development

02662 Building user interfaces before writing code saves time and money. KADOR, J. *Syst. Dev.* **8,** 12, (Dec. 1988) 6–7.

## Systems Analysis Modeling Simulation

02663 Performance evaluation of simulators. SCHMIDT, B. *Syst. Anal. Model. Simul.* **3,** 3, (Oct. 1986) 241–247.

02664 Man-machine procedures of decision making under uncertainty based on linear programming. BORISOV, A.; AND VETROV, A. *Syst. Anal. Model. Simul.* **3,** 3, (Oct. 1986) 289–292.

02665 Linearization of the dynamic transfer response of time invariant nonlinear systems—in connection with the parallel information processing in living organisms. BALLA, K. *Syst. Anal. Model. Simul.* **4,** 1, (Jan. 1987) 53–59.

02666 Visuomotor control by a combined position- and speedservo. Theoretical considerations and experimental results in man. LÄSSIG, P.; KIRMSE, W.; AND YEKOYE, A. *Syst. Anal. Model. Simul.* **4,** 4, (Sept. 1987) 321–334.

02667 ATLANTIS—a software simulator for behavior analysis of protocol specifications and their target implementations. FISCHER, J. *Syst. Anal. Model. Simul.* **5,** 3, (Sept. 1988) 181–213.

02668 BNETD—A modelling tool to computer systems performance evaluation. IRMSCHER, K. *Syst. Anal. Model. Simul.* **5,** 3, (Sept. 1988) 233–241.

**02669** The KOMPLEX performance prediction tool. LEHMANN, D.; AND BERGHOLZ, G. *Syst. Anal. Model. Simul.* **5**, 3, (Sept. 1988) 243–251.

**02670** SATURN—a tool for modelling and performance evaluation of computer systems. BURGHARDT, F.; AND WIRTH, K. *Syst. Anal. Model. Simul.* **5**, 3, (Sept. 1988) 273–282.

## Technique et Science Informatiques

**02671** Natural language and computers: a general survey of written text interpretation methods. COULON, D.; AND KAYSER, D. *Tech. Sci. Inf.* **5**, 2, (March 1986) 103–128.

## Technometrics

**02672** Brushing scatterplots. BECKER, R.; AND CLEVELAND, W. *Technometrics* **29**, 2, (May 1, 1987) 127–142.

## Telematics and Informatics

**02673** The development of an intelligent user interface for NASA's scientific databases. CAMPBELL, W.; AND ROELOFS, L. *Telem. Inf.* **3**, 3, (Oct. 1986) 177–190.

**02674** The mission operators planning assistant. SCHUETZLE, J. *Telem. Inf.* **4**, 4, (January 2, 1987) 241–251.

**02675** The second generation intelligent user interface for the crustal dynamics data information system. SHORT JR., N.; AND WATTAWA, S. *Telem. Inf.* **5**, 3, (November 1988) 253–268.

**02676** Understanding cable subscribership as telecommunications behavior. LAROSE, R.; AND ATKIN, D. *Telem. Inf.* **5**, 4, (December 1988) 377–388.

**02677** Interaction of CMC with video telecourses for distance education. BELLMAN, B. *Telem. Inf.* **5**, 4, (December 1988) 389–395.

**02678** Electronic communications and collaboration: the emerging model for computer aided communications in science and medicine. LERCH, I. *Telem. Inf.* **5**, 4, (December 1988) 397–413.

**02679** Communications technology and the public sector: understanding the process of adoption. BRANSFORD, L. *Telem. Inf.* **5**, 4, (December 1988) 431–435.

**02680** Threat to privacy: the federal government's use of personal information in the new communication environment. APOSTOLOU, G. *Telem. Inf.* **5**, 4, (December 1988) 451–459.

## Transactions of the Society for Computer Simulation

**02681** Development and sensitivity analysis of adaptive predictor for human eye movement model. HARVEY, D.; AND BAHILL, A. *Trans. Soc. Comput. Simul.* **2**, 4, (Dec. 1985) 275–292.

**02682** Power plant simulation and reactor safety. HETRICK, D. *Trans. Soc. Comput. Simul.* **3**, 3, (July 1986) 173–194.

**02683** A compact model of a power house boiler. SURGENOR, B.; AND DOLEMAN, E. *Trans. Soc. Comput. Simul.* **4**, 4, (Oct. 1987) 271–297.

## University Computing

**02684** The measurement of the performance of communications protocols from the user's viewpoint. PATTINSON, C. *Univ. Comput.* **8**, 1, (Spring 1986) 37–41.

**02685** Computer Board Forum. GILMOUR, A. *Univ. Comput.* **8**, 1, (Spring 1986) 55–58.

**02686** The provision of terminal-based user support. ANSTEY, P. *Univ. Comput.* **9**, 1, (March 1, 1987) 40–44.

**02687** Developments in one-line information systems. CUNNINGHAM, D. *Univ. Comput.* **9**, 2, (June 1, 1987) 76–80.

**02688** Computing facilities in the MRC clinical research centre. RYSAVY, F. *Univ. Comput.* **9**, 2, (June 1, 1987) 87–92.

**02689** Where have all the girls gone? LOVERGROVE, G.; AND HALL, W. *Univ. Comput.* **9**, 4, (Dec. 1987) 207–210.

# Proceedings

Proceedings are listed by main entry (indicated by §) in alphabetical order by publisher and followed by the contents in page number order. Each main entry contains the title, location and date of conference, with additional bibliographic information. Please note that all prices reflect the price upon original publication and should be used only as a guide.

02690 § Empirical studies of programmers. Papers presented at the first workshop on empirical studies of programmers (Washington, DC, June 5-6, 1986), SOLOWAY, E.; AND IYENGAR, S. (Eds.) Ablex Publishing Corp., Norwood, NJ, 1986, 268 pp., $37.50, ISBN 0-89391-388-X.

02691 Empirical studies of programmers: the territory, paths, and destination. SHNEIDERMAN, B. See 02690. 1-12.
HCI-0172 Processes in computer program comprehension. WEIDENBECK, S. See 02690. 48-57.
HCI-0179 Cognitive processes in program comprehension. LETOVSKY, S. See 02690. 58-79.
HCI-0173 Mental models and software maintenance. LITTMAN, D.; PINTO, J.; LETOVSKY, S.; AND SOLOWAY, E. See 02690. 80-98.
HCI-0174 Programmer/nonprogrammer differences in specifying procedures to people and computers. ONORATO, L.; AND SCHVANEVELDT, R. See 02690. 128-137.
HCI-0175 The effects of program-dependent and program-independent deletions on software cloze tests. THOMAS, M.; AND ZWEBEN, S. See 02690. 138-152.
HCI-0176 Experimental evaluation of program quality using external metrics. HAROLD, F. See 02690. 153-167.
HCI-0155 An empirical study of the effects of modularity on program modifiability. KORSON, T.; AND VAISHNAVI, V. See 02690. 168-186.
HCI-0177 Fragile knowledge and neglected strategies in novice programmers. PERKINS, D.; AND MARTIN, F. See 02690. 213-229.
HCI-0178 Analyzing the high frequency bugs in novice programs. SPOHRER, J.; AND SOLOWAY, E. See 02690. 230-251.
02692 A plan for empirical studies of programmers. BASILI, V. See 02690. 252-255.
HCI-0038 § Human factors and interactive computer systems. Proc. of the NYU symposium on user interfaces (New York, May 26-28, 1982), VASSILIOU, Y. (Ed.) [Human/computer interaction series] Ablex Publishing Corp., Norwood, NJ, 1984, 287 pp., $34.50, ISBN 0-89391-182-8.
HCI-0186 The future of interactive systems and the emergence of direct manipulation. SHNEIDERMAN, B. See HCI-0038. 1-28.
HCI-0230 Organizing for human factors. THOMAS, J. See HCI-0038. 29-46.
HCI-0254 Query languages—a taxonomy. VASSILIOU, Y.; AND JARKE, M. See HCI-0038. 47-81.
HCI-0133 Graphical user interfaces. HEROT, C. See HCI-0038. 83-103.
02693 A multi media approach to the user interface. MCDONALD, N. See HCI-0038. 105-116.
HCI-0233 Querying external databases. LOCKHOVSKY, F.; AND TSICHRITZIS, D. See HCI-0038. 117-140.
02694 Ergonomic considerations in the design of command languages. SCHNEIDER, M. See HCI-0038. 141-161.
HCI-0255 Using restricted natural language for data retrieval: a plan for field evaluation. TURNER, J.; JARKE, M.; STOHR, F.; AND VASSILIOU, Y. See HCI-0038. 163-190.
02695 User interfaces for problem solving support. BARBER, G. See HCI-0038. 191-205.
HCI-0286 The user interface of a personal calendar program. GREIF, I. See HCI-0038. 207-222.
HCI-0136 A general user interface for creating and displaying tree-structures, hierarchies, decision trees, and nested menus. REITMAN-OLSON, J.; WHITTEN, W.; AND GRUENENFELDER, T. See HCI-0038. 223-241.
HCI-0305 Interface design in computerized conferencing systems: a personal view. TUROFF, M. See HCI-0038. 243-259.
HCI-0107 Consistent user interface. OTTE, F. See HCI-0038. 261-275.
02696 § Human and Machine Vision II. Papers from the second workshop Vol. 13 (Montreal, Quebec, Canada, Aug. 1-3, 1984), ROSENFELD, A. (Ed.) Academic Press, Inc., San Diego, CA, 1986, 364 pp., ISBN 0-12-597345-4.

| | |
|---|---|
| 02697 | Perception of transparency in man and machine. BECK, J. See 02696. 1-12. |
| 02698 | Human image understanding: recent research and a theory. BIEDERMAN, I. See 02696. 13-57. |
| 02699 | Describing surfaces. BRADY, M.; PONCE, J.; YUILLE, A.; AND ASADA, H. See 02696. 58-85. |
| 02700 | Connectionist models and parallelism in high level vision. FELDMAN, J. See 02696. 86-108. |
| 02701 | Toward a theory of the perceived spatial layout of scenes. HABER, R. See 02696. 109-148. |
| 02702 | Generative systems of analyzers. LEYTON, M. See 02696. 149-189. |
| 02703 | Early vision: from computational structure to algorithms and parallel hardware. POGGIO, T. See 02696. 190-206. |
| 02704 | Codon constraints on closed 2D shapes. RICHARDS, W.; AND HOFFMAN, D. See 02696. 207-223. |
| 02705 | Environment-centered and viewer-centered perception of surface orientation. SEDGWICK, H.; AND LEVY, S. See 02696. 224-236. |
| 02706 | Perception of organization in a random stimulus. SMITH, B. See 02696. 237-242. |
| 02707 | Autonomous scene description with range imagery. SMITH, D.; AND KANADE, T. See 02696. 243-255. |
| 02708 | Intelligible encoding of ASL image sequences at extremely low information rates. SPERLING, G.; LANDY, M.; COHEN, Y.; AND PAVEL, M. See 02696. 256-312. |
| 02709 | Preattentive processing in vision. TREISMAN, A. See 02696. 313-334. |
| 02710 § | New applications of data bases. Proc. of the ICOD-2 workshop (Cambridge, UK, Sept. 2-3, 1983), GARDARIN, G.; AND GELENBE, E. (Eds.) Academic Press, Inc., San Diego, CA, 1984, 273 pp., $25, ISBN 0-12-275550-2. |
| HCI-0374 | Managing the semantic content of graphical data. BROYAYE, P.; PUDET, T.; AND VICARD, J. See 02710. 63-84. |
| HCI-0338 | A natural language front end to databases with evaluative feedback. BOGURAEV, B.; AND SPARCK JONES, K. See 02710. 159-182. |
| 02711 § | Expert systems & their applications. 5th International Workshop Vol. 2 (Avignon, France, May 13-15, 1985), RAULT, J. (Ed.) Agence de l'Informatique, Paris La Défense, France, 1987, 1346 pp., ISBN 2-86851-033-X. |
| 02712 | NLI-ESD: An expert natural language interface to a statistical data bank. BUCCI, P.; LELLA, G.; AND PAVAN, S. See 02711. 667-671. |
| 02713 | The ANALYST—A workstation for analysis and design. STEPHENS, M.; AND WHITEHEAD, K. See 02711. 745-763. |
| 02714 | The polarisation approach to intelligent artifacts. KABLESHKOV, S. See 02711. 1323-1338. |
| 02715 § | Expert systems & their applications. 6th International Workshop Vol. 2 (Avignon, France, April 28-30, 1986), RAULT, J. (Ed.) Agence de l'Informatique, Paris La Défense, France, 1987, 1575 pp., ISBN 2-86851-033-X. |
| 02716 | The HORSES project and its perspectives in knowledge engineering. BOY, G. See 02715. 1405-1414. |
| 02717 § | Expert Systems & Their Applications. 6th Internation Workshop Vol. 1 (Avignon, France, April 28-30, 1986), RAULT, J. (Ed.) Agence de l'Informatique, Paris La Défense, France, 1987, 848 pp., ISBN 2-86851-033-X. |
| 02718 | Expert system tool evaluation. GILMORE, J.; AND HOWARD, C. See 02717. 437-459. |
| 02719 | A planning system for a cognitive problem. BOTTINO, R.; MARTINOLI, A.; AND RONCAROLO, L. See 02717. 743-756. |
| 02720 § | Advances in Cognitive Science. (Los Angeles, May 1985), KOCHEN, M.; AND HASTINGS, H. (Eds.) Amer. Assn. for Advancement of Science, Washington, DC, 1988, 283 pp., ISBN 0-8133-7471-5. |
| 02721 | Advances in cognitive science. KOCHEN, M.; AND HASTINGS, H. See 02720. 1-6. |
| 02722 | Order and disorder in knowledge structures. KOCHEN, M. See 02720. 241-271. |
| 02723 § | Neural Networks for Computing. AIP Conference Proceedings 151 (Snowbird, UTAH, April 13-16, 1986), DENKER, J. (Ed.) American Institute of Physics, New York, NY, 1987, 445 pp., 60.50, ISBN 0-88318-351-X. |
| 02724 | Concepts in connectionist models. ANDERSON, J.; AND MURPHY, G. See 02723. 17-22. |
| 02725 | Bifurcation analysis of oscillating network model of pattern recognition in the rabbit olfactory bulb. BAIRD, B. See 02723. 29-34. |

02726 Generalizing back propagation to computation. BAUM, E. See 02723. 47-52.
02727 Influence of noise on the behavior of an autoassociative neural network. BUHMANN, J.; AND SCHULTEN, K. See 02723. 71-76.
02728 Absolutely stable learning of recognition codes by a self-organizing neural network. CARPENTER, G.; AND GROSSBERG, S. See 02723. 77-85.
02729 High order correlation model for associative memory. CHEN, H.; LEE, Y.; SUN, G.; LEE, H.; MAXWELL, T.; AND GILES, C. See 02723. 86-99.
02730 Coupled mode theory for neural networks. COHEN, M. See 02723. 100-109.
02731 A model for cortical function. COLVIN, M.; EECKMAN, F.; AND TROMP, J. See 02723. 110-114.
02732 Neural network refinements and extensions. DENKER, J. See 02723. 121-128.
02733 Optical analog of two-dimensional neural networks and their application in recognition of radar targets. FARHAT, N.; MIYAHARA, S.; AND LEE, K. See 02723. 146-152.
02734 Application of neural network algorithms and architectures to correlation/tracking and identification. GARDNER, S. See 02723. 153-157.
02735 Hopfield model applied to vowel and consonant discrimination. GOLD, B. See 02723. 158-164.
02736 Lyapunov function for parallel neural networks. GOLES, E.; AND VICHNIAC, G. See 02723. 165-181.
02737 A dynamic model of olfactory discrimination. GRAJSKI, K.; AND FREEMAN, W. See 02723. 188-193.
02738 A comparison of neural network and matched filter processing for detecting lines in images. GRANT, P.; AND SAGE, J. See 02723. 194-199.
02739 Motion correspondence and analog networks. GRZYWACX, N.; AND YUILLE, A. See 02723. 200-205.
02740 Memory networks with asymmetric bonds. HERTZ, J.; GRINSTEIN, G.; AND SOLLA, S. See 02723. 212-218.
02741 Neurons with hysteresis form a network that can learn without any changes in synaptic connection strengths. HOFFMAN, G.; AND BENSON, M. See 02723. 219-226.
02742 Parallel structures in human and computer memory. KANERVA, P. See 02723. 247-258.
02743 A drive-reinforcement model of single neuron function: An alternative to the Hebbian neuronal model. KLOPF, A. See 02723. 265-270.
02744 Representation of sensory information in self-organizing feature maps. KOHONEN, T.; AND MÄKISARA, K. See 02723. 271-276.
02745 Differential Hebbian learning. KOSCO, B. See 02723. 277-282.
02746 Programming a massively parallel, computation universal system: Static behavior. LAPEDES, A.; AND FARBER, R. See 02723. 283-298.
02747 Nonlinear dynamics of artificial neural systems. MAXWELL, T.; GILES, C.; LEE, Y.; AND CHEN, H. See 02723. 299-304.
02748 A neural network model for the mechanism of pattern information processing. MIYAKE, S.; AND FUKUSHIMA, K. See 02723. 305-308.
02749 A preliminary analysis of recursively generated networks. MJOLSNESS, E.; AND SHARP, D. See 02723. 309-314.
02750 Error correction and asymmetry in a binary memory matrix. MOOPENN, A.; KHANNA, S.; LAMBE, J.; AND THAKOOR, A. See 02723. 315-320.
02751 A machine for neural computation of acoustical patterns with application to real time speech recognition. MUELLER, P.; AND LAZZARO, J. See 02723. 321-326.
02752 A comparison of algorithms for neuron-like cells. PARKER, D. See 02723. 327-332.
02753 Tensor network theory and its application in computer modeling of the metaorganization of sensorimotor hierarchies of gaze. PELLIONISZ, A. See 02723. 339-344.
02754 Digial signal processor accelerators for neural network simulations. PENZ, P.; AND WIGGINS, R. See 02723. 345-355.
02755 Designing a neural network satisfying a given set of constraints. PERSONNAZ, L.; GUYON, I.; AND DREYFUS, G. See 02723. 356-359.
02756 A simple selectionist learning rule for neural networks. PERSONNAZ, L.; GUYON, I.; JOHANNET, A.; DREYFUS, G.; AND TOULOUSE, G. See 02723. 360-363.
02757 Nonlinear discriminant functions and associative memories. PSALTIS, D.; AND PARK, C. See 02723. 370-375.

02758 Topology conserving mappings for learning motor tasks. RITTER, H.; AND SCHULTEN, K. See 02723. 376-380.
02759 Forgetting as a way to improve neural-net behavior. SASIELA, R. See 02723. 386-391.
02760 Higher-order Boltzmann machines. SEJNOWSKI, T. See 02723. 398-403.
02761 Firing response of a neural model with threshold modulation and neural dynamics. SIBANI, P. See 02723. 404-407.
02762 VLSI architectures for implementation of neural networks. SIVILOTTI, M.; EMERLING, M.; AND MEAD, C. See 02723. 408-413.
02763 A layered neural network model applied to the auditory system. TRAVIS, B. See 02723. 432-439.
HCI-0084 § The computer culture. Proc. of a symposium to explore the computer's impact on society (Loudonville, NY, 1981), DONNELLY, D. (Ed.) Associated University Presses, Cranbury, NJ, 1985, 176 pp., $24.50, ISBN 0-8386-3220-3.
HCI-0348 Postscript: computers and the modeling of mind. HOCKENOS, W. See HCI-0084. 153-166.
02764 § Artificial Intelligence and Law. Proceedings of the First International Conference (Boston, MA, May 27-29, 1987), Association for Computing Machinery, New York, NY, 1987, 257 pp., $16, ISBN 0-89791-230-6.
02765 Expert systems in law: out of the research laboratory and into the marketplace. SUSSKIND, R. See 02764. 1-8.
02766 Expert systems in law: The datalex project. GREENLEAF, G.; MOWBRAY, A.; AND TYREE, A. See 02764. 9-17.
02767 Explanation for an expert system that performs estate planning. SCHLOBOHM, D.; AND WATERMAN, D. See 02764. 18-27.
02768 A process specification of expert lawyer reasoning. O'NEIL, D. See 02764. 52-59.
02769 A case-based system for trade secrets law. RISSLAND, E.; AND ASHLEY, K. See 02764. 60-66.
02770 Ashley,K. D.-But, see, accord: generating blue book citations in HYPO. ASHLEY, K.; AND RISSLAND, E. See 02764. 67-74.
02771 The application of expert systems technology to case-based law. SMITH, J.; AND DEEDMAN, C. See 02764. 84-93.
02772 A connectionist approach to conceptual information retrieval. BELEW, R. See 02764. 116-126.
02773 An expert system for screening employee pension plans for the Internal Revenue Service. GRDY, G.; AND PATIL, R. See 02764. 137-144.
02774 Legal reasoning in 3-D. BELZER, M. See 02764. 155-163.
02775 Knowledge representation in "Default": An attempt to classify general types of knowledge used by legal experts. PURDY, R. See 02764. 199-208.
02776 Precedent-based legal reasoning and knowledge acquisition in contract law: A process model. GOLDMAN, S.; DYER, M.; AND FLOWERS, M. See 02764. 210-221.
02777 Reasoning about 'hard' cases in Talmudic law. WEINER, S. See 02764. 222-230.
02778 Oblog-2: A hybrid knowledge representation system for defeasible reasoning. GORDON, T. See 02764. 231-239.
02779 Legal data modeling: The prohibited transaction exemption analyst. BELLAIRS, K. See 02764. 252-257.
02780 § ACM SIGDOC '85. Proceedings of the Fourth International Conference on Systems Documentation (Cornell University, Ithaca, NY, June 18-21, 1985), PATTERSON, D. (Chr.) Association for Computing Machinery, New York, NY, 1986, 168 pp., $16.00, ISBN 0-89791-186-5.
02781 Separating content from form: A language for formatting on-line documentation and dialog. WIECHA, C.; AND HENRION, M. See 02780. 1-7.
02782 Computer user manuals in print: Do they have a future? MCKEE, J. See 02780. 8-14.
02783 An informal overview of CUINFO (Cornell's computer-based bulletin board). WORONA, S. See 02780. 71-77.
02784 Help texts vs. help mechanisms: A new mandate for documentation writers. BORENSTEIN, N. See 02780. 78-83.
02785 Multilingual programming: Coordinating programs, user interfaces, on-line help and documentation. PERLMAN, G. See 02780. 123-129.
02786 Dynamic screens and static paper. SMITH, S. See 02780. 139-145.
02787 § ACTES/Proceedings Symposium 1988 ACM SIGSMAll/PC. (Cannes, France, May 4-6, 1988), JOLOBOFF, V. (Chr.) Association for Computing Machinery, New York, NY, 1988, 196 pp..

02788  A highly integrated tool set for program development support. ENGELS, G.; JANNING, T.; AND SCHÄFER, W. See 02787. 1-10.

02789  Affect-chaining and dependency oriented flow analysis applied to queries of programs. KAMKAR, M.; SHAHMEHRI, N.; AND FRITZSON, P. See 02787. 36-44.

02790  ALIEN: a programming environment generator for personal computers. SCHROEDER, U.; AND SPINNER, A. See 02787. 45-52.

02791  A user interface for database creation use and maintenance. HECKER, G.; AND UNGER, E. See 02787. 176-186.

02792  Iconic shells for multitasking workstations. BEAUDOUIN-LAFON, M.; AND KARSENTY, S. See 02787. 187-196.

02793 §  APL in transition. (Dallas, Texas, May 10-14, 1987), HALIBURTON, J. (Ed.) Association for Computing Machinery, New York, NY, 1987, 512 pp., $37.00, ISBN 0-89791-226-8.

02794  Application screen management: an APL2 approach. DEERHAKE, S. See 02793. 94-102.

02795  Screen management in the "real world". STAWICK, E. See 02793. 292-299.

02796  Design of a new user interface for APL. HOWLAND, J. See 02793. 469-477.

02797 §  APL88. Conference Proceedings (Sydney, Australia, February 1-5, 1988), DICKEY, L.; AND SHAW, L. (Eds.) Association for Computing Machinery, New York, NY, 1987, 349 pp., $28.00, ISBN 0-89791-253-5.

02798  Parametric Fourier image characterization toolkit. ALONSO, J. See 02797. 5-9.

02799  APL: The language of science and management. EISNER, A.; YIONOULIS, S.; PLATT, J.; AND JERNIGAN, R. See 02797. 107-112.

02800  Innovation of decision support system-matplan based on structure matrix supported by APL. TOYAMA, T.; AND YAUDA, M. See 02797. 318-328.

02801 §  Communications and architecture & protocols. (August 5-7, 1986, Stowe, VT), KOSINSKY, W.; GARCIA-LUNA, J.; AND KUO, F. (Eds.) Association for Computing Machinery, New York, NY, 1986, 414 pp., $24.

02802  An architecture for a multimedia teleconferencing system. AGUILAR, L.; GARCIA-LUNA-ACEVES, J.; MORAN, D.; CRAIGHILL, E.; AND BRUNGARDT, R. See 02801. 126-136.

02803 §  Computer personnel research. Proceedings of the twenty-first annual conference (Minneapolis, MN, May 2-3, 1985), WETHERBE, J. (Ed.) Association for Computing Machinery, New York, NY, 1985, 207 pp., $18, ISBN 0-89791-156-3.

02804  GDSS: a brief look at a new concept in decision support. DESANCTIS, G.; AND GALLUPE, B. See 02803. 24-28.

02805  Mainframe and microcomputer-based business graphics: end user computing comparisons and trends. LEHMAN, J.; AND VOGEL, D. See 02803. 66-73.

02806  Linking mechanism supporting end-user computing. ZMUD, R.; AND LIND, M. See 02803. 74-80.

02807  User development of applications: a study of a model of success. RIVARD, S.; AND HUFF, S. See 02803. 81-90.

02808  A program development system for the casual programmer. PARKER, J. See 02803. 172-180.

02809 §  Computer science education. Papers of the seventeenth SIGCSE technical symposium (Cincinnati, Ohio, Feb. 6-7, 1986), LITTLE, J.; AND CASSEL, L. (Eds.) Association for Computing Machinery, New York, NY, 1986, 336 pp., $28, ISBN 0-89791-178-4.

HCI-0433  Adult learners: away with computerphobia. KNELLER, G. See 02809. 34-37.

HCI-0120  The influence of color on program readability and comprehensibility. RAMBALLY, G. See 02809. 173-181.

02810 §  Computer Graphics. Proceedings of SIGGRAPH 88 15th Annual Conference (Atlanta, Georgia, August 1-5, 1988), BEACH, R. (Ed.) Association for Computing Machinery, New York, NY, 1988, 356 pp., ISBN 0-89791-275-6.

02811  Conman: a visual programming language for interactive graphics. HAEBERLI, P. See 02810. 103-112.

02812  Graphical search and replace. KURLANDER, D.; AND BIER, E. See 02810. 113-120.

02813  A study in interactive 3-D rotation using 2-D control devices. CHEN, M.; MOUNTFORD, S.; AND SELLEN, A. See 02810. 121-129.

02814  High-performance polygon rendering. AKELEY, K.; AND JERMOLUK, T. See 02810. 239-246.

02815  Virtual graphics. VOORHIES, D.; KIRK, D.; AND LATHROP, O. See 02810. 247-254.

02816 A display system for the Stellar Graphics Supercomputer Model GS1000. APGAR, B.; BERSACK, B.; AND MAMMEN, A. See 02810. 255-262.
02817 Motion interpolation by optimal control. BROTMAN, L.; AND NETRAVALI, A. See 02810. 309-315.
02818 Getting graphics in gear: graphics and dynamics in driving simulation. DEYO, R.; BRIGGS, J.; AND DOENGES, P. See 02810. 317-326.
02819 Applications of computer graphics to the visualization of meteorological data. PAPATHOMAS, T.; SCHIAVONE, J.; AND JULESZ, B. See 02810. 327-334.
02820 A hand biomechanics workstation. THOMPSON, D.; BUDFORD JR, W.; MYERS, L.; GIURINTANO, D.; AND BREWER III, J. See 02810. 335-343.
02821 § Computer-Supported Cooperative Work. CSCW 88: Proceedings of the Conference (Portland, OR, Sept. 26-28, 1988), GREIF, I. (Chr.) Association for Computing Machinery, New York, NY, 1988, 395 pp., ISBN 0-89791-282-9.
02822 Design of a multi-media vehicle for social browsing. ROOT, R. See 02821. 25-38.
02823 Guided tours and tabletops: tools for communicating in a hypertext environment. TRIGG, R. See 02821. 216-226.
02824 Capturing the capture concepts: a case study in the design of computer-supported meeting environments. MANTEI, M. See 02821. 257-270.
02825 Children's collaborative use of a computer microworld. SINGER, J.; BEHREND, S.; AND ROSCHELLE, J. See 02821. 271-281.
02826 Collaborative learning in a virtual classroom: highlights of findings. HILTZ, S. See 02821. 282-290.
02827 Cooperative work in the Andrew message system. BORENSTEIN, N.; AND THYBERG, C. See 02821. 306-323.
02828 § Design Automation. 24th ACM/IEEE Conference Proceedings (Miami Beach, FL, June 28-July 1, 1987), O'NEILL, A.; AND THOMAS, D. Association for Computing Machinery, New York, NY, 1987, 840 pp., $47, ISBN 0-8186-0781-5.
02829 PHRAN-SPAN: a natural language interface for system specifications. GRANACKI, J.; AND PARKER, A. See 02828. 416-422.
02830 VISION: VHDL induced schematic imaging on net-lists. CHUN, R.; CHANG, K.; AND McNAMEE, L. See 02828. 436-442.
02831 § Document Processing Systems. Proceedings of the ACM Conference (Santa Fe, New Mexico, December 5-9, 1988), SOLEM, A. (Chr.) Association for Computing Machinery, New York, NY, 1988, 195 pp., ISBN 0-89791-291-8.
02832 Hypertext engineering: practical methods for creating a compact disk encyclopedia. GLUSHKO, R.; WEAVER, M.; COONAN, T.; AND LINCOLN, J. See 02831. 11-19.
02833 Conceptual documents: a mechanism for specifying active views in hypertext. NANARD, J.; NANARD, M.; AND RICHY, H. See 02831. 37-42.
02834 Adding browsing semantics to the hypertext model. STOTTS, P.; AND FURUTA, R. See 02831. 43-50.
02835 The design of a document database. CLIFTON, C.; AND GARCIE-MOLINA, H. See 02831. 125-134.
02836 A library for incremental update of bitmap images. DOBKIN, D.; KOUTSOFIOS, E.; AND PIKE, R. See 02831. 153-158.
02837 § History of Medical Informatics. Proceedings of ACM conference on the History of Medical Informatics (Bethesda, MD, Nov. 5-6, 1987), BLUM, B. (Ed.) Association for Computing Machinery, New York, NY, 1987, 206 pp., $14, ISBN 0-89791-248-9.
02838 In praise of computing. LINDBERG, D. See 02837. 1-4.
02839 How DENDRAL was conceived and born. LEDERBERG, J. See 02837. 5-19.
02840 Planting the seeds. WAXMAN, B. See 02837. 27-29.
02841 Medical informatics: a personal view of sowing the seeds. LEDLEY, R. See 02837. 31-41.
02842 History of the development of medical information systems at the Laboratory of Computer Science at Massachusetts General Hospital. BARNETT, G. See 02837. 43-49.
02843 The LINC was early and small. CLARK, W. See 02837. 51-73.
02844 The UCLA Brain Research Institute data processing laboratory. ESTRIN, T. See 02837. 75-83.

02845   The history of the use of computers in the interpretation of radiological images. LODWICK, G. See 02837. 85-94.
02846   Recollections on the processing of biomedical signals. COX JR., J. See 02837. 95-103.
02847   Perspectives over forty years. WEED, L. See 02837. 105-115.
02848   An historical perspective on clinical laboratory information systems. LINCOLN, T. See 02837. 117-121.
02849   Health care information systems: a personal historic review. COLLEN, M. See 02837. 123-136.
02850   The perception of system and the reduction of uncertainty. FLAGLE, C. See 02837. 137-142.
02851   History of the TDS medical information system. HODGE, M. See 02837. 143-152.
02852   Patient management systems: the early years. HAMMOND, W. See 02837. 153-164.
02853   The background of INTERNIST I and QMR. MYERS, J. See 02837. 195-197.
02854 § Human factors in computing systems. CHI'86 Conference Proceedings (Boston, April 13-17, 1986), MANTEI, M.; AND ORBETON, P. (Eds.) Association for Computing Machinery, New York, NY, 1986, 362 pp., $27, ISBN 0-89791-180-6.
02855 § Human factors in computing systems and graphics interface. CHI/GI 1987 conference proceedings (Toronto, Canada, April 5-9, 1987), CARROLL, J.; AND TANNER, P. (Eds.) Association for Computing Machinery, New York, NY, 1987, 344 pp., $20, ISBN 089791-213-6.
02856 § Human Factors in Computing Systems. Conference Proceedings (Washington, D. C., May 15-19, 1988), O'HARE, J. (Ed.) Association for Computing Machinery, New York, NY, 1988, 292 pp., ISBN 0-201-14237-6.
02857   Grasping reality through illusion—interactive graphics serving science. BROOKS, F. See 02856. 1-11.
02858   Exploratory evaluation of a planar foot-operated cursor-positioning device. PEARSON, G.; AND WEISER, M. See 02856. 13-18.
02859   An improved automatic lipreading system to enhance speech recognition. PETAJAN, E.; BISCHOFF, B.; BODOFF, D.; AND BROOKE, N. See 02856. 19-25.
02860   Improving the accuracy of touch screens: an experimental evaluation of three strategies. POTTER, R.; WELDON, L.; AND SHNEIDERMAN, B. See 02856. 27-32.
02861   Perspectives on algorithm animation. BROWN, M. See 02856. 33-38.
02862   A graphical programming language interface for an intelligent LISP tutor. REISER, B.; FRIEDMANN, P.; GEVINS, J.; KIMBERG, D.; AND RANNEY, M. See 02856. 39-44.
02863   Users' preferences among different techniques for displaying the evaluation of LISP functions in an interactive debugger. HARY, J.; COHAN, L.; AND DARNELL, M. See 02856. 45-50.
02864   Retrieval systems for the information seeker: can the role of the intermediary be automated? BORGMAN, C.; BELKIN, N.; CROFT, W.; LESK, M.; AND LANDAUER, T. See 02856. 51-53.
02865   Transferring skills from training to the actual work situation: the role of task application knowledge, action styles and job decision latitude. VON PAPSTEIN, P.; AND FRESE, M. See 02856. 55-60.
02866   A case study of CSCW in a dispersed organization. CARASIK, R.; AND GRANTHAM, C. See 02856. 61-66.
02867   A knowledge-based user interface management system. FOLEY, J.; GIBBS, C.; AND KOVACEVIC, S. See 02856. 67-72.
02868   A grammar-based approach to automatic generation of user-interface dialogues. SCOTT, M.; AND YAP, S. See 02856. 73-78.
02869   The design of auditory interfaces for visually disabled users. EDWARDS, A. See 02856. 83-88.
02870   Multifunctional cursor for direct manipulation user interfaces. MULLER, M. See 02856. 89-94.
02871   An empirical comparison of pie vs. linear menus. CALLAHAN, J.; HOPKINS, D.; WEISER, M.; AND SHNEIDERMAN, B. See 02856. 95-100.
02872   Color-coding categories in menus. MCDONALD, J.; MOLANDER, M.; AND NOEL, R. See 02856. 101-106.
02873   Transfer between menu systems. FOLTZ, P.; DAVIES, S.; POLSON, P.; AND KIERAS, D. See 02856. 107-112.
02874   Computer-supported cooperative work: breakthroughs for user acceptance. GREIF, I.; BROWN, J.; DYSON, E.; KAPOR, M.; AND MALONE, T. See 02856. 113-114.
02875   The data model is the heart of interface design. AKSCYN, R.; YODER, E.; AND MCCRACKEN, D. See 02856. 115-120.

02876  Navigating integrated facilities: initiating and terminating interaction sequences. BARNARD, P.; MACLEAN, A.; AND WILSON, M. See 02856. 121-129.

02877  Pictures and category labels as navigational aids for catalog browsing. EGIDO, C.; AND PATTERSON, J. See 02856. 127-132.

02878  Video: Data for studying human-computer interaction. MACKAY, W.; GUINDON, R.; MANTEL, M.; SUCHMAN, L.; AND TATAR, D. See 02856. 133-137.

02879  Choosing between methods: analysing the user's decision space in terms of schemas and linear models. YOUNG, R.; AND MACLEAN, A. See 02856. 139-143.

02880  A general user modelling facility. KASS, R.; AND FININ, T. See 02856. 145-150.

02881  Misconceived misconceptions? MASSON, M.; HILL, W.; CONNER, J.; AND GUIDON, R. See 02856. 151-156.

02882  Integrating human factors and software development. GRUDIN, J.; CARROLL, J.; EHRLICH, S.; GRISHAM, M.; AND HERSH, H. See 02856. 157-159.

02883  Groupware: interface design for meetings. MANTEI, M.; SUCHMAN, L.; DESANCTIS; APPLEGATE, L.; AND JARVENPAA, S. See 02856. 161-163.

02884  A new conceptual model for interactive user recovery and command reuse facilities. YANG, Y. See 02856. 165-170.

02885  How users repeat their actions on computers: principles for design of history mechanisms. GREENBERG, S.; AND WITTEN, I. See 02856. 171-178.

02886  Planning for advising. MCKENDREE, J.; AND ZABACK, J. See 02856. 179-184.

02887  Justified advice: a semi-naturalistic study of advisory strategies. HILL, W.; AND MILLER, J. See 02856. 185-190.

02888  How to interface to advisory systems? Users request help with a very simple language. GUINDON, R. See 02856. 191-196.

02889  UIMSs: threat or menace? ROSENBERG, J.; HILL, R.; MILLER, J.; SCHULERT, A.; AND SHEWMAKE, D. See 02856. 197-200.

02890  Designing keybindings to be easy to learn and resistant to forgetting even when the set of commands is large. WALKER, N.; AND OLSON, J. See 02856. 201-206.

02891  Effects of interface design upon user productivity. BAILEY, W.; KNOX, S.; AND LYNCH, E. See 02856. 207-212.

02892  Development of an instrument measuring user satisfaction of the human-computer interface. CHIN, J.; DIEHL, V.; AND NORMAN, L. See 02856. 213-218.

02893  Public Law 99-506, "Section 508" Electronic Equipment Accessibility for disabled workers. LADNER, R.; MCDONOUGH, F.; ROTH, W.; SCADDEN, L.; AND VANDERHEIDEN, G. See 02856. 219-222.

02894  Multimodal response planning: an adaptive rule based approach. JR. GARGAN, R.; SULLIVAN, J.; AND TYLER, S. See 02856. 229-234.

02895  SAUCI: a knowledge-based interface architecture. TYLER, S. See 02856. 235-240.

02896  Task-oriented parsing - a diagnostic method to be used adaptive systems. HOPPE, H. See 02856. 241-247.

02897  Plan-based representations of pascal and fortran code. YU, C.; AND ROBERTSON, S. See 02856. 251-256.

02898  Providing the requisite knowledge via software documentation. PINTO, J.; AND SOLOWAY, E. See 02856. 257-261.

02899  Control of cognitive processes during software design: what tools are needed? GUINDON, R.; AND CURTIS, B. See 02856. 263-268.

02900  Travel around a learning support environment: rambling, orienteering or touring? HAMMOND, N.; AND ALLINSON, L. See 02856. 269-273.

02901  Using latent semantic analysis to improve access to textual information. DUMAIS, S.; FURNAS, G.; LANDAUER, T.; DEERWESTER, S.; AND HARSHMAN, R. See 02856. 281-285.

02902  Online help systems: design and implementation issues (panel). KEARSLEY, G.; CAMPBELL, R.; ELKERTON, J.; JUDD, W.; AND WALKER, J. See 02856. 287-288.

02903 § Human Factors in Computing Systems. CHI '89 'Wings For The Mind' Conference Proceedings (Austin, TX, April 30–May 4, 1989), BICE, K.; AND LEWIS, C. (Eds.) Association for Computing Machinery, New York, NY, 1989, 397 pp., ISBN 0-201-50400-6.

02904 § Hypercube Concurrent Computers and Applications. The Third Conference. Volume 1: Architecture, Software, Computer Systems and General Issues (Pasadena, CA, Jan. 19-20, 1988), Fox, G. (Ed.) Association for Computing Machinery, New York, NY, 1988, 895 pp., ISBN 0-89791-278-0.
02905  A dataflow-based APL for the hypercube. Mazer, A. See 02904. 505-512.
02906  g - A compact language for real-time graphics. Furmanski, W.; and Gates, D. See 02904. 749-759.
02907  Interactive performance display and debugging using the NCUBE real-time graphicssystem. Morison, R. See 02904. 760-765.
02908 § Hypercube Concurrent Computers and Applications; vol. 2. The Third Conference (Pasadena, CA, Jan. 19-20, 1988), Fox, G. (Ed.) Association for Computing Machinery, New York, NY, 1988, 1787 pp., ISBN 0-89791-278-0.
02909  DIME: a programming environment for unstructured triangular meshes on a distributed-memory parallel processor. Williams, R. See 02908. 1770-1787.
02910 § Industrial & Engineering Applications of Artificial Intelligence & Expert Systems. First International Conference (IEA/AIE—88) (Univ. of Tennessee Space Institute, Tullahoma, TN, June 1–3, 1988), Ali, M. (Ed.) Association for Computing Machinery, New York, NY, 1988, 636 pp., ISBN 0-89791-271-3.
02911  Generic expert system shell for diagnostic reasoning. Chu, W. See 02910. 7-12.
02912  Expert diagnostic system. Khaksari, G. See 02910. 43-53.
02913  The ISA expert system: a prototype system for failure diagnosis on the space station. Marsh, C. See 02910. 60-74.
02914  Using hypertext to overcome the knowledge base development bottleneck: a case study. Roehl, E.; and Hill, C. See 02910. 80-82.
02915  PISCES: an expert system for coal fired power plant monitoring and diagnostics. Washington, E.; and Ali, M. See 02910. 87-93.
02916  Sherlock—a system for diagnosing power distribution ring network faults. Wong, K.; Tsang, C.; and Chan, W. See 02910. 109-115.
02917  Approximate spatial reasoning. Dutta, S. See 02910. 126-140.
02918  INQUEST: A prototype intelligence tool. Hillman, D. See 02910. 147-156.
02919  Goal-directed semantic tutor. Koh, H.; and Wu, D. See 02910. 171-176.
02920  The responsive system: a new challenge for AI. Kurstedt, H.; Lee, K.; Mendes, P.; and Berube, S. See 02910. 177-184.
02921  SIMS: a uniform environment for planning and performing user's tasks. Pavlin, J.; and Bates, R. See 02910. 195-200.
02922  Symbiotic systems for complex problems. Sciabin, M.; Bisanz, S.; Lakeman, G.; and Place, S. See 02910. 219-228.
02923  Experience of constructing a fault localisation expert system using an AI toolkit. Inder, R. See 02910. 229-239.
02924  Knowledge base applications with software engineering: a tool for requirements specifications. Cordes, D.; and Carver, D. See 02910. 266-272.
02925  Improving performance of an electrical power expert system with genetic algorithms. Goodloe, M.; and Graves, S. See 02910. 298-305.
02926  A blackboard architecture for problem solving and machine learning in an expert system for power system voltage control. Gupta, U.; and Lee, S. See 02910. 306-316.
02927  A rule-based system for interactive proposal evaluation. Helman, D.; and Burke, J. See 02910. 317-323.
02928  The development of an automated flight test management system for flight test planning and monitoring. Hewett, M.; Tartt, D.; Duke, E.; Antoniewicz, R.; and Agarwal, A. See 02910. 324-333.
02929  SMARTGEN: the implementation of an expert system for the generation of digital logic diagnostic tests. Karim, A.; and Szygenda, S. See 02910. 355-360.
02930  The network control assistant (NCA), a real-time prototype expert system for network management. Kosieniak, P.; Mathis, V.; St. Jacques, M.; and Stevens, D. See 02910. 367-379.

02931 Automated design and analysis system for design of custom orthopedic implants. DOOLEY, R.; HEIMKE, G.; DINGANKAR, A.; BERG, E.; AND KIMBROUGH, E. See 02910. 405-412.
02932 Applications of an AI design shell ENGINEOUS to advanced engineering products. RUSSO, C.; AND POWELL, D. See 02910. 413-420.
02933 Process design of oil and gas production facilities using expert systems. AGHILI, H.; MONTGOMERY, G.; AMLANI, A.; AND SHAH, J. See 02910. 421-429.
02934 Process control with the G2 real-time expert system. MOORE, R.; LINDENFILZER, P.; HAWKINSON, L.; AND MATTHEWS, B. See 02910. 492-497.
02935 ProCEED: an expert system for multivariate process control systems design. CHAWLA, V.; RAGADE, R.; AND DESHPANDE, P. See 02910. 498-506.
02936 GTEX—A group technology expert system. BONANI, L.; CALVO, P.; AND CONTRI, G. See 02910. 514-521.
02937 An expert database for material and production planning. PRASAD, B. See 02910. 530-539.
02938 A comparison of the artistic aspects of various industrial robots. APOSTOLOS, M. See 02910. 548-552.
02939 A mission planning architecture for an autonomous vehicle. HALL, M.; AND BENOKRAITIS, V. See 02910. 582-589.
02940 Evaluating the impact of camera placement on teleoperator efficiency. PISANICH, G.; PREVOST, M.; AND HALL, S. See 02910. 629-637.
02941 § Industrial & Engineering Applications of Artificial Intelligence & Expert Systems. The First International Conference on IEA/AIE-88 (Tullahoma, Tennessee, June 1-3, 1988), ALI, M. (Chr.) Association for Computing Machinery, New York, NY, 1988, 1189 pp., ISBN 0-89791-271-3.
02942 Hierarchical scene structure representations to facilitate image understanding. MAREN, A.; AND ALI, M. See 02941. 657-667.
02943 Automatic acquisition of domain and procedural knowledge. FERBER, H.; AND ALI, M. See 02941. 762-771.
02944 Generic diagnostic knowledge acquisition tool. LIMBEK, B. See 02941. 772-777.
02945 Use of metaknowledge in the verification of knowledge-based systems. MORELL, L. See 02941. 847-857.
02946 Graphics-based qualitative simulation generator for power distribution systems. LI, X.; JIANG, J.; CANTWELL, J.; BOURNE, J.; AND KAWAMURA, K. See 02941. 877-884.
02947 Understanding text with an accompanying diagram. BULKO, W. See 02941. 894-898.
02948 A computer training tool using Chinese natural language. LI, P.; AND CHEN, J. See 02941. 899-904.
02949 Interacting with expert systems. REDDY, Y. See 02941. 905-916.
02950 SIMTALK: Pros and cons of natural language for manufacturing simulation. RUMMEL, P. See 02941. 917-921.
02951 Providing natural language assistance in locating objects: a general model for information selection and generation. SMITH, R. See 02941. 922-931.
02952 The design of a traffic control expert system for long distance network contingencies. CHANG, C.; CHUNG, C.; AND WANG, J. See 02941. 932-939.
02953 Multi-Input fuzzy inference engine on a systolic array. MANZOUL, M.; AND RAO, V. See 02941. 958-964.
02954 The actem model for decision modelling in a scene management system. MOULIN, B. See 02941. 965-974.
02955 Lets "Deep-Six" our reference manuals. LEARY, E. See 02941. 1016-1023.
02956 EPVM: An expert patient-ventilator manager for chemical warfare casualties. SINGH, R.; AND ROTH, B. See 02941. 1024-1032.
02957 A generic strategy for diagnostic assistance: the technician's assistant. MCBETH, M.; COLLINS, G.; BOURNE, J.; BRODERSEN, A.; AND HOFMANN, M. See 02941. 1040-1043.
02958 CAD Data management using object-oriented paradigms. HONG, B.; AND LEE, S. See 02941. 1044-1048.
02959 Design of an AI-Based self-sustaining habitats control system. KIM, T.; MIGNON, G.; AND ZEIGLER, B. See 02941. 1059-1065.
02960 Using a top-down and bottom-up strategy to analyze high resolution aerial photographs of urban areas. PHILLIPS, D. See 02941. 1139-1145.
02961 Character recognition of cursive scripts. HYDER, S.; AND KHOUJAH, A. See 02941. 1146-1150.
02962 Using design expertise to develop an expert system. MYCHALTCHOUK, P.; AND BERNARD, J. See 02941. 1157-1162.

## PROCEEDINGS

**02963** Some considerations on intelligent tutoring systems. VANTAGGIATO, A. See 02941. 1163-1167.

**02964** PC Version of a knowledge-based expert system with voice interface. BALARAM, M. See 02941. 1168-1173.

**02965** Logic programmable natural language processor of a knowledge-base management system. MATSUO, M.; ARIMA, K.; FREIHEIT, F.; AND HUBBARD, K. See 02941. 1174-1182.

**02966** Knowledge-based interface to manufacturing computer systems. WILSON DR., D.; AND KNIGHT DR., D. See 02941. 1183-1189.

**02967** § Industrial & Engineering Applications of Artificial Intelligence & Expert Systems: vol. I. The Second International Conference (Tullahoma, TN, June 6–9, 1989), ALI, M. (Ed.) Association for Computing Machinery, New York, NY, 1989, 517 pp., $37.50, ISBN 0-89791-320-5.

**02968** Concept demonstration of the use of interactive fault diagnosis and isolation for TF30 engines. FORSYTH, G.; AND LARKIN, M. See 02967. 15-20.

**02969** SPA: a systems for diagnosis of computer performance problems. DAWSON, J.; AND SHUBIN, H. See 02967. 54-57.

**02970** Applications of qualitative modeling to knowledge-based risk assessment studies. BISWAS, G.; DEBELAK, K.; AND KAWAMURA, K. See 02967. 92-101.

**02971** Artificial intelligence techniques applied to maintenance management. RAY, A.; AND MURTY, M. See 02967. 112-118.

**02972** NetGraph: an object-oriented graphical toolset for risk assessment. UCKUN, S.; DAWANT, B.; AND KAWAMURA, K. See 02967. 119-125.

**02973** An object-oriented expert system for coal-fired MHD power plant fault monitoring and diagnosis. WASHINGTON, E.; AND ALI, M. See 02967. 146-153.

**02974** Jet engine technical advisor (JETA). ABU-HAKIMA, S.; DAVIDSON, P.; HALASZ, M.; AND PHAN, S. See 02967. 154-160.

**02975** An interactive tolerance system. EYADA, O.; IOANNOU, Y.; AND ONG, J. See 02967. 178-184.

**02976** Hierarchical scheduling in an intelligent environmental control system. KIM, T.; AND ZEIGLER, B. See 02967. 310-317.

**02977** Plant scheduling expert system for batch processing. KAMINSKY, W.; AND WESTERGREN, B. See 02967. 348-355.

**02978** Planning as feedback to designers. MILLS, J.; SEKINE, Y.; WYSOCKI, E.; FURTH, W.; OTWELL, K.; JAMESON, S.; AND BURZIO, A. See 02967. 374-381.

**02979** DORUS: an architecture for dynamic optimal resource utilization systems. ULUG, S.; BOWEN, B.; AND ACHESON, A. See 02967. 428-434.

**02980** A process oriented approach to an intelligent design aid. BAKER, K.; BALL, L.; CULVERHOUSE, P.; EVANS, D.; AND JAGODZINSKI, A. See 02967. 479-485.

**02981** Computer aided concurrent design for printed wiring boards. MARTIN, C.; AND HUTCHISON, K. See 02967. 493-499.

**02982** § Industrial & Engineering Applications of Artificial Intelligence & Expert Systems: vol. II. The Second International Conference (Tullahoma, TN, June 6–9, 1989), MUNNIS, A. (Ed.) Association for Computing Machinery, New York, NY, 1989, 1108 pp., $37.50, ISBN 0-89791-320-5.

**02983** An operations advisor for an on-line computer banking system with graphics interface. ISHII, S.; ABE, T.; HIDAI, Y.; AND TANAKA, A. See 02982. 568-576.

**02984** Object oriented rapid prototyping with G2. MOORE, R.; STANLEY, G.; AND ROSENOF, H. See 02982. 620-631.

**02985** Extending knowledge-based systems through closely-coupled graphics and windows. WONG, S.; AND WILSON, J. See 02982. 770-774.

**02986** An advisory system for digital logic simulation. ANTAO, B.; CANTWELL, J.; BRODERSEN, A.; AND BOURNE, J. See 02982. 775-778.

**02987** A knowledge representation for natural language understanding. PHARR, W. See 02982. 859-865.

**02988** A dialog based interface to a design knowledge base that understands user design-intentions. MOHAN, L.; AND KASHYAP, R. See 02982. 952-960.

02989  Delphi: an intelligent interface for a dolphin communication laboratory. LANGTON, K.; MCLEISH, M.; PHILLIPS, D.; AND HERMAN, L. See 02982. 969-976.

02990  Intelligent interfaces for secure multilevel database systems. WONG, J.; J., S.; AND NULL, L. See 02982. 977-981.

02991  Embedded training in AI technology through an expert system interface: an alarm processor application. MACGREGOR, D.; VALENTA, W.; TONN, B.; AND GOELTZ, R. See 02982. 982-990.

02992  Towards reasoning visualization in expert systems. SELIG, W.; AND JOHANNES, J. See 02982. 1001-1007.

02993  An intelligent tutoring system for basic set theory. XIA, J.; AND BISWAS, G. See 02982. 1008-1017.

02994  A prototype autonomous agent for crew and equipment retrieval in space. ERICKSON, J.; PHINNEY, D.; NORSWORTHY, R.; ZACKSENHOUSE, M.; HARTNESS, K.; PHAM, T.; MERKEL, L.; AND TU, E. See 02982. 1052-1058.

02995  Developing intelligent simulation language to support telerobotic workstation activities. NTUEN, C.; PARK, E.; FERGUSON, G.; AND ROBERTS, R. See 02982. 1073-1081.

02996 §  Management of Information Systems Personnel. Proceedings of the 1988 ACM SIGCPR conference (College Park, Maryland, April 7-8, 1988), AWAD, E. (Chr.) Association for Computing Machinery, New York, NY, 1988, 216 pp., $19.00, ISBN 0-89791-262-4.

02997  Information systems skills requirements: 1980 & 1988. CHENEY, O. See 02996. 1-7.

02998  The systems analyst of the 1990's. MCCUBBRAY, D. See 02996. 8-16.

02999  Perceptions of the CIS graduate's workstyle: undergraduate business students versus CIS faculty. MAWHINNEY, C.; CALE, E.; AND CALLAGHAN, D. See 02996. 17-21.

03000  Electronic monitoring and the redundancy of control systems: The role of the supervisor. EISENMAN, E. See 02996. 22-32.

03001  Adequate documentation of user-developed applications: a new challenge for end-user computing management. PIERSON, J.; FORCHT, K.; AND SHORTER, J. See 02996. 42-45.

03002  An evaluation and selection methodology of microcomputer training software: Implications for human resource managers and computer personnel. RUSHINEK, S.; AND RUSHINEK, A. See 02996. 46-49.

03003  Motivations and behaviors of software professionals. RUBIN, H.; AND HERNANDEZ, E. See 02996. 62-71.

03004  Causes of motivational problems among AI managers. COUGER, J.; AND MCINTYRE, S. See 02996. 72-77.

03005  Making computer tasks at work more playful: Implications for systems analysts and designers. WEBSTER, J. See 02996. 78-87.

03006  Perspectives on the academic preparation of MIS professionals. TRENT, R. See 02996. 119-119.

03007  Managers who personally use information technology frequently: a profile of some invisible computer personnel. FERRATT, T.; DUNNE, E.; AND YOUNG, S. See 02996. 120-127.

03008  Analysis and design skills required by end-users in small organizations. SCHELL, G. See 02996. 128-132.

03009  The importance of individual differences in end-user training: The case for learning style. BOSTROM, R.; OLFMAN, L.; AND SEIN, M. See 02996. 133-144.

03010  Developing awareness of computer ethics. FORCHT, K.; PIERSON, J.; AND BAUMAN, B. See 02996. 142-143.

03011  Evaluating performance appraisal systems for IS personnel. ZAWACKI, R.; AND COUGER, J. See 02996. 144-147.

03012  An update measure of supervisor-rated job performance for programmer/analysis. GOLDSTEIN, D. See 02996. 148-152.

03013  The experimental validation of a programmer productivity measure. DANAHER, M.; MUNSON, J.; AND COULTER, N. See 02996. 153-156.

03014  Increase organizational effectiveness: Support self-managed IS development teams. NOSEK, J. See 02996. 157-166.

03015  Repositioning the information systems management function: Implications for information systems personnel. LEVINSON, N. See 02996. 167-175.

03016  Negotiating IS: Observations on changes in structure from a negotiated order perspective. GASH, D. See 02996. 176-182.

03017  Recent trends in information systems law. ESPOSITO, B.; WALTON, C.; AND WALTON, S. See 02996. 183-187.

**03018** The two cultures in computing. HAROLD, F. See 02996. 188-191.
**03019** Instilling professionalism in a software development organization. WEISERT, C. See 02996. 192-198.
**03020** Male/female programmer and systems analyst Job performance. WILLOUGHBY, T.; AND HUGHES, J. See 02996. 200-201.
**03021** Moderating effects of age, education, and tenure on the job satisfaction-job performance relationship. WOODRUFF, C. See 02996. 202-206.
**03022** An investigation into the existence of subgroup concept in information systems personnel management. AHN, J.; AND LEE, S. See 02996. 207-210.
**03023** Need of electronic tools in educational programmers and the impact in developing countries. SUBRAHMAN-YAM, Y. See 02996. 211-216.
**03024** § Measurement and Modeling of Computer Systems. Proceedings of the 1988 ACM SIGMETRICS Conference (Santa Fe, New Mexico, May 24-27, 1988), SMITH, C. (Chr.) Association for Computing Machinery, New York, NY, 1988, 282 pp., $23.00, ISBN 0-89791-254-3.
**03025** Monitoring and performance measuring distributed systems during operation. WYBRANIETZ, D.; AND HABAN, D. See 03024. 197-206.
**03026** § Methodologies for intelligent systems. Proceedings of the ACM SIGART international symposium (Knoxville, TN, Oct. 22-24, 1986), RAS, Z.; AND ZEMANKOVA, M. (Eds.) Association for Computing Machinery, New York, NY, 1986, 450 pp., $33, ISBN 0-89791-206-3.
**03027** A knowledge-based approach to online document retrieval system design. BISWAS, G.; BEZDEK, J.; AND OAKMAN, R. See 03026. 112-120.
**03028** Towards an intelligent and personalized retrieval system. MYAENG, S.; AND KORFHAGE, R. See 03026. 121-129.
**03029** Logical foundations for knowledge representation in intelligent systems. GAINES, B. See 03026. 366-380.
**03030** § Object-oriented programming systems, languages and applications. OOPSLA'86 conference proceedings (Portland, Oregon, Sept. 29-Oct. 2, 1986), MEYROWITZ, N. (Ed.) Association for Computing Machinery, New York, NY, 1986, 508 pp., $37.00, ISBN 0-89791-204-7.
**03031** Mach and Matchmaker: kernel and language support for object-oriented distributed systems. JONES, M.; AND RASHID, R. See 03030. 67-77.
**03032** Impulse-86: a substrate for object-oriented interface design. SMITH, R.; DINITZ, R.; AND BARTH, P. See 03030. 167-176.
**03033** Experience with Flamingo: a distributed, object-oriented user interface system. ANDERSON, D. See 03030. 177-185.
**03034** Encapsulators: a new software paradigm in Smalltalk-80. PASCOE, G. See 03030. 341-346.
**03035** § Object-oriented programming systems, languages and applications. OOPSLA '88 Conference Proceedings (San Diego, CA, Sept. 25-30, 1988), MEYROWITZ, N. (Ed.) Association for Computing Machinery, New York, NY, 1988, 390 pp., ISBN 0-89791-284-5.
**03036** § Office Information Systems. Conference Sponsored by ACM SIGOIS and IEEECS TC-OA (Palo Alto, California, March 23-25, 1988), ALLEN, R. (Ed.) Association for Computing Machinery, New York, NY, 1988, 315 pp., $25.00, ISBN 089791-261-6.
**03037** The rapport multimedia conferencing system. AHUJA, S.; ENSOR, J.; AND HORN, D. See 03036. 1-8.
**03038** How can groups communicate when they use different languages? LEE, J.; AND MALONE, T. See 03036. 22-29.
**03039** OTM: specifying office tasks. LOCHOVSKY, F.; HOGG, J.; MENDELZON, A.; AND WEISER, S. See 03036. 46-54.
**03040** Computers' impact on productivity and work life. DUMAIS, S.; KRAUT, R.; AND KOCH, S. See 03036. 88-95.
**03041** The impact of electronic mail on managerial and organizational communications. SUMNER, M. See 03036. 96-109.
**03042** The influence of training on use of end-user software. OLFMAN, L.; AND BOSTROM, R. See 03036. 110-117.
**03043** Playing the language-games of design and use-on skill and participation. EHN, P. See 03036. 142-157.
**03044** Social choice theory and distributed decision making. URKEN, A. See 03036. 158-168.
**03045** Employing voice back channels of facilitate audio document retrieval. SCHMANDT, C. See 03036. 213-218.

03046   Browsing within time-driven multimedia documents. CHRISTODULAKIS, S.; AND GRAHAM, S. See 03036. 219-227.
03047   Interactive retrieval office documents. CROFT, W.; AND KROVETZ, R. See 03036. 228-235.
03048 § Practical Software Development Environments. Proceedings of the ACM SIGSOFT/SIGPLAN Software Engineering Symposium (Palo Alto, California, Dec. 9-11, 1986), HENDERSON, P. (Ed.) Association for Computing Machinery, New York, NY, 1987, 227 pp., 19.00, ISBN 0-8979-212-8.
03049   Integral-C—a practical environment for C programming. ROSS, G. See 03048. 42-48.
03050   Experience with a data base of programs. BELKATIR, N.; AND ESTUBLIER, J. See 03048. 84-91.
03051   AWB-ADE: an application development environment for interactive, integrated systems. CHILDS, C.; AND VOKOLOS, F. See 03048. 111-120.
03052   Implementing a user interface as a system of attributes. KING, R.; AND HUDSON, S. See 03048. 143-149.
03053   Dost: an environment to support automatic generation of user interfaces. DEWAN, P.; AND SOLOMON, M. See 03048. 150-159.
03054   A structural approach to the maintenance of structure-oriented environments. STAUDT, B.; KRUEGER, C.; AND GARLAN, D. See 03048. 160-170.
03055   A methodology for evaluating environments. WEIDERMAN, N.; HABERMANN, A.; BORGER, M.; AND KLEIN, M. See 03048. 199-207.
03056   The kernel of a generic software development environment. VAN LAMSWEERDE, A.; BUYSE, M.; DELCOURT, B.; DELOR, E.; ERVIER, M.; AND SCHAYES, M. See 03048. 208-217.
03057   A foundation for programming environments. REPPY, J.; AND GANSNER, E. See 03048. 218-227.
03058 § Programming Language design and Implementation. SIGPLAN'88 Conference (Atlanta, Georgia, June 22-24, 1988), WEXELBLAT, R. Association for Computing Machinery, New York, NY, 1988, 338 pp., ISBN 0-89791-269-1.
03059   Design and implementation of the UW Illustrated compiler. ANDREWS, K.; HENRY, R.; AND YAMAMOTO, W. See 03058. 105-114.
03060   Debugging concurrent processes: a case study. STONE, J. See 03058. 145-153.
03061   Multiprocessor Smalltalk: a case study of a multiprocessor-based programming environment. PALLAS, J.; AND UNGAR, D. See 03058. 268-277.
03062 § Research & Development in Information Retrieval. Eleventh International Conference (Grenoble, France, June 13-15, 1988), CHIARAMELLA, Y. (Ed.) Association for Computing Machinery, New York, NY, 1988, 677 pp., ISBN 2-7061-0309-4.
03063   How do the experts do it? The use of ethnographic methods as an aid to understanding the cognitive processing and retrieval of large bodies of text. CASE, D. See 03062. 127-133.
03064   On the nature and fuction of explanation in intelligent information retrieval. BELKIN, N. See 03062. 135-145.
03065   Information retrieval using impression of documents as a clue. HIRABAYASHI, F.; MATOBA, H.; AND KASAHARA, Y. See 03062. 233-244.
03066   Concept based retrieval in classical IR systems. GIGER, H. See 03062. 275-289.
03067   Towards interactive query expansion. HARMAN, D. See 03062. 321-331.
03068   Retrieval based on user behaviour. KOK, A.; AND BOTMAN, A. See 03062. 343-357.
03069   Some measures and procedures for evaluation of the user interface in an information retrieval system. TAGUE, J.; AND SCHULTZ, R. See 03062. 371-385.
03070   IR-NLI II: applying man-machine interaction and artificial intelligence conceptsto information retrieval. BRAJNIK, G.; GUIDA, G.; AND TASSO, C. See 03062. 387-399.
03071   Integrated information retrieval for law in a hypertext environment. WILSON, E. See 03062. 663-677.
03072 § Research and development in information retrieval. Proceedings of the Tenth Annual International ACMSIGIR Conference (New Orleans, LA, June 3-5, 1987), YU, C.; AND VAN RIJSBERGEN, C. (Eds.) Association for Computing Machinery, New York, NY, 1987, 317 pp., $19, ISBN 0-89791-232-2.
03073   Informational zooming: an interaction model for the graphical access to text knowledge bases. THIEL, U.; AND HAMMWOHNER, R. See 03072. 45-56.

03074 Generating an individualized user interface. TAGUE, J. See 03072. 57-60.
03075 Why do some people have more difficulty learning to use an information retrieval system than others? BORGMAN, C. See 03072. 61-71.
03076 Illustrated description of an interactive knowledge based indexing system. HUMPHREY, S. See 03072. 73-90.
03077 Optimal determination of user-oriented clusters. DEOGUN, J.; AND RAGHAVAN, V. See 03072. 140-146.
03078 A retrieval system for on-line English-Japanese dictionaries. ITO, T.; AND KUBOTA, M. See 03072. 181-186.
03079 An advanced full-text retrieval and analysis system. SMITH, J.; WEISS, S.; AND FERGUSON, G. See 03072. 187-195.
03080 § Symsac '86. Proceedings of the 1986 symposium on symbolic and algebraic computation (Waterloo, Ont., Canada, July 21-23, 1986), CHAR, B. (Ed.) Association for Computing Machinery, New York, NY, 1986, 254 pp., $21, ISBN 0-89791-199-7.
03081 Iris: design of a user interface program for symbolic algebra. LEONG, B. See 03080. 1-6.
03082 MathScribe: a user interface for computer algebra systems. SMITH, C.; AND SOIFFER, N. See 03080. 7-13.
03083 PowerMath—A system for the Macintosh. DAVENPORT, J.; AND ROTH, C. See 03080. 13-15.
03084 § Symsac '86—Proceedings of the 1986 symposium on symbolic and algebraic manipulation. (Waterloo, Ont., Canada, July 21-23, 1986), CHAR, B. (Ed.) Association for Computing Machinery, New York, NY, 1986, 254 pp., $21, ISBN 0-89791-199-7.
03085 Iris: design of an user interface program for symbolic algebra. LEONG, B. See 03084. 1-6.
03086 MathScribe: a user interface for computer algebra systems. SMITH, C.; AND SOIFFER, N. See 03084. 7-12.
03087 Alkahest III: automatic analysis of periodic weakly nonlinear ODEs. FITCH, J.; NORMAN, A.; AND MOORE, M. See 03084. 34-38.
03088 Dialogue in REDUCE: experience and development. KRYUKOV, A. See 03084. 107-109.
03089 § SIGMOD International Conference on Management of Data. Proceedings (Chicago, Illinois, June 1-3), BORAL, H.; AND LARSON, P. (Eds.) Association for Computing Machinery, New York, NY, 1988, 443 pp., $33.00, ISBN 0-89791-268-3.
03090 A design data manager. ALHO, K.; PELTONEN, H.; MÄNTYLÄ, M.; AND SULONEN, R. See 03089. 202-202.
03091 § The history of personal workstations. Proceedings of the ACM Conference (Palo Alto, CA, Jan. 9-10, 1986), WHITE, J.; AND ANDERSON, K. (Eds.) Association for Computing Machinery, New York, NY, 1986, 198 pp., ISBN 0-89791-176-8.
03092 Toward a history of (personal) workstations. BELL, G. See 03091. 1-17.
03093 A personal view of the personal work station: some firsts in the Fifties. ROSS, D. See 03091. 19-48.
03094 The augmented knowledge workshop. ENGLEBART, D. See 03091. 73-83.
03095 Personal distributed computing: the Alto and Ethernet hardware. THACKER, C. See 03091. 87-100.
03096 Personal distributed computing: the Alto and Ethernet software. LAMPSON, B. See 03091. 101-131.
03097 A history of the Promis technology: an effective human interface. SCHULTZ, J. See 03091. 159-182.
03098 User technology—from pointing to pondering. CARD, S.; AND MORAN, T. See 03091. 183-198.
03099 § The 1987 ACM SIGBDP-SIGCPR Conference. (Coral Gables, Florida, March 5-6, 1987), AWAD, E. (Ed.) Association for Computing Machinery, New York, NY, 1987, 235 pp., $20.00, ISBN 0-89791-222-5.
03100 A consultation system for information center resource allocation. HELTNE, M.; VINZE, A.; KONSYNSKI, B.; AND NUNAMAKER JR., J. See 03099. 20-44.
03101 Expert system applications in customer service. SCHON, S.; AND HELFERICH, O. See 03099. 140-162.
03102 § Twenty-five years of electronic design automation. A compendium of papers from the Design Automation Conference (,), NEWTON, A. Association for Computing Machinery, New York, NY, 1988, 630 pp., ISBN 0-89791-267-5.
03103 Sketchpad a man-machine graphical communication system. SUTHERLAND, I. See 03102. 507-524.
03104 Incorporating the human factor in color CAD systems. FROME, F. See 03102. 554-560.
03105 § User Interface Software. Proceedings of the ACM SIGGRAPH Symposium (Alberta, Canada, October 17-19, 1988), GREEN, M. (Chr.) Association for Computing Machinery, New York, NY, 1988, 230 pp., ISBN 0-89791-283-7.
03106 EDGE - a graph based tool for specifying interaction. KLEYN, M.; AND CHAKRAVARTY, I. See 03105. 1-14.

03107  State trees as structured finite state machines for user interfaces. RUMBAUGH, J. See 03105. 15-29.
03108  Extensions to C for interface programming. RHYNE, J. See 03105. 30-45.
03109  An overview of the C toolkit. McCORMACK, J.; AND ASENTE, P. See 03105. 46-55.
03110  The architecture of a user interface toolkit. BINDING, C. See 03105. 56-65.
03111  Event-driven user interfaces based on quasi-parallelism. HAUGE, T.; NORDGARD, I.; OSCARSSON, D.; AND RAEDER, G. See 03105. 66-76.
03112  The mirage rapid interface prototyping system. McDONALD, J.; VANDENBERG, P.; AND SMARTT, M. See 03105. 77-84.
03113  Clue: a common lisp user interface environment. KIMBROUGH, K.; AND OREN, L. See 03105. 85-94.
03114  UNIX Emacs: a retrospective (lessons for flexible system design). BORENSTEIN, N.; AND GOSLING, J. See 03105. 95-101.
03115  Interface usage measurements in a user interface management system. OLSEN, D.; AND HALVERSEN, B. See 03105. 102-108.
03116  Designing the interface designer's interface. SINGH, G.; AND GREEN, M. See 03105. 109-116.
03117  ACE: a color expert system for user interface design. MEIER, B. See 03105. 117-128.
03118  XY-WINS: an integraded environment for developing graphical user interfaces. GIACALONE, A. See 03105. 129-143.
03119  Building interfaces interactively. SMITH, D. See 03105. 144-151.
03120  Building user interfaces by direct manipulation. CARDELLI, L. See 03105. 152-166.
03121  Using active data in a UIMS. HENRY, T.; AND HUDSON, S. See 03105. 167-178.
03122  Applying a theory of graphical presentation to the graphic design of user interfaces. M ACKINLAY, J. See 03105. 179-189.
03123  Dynamic construction of animated help from application context. SUKAVIRIYA, P. See 03105. 190-202.
03124  XVISION: a comprehensive software system for image processing research, education, and applications. TERAN, M.; RASURE, J.; ARGIRO, D.; HALLETT, S.; NEHER, R.; YOUNG, M.; AND WILSON, S. See 03105. 203-210.
03125  A portable user interface for a scientific programming environment. GUARNA, V.; AND GAUR, Y. See 03105. 211-220.
03126  JACK: a toolkit for manipulating articulated figures. PHILLIPS, C.; AND BADLER, N. See 03105. 221-229.
03127 §  User Services. Proc. of the ACM SIGUCCS Conference XV (Kansas City, MO, Sept. 27-30, 1987), HUTCHISON, L. (Ed.) Association for Computing Machinery, New York, NY, 1987, 504 pp., $38, ISBN 0-89791-241-1.
03128  Le Menu: changing the user interface on a local area network. BOESHARR, D. See 03127. 19-20.
03129  Captive...a new tool. HALLER, R.; AND KOVAL, G. See 03127. 237-245.
03130 §  User Services Conference. Proceedings of the sixteenth ACM SIGUCCS Conference (Hyatt Regency Long Beach, Long Beach, CA, October 30 - November 2, 1988), CRANE, P. (Ed.) Association for Computing Machinery, New York, NY, 1988, 444 pp., ISBN 0-89791-286-1.
03131  Why desktop publishing is not a panacea. PURCELL, P. See 03130. 19-21.
03132  User services—a british perspective. MORROW, T. See 03130. 41-47.:4T03133I didn't even know it was user services. PRATTO, M.; AND MARTIN, J. See 03130. 49-53.
03134  CAREing for users at Syracuse University. DERR, B.; AND LADD, C. See 03130. 71-75.
03135  The crystal ball of research: how to use it to learn about the user community. GRAJEK, S. See 03130. 77-80.
03136  Charting the course of a user survey that will rock the boat. STAGER, S. See 03130. 81-89.
03137  An empirical study of user satisfaction with a microcomputer-based campus-wide. FOLEY, T.; AND NEWMAN, M. See 03130. 91-100.
03138  From user to client services; making the transition for supercomputing. GOODWIN, S.; AND VUKELICH, J. See 03130. 111-115.
03139  The evolution of user services. GARRET, R. See 03130. 131-137.
03140  New wine in old skins, or, was all this ferment really necessary? WEBSTER, S. See 03130. 139-144.
03141  Software engineering meets user services: a methodology for developing user. MAYNE, R. See 03130. 151-163.

**03142** Establishing a computing assistance centre. NIGHTINGALE, J. See 03130. 165-171.
**03143** The many faces of faculty computing assistance. KENT, P.; AND RUFFO, B. See 03130. 173-176.
**03144** Learning the ways: the enculturation of SDSC users. JOVANOVIC, M. See 03130. 179-183.
**03145** Super consulting for supercomputer users: a philosophy of user support. HILINSKI, T. See 03130. 185-187.
**03146** Information in the air and in the wave. WAGGONER, J. See 03130. 189-191.
**03147** Supercomputer applications: helping users cope with tough programming problems. ROGERS, J. See 03130. 197-199.
**03148** How to build a help desk that floats. DEAVERS-CLASPELL, P. See 03130. 219-223.
**03149** Starting and maintaining a computing resource center: lessons we've learned. O'BRIEN, L. See 03130. 229-233.
**03150** Still sailing (and bailing): managing unexpected change in user support. JOHNSON, E. See 03130. 235-241.
**03151** Advisor—an electronic mail consulting service. THYBERG, C. See 03130. 247-255.
**03152** Local area networks: sailing from the past to the present and into the future. GELMAN, T. See 03130. 303-311.
**03153** A new model for user services: distributed support. PEAR, M. See 03130. 323-327.
**03154** Hypermedia: a face lift for presentation research and development: a user services function. BARONE, R. See 03130. 359-361.
**03155** Hypermedia, help and how-to. ELLS, R. See 03130. 363-368.
**03156** Teaching users to fish: hooks, lines and sinkers for reading computer documentat. TROLL, D. See 03130. 377-382.
**03157** A suppport strategy for users of a campus-wide local area network. POLTZ, S.; SMITH, S.; AND BALLOWE, D. See 03130. 387-392.
**03158** Desktop publishing and user services; moment in the evolution of user support documentation at UNH. BLACK, M. See 03130. 401-404.
**03159** The evolution of microcomputer laboratory services at the University of Notre Dame. See 03130. 423-425.
**03160** Three steps of better documentation. CUNNINGHAM, B.; AND COMMISSO, M. See 03130. 427-433.
**03161** User services consulting supportr tools at the NASA numerical aerodynamic simula. WILLARD, C.; MIDDLECOFF, J.; HART, L.; AND ECKERT, R. See 03130. 437-442.
**03162** § AFIPS Conference Proceedings; vol. 55 1986 National Computer Conference. (Las Vegas, Nevada, June 16-19, 1986), MATTOX, A. (Ed.) AFIPS Press, Arlington, VA, 1986, 566 pp., ISBN 0-88283-049-X.
**03163** Testing for usability. POTOSNAK, K.; AND KOFFLER, R. See 03162. 77-84.
**03164** Human interfaces in a legal expert system. SPROWL, J.; APPLEGATE, K.; EVENS, M.; RUEB, R.; AND HARR, H. See 03162. 135-142.
**03165** Design issues of an intelligent workstation for the office. NAFFAH, N.; WHITE, G.; AND GIBBS, S. See 03162. 153-159.
**03166** Organizational videotex: information services for the end user. FINN, A. See 03162. 161-169.
**03167** Reasoning about knowledge: an overview. HALPERN, J. See 03162. 219-228.
**03168** Project source file management under the UNIX operating system. FILIPSKI, A.; AND DION, L. See 03162. 267-271.
**03169** Shifting to a higher gear in a natural language system. THOMPSON, B.; AND THOMPSON, F. See 03162. 349-354.
**03170** GRASS3, a language for interactive graphics. DONATO, N. See 03162. 355-359.
**03171** The star user interface: an overview. SMITH, D.; IRBY, C.; KIMBALL, R.; AND HARSLEM, E. See 03162. 383-396.
**03172** Advanced office systems: An empirical look at use and satisfaction. BIKSON, T.; AND GUTEK, B. See 03162. 421-430.
**03173** § Expert database systems. Proceedings from the first international workshop (Kiawah Island, SC, Oct. 24-27, 1984), KERSCHBERG, L. (Ed.) Benjamin/Cummings Publ. Co., Inc., Menlo Park, CA, 1986, 701 pp., $41.95, ISBN 0-8053-3270-7.
**03174** An interactive data dictionary facility for CAD/CAM data bases. CAMMARATA, S.; AND MELKANOFF, M. See 03173. 423-440.

03175 Distributed database considerations in an expert system for radar analysis. CROMARTY, A.; ADAMS, T.; WILSON, G.; CUNNINGHAM, J.; TOLLANDER, C.; AND GRINBERG, M. See 03173. 505-524.

03176 A temporal logic for reasoning about changing data bases in the context of natural language question-answering. MAYS, E. See 03173. 559-578.

03177 The IRUS transportable natural language database interface. BATES, M.; MOSER, M.; AND STALLARD, D. See 03173. 617-630.

03178 Anticipating false implicatures: cooperative responses in question-answer systems. HIRSCHBERG, J. See 03173. 631-638.

03179 Supporting natural language database update by modeling real world actions. SALVETER, S. See 03173. 639-658.

03180 § Ada-components: libraries and tools. Proceedings of the Ada-Europe International Conference (Stockholm, Sweden, May 26–28, 1987), TAFVELIN, S. (Ed.) Cambridge University Press, New York, NY, 1987, 292 pp., ISBN 0-521-34636-3.

03181 Ecilpse—an APSE based on PCTE. PIERCE, R. See 03180. 32-45.

HCI-0100 SKETCHER, an interactive, graphical Ada software tool—its development and use. BRINTZENHOFF, A. See 03180. 209-222.

HCI-0098 Ada-based executable modelling of distributed systems. BRUNO, G.; AND BALSAMO, A. See 03180. 279-292.

03182 § Document manipulation and typography. Proceedings of the International Conference on Electronic Publishing (Nice, France, April 20–22, 1988), VAN VLIET, J. (Ed.) [Cambridge series on electronic publishing] Cambridge University Press, New York, NY, 1988, 288 pp., $47.50, ISBN 0-521-36294-6.

HCI-0404 Visual structure and the transmission of meaning. SOUTHALL, R. See 03182. 35-45.

HCI-0403 Image processing aspects of type. MORRIS, R. See 03182. 139-155.

03183 Drag: a graph drawing system. TRICKEY, H. See 03182. 171-182.

03184 Abstraction and integration in IDE, an editing and formatting environment. KAPLAN, M. See 03182. 193-204.

03185 An introduction to Gargoyle: an interactive illustration tool. PIER, K.; BIER, E.; AND STONE, M. See 03182. 223-238.

03186 Vidura—an interactive multilingual publishing system—specification & design. NATH, S.; PATTANAIK, S.; AND MUDUR, S. See 03182. 249-260.

HCI-0402 Synthesis of print-quality cursive script based on a model of the human handwriting mechanism. DOOIJES, E. See 03182. 261-273.

03187 Chinese character processing system based on character-root combination and gra phic processing. CUN-CHANG, F.; AND ZINI, P. See 03182. 275-286.

03188 § Expert systems 85. Proc. of the fifth technical conference of the British Computer Society Specialist Group on Expert Systems (Univ. of Warwick, Warwick, UK, Dec. 17-19, 1985), MERRY, M. (Ed.) [British Computer Society workshop series] Cambridge University Press, New York, NY, 1986, 334 pp., $39.50, ISBN 0-521-32596-X.

HCI-0326 What do users ask? Some thoughts on diagnostic advice. KIDD, A. See 03188. 9-19.

HCI-0362 O-Plan: control in the open planning architecture. CURRIE, K.; AND TATE, A. See 03188. 225-240.

HCI-0319 Acquisition of control and domain knowledge by watching in a blackboard environment. BOYLE, C. See 03188. 273-286.

03189 § People and computers III. Proceedings of Third Conference of the British Computer Society Human-Interactio (Univ. of Exeter, Exeter, UK, Sept. 7–11, 1987), DIAPER, D.; AND WINDER, R. (Eds.) Cambridge University Press, New York, NY, 1987, 379 pp., $79.50, ISBN 0521-35197-9.

03190 Formally-based techniques for dialogue design. ALEXANDER, H. See 03189. 1-214.

03191 The incorporation of early interface evaluation into command language grammar specifications. SHARRATT, B. See 03189. 11-28.

03192 Human factors and the problems of evaluation in the design of speech systems interfaces. JONES, D.; HAPESHI, K.; AND FRANKISH, C. See 03189. 41-49.

## PROCEEDINGS

03193   Patterned systems design—HCI in commercial data processing. SHARROCK, B. See 03189. 53-60.
03194   Describing a product opportunity: a method of understanding the users' environment. HUTT, A.; DONNELLY, N.; MACAULAY, L.; FOWLER, C.; AND TWIGGER, D. See 03189. 61-74.
03195   The travel metaphor as design principle and training aid for navigating around complex systems. HAMMOND, N.; AND ALLINSON, L. See 03189. 75-90.
03196   Human factors in systems design: a case study. REYNOLDS, C. See 03189. 93-102.
03197   A flexible negotiable interactive learning environment. FERM, R.; KINDBORG, M.; AND KOLLERBAUER, A. See 03189. 103-113.
03198   The Drexel disk: an electronic "Guidebook". HEWETT, T. See 03189. 115-129.
03199   Preliminary analysis for design. KEANE, M.; AND JOHNSON, P. See 03189. 133-146.
03200   Refining early design decisions with a black-box model. MONK, A.; AND DIX, A. See 03189. 147-158.
03201   Pictorial knowledge bases. BARKER, P.; AND MANJI, K. See 03189. 161-173.
03202   Visual languages and human computer interaction. KINDBORG, M.; AND KOLLERBAUR, A. See 03189. 175-187.
03203   Video browsing and system response time. PATTERSON, J.; AND EGIDO, C. See 03189. 189-198.
03204   The myth of the infinitely fast machine. DIX, A. See 03189. 215-228.
03205   INTERA/P: a user interface prototyping tool. HASHIMOTO, O.; AND MIYAI, H. See 03189. 229-244.
03206   Designing electronic paper to fit user requirements. THOMAS, C. See 03189. 247-257.
03207   Automation—implications for knowledge retention as a function of operator control responsibility. NARBOROUGH-HALL, C. See 03189. 269-282.
03208   A human-computer interface for control system design. BARKER, H.; TOWNSEND, P.; JOBLING, C.; GRANT, P.; AND CHEN, M. See 03189. 283-293.
03209   Parcel sorting by speech recognition: human factors issues. FRANKISH, C.; JONES, D.; MADDEN, C.; WAIGHT, K.; AND STODDART, J. See 03189. 295-303.
03210   Expert systems—interface insight. MORRIS, A. See 03189. 307-324.
03211   Some critical remarks on abstractions for adaptable dialogue managers. COCKTON, G. See 03189. 325-343.
03212   An evaluation of the effectiveness of the adaptive interface module (AIM) in matching dialogues to users. FOWLER, C.; MACAULAY, L.; AND SIRIPOKSUP, S. See 03189. 345-359.
03213   Planning in the context of human-computer interaction. YOUNG, R.; AND SIMON, T. See 03189. 363-370.
03214   Knowledge acquisition and conceptual models: a cognitive analysis of the interface. DILLION, A. See 03189. 371-379.
03215 § People and computers IV. Proceedings of the Fourth Conference of the British Computer Society (Univ. of Manchester, UK, Sept. 5–6, 1988), JONES, D.; AND WINDER, R. (Eds.) Cambridge University Press, New York, NY, 1988, 594 pp., $79.50, ISBN 0-521-36553-8.
03216   Computers for the people: HCI in prospect. An introduction to the HCI '88 conference. JONES, D. See 03215. 7-10.
03217   Implications of current design practice for the use of HCI techniques. BELLOTTI, V. See 03215. 13-34.
03218   Task-related knowledge structures: analysis, modelling and application. JOHNSON, P.; JOHNSON, H.; WADDINGTON, R.; AND SHOULS, A. See 03215. 35-62.
03219   Abstract, generic models of interactive systems. DIX, A. See 03215. 63-77.
HCI-0245   Analysing the scope of cognitive models in human-computer interaction: a trade-off approach. SIMON, T. See 03215. 79-93.
03220   The design and evaluation of an animated programming environment. HEERJEE, K.; SWANSTON, M.; MILLER, C.; AND SAMSON, W. See 03215. 97-109.
03221   The representation of user interface style. NEWMAN, W. See 03215. 123-143.
03222   Some experiences in integrating specification of human computer interaction within a structured system development method. SUTCLIFFE, A. See 03215. 145-160.
03223   Humans, computers, and contracts. GUNDRY, A. See 03215. 161-175.
HCI-0284   A user oriented design process for user recovery and command reuse support. YANG, Y. See 03215. 179-198.

03224  Issues governing the suitability of programming languages for programming tasks. PETRE, M.; AND WINDER, R. See 03215. 199-215.
03225  SEE: a safe editing environment; human-computer interaction for programmers. HARRIS, J. See 03215. 217-233.
03226  User-driven adaptive behaviour, a comparative evaluation and an inductive analysis. BROOKS, A.; AND THORBURN, C. See 03215. 237-255.
03227  Contextual structure analysis of microcomputer manuals. CHIMURA, H.; KATO, H.; MITANI, H.; AND SATO, T. See 03215. 257-274.
03228  Information flow in a user interface: the effect of experience and context on the recall of MacWrite screens. MAYES, J.; DRAPER, S.; MCGREGOR, A.; AND OATLEY, K. See 03215. 275-289.
03229  Can cognitive complexity theory (CCT) produce an adequate measure of system usability? KNOWLES, C. See 03215. 291-307.
HCI-0447  Training for optimising transfer between word processors. POLLOCK, C. See 03215. 309-328.
03230  Measuring user satisfaction. KIRAKOWSKI, J.; AND CORBETT, M. See 03215. 329-338.
03231  A review of human performance and preferences with different input devices to computer systems. MILNER, N. See 03215. 341-362.
03232  A gesture based text editor. WELBOURN, L.; AND WHITROW, R. See 03215. 363-371.
03233  Towards the construction of a maximally-contrasting set of colours. VAN LAAR, D.; AND FLAVELL, R. See 03215. 373-389.
03234  Gripe: a graphical interface to a knowledge based system which reasons about protein topology. SEIFERT, K.; AND RAWLINGS, C. See 03215. 391-406.
HCI-0375  Graphical prototyping of graphical tools. ENGLAND, D. See 03215. 407-420.
03235  A comparison of hypertext, scrolling and folding as mechanisms for program browsing. MONK, A.; WALSH, P.; AND DIX, A. See 03215. 421-435.
03236  Hypertext tips: experiences in developing a hypertext tutorial. HARDMAN, L. See 03215. 437-451.
03237  Optimum display arrangements for presenting visual reminders. FINDLAY, J.; DAVIES, S.; KENTRIDGE, R.; LAMBERT, A.; AND KELLY, J. See 03215. 453-464.
03238  Flexible intelligent interactive-video. WEBB, T.; AND JAMESON, D. See 03215. 465-476.
03239  The application of cognitive psychology to CAD. DILLON, A.; AND SWEENEY, M. See 03215. 477-488.
03240  How much is enough? A study of user command repertoires. ANSTEY, P. See 03215. 491-507.
03241  Generative transition networks: a new communication control abstraction. COCKTON, G. See 03215. 509-527.
HCI-0357  Text processing by speech: dialogue design and usability issues in the provision of a system for disabled users. HEWITT, J.; AND FURNER, S. See 03215. 529-544.
03242  User requirements for expert system explanation: what, why and when? ROGERS, Y. See 03215. 547-564.
HCI-0337  Knowledge elicitation: dissociating conscious reflections from automatic processes. STEVENSON, R.; MANKTELOW, K.; AND HOWARD, M. See 03215. 565-579.
03243  GOMS meets STRIPS: the integration of planning with skilled procedure execution in human-computer interaction. SIMON, T.; AND YOUNG, R. See 03215. 581-594.
03244 §  People and computers: designing for usability. Proceedings of the Second Conference of the British Computer Society, human computer interaction specialist group (York, UK, Sept. 23-26, 1986), HARRISON, M.; AND MONK, A. (Eds.) Cambridge University Press, New York, NY, 1986, ISBN 0-521-33259-1.
03245  People and computers: designing for usability. LONG, J. See 03244. 3-23.
03246  Formal methods and the design of effective user interfaces. SUFRIN, B. See 03244. 24-43.
03247  Ergonomics in design for usability. SHACKEL, B. See 03244. 44-64.
03248  Understanding the nature of the office for the design of third wave office systems. BJORN-ANDERSEN, N. See 03244. 65-77.
03249  Ease of use - the ultimate deception. THIMBLEBY, H. See 03244. 78-94.
03250  Human factors in the Columbus space station. ALEXANDER, I.; MORRISROE, G.; NORRIS, P.; AND TINDELL, A. See 03244. 97-114.

03251   Tools for management and support of multiple constraints in a writer's assistant. O'MALLEY, K.; AND SHARPLES, M. See 03244. 115-131.

03252   MacCadd - an enabling software method support tool. JONES, J. See 03244. 132-154.

03253   ECS - A technique for the formal specification and rapid prototyping of human-computer interaction. ALEXANDER, H. See 03244. 157-179.

03254   Rapid prototyping of dialogue for human factors research: the EASIE approach. MACLEAN, A.; BARNARD, P.; AND WILSON, M. See 03244. 180-195.

03255   The role of iterative evaluation in designing systems for usability. HEWETT, T. See 03244. 196-214.

03256   Toward the successful design and implementation of computer based management information systems in small companies. WROE, B. See 03244. 217-234.

03257   A study of group interaction over a computer-based message system. WILBUR, S.; RUBIN, T.; AND LEE, S. See 03244. 235-248.

03258   Usability engineering in office product development. BROOKE, J. See 03244. 249-259.

03259   Identifying the knowledge requirements of an expert system's natural language processing interface. DIAPER, D. See 03244. 263-280.

03260   Design and evaluation of the AID adaptive front-end to Telecom Gold. TOTTERDELL, P.; AND COOPER, P. See 03244. 281-295.

03261   Plan recognition for intelligent monitoring. DAVENPORT, C.; AND WEIR, G. See 03244. 296-315.

03262   Application modelling in a user interface management system. ALTY, J.; AND MCKELL, P. See 03244. 319-335.

03263   The design of two innovative user interfaces. THIMBLEBY, H. See 03244. 336-351.

03264   Principles and interaction models for window managers. DIX, A.; AND HARRISON, M. See 03244. 352-366.

03265   Modelling generic user-interfaces with functional programs. COOK, S. See 03244. 369-385.

03266   Text representation and manipulation in a mouse-driven interface. TOOK, R. See 03244. 386-401.

03267   Proving properties of interactive systems. ANDERSON, S. See 03244. 402-416.

03268   Where do we draw the line? - Derivation and evaluation of user interface software separation rules. COCKTON, G. See 03244. 417-431.

03269   A viewdata-structure editor designed around a task/action mapping. YOUNG, R.; AND HARRIS, J. See 03244. 435-446.

03270   The use of complexity theory in evaluating interfaces. KISS, G.; AND PINDER, R. See 03244. 447-463.

03271   User programs: a way to match computer systems and human cognition. RUNCIMAN, C.; AND HAMMOND, N. See 03244. 464-481.

03272   Using an expert system to convey HCI information. WILSON, M.; BARNARD, P.; AND MACLEAN, A. See 03244. 482-497.

03273   New technology work aids for the physically disabled. HOWEY, K. See 03244. 501-526.

03274   Structural visibility and program comprehension. GILMORE, D. See 03244. 527-545.

03275   Voice versus keyboard: use of a comparative analysis of learning to identify skill requirements of input devices. JOHNSON, P.; LONG, J.; AND VISICK, D. See 03244. 546-562.

03276   Empirical evaluation of map interfaces. HITCH, G.; SUTCLIFFE, A.; BOWERS, J.; AND ECCLES, L. See 03244. 565-585.

03277   Evaluating the meaningfulness of icon sets to represent command operations. ROGERS, Y. See 03244. 586-603.

03278   Optimizing the usability of computer-generated displays. TULLIS, T. See 03244. 604-613.

03279 §   Proc. of the third British national conference on databases (BNCOD3). (Leeds, UK, July 11-13, 1984), LONGSTAFF, J. (Ed.) [British Computer Society workshop series] Cambridge University Press, New York, NY, 1984, 263 pp., ISBN 0-521-26841-9.

03280   Integrating data and metadata to enhance the user interface. JOHNSON, R. See 03279. 29-39.

HCI-0253   HERCULES: database query using natural language fragments. CUFF, R. See 03279. 133-149.

03281   An approach to interactive definition of database views. LAENDER, A. See 03279. 173-185.

03282 § Proceedings of the fourth British national conference on databases (BNCOD 4). (Univ. of Keele, UK, July 10-12, 1985), GRUNDY, A. (Ed.) [British Computer Society workshop series] Cambridge University Press, New York, NY, 1985, 229 pp., $44.50, ISBN 0-521-32020-8.

03283 The integration of the network and relational approaches in a DBMS. D'APPOLLONIO, V.; FUGGETTA, A.; NEGRI, M.; AND PELAGATTI, G. See 03282. 177-197.

HCI-0117 Some observations on user interface design and user performance. NEWMAN, A.; AND SETHI, J. See 03282. 199-213.

03284 § Proceedings of the Fifth British National Conference on Databases (BNCOD 5). (Univ. of Kent at Canterbury, Canterbury, UK, July 14-16, 1986), OXBORROW, E. Cambridge University Press, New York, NY, 1986, 199 pp., ISBN 0-521-33260-5.

03285 Knowledge base enhancements to relational databases. YEO, C.; THORPE, J.; AND LONGSTAFF, J. See 03284. 87-103.

03286 Database maps. SUTCLIFFE, A. See 03284. 155-165.

03287 § Research and development in information retrieval. Proc. of the third joint BCS and ACM symposium (King's College, Cambridge, July 2-6, 1984), VAN RIJSBERGEN, C. (Ed.) [The British Computer Society workshop series] Cambridge University Press, New York, NY, 1984, 433 pp., $49.50, ISBN 0-521-26865-6.

HCI-0263 An interactive database end user facility for the definition and manipulation of forms. LAENDER, A.; AND STOCKER, P. See 03287. 41-54.

HCI-0323 Knowledge based systems versus thesaurus : an architecture problem about expert systems design. DEFUDE, B. See 03287. 267-280.

HCI-0267 Computing text constituency: an algorithmic approach to the generation of text graphs. HAHN, U.; AND REIMER, U. See 03287. 343-368.

03288 § Graphics Interface '86/Vision Interface '86. Proceedings (Vancouver, B.C., Canada, May 26-30, 1986), WEIN, M.; AND KIDD, E. (Eds.) Canadian Information Processing Society, Toronto, Ontario, Canada, 1986, 402 pp., $35, ISBN 0713-5424.

03289 An editing model for generating graphical user interfaces. OLSEN, D. See 03288. 66-70.

03290 Automatic generation of graphical user interfaces. SINGH, G.; AND GREEN, M. See 03288. 71-76.

03291 Animating human figures: perspectives and directions. BADLER, N. See 03288. 115-120.

03292 The interactive specification of human animation. RISDALE, G.; HEWITT, S.; AND CALVERT, T. See 03288. 121-130.

03293 Speech and expression: a computer solution to face animation. PEARCE, A.; WYVILL, B.; WYVILL, G.; AND HILL, D. See 03288. 136-140.

03294 Virya—a motion control editor for kinematic and dynamic animation. WILHELMS, J. See 03288. 141-146.

03295 Near-real-time control of human figure models. ARMSTRONG, W.; GREEN, M.; AND LAKE, R. See 03288. 147-151.

03296 Interactive 3-D modeling with personal computers. THORNTON, R.; AND GLASS, G. See 03288. 180-185.

03297 Psychology and the user interface: science is soft at the frontier. CARROLL, J. See 03288. 186-187.

03298 Learning graphics programming by direct communication. TUORI, M.; AND POINTING, T. See 03288. 188-192.

03299 Eliminating the dichotomy between scripting and interaction. SCHLAG, J. See 03288. 202-206.

03300 Part structure for 3-D sketching. PENTLAND, A. See 03288. 223-228.

03301 Interfacing image processing and computer graphics systems using an artificial visual system. COGGINS, J.; FOGARTY, K.; AND FAY, F. See 03288. 229-234.

03302 A knowledge-based approach to computer vision systems. LEVINE, M.; AND HONG, W. See 03288. 260-265.

03303 Image segmentation based on color and texture gradient. NGUYEN, P. See 03288. 267-272.

03304 Principle of visual color coding applied to satellite images. LEFEVRE-FONOLLOSA, M.; AND CRUCHANT, H. See 03288. 284-286.

03305 Selection and use of image features for segmentation of boundary images. WALTERS, D. See 03288. 318-324.

03306 Cortical representation of texture primitives. WALFORD, A.; AND JERNIGAN, M. See 03288. 325-330.

## PROCEEDINGS

03307    Speeded phase discrimination: evidence for global to local processing. BARR, J. See 03288. 331-336.
03308    Correspondence in apparent motion: defining the heuristics. GREEN, M. See 03288. 337-342.
03309    Coupling visual and dynamic features to study handwritten signatures. BRAULT, J.; AND PLAMONDON, R. See 03288. 375-379.
03310    Reconstruction and display of the retina. SLOAN, K.; MEYERS, D.; AND CURCIO, C. See 03288. 385-389.
HCI-0052 §  Artificial and human intelligence. Proc. of the international NATO symposium (Lyon, France, Oct. 1981), ELITHORN, A.; AND BANERJI, R. (Eds.) Elsevier North-Holland, Inc., New York, NY, 1984, 344 pp., $40, ISBN 0-444-86545-4.
03311    GPS and the psychology of th Rubik cubist: a study in reasoning about actions. BANERJI, R. See HCI-0052. 67-79.
HCI-0353  A framework of a mechanical translation between Japanese and English by analogy principle. NAGAO, M. See HCI-0052. 173-180.
HCI-0239  Approaches to human reasoning: an analytic framework. STERNBERG, R.; AND LASAGA, M. See HCI-0052. 213-227.
HCI-0240  The distributed processing of knowledge and belief in the human brain. LAVOREL, P. See HCI-0052. 229-238.
03312    Common and uncommon issues in artificial intelligence an psychology. STERNBERG, R. See HCI-0052. 281-288.
HCI-0322  Reasoning in natural language for designing a data base. COLOMBETTI, M.; GUIDA, G.; PERNICI, B.; AND SOMALVICO, M. See HCI-0052. 297-314.
03313 §  Computer science and statistics. Proceedings of the Seventeenth Symposium on the interface of computer sciences and statistics (Lexington, KY, March 1985), ALLEN, D. (Ed.) Elsevier North-Holland, Inc., New York, NY, 1986, 342 pp., $65, ISBN 0-444-70018-8.
03314    Measuring the performance of statisticians with statistical software. NASH, J. See 03313. 161-165.
03315    Essential ingredients for a statistical workstation. BOARDMAN, T. See 03313. 169-175.
03316    Statistical software, graphics and future workstations for data analysis. BECKER, R.; CHAMBERS, J.; AND WILKS, A. See 03313. 177-181.
03317    The Monte Carlo processor: designing and implementing a language for Monte Carlo work. GRIER, D. See 03313. 217-221.
03318    An iterative approach to improving data analysis in the classroom. KOPSCO, D.; MCKENZIE JR., J.; AND RYBOLT, W. See 03313. 315-323.
03319 §  Computer-based message services. Proc. of the IFIP WG 6.5 working conference (Nottingham, UK, May 1-4, 1984), SMITH, H. (Ed.) Elsevier North-Holland, Inc., New York, NY, 1984, 340 pp., $40.50, ISBN 0-444-87621-9.
HCI-0306  A user agent for multiple computer-based message services. KAYE, A.; AND MCDOWELL, R. See 03319. 127-136.
03320    User friendly interface for messaging systems. ROCKENBACH TAROUCO, L. See 03319. 167-174.
03321 §  Motion: representation and perception. Proc. of the ACM SIGGRAPH/SIGART interdisciplinary workshop (Toronto, Ont., Canada, 1983), BADLER, N.; AND TSOTSOS, J. (Chrs.) Elsevier North-Holland, Inc., New York, NY, 1986, 345 pp., ISBN 0-444-01079-3.
03322    How human perception deals with motion. WALLACH, H. See 03321. 1-19.
03323    The scope of research on motion: sensations, perception, representation and generation. TSOTSOS, J. See 03321. 20-25.
03324    The fox and the forest: toward a type I/type II constraint for early optical flow. ZUCKER, S. See 03321. 29-62.
03325    Motion perception: second thoughts on the correspondence problem. MATHER, G.; AND ANSTIS, S. See 03321. 63-78.
03326    The representation and perception of geometric structure in moving visual patterns. LAPPIN, J. See 03321. 79-92.
03327    The perception of coherent motion in two-dimensional patterns. ADELSON, E.; AND MOVSHON, J. See 03321. 93-98.

**03328** Real and apparent motion: one mechanism or two? GREEN, M.; AND VON GRUNAU, M. See 03321. 99-104.
**03329** Coherent global motion percepts from stochastic local motions. WILLIAMS, D.; AND SEKULER, R. See 03321. 105-106.
**03330** Optical flow. NEUMANN, B. See 03321. 109-120.
**03331** Computing the velocity field along contours. HILDRETH, E. See 03321. 121-127.
**03332** Determining the instantaneous axis of translation from optic flow generated by arbitrary sensot motion. RIEGER, J.; AND LAWTON, D. See 03321. 128-136.
**03333** Complex logarithmic mapping and the focus of expansion. JAIN, R. See 03321. 137-144.
**03334** Adapting optical-flow to measure object motion in reflectance and X-ray image sequences. CORNELIUS, N.; AND KANADE, T. See 03321. 145-153.
**03335** On the estimation of dense displacement vector fields from image sequences. NAGEL, H. See 03321. 154-160.
**03336** Motion and time-varying imagery. AGGARWAL, J. See 03321. 163-170.
**03337** Tracking three-dimensional moving light displays. JENKIN, M. See 03321. 171-175.
**03338** Determining motion parameters for scenes with translation and rotation. JERIAN, C.; AND JAIN, R. See 03321. 176-182.
**03339** Determining 3-D motion parameters of a rigid body: a vector-geometrical approach. YEN, B.; AND HUANG, T. See 03321. 183-195.
**03340** A hybrid approach to structure-from-motion. BOBICK, A. See 03321. 196-214.
**03341** Multicomputer architectures for real-time perception. UHR, L. See 03321. 215-223.
**03342** Motion from continuous or discontinuous arrangements. KOLERS, P. See 03321. 227-241.
**03343** Perception of rotation in depth: the psychophysical evidence. BRAUNSTEIN, M. See 03321. 242-247.
**03344** The cross-ratio and the perception of motion and structure. SIMPSON, W. See 03321. 248-252.
**03345** Selective attention to aspects of motion configurations: common vs. relative motion. POMERANTZ, J.; AND TOTH, N. See 03321. 253-263.
**03346** Perceiving and recovering structure from events. CUTTING, J. See 03321. 264-270.
**03347** Motion analysis of grammatical processes in a visual-gestural language. POIZNER, H.; KLIMA, E.; BELLUGI, U.; AND LIVINGSTON, R. See 03321. 271-292.
**03348** Motion graphics, description and control. BADLER, N. See 03321. 295-302.
**03349** "Graphical marionette". GINSBERG, C.; AND MAXWELL, D. See 03321. 303-310.
**03350** A multiple track animator system for motion synchronization. FORTIN, D.; LAMY, J.; AND THALMAN, D. See 03321. 311-317.
**03351** Knowledge-based animation. ZELTZER, D. See 03321. 318-323.
**03352** 3-D balance in legged locomotion: modeling and simulation for the one-legged case. MURTHY, S.; AND RAIBERT, M. See 03321. 324-331.
**03353** Representing and reasoning about change. SIMMONS, R.; AND DAVIS, R. See 03321. 332-343.
**03354** § Office Systems. Proceedings of the IFIP TC 8 working conference on office systems (Helsinki, Finland, Sept. 29-Oct. 2, 1985), VERRIJN-STUART, A.; AND HIRSCHHEIM, R. (Eds.) Elsevier North-Holland, Inc., New York, NY, 1986, 199 pp., $38, ISBN 0-444-70105-2.
**03355** Trends in office modeling. BRACCHI, G.; AND PERNICI, B. See 03354. 77-97.
**03356** Architectural implications of office systems. UHLIG, R.; AND EMERSON, R. See 03354. 99-128.
**03357** Human factors in office systems. DAMODARAN, L. See 03354. 129-142.
**03358** Organizational implications of office systems: toward a critical social action perspective. KLEIN, H. See 03354. 143-159.
**03359** Security of office systems. FINCH, J. See 03354. 161-175.
**03360** Implementation of office systems. BJORN-ANDERSEN, N. See 03354. 177-191.
**03361** § Theory and practice of software technology. Proc. international seminars on software engineering (Capri, Italy, 1980 & 1982), FERRARI, D.; BOLOGNANI, M.; AND GOGUEN, J. (Eds.) Elsevier North-Holland, Inc., New York, NY, 1983, 245 pp., $46.75, ISBN 0-444-86647-7.

HCI-0158  Towards an integration between language and software development environment. MONTANARI, U. See 03361. 195-202.
03362 §  Ergonomics of Hybrid Automated Systems I. Proceedings of the First International Conference (Louisville, Kentucky, August 15-18, 1988), KARWOWSKI, W. (Ed.) Elsevier Sci. Pub. B. V., Amsterdam, The Netherlands, 1988, 772 pp., ISBN 0-444-70486-8.
03363  Issues in modeling supervisory control in flexible manufacturing systems. SHARIT, J. See 03362. 3-13.
03364  Human supervisory control in discrete manufacturing: Translating the paradigm. SANDERSON, P. See 03362. 15-22.
03365  Custos IPSE: Towards a theory of the supervisor. MORAY, N. See 03362. 23-29.
03366  The effects of the supervisor's knowledge in a complex automated system. YAN, X.; WEN, Z.; AND YIQUAN, Z. See 03362. 31-36.
03367  Sources of Difficulty in troubleshooting automated manufacturing systems. BEREITER, S. See 03362. 37-50.
03368  Towards a new theory of job design. BLUMBERG, M. See 03362. 53-59.
03369  Human implications of technological change. GREATREX, M. See 03362. 61-70.
03370  Sociotechnical design of advanced manufacturing systems. SCHILLING, A. See 03362. 71-77.
03371  Structure and policy in computer integrated manufacturing systems: human factors implications. BRENNAN, L. See 03362. 85-92.
03372  Towards a framework for identifying organizationally-compatible AMT. MAJCHRZAK, A. See 03362. 93-99.
03373  Stress, coping, and worker well-being in computer-aided manufacturing: A field investigation of a CNC machine shop. EDWARDS, J. See 03362. 101-108.
03374  The impact of advanced manufacturing in work organization: The Portugese case of the plastic moulding industry. MONIZ, A. See 03362. 109-116.
03375  Design of distribution of production control functions between humans and artificially intelligent devices. PAWLOWSKI, E. See 03362. 117-123.
03376  Product engineering in the CIM environment. HOERGER, C. See 03362. 125-132.
03377  CIM and manufacturing industry in the north east of England: A survey of some current issues. KIMBLE, C.; AND PRABHU, V. See 03362. 133-140.
03378  Models for design of computer integrated manufacturing systems. RASMUSSEN, J. See 03362. 143-143.
03379  Human and computer aided manufacturing: The end of taylorism? KIDD, P. See 03362. 145-152.
03380  Differential organization impacts of the transition from stand-alone to integrated flexible production. MAJCHRZAK, A.; AND RAHIMI, M. See 03362. 153-159.
03381  A search for machine/human compatibility in manufacturing systems. BISHOP, A.; AND LUND, R. See 03362. 161-166.
03382  Designing hybrid automated manufacturing systems: A European perspective. CORBETT, J. See 03362. 167-172.
03383  Macro-ergonomics and the computer-integrated enterprise. SINCLAIR, M. See 03362. 173-178.
03384  The man-machine integration. HOSEIN, R. See 03362. 179-185.
03385  Further division of reintegration of mental labour? CAD/CAP and work in design and work preparation shops. MANSKE, F.; AND WOLF, H. See 03362. 187-193.
03386  Beyond software ergonomics? Human control of automated systems. WILLIAMS, T. See 03362. 195-200.
03387  Human factor issues in teleoperated systems. NTUEN, C.; AND PARK, E. See 03362. 203-210.
03388  A conceptual dependency network approach to multi-task assignments in man-machine (teleoperated) systems. NTEUN, C.; AND PARK, E. See 03362. 211-217.
03389  A study on an error recovery expert system using a superimposer and a digitizer in the advanced teleoperator system. LEE, S.; NAGAMACHI, M.; AND LEE, C. See 03362. 219-226.
03390  Static stereo vision depth distortions in teleoperation. DINER, D.; AND SYDOW, M. See 03362. 227-232.
03391  Human visual requirements for control and monitoring of a space telerobot. SMITH, R. See 03362. 233-240.
03392  Illumination requirements for operating a space remote manipulator. CHANDLEE, G.; SMITH, R.; AND WHEELWRIGHT, C. See 03362. 241-248.
03393  Ergonomics of hybrid intelligence. SALVENDY, G. See 03362. 251-257.

03394 An approach to knowledge elicitation in scheduling FMS: Toward a hybrid intelligent system. TABE, T.; YAMAMURO, S.; AND SALVENDY, G. See 03362. 259-266.
03395 Interactive aspects of knowledge representations. SPEED, R.; AND APPLETON, E. See 03362. 267-274.
03396 Human-computer-software interaction (HCSI) strategy in the design of global intelligent computer integrated management (ICIM) systems. TANAKA, Y.; AND TANAKA, K. See 03362. 283-290.
03397 Humane: A designer's assistant for modeling and evaluating function allocation options. MADNI, A. See 03362. 291-302.
03398 Decision support using qualitative evidence. ZIMMER, A. See 03362. 303-310.
03399 Human-machine interface in remote monitoring and control of flexible manufacturing systems. BOUBEKRI, N.; KHALIL, T.; AND KABUKA, M. See 03362. 311-318.
03400 Design of individual adaptive man-computer dialogues in the hybrid intelligence systems. VENDA, V. See 03362. 319-327.
03401 Human nature and robot nature. PARSONS, H. See 03362. 331-364.
03402 U.S. Army field robotics focus and key technology issues. HODGE, D. See 03362. 365-371.
03403 Robot vs. human operator for speed, precision and other aspects. KENGSKOOL, K.; MARTINEZ, S.; AND COBAUGH, P. See 03362. 373-380.
03404 Individualizing the man-machine interface. MACGREGOR, R.; KING, K.; AND CLARKE, R. See 03362. 375-381.
03405 Human response to unexpected robot movements at selected slow speeds. ETHERTON, J.; BEAUCHAMP, Y.; NUNEZ, G.; AND AHLUWALIA, R. See 03362. 381-389.
03406 Ten fatal accidents due to robots in Japan. NAGAMACHI, M. See 03362. 391-396.
03407 Some recent documentation of robotic safety from Sweden. PARSONS, H. See 03362. 397-402.
03408 Methods for field evaluation of safety in a robotics workplace. HELANDER, M.; AND KARWAN, M. See 03362. 403-410.
03409 Unexpected motion hazard exposures on a large robotic assembly. ETHERTON, J. See 03362. 411-419.
03410 Human perception of the work envelope of an industrial robot. KARWOWSKI, W.; PARSAEI, H.; NASH, M.; AND RAHIMI, M. See 03362. 421-428.
03411 Development of a human engineering design standard for robot teach pendants. COUSINS, S. See 03362. 429-436.
03412 A study on the safety operation of robots using monitor hold. FUKAYA, K. See 03362. 437-444.
03413 Man-machine interfaces for mobile robotic systems. MEIERAN, H. See 03362. 447-454.
03414 100 Percent assured performance for robotic assistive devices for handicapped and elderly persons. BLATT, S.; AND MEIERAN, H. See 03362. 455-459.
03415 Standards requirements for mobile robotic systems. MEIERAN, H. See 03362. 461-465.
03416 Critical issues in the safety of software-dominant automated systems. RAHIMI, M. See 03362. 469-476.
03417 Overview of research issues in robot safety. GRAHAM, J. See 03362. 477-482.
03418 Safety considerations in robot design. RYAN, J. See 03362. 483-490.
03419 A study on safety evaluation index and industrial accident analysis from the viewpoint of the safety confirmation type. UMEZAKI, S.; AND SUGIMOT, N. See 03362. 491-498.
03420 Interactive error recovery expert system for robot with voice recognition subsystem. LEE, C.; LEE, S.; AND KOO, C. See 03362. 499-504.
03421 A study of fail-safe technology. FUTSUHARA, K.; SUGIMOTO, N.; AND MUKAIDONO, M. See 03362. 505-512.
03422 A study of intrinsic safety asymmetrical actuator. SIMIZU, S.; AND SUGIMOTO, N. See 03362. 513-519.
03423 AGV safety system designed for preventing hazardous human contact. KUMEKAWA, S.; AND SUGIMOTO, N. See 03362. 521-528.
03424 A study of auditory warning alarms evaluation for automated guided vehicles. EGAWA, Y. See 03362. 529-536.
03425 Construction and examples of sensor in safe working system. SUGIMOTO, N.; FUTSUHARA, K.; AND MUKAIDONO, M. See 03362. 537-544.
03426 Pneumatic manipulating system provided with active compliance function. IKEDA, H.; AND SUGIMOTO, N. See 03362. 545-552.

03427 Experiences from the use of an intelligent safety sensor with industrial robots. KUIVANEN, R. See 03362. 553-558.

03428 Performance evaluation of three pressure mats as robot workstation safety sensors. TIAN, J.; AND SNECKENBERGER, J. See 03362. 559-565.

03429 The evaluation of selected ergonomical factors by production automation growth. PACHOLSKI, L.; AND JOZEFOWSKA, J. See 03362. 569-575.

03430 An evaluation of production systems from the ergonomic viewpoint: a plea for an integral approach to design. KRAGT, H. See 03362. 577-583.

03431 Process control and people at General Motors' Delta engine plant. BLACHE, K.; STEWART, K.; ZIMMERMAN, R.; SHAULL, J.; BENNER, R.; AND HUMPHREYS, P. See 03362. 585-597.

03432 Gribs—an approach to a realistic realtime simulation of human arm motion. BULLINGER, H.; KAY, L.; AND MENGES, R. See 03362. 599-606.

03433 Implementation plan for the use of on-line fiber analysis in the textile industry. MOGAHZY, Y.; REED, M.; AND LYNCH, W. See 03362. 607-614.

03434 Development of a continuous finishing line to improve working conditions. SCHNAUBER, H. See 03362. 615-629.

03435 Effects of automation on occupational safety & health. RAOUF, A. See 03362. 631-638.

03436 Health and productivity issues of CAD/CAM systems. SMITH, A. See 03362. 639-644.

03437 The impact of automation on musculoskeletal disorders. PUTZ-ANDERSON, V. See 03362. 645-651.

03438 Occupational accidents to the hand: A comparison of factory and nonfactory injuries. KASDAN, M. See 03362. 653-656.

03439 Accident analysis of blind production workers. NTUEN, C.; AND SIMPSON, K. See 03362. 657-662.

03440 Acting-out and burn-out behaviours of operators monitoring automated systems. MAREK, T.; FAFROWICZ, M.; AND NOWOROL, C. See 03362. 663-670.

03441 Optimum stresses and strains represented by examples from shop practice. SCHNAUBER, H. See 03362. 671-687.

03442 The social cybernetics of human interaction with automated systems. SMITH, T.; AND SMITH, K. See 03362. 691-711.

03443 Computerized manufacturing technology and work organization effects on labor relations and worker satisfaction. CARLOPIO, J. See 03362. 713-717.

03444 Union acceptance of automation technology: A case study. WHITMAN, K. See 03362. 719-722.

03445 Human aspects of automated assembly lines. PRUSSAK, W. See 03362. 723-728.

03446 Human factors in automating manufacturing systems in India. KOCHAR, I. See 03362. 729-734.

03447 The economic evaluation on implementation industrial robot from user point of view. LU, I.; AND TSENG, H. See 03362. 735-742.

03448 "Automation, robotization in particular, is always economically desirable"—fact or fiction? MITAL, A.; AND GENAIDY, A. See 03362. 743-750.

03449 Ergonomic evaluation of safety devices in robotic systems. NANTHAVANIJ, S.; AND ABDEL-MALEK, I. See 03362. 753-760.

03450 Human aspects of QC circle movement in Japanese manufacturing: Natures and problems. YUI, H.; AND MORI, K. See 03362. 761-768.

03451 § Reliability and robustness of engineering software. Edited papers presented at the 1st International Conference (Como, Italy, Sept. 1987), BREBBIA, C.; AND KERAMIDAS, G. (Eds.) Elsevier Sci. Pub. B. V., Amsterdam, The Netherlands, 1987, 537 pp., $175.50, ISBN 0-444-98948-X.

03452 An extended relational database model based on user views. PERNUL, G. See 03451. 177-192.

03453 Human interface in structural analysis software. SPAGNUOLO, R. See 03451. 195-207.

03454 § Human-computer interaction. Proceedings of the Second IFIP conference (Univ. of Stuttgart, W. Germany, Sept. 1-4, 1987), BULLINGER, H.; AND SHACKEL, B. (Eds.) Elsevier Sci. Publ. Co., New York, NY, 1987, ISBN 0-444-70304-7.

**03455** § Applications Track. Proceedings of the Twenty-First Annual Hawaii International Conference (Kailua-Kona, Hawaii, January 5-8, 1988), SPRAGUE JR., R. (Ed.) IEEE Computer Society, Washington, DC, 1988, 297 pp., ISBN 0-8186-0844-7.
**03456** The influence of individual differences on the reading of computer programs. CROSBY, M. See 03455. 64-68.
**03457** POEM: An office system for international use. HAHN, J.; SCHINDLER, S.; AND ZINGLER, K. See 03455. 87-93.
**03458** Tele-cybernetics: implications for the international marketplace. MIHRAM, G.; AND MIHRAM, D. See 03455. 102-111.
**03459** The information technology champion: aiding and abetting, care and feeding. BEATH, C.; AND IVES, B. See 03455. 115-123.
**03460** Problems among managers of AI personnel. COUGER, J.; AND MCINTYRE, S. See 03455. 157-161.
**03461** § Decision Support and Knowledge Based Systems Track. Proceedings of the Twenty-First Annual Hawaii International Conference (Kailua-Kona, Hawaii, January 5-8, 1988), KONSYNSKI, B. (Ed.) IEEE Computer Society, Washington, DC, 1988, 533 pp., ISBN 0-8186-0843-9.
**03462** The role of memory in intelligent information systems. PARADICE, D. See 03461. 2-9.
**03463** An investigation of performance, productivity, and rationality in multi-criteria decision making. VOLONINO, L.; AND KIRS, P. See 03461. 10-18.
**03464** Crisis planning systems: tools for intelligent action. NUNAMAKER, J.; WEBER, E.; SMITH, C.; AND CHEN, M. See 03461. 25-34.
**03465** A framework of composite information systems for strategic advantage. MADNICK, S.; AND WANG, Y. See 03461. 35-43.
**03466** Automated document distribution using AI based workstations and knowledge based servers. MARTINEZ, R.; AND MOHAMED, S. See 03461. 61-67.
**03467** Ontological analysis of document usage: an exploratory study. TONGE, F. See 03461. 68-76.
**03468** An expert system framework for forecasting method selection. KUMAR, S.; AND HSU, C. See 03461. 86-95.
**03469** Perceptions of system effectiveness as viewed by executives, users, and information specialists. MCLEOD, R.; AND BENDER, D. See 03461. 106-115.
**03470** User perceptions of DSS restrictiveness: an experiment. SILVER, M. See 03461. 116-124.
**03471** Systems for cooperative work and group decision making: status of use and problems in development. KRAEMER, K.; AND KING, J. See 03461. 137-148.
**03472** On building future decision support systems. KANDT, K. See 03461. 197-206.
**03473** Flexible user interface decision support systems. HOLSAPPLE, C.; PARK, S.; STANSIFER, R.; AND WINSTON, A. See 03461. 217-222.
**03474** When and how cognitive style impacts decision making. KOTTEMANN, J.; AND REMUS, W. See 03461. 223-232.
**03475** Handling textual information in a GDSS database: experience with the Arizona analyst information system. MCHENRY, W.; LYNCH, K.; AND DOODMAN, S. See 03461. 232-239.
**03476** The impact of "Messy" data on group decision making. VODEL, D. See 03461. 240-246.
**03477** A study of conflict in group design activities: implications for computer-supported cooperative work environments. ELAM, J.; AND WALZ, D. See 03461. 247-254.
**03478** Knowledge-based support of cooperative activities. CROFT, W.; AND LEFKOWITZ, L. See 03461. 312-318.
**03479** Knowledge representation for model libraries. MANNINO, M.; GREENBERG, B.; AND HONG, S. See 03461. 349-355.
**03480** An architecture for active DSS. MANHEIM, M. See 03461. 356-365.
**03481** Structured what if analysis in DSS models. PHILIPPAKIS, A. See 03461. 366-370.
**03482** A longitudinal study of spreadsheet program use. CARLSSON, S. See 03461. 371-380.
**03483** A box structured methodology for solving business problems. BANDYOPADHYAY, S.; AND HEVNER, A. See 03461. 387-395.
**03484** GMMS: global model management system: a conceptional design framework for model management systems for distributed decision support systems. ADAMS, D.; AND HALE, D. See 03461. 411-417.
**03485** Composite models in symms. MUHANNA, W.; AND PICK, R. See 03461. 418-427.
**03486** Decision support for reasoning about values. WIDMEYER, G. See 03461. 445-457.
**03487** Reasoning in model management systems. LIANG, T. See 03461. 461-470.

**03488** On representation schemes for electronic promising. KIMBROUGH, S. See 03461. 486-495.
**03489** Conceptual information extraction form financial news. RAU, L. See 03461. 501-509.
**03490** A financial investment assistant. KANDT, K.; AND YUENGER, P. See 03461. 510-517.
**03491** § Exploring technology: today and tomorrow. Proceedings of the 1987 Fall Joint Computer Conference (Dallas, TX, Oct. 25-29, 1987), SZYGENDA, S. (Chr.) IEEE Computer Society, Washington, DC, 1987, 763 pp., $100, ISBN 0-8186-0811-0.
**03492** Express—rapid prototyping and product development via integrated knowledge-based executable specifications. TOPPING, P.; MCINROY, J.; LIVLEY, W.; AND SHEPPARD, S. See 03491. 3-9.
**03493** Visual programming—toward realization of user-friendly programming environments. ICHIKAWA, T.; AND HIRAKAWA, M. See 03491. 129-137.
**03494** The software structure of extended nucleus based on BTRON specification. KOBAYASHI, M.; TAKENOUCHI, S.; KUSHIKI, Y.; AND SAKAMURA, K. See 03491. 153-158.
**03495** Report on German Joint Venture Tool Integration Projects. MERBETH, G. See 03491. 214-218.
**03496** Building a visual designer's environment. GRAF, M. See 03491. 287-297.
**03497** Out of Flatland: towards 3-D visual programming. GLINERT, E. See 03491. 292-299.
**03498** A dietary recommendation expert system using OPS5. KOA, C.; AND HWANG, C. See 03491. 658-663.
**03499** § Proceedings of the 21st Annual Simulation Symposium. (Tampa, FL, March 16-18, 1988), ABRAMS, M. (Ed.) IEEE Computer Society, Washington, DC, 1988, 243 pp., ISBN 0-8186-0845-5.
**03500** Using distributed simulation for distributed application development. MUHLHAUSER, M. See 03499. 189-206.
**03501** § Simulation. The 20th Annual Symposium (Tampa, FL, March 11-13, 1987), GAGLIANO, R. (Ed.) IEEE Computer Society, Washington, DC, 1987, 235 pp., $50, ISBN 0-8186-0766-1.
**03502** The MIRRORS/II simulator. D'AUTRECHY, C.; AND REGGIA, J. See 03501. 121-132.
**03503** Visual simulation. CLAPP, R. See 03501. 197-214.
**03504** § Software Engineering. Proceedings of the 9th International Conference (Monterey, CA, March 30-April 2), RIDDLE, W. (Chr.) IEEE Computer Society, Washington, DC, 1987, 399 pp., $60, ISBN 0-89791-216-0.
**03505** Human-computer communication meets software engineering. RATHKE, C. See 03504. 216-224.
**03506** Tool interfaces in integrated project support environments. HALL, A. See 03504. 289-290.
**03507** § Software Engineering. 10th International Conference (Singapore, April 11-15, 1988), NAM, T. (Chr.) IEEE Computer Society, Washington, DC, 1988, 459 pp., ISBN 0-89791-258-6.
**03508** Software engineering for distributed applications: the design project. MUHLHÄUSER, M. See 03507. 93-101.
**03509** A programming environment supporting reuse of object-oriented software. TARUMI, H.; AGUSA, K.; AND OHNO, Y. See 03507. 265-273.
**03510** Enhancing program readability and comprehensibility with tools for program visualization. BAECKER, R. See 03507. 356-366.
**03511** Design principles behind Chiron: a UIMS for software environments. YOUNG, M.; TAYLOR, R.; TROUP, D.; AND KELLY, C. See 03507. 367-376.
**03512** The space station information system and software support environment. PITTMAN, C. See 03507. 455-458.
**03513** § Software Track. Proceedings of the Twenty-First Annual Hawaii International Conference (Kailua-Kona, Hawaii, January 5-8, 1988), SHRIVER, B. (Ed.) IEEE Computer Society, Washington, DC, 1988, 806 pp., ISBN 0-8186-0842-0.
**03514** Structured message passing on a shared-memory multiprocessor. LEBLANC, T. See 03513. 188-194.
**03515** Management of distributed applications in large networks. FLAVIN, R.; AND WILLIFORD, J. See 03513. 232-241.
**03516** Extending the DARTS software design method to distributed real time applications. GOMAA, E. See 03513. 252-261.
**03517** Quill: An extensible system for editing documents of mixed type. CHAMBERLIN, D.; HASSELMEIER, H.; LUNIEWSKI, A.; PARIS, D.; WADE, B.; AND ZOLLIKER, M. See 03513. 317-326.
**03518** Multiple representation document development (extende abstract). CHEN, P.; AND HARRISON, M. See 03513. 327-336.

03519   A hypertext system to manage software life cycle documents. GARG, P.; AND SCACCHI, W. See 03513. 337-346.
03520   FolioPub: A publication management system. SCHICHTER, J. H.; AND MILLER, L. See 03513. 347-354.
03521   Supporting document development with concordia. WALKER, J. See 03513. 355-364.
03522   Language level persistence for an object-oriented application programming platform. KEMPF, J.; PAEPCKE, A.; BEACH, B.; MOHAN, J.; MAHBOD, B.; AND SNYDER, A. See 03513. 424-433.
03523   Prototyping user interfaces for applications depicted by graphs. BEAUODOUIN-LAFON, M.; AND KARSENTY, S. See 03513. 436-445.
03524   The control structure diagram: an automated graphical representation for software. CROSS II, J.; AND SHEPPARD, S. See 03513. 446-454.
03525   An environment for understanding programs. CLEVELAND, L. See 03513. 500-509.
03526   Segue: Support for distributed graphical interfaces. SCHAFFNER, S.; AND BORKAN, M. See 03513. 621-629.
03527   The PFG environment: parallel programming with petri net semantics. STOTTS, P. See 03513. 630-638.
03528   Building interprocess communication models using Stile. STOVSKY, M.; AND WEIDE, B. See 03513. 639-647.
03529   A visual programming language designed for automatic programming. SHU, N. See 03513. 662-671.
03530   An efficient high-level man-machine interface. UKELSON, J.; AND RODEH, M. See 03513. 672-681.
03531   Investigations into a command and response language interface. BULGREN, W.; WALLACE, V.; AND VAN DE LIEFVOORT, A. See 03513. 684-693.
03532   A graphical entity-relationship database browser. BURNS, L.; ARCHIBALD, J.; AND MALHOTRA, A. See 03513. 694-704.
03533   A consideration of learning in speech recognition from the viewpoint of AI class-description learning. TAKEBAYASHI, Y. See 03513. 705-714.
03534   Connections in context: The intermedia system. YANKELOVICH, N.; HAAN, B.; AND DRUCKER, S. See 03513. 715-724.
03535   jThe assessment of human/computer performance: a case for connectivity. BANKS, W.; SCHULTZ JR., E.; AND CRANE, E. See 03513. 725-731.
03536   Grand computer conferencing: What have we learned? WILLIFORD, J.; SANTERO, B.; AND FLAVIN, R. See 03513. 732-744.
03537   A processing system for program specifications in a natural language. SEKI, H.; NABIKA, E.; MATSUMURA, T.; SUGIYAMA, Y.; FUJII, M.; TORII, K.; AND KASAMI, T. See 03513. 754-763.
03538   The design of a flexible distributed testbeb for communication systems. THOET, W.; HAUSER, J.; AND BAKER, D. See 03513. 773-781.
03539   A cost model for estimating the costs of developing software in the Ada programming language. KANE, P.; LEUCI, N.; AND REIFER, D. See 03513. 782-799.
03540 § Supercomputing'88. (Orlando, Florida, November 14-18, 1988), MICHAEL, G. (Chr.) IEEE Computer Society, Washington, DC, 1988, 458 pp., ISBN 0-8186-0882-X.
03541   HORSE: a simulation of the horizon supercomputer. KOPETZKY, D. See 03540. 53-54.
03542   Interactive scientific visualization and parallel display techniques. SETHIAN, J.; SALEM, J.; AND GHONIEM, A. See 03540. 132-139.
03543   Design and implementation of a supercomputer frame buffer system. FOWLER, J.; AND MCGROWEN, A. See 03540. 140-147.
03544 § Conference on software maintenance–1985. (Sheraton Inn Washington-Northwest, Nov. 11-13, 1985), ZVEGINTZOV, N. (Chr.) IEEE Press, New York, NY, 1985, 239 pp., ISBN 0-8186-0648-7.
03545   Display strategies for program browsing. SHNEIDERMAN, B.; SHAFER, P.; SIMON, R.; AND WELDON, L. See 03544. 136-143.
03546 § Advances in artificial intelligence. (University of Edinburgh, April 6-10, 1987), HALLAM, J.; AND MELLISH, C. (Eds.) John Wiley & Sons, Inc., New York, NY, 1987, 290 pp., ISBN 0-471-91549-1.
03547   Connectionism and cognitive science. CLARK, A. See 03546. 3-15.
03548   Intelligent machines: What chance? KELLY, J. See 03546. 17-32.
03549   The lexicon, grammatical categories and temporal reasoning. NAKHIMOVSKY, A. See 03546. 35-48.

## PROCEEDINGS

03550    The alternatives allowed by a rectangularity postulate, and a pragmatic approach to interpreting motion. COWIE, R. See 03546. 109-121.
03551    A natural language interface for expert systems: system architecture. FROST, D. See 03546. 157-168.
03552    Transfer of learning in inference problems. CONWAY, M.; AND KAHNEY, H. See 03546. 239-250.
03553    The subjective ascription of belief to agents. BALLIM, A. See 03546. 267-278.
03554    Knowing that and knowing what. RAMSAY, A. See 03546. 279-290.
03555 § Progress in artificial intelligence. Selected and updated papers from the proceedings of the 1982 European conference (Orsay, France, 1982), STEELS, L.; AND CAMPBELL, J. (Eds.) [Ellis Horwood series in artificial intelligence] John Wiley & Sons, Inc., New York, NY, 1985, 320 pp., $39.95, ISBN 0-470-20171-1.
HCI-0360    Naive algorithm design techniques—a case study. KANT, E.; AND NEWELL, A. See 03555. 41-51.
03556 § Optical information systems '86. (Arlington, Virginia, Dec. 9-11. 1986), ROTH, J. (Ed.) Meckler Publishing, Westport, CT, 1986, 299 pp., ISBN 0-88736-113-7.
03557    Videotex and online services: competition or collateral. ARLEN, G. See 03556. 42-47.
03558    Integrating CD-ROM with printed and online services: a silver platter end-user perspective. BEZANSON, D. See 03556. 76-83.
03559 § Theoretical aspects of reasoning about knowledge. Proceedings of the 1986 Conference (Monterey,California, March 19-22, 1986), HALPERN, J. (Ed.) Morgan-Kaufmann, Palo Alto, CA, 1986, 408 pp., $18.95, ISBN 0-934613-04-4.
03560    What awareness isn't: a sentential view of implicit and explicit belief. KONOLIGE, K. See 03559. 241-250.
03561 § The fourth international symposium. (Univ. of California, Santa Cruz, Aug. 9—14, 1987), BOLLES, R.; AND ROTH, B. (Eds.) [MIT Press series in artificial intelligence] MIT Press, Cambridge, MA, 1988, 520 pp., $, ISBN 0-262-02272-9.
03562    MEISTER: a model enhanced intelligent and skillful teleoperational robot system. SATO, T.; AND HIRAI, S. See 03561. 155-162.
03563    Generic surface interpretation: observability model. BINFORD, T. See 03561. 265-272.
03564    Issues in the design of off-line programming systems. CRAIG, J. See 03561. 379-389.
03565    Concept for a model databased remote maintenance system. ASANO, K. See 03561. 401-410.
03566 § Methods for designing software to fit human needs and capabilities. Proceedings of the workshop on software human factors (Washington, DC, 1983), ANDERSON, N.; AND OLSON, J. (Eds.) National Academy Press, Washington, DC, 1985, 34 pp..
03567 § Computer culture: the scientific, intellectual, and social impact of the computer. Proc. of a symposium (New York, April 5-8, 1983), PAGELS, H. (Ed.) [Annals of The New York Academy of Sciences, Vol. 426] New York Academy of Sciences, New York, NY, 1984, 288 pp., $66, ISBN 0-89766-244-X.
HCI-0390    Selective networks and recognition automata. REEKE, G.; AND EDELMAN, G. See 03567. 181-201.
HCI-0195    Taming and civilizing computers. CHAPANIS, A. See 03567. 202-219.
HCI-0443    Computer-assisted negotiations: a case history from the law of the sea negotiations and speculation regarding future uses. STRAUS, D. See 03567. 234-265.
03568 § CAD and robotics in architecture and construction. Proceedings of the Joint International Conference (Marseilles, France, June 25-27, 1986), GIRAUD, C. (Ath.) QUINTRAND, P. (Ed.) Nichols Publishing Co., New York, NY, 1986, 287 pp., ISBN 0-89397-258-4.
03569    Evolution of a robotic excavator. WHITTAKER, W.; AND MOTAZED, B. See 03568. 233-239.
03570 § Artificial Intelligence and Information-Control systems of Robots-87. (Smolenice, Czechoslovakia, October 19-23, 1987), PLANDER, I. (Ed.) North-Holland Publishing Co., Amsterdam, The Netherlands, 1987, 499 pp., ISBN 0-444-70303-9.
03571    On one aspect of natural-language based knowledge acquisition. HAJIČOVÁ, E.; AND SGALL, P. See 03570. 49-54.
03572    Knowledge acquisition via a graphical interface. CONSOLE, L.; FOSSA, M.; AND TORASSO, P. See 03570. 173-177.
03573    Object-oriented signal processing systems. KARJALAINEN, M. See 03570. 275-279.
03574    A rule-based system for fuzzy natural language robot control. KRATCHANOV, K.; AND STANEV, I. See 03570. 305-309.

**03575** A functional model of questions for natural language processing systems. MANDUTIANU, S. See 03570. 321-325.
**03576** The semantic language episode understanding. MATTIELIGH, A. See 03570. 339-342.
**03577** § Computer security: a global challenge. Proceedings of the 2nd IFIP international conference (Toronto, Ontario, Canada, Sept. 10-12, 1984), FINCH, J.; AND DOUGALL, E. (Eds.) North-Holland Publishing Co., Amsterdam, The Netherlands, 1984, 580 pp., ISBN 0-444-87618-9.
**03578** The integrity lock support environment. GRAUBART, R.; AND KRAMER, S. See 03577. 249-267.
**03579** § Database Security: Status and Prospects. (Annapolis, Maryland, October 1987), LANDWEHR, C. (Ed.) North-Holland Publishing Co., Amsterdam, The Netherlands, 1988, 331 pp., ISBN 0-444-70479-5.
**03580** Lessons learned from modeling a secure multilevel relational database system. DENNING, D. See 03579. 35-43.
**03581** Inference control via query restriction vs. data modification: a perspective. MATLOFF, N. See 03579. 159-166.
**03582** Modelling and controlling user inference. COX, L. See 03579. 167-171.
**03583** Privacy respecting permissions and rights. BISKUP, J. See 03579. 173-185.
**03584** Role-based security in data base management systems. LOCHOVSKY, F.; AND WOO, C. See 03579. 209-222.
**03585** Status of trusted DBMS interpretations. HALE, M. See 03579. 263-268.
**03586** § Fifth generation computer architectures. Proc. of the IFIP TC 10 working conference (Manchester, UK, July 15-18, 1985), WOODS, J. (Ed.) North-Holland Publishing Co., Amsterdam, The Netherlands, 1986, 355 pp., $46.25, ISBN 0-444-87987-0.
**03587** The FAIM-1 user interface—human engineering for the fifth generation. COHEN, S.; DAVIS, A.; AND ROBINSON, S. See 03586. 257-273.
**03588** § Information processing 86. Proceedings of the IFIP World Computer Congress (Dublin, Ireland, Sept. 1-5, 1986), KUGLER, H. (Ed.) North-Holland Publishing Co., Amsterdam, The Netherlands, 1986, ISBN 0-444-70077-3.
**03589** § Man-computer interaction research (MACINTER-I): Proceedings of the first network. seminar of The International Union of Psychological Science (IUPsyS) (Berlin, German Democratic Republic, October 16-19, 1984), KLIX, F.; AND WANDKE, H. (Eds.) North-Holland Publishing Co., Amsterdam, The Netherlands, 1986, 474 pp., 83.25, ISBN 0-444-87910-2.
**03590** MACINTER—aim and goal. KLIX, F. See 03589. 3-19.
**03591** Cognitive ergonomics: an approach for the design of user-oriented interactive systems. STREITZ, N. See 03589. 21-33.
**03592** An approach to metacommunication in human-computer interaction. TAUBER, M. See 03589. 35-49.
**03593** Personality traits of the worker within the :20man-machine" system at automated production. GENOV, P. See 03589. 51-57.
**03594** Analysis of the competence of operators confronting new technologies: some methodological problems and some results. DE MONTMOLLIN, M. See 03589. 59-63.
**03595** Methodological problems of designing dialogue-oriented components in information systems. FUCHS-KITTOWSKI, K.; KOITZ, K.; AND RUDECK, C. See 03589. 65-70.
**03596** Smaller sizes-changing roles: new dimensions of the man-computer interactions. GELLÉI, P. See 03589. 71-75.
**03597** Exploratory investigations in acquiring and using information in interactive problem solving. KRAUSE, B.; AND HAGENDORF, H. See 03589. 79-87.
**03598** Necessary contributions of cognitive psychology to computer knowledge representation and manipulation systems. HELBIG, H. See 03589. 89-96.
**03599** Memory research and knowledge engineering. KLIX, F. See 03589. 97-116.
**03600** Psychological methods for assembling procedures in text management systems. HOFFMAN, J.; ZIESSLER, M.; AND SEIFERT, R. See 03589. 117-123.
**03601** Internal representation of externally stored information. SCHÖPFLUG, W. See 03589. 125-130.

03602 Problems in the design of information retrieval systems: user competence and information complexity. BATTMANN, W. See 03589. 131-138.

03603 Computer assisted knowledge acquisition: towards a laboratory for protocol analysis of user dialogues. DZIDA, W. See 03589. 139-150.

03604 Effectiveness of training as a function of the teacher knowledge structure. SCHINDLER, R.; AND FISCHER, F. See 03589. 151-159.

03605 Designing learning processes for work activities in automated technologies. MATERN, B. See 03589. 161-172.

03606 System issues in problem solving research. SCANDURA, J. See 03589. 173-183.

03607 Understanding learning problems in computer aided tasks. WAERN, Y. See 03589. 185-193.

03608 Learning styles in conversation—a practical application of Pask's learning theory to human-computer interaction. VAN DER VEER, G.; AND BEISHUIZEN, J. See 03589. 195-205.

03609 Machine adaption to psychological differences among users in instructive information exchanges with computers. ROTHKOPF, E. See 03589. 209-220.

03610 On complexity of command-entry in man-computer dialogues. WANDKE, H.; AND SCHULZ, J. See 03589. 221-233.

03611 Intuitive representations and interaction languages: an exploratory experiment. SCAPIN, D. See 03589. 235-248.

03612 Computer languages: everything you always wanted to know but no one can tell you. GREEN, T. See 03589. 249-259.

03613 Design of programming languages under psychological aspects. SCHMITT, R.; SCHULZ, E.; AND FRANK, E. See 03589. 261-271.

03614 Problem oriented design of interaction structures. KIESEWETTER, H. See 03589. 273-283.

03615 User requirements in natural language communication with database systems. KOCH, U. See 03589. 285-293.

03616 The efficiency of letter perception in function of color combinations: a study of video-screen colors. D'YDEWALLE, G.; VAN RENSBERGEN, J.; AND HUYS, J. See 03589. 295-300.

03617 On the temporal stability of signal detection processes. NACHREINER, F.; BAER, K.; AND ZDOBYCH, A. See 03589. 301-306.

03618 Coding of information in man-computer systems based on cognitive task analysis. WETZENSTEIN-OLLENSCHLÄGER,; AND SCHEIDEREITER, U. See 03589. 307-319.

03619 Visualization of process information in improving work orientation. NORROS, L.; KAUTTO, A.; AND RANTA, J. See 03589. 321-329.

03620 Experimental and theoretical analysis of visual search activities. CHALUPA, B. See 03589. 331-338.

03621 Alternative information presentation is a contribution to user centered dialogue design. RAUM, H. See 03589. 339-348.

03622 Effects of computerization on job demands and stress: the correspondence of subjective and objective data. LEPPÄNEN, A.; KALIMO, R.; AND HUUHTANEN, P. See 03589. 351-356.

03623 Assessment of mental load for different strategies of man-computer dialogue by means of the heart rate power spectrum. ZIMMER, K.; AND GUGULJANOVA, B. See 03589. 357-363.

03624 Performance in cognitive tasks and cardiovascular parameters as indicators of mental load. QUAAS, P.; RICHTER, P.; AND SCHIRMER, F. See 03589. 365-372.

03625 Influences of mental load on reaction times in man-computer dialogues. KÜHN, F.; SCHMIDT, K.; SCHOO, K.; AND KLEINBECK, U. See 03589. 373-381.

03626 Some remarks on a measure of computer operator workload: changes in pupil reflex. MAREK, T.; AND NOWOROL, C. See 03589. 383-388.

03627 Subjective load in introducing visual display units. WOLFF, T.; HUGLER, H.; SELLE, H.; WEIMANN, J.; AND SCHULZ, E. See 03589. 389-400.

03628 Job organization and allocation of functions between man and computer: I analysis and assessment. HACKER, W.; AND SCHÖFELDER, E. See 03589. 403-419.

03629 Job organization and allocation of functions between man and computer: II. job organization. ULICH, E.; AND TROY, N. See 03589. 421-427.

03630 Psychological principles for allocation of functions in man-robot system. TIMPE, K. See 03589. 429-437.
03631 Social psychological prerequisites and consequences of new information technologies. WILPERT, B.; AND RUIZ QUINTANILLA, S. See 03589. 439-444.
03632 What should be computerized? Cognitive demands of mental routine tasks and mental load. HACKER, W. See 03589. 445-461.
03633 § Methodologies for intelligent systems. Proceeding of the Second International Symposium (Charlotte, NC, Oct. 14-17, 1987), RAS, Z.; AND ZEMANKOVA, M. (Eds.) North-Holland Publishing Co., Amsterdam, The Netherlands, 1987, 509 pp., ISBN 0-444-01295-8.
03634 Human-computer interaction in the game of Go. KIERULF, A. See 03633. 481-487.
03635 A methodology for dynamic task allocation in man-machine system. PARKER, L.; AND PIN, F. See 03633. 488-495.
03636 Knowledge structures for intelligent interaction. GAINES, B. See 03633. 496-207.
03637 § Networks in office automation. Proc. of the IFIP TC 6 international in-depth symposium (Sofia, Bulgaria, Sept. 25-30, 1984), BOYANOV, K. (Ed.) North-Holland Publishing Co., Amsterdam, The Netherlands, 1985, 281 pp., ISBN 0-444-87715-0.
03638 An implementation of OSI protocols in SM-4 host computers. DIMITROV, S.; DIMITROVA, B.; MINDOV, J.; AND GOTCHEVA, T. See 03637. 21-29.
03639 A biparty grammar as a tool for defining a man-machine dialogue. MANOLESCU, G.; CONSTANTINESCU, R.; LEPĂDATU, A.; LEPĂDATU, C.; AND TUDOR, A. See 03637. 71-80.
03640 § System design for human development and productivity: participation and beyond. The IFIP TC 9/WG 9.1 Working Conference on system design for human development and productivity: participation and beyond (Berlin, German Democratic Republic, May 12-15, 1986), FUCHS-KITTOWSKI, K.; KOLM, P.; AND MATHIASSEN, L. (Eds.) North-Holland Publishing Co., Amsterdam, The Netherlands, 1987, 461 pp., ISBN 0-444-70251-2.
03641 Integrative participation—a challenge to the development of informatics. FUCHS-KITTOWSKI, K.; AND WENZLAFF, B. See 03640. 3-17.
03642 The design of information processing systems in relation to users. BAZEWICZ, M.; AND STUCHLIK, F. See 03640. 19-32.
03643 Some aspects of user-oriented dialogue design. ULICH, E. See 03640. 33-47.
03644 Systems, processes, and structures. MATHIASSEN, L. See 03640. 49-61.
03645 Seven mortal sins of systems work. LYYTINEN, K.; AND LEHTINEN, E. See 03640. 63-79.
03646 User-centered system design: design of mental tasks. HACKER, W. See 03640. 81-90.
03647 Who is user and who is affected: a proposal to better semantics. STEINMÜLLER, W. See 03640. 91-105.
03648 The importance of work organization by systems design. DÖRR, G.; AND KARLSEN, T. See 03640. 107-117.
03649 Contrastive analysis of the relationship of man and computer as a basis of system design. VOLPERT, W. See 03640. 119-128.
03650 Participation, organizational choices and time-economy: some theoretical questions. MANACORDA, P. See 03640. 129-139.
03651 The office between humanization and control. WAGNER, I. See 03640. 141-154.
03652 User participation from the point of view of the workers and trade union policy. BRIEFS, U. See 03640. 155-159.
03653 Different perspectives: What are they and how can they be used? NURMINEN, M. See 03640. 163-175.
03654 User or development of information systems: Which is more fundamental? NURMINEN, M.; KALMI, R.; KARHU, P.; AND NIEMELÄ, J. See 03640. 187-196.
03655 Transparency and system design. KOLM, P. See 03640. 199-208.
03656 System design for local authorities: participation based on "information contracts". CIBORRA, C.; GASBARRI, G.; AND MAGGIOLINI, P. See 03640. 219-236.
03657 Report from the working group on "goals and strategies of trade unions and other social groups in systems design for human development and productivity.". KOLM, P. See 03640. 245-246.

03658 Participative design and requirements on planning, software engineering and education. KOEHLI, S. See 03640. 263-269.

03659 Procedures for participation in planning, developing and operating information systems. REUTER, W. See 03640. 271-275.

03660 Establishing structures of requirements for the application of automated information processing (AIP)—an approach for the development of computer-aided systems. BELKE, W.; AND SCHIEMENTZ, W. See 03640. 277-284.

03661 Generation of visions in systems development: a supplement to the tool box. KENSING, F. See 03640. 285-301.

03662 How to improve pragmatic quality of information systems. SANDSTRÖM, G. See 03640. 303-318.

03663 Participation in the development of software and the utilisation of standard software. FALCK, M. See 03640. 331-337.

03664 Report from the working group on "methods and tools in system design for, with and by the users". FLOYD, C. See 03640. 339-342.

03665 Experiences in participative systems design. MAMBREY, P.; OPPERMANN, R.; AND TEPPER, A. See 03640. 345-357.

03666 Intentional and operational aspects of decision behaviour and their modelling. DAHME, C.; AND HAGER, T. See 03640. 359-370.

03667 Report from the working group on "socialist experience with modelling and using systems". LAUENROTH, H. See 03640. 383-385.

03668 Report from the working group on "experience with participation: application in administration and health care". DOCHERTY, P. See 03640. 415-417.

03669 Some aspects of knowledge processing and participation. FELLIEN, A. See 03640. 421-424.

03670 Some aspects of communication in the natural language and user's involvement in software development. MORAVCIK, O.; AND STRAKA, M. See 03640. 425-435.

03671 Work design instead of system design. RÖDIGER, K.; AND NULLMEIER, E. See 03640. 439-445.

03672 On the detection of social effects in man-computer interaction—a contribution to systems design. PILGRIM, J. See 03640. 447-453.

03673 A roundtable discussion on women, computers and participation. FALCK, M.; GENSIOR, S.; MANACORDA, P.; MEIER, U.; PAETZOLD, G.; WAGNER, I.; AND WENZLAFF, R. See 03640. 457-461.

03674 § Women, work and computerization: opportunities and disadvantages. (Riva del Sole, Tuscany, Italy, September 17-21, 1984), OLERUP, A.; SCHNEIDER, L.; AND MONOD, E. (Eds.) North-Holland Publishing Co., Amsterdam, The Netherlands, 1986, 372 pp., $48.25, ISBN 0-444-87864-5.

03675 System development in a women's perspective. NIELSEN, G.; AND THOMSEN, K. See 03674. 187-194.

03676 § Work with display units 86. Selected papers from the International Scientific Conference (Stockholm, Sweden, May 12-15, 1986), KNAVE, B.; AND WIDEBÄCK, P. (Eds.) North-Holland Publishing Co., Amsterdam, The Netherlands, 1987, 877 pp., $85, ISBN 0-444-70171-0.

03677 VDTs and health—fact or fancy? BONNELL, J. See 03676. 3-5.

03678 Health impact of work with visual display terminals. SUESS, M. See 03676. 6-15.

03679 Determinants of the VDU operator's well-being. POT, F.; PADMOS, P.; AND BROUWERS, A. See 03676. 16-25.

03680 Environmental stressors and perceived health symptoms among office workers. PREZANT, B.; AND KLEINMAN, G. See 03676. 26-37.

03681 Repetition strain injury in Australian VDU users. ROWE, S.; OXENBURGH, M.; AND DOUGLAS, D. See 03676. 38-41.

03682 Eye Fatigue among VDU users and non-VDU users. LEVY, F.; AND RAMBERG, G. See 03676. 42-52.

03683 Intraocular pressure during VDT work. GRIGNOLO, F.; DI BARI, A.; BROGLIATTI, B.; AND MAINA, G. See 03676. 53-59.

03684 Radiation emissions from VDUs. PAULSSON, L. See 03676. 63-68.

03685 Health hazards assessment of radio frequency electromagnetic fields emitted by video display terminals. GUY, A. See 03676. 69-80.

03686 Pregnancy and VDT work—an evaluation of the state of the art. BERGQVIST, U. See 03676. 87-93.
03687 Video display terminals—electromagnetic radiation and health. FRANKENHAEUSER, B. See 03676. 91-84.
03688 Birth defect, spontaneous abortion and work with VDUs. MCDONNALD, A. See 03676. 94-95.
03689 Birth defects, course of pregnancy, and work with VDUs: a Finnish case-referent study. KURPPA, K.; HOLMBERG, P.; RANTALA, K.; NURMINEN, T.; AND SAXEN, L. See 03676. 96-103.
03690 Pregnancy outcome and VDU-work in a cohort of insurance clerks. WESTERHOLM, P.; AND ERICSON, A. See 03676. 104-110.
03691 Video display terminals and birth defects. A study of pregnancy outcomes of employees of the Postal-Giro Center, Oslo, Norway. BJERKEDAL, T.; AND EGENAES, J. See 03676. 111-114.
03692 Task-load and endocrinological risk for pregnancy in women VDU operators. MIKOLAJCZYK, H.; INDULSKI, J.; KAMEDULA, T.; PAWLACZYK, M.; AND WALICKA, L. See 03676. 115-121.
03693 Some physical factors at VDT work stations and ski problems. BERGQVIST, U.; WIBOM, R.; AND NYLÉN, P. See 03676. 143-150.
03694 Facial particle exposure in the VDU environment: the role of static electricity. WEDBERG, W. See 03676. 151-159.
03695 A Rosacea-like skin rash in VDU-operators. STENBERG, B. See 03676. 160-164.
03696 VDT work and the skin. LIDÉN, C.; AND WAHLBERG, J. See 03676. 165-168.
03697 Skin paroblems from VDT work-a summary. SWANBECK, G. See 03676.
03698 Human factors considerations in the design of a VDU for visually impaired persons. KELLY, G.; PSY, B.; AND ROSS, D. See 03676. 173-182.
03699 VDU-work and dyslexia. a case report. KNUTSSON, A. See 03676. 183-186.
03700 Psychological aspects on blind peoples's reading of radio-distributed daily newspapers. HJELMQUIST, E.; JANSSON, B.; AND TORELL, G. See 03676. 187-201.
03701 Study of visual performance on a multi-color VDU of color defective and normal Trichromatic subjects. VERRIEST, G.; ANDREW, I.; AND UVIJLS, A. See 03676. 202-207.
03702 Influence of age on performance and health of VDU workers. ONG, C.; AND PHOON, W. See 03676. 211-215.
03703 Short- and long-term effects of extreme physical inactivity. A review. KILBOM, A. See 03676. 219-228.
03704 On the significance of physical activity on sedentary work. WINKEL, J. See 03676. 229-236.
03705 Inactivity, night work, and fatigue. ÅKERSTEDT, T.; TORSVALL, L.; GILLANDER, K.; AND KNUTSSON, A. See 03676. 237-242.
03706 The back during prolonged sitting. HANSSON, T. See 03676. 243-245.
03707 Preferred settings in VDT work: The Zürich Experience. LÄUBLI, T. See 03676. 249-262.
03708 Subject reports about musculoskeletal discomfort in VDU work as a complex phenomenon. ZEIER, H.; MION, H.; LÄUBLI, T.; THOMAS, C.; AND FASSER, W. See 03676. 263-278.
03709 VDUs and musculo-skeletal problems at the Australian National University. A case study. BAMMER, G. See 03676. 279-287.
03710 Generation of muscle tension related to a demand of continuing attention. WAERSTED, M.; BJORKLUND, R.; AND WESTGAARD, R. See 03676. 288-293.
03711 Task and the adjustment of ergonomic chairs. DAINOFF, M.; AND MARK, L. See 03676. 294-302.
03712 Equipment and workstation design for banking services. SALOVAARA, J. See 03676. 305-310.
03713 On the design of dealing desks. TRICKETT, T. See 03676. 311-319.
03714 The effect of VDU on the interior design of offices. ISHAI, E. See 03676. 320-328.
03715 Lighting for visual display unit workplaces. BJORSET, H. See 03676. 331-339.
03716 Lighting the display or displaying the lighting. BOYCE, P. See 03676. 340-349.
03717 Lighting the electronic office. VAN OOYEN, M.; AND BEGEMANN, S. See 03676. 350-356.
03718 Work at video display terminals among office employees: visual ergonomics and lighting. WIBOM, R.; AND CARLSSON, L. See 03676. 357-367.
03719 Recent results on the illumination of VDU and CAD workstations. ROLL, K. See 03676. 368-375.
03720 Non-visual effects of visual surroundings. KÜLLER, R. See 03676. 376-381.
03721 Improving the VDU workplace by introducing a physiologically optimized bright-background screen with dark characters: advantages and requirements. BAUER, D. See 03676. 382-393.

03722 Display image characteristics and visual response. TAYLOR, S.; AND RUPP, B. See 03676. 394-403.
03723 Matching display characteristics to human visual capacity. MURCH, G.; AND BEATON, R. See 03676. 407-411.
03724 Criteria for the subjective quality of visual display units. ROUFS, J.; LEEMAKERS, M.; AND BOSCHMAN, M. See 03676. 412-417.
03725 Colors in video displays. TONNQUIST, G. See 03676. 418-429.
03726 A colour atlas for graphical displays. DEREFELDT, G.; AND HEDIN, C. See 03676. 430-437.
03727 Colour on displays—boon or curse? VAN NES, F. See 03676. 438-440.
03728 The effect of VDT symbol characteristics on operator performance and visual comfort. BLEWETT, V. See 03676. 441-444.
03729 Visual phenomena and their relation to top luminance, phosphor persistence time and contrast polarity. NYLÉN, P.; AND BERGQVIST, U. See 03676. 445-448.
03730 Temporal and spatial stability in visual displays. ERIKSSON, S.; AND BÄCKSTRÖM, L. See 03676. 461-473.
03731 Influence of CRT refresh rates on accommodation aftereffects. TAKEDA, T.; FUKUI, Y.; AND IIDA, T. See 03676. 474-482.
03732 Sensitivity to light and visual strain in VDT operators: basic data for the design of work stations. MEYER, J.; REY, P.; SCHIRA, J.; AND BOUSQUET, A. See 03676. 485-489.
03733 Are there subtle changes in vision after use of VDTs? WOO, G.; STRONG, G.; IRVING, E.; AND ING, B. See 03676. 490-503.
03734 Visual impairment and subjective ocular symptomatology in VDT operators. RUBINO, G.; MAINA, G.; SONNINO, A.; GRIGNOLO, F.; AND PESCE, F. See 03676. 504-511.
03735 Effects on visual accommodation and subjective visual discomfort from VDT work intensified through split screen technique. ÖSTBERG, O.; AND SMITH, M. See 03676. 512-521.
03736 Work distance and optical correction. PALM, B. See 03676. 522-525.
03737 Is the resting state of our eyes a favorable viewing distance for VDU-work? JASCHINSKI-KRUZA, W. See 03676. 526-538.
03738 Vision monitoring of VDU operators and relaxation of visual stress by means of a laser speckle system. FRANZÉN, O.; RICHTER, H.; AND VON SANDOR, R. See 03676. 539-551.
03739 VDU work, refractive errors and binocular vision. JÄRVINEN, E.; AND MÄKITIE, J. See 03676. 552-555.
03740 Refraction in VDU operators—a comparison with other professions. NYMAN, K. See 03676. 556-561.
03741 How identify organizational factors crucial of VDU-health? A context-oriented method approach. WESTLANDER, G. See 03676. 565-577.
03742 Psychosocial work environment and use of visual display terminals:8mfrom theoretical model to action. BRADLEY, G. See 03676. 578-590.
03743 On the user's opinion about systems design. ROGARD, V. See 03676. 591-594.
03744 Identification and prevention of work-related mental and psycho-somatic disorders among two categories of VDU users. WRIGHT, I. See 03676. 595-604.
03745 Comparison of well-being among non-machine interactive clerical workers and full-time and part-time VDT users and typists. STELLMAN, J.; KLITZMAN, S.; GORDON, G.; AND SNOW, B. See 03676. 605-613.
03746 Office automation and work organization: making use of the scope of choice. SYDOW, J. See 03676. 614-623.
03747 the role of user prototyping in the system design process. HARKER, S. See 03676. 624-634.
03748 Use of an entire workforce as computer. GREENE, R. See 03676. 635-639.
03749 Office automation as an opportunity for an organizational check-up. VISCIOLA, M.; RIZZO, A.; AND BAGNARA, S. See 03676. 640-647.
03750 Automation and work culture. HAUG, F. See 03676. 648-652.
03751 Analyzing and improving VDU working conditions: workers' education. DESNOYERS, L. See 03676. 655-664.
03752 Workers education and user participation in the development of protective policies for VDT operators. BAKER, R.; AND STOCK, L. See 03676. 665-669.
03753 Trends in U.S. user policies for VDT work. WESTIN, A. See 03676. 670-681.
03754 Characterization of VDT work. YAMAMOTO, S.; AND NORO, K. See 03676. 685-694.

**03755** VDT technology: psychosocial and stress concerns. SMITH, M.; CARAYON, P.; AND MEIZIO, K. See 03676. 695-712.

**03756** A model for evaluating stress effects of work with display units. HANCOCK, P.; AND ROSENBERG, S. See 03676.

**03757** Growth and challenge VS wear and tear of humans in computer mediated work. JOHANSSON, G. See 03676. 725-731.

**03758** Work content, stress and health in computer-mediated work: a seven year follow-up study. ARONSSON, G.; AND JOHANSSON, G. See 03676. 732-738.

**03759** Focusing variability during visual work. HEDMAN, L.; AND BRIEM, V. See 03676. 739-744.

**03760** Mental fatigue of VDU operators induced by monotonous and various tasks. MAREK, T.; AND NORWOROL, C. See 03676. 745-755.

**03761** Data entry task on VDU: underload or overload. FLORU, R.; AND CAIL, F. See 03676. 756-767.

**03762** Videocoding - a highly monotonous VDU work in a new technique for mail sorting. WENNBERG, A.; AND VOSS, M. See 03676. 768-777.

**03763** Qualified CAD work: an intensive case study. HEDMAN, L. See 03676. 778-785.

**03764** Process control software design: how will the operators work? DANIELLOU, F. See 03676. 786-789.

**03765** An evaluation of mood disturbances and somatic discomfort under slow computer-response time and incentive-pay conditions. SCHLEIFER, L. See 03676. 793-802.

**03766** The applicability of eye movement analysis in the ergonomic evaluation of human-computer interaction. GRAF, W.; SIEL, F.; VAN DER HEIDEN, G.; AND KRÜGER, H. See 03676. 803-808.

**03767** Eye-head coordination and information uptake during text processing. FLEISCHER, A. See 03676. 809-821.

**03768** Effect of visual presentation of different dialogue structures on human-computer interaction. KASTER, J.; AND WIDDEL, H. See 03676. 822-830.

**03769** Touch screen, cursor keys and mouse interaction. AHLSTRÖM, B.; AND LENMAN, S. See 03676. 831-837.

**03770** Naming errors and automatic error correction in human-computer interaction. LENMAN, S.; AND MARMOLIN, H. See 03676. 838-846.

**03771** User interface in new PC software. LAESTADIUS, H. See 03676. 847-850.

**03772** Formal specification of user interfaces: two application studies. JORGENSEN, A.; NIELSEN, L.; AND CARSTENSEN, P. See 03676. 851-859.

**03773** Where is the action in human-computer interaction? MORAN, T. See 03676. 860-861.

**03774** User-friendliness - from sugar to symbiosis. WAERN, Y. See 03676. 862-874.

**03775** § Crystallographic Computing 4. Techniques and new technologies (Adelaide, Australia, August 22-29, 1987), ISAACS, N.; AND TAYLOR, M. (Eds.) Oxford University Press, Inc., New York, NY, 1988, 464 pp., $70.00, ISBN 0-19-855282-3.

**03776** Programming for interactive structure analysis. GABE, E. See 03775. 381-392.

**03777** § The Universal Turing Machine. A half-century survey (Berlin, 1988), HERKEN, R. (Ed.) Oxford University Press, Inc., New York, NY, 1988, 661 pp., ISBN 0-19-853741-7.

**03778** On the physics and mathematics of thought. PENROSE, R. See 03777. 491-522.

**03779** § Advanced programming environments. An international workshop (Trondheim, Norway, June 16-18, 1986), CONRADI, R.; DIDRIKSEN, T.; AND WANVIK, D. (Eds.) Springer-Verlag, Berlin, West Germany, 1986, 604 pp., ISBN 0-387-17189-4.

**03780** Context-sensitive editing with PSG environments. BAHLKE, R.; AND SNELTING, G. See 03779. 26-38.

**03781** On the usefulness of syntax directed editors. LANG, B. See 03779. 47-51.

**03782** IDL: past experience and new ideas. NEWCOMER, J. See 03779. 257-289.

**03783** Supporting flexible and efficient tool integration. SNODGRASS, R.; AND SHANNON, K. See 03779. 290-313.

**03784** Views for tools in integrated environments. GARLAN, D. See 03779. 314-343.:3T03785Advances in computer graphics hardware I. (Lisbon, Portugal, Aug. 1986), STRASSER, W. (Ed.) Springer-Verlag, Berlin, West Germany, 1987, 145 pp., ISBN 0-387-18222-5.

**03786** Display architecture for VLSI-based graphics workstations. TEN HAGEN, P.; KUIJK, A.; AND TRIENEKENS, C. See 03785. 3-16.

03787 Looking at workstation architectures from the viewpoint of interaction. KRÖMKER, D. See 03785. 27-37.

03788 § Decision support systems: theory and application. Proc. of the NATO Advanced Study Institute (Acquafredda di Maratea, Italy, June 3-14, 1985), HOLSAPPLE, C.; AND WHINSTON, A. (Eds.) Springer-Verlag, Berlin, West Germany, 1987, 500 pp., ISBN 0-387-17774-4.

03789 Characteristics of a successful DSS user's needs vs. builder's needs. GHIASEDDIN, N. See 03788. 159-184.

03790 § ECOOP '87. European conference on object-oriented programming (Paris, France, June 15–17, 1987), BÉZIVIN, J.; HULLOT, J.; COINTE, P.; AND LIEBERMAN, H. (Eds.) Springer-Verlag, Berlin, West Germany, 1987, 273 pp., ISBN 0-387-18353-1.

03791 The construction of user interfaces and the object paradigm. COUTAZ, J. See 03790. 121-130.

03792 The filter browser defining interfaces graphically. EGE, R.; MAIER, D.; AND BORNING, A. See 03790. 140-150.

03793 § ECOOP '88 (European Conference on Object-Oriented Programming). (Oslo, Norway, Aug. 15–17, 1988), GJESSING, S.; AND NYGAARD, K. (Eds.) [Lecture notes in computer science: 322] Springer-Verlag, Berlin, West Germany, 1988, 410 pp., $31.40, ISBN 0-387-50053-7.

03794 The Mjølner environment: direct interaction with abstractions. HEDIN, G.; AND MAGNUSSON, B. See 03793. 41-54.

03795 § ESEC '87. Proc. of the 1st European Software Engineering Conference (Strasbourg, France, Sept. 9-11, 1987), NICHOLS, H.; AND SIMPSON, D. (Eds.) Springer-Verlag, Berlin, West Germany, 1987, 404 pp., $33.30, ISBN 0-387-18712-X.

03796 PantaPM: an integrated software development environment. OSWALD, H. See 03795. 12-20.

03797 Knowledge-based editors for directed graphs. TICHY, W.; AND NEWBERY, F. See 03795. 101-109.

03798 A user interface design tool. ENGLAND, D. See 03795. 110-117.

03799 Interaction models and the principled design of interactive systems. DIX, A.; HARRISON, M.; RUNCIMAN, C.; AND THIMBLEBY, H. See 03795. 118-126.

03800 Using data flow specifications and interactive editing in the operating system user interface. SZWILLUS, G. See 03795. 149-157.

03801 SPECIF-X: a tool for CASE. LISSANDRE, M.; AND DEVAULX, B. See 03795. 279-287.

03802 ProMod at the age of 5. HRUSCHKA, P. See 03795. 288-296.

03803 A set of tools supporting the software design based on SDL. TEMPEL, H. See 03795. 348-356.

03804 § Information systems: failure analysis. Proc. of the NATO Advanced Research Workshop (Bad Windsheim, W. Germany, Aug. 18–22, 1986), WISE, J.; AND DEBONS, A. (Eds.) Springer-Verlag, Berlin, West Germany, 1987, 338 pp., ISBN 0-387-17800-7.

03805 Factors in the investigation of human error in accident causation. BARNETT, M. See 03804. 79-83.

03806 Management strategies and information failure. WESTRUM, R. See 03804. 109-127.

03807 Investigating sources of error in the management of crises: theoretical assumptions and a methodological approach. JANIS, I. See 03804. 129-162.

03808 Fallible humans and vulnerable systems: lessons learned from aviation. WIENER, E. See 03804. 163-181.

03809 Human reliability in information systems. DHILLON, B. See 03804. 183-189.

03810 Error auditing in air traffic control. EMPSON, J. See 03804. 191-198.

03811 Failure analysis of information systems: reflections on the use of expert systems in information systems. HOLLNAGEL, E. See 03804. 199-204.

03812 Fault management, knowledge support, and responsibility in man-machine systems. JOHANNSEN, G. See 03804. 205-209.

03813 An interactionist's view of system pathology. REASON, J. See 03804. 211-220.

03814 Mental models and failures in human-machine systems. VAN DER VEER, G. See 03804. 221-230.

03815 Failure analysis of information systems in small manufacturing enterprises: the importance of the human interface. CORREIA, A. See 03804. 305-310.

03816 § Logic programming '86. The 5th Conference (Tokyo, Japan, June 23-26, 1986), WADA, E. (Ed.) Springer-Verlag, Berlin, West Germany, 1987, 179 pp., ISBN 0-387-18024-9.

03817 Plan-based text generation in an on-line help system. KAKIUCHI, T.; UEHARA, K.; AND TOYODA, J. See 03816. 1-11.

03818  Logic interface system on navigational database systems. TAKIZAWA, M.; ITOH, H.; AND MORIYA, K. See 03816. 70-80.

03819 § Parallel algorithms and architectures. Proc. of an international workshop (Suhl, E. Germany, May 25-30, 1987), ALBRECHT, A.; JUNG, H.; AND MEHLHORN, K. (Eds.) Springer-Verlag, Berlin, West Germany, 1987, 205 pp., ISBN 0-387-18099-0.

03820  Parallel in sequence—towards the architecture of an elementary cortical processor. KOERNER, E.; TAUDA, I.; AND SHIMIZU, H. See 03819. 37-47.

03821 § TRON Project 1987—Open-architecture computer systems. Proc. of the Third TRON Project Symposium (Tokyo, Japan, Nov. 13, 1987), SAKAMURA, K. (Ed.) Springer-Verlag, Berlin, West Germany, 1987, 307 pp., ISBN 0-387-70027-7.

03822 § Uncertainty in knowledge-based systems. International Conference on Information. Processing and Management of Uncertainty in Knowledge-Based Systems (Paris, France, June 30-July 4, 1986), BOUCHON, B.; AND YAGER, R. (Eds.) Springer-Verlag, Berlin, West Germany, 1987, 405 pp., ISBN 0-387-18579-8.

03823  On the management of information imperfection in knowledge based systems. SAGE, A. See 03822. 3-29.

03824  An investigation of pictographic form in relation to mechanisms of knowledge acquisition. BONAVENTURA, M.; AND FAIRHURST, M. See 03822. 319-328.

03825  Modeling uncertainty in human perception. LIGOMENIDES, P. See 03822. 337-346.

03826 § Visualization in programming. 5th Interdisciplinary Workshop in Informatics and. Psychology. Selected contributions (Schärding, Austria, May 20-23, 1986), GORNY, P.; AND TAUBER, M. (Eds.) Springer-Verlag, Berlin, West Germany, 1987, 210 pp., ISBN 0-387-18507-0.

03827  The role of mental models in programming: from experiment to requirements for an interactive system. ACKERMANN, D.; AND STELOVSKY, J. See 03826. 53-69.

03828  How people comprehend unknown system structures: conceptual primitives in systems' surface representations. ROHR, G. See 03826. 89-105.:4T03829On visual interfaces and their conceptual analysis. TAUBER, M. See 03826. 106-123.

03830  On the design of a graphical transition network editor. MCDAID, E.; AND GUEST, S. See 03826. 142-150.

03831 § VDM '87: VDM—a formal method at work. VDM-Europe Symposium 1987 (Brussels, Belgium, March 23-26, 1987), BJORNER, D.; AND JONES, C. (Eds.) Springer-Verlag, Berlin, West Germany, 1987, 422 pp., ISBN 0-387-17654-3.

03832  Support environments for VDM. JONES, K. See 03831. 110-117.

03833 § Advanced computing concepts and techniques in control engineering. Proceedings of the NATO Advanced Study Institute on The Application of Advanced Computing Concepts and Techniques in Control Engineering (Ciocco, Italy, Sept. 14-25, 1987), DENHAM, M.; AND LAUB, A. (Eds.) Springer-Verlag New York, Inc., New York, NY, 1988, 518 pp., ISBN 0-387-50037-5.

03834  Qualitative modeling of physical systems for knowledge based control. LEITCH, R. See 03833. 31-51.

03835  A design environment for computer-aided control system design via multi-objective optimisation. GRACE, A.; AND FLEMING, P. See 03833. 497-512.

03836 § Advanced Computer Graphics. Proceedings of Computer Graphics Tokyo '86 (Tokyo, Japan, 1986), KUNII, T. (Ed.) Springer-Verlag New York, Inc., New York, NY, 1986, 504 pp., $89.00, ISBN 4-431-70011-0.

03837  Interactive solid modeling in hut design. MÄNTYLÄ, M.; AND RANTA, M. See 03836. 34-49.

03838  Interaction with IBS: an Icon-based system. ERRADI, M.; AND FRASSON, C. See 03836. 159-171.

03839  A new graphics user interface for accessing a database. WU, C. See 03836. 203-219.

03840  Visual business graphics query interface. HUANG, K. See 03836. 233-243.

03841 § Advances in object-oriented database systems. Lecture notes in computer science (Bad Münster am Stein-Edernburg, W. Germany, September 27-30, 1988), DITTRICH, K. (Ed.) Springer-Verlag New York, Inc., New York, NY, 1988, 373 pp., ISBN 0-387-50345-5.

03842  A distributed object server. PORTER, H.; ECKLUND, E.; ECKLUND, D.; ANDERSON, T.; AND SCHNEIDER, B. See 03841. 43-59.

03843  A model for an object management system for software engineering environments. PETRY, E. See 03841. 262-267.

**03844** Multiple inheritance and genericity for the integration of a database management system in an object-oriented approach. FRANK, A. See 03841. 268-273.

**03845** ROSE: An object-oriented database system for interactive computer graphics applications. HARDWICK, M.; AND SPOONER, D. See 03841. 340-345.

**03846** § Applicable algebra, error-correcting codes, combinatorics and computer algebra. Proceedings of the 4th International Conference, AAECC-4 (Karlsruhe, W. Germany, Sept. 23–26, 1986), BETH, T.; AND CLAUSEN, M. (Eds.) [Lecture notes in computer science, no. 307] Springer-Verlag New York, Inc., New York, NY, 1988, 214 pp., $21.80, ISBN 0-387-19200-X.

**03847** Integration of graphical tools in a computer algebra system. BITTENCOURT, G. See 03846. 13-24.

**03848** § Applied algebra, algorithmics and error-correcting codes. Proceedings of the 2nd international conference, AAECC-2 (Toulouse, France, Oct. 1-5, 1984), POLI, A. (Ed.) Springer-Verlag New York, Inc., New York, NY, 1986, 265 pp., ISBN 0-387-16767-6.

**03849** Some design principles for a mathematical knowledge representation system: a new approach to scientific calculation. CALMET, J.; AND BERGMAN, M. See 03848. 253-265.

**03850** § Computational Geometry and its Applications. Proceedings on International Workshop on Computational Geometry (Würzburg, W. Germany, March 24-25, 1988), NOLTEMEIER, H. (Ed.) [Lecture Notes in Computer Science: 333] Springer-Verlag New York, Inc., New York, NY, 1988, 252 pp., ISBN 0-387-50335-8.

**03851** Automatizing geometric proofs and constructions. BRÜDERLIN, B. See 03850. 232-252.

**03852** § Computer graphics 1987. CG International '87 (Karuizawa, Japan, May 25-28, 1987), KUNII, T. (Ed.) Springer-Verlag New York, Inc., New York, NY, 1987, 491 pp., ISBN 4-431-70022-6.

**03853** A simple, general method for ray tracing bicubic surfaces. LEVNER, G.; TASSINARI, P.; AND MARINI, D. See 03852. 285-302.

**03854** HutWindows: an improved architecture for a user interface management system. KOIVUNEN, M.; AND MÄNTYLÄ, M. See 03852. 393-406.

**03855** A gestural representation of the process of composing Chinese temples. MAKKUNI, R. See 03852. 407-426.

**03856** § Computer-generated images: the state of the art. Proceedings of Graphics Interface '85 (Montreal, Canada, May 27-31, 1985), MAGNENAT-THALMANN, N.; AND THALMANN, D. (Eds.) Springer-Verlag New York, Inc., New York, NY, 1985, 497 pp., $75, ISBN 4-431-70010-2.

**03857** Geometric continuity with interpolating Bézier curves. FOURNIER, A.; AND BARSKY, B. See 03856. 153-158.

**03858** ANIMENGINE: an engineering animation system. NOMA, T.; AND KUNII, T. See 03856. 189-202.

**03859** Towards an integrated view of 3-D computer animation. ZELTZER, D. See 03856. 230-248.

**03860** The interactive planning work station: a graphics-based UNIX tool for application users and developers. BOURNIQUE, R.; CANDREA, R.; AND HARTMAN, D. See 03856. 269-277.

**03861** The Higgens UIMS and its efficient implementation of Undo. HUDSON, S.; AND KING, R. See 03856. 278-290.

**03862** Graphics interaction in databases. FRASSON, C.; AND ERRADI, M. See 03856. 291-301.

**03863** Interface abstractions for an *naplps* page creation system. CHANG, E. See 03856. 302-306.

**03864** Colour coding scales and computer graphics. HEATH, A.; AND FLAVELL, R. See 03856. 307-318.

**03865** An innovative user interface for microcomputer-based computer-aided design. LICHTEN, L.; AND EATON, R. See 03856. 321-329.

**03866** Low cost geometric modelling system for CAM. NGAI, W.; AND CHAN, Y. See 03856. 342-355.

**03867** The CADME approach to the interface of solid modellers. BIZZOZERO, C.; AND CUGINI, U. See 03856. 356-364.

**03868** Heuristic rules for visualization. SCHOLL, L. See 03856. 386-391.

**03869** A graphics interface for interactive simulation of packet-switched networks. HOULE, J.; AND RICHARDSON, L. See 03856. 411-418.

**03870** How map designers can represent their ideas in thematic maps: effective user interfaces for thematic map design. YAMAHIRA, T.; KASAHARA, Y.; AND TSURUTANI, T. See 03856. 457-468.

**03871** Challenges in the application of graphics technology to the management of geographic information. CRAIN, I.; AND MACDONALD, C. See 03856. 469-477.

**03872** § Concepts in user interfaces: a reference model for command and response languages. (,), IFIP WORKING GROUP 2.7 (Ath.) BEECH, D. (Ed.) Springer-Verlag New York, Inc., New York, NY, 1986, 115 pp., ISBN 0-387-16791-9.

**03873** § Concurrency 88. International Conference on Concurrency (Hamburg, W. Germany, October 18-19, 1988), VOGT, F. (Ed.) Springer-Verlag New York, Inc., New York, NY, 1988, 400 pp., ISBN 0-387-50403-6.

**03874** A logic-functional approach to the execution of CCS specifications modulo behavioural equivalences. GNESI, S.; INVERARDI, P.; AND NESI, M. See 03873. 181-196.

**03875** § Designing computer-based learning materials. Proceedings of the NATO Advanced Study Institute on Learning Physics and Mathematics via computers (San Miniato, Italy, July 15-26, 1985), WEINSTOCK, H.; AND BORK, A. (Eds.) Springer-Verlag New York, Inc., New York, NY, 1986, 285 pp., $65.50, ISBN 0-387-16080-9.

**03876** Current research in the psychology of learning and teaching. SHULMAN, L.; AND RINGSTAFF, C. See 03875. 1-31.

**03877** Overcoming conceptual difficulties in physical science through computer-based Socratic dialogs. ARONS, A. See 03875. 33-66.

**03878** Pedagogical development of computer-based learning material. BORK, A. See 03875. 67-94.

**03879** Integrating physics and computer education in a single process. SASSI, E. See 03875. 183-207.

**03880** The computer as an integral part of the laboratory. PITRE, J. See 03875. 235-259.

**03881** § Experiences with Distributed Systems. Proceedings of the International Workshop (Kaiserslautern, FRG, September 28-30, 1987), GOOS, G.; AND HARTMANIS, J. (Eds.) [Lecture notes in computer science, no. 309] Springer-Verlag New York, Inc., New York, NY, 1988, 291 pp., ISBN 0-387-19333-2.

**03882** Experiences with the development of a portable network operating system. HOLLBERG, U.; MATTES, B.; SCHILL, A.; SCHMUTZ, H.; AND SCHONER, B. See 03881. 52-88.

**03883** § ESOP 86. Proc. of the European symposium on programming (Saarbrücken, Federal Republic of Germany, March 17 - 19, 1986), ROBINET, E.; AND WILHELM, R. (Eds.) Springer-Verlag New York, Inc., New York, NY, 1986, 374 pp., ISBN -540-16442-1.

**03884** Specification of a tool for viewing program text. SALMINEN, A. See 03883. 250-261.

**03885** § Graph-theoretic concepts in computer science. Proceedings of the International Workshop WG '87 (Kloster Banz/Staffelstein, W. Germany, June 29–July 1, 1987), SCHNEIDER, H. (Ath.) GÖTTLER, H. (Ed.) [Lecture notes in computer science: 314] Springer-Verlag New York, Inc., New York, NY, 1988, 254 pp., ISBN 0-387-19422-3.

**03886** Graph-theoretical tools and their use in a practical distributed operating system design case. WEDDE, H.; AND DANIELS, D. See 03885. 186-205.

**03887** § Human-computer interaction: psychonomic aspects. Conference of the Dutch Psychonomic Society (Free Univ., Amsterdam, 1988), VAN DER VEER, G.; AND MULDER, G. Springer-Verlag New York, Inc., New York, NY, 1988, 458 pp., ISBN 0-387-18901-7.

**03888** Introduction: human-computer interaction: psychonomic aspects. VAN DER VEER, G.; AND MULDER, G. (Eds.) See 03887. 1-11.

**03889** The legibility of visual display texts. VAN NES, F. See 03887. 14-25.

**03890** The use of color in visual displays. DE WEERT, C. See 03887. 26-40.

**03891** Visual fatigue with work on visual display units: the current state of knowledge. PADMOS, P. See 03887. 41-52.

**03892** Visual comfort as a criterion for designing display units. ROUFS, J.; BOSCHMAN, M.; AND LEERMAKERS, M. See 03887. 53-74.

**03893** Displaying statistical information—ergonomic considerations. MOLENAAR, I. See 03887. 76-88.

**03894** Factors influencing the detection of trend deviations on VDTs. WHITE, T.; AND VAN SCHAIK, P. See 03887. 89-102.

03895  Visual presentation of text: the process of reading from a psycholinguistic perspective. NOORDMAN, L. See 03887. 104-124.
03896  The effect on reading speed of word divisions at the end of a line. NAS, G. See 03887. 125-143.
03897  Document processing. BOUMA, L.; BRUIJNING, J.; AND VAN VLIET, J. See 03887. 144-169.
03898  A comparison of presentation and representation: linguistic and pictorial. JORNA, R. See 03887. 172-185.
03899  Structuring knowledge in a graph. STOKMAN, F.; AND DE VRIES, P. See 03887. 186-206.
03900  Knowledge representation techniques in artificial intelligence: an overview. DE SMEDT, K. See 03887. 207-222.
03901  Tree doctor, a software package for graphical manipulation and animation of tree structures. DESAIN, P. See 03887. 223-236.
03902  Textvision: elicitation and acquisition of conceptual knowledge by graphic representation and multiwindowing. KOMMERS, P. See 03887. 237-249.
03903  Development of mental models of an office system: a field study on an introductory course. VAN DER VEER, G.; AND FELT, M. See 03887. 250-272.
03904  Artificial intelligence and cognitive psychology: a new look at human factors. BREÉ, D. See 03887. 274-289.
03905  Knowledge and expertise in expert systems. WIELINGA, B.; AND BREDEWEG, B. See 03887. 290-297.
03906  Architectures for production systems: an inside look for those who study human-computer interaction. JAMESON, A. See 03887. 298-297.
03907  A provisional evaluation of a new chord keyboard, the Velotype. VAN NOORDEN, L. See 03887. 318-333.
03908  Real-time processing of cursive writing and sketched graphics. THOMASSEN, A. See 03887. 334-352.
03909  Automatic identification of writers. MAARSE, F.; SCHOMAKER, L.; AND TEULINGS, H. See 03887. 353-360.
03910  The use of speech in man-machine interaction. POLS, L. See 03887. 361-372.
03911  Search strategies in internal and external memories. BEISHUIZEN, J. See 03887. 374-391.
03912  Keywords instead of hierarchical menus. WEERDMEESTER, B. See 03887. 392-403.
03913  Natural language communication with computers: some problems, perspectives, and new directions. BUNT, H. See 03887. 406-442.
03914 § International conference on database theory. Proceedings (Rome, Italy, Sept. 8-10, 1986), AUSIELLO, G.; AND ATZENI, P. (Eds.) Springer-Verlag New York, Inc., New York, NY, 1986, 444 pp., $30.60, ISBN 0-387-17187-8.
03915  Unsolvable problems related to the view integration approach. CONVENT, B. See 03914. 141-156.
03916 § Logic programming '85. Proceedings of the 4th conference (Tokyo, Japan, July 1-3, 1985), WADA, E. (Ed.) Springer-Verlag New York, Inc., New York, NY, 1986, 311 pp., ISBN 0-387-16479-0.
03917  A travel consultation system: towards a smooth conversation in Japanese. SUZUKI, H.; KIYONO, M.; KOUGO, S.; TAKAHASHI, M.; MOTOIKE, S.; AND NIKI, T. See 03916. 226-235.
03918  KRIP: a knowledge representation system for laws relating to industrial property. NITTA, K.; AND NAGAO, J. See 03916. 276-286.
03919 § Logic programming '87. Proceedings of the 6th Conference (Tokyo, Japan, June 22-24, 1987), FURUKAWA, K.; TANAKA, H.; AND FUJISAKI, T. (Eds.) [Lecture Notes in Computer Science, no. 315] Springer-Verlag New York, Inc., New York, NY, 1988, 327 pp., $25.70, ISBN 0-387-19426-6.
03920  Analogical program synthesis from program components. IMANAKA, T.; UEHARA, K.; AND TOYODA, J. See 03919. 60-79.
03921  Manipulation of embedded context using the multiple world mechanism. KURATA, A.; AND NAKASHIMA, H. See 03919. 252-263.
03922  Generating natural language responses appropriate to conversational situations—in the case of Japanese. NOGUCHI, N.; TAKAHASHI, M.; AND YASUKAWA, H. See 03919. 264-283.
03923 § Methodology of window management. Proceedings of an Alvey Workshop (Cosener's House, Abingdon, UK, April 29-May 1, 1985), HOPGOOD, F.; DUCE, D.; FIELDING, E.; ROBINSON, K.; AND WILLIAMS, A. (Eds.) Springer-Verlag New York, Inc., New York, NY, 1986, 250 pp., 34.50, ISBN 3-540-16116-3.
03924  Introducing windows to Unix: user expectations. PROSSER, C. See 03923. 9-13.
03925  A comparison of some window managers. WILLIAMS, T. See 03923. 15-33.

03926 Ten years of window systems—a retrospective view. TEITELMAN, W. See 03923. 35-46.
03927 SunDew—a distributed and extensible window system. GOSLING, J. See 03923. 47-57.
03928 Issues in window management design and implementation. MYERS, B. See 03923. 59-71.
03929 A modular window system for Unix. SWEETMAN, D. See 03923. 73-79.
03930 Windows, viewports and structured display files. PROSSER, C. See 03923. 97-100.
03931 Partitioning of function in window systems. GOSLING, J. See 03923. 101-106.
03932 System aspects of low-cost bitmapped displays. ROSENTHAL, D.; AND GOSLING, J. See 03923. 107-113.
03933 A window manager for bitmapped displays and Unix. GOSLING, J.; AND ROSENTHAL, D. See 03923. 115-128.
03934 Application program interface working group discussions. See 03923. 141-144.
03935 Application program interface working group final report. See 03923. 145-173.
03936 User interface working group discussions. See 03923. 175-180.
03937 User interface working group final report. See 03923. 181-194.
03938 Architecture working group discussions. See 03923. 195-202.
03939 Architecture working group final report. See 03923. 203-209.
03940 Application program interface task group. See 03923. 211-215.
03941 Structures task group. See 03923. 217-223.
03942 Future work. See 03923. 227-230.
03943 § MFDBS 87. Proceedings on Mathematical Fundamentals of Database Systems (Dresden, E. Germany, Jan. 19–23, 1987), BISKUP, J.; DEMETROVICS, J.; PAREDAENS, J.; AND THALHEIM, B. (Eds.) [Lecture notes in computer science: 305] Springer-Verlag New York, Inc., New York, NY, 1988, 247 pp., ISBN 0-387-19121-6.
03944 Data manipulation languages for the universal relation view DURST. BISKUP, J.; AND BRÜGGEMANN, H. See 03943. 20-41.
03945 On global context dependencies and their properties (extended abstract). D'ATRI, A.; DI FELICE, P.; LAKSHMANAN, V.; AND MOSCARINI, M. See 03943. 71-79.
03946 Design tools for large relational database systems. THALHEIM, B. See 03943. 210-224.
03947 § Natural Language at the Computer. Scientific Symposium on Syntax and Semantics (Heidelberg, W. Germany, February 25, 1988), BLASER, A. (Ed.) Springer-Verlag New York, Inc., New York, NY, 1988, 176 pp., ISBN 0-387-50011-1.
03948 Computational linguistics: issues and solutions. KING, M. See 03947. 9-30.
03949 § Neural computers. Proceedings of the NATO Advanced Research Workshop (Neuss, W. Germany, Sept. 28-Oct.2, 1987), ECKMILLER, R.; AND V. D. MALSBURG, C. (Eds.) Springer-Verlag New York, Inc., New York, NY, 1988, 566 pp., ISBN 0-387-18724-3.
03950 Structured neural networks in nature and in computer science. FELDMAN, J. See 03949. 17-21.
03951 Conventional fault-tolerance and neural computers. MOORE, W. See 03949. 29-37.
03952 Parallelism and redundancy in neural networks. SEELEN, W.; AND MALLOT, H. See 03949. 51-60.
03953 Relational models in natural and artificial vision. BIENENSTOCK, E. See 03949. 61-70.
03954 Mapping images to a hierarchical data structure—a way to knowledge-based pattern recognition. HARTMANN, G. See 03949. 91-100.
03955 Design principles for a front-end visual systems. KOENDERINK, J. See 03949. 111-118.
03956 Why cortices? Neural computation in the vertebrate visual system. MALLOT, H. See 03949. 129-138.
03957 A cortical network model for early vision processing. MOLLER, P.; NYLÉN, M.; AND HERTZ, J. See 03949. 139-148.
03958 Image segregation by motion: cortical mechanisms and implementation in neural networks. ORBAN, G.; AND GULYÁS, B. See 03949. 149-158.
03959 On the acquisition of object concepts from sensory data. PHILLIPS, W.; HANCOCK, P.; WILLSON, N.; AND SMITH, L. See 03949. 159-168.
03960 Neural computers in vision: processing of high dimensional data. ZEEVI, Y.; AND GINOSAR, R. See 03949. 169-178.

03961 Computational networks in early vision: from orientation selection to optical flow. ZUCKER, S.; AND IVERSON, L. See 03949. 179-188.

03962 Exploring three possibilities in network design: spontaneous node activity, node plasticity and temporal coding. TORRAS I GENÍS, C. See 03949. 301-309.

03963 Spatial and temporal transformations in visuo-motor coordination. DROULEZ, J.; AND BERTHOZ, A. See 03949. 345-357.

03964 Neural networks for motor program generation. ECKMILLER, R. See 03949. 359-370.

03965 Innate and learned components in a simple visuo-motor reflex. HOFFMANN, K. See 03949. 371-380.

03966 Tensor geometry: a language of brains & neurocomputers. Generalized coordinates in neuroscience & robotics. PELLIONISZ, A. See 03949. 381-391.

03967 Extending Kohonen's self-organizing mapping algorithms to learn ballistic movements. RITTER, H.; AND SCHULTEN, K. See 03949. 393-406.

03968 Limited interconnectivity in synthetic neural systems. AKERS, L.; WALKER, M.; FERRY, D.; AND GRONDIN, R. See 03949. 407-416.

03969 Dynamical properties of a new type of neural network. COTTERILL, R. See 03949. 425-433.

03970 Control of the immune response. WEISBUCH, G.; AND ATLAN, H. See 03949. 497-501.

03971 § Parcella '88: Fourth International Workshop on Parallel Processing by Cellular Automata and Arrays. (Berlin, E. Germany, October 17-21, 1988), LEGENDI, T.; AND SCHENDEL, U. (Eds.) [Lecture Notes in Computer Science: 342] Springer-Verlag New York, Inc., New York, NY, 1989, 380 pp., ISBN 0-387-50647-0.

03972 Control of sensory processing - a hypothesis on and simulation of the architecture of an elementary cortical processor. KOERNER, E.; GROSS, M.; RICHTER, A.; AND SHIMIZU, H. See 03971. 291-297.

03973 § Petri nets: applications and relationships to other models of concurrency. Advances in Petri nets 1986, part II (Bad Honnef, Sept. 8-19, 1986), BRAUER, W.; REISIG, W.; AND ROZENBERG, G. (Eds.) Springer-Verlag New York, Inc., New York, NY, 1987, 516 pp., ISBN 0-387-17906-2.

03974 Human-machine interaction and role/function/action-nets. OBERQUELLE, H. See 03973. 171-190.

03975 Nets in office automation. VOSS, K. See 03973. 234-257.

03976 § Pictorial information systems in medicine. Proceedings of the NATO Advanced Study Institute (NATO ASI Series) (Braulage,Federal Republic of Germany, August 27-September 7, 1984), HÖHNE, K. (Ed.) Springer-Verlag New York, Inc., New York, NY, 1986, 524 pp., ISBN 3-540-13921-4.

03977 On the architecture for pictorial information systems. MEYER-EBRECHT, D. See 03976. 151-179.

03978 Psychovisual issues in the display of medical images. PIZER, S. See 03976. 211-233.

03979 Issues in the design of human-computer interfaces. NIEVERGELT, J. See 03976. 251-262.

03980 Software tools for the development of pictorial information systems in medicine—the ISQL experience. ASSMANN, K.; VENEMA, R.; AND HÖHNE, K. See 03976. 333-356.

03981 § Product data interfaces in CAD/CAM applications: design, implementation and experiences. Proc. of a seminar of the ZGDV (Technical Univ. of Darmstadt, Darmstadt, W. Germany, Dec. 1984-Feb. 1985), ENCARNAÇÃO, J.; SCHUSTER, R.; AND VÖGE, E. (Eds.) [Special series on symbolic computation] Springer-Verlag New York, Inc., New York, NY, 1986, 254 pp., $68, ISBN 0-387-15118-4.

HCI-0416 Goals in the application of CAD interfaces. VÖGE, E. See 03981. 1-12.

HCI-0419 Interfaces and data transfer formats in computer graphics systems. ENCARNAÇÃO, J. See 03981. 13-33.

HCI-0413 CAD/CAM: integration in the automobile industry. WILFERT, H.; AND SEELAND, H. See 03981. 34-62.

HCI-0418 Interfaces for CAD applications. PASEMANN, K. See 03981. 63-71.

HCI-0417 Graphical standards. ENDERLE, G. See 03981. 74-82.

03982 GKSGRAL—software and hardware realizations of the graphical kernel system. CULLMANN, N.; AND PFAFF, G. See 03981. 101-113.

HCI-0420 VDAFS—a pragmatic interface for the exchange of sculptured surface data. RENZ, W. See 03981. 144-149.

HCI-0421 Approximation methods used in the exchange of geometric information via the VDA/VDMA surface interface. NOWACKI, H.; AND DANNENBERG, L. See 03981. 150-159.:4THCI-0422A tentative implementation of VDAFS. HOPERT, D.; AND WEISSBARTH, T. See 03981. 160-166.

03983     Implementation of a VDA interface in the CAD system STRIM 100. DE MARNÉ, K. See 03981. 167-175.
HCI-0423     Testing and validation of IGES processors. GRABOWSKI, H.; AND GLATZ, R. See 03981. 221-235.
HCI-0039 § Readings on cognitive ergonomics - mind and computers. Proc. of the 2nd European conference (Gmunden, Austria, Sept. 10-14, 1984), VAN DER VEER, G.; TAUBER, M.; GREEN, T.; AND GORNY, P. (Eds.) [Lecture notes in computer science 178] Springer-Verlag New York, Inc., New York, NY, 1984, 269 pp., ISBN 0-387-13394-1.
HCI-0188     Representational frameworks and models for human-computer interfaces. ROHR, G.; AND TAUBER, M. See HCI-0039. 8-25.
HCI-0182     On models and modelling in human-computer co-operation. OBERQUELLE, H. See HCI-0039. 26-43.
HCI-0097     Information systems design methodologies and their compliance with cognitive ergonomy. TRAÜNMULLER, R. See HCI-0039. 44-61.
HCI-0241     Human cognition and human computer interaction. SCHNEIDER, W.; LIND, M.; ALLARD, R.; AND SANDBLAD, B. See HCI-0039. 76-80.
HCI-0108     Active help systems. FISCHER, G.; LEMKE, A.; AND SCHWAB, T. See HCI-0039. 116-131.
HCI-0164     Fatal error in pass zero: how not to confuse novices. DU BOULAY, B.; AND MATTHEW, I. See HCI-0039. 132-141.
HCI-0379     Real time graphic simulation of visual effects of egomotion. PERUCH, P.; CAVALLO, V.; DEUTSCH, C.; AND PAILHOUS, J. See HCI-0039. 192-199.
03984     From surface form to the structure of the interface - studies in human computer interaction at INRIA. FALZON, P. See HCI-0039. 205-216.
03985 § Real-time object measurement and classification. Proceedings of the NATO Advanced Research workshop (Maratea, Italy, Aug. 31-Sept. 3, 1987), JAIN, A. (Ed.) Springer-Verlag New York, Inc., New York, NY, 1988, 407 pp., ISBN 0-387-18766-9.
03986     A flexible and intelligent system for fast measurements in binary images for in-line robotic control. BACKER, E.; AND GERBRANDS, J. See 03985. 25-40.
03987 § Recent advances in speech understanding and dialog systems. Proceedings of the NATO Advanced Study Institute on Recent Advances in Speech Understanding and Dialog Systems (W. Germany, July 5-18, 1987), NIEMANN, H.; LANG, M.; AND SAGERER, G. [NATO Advanced Science Institute] Springer-Verlag New York, Inc., New York, NY, 1988, 521 pp., ISBN 0-387-19245-X.
03988     The use of prosodic parameters in automatic speech recognition. VAISSIÈRE, J. See 03987. 71-99.
03989     Prosodic features in German speech: stress assignment by man and machine. NÖTH, E.; NIEMANN, H.; AND SCHMÖLZ, S. See 03987. 101-106.
03990     Recognition of speech using temporal decomposition. CHOLLET, G.; AHLBOM, G.; AND BIMBOT, F. See 03987. 107-110.
03991     Phonetic segmentation using psychoacoustic speech parameters. MARTENS, J. See 03987. 135-139.
03992     Morphological representation of speech knowledge for automatic speech recognition systems. PALAKAL, M. See 03987. 141-146.
03993     Speaker-independent automatic recognition of plosive sound in letters and digits. CARDIN, R. See 03987. 147-151.
03994     Primary perceptual units in word recognition. SENDLMEIER, W. See 03987. 165-169.
03995     Computer recognition of spoken letters and digits. DE MORI, R. See 03987. 207-233.
03996     Real-time large vocabulary word recognition via diphone spotting and multiprocessor implementation. SCAGLIOLA, C.; CAROSSINO, A.; COLLA, A.; FAVARETO, C.; PEDRAZZI, P.; SCIARRA, D.; AND VICENZI, C. See 03987. 273-278.
03997     Recent results on the application of a metric-space search algorithm (AESA) to multispeaker data. VIDAL, E.; AND LLORET, M. See 03987. 285-290.
03998     An experimental environment for generating word hypotheses in continuous speech. KUNZMANN, S.; KUHN, T.; AND NIEMANN, H. See 03987. 311-316.
03999     Dynamic spectral adaptation of automatic speech recognizers to new speakers. CHOLLET, G.; AND CHOUKRI, K. See 03987. 335-338.

## PROCEEDINGS

**04000** On-line interpretation in speech understanding and dialogue systems. BUNT, H. See 03987. 349-395.
**04001** Knowledge based systems for speech understanding. SAGERER, G.; AND KUMMERT, F. See 03987. 421-458.
**04002** Recognition of speaker-dependent continuous speech with Keal-Nevezh. MERCIER, G.; COZANNET, A.; AND VAISSIÈRE, J. See 03987. 459-463.
**04003** Modification of Earley's algorithm for speech recognition. PAESELER, A. See 03987. 465-472.
**04004** Merging acoustics and linguistics in speech understanding. NIEDERMAIR, G. See 03987. 479-484.
**04005** Experimentation in the specification of an oral dialogue. GUYOMARD, M.; AND SIROUX, J. See 03987. 497-501.
**04006** § Sensors and sensory systems for advanced robots. Proceedings of a NATO Advanced Research Workshop (Maratea, Italy, April 28–May 3, 1986), DARIO, P. (Ed.) [NATO ASI series] Springer-Verlag New York, Inc., New York, NY, 1988, 597 pp., $120.00, ISBN 0-387-19089-9.
**04007** The central nervous system as a low and high level control system. ALBUS, J. See 04006. 3-20.
**04008** Proprioceptive feedback for sensory-motor control. HULLIGER, M. See 04006. 21-47.
**04009** Physiology and psychophysics in taste and smell. PERSAUD, K.; DESIMONE, J.; AND HECK, G. See 04006. 49-70.
**04010** The physiology and psychophysics of touch. LEDERMAN, S.; AND BROWSE, R. See 04006. 71-91.
**04011** Steps toward making robots see. BRADY, M. See 04006. 95-123.
**04012** An overview of local environment sensing in robotics applications. ESPIAU, B. See 04006. 125-151.
**04013** Force and tactile sensing for robots. DARIO, P.; BERGAMASCO, M.; AND FIORILLO, A. See 04006. 153-185.
**04014** Analogs of biological tissues for mechanoelectrical transduction: tactile sensors and muscle-like actuators. DE ROSSI, D.; DOMENICI, C.; AND CHIARELLI, P. See 04006. 201-218.
**04015** Gas sensors: towards an artificial nose. PELOSI, P.; AND PERSAUD, K. See 04006. 361-381.
**04016** Integration of robot sensory systems. JAYAWANT, B. See 04006. 417-422.
**04017** Active vision: integration of fixed and mobile cameras. MORASSO, P.; SANDINI, G.; AND TISTARELLI, M. See 04006. 449-462.
**04018** An iterative and interactive simulation method to reconstruct unknown inputs contributing to known outputs of neuronal systems. HULLIGER, M. See 04006. 561-569.
**04019** § Signal processing and pattern recognition in nondestructive evaluation of materials. Proceedings of a NATO Advanced Research Workshop held within the activities of the NATO Special Programme on Sensory Systems for Robotic Control (Lac Beauport, Quebec, Canada, Aug. 19–22, 1987), CHEN, C. [NATO ASI series F: vol. 44] Springer-Verlag New York, Inc., New York, NY, 1988, 344 pp., ISBN 0-387-19100-3.
**04020** The effects of limited data in multi-frequency reflection diffraction tomography. SOUMEKH, M. See 04019. 231-239.
**04021** Parameter estimation in array processing. BÖHME, J. See 04019. 307-325.
**04022** § Software Engineering Education. Lecture Notes in Computer Science (Fairfax, Virginia, April 28-29, 1988), FORD, G. (Ed.) Springer-Verlag New York, Inc., New York, NY, 1988, 207 pp., ISBN 0-387-96854-7.
**04023** Teaching the tricks of the trade. BENTLEY, J. See 04022. 1-8.
**04024** Stategic imperatives in software engineering education. MILLS, H. See 04022. 9-19.
**04025** Undergraduate software engineering education. RICHARDSON, W. See 04022. 121-144.
**04026** Software tools at the University: Why, What and How. WERTH, L. See 04022. 169-186.
**04027** A scarce resource in undergraduate software engineering courses: user interface design materials. LEVENTHAL, L.; AND MYNATT, B. See 04022. 187-198.
**04028** § Third international conference on logic programming. Proceedings (London, UK, July 14-18, 1986), SHAPIRO, E. (Ed.) Springer-Verlag New York, Inc., New York, NY, 1986, 720 pp., ISBN 0-387-16492-8.
**04029** A new approach for introducing Prolog to naive users. MALER, O.; SCHERZ, Z.; AND SHAPIRO, E. See 04028. 544-551.
**04030** § Uncertainty and intelligent systems. Proceedings of the 2nd International Conference on Information Processing and Management of Uncertainty in Knowledge-Based Systems (Urbino, Italy, July 1988), GOOS, G.; AND HARTMANIS, J. (Eds.) [Lecture Notes in Computer Science: 313] Springer-Verlag New York, Inc., New York, NY, 1988, 408 pp., ISBN 0-387-19402-9.

04031   A study of Arab computer users: a special case of a general HCI methodology. KALLALA, M.; AND BELLIN, W. See 04030. 338-350.
04032 § Visualization in programming. 5th Interdisciplinary Workshop in informatics and psychology (Scharding, Austria, May 20-23, 1986), GORNY, P.; AND JAUBER, M. (Eds.) Springer-Verlag New York, Inc., New York, NY, 1986, ISBN 0-387-18507-0.
04033 § VDM—The Way Ahead. Proceedings of the 2nd VDM-Europe Symposium (Dublin, Ireland, September 11-16, 1988), GOOS, G.; AND HARTMANIS, J. (Eds.) [Lecture notes in computer science, no. 328] Springer-Verlag New York, Inc., New York, NY, 1988, 499 pp., ISBN 0-387-50214-9.
04034   The B tool. ABRAIAL, J. See 04033. 86-87.
04035   A support system for formal reasoning: requirements and status. JONES, C.; AND LINDSAY, P. See 04033. 139-152.
04036   The VIP VDM specification language. MIDDELBURG, K. See 04033. 187-201.
04037   Muffin: a user interface design experiment for a theorem proving assistant. JONES, C.; AND MOORE, R. See 04033. 337-375.
04038   The use of VDM on the specification of Chinese characters. TEO, G.; AND MAC, M. See 04033. 476-499.
04039 § Future Trends in Information Science and Technology. Proceedings of the Silver Jubilee Conference (City Univ., London, January 16, 1987), YATES-MERCER, P. (Ed.) Taylor Graham Publishers, London, UK, 1988, 123 pp., $35.00, ISBN 0-947568-20-4.
04040   Online library catalogues as information retrieval systems: what can we learn from research? HILDRETH, C. See 04039. 9-25.
04041   Practical applications of optical disk image systems in document management. PLUME, T. See 04039. 26-37.
04042   Intelligent interfaces for information retrieval systems: architecture problems in the construction of expert systems for document retrieval. JONES, K. See 04039. 47-73.
04043 § Integrating text with non-text:a picture is worth 1k words. Proceedings of the I. nstitute of Information Scientists Text Retrieval '85 Conference (,), KIMBERLEY, R. (Ed.) Taylor Graham Publishers, London, UK, 1986, 120 pp., 26.50, ISBN 0-947568-07-7.
04044   Integrating graphics and text in computer products. RHIND, D. See 04043. 77-81.
04045   Information retrieval: the future. EDWARDS, K. See 04043. 109-117.
04046 § New horizons for the information profession: meeting the challenge of change. Proceedings of the Annual Conference of the Institute of Information Scientists (Coventry, England, 1987), DYER, H.; AND TSENG, G. (Eds.) Taylor Graham Publishers, London, UK, 1988, 225 pp., $34.00, ISBN 0-947568-32-8.
04047   Interfaces and on-line reading. FORRESTER, M. See 04046. 97-112.
04048   Human factors of changing information science technology. ROBERTSON, P. See 04046. 173-178.

# DOCTORAL THESES

The doctoral disserations are listed in alphabetical order by publisher, which is usually the granting institution. UMI order number is also provided.

04049   SAMAD, T. Towards a natural language interface for computer aided design. Carnegie-Mellon University, Pittsburgh, PA, 1986, UMI Order No. GAX86-16520.
04050   GOWDA, R. Influence of individual characteristics and group cohesiveness on programmer productivity. College of Business Administration, Atlanta, GA, 1988, Order No. GAX88-20750.
04051   PARIS, C. The use of explicit user models in text generation: tailoring to a user's level of expertise. Columbia University, New York, NY, Order No: GAX88-15690.

## DOCTORAL THESES

04052 SCHNEIER, C. Effects of an immediate feedback tool on designer productivity and design usability. Georgia Institute of Technology, Atlanta, GA, 1987, UMI Order No. GAX87-18463.

04053 KAZEMIAN, F. A formal specification for a user interface for office automation. Kansas State Univ., Manhattan, KS, 1987, UMI Order No. GAX87-08663.

04054 LOKEN-KIM, K. Error detection and correction in a speech recognition system: a knowledge based system approach. N. C. State Univ. at Raleigh, Raleigh, NC, Order No: GAX88-15557.

04055 SHAPIRO, G. (Ed.) Nested window flow controls with packet fragmentation. N. C. State Univ. at Raleigh, Raleigh, NC, Order No: GAX88-21779.

04056 ASENTE, P. Editing graphical objects using procedural representations. Stanford University, Stanford, CA, Order No: GAX88-08345.

04057 NGWENYAMA, O. Fundamental issues of knowledge acquisition: toward a human action perspective of knowledge systems. State Univ. of New York at Binghamton, Binghamton, NY, Order No: GAX88-25946.

04058 SNELL, J. A systems model of cognition for improving human factors of computing environments. State Univ. of New York at Binghamton, Binghamton, NY, 1986, UMI Order No. GAX86-27918.

04059 OPPENHEIMER, C. (Ed.) Reasons for computer utilization reluctance by teachers with computer training. Temple Univ., Philadelphia, PA, Order NoAX88-18829.

04060 OWAIED, H. (Ed.) A computer assisted learning system for reliability engineering. Univ. of Bradford, Bradford, UK, Order No: GAXDX-82833.

04061 FERRIN, T. MIDAS: molecular interactive display and simulation. Univ. of California at San Francisco, San Francisco, CA, 1987, UMI Order No. GAX87-08445.

04062 SATTLER, D. Programming in Basic or Logo: effect on critical thinking skills. Univ. of New Mexico, Albuquerque, NM, 1987, UMI Order No. GAX87-20773.

04063 WISHART, J. (Ed.) User involvement with microcomputer software. Univ. of Surrey, Surrey, UK, Order No: GAXDX-83027.

04064 REEVE, D. (Ed.) A comparison of the effects of computer-assisted instruction, interactive video, and traditional instruction on third-grade students in art education. University of Alabama in Huntsville, Huntsville, AL, Order No: GAX88-21829.

04065 SMITH, T. Assessing the usability of user interfaces: guidance and online help features. University of Arizona, Tucson, AZ, Order No: GAX88-09947.

04066 KLEFSTAD, R. Maintaining a uniform user interface for an Ada programming environment. University of California at Irvine, Irvine, CA, 1988,Order No. GAX88-20199.

04067 MUELLER, E. Daydreaming and computation: a computer model of everyday creativity, learning and emotions in the human stream of thought. University of California at Los Angeles, Los Angeles, CA, 1987, UMI Order No. GAX87-13872.

04068 WORLEY, D. A methodology, specification language, and automated support environment for comluter-aided design systems. University of California at Los Angeles, Los Angeles, CA, 1986, UMI Order No. GAX86-21157.

04069 MIYATA, Y. The learning and planning of actions. University of California at San Diego, La Jolla, CA, 1988,Order No. GAX88-17183.

04070 GLOVER, D. Experimentation with an adaptive search strategy for solving a keyboard design/configuration problem. University of Iowa, Iowa City, IA, 1986, UMI Order No. GAX86-22767.

04071 LEVI, S. A methodology for designing distributed, fault-tolerant, and reactive real-time operating systems. University of Maryland, College Park, MD, 1988,Order No. GAX88-18423.

04072 IBERALL, A. A neural model of human prehension. University of Massachusetts, Amherst, MA, 1987, UMI Order No. GAX87-10462.

04073 LILLY, P. Automatic contour definition on left ventriculograms by image evidence and a multiple template-based model. University of Michigan, Ann Arbor, MI, 1987, UMI Order No. GAX87-12163.

04074 GRANOR, T. A user interface mangement system generator. University of Pennsylvania, Philadelphia, PA, 1986, UMI Order No. GAX86-14805.

**04075** DORSEY, P. An investigation of the effectiveness of communication between systems analysts and end users in the design of large computer systems. University of Utah, Salt Lake City, UT, 1988,Order No: GAX88-16831.

**04076** MUTKA, M. Sharing in a privately owned workstation environment. University of Wisconsin, Madison, WI, 1988,Order No. GAX88-17140.

**04077** WEST, D. (Ed.) Culture, cognitive, and connectionism: Towards an hermeneutic anthropology of mind. University of Wisconsin, Madison, WI, Order No: GAX88-17155.

**04078** NAPOLIELLO, M. A study of managerial computer users: the impact of user sophistication on decision structure and attributes of decision-related information (end user). Virginia Polytech Inst. & State Univ., Blacksburg, VA, 1987, UMI Order No. GAX87-21992.

# PART 3

# INDEXES

| | |
|---|---|
| Author Index | 519 |
| Keyword Index | 697 |
| ACM *CR* Classification System | 929 |
| Category Index | 947 |
| Proper Noun Index | 1160 |
| Reviewer Index | 1172 |
| Periodicals Cited | 1186 |

Key
- • Book
- § Proceedings
- † Reviewed item

# Author Index

All authors of each item are listed alphabetically in this index. Titles are given for easy reference. Find the full citation in the Bibliography by accession number. Those numbers prefixed with "HCI" may be looked up in the Review section. Bulleted items are books. The symbol § indicates an entire proceedings entry.

**Åkerstedt, T.**
Inactivity, night work, and fatigue. 03705

**Aaronson, A.**
Learning by doing with simulated intelligent help. HCI-0229 †

**Aaronson, A. P.**
Learning by doing with simulated intelligent help. 0132

**Aasman, J.**
Operator effort and the measurement of heart-rate variability. 01736

**Abdel-Malek, A.**
Modeling of task-dependent characteristics of human operator dynamics during pursuit manual tracking. 01859

**Abdel-Malek, L.**
Ergonomic evaluation of safety devices in robotic systems. 03449

**Abdel-Moty, E.**
Computerized design and analysis of sitting workplace. 01506

**Abdollahi, M.**
Image compression using polylines. 02533

**Abe, O.**
Directed graph representations of association structures: A systematic approach. 01862

**Abe, T.**
An operations advisor for an on-line computer banking system with graphics interface. 02983

**Abel, J. F.**
Interactive color graphical postprocessing as a unifying influence in numerical analysis research. 01684

**Abel, M. J.**
Report on the Collaborative Technology Developers' Workshop. 0994

**Abelson, H.**
Boxer: a reconstructible computational medium. HCI-0121 †

**Abernethy, C. N.**
Experimental results do not support some ergonomic standards for computer video terminal design. HCI-0428 †

**Abraial, J. R.**
The B tool. 04034

**Abrams, M. A. (Ed.)**
Proceedings of the 21st Annual Simulation Symposium. § 03499

**Abu-Hakima, S.**
Jet engine technical advisor (JETA). 02974

**Abu-Mostafa, Y. S. (Ed.)**
Complexity in information theory. ● 0003

**Acheson, A.**
DORUS: an architecture for dynamic optimal resource utilization systems. 02979

**Ackerman, P. L.**
Automatic and controlled processing theory and its applications to human factors problems. 0402

**Ackermann, D.**
The chances of individualization in human-computer interaction and its consequences. 0309
The role of mental models in programming: from experiment to requirements for an interactive system. 03827

**Adams, D. A.**
GMMS: global model management system: a conceptional design framework for model management systems for distributed decision support systems. 03484

**Adams, E.**
Dbxtool: A window-based symbolic debugger for sun workstations. 02614

**Adams, L.**
High performance interactive graphics: modeling, rendering and animating for IBM PCs and compatibles. ● HCI-0071 †

**Adams, T. L.**
Distributed database considerations in an expert system for radar analysis. 03175

**Adelman, L.**
Distributed tactical decisionmaking: conceptual framework and empirical results. 01885

An empirical investigation as to the need for multicomponent decision models. 01898

**Adelsberger, H.**
Environments: Austria compared to the United States. 01026

**Adelson, E. H.**
The perception of coherent motion in two-dimensional patterns. 03327

**Agarwal, A. K.**
The development of an automated flight test management system for flight test planning and monitoring. 02928

**Agarwal, R.**
A preliminary specification of an on-line expert help system. 01930

**Aggarwal, J. K.**
Motion and time-varying imagery. 03336

**Aghili, H.**
Process design of oil and gas production facilities using expert systems. 02933

**Agosti, M.**
Design of personal information retrieval systems. 02032

**Aguilar, L.**
An architecture for a multimedia teleconferencing system. 02802

**Agusa, K.**
A programming environment supporting reuse of object-oriented software. 03509

**Ahituv, N.**
Principles of information systems for management (2nd ed.). ● 0005

**Ahlbom, G.**
Recognition of speech using temporal decomposition. 03990

**Ahlström, B.**
Touch screen, cursor keys and mouse interaction. 03769

**Ahluwalia, R.**
Human response to unexpected robot movements at selected slow speeds. 03405

**Ahn, J. H.**
An investigation into the existence of subgroup concept in information systems personnel management. 03022

**Aho, A. V.**
The AWK programming language. ● HCI-0020 †

**Ahrens, J. D.**
An experiment to test user validation of requirements: data-flow diagrams vs task-oriented menus. 02131

**Ahuja, S. R.**
The rapport multimedia conferencing system. 03037

**Aiken, A.**
A development environment for horizontal microcode programs. 01079

**Aiken, R. M.**
Retraining high school teachers to teach computer science—observations on the first course. 01030

**Ainsworth, W. A.**
Optimization of string length for spoken digit input with error correction. 02185

**Airenti, G.**
Functional modelling in the execution of actions. 01485

**Akagi, K.**
Experimental results do not support some ergonomic standards for computer video terminal design. HCI-0428 †

**Akaho, E.**
Comparison of manual and online searches of chemical abstracts. 02265

**Akeley, K.**
High-performance polygon rendering. 02814

**Aken, R.**
Computer-assisted instruction in academic libraries. 02282

**Akers, L. A.**
Limited interconnectivity in synthetic neural systems. 03968

**Akin, O.**
Structure of a directory space: a case study with a UNIX operating system. 02138
Efficient computer-user interface in electronic mail systems. HCI-0118 †

**Akman, V. (Ed.)**
Intelligent CAD systems II: implementational issues. ● 0006

**Akscyn, R.**
Collaboration in KMS, a shared hypermedia system. 0807
The data model is the heart of interface design. 02875

**Akscyn, R. M.**
Experience with the ZOG human-computer interface system. HCI-0246 †

**Alagar, V. S.**
A human approach to the technological challenges in data security. 01543

**Alavi, M.**
User-developed DSS: steps toward quality control. 0461
Strategies for end-user computing: An integrative framework. 02348

**Alberico, R.**
Front end games. 02599
Where person meets machine. 02601
User-supported artificial intelligence. 02602

**Albrecht, A. (Ed.)**
Parallel algorithms and architectures. § 03819

**Albritton, R. L.**
Investigating computer anxiety in an academic library. 02047

**Albus, J. S.**
The central nervous system as a low and high level control system. 04007

**Aleksander, I.**
The management of advanced information technology. 0226
Neural computing: ideas from the brain. 01379
Decision and intelligence. ● HCI-0068 †

**Alexander, H.**
Comments on "formal specification of user interfaces: a comparison and evaluation of four axiomatic approaches". 01847
Formally-based techniques for dialogue design. 03190

ECS - A technique for the formal specification and rapid prototyping of human-computer interaction. 03253
Formally-based tools and techniques for human-computer dialogues. ● HCI-0021 †

**Alexander, I.**
Human factors in the Columbus space station. 03250

**Alexander, J.**
Interactive data visualization. 01986

**Alexander, J. H.**
Painless panes for Smalltalk windows. 01118

**Alexander, R. A.**
Cognitive processing differences between novice and expert computer programmers. 02145

**Alfaro, L.**
Why reading was slower from CRT displays than from paper. 0797
Reading is slower from CRT displays than from paper: attempts to isolate a single-variable explanation. 01743
Reading from CRT displays can be as fast as reading from paper. 01758

**Alfize, A. R.**
Rule-based reasoning as Boolean transformations. 01901

**Alho, K.**
A design data manager. 03090

**Ali, D.**
A graphical database interface. 01511

**Ali, M.**
PISCES: an expert system for coal fired power plant monitoring and diagnostics. 02915
Hierarchical scene structure representations to facilitate image understanding. 02942
Automatic acquisition of domain and procedural knowledge. 02943
An object-oriented expert system for coal-fired MHD power plant fault monitoringand diagnosis. 02973

**Ali, M. (Chair.)**
Industrial & Engineering Applications of Artificial Intelligence & Expert Systems. § 02941

**Ali, M. (Ed.)**
Industrial & Engineering Applications of Artificial Intelligence & Expert Systems. § 02910
Industrial & Engineering Applications of Artificial Intelligence & Expert Systems: vol. I. § 02967

**Ali, S. M.**
A new algorithm for extracting the interior of bounded regions based on chain coding. 01469

**Allard, R.**
Human cognition and human computer interaction. HCI-0241 †

**Allen, B. S.**
A theoretical framework for interactivating linear video. 02284
Expert systems and interactive video tutorials: separating strategies from subject matter. 02293

**Allen, D. C.**
Application of the butterfly parallel processor in artificial intelligence. 0489

**Allen, D. M. (Ed.)**
Computer science and statistics. § 03313

**Allen, G. H.**
A VLSI interactive layout editor (VILE). 02611

**Allen, J.**
Analyzing intention in utterances. 0391

**Allen, J. A.**
Maintenance training simulator fidelity and individual differences in transfer of training. 01722

**Allen, P.**
Program generation for Ada—a case study. 02634

**Allen, R. B. (Ed.)**
Office Information Systems. § 03036

**Allen, R. H.**
A multiparadigm user interface for intelligent CAD systems. 0716

**Allgayer, J.**
XTRA: a natural-language access system to expert systems. 02244

**Allinson, L.**
Travel around a learning support environment: rambling, orienteering or touring? 02900
The travel metaphor as design principle and training aid for navigating around complex systems. 03195

**Allwood, C. M.**
Novices on the computer: a review of the literature. 02129
Analogy and other sources of difficulty in novices' very first text-editing. 02148
Question asking when learning a text-editing system. 02202

**Almes, G. T.**
Edmas: an object-oriented, locally distributed mail system. 01857

**Almy, T.**
Compiling Forth for performance. 02309
Pride-II physical layout program of modifying Forth for "non-believers". 02312

**Aloimonos, J.**
Shape from texture. 01278

**Alonso, J. R.F.**
Parametric Fourier image characterization toolkit. 02798

**Alpern, B.**
Graph attribution as a specification paradigm. 01138

**Alschuler, L.**
Hand-crafted hypertext-lessons from the ACM experiment. 0128

**Altheide, D. L.**
Keyboarding as a social form. 01551

**Alty, J. L.**
Microtechnology and user friendly systems—the CONNECT dialogue executor. 02382
Application modelling in a user interface management system. 03262

**Amadi, A. O.**
Viewdata in the office—user-friendly page identification. 02334

**Amano, K.**
A supporting system for effective construction and sharing of scientific databases by general researchers. HCI-0262 †

**Ambler, A. L.**
Experience with a functional layered multicomputer architecture for interactive processing. 02402

**Ambron, S.**
Interactive multimedia. ● 0011

**Amell, J. R.**
Capacity equivalence curves: a double trade-off curve method for equating task performance. 01796

**Amendola, A.**
Modelling operators in accident conditions: advances and perspectives on a cognitive model. 02169

**Amlani, A.**
Process design of oil and gas production facilities using expert systems. 02933

**Ammann, A.**
Office-by-example: an integrated office system and database manager. 01159

**Ammeraal, L.**
Interactive 3D computer graphics. ● 0012
Graphics programming in Turbo C. ● 0013

**Ammons, J. C.**
A supervisory control paradigm for real-time control of flexible manufacturing systems. 01205

**Amoroso, D. L.**
Organizational issues of end-user computing. 01638
Examining the duality role of I.S. executives: a study of I.S. issues. 01953
Organizational factors affecting the success of end-user computing. 02344

**Anand, N.**
Clarify function! 01122

**Ananiashvili, G. G.**
Algebraic approach to the problem of addressation. 01488

**Andersen, P. B./.**
Semiotics and informatics: computers as media. 0448

**Anderson, D. B.**
Experience with Flamingo: a distributed, object-oriented user interface system. 03033

**Anderson, D. Z.**
Optical systems that imitate human memory. 01576

**Anderson, E. E.**
The implementation of information systems for workers: a structural equation model. 01948

**Anderson, H.**
Why artificial intelligence isn't (yet). 01175

**Anderson, J.**
The acquisition of grammar. 0353
Designing with constraints. 0467
Production systems, learning, and tutoring. 0487
Neural networks and NP-complete optimization problems; a performance study on the graph bisection problem. 01339
How technology brings blind people into the workplace. 01705

**Anderson, J. A.**
Software for neural networks. 0770
Psychological concepts in a parallel system. 02564
Concepts in connectionist models. 02724

**Anderson, J. R.**
Effect of practice on knowledge and use of basic Lisp. 0210
The LISP tutor: it approaches the effectiveness of a human tutor. HCI-0431 †
The automated tutoring of introductory computer programming. HCI-0438 †

**Anderson, K. (Ed.)**
The history of personal workstations. § 03091

**Anderson, M.**
A comparison of menu selection techniques: touch panel, mouse and keyboard. 02122

**Anderson, M. P.**
Pygmalion at the interface. HCI-0349 †

**Anderson, N. S.**
Methods for designing software to fit human needs and capabilities (excerpt). 0079

**Anderson, N. S. (Ed.)**
Methods for designing software to fit human needs and capabilities. § 03566

**Anderson, S.**
Proving properties of interactive systems. 03267

**Anderson, T. L.**
Panel: user interfaces and database management systems. 01082
A distributed object server. 03842

**Andersson, E.**
Automatic construction of surfaces with prescribed shape. 01474

**Andersson, R.**
Automatic construction of surfaces with prescribed shape. 01474

**André, P.**
Robot components and systems. ● HCI-0068 †

**Andrew, I.**
Study of visual performance on a multi-color VDU of color defective and normal Trichromatic subjects. 03701

**Andrews, K.**
Design and implementation of the UW Illustrated compiler. 03059

**Andriole, S. J.**
Graphic equivalence, graphic explanations, and embedded process modeling for enhanced user-system interaction. 01888
Storyboard prototyping: a new approach to user requirements analysis. ● HCI-0005 †

**Angell, I. O.**
GENIE-M: A generator for multimedia information environments. 0268

**Anstey, P.**
Computing advice at a distance: the 'remote advisory' concept. 02617
The provision of terminal-based user support. 02686
How much is enough? A study of user command repertoires. 03240

**Anstis, S.**
Motion perception: second thoughts on the correspondence problem. 03325

**Antao, B. A.**
An advisory system for digital logic simulation. 02986

**Antill, L.**
Information systems definition: the Multiview approach. ● HCI-0085 †

**Antoniewicz, R. F.**
The development of an automated flight test management system for flight test planning and monitoring. 02928

**Anzai, Y.**
Doing, understanding, and learning in problem solving. 0480

**Anzenhofer, K.**
Information systems user–designer communication problems. 01938

**Apgar, B.**
A display system for the Stellar Graphics Supercomputer Model GS1000. 02816

**Apostolos, M. K.**
A comparison of the artistic aspects of various industrial robots. 02938

**Apostolou, G. L.**
Threat to privacy: the federal government's use of personal information in the new communication environment. 02680

**Appelt, D.**
Transportability and generality in a natural-language interface system. 0394

**Appelt, D. E.**
TEAM: an experiment in the design of transportable natural-language interfaces. HCI-0351 †

**Apperley, M. D.**
Lean cuisine: a low fat notation for menus. 02062

**Applegate, K.**
Human interfaces in a legal expert system. 03164

**Applegate, L.**
Groupware: interface design for meetings. 02883

**Applerley, M. D.**
Designing the "cockpit": the application of a human-centered design philosophy to make optimization systems accessible. 01016

**Appleton, E.**
Interactive aspects of knowledge representations. 03395

**Arabyan, A.**
Modeling of control and learning in a stepping motion. 01250

**Aral, Z.**
Non-intrusive and interactive profiling in parasight. 01123

**Arbib, M. A.**
Vision, brain, and cooperative computation: an overview. 0015
Depth and detours: an essay on visually guided behavior. 0018
Schemas that integrate vision and touch for hand control. 0026
Brains, machines, and mathematics (2nd ed.). ● HCI-0034 †
In search of the person: philosophical explorations in cognitive science. ● HCI-0062 †
From schema theory to computational (neuro-)linguistics. HCI-0345 †

**Arbib, M. A. (Ed.)**
Vision, brain, and cooperative computation. ● 0014

**Archer, N. P.**
End user software selection. 02434

**Archibald, J. L.**
A graphical entity-relationship database browser. 03532

**Arden, M. J.**
The NeWS book: an introduction to the network/extensible window system. ● 0358

**Arditi, A.**
Computing for the blind user. 01287

**Aretz, A. J.**
Color computer graphics in military cockpits. 0261

**Argiro, D.**
XVISION: a comprehensive software system for image processing research, education, and applications. 03124

**Argote, L.**
The human side of robotics: how workers react to a robot. 0443

**Ariav, G.**
Designing conceptual models of dialog: a case for dialog charts. 0968
Panel: user interfaces and database management systems. 01082

**Arima, K.**
Logic programmable natural language processor of a knowledge-base management system. 02965

**Arinze, B.**
Develping decision support systems from a model of the DSS/user interface. 0253

**Arlen, G. H.**
Videotex and online services: competition or collateral. 03557

**Armistead, L. P.**
Creative computer problem solving. 01584

**Armstrong, C. J.**
OST— a training package for end-users of online systems. 02568

**Armstrong, P.**
Producing resource discs—the Domesday project experience. 0514

**Armstrong, W. W.**
Near-real-time control of human figure models. 01829
Near-real-time control of human figure models. 03295

**Arnaut, L. Y.**
Optimizing the touch tablet: the effects of control display gain and method of cursor control. 01730
An empirical comparison of model-based and explicit communication for dynamic human-computer task allocation. 02109

**Arnett, K. P.**
Including a user interface management system (UIMS) in the performance relationship model. 01000

**Arnold, B.**
User errors in human—computer interaction. 0313

**Arnold, L. M.**
Item selection from menus: the influence of menu organization, query interpretation, and programming experience on selection strategies. 01011

**Arnold, S. E.**
End-users: Dreams or dollars. 02519

**Arons, A. B.**
Overcoming conceptual difficulties in physical science through computer-based Socratic dialogs. 03877

**Aronsson, G.**
Work content, stress and health in computer-mediated work: a seven year follow-up study. 03758

**Arora, J. S.**
SMART: Scientific database management and engineering analysis routines and tools. 01166

**Arthur, J. D.**
A descriptive/prescriptive model for menu-based interaction. 02120
An interactive environment for tool selection, specification and composition. 02141
Toward a formal specification of menu-based systems. 02400

**Arthur, L. J.**
UNIX shell programming. ● HCI-0027 †

**Asada, H.**
Describing surfaces. 02699

**Asano, K.**
Concept for a model databased remote maintenance system. 03565

**Asanuma, C.**
Certain aspects of the anatomy and physiology of the cerebral cortex. 0636

**Asente, P.**
An overview of the C toolkit. 03109

**Asente, P. J.**
Editing graphical objects using procedural representations. 04056

**Asfahl, C. R.**
An industrial chemical hazards database with a natural language interface: an application of artificial intelligence. 01533

**Asfour, S.**
A comprehensive data base for the design of manual materials handling. 01510

**Asfour, S. S.**
A knowledge-based system for assessment of human physiological abilities in manual lifting tasks. 01519
Review and evaluation of physiological cost prediction models for manual materials handling. 01757

**Ashby, F. G.**
Counting and timing models in psychophysics and the conjoint Weber's law. 02368

**Ashley, K. D.**
A case-based system for trade secrets law. 02769
Ashley, K. D.-But, see, accord: generating blue book citations in HYPO. 02770

**Ashton, P. J.**
Instrumenting systems to measure components of interactive response times. 01230

**Assmann, K.**
Software tools for the development of pictorial information systems in medicine—the ISQL experience. 03980

**Assunto, K.**
Socio-tech: what is it (and why should we care)? 0908

**Astrahan, M. M.**
System R: a relational approach to database management. 0709

**AT&T, C.**
UNIX system V: release 3.0 Intel 80286/80386 computer version: system administrator's guide. ● 0031

**Atal, B. S.**
Linear predictive coding of speech. 0289

**Athale (Ed.)**
Neural network models for optical computing. ● 0032

**Atkin, D.**
Understanding cable subscribership as telecommunications behavior. 02676

**Atkinson, M. P. (Ed.)**
Data types and persistence. ● 0033

**Atlan, H.**
Control of the immune response. 03970

**Atwood, M. E.**
NYNEX intelligent systems group. 0814

**Atzeni, P. (Ed.)**
International conference on database theory. § 03914

**Aucella, A.**
Voice: technology searching for communication needs. 0808

**Aucella, A. F.**
Voice messaging enhancing the user interface design based on field performance. 0913

**Ausiello, G. (Ed.)**
International conference on database theory. § 03914

**Austin, J.**
Pixel-planes 4: a summary. 0495

**Aviad, Z.**
Computing human oriented descriptions. 02020

**Avison, D. E.**
Information systems definition: the Multiview approach. ● HCI-0085 †

**Awad, E. M. (Chair.)**
Management of Information Systems Personnel. § 02996

**Awad, E. M. (Ed.)**
The 1987 ACM SIGBDP-SIGCPR Conference. § 03099

**Aykin, N.**
A simultaneous regression model for double stimulation tasks. 01726

**Ayoub, M.**
Ergonomic job design in frequent manual lifting tasks: a microcomputer-based model. 01532

**Ayton, P.**
A general purpose computer aid to judgemental forecasting: Rationale and procedure. 01665

**Azevedo, J. A.**
ISPF: the strategic dailog manager. ● 0035

**Azubuike, A. A.**
The computer as mask: a problem of inadequate human interaction examined with particular regard to online public access catalogues. 02337

**Bäckström, L.**
Temporal and spatial stability in visual displays. 03730

**Babka, O.**
Processor for man-machine natural-language-like communication. 01484

**Babu, A. J.C.**
A human factors design investigation of a computerized layout system of text-graphic technical materials. 01779

**Babu, A. J.G.**
Modelling the human factors aspects of a computer-based text-graphics layout system. 01518
Effects of graphic boundaries in tabular displays: a human factors evaluation. 01526

**Bach, M. J.**
The design of the UNIX operating system. ● HCI-0026 †

**Backer, E.**
A flexible and intelligent system for fast measurements in binary images for in-line robotic control. 03986

**Badler, N. I.**
JACK: a toolkit for manipulating articulated figures. 03126
Animating human figures: perspectives and directions. 03291
Motion graphics, description and control. 03348

**Badler, N. I. (Chair.)**
Motion: representation and perception. § 03321

**Baeck, K.**
The SIMONA project: the introduction of information processing in labour market administration. 0248

**Baecker, R.**
A vision of education in user-centered system and interface design. 0985
Enhancing program readability and comprehensibility with tools for program visualization. 03510

**Baecker, R. M.**
Towards a characterization of graphical interaction. 0074

**Baecker, R. M. (Ed.)**
Human-computer interaction. ● 0036

**Baek, Y. K.**
Color, graphics, and animation in a computer-assisted learning tutorial lesson. 02294

**Baer, K.**
On the temporal stability of signal detection processes. 03617

**Baer, V. E.H.**
Computers as composition tools: a case study of student attitudes. 02296

**Baert, P.**
The silent force of the screen. A research note on the impact of microelectronics on work autonomy among clerical workers in public administration. 01437

**Baggett, P.**
Conceptualizing in assembly tasks. 01776

**Bagnara, S.**
Human error detection processes. 02166
Office automation as an opportunity for an organizational check-up. 03749

**Bahill, A. T.**
Open-loop experiments for modeling the human eye movement system. 01870
Development and sensitivity analysis of adaptive predictor for human eye movement model. 02681

**Bahlke, R.**
The PSG—programming system generator. 01098
Context-sensitive editing with PSG environments. 03780

**Bailey, C. D.**
Forgetting and the learning curve: a laboratory study. 02484

**Bailey, D.**
PHIGS: a standard, dynamic, interactive graphics interface. 01826

**Bailey, R. W.**
Human performance engineering: using human factors/ergonomics to achieve computer system usability (2nd ed.). ● HCI-0042 †

**Bailey, W. A.**
Learning and transfer of measurement tasks. 0832
Directed dialogue protocols: verbal data for user interface design. 0866
Effects of interface design upon user productivity. 02891

**Baird Jr., L. L.**
The moral cracker? 01546

**Baird, B.**
Nonlinear dynamics of pattern formation and pattern recognition in the rabbit olfactory bulb. 02558
Bifurcation analysis of oscillating network model of pattern recognition in the rabbit olfactory bulb. 02725

**Baker, D.**
The design of a flexible distributed testbeb for communication systems. 03538

**Baker, K. D.**
A process oriented approach to an intelligent design aid. 02980

**Baker, M. A.**
The changing workplace: A guide to managing the people, organizational, and regulatory aspects of office technology (book excerpt). 0044

**Baker, M. P.**
Computer graphics. ● HCI-0069 †

**Baker, R.**
Workers education and user participation in the development of protective policies for VDT operators. 03752

**Baker, W.**
Socio-tech: what is it (and why should we care)? 0908

**Bakk, J.**
Improving speaker consistency in an automatic speech recognition framework. 01448

**Balaceanu, C.**
Simplicial differential geometric theory for language cortical dynamics. 01698

**Balaram, M.**
PC Version of a knowledge-based expert system with voice interface. 02964

**Baldwin, J. F.**
Concept learning from examples and counter examples. 02229

**Bales, V.**
Information management—the realities. 01377

**Ball, L. J.**
A process oriented approach to an intelligent design aid. 02980

**Balla, K.**
Linearization of the dynamic transfer response of time invariant nonlinear systems—in connection with the parallel information processing in living organisms. 02665

**Ballantine, R.**
Dialing a name: alphabetic entry through a telephone keypad. 0973

**Ballard, D. H.**
Cortical connections and parallel processing: structure and function. 0028
Interpolation coding: A representation for numbers in neural models. 01271

**Ballim, A.**
The subjective ascription of belief to agents. 03553

**Ballou, N.**
Data model issues for object-oriented applications. 0712
Data model issues for object-oriented applications. 01157

**Ballowe, D. W.**
A suppport strategy for users of a campus-wide local area network. 03157

**Balma, P.**
The world of GEM. ● 0396

**Balsamo, A.**
Ada-based executable modelling of distributed systems. HCI-0098 †

**Bammer, G.**
VDUs and musculo-skeletal problems at the Australian National University. A case study. 03709

**Banbury, J.**
Towards a framework for systems analysis practice. 0155

**Bandai, A.**
Comparison of manual and online searches of chemical abstracts. 02265

**Bandyopadhyay, S.**
A box structured methodology for solving business problems. 03483

**Banerjee, J.**
Data model issues for object-oriented applications. 0712
Data model issues for object-oriented applications. 01157

**Banerji, R. (Ed.)**
Artificial and human intelligence. § HCI-0052 †

**Banerji, R. B.**
GPS and the psychology of th Rubik cubist: a study in reasoning about actions. 03311

**Banks, W. P.**
Visual fatigue and spatial frequency adaptation to video displays of text. 01721

**Banks, W. W.**
jThe assessment of human/computer performance: a case for connectivity. 03535

**Baptista, G.**
A high accuracy algorithm for recognition of handwritten numerals. 02532

**Bara, B. G. (Ed.)**
Computational models of natural language processing. ● 0095

**Barakett, J.**
The effects of computer use in early childhood socialization. 0793

**Barbary, C. L.**
A database primer on natural language. 02413

**Barber, G. R.**
User interfaces for problem solving support. 02695

**Barber, T. J.**
Interactive critical path analysis (ICPA)—microcomputer implementation of a project management and knowledge engineering tool. HCI-0445 †

**Bareiss, E. R.**
Protos: an examplar-based learning apprentice. 02210

**Barfield, W.**
The mental rotation and perceived realism of computer-generated three-dimensional images. 02213

**Barid, B. J.**
The moral cracker? 01546

**Bariff, M. L.**
A study of user interface aids for model-oriented decision support systems. 02479

**Barker, H. A.**
A man-machine interface for computer-aided and simulation of control systems. 01237
A human-computer interface for control system design. 03208

**Barker, P. G.**
Pictorial dialogue methods. 02251
Pictorial knowledge bases. 03201
Pictorial interfaces to data bases. HCI-0116 †

**Barki, H.**
Change, attitude to change, and decision support system success. HCI-0296 †

**Barlow, J.**
Interacting with computers. 02061

**Barlow, J. F.**
Structuring informal information. 02426

**Barn, B. S.**
Graphical interaction management. 01390

**Barnard, D. T.**
Holophrasted displays in an interactive environment. HCI-0105 †

**Barnard, P.**
Approximate modelling of cognitive activity: towards an expert system design aid. 0801
The elicitation of system knowledge by picture probes. 0921
How would your favourite user model cope with these scenarios? 0999
Approximate modelling of cognitive activity with an expert system: a theory-based strategy for developing an interactive design tool. 01415
Navigating integrated facilities: initiating and terminating interaction sequences. 02876
Rapid prototyping of dialogue for human factors research: the EASIE approach. 03254
Using an expert system to convey HCI information. 03272

**Barnard, P. J.**
Cognitive resources and the learning of human-computer dialogs. 0209

**Barnes, J.**
A user perspective on computer-assisted translation for Minority languages. 01557

**Barnes, V.**
Reading is slower from CRT displays than from paper: attempts to isolate a single-variable explanation. 01743
Cursor movement during text editing. HCI-0113 †

**Barnett, B. J.**
Display proximity in multicue information integration: the benefits of boxes. 01763

**Barnett, G. O.**
History of the development of medical information systems at the Laboratory of Computer Science at Massachusetts General Hospital. 02842

**Barnett, M. L.**
Factors in the investigation of human error in accident causation. 03805

**Baroff, J.**
Direct manipulation user interfaces for expert systems. 0429

**Baron, N. S.**
Language, sublanguage, and the promise of machine translation. 01554

**Baron, R.**
A dedicated microcomputer for handwritten interaction with a software tool: system prototyping. HCI-0119 †

**Baronas, A.**
Restoring a sense of control during implementation: how user involvement leads to system acceptance. 02509

**Barone, R.**
Hypermedia: a face lift for presentation research and development: a user services function. 03154

**Baroudi, J. J.**
A short-form measure of user information satisfaction: a psychometric evaluation and notes on use. 02351
An empirical study of the impact of user involvement on system usage and information satisfaction. HCI-0448 †

**Barr, J. M.**
Speeded phase discrimination: evidence for global to local processing. 03307

**Barrett, E.**
Introduction: a new paradigm for writing with and for the computer. 0099
The on-line environment and in-house training. 0106
Textual intervention, collaboration, and the online environment. 0126

**Barrett, E. (Ed.)**
Text, context, and hypertext: writing with and for the computer. ● 0098
The society of text: hypertext, hypermedia, and the social construction of information. ● 0111

**Barry, P. L.**
Implementation of a multirule, multistage quality control program in a clinical laboratory computer system. 02380

**Barschdorff, D.**
Real-time failure detection on complex mechanical structures via parallel data processing. 01561

**Barsky, B. A.**
Geometric continuity with interpolating Bézier curves. 03857

**Barstow, D.**
An experiment in knowledge-based automatic programming. 0613

**Barstow, T. R.**
DOMAIN/DELPHI: retrieving documents online. 0906

**Bartee, T. C.**
Expert systems and artificial intelligence. ● 0133

**Barth, P.**
Impulse-86: a substrate for object-oriented interface design. 03032

**Barth, P. S.**
A substrate for object-oriented interface design. 0691

**Barto, A. G.**
An approach to learning control surfaces by connectionist systems. 0030

**Barton, B. F.**
User-friendly password methods for computer-mediated information systems. HCI-0167 †

**Barton, M. S.**
User-friendly password methods for computer-mediated information systems. HCI-0167 †

**Barzel, R.**
Two-bit graphics. HCI-0372 †

**Baselli, G.**
Single sweep analysis of visual evoked potentials through a model of parametric identification. 01261

**Basevi, E.**
Some remarks on videotex interaction. How to write for a new reader. 01433

**Basili, V. R.**
A plan for empirical studies of programmers. 02692

**Bass, L. J.**
A generalized user interface for applications programs (II). HCI-0112 †
An approach to user specification of interactive display interfaces. HCI-0137 †

**Bass, R. M.**
Design of an integral computer-based wheelchair controller/linear synchronous motor system. 02378

**Bates, M.**
Designing a practical interface. 01174
How to choose natural language software. 01183
The IRUS transportable natural language database interface. 03177

**Bates, R. L.**
SIMS: a uniform environment for planning and performing user's tasks. 02921

**Bateson, A.**
Cognitive processing differences between novice and expert computer programmers. 02145

**Batista, E. J.**
Putting on a show: using computer graphics to train end-users. 02520

**Batsell, R. R.**
Impact of a restricted natural language interface on ease of learning and productivity. 01334

**Battmann, W.**
Problems in the design of information retrieval systems: user competence and information complexity. 03602

**Baudelaire, P.**
Planar maps: an interaction paradigm for graphic design. 0873:1PBauer, D.
Improving the VDU workplace by introducing a physiologically optimized bright-background screen with dark characters: advantages and requirements. 03721

**Bauer, L. O.**
Effects of information-processing demands on physiological response patterns. 01740

**Bauer, M.**
The emerging role of workstations in the library environment. 02467

**Bauerfeld, W.**
Session on the requirements of international user groups. 01431

**Baum, E. B.**
Generalizing back propagation to computation. 02726

**Bauman, B. M.**
Developing awareness of computer ethics. 03010

**Bawden, D.**
Information systems and the stimulation of creativity. 02327
The foreign language barrier: a study among pharmaceutical research workers. 02333

**Baxter, C.**
Bat brushes: on the uses of six position and orientation parameters in a paint program. 0846

**Baykan, C.**
Structure of a directory space: a case study with a UNIX operating system. 02138

**Bazewicz, M.**
The design of information processing systems in relation to users. 03642

**Bérubé, C.**
The management of the end-user environment: an empirical investigation. 01937

**Bézivin, J. (Ed.)**
ECOOP '87. § 03790

**Beach, B.**
Language level persistence for an object-oriented application programming platform. 03522

**Beach, R. J. (Ed.)**
Computer Graphics. § 02810

**Beard, J. W.**
A taxonomy for the study of human factors in management information systems. HCI-0205 †

**Beason, P. S.**
Introduction to Windows programming. ● HCI-0013 †

**Beath, C. M.**
The information technology champion: aiding and abetting, care and feeding. 03459

**Beaton, R. J.**
Matching display characteristics to human visual capacity. 03723

**Beatty, J. C.**
Using color dimensions to display data dimensions. 01766
An experimental comparison of RGB, YIQ, LAB, HSV, and opponent color models. HCI-0381 †

**Beauchamp, Y.**
Human response to unexpected robot movements at selected slow speeds. 03405

**Beauclair, R. A.**
Current and future uses of the group decision support system technology: report on a recent empirical study. 02355

**Beaudouin-Lafon, M.**
User interface support for the integration of software tools: an iconic model of interaction. 01139
Iconic shells for multitasking workstations. 02792

**Beaumont, J. G.**
The effect of microcomputer presentation and response medium on digit span. 02090
Speed of response using keyboard and screen-based microcomputer response media. HCI-0192 :8E

**Beauodouin-Lafon, M.**
Prototyping user interfaces for applications depicted by graphs. 03523

**Bechtold, J. S.**
On-line tutorials: What kind of inference leads to the most effective learning? 0823

**Beck, D.**
Development and evaluation of direct manipulation lists (poster session). 0993

**Beck, J.**
Perception of transparency in man and machine. 02697
Perception of transparency in man and machine. HCI-0367 †

**Beck, K.**
Diagramming objects. 01177

**Becker, H. S.**
A novice user's interface to information retrieval systems. HCI-0219 †

**Becker, R. A.**
Brushing scatterplots. 02672
Statistical software, graphics and future workstations for data analysis. 03316

**Beech, D. (Ed.)**
Concepts in user interfaces: a reference model for command and response languages. § 03872
Concepts in user interfaces: a reference model for command and response languages. • HCI-0032 †

**Beeman, W.**
Social science and system design: interdisciplinary collaborations. 0833

**Beesley, K. R.**
Machine assisted translation with a human face. 01627

**Beeson Spillers, B.**
The effects of gender and age on preschool children's choice of the computer as a child-selected activity. 02450

**Befrosian, S. D.**
Effect of fuzzy membership on recognition of gray level images. 02539

**Begeman, M. L.**
gIBIS: a hypertext tool for exploratory policy discussion. HCI-0300 †

**Begemann, S. H.A.**
Lighting the electronic office. 03717

**Begg, I. M.**
Authoring systems for ICAI. 0469

**Behar, E.**
Preserving the integrity of the medium: a method of measuring visual and auditory comprehension of electronic media. 02084

**Beheshtian, M.**
Strategies for managing user developed systems. 01923

**Behrend, S. D.**
Children's collaborative use of a computer microworld. 02825

**Beilken, C.**
A spreadsheet interface for logic programming. 0822

**Beiser, K.**
Real librarians don't program...do they? 02600

**Beishuizen, J.**
Search strategies in internal and external memories. 03911

**Beishuizen, J. J.**
Learning styles in conversation—a practical application of Pask's learning theory to human-computer interaction. 03608

**Belady, L. A.**
The Japanese and software: is it a good match? HCI-0429 †

**Belardo, S.**
The feature chart: A tool for communicating the analysis for a decision support system. 01913

**Belew, R. K.**
A connectionist approach to conceptual information retrieval. 02772

**Belkatir, N.**
Experience with a data base of programs. 03050

**Belke, W.**
Establishing structures of requirements for the application of automated information processing (AIP)—an approach for the development of computer-aided systems. 03660

**Belkin, N. J.**
Knowledge elicitation using discourse analysis. 02152
Research on information interaction and intelligent information provision mechanisms. 02328
Retrieval systems for the information seeker: can the role of the intermediary be automated? 02864

On the nature and fuction of explanation in intelligent information retrieval. 03064

**Bell, D. A.**
Employment skills for the robot age. 0442

**Bell, G.**
Toward a history of (personal) workstations. 03092

**Bell, P. C.**
Visual interactive simulation - history, recent developments, and major issues. 02585

**Bell, S.**
Electronic information systems analysis. Present and future information systems use by academics involved in development studies. 02323

**Bellairs, K.**
Legal data modeling: The prohibited transaction exemption analyst. 02779

**Bellardo, T.**
An investigation of online searcher traits and their relationship to search outcomes. 02447

**Bellin, W.**
A study of Arab computer users: a special case of a general HCI methodology. 04031

**Bellman, B. L.**
Interaction of CMC with video telecourses for distance education. 02677

**Bellotti, V.**
Implications of current design practice for the use of HCI techniques. 03217

**Bellugi, U.**
Motion analysis of grammatical processes in a visual-gestural language. 03347

**Belz, F. C.**
Foundations for the Arcadia environment architecture. 01135

**Belzer, M.**
Legal reasoning in 3-D. 02774

**Bemis, S. V.**
Operator performance as a function of type of display: conventional versus perspective. 01769

**Ben-Arieh, D.**
Product and process design in intelligent CAD workstations. 0009

**Ben-Eli, M. U.**
The way you look determines what you see (or self-organization in management and society). 01614

**Benbasat, I.**
A structured approach to designing human-computer dialogues. HCI-0106 †
An experimental program investigating color-enhanced and graphical information presentation: an integration of the findings. HCI-0196 †

**Bench-Capon, T. J.M.**
People interact through computers not with them. 02060

**Bender, D. H.**
Perceptions of system effectiveness as viewed by executives, users, and information specialists. 03469

**Benjamin, J.**
The impact of menus and command-level feedback on learners' acquisition of data base language skills. 01041

**Bennaton, J.**
Off-line programming of robots using 3D graphical simulation system. 0602

**Benner, R. D.**
Process control and people at General Motors' Delta Engine Plant. 01905
Process control and people at General Motors' Delta engine plant. 03431

**Bennett, I.**
SOFTLIB—A documentation management system. HCI-0149 †

**Bennett, J.**
Report on the workshop on analytical models. 01001
Tools and methodology for user interface development. 01057

**Bennett, J. L.**
Collaboration of UIMS designers and human factors specialists. 01060

**Bennett, K. B.**
Human interaction with an "intelligent" machine. 02163

**Bennett, T. J.A.**
Self-organizing systems and transformational-generative (TG) grammar. 01619

**Bennett, W.**
Generating highly interactive user interfaces. 0865

**Bennett, W. S.**
Human language and computers. 01550

**Benokraitis, V. J.**
A mission planning architecture for an autonomous vehicle. 02939

**Benson, D.**
IRX: an information retrieval system for experimentation and user applications. 01076

**Benson, G. P.**
Classifying sensory inspectors with heterogeneous inspection-error probabilities. 02396

**Benson, M. W.**
A teachable neural network based on an unorthodox neuron. 02561
Neurons with hysteresis form a network that can learn without any changes in synaptic connection strengths. 02741

**Bentley, J.**
Teaching the tricks of the trade. 04023

**Benyon, D.**
Experience with adaptive interfaces. 01417

**Berce, J.**
Graphics fundamentals for a PCB-CAD PC system. 02494

**Bereiter, S. R.**
Sources of Difficulty in troubleshooting automated manufacturing systems. 03367

**Berg, E.**
Automated design and analysis system for design of custom orthopedic implants. 02931

**Berg, W. K.**
Changes in electromyographic activity associated with occupational stress and poor performance in the workplace. 01734

**Bergadano, F.**
Automated concept acquisition in noisy environments. 01841
Knowledge representation and use in pattern analysis. 02030

**Bergamasco, M.**
Force and tactile sensing for robots. 04013

**Bergen, J. R.**
Textons, the fundamental elements in preattentive vision and perception of textures. 0297

**Berger-Vachon, C.**
An evaluation of auditory performances in patients with Cochlear implants. 02658

**Bergeron, F.**
The management of the end-user environment: an empirical investigation. 01937

**Bergerud, M.**
Computers for managing information. ● 0141

**Bergholz, G.**
The KOMPLEX performance prediction tool. 02669

**Bergman, H.**
No effect of noise on vigilance performance? 01724

**Bergman, M.**
Some design principles for a mathematical knowledge representation system: a new approach to scientific calculation. 03849

**Bergqvist, U.**
Pregnancy and VDT work—an evaluation of the state of the art. 03686
Some physical factors at VDT work stations and ski problems. 03693
Visual phenomena and their relation to top luminance, phosphor persistence time and contrast polarity. 03729

**Beringer, D.**
Goodness of fit in the user-computer interface: A hierarchical control framework related to "friendliness". 01868

**Berkowitz, G. C.**
An approach to a mathematics of phenomena: canonical aspects of reentrant form eigenbehavior in the extended calculus of indications. 01621

**Berman, S.**
A semantic data model as the basis for an automated database design tool. 02036

**Bernard, J.**
Using design expertise to develop an expert system. 02962

**Berndt, R. S.**
Competitive dynamics in a dual-route connectionist model of print-to-sound transformation. 01341

**Bernhardt, R.**
Computer aided application program synthesis for industrial robots. 0606

**Bernius, M. T.**
Simps: Secondary ion mass image processing system. 02267

**Bernold, T.**
User interfaces: gateway or bottleneck. ● 0142

**Berry, R. E.**
A book on C. ● 0143
Common user access—a consistent and usable human-computer interface for the SAA environments. 01819

**Bersack, B.**
A display system for the Stellar Graphics Supercomputer Model GS1000. 02816

**Bersini, U.**
Modelling operators in accident conditions: advances and perspectives on a cognitive model. 02169

**Berthoz, A.**
Spatial and temporal transformations in visuo-motor coordination. 03963

**Bertino, E.**
View management in distributed data base systems. 0218

**Bertrand-Gastaldy, S.**
Improved design of graphic displays in thesauri—through technology and ergonomics. 02297

**Berube, S.**
The responsive system: a new challenge for AI. 02920

**Besen, S. M.**
Private copying, reproduction costs, and the supply of intellectual property. 01988

**Beshers, G.**
Maintained and constructor attributes. 01099

**Beth, T. (Ed.)**
Applicable algebra, error-correcting codes, combinatorics and computer algebra. § 03846

**Bethune, J. D.**
Modern drafting: an introduction to CAD. ● HCI-0077 †

**Betts, B.**
Goals and objectives for user interface software. 01056

**Beuter, A.**
Modeling of control and learning in a stepping motion. 01250

**Bevan, N.**
User system interaction standards. 01386

**Bever, T. G.**
The relation between linguistic structure and associative theories of language learning models: constructive critique of some connectionist learning models. 0591

**Bewley, W. L.**
Human factors testing in the design of Xerox's 8010 "Star" office workstation. 0090

**Beynon, M.**
A definitive programming approach to the implementation of CAD software. 0008

**Bez, H. E.**
WIMP interface for Unix. 01973
An icon-driven end-user interface to UNIX. 02089

On methods for interface specification and design. 02114

**Bezanson, D.**
Integrating CD-ROM with printed and online services: a silver platter end-user perspective. 03558

**Bezdek, J. C.**
A knowledge-based approach to online document retrieval system design. 03027

**Bhabuta, L.**
Standards and system development. 01629

**Bhushan, A.**
The workstation: the interpress page and document description language. 01356

**Bias, R. G.**
AIX usability enhancements and human factors. 01817

**Bice, K. (Ed.)**
Human Factors in Computing Systems. § 02903

**Biederman, I.**
Human image understanding: recent research and a theory. 02698

**Biemans, F. P.M.**
The design of distributed transport systems as a major standard interface in computer integrated manufacturing. 01564

**Bienenstock, E.**
Relational models in natural and artificial vision. 03953

**Bienkowski, T. L.**
A comprehensive data base for the design of manual materials handling. 01510

**Bier, E.**
An introduction to Gargoyle: an interactive illustration tool. 03185

**Bier, E. A.**
Snap-dragging. 01052
Graphical search and replace. 02812

**Biermann, A. W.**
Natural language with discrete speech as a mode for human-to-machine. HCI-0355 †

**Biggerstaff, T. J.**
Systems software tools. ● HCI-0030 †

**Biggs, W. D.**
Student perceptions of skill acquisition through cases and a general management simulation. 02589

**Bijl, A.**
Making drawings talk: pictures in minds and machines. 01392

**Bikson, T.**
Tools for supporting cooperative work near and far: highlights from the CSCW conference. 0879

**Bikson, T. K.**
Advanced office systems: An empirical look at use and satisfaction. 03172

**Billingsley, P.**
The standard factor. 01003

**Bills, L. G.**
User interfaces for CD'ROM PACs. 02466

**Bilodeau, I. M.**
Comparison of video game and conventional test performance. 02594

**Bimbot, F.**
Recognition of speech using temporal decomposition. 03990

**Binaghi, E.**
An abstract description generator for the reliability analysis in the design of real time systems. 02490

**Binding, C.**
Reference models, window systems, and concurrency. 01058
The architecture of a user interface toolkit. 03110

**Binford, T. O.**
Generic surface interpretation: observability model. 03563

**Bisanz, S.**
Symbiotic systems for complex problems. 02922

**Bisberg, C.**
Peopleware. 02557

**Bischoff, B.**
An improved automatic lipreading system to enhance speech recognition. 02859

**Bishop, A. B.**
A search for machine/human compatibility in manufacturing systems. 03381

**Bishop, P.**
Fifth generation computers: concepts, implementations and uses. ● HCI-0001 †

**Biskup, J.**
Privacy respecting permissions and rights. 03583
Data manipulation languages for the universal relation view DURST. 03944

**Biskup, J. (Ed.)**
MFDBS 87. § 03943

**Bisseret, A.**
The ergonomics psychology project at Inria. 0844

**Bissett, A.**
An external data structure tool for Pascal. 02495

**Biswas, G.**
Applications of qualitative modeling to knowledge-based risk assessment studies. 02970
An intelligent tutoring system for basic set theory. 02993
A knowledge-based approach to online document retrieval system design. 03027

**Bittencourt, G.**
Integration of graphical tools in a computer algebra system. 03847

**Bittner, A. C.**
Estimating reliability with small samples: increased precision with averaged correlations. 01728

**Bizzozero, C.**
The CADME approach to the interface of solid modellers. 03867

**Bjerkedal, T.**
Video display terminals and birth defects. A study of pregnancy outcomes of employees of the Postal-Giro Center, Oslo, Norway. 03691

**Bjorklund, R.**
Generation of muscle tension related to a demand of continuing attention. 03710

**Bjorn-Andersen, N.**
Understanding the nature of the office for the design of third wave office systems. 03248
Implementation of office systems. 03360

**Bjorn-Anderson, N.**
Are 'human factors' human? 01407

**Bjorner, D. (Ed.)**
VDM '87: VDM—a formal method at work. § 03831

**Bjorset, H.**
Lighting for visual display unit workplaces. 03715

**Blaazer, C.**
OA: bridging the language gap. 01376

**Blache, K. M.**
Process control and people at General Motors' Delta Engine Plant. 01905
Process control and people at General Motors' Delta engine plant. 03431

**Black, E. W.**
An experiment in computational discrimination of English word senses. 01813

**Black, J. B.**
Software psychology: the need for an interdisciplinary program. 0052
On-line tutorials: What kind of inference leads to the most effective learning? 0823
Goal and plan knowledge representations: from stories to text editors and programs. HCI-0183 †

**Black, M.**
Desktop publishing and user services; moment in the evolution of user support documentation at UNH. 03158

**Blackler, F.**
Information technology & people: designing for the future. ● 0144
Management, organizations and the new technologies. 0145

**Blackman, H. S.**
The user-computer interface in process control: a human factors engineering handbook. ● 0341

**Blackshaw, L.**
Search success and expectations with a computer interface. 01995

**Bladon, A.**
Acoustic phonetics, auditory phonetics, speaker sex and speech recognition: a thread. 0288

**Blahut, N. W.**
Adapting expert systems to simulation training of process operators. 02056

**Blair, D. C.**
Indeterminacy in the subject access to documents. 01993

**Blank, D.**
A comparison of children's reading comprehension and reading rates at three text presentation speeds on a CRT. 02280

**Blanning, R. W.**
An entity-relationship framework for information resource management. 01943

**Blaser, A. (Ed.)**
Natural Language at the Computer. § 03947

**Blasgen, M. W.**
System R: a relational approach to database management. 0709

**Blatt, S. E.**
100 Percent assured performance for robotic assistive devices for handicapped and elderly persons. 03414

**Blazek, Z.**
Microcomputer hardware education at a Czechoslovakian Technical University. 02488

**Bleser, T.**
Tools and methodology for user interface development. 01057

**Bleser, T. W.**
Design and implementation of an object-oriented user interface management system. 0412
An object-oriented user interface management system. 01055

**Blesser, B.**
Interactive recognition of handprinted characters for computer input. 0940

**Blewett, V.**
The effect of VDT symbol characteristics on operator performance and visual comfort. 03728

**Blinowska, K. J.**
A study of stability of electrocortical rhythm generators. 01258

**Blois, M. S.**
Evaluating RECONSIDER: a computer program for diagnostic prompting. HCI-0410 †

**Blokdijk, A.**
Planning and design of information systems. ● HCI-0045 †

**Blokdijk, P.**
Planning and design of information systems. ● HCI-0045 †

**Blomberg, J. L.**
The variable impact of computer technologies on the organization of work activities. 0388

**BloomBecker, J. J.B.**
Computer ethics: an antidote to despair. 0791

**Blount, G. N.**
Initial work on a system-independent computer model of a 3D anthropomorphic dummy. 01476

**Bluff, K.**
Self-modifying production system model of cognitive development. 0486

**Blum, B. I. (Ed.)**
History of Medical Informatics. § 02837

**Blumberg, M.**
Towards a new theory of job design. 03368

**Bly, S. A.**
Communicating with sound. 0067
A comparison of tiled and overlapping windows. 0904

**Blythe, J.**
Generalization and noise. 02155

**Böhme, J. F.**
Parameter estimation in array processing. 04021

**Bösser, T.**
Learning in man-computer interaction: a review of the literature. 0151

**Boardman, J. T.**
Interactive critical path analysis (ICPA)—microcomputer implementation of a project management and knowledge engineering tool. HCI-0445 †

**Boardman, T. J.**
Essential ingredients for a statistical workstation. 03315

**Bobick, A.**
A hybrid approach to structure-from-motion. 03340

**Bobrow, D.**
GUS, a frame driven dialog system. 0395

**Bobrow, D. G.**
Beyond the chalkboard: computer support for collaboration and problem solving inmeetings (Reprint). 0376
DARN: Toward a community memory for diagnosis and repair tasks. 0428
Common LISP object system specification X3J13 Document 88-002R. 01121
WYSIWIS revised: early experiences with multiuser interfaces. 01158
Beyond the chalkboard: computer support for collaboration and problem solving in meetings. HCI-0312 †

**Bocker, H. D.**
The enhancement of understanding through visual representations. 0898

**Boddy, D.**
Information technology and the experience of work. 0041

**Boden, M. A.**
Computer models of mind: computational approaches in theoretical psychology. ● 0152

**Bodendorf, F.**
A method framework for the statistical package SPSS/PC+ to support occasional users. 01202

**Bodoff, D.**
An improved automatic lipreading system to enhance speech recognition. 02859

**Boehm-Davis, D. A.**
The effects of structured, multi-level documentation. 0907

**Boesharr, D. K.**
Le Menu: changing the user interface on a local area network. 03128

**Boettcher, K. L.**
Distributed decisionmaking with constrained decisionmakers: a case study. 01886

**Boff, K. R.**
Information transfer rate with serial and simultaneous visual display formats. 01770

**Boguraev, B. K.**
A natural language front end to databases with evaluative feedback. HCI-0338 †

**Bohn, L. S.**
DOMAIN/DELPHI: retrieving documents online. 0906

**Boies, s.**
Generating highly interactive user interfaces. 0865

**Boies, S.**
Managing the design of user-computer interfaces. 0936

**Boies, S. J.**
Speech filing—An office system for principals. 0037
Rapid prototyping and system development: examination of an interface toolkit for voice and telephony applications. 0918
The 1984 Olympic Message System: a test of behavioral principles of system design. HCI-0125 †

**Bois, S. J.**
Human factors challenges in creating a principal support office system—The speh filing system approach. 0038

**Boland Jr., R. J.**
The in-formation of information systems. 0159

**Boland Jr., R. J. (Ed.)**
Critical issues in information systems research. ● 0153

**Bolc, L.**
Natural language interface to the question-answering system for physicians. 01478
A natural language information retrieval system with extentions towards fuzzy reasoning. HCI-0281 †

**Bolc, L. (Ed.)**
Cooperative interfaces to information systems. ● 0160
Cooperative interfaces to information systems. ● HCI-0066 †

**Boles, D. B.**
Display formatting in information integration and nonintegration tasks. 01750

**Bolles, R. C.**
Perceptual organization and curve partitioning. 01838

**Bolles, R. C. (Ed.)**
The fourth international symposium. § 03561

**Bolmarcich, A.**
Office-by-example: an integrated office system and database manager. 01159

**Bolocan, D.**
Q & A simplified. ● 0167

**Bolognani, M. (Ed.)**
Theory and practice of software technology. § 03361

**Bolt, R. A.**
Conversing and computers. 0092

**Bolton, D. L.**
ER model clustering as an aid for user communication and documentation in database design. 01331

**Boman, M.**
Automatic construction of surfaces with prescribed shape. 01474

**Bonani, L.**
GTEX—A group technology expert system. 02936

**Bonasso, R. P.**
Military systems. 0138

**Bonaventura, M.**
An investigation of pictographic form in relation to mechanisms of knowledge acquisition. 03824

**Bond, A. H. (Ed.)**
Distributed Artificial Intelligence. ● 0168

**Bonder, S.**
Capturing expertise: Some approaches to modeling command decisionmaking in combat analysis. 01883

**Bonnell, J. A.**
VDTs and health—fact or fancy? 03677

**Bonner, P.**
User interface wars: the next wave. 02544
Building a great windows system. 02550

**Boose, J. H.**
ETS—a system for the transfer of human expertise. 0491
Refining problem-solving knowledge in repertory grids using a consultation mechanism. 02205
Expertise transfer for expert system design. ● HCI-0059 †
Expertise transfer and complex problems: using AQUINAS as a knowledge-acquisition workbench for knowledge-based systems. HCI-0336 †

**Booth, K. S.**
On the parameters of human visual performance: an investigation of the benefits of antialiasing. 0799

**Boral, H. (Ed.)**
SIGMOD International Conference on Management of Data. § 03089

**Borenstein, N. S.**
Help texts vs. help mechanisms: A new mandate for documentation writers. 01047
Help texts vs. help mechanisms: A new mandate for documentation writers. 02784
Cooperative work in the Andrew message system. 02827
UNIX Emacs: a retrospective (lessons for flexible system design). 03114

**Borger, M. W.**
A methodology for evaluating environments. 03055

**Borgman, C.**
The study of user behavior on information retrieval systems. 01046
Why do some people have more difficulty learning to use an information retrieval system than others? 03075

**Borgman, C. L.**
All users of information retrieval systems are not created equal: an exploration into individual differences. 02011
The user's mental model of an information retrieval system: an experiment on a prototype online catalog. 02099
The design and evaluation of a front-end user interface for energy researchers. 02453
Retrieval systems for the information seeker: can the role of the intermediary be automated? 02864

**Borisov, A. N.**
Man-machine procedures of decision making under uncertainty based on linear programming. 02664

**Borisyuk, G. N.**
Short-term memory as a metastable state.III. Diffusion approximation. 01611

**Borisyuk, R. M.**
Short-term memory as a metastable state.III. Diffusion approximation. 01611

**Bork, A.**
Lessons from computer-based learning. 0503
Pedagogical development of computer-based learning material. 03878

**Bork, A. (Ed.)**
Designing computer-based learning materials. § 03875

**Borkan, M.**
Segue: support for distributed graphical interfaces. 01369
Segue: Support for distributed graphical interfaces. 03526

**Borning, A.**
Defining constraints graphically. 0910
Constraint hierarchies. 01114
Constraint-based tools for building user interfaces. 01153
The filter browser defining interfaces graphically. 03792

**Borning, A. H.**
A prototype electronic encyclopedia. HCI-0278 †

**Borras, P.**
Centaur: the system. 01136

**Borretty, R.**
Methodological problems of field-research on workplaces in offices. 0249

**Boschman, M. C.**
Criteria for the subjective quality of visual display units. 03724
Visual comfort as a criterion for designing display units. 03892

**Bose, S.**
Prototypes from standard user interface management systems. 01370

**Bostrom, R. P.**
Successful application of communication techniques to improve the systems development process. 01952
The importance of individual differences in end-user training: The case for learning style. 03009
The influence of training on use of end-user software. 03042

**Bostyn, Y.**
The SIMONA project: the introduction of information processing in labour market administration. 0248

**Botman, A. M.**
Retrieval based on user behaviour. 03068

**Bottino, R. M.**
A planning system for a cognitive problem. 02719

**Bottle, R. T.**
Managers' reading habits in the electronics industry. 02339

**Boubekri, N.**
Human-machine interface in remote monitoring and control of flexible manufacturing systems. 03399

**Bouchon, B. (Ed.)**
Uncertainty in knowledge-based systems. International Conference on Information. § 03822

**Boucsein, W.**
Psychophysiological investigation of stress induced by temporal factors in human-computer interaction. 0311

**Bouma, L. G.**
Document processing. 03897

**Bourne, J. R.**
Graphics-based qualitative simulation generator for power distribution systems. 02946
A generic strategy for diagnostic assistance: the technician's assistant. 02957
An advisory system for digital logic simulation. 02986

**Bournique, R.**
The interactive planning work station: a graphics-based UNIX tool for application users and developers. 03860
Specification and generation of variable, personalized graphical interfaces. HCI-0134 †

**Bousquet, A.**
Sensitivity to light and visual strain in VDT operators: basic data for the design of work stations. 03732

**Bovair, S.**
Transfer between text editors. 0804

**Bovey, J. D.**
Interactive document display and its use in information retrieval. 02300
Weighting, ranking and relevance feedback in a front-end system. 02329
A debugger for a graphical workstation. 02623

**Bowe, F.**
Making computers accessible to disabled people. 0094

**Bowen, B. A.**
DORUS; an architecture for dynamic optimal resource utilization systems. 02979

**Bowen, D. H.**
Primary journals today and tomorrow. 02264

**Bowers, J. M.**
Empirical evaluation of map interfaces. 03276

**Bowman, J. C.**
Dow Chemical makes continuous improvement part of everyone's job. 01908

**Box, T. M.**
Team cohesion effects on business game performance. 02597

**Boy, G. A.**
Operator assistant systems. 02165
The HORSES project and its perspectives in knowledge engineering. 02716

**Boyanov, K. (Ed.)**
Networks in office automation. § 03637

**Boyce, P. R.**
Lighting the display or displaying the lighting. 03716

**Boyd, G.**
Why do instructional designers need conversation theory? 0506
Conversation theory as a basis for instructional design. 0507

**Boyes, L.**
Transfer between word processing systems. 0899

**Boyle, C. D.**
Acquisition of control and domain knowledge by watching in a blackboard environment. HCI-0319 †

**Brädli, N.**
Exchange of solid models: current state and future trends. 01475

**Bracchi, G.**
The design requirements of office systems. 0757
Trends in office modeling. 03355

**Bracchi, G. (Ed.)**
Trends in information systems. • 0498

**Bracha, G.**
GCI—a tool for developing interactive CAD user interfaces. 02625

**Bradbard, D. A.**
The effects of relational and entity-relationship data models on query performance of end users. 02247

**Bradley, G.**
Psychosocial work environment and use of visual display terminals:8mfrom theoretical model to action. 03742

**Bradshaw, J. M.**
Expertise transfer and complex problems: using AQUINAS as a knowledge-acquisition workbench for knowledge-based systems. HCI-0336 †

**Brady, J. T.**
A theory of productivity in the creative process. 01824

**Brady, L. M.**
Dow Chemical makes continuous improvement part of everyone's job. 01908

**Brady, M.**
An extremum principle for shape from contour. 0024
Describing surfaces. 02699
Steps toward making robots see. 04011

**Brajnik, G.**
An expert interface for effective man-machine interaction. 0166
User modeling in intelligent information retrieval. 01994
IR-NLI II: applying man-machine interaction and artificial intelligence conceptsto information retrieval. 03070

**Bramwell, B.**
A system for interactive viewing of structured documents. HCI-0400 †

**Brancheau, J. C.**
Managing information systems for effectiveness and humanity: applying research of organizational behavior. 01932

**Brand, S.**
Mondo media. 02552

**Brannen, J. P.**
Expanding the domain of systems analysis. 02587

**Bransford, L. A.**
Communications technology and the public sector: understanding the process of adoption. 02679

**Bratt, P.**
Some issues related to the design and development of an interactive video disc. 01497

**Brauer, W. (Ed.)**
Petri nets: applications and relationships to other models of concurrency. § 03973

**Brault, J.**
Coupling visual and dynamic features to study handwritten signatures. 03309

**Braun, T. H.**
The age of the end-user and the shift from corporate MIS to corporate DSS. 01676

**Braune, R.**
A psychophysiological assessment of operator workload during simulated flight missions. 01735

**Braunstein, M. L.**
Perception of rotation in depth: the psychophysical evidence. 03343

**Breaux, E. H.**
A mixed-initiative workbench for knowledge acquisition. 02154

**Brebbia, C. A. (Ed.)**
Reliability and robustness of engineering software. § 03451

**Bredeweg, B.**
Knowledge and expertise in expert systems. 03905

**Bree, G. M.**
A teachable neural network based on an unorthodox neuron. 02561

**Breé, D. S.**
Artificial intelligence and cognitive psychology: a new look at human factors. 03904

**Brennan, J. J.**
Understanding and validating results in model-based decision support systems. 01666

**Brennan, L.**
Structure and policy in computer integrated manufacturing systems: human factors implications. 03371

**Brereton, P. (Ed.)**
Software engineering environments. • 0172

**Brewer III, J. A.**
A hand biomechanics workstation. 02820

**Brewer, B.**
The look and feel . . . and sound of the user interface. 01315

**Bridgeman, B.**
Development of a hand-held computerized vocabulary tutor. 02468

**Bridger, R. S.**
Some cognitive aspects of interface design in a two-variable optimization task. HCI-0111 †

**Briefs, U.**
User participation from the point of view of the workers and trade union policy. 03652

**Briem, V.**
Focusing variability during visual work. 03759

**Briggs, J. A.**
Getting graphics in gear: graphics and dynamics in driving simulation. 02818

**Briggs, J. S.**
Generating reversible programs. 02620

**Briggs, P.**
Usability assessment for the office: methodological choices and their implications. 0318
What we know and what we need to know: the user model versus the user's model in human-computer interaction. 01243

**Brigham, F. R.**
Human factors support for product development. 01681

**Brinkman, J.**
Processing demands, effort, and individual differences in four different vigilance tasks. 01801

**Brinkman, J. A.**
No effect of noise on vigilance performance? 01724

**Brintzenhoff, A. L.**
SKETCHER, an interactive, graphical Ada software tool—its development and use. HCI-0100 †

**Bristow, G. (Ed.)**
Electronic speech recognition: techniques, technology, and applications. • 0174

**Brittain, J. L.**
The AutoCAD productivity book: tapping the hidden power of AutoCAD: 2nd edition. • 0668
The AutoCAD productivity book: tapping the hidden power of AutoCAD. • HCI-0076 †

**Brittain, S.**
Understanding natural languages. 01172

**Britts, S.**
Dialog management in interactive systems: a comparative survey. 0949

**Brobst, S. A.**
Intelligent information-sharing systems. 01322

**Brock, K.**
From database to hypertext via electronic publishing: an information odyssey. 0122

**Brock, P. J.**
Unified interactive geometric modeller for simulating highly complex environments. 01472

**Brockmann, R. J.**
From database to hypertext via electronic publishing: an information odyssey. 0122

**Brodersen, A. J.**
A generic strategy for diagnostic assistance: the technician's assistant. 02957
An advisory system for digital logic simulation. 02986

**Brodie, M. L. (Ed.)**
On knowledge base management systems: integrating artificial intelligence and d atabase technologies. • 0180

**Brody, H.**
NEXT. 02546
The body in question: how to stay healthy at the PC. 02548

**Broekstra, G.**
Organizational humanity and architecture: Duality and complementarity of papa-logic and mama-logic in managerial conceptualizations of change. 01609

**Brogliatti, B.**
Intraocular pressure during VDT work. 03683

**Bronsvoort, W. F.**
Geometric modelling. 0236

**Brooke, J. B.**
Usability engineering in office product development. 03258

**Brooke, J. D.**
A multivariate solution for cyclic data, applied in modelling locomotor forces. 01252

**Brooke, N. M.**
An improved automatic lipreading system to enhance speech recognition. 02859

**Brookes, A.**
Detecting structure by symbolic constructions on tokens. 01466

**Brooking, A. G.**
The analysis phase in development of knowledge based systems. 0324

**Brooks, A.**
Microtechnology and user friendly systems—the CONNECT dialogue executor. 02382
User-driven adaptive behaviour, a comparative evaluation and an inductive analysis. 03226

**Brooks, F. P.**
Grasping reality through illusion—interactive graphics serving science. 02857

**Brooks, H. M.**
Knowledge elicitation using discourse analysis. 02152
Research on information interaction and intelligent information provision mechanisms. 02328

**Brooks, R. E.**
Software psychology: the need for an interdisciplinary program. 0052

**Brosda, V.**
Update and retrieval in a relational database through a universal schema interface. HCI-0260 †

**Brotman, L. S.**
Motion interpolation by optimal control. 02817

**Brouwers, A.**
Determinants of the VDU operator's well-being. 03679

**Brown, A. D.**
Computer-aided hierarchical diagrams. HCI-0160 †

**Brown, C.**
Management, organizations and the new technologies. 0145

**Brown, C. M.**
Human-computer interface design guidelines. ● 0184
Human-computer interface design guidelines. ● HCI-0011 †

**Brown, D. C.**
Knowledge and control for a mechanical design expert system. HCI-0320 †

**Brown, J. R.**
Programming the user interface principles and examples. ● 0185

**Brown, J. S.**
The computer as a tool for learning through reflection. 0535
Human computer interaction in the year 2000. 0924
A science of information for the information age. 01285
Computer-supported cooperative work: breakthroughs for user acceptance. 02874

**Brown, L.**
Digital waveform sampling rate converter. 01578

**Brown, M. H.**
Algorithm animation. ● 0186
Exploring algorithms using Balsa-II. 01367
Perspectives on algorithm animation. 02861

**Brown, M. L.**
An experiment into the use of auditory cues to reduce visual workload. 0877

**Brown, P. J.**
Presenting documents on workstation screens. 0267
Interactive document display and its use in information retrieval. 02300

**Brown, P. J. (Ed.)**
Interactive documentation. 02612

**Brownbridge, G.**
The doctor's use of a computer in the consulting room: an analysis. HCI-0409 †

**Browne, D. P.**
A self-regulating adaptive system. 0829
The formal specification of adaptive user interfaces using command language grammar. 0925

**Browning, I.**
Biological aspects of neural nets. 02311

**Browse, R. A.**
The physiology and psychophysics of touch. 04010

**Broyaye, P.**
Managing the semantic content of graphical data. HCI-0374 †

**Brüderlin, B.**
Automatizing geometric proofs and constructions. 03851

**Brüggemann, H. H.**
Data manipulation languages for the universal relation view DURST. 03944

**Bruce, B.**
Generation as a social action. 0389

**Bruce, M.**
Learning in British Airways-A case of putting people first. 02572

**Bruck, K.**
A personal computer based graphic workstation. 02493

**Bruijning, J.**
Evaluation and intergration of specification languages. 01430
Document processing. 03897

**Brumm, D. B.**
A stand-alone Forth system. 02310

**Brungardt, R.**
An architecture for a multimedia teleconferencing system. 02802

**Bruno, G.**
Ada-based executable modelling of distributed systems. HCI-0098 †

**Bruno, R.**
Compact disc–interactive. 0680

**Bryant, P.**
Intelligence and children's development. 0360

**Bryden, M. P.**
On the parameters of human visual performance: an investigation of the benefits of antialiasing. 0799

**Bucci, P.**
NLI-ESD: An expert natural language interface to a statistical data bank. 02712

**Buchanan, B. G.**
Design of knowledge-based systems with a knowledge-based assistant. 01853
Knowledge base refinement by monitoring abstract control knowledge. 02160

**Buchanan, D. A.**
Information technology and the experience of work. 0041

**Buchberger, E.**
DATENBANK-DIALOG: a German language interface for relational databases. 01208

**Buchs, D.**
EM2—a Modula-2 programming environment. 02392

**Buckingham, H. W., Jr.**
Language, the mind, and psychophysical parallelism. 0357

**Buckland, J. A.**
Supporting the microcomputer end user. 0187

**Buckley, P.**
Cognitive optimisation of Videotex dialogues: a formal—empirical approach. 0320

**Budford Jr, W. L.**
A hand biomechanics workstation. 02820

**Buede, D. M.**
Concept design of a program manager's decision support system. 0660

**Buffa, M. G.**
Issues limiting the acceptance of user interfaces using gesture input and handwriting character recognition. 0845

**Buffardi, L. C.**
Maintenance training simulator fidelity and individual differences in transfer of training. 01722

**Buhmann, J.**
Influence of noise on the behavior of an autoassociative neural network. 02727

**Bui, T. X.**
Communications design for Co-oP: a group decision support system. HCI-0297 †

**Buie, E. A.**
Bibliography: Individual differences and computer-human interaction. 0890

**Bulgren, W. G.**
Problems, problems, problems... 02407
Investigations into a command and response language interface. 03531

**Bulko, W. C.**
Understanding text with an accompanying diagram. 02947

**Bullen, C.**
Thinking ahead: what to expect from teleconferencing (Reprint). 0372

**Bullen, C. V.**
Company experiences with end-user computing. 0460

**Bullinger, H.**
Principles and illustrations of dialogue design. 0188
Software ergonomics: advances and applications. • HCI-0012 †

**Bullinger, H. (Ed.)**
Software ergonomics: advocations & applications for the human computer interface. • 0193
Human-computer interaction. § 03454

**Bullinger, H. J.**
Gribs—an approach to a realistic realtime simulation of human arm motion. 03432

**Bundy, A.**
What stories should we tell novice PROLOG programmers? 0421

**Buneman, P. (Ed.)**
Data types and persistence. • 0033

**Bunke, H. (Ed.)**
Syntactic and structural pattern recognition. • 0292

**Bunt, H.**
On-line interpretation in speech understanding and dialogue systems. 04000

**Bunt, H. C.**
Natural language communication with computers: some problems, perspectives, and new directions. 03913

**Buntrock, R. E.**
Cost effectiveness of on-line searching of chemical information: an industrial viewpoint. 0195

**Burbidge, J. L.**
A drafted PM glossary. 0625

**Burch, J. G.**
Designing information systems for people. 02411

**Burge, R. E.**
A new algorithm for extracting the interior of bounded regions based on chain coding. 01469

**Burger, J.**
Considerations for the development of natural-language interfaces to database management systems. 0161

**Burger, M.**
Embedding graphics into documents by using a graphic-editor. 0266

**Burgess, C.**
User facilities for engineering support stations. 01512

**Burgess, C. G.**
A graphical database interface. 01511
Helping users use UNIX. 01529

**Burgess, R. C.**
User-interface design for a clinical neurophysiological intensive monitoring system. 0881

**Burghardt, F.**
SATURN—a tool for modelling and performance evaluation of computer systems. 02670

**Burke, J. S.**
A rule-based system for interactive proposal evaluation. 02927

**Burke, M. G.**
A practical method for LR and LL syntactic error diagnosis and recovery. HCI-0163 †

**Burkhardt, H.**
Improving human/computer interactions. 0759

**Burlingame, D.**
Goals and objectives for user interface software. 01056

**Burnett, N.**
Dp and the disabled. 01646

**Burnett, R. C.**
A case study of user interface management system development and application. 0836

**Burnie, J.**
Microcomputing in motion analysis. 02384

**Burns, A.**
ADDS-a dialogue development system for the Ada programming language. 02102
The construction of information management system prototypes in Ada. 02613
Program generation for Ada—a case study. 02634

**Burns, J. R.**
Conceptual design of decision support systems utilizing management science models. 0658

**Burns, L. M.**
A graphical entity-relationship database browser. 03532

**Burns, M. J.**
Formatting space-related displays to optimize expert and nonexpert user performance. 0927

**Burr, B. J.**
Evaluation of mouse, rate-controlled isometric joystick, step keys, and text keys, for text selection on a CRT. 0064

**Burr, D.**
Visual analysis during motion. 0020

**Burstein, G.**
Simplicial differential geometric theory for language cortical dynamics. 01698

**Burt, P. J.**
The interdependence of temporal and spatial information in early vision. 0023

**Burt, P. V.**
The effects of entry arrangement in search times: a cross-generational study. 02048

**Burtin, J. K.**
Adolescents' chunking of computer programs. 01586

**Burton, J. K.**
Creative computer problem solving. 01584

Computer programming and generalized problem-solving skills: in search of direction. 01585
The relationship of computer programming and mathematics in secondary students. 01588

**Bury, K. F.**
Usability testing in the real world. 0917

**Burzio, A.**
Planning as feedback to designers. 02978

**Busemeyer, J. R.**
Psychological models of deferred decision making. 02370

**Bush, C. M.**
In search of the perfect programmer. 01648

**Bush, V.**
As we may think (Reprint). 0367

**Butcher, D. R.**
The seacher/information interface project—final report. 02341

**Butcher, M. D.**
A graded interface for novice/expert interaction. 0270

**Butcher, P. G.**
Computer-assisted learning and interactive video. 0504

**Butera, W.**
Coding image sequences for interactive retrieval. 01330

**Butler, C. J.**
Turbo pascal windowing system. 01306

**Butler, K.**
Report on the workshop on analytical models. 01001

**Butler, K. A.**
Use of psychometric tools for knowledge acquistion: a case study. 0323

**Buttigieg, M. A.**
Reader-controlled computerized presentation of text. 01785

**Buxton, B.**
Drama and personality in user interface design. 0830

**Buxton, H.**
Towards computer vision. 0564

**Buxton, W.**
There's more to interaction than meets the eye: Some issues in manual. 0062
Issues and techniques in touch-sensitive tablet input. 0063
Communicating with sound. 0067
Towards a comprehensive user interface management system. 0081
Creating highly-interactive and graphical user interfaces by demonstration. 0084
The computer as musical accompanist. 0897
Human computer interaction in the year 2000. 0924
A study in two-handed input. 0933
A directory of sources for interactive technologies. 0941
Creating highly-interactive and graphical user interfaces by demonstration. 01054

**Buxton, W. A.S.**
Human-computer interaction. • 0036

**Buyse, M.**
The kernel of a generic software development environment. 03056

**Byerley, P. F.**
Design of user-system interfaces using a cognitive design aid. 01682

**Byrd, J.**
The world of GEM. • 0396

**Byrne, K. E.**
Insights on the implementation of a computer-based message system. 01917

**Bysouth, P. (Ed.)**
The economics of online. • 0194

**Çakir, A.**
Ergonomic features of interactive systems—the interdependency of software and hardware. 0312

**Cacciabue, P. C.**
Modelling operators in accident conditions: advances and perspectives on a cognitive model. 02169

**Caelli, T.**
Visual pattern recognition in humans: I. Evidence for adaptive filtering. 01274

**Caelli, T. M.**
On the identification of neural responses. 01260
On the minimum number of templates required for shift, rotation and size invariant pattern recognition. 02531

**Cail, F.**
Data entry task on VDU: underload or overload. 03761

**Calder, P. R.**
Composing user interfaces with InterViews. HCI-0131 †

**Cale Jr., E. G.**
Measuring implementation outcome: beyond success and failure. 01933

**Cale, E. G.**
Perceptions of the CIS graduate's workstyle: undergraduate business students versus CIS faculty. 02999

**Caley, M. T.**
Recursive complementarity in the cybernetics of education. 01598

**Call, L. A.**
CLAM- an open system for graphical user interfaces. 01117

**Callaghan, D. R.**
Perceptions of the CIS graduate's workstyle: undergraduate business students versus CIS faculty. 02999

**Callahan, J.**
An empirical comparison of pie vs. linear menus. 02871

**Calloway, L.**
Designing conceptual models of dialog: a case for dialog charts. 0968

**Calmet, J.**
Some design principles for a mathematical knowledge representation system: a new approach to scientific calculation. 03849

**Calvert, T. W.**
The interactive specification of human animation. 03292

**Calvo, P.**
GTEX—A group technology expert system. 02936

**Cameron, K.**
Computer assisted language learning: program structure and principles. ● 0196
A study of organizational effectiveness and its predictors. 02471

**Cammarata, S.**
Extending a relational database with deferred referential integrity checking and intelligent joins. 01089

**Cammarata, S. J.**
An interactive data dictionary facility for CAD/CAM data bases. 03174

**Campagnoni, F. R.**
Information retrieval using a hypertext-based help system. 01155

**Campbell, D. B.**
Representations of perceived relations among the properties and variables of a complex system. 01892

**Campbell, G.**
The effectiveness of a keystroke line in interactive tutorials. 0969

**Campbell, I.**
Emeraude portable common tool environment. 01970

**Campbell, J. A.**
Perspectives in artificial intelligence vol. 2: machine translation, NLP, databases and computer-aided instruction. ● 0198

**Campbell, J. A. (Ed.)**
Progress in artificial intelligence. § 03555

**Campbell, R.**
Experience with contextual field research. 0802
Maintained and constructor attributes. 01099

**Campbell, R. L.**
Online help systems: design and implementation issues (panel). 02902

**Campbell, W. J.**
The development of an intelligent user interface for NASA's scientific databases. 02673

**Camstra, B.**
A question of delivery—an outline classification of interactive video delivery systems. 0510

**Cañas, A. J.**
Measuring the effectiveness of personal database structures. 02246

**Candrea, R.**
The interactive planning work station: a graphics-based UNIX tool for application users and developers. 03860

**Canter, D.**
Variations in user involvement with educational software. 01498

**Cantwell, J. R.**
Graphics-based qualitative simulation generator for power distribution systems. 02946
An advisory system for digital logic simulation. 02986

**Caplinger, M.**
Structured editor support for modularity and data abstraction. 01105
An information system based on distributed objects. 01116

**Capurro, R.**
Moral issues in information science. 02321

**Carasik, R. P.**
A case study of CSCW in a dispersed organization. 02866

**Carayon, P.**
VDT technology: psychosocial and stress concerns. 03755

**Carberry, S.**
Modeling the user's plans and goals. 01349

**Card, S.**
Rooms: the use of multiple virtual workspaces to reduce space contention in a window-based graphical user interface. 01151
User technology—from pointing to pondering. 03098

**Card, S. K.**
Human limits and the VDT computer interface (excerpt). 0054
The keystroke-level model for user performance time with interactive systems. 0055
Computer text-editing: an information-processing analysis of a routine cognitive skill. 0056
Evaluation of mouse, rate-controlled isometric joystick, step keys, and text keys, for text selection on a CRT. 0064
Window-based computer dialogues. 0071
User technology: from pointing to pondering. 0350
A multiple, virtual-workspace interface to support user task switching. 0813
How do experienced information lens users use rules? 0854

**Cardelli, L.**
Building user interfaces by direct manipulation. 03120

**Cardin, R.**
Speaker-independent automatic recognition of plosive sound in letters and digits. 03993

**Carey, J. M. (Ed.)**
Human factors in management information systems. ● 0200

**Carey, T.**
The gift of good design tools. 0411

**Carle, A.**
Graph attribution as a specification paradigm. 01138

**Carlopio, J.**
Computerized manufacturing technology and work organization effects on labor relations and worker satisfaction. 03443

**Carlson, P. A.**
Hypertext: a way of incorporating user feedback into online documentation. 0102
Hypertext and intelligent interfaces for text retrieval. 0115

**Carlsson, L. W.**
Work at video display terminals among office employees: visual ergonomics and lighting. 03718

**Carlsson, S. A.**
A longitudinal study of spreadsheet program use. 02354
A longitudinal study of spreadsheet program use. 03482

**Caro, D. H.**
Strategic management of technostress: The chaining of Prometheus. HCI-0452 †

**Caron, A.**
Morphologic machines and conservative networks. 01604

**Carossino, A.**
Real-time large vocabulary word recognition via diphone spotting and multiprocessor implementation. 03996

**Carpenter, G. A.**
The ART of adaptive pattern recognition by a self-organizing neural network. 01364
Absolutely stable learning of recognition codes by a self-organizing neural network. 02728

**Carpenter, S.**
Multimodal detection and recognition performance of sonar operators. 01709

**Carr, H. H.**
An investigation of the effects of age, size, and hardware option on the critical success factors applicable to information centers. 02352

**Carré, R.**
Distinctive regions and modes: a new theory of speech production. 02659

**Carrithers, C.**
Training wheels in a user interface. HCI-0208 †

**Carroll, J.**
Integrating human factors and software development. 02882
Learning by doing with simulated intelligent help. HCI-0229 †

**Carroll, J. M.**
Learning to use word processors: problems and prospects. 0059
Learning to use a word processor: by doing, by thinking, and by knowing. 0060
Minimalist design for active users. 0086
The adventure of getting to know a computer. 0088
Learning by doing with simulated intelligent help. 0132

Five gambits for the advisory interface dilemma. 0314
Artifact as theory-nexus: hermeneutics meets theory-based design. 0798
On-line tutorials: What kind of inference leads to the most effective learning? 0823
The role of laboratory experiments in HCI: help, hindrance, or ho-hum? 0863
Advising roles of a computer consultant. 0896
Interface design issues for advice-giving expert systems. 01321
Metaphor, computing systems, and active learning. 02091
Prompting, feedback and error correction in the design of a scenario machine. 02176
Psychology and the user interface: science is soft at the frontier. 03297
LisaLearning. HCI-0092 †
Training wheels in a user interface. HCI-0208 †
Learning to use a word processor: by doing, by thinking, and by knowing. HCI-0292 †
Paradox of the active user. HCI-0434 †

**Carroll, J. M. (Ed.)**
Interfacing thought: cognitive aspects of human-computer interaction. • 0206
Interfacing thought: cognitive aspects of human-computer interaction. • 0207
Mental models in human-computer interaction: research issues about what the user of software knows. • 0214
Human factors in computing systems and graphics interface. § 02855

**Carstensen, P. H.**
Formal specification of user interfaces: two application studies. 03772

**Carter, J. A., Jr.**
A taxonomy of user-oriented functions. 02104

**Carter, R. C.**
Beware the reliability of slope scores for individuals. 01727

**Cartmell, J.**
The evaluation of project support environments for the STARTS user guide. 0173

**Cartwright, A.**
A definitive programming approach to the implementation of CAD software. 0008

**Cartwright, G. P.**
Efficacy of higher cognitive and factual questions in computer assisted instruction modules. 02278

**Caruso, D.**
Breaking away. 02553

**Carver, D. L.**
Programmer variations in software debugging approaches. 02250
Knowledge base applications with software engineering: a tool for requirements specifications. 02924

**Casali, J. G.**
Effects of visual display and motion system delays on operator performance and ueasiness in a driving simulator. 01772

**Case, D. O.**
The design and evaluation of a front-end user interface for energy researchers. 02453
How do the experts do it? The use of ethnographic methods as an aid to understanding the cognitive processing and retrieval of large bodies of text. 03063

**Cassel, L. N. (Ed.)**
Computer science education. § 02809

**Castelfranchi, C.**
Knowledge representation and natural language: extending the expressive power of proposition nodes. 0096

**Caswell, S. A.**
Oil and water? 01654

**Caters, C. D.**
Expert systems and interactive video tutorials: separating strategies from subject matter. 02293

# AUTHOR INDEX

**Cattell, R. G.G.**
Entity-relationship database user interfaces. 0711

**Caudill, M.**
Neural networks primer, part I. 01178
Neural networks primer, Part II. 01181
Neural networks primer, part III. 01182
Neural networks primer, part IV. 01188
Neural networks primer, Part VII. 01192

**Cauzinille-Marmèche, E.**
Experimental data for the design of a microworld-based system for algebra. 0543

**Cavallo, V.**
Real time graphic simulation of visual effects of egomotion. HCI-0379 †

**Cavestro, W.**
Automation, work organization and skills: the case of numerical control. 01234

**Cawkell, A. E.**
The real information society: present situation and some forecasts. 02322

**Cawsey, A.**
Expanatory dialogues. 02063

**CBEMA**
Guide to the draft American national standard for human factors engineering of visual display terminal workstations. 01549

**Cecala, A. J.**
Designing a quality voice: an analysis of listeners' reactions to synthetic voices. 0914

**Cedar, T.**
Person-to-person communication in an applied research/service delivery setting. 02445

**Cercone, N.**
Computational linguistics. ● 0215
Providing quality responses with natural language interfaces: the null value problem. 01848

**Cerutti, S.**
Single sweep analysis of visual evoked potentials through a model of parametric identification. 01261

**Cerveny, R. P.**
A laboratory study of user characteristics and decision-making performance in end-user computing. HCI-0301 †

**Chabay, R. W.**
Socializing the intelligent tutor: bringing empathy to computer tutors. 0541

**Chakravarty, I.**
EDGE - a graph based tool for specifying interaction. 03106

**Chalupa, B.**
Experimental and theoretical analysis of visual search activities. 03620

**Chamberlin, D. D.**
System R: a relational approach to database management. 0709
Quill: An extensible system for editing documents of mixed type. 03517
Document convergence in an interactive formatting system. HCI-0405 †

**Chambers, J. M.**
Statistical software, graphics and future workstations for data analysis. 03316

**Chamoux, J. P.**
Data security and confidentiality in Europe. HCI-0450 †

**Chan, K.**
Reading self-paced moving text on a computer display. 01777

**Chan, P.**
The human factors of computer graphics interaction techniques. HCI-0377 †

**Chan, W. Y.**
Sherlock—a system for diagnosing power distribution ring network faults. 02916

**Chan, Y. K.**
Low cost geometric modelling system for CAM. 03866

**Chandlee, G. O.**
Illumination requirements for operating a space remote manipulator. 03392

**Chandrasekar, R.**
Interactive communication of sentential structure and content: an alternative approach to man-machine communication. 02220

**Chandrasekaran, B.**
Knowledge and control for a mechanical design expert system. HCI-0320 †

**Chang, C.**
The design of a traffic control expert system for long distance network contingencies. 02952

**Chang, E.**
Interface abstractions for an *naplps* page creation system. 03863

**Chang, K.**
VISION: VHDL induced schematic imaging on net-lists. 02830

**Chang, L. W.**
Study of combination of belief intevals in lattice-structured networks. 02223

**Chang, S.**
Icon semantics—a formal approach to icon system design. HCI-0161 †
An image processing language with ICON-assisted navigation. HCI-0387 †

**Chapanis, A.**
Interactive human communication (Reprint). 0371
Some generalizations about generalization. 01775
Taming and civilizing computers. HCI 0195 †

**Chapman, L. J.**
Preventing back strain. 0047

**Char, B. W. (Ed.)**
Symsac '86. § 03080
Symsac '86—Proceedings of the 1986 symposium on symbolic and algebraic manipulation. § 03084

**Char, M. B.S.**
The cybernetic principle: its transdisciplinarity to science and religion and the challenging task. 01596

**Charniak, E.**
Motivation analysis, abductive unification, and nonmonotonic equality. 01211

**Chase, P.**
VM/CMS: a user's guide. ● HCI-0028 †

**Chaudhuri, B. B.**
Interactive curve drawing by segmented Bezier approximation with a control parameter. 02535

**Chawla, V. K.**
ProCEED: an expert system for multivariate process control systems design. 02935

**Chechile, R. A.**
The effects of syntactic complexity on the human-computer interaction. 01708
Modeling the Cognitive content of displays. 01800

**Chen, C. H.**
Signal processing and pattern recognition in nondestructive evaluation of materials. § 04019

**Chen, H.**
IBM 3270 full screen interactive programming without CICS. 01040
Factors affecting the readability of moving text on a computer display. 01764
Reading self-paced moving text on a computer display. 01777

**Chen, H. H.**
Machine learning using a higher order correlation network. 02563
High order correlation model for associative memory. 02729
Nonlinear dynamics of artificial neural systems. 02747

**Chen, J.**
A computer training tool using Chinese natural language. 02948

**Chen, K.**
A computer aided design system for artistic chinese fonts. 02455

**Chen, K. C.**
A group model of form recognition under plane similarity transformations. 02366

**Chen, M.**
PLEXACT: an architecture & design of a knowledge-based system for information systems development. 01020
A man-machine interface for computer-aided and simulation of control systems. 01237
A group model of form recognition under plane similarity transformations. 02366
A study in interactive 3-D rotation using 2-D control devices. 02813
A human-computer interface for control system design. 03208
Crisis planning systems: tools for intelligent action. 03464

**Chen, N. S.**
Effect of fuzzy membership on recognition of gray level images. 02539

**Chen, P.**
Multiple representation document development (extende abstract). 03518

**Cheney, O. H.**
Information systems skills requirements: 1980 & 1988. 02997

**Cheney, P. H.**
Educating the CBIS user: a case analysis. 0778
Examining the duality role of I.S. executives: a study of I.S. issues. 01953
A tool for measuring analysis end user computing. 02000
Organizational factors affecting the success of end-user computing. 02344
Training end users: an exploratory study. 02506

**Cheng, C.**
Microcomputer-based user interface. 02044

**Cherry, J. M.**
An experimental evaluation of prefix and postfix notation in command language sytax. 02110

**Chiaramella, Y. (Ed.)**
Research & Development in Information Retrieval. § 03062

**Chiarelli, P.**
Analogs of biological tissues for mechanoelectrical transduction: tactile sensors and muscle-like actuators. 04014

**Chignell, M. H.**
Adaptive control in human-machine systems. 0405
Knowledge-based search tactics for an intelligent intermediary system. HCI-0277 †
Strategic issues in knowledge engineering. HCI-0317 †

**Childs, C.**
AWB-ADE: an application development environment for interactive, integrated systems. 03051

**Chimura, H.**
Contextual structure analysis of microcomputer manuals. 03227

**Chin, D.**
The relationship between user models and discourse models. 01353

**Chin, D. N.**
User modeling in UC, the UNIX consultant. 0894
The Berkeley UNIX consultant project. 01355

**Chin, J. P.**
Development of an instrument measuring user satisfaction of the human-computer interface. 02892

**Chiu, S. L.**
Task compatibility of manipulator postures. 02258

**Choi, U. J.**
Inference control mechanism for statistical database frequency-imposed data distortions. 02449

**Choi, W.**
A visual shell interface to a database. 02640

**Chollet, G.**
Recognition of speech using temporal decomposition. 03990
Dynamic spectral adaptation of automatic speech recognizers to new speakers. 03999

**Chong, J.**
Visual accommodation and target detection in the vicinity of a window post. 01802

**Chong, P. S.**
Using worker's survey to improve production. 02566

**Choobineh, J.**
Formflex: a user interface tool for forms definition and management. 0204

**Chorafas, D. N.**
Interactive workstations. ● 0216

**Chou, H.**
Data model issues for object-oriented applications. 0712
Data model issues for object-oriented applications. 01157

**Choukri, K.**
Dynamic spectral adaptation of automatic speech recognizers to new speakers. 03999

**Chow, Y.**
Fabrik: a visual programming environment. 01130

**Chowdhary, D. M.**
Generalized query-by-rule: a heterogeneous database query language. HCI-0252 †

**Chrisment, C. Y.**
Advanced databases multi-media interface. 0418

**Christie, B.**
Applying cognitive psychology to user-interface design. ● 0325
Introduction. 0326
The role of cognitive psychology in user-interface design. 0327
Assessment of trends in the technology and techniques of human-computer interaction. 0335
Future directions. 0336
Office systems. HCI-0291 †

**Christodoulakis, S.**
The multimedia object presentation manager of MINOS: a symmetric approach. 01083
Design and performance considerations for an optical disk-based, multimedia object server. HCI-0265 †

**Christodulakis, S.**
Browsing within time-driven multimedia documents. 03046

**Chrysler, E.**
An expert system for system design. 02441

**Chryssolouris, G.**
MADEMA: an approach to intelligent manufacturing systems. 01318

**Chu, W.**
Generic expert system shell for diagnostic reasoning. 02911

**Chu, W. W. (Ed.)**
Distributed systems, Vol. II: distributed data base systems. ● 0217

**Chun, R. K.**
VISION: VHDL induced schematic imaging on net-lists. 02830

**Chung, C.**
The design of a traffic control expert system for long distance network contingencies. 02952

**Churchland, P. S.**
Neurophilosophy: toward a unified science of the mind-brain. ● 0219

**Ciarcia, S.**
The BCC180 multitasking controller part 3: memory management and windowing. 01295
Computers on the brain, part 1. 01296
Error-free fractions. 01297
Computers on the brain, part 2. 01298

**Ciborra, C.**
System design for local authorities: participation based on "information contracts". 03656

**Citrenbaum, R.**
Selecting a shell. 01176

**Claisse, G.**
The telephone in question: questions on communication. 01436

**Clancey, W. J.**
Qualitative student models. 0721
Knowledge base refinement by monitoring abstract control knowledge. 02160

**Clapp, R. E.**
Visual simulation. 03503

**Clark, A.**
Connectionism and cognitive science. 03547

**Clark, D. P.**
AI/learn: an interactive videodisk system for teaching medical concepts and reasoning. 02381

**Clark, J. D.**
The influence of programmers' cognitive complexity on program comprehension and modification. 02245

**Clark, W. A.**
The LINC was early and small. 02843

**Clarke, A. A.**
A three-level human-computer interface model. 02112

**Clarke, D. D.**
User systems analysis: a user oriented approach to computer systems analysis, design, and implementation. ● 0454
A multidimensional approach to the measurement of human-computer performance. 01410

**Clarke, L. A.**
Foundations for the Arcadia environment architecture. 01135

**Clarke, M.**
Back to basics: Simple but high-quality text pagination systems. 0271

**Clarke, R. J.**
Individualizing the man-machine interface. 03404

**Clausen, M. (Ed.)**
Applicable algebra, error-correcting codes, combinatorics and computer algebra. § 03846

**Clayton, N.**
Investigating computer anxiety in an academic library. 02047

**Cleal, D. M.**
Knowledge-based systems: implications for human-computer interfaces. ● HCI-0060 †

**Cleaves, D. A.**
Cognitive biases and corrective techniques: proposals for improving elicitation procedures for knowledge-based systems. 02153

**Clegg, C.**
Managing factory automation. 0146

**Clemen, R. T.**
Combining overlapping information. 02477

**Clemens, R.**
Experiences with off-line robot programming via standardized interfaces. 0601

**Clemensin, G.**
Querying the French *Yellow Pages*: natural language access to the directory. 02007

**Clement, A.**
Evolution of an organizational interface: the new business department at a large insurance firm (Reprint). 0382

**Clement, C. A.**
Mapping the cognitive demands of learning to program. 0579

**Clement, D.**
Centaur: the system. 01136

**Clements, P. J.**
Systematic evaluation strategies for computer-based music instruction systems. 02275

**Clemons, E. K.**
Competition and cooperation in information systems innovation. 01941

**Cleveland, L.**
An environment for understanding programs. 03525

**Cleveland, W. S.**
An experiment in graphical perception. 02125
Brushing scatterplots. 02672
The elements of graphing data. ● HCI-0035 †

**Clifford, J.**
Natural language querying of historical data bases. 01354

**Clifton, C.**
The design of a document database. 02835

**Coats, R. B.**
Man-computer interfaces: an introduction to software design and implementation. ● 0220

**Cobaugh, P.**
Robot vs. human operator for speed, precision and other aspects. 03403

**Cobb, R. E.**
The database designer's workbench. HCI-0249 †

**Coble, C. R.**
Personality characteristics of junior high school students successful with computers. 01592

**Cochrane, L.**
Studying depth cues in a three-dimensional computer graphics workstation. 02117

**Cockton, G.**
Interaction ergonomics, control and separation: open problems in user interface management. 01962
Some critical remarks on abstractions for adaptable dialogue managers. 03211
Generative transition networks: a new communication control abstraction. 03241
Where do we draw the line? - Derivation and evaluation of user interface software separation rules. 03268

**Cody, W. J.**
On the design of man-machine systems: principles, practices and prospects. 01236

**Coggins, J. M.**
Interfacing image processing and computer graphics systems using an artificial visual system. 03301

**Cohan, L. A.**
Navigational aids and learning styles: structural optimal training for computer users. 0970
Users' preferences among different techniques for displaying the evaluation of LISP functions in an interactive debugger. 02863

**Cohen, K. C.**
Creating consistency in the user interface: opinions and procedures of software developments experts. 01012

**Cohen, M.**
Coupled mode theory for neural networks. 02730

**Cohen, M. D.**
Intelligent information-sharing systems. 01322

**Cohen, M. F.**
An experimental evaluation of computer graphics imagery. HCI-0373 †

**Cohen, P.**
Elements of a plan-based theory of speech acts. 0390

**Cohen, P. R.**
Synergistic use of direct manipulation and natural language. 0857

**Cohen, R.**
The relationship between user models and discourse models. 01353
Formative evaluation of pre-Logo programming environments: a collaborative effort of researchers, teachers, and children. 02292

**Cohen, S.**
An architecture of a distributed window system and its FCP implementation. 0676
Rule base management using meta knowledge. 01081
The FAIM-1 user interface—human engineering for the fifth generation. 03587

**Cohen, Y.**
Intelligible encoding of ASL image sequences at extremely low information rates. 02708

**Cohn, A. G. (Ed.)**
Artificial intelligence and its applications. ● 0221

**Cohrs, D. L.**
CLAM- an open system for graphical user interfaces. 01117

**Coiffet, P.**
Teleoperations and robotics: applications and technology. ● HCI-0068 †
Modelling and control. ● HCI-0068 †
Interaction with the environment. ● HCI-0068 †
Teleoperations and robotics: evolution and development. ● HCI-0068 †

## AUTHOR INDEX

**Indexes and bibliography.** ● HCI-0068 †
**Cointe, P. (Ed.)**
ECOOP '87. § 03790
**Colbourn, C. J.**
The role of social processes in children's microcomputer use. 0471
**Cole, W. G.**
Understanding Bayesian reasoning via graphical displays. 0884
**Colgan, L.**
Designing the "cockpit": the application of a human-centered design philosophy to make optimization systems accessible. 01016
**Colla, A. M.**
Real-time large vocabulary word recognition via diphone spotting and multiprocessor implementation. 03996
**Colle, H. A.**
Capacity equivalence curves: a double trade-off curve method for equating task performance. 01796
**Collen, M. F.**
Health care information systems: a personal historic review. 02849
**Colligan, M. J.**
Long workdays versus restdays: assessing fatigue and alertness with a portable performance. 01778
**Collins, A.**
The computer as a tool for learning through reflection. 0535
**Collins, A. (Ed.)**
Readings in cognitive science: a perspective from psychology & artificial intelligence. ● 0223
**Collins, G. C.**
A generic strategy for diagnostic assistance: the technician's assistant. 02957
**Collura, T. F.**
User-interface design for a clinical neurophysiological intensive monitoring system. 0881
**Collyer, S. C.**
Spatial requirements for visual simulation of aircraft at real-world distances. 01768

**Colombetti, M.**
Functional modelling in the execution of actions. 01485
Reasoning in natural language for designing a data base. HCI-0322 †
**Colvin, M. E.**
A model for cortical function. 02731
**Comer, D.**
Operating system design. Vol. 1: the XINU approach (PC edition). ● HCI-0029 †
**Comer, D. E.**
An interactive environment for tool selection, specification and composition. 02141
**Commisso, M. B.**
Three steps of better documentation. 03160
**Condie, L.**
Communication methods of the vocally disabled: a review. 0783
**Conklin, J.**
Hypertext: an introduction and survey (Reprint). 0378
Hypertext: an introduction and survey. 01360
gIBIS: a hypertext tool for exploratory policy discussion. HCI-0300 †
**Conley, W.**
Pygmalion at the interface. HCI-0349 †
**Conlin, C.**
The three c's: children, computers, and communication. ● 0713
**Conner, J.**
Misconceived misconceptions? 02881
**Conner, M. H.**
Andrew: a distributed personal computing environment. HCI-0091 †
**Connors, T.**
Equivalence of views by query capacity. 02271
**Conrad, M.**
The lure of molecular computing. 01833
**Conradi, R. (Ed.)**
Advanced programming environments. § 03779

**Console, L.**
Knowledge acquisition via a graphical interface. 03572
**Constantinescu, R.**
A biparty grammar as a tool for defining a man-machine dialogue. 03639
**Contri, G.**
GTEX—A group technology expert system. 02936
**Convent, B.**
Unsolvable problems related to the view integration approach. 03915
**Conway, M.**
Transfer of learning in inference problems. 03552
**Cook, C. (Ed.)**
Computers, cognition, and development: issues for psychology and education. ● 0643
**Cook, J.**
Human intelligence models and their implications for expert system structure and research. 01242
**Cook, P.**
Project Nick: meetings augmentation and analysis. HCI-0156 †
**Cook, S.**
Modelling generic user-interfaces with functional programs. 03265
**Cooke, D. J.**
On methods for interface specification and design. 02114
**Cooke, M. P.**
A computer model of peripheral auditory processing incorporating phase-locking, suppression and adaptation effects. 02650
**Cooke, N. J.**
Effects of computer programming experience on network representations of abstract programming concepts. 02204
**Cooke, N. M.**
The application of psychological scaling techniques to knowledge elicitation for knowledge-based systems. 02139

**Cooley, M.**
Creativity, skill and human-centered systems. 0346

**Cooling, J. E.**
Real-time interfacing: engineering aspects of microprocessor peripheral systems. ● 0224

**Coombs, M. J.**
The MDR algorithm and its application to the generation of explanations for novel events. 02174

**Coonan, T. A.**
Hypertext engineering: practical methods for creating a compact disk encyclopedia. 02832

**Cooper, L. (Ed.)**
Neural connections, mental computation. ● 0229

**Cooper, L. N.**
Brain research: theory and experiment. 01575

**Cooper, M. B.**
Man-machine interface issues in the construction and use of an expert system. HCI-0212 †

**Cooper, P.**
Expert systems in management science. 01689
Design and evaluation of the AID adaptive front-end to Telecom Gold. 03260

**Coote, A.**
Human and computer involvement in simulation. 02593

**Coovert, M. D.**
Preferences for power in expert systems by novice users. 0971
Problem solving performance and display preference for information displays depicting numerical functions. 0978

**Copp, E.**
Methods improvement kit uses IE technique to simplify work. 01909

**Corbett, J. M.**
Designing hybrid automated manufacturing systems: A European perspective. 03382

**Corbett, M.**
Measuring user satisfaction. 03230

**Corbin, D. S.**
The end user attack: Will the real computer professionals stand up and fight. 02424
Strategic IRM plan: user involvement spells success. 02432

**Cordell II, R. Q.**
Advanced interactive executive program development environment. 01816

**Cordell, A. J.**
The uneasy eighties: the transition to an information society. 0792

**Cordes, D. W.**
Knowledge base applications with software engineering: a tool for requirements specifications. 02924

**Corman, L. S.**
User programmer and costs of the misinformed user. 02415

**Cornelius, N.**
Adapting optical-flow to measure object motion in reflectance and X-ray image sequences. 03334

**CORPORATE**
Are video displays a health hazard? 01980

**Correia, A. M.R.**
Failure analysis of information systems in small manufacturing enterprises: the importance of the human interface. 03815

**Corter, J. E.**
Use of psychometric tools for knowledge acquistion: a case study. 0323

**Cotsaftis, M.**
Modeling of robot system dynamics for CAD based robot programming. 0605

**Cotterell, A.**
Advanced information technology in the new industrial society: the Kingston seminars. ● 0225

**Cotterill, R. M.J.**
Dynamical properties of a new type of neural network. 03969

**Cotterman, W. W.**
User cube: a taxonomy of end users. 01335

**Cottin, G.**
PLEIADE: A system for interactive manipulation of structured documents. 0265

**Couchman, D. H.**
Improving visual performance through volitional focus control. 01744

**Couger, J. D.**
Environments: Austria compared to the United States. 01026
Stress. 01651
Key human resource issues in IS in the 1990s: Views of IS executives versus human resource executives. 01939
Motivation norms of knowledge engineers compared to those of software engineers. 02349
Motivators vs. demotivators in the IS environment. 02433
Causes of motivational problems among AI managers. 03004
Evaluating performance appraisal systems for IS personnel. 03011
Problems among managers of AI personnel. 03460

**Coulbeck, B.**
A systems approach to extended GINAS applications. 0228

**Coulbeck, B. (Ed.)**
Computer applications in water supply: vol. 1—systems analysis and simulation. ● 0227

**Coulon, D.**
Natural language and computers: a general survey of written text interpretation methods. 02671

**Coulter, N.**
The experimental validation of a programmer productivity measure. 03013

**Counte, M. A.**
The effects of a computerized information system on a hospital. 01553

**Coupland, J.**
Improving human/computer interactions. 0759

**Courtney, J. e., Jr.**
SmartSLIM: a DSS for controlling biases during problem formulation. 0203

**Courtney, J. F.**
A conceptual architecture for generalized decision support system software. 0659
The impact of DSS on organizational communication. HCI-0294 †

**Courtney, J. F., Jr.**
Controlling bias in user assertions in expert decision support systems for problem formulation. 02343

**Cousins, S.**
Automatic menu generation. 0774

**Cousins, S. A.**
Development of a human engineering design standard for robot teach pendants. 03411

**Coutaz, J.**
The construction of user interfaces and the object paradigm. 03791
Abstractions for user interface design. HCI-0114 †

**Cove, J. F.**
Online text retrieval via browsing. 01999

**Coventry, L.**
Some effects of cognitive style on learning UNIX. 02252

**Cowan, W. B.**
On the parameters of human visual performance: an investigation of the benefits of antialiasing. 0799
Color in user interface design: functionally and aesthetics. 0803
An experimental comparison of RGB, YIQ, LAB, HSV, and opponent color models. HCI-0381 †

**Cowie, R.**
The alternatives allowed by a rectangularity postulate, and a pragmatic approach to interpreting motion. 03550

**Cox Jr., J. R.**
Recollections on the processing of biomedical signals. 02846

**Cox, J. L.**
System user/system implementer: a joint responsibility for success. 01535

**Cox, L. H.**
Modelling and controlling user inference. 03582

**Cox, S.**
Interactive graphics in GPSS/PC. 02586

**Coyne, M.**
A help system for command driven applications. 01050

**Cozannet, A.**
Recognition of speaker-dependent continuous speech with Keal-Nevezh. 04002

**Crabb, D.**
The Mac interface: showing its age. 01311

**Craig, J. J.**
Issues in the design of off-line programming systems. 03564

**Craighill, E.**
An architecture for a multimedia teleconferencing system. 02802

**Crain, I. K.**
Challenges in the application of graphics technology to the management of geographic information. 03871

**Crane, C. D.**
Off-line programming and path generation for robot manipulators. 0603

**Crane, E.**
jThe assessment of human/computer performance: a case for connectivity. 03535

**Crane, G.**
The Perseus project: an interactive curriculum on classical greek civilization. 01680

**Crane, H. D.**
Issues limiting the acceptance of user interfaces using gesture input and handwriting character recognition. 0845

**Crane, P. (Ed.)**
User Services Conference. § 03130

**Crawford, R. G.**
A novice user's interface to information retrieval systems. HCI-0219 †

**Crawford, W.**
Common sense and user interfaces: issues beyond the keyboard. 02465
Testing bibliographic displays for online catalogs. HCI-0285 †

**Crawshaw, H. S.**
Managers' reading habits in the electronics industry. 02339

**Creed, A.**
Efforts of display format on proof-reading with VDUs. 01246

**Crick, F. H.C.**
Certain aspects of the anatomy and physiology of the cerebral cortex. 0636

**Cristiano, L. K.**
Methodology for comparative selection of interactive database interface types. 01005

**Crocker, S. D.**
The Greenblatt chess program. 0527

**Croft, W. B.**
Knowledge-based support of cooperative activities. 0171
Support for browsing in an intelligent text retrieval system. 02240
Retrieval systems for the information seeker: can the role of the intermediary be automated? 02864
Interactive retrieval office documents. 03047
Knowledge-based support of cooperative activities. 03478
The role of context and adaptation in user interfaces. HCI-0109 †

**Cromarty, A. S.**
Distributed database considerations in an expert system for radar analysis. 03175

**Crombie, I. K.**
An investigation of data entry methods with a personal computer. 01490

**Crookall, D.**
Human and computer involvement in simulation. 02593

**Crookes, D.**
Online searching using speech as a man/machine interface. 02013
Voice input/output interface for online searching: some design and human factor onsiderations. 02335

**Crosby, M. E.**
The influence of individual differences on the reading of computer programs. 03456

**Cross II, J. H.**
The control structure diagram: an automated graphical representation for software. 03524

**Cross, T. B.**
The soft side of software: a management approach to computer documentation. ● HCI-0016 †

**Crowe, M. K.**
Dynamic compilation in the Unix environment. 02621

**Crowley, T. R.**
Diamond: a multimedia message system built on a distributed architecture (Reprint). 0380
Diamond: A multimedia message system built on a distributed architecture. 0574

**Crowston, K.**
Cognitive science and organizational design: a case study of computer conferencing (Reprint). 0386
How do experienced information lens users use rules? 0854
Intelligent software agents. 01303

**Cruchant, H.**
Principle of visual color coding applied to satellite images. 03304

**Crypton**
A boy and his brain machine. 02575

**Cuadra, C. A.**
History offers clues to the future: user control returns. 02517

**Cuena, J. (Ed.)**
Perspectives in artificial intelligence vol. 2: machine translation, NLP, databases and computer-aided instruction. ● 0198

**Cuff, R. N.**
HERCULES: database query using natural language fragments. HCI-0253 †

**Cugini, U.**
The CADME approach to the interface of solid modellers. 03867

**Culicover, P. (Ed.)**
Neural connections, mental computation. ● 0229

**Cullmann, N.**
GKSGRAL—software and hardware realizations of the graphical kernel system. 03982

**Culnan, M. J.**
The dimensions of perceived accessibility to information: Implications for the delivery of information systems and services. 02448
The dimensions of accessibility to online information: implications for implementing office information systems. HCI-0304 †

**Culverhouse, P. F.**
A process oriented approach to an intelligent design aid. 02980

**Cumming, G.**
QWERTY and keyboard reform: the soft keyboard option. HCI-0190 †

**Cun-Chang, F.**
Chinese character processing system based on character-root combination and graphic processing. 03187

**Cunniff, N.**
Graphical vs. textual representation: an empirical study of novices' program comprehension. 0566

**Cunningham, B.**
Three steps of better documentation. 03160

**Cunningham, D. J.**
Developments in one-line information systems. 02687

**Cunningham, J. F.**
Distributed database considerations in an expert system for radar analysis. 03175

**Cunningham, S.**
Programming the user interface principles and examples. ● 0185

**Cunningham, W.**
Diagramming objects. 01177

**Cuomo, D. L.**
A cognitively based methodology for evaluating human performance in the computer-aided design task domain. 01240

**Cuppens, F.**
How to recognize interesting topics to provide cooperative answering. 02043

**Curcio, C. A.**
Reconstruction and display of the retina. 03310

**Cure, K.**
Man is not a robot. 0445

**Curley, K. F.**
Measuring implementation outcome: beyond success and failure. 01933

**Currie, K.**
O-Plan: control in the open planning architecture. HCI-0362 †

**Curth, M. A.**
APL: a problem-oriented introduction. ● 0230

**Curtis, B.**
Software psychology: the need for an interdisciplinary program. 0052
CHI research at MCC. 0842
Human computer interaction in the year 2000. 0924
Control of cognitive processes during software design: what tools are needed? 02899

**Cushman, W. H.**
Reading from microfiche, a VDT, and the printed page: subjective fatigue and performance. 01712

**Cutting, J. E.**
Perceiving and recovering structure from events. 03346

**Cutts, J. H.**
AI/learn: an interactive videodisk system for teaching medical concepts and reasoning. 02381

**Cuypers, C.**
The silent force of the screen. A research note on the impact of microelectronics on work autonomy among clerical workers in public administration. 01437

**Czaja, S. J.**
A simultaneous regression model for double stimulation tasks. 01726

**D'Appollonio, V.**
The integration of the network and relational approaches in a DBMS. 03283

**D'Atri, A.**
On global context dependencies and their properties (extended abstract). 03945

**D'Autrechy, C. L.**
The MIRRORS/II simulator. 03502

**d'Ydewalle, G.**
The efficiency of letter perception in function of color combinations: a study of video-screen colors. 03616

**Dähler, J.**
A graphical tool for the design and prototyping of distributed systems. 01146

**Dabbagh, H. I.**
'Transparent' interfacing of speech recognizers to microcomputers. 02497

**Daduna, J. R.**
A decision support system for vehicle scheduling in public transport. 0339

**Daft, R. L.**
Message equivocality, media selection and manager performance: implications for information systems. 02505

**Dahlberg, B.**
Automatic construction of surfaces with prescribed shape. 01474

**Dahme, C.**
Intentional and operational aspects of decision behaviour and their modelling. 03666

**Dainoff, M. J.**
Task and the adjustment of ergonomic chairs. 03711

**Dalrymple, M.**
Synergistic use of direct manipulation and natural language. 0857

**Dalton, D. w.**
How effective is interactive video in improving performance and attitude? 0278

**Dalton, D. W.**
The efficacy of computer-assisted video instruction on rule learning and attitudes. 02286

**Damerau, F. J.**
An interactive customization program for a natural language database query system. 0163
Prospects for knowledge-based customization of natural languages query systems. 02008

**Damodaran, L.**
Human factors in office systems. 03357

**Damper, R.**
'Transparent' interfacing of speech recognizers to microcomputers. 02497

**Damper, R. I.**
Voice-input aids for the physically disabled. HCI-0089 †

**Danaher, M.**
The experimental validation of a programmer productivity measure. 03013

**Dance, J. R.**
The run-time structure of UIMS-supported applications. 01059
Marcosby example in a graphical UIMS. 01831

**Daniellou, F.**
Process control software design: how will the operators work? 03764

**Daniels, D. C.**
Graph-theoretical tools and their use in a practical distributed operating system design case. 03886

**Daniels, P. J.**
Knowledge elicitation using discourse analysis. 02152
Cognitive models in information retrieval—an evaluative review. 02298
Research on information interaction and intelligent information provision mechanisms. 02328

**Danilowicz, C.**
Users and experts in the document retrieval system model. HCI-0270 †

**Dannenberg, L.**
Approximation methods used in the exchange of geometric information via the VDA/VDMA surface interface. HCI-0421 †

**Dannenberg, R.**
The computer as musical accompanist. 0897

**Danzig, P.**
A visual shell interface to a database. 02640

**Dario, P.**
Force and tactile sensing for robots. 04013

**Dario, P. (Ed.)**
Sensors and sensory systems for advanced robots. § 04006

**Darnell, M. J.**
Users' preferences among different techniques for displaying the evaluation of LISP functions in an interactive debugger. 02863

**Davenport, C.**
Plan recognition for intelligent monitoring. 03261

**Davenport, G.**
Virtual video editing in interactive multimedia applications. 01326

**Davenport, J. H.**
PowerMath—A system for the Macintosh. 03083

**Davenport, T. H.**
How executives can shape their company's information systems. 01707

**Davey, K. R.**
Design of an integral computer-based wheelchair controller/linear synchronous motor system. 02378

**Davidove, E. A.**
Design and production of videodisc programming. 0276

**Davidson, C. H.**
Improved design of graphic displays in thesauri—through technology and ergonomics. 02297

**Davidson, P.**
Jet engine technical advisor (JETA). 02974

**Davies, A. C.**
Graphbug - a microprocessor software debugging tool. 02496

**Davies, C. G.**
MAJIC—an integrated program support environment. 01960

**Davies, D.**
User-network interfaces. 01384

**Davies, G.**
A coherent specification method for the human interface to documentation systems. 0269

**Davies, I.**
ISPBXs and terminals. 01385

**Davies, S. E.**
Transfer between menu systems. 02873

**Davies, S. P.**
Optimum display arrangements for presenting visual reminders. 03237

**Davis, A.**
The FAIM-1 user interface—human engineering for the fifth generation. 03587

**Davis, G. K.**
Ada-embedded SQL: the options. 0763

**Davis, J. E.**
Robot simulation and off-line programming—an integrated CAE-CAD approach. 0599

**Davis, M. H.**
Investigations in multimedia design documentation. 0116

**Davis, R.**
Representing and reasoning about change. 03353

**Davis, R. D.**
The architecture of an inexpensive and portable talking-tactile terminal to aid the visually handicapped. 01452
An inexpensive and portable talking-tactile terminal for the visually handicapped. 02377

**Davis, R. H.**
The automated solution of logic puzzles. 02015

**Dawant, B.**
NetGraph: an object-oriented graphical toolset for risk assessment. 02972

**Dawson, J.**
SPA: a systems for diagnosis of computer performance problems. 02969

**Day, r.**
A user interface for deaf-blind people (preliminary report). 0794

**Dayton, T.**
Adapting menu layout to tasks. 02182
Theoretical training and problem detection in a computerized database retrieval task. 02239

**de Alberdi, M.**
Computer assisted video analysis system. 01683

**de Corte, W.**
The algorithmic approach in ergonomics: the case of optimal colours and ambients for display work. 0247

**De Corte, W.**
Optimal colors, phosphors, and illuminant characteristics of CRT displays: the algorithmic approach. 01710

**de Giacomo, P.**
Evolution of interactional human behavior with age: a theoretical/experimental approach. 01618

**de Keyser, R. M.C.**
Personal computer training software for adaptive control. 02262

**De Keyser, V.**
How can computer-based visual displays aid operators? 02162

**de Kleer, J.**
DARN: Toward a community memory for diagnosis and repair tasks. 0428

**De Long, D. W.**
Executive support systems: the emergence of top management computer use. ● HCI-0049 †

**de Marné, K.**
Implementation of a VDA interface in the CAD system STRIM 100. 03983

**de Montmollin, M.**
Analysis of the competence of operators confronting new technologies: some methodological problems and some results. 03594

**de Mori, R.**
Computer recognition of spoken letters and digits. 03995

**De Mori, R.**
Rule-based detection of speech features for automatic speech recognition. 0419
An expert system for mapping acoustic cues into phonetic features. HCI-0328 †

**De Rossi, D.**
Analogs of biological tissues for mechanoelectrical transduction: tactile sensors and muscle-like actuators. 04014

**de Ruiter, M. M. (Ed.)**
Advances in Computer Graphics III. ● 0231

**de Schampheleire, J.**
The silent force of the screen. A research note on the impact of microelectronics on work autonomy among clerical workers in public administration. 01437

**de Schutter, J.**
CAD Based verification and refinement of high level compliant motion primitives. 0600

**De Smedt, K.**
Knowledge representation techniques in artificial intelligence: an overview. 03900

**De Soete, G.**
A perceptual study of the Flury-Riedwyl faces for graphically displaying multivariate data. 02126

**de Stricker, U.**
A menu interface to formulate boolean logic-can it be done? 02034

**de Vries, P. H.**
Structuring knowledge in a graph. 03899

**De Vries, R.**
Image processing with personal computers. 02581

**de Weert, C. M.M.**
The use of color in visual displays. 03890

**De, P.**
Adaptive information systems control: A reliability-based approach. 02345

**De, S.**
Providing effective decision support: modeling users and their requirements. 01668
Temporal semantics and natural language processing in a decision support system. 02038
Natural language query processing in a temporal database. HCI-0257 †

**Dean, B. V.**
Optimal allocation of a work force in a toxic substance environment. 01534

**Dean, J.**
Computers and children's historical thinking and understanding. 0283
Pupils, computers and history teaching. 0746

**Dearholt, D. W.**
A formal interface design methodology based on user knowledge. 0929

**Deavers-Claspell, P.**
How to build a help desk that floats. 03148

**Debelak, K. A.**
Applications of qualitative modeling to knowledge-based risk assessment studies. 02970

**DeBloois, M.**
Anticipating compact disc-interactive (CD-I): ten guidelines for prospective authors. 0280

**Debons, A. (Ed.)**
Information systems: failure analysis. § 03804

**Debus, G. (Ed.)**
The psychology of work and organization: current trends and issues. ● 0239

**Decyk, V. K.**
Supercomputers in the classroom. 01577

**Dede, C.**
A review and synthesis of recent research in intelligent computer-assisted instruction. 02108

**Deedman, C.**
The application of expert systems technology to case-based law. 02771

**Deerhake, S.**
Application screen management: an APL2 approach. 02794

**Deerwester, S.**
The engineering information system: a guided tour. 02046
Using latent semantic analysis to improve access to textual information. 02901

**Defude, B.**
Knowledge based systems versus thesaurus : an architecture problem about expert systems design. HCI-0323 †

**Dehdashti, P.**
Evaluation of mental models and meta models through interactions between users and helpers about software usage problems. 0972

**Deisenroth, M. P.**
An interactive programming system for the IBM 7545 robot. 01517

**DeKlerk, P.**
A mixed-initiative workbench for knowledge acquisition. 02154

**Delcourt, B.**
The kernel of a generic software development environment. 03056

**Delgado, A. E.**
A logical model of co-operative processes in cerebral dynamics. 01615
The fuzzy paradigm for knowledge representation in cerebral dynamics. 01699

**Delor, E.**
The kernel of a generic software development environment. 03056

**Demers, A.**
Attribute propagation by message passing. 01100

**Demetrovics, J. (Ed.)**
MFDBS 87. § 03943

**Demetrulias, D. M.**
Assessing gender bias in computer software. 01591

**DeMichiel, L. G.**
Common LISP object system specification X3J13 Document 88-002R. 01121

**Demolombe, R.**
How to recognize interesting topics to provide cooperative answering. 02043

**Denham, M. J. (Ed.)**
Advanced computing concepts and techniques in control engineering. § 03833

**Denicoff, M.**
AI development and the Office of Naval Research. 0140

**Denker, J. S.**
Neural network models of learning and adaptation. 02560
Neural network refinements and extensions. 02732

**Denker, J. S. (Ed.)**
Neural Networks for Computing. § 02723

**Dennett, D. C.**
Designing intelligence. 0361

**Denning, D. E.**
Lessons learned from modeling a secure multilevel relational database system. 03580

**Dennis, I.**
Efforts of display format on proof-reading with VDUs. 01246

**Dennis, J. E., Jr.**
Curve tailoring with interactive computer. 01209

**Densmore, O. M.**
A user-interface toolkit in object-oriented PostScript. 01391

**Deogun, J.**
Optimal determination of user-oriented clusters. 03077

**Derefeldt, G.**
A colour atlas for graphical displays. 03726

**DeRidder, M.**
Technology transfer: a new computer-based system. HCI-0203 †

**Derr, B.**
CAREing for users at Syracuse University. 03134

**Desai, B. C.**
A natural language interface to a multiple databased office information system. 01094
Non-first normal form universal relations: an application to information retrieval systems. 02039

**Desai, H. B.**
Computer anxiety: sex, race and age. 02133

**Desain, P.**
Tree doctor, a software package for graphical manipulation and animation of tree structures. 03901

**DeSanctis**
Groupware: interface design for meetings. 02883

**DeSanctis, G.**
GDSS: a brief look at a new concept in decision support. 02804
Understanding the effectiveness of computer graphics for decision support: a cumulative experimental approach. HCI-0215 †

**Deschamps, I.**
Managerial influence in the implementation of new technology. 02481

**Desharnais, J.**
A new approach to cursor movements in user interfaces of integrated programming environments. 01974

**Deshpande, P. B.**
ProCEED: an expert system for multivariate process control systems design. 02935

**DeSimone, J. A.**
Physiology and psychophysics in taste and smell. 04009

**Desnoyers, L.**
Analyzing and improving VDU working conditions: workers' education. 03751

**DeSoi, J. F.**
Graphical specification of user interfaces with behavior abstraction. 0840

**Despeyroux, T.**
Centaur: the system. 01136

**Detweiler, M.**
The role of practice in dual-task performance: toward workload modeling in a connectionist/control architecture. 01790

**Deutsch, C.**
Real time graphic simulation of visual effects of egomotion. HCI-0379 †

**DeVaulx, B.**
SPECIF-X: a tool for CASE. 03801

**Devlin, B. A.**
An architecture for a business and information system. 01818

**Dewan, P.**
Dost: an environment to support automatic generation of user interfaces. 03053

**Dexter, A. S.**
An experimental program investigating color-enhanced and graphical information presentation: an integration of the findings. HCI-0196 †

**Deyo, R.**
Getting graphics in gear: graphics and dynamics in driving simulation. 02818

**Dhillon, B. S.**
Human reliability in information systems. 03809

**Di Bari, A.**
Intraocular pressure during VDT work. 03683

**Di Eugenio, B.**
Cooperative behaviour in the FIDO system. 02041

**Di Felice, P.**
On global context dependencies and their properties (extended abstract). 03945

**Di Manzo, M.**
A first order theory of common sense object positioning. 01563

**Diaper, D.**
Interacting with computers. 02061

Identifying the knowledge requirements of an expert system's natural language processing interface. 03259

**Diaper, D. (Ed.)**
People and computers III. § 03189

**Diaper, D. Dr. (Ed.)**
Interacting with Computers. HCI-0207 †

**Dickey, L. J. (Ed.)**
APL88. § 02797

**Dickson, G. W.**
Understanding the effectiveness of computer graphics for decision support: a cumulative experimental approach. HCI-0215 †

**Didriksen, T. M. (Ed.)**
Advanced programming environments. § 03779

**Diebert, T. R.**
Predicting end-user acceptance of microcomputers in the workplace. 02147

**Diederich, J.**
KRITON: a knowledge-acquisition tool for expert systems. HCI-0327 †

**Diehl, V. A.**
Development of an instrument measuring user satisfaction of the human-computer interface. 02892

**Diekmann, V.**
Uncertainty analysis of human EEG spectra: A multivariate information theoretical method for the analysis of brain activity. 01270

**Dight, J.**
Grow your own programmers. 01663

**Dillion, A.**
Knowledge acquisition and conceptual models: a cognitive analysis of the interface. 03214

**Dillon, A.**
Reading from paper versus reading from screen. 01416
The application of cognitive psychology to CAD. 03239

**Dimitrov, S.**
An implementation of OSI protocols in SM-4 host computers. 03638

**Dimitrova, B.**
An implementation of OSI protocols in SM-4 host computers. 03638

**Diner, D. B.**
Static stereo vision depth distortions in teleoperation. 03390

**Dingankar, A.**
Automated design and analysis system for design of custom orthopedic implants. 02931

**Dingus, V. R.**
Tennessee Eastman employee teamwork raises quality, customer service. 01907

**Dinitz, R.**
Impulse-86: a substrate for object-oriented interface design. 03032

**Dion, L. C.**
Project source file management under the UNIX operating system. 03168

**diSessa, A. A.**
Artificial worlds and real experience. 0518
Boxer: a reconstructible computational medium. HCI-0121 †

**Dittrich, K. R. (Ed.)**
Advances in object-oriented database systems. § 03841

**Dix, A.**
Refining early design decisions with a black-box model. 03200
Abstract, generic models of interactive systems. 03219

**Dix, A. J.**
The myth of the infinitely fast machine. 03204
A comparison of hypertext, scrolling and folding as mechanisms for program browsing. 03235
Principles and interaction models for window managers. 03264
Interaction models and the principled design of interactive systems. 03799

**Dix, T. I.**
Support for graphs of processes in a command interpreter. 02633

**Dixon, D.**
Life before the chips: simulating digital video interactive technology. 01328

**Dixon, P. W.**
The effects of display formats on information systems design. 02357

**Dmitrevich, G. D.**
An approach to CAD system performance evaluation. HCI-0414 †

**Dmitrov, D.**
Software development approach in FMS. 01567

**Dörr, G.**
Barriers to plant transparency, barriers to plant rigidity—A sketch of the problems posed by the radical changes in work forms in the machine-building industry. 01562
The importance of work organization by systems design. 03648

**Doane, S.**
University of Colorado at Boulder, Institute of cognitive science. 0811

**Dobkin, D.**
A library for incremental update of bitmap images. 02836

**Docherty, P.**
System design for human development and productivity: participation and beyond. § 03640

**Docherty, P.**
Report from the working group on "experience with participation: application in administration and health care". 03668

**Dodonov, S. B.**
Interactive CAD/CAM in engineering industry. 01571

**Doenges, P.**
Getting graphics in gear: graphics and dynamics in driving simulation. 02818

**Doi, M.**
A document layout system using automatic document architecture extraction. 0882

**Doland, V. M.**
Hypermedia as an interpretive act. 01806

**Doleman, E. A.**
A compact model of a power house boiler. 02683

**Dolk, D. R.**
A generalized model management system for mathematical programming. HCI-0302 †

**Doll, W. J.**
The quality of user documentation. 01924
Encouraging user management participation in systems design. 01926
The measurement of end-user computing satisfaction. 02510

**Domas, K.**
Task allocation between humans and robots in manufacturing. 0559

**Domenici, C.**
Analogs of biological tissues for mechanoelectrical transduction: tactile sensors and muscle-like actuators. 04014

**Dominick, W. D.**
A survey of formal tools and models for developing user interfaces. 02207

**Donaho, J. E. D.**
Ada-embedded SQL: the options. 0763

**Donahue, J.**
Integration mechanisms in Cedar. 01110
Whiteboards: a graphical database tool. HCI-0289 †

**Donato, N.**
GRASS3, a language for interactive graphics. 03170

**Donnell, M. L.**
Fuzzy decision analysis. 0650

**Donnelly, D. P. (Ed.)**
The computer culture. § HCI-0084 †

**Donnelly, N.**
Describing a product opportunity: a method of understanding the users' environment. 03194

**Doodman, S. E.**
Handling textual information in a GDSS database: experience with the Arizona analyst information system. 03475

**Dooijes, E. H.**
Synthesis of print-quality cursive script based on a model of the human handwriting mechanism. HCI-0402 †

**Doolen, G.**
Machine learning using a higher order correlation network. 02563

**Dooley, R. L.**
Automated design and analysis system for design of custom orthopedic implants. 02931

**Dorsey, P. R.**
An investigation of the effectiveness of communication between systems analysts and end users in the design of large computer systems. 04075

**Dos Santos, B. L.**
A framework for designing adaptive DSS Interfaces. 01672
Differences in analyst's attitudes towards information systems development: evidence and implications. 01935
A study of user interface aids for model-oriented decision support systems. 02479

**Doss, H.**
Computer aids for vision and employment (CAVE). 0976

**Doster, W.**
Issues limiting the acceptance of user interfaces using gesture input and handwriting character recognition. 0845

**Dougall, A.**
Computer-based microworlds—a definition to aid design. HCI-0432 †

**Dougall, E. G. (Ed.)**
Computer security: a global challenge. § 03577

**Douglas, D.**
Repetition strain injury in Australian VDU users. 03681

**Doukidis, G. I.**
Developing and running expert systems with PESYS. 01690

**Doukidis, G. I. (Ed.)**
Knowledge based management support systems. ● 0252

**Doumeingts, G.**
Systems analysis techniques. 0622

**Dowling, R.**
A question of delivery—an outline classification of interactive video delivery systems. 0510

**Dowling, T.**
User-oriented suggestions for floating-point and complex-arithmetic Forth standard extensions. 02306

**Downing, J. V.**
The effects of panel arrangements and locus of attention on performance. 01759

**Downs, C. G.**
Representing the structure of jobs in job analysis. 02181

**Downton, A. C.**
On-line recognition of Pitman's hand-written shorthand—an evaluation of potential. 02111

**Doyle, K.**
Fabrik: a visual programming environment. 01130

**Drang, D. E.**
A comprehensive guide to AI and expert systems. ● HCI-0058 †

**Draper, S. W.**
Software engineering for user interfaces. 01854
Information flow in a user interface: the effect of experience and context on the recall of MacWrite screens. 03228

**Dray, S.**
Socio-tech: what is it (and why should we care)? 0908

**Dress, W. B.**
High performance neural networks. 02313

**Dressler, T.**
Real-time failure detection on complex mechanical structures via parallel data processing. 01561

**Dreyfus, G.**
Designing a neural network satisfying a given set of constraints. 02755
A simple selectionist learning rule for neural networks. 02756

**Drösler, J.**
The psychophysical function of binocular space perception. 02375

**Droulez, J.**
Spatial and temporal transformations in visuo-motor coordination. 03963

**Drucker, S. M.**
Connections in context: The intermedia system. 03534

**Drury, C. G.**
A simultaneous regression model for double stimulation tasks. 01726
A human factors design investigation of a computerized layout system of text-graphic technical materials. 01779

**du Boulay, B.**
Fatal error in pass zero: how not to confuse novices. HCI-0164 †

**Duce, D. A. (Ed.)**
Advances in computer graphics II. ● 0437
Methodology of window management. § 03923

**Duchastel, P.**
Computer text access. 01493

**Duffy, J.**
Off-line programming and path generation for robot manipulators. 0603

**Duffy, T. M.**
The evaluation of online help systems: a conceptual model. 0129

**Dufourd, J.**
Construction of interactive programs in computer graphics. 01398

**Duggal, J.**
Ergonomic job design in frequent manual lifting tasks: a microcomputer-based model. 01532

**Duisberg, R.**
Constraint hierarchies. 01114
Constraint-based tools for building user interfaces. 01153

**Duisberg, R. A.**
Animated graphical interfaces using temporal constraints. 0909

**Duke, E. L.**
The development of an automated flight test management system for flight test planning and monitoring. 02928

**Dumais, S.**
Computers' impact on productivity and work life. 03040

**Dumais, S. T.**
Using latent semantic analysis to improve access to textual information. 02901
The vocabulary problem in human-system communication. HCI-0224 †
The spatial metaphor for user interfaces: experimental tests of reference by location versus name. HCI-0268 †
Computerization, productivity, and quality of work-life. HCI-0441 †

**Dumas, J. S.**
Stimulating change through usability testing. 01006
Designing user interfaces for software. ● HCI-0010 †

**Duncan, E. B.**
Structuring knowledge bases for designers of learning materials. 01807

**Dunfee, W. P.**
Designing SAA applications and user interfaces. 01821

**Dunlap, W. P.**
Estimating reliability with small samples: increased precision with averaged correlations. 01728
Spatial requirements for visual simulation of aircraft at real-world distances. 01768

Comparison of video game and conventional test performance. 02594

**Dunne, E. J.**
Managers who personally use information technology frequently: a profile of some invisible computer personnel. 03007

**Dunsmore, H. E.**
Cognitive issues in the process of software development: review and reappraisal. 02222

**Dupont, P. B.**
Electronic calendars in the office: an assessment of user needs and current technology. HCI-0287 †

**Durham, I.**
DRAT: A program for maintaining listings. 02401

**Durham, T. W.**
Personality characteristics of junior high school students successful with computers. 01592

**Durrani, O.**
Designer labyrinths: text mazes for language learners. 0197

**Durrett, H. J.**
Color and the instructional use of the computer. 0263

**Durrett, H. J. (Ed.)**
Color and the computer. ● 0254

**Dutta, A.**
Reasoning with imprecise knowledge in expert systems. 02018

**Dutta, S.**
Interactive curve drawing by segmented Bezier approximation with a control parameter. 02535
Approximate spatial reasoning. 02917

**Dutton, B.**
End-user searching—What are the implications? 01224

**Dutton, B. G.**
Introducing information technology: experiences of a large industrial unit. 01217

**Dutton, W. H.**
A tolerance for surveillance: American public opinion concerning privacy and civil liberties. 0524

The diffusion and impacts of information technology in households. 0754

**Dwelly, A.**
Reference models, window systems, and concurrency. 01058
Synchronizing the I/O behavior of functional programs with feedback. 02016

**Dybvig, R. K.**
A semantic editor. 01101

**Dyer, H. (Ed.)**
New horizons for the information profession: meeting the challenge of change. § 04046

**Dyer, M.**
Recognizing and responding to plan-oriented misconceptions. 01350

**Dyer, M. C.**
Precedent-based legal reasoning and knowledge acquisition in contract law: A process model. 02776

**Dyn, N.**
Identification of MGB cells by Volterra kernels. III. A glance into the black box. 01259

**Dyson, E.**
Computer-supported cooperative work: breakthroughs for user acceptance. 02874

**Dzida, W.**
On tools and interfaces. 0316
The development of ergonomic standards. 0987
Computer assisted knowledge acquisition: towards a laboratory for protocol analysis of user dialogues. 03603

**Dzida, W. (Ed.)**
Psychological issues of human-computer interaction in the work place. ● 0305

**Earnshaw, R. A. (Ed.)**
Workstations and publication systems. ● 0264

**Eason, K. D.**
The supplier's role in the design of products for organisations. 01412

**Easterby, R.**
Trillium: an interface design prototyping tool. 01965

**Eastlake, D. E., III**
The Greenblatt chess program. 0527

**Eaton, R.**
An innovative user interface for microcomputer-based computer-aided design. 03865

**Eberhardt, J.**
Formative design evaluation of superbook. 01154

**Eberts, R.**
Human computer interaction. 0404

**Eberts, R. E.**
Comparison of speech and pictorial displays in a cockpit environment. 01731
Internal models, tracking strategies and dual-task performance. 01751

**Ebihara, S.**
An acoustic of pathological voice and its application to the evaluation of laryngeal pathology. 02644

**Eccles, L. M.**
Empirical evaluation of map interfaces. 03276

**Eckert, R.**
User services consulting supportr tools at the NASA numerical aerodynamic simula. 03161

**Ecklund, D. J.**
A distributed object server. 03842

**Ecklund, E. F.**
The proteus bibliography: Representation and interactive display in databases. 01085
A distributed object server. 03842

**Eckmiller, R.**
Neural networks for motor program generation. 03964

**Eckmiller, R. (Ed.)**
Neural computers. § 03949

**Eddins, J. M.**
Computer analysis of students' procedural "bugs" in an arithmetic domain. 02273

**Eddison, E. B.**
Choreography for technology and humans. 02518

**Edel, M.**
The tinkertoy graphical programming environment. 01850

**Edelman, G. M.**
Selective networks and recognition automata. HCI-0390 †

**Edelman, S.**
Line connectivity algorithms for an asynchronous pyramid computer. 01468

**Edelmann, H.**
APL: a problem-oriented introduction. ● 0230

**Edelson, B.**
A comprehensive guide to AI and expert systems. ● HCI-0058 †

**Eden, C.**
Computer decision support for senior managers: encouraging exploration. HCI-0298 †

**Edmonds, E.**
Negative knowledge towards a strategy for asking in logic programming. 02115

**Edmonds, E. A.**
Support for tentative design: incorporating the screen image, as a graphical object, into PROLOG. 02116

**Edmunds, G.**
Teaching software engineering at university. 01968

**Edmundson, R. H.**
Graphical data presentation for decision support systems. 01229
The accuracy of combining judgemental and statistical forecasts. 02474

**Educational Technology Publica**
Interactive video: vol. 1. ● HCI-0081 †

**Edward, P.**
Information processing today, with applications. ● 0568

**Edwards, A. D. N.**
Modelling blind users' interactions with an auditory computer interface. 02237
The design of auditory interfaces for visually disabled users. 02869

**Edwards, H. M.**
Experiences in use of SSADM: series of case studies. Part 1: first time users. 01976
Experiences in use of SSADM: series of case studies. Part 2: experienced users. 01977

**Edwards, J. L.**
Evaluating the intelligence in dialogue systems. 02194
Surveying projects on intelligent dialogue. 02197
Toward intelligent dialogue with ISIS. 02198

**Edwards, J. R.**
Stress, coping, and worker well-being in computer-aided manufacturing: A field investigation of a CNC machine shop. 03373

**Edwards, K.**
Information retrieval: the future. 04045

**Edwards, P.**
Information processing today, with applications. ● 0567
Information processing today, with applications and BASIC. ● 0569
Information processing today, with applications and BASIC: updat 87/88. ● 0570
Principles of information processing. ● 0571
Principles of information processing with applications and BASIC. ● 0572
The system understands. 01659
The designing mind. 01661

**Eeckman, F. H.**
A model for cortical function. 02731

**Efe, K.**
The problem of levels and automatic response generation in a "Let's Talk AboutIt" strategy. 0410
A proposed solution to the problem of levels in error-message generation. HCI-0126 †

**Efstathiou, J.**
Intelligent machines for process control. 0362
Introduction to expert systems. 02261

**Egan, D. E.**
TNT: a talking tutor 'n' trainer for teaching use of interactive computer systems. 0895
Formative design evaluation of superbook. 01154
Improving speaker consistency in an automatic speech recognition framework. 01448

**Egawa, Y.**
A study of auditory warning alarms evaluation for automated guided vehicles. 03424

**Ege, R. K.**
The filter browser defining interfaces graphically. 03792

**Egenaes, J.**
Video display terminals and birth defects. A study of pregnancy outcomes of employees of the Postal-Giro Center, Oslo, Norway. 03691

**Eggert, A. A.**
Implementation of a multirule, multistage quality control program in a clinical laboratory computer system. 02380

**Eggleston, R. G.**
Modeling the Cognitive content of displays. 01800

**Egido, C.**
Relationships and tasks in scientific research collaborations (Reprint). 0387
Pictures and category labels as navigational aids for catalog browsing. 02877
Video browsing and system response time. 03203

**Ehn, P.**
Playing the language-games of design and use-on skill and participation. 03043

**Ehrenfeucht, A.**
Conceptualizing in assembly tasks. 01776

**Ehrich, R.**
Tools and methodology for user interface development. 01057

**Ehrlich, K.**
Software psychology: the need for an interdisciplinary program. 0052
User interface design: Are human factors principles used? 0886
Information retrieval using a hypertext-based help system. 01155

**Ehrlich, S.**
Integrating human factors and software development. 02882

**Ehrlich, S. F.**
Positioning human factors in the user interface development chain. 0835
Tools for supporting cooperative work near and far: highlights from the CSCW conference. 0879
Voice messaging enhancing the user interface design based on field performance. 0913
Strategies for encouraging successful adoption of office communication systems. HCI-0307 †

**Einbu, J. M.**
An architectural approach to improved program maintainability. 02627

**Einhorn, D. A.**
Putting on a show: using computer graphics to train end-users. 02520

**Eisenberg, M.**
Is the unified keyboard better? 0768

**Eisenman, E. J.**
Electronic monitoring and the redundancy of control systems: The role of the supervisor. 03000

**Eisner, A.**
APL: The language of science and management. 02799

**Ejiri, M.**
An automatic wafer inspection system using pipelined image processing techniques. 01840

**Ekkers, R. J.**
Image processing with personal computers. 02581

**Eklundh, K. S.**
Experimental evaluation of dialogue types for data entry. HCI-0115 †

**Elam, J. J.**
Understanding and validating results in model-based decision support systems. 01666

A study of conflict in group design activities: implications for computer-supported cooperative work environments. 03477

**Elata, S.**
A priori analysis of natural language queries. 02006

**Eliasson, M.**
Analogy and other sources of difficulty in novices' very first text-editing. 02148
Question asking when learning a text-editing system. 02202

**Elithorn, A. (Ed.)**
Artificial and human intelligence. § HCI-0052 †

**Elkerton, J.**
Development and evaluation of direct manipulation lists (poster session). 0993
Online help systems: design and implementation issues (panel). 02902

**Ellidon, C.**
Portfolio: kaleidoscopic visions. 02551

**Elliott, C. S.**
Barriers to factory automation. 01906

**Ellis, C.**
Project Nick: meetings augmentation and analysis. HCI-0156 †

**Ellis, C. A.**
Office information systems and computer science (Reprint). 0373
Concurrency control in groupware systems. 01090

**Ellis, D.**
A behavioral approach to information retrieval system design. 02304

**Ellis, S. R.**
Statistical dependency in visual scanning. 01719
The effect of perspective geometry on judged direction in spatial information instruments. 01720
Perspective traffic display format and airline pilot traffic avoidance. 01748

The emergence of Zipf's law: Spontaneous encoding optimization by users of a command language. 01875

**Ells, R.**
Hypermedia, help and how-to. 03155

**Ellzey, R. S.**
Computer systems software: the programmer/machine interface. ● HCI-0361 †

**Elmaghraby, A. S.**
A prolog simulation for a Delphi-based problem solver. 01141

**Elman, J. L.**
Interactive processes in speech perception: the TRACE model. 0631

**Elmroth, T.**
Automatic construction of surfaces with prescribed shape. 01474

**Eloranta, E.**
User interface. 0621

**Elshennawy, A. K.**
Human-computer interaction in manufacturing. 01522

**Emerling, M. R.**
VLSI architectures for implementation of neural networks. 02762

**Emerson, R. S.**
Architectural implications of office systems. 03356

**Emmerich, K. A.**
Implementation of a multirule, multistage quality control program in a clinical laboratory computer system. 02380

**Empson, J.**
Error auditing in air traffic control. 03810

**Encarnação, J.**
Interfaces and data transfer formats in computer graphics systems. HCI-0419 †

**Encarnação, J. (Ed.)**
Product data interfaces in CAD/CAM applications: design, implementation and experiences. § 03981

**Enderle, G.**
Graphical standards. HCI-0417 †

**Engelbart, D.**
Working together. 01300

**Engelbart, D. C.**
A conceptual framework for the augmentation of man's intellect (Reprint). 0368
Toward high-performance knowledge workers (Reprint). 0369
Authorship provisions in AUGMENT (Reprint). 0370
A research center for augmenting human intellect. HCI-0334 †

**Engelbeck, G.**
The effects of device technology on the usability of advanced telephone functions. 0876
A test of a common elements theory of transfer. 0901
Modes survey. 0963
Modes survey results. 0998

**Engels, G.**
A highly integrated tool set for program development support. 02788

**England, D.**
A user interface design tool. 03798
Graphical prototyping of graphical tools. HCI-0375 †

**England, N.**
A graphics system architecture for interactive application-specific display functions. 01822

**Englebart, D.**
The augmented knowledge workshop. 03094

**English, W. K.**
Evaluation of mouse, rate-controlled isometric joystick, step keys, and text keys, for text selection on a CRT. 0064
A research center for augmenting human intellect. HCI-0334 †

**Engmann, R.**
Generation of file processing programs based on JSP. 02639

**Enkawa, T.**
Underlying dimensions of human problem solving and learning: implications for personnel selection, training tasks design and expert system. 02225

**Ennals, R. (Ed.)**
Information technology and education: the changing school. ● 0282

**Enomoto, N.**
Fuzzy control of a mobile robot for obstacle avoidance. 02025

**Ensor, J. R.**
The rapport multimedia conferencing system. 03037

**Epstein, D.**
A smalltalk window system based on constraints. 01128

**Epstein, R. G.**
Retraining high school teachers to teach computer science—observations on the first course. 01030

**Er-radi, M.**
Principles of an icons-based language. 01080

**Erbach, G.**
Online use and end-users in media and advertising: an overview. 01216
End-users: threat, challenge or myth? 01221
Time-life, world reporter and the secretary: experiments with end-users. 02325

**Erickson, J. D.**
A prototype autonomous agent for crew and equipment retrieval in space. 02994

**Erickson, T.**
"My user interface is the best because...". 0856
Interfaces for cooperative work: an eclectic look at CSCW '88. 01009

**Ericson, A.**
Pregnancy outcome and VDU-work in a cohort of insurance clerks. 03690

**Eriksson, S.**
Temporal and spatial stability in visual displays. 03730

**Erlandsen, J.**
Intelligent help systems. 01959

**Erlbaum, M.**
Evaluating RECONSIDER: a computer program for diagnostic prompting. HCI-0410 †

**Ero, J.**
User interface management systems. 0233

**Erradi, M.**
Interaction with IBS: an Icon-based system. 03838
Graphics interaction in databases. 03862

**Ervier, M.**
The kernel of a generic software development environment. 03056

**Ervin, S.**
Designing with constraints. 0467

**Espiau, B.**
An overview of local environment sensing in robotics applications. 04012

**Esposito, B. K.**
Recent trends in information systems law. 03017

**Estes, J. E.**
But what will the workers do? simulating what the workers do to us when we do what we do to them. 02590

**Estrin, T.**
The UCLA Brain Research Institute data processing laboratory. 02844

**Estublier, J.**
Experience with a data base of programs. 03050

**Eswaran, K. P.**
System R: a relational approach to database management. 0709

**Etherton, J.**
Human response to unexpected robot movements at selected slow speeds. 03405
Unexpected motion hazard exposures on a large robotic assembly. 03409

**Etter, D.**
Digital waveform sampling rate converter. 01578

**Evans, D. J.**
A process oriented approach to an intelligent design aid. 02980

**Evans, J.**
Interpretation of natural language database queries using optimization methods. 01861

**Evans, S. J.**
An error correcting protocol for medical expert systems. 02143

**Evans, S. M.**
CHI '88 poster session papers and abstracts. 0992

**Evans, T. G.**
A heuristic program to solve geometric-analogy problems. 0299

**Evanson, S.**
How to talk to an expert. 01180

**Evens, M.**
Human interfaces in a legal expert system. 03164

**Evrenol, M.**
The design of a user friendly interactive personal computer package for quality control charts, project management, and linear programming applications. 01521

**Ewing, J.**
An experimental comparison of a mouse and arrow-jump keys for an interactive encyclopedia. 02098

**Ewry, M. E.**
Capacity equivalence curves: a double trade-off curve method for equating task performance. 01796

**Extejt, M. M.**
Expert systems as human resource management decision tools. 02440

**Eyada, O. K.**
An interactive tolerance system. 02975

**Eyles, J.**
Pixel-planes 4: a summary. 0495

**Eysel, U. T.**
Quantitative determination of orientational and directional components in the response of visual cortical cells to moving stimuli. 01268

**Ezzell, B.**
Programming the IBM User Interface: Using Turbo Pascal. ● 0286

**Fähnrich, K. P.**
How to design dialogue systems for large computer applications. 0189

**Fafrowicz, M.**
Acting-out and burn-out behaviours of operators monitoring automated systems. 03440

**Fagan, L. M.**
Graphical specification of procedural knowledge for an expert system. 0427

**Fahnrich, K. P.**
Learning and transfer for text and graphics editing with a direct manipulation interface. 0900

**Fainter, R. G.**
GENIE: a modifiable computer-based task for experiments in human-computer interaction. HCI-0194 †

**Fairbairn, J.**
Non-strict languages-programming and implementation. 01418

**Fairchild, K.**
The tourist artificial reality. 0868

**Fairhall, D.**
In search of searching skills. HCI-0274 †

**Fairhurst, M. C.**
An investigation of pictographic form in relation to mechanisms of knowledge acquisition. 03824

**Falck, M.**
Participation in the development of software and the utilisation of standard software. 03663
A roundtable discussion on women, computers and participation. 03673

**Falcone, J. R.**
A programmable interface language for heterogeneous distributed systems. HCI-0094 †

**Falkenberg, E.**
Representation of dynamic features in a conceptual schema. 01231

**Fallside, F. (Ed.)**
Computer speech processing. ● 0287

**Faloutsos, C.**
Design and performance considerations for an optical disk-based, multimedia object server. HCI-0265 †

**Falzon, P.**
From surface form to the structure of the interface - studies in human computer interaction at INRIA. 03984

**Fanty, M. A.**
Computing with structured neural networks. 01365
Computing with structured connectionist networks. HCI-0314 †

**Farber, R.**
A self-optimizing, nonsymmetrical neural net for content addressable memory and pattern recognition. 02562
Programming a massively parallel, computation universal system: Static behavior. 02746

**Farhat, N. H.**
Optical analog of two-dimensional neural networks and their application in recognition of radar targets. 02733

**Farhoosh, H.**
CNS-HLS mapping using fuzzy sets. HCI-0380 †

**Farkash, A.**
How can cognitive psychology help solve an artificial intelligence problem? 01480

**Farmer, J. D.**
The immune system, adaptation, and machine learning. 02559

**Farmer, M.**
Live-Net in education. 01381

**Farooq, M. U.**
A survey of formal tools and models for developing user interfaces. 02207

**Farrand, A. B.**
"My user interface is the best because...". 0856

**Farrell, J. E.**
Window-based computer dialogues. 0071

**Farrell, R. L.**
Capturing expertise: Some approaches to modeling command decisionmaking in combat analysis. 01883

**Farreny, H.**
Decision and intelligence. ● HCI-0068 †

**Fasser, W.**
Subject reports about musculoskeletal discomfort in VDU work as a complex phenomenon. 03708

**Fast, L.**
Dialing a name: alphabetic entry through a telephone keypad. 0973

**Fatmi, H. A.**
Time, structure and levels of consciousness. 01608

**Faught, W. S.**
Applications of AI in engineering. HCI-0321 †

**Favareto, C.**
Real-time large vocabulary word recognition via diphone spotting and multiprocessor implementation. 03996

**Fay, F. S.**
Interfacing image processing and computer graphics systems using an artificial visual system. 03301

**Feibig, P.**
Digital waveform sampling rate converter. 01578

**Feider, M. S.**
The linear file—restrictions on online information use: a searcher's perspective. 01634

**Feinberg, W. E.**
The inept and the computer revolution: some clues from other innovations. 01552

**Feldman, J. A.**
A functional model of vision and space. 0027
Computing with structured neural networks. 01365
Connectionist models and parallelism in high level vision. 02700
Structured neural networks in nature and in computer science. 03950
Computing with structured connectionist networks. HCI-0314 †
Connectionist models and parallelism in high level vision. HCI-0363 †

**Fell, H.**
An authoring system for the creation of interfaces for disabled users. 0974

**Fellers, J.**
Key factors in knowledge acquisition. 01019

**Fellien, A.**
Some aspects of knowledge processing and participation. 03669

**Fels, D.**
User interface primitives to allow full functional use of computers by physically disabled persons. 0979

**Felt, M. A.M.**
Development of mental models of an office system: a field study on an introductory course. 03903

**Ferber, H. J.**
Automatic acquisition of domain and procedural knowledge. 02943

**Ferguson, G.**
Developing intelligent simulation language to support telerobotic workstation activities. 02995
An advanced full-text retrieval and analysis system. 03079

**Ferm, R.**
A flexible negotiable interactive learning environment. 03197

**Ferrari, D. (Ed.)**
Theory and practice of software technology. § 03361

**Ferraté, G. (Ed.)**
Syntactic and structural pattern recognition. ● 0292

**Ferratt, T. W.**
Are information systems people different? An investigation of how they are and should be managed. 02511
Managers who personally use information technology frequently: a profile of some invisible computer personnel. 03007

**Ferrier, L.**
An authoring system for the creation of interfaces for disabled users. 0974

**Ferrin, T. E.**
The MIDAS database system. 02387
The MIDAS display system. 02388
MIDAS: molecular interactive display and simulation. 04061

**Ferrington, L.**
The economics of UNIX workstations. 01312

**Ferris, J. T.**
Putting Texas on disc. 01316

**Ferry, D. K.**
Limited interconnectivity in synthetic neural systems. 03968

**Feurzeig, W.**
Algebra slaves and agents in a Logo-based mathematics curriculum. 0517

**Fiadeiro, J.**
Specification and verification of database dynamics. HCI-0251 †

**Fidelman, U.**
Ordinals and the hemispheres of the brain. 01620

**Fidge, C. J.**
A LISP implementation of the model for 'communicating sequential processes'. 02632

**Field, D.**
Towards universality of access: interfacing physically disabled students to the Icon educational microcomputer. 0821

**Fielding, E. V. (Ed.)**
Methodology of window management. § 03923

**Filipski, A.**
Project source file management under the UNIX operating system. 03168

**Finch, J. H.**
Security of office systems. 03359

**Finch, J. H. (Ed.)**
Computer security: a global challenge. § 03577

**Findlay, J. M.**
Optimum display arrangements for presenting visual reminders. 03237

**Finin, T.**
VP$^2$: the role of user modelling in correcting errors in second language learning. 0222

Modeling the user in natural language systems. 01348
A general user modelling facility. 02880

**Finkel, R. A.**
An operating systems vade mecum: 2nd edition. ● HCI-0025 †

**Finn, A. T.**
Organizational videotex: information services for the end user. 03166

**Finn, G. G.**
An experimental multimedia mail system. HCI-0309 †

**Finn, R.**
Why reading was slower from CRT displays than from paper. 0797
Reading is slower from CRT displays than from paper: attempts to isolate a single-variable explanation. 01743
Reading from CRT displays can be as fast as reading from paper. 01758

**Finnie, G. R.**
Is top-down natural? Some experimental results from non-procedural languages. 02123

**Fiorillo, A.**
Force and tactile sensing for robots. 04013

**Firschein, O.**
Questions, intelligence, and intelligent behavior. 01540
Questions, intelligence and intelligent behavior. 01542

**Firschein, O. (Ed.)**
Readings in computer vision: issues, problems, principles, and paradigms. ● 0206

**Fischer, F.**
Effectiveness of training as a function of the teacher knowledge structure. 03604

**Fischer, G.**
Knowledge-based systems and communication between computers and human beings. 0192
Enhancing incremental learning processes with knowledge-based systems. 0538

University of Colorado at Boulder, Institute of cognitive science. 0811
Design environments for constructive and argumentative design. 0864
Helgon: extending the retrieval by reformulation paradigm. 0880
The enhancement of understanding through visual representations. 0898
Goals and objectives for user interface software. 01056
An object-oriented construction and tool kit for human-computer communication. 01061
Active help systems. HCI-0108 †

**Fischer, J.**
ATLANTIS—a software simulator for behavior analysis of protocol specificationsand their target implementations. 02667

**Fischer, P. M.**
Improvement of the acquisition of knowledge by informing feedback. 0540

**Fischhoff, B.**
Search success and expectations with a computer interface. 01995
Creating categories for databases. 02149
Calibrating databases. HCI-0269 †

**Fischler, M. A.**
Questions, intelligence, and intelligent behavior. 01540
Questions, intelligence and intelligent behavior. 01542
Perceptual organization and curve partitioning. 01838

**Fischler, M. A. (Ed.)**
Readings in computer vision: issues, problems, principles, and paradigms. ● 0296

**Fischlin, A.**
Automated construction of interactive learning programs in Modula-2. 01500

**Fisher, D. L.**
Visual Displays: the highlighting Paradox. 01799

**Fisher, G.**
Student-oriented features of an interactive programming environment. 01036

**Fisher, G. A.**
A practical method for LR and LL syntactic error diagnosis and recovery. HCI-0163 †

**Fisk, A. D.**
Automatic and controlled processing theory and its applications to human factors problems. 0402
Training consistent task components: application of automatic and controlled processing theory to industrial task training. 01742
The role of stimulus-to-rule consistency in learning rapid application of spatial rules. 01765
Examination of the role of "higher order" consistency in skill development. 01791

**Fitch, J.**
Alkahest III: automatic analysis of periodic weakly nonlinear ODEs. 03087

**Fitter, M.**
The doctor's use of a computer in the consulting room: an analysis. HCI-0409 †

**Fitzgibbon, L.**
Structural displays as learning aids. 02188

**Fitzpatrick, L.**
IRX: an information retrieval system for experimentation and user applications. 01076

**Flach, L.**
A serial interface for process control. 02383

**Flagle, C. D.**
The perception of system and the reduction of uncertainty. 02850

**Flash, T.**
The control of hand equilibrium trajectories in multi-joint arm movements. 01275

**Flashner, H.**
Modeling of control and learning in a stepping motion. 01250

**Flavell, R.**
Towards the construction of a maximally-contrasting set of colours. 03233

**Flavell, R. B.**
Colour coding scales and computer graphics. 03864

**Flavin, R. A.**
Management of distributed applications in large networks. 03515
Grand computer conferencing: What have we learned? 03536

**Fleischer, A. G.**
Eye-head coordination and information uptake during text processing. 03767

**Fleischman, R. N.**
The effects of syntactic complexity on the human-computer interaction. 01708
Modeling the Cognitive content of displays. 01800

**Fleisher, A.**
Designing with constraints. 0467

**Fleming, P. J.**
A design environment for computer-aided control system design via multi-objective optimisation. 03835

**Flood, R. L.**
Cybernetics and organization theory: a critical review. 01617

**Flores, F. (Ed.)**
Understanding computers and cognition. ● HCI-0054 †

**Floru, R.**
Data entry task on VDU: underload or overload. 03761

**Flowers, M.**
Recognizing and responding to plan-oriented misconceptions. 01350
Precedent-based legal reasoning and knowledge acquisition in contract law: A process model. 02776

**Floyd, C.**
Report from the working group on "methods and tools in system design for, with and by the users". 03664

**Floyd, R.**
Toward interactive design of correct programs. 0614

**Flynn, G. J.**
Medicine in the age of the computer. ● HCI-0075 †

**Fodor, J. A.**
Connectionism and cognitive architecture: a critical analysis. 0589

**Foehr, T.**
The soft side of software: a management approach to computer documentation. ● HCI-0016 †

**Fogarty, K. E.**
Interfacing image processing and computer graphics systems using an artificial visual system. 03301

**Foley, J.**
User interface strategies '88 (Videotape). ● 0684
Managing the design of user-computer interfaces. 0936
Goals and objectives for user interface software. 01056
Transformations on a formal specification of user-computer interfaces. 01062
The mental rotation and perceived realism of computer-generated three-dimensional images. 02213
A knowledge-based user interface management system. 02867

**Foley, J. D.**
James D. Foley, Oct. 12: user interface strategies '88. ● 0303
Interfaces for advanced computing. 02578
Fundamentals of interactive computer graphics. ● HCI-0069 †
The human factors of computer graphics interaction techniques. HCI-0377 †

**Foley, P.**
Temporal resolution: an insight into the video display terminal (VDT) "problem". 01754

**Foley, T. J.**
An empirical study of user satisfaction with a microcomputer-based campus-wide. 03137

**Foltz, P. W.**
Transfer between menu systems. 02873

**Fontenier, G.**
Architectures of graphic processors for interactive 2D graphics. 01395

**Foote-Lenox, T.**
Ergonomic guidelines for computerized user interfaces. 01449

**Forcht, K. A.**
Documentation for user-developed applications with high documentation requirements. 01049
Adequate documentation of user-developed applications: a new challenge for end-user computing management. 03001
Developing awareness of computer ethics. 03010

**Ford, D. R.**
An expert manufacturing simulation system. 02584

**Ford, G. A. (Ed.)**
Software Engineering Education. § 04022

**Ford, R.**
Abstract data type development and implementation: an example. HCI-0162 †

**Fordyce, K. J.**
Looking at worksheet modeling through expert system eyes. 0696

**Forer, P.**
Symbiotic software: development and usage issues on stand-alone and networked systems. 0474

**Forgie, D.**
Technological development and the integrated workstation. 01313

**Forrest, B. M.**
Implementing neural network models on parallel computers. 01403

**Forrest, J.**
An external data structure tool for Pascal. 02495

**Forrester, M.**
Interfaces and on-line reading. 04047

**Forsdick, H. C.**
Diamond: a multimedia message system built on a distributed architecture (Reprint). 0380
Diamond: A multimedia message system built on a distributed architecture. 0574

**Forshaw, M. R. B.**
Pattern storage and associative memory in quasi-neural network. 02537

**Forsyth, G. F.**
Concept demonstration of the use of interactive fault diagnosis and isolation for TF30 engines. 02968

**Fortin, D.**
A multiple track animator system for motion synchronization. 03350

**Fosdick, H.**
Using IBM's ISPF dialog manager: under MSV, VM, and VSE. ● 0304

**Foss, C. L.**
Tools for reading and browsing hypertext. 02014

**Foss, D. J.**
On comprehending a computer manual: analysis of variables affecting performance. 02135
Technology transfer: a new computer-based system. HCI-0203 †

**Fossa, M.**
Knowledge acquisition via a graphical interface. 03572

**Fossum, T. V.**
Operating system design. Vol. 1: the XINU approach (PC edition). ● HCI-0029 †

**Foster, G.**
Beyond the chalkboard: computer support for collaboration and problem solving in meetings (Reprint). 0376
WYSIWIS revised: early experiences with multiuser interfaces. 01158
Beyond the chalkboard: computer support for collaboration and problem solving in meetings. HCI-0312 †

**Foster, J.**
Online searching: a five star review of research. 01314

**Foster, S. H.**
Development of a three-dimensional auditory display system. 0980

**Fournier, A.**
Geometric continuity with interpolating Bézier curves. 03857

**Fowler, C.**
Human factors in the IT specification process. 01372
Describing a product opportunity: a method of understanding the users' environment. 03194

**Fowler, C. J. H.**
An evaluation of the effectiveness of the adaptive interface module (AIM) in matching dialogues to users. 03212

**Fowler, J. D.**
Design and implementation of a supercomputer frame buffer system. 03543

**Fox, B.**
Social science and system design: interdisciplinary collaborations. 0833

**Fox, E. A.**
The coming revolution in interactive digital video. 01325

**Fox, G. (Ed.)**
Hypercube Concurrent Computers and Applications. § 02904
Hypercube Concurrent Computers and Applications; vol. 2. § 02908

**Foxley, E.**
A flexible synonym interface with application examples in CAL and help environments. 01404
Music—a language for typesetting music scores. 02622

**Franaszczuk, P. J.**
A study of stability of electrocortical rhythm generators. 01258

**Francesco, N.**
Interactive videodiscs control and computer-based training on the Apple Macintosh. 02305

**Francez, N.**
An environment for logic programming. 01106

**Frank, A. U.**
Multiple inheritance and genericity for the integration of a database management system in an object-oriented approach. 03844

**Frank, E.**
Design of programming languages under psychological aspects. 03613

**Frank, J.**
Quality control of personal computing. 02443

**Frank, L. H.**
Effects of visual display and motion system delays on operator performance and ueasiness in a driving simulator. 01772

**Frank, S. J.**
What AI practitioners should know about the law, part 2. 01197

**Frankenhaeuser, B.**
Video display terminals—electromagnetic radiation and health. 03687

**Frankish, C.**
Human factors and the problems of evaluation in the design of speech systems interfaces. 03192

**Frankish, C. R.**
Parcel sorting by speech recognition: human factors issues. 03209

**Franz, C. R.**
Strategies for research on information systems in organizations. A critical analysis of research purpose and time frame. 0158

**Franzén, O.**
Vision monitoring of VDU operators and relaxation of visual stress by means of a laser speckle system. 03738

**Franzen, J. M.**
A model-based monitor of human sleep stages. 01269

**Fraser, P.**
An annotated bibliography on user interface design. 01004

**Fraser, R.**
Improving human/computer interactions. 0759

**Frasson, C.**
Principles of an icons-based language. 01080
DYNABOARD: user animated display of deductive proofs in mathematics. 02221
Interaction with IBS: an Icon-based system. 03838
Graphics interaction in databases. 03862

**Frazier, L.**
The mapping between grammar and processor. HCI-0346 †

**Freburger, K.**
RAPID: Prototyping control panel interfaces. 01120

**Frederick, D. K.**
An expert system architecture for computer-aided control engineering. 0662

**Freeland, R.**
dBUG III offers source level solutions. 01641

**Freeland, R. R.**
dANALYST attempts to do it all. 01640

**Freeling, A. N. S.**
A philosophical basis for decision aiding. 0649
Fuzzy sets and decision analysis. 0651

**Freeman-Benson, B.**
Constraint hierarchies. 01114

**Freeman, W. J.**
Simulation of chaotic EEG patterns with a dynamic model of the olfactory system. 01263
A dynamic model of olfactory discrimination. 02737

**Freiheit, F.**
Logic programmable natural language processor of a knowledge-base management system. 02965

**Frenkel, K. A.**
The next generation of interactive technologies. HCI-0384 †

**Frese, M.**
A theory of control and complexity: implications for software design and integration of computer systems into the work place. 0315
Transferring skills from training to the actual work situation: the role of task application knowledge, action styles and job decision latitude. 02865

**Frese, M. (Ed.)**
Psychological issues of human-computer interaction in the work place. ● 0305

**Freuder, E. C.**
The complexity of some polynomial network consistency algorithms for constraint satisfaction problems. HCI-0361 †

**Freund, D. D.**
An interactive procedure for constructing line and circle tangencies. 01823

**Friday, K. K.**
How well do you write user documentation? 02442

**Friedman, A.**
Task-sharing within and between hemispheres: a multiple-resources approach. 01795

**Friedman, C.**
Transporting the linguistic string project system from a medical to a Navy domain. HCI-0352 †

**Friedman, M.**
Access-control software. 01911

**Friedmann, K.**
The effect of adding symbols to written warning labels on user behavior and recall. 01788

**Friedmann, P.**
A graphical programming language interface for an intelligent LISP tutor. 02862

**Friis, S.**
Action research on systems development: case study of changing actor roles. 0788

**Fritter, M. J.**
The development and use of information technology in health care. HCI-0408 †

**Fritzson, P.**
Affect-chaining and dependency oriented flow analysis applied to queries of programs. 02789

**Frixone, M.**
Are there individual concepts? Proper names and individual concepts in SI-Nets. 02233

**Frohlich, D. M.**
Conversational resources for situated action. 0861

**Frohn, H.**
A self-organizing neural network sharing features of the mammalian visual system. 01248

**Frome, F. S.**
Incorporating the human factor in color CAD systems. 03104

**Frost, D.**
A natural language interface for expert systems: system architecture. 03551

**Frost, J.**
Design factors for successful videodisc-based instruction. 0277

**Frude, N.**
Information technology in the home: promises as yet unrealized. HCI-0425 †

**Fry, J. P.**
A practical approach to transforming extended ER diagrams into the relational model. 02022
The database designer's workbench. HCI-0249 †

**Frye, D.**
Interface design: a neglected issue in educational software. 0826

**Frysinger, L.**
Communicating with sound. 0067

**Fu, K.**
Modeling rule-based systems by stochastic programmed production systems. 02017

**Fuchs-Kittowski, K.**
Methodological problems of designing dialogue-oriented components in information systems. 03595
Integrative participation—a challenge to the development of informatics. 03641

**Fuchs-Kittowski, K. (Ed.)**
System design for human development and productivity: participation and beyond. § 03640

**Fuchs, H.**
Pixel-planes 4: a summary. 0495

**Fuerst, W. L.**
Effect of computer knowledge on user performance over time. 01975
Using computer knowledge in the design of interactive systems. 02137

**Fuggetta, A.**
The integration of the network and relational approaches in a DBMS. 03283

**Fuhrmann, G.**
Arithmetic codes resembling neural encoding. 02021

**Fujii, M.**
Comparison of manual and online searches of chemical abstracts. 02265
A processing system for program specifications in a natural language. 03537

**Fujisaki, T. (Ed.)**
Logic programming '87. § 03919

**Fujita, S.**
"Structure—reaction type" paradigm in the conventional methods of describing organic reactions and the concept of imaginary transitions structures overcoming this paradigm. 02268

**Fukaya, K.**
A study on the safety operation of robots using monitor hold. 03412

**Fukui, M.**
A document layout system using automatic document architecture extraction. 0882

**Fukui, Y.**
Influence of CRT refresh rates on accommodation aftereffects. 03731

**Fukushima, K.**
A neural network model for the mechanism of pattern information processing. 02748
A neural network for visual pattern recognition. HCI-0391 †

**Fuller, R. F.**
Setting up an interactive videodisc project. 0502

**Fulton, M. A.**
A research model for studying the gender/power aspects of human-computer communication. HCI-0193 †

**Fum, D.**
A propositional language for text representation. 0097

**Funke, J.**
Using simulation to study complex problem solving: a review of studies in the FRG. 02598

**Furedy, J. J.**
Beyond heart rate in the cardiac psychophysiological assessment of mental effort: the T-wave amplitude component of the electrocardiogram. 01738

**Furmanski, W.**
g - A compact language for real-time graphics. 02906

**Furnas, G. W.**
Generalized fisheye views. 0893
Using latent semantic analysis to improve access to textual information. 02901
The vocabulary problem in human-system communication. HCI-0224 †

**Furner, S.**
Text processing by speech: dialogue design and usability issues in the provision of a system for disabled users. HCI-0357 †

**Furth, W.**
Planning as feedback to designers. 02978

**Furui, S.**
Research on individuality features in speech waves and automatic speaker recognition techniques. 02645

**Furukawa, K. (Ed.)**
Logic programming '87. § 03919

**Furuta, R.**
Adding browsing semantics to the hypertext model. 02834

**Futsuhara, K.**
A study of fail-safe technology. 03421
Construction and examples of sensor in safe working system. 03425

**Gabe, E.**
Programming for interactive structure analysis. 03776

**Gabriel, R. P.**
Common LISP object system specification X3J13 Document 88-002R. 01121

**Gagliano, R. A. (Ed.)**
Simulation. § 03501
**Gaglio, S.**
Are there individual concepts? Proper names and individual concepts in SI-Nets. 02233
**Gaines, B.**
Knowledge structures for intelligent interaction. 03636
**Gaines, B. R.**
From timesharing to the sixth generation: the development of human-computer interaction. Part I. 02097
Foundations of dialog engineering: the development of human-computer interaction. Part II. 02100
KITTEN: knowledge initiation and transfer tools for experts and novices. 02159
Integration issues in knowledge support system. 02253
Logical foundations for knowledge representation in intelligent systems. 03029
**Gait, J.**
A debugger for concurrent programs. HCI-0142 †
An aspect of aesthetics in human-computer communications: pretty windows. HCI-0213 †
**Galdes, B.**
Knowledge-based search tactics for an intelligent intermediary system. HCI-0277 †
**Gale, A. W. (Ed.)**
Artificial intelligence and statistics. ● 0321
**Galegher, J.**
Relationships and tasks in scientific research collaborations (Reprint). 0387
**Gall, D.**
Embedding graphics into documents by using a graphic-editor. 0266
**Gallagher, R. S.**
Developing computer aided design technology in China. 0942
**Gallop, J. R.**
Computer graphics language bindings: programmer interface standards. 01473

User interface management and graphics standards. 01964
**Gallupe, B.**
GDSS: a brief look at a new concept in decision support. 02804
**Galotti, K. M.**
What non-programmers know about programming: natural language procedure specification. HCI-0211 †
**Gammerman, A.**
A hybrid approach to deductive uncertain inference. 02191
**Ganapathy, S. K.**
A synthetic visual environment with hand gesturing and voice input. 0858
**Gangnet, M.**
Planar maps: an interaction paradigm for graphic design. 0873
**Gangon, W. F., III**
What non-programmers know about programming: natural language procedure specification. HCI-0211 †
**Gansner, E. R.**
A foundation for programming environments. 03057
**Garcia-Luna-Aceves, J. J.**
An architecture for a multimedia teleconferencing system. 02802
**Garcia-Luna, J. J. (Ed.)**
Communications and architecture & protocols. § 02801
**Garcie-Molina, H.**
The design of a document database. 02835
**Gardarin, G. (Ed.)**
New applications of data bases. § 02710
**Garden, A.**
Behavioural and organisational factors involved in the turnover of high tech professionals. 01024
Maintaining the spirit of excitement in growing companies. 01025
**Gardenfors, P.**
Decision making with unreliable probabilities. 0652
**Gardiner, M. M.**
Applying cognitive psychology to user-interface design. ● 0325

Introduction. 0326
The role of cognitive psychology in user-interface design. 0327
Principles from the psychology of memory: Part II-Episodic and semantic memory. 0331
Design guidelines. 0334
Assessment of trends in the technology and techniques of human-computer interaction. 0335
Future directions. 0336
Office systems. HCI-0291 †
**Gardner, A. v.d.L.**
An artificial intelligence approach to legal reasoning. ● HCI-0061 †
**Gardner, D. G.**
Stress. 01651
**Gardner, E. P.**
Establishing user-centered criteria for information systems: a software ergonomics perspective. 01920
**Gardner, S.**
Application of neural network algorithms and architectures to correlation/tracking and identification. 02734
**Garg-Janardan, C.**
The contribution of cognitive engineering to the effective design and use of information systems. 02033
**Garg, P. K.**
A hypertext system to manage software life cycle documents. 03519
**Garhart, C.**
The accuracy of cognitive monitoring during computer-based instruction. 02281
**Garlan, D.**
A structural approach to the maintenance of structure-oriented environments. 03054
Views for tools in integrated environments. 03784
**Garratt, P. W.**
Teaching software engineering at university. 01968

**Garret, R. B.**
The evolution of user services. 03139

**Garrett, P. H.**
Computer interface engineering with model-based analysis. • 0337

**Garrison, J. W.**
The erotetic logic of problem-solving inquiry. 01583

**Garth, S.**
An integrated system for neural network simulations. 0771

**Garvey, P. M.**
The effects of target wavelength on dynamic visual acuity under photopic and scotopic viewing. 01762

**Garza, J. F.**
Data model issues for object-oriented applications. 0712
Data model issues for object-oriented applications. 01157

**Gasbarri, G.**
System design for local authorities: participation based on "information contr cts". 03656

**Gasen, J. B.**
Measuring change in the programming process. 02242

**Gash, D. C.**
Negotiating IS: Observations on changes in structure from a negotiated order perspective. 03016

**Gash, S.**
Personal transferable skills for the modern information professional: a discussion paper. 02338

**Gasser, L. (Ed.)**
Distributed Artificial Intelligence. • 0168

**Gates, D.**
g - A compact language for real-time graphics. 02906

**Gattiker, U. E.**
Technology adaptation: a typology for strategic human resource management. 01238

**Gaul, W. (Ed.)**
Data, expert knowledge and decisions. • 0338

**Gaulding, J.**
Using "word-knowledge" reasoning for question answering. 0131

**Gaur, Y.**
A portable user interface for a scientific programming environment. 03125

**Gayeski, D. M.**
Interactive Toolkit. • 0340

**Gaylin, K. B.**
How are windows used? Some notes on creating an empirically-based windowing benchmark task. 0903

**Geary, M.**
Spying on windows. 01290

**Gediga, G.**
A critique and empirical investigation of the "One-Best-Way-Models" in human-computer interaction. 0317

**Geiger, H.**
A self-organizing neural network sharing features of the mammalian visual system. 01248

**Geissman, J. R.**
Selecting a shell. 01176

**Gelenbe, E. (Ed.)**
New applications of data bases. § 02710

**Golléi, P.**
Smaller sizes-changing roles: new dimensions of the man-computer interactions. 03596

**Gelman, T. P.**
Local area networks: sailing from the past to the present and into the future. 03152

**Gen, M.**
Interactive multiple objective linear programming system implemented on a microcomputer. 01508

**Genaidy, A.**
Ergonomic job design in frequent manual lifting tasks: a microcomputer-based model. 01532

**Genaidy, A. M.**
A comprehensive data base for the design of manual materials handling. 01510

A knowledge-based system for assessment of human physiological abilities in manual lifting tasks. 01519
Review and evaluation of physiological cost prediction models for manual materials handling. 01757
"Automation, robotization in particular, is always economically desirable"—fact or fiction? 03448

**Genesereth, M. R.**
Cooperation without communication. 0169
Deals among rational agents. 0170

**Genov, P.**
Personality traits of the worker within the :20man-machine" system at automated production. 03593

**Gensior, S.**
A roundtable discussion on women, computers and participation. 03673

**Gent, A. C.**
Managers' reading habits in the electronics industry. 02339

**Gentry, D.**
A user interface for deaf-blind people (preliminary report). 0794

**George, P.**
User-derived impact analysis as a tool for usability engineering. 0922

**Gerber, P.**
A graphical tool for the design and prototyping of distributed systems. 01146

**Gerbrands, J. J.**
A flexible and intelligent system for fast measurements in binary images for in-line robotic control. 03986

**Gerlach, V. S.**
Designing interactive, responsive instruction: a set of procedures. 0274

**Gersting, J.**
Reference model for DBMS user facility. 01086

**Gertman, D. I.**
The user-computer interface in process control: a human factors engineering handbook. • 0341

**Gertner, I.**
Non-intrusive and interactive profiling in parasight. 01123

**Getts, J.**
Jeff Garbers and the ergonomics of software. 01420

**Gettys, C. F.**
Theoretical training and problem detection in a computerized database retrieval task. 02239

**Gettys, J.**
The X window system. HCI-0370 †

**Gevins, J.**
A graphical programming language interface for an intelligent LISP tutor. 02862

**Gfeller, M.**
Open fullscreen systems. 0766

**Ghallab, M.**
Decision and intelligence. ● HCI-0068 †

**Ghiaseddin, N.**
Characteristics of a successful DSS user's needs vs. builder's needs. 03789

**Ghitman, J. M.**
Practices of novices and experts in critical inquiry. 0585

**Ghoniem, A. F.**
Interactive scientific visualization and parallel display techniques. 03542

**Ghosh, S.**
Implementation of a Prolog-INGRES interface. 01087

**Giacalone, A.**
XY-WINS: an integraded environment for developing graphical user interfaces. 03118

**Giannakopoulos, F.**
Characteristics of neuronal systems in the visual cortex. 01255

**Gibbs, C.**
A knowledge-based user interface management system. 02867

**Gibbs, S.**
Design issues of an intelligent workstation for the office. 03165

**Gibbs, S. J.**
LIZA: an extensible groupware toolkit. 0805

Concurrency control in groupware systems. 01090

**Gibson, J.**
POP-11: an AI programming language. 0748

**Gibson, M. L.**
User programmer and costs of the misinformed user. 02415
Components of user work stations. 02427
The user designer/developer and the user work station. 02431

**Gielen, C. C.A.M.**
A model of the motor servo: Incorporating nonlinear spindle receptor and muscle mechanical properties. 01273

**Giffin, W. C.**
Modeling fault diagnosis as the activation and use of a frame system. 01729

**Giger, H. P.**
Concept based retrieval in classical IR systems. 03066

**Giles, C. L.**
Machine learning using a higher order correlation network. 02563
High order correlation model for associative memory. 02729
Nonlinear dynamics of artificial neural systems. 02747

**Gillan, D. J.**
NASA Johnson Space Center, Human-Computer Interaction. 0815
Models of user interactions with graphical interfaces: 1. statistical. 0883

**Gillander, K.**
Inactivity, night work, and fatigue. 03705

**Gillman, A.**
Computing for the blind user. 01287

**Gilman, F.**
Direct manipulation user interfaces for expert systems. 0429

**Gilmore, B.**
A user view of virtual terminal standardisation. 01432

**Gilmore, D. J.**
Comprehension and recall of miniature programs. 02087

Structural visibility and program comprehension. 03274

**Gilmore, J. F.**
Expert system tool evaluation. 02718

**Gilmore, W. E.**
The user-computer interface in process control: a human factors engineering handbook. ● 0341

**Gilmour, A.**
Computer Board Forum. 02685

**Gilnert, E. P.**
PICT: an interactive graphical programming environment. HCI-0143 †

**Gilroy, F. D.**
Computer anxiety: sex, race and age. 02133

**Gimpel, M.**
A user-unfriendly WELCOME. 02603

**Ginosar, R.**
Neural computers in vision: processing of high dimensional data. 03960

**Ginsberg, C. M.**
"Graphical marionette". 03349

**Ginsberg, M. L.**
Cooperation without communication. 0169
Reasoning about action II: the qualification problem. 01213

**Giordana, A.**
Automated concept acquisition in noisy environments. 01841
Knowledge representation and use in pattern analysis. 02030
An expert system for mapping acoustic cues into phonetic features. HCI-0328 †

**Gipps, P. G.**
The role of computer graphics in validating simulation models. 02486

**Girard, M.**
Interactive design of 3D computer-animated legged animal motion. 01828

**Giraud, C.**
CAD and robotics in architecture and construction. § 03568

**Gisiger, H.**
A graphical tool for the design and prototyping of distributed systems. 01146

**Gitomer, D. H.**
Error analysis and tutor design. 02469

**Gittins, D.**
Icon-based human-computer interaction. 02113

**Gittins, D. T.**
An icon-driven end-user interface to UNIX. 02089
On methods for interface specification and design. 02114

**Giurintano, D. J.**
A hand biomechanics workstation. 02820

**Gjessing, S. (Ed.)**
ECOOP '88 (European Conference on Object-Oriented Programming). § 03793

**Glasgow III, J. C.**
YANLI: a powerful natural language front-end tool. 01194

**Glass, B.**
Hard disk interfaces. 01307

**Glass, G. J.**
Interactive 3-D modeling with personal computers. 03296

**Glass, L. B.**
Digital video interactive. 01308

**Glath, R. M.**
The case of the "Gerbil Virus" that wasn't. 01548

**Glatz, R.**
Testing and validation of IGES processors. HCI-0423 †

**Glenn, K. G.**
From vision science to HDTV: bridging the gap. 01981

**Glenn, W. E.**
From vision science to HDTV: bridging the gap. 01981

**Glickman, A. S.**
Color displays for medical imaging. 0262

**Glimm, J.**
A Computational model for interfaces. 01163

**Glinert, E.**
The MAGNEX text editor for the Comodore Amiga personal computer. 0782

**Glinert, E. P.**
An experiment into the use of auditory cues to reduce visual workload. 0877
Out of Flatland: towards 3-D visual programming. 03497

**Glover, D. E.**
Experimentation with an adaptive search strategy for solving a keyboard design/configuration problem. 04070

**Glushko, R. J.**
Hypertext engineering: practical methods for creating a compact disk encyclopedia. 02832

**Gnesi, S.**
A logic-functional approach to the execution of CCS specifications modulo behavioural equivalences. 03874

**Göranzon, B.**
The practice of the use of computers. A paradoxical encounter between different traditions of knowledge. 0343

**Göranzon, B. (Ed.)**
Knowledge, skill and artificial intelligence. ● 0342

**Göttler, H. (Ed.)**
Graph-theoretic concepts in computer science. § 03885

**Goddard, N. H.**
Computing with structured neural networks. 01365
Computing with structured connectionist networks. HCI-0314 †

**Godden, K.**
Portability of syntax and semantics in DATALOG. HCI-0340 †

**Godhelp, H.**
Effects of vehicle handling characteristics on driving strategy. 01773

**Goeltz, R.**
Embedded training in AI technology through an expert system interface: an alarm processor application. 02991

**Goguelin, P.**
Ergonomics and organizational consulting: accentuation or neglect of psychology. 0242

**Goguen, J. (Ed.)**
Theory and practice of software technology. § 03361

**Gold, B.**
Hopfield model applied to vowel and consonant discrimination. 02735

**Gold, P. Dr.**
A powerful solution meets an overwhelming problem. 02053

**Goldberg, A. (Ed.)**
A history of personal workstations. ● 0347

**Golden, J. B.**
Artificial intelligence systems. 0683

**Goldenberg, S.**
An environment for logic programming. 01106

**Goldenson, D. R.**
Fine tuning selection semantics in a structure editor based programming environment: some experimental results. 0975

**Goldman, S. R.**
Precedent-based legal reasoning and knowledge acquisition in contract law: A process model. 02776

**Goldstein, C.**
IRX: an information retrieval system for experimentation and user applications. 01076

**Goldstein, D. K.**
The effects of task differences on the work satisfaction, job characteristics, and role perceptions of programmer/analysts. 02359
An update measure of supervisor-rated job performance for programmer/analysis. 03012

**Goldstein, M.**
GISD: a graphical interactive system for conceptual database design. 02042

**Goldstein, R.**
Effects of information-processing demands on physiological response patterns. 01740

**Goldstein, T. C.**
A smalltalk implementation of an intelligent operator's associate. 01132

**Goldszmidt, G.**
Interactive blackbox debugging for concurrent languages. 01134

**Golen, S.**
Communication barriers in microcomputer—based courses. 01319

**Goles, E.**
Lyapunov function for parallel neural networks. 02736

**Gomaa, E.**
Extending the DARTS software design method to distributed real time applications. 03516

**Gomer, F. E.**
Changes in electromyographic activity associated with occupational stress and poor performance in the workplace. 01734

**Gomes, C. S.**
Posture and VDU operator satisfaction. 0988

**Gomez, L. M.**
Formative design evaluation of superbook. 01154
The vocabulary problem in human-system communication. HCI-0224 †

**Good, M.**
Experience with contextual field research. 0802
User-derived impact analysis as a tool for usability engineering. 0922
Articulating the experience of transparency: an example of field research techniques. 0977
Seven experiences with contextual field research. 0996

**Goodfellow, M. J.**
whim, the window handler and input manager. 01825

**Goodloe, M.**
Improving performance of an electrical power expert system with genetic algorithms. 02925

**Goodman, B. A.**
Reference identification and reference identification failures. 01345

**Goodman, P. S.**
The human side of robotics: how workers react to a robot. 0443

**Goodwin, M.**
User interfaces in C: programmer's guide to state-of-the-art interfaces. ● 0351

**Goodwin, S. S.**
From user to client services; making the transition for supercomputing. 03138

**Goos, G. (Ed.)**
Experiences with Distributed Systems. § 03881
Uncertainty and intelligent systems. § 04030
VDM—The Way Ahead. § 04033

**Gopnik, I. (Ed.)**
From models to modules: studies in cognitive science from the McGill workshops. ● 0352

**Gopnik, M. (Ed.)**
From models to modules: studies in cognitive science from the McGill workshops. ● 0352

**Goransson, B.**
The interface is often not the problem. 0837

**Gordon, C. L.**
The information center approach for developing computer-based information systems. 01929

**Gordon, G.**
Comparison of well-being among non-machine interactive clerical workers and full-time and part-time VDT users and typists. 03745

**Gordon, S.**
The human factor in expert systems. 01179

**Gordon, T. F.**
Oblog-2: A hybrid knowledge representation system for defeasible reasoning. 02778

**Gorn, S. (Ed.)**
Informatics (computer and information science): its ideology, methodology, and sociology. HCI-0086 †

**Gorny, P. (Ed.)**
Visualization in programming. 5th Interdisciplinary Workshop in Informatics and. § 03826
Visualization in programming. § 04032
Readings on cognitive ergonomics - mind and computers. § HCI-0039 †

**Gosling, J.**
The NeWS book: an introduction to the network/extensible window system. ● 0358
UNIX Emacs: a retrospective (lessons for flexible system design). 03114
SunDew—a distributed and extensible window system. 03927
Partitioning of function in window systems. 03931
System aspects of low-cost bitmapped displays. 03932
A window manager for bitmapped displays and Unix. 03933

**Gotcheva, T.**
An implementation of OSI protocols in SM-4 host computers. 03638

**Gotlieb, C. C.**
Evolution of an organizational interface: the new business department at a large insurance firm (Reprint). 0382

**Gould, J.**
Generating highly interactive user interfaces. 0865

**Gould, J. D.**
Speech filing—An office system for principals. 0037
Human factors challenges in creating a principal support office system—The speh filing system approach. 0038
Designing for usability: Key principles and what designers think. 0078
Why reading was slower from CRT displays than from paper. 0797

Rapid prototyping and system development: examination of an interface toolkit for voice and telephony applications. 0918
Reading is slower from CRT displays than from paper: attempts to isolate a single-variable explanation. 01743
Reading from CRT displays can be as fast as reading from paper. 01758
Cursor movement during text editing. HCI-0113 †
The 1984 Olympic Message System: a test of behavioral principles of system design. HCI-0125 †
Behavioral experiments on handmarkings. HCI-0201 †
Designing for usability: key principles and what designers think. HCI-0231 †

**Goussous, A. S.**
Graphbug - a microprocessor software debugging tool. 02496

**Govindaraj, T.**
A supervisory control paradigm for real-time control of flexible manufacturing systems. 01205
A rule-based model for the human operator in a time-constrained competing-task environment. 01877
Qualitative approximation methodology for modeling and simulation of large dynamic systems: Applications to a Marine power plant. 01900
A model of fault diagnosis performance of expert marine engineers. 02199

**Gowda, R. G.**
Influence of individual characteristics and group cohesiveness on programmer productivity. 04050

**Goyal, P.**
Non-first normal form universal relations: an application to information retrieval systems. 02039

**Grabowski, H.**
Testing and validation of IGES processors. HCI-0423 †

**Grace, A. C.W.**
A design environment for computer-aided control system design vi multi-objective optimisation. 03835

**Graf, H. P.**
VLSI implementation of a neural network model. 01363

**Graf, M.**
Building a visual designer's environment. 03496
Project Nick: meetings augmentation and analysis. HCI-0156 †

**Graf, W.**
The applicability of eye movement analysis in the ergonomic evaluation of human-computer interaction. 03766

**Graham, J. H.**
Overview of research issues in robot safety. 03417

**Graham, P.**
Graphic objects. 01190

**Graham, S.**
Browsing within time-driven multimedia documents. 03046

**Grajek, S.**
The crystal ball of research: how to use it to learn about the user community. 03135

**Grajski, K. A.**
A dynamic model of olfactory discrimination. 02737

**Granacki, J. J.**
PHRAN-SPAN: a natural language interface for system specifications. 02829

**Granor, T. E.**
The run-time structure of UIMS-supported applications. 01059
A user interface mangement system generator. 04074

**Grant, K. R.**
The information lens: an intelligent system for information sharing in organizations. 0891
Intelligent information-sharing systems. 01322

Semistructured messages are surprisingly useful for computer-supported coordination. HCI-0290 †

**Grant, P. M.**
A comparison of neural network and matched filter processing for detecting lines in images. 02738

**Grant, P. W.**
A man-machine interface for computer-aided and simulation of control systems. 01237
A human-computer interface for control system design. 03208

**Grantham, C. E.**
A case study of CSCW in a dispersed organization. 02866

**Grassia, J.**
Direct comparison of the relative efficiency on intuitive and analytical cognition. 01896

**Graubart, R. D.**
The integrity lock support environment. 03578

**Graves, S.**
Improving performance of an electrical power expert system with genetic algorithms. 02925

**Gray, J.**
The role of menu titles as a navigational aid in hierarchical menus. 0888

**Gray, J. N.**
System R: a relational approach to database management. 0709

**Gray, M.**
POP-11 for everyone. 0749
UNIX and the naive user: children meet a grown-up operating system. 0752

**Gray, P. D.**
Experience with chisl, a configurable hierarchical interface specification language. 01397
Dynamic reconfigurability for fast prototyping of user interfaces. 02609

**Grdy, G.**
An expert system for screening employee pension plans for the Internal Revenue Service. 02773

**Greatrex, M. D.**
Human implications of technological change. 03369

**Greaves, W.**
User investigation into practical systems. 01458

**Greco, G.**
The fuzzy logic of text understanding. 01701

**Green, G. I.**
Effects of decision support training and cognitive style on decision process attributes. 02346

**Green, M.**
A high-level user interface management system. 0838
Goals and objectives for user interface software. 01056
Directions for user interface management systems research. 01063
A survey of three dialogue models. 01152
Near-real-time control of human figure models. 01829
Designing the interface designer's interface. 03116
Automatic generation of graphical user interfaces. 03290
Near-real-time control of human figure models. 03295
Correspondence in apparent motion: defining the heuristics. 03308
Real and apparent motion: one mechanism or two? 03328

**Green, M. (Chair.)**
User Interface Software. § 03105

**Green, P.**
Human factors in computer systems: some useful readings. 0957

**Green, S.**
THESYS—implementation of a knowledge-based design system with multiple viewpoints. 0010

**Green, T. R.**
Organization and learnability in computer languages. 02085
Perceptual structure cueing in a simple command language. 02086
Comprehension and recall of miniature programs. 02087
Speech-controlled text-editing: effects of input modality and of command structure. HCI-0397 †

**Green, T. R. (Ed.)**
Readings on cognitive ergonomics - mind and computers. § HCI-0039 †

**Green, T. R.G.**
Programmable user models for predictive evaluation of interface designs. 0800
Cognitive aspects of HCI. 01371
The structure of command languages: an experiment on task-action grammar. 02224
Computer languages: everything you always wanted to know but no one can tell you. 03612

**Greenberg, B. S.**
Knowledge representation for model libraries. 03479

**Greenberg, D. P.**
Perceptual color spaces for computer graphics. 0258
Unified interactive geometric modeller for simulating highly complex environments. 01472
Interactive color graphical postprocessing as a unifying influence in numerical analysis research. 01684
An experimental evaluation of computer graphics imagery. HCI-0373 †

**Greenberg, D. R.**
An approach to a mathematics of phenomena: canonical aspects of reentrant form eigenbehavior in the extended calculus of indications. 01621

**Greenberg, H. J.**
A natural language discourse model to explain linear programming models and solutions. 01671

**Greenberg, M.**
The VDTs are here: health hazard and all. 02439

**Greenberg, S.**
User interfaces for office systems. 0756
The 1988 CSCW: trip report. 01008
How users repeat their actions on computers: principles for design of history mechanisms. 02885

**Greenblatt, R. D.**
The Greenblatt chess program. 0527

**Greene, E.**
Grid analysis: continuing the search for a metric of shape. 02367

**Greene, R. T.**
Use of an entire workforce as computer. 03748

**Greenleaf, G.**
Expert systems in law: The datalex project. 02766

**Greenstein, J.**
Two simulation studies investigating means of human-computer communication for dynamic task allocation. 01882

**Greenstein, J. S.**
Optimizing the touch tablet: the effects of control display gain and method of cursor control. 01730
Application of a mathematical model of human decisionmaking for human-computer communication. 01866
An empirical comparison of model-based and explicit communication for dynamic human-computer task allocation. 02109

**Greer, T.**
Pixel-planes 4: a summary. 0495

**Gregory, R.**
Intelligence based on knowledge—knowledge based on intelligence. 0359

**Gregory, R. L. (Ed.)**
Creative intelligences. ● HCI-0056 †

**Greif, I.**
Computer-based real-time conferencing systems (Reprint). 0377
Data sharing in group work (Reprint). 0379
Computer-supported cooperative work: breakthroughs for user acceptance. 02874
The user interface of a personal calendar program. HCI-0286 †

**Greif, I. (Chair.)**
Computer-Supported Cooperative Work. § 02821

**Greif, I. (Ed.)**
Computer-supported cooperative work: a book of readings. ● 0366

# AUTHOR INDEX

**Greif, S.**
A critique and empirical investigation of the "One-Best-Way-Models" in human-computer interaction. 0317

**Grice, R. A.**
Information development is part of product development—not an afterthought. 0103
Online information: what do people want? What do people need? 0113

**Grier, D. G.**
The Monte Carlo processor: designing and implementing a language for Monte Carlo work. 03317

**Gries, D.**
A new notion of encapsulation. 01104

**Griffith, D.**
Computer aids for vision and employment (CAVE). 0976

**Griffiths, M.**
Inactive video at work. 02571

**Griffiths, P. P.**
System R: a relational approach to database management. 0709

**Grignolo, F. M.**
Intraocular pressure during VDT work. 03683
Visual impairment and subjective ocular symptomatology in VDT operators. 03734

**Grimes, J.**
User interface design: Are human factors principles used? 0886

**Grimes, J. E.**
An interaction between morphology and discourse. 0355

**Grinberg, M. R.**
Distributed database considerations in an expert system for radar analysis. 03175

**Grinstein, G.**
Memory networks with asymmetric bonds. 02740

**Grischkowsky, N.**
Reading is slower from CRT displays than from paper: attempts to isolate a single-variable explanation. 01743

**Grischow, C.**
A user-friendly interface to Kendrick's DUAL code. 01447

**Grisham, M.**
Integrating human factors and software development. 02882

**Grishin, V. G.**
Algorithm for interactive forming matrix data representation and estimation of its efficiency. 02536

**Gröneveld, E. W.**
A model-based monitor of human sleep stages. 01269

**Grobelny, J.**
The fuzzy approach to facilities layout problems. 01697

**Groen, F. C.A.**
Image processing with personal computers. 02581

**Groeneweg, J.**
Accidents at sea: multiple causes and impossible consequences. 02168

**Grondin, R. O.**
Limited interconnectivity in synthetic neural systems. 03968

**Gros, P.**
Architectures of graphic processors for interactive 2D graphics. 01395

**Gross, M.**
Designing with constraints. 0467
Control of sensory processing - a hypothesis on and simulation of the architecture of an elementary cortical processor. 03972

**Grossberg, S.**
The ART of adaptive pattern recognition by a self-organizing neural network. 01364
Absolutely stable learning of recognition codes by a self-organizing neural network. 02728

**Grossner, C. P.**
An intelligent braille display device. 01832

**Grosz, B. J.**
Natural-language interfaces. 0693
Natural-language interfaces. 0720
Attention, intention, and the structure of discourse. 01344
TEAM: an experiment in the design of transportable natural-language interfaces. HCI-0351 †

**Grosz, B. J. (Ed.)**
Annual review of computer science vol. 1, 1986. ● 0719
Readings in natural language processing. ● HCI-0067 †

**Groz, R.**
Attacking a complex distributed algorithm from different sides: an experience wih complementary validation tools. 01429

**Grudin, J.**
Positioning human factors in the user interface development chain. 0835
User interface design in large corporations: coordination and communication across disciplines. 0853
Designing in the dark: logics that compete with the user. 0928
The standards factor. 0965
CSCW'88: report on the conference & review of the proceedings. 01002
Perils and pitfalls. 01302
The case against user interface consistency. 01333
Integrating human factors and software development. 02882

**Gruenenfelder, T. M.**
A general user interface for creating and displaying tree-structures, hierarchies, decision trees, and nested menus. HCI-0136 †

**Grundy, A. F. (Ed.)**
Proceedings of the fourth British national conference on databases (BNCOD 4). § 03282

**Grune, D.**
A programmer-friendly LL(1) parser generator. 02626

**Grupen, R. A.**
A survey of general-purpose manipulation. 02259

**Grzywacx, N. M.**
Motion correspondence and analog networks. 02739

**Guadango, N. S.**
Impact of a restricted natural language interface on ease of learning and productivity. 01334

**Guan, Y.**
An interactive biomolecule graphics system. 02386

**Guarna, V. A.**
A portable user interface for a scientific programming environment. 03125

**Guarna, V. A., Jr.**
GMB: a tool for manipulating and animating graph data structures. 02636

**Guastello, S. J.**
Mathematical modeling of fatigue in physically demanding jobs. 02363

**Gudes, E.**
GISD: a graphical interactive system for conceptual database design. 02042
GCI—a tool for developing interactive CAD user interfaces. 02625

**Guenthner, F.**
A theory for the representation of knowledge. 01811

**Guerin, B.**
Distinctive regions and modes: a new theory of speech production. 02659

**Guest, S.**
An interdisciplinary approach to human factors in telematic systems. A review of the problems and possible solutions by a COST-11 ter working group. 01440

**Guest, S. P.**
On the design of a graphical transition network editor. 03830

**Gueutal, H. G.**
Utilizing high technology: computer-aided-design and user performance. 01954

**Guguljanova, B.**
Assessment of mental load for different strategies of man-computer dialogue by means of the heart rate power spectrum. 03623

**Guida, G.**
A propositional language for text representation. 0097
An expert interface for effective man-machine interaction. 0166

User modeling in intelligent information retrieval. 01994
IR-NLI II: applying man-machine interaction and artificial intelligence conceptsto information retrieval. 03070
Reasoning in natural language for designing a data base. HCI-0322 †

**Guida, G. (Ed.)**
Computational models of natural language processing. ● 0095

**Guidon, R.**
Misconceived misconceptions? 02881

**Guillemette, R. A.**
Development and validation of a reader-based documentation measure. 02236
Application software documentation. 02418

**Guinchiglia, F.**
A first order theory of common sense object positioning. 01563

**Guindon, R.**
Video: Data for studying human-computer interaction. 02878
How to interface to advisory systems? Users request help with a very simple language. 02888
Control of cognitive processes during software design: what tools are needed? 02899

**Gulledge Jr., T. R.**
A model of the controller responses of the human temperature regulating system to changes in water temperature. 02487

**Gulyás, B.**
Image segregation by motion: cortical mechanisms and implementation in neural networks. 03958

**Gundry, A. J.**
Humans, computers, and contracts. 03223

**Gunzenhäuser, R.**
Knowledge-based human-computer interfaces and software ergonomics. 0191

**Gunzenhäuser, R. (Ed.)**
Software ergonomics: advances and applications. ● HCI-0012 †

**Gupta, N. K.**
Computer-aided engineering (CAE) for system analysis. 0663

**Gupta, U. K.**
A blackboard architecture for problem solving and machine learning in an expert system for power system voltage control. 02926

**Gutek, B. A.**
Advanced office systems: An empirical look at use and satisfaction. 03172

**Gutierrez, O.**
Prototyping techniques for different problem contexts. 0862

**Guy, A. W.**
Health hazards assessment of radio frequency electromagnetic fields emitted by video display terminals. 03685

**Guy, D. P.**
'Transparent' interfacing of speech recognizers to microcomputers. 02497

**Guynes, J. L.**
Impact of system response time on state anxiety. HCI-0228 †

**Guyomard, M.**
Experimentation in the specification of an oral dialogue. 04005

**Guyon, I.**
Designing a neural network satisfying a given set of constraints. 02755
A simple selectionist learning rule for neural networks. 02756

**Guzaitis, J.**
The world of GEM. ● 0396

**Gwei, G. M.**
A flexible synonym interface with application examples in CAL and help environments. 01404

**Gwyn, R. (Ed.)**
Information technology and education: the changing school. ● 0282

**Haan, B. J.**
Connections in context: The intermedia system. 03534

**Haas, C.**
Reading and writing with computers: a framework for explaining differences in performance. HCI-0204 †

**Haas, L. M.**
View management in distributed data base systems. 0218

**Haas, N.**
The effects of orienting objectives and review on learning from interactive video. 02287

**Haas, S. W.**
The flexibility of case grammar representations: a porting procedure for natural language interfaces. 02255

**Haban, D.**
Monitoring and performance measuring distributed systems during operation. 03025

**Haber, R. N.**
Toward a theory of the perceived spatial layout of scenes. 02701

**Habermann, A. N.**
A methodology for evaluating environments. 03055

**Habinek, J. K.**
A Multilevel menu-driven user interface: Design and evaluation through simulation. HCI-0170 †

**Hachimura, K.**
A system for the representation of human body movement from dance scores. 02540

**Hackathorn, R. D.**
End-user computing by top executives. 0780

**Hacker, W.**
Complete vs. incomplete working tasks—a concept and its verification. 0241
Computerization versus computer aided mental. 0308
Job organization and allocation of functions between man and computer: I analysis and assessment. 03628
What should be computerized? Cognitive demands of mental routine tasks and mental load. 03632
User-centered system design: design of mental tasks. 03646

**Haeberli, P. E.**
Conman: a visual programming language for interactive graphics. 02811

**Hafner, C. D.**
Portability of syntax and semantics in DATALOG. HCI-0340 †

**Hagendorf, H.**
Exploratory investigations in acquiring and using information in interactive problem solving. 03597

**Hager, T.**
Intentional and operational aspects of decision behaviour and their modelling. 03666

**Hagmann, R. B.**
The structure of Cedar. 01109

**Hahn, J.**
The committee support system. 01460
POEM: An office system for international use. 03457

**Hahn, U.**
Computing text constituency: an algorithmic approach to the generation of text graphs. HCI-0267 †

**Hair, D. C.**
Generalization, consistency, and control. 0796

**Hajek, P.**
Combining functions for certainty degrees in consulting systems. 02092

**Hajičová, E.**
On one aspect of natural-language based knowledge acquisition. 03571

**Hajnicz, E.**
Absolute dates and relative dates in an inferential system on temporal dependencies between events. 02235

**Haken, H.**
Information compression in biological systems. 01253

**Hakkinen, M. T.**
GENIE: a modifiable computer-based task for experiments in human-computer interaction. HCI-0194 †

**Halasz, F. G.**
Notecards in a nutshell. 0810
Reflections on NoteCards: seven issues for the next generation of hypermedia systems. HCI-0293 †

**Halasz, M.**
Jet engine technical advisor (JETA). 02974

**Hale, D. P.**
GMMS: global model management system: a conceptional design framework for model management systems for distributed decision support systems. 03484

**Hale, M. W.**
Status of trusted DBMS interpretations. 03585

**Hales, G. W.**
The disabled. 0148

**Haliburton, J. (Ed.)**
APL in transition. § 02793

**Hall, A.**
The evaluation of project support environments for the STARTS user guide. 0173
Tool interfaces in integrated project support environments. 03506

**Hall, M. R.**
A mission planning architecture for an autonomous vehicle. 02939

**Hall, R.**
Distributed tactical decisionmaking: conceptual framework and empirical results. 01885

**Hall, S. B.**
Evaluating the impact of camera placement on teleoperator efficiency. 02940

**Hall, W.**
Where have all the girls gone? 02689
The art of programming. HCI-0095 †

**Hall, W. S.**
Theoretical issues in the investigation of words of internal report. 0354

**Hallam, J. (Ed.)**
Advances in artificial intelligence. § 03546

**Haller, R. I.**
Captive...a new tool. 03129

**Hallett, S.**
XVISION: a comprehensive software system for image processing research, education, and applications. 03124

**Halperin, M.**
Datastream: numeric data—all you can use at a fixed price. 02525

**Halpern, J. Y.**
Reasoning about knowledge: an overview. 03167

**Halpern, J. Y. (Ed.)**
Theoretical aspects of reasoning about knowledge. § 03559

**Halpern, P.**
An incidence-matrix-driven panel system for the IBM PC. 01814

**Halpin, S. M.**
Adaptive user interfaces for planning and decision aids in $C^3I$ systems. 01887

**Halstead-Nussloch, R.**
The design of phone-based interfaces for consumers. 0878
Shaping user input: a strategy for natural language dialogue design. 02067

**Halton, T. B.**
Designing screens for people to use easily. 01531

**Halversen, B. W.**
Interface usage measurements in a user interface management system. 03115

**Hamm, R. M.**
Direct comparison of the relative efficiency on intuitive and analytical cognition. 01896

**Hammer, J. M.**
Aiding the operator during novel fault diagnosis. 01858
Significance testing of rules in rule-based models of human problem solving. 01867
Analysis of user procedural compliance in controlling a simulated process. 01879
A display editor with random access and continuous control. HCI-0140 †

**Hammer, M.**
How executives can shape their company's information systems. 01707

**Hammond, K. R.**
Direct comparison of the relative efficiency on intuitive and analytical cognition. 01896

**Hammond, N.**
The role of cognitive psychology in user-interface design. 0327
Principles from the psychology of skill acquisition. 0332
Travel around a learning support environment: rambling, orienteering or touring? 02900
The travel metaphor as design principle and training aid for navigating around complex systems. 03195
User programs: a way to match computer systems and human cognition. 03271

**Hammond, W. E.**
Patient management systems: the early years. 02852

**Hammwohner, R.**
Informational zooming: an interaction model for the graphical access to text knowledge bases. 03073

**Hampson, S. E.**
Disjunctive models of boolean category learning. 01262

**Hampton, J. A.**
Principles from the psychology of language. 0333

**Hancock, M.**
Subject searching behaviour at the library catalogue and at the shelves: implications for online interactive catalogues. 02302

**Hancock, P. A.**
Human Factors Psychology. ● 0397
Adaptive control in human-machine systems. 0405
A model for evaluating stress effects of work with display units. 03756

**Hancock, P. J.B.**
On the acquisition of object concepts from sensory data. 03959

**Handloser, F. T.**
Prototypes from standard user interface management systems. 01370

**Hanna, J.**
Logic for learning. 0284

Learning environment criteria. 0285

**Hannabuss, S.**
A folklore view of information. 01222
Dialogue and the search for information. 01223

**Hannafin, M.**
The accuracy of cognitive monitoring during computer-based instruction. 02281

**Hannafin, M. J.**
The effects of orienting, processing, and practicing activities on learning from interactive video. 02289

**Hanrahan, M.**
Office-by-example: an integrated office system and database manager. 01159

**Hansen, G. W.**
Procedural and non-procedural query languages revisited: a comparison of relational algebra and relational calculus. 02146
Human performance in relational algebra, tuple calculus, and domain calculus. 02208

**Hansen, J. V.**
Procedural and non-procedural query languages revisited: a comparison of relational algebra and relational calculus. 02146
Human performance in relational algebra, tuple calculus, and domain calculus. 02208

**Hansen, W. J.**
Reading and writing with computers: a framework for explaining differences in performance. HCI-0204 †

**Hanson, A. R.**
Vision, brain, and cooperative computation: an overview. 0015

**Hanson, A. R. (Ed.)**
Vision, brain, and cooperative computation. ● 0014

**Hanson, R.**
Toward hypertext publishing. 01075

**Hanson, S. J.**
Programmer perceptions of productivity and programming tools. HCI-0099 †

**Hansson, T.**
The back during prolonged sitting. 03706

**Hapeshi, K.**
Human factors and the problems of evaluation in the design of speech systems interfaces. 03192

**Happ, A. L.**
Creating consistency in the user interface: opinions and procedures of software developments experts. 01012

**Harandi, M. T.**
Rule base management using meta knowledge. 01081

**Harbeson, M. M.**
Beware the reliability of slope scores for individuals. 01727

**Harbusch, K.**
XTRA: a natural-language access system to expert systems. 02244

**Hardman, L.**
Evaluating the usability of the Glasgow online. 01808
Hypertext tips: experiences in developing a hypertext tutorial. 03236

**Hardwick, M.**
ROSE: An object-oriented database system for interactive computer graphics applications. 03845

**Hare, D. F.**
The PegaSys System: pictures as formal documentation of large programs. HCI-0146 †

**Harhen, J.**
MRP/MRP II. 0620

**Harke, U.**
Embedding graphics into documents by using a graphic-editor. 0266

**Harker, S.**
The use of prototyping and simulation in the development of large-scale applications. 01411
The supplier's role in the design of products for organisations. 01412

**Harker, S. D.P.**
the role of user prototyping in the system design process. 03747

**Harless, W. G.**
An interactive videodisc drama: The case of Frank hall. 02285

**Harman, D.**
IRX: an information retrieval system for experimentation and user applications. 01076
Towards interactive query expansion. 03067

**Harms, J.**
EM2—a Modula-2 programming environment. 02392

**Harold, F. G.**
The two cultures in computing. 03018
Experimental evaluation of program quality using external metrics. HCI-0176 †

**Harper-Marinick, M.**
Designing interactive, responsive instruction: a set of procedures. 0274

**Harr, H.**
Human interfaces in a legal expert system. 03164

**Harrap, C.**
Enhancing search results by editing, analysis and packaging. 02035

**Harris, J. E.**
A viewdata-structure editor designed around a task/action mapping. 03269

**Harris, J. R.**
SEE: a safe editing environment; human-computer interaction for programmers. 03225

**Harris, K.**
Online use and end-users in media and advertising: an overview. 01216
End-users: threat, challenge or myth? 01221
Time-life, world reporter and the secretary: experiments with end-users. 02325

**Harris, L. R.**
Natural languages. 0136

**Harris, M.**
The IE's future role in improving knowledge. 01903

**Harris, M. D.**
Introduction to natural language processing. ● HCI-0065 †

**Harrison, M. A.**
Multiple representation document development (extende abstract). 03518

**Harrison, M. D.**
Principles and interaction models for window managers. 03264
Interaction models and the principled design of interactive systems. 03799

**Harrison, M. D. (Ed.)**
People and computers: designing for usability. § 03244

**Harrison, P.**
Evaluating RECONSIDER: a computer program for diagnostic prompting. HCI-0410 †

**Harshman, R.**
Using latent semantic analysis to improve access to textual information. 02901

**Harslem, E.**
Designing the star user interface. 0089
The star user interface: an overview. 03171

**Hart, A.**
The political economy of interactive video in British higher education. 0512

**Hart, L.**
User services consulting supportr tools at the NASA numerical aerodynamic simula. 03161

**Harter, S. P.**
Online information retrieval: concepts, principles, and techniques. ●HCI-0046 †

**Hartley, R. T.**
The MDR algorithm and its application to the generation of explanations for novel events. 02174

**Hartman, D.**
The interactive planning work station: a graphics-based UNIX tool for application users and developers. 03860

**Hartmanis, J. (Ed.)**
Experiences with Distributed Systems. § 03881
Uncertainty and intelligent systems. § 04030

VDM—The Way Ahead. § 04033

**Hartmann, G.**
Mapping images to a hierarchical data structure—a way to knowledge-based pattern recognition. 03954

**Hartness, K. T.**
A prototype autonomous agent for crew and equipment retrieval in space. 02994

**Hartson, H. R.**
Task-oriented representation of asynchronous user interfaces. 0851
An interactive environment for dialogue development: its design, use and evaluation; or, is aide useful? 0920
Human-computer interface development: concepts and systems for its management. HCI-0444 †

**Hartson, H. R. (Ed.)**
Advances in human-computer interaction. ● 0407

**Harvey, D. R.**
Open-loop experiments for modeling the human eye movement system. 01870
Development and sensitivity analysis of adaptive predictor for human eye movement model. 02681

**Harvey, W. A.**
Automating knowledge acquisition for aerial image interpretation. 01470

**Harwood, K.**
Temporal resolution: an insight into the video display terminal (VDT) "problem". 01754

**Hary, J. M.**
Users' preferences among different techniques for displaying the evaluation of LISP functions in an interactive debugger. 02863

**Haselager, P.**
An interdisciplinary approach to human factors in telematic systems. A review of the problems and possible solutions by a COST-11 ter working group. 01440

**Haselkorn, M. P.**
The future of "writing" for the computer industry. HCI-0150 †

**Hasell, M. J.**
Community design and gaming/simulation: Comparison of communications techniques in participatory design sessions. 02596

**Hasemer, T.**
A very friendly software environment for SOLO. 0743

**Hashimoto, O.**
INTERA/P: a user interface prototyping tool. 03205

**Haskell, G.**
Multimodal detection and recognition performance of sonar operators. 01709

**Hasselmeier, H. F.**
Quill: An extensible system for editing documents of mixed type. 03517

**Hastings, H. M.**
Advances in cognitive science. 02721

**Hastings, H. M. (Ed.)**
Advances in Cognitive Science. § 02720

**Hatcher, M. E.**
Predicting end-user acceptance of microcomputers in the workplace. 02147

**Hativa, N.**
The microcomputer as a classroom audio visual device: the concept, and prospects. HCI-0223 †

**Haton, J.**
Artificial intelligence techniques in man–machine communication. 01459

**Haton, J. (Ed.)**
Fundamentals in computer understanding: speech and vision. ● 0416

**Haton, M.**
Artificial intelligence techniques in man–machine communication. 01459

**Haug, F.**
Automation and work culture. 03750

**Hauge, T.**
Event-driven user interfaces based on quasi-parallelism. 03111

**Haupt, B.**
Why reading was slower from CRT displays than from paper. 0797
Reading from CRT displays can be as fast as reading from paper. 01758

**Hauptmann, A. G.**
Speech and gestures for graphic image manipulation. 0859
Talking to computers: an empirical investigation. 02186

**Hauser, J.**
The design of a flexible distributed testbeb for communication systems. 03538

**Hausser, R.**
Left-associative grammar: an informal outline. 01558

**Hawaleshka, O.**
User friendly micro computer program for solving fractional and linear programming problems. 01509

**Hawk, S. R.**
Differences in analyst's attitudes towards information systems development: evidence and implications. 01935

**Hawkins, D. J.**
Multidimensional attribute analyhsis and pattern recognition for seismic interpretation. 02530

**Hawkins, J.**
The interpretation of Logo in practice. 0576
Logo and development of thinking skills. 0582
Informing the design of software through context-based research. 0584
Practices of novices and experts in critical inquiry. 0585

**Hawkinson, L.**
Process control with the G2 real-time expert system. 02934

**Hawley, P. M.**
TNT: a talking tutor 'n' trainer for teaching use of interactive computer systems. 0895

**Hawley, R. (Ed.)**
Artificial intelligence programming environments. ● 0420

**Hayden, B. A.**
Understanding & using application software. ● 0626

**Haydon, G. B.**
A unification of software and hardware; a new tool for human thought. 02314

**Hayes, B. C.**
Assaying and isolating individual differences in searching a hierarchical file system. 01747

**Hayes, P. J.**
Using a knowledge base to drive an expert system interface with a natural language component. 0430
Classifying users: a hard look at some controversial issues. 0902

**Haylett, G. M.**
Advanced diagnostics: a PASCAL interactive system. 01958

**Hays, H. D.**
Interactive graphics: a tool for beginning programming students in discovering solutions to novel problems. 01038

**Hays, R. T.**
Maintenance training simulator fidelity and individual differences in transfer of training. 01722

**Hearn, D.**
Computer graphics. ● HCI-0069 †

**Heath, A. M.**
Colour coding scales and computer graphics. 03864

**Heather, M.**
Cybernetic consciousness. 01605

**Heaton, N. (Ed.)**
Designing end-user interfaces: state of the art report 15.8. ● 0422

**Heaton, N. O.**
Knowledge-based systems: implications for human-computer interfaces. ● HCI-0060 †

**Hecht-Nielsen, R.**
Neurocomputing. 01836

**Heck, G. L.**
Physiology and psychophysics in taste and smell. 04009

**Hecker, G.**
A user interface for database creation use and maintenance. 02791

**Hedeen, A.**
The effects of restricted syntax on menu-based interaction. 0775

**Hedin, C.**
A colour atlas for graphical displays. 03726
Experimental evaluation of dialogue types for data entry. HCI-0115 †

**Hedin, G.**
The Mjo:.KC /lner environment: direct interaction with abstractions. 03794

**Hedman, L.**
Focusing variability during visual work. 03759

**Hedman, L. R.**
Qualified CAD work: an intensive case study. 03763

**Heerjee, K. B.**
The design and evaluation of an animated programming environment. 03220

**Hefley, W. E.**
Designing real-time, decision support computer-human interaction. 0982

**Heibert-Dodd, K. L.**
Expanding the domain of systems analysis. 02587

**Heid, J.**
Power windows: maximizing the speed and performance of Windows 2.0 & Windows 386. ● 0423

**Heidlage, J. F.**
Natural language with discrete speech as a mode for human-to-machine. HCI-0355 †

**Heikkila, J.**
Strategies for managing end user computing. 02436

**Heikkilá, J.**
The dual role of information centers: an assessment of end user computing management strategies. 01942

**Heimke, G.**
Automated design and analysis system for design of custom orthopedic implants. 02931

**Heine, M. H.**
A logic assistant for the database searcher. 02001

**Heines, J. M.**
Screen design strategies for computer-assisted instruction. ● 0424

**Heinrich, S.**
An expert system for system design. 02441

**Heinz, W.**
DATENBANK-DIALOG: a German language interface for relational databases. 01208

**Heise, G. F.**
Barriers to cooperative computerized circulation systems in public libraries. 02573

**Hekmatpour, S.**
A notation for specifying menus. 01111

**Helander, M. G.**
Task allocation between humans and robots in manufacturing. 0559
Methods for field evaluation of safety in a robotics workplace. 03408

**Helbig, H.**
Necessary contributions of cognitive psychology to computer knowledge representation and manipulation systems. 03598

**Held, J.**
Computer aided application program synthesis for industrial robots. 0606

**Helferich, O. K.**
Expert system applications in customer service. 03101

**Helgerson, L. W.**
User interfaces for CD'ROM PACs. 02466

**Helman, D.**
A rule-based system for interactive proposal evaluation. 02927

**Heltne, M. M.**
ICE: information center expert: a consultation system for resource allocation. 0781

A consultation system for information center resource allocation. 03100

**Henderson Jr., A.**
A multiple, virtual-workspace interface to support user task switching. 0813

**Henderson Jr., D. A.**
The Trillium user interface design environment. 0082
The Trillium user interface design environment. 0919

**Henderson, D. A., Jr.**
Rooms: the use of multiple virtual workspaces to reduce space contention in a window-based graphical user interface. 01151

**Henderson, P. (Ed.)**
Practical Software Development Environments. § 03048

**Henderson, T. C.**
A survey of general-purpose manipulation. 02259

**Hendler, J. (Ed.)**
Expert systems: the user interface. • 0433

**Hendler, J. A.**
Introduction: designing interfaces for expert systems. 0426

**Hendler, J. A. (Ed.)**
Expert systems: the user interface. • 0425

**Hendrick, H. W.**
Human factors in organizational design and management. 0406

**Hendrickson, J. J.**
Performance, preference, and visual scan patterns on a menu-based system: implications for interface design. 0855

**Hendriks, L.**
Processing demands, effort, and individual differences in four different vigilance tasks. 01801

**Hendrix, G.**
Developing a natural language interface to complex data. 0393

**Henik, A.**
Radiation detection by ear and by eye. 01732

**Henneman, R. L.**
Measures of human problem solving performance in fault diagnosis tasks. 0655

**Henny, C.**
Trends in printer technology. 01624

**Henrion, M.**
Separating content from form: A language for formatting on-line documentation and dialog. 02781

**Henry, R. R.**
Design and implementation of the UW Illustrated compiler. 03059

**Henry, T. R.**
Using active data in a UIMS. 03121

**Hensel, H.**
Standardization aspects on software for CAD of control systems. 01565

**Henty, M.**
The user at the online catalogue. 02462

**Her, C.**
An experimental study of Chinese information displays on VDTs. 01784

**Herczeg, M.**
Knowledge-based systems and communication between computers and human beings. 0192

**Herken, R. (Ed.)**
The Universal Turing Machine. § 03777

**Herman, G. T.**
Manipulation of 3D imagery. 0557

**Herman, I.**
Managing multiple context-frames through GKS. 01389

**Herman, L. M.**
Delphi: an intelligent interface for a dolphin communication laboratory. 02989

**Hernandez, E. F.**
Motivations and behaviors of software professionals. 03003

**Herot, C. F.**
Graphical user interfaces. HCI-0133 †

**Herrstrom, D. S.**
Hypertext in context. 0114

**Herschberg, I. S.**
The hackers' comfort. 01544

**Hersh, H.**
The human factor: Designing computer systems for people. 0076
Integrating human factors and software development. 02882

**Hertz, J. A.**
Memory networks with asymmetric bonds. 02740
A cortical network model for early vision processing. 03957

**Hertzberger, L. O.**
The architecture of fifth generation inference computers. HCI-0093 †

**Hesketh, B.**
An application of computerized fuzzy graphics rating scale to the psychological measurement of individual differences. 02200

**Hesketh, T.**
An application of computerized fuzzy graphics rating scale to the psychological measurement of individual differences. 02200

**Hess, R. A.**
Automation effects in a multiloop manual control system. 01865
A qualitative model of human interaction with complex dynamic systems. 01891

**Hetrick, D. L.**
Power plant simulation and reactor safety. 02682

**Hevner, A. R.**
A box structured methodology for solving business problems. 03483
Executive workstations: issues and requirements. HCI-0288 †

**Hewett, M.**
The development of an automated flight test management system for flight test planning and monitoring. 02928

**Hewett, T.**
Tools and methodology for user interface development. 01057

**Hewett, T. J.**
The Drexel disk: an electronic "Guidebook". 03198

**Hewett, T. T.**
On designing for usability: an application of four key principles. 0923
The role of iterative evaluation in designing systems for usability. 03255

**Hewitt, C.**
Concurrency in intelligent systems. 01169

**Hewitt, J.**
Text processing by speech: dialogue design and usability issues in the provision of a system for disabled users. HCI-0357 †

**Hewitt, S.**
The interactive specification of human animation. 03292

**Hidai, Y.**
An operations advisor for an on-line computer banking system with graphics interface. 02983

**Higgs, M.**
The evaluation of project support environments for the STARTS user guide. 0173

**Highsmith, A. L.**
Library processing systems and the man/machine interface. 02045

**Hiki, S.**
Influence of palate shape on lingual articulation. 02642

**Hilbush, M. R.**
Experiencing artificial intelligence: an interactive approach to the IBM PC. • 0550
Experiencing artificial intelligence: an interactive approach for the APPLE. • 0551

**Hildreth, C.**
Online library catalog systems: an analysis of user errors. 02128

**Hildreth, C. R.**
Online library catalogues as information retrieval systems: what can we learn from research? 04040

**Hildreth, E. C.**
Computing the velocity field along contours. 03331

**Hilinski, T. E.**
Super consulting for supercomputer users: a philosophy of user support. 03145

**Hill, C. R.**
Using hypertext to overcome the knowledge base development bottleneck: a case study. 02914

**Hill, D.**
Speech and expression: a computer solution to face animation. 03293

**Hill, M. D.**
Effects of breadth, depth and number responses on computer menu search performance. 02192

**Hill, R.**
Issues and techniques in touch-sensitive tablet input. 0063
UIMSs: threat or menace? 02889

**Hill, R. D.**
The run-time structure of UIMS-supported applications. 01059
Some important features and issues in user interface management systems. 01064
Supporting concurrency, communication, and synchronization in human-computer interaction—the Sassafras UIMS. HCI-0102 †

**Hill, W. C.**
How some advice fails. 0824
Misconceived misconceptions? 02881
Justified advice: a semi-naturalistic study of advisory strategies. 02887

**Hillis, W. D.**
Parallel computers for AI databases. 0183

**Hillman, D.**
INQUEST: A prototype intelligence tool. 02918

**Hillyard, S. A.**
The spatial allocation of visual attention as indexed by event-related brain potentials. 01739

**Hiltz, S. R.**
Learning modes and subsequent use of computer-mediated communication systems. 0912
Collaborative learning in a virtual classroom: highlights of findings. 02826
Online communities. • HCI-0051 †

**Hines, W. G. S.**
A multivariate solution for cyclic data, applied in modelling locomotor forces. 01252

**Hino, K.**
An object-oriented framework of pattern recognition systems. 01133

**Hinrichs, E. W.**
Tense, qualifiers, and contexts. 01346

**Hintikka, J.**
Model minimization—an alternative to circumscription. 02263

**Hinton, G. E.**
Schemata and sequential thought processes in PDP models. 0630
Learning in parallel networks: simulating learning in a probabilistic system. HCI-0332 †

**Hinton, G. E. (Ed.)**
Neural network architectures for artificial intelligence. • 0434

**Hirabayashi, F.**
Information retrieval using impression of documents as a clue. 03065

**Hirai, S.**
MEISTER: a model enhanced intelligent and skillful teleoperational robot system. 03562

**Hirakawa, M.**
Visual programming—toward realization of user-friendly programming environments. 03493
ARES: a relational database with the capability of performing flexible interpretation of queries. HCI-0248 †

**Hird, E.**
Operator work load: when is enough enough? HCI-0222 †

**Hirsch, B.**
Production control in the aircraft industry. 0624

**Hirsch, M.**
The Logix system user manual version 1.21. 0675

**Hirsch, P.**
Interfaces for knowledge-base builders' control knowledge and application-specific procedures. 01810

**Hirschberg, J.**
Anticipating false implicatures: cooperative responses in question-answer systems. 03178

**Hirschheim, R.**
Issues and approaches to appraising technological change in the office: A consequentialist perspective. 0043
Information systems and user resistance: theory and practice. 01409

**Hirschheim, R. A.**
Office automation: a social and organizational perspective. ● HCI-0048 †

**Hirschheim, R. A. (Ed.)**
Critical issues in information systems research. ● 0153
Office Systems. § 03354

**Hitch, G. J.**
Principles from the psychology of memory: Part I-Working memory. 0330
Empirical evaluation of map interfaces. 03276

**Hitchcock, R. J.**
Perspective traffic display format and airline pilot traffic avoidance. 01748
The emergence of Zipf's law: Spontaneous encoding optimization by users of a command language. 01875

**Hix, D.**
Human-computer interface development: concepts and systems for its management. HCI-0444 †

**Hix, D. (Ed.)**
Advances in human-computer interaction. ● 0407

**Hix, D. H.**
An interactive environment for dialogue development: its design, use and evaluation; or, is aide useful? 0920

**Hjelmquist, E.**
Psychological aspects on blind peoples's reading of radio-distributed daily newspapers. 03700

**Ho, C. P.**
The effects of orienting objectives and review on learning from interactive video. 02287

**Ho, F.**
The multimedia object presentation manager of MINOS: a symmetric approach. 01083

**Höhne, K. H.**
Software tools for the development of pictorial information systems in medicine—the ISQL experience. 03980

**Höhne, K. H. (Ed.)**
Pictorial information systems in medicine. § 03976

**Hörtnagel, C.**
DATENBANK-DIALOG: a German language interface for relational databases. 01208

**Hoc, J.**
Cognitive psychology of planning. ● 0435
Strategies in controlling a continuous process with long response latencies: needs for computer support to diagnosis. 02217

**Hochberg, J.**
Machines should not see as people do, but must know how people see. 01465

**Hochgesang, G.**
Office-by-example: an integrated office system and database manager. 01159

**Hockenos, W.**
Postscript: computers and the modeling of mind. HCI-0348 †

**Hodge, D. C.**
U.S. Army field robotics focus and key technology issues. 03402

**Hodge, M. H.**
History of the TDS medical information system. 02851

**Hodges, M. E.**
Investigations in multimedia design documentation. 0116

**Hoeber, T.**
:20My user interface is the best because...". 0856
Face to face with Open Look. 01305

**Hoeppner, W.**
Talking it over: the natural language dialog system HAM-ANS. 0165

**Hoerger, C. R.B.**
Product engineering in the CIM environment. 03376

**Hoffman, D. D.**
Codon constraints on closed 2D shapes. 02704

**Hoffman, G. W.**
Neurons with hysteresis form a network that can learn without any changes in synaptic connection strengths. 02741

**Hoffman, J.**
Psychological methods for assembling procedures in text management systems. 03600

**Hoffman, R.**
The problem of extracting the knowledge of experts. 01195
Computer quantification of delta activity in sleep EEG. 01491

**Hoffmann, C. M.**
Model generation and modification for dynamic systems from geometric data. 0604

**Hoffmann, G. W.**
A teachable neural network based on an unorthodox neuron. 02561

**Hoffmann, K.**
Innate and learned components in a simple visuo-motor reflex. 03965

**Hoffmann, T. R.**
Managing information systems for effectiveness and humanity: applying research of organizational behavior. 01932

**Hofmann, M. O.**
A generic strategy for diagnostic assistance: the technician's assistant. 02957

**Hogg, I.**
Authoring systems for ICAI. 0469

**Hogg, J. S.**
OTM: specifying office tasks. 03039

**Hogley, J. R.**
Will you be replaced by a knowledge base? 02055

**Hokansson, N. C. I.**
Change and the systems person. 02417

**Holcomb, R.**
The effect of windows on man-machine interfaces. 01048

**Holdaway, K.**
User system interaction standards. 01386

**Hollan, J.**
CHI research at MCC. 0842

**Hollan, J. D.**
Direct manipulation interfaces (excerpt). 0073

**Holland, J. H.**
Induction: processes of inference, learning, and discovery. • HCI-0064 †

**Hollands, J. G.**
Menu organization and user expertise in information search tasks. 01761

**Hollberg, U.**
Experiences with the development of a portable network operating system. 03882

**Holligan, P. J.**
Access to academic networks. • HCI-0050 †

**Hollnagel, E.**
Cognitive engineering in complex dynamic worlds. • 0436
Cognitive systems engineering: new wine in new bottles. 02078
Information and reasoning in intelligent decision support systems. 02173
Failure analysis of information systems: reflections on the use of expert systems in information systems. 03811
Cognitive models, cognitive tasks, and information retrieval. HCI-0331 †

**Holm, J.**
Intelligent help systems. 01959

**Holman, C. L.**
Edmas: an object-oriented, locally distributed mail system. 01857

**Holmberg, P. C.**
Birth defects, course of pregnancy, and work with VDUs: a Finnish case-referent study. 03689

**Holmes, J. N.**
A parallel formant synthesizer for machine voice output. HCI-0396 †

**Holsapple, C. W.**
A framework for designing adaptive DSS Interfaces. 01672
Flexible user interface decision support systems. 03473

**Holsapple, C. W. (Ed.)**
Decision support systems: theory and application. § 03788

**Holsti, N.**
A session editor with incremental execution functions. 02637

**Holt, R. W.**
The effects of structured, multi-level documentation. 0907

**Holton, D.**
Reading from screen versus paper: there is no difference. 02175

**Holtzblatt, K. A.**
Articulating the experience of transparency: an example of field research techniques. 0977

**Holynski, M.**
User-adaptive computer graphics. 02209

**Holyoak, K. J.**
Induction: processes of inference, learning, and discovery. • HCI-0064 †

**Honda, N.**
Multivariate data representation and analysis by face pattern using facial expression characteristics. HCI-0394 †

**Hong, B.**
CAD Data management using object-oriented paradigms. 02958

**Hong, S. N.**
Knowledge representation for model libraries. 03479

**Hong, W.**
A knowledge-based approach to computer vision systems. 03302

**Hooper, K.**
Interactive multimedia. • 0011

**Hopcroft, J. E.**
Model generation and modification for dynamic systems from geometric data. 0604

**Hopert, D.**
A tentative implementation of VDAFS. HCI-0422 †

**Hopfield, J. J.**
Collective computation, content-addressable memory, and optimization problems. 0004

**Hopgood, F. R. (Ed.)**
Methodology of window management. § 03923

**Hopgood, F. R.A. (Ed.)**
Advances in computer graphics II. • 0437

**Hopkins, D.**
An empirical comparison of pie vs. linear menus. 02871

**Hopkins, R. H.**
Representations of perceived relations among the properties and variables of a complex system. 01892

**Hoppe, H. U.**
Cognitive user interface laboratory, GMD-IPSI. 0870
Learning and transfer for text and graphics editing with a direct manipulation interface. 0900
Task-oriented parsing - a diagnostic method to be used adaptive systems. 02896

**Horacek, H.**
Choice of words in the generation process of a natural language interface. 01206

**Horaud, R.**
New methods for matching 3-D objects with single perspective views. 01844

**Horn, D. N.**
The rapport multimedia conferencing system. 03037

**Horowitz, E. (Ed.)**
Programming languages: a grand tour (2nd ed.). • HCI-0018 †

**Horton, W.**
From database to hypertext via electronic publishing: an information odyssey. 0122

**Horwitz, S.**
Relations and attributes. 01103

**Hosein, R. W.**
The man-machine integration. 03384

**Hosie, P.**
Adopting interactive videodisc technology for education. 0272

**Hosni, Y.**
Knowledge-based system for task analysis and reliability enhancement. 01516

**Houghton, R.**
Characteristics and functions of software environments: an overview. 01145

**Houk, J. C.**
A model of the motor servo: Incorporating nonlinear spindle receptor and muscle mechanical properties. 01273

**Houle, J. L.**
A graphics interface for interactive simulation of packet-switched networks. 03869

**Houri, A.**
The Logix system user manual version 1.21. 0675

**House, D. H.**
Depth and detours: an essay on visually guided behavior. 0018

**Hovy, E. H.**
Language generation by computer. HCI-0342 †

**Howard, C.**
Expert system tool evaluation. 02718

**Howard, G. S.**
User's complaints: Information system problems from the user's perspective. 02416
Computer anxiety in management: myth or reality? HCI-0232 †

**Howard, J. H.**
Andrew: a distributed personal computing environment. HCI-0091 †

**Howard, M. J.**
Knowledge elicitation: dissociating conscious reflections from automatic processes. HCI-0337 †

**Howard, R.**
Systems design and social responsibility: the political implications of "computer-supported cooperative work". A commentary. 02516

**Howard, R. A.**
Decision analysis: practice and promise. 02480

**Howarth, I.**
Psychology and information technology. HCI-0225 †

**Howe, C. L.**
Getting straight again. 01658

**Howey, K.**
New technology work aids for the physically disabled. 03273

**Howland, J. E.**
Design of a new user interface for APL. 02796

**Hoyle, B. S.**
PC networks: usage and graphics tutorials. 01499

**Hruschka, P.**
ProMod at the age of 5. 03802

**Hsu, C.**
Adaptive information systems control: A reliability-based approach. 02345
An expert system framework for forecasting method selection. 03468

**Hu, D.**
C/C++ for expert systems: "unleashes the power of a artificial intelligence". ● 0439

**Huang, C. C.**
The MIDAS database system. 02387
The MIDAS display system. 02388

**Huang, K.**
Reference models, window systems, and concurrency. 01058
Office-by-example: an integrated office system and database manager. 01159

**Huang, K. T.**
Visual business graphics query interface. 03840

**Huang, T. S.**
Determining 3-D motion parameters of a rigid body: a vector-geometrical approach. 03339

**Hubbard, K.**
Logic programmable natural language processor of a knowledge-base management system. 02965

**Hubbard, W. E.**
VLSI implementation of a neural network model. 01363

**Hubbold, R. J. (Ed.)**
Advances in computer graphics II. ● 0437

**Huber, P. J.**
Environments for supporting statistical strategy. 0322

**Hudlicka, E.**
Visual system browser. 0995

**Hudson, K.**
Introducing CAL: a practical guide to writing computer-assisted learning programs. ● HCI-0079 †

**Hudson, S.**
Implementing a user interface as a system of attributes. 03052

**Hudson, S. E.**
The run-time structure of UIMS-supported applications. 01059
UIMS support for direct manipulation interfaces. 01065
Semantic feedback in the Higgens UIMS. 01851
Using active data in a UIMS. 03121
The Higgens UIMS and its efficient implementation of Undo. 03861
A generator of direct manipulation office systems. HCI-0250 †

**Huff, S. L.**
Microcomputer applications: an empirical look at usage. 01949
Expansion and control of end-user computing. 02347
User development of applications: a study of a model of success. 02807
Change, attitude to change, and decision support system success. HCI-0296 †

# AUTHOR INDEX

**Huffman, G. D.**
User facilities for engineering support stations. 01512

**Hug, M. A.**
Libraries as programs preserved within compiler continuations. 01102

**Hughes, C. T.**
Effects of decision support training and cognitive style on decision process attributes. 02346

**Hughes, G. T.**
Managing the work station environment. 02430
The user designer/developer and the user work station. 02431

**Hughes, J. A.**
Male/female programmer and systems analyst Job performance. 03020

**Hugler, H.**
Subjective load in introducing visual display units. 03627

**Hull, M. E. C.**
Uniforms: an automatic forms facility. 01628

**Hull, R.**
Relative information capacity of simple relational database schemata. 02579

**Hulliger, M.**
Proprioceptive feedback for sensory-motor control. 04008
An iterative and interactive simulation method to reconstruct unknown inputs contributing to known outputs of neuronal systems. 04018

**Hullot, J. (Ed.)**
ECOOP '87. § 03790

**Hulme, A. J.**
Professional education and subsequent careers in library/information work: a follow-up study of former students on the MA/MSc information studies course at the University of Sheffield. 02336

**Humbert, G.**
Production control in the aircraft industry. 0624

**Humphrey, S.**
Illustrated description of an interactive knowledge based indexing system. 03076

**Humphreys, P. A.**
Process control and people at General Motors' Delta engine plant. 03431

**Humphries, C.**
Implications for education and training. HCI-0430 †

**Humrich, A.**
Problems associated with the off-line programming of robots. 01241
Studying depth cues in a three-dimensional computer graphics workstation. 02117

**Hung, M. S.**
Network generation using the Prufer code. 01536

**Hunt, R. G.**
Propaedeutics of decision-making: supporting managerial learning and innovation. 01667

**Hunt, R. M.**
A fuzzy rule-based model of human problem solving. 0656
Search technology, Inc. 0872
A fuzzy rule-based model of human problem solving. HCI-0359 †

**Hunt, V. R.**
The FAA's Advanced Automation System: strategies for future air traffic control systems. 01357

**Hunter, D.**
Causality and maximum entropy updating. 02076

**Huntzinger, R.**
IRX: an information retrieval system for experimentation and user applications. 01076

**Hurley, W. D.**
Design and implementation of an object-oriented user interface management system. 0412
An object-oriented user interface management system. 01055

**Husband, T. M. (Ed.)**
Education and training in robotics. • 0440

**Hutchins, E. L.**
Direct manipulation interfaces (excerpt). 0073

**Hutchison, K. K.**
Computer aided concurrent design for printed wiring boards. 02981

**Hutchison, L. (Ed.)**
User Services. § 03127

**Hutchison, S. E. (Ed.)**
Computers : the user perspective. • 0705

**Hutt, A.**
Human factors in the IT specification process. 01372
Describing a product opportunity: a method of understanding the users' environment. 03194

**Huuhtanen, P.**
Effects of computerization on job demands and stress: the correspondence of subjective and objective data. 03622

**Huys, J.**
The efficiency of letter perception in function of color combinations: a study of video-screen colors. 03616

**Hwang, C. J.**
A dietary recommendation expert system using OPS5. 03498

**Hwang, S.**
An experimental study of Chinese information displays on VDTs. 01784
Human supervisory control in flexible manufacturing systems: Allocation of functions and system size. 02456

**Hyder, D. A.**
System user/system implementer: a joint responsibility for success. 01535

**Hyder, S. S.**
Character recognition of cursive scripts. 02961

**Hyman, M. I.**
Microsoft windows 2.0 program development. • 0446

**Iberall, A. R.**
A neural model of human prehension. 04072

**Iberall, T.**
Schemas that integrate vision and touch for hand control. 0026

**Ichikawa, T.**
A high level language-based computing enviornment to support production and execution of reliable programs. 01855
Visual programming—toward realization of user-friendly programming environments. 03493
ARES: a relational database with the capability of performing flexible interpretation of queries. HCI-0248 †
An image processing language with ICON-assisted navigation. HCI-0387 †

**Ida, K.**
Interactive multiple objective linear programming system implemented on a microcomputer. 01508

**IFIP Working Group 2.7**
Concepts in user interfaces: a reference model for command and response languages. § 03872

**Igbaria, M.**
Microcomputer applications: an empirical look at usage. 01949

**Ihara, J.**
Extension of conditional probability and measures of belief and disbelief in a hypothesis based on uncertain evidence. 01846

**Iida, T.**
Influence of CRT refresh rates on accommodation aftereffects. 03731

**Iivari, J.**
Impact of prototyping on user information satisfaction during the IS specification phase. 01955

**Ikeda, H.**
Pneumatic manipulating system provided with active compliance function. 03426

**Imam, I.**
Robot simulation and off-line programming—an integrated CAE-CAD approach. 0599

**Imanaka, T.**
Analogical program synthesis from program components. 03920

**Ince, D. C.**
A coherent specification method for the human interface to documentation systems. 0269

**Incerpi, J.**
Centaur: the system. 01136

**Inder, R.**
Experience of constructing a fault localisation expert system using an AI toolkit. 02923

**Indow, T.**
Alleys on an apparent frontoparallel plane. 02374

**Indulski, J.**
Task-load and endocrinological risk for pregnancy in women VDU operators. 03692

**Infante, C.**
CRTs—present and future. 01985

**Ing, B.**
Are there subtle changes in vision after use of VDTs? 03733

**Ingalls, D.**
Fabrik: a visual programming environment. 01130

**Ingraffea, A. R.**
Interactive color graphical postprocessing as a unifying influence in numerical analysis research. 01684
An interactive approach to local remeshing around a propagating crack. 01685

**Ingwersen, P.**
User requirements—empirical research and information systems design. 0450
Towards a new research paradigm in information retrieval. HCI-0273 †

**Ingwersen, P. (Ed.)**
Information technology and information use: towards a unified view of information and information technology. • 0447

**Innocent, P.**
The many faces of HMI. 01382
An interdisciplinary approach to human factors in telematic systems. A review of the problems and possible solutions by a COST-11 ter working group. 01440

**Inverardi, P.**
A logic-functional approach to the execution of CCS specifications modulo behavioural equivalences. 03874

**Ioannou, Y. A.**
An interactive tolerance system. 02975

**Irby, C.**
Designing the star user interface. 0089
The star user interface: an overview. 03171

**Irish, P. M.**
Supporting collaboration in hypermedia: issues and experiences. 0117
Supporting collaboration in Hypermedia: issues and experiences. 02454

**Irmscher, K.**
BNETD—A modelling tool to computer systems performance evaluation. 02668

**Irving, A.**
Preparing new generations for the information age. 0453

**Irving, E.**
Are there subtle changes in vision after use of VDTs? 03733

**Irving, J. M.**
An investigation of data entry methods with a personal computer. 01490

**Isaacs, N. W. (Ed.)**
Crystallographic Computing 4. § 03775

**Isaacs, R. I.**
Design of computer programs for the physically handicapped. HCI-0096 †

**Iseku, O.**
Applying direct manipulation concepts. 01143

**Iselin, E. R.**
Conditional statements, looping constructs, and program comprehension: an experiments study. 02177

**Ishai, E.**
The effect of VDU on the interior design of offices. 03714

**Ishii, S.**
An operations advisor for an on-line computer banking system with graphics interface. 02983

**Ishikawa, T.**
The man-machine interface aspect of an automatic classification numbering system in a computerized library system. 02316

**Isotani, R.**
Self-organizing system obtaining communication ability primitive model for language generation. 01279

**Itakura, F.**
Speech analysis and synthesis methods developed at ECL in NTT-From LPC to LSP-. 02646

**Ito, T.**
CRT picture vibration caused by low-frequency magnetic field and its reduction method. 01987
A retrieval system for on-line English-Japanese dictionaries. 03078

**Itoh, H.**
Influence of palate shape on lingual articulation. 02642
Logic interface system on navigational database systems. 03818

**Ivancevich, J. M.**
An empirical study of occupational stress, attitudes and health among information systems personnel. HCI-0451 †

**Iverson, L.**
Computational networks in early vision: from orientation selection to optical flow. 03961

**Ives, B.**
The information technology champion: aiding and abetting, care and feeding. 03459
An empirical study of the impact of user involvement on system usage and information satisfaction. HCI-0448 †

**Iwai, I.**
A document layout system using automatic document architecture extraction. 0882

**Iwai, S.**
A similarity-based reasoning model for intelligent interfaces. 01503

**Iyengar, S. (Ed.)**
Empirical studies of programmers. § 02690

**Izumida, Y.**
A practical natural language interface to databases. 0199

**J. S.**
Assessing the impact of human factors on data processing inspection errors. 01527

**J., S.**
Intelligent interfaces for secure multilevel database systems. 02990

**Järvinen, E.**
VDU work, refractive errors and binocular vision. 03739

**Jármai, K.**
Application of decision support system on sandwich beams, verified by experiments. 01572

**Jablonowski, D.**
GMB: a tool for manipulating and animating graph data structures. 02636

**Jackel, L. D.**
VLSI implementation of a neural network model. 01363

**Jackson, A. R.H.**
End-user searching of CAS ONLINE. Results of a cooperative experiment between Imperial Chemical Industries and Chemical Abstracts Services. 02269

**Jackson, C.**
Videodisc and videotex: love-match or passing acquaintance? 0515

**Jackson, F.**
Tenuring policies for generation-based storage reclamation. 01124

**Jackson, J. C.**
Circling: a method of mouse-based selection without button presses. 0847

**Jackson, J. V.**
Idea for a mind. 0773

**Jackson, M. C.**
Cybernetics and organization theory: a critical review. 01617

**Jackson, P.**
On the application of rule-based techniques to the design of advice giving systems. HCI-0315 †

**Jackson, T. E.**
Developing the technology for intelligent maintenance advisors. 02276

**Jacob, M. E.**
The moving target: future trends in networking. 01282

**Jacob, R. J.K.**
A specification language for direct-manipulation user interfaces. HCI-0123 †

**Jacob, V. S.**
An analysis of human and computer decision-making capabilities. 01951

**Jacobs, C. J.H.**
A programmer-friendly LL(1) parser generator. 02626

**Jacobs, E. C.**
User-interface design for a clinical neurophysiological intensive monitoring system. 0881

**Jacobs, P. S.**
Knowledge-intensive natural language generation. HCI-0343 †

**Jacobs, S. M.**
CHI '88 Workshop on Real Time, decision support computer-human interaction. 0991

**Jacobsen, A. R.**
The effects of set size on color matching using CRT displays. 01711

**Jacobson, L. D.**
Joint spatial/spatial-frequency representation. 02580

**Jagacinski, R. J.**
Describing movement control at two levels of abstraction. 0403

**Jagannathan, V.**
A fuzzy knowledge base of an expert system for analysis of manual lifting tasks. 01693

**Jagodzinski, A. P.**
A multidimensional approach to the measurement of human-computer performance. 01410
A process oriented approach to an intelligent design aid. 02980

**Jagodzinski, P.**
User systems analysis: a user oriented approach to computer systems analysis, design, and implementation. ● 0454

**Jain, A. K. (Ed.)**
Real-time object measurement and classification. § 03985

**Jain, R.**
Complex logarithmic mapping and the focus of expansion. 03333
Determining motion parameters for scenes with translation and rotation. 03338

**Jakobsson, M.**
Autocompletion in full text transaction entry: a method for humanized input. 0934

**James, G.**
The ethics of automated publishing systems (a response to Dr. Brockmann). HCI-0425A †

**Jameson, A.**
Architectures for production systems: an inside look for those who study human-computer interaction. 03906

**Jameson, D. G.**
Flexible intelligent interactive-video. 03238

**Jameson, S.**
Planning as feedback to designers. 02978

**Janas, J. M.**
The semantics-based natural language interface to relational databases. 0164

**Janes, V.**
Microcomputer hardware education at a Czechoslovakian Technical University. 02488

**Janik, A.**
Tacit knowledge, working life and scientific method. 0345

**Janis, I. L.**
Investigating sources of error in the management of crises: theoretical assumptions and a methodological approach. 03807

**Janning, T.**
A highly integrated tool set for program development support. 02788

**Janosky, B.**
Online library catalog systems: an analysis of user errors. 02128

**Jansen, F. W.**
A multi-processor workstation with a logic-enhanced distributed frame buffer. 0496

**Janson, M.**
Applying a pilot system and prototyping approach to systems development and implementation. 01915

**Janssen, A. J.M.W.**
A model-based monitor of human sleep stages. 01269

**Janssens, B.**
Scaling relationships in back-propagation learning. 01338

**Jansson, B.**
Psychological aspects on blind peoples's reading of radio-distributed daily newspapers. 03700

**Jao, S. Y.**
SMART: Scientific database management and engineering analysis routines and tools. 01166

**Jard, C.**
Attacking a complex distributed algorithm from different sides: an experience wih complementary validation tools. 01429

**Jarke, M.**
Studies in the evaluation of a domain-independent natural language query system. 0162
Managers, micros and mainframes: integrating systems for end-users. ● 0455
Managers, micros and mainframes: an introduction. 0456
A framework for choosing a database query language. 0761
Query languages—a taxonomy. HCI-0254 †
Using restricted natural language for data retrieval: a plan for field evaluation. HCI-0255 †
Communications design for Co-oP: a group decision support system. HCI-0297 †

**Jarke, M. (Ed.)**
Cooperative interfaces to information systems. ● 0160
Cooperative interfaces to information systems. ● HCI-0066 †

**Jarvenpaa, S.**
Groupware: interface design for meetings. 02883

**Jarvenpaa, S. L.**
The effect of task demands and graphical format on information processing strategies. 02482

**Jarvis, L. E.**
The MIDAS database system. 02387
The MIDAS display system. 02388

**Jaschinski-Kruza, W.**
Is the resting state of our eyes a favorable viewing distance for VDU-work? 03737

**Jauber, M. J. (Ed.)**
Visualization in programming. § 04032

**Jay, M.**
The role of the primate superior colliculus in sensorimotor integration. 0017

**Jayaraman, R.**
A workcell application design environment (WADE). 0598
An interactive programming system for the IBM 7545 robot. 01517

**Jayawant, B. V.**
Integration of robot sensory systems. 04016

**Jaynes, J. T.**
Limited freedom: linear reflections on nonlinear texts. 0121
DOMAIN/DELPHI: retrieving documents online. 0906

**Jeakins, D.**
Computer quantification of delta activity in sleep EEG. 01491

**Jelinek, J.**
An appropriate representation for early vision. 02542

**Jenkin, M.**
Tracking three-dimensional moving light displays. 03337

**Jenkins, G. H.**
Education requirements for the entry level business systems analyst. 02409

**Jenkins, M.**
Capacity equivalence curves: a double trade-off curve method for equating task performance. 01796

**Jenkins, M. A.**
Q'Nial: a portable interpreter for the nested interactive array language, Nial. 02635

**Jenkins, R.**
Profile data acquisition for the JCPDS-ICDD database s. 01232

**Jensen-Bjørn, R.**
Intelligent interfaces to Nordic data bases. 0738

**Jerian, C.**
Determining motion parameters for scenes with translation and rotation. 03338

**Jermoluk, T.**
High-performance polygon rendering. 02814

**Jernigan, M. E.**
Cortical representation of texture primitives. 03306

**Jernigan, R.**
APL: The language of science and management. 02799

**Jerrams-Smith, J.**
An attempt to incorporate expertise about users into an intelligent interface for Unix. 02248

**Jiang, J.**
Graphics-based qualitative simulation generator for power distribution systems. 02946

**Jih, W. J. K.**
The effects of relational and entity-relationship data models on query performance of end users. 02247

**Jin, Z. P.**
An appropriate representation for early vision. 02542

**Jobling, C. P.**
A man-machine interface for computer-aided and simulation of control systems. 01237
A human-computer interface for control system design. 03208

**Johannes, J. D.**
Towards reasoning visualization in expert systems. 02992

**Johannet, A.**
A simple selectionist learning rule for neural networks. 02756

**Johannsen, G.**
Fault management, knowledge support, and responsibility in man-machine systems. 03812

**Johansen, R.**
Thinking ahead: what to expect from teleconferencing (Reprint). 0372

**Johansson, B.**
Automatic construction of surfaces with prescribed shape. 01474

**Johansson, G.**
Growth and challenge VS wear and tear of humans in computer mediated work. 03757
Work content, stress and health in computer-mediated work: a seven year follow-up study. 03758

**John, B. E.**
Predicting the time to recall computer command abbreviations. 0806
Cumulating the science of HCI: from s-R compatibility to transcription typing. 0831
The role of laboratory experiments in HCI: help, hindrance, or ho-hum? 0863

**John, N. W.**
The controller animation system. 01402

**Johnsen, S.**
An industrial chemical hazards database with a natural language interface: an application of artificial intelligence. 01533

**Johnson-Laird, P. N.**
The computer and the mind. ● 0462
The computer and the mind: an introduction to cognitive science. ● 0463
Mental models in cognitive science. 0647
Mental models: towards a cognitive science of language, inference, and consciousness. ● HCI-0063 †
Semantic primitives or meaning postulates: mental models or propositional representation? HCI-0339 †

**Johnson, D. W.**
A scale for assessing student attitudes toward computers preliminary findings. 01579

**Johnson, E. L.**
Still sailing (and bailing): managing unexpected change in user support. 03150

**Johnson, G.**
Evaluating usability of human-computer interfaces: a practical method. ● 0608

**Johnson, H.**
Task-related knowledge structures: analysis, modelling and application. 03218

**Johnson, J.**
How faithfully should the electronic office simulate real one? 0958
Modes survey. 0963
Modes survey results. 0998

**Johnson, J. H.**
Star, maximal rectangles, lattices: a new perspective on Q-analysis. 02105

**Johnson, P.**
Preliminary analysis for design. 03199
Task-related knowledge structures: analysis, modelling and application. 03218
Voice versus keyboard: use of a comparative analysis of learning to identify skill requirements of input devices. 03275

**Johnson, R. E.**
An interactive environment for object-oriented music composition and sound synthesis. 01131

**Johnson, R. G.**
Integrating data and metadata to enhance the user interface. 03280

**Johnson, R. T.**
A scale for assessing student attitudes toward computers preliminary findings. 01579

**Johnson, S. B.**
Mathematical building blocks. 01173

**Joice, J. R.**
The foreign language barrier: a study among pharmaceutical research workers. 02333

**Joloboff, V. (Chair.)**
ACTES/Proceedings Symposium 1988 ACM SIGSMAll/PC. § 02787

**Jonassen, D. H.**
Interactive lesson designs: a taxonomy. 0273
Hypertext/hypermedia. • HCI-0047 †

**Jonassen, D. H. (Ed.)**
Instructional designs for microcomputer courseware. • 0464

**Jones, C. B.**
A support system for formal reasoning: requirements and status. 04035
Muffin: a user interface design experiment for a theorem proving assistant. 04037

**Jones, C. B. (Ed.)**
VDM '87: VDM—a formal method at work. § 03831

**Jones, D.**
Ada info: apologies to TEXT_10. 02395
Human factors and the problems of evaluation in the design of speech systems interfaces. 03192
Computers for the people: HCI in prospect. An introduction to the HCI '88 conference. 03216

**Jones, D. M.**
Parcel sorting by speech recognition: human factors issues. 03209

**Jones, D. M. (Ed.)**
People and computers IV. § 03215

**Jones, J.**
Priniciples from the psychology of thinking and mental models. 0329
MacCadd - an enabling software method support tool. 03252

**Jones, K.**
Simulations and anxiety related to public speaking. 02592

**Jones, K. D.**
Support environments for VDM. 03832

**Jones, K. S.**
The relationship between user models and discourse models. 01353
Intelligent interfaces for information retrieval systems: architecture problems in the construction of expert systems for document retrieval. 04042

**Jones, M. B.**
Comparison of video game and conventional test performance. 02594
Mach and Matchmaker: kernel and language support for object-oriented distributed systems. 03031

**Jones, M. L.**
Summarizing natural language database responses. 01343

**Jones, M. S.**
Human-computer interaction: a design guide. • HCI-0041 †

**Jones, P. M.**
A smalltalk implementation of an intelligent operator's associate. 01132

**Jones, R. L.**
STATUS with IQ—escaping from the Boolean straitjacket. 02569

**Jones, S.**
User performance with command, menu, and iconic interfaces. 0414
Articulating the experience of transparency: an example of field research techniques. 0977

**Jones, W. P.**
The memory extender personal filing system. 0930
The spatial metaphor for user interfaces: experimental tests of reference by location versus name. HCI-0268 †
On the applied use of human memory models: the memory extender personal filing system. HCI-0271 †

**Jorde-Bloom, P.**
Self-efficacy expectations as a predictor of computer use: a look at early childhood administrators. 01590

**Jorgensen, A. H.**
Formal specification of user interfaces: two application studies. 03772

**Jorgensen, C. C.**
Catching knowledge in neural nets. 01171

**Jorna, R.**
A comparison of presentation and representation: linguistic and pictorial. 03898

**Josefson, I.**
Knowledge and experience. 01207

**Josefson, I. (Ed.)**
Knowledge, skill and artificial intelligence. • 0342

**Joseph, R. L.**
A mixed-initiative workbench for knowledge acquisition. 02154

**Josin, G.**
Integrating neural networks with robots. 01187

**Jovanovic, M.**
Learning the ways: the enculturation of SDSC users. 03144

**Joyce, J.**
Monitoring distributed systems. HCI-0169 †

**Jozefowska, J.**
The evaluation of selected ergonomical factors by production automation growth. 03429

**Jr. Gargan, R. A.**
Multimodal response planning: an adaptive rule based approach. 02894

**Judd, W.**
Online help systems: design and implementation issues (panel). 02902

**Julesz, B.**
Textons, the fundamental elements in preattentive vision and perception of textures. 0297

Applications of computer graphics to the visualization of meteorological data. 02819

**Jun, S.**
The diffusion and impacts of information technology in households. 0754

**Jung, H. (Ed.)**
Parallel algorithms and architectures. § 03819

**Jungert, E.**
An image processing language with ICON-assisted navigation. HCI-0387 †

**Jurgen, R. K.**
The specialties. 01835

**Justice, J. H.**
Multidimensional attribute analyhsis and pattern recognition for seismic interpretation. 02530

**Kableshkov, S.**
The polarisation approach to intelligent artifacts. 02714

**Kabuka, M.**
Human-machine interface in remote monitoring and control of flexible manufacturing systems. 03399

**Kador, J.**
Building user interfaces before writing code saves time and money. 02662

**Kahn, G.**
Centaur: the system. 01136

**Kahn, G. S.**
A mixed-initiative workbench for knowledge acquisition. 02154

**Kahn, K.**
Beyond the chalkboard: computer support for collaboration and problem solving inmeetings (Reprint). 0376
A grammar kit in PROLOG. 0745
Beyond the chalkboard: computer support for collaboration and problem solving in meetings. HCI-0312 †

**Kahn, R.**
Later years at IPTO. 0139

**Kahney, H.**
Modelling novice programmer behaviour. 0744
Modelling novice programmer behaviour. 0751

Transfer of learning in inference problems. 03552

**Kaisler, S. H.**
INTERLISP: the language and its usage. ● HCI-0022 †

**Kaivers, R.**
Communication analysis in the company. 01435

**Kajberg, L. (Ed.)**
Information technology and information use: towards a unified view of information and information technology. ● 0447

**Kakiuchi, T.**
Plan-based text generation in an on-line help system. 03817

**Kalay, Y. E. (Ed.)**
Principles of computer-aided design: computability of design. ● 0465

**Kalimo, R.**
Effects of computerization on job demands and stress: the correspondence of subjective and objective data. 03622

**Kalita, J. K.**
Summarizing natural language database responses. 01343

**Kallala, M.**
A study of Arab computer users: a special case of a general HCI methodology. 04031

**Kalmi, R.**
User or development of information systems: Which is more fundamental? 03654

**Kaltenbach, M.**
DYNABOARD: user animated display of deductive proofs in mathematics. 02221

**Kamae, T.**
Visual terminals and user interfaces. 01686

**Kamedula, T.**
Task-load and endocrinological risk for pregnancy in women VDU operators. 03692

**Kaminsky, W.**
Plant scheduling expert system for batch processing. 02977

**Kamkar, M.**
Affect-chaining and dependency oriented flow analysis applied to queries of programs. 02789

**Kammersgaard, J.**
Four different perspectives on human-computer interaction. 02180

**Kamouri, A. L.**
Training by exploration: facilitating the transfer of procedural knowledge through analogical reasoning. 02103
Which way to computer literacy, programming or applications experience? 02127

**Kamouri, J.**
Training by exploration: facilitating the transfer of procedural knowledge through analogical reasoning. 02103

**Kanade, T.**
Autonomous scene description with range imagery. 02707
Adapting optical-flow to measure object motion in reflectance and X-ray image sequences. 03334

**Kandel, A.**
Implementing imprecision in information systems. HCI-0259 †

**Kandt, K.**
On building future decision support systems. 03472
A financial investment assistant. 03490

**Kane, P. T.**
A cost model for estimating the costs of developing software in the Ada programming language. 03539

**Kane, R. M.**
A case example of human factors in product definition: needs finding for a voice output workstation for the blind. 0819

**Kanerva, P.**
Parallel structures in human and computer memory. 02742

**Kang, T. J.**
Reader-controlled computerized presentation of text. 01785

**Kani, K.**
Eye movement analysis system using fundus images. HCI-0243 †

**Kant, E.**
Naive algorithm design techniques—a case study. HCI-0360 †

**Kantorowitz, E.**
The adaptable user interface. 01337

**Kantowitz, B. H.**
Mental workload. 0400
Likelihood alarm displays. 01783

**Kantowitz, S. C.**
Likelihood alarm displays. 01783

**Kao, M.**
Providing quality responses with natural language interfaces: the null value problem. 01848

**Kaplan, G.**
Realism in synthetic speech. 0066

**Kaplan, M.**
Abstraction and integration in IDE, an editing and formatting environment. 03184

**Kapor, M.**
Computer-supported cooperative work: breakthroughs for user acceptance. 02874

**Kappler, W.**
Effects of vehicle handling characteristics on driving strategy. 01773

**Karat, J.**
Transfer between word processing systems. 0899
A comparison of menu selection techniques: touch panel, mouse and keyboard. 02122

**Karhu, P.**
User or development of information systems: Which is more fundamental? 03654

**Karim, A.**
SMARTGEN: the implementation of an expert system for the generation of digital logic diagnostic tests. 02929

**Karimi, J.**
User interface design from a real time perspective. 01323

**Kariya, K.**
Eye movement analysis system using fundus images. HCI-0243 †

**Karjalainen, M.**
Impact of prototyping on user information satisfaction during the IS specification phase. 01955
Object-oriented signal processing systems. 03573

**Karlsen, T. K.**
The importance of work organization by systems design. 03648

**Karrat, J.**
Report on the workshop on analytical models. 01001

**Karsenty, S.**
Iconic shells for multitasking workstations. 02792
Prototyping user interfaces for applications depicted by graphs. 03523

**Karshmer, A. I.**
An overview of $T^3$-PBE. 0784
The architecture of an inexpensive and portable talking-tactile terminal to aid the visually handicapped. 01452
An inexpensive and portable talking-tactile terminal for the visually handicapped. 02377

**Karten, N.**
Managing end user computing when the only constant is change. 02425

**Karwan, M. H.**
Methods for field evaluation of safety in a robotics workplace. 03408

**Karwowski, W.**
Towards the development of human work-performance standards in futuristic man-machine systems: a fuzzy modeling approach. 01692
A fuzzy knowledge base of an expert system for analysis of manual lifting tasks. 01693
Human perception of the work envelope of an industrial robot. 03410

**Karwowski, W. (Ed.)**
Ergonomics of Hybrid Automated Systems I. § 03362

**Kasahara, Y.**
Designing optimum CRT text blinking video image presentation. 0795

Information retrieval using impression of documents as a clue. 03065
How map designers can represent their ideas in thematic maps: effective user interfaces for thematic map design. 03870

**Kasami, T.**
A processing system for program specifications in a natural language. 03537

**Kasdan, M. L.**
Occupational accidents to the hand: A comparison of factory and nonfactory injuries. 03438

**Kashyap, R. L.**
Study of combination of belief intevals in lattice-structured networks. 02223
A dialog based interface to a design knowledge base that understands user design-intentions. 02988

**Kasik, D.**
Goals and objectives for user interface software. 01056

**Kaske, N. K.**
A comparative study of subject searching in an OPAC among branch libraries of a university library system. 02050

**Kasper, G. M.**
The effect of presentation media on recipient performance in text-based information systems. 02350
A laboratory study of user characteristics and decision-making performance in end-user computing. HCI-0301 †

**Kass, R.**
Modeling the user in natural language systems. 01348
A general user modelling facility. 02880

**Kaster, J.**
Effect of visual presentation of different dialogue structures on human-computer interaction. 03768

**Kasuya, H.**
An acoustic of pathological voice and its application to the evaluation of laryngeal pathology. 02644

**Katke, W.**
Interfaces for knowledge-base builders' control knowledge and application-specific procedures. 01810

**Kato, H.**
Contextual structure analysis of microcomputer manuals. 03227

**Kato, T.**
What "question-asking protocols" can say about the user interface. 02130

**Katsuya, A.**
Directed graph representations of association structures: A systematic approach. 01862

**Katz, A. R.**
An experimental multimedia mail system. HCI-0309 †

**Katz, B.**
Text processing with the START natural language system. 0100
Using "word-knowledge" reasoning for question answering. 0131

**Katz, S.**
Interactive blackbox debugging for concurrent languages. 01134

**Katzeff, C.**
Dealing with a database query language in a new situation. 02119
The effect of different conceptual models using reasoning in a database query writing task. 02201

**Katzenellenbogen, D.**
An architecture of a distributed window system and its FCP implementation. 0676

**Katzin, E.**
How to write a really good user's manual. ● HCI-0017 †

**Kauffmann, J.**
Robot components and systems. ● HCI-0068 †

**Kaufman, A.**
A two-dimensional frame buffer processor. 0494

**Kautto, A.**
Visualization of process information in improving work orientation. 03619

**Kavalerchik, B. Y.**
The selection of a servicing discipline in a multiterminal conversational information retrieval system. 01233

**Kawai, H.**
Eye movement analysis system using fundus images. HCI-0243 †

**Kawamoto, A. H.**
Mechanisms of sentence processing: assigning roles to constituents. 0635

**Kawamura, K.**
Graphics-based qualitative simulation generator for power distribution systems. 02946
Applications of qualitative modeling to knowledge-based risk assessment studies. 02970
NetGraph: an object-oriented graphical toolset for risk assessment. 02972

**Kay, D. S.**
Prompting, feedback and error correction in the design of a scenario machine. 02176
Goal and plan knowledge representations: from stories to text editors and programs. HCI-0183 †

**Kay, L.**
Gribs—an approach to a realistic realtime simulation of human arm motion. 03432

**Kaya, A.**
Continuous processing of images through user sketched functional blocks. 01399

**Kaye, A. R.**
Insights on the implementation of a computer-based message system. 01917
Electronic calendars in the office: an assessment of user needs and current technology. HCI-0287 †
A user agent for multiple computer-based message services. HCI-0306 †

**Kayser, D.**
Natural language and computers: a general survey of written text interpretation methods. 02671

**Kayser, K.**
Application of structural pattern recognition in histopathology. 0295

**Kazanides, P.**
A multiprocessor system for real-time robotic control. 02023

**Kazemian, F.**
A formal specification for a user interface for office automation. 04053

**Keane, M.**
Preliminary analysis for design. 03199

**Keane, M. T.**
Analogical problem solving. ● HCI-0044 †

**Kearlsey, G.**
Authoring considerations for hypertext. 01679

**Kearns, C. F.**
Interactive microcomputer programs for linear and non-linear static analysis of frameworks. 01165

**Kearsely, G. P.**
Design factors for successful videodisc-based instruction. 0277

**Kearsley, G.**
Hypertext hands-on!: an introduction to a new way of organizing and accessing information. ● 0686
Online help systems: design and implementation issues (panel). 02902
Online help systems: design and implementation. ● HCI-0009 †
Authoring: a guide to the design of instructional software. ● HCI-0031 †

**Kearsley, G. P. (Ed.)**
Artificial intelligence and instruction: Applications and methods. ● 0468

**Kedzierski, B. I.**
Communication and management support in system development environments (Reprint). 0374

**Kee, B. A.**
Modern drafting: an introduction to CAD. ● HCI-0077 †

**Keene, S. E.**
Common LISP object system specification X3J13 Document 88-002R. 01121

**Kelemen, J.**
Two notes concerning the society theory of thinking. 01479

**Keller, T.**
Computers for managing information. ● 0141
Communication barriers in microcomputer—based courses. 01319

**Kelley, J. F.**
Videotex information packagers: a field study aimed at tomorrow's videotex authoring interface. 0962

**Kellogg, W.**
The designer as user: building requirements for design tools from design practice. HCI-0129 †

**Kellogg, W. A.**
Artifact as theory-nexus: hermeneutics meets theory-based design. 0798
Designing for designers: an analysis of design practice in the real world. 0839

**Kelly-Bootle, S.**
HIC: the human interface column. 01422
Orthodox dialectical interfaces. 01423

**Kelly, C. D.**
Design principles behind Chiron: a UIMS for software environments. 03511

**Kelly, G. W.**
Design of an integral computer-based wheelchair controller/linear synchronous motor system. 02378
Human factors design of a video monitor emulator and display (VMED) for visuallyimpaired computer users. 02379
Human factors considerations in the design of a VDU for visually impaired persons. 03698

**Kelly, J.**
Optimum display arrangements for presenting visual reminders. 03237

Intelligent machines: What chance? 03548

**Kelly, M. J.**
Performance measurement during simulated air-to-air combat. 01787

**Kelly, P. A.**
Hesitations in continuous tracking induced by a concurrent discrete task. 01745

**Kemp, B.**
A model-based monitor of human sleep stages. 01269

**Kemp, N.**
Attitudes to information technology. 0150

**Kempf, J.**
Language level persistence for an object-oriented application programming platform. 03522

**Kempf, R.**
Teaching object-oriented programming with the KEE system. 01113

**Kendzierski, N.**
Human-computer interaction department, Hewlett-Packard Laboratories. 0869

**Kengskool, K.**
Robot vs. human operator for speed, precision and other aspects. 03403

**Kennard, A.**
The 'window' terminal. 01405

**Kennedy, R. S.**
Spatial requirements for visual simulation of aircraft at real-world distances. 01768

**Kensing, F.**
Generation of visions in systems development: a supplement to the tool box. 03661

**Kent, P.**
The many faces of faculty computing assistance. 03143

**Kent, W. A. (Ed.)**
Computer assisted learning in the humanities and social sciences. ● 0470

**Kentridge, R.**
Optimum display arrangements for presenting visual reminders. 03237

**Keramidas, G. A. (Ed.)**
Reliability and robustness of engineering software. § 03451

**Kerber, K. W.**
Attitudes towards specific uses of the computers quantitative, decision-making and record-keeping applications. HCI-0234 †

**Kern, G. M.**
The influence of personality on self-paced instruction. 02291

**Kernighan, B. W.**
The AWK programming language. ● HCI-0020 †

**Kerr, D.**
Putting Texas on disc. 01316

**Kerr, J.**
Turbo windows. 01421

**Kerr, R. K.**
Use of object-oriented programming in a time series analysis system. 01112

**Kerr, S. T.**
Goals and objectives for user interface software. 01056

**Kerschberg, L. (Ed.)**
Expert database systems. § 03173

**Kersten, G. E.**
On two roles decision support systems can play in negotiations. 01998

**Kersten, M. L.**
Developing interactive information systems with the user software engineering methodology. 0077
Developing interactive information systems with the user software engineering methodology. 01856

**Keyes, E.**
Technology + design + research = information design. 0107

**Keyes, J.**
Wall Street speaks English. 01184

**Khaksari, G. H.**
Expert diagnostic system. 02912

**Khalil, O. E.**
The influence of programmers' cognitive complexity on program comprehension and modification. 02245

**Khalil, T. M.**
Computerized design and analysis of sitting workplace. 01506
Biomechanical evaluation of lifting tasks: a microcomputer-based model. 01524
Human-machine interface in remote monitoring and control of flexible manufacturing systems. 03399

**Khanna, S. K.**
Error correction and asymmetry in a binary memory matrix. 02750

**Khorasani, A.**
Office-by-example: an integrated office system and database manager. 01159

**Khoujah, A.**
Character recognition of cursive scripts. 02961

**Kicsales, G.**
Common LISP object system specification X3J13 Document 88-002R. 01121

**Kidd, A. L.**
Man-machine interface issues in the construction and use of an expert system. HCI-0212 †
What do users ask? Some thoughts on diagnostic advice. HCI-0326 †

**Kidd, E. M. (Ed.)**
Graphics Interface '86/Vision Interface '86. § 03288

**Kidd, P. T.**
Human and computer aided manufacturing: The end of taylorism? 03379

**Kido, K.**
Recognition of phonemes using time-spectrum pattern. 02648

**Kieras, D.**
Transfer between text editors. 0804

**Kieras, D. E.**
Transfer between menu systems. 02873

**Kierulf, A.**
Human-computer interaction in the game of Go. 03634

**Kiesewetter, H.**
Problem oriented design of interaction structures. 03614

**Kiesler, S.**
Social psychological aspects of computer-mediated communication (Reprint). 0384
Reducing social context cues: electronic mail in organizational communication (Reprint). 0385
Reducing social context cues: electronic mail in organizational communication. 02473

**Kiger, J. I.**
The depth/breadth trade-off in the design of menu-driven user interfaces. HCI-0135 †

**Kikuchi, Y.**
An acoustic of pathological voice and its application to the evaluation of laryngeal pathology. 02644

**Kilbom, A.**
Short- and long-term effects of extreme physical inactivity. A review. 03703

**Kilgour, A.**
Theory and practice in user interface management systems. 01961

**Kilgour, A. C.**
Experience with chisl, a configurable hierarchical interface specification language. 01397
Dynamic reconfigurability for fast prototyping of user interfaces. 02609

**Kim, C. E.**
Digital parallelism, perpendicularity, and rectangles. 01843

**Kim, E.**
An exploratory contingency model of user participation and MIS use. 01919

**Kim, H.**
Data model issues for object-oriented applications. 0712
Data model issues for object-oriented applications. 01157
Evaluating RECONSIDER: a computer program for diagnostic prompting. HCI-0410 †

**Kim, S.**
Graphic invention for user interfaces: an experimental course in user-interface design. 0950

**Kim, T. G.**
Design of an AI-Based self-sustaining habitats control system. 02959
Hierarchical scheduling in an intelligent environmental control system. 02976

**Kim, W.**
Object-oriented concepts, databases, and applications. • 0475
Data model issues for object-oriented applications. 0712
An object-oriented approach to multimedia databases. 01084
Data model issues for object-oriented applications. 01157

**Kimball, R.**
Designing the star user interface. 0089
The star user interface: an overview. 03171

**Kimberg, D. Y.**
A graphical programming language interface for an intelligent LISP tutor. 02862

**Kimberley, R. (Ed.)**
Integrating text with non-text: a picture is worth 1k words. Proceedings of the I. § 04043

**Kimble, C.**
CIM and manufacturing industry in the north east of England: A survey of some current issues. 03377

**Kimbrough, E.**
Automated design and analysis system for design of custom orthopedic implants. 02931

**Kimbrough, K.**
Clue: a common lisp user interface environment. 03113

**Kimbrough, S. O.**
On representation schemes for electronic promising. 03488

**Kimerer, B. S.**
A user interface for multiple-process, turnkey systems targeted for the novice user. 0911

**Kinahan, P. E.**
A teachable neural network based on an unorthodox neuron. 02561

**Kincaid, C. M.**
Electronic calendars in the office: an assessment of user needs and current technology. HCI-0287 †

**Kindborg, M.**
A flexible negotiable interactive learning environment. 03197
Visual languages and human computer interaction. 03202

**King, B.**
A closed-loop causal model of workload based on a comparison of fuzzy and crisp measurement techniques. 01746

**King, J. L.**
Systems for cooperative work and group decision making: status of use and problems in development. 03471

**King, K. F.**
Individualizing the man-machine interface. 03404

**King, L.**
Users are people too. 01653

**King, M.**
Environments for Eurota. 02514
Computational linguistics: issues and solutions. 03948

**King, R.**
Semantic feedback in the Higgens UIMS. 01851
Implementing a user interface as a system of attributes. 03052
The Higgens UIMS and its efficient implementation of Undo. 03861
A generator of direct manipulation office systems. HCI-0250 †

**King, R. T.**
Cognitive user interface laboratory, GMD-IPSI. 0870

**King, W. F.**
System R: a relational approach to database management. 0709

**Kingdom, F.**
Effect of pixel height, display height, and vertical resolution on the detection of a simple vertical line signal in visual noise. 01753

**Kinkead, R.**
Voice: technology searching for communication needs. 0808

**Kinnell, S. K.**
An online interface within a hypertext system: project Jefferson's electronic notebook. 02524

**Kinnucan, M. T.**
The effects of entry arrangement in search times: a cross-generational study. 02048

**Kinsley, K.**
Reference model for DBMS user facility. 01086

**Kinukawa, H.**
A natural language interface processor based on the hierarchical-tree structure model of relation tables. 02315

**Kirakowski, J.**
Measuring user satisfaction. 03230

**Kirchhoff, U.**
Computer aided application program synthesis for industrial robots. 0606

**Kirillov, A. B.**
Short-term memory as a metastable state.III. Diffusion approximation. 01611

**Kirilov, A. S.**
A personal computer based graphic workstation. 02493

**Kiritani, S.**
X-ray microbeam method for measurement of articulatory dynamics-techniques and results. 02641

**Kirk, D.**
Virtual graphics. 02815

**Kirkham, J. A.**
The construction of information management system prototypes in Ada. 02613

**Kirkman, J.**
How "friendly" is your writing for readers around the world? 0110

**Kirkpatrick, J.**
Algebras for nested relations. 01623

**Kirmse, W.**
Visuomotor control by a combined position- and speedservo. Theoretical considerations and experimental results in man. 02666

**Kirs, P.**
An investigation of performance, productivity, and rationality in multi-criteria decision making. 03463

**Kirsch, J.**
Investment in computer-product documentation: causes and effects. 0105
Trends in the emerging profession of technical communciation. 0123

**Kiss, G.**
The use of complexity theory in evaluating interfaces. 03270

**Kitajima, M.**
A formal representation system for the human-computer interaction process. 02241

**Kitakaze, S.**
Designing optimum CRT text blinking video image presentation. 0795

**Kiyono, M.**
A travel consultation system: towards a smooth conversation in Japanese. 03917

**Kjerulff, K.**
The effects of a computerized information system on a hospital. 01553

**Klahr, D.**
Learning, development, and production systems. 0479
Self-modifying production system model of cognitive development. 0486
Instructionless learning about a complex device: the paradigm and observations. HCI-0333 †

**Klahr, D. (Ed.)**
Production system models of learning and development. ● 0478

**Klapp, S. T.**
Short-term memory limits in human performance. 0398

**Hesitations** in continuous tracking induced by a concurrent discrete task. 01745
Multiple resources for processing and storage in short-term working memory. 01794

**Klefstad, R. O.**
Maintaining a uniform user interface for an Ada programming environment. 04066

**Klein, E.**
GRAFLOG: understanding drawings through natural language. 01396

**Klein, H. K.**
Issues and approaches to appraising technological change in the office: A consequentialist perspective. 0043
Organizational implications of office systems: toward a critical social action perspective. 03358

**Klein, J. A.**
The human costs of manufacturing reform. 01706

**Klein, J. D.**
A comparison of a microcomputer progressive state drill and flashcards for learning paired associates. 02295

**Klein, M.**
Information politics. 01656

**Klein, M. H.**
A methodology for evaluating environments. 03055

**Klein, R.**
Who's behind the help desk? 01632

**Kleinbeck, U.**
Influences of mental load on reaction times in man-computer dialogues. 03625

**Kleinman, G. D.**
Environmental stressors and perceived health symptoms among office workers. 03680

**Kleinmuntz, D. N.**
Human decision processes: Heuristics and task structure. 0401

**Klem, G. H.**
User-interface design for a clinical neurophysiological intensive monitoring system. 0881

**Klemp, J. B.**
Computing needs in thunderstorm modeling: supercomputers and interactive graphics. 0730

**Klepper, R.**
Information systems strategy and end-user application development. 01637
The impact of information systems strategy on end user computing. 02423

**Klerer, M.**
User-oriented computer languages: analysis and design. ● HCI-0019 †
Experimental study of a two-dimensional language vs. FORTRAN for first-course progammers. HCI-0171 †

**Kleyn, M. F.**
EDGE - a graph based tool for specifying interaction. 03106

**Klima, E. S.**
Motion analysis of grammatical processes in a visual-gestural language. 03347

**Kline, J. S.**
Development of the wedding planner—extensions to reach a young audience. 01502

**Klingholz, F.**
The measurement of the signal-to-noise ratio (SNR) in continuous speech. 02654

**Klinner, P. A.**
How well do you write user documentation? 02442

**Klitzman, S.**
Comparison of well being among non-machine interactive clerical workers and full-time and part-time VDT users and typists. 03745

**Klix, F.**
MACINTER—aim and goal. 03590
Memory research and knowledge engineering. 03599

**Klix, F. (Ed.)**
Man-computer interaction research (MACINTER-I): Proceedings of the first network. § 03589

**Klopf, A. H.**
A drive-reinforcement model of single neuron function: An alternative to the Hebbian neuronal model. 02743

**Klopfenstein, B. C.**
Forecasting consumer adoption of information technology and services—lessons from home video forecasting. 02451

**Kloster, G. V.**
Engineering the man-machine interface for air traffic control. 01358

**Knave, B. (Ed.)**
Work with display units 86. § 03676

**Kneller, G. R.**
Adult learners: away with computerphobia. HCI-0433 †

**Knez, M.**
Competition and cooperation in information systems innovation. 01941

**Knight Dr., D. O.**
Knowledge-based interface to manufacturing computer systems. 02966

**Knight, D. O.**
Smart help for operator performance. 01528

**Knittle, D. L.**
Establishing user-centered criteria for information systems: a software ergonomics perspective. 01920

**Knopik, T.**
Knowledge-based human-computer interfaces and software ergonomics. 0191

**Knowles, C.**
Can cognitive complexity theory (CCT) produce an adequate measure of system usability? 03229

**Knox, S. T.**
Directed dialogue protocols: verbal data for user interface design. 0866
Effects of interface design upon user productivity. 02891

**Knuth, D. E.**
Literate programming. HCI-0148 †

**Knutson, S. J.**
Preventing back strain. 0047
**Knutsson, A.**
VDU-work and dyslexia. a case report. 03699
Inactivity, night work, and fatigue. 03705
**Ko, S. H.**
Showing programs on a screen. HCI-0141 †
**Koa, C.**
A dietary recommendation expert system using OPS5. 03498
**Kobayashi, M.**
The software structure of extended nucleus based on BTRON specification. 03494
**Kobayashi, T.**
Estimating articulatory motion from speech wave. 02643
**Kobsa, A.**
The relationship between user models and discourse models. 01353
XTRA: a natural-language access system to expert systems. 02244
**Kobus, D. A.**
Multimodal detection and recognition performance of sonar operators. 01709
**Koch, C.**
Computational vision and regularization theory. 0301
**Koch, S.**
Computers' impact on productivity and work life. 03040
Computerization, productivity, and quality of work-life. HCI-0441 †
**Koch, S. E.**
The interactionist perspective on computer implementation. 0785
**Koch, U.**
User requirements in natural language communication with database systems. 03615
**Kochar, I. S.**
Human factors in automating manufacturing systems in India. 03446
**Kochen, M.**
How well do we acknowledge intellectual debts? 02299
Advances in cognitive science. 02721
Order and disorder in knowledge structures. 02722
**Kochen, M. (Ed.)**
Advances in Cognitive Science. § 02720
**Kodratoff, Y.**
Generalization and noise. 02155
**Koehli, S.**
Participative design and requirements on planning, software engineering and education. 03658
**Koelega, H. S.**
No effect of noise on vigilance performance? 01724
Processing demands, effort, and individual differences in four different vigilance tasks. 01801
**Koenderink, J. J.**
Representation of local geometry in the visual system. 01249
Facts on optic flow. 01257
Design principles for a front-end visual systems. 03955
**Koenig, J. A.**
ER model clustering as an aid for user communication and documentation in database design. 01331
**Koenig, M. E.**
The convergence of Moore's/Mooers' laws. 01996
**Koerner, E.**
Parallel in sequence—towards the architecture of an elementary cortical processor. 03820
Control of sensory processing - a hypothesis on and simulation of the architecture of an elementary cortical processor. 03972
**Koffler, R. P.**
Testing for usability. 03163
**Koh, H.**
Goal-directed semantic tutor. 02919
**Kohonen, T.**
The "neural" phonetic typewriter. 01361
Representation of sensory information in self-organizing feature maps. 02744

**Koitz, K.**
Methodological problems of designing dialogue-oriented components in information systems. 03595
**Koivunen, M.**
HutWindows: an improved architecture for a user interface management system. 01830
**Koivunen, M. R.**
HutWindows: an improved architecture for a user interface management system. 03854
**Kojima, K.**
Information detective: a workstation for exploring three dimensional information space. 01010
**Kok, A. J.**
Retrieval based on user behaviour. 03068
**Kokjer, K. J.**
The information capacity of the human fingertip. 01893
**Kolers, P. A.**
Motion from continuous or discontinuous arrangements. 03342
**Kollerbauer, A.**
A flexible negotiable interactive learning environment. 03197
**Kollerbaur, A.**
Visual languages and human computer interaction. 03202
**Kolluri, S. P.**
Simulation of CNC controller features in graphics-based programming. 01568
**Kolm, P.**
Transparency and system design. 03655
Report from the working group on "goals and strategies of trade unions and other social groups in systems design for human development and productivity.". 03657
**Kolm, P. (Ed.)**
System design for human development and productivity: participation and beyond. § 03640

**Kommers, P. A.M.**
Textvision: elicitation and acquisition of conceptual knowledge by graphic representation and multiwindowing. 03902

**Komorowski, H. J.**
A model and an implementation of a logic programming environment. 01107

**Konolige, K.**
On the relation between default and autoepistemic logic. 01214
What awareness isn't: a sentential view of implicit and explicit belief. 03560

**Konstam, A.**
A help system for command driven applications. 01050

**Konsynski, B.**
Dialogue management: support for dialogue independence. 02512

**Konsynski, B. R.**
ICE: information center expert: a consultation system for resource allocation. 0781
PLEXACT: an architecture & design of a knowledge-based system for information systems development. 01020
A consultation system for information center resource allocation. 03100

**Konsynski, B. R. (Ed.)**
Decision Support and Knowledge Based Systems Track. § 03461

**Koo, C. S.**
Interactive error recovery expert system for robot with voice recognition subsystem. 03420

**Koopman, B. O.**
An empirical formula for visual search. 02526

**Koopmans-van Beinum, F. J.**
Perceptual normalization of the vowels of a man and a child in various contexts. 02656

**Kopetzky, D. J.**
HORSE: a simulation of the horizon supercomputer. 03541

**Kopp, E. F.**
A plan for evaluating usability of software products. HCI-0449 †

**Koppa, R. J.**
User computer interface guidelines research for keyboards and function keys. 0201

**Kopsco, D. P.**
An iterative approach to improving data analysis in the classroom. 03318

**Korfhage, R. R.**
Towards an intelligent and personalized retrieval system. 03028

**Korn, G.**
One hundred differential equations execute directly on the IBM PC. 02582

**Korncoff, A. R.**
Will you be replaced by a knowledge base? 02055

**Korson, T. D.**
An empirical study of the effects of modularity on program modifiability. HCI-0155 †

**Kosar, R. P.**
Adapting expert systems to simulation training of process operators. 02056

**Kosco, B.**
Differential Hebbian learning. 02745

**Kosieniak, P. M.**
The network control assistant (NCA), a real-time prototype expert system for network management. 02930

**Kosinsky, W. (Ed.)**
Communications and architecture & protocols. § 02801

**Kosko, B.**
Constructing an associative memory. 01289
Hidden patterns in combined and adaptive knowledge networks. 02073

**Kottemann, J. E.**
When and how cognitive style impacts decision making. 03474
Anatomy of a compact user interface development tool. HCI-0104 †

**Koubek, R. J.**
Cognitive issues in the process of software development: review and reappraisal. 02222

**Kougo, S.**
A travel consultation system: towards a smooth conversation in Japanese. 03917:1PKoutsofios, E.
A library for incremental update of bitmap images. 02836

**Kovacevic, S.**
A knowledge-based user interface management system. 02867

**Koval, G. M.**
Captive...a new tool. 03129

**Kovalenko, Y. I.**
Short-term memory as a metastable state.III. Diffusion approximation. 01611

**Koved, L.**
Embedded menus: selecting items in context. 01320

**Kowalczyk, M.**
A study of stability of electrocortical rhythm generators. 01258

**Kowalik, J. (Ed.)**
Parallel computation and computers for artificial intelligence. ● 0488

**Kowalik, S. J. (Ed.)**
Knowledge based problem solving. ● 0490

**Kowalski, A.**
A natural language information retrieval system with extentions towards fuzzy reasoning. HCI-0281 †

**Kozlowska, M.**
A natural language information retrieval system with extentions towards fuzzy reasoning. HCI-0281 †

**Kraemer, K. L.**
Systems for cooperative work and group decision making: status of use and problems in development. 03471

**Kraft, M. A.**
Designing a user manual to support an in-house database. 01635

**Kragt, H.**
An evaluation of production systems from the ergonomic viewpoint: a plea for an integral approach to design. 03430

**Kralj, M. M.**
Cognitive impacts of the user interface. 0432

**Kramer, A.**
Constraint hierarchies. 01114

**Kramer, A. F.**
A psychophysiological assessment of operator workload during simulated flight missions. 01735

**Kramer, S.**
The integrity lock support environment. 03578

**Krasner, G. E.**
A cookbook for using the model-view controller user interface paradigm in Smalltalk-80. 02390

**Krasner, H.**
CSCW '86 Conference summary report. 0955

**Kratchanov, K.**
A rule-based system for fuzzy natural language robot control. 03574

**Krause, B.**
Exploratory investigations in acquiring and using information in interactive problem solving. 03597

**Krause, J.**
Studies in the evaluation of a domain-independent natural language query system. 0162

**Krause, M.**
Beware the reliability of slope scores for individuals. 01727

**Kraut, R.**
Relationships and tasks in scientific research collaborations (Reprint). 0387
Computers' impact on productivity and work life. 03040

**Kraut, R. E.**
Computerization, productivity, and quality of work-life. HCI-0441 †

**Krauth, W.**
Basins of attraction in a perceptron-like neural network. 01340

**Krejčí, F.**
An alternative approach to the conceptual database design using fragments of nat. 01481

**Kretchman, L.**
Keyboarding for personal computer use. • 0492

**Kreuzig, A.**
Methodological problems of field-research on workplaces in offices. 0249

**Krishna, G.**
Structural aspects of semantic-directed clusters. 02534

**Krishnamurthy, R.**
Office-by-example: an integrated office system and database manager. 01159

**Krishnaswamy, R.**
Digital parallelism, perpendicularity, and rectangles. 01843

**Krömker, D.**
Looking at workstation architectures from the viewpoint of interaction. 03787

**Krotkov, E. P.**
Visual hyperacuity: representation and computation of high precision position information. HCI-0393 †

**Krovetz, R.**
Interactive retrieval office documents. 03047

**Krüger, H.**
The applicability of eye movement analysis in the ergonomic evaluation of human-computer interaction. 03766

**Krueger, C. W.**
A structural approach to the maintenance of structure-oriented environments. 03054

**Krueger, M.**
Drama and personality in user interface design. 0830

**Kruk, R. S.**
Reader-controlled computerized presentation of text. 01785

**Krull, R.**
Designing online information. HCI-0152 †

**Krushinsky, D.**
A personal computer based graphic workstation. 02493

**Kruzydlowska, A.**
ORGPLAN an information-decisive aid system to resolving organizing problems. 01573

**Kryukov, A. P.**
Dialogue in REDUCE: experience and development. 03088

**Kryukov, V. I.**
Short-term memory as a metastable state.III. Diffusion approximation. 01611

**Kuihn, F. N.**
Influences of mental load on reaction times in man-computer dialogues. 03625

**Küller, R.**
Non-visual effects of visual surroundings. 03720

**Kündig, A.**
A graphical tool for the design and prototyping of distributed systems. 01146

**Kubota, M.**
A retrieval system for on-line English-Japanese dictionaries. 03078

**Kugler, H. (Ed.)**
Information processing 86. § 03588

**Kuhlthau, C. C.**
Perceptions of the information search process in libraries: a study of changes from high school through college. 02002

**Kuhn, T.**
An experimental environment for generating word hypotheses in continuous speech. 03998

**Kuijk, A. A.M.**
Display architecture for VLSI-based graphics workstations. 03786

**Kuijk, A. A.M. (Ed.)**
Advances in computer graphics hardware II. • 0493

**Kuivanen, R.**
Experiences from the use of an intelligent safety sensor with industrial robots. 03427

**Kulkarni, K. M.**
A high accuracy algorithm for recognition of handwritten numerals. 02532

**Kulkarni, U. D.**
A stand-alone Forth system. 02310

**Kullback, J. H.**
A framework for task cooperation within systems containing intelligent components. 01884

**Kumar, A.**
Mapping the manipulator workspace using interactive computer graphics. 02257

**Kumar, K.**
User cube: a taxonomy of end users. 01335

**Kumar, S.**
An expert system framework for forecasting method selection. 03468

**Kumekawa, S.**
AGV safety system designed for preventing hazardous human contact. 03423

**Kummert, F.**
Knowledge based systems for speech understanding. 04001

**Kundu, M. K.**
Thresholding for edge detection using human psychovisual phenomena. 02538

**Kunii, T. (Ed.)**
Advanced Computer Graphics. § 03836

**Kunii, T. L.**
ANIMENGINE: an engineering animation system. 03858

**Kunii, T. L. (Ed.)**
Computer graphics 1987. § 03852

**Kunzmann, S.**
An experimental environment for generating word hypotheses in continuous speech. 03998

**Kuo, F.**
User interface design from a real time perspective. 01323
Dialogue management: support for dialogue independence. 02512

**Kuo, F. F. (Ed.)**
Communications and architecture & protocols. § 02801

**Kuo, F. Y.**
An object-oriented approach to the design of a mail system for a heterogeneous environment. 01944

**Kurata, A.**
Manipulation of embedded context using the multiple world mechanism. 03921

**Kurland, D. M.**
Mapping the cognitive demands of learning to program. 0579
On the cognitive effects of learning computer programming. 0581
Logo and development of thinking skills. 0582
Informing the design of software through context-based research. 0584

**Kurlander, D.**
Graphical search and replace. 02812

**Kurppa, K.**
Birth defects, course of pregnancy, and work with VDUs: a Finnish case-referent study. 03689

**Kurshan, B. L.**
VAX-BASIC with structured problem solving: 2nd edition. ● 0725

**Kurstedt, H.**
The responsive system: a new challenge for AI. 02920

**Kushelevsky, A.**
Radiation detection by ear and by eye. 01732

**Kushiki, Y.**
The software structure of extended nucleus based on BTRON specification. 03494

**Kuznetsov, H.**
A human-computer interactive design program for a multisolution nonlinear problem. 01168

**Kykodym, N.**
TA: Can it improve worker satisfaction with organizational decision-making? 02414

**L'Hote, F.**
Robot components and systems. ● HCI-0068 †

**La Brecque, M.**
Retinex: physics and the theory of color vision. 01574

**Lässig, P.**
Visuomotor control by a combined position- and speedservo. Theoretical considerations and experimental results in man. 02666

**Läubli, T.**
Preferred settings in VDT work: The Zürich Experience. 03707
Subject reports about musculoskeletal discomfort in VDU work as a complex phenomenon. 03708

**Lánská, V.**
Diffusion approximation of the neuronal model with synaptic reversal potentials. 01254

**Lánský, P.**
Statistical inference on spontaneous neuronal discharge patterns. I. Single neuron. 01247

**Lánský, P. L.**
Diffusion approximation of the neuronal model with synaptic reversal potentials. 01254

**Lachman, R.**
Comprehensino aids for on-line reading of expository text. 01798

**Lachter, J.**
The relation between linguistic structure and associative theories of language learning models: constructive critique of some connectionist learning models. 0591

**Laczik, B.**
A multiparadigm user interface for intelligent CAD systems. 0716

**Ladd, C.**
CAREing for users at Syracuse University. 03134

**Ladefoged, P.**
The phonetic basis for computer speech processing. HCI-0358 †

**Ladner, R.**
A user interface for deaf-blind people (preliminary report). 0794

**Ladner, R. E.**
Public Law 99-506, "Section 508" Electronic Equipment Accessibility for disabled workers. 02893

**Laender, A. H.F.**
An approach to interactive definition of database views. 03281
An interactive database end user facility for the definition and manipulation of forms. HCI-0263 †

**Laestadius, H.**
User interface in new PC software. 03771

**Laface, P.**
An expert system for mapping acoustic cues into phonetic features. HCI-0328 †

**Lafferty, E. L.**
Space. 0134

**Lagodimos, A. G.**
Interactive computer program for the selection of interference fits. HCI-0406 †

**Lai, K.**
Object lens: a "spreadsheet" for cooperative work. HCI-0206 †
Semistructured messages are surprisingly useful for computer-supported coordination. HCI-0290 †

**Laine, U. K.**
Higher pole correction in vocal tract models and terminal analogs. 02657

**Laird, A.**
Hyperbiorhythms. 02470

**Laird, J.**
Universal subgoaling and chunking: the automatic generation and learning of goal hierarchies. ● 0497

**Laird, R. K.**
Emerging communications technology paradigms. 02320

**Lake, R.**
Near-real-time control of human figure models. 01829
Near-real-time control of human figure models. 03295

**Lakeman, G.**
Symbiotic systems for complex problems. 02922

**Lakin, F.**
A performing medium for working group graphics. HCI-0383 †

**Lakshmanan, V. S.**
On global context dependencies and their properties (extended abstract). 03945

**LaLomia, M. J.**
Problem solving performance and display preference for information displays depicting numerical functions. 0978

**LaLonde, W.**
Graphics through the looking glass. 02391

**LaLonde, W. R.**
A smalltalk window system based on constraints. 01128

**Lam, L.**
Rule-based detection of speech features for automatic speech recognition. 0419

**Lam, N.**
Optimizing the structure of database menu indexes: a decision model of menu search. 01716

**Lamb, D. A.**
An annotated bibliography on user interface design. 01004
DRAT: A program for maintaining listings. 02401

**Lamb, L.**
X window system user's guide for version 11: vol. 3. ● 0562

**Lamb, M. R.**
Towards a comprehensive user interface management system. 0081

**Lamba, T. S.**
Natural language interface based on keyword extraction using AWK. 02498

**Lambe, J.**
Electronic implementation of associative memory based on neural network models. 01895
Error correction and asymmetry in a binary memory matrix. 02750

**Lambert, A. J.**
Optimum display arrangements for presenting visual reminders. 03237

**Lampson, B.**
Personal distributed computing: the Alto and Ethernet software. 03096

**Lampson, B. W. (Ed.)**
Annual review of computer science vol. 1, 1986. ● 0719

**Lamy, J. F.**
A multiple track animator system for motion synchronization. 03350

**Lancaster, F. W.**
The evaluation of information services: a typology. 0452

**Land, F. (Ed.)**
Knowledge based management support systems. ● 0252

**Landau, J. A.**
An error correcting protocol for medical expert systems. 02143

**Landauer, T.**
Human computer interaction in the year 2000. 0924

**Landauer, T. K.**
The role of laboratory experiments in HCI: help, hindrance, or ho-hum? 0863
Formative design evaluation of superbook. 01154
Retrieval systems for the information seeker: can the role of the intermediary be automated? 02864
Using latent semantic analysis to improve access to textual information. 02901
The vocabulary problem in human-system communication. HCI-0224 †
Relations between cognitive psychology and computer system design. HCI-0244 †

**Landwehr, C. E. (Ed.)**
Database Security: Status and Prospects. § 03579

**Landy, F. J.**
Human—computer interactions in the workplace: psychosocial aspects of VDT use. 0306

# AUTHOR INDEX

**Landy, M.**
Intelligible encoding of ASL image sequences at extremely low information rates. 02708
**Lane, A.**
Domesticating microsoft windows. 01309
**Lane, D. M.**
Impact of a restricted natural language interface on ease of learning and productivity. 01334
**Lang, B.**
Centaur: the system. 01136
On the usefulness of syntax directed editors. 03781
**Lang, M.**
Recent advances in speech understanding and dialog systems. § 03987
**Lange, B. M.**
Some strategies of reuse in an object-oriented programming environment. 0820
**Langefors, B. (Ed.)**
Trends in information systems. • 0498
**Langley, P.**
Learning, development, and production systems. 0479
A general theory of discrimination learning. 0481
Psychological evaluation of path hypotheses in cognitive diagnosis. 0537
**Langley, P. (Ed.)**
Production system models of learning and development. • 0478
**Langridge, R.**
The MIDAS database system. 02387
The MIDAS display system. 02388
**Langton, K. B.**
Delphi: an intelligent interface for a dolphin communication laboratory. 02989
**Lanning, S.**
Beyond the chalkboard: computer support for collaboration and problem solving inmeetings (Reprint). 0376
WYSIWIS revised: early experiences with multiuser interfaces. 01158
Beyond the chalkboard: computer support for collaboration and problem solving in meetings. HCI-0312 †
**Lansdown, J.**
Computer graphics: A tool for the artist, designer and amateur. 0235
**Lansner, J.**
Steel yields in Pa. 01649
**Lantz, K. A.**
An experiment in integrated multimedia conferencing. 0381
On user interface reference models. 0946
Reference models, window systems, and concurrency. 01058
Multi-process structuring of user interface software. 01066
**Lapedes, A.**
A self-optimizing, nonsymmetrical neural net for content addressable memory and pattern recognition. 02562
Programming a massively parallel, computation universal system: Static behavior. 02746
**Lappin, J. S.**
The representation and perception of geometric structure in moving visual patterns. 03326
**Large, J. A.**
OST— a training package for end-users of online systems. 02568
**Larkin, I. N.**
The user is always right. 01966
**Larkin, M. D.**
Concept demonstration of the use of interactive fault diagnosis and isolation for TF30 engines. 02968
**LaRose, R.**
Understanding cable subscribership as telecommunications behavior. 02676
**Larsen, H. L.**
KIWI: knowledge-based user-friendly system for the utilization of information bases. 0739
**Larsen, J. F.**
Human aspects of factory modernization. 01513
**Larsen, S. S.**
Understanding & using application software. • 0626

**Larson, J. A.**
A visual approach to browsing in a database environment. HCI-0258 †
**Larson, P. (Ed.)**
SIGMOD International Conference on Management of Data. § 03089
**Lasaga, M. I.**
Approaches to human reasoning: an analytic framework. HCI-0239 †
**Lashley, C.**
An experimental comparison of tabular and graphic data presentation. HCI-0236 †
**Lasseter, J.**
Principles of traditional animation applied to 3D computer animation. 01072
**Lassiter, D. L.**
Changes in electromyographic activity associated with occupational stress and poor performance in the workplace. 01734
**Lassudrie, C.**
Attacking a complex distributed algorithm from different sides: an experience wih complementary validation tools. 01429
**Last, R. W.**
Artificial intelligence techniques in language learning. • 0500
**Lathrop, O.**
Virtual graphics. 02815
**Latrille, J.**
Socio-technical aspects of electronic mail implementation. 01439
**Laub, A. J. (Ed.)**
Advanced computing concepts and techniques in control engineering. § 03833
**Lauenroth, H. G.**
Report from the working group on "socialist experience with modelling and using systems". 03667
**Laughery, K. R., Jr.**
Human factors in software engineering: a review of the literature. HCI-0157 †

**Laughery, K. R., Sr.**
Human factors in software engineering: a review of the literature. HCI-0157 †

**Laurel, B.**
Drama and personality in user interface design. 0830

**Laurent, D.**
Geomatic: a 3-D graphic relief simulation system. HCI-0395 †

**Laurgeau, C.**
Logic and programming. • HCI-0068 †

**Laurillard, D.**
Pedagogical design for interactive video. 0505

**Laurillard, D. (Ed.)**
Interactive media: working methods and practical applications. • 0501

**Lavorel, P. M.**
The distributed processing of knowledge and belief in the human brain. HCI-0240 †

**Lawler, B.**
Designing computer-based microworlds. 0742

**Lawler, R. W. (Ed.)**
Artificial intelligence and education; vol. 1: learning environments and tutoring systems. • 0516

**Lawrence, K.**
Artificial intelligence in the man/machine interface. 01626

**Lawrence, M. J.**
The accuracy of combining judgemental and statistical forecasts. 02474

**Lawton, D.**
Computational techniques in motion processing. 0025

**Lawton, D. T.**
Determining the instantaneous axis of translation from optic flow generated by arbitrary sensot motion. 03332

**Layne, B. H.**
Color, graphics, and animation in a computer-assisted learning tutorial lesson. 02294

**Lazzaro, J.**
A machine for neural computation of acoustical patterns with application to real time speech recognition. 02751

**Lea, W. A.**
The elements of speech recognition. 0176

**Leary, E.**
Lets "Deep-Six" our reference manuals. 02955

**Leben, J.**
Principles of data communication. • 0547

**LeBert, J. J.**
Advanced interactive cobol for micros: a practical approach. • 0521
Advanced interactive COBOL for micros: a practical approach. • 0522

**LeBlanc, T. J.**
Structured message passing on a shared-memory multiprocessor. 03514

**LeBold, W. K.**
Cognitive issues in the process of software development: review and reappraisal. 02222

**LeClair, S. R.**
Interactive learning: a multiexpert paradigm for acquiring new knowledge. 0776

**Lederberg, J.**
How DENDRAL was conceived and born. 02839

**Lederer, A. L.**
Validation of a Jungian instrument for MIS research. 01022
Some design guidelines for an information center to support office information systems. 01093

**Lederman, L. C.**
The marble company: The design and implementation of a simulation board game. 02595

**Lederman, S. J.**
The physiology and psychophysics of touch. 04010

**Ledgard, H.**
Misconception in human factors. 0758

**Ledley, R. S.**
Medical informatics: a personal view of sowing the seeds. 02841

**Lee, A. S.C.**
AI/learn: an interactive videodisk system for teaching medical concepts and reasoning. 02381

**Lee, A. Y.**
Learning and transfer of measurement tasks. 0832

**Lee, C.**
Knowledge-based system for task analysis and reliability enhancement. 01516

**Lee, C. H.**
Human-computer interaction in manufacturing. 01522

**Lee, C. M.**
A study on an error recovery expert system using a superimposer and a digitizer in the advanced teleoperator system. 03389
Interactive error recovery expert system for robot with voice recognition subsystem. 03420

**Lee, D. T.**
Personal computing for decision support. HCI-0299 †

**Lee, E.**
An empirical investigation of two electronic mail systems. 01239
Optimizing the structure of database menu indexes: a decision model of menu search. 01716
Menu search: random or systematic? 02144

**Lee, E. S.**
A feature matching approach to the retrieval of graphical information. 01245

**Lee, G.**
From arcane ASCII to the printed page - computer basics. 01148

**Lee, H. H.**
SMART: Scientific database management and engineering analysis routines and tools. 01166

**Lee, H. Y.**
Machine learning using a higher order correlation network. 02563
High order correlation model for associative memory. 02729

**Lee, J.**
GRAFLOG: understanding drawings through natural language. 01396
An exploratory contingency model of user participation and MIS use. 01919
How can groups communicate when they use different languages? 03038

**Lee, J. M.**
The effects of 3D imagery on managerial data interpretation. 02502

**Lee, K.**
The responsive system: a new challenge for AI. 02920

**Lee, K. S.**
Optical analog of two-dimensional neural networks and their application in recognition of radar targets. 02733

**Lee, N. S.**
$DM^2$: an algorithm for diagnostic reasoning that combines analytical models and experiential knowledge. 02190

**Lee, S.**
CAD Data management using object-oriented paradigms. 02958
An investigation into the existence of subgroup concept in information systems personnel management. 03022
A study of group interaction over a computer-based message system. 03257

**Lee, S. C.**
A blackboard architecture for problem solving and machine learning in an expert system for power system voltage control. 02926

**Lee, S. Y.**
A study on an error recovery expert system using a superimposer and a digitizer in the advanced teleoperator system. 03389
Interactive error recovery expert system for robot with voice recognition subsystem. 03420

**Lee, Y. C.**
Machine learning using a higher order correlation network. 02563
High order correlation model for associative memory. 02729
Nonlinear dynamics of artificial neural systems. 02747

**Leedham, C. G.**
On-line recognition of Pitman's hand-written shorthand—an evaluation of potential. 02111

**Leeds, J. L.**
Operator performance as a function of type of display: conventional versus perspective. 01769

**Leemakers, M. A.M.**
Criteria for the subjective quality of visual display units. 03724

**Leemon, J.**
Assessment of an effort to integrate computer functions in an engineering design firm. 0779

**Leermakers, M. A.M.**
Visual comfort as a criterion for designing display units. 03892

**Lefevre-Fonollosa, M.**
Principle of visual color coding applied to satellite images. 03304

**LeFevre, A. M.**
Planning for hospital information systems using the Lancaster Soft Systems methodology. 01228

**Lefkowitz, L. S.**
Knowledge-based support of cooperative activities. 0171
Knowledge-based support of cooperative activities. 03478

**Lefons, E.**
Evolution of interactional human behavior with age: a theoretical/experimental approach. 01618

**Lefrere, P.**
On the application of rule-based techniques to the design of advice giving systems. HCI-0315 †

**Legendi, T. (Ed.)**
Parcella '88: Fourth International Workshop on Parallel Processing by Cellular Automata and Arrays. § 03971

**Leggett, J.**
Verifying identity via keystroke characteristics. 02178

An empirical investigation of voice as an input modality for computer programming. HCI-0237 †

**Lehman, J.**
Mainframe and microcomputer-based business graphics: end user computing comparisons and trends. 02805
Mainframe and microcomputer-based business graphics: What satisfies users? HCI-0216 †

**Lehman, J. A.**
Business graphics trends, two years later. 01945

**Lehman, S.**
The changing workplace: A guide to managing the people, organizational, and regulatory aspects of office technology (book excerpt). 0044

**Lehmann, D.**
The KOMPLEX performance prediction tool. 02669

**Lehmann, H.**
A theory for the representation of knowledge. 01811

**Lehmann, W. P.**
Human language and computers. 01550

**Lehner, P.**
An empirical investigation as to the need for multicomponent decision models. 01898

**Lehner, P. E.**
Cognitive impacts of the user interface. 0432
Cognitive factors in user/expert-system interaction. 01733
Distributed tactical decisionmaking: conceptual framework and empirical results. 01885

**Lehtinen, E.**
Action based model of information system. 02037
Seven mortal sins of systems work. 03645

**Lehtman, H.**
Working together. 01300

**Leifer, R.**
Information systems development success: Perspectives from project team participants. 02501

**Leigh, W.**
A graphical database interface. 01511
User facilities for engineering support stations. 01512
Interpretation of natural language database queries using optimization methods. 01861

**Leiser, R. G.**
Design of user-system interfaces using a cognitive design aid. 01682
Exploiting convergence to improve natural language understanding. 02071

**Leitch, R.**
Qualitative modeling of physical systems for knowledge based control. 03834

**Leitheiser, R. L.**
Service support levels: An organizational approach to end-user computing. 02503

**Leiweber, D.**
Finance. 0135

**Lella, G.**
NLI-ESD: An expert natural language interface to a statistical data bank. 02712

**LeMay, M.**
Operator work load: when is enough enough? HCI-0222 †

**Lemke, A.**
Active help systems. HCI-0108 †

**Lengel, R. H.**
Message equivocality, media selection and manager performance: implications for information systems. 02505

**Lenman, S.**
Touch screen, cursor keys and mouse interaction. 03769
Naming errors and automatic error correction in human-computer interaction. 03770

**Leonard-Barton, D.**
Putting expert systems to work. 01704
Managerial influence in the implementation of new technology. 02481

**Leong, B. L.**
Iris: design of a user interface program for symbolic algebra. 03081
Iris: design of an user interface program for symbolic algebra. 03085

**Lepădatu, A.**
A biparty grammar as a tool for defining a man-machine dialogue. 03639

**Lepădatu, C.**
A biparty grammar as a tool for defining a man-machine dialogue. 03639

**Leppänen, A.**
Effects of computerization on job demands and stress: the correspondence of subjective and objective data. 03622

**Lepper, M. R.**
Socializing the intelligent tutor: bringing empathy to computer tutors. 0541

**Lequesne, P. N.**
Individual and organizational factors and the design of IPSEs. 01408

**Lerch, F. J.**
Skilled financial planning: the cost of translating ideas into action. 0834

**Lerch, I. A.**
Electronic communications and collaboration: the emerging model for computer aided communications in science and medicine. 02678

**Lerner, E. J.**
Realism in synthetic speech. 0066

**Lesgold, A. (Ed.)**
Learning Issues for Intelligent Tutoring Systems. • 0534
Learning issues for intelligent tutoring systems. • 0545

**Lesk, M. E.**
Retrieval systems for the information seeker: can the role of the intermediary be automated? 02864

**Letovsky, S.**
Cognitive processes in program comprehension. 02403
Mental models and software maintenance. 02404
Mental models and software maintenance. HCI-0173 †
Cognitive processes in program comprehension. HCI-0179 †

**Letts, S.**
The use of the IBM personal computer in the man-machine interface to a nuclear research accelerator. 01454

**Leuci, N. D.**
A cost model for estimating the costs of developing software in the Ada programming language. 03539

**Leung, C.**
Application frameworks: experience with MacApp. 01039

**Levas, A.**
A workcell application design environment (WADE). 0598

**Leventhal, L.**
Profile of undergraduate software engineering courses: results from a survey. 01035

**Leventhal, L. M.**
Software development snapshots: A preliminary investigation. 0959
Experience of programming beauty: some patterns of programming aesthetics. 02184
A scarce resource in undergraduate software engineering courses: user interface design materials. 04027

**Levi, S.**
A methodology for designing distributed, fault-tolerant, and reactive real-time operating systems. 04071

**Levialdi, S.**
An image processing language with ICON-assisted navigation. HCI-0387 †

**Levin, J. A.**
Learning with interactive media: dynamic support for students and teachers. 0519

**Levine, E. H.**
Information science and the PSI phenomenon. 01281

# AUTHOR INDEX

**Levine, L. B.**
Consulting skills for technical writers. 0124
Corporate culture, technical documentation, and organization diagnosis. HCI-0151 †

**Levine, M. D.**
A knowledge-based approach to computer vision systems. 03302

**Levine, R. I.**
A comprehensive guide to AI and expert systems. ● HCI-0058 †

**Levinson, N. S.**
Repositioning the information systems management function: Implications for information systems personnel. 03015

**Levitan, K. B. (Ed.)**
Government infostructures: a guide to the networks of information resources and technologies at federal, state, and local levels. ● 0523

**Levner, G.**
A simple, general method for ray tracing bicubic surfaces. 03853

**Levy, D. (Ed.)**
Computer chess compendium. ● 0526

**Levy, F.**
Eye Fatigue among VDU users and non-VDU users. 03682

**Levy, S.**
Environment-centered and viewer-centered perception of surface orientation. 02705
The 1984 Olympic Message System: a test of behavioral principles of system design. HCI-0125 †
Environment-centered and viewer-centered perception of surface orientation. HCI-0392 †

**Lewart, D. K.**
TNT: a talking tutor 'n' trainer for teaching use of interactive computer systems. 0895

**Lewerentz, C.**
Extended programming in the large in a software development environment. HCI-0101 †

**Lewis, C.**
Designing for usability: Key principles and what designers think. 0078

Designing for error. 0087
Learning about computers and learning about mathematics. 0208
Introduction: designing interfaces for expert systems. 0426
Composition of production. 0485
Generalization, consistency, and control. 0796
A model of mental model construction. 0931
Cursor movement during text editing. HCI-0113 †
Designing for usability: key principles and what designers think. HCI-0231 †

**Lewis, C. (Ed.)**
Human Factors in Computing Systems. § 02903

**Lewis, C. H.**
Learning to use word processors: problems and prospects. 0059

**Lewis, C. M.**
Significance testing of rules in rule-based models of human problem solving. 01867

**Lewis, E.**
Technology + design + research = information design. 0107

**Lewis, J. R.**
Slot versus insertion magnetic stripe readers: user performance and preference. 01756

**Lewis, M. B.**
Fine tuning selection semantics in a structure editor based programming environment: some experimental results. 0975

**Lewis, R.**
Models of user interactions with graphical interfaces: 1. statistical. 0883

**Lewis, R. (Ed.)**
Computer assisted learning in the humanities and social sciences. ● 0470

**Lewis, T. G.**
Prototypes from standard user interface management systems. 01370

**Leyton, M.**
Generative systems of analyzers. 01461
Nested structures of control: an intuitive view. 01464

Principles of information structure common to six levels of the human cognitive system. 02019
A theory of information structure. I. General principles. 02361
A theory of information structure. II. A theory of perceptual organization. 02362
A limitation theorem for the differentiable prototypification of shape. 02365
Generative systems of analyzers. 02702

**Li, P. Y.**
A computer training tool using Chinese natural language. 02948

**Li, X.**
Graphics-based qualitative simulation generator for power distribution systems. 02946

**Liang, T.**
Reasoning in model management systems. 03487

**Liberati, D.**
Single sweep analysis of visual evoked potentials through a model of parametric identification. 01261

**Liberatore, M. J.**
The effects of display formats on information systems design. 02357

**Lichten, L.**
An innovative user interface for microcomputer-based computer-aided design. 03865

**Licklider, J. C. R.**
Some reflections on early history. 0348

**Lickorish, A.**
Multi-window displays for readers of lengthy texts. 02142

**Lidén, C.**
VDT work and the skin. 03696

**Liégeois, A.**
Performance and computer-aided design. ● HCI-0068 †

**Lieberman, H.**
An example-base environment for beginning programmers. 0520

**Lieberman, H. (Ed.)**
ECOOP '87. § 03790

**Liebman, J. S.**
Implementation issues for operations research software. 01537

**Liew, C. J.**
Inference control mechanism for statistical database frequency-imposed data distortions. 02449

**Liew, C. K.**
Inference control mechanism for statistical database frequency-imposed data distortions. 02449

**Light, P. H.**
The role of social processes in children's microcomputer use. 0471

**Ligier, Y.**
EM2—a Modula-2 programming environment. 02392

**Ligomenides, P. A.**
Notions and dynamics of information. 02319
Modeling uncertainty in human perception. 03825

**Lilly, P. M.**
Automatic contour definition on left ventriculograms by image evidence and a multiple template-based model. 04073

**Limbek, B. E.**
Generic diagnostic knowledge acquisition tool. 02944

**Lin, C. C.**
Implementation of a Prolog-INGRES interface. 01087

**Lin, F.**
Cognitive science and organizational design: a case study of computer conferencing (Reprint). 0386

**Lin, J.**
Attitudes toward unauthorized software copying: general public vs. business faculty member. 01142

**Lin, X.**
An interactive system SDI on microcomputer. 02272

**Lincoln, J. E.**
Hypertext engineering: practical methods for creating a compact disk encyclopedia. 02832

**Lincoln, T. L.**
An historical perspective on clinical laboratory information systems. 02848

**Lind, M.**
The interface is often not the problem. 0837
Human cognition and human computer interaction. HCI-0241 †

**Lind, M. R.**
Linking mechanism supporting end-user computing. 02806

**Lindberg, D. A.B.**
In praise of computing. 02838

**Linde, L.**
On search in an incomplete database. HCI-0214 †

**Lindenfilzer, P.**
Process control with the G2 real-time expert system. 02934

**Lindquist, T. E.**
GENIE: a modifiable computer-based task for experiments in human-computer interaction. HCI-0194 †

**Lindsay, B. G.**
View management in distributed data base systems. 0218

**Lindsay, P. A.**
A support system for formal reasoning: requirements and status. 04035

**Lindsay, R. K.**
Linguistic knowledge as expertise. 02077

**Lines, B. M.**
A model for assessing the performance of a local area network employing technical office protocol (TOP) as part of MAP/TOP network in a computer integrated manufacturing (CIM) research project, for the transmission of real time interactive speech. 02491

**Ling, Y.**
Simps: Secondary ion mass image processing system. 02267

**Linnainmaa, S.**
Icecream, transportable software for creating friendly human interfaces. 02615

**Linsker, R.**
Self-organization in a perceptual network. 01366

**Lintern, G.**
Simulator design and instructional features for air-to-ground attack: a transfer study. 01804

**Linton, A.**
A communication system supporting large datagrams on a local area network. HCI-0166 †

**Linton, M. A.**
Composing user interfaces with InterViews. HCI-0131 †

**Lippman, A.**
Coding image sequences for interactive retrieval. 01330

**Lippmann, R. P.**
An introduction to computing with neural nets. 0769

**Lisca, L.**
An abstract description generator for the reliability analysis in the design of real time systems. 02490

**Lissandre, M.**
SPECIF-X: a tool for CASE. 03801

**Little, J. C. (Ed.)**
Computer science education. § 02809

**Littman, D. C.**
Modelling human expertise in knowledge engineering: some preliminary observations. 02134
Mental models and software maintenance. 02404
Mental models and software maintenance. HCI-0173 †

**Liu, J. P.**
Utilizing the trend of end user development. 02444

**Liu, X.**
A hybrid approach to deductive uncertain inference. 02191

**Liu, Y.**
Codes and modalities in multiple resources: a success and a qualification. 01793

**Liu, Z.**
On the minimum number of templates required for shift, rotation and size invariant pattern recognition. 02531

# AUTHOR INDEX

**Lively, W. M.**
Graphical specification of user interfaces with behavior abstraction. 0840

**Liverpool, P. R.**
TA: Can it improve worker satisfaction with organizational decision-making? 02414

**Livingston, R. B.**
Motion analysis of grammatical processes in a visual-gestural language. 03347

**Livley, W.**
Express—rapid prototyping and product development via integrated knowledge-based executable specifications. 03492

**Lloret, M. J.**
Recent results on the application of a metric-space search algorithm (AESA) to multispeaker data. 03997

**Lloyd, E. L.**
One-layer routing without component constraints. HCI-0090 †

**Lloyd, S. J.**
The role of stimulus-to-rule consistency in learning rapid application of spatial rules. 01765

**Löwgren, J.**
History, state and future of user interface management systems. 0966

**Lochbaum, C. C.**
Formative design evaluation of superbook. 01154

**Lochovsky, F. H.**
OTM: specifying office tasks. 03039
Role-based security in data base management systems. 03584

**Lochovsky, F. H. (Ed.)**
Object-oriented concepts, databases, and applications. ● 0475

**Locke, M.**
Off-line programming and path generation for robot manipulators. 0603

**Lockhovsky, F. H.**
Querying external databases. HCI-0233 †

**Lockwood, R.**
Graphics. 02554

**Lodwick, G. S.**
The history of the use of computers in the interpretation of radiological images. 02845

**Loewenstein, G. F.**
Frames of mind in intertemporal choice. 02478

**Logan, G. D.**
Automaticity, resources, and memory: theoretical controversies and practical implications. 01792

**Loken-Kim, K.**
Error detection and correction in a speech recognition system: a knowledge based system approach. 04054

**Lomow, G.**
Monitoring distributed systems. HCI-0169 †

**Long, G. M.**
The effects of target wavelength on dynamic visual acuity under photopic and scotopic viewing. 01762

**Long, J.**
Cognitive optimisation of Videotex dialogues: a formal—empirical approach. 0320
Some cognitive aspects of interface design in a two-variable optimization task. HCI-0111 †
Information technology and home-based services: improving the usability of teleshopping. HCI-0226 †

**Long, J. B.**
People and computers: designing for usability. 03245
Voice versus keyboard: use of a comparative analysis of learning to identify skill requirements of input devices. 03275

**Longstaff, J.**
Knowledge base enhancements to relational databases. 03285

**Longstaff, J. (Ed.)**
Proc. of the third British national conference on databases (BNCOD3). § 03279

**Longuet-Higgins, C.**
Tones of voice: the role of intonation in computer speech understanding. HCI-0356 †

**Looney, C. G.**
Rule-based reasoning as Boolean transformations. 01901

**Lootsteen, P.**
Acquisition of process control skills. 01878

**Lopez, L.**
An incidence-matrix-driven panel system for the IBM PC. 01814

**Lorenz, V.**
Help systems-assisting the user. 01201

**Lorie, R. A.**
System R: a relational approach to database management. 0709

**Loucks, L. K.**
Advanced interactive executive (AIX) operating system overview. 01815

**Lougenia Anderson, T.**
The proteus bibliography: Representation and interactive display in databases. 01085

**Louis, M. R.**
Restoring a sense of control during implementation: how user involvement leads to system acceptance. 02509

**Lounamaa, P. H.**
Adaptive coordination of a learning team. 02475

**Love, W.**
Human-computer interface recording. 01414

**Loveless, R. L. (Ed.)**
The computer revolution and the arts. ● 0529

**Lovergrove, G.**
Where have all the girls gone? 02689

**Low, Y. P.**
GENIE-M: A generator for multimedia information environments. 0268

**Loy, S. L.**
The impact of DSS on organizational communication. HCI-0294 †

**Lozinskii, E.**
Computing human oriented descriptions. 02020

**Lu, I. Y.**
The economic evaluation on implementation industrial robot from user point of view. 03447

**Lucash, R. M.**
Legal liability for malfunction and misuse of expert systems. 0939

**Luchetti, R.**
Your office is where you are. 01703

**Luck, K.**
CAD system GISK for interactive graphical modelling of planar mechanisms. 01570

**Ludolph, F.**
Fabrik: a visual programming environment. 01130

**Luebking, S.**
A change of mind or the story of Fuzzies in Purgatory. 0961
Once more, with meaning. 0967

**Luey, B.**
Technology and the author's labour. 02574

**Luff, P.**
Conversational resources for situated action. 0861

**Luk, W.**
Providing quality responses with natural language interfaces: the null value problem. 01848

**Lumia, R.**
CAD-based off-line programming applied to a cleaning and deburring workstation. 0607

**Lund, P. H.**
Understanding & using application software. ● 0626

**Lund, R. L.**
A search for machine/human compatibility in manufacturing systems. 03381

**Luniewski, A. W.**
Quill: An extensible system for editing documents of mixed type. 03517

**Lunn, R.**
Visual fatigue and spatial frequency adaptation to video displays of text. 01721

**Lunney, D.**
Communicating with sound. 0067

**Luria, M.**
The Berkeley UNIX consultant project. 01355

**Luria, S. M.**
The effects of set size on color matching using CRT displays. 01711

**Luther, A.**
Digital video interactive. 0681

**Luther, W.**
An object-oriented approach to multimedia databases. 01084

**Lutz, J.**
Personality characteristics of junior high school students successful with computers. 01592

**Luzadder, W. J.**
Fundamentals of engineering drawing: with an introduction to interactive computer graphics for design and production, (9th ed.). ● 0531

**Lynch, E. F.**
Directed dialogue protocols: verbal data for user interface design. 0866
Effects of interface design upon user productivity. 02891

**Lynch, G.**
Experience with contextual field research. 0802
In search of a user interface reference model. 0944

**Lynch, K. J.**
Handling textual information in a GDSS database: experience with the Arizona analyst information system. 03475

**Lynch, W. K.**
Implementation plan for the use of on-line fiber analysis in the textile industry. 03433

**Lynn, M. P.**
Expert systems as human resource management decision tools. 02440

**Lynne, K. J.**
Computing with structured connectionist networks. HCI-0314 †

**Lyons, D.**
Schemas that integrate vision and touch for hand control. 0026

**Lyons, N. P.**
An empirical approach to the evaluation of icons. 01013

**Lyons, T. G.**
Selecting an Ada environment. ● HCI-0015 †

**Lyytinen, K.**
Action based model of information system. 02037
Seven mortal sins of systems work. 03645

**Ma, P.**
A graphics interface for linear programming. 01332

**Mäkisara, K.**
Representation of sensory information in self-organizing feature maps. 02744

**Mäkitie, J.**
VDU work, refractive errors and binocular vision. 03739

**Mäntylä, M.**
A design data manager. 03090
Interactive solid modeling in hut design. 03837
HutWindows: an improved architecture for a user interface management system. 03854

**Maarse, F. J.**
Automatic identification of writers. 03909

**Maas, R. E.**
Natural-language interface for an instructable robot. HCI-0324 †

**Maass, S.**
Designing for designers: an analysis of design practice in the real world. 0839
The designer as user: building requirements for design tools from design practice. HCI-0129 †

**Mably, C.**
Interactive video as a school resource: Rolls-Royce or Model T Ford? 0513

**Mac, M.**
The use of VDM on the specification of Chinese characters. 04038

**MacArthur, C. A.**
Learning disabled students' difficulties in learning to use a word processor: implications for design. 0889
Using interactive videotaped-based instruction to teach on-the-job social skills to handicapped adolescents. 02288

**Macaskill, M. J.**
Weighting, ranking and relevance feedback in a front-end system. 02329

**Macaulay, L.**
Human factors in the IT specification process. 01372
Describing a product opportunity: a method of understanding the users' environment. 03194

**Macaulay, L. A.**
An evaluation of the effectiveness of the adaptive interface module (AIM) in matching dialogues to users. 03212

**MacCallum, K.**
THESYS—implementation of a knowledge-based design system with multiple viewpoints. 0010

**MacCrimmon, K. R.**
Expert systems and creativity. 0553

**MacDonald, C. I.**
Challenges in the application of graphics technology to the management of geographic information. 03871

**Macfarlane, K. N.**
A study of an advance organizer as a technique for teaching computer programming concepts. 01042

**MacGregor, D.**
Search success and expectations with a computer interface. 01995
Embedded training in AI technology through an expert system interface: an alarm processor application. 02991
Calibrating databases. HCI-0269 †

**MacGregor, J.**
An empirical investigation of two electronic mail systems. 01239
Optimizing the structure of database menu indexes: a decision model of menu search. 01716

Menu search: random or systematic? 02144

**MacGregor, J. N.**
A feature matching approach to the retrieval of graphical information. 01245

**MacGregor, R. C.**
Individualizing the man-machine interface. 03404

**Machlup, F. (Ed.)**
The study of information: interdisciplinary messages. ● HCI-0036 †

**MacIntyre, F.**
User-oriented suggestions for floating-point and complex-arithmetic Forth standard extensions. 02306

**Mack, R. L.**
Learning to use word processors: problems and prospects. 0059
Learning to use a word processor: by doing, by thinking, and by knowing. 0060
Metaphor, computing systems, and active learning. 02091
Learning to use a word processor: by doing, by thinking, and by knowing. HCI-0292 †

**MacKay, S. A.**
A multitasking switchboard approach to user interface management. 01053

**Mackay, W.**
Tools for supporting cooperative work near and far: highlights from the CSCW conference. 0879

**Mackay, W. E.**
How do experienced information lens users use rules? 0854
Virtual video editing in interactive multimedia applications. 01326
Video: Data for studying human-computer interaction. 02878
Diversity in the use of electronic mail: a preliminary inquiry. HCI-0310 †

**Mackinlay, J.**
Automating the design of graphical presentations of relational information. 01150

Applying a theory of graphical presentation to the graphic design of user interfaces. 03122

**Mackworth, A. K.**
The complexity of some polynomial network consistency algorithms for constraint satisfaction problems. HCI-0361 †

**MacLachlan, J.**
Psychologically based techniques for improving learning within computerized tutorials. 02277
The effects of 3D imagery on managerial data interpretation. 02502

**Maclean, A.**
Approximate modelling of cognitive activity with an expert system: a theory-based strategy for developing an interactive design tool. 01415

**MacLean, A.**
Approximate modelling of cognitive activity: towards an expert system design aid. 0801
Design rationale: the argument behind the artifact. 0860
The elicitation of system knowledge by picture probes. 0921
Human factors and the design of user interface management systems: EASIE as a case study. 01963
Navigating integrated facilities: initiating and terminating interaction sequences. 02876
Choosing between methods: analysing the user's decision space in terms of schemas and linear models. 02879
Rapid prototyping of dialogue for human factors research: the EASIE approach. 03254
Using an expert system to convey HCI information. 03272

**Macleod, I. A.**
Holophrasted displays in an interactive environment. HCI-0105 †

**Macmillan, C. J. B.**
The erotetic logic of problem-solving inquiry. 01583

**MacMillan, H.**
User interface primitives to allow full functional use of computers by physically disabled persons. 0979

**MacMorrow, N.**
Do VDU's make you sick? 01219
Are you sitting comfortably? 01220

**Macphail, E.**
Creativity, intelligence and evolution. 0365

**MacWhinney, B.**
The acquisition of grammar. 0353

**Madden, C.**
Parcel sorting by speech recognition: human factors issues. 03209

**Maddox, M. E.**
The effect of number ordering and orientation on marking speed and errors for mark-sensed labels. 01717

**Madhavji, N. H.**
A new approach to cursor movements in user interfaces of integrated programming environments. 01974

**Madni, A. M.**
The role of human factors in expert systems design and acceptance. 01780
Humane: A designer's assistant for modeling and evaluating function allocation options. 03397

**Madnick, S. E.**
A framework of composite information systems for strategic advantage. 03465

**Maeda, H.**
A fuzzy decision-making method and its application to a company choice problem. 02029

**Maeda, M.**
A design for a fuzzy logic controller. 02028

**Maehana, Y.**
CRT picture vibration caused by low-frequency magnetic field and its reduction method. 01987

**Magal, S. R.**
An investigation of the effects of age, size, and hardware option on the critical success factors applicable to information centers. 02352

**Maggiolini, P. C.**
System design for local authorities: participation based on "information contracts". 03656

**Magliaro, S.**
Computer programming and generalized problem-solving skills: in search of direction. 01585
Adolescents' chunking of computer programs. 01586

**Magnenat-Thalmann, N. (Ed.)**
Computer-generated images: the state of the art. § 03856

**Magnusson, B.**
The Mjølner environment: direct interaction with abstractions. 03794

**Magrass, Y.**
Computer literacy: the pigeonhole principle. 0789

**Magrez, P.**
Epistemic necessity, possibility, and truth. Tools for dealing with imprecision and uncertainty in fuzzy knowledge-based systems. 02075

**Mahbod, B.**
Language level persistence for an object-oriented application programming platform. 03522

**Mahmood, M. A.**
System development methods—a comparative investigation. 02504
Impact of design methods on decision support systems success: an empirical assessment. HCI-0303 †

**Maida, A. S.**
Selecting a humanly understandable knowledge representation for reasoning about knowledge. HCI-0330 †

**Maier, D.**
The proteus bibliography: Representation and interactive display in databases. 01085
The filter browser defining interfaces graphically. 03792

**Maigret, B.**
MOL3D, a modular and interactive program for molecular modeling and conformational analysis: I—basic modules. 02389

**Maina, G.**
Intraocular pressure during VDT work. 03683
Visual impairment and subjective ocular symptomatology in VDT operators. 03734

**Maio, D.**
A modular user-oriented decision support for physical database design. 01669

**Mair, P.**
The evaluation of project support environments for the STARTS user guide. 0173

**Majchrzak, A.**
Towards a framework for identifying organizationally-compatible AMT. 03372
Differential organization impacts of the transition from stand-alone to integrated flexible production. 03380

**Makino, S.**
Recognition of phonemes using time-spectrum pattern. 02648

**Makinouchi, A.**
A practical natural language interface to databases. 0199

**Makkuni, R.**
A gestural representation of the process of composing Chinese temples. 03855

**Malamud, C.**
DEC networks and architectures. • HCI-0003 †

**Maler, O.**
A new approach for introducing Prolog to naive users. 04029

**Malhotra, A.**
A graphical entity-relationship database browser. 03532

**Mallot, H. A.**
Characteristics of neuronal systems in the visual cortex. 01255
Parallelism and redundancy in neural networks. 03952

Why cortices? Neural computation in the vertebrate visual system. 03956

**Malloy, R.**
DOS 4.0. 01299

**Malone, T.**
User interface strategies '88 (Videotape). ● 0684
Computer-supported cooperative work: breakthroughs for user acceptance. 02874

**Malone, T. W.**
Computer support for organizations: toward an organizational science. 0211
Cognitive science and organizational design: a case study of computer conferencing (Reprint). 0386
Thomas W. Malone, Oct. 5: user interface strategies '88. ● 0532
Center for coordination science, MIT. 0841
How do experienced information lens users use rules? 0854
The information lens: an intelligent system for information sharing in organizations. 0891
Intelligent software agents. 01303
Intelligent information-sharing systems. 01322
How can groups communicate when they use different languages? 03038
Heuristics for designing enjoyable user interfaces: lessons from computer games. HCI-0132 †
Object lens: a "spreadsheet" for cooperative work. HCI-0206 †
Semistructured messages are surprisingly useful for computer-supported coordination. HCI-0290 †

**Maloney, L. T,**
Color constancy: a method for recovering surface spectral reflectance. 0298

**Malouf, D. B.**
Using interactive videotaped-based instruction to teach on-the-job social skills to handicapped adolescents. 02288

**Mambrey, P.**
Experiences in participative systems design. 03665

**Mammen, A.**
A display system for the Stellar Graphics Supercomputer Model GS1000. 02816

**Manacorda, P.**
A roundtable discussion on women, computers and participation. 03673

**Manacorda, P. M.**
Participation, organizational choices and time-economy: some theoretical questions. 03650

**Manago, M.**
Generalization and noise. 02155

**Manaster-Ramer, A.**
Linguistic knowledge as expertise. 02077

**Manatyla, M.**
HutWindows: an improved architecture for a user interface management system. 01830

**Mancini, G.**
Cognitive engineering in complex dynamic worlds. ● 0436
Modelling operators in accident conditions: advances and perspectives on a cognitive model. 02169
Models of the decision maker in unforeseen accidents. 02172

**Mancuso, J. C.**
Cognition & personal structure. ● 0533

**Mandell, S. F.**
Resistance to computerization: an examination of the relationship between resistance and the cognitive style of the clinician. HCI-0407 †

**Mandeville, D. E.**
Job characteristic perceptions of manual drafting and CADD: A field study of the effects of computerization on drafting & design personnel. 01523

**Mandl, H.**
Improvement of the acquisition of knowledge by informing feedback. 0540

**Mandl, H. (Ed.)**
Learning Issues for Intelligent Tutoring Systems. ● 0534

Learning issues for intelligent tutoring systems. ● 0545

**Mandutianu, S.**
A functional model of questions for natural language processing systems. 03575

**Mangun, G. R. R.**
The spatial allocation of visual attention as indexed by event-related brain potentials. 01739

**Manheim, M. L.**
An architecture for active DSS. 03480

**Manheimer, J. M.**
A case study of user interface management system development and application. 0836

**Manji, K. A.**
Pictorial dialogue methods. 02251
Pictorial knowledge bases. 03201

**Manktelow, K.**
Priniciples from the psychology of thinking and mental models. 0329

**Manktelow, K. I.**
Knowledge elicitation: dissociating conscious reflections from automatic processes. HCI-0337 †

**Mann, R. I.**
Organizational factors affecting the success of end-user computing. 02344

**Mann, T. L.**
Analysis of user procedural compliance in controlling a simulated process. 01879

**Manninen, M.**
Task-oriented approach to interactive control of heavy-duty manipulators based on coarse scene description. ● 0546

**Manninen, O.**
Changes in prosodic features of speech due to environmental factors. 02651

**Mannino, M. V.**
Knowledge representation for model libraries. 03479

**Manolescu, G.**
A biparty grammar as a tool for defining a man-machine dialogue. 03639

**Mansfield, U. (Ed.)**
The study of information: interdisciplinary messages. • HCI-0036 †

**Manske, F.**
Further division of reintegration of mental labour? CAD/CAP and work in design and work preparation shops. 03385

**Mansur, D. L.**
Communicating with sound. 0067

**Mantei, M.**
Capturing the capture concepts: a case study in the design of computer-supported meeting environments. 02824
Groupware: interface design for meetings. 02883

**Mantei, M. (Ed.)**
Human factors in computing systems. § 02854

**Mantei, M. M.**
Skilled financial planning: the cost of translating ideas into action. 0834
Cost/benefit analysis for incorporating human factors in the software lifecycle. HCI-0127 †

**Mantel, M. M.**
Video: Data for studying human-computer interaction. 02878

**Manzoul, M. A.**
Multi-Input fuzzy inference engine on a systolic array. 02953

**Marburger, H.**
Talking it over: the natural language dialog system HAM-ANS. 0165

**March, J. G.**
Adaptive coordination of a learning team. 02475

**March, S. T.**
End-user computing environments—finding a balance between productivity and control. 01927

**Marchal, A.**
Coproduction: evidence from EPG data. 02660

**Marchionini, G.**
Making the transition from print to electronic encyclopaedias: adapation of mental models. 02238
Information-seeking strategies of novices using a full-text electronic encyclopedia. 02452

**Marcus, A.**
Color in user interface design: functionally and aesthetics. 0803
Graphic design for computer graphics. HCI-0376 †

**Marek, T.**
Acting-out and burn-out behaviours of operators monitoring automated systems. 03440
Some remarks on a measure of computer operator workload: changes in pupil reflex. 03626
Mental fatigue of VDU operators induced by monotonous and various tasks. 03760

**Maren, A. J.**
Conference report: IEEE 1'st Int'l conference on neural networks. 0772
Hierarchical scene structure representations to facilitate image understanding. 02942

**Margulius, D. L.**
Videotex redux. 02545

**Marini, D.**
A simple, general method for ray tracing bicubic surfaces. 03853

**Maritorena, C.**
Presentation of a description language for office tasks. 01434

**Mark, L. S.**
Task and the adjustment of ergonomic chairs. 03711

**Marks, A.**
Using low-cost workstations to investigate computer networks and distributed systems. HCI-0437 †

**Marks, S.**
High tech, high stress? 01652

**Markus, M. L.**
Power, politics, and MIS implementation. 0042

**Marmarelis, V. Z.**
Modeling of task-dependent characteristics of human operator dynamics during pursuit manual tracking. 01859

**Marmolin, H.**
Naming errors and automatic error correction in human-computer interaction. 03770
Experimental evaluation of dialogue types for data entry. HCI-0115 †

**Marr, D.**
Visual information processing: artificial intelligence and the sensorium of sight. 0300

**Marras, W. S.**
Measurement of seat pressure distribution. 01760

**Marsden, J. R.**
End user—IS design professional interaction—information exchange for firm profit or end user satisfaction? 01936

**Marsh, C. A.**
The ISA expert system: a prototype system for failure diagnosis on the space station. 02913

**Marsh, C. E.**
Local work station concepts in a small distributed system. 02054

**Marsh, E.**
Transporting the linguistic string project system from a medical to a Navy domain. HCI-0352 †

**Marshall, C.**
Design guidelines. 0334
Assessment of trends in the technology and techniques of human-computer interaction. 0335

**Marshall, G.**
Interactive critical path analysis (ICPA)—microcomputer implementation of a project management and knowledge engineering tool. HCI-0445 †

**Marshall, J. C.**
Microcomputer software. 2. Scientific and technical word processing on a personal computer: has the time come? 02266

**Marsland, P. M.**
Competitive dynamics in a dual-route connectionist model of print-to-sound transformation. 01341

**Marslen-Wilson, W. D.**
Aspects of human speech understanding. 0290

**Marstrand, P. K. (Ed.)**
Creative intelligences. ● HCI-0056 †

**Martens, J.**
Phonetic segmentation using psychoacoustic speech parameters. 03991

**Martin, A.**
Human and computer involvement in simulation. 02593

**Martin, C. C.**
Computer aided concurrent design for printed wiring boards. 02981

**Martin, C. F.**
User-centered requirements analysis. ● HCI-0004 †

**Martin, F.**
Fragile knowledge and neglected strategies in novice programmers. HCI-0177 †

**Martin, G.**
Human performance evaluation of digitizer pucks for computer input of spatial information. 01774

**Martin, G. L.**
The utility of speech input in user-computer interfaces. 02230

**Martin, J.**
Principles of data communication. ● 0547
The Berkeley UNIX consultant project. 01355

**Martin, J. H.**
I didn't even know it was user services. 03133

**Martin, L. M.W.**
Teachers' adoption of multimedia technologies for science and mathematics instruction. 0577

**Martin, M. P.**
Adaptive general audience models: a research framework. 0202
Effect of computer knowledge on user performance over time. 01975

Using computer knowledge in the design of interactive systems. 02137
The human connection in systems design. 02410
Human factors principles. 02419
Designing systems for change. 02420
Prototypes for user training. 02421

**Martin, P.**
Transportability and generality in a natural-language interface system. 0394

**Martin, P. A.**
TEAM: an experiment in the design of transportable natural-language interfaces. HCI-0351 †

**Martinez, R.**
Automated document distribution using AI based workstations and knowledge based servers. 03466

**Martinez, S. E.**
Robot vs. human operator for speed, precision and other aspects. 03403

**Martinoli, A.**
A planning system for a cognitive problem. 02719

**Martins, J. S.B.**
A Unix distributed application support suitable for mini and microcomputer based systems. 02489

**Mason, J. A.**
Evaluating the intelligence in dialogue systems. 02194
Surveying projects on intelligent dialogue. 02197
Toward intelligent dialogue with ISIS. 02198

**Mason, M. V.**
Adaptive command prompting in an on-line documentation. 02121
Experimental adaptive interface. HCI-0139 †

**Massello, J.**
Implementing computer-mediated communication technologies: a technoacceptance approach to critical mass utilization. 01931

**Massey, D. G.**
Hypertext in context. 0114

**Massicote, M.**
Improved browsable displays for online subject access. 02051

**Masson, M. E.J.**
Misconceived misconceptions? 02881

**Massoni, J. B.**
Advanced interactive cobol for micros: a practical approach. ● 0521

**Masui, S.**
Manual control of an intrinsically unstable system and its modeling by fuzzy logic. 02026

**Matern, B.**
Designing learning processes for work activities in automated technologies. 03605

**Mather, G.**
Motion perception: second thoughts on the correspondence problem. 03325

**Matheus, C.**
Catching knowledge in neural nets. 01171

**Mathiassen, L.**
Systems, processes, and structures. 03644

**Mathiassen, L. (Ed.)**
System design for human development and productivity: participation and beyond. § 03640

**Mathieu, J.**
Experimental data for the design of a microworld-based system for algebra. 0543

**Mathis, V.**
The network control assistant (NCA), a real-time prototype expert system for network management. 02930

**Mathisen, K. S.**
Issues in research on clinical computer applications for mental health. 01560

**Matiasek, J.**
DATENBANK-DIALOG: a German language interface for relational databases. 01208

**Matin, E.**
Information transfer rate with serial and simultaneous visual display formats. 01770

**Matloff, N. S.**
Inference control via query restriction vs. data modification: a perspective. 03581

**Matoba, H.**
Information retrieval using impression of documents as a clue. 03065

**Matsumoto, G.**
Neurocomputing—neurons as microcomputers. 01691

**Matsumoto, H.**
Vowel normalization by frequency warped spectral matching. 02649

**Matsumura, T.**
A processing system for program specifications in a natural language. 03537

**Matsuo, M.**
Logic programmable natural language processor of a knowledge-base management system. 02965

**Matta, K. F.**
The influence of personality on self-paced instruction. 02291

**Mattes, B.**
Experiences with the development of a portable network operating system. 03882

**Matthew, I.**
Fatal error in pass zero: how not to confuse novices. HCI-0164 †

**Matthews, B.**
Process control with the G2 real-time expert system. 02934

**Matthews, M. L.**
The influence of visual workload history on visual performance. 01725

**Mattieligh, A.**
The semantic language episode understanding. 03576

**Mattox, A. (Ed.)**
AFIPS Conference Proceedings; vol. 55 1986 National Computer Conference. § 03162

**Maulsby, D. L.**
Inducing programs in a direct-manipulation environment. 0816

**Mawby, R.**
Mapping the cognitive demands of learning to program. 0579
Practices of novices and experts in critical inquiry. 0585

**Mawhinney, C. H.**
Validation of a Jungian instrument for MIS research. 01022
Perceptions of the CIS graduate's workstyle: undergraduate business students versus CIS faculty. 02999

**Maxwell, D.**
"Graphical marionette". 03349

**Maxwell, T.**
Machine learning using a higher order correlation network. 02563
High order correlation model for associative memory. 02729
Nonlinear dynamics of artificial neural systems. 02747

**May, J. G.**
Spatial requirements for visual simulation of aircraft at real-world distances. 01768

**May, M.**
KRITON: a knowledge-acquisition tool for expert systems. HCI-0327 †

**Mayer, R. E.**
Cognitive aspects of learning and using a programming language. HCI-0439 †

**Mayes, J. T.**
Information flow in a user interface: the effect of experience and context on the recall of MacWrite screens. 03228

**Mayfield, J.**
The Berkeley UNIX consultant project. 01355

**Mayhew, L. B.**
Increasing productivity with ISPF/APL2. 0767

**Maynard, J. F.**
An economical approach to modeling speech recognition accuracy. HCI-0354 †

**Mayne, R.**
Software engineering meets user services: a methodology for developing user. 03141

**Mayoh, B.**
Are machines as good as people in drawing conclusions from knowledge represented in catalogues, data bases and expert systems? 0736
On formalisms. 01280

**Mays, E.**
A temporal logic for reasoning about changing data bases in the context of natural language question-answering. 03176

**Mazer, A. S.**
A dataflow-based APL for the hypercube. 02905

**Mazur, S. A.**
LisaLearning. HCI-0092 †

**McBain, A.**
ISPBXs and terminals. 01385

**McBeth, M. B.**
A generic strategy for diagnostic assistance: the technician's assistant. 02957

**McBride, D. J.**
Understanding the effectiveness of computer graphics for decision support: a cumulative experimental approach. HCI-0215 †

**McBryan, O. A.**
A Computational model for interfaces. 01163

**McCall, R.**
Design environments for constructive and argumentative design. 0864

**McCalla, G. I.**
Summarizing natural language database responses. 01343

**McCammon, I. D.**
A survey of general-purpose manipulation. 02259

**McCann, C. A.**
ISIS: the interactive spatial information system. 02193

**McCauley, M. E.**
System design for speech recognition and generation. 0065

**McClelland, J. L.**
Parallel distributed processing: explorations in the microstructures of cognition; Vol. 2: Psychological and biological models. ● 0629
Schemata and sequential thought processes in PDP models. 0630
Interactive processes in speech perception: the TRACE model. 0631
The programmable blackboard model of reading. 0632
A distributed model of human learning and memory. 0633
On learning the past tenses of English verbs. 0634
Mechanisms of sentence processing: assigning roles to constituents. 0635
Amnesia and distrubuted memory. 0641

**McConnell, G.**
Interactive microcomputer programs for linear and non-linear static analysis of frameworks. 01165

**McCormack, J.**
An overview of the C toolkit. 03109

**McCormick, S.**
Some issues related to the design and development of an interactive video disc. 01497

**McCoy, K. F.**
Reasoning on a highlighted user model to respond to misconceptions. 01351

**McCoy, L. P.**
Computer programming and general problem solving by secondary students. 01587
The relationship of computer programming and mathematics in secondary students. 01588

**McCoy, L. S.**
Interfacing Ada and relational databases. 0762

**McCracken, D.**
Collaboration in KMS, a shared hypermedia system. 0807
The data model is the heart of interface design. 02875

**McCracken, D. L.**
Experience with the ZOG human-computer interface system. HCI-0246 †

**McCubbray, D. J.**
The systems analyst of the 1990's. 02998

**McDaid, E.**
An interdisciplinary approach to human factors in telematic systems. A review of the problems and possible solutions by a COST-11 ter working group. 01440

**McDaid, E. G.**
On the design of a graphical transition network editor. 03830

**McDonald, C.**
Support for graphs of processes in a command interpreter. 02633

**McDonald, C. S.**
fsh—a functional UNIX command interpreter. 02624

**McDonald, D. R.**
Adapting menu layout to tasks. 02182

**McDonald, J. E.**
A formal interface design methodology based on user knowledge. 0929
A comparison of menu selection techniques: touch panel, mouse and keyboard. 02122
The application of psychological scaling techniques to knowledge elicitation for knowledge-based systems. 02139
Adapting menu layout to tasks. 02182
Color-coding categories in menus. 02872
The mirage rapid interface prototyping system. 03112

**McDonald, N.**
Reference model for DBMS user facility. 01086

**McDonald, N. H.**
A multi media approach to the user interface. 02693

**McDonnald, A. D.**
Birth defect, spontaneous abortion and work with VDUs. 03688

**McDonough, F. A.**
Public Law 99-506, "Section 508" Electronic Equipment Accessibility for disabled workers. 02893

**McDougall, J.**
User interface primitives to allow full functional use of computers by physically disabled persons. 0979

**McDowell, R.**
A user agent for multiple computer-based message services. HCI-0306 †

**McEnery, A. M.**
People interact through computers not with them. 02060

**McGee, D. W.**
Mathematical modeling of fatigue in physically demanding jobs. 02363

**McGehe, J. D.**
Designing SAA applications and user interfaces. 01821

**McGill, R.**
An experiment in graphical perception. 02125

**McGreevy, M. W.**
The effect of perspective geometry on judged direction in spatial information instruments. 01720
Perspective traffic display format and airline pilot traffic avoidance. 01748

**McGregor, A. M.**
Information flow in a user interface: the effect of experience and context on the recall of MacWrite screens. 03228

**McGrowen, A. F.**
Design and implementation of a supercomputer frame buffer system. 03543

**McGuire, T. W.**
Social psychological aspects of computer-mediated communication (Reprint). 0384

**McGuire, W.**
Interactive color graphical postprocessing as a unifying influence in numerical analysis research. 01684

**McHenry, W. K.**
Handling textual information in a GDSS database: experience with the Arizona analyst information system. 03475

**McInroy, J.**
Express—rapid prototyping and product development via integrated knowledge-based executable specifications. 03492

**McIntyre, S. C.**
Motivation norms of knowledge engineers compared to those of software engineers. 02349
Causes of motivational problems among AI managers. 03004
Problems among managers of AI personnel. 03460

**McJones, P. R.**
System R: a relational approach to database management. 0709

**McKee, J. B.**
Computer user manuals in print: Do they have a future? 02782

**McKell, P.**
Application modelling in a user interface management system. 03262

**McKendree, J.**
Effect of practice on knowledge and use of basic Lisp. 0210
Advising roles of a computer consultant. 0896
Interface design issues for advice-giving expert systems. 01321
Planning for advising. 02886

**McKenzie Jr., J. D.**
An iterative approach to improving data analysis in the classroom. 03318

**McKeown Jr., D. M.**
Automating knowledge acquisition for aerial image interpretation. 01470

**McKeown, K. R.**
Using focus to constrain language generation. HCI-0341 †

**McKnight, C.**
Reading from paper versus reading from screen. 01416

**McLean, C. R.**
Interface concepts for plug-compatible production management systems. 01566

**McLeish, M. D.**
Delphi: an intelligent interface for a dolphin communication laboratory. 02989

**McLeod, R. J.**
Perceptions of system effectiveness as viewed by executives, users, and information specialists. 03469

**McMath, C. F.**
A graphical thesaurus-based information retrieval system. 02243

**McNally, B. D.**
Automation effects in a multiloop manual control system. 01865

**McNamee, L. P.**
VISION: VHDL induced schematic imaging on net-lists. 02830

**McNelis, K.**
Preferences for power in expert systems by novice users. 0971

**McPeters, D. L.**
The influence of rule-generated stress on computer-synthesized speech. 02081

**McPherson, M. G.**
Enhancing search results by editing, analysis and packaging. 02035

**McQuarrie, E. F.**
The computer imperative among owners of home computers: explanation by social factors. HCI-0217 †

**McShan, D. L.**
Color displays for medical imaging. 0262

**Méndez, A.**
An analysis of humanists' requests received by an information service for the humanities. 02318

**Mézard, M.**
Basins of attraction in a perceptron-like neural network. 01340

**Meacham, W.**
Build your own user interface. 01419

**Mead, C. A.**
VLSI architectures for implementation of neural networks. 02762

**Meadow, C. T.**
On designing for usability: an application of four key principles. 0923
Comment on some recent comments on information retrieval. 01074
OAKDEC, a program for studying the effects on users of a procedural expert system for database searching. 02003
The design and evaluation of a front-end user interface for energy researchers. 02453

**Meadow, R. G.**
A tolerance for surveillance: American public opinion concerning privacy and civil liberties. 0524

**Meadows, S.**
An assessment of the major computerised databases relating to disabled people in the UK and Scandinavia. 02326

**Meads, J.**
The standards factor. 0938
In search of a user interface reference model. 0944
The standards factor. 0952
The standards factor. 0986
The run-time structure of UIMS-supported applications. 01059

**Meads, J. A.**
Friendly or frivolous? 01650

**Medewitz, J. N.**
Impact of design methods on decision support systems success: an empirical assessment. HCI-0303 †

**Meehan, J. W.**
Magnification effects with imaging displays depend on scene content and viewing condition. 01786

**Meekings, B. A.E.**
A book on C. ● 0143

**Mehl, J. W.**
System R: a relational approach to database management. 0709

**Mehlenbacher, B.**
The evaluation of online help systems: a conceptual model. 0129

**Mehler, J. (Ed.)**
Connections and symbols. • 0588

**Mehlhorn, K. (Ed.)**
Parallel algorithms and architectures. § 03819

**Mehrabanzad, S.**
An experimental comparison of a mouse and arrow-jump keys for an interactive encyclopedia. 02098

**Meier, B. J.**
ACE: a color expert system for user interface design. 03117

**Meier, M.**
Interfaces for knowledge-base builders' control knowledge and application-specific procedures. 01810

**Meier, U.**
A roundtable discussion on women, computers and participation. 03673

**Meieran, H. B.**
Man-machine interfaces for mobile robotic systems. 03413
100 Percent assured performance for robotic assistive devices for handicapped and elderly persons. 03414
Standards requirements for mobile robotic systems. 03415

**Meijs, W.**
Lexical organisation from three different angles. 01199

**Mein, B.**
Issuing each undergraduate student a personal computer: living with it for three years. 01028

**Meinhard, A.**
Help systems-assisting the user. 01201

**Meizio, K.**
VDT technology: psychosocial and stress concerns. 03755

**Melkanoff, M. A.**
An interactive data dictionary facility for CAD/CAM data bases. 03174

**Mellish, C. (Ed.)**
Advances in artificial intelligence. § 03546

**Meltzer, D.**
Designing a practical interface. 01174

**Mendelzon, A. O.**
OTM: specifying office tasks. 03039

**Mendes, P.**
The responsive system: a new challenge for AI. 02920

**Menges, R.**
Gribs—an approach to a realistic realtime simulation of human arm motion. 03432

**Merbeth, G.**
Report on German Joint Venture Tool Integration Projects. 03495

**Mercier, G.**
Recognition of speaker-dependent continuous speech with Keal-Nevezh. 04002

**Meredith, G.**
The tourist artificial reality. 0868

**Merikle, P. M.**
Menu organization and user expertise in information search tasks. 01761

**Merkel, L. F.**
A prototype autonomous agent for crew and equipment retrieval in space. 02994

**Merrifield, R. M.**
Visual parameters for color CRTs. 0257

**Merriman, M. F.**
Automated interactive simulation modeling system: AISIM. 02399

**Merry, M. (Ed.)**
Expert systems 85. § 03188

**Mestre, D.**
Visual control of displacement at slow speeds. 01797

**Metsisto, T. J.**
How executives can shape their company's information systems. 01707

**Metzler, D. P.**
The flexibility of case grammar representations: a porting procedure for naturallanguage interfaces. 02255

**Meyer-Ebrecht, D.**
On the architecture for pictorial information systems. 03977

**Meyer, B.**
Showing programs on a screen. HCI-0141 †

**Meyer, B. C.**
A graphics interface to an engineering economy program. 01520

**Meyer, D.**
Power and credibility in office automation. 01657

**Meyer, G. W.**
Perceptual color spaces for computer graphics. 0258
An experimental evaluation of computer graphics imagery. HCI-0373 †

**Meyer, J.**
Sensitivity to light and visual strain in VDT operators: basic data for the design of work stations. 03732

**Meyer, K.**
A user interface for deaf-blind people (preliminary report). 0794

**Meyer, N. D.**
Efficiency vs. effectiveness. 01092

**Meyers, D.**
Reconstruction and display of the retina. 03310

**Meyrowitz, N.**
The missing link: why we're all doing hypertext wrong. 0118
Reading and writing the electronic book. HCI-0282 †

**Meyrowitz, N. (Ed.)**
Object-oriented programming systems, languages and applications. § 03030
Object-oriented programming systems, languages and applications. § 03035

**Mezrich, J. J.**
Communicating with sound. 0067

**Michael, G. A. (Chair.)**
Supercomputing'88. § 03540

**Michaels, D. L.**
Technology's impact on library interior planning. 02464

**Michielsen, K.**
A PC policy primer. 01660

**Middelburg, K.**
The VIP VDM specification language. 04036

**Middlecoff, J.**
User services consulting supportr tools at the NASA numerical aerodynamic simula. 03161

**Middleton, A. G.**
Mental gymnastics of sequential programming. 01971

**Mignon, G.**
Design of an AI-Based self-sustaining habitats control system. 02959

**Mihram, D.**
Tele-cybernetics: implications for the international marketplace. 03458

**Mihram, G. A.**
Tele-cybernetics: implications for the international marketplace. 03458

**Mikealain, H. H.**
Changes in contrast sensitivity function produced by VDT use. 02189

**Mikolajczyk, H.**
Task-load and endocrinological risk for pregnancy in women VDU operators. 03692

**Miles, J. W. G.**
Student perceptions of skill acquisition through cases and a general management simulation. 02589

**Miller-Souviney, B.**
Learning with interactive media: dynamic support for students and teachers. 0519

**Miller, B. P.**
CLAM- an open system for graphical user interfaces. 01117

**Miller, C. J.**
The design and evaluation of an animated programming environment. 03220

**Miller, D.**
Chief executive personality and corporate strategy and structure in small firms. 02472

**Miller, D. C.**
CD ROM joins the new media homesteaders. 0281

**Miller, G.**
Capturing expertise: Some approaches to modeling command decisionmaking in combat analysis. 01883

**Miller, G. (Ed.)**
Knowledge based management support systems. ● 0252

**Miller, J.**
UIMSs: threat or menace? 02889

**Miller, J. R.**
Justified advice: a semi-naturalistic study of advisory strategies. 02887

**Miller, K.**
Abstract data type development and implementation: an example. HCI-0162 †

**Miller, L. J.**
FolioPub: A publication management system. 03520

**Miller, P.**
Transportable applications environment (TAE) plus experiences in "Object"-ively modernizing a user interface environment. 01126

**Miller, R. A.**
Describing movement control at two levels of abstraction. 0403
A discrete control model of operator function: A methodology for information dislay design. 01874

**Miller, T.**
Two views of generality. 01876

**Mills, C.**
Usability testing in the real world. 0917

**Mills, C. B.**
Usability testing in the real world. 0951
Usability testing in the real world. 0953
Reading text from computer screens. HCI-0088 †

**Mills, H.**
Stategic imperatives in software engineering education. 04024

**Mills, J.**
Planning as feedback to designers. 02978

**Milne, W. J.**
A practical approach to data modelling in spatial applications. 02616

**Milner, M.**
User interface primitives to allow full functional use of computers by physically disabled persons. 0979

**Milner, N. P.**
A review of human performance and preferences with different input devices to computer systems. 03231

**Minch, R. P.**
Conceptual design of decision support systems utilizing management science models. 0658

**Mindov, J.**
An implementation of OSI protocols in SM-4 host computers. 03638

**Minuto, A.**
Why reading was slower from CRT displays than from paper. 0797
Reading is slower from CRT displays than from paper: attempts to isolate a single-variable explanation. 01743
Reading from CRT displays can be as fast as reading from paper. 01758

**Mion, H.**
Subject reports about musculoskeletal discomfort in VDU work as a complex phenomenon. 03708

**Mira, J.**
A logical model of co-operative processes in cerebral dynamics. 01615
The fuzzy paradigm for knowledge representation in cerebral dynamics. 01699

**Misra, M.**
Advanced interactive executive program development environment. 01816

**Mital, A.**
Towards the development of human work-performance standards in futuristic man-machine systems: a fuzzy modeling approach. 01692

"Automation, robotization in particular, is always economically desirable"—fact or fiction? 03448

**Mitani, H.**
Contextual structure analysis of microcomputer manuals. 03227

**Mitchell, C. M.**
A smalltalk implementation of an intelligent operator's associate. 01132
A supervisory control paradigm for real-time control of flexible manufacturing systems. 01205
A discrete control model of operator function: A methodology for information dislay design. 01874
Cognitive attributes: implications for display design in supervisory control systems. HCI-0242 †

**Mitchell, J.**
Dynamic versus static menus: an exploratory comparison. 0997

**Mitchell, J. A.**
AI/learn: an interactive videodisk system for teaching medical concepts and reasoning. 02381

**Mitiche, A.**
On kineopsis and cimputation of structure and motion. 01839

**Mitrani, M.**
On-line tutorials: What kind of inference leads to the most effective learning? 0823

**Mitraszewski, P.**
A study of stability of electrocortical rhythm generators. 01258

**Mittal, S.**
DARN: Toward a community memory for diagnosis and repair tasks. 0428

**Mittelstaedt, K. M.**
CAD data exchange. 0237

**Mittelstaedt, M.**
Exchange of solid models: current state and future trends. 01475

**Miyahara, S.**
Optical analog of two-dimensional neural networks and their application in recognition of radar targets. 02733

**Miyai, H.**
INTERA/P: a user interface prototyping tool. 03205

**Miyake, K.**
Traffic study on primary rate ISDN user-network interface. 01442

**Miyake, S.**
A neural network model for the mechanism of pattern information processing. 02748

**Miyamoto, S.**
Directed graph representations of association structures: A systematic approach. 01862

**Miyata, Y.**
The learning and planning of actions. 04069

**Mjolsness, E.**
A preliminary analysis of recursively generated networks. 02749

**Möhler, W.**
Visual information pick-up in a simulated driving situation. 0251

**Mochida, A.**
A supporting system for effective construction and sharing of scientific databases by general researchers. HCI-0262 †

**Mockler, J.**
Preserving the integrity of the medium: a method of measuring visual and auditory comprehension of electronic media. 02084

**Mody, A.**
Firm strategies for costly engineering learning. 02485

**Moens, M.**
Temporal ontology and temporal reference. 01347

**Moffett, R. J.**
Distributed tactical decisionmaking: conceptual framework and empirical results. 01885

**Mogahzy, Y. E.**
Implementation plan for the use of on-line fiber analysis in the textile industry. 03433

**Mohamed, A.**
User friendly micro computer program for solving fractional and linear programming problems. 01509

**Mohamed, S.**
Automated document distribution using AI based workstations and knowledge based servers. 03466

**Mohan, J.**
Language level persistence for an object-oriented application programming platform. 03522

**Mohan, L.**
A dialog based interface to a design knowledge base that understands user design-intentions. 02988

**Mohan, R.**
Using perceptual organization to extract 3-D structures. 01842

**Moher, T. G.**
Some strategies of reuse in an object-oriented programming environment. 0820

**Moily, J. P.**
A preliminary specification of an on-line expert help system. 01930

**Molander, M. E.**
Color-coding categories in menus. 02872

**Molander, P.**
Induction of categories: The problem of multiple equilibria. 02360

**Molenaar, I. W.**
Displaying statistical information—ergonomic considerations. 03893

**Molich, R.**
Teaching user interface design based on usability engineering. 01007

**Moll, T.**
On methods of analysis of mental models and the evaluation of interactive computer systems. 0319

**Moller, P.**
A cortical network model for early vision processing. 03957

**Monden, N.**
A high level language-based computing enviornment to support production and execution of reliable programs. 01855

**Monien, B.**
The ring machine. 01483

**Moniz, A. B.**
The impact of advanced manufacturing in work organization: The Portuguese case of the plastic moulding industry. 03374

**Monk, A.**
How and when to collect behavioural data. 0050
Statistical evaluation of behavioural data. 0051
Mode errors: a user-centered analysis and some preventative measures using keying-contingent sound. 02107

**Monk, A. F.**
Refining early design decisions with a black-box model. 03200
A comparison of hypertext, scrolling and folding as mechanisms for program browsing. 03235
Reading continuous text from a one-line visual display. HCI-0187 †

**Monk, A. F. (Ed.)**
People and computers: designing for usability. § 03244

**Monnis, A. (Ed.)**
Industrial & Engineering Applications of Artificial Intelligence & Expert Systems: vol. II. § 02982

**Monod, E. (Ed.)**
Women, work and computerization: opportunities and disadvantages. § 03674

**Montanari, U.**
Towards an integration between language and software development environment. HCI-0158 †

**Montazemi, A. R.**
The effects of modes of information presentation on decision-making: a review and meta-analysis. 02358

**Montgomery, G.**
Process design of oil and gas production facilities using expert systems. 02933

**Moody, G. H.**
Bringing image processing into focus. 01317

**Moody, L. E.**
Human factors design of a video monitor emulator and display (VMED) for visually impaired computer users. 02379

**Moon, D. A.**
Common LISP object system specification X3J13 Document 88-002R. 01121

**Mooney, J. D.**
Lessons from the MOSI project. 01450

**Moopenn, A.**
Electronic implementation of associative memory based on neural network models. 01895
Error correction and asymmetry in a binary memory matrix. 02750

**Moore, G.**
Expansion and control of end-user computing. 02347

**Moore, J. C.**
An analysis of human and computer decision-making capabilities. 01951

**Moore, J. D.**
Responding to "HUH?": answering vaguely articulated follow-up questions. 0825

**Moore, J. L.**
Enhancing PIXIE's tutoring capabilities. 02187

**Moore, M. A.**
Alkahest III: automatic analysis of periodic weakly nonlinear ODEs. 03087

**Moore, R.**
Process control with the G2 real-time expert system. 02934
Object oriented rapid prototyping with G2. 02984
Muffin: a user interface design experiment for a theorem proving assistant. 04037

**Moore, R. E. (Ed.)**
Reliability in computing: the role of interval methods in scientific computing. ● 0548

**Moore, W. R.**
Conventional fault-tolerance and neural computers. 03951

**Moran, D.**
An architecture for a multimedia teleconferencing system. 02802

**Moran, D. B.**
Synergistic use of direct manipulation and natural language. 0857

**Moran, T.**
User technology—from pointing to pondering. 03098
Where is the action in human-computer interaction? 03773

**Moran, T. P.**
The keystroke-level model for user performance time with interactive systems. 0055
Computer text-editing: an information-processing analysis of a routine cognitive skill. 0056
The evaluation of text editors: Methodology and empirical results. 0058
User technology: from pointing to pondering. 0350
Notecards in a nutshell. 0810
What is EuroParc? 0812
Design rationale: the argument behind the artifact. 0860
The evaluation of text editors: methodology and empirical results. HCI-0209 †

**Morandi, M.**
Posture and VDU operator satisfaction. 0988

**Morariu, J.**
Human factors for design and evaluation of software. 01283

**Morasso, P.**
Active vision: integration of fixed and mobile cameras. 04017

**Moravcik, O.**
Some aspects of communication in the natural language and user's involvement in software development. 03670

**Moray, N.**
Spectral analysis of sinus arrhythmia: a measure of mental effort. 01737
A closed-loop causal model of workload based on a comparison of fuzzy and crisp measurement techniques. 01746

Acquisition of process control skills. 01878
Intelligent aids, mental models, and the theory of machines. 02171
Custos IPSE: Towards a theory of the supervisor. 03365

**Morch, A.**
Design environments for constructive and argumentative design. 0864

**More, E. A.**
Emerging communications technology paradigms. 02320

**Morehead, D. R.**
The value of information and computer-aided information seeking: problem formulation and application to fiction retrieval. 01989

**Morell, J. A.**
Assessment of an effort to integrate computer functions in an engineering design firm. 0779

**Morell, L. J.**
Use of metaknowledge in the verification of knowledge-based systems. 02945

**Moreno-Díaz, R.**
The fuzzy paradigm for knowledge representation in cerebral dynamics. 01699

**Morgan, M. A.**
Job histories as predictors of career success in management information systems. 01021

**Morgan, M. F.**
On the parameters of human visual performance: an investigation of the benefits of antialiasing. 0799

**Morgon, A.**
An evaluation of auditory performances in patients with Cochlear implants. 02658

**Mori, K.**
Human aspects of QC circle movement in Japanese manufacturing: Natures and problems. 03450

**Moriconi, M.**
The PegaSys System: pictures as formal documentation of large programs. HCI-0146 †

**Morik, K.**
Talking it over: the natural language dialog system HAM-ANS. 0165
The relationship between user models and discourse models. 01353
Customers' requirements for natural language systems: results of an inquiry. HCI-0426 †

**Morison, R.**
Interactive performance display and debugging using the NCUBE real-time graphics system. 02907

**Moriya, K.**
Logic interface system on navigational database systems. 03818

**Morone, J. J.**
Experiencing artificial intelligence: an interactive approach to the IBM PC. ● 0550
Experiencing artificial intelligence: an interactive approach for the APPLE. ● 0551

**Morrel-Samuels, P.**
The use of hand-drawn gestures for text editing. 02151

**Morris, A.**
Expert systems—interface insight. 03210

**Morris, A. H.**
The effect of presentation media on recipient performance in text-based information systems. 02350

**Morris, D.**
Human-computer interface recording. 01414

**Morris, J. H.**
Andrew: a distributed personal computing environment. HCI-0091 †

**Morris, N. M.**
The effects of type of knowledge upon human problem solving in a process control task. 0657
Conceptual design of a human error tolerant interface for complex engineering systems. 01235
Understanding and enhancing user acceptance of computer. 01889

**Morris, R. A.**
Image processing aspects of type. HCI-0403 †

**Morrison, D. L.**
Speech-controlled text-editing: effects of input modality and of command structure. HCI-0397 †

**Morrison, G. H.**
Simps: Secondary ion mass image processing system. 02267

**Morrison, R. (Ed.)**
Data types and persistence. ● 0033

**Morrison, R. C.**
Communicating with sound. 0067

**Morrison, W.**
Communicating with users during systems development. 01972

**Morrisroe, G.**
Human factors in the Columbus space station. 03250

**Morrissey, T. P.**
PHIGS: a standard, dynamic, interactive graphics interface. 01826

**Morrow, T.**
User services—a british perspective. 03132

**Morse, L. C.**
Needs and perceived needs of electronic workstations by engineering project managers. 01515

**Morton, T. E.**
Callisto: an intelligent project management system (Reprint). 0375

**Moscarini, M.**
On global context dependencies and their properties (extended abstract). 03945

**Moser, J.**
Documentation for user-developed applications with high documentation requirements. 01049

**Moser, M. G.**
The IRUS transportable natural language database interface. 03177

**Motazed, B.**
Evolution of a robotic excavator. 03569

**Motet, S.**
Geomatic: a 3-D graphic relief simulation system. HCI-0395 †

**Motoike, S.**
A travel consultation system: towards a smooth conversation in Japanese. 03917

**Motowidlo, S.**
Human—computer interactions in the workplace: psychosocial aspects of VDT use. 0306

**Moulden, B.**
Effect of pixel height, display height, and vertical resolution on the detection of a simple vertical line signal in visual noise. 01753

**Moulin, B.**
The actem model for decision modelling in a scene management system. 02954

**Mount, R. P.**
What users want. 01443

**Mountford, S. J.**
Drama and personality in user interface design. 0830
A study in interactive 3-D rotation using 2-D control devices. 02813

**Mourino, M.**
Interactive graphic editor for analysis and enhancement of medical images. 01492

**Movshon, J. A.**
The perception of coherent motion in two-dimensional patterns. 03327

**Mowbray, A.**
Expert systems in law: The datalex project. 02766

**Mowforth, P. H.**
An appropriate representation for early vision. 02542

**Mozes, E.**
A deductive database based on Aristotelian logic. 02398

**Mrayati, M.**
Distinctive regions and modes: a new theory of speech production. 02659

**Mrózek, A.**
Rough sets and dependency analysis among attributes in computer implementations of expert's inference models. 02231

**Mruk, C. J.**
Communication issues among psychologists working with computers: a view from the top. 02606

**Mucci, M. A.**
Using worker's survey to improve production. 02566

**Muchnick, S. S.**
Dbxtool: A window-based symbolic debugger for sun workstations. 02614

**Mudur, S. P.**
Vidura—an interactive multilingual publishing system—specification & design. 03186

**Mueller, E. T.**
Daydreaming and computation: a computer model of everyday creativity, learning and emotions in the human stream of thought. 04067

**Mueller, P.**
A machine for neural computation of acoustical patterns with application to real time speech recognition. 02751

**Muhanna, W. A.**
Composite models in symms. 03485

**Muhlhäuser, M. D.**
Software engineering for distributed applications: the design project. 03508

**Muhlhauser, M.**
Using distributed simulation for distributed application development. 03500

**Muir, B. M.**
Trust between humans and machines, and the design of decision aids. 02164

**Mukaidono, M.**
A study of fail-safe technology. 03421
Construction and examples of sensor in safe working system. 03425

**Mulder, G.**
Operator effort and the measurement of heart-rate variability. 01736
Human-computer interaction: psychonomic aspects. § 03887

**Mulder, G. Dr. (Ed.)**
Introduction: human-computer interaction: psychonomic aspects. 03888

**Mulder, L. J.M.**
Operator effort and the measurement of heart-rate variability. 01736

**Mulder, M. C. (Ed.)**
Special Issue: The FAA's Advanced Automation Program. HCI-0424 †

**Mulholland, N. O.**
A fuzzy knowledge base of an expert system for analysis of manual lifting tasks. 01693

**Muller, M. J.**
Multifunctional cursor for direct manipulation user interfaces. 02870

**Mullin, A. W.**
Preparing for new technology. 0444

**Mumford, E.**
Managerial expert systems and organizational change: some critical research issues. 0157
Participation–from Aristotle to today. 0499

**Mumpower, J. L. (Ed.)**
Expert judgment and expert systems. ● 0552

**Muncher, E.**
A test of a common elements theory of transfer. 0901

**Munro, M. C.**
Expansion and control of end-user computing. 02347

**Munro, P. W.**
State-dependent factors influencing neural plasticity: a partial account of the. 0640

**Munson, J.**
The experimental validation of a programmer productivity measure. 03013

**Murakami, S.**
A design for a fuzzy logic controller. 02028
A fuzzy decision-making method and its application to a company choice problem. 02029

**Murayama, Y.**
Manual control of an intrinsically unstable system and its modeling by fuzzy logic. 02026

**Murch, G.**
Color displays and color science. 0255

**Murch, G. M.**
Colour graphics—Blessing or Ballyhoo? 0061
Human factors of color displays. 0438
Human factors and flat panels challenge the CRT. 01982
Matching display characteristics to human visual capacity. 03723
Physiological principles for the effective use of color. HCI-0378 †

**Murphy, C. M.**
Network generation using the Prufer code. 01536

**Murphy, E. D.**
Cognitive attributes: implications for display design in supervisory control systems. HCI-0242 †

**Murphy, F. H.**
A graphics interface for linear programming. 01332

**Murphy, G. L.**
Psychological concepts in a parallel system. 02564
Concepts in connectionist models. 02724

**Murphy, M. D.**
Cognitive processing differences between novice and expert computer programmers. 02145

**Murphy, P. A.**
A comparison of children's reading comprehension and reading rates at three text presentation speeds on a CRT. 02280

**Murphy, P. T.**
An architecture for a business and information system. 01818

**Murray, D.**
Experience with adaptive interfaces. 01417

**Murray, T. J.**
A preliminary specification of an on-line expert help system. 01930

**Murthy, S. S.**
3-D balance in legged locomotion: modeling and simulation for the one-legged case. 03352

**Murthy, V. S.**
Business graphics trends, two years later. 01945

**Murty, M. N.**
Structural aspects of semantic-directed clusters. 02534

**Murty, M. S.S.N.**
Artificial intelligence techniques applied to maintenance management. 02971

**Musen, M. A.**
Graphical specification of procedural knowledge for an expert system. 0427
Conceptual models of interacitve knowledge acquisition tools. 02457

**Mustafa Pulat, B.**
Ergonomic improvements boost AS/RS performance. 01904

**Muter, P.**
Reader-controlled computerized presentation of text. 01785

**Mutka, M. W.**
Sharing in a privately owned workstation environment. 04076

**Myaeng, S. H.**
Towards an intelligent and personalized retrieval system. 03028

**Mychaltchouk, P.**
Using design expertise to develop an expert system. 02962

**Mycielski, J.**
A model of the neocortex. 01164
Can mathematics explain natural intelligence? 02565

**Myers, B.**
A study in two-handed input. 0933
A user interface toolkit based on graphical objects and constraints. 01125
Issues in window management design and implementation. 03928

**Myers, B. A.**
Creating highly-interactive and graphical user interfaces by demonstration. 0084
Encapsulating interactive behaviors. 0874
Creating highly-interactive and graphical user interfaces by demonstration. 01054
The run-time structure of UIMS-supported applications. 01059
Gaining general acceptance for UIMSs. 01067
Creating user interfaces by demonstration. ● HCI-0008 †

**Myers, G.**
Qualities of a good forms designer. 02412

**Myers, G. L.**
Training consistent task components: application of automatic and controlled processing theory to industrial task training. 01742

**Myers, J. D.**
The background of INTERNIST I and QMR. 02853

**Myers, L. M.**
A hand biomechanics workstation. 02820

**Myers, W.**
Ada: first users—pleased; prospective users—still hesitant. HCI-0159 †

**Mykytyn Jr., P. P.**
An empirical investigation of DSS usage and the user's perception of DSS training. 01934

**Myler, H. R.**
The architecture of an inexpensive and portable talking-tactile terminal to aid the visually handicapped. 01452
An inexpensive and portable talking-tactile terminal for the visually handicapped. 02377

**Mylonas, E.**
The Perseus project: an interactive curriculum on classical greek civilization. 01680

**Mylopoulos, J. (Ed.)**
On knowledge base management systems: integrating artificial intelligence and d atabase technologies. ● 0180

**Mynatt, B.**
Profile of undergraduate software engineering courses: results from a survey. 01035

**Mynatt, B. T.**
A study of an advance organizer as a technique for teaching computer programming concepts. 01042
Which way to computer literacy, programming or applications experience? 02127
A scarce resource in undergraduate software engineering courses: user interface design materials. 04027

**Nabika, E.**
A processing system for program specifications in a natural language. 03537

**Naccache, N. J.**
An investigation into the skeletonization approach of Hilditch. HCI-0388 †

**Nachreiner, F.**
On the temporal stability of signal detection processes. 03617

**Nadal, J.**
Basins of attraction in a perceptron-like neural network. 01340

**Nadin, M.**
Interface design and evaluation—Semiotic implications. 0409

**Naffah, N.**
Design issues of an intelligent workstation for the office. 03165

**Nagai, Y.**
Fuzzy control of a mobile robot for obstacle avoidance. 02025

**Nagamachi, M.**
A study on an error recovery expert system using a superimposer and a digitizer in the advanced teleoperator system. 03389
Ten fatal accidents due to robots in Japan. 03406

**Nagao, J.**
KRIP: a knowledge representation system for laws relating to industrial property. 03918

**Nagao, M.**
A framework of a mechanical translation between Japanese and English by analogy principle. HCI-0353 †

**Nagel, H. H.**
On the estimation of dense displacement vector fields from image sequences. 03335

**Nagy, W. E.**
Theoretical issues in the investigation of words of internal report. 0354

**Najah, M.**
Pictorial interfaces to data bases. HCI-0116 †

**Nakamura, K.**
A similarity-based reasoning model for intelligent interfaces. 01503

**Nakamura, O.**
Resource management scheme in distributed environments. 01018

**Nakano, K.**
Self-organizing system obtaining communication ability primitive model for language generation. 01279

**Nakashima, H.**
Manipulation of embedded context using the multiple world mechanism. 03921

**Nakatani, L. H.**
TNT: a talking tutor 'n' trainer for teaching use of interactive computer systems. 0895

**Nakayama, K.**
Directed graph representations of association structures: A systematic approach. 01862

**Nakayama, Y.**
Mathematical formula editor for CAI. 0885

**Nakhimovsky, A.**
The lexicon, grammatical categories and temporal reasoning. 03549

**Nam, T. N. (Chair.)**
Software Engineering. § 03507

**Nanard, J.**
PLEIADE: A system for interactive manipulation of structured documents. 0265
Conceptual documents: a mechanism for specifying active views in hypertext. 02833

**Nanard, M.**
PLEIADE: A system for interactive manipulation of structured documents. 0265
Conceptual documents: a mechanism for specifying active views in hypertext. 02833

**Nanthavanij, S.**
Ergonomic evaluation of safety devices in robotic systems. 03449

**Napier, H. A.**
Impact of a restricted natural language interface on ease of learning and productivity. 01334
An empirical study of occupational stress, attitudes and health among information systems personnel. HCI-0451 †

**Napoliello, M. F.**
A study of managerial computer users: the impact of user sophistication on decision structure and attributes of decision-related information (end user). 04078

**Narborough-Hall, C. S.**
Automation—implications for knowledge retention as a function of operator control responsibility. 03207

**Nas, G. L. J.**
The effect on reading speed of word divisions at the end of a line. 03896

**Nash, J. C.**
Measuring the performance of statisticians with statistical software. 03314

**Nash, M.**
Human perception of the work envelope of an industrial robot. 03410

**Nash, S. H.**
People and organizations in software production: a review of the literature. 01023
A map of the world of software-related standards, guidelines, and recommended practices. 01453

**Nath, S.**
Vidura—an interactive multilingual publishing system—specification & design. 03186

**Naumann, S.**
Towards universality of access: interfacing physically disabled students to the Icon educational microcomputer. 0821

**Naumienko, B. J.**
Simulations of behavior in competitive situations. 02591

**Naumienko, E. Z.**
Simulations of behavior in competitive situations. 02591

**Nazareth, D.**
Issues in the verification of knowledge in rule-based systems. 02226

**Neal, L. R.**
A system for example-based programming. 0818
Cognition-sensitive design and user modeling for syntax-directed editors. 0828

**Necco, C. R.**
The information center approach for developing computer-based information systems. 01929
Use of fourth generation languages: application development and documentation problems. 02435

**Neches, R.**
Learning, development, and production systems. 0479
Learning through incremental refinement of procedures. 0482
Knowledge-based tools to promote shared goals and terminology between interface designers. 01160

**Neches, R. (Ed.)**
Production system models of learning and development. ● 0478

**Neghabat, M.**
A model of the controller responses of the human temperature regulating system to changes in water temperature. 02487

**Negri, M.**
The integration of the network and relational approaches in a DBMS. 03283

**Neher, R.**
XVISION: a comprehensive software system for image processing research, education, and applications. 03124

**Neilson, M. D.**
Speech motor control and stuttering: a computational model of adaptive sensory-motor processing. 02655

**Neilson, P. D.**
Speech motor control and stuttering: a computational model of adaptive sensory-motor processing. 02655

**Neimark, J.**
Dp and the disabled. 01646

**Nelson, C.**
Design guidelines. 0334

**Nelson, D.**
Interactive video—a producer's medium. 0511

**Nelson, M. J.**
Correlation of term usage and term indexing frequencies. 02004

**Nelson, P. P.**
Model of the neuro-muscular recruitment example of the extensor digitorum communis muscle in man: I—identification of motoneurons and of muscular fibers. 01595

**Nelson, R. R.**
Educating the CBIS user: a case analysis. 0778
A tool for measuring analysis end user computing. 02000
Strategies for end-user computing: An integrative framework. 02348
Training end users: an exploratory study. 02506

**Nelson, S. J.**
Evaluating RECONSIDER: a computer program for diagnostic prompting. HCI-0410 †

**Nelson, T. H.**
Hyperwelcome. 01805

**Nelson, W. A.**
Problem solving and software design. 01589

**Nemes, L.**
Information control problems in manufacturing. ● 0554

**Neri, D. F.**
The effects of set size on color matching using CRT displays. 01711

**Nerson, J.**
Showing programs on a screen. HCI-0141 †

**Nesbit, J. C.**
The accuracy of approximate string matching algorithms. 02279

**Nesher, P.**
Comparison of student performance in artihmetic exercises TOAM us paper-and-pencil testing. 02249

**Nesi, M.**
A logic-functional approach to the execution of CCS specifications modulo behavioural equivalences. 03874

**Netick, A.**
Hesitations in continuous tracking induced by a concurrent discrete task. 01745
Multiple resources for processing and storage in short-term working memory. 01794

**Netravali, A. N.**
Motion interpolation by optimal control. 02817

**Neumann, B.**
Optical flow. 03330

**Neumann, S.**
Principles of information systems for management (2nd ed.). ● 0005

**Neuwirth, C. M.**
Techniques of user message design: developing a user message system to support cooperative work. 0127

**Nevatia, R.**
Using perceptual organization to extract 3-D structures. 01842

**Newbery, F. J.**
Knowledge-based editors for directed graphs. 03797

**Newcomer, J.**
IDL: past experience and new ideas. 03782

**Newcomer, J. M.**
DRAT: A program for maintaining listings. 02401

**Newcomer, L. R.**
Schaum's outline of theories and problems of programming with advanced structured COBOL with file processing structured systems deveopment and interactive cons. ● 0555

**Newell, A.**
The keystroke-level model for user performance time with interactive systems. 0055
Computer text-editing: an information-processing analysis of a routine cognitive skill. 0056
Learning by chunking: a production system model of practice. 0483
Universal subgoaling and chunking: the automatic generation and learning of goal hierarchies. ● 0497
Predicting the time to recall computer command abbreviations. 0806
Cumulating the science of HCI: from s-R compatibility to transcription typing. 0831
Naive algorithm design techniques—a case study. HCI-0360 †

**Newhouse, V. L. (Ed.)**
Progress in medical imaging. ● 0556

**Newman, A.**
Some observations on user interface design and user performance. HCI-0117 †

**Newman, D.**
Functional environments for microcomputers in education. 0578

**Newman, M.**
Professional and expert systems: a meeting of minds. 0790
Information systems and user resistance: theory and practice. 01409

**Newman, M. A.**
An empirical study of user satisfaction with a microcomputer-based campus-wide. 03137

**Newman, W. M.**
The representation of user interface style. 03221

**Newman, W. M. (Ed.)**
Principles of interactive computer graphics (2nd ed.). ● HCI-0069 †

**Newsome, S. L.**
An experiment into the use of auditory cues to reduce visual workload. 0877
Navigational aids and learning styles: structural optimal training for computer users. 0970

**Newstead, S.**
Efforts of display format on proof-reading with VDUs. 01246

**Newton, A. R.**
Twenty-five years of electronic design automation. § 03102

**Ngai, W. B.**
Low cost geometric modelling system for CAM. 03866

**Nguyen, D. T.**
Prediction of the smallest channel in early human vision. 01894

**Nguyen, P. T.**
Image segmentation based on color and texture gradient. 03303

**Ngwenyama, O. K.**
Fundamental issues of knowledge acquisition: toward a human action perspective of knowledge systems. 04057

**Nichol, J.**
Computers and children's historical thinking and understanding. 0283
Pupils, computers and history teaching. 0746

**Nicholas, D.**
Online use and end-users in media and advertising: an overview. 01216
End-users: threat, challenge or myth? 01221
Time-life, world reporter and the secretary: experiments with end-users. 02325

**Nichols, H. (Ed.)**
ESEC '87. § 03795

**Nicholson, R. T.**
Usage patterns in an integrated voice and data communications system. HCI-0311 †

**Nickerson, R. S.**
On conversational interaction with computers. 0091
Counting, computing, and the representation of numbers. 01771

**Nicolau, A.**
A development environment for horizontal microcode programs. 01079

**Nicolson, J.**
JDB: an adaptable interface for debugging. 02628

**Nicu, M. D.**
Simplicial differential geometric theory for language cortical dynamics. 01698

**Niedermair, G. T.**
Merging acoustics and linguistics in speech understanding. 04004

**Nielsen, G. M.**
System development in a women's perspective. 03675

**Nielsen, J.**
'This is a very unpredictable machine': on computers and human cognition. 0364
Computer-support cooperative work. 0956
Classification of dialog techniques. 0960
Interact '87. 0964
CHI '88 trip report. 0981
Coordinating user interfaces for consistency. 0990
Teaching user interface design based on usability engineering. 01007
A virtual protocol model for computer-human interaction. 02106

**Nielsen, L. C.**
Formal specification of user interfaces: two application studies. 03772

**Niemann, H.**
Recent advances in speech understanding and dialog systems. § 03987
Prosodic features in German speech: stress assignment by man and machine. 03989
An experimental environment for generating word hypotheses in continuous speech. 03998

**Niemelä, J.**
User or development of information systems: Which is more fundamental? 03654

**Nieper-Lemke, H.**
Helgon: extending the retrieval by reformulation paradigm. 0880

**Nieper, H.**
The enhancement of understanding through visual representations. 0898

**Nierstrasz, O.**
Directions in object-oriented research. 0477

**Nievergelt, J.**
Sites, modes, and trails: Telling the user of an interactive system where he is, what he can do, and how to get to places (excerpt). 0068
Issues in the design of human-computer interfaces. 03979

**Nightingale, J. H.**
Establishing a computing assistance centre. 03142

**Nikhil, R. S.**
Functional databases, functional languages. 0034

**Niki, T.**
A travel consultation system: towards a smooth conversation in Japanese. 03917

**Nilsson, N. J. (Ed.)**
Annual review of computer science vol. 1, 1986. ● 0719

**Nisbett, R. E.**
Induction: processes of inference, learning, and discovery. ● HCI-0064 †

**Nishida, S.**
Speech recognition enhancement by lip information. 0915

**Nishihara, H. K.**
Visual information processing: artificial intelligence and the sensorium of sight. 0300

**Nissen, J. C.**
Selecting an Ada environment. ● HCI-0015 †

**Nitsche, W.**
Real-time failure detection on complex mechanical structures via parallel data processing. 01561

**Nitta, K.**
KRIP: a knowledge representation system for laws relating to industrial property. 03918

**Nitta, S.**
CRT picture vibration caused by low-frequency magnetic field and its reduction method. 01987

**Nitta, Y.**
Problems of machine translation system - effect of cultural differences on sentence structure. 01687

**Niwa, K.**
A knowledge-based human-computer cooperative system for ill-structured management domains. 01873

**Nix, R. P.**
Editing by example. HCI-0398 †

**Nöth, E.**
Prosodic features in German speech: stress assignment by man and machine. 03989

**Noah, W. W.**
Adaptive user interfaces for planning and decision aids in $C^3I$ systems. 01887

**Noel, R. W.**
Color-coding categories in menus. 02872

**Noerr, K. T.**
Can finding information be easy, fun and successful? 02324

**Nof, S. Y. (Ed.)**
Robotics and Material Flow. ● 0558

**Noguchi, N.**
Generating natural language responses appropriate to conversational situations—in the case of Japanese. 03922

**Noguez, G.**
A Unix distributed application support suitable for mini and microcomputer based systems. 02489

**Nolan, F.**
The nature of speech. 0175

**Nolan, M. D.**
Simulator design and instructional features for air-to-ground attack: a transfer study. 01804

**Noll, A. M.**
Videotex: anatomy of a failure. HCI-0313 †

**Noltemeier, H. (Ed.)**
Computational Geometry and its Applications. § 03850

**Noma, T.**
ANIMENGINE: an engineering animation system. 03858

**Nonnenmacher, T. F.**
A scaling model for dichotomous branching processes. 01264

**Noordman, L. G.M.**
Visual presentation of text: the process of reading from a psycholinguistic perspective. 03895

**Nordgard, I.**
Event-driven user interfaces based on quasi-parallelism. 03111

**Noreault, T.**
Designing a CD ROM information structure. 0682

**Norman, A.**
Alkahest III: automatic analysis of periodic weakly nonlinear ODEs. 03087

**Norman, D.**
User interface strategies '88 (Videotape). ● 0684

**Norman, D. A.**
Some observations on mental models. 0057
Direct manipulation interfaces (excerpt). 0073
Design principles for human-computer interfaces. 0075
Designing for error. 0087
Donald A. Norman, Oct. 12: user interface strategies '88. ● 0560
Reflections on cognition and parallel distributed. 0642
Software engineering for user interfaces. 01854
Stages and levels in human-machine interaction. HCI-0189 †
Cognitive engineering—cognitive science. HCI-0200 †

**Norman, K. L.**
Cognitive layouts of windows and multiple screens for user interfaces. HCI-0122 †

**Norman, L. K.**
Development of an instrument measuring user satisfaction of the human-computer interface. 02892

**Norman, M.**
The formal specification of adaptive user interfaces using command language grammar. 0925

**Noro, K.**
Characterization of VDT work. 03754

**Norris-Sherborn, A.**
A practical approach to data modelling in spatial applications. 02616

**Norris, P.**
Human factors in the Columbus space station. 03250

**Norros, L.**
Visualization of process information in improving work orientation. 03619

**Norsworthy, R. S.**
A prototype autonomous agent for crew and equipment retrieval in space. 02994

**North, J.**
Reference model for DBMS user facility. 01086

**Norton, R. A.**
Starting end-users. 01215

**Norwich, K. H.**
An error correcting protocol for medical expert systems. 02143

**Norworol, C.**
Mental fatigue of VDU operators induced by monotonous and various tasks. 03760

**Nosek, J. T.**
User validation of information systems requirements: some empirical results. 01852
An experiment to test user validation of requirements: data-flow diagrams vs task-oriented menus. 02131
Increase organizational effectiveness: Support self-managed IS development teams. 03014

**Nowacki, H.**
Approximation methods used in the exchange of geometric information via the VDA/VDMA surface interface. HCI-0421 †

**Nowaczyk, R. H.**
The relationship of problem-solving ability and course performance among novice programmers. HCI-0435 †

**Noworol, C.**
Acting-out and burn-out behaviours of operators monitoring automated systems. 03440
Some remarks on a measure of computer operator workload: changes in pupil reflex. 03626

**Nteun, C. A.**
A conceptual dependency network approach to multi-task assignments in man-machine (teleoperated) systems. 03388

**Ntuen, C. A.**
Developing intelligent simulation language to support telerobotic workstation activities. 02995
Human factor issues in teleoperated systems. 03387
Accident analysis of blind production workers. 03439

**Null, L. M.**
Intelligent interfaces for secure multilevel database systems. 02990

**Nullmeier, E.**
The limitations of task complexity through information technologies: results of a field study. 0307
Work design instead of system design. 03671

**Nunamaker Jr., J. F.**
ICE: information center expert: a consultation system for resource allocation. 0781
PLEXACT: an architecture & design of a knowledge-based system for information systems development. 01020
A consultation system for information center resource allocation. 03100

**Nunamaker, J. F.**
Crisis planning systems: tools for intelligent action. 03464

**Nunez, G.**
Human response to unexpected robot movements at selected slow speeds. 03405

**Nurminen, M. I.**
Different perspectives: What are they and how can they be used? 03653
User or development of information systems: Which is more fundamental? 03654

**Nurminen, T.**
Birth defects, course of pregnancy, and work with VDUs: a Finnish case-referent study. 03689

**Nutt, G. J.**
Office information systems and computer science (Reprint). 0373

**Nwankwo, H. H.**
Formatting alphanumeric crt displays. 02140

**Nyberg, K. A.**
Using representation clauses as an operating system interface. 0764

**Nye, A.**
Xlib programming manual for version 11: Vol. 1. ● 0561

**Nye, J. B.**
User interaction with the authority structure of the online catalog: results of a survey. 02049

**Nygaard, K. (Ed.)**
ECOOP '88 (European Conference on Object-Oriented Programming). § 03793

**Nykodym, N.**
Selection systems for sales representatives. 02408

**Nylén, M.**
A cortical network model for early vision processing. 03957

**Nylén, P.**
Some physical factors at VDT work stations and ski problems. 03693
Visual phenomena and their relation to top luminance, phosphor persistence time and contrast polarity. 03729

**Nyman, K. G.**
Refraction in VDU operators—a comparison with other professions. 03740

**Östberg, O.**
Effects on visual accommodation and subjective visual discomfort from VDT work intensified through split screen technique. 03735

**Özgüc, B.**
Continuous processing of images through user sketched functional blocks. 01399

**O'Brien, B.**
Opening Windows. ● HCI-0007 †

**O'Brien, L.**
Starting and maintaining a computing resource center: lessons we've learned. 03149

**O'Callaghan, J. F.**
The application of scene synthesis techniques to the display of multidimensional image data. HCI-0371 †

**O'Connor, M. J.**
The accuracy of combining judgemental and statistical forecasts. 02474

**O'Donnell, D. J.**
End-user computing environments—finding a balance between productivity and control. 01927

**O'Donnell, J. T.**
Dialogues: a basis for constructing programming environments. 01097

**O'Hara-Hines, R. J.**
A multivariate solution for cyclic data, applied in modelling locomotor forces. 01252

**O'Hare, J. J. (Ed.)**
Human Factors in Computing Systems. § 02856

**O'Keefe, R. M.**
An interactive simulation description interpreter. 01538
Visual interactive simulation - history, recent developments, and major issues. 02585

**O'Leary, D. E.**
On the representation and the impact of reliability on expert system weights. 02211

**O'Malley, C.**
Unix: tomorrow's operating system? 02555
What's new in personal information managers. 02556

**O'Malley, K.**
Tools for management and support of multiple constraints in a writer's assistant. 03251

**O'Mara, R.**
Implementation of the Geac circulation system within the CLANN network. 02458

**O'Neil, D. P.**
A process specification of expert lawyer reasoning. 02768

**O'Neil, M. A.**
GPROC—an integrated system for the processing of numerical scientific data. 02631

**O'Neill, A.**
Design Automation. § 02828

**O'Reilly, J. E.**
Enhancing search results by editing, analysis and packaging. 02035

**O'Reilly, T.**
X window system user's guide for version 11: vol. 3. ● 0562

**O'Shea, T.**
Cognitive economy in physics reasoning: implications for designing instructional materials. 0542

**Oakley, B.**
An overview of research and co-operation in advanced information technology. HCI-0442 †

**Oakman, R. L.**
A knowledge-based approach to online document retrieval system design. 03027

**Oatley, K.**
Information flow in a user interface: the effect of experience and context on the recall of MacWrite screens. 03228

**Oberquelle, H.**
Human-machine interaction and role/function/action-nets. 03974
On models and modelling in human-computer co-operation. HCI-0182 †

**Oborne, D.**
Information technology & people: designing for the future. ● 0144

**Oborne, D. J.**
Ergonomics and the new technologies. 0147
Reading from screen versus paper: there is no difference. 02175

**Offen, R. J. (Ed.)**
VLSI image processing. ● 0563

**Ofori-Dwumfuo, G. O.**
Using a cognitive model of dialogue for reference retrieval. 02317

**Oğuztöreli, M. N.**
On the identification of neural responses. 01260

**Ogawa, S.**
An acoustic of pathological voice and its application to the evaluation of laryngeal pathology. 02644

**Ogden, W. C.**
A cognitive model of database querying: a tool for novice instruction. 0905

**Ogozalek, V.**
Comparison of elderly and younger users on keyboard and voice input computer-based composition tasks. 0916

**Ogozalek, V. Z.**
A comparison of male and female computer science students' attitudes toward computers. 01045

**Ohki, M.**
Spreadsheets with incremental queries as a user interface for logic programming. 02515

**Ohlsson, S.**
Truth versus appropriateness: relating declarative to procedural knowledge. 0484
Psychological evaluation of path hypotheses in cognitive diagnosis. 0537

**Ohmori, T.**
Self-organizing system obtaining communication ability primitive model for language generation. 01279

**Ohno, Y.**
A system for the representation of human body movement from dance scores. 02540
A programming environment supporting reuse of object-oriented software. 03509

**Ohsato, A.**
Convexly combined fuzzy relational equations and several aspects of their application to fuzzy information processing. 02027

**Ohta, H.**
Classifying sensory inspectors with heterogeneous inspection-error probabilities. 02396

**Ohuchi, Y.**
An automatic wafer inspection system using pipelined image processing techniques. 01840

**Oi, K.**
Directed graph representations of association structures: A systematic approach. 01862

**Ojala, M.**
Views on end-user searching. HCI-0283 †

**Okey, R. E.**
Initial work on a system-independent computer model of a 3D anthropomorphic dummy. 01476

**Olerup, A. (Ed.)**
Women, work and computerization: opportunities and disadvantages. § 03674

**Olfman, L.**
The importance of individual differences in end-user training: The case for learning style. 03009
The influence of training on use of end-user software. 03042

**Olsen Jr., D. R.**
Larger issues in user interface management. 01068

**Olsen, D.**
Goals and objectives for user interface software. 01056

**Olsen, D. R.**
Interface usage measurements in a user interface management system. 03115

**Olsen, D. R., Jr.**
A programming language basis for user interface. 0849
An editing model for generating graphical user interfaces. 03289
MIKE: the menu interaction kontrol environment. HCI-0124 †
Pushdown automata for user interface management. HCI-0382 †

**Olsen, J. D. R.**
Editing templates: a user interface generation tool. 01827
Marcosby example in a graphical UIMS. 01831

**Olsen, S. E.**
Development of a term association interface for browsing bibliographic data bases based on end users' word associations. HCI-0266 †

**Olson, A. T.**
Computer, quantized time and human duration. 01593

**Olson, G. M.**
Cognitive science and machine intelligence laboratory, University of Michigan. 0843

**Olson, G. M. (Ed.)**
Empirical studies of programmers: second workshop. ● 0565

**Olson, J. M.**
Color and the computer in cartography. HCI-0386 †

**Olson, J. R.**
Methods for designing software to fit human needs and capabilities (excerpt). 0079
Skilled financial planning: the cost of translating ideas into action. 0834
Designing keybindings to be easy to learn and resistant to forgetting even when the set of commands is large. 02890
Cognitive analysis of people's use of software. HCI-0199 †

**Olson, J. R. (Ed.)**
Mental models in human-computer interaction: research issues about what the user of software knows. ● 0214
Methods for designing software to fit human needs and capabilities. § 03566

**Olson, L.**
Computer-assisted instruction in academic libraries. 02282

**Olson, M. H.**
An empirical study of the impact of user involvement on system usage and information satisfaction. HCI-0448 †

**Oman, P. W.**
Posture and VDU operator satisfaction. 0988

**Omori, S.**
A model and an implementation of a logic programming environment. 01107

**Ong, C.**
Influence of age on performance and health of VDU workers. 03702

**Ong, J. B.**
An interactive tolerance system. 02975

**Onisawa, T.**
An approach to human reliability on man-machine systems using error possibility. 01702
A representation of human reliability using fuzzy concepts. 02024

**Onorato, L. A.**
Programmer-nonprogrammer differences in specifying procedures to people and computers. 02405
Programmer/nonprogrammer differences in specifying procedures to people and computers. HCI-0174 †

**Oosterlinck, A.**
Critical review of visual inspection. 02260

**Oppenheimer, C. G. (Ed.)**
Reasons for computer utilization reluctance by teachers with computer training. 04059

**Opper, S.**
A groupware toolbox. 01304

**Oppermann, R.**
Experiences in participative systems design. 03665

**Oransky, N. A.**
Examination of the role of "higher order" consistency in skill development. 01791

**Orban, G. A.**
Image segregation by motion: cortical mechanisms and implementation in neural networks. 03958

**Orbeton, P. (Ed.)**
Human factors in computing systems. § 02854

**Ord, J. G.**
Who's joking? The information system at play. 02066

**Oren, L.**
Clue: a common lisp user interface environment. 03113

**Orey III, M. A.**
Computer programming and general problem solving by secondary students. 01587

**Oriol, W. E.**
Information and the "Aging Network". 0525

**Orlikowski, W. J.**
A short-form measure of user information satisfaction: a psychometric evaluation and notes on use. 02351

**Orr, C. (Ed.)**
Computer applications in water supply: vol. 1—systems analysis and simulation. ● 0227

**Orr, C. H.**
A systems approach to extended GINAS applications. 0228

**Orwick, P.**
DOMAIN/DELPHI: retrieving documents online. 0906

**Oscarsson, D.**
Event-driven user interfaces based on quasi-parallelism. 03111

**Osiander, U.**
A method framework for the statistical package SPSS/PC+ to support occasional users. 01202

**Osin, L.**
Comparison of student performance in artihmetic exercises TOAM us paper-and-pencial testing. 02249

**Osterweil, L.**
Foundations for the Arcadia environment architecture. 01135

**Ostroff, D.**
Selection devices for users of an electronic encyclopedia: an empirical comparison of four possibilities. 02009
An experimental comparison of a mouse and arrow-jump keys for an interactive encyclopedia. 02098

**Oswald, H.**
PantaPM: an integrated software development environment. 03796

**Ott, A.**
Real time speech synthesis—development and employment. 01482

**Otte, F. H.**
Consistent user interface. HCI-0107 †

**Otwell, K.**
Planning as feedback to designers. 02978

**Owaied, H. H. (Ed.)**
A computer assisted learning system for reliability engineering. 04060

**Owen, T.**
Information processing today, with applications. ● 0567

**Owens, T.**
Information processing today, with applications. ● 0568
Information processing today, with applications and BASIC. ● 0569
Information processing today, with applications and BASIC: updat 87/88. ● 0570
Principles of information processing. ● 0571
Principles of information processing with applications and BASIC. ● 0572

**Oxborrow, E. A.**
Proceedings of the Fifth British National Conference on Databases (BNCOD 5). § 03284

**Oxenburgh, M.**
Repetition strain injury in Australian VDU users. 03681

**Paap, K. R.**
A formal interface design methodology based on user knowledge. 0929
The optimal number of menu options per panel. 01715

**Pacholski, L.**
The evaluation of selected ergonomical factors by production automation growth. 03429

**Packard, N. H.**
The immune system, adaptation, and machine learning. 02559

**Paddock, C. E.**
A critical view of factors affecting successful application of normative and socio-technical systems development approaches. 01914
Open versus closed minds: the effect of dogmatism on an analyst's problem-solving behavior. HCI-0446 †

**Padmos, P.**
Determinants of the VDU operator's well-being. 03679
Visual fatigue with work on visual display units: the current state of knowledge. 03891

**Paepcke, A.**
Language level persistence for an object-oriented application programming platform. 03522

**Paeseler, A.**
Modification of Earley's algorithm for speech recognition. 04003

**Paetzold, G.**
A roundtable discussion on women, computers and participation. 03673

**Pagels, H. R. (Ed.)**
Computer culture: the scientific, intellectual, and social impact of the computer. § 03567

**Pailhous, J.**
Real time graphic simulation of visual effects of egomotion. HCI-0379 †

**Pain, H.**
What stories should we tell novice PROLOG programmers? 0421
**Pajak, J.**
Acquisition of process control skills. 01878
**Pal, N. R.**
Segmentation using contrast and homogeneity measures. 02543
**Pal, S. K.**
Thresholding for edge detection using human psychovisual phenomena. 02538
Segmentation using contrast and homogeneity measures. 02543
**Palakal, M. J.**
Morphological representation of speech knowledge for automatic speech recognition systems. 03992
**Pallas, J.**
Multiprocessor Smalltalk: a case study of a multiprocessor-based programming environment. 03061
**Palm, B.**
Work distance and optical correction. 03736
**Palmer, J.**
The evaluation of online help systems: a conceptual model. 0129
**Palmer, T. R.**
GRAPE programming environment. 01967
**Palumbo, D. B.**
Problem solving: a behavioral interpretation. 01582
**Pan, S.**
Temporal semantics and natural language processing in a decision support system. 02038
Natural language query processing in a temporal database. HCI-0257 †
**Panzieri, F.**
A communication system supporting large datagrams on a local area network. HCI-0166 †
**Papathomas, T. V.**
Applications of computer graphics to the visualization of meteorological data. 02819

**Papazoglou, M. P.**
A portable query language for small scale systems. 02492
**Pape, D. L.**
STATUS with IQ—escaping from the Boolean straitjacket. 02569
**Paradice, D. B.**
SmartSLIM: a DSS for controlling biases during problem formulation. 0203
Controlling bias in user assertions in expert decision support systems for problem formulation. 02343
The role of memory in intelligent information systems. 03462
**Paradis, J.**
The on-line environment and in-house training. 0106
**Paradis, M.**
The optimal level of abstraction for models of cerebral representation of language processes: the state of the question. 0356
**Paredaens, J. (Ed.)**
MFDBS 87. § 03943
**Parent, M.**
Logic and programming. ● HCI-0068 †
**Parer, D.**
The design and construction of a vital database. 02460
**Paris, C. L.**
Tailoring object descriptions to a user's level of expertise. 01352
The use of explicit user models in text generation: tailoring to a user's level of expertise. 04051
**Paris, D. P.**
Quill: An extensible system for editing documents of mixed type. 03517
**Paris, J. B.**
On the applicability of maximum entropy to inexact reasoning. 02074
**Parisi, D.**
Knowledge representation and natural language: extending the expressive power of proposition nodes. 0096
**Park, C. H.**
Nonlinear discriminant functions and associative memories. 02757

**Park, E. H.**
Developing intelligent simulation language to support telerobotic workstation activities. 02995
Human factor issues in teleoperated systems. 03387
A conceptual dependency network approach to multi-task assignments in man-machine (teleoperated) systems. 03388
**Park, S.**
Flexible user interface decision support systems. 03473
**Parker, A. C.**
PHRAN-SPAN: a natural language interface for system specifications. 02829
**Parker, D. B.**
A comparison of algorithms for neuron-like cells. 02752
**Parker, D. L.**
Simulator design and instructional features for air-to-ground attack: a transfer study. 01804
**Parker, J.**
The 'window' terminal. 01405
A program development system for the casual programmer. 02808
**Parker, L. E.**
A methodology for dynamic task allocation in man-machine system. 03635
**Parker, S. C.**
An industrial chemical hazards database with a natural language interface: an application of artificial intelligence. 01533
**Parker, T.**
Tools for buidling interfaces. 01426
**Parkhurst, B.**
"My user interface is the best because...". 0856
**Parkinson, S. R.**
Considerations of menu structure and communication rate for the design of computer menu displays. 02124
Effects of breadth, depth and number responses on computer menu search performance. 02192
**Parsaei, H. R.**
Human perception of the work envelope of an industrial robot. 03410

## AUTHOR INDEX

**Parsons, H. M.**
Human nature and robot nature. 03401
Some recent documentation of robotic safety from Sweden. 03407

**Partridge, C.**
Innovations in Internetworking. • 0573

**Pascoe, G. A.**
Encapsulators: a new software paradigm in Smalltalk-80. 03034

**Pascual, V.**
Centaur: the system. 01136

**Pasemann, K.**
Interfaces for CAD applications. HCI-0418 †

**Pask, G.**
Why do instructional designers need conversation theory? 0506
Conversation theory as a basis for instructional design. 0507

**Patel, M. S.**
Mapping the manipulator workspace using interactive computer graphics. 02257

**Patil, R. S.**
An expert system for screening employee pension plans for the Internal Revenue Service. 02773

**Patnaik, L. M.**
Generalized query-by-rule: a heterogeneous database query language. HCI-0252 †

**Patrick, A.**
Conversational hypertext: information access through natural language dialogues with computers. 0867

**Patrick, J.**
Structural displays as learning aids. 02188

**Pattanaik, S. N.**
Vidura—an interactive multilingual publishing system—specification & design. 03186

**Patterson, D. (Chair.)**
ACM SIGDOC '85. § 02780

**Patterson, J.**
Pictures and category labels as navigational aids for catalog browsing. 02877

**Patterson, J. F.**
Video browsing and system response time. 03203

**Pattinson, C.**
The measurement of the performance of communications protocols from the user's viewpoint. 02684

**Pattison, E. M.**
Planning for hospital information systems using the Lancaster Soft Systems methodology. 01228

**Pattou, D.**
MOL3D, a modular and interactive program for molecular modeling and conformational analysis: I—basic modules. 02389

**Paul, R. L.**
Touchscreen usage in plant computer systems: a case study. 01530

**Paulanka, B. J.**
A regression model to identify successful learner traits with CAI. 02376

**Paulsson, L.**
Radiation emissions from VDUs. 03684

**Paulton, J.**
Pixel-planes 4: a summary. 0495

**Pavan, S.**
NLI-ESD: An expert natural language interface to a statistical data bank. 02712

**Pavel, M.**
Window-based computer dialogues. 0071
Intelligible encoding of ASL image sequences at extremely low information rates. 02708

**Pavesi, G.**
Single sweep analysis of visual evoked potentials through a model of parametric identification. 01261

**Pavlidis, T.**
Problems in recognition of drawings. 0294

**Pavlidis, T. (Ed.)**
Syntactic and structural pattern recognition. • 0292

**Pavlin, J.**
SIMS: a uniform environment for planning and performing user's tasks. 02921

**Pavri, F. N.**
Microcomputer applications: an empirical look at usage. 01949

**Pawlaczyk, M.**
Task-load and endocrinological risk for pregnancy in women VDU operators. 03692

**Pawlowski, E.**
Design of distribution of production control functions between humans and artificially intelligent devices. 03375

**Paxton, A. L.**
The application of human factors to the needs of the novice computer user. 02079

**Payne, S. J.**
Organization and learnability in computer languages. 02085
Perceptual structure cueing in a simple command language. 02086
The structure of command languages: an experiment on task-action grammar. 02224
Speech-controlled text-editing: effects of input modality and of command structure. HCI-0397 †

**Paz, N.**
User facilities for engineering support stations. 01512

**PDP Research Group**
Parallel distributed processing: explorations in the microstructures of cognition; Vol. 2: Psychological and biological models. • 0629

**Pea, R. D.**
Mapping the cognitive demands of learning to program. 0579
Integrated human and computer intelligence. 0580
On the cognitive effects of learning computer programming. 0581
Logo and development of thinking skills. 0582

**Pea, R. D. (Ed.)**
Mirrors of minds: patterns of experience in educational computing. • 0575

**Pear, M.**
Social science and system design: interdisciplinary collaborations. 0833

**Pear, M. R.**
A new model for user services: distributed support. 03153

**Pearce, A.**
Speech and expression: a computer solution to face animation. 03293

**Pearson, G.**
Of moles and men: the design of foot controls for workstations. 0935
Exploratory evaluation of a planar foot-operated cursor-positioning device. 02858

**Pearson, T.**
Direct comparison of the relative efficiency on intuitive and analytical cognition. 01896

**Peckham, J.**
Human factors in speech recognition. 0177

**Pedersen, G.**
Perception and acceptance of a local area network and electronic mail. 01284

**Pedrazzi, P.**
Real-time large vocabulary word recognition via diphone spotting and multiprocessor implementation. 03996

**Pejtersen, A. M.**
User requirements—empirical research and information systems design. 0450
Design and test of a database for fiction, based on an analysis of children's search behavior. 0451
The value of information and computer-aided information seeking: problem formulation and application to fiction retrieval. 01989
Development of a term association interface for browsing bibliographic data bases based on end users' word associations. HCI-0266 †

**Pejtersen, A. M. (Ed.)**
Information technology and information use: towards a unified view of information and information technology. ● 0447

**Pelagatti, G.**
The integration of the network and relational approaches in a DBMS. 03283

**Pellionisz, A. J.**
Tensor network theory and its application in computer modeling of the metaorganization of sensorimotor hierarchies of gaze. 02753
Tensor geometry: a language of brains & neurocomputers. Generalized coordinates in neuroscience & robotics. 03966

**Pelosi, P.**
Gas sensors: towards an artificial nose. 04015

**Peltonen, H.**
A design data manager. 03090

**Penning, L. J.**
LSP-automatic translation and information technology. 02513

**Penny, J. P.**
Instrumenting systems to measure components of interactive response times. 01230

**Pennycook, B. W.**
Computer-music interfaces: a survey. HCI-0412 †

**Penrose, R.**
On the physics and mathematics of thought. 03778

**Pentland, A. P.**
Perceptual organization and the representation of natural form. 0302
A new sense for depth of field. 01845
Part structure for 3-D sketching. 03300

**Penz, P. A.**
Digial signal processor accelerators for neural network simulations. 02754

**Penzias, A.**
Ideas and information: managing in a high-tech world. ● 0586

**Perby, M.**
Computerization and skill in local weather forecasting. 0344

**Percival, D. B.**
Use of object-oriented programming in a time series analysis system. 01112

**Percy, T.**
The importance of good relations. 01645

**Pereira, F.**
Transportability and generality in a natural-language interface system. 0394

**Pereira, F. C.**
Synergistic use of direct manipulation and natural language. 0857

**Pereira, F. C.N.**
TEAM: an experiment in the design of transportable natural-language interfaces. HCI-0351 †

**Perelson, A. S.**
The immune system, adaptation, and machine learning. 02559

**Peretto, P.**
Stochastic dynamics of neural networks. 01863

**Perez, E.**
Preserving the integrity of the medium: a method of measuring visual and auditory comprehension of electronic media. 02084

**Perez, E. C.**
Student evaluation of motivational and learning attributes of microcomputer soft. 02274

**Perkins, B.**
Apollo domain series 3000. 01170

**Perkins, D. N.**
Fragile knowledge and neglected strategies in novice programmers. HCI-0177 †

**Perkins, J.**
Design of computer programs for the physically handicapped. HCI-0096 †

**Perlman, G.**
Making the right choices with menus. 0070
Designing menu display format to match input device format. 0983

Natural artificial languages: low level processes. 02082
Multilingual programming: Coordinating programs, user interfaces, on-line help and documentation. 02785

**Pernici, B.**
The design requirements of office systems. 0757
Trends in office modeling. 03355
Reasoning in natural language for designing a data base. HCI-0322 †

**Pernul, G.**
An extended relational database model based on user views. 03452

**Perrault, C. R.**
Elements of a plan-based theory of speech acts. 0390
Analyzing intention in utterances. 0391
Natural-language interfaces. 0693
Natural-language interfaces. 0720

**Perry, S.**
A VLSI interactive layout editor (VILE). 02611

**Perry, T. S.**
Of mice and menus: designing the user-friendly interface. 01837

**Persaud, K.**
Gas sensors: towards an artificial nose. 04015

**Persaud, K. C.**
Physiology and psychophysics in taste and smell. 04009

**Personnaz, L.**
Designing a neural network satisfying a given set of constraints. 02755
A simple selectionist learning rule for neural networks. 02756

**Peruch, P.**
Real time graphic simulation of visual effects of egomotion. HCI-0379 †

**Pesce, F.**
Visual impairment and subjective ocular symptomatology in VDT operators. 03734

**Petajan, E.**
An improved automatic lipreading system to enhance speech recognition. 02859

**Peters, B. F.**
Online searching using speech as a man/machine interface. 02013

**Peterson, C.**
Neural networks and NP-complete optimization problems; a performance study on the graph bisection problem. 01339

**Peterson, D. J.**
Directories, DOS, and hard disks: impact on the user. 02604

**Peterson, J. G.**
Strategic issues in knowledge engineering. HCI-0317 †

**Peterson, J. L.**
4.2BSD and 4.3BSD as examples of the UNIX system. HCI-0165 †
A note on undetected typing errors. HCI-0399 †

**Peterson, L. L.**
The profile naming service. 01149
Dragonmail: an exercise in distributed computing. 02630

**Peterson, N. S.**
Representations of perceived relations among the properties and variables of a complex system. 01892

**Peterson, T. O.**
A taxonomy for the study of human factors in management information systems. HCI-0205 †

**Petit, E. J.**
Analysis of the performance of a genetic algorithm-based system for message classification in noisy environments. 02156

**Petit, M. J.**
Analysis of the performance of a genetic algorithm-based system for message classification in noisy environments. 02156

**Petre, M.**
Issues governing the suitability of programming languages for programming tasks. 03224

**Petrel, J.**
Fundamentals of psychosomatic transduction. 01594

**Petry, E.**
A model for an object management system for software engineering environments. 03843

**Pettersson, E.**
The interface is often not the problem. 0837

**Petzold, C.**
Programming the OS/2 presentation manager. ● 0587

**Pew, R.**
Socio-tech: what is it (and why should we care)? 0908

**Pfaff, G.**
GKSGRAL—software and hardware realizations of the graphical kernel system. 03982

**Pfitzmann, A.**
Networks without user observability. 01545

**Pham, D. T.**
Image compression using polylines. 02533

**Pham, T. T.**
A prototype autonomous agent for crew and equipment retrieval in space. 02994

**Phan, S.**
Jet engine technical advisor (JETA). 02974

**Pharr, W.**
A knowledge representation for natural language understanding. 02987

**Philip, G.**
Online searching using speech as a man/machine interface. 02013
Man—machine interaction by voice: developments in speech technology. Part I: The state-of-the-art. 02331
Man—machine interaction by voice: developments in speech technology. Part 2: general applications and potential applications in libraries and information services. 02332
Voice input/output interface for online searching: some design and human factor onsiderations. 02335

**Philippakis, A. S.**
Structured what if analysis in DSS models. 03481

**Philips International, I. (Ed.)**
Compact disc-interactive: a designer's overview. ● HCI-0078 †

**Phillips, B.**
IBM DOS 4.0: a bridge to OS/2. 02523

**Phillips, C. B.**
JACK: a toolkit for manipulating articulated figures. 03126

**Phillips, D.**
Using a top-down and bottom-up strategy to analyze high resolution aerial photographs of urban areas. 02960

**Phillips, D. F.**
Delphi: an intelligent interface for a dolphin communication laboratory. 02989

**Phillips, L. D. (Ed.)**
Expert judgment and expert systems. ● 0552

**Phillips, M. D.**
The quantification of operational suitability. 01359

**Phillips, R.**
Improving human/computer interactions. 0759
Human-computer interface recording. 01414
Magic PC- the "UN-LANGUAGE" approach. 01639

**Phillips, T. L.**
The effects of orienting, processing, and practicing activities on learning from interactive video. 02289

**Phillips, W. A.**
On the acquisition of object concepts from sensory data. 03959

**Phinney, D. E.**
A prototype autonomous agent for crew and equipment retrieval in space. 02994

**Phoon, W.**
Influence of age on performance and health of VDU workers. 03702

**Piasecki, S.**
ORGPLAN an information-decisive aid system to resolving organizing problems. 01573

**Picciotto, M.**
Interactive video in language learning. 01380

**Pich, B.**
An error correcting protocol for medical expert systems. 02143

**Pick, R. A.**
Composite models in symms. 03485

**Pickering, J. A.**
Touch-sensitive screens: the technologies and their application. HCI-0087 †

**Pickering, T.**
Office automation—can it be justified? 01383

**Pickett, M.**
The evaluation of project support environments for the STARTS user guide. 0173

**Pier, K.**
An introduction to Gargoyle: an interactive illustration tool. 03185

**Pierce, R. H.**
Ecilpse—an APSE based on PCTE. 03181

**Pierson, J. K.**
Documentation for user-developed applications with high documentation requirements. 01049
Adequate documentation of user-developed applications: a new challenge for end-user computing management. 03001
Developing awareness of computer ethics. 03010

**Pike, D.**
An integrated system for neural network simulations. 0771

**Pike, R.**
A library for incremental update of bitmap images. 02836

**Pilant, W. L.**
A PC-interactives stereonet plotting program. 01504

**Pilgrim, J.**
On the interaction of man and EDP use as work activity. 02094
On the detection of social effects in man-computer interaction—a contribution to systems design. 03672
On the purpose and analysis of EDP user systems. HCI-0218 †

**Pin, F. G.**
A methodology for dynamic task allocation in man-machine system. 03635

**Pincus, K.**
Artificial intelligence systems. 0683

**Pincus, M.**
Artificial intelligence systems. 0683

**Pinder, R.**
The use of complexity theory in evaluating interfaces. 03270

**Pineda, F. J.**
Dynamics and architecture for neural computation. 02270

**Pineda, L. A.**
GRAFLOG: understanding drawings through natural language. 01396

**Pingry, D. E.**
End user—IS design professional interaction—information exchange for firm profit or end user satisfaction? 01936

**Pinker, S.**
On language and connectionism: analysis of a parallel distributed processing model of language acquisition. 0590

**Pinker, S. (Ed.)**
Connections and symbols. ● 0588

**Pinsonneault, L.**
A new approach to cursor movements in user interfaces of integrated programming environments. 01974

**Pinter, R. Y.**
An environment for logic programming. 01106

**Pinto, J.**
Mental models and software maintenance. 02404
Providing the requisite knowledge via software documentation. 02898
Mental models and software maintenance. HCI-0173 †

**Piotrowski, J. A.**
The small computer assisted lecturing system. 01043

**Pircher, P. A.**
Developing interactive information systems with the user software engineering methodology. 0077

Developing interactive information systems with the user software engineering methodology. 01856

**Pisanich, G. M.**
Evaluating the impact of camera placement on teleoperator efficiency. 02940

**Pitre, J. M.**
The computer as an integral part of the laboratory. 03880

**Pittman, C. W.**
The space station information system and software support environment. 03512

**Pitz, G. F.**
Judgement and decision: theory and application. 0648

**Pizer, S. M.**
Psychovisual issues in the display of medical images. 03978

**Pizlo, Z.**
Physiology based simulation model of triangle shape recognition. 01277

**Place, S.**
Symbiotic systems for complex problems. 02922

**Plamondon, B. D.**
Describing movement control at two levels of abstraction. 0403

**Plamondon, R.**
Coupling visual and dynamic features to study handwritten signatures. 03309
A dedicated microcomputer for handwritten interaction with a software tool: system prototyping. HCI-0119 †

**Plander, I. (Ed.)**
Artificial Intelligence and Information-Control systems of Robots-87. § 03570

**Plante, B. L.**
On the parameters of human visual performance: an investigation of the benefits of antialiasing. 0799

**Plantinga, E. P. O.**
Creating the domain of discourse: ontology and inventory. 02158

**Plass, M.**
The workstation: the interpress page and document description language. 01356

**Platt, J. A.**
APL: The language of science and management. 02799

**Pliske, R.**
An empirical investigation as to the need for multicomponent decision models. 01898

**Pliskin, N.**
End-user prototyping: sophisticated users supporting system development. 01636
Responsibility sharing between sophisticated users and professionals in structured prototyping. 01978
Interacting with electronic mail can be a dream or a night: a user's point of view. 02069

**Plume, T.**
Practical applications of optical disk image systems in document management. 04041

**Podorowsky, G.**
A practical guide to the first time user/systems developer. 02437

**Poggio, T.**
Computational vision and regularization theory. 0301
Early vision: from computational structure to algorithms and parallel hardware. 02703
Early vision: from computational structure to algorithms and parallel hardware. HCI-0365 †

**Poh, K. L.**
A user-friendly program of human judgments in engineering decision analysis. 01167

**Pointing, T.**
Learning graphics programming by direct communication. 03298

**Poizner, H.**
Motion analysis of grammatical processes in a visual-gestural language. 03347

**Polacsek-Vancso, K.**
Automated construction of interactive learning programs in Modula-2. 01500

**Poli, A. (Ed.)**
Applied algebra, algorithmics and error-correcting codes. § 03848

**Polinsky, A. J.**
Unified interactive geometric modeller for simulating highly complex environments. 01472

**Pollack, J.**
Preserving the integrity of the medium: a method of measuring visual and auditory comprehension of electronic media. 02084

**Pollock, C.**
Training for optimising transfer between word processors. HCI-0447 †

**Pollock, R. J.**
A natural language interface to a multiple databased office information system. 01094

**Pols, L. C.W.**
Perceptual normalization of the vowels of a man and a child in various contexts. 02656
The use of speech in man-machine interaction. 03910

**Polson, M. C.**
Task-sharing within and between hemispheres: a multiple-resources approach. 01795

**Polson, M. C. (Ed.)**
Foundations of intelligent tutoring systems. ● 0592

**Polson, P.**
Report on the workshop on analytical models. 01001

**Polson, P. G.**
Transfer between text editors. 0804
Learning and transfer of measurement tasks. 0832
A test of a common elements theory of transfer. 0901
Transfer between menu systems. 02873
A quantitative theory of human-computer interaction. HCI-0198 †

**Poltrock, S. E.**
Innovation in user interface development: obstacles and opportunities. 0852
User interface design in large corporations: coordination and communication across disciplines. 0853

Graphic interfaces for knowledge-based system development. 0892
**Poltz, S. M.**
A suppport strategy for users of a campus-wide local area network. 03157
**Polynter, D.**
Variability in brightness matching of colored lights. 01767
**Pomerantz, J. R.**
Selective attention to aspects of motion configurations: common vs. relative motion. 03345
**Ponce, J.**
Describing surfaces. 02699
**Pope, S. T.**
A cookbook for using the model-view controller user interface paradigm in Smalltalk-80. 02390
**Porter, B. W.**
Protos: an examplar-based learning apprentice. 02210
**Porter, H. H.**
A distributed object server. 03842
**Porter, L. R.**
Managing the diffusion of end-user computing technologies: a fifties mindset with eighties tools. 0459
**Pospelov, D. A.**
Fuzzy reasoning in pseudo-physical logics. 01695
**Post, F. H.**
Geometric modelling. 0236
**Postel, J. B.**
An experimental multimedia mail system. HCI-0309 †
**Pot, F.**
Determinants of the VDU operator's well-being. 03679
**Potosky, J.**
Retraining high school teachers to teach computer science—observations on the first course. 01030
**Potosnak, K.**
Classifying users: a hard look at some controversial issues. 0902
**Potosnak, K. M.**
Testing for usability. 03163

**Potter, A.**
Direct manipulation interfaces. 01191
**Potter, R. L.**
Improving the accuracy of touch screens: an experimental evaluation of three strategies. 02860
**Potter, S.**
The ECLIPSE user interface. 02638
**Powell, D. J.**
Applications of an AI design shell ENGINEOUS to advanced engineering products. 02932
**Powell, J.**
Tools for buidling interfaces. 01426
**Powell, M. S.**
An input/output primitive for object-oriented systems. 01969
Strongly typed user interfaces in an abstract data store. 02618
**Powell, W. B.**
Design and implementation of an interactive optimization system for network design in the motor carrier industry. 02528
**Power, D. J.**
Executive workstations: issues and requirements. HCI-0288 †
**Powers, M.**
An experimental comparison of tabular and graphic data presentation. HCI-0236 †
**Prabhakaran, N.**
Representation of dynamic features in a conceptual schema. 01231
**Prabhu, V. P.**
CIM and manufacturing industry in the north east of England: A survey of some current issues. 03377
**Pracht, W. E.**
GISMO: A visual problem-structuring and knowledge-organization tool. 01871
**Prasad, B. G.**
An expert database for material and production planning. 02937
**Prasad, K. V.K.K.**
Natural language interface based on keyword extraction using AWK. 02498

**Pratt, G. E.C.**
Using the micro-computer to simplify database access: designing interfaces to complex files. HCI-0275 †
**Pratto, M. R.**
I didn't even know it was user services. 03133
**Prazdny, K.**
Vertical disparity nulling in random-dot stereograms. 01256
**Preece, J.**
A coherent specification method for the human interface to documentation systems. 0269
**Prekumar, G.**
A cognitive study of the decision-making process in a business context: implications for design of expert systems. 02256
**Prevost, M. P.**
Evaluating the impact of camera placement on teleoperator efficiency. 02940
**Prezant, B. D.**
Environmental stressors and perceived health symptoms among office workers. 03680
**Price, J.**
Creating a style for online help. HCI-0154 †
**Price, K.**
Anything you can do, I can do better (no you can't). 01462
**Prikhodko, V. I.**
A personal computer based graphic workstation. 02493
**Primov, G. V.**
A survey on systems informational paradigm to the psychic. 01606
A holography-based computer-aided translation system-conceptual analysis. 01607
**Prins, J.**
A new notion of encapsulation. 01104
**Probst, D.**
Rule-based detection of speech features for automatic speech recognition. 0419

**Probst, G. J.B.**
The way you look determines what you see (or self-organization in management and society). 01614

**Prochner, L.**
The effects of computer use in early childhood socialization. 0793

**Prochnow, D.**
Chip talk: projects in speech synthesis. ● HCI-0002 †

**Proeger, L. D.**
Capturing expertise: Some approaches to modeling command decisionmaking in combat analysis. 01883

**Proserpio, A.**
An abstract description generator for the reliability analysis in the design of real time systems. 02490

**Prosser, C.**
Introducing windows to Unix: user expectations. 03924
Windows, viewports and structured display files. 03930

**Prussak, W. J.**
Human aspects of automated assembly lines. 03445

**Pryor, R.**
An application of computerized fuzzy graphics rating scale to the psychological measurement of individual differences. 02200

**Psaltis, D.**
Nonlinear discriminant functions and associative memories. 02757

**Psy, B. S.**
Human factors considerations in the design of a VDU for visually impaired persons. 03698

**Pudet, T.**
Managing the semantic content of graphical data. HCI-0374 †

**Puetz, G. H.**
The design of a user friendly engineering economy analysis package for a microcomputer. 01507

**Pugh, J.**
Graphics through the looking glass. 02391

**Pugh, J. R.**
Application frameworks: experience with MacApp. 01039

**Pugh, W. J.**
Designing a user manual to support an in-house database. 01635

**Pulat, B. M.**
A workstation assessor for crew operations-WOSTAS. 02093
Formatting alphanumeric crt displays. 02140

**Pulat, P. S.**
A workstation assessor for crew operations-WOSTAS. 02093

**Pulford, K.**
The evaluation of project support environments for the STARTS user guide. 0173

**Pulkkis, G.**
An approach to CAD system performance evaluation. HCI-0414 †

**Pullinger, D. J.**
Moral judgements in designing better systems. 02064

**Purcell, P. J.**
Why desktop publishing is not a panacea. 03131

**Purcell, R.**
User orientation for the electronic encyclopedia. 02605

**Purdy, R. D.**
Knowledge representation in "Default": An attempt to classify general types of knowledge used by legal experts. 02775

**Purtilo, J.**
Polylith: an environment to support management of tool interfaces. 01096

**Putz-Anderson, V.**
The impact of automation on musculoskeletal disorders. 03437

**Putzolu, G. R.**
System R: a relational approach to database management. 0709

**Pylyshyn, Z. W.**
Connectionism and cognitive architecture: a critical analysis. 0589
Computation and cognition: toward a foundation for cognitive science. ● 0593

Information science: its roots and relation as viewed from the perspective of cognitive science. HCI-0185 †

**QED Information Sciences, I. W**
Critical issues in information processing management and technology: vol. 6. ● 0594

**Quaas, P.**
Performance in cognitive tasks and cardiovascular parameters as indicators of mental load. 03624

**Quaddua, M. A.**
A user-friendly program of human judgments in engineering decision analysis. 01167

**Quarterman, J. S.**
4.2BSD and 4.3BSD as examples of the UNIX system. HCI-0165 †

**Quedens, G.**
Introduction to Windows programming. ● HCI-0013 †

**Quercia, V.**
X window system user's guide for version 11: vol. 3. ● 0562

**Quilici, A.**
Recognizing and responding to plan-oriented misconceptions. 01350

**Quinlan, J. R.**
Simplifying decision trees. 02157

**Quinn, L.**
Intelligent interfaces: user models and planners. 0932

**Quintrand, P. (Ed.)**
CAD and robotics in architecture and construction. § 03568

**Raban, A.**
Word processing techniques and user learning preferences. 0984

**Rada, R.**
Interacting with computers. 02061
A graphical thesaurus-based information retrieval system. 02243

**Radhakrishnan, T.**
An intelligent braille display device. 01832

**Radil, T.**
Statistical inference on spontaneous neuronal discharge patterns. I. Single neuron. 01247

**Radin, S.**
Using interactive videotaped-based instruction to teach on-the-job social skills to handicapped adolescents. 02288

**Raeder, G.**
Event-driven user interfaces based on quasi-parallelism. 03111

**Ragade, R. K.**
ProCEED: an expert system for multivariate process control systems design. 02935

**Ragan, R. R.**
CONTEXT: an on-line documentation system. HCI-0280 †

**Raghavan, V.**
Optimal determination of user-oriented clusters. 03077

**Rahbari, H.**
A multi-purpose system for alpha-numeric input to computers via a reduced keyboard. 02118

**Rahimi, M.**
Differential organization impacts of the transition from stand-alone to integrated flexible production. 03380
Human perception of the work envelope of an industrial robot. 03410
Critical issues in the safety of software-dominant automated systems. 03416

**Rahtz, S. (Ed.)**
Information technology in the humanities: tools, techniques and applications. ● 0595

**Raibert, M. H.**
3-D balance in legged locomotion: modeling and simulation for the one-legged case. 03352

**Rainey, L. B.**
Design of a control room for the air force logistics command (AFLC) command, control,and communication and intelligence ($C^3I$) system. 01612

**Rains, K.**
Posture and VDU operator satisfaction. 0988

**Ralescu, A. L.**
Concept learning from examples and counter examples. 02229

**Ram, B.**
Evaluating formatted alphanumeric displays. 01525

**Ramachandra, P.**
Extending a relational database with deferred referential integrity checking andintelligent joins. 01089

**Ramadan, M.**
Biomechanical evaluation of lifting tasks: a microcomputer-based model. 01524

**Ramakrishna, K.**
Preferences for power in expert systems by novice users. 0971

**Ramani, S.**
Interactive communication of sentential structure and content: an alternative approach to man-machine communication. 02220

**Ramaprasad, A.**
Cognitive process as a basis for MIS and DSS design. 02476

**Rambally, G. K.**
Human factors in CAI design. 01494
The influence of color on program readability and comprehensibility. HCI-0120 †

**Rambally, R. S.**
Human factors in CAI design. 01494

**Ramberg, G.**
Eye Fatigue among VDU users and non-VDU users. 03682

**Ramey, J.**
Escher effects in online text. 0130

**Ramsay, A.**
Knowing that and knowing what. 03554

**Ramsey, H. R.**
Software psychology: the need for an interdisciplinary program. 0052

**Ramsower, R. M.**
Telecommuting the organizational and behavioral effects of working at home. ● 0596

**Ranauro, R. P.**
The moral cracker? 01546

**Randall, E. W.**
A serial interface for process control. 02383

**Rankin, P.**
Designing the "cockpit": the application of a human-centered design philosophy to make optimization systems accessible. 01016

**Ranney, M.**
A graphical programming language interface for an intelligent LISP tutor. 02862

**Ranta, J.**
Visualization of process information in improving work orientation. 03619

**Ranta, M.**
Interactive solid modeling in hut design. 03837

**Rantala, K.**
Birth defects, course of pregnancy, and work with VDUs: a Finnish case-referent study. 03689

**Rao, D. R.**
Structure of a directory space: a case study with a UNIX operating system. 02138
Efficient computer-user interface in electronic mail systems. HCI-0118 †

**Rao, R.**
How do experienced information lens users use rules? 0854
Semistructured messages are surprisingly useful for computer-supported coordination. HCI-0290 †

**Rao, V. B.**
Multi-Input fuzzy inference engine on a systolic array. 02953

**Raouf, A.**
Effects of automation on occupational safety & health. 03435

**Rapaport, M.**
Designing with databases. 01425

**Rapoport, A.**
Psychological models of deferred decision making. 02370

**Rappaport, A. T.**
Cognitive primitives. 02214

**Ras, Z. W. (Ed.)**
Methodologies for intelligent systems. § 03026
Methodologies for intelligent systems. § 03633

**Rashid, R. F.**
Mach and Matchmaker: kernel and language support for object-oriented distributed systems. 03031

**Raskin, J.**
Systemic implications of leap and an improved two-part cursor. 0848

**Rasmussen, J.**
Skills, rules, and knowledge; signals, signs, and symbols, and other distinctions in human performance models. 0654
Coping with human errors through system design: implications for ecological interface design. 02254
Models for design of computer integrated manufacturing systems. 03378

**Rastegary, H.**
Human—computer interactions in the workplace: psychosocial aspects of VDT use. 0306

**Rasure, J.**
XVISION: a comprehensive software system for image processing research, education, and applications. 03124

**Ratcliff, B.**
An empirical investigation into problem decomposition strategies used in program design. HCI-0103 †

**Ratcliff, R.**
A note on mimicking additive reaction time models. 02373

**Rathke, C.**
Human-computer communication meets software engineering. 03505

**Rau, L. F.**
Conceptual information extraction form financial news. 03489

**Rauf, R. C.**
Designing SAA applications and user interfaces. 01821

**Rault, J. (Ed.)**
Expert systems & their applications. § 02711
Expert systems & their applications. § 02715
Expert Systems & Their Applications. § 02717

**Raum, H.**
Alternative information presentation is a contribution to user centered dialogue design. 03621

**Ravani, B. (Ed.)**
CAD Based Programming for Sensory Robots. ● 0597

**Ravden, S.**
Evaluating usability of human-computer interfaces: a practical method. ● 0608

**Ravi, S. S.**
One-layer routing without component constraints. HCI-0090 †

**Rawlings, C.**
Gripe: a graphical interface to a knowledge based system which reasons about protein topology. 03234

**Ray, A. K.**
Artificial intelligence techniques applied to maintenance management. 02971

**Raymond, D. R.**
Measuring the effectiveness of personal database structures. 02246

**Rayner, K. (Ed.)**
Eye movements in reading: perceptual and language processes. ● 0609

**Raz, Y.**
Interactive L systems with a fast local growth. 01673

**Rock-Evans, R.**
An introduction to data and activity analysis. ● 0610

**Reader, A. V.**
The memory channel machine: part of a proposed learning machine. 01602

**Reardon, D. F.**
Personal transferable skills for the modern information professional: a discussion paper. 02338

**Reason, J.**
Cognitive aids in process environments: prostheses or tools? 02161
An interactionist's view of system pathology. 03813

**Reber, J.**
CAD system GISK for interactive graphical modelling of planar mechanisms. 01570

**Reddig, C.**
XTRA: a natural-language access system to expert systems. 02244

**Reddy, U. S.**
Transformational derivation of programs using the focus system. 01140

**Reddy, Y. B.**
Interacting with expert systems. 02949

**Redmond, R. T.**
Measuring change in the programming process. 02242

**Redwine, S. T., Jr.**
People and organizations in software production: a review of the literature. 01023
A map of the world of software-related standards, guidelines, and recommended practices. 01453

**Reed, M. W.**
Implementation plan for the use of on-line fiber analysis in the textile industry. 03433

**Reed, P.**
Usability testing in the real world. 0917

**Reeke, G. N., Jr.**
Selective networks and recognition automata. HCI-0390 †

**Reeve, D. B. (Ed.)**
A comparison of the effects of computer-assisted instruction, interactive video, and traditional instruction on third-grade students in art education. 04064

**Reeves, M.**
MINID—a BASIC program to assist in the optical identification of minerals in thin section. 01505

**Reeves, T. C.**
Research and evaluation models for the study of interactive video. 02283

**Reggia, J. A.**
Competitive dynamics in a dual-route connectionist model of print-to-sound transformation. 01341
Analysis of competition-based spreading activation in connectionist models. 02179
The MIRRORS/II simulator. 03502

**Regoczei, S.**
Creating the domain of discourse: ontology and inventory. 02158

**Reichman-Adar, R.**
Extended person-machine interface. HCI-0344 †

**Reifer, D. J.**
A cost model for estimating the costs of developing software in the Ada programming language. 03539

**Reilly, R.**
Ill-formedness and miscommunication in person-machine dialogue. 01957

**Reilly, R. G. (Ed.)**
Communication failure in dialogue and discourse: detection and repair processes. ● 0611

**Reimer, U.**
Computing text constituency: an algorithmic approach to the generation of text graphs. HCI-0267 †

**Rein, G.**
Project Nick: meetings augmentation and analysis. HCI-0156 †

**Rein, G. L.**
Report on the Collaborative Technology Developers' Workshop. 0994

**Reinke, W.**
Uncertainty analysis of human EEG spectra: A multivariate information theoretical method for the analysis of brain activity. 01270

**Reiser, B. J.**
A graphical programming language interface for an intelligent LISP tutor. 02862
The LISP tutor: it approaches the effectiveness of a human tutor. HCI-0431 †

**Reisig, W. (Ed.)**
Petri nets: applications and relationships to other models of concurrency. § 03973

**Reising, J. M.**
Color computer graphics in military cockpits. 0261

**Reisner, P.**
HCI, what is it and what research is needed? 0212

**Reiss, S. P.**
PECAN: program development systems that support multiple views. HCI-0145 †

**Reithinger, N.**
XTRA: a natural-language access system to expert systems. 02244

**Reitman-Olson, J. S.**
A general user interface for creating and displaying tree-structures, hierarchies, decision trees, and nested menus. HCI-0136 †

**Remde, J. R.**
Formative design evaluation of superbook. 01154

**Remington, R.**
On the selection and evaluation of visual display symbology: factors influencing search and identification times. 01718

**Remus, W. E.**
When and how cognitive style impacts decision making. 03474

**Renbao, Z.**
An interactive system SDI on microcomputer. 02272

**Renc, Z.**
Decision trees: a contribution to automatic interpretation of GUHA results. HCI-0329 †

**Renn, O. (Ed.)**
Expert judgment and expert systems. ● 0552

**Rentschler, I.**
Visual pattern recognition in humans: I. Evidence for adaptive filtering. 01274

**Renz, W.**
VDAFS—a pragmatic interface for the exchange of sculptured surface data. HCI-0420 †

**Reppy, J. H.**
A foundation for programming environments. 03057

**Reps, T. W.**
The synthesizer generator: a system for constructing language-based editors. ● HCI-0024 †
The synthesizer generator reference manual (3rd ed.). ● HCI-0024 †

**Restian, A.**
The cybernetic mechanisms of stress. 01599
The informational substrata of psychic illnesses. 01600

**Restivo, A.**
Some applications of a theorem of Shirshov to language theory. HCI-0181 †

**Rettig, M.**
How to choose natural language software. 01183

**Retz-Schmidt, G.**
Various views on spatial prepositions. 01196

**Reutenauer, C.**
Some applications of a theorem of Shirshov to language theory. HCI-0181 †

**Reuter, W.**
Procedures for participation in planning, developing and operating information systems. 03659

**Revesman, M.**
Two simulation studies investigating means of human-computer communication for dynamic task allocation. 01882

**Revesman, M. E.**
Application of a mathematical model of human decisionmaking for human-computer communication. 01866
An empirical comparison of model-based and explicit communication for dynamic human-computer task allocation. 02109

**Rey, P.**
Sensitivity to light and visual strain in VDT operators: basic data for the design of work stations. 03732

**Reynolds, C. F.**
Human factors in systems design: a case study. 03196
The use of colour in language syntax analysis. HCI-0385 †

**Reynolds, J. K.**
An experimental multimedia mail system. HCI-0309 †

**Rhind, D.**
Integrating graphics and text in computer products. 04044

**Rhine, L.**
Effects of the adoption of an integrated online system on a technical services department. 02463

**Rhyne, J.**
Issues limiting the acceptance of user interfaces using gesture input and handwriting character recognition. 0845
Tools and methodology for user interface development. 01057
Dialogue management for gestural interfaces. 01069

**Rhyne, J. R.**
Extensions to C for interface programming. 03108

**Rice, R. E.**
Applying the human relations perspective to the study of new media. 0787

**Rich, C.**
The programmer's apprentices: a research overview. 01368

**Rich, C. (Ed.)**
Readings in artificial intelligence and software engineering. • 0612

**Rich, E.**
Natural-language interfaces. 0069

**Richards, J. N. J.**
On methods for interface specification and design. 02114

**Richards, J. T.**
Rapid prototyping and system development: examination of an interface toolkit for voice and telephony applications. 0918
The 1984 Olympic Message System: a test of behavioral principles of system design. HCI-0125 †

**Richards, P. S.**
A scale for assessing student attitudes toward computers preliminary findings. 01579

**Richards, R. M.**
Documentation in a user work station environment. 02429

**Richards, T.**
An online interface within a hypertext system: project Jefferson's electronic notebook. 02524

**Richards, W.**
Codon constraints on closed 2D shapes. 02704

**Richards, W. (Ed.)**
Image understanding 1985-86. • 0615

**Richards, W. A. (Ed.)**
Natural computation: selected readings. • 0617

**Richardson, J.**
Reading from paper versus reading from screen. 01416

**Richardson, J. J.**
Developing the technology for intelligent maintenance advisors. 02276

**Richardson, J. J. (Ed.)**
Foundations of intelligent tutoring systems. • 0592

**Richardson, L.**
A graphics interface for interactive simulation of packet-switched networks. 03869

**Richardson, W. E.**
Undergraduate software engineering education. 04025

**Richter, A.**
Control of sensory processing - a hypothesis on and simulation of the architecture of an elementary cortical processor. 03972

**Richter, H.**
Vision monitoring of VDU operators and relaxation of visual stress by means of a laser speckle system. 03738

**Richter, P.**
Performance in cognitive tasks and cardiovascular parameters as indicators of mental load. 03624

**Richy, H.**
Conceptual documents: a mechanism for specifying active views in hypertext. 02833

**Riddle, W. E. (Chair.)**
Software Engineering. § 03504

**Ridgway, D. F.**
A C Interface. 01294

**Ridgway, J.**
Improving human/computer interactions. 0759

**Rieger, J.**
Computational techniques in motion processing. 0025

**Rieger, J. H.**
Determining the instantaneous axis of translation from optic flow generated by arbitrary sensot motion. 03332

**Riel, M. M.**
Learning with interactive media: dynamic support for students and teachers. 0519

**Ries, D. A.**
Distributed databases and distributed processing between personal computers and mainframes. 0458

**Righter, D. A.**
Programming the mouse in Turbo Pascal 4.0. 02393

**Ringle, M. D.**
Shaping user input: a strategy for natural language dialogue design. 02067

**Ringstaff, C.**
Current research in the psychology of learning and teaching. 03876

**Ringuest, J. L.**
A model of the controller responses of the human temperature regulating system to changes in water temperature. 02487

**Ripley, G. D.**
DVI—a digital multimedia technology. 01327

**Risdale, G.**
The interactive specification of human animation. 03292

**Rissland, E. L.**
Ingredients of intelligent user interfaces. 0093
Ingredients of intelligent user interfaces. 02088
A case-based system for trade secrets law. 02769
Ashley, K. D.-But, see, accord: generating blue book citations in HYPO. 02770

**Ritter, H.**
Topology conserving mappings for learning motor tasks. 02758
Extending Kohonen's self-organizing mapping algorithms to learn ballistic movements. 03967

**Rivard, S.**
User development of applications: a study of a model of success. 02807

**Rivers, R.**
Embedded user model-where next? 02059

**Rizzo, A.**
Human error detection processes. 02166
Office automation as an opportunity for an organizational check-up. 03749

**Rödiger, K. H.**
Work design instead of system design. 03671

**Roach, J. W.**
Representing and using metacommunication to control speakers' relationships in natural-language dialogue. 02136

**Roberts, L. A.**
Improving speaker consistency in an automatic speech recognition framework. 01448

**Roberts, M.**
Twelve neural network cliches. 01186
A multi-purpose system for alpha-numeric input to computers via a reduced keyboard. 02118

**Roberts, R.**
Developing intelligent simulation language to support telerobotic workstation activities. 02995

**Roberts, S. M.**
An incidence-matrix-driven panel system for the IBM PC. 01814

**Roberts, T.**
Usability testing in the real world. 0917

**Roberts, T. L.**
The evaluation of text editors: Methodology and empirical results. 0058
Human factors testing in the design of Xerox's 8010 "Star" office workstation. 0090
The effects of device technology on the usability of advanced telephone functions. 0876
The evaluation of text editors: methodology and empirical results. HCI-0209 †

**Roberts, W.**
'Remember to lock the door': MMI and the hacker. 01910

**Roberts, W. T.**
A formal specification of the QMS message system: the underlying abstract model. 01406

**Robertson, G. G.**
Diamond: a multimedia message system built on a distributed architecture (Reprint). 0380
Diamond: A multimedia message system built on a distributed architecture. 0574

**Robertson, I.**
Interactive video in language learning. 01380

**Robertson, P. J.**
Human factors of changing information science technology. 04048

**Robertson, P. K.**
The application of scene synthesis techniques to the display of multidimensional image data. HCI-0371 †

**Robertson, S. E.**
Weighting, ranking and relevance feedback in a front-end system. 02329

**Robertson, S. P.**
Plan-based representations of pascal and fortran code. 02897

**Robey, D.**
Strategies for research on information systems in organizations. A critical analysis of research purpose and time frame. 0158

**Robinet, E. (Ed.)**
ESOP 86. § 03883

**Robinson, C. P.**
Comparison of speech and pictorial displays in a cockpit environment. 01731

**Robinson, D. A.**
Why visuomotor systems don't like negative feedback and how they avoid it. 0016

**Robinson, J.**
ADDS-a dialogue development system for the Ada programming language. 02102

**Robinson, K. (Ed.)**
Methodology of window management. § 03923

**Robinson, P.**
A model for graphical interaction. 02610

**Robinson, S.**
The FAIM-1 user interface—human engineering for the fifth generation. 03587

**Rocha, A. F.**
The fuzzy logic of text understanding. 01701

**Rockart, J. F.**
Executive support systems: the emergence of top management computer use. ● HCI-0049 †

**Rockenbach Tarouco, L. M.**
User friendly interface for messaging systems. 03320

**Rockwell, T. H.**
Modeling fault diagnosis as the activation and use of a frame system. 01729

**Rodden, T.**
Interacting with an active, integrated environment. 01137

**Rodeh, M.**
An efficient high-level man-machine interface. 03530

**Rodman, R. D.**
Natural language with discrete speech as a mode for human-to-machine. HCI-0355 †

**Roe, R.**
User errors in human—computer interaction. 0313

**Roe, R. A.**
Automation in public libraries: effects on the organization, quality of working life, and quality of services. 0246

**Roediger, K.**
The limitations of task complexity through information technologies: results of a field study. 0307

**Roehl, E. A.**
Using hypertext to overcome the knowledge base development bottleneck: a case study. 02914

**Roelofs, L. H.**
The development of an intelligent user interface for NASA's scientific databases. 02673

**Roesner, H.**
Expert systems for commercial use. 0666

**Rogard, V.**
On the user's opinion about systems design. 03743

**Rogers, A.**
Attribute propagation by message passing. 01100

**Rogers, D. F.**
Procedural elements for computer graphics. • HCI-0069 †

**Rogers, E. M.**
The diffusion and impacts of information technology in households. 0754

**Rogers, J.**
Supercomputer applications: helping users cope with tough programming problems. 03147

**Rogers, T. R.**
Entity-relationship database user interfaces. 0711

**Rogers, Y.**
Pictorial representations of abstract concepts relating to human-computer interaction. 0947
Icons at the interface: their usefulness. 02065
User requirements for expert system explanation: what, why and when? 03242
Evaluating the meaningfulness of icon sets to represent command operations. 03277

**Rohr, G.**
How people comprehend unknown system structures: conceptual primitives in systems' surface representations. 03828
Representational frameworks and models for human-computer interfaces. HCI-0188 †

**Roland, E. F.**
System design for speech recognition and generation. 0065

**Roll, K.**
Recent results on the illumination of VDU and CAD workstations. 03719

**Rolstadås, A.**
Production management systems. 0619

**Rolstadas, A. (Ed.)**
Computer-aided production management IFIP. • 0618

**Roncarolo, L.**
A planning system for a cognitive problem. 02719

**Root, R. W.**
Design of a multi-media vehicle for social browsing. 02822

**Roper, P.**
Investigating computer anxiety in an academic library. 02047

**Rosa, R. R.**
Long workdays versus restdays: assessing fatigue and alertness with a portable performance. 01778

**Roschelle, J.**
Children's collaborative use of a computer microworld. 02825

**Roscoe, S. N.**
An integrated display for vertical and translational flight: eight factors affecting pilot performance. 01714
Improving visual performance through volitional focus control. 01744
Spatial misorientation exacerbated by collimated virtual flight display. 01979

**Rose, M. T.**
MH: a multifarious user agent. 01428

**Rose, S.**
A user interface for deaf-blind people (preliminary report). 0794

**Rosemann, H.**
Some principles of perceptual and cognitive psychology applied to the design of help menus. 01200

**Rosen, B.**
Graph attribution as a specification paradigm. 01138

**Rosen, D.**
History in the making: a report from Microsoft's First International Conference on CD ROM. 0279

**Rosenberg, D. J.**
Human performance evaluation of digitizer pucks for computer input of spatial information. 01774

**Rosenberg, J.**
UIMSs: threat or menace? 02889

**Rosenberg, J. K.**
A comparison of tiled and overlapping windows. 0904

**Rosenberg, S. M.**
A model for evaluating stress effects of work with display units. 03756

**Rosenblad, K.**
Preserving the integrity of the medium: a method of measuring visual and auditory comprehension of electronic media. 02084

**Rosenblitt, D.**
How do experienced information lens users use rules? 0854
Semistructured messages are surprisingly useful for computer-supported coordination. HCI-0290 †

**Rosenbloom, P.**
Learning by chunking: a production system model of practice. 0483
Universal subgoaling and chunking: the automatic generation and learning of goal hierarchies. • 0497

**Rosenfeld, A.**
Recognizing unexpected objects: a proposed approach. HCI-0389 †

**Rosenfeld, A. (Ed.)**
Human and Machine Vision II. § 02696

**Rosenof, H.**
Object oriented rapid prototyping with G2. 02984

**Rosenschein, J. S.**
Cooperation without communication. 0169
Deals among rational agents. 0170

**Rosenthal, D.**
System aspects of low-cost bitmapped displays. 03932
A window manager for bitmapped displays and Unix. 03933

**Rosenthal, D. S.**
Andrew: a distributed personal computing environment. HCI-0091 †

**Rosenthal, D. S.H.**
The NeWS book: an introduction to the network/extensible window system. • 0358
A user-interface toolkit in object-oriented PostScript. 01391

**Rosenthal, N. R.**
Assessing gender bias in computer software. 01591

**Rosinski, R. R.**
Programmer perceptions of productivity and programming tools. HCI-0099 †

**Roske-Hofstrand, R. J.**
Circling: a method of mouse-based selection without button presses. 0847
The optimal number of menu options per panel. 01715

**Ross, D.**
A personal view of the personal work station: some firsts in the Fifties. 03093

**Ross, D. A.**
Design of an integral computer-based wheelchair controller/linear synchronous motor system. 02378
Human factors design of a video monitor emulator and display (VMED) for visuallyimpaired computer users. 02379
Human factors considerations in the design of a VDU for visually impaired persons. 03698

**Ross, G.**
Integral-C—a practical environment for C programming. 03049

**Ross, J.**
Visual analysis during motion. 0020

**Ross, J. W.**
Windows for BASIC. 01292

**Ross, R.**
VDTs: are they safe? 02549

**Ross, S. C.**
Understanding & using application software. • 0626

**Rosseel, E.**
The impact of changes in work ethics upon organizational life. 0250

**Rosson, M. B.**
Designing for designers: an analysis of design practice in the real world. 0839
Classifying users: a hard look at some controversial issues. 0902
Designing a quality voice: an analysis of listeners' reactions to synthetic voices. 0914
On comprehending a computer manual: analysis of variables affecting performance. 02135

The designer as user: building requirements for design tools from design practice. HCI-0129 †
Paradox of the active user. HCI-0434 †

**Roth, B. (Ed.)**
The fourth international symposium. § 03561

**Roth, B. D.**
EPVM: An expert patient-ventilator manager for chemical warfare casualties. 02956

**Roth, C. E.**
PowerMath—A system for the Macintosh. 03083

**Roth, E. M.**
Cognitive engineering: human problem solving with tools. 01781
Human interaction with an "intelligent" machine. 02163

**Roth, J. P. (Ed.)**
Optical information systems '86. § 03556

**Roth, M.**
Algebras for nested relations. 01623

**Roth, R. W.**
Dealing with disparate audiences in computer science courses using a project group within a traditional class. 01031

**Roth, S. F.**
Callisto: an intelligent project management system (Reprint). 0375

**Roth, W.**
Public Law 99-506, "Section 508" Electronic Equipment Accessibility for disabled workers. 02893

**Rothermel, K.**
A communication mechanism supporting actions. 01441

**Rothkopf, E. Z.**
Machine adaption to psychological differences among users in instructive information exchanges with computers. 03609

**Roucoux, J.**
Education and training in office technology. 02330

**Roufs, J. A.F.**
Visual comfort as a criterion for designing display units. 03892

**Roufs, J. A. J.**
Criteria for the subjective quality of visual display units. 03724

**Rouse, S. H.**
Human information seeking and design of information systems. HCI-0184 †

**Rouse, W. B.**
Models of human problem solving: detection, diagnosis, and compensation for system failures. 0653
Measures of human problem solving performance in fault diagnosis tasks. 0655
A fuzzy rule-based model of human problem solving. 0656
The effects of type of knowledge upon human problem solving in a process control task. 0657
Conceptual design of a human error tolerant interface for complex engineering systems. 01235
On the design of man-machine systems: principles, practices and prospects. 01236
Adaptive aiding for human/computer control. 01782
Aiding the human decisionmaker through the knowledge-based sciences. 01880
Understanding and enhancing user acceptance of computer. 01889
The value of information and computer-aided information seeking: problem formulation and application to fiction retrieval. 01989
On meanings menus for measurement: disentangling evaluative issues in system design. 01997
Human information seeking and design of information systems. HCI-0184 †
A note on the nature of creativity in engineering: implications for supporting system design. HCI-0220 †
A fuzzy rule-based model of human problem solving. HCI-0359 †

**Rowe, F.**
The telephone in question: questions on communication. 01436

**Rowe, L. A.**
Database portals: a new application program interface. 0707
"Fill-in-Form" programming. 0710
A visual shell interface to a database. 02640

**Rowe, N. C.**
Modelling degrees of item interest for a general database query system. 02083

**Rowe, S.**
Repetition strain injury in Australian VDU users. 03681

**Roweth, D.**
Implementing neural network models on parallel computers. 01403

**Rowley, J. E.**
The seacher/information interface project—final report. 02341

**Rowley, P.**
Issues and techniques in touch-sensitive tablet input. 0063

**Rozenberg, G. (Ed.)**
Petri nets: applications and relationships to other models of concurrency. § 03973

**Rubel, M.**
Programming the dBASE III Plus user interface. ● 0627

**Rubens, P.**
Online information, hypermedia, and the idea of literacy. 0112
Designing online information. HCI-0152 †

**Rubin, D. C.**
Natural language with discrete speech as a mode for human-to-machine. HCI-0355 †

**Rubin, H. I.**
Motivations and behaviors of software professionals. 03003

**Rubin, K. S.**
A smalltalk implementation of an intelligent operator's associate. 01132

**Rubin, T.**
User interface design for computer systems. ● 0628
Human factors in computer based message systems. 01374

A study of group interaction over a computer-based message system. 03257

**Rubino, G. F.**
Visual impairment and subjective ocular symptomatology in VDT operators. 03734

**Rubinstein, R.**
The human factor: Designing computer systems for people. 0076
Digital typography: an introduction to type and composition for computer system design. ● HCI-0074 †

**Rudeck, C.**
Methodological problems of designing dialogue-oriented components in information systems. 03595

**Rudisill, M.**
NASA Johnson Space Center, Human-Computer Interaction. 0815
Models of user interactions with graphical interfaces: 1. statistical. 0883
Formatting space-related displays to optimize expert and nonexpert user performance. 0927

**Rudnicky, A. I.**
Talking to computers: an empirical investigation. 02186

**Rueb, R.**
Human interfaces in a legal expert system. 03164

**Ruedisueli, L. W.**
TNT: a talking tutor 'n' trainer for teaching use of interactive computer systems. 0895

**Ruffo, b.**
The many faces of faculty computing assistance. 03143

**Ruhmann, I.**
KRITON: a knowledge-acquisition tool for expert systems. HCI-0327 †

**Ruiz Quintanilla, S. A.**
Social psychological prerequisites and consequences of new information technologies. 03631

**Rumbaugh, J.**
State trees as structured finite state machines for user interfaces. 03107

**Rumelhart, D. E.**
Parallel distributed processing: explorations in the microstructures of cognition; Vol. 2: Psychological and biological models. ● 0629
A distributed model of human learning and memory. 0633
On learning the past tenses of English verbs. 0634
Amnesia and distrubuted memory. 0641

**Rumlehart, D. E.**
Schemata and sequential thought processes in PDP models. 0630

**Rummel, P. A.**
SIMTALK: Pros and cons of natural language for manufacturing simulation. 02950

**Rump, S. M.**
Algorithms for verified inclusions—theory and practice. 0549

**Rumsey, D.**
User-network interfaces. 01384

**Runciman, C.**
User programs: a way to match computer systems and human cognition. 03271
Interaction models and the principled design of interactive systems. 03799
Equal opportunity interactive systems. HCI-0168 †

**Rupp, B. A.**
Display image characteristics and visual response. 03722

**Rushby, N.**
From trigger video to videodisc: a case study in interpersonal skills. 0508

**Rushinek, A.**
The effects of sources of applications programs on user satisfaction: an empirical study of micro, mini & mainframe computers using an interactive artificial intelligence expert-system. 01601

The influence of troubleshooting, education, and documentation on computer user satisfaction. 01869
A methodology for interactive evaluation of user reactions to software packages:an empirical analysis of system performance, interaction, and run time. 02080
Produciton and inventory management software packages related to user reactions. 02567
An evaluation and selection methodology of microcomputer training software: Implications for human resource managers and computer personnel. 03002
The effects of communication monitors on user satisfaction. HCI-0221 †
What makes users happy? HCI-0427 †

**Rushinek, S.**
The influence of troubleshooting, education, and documentation on computer user satisfaction. 01869

**Rushinek, S. F.**
The effects of sources of applications programs on user satisfaction: an empirical study of micro, mini & mainframe computers using an interactive artificial intelligence expert-system. 01601
A methodology for interactive evaluation of user reactions to software packages:an empirical analysis of system performance, interaction, and run time. 02080
Produciton and inventory management software packages related to user reactions. 02567
An evaluation and selection methodology of microcomputer training software: Implications for human resource managers and computer personnel. 03002
The effects of communication monitors on user satisfaction. HCI-0221 †
What makes users happy? HCI-0427 †

**Rushmeier, H. E.**
An experimental evaluation of computer graphics imagery. HCI-0373 †

**Rusinek, H.**
Interactive graphic editor for analysis and enhancement of medical images. 01492

**Ruske, R.**
Structure of German syllable initial and final consonant clusters based on articulatory features. 02652

**Russell, D. M.**
Intelligent interfaces: user models and planners. 0932

**Russo, C. J.**
Applications of an AI design shell ENGINEOUS to advanced engineering products. 02932

**Russotti, J.**
Multimodal detection and recognition performance of sonar operators. 01709

**Ruth, J. C.**
System design for speech recognition and generation. 0065

**Ruth, S.**
Establishing user-centered criteria for information systems: a software ergonomics perspective. 01920

**Rutkowska, J. C. (Ed.)**
Computers, cognition, and development: issues for psychology and education. ● 0643

**Ruttkay, Z.**
Multi-media presentation in CAD systems. 0007
A multiparadigm user interface for intelligent CAD systems. 0716

**Ruud, W. N.**
Selection systems for sales representatives. 02408
TA: Can it improve worker satisfaction with organizational decision-making? 02414

**Ryan, J. P.**
Safety considerations in robot design. 03418

**Rybolt, W. H.**
An iterative approach to improving data analysis in the classroom. 03318

**Rychlik, P.**
The use of modal default reasoning in information systems. 02095

**Rysavy, F. R.**
Computing facilities in the MRC clinical research centre. 02688

**Sááksjárvi, M.**
The dual role of information centers: an assessment of end user computing management strategies. 01942

**Saaksjarvi, M.**
Strategies for managing end user computing. 02436

**Saariluoma, P.**
Visual information chunking in spreadsheet calculation. 02232

**Saarinen, T.**
The dual role of information centers: an assessment of end user computing management strategies. 01942
Strategies for managing end user computing. 02436

**Saaty, T. L.**
Speculating on the future of mathematics. 01210

**Sacerdoti, E.**
Developing a natural language interface to complex data. 0393

**Sachs, N. J.**
Judgement and decision: theory and application. 0648

**Sadoski, D. M.**
The effects of syntactic complexity on the human-computer interaction. 01708

**Sadri, F.**
Non-first normal form universal relations: an application to information retrieval systems. 02039

**Safayeni, F.**
An empirical investigation of two electronic mail systems. 01239

**Safayeni, F. R.**
Measuring the effectiveness of personal database structures. 02246

**Saffin, R. F.**
Design of user-system interfaces using a cognitive design aid. 01682

**Sagalowicz, D.**
Developing a natural language interface to complex data. 0393

**Sagan, J.**
Application input drivers. 01291

**Sage, A. P.**
An overview of system design for human interaction. 0646
ARIADNE: A knowledge-based interactive system for planning and decision support. 0661
A similarity-based reasoning model for intelligent interfaces. 01503
ARIADNE: a knowledge-based interactive system for planning and decision support. 01860
Aiding the human decisionmaker through the knowledge-based sciences. 01880
Information systems engineering for distributed decisionmaking. 01899
On the management of information imperfection in knowledge based systems. 03823

**Sage, A. P. (Ed.)**
System design for human interaction. • 0644
System design for human interaction. • 0645

**Sage, J. P.**
A comparison of neural network and matched filter processing for detecting lines in images. 02738

**Sagerer, G.**
Recent advances in speech understanding and dialog systems. § 03987
Knowledge based systems for speech understanding. 04001

**Sagie, I.**
Computer-aided modeling and planning (CAMP). HCI-0415 †

**Sagisaka, Y.**
Composite phoneme units for the speech synthesis of Japanese. 02647

**Sahlin, N. E.**
Decision making with unreliable probabilities. 0652

**Saint-Dizier, P.**
An approach to natural-language semantics in logic programming. 02342

**Saito, N.**
Resource management scheme in distributed environments. 01018

**Saitta, L.**
Automated concept acquisition in noisy environments. 01841
Knowledge representation and use in pattern analysis. 02030
An expert system for mapping acoustic cues into phonetic features. HCI-0328 †

**Sajaniemi, J.**
Visual information chunking in spreadsheet calculation. 02232

**Saka, T. T.**
Computer work skills training for persons with developmental disabilities. 01559

**Sakaguchi, Y.**
Self-organizing system obtaining communication ability primitive model for language generation. 01279

**Sakamura, K.**
The software structure of extended nucleus based on BTRON specification. 03494

**Sakamura, K. (Ed.)**
TRON Project 1987—Open-architecture computer systems. § 03821

**Sakata, S.**
A distributed interoffice mail system. HCI-0308 †

**Sakawa, M.**
Interactive fuzzy decision-making for multi-objective nonlinear programming using reference membership intervals. HCI-0295 †

**Sala, E.**
Preferences for power in expert systems by novice users. 0971

**Salama, R.**
Linkage versus integration for binding database and interactive graphics systems. 02040
Linkage versus integration for binding database and interactive graphics systems. 02406

**Salas, E.**
Problem solving performance and display preference for information displays depicting numerical functions. 0978

**Salasin, J.**
Person-to-person communication in an applied research/service delivery setting. 02445

**Salaun, J.**
Behavioral experiments on handmarkings. HCI-0201 †

**Saleh, B.**
A model for the fading of stabilized images in a visual system. 01864

**Salem, J. B.**
Interactive scientific visualization and parallel display techniques. 03542

**Salesin, D.**
Two-bit graphics. HCI-0372 †

**Salisbury, D. F.**
A comparison of a microcomputer progressive state drill and flashcards for learning paired associates. 02295

**Salloway, J. C.**
The effects of a computerized information system on a hospital. 01553

**Salmad, T.**
A natural language interface for computer-aided design. • 0664

**Salminen, A.**
Specification of a tool for viewing program text. 03884

**Salovaara, J.**
Equipment and workstation design for banking services. 03712

**Salvendy, G.**
Human intelligence models and their implications for expert system structure and research. 01242
The contribution of cognitive engineering to the effective design and use of information systems. 02033
Cognitive issues in the process of software development: review and reappraisal. 02222
Underlying dimensions of human problem solving and learning: implications for personnel selection, training tasks design and expert system. 02225
Ergonomics of hybrid intelligence. 03393

An approach to knowledge elicitation in scheduling FMS: Toward a hybrid intelligent system. 03394

**Salveter, S.**
Supporting natural language database update by modeling real world actions. 03179

**Samad, T.**
Towards a natural language interface for computer aided design. 04049

**Samet, P. A.**
A computing service using linked minis. 01674

**Samson, W. B.**
The design and evaluation of an animated programming environment. 03220

**Samuelson, P.**
Protecting user interfaces through copyright: the debate. 0827
Why the look and feel of software user interfaces should not be protected by copyright law. 01324

**Sanchez, P.**
An experimental comparison of tabular and graphic data presentation. HCI-0236 †

**Sandahl, K.**
The migration of expert systems into the production environment. 0740

**Sandberg, B.**
Preserving the integrity of the medium: a method of measuring visual and auditory comprehension of electronic media. 02084

**Sandblad, B.**
The interface is often not the problem. 0837
Human cognition and human computer interaction. HCI-0241 †

**Sanders, A. F.**
Contexts and conflicts between ergonomics and industrial psychology. 0240

**Sanders, G. L.**
Definitional distinctions and implications for managing end user computing. 01946

The impact of DSS on organizational communication. HCI-0294 †

**Sanders, L. G.**
Propaedeutics of decision-making: supporting managerial learning and innovation. 01667

**Sanders, M. S.**
The effects of panel arrangements and locus of attention on performance. 01759

**Sanderson, P. M.**
Human supervisory control in discrete manufacturing: Translating the paradigm. 03364

**Sandford, J.**
The mental rotation and perceived realism of computer-generated three-dimensional images. 02213

**Sandini, G.**
VIS: a virtual image system for image-understanding research. 02629
Active vision: integration of fixed and mobile cameras. 04017

**Sandström, G.**
How to improve pragmatic quality of information systems. 03662

**Sanfeliu, A. (Ed.)**
Syntactic and structural pattern recognition. • 0292

**Sanford, D. L.**
Representing and using metacommunication to control speakers' relationships in natural-language dialogue. 02136

**Santaella, E. M.**
Toward native language software for information management. HCI-0138 †

**Santero, B. A.**
Grand computer conferencing: What have we learned? 03536

**Santha, M.**
Relativized Arthur-Merlin versus Merlin-Arthur games. 01912

**Santos, M. R.**
The fuzzy decodings of educative texts. 01700

**Sanwal, M.**
Methodology for end user computing in development administration. 01956

**Saracevic, T.**
Processes and problems in information consolidation. 01992

**Sarin, S.**
Computer-based real-time conferencing systems (Reprint). 0377
Data sharing in group work (Reprint). 0379
Evaluating formatted alphanumeric displays. 01525

**Sartori, C.**
A modular user-oriented decision support for physical database design. 01669

**Sasiela, R. J.**
Forgetting as a way to improve neural-net behavior. 02759

**Sasnett, R. M.**
Investigations in multimedia design documentation. 0116

**Sasseville, A. M.**
Modeling the Cognitive content of displays. 01800

**Sassi, E.**
Integrating physics and computer education in a single process. 03879

**Sastry, M.**
Reference model for DBMS user facility. 01086

**Sathi, A.**
Callisto: an intelligent project management system (Reprint). 0375

**Sato, H.**
Composite phoneme units for the speech synthesis of Japanese. 02647

**Sato, T.**
Contextual structure analysis of microcomputer manuals. 03227
MEISTER: a model enhanced intelligent and skillful teleoperational robot system. 03562

**Sattler, D. M.**
Programming in Basic or Logo: effect on critical thinking skills. 04062

**Satyanarayanan, M.**
Andrew: a distributed personal computing environment. HCI-0091 †

**Sauer, C. H.**
Advanced interactive executive (AIX) operating system overview. 01815

**Saunders, D.**
Human and computer involvement in simulation. 02593

**Sauter, S. L.**
Preventing back strain. 0047

**Savage, R. E.**
A Multilevel menu-driven user interface: Design and evaluation through simulation. HCI-0170 †

**Savenye, W.**
The effects of orienting objectives and review on learning from interactive video. 02287

**Savory, S. (Ed.)**
Artificial intelligence and expert systems. ● 0665

**Savoy, J.**
The electronic book Ebook3. 02234

**Savoy, R. L.**
Contingent aftereffects and isoluminance: psychophysical evidence for separation of color, orientation, and motion. 01463

**Sawada, D.**
Computer, quantized time and human duration. 01593
Recursive complementarity in the cybernetics of education. 01598

**Sawyer, D.**
Display legibility guidelines: a design aid. 01983

**Sawyer, P.**
Interacting with an active, integrated environment. 01137
Direct manipulation of an object store. 02608

**Sawyer, S. C. (Ed.)**
Computers : the user perspective. ● 0705

**Saxberg, B. V. H.**
Projected free fall trajectories. I. Theory and simulation. 01265
Projected free fall trajectories. II. Human experiments. 01266

**Saxen, L.**
Birth defects, course of pregnancy, and work with VDUs: a Finnish case-referent study. 03689

**Scacchi, W.**
A hypertext system to manage software life cycle documents. 03519

**Scadden, L. A.**
Public Law 99-506, "Section 508" Electronic Equipment Accessibility for disabled workers. 02893

**Scagliola, C.**
Real-time large vocabulary word recognition via diphone spotting and multiprocessor implementation. 03996

**Scalas, M. R.**
A modular user-oriented decision support for physical database design. 01669

**Scaletti, C. A.**
An interactive environment for object-oriented music composition and sound synthesis. 01131

**Scandura, J. M.**
System issues in problem solving research. 03606

**Scane, R.**
Key areas of cognitive psychology: a historical perspective. 0328

**Scanlan, D.**
Data-structures students may prefer to learn algorithms using graphical methods. 01032

**Scanlon, E.**
Cognitive economy in physics reasoning. implications for designing instructional materials. 0542

**Scapin, D. L.**
Ergonomic aspects of man-machine communications. 0417
Intuitive representations and interaction languages: an exploratory experiment. 03611

**Scarr, A. J.**
Interactive computer program for the selection of interference fits. HCI-0406 †

**Schäfer, W.**
A highly integrated tool set for program development support. 02788

**Schaaf, R. W.**
Diamond: a multimedia message system built on a distributed architecture (Reprint). 0380
Diamond: A multimedia message system built on a distributed architecture. 0574

**Schach, S. R.**
An almost path-free very high-level interactive data manipulation language for a microcomputer-based database system. HCI-0261 †

**Schader, M. (Ed.)**
Data, expert knowledge and decisions. • 0338

**Schaefer, A. T.**
The AutoCAD productivity book: tapping the hidden power of AutoCAD. • HCI-0076 †

**Schaefer, R. E.**
Thinking: information processing, mathematical models and computer simulation. • 0667

**Schaefer, T. A.**
The AutoCAD productivity book: tapping the hidden power of AutoCAD: 2nd edition. • 0668

**Schafer, C.**
Transfer between word processing systems. 0899

**Schaffner, S. C.**
Segue: support for distributed graphical interfaces. 01369
Segue: Support for distributed graphical interfaces. 03526

**Schang, T.**
Rule base management using meta knowledge. 01081

**Schank, R. C.**
Language generation by computer. HCI-0342 †

**Schappo, A.**
Support for tentative design: incorporating the screen image, as a graphical object, into PROLOG. 02116

**Schardt, L. P.**
Integrated software-design: a work-oriented approach to the humanization of computerized clerical tasks. 0243

**Schaub, B.**
Teachware for power engineering education. 01203

**Schayes, M. C.**
The kernel of a generic software development environment. 03056

**Scheidereiter, U.**
Coding of information in man-computer systems based on cognitive task analysis. 03618

**Scheidler, W.**
Visual pattern recognition in humans: I. Evidence for adaptive filtering. 01274

**Scheifler, R. W.**
X Protocol reference manual for version II: vol. 0. • 0669
The X window system. HCI-0370 †

**Schell, G.**
Analysis and design skills required by end-users in small organizations. 03008

**Schena, A.**
An intelligent braille display device. 01832

**Schendel, U. (Ed.)**
Parcella '88: Fourth International Workshop on Parallel Processing by Cellular Automata and Arrays. § 03971

**Scherz, Z.**
A new approach for introducing Prolog to naive users. 04029

**Schiavone, J. A.**
Applications of computer graphics to the visualization of meteorological data. 02819

**Schichter, J. H.**
FolioPub: A publication management system. 03520

**Schiel, U.**
The problem of identification. 01088

**Schiementz, W.**
Establishing structures of requirements for the application of automated information processing (AIP)—an approach for the development of computer-aided systems. 03660

**Schildt, H.**
OS/2 programming: an introduction. • 0670

**Schill, A.**
Experiences with the development of a portable network operating system. 03882

**Schilling, A.**
Sociotechnical design of advanced manufacturing systems. 03370

**Schindler, R.**
Effectiveness of training as a function of the teacher knowledge structure. 03604

**Schindler, S.**
POEM: An office system for international use. 03457

**Schira, J.**
Sensitivity to light and visual strain in VDT operators: basic data for the design of work stations. 03732

**Schirmer, F.**
Performance in cognitive tasks and cardiovascular parameters as indicators of mental load. 03624

**Schkade, D.**
The human side of robotics: how workers react to a robot. 0443

**Schkade, L. L.**
In search of the perfect programmer. 01648

**Schlag, J. F.**
Eliminating the dichotomy between scripting and interaction. 03299

**Schlager, M. S.**
A cognitive model of database querying: a tool for novice instruction. 0905

**Schleifer, L. M.**
An evaluation of mood disturbances and somatic discomfort under slow computer-response time and incentive-pay conditions. 03765

**Schlichting, C.**
Multimodal detection and recognition performance of sonar operators. 01709

**Schlobohm, D. A.**
Explanation for an expert system that performs estate planning. 02767

**Schloss, C. N.**
Efficacy of higher cognitive and factual questions in computer assisted instruction modules. 02278

**Schloss, P. J.**
Efficacy of higher cognitive and factual questions in computer assisted instruction modules. 02278

**Schmalhofer, F.**
Expert systems as cognitive tools for human decision making. HCI-0227 †

**Schmandt, C.**
Employing voice back channels of facilitate audio document retrieval. 03045

**Schmell, R. W.**
An experimental evaluation of the impact of data display format on recall performance. HCI-0202 †

**Schmidt, A. L.**
Effects of experience and comprehension on reading time and memory for computer programs. HCI-0197 †

**Schmidt, B.**
Performance evaluation of simulators. 02663

**Schmidt, K. H.**
Influences of mental load on reaction times in man-computer dialogues. 03625

**Schmitt, R.**
Design of programming languages under psychological aspects. 03613

**Schmölz, S.**
Prosodic features in German speech: stress assignment by man and machine. 03989

**Schmucker, K. J.**
MacApp: An application framework. 0083

**Schmutz, H.**
Experiences with the development of a portable network operating system. 03882

**Schnauber, H.**
Development of a continuous finishing line to improve working conditions. 03434
Optimum stresses and strains represented by examples from shop practice. 03441

**Schneider, B.**
A distributed object server. 03842

**Schneider, H.**
Graph-theoretic concepts in computer science. § 03885

**Schneider, L. (Ed.)**
Women, work and computerization: opportunities and disadvantages. § 03674

**Schneider, M. L.**
Classifying users: a hard look at some controversial issues. 0902
Ergonomic considerations in the design of command languages. 02694

**Schneider, M. L. (Ed.)**
Human factors in computer systems. ● 0718
Human factors in computer systems. ● HCI-0037 †

**Schneider, W.**
Automatic and controlled processing theory and its applications to human factors problems. 0402
The role of practice in dual-task performance: toward workload modeling in a connectionist/control architecture. 01790
Human cognition and human computer interaction. HCI-0241 †

**Schneier, C. A.**
Effects of an immediate feedback tool on designer productivity and design usability. 04052

**Schöfelder, E.**
Job organization and allocation of functions between man and computer: I analysis and assessment. 03628

**Schönfeld, W.**
A theory for the representation of knowledge. 01811

**Schöpflug, W.**
Internal representation of externally stored information. 03601

**Schoemaker, P. J. H.**
A probabilistic dominance measure for binary choices: analytic aspects of a multi-attribute random weights model. 02372

**Schoen, E.**
Design of knowledge-based systems with a knowledge-based assistant. 01853

**Schoenberg, V.**
Generalization, consistency, and control. 0796

**Scholl, L. R.**
Heuristic rules for visualization. 03868

**Scholtz, J.**
Beacons an initial program comprehension. 01014

**Scholtz, J. C.**
A transfer of skill between programming languages. 01015

**Schomaker, L. R. B.**
Automatic identification of writers. 03909

**Schon, S.**
Expert system applications in customer service. 03101

**Schoner, B.**
Experiences with the development of a portable network operating system. 03882

**Schoo, K. C.**
Influences of mental load on reaction times in man-computer dialogues. 03625

**Schoonard, J.**
The 1984 Olympic Message System: a test of behavioral principles of system design. HCI-0125 †

**Schouten, H. J.**
Dialogue cell resource model and basic dialogue cells. 01400

**Schrack, G.**
CNS-HLS mapping using fuzzy sets. HCI-0380 †

**Schrettenbrunner, H. L.**
Evaluation of a program on "distance". 0472

**Schröder, M.**
Evaluating user utterances in natural language interfaces to databases. 01486

**Schroeder, U.**
ALIEN: a programming environment generator for personal computers. 02790

**Schroer, B. J.**
An expert manufacturing simulation system. 02584

**Schroiff, H. W.**
Visual information pick-up in a simulated driving situation. 0251

**Schroiff, H. W. (Ed.)**
The psychology of work and organization: current trends and issues. ● 0239

**Schroit, D.**
Human factors testing in the design of Xerox's 8010 "Star" office workstation. 0090

**Schubert, J. N.**
Student perceptions of skill acquisition through cases and a general management simulation. 02589

**Schuetzle, J. G.**
The mission operators planning assistant. 02674

**Schulert, A.**
The run-time structure of UIMS-supported applications. 01059
UIMSs: threat or menace? 02889

**Schulten, K.**
Influence of noise on the behavior of an autoassociative neural network. 02727
Topology conserving mappings for learning motor tasks. 02758
Extending Kohonen's self-organizing mapping algorithms to learn ballistic movements. 03967

**Schultz Jr., E. E.**
jThe assessment of human/computer performance: a case for connectivity. 03535

**Schultz, A. C.**
The effects of structured, multi-level documentation. 0907

**Schultz, J.**
A history of the Promis technology: an effective human interface. 03097

**Schultz, R.**
Selecting a shell. 01176
Evaluation of the user interface in an information retrieval system: a model. 02012
Some measures and procedures for evaluation of the user interface in an information retrieval system. 03069

**Schulz, E.**
Design of programming languages under psychological aspects. 03613
Subjective load in introducing visual display units. 03627

**Schulz, J.**
On complexity of command-entry in man-computer dialogues. 03610

**Schur, H.**
The foreign language barrier: a study among pharmaceutical research workers. 02333

**Schuster, E.**
$VP^2$: the role of user modelling in correcting errors in second language learning. 0222
The relationship between user models and discourse models. 01353

**Schuster, R. (Ed.)**
Product data interfaces in CAD/CAM applications: design, implementation and experiences. § 03981

**Schvaneveld, W.**
Effects of computer programming experience on network representations of abstract programming concepts. 02204

**Schvaneveldt, R. W.**
A formal interface design methodology based on user knowledge. 0929
Programmer-nonprogrammer differences in specifying procedures to people and computers. 02405

Programmer/nonprogrammer differences in specifying procedures to people and computers. HCI-0174 †

**Schwab, A.**
Teachware for power engineering education. 01203

**Schwab, T.**
Active help systems. HCI-0108 †

**Schwalbe, P.**
The interface is often not the problem. 0837

**Schwartz, J. P.**
A framework for task cooperation within systems containing intelligent components. 01884

**Schwartz, R. B.**
User validation of information systems requirements: some empirical results. 01852

**Schwartz, T. A.**
The AT&T soft touch-sensitive screen. 01226

**Schwartz, T. J.**
Twelve-product wrap-up: neural networks. 01189

**Schwarz, M. W.**
An experimental comparison of RGB, YIQ, LAB, HSV, and opponent color models. HCI-0381 †

**Schweder, H. A.**
The changing workplace: A guide to managing the people, organizational, and regulatory aspects of office technology (book excerpt). 0044

**Sciabin, M.**
Symbiotic systems for complex problems. 02922

**Sciarra, D.**
Real-time large vocabulary word recognition via diphone spotting and multiprocessor implementation. 03996

**Scneiderman, B.**
Embedded menus: selecting items in context. 01320

**Scott, M. L.**
A grammar-based approach to automatic generation of user-interface dialogues. 02868

# AUTHOR INDEX [SHACKEL, B. (ED.)]

**Scown, S. J.**
Artificial intelligence and natural language systems. 01541

**Sculley, J.**
Interactive multimedia. ● 0011

**Seabrook, R. H.**
The user interface in a hypertext, multiwindow program browser. 02072

**Seagle, J. P.**
The feature chart: A tool for communicating the analysis for a decision support system. 01913

**Sechi, G. R.**
An abstract description generator for the reliability analysis in the design of real time systems. 02490

**Seck, R.**
Structure of German syllable initial and final consonant clusters based on articulatory features. 02652

**Sedgwick, H. A.**
Environment-centered and viewer-centered perception of surface orientation. 02705
Environment-centered and viewer-centered perception of surface orientation. HCI-0392 †

**Seeland, H.**
CAD/CAM: integration in the automobile industry. HCI-0413 †

**Seelen, W. v.**
Parallelism and redundancy in neural networks. 03952

**Seidenberg, M. S.**
Modularity and lexical access. HCI-0350 †

**Seidman, S. B.**
Analysis of competition-based spreading activation in connectionist models. 02179

**Seifert, K.**
Gripe: a graphical interface to a knowledge based system which reasons about protein topology. 03234

**Seifert, R.**
Psychological methods for assembling procedures in text management systems. 03600

**Seilheimer, S. D.**
Importance of the human factor in the information system life cycle. 02422

**Sein, M. K.**
The importance of individual differences in end-user training: The case for learning style. 03009

**Sejnowski, T. J.**
Open questions about computation in cerebral cortex. 0637
Higher-order Boltzmann machines. 02760

**Seki, H.**
A processing system for program specifications in a natural language. 03537

**Sekiguchi, T.**
Convexly combined fuzzy relational equations and several aspects of their application to fuzzy information processing. 02027

**Sekine, Y.**
Planning as feedback to designers. 02978

**Sekuler, R.**
Coherent global motion percepts from stochastic local motions. 03329

**Selby, R. W.**
Foundations for the Arcadia environment architecture. 01135

**Self, J. (Ed.)**
Artificial intelligence & human learning: intelligent computer-aided instruction. ● 0671

**Selfridge, M.**
Integrated processing produces robust understanding. 01342

**Selig, W. J.**
Towards reasoning visualization in expert systems. 02992

**Selkirk, E. O.**
Phonology and syntax: the relationship between sound and structure. ● 0672

**Selle, H. J.**
Subjective load in introducing visual display units. 03627

**Sellen, A.**
A study in interactive 3-D rotation using 2-D control devices. 02813

**Sellis, T.**
Implementation of a Prolog-INGRES interface. 01087

**Sena, J. A.**
Applying software engineering principles to the user application interface. HCI-0130 †

**Sendlmeier, W. F.**
Primary perceptual units in word recognition. 03994

**Senker, P. J.**
Coping with new technology: the need for training. 0441

**Senn, J. A.**
Information systems in management: 3rd edition. ● 0673

**Sernadas, A.**
Specification and verification of database dynamics. HCI-0251 †

**Sethi, A. S.**
Strategic management of technostress: The chaining of Prometheus. HCI-0452 †

**Sethi, J.**
Some observations on user interface design and user performance. HCI-0117 †

**Sethi, V.**
Some design guidelines for an information center to support office information systems. 01093

**Sethian, J. A.**
Interactive scientific visualization and parallel display techniques. 03542

**Setíkovská, L.**
Decision trees: a contribution to automatic interpretation of GUHA results. HCI-0329 †

**Sewell, W.**
Observations of end user online searching behavior over eleven years. HCI-0235 †

**Sgall, P.**
On one aspect of natural-language based knowledge acquisition. 03571

**Shackel, B.**
Ergonomics in design for usability. 03247

**Shackel, B. (Ed.)**
Human-computer interaction. § 03454

**Shafer, D.**
Mac programming tools: prototyper version 2.0 eases interface design. 02394

**Shafer, P.**
Display strategies for program browsing. 03545

**Shafto, M. (Ed.)**
How we know. ● HCI-0053 †

**Shah, J.**
Process design of oil and gas production facilities using expert systems. 02933

**Shah, S. C.**
Computer-aided engineering (CAE) for system analysis. 0663

**Shahmehri, N.**
Affect-chaining and dependency oriented flow analysis applied to queries of programs. 02789

**Shane, D.**
Extending a relational database with deferred referential integrity checking andintelligent joins. 01089

**Shannon, K.**
Supporting flexible and efficient tool integration. 03783

**Shapiro, D. I.**
Human specifics fuzzy categories and counteraction in decision making problems. 01696

**Shapiro, E.**
Concurrent Prolog: collected papers. ● 0674
The Logix system user manual version 1.21. 0675
An architecture of a distributed window system and its FCP implementation. 0676
Object oriented programming in Concurrent Prolog. 0677
A new approach for introducing Prolog to naive users. 04029

**Shapiro, E. (Ed.)**
Third international conference on logic programming. § 04028

**Shapiro, G. W. (Ed.)**
Nested window flow controls with packet fragmentation. 04055

**Sharit, J.**
A cognitively based methodology for evaluating human performance in the computer-aided design task domain. 01240
The use of measures of entropy in evaluating human supervisory control of a manufacturing system. 01897
Issues in modeling supervisory control in flexible manufacturing systems. 03363

**Sharp, D. H.**
A preliminary analysis of recursively generated networks. 02749

**Sharpe, D.**
Human factors in teaching. 0989

**Sharples, M.**
Tools for management and support of multiple constraints in a writer's assistant. 03251

**Sharratt, B.**
The formal specification of adaptive user interfaces using command language grammar. 0925
The incorporation of early interface evaluation into command language grammar specifications. 03191

**Sharrock, B.**
Patterned systems design—HCI in commercial data processing. 03193

**Shaull, J. E.**
Process control and people at General Motors' Delta Engine Plant. 01905
Process control and people at General Motors' Delta engine plant. 03431

**Shaw, A. C.**
Speech-controlled text-editing: effects of input modality and of command structure. HCI-0397 †

**Shaw, L. C. (Ed.)**
APL88. § 02797

**Shaw, M.**
An input-output model of interactive systems. 0926

**Shaw, M. L. G.**
From timesharing to the sixth generation: the development of human-computer interaction. Part I. 02097
Foundations of dialog engineering: the development of human-computer interaction. Part II. 02100
KITTEN: knowledge initiation and transfer tools for experts and novices. 02159
Validation in a knowledge support system: construing and consistency with multiple experts. 02203

**Shcultz, J.**
A history of the promis technology: an effective human interface. 0349

**Shea, S.**
Designing a practical interface. 01174

**Sheck, S.**
An experimental comparison of a mouse and arrow-jump keys for an interactive encyclopedia. 02098

**Sheer, R.**
User-developers: the new software resource. 02052

**Sheffi, Y.**
Design and implementation of an interactive optimization system for network design in the motor carrier industry. 02528

**Sheffield, J.**
The effects of bargaining orientation and communication medium on negotiations in the bilateral monopoly task: a comparison of decision room and computer conferencing communication media. 0809

**Sheil, B. A.**
The psychological study of programming. 0053

**Sheingold, K.**
The microcomputer as a symbolic medium. 0583

**Sheingold, K. (Ed.)**
Mirrors of minds: patterns of experience in educational computing. ● 0575

**Shekar, B.**
Structural aspects of semantic-directed clusters. 02534

**Shema, D. B.**
Refining problem-solving knowledge in repertory grids using a consultation mechanism. 02205

**Shepherd, M. A.**
A common interface for accessing document retrieval systems and dbms for retrieval of bibliographic data. 01990

**Sheppard, D. J.**
Simulator design and instructional features for air-to-ground attack: a transfer study. 01804

**Sheppard, S.**
Express—rapid prototyping and product development via integrated knowledge-based executable specifications. 03492

**Sheppard, S. (Ed.)**
Empirical studies of programmers: second workshop. ● 0565

**Sheppard, S. V.**
Graphical specification of user interfaces with behavior abstraction. 0840
The control structure diagram: an automated graphical representation for software. 03524

**Sherman, C.**
The CD ROM handbook. ● 0678

**Sherman, D.**
Towards a comprehensive user interface management system. 0081

**Sherman, M.**
Using low-cost workstations to investigate computer networks and distributed systems. HCI-0437 †

**Sherman, T. M.**
A brief review of developments in problem solving. 01581

**Sherwin, L. C.**
Designing menu display format to match input device format. 0983

**Shewmake, D.**
UIMSs: threat or menace? 02889

**Shewmake, D. T.**
Developing interactive information systems with the user software engineering methodology. 0077

Developing interactive information systems with the user software engineering methodology. 01856

**Shiflet, A. B.**
A historical perspective for teaching. 01033

**Shimizu, H.**
Parallel in sequence—towards the architecture of an elementary cortical processor. 03820
Control of sensory processing - a hypothesis on and simulation of the architecture of an elementary cortical processor. 03972

**Shinar, D.**
Alternative option selection methods in menu-driven computer programs. 01755

**Shinghal, R.**
An investigation into the skeletonization approach of Hilditch. HCI-0388 †

**Shipp, K. O.**
Designing SAA applications and user interfaces. 01821

**Shirai, K.**
Estimating articulatory motion from speech wave. 02643

**Shirk, H. N.**
Technical writers as computer scientists: the challenges of online documentation. HCI-0153 †

**Shlechter, T. M.**
An examination of the research evidence for computer-based instruction. 0415

**Shmandt, C.**
Voice: technology searching for communication needs. 0808

**Shneiderman, B.**
Direct manipulation: A step beyond programming languages. 0072
Reflections on authoring, editing, and managing hypertext. 0119
Direct manipulation user interfaces for expert systems. 0429
User interface strategies '88 (Videotape). ● 0684
Ben Shneiderman, Oct. 5,12: user interface strategies '88. ● 0685
Hypertext hands-on!: an introduction to a new way of organizing and accessing information. ● 0686

Response time and display rate in human performance with computers. 0760
Human-computer interaction lab, University of Maryland. 0871
Human-computer interaction research at the university of Maryland. 0887
Learning disabled students' difficulties in learning to use a word processor: implications for design. 0889
Seven plus or minus two central issues in human-computer interaction. 0937
No members, no officers, no dues: A ten year history of the software psychology society. 0943
Dynamic versus static menus: an exploratory comparison. 0997
Applying direct manipulation concepts. 01143
Selection devices for users of an electronic encyclopedia: an empirical comparison of four possibilities. 02009
The user interface in a hypertext, multiwindow program browser. 02072
An experimental comparison of a mouse and arrow-jump keys for an interactive encyclopedia. 02098
A comparison of children's reading comprehension and reading rates at three text presentation speeds on a CRT. 02280
Empirical studies of programmers: the territory, paths, and destination. 02691
Improving the accuracy of touch screens: an experimental evaluation of three strategies. 02860
An empirical comparison of pie vs. linear menus. 02871
Display strategies for program browsing. 03545
Designing the user interface: strategies for effective human-computer interaction. ● HCI-0006 †
Cognitive layouts of windows and multiple screens for user interfaces. HCI-0122 †

The future of interactive systems and the emergence of direct manipulation. HCI-0186 †
An experimental comparison of tabular and graphic data presentation. HCI-0236 †

**Shneiderman, B. Dr.**
Designing the user interface (Videotape). ● 0687
Designing the user interface: professional development courses from the Univ. of Maryland. ● 0688
Designing the user interface: supplemental materials. ● 0689

**Shorrock, B.**
Patterned systems design. 01625

**Short Jr., N.**
The second generation intelligent user interface for the crustal dynamics data information system. 02675

**Short, L. E.**
Are information systems people different? An investigation of how they are and should be managed. 02511

**Shorter, J.**
Adequate documentation of user-developed applications: a new challenge for end-user computing management. 03001

**Shortliffe, E. H.**
Graphical specification of procedural knowledge for an expert system. 0427

**Shouls, A.**
Task-related knowledge structures: analysis, modelling and application. 03218

**Shoval, P.**
End-user prototyping: sophisticated users supporting system development. 01636
Responsibility sharing between sophisticated users and professionals in structured prototyping. 01978
GISD: a graphical interactive system for conceptual database design. 02042
Comparison of decision support strategies in expert consultation systems. 02101

**Shrager, J.**
Instructionless learning about a complex device: the paradigm and observations. HCI-0333 †

**Shrier, S.**
A framework for task cooperation within systems containing intelligent components. 01884

**Shriner, R.**
Positioning human factors in the user interface development chain. 0835

**Shriver, B. (Ed.)**
Research directions in object-oriented programming. ● 0690

**Shriver, B. D. (Ed.)**
Software Track. § 03513

**Shrobe, H. E. (Ed.)**
Exploring artificial intelligence. ● 0692

**Shu, N. C.**
A visual programming language designed for automatic programming. 03529

**Shu, N. C. (Ed.)**
Visual programming. ● 0694

**Shubin, H.**
SPA: a systems for diagnosis of computer performance problems. 02969

**Shuey, D.**
PHIGS: a standard, dynamic, interactive graphics interface. 01826

**Shulman, L. S.**
Current research in the psychology of learning and teaching. 03876

**Shute, S. J.**
Knowledge-based search tactics for an intelligent intermediary system. HCI-0277 †

**Shyong, S.**
An interactive simulator for the designing of woven fabric structures second place. 02583

**Sibani, P.**
Firing response of a neural model with threshold modulation and neural dynamics. 02761

**Sibert, J.**
Issues limiting the acceptance of user interfaces using gesture input and handwriting character recognition. 0845
Tools and methodology for user interface development. 01057

**Sibert, J. L.**
Design and implementation of an object-oriented user interface management system. 0412
An object-oriented user interface management system. 01055

**Siddiqi, J. I.**
An empirical investigation into problem decomposition strategies used in program design. HCI-0103 †

**Sideridis, A.**
Informatics and municipalities: the Greek approach. 01940

**Sidner, C. L.**
Attention, intention, and the structure of discourse. 01344

**Siegel, J.**
Social psychological aspects of computer-mediated communication (Reprint). 0384

**Siel, F.**
The applicability of eye movement analysis in the ergonomic evaluation of human-computer interaction. 03766

**Sievert, M.**
Investigating computer anxiety in an academic library. 02047

**Siil, I.**
Real time speech synthesis—development and employment. 01482

**Silberschatz, A.**
4.2BSD and 4.3BSD as examples of the UNIX system. HCI-0165 †

**Siler, W.**
Patterns of inductive reasoning in a parallel expert system. 02219

**Silver, M. S.**
User perceptions of decision support system restrictiveness: an experiment. 02353
Descriptive analysis for computer-based decision support. 02527

**User perceptions of DSS restrictiveness: an experiment.** 03470

**Silver, N. C.**
Estimating reliability with small samples: increased precision with averaged correlations. 01728

**Silver, R.**
Libraries as programs preserved within compiler continuations. 01102

**Silverman, B. G. (Ed.)**
Expert systems for business. ● 0695

**Silverman, W.**
The Logix system user manual version 1.21. 0675

**Silverstein, L. D.**
Human factors for color display systems: concepts, methods, and research. 0256
Changes in electromyographic activity associated with occupational stress and poor performance in the workplace. 01734

**Silvestri, A.**
Evolution of interactional human behavior with age: a theoretical/experimental approach. 01618

**Sime, M.**
The doctor's use of a computer in the consulting room: an analysis. HCI-0409 †

**Sime, M. E.**
Perceptual structure cueing in a simple command language. 02086

**Simizu, S.**
A study of intrinsic safety asymmetrical actuator. 03422

**Simkens, P.**
CAD Based verification and refinement of high level compliant motion primitives. 0600

**Simmons, R. G.**
Representing and reasoning about change. 03353

**Simon, R.**
Direct manipulation user interfaces for expert systems. 0429
Display strategies for program browsing. 03545

**Simon, T.**
Programmable user models for predictive evaluation of interface designs. 0800
How would your favourite user model cope with these scenarios? 0999
Planning in the context of human-computer interaction. 03213
GOMS meets STRIPS: the integration of planning with skilled procedure execution in human-computer interaction. 03243
Analysing the scope of cognitive models in human-computer interaction: a trade-off approach. HCI-0245 †

**Simons, G. L.**
Is man a robot? ● 0697

**Simpson, C.**
System design for speech recognition and generation. 0065

**Simpson, D. (Ed.)**
ESEC '87. § 03795

**Simpson, H.**
Programming the Macintosh User Interface. ● 0698
Developing effective user documentation: a human factors approach. ● 0699

**Simpson, K. L.**
Accident analysis of blind production workers. 03439

**Simpson, W. A.**
The cross-ratio and the perception of motion and structure. 03344

**Sinclair, M. A.**
Macro-ergonomics and the computer-integrated enterprise. 03383

**Sindelar, P. T.**
Efficacy of higher cognitive and factual questions in computer assisted instruction modules. 02278

**Singer, J.**
Children's collaborative use of a computer microworld. 02825

**Singer, W.**
A self-organizing neural network sharing features of the mammalian visual system. 01248

**Singh, G.**
A high-level user interface management system. 0838
Designing the interface designer's interface. 03116
Automatic generation of graphical user interfaces. 03290

**Singh, R. N.P.**
EPVM: An expert patient-ventilator manager for chemical warfare casualties. 02956

**Siochi, A. C.**
Task-oriented representation of asynchronous user interfaces. 0851

**Sipior, J. C.**
Definitional distinctions and implications for managing end user computing. 01946

**Sirevaag, E. J.**
A psychophysiological assessment of operator workload during simulated flight missions. 01735

**Siripoksup, S.**
An evaluation of the effectiveness of the adaptive interface module (AIM) in matching dialogues to users. 03212

**Siroux, J.**
Experimentation in the specification of an oral dialogue. 04005

**Sisson, N.**
Dialogue management reference model. 0945
Considerations of menu structure and communication rate for the design of computer menu displays. 02124
Effects of breadth, depth and number responses on computer menu search performance. 02192

**Sistrunk, F.**
Part-task training strategies in simulated carrier landing final-approach training. 01741

**Sivilotti, M. A.**
VLSI architectures for implementation of neural networks. 02762

**Skedsvold, P. R.**
Examination of the role of "higher order" consistency in skill development. 01791

**Skwarecki, E.**
The automated tutoring of introductory computer programming. HCI-0438 †

**Slamecka, V.**
Toward native language software for information management. HCI-0138 †

**Slater, J. B., Dr.**
Staying afloat—a collective enterprise. 01147

**Slater, M.**
A top down method for interactive drawing. 01401

**Slator, B. M.**
Pygmalion at the interface. HCI-0349 †

**Slatter, P. E.**
Building expert systems: cognitive emulation. ● 0700

**Sleeman, D.**
Enhancing PIXIE's tutoring capabilities. 02187
UMFE: a user modelling front-end subsystem. HCI-0325 †

**Slind, K.**
Monitoring distributed systems. HCI-0169 †

**Slivka, R.**
Unified interactive geometric modeller for simulating highly complex environments. 01472

**Sloan, K. R., Jr.**
Reconstruction and display of the retina. 03310

**Slocum, J.**
Developing a natural language interface to complex data. 0393

**Sloman, A.**
Beginners need powerful systems. 0747

**Slottow, J. F.**
Supercomputers in the classroom. 01577

**Smarr, L.**
The computational science revolution: technology, methodology, and sociology. 0728

**Smart, J.**
The ECLIPSE user interface. 02638

**Smartt, M. J.**
The mirage rapid interface prototyping system. 03112

**Smets, P.**
Epistemic necessity, possibility, and truth. Tools for dealing with imprecision and uncertainty in fuzzy knowledge-based systems. 02075

**Smith-Kerker, P. L.**
AIX usability enhancements and human factors. 01817
On comprehending a computer manual: analysis of variables affecting performance. 02135

**Smith, A. D.**
Health and productivity issues of CAD/CAM systems. 03436

**Smith, B. J.**
Perception of organization in a random stimulus. 02706
Perception of organization in a random stimulus. HCI-0364 †

**Smith, B. T.**
A semantic editor. 01101

**Smith, C. A.P.**
Crisis planning systems: tools for intelligent action. 03464

**Smith, C. J.**
MathScribe: a user interface for computer algebra systems. 03082
MathScribe: a user interface for computer algebra systems. 03086

**Smith, C. U. (Chair.)**
Measurement and Modeling of Computer Systems. § 03024

**Smith, D. C.**
Designing the star user interface. 0089
The star user interface: an overview. 03171

**Smith, D. E.**
Reasoning about action II: the qualification problem. 01213

**Smith, D. N.**
Building interfaces interactively. 03119

**Smith, D. R.**
Autonomous scene description with range imagery. 02707

**Smith, F. D.**
Andrew: a distributed personal computing environment. HCI-0091 †

**Smith, F. J.**
Online searching using speech as a man/machine interface. 02013

Voice input/output interface for online searching: some design and human factor onsiderations. 02335

**Smith, G.**
A FORTRAN input program generator. 01227

**Smith, H. T. (Ed.)**
Computer-based message services. § 03319

**Smith, J.**
An advanced full-text retrieval and analysis system. 03079

**Smith, J. C.**
The application of expert systems technology to case-based law. 02771

**Smith, K. C.**
Towards a comprehensive user interface management system. 0081

**Smith, K. H.**
Training by exploration: facilitating the transfer of procedural knowledge through analogical reasoning. 02103
Which way to computer literacy, programming or applications experience? 02127

**Smith, K. U.**
The social cybernetics of human interaction with automated systems. 03442

**Smith, L. C.**
Knowledge-based systems, artificial intelligence and human factors. 0449

**Smith, L. M.**
Applying software engineering principles to the user application interface. HCI-0130 †

**Smith, L. S.**
On the acquisition of object concepts from sensory data. 03959

**Smith, M. J.**
Human factors issues in VDT use: Environmental and workstation design considerations. 0046

Effects on visual accommodation and subjective visual discomfort from VDT work intensified through split screen technique. 03735
VDT technology: psychosocial and stress concerns. 03755
Human factors issues in VDT use: environmental and workstation design considerations. HCI-0210 †

**Smith, O. R.**
Human intelligence models and their implications for expert system structure and research. 01242

**Smith, P.**
Experiences in use of SSADM: series of case studies. Part 1: first time users. 01976
Experiences in use of SSADM: series of case studies. Part 2: experienced users. 01977

**Smith, P. J.**
Modeling fault diagnosis as the activation and use of a frame system. 01729
Online library catalog systems: an analysis of user errors. 02128
Knowledge-based search tactics for an intelligent intermediary system. HCI-0277 †

**Smith, P. L.**
The accumulator model of two-choice discrimination. 02371

**Smith, R. B.**
Experiences with the alternate reality kit: an example of the tension between literalism and magic. 0817

**Smith, R. C.**
The creation of an integrated IVD curriculum. 0509

**Smith, R. D.**
Computer anxiety in management: myth or reality? HCI-0232 †

**Smith, R. G.**
A substrate for object-oriented interface design. 0691
Design of knowledge-based systems with a knowledge-based assistant. 01853
Impulse-86: a substrate for object-oriented interface design. 03032

**Smith, R. L.**
Human visual requirements for control and monitoring of a space telerobot. 03391
Illumination requirements for operating a space remote manipulator. 03392

**Smith, R. W.**
Providing natural language assistance in locating objects: a general model for information selection and generation. 02951

**Smith, S. B.**
Dynamic screens and static paper. 02786

**Smith, S. R.**
Holophrasted displays in an interactive environment. HCI-0105 †

**Smith, S. W.**
A suppport strategy for users of a campus-wide local area network. 03157

**Smith, T.**
Project Nick: meetings augmentation and analysis. HCI-0156 †

**Smith, T. J.**
The social cybernetics of human interaction with automated systems. 03442

**Smith, T. W.**
Assessing the usability of user interfaces: guidance and online help features. 04065

**Smith, W.**
Ergonomic vision. 0259
Color in user interface design: functionally and aesthetics. 0803

**Smithin, T.**
Computer decision support for senior managers: encouraging exploration. HCI-0298 †

**Smolensky, P.**
Schemata and sequential thought processes in PDP models. 0630
Neural and conceptual interpretation of PDP models. 0638
Social science and system design: interdisciplinary collaborations. 0833

**Sneckenberger, J. E.**
Performance evaluation of three pressure mats as robot workstation safety sensors. 03428

**Snelbecker, G.**
Retraining high school teachers to teach computer science—observations on the first course. 01030

**Snell, J.**
A systems model of cognition for improving human factors of computing environments. 04058

**Snelting, G.**
The PSG—programming system generator. 01098
Context-sensitive editing with PSG environments. 03780

**Snodgrass, R.**
Supporting flexible and efficient tool integration. 03783

**Snodgrass, R. (Ed.)**
Automating interfaces in a software system. ● 0701

**Snow, B. R.**
Comparison of well-being among non-machine interactive clerical workers and full-time and part-time VDT users and typists. 03745

**Snowberry, K.**
Considerations of menu structure and communication rate for the design of computer menu displays. 02124

**Snyder, A.**
Language level persistence for an object-oriented application programming platform. 03522

**Snyder, C. A.**
The effects of relational and entity-relationship data models on query performance of end users. 02247

**Snyder, K. R.**
Barriers to factory automation. 01906

**Snyder, S.**
Interfaces for knowledge-base builders' control knowledge and application-specific procedures. 01810

**Sockut, G.**
Office-by-example: an integrated office system and database manager. 01159

**Soiffer, N.**
MathScribe: a user interface for computer algebra systems. 03082
MathScribe: a user interface for computer algebra systems. 03086

**Sojka, D.**
Shucking Dp. 01644

**Solem, A. (Chair.)**
Document Processing Systems. § 02831

**Solla, S. A.**
Memory networks with asymmetric bonds. 02740

**Solomon, M.**
Dost: an environment to support automatic generation of user interfaces. 03053

**Soloway, E.**
Interface design: a neglected issue in educational software. 0826
Mental models and software maintenance. 02404
Providing the requisite knowledge via software documentation. 02898
Mental models and software maintenance. HCI-0173 †
Analyzing the high frequency bugs in novice programs. HCI-0178 †

**Soloway, E. (Ed.)**
Empirical studies of programmers: second workshop. ● 0565
Empirical studies of programmers. § 02690

**Soloway, E. M.**
Software psychology: the need for an interdisciplinary program. 0052
Goal and plan knowledge representations: from stories to text editors and programs. HCI-0183 †

**Somalvico, M.**
Reasoning in natural language for designing a data base. HCI-0322 †

**Sommerville, I.**
An information retrieval system for software components. 01077
Interacting with an active, integrated environment. 01137

Direct manipulation of an object store. 02608
The ECLIPSE user interface. 02638
SOFTLIB—A documentation management system. HCI-0149 †

**Sonnino, A.**
Visual impairment and subjective ocular symptomatology in VDT operators. 03734

**Soop, K.**
Bringing graphic dialogues to APL. 0765

**Sorenson, P. F.**
An empirical approach to the evaluation of icons. 01013

**Sorkin, R. D.**
Likelihood alarm displays. 01783

**Sormunen, E.**
A knowledge-based intermediary system for information retrieval. 0737

**Soucek, B. (Ed.)**
Nueral & massively parallel computers: the sixth generation. ● 0702

**Soumekh, M.**
The effects of limited data in multi-frequency reflection diffraction tomography. 04020

**Souter, G. A. (Ed.)**
The disconnection: how to interface computers and video. ● 0703

**Southall, R.**
Visual structure and the transmission of meaning. HCI-0404 †

**Sowa, J. F.**
Implementing a semantic interpreter using conceptual graphs. 01812
Conceptual structures: information processing in mind and machine. ● HCI-0057 †

**Spagnuolo, R.**
Human interface in structural analysis software. 03453

**Sparck Jones, K.**
Architecture problems in the construction of expert systems for document retrieval. HCI-0272 †
A natural language front end to databases with evaluative feedback. HCI-0338 †

**Sparck-Jones, K. (Ed.)**
Readings in natural language processing. ● HCI-0067 †

**Sparks, D. L.**
The role of the primate superior colliculus in sensorimotor integration. 0017

**Sparks, M. R.**
Computer graphics language bindings: programmer interface standards. 01473

**Speed, R. C.B.**
Interactive aspects of knowledge representations. 03395

**Spence, J. W.**
End user computing—the human interface. 02428

**Spence, R.**
Designing the "cockpit": the application of a human-centered design philosophy to make optimization systems accessible. 01016
More on the mouse. 01642
Lean cuisine: a low fat notation for menus. 02062

**Spencer, R. H.**
Computer usability testing & evaluation. ● HCI-0014 †

**Spenke, M.**
A spreadsheet interface for logic programming. 0822

**Sperandio, J. C.**
Ergonomic aspects of man-machine communications. 0417

**Sperber, D.**
Relevance: communication and cognition. ● 0704

**Sperling, G.**
Intelligible encoding of ASL image sequences at extremely low information rates. 02708

**Spiegler, I.**
A priori analysis of natural language queries. 02006

**Spilotro, F.**
Design of personal information retrieval systems. 02032

**Spinas, P.**
VDU—work and user—friendly human—computer interaction: analysis of dialogue structures. 0310

**Spine, T. M.**
User-derived impact analysis as a tool for usability engineering. 0922
An economical approach to modeling speech recognition accuracy. HCI-0354 †

**Spinelli, D. N.**
A trace of memory: an evolutionary perspective on the visual system. 0019

**Spinelli, G.**
Are there individual concepts? Proper names and individual concepts in SI-Nets. 02233

**Spinner, A.**
ALIEN: a programming environment generator for personal computers. 02790

**Spohrer, J. G.**
Analyzing the high frequency bugs in novice programs. HCI-0178 †

**Spooner, D. L.**
ROSE: An object-oriented database system for interactive computer graphics applications. 03845

**Sprague Jr., R. H. (Ed.)**
Applications Track. § 03455

**Springer, T. J.**
The statutes and standards movement. 0049

**Sproull, L.**
Reducing social context cues: electronic mail in organizational communication (Reprint). 0385
Reducing social context cues: electronic mail in organizational communication. 02473

**Sproull, R. F.**
Principles of interactive computer graphics (2nd ed.). ● HCI-0069 †
Device-independent graphics: with examples from IBM personal computers. ● HCI-0070 †

**Sprowl, J.**
Human interfaces in a legal expert system. 03164

**Spur, G.**
Computer aided application program synthesis for industrial robots. 0606

**Squires, D.**
Computer-based microworlds—a definition to aid design. HCI-0432 †

**Srebro, R.**
Radiation detection by ear and by eye. 01732

**Sridhar, S.**
Configuring stand-alone smalltalk-80 applications. 01129

**Sridharan, N. S.**
Application of the butterfly parallel processor in artificial intelligence. 0489

**St. Jacques, M.**
The network control assistant (NCA), a real-time prototype expert system for network management. 02930

**St. Pierre, F.**
Towards universality of access: interfacing physically disabled students to the Icon educational microcomputer. 0821

**Stager, S.**
Charting the course of a user survey that will rock the boat. 03136

**Stahl, B.**
The trouble with application generators. 01662

**Stallard, D.**
The IRUS transportable natural language database interface. 03177

**Stallings, W. D. (Ed.)**
Computers : the user perspective. ● 0705

**Stamper, R.**
Semantics. 0154

**Standera, O. L.**
Electronic publishing. The predicament of occasional users in the editorial proc. 02446

**Stanev, I.**
A rule-based system for fuzzy natural language robot control. 03574

**Stanley, G.**
Object oriented rapid prototyping with G2. 02984

**Stansifer, R. D.**
Flexible user interface decision support systems. 03473

**Stanton, J. A.**
User satisfaction: A vital management issue. 01678

**Stark, J.**
Successful use of CADCAM—a combination of technology, organization, and people. 01569

**Stark, L.**
Muscle models: what is gained and what is lost by varying model complexity. 01251
Statistical dependency in visual scanning. 01719

**Stassen, H. G.**
Human supervisor modelling: some new developments. 02170

**Staudt, B. J.**
A structural approach to the maintenance of structure-oriented environments. 03054

**Stawick, E. W.**
Screen management in the "real world". 02795

**Steedman, M.**
Temporal ontology and temporal reference. 01347

**Steels, L. (Ed.)**
Progress in artificial intelligence. § 03555

**Steenstrup, M.**
Computational techniques in motion processing. 0025

**Stefferud, E. A.**
MH: a multifarious user agent. 01428

**Stefik, M.**
Beyond the chalkboard: computer support for collaboration and problem solving inmeetings (Reprint). 0376
WYSIWIS revised: early experiences with multiuser interfaces. 01158
Beyond the chalkboard: computer support for collaboration and problem solving in meetings. HCI-0312 †

**Steil, G. M.**
On the identification of neural responses. 01260

**Steinbrinck, T.**
Necessary functions of institutions for test and certification from the viewpoint of users in IT. 01456

**Steiner, D. D.**
Graphic interfaces for knowledge-based system development. 0892

**Steinhauer, G. D.**
Artificial behavior: computer simulation of psychological processes. ● HCI-0073 †

**Steinmüller, W.**
Who is user and who is affected: a proposal to better semantics. 03647

**Stellman, J. M.**
Comparison of well-being among non-machine interactive clerical workers and full-time and part-time VDT users and typists. 03745

**Stelovsky, J.**
A system for specification and rapid prototyping of application command languages. 01849
The role of mental models in programming: from experiment to requirements for an interactive system. 03827

**Stelzner, M.**
The evolution of interface requirements for expert systems. 0431
Teaching object-oriented programming with the KEE system. 01113

**Stenberg, B.**
A Rosacea-like skin rash in VDU-operators. 03695

**Stengl, M.**
Open fullscreen systems. 0766

**Stephens, M.**
The ANALYST—A workstation for analysis and design. 02713

**Sterman, J. D.**
Modeling managerial behavior: misperceptions of feedback in a dynamic decision making experiment. 02483

**Stern, H. I.**
Alternative option selection methods in menu-driven computer programs. 01755

**Stern, H. L.**
Comparison of Windowing Systems. 01293

**Stern, J. A.**
Effects of information-processing demands on physiological response patterns. 01740

**Sternberg, R. J.**
Common and uncommon issues in artificial intelligence an psychology. 03312
Approaches to human reasoning: an analytic framework. HCI-0239 †

**Stevens, D.**
The network control assistant (NCA), a real-time prototype expert system for network management. 02930

**Stevens, J. K.**
Reverse engineering the brain. HCI-0368 †

**Stevens, K. A.**
Detecting structure by symbolic constructions on tokens. 01466

**Stevens, R. I.**
The case of the rejected applicants. 02438

**Stevens, S. M.**
Intelligent interactive video simulation of a code inspection. 01329

**Stevenson, R. J.**
Knowledge elicitation: dissociating conscious reflections from automatic processes. HCI-0337 †

**Stewart, D. A.**
A multitasking switchboard approach to user interface management. 01053

**Stewart, J. A.**
How to manage educational computing initiatives-lessons from the first five years of Project Athena at MIT. 0125

**Stewart, K. C.**
Process control and people at General Motors' Delta Engine Plant. 01905
Process control and people at General Motors' Delta engine plant. 03431

**Stewart, L. P.**
The marble company: The design and implementation of a simulation board game. 02595

**Sticha, P. J.**
Models of procedural control for human performance simulation. 01752

**Stillman, R.**
Interfaces for knowledge-base builders' control knowledge and application-specific procedures. 01810

**Stimmel, D. T.**
Color and the instructional use of the computer. 0263

**Stock, L.**
Workers education and user participation in the development of protective policies for VDT operators. 03752

**Stock, O.**
Knowledge representation and natural language: extending the expressive power of proposition nodes. 0096

**Stocker, P. M.**
An interactive database end user facility for the definition and manipulation of forms. HCI-0263 †

**Stoddart, J.**
Parcel sorting by speech recognition: human factors issues. 03209

**Stohr, E. A.**
A graphics interface for linear programming. 01332
Using restricted natural language for data retrieval: a plan for field evaluation. HCI-0255 †

**Stokman, F. N.**
Structuring knowledge in a graph. 03899

**Stone, J. M.**
Debugging concurrent processes: a case study. 03060

**Stone, M.**
An introduction to Gargoyle: an interactive illustration tool. 03185

**Stone, M. C.**
Snap-dragging. 01052

**Stone, P. J.**
Your office is where you are. 01703

**Stonebraker, M.**
Database portals: a new application program interface. 0707
Readings in database systems. ● 0708

**Stonebraker, M. (Ed.)**
The INGRES papers: anatomy of a relational database system. ● 0706

**Stonier, T.**
The three c's: children, computers, and communication. ● 0713

**Stott, J. W.**
Anatomy of a compact user interface development tool. HCI-0104 †

**Stotts, P. D.**
Adding browsing semantics to the hypertext model. 02834
The PFG environment: parallel programming with petri net semantics. 03527

**Stovsky, M. P.**
Building interprocess communication models using Stile. 03528

**Straka, M.**
Some aspects of communication in the natural language and user's involvement in software development. 03670

**Strasser, W. (Ed.)**
Advances in computer graphics hardware II. ● 0493
Advances in computer graphics hardware I. § 03785

**Strassmann, P. A.**
The real cost of OA. 01647

**Straub Jr., D. W.**
Current and future uses of the group decision support system technology: report on a recent empirical study. 02355

**Straub, D. W., Jr.**
Information technologies for the 1990's: an orgnizational impact perspective. 01336

**Straus, D. B.**
Computer-assisted negotiations: a case history from the law of the sea negotiations and speculation regarding future uses. HCI-0443 †

**Streeter, L. A.**
How to tell people where to go: comparing navigational aids. 02096

**Streitz, N. A.**
Cognitive ergonomics and human computer interaction. 0245
Mental models and metaphors: implications for the design of adaptive user-system interfaces. 0539
Cognitive ergonomics: an approach for the design of user-oriented interactive systems. 03591

**Strelich, T.**
The Software Life Cycle Support Environment (SLCSE): a computer based framework for developing software systems. HCI-0147 †

**Strelnikov, Y. N.**
An approach to CAD system performance evaluation. HCI-0414 †

**Striženec, M.**
The contemporary psychology of thinking and expert systems. 01487

**Strong, G.**
Are there subtle changes in vision after use of VDTs? 03733

**Stroud, N.**
Implementing neural network models on parallel computers. 01403

**Strzalkowski, T.**
Natural language interface to the question-answering system for physicians. 01478
A natural language information retrieval system with extentions towards fuzzy reasoning. HCI-0281 †

**Stuart, A. (Ed.)**
Screen input/output programming techniques using Turbo Pascal. ● 0714

**Stuchlik, F.**
The design of information processing systems in relation to users. 03642

**Stull, E.**
Reference model for DBMS user facility. 01086

**Stuller, P. J.**
Power plant simulation using a distributed control system. 02057

**Stutz, J.**
A methodology for interactive evaluation of user reactions to software packages:an empirical analysis of system performance, interaction, and run time. 02080

**Su, Y. D.**
A model of fault diagnosis performance of expert marine engineers. 02199

**Subrahmanyam, Y. V.**
Need of electronic tools in educational programmers and the impact in developing countries. 03023

**Suchman, L.**
Beyond the chalkboard: computer support for collaboration and problem solving inmeetings (Reprint). 0376
Social science and system design: interdisciplinary collaborations. 0833
Video: Data for studying human-computer interaction. 02878
Groupware: interface design for meetings. 02883
Beyond the chalkboard: computer support for collaboration and problem solving in meetings. HCI-0312 †

**Suchman, L. A.**
Plans and situated actions: the problem of human-machine communication. ● HCI-0040 †

**Sudarsky, O.**
The adaptable user interface. 01337

**Suess, M. J.**
Health impact of work with visual display terminals. 03678

**Suetens, P.**
Critical review of visual inspection. 02260

**Suffell, C.**
Initial work on a system-independent computer model of a 3D anthropomorphic dummy. 01476

**Sufrin, B.**
Towards the formal specification of a simple programming support environment. 02607
Formal methods and the design of effective user interfaces. 03246

**Sugamura, N.**
Speech analysis and synthesis methods developed at ECL in NTT-From LPC to LSP-. 02646

**Sugaya, H.**
A system for specification and rapid prototyping of application command languages. 01849

**Sugimot, N.**
A study on safety evaluation index and industrial accident analysis from the viewpoint of the safety confirmation type. 03419

**Sugimoto, F.**
Multivariate data representation and analysis by face pattern using facial expression characteristics. HCI-0394 †

**Sugimoto, N.**
A study of fail-safe technology. 03421
A study of intrinsic safety asymmetrical actuator. 03422
AGV safety system designed for preventing hazardous human contact. 03423
Construction and examples of sensor in safe working system. 03425
Pneumatic manipulating system provided with active compliance function. 03426

**Sugimoto, S.**
A knowledge-based system with audio-visual aids. 02068

**Sugiyama, K.**
A cognitive approach for graph drawing. 01616

**Sugiyama, Y.**
A processing system for program specifications in a natural language. 03537

**Sukaviriya, P.**
Dynamic construction of animated help from application context. 03123

**Sullivan, J. W.**
Synergistic use of direct manipulation and natural language. 0857
Multimodal response planning: an adaptive rule based approach. 02894

**Sullivan, P.**
Writers as total desktop publishers: developing a conceptual approach to training. 0108

**Sulonen, R.**
A design data manager. 03090

**Summer, T. A.**
KIDS. 02547

**Summers, W.**
IBM 3270 full screen interactive programming without CICS. 01040

**Sumner, M.**
The impact of menus and command-level feedback on learners' acquisition of data base language skills. 01041
Information systems strategy and end-user application development. 01637
The impact of electronic mail on managerial and organizational communications. 03041

**Sumner, M. R.**
The impact of information systems strategy on end user computing. 02423

**Sun, G. Z.**
Machine learning using a higher order correlation network. 02563
High order correlation model for associative memory. 02729

**Suppes, P.**
Natural-language interface for an instructable robot. HCI-0324 †

**Surgenor, B. W.**
A compact model of a power house boiler. 02683

**Susskind, R. E.**
Expert systems in law: out of the research laboratory and into the marketplace. 02765

**Sutcliffe, A.**
Task analysis, systems analysis and design: symbiosis or synthesis? 02058

Some experiences in integrating specification of human computer interaction within a structured system development method. 03222
Human-computer interface design. HCI-0043 †

**Sutcliffe, A. G.**
MAJIC—an integrated program support environment. 01960
Empirical evaluation of map interfaces. 03276
Database maps. 03286

**Suter, V.**
From arcane ASCII to the printed page - computer basics. 01148

**Sutherland, I. E.**
Sketchpad a man-machine graphical communication system. 03103

**Sutherland, W. R.**
Device-independent graphics: with examples from IBM personal computers. ● HCI-0070 †

**Suzuki, H.**
A travel consultation system: towards a smooth conversation in Japanese. 03917

**Svarovski, S. G.**
Usage of linguistic variable concept for human operator modelling. 01694

**Sviokla, J. J.**
Putting expert systems to work. 01704

**Swanbeck, G.**
Skin paroblems from VDT work-a summary. 03697

**Swanson, N. E.**
Open versus closed minds: the effect of dogmatism on an analyst's problem-solving behavior. HCI-0446 †

**Swanston, M. T.**
The design and evaluation of an animated programming environment. 03220

**Sweeney, M.**
The application of cognitive psychology to CAD. 03239

**Sweeney, P.**
Graph attribution as a specification paradigm. 01138

**Sweet, J. N.**
Office-by-example: an integrated office system and database manager. 01159

**Sweet, J. N.**
MH: a multifarious user agent. 01428

**Sweet, R. E.**
The Mesa programming environment. 01108

**Sweetland, J.**
Beta tests and end-user surveys: are they valid? 01631

**Sweetman, D.**
A modular window system for Unix. 03929

**Swierczkowski, S.**
A model of the neocortex. 01164

**Swineheart, D. C.**
The structure of Cedar. 01109

**Sydow, J.**
Office automation and work organization: making use of the scope of choice. 03746

**Sydow, M. V.**
Static stereo vision depth distortions in teleoperation. 03390

**Sykes, D.**
Technology + design + research = information design. 0107

**Sykes, E. A.**
A user preference guided approach to conflict resolution in rule-based expert systems. 01872

**Sylla, C.**
Modelling the human factors aspects of a computer-based text-graphics layout system. 01518
A human factors design investigation of a computerized layout system of text-graphic technical materials. 01779

**Sylvester, W. A.**
Human aspects of factory modernization. 01513

**Szczur, M. R.**
Transportable applications environment (TAE) plus experiences in "Object"-ively modernizing a user interface environment. 01126

**Szekely, P.**
Separating the user interface from the functionality of application programs. 0948
A user interface toolkit based on graphical objects and constraints. 01125

**Szpak, M. D.**
ISDN and the move to integrated communications—an introduction. 01455

**Szwillus, G.**
Using data flow specifications and interactive editing in the operating system user interface. 03800

**Szygenda, S. (Chair.)**
Exploring technology: today and tomorrow. § 03491

**Szygenda, S. A.**
SMARTGEN: the implementation of an expert system for the generation of digital logic diagnostic tests. 02929

**T. R.**
Assessing the impact of human factors on data processing inspection errors. 01527

**Tabata, K.**
A knowledge-based system with audio-visual aids. 02068

**Tabe, T.**
An approach to knowledge elicitation in scheduling FMS: Toward a hybrid intelligent system. 03394

**Tafvelin, S. (Ed.)**
Ada-components: libraries and tools. § 03180

**Tagg, R.**
...from the end user angle. 01378

**Taggart, W. M.**
A human information processing model of the managerial mind: some MIS implications. 0205

**Tague, J.**
Evaluation of the user interface in an information retrieval system: a model. 02012
Some measures and procedures for evaluation of the user interface in an information retrieval system. 03069

Generating an individualized user interface. 03074

**Taillard, J.**
Robot components and systems. • HCI-0068 †

**Tainsh, M. A.**
The concept of an information management system and its use within design studies. 01244

**Tait, A.**
Helping the disabled. 01445

**Tait, P.**
The effect of user involvement on system success: a contingency approach. 02508

**Takahashi, M.**
A travel consultation system: towards a smooth conversation in Japanese. 03917
Generating natural language responses appropriate to conversational situations—in the case of Japanese. 03922

**Takebayashi, Y.**
A document layout system using automatic document architecture extraction. 0882
A consideration of learning in speech recognition from the viewpoint of AI class-description learning. 03533

**Takeda, T.**
Influence of CRT refresh rates on accommodation aftereffects. 03731

**Takenouchi, S.**
The software structure of extended nucleus based on BTRON specification. 03494

**Takeuchi, A.**
Object oriented programming in Concurrent Prolog. 0677
Spreadsheets with incremental queries as a user interface for logic programming. 02515

**Takeuchi, T.**
Fuzzy control of a mobile robot for obstacle avoidance. 02025

**Takizawa, M.**
Logic interface system on navigational database systems. 03818

**Talbot, M.**
Speech and language-based interaction with machines: towards the conversational computer. ● 0724

**Talley, W. T.**
Display legibility guidelines: a design aid. 01983

**Tally, R.**
Perception and acceptance of a local area network and electronic mail. 01284

**Talyor, R. N.**
Foundations for the Arcadia environment architecture. 01135

**Tamaru, R. S.**
A graphical thesaurus-based information retrieval system. 02243

**Tamine, J.**
Successful implementation of an office system. 01438

**Tamura, S.**
Eye movement analysis system using fundus images. HCI-0243 †

**Tan, K. C.**
Visual Displays: the highlighting Paradox. 01799

**Tanaka, A.**
An operations advisor for an on-line computer banking system with graphics interface. 02983

**Tanaka, E.**
A string correction method based on the context-dependent similarity. 0293

**Tanaka, H. (Ed.)**
Logic programming '87. § 03919

**Tanaka, K.**
Manual control of an intrinsically unstable system and its modeling by fuzzy logic. 02026
Human-computer-software interaction (HCSI) strategy in the design of global intelligent computer integrated management (ICIM) systems. 03396

**Tanaka, M.**
A high level language-based computing enviornment to support production and execution of reliable programs. 01855

**Tanaka, Y.**
Human-computer-software interaction (HCSI) strategy in the design of global intelligent computer integrated management (ICIM) systems. 03396

**Tanenbaum, A. S.**
A UNIX clone with source code for operating systems courses. 01095

**Tanenhaus, M. K.**
Modularity and lexical access. HCI-0350 †

**Tang, J. C.**
Tools for supporting cooperative work near and far: highlights from the CSCW conference. 0879

**Taniguchi, Y.**
An automatic wafer inspection system using pipelined image processing techniques. 01840

**Tanimoto, S. L.**
PICT: an interactive graphical programming environment. HCI-0143 †

**Tanner, P. P.**
A multitasking switchboard approach to user interface management. 01053
Reference models, window systems, and concurrency. 01058
Multi-thread input. 01070

**Tanner, P. P. (Ed.)**
Human factors in computing systems and graphics interface. § 02855

**Tarlton, M. A.**
Pogo: a declarative representation system for graphics. 0476

**Tarlton, P. N.**
Pogo: a declarative representation system for graphics. 0476
Graphic interfaces for knowledge-based system development. 0892

**Tartt, D.**
The development of an automated flight test management system for flight test planning and monitoring. 02928

**Tarumi, H.**
A programming environment supporting reuse of object-oriented software. 03509

**Tassinari, P.**
A simple, general method for ray tracing bicubic surfaces. 03853

**Tasso, C.**
A propositional language for text representation. 0097
An expert interface for effective man-machine interaction. 0166
User modeling in intelligent information retrieval. 01994
IR-NLI II: applying man-machine interaction and artificial intelligence conceptsto information retrieval. 03070

**Tatar, D.**
WYSIWIS revised: early experiences with multiuser interfaces. 01158

**Tatar, D. G.**
Video: Data for studying human-computer interaction. 02878

**Tate, A.**
O-Plan: control in the open planning architecture. HCI-0362 †

**Tatro, J. S.**
An integrated display for vertical and translational flight: eight factors affecting pilot performance. 01714

**Tatsuoka, K. K.**
Computer analysis of students' procedural "bugs" in an arithmetic domain. 02273

**Tauber, M. J.**
An approach to metacommunication in human-computer interaction. 03592
On visual interfaces and their conceptual analysis. 03829
Representational frameworks and models for human-computer interfaces. HCI-0188 †

**Tauber, M. J. (Ed.)**
Visualization in programming. 5th Interdisciplinary Workshop in Informatics and. § 03826
Readings on cognitive ergonomics - mind and computers. § HCI-0039 †

**Tauda, I.**
Parallel in sequence—towards the architecture of an elementary cortical processor. 03820

**Taylor, J.**
Socio-tech: what is it (and why should we care)? 0908
Expert systems—where do we go from here? HCI-0318 †

**Taylor, J. H.**
An expert system architecture for computer-aided control engineering. 0662

**Taylor, M.**
Voice input applications in aerospace. 0179

**Taylor, M. J.**
Microcomputing in motion analysis. 02384

**Taylor, M. M.**
ISIS: the interactive spatial information system. 02193
Layered protocols for computer-human dialogue. 1: principles. 02195
Layered protocols for computer-human dialogue. 11: some practical issues. 02196

**Taylor, M. R. (Ed.)**
Crystallographic Computing 4. § 03775

**Taylor, R. N.**
Design principles behind Chiron: a UIMS for software environments. 03511

**Taylor, R. P.**
Graphical vs. textual representation: an empirical study of novices' program comprehension. 0566

**Taylor, S. E.**
Display image characteristics and visual response. 03722

**Tecosky, J.**
Interfacing standards for recognisers. 0178

**Teitelbaum, S.**
Observations of end-user online searching behavior over eleven years. HCI-0235 †

**Teitelbaum, T.**
Relations and attributes. 01103
The synthesizer generator: a system for constructing language-based editors. ● HCI-0024 †
The synthesizer generator reference manual (3rd ed.). ● HCI-0024 †

**Teitelman, W.**
Ten years of window systems—a retrospective view. 03926

**Tekfi, C.**
Readability formulas: An overview. 02301

**Telem, M.**
Information requirements specification II: Brainstorming collective decision-making technique. 02005

**Tello, E. R.**
Between man and machine. HCI-0128 †

**Tempel, H. G.**
A set of tools supporting the software design based on SDL. 03803

**Templeton, M.**
Considerations for the development of natural-language interfaces to database management systems. 0161

**ten Hagen, P. J.**
Logical input devices and interaction. 01393
Display architecture for VLSI-based graphics workstations. 03786

**ten Hagen, P. J.W.**
Dialogue cell resource model and basic dialogue cells. 01400

**ten Hagen, P. J.W. (Ed.)**
Intelligent CAD systems II: implementational issues. ● 0006
Intelligent CAD systems I: theoretical and methodological aspects. ● 0715

**Ten Horn, L, A.**
Automation in public libraries: effects on the organization, quality of working life, and quality of services. 0246

**TenBrink, T.**
AI/learn: an interactive videodisk system for teaching medical concepts and reasoning. 02381

**Tenney, R. R.**
Distributed decisionmaking with constrained decisionmakers: a case study. 01886

**Tenny, T.**
Leadership style vs. succssus in student chief programmer teams. 01029

**Teo, G. S.**
The use of VDM on the specification of Chinese characters. 04038

**Teorey, T. J.**
ER model clustering as an aid for user communication and documentation in database design. 01331
A practical approach to transforming extended ER diagrams into the relational model. 02022
Cost/benefit analysis for incorporating human factors in the software lifecycle. HCI-0127 †
The database designer's workbench. HCI-0249 †

**Tepper, A.**
Experiences in participative systems design. 03665

**Teran, M.**
XVISION: a comprehensive software system for image processing research, education, and applications. 03124

**Terano, T.**
Manual control of an intrinsically unstable system and its modeling by fuzzy logic. 02026

**Terry, J. E.**
Graphical data presentation for decision support systems. 01229

**Tesauro, G.**
Scaling relationships in back-propagation learning. 01338

**Teullngs, H.**
Automatic identification of writers. 03909

**Teunissen, W.**
IDECAP: interactive pictorial information system for demographic and environmental planning applications. HCI-0411 †

**Thacker, C.**
Personal distributed computing: the Alto and Ethernet hardware. 03095

**Thacker, P.**
Effects of graphic boundaries in tabular displays: a human factors evaluation. 01526

**Thagard, P. R.**
Induction: processes of inference, learning, and discovery. ● HCI-0064 †

**Thakoor, A. P.**
Electronic implementation of associative memory based on neural network models. 01895
Error correction and asymmetry in a binary memory matrix. 02750

**Thalheim, B.**
Design tools for large relational database systems. 03946

**Thalheim, B. (Ed.)**
MFDBS 87. § 03943

**Thalman, D.**
A multiple track animator system for motion synchronization. 03350

**Thalmann, D. (Ed.)**
Computer-generated images: the state of the art. § 03856

**Tharp, A. L.**
Let's motivate! 01034
The effect of windows on man-machine interfaces. 01048
The influence of rule-generated stress on computer-synthesized speech. 02081

**The ARBEN Group Inc.**
Principles of data communication. ● 0547

**Theaker, C. J.**
Human-computer interface recording. 01414

**Theodoridou, M.**
The multimedia object presentation manager of MINOS: a symmetric approach. 01083

**Theoto, M.**
The fuzzy decodings of educative texts. 01700

**Thesen, A.**
Goodness of fit in the user-computer interface: A hierarchical control framework related to "friendless". 01868

**Thiel, U.**
Informational zooming: an interaction model for the graphical access to text knowledge bases. 03073

**Thieme, R. H.**
Human intelligence models and their implications for expert system structure and research. 01242

**Thimbleby, H.**
User interface design and formal methods. 01373
The design of a terminal independent package. 02619
Equal opportunity interactive systems. HCI-0168 †

**Thimbleby, H. W.**
Ease of use - the ultimate deception. 03249
The design of two innovative user interfaces. 03263
Interaction models and the principled design of interactive systems. 03799

**Thoet, W.**
The design of a flexible distributed testbeb for communication systems. 03538

**Thomas, A. L.**
VLSI for solid modelling. 0232

**Thomas, C.**
Designing electronic paper to fit user requirements. 03206
Subject reports about musculoskeletal discomfort in VDU work as a complex phenomenon. 03708

**Thomas, D.**
Design Automation. § 02828

**Thomas, J.**
Human computer interaction in the year 2000. 0924
Goals and objectives for user interface software. 01056

**Thomas, J. C.**
Human factors and artificial intelligence. 0408
Organizing for human factors. HCI-0230 †

**Thomas, J. C. (Ed.)**
Human factors in computer systems. ● 0718

Human factors in computer systems. ● HCI-0037 †

**Thomas, J. R. (Ed.)**
Artificial intelligence and its applications. ● 0221

**Thomas, M.**
Modeling fault diagnosis as the activation and use of a frame system. 01729
The effects of program-dependent and program-independent deletions on software cloze tests. HCI-0175 †

**Thomas, R. C.**
Experimental adaptive interface. HCI-0139 †

**Thomas, R. H.**
Diamond: a multimedia message system built on a distributed architecture (Reprint). 0380
Diamond: A multimedia message system built on a distributed architecture. 0574

**Thomassen, A. J.W.M.**
Real-time processing of cursive writing and sketched graphics. 03908

**Thompson, B. H.**
Shifting to a higher gear in a natural language system. 03169
ASK is transportable in half a dozen ways. HCI-0279 †

**Thompson, C. L.**
Weighting, ranking and relevance feedback in a front-end system. 02329

**Thompson, D. E.**
Capturing expertise: Some approaches to modeling command decisionmaking in combat analysis. 01883
A hand biomechanics workstation. 02820

**Thompson, F. B.**
Shifting to a higher gear in a natural language system. 03169
ASK is transportable in half a dozen ways. HCI-0279 †

**Thompson, J. B.**
Experiences in use of SSADM: series of case studies. Part 1: first time users. 01976
Experiences in use of SSADM: series of case studies. Part 2:

experienced users. 01977

**Thompson, N. G.A.**
The effects of relational and entity-relationship data models on query performance of end users. 02247

**Thompson, P.**
Subjective probability and information retrieval: a review of the psychological literature. 02303

**Thompson, R.**
SOFTLIB—A documentation management system. HCI-0149 †

**Thompson, R. H.**
Support for browsing in an intelligent text retrieval system. 02240

**Thompson, R. L.**
Examining the duality role of I.S. executives: a study of I.S. issues. 01953

**Thomsen, K. S.**
System development in a women's perspective. 03675

**Thorburn, C.**
User-driven adaptive behaviour, a comparative evaluation and an inductive analysis. 03226

**Thornton, D. C.**
Spectral analysis of sinus arrhythmia: a measure of mental effort. 01737

**Thornton, R. W.**
Interactive 3-D modeling with personal computers. 03296

**Thorp, R. G.**
The foreign language barrier: a study among pharmaceutical research workers. 02333

**Thorpe, J.**
Knowledge base enhancements to relational databases. 03285

**Thurow, W. D.**
Production control in car industry. 0623

**Thyberg, C. A.**
Cooperative work in the Andrew message system. 02827
Advisor—an electronic mail consulting service. 03151

**Tian, J.**
Performance evaluation of three pressure mats as robot workstation safety sensors. 03428

**Tichy, W. F.**
Knowledge-based editors for directed graphs. 03797

**Timmer, H. J.**
A plan for evaluating usability of software products. HCI-0449 †

**Timpe, K. P.**
Psychological principles for allocation of functions in man-robot system. 03630

**Tindell, A.**
Human factors in the Columbus space station. 03250

**Tiomkin, M.**
An environment for logic programming. 01106

**Tissen, A.**
Cognitive user interface laboratory, GMD-IPSI. 0870

**Tistarelli, M.**
Active vision: integration of fixed and mobile cameras. 04017

**Tito, C.**
Broderbund Software, Inc. v. Unison World, Inc. 648 F. Supp. 1127 (1986). 01477

**Titus, G. J.**
The effects of display formats on information systems design. 02357

**Todd, P.**
An experimental program investigating color-enhanced and graphical information presentation: an integration of the findings. HCI-0196 †

**Todorov, N.**
Software development approach in FMS. 01567

**Tognazzini, B.**
Usability testing in the real world. 0917

**Tollander, C. J.**
Distributed database considerations in an expert system for radar analysis. 03175

**Tomabechi, H.**
The direct memory access paradigm and its applications to natural language processing. 01489

**Tombaugh, J.**
Multi-window displays for readers of lengthy texts. 02142

**Tomita, M.**
The direct memory access paradigm and its applications to natural language processing. 01489

**Tomiyama, T. (Ed.)**
Intelligent CAD systems I: theoretical and methodological aspects. ● 0715

**Tomlinson, R. S.**
Diamond: a multimedia message system built on a distributed architecture (Reprint). 0380
Diamond: A multimedia message system built on a distributed architecture. 0574

**Tompa, F. W.**
Measuring the effectiveness of personal database structures. 02246

**Tompkins, J. S.**
Gossip as creativity. 02576

**Tong, L. C.**
The engineering of a translator workstation. 01555

**Tonge, F.**
Ontological analysis of document usage: an exploratory study. 03467

**Tonn, B.**
Embedded training in AI technology through an expert system interface: an alarm processor application. 02991

**Tonnquist, G.**
Colors in video displays. 03725

**Took, R.**
Text representation and manipulation in a mouse-driven interface. 03266

**Topping, P.**
Express—rapid prototyping and product development via integrated knowledge-based executable specifications. 03492

**Torasso, P.**
Knowledge acquisition via a graphical interface. 03572

**Torell, G.**
Psychological aspects on blind peoples's reading of radio-distributed daily newspapers. 03700

**Torii, K.**
A processing system for program specifications in a natural language. 03537

**Torkzadeh, G.**
The quality of user documentation. 01924
The quality of user documentation: an instrument validation. 02356
The measurement of end-user computing satisfaction. 02510

**Torrance, K. E.**
An experimental evaluation of computer graphics imagery. HCI-0373 †

**Torras i Genís, C.**
Exploring three possibilities in network design: spontaneous node activity, node plasticity and temporal coding. 03962

**Torras i Genis, C.**
Neural network model with rhythm-assimilation capacity. 01881

**Torre, V.**
Computational vision and regularization theory. 0301

**Torsvall, L.**
Inactivity, night work, and fatigue. 03705

**Tortora, G.**
An image processing language with ICON-assisted navigation. HCI-0387 †

**Toth, N.**
Selective attention to aspects of motion configurations: common vs. relative motion. 03345

**Totterdell, P.**
Design and evalution of the AID adaptive front-end to Telecom Gold. 03260

**Toubache, K.**
A new approach to cursor movements in user interfaces of integrated programming environments. 01974

**Toulouse, G.**
A simple selectionist learning rule for neural networks. 02756

**Toulouse, J.**
Chief executive personality and corporate strategy and structure in small firms. 02472

**Townsend, P.**
A man-machine interface for computer-aided and simulation of control systems. 01237
A human-computer interface for control system design. 03208

**Toyama, T.**
Innovation of decision support system-matplan based on structure matrix supported by APL. 02800

**Toyoda, J.**
Plan-based text generation in an on-line help system. 03817
Analogical program synthesis from program components. 03920

**Traiger, I. L.**
System R: a relational approach to database management. 0709

**Traünmuller, R.**
Information systems design methodologies and their compliance with cognitive ergonomy. HCI-0097 †

**Traub, D. C.**
An historical perspective of CD ROM. 0679

**Traub, J. F. (Ed.)**
Annual review of computer science vol. 1, 1986. ● 0719

**Travers, V. M.**
Diamond: a multimedia message system built on a distributed architecture (Reprint). 0380
Diamond: A multimedia message system built on a distributed architecture. 0574

**Travis, B. J.**
A layered neural network model applied to the auditory system. 02763

**Treaster, D.**
Measurement of seat pressure distribution. 01760

**Treger, M.**
An interactive modeling program for DNA. 02385

**Trehub, A.**
Visual-cognitive neuronal networks. 0029

**Treisman, A.**
Features and objects in visual processing. 02577
Preattentive processing in vision. 02709
Preattentive processing in vision. HCI-0366 †

**Trelease, R. B.**
Connectionism, cybernetics, and the cerebellum. 01185

**Trenner, L.**
A comparative survey of the friendliness of online 'help' in interactive information. 02010

**Trent, R. H.**
Perspectives on the academic preparation of MIS professionals. 03006

**Treu, S.**
Adaptive interface design: a symmetric model and a knowledge-based implementation. 01091
An interface architecture to provide adaptive task-specific context for the user. 02228
Specification and generation of variable, personalized graphical interfaces. HCI-0134 †

**Trevellyan, R.**
A self-regulating adaptive system. 0829

**Trevino, L. K.**
Message equivocality, media selection and manager performance: implications for information systems. 02505

**Trickett, T. W.**
On the design of dealing desks. 03713

**Trickey, H.**
Drag: a graph drawing system. 03183

**Trienekens, C. G.**
Display architecture for VLSI-based graphics workstations. 03786

**Trigg, R. H.**
Supporting collaboration in hypermedia: issues and experiences. 0117
Notecards in a nutshell. 0810
Guided tours and tabletops: tools for communicating in a hypertext environment. 01161
Supporting collaboration in Hypermedia: issues and experiences. 02454
Guided tours and tabletops: tools for communicating in a hypertext environment. 02823
TEXTNET: a network-based approach to text handling. HCI-0401 †

**Triggs, T. J.**
Magnification effects with imaging displays depend on scene content and viewing condition. 01786
Visual accommodation and target detection in the vicinity of a window post. 01802

**Trinkaus, J.**
The VDTs are here: health hazard and all. 02439

**Tripp, D. G.**
Instrumenting systems to measure components of interactive response times. 01230

**Tripp, R. S.**
Design of a control room for the air force logistics command (AFLC) command, control, and communication and intelligence ($C^3I$) system. 01612

**Tripp, S. D.**
The effects of orienting, processing, and practicing activities on learning from interactive video. 02289

**Trippner, D. E. E.**
CAD data exchange. 0237

**Trivedi, S. S.**
Manipulation of 3D imagery. 0557

**Troll, D. A.**
Teaching users to fish: hooks, lines and sinkers for reading computer documentat. 03156

**Tromp, J. W.**
A model for cortical function. 02731

**Trost, H.**
DATENBANK-DIALOG: a German language interface for relational databases. 01208

**Troup, D. B.**
Design principles behind Chiron: a UIMS for software environments. 03511

**Troy, N.**
Job organization and allocation of functions between man and computer: II.job organization. 03629

**Trumbly, J. E.**
Including a user interface management system (UIMS) in the performance relationship model. 01000

**Tsai, N. W.**
The information center approach for developing computer-based information systems. 01929
Use of fourth generation languages: application development and documentation problems. 02435

**Tsang, C. P.**
Sherlock—a system for diagnosing power distribution ring network faults. 02916

**Tsatsoulis, C.**
Modeling rule-based systems by stochastic programmed production systems. 02017

**Tseng, A. A.**
Simulation of CNC controller features in graphics-based programming. 01568

**Tseng, G. (Ed.)**
New horizons for the information profession: meeting the challenge of change. § 04046

**Tseng, H. C.**
The economic evaluation on implementation industrial robot from user point of view. 03447

**Tsichritzis, D. C.**
Directions in object-oriented research. 0477
Querying external databases. HCI-0233 †

**Tsoi, K.**
Factors affecting the readability of moving text on a computer display. 01764
Reading self-paced moving text on a computer display. 01777

**Tsotsos, J. K.**
The scope of research on motion: sensations, perception, representation and generation. 03323

**Tsotsos, J. K. (Chair.)**
Motion: representation and perception. § 03321

**Tsubotani, H.**
A high level language-based computing enviornment to support production and execution of reliable programs. 01855

**Tsur, S.**
An environment for logic programming. 01106

**Tsurutani, T.**
How map designers can represent their ideas in thematic maps: effective user interfaces for thematic map design. 03870

**Tu, E. Y.**
A prototype autonomous agent for crew and equipment retrieval in space. 02994

**Tucker, D.**
Patterns of inductive reasoning in a parallel expert system. 02219

**Tucker, H. A.**
Desktop publishing. 0238

**Tucker, T. W.**
Local work station concepts in a small distributed system. 02054

**Tudor, A.**
A biparty grammar as a tool for defining a man-machine dialogue. 03639

**Tullis, T. S.**
A system for evaluating screen formats: Research and application. 0413
Optimizing the usability of computer-generated displays. 03278

**Tulunay-Keesey, U.**
A model for the fading of stabilized images in a visual system. 01864
**Tuori, M.**
Learning graphics programming by direct communication. 03298
**Tuori, M. I.**
ISIS: the interactive spatial information system. 02193
**Turbak, F. A.**
The information lens: an intelligent system for information sharing in organizations. 0891
Intelligent information-sharing systems. 01322
**Turkle, S.**
The second self: computers and the human spirit. ● HCI-0082 †
**Turksen, B.**
A closed-loop causal model of workload based on a comparison of fuzzy and crisp measurement techniques. 01746
**Turner, E. J.**
The application of human factors to the needs of the novice computer user. 02079
**Turner, J. A.**
Understanding the elements of system design. 0156
Using restricted natural language for data retrieval: a plan for field evaluation. HCI-0255 †
Computer mediated work: the interplay between technology and structured jobs. HCI-0440 †
**Turoff, M.**
The rational, the pragmatic and the inquiry process: The social study of information- communication systems. 0786
Interface design in computerized conferencing systems: a personal view. HCI-0305 †
**Turpin, J. A.**
The effect of number ordering and orientation on marking speed and errors for mark-sensed labels. 01717
**Turtle, H.**
Designing a CD ROM information structure. 0682
**Tuten, P.**
Claris CAD. 01310

**Tuttle, M. S.**
Evaluating RECONSIDER: a computer program for diagnostic prompting. HCI-0410 †
**Twigger, D.**
Describing a product opportunity: a method of understanding the users' environment. 03194
**Tykodi, T. A.**
Which way to computer literacy, programming or applications experience? 02127
**Tyldesley, D. A.**
Employing usability engineering in the development of office products. 01413
**Tyler, L. K.**
The sequential organization of spoken word recognition. 0291
**Tyler, S. W.**
Adaptive interface design: a symmetric model and a knowledge-based implementation. 01091
An interface architecture to provide adaptive task-specific context for the user. 02228
Multimodal response planning: an adaptive rule based approach. 02894
SAUCI: a knowledge-based interface architecture. 02895
**Tylutki, G.**
Building a self-modifying user interface. 01424
**Tyree, A. L.**
Expert systems in law: The datalex project. 02766
**Tzelgov, J.**
Radiation detection by ear and by eye. 01732
**Uchiyama, N.**
The fuzzy decodings of educative texts. 01700
**Uckun, S.**
NetGraph: an object-oriented graphical toolset for risk assessment. 02972
**Udupa, J. K.**
Manipulation of 3D imagery. 0557
**Uebe, G.**
A user-friendly interface to Kendrick's DUAL code. 01447

**Ueda, T.**
A distributed interoffice mail system. HCI-0308 †
**Uehara, K.**
Plan-based text generation in an on-line help system. 03817
Analogical program synthesis from program components. 03920
**Uhlig, R. P.**
Architectural implications of office systems. 03356
**Uhlir, S.**
Enabling the user interface. 01820
**Uhr, L.**
Multicomputer architectures for real-time perception. 03341
**Ukelson, J.**
An efficient high-level man-machine interface. 03530
**Ukkonen, E.**
Algorithms for approximate string matching. HCI-0180 †
**Ulich, E.**
The chances of individualization in human-computer interaction and its consequences. 0309
Job organization and allocation of functions between man and computer: II.job organization. 03629
Some aspects of user-oriented dialogue design. 03643
**Ulich, E. (Ed.)**
Psychological issues of human-computer interaction in the work place. ● 0305
**Ullman, S.**
Visual routines. 0616
**Ullman, S. (Ed.)**
Image understanding 1985-86. ● 0615
**Ullner, M. K.**
Device-independent graphics: with examples from IBM personal computers. ● HCI-0070 †
**Ulug, S.**
DORUS: an architecture for dynamic optimal resource utilization systems. 02979
**Umanath, N. S.**
An experimental evaluation of the impact of data display format on recall performance. HCI-0202 †

**Umezaki, S.**
A study on safety evaluation index and industrial accident analysis from the viewpoint of the safety confirmation type. 03419

**Umpleby, S. A.**
Self-authorization: A characteristic of some elements in certain self-organizing systems. 01610

**Underwood, G.**
The computer in the classroom: a force for change? 0149

**Underwood, J. D.M.**
The computer in the classroom: a force for change? 0149

**Ungar, D.**
Tenuring policies for generation-based storage reclamation. 01124
Multiprocessor Smalltalk: a case study of a multiprocessor-based programming environment. 03061

**Unger, B.**
Monitoring distributed systems. HCI-0169 †

**Unger, E. A.**
A user interface for database creation use and maintenance. 02791

**Unrein, J. T.**
Theoretical training and problem detection in a computerized database retrieval task. 02239

**Upchurch, R. L.**
Computer literacy: the pigeonhole principle. 0789

**Uppuluri, V. R.R. (Ed.)**
Expert judgment and expert systems. ● 0552

**Urieli, I.**
REPTIL promoting dialog between humanoid and computer. 02307

**Urken, A. B.**
Social choice theory and distributed decision making. 03044

**Uvijls, A.**
Study of visual performance on a multi-color VDU of color defective and normal Trichromatic subjects. 03701

**v. d. Malsburg, C. (Ed.)**
Neural computers. § 03949

**Vaishnavi, V. K.**
An empirical study of the effects of modularity on program modifiability. HCI-0155 †

**Vaissière, J.**
The use of prosodic parameters in automatic speech recognition. 03988
Recognition of speaker-dependent continuous speech with Keal-Nevezh. 04002

**Valenta, W.**
Embedded training in AI technology through an expert system interface: an alarm processor application. 02991

**Valentine, M.**
The automated solution of logic puzzles. 02015

**Valentini, F. A.**
Model of the neuro-muscular recruitment example of the extensor digitorum communis muscle in man: I—identification of motoneurons and of muscular fibers. 01595

**van Bergem, D. R.**
Perceptual normalization of the vowels of a man and a child in various contexts. 02656

**van Biljon, W. R.**
Extending Petri nets for specifying man-machine dialogues. 02183

**Van Camp, A. J.**
How good an Online searcher are you? Twenty questions about BIOSIS previews. 02521

**van Dam, A.**
Reading and writing the electronic book. HCI-0282 †
The electronic classroom: workstations for teaching. HCI-0436 †

**Van Dam, A.**
Fundamentals of interactive computer graphics. ● HCI-0069 †

**van de Liefvoort, A.**
Investigations into a command and response language interface. 03531

**van den Berg, R. J.H.**
The effect of varying voice and noise parameters on the perception of voicing in Dutch two-obstruent sequences. 02653

**van den Bos, J.**
IDECAP: interactive pictorial information system for demographic and environmental planning applications. HCI-0411 †

**Van Den Bos, J.**
Abstract interaction tools: a language for user interface management systems. 01162

**van der Heiden, G.**
The applicability of eye movement analysis in the ergonomic evaluation of human-computer interaction. 03766

**van der Meulen, P. S.**
INSIST: Interactive Simulation in Smalltalk. 01119

**van der Veer, G. C.**
An interdisciplinary approach to human factors in telematic systems. A review of the problems and possible solutions by a COST-11 ter working group. 01440
Learning styles in conversation—a practical application of Pask's learning theory to human-computer interaction. 03608
Human-computer interaction: psychonomic aspects. § 03887
Development of mental models of an office system: a field study on an introductory course. 03903

**van der Veer, G. C. (Ed.)**
Readings on cognitive ergonomics - mind and computers. § HCI-0039 †

**Van der Veer, G. C.**
Mental models and failures in human-machine systems. 03814

**van der Veer, G. C., Dr. (Ed.)**
Introduction: human-computer interaction: psychonomic aspects. 03888

**van der Vlist, R.**
Automatic information processing activities and operational decision making: a case study of consequence. 01950

**van Doom, A. J.**
Representation of local geometry in the visual system. 01249
Facts on optic flow. 01257

**Van Dyke, C.**
Binary jargon: the metaphoric language of computing. 01044

**van Emden, M. H.**
Spreadsheets with incremental queries as a user interface for logic programming. 02515

**Van Epps, T. J.**
A structure for enhancing user participation in model development. 01514

**van Hoeve, F.**
Generation of file processing programs based on JSP. 02639

**van Laar, D.**
Towards the construction of a maximally-contrasting set of colours. 03233

**van Lamsweerde, A.**
The kernel of a generic software development environment. 03056

**van Liere, R.**
User interface management systems. 0233
Logical input devices and interaction. 01393

**van Naelten, M.**
IDECAP: interactive pictorial information system for demographic and environmental planning applications. HCI-0411 †

**van Nes, F. L.**
Colour on displays—boon or curse? 03727
The legibility of visual display texts. 03889

**van Noorden, L. P.A.S.**
A provisional evaluation of a new chord keyboard, the Velotype. 03907

**van Ooyen, M. H.F.**
Lighting the electronic office. 03717

**van Peer, W.**
Reading, culture and modern mass media. 02340

**Van Praag, J.**
Comparison of elderly and younger users on keyboard and voice input computer-based composition tasks. 0916

**van Rensbergen, J.**
The efficiency of letter perception in function of color combinations: a study of video-screen colors. 03616

**van Rijsbergen, C. J. (Ed.)**
Research and development in information retrieval. § 03287

**Van Rijsbergen, C. J. (Ed.)**
Research and development in information retrieval. § 03072

**Van Rotterdam, A.**
Electric and magnetic fields of the brain computed by way of a discrete systems analytical approach: Theory and validation. 01276

**van Schaik, P.**
Factors influencing the detection of trend deviations on VDTs. 03894

**Van Slyke, D. A.**
Error analysis and tutor design. 02469

**van Vliet, J. C.**
Document processing. 03897

**van Vliet, J. C. (Ed.)**
Document manipulation and typography. § 03182

**Van Wert, P. D.**
Strategies for managing user developed systems. 01923

**Van Wetering, J.**
Mainframe and microcomputer-based business graphics: What satisfies users? HCI-0216 †

**van Wijk, J. J.**
SML: a solid modelling language. 01471

**Vance, M.**
Computer crime. ● 0722

**Vandenberg, P. D.J.**
The mirage rapid interface prototyping system. 03112

**Vanderheiden, G. C.**
Public Law 99-506, "Section 508" Electronic Equipment Accessibility for disabled workers. 02893

**VanLehn, K.**
Toward a theory of impasse-driven learning. 0536

**Vantaggiato, A.**
Some considerations on intelligent tutoring systems. 02963

**Vargas, E. A.**
Problem solving: a behavioral interpretation. 01582

**Vaske, J.**
User interface design: Are human factors principles used? 0886

**Vassiliou, Y.**
Studies in the evaluation of a domain-independent natural language query system. 0162
A framework for choosing a database query language. 0761
Query languages—a taxonomy. HCI-0254 †
Using restricted natural language for data retrieval: a plan for field evaluation. HCI-0255 †

**Vassiliou, Y. (Ed.)**
Human factors and interactive computer systems. § HCI-0038 †

**Vaumoron, J. A.**
Two-level data banks for translators. 01556

**Veerkamp, P. J. (Ed.)**
Intelligent CAD systems II: implementational issues. ● 0006

**Vegdahl, S. R.**
The design of an interactive compiler for optimizing microprograms. 01078

**Vencovská, A.**
On the applicability of maximum entropy to inexact reasoning. 02074

**Venda, V. F.**
Design of individual adaptive man-computer dialogues in the hybrid intelligence systems. 03400

**Venema, R.**
Software tools for the development of pictorial information systems in medicine—the ISQL experience. 03980

**Vener, A.**
The MAGNEX text editor for the Comodore Amiga personal computer. 0782

**Ventriglia, F.**
Kinetic theory of "hot" neural systems. 01613

**Verbaten, M. N.**
Processing demands, effort, and individual differences in four different vigilance tasks. 01801

**Verburg, G.**
Towards universality of access: interfacing physically disabled students to the Icon educational microcomputer. 0821

**Verin, L. L.**
Algorithm for interactive forming matrix data representation and estimation of its efficiency. 02536

**Vermeulen, J.**
Effects of functionally or topographically presented process schemes on operator performance. 01749

**Vernon, D.**
VIS: a virtual image system for image-understanding research. 02629

**Vernoy, M. W.**
Simultaneous adaptation to size, distance, and curvature underwater. 01803

**Verplank, B.**
Graphic invention for user interfaces: an experimental course in user-interface design. 0950

**Verplank, W. L.**
Designing the star user interface. 0089
Human factors testing in the design of Xerox's 8010 "Star" office workstation. 0090

**Verriest, G.**
Study of visual performance on a multi-color VDU of color defective and normal Trichromatic subjects. 03701

**Verrijn-Stuart, A. A.**
Information systems user–designer communication problems. 01938

**Verrijn-Stuart, A. A. (Ed.)**
Trends in information systems. • 0498
Office Systems. § 03354

**Vertelney, L.**
Drama and personality in user interface design. 0830

**Vertut, J.**
Teleoperations and robotics: applications and technology. • HCI-0068 †
Teleoperations and robotics: evolution and development. • HCI-0068 †

**Veryard, R.**
Demanding higher productivity. 01630

**Vessey, I.**
On matching programmers' chunks with program structures: an empirical investigation. 02150
Toward a theory of computer program bugs: an empirical test. 02216
The effect of user involvement on system success: a contingency approach. 02508

**Veth, B.**
An integrated data description language for coding design knowledge. 0717

**Vetrov, A. N.**
Man-machine procedures of decision making under uncertainty based on linear programming. 02664

**Vetschera, R.**
An interactive outranking system for multi-attribute decision making. 01539

**Vibet, C.**
Modeling of robot system dynamics for CAD based robot programming. 0605

**Vicard, J.**
Managing the semantic content of graphical data. HCI-0374 †

**Vicente, K.**
Coping with human errors through system design: implications for ecological interface design. 02254

**Vicente, K. J.**
Spectral analysis of sinus arrhythmia: a measure of mental effort. 01737
Assaying and isolating individual differences in searching a hierarchical file system. 01747
Accommodating individual differences in searching a hierarchical file system. 02212

**Vicenzi, C.**
Real-time large vocabulary word recognition via diphone spotting and multiprocessor implementation. 03996

**Vichniac, G. Y.**
Lyapunov function for parallel neural networks. 02736

**Vickers, D.**
The accumulator model of two-choice discrimination. 02371

**Vickery, A.**
An intelligent interface for online interaction. HCI-0264 †

**Vidal, E.**
Recent results on the application of a metric-space search algorithm (AESA) to multispeaker data. 03997

**Vidulich, M. A.**
Speech responses and dual-task performance: better time-sharing or asymmetric transfer? 01789

**Viera, C.**
Effects of breadth, depth and number responses on computer menu search performance. 02192

**Vilkman, E.**
Changes in prosodic features of speech due to environmental factors. 02651

**Villeda, R.**
Optimal allocation of a work force in a toxic substance environment. 01534

**Vincent, P. J.**
A natural language interface to a multiple databased office information system. 01094

**Vining, G. W.**
The IE's future role in improving knowledge. 01903

**Vinze, A. S.**
ICE: information center expert: a consultation system for resource allocation. 0781
A consultation system for information center resource allocation. 03100

**Virgin, L.**
Understanding and evaluating a computer graphics display. 01984

**Visciola, M.**
Human error detection processes. 02166
Office automation as an opportunity for an organizational check-up. 03749

**Viscuso, S. R.**
Software for neural networks. 0770

**Visick, D.**
Voice versus keyboard: use of a comparative analysis of learning to identify skill requirements of input devices. 03275

**Visikirsky, V. A.**
Interactive CAD/CAM in engineering industry. 01571

**Vissides, J. M.**
Composing user interfaces with InterViews. HCI-0131 †

**Vitello, D.**
How to tell people where to go: comparing navigational aids. 02096

**Vlaeminke, I.**
Man-computer interfaces: an introduction to software design and implementation. ● 0220

**Vöge, E.**
Goals in the application of CAD interfaces. HCI-0416 †

**Vöge, E. (Ed.)**
Product data interfaces in CAD/CAM applications: design, implementation and experiences. § 03981

**Vodel, D. R.**
The impact of "Messy" data on group decision making. 03476

**Voelcker, J.**
Instrumentation. 01834
Of mice and menus: designing the user-friendly interface. 01837

**Vogel, D.**
Mainframe and microcomputer-based business graphics: end user computing comparisons and trends. 02805
Mainframe and microcomputer-based business graphics: What satisfies users? HCI-0216 †

**Vogt, E. E.**
Managing the PC revolution. 01643

**Vogt, F. H. (Ed.)**
Concurrency 88. § 03873

**Voigt, K.**
A personal computer based graphic workstation. 02493

**Vokolos, F. I.**
AWB-ADE: an application development environment for interactive, integrated systems. 03051

**Vold, T. G.**
A single-board Forth computer with versatile analog I/O circuitry. 02308

**Volonino, L.**
An investigation of performance, productivity, and rationality in multi-criteria decision making. 03463

**Volper, D. J.**
Disjunctive models of boolean category learning. 01262

**Volpert, W.**
Contrastive analysis of the relationship of man and computer as a basis of system design. 03649

**von Benda, H.**
Practical experience in designing software ergonomic projects for large application systems. 0190

**von Grunau, M.**
Real and apparent motion: one mechanism or two? 03328

**von Papstein, P.**
Transferring skills from training to the actual work situation: the role of task application knowledge, action styles and job decision latitude. 02865

**von Sandor, R.**
Vision monitoring of VDU operators and relaxation of visual stress by means of a laser speckle system. 03738

**von Seelen, W.**
Characteristics of neuronal systems in the visual cortex. 01255

**Voogt, J.**
Computer literacy in secondary education: the performance and engagement of girls. 01495

**Voorhies, D.**
Virtual graphics. 02815

**Vornberger, O.**
The ring machine. 01483

**Voss, K.**
Nets in office automation. 03975

**Voss, M.**
Videocoding - a highly monotonous VDU work in a new technique for mail sorting. 03762

**Vossen, G.**
Update and retrieval in a relational database through a universal schema interface. HCI-0260 †

**Vukelich, J. C.**
From user to client services; making the transition for supercomputing. 03138

**Wada, E. (Ed.)**
Logic programming '86. § 03816
Logic programming '85. § 03916

**Waddington, R.**
Task-related knowledge structures: analysis, modelling and application. 03218

**Waddle, V.**
Office-by-example: an integrated office system and database manager. 01159

**Wade, B. W.**
System R: a relational approach to database management. 0709
Quill: An extensible system for editing documents of mixed type. 03517

**Waern, Y.**
Understanding learning problems in computer aided tasks. 03607
User-friendliness - from sugar to symbiosis. 03774

**On search in an incomplete database.** HCI-0214 †

**Waersted, M.**
Generation of muscle tension related to a demand of continuing attention. 03710

**Wagenaar, W. A.**
The psychological costs of master computer. 01655
Accidents at sea: multiple causes and impossible consequences. 02168

**Waggoner, J.**
Information in the air and in the wave. 03146

**Wagner, C.**
Expert systems and creativity. 0553

**Wagner, I.**
The office between humanization and control. 03651
A roundtable discussion on women, computers and participation. 03673

**Wahlberg, J. E.**
VDT work and the skin. 03696

**Wahlster, W.**
The relationship between user models and discourse models. 01353

**Waid, C. C.**
A probabilistic dominance measure for binary choices: analytic aspects of a multi-attribute random weights model. 02372

**Waidner, M.**
Networks without user observability. 01545

**Waight, K.**
Parcel sorting by speech recognition: human factors issues. 03209

**Wakita, H.**
Vowel normalization by frequency warped spectral matching. 02649

**Waksman, P.**
Grid analysis: continuing the search for a metric of shape. 02367

**Waldern, J. D.**
Studying depth cues in a three-dimensional computer graphics workstation. 02117

**Waldrop, M. M.**
Man-made minds: the promise of artificial intelligence. ● HCI-0055 †

**Waldschmidt, H.**
An editor for constructing graphics with $T_EX$. 01394

**Waldstein, R. K.**
*Library*—An electronic ordering system. 01991

**Walford, A. E.J.**
Cortical representation of texture primitives. 03306

**Walicka, L.**
Task-load and endocrinological risk for pregnancy in women VDU operators. 03692

**Walker, J.**
Online help systems: design and implementation issues (panel). 02902

**Walker, J. H.**
Authoring tools for complex document sets. 0120
Supporting document development with concordia. 03521

**Walker, M. R.**
Limited interconnectivity in synthetic neural systems. 03968

**Walker, N.**
Designing keybindings to be easy to learn and resistant to forgetting even when the set of commands is large. 02890

**Walker, R.**
Why users must co-operate internationally on standardization. 01457

**Walker, R. A.**
Computer-aided engineering (CAE) for system analysis. 0663

**Wall, M. L.**
Smart help for operator performance. 01528

**Wall, T. D.**
Managing factory automation. 0146

**Wallace, D.**
Characteristics and functions of software environments: an overview. 01145

**Wallace, D. J.**
Implementing neural network models on parallel computers. 01403

**Wallace, I.**
Self-modifying production system model of cognitive development. 0486

**Wallace, S.**
Fabrik: a visual programming environment. 01130

**Wallace, V. L.**
Investigations into a command and response language interface. 03531
The human factors of computer graphics interaction techniques. HCI-0377 †

**Wallace, W. A.**
The effects of 3D imagery on managerial data interpretation. 02502

**Wallach, H.**
How human perception deals with motion. 03322

**Wallers, J. A.**
A case study of user interface management system development and application. 0836

**Walmisley, P.**
The use and misuse of VDU'S. 01375

**Walsh, B. C.**
Online text retrieval via browsing. 01999

**Walsh, P.**
A comparison of hypertext, scrolling and folding as mechanisms for program browsing. 03235

**Walsham, G.**
A survey of information technology in the U.K. service sector. 01916

**Walters, D.**
Selection of image primitives for general-purpose visual processing. 01467
Selection and use of image features for segmentation of boundary images. 03305

**Walton, C.**
Recent trends in information systems law. 03017

**Walton, S.**
Recent trends in information systems law. 03017

**Walton, T.**
Intelligence and the man-machine interface. 0363

**Waly, S. M.**
A comprehensive data base for the design of manual materials handling. 01510

**Walz, D.**
A study of conflict in group design activities: implications for computer-supported cooperative work environments. 03477

**Wand, Y.**
A structured approach to designing human-computer dialogues. HCI-0106 †

**Wandell, B. A.**
Color constancy: a method for recovering surface spectral reflectance. 0298

**Wandke, H.**
On complexity of command-entry in man-computer dialogues. 03610

**Wandke, H. (Ed.)**
Man-computer interaction research (MACINTER-I): Proceedings of the first network. § 03589

**Wang, J.**
The design of a traffic control expert system for long distance network contingencies. 02952

**Wang, M.**
On the interface between the high level languages and Chinese character information. 01451
An experimental study of Chinese information displays on VDTs. 01784

**Wang, M. S.**
A conceptual architecture for generalized decision support system software. 0659

**Wang, P. S.**
GI/S: A graphical user interface for symbolic computation systems. 02397

**Wang, P. Y.**
Analysis of competition-based spreading activation in connectionist models. 02179

**Wang, S.**
The effects of modes of information presentation on decision-making: a review and meta-analysis. 02358

**Wang, Y. R.**
A framework of composite information systems for strategic advantage. 03465

**Wanvik, D. H. (Ed.)**
Advanced programming environments. § 03779

**Ward, J. R.**
Interactive recognition of handprinted characters for computer input. 0940

**Ward, R. D.**
Natural language processing and the language-impaired. 02570

**Ware, C.**
Bat brushes: on the uses of six position and orientation parameters in a paint program. 0846
Using color dimensions to display data dimensions. 01766

**Warfield, J. N.**
The magical number three—plus or minus zero. 01622

**Warman, A. R.**
GENIE-M: A generator for multimedia information environments. 0268

**Warr, W. A.**
End-user searching of CAS ONLINE. Results of a cooperative experiment between Imperial Chemical Industries and Chemical Abstracts Services. 02269

**Warren, D. L.**
Formatting space-related displays to optimize expert and nonexpert user performance. 0927

**Warrick, D.**
Stress. 01651

**Washington, E. S.**
PISCES: an expert system for coal fired power plant monitoring and diagnostics. 02915
An object-oriented expert system for coal-fired MHD power plant fault monitoringand diagnosis. 02973

**Wasserman, A. I.**
Developing interactive information systems with the user software engineering methodology. 0077
Extending state transition diagrams for the specification of human-computer interaction. 0080
Developing interactive information systems with the user software engineering methodology. 01856
Extending state transition diagrams for the specification of human-computer interaction. HCI-0191 †

**Wasti, H. A.**
A multiprocessor system for real-time robotic control. 02023

**Watanabe, H.**
Heuristic graph displayer for G-BASE. 02227

**Watanabe, S.**
Pattern recognition: human and mechanical. ● HCI-0072 †

**Waterman, D. A.**
Explanation for an expert system that performs estate planning. 02767

**Waters, D.**
Assessing the impacts of new technology on library employees. 02459

**Waters, F. C.H.**
AIX usability enhancements and human factors. 01817

**Waters, R. C.**
The programmer's apprentices: a research overview. 01368

**Waters, R. C. (Ed.)**
Readings in artificial intelligence and software engineering. ● 0612

**Waterton, K.**
A closed-loop causal model of workload based on a comparison of fuzzy and crisp measurement techniques. 01746

**Waterworth (Ed.)**
Speech & language based interaction with machines. ● 0723

**Waterworth, J. A.**
Speech and language-based interaction with machines: towards the conversational computer. ● 0724

**Watson, B.**
Designing a CD ROM information structure. 0682

**Watson, S. L.**
OS/2 query manager overview and prompted interface. 01809

**Watson, S. R.**
Fuzzy decision analysis. 0650

**Watson, V.**
System R: a relational approach to database management. 0709

**Watt, R. J.**
An outline of the primal sketch in human vision. 02541

**Wattawa, S. L.**
The second generation intelligent user interface for the crustal dynamics data information system. 02675

**Watters, C.**
A common interface for accessing document retrieval systems and dbms for retrieval of bibliographic data. 01990

**Watts, T. D.**
Some historical currents concerning the 'societal learning' approach to policy and planning. 01603

**Wawrzynek, P. A.**
An interactive approach to local remeshing around a propagating crack. 01685

**Waxman, B. D.**
Planting the seeds. 02840

**Way, E. C.**
Implementing a semantic interpreter using conceptual graphs. 01812

**Weaver, C. A.**
Concept design of a program manager's decision support system. 0660

**Weaver, M. D.**
Hypertext engineering: practical methods for creating a compact disk encyclopedia. 02832

**Webb, J. M.**
An empirical approach to the evaluation of icons. 01013

**Webb, T.**
Flexible intelligent interactive-video. 03238

**Webber, B. L.**
Natural language processing: a survey. 0181
Questions, answers, and responses: interacting with knowledge base systems. 0182

**Webber, B. L. (Ed.)**
Readings in natural language processing. • HCI-0067 †

**Weber, E. S.**
Crisis planning systems: tools for intelligent action. 03464

**Weber, E. U.**
Expectation and variance of item resemblance distributions in a convolution-correction model of distributed memory. 02369

**Weber, G.**
FINGER—Formalizing Interaction for Gesture Recognition. 01017

**Webster, B.**
A simple windowing system, part 1: basic principles. 01286

**Webster, J.**
Making computer tasks at work more playful: Implications for systems analysts and designers. 03005

**Webster, S.**
New wine in old skins, or, was all this ferment really necessary? 03140

**Wechsler, H.**
Joint spatial/spatial-frequency representation. 02580

**Weck, M.**
Experiences with off-line robot programming via standardized interfaces. 0601

**Wedberg, W. C.**
Facial particle exposure in the VDU environment: the role of static electricity. 03694

**Wedde, H. F.**
Graph-theoretical tools and their use in a practical distributed operating system design case. 03886

**Wedekind, J.**
Computer-aided model building. 0544

**Wedman, J. F.**
Citation patterns in the computer-based instruction literature. 02290

**Weed, L. L.**
Perspectives over forty years. 02847

**Weerdmeester, B. A.**
Keywords instead of hierarchical menus. 03912

**Wegner, P.**
Research directions in object-oriented programming. • 0690

**Wehrhahn, C.**
Comparison of color sensation in dichoptic and in normal vision. 01272

**Wei, G.**
ER model clustering as an aid for user communication and documentation in database design. 01331

**Weide, B. W.**
Building interprocess communication models using Stile. 03528

**Weidenbeck, S.**
Processes in computer program comprehension. HCI-0172 †

**Weiderman, N. H.**
A methodology for evaluating environments. 03055

**Weimann, J.**
Subjective load in introducing visual display units. 03627

**Weimer, D.**
A synthetic visual environment with hand gesturing and voice input. 0858

**Wein, M.**
A multitasking switchboard approach to user interface management. 01053

**Wein, M. (Ed.)**
Graphics Interface '86/Vision Interface '86. § 03288

**Weinberger, P. J.**
The AWK programming language. • HCI-0020 †

**Weiner, S. S.**
Reasoning about 'hard' cases in Talmudic law. 02777

**Weinman, D. G.**
VAX-BASIC with structured problem solving: 2nd edition. ● 0725

**Weinroth, G. J.**
User's complaints: Information system problems from the user's perspective. 02416

**Weinstock, H. (Ed.)**
Designing computer-based learning materials. § 03875

**Weir, G.**
Plan recognition for intelligent monitoring. 03261

**Weir, G. R. S.**
Learning from a plan-based interface. 01496

**Weisbuch, G.**
Control of the immune response. 03970

**Weiser, M.**
Of moles and men: the design of foot controls for workstations. 0935
Exploratory evaluation of a planar foot-operated cursor-positioning device. 02858
An empirical comparison of pie vs. linear menus. 02871
TEXTNET: a network-based approach to text handling. HCI-0401 †

**Weiser, S. P.**
OTM: specifying office tasks. 03039

**Weisert, C.**
Instilling professionalism in a software development organization. 03019

**Weisgerber, S.**
Transfer between word processing systems. 0899

**Weiskamp, K.**
Advanced Turbo C programming. ● 0726

**Weiss, E. H.**
Usability: stereotypes and traps. 0104

**Weiss, I. R.**
Strategies for end-user computing: An integrative framework. 02348

**Weiss, J. J.**
Fuzzy decision analysis. 0650

**Weiss, P. E.H.**
Breaking the grip of user manuals. 01051

**Weiss, S.**
An advanced full-text retrieval and analysis system. 03079

**Weissbarth, T.**
A tentative implementation of VDAFS. HCI-0422 †

**Weisstein, N.**
Figure-ground organization affects the early visual processing. 0021

**Welbourn, L. K.**
A gesture based text editor. 03232

**Weldon, L.**
Display strategies for program browsing. 03545

**Weldon, L. J.**
Improving the accuracy of touch screens: an experimental evaluation of three strategies. 02860
Reading text from computer screens. HCI-0088 †
Cognitive layouts of windows and multiple screens for user interfaces. HCI-0122 †

**Welland, R.**
The ECLIPSE user interface. 02638
SOFTLIB—A documentation management system. HCI-0149 †

**Weller, H. G.**
Interactivity in microcomputer-based instruction: its essential elements and how it can be enhanced. 0275

**Wellner, P. D.**
Statemaster: A UIMS based on statechart for prototyping and target implementation. 0850

**Wells, M. B.**
Libraries as programs preserved within compiler continuations. 01102

**Wells, T. L.**
Hypertext as a means for knowledge acquisition. 0777

**Welsh, D.**
Codes and cryptography. ● HCI-0033 †

**Wen, Z. S.**
The effects of the supervisor's knowledge in a complex automated system. 03366

**Wenger, E.**
Artificial intelligence and tutoring systems: computational and cognitive approaches to the communication of knowledge. ● HCI-0080 †

**Wennberg, A.**
Videocoding - a highly monotonous VDU work in a new technique for mail sorting. 03762

**Wenzel, E. M.**
Development of a three-dimensional auditory display system. 0980

**Wenzlaff, B.**
Integrative participation—a challenge to the development of informatics. 03641

**Wenzlaff, R.**
A roundtable discussion on women, computers and participation. 03673

**Werbos, P. J.**
Building and understanding adaptive systems: a statistical/numerical approach to factory automation and brain research. 01890

**Werth, L. H.**
Integrating software engineering into an intermediate programming class. 01037
Software tools at the University: Why, What and How. 04026

**West, D. (Ed.)**
Culture, cognitive, and connectionism: Towards an hermeneutic anthropology of mind. 04077

**Westergren, B. A.**
Plant scheduling expert system for batch processing. 02977

**Westerholm, P.**
Pregnancy outcome and VDU-work in a cohort of insurance clerks. 03690

**Westgaard, R. H.**
Generation of muscle tension related to a demand of continuing attention. 03710

**Westgard, J. O.**
Implementation of a multirule, multistage quality control program in a clinical laboratory computer system. 02380

**Westin, A. F.**
The changing workplace: A guide to managing the people, organizational, and regulatory aspects of office technology (book excerpt). 0044
Trends in U.S. user policies for VDT work. 03753

**Westlander, G.**
How identify organizational factors crucial of VDU-health? A context-oriented method approach. 03741

**Westmore, R. J.**
A window-based graphics frame store architecture. HCI-0369 †

**Westof, E.**
An interactive modeling program for DNA. 02385

**Westrum, R.**
Management strategies and information failure. 03806

**Westwater, J.**
Starting end-users. 01215

**Wetherbe, J. C.**
Information technologies for the 1990's: an orgnizational impact perspective. 01336
Service support levels: An organizational approach to end-user computing. 02503
An empirical study of occupational stress, attitudes and health among information systems personnel. HCI-0451 †

**Wetherbe, J. C. (Ed.)**
Computer personnel research. § 02803

**Wetzel, G. F.**
Problems, problems, problems... 02407

**Wetzel, P.**
FINGER—Formalizing Interaction for Gesture Recognition. 01017

**Wetzenstein-Ollenschläger,**
Coding of information in man-computer systems based on cognitive task analysis. 03618

**Wexelblat, A.**
The tourist artificial reality. 0868

**Wexelblat, R. L.**
On interface requirements for expert systems. 01198
Programming Language design and Implementation. § 03058

**Weydert, J.**
Sites, modes, and trails: Telling the user of an interactive system where he is, what he can do, and how to get to places (excerpt). 0068

**Weyer, S. A.**
A prototype electronic encyclopedia. HCI-0278 †

**Whalen, T.**
Conversational hypertext: information access through natural language dialogues with computers. 0867

**Whalley, P.**
A general purpose computer aid to judgemental forecasting: Rationale and procedure. 01665

**Whang, K.**
Office-by-example: an integrated office system and database manager. 01159

**Wheelwright, C. D.**
Illumination requirements for operating a space remote manipulator. 03392

**Whinston, A.**
Temporal semantics and natural language processing in a decision support system. 02038

**Whinston, A. B.**
An analysis of human and computer decision-making capabilities 01951
Natural language query processing in a temporal database. HCI-0257 †

**Whinston, A. B. (Ed.)**
Decision support systems: theory and application. § 03788

**White III, C. C.**
ARIADNE: A knowledge-based interactive system for planning and decision support. 0661

**White, A.**
Dealing with disparate audiences in computer science courses using a project group within a traditional class. 01031

**White, C. A.**
An approach to a mathematics of phenomena: canonical aspects of reentrant form eigenbehavior in the extended calculus of indications. 01621

**White, C. C.**
A user preference guided approach to conflict resolution in rule-based expert systems. 01872

**White, C. C., III**
ARIADNE: a knowledge-based interactive system for planning and decision support. 01860

**White, G.**
Design issues of an intelligent workstation for the office. 03165

**White, G. M.**
Interactive timetabling in universities. 01501

**White, J. R. (Ed.)**
The history of personal workstations. § 03091

**White, K. B.**
Implementing computer-mediated communication technologies: a technoacceptance approach to critical mass utilization. 01931
Information systems development success: Perspectives from project team participants. 02501

**White, M. A.**
Preserving the integrity of the medium: a method of measuring visual and auditory comprehension of electronic media. 02084
Student evaluation of motivational and learning attributes of microcomputer soft. 02274

**White, N.**
Using restricted natural language for data retrieval: a plan for field evaluation. HCI-0255 †

**White, N. H.**
Advanced diagnostics: a PASCAL interactive system. 01958

**White, T. N.**
Factors influencing the detection of trend deviations on VDTs. 03894

**Whitehead, K.**
The ANALYST—A workstation for analysis and design. 02713

**Whiteside, J.**
Improving human-computer interaction—a quest for cognitive science. 0213
User performance with command, menu, and iconic interfaces. 0414
The role of laboratory experiments in HCI: help, hindrance, or ho-hum? 0863
User-derived impact analysis as a tool for usability engineering. 0922

**Whiteside, J. A.**
Classifying users: a hard look at some controversial issues. 0902

**Whitkey, E. A.**
Developing and running expert systems with PESYS. 01690

**Whitman, K. A.**
Union acceptance of automation technology: A case study. 03444

**Whitney, D.**
The evaluation of project support environments for the STARTS user guide. 0173

**Whitrow, R. J.**
A gesture based text editor. 03232

**Whittaker, A. D.**
Human intelligence models and their implications for expert system structure and research. 01242

**Whittaker, W. L.**
Evolution of a robotic excavator. 03569

**Whitten, W. B., II**
A general user interface for creating and displaying tree-structures, hierarchies, decision trees, and nested menus. HCI-0136 †

**Whittington, J.**
How would your favourite user model cope with these scenarios? 0999

**Wibom, R.**
Some physical factors at VDT work stations and ski problems. 03693

**Wibom, R. I.**
Work at video display terminals among office employees: visual ergonomics and lighting. 03718

**Wichansky, A.**
Voice: technology searching for communication needs. 0808
Usability testing in the real world. 0917

**Wickens, C. D.**
Attention. 0399
Display formatting in information integration and nonintegration tasks. 01750
Display proximity in multicue information integration: the benefits of boxes. 01763
Codes and modalities in multiple resources: a success and a qualification. 01793

**Widdel, H.**
Effect of visual presentation of different dialogue structures on human-computer interaction. 03768

**Widebäck, P. (Ed.)**
Work with display units 86. § 03676

**Widmeyer, G.**
Decision support for reasoning about values. 03486

**Widom, J.**
Whiteboards: a graphical database tool. HCI-0289 †

**Widrow, B.**
Neural nets for adaptive filtering and adaptive pattern recognition. 01362

**Wiecha, C.**
Generating highly interactive user interfaces. 0865
Separating content from form: A language for formatting on-line documentation and dialog. 02781

**Wiedenbeck, S.**
Beacons an initial program comprehension. 01014
Beacons in computer program comprehension. 02132
Learning iteration recursion from examples. 02215

**Wiejak, J.**
Towards computer vision. 0564

**Wielinga, B. J.**
Knowledge and expertise in expert systems. 03905

**Wiener, E. L.**
Fallible humans and vulnerable systems: lessons learned from aviation. 03808

**Wier, C. C.**
Protos: an examplar-based learning apprentice. 02210

**Wierwille, W. W.**
Effects of visual display and motion system delays on operator performance and uneasiness in a driving simulator. 01772

**Wigand, R. T.**
Integrated communications and work efficiency: impacts on organizational structure and power. 02031

**Wigert-Johnston, M. E.**
Color graphic displays for network planning and design. 0260

**Wiggins, E. S.**
Development of the wedding planner—extensions to reach a young audience. 01502

**Wiggins, R.**
Digital signal processor accelerators for neural network simulations. 02754

**Wightman, D. C.**
Part-task training strategies in simulated carrier landing final-approach training. 01741

**Wightman, F. L.**
Development of a three-dimensional auditory display system. 0980

**Wiginton, J. C.**
Designing screens for people to use easily. 01531

**Wilbur, S.**
A study of group interaction over a computer-based message system. 03257

**Wileden, J. C.**
Foundations for the Arcadia environment architecture. 01135

**Wilensky, R.**
Points: a theory of the structure of stories in memory. 0392
The Berkeley UNIX consultant project. 01355
LISPcraft. ● HCI-0023 †

**Wilfert, H. G.**
CAD/CAM: integration in the automobile industry. HCI-0413 †

**Wilhelm, R. (Ed.)**
ESOP 86. § 03883

**Wilhelms, J.**
Virya—a motion control editor for kinematic and dynamic animation. 03294

**Wilhelmson, R. B. (Ed.)**
High-speed computing: scientific applications and algorithm design. ● 0727

**Wilkins, A.**
Intermittent illumination from visual display units and fluorescent lighting affects movements of the eyes across text. 01713

**Wilkins, D.**
Using patterns and plans in chess. 0528

**Wilkins, D. C.**
Knowledge base refinement by monitoring abstract control knowledge. 02160

**Wilkins, P. R.**
Selection systems for sales representatives. 02408

**Wilkinson, M. A.**
The effects of entry arrangement in search times: a cross-generational study. 02048

**Wilks, A. R.**
Statistical software, graphics and future workstations for data analysis. 03316

**Willard, C.**
User services consulting supportr tools at the NASA numerical aerodynamic simula. 03161

**Willard, P.**
Microcomputer availability to public library clients. 02461

**Williams, A. R.**
The effects of gender and age on preschool children's choice of the computer as a child-selected activity. 02450

**Williams, A. S. (Ed.)**
Methodology of window management. § 03923

**Williams, D.**
On the selection and evaluation of visual display symbology: factors influencing search and identification times. 01718

**Williams, D. W.**
Coherent global motion percepts from stochastic local motions. 03329

**Williams, G.**
Verifying identity via keystroke characteristics. 02178
An empirical investigation of voice as an input modality for computer programming. HCI-0237 †

**Williams, M. D.**
The evolution of interface requirements for expert systems. 0431
What makes RABBIT run? HCI-0256 †

**Williams, M. E.**
Transparent information systems through gateways, front ends, intermediaries, and interfaces. HCI-0276 †

**Williams, P. S.**
Processing demands, training, and the vigilance decrement. 01723

**Williams, R. D.**
DIME: a programming environment for unstructured triangular meshes on a distributed-memory parallel processor. 02909

**Williams, T.**
Advanced computers. 01387
Windowlike user interfaces link systems and applications. 01388
A comparison of some window managers. 03925

**Williams, T. A.**
Beyond software ergonomics? Human control of automated systems. 03386

**Williams, T. J.**
One view of the future of industrial control. 01921

**Williford, J. D.**
Management of distributed applications in large networks. 03515
Grand computer conferencing: What have we learned? 03536

**Williges, B. H.**
System design for speech recognition and generation. 0065
An economical approach to modeling speech recognition accuracy. HCI-0354 †

**Williges, R. C.**
Assaying and isolating individual differences in searching a hierarchical file system. 01747
Accommodating individual differences in searching a hierarchical file system. 02212

**Willis, P.**
Graphical interaction management. 01390

**Willis, P. J.**
The controller animation system. 01402

**Willoughby, T. C.**
Male/female programmer and systems analyst Job performance. 03020

**Willshire, M. J.**
Human factors in teaching. 0989

**Willson, N. J.**
On the acquisition of object concepts from sensory data. 03959

**Wilpert, B.**
Social psychological prerequisites and consequences of new information technologies. 03631

**Wilpon, J. G.**
Improving speaker consistency in an automatic speech recognition framework. 01448

**Wilson Dr., D.**
Knowledge-based interface to manufacturing computer systems. 02966

**Wilson, D.**
Relevance: communication and cognition. ● 0704

**Wilson, E.**
Integrated information retrieval for law in a hypertext environment. 03071

**Wilson, G. A.**
Distributed database considerations in an expert system for radar analysis. 03175

**Wilson, G. V.**
Implementing neural network models on parallel computers. 01403

**Wilson, I.**
Problems associated with the off-line programming of robots. 01241

**Wilson, J. L.**
Extending knowledge-based systems through closely-coupled graphics and windows. 02985

**Wilson, M.**
Approximate modelling of cognitive activity: towards an expert system design aid. 0801
The elicitation of system knowledge by picture probes. 0921
Approximate modelling of cognitive activity with an expert system: a theory-based strategy for developing an interactive design tool. 01415
Navigating integrated facilities: initiating and terminating interaction sequences. 02876
Rapid prototyping of dialogue for human factors research: the EASIE approach. 03254
Using an expert system to convey HCI information. 03272

**Wilson, S.**
XVISION: a comprehensive software system for image processing research, education, and applications. 03124

**Wilson, T.**
"My user interface is the best because...". 0856

**Wilson, T. D.**
Professional education and subsequent careers in library/information work: a follow-up study of former students on the MA/MSc information studies course at the University of Sheffield. 02336

**Wilson, T. P.**
Uniforms: an automatic forms facility. 01628

**Wilton, J. A.**
User behaviour in computer networked groups. 0473

**Winarsky, N.**
Interactive data visualization. 01986

**Winder, J.**
The value of downloading for database users and database producers. 01218

**Winder, R.**
Modelling 8-bit microprocessors for a general-purpose simulator. 02499
JDB: an adaptable interface for debugging. 02628
Issues governing the suitability of programming languages for programming tasks. 03224

**Winder, R. (Ed.)**
People and computers III. § 03189
People and computers IV. § 03215

**Winder, R. L.**
An icon-driven end-user interface to UNIX. 02089

**Windsor, J. C.**
Documentation in a user work station environment. 02429

**Winer, E. A.**
Operator performance as a function of type of display: conventional versus perspective. 01769

**Winfree, D.**
Computer aids for vision and employment (CAVE). 0976

**Winiarski, M. E.**
What the help desk needs from you. 01633

**Winkel, J.**
On the significance of physical activity on sedentary work. 03704

**Winkelmann, B.**
Evaluating RECONSIDER: a computer program for diagnostic prompting. HCI-0410 †

**Winkler, C.**
Battling for new roles. 01664

**Winograd, T.**
A language/action perspective on the design of cooperative work (Reprint). 0383
Where the action is. 01301

**Winograd, T. (Ed.)**
Understanding computers and cognition. ● HCI-0054 †

**Winship, W. S.**
Ergonomic improvements boost AS/RS performance. 01904

**Winston, A. B.**
Flexible user interface decision support systems. 03473

**Winter, E.**
Requirements checklist for a system development workstation. 01144

**Winter, R.**
Neural nets for adaptive filtering and adaptive pattern recognition. 01362

**Winters, J. M.**
Muscle models: what is gained and what is lost by varying model complexity. 01251

**Wirfs-Brock, R.**
An integrated color smalltalk-80 system. 01127

**Wirth, K. D.**
SATURN—a tool for modelling and performance evaluation of computer systems. 02670

**Wise, J. A. (Ed.)**
Information systems: failure analysis. § 03804

**Wishart, J.**
Variations in user involvement with educational software. 01498

**Wishart, J. (Ed.)**
User involvement with microcomputer software. 04063

**Wisher, R.**
Development of a hand-held computerized vocabulary tutor. 02468

**Wisniewski, E. J.**
Software for neural networks. 0770

**Wisskirchen, P.**
Object-oriented graphics. 0234

**Withrow, R.**
Knowledge-based system for task analysis and reliability enhancement. 01516

**Witiak, J.**
What is the role of the intermediary in end-user training? 02522

**Witten, I. H.**
User interfaces for office systems. 0756
Inducing programs in a direct-manipulation environment. 0816
How users repeat their actions on computers: principles for design

## AUTHOR INDEX

of history mechanisms. 02885
A system for interactive viewing of structured documents. HCI-0400 †

**Wixon, D.**
Improving human-computer interaction—a quest for cognitive science. 0213
User performance with command, menu, and iconic interfaces. 0414

**Wixson, L. E.**
Automating knowledge acquisition for aerial image interpretation. 01470

**Wörg0tter, F.**
Quantitative determination of orientational and directional components in the response of visual cortical cells to moving stimuli. 01268

**Woelk, D.**
Data model issues for object-oriented applications. 0712
An object-oriented approach to multimedia databases. 01084
Data model issues for object-oriented applications. 01157

**Wohl, A. D.**
Designing advanced workstations. 0457

**Wojtowicz, J.**
Multimodal detection and recognition performance of sonar operators. 01709

**Wolf, A. L.**
Foundations for the Arcadia environment architecture. 01135

**Wolf, C. G.**
The role of laboratory experiments in HCI: help, hindrance, or ho-hum? 0863
The role of laboratory experiments in HCI: help, hindrance, or ho-hum? 0863
The use of hand-drawn gestures for text editing. 02151

**Wolf, D. J.**
Working with Lotus HAL: a 1-2-3 user's guide. ● 0731

**Wolf, G.**
Parcella '88: Fourth International Workshop on Parallel Processing by Cellular Automata and Arrays. § 03971

**Wolf, H.**
Further division of reintegration of mental labour? CAD/CAP and work in design and work preparation shops. 03385

**Wolfe, J.**
Team cohesion effects on business game performance. 02597

**Wolfe, O. B.**
User friendly micro computer program for solving fractional and linear programming problems. 01509

**Wolfe, R. F.**
Advanced interactive executive program development environment. 01816

**Wolff, T.**
Subjective load in introducing visual display units. 03627

**Wollberg, Z.**
Identification of MGB cells by Volterra kernels. III. A glance into the black box. 01259

**Wolovich, W. A.**
A multiprocessor system for real-time robotic control. 02023

**Wong, E.**
Figure-ground organization affects the early visual processing. 0021

**Wong, G.**
Multidimensional attribute analyhsis and pattern recognition for seismic interpretation. 02530

**Wong, J. S.**
Intelligent interfaces for secure multilevel database systems. 02990

**Wong, K. P.**
Sherlock—a system for diagnosing power distribution ring network faults. 02916

**Wong, S. K.S.**
Interactive timetabling in universities. 01501

**Wong, S. T.**
Extending knowledge-based systems through closely-coupled graphics and windows. 02985

**Wonsiewicz, S. A.**
How to tell people where to go: comparing navigational aids. 02096

**Woo, C. C.**
Role-based security in data base management systems. 03584

**Woo, G. C.**
Are there subtle changes in vision after use of VDTs? 03733

**Wood-Harper, A. T.**
Information systems definition: the Multiview approach. ● HCI-0085 †

**Wood, C. A.**
Experience with chisl, a configurable hierarchical interface specification language. 01397
Dynamic reconfigurability for fast prototyping of user interfaces. 02609

**Wood, C. C.**
The human immune system as an information systems security reference model. 01547

**Wood, M.**
An information retrieval system for software components. 01077

**Wood, M. (Ed.)**
The development of a postmodern self: a computer-assisted comparative analysis of personal documents. ● 0732

**Wood, P. T.**
An almost path-free very high-level interactive data manipulation language for a microcomputer-based database system. HCI-0261 †

**Wood, R. W.**
Systematic evaluation strategies for computer-based music instruction systems. 02275

**Woodbury, R. F.**
Strategies for interactive design systems. 0466

**Woodcock, J.**
Towards the formal specification of a simple programming support environment. 02607

**Woodman, M.**
A coherent specification method for the human interface to documentation systems. 0269

**Woodruff, C. K.**
Moderating effects of age, education, and tenure on the job satisfaction-job performance relationship. 03021

**Woods, D. D.**
Cognitive engineering in complex dynamic worlds. ● 0436
Cognitive technologies: The design of joint human-machine cognitive systems. 01193
Cognitive engineering: human problem solving with tools. 01781
Cognitive systems engineering: new wine in new bottles. 02078
Human interaction with an "intelligent" machine. 02163
Cognitive engineering in complex dynamic worlds. 02167
Visual momentum: a concept to improve the cognitive coupling of person and computer. HCI-0238 †

**Woods, D. J.**
Curve tailoring with interactive computer. 01209

**Woods, J. V. (Ed.)**
Fifth generation computer architectures. § 03586

**Woods, W. A.**
Knowledge representation. 0137

**Woods, W. A. (Ed.)**
Computer speech processing. ● 0287

**Woodson, W. E.**
Human factors reference guide for electronics and computer professionals. ● 0733
Human factors reference guide for electronics and computer professionals. ● 0734

**Woodward, B.**
Validation in a knowledge support system: construing and consistency with multiple experts. 02203

**Woodward, T.**
Information retrieval using micros. 01225

**Woolf, M.**
Constraint hierarchies. 01114

**Worley, D. R.**
A methodology, specification language, and automated support environment for com1uter-aided design systems. 04068

**Wormell, I. (Ed.)**
Knowledge engineering: expert systems and information retrieval. ● 0735

**Worona, S.**
An informal overview of CUINFO (Cornell's computer-based bulletin board). 02783

**Wozny, L. a.**
The application of metaphor, analogy, and conceptual models in computer systems. 02070

**Wray, S. C.**
Non-strict languages-programming and implementation. 01418

**Wright, G.**
A general purpose computer aid to judgemental forecasting: Rationale and procedure. 01665

**Wright, I.**
Identification and prevention of work-related mental and psycho-somatic disorders among two categories of VDU users. 03744

**Wright, M.**
Interactive video—a producer's medium. 0511

**Wright, P.**
Manual Dexterity: A user-oriented approach to creating computer documentation. 0085
Experience with contextual field research. 0802
Multi-window displays for readers of lengthy texts. 02142

**Wrobel, S.**
Design goals for sloppy modeling systems. 02206

**Wroe, B.**
Toward the successful design and implementation of computer based management information systems in small companies. 03256

**Wu, C. T.**
A new graphics user interface for accessing a database. 03839

**Wu, D. M.**
Goal-directed semantic tutor. 02919

**Wu, J.**
An interactive biomolecule graphics system. 02386

**Wu, W.**
A computer aided design system for artistic chinese fonts. 02455

**Wybranietz, D.**
Monitoring and performance measuring distributed systems during operation. 03025

**Wyle, M. F.**
A comparison of textual information retention from CRT terminals and paper. 0954

**Wysocki, E.**
Planning as feedback to designers. 02978

**Wyvill, B.**
Speech and expression: a computer solution to face animation. 03293

**Wyvill, G.**
Speech and expression: a computer solution to face animation. 03293

**Xia, J.**
An intelligent tutoring system for basic set theory. 02993

**Xu, Y.**
An acoustic-phonetic oriented system for synthesizing Chinese. 02661

**Yager, R. (Ed.)**
Uncertainty in knowledge-based systems. International Conference on Information. § 03822

**Yager, R. R.**
General multiple-objective decision functions and linguistically quantified statements. HCI-0110 †
Measuring the quality of linguistic forecasts. HCI-0247 †

**Yamaguchi, K.**
A document layout system using automatic document architecture extraction. 0882

**Yamahira, T.**
How map designers can represent their ideas in thematic maps: effective user interfaces for thematic map design. 03870

**Yamamoto, S.**
Characterization of VDT work. 03754

**Yamamoto, W. K.**
Design and implementation of the UW Illustrated compiler. 03059

**Yamamuro, S.**
An approach to knowledge elicitation in scheduling FMS: Toward a hybrid intelligent system. 03394

**Yamashita, D.**
Evaluating RECONSIDER: a computer program for diagnostic prompting. HCI-0410 †

**Yamazaki, T.**
Non-Reimannian approach to geometry of visual space: An application of affinely connected geometry to visual alleys and horopter. 02364

**Yan, X.**
The effects of the supervisor's knowledge in a complex automated system. 03366

**Yang, C.**
A computer aided design system for artistic chinese fonts. 02455

**Yang, D.**
A practical approach to transforming extended ER diagrams into the relational model. 02022

**Yang, S.**
Prototypes from standard user interface management systems. 01370
An acoustic-phonetic oriented system for synthesizing Chinese. 02661

**Yang, Y.**
A new conceptual model for interactive user recovery and command reuse facilities. 02884

Undo support models. HCI-0144 †
A user oriented design process for user recovery and command reuse support. HCI-0284 †

**Yankelovich, N.**
Connections in context: The intermedia system. 03534
Reading and writing the electronic book. HCI-0282 †

**Yano, H.**
Interactive fuzzy decision-making for multi-objective nonlinear programming using reference membership intervals. HCI-0295 †

**Yap, C. S.**
A survey of information technology in the U.K. service sector. 01916

**Yap, S.**
A grammar-based approach to automatic generation of user-interface dialogues. 02868

**Yasdi, R.**
An expert system for conceptual schema design: a machine learning approach. HCI-0335 †

**Yasukawa, H.**
Generating natural language responses appropriate to conversational situations—in the case of Japanese. 03922

**Yates-Mercer, P. A.**
Education and training in office technology. 02330

**Yates-Mercer, P. A. (Ed.)**
Future Trends in Information Science and Technology. § 04039

**Yates, G.**
Concept design of a program manager's decision support system. 0660

**Yates, K. E.**
Simulator design and instructional features for air-to-ground attack: a transfer study. 01804

**Yauda, M.**
Innovation of decision support system-matplan based on structure matrix supported by APL. 02800

**Yaverbaum, G. J.**
An evaluation of a realistic approach to MIS. 01027

Critical factors in the user environment: an experimental study of users, organizations and tasks. 02507

**Yazdani, M. (Ed.)**
Artificial intelligence and education; vol. 1: learning environments and tutoring systems. ● 0516
New horizons in educational computing. ● 0741
New horizons in educational computing. ● 0750

**Yeap, W. K.**
Towards a computational theory of cognitive maps. 01212

**Yekoye, A.**
Visuomotor control by a combined position- and speedservo. Theoretical considerations and experimental results in man. 02666

**Yemini, S.**
Interactive blackbox debugging for concurrent languages. 01134

**Yen, B. L.**
Determining 3-D motion parameters of a rigid body: a vector-geometrical approach. 03339

**Yeo, C.**
Knowledge base enhancements to relational databases. 03285

**Yeshurun, Y.**
Identification of MGB cells by Volterra kernels. III. A glance into the black box. 01259

**Yionoulis, S. M.**
APL: The language of science and management. 02799

**Yiquan, Z.**
The effects of the supervisor's knowledge in a complex automated system. 03366

**Yoda, H.**
An automatic wafer inspection system using pipelined image processing techniques. 01840

**Yoder, E.**
Collaboration in KMS, a shared hypermedia system. 0807
The data model is the heart of interface design. 02875

**Yong, Y.**
Handprinted chinese character recognition via neural networks. 02529

**Yoon, W. C.**
Aiding the operator during novel fault diagnosis. 01858

**York, B. W.**
An overview of T³-PBE. 0784

**Yoshida, N.**
An object-oriented framework of pattern recognition systems. 01133

**Yoshino, T.**
A practical natural language interface to databases. 0199

**Yound, M.**
Foundations for the Arcadia environment architecture. 01135

**Young, D. A.**
GI/S: A graphical user interface for symbolic computation systems. 02397

**Young, E. S.**
Man—machine interaction by voice: developments in speech technology. Part I: The state-of-the-art. 02331
Man—machine interaction by voice: developments in speech technology. Part 2: general applications and potential applications in libraries and information services. 02332

**Young, K.**
Off-line programming of robots using 3D graphical simulation system. 0602

**Young, L. F.**
The metaphor machine: a database method for creativity support. 01670
A systems architecture for supporting senior managers' messy tasks. 01928
Decision support systems for workers: a bridge to advancing productivity. 01947

**Young, M.**
XVISION: a comprehensive software system for image processing research, education, and applications. 03124

Design principles behind Chiron: a UIMS for software environments. 03511

**Young, R. L.**
A substrate for object-oriented interface design. 0691
An object-oriented framework for interactive data graphics. 01115

**Young, R. M.**
Programmable user models for predictive evaluation of interface designs. 0800
Design rationale: the argument behind the artifact. 0860
How would your favourite user model cope with these scenarios? 0999
Choosing between methods: analysing the user's decision space in terms of schemas and linear models. 02879
Planning in the context of human-computer interaction. 03213
GOMS meets STRIPS: the integration of planning with skilled procedure execution in human-computer interaction. 03243
A viewdata-structure editor designed around a task/action mapping. 03269

**Young, S.**
Managers who personally use information technology frequently: a profile of some invisible computer personnel. 03007

**Youngblood, G.**
The new renaissance: art, science and universal machine. 0530

**Younggren, G.**
Using an object-oriented programming language to create audience-driven hypermedia environments. 0101

**Yu, C.**
Plan-based representations of pascal and fortran code. 02897

**Yu, C. T. (Ed.)**
Research and development in information retrieval. § 03072

**Yu, K.**
Object lens: a "spreadsheet" for cooperative work. HCI-0206 †

**Yuen, P. E.J.**
Microcomputing in motion analysis. 02384

**Yuenger, P.**
A financial investment assistant. 03490

**Yui, H.**
Human aspects of QC circle movement in Japanese manufacturing: Natures and problems. 03450

**Yuille, A.**
An extremum principle for shape from contour. 0024
A method for computing spectral reflectance. 01267
Describing surfaces. 02699

**Yuille, A. L.**
Motion correspondence and analog networks. 02739

**Yuschik, M.**
A case example of human factors in product definition: needs finding for a voice output workstation for the blind. 0819

**Zaback, J.**
Planning for advising. 02886

**Zabusky, N. J.**
Coherent and chaotic structures in 2D vortex dynamics: progress and problems. 0729

**Zackin, A.**
Enhanced console driver. 01288

**Zacksenhouse, M.**
A prototype autonomous agent for crew and equipment retrieval in space. 02994

**Zadeck, F. K.**
Attribute propagation by message passing. 01100

**Zadeck, K.**
Graph attribution as a specification paradigm. 01138

**Zaki, M.**
Design of a graphics interface for computer-based biomedical applications. 01427
Linkage versus integration for binding database and interactive

graphics systems. 02040
Linkage versus integration for binding database and interactive graphics systems. 02406

**Zanden, B. T.**
Constraint grammars–a new model for specifying graphical applications. 0875

**Zawacki, R. A.**
Stress. 01651
Evaluating performance appraisal systems for IS personnel. 03011

**Zdobych, A.**
On the temporal stability of signal detection processes. 03617

**Zdravchev, L. (Ed.)**
Information technology and education: the changing school. ● 0282

**Zeevi, Y. Y.**
Neural computers in vision: processing of high dimensional data. 03960

**Zeier, H.**
Subject reports about musculoskeletal discomfort in VDU work as a complex phenomenon. 03708

**Zeigler, B. P.**
Hierarchical, modular discrete-event modelling in an object-oriented environment. 02588
Design of an AI-Based self-sustaining habitats control system. 02959
Hierarchical scheduling in an intelligent environmental control system. 02976

**Zeleznikar, A. P.**
Principles of information. 01597

**Zellweger, A.**
The FAA's Advanced Automation System: strategies for future air traffic control systems. 01357
Engineering the man-machine interface for air traffic control. 01358

**Zellweger, P. T.**
The structure of Cedar. 01109

**Zeltzer, D.**
Knowledge-based animation. 03351

Towards an integrated view of 3-D computer animation. 03859

**Zemankova, M.**
Implementing imprecision in information systems. HCI-0259 †

**Zemankova, M. (Ed.)**
Methodologies for intelligent systems. § 03026
Methodologies for intelligent systems. § 03633

**Zhaoyang, R.**
An interactive system SDI on microcomputer. 02272

**Zheng, Q.**
An interactive biomolecule graphics system. 02386

**Ziarko, W.**
An expert system for conceptual schema design: a machine learning approach. HCI-0335 †

**Ziegler, J. E.**
Learning and transfer for text and graphics editing with a direct manipulation interface. 0900

**Ziessler, M.**
Psychological methods for assembling procedures in text management systems. 03600

**Zimmer, A. C.**
Decision support using qualitative evidence. 03398
A model for the interpretation of verbal predictions. HCI-0316 †

**Zimmer, K. W.**
Assessment of mental load for different strategies of man-computer dialogue by means of the heart rate power spectrum. 03623

**Zimmer, W.**
Managing the design of user-computer interfaces. 0936

**Zimmerman, M.**
Are writers obsolete in the computer industry? 0109

**Zimmerman, R. L.**
Process control and people at General Motors' Delta Engine Plant. 01905
Process control and people at General Motors' Delta engine plant. 03431

**Zimolong, B.**
Evaluation of expert systems for decision support. 0244

**Zingler, K.**
POEM: An office system for international use. 03457

**Zini, P.**
Chinese character processing system based on character-root combination and graphic processing. 03187

**Zipser, D.**
Biologically plausible models of place recognition and goal location. 0639

**Zirk, D. A.**
Cognitive factors in user/expert-system interaction. 01733
Distributed tactical decisionmaking: conceptual framework and empirical results. 01885

**Zlatuška, J.**
An alternative approach to the conceptual database design using fragments of nat. 01481

**Zloof, M.**
Office-by-example: an integrated office system and database manager. 01159

**Zmud, R. W.**
Linking mechanism supporting end-user computing. 02806

**Zoeppritz, M.**
A framework for investigating language-mediated interaction with machines. HCI-0347 †

**Zoller, P.**
Determination of work contexts—an important aspect of future user interfaces. 01204

**Zolliker, M. L.**
Quill: An extensible system for editing documents of mixed type. 03517

**Zorkoczy, P. (Ed.)**
Oxford Surveys in Information Technology. ● 0753

**Zorkoczy, P. I. (Ed.)**
Oxford surveys in information technology; vol. 2, 1985. ● 0755

**Zuboff, S.**
In the age of the smart machine: the future of work and power. ● HCI-0083 †

**Zucker, S. W.**
The diversity of perceptual grouping. 0022
The fox and the forest: toward a type I/type II constraint for early optical flow. 03324
Computational networks in early vision: from orientation selection to optical flow. 03961

**Zuk, D.**
The effects of microcomputers on children's attention to reading. 01580

**Zunde, P.**
Development of a term association interface for browsing bibliographic data bases based on end users' word associations. HCI-0266 †

**Zurfluh, G.**
Advanced databases multi-media interface. 0418

**Zvegintzov, N. (Chair.)**
Conference on software maintenance–1985. § 03544

**Zwahlen, H. T.**
The design of a user friendly engineering economy analysis package for a microcomputer. 01507
The design of a user friendly interactive personal computer package for quality control charts, project management, and linear programming applications. 01521

**Zweben, S.**
The effects of program-dependent and program-independent deletions on software cloze tests. HCI-0175 †

**Zwick, R.**
Combining stochastic uncertainty and linguistic inexactness: theory and experimental evaluation of four fuzzy probability models. 02218

# Keyword Index

Each keyword in the title of the cited item is displayed in alphabetic order with the titles and identification numbers grouped underneath. The keyword has been extracted from the title and an asterisk appears in its place. This technique is sometimes called keyword out of context, or KWOC. The title is listed under each of the keywords; however not every word in the title is a keyword. Many common or uninformative words do not appear. For example, headings for "of," "computer," or "human" do not appear. To use the Keyword Index, think through the subject, determining the words to be searched that best define the major concepts. Think of spelling variants and alternative singular, plural and other grammatical forms. Consider whether related terms, more general, or more specific terms are associated with the concept. Then look up the words alphabetically, noting the identification number of each "hit." The full citations are available in the Bibliography. Items with an "HCI" number have reviews that can be located by number in the Review Section. A combination keyword and category search will improve the results of a subject search.

**ABILITIES**
A knowledge-based system for assessment of human physiological * in manual lifting tasks 01519

**ABILITY**
Self-organizing system obtaining communication * primitive model for language generation 01279
The relationship of problem-solving * and course performance among novice programmers HCI-0435 †

**ABORTION**
Birth defect, spontaneous * and work with VDUs 036880410

**ACADEMICS**
Electronic information systems analysis. Present and future information systems use by * involved in development studies 02323

**ACCELERATOR**
The use of the IBM personal computer in the man-machine interface to a nuclear research * 01454

**ACCELERATORS**
Digial signal processor * for neural network simulations 02754

**ACCENTUATION**
Ergonomics and organizational consulting: * or neglect of psychology 0242

**ACCESSIBILITY**
The dimensions of perceived * to information: Implications for the delivery if information systems and services 02448
Public Law 99-506, "Section 508" Electronic Equipment * for disabled workers 02893
The dimensions of * to online information: implications for implementing office information systems HCI-0304 †

**ACCESSIBLE**
Making computers * to disabled people 0094
Designing the "cockpit": the application of a human-centered design philosophy to make optimization systems * 01016

**ACCIDENT**
Modelling operators in * conditions: advances and perspectives on a cognitive model 02169
A study on safety evaluation index and industrial * analysis from the viewpoint of the safety confirmation type 03419
* analysis of blind production workers 03439
Factors in the investigation of human error in * causation 03805

**ACCIDENTS**
* at sea: multiple causes and impossible consequences 02168
Models of the decision maker in unforeseen * 02172
Ten fatal * due to robots in Japan 03406
Occupational * to the hand: A comparison of factory and nonfactory injuries 03438

**ACCOMMODATION**
Visual * and target detection in the vicinity of a window post 01802
Influence of CRT refresh rates on * aftereffects 03731

Effects on visual * and subjective visual discomfort from VDT work intensified through split screen technique 03735

**ACCOMPANIST**
The computer as musical * 0897

**ACCOMPANYING**
Understanding text with an * diagram 02947

**ACCORD**
Ashley,K. D.-But, see, *: generating blue book citations in HYPO 02770

**ACCUMULATOR**
The * model of two-choice discrimination 02371

**ACE**
*: a color expert system for user interf* design 03117

**ACKNOWLEDGE**
How well do we * intellectual debts? 02299

**ACM**
Hand-crafted hypertext-lessons from the * experiment 0128
* SIGUCCS User Services Conference XIV 01925
* SIGDOC '85 § 02780
ACTES/Proceedings Symposium 1988 * SIGSMAll/PC § 02787
The 1987 * SIGBDP-SIGCPR Conference § 03099

**ACOUSTICAL**
A machine for neural computation of * patterns with application to real time speech recognition 02751

**ACOUSTICS**
Merging * and linguistics in speech understanding 04004

**ACQUIRING**
Interactive learning: a multiexpert paradigm for * new knowledge 0776
Exploratory investigations in * and using information in interactive problem solving 03597

**ACQUISITION**
Principles from the psychology of skill * 0332
The * of grammar 0353
Improvement of the * of knowledge by informing feedback 0540
On language and connectionism: analysis of a parallel distributed processing model of language * 0590
Hypertext as a means for knowledge * 0777
Key factors in knowledge * 01019
The impact of menus and command-level feedback on learners' * of data base language skills 01041
Profile data * for the JCPDS-ICDD database s 01232
Automating knowledge * for aerial image interpretation 01470
Automated concept * in noisy environments 01841
* of process control skills 01878
A mixed-initiative workbench for knowledge * 02154
Conceptual models of interacitve knowledge * tools 02457
Student perceptions of skill * through cases and a general management simulation 02589
Precedent-based legal reasoning and knowledge * in contract law: A process model 02776
Automatic * of domain and procedural knowledge 02943
Generic diagnostic knowledge * tool 02944
Knowledge * and conceptual models: a cognitive analysis of the interface 03214
On one aspect of natural-language based knowledge * 03571
Knowledge * via a graphical interface 03572
Computer assisted knowledge *: towards a laboratory for protocol analysis of user dialogues 03603
An investigation of pictographic form in relation to mechanisms of knowledge * 03824
Textvision: elicitation and * of conceptual knowledge by graphic representation and multiwindowing 03902
On the * of object concepts from sensory data 03959
Fundamental issues of knowledge *: toward a human action perspective of knowledge systems 04057
* of control and domain knowledge by watching in a blackboard environment HCI-0319 †
KRITON: a knowledge-* tool for expert systems HCI-0327 †
Expertise transfer and complex problems: using AQUINAS as a knowledge-* workbench for knowledge-based systems HCI-0336 †

**ACT**
Hypermedia as an interpretive * 01806

**ACTEM**
The * model for decision modelling in a scene management system 02954

**ACTES**
*/Proceedings Symposium 1988 ACM SIGSMAll/PC § 02787

**ACTIVATION**
Modeling fault diagnosis as the * and use of a frame system 01729
Analysis of competition-based spreading * in connectionist models 02179

**ACTOR**
Action research on systems development: case study of changing * roles 0788

**ACTS**
Elements of a plan-based theory of speech * 0390

**ACTUATOR**
A study of intrinsic safety asymmetrical * 03422

**ACTUATORS**
Analogs of biological tissues for mechanoelectrical transduction: tactile sensors and muscle-like * 04014

**ACUITY**
The effects of target wavelength on dynamic visual * under photopic and scotopic viewing 01762

**ADA**
Interfacing * and relational databases 0762
*-embedded SQL: the options 0763
ADDS-a dialogue development system for the * programming language 02102
* info: apologies to TEXT_10 02395

# KEYWORD INDEX

The construction of information management system prototypes in * 02613
Program generation for *—a case study 02634
*-components: libraries and tools § 03180
Maintaining a uniform user interface for an * programming environment 04066
Selecting an * environment ● HCI-0015 †
*-based executable modelling of distributed systems HCI-0098 †
SKETCHER, an interactive, graphical * software tool—its development and use HCI-0100 †
*: first users—pleased; prospective users—still hesitant HCI-0159 †

## ADAPTATION
Making the transition from print to electronic encyclopaedias: * of mental models 02238
Machine * to psychological differences among users in instructive information exchanges with computers 03609

## ADAPTIVE
* general audience models: a research framework 0202
* control in human-machine systems 0405
Mental models and metaphors: implications for the design of *user-system interfaces 0539
A self-regulating * system 0829
The formal specification of * user interfaces using command language grammar 0925
* interface design: a symmetric model and a knowledge-based implementation 01091
Visual pattern recognition in humans: I. Evidence for * filtering 01274
Neural nets for * filtering and * pattern recognition 01362
The ART of * pattern recognition by a self-organizing neural network 01364
Experience with * interfaces 01417
A framework for designing * DSS Interfaces 01672
* aiding for human/computer control 01782

* user interfaces for planning and decision aids in C³I systems 01887
Building and understanding * systems: a statistical/numerical approach to factory automation and brain research 01890
Hidden patterns in combined and * knowledge networks 02073
* command prompting in an on-line documentation 02121
User-* computer graphics 02209
An interface architecture to provide * task-specific context for the user 02228
Personal computer training software for * control 02262
* information systems control: A reliability-based approach 02345
* coordination of a learning team 02475
Speech motor control and stuttering: a computational model of *sensory-motor processing 02655
Development and sensitivity analysis of * predictor for human eye movement model 02681
Multimodal response planning: an * rule based approach 02894
Task-oriented parsing - a diagnostic method to be used * systems 02896
An evaluation of the effectiveness of the * interface module (AIM) in matching dialogues to users 03212
User-driven * behaviour, a comparative evaluation and an inductive analysis 03226
Design and evaluation of the AID * front-end to Telecom Gold 03260
Design of individual * man-computer dialogues in the hybrid intelligence systems 03400
Experimentation with an * search strategy for solving a keyboard design/configuration problem 04070
Experimental * interface HCI-0139 †

## ADDRESSABLE
Collective computation, content-* memory, and optimization problems 0004
A self-optimizing, nonsymmetrical neural net for content * memory and pattern recognition 02562

## ADDRESSATION
Algebraic approach to the problem of * 01488

## ADE
AWB-*: an application development environment for interactive, integrated systems 03051

## ADJUSTMENT
Task and the * of ergonomic chairs 03711

## ADMINISTRATOR
UNIX system V: release 3.0 Intel 80286/80386 computer version: system *'s guide ● 0031

## ADMINISTRATORS
Self-efficacy expectations as a predictor of computer use: a look at early childhood * 01590

## ADOLESCENTS
*' chunking of computer programs 01586
Using interactive videotaped-based instruction to teach on-the-job social skills to handicapped * 02288

## ADOPTING
* interactive videodisc technology for education 0272

## ADOPTION
Teachers' * of multimedia technologies for science and mathematics instruction 0577
Forecasting consumer * of information technology and services—lessons from home video forecasting 02451
Effects of the * of an integrated online system on a technical services department 02463
Communications technology and the public sector: understanding the process of * 02679
Strategies for encouraging successful * of office communication systems HCI-0307 †

## ADVANCE
A study of an * organizer as a technique for teaching computer programming concepts 01042

## ADVANTAGE
A framework of composite information systems for strategic * 03465

## ADVENTURE
The * of getting to know a computer 0088

## ADVERTISING
Online use and end-users in media and *: an overview 01216

## ADVICE
How some * fails 0824
Interface design issues for *-giving expert systems 01321
Computing * at a distance: the 'remote advisory' concept 02617
Justified *: a semi-naturalistic study of advisory strategies 02887
On the application of rule-based techniques to the design of * giving systems HCI-0315 †
What do users ask? Some thoughts on diagnostic * HCI-0326 †

## ADVISOR
Jet engine technical * (JETA) 02974
An operations * for an on-line computer banking system with graphics interface 02983
*—an electronic mail consulting service 03151

## ADVISORS
Developing the technology for intelligent maintenance * 02276

## ADVOCATIONS
Software ergonomics: * & applications for the human computer interface ● 0193

## AERIAL
Automating knowledge acquisition for * image interpretation 01470

## AERODYNAMIC
User services consulting supportr tools at the NASA numerical * simula 03161

## AESA
Recent results on the application of a metric-space search algorithm (*) to multispeaker data 03997

## AESTHETICS
Color in user interface design: functionally and * 0803
Experience of programming beauty: some patterns of programming * 02184
An aspect of * in human-computer communications: pretty windows HCI-0213 †

## AFFINELY
Non-Reimannian approach to geometry of visual space: An application of *connected geometry to visual alleys and horopter 02364

## AFIPS
* Conference Proceedings; vol. 55 1986 National Computer Conference § 03162

## AFLC
Design of a control room for the air force logistics command (*) command, control,and communication and intelligence ($C^3I$) system 01612

## AFLOAT
Staying *—a collective enterprise 01147

## AFTEREFFECTS
Contingent * and isoluminance: psychophysical evidence for separation of color, orientation, and motion 01463
Influence of CRT refresh rates on accommodation * 03731

## AFTERTHOUGHT
Information development is part of product development—not an * 0103

## AGENTS
Deals among rational * 0170
Algebra slaves and * in a Logo-based mathematics curriculum 0517
Intelligent software * 01303
The subjective ascription of belief to * 03553

## AGV
* safety system designed for preventing hazardous human contact 03423

## AI
* development and the Office of Naval Research 0140
Parallel computers for * databases 0183
POP-11: an * programming language 0748
What * practitioners should know about the law, part 2 01197
*/learn: an interactive videodisk system for teaching medical concepts and reasoning 02381
The responsive system: a new challenge for * 02920
Experience of constructing a fault localisation expert system using an *toolkit 02923
Applications of an * design shell ENGINEOUS to advanced engineering products 02932
Design of an *-Based self-sust*ning habitats control system 02959
Embedded tr*ning in * technology through an expert system interface: an alarm processor application 02991
Causes of motivational problems among * managers 03004
Problems among managers of * personnel 03460
Automated document distribution using * based workstations and knowledge based servers 03466
A consideration of learning in speech recognition from the viewpoint of *class-description learning 03533
A comprehensive guide to * and expert systems ● HCI-0058 †
Applications of * in engineering HCI-0321 †

## AID
Approximate modelling of cognitive activity: towards an expert system design * 0801
The role of menu titles as a navigational * in hierarchical menus 0888
ER model clustering as an * for user communication and documentation in database design 01331
The architecture of an inexpensive and portable talking-tactile terminal to *the visually handicapped 01452
ORGPLAN an information-decisive * system to resolving organizing problems 01573
A general purpose computer * to judgemental forecasting: Rationale and procedure 01665
Design of user-system interfaces using a cognitive design * 01682
Display legibility guidelines: a design * 01983
How can computer-based visual displays * operators? 02162

A process oriented approach to an intelligent design * 02980
The travel metaphor as design principle and training * for navigating around complex systems 03195
Design and evaluation of the * adaptive front-end to Telecom Gold 03260
Computer-based microworlds—a definition to * design HCI-0432 †

## AIDS
Navigational * and learning styles: structural optimal training for computer users 0970
Computer * for vision and employment (CAVE) 0976
Comprehensino * for on-line reading of expository text 01798
Adaptive user interfaces for planning and decision * in $C^3I$ systems 01887
A knowledge-based system with audio-visual * 02068
How to tell people where to go: comparing navigational * 02096
Cognitive * in process environments: prostheses or tools? 02161
Trust between humans and machines, and the design of decision * 02164
Intelligent *, mental models, and the theory of machines 02171
Structural displays as learning * 02188
A study of user interface * for model-oriented decision support systems 02479
Pictures and category labels as navigational * for catalog browsing 02877
New technology work * for the physically disabled 03273
Voice-input * for the physically disabled HCI-0089 †

## AIP
Establishing structures of requirements for the application of automated information processing (*)—an approach for the development of computer-aided systems 03660

## AIR
The FAA's Advanced Automation System: strategies for future * traffic control systems 01357
Engineering the man-machine interface for * traffic control 01358
Design of a control room for the * force logistics command (AFLC) command, control, and communication and intelligence ($C^3I$) system 01612
Performance measurement during simulated *-to-* combat 01787
Simulator design and instructional features for *-to-ground attack: a transfer study 01804
Information in the * and in the wave 03146
Error auditing in * traffic control 03810

## AIRCRAFT
Production control in the * industry 0624
Spatial requirements for visual simulation of * at real-world distances 01768

## AIRLINE
Perspective traffic display format and * pilot traffic avoidance 01748

## AIRWAYS
Learning in British *-A case of putting people first 02572

## AISIM
Automated interactive simulation modeling system: * 02399

## AIX
Advanced interactive executive (*) operating system overview 01815
* usability enhancements and human factors 01817

## ALARMS
A study of auditory warning * evaluation for automated guided vehicles 03424

## ALERTNESS
Long workdays versus restdays: assessing fatigue and * with a portable performance 01778

## ALGEBRA
* slaves and agents in a Logo-based mathematics curriculum 0517

Experimental data for the design of a microworld-based system for * 0543
Procedural and non-procedural query languages revisited: a comparison of relational * and relational calculus 02146
Human performance in relational *, tuple calculus, and domain calculus 02208
Iris: design of a user interface program for symbolic * 03081
MathScribe: a user interface for computer * systems 03082
Iris: design of an user interface program for symbolic * 03085
MathScribe: a user interface for computer * systems 03086
Applicable *, error-correcting codes, combinatorics and computer * § 03846
Integration of graphical tools in a computer * system 03847
Applied *, algorithmics and error-correcting codes § 03848

## ALGEBRAIC
* approach to the problem of addressation 01488
Symsac '86—Proceedings of the 1986 symposium on symbolic and *manipulation § 03084

## ALGEBRAS
* for nested relations 01623

## ALGORITHMIC
The * approach in ergonomics: the case of optimal colours and ambients for display work 0247
Computing text constituency: an * approach to the generation of text graphs HCI-0267 †

## ALGORITHMICS
Applied algebra, * and error-correcting codes § 03848

## ALIEN
*: a programming environment generator for personal computers 02790

## ALKAHEST
* III: automatic analysis of periodic weakly nonlinear ODEs 03087

## ALLEYS
Non-Reimannian approach to geometry of visual space: An application of affinely connected geometry to visual * and horopter 02364

* on an apparent frontoparallel plane 02374

## ALLOCATION
Task * between humans and robots in manufacturing 0559

ICE: information center expert: a consultation system for resource * 0781

Optimal * of a work force in a toxic substance environment 01534

The spatial * of visual attention as indexed by event-related brain potentials 01739

Two simulation studies investigating means of human-computer communication for dynamic task * 01882

An empirical comparison of model-based and explicit communication for dynamic human-computer task * 02109

Human supervisory control in flexible manufacturing systems: * of functions and system size 02456

A consultation system for information center resource * 03100

Humane: A designer's assistant for modeling and evaluating function *options 03397

Job organization and * of functions between man and computer: I analysis and assessment 03628

Job organization and * of functions between man and computer: II.job organization 03629

Psychological principles for * of functions in man-robot system 03630

A methodology for dynamic task * in man-machine system 03635

## ALPHABETIC
Dialing a name: * entry through a telephone keypad 0973

## ALPHANUMERIC
Evaluating formatted * displays 01525

Formatting * crt displays 02140

## AMATEUR
Computer graphics: A tool for the artist, designer and * 0235

## AMBIENTS
The algorithmic approach in ergonomics: the case of optimal colours and * for display work 0247

## AMIGA
The MAGNEX text editor for the Comodore * personal computer 0782

## AMNESIA
* and distrubuted memory 0641

## AMPLITUDE
Beyond heart rate in the cardiac psychophysiological assessment of mental effort: the T-wave * component of the electrocardiogram 01738

## AMT
Towards a framework for identifying organizationally-compatible * 03372

## ANALOG
A single-board Forth computer with versatile * I/O circuitry 02308

Optical * of two-dimensional neural networks and their application in recognition of radar targets 02733

Motion correspondence and * networks 02739

## ANALOGICAL
Training by exploration: facilitating the transfer of procedural knowledge through * reasoning 02103

* program synthesis from program components 03920

* problem solving ● HCI-0044 †

## ANALOGS
Higher pole correction in vocal tract models and terminal * 02657

* of biological tissues for mechanoelectrical transduction: tactile sensors and muscle-like actuators 04014

## ANALOGY
A heuristic program to solve geometric-* problems 0299

The application of metaphor, *, and conceptual models in computer systems 02070

* and other sources of difficulty in novices' very first text-editing 02148

A framework of a mechanical translation between Japanese and English by *principle HCI-0353 †

## ANALYSIS
Multidimensional attribute * and pattern recognition for seismic interpretation 02530

## ANALYSING
Choosing between methods: * the user's decision space in terms of schemas and linear models 02879

* the scope of cognitive models in human-computer interaction: a trade-off approach HCI-0245 †

## ANALYST
Differences in *'s attitudes towards information systems development: evidence and implications 01935

Education requirements for the entry level business systems * 02409

The *—A workstation for analysis and design 02713

Legal data modeling: The prohibited transaction exemption * 02779

The systems * of the 1990's 02998

Male/female programmer and systems * Job performance 03020

Handling textual information in a GDSS database: experience with the Arizona * information system 03475

Open versus closed minds: the effect of dogmatism on an *'s problem-solving behavior HCI-0446 †

## ANALYSTS
The effects of task differences on the work satisfaction, job characteristics, nd role perceptions of programmer/a* 02359

Making computer tasks at work more playful: Implications for systems *and designers 03005

An investigation of the effectiveness of communication between systems *and end users in the design of large computer systems 04075

## ANALYZERS
Generative systems of * 01461

Generative systems of * 02702

**ANALYZING**
* intention in utterances 0391
* and improving VDU working conditions: workers' education 03751
* the high frequency bugs in novice programs HCI-0178 †

**ANIMAL**
Interactive design of 3D computer-animated legged * motion 01828

**ANIMATING**
GMB: a tool for manipulating and * graph data structures 02636
* human figures: perspectives and directions 03291
High performance interactive graphics: modeling, rendering and * for IBM PCs and compatibles ● HCI-0071 †

**ANIMATION**
Algorithm * ● 0186
Principles of traditional * applied to 3D computer * 01072
The controller * system 01402
Color, graphics, and * in a computer-assisted learning tutorial lesson 02294
Perspectives on algorithm * 02861
The interactive specification of human * 03292
Speech and expression: a computer solution to face * 03293
Virya—a motion control editor for kinematic and dynamic * 03294
Knowledge-based * 03351
ANIMENGINE: an engineering * system 03858
Towards an integrated view of 3-D computer * 03859
Tree doctor, a software package for graphical manipulation and * of tree structures 03901

**ANIMATOR**
A multiple track * system for motion synchronization 03350

**ANIMENGINE**
*: an engineering animation system 03858

**ANS**
Talking it over: the natural language dialog system HAM-* 0165

**ANSWERING**
Using "word-knowledge" reasoning for question * 0131
Responding to "HUH?": * vaguely articulated follow-up questions 0825
Natural language interface to the question-* system for physicians 01478
How to recognize interesting topics to provide cooperative * 02043
A temporal logic for reasoning about changing data bases in the context of natural language question-* 03176

**ANTHROPOLOGY**
Culture, cognitive, and connectionism: Towards an hermeneutic * of mind 04077

**ANTHROPOMORPHIC**
Initial work on a system-independent computer model of a 3D *dummy 01476

**ANTIALIASING**
On the parameters of human visual performance: an investigation of the benefits of * 0799

**ANTICIPATING**
* compact disc-interactive (CD-I): ten guidelines for prospective authors 0280
* false implicatures: cooperative responses in question-answer systems 03178

**ANTIDOTE**
Computer ethics: an * to despair 0791

**ANXIETY**
Investigating computer * in an academic library 02047
Computer *: sex, race and age 02133
Simulations and * related to public speaking 02592
Impact of system response t..ne on state * HCI-0228 †
Computer * in management: myth or reality? HCI-0232 †

**APL**
*: a problem-oriented introduction ● 0230
Bringing graphic dialogues to * 0765
* in transition § 02793

Design of a new user interface for * 02796
*: The language of science and management 02799
Innovation of decision support system-matplan based on structure matrix supported by * 02800
A dataflow-based * for the hypercube 02905

**APL2**
Increasing productivity with ISPF/* 0767
Application screen management: an * approach 02794

**APL88**
* § 02797

**APOLLO**
* domain series 3000 01170

**APOLOGIES**
Ada info: * to TEXT_10 02395

**APPARENT**
Alleys on an * frontoparallel plane 02374
Correspondence in * motion: defining the heuristics 03308
Real and * motion: one mechanism or two? 03328

**APPLICANTS**
The case of the rejected * 02438

**APPRENTICE**
Protos: an examplar-based learning * 02210

**APPRENTICES**
The programmer's *: a research overview 01368

**APPROPRIATENESS**
Truth versus *: relating declarative to procedural knowledge 0484

**APPROXIMATE**
* modelling of cognitive activity: towards an expert system design aid 0801
* modelling of cognitive activity with an expert system: a theory-based strategy for developing an interactive design tool 01415
The accuracy of * string matching algorithms 02279
* spatial reasoning 02917
Algorithms for * string matching HCI-0180 †

## APPROXIMATION
Diffusion * of the neuronal model with synaptic reversal potentials 01254
Short-term memory as a metastable state.III. Diffusion * 01611
Qualitative * methodology for modeling and simulation of large dynamic systems: Applications to a Marine power plant 01900
Interactive curve drawing by segmented Bezier * with a control parameter 02535
* methods used in the exchange of geometric information via the VDA/VDMA surface interface HCI-0421 †

## APSE
Ecilpse—an * based on PCTE 03181

## AQUINAS
Expertise transfer and complex problems: using * as a knowledge-acquisition workbench for knowledge-based systems HCI-0336 †

## ARAB
A study of * computer users: a special case of a general HCI methodology 04031

## ARCADIA
Foundations for the * environment architecture 01135

## ARCANE
From * ASCII to the printed page - computer basics 01148

## ARCHITECTURAL
An * approach to improved program maintainability 02627
* implications of office systems 03356

## ARCHITECTURE
Diamond: a multimedia message system built on a distributed *(Reprint) 0380
Diamond: A multimedia message system built on a distributed * 0574
Connectionism and cognitive *: a critical analysis 0589
A conceptual * for generalized decision support system software 0659
An expert system * for computer-aided control engineering 0662

An * of a distributed window system and its FCP implementation 0676
A document layout system using automatic document * extraction 0882
PLEXACT: an * & design of a knowledge-based system for information systems development 01020
Foundations for the Arcadia environment * 01135
The * of an inexpensive and portable talking-tactile terminal to aid the visually handicapped 01452
Organizational humanity and *: Duality and complementarity of papa-logic and mama-logic in managerial conceptualizations of change 01609
The role of practice in dual-task performance: toward workload modeling in a connectionist/control * 01790
An * for a business and information system 01818
A graphics system * for interactive application-specific display functions 01822
HutWindows: an improved * for a user interface management system 01830
A systems * for supporting senior managers' messy tasks 01928
An interface * to provide adaptive task-specific context for the user 02228
Dynamics and * for neural computation 02270
Experience with a functional layered multicomputer * for interactive processing 02402
Communications and * & protocols § 02801
An * for a multimedia teleconferencing system 02802
SAUCI: a knowledge-based interface * 02895
A blackboard * for problem solving and machine learning in an expert system for power system voltage control 02926
A mission planning * for an autonomous vehicle 02939
DORUS: an * for dynamic optimal resource utilization systems 02979

The * of a user interface toolkit 03110
An * for active DSS 03480
A natural language interface for expert systems: system * 03551
CAD and robotics in * and construction § 03568
Display * for VLSI-based graphics workstations 03786
Parallel in sequence—towards the * of an elementary cortical processor 03820
TRON Project 1987—Open-* computer systems § 03821
HutWindows: an improved * for a user interface management system 03854
* working group discussions 03938
* working group final report 03939
Control of sensory processing - a hypothesis on and simulation of the * of an elementary cortical processor 03972
On the * for pictorial information systems 03977
Intelligent interfaces for information retrieval systems: * problems in the construction of expert systems for document retrieval 04042
The * of fifth generation inference computers HCI-0093 †
* problems in the construction of expert systems for document retrieval HCI-0272 †
Knowledge based systems versus thesaurus : an * problem about expert systems design HCI-0323 †
O-Plan: control in the open planning * HCI-0362 †
A window-based graphics frame store * HCI-0369 †

## ARCHITECTURES
Neural network * for artificial intelligence ● 0434
* of graphic processors for interactive 2D graphics 01395
Application of neural network algorithms and * to correlation/tracking and identification 02734
VLSI * for implementation of neural networks 02762
Multicomputer * for real-time perception 03341
Fifth generation computer * § 03586

# KEYWORD INDEX [ARTIFICIAL]

Looking at workstation * from the viewpoint of interaction 03787
Parallel algorithms and * § 03819
* for production systems: an inside look for those who study human-computer interaction 03906
DEC networks and * ● HCI-0003 †

## ARES
*: a relational database with the capability of performing flexible interpretation of queries HCI-0248 †

## ARGUMENT
Design rationale: the * behind the artifact 0860

## ARGUMENTATIVE
Design environments for constructive and * design 0864

## ARIADNE
*: A knowledge-based interactive system for planning and decision support 0661
*: a knowledge-based interactive system for planning and decision support 01860

## ARISTOTELIAN
A deductive database based on * logic 02398

## ARISTOTLE
Participation–from * to today 0499

## ARITHMETIC
* codes resembling neural encoding 02021
Computer analysis of students' procedural "bugs" in an * domain 02273
User-oriented suggestions for floating-point and complex-* Forth standard extensions 02306

## ARMY
U.S. * field robotics focus and key technology issues 03402

## ARRAY
Q'Nial: a portable interpreter for the nested interactive * language, Nial 02635
Multi-Input fuzzy inference engine on a systolic * 02953
Parameter estimation in * processing 04021

## ARRAYS
Parcella '88: Fourth International Workshop on Parallel Processing by Cellular Automata and * § 03971

## ARRHYTHMIA
Spectral analysis of sinus *: a measure of mental effort 01737

## ARROW
An experimental comparison of a mouse and *-jump keys for an interactive encyclopedia 02098

## ART
User interfaces in C: programmer's guide to state-of-the-* interfaces ● 0351
Designing end-user interfaces: state of the * report 15.8 ● 0422
The new renaissance: *, science and universal machine 0530
The * of adaptive pattern recognition by a self-organizing neural network 01364
Man—machine interaction by voice: developments in speech technology. P* I: The state-of-the-* 02331
Pregnancy and VDT work—an evaluation of the state of the * 03686
Computer-generated images: the state of the * § 03856
A comparison of the effects of computer-assisted instruction, interactive video, and traditional instruction on third-grade students in * education 04064
The * of programming HCI-0095 †

## ARTICULATING
* the experience of transparency: an example of field research techniques 0977

## ARTICULATION
Influence of palate shape on lingual * 02642

## ARTICULATORY
X-ray microbeam method for measurement of * dynamics-techniques and results 02641
Estimating * motion from speech wave 02643
Structure of German syllable initial and final consonant clusters based on * features 02652

## ARTIFACT
* as theory-nexus: hermeneutics meets theory-based design 0798
Design rationale: the argument behind the * 0860

## ARTIFACTS
The polarisation approach to intelligent * 02714

## ARTIFICIAL
Expert systems and * intelligence ● 0133
Distributed * Intelligence ● 0168
On knowledge base management systems: integrating * intelligence and d atabase technologies ● 0180
Perspectives in * intelligence vol. 2: machine translation, NLP, databases and computer-aided instruction ● 0198
* intelligence and its applications ● 0221
Readings in cognitive science: a perspective from psychology & *intelligence ● 0223
Visual information processing: * intelligence and the sensorium of sight 0300
* intelligence and statistics ● 0321
Knowledge, skill and * intelligence ● 0342
Human factors and * intelligence 0408
* intelligence programming environments ● 0420
Neural network architectures for * intelligence ● 0434
C/C++ for expert systems: "unleashes the power of a * intelligence" ● 0439
Knowledge-based systems, * intelligence and human factors 0449
* intelligence and instruction: Applications and methods ● 0468
Parallel computation and computers for * intelligence ● 0488
Application of the butterfly parallel processor in * intelligence 0489
* intelligence techniques in language learning ● 0500
* intelligence and education; vol. 1: learning environments and tutoring systems ● 0516
* worlds and real experience 0518

Experiencing * intelligence: an interactive approach to the IBM PC ● 0550
Experiencing * intelligence: an interactive approach for the APPLE ● 0551
Readings in * intelligence and software engineering ● 0612
* intelligence and expert systems ● 0665
* intelligence & human learning: intelligent computer-aided instruction ● 0671
* intelligence systems 0683
Exploring * intelligence ● 0692
The tourist * reality 0868
Why * intelligence isn't (yet) 01175
* intelligence techniques in man–machine communication 01459
How can cognitive psychology help solve an * intelligence problem? 01480
An industrial chemical hazards database with a natural language interface: an application of * intelligence 01533
* intelligence and natural language systems 01541
The effects of sources of applications programs on user satisfaction: an empirical study of micro, mini & mainframe computers using an interactive * intelligence expert-system 01601
* intelligence in the man/machine interface 01626
Language and * intelligence conference report 01688
Natural * languages: low level processes 02082
User-supported * intelligence 02602
Nonlinear dynamics of * neural systems 02747
* Intelligence and Law § 02764
Industrial & Engineering Applications of * Intelligence & Expert Systems § 02910
Industrial & Engineering Applications of * Intelligence & Expert Systems § 02941
Industrial & Engineering Applications of * Intelligence & Expert Systems: vol. I § 02967
* intelligence techniques applied to maintenance management 02971

Industrial & Engineering Applications of * Intelligence & Expert Systems: vol. II § 02982
IR-NLI II: applying man-machine interaction and * intelligence conceptsto information retrieval 03070
Interfacing image processing and computer graphics systems using an *visual system 03301
Common and uncommon issues in * intelligence an psychology 03312
Advances in * intelligence § 03546
Progress in * intelligence § 03555
* Intelligence and Information-Control systems of Robots-87 § 03570
Knowledge representation techniques in * intelligence: an overview 03900
* intelligence and cognitive psychology: a new look at human factors 03904
Relational models in natural and * vision 03953
Gas sensors: towards an * nose 04015
* and human intelligence § HCI-0052 †
Man-made minds: the promise of * intelligence ● HCI-0055 †
An * intelligence approach to legal reasoning ● HCI-0061 †
* behavior: computer simulation of psychological processes ● HCI-0073 †
* intelligence and tutoring systems: computational and cognitive approaches to the communication of knowledge ● HCI-0080 †

**ARTIST**
Computer graphics: A tool for the *, designer and amateur 0235

**ARTS**
The computer revolution and the * ● 0529

**ASCII**
From arcane * to the printed page - computer basics 01148

**ASCRIPTION**
The subjective * of belief to agents 03553

**ASKING**
Negative knowledge towards a strategy for * in logic programming 02115

What "question-* protocols" can say about the user interface 02130
Question * when learning a text-editing system 02202

**ASL**
Intelligible encoding of * image sequences at extremely low information rates 02708

**ASSAYING**
* and isolating individual differences in searching a hierarchical file system 01747

**ASSEMBLING**
Psychological methods for * procedures in text management systems 03600

**ASSEMBLY**
Conceptualizing in * tasks 01776
Unexpected motion hazard exposures on a large robotic * 03409
Human aspects of automated * lines 03445

**ASSERTIONS**
Controlling bias in user * in expert decision support systems for problem formulation 02343

**ASSESSOR**
A workstation * for crew operations-WOSTAS 02093

**ASSIGNING**
Mechanisms of sentence processing: * roles to constituents 0635

**ASSIGNMENT**
Prosodic features in German speech: stress * by man and machine 03989

**ASSIGNMENTS**
A conceptual dependency network approach to multi-task * in man-machine (teleoperated) systems 03388

**ASSIMILATION**
Neural network model with rhythm-* capacity 01881

**ASSISTING**
Help systems-* the user 01201

**ASSISTIVE**
100 Percent assured performance for robotic * devices for handicapped and elderly persons 03414

## ASSOCIATION
Directed graph representations of * structures: A systematic approach 01862

Development of a term * interface for browsing bibliographic data bases based on end users' word * HCI-0266 †

## ASSOCIATIONS
Development of a term association interface for browsing bibliographic data bases based on end users' word * HCI-0266 †

## ASSOCIATIVE
The relation between linguistic structure and * theories of language learning models: constructive critique of some connectionist learning models 0591

Constructing an * memory 01289

Left-* grammar: an informal outline 01558

Electronic implementation of * memory based on neural network models 01895

Pattern storage and * memory in quasi-neural network 02537

High order correlation model for * memory 02729

Nonlinear discriminant functions and * memories 02757

## ASSUMPTIONS
Investigating sources of error in the management of crises: theoretical * and a methodological approach 03807

## ASSURED
100 Percent * performance for robotic assistive devices for handicapped and elderly persons 03414

## ASYMMETRIC
Speech responses and dual-task performance: better time-sharing or *transfer? 01789

Memory networks with * bonds 02740

## ASYMMETRICAL
A study of intrinsic safety * actuator 03422

## ASYMMETRY
Error correction and * in a binary memory matrix 02750

## ASYNCHRONOUS
Task-oriented representation of * user interfaces 0851

Line connectivity algorithms for an * pyramid computer 01468

## ATHENA
How to manage educational computing initiatives-lessons from the first five years of Project * at MIT 0125

## ATLANTIS
*—a software simulator for behavior analysis of protocol specificationsand their target implementations 02667

## ATLAS
A colour * for graphical displays 03726

## ATTACK
Simulator design and instructional features for air-to-ground *: a transfer study 01804

The end user *: Will the real computer professionals stand up and fight 02424

## ATTACKING
* a complex distributed algorithm from different sides: an experience wih complementary validation tools 01429

## ATTITUDE
How effective is interactive video in improving performance and * 0278

Change, * to change, and decision support system success HCI-0296 †

## ATTRACTION
Basins of * in a perceptron-like neural network 01340

## ATTRIBUTE
* propagation by message passing 01100

An interactive outranking system for multi-* decision making 01539

A probabilistic dominance measure for binary choices: analytic aspects of a multi-* random weights model 02372

Multidimensional * analyhsis and pattern recognition for seismic interpretation 02530

## ATTRIBUTES
Maintained and constructor * 01099

Relations and * 01103

Rough sets and dependency analysis among * in computer implementations of expert's inference models 02231

Student evaluation of motivational and learning * of microcomputer soft 02274

Effects of decision support training and cognitive style on decision process * 02346

Implementing a user interface as a system of * 03052

A study of managerial computer users: the impact of user sophistication on decision structure and * of decision-related information (end user) 04078

Cognitive *: implications for display design in supervisory control systems HCI-0242 †

## ATTRIBUTION
Graph * as a specification paradigm 01138

## AUDIENCE
Using an object-oriented programming language to create *-driven hypermedia environments 0101

Adaptive general * models: a research framework 0202

Development of the wedding planner—extensions to reach a young * 01502

## AUDIO
A knowledge-based system with *-visual aids 02068

Employing voice back channels of facilitate * document retrieval 03045

The microcomputer as a classroom * visual device: the concept, and prospects HCI-0223 †

## AUDITING
Error * in air traffic control 03810

## AUDITORY
Acoustic phonetics, * phonetics, speaker sex and speech recognition: a thread 0288

An experiment into the use of * cues to reduce visual workload 0877

Development of a three-dimensional * display system 0980

Preserving the integrity of the medium: a method of measuring visual and * comprehension of electronic media 02084

Modelling blind users' interactions with an * computer interface 02237

A computer model of peripheral * processing incorporating phase-locking, suppression and adaptation effects 02650

An evaluation of * performances in patients with Cochlear implants 02658

A layered neural network model applied to the * system 02763

The design of * interfaces for visually disabled users 02869

A study of * warning alarms evaluation for automated guided vehicles 03424

## AUGMENT
Authorship provisions in * (Reprint) 0370

## AUGMENTATION
A conceptual framework for the * of man's intellect (Reprint) 0368

Project Nick: meetings * and analysis HCI-0156 †

## AUGMENTED
The * knowledge workshop 03094

## AUGMENTING
A research center for * human intellect HCI-0334 †

## AUTHOR
Technology and the *'s labour 02574

## AUTHORING
Reflections on *, editing, and managing hypertext 0119

* tools for complex document sets 0120

* systems for ICAI 0469

Videotex information packagers: a field study aimed at tomorrow's videotex * interface 0962

An * system for the creation of interfaces for disabled users 0974

* considerations for hypertext 01679

*: a guide to the design of instructional software ● HCI-0031 †

## AUTHORITY
User interaction with the * structure of the online catalog: results of a survey 02049

## AUTHORIZATION
Self-*: A characteristic of some elements in certain self-organizing systems 01610

## AUTHORS
Anticipating compact disc-interactive (CD-I): ten guidelines for prospective * 0280

## AUTHORSHIP
* provisions in AUGMENT (Reprint) 0370

## AUTOASSOCIATIVE
Influence of noise on the behavior of an * neural network 02727

## AUTOCAD
The * productivity book: tapping the hidden power of *: 2nd edition ● 0668

The * productivity book: tapping the hidden power of * ● HCI-0076 †

## AUTOCOMPLETION
* in full text transaction entry: a method for humanized input 0934

## AUTOEPISTEMIC
On the relation between default and * logic 01214

## AUTOMATA
Parcella '88: Fourth International Workshop on Parallel Processing by Cellular * and Arrays § 03971

Pushdown * for user interface management HCI-0382 †

Selective networks and recognition * HCI-0390 †

## AUTOMATED
* construction of interactive learning programs in Modula-2 01500

* concept acquisition in noisy environments 01841

The * solution of logic puzzles 02015

A semantic data model as the basis for an * database design tool 02036

* interactive simulation modeling system: AISIM 02399

Retrieval systems for the information seeker: can the role of the intermediary be * 02864

The development of an * flight test management system for flight test planning and monitoring 02928

* design and analysis system for design of custom orthopedic implants 02931

Ergonomics of Hybrid * Systems I § 03362

The effects of the supervisor's knowledge in a complex * system 03366

Sources of Difficulty in troubleshooting * manufacturing systems 03367

Designing hybrid * manufacturing systems: A European perspective 03382

Beyond software ergonomics? Human control of * systems 03386

Critical issues in the safety of software-dominant * systems 03416

A study of auditory warning alarms evaluation for * guided vehicles 03424

Acting-out and burn-out behaviours of operators monitoring * systems 03440

The social cybernetics of human interaction with * systems 03442

Human aspects of * assembly lines 03445

* document distribution using AI based workstations and knowledge based servers 03466

The control structure diagram: an * graphical representation for software 03524

Personality traits of the worker within the :20man-machine" system at * production 03593

Designing learning processes for work activities in * technologies 03605

Establishing structures of requirements for the application of *information processing (AIP)—an approach for the development of computer-aided systems 03660

A methodology, specification language, and * support environment for com1uter-aided design systems 04068

The ethics of * publishing systems (a response to Dr. Brockmann) HCI-0170 †
The * tutoring of introductory computer programming HCI-0438 †

## AUTOMATICITY
*, resources, and memory: theoretical controversies and practical implications 01792

## AUTOMATING
* interfaces in a software system ● 0701
* the design of graphical presentations of relational information 01150
* knowledge acquisition for aerial image interpretation 01470
Human factors in * manufacturing systems in India 03446

## AUTOMATIZING
* geometric proofs and constructions 03851

## AUTOMOBILE
CAD/CAM: integration in the * industry HCI-0413 †

## AUTONOMOUS
* scene description with range imagery 02707
A mission planning architecture for an * vehicle 02939
A prototype * agent for crew and equipment retrieval in space 02994

## AUTONOMY
The silent force of the screen. A research note on the impact of microelectronics on work * among clerical workers in public administration 01437

## AVAILABILITY
Microcomputer * to public library clients 02461

## AVERAGED
Estimating reliability with small samples: increased precision with *correlations 01728

## AWARENESS
Developing * of computer ethics 03010
What * isn't: a sentential view of implicit and explicit belief 03560

## AWB
*-ADE: an application development environment for interactive, integrated systems 03051

## AWK
Natural language interface based on keyword extraction using * 02498
The * programming language ● HCI-0020 †

## AXIOMATIC
Comments on "formal specification of user interfaces: a comparison and evaluation of four * approaches" 01847

## AXIS
Determining the instantaneous * of translation from optic flow generated by rbitrary sensot motion 03332

## BACKGROUND
The * of INTERNIST I and QMR 02853
Improving the VDU workplace by introducing a physiologically optimized bright-* screen with dark characters: advantages and requirements 03721

## BAILING
Still sailing (and *): managing unexpected change in user support 03150

## BALANCE
End-user computing environments—finding a * between productivity and control 01927
3-D * in legged locomotion: modeling and simulation for the one-legged case 03352

## BALL
The crystal * of research: how to use it to learn about the user community 03135

## BALLISTIC
Extending Kohonen's self-organizing mapping algorithms to learn *movements 03967

## BALLYHOO
Colour graphics—Blessing or * 0061

## BALSA
Exploring algorithms using *-II 01367

## BANK
NLI-ESD: An expert natural language interface to a statistical data * 02712

## BANKING
An operations advisor for an on-line computer * system with graphics interface 02983
Equipment and workstation design for * services 03712

## BANKS
Two-level data * for translators 01556

## BARGAINING
The effects of * orientation and communication medium on negotiations in the bilateral monopoly task: a comparison of decision room and computer conferencing communication media 0809

## BARRIER
The foreign language *: a study among pharmaceutical research workers 02333

## BARRIERS
Communication * in microcomputer—based courses 01319
* to plant transparency, * to plant rigidity—A sketch of the problems posed by the radical changes in work forms in the machine-building industry 01562
* to factory automation 01906
* to cooperative computerized circulation systems in public libraries 02573

## BASES
Are machines as good as people in drawing conclusions from knowledge represented in catalogues, data * and expert systems? 0736
Intelligent interfaces to Nordic data * 0738
KIWI: knowledge-based user-friendly system for the utilization of information * 0739
Natural language querying of historical data * 01354

Structuring knowledge * for designers of learning materials 01807
New applications of data * § 02710
Informational zooming: an interaction model for the graphical access to text knowledge * 03073
An interactive data dictionary facility for CAD/CAM data * 03174
A temporal logic for reasoning about changing data * in the context of natural language question-answering 03176
Pictorial knowledge * 03201
Pictorial interfaces to data * HCI-0116 †
Development of a term association interface for browsing bibliographic data * based on end users' word associations HCI-0266 †

**BASIC**
Effect of practice on knowledge and use of * Lisp 0210
Information processing today, with applications and * ● 0569
Information processing today, with applications and *: updat 87/88 ● 0570
Principles of information processing with applications and * ● 0572
VAX-* with structured problem solving: 2nd edition ● 0725
A simple windowing system, part 1: * principles 01286
Windows for * 01292
Dialogue cell resource model and * dialogue cells 01400
MINID—a * program to assist in the optical identification of minerals in thin section 01505
An intelligent tutoring system for * set theory 02993
Sensitivity to light and visual strain in VDT operators: * data for the design of work stations 03732
Programming in * or Logo: effect on critical thinking skills 04062

**BASICS**
Back to *: Simple but high-quality text pagination systems 0271
From arcane ASCII to the printed page - computer * 01148

**BASINS**
* of attraction in a perceptron-like neural network 01340

**BAT**
* brushes: on the uses of six position and orientation parameters in a paint program 0846

**BATCH**
Plant scheduling expert system for * processing 02977

**BAYESIAN**
Understanding * reasoning via graphical displays 0884

**BCC180**
The * multitasking controller part 3: memory management and windowing 01295

**BCS**
* human—computer interaction conference 01922

**BEACONS**
* an initial program comprehension 01014
* in computer program comprehension 02132

**BEAMS**
Application of decision support system on sandwich *, verified by experiments 01572

**BEAUTY**
Experience of programming *: some patterns of programming aesthetics 02184

**BEHAVIORAL**
Telecommuting the organizational and * effects of working at home ● 0596
Problem solving: a * interpretation 01582
A * approach to information retrieval system design 02304
The 1984 Olympic Message System: a test of * principles of system design HCI-0125 †
* experiments on handmarkings HCI-0201 †

**BEHAVIORS**
Encapsulating interactive * 0874
Motivations and * of software professionals 03003

**BEHAVIOUR**
User * in computer networked groups 0473

Modelling novice programmer * 0744
Modelling novice programmer * 0751
Cooperative * in the FIDO system 02041
Subject searching * at the library catalogue and at the shelves: implications for online interactive catalogues 02302
Retrieval based on user * 03068
User-driven adaptive *, a comparative evaluation and an inductive analysis 03226
Intentional and operational aspects of decision * and their modelling 03666

**BEHAVIOURAL**
How and when to collect * data 0050
Statistical evaluation of * data 0051
* and organisational factors involved in the turnover of high tech professionals 01024
A logic-functional approach to the execution of CCS specifications modulo * equivalences 03874

**BEHAVIOURS**
Acting-out and burn-out * of operators monitoring automated systems 03440

**BEINGS**
Knowledge-based systems and communication between computers and human * 0192

**BELIEF**
Extension of conditional probability and measures of * and dis* in a hypothesis based on uncertain evidence 01846
Study of combination of * intevals in lattice-structured networks 02223
The subjective ascription of * to agents 03553
What awareness isn't: a sentential view of implicit and explicit * 03560
The distributed processing of knowledge and * in the human brain HCI-0240 †

**BEN**
* Shneiderman, Oct. 5,12: user interface strategies '88 ● 0685

# KEYWORD INDEX [BLACKBOARD]

## BENCHMARK
How are windows used? Some notes on creating an empirically-based windowing * task 0903

## BENEFIT
Cost/* analysis for incorporating human factors in the software lifecycle HCI-0127 †

## BERKELEY
The * UNIX consultant project 01355

## BEZIER
Interactive curve drawing by segmented * approximation with a control parameter 02535

## BIAS
Assessing gender * in computer software 01591
Controlling * in user assertions in expert decision support systems for problem formulation 02343

## BIASES
SmartSLIM: a DSS for controlling * during problem formulation 0203
Cognitive * and corrective techniques: proposals for improving elicitation procedures for knowledge-based systems 02153

## BIBLIOGRAPHIC
A common interface for accessing document retrieval systems and dbms for retrieval of * data 01990
Development of a term association interface for browsing * data bases based on end users' word associations HCI-0266 †
Testing * displays for online catalogs HCI-0285 †

## BIBLIOGRAPHY
*: Individual differences and computer-human interaction 0890
An annotated * on user interface design 01004
* of software tools for user interface development 01071
The proteus *: Representation and interactive display in databases 01085
Indexes and * ● HCI-0068 †

## BICUBIC
A simple, general method for ray tracing * surfaces 03853

## BIFURCATION
* analysis of oscillating network model of pattern recognition in the rabbit olfactory bulb 02725

## BILATERAL
The effects of bargaining orientation and communication medium on negotiations in the * monopoly task: a comparison of decision room and computer conferencing communication media 0809

## BINARY
* jargon: the metaphoric language of computing 01044
A probabilistic dominance measure for * choices: analytic aspects of a multi-attribute random weights model 02372
Error correction and asymmetry in a * memory matrix 02750
A flexible and intelligent system for fast measurements in * images for in-line robotic control 03986

## BINDING
Linkage versus integration for * database and interactive graphics systems 02040
Linkage versus integration for * database and interactive graphics systems 02406

## BINDINGS
Computer graphics language *: programmer interface standards 01473

## BINOCULAR
The psychophysical function of * space perception 02375
VDU work, refractive errors and * vision 03739

## BIOLOGICAL
Parallel distributed processing: explorations in the microstructures of cognition; Vol. 2: Psychological and * models ● 0629
Information compression in * systems 01253
* aspects of neural nets 02311
Analogs of * tissues for mechanoelectrical transduction: tactile sensors and muscle-like actuators 04014

## BIOLOGICALLY
* plausible models of place recognition and goal location 0639

## BIOMECHANICAL
* evaluation of lifting tasks: a microcomputer-based model 01524

## BIOMECHANICS
A hand * workstation 02820

## BIOMEDICAL
Design of a graphics interface for computer-based * applications 01427
Recollections on the processing of * signals 02846

## BIOMOLECULE
An interactive * graphics system 02386

## BIOSIS
How good an Online searcher are you? Twenty questions about * previews 02521

## BIPARTY
A * grammar as a tool for defining a man-machine dialogue 03639

## BISECTION
Neural networks and NP-complete optimization problems; a performance study on the graph * problem 01339

## BIT
Modelling 8-* microprocessors for a general-purpose simulator 02499
Two-* graphics HCI-0372 †

## BITMAP
A library for incremental update of * images 02836

## BITMAPPED
System aspects of low-cost * displays 03932
A window manager for * displays and Unix 03933

## BLACK
Refining early design decisions with a *-box model 03200

## BLACKBOARD
The programmable * model of reading 0632
A * architecture for problem solving and machine learning in an expert system for power system voltage control 02926

711

Acquisition of control and domain knowledge by watching in a *environment HCI-0319 †

**BLACKBOX**
Interactive * debugging for concurrent languages 01134

**BLIND**
A user interface for deaf-* people (preliminary report) 0794
A case example of human factors in product definition: needs finding for a voice output workstation for the * 0819
Computing for the * user 01287
How technology brings * people into the workplace 01705
Modelling * users' interactions with an auditory computer interface 02237
Accident analysis of * production workers 03439
Psychological aspects on * peoples's reading of radio-distributed daily newspapers 03700

**BLINKING**
Designing optimum CRT text * video image presentation 0795

**BLOCKS**
Mathematical building * 01173
Continuous processing of images through user sketched functional * 01399

**BNCOD**
Proceedings of the fourth British national conference on databases (* 4) § 03282
Proceedings of the Fifth British National Conference on Databases (* 5) § 03284

**BNCOD3**
Proc. of the third British national conference on databases (* § 03279

**BNETD**
*—A modelling tool to computer systems performance evaluation 02668

**BOARD**
A single-* Forth computer with versatile analog I/O circuitry 02308
The marble company: The design and implementation of a simulation * game 02595

Computer * Forum 02685
An informal overview of CUINFO (Cornell's computer-based bulletin * 02783

**BOARDS**
Computer aided concurrent design for printed wiring * 02981

**BOAT**
Charting the course of a user survey that will rock the * 03136

**BODIES**
How do the experts do it? The use of ethnographic methods as an aid to understanding the cognitive processing and retrieval of large * of text 03063

**BODY**
A system for the representation of human * movement from dance scores 02540
The * in question: how to stay healthy at the PC 02548
Determining 3-D motion parameters of a rigid *: a vector-geometrical approach 03339

**BOILER**
A compact model of a power house * 02683

**BOLTZMANN**
Higher-order * machines 02760

**BONDS**
Memory networks with asymmetric * 02740

**BOOLEAN**
Disjunctive models of * category learning 01262
Rule-based reasoning as * transformations 01901
A menu interface to formulate * logic-can it be done? 02034
STATUS with IQ—escaping from the * straitjacket 02569

**BOTTLENECK**
User interfaces: gateway or * ● 0142
Using hypertext to overcome the knowledge base development *: a case study 02914

**BOTTLES**
Cognitive systems engineering: new wine in new * 02078

**BOUNDARIES**
Effects of graphic * in tabular displays: a human factors evaluation 01526

**BOUNDARY**
Selection and use of image features for segmentation of * images 03305

**BOUNDED**
A new algorithm for extracting the interior of * regions based on chain coding 01469

**BOXER**
*: a reconstructible computational medium HCI-0121 †

**BOXES**
Display proximity in multicue information integration: the benefits of * 01763

**BRAILLE**
An intelligent * display device 01832

**BRAIN**
Vision, *, and cooperative computation ● 0014
Vision, *, and cooperative computation: an overview 0015
Neurophilosophy: toward a unified science of the mind-* ● 0219
Uncertainty analysis of human EEG spectra: A multivariate information theoretical method for the analysis of * activity 01270
Electric and magnetic fields of the * computed by way of a discrete systems analytical approach: Theory and validation 01276
Computers on the *, part 1 01296
Computers on the *, part 2 01298
Neural computing: ideas from the * 01379
* research: theory and experiment 01575
Ordinals and the hemispheres of the * 01620
The spatial allocation of visual attention as indexed by event-related *potentials 01739
Building and understanding adaptive systems: a statistical/numerical approach to factory automation and * research 01890
A boy and his * machine 02575
The UCLA * Research Institute data processing laboratory 02844
The distributed processing of knowledge and belief in the human * HCI-0240 †

Reverse engineering the *
HCI-0368 †
**BRAINS**
Tensor geometry: a language of * & neurocomputers. Generalized coordinates in neuroscience & robotics 03966
*, machines, and mathematics (2nd ed.) • HCI-0034 †
**BRAINSTORMING**
Information requirements specification II: * collective decision-making technique 02005
**BRANCH**
A comparative study of subject searching in an OPAC among * libraries of a university library system 02050
**BRANCHING**
A scaling model for dichotomous * processes 01264
**BREADTH**
Effects of *, depth and number responses on computer menu search performance 02192
The depth/* trade-off in the design of menu-driven user interfaces HCI-0135 †
**BREAKTHROUGHS**
Computer-supported cooperative work: * for user acceptance 02874
**BRIDGE**
Decision support systems for workers: a * to advancing productivity 01947
IBM DOS 4.0: a * to OS/2 02523
**BROCKMANN**
The ethics of automated publishing systems (a response to Dr. * HCI-0170 †
**BRODERBUND**
* Software, Inc. v. Unison World, Inc. 648 F. Supp. 1127 (1986). 01477
**BROWSABLE**
Improved * displays for online subject access 02051
**BROWSER**
Visual system * 0995
The user interface in a hypertext, multiwindow program * 02072
A graphical entity-relationship database * 03532

The filter * defining interfaces graphically 03792
**BROWSING**
Online text retrieval via * 01999
Tools for reading and * hypertext 02014
Support for * in an intelligent text retrieval system 02240
Design of a multi-media vehicle for social * 02822
Adding * semantics to the hypertext model 02834
Pictures and category labels as navigational aids for catalog * 02877
* within time-driven multimedia documents 03046
Video * and system response time 03203
A comparison of hypertext, scrolling and folding as mechanisms for program * 03235
Display strategies for program * 03545
A visual approach to * in a database environment HCI-0258 †
Development of a term association interface for * bibliographic data bases based on end users' word associations HCI-0266 †
**BRUSHES**
Bat *: on the uses of six position and orientation parameters in a paint program 0846
**BRUSHING**
* scatterplots 02672
**BTRON**
The software structure of extended nucleus based on * specification 03494
**BUFFER**
A two-dimensional frame * processor 0494
A multi-processor workstation with a logic-enhanced distributed frame * 0496
Design and implementation of a supercomputer frame * system 03543
**BUGS**
Toward a theory of computer program *: an empirical test 02216
Analyzing the high frequency * in novice programs HCI-0178 †

**BUIDLING**
Tools for * interfaces 01426
**BUILD**
* your own user interface 01419
How to * a help desk that floats 03148
**BUILDING**
Computer-aided model * 0544
* expert systems: cognitive emulation • 0700
Constraint-based tools for * user interfaces 01153
Mathematical * blocks 01173
* a self-modifying user interface 01424
* and understanding adaptive systems: a statistical/numerical approach to factory automation and brain research 01890
* a great windows system 02550
* user interfaces before writing code saves time and money 02662
* interfaces interactively 03119
* user interfaces by direct manipulation 03120
On * future decision support systems 03472
* a visual designer's environment 03496
* interprocess communication models using Stile 03528
The designer as user: * requirements for design tools from design practice HCI-0129 †
**BULB**
Nonlinear dynamics of pattern formation and pattern recognition in the rabbit olfactory * 02558
Bifurcation analysis of oscillating network model of pattern recognition in the rabbit olfactory * 02725
**BULLETIN**
An informal overview of CUINFO (Cornell's computer-based * board) 02783
**BURN**
Acting-out and *-out behaviours of operators monitoring automated systems 03440
**BUTTERFLY**
Application of the * parallel processor in artificial intelligence 0489

## C++

C/* for expert systems: "unleashes the power of a artificial intelligence" ● 0439

## CABLE

Understanding * subscribership as telecommunications behavior 02676

## CAD

Intelligent * systems II: implementational issues ● 0006
Multi-media presentation in * systems 0007
A definitive programming approach to the implementation of * software 0008
Product and process design in intelligent * workstations 0009
* data exchange 0237
* Based Programming for Sensory Robots ● 0597
Robot simulation and off-line programming—an integrated CAE-* approach 0599
* Based verification and refinement of high level compliant motion primitives 0600
Modeling of robot system dynamics for * based robot programming 0605
*-based off-line programming applied to a cleaning and deburring workstation 0607
Intelligent * systems I: theoretical and methodological aspects ● 0715
A multiparadigm user interface for intelligent * systems 0716
Claris * 01310
Standardization aspects on software for * of control systems 01565
* system GISK for interactive graphical modelling of planar mechanisms 01570
Interactive */CAM in engineering industry 01571
Graphics fundamentals for a PCB-* PC system 02494
GCI—a tool for developing interactive * user interfaces 02625
* Data management using object-oriented paradigms 02958
Incorporating the human factor in color * systems 03104
An interactive data dictionary facility for */CAM data bases 03174
The application of cognitive psychology to * 03239
Further division of reintegration of mental labour? */CAP and work in design nd work preparation shops 03385
Health and productivity issues of */CAM systems 03436
* and robotics in architecture and construction § 03568
Recent results on the illumination of VDU and * workstations 03719
Qualified * work: an intensive case study 03763
Product data interfaces in */CAM applications: design, implementation and experiences § 03981
Implementation of a VDA interface in the * system STRIM 100 03983
Modern drafting: an introduction to * ● HCI-0077 †
*/CAM: integration in the automobile industry HCI-0413 †
An approach to * system performance evaluation HCI-0414 †
Goals in the application of * interfaces HCI-0416 †
Interfaces for * applications HCI-0418 †

## CADCAM

Successful use of *—a combination of technology, organization, and people 01569

## CADD

Job characteristic perceptions of manual drafting and *: A field study of the effects of computerization on drafting & design personnel 01523

## CADME

The * approach to the interface of solid modellers 03867

## CAE

Robot simulation and off-line programming—an integrated *-CAD approach 0599
Computer-aided engineering (*) for system analysis 0663

## CAI

Mathematical formula editor for * 0885
Human factors in * design 01494
A regression model to identify successful learner traits with * 02376

## CAL

A flexible synonym interface with application examples in * and help environments 01404
Introducing *: a practi* guide to writing computer-assisted learning programs ● HCI-0079 †

## CALCULATION

Visual information chunking in spreadsheet * 02232
Some design principles for a mathematical knowledge representation system: a new approach to scientific * 03849

## CALCULUS

An approach to a mathematics of phenomena: canonical aspects of reentrant form eigenbehavior in the extended * of indications 01621
Procedural and non-procedural query languages revisited: a comparison of relational algebra and relational * 02146
Human performance in relational algebra, tuple *, and domain * 02208

## CALENDAR

The user interface of a personal * program HCI-0286 †

## CALENDARS

Electronic * in the office: an assessment of user needs and current technology HCI-0287 †

## CALIBRATING

* databases HCI-0269 †

## CALLISTO

*: an intelligent project management system (Reprint) 0375

## CAM

Interactive CAD/* in engineering industry 01571
An interactive data dictionary facility for CAD/* data bases 03174
Health and productivity issues of CAD/* systems 03436

# KEYWORD INDEX [CBIS]

Low cost geometric modelling system for * 03866
Product data interfaces in CAD/* applications: design, implementation and experiences § 03981
CAD/*: integration in the automobile industry HCI-0413 †

**CAMERA**
Evaluating the impact of * placement on teleoperator efficiency 02940

**CAMERAS**
Active vision: integration of fixed and mobile * 04017

**CAMP**
Computer-aided modeling and planning (* HCI-0415 †

**CAMPUS**
An empirical study of user satisfaction with a microcomputer-based *-wide 03137
A suppport strategy for users of a *-wide local area network 03157

**CANONICAL**
An approach to a mathematics of phenomena: * aspects of reentrant form eigenbehavior in the extended calculus of indications 01621

**CAP**
Further division of reintegration of mental labour? CAD/* and work in design nd work preparation shops 03385

**CAPTIVE**
*...a new tool 03129

**CAPTURE**
Capturing the * concepts: a case study in the design of computer-supported meeting environments 02824

**CAR**
Production control in * industry 0623

**CARDIAC**
Beyond heart rate in the * psychophysiological assessment of mental effort: the T-wave amplitude component of the electrocardiogram 01738

**CARDIOVASCULAR**
Performance in cognitive tasks and * parameters as indicators of mental load 03624

**CAREER**
Job histories as predictors of * success in management information systems 01021

**CAREERS**
Professional education and subsequent * in library/information work: a follow-up study of former students on the MA/MSc information studies course at the University of Sheffield 02336

**CAREING**
* for users at Syracuse University 03134

**CARRIER**
Part-task training strategies in simulated * landing final-approach training 01741
Design and implementation of an interactive optimization system for network design in the motor * industry 02528

**CARTOGRAPHY**
Color and the computer in * HCI-0386 †

**CAS**
End-user searching of * ONLINE. Results of a cooperative experiment between Imperial Chemical Industries and Chemical Abstracts Services 02269

**CASUALTIES**
EPVM: An expert patient-ventilator manager for chemical warfare * 02956

**CATALOG**
User interaction with the authority structure of the online *: results of a survey 02049
The user's mental model of an information retrieval system: an experiment on a prototype online * 02099
Online library * systems: an analysis of user errors 02128
Pictures and category labels as navigational aids for * browsing 02877

**CATALOGS**
Testing bibliographic displays for online * HCI-0285 †

**CATALOGUES**
Are machines as good as people in drawing conclusions from knowledge represented in *, data bases and expert systems? 0736
Subject searching behaviour at the library catalogue and at the shelves: implications for online interactive * 02302
The computer as mask: a problem of inadequate human interaction examined with particular regard to online public access * 02337
Online library * as information retrieval systems: what can we learn from research? 04040

**CATCHING**
* knowledge in neural nets 01171

**CATEGORIES**
Human specifics fuzzy * and counteraction in decision making problems 01696
Creating * for databases 02149
Induction of *: The problem of multiple equilibria 02360
Color-coding * in menus 02872
The lexicon, grammatical * and temporal reasoning 03549
Identification and prevention of work-related mental and psycho-somatic disorders among two * of VDU users 03744

**CATEGORY**
Disjunctive models of boolean * learning 01262
Pictures and * labels as navigational aids for catalog browsing 02877

**CAUSAL**
A closed-loop * model of workload based on a comparison of fuzzy and crisp measurement techniques 01746

**CAUSALITY**
* and maximum entropy updating 02076

**CAUSATION**
Factors in the investigation of human error in accident * 03805

**CBIS**
Educating the * user: a case analysis 0778

## CCS
A logic-functional approach to the execution of * specifications modulo behavioural equivalences 03874

## CCT
Can cognitive complexity theory (*) produce an adequate measure of system usability? 03229

## CEDAR
The structure of * 01109
Integration mechanisms in * 01110

## CELL
Dialogue * resource model and basic dialogue * 01400

## CELLS
Identification of MGB * by Volterra kernels. III. A glance into the black box 01259
Quantitative determination of orientational and directional components in the response of visual cortical * to moving stimuli 01268
Dialogue cell resource model and basic dialogue * 01400
A comparison of algorithms for neuron-like * 02752

## CELLULAR
Parcella '88: Fourth International Workshop on Parallel Processing by *Automata and Arrays § 03971

## CENTAUR
*: the system 01136

## CENTERED
Creativity, skill and human-* systems 0346
A vision of education in user-* system and interface design 0985
Designing the "cockpit": the application of a human-* design philosophy to make optimization systems accessible 01016
Establishing user-* criteria for information systems: a software ergonomics perspective 01920
Mode errors: a user-* analysis and some preventative measures using keying-contingent sound 02107
Environment-* and viewer-* perception of surface orientation 02705

Alternative information presentation is a contribution to user *dialogue design 03621
User-* system design: design of mental tasks 03646
User-* requirements analysis ● HCI-0004 †
Environment-* and viewer-* perception of surface orientation HCI-0392 †

## CENTRE
Computing facilities in the MRC clinical research * 02688
Establishing a computing assistance * 03142

## CEREBELLUM
Connectionism, cybernetics, and the * 01185

## CEREBRAL
The optimal level of abstraction for models of * representation of language processes: the state of the question 0356
Certain aspects of the anatomy and physiology of the * cortex 0636
Open questions about computation in * cortex 0637
A logical model of co-operative processes in * dynamics 01615
The fuzzy paradigm for knowledge representation in * dynamics 01699

## CERTAINTY
Combining functions for * degrees in consulting systems 02092

## CERTIFICATION
Necessary functions of institutions for test and * from the viewpoint of users in IT 01456

## CHAIN
Positioning human factors in the user interface development * 0835

## CHAINING
Affect-* and dependency oriented flow analysis applied to queries of programs 02789
Strategic management of technostress: The * of Prometheus HCI-0452 †

## CHAIRS
Task and the adjustment of ergonomic * 03711

## CHALKBOARD
Beyond the *: computer support for collaboration and problem solving inmeetings (Reprint) 0376
Beyond the *: computer support for collaboration and problem solving in meetings HCI-0312 †

## CHANCES
The * of individualization in human-computer interaction and its consequences 0309

## CHANGING
The * workplace: A guide to managing the people, organizational, and regulatory aspects of office technology (book excerpt) 0044
Information technology and education: the * school ● 0282
Action research on systems development: case study of * actor roles 0788
Le Menu: * the user interface on a local area network 03128
A temporal logic for reasoning about * data bases in the context of natural language question-answering 03176
Smaller sizes-* roles: new dimensions of the man-computer interactions 03596
Human factors of * information science technology 04048

## CHANNEL
The memory * machine: part of a proposed learning machine 01602
Prediction of the smallest * in early human vision 01894

## CHANNELS
Employing voice back * of facilitate audio document retrieval 03045

## CHAOTIC
Coherent and * structures in 2D vortex dynamics: progress and problems 0729
Simulation of * EEG patterns with a dynamic model of the olfactory system 01263

## CHARACTER
Issues limiting the acceptance of user interfaces using gesture input and handwriting * recognition 0845

On the interface between the high level languages and Chinese *information 01451
Handprinted chinese * recognition via neural networks 02529
* recognition of cursive scripts 02961
Chinese * processing system based on *-root combination and gra phic processing 03187

## CHARACTERS
Interactive recognition of handprinted * for computer input 0940
Improving the VDU workplace by introducing a physiologically optimized bright-background screen with dark *: advantages and requirements 03721
The use of VDM on the specification of Chinese * 04038

## CHART
The feature *: A tool for communicating the analysis for a decision support system 01913

## CHARTING
* the course of a user survey that will rock the boat 03136

## CHARTS
Designing conceptual models of dialog: a case for dialog * 0968
The design of a user friendly interactive personal computer package for quality control *, project management, and linear programming applications 01521

## CHECK
Office automation as an opportunity for an organizational *-up 03749

## CHECKING
Extending a relational database with deferred referential integrity *andintelligent joins 01089

## CHECKLIST
Requirements * for a system development workstation 01144

## CHEMICAL
Cost effectiveness of on-line searching of * information: an industrial viewpoint 0195
An industrial * hazards database with a natural language interface: an application of artificial intelligence 01533

Dow * makes continuous improvement part of everyone's job 01908
Comparison of manual and online searches of * abstracts 02265
End-user searching of CAS ONLINE. Results of a cooperative experiment between Imperial * Industries and * Abstracts Services 02269
EPVM: An expert patient-ventilator manager for * warfare casualties 02956

## CHESS
Computer * compendium ● 0526
The Greenblatt * program 0527
Using patterns and plans in * 0528

## CHI
* research at MCC 0842
* '88 trip report 0981
* '88 Workshop on Real Time, decision support computer-human interaction 0991
* '88 poster session papers and abstracts 0992
* '86 - human factors in computing systems 01918

## CHILDHOOD
The effects of computer use in early * socialization 0793
Self-efficacy expectations as a predictor of computer use: a look at early * administrators 01590

## CHINA
Developing computer aided design technology in * 0942

## CHINESE
On the interface between the high level languages and * character information 01451
An experimental study of * information displays on VDTs 01784
A computer aided design system for artistic * fonts 02455
Handprinted * character recognition via neural networks 02529
An acoustic-phonetic oriented system for synthesizing * 02661
A computer training tool using * natural language 02948

* character processing system based on character-root combination and gra phic processing 03187
A gestural representation of the process of composing * temples 03855
The use of VDM on the specification of * characters 04038

## CHIP
* talk: projects in speech synthesis ● HCI-0002 †

## CHIPS
Life before the *: simulating digital video interactive technology 01328

## CHIRON
Design principles behind *: a UIMS for software environments 03511

## CHISL
Experience with *, a configurable hierarchical interface specification language 01397

## CHORD
A provisional evaluation of a new * keyboard, the Velotype 03907

## CHOREOGRAPHY
* for technology and humans 02518

## CHUNKING
Learning by *: a production system model of practice 0483
Universal subgoaling and *: the automatic generation and learning of goal hierarchies ● 0497
Adolescents' * of computer programs 01586
Visual information * in spreadsheet calculation 02232

## CHUNKS
On matching programmers' * with program structures: an empirical investigation 02150

## CICS
IBM 3270 full screen interactive programming without * 01040

## CIM
A model for assessing the performance of a local area network employing technical office protocol (TOP) as part of MAP/TOP network in a computer integrated manufacturing (*) research project, for the

transmission of real time interactive speech 02491
Product engineering in the * environment 03376
* and manufacturing industry in the north east of England: A survey of some current issues 03377

**CIRCLE**
An interactive procedure for constructing line and * tangencies 01823
Human aspects of QC * movement in Japanese manufacturing: Natures and problems 03450

**CIRCLING**
*: a method of mouse-based selection without button presses 0847

**CIRCUITRY**
A single-board Forth computer with versatile analog I/O * 02308

**CIRCULATION**
Implementation of the Geac * system within the CLANN network 02458
Barriers to cooperative computerized * systems in public libraries 02573

**CIRCUMSCRIPTION**
Model minimization—an alternative to * 02263

**CIS**
Perceptions of the * graduate's workstyle: undergraduate business students versus * faculty 02999

**CITATION**
* patterns in the computer-based instruction literature 02290

**CITATIONS**
Ashley, K. D.-But, see, accord: generating blue book * in HYPO 02770

**CIVIL**
A tolerance for surveillance: American public opinion concerning privacy and * liberties 0524

**CIVILIZATION**
The Perseus project: an interactive curriculum on classical greek * 01680

**CIVILIZING**
Taming and * computers HCI-0195 †

**CLAM**
*- an open system for graphical user interfaces 01117

**CLANN**
Implementation of the Geac circulation system within the * network 02458

**CLARIS**
* CAD 01310

**CLASSIFICATION**
A question of delivery—an outline * of interactive video delivery systems 0510
* of dialog techniques 0960
Analysis of the performance of a genetic algorithm-based system for message * in noisy environments 02156
The man-machine interface aspect of an automatic * numbering system in a computerized library system 02316
Real-time object measurement and * § 03985

**CLASSIFY**
Knowledge representation in "Default": An attempt to * general types of knowledge used by legal experts 02775

**CLASSIFYING**
* users: a hard look at some controversial issues 0902
* sensory inspectors with heterogeneous inspection-error probabilities 02396

**CLASSROOM**
The computer in the *: a force for change? 0149
Supercomputers in the * 01577
Collaborative learning in a virtual *: highlights of findings 02826
An iterative approach to improving data analysis in the * 03318
The microcomputer as a * audio visual device: the concept, and prospects HCI-0223 †
The electronic *: workstations for teaching HCI-0436 †

**CLAUSES**
Using representation * as an operating system interface 0764

**CLEANING**
CAD-based off-line programming applied to a * and deburring workstation 0607

**CLERICAL**
Integrated software-design: a work-oriented approach to the humanization of computerized * tasks 0243
The silent force of the screen. A research note on the impact of microelectronics on work autonomy among * workers in public administration 01437
Comparison of well-being among non-machine interactive * workers and full-time and part-time VDT users and typists 03745

**CLERKS**
Pregnancy outcome and VDU-work in a cohort of insurance * 03690

**CLIBRARY**
:*—An electronic ordering system 01991

**CLICHES**
Twelve neural network * 01186

**CLIENTS**
Microcomputer availability to public library * 02461

**CLINICAL**
User-interface design for a * neurophysiological intensive monitoring system 0881
Issues in research on * computer applications for mental health 01560
Implementation of a multirule, multistage quality control program in a *laboratory computer system 02380
Computing facilities in the MRC * research centre 02688
An historical perspective on * laboratory information systems 02848

**CLINICIAN**
Resistance to computerization: an examination of the relationship between resistance and the cognitive style of the * HCI-0407 †

**CLONE**
A UNIX * with source code for operating systems courses 01095

# KEYWORD INDEX [COGNITION]

## CLOSED
A *-loop causal model of workload based on a comparison of fuzzy and crisp measurement techniques 01746

Codon constraints on * 2D shapes 02704

Open versus * minds: the effect of dogmatism on an analyst's problem-solving behavior HCI-0446 †

## CLOSELY
Extending knowledge-based systems through *-coupled graphics and windows 02985

## CLOZE
The effects of program-dependent and program-independent deletions on software * tests HCI-0175 †

## CLUE
Information retrieval using impression of documents as a * 03065

*: a common lisp user interface environment 03113

## CLUES
The inept and the computer revolution: some * from other innovations 01552

History offers * to the future: user control returns 02517

## CLUSTERING
ER model * as an aid for user communication and documentation in database design 01331

## CLUSTERS
Structural aspects of semantic-directed * 02534

Structure of German syllable initial and final consonant * based on articulatory features 02652

Optimal determination of user-oriented * 03077

## CMC
Interaction of * with video telecourses for distance education 02677

## CMS
VM/*: a user's guide ● HCI-0028 †

## CNAPLPS
Interface abstractions for an :* page creation system 03863

## CNC
Simulation of * controller features in graphics-based programming 01568

Stress, coping, and worker well-being in computer-aided manufacturing: A field investigation of a * machine shop 03373

## COAL
PISCES: an expert system for * fired power plant monitoring and diagnostics 02915

An object-oriented expert system for *-fired MHD power plant fault monitoringand diagnosis 02973

## COARSE
Task-oriented approach to interactive control of heavy-duty manipulators based on * scene description ● 0546

## COBOL
Advanced interactive * for micros: a practical approach ● 0521

Advanced interactive * for micros: a practical approach ● 0522

Schaum's outline of theories and problems of programming with advanced structured * with file processing structured systems deveolpment and interactive cons ● 0555

## COCKPITS
Color computer graphics in military * 0261

## CODE
A UNIX clone with source * for operating systems courses 01095

Intelligent interactive video simulation of a * inspection 01329

A user-friendly interface to Kendrick's DUAL * 01447

Network generation using the Prufer * 01536

Building user interfaces before writing * saves time and money 02662

Plan-based representations of pascal and fortran * 02897

## CODES
* and modalities in multiple resources: a success and a qualification 01793

Arithmetic * resembling neural encoding 02021

Absolutely stable learning of recognition * by a self-organizing neural network 02728

Applicable algebra, error-correcting *, combinatorics and computer algebra § 03846

Applied algebra, algorithmics and error-correcting * § 03848

* and cryptography ● HCI-0033 †

## CODING
Linear predictive * of speech 0289

An integrated data description language for * design knowledge 0717

Interpolation *: A representation for numbers in neural models 01271

* image sequences for interactive retrieval 01330

A new algorithm for extracting the interior of bounded regions based on chain * 01469

Color-* categories in menus 02872

Principle of visual color * applied to satellite images 03304

* of information in man-computer systems based on cognitive task analysis 03618

Colour * scales and computer graphics 03864

Exploring three possibilities in network design: spontaneous node activity, node plasticity and temporal * 03962

## CODON
* constraints on closed 2D shapes 02704

## COGNITION
'This is a very unpredictable machine': on computers and human * 0364

* & personal structure ● 0533

Computation and *: toward a foundation for cognitive science ● 0593

Parallel distributed processing: explorations in the microstructures of *; Vol. 2: Psychological and biological models ● 0629

Reflections on * and parallel distributed 0642

719

Computers, *, and development: issues for psychology and education ● 0643
Relevance: communication and * ● 0704
*-sensitive design and user modeling for syntax-directed editors 0828
Direct comparison of the relative efficiency on intuitive and analytical * 01896
User programs: a way to match computer systems and human * 03271
A systems model of * for improving human factors of computing environments 04058
Understanding computers and * ● HCI-0054 †
Human * and human computer interaction HCI-0241 †

## COGNITIVE

Visual-* neuronal networks 0029
Computer text-editing: an information-processing analysis of a routine * skill 0056
Interfacing thought: * aspects of human-computer interaction ● 0206
Interfacing thought: * aspects of human-computer interaction ● 0207
* resources and the learning of human-computer dialogs 0209
Improving human-computer interaction—a quest for * science 0213
Readings in * science: a perspective from psychology & artificial intelligence ● 0223
* ergonomics and human computer interaction 0245
* optimisation of Videotex dialogues: a formal—empirical approach 0320
Applying * psychology to user-interface design ● 0325
The role of * psychology in user-interface design 0327
Key areas of * psychology: a historical perspective 0328
From models to modules: studies in * science from the McGill workshops ● 0352
* science and organizational design: a case study of computer conferencing (Reprint) 0386

* impacts of the user interface 0432
* psychology of planning ● 0435
* engineering in complex dynamic worlds ● 0436
The computer and the mind: an introduction to * science ● 0463
Self-modifying production system model of * development 0486
Psychological evaluation of path hypotheses in * diagnosis 0537
* economy in physics reasoning: implications for designing instructional materials 0542
Mapping the * demands of learning to program 0579
On the * effects of learning computer programming 0581
Connectionism and * architecture: a critical analysis 0589
Computation and cognition: toward a foundation for * science ● 0593
Mental models in * science 0647
Building expert systems: * emulation ● 0700
Approximate modelling of * activity: towards an expert system design aid 0801
University of Colorado at Boulder, Institute of * science 0811
* science and machine intelligence laboratory, University of Michigan 0843
* user interface laboratory, GMD-IPSI 0870
A * model of database querying: a tool for novice instruction 0905
* technologies: The design of joint human-machine * systems 01193
Some principles of perceptual and * psychology applied to the design of help menus 01200
Towards a computational theory of * maps 01212
* aspects of HCI 01371
Approximate modelling of * activity with an expert system: a theory-based strategy for developing an interactive design tool 01415
How can * psychology help solve an artificial intelligence problem? 01480
A * approach for graph drawing 01616
Design of user-system interfaces using a * design aid 01682

* factors in user/expert-system interaction 01733
* engineering: human problem solving with tools 01781
Modeling the * content of displays 01800
Principles of information structure common to six levels of the human *system 02019
The contribution of * engineering to the effective design and use of information systems 02033
* systems engineering: new wine in new bottles 02078
* processing differences between novice and expert computer programmers 02145
* biases and corrective techniques: proposals for improving elicitation procedures for knowledge-based systems 02153
* aids in process environments: prostheses or tools? 02161
* engineering in complex dynamic worlds 02167
Modelling operators in accident conditions: advances and perspectives on a * model 02169
* primitives 02214
* issues in the process of software development: review and reappraisal 02222
The influence of programmers' * complexity on program comprehension and modification 02245
Some effects of * style on learning UNIX 02252
A * study of the decision-making process in a business context: implications for design of expert systems 02256
Efficacy of higher * and factual questions in computer assisted instruction modules 02278
The accuracy of * monitoring during computer-based instruction 02281
* models in information retrieval—an evaluative review 02298
Using a * model of dialogue for reference retrieval 02317
Effects of decision support training and * style on decision process attributes 02346

# KEYWORD INDEX [COLOR]

* processes in program comprehension 02403
* process as a basis for MIS and DSS design 02476
A planning system for a * problem 02719
Advances in * Science § 02720
Advances in * science 02721
Control of * processes during software design: what tools are needed? 02899
How do the experts do it? The use of ethnographic methods as an aid to understanding the * processing and retrieval of large bodies of text 03063
Knowledge acquisition and conceptual models: a * analysis of the interface 03214
Can * complexity theory (CCT) produce an adequate measure of system usability? 03229
The application of * psychology to CAD 03239
When and how * style impacts decision making 03474
Connectionism and * science 03547
* ergonomics: an approach for the design of user-oriented interactive systems 03591
Necessary contributions of * psychology to computer knowledge representation and manipulation systems 03598
Coding of information in man-computer systems based on * task analysis 03618
Performance in * tasks and cardiovascular parameters as indicators of mental load 03624
What should be computerized? * demands of mental routine tasks and mental load 03632
Artificial intelligence and * psychology: a new look at human factors 03904
Culture, *, and connectionism: Towards an hermeneutic anthropology of mind 04077
Readings on * ergonomics - mind and computers § HCI-0039 †
In search of the person: philosophical explorations in * science ● HCI-0062 †

Mental models: towards a * science of language, inference, and consciousness ● HCI-0063 †
Artificial intelligence and tutoring systems: computational and *approaches to the communication of knowledge ● HCI-0080 †
Information systems design methodologies and their compliance with *ergonomy HCI-0097 †
Some * aspects of interface design in a two-variable optimization task HCI-0111 †
* layouts of windows and multiple screens for user interfaces HCI-0122 †
* processes in program comprehension HCI-0179 †
Information science: its roots and relation as viewed from the perspective of * science HCI-0185 †
* analysis of people's use of software HCI-0199 †
* engineering—* science HCI-0200 †
Expert systems as * tools for human decision making HCI-0227 †
Visual momentum: a concept to improve the * coupling of person and computer HCI-0238 †
* attributes: implications for display design in supervisory control systems HCI-0242 †
Relations between * psychology and computer system design HCI-0244 †
Analysing the scope of * models in human-computer interaction: a trade-off approach HCI-0245 †
* models, * tasks, and information retrieval HCI-0331 †
Resistance to computerization: an examination of the relationship between resistance and the * style of the clinician HCI-0407 †
* aspects of learning and using a programming language HCI-0439 †

## COGNITIVELY
A * based methodology for evaluating human performance in the computer-aided design task domain 01240

## COHERENT
A * specification method for the human interface to documentation systems 0269
* and chaotic structures in 2D vortex dynamics: progress and problems 0729
The perception of * motion in two-dimensional patterns 03327
* global motion percepts from stochastic local motions 03329

## COHESIVENESS
Influence of individual characteristics and group * on programmer productivity 04050

## COLLABORATIONS
Relationships and tasks in scientific research * (Reprint) 0387
Social science and system design: interdisciplinary * 0833

## COLLATERAL
Videotex and online services: competition or * 03557

## COLLICULUS
The role of the primate superior * in sensorimotor integration 0017

## COLLIMATED
Spatial misorientation exacerbated by * virtual flight display 01979

## COLOR
* and the computer ● 0254
* displays and * science 0255
Human factors for * display systems: concepts, methods, and research 0256
Visual parameters for * CRTs 0257
Perceptual * spaces for computer graphics 0258
* graphic displays for network planning and design 0260
* computer graphics in military cockpits 0261
* displays for medical imaging 0262
* and the instructional use of the computer 0263
* constancy: a method for recovering surface spectral reflectance 0298
Human factors of * displays 0438
* in user interface design: functionally and aesthetics 0803
An integrated * smalltalk-80 system 01127

# [COLORED] KEYWORD INDEX

Comparison of * sensation in dichoptic and in normal vision 01272

Contingent aftereffects and isoluminance: psychophysical evidence for separation of *, orientation, and motion 01463

Retinex: physics and the theory of * vision 01574

Interactive * graphical postprocessing as a unifying influence in numerical analysis research 01684

The effects of set size on * matching using CRT displays 01711

Using * dimensions to display data dimensions 01766

*, graphics, and animation in a computer-assisted learning tutorial lesson 02294

*-coding categories in menus 02872

Incorporating the human factor in * CAD systems 03104

ACE: a * expert system for user interface design 03117

Image segmentation based on * and texture gradient 03303

Principle of visual * coding applied to satellite images 03304

The efficiency of letter perception in function of * combinations: a study of video-screen * 03616

Study of visual performance on a multi-* VDU of * defective and normal Trichromatic subjects 03701

The use of * in visual displays 03890

The influence of * on program readability and comprehensibility HCI-0120 †

An experimental program investigating *-enhanced and graphical information presentation: an integration of the findings HCI-0196 †

Physiological principles for the effective use of * HCI-0378 †

An experimental comparison of RGB, YIQ, LAB, HSV, and opponent * models HCI-0381 †

* and the computer in cartography HCI-0386 †

## COLORED
Variability in brightness matching of * lights 01767

## COLORS
Optimal *, phosphors, and illuminant characteristics of CRT displays: the lgorithmic approach 01710

The efficiency of letter perception in function of color combinations: a study of video-screen * 03616

* in video displays 03725

## COLOUR
* graphics—Blessing or Ballyhoo? 0061

A * atlas for graphical displays 03726

* on displays—boon or curse? 03727

* coding scales and computer graphics 03864

The use of * in language syntax analysis HCI-0385 †

## COLOURS
The algorithmic approach in ergonomics: the case of optimal * and ambients for display work 0247

Towards the construction of a maximally-contrasting set of * 03233

## COMBAT
Performance measurement during simulated air-to-air * 01787

Capturing expertise: Some approaches to modeling command decisionmaking in * analysis 01883

## COMBINATIONS
The efficiency of letter perception in function of color *: a study of video-screen colors 03616

## COMBINATORICS
Applicable algebra, error-correcting codes, * and computer algebra § 03846

## COMFORTABLY
Are you sitting * 01220

## COMMAND
User performance with *, menu, and iconic interfaces 0414

Predicting the time to recall computer * abbreviations 0806

The formal specification of adaptive user interfaces using * language grammar 0925

The impact of menus and *-level feedback on learners' acquisition of data base language skills 01041

A help system for * driven applications 01050

Design of a control room for the air force logistics * (AFLC) *, control,and communication and intelligence ($C^3I$) system 01612

A system for specification and rapid prototyping of application *languages 01849

The emergence of Zipf's law: Spontaneous encoding optimization by users of a * language 01875

Capturing expertise: Some approaches to modeling * decisionmaking in combat analysis 01883

Perceptual structure cueing in a simple * language 02086

An experimental evaluation of prefix and postfix notation in * language sytax 02110

Adaptive * prompting in an on-line documentation 02121

The structure of * languages: an experiment on task-action grammar 02224

fsh—a functional UNIX * interpreter 02624

Support for graphs of processes in a * interpreter 02633

Ergonomic considerations in the design of * languages 02694

A new conceptual model for interactive user recovery and * reuse facilities 02884

The incorporation of early interface evaluation into * language grammar specifications 03191

How much is enough? A study of user * repertoires 03240

Evaluating the meaningfulness of icon sets to represent * operations 03277

Investigations into a * and response language interface 03531

On complexity of *-entry in man-computer dialogues 03610

Concepts in user interfaces: a reference model for * and response languages § 03872

# KEYWORD INDEX [COMMUNICATION]

Concepts in user interfaces: a reference model for * and response languages ● HCI-0032 †
A user oriented design process for user recovery and * reuse support HCI-0284 †
Speech-controlled text-editing: effects of input modality and of *structure HCI-0397 †

## COMMANDS
Designing keybindings to be easy to learn and resistant to forgetting even when the set of * is large 02890

## COMMENTARY
Systems design and social responsibility: the political implications of "computer-supported cooperative work". A * 02516

## COMMERCIAL
Expert systems for * use 0666
Patterned systems design—HCI in * data processing 03193

## COMMUNCIATION
Trends in the emerging profession of technical * 0123

## COMMUNICATE
How can groups * when they use different languages? 03038

## COMMUNICATION
Cooperation without * 0169
Knowledge-based systems and * between computers and human beings 0192
Interactive human * (Reprint) 0371
* and management support in system development environments (Reprint) 0374
Social psychological aspects of computer-mediated * (Reprint) 0384
Reducing social context cues: electronic mail in organizational *(Reprint) 0385
Principles of data * ● 0547
* failure in dialogue and discourse: detection and repair processes ● 0611
Relevance: * and cognition ● 0704
The three c's: children, computers, and * ● 0713
* methods of the vocally disabled: a review 0783

The rational, the pragmatic and the inquiry process: The social study of information- * systems 0786
Voice: technology searching for * needs 0808
The effects of bargaining orientation and * medium on negotiations in the bilateral monopoly task: a comparison of decision room and computer conferencing * media 0809
User interface design in large corporations: coordination and *across disciplines 0853
Learning modes and subsequent use of computer-mediated * systems 0912
An object-oriented construction and tool kit for human-computer * 01061
Self-organizing system obtaining * ability primitive model for language generation 01279
* barriers in microcomputer—based courses 01319
ER model clustering as an aid for user * and documentation in database design 01331
* analysis in the company 01435
The telephone in question: questions on * 01436
A * mechanism supporting actions 01441
Artificial intelligence techniques in man–machine * 01459
Processor for man-machine natural-language-like * 01484
Design of a control room for the air force logistics command (AFLC) command, control, and * and intelligence ($C^3I$) system 01612
Application of a mathematical model of human decisionmaking for human-computer * 01866
Two simulation studies investigating means of human-computer * for dynamic task allocation 01882
Implementing computer-mediated * technologies: a technoacceptance approach to critical mass utilization 01931
Information systems user–designer * problems 01938
Successful application of * techniques to improve the systems development process 01952

An empirical comparison of model-based and explicit * for dynamic human-computer task allocation 02109
Considerations of menu structure and * rate for the design of computer menu displays 02124
Interactive * of sentential structure and content: an alternative approach to man-machine * 02220
Person-to-person * in an applied research/service delivery setting 02445
Reducing social context cues: electronic mail in organizational * 02473
* issues among psychologists working with computers: a view from the top 02606
Threat to privacy: the federal government's use of personal information in the new * environment 02680
Delphi: an intelligent interface for a dolphin * laboratory 02989
Sketchpad a man-machine graphical * system 03103
Generative transition networks: a new * control abstraction 03241
Learning graphics programming by direct * 03298
Human-computer * meets software engineering 03505
Building interprocess * models using Stile 03528
The design of a flexible distributed testbeb for * systems 03538
User requirements in natural language * with database systems 03615
Some aspects of * in the natural language and user's involvement in software development 03670
Natural language * with computers: some problems, perspectives, and new directions 03913
An investigation of the effectiveness of * between systems analysts and end users in the design of large computer systems 04075
Plans and situated actions: the problem of human-machine * ● HCI-0040 †

Artificial intelligence and tutoring systems: computational and cognitive approaches to the * of knowledge ● HCI-0080 †
Supporting concurrency, *, and synchronization in human-computer interaction—the Sassafras UIMS HCI-0102 †
A * system supporting large datagrams on a local area network HCI-0166 †
A research model for studying the gender/power aspects of human-computer * HCI-0193 †
The effects of * monitors on user satisfaction HCI-0221 †
The vocabulary problem in human-system * HCI-0224 †
The impact of DSS on organizational * HCI-0294 †
Strategies for encouraging successful adoption of office * systems HCI-0307 †

**COMMUNICATIONS**
Ergonomic aspects of man-machine * 0417
ISDN and the move to integrated *—an introduction 01455
Integrated * and work efficiency: impacts on organizational structure and power 02031
Emerging * technology paradigms 02320
Community design and gaming/simulation: Comparison of *techniques in participatory design sessions 02596
Electronic * and collaboration: the emerging model for computer aided * in science and medicine 02678
* technology and the public sector: understanding the process of adoption 02679
The measurement of the performance of * protocols from the user's viewpoint 02684
* and architecture & protocols § 02801
The impact of electronic mail on managerial and organizational * 03041
An aspect of aesthetics in human-computer *: pretty windows HCI-0213 †

* design for Co-oP: a group decision support system HCI-0297 †
Usage patterns in an integrated voice and data * system HCI-0311 †

**COMMUNIS**
Model of the neuro-muscular recruitment example of the extensor digitorum * muscle in man: I—identification of motoneurons and of muscular fibers 01595

**COMMUNITY**
DARN: Toward a * memory for diagnosis and repair tasks 0428
* design and gaming/simulation: Comparison of communications techniques in participatory design sessions 02596

**COMODORE**
The MAGNEX text editor for the * Amiga personal computer 0782

**COMPACT**
Anticipating * disc-interactive (CD-I): ten guidelines for prospective authors 0280
* disc–interactive 0680
A * model of a power house boiler 02683
Hypertext engineering: practical methods for creating a * disk encyclopedia 02832
g - A * language for real-time graphics 02906
* disc-interactive: a designer's overview ● HCI-0078 †
Anatomy of a * user interface development tool HCI-0104 †

**COMPARISONS**
Mainframe and microcomputer-based business graphics: end user computing * and trends 02805

**COMPATIBILITY**
Cumulating the science of HCI: from s-R * to transcription typing 0831
Task * of manipulator postures 02258
A search for machine/human * in manufacturing systems 03381

**COMPATIBLES**
High performance interactive graphics: modeling, rendering and animating for IBM PCs and * ● HCI-0071 †

**COMPENDIUM**
Computer chess * ● 0526

**COMPILATION**
Dynamic * in the Unix environment 02621

**COMPILER**
The design of an interactive * for optimizing microprograms 01078
Libraries as programs preserved within * continuations 01102
Design and implementation of the UW Illustrated * 03059

**COMPLAINTS**
User's *: Information system problems from the user's perspective 02416

**COMPLEMENTARITY**
Recursive * in the cybernetics of education 01598
Organizational humanity and architecture: Duality and * of papa-logic and mama-logic in managerial conceptualizations of change 01609

**COMPLEMENTARY**
Attacking a complex distributed algorithm from different sides: an experience wih * validation tools 01429

**COMPLEXITY**
* in information theory ● 0003
The limitations of task * through information technologies: results of a field study 0307
A theory of control and *: implications for software design and integration of computer systems into the work place 0315
The effects of syntactic * on the human-computer interaction 01708
The influence of programmers' cognitive * on program comprehension and modification 02245
Can cognitive * theory (CCT) produce an adequate measure of system usability? 03229
The use of * theory in evaluating interfaces 03270
Problems in the design of information retrieval systems: user competence and information * 03602

On * of command-entry in man-computer dialogues 03610
The * of some polynomial network consistency algorithms for constraint satisfaction problems HCI-0361 †

**COMPLIANT**
CAD Based verification and refinement of high level * motion primitives 0600

**COMPONENTS**
An information retrieval system for software * 01077
Instrumenting systems to measure * of interactive response times 01230
Quantitative determination of orientational and directional * in the response of visual cortical cells to moving stimuli 01268
Training consistent task *: application of automatic and controlled processing theory to industrial task training 01742
A framework for task cooperation within systems containing intelligent * 01884
* of user work stations 02427
Ada-*: libraries and tools § 03180
Methodological problems of designing dialogue-oriented * in information systems 03595
Analogical program synthesis from program * 03920
Innate and learned * in a simple visuo-motor reflex 03965
Robot * and systems ● HCI-0068 †

**COMPREHEND**
How people * unknown system structures: conceptual primitives in systems' surface representations 03828

**COMPREHENDING**
On * a computer manual: analysis of variables affecting performance 02135

**COMPREHENSIBILITY**
Enhancing program readability and * with tools for program visualization 03510
The influence of color on program readability and * HCI-0120 †

**COMPREHENSINO**
* aids for on-line reading of expository text 01798

**COMPRESSION**
Information * in biological systems 01253
Image * using polylines 02533

**COMPUTABILITY**
Principles of computer-aided design: * of design ● 0465

**COMPUTERPHOBIA**
Adult learners: away with * HCI-0433 †

**COM1UTER**
A methodology, specification language, and automated support environment for *-aided design systems 04068

**CONCEIVED**
How DENDRAL was * and born 02839

**CONCEPTSTO**
IR-NLI II: applying man-machine interaction and artificial intelligence * information retrieval 03070

**CONCEPTUALIZATIONS**
Organizational humanity and architecture: Duality and complementarity of papa-logic and mama-logic in managerial * of change 01609

**CONCEPTUALIZING**
* in assembly tasks 01776

**CONCORDIA**
Supporting document development with * 03521

**CONCURRENCY**
Reference models, window systems, and * 01058
* control in groupware systems 01090
* in intelligent systems 01169
* 88 § 03873
Petri nets: applications and relationships to other models of * § 03973
Supporting *, communication, and synchronization in human-computer interaction—the Sassafras UIMS HCI-0102 †

**CONFERENCING**
Computer-based real-time * systems (Reprint) 0377
An experiment in integrated multimedia * 0381

Cognitive science and organizational design: a case study of computer * (Reprint) 0386
The effects of bargaining orientation and communication medium on negotiations in the bilateral monopoly task: a comparison of decision room and computer * communication media 0809
The rapport multimedia * system 03037
Grand computer *: What have we learned? 03536
Interface design in computerized * systems: a personal view HCI-0305 †

**CONFIDENTIALITY**
Data security and * in Europe HCI-0450 †

**CONFIGURABLE**
Experience with chisl, a * hierarchical interface specification language 01397

**CONFIGURATIONS**
Selective attention to aspects of motion *: common vs. relative motion 03345

**CONFIGURING**
* stand-alone smalltalk-80 applications 01129

**CONFLICT**
A user preference guided approach to * resolution in rule-based expert systems 01872
A study of * in group design activities: implications for computer-supported cooperative work environments 03477

**CONFLICTS**
Contexts and * between ergonomics and industrial psychology 0240

**CONFORMATIONAL**
MOL3D, a modular and interactive program for molecular modeling and * analysis: I—basic modules 02389

**CONFRONTING**
Analysis of the competence of operators * new technologies: some methodological problems and some results 03594

## CONMAN
*: a visual programming language for interactive graphics 02811

## CONNECTIONISM
* and cognitive architecture: a critical analysis 0589
On language and *: analysis of a parallel distributed processing model of language acquisition 0590
*, cybernetics, and the cerebellum 01185
* and cognitive science 03547
Culture, cognitive, and *: Towards an hermeneutic anthropology of mind 04077

## CONNECTIVITY
Line * algorithms for an asynchronous pyramid computer 01468
jThe assessment of human/computer performance: a case for * 03535

## CONS
Schaum's outline of theories and problems of programming with advanced structured COBOL with file processing structured systems deveolpment and interactive * ● 0555
SIMTALK: Pros and * of natural language for manufacturing simulation 02950

## CONSCIOUS
Knowledge elicitation: dissociating * reflections from automatic processes HCI-0337 †

## CONSCIOUSNESS
Cybernetic * 01605
Time, structure and levels of * 01608
Mental models: towards a cognitive science of language, inference, and * ● HCI-0063 †

## CONSEQUENCE
Automatic information processing activities and operational decision making: a case study of * 01950

## CONSEQUENTIALIST
Issues and approaches to appraising technological change in the office: A * perspective 0043

## CONSERVING
Topology * mappings for learning motor tasks 02758

## CONSOLE
Enhanced * driver 01288

## CONSOLIDATION
Processes and problems in information * 01992

## CONSONANT
Structure of German syllable initial and final * clusters based on articulatory features 02652
Hopfield model applied to vowel and * discrimination 02735

## CONSTANCY
Color *: a method for recovering surface spectral reflectance 0298

## CONSTITUENCY
Computing text *: an algorithmic approach to the generation of text graphs HCI-0267 †

## CONSTRAIN
Using focus to * language generation HCI-0341 †

## CONSTRAINED
A rule-based model for the human operator in a time-* competing-task environment 01877
Distributed decisionmaking with * decisionmakers: a case study 01886

## CONSTRAINT
* grammars–a new model for specifying graphical applications 0875
* hierarchies 01114
*-based tools for building user interfaces 01153
The fox and the forest: toward a type I/type II * for early optical flow 03324
The complexity of some polynomial network consistency algorithms for *satisfaction problems HCI-0361 †

## CONSTRAINTS
Designing with * 0467
Animated graphical interfaces using temporal * 0909
Defining * graphically 0910
A user interface toolkit based on graphical objects and * 01125
A smalltalk window system based on * 01128
Codon * on closed 2D shapes 02704
Designing a neural network satisfying a given set of * 02755
Tools for management and support of multiple * in a writer's assistant 03251
One-layer routing without component * HCI-0090 †

## CONSTRUCTOR
Maintained and * attributes 01099

## CONSTRUING
Validation in a knowledge support system: * and consistency with multiple experts 02203

## CONSULTANT
User modeling in UC, the UNIX * 0894
Advising roles of a computer * 0896
The Berkeley UNIX * project 01355

## CONSULTATION
ICE: information center expert: a * system for resource allocation 0781
Comparison of decision support strategies in expert * systems 02101
Refining problem-solving knowledge in repertory grids using a *mechanism 02205
A * system for information center resource allocation 03100
A travel * system: towards a smooth conversation in Japanese 03917

## CONSULTING
* skills for technical writers 0124
Ergonomics and organizational *: accentuation or neglect of psychology 0242
Combining functions for certainty degrees in * systems 02092
Super * for supercomputer users: a philosophy of user support 03145
Advisor—an electronic mail * service 03151
User services * supportr tools at the NASA numerical aerodynamic simula 03161
The doctor's use of a computer in the * room: an analysis HCI-0409 †

## CONSUMER
Forecasting * adoption of information technology and services—lessons from home video forecasting 02451

## CONTENT
Collective computation, *-addressable memory, and optimization problems 0004
Magnification effects with imaging displays depend on scene * and viewing condition 01786
Modeling the Cognitive * of displays 01800
Interactive communication of sentential structure and *: an alternative approach to man-machine communication 02220
A self-optimizing, nonsymmetrical neural net for * addressable memory and pattern recognition 02562
Separating * from form: A language for formatting on-line documentation and dialog 02781
Work *, stress and health in computer-mediated work: a seven year follow-up study 03758
Managing the semantic * of graphical data HCI-0374 †

## CONTEXTS
* and conflicts between ergonomics and industrial psychology 0240
Prototyping techniques for different problem * 0862
Determination of work *—an important aspect of future user interfaces 01204
Tense, qualifiers, and * 01346

## CONTEXTUAL
Experience with * field research 0802
Seven experiences with * field research 0996
* structure analysis of microcomputer manuals 03227

## CONTINGENCIES
The design of a traffic control expert system for long distance network * 02952

## CONTINGENCY
An exploratory * model of user participation and MIS use 01919

The effect of user involvement on system success: a * approach 02508

## CONTINGENT
* aftereffects and isoluminance: psychophysical evidence for separation of color, orientation, and motion 01463
Mode errors: a user-centered analysis and some preventative measures using keying-* sound 02107

## CONTINUATIONS
Libraries as programs preserved within compiler * 01102

## CONTINUITY
Geometric * with interpolating Bézier curves 03857

## CONTOUR
An extremum principle for shape from * 0024
Automatic * definition on left ventriculograms by image evidence and a multiple template-based model 04073

## CONTOURS
Computing the velocity field along * 03331

## CONTRACT
Precedent-based legal reasoning and knowledge acquisition in * law: A process model 02776

## CONTRACTS
Humans, computers, and * 03223
System design for local authorities: participation based on "information *" 03656

## CONTRASTING
Towards the construction of a maximally-* set of colours 03233

## CONTRASTIVE
* analysis of the relationship of man and computer as a basis of system design 03649

## CONTRIBUTING
An iterative and interactive simulation method to reconstruct unknown inputs * to known outputs of neuronal systems 04018

## CONTROLLED
Evaluation of mouse, rate-* isometric joystick, step keys, and text keys, for text selection on a CRT 0064
Automatic and * processing theory and its applications to human factors problems 0402
Training consistent task components: application of automatic and *processing theory to industrial task training 01742
Reader-* computerized presentation of text 01785
Speech-* text-editing: effects of input modality and of command structure HCI-0397 †

## CONTROLLER
The BCC180 multitasking * part 3: memory management and windowing 01295
The * animation system 01402
Simulation of CNC * features in graphics-based programming 01568
A design for a fuzzy logic * 02028
Design of an integral computer-based wheelchair */linear synchronous motor system 02378
A cookbook for using the model-view * user interface paradigm in Smalltalk-80 02390
A model of the * responses of the human temperature regulating system to changes in water temperature 02487

## CONTROLLING
SmartSLIM: a DSS for * biases during problem formulation 0203
Analysis of user procedural compliance in * a simulated process 01879
Strategies in * a continuous process with long response latencies: needs for computer support to diagnosis 02217
* bias in user assertions in expert decision support systems for problem formulation 02343
Modelling and * user inference 03582

## CONTROVERSIES
Automaticity, resources, and memory: theoretical * and practical implications 01792

## CONVERGENCE
The * of Moore's/Mooers' laws 01996
Exploiting * to improve natural language understanding 02071
Document * in an interactive formatting system HCI-0405 †

## CONVERSATION
Why do instructional designers need * theory? 0506
* theory as a basis for instructional design 0507
Learning styles in *—a practical application of Pask's learning theory to human-computer interaction 03608
A travel consultation system: towards a smooth * in Japanese 03917

## CONVERSING
* and computers 0092

## CONVERTER
Digital waveform sampling rate * 01578

## CONVEXLY
* combined fuzzy relational equations and several aspects of their application to fuzzy information processing 02027

## CONVEY
Using an expert system to * HCI information 03272

## CONVOLUTION
Expectation and variance of item resemblance distributions in a *-correction model of distributed memory 02369

## COORDINATES
Tensor geometry: a language of brains & neurocomputers. Generalized *in neuroscience & robotics 03966

## COORDINATING
* user interfaces for consistency 0990
Multilingual programming: * programs, user interfaces, on-line help nd documentation 02785

## COORDINATION
Center for * science, MIT 0841

User interface design in large corporations: * and communication across disciplines 0853
Adaptive * of a learning team 02475
Eye-head * and information uptake during text processing 03767
Spatial and temporal transformations in visuo-motor * 03963
Semistructured messages are surprisingly useful for computer-supported * HCI-0290 †

## COPE
How would your favourite user model * with these scenarios? 0999
Supercomputer applications: helping users * with tough programming problems 03147

## COPRODUCTION
*: evidence from EPG data 02660

## COPYING
Attitudes toward unauthorized software *: general public vs. business faculty member 01142
Private *, reproduction costs, and the supply of intellectual property 01988

## COPYRIGHT
Protecting user interfaces through *: the debate 0827
Why the look and feel of software user interfaces should not be protected by * law 01324

## CORPORATE
The age of the end-user and the shift from * MIS to * DSS 01676
Chief executive personality and * strategy and structure in small firms 02472
* culture, technical documentation, and organization diagnosis HCI-0151 †

## CORPORATIONS
User interface design in large *: coordination and communication across disciplines 0853

## CORRECT
Toward interactive design of * programs 0614

## CORRECTION
A string * method based on the context-dependent similarity 0293
Prompting, feedback and error * in the design of a scenario machine 02176
Optimization of string length for spoken digit input with error * 02185
Expectation and variance of item resemblance distributions in a convolution-* model of distributed memory 02369
Higher pole * in vocal tract models and terminal analogs 02657
Error * and asymmetry in a binary memory matrix 02750
Work distance and optical * 03736
Naming errors and automatic error * in human-computer interaction 03770
Error detection and * in a speech recognition system: a knowledge based system approach 04054

## CORRECTIVE
Cognitive biases and * techniques: proposals for improving elicitation procedures for knowledge-based systems 02153

## CORRELATION
* of term usage and term indexing frequencies 02004
Machine learning using a higher order * network 02563
High order * model for associative memory 02729
Application of neural network algorithms and architectures to */tracking and identification 02734

## CORRELATIONS
Estimating reliability with small samples: increased precision with averaged * 01728

## CORTICES
Why *? Neural computation in the vertebrate visual system 03956

## COST
* effectiveness of on-line searching of chemical information: an industrial viewpoint 0195
Skilled financial planning: the * of translating ideas into action 0834

# KEYWORD INDEX

[CRT]

An interdisciplinary approach to human factors in telematic systems. A review of the problems and possible solutions by a *-11 ter working group 01440
The real * of OA 01647
Review and evaluation of physiological * prediction models for manual materials handling 01757
A * model for estimating the *s of developing software in the Ada programming language 03539
Low * geometric modelling system for CAM 03866
System aspects of low-* bitmapped displays 03932
*/benefit analysis for incorporating human factors in the software lifecycle HCI-0127 †
Using low-* workstations to investigate computer networks and distributed systems HCI-0437 †

## COSTLY
Firm strategies for * engineering learning 02485

## COSTS
The psychological * of master computer 01655
The human * of manufacturing reform 01706
Private copying, reproduction *, and the supply of intellectual property 01988
User programmer and * of the misinformed user 02415
A cost model for estimating the * of developing software in the Ada programming language 03539

## COUNTERACTION
Human specifics fuzzy categories and * in decision making problems 01696

## COUPLED
* mode theory for neural networks 02730
Extending knowledge-based systems through closely-* graphics and windows 02985

## COUPLING
* visual and dynamic features to study handwritten signatures 03309

Visual momentum: a concept to improve the cognitive * of person and computer HCI-0238 †

## COURSES
Designing the user interface: professional development * from the Univ. of Maryland ● 0688
Dealing with disparate audiences in computer science * using a project group within a traditional class 01031
Profile of undergraduate software engineering *: results from a survey 01035
A UNIX clone with source code for operating systems * 01095
Communication barriers in microcomputer—based * 01319
A scarce resource in undergraduate software engineering *: user interface design materials 04027

## COURSEWARE
Instructional designs for microcomputer * ● 0464

## CRACK
An interactive approach to local remeshing around a propagating * 01685

## CRACKER
The moral * 01546

## CRAFTED
Hand-* hypertext-lessons from the ACM experiment 0128

## CREATE
Using an object-oriented programming language to * audience-driven hypermedia environments 0101

## CREATIVITY
*, skill and human-centered systems 0346
*, intelligence and evolution 0365
Expert systems and * 0553
The metaphor machine: a database method for * support 01670
Information systems and the stimulation of * 02327
Gossip as * 02576
Daydreaming and computation: a computer model of everyday *, learning nd emotions in the human stream of thought 04067
A note on the nature of * in engineering: implications for

supporting system design HCI-0220 †

## CREDIBILITY
Power and * in office automation 01657

## CRIME
Computer * ● 0722

## CRISIS
* planning systems: tools for intelligent action 03464

## CRITERIA
Learning environment * 0285
Establishing user-centered * for information systems: a software ergonomics perspective 01920
An investigation of performance, productivity, and rationality in multi-* decision making 03463
* for the subjective quality of visual display units 03724

## CRT
Evaluation of mouse, rate-controlled isometric joystick, step keys, and text keys, for text selection on a * 0064
Designing optimum * text blinking video image presentation 0795
Why reading was slower from * displays than from paper 0797
A comparison of textual information retention from * terminals and paper 0954
Optimal colors, phosphors, and illuminant characteristics of * displays: the lgorithmic approach 01710
The effects of set size on color matching using * displays 01711
Reading is slower from * displays than from paper: attempts to isolate a single-variable explanation 01743
Reading from * displays can be as fast as reading from paper 01758
Human factors and flat panels challenge the * 01982
* picture vibration caused by low-frequency magnetic field and its reduction method 01987
Formatting alphanumeric * displays 02140
A comparison of children's reading comprehension and reading rates at three text presentation speeds on a * 02280

[CRTS]

Influence of * refresh rates on accommodation aftereffects 03731

**CRTS**
Visual parameters for color * 0257
*—present and future 01985

**CRUCIAL**
How identify organizational factors * of VDU-health? A context-oriented method approach 03741

**CRUSTAL**
The second generation intelligent user interface for the * dynamics data information system 02675

**CRYSTAL**
The * ball of research: how to use it to learn about the user community 03135

**CRYSTALLOGRAPHIC**
* Computing 4 § 03775

**CSCW**
Tools for supporting cooperative work near and far: highlights from the *conference 0879
* '86 Conference summary report 0955
*'88: report on the conference & review of the proceedings 01002
The 1988 *: trip report 01008
Interfaces for cooperative work: an eclectic look at * '88 01009
A case study of * in a dispersed organization 02866

**CUBE**
User *: a taxonomy of end users 01335

**CUBIST**
GPS and the psychology of th Rubik *: a study in reasoning about actions 03311

**CUEING**
Perceptual structure * in a simple command language 02086

**CUES**
Reducing social context *: electronic mail in organizational communication (Reprint) 0385
An experiment into the use of auditory * to reduce visual workload 0877
Studying depth * in a three-dimensional computer graphics workstation 02117

Reducing social context *: electronic mail in organizational communication 02473
An expert system for mapping acoustic * into phonetic features HCI-0328 †

**CUINFO**
An informal overview of * (Cornell's computer-based bulletin board) 02783

**CUISINE**
Lean *: a low fat notation for menus 02062

**CULTURE**
Reading, * and modern mass media 02340
Computer *: the scientific, intellectual, and social impact of the computer § 03567
Automation and work * 03750
*, cognitive, and connectionism: Towards an hermeneutic anthropology of mind 04077
The computer * § HCI-0084 †
Corporate *, technical documentation, and organization diagnosis HCI-0151 †

**CULTURES**
The two * in computing 03018

**CUMULATING**
* the science of HCI: from s-R compatibility to transcription typing 0831

**CURRENTS**
Some historical * concerning the 'societal learning' approach to policy and planning 01603

**CURRICULUM**
The creation of an integrated IVD * 0509
Algebra slaves and agents in a Logo-based mathematics * 0517
The Perseus project: an interactive * on classical greek civilization 01680

**CURSE**
Colour on displays—boon or * 03727

**CURSOR**
Systemic implications of leap and an improved two-part * 0848
Optimizing the touch tablet: the effects of control display gain and method of * control 01730

A new approach to * movements in user interfaces of integrated programming environments 01974
Exploratory evaluation of a planar foot-operated *-positioning device 02858
Multifunctional * for direct manipulation user interfaces 02870
Touch screen, * keys and mouse interaction 03769
* movement during text editing HCI-0113 †

**CURVATURE**
Simultaneous adaptation to size, distance, and * underwater 01803

**CURVE**
* tailoring with interactive computer 01209
Capacity equivalence *s: a double trade-off * method for equating task performance 01796
Perceptual organization and * partitioning 01838
Forgetting and the learning *: a laboratory study 02484
Interactive * drawing by segmented Bezier approximation with a control parameter 02535

**CUSTOM**
Automated design and analysis system for design of * orthopedic implants 02931

**CUSTOMER**
Tennessee Eastman employee teamwork raises quality, * service 01907
Expert system applications in * service 03101

**CUSTOMERS**
*' requirements for natural language systems: results of an inquiry HCI-0426 †

**CUSTOMIZATION**
An interactive * program for a natural language database query system 0163
Prospects for knowledge-based * of natural languages query systems 02008

**CUSTOS**
* IPSE: Towards a theory of the supervisor 03365

# KEYWORD INDEX [DEBUGGING]

## CYBERNETIC
The * principle: its transdisciplinarity to science and religion and the challenging task 01596
The * mechanisms of stress 01599
* consciousness 01605

## CYBERNETICS
Connectionism, *, and the cerebellum 01185
Recursive complementarity in the * of education 01598
* and organization theory: a critical review 01617
The social * of human interaction with automated systems 03442
Tele-*: implications for the international marketplace 03458

## CYCLE
Importance of the human factor in the information system life * 02422
A hypertext system to manage software life * documents 03519
The Software Life * Support Environment (SLCSE): a computer based framework for developing software systems HCI-0147 †

## CYCLIC
A multivariate solution for * data, applied in modelling locomotor forces 01252

## CZECHOSLOVAKIAN
Microcomputer hardware education at a * Technical University 02488

## DAILOG
ISPF: the strategic * manager ● 0035

## DAME
The evolution of microcomputer laboratory services at the University of Notre * 03159

## DANALYST
* attempts to do it all 01640

## DANCE
A system for the representation of human body movement from * scores 02540

## DANGERS
The dubious * of VDT radiation 01902

## DARK
Designing in the *: logics that compete with the user 0928
Improving the VDU workplace by introducing a physiologically optimized bright-background screen with * characters: advantages and requirements 03721

## DARN
*: Toward a community memory for diagnosis and repair tasks 0428

## DARTS
Extending the * software design method to distributed real time applications 03516

## DATABASED
A natural language interface to a multiple * office information system 01094
Concept for a model * remote maintenance system 03565

## DATAFLOW
A *-based APL for the hypercube 02905

## DATAGRAMS
A communication system supporting large * on a local area network HCI-0166 †

## DATALEX
Expert systems in law: The * project 02766

## DATALOG
Portability of syntax and semantics in * HCI-0340 †

## DATASTREAM
*: numeric data—all you can use at a fixed price 02525

## DATENBANK
*-DIALOG: a German language interface for relational databases 01208

## DATES
Absolute * and relative * in an inferential system on temporal dependencies between events 02235

## DAYDREAMING
* and computation: a computer model of everyday creativity, learning nd emotions in the human stream of thought 04067

## DBASE
Programming the * III Plus user interface ● 0627

## DBMS
Reference model for * user facility 01086
A common interface for accessing document retrieval systems and * for retrieval of bibliographic data 01990
The integration of the network and relational approaches in a * 03283
Status of trusted * interpretations 03585

## DBUG
* III offers source level solutions 01641

## DBXTOOL
*: A window-based symbolic debugger for sun workstations 02614

## DEAF
A user interface for *-blind people (preliminary report) 0794

## DEBATE
Protecting user interfaces through copyright: the * 0827

## DEBUGGER
Dbxtool: A window-based symbolic * for sun workstations 02614
A * for a graphical workstation 02623
Users' preferences among different techniques for displaying the evaluation of LISP functions in an interactive * 02863
A * for concurrent programs HCI-0142 †

## DEBUGGING
Interactive blackbox * for concurrent languages 01134
Programmer variations in software * approaches 02250
Graphbug - a microprocessor software * tool 02496
JDB: an adaptable interface for * 02628
Interactive performance display and * using the NCUBE real-time graphicssystem 02907
* concurrent processes: a case study 03060

## DEBURRING
CAD-based off-line programming applied to a cleaning and * workstation 0607

## DECEPTION
Ease of use - the ultimate * 03249

## DECISION
Evaluation of expert systems for * support 0244
Develping * support systems from a model of the DSS/user interface 0253
A * support system for vehicle scheduling in public transport 0339
Human * processes: Heuristics and task structure 0401
Judgement and *: theory and application 0648
A philosophical basis for * aiding 0649
Fuzzy * analysis 0650
Fuzzy sets and * analysis 0651
* making with unreliable probabilities 0652
Conceptual design of * support systems utilizing management science models 0658
A conceptual architecture for generalized * support system software 0659
Concept design of a program manager's * support system 0660
ARIADNE: A knowledge-based interactive system for planning and * support 0661
The effects of bargaining orientation and communication medium on negotiations in the bilateral monopoly task: a comparison of * room and computer conferencing communication media 0809
Designing real-time, * support computer-human interaction 0982
CHI '88 Workshop on Real Time, * support computer-human interaction 0991
A user-friendly program of human judgments in engineering * analysis 01167

Graphical data presentation for * support systems 01229
An interactive outranking system for multi-attribute * making 01539
Application of * support system on sandwich beams, verified by experiments 01572
Understanding and validating results in model-based * support systems 01666
Propaedeutics of *-making: supporting managerial learning and innovation 01667
Providing effective * support: modeling users and their requirements 01668
A modular user-oriented * support for physical database design 01669
Human specifics fuzzy categories and counteraction in * making problems 01696
Optimizing the structure of database menu indexes: a * model of menu search 01716
ARIADNE: a knowledge-based interactive system for planning and * support 01860
Adaptive user interfaces for planning and * aids in $C^3I$ systems 01887
An empirical investigation as to the need for multicomponent * models 01898
The feature chart: A tool for communicating the analysis for a * support system 01913
* support systems for workers: a bridge to advancing productivity 01947
Automatic information processing activities and operational * making: a case study of consequence 01950
An analysis of human and computer *-making capabilities 01951
On two roles * support systems can play in negotiations 01998
Information requirements specification II: Brainstorming collective *-making technique 02005
A fuzzy *-making method and its application to a company choice problem 02029

Temporal semantics and natural language processing in a * support system 02038
Comparison of * support strategies in expert consultation systems 02101
Simplifying * trees 02157
Trust between humans and machines, and the design of * aids 02164
Models of the * maker in unforeseen accidents 02172
Information and reasoning in intelligent * support systems 02173
A cognitive study of the *-making process in a business context: implications for design of expert systems 02256
Controlling bias in user assertions in expert * support systems for problem formulation 02343
Effects of * support training and cognitive style on * process attributes 02346
User perceptions of * support system restrictiveness: an experiment 02353
Current and future uses of the group * support system technology: report on a recent empirical study 02355
The effects of modes of information presentation on *-making: a review and meta-analysis 02358
Psychological models of deferred * making 02370
TA: Can it improve worker satisfaction with organizational *-making? 02414
Expert systems as human resource management * tools 02440
A study of user interface aids for model-oriented * support systems 02479
* analysis: practice and promise 02480
Modeling managerial behavior: misperceptions of feedback in a dynamic *making experiment 02483
Descriptive analysis for computer-based * support 02527
Man-machine procedures of * making under uncertainty based on linear programming 02664

Innovation of * support system-matplan based on structure matrix supported by APL 02800
GDSS: a brief look at a new concept in * support 02804
Transferring skills from training to the actual work situation: the role of task application knowledge, action styles and job * latitude 02865
Choosing between methods: analysing the user's * space in terms of schemas and linear models 02879
The actem model for * modelling in a scene management system 02954
Social choice theory and distributed * making 03044
* support using qualitative evidence 03398
* Support and Knowledge Based Systems Track § 03461
An investigation of performance, productivity, and rationality in multi-criteria * making 03463
Systems for cooperative work and group * making: status of use and problems in development 03471
On building future * support systems 03472
Flexible user interface * support systems 03473
When and how cognitive style impacts * making 03474
The impact of "Messy" data on group * making 03476
GMMS: global model management system: a conceptual design framework for model management systems for distributed * support systems 03484
* support for reasoning about values 03486
Intentional and operational aspects of * behaviour and their modelling 03666
* support systems: theory and application § 03788
A study of managerial computer users: the impact of user sophistication on * structure and attributes of *-related information (end user) 04078
* and intelligence ● HCI-0068 †

General multiple-objective * functions and linguistically quantified statements HCI-0110 †
A general user interface for creating and displaying tree-structures, hierarchies, * trees, and nested menus HCI-0136 †
Understanding the effectiveness of computer graphics for * support: a cumulative experimental approach HCI-0215 †
Expert systems as cognitive tools for human * making HCI-0227 †
Attitudes towards specific uses of the computers quantitative, *-making and record-keeping applications HCI-0234 †
Interactive fuzzy *-making for multi-objective nonlinear programming using reference membership intervals HCI-0295 †
Change, attitude to change, and * support system success HCI-0296 †
Communications design for Co-oP: a group * support system HCI-0297 †
Computer * support for senior managers: encouraging exploration HCI-0298 †
Personal computing for * support HCI-0299 †
A laboratory study of user characteristics and *-making performance in end-user computing HCI-0301 †
Impact of design methods on * support systems success: an empirical assessment HCI-0303 †
* trees: a contribution to automatic interpretation of GUHA results HCI-0329 †

**DECISIONMAKER**
Aiding the human * through the knowledge-based sciences 01880

**DECISIONMAKERS**
Distributed decisionmaking with constrained *: a case study 01886

**DECISIONMAKING**
Application of a mathematical model of human * for human-computer communication 01866

Capturing expertise: Some approaches to modeling command * in combat analysis 01883
Distributed tactical *: conceptual framework and empirical results 01885
Distributed * with constrained decisionmakers: a case study 01886
Information systems engineering for distributed * 01899

**DECISIONS**
Data, expert knowledge and * ● 0338
Refining early design * with a black-box model 03200

**DECISIVE**
ORGPLAN an information-* aid system to resolving organizing problems 01573

**DECLARATIVE**
Pogo: a * representation system for graphics 0476
Truth versus appropriateness: relating * to procedural knowledge 0484

**DECODINGS**
The fuzzy * of educative texts 01700

**DECOMPOSITION**
Recognition of speech using temporal * 03990
An empirical investigation into problem * strategies used in program design HCI-0103 †

**DECREMENT**
Processing demands, training, and the vigilance * 01723

**DEDUCTIVE**
A hybrid approach to * uncertain inference 02191
DYNABOARD: user animated display of * proofs in mathematics 02221
A * database based on Aristotelian logic 02398

**DEFAULT**
On the relation between * and autoepistemic logic 01214
The use of modal * reasoning in information systems 02095

**DEFEASIBLE**
Oblog-2: A hybrid knowledge representation system for * reasoning 02778

**DEFECT**
Birth *, spontaneous abortion and work with VDUs 03688

**DEFECTIVE**
Study of visual performance on a multi-color VDU of color * and normal Trichromatic subjects 03701

**DEFECTS**
Birth *, course of pregnancy, and work with VDUs: a Finnish case-referent study 03689
Video display terminals and birth *. A study of pregnancy outcomes of employees of the Postal-Giro Center, Oslo, Norway 03691

**DEFINITIONAL**
* distinctions and implications for managing end user computing 01946

**DEFINITIVE**
A * programming approach to the implementation of CAD software 0008

**DELETIONS**
The effects of program-dependent and program-independent * on software cloze tests HCI-0175 †

**DELTA**
Computer quantification of * activity in sleep EEG 01491
Process control and people at General Motors' * Engine Plant 01905
Process control and people at General Motors' * engine plant 03431

**DEMANDING**
* higher productivity 01630
Mathematical modeling of fatigue in physically * jobs 02363

**DEMANDS**
Mapping the cognitive * of learning to program 0579
Processing *, training, and the vigilance decrement 01723
Effects of information-processing * on physiological response patterns 01740
Processing *, effort, and individual differences in four different vigilance tasks 01801
The effect of task * and graphical format on information processing strategies 02482

Effects of computerization on job * and stress: the correspondence of subjective and objective data 03622
What should be computerized? Cognitive * of mental routine tasks and mental load 03632

**DEMOGRAPHIC**
IDECAP: interactive pictorial information system for * and environmental planning applications HCI-0411 †

**DEMOTIVATORS**
Motivators vs. * in the IS environment 02433

**DENSE**
On the estimation of * displacement vector fields from image sequences 03335

**DEPENDENCIES**
Absolute dates and relative dates in an inferential system on temporal * between events 02235
On global context * and their properties (extended abstract) 03945

**DEPENDENCY**
Statistical * in visual scanning 01719
Rough sets and * analysis among attributes in computer implementations of expert's inference models 02231
Affect-chaining and * oriented flow analysis applied to queries of programs 02789
A conceptual * network approach to multi-task assignments in man-machine (teleoperated) systems 03388

**DEPICTED**
Prototyping user interfaces for applications * by graphs 03523

**DEPICTING**
Problem solving performance and display preference for information displays * numerical functions 0978

**DEPTH**
* and detours: an essay on visually guided behavior 0018
A new sense for * of field 01845
Studying * cues in a three-dimensional computer graphics workstation 02117

Effects of breadth, * and number responses on computer menu search performance 02192
Perception of rotation in *: the psychophysical evidence 03343
Static stereo vision * distortions in teleoperation 03390
The */breadth trade-off in the design of menu-driven user interfaces HCI-0135 †

**DESCRIPTIVE**
A */prescriptive model for menu-based interaction 02120
* analysis for computer-based decision support 02527

**DESIGNER**
* labyrinths: text mazes for language learners 0197
Computer graphics: A tool for the artist, * and amateur 0235
Qualities of a good forms * 02412
The user */developer and the user work station 02431
Designing the interface *'s interface 03116
Humane: A *'s assistant for modeling and evaluating function allocation options 03397
Building a visual *'s environment 03496
Effects of an immediate feedback tool on * productivity and design usability 04052
Compact disc-interactive: a *'s overview ● HCI-0078 †
The * as user: building requirements for design tools from design practice HCI-0129 †
The database *'s workbench HCI-0249 †

**DESIGNERS**
Designing for usability: Key principles and what * think 0078
Why do instructional * need conversation theory? 0506
Designing for *: an analysis of design practice in the real world 0839
Collaboration of UIMS * and human factors specialists 01060
Knowledge-based tools to promote shared goals and terminology between interface * 01160
Structuring knowledge bases for * of learning materials 01807

Planning as feedback to * 02978
Making computer tasks at work more playful: Implications for systems analysts and * 03005
How map * can represent their ideas in thematic maps: effective user interfaces for thematic map design 03870
Designing for usability: key principles and what * think HCI-0231 †

**DESIGNING**

The human factor: * computer systems for people 0076
* for usability: Key principles and what designers think 0078
Methods for * software to fit human needs and capabilities (excerpt) 0079
* for error 0087
* the star user interface 0089
Information technology & people: * for the future ● 0144
Practical experience in * software ergonomic projects for large application systems 0190
* interactive, responsive instruction: a set of procedures 0274
* intelligence 0361
* end-user interfaces: state of the art report 15.8 ● 0422
Introduction: * interfaces for expert systems 0426
* advanced workstations 0457
* with constraints 0467
Cognitive economy in physics reasoning: implications for *instructional materials 0542
* a CD ROM information structure 0682
* the user interface (Videotape) ● 0687
* the user interface: professional development courses from the Univ. of Maryland ● 0688
* the user interface: supplemental materials ● 0689
* computer-based microworlds 0742
* optimum CRT text blinking video image presentation 0795
* for designers: an analysis of design practice in the real world 0839
* a quality voice: an analysis of listeners' reactions to synthetic voices 0914
On * for usability: an application of four key principles 0923

* in the dark: logics that compete with the user 0928
* conceptual models of dialog: a case for dialog charts 0968
* real-time, decision support computer-human interaction 0982
* menu display format to match input device format 0983
* the "cockpit": the application of a human-centered design philosophy to make optimization systems accessible 01016
* a practical interface 01174
* with databases 01425
* screens for people to use easily 01531
* a user manual to support an in-house database 01635
The * mind 01661
A framework for * adaptive DSS Interfaces 01672
* SAA applications and user interfaces 01821
Of mice and menus: * the user-friendly interface 01837
Moral judgements in * better systems 02064
* information systems for people 02411
* systems for change 02420
An interactive simulator for the * of woven fabric structures second place 02583
* a neural network satisfying a given set of constraints 02755
* keybindings to be easy to learn and resistant to forgetting even when the set of commands is large 02890
* the interface designer's interface 03116
* electronic paper to fit user requirements 03206
People and computers: * for usability § 03244
People and computers: * for usability 03245
The role of iterative evaluation in * systems for usability 03255
The Monte Carlo processor: * and implementing a language for Monte Carlo work 03317
* hybrid automated manufacturing systems: A European perspective 03382

Methods for * software to fit human needs and capabilities § 03566
Methodological problems of * dialogue-oriented components in information systems 03595
* learning processes for work activities in automated technologies 03605
* computer-based learning materials § 03875
Visual comfort as a criterion for * display units 03892
A methodology for * distributed, fault-tolerant, and reactive real-time operating systems 04071
* the user interface: strategies for effective human-computer interaction ● HCI-0006 †
* user interfaces for software ● HCI-0010 †
A structured approach to * human-computer dialogues HCI-0106 †
Heuristics for * enjoyable user interfaces: lessons from computer games HCI-0132 †
* online information HCI-0152 †
* for usability: key principles and what designers think HCI-0231 †
Using the micro-computer to simplify database access: * interfaces to complex files HCI-0275 †
Reasoning in natural language for * a data base HCI-0322 †

**DESIRABLE**

"Automation, robotization in particular, is always economically *"—fact or fiction? 03448

**DESKS**

On the design of dealing * 03713

**DESKTOP**

Writers as total * publishers: developing a conceptual approach to training 0108
* publishing 0238
Why * publishing is not a panacea 03131
* publishing and user services; moment in the evolution of user support documentation at UNH 03158

**DESPAIR**

Computer ethics: an antidote to * 0791

[DESTINATION]

## DESTINATION
Empirical studies of programmers: the territory, paths, and * 02691

## DETECTION
Rule-based * of speech features for automatic speech recognition 0419

Communication failure in dialogue and discourse: * and repair processes ● 0611

Models of human problem solving: *, diagnosis, and compensation for system failures 0653

Real-time failure * on complex mechanical structures via parallel data processing 01561

Multimodal * and recognition performance of sonar operators 01709

Radiation * by ear and by eye 01732

Effect of pixel height, display height, and vertical resolution on the * of a simple vertical line signal in visual noise 01753

Visual accommodation and target * in the vicinity of a window post 01802

Human error * processes 02166

Theoretical training and problem * in a computerized database retrieval task 02239

Thresholding for edge * using human psychovisual phenomena 02538

On the temporal stability of signal * processes 03617

On the * of social effects in man-computer interaction—a contribution to systems design 03672

Factors influencing the * of trend deviations on VDTs 03894

Error * and correction in a speech recognition system: a knowledge based system approach 04054

## DETERMINANTS
* of the VDU operator's well-being 03679

## DETOURS
Depth and *: an essay on visually guided behavior 0018

## DEVELOPMENT
Information * is part of product *—not an afterthought 0103

AI * and the Office of Naval Research 0140

Considerations for the * of natural-language interfaces to database management systems 0161

The analysis phase in * of knowledge based systems 0324

Intelligence and children's * 0360

Communication and management support in system * environments (Reprint) 0374

Microsoft windows 2.0 program * ● 0446

Symbiotic software: * and usage issues on stand-alone and networked systems 0474

Production system models of learning and * ● 0478

Learning, *, and production systems 0479

Self-modifying production system model of cognitive * 0486

Logo and * of thinking skills 0582

Computers, cognition, and *: issues for psychology and education ● 0643

Designing the user interface: professional * courses from the Univ. of Maryland ● 0688

The * of a postmodern self: a computer-assisted comparative analysis of personal documents ● 0732

Action research on systems *: case study of changing actor roles 0788

Positioning human factors in the user interface * chain 0835

A case study of user interface management system * and application 0836

Innovation in user interface *: obstacles and opportunities 0852

Graphic interfaces for knowledge-based system * 0892

Rapid prototyping and system *: examination of an interface toolkit for voice and telephony applications 0918

An interactive environment for dialogue *: its design, use and evaluation; or, is aide useful? 0920

Software * snapshots: A preliminary investigation 0959

* of a three-dimensional auditory display system 0980

The * of ergonomic standards 0987

* and evaluation of direct manipulation lists (poster session) 0993

PLEXACT: an architecture & design of a knowledge-based system for information systems * 01020

Tools and methodology for user interface * 01057

Bibliography of software tools for user interface * 01071

A * environment for horizontal microcode programs 01079

Requirements checklist for a system * workstation 01144

Technological * and the integrated workstation 01313

The use of prototyping and simulation in the * of large-scale applications 01411

Employing usability engineering in the * of office products 01413

Some issues related to the design and * of an interactive video disc 01497

* of the wedding planner—extensions to reach a young audience 01502

A structure for enhancing user participation in model * 01514

Software * approach in FMS 01567

Standards and system * 01629

End-user prototyping: sophisticated users supporting system * 01636

Information systems strategy and end-user application * 01637

Human factors support for product * 01681

Towards the * of human work-performance standards in futuristic man-machine systems: a fuzzy modeling approach 01692

Examination of the role of "higher order" consistency in skill * 01791

Advanced interactive executive program * environment 01816

A critical view of factors affecting successful application of normative and socio-technical systems * approaches 01914

Applying a pilot system and prototyping approach to systems * and implementation 01915

KEYWORD INDEX

# KEYWORD INDEX [DEVELOPMENT]

Differences in analyst's attitudes towards information systems *: evidence and implications 01935
Successful application of communication techniques to improve the systems * process 01952
Methodology for end user computing in * administration 01956
Communicating with users during systems * 01972
From timesharing to the sixth generation: the * of human-computer interaction. Part I 02097
Foundations of dialog engineering: the * of human-computer interaction. Part II 02100
ADDS-a dialogue * system for the Ada programming language 02102
Cognitive issues in the process of software *: review and reappraisal 02222
* and validation of a reader-based documentation measure 02236
Electronic information systems analysis. Present and future information systems use by academics involved in * studies 02323
Use of fourth generation languages: application * and documentation problems 02435
Utilizing the trend of end user * 02444
* of a hand-held computerized vocabulary tutor 02468
Information systems * success: Perspectives from project team participants 02501
System * methods—a comparative investigation 02504
The * of an intelligent user interface for NASA's scientific databases 02673
* and sensitivity analysis of adaptive predictor for human eye movement model 02681
A highly integrated tool set for program * support 02788
User * of applications: a study of a model of success 02807
A program * system for the casual programmer 02808

History of the * of medical information systems at the Laboratory of Computer Science at Massachusetts General Hospital 02842
Integrating human factors and software * 02882
* of an instrument measuring user satisfaction of the human-computer interface 02892
Using hypertext to overcome the knowledge base * bottleneck: a case study 02914
The * of an automated flight test management system for flight test planning and monitoring 02928
Increase organizational effectiveness: Support self-managed IS * teams 03014
Instilling professionalism in a software * organization 03019
Practical Software * Environments § 03048
AWB-ADE: an application * environment for interactive, integrated systems 03051
The kernel of a generic software * environment 03056
Research & * in Information Retrieval § 03062
Research and * in information retrieval § 03072
Dialogue in REDUCE: experience and * 03088
Hypermedia: a face lift for presentation research and *: a user services function 03154
Some experiences in integrating specification of human computer interaction within a structured system * method 03222
Usability engineering in office product * 03258
Research and * in information retrieval § 03287
* of a human engineering design standard for robot teach pendants 03411
* of a continuous finishing line to improve working conditions 03434
Systems for cooperative work and group decision making: status of use and problems in * 03471
Express—rapid prototyping and product * via integrated knowledge-based executable specifications 03492
Using distributed simulation for distributed application * 03500
Multiple representation document * (extende abstract) 03518
Supporting document * with concordia 03521
System design for human * and productivity: participation and beyond § 03640
Integrative participation—a challenge to the * of informatics 03641
User or * of information systems: Which is more fundamental? 03654
Report from the working group on "goals and strategies of trade unions and other social groups in systems design for human * and productivity." 03657
Establishing structures of requirements for the application of automated information processing (AIP)—an approach for the * of computer-aided systems 03660
Generation of visions in systems *: a supplement to the tool box 03661
Participation in the * of software and the utilisation of standard software 03663
Some aspects of communication in the natural language and user's involvement in software * 03670
System * in a women's perspective 03675
Workers education and user participation in the * of protective policies for VDT operators 03752
PantaPM: an integrated software * environment 03796
Pedagogical * of computer-based learning material 03878
Experiences with the * of a portable network operating system 03882
* of mental models of an office system: a field study on an introductory course 03903
Software tools for the * of pictorial information systems in medicine—the ISQL experience 03980
Teleoperations and robotics: evolution and * ● HCI-0068 †

737

SKETCHER, an interactive, graphical Ada software tool—its * and use HCI-0100 †

Extended programming in the large in a software * environment HCI-0101 †

Anatomy of a compact user interface * tool HCI-0104 †

PECAN: program * systems that support multiple views HCI-0145 †

Towards an integration between language and software * environment HCI-0158 †

Abstract data type * and implementation: an example HCI-0162 †

* of a term association interface for browsing bibliographic data bases based on end users' word associations HCI-0266 †

The * and use of information technology in health care HCI-0408 †

Human-computer interface *: concepts and systems for its management HCI-0444 †

## DEVELOPING

* decision support systems from a model of the DSS/user interface 0253

## DEVELOPMENT

Schaum's outline of theories and problems of programming with advanced structured COBOL with file processing structured systems * and interactive cons ● 0555

## DEVIATIONS

Factors influencing the detection of trend * on VDTs 03894

## DEVICE

The effects of * technology on the usability of advanced telephone functions 0876

Designing menu display format to match input * format 0983

An intelligent braille display * 01832

Exploratory evaluation of a planar foot-operated cursor-positioning * 02858

*-independent graphics: with examples from IBM personal computers ● HCI-0070 †

The microcomputer as a classroom audio visual *: the concept, and prospects HCI-0223 †

Instructionless learning about a complex *: the paradigm and observations HCI-0333 †

## DEXTERITY

Manual *: A user-oriented approach to creating computer documentation 0085

## DIAGNOSING

Sherlock—a system for * power distribution ring network faults 02916

## DIAGNOSIS

DARN: Toward a community memory for * and repair tasks 0428

Psychological evaluation of path hypotheses in cognitive * 0537

Models of human problem solving: detection, *, and compensation for system failures 0653

Measures of human problem solving performance in fault * tasks 0655

Modeling fault * as the activation and use of a frame system 01729

Aiding the operator during novel fault * 01858

A model of fault * performance of expert marine engineers 02199

Strategies in controlling a continuous process with long response latencies: needs for computer support to * 02217

The ISA expert system: a prototype system for failure * on the space station 02913

Concept demonstration of the use of interactive fault * and isolation for TF30 engines 02968

SPA: a systems for * of computer performance problems 02969

An object-oriented expert system for coal-fired MHD power plant fault monitoringand * 02973

Corporate culture, technical documentation, and organization * HCI-0151 †

A practical method for LR and LL syntactic error * and recovery HCI-0163 †

## DIAGNOSTIC

$DM^2$: an algorithm for * reasoning that combines analytical models and experiential knowledge 02190

Task-oriented parsing - a * method to be used adaptive systems 02896

Generic expert system shell for * reasoning 02911

Expert * system 02912

SMARTGEN: the implementation of an expert system for the generation of digital logic * tests 02929

Generic * knowledge acquisition tool 02944

A generic strategy for * assistance: the technician's assistant 02957

What do users ask? Some thoughts on * advice HCI-0326 †

Evaluating RECONSIDER: a computer program for * prompting HCI-0410 †

## DIAGNOSTICS

Advanced *: a PASCAL interactive system 01958

PISCES: an expert system for coal fired power plant monitoring and * 02915

## DIALECTICAL

Orthodox * interfaces 01423

## DIAMOND

*: a multimedia message system built on a distributed architecture (Reprint) 0380

*: A multimedia message system built on a distributed architecture 0574

## DICHOPTIC

Comparison of color sensation in * and in normal vision 01272

## DICHOTOMOUS

A scaling model for * branching processes 01264

## DICHOTOMY

Eliminating the * between scripting and interaction 03299

## DICTIONARIES

A retrieval system for on-line English-Japanese * 03078

## DICTIONARY

An interactive data * facility for CAD/CAM data bases 03174

## DIETARY

A * recommendation expert system using OPS5 03498

## DIFFERENTIABLE

A limitation theorem for the * prototypification of shape 02365

# KEYWORD INDEX [DISABLED]

## DIFFERENTIAL
Simplicial * geometric theory for language cortical dynamics 01698
One hundred * equations execute directly on the IBM PC 02582
* Hebbian learning 02745
* organization impacts of the transition from stand-alone to integrated flexible production 03380

## DIFFRACTION
The effects of limited data in multi-frequency reflection * tomography 04020

## DIFFUSION
Managing the * of end-user computing technologies: a fifties mindset with eighties tools 0459
The * and impacts of information technology in households 0754
* approximation of the neuronal model with synaptic reversal potentials 01254
Short-term memory as a metastable state.III. * approximation 01611

## DIGIAL
* signal processor accelerators for neural network simulations 02754

## DIGIT
The effect of microcomputer presentation and response medium on * span 02090
Optimization of string length for spoken * input with error correction 02185

## DIGITAL
* video interactive 0681
* video interactive 01308
The coming revolution in interactive * video 01325
DVI—a * multimedia technology 01327
Life before the chips. simulating * video interactive technology 01328
* waveform sampling rate converter 01578
* parallelism, perpendicularity, and rectangles 01843
SMARTGEN: the implementation of an expert system for the generation of *logic diagnostic tests 02929
An advisory system for * logic simulation 02986

* typography: an introduction to type and composition for computer system design ● HCI-0074 †

## DIGITORUM
Model of the neuro-muscular recruitment example of the extensor *communis muscle in man: I—identification of motoneurons and of muscular fibers 01595

## DIGITS
Speaker-independent automatic recognition of plosive sound in letters and * 03993
Computer recognition of spoken letters and * 03995

## DILEMMA
Five gambits for the advisory interface * 0314

## DIME
*: a programming environment for unstructured triangular meshes on a distributed-memory parallel processor 02909

## DIMENSIONAL
A two-* frame buffer processor 0494
Development of a three-* auditory display system 0980
Information detective: a workstation for exploring three *information space 01010
Studying depth cues in a three-* computer graphics workstation 02117
The mental rotation and perceived realism of computer-generated three-* images 02213
Optical analog of two-* neural networks and their application in recognition of radar targets 02733
The perception of coherent motion in two-* patterns 03327
Tracking three-* moving light displays 03337
Neural computers in vision: processing of high * data 03960
Experimental study of a two-* language vs. FORTRAN for first-course progammers HCI-0171 †

## DIPHONE
Real-time large vocabulary word recognition via * spotting and multiprocessor implementation 03996

## DIRECTIONAL
Quantitative determination of orientational and * components in the response of visual cortical cells to moving stimuli 01268

## DIRECTLY
One hundred differential equations execute * on the IBM PC 02582

## DIRECTORIES
*, DOS, and hard disks: impact on the user 02604

## DIRECTORY
A * of sources for interactive technologies 0941
Querying the French *Yellow Pages*: natural language access to the * 02007
Structure of a * space: a case study with a UNIX operating system 02138

## DISABILITIES
Computer work skills training for persons with developmental * 01559

## DISABLED
Making computers accessible to * people 0094
The * 0148
Communication methods of the vocally *: a review 0783
Towards universality of access: interfacing physically * students to the Icon educational microcomputer 0821
Learning * students' difficulties in learning to use a word processor: implications for design 0889
An authoring system for the creation of interfaces for * users 0974
User interface primitives to allow full functional use of computers by physically * persons 0979
Helping the * 01445
Dp and the * 01646
An assessment of the major computerised databases relating to * people in the UK and Scandinavia 02326

Headstart—a lifeline for the * 02500
The design of auditory interfaces for visually * users 02869
Public Law 99-506, "Section 508" Electronic Equipment Accessibility for * workers 02893
New technology work aids for the physically * 03273
Voice-input aids for the physically * HCI-0089 †
Text processing by speech: dialogue design and usability issues in the provision of a system for * users HCI-0357 †

## DISADVANTAGES
Women, work and computerization: opportunities and * § 03674

## DISBELIEF
Extension of conditional probability and measures of belief and * in a hypothesis based on uncertain evidence 01846

## DISC
Anticipating compact *-interactive (CD-I): ten guidelines for prospective authors 0280
Compact *-interactive 0680
Putting Texas on * 01316
Compact *-interactive: a designer's overview ● HCI-0078 †

## DISCHARGE
Statistical inference on spontaneous neuronal * patterns. I. Single neuron 01247

## DISCIPLINES
User interface design in large corporations: coordination and communication across * 0853

## DISCOMFORT
Subject reports about musculoskeletal * in VDU work as a complex phenomenon 03708
Effects on visual accommodation and subjective visual * from VDT work intensified through split screen technique 03735
An evaluation of mood disturbances and somatic * under slow computer-response time and incentive-pay conditions 03765

## DISCONNECTION
The *: how to interface computers and video ● 0703

## DISCONTINUOUS
Motion from continuous or * arrangements 03342

## DISCOVERY
Induction: processes of inference, learning, and * ● HCI-0064 †

## DISCRIMINANT
Nonlinear * functions and associative memories 02757

## DISCRIMINATION
A general theory of * learning 0481
An experiment in computational * of English word senses 01813
The accumulator model of two-choice * 02371
Hopfield model applied to vowel and consonant * 02735
A dynamic model of olfactory * 02737
Speeded phase *: evidence for global to local processing 03307

## DISCS
Producing resource *—the Domesday project experience 0514

## DISENTANGLING
On meanings menus for measurement: * evaluative issues in system design 01997

## DISJUNCTIVE
* models of boolean category learning 01262

## DISK
Hard * interfaces 01307
Hypertext engineering: practical methods for creating a compact *encyclopedia 02832
The Drexel *: an electronic "Guidebook" 03198
Practical applications of optical * image systems in document management 04041
Design and performance considerations for an optical *-based, multimedia object server HCI-0265 †

## DISKS
Directories, DOS, and hard *: impact on the user 02604

## DISLAY
A discrete control model of operator function: A methodology for information * design 01874

## DISORDER
Order and * in knowledge structures 02722

## DISPARITY
Vertical * nulling in random-dot stereograms 01256

## DISPERSED
A case study of CSCW in a * organization 02866

## DISPLACEMENT
Visual control of * at slow speeds 01797
On the estimation of dense * vector fields from image sequences 03335

## DISPLAY
Guide to the Draft American National Standard for Human Factors Engineering of Visual * Terminal Workstations 0048
The algorithmic approach in ergonomics: the case of optimal colours and ambients for * work 0247
Human factors for color * systems: concepts, methods, and research 0256
Response time and * rate in human performance with computers 0760
Problem solving performance and * preference for information *s depicting numerical functions 0978
Development of a three-dimensional auditory * system 0980
Designing menu * format to match input device format 0983
The proteus bibliography: Representation and interactive * in databases 01085
Efforts of * format on proof-reading with VDUs 01246
Guide to the draft American national standard for human factors engineering of visual * terminal workstations 01549
Intermittent illumination from visual * units and fluorescent lighting affects movements of the eyes across text 01713
An integrated * for vertical and translational flight: eight factors affecting pilot performance 01714

KEYWORD INDEX [DISPLAYS]

On the selection and evaluation of visual * symbology: factors influencing search and identification times 01718
Optimizing the touch tablet: the effects of control * gain and method of cursor control 01730
Perspective traffic * format and airline pilot traffic avoidance 01748
* formatting in information integration and nonintegration tasks 01750
Effect of pixel height, * height, and vertical resolution on the detection of a simple vertical line signal in visual noise 01753
Temporal resolution: an insight into the video * terminal (VDT) "problem" 01754
* proximity in multicue information integration: the benefits of boxes 01763
Factors affecting the readability of moving text on a computer * 01764
Using color dimensions to * data dimensions 01766
Operator performance as a function of type of *: conventional versus perspective 01769
Information transfer rate with serial and simultaneous visual * formats 01770
Effects of visual * and motion system delays on operator performance and ueasiness in a driving simulator 01772
Reading self-paced moving text on a computer * 01777
A graphics system architecture for interactive application-specific *functions 01822
An intelligent braille * device 01832
Spatial misorientation exacerbated by collimated virtual flight * 01979
* legibility guidelines: a design aid 01983
Understanding and evaluating a computer graphics * 01984
DYNABOARD: user animated * of deductive proofs in mathematics 02221
Interactive document * and its use in information retrieval 02300

The effects of * formats on information systems design 02357
Human factors design of a video monitor emulator and * (VMED) for visuallyimpaired computer users 02379
The MIDAS * system 02388
A * system for the Stellar Graphics Supercomputer Model GS1000 02816
Interactive performance * and debugging using the NCUBE real-time graphicssystem 02907
Optimum * arrangements for presenting visual reminders 03237
Reconstruction and * of the retina 03310
Interactive scientific visualization and parallel * techniques 03542
* strategies for program browsing 03545
Subjective load in introducing visual * units 03627
Work with * units 86 § 03676
Health impact of work with visual * terminals 03678
Health hazards assessment of radio frequency electromagnetic fields emitted by video * terminals 03685
Video * terminals—electromagnetic radiation and health 03687
Video * terminals and birth defects. A study of pregnancy outcomes of employees of the Postal-Giro Center, Oslo, Norway 03691
Lighting for visual * unit workplaces 03715
Lighting the * or *ing the lighting 03716
Work at video * terminals among office employees: visual ergonomics and lighting 03718
* image characteristics and visual response 03722
Matching * characteristics to human visual capacity 03723
Criteria for the subjective quality of visual * units 03724
Psychosocial work environment and use of visual * terminals:8mfrom theoretical model to action 03742
A model for evaluating stress effects of work with * units 03756

* architecture for VLSI-based graphics workstations 03786
The legibility of visual * texts 03889
Visual fatigue with work on visual * units: the current state of knowledge 03891
Visual comfort as a criterion for designing * units 03892
Windows, viewports and structured * files 03930
Psychovisual issues in the * of medical images 03978
MIDAS: molecular interactive * and simulation 04061
An approach to user specification of interactive * interfaces HCI-0137 †
A * editor with random access and continuous control HCI-0140 †
Reading continuous text from a one-line visual * HCI-0187 †
An experimental evaluation of the impact of data * format on recall performance HCI-0202 †
Cognitive attributes: implications for * design in supervisory control systems HCI-0242 †
The application of scene synthesis techniques to the * of multidimensional image data HCI-0371 †

**DISPLAYER**

Heuristic graph * for G-BASE 02227

**DISPLAYING**

A perceptual study of the Flury-Riedwyl faces for graphically *multivariate data 02126
Users' preferences among different techniques for * the evaluation of LISP functions in an interactive debugger 02863
Lighting the display or * the lighting 03716
* statistical information—ergonomic considerations 03893
A general user interface for creating and * tree-structures, hierarchies, decision trees, and nested menus HCI-0136 †

**DISPLAYS**

Color * and color science 0255

[DISSOCIATING]        KEYWORD INDEX

Color graphic * for network planning and design 0260
Color * for medical imaging 0262
Human factors of color * 0438
Why reading was slower from CRT * than from paper 0797
Understanding Bayesian reasoning via graphical * 0884
Formatting space-related * to optimize expert and nonexpert user performance 0927
Problem solving performance and display preference for information *depicting numerical functions 0978
Evaluating formatted alphanumeric * 01525
Effects of graphic boundaries in tabular *: a human factors evaluation 01526
Optimal colors, phosphors, and illuminant characteristics of CRT *: the lgorithmic approach 01710
The effects of set size on color matching using CRT * 01711
Visual fatigue and spatial frequency adaptation to video * of text 01721
Comparison of speech and pictorial * in a cockpit environment 01731
Reading is slower from CRT * than from paper: attempts to isolate a single-variable explanation 01743
Reading from CRT * can be as fast as reading from paper 01758
Likelihood alarm * 01783
An experimental study of Chinese information * on VDTs 01784
Magnification effects with imaging * depend on scene content and viewing condition 01786
Visual *: the highlighting Paradox 01799
Modeling the Cognitive content of * 01800
Are video * a health hazard? 01980
Improved browsable * for online subject access 02051
Considerations of menu structure and communication rate for the design of computer menu * 02124
Formatting alphanumeric crt * 02140
Multi-window * for readers of lengthy texts 02142
How can computer-based visual * aid operators? 02162

Structural * as learning aids 02188
Improved design of graphic * in thesauri—through technology and ergonomics 02297
Optimizing the usability of computer-generated * 03278
Tracking three-dimensional moving light * 03337
Colors in video * 03725
A colour atlas for graphical * 03726
Colour on *—boon or curse? 03727
Temporal and spatial stability in visual * 03730
The use of color in visual * 03890
System aspects of low-cost bitmapped * 03932
A window manager for bitmapped * and Unix 03933
Holophrasted * in an interactive environment HCI-0105 †
Testing bibliographic * for online catalogs HCI-0285 †

**DISSOCIATING**
Knowledge elicitation: * conscious reflections from automatic processes HCI-0337 †

**DISTINCTIONS**
Skills, rules, and knowledge; signals, signs, and symbols, and other * in human performance models 0654
Definitional * and implications for managing end user computing 01946

**DISTINCTIVE**
* regions and modes: a new theory of speech production 02659

**DISTORTIONS**
Inference control mechanism for statistical database frequency-imposed data * 02449
Static stereo vision depth * in teleoperation 03390

**DISTRIBUTION**
Measurement of seat pressure * 01760
Sherlock—a system for diagnosing power * ring network faults 02916
Graphics-based qualitative simulation generator for power * systems 02946
Design of * of production control functions between humans and artificially intelligent devices 03375

Automated document * using AI based workstations and knowledge based servers 03466

**DISTRUBUTED**
Amnesia and * memory 0641

**DIVISION**
Further * of reintegration of mental labour? CAD/CAP and work in design nd work preparation shops 03385

**DIVISIONS**
The effect on reading speed of word * at the end of a line 03896

**DNA**
An interactive modeling program for * 02385

**DOCTOR**
Tree *, a software package for graphical manipulation and animation of tree structures 03901
The *'s use of a computer in the consulting room: an analysis HCI-0409 †

**DOCUMENT**
Authoring tools for complex * sets 0120
A * layout system using automatic * architecture extraction 0882
Writing to be searched: A workshop on * creation principles 01073
Common LISP object system specification X3J13 * 88-002R 01121
The workstation: the interpress page and * description language 01356
A common interface for accessing * retrieval systems and dbms for retrieval of bibliographic data 01990
Interactive * display and its use in information retrieval 02300
* Processing Systems § 02831
The design of a * database 02835
A knowledge-based approach to online * retrieval system design 03027
Employing voice back channels of facilitate audio * retrieval 03045
* manipulation and typography § 03182
Automated * distribution using AI based workstations and knowledge based servers 03466

742

Ontological analysis of * usage: an exploratory study 03467
Multiple representation * development (extende abstract) 03518
Supporting * development with concordia 03521
* processing 03897
Practical applications of optical disk image systems in * management 04041
Intelligent interfaces for information retrieval systems: architecture problems in the construction of expert systems for * retrieval 04042
Users and experts in the * retrieval system model HCI-0270 †
Architecture problems in the construction of expert systems for *retrieval HCI-0272 †
* convergence in an interactive formatting system HCI-0405 †

**DOCUMENTATION**
Teaching users to fish: hooks, lines and sinkers for reading computer * 03156

**DOCUMENTATION**
Manual Dexterity: A user-oriented approach to creating computer * 0085
Hypertext: a way of incorporating user feedback into online * 0102
Investment in computer-product *: causes and effects 0105
Investigations in multimedia design * 0116
A coherent specification method for the human interface to * systems 0269
Developing effective user *: a human factors approach ● 0699
The effects of structured, multi-level * 0907
Help texts vs. help mechanisms: A new mandate for * writers 01047
* for user-developed applications with high *requirements 01049
ER model clustering as an aid for user communication and * in database design 01331
The influence of troubleshooting, education, and * on computer user satisfaction 01869
The quality of user * 01924

Adaptive command prompting in an on-line * 02121
Development and validation of a reader-based * measure 02236
The quality of user *: an instrument validation 02356
Application software * 02418
* in a user work station environment 02429
Use of fourth generation languages: application development and *problems 02435
How well do you write user * 02442
Interactive * 02612
Separating content from form: A language for formatting on-line *and dialog 02781
Help texts vs. help mechanisms: A new mandate for * writers 02784
Multilingual programming: Coordinating programs, user interfaces, on-line help nd d* 02785
Providing the requisite knowledge via software * 02898
Adequate * of user-developed applications: a new challenge for end-user computing management 03001
Desktop publishing and user services; moment in the evolution of user support * at UNH 03158
Three steps of better * 03160
Some recent * of robotic safety from Sweden 03407
The soft side of software: a management approach to computer * ● HCI-0016 †
The PegaSys System: pictures as formal * of large programs HCI-0146 †
SOFTLIB—A * management system HCI-0149 †
Corporate culture, technical *, and organization diagnosis HCI-0151 †
Technical writers as computer scientists: the challenges of online * HCI-0153 †
CONTEXT: an on-line * system HCI-0280 †

**DOCUMENTS**
PLEIADE: A system for interactive manipulation of structured * 0265

Embedding graphics into * by using a graphic-editor 0266
Presenting * on workstation screens 0267
The development of a postmodern self: a computer-assisted comparative analysis of personal * ● 0732
DOMAIN/DELPHI: retrieving * online 0906
Indeterminacy in the subject access to * 01993
Conceptual *: a mechanism for specifying active views in hypertext 02833
Browsing within time-driven multimedia * 03046
Interactive retrieval office * 03047
Information retrieval using impression of * as a clue 03065
Quill: An extensible system for editing * of mixed type 03517
A hypertext system to manage software life cycle * 03519
A system for interactive viewing of structured * HCI-0400 †

**DOGMATISM**
Open versus closed minds: the effect of * on an analyst's problem-solving behavior HCI-0446 †

**DOLLARS**
End-users: Dreams or * 02519

**DOLPHIN**
Delphi: an intelligent interface for a * communication laboratory 02989

**DOMAIN**
Studies in the evaluation of a *-independent natural language query system 0162
*/DELPHI: retrieving documents online 0906
Apollo * series 3000 01170
A cognitively based methodology for evaluating human performance in the computer-aided design task * 01240
Creating the * of discourse: ontology and inventory 02158
Human performance in relational algebra, tuple calculus, and * calculus 02208
Computer analysis of students' procedural "bugs" in an arithmetic * 02273

[DOMAINS]

Expanding the * of systems analysis 02587
Automatic acquisition of * and procedural knowledge 02943
Acquisition of control and * knowledge by watching in a blackboard environment HCI-0319 †
Transporting the linguistic string project system from a medical to a Navy * HCI-0352 †

**DOMAINS**
A knowledge-based human-computer cooperative system for ill-structured management * 01873

**DOMESDAY**
Producing resource discs—the * project experience 0514

**DOMINANCE**
A probabilistic * measure for binary choices: analytic aspects of a multi-attribute random weights model 02372

**DOMINANT**
Critical issues in the safety of software-* automated systems 03416

**DORUS**
*: an architecture for dynamic optimal resource utilization systems 02979

**DOS**
* 4.0 01299
IBM * 4.0: a bridge to OS/2 02523
Directories, *, and hard disks: impact on the user 02604

**DOST**
*: an environment to support automatic generation of user interfaces 03053

**DOT**
Vertical disparity nulling in random-* stereograms 01256

**DOWN**
A top * method for interactive drawing 01401
Is top-* natural? Some experimental results from non-procedural languages 02123
Using a top-* and bottom-up strategy to analyze high resolution aerial photographs of urban areas 02960

**DOWNLOADING**
The value of * for database users and database producers 01218

**DRAFT**
Guide to the * American National Standard for Human Factors Engineering of Visual Display Terminal Workstations 0048
Guide to the * American national standard for human factors engineering of visual display terminal workstations 01549

**DRAFTED**
A * PM glossary 0625

**DRAFTING**
Job characteristic perceptions of manual * and CADD: A field study of the effects of computerization on * & design personnel 01523
Modern *: an introduction to CAD ● HCI-0077 †

**DRAGGING**
Snap-* 01052

**DRAGONMAIL**
*: an exercise in distributed computing 02630

**DRAMA**
* and personality in user interface design 0830
An interactive videodisc *: The case of Frank hall 02285

**DRAT**
*: A program for maintaining listings 02401

**DRAW**
Where do we * the line? - Derivation and evaluation of user interface software separation rules 03268

**DRAWING**
Fundamentals of engineering *: with an introduction to interactive computer graphics for design and production, (9th ed.) ● 0531
Are machines as good as people in * conclusions from knowledge represented in catalogues, data bases and expert systems? 0736
A top down method for interactive * 01401
A cognitive approach for graph * 01616
Interactive curve * by segmented Bezier approximation with a control parameter 02535

KEYWORD INDEX

Drag: a graph * system 03183

**DRAWINGS**
Problems in recognition of * 0294
Making * talk: pictures in minds and machines 01392
GRAFLOG: understanding * through natural language 01396

**DREAMS**
End-users: * or dollars 02519

**DREXEL**
The * disk: an electronic "Guidebook" 03198

**DRILL**
A comparison of a microcomputer progressive state * and flashcards for learning paired associates 02295

**DRIVE**
Using a knowledge base to * an expert system interface with a natural language component 0430
A *-reinforcement model of single neuron function: An alternative to the Hebbian neuronal model 02743

**DRIVER**
Enhanced console * 01288

**DRIVERS**
Application input * 01291

**DRIVING**
Visual information pick-up in a simulated * situation 0251
Effects of visual display and motion system delays on operator performance and ueasiness in a * simulator 01772
Effects of vehicle handling characteristics on * strategy 01773
Getting graphics in gear: graphics and dynamics in * simulation 02818

**DSS**
SmartSLIM: a * for controlling biases during problem formulation 0203
Develping decision support systems from a model of the */user interface 0253
User-developed *: steps toward quality control 0461
A framework for designing adaptive * Interfaces 01672

An empirical investigation of * usage and the user's perception of *training 01934
Cognitive process as a basis for MIS and * design 02476
User perceptions of * restrictiveness: an experiment 03470
An architecture for active * 03480
Structured what if analysis in * models 03481
Characteristics of a successful * user's needs vs. builder's needs 03789
The impact of * on organizational communication HCI-0294 †

**DUAL**
Competitive dynamics in a *-route connectionist model of print-to-sound transformation 01341
A user-friendly interface to Kendrick's * code 01447
Internal models, tracking strategies and *-task performance 01751
Speech responses and *-task performance: better time-sharing or asymmetric transfer? 01789
The role of practice in *-task performance: toward workload modeling in a connectionist/control architecture 01790
The * role of information centers: an assessment of end user computing management strategies 01942

**DUALITY**
Organizational humanity and architecture: * and complementarity of papa-logic and mama-logic in managerial conceptualizations of change 01609
Examining the * role of I.S. executives: a study of I.S. issues 01953

**DUMMY**
Initial work on a system-independent computer model of a 3D anthropomorphic * 01476

**DURST**
Data manipulation languages for the universal relation view * 03944

**DUTY**
Task-oriented approach to interactive control of heavy-* manipulators based on coarse scene description ● 0546

**DVI**
*—a digital multimedia technology 01327

**DYNABOARD**
*: user animated display of deductive proofs in mathematics 02221

**DYNAMIC**
Cognitive engineering in complex * worlds ● 0436
Learning with interactive media: * support for students and teachers 0519
Model generation and modification for * systems from geometric data 0604
* versus static menus: an exploratory comparison 0997
Representation of * features in a conceptual schema 01231
Simulation of chaotic EEG patterns with a * model of the olfactory system 01263
The effects of target wavelength on * visual acuity under photopic and scotopic viewing 01762
PHIGS: a standard, *, interactive graphics interface 01826
Two simulation studies investigating means of human-computer communication for * task allocation 01882
A qualitative model of human interaction with complex * systems 01891
Qualitative approximation methodology for modeling and simulation of large * systems: Applications to a Marine power plant 01900
An empirical comparison of model-based and explicit communication for *human-computer task allocation 02109
Cognitive engineering in complex * worlds 02167
Modeling managerial behavior: misperceptions of feedback in a * decision making experiment 02483
* reconfigurability for fast prototyping of user interfaces 02609
* compilation in the Unix environment 02621
Linearization of the * transfer response of time invariant nonlinear systems—in connection with the parallel information processing in living organisms 02665
A * model of olfactory discrimination 02737
* screens and static paper 02786
DORUS: an architecture for * optimal resource utilization systems 02979
* construction of animated help from application context 03123
Virya—a motion control editor for kinematic and * animation 03294
Coupling visual and * features to study handwritten signatures 03309
A methodology for * task allocation in man-machine system 03635
* spectral adaptation of automatic speech recognizers to new speakers 03999

**DYNAMICS**
Modeling of robot system * for CAD based robot programming 0605
Coherent and chaotic structures in 2D vortex *: progress and problems 0729
Competitive * in a dual-route connectionist model of print-to-sound transformation 01341
A logical model of co-operative processes in cerebral * 01615
Simplicial differential geometric theory for language cortical * 01698
The fuzzy paradigm for knowledge representation in cerebral * 01699
Modeling of task-dependent characteristics of human operator * during pursuit manual tracking 01859
Stochastic * of neural networks 01863

* and architecture for neural computation 02270
Notions and * of information 02319
Nonlinear * of pattern formation and pattern recognition in the rabbit olfactory bulb 02558
X-ray microbeam method for measurement of articulatory *-techniques and results 02641
The second generation intelligent user interface for the crustal * data information system 02675
Nonlinear * of artificial neural systems 02747
Firing response of a neural model with threshold modulation and neural * 02761
Getting graphics in gear: graphics and * in driving simulation 02818
Specification and verification of database * HCI-0251 †

## DYSLEXIA
VDU-work and *. a case report 03699

## EAR
Radiation detection by * and by eye 01732

## EARLEY
Modification of *'s algorithm for speech recognition 04003

## EASIE
Human factors and the design of user interface management systems: * as a case study 01963
Rapid prototyping of dialogue for human factors research: the * approach 03254

## EASTMAN
Tennessee * employee teamwork raises quality, customer service 01907

## EBOOK3
The electronic book * 02234

## ECILPSE
*—an APSE based on PCTE 03181

## ECL
Speech analysis and synthesis methods developed at * in NTT-From LPC to LSP- 02646

## ECLIPSE
The * user interface 02638

## ECOLOGICAL
Coping with human errors through system design: implications for *interface design 02254

## ECONOMIC
The * evaluation on implementation industrial robot from user point of view 03447

## ECONOMICAL
An * approach to modeling speech recognition accuracy HCI-0354 †

## ECONOMICALLY
"Automation, robotization in particular, is always *desirable"—fact or fiction? 03448

## ECONOMY
The political * of interactive video in British higher education 0512
Cognitive * in physics reasoning: implications for designing instructional materials 0542
The design of a user friendly engineering * analysis package for a microcomputer 01507
A graphics interface to an engineering * program 01520
Participation, organizational choices and time-*: some theoretical questions 03650

## ECOOP
* '87 § 03790
* '88 (European Conference on Object-Oriented Programming) § 03793

## ECS
* - A technique for the formal specification and rapid prototyping of human-computer interaction 03253

## EDITING
Computer text-*: an information-processing analysis of a routine cognitive skill 0056
Reflections on authoring, *, and managing hypertext 0119
Learning and transfer for text and graphics * with a direct manipulation interface 0900
Virtual video * in interactive multimedia applications 01326
* templates: a user interface generation tool 01827
Enhancing search results by *, analysis and packaging 02035
Analogy and other sources of difficulty in novices' very first text-* 02148

The use of hand-drawn gestures for text * 02151
Question asking when learning a text-* system 02202
Abstraction and integration in IDE, an * and formatting environment 03184
SEE: a safe * environment; human-computer interaction for programmers 03225
An * model for generating graphical user interfaces 03289
Quill: An extensible system for * documents of mixed type 03517
Context-sensitive * with PSG environments 03780
Using data flow specifications and interactive * in the operating system user interface 03800
* graphical objects using procedural representations 04056
Cursor movement during text * HCI-0113 †
Speech-controlled text-*: effects of input modality and of command structure HCI-0397 †
* by example HCI-0398 †

## EDITOR
Embedding graphics into documents by using a graphic-* 0266
The MAGNEX text * for the Comodore Amiga personal computer 0782
Mathematical formula * for CAI 0885
Fine tuning selection semantics in a structure * based programming environment: some experimental results 0975
A semantic * 01101
Structured * support for modularity and data abstraction 01105
An * for constructing graphics with $T_EX$ 01394
Interactive graphic * for analysis and enhancement of medical images 01492
A VLSI interactive layout * (VILE) 02611
A session * with incremental execution functions 02637
A gesture based text * 03232
A viewdata-structure * designed around a task/action mapping 03269

Virya—a motion control * for kinematic and dynamic animation 03294
On the design of a graphical transition network * 03830
A display * with random access and continuous control HCI-0140 †

**EDITORS**
The evaluation of text *: Methodology and empirical results 0058
Transfer between text * 0804
Cognition-sensitive design and user modeling for syntax-directed * 0828
On the usefulness of syntax directed * 03781
Knowledge-based * for directed graphs 03797
The synthesizer generator: a system for constructing language-based * ● HCI-0024 †
Goal and plan knowledge representations: from stories to text * and programs HCI-0183 †
The evaluation of text *: methodology and empirical results. HCI-0209 †

**EDMAS**
*: an object-oriented, locally distributed mail system 01857

**EDUCATING**
* the CBIS user: a case analysis 0778

**EDUCATION**
Adopting interactive videodisc technology for * 0272
Information technology and *: the changing school ● 0282
* and training in robotics ● 0440
The political economy of interactive video in British higher * 0512
Artificial intelligence and *; vol. 1: learning environments and tutoring systems ● 0516
Functional environments for microcomputers in * 0578
Computers, cognition, and development: issues for psychology and * ● 0643
A vision of * in user-centered system and interface design 0985
Teachware for power engineering * 01203
Live-Net in * 01381

Computer literacy in secondary *: the performance and engagement of girls 01495
Recursive complementarity in the cybernetics of * 01598
The influence of troubleshooting, *, and documentation on computer user satisfaction 01869
* and training in office technology 02330
Professional * and subsequent careers in library/information work: a follow-up study of former students on the MA/MSc information studies course at the University of Sheffield 02336
* requirements for the entry level business systems analyst 02409
Microcomputer hardware * at a Czechoslovakian Technical University 02488
Interaction of CMC with video telecourses for distance * 02677
Computer science * § 02809
Moderating effects of age, *, and tenure on the job satisfaction-job performance relationship 03021
XVISION: a comprehensive software system for image processing research, *, and applications 03124
Participative design and requirements on planning, software engineering and * 03658
Analyzing and improving VDU working conditions: workers' * 03751
Workers * and user participation in the development of protective policies for VDT operators 03752
Integrating physics and computer * in a single process 03879
Software Engineering * § 04022
Stategic imperatives in software engineering * 04024
Undergraduate software engineering * 04025
A comparison of the effects of computer-assisted instruction, interactive video, and traditional instruction on third-grade students in art * 04064
Implications for * and training HCI-0430 †

**EDUCATIVE**
The fuzzy decodings of * texts 01700

**EEG**
Simulation of chaotic * patterns with a dynamic model of the olfactory system 01263
Uncertainty analysis of human * spectra: A multivariate information theoretical method for the analysis of brain activity 01270
Computer quantification of delta activity in sleep * 01491

**EFFECTIVENESS**
Cost * of on-line searching of chemical information: an industrial viewpoint 0195
The * of a keystroke line in interactive tutorials 0969
Efficiency vs. * 01092
Managing information systems for * and humanity: applying research of organizational behavior 01932
Measuring the * of personal database structures 02246
A study of organizational * and its predictors 02471
Increase organizational *: Support self-managed IS development teams 03014
An evaluation of the * of the adaptive interface module (AIM) in matching dialogues to users 03212
Perceptions of system * as viewed by executives, users, and information specialists 03469
* of training as a function of the teacher knowledge structure 03604
An investigation of the * of communication between systems analysts and end users in the design of large computer systems 04075
Understanding the * of computer graphics for decision support: a cumulative experimental approach HCI-0215 †
The LISP tutor: it approaches the * of a human tutor HCI-0431 †

## EFFICACY
Self-* expectations as a predictor of computer use: a look at early childhood administrators 01590
* of higher cognitive and factual questions in computer assisted instruction modules 02278
The * of computer-assisted video instruction on rule learning and attitudes 02286

## EGOMOTION
Real time graphic simulation of visual effects of * HCI-0379 †

## EIGENBEHAVIOR
An approach to a mathematics of phenomena: canonical aspects of reentrant form * in the extended calculus of indications 01621

## EIGHTIES
Managing the diffusion of end-user computing technologies: a fifties mindset with * tools 0459
The uneasy *: the transition to an information society 0792

## ELECTRIC
* and magnetic fields of the brain computed by way of a discrete systems analytical approach: Theory and validation 01276

## ELECTRICAL
Improving performance of an * power expert system with genetic algorithms 02925

## ELECTRICITY
Facial particle exposure in the VDU environment: the role of static * 03694

## ELECTROCARDIOGRAM
Beyond heart rate in the cardiac psychophysiological assessment of mental effort: the T-wave amplitude component of the * 01738

## ELECTROCORTICAL
A study of stability of * rhythm generators 01258

## ELECTROMAGNETIC
Health hazards assessment of radio frequency * fields emitted by video display terminals 03685

## ELECTROMYOGRAPHIC
Changes in * activity associated with occupational stress and poor performance in the workplace 01734

## ELECTRONIC
From database to hypertext via * publishing: an information odyssey 0122
* speech recognition: techniques, technology, and applications ● 0174
Reducing social context cues: * mail in organizational communication (Reprint) 0385
How faithfully should the * office simulate real one? 0958
An empirical investigation of two * mail systems 01239
Perception and acceptance of a local area network and * mail 01284
Socio-technical aspects of * mail implementation 01439
Needs and perceived needs of * workstations by engineering project managers 01515
* implementation of associative memory based on neural network models 01895
*Library*—An * ordering system 01991
Selection devices for users of an * encyclopedia: an empirical comparison of four possibilities 02009
Interacting with * mail can be a dream or a night: a user's point of view 02069
Preserving the integrity of the medium: a method of measuring visual and auditory comprehension of * media 02084
The * book Ebook3 02234
Making the transition from print to * encyclopaedias: adapation of mental models 02238
* information systems analysis. Present and future information systems use by academics involved in development studies 02323
* publishing: The predicament of occasional users in the editorial proc 02446
Information-seeking strategies of novices using a full-text *encyclopedia 02452
Reducing social context cues: * mail in organizational communication 02473
An online interface within a hypertext system: project Jefferson's *notebook 02524

User orientation for the * encyclopedia 02605
* communications and collaboration: the emerging model for computer aided communications in science and medicine 02678
Public Law 99-506, "Section 508" * Equipment Accessibility for disabled workers 02893
* monitoring and the redundancy of control systems: The role of the supervisor 03000
Need of * tools in educational programmers and the impact in developing countries 03023
The impact of * mail on managerial and organizational communications 03041
Twenty-five years of * design automation § 03102
Advisor—an * mail consulting service 03151
The Drexel disk: an * "Guidebook" 03198
Designing * paper to fit user requirements 03206
On representation schemes for * promising 03488
Lighting the * office 03717
Efficient computer-user interface in * mail systems HCI-0118 †
A prototype * encyclopedia HCI-0278 †
Reading and writing the * book HCI-0282 †
* calendars in the office: an assessment of user needs and current technology HCI-0287 †
Diversity in the use of * mail: a preliminary inquiry HCI-0310 †
The * classroom: workstations for teaching HCI-0436 †

## ELECTRONICS
Human factors reference guide for * and computer professionals ● 0733
Human factors reference guide for * and computer professionals ● 0734
Managers' reading habits in the * industry 02339

## ELEMENTS
Understanding the * of system design 0156
The * of speech recognition 0176

Interactivity in microcomputer-based instruction: its essential * and how it can be enhanced 0275
Textons, the fundamental * in preattentive vision and perception of textures 0297
* of a plan-based theory of speech acts 0390
A test of a common * theory of transfer 0901
Self-authorization: A characteristic of some * in certain self-organizing systems 01610
The * of graphing data ● HCI-0035 †
Procedural * for computer graphics ● HCI-0069 †

### ELICITATION
The * of system knowledge by picture probes 0921
The application of psychological scaling techniques to knowledge *for knowledge-based systems 02139
Knowledge * using discourse analysis 02152
Cognitive biases and corrective techniques: proposals for improving *procedures for knowledge-based systems 02153
An approach to knowledge * in scheduling FMS: Toward a hybrid intelligent system 03394
Textvision: * and acquisition of conceptual knowledge by graphic representation and multiwindowing 03902
Knowledge *: dissociating conscious reflections from automatic processes HCI-0337 †

### ELIMINATING
* the dichotomy between scripting and interaction 03299

### EMACS
UNIX *: a retrospective (lessons for flexible system design) 03114

### EMBEDDED
Ada-* SQL: the options 0763
* menus: selecting items in context 01320
Graphic equivalence, graphic explanations, and * process modeling for enhanced user-system interaction 01888
* user model-where next? 02059

* training in AI technology through an expert system interface: an alarm processor application 02991
Manipulation of * context using the multiple world mechanism 03921

### EMERAUDE
* portable common tool environment 01970

### EMERGENCE
The * of Zipf's law: Spontaneous encoding optimization by users of a command language 01875
Executive support systems: the * of top management computer use ● HCI-0049 †
The future of interactive systems and the * of direct manipulation HCI-0186 †

### EMISSIONS
Radiation * from VDUs 03684

### EMITTED
Health hazards assessment of radio frequency electromagnetic fields * by video display terminals 03685

### EMOTIONS
Daydreaming and computation: a computer model of everyday creativity, learning nd e*in the human stream of thought 04067

### EMPATHY
Socializing the intelligent tutor: bringing * to computer tutors 0541

### EMPIRICALLY
How are windows used? Some notes on creating an *-based windowing benchmark task 0903

### EMPLOYEE
Tennessee Eastman * teamwork raises quality, customer service 01907
An expert system for screening * pension plans for the Internal Revenue Service 02773

### EMPLOYEES
Assessing the impacts of new technology on library * 02459
Video display terminals and birth defects. A study of pregnancy outcomes of * of the Postal-Giro Center, Oslo, Norway 03691

Work at video display terminals among office *: visual ergonomics and lighting 03718

### EMPLOYMENT
* skills for the robot age 0442
Computer aids for vision and * (CAVE) 0976
Real time speech synthesis—development and * 01482

### EMULATION
Building expert systems: cognitive * ● 0700

### EMULATOR
Human factors design of a video monitor * and display (VMED) for visuallyimpaired computer users 02379

### EM2
*—a Modula-2 programming environment 02392

### ENABLING
* the user interface 01820
MacCadd - an * software method support tool 03252

### ENCAPSULATING
* interactive behaviors 0874

### ENCAPSULATION
A new notion of * 01104

### ENCAPSULATORS
*: a new software paradigm in Smalltalk-80 03034

### ENCODING
The emergence of Zipf's law: Spontaneous * optimization by users of a command language 01875
Arithmetic codes resembling neural * 02021
Intelligible * of ASL image sequences at extremely low information rates 02708

### ENCOUNTER
The practice of the use of computers. A paradoxical * between different traditions of knowledge 0343

### ENCULTURATION
Learning the ways: the * of SDSC users 03144

## ENCYCLOPAEDIAS

Making the transition from print to electronic *: adapation of mental models 02238

## ENCYCLOPEDIA

Selection devices for users of an electronic *: an empirical comparison of four possibilities 02009

An experimental comparison of a mouse and arrow-jump keys for an interactive * 02098

Information-seeking strategies of novices using a full-text electronic * 02452

User orientation for the electronic * 02605

Hypertext engineering: practical methods for creating a compact disk * 02832

A prototype electronic * HCI-0278 †

## END-USER

Supporting the microcomputer * user 0187

Designing *-user interfaces: state of the art report 15.8 ● 0422

Managers, micros and mainframes: integrating systems for *-users ● 0455

Managing the diffusion of *-user computing technologies: a fifties mindset with eighties tools 0459

Company experiences with *-user computing 0460

*-user computing by top executives 0780

Starting *-users 01215

Online use and *-users in media and advertising: an overview 01216

*-users: threat, challenge or myth? 01221

*-user searching—What are the implications? 01224

User cube: a taxonomy of * users 01335

...from the * user angle 01378

Supporting * users in the office 01444

Beta tests and *-user surveys: are they valid? 01631

*-user prototyping: sophisticated users supporting system development 01636

Information systems strategy and *-user application development 01637

Organizational issues of *-user computing 01638

The age of the *-user and the shift from corporate MIS to corporate DSS 01676

*-user computing environments—finding a balance between productivity and control 01927

* user—IS design professional interaction—information exchange for firm profit or * user satisfaction? 01936

The management of the *-user environment: an empirical investigation 01937

The dual role of information centers: an assessment of * user computing management strategies 01942

Definitional distinctions and implications for managing * user computing 01946

Methodology for * user computing in development administration 01956

A tool for measuring analysis * user computing 02000

An icon-driven *-user interface to UNIX 02089

Predicting *-user acceptance of microcomputers in the workplace 02147

The effects of relational and entity-relationship data models on query performance of * users 02247

*-user searching of CAS ONLINE. Results of a cooperative experiment between Imperial Chemical Industries and Chemical Abstracts Services 02269

Time-life, world reporter and the secretary: experiments with *-users 02325

Organizational factors affecting the success of *-user computing 02344

Expansion and control of *-user computing 02347

Strategies for *-user computing: An integrative framework 02348

The impact of information systems strategy on * user computing 02423

The * user attack: Will the real computer professionals stand up and fight 02424

Managing * user computing when the only constant is change 02425

* user computing—the human interface 02428

* user software selection 02434

Strategies for managing * user computing 02436

Utilizing the tr* of * user development 02444

The design and evaluation of a front-* user interface for energy researchers 02453

Service support levels: An organizational approach to *-user computing 02503

Training * users: an exploratory study 02506

The measurement of *-user computing satisfaction 02510

*-users: Dreams or dollars 02519

Putting on a show: using computer graphics to train *-users 02520

What is the role of the intermediary in *-user training? 02522

OST— a training package for *-users of online systems 02568

Front * games 02599

Mainframe and microcomputer-based business graphics: * user computing comparisons and tr* 02805

Linking mechanism supporting *-user computing 02806

Adequate documentation of user-developed applications: a new challenge for *-user computing management 03001

Analysis and design skills required by *-users in small organizations 03008

The importance of individual differences in *-user training: The case for learning style 03009

The influence of training on use of *-user software 03042

Organizational videotex: information services for the * user 03166

Design and evalution of the AID adaptive front-* to Telecom Gold 03260

Human and computer aided manufacturing: The * of taylorism? 03379

Integrating CD-ROM with printed and online services: a silver platter *-user perspective 03558

An investigation of the effectiveness of communication between systems analysts and * users in the design of large computer systems 04075

A study of managerial computer users: the impact of user sophistication on decision structure and attributes of decision-related information (* user) 04078

Observations of *-user online searching behavior over eleven years HCI-0235 †

An interactive database * user facility for the definition and manipulation of forms HCI-0263 †

Development of a term association interface for browsing bibliographic data bases based on * users' word associations HCI-0266 †

Views on *-user searching HCI-0283 †

A laboratory study of user characteristics and decision-making performance in *-user computing HCI-0301 †

## ENDOCRINOLOGICAL

Task-load and * risk for pregnancy in women VDU operators 03692

## ENDS

Transparent information systems through gateways, front *, intermediaries, and interfaces HCI-0276 †

## ENERGY

The design and evaluation of a front-end user interface for * researchers 02453

## ENGAGEMENT

Computer literacy in secondary education: the performance and * of girls 01495

## ENGINE

Process control and people at General Motors' Delta * Plant 01905

Multi-Input fuzzy inference * on a systolic array 02953

Jet * technical advisor (JETA) 02974

Process control and people at General Motors' Delta * plant 03431

## ENGINEERING

Guide to the Draft American National Standard for Human Factors * of Visual Display Terminal Workstations 0048

Developing interactive information systems with the user software *methodology 0077

Software * environments ● 0172

Real-time interfacing: * aspects of microprocessor peripheral systems ● 0224

Computer interface * with model-based analysis ● 0337

The user-computer interface in process control: a human factors *handbook ● 0341

Cognitive * in complex dynamic worlds ● 0436

Fundamentals of * drawing: with an introduction to interactive computer graphics for design and production, (9th ed.) ● 0531

Readings in artificial intelligence and software * ● 0612

An expert system architecture for computer-aided control * 0662

Computer-aided * (CAE) for system analysis 0663

Knowledge *: expert systems and information retrieval ● 0735

Assessment of an effort to integrate computer functions in an *design firm 0779

User-derived impact analysis as a tool for usability * 0922

Teaching user interface design based on usability * 01007

Profile of undergraduate software * courses: results from a survey 01035

Integrating software * into an intermediate programming class 01037

SMART: Scientific database management and * analysis routines and tools 01166

A user-friendly program of human judgments in * decision analysis 01167

Teachware for power * education 01203

Conceptual design of a human error tolerant interface for complex *systems 01235

* the man-machine interface for air traffic control 01358

Employing usability * in the development of office products 01413

The design of a user friendly * economy analysis package for a microcomputer 01507

User facilities for * support stations 01512

Needs and perceived needs of electronic workstations by * project managers 01515

A graphics interface to an * economy program 01520

Guide to the draft American national standard for human factors * of visual display terminal workstations 01549

The * of a translator workstation 01555

Interactive CAD/CAM in * industry 01571

Cognitive *: human problem solving with tools 01781

Software * for user interfaces 01854

Developing interactive information systems with the user software *methodology 01856

Information systems * for distributed decisionmaking 01899

Teaching software * at university 01968

The contribution of cognitive * to the effective design and use of information systems 02033

The * information system: a guided tour 02046

Cognitive systems *: new wine in new bottles 02078

Foundations of dialog *: the development of human-computer interaction. Part II 02100

Modelling human expertise in knowledge *: some preliminary observations 02134

Cognitive * in complex dynamic worlds 02167
Firm strategies for costly * learning 02485
The HORSES project and its perspectives in knowledge * 02716
Hypertext *: practical methods for creating a compact disk encyclopedia 02832
Industrial & * Applications of Artificial Intelligence & Expert Systems § 02910
Knowledge base applications with software *: a tool for requirements specifications 02924
Applications of an AI design shell ENGINEOUS to advanced * products 02932
Industrial & * Applications of Artificial Intelligence & Expert Systems § 02941
Industrial & * Applications of Artificial Intelligence & Expert Systems: vol. I § 02967
Industrial & * Applications of Artificial Intelligence & Expert Systems: vol. II § 02982
Software * meets user services: a methodology for developing user 03141
Usability * in office product development 03258
Product * in the CIM environment 03376
Development of a human * design standard for robot teach pendants 03411
Reliability and robustness of * software § 03451
Software * § 03504
Human-computer communication meets software * 03505
Software * § 03507
Software * for distributed applications: the design project 03508
The FAIM-1 user interface—human * for the fifth generation 03587
Memory research and knowledge * 03599
Participative design and requirements on planning, software * and education 03658
Advanced computing concepts and techniques in control * § 03833

A model for an object management system for software * environments 03843
ANIMENGINE: an * animation system 03858
Software * Education § 04022
Stategic imperatives in software * education 04024
Undergraduate software * education 04025
A scarce resource in undergraduate software * courses: user interface design materials 04027
A computer assisted learning system for reliability * 04060
Human performance *: using human factors/ergonomics to achieve computer system usability (2nd ed.) ● HCI-0042 †
Applying software * principles to the user application interface HCI-0130 †
Human factors in software *: a review of the literature HCI-0157 †
Cognitive *—cognitive science HCI-0200 †
A note on the nature of creativity in *: implications for supporting system design HCI-0220 †
Strategic issues in knowledge * HCI-0317 †
Applications of AI in * HCI-0321 †
Reverse * the brain HCI-0368 †
Interactive critical path analysis (ICPA)—microcomputer implementation of a project management and knowledge * tool HCI-0445 †

**ENGINEERS**
A model of fault diagnosis performance of expert marine * 02199
Motivation norms of knowledge * compared to those of software * 02349

**ENGINEOUS**
Applications of an AI design shell * to advanced engineering products 02932

**ENGINES**
Concept demonstration of the use of interactive fault diagnosis and isolation for TF30 * 02968

**ENGLAND**
CIM and manufacturing industry in the north east of *: A survey of some current issues 03377

**ENGLISH**
On learning the past tenses of * verbs 0634
Wall Street speaks * 01184
An experiment in computational discrimination of * word senses 01813
A retrieval system for on-line *-Japanese dictionaries 03078
A framework of a mechanical translation between Japanese and * by analogy principle HCI-0353 †

**ENTITY**
*-relationship database user interfaces 0711
An *-relationship framework for information resource management 01943
The effects of relational and *-relationaship data models on query performance of end users 02247
A graphical *-relationship database browser 03532

**ENTROPY**
The use of measures of * in evaluating human supervisory control of a manufacturing system 01897
On the applicability of maximum * to inexact reasoning 02074
Causality and maximum * updating 02076

**ENTRY**
Autocompletion in full text transaction *: a method for humanized input 0934
Dialing a name: alphabetic * through a telephone keypad 0973
An investigation of data * methods with a personal computer 01490
The effects of * arrangement in search times: a cross-generational study 02048
Education requirements for the * level business systems analyst 02409
On complexity of command-* in man-computer dialogues 03610
Data * task on VDU: underload or overload 03761

Experimental evaluation of dialogue types for data * HCI-0115 †

**ENVELOPE**
Human perception of the work * of an industrial robot 03410

**ENVIRONMENT**
The Socio/Political * 0040
The physical * 0045
The Trillium user interface design * 0082
The on-line * and in-house training 0106
Textual intervention, collaboration, and the online * 0126
Learning * criteria 0285
An example-base * for beginning programmers 0520
A workcell application design * (WADE) 0598
The migration of expert systems into the production * 0740
A very friendly software * for SOLO 0743
Inducing programs in a direct-manipulation * 0816
Some strategies of reuse in an object-oriented programming * 0820
A synthetic visual * with hand gesturing and voice input 0858
The Trillium user interface design * 0919
An interactive * for dialogue development: its design, use and evaluation; or, is aide useful? 0920
Fine tuning selection semantics in a structure editor based programming *: some experimental results 0975
Student-oriented features of an interactive programming * 01036
A development * for horizontal microcode programs 01079
Polylith: an * to support management of tool interfaces 01096
An * for logic programming 01106
A model and an implementation of a logic programming * 01107
The Mesa programming * 01108
Transportable applications * (TAE) plus experiences in "Object"-ively modernizing a user interface * 01126

Fabrik: a visual programming * 01130
An interactive * for object-oriented music composition and sound synthesis 01131
Foundations for the Arcadia * architecture 01135
Interacting with an active, integrated * 01137
Guided tours and tabletops: tools for communicating in a hypertext * 01161
Optimal allocation of a work force in a toxic substance * 01534
Comparison of speech and pictorial displays in a cockpit * 01731
Advanced interactive executive program development * 01816
The tinkertoy graphical programming * 01850
A rule-based model for the human operator in a time-constrained competing-task * 01877
The management of the end-user *: an empirical investigation 01937
An object-oriented approach to the design of a mail system for a heterogeneous * 01944
MAJIC—an integrated program support * 01960
GRAPE programming * 01967
Emeraude portable common tool * 01970
An interactive * for tool selection, specification and composition 02141
EM2—a Modula-2 programming * 02392
Documentation in a user work station * 02429
Managing the work station * 02430
Motivators vs. demotivators in the IS * 02433
The emerging role of workstations in the library * 02467
Critical factors in the user *: an experimental study of users, organizations and tasks 02507
Hierarchical, modular discrete-event modelling in an object-oriented * 02588
Towards the formal specification of a simple programming support * 02607
Dynamic compilation in the Unix * 02621

Threat to privacy: the federal government's use of personal information in the new communication * 02680
*-centered and viewer-centered perception of surface orientation 02705
ALIEN: a programming * generator for personal computers 02790
Guided tours and tabletops: tools for communicating in a hypertext * 02823
Travel around a learning support *: rambling, orienteering or touring? 02900
DIME: a programming * for unstructured triangular meshes on a distributed-memory parallel processor 02909
SIMS: a uniform * for planning and performing user's tasks 02921
Integral-C—a practical * for C programming 03049
AWB-ADE: an application development * for interactive, integrated systems 03051
Dost: an * to support automatic generation of user interfaces 03053
The kernel of a generic software development * 03056
Multiprocessor Smalltalk: a case study of a multiprocessor-based programming * 03061
Integrated information retrieval for law in a hypertext * 03071
Clue: a common lisp user interface * 03113
XY-WINS: an integraded * for developing graphical user interfaces 03118
A portable user interface for a scientific programming * 03125
Abstraction and integration in IDE, an editing and formatting * 03184
Describing a product opportunity: a method of understanding the users' * 03194
A flexible negotiable interactive learning * 03197
The design and evaluation of an animated programming * 03220
SEE: a safe editing *; human-computer interaction for programmers 03225

[ENVIRONMENTAL]

Product engineering in the CIM * 03376
Building a visual designer's * 03496
A programming * supporting reuse of object-oriented software 03509
The space station information system and software support * 03512
An * for understanding programs 03525
The PFG *: parallel programming with petri net semantics 03527
The integrity lock support * 03578
Facial particle exposure in the VDU *: the role of static electricity 03694
Psychosocial work * and use of visual display terminals:8mfrom theoretical model to action 03742
The Mjo:.KC /lner *: direct interaction with abstractions 03794
PantaPM: an integrated software development * 03796
A design * for computer-aided control system design via multi-objective optimisation 03835
An experimental * for generating word hypotheses in continuous speech 03998
An overview of local * sensing in robotics applications 04012
Maintaining a uniform user interface for an Ada programming * 04066
A methodology, specification language, and automated support * for com1uter-aided design systems 04068
Sharing in a privately owned workstation * 04076
Selecting an Ada * ● HCI-0015 †
Interaction with the * ● HCI-0068 †
Andrew: a distributed personal computing * HCI-0091 †
Extended programming in the large in a software development * HCI-0101 †
Holophrasted displays in an interactive * HCI-0105 †
MIKE: the menu interaction kontrol * HCI-0124 †
PICT: an interactive graphical programming * HCI-0143 †

The Software Life Cycle Support * (SLCSE): a computer based framework for developing software systems HCI-0147 †
Towards an integration between language and software development * HCI-0158 †
A visual approach to browsing in a database * HCI-0258 †
Acquisition of control and domain knowledge by watching in a blackboard * HCI-0319 †
*-centered and viewer-centered perception of surface orientation HCI-0392 †

**ENVIRONMENTAL**

Human factors issues in VDT use: * and workstation design considerations 0046
Changes in prosodic features of speech due to * factors 02651
Hierarchical scheduling in an intelligent * control system 02976
* stressors and perceived health symptoms among office workers 03680
Human factors issues in VDT use: * and workstation design considerations HCI-0210 †
IDECAP: interactive pictorial information system for demographic and * planning applications HCI-0411 †

**ENVIRONMENTS**

Using an object-oriented programming language to create audience-driven hypermedia * 0101
Software engineering * ● 0172
The evaluation of project support * for the STARTS user guide 0173
GENIE-M: A generator for multimedia information * 0268
* for supporting statistical strategy 0322
Communication and management support in system development *(Reprint) 0374
Artificial intelligence programming * ● 0420
Artificial intelligence and education; vol. 1: learning * and tutoring systems ● 0516
Functional * for microcomputers in education 0578

Design * for constructive and argumentative design 0864
Resource management scheme in distributed * 01018
*: Austria compared to the United States 01026
Dialogues: a basis for constructing programming * 01097
Characteristics and functions of software *: an overview 01145
A flexible synonym interface with application examples in CAL and help * 01404
Unified interactive geometric modeller for simulating highly complex * 01472
Common user access—a consistent and usable human-computer interface for the SAA * 01819
Automated concept acquisition in noisy * 01841
End-user computing *—finding a balance between productivity and control 01927
A new approach to cursor movements in user interfaces of integrated programming * 01974
Analysis of the performance of a genetic algorithm-based system for message classification in noisy * 02156
Cognitive aids in process *: prostheses or tools? 02161
Formative evaluation of pre-Logo programming *: a collaborative effort of researchers, teachers, and children 02292
* for Eurota 02514
Capturing the capture concepts: a case study in the design of computer-supported meeting * 02824
Practical Software Development * § 03048
A structural approach to the maintenance of structure-oriented * 03054
A methodology for evaluating * 03055
A foundation for programming * 03057
A study of conflict in group design activities: implications for computer-supported cooperative work * 03477

Visual programming—toward realization of user-friendly programming * 03493
Tool interfaces in integrated project support * 03506
Design principles behind Chiron: a UIMS for software * 03511
Advanced programming * § 03779
Context-sensitive editing with PSG * 03780
Views for tools in integrated * 03784
Support * for VDM 03832
A model for an object management system for software engineering * 03843
A systems model of cognition for improving human factors of computing * 04058

## EPG
Coproduction: evidence from * data 02660

## EPISODE
The semantic language * understanding 03576

## EPISODIC
Principles from the psychology of memory: Part II-* and semantic memory 0331

## EPVM
*: An expert patient-ventilator manager for chemical warfare casualties 02956

## EQUATING
Capacity equivalence curves: a double trade-off curve method for * task performance 01796

## EQUILIBRIA
Induction of categories: The problem of multiple * 02360

## EQUILIBRIUM
The control of hand * trajectories in multi-joint arm movements 01275

## EQUIVALENCE
Capacity * curves: a double trade-off curve method for equating task performance 01796
Graphic *, graphic explanations, and embedded process modeling for enhanced user-system interaction 01888
* of views by query capacity 02271

## EQUIVALENCES
A logic-functional approach to the execution of CCS specifications modulo behavioural * 03874

## EQUIVOCALITY
Message *, media selection and manager performance: implications for information systems 02505

## ERGONOMIC
Practical experience in designing software * projects for large application systems 0190
* vision 0259
* features of interactive systems—the interdependency of software and hardware 0312
* aspects of man-machine communications 0417
The development of * standards 0987
* guidelines for computerized user interfaces 01449
* job design in frequent manual lifting tasks: a microcomputer-based model 01532
* improvements boost AS/RS performance 01904
* considerations in the design of command languages 02694
An evaluation of production systems from the * viewpoint: a plea for an integral approach to design 03430
* evaluation of safety devices in robotic systems 03449
Task and the adjustment of * chairs 03711
The applicability of eye movement analysis in the * evaluation of human-computer interaction 03766
Experimental results do not support some * standards for computer video terminal design HCI-0428 †

## ERGONOMICAL
The evaluation of selected * factors by production automation growth 03429

## ERGONOMICS
* and the new technologies 0147
Knowledge-based human-computer interfaces and software * 0191

Software *: advocations & applications for the human computer interface ● 0193
Contexts and conflicts between * and industrial psychology 0240
* and organizational consulting: accentuation or neglect of psychology 0242
Cognitive * and human computer interaction 0245
The algorithmic approach in *: the case of optimal colours and ambients for display work 0247
The * psychology project at Inria 0844
Jeff Garbers and the * of software 01420
Establishing user-centered criteria for information systems: a software * perspective 01920
Interaction *, control and separation: open problems in user interface management 01962
Improved design of graphic displays in thesauri—through technology and * 02297
* in design for usability 03247
* of Hybrid Automated Systems I § 03362
Macro-* and the computer-integrated enterprise 03383
Beyond software *? Human control of automated systems 03386
* of hybrid intelligence 03393
Cognitive *: an approach for the design of user-oriented interactive systems 03591
Work at video display terminals among office employees: visual * and lighting 03718
Software *: advances and applications ● HCI-0012 †
Readings on cognitive * - mind and computers § HCI-0039 †
Human performance engineering: using human factors/* to achieve computer system usability (2nd ed.) ● HCI-0042 †

## ERGONOMY
Information systems design methodologies and their compliance with cognitive * HCI-0097 †

**EROTETIC**
The * logic of problem-solving inquiry 01583

**ERROR**
Designing for * 0087
Conceptual design of a human * tolerant interface for complex engineering systems 01235
*-free fractions 01297
An approach to human reliability on man-machine systems using * possibility 01702
An * correcting protocol for medical expert systems 02143
Human * detection processes 02166
Prompting, feedback and * correction in the design of a scenario machine 02176
Optimization of string length for spoken digit input with * correction 02185
Classifying sensory inspectors with heterogeneous inspection-* probabilities 02396
* analysis and tutor design 02469
* correction and asymmetry in a binary memory matrix 02750
A study on an * recovery expert system using a superimposer and a digitizer in the advanced teleoperator system 03389
Interactive * recovery expert system for robot with voice recognition subsystem 03420
Naming *s and automatic * correction in human-computer interaction 03770
Factors in the investigation of human * in accident causation 03805
Investigating sources of * in the management of crises: theoretical assumptions and a methodological approach 03807
* auditing in air traffic control 03810
Applicable algebra, *-correcting codes, combinatorics and computer algebra § 03846
Applied algebra, algorithmics and *-correcting codes § 03848
* detection and correction in a speech recognition system: a knowledge based system approach 04054

A proposed solution to the problem of levels in *-message generation HCI-0126 †
A practical method for LR and LL syntactic * diagnosis and recovery HCI-0163 †
Fatal * in pass zero: how not to confuse novices HCI-0164 †

**ERRORS**
VP$^2$: the role of user modelling in correcting * in second language learning 0222
User * in human—computer interaction 0313
Assessing the impact of human factors on data processing inspection * 01527
The effect of number ordering and orientation on marking speed and * for mark-sensed labels 01717
Mode *: a user-centered analysis and some preventative measures using keying-contingent sound 02107
Online library catalog systems: an analysis of user * 02128
Coping with human * through system design: implications for ecological interface design 02254
VDU work, refractive * and binocular vision 03739
Naming * and automatic error correction in human-computer interaction 03770
A note on undetected typing * HCI-0399 †

**ESCHER**
* effects in online text 0130

**ESD**
NLI-*: An expert natural language interface to a statistical data bank 02712

**ESEC**
* '87 § 03795

**ESOP**
* 86 § 03883

**ETHERNET**
Personal distributed computing: the Alto and * hardware 03095
Personal distributed computing: the Alto and * software 03096

**ETHICS**
The impact of changes in work * upon organizational life 0250

Computer *: an antidote to despair 0791
Developing awareness of computer * 03010
The * of automated publishing systems (a response to Dr. Brockmann) HCI-0170 †

**ETHNOGRAPHIC**
How do the experts do it? The use of * methods as an aid to understanding the cognitive processing and retrieval of large bodies of text 03063

**ETS**
*—a system for the transfer of human expertise 0491

**EUROPARC**
What is * 0812

**EUROPE**
Data security and confidentiality in * HCI-0450 †

**EUROPEAN**
Designing hybrid automated manufacturing systems: A * perspective 03382
ECOOP '88 (* Conference on Object-Oriented Programming) § 03793

**EUROTA**
Environments for * 02514

**EVALUATING**
A system for * screen formats: Research and application 0413
* usability of human-computer interfaces: a practical method ● 0608
A cognitively based methodology for * human performance in the computer-aided design task domain 01240
* user utterances in natural language interfaces to databases 01486
* formatted alphanumeric displays 01525
* the usability of the Glasgow online 01808
The use of measures of entropy in * human supervisory control of a manufacturing system 01897
Understanding and * a computer graphics display 01984
* the intelligence in dialogue systems 02194

\* the impact of camera placement on teleoperator efficiency 02940
\* performance appraisal systems for IS personnel 03011
A methodology for \* environments 03055
The use of complexity theory in \* interfaces 03270
\* the meaningfulness of icon sets to represent command operations 03277
Humane: A designer's assistant for modeling and \* function allocation options 03397
A model for \* stress effects of work with display units 03756
\* RECONSIDER: a computer program for diagnostic prompting HCI-0410 †
A plan for \* usability of software products HCI-0449 †

## EVALUATION

Statistical \* of behavioural data 0051
The \* of text editors: Methodology and empirical results 0058
\* of mouse, rate-controlled isometric joystick, step keys, and text keys, for text selection on a CRT 0064
The \* of online help systems: a conceptual model 0129
Studies in the \* of a domain-independent natural language query system 0162
The \* of project support environments for the STARTS user guide 0173
\* of expert systems for decision support 0244
On methods of analysis of mental models and the \* of interactive computer systems 0319
Interface design and \*—Semiotic implications 0409
The \* of information services: a typology 0452
\* of a program on "distance" 0472
Psychological \* of path hypotheses in cognitive diagnosis 0537
Programmable user models for predictive \* of interface designs 0800
An interactive environment for dialogue development: its design, use and \*; or, is aide useful? 0920

\* of mental models and meta models through interactions between users nd helpers about software usage problems 0972
Development and \* of direct manipulation lists (poster session) 0993
An empirical approach to the \* of icons 01013
An \* of a realistic approach to MIS 01027
Formative design \* of superbook 01154
Human factors for design and \* of software 01283
\* and intergration of specification languages 01430
Biomechanical \* of lifting tasks: a microcomputer-based model 01524
Effects of graphic boundaries in tabular displays: a human factors \* 01526
On the selection and \* of visual display symbology: factors influencing search and identification times 01718
Review and \* of physiological cost prediction models for manual materials handling 01757
Human performance \* of digitizer pucks for computer input of spatial information 01774
Comments on "formal specification of user interfaces: a comparison and \* of four axiomatic approaches" 01847
\* of the user interface in an information retrieval system: a model 02012
A methodology for interactive \* of user reactions to software packages:an empirical analysis of system performance, interaction, and run time 02080
An experimental \* of prefix and postfix notation in command language sytax 02110
On-line recognition of Pitman's hand-written shorthand—an \* of potential 02111
Combining stochastic uncertainty and linguistic inexactness: theory and experimental \* of four fuzzy probability models 02218

Student \* of motivational and learning attributes of microcomputer soft 02274
Systematic \* strategies for computer-based music instruction systems 02275
Research and \* models for the study of interactive video 02283
Formative \* of pre-Logo programming environments: a collaborative effort of researchers, teachers, and children 02292
A short-form measure of user information satisfaction: a psychometric \* and notes on use 02351
The design and \* of a front-end user interface for energy researchers 02453
An acoustic of pathological voice and its application to the \* of laryngeal pathology 02644
An \* of auditory performances in patients with Cochlear implants 02658
Performance \* of simulators 02663
BNETD—A modelling tool to computer systems performance \* 02668
SATURN—a tool for modelling and performance \* of computer systems 02670
Expert system tool \* 02718
Exploratory \* of a planar foot-operated cursor-positioning device 02858
Improving the accuracy of touch screens: an experimental \* of three strategies 02860
Users' preferences among different techniques for displaying the \* of LISP functions in an interactive debugger 02863
A rule-based system for interactive proposal \* 02927
An \* and selection methodology of microcomputer training software: Implications for human resource managers and computer personnel 03002
Some measures and procedures for \* of the user interface in an information retrieval system 03069

The incorporation of early interface * into command language grammar specifications 03191
Human factors and the problems of * in the design of speech systems interfaces 03192
An * of the effectiveness of the adaptive interface module (AIM) in matching dialogues to users 03212
The design and * of an animated programming environment 03220
User-driven adaptive behaviour, a comparative * and an inductive analysis 03226
The role of iterative * in designing systems for usability 03255
Where do we draw the line? - Derivation and * of user interface software separation rules 03268
Empirical * of map interfaces 03276
Methods for field * of safety in a robotics workplace 03408
A study on safety * index and industrial accident analysis from the viewpoint of the safety confirmation type 03419
A study of auditory warning alarms * for automated guided vehicles 03424
Performance * of three pressure mats as robot workstation safety sensors 03428
The * of selected ergonomical factors by production automation growth 03429
An * of production systems from the ergonomic viewpoint: a plea for an integral approach to design 03430
The economic * on implementation industrial robot from user point of view 03447
Ergonomic * of safety devices in robotic systems 03449
Pregnancy and VDT work—an * of the state of the art 03686
An * of mood disturbances and somatic discomfort under slow computer-response time and incentive-pay conditions 03765
The applicability of eye movement analysis in the ergonomic * of human-computer interaction 03766
A provisional * of a new chord keyboard, the Velotype 03907

Signal processing and pattern recognition in nondestructive * of materials § 04019
Computer usability testing & * ● HCI-0014 †
Experimental * of dialogue types for data entry HCI-0115 †
A Multilevel menu-driven user interface: Design and * through simulation HCI-0170 †
Experimental * of program quality using external metrics HCI-0176 †
An experimental * of the impact of data display format on recall performance HCI-0202 †
The * of text editors: methodology and empirical results. HCI-0209 †
Using restricted natural language for data retrieval: a plan for field * HCI-0255 †
An experimental * of computer graphics imagery HCI-0373 †
An approach to CAD system performance * HCI-0414 †

**EVALUATIVE**
On meanings menus for measurement: disentangling * issues in system design 01997
Cognitive models in information retrieval—an * review 02298
A natural language front end to databases with * feedback HCI-0338 †

**EVALUATION**
Design and * of the AID adaptive front-end to Telecom Gold 03260

**EVENT**
The spatial allocation of visual attention as indexed by *-related brain potentials 01739
Hierarchical, modular discrete-* modelling in an object-oriented environment 02588
*-driven user interfaces based on quasi-parallelism 03111

**EVENTS**
The MDR algorithm and its application to the generation of explanations for novel * 02174
Absolute dates and relative dates in an inferential system on temporal dependencies between * 02235
Perceiving and recovering structure from * 03346

**EVERYDAY**
Daydreaming and computation: a computer model of * creativity, learning nd emotions in the human stream of thought 04067

**EVERYONE**
POP-11 for * 0749
Dow Chemical makes continuous improvement part of *'s job 01908

**EVIDENCE**
An examination of the research * for computer-based instruction 0415
Visual pattern recognition in humans: I. * for adaptive filtering 01274
Contingent aftereffects and isoluminance: psychophysical * for separation of color, orientation, and motion 01463
Extension of conditional probability and measures of belief and disbelief in a hypothesis based on uncertain * 01846
Differences in analyst's attitudes towards information systems development: * and implications 01935
Coproduction: * from EPG data 02660
Speeded phase discrimination: * for global to local processing 03307
Perception of rotation in depth: the psychophysical * 03343
Decision support using qualitative * 03398
Automatic contour definition on left ventriculograms by image * and a multiple template-based model 04073

**EVOLUTIONARY**
A trace of memory: an * perspective on the visual system 0019

**EXACERBATED**
Spatial misorientation * by collimated virtual flight display 01979

**EXAMPLAR**
Protos: an *-based learning apprentice 02210

**EXCAVATOR**
Evolution of a robotic * 03569

**EXCERPT**
The changing workplace: A guide to managing the people, organizational, and regulatory aspects of office technology (book * 0044
Human limits and the VDT computer interface (* 0054
Sites, modes, and trails: Telling the user of an interactive system where he is, what he can do, and how to get to places (* 0068
Direct manipulation interfaces (* 0073
Methods for designing software to fit human needs and capabilities (* 0079

**EXCHANGES**
Machine adaption to psychological differences among users in instructive information * with computers 03609

**EXCITEMENT**
Maintaining the spirit of * in growing companies 01025

**EXECUTABLE**
Express—rapid prototyping and product development via integrated knowledge-based * specifications 03492
Ada-based * modelling of distributed systems HCI-0098 †

**EXECUTE**
One hundred differential equations * directly on the IBM PC 02582

**EXECUTION**
Functional modelling in the * of actions 01485
A high level language-based computing enviornment to support production and * of reliable programs 01855
A session editor with incremental * functions 02637
GOMS meets STRIPS: the integration of planning with skilled procedure *in human-computer interaction 03243
A logic-functional approach to the * of CCS specifications modulo behavioural equivalences 03874

**EXECUTOR**
Microtechnology and user friendly systems—the CONNECT dialogue * 02382

**EXEMPTION**
Legal data modeling: The prohibited transaction * analyst 02779

**EXISTENCE**
An investigation into the * of subgroup concept in information systems personnel management 03022

**EXPANATORY**
* dialogues 02063

**EXPANSION**
* and control of end-user computing 02347
Towards interactive query * 03067
Complex logarithmic mapping and the focus of * 03333

**EXPECT**
Thinking ahead: what to * from teleconferencing (Reprint) 0372

**EXPECTATIONS**
Self-efficacy * as a predictor of computer use: a look at early childhood administrators 01590
Search success and * with a computer interface 01995
Introducing windows to Unix: user * 03924

**EXPERIENCES**
Supporting collaboration in hypermedia: issues and * 0117
Company * with end-user computing 0460
* with off-line robot programming via standardized interfaces 0601
* with the alternate reality kit: an example of the tension between literalism and magic 0817
Seven * with contextual field research 0996
Transportable applications environment (TAE) plus * in "Object"-ively modernizing a user interface environment 01126
WYSIWIS revised: early * with multiuser interfaces 01158
Introducing information technology: * of a large industrial unit 01217
* in use of SSADM: series of case studies. Part 1: first time users 01976
* in use of SSADM: series of case studies. Part 2: experienced users 01977
Supporting collaboration in Hypermedia: issues and * 02454

Some * in integrating specification of human computer interaction within a structured system development method 03222
Hypertext tips: * in developing a hypertext tutorial 03236
* from the use of an intelligent safety sensor with industrial robots 03427
* in participative systems design 03665
* with Distributed Systems § 03881
* with the development of a portable network operating system 03882
Product data interfaces in CAD/CAM applications: design, implementation and * § 03981

**EXPERIENCING**
* artificial intelligence: an interactive approach to the IBM PC ● 0550
* artificial intelligence: an interactive approach for the APPLE ● 0551

**EXPERIENTIAL**
$DM^2$: an algorithm for diagnostic reasoning that combines analytical models and * knowledge 02190

**EXPERIMENTAL**
* data for the design of a microworld-based system for algebra 0543
Graphic invention for user interfaces: an * course in user-interface design 0950
Fine tuning selection semantics in a structure editor based programming environment: some * results 0975
Evolution of interactional human behavior with age: a theoretical/*pproach 01618
An * study of Chinese information displays on VDTs 01784
An * comparison of a mouse and arrow-jump keys for an interactive encyclopedia 02098
An * evaluation of prefix and postfix notation in command language sytax 02110
Is top-down natural? Some * results from non-procedural languages 02123
Combining stochastic uncertainty and linguistic inexactness: theory and * evaluation of four fuzzy probability models 02218

759

[EXPERIMENTATION]

Critical factors in the user environment: an * study of users, organizations and tasks 02507
Visuomotor control by a combined position- and speedservo. Theoretical considerations and * results in man 02666
Improving the accuracy of touch screens: an * evaluation of three strategies 02860
The * validation of a programmer productivity measure 03013
* and theoretical analysis of visual search activities 03620
An * environment for generating word hypotheses in continuous speech 03998
* evaluation of dialogue types for data entry HCI-0115 †
* adaptive interface HCI-0139 †
* study of a two-dimensional language vs. FORTRAN for first-course progammers HCI-0171 †
* evaluation of program quality using external metrics HCI-0176 †
An * program investigating color-enhanced and graphical information presentation: an integration of the findings HCI-0196 †
An * evaluation of the impact of data display format on recall performance HCI-0202 †
Understanding the effectiveness of computer graphics for decision support: a cumulative * approach HCI-0215 †
An * comparison of tabular and graphic data presentation HCI-0236 †
The spatial metaphor for user interfaces: * tests of reference by location versus name HCI-0268 †
An * multimedia mail system HCI-0309 †
An * evaluation of computer graphics imagery HCI-0373 †
An * comparison of RGB, YIQ, LAB, HSV, and opponent color models HCI-0381 †
* results do not support some ergonomic standards for computer video terminal design HCI-0428 †

**EXPERIMENTATION**
IRX: an information retrieval system for * and user applications 01076
* in the specification of an oral dialogue 04005
* with an adaptive search strategy for solving a keyboard design/configuration problem 04070

**EXPERTISE**
ETS—a system for the transfer of human * 0491
Tailoring object descriptions to a user's level of * 01352
Menu organization and user * in information search tasks 01761
Capturing *: Some approaches to modeling command decisionmaking in combat analysis 01883
Linguistic knowledge as * 02077
Modelling human * in knowledge engineering: some preliminary observations 02134
An attempt to incorporate * about users into an intelligent interface for Unix 02248
Using design * to develop an expert system 02962
Knowledge and * in expert systems 03905
The use of explicit user models in text generation: tailoring to a user's level of * 04051
* transfer for expert system design ● HCI-0059 †
* transfer and complex problems: using AQUINAS as a knowledge-acquisition workbench for knowledge-based systems HCI-0336 †

**EXPERTS**
Practices of novices and * in critical inquiry 0585
Creating consistency in the user interface: opinions and procedures of software developments * 01012
The problem of extracting the knowledge of * 01195
KITTEN: knowledge initiation and transfer tools for * and novices 02159
Validation in a knowledge support system: construing and consistency with multiple * 02203

Knowledge representation in "Default": An attempt to classify general types of knowledge used by legal * 02775
How do the * do it? The use of ethnographic methods as an aid to understanding the cognitive processing and retrieval of large bodies of text 03063
Users and * in the document retrieval system model HCI-0270 †

**EXPLANATION**
Reading is slower from CRT displays than from paper: attempts to isolate a single-variable * 01743
* for an expert system that performs estate planning 02767
On the nature and fuction of * in intelligent information retrieval 03064
User requirements for expert system *: what, why and when? 03242
The computer imperative among owners of home computers: * by social factors HCI-0217 †

**EXPLANATIONS**
Graphic equivalence, graphic *, and embedded process modeling for enhanced user-system interaction 01888
The MDR algorithm and its application to the generation of * for novel events 02174

**EXPLOITING**
* convergence to improve natural language understanding 02071

**EXPLORATION**
All users of information retrieval systems are not created equal: an * into individual differences 02011
Training by *: facilitating the transfer of procedural knowledge through analogical reasoning 02103
Computer decision support for senior managers: encouraging * HCI-0298 †

**EXPLORATORY**
Dynamic versus static menus: an * comparison 0997
An * contingency model of user participation and MIS use 01919

Training end users: an * study 02506
* evaluation of a planar foot-operated cursor-positioning device 02858
Ontological analysis of document usage: an * study 03467
* investigations in acquiring and using information in interactive problem solving 03597
Intuitive representations and interaction languages: an * experiment 03611
gIBIS: a hypertext tool for * policy discussion HCI-0300 †

**EXPOSITORY**
Comprehensino aids for on-line reading of * text 01798

**EXPOSURE**
Facial particle * in the VDU environment: the role of static electricity 03694

**EXPOSURES**
Unexpected motion hazard * on a large robotic assembly 03409

**EXTENDE**
Multiple representation document development (* abstract) 03518

**EXTENDER**
The memory * personal filing system 0930
On the applied use of human memory models: the memory * personal filing system HCI-0271 †

**EXTENSIBLE**
The NeWS book: an introduction to the network/* window system ● 0358
LIZA: an * groupware toolkit 0805
Quill: An * system for editing documents of mixed type 03517
SunDew—a distributed and * window system 03927

**EXTENSOR**
Model of the neuro-muscular recruitment example of the * digitorum communis muscle in man: I—identification of motoneurons and of muscular fibers 01595

**EXTENTIONS**
A natural language information retrieval system with * towards fuzzy reasoning HCI-0281 †

**EXTERNALLY**
Internal representation of * stored information 03601

**EXTRACT**
Using perceptual organization to * 3-D structures 01842

**EXTRACTING**
The problem of * the knowledge of experts 01195
A new algorithm for * the interior of bounded regions based on chain coding 01469

**EXTRACTION**
A document layout system using automatic document architecture * 0882
Natural language interface based on keyword * using AWK 02498
Conceptual information * form financial news 03489

**EXTREME**
Short- and long-term effects of * physical inactivity. A review 03703

**EXTREMUM**
An * principle for shape from contour 0024

**EYE**
There's more to interaction than meets the *: Some issues in manual 0062
* movements in reading: perceptual and language processes ● 0609
Radiation detection by ear and by * 01732
Open-loop experiments for modeling the human * movement system 01870
Development and sensitivity analysis of adaptive predictor for human *movement model 02681
* Fatigue among VDU users and non-VDU users 03682
The applicability of * movement analysis in the ergonomic evaluation of human-computer interaction 03766
*-head coordination and information uptake during text processing 03767
* movement analysis system using fundus images HCI-0243 †

**EYES**
Looking at worksheet modeling through expert system * 0696

Intermittent illumination from visual display units and fluorescent lighting affects movements of the * across text 01713
Is the resting state of our * a favorable viewing distance for VDU-work? 03737

**FABRIC**
An interactive simulator for the designing of woven * structures second place 02583

**FABRIK**
*: a visual programming environment 01130

**FACE**
* to * with Open Look 01305
Machine assisted translation with a human * 01627
Hypermedia: a * lift for presentation research and development: a user services function 03154
Speech and expression: a computer solution to * animation 03293
Multivariate data representation and analysis by * pattern using facial expression characteristics HCI-0394 †

**FACIAL**
* particle exposure in the VDU environment: the role of static electricity 03694
Multivariate data representation and analysis by face pattern using *expression characteristics HCI-0394 †

**FACILITATING**
Training by exploration: * the transfer of procedural knowledge through analogical reasoning 02103

**FACULTY**
Attitudes toward unauthorized software copying: general public vs. business * member 01142
Perceptions of the CIS graduate's workstyle: undergraduate business students versus CIS * 02999
The many faces of * computing assistance 03143

**FAILURE**
Communication * in dialogue and discourse: detection and repair processes ● 0611

Real-time * detection on complex mechanical structures via parallel data processing 01561
Measuring implementation outcome: beyond success and * 01933
The ISA expert system: a prototype system for * diagnosis on the space station 02913
Information systems: * analysis § 03804
Management strategies and information * 03806
* analysis of information systems: reflections on the use of expert systems in information systems 03811
* analysis of information systems in small manufacturing enterprises: the importance of the human interface 03815
Videotex: anatomy of a * HCI-0313 †

## FAILURES
Models of human problem solving: detection, diagnosis, and compensation for system * 0653
Reference identification and reference identification * 01345
Mental models and * in human-machine systems 03814

## FAIM
The *-1 user interface—human engineering for the fifth generation 03587

## FAITHFULLY
How * should the electronic office simulate real one? 0958

## FALLIBLE
* humans and vulnerable systems: lessons learned from aviation 03808

## FALSE
Anticipating * implicatures: cooperative responses in question-answer systems 03178

## FAT
Lean cuisine: a low * notation for menus 02062

## FATAL
Ten * accidents due to robots in Japan 03406
* error in pass zero: how not to confuse novices HCI-0164 †

## FATIGUE
Reading from microfiche, a VDT, and the printed page: subjective * and performance 01712
Visual * and spatial frequency adaptation to video displays of text 01721
Long workdays versus restdays: assessing * and alertness with a portable performance 01778
Mathematical modeling of * in physically demanding jobs 02363
Eye * among VDU users and non-VDU users 03682
Inactivity, night work, and * 03705
Mental * of VDU operators induced by monotonous and various tasks 03760
Visual * with work on visual display units: the current state of knowledge 03891

## FAULT
Measures of human problem solving performance in * diagnosis tasks 0655
Modeling * diagnosis as the activation and use of a frame system 01729
Aiding the operator during novel * diagnosis 01858
A model of * diagnosis performance of expert marine engineers 02199
Experience of constructing a * localisation expert system using an AI toolkit 02923
Concept demonstration of the use of interactive * diagnosis and isolation for TF30 engines 02968
An object-oriented expert system for coal-fired MHD power plant *monitoringand diagnosis 02973
* management, knowledge support, and responsibility in man-machine systems 03812
Conventional *-tolerance and neural computers 03951
A methodology for designing distributed, *-tolerant, and reactive real-time operating systems 04071

## FAULTS
Sherlock—a system for diagnosing power distribution ring network * 02916

## FAVORABLE
Is the resting state of our eyes a * viewing distance for VDU-work? 03737

## FAVOURITE
How would your * user model cope with these scenarios? 0999

## FCP
An architecture of a distributed window system and its * implementation 0676

## FEDERAL
Government infostructures: a guide to the networks of information resources and technologies at *, state, and local levels ● 0523
Threat to privacy: the * government's use of personal information in the new communication environment 02680

## FEEDBACK
Why visuomotor systems don't like negative * and how they avoid it 0016
Hypertext: a way of incorporating user * into online documentation 0102
Improvement of the acquisition of knowledge by informing * 0540
The impact of menus and command-level * on learners' acquisition of data base language skills 01041
Semantic * in the Higgens UIMS 01851
Synchronizing the I/O behavior of functional programs with * 02016
Prompting, * and error correction in the design of a scenario machine 02176
Weighting, ranking and relevance * in a front-end system 02329
Modeling managerial behavior: misperceptions of * in a dynamic decision making experiment 02483
Planning as * to designers 02978
Proprioceptive * for sensory-motor control 04008
Effects of an immediate * tool on designer productivity and design usability 04052
A natural language front end to databases with evaluative * HCI-0338 †

## FEEDING
The information technology champion: aiding and abetting, care and * 03459

## FEEL
The look and * . . . and sound of the user interface 01315
Why the look and * of software user interfaces should not be protected by copyright law 01324

## FEMALE
A comparison of male and * computer science students' attitudes toward computers 01045
Male/* programmer and systems analyst Job performance 03020

## FERMENT
New wine in old skins, or, was all this * really necessary? 03140

## FIBER
Implementation plan for the use of on-line * analysis in the textile industry 03433

## FIBERS
Model of the neuro-muscular recruitment example of the extensor digitorum communis muscle in man: I—identification of motoneurons and of muscular * 01595

## FICTION
Design and test of a database for *, based on an analysis of children's search behavior 0451
The value of information and computer-aided information seeking: problem formulation and application to * retrieval 01989
"Automation, robotization in particular, is always economically desirable"—fact or * 03448

## FIDELITY
Maintenance training simulator * and individual differences in transfer of training 01722

## FIDO
Cooperative behaviour in the * system 02041

## FIFTIES
Managing the diffusion of end-user computing technologies: a * mindset with eighties tools 0459

## FIGURE
*-ground organization affects the early visual processing 0021
Near-real-time control of human * models 01829
Near-real-time control of human * models 03295

## FIGURES
JACK: a toolkit for manipulating articulated * 03126
Animating human *: perspectives and directions 03291

## FILE
Schaum's outline of theories and problems of programming with advanced structured COBOL with * processing structured systems deveolpment and interactive cons ● 0555
The linear *—restrictions on online information use: a searcher's perspective 01634
Assaying and isolating individual differences in searching a hierarchical *system 01747
Accommodating individual differences in searching a hierarchical * system 02212
Generation of * processing programs based on JSP 02639
Project source * management under the UNIX operating system 03168

## FILES
Windows, viewports and structured display * 03930
Using the micro-computer to simplify database access: designing interfaces to complex * HCI-0275 †

## FILING
Speech *—An office system for principals 0037
Human factors challenges in creating a principal support office system—The speh * system approach 0038
The memory extender personal * system 0930

## FILTER
A comparison of neural network and matched * processing for detecting lines in images 02738
The * browser defining interfaces graphically 03792

## FILTERING
Visual pattern recognition in humans: I. Evidence for adaptive * 01274
Neural nets for adaptive * and adaptive pattern recognition 01362

## FINANCE
* 0135

## FINANCIAL
Skilled * planning: the cost of translating ideas into action 0834
Conceptual information extraction form * news 03489
A * investment assistant 03490

## FINDINGS
A scale for assessing student attitudes toward computers preliminary * 01579
Collaborative learning in a virtual classroom: highlights of * 02826
An experimental program investigating color-enhanced and graphical information presentation: an integration of the * HCI-0196 †

## FINGER
*—Formalizing Interaction for Gesture Recognition 01017

## FINGERTIP
The information capacity of the human * 01893

## FINISHING
Development of a continuous * line to improve working conditions 03434

## FINITE
State trees as structured * state machines for user interfaces 03107

## FIRED
PISCES: an expert system for coal * power plant monitoring and diagnostics 02915
An object-oriented expert system for coal-* MHD power plant fault monitoringand diagnosis 02973

## FIRING
* response of a neural model with threshold modulation and neural dynamics 02761

**FISH**
Teaching users to *: hooks, lines and sinkers for reading computer documentat 03156

**FISHEYE**
Generalized * views 0893

**FITS**
Interactive computer program for the selection of interference * HCI-0406 †

**FIXED**
Datastream: numeric data—all you can use at a * price 02525
Active vision: integration of * and mobile cameras 04017

**FLAMINGO**
Experience with *: a distributed, object-oriented user interface system 03033

**FLASHCARDS**
A comparison of a microcomputer progressive state drill and * for learning paired associates 02295

**FLAT**
Human factors and * panels challenge the CRT 01982

**FLATLAND**
Out of *: towards 3-D visual programming 03497

**FLEXIBILITY**
The * of case grammar representations: a porting procedure for naturallanguage interfaces 02255

**FLIGHT**
An integrated display for vertical and translational *: eight factors affecting pilot performance 01714
A psychophysiological assessment of operator workload during simulated *missions 01735
Spatial misorientation exacerbated by collimated virtual * display 01979
The development of an automated * test management system for * test planning and monitoring 02928

**FLOATING**
User-oriented suggestions for *-point and complex-arithmetic Forth standard extensions 02306

**FLOATS**
How to build a help desk that * 03148

**FLOW**
Robotics and Material * ● 0558
Facts on optic * 01257
An experiment to test user validation of requirements: data-* diagrams vs task-oriented menus 02131
Affect-chaining and dependency oriented * analysis applied to queries of programs 02789
Information * in a user interface: the effect of experience and context on the recall of MacWrite screens 03228
The fox and the forest: toward a type I/type II constraint for early optical * 03324
Optical * 03330
Determining the instantaneous axis of translation from optic * generated by rbitrary sensot motion 03332
Adapting optical-* to measure object motion in reflectance and X-ray image sequences 03334
Using data * specifications and interactive editing in the operating system user interface 03800
Computational networks in early vision: from orientation selection to optical * 03961
Nested window * controls with packet fragmentation 04055

**FLUORESCENT**
Intermittent illumination from visual display units and * lighting affects movements of the eyes across text 01713

**FLURY**
A perceptual study of the *-Riedwyl faces for graphically displaying multivariate data 02126

**FMS**
Software development approach in * 01567
An approach to knowledge elicitation in scheduling *: Toward a hybrid intelligent system 03394

**FOCUSING**
* variability during visual work 03759

**FOLDING**
A comparison of hypertext, scrolling and * as mechanisms for program browsing 03235

**FOLEY**
James D. *, Oct. 12: user interface strategies '88 ● 0303

**FOLIOPUB**
*: A publication management system 03520

**FOLKLORE**
A * view of information 01222

**FOLLOW**
Responding to "HUH?": answering vaguely articulated *-up questions 0825
Professional education and subsequent careers in library/information work: a *-up study of former students on the MA/MSc information studies course at the University of Sheffield 02336
Work content, stress and health in computer-mediated work: a seven year *-up study 03758

**FONTS**
A computer aided design system for artistic chinese * 02455

**FOOT**
Of moles and men: the design of * controls for workstations 0935
Exploratory evaluation of a planar *-operated cursor-positioning device 02858

**FORD**
Interactive video as a school resource: Rolls-Royce or Model T * 0513

**FOREST**
The fox and the *: toward a type I/type II constraint for early optical flow 03324

**FORGETTING**
* and the learning curve: a laboratory study 02484
* as a way to improve neural-net behavior 02759
Designing keybindings to be easy to learn and resistant to * even when the set of commands is large 02890

## FORMAL
Cognitive optimisation of Videotex dialogues: a *—empirical approach 0320
The * specification of adaptive user interfaces using command language grammar 0925
A * interface design methodology based on user knowledge 0929
Transformations on a * specification of user-computer interfaces 01062
User interface design and * methods 01373
A * specification of the QMS message system: the underlying abstract model 01406
A survey of * tools and models for developing user interfaces 02207
A * representation system for the human-computer interaction process 02241
Toward a * specification of menu-based systems 02400
Towards the * specification of a simple programming support environment 02607
* methods and the design of effective user interfaces 03246
ECS - A technique for the * specification and rapid prototyping of human-computer interaction 03253
* specification of user interfaces: two application studies 03772
VDM '87: VDM—a * method at work § 03831
A support system for * reasoning: requirements and status 04035
A * specification for a user interface for office automation 04053
The PegaSys System: pictures as * documentation of large programs IICI-0146 |
Icon semantics—a * approach to icon system design HCI-0161 †

## FORMALISMS
On * 01280

## FORMANT
A parallel * synthesizer for machine voice output HCI-0396 †

## FORMAT
Designing menu display * to match input device * 0983
Efforts of display * on proof-reading with VDUs 01246
Perspective traffic display * and airline pilot traffic avoidance 01748
The effect of task demands and graphical * on in*ion processing strategies 02482
An experimental evaluation of the impact of data display * on recall performance HCI-0202 †

## FORMATS
A system for evaluating screen *: Research and application 0413
Information transfer rate with serial and simultaneous visual display * 01770
The effects of display * on information systems design 02357
Interfaces and data transfer * in computer graphics systems HCI-0419 †

## FORMATTED
Evaluating * alphanumeric displays 01525

## FORMATTING
* space-related displays to optimize expert and nonexpert user performance 0927
Display * in information integration and nonintegration tasks 01750
* alphanumeric crt displays 02140
Separating content from form: A language for * on-line documentation and dialog 02781
Abstraction and integration in IDE, an editing and * environment 03184
Document convergence in an interactive * system HCI-0405 †

## FORMEDNESS
Ill-* and miscommunication in person-machine dialogue 01957

## FORMFLEX
*: a user interface tool for forms definition and management 0204

## FORMULA
Mathematical * editor for CAI 0885
An empirical * for visual search 02526

## FORMULATE
A menu interface to * boolean logic-can it be done? 02034

## FORTH
User-oriented suggestions for floating-point and complex-arithmetic *standard extensions 02306
A single-board * computer with versatile analog I/O circuitry 02308
Compiling * for performance 02309
A stand-alone * system 02310
Pride-II physical layout program of modifying * for "non-believers" 02312

## FORTRAN
A * input program generator 01227
Plan-based representations of pascal and * code 02897
Experimental study of a two-dimensional language vs. * for first-course progammers HCI-0171 †

## FOURIER
Parametric * image characterization toolkit 02798

## FOX
The * and the forest: toward a type I/type II constraint for early optical flow 03324

## FRACTIONAL
User friendly micro computer program for solving * and linear programming problems 01509

## FRACTIONS
Error-free * 01297

## FRAGILE
* knowledge and neglected strategies in novice programmers HCI-0177 †

## FRAGMENTATION
Nested window flow controls with packet * 04055

## FRAGMENTS
An alternative approach to the conceptual database design using * of nat 01481
HERCULES: database query using natural language * HCI-0253 †

## FRAMES
Managing multiple context-* through GKS 01389
* of mind in intertemporal choice 02478

## FRAMEWORKS
Application *: experience with MacApp 01039
Interactive microcomputer programs for linear and non-linear static analysis of * 01165
Representational * and models for human-computer interfaces HCI-0188 †

## FREEDOM
Limited *: linear reflections on nonlinear texts 0121

## FRENCH
Querying the * *Yellow Pages*: natural language access to the directory 02007

## FREQUENCIES
Correlation of term usage and term indexing * 02004

## FREQUENCY
Visual fatigue and spatial * adaptation to video displays of text 01721
CRT picture vibration caused by low-* magnetic field and its reduction method 01987
Inference control mechanism for statistical database *-imposed data distortions 02449
Joint spatial/spatial-* representation 02580
Vowel normalization by * warped spectral matching 02649
Health hazards assessment of radio * electromagnetic fields emitted by video display terminals 03685
The effects of limited data in multi-* reflection diffraction tomography 04020
Analyzing the high * bugs in novice programs HCI-0178 †

## FREQUENT
Ergonomic job design in * manual lifting tasks: a microcomputer-based model 01532

## FRG
Using simulation to study complex problem solving: a review of studies in the * 02598

## FRIVOLOUS
Friendly or * 01650

## FRONTIER
Psychology and the user interface: science is soft at the * 03297

## FRONTOPARALLEL
Alleys on an apparent * plane 02374

## FSH
*—a functional UNIX command interpreter 02624

## FUCTION
On the nature and * of explanation in intelligent information retrieval 03064

## FULLSCREEN
Open * systems 0766

## FUNCTION
Cortical connections and parallel processing: structure and * 0028
User computer interface guidelines research for keyboards and * keys 0201
Clarify * 01122
Operator performance as a * of type of display: conventional versus perspective 01769
A discrete control model of operator *: A methodology for information dislay design 01874
Changes in contrast sensitivity * produced by VDT use 02189
The psychophysical * of binocular space perception 02375
A model for cortical * 02731
Lyapunov * for parallel neural networks 02736
A drive-reinforcement model of single neuron *: An alternative to the Hebbian neuronal model 02743
Repositioning the information systems management *: Implications for information systems personnel 03015
Hypermedia: a face lift for presentation research and development: a user services * 03154
Automation—implications for knowledge retention as a * of operator control responsibility 03207
Humane: A designer's assistant for modeling and evaluating * allocation options 03397

Pneumatic manipulating system provided with active compliance * 03426
Effectiveness of training as a * of the teacher knowledge structure 03604
The efficiency of letter perception in * of color combinations: a study of video-screen colors 03616
Partitioning of * in window systems 03931
Human-machine interaction and role/*/action-nets 03974

## FUNCTIONAL
A * model of vision and space 0027
* databases, * languages 0034
* environments for microcomputers in education 0578
User interface primitives to allow full * use of computers by physically disabled persons 0979
Continuous processing of images through user sketched * blocks 01399
* modelling in the execution of actions 01485
Synchronizing the I/O behavior of * programs with feedback 02016
Experience with a * layered multicomputer architecture for interactive processing 02402
fsh—a * UNIX command interpreter 02624
Modelling generic user-interfaces with * programs 03265
A * model of questions for natural language processing systems 03575
A logic-* approach to the execution of CCS specifications modulo behavioural equivalences 03874

## FUNCTIONALITY
Separating the user interface from the * of application programs 0948

## FUNCTIONALLY
Color in user interface design: * and aesthetics 0803
Effects of * or topographically presented process schemes on operator performance 01749

## FUNCTIONS
Assessment of an effort to integrate computer * in an engineering design firm 0779

# KEYWORD INDEX [FUZZY]

The effects of device technology on the usability of advanced telephone * 0876
Problem solving performance and display preference for information displays depicting numerical * 0978
Characteristics and * of software environments: an overview 01145
Necessary * of institutions for test and certification from the viewpoint of users in IT 01456
A graphics system architecture for interactive application-specific display * 01822
Combining * for certainty degrees in consulting systems 02092
A taxonomy of user-oriented * 02104
Human supervisory control in flexible manufacturing systems: Allocation of * and system size 02456
A session editor with incremental execution * 02637
Nonlinear discriminant * and associative memories 02757
Users' preferences among different techniques for displaying the evaluation of LISP * in an interactive debugger 02863
Design of distribution of production control * between humans and artificially intelligent devices 03375
Job organization and allocation of * between man and computer: I analysis and assessment 03628
Job organization and allocation of * between man and computer: II.job organization 03629
Psychological principles for allocation of * in man-robot system 03630
General multiple-objective decision * and linguistically quantified statements HCI-0110 †

## FUNDUS

Eye movement analysis system using * images HCI-0243 †

## FUTURE

Information technology & people: designing for the * ● 0144
* directions 0336
History, state and * of user interface management systems 0966

Determination of work contexts—an important aspect of * user interfaces 01204
Speculating on the * of mathematics 01210
The moving target: * trends in networking 01282
The FAA's Advanced Automation System: strategies for * air traffic control systems 01357
Exchange of solid models: current state and * trends 01475
The IE's * role in improving knowledge 01903
One view of the * of industrial control 01921
CRTs—present and * 01985
Electronic information systems analysis. Present and * information systems use by academics involved in development studies 02323
Current and * uses of the group decision support system technology: report on a recent empirical study 02355
History offers clues to the *: user control returns 02517
Computer user manuals in print: Do they have a * 02782
Statistical software, graphics and * workstations for data analysis 03316
On building * decision support systems 03472
* work 03942
* Trends in Information Science and Technology § 04039
Information retrieval: the * 04045
In the age of the smart machine: the * of work and power ● HCI-0083 †
The * of "writing" for the computer industry HCI-0150 †
The * of interactive systems and the emergence of direct manipulation HCI-0186 †
Computer-assisted negotiations: a case history from the law of the sea negotiations and speculation regarding * uses HCI-0443 †

## FUTURISTIC

Towards the development of human work-performance standards in *man-machine systems: a fuzzy modeling approach 01692

## FUZZIES

A change of mind or the story of * in Purgatory 0961

## FUZZY

* decision analysis 0650
* sets and decision analysis 0651
A * rule-based model of human problem solving 0656
Towards the development of human work-performance standards in futuristic man-machine systems: a * modeling approach 01692
A * knowledge base of an expert system for analysis of manual lifting tasks 01693
* reasoning in pseudo-physical logics 01695
Human specifics * categories and counteraction in decision making problems 01696
The * approach to facilities layout problems 01697
The * paradigm for knowledge representation in cerebral dynamics 01699
The * decodings of educative texts 01700
The * logic of text understanding 01701
A representation of human reliability using * concepts 02024
* control of a mobile robot for obstacle avoidance 02025
Manual control of an intrinsically unstable system and its modeling by *logic 02026
Convexly combined * relational equations and several aspects of their application to * information processing 02027
A design for a * logic controller 02028
A * decision-making method and its application to a company choice problem 02029
Epistemic necessity, possibility, and truth. Tools for dealing with imprecision and uncertainty in * knowledge-based systems 02075
An application of computerized * graphics rating scale to the psychological measurement of individual differences 02200

767

Combining stochastic uncertainty and linguistic inexactness: theory and experimental evaluation of four * probability models 02218
Effect of * membership on recognition of gray level images 02539
Multi-Input * inference engine on a systolic array 02953
A rule-based system for * natural language robot control 03574
A natural language information retrieval system with extentions towards *reasoning HCI-0281 †
Interactive * decision-making for multi-objective nonlinear programming using reference membership intervals HCI-0295 †
A * rule-based model of human problem solving HCI-0359 †
CNS-HLS mapping using * sets HCI-0380 †

## GAME
Comparison of video * and conventional test performance 02594
The marble company: The design and implementation of a simulation board * 02595
Team cohesion effects on business * performance 02597
Human-computer interaction in the * of Go 03634

## GAMES
Relativized Arthur-Merlin versus Merlin-Arthur * 01912
Front end * 02599
Playing the language-* of design and use-on skill and participation 03043
Heuristics for designing enjoyable user interfaces: lessons from computer * HCI-0132 †

## GAMING
Community design and */simulation: Comparison of communications techniques in participatory design sessions 02596

## GARBERS
Jeff * and the ergonomics of software 01420

## GARGOYLE
An introduction to *: an interactive illustration tool 03185

## GAS
Process design of oil and * production facilities using expert systems 02933
* sensors: towards an artificial nose 04015

## GATEWAY
User interfaces: * or bottleneck ● 0142

## GATEWAYS
Transparent information systems through *, front ends, intermediaries, and interfaces HCI-0276 †

## GAZE
Tensor network theory and its application in computer modeling of the metaorganization of sensorimotor hierarchies of * 02753

## GCI
*—a tool for developing interactive CAD user interfaces 02625

## GDSS
*: a brief look at a new concept in decision support 02804
Handling textual information in a * database: experience with the Arizona analyst information system 03475

## GEAC
Implementation of the * circulation system within the CLANN network 02458

## GEM
The world of * ● 0396

## GENDER
Assessing * bias in computer software 01591
The effects of * and age on preschool children's choice of the computer as a child-selected activity 02450
A research model for studying the */power aspects of human-computer communication HCI-0193 †

## GENERALITY
Transportability and * in a natural-language interface system 0394
Two views of * 01876

## GENERALIZATIONS
Some * about generalization 01775

## GENERALIZED
A conceptual architecture for * decision support system software 0659
* fisheye views 0893
Computer programming and * problem-solving skills: in search of direction 01585
Tensor geometry: a language of brains & neurocomputers. * coordinates in neuroscience & robotics 03966
A * user interface for applications programs (II) HCI-0112 †
* query-by-rule: a heterogeneous database query language HCI-0252 †
A * model management system for mathematical programming HCI-0302 †

## GENERALIZING
* back propagation to computation 02726

## GENERATIONS
Preparing new * for the information age 0453

## GENERATIVE
* systems of analyzers 01461
Self-organizing systems and transformational-* (TG) grammar 01619
* systems of analyzers 02702
* transition networks: a new communication control abstraction 03241

## GENERATOR
GENIE-M: A * for multimedia information environments 0268
The PSG—programming system * 01098
A FORTRAN input program * 01227
An abstract description * for the reliability analysis in the design of real time systems 02490
A programmer-friendly LL(1) parser * 02626
ALIEN: a programming environment * for personal computers 02790
Graphics-based qualitative simulation * for power distribution systems 02946
A user interface mangement system * 04074

The synthesizer *: a system for constructing language-based editors ● HCI-0024 †
A * of direct manipulation office systems HCI-0250 †

**GENERATORS**
A study of stability of electrocortical rhythm * 01258
The trouble with application * 01662

**GENERIC**
* expert system shell for diagnostic reasoning 02911
* diagnostic knowledge acquisition tool 02944
A * strategy for diagnostic assistance: the technician's assistant 02957
The kernel of a * software development environment 03056
Abstract, * models of interactive systems 03219
Modelling * user-interfaces with functional programs 03265
* surface interpretation: observability model 03563

**GENERICITY**
Multiple inheritance and * for the integration of a database management system in an object-oriented approach 03844

**GENETIC**
Analysis of the performance of a * algorithm-based system for message classification in noisy environments 02156
Improving performance of an electrical power expert system with *algorithms 02925

**GENIE**
*-M: A generator for multimedia information environments 0268
*: a modifiable computer-based task for experiments in human-computer interaction HCI-0194 †

**GEOGRAPHIC**
Challenges in the application of graphics technology to the management of * information 03871

**GEOMATIC**
*: a 3-D graphic relief simulation system HCI-0395 †

**GEOMETRIC**
* modelling 0236
A heuristic program to solve *-analogy problems 0299
Model generation and modification for dynamic systems from * data 0604
Unified interactive * modeller for simulating highly complex environments 01472
Simplicial differential * theory for language cortical dynamics 01698
The representation and perception of * structure in moving visual patterns 03326
Automatizing * proofs and constructions 03851
* continuity with interpolating Bézier curves 03857
Low cost * modelling system for CAM 03866
Approximation methods used in the exchange of * information via the VDA/VDMA surface interface HCI-0421 †

**GEOMETRICAL**
Determining 3-D motion parameters of a rigid body: a vector-* approach 03339

**GEOMETRY**
Representation of local * in the visual system 01249
The effect of perspective * on judged direction in spatial information instruments 01720
Non-Reimannian approach to * of visual space: An application of affinely connected * to visual alleys and horopter 02364
Computational * and its Applications § 03850
Tensor *: a language of brains & neurocomputers. Generalized coordinates in neuroscience & robotics 03966

**GERMAN**
DATENBANK-DIALOG: a * language interface for relational databases 01208
Structure of * syllable initial and final consonant clusters based on articulatory features 02652
Report on * Joint Venture Tool Integration Projects 03495
Prosodic features in * speech: stress assignment by man and machine 03989

**GESTURAL**
Dialogue management for * interfaces 01069
Motion analysis of grammatical processes in a visual-* language 03347
A * representation of the process of composing Chinese temples 03855

**GESTURE**
Issues limiting the acceptance of user interfaces using * input and handwriting character recognition 0845
FINGER—Formalizing Interaction for * Recognition 01017
A * based text editor 03232

**GESTURES**
Speech and * for graphic image manipulation 0859
The use of hand-drawn * for text editing 02151

**GESTURING**
A synthetic visual environment with hand * and voice input 0858

**GIBIS**
*: a hypertext tool for exploratory policy discussion HCI-0300 †

**GIFT**
The * of good design tools 0411

**GINAS**
A systems approach to extended * applications 0228

**GIRLS**
Computer literacy in secondary education: the performance and engagement of * 01495
Where have all the * gone? 02689

**GIRO**
Video display terminals and birth defects. A study of pregnancy outcomes of employees of the Postal-* Center, Oslo, Norway 03691

**GISD**
*: a graphical interactive system for conceptual database design 02042

**GISK**
CAD system * for interactive graphical modelling of planar mechanisms 01570

## GISMO
*: A visual problem-structuring and knowledge-organization tool 01871

## GIVING
Interface design issues for advice-* expert systems 01321

## GKS
Managing multiple context-frames through * 01389

## GKSGRAL
*—software and hardware realizations of the graphical kernel system 03982

## GLASGOW
Evaluating the usability of the * online 01808

## GLOBAL
Speeded phase discrimination: evidence for * to local processing 03307
Coherent * motion percepts from stochastic local motions 03329
Human-computer-software interaction (HCSI) strategy in the design of *intelligent computer integrated management (ICIM) systems 03396
GMMS: * model management system: a conceptional design framework for model management systems for distributed decision support systems 03484
Computer security: a * challenge § 03577
On * context dependencies and their properties (extended abstract) 03945

## GLOSSARY
A drafted PM * 0625

## GMB
*: a tool for manipulating and animating graph data structures 02636

## GMD
Cognitive user interface laboratory, *-IPSI 0870

## GMMS
*: global model management system: a conceptional design framework for model management systems for distributed decision support systems 03484

## GOAL
Universal sub*ing and chunking: the automatic generation and learning of * hierarchies ● 0497
Biologically plausible models of place recognition and * location 0639
*-directed semantic tutor 02919
MACINTER—aim and * 03590
* and plan knowledge representations: from stories to text editors and programs HCI-0183 †

## GOMS
* meets STRIPS: the integration of planning with skilled procedure execution in human-computer interaction 03243

## GONE
Where have all the girls * 02689

## GOODNESS
* of fit in the user-computer interface: A hierarchical control framework related to "friendless" 01868

## GOSSIP
* as creativity 02576

## GOVERNMENT
* infostructures: a guide to the networks of information resources and technologies at federal, state, and local levels ● 0523
Threat to privacy: the federal *'s use of personal information in the new communication environment 02680

## GPROC
*—an integrated system for the processing of numerical scientific data 02631

## GPS
* and the psychology of th Rubik cubist: a study in reasoning about actions 03311

## GPSS
Interactive graphics in */PC 02586

## GRA
Chinese character processing system based on character-root combination and *phic processing 03187

## GRADED
A * interface for novice/expert interaction 0270

## GRADIENT
Image segmentation based on color and texture * 03303

## GRAFLOG
*: understanding drawings through natural language 01396

## GRAMMAR
The acquisition of * 0353
A * kit in PROLOG 0745
The formal specification of adaptive user interfaces using command language * 0925
Left-associative *: an informal outline 01558
Self-organizing systems and transformational-generative (TG) * 01619
The structure of command languages: an experiment on task-action * 02224
The flexibility of case * representations: a porting procedure for naturallanguage interfaces 02255
A *-based approach to automatic generation of user-interface dialogues 02868
The incorporation of early interface evaluation into command language *specifications 03191
A biparty * as a tool for defining a man-machine dialogue 03639
The mapping between * and processor HCI-0346 †

## GRAMMARS
Constraint *–a new model for specifying graphical applications 0875

## GRAMMATICAL
Motion analysis of * processes in a visual-gestural language 03347
The lexicon, * categories and temporal reasoning 03549

## GRAPE
* programming environment 01967

## GRAPH
* attribution as a specification paradigm 01138
Neural networks and NP-complete optimization problems; a performance study on the * bisection problem 01339

# KEYWORD INDEX [GRAPHICAL]

A cognitive approach for * drawing 01616
Directed * representations of association structures: A systematic approach 01862
Heuristic * displayer for G-BASE 02227
GMB: a tool for manipulating and animating * data structures 02636
EDGE - a * based tool for specifying interaction 03106
Drag: a * drawing system 03183
*-theoretic concepts in computer science § 03885
*-theoretical tools and their use in a practical distributed operating system design case 03886
Structuring knowledge in a * 03899

## GRAPHBUG
* - a microprocessor software debugging tool 02496

## GRAPHIC
Color * displays for network planning and design 0260
Embedding *s into documents by using a *-editor 0266
Bringing * dialogues to APL 0765
Speech and gestures for * image manipulation 0859
Planar maps: an interaction paradigm for * design 0873
* interfaces for knowledge-based system development 0892
* invention for user interfaces: an experimental course in user-interface design 0950
* objects 01190
Architectures of * processors for interactive 2D * 01395
Interactive * editor for analysis and enhancement of medical images 01492
Effects of * boundaries in tabular displays: a human factors evaluation 01526
A human factors design investigation of a computerized layout system of text-* technical materials 01779
* equivalence, * explanations, and embedded process modeling for enhanced user-system interaction 01888
Improved design of * displays in thesauri—through technology and ergonomics 02297

A personal computer based * workstation 02493
Applying a theory of *al presentation to the * design of user interfaces 03122
Textvision: elicitation and acquisition of conceptual knowledge by *representation and multiwindowing 03902
An experimental comparison of tabular and * data presentation HCI-0236 †
* design for computer * HCI-0376 †
Real time * simulation of visual effects of egomotion HCI-0379 †
Geomatic: a 3-D * relief simulation system HCI-0395 †

## GRAPHICAL
Towards a characterization of * interaction 0074
Creating highly-interactive and * user interfaces by demonstration 0084
* specification of procedural knowledge for an expert system 0427
* vs. textual representation: an empirical study of novices' program comprehension 0566
Off-line programming of robots using 3D * simulation system 0602
* specification of user interfaces with behavior abstraction 0840
Constraint grammars—a new model for specifying * applications 0875
Models of user interactions with * interfaces: 1. statistical 0883
Understanding Bayesian reasoning via * displays 0884
Animated * interfaces using temporal constraints 0909
Data-structures students may prefer to learn algorithms using * methods 01032
Creating highly-interactive and * user interfaces by demonstration 01054
CLAM- an open system for * user interfaces 01117
A user interface toolkit based on * objects and constraints 01125
A * tool for the design and prototyping of distributed systems 01146

Automating the design of * presentations of relational information 01150
Rooms: the use of multiple virtual workspaces to reduce space contention in a window-based * user interface 01151
* data presentation for decision support systems 01229
A feature matching approach to the retrieval of * information 01245
Segue: support for distributed * interfaces 01369
* interaction management 01390
A * database interface 01511
CAD system GISK for interactive * modelling of planar mechanisms 01570
Interactive color * postprocessing as a unifying influence in numerical analysis research 01684
Marcosby example in a * UIMS 01831
The tinkertoy * programming environment 01850
GISD: a * interactive system for conceptual database design 02042
Support for tentative design: incorporating the screen image, as a *object, into PROLOG 02116
An experiment in * perception 02125
A * thesaurus-based information retrieval system 02243
GI/S: A * user interface for symbolic computation systems 02397
The effect of task demands and * format on information processing strategies 02482
A model for * interaction 02610
A debugger for a * workstation 02623
* search and replace 02812
A * programming language interface for an intelligent LISP tutor 02862
NetGraph: an object-oriented * toolset for risk assessment 02972
Informational zooming: an interaction model for the * access to text knowledge bases 03073
Sketchpad a man-machine * communication system 03103

XY-WINS: an integraded environment for developing * user interfaces 03118
Applying a theory of * presentation to the graphic design of user interfaces 03122
Gripe: a * interface to a knowledge based system which reasons about protein topology 03234
An editing model for generating * user interfaces 03289
Automatic generation of * user interfaces 03290
The control structure diagram: an automated * representation for software 03524
Segue: Support for distributed * interfaces 03526
A * entity-relationship database browser 03532
Knowledge acquisition via a * interface 03572
A colour atlas for * displays 03726
On the design of a * transition network editor 03830
Integration of * tools in a computer algebra system 03847
Tree doctor, a software package for * manipulation and animation of tree structures 03901
GKSGRAL—software and hardware realizations of the * kernel system 03982
Editing * objects using procedural representations 04056
SKETCHER, an interactive, * Ada software tool—its development and use HCI-0100 †
* user interfaces HCI-0133 †
Specification and generation of variable, personalized * interfaces HCI-0134 †
PICT: an interactive * programming environment HCI-0143 †
An experimental program investigating color-enhanced and * information presentation: an integration of the findings HCI-0196 †
Whiteboards: a * database tool HCI-0289 †
Managing the semantic content of * data HCI-0374 †
* prototyping of * tools HCI-0375 †
* standards HCI-0417 †

## GRAPHICALLY
Defining constraints * 0910
A perceptual study of the Flury-Riedwyl faces for * displaying multivariate data 02126
The filter browser defining interfaces * 03792

## GRAPHICSSYSTEM
Interactive performance display and debugging using the NCUBE real-time * 02907

## GRAPHING
The elements of * data ● HCI-0035 †

## GRAPHS
Implementing a semantic interpreter using conceptual * 01812
Support for * of processes in a command interpreter 02633
Prototyping user interfaces for applications depicted by * 03523
Knowledge-based editors for directed * 03797
Computing text constituency: an algorithmic approach to the generation of text * HCI-0267 †

## GRASPING
* reality through illusion—interactive graphics serving science 02857

## GRASS3
*, a language for interactive graphics 03170

## GRAY
Effect of fuzzy membership on recognition of * level images 02539

## GREEK
The Perseus project: an interactive curriculum on classical * civilization 01680
Informatics and municipalities: the * approach 01940

## GREENBLATT
The * chess program 0527

## GRIBS
*—an approach to a realistic realtime simulation of human arm motion 03432

## GRID
* analysis: continuing the search for a metric of shape 02367

## GRIDS
Refining problem-solving knowledge in repertory * using a consultation mechanism 02205

## GRIP
Breaking the * of user manuals 01051

## GRIPE
*: a graphical interface to a knowledge based system which reasons about protein topology 03234

## GROUPS
User behaviour in computer networked * 0473
Session on the requirements of international user * 01431
How can * communicate when they use different languages? 03038
Report from the working group on "goals and strategies of trade unions and other social * in systems design for human development and productivity." 03657

## GROUPWARE
LIZA: an extensible * toolkit 0805
Concurrency control in * systems 01090
A * toolbox 01304
*: interface design for meetings 02883

## GS1000
A display system for the Stellar Graphics Supercomputer Model * 02816

## GTEX
*—A group technology expert system 02936

## GUHA
Decision trees: a contribution to automatic interpretation of * results HCI-0329 †

## GUIDANCE
Assessing the usability of user interfaces: * and online help features 04065

## GUIDED
Depth and detours: an essay on visually * behavior 0018
* tours and tabletops: tools for communicating in a hypertext environment 01161

A user preference * approach to conflict resolution in rule-based expert systems 01872
The engineering information system: a * tour 02046
* tours and tabletops: tools for communicating in a hypertext environment 02823
A study of auditory warning alarms evaluation for automated * vehicles 03424

## GUS
*, a frame driven dialog system 0395

## GYMNASTICS
Mental * of sequential programming 01971

## HABITATS
Design of an AI-Based self-sustaining * control system 02959

## HABITS
Managers' reading * in the electronics industry 02339

## HACKER
'Remember to lock the door': MMI and the * 01910

## HACKERS
The *' comfort 01544

## HAL
Working with Lotus *: a 1-2-3 user's guide ● 0731

## HAM
Talking it over: the natural language dialog system *-ANS 0165

## HAND
Schemas that integrate vision and touch for * control 0026
*-crafted hypertext-lessons from the ACM experiment 0128
A synthetic visual environment with * gesturing and voice input 0858
The control of * equilibrium trajectories in multi-joint arm movements 01275
On-line recognition of Pitman's *-written short*—an evaluation of potential 02111
The use of *-drawn gestures for text editing 02151
Development of a *-held computerized vocabulary tutor 02468
A * biomechanics workstation 02820

Occupational accidents to the *: A comparison of factory and nonfactory injuries 03438

## HANDBOOK
The user-computer interface in process control: a human factors engineering * ● 0341
The CD ROM * ● 0678

## HANDED
A study in two-* input 0933

## HANDICAPPED
The architecture of an inexpensive and portable talking-tactile terminal to aid the visually * 01452
Using interactive videotaped-based instruction to teach on-the-job social skills to * adolescents 02288
An inexpensive and portable talking-tactile terminal for the visually * 02377
100 Percent assured performance for robotic assistive devices for *and elderly persons 03414
Design of computer programs for the physically * HCI-0096 †

## HANDLER
whim, the window * and input manager 01825

## HANDMARKINGS
Behavioral experiments on * HCI-0201 †

## HANDPRINTED
Interactive recognition of * characters for computer input 0940
* chinese character recognition via neural networks 02529

## HAPPY
What makes users * HCI-0427 †

## HAZARD
Are video displays a health * 01980
The VDTs are here: health * and all 02439
Unexpected motion * exposures on a large robotic assembly 03409

## HAZARDOUS
AGV safety system designed for preventing * human contact 03423

## HAZARDS
An industrial chemical * database with a natural language interface: an application of artificial intelligence 01533
Health * assessment of radio frequency electromagnetic fields emitted by video display terminals 03685

## HCI
*, what is it and what research is needed? 0212
Cumulating the science of *: from s-R compatibility to transcription typing 0831
The role of laboratory experiments in *: help, hindrance, or ho-hum? 0863
Cognitive aspects of * 01371
Computers for the people: * in prospect. An introduction to the * '88 conference 03216
Implications of current design practice for the use of * techniques 03217
Using an expert system to convey * information 03272

## HCSI
Human-computer-software interaction (*) strategy in the design of global intelligent computer integrated management (ICIM) systems 03396

## HDTV
From vision science to *: bridging the gap 01981

## HEAD
Eye-* coordination and information uptake during text processing 03767

## HEADSTART
*—a lifeline for the disabled 02500

## HEALTH
VDUs can ruin your * 01446
Issues in research on clinical computer applications for mental * 01560
Are video displays a * hazard? 01980
The VDTs are here: * hazard and all 02439
* care information systems: a personal historic review 02849
Effects of automation on occupational safety & * 03435

* and productivity issues of CAD/CAM systems 03436
Report from the working group on "experience with participation: application in administration and * care" 03668
VDTs and *—fact or fancy? 03677
* impact of work with visual display terminals 03678
Environmental stressors and perceived * symptoms among office workers 03680
* hazards assessment of radio frequency electromagnetic fields emitted by video display terminals 03685
Video display terminals—electromagnetic radiation and * 03687
Influence of age on performance and * of VDU workers 03702
How identify organizational factors crucial of VDU-*? A context-oriented method approach 03741
Work content, stress and * in computer-mediated work: a seven year follow-up study 03758
The development and use of information technology in * care HCI-0408 †
An empirical study of occupational stress, attitudes and * among information systems personnel HCI-0451 †

**HEALTHY**
The body in question: how to stay * at the PC 02548

**HEART**
Operator effort and the measurement of *-rate variability 01736
Beyond * rate in the cardiac psychophysiological assessment of mental effort: the T-wave amplitude component of the electrocardiogram 01738
The data model is the * of interface design 02875
Assessment of mental load for different strategies of man-computer dialogue by means of the * rate power spectrum 03623

**HEAVY**
Task-oriented approach to interactive control of *-duty manipulators based on coarse scene description ● 0546

**HEBBIAN**
A drive-reinforcement model of single neuron function: An alternative to the * neuronal model 02743
Differential * learning 02745

**HEIGHT**
Effect of pixel *, display *, and vertical resolution on the detection of a simple vertical line signal in visual noise 01753

**HELGON**
*: extending the retrieval by reformulation paradigm 0880

**HEMISPHERES**
Ordinals and the * of the brain 01620
Task-sharing within and between *: a multiple-resources approach 01795

**HERCULES**
*: database query using natural language fragments HCI-0253 †

**HERMENEUTIC**
Culture, cognitive, and connectionism: Towards an * anthropology of mind 04077

**HERMENEUTICS**
Artifact as theory-nexus: * meets theory-based design 0798

**HESITANT**
Ada: first users—pleased; prospective users—still * HCI-0159 †

**HESITATIONS**
* in continuous tracking induced by a concurrent discrete task 01745

**HEURISTIC**
A * program to solve geometric-analogy problems 0299
* graph displayer for G-BASE 02227
* rules for visualization 03868

**HEURISTICS**
Human decision processes: * and task structure 0401
Correspondence in apparent motion: defining the * 03308

* for designing enjoyable user interfaces: lessons from computer games HCI-0132 †

**HIC**
*: the human interface column 01422

**HIDDEN**
The AutoCAD productivity book: tapping the * power of AutoCAD: 2nd edition ● 0668
* patterns in combined and adaptive knowledge networks 02073
The AutoCAD productivity book: tapping the * power of AutoCAD ● HCI-0076 †

**HIERARCHIES**
Universal subgoaling and chunking: the automatic generation and learning of goal * ● 0497
Constraint * 01114
Tensor network theory and its application in computer modeling of the metaorganization of sensorimotor * of gaze 02753
A general user interface for creating and displaying tree-structures, *, decision trees, and nested menus HCI-0136 †

**HIGGENS**
Semantic feedback in the * UIMS 01851
The * UIMS and its efficient implementation of Undo 03861

**HILDITCH**
An investigation into the skeletonization approach of * HCI-0388 †

**HINDRANCE**
The role of laboratory experiments in HCI: help, *, or ho-hum? 0863

**HISTOPATHOLOGY**
Application of structural pattern recognition in * 0295

**HISTORIC**
Health care information systems: a personal * review 02849

**HISTORICAL**
A * and intellectual perspective of the context of human computer interaction 0039
Computers and children's * thinking and understanding 0283
Key areas of cognitive psychology: a * perspective 0328

An * perspective of CD ROM 0679
A * perspective for teaching 01033
Natural language querying of * data bases 01354
Some * currents concerning the 'societal learning' approach to policy and planning 01603
An * perspective on clinical laboratory information systems 02848

**HLS**
CNS-* mapping using fuzzy sets HCI-0380 †

**HMI**
The many faces of * 01382

**HOLOGRAPHY**
A *-based computer-aided translation system-conceptual analysis 01607

**HOLOPHRASTED**
* displays in an interactive environment HCI-0105 †

**HOMESTEADERS**
CD ROM joins the new media * 0281

**HOMOGENEITY**
Segmentation using contrast and * measures 02543

**HOOKS**
Teaching users to fish: *, lines and sinkers for reading computer documentat 03156

**HOPFIELD**
* model applied to vowel and consonant discrimination 02735

**HORIZON**
HORSE: a simulation of the * supercomputer 03541

**HORIZONS**
New * in educational computing ● 0741
New * in educational computing ● 0750
New * for the information profession: meeting the challenge of change § 04046

**HORIZONTAL**
A development environment for * microcode programs 01079

**HOROPTER**
Non-Reimannian approach to geometry of visual space: An application of affinely connected geometry to visual alleys and * 02364

**HORSES**
The * project and its perspectives in knowledge engineering 02716

**HOSPITAL**
Planning for * information systems using the Lancaster Soft Systems methodology 01228
The effects of a computerized information system on a * 01553
History of the development of medical information systems at the Laboratory of Computer Science at Massachusetts General * 02842

**HOST**
An implementation of OSI protocols in SM-4 * computers 03638

**HOUSEHOLDS**
The diffusion and impacts of information technology in * 0754

**HSV**
An experimental comparison of RGB, YIQ, LAB, *, and opponent color models HCI-0381 †

**HUM**
The role of laboratory experiments in HCI: help, hindrance, or ho-* 0863

**HUMANISTS**
An analysis of *' requests received by an information service for the humanities 02318

**HUMANITIES**
Computer assisted learning in the * and social sciences ● 0470
Information technology in the *: tools, techniques and applications ● 0595
An analysis of humanists' requests received by an information service for the * 02318

**HUMANITY**
Organizational * and architecture: Duality and complementarity of papa-logic and mama-logic in managerial conceptualizations of change 01609
Managing information systems for effectiveness and *: applying research of organizational behavior 01932

**HUMANIZATION**
Integrated software-design: a work-oriented approach to the * of computerized clerical tasks 0243
The office between * and control 03651

**HUMANIZED**
Autocompletion in full text transaction entry: a method for * input 0934

**HUMANLY**
Selecting a * understandable knowledge representation for reasoning about knowledge HCI-0330 †

**HUMANOID**
REPTIL-promoting dialog between * and computer 02307

**HUMANS**
Task allocation between * and robots in manufacturing 0559
Visual pattern recognition in *: I. Evidence for adaptive filtering 01274
Trust between * and machines, and the design of decision aids 02164
Choreography for technology and * 02518
*, computers, and contracts 03223
Design of distribution of production control functions between * and artificially intelligent devices 03375
Growth and challenge VS wear and tear of * in computer mediated work 03757
Fallible * and vulnerable systems: lessons learned from aviation 03808

**HUTWINDOWS**
*: an improved architecture for a user interface management system 01830
*: an improved architecture for a user interface management system 03854

**HYBRID**
A * approach to deductive uncertain inference 02191

Oblog-2: A * knowledge representation system for defeasible reasoning 02778
A * approach to structure-from-motion 03340
Ergonomics of * Automated Systems I § 03362
Designing * automated manufacturing systems: A European perspective 03382
Ergonomics of * intelligence 03393
An approach to knowledge elicitation in scheduling FMS: Toward a *intelligent system 03394
Design of individual adaptive man-computer dialogues in the * intelligence systems 03400

## HYPERACUITY
Visual *: representation and computation of high precision position information HCI-0393 †

## HYPERBIORHYTHMS
* 02470

## HYPERCUBE
* Concurrent Computers and Applications § 02904
A dataflow-based APL for the * 02905
* Concurrent Computers and Applications; vol. 2 § 02908

## HYPERMEDIA
Using an object-oriented programming language to create audience-driven * environments 0101
The society of text: hypertext, *, and the social construction of information ● 0111
Online information, *, and the idea of literacy 0112
Supporting collaboration in *: issues and experiences 0117
Collaboration in KMS, a shared * system 0807
* as an interpretive act 01806
Supporting collaboration in *: issues and experiences 02454
*: a face lift for presentation research and development: a user services function 03154
*, help and how-to 03155
Hypertext/* ● HCI-0047 †

Reflections on NoteCards: seven issues for the next generation of *systems HCI-0293 †

## HYPERTEXT
Text, context, and *: writing with and for the computer ● 0098
*: a way of incorporating user feedback into online documentation 0102
The society of text: *, hypermedia, and the social construction of information ● 0111
* in context 0114
* and intelligent interfaces for text retrieval 0115
The missing link: why we're all doing * wrong 0118
Reflections on authoring, editing, and managing * 0119
From database to * via electronic publishing: an information odyssey 0122
Hand-crafted *-lessons from the ACM experiment 0128
*: an introduction and survey (Reprint) 0378
* hands-on!: an introduction to a new way of organizing and accessing information ● 0686
* as a means for knowledge acquisition 0777
Conversational *: information access through natural language dialogues with computers 0867
Toward * publishing 01075
Information retrieval using a *-based help system 01155
Guided tours and tabletops: tools for communicating in a * environment 01161
*: an introduction and survey 01360
Authoring considerations for * 01679
Tools for reading and browsing * 02014
The user interface in a *, multiwindow program browser 02072
An online interface within a * system: project Jefferson's electronic notebook 02524
Guided tours and tabletops: tools for communicating in a * environment 02823
* engineering: practical methods for creating a compact disk encyclopedia 02832

Conceptual documents: a mechanism for specifying active views in * 02833
Adding browsing semantics to the * model 02834
Using * to overcome the knowledge base development bottleneck: a case study 02914
Integrated information retrieval for law in a * environment 03071
A comparison of *, scrolling and folding as mechanisms for program browsing 03235
* tips: experiences in developing a * tutorial 03236
A * system to manage software life cycle documents 03519
*/hypermedia ● HCI-0047 †
gIBIS: a * tool for exploratory policy discussion HCI-0300 †

## HYPERWELCOME
* 01805

## HYPO
Ashley, K. D.-But, see, accord: generating blue book citations in * 02770

## IBM
Programming the * User Interface: Using Turbo Pascal ● 0286
Using *'s ISPF dialog manager: under MSV, VM, and VSE ● 0304
Experiencing artificial intelligence: an interactive approach to the * PC ● 0550
* 3270 full screen interactive programming without CICS 01040
The use of the * personal computer in the man-machine interface to a nuclear research accelerator 01454
An interactive programming system for the * 7545 robot 01517
An incidence-matrix-driven panel system for the * PC 01814
* DOS 4.0: a bridge to OS/2 02523
One hundred differential equations execute directly on the * PC 02582
Device-independent graphics: with examples from * personal computers ● HCI-0070 †

# KEYWORD INDEX

High performance interactive graphics: modeling, rendering and animating for * PCs and compatibles ● HCI-0071 †

## IBS
Interaction with *: an Icon-based system 03838

## ICAI
Authoring systems for * 0469

## ICDD
Profile data acquisition for the JCPDS-* database s 01232

## ICE
*: information center expert: a consultation system for resource allocation 0781

## ICECREAM
*, transportable software for creating friendly human interfaces 02615

## ICIM
Human-computer-software interaction (HCSI) strategy in the design of global intelligent computer integrated management (*) systems 03396

## ICON
Towards universality of access: interfacing physically disabled students to the * educational microcomputer 0821
An *-driven end-user interface to UNIX 02089
*-based human-computer interaction 02113
Evaluating the meaningfulness of * sets to represent command operations 03277
Interaction with IBS: an *-based system 03838
* semantics—a formal approach to * system design HCI-0161 †
An image processing language with *-assisted navigation HCI-0387 †

## ICONIC
User performance with command, menu, and * interfaces 0414
User interface support for the integration of software tools: an * model of interaction 01139
* shells for multitasking workstations 02792

## ICONS
An empirical approach to the evaluation of * 01013

Principles of an *-based language 01080
* at the interface: their usefulness 02065

## ICPA
Interactive critical path analysis (*)—microcomputer implementation of a project management and knowledge engineering tool HCI-0445 †

## IDE
Abstraction and integration in *, an editing and formatting environment 03184

## IDECAP
*: interactive pictorial information system for demographic and environmental planning applications HCI-0411 †

## IDENTIFICATION
The problem of * 01088
* of MGB cells by Volterra kernels. III. A glance into the black box 01259
On the * of neural responses 01260
Single sweep analysis of visual evoked potentials through a model of parametric * 01261
Reference * and reference * failures 01345
MINID—a BASIC program to assist in the optical * of minerals in thin section 01505
On the selection and evaluation of visual display symbology: factors influencing search and * times 01718
Viewdata in the office—user-friendly page * 02334
Application of neural network algorithms and architectures to correlation/tracking and * 02734
* and prevention of work-related mental and psycho-somatic disorders among two categories of VDU users 03744
Automatic * of writers 03909

## IDENTIFY
A regression model to * successful learner traits with CAI 02376
Voice versus keyboard: use of a comparative analysis of learning to *skill requirements of input devices 03275

How * organizational factors crucial of VDU-health? A context-oriented method approach 03741

## IDENTITY
Verifying * via keystroke characteristics 02178

## IDEOLOGY
Informatics (computer and information science): its *, methodology, and sociology HCI-0086 †

## IDL
*: past experience and new ideas 03782

## IEEE
Second * Conference on Computer Workstations: proceedings ● 0002
Conference report: * 1'st Int'l conference on neural networks 0772

## IGES
Testing and validation of * processors HCI-0423 †

## ILLNESSES
The informational substrata of psychic * 01600

## ILLUMINANT
Optimal colors, phosphors, and * characteristics of CRT displays: the lgorithmic approach 01710

## ILLUMINATION
Intermittent * from visual display units and fluorescent lighting affects movements of the eyes across text 01713
* requirements for operating a space remote manipulator 03392
Recent results on the * of VDU and CAD workstations 03719

## ILLUSION
Grasping reality through *—interactive graphics serving science 02857

## ILLUSTRATION
An introduction to Gargoyle: an interactive * tool 03185

## IMAGE
VLSI * processing ● 0563
* understanding 1985-86 ● 0615
Designing optimum CRT text blinking video * presentation 0795
Speech and gestures for graphic * manipulation 0859

# [IMAGERY]

Bringing * processing into focus 01317
Coding * sequences for interactive retrieval 01330
Selection of * primitives for general-purpose visual processing 01467
Automating knowledge acquisition for aerial * interpretation 01470
An automatic wafer inspection system using pipelined * processing techniques 01840
Support for tentative design: incorporating the screen *, as a graphical object, into PROLOG 02116
Simps: Secondary ion mass * processing system 02267
* compression using polylines 02533
* processing with personal computers 02581
VIS: a virtual * system for *-understanding research 02629
Human * understanding: recent research and a theory 02698
Intelligible encoding of ASL * sequences at extremely low information rates 02708
Parametric Fourier * characterization toolkit 02798
Hierarchical scene structure representations to facilitate * understanding 02942
XVISION: a comprehensive software system for * processing research, education, and applications 03124
Interfacing * processing and computer graphics systems using an artificial visual system 03301
* segmentation based on color and texture gradient 03303
Selection and use of * features for segmentation of boundary * 03305
On the estimation of dense displacement vector fields from * sequences 03335
Display * characteristics and visual response 03722
* segregation by motion: cortical mechanisms and implementation in neural networks 03958
Practical applications of optical disk * systems in document management 04041

Automatic contour definition on left ventriculograms by * evidence and a multiple template-based model 04073
The application of scene synthesis techniques to the display of multidimensional * data HCI-0371 †
An * processing language with ICON-assisted navigation HCI-0387 †
* processing aspects of type HCI-0403 †

## IMAGERY
Manipulation of 3D * 0557
The effects of 3D * on managerial data interpretation 02502
Autonomous scene description with range * 02707
Motion and time-varying * 03336
An experimental evaluation of computer graphics * HCI-0373 †

## IMAGES
Continuous processing of * through user sketched functional blocks 01399
Interactive graphic editor for analysis and enhancement of medical * 01492
A model for the fading of stabilized * in a visual system 01864
The mental rotation and perceived realism of computer-generated three-dimensional * 02213
Effect of fuzzy membership on recognition of gray level * 02539
A comparison of neural network and matched filter processing for detecting lines in * 02738
A library for incremental update of bitmap * 02836
The history of the use of computers in the interpretation of radiological * 02845
Principle of visual color coding applied to satellite * 03304
Selection and use of image features for segmentation of boundary * 03305
Computer-generated *: the state of the art § 03856
Mapping * to a hierarchical data structure—a way to knowledge-based pattern recognition 03954

# KEYWORD INDEX

Psychovisual issues in the display of medical * 03978
A flexible and intelligent system for fast measurements in binary * for in-line robotic control 03986
Eye movement analysis system using fundus * HCI-0243 †

## IMAGINARY
"Structure—reaction type" paradigm in the conventional methods of describing organic reactions and the concept of * transitions structures overcoming this paradigm 02268

## IMAGING
Color displays for medical * 0262
Progress in medical * ● 0556
Magnification effects with * displays depend on scene content and viewing condition 01786
VISION: VHDL induced schematic * on net-lists 02830

## IMITATE
Optical systems that * human memory 01576

## IMMUNE
The human * system as an information systems security reference model 01547
The * system, adaptation, and machine learning 02559
Control of the * response 03970

## IMPAIRED
Natural language processing and the language-* 02570
Human factors considerations in the design of a VDU for visually *persons 03698

## IMPAIRMENT
Visual * and subjective ocular symptomatology in VDT operators 03734

## IMPASSE
Toward a theory of *-driven learning 0536

## IMPERATIVE
The computer * among owners of home computers: explanation by social factors HCI-0217 †

## IMPERATIVES
Stategic * in software engineering education 04024

## IMPERFECTION
On the management of information * in knowledge based systems 03823

## IMPLANTS
An evaluation of auditory performances in patients with Cochlear * 02658
Automated design and analysis system for design of custom orthopedic * 02931

## IMPLEMENTATIONAL
Intelligent CAD systems II: * issues ● 0006

## IMPLEMENTER
System user/system *: a joint responsibility for success 01535

## IMPLICATURES
Anticipating false *: cooperative responses in question-answer systems 03178

## IMPOSED
Inference control mechanism for statistical database frequency-* data distortions 02449

## IMPRECISE
Reasoning with * knowledge in expert systems 02018

## IMPRECISION
Epistemic necessity, possibility, and truth. Tools for dealing with *and uncertainty in fuzzy knowledge-based systems 02075
Implementing * in information systems HCI-0259 †

## IMPRESSION
Information retrieval using * of documents as a clue 03065

## IMPULSE
*-86: a substrate for object-oriented interface design 03032

## INACTIVE
* video at work 02571

## INACTIVITY
Short- and long-term effects of extreme physical *. A review 03703
*, night work, and fatigue 03705

## INADEQUATE
The computer as mask: a problem of * human interaction examined with particular regard to online public access catalogues 02337

## INCENTIVE
An evaluation of mood disturbances and somatic discomfort under slow computer-response time and *-pay conditions 03765

## INCOMPLETE
Complete vs. * working tasks—a concept and its verification 0241
On search in an * database HCI-0214 †

## INCORPORATE
An attempt to * expertise about users into an intelligent interface for Unix 02248

## INCORPORATING
Hypertext: a way of * user feedback into online documentation 0102
A model of the motor servo: * nonlinear spindle receptor and muscle mechanical properties 01273
Support for tentative design: * the screen image, as a graphical object, into PROLOG 02116
A computer model of peripheral auditory processing * phase-locking, suppression and adaptation effects 02650
* the human factor in color CAD systems 03104
Cost/benefit analysis for * human factors in the software lifecycle HCI-0127 †

## INCORPORATION
The * of early interface evaluation into command language grammar specifications 03191

## INCREASE
* organizational effectiveness: Support self-managed IS development teams 03014

## INCREASED
Estimating reliability with small samples: * precision with averaged correlations 01728

## INCREASING
* productivity with ISPF/APL2 0767

## INCREMENTAL
Learning through * refinement of procedures 0482
Enhancing * learning processes with knowledge-based systems 0538

## INDEPENDENCE
Spreadsheets with * queries as a user interface for logic programming 02515
A session editor with * execution functions 02637
A library for * update of bitmap images 02836

## INDEPENDENCE
Dialogue management: support for dialogue * 02512

## INDEPENDENT
Studies in the evaluation of a domain-* natural language query system 0162
Initial work on a system-* computer model of a 3D anthropomorphic dummy 01476
The design of a terminal * package 02619
Speaker-* automatic recognition of plosive sound in letters and digits 03993
Device-* graphics: with examples from IBM personal computers ● HCI-0070 †
The effects of program-dependent and program-* deletions on software cloze tests HCI-0175 †

## INDETERMINACY
* in the subject access to documents 01993

## INDEX
A study on safety evaluation * and industrial accident analysis from the viewpoint of the safety confirmation type 03419

## INDEXED
The spatial allocation of visual attention as * by event-related brain potentials 01739

## INDEXES
Optimizing the structure of database menu *: a decision model of menu search 01716
* and bibliography ● HCI-0068 †

## INDEXING
Correlation of term usage and term * frequencies 02004
Illustrated description of an interactive knowledge based * system 03076

## INDIA
Human factors in automating manufacturing systems in * 03446

## INDICATIONS
An approach to a mathematics of phenomena: canonical aspects of reentrant form eigenbehavior in the extended calculus of * 01621

## INDICATORS
Performance in cognitive tasks and cardiovascular parameters as * of mental load 03624

## INDIVIDUAL
Bibliography: * differences and computer-human interaction 0890
* and organizational factors and the design of IPSEs 01408
Maintenance training simulator fidelity and * differences in transfer of training 01722
Assaying and isolating * differences in searching a hierarchical file system 01747
Processing demands, effort, and * differences in four different vigilance tasks 01801
All users of information retrieval systems are not created equal: an exploration into * differences 02011
An application of computerized fuzzy graphics rating scale to the psychological measurement of * differences 02200
Accommodating * differences in searching a hierarchical file system 02212
Are there * concepts? Proper names and * concepts in SI-Nets 02233
The importance of * differences in end-user training: The case for learning style 03009
Design of * adaptive man-computer dialogues in the hybrid intelligence systems 03400
The influence of * differences on the reading of computer programs 03456
Influence of * characteristics and group cohesiveness on programmer productivity 04050

## INDIVIDUALITY
Research on * features in speech waves and automatic speaker recognition techniques 02645

## INDIVIDUALIZATION
The chances of * in human-computer interaction and its consequences 0309

## INDIVIDUALIZED
Generating an * user interface 03074

## INDIVIDUALIZING
* the man-machine interface 03404

## INDIVIDUALS
Beware the reliability of slope scores for * 01727

## INDUCED
Psychophysiological investigation of stress * by temporal factors in human-computer interaction 0311
Hesitations in continuous tracking * by a concurrent discrete task 01745
VISION: VHDL * schematic imaging on net-lists 02830
Mental fatigue of VDU operators * by monotonous and various tasks 03760

## INDUCING
* programs in a direct-manipulation environment 0816

## INDUCTION
* of categories: The problem of multiple equilibria 02360
*: processes of inference, learning, and discovery ● HCI-0064 †

## INDUCTIVE
Patterns of * reasoning in a parallel expert system 02219
User-driven adaptive behaviour, a comparative evaluation and an *analysis 03226

## INDUSTRIAL
Cost effectiveness of on-line searching of chemical information: an *viewpoint 0195
Advanced information technology in the new * society: the Kingston seminars ● 0225
Contexts and conflicts between ergonomics and * psychology 0240
Computer aided application program synthesis for * robots 0606
Introducing information technology: experiences of a large * unit 01217
An * chemical hazards database with a natural language interface: an application of artificial intelligence 01533
Training consistent task components: application of automatic and controlled processing theory to * task training 01742
One view of the future of * control 01921
* & Engineering Applications of Artificial Intelligence & Expert Systems § 02910
A comparison of the artistic aspects of various * robots 02938
* & Engineering Applications of Artificial Intelligence & Expert Systems § 02941
* & Engineering Applications of Artificial Intelligence & Expert Systems: vol. I § 02967
* & Engineering Applications of Artificial Intelligence & Expert Systems: vol. II § 02982
Human perception of the work envelope of an * robot 03410
A study on safety evaluation index and * accident analysis from the viewpoint of the safety confirmation type 03419
Experiences from the use of an intelligent safety sensor with * robots 03427
The economic evaluation on implementation * robot from user point of view 03447
KRIP: a knowledge representation system for laws relating to * property 03918

## INDUSTRIES
End-user searching of CAS ONLINE. Results of a cooperative experiment between Imperial Chemical * and Chemical Abstracts Services 02269

## INDUSTRY
Are writers obsolete in the computer * 0109
Production control in car * 0623
Production control in the aircraft * 0624

Barriers to plant transparency, barriers to plant rigidity—A sketch of the problems posed by the radical changes in work forms in the machine-building * 01562
Interactive CAD/CAM in engineering * 01571
Managers' reading habits in the electronics * 02339
Design and implementation of an interactive optimization system for network design in the motor carrier * 02528
The impact of advanced manufacturing in work organization: The Portuguese case of the plastic moulding * 03374
CIM and manufacturing * in the north east of England: A survey of some current issues 03377
Implementation plan for the use of on-line fiber analysis in the textile * 03433
The future of "writing" for the computer * HCI-0150 †
CAD/CAM: integration in the automobile * HCI-0413 †

### INEPT
The * and the computer revolution: some clues from other innovations 01552

### INEXACT
On the applicability of maximum entropy to * reasoning 02074

### INEXACTNESS
Combining stochastic uncertainty and linguistic *: theory and experimental evaluation of four fuzzy probability models 02218

### INEXPENSIVE
The architecture of an * and portable talking-tactile terminal to aid the visually handicapped 01452
An * and portable talking-tactile terminal for the visually handicapped 02377

### INFERENCE
On-line tutorials: What kind of * leads to the most effective learning? 0823
Statistical * on spontaneous neuronal discharge patterns. I. Single neuron 01247
A hybrid approach to deductive uncertain * 02191
Rough sets and dependency analysis among attributes in computer implementations of expert's * models 02231
* control mechanism for statistical database frequency-imposed data distortions 02449
Multi-Input fuzzy * engine on a systolic array 02953
Transfer of learning in * problems 03552
* control via query restriction vs. data modification: a perspective 03581
Modelling and controlling user * 03582
Mental models: towards a cognitive science of language, *, and consciousness ● HCI-0063 †
Induction: processes of *, learning, and discovery ● HCI-0064 †
The architecture of fifth generation * computers HCI-0093 †

### INFERENTIAL
Absolute dates and relative dates in an * system on temporal dependencies between events 02235

### INFINITELY
The myth of the * fast machine 03204

### INFLUENCE
Item selection from menus: the * of menu organization, query interpretation, and programming experience on selection strategies 01011
Interactive color graphical postprocessing as a unifying * in numerical analysis research 01684
The * of visual workload history on visual performance 01725
The * of troubleshooting, education, and documentation on computer user satisfaction 01869
The * of rule-generated stress on computer-synthesized speech 02081
The * of programmers' cognitive complexity on program comprehension and modification 02245
The * of personality on self-paced instruction 02291
Managerial * in the implementation of new technology 02481
* of palate shape on lingual articulation 02642
* of noise on the behavior of an autoassociative neural network 02727
The * of training on use of end-user software 03042
The * of individual differences on the reading of computer programs 03456
* of age on performance and health of VDU workers 03702
* of CRT refresh rates on accommodation aftereffects 03731
* of individual characteristics and group cohesiveness on programmer productivity 04050
The * of color on program readability and comprehensibility HCI-0120 †

### INFLUENCES
* of mental load on reaction times in man-computer dialogues 03625

### INFLUENCING
State-dependent factors * neural plasticity: a partial account of the 0640
On the selection and evaluation of visual display symbology: factors * search and identification times 01718
Factors * the detection of trend deviations on VDTs 03894

### INFO
Ada *: apologies to TEXT_10 02395

### INFORMAL
Left-associative grammar: an * outline 01558
Structuring * information 02426
An * overview of CUINFO (Cornell's computer-based bulletin board) 02783

### INFORMATICS
Semiotics and *: computers as media 0448
* and municipalities: the Greek approach 01940
History of Medical * § 02837

[INFORMATIONAL]

Medical *: a personal view of sowing the seeds 02841
Integrative participation—a challenge to the development of * 03641
Visualization in programming. 5th Interdisciplinary Workshop in * and § 03826
* (computer and information science): its ideology, methodology, and sociology HCI-0086 †

**INFORMATIONAL**
The * substrata of psychic illnesses 01600
A survey on systems * paradigm to the psychic 01606
* zooming: an interaction model for the graphical access to text knowledge bases 03073

**INFORMING**
Improvement of the acquisition of knowledge by * feedback 0540
* the design of software through context-based research 0584

**INFOSTRUCTURES**
Government *: a guide to the networks of information resources and technologies at federal, state, and local levels ● 0523

**INGREDIENTS**
* of intelligent user interfaces 0093
* of intelligent user interfaces 02088
Essential * for a statistical workstation 03315

**INGRES**
The * papers: anatomy of a relational database system ● 0706
Implementation of a Prolog-* interface 01087

**INHERITANCE**
Multiple * and genericity for the integration of a database management system in an object-oriented approach 03844

**INITIATING**
Navigating integrated facilities: * and terminating interaction sequences 02876

**INITIATION**
KITTEN: knowledge * and transfer tools for experts and novices 02159

**INITIATIVE**
A mixed-* workbench for knowledge acquisition 02154

**INITIATIVES**
How to manage educational computing *-lessons from the first five years of Project Athena at MIT 0125

**INJURIES**
Occupational accidents to the hand: A comparison of factory and nonfactory * 03438

**INJURY**
Repetition strain * in Australian VDU users 03681

**INMEETINGS**
Beyond the chalkboard: computer support for collaboration and problem solving * (Reprint) 0376

**INNATE**
* and learned components in a simple visuo-motor reflex 03965

**INNOVATIONS**
* in Internetworking ● 0573
The inept and the computer revolution: some clues from other * 01552

**INPUT**
Issues and techniques in touch-sensitive tablet * 0063
Voice * applications in aerospace 0179
Screen */output programming techniques using Turbo Pascal ● 0714
Issues limiting the acceptance of user interfaces using gesture * and handwriting character recognition 0845
A synthetic visual environment with hand gesturing and voice * 0858
Comparison of elderly and younger users on keyboard and voice *computer-based composition tasks 0916
An *-output model of interactive systems 0926
A study in two-handed * 0933
Autocompletion in full text transaction entry: a method for humanized * 0934
Interactive recognition of handprinted characters for computer * 0940

Designing menu display format to match * device format 0983
Multi-thread * 01070
A FORTRAN * program generator 01227
Application * drivers 01291
Logical * devices and interaction 01393
Human performance evaluation of digitizer pucks for computer * of spatial information 01774
whim, the window handler and * manager 01825
An */output primitive for object-oriented systems 01969
Shaping user *: a strategy for natural language dialogue design 02067
A multi-purpose system for alpha-numeric * to computers via a reduced keyboard 02118
Optimization of string length for spoken digit * with error correction 02185
The utility of speech * in user-computer interfaces 02230
Voice */output interface for online searching: some design and human factor onsiderations 02335
Multi-* fuzzy inference engine on a systolic array 02953
A review of human performance and preferences with different * devices to computer systems 03231
Voice versus keyboard: use of a comparative analysis of learning to identify skill requirements of * devices 03275
Voice-* aids for the physically disabled HCI-0089 †
An empirical investigation of voice as an * modality for computer programming HCI-0237 †
Speech-controlled text-editing: effects of * modality and of command structure HCI-0397 †

**INPUTS**
An iterative and interactive simulation method to reconstruct unknown *contributing to known outputs of neuronal systems 04018

# KEYWORD INDEX

[INTEGRADED]

## INQUEST
*: A prototype intelligence tool 02918

## INQUIRY
Practices of novices and experts in critical * 0585
The rational, the pragmatic and the * process: The social study of information- communication systems 0786
The erotetic logic of problem-solving * 01583
Diversity in the use of electronic mail: a preliminary * HCI-0310 †
Customers' requirements for natural language systems: results of an * HCI-0426 †

## INRIA
The ergonomics psychology project at * 0844
From surface form to the structure of the interface - studies in human computer interaction at * 03984

## INSERTION
Slot versus * magnetic stripe readers: user performance and preference 01756

## INSIGHT
Temporal resolution: an * into the video display terminal (VDT) "problem" 01754
Expert systems—interface * 03210

## INSIGHTS
* on the implementation of a computer-based message system 01917

## INSIST
*: Interactive Simulation in Smalltalk 01119

## INSPECTION
Intelligent interactive video simulation of a code * 01329
Assessing the impact of human factors on data processing * errors 01527
An automatic wafer * system using pipelined image processing techniques 01840
Critical review of visual * 02260
Classifying sensory inspectors with heterogeneous *-error probabilities 02396

## INSPECTORS
Classifying sensory * with heterogeneous inspection-error probabilities 02396

## INSTANTANEOUS
Determining the * axis of translation from optic flow generated by rbitrary sensot motion 03332

## INSTEAD
Work design * of system design 03671
Keywords * of hierarchical menus 03912

## INSTILLING
* professionalism in a software development organization 03019

## INSTRUCTABLE
Natural-language interface for an * robot HCI-0324 †

## INSTRUCTION
Perspectives in artificial intelligence vol. 2: machine translation, NLP, databases and computer-aided * ● 0198
Designing interactive, responsive *: a set of procedures 0274
Interactivity in microcomputer-based *: its essential elements and how it can be enhanced 0275
Design factors for successful videodisc-based * 0277
An examination of the research evidence for computer-based * 0415
Screen design strategies for computer-assisted * ● 0424
Artificial intelligence and *: Applications and methods ● 0468
Teachers' adoption of multimedia technologies for science and mathematics * 0577
Artificial intelligence & human learning: intelligent computer-aided * ● 0671
A cognitive model of database querying: a tool for novice * 0905
A review and synthesis of recent research in intelligent computer-assisted * 02108
Systematic evaluation strategies for computer-based music * systems 02275

Efficacy of higher cognitive and factual questions in computer assisted * modules 02278
The accuracy of cognitive monitoring during computer-based * 02281
Computer-assisted * in academic libraries 02282
The efficacy of computer-assisted video * on rule learning and attitudes 02286
Using interactive videotaped-based * to teach on-the-job social skills to handicapped adolescents 02288
Citation patterns in the computer-based * literature 02290
The influence of personality on self-paced * 02291
A comparison of the effects of computer-assisted *, interactive video, and traditional * on third-grade students in art education 04064

## INSTRUCTIONLESS
* learning about a complex device: the paradigm and observations HCI-0333 †

## INSTRUCTIVE
Machine adaption to psychological differences among users in *information exchanges with computers 03609

## INSTRUMENTATION
* 01834

## INSTRUMENTING
* systems to measure components of interactive response times 01230

## INSTRUMENTS
The effect of perspective geometry on judged direction in spatial information * 01720

## INSURANCE
Evolution of an organizational interface: the new business department at a large * firm (Reprint) 0382
Pregnancy outcome and VDU-work in a cohort of * clerks 03690

## INTEGRADED
XY-WINS: an * environment for developing graphical user interfaces 03118

## INTEGRAL

Design of an * computer-based wheelchair controller/linear synchronous motor system 02378
*-C—a practical environment for C programming 03049
An evaluation of production systems from the ergonomic viewpoint: a plea for an * approach to design 03430
The computer as an * part of the laboratory 03880

## INTEGRATE

Schemas that * vision and touch for hand control 0026
Assessment of an effort to * computer functions in an engineering design firm 0779

## INTEGRATED

* software-design: a work-oriented approach to the humanization of computerized clerical tasks 0243
An experiment in * multimedia conferencing 0381
The creation of an * IVD curriculum 0509
* human and computer intelligence 0580
Robot simulation and off-line programming—an * CAE-CAD approach 0599
An * data description language for coding design knowledge 0717
An * system for neural network simulations 0771
An * color smalltalk-80 system 01127
Interacting with an active, * environment 01137
Office-by-example: an * office system and database manager 01159
Technological development and the * workstation 01313
* processing produces robust understanding 01342
ISDN and the move to * communications—an introduction 01455
The design of distributed transport systems as a major standard interface in computer * manufacturing 01564
An * display for vertical and translational flight: eight factors affecting pilot performance 01714
MAJIC—an * program support environment 01960
A new approach to cursor movements in user interfaces of * programming environments 01974
* communications and work efficiency: impacts on organizational structure and power 02031
Effects of the adoption of an * online system on a technical services department 02463
A model for assessing the performance of a local area network employing technical office protocol (TOP) as part of MAP/TOP network in a computer * manufacturing (CIM) research project, for the transmission of real time interactive speech 02491
GPROC—an * system for the processing of numerical scientific data 02631
A highly * tool set for program development support 02788
Navigating * facilities: initiating and terminating interaction sequences 02876
AWB-ADE: an application development environment for interactive, *systems 03051
* information retrieval for law in a hypertext environment 03071
Structure and policy in computer * manufacturing systems: human factors implications 03371
Models for design of computer * manufacturing systems 03378
Differential organization impacts of the transition from stand-alone to * flexible production 03380
Macro-ergonomics and the computer-* enterprise 03383
Human-computer-software interaction (HCSI) strategy in the design of global intelligent computer * management (ICIM) systems 03396
Express—rapid prototyping and product development via *knowledge-based executable specifications 03492
Tool interfaces in * project support environments 03506
Views for tools in * environments 03784
PantaPM: an * software development environment 03796
Towards an * view of 3-D computer animation 03859
Usage patterns in an * voice and data communications system HCI-0311 †

## INTEGRATING

On knowledge base management systems: * artificial intelligence and d atabase technologies ● 0180
Managers, micros and mainframes: * systems for end-users ● 0455
* software engineering into an intermediate programming class 01037
* neural networks with robots 01187
* human factors and software development 02882
Some experiences in * specification of human computer interaction within a structured system development method 03222
* data and metadata to enhance the user interface 03280
* CD-ROM with printed and online services: a silver platter end-user perspective 03558
* physics and computer education in a single process 03879
* text with non-text:a picture is worth 1k words. Proceedings of the I § 04043
* graphics and text in computer products 04044

## INTEGRATION

The role of the primate superior colliculus in sensorimotor * 0017
A theory of control and complexity: implications for software design and * of computer systems into the work place 0315
* mechanisms in Cedar 01110
User interface support for the * of software tools: an iconic model of interaction 01139
Display formatting in information * and non* tasks 01750
Display proximity in multicue information *: the benefits of boxes 01763

Linkage versus * for binding database and interactive graphics systems 02040
* issues in knowledge support system 02253
Linkage versus * for binding database and interactive graphics systems 02406
Abstraction and * in IDE, an editing and formatting environment 03184
GOMS meets STRIPS: the * of planning with skilled procedure execution in human-computer interaction 03243
The * of the network and relational approaches in a DBMS 03283
The man-machine * 03384
Report on German Joint Venture Tool * Projects 03495
Supporting flexible and efficient tool * 03783
Multiple inheritance and genericity for the * of a database management system in an object-oriented approach 03844
* of graphical tools in a computer algebra system 03847
Unsolvable problems related to the view * approach 03915
* of robot sensory systems 04016
Active vision: * of fixed and mobile cameras 04017
Towards an * between language and software development environment HCI-0158 †
An experimental program investigating color-enhanced and graphical information presentation: an * of the findings HCI-0196 †
CAD/CAM: * in the automobile industry HCI-0413 †

## INTEGRATIVE
Strategies for end-user computing: An * framework 02348
* participation—a challenge to the development of informatics 03641

## INTEGRITY
Extending a relational database with deferred referential * checking andintelligent joins 01089
Preserving the * of the medium: a method of measuring visual and auditory comprehension of electronic media 02084
The * lock support environment 03578

## INTEL
UNIX system V: release 3.0 * 80286/80386 computer version: system administrator's guide ● 0031

## INTELLECT
A conceptual framework for the augmentation of man's * (Reprint) 0368
A research center for augmenting human * HCI-0334 †

## INTELLECTUAL
A historical and * perspective of the context of human computer interaction 0039
Private copying, reproduction costs, and the supply of * property 01988
How well do we acknowledge * debts? 02299
Computer culture: the scientific, *, and social impact of the computer § 03567

## INTELLIGENCE
Expert systems and artificial * ● 0133
Distributed Artificial * ● 0168
On knowledge base management systems: integrating artificial * and d atabase technologies ● 0180
Perspectives in artificial * vol. 2: machine translation, NLP, databases and computer-aided instruction ● 0198
Artificial * and its applications ● 0221
Readings in cognitive science: a perspective from psychology & artificial * ● 0223
Visual information processing: artificial * and the sensorium of sight 0300
Artificial * and statistics ● 0321
Knowledge, skill and artificial * ● 0342
* based on knowledge—knowledge based on * 0359
* and children's development 0360
Designing * 0361
* and the man-machine interface 0363

Creativity, * and evolution 0365
Human factors and artificial * 0408
Artificial * programming environments ● 0420
Neural network architectures for artificial * ● 0434
C/C++ for expert systems: "unleashes the power of a artificial *" ● 0439
Knowledge-based systems, artificial * and human factors 0449
Artificial * and instruction: Applications and methods ● 0468
Parallel computation and computers for artificial * ● 0488
Application of the butterfly parallel processor in artificial * 0489
Artificial * techniques in language learning ● 0500
Artificial * and education; vol. 1: learning environments and tutoring systems ● 0516
Experiencing artificial *: an interactive approach to the IBM PC ● 0550
Experiencing artificial *: an interactive approach for the APPLE ● 0551
Integrated human and computer * 0580
Readings in artificial * and software engineering ● 0612
Artificial * and expert systems ● 0665
Artificial * & human learning: intelligent computer-aided instruction ● 0671
Artificial * systems 0683
Exploring artificial * ● 0692
Cognitive science and machine * laboratory, University of Michigan 0843
Why artificial * isn't (yet) 01175
Human * models and their implications for expert system structure and research 01242
Artificial * techniques in man–machine communication 01459
How can cognitive psychology help solve an artificial * problem? 01480
An industrial chemical hazards database with a natural language interface: an application of artificial * 01533

[INTELLIGENCES]

Questions, *, and intelligent behavior 01540
Artificial * and natural language systems 01541
Questions, * and intelligent behavior 01542
The effects of sources of applications programs on user satisfaction: an empirical study of micro, mini & mainframe computers using an interactive artificial * expert-system 01601
Design of a control room for the air force logistics command (AFLC) command, control, and communication and * (C³I) system 01612
Artificial * in the man/machine interface 01626
Language and artificial * conference report 01688
Evaluating the * in dialogue systems 02194
Can mathematics explain natural * 02565
User-supported artificial * 02602
Artificial * and Law § 02764
Industrial & Engineering Applications of Artificial * & Expert Systems § 02910
INQUEST: A prototype * tool 02918
Industrial & Engineering Applications of Artificial * & Expert Systems § 02941
Industrial & Engineering Applications of Artificial * & Expert Systems: vol. I § 02967
Artificial * techniques applied to maintenance management 02971
Industrial & Engineering Applications of Artificial * & Expert Systems: vol. II § 02982
IR-NLI II: applying man-machine interaction and artificial *concepts to information retrieval 03070
Common and uncommon issues in artificial * an psychology 03312
Ergonomics of hybrid * 03393
Design of individual adaptive man-computer dialogues in the hybrid *systems 03400
Advances in artificial * § 03546
Progress in artificial * § 03555

Artificial * and Information-Control systems of Robots-87 § 03570
Knowledge representation techniques in artificial *: an overview 03900
Artificial * and cognitive psychology: a new look at human factors 03904
Artificial and human * § HCI-0052 †
Man-made minds: the promise of artificial * ● HCI-0055 †
An artificial * approach to legal reasoning ● HCI-0061 †
Decision and * ● HCI-0068 †
Artificial * and tutoring systems: computational and cognitive approaches to the communication of knowledge ● HCI-0080 †

**INTELLIGENCES**
Creative * ● HCI-0056 †

**INTELLIGENT**
* CAD systems II: implementational issues ● 0006
Product and process design in * CAD workstations 0009
Ingredients of * user interfaces 0093
Hypertext and * interfaces for text retrieval 0115
Learning by doing with simulated * help 0132
* machines for process control 0362
Callisto: an * project management system (Reprint) 0375
Learning Issues for * Tutoring Systems ● 0534
Socializing the * tutor: bringing empathy to computer tutors 0541
Learning issues for * tutoring systems ● 0545
Foundations of * tutoring systems ● 0592
Artificial intelligence & human learning: * computer-aided instruction ● 0671
* CAD systems I: theoretical and methodological aspects ● 0715
A multiparadigm user interface for * CAD systems 0716
* interfaces to Nordic data bases 0738
NYNEX * systems group 0814
The information lens: an * system for information sharing in organizations 0891

* interfaces: user models and planners 0932
A smalltalk implementation of an * operator's associate 01132
Concurrency in * systems 01169
* software agents 01303
MADEMA: an approach to * manufacturing systems 01318
* information-sharing systems 01322
* interactive video simulation of a code inspection 01329
A similarity-based reasoning model for * interfaces 01503
Questions, intelligence, and * behavior 01540
Questions, intelligence and * behavior 01542
An * braille display device 01832
A framework for task cooperation within systems containing *components 01884
* help systems 01959
User modeling in * information retrieval 01994
Ingredients of * user interfaces 02088
A review and synthesis of recent research in * computer-assisted instruction 02108
* aids, mental models, and the theory of machines 02171
Information and reasoning in * decision support systems 02173
Surveying projects on * dialogue 02197
Toward * dialogue with ISIS 02198
Support for browsing in an * text retrieval system 02240
An attempt to incorporate expertise about users into an * interface for Unix 02248
Developing the technology for * maintenance advisors 02276
Research on information interaction and * information provision mechanisms 02328
The development of an * user interface for NASA's scientific databases 02673
The second generation * user interface for the crustal dynamics data information system 02675
The polarisation approach to * artifacts 02714

# KEYWORD INDEX [INTERACTIVE]

A graphical programming language interface for an * LISP tutor 02862
Some considerations on * tutoring systems 02963
Hierarchical scheduling in an * environmental control system 02976
A process oriented approach to an * design aid 02980
Delphi: an * interface for a dolphin communication laboratory 02989
* interfaces for secure multilevel database systems 02990
An * tutoring system for basic set theory 02993
Developing * simulation language to support telerobotic workstation activities 02995
Methodologies for * systems § 03026
Towards an * and personalized retrieval system 03028
Logical foundations for knowledge representation in * systems 03029
On the nature and fuction of explanation in * information retrieval 03064
Design issues of an * workstation for the office 03165
Flexible * interactive-video 03238
Plan recognition for * monitoring 03261
Design of distribution of production control functions between humans and artificially * devices 03375
An approach to knowledge elicitation in scheduling FMS: Toward a hybrid * system 03394
Human-computer-software interaction (HCSI) strategy in the design of global * computer integrated management (ICIM) systems 03396
Experiences from the use of an * safety sensor with industrial robots 03427
The role of memory in * information systems 03462
Crisis planning systems: tools for * action 03464
* machines: What chance? 03548
MEISTER: a model enhanced * and skillful teleoperational robot system 03562

Methodologies for * systems § 03633
Knowledge structures for * interaction 03636
A flexible and * system for fast measurements in binary images for in-line robotic control 03986
Uncertainty and * systems § 04030
* interfaces for information retrieval systems: architecture problems in the construction of expert systems for document retrieval 04042
Learning by doing with simulated * help HCI-0229 †
An * interface for online interaction HCI-0264 †
Knowledge-based search tactics for an * intermediary system HCI-0277 †

## INTELLIGIBLE
* encoding of ASL image sequences at extremely low information rates 02708

## INTENSIFIED
Effects on visual accommodation and subjective visual discomfort from VDT work * through split screen technique 03735

## INTENSIVE
User-interface design for a clinical neurophysiological * monitoring system 0881
Qualified CAD work: an * case study 03763
Knowledge-* natural language generation HCI-0343 †

## INTENTION
Analyzing * in utterances 0391
Attention, *, and the structure of discourse 01344

## INTENTIONAL
* and operational aspects of decision behaviour and their modelling 03666

## INTERA
*/P: a user interface prototyping tool 03205

## INTERACT
* '87 0964
People * through computers not with them 02060

## INTERACTING
Questions, answers, and responses: * with knowledge base systems 0182
* with an active, integrated environment 01137
* with computers 02061
* with electronic mail can be a dream or a night: a user's point of view 02069
* with expert systems 02949

## INTERACTIONAL
Evolution of * human behavior with age: a theoretical/experimental approach 01618

## INTERACTIONIST
The * perspective on computer implementation 0785
An *'s view of system pathology 03813

## INTERACTIVATING
A theoretical framework for * linear video 02284

## INTERACTIVE
* multimedia ● 0011
* 3D computer graphics ● 0012
The keystroke-level model for user performance time with * systems 0055
Sites, modes, and trails: Telling the user of an * system where he is, what he can do, and how to get to places (excerpt) 0068
Developing * information systems with the user software engineering methodology 0077
Creating highly-* and graphical user interfaces by demonstration 0084
An * customization program for a natural language database query system 0163
* workstations ● 0216
PLEIADE: A system for * manipulation of structured documents 0265
Adopting * videodisc technology for education 0272
* lesson designs: a taxonomy 0273
Designing *, responsive instruction: a set of procedures 0274
How effective is * video in improving performance and attitude? 0278

Anticipating compact disc-* (CD-I): ten guidelines for prospective authors 0280
Ergonomic features of * systems—the interdependency of software and hardware 0312
On methods of analysis of mental models and the evaluation of *computer systems 0319
* Toolkit ● 0340
* human communication (Reprint) 0371
Strategies for * design systems 0466
* media: working methods and practical applications ● 0501
Setting up an * videodisc project 0502
Computer-assisted learning and * video 0504
Pedagogical design for * video 0505
A question of delivery—an outline classification of * video delivery systems 0510
* video—a producer's medium 0511
The political economy of * video in British higher education 0512
* video as a school resource: Rolls-Royce or Model T Ford? 0513
Learning with * media: dynamic support for students and teachers 0519
Advanced * cobol for micros: a practical approach ● 0521
Advanced * COBOL for micros: a practical approach ● 0522
Fundamentals of engineering drawing: with an introduction to *computer graphics for design and production, (9th ed.) ● 0531
Task-oriented approach to * control of heavy-duty manipulators based on coarse scene description ● 0546
Experiencing artificial intelligence: an * approach to the IBM PC ● 0550
Experiencing artificial intelligence: an * approach for the APPLE ● 0551
Schaum's outline of theories and problems of programming with advanced structured COBOL with file processing structured systems deveolpment and * cons ● 0555
Toward * design of correct programs 0614

* processes in speech perception: the TRACE model 0631
ARIADNE: A knowledge-based * system for planning and decision support 0661
Digital video * 0681
Computing needs in thunderstorm modeling: supercomputers and *graphics 0730
* learning: a multiexpert paradigm for acquiring new knowledge 0776
Generating highly * user interfaces 0865
Encapsulating * behaviors 0874
TNT: a talking tutor 'n' trainer for teaching use of * computer systems 0895
An * environment for dialogue development: its design, use and evaluation; or, is aide useful? 0920
An input-output model of * systems 0926
* recognition of handprinted characters for computer input 0940
A directory of sources for * technologies 0941
Dialog management in * systems: a comparative survey 0949
The effectiveness of a keystroke line in * tutorials 0969
Methodology for comparative selection of * database interface types 01005
Student-oriented features of an * programming environment 01036
* graphics: a tool for beginning programming students in discovering solutions to novel problems 01038
IBM 3270 full screen * programming without CICS 01040
Creating highly-* and graphical user interfaces by demonstration 01054
The design of an * compiler for optimizing microprograms 01078
The proteus bibliography: Representation and * display in databases 01085
An object-oriented framework for * data graphics 01115
INSIST: * Simulation in Smalltalk 01119

Non-intrusive and * profiling in parasight 01123
An * environment for object-oriented music composition and sound synthesis 01131
* blackbox debugging for concurrent languages 01134
* microcomputer programs for linear and non-linear static analysis of frameworks 01165
A human-computer * design program for a multisolution nonlinear problem 01168
Curve tailoring with * computer 01209
Instrumenting systems to measure components of * response times 01230
Digital video * 01308
The coming revolution in * digital video 01325
Virtual video editing in * multimedia applications 01326
Life before the chips: simulating digital video * technology 01328
Intelligent * video simulation of a code inspection 01329
Coding image sequences for * retrieval 01330
* video in language learning 01380
Architectures of graphic processors for * 2D graphics 01395
Construction of * programs in computer graphics 01398
A top down method for * drawing 01401
Approximate modelling of cognitive activity with an expert system: a theory-based strategy for developing an * design tool 01415
Unified * geometric modeller for simulating highly complex environments 01472
* graphic editor for analysis and enhancement of medical images 01492
Some issues related to the design and development of an * video disc 01497
Automated construction of * learning programs in Modula-2 01500
* timetabling in universities 01501

# KEYWORD INDEX

[INTERACTIVE]

* multiple objective linear programming system implemented on a microcomputer 01508
An * programming system for the IBM 7545 robot 01517
The design of a user friendly * personal computer package for quality control charts, project management, and linear programming applications 01521
An * simulation description interpreter 01538
An * outranking system for multi-attribute decision making 01539
CAD system GISK for * graphical modelling of planar mechanisms 01570
* CAD/CAM in engineering industry 01571
The effects of sources of applications programs on user satisfaction: an empirical study of micro, mini & mainframe computers using an *artificial intelligence expert-system 01601
* L systems with a fast local growth 01673
The Perseus project: an * curriculum on classical greek civilization 01680
* color graphical postprocessing as a unifying influence in numerical analysis research 01684
An * approach to local remeshing around a propagating crack 01685
Advanced * executive (AIX) operating system overview 01815
Advanced * executive program development environment 01816
A graphics system architecture for * application-specific display functions 01822
An * procedure for constructing line and circle tangencies 01823
PHIGS: a standard, dynamic, * graphics interface 01826
* design of 3D computer-animated legged animal motion 01828
Developing * information systems with the user software engineering methodology 01856
ARIADNE: a knowledge-based * system for planning and decision support 01860

Advanced diagnostics: a PASCAL * system 01958
* data visualization 01986
A comparative survey of the friendliness of online 'help' in *information 02010
Linkage versus integration for binding database and * graphics systems 02040
GISD: a graphical * system for conceptual database design 02042
A methodology for * evaluation of user reactions to software packages:an empirical analysis of system performance, interaction, and run time 02080
Using computer knowledge in the design of * systems 02137
An * environment for tool selection, specification and composition 02141
ISIS: the * spatial information system 02193
* communication of sentential structure and content: an alternative approach to man-machine communication 02220
Mapping the manipulator workspace using * computer graphics 02257
An * system SDI on microcomputer 02272
Research and evaluation models for the study of * video 02283
An * videodisc drama: The case of Frank hall 02285
The effects of orienting objectives and review on learning from *video 02287
Using * videotaped-based instruction to teach on-the-job social skills to handicapped adolescents 02288
The effects of orienting, processing, and practicing activities on learning from * video 02289
Expert systems and * video tutorials: separating strategies from subject matter 02293
* document display and its use in information retrieval 02300
Subject searching behaviour at the library catalogue and at the shelves: implications for online * catalogues 02302

* videodiscs control and computer-based training on the Apple Macintosh 02305
AI/learn: an * videodisk system for teaching medical concepts and reasoning 02381
An * modeling program for DNA 02385
An * biomolecule graphics system 02386
MOL3D, a modular and * program for molecular modeling and conformational analysis: I—basic modules 02389
Automated * simulation modeling system: AISIM 02399
Experience with a functional layered multicomputer architecture for *processing 02402
Linkage versus integration for binding database and * graphics systems 02406
A model for assessing the performance of a local area network employing technical office protocol (TOP) as part of MAP/TOP network in a computer integrated manufacturing (CIM) research project, for the transmission of real time * speech 02491
Design and implementation of an * optimization system for network design in the motor carrier industry 02528
* curve drawing by segmented Bezier approximation with a control parameter 02535
Algorithm for * forming matrix data representation and estimation of its efficiency 02536
An * simulator for the designing of woven fabric structures second place 02583
Visual * simulation - history, recent developments, and major issues 02585
* graphics in GPSS/PC 02586
A VLSI * layout editor (VILE) 02611
* documentation 02612
GCI—a tool for developing * CAD user interfaces 02625
Q'Nial: a portable interpreter for the nested * array language, Nial 02635

Conman: a visual programming language for * graphics 02811
A study in * 3-D rotation using 2-D control devices 02813
Users' preferences among different techniques for displaying the evaluation of LISP functions in an * debugger 02863
A new conceptual model for * user recovery and command reuse facilities 02884
* performance display and debugging using the NCUBE real-time graphicssystem 02907
A rule-based system for * proposal evaluation 02927
Concept demonstration of the use of * fault diagnosis and isolation for TF30 engines 02968
An * tolerance system 02975
* retrieval office documents 03047
AWB-ADE: an application development environment for *, integrated systems 03051
Towards * query expansion 03067
Illustrated description of an * knowledge based indexing system 03076
GRASS3, a language for * graphics 03170
An * data dictionary facility for CAD/CAM data bases 03174
An introduction to Gargoyle: an * illustration tool 03185
Vidura—an * multilingual publishing system—specification & design 03186
A flexible negotiable * learning environment 03197
Abstract, generic models of * systems 03219
Flexible intelligent *-video 03238
Proving properties of * systems 03267
An approach to * definition of database views 03281
The * specification of human animation 03292
* 3-D modeling with personal computers 03296
* aspects of knowledge representations 03395
* error recovery expert system for robot with voice recognition subsystem 03420

* scientific visualization and parallel display techniques 03542
Cognitive ergonomics: an approach for the design of user-oriented *systems 03591
Exploratory investigations in acquiring and using information in *problem solving 03597
Comparison of well-being among non-machine * clerical workers and full-time and part-time VDT users and typists 03745
Programming for * structure analysis 03776
Interaction models and the principled design of * systems 03799
Using data flow specifications and * editing in the operating system user interface 03800
The role of mental models in programming: from experiment to requirements for an * system 03827
* solid modeling in hut design 03837
ROSE: An object-oriented database system for * computer graphics applications 03845
The * planning work station: a graphics-based UNIX tool for application users and developers 03860
A graphics interface for * simulation of packet-switched networks 03869
An iterative and * simulation method to reconstruct unknown inputs contributing to known outputs of neuronal systems 04018
MIDAS: molecular * display and simulation 04061
A comparison of the effects of computer-assisted instruction, *video, and traditional instruction on third-grade students in art education 04064
Human factors and * computer systems § HCI-0038 †
Principles of * computer graphics (2nd ed.) ● HCI-0069 †
High performance * graphics: modeling, rendering and animating for IBM PCs and compatibles ● HCI-0071 †

Compact disc-*: a designer's overview ● HCI-0078 †
* video: vol. 1 ● HCI-0081 †
SKETCHER, an *, graphical Ada software tool—its development and use HCI-0100 †
Holophrasted displays in an * environment HCI-0105 †
An approach to user specification of * display interfaces HCI-0137 †
PICT: an * graphical programming environment HCI-0143 †
Equal opportunity * systems HCI-0168 †
The future of * systems and the emergence of direct manipulation HCI-0186 †
An almost path-free very high-level * data manipulation language for microcomputer-based database system HCI-0261 †
An * database end user facility for the definition and manipulation of forms HCI-0263 †
* fuzzy decision-making for multi-objective nonlinear programming using reference membership intervals HCI-0295 †
The next generation of * technologies HCI-0384 †
A system for * viewing of structured documents HCI-0400 †
Document convergence in an * formatting system HCI-0405 †
* computer program for the selection of interference fits HCI-0406 †
IDECAP: * pictorial information system for demographic and environmental planning applications HCI-0411 †
* critical path analysis (ICPA)—microcomputer implementation of a project management and knowledge engineering tool HCI-0445 †

**INTERACTIVELY**
Building interfaces * 03119

**INTERACTIVES**
A PC-* stereonet plotting program 01504

**INTERACTIVITY**
* in microcomputer-based instruction: its essential elements and how it can be enhanced 0275

# KEYWORD INDEX [INTERPRETIVE]

**INTERCONNECTIVITY**
Limited * in synthetic neural systems 03968

**INTERDEPENDENCE**
The * of temporal and spatial information in early vision 0023

**INTERDEPENDENCY**
Ergonomic features of interactive systems—the * of software and hardware 0312

**INTERESTING**
How to recognize * topics to provide cooperative answering 02043

**INTERFACING**
* standards for recognisers 0178
* thought: cognitive aspects of human-computer interaction ● 0206
* thought: cognitive aspects of human-computer interaction ● 0207
Real-time *: engineering aspects of microprocessor peripheral systems ● 0224
* Ada and relational databases 0762
Towards universality of access: * physically disabled students to the Icon educational microcomputer 0821
'Transparent' * of speech recognizers to microcomputers 02497
* image processing and computer graphics systems using an artificial visual system 03301

**INTERFERENCE**
Interactive computer program for the selection of * fits HCI-0406 †

**INTERIOR**
A new algorithm for extracting the * of bounded regions based on chain coding 01469
Technology's impact on library * planning 02464
The effect of VDU on the * design of offices 03714

**INTERLISP**
*: the language and its usage ● HCI-0022 †

**INTERMEDIA**
Connections in context: The * system 03534

**INTERMEDIARIES**
Transparent information systems through gateways, front ends, *, and interfaces HCI-0276 †

**INTERMEDIARY**
A knowledge-based * system for information retrieval 0737
What is the role of the * in end-user training? 02522
Retrieval systems for the information seeker: can the role of the *be automated? 02864
Knowledge-based search tactics for an intelligent * system HCI-0277 †

**INTERMITTENT**
* illumination from visual display units and fluorescent lighting affects movements of the eyes across text 01713

**INTERNATIONALLY**
Why users must co-operate * on standardization 01457

**INTERNETWORKING**
Innovations in * ● 0573

**INTERNIST**
The background of * I and QMR 02853

**INTEROFFICE**
A distributed * mail system HCI-0308 †

**INTERPERSONAL**
From trigger video to videodisc: a case study in * skills 0508

**INTERPOLATING**
Geometric continuity with * Bézier curves 03857

**INTERPOLATION**
* coding: A representation for numbers in neural models 01971
Motion * by optimal control 02817

**INTERPRESS**
The workstation: the * page and document description language 01356

**INTERPRETATION**
The * of Logo in practice 0576
Neural and conceptual * of PDP models 0638
Item selection from menus: the influence of menu organization, query *, and programming experience on selection strategies 01011
Automating knowledge acquisition for aerial image * 01470
Problem solving: a behavioral * 01582
* of natural language database queries using optimization methods 01861
The effects of 3D imagery on managerial data * 02502
Multidimensional attribute analyhsis and pattern recognition for seismic * 02530
Natural language and computers: a general survey of written text *methods 02671
The history of the use of computers in the * of radiological images 02845
Generic surface *: observability model 03563
On-line * in speech understanding and dialogue systems 04000
ARES: a relational database with the capability of performing flexible * of queries HCI-0248 †
A model for the * of verbal predictions HCI-0316 †
Decision trees: a contribution to automatic * of GUHA results HCI-0329 †

**INTERPRETATIONS**
Status of trusted DBMS * 03585

**INTERPRETER**
An interactive simulation description * 01538
Implementing a semantic * using conceptual graphs 01812
fsh—a functional UNIX command * 02624
Support for graphs of processes in a command * 02633
Q'Nial: a portable * for the nested interactive array language, Nial 02635

**INTERPRETING**
The alternatives allowed by a rectangularity postulate, and a pragmatic approach to * motion 03550

**INTERPRETIVE**
Hypermedia as an * act 01806

791

**INTERPROCESS**
Building * communication models using Stile 03528

**INTERTEMPORAL**
Frames of mind in * choice 02478

**INTERVAL**
Reliability in computing: the role of * methods in scientific computing ● 0548

**INTERVALS**
Interactive fuzzy decision-making for multi-objective nonlinear programming using reference membership * HCI-0295 †

**INTERVENTION**
Textual *, collaboration, and the online environment 0126

**INTERVALS**
Study of combination of belief * in lattice-structured networks 02223

**INTONATION**
Tones of voice: the role of * in computer speech understanding HCI-0356 †

**INTRAOCULAR**
* pressure during VDT work 03683

**INTRUSIVE**
Non-* and interactive profiling in parasight 01123

**INTUITIVE**
Nested structures of control: an * view 01464
Direct comparison of the relative efficiency on * and analytical cognition 01896
* representations and interaction languages: an exploratory experiment 03611

**INVARIANT**
On the minimum number of templates required for shift, rotation and size * pattern recognition 02531
Linearization of the dynamic transfer response of time * nonlinear systems—in connection with the parallel information processing in living organisms 02665

**INVENTION**
Graphic * for user interfaces: an experimental course in user-interface design 0950

**INVENTORY**
Creating the domain of discourse: ontology and * 02158
Produciton and * management software packages related to user reactions 02567

**INVESTIGATE**
Using low-cost workstations to * computer networks and distributed systems HCI-0437 †

**INVESTIGATING**
Two simulation studies * means of human-computer communication for dynamic task allocation 01882
* computer anxiety in an academic library 02047
* sources of error in the management of crises: theoretical assumptions and a methodological approach 03807
An experimental program * color-enhanced and graphical information presentation: an integration of the findings HCI-0196 †
A framework for * language-mediated interaction with machines HCI-0347 †

**INVESTMENT**
* in computer-product documentation: causes and effects 0105
A financial * assistant 03490

**ION**
Simps: Secondary * mass image processing system 02267

**IPSE**
Custos *: Towards a theory of the supervisor 03365

**IPSES**
Individual and organizational factors and the design of * 01408

**IPSI**
Cognitive user interface laboratory, GMD-* 0870

**IPTO**
Later years at * 0139

**IQ**
STATUS with *—escaping from the Boolean straitjacket 02569

**IRIS**
*: design of a user interface program for symbolic algebra 03081

*: design of an user interface program for symbolic algebra 03085

**IRM**
Strategic * plan: user involvement spells success 02432

**IRUS**
The * transportable natural language database interface 03177

**IRX**
*: an information retrieval system for experimentation and user applications 01076

**ISA**
The * expert system: a prototype system for failure diagnosis on the space station 02913

**ISDN**
Traffic study on primary rate * user-network interface 01442
* and the move to integrated communications—an introduction 01455

**ISIS**
*: the interactive spatial information system 02193
Toward intelligent dialogue with * 02198

**ISOLATING**
Assaying and * individual differences in searching a hierarchical file system 01747

**ISOLATION**
Concept demonstration of the use of interactive fault diagnosis and *for TF30 engines 02968

**ISOLUMINANCE**
Contingent aftereffects and *: psychophysical evidence for separation of color, orientation, and motion 01463

**ISOMETRIC**
Evaluation of mouse, rate-controlled * joystick, step keys, and text keys, for text selection on a CRT 0064

**ISPBXS**
* and terminals 01385

**ISPF**
*: the strategic dailog manager ● 0035

Using IBM's * dialog manager: under MSV, VM, and VSE ● 0304
Increasing productivity with */APL2 0767

**ISQL**
Software tools for the development of pictorial information systems in medicine—the * experience 03980

**ISSUING**
* each undergraduate student a personal computer: living with it for three years 01028

**ITERATION**
Learning * recursion from examples 02215

**ITERATIVE**
The role of * evaluation in designing systems for usability 03255
An * approach to improving data analysis in the classroom 03318
An * and interactive simulation method to reconstruct unknown inputs contributing to known outputs of neuronal systems 04018

**IVD**
The creation of an integrated * curriculum 0509

**JAPANESE**
Composite phoneme units for the speech synthesis of * 02647
A retrieval system for on-line English-* dictionaries 03078
Human aspects of QC circle movement in * manufacturing: Natures and problems 03450
A travel consultation system: towards a smooth conversation in * 03917
Generating natural language responses appropriate to conversational situations—in the case of * 03922
A framework of a mechanical translation between * and English by analogy principle HCI-0353 †
The * and software: is it a good match? HCI-0429 †

**JARGON**
Binary *: the metaphoric language of computing 01044

**JCPDS**
Profile data acquisition for the *-ICDD database s 01232

**JDB**
*: an adaptable interface for debugging 02628

**JEFFERSON**
An online interface within a hypertext system: project *'s electronic notebook 02524

**JETA**
Jet engine technical advisor (* 02974

**JOB**
* histories as predictors of career success in management information systems 01021
* characteristic perceptions of manual drafting and CADD: A field study of the effects of computerization on drafting & design personnel 01523
Ergonomic * design in frequent manual lifting tasks: a microcomputer-based model 01532
Dow Chemical makes continuous improvement part of everyone's * 01908
Representing the structure of *s in * analysis 02181
Using interactive videotaped-based instruction to teach on-the-* social skills to handicapped adolescents 02288
The effects of task differences on the work satisfaction, * characteristics, nd role perceptions of programmer/analysts 02359
Transferring skills from training to the actual work situation: the role of task application knowledge, action styles and * decision latitude 02865
An update measure of supervisor-rated * performance for programmer/analysis 03012
Male/female programmer and systems analyst * performance 03020
Moderating effects of age, education, and tenure on the * satisfaction-*performance relationship 03021

Towards a new theory of * design 03368
Effects of computerization on * demands and stress: the correspondence of subjective and objective data 03622
* organization and allocation of functions between man and computer: I analysis and assessment 03628
* organization and allocation of functions between man and computer: II.*organization 03629

**JOBS**
Representing the structure of * in job analysis 02181
Mathematical modeling of fatigue in physically demanding * 02363
Computer mediated work: the interplay between technology and structured * HCI-0440 †

**JOINS**
CD ROM * the new media homesteaders 0281
Extending a relational database with deferred referential integrity checking andintelligent * 01089

**JOKING**
Who's *? The information system at play 02066

**JOYSTICK**
Evaluation of mouse, rate-controlled isometric *, step keys, and text keys, for text selection on a CRT 0064

**JSP**
Generation of file processing programs based on * 02639

**JTHE**
* assessment of human/computer performance: a case for connectivity 03535

**JUDGED**
The effect of perspective geometry on * direction in spatial information instruments 01720

**JUDGEMENT**
* and decision: theory and application 0648

**JUDGEMENTAL**
A general purpose computer aid to * forecasting: Rationale and procedure 01665

The accuracy of combining * and statistical forecasts 02474

**JUDGEMENTS**
Moral * in designing better systems 02064

**JUMP**
An experimental comparison of a mouse and arrow-* keys for an interactive encyclopedia 02098

**JUNGIAN**
Validation of a * instrument for MIS research 01022

**JUNIOR**
Personality characteristics of * high school students successful with computers 01592

**JUSTIFIED**
Office automation—can it be * 01383
* advice: a semi-naturalistic study of advisory strategies 02887

**KALEIDOSCOPIC**
Portfolio: * visions 02551

**KC**
The Mjo:.* /lner environment: direct interaction with abstractions 03794

**KEAL**
Recognition of speaker-dependent continuous speech with *-Nevezh 04002

**KEE**
Teaching object-oriented programming with the * system 01113

**KENDRICK**
A user-friendly interface to *'s DUAL code 01447

**KERNEL**
Mach and Matchmaker: * and language support for object-oriented distributed systems 03031
The * of a generic software development environment 03056
GKSGRAL—software and hardware realizations of the graphical * system 03982

**KERNELS**
Identification of MGB cells by Volterra *. III. A glance into the black box 01259

**KEY**
Designing for usability: * principles and what designers think 0078
* areas of cognitive psychology: a historical perspective 0328
On designing for usability: an application of four * principles 0923
* factors in knowledge acquisition 01019
* human resource issues in IS in the 1990s: Views of IS executives versus human resource executives 01939
U.S. Army field robotics focus and * technology issues 03402
Designing for usability: * principles and what designers think HCI-0231 †

**KEYBINDINGS**
Designing * to be easy to learn and resistant to forgetting even when the set of commands is large 02890

**KEYBOARD**
Is the unified * better? 0768
Comparison of elderly and younger users on * and voice input computer-based composition tasks 0916
A multi-purpose system for alpha-numeric input to computers via a reduced * 02118
A comparison of menu selection techniques: touch panel, mouse and * 02122
Common sense and user interfaces: issues beyond the * 02465
Voice versus *: use of a comparative analysis of learning to identify skill requirements of input devices 03275
A provisional evaluation of a new chord *, the Velotype 03907
Experimentation with an adaptive search strategy for solving a *design/configuration problem 04070
QWERTY and * reform: the soft * option HCI-0190 †
Speed of response using * and screen-based microcomputer response media HCI-0192 †

**KEYBOARDING**
* for personal computer use ● 0492
* as a social form 01551

**KEYBOARDS**
User computer interface guidelines research for * and function keys 0201

**KEYING**
Mode errors: a user-centered analysis and some preventative measures using *-contingent sound 02107

**KEYPAD**
Dialing a name: alphabetic entry through a telephone * 0973

**KEYS**
Evaluation of mouse, rate-controlled isometric joystick, step *, and text *, for text selection on a CRT 0064
User computer interface guidelines research for keyboards and function * 0201
An experimental comparison of a mouse and arrow-jump * for an interactive encyclopedia 02098
Touch screen, cursor * and mouse interaction 03769

**KEYSTROKE**
The *-level model for user performance time with interactive systems 0055
The effectiveness of a * line in interactive tutorials 0969
Verifying identity via * characteristics 02178

**KEYWORD**
Natural language interface based on * extraction using AWK 02498

**KEYWORDS**
* instead of hierarchical menus 03912

**KINEMATIC**
Virya—a motion control editor for * and dynamic animation 03294

**KINEOPSIS**
On * and cimputation of structure and motion 01839

**KINETIC**
* theory of "hot" neural systems 01613

# KEYWORD INDEX [KNOWLEDGE]

**KINGSTON**
Advanced information technology in the new industrial society: the *seminars ● 0225

**KITTEN**
*: knowledge initiation and transfer tools for experts and novices 02159

**KIWI**
*: knowledge-based user-friendly system for the utilization of information bases 0739

**KMS**
Collaboration in *, a shared hypermedia system 0807

**KNOWING**
* that and * what 03554

**KNOWLEDGE**
THESYS—implementation of a *-based design system with multiple viewpoints 0010
* representation and natural language: extending the expressive power of proposition nodes 0096
Using "word-*" reasoning for question answering 0131
* representation 0137
*-based support of cooperative activities 0171
On * base management systems: integrating artificial intelligence and d atabase technologies ● 0180
Questions, answers, and responses: interacting with * base systems 0182
*-based human-computer interfaces and software ergonomics 0191
*-based systems and communication between computers and human beings 0192
Effect of practice on * and use of basic Lisp 0210
* based management support systems ● 0252
Use of psychometric tools for * acquistion: a case study 0323
The analysis phase in development of * based systems 0324
Data, expert * and decisions ● 0338
*, skill and artificial intelligence ● 0342
The practice of the use of computers. A paradoxical encounter between different traditions of * 0343
Tacit *, working life and scientific method 0345
Intelligence based on *—* based on intelligence 0359
Toward high-performance * workers (Reprint) 0369
Graphical specification of procedural * for an expert system 0427
Using a * base to drive an expert system interface with a natural language component 0430
*-based systems, artificial intelligence and human factors 0449
Truth versus appropriateness: relating declarative to procedural * 0484
* based problem solving ● 0490
Enhancing incremental learning processes with *-based systems 0538
Improvement of the acquisition of * by informing feedback 0540
An experiment in *-based automatic programming 0613
Skills, rules, and *; signals, signs, and symbols, and other distinctions in human performance models 0654
The effects of type of * upon human problem solving in a process control task 0657
ARIADNE: A *-based interactive system for planning and decision support 0661
An integrated data description language for coding design * 0717
* engineering: expert systems and information retrieval ● 0735
Are machines as good as people in drawing conclusions from *represented in catalogues, data bases and expert systems? 0736
A *-based intermediary system for information retrieval 0737
KIWI: *-based user-friendly system for the utilization of information bases 0739
Interactive learning: a multiexpert paradigm for acquiring new * 0776
Hypertext as a means for * acquisition 0777
Graphic interfaces for *-based system development 0892
The elicitation of system * by picture probes 0921
A formal interface design methodology based on user * 0929
Key factors in * acquisition 01019
PLEXACT: an architecture & design of a *-based system for information systems development 01020
Rule base management using meta * 01081
Adaptive interface design: a symmetric model and a *-based implementation 01091
*-based tools to promote shared goals and terminology between interface designers 01160
Catching * in neural nets 01171
The problem of extracting the * of experts 01195
* and experience 01207
Automating * acquisition for aerial image interpretation 01470
*-based system for task analysis and reliability enhancement 01516
A *-based system for assessment of human physiological abilities in manual lifting tasks 01519
A fuzzy * base of an expert system for analysis of manual lifting tasks 01693
The fuzzy paradigm for * representation in cerebral dynamics 01699
Structuring * bases for designers of learning materials 01807
Interfaces for *-base builders' control * and application-specific procedures 01810
A theory for the representation of * 01811
Design of *-based systems with a *-based assistant 01853
ARIADNE: a *-based interactive system for planning and decision support 01860
GISMO: A visual problem-structuring and *-organization tool 01871
A *-based human-computer cooperative system for ill-structured management domains 01873

[KNOWLEDGE]

Aiding the human decisionmaker through the *-based sciences 01880
The IE's future role in improving * 01903
Effect of computer * on user performance over time 01975
Prospects for *-based customization of natural languages query systems 02008
Reasoning with imprecise * in expert systems 02018
* representation and use in pattern analysis 02030
Will you be replaced by a * base? 02055
A *-based system with audio-visual aids 02068
Hidden patterns in combined and adaptive * networks 02073
Epistemic necessity, possibility, and truth. Tools for dealing with imprecision and uncertainty in fuzzy *-based systems 02075
Linguistic * as expertise 02077
Training by exploration: facilitating the transfer of procedural *through analogical reasoning 02103
Negative * towards a strategy for asking in logic programming 02115
Modelling human expertise in * engineering: some preliminary observations 02134
Using computer * in the design of interactive systems 02137
The application of psychological scaling techniques to * elicitation for *-based systems 02139
* elicitation using discourse analysis 02152
Cognitive biases and corrective techniques: proposals for improving elicitation procedures for *-based systems 02153
A mixed-initiative workbench for * acquisition 02154
KITTEN: * initiation and transfer tools for experts and novices 02159
* base refinement by monitoring abstract control * 02160
DM²: an algorithm for diagnostic reasoning that combines analytical models and experiential * 02190

Validation in a * support system: construing and consistency with multiple experts 02203
Refining problem-solving * in repertory grids using a consultation mechanism 02205
Issues in the verification of * in rule-based systems 02226
Integration issues in * support system 02253
Motivation norms of * engineers compared to those of software engineers 02349
Conceptual models of interacitve * acquisition tools 02457
The HORSES project and its perspectives in * engineering 02716
Order and disorder in * structures 02722
* representation in "Default": An attempt to classify general types of * used by legal experts 02775
Precedent-based legal reasoning and * acquisition in contract law: A process model 02776
Oblog-2: A hybrid * representation system for defeasible reasoning 02778
Transferring skills from training to the actual work situation: the role of task application *, action styles and job decision latitude 02865
A *-based user interface management system 02867
SAUCI: a *-based interface architecture 02895
Providing the requisite * via software documentation 02898
Using hypertext to overcome the * base development bottleneck: a case study 02914
* base applications with software engineering: a tool for requirements specifications 02924
Automatic acquisition of domain and procedural * 02943
Generic diagnostic * acquisition tool 02944
Use of meta* in the verification of *-based systems 02945
PC Version of a *-based expert system with voice interface 02964
Logic programmable natural language processor of a *-base management system 02965

KEYWORD INDEX

*-based interface to manufacturing computer systems 02966
Applications of qualitative modeling to *-based risk assessment studies 02970
Extending *-based systems through closely-coupled graphics and windows 02985
A * representation for natural language understanding 02987
A dialog based interface to a design * base that understands user design-intentions 02988
A *-based approach to online document retrieval system design 03027
Logical foundations for * representation in intelligent systems 03029
Informational zooming: an interaction model for the graphical access to text * bases 03073
Illustrated description of an interactive * based indexing system 03076
The augmented * workshop 03094
Reasoning about *: an overview 03167
Pictorial * bases 03201
Automation—implications for * retention as a function of operator control responsibility 03207
* acquisition and conceptual models: a cognitive analysis of the interface 03214
Task-related * structures: analysis, modelling and application 03218
Gripe: a graphical interface to a * based system which reasons about protein topology 03234
Identifying the * requirements of an expert system's natural language processing interface 03259
* base enhancements to relational databases 03285
A *-based approach to computer vision systems 03302
*-based animation 03351
The effects of the supervisor's * in a complex automated system 03366
An approach to * elicitation in scheduling FMS: Toward a hybrid intelligent system 03394

Interactive aspects of * representations 03395
Decision Support and * Based Systems Track § 03461
Automated document distribution using AI based workstations and *based servers 03466
*-based support of cooperative activities 03478
* representation for model libraries 03479
Express—rapid prototyping and product development via integrated *-based executable specifications 03492
Theoretical aspects of reasoning about * § 03559
On one aspect of natural-language based * acquisition 03571
* acquisition via a graphical interface 03572
Necessary contributions of cognitive psychology to computer *representation and manipulation systems 03598
Memory research and * engineering 03599
Computer assisted * acquisition: towards a laboratory for protocol analysis of user dialogues 03603
Effectiveness of training as a function of the teacher * structure 03604
* structures for intelligent interaction 03636
Some aspects of * processing and participation 03669
*-based editors for directed graphs 03797
Fault management, * support, and responsibility in man-machine systems 03812
Uncertainty in *-based systems. International Conference on Information § 03822
On the management of information imperfection in * based systems 03823
An investigation of pictographic form in relation to mechanisms of *acquisition 03824
Qualitative modeling of physical systems for * based control 03834
Some design principles for a mathematical * representation system: a new approach to scientific calculation 03849

Visual fatigue with work on visual display units: the current state of * 03891
Structuring * in a graph 03899
* representation techniques in artificial intelligence: an overview 03900
Textvision: elicitation and acquisition of conceptual * by graphic representation and multiwindowing 03902
* and expertise in expert systems 03905
KRIP: a * representation system for laws relating to industrial property 03918
Mapping images to a hierarchical data structure—a way to *-based pattern recognition 03954
Morphological representation of speech * for automatic speech recognition systems 03992
* based systems for speech understanding 04001
Error detection and correction in a speech recognition system: a *based system approach 04054
Fundamental issues of * acquisition: toward a human action perspective of * systems 04057
*-based systems: implications for human-computer interfaces ● HCI-0060 †
Artificial intelligence and tutoring systems: computational and cognitive approaches to the communication of * ● HCI-0080 †
Fragile * and neglected strategies in novice programmers HCI-0177 †
Goal and plan * representations: from stories to text editors and programs HCI-0183 †
The distributed processing of * and belief in the human brain HCI-0240 †
*-based search tactics for an intelligent intermediary system HCI-0277 †
Strategic issues in * engineering HCI-0317 †
Acquisition of control and domain * by watching in a blackboard environment HCI-0319 †
* and control for a mechanical design expert system HCI-0320 †

* based systems versus thesaurus : an architecture problem about expert systems design HCI-0323 †
KRITON: a *-acquisition tool for expert systems HCI-0327 †
Selecting a humanly understandable * representation for reasoning about * HCI-0330 †
Expertise transfer and complex problems: using AQUINAS as a *-acquisition workbench for *-based systems HCI-0336 †
* elicitation: dissociating conscious reflections from automatic processes HCI-0337 †
*-intensive natural language generation HCI-0343 †
Interactive critical path analysis (ICPA)—microcomputer implementation of a project management and * engineering tool HCI-0445 †

**KOHONEN**
Extending *'s self-organizing mapping algorithms to learn ballistic movements 03967

**KOMPLEX**
The * performance prediction tool 02669

**KONTROL**
MIKE: the menu interaction * environment HCI-0124 †

**KRIP**
*: a knowledge representation system for laws relating to industrial property 03918

**KRITON**
*: a knowledge-acquisition tool for expert systems HCI-0327 †

**LABELS**
The effect of number ordering and orientation on marking speed and errors for mark-sensed * 01717
The effect of adding symbols to written warning * on user behavior and recall 01788
Pictures and category * as navigational aids for catalog browsing 02877

**LABOR**
Computerized manufacturing technology and work organization effects on *relations and worker satisfaction 03443

## LABOUR

The SIMONA project: the introduction of information processing in * market administration 0248

Technology and the author's * 02574

Further division of reintegration of mental *? CAD/CAP and work in design nd work preparation shops 03385

## LANCASTER

Planning for hospital information systems using the * Soft Systems methodology 01228

## LANDING

Part-task training strategies in simulated carrier * final-approach training 01741

## LANGUAGE

Natural-* interfaces 0069

Computational models of natural * processing ● 0095

Knowledge representation and natural *: extending the expressive power of proposition nodes 0096

A propositional * for text representation 0097

Text processing with the START natural * system 0100

Using an object-oriented programming * to create audience-driven hypermedia environments 0101

Considerations for the development of natural-* interfaces to database management systems 0161

Studies in the evaluation of a domain-independent natural * query system 0162

An interactive customization program for a natural * database query system 0163

The semantics-based natural * interface to relational databases 0164

Talking it over: the natural * dialog system HAM-ANS 0165

Natural * processing: a survey 0181

Computer assisted * learning: program structure and principles ● 0196

Designer labyrinths: text mazes for * learners 0197

A practical natural * interface to databases 0199

Principles from the psychology of * 0333

The optimal level of abstraction for models of cerebral representation of * processes: the state of the question 0356

*, the mind, and psychophysical parallelism 0357

A */action perspective on the design of cooperative work (Reprint) 0383

Developing a natural * interface to complex data 0393

Transportability and generality in a natural-* interface system 0394

Using a knowledge base to drive an expert system interface with a natural * component 0430

Artificial intelligence techniques in * learning ● 0500

On * and connectionism: analysis of a parallel distributed processing model of * acquisition 0590

The relation between linguistic structure and associative theories of *learning models: constructive critique of some connectionist learning models 0591

Eye movements in reading: perceptual and * processes ● 0609

A natural * interface for computer-aided design ● 0664

Natural-* interfaces 0693

An integrated data description * for coding design knowledge 0717

Natural-* interfaces 0720

Speech & * based interaction with machines ● 0723

Speech and *-based interaction with machines: towards the conversational computer ● 0724

POP-11: an AI programming * 0748

A framework for choosing a database query * 0761

A programming * basis for user interface 0849

Synergistic use of direct manipulation and natural * 0857

Conversational hypertext: information access through natural * dialogues with computers 0867

The formal specification of adaptive user interfaces using command *grammar 0925

The impact of menus and command-level feedback on learners' acquisition of data base * skills 01041

Binary jargon: the metaphoric * of computing 01044

Principles of an icons-based * 01080

A natural * interface to a multiple databased office information system 01094

Abstract interaction tools: a * for user interface management systems 01162

How to choose natural * software 01183

YANLI: a powerful natural * front-end tool 01194

Choice of words in the generation process of a natural * interface 01206

DATENBANK-DIALOG: a German * interface for relational databases 01208

Self-organizing system obtaining communication ability primitive model for * generation 01279

Impact of a restricted natural * interface on ease of learning and productivity 01334

Summarizing natural * database responses 01343

Modeling the user in natural * systems 01348

Natural * querying of historical data bases 01354

The workstation: the interpress page and document description * 01356

OA: bridging the * gap 01376

Interactive video in * learning 01380

GRAFLOG: understanding drawings through natural * 01396

Experience with chisl, a configurable hierarchical interface specification * 01397

Presentation of a description * for office tasks 01434

SML: a solid modelling * 01471

Computer graphics * bindings: programmer interface standards 01473

# KEYWORD INDEX [LANGUAGE]

Natural * interface to the question-answering system for physicians 01478

Processor for man-machine natural-*-like communication 01484

Evaluating user utterances in natural * interfaces to databases 01486

The direct memory access paradigm and its applications to natural *processing 01489

An industrial chemical hazards database with a natural * interface: an application of artificial intelligence 01533

Artificial intelligence and natural * systems 01541

Human * and computers 01550

*, sub*, and the promise of machine translation 01554

Magic PC- the "UN-*" approach 01639

A natural * discourse model to explain linear programming models and solutions 01671

* and artificial intelligence conference report 01688

Simplicial differential geometric theory for * cortical dynamics 01698

Providing quality responses with natural * interfaces: the null value problem 01848

A high level *-based computing enviornment to support production and execution of reliable programs 01855

Interpretation of natural * database queries using optimization methods 01861

The emergence of Zipf's law: Spontaneous encoding optimization by users of a command * 01875

A priori analysis of natural * queries 02006

Querying the French *Yellow Pages*: natural * access to the directory 02007

Temporal semantics and natural * processing in a decision support system 02038

Shaping user input: a strategy for natural * dialogue design 02067

Exploiting convergence to improve natural * understanding 02071

Perceptual structure cueing in a simple command * 02086

ADDS-a dialogue development system for the Ada programming * 02102

An experimental evaluation of prefix and postfix notation in command *sytax 02110

Dealing with a database query * in a new situation 02119

Representing and using metacommunication to control speakers' relationships in natural-* dialogue 02136

XTRA: a natural-* access system to expert systems 02244

A natural * interface processor based on the hierarchical-tree structure model of relation tables 02315

The foreign * barrier: a study among pharmaceutical research workers 02333

An approach to natural-* semantics in logic programming 02342

A database primer on natural * 02413

A portable query * for small scale systems 02492

Natural * interface based on keyword extraction using AWK 02498

Natural * processing and the *-impaired 02570

Music—a * for typesetting music scores 02622

Q'Nial: a portable interpreter for the nested interactive array *, Nial 02635

Natural * and computers: a general survey of written text interpretation methods 02671

NLI-ESD: An expert natural * interface to a statistical data bank 02712

Separating content from form: A * for formatting on-line documentation and dialog 02781

APL: The * of science and management 02799

Conman: a visual programming * for interactive graphics 02811

PHRAN-SPAN: a natural * interface for system specifications 02829

A graphical programming * interface for an intelligent LISP tutor 02862

How to interface to advisory systems? Users request help with a very simple * 02888

g - A compact * for real-time graphics 02906

A computer training tool using Chinese natural * 02948

SIMTALK: Pros and cons of natural * for manufacturing simulation 02950

Providing natural * assistance in locating objects: a general model for information selection and generation 02951

Logic programmable natural * processor of a knowledge-base management system 02965

A knowledge representation for natural * understanding 02987

Developing intelligent simulation * to support telerobotic workstation activities 02995

Mach and Matchmaker: kernel and * support for object-oriented distributed systems 03031

Playing the *-games of design and use-on skill and participation 03043

Programming * design and Implementation § 03058

Shifting to a higher gear in a natural * system 03169

GRASS3, a * for interactive graphics 03170

A temporal logic for reasoning about changing data bases in the context of natural * question-answering 03176

The IRUS transportable natural * database interface 03177

Supporting natural * database update by modeling real world actions 03179

The incorporation of early interface evaluation into command * grammar specifications 03191

Identifying the knowledge requirements of an expert system's natural *processing interface 03259

The Monte Carlo processor: designing and implementing a * for Monte Carlo work 03317

799

[LANGUAGES]

Motion analysis of grammatical processes in a visual-gestural * 03347
* level persistence for an object-oriented application programming platform 03522
A visual programming * designed for automatic programming 03529
Investigations into a command and response * interface 03531
A processing system for program specifications in a natural * 03537
A cost model for estimating the costs of developing software in the Ada programming * 03539
A natural * interface for expert systems: system architecture 03551
On one aspect of natural-* based knowledge acquisition 03571
A rule-based system for fuzzy natural * robot control 03574
A functional model of questions for natural * processing systems 03575
The semantic * episode understanding 03576
User requirements in natural * communication with database systems 03615
Some aspects of communication in the natural * and user's involvement in software development 03670
Natural * communication with computers: some problems, perspectives, and new directions 03913
Generating natural * responses appropriate to conversational situations—in the case of Japanese 03922
Natural * at the Computer § 03947
Tensor geometry: a * of brains & neurocomputers. Generalized coordinates in neuroscience & robotics 03966
The VIP VDM specification * 04036
Towards a natural * interface for computer aided design 04049
A methodology, specification *, and automated support environment for com1uter-aided design systems 04068

The AWK programming * ● HCI-0020 †
INTERLISP: the * and its usage ● HCI-0022 †
The synthesizer generator: a system for constructing *-based editors ● HCI-0024 †
Mental models: towards a cognitive science of *, inference, and consciousness ● HCI-0063 †
Introduction to natural * processing ● HCI-0065 †
Readings in natural * processing ● HCI-0067 †
A programmable interface * for heterogeneous distributed systems HCI-0094 †
A specification * for direct-manipulation user interfaces HCI-0123 †
Toward native * software for information management HCI-0138 †
Towards an integration between * and software development environment HCI-0158 †
Experimental study of a two-dimensional * vs. FORTRAN for first-course progammers HCI-0171 †
Some applications of a theorem of Shirshov to * theory HCI-0181 †
What non-programmers know about programming: natural * procedure specification HCI-0211 †
Generalized query-by-rule: a heterogeneous database query * HCI-0252 †
HERCULES: database query using natural * fragments HCI-0253 †
Using restricted natural * for data retrieval: a plan for field evaluation HCI-0255 †
Natural * query processing in a temporal database HCI-0257 †
An almost path-free very high-level interactive data manipulation * for microcomputer-based database system HCI-0261 †
A natural * information retrieval system with extentions towards fuzzy reasoning HCI-0281 †
Reasoning in natural * for designing a data base HCI-0322 †

Natural-* interface for an instructable robot HCI-0324 †
A natural * front end to databases with evaluative feedback HCI-0338 †
Using focus to constrain * generation HCI-0341 †
* generation by computer HCI-0342 †
Knowledge-intensive natural * generation HCI-0343 †
A framework for investigating *-mediated interaction with machines HCI-0347 †
TEAM: an experiment in the design of transportable natural-* interfaces HCI-0351 †
Natural * with discrete speech as a mode for human-to-machine HCI-0355 †
The use of colour in * syntax analysis HCI-0385 †
An image processing * with ICON-assisted navigation HCI-0387 †
Customers' requirements for natural * systems: results of an inquiry HCI-0426 †
Cognitive aspects of learning and using a programming * HCI-0439 †

**LANGUAGES**

Functional databases, functional * 0034
Direct manipulation: A step beyond programming * 0072
Natural * 0136
A transfer of skill between programming * 01015
Interactive blackbox debugging for concurrent * 01134
Understanding natural * 01172
Non-strict *-programming and implementation 01418
Evaluation and intergration of specification * 01430
On the interface between the high level * and Chinese character information 01451
A user perspective on computer-assisted translation for Minority * 01557
A system for specification and rapid prototyping of application command * 01849

800

# KEYWORD INDEX [LAYOUTS]

Prospects for knowledge-based customization of natural * query systems 02008

Natural artificial *: low level processes 02082

Organization and learnability in computer * 02085

Is top-down natural? Some experimental results from non-procedural * 02123

Procedural and non-procedural query * revisited: a comparison of relational algebra and relational calculus 02146

The structure of command *: an experiment on task-action grammar 02224

Use of fourth generation *: application development and documentation problems 02435

Ergonomic considerations in the design of command * 02694

Object-oriented programming systems, * and applications § 03030

Object-oriented programming systems, * and applications § 03035

How can groups communicate when they use different * 03038

Visual * and human computer interaction 03202

Issues governing the suitability of programming * for programming tasks 03224

Intuitive representations and interaction *: an exploratory experiment 03611

Computer *: everything you always wanted to know but no one can tell you 03612

Design of programming * under psychological aspects 03613

Concepts in user interfaces: a reference model for command and response * § 03872

Data manipulation * for the universal relation view DURST 03944

Programming *: a grand tour (2nd ed.) ● HCI-0018 †

User-oriented computer *: analysis and design ● HCI-0019 †

Concepts in user interfaces: a reference model for command and response * ● HCI-0032 †

Query *—a taxonomy HCI-0254 †

## LARYNGEAL
An acoustic of pathological voice and its application to the evaluation of * pathology 02644

## LASER
Vision monitoring of VDU operators and relaxation of visual stress by means of l*speckle system 03738

## LATENCIES
Strategies in controlling a continuous process with long response *: needs for computer support to diagnosis 02217

## LATITUDE
Transferring skills from training to the actual work situation: the role of task application knowledge, action styles and job decision * 02865

## LATTICE
Study of combination of belief intevals in *-structured networks 02223

## LATTICES
Star, maximal rectangles, *: a new perspective on Q-analysis 02105

## LAW
What AI practitioners should know about the *, part 2 01197

Why the look and feel of software user interfaces should not be protected by copyright * 01324

The emergence of Zipf's *: Spontaneous encoding optimization by users of a command language 01875

Counting and timing models in psychophysics and the conjoint Weber's * 02368

Artificial Intelligence and * § 02704

Expert systems in *: out of the research laboratory and into the marketplace 02765

Expert systems in *: The datalex project 02766

A case-based system for trade secrets * 02769

The application of expert systems technology to case-based * 02771

Precedent-based legal reasoning and knowledge acquisition in contract *: A process model 02776

Reasoning about 'hard' cases in Talmudic * 02777

Public * 99-506, "Section 508" Electronic Equipment Accessibility for disabled workers 02893

Recent trends in information systems * 03017

Integrated information retrieval for * in a hypertext environment 03071

Computer-assisted negotiations: a case history from the * of the sea negotiations and speculation regarding future uses HCI-0443 †

## LAWYER
A process specification of expert * reasoning 02768

## LAYERED
* protocols for computer-human dialogue. 1: principles 02195

* protocols for computer-human dialogue. 11: some practical issues 02196

Experience with a functional * multicomputer architecture for interactive processing 02402

A * neural network model applied to the auditory system 02763

## LAYOUT
A document * system using automatic document architecture extraction 0882

Modelling the human factors aspects of a computer-based text-graphics *system 01518

The fuzzy approach to facilities * problems 01697

A human factors design investigation of a computerized * system of text-graphic technical materials 01779

Adapting menu * to tasks 02182

Pride-II physical * program of modifying Forth for "non-believers" 02312

A VLSI interactive * editor (VILE) 02611

Toward a theory of the perceived spatial * of scenes 02701

## LAYOUTS
Cognitive * of windows and multiple screens for user interfaces HCI-0122 †

801

[LEADERSHIP]          KEYWORD INDEX

**LEADERSHIP**
* style vs. succssus in student chief programmer teams 01029

**LEADS**
On-line tutorials: What kind of inference * to the most effective learning? 0823
Restoring a sense of control during implementation: how user involvement *to system acceptance 02509

**LEAN**
* cuisine: a low fat notation for menus 02062

**LEAP**
Systemic implications of * and an improved two-part cursor 0848

**LEARNABILITY**
Organization and * in computer languages 02085

**LEARNED**
Innate and * components in a simple visuo-motor reflex 03965

**LEARNER**
A regression model to identify successful * traits with CAI 02376

**LEARNERS**
Designer labyrinths: text mazes for language * 0197
The impact of menus and command-level feedback on *' acquisition of data base language skills 01041
Adult *: away with computerphobia HCI-0433 †

**LEARNING**
An approach to * control surfaces by connectionist systems 0030
* to use word processors: problems and prospects 0059
* to use a word processor: by doing, by thinking, and by knowing 0060
* by doing with simulated intelligent help 0132
* in man-computer interaction: a review of the literature 0151
Computer assisted language *: program structure and principles ● 0196
* about computers and * about mathematics 0208
Cognitive resources and the * of human-computer dialogs 0209

$VP^2$: the role of user modelling in correcting errors in second language * 0222
Logic for * 0284
* environment criteria 0285
Computer assisted * in the humanities and social sciences ● 0470
Production system models of * and development ● 0478
*, development, and production systems 0479
Doing, understanding, and * in problem solving 0480
A general theory of discrimination * 0481
* through incremental refinement of procedures 0482
* by chunking: a production system model of practice 0483
Production systems, *, and tutoring 0487
Universal subgoaling and chunking: the automatic generation and * of goal hierarchies ● 0497
Artificial intelligence techniques in language * ● 0500
Lessons from computer-based * 0503
Computer-assisted * and interactive video 0504
Artificial intelligence and education; vol. 1: * environments and tutoring systems ● 0516
* with interactive media: dynamic support for students and teachers 0519
* Issues for Intelligent Tutoring Systems ● 0534
The computer as a tool for * through reflection 0535
Toward a theory of impasse-driven * 0536
Enhancing incremental * processes with knowledge-based systems 0538
* issues for intelligent tutoring systems ● 0545
Mapping the cognitive demands of * to program 0579
On the cognitive effects of * computer programming 0581
The relation between linguistic structure and associative theories of language * models: constructive critique of some connectionist * models 0591

A distributed model of human * and memory 0633
On * the past tenses of English verbs 0634
Artificial intelligence & human *: intelligent computer-aided instruction ● 0671
Interactive *: a multiexpert paradigm for acquiring new knowledge 0776
* and transfer of measurement tasks 0832
* disabled students' difficulties in * to use a word processor: implications for design 0889
* and transfer for text and graphics editing with a direct manipulation interface 0900
* modes and subsequent use of computer-mediated communication systems 0912
Navigational aids and * styles: structural optimal training for computer users 0970
Word processing techniques and user * preferences 0984
Modeling of control and * in a stepping motion 01250
Disjunctive models of boolean category * 01262
Impact of a restricted natural language interface on ease of * and productivity 01334
Scaling relationships in back-propagation * 01338
Interactive video in language * 01380
* from a plan-based interface 01496
Automated construction of interactive * programs in Modula-2 01500
The memory channel machine: part of a proposed * machine 01602
Some historical currents concerning the 'societal *' approach to policy and planning 01603
Propaedeutics of decision-making: supporting managerial * and innovation 01667
The role of stimulus-to-rule consistency in * rapid application of spatial rules 01765
Structuring knowledge bases for designers of * materials 01807

802

Metaphor, computing systems, and active * 02091
Structural displays as * aids 02188
Question asking when * a text-editing system 02202
Protos: an examplar-based * apprentice 02210
* iteration recursion from examples 02215
Underlying dimensions of human problem solving and *: implications for personnel selection, training tasks design and expert system 02225
Concept * from examples and counter examples 02229
Some effects of cognitive style on * UNIX 02252
Student evaluation of motivational and * attributes of microcomputer soft 02274
Psychologically based techniques for improving * within computerized tutorials 02277
The efficacy of computer-assisted video instruction on rule * and attitudes 02286
The effects of orienting objectives and review on * from interactive video 02287
The effects of orienting, processing, and practicing activities on *from interactive video 02289
Color, graphics, and animation in a computer-assisted * tutorial lesson 02294
A comparison of a microcomputer progressive state drill and flashcards for * paired associates 02295
Adaptive coordination of a * team 02475
Forgetting and the * curve: a laboratory study 02484
Firm strategies for costly engineering * 02485
The immune system, adaptation, and machine * 02559
Neural network models of * and adaptation 02560
Machine * using a higher order correlation network 02563
* in British Airways-A case of putting people first 02572
Absolutely stable * of recognition codes by a self-organizing neural network 02728

Differential Hebbian * 02745
A simple selectionist * rule for neural networks 02756
Topology conserving mappings for * motor tasks 02758
Collaborative * in a virtual classroom: highlights of findings 02826
Travel around a * support environment: rambling, orienteering or touring? 02900
A blackboard architecture for problem solving and machine * in an expert system for power system voltage control 02926
The importance of individual differences in end-user training: The case for * style 03009
Why do some people have more difficulty * to use an information retrieval system than others? 03075
* the ways: the enculturation of SDSC users 03144
A flexible negotiable interactive * environment 03197
Voice versus keyboard: use of a comparative analysis of * to identify skill requirements of input devices 03275
* graphics programming by direct communication 03298
A consideration of * in speech recognition from the viewpoint of AI class-description * 03533
Transfer of * in inference problems 03552
Designing * processes for work activities in automated technologies 03605
Understanding * problems in computer aided tasks 03607
* styles in conversation—a practical application of Pask's *theory to human-computer interaction 03608
Designing computer-based * materials § 03875
Current research in the psychology of * and teaching 03876
Pedagogical development of computer-based * material 03878
A computer assisted * system for reliability engineering 04060
Daydreaming and computation: a computer model of everyday creativity, *nd emotions in the human stream of thought 04067
The * and planning of actions 04069
Induction: processes of inference, *, and discovery ● HCI-0064 †
Introducing CAL: a practical guide to writing computer-assisted *programs ● HCI-0079 †
* by doing with simulated intelligent help HCI-0229 †
* to use a word processor: by doing, by thinking, and by knowing HCI-0292 †
* in parallel networks: simulating * in a probabilistic system HCI-0332 †
Instructionless * about a complex device: the paradigm and observations HCI-0333 †
An expert system for conceptual schema design: a machine * approach HCI-0335†
Cognitive aspects of * and using a programming language HCI-0439 †

**LECTURING**
The small computer assisted * system 01043

**LEGAL**
* liability for malfunction and misuse of expert systems 0939
* reasoning in 3-D 02774
Knowledge representation in "Default": An attempt to classify general types of knowledge used by * experts 02775
Precedent-based * reasoning and knowledge acquisition in contract law: A process model 02776
* data modeling: The prohibited transaction exemption analyst 02779
Human interfaces in a * expert system 03164
An artificial intelligence approach to * reasoning ● HCI-0061 †

**LEGGED**
Interactive design of 3D computer-animated * animal motion 01828
3-D balance in * locomotion: modeling and simulation for the one-*case 03352

## LEGIBILITY
Display * guidelines: a design aid 01983
The * of visual display texts 03889

## LENGTHY
Multi-window displays for readers of * texts 02142

## LENS
How do experienced information * users use rules? 0854
The information *: an intelligent system for information sharing in organizations 0891
Object *: a "spreadsheet" for cooperative work HCI-0206 †

## LESSON
Interactive * designs: a taxonomy 0273
Color, graphics, and animation in a computer-assisted learning tutorial * 02294

## LETTERS
Speaker-independent automatic recognition of plosive sound in * and digits 03993
Computer recognition of spoken * and digits 03995

## LEXICAL
* organisation from three different angles 01199
Modularity and * access HCI-0350 †

## LEXICON
The *, grammatical categories and temporal reasoning 03549

## LIABILITY
Legal * for malfunction and misuse of expert systems 0939

## LIBERTIES
A tolerance for surveillance: American public opinion concerning privacy and civil * 0524

## LIBRARIANS
Real * don't program...do they? 02600

## LIBRARIES
Automation in public *: effects on the organization, quality of working life, and quality of services 0246
* as programs preserved within compiler continuations 01102
Perceptions of the information search process in *: a study of changes from high school through college 02002
A comparative study of subject searching in an OPAC among branch * of a university library system 02050
Computer-assisted instruction in academic * 02282
Man—machine interaction by voice: developments in speech technology. Part 2: general applications and potential applications in * and information services 02332
Barriers to cooperative computerized circulation systems in public * 02573
Ada-components: * and tools § 03180
Knowledge representation for model * 03479

## LIBRARY
* processing systems and the man/machine interface 02045
Investigating computer anxiety in an academic * 02047
A comparative study of subject searching in an OPAC among branch libraries of a university * system 02050
Online * catalog systems: an analysis of user errors 02128
Subject searching behaviour at the * catalogue and at the shelves: implications for online interactive catalogues 02302
The man-machine interface aspect of an automatic classification numbering system in a computerized * system 02316
Professional education and subsequent careers in */information work: a follow-up study of former students on the MA/MSc information studies course at the University of Sheffield 02336
Assessing the impacts of new technology on * employees 02459
Microcomputer availability to public * clients 02461
Technology's impact on * interior planning 02464
The emerging role of workstations in the * environment 02467
A * for incremental update of bitmap images 02836
Online * catalogues as information retrieval systems: what can we learn from research? 04040

## LIFECYCLE
Cost/benefit analysis for incorporating human factors in the software * HCI-0127 †

## LIFELINE
Headstart—a * for the disabled 02500

## LIFTING
A knowledge-based system for assessment of human physiological abilities in manual * tasks 01519
Biomechanical evaluation of * tasks: a microcomputer-based model 01524
Ergonomic job design in frequent manual * tasks: a microcomputer-based model 01532

## LIGHT
Tracking three-dimensional moving * displays 03337
Sensitivity to * and visual strain in VDT operators: basic data for the design of work stations 03732

## LIGHTING
Intermittent illumination from visual display units and fluorescent *affects movements of the eyes across text 01713
* for visual display unit workplaces 03715
* the display or displaying the * 03716
* the electronic office 03717
Work at video display terminals among office employees: visual ergonomics and * 03718

## LIGHTS
Variability in brightness matching of colored * 01767

## LIKELIHOOD
* alarm displays 01783

## LIMITATION
A * theorem for the differentiable prototypification of shape 02365

## LIMITS
Human * and the VDT computer interface (excerpt) 0054

# KEYWORD INDEX [LINGUISTIC]

Short-term memory * in human performance 0398

## LINC
The * was early and small 02843

## LINE
The on-* environment and in-house training 0106
Cost effectiveness of on-* searching of chemical information: an industrial viewpoint 0195
Robot simulation and off-* programming—an integrated CAE-CAD approach 0599
Experiences with off-* robot programming via standardized interfaces 0601
Off-* programming of robots using 3D graphical simulation system 0602
Off-* programming and path generation for robot manipulators 0603
CAD-based off-* programming applied to a cleaning and deburring workstation 0607
On-* tutorials: What kind of inference leads to the most effective learning? 0823
The effectiveness of a keystroke * in interactive tutorials 0969
Problems associated with the off-* programming of robots 01241
* connectivity algorithms for an asynchronous pyramid computer 01468
Effect of pixel height, display height, and vertical resolution on the detection of a simple vertical * signal in visual noise 01753
Comprehensino aids for on-* reading of expository text 01798
An interactive procedure for constructing * and circle tangencies 01823
A preliminary specification of an on-* expert help system 01930
On-* recognition of Pitman's hand-written shorthand—an evaluation of potential 02111
Adaptive command prompting in an on-* documentation 02121
Developments in one-* information systems 02687

Separating content from form: A language for formatting on-* documentation and dialog 02781
Multilingual programming: Coordinating programs, user interfaces, on-* help nd documentation 02785
An operations advisor for an on-* computer banking system with graphics interface 02983
A retrieval system for on-* English-Japanese dictionaries 03078
Where do we draw the *? - Derivation and evaluation of user interface software separation rules 03268
Implementation plan for the use of on-* fiber analysis in the textile industry 03433
Development of a continuous finishing * to improve working conditions 03434
Issues in the design of off-* programming systems 03564
Plan-based text generation in an on-* help system 03817
A flexible and intelligent system for fast measurements in binary images for in-* robotic control 03986
On-* interpretation in speech understanding and dialogue systems 04000
Interfaces and on-* reading 04047
Reading continuous text from a one-* visual display HCI-0187 †
CONTEXT: an on-* documentation system HCI-0280 †

## LINEAR
Limited freedom: * reflections on non* texts 0121
* predictive coding of speech 0289
Interactive microcomputer programs for * and non-* static analysis of frameworks 01165
A graphics interface for * programming 01332
Interactive multiple objective * programming system implemented on a microcomputer 01508
User friendly micro computer program for solving fractional and *programming problems 01509

The design of a user friendly interactive personal computer package for quality control charts, project management, and * programming applications 01521
The * file—restrictions on online information use: a searcher's perspective 01634
A natural language discourse model to explain * programming models and solutions 01671
A theoretical framework for interactivating * video 02284
Design of an integral computer-based wheelchair controller/* synchronous motor system 02378
Man-machine procedures of decision making under uncertainty based on *programming 02664
An empirical comparison of pie vs. * menus 02871
Choosing between methods: analysing the user's decision space in terms of schemas and * models 02879

## LINEARIZATION
* of the dynamic transfer response of time invariant nonlinear systems—in connection with the parallel information processing in living organisms 02665

## LINES
A comparison of neural network and matched filter processing for detecting * in images 02738
Teaching users to fish: hooks, * and sinkers for reading computer documentat 03156
Human aspects of automated assembly * 03445

## LINGUAL
Influence of palate shape on * articulation 02642

## LINGUISTIC
The relation between * structure and associative theories of language learning models: constructive critique of some connectionist learning models 0591
Usage of * variable concept for human operator modelling 01694
* knowledge as expertise 02077

Combining stochastic uncertainty and * inexactness: theory and experimental evaluation of four fuzzy probability models 02218
A comparison of presentation and representation: * and pictorial 03898
Measuring the quality of * forecasts HCI-0247 †
Transporting the * string project system from a medical to a Navy domain HCI-0352 †

## LINGUISTICALLY
General multiple-objective decision functions and * quantified statements HCI-0110 †

## LINGUISTICS
Computational * ● 0215
Computational *: issues and solutions 03948
Merging acoustics and * in speech understanding 04004
From schema theory to computational (neuro-)* HCI-0345 †

## LINK
The missing *: why we're all doing hypertext wrong 0118
Windowlike user interfaces * systems and applications 01388

## LINKAGE
* versus integration for binding database and interactive graphics systems 02040
* versus integration for binding database and interactive graphics systems 02406

## LINKED
A computing service using * minis 01674

## LINKING
* mechanism supporting end-user computing 02806

## LIP
Speech recognition enhancement by * information 0915

## LIPREADING
An improved automatic * system to enhance speech recognition 02859

## LISALEARNING
* HCI-0092 †

## LISP
Effect of practice on knowledge and use of basic * 0210
Common * object system specification X3J13 Document 88-002R 01121
A * implementation of the model for 'communicating sequential processes' 02632
A graphical programming language interface for an intelligent * tutor 02862
Users' preferences among different techniques for displaying the evaluation of * functions in an interactive debugger 02863
Clue: a common * user interface environment 03113
The * tutor: it approaches the effectiveness of a human tutor HCI-0431 †

## LISPCRAFT
* ● HCI-0023 †

## LISTENERS
Designing a quality voice: an analysis of *' reactions to synthetic voices 0914

## LISTINGS
DRAT: A program for maintaining * 02401

## LISTS
Development and evaluation of direct manipulation * (poster session) 0993
VISION: VHDL induced schematic imaging on net-* 02830

## LITERACY
Online information, hypermedia, and the idea of * 0112
Computer *: the pigeonhole principle 0789
Computer * in secondary education: the performance and engagement of girls 01495
Which way to computer *, programming or applications experience? 02127

## LITERALISM
Experiences with the alternate reality kit: an example of the tension between * and magic 0817

## LITERATE
* programming HCI-0148 †

## LITERATURE
Human foundations of advanced computing technology: the guide to the select * 0001
Learning in man-computer interaction: a review of the * 0151
People and organizations in software production: a review of the * 01023
Novices on the computer: a review of the * 02129
Citation patterns in the computer-based instruction * 02290
Subjective probability and information retrieval: a review of the psychological * 02303
Human factors in software engineering: a review of the * HCI-0157 †

## LIZA
*: an extensible groupware toolkit 0805

## LL
A programmer-friendly *(1) parser generator 02626
A practical method for LR and * syntactic error diagnosis and recovery HCI-0163 †

## LOCALISATION
Experience of constructing a fault * expert system using an AI toolkit 02923

## LOCATING
Providing natural language assistance in * objects: a general model for information selection and generation 02951

## LOCK
'Remember to * the door': MMI and the hacker 01910
The integrity * support environment 03578

## LOCKING
A computer model of peripheral auditory processing incorporating phase-*, suppression and adaptation effects 02650

## LOCOMOTION
3-D balance in legged *: modeling and simulation for the one-legged case 03352

## LOCOMOTOR
A multivariate solution for cyclic data, applied in modelling * forces 01252

## LOCUS
The effects of panel arrangements and * of attention on performance 01759

## LOGARITHMIC
Complex * mapping and the focus of expansion 03333

## LOGIC
* for learning 0284
A multi-processor workstation with a *-enhanced distributed frame buffer 0496
A spreadsheet interface for * programming 0822
An environment for * programming 01106
A model and an implementation of a * programming environment 01107
On the relation between default and autoepistemic * 01214
The erotetic * of problem-solving inquiry 01583
Organizational humanity and architecture: Duality and complementarity of papa-* and mama-* in managerial conceptualizations of change 01609
The fuzzy * of text understanding 01701
A * assistant for the database searcher 02001
The automated solution of * puzzles 02015
Manual control of an intrinsically unstable system and its modeling by fuzzy * 02026
A design for a fuzzy * controller 02028
A menu interface to formulate boolean *-can it be done? 02034
Negative knowledge towards a strategy for asking in * programming 02115
An approach to natural-language semantics in * programming 02342
A deductive database based on Aristotelian * 02398
Spreadsheets with incremental queries as a user interface for * programming 02515
SMARTGEN: the implementation of an expert system for the generation of digital * diagnostic tests 02929
* programmable natural language processor of a knowledge-base management system 02965
An advisory system for digital * simulation 02986
A temporal * for reasoning about changing data bases in the context of natural language question-answering 03176
* programming '86 § 03816
* interface system on navigational database systems 03818
A *-functional approach to the execution of CCS specifications modulo behavioural equivalences 03874
* programming '85 § 03916
* programming '87 § 03919
Third international conference on * programming § 04028
* and programming ● HCI-0068 †

## LOGICS
Designing in the dark: * that compete with the user 0928
Fuzzy reasoning in pseudo-physical * 01695

## LOGISTICS
Design of a control room for the air force * command (AFLC) command, control,and communication and intelligence ($C^3I$) system 01612

## LOGIX
The * system user manual version 1.21 0675

## LOGO
Algebra slaves and agents in a *-based mathematics curriculum 0517
The interpretation of * in practice 0576
* and development of thinking skills 0582
Formative evaluation of pre-* programming environments: a collaborative effort of researchers, teachers, and children 02292
Programming in Basic or *: effect on critical thinking skills 04062

## LONGITUDINAL
A * study of spreadsheet program use 02354
A * study of spreadsheet program use 03482

## LOOP
A closed-* causal model of workload based on a comparison of fuzzy and crisp measurement techniques 01746
Open-* experiments for modeling the human eye movement system 01870

## LOOPING
Conditional statements, * constructs, and program comprehension: an experiments study 02177

## LOTUS
Working with * HAL: a 1-2-3 user's guide ● 0731

## LPC
Speech analysis and synthesis methods developed at ECL in NTT-From * to LSP- 02646

## LSP
*-automatic translation and information technology 02513

## LYAPUNOV
* function for parallel neural networks 02736

## MA
Professional education and subsequent careers in library/information work: a follow-up study of former students on the */MSc information studies course at the University of Sheffield 02336

## MAC
The * interface: showing its age 01311
* programming tools: prototyper version 2.0 eases interface design 02394

## MACAPP
*: An application framework 0083
Application frameworks: experience with * 01039

## MACCADD
* - an enabling software method support tool 03252

## MACHINE
An expert interface for effective man-* interaction 0166
Perspectives in artificial intelligence vol. 2: * translation, NLP, databases and computer-aided instruction ● 0198
Intelligence and the man-* interface 0363
'This is a very unpredictable *': on computers and human cognition 0364
Adaptive control in human-* systems 0405
Ergonomic aspects of man-* communications 0417
The new renaissance: art, science and universal * 0530
Cognitive science and * intelligence laboratory, University of Michigan 0843
The effect of windows on man-* interfaces 01048
Cognitive technologies: The design of joint human-* cognitive systems 01193
On the design of man-* systems: principles, practices and prospects 01236
A man-* interface for computer-aided and simulation of control systems 01237
Engineering the man-* interface for air traffic control 01358
The use of the IBM personal computer in the man-* interface to a nuclear research accelerator 01454
The ring * 01483
Processor for man-* natural-language-like communication 01484
Language, sublanguage, and the promise of * translation 01554
Barriers to plant transparency, barriers to plant rigidity—A sketch of the problems posed by the radical changes in work forms in the *-building industry 01562
The memory channel *: part of a proposed learning * 01602
Artificial intelligence in the man/* interface 01626

* assisted translation with a human face 01627
The metaphor *: a database method for creativity support 01670
Problems of * translation system - effect of cultural differences on sentence structure 01687
Towards the development of human work-performance standards in futuristic man-* systems: a fuzzy modeling approach 01692
An approach to human reliability on man-* systems using error possibility 01702
Ill-formedness and miscommunication in person-* dialogue 01957
Online searching using speech as a man/* interface 02013
Library processing systems and the man/* interface 02045
Human interaction with an "intelligent" * 02163
Prompting, feedback and error correction in the design of a scenario * 02176
Extending Petri nets for specifying man-* dialogues 02183
Interactive communication of sentential structure and content: an alternative approach to man-* communication 02220
The man-* interface aspect of an automatic classification numbering system in a computerized library system 02316
The immune system, adaptation, and * learning 02559
* learning using a higher order correlation network 02563
A boy and his brain * 02575
Where person meets * 02601
Man-* procedures of decision making under uncertainty based on linear programming 02664
Human and * Vision II § 02696
Perception of transparency in man and * 02697
A * for neural computation of acoustical patterns with application to real time speech recognition 02751
A blackboard architecture for problem solving and * learning in

an expert system for power system voltage control 02926
IR-NLI II: applying man-* interaction and artificial intelligence conceptsto information retrieval 03070
Sketchpad a man-* graphical communication system 03103
The myth of the infinitely fast * 03204
Stress, coping, and worker well-being in computer-aided manufacturing: A field investigation of a CNC * shop 03373
A search for */human compatibility in manufacturing systems 03381
The man-* integration 03384
A conceptual dependency network approach to multi-task assignments in man-* (teleoperated) systems 03388
Human-* interface in remote monitoring and control of flexible manufacturing systems 03399
Individualizing the man-* interface 03404
Man-* interfaces for mobile robotic systems 03413
An efficient high-level man-* interface 03530
Personality traits of the worker within the :20man-*'' system at automated production 03593
* adaption to psychological differences among users in instructive information exchanges with computers 03609
A methodology for dynamic task allocation in man-* system 03635
A biparty grammar as a tool for defining a man-* dialogue 03639
Comparison of well-being among non-* interactive clerical workers and full-time and part-time VDT users and typists 03745
The Universal Turing * § 03777
Fault management, knowledge support, and responsibility in man-* systems 03812
Mental models and failures in human-* systems 03814
The use of speech in man-* interaction 03910
Human-* interaction and role/function/action-nets 03974

Prosodic features in German speech: stress assignment by man and * 03989
Plans and situated actions: the problem of human-* communication ● HCI-0040 †
Conceptual structures: information processing in mind and * ● HCI-0057 †
In the age of the smart *: the future of work and power ● HCI-0083 †
Between man and * HCI-0128 †
Stages and levels in human-* interaction HCI-0189 †
Man-* interface issues in the construction and use of an expert system HCI-0212 †
An expert system for conceptual schema design: a * learning approach HCI-0335 †
Extended person-* interface HCI-0344 †
Natural language with discrete speech as a mode for human-to-* HCI-0355 †
Computer systems software: the programmer/* interface ● HCI-0361 †
Perception of transparency in man and * HCI-0367 †
A parallel formant synthesizer for * voice output HCI-0396 †

## MACHINES

Intelligent * for process control 0362
Speech & language based interaction with * ● 0723
Speech and language-based interaction with *: towards the conversational computer ● 0724
Are * as good as people in drawing conclusions from knowledge represented in catalogues, data bases and expert systems? 0736
Making drawings talk: pictures in minds and * 01392
* should not see as people do, but must know how people see 01465
Morphologic * and conservative networks 01604
Trust between humans and *, and the design of decision aids 02164
Intelligent aids, mental models, and the theory of * 02171
Higher-order Boltzmann * 02760

State trees as structured finite state * for user interfaces 03107
Intelligent *: What chance? 03548
Brains, *, and mathematics (2nd ed.) ● HCI-0034 †
A framework for investigating language-mediated interaction with * HCI-0347 †

## MACINTER

Man-computer interaction research (*-I): Proceedings of the first network § 03589
*—aim and goal 03590

## MACINTOSH

Programming the * User Interface ● 0698
Interactive videodiscs control and computer-based training on the Apple * 02305
PowerMath—A system for the * 03083

## MACWRITE

Information flow in a user interface: the effect of experience and context on the recall of * screens 03228

## MADEMA

*: an approach to intelligent manufacturing systems 01318

## MAGICAL

The * number three—plus or minus zero 01622

## MAGNETIC

Electric and * fields of the brain computed by way of a discrete systems analytical approach: Theory and validation 01276
Slot versus insertion * stripe readers: user performance and preference 01756
CRT picture vibration caused by low-frequency * field and its reduction method 01987

## MAGNEX

The * text editor for the Comodore Amiga personal computer 0782

## MAGNIFICATION

* effects with imaging displays depend on scene content and viewing condition 01786

## MAIL

Reducing social context cues: electronic * in organizational communication (Reprint) 0385

An empirical investigation of two electronic * systems 01239
Perception and acceptance of a local area network and electronic * 01284
Socio-technical aspects of electronic * implementation 01439
Edmas: an object-oriented, locally distributed * system 01857
An object-oriented approach to the design of a * system for a heterogeneous environment 01944
Interacting with electronic * can be a dream or a night: a user's point of view 02069
Reducing social context cues: electronic * in organizational communication 02473
The impact of electronic * on managerial and organizational communications 03041
Advisor—an electronic * consulting service 03151
Videocoding - a highly monotonous VDU work in a new technique for * sorting 03762
Efficient computer-user interface in electronic * systems HCI-0118 †
A distributed interoffice * system HCI-0308 †
An experimental multimedia * system HCI-0309 †
Diversity in the use of electronic *: a preliminary inquiry HCI-0310 †

## MAINFRAME

The effects of sources of applications programs on user satisfaction: an empirical study of micro, mini & * computers using an interactive artificial intelligence expert-system 01601
* and microcomputer-based business graphics: end user computing comparisons and trends 02805
* and microcomputer-based business graphics: What satisfies users? HCI-0216 †

## MAINFRAMES

Managers, micros and *: integrating systems for end-users ● 0455
Managers, micros and *: an introduction 0456

[MAINTAINABILITY]

Distributed databases and distributed processing between personal computers and * 0458

**MAINTAINABILITY**
An architectural approach to improved program * 02627

**MAINTAINED**
* and constructor attributes 01099

**MAJIC**
*—an integrated program support environment 01960

**MALE**
A comparison of * and fe* computer science students' attitudes toward computers 01045
*/fe* programmer and systems analyst Job performance 03020

**MALFUNCTION**
Legal liability for * and misuse of expert systems 0939

**MALONE**
Thomas W. *, Oct. 5: user interface strategies '88 ● 0532

**MAMA**
Organizational humanity and architecture: Duality and complementarity of papa-logic and *-logic in managerial conceptualizations of change 01609

**MAMMALIAN**
A self-organizing neural network sharing features of the * visual system 01248

**MANAGED**
Are information systems people different? An investigation of how they are and should be * 02511
Increase organizational effectiveness: Support self-* IS development teams 03014

**MANAGER**
ISPF: the strategic dailog * ● 0035
Using IBM's ISPF dialog *: under MSV, VM, and VSE ● 0304
Programming the OS/2 presentation * ● 0587
Concept design of a program *'s decision support system 0660
The multimedia object presentation * of MINOS: a symmetric approach 01083
Office-by-example: an integrated office system and database * 01159

OS/2 query * overview and prompted interface 01809
whim, the window handler and input * 01825
Message equivocality, media selection and * performance: implications for information systems 02505
EPVM: An expert patient-ventilator * for chemical warfare casualties 02956
A design data * 03090
A window * for bitmapped displays and Unix 03933

**MANAGERIAL**
* expert systems and organizational change: some critical research issues 0157
A human information processing model of the * mind: some MIS implications 0205
Organizational humanity and architecture: Duality and complementarity of papa-logic and mama-logic in * conceptualizations of change 01609
Propaedeutics of decision-making: supporting * learning and innovation 01667
* influence in the implementation of new technology 02481
Modeling * behavior: misperceptions of feedback in a dynamic decision making experiment 02483
The effects of 3D imagery on * data interpretation 02502
The impact of electronic mail on * and organizational communications 03041
A study of * computer users: the impact of user sophistication on decision structure and attributes of decision-related information (end user) 04078

**MANAGERS**
*, micros and mainframes: integrating systems for end-users ● 0455
*, micros and mainframes: an introduction 0456
Needs and perceived needs of electronic workstations by engineering project * 01515

A systems architecture for supporting senior *' messy tasks 01928
*' reading habits in the electronics industry 02339
What's new in personal information * 02556
An evaluation and selection methodology of microcomputer training software: Implications for human resource * and computer personnel 03002
Causes of motivational problems among AI * 03004
* who personally use information technology frequently: a profile of some invisible computer personnel 03007
Some critical remarks on abstractions for adaptable dialogue * 03211
Principles and interaction models for window * 03264
Problems among * of AI personnel 03460
A comparison of some window * 03925
Computer decision support for senior *: encouraging exploration HCI-0298 †

**MANAGING**
The changing workplace: A guide to * the people, organizational, and regulatory aspects of office technology (book excerpt) 0044
Reflections on authoring, editing, and * hypertext 0119
Computers for * information ● 0141
* factory automation 0146
* the diffusion of end-user computing technologies: a fifties mindset with eighties tools 0459
Ideas and information: * in a high-tech world ● 0586
* the design of user-computer interfaces 0936
* multiple context-frames through GKS 01389
* the PC revolution 01643
Strategies for * user developed systems 01923
* information systems for effectiveness and humanity: applying research of organizational behavior 01932

# KEYWORD INDEX [MANUFACTURING]

Definitional distinctions and implications for * end user computing 01946
* end user computing when the only constant is change 02425
* the work station environment 02430
Strategies for * end user computing 02436
Still sailing (and bailing): * unexpected change in user support 03150
* the semantic content of graphical data HCI-0374 †

## MANDATE
Help texts vs. help mechanisms: A new * for documentation writers 01047
Help texts vs. help mechanisms: A new * for documentation writers 02784

## MANIPULATION
Direct *: A step beyond programming languages 0072
Direct * interfaces (excerpt) 0073
PLEIADE: A system for interactive * of structured documents 0265
Direct * user interfaces for expert systems 0429
* of 3D imagery 0557
Inducing programs in a direct-* environment 0816
Synergistic use of direct * and natural language 0857
Speech and gestures for graphic image * 0859
Learning and transfer for text and graphics editing with a direct *interface 0900
Development and evaluation of direct * lists (poster session) 0993
UIMS support for direct * interfaces 01065
Applying direct * concepts 01143
Direct * interfaces 01191
A survey of general-purpose * 02259
Direct * of an object store 02608
Multifunctional cursor for direct * user interfaces 02870
Symsac '86—Proceedings of the 1986 symposium on symbolic and algebraic * § 03084
Building user interfaces by direct * 03120

Document * and typography § 03182
Text representation and * in a mouse-driven interface 03266
Necessary contributions of cognitive psychology to computer knowledge representation and * systems 03598
Tree doctor, a software package for graphical * and animation of tree structures 03901
* of embedded context using the multiple world mechanism 03921
Data * languages for the universal relation view DURST 03944
A specification language for direct-* user interfaces HCI-0123 †
The future of interactive systems and the emergence of direct * HCI-0186 †
A generator of direct * office systems HCI-0250 †
An almost path-free very high-level interactive data * language for microcomputer-based database system HCI-0261 †
An interactive database end user facility for the definition and *of forms HCI-0263 †

## MANIPULATOR
Mapping the * workspace using interactive computer graphics 02257
Task compatibility of * postures 02258
Illumination requirements for operating a space remote * 03392

## MANIPULATORS
Task-oriented approach to interactive control of heavy-duty * based on coarse scene description ● 0546
Off-line programming and path generation for robot * 0603

## MANUAL
* Dexterity: A user-oriented approach to creating computer documentation 0085
Xlib programming * for version 11: Vol. 1 ● 0561
X Protocol reference * for version II: vol. 0 ● 0669
The Logix system user * version 1.21 0675

A comprehensive data base for the design of * materials handling 01510
A knowledge-based system for assessment of human physiological abilities in * lifting tasks 01519
Job characteristic perceptions of * drafting and CADD: A field study of the effects of computerization on drafting & design personnel 01523
Ergonomic job design in frequent * lifting tasks: a microcomputer-based model 01532
Designing a user * to support an in-house database 01635
A fuzzy knowledge base of an expert system for analysis of * lifting tasks 01693
Review and evaluation of physiological cost prediction models for *materials handling 01757
Modeling of task-dependent characteristics of human operator dynamics during pursuit * tracking 01859
Automation effects in a multiloop * control system 01865
* control of an intrinsically unstable system and its modeling by fuzzy logic 02026
On comprehending a computer *: analysis of variables affecting performance 02135
Comparison of * and online searches of chemical abstracts 02265
How to write a really good user's * ● HCI-0017 †
The synthesizer generator reference * (3rd ed.) ● HCI-0024 †

## MANUALS
Breaking the grip of user * 01051
Computer user * in print: Do they have a future? 02782
Lets "Deep-Six" our reference * 02955
Contextual structure analysis of microcomputer * 03227

## MANUFACTURING
Information control problems in * ● 0554

811

[MAP]

Task allocation between humans and robots in * 0559
A supervisory control paradigm for real-time control of flexible *systems 01205
MADEMA: an approach to intelligent * systems 01318
Human-computer interaction in * 01522
The design of distributed transport systems as a major standard interface in computer integrated * 01564
The human costs of * reform 01706
The use of measures of entropy in evaluating human supervisory control of a * system 01897
Human supervisory control in flexible * systems: Allocation of functions and system size 02456
A model for assessing the performance of a local area network employing technical office protocol (TOP) as part of MAP/TOP network in a computer integrated * (CIM) research project, for the transmission of real time interactive speech 02491
An expert * simulation system 02584
SIMTALK: Pros and cons of natural language for * simulation 02950
Knowledge-based interface to * computer systems 02966
Issues in modeling supervisory control in flexible * systems 03363
Human supervisory control in discrete *: Translating the paradigm 03364
Sources of Difficulty in troubleshooting automated * systems 03367
Sociotechnical design of advanced * systems 03370
Structure and policy in computer integrated * systems: human factors implications 03371
Stress, coping, and worker well-being in computer-aided *: A field investigation of a CNC machine shop 03373
The impact of advanced * in work organization: The Portuguese case of the plastic moulding industry 03374

CIM and * industry in the north east of England: A survey of some current issues 03377
Models for design of computer integrated * systems 03378
Human and computer aided *: The end of taylorism? 03379
A search for machine/human compatibility in * systems 03381
Designing hybrid automated * systems: A European perspective 03382
Human-machine interface in remote monitoring and control of flexible * systems 03399
Computerized * technology and work organization effects on labor relations and worker satisfaction 03443
Human factors in automating * systems in India 03446
Human aspects of QC circle movement in Japanese *: Natures and problems 03450
Failure analysis of information systems in small * enterprises: the importance of the human interface 03815

MAP
A * of the world of software-related standards, guidelines, and recommended practices 01453
A model for assessing the performance of a local area network employing technical office protocol (TOP) as part of */TOP network in a computer integrated manufacturing (CIM) research project, for the transmission of real time interactive speech 02491
Empirical evaluation of * interfaces 03276
How * designers can represent their ideas in thematic *s: effective user interfaces for thematic * design 03870

MAPPING
* the cognitive demands of learning to program 0579
* the manipulator workspace using interactive computer graphics 02257

KEYWORD INDEX

A viewdata-structure editor designed around a task/action * 03269
Complex logarithmic * and the focus of expansion 03333
* images to a hierarchical data structure—a way to knowledge-based pattern recognition 03954
Extending Kohonen's self-organizing * algorithms to learn ballistic movements 03967
An expert system for * acoustic cues into phonetic features HCI-0328 †
The * between grammar and processor HCI-0346 †
CNS-HLS * using fuzzy sets HCI-0380 †

MAPPINGS
Topology conserving * for learning motor tasks 02758

MAPS
Planar *: an interaction paradigm for graphic design 0873
Towards a computational theory of cognitive * 01212
Representation of sensory information in self-organizing feature * 02744
Database * 03286
How map designers can represent their ideas in thematic *: effective user interfaces for thematic map design 03870

MARBLE
The * company: The design and implementation of a simulation board game 02595

MARCOSBY
* example in a graphical UIMS 01831

MARINE
Qualitative approximation methodology for modeling and simulation of large dynamic systems: Applications to a * power plant 01900
A model of fault diagnosis performance of expert * engineers 02199

MARIONETTE
"Graphical *" 03349

## MARKET
The SIMONA project: the introduction of information processing in labour *administration 0248

## MARKETPLACE
Tele-cybernetics: implications for the international * 03458

## MARKING
The effect of number ordering and orientation on * speed and errors for mark-sensed labels 01717

## MASK
The computer as *: a problem of inadequate human interaction examined with particular regard to online public access catalogues 02337

## MASS
Implementing computer-mediated communication technologies: a technoacceptance approach to critical * utilization 01931
Simps: Secondary ion * image processing system 02267
Reading, culture and modern * media 02340

## MASSACHUSETTS
History of the development of medical information systems at the Laboratory of Computer Science at * General Hospital 02842

## MASSIVELY
Nueral & * parallel computers: the sixth generation ● 0702
Programming a * parallel, computation universal system: Static behavior 02746

## MATCH
Videodisc and videotex: love-* or passing acquaintance? 0515
Designing menu display format to * input device format 0983
User programs: a way to * computer systems and human cognition 03271
The Japanese and software: is it a good * HCI-0429 †

## MATCHED
A comparison of neural network and * filter processing for detecting lines in images 02738

## MATCHING
A feature * approach to the retrieval of graphical information 01245
The effects of set size on color * using CRT displays 01711
Variability in brightness * of colored lights 01767
New methods for * 3-D objects with single perspective views 01844
On * programmers' chunks with program structures: an empirical investigation 02150
The accuracy of approximate string * algorithms 02279
Vowel normalization by frequency warped spectral * 02649
An evaluation of the effectiveness of the adaptive interface module (AIM) in * dialogues to users 03212
* display characteristics to human visual capacity 03723
Algorithms for approximate string * HCI-0180 †

## MATCHMAKER
Mach and *: kernel and language support for object-oriented distributed systems 03031

## MATHEMATICS
Learning about computers and learning about * 0208
Algebra slaves and agents in a Logo-based * curriculum 0517
Teachers' adoption of multimedia technologies for science and *instruction 0577
Speculating on the future of * 01210
The relationship of computer programming and * in secondary students 01588
An approach to a * of phenomena: canonical aspects of reentrant form eigenbehavior in the extended calculus of indications 01621
DYNABOARD: user animated display of deductive proofs in * 02221
Can * explain natural intelligence? 02565
On the physics and * of thought 03778
Brains, machines, and * (2nd ed.) ● HCI-0034 †

## MATHSCRIBE
*: a user interface for computer algebra systems 03082
*: a user interface for computer algebra systems 03086

## MATPLAN
Innovation of decision support system-* based on structure matrix supported by APL 02800

## MATRIX
An incidence-*-driven panel system for the IBM PC 01814
Algorithm for interactive forming * data representation and estimation of its efficiency 02536
Error correction and asymmetry in a binary memory * 02750
Innovation of decision support system-matplan based on structure *supported by APL 02800

## MATS
Performance evaluation of three pressure * as robot workstation safety sensors 03428

## MAXIMALLY
Towards the construction of a *-contrasting set of colours 03233

## MAXIMIZING
Power windows: * the speed and performance of Windows 2.0 & Windows 386 ● 0423

## MAXIMUM
On the applicability of * entropy to inexact reasoning 02074
Causality and * entropy updating 02076

## MAZES
Designer labyrinths: text * for language learners 0197

## MCC
CHI research at * 0842

## MCGILL
From models to modules: studies in cognitive science from the * workshops ● 0352

## MDR
The * algorithm and its application to the generation of explanations for novel events 02174

## MEANINGFULNESS
Evaluating the * of icon sets to represent command operations 03277

813

## MECHANISM

A communication * supporting actions 01441
Refining problem-solving knowledge in repertory grids using a consultation * 02205
Inference control * for statistical database frequency-imposed data distortions 02449
A neural network model for the * of pattern information processing 02748
Linking * supporting end-user computing 02806
Conceptual documents: a * for specifying active views in hypertext 02833
Real and apparent motion: one * or two? 03328
Manipulation of embedded context using the multiple world * 03921
Synthesis of print-quality cursive script based on a model of the human handwriting * HCI-0402 †

## MECHANOELECTRICAL

Analogs of biological tissues for * transduction: tactile sensors and muscle-like actuators 04014

## MEDIA

Multi-* presentation in CAD systems 0007
CD ROM joins the new * homesteaders 0281
Advanced databases multi-* interface 0418
Semiotics and informatics: computers as * 0448
Interactive *: working methods and practical applications ● 0501
Learning with interactive *: dynamic support for students and teachers 0519
Applying the human relations perspective to the study of new * 0787
The effects of bargaining orientation and communication medium on negotiations in the bilateral monopoly task: a comparison of decision room and computer conferencing communication * 0809
Online use and end-users in * and advertising: an overview 01216

Preserving the integrity of the medium: a method of measuring visual and auditory comprehension of electronic * 02084
Reading, culture and modern mass * 02340
The effect of presentation * on recipient performance in text-based information systems 02350
Message equivocality, * selection and manager performance: implications for information systems 02505
Mondo * 02552
A multi * approach to the user interface 02693
Design of a multi-* vehicle for social browsing 02822
Speed of response using keyboard and screen-based microcomputer response * HCI-0192 †

## MEDIATED

Social psychological aspects of computer-* communication (Reprint) 0384
Learning modes and subsequent use of computer-* communication systems 0912
Implementing computer-* communication technologies: a technoacceptance approach to critical mass utilization 01931
Growth and challenge VS wear and tear of humans in computer * work 03757
Work content, stress and health in computer-* work: a seven year follow-up study 03758
User-friendly password methods for computer-* information systems HCI-0167 †
A framework for investigating language-* interaction with machines HCI-0347 †
Computer * work: the interplay between technology and structured jobs HCI-0440 †

## MEDICAL

Color displays for * imaging 0262
Progress in * imaging ● 0556
Interactive graphic editor for analysis and enhancement of * images 01492

An error correcting protocol for * expert systems 02143
AI/learn: an interactive videodisk system for teaching * concepts and reasoning 02381
History of * Informatics § 02837
* informatics: a personal view of sowing the seeds 02841
History of the development of * information systems at the Laboratory of Computer Science at Massachusetts General Hospital 02842
History of the TDS * information system 02851
Psychovisual issues in the display of * images 03978
Transporting the linguistic string project system from a * to a Navy domain HCI-0352 †

## MEDICINE

Electronic communications and collaboration: the emerging model for computer aided communications in science and * 02678
Pictorial information systems in * § 03976
Software tools for the development of pictorial information systems in *—the ISQL experience 03980
* in the age of the computer ● HCI-0075 †

## MEDIUM

Interactive video—a producer's * 0511
The microcomputer as a symbolic * 0583
The effects of bargaining orientation and communication * on negotiations in the bilateral monopoly task: a comparison of decision room and computer conferencing communication media 0809
Preserving the integrity of the *: a method of measuring visual and auditory comprehension of electronic media 02084
The effect of microcomputer presentation and response * on digit span 02090
Boxer: a reconstructible computational * HCI-0121 †

A performing * for working group graphics HCI-0383 †

**MEISTER**

*: a model enhanced intelligent and skillful teleoperational robot system 03562

**MEMBER**

Attitudes toward unauthorized software copying: general public vs. business faculty * 01142

**MEMORIES**

Nonlinear discriminant functions and associative * 02757

Search strategies in internal and external * 03911

**MEMORY**

Collective computation, content-addressable *, and optimization problems 0004

A trace of *: an evolutionary perspective on the visual system 0019

Principles from the psychology of *: Part I-Working * 0330

Principles from the psychology of *: Part II-Episodic and semantic * 0331

Points: a theory of the structure of stories in * 0392

Short-term * limits in human performance 0398

DARN: Toward a community * for diagnosis and repair tasks 0428

A distributed model of human learning and * 0633

Amnesia and distrubuted * 0641

The * extender personal filing system 0930

Constructing an associative * 01289

The BCC180 multitasking controller part 3: * management and windowing 01295

The direct * access paradigm and its applications to natural language processing 01489

Optical systems that imitate human * 01576

The * channel machine: part of a proposed learning machine 01602

Short-term * as a metastable state.III. Diffusion approximation 01611

Automaticity, resources, and *: theoretical controversies and practical implications 01792

Multiple resources for processing and storage in short-term working * 01794

Electronic implementation of associative * based on neural network models 01895

Expectation and variance of item resemblance distributions in a convolution-correction model of distributed * 02369

Pattern storage and associative * in quasi-neural network 02537

A self-optimizing, nonsymmetrical neural net for content addressable * and pattern recognition 02562

High order correlation model for associative * 02729

* networks with asymmetric bonds 02740

Parallel structures in human and computer * 02742

Error correction and asymmetry in a binary * matrix 02750

DIME: a programming environment for unstructured triangular meshes on a distributed-* parallel processor 02909

The role of * in intelligent information systems 03462

Structured message passing on a shared-* multiprocessor 03514

* research and knowledge engineering 03599

Effects of experience and comprehension on reading time and * for computer programs HCI-0197 †

On the applied use of human * models: the * extender personal filing system HCI-0271 †

**MENACE**

UIMSs: threat or * 02889

**MENTAL**

Some observations on * models 0057

* models in human-computer interaction: research issues about what the user of software knows ● 0214

Neural connections, * computation ● 0229

Computerization versus computer aided * 0308

On methods of analysis of * models and the evaluation of interactive computer systems 0319

Priniciples from the psychology of thinking and * models 0329

* workload 0400

* models and metaphors: implications for the design of adaptive user-system interfaces 0539

* models in cognitive science 0647

A model of * model construction 0931

Evaluation of * models and meta models through interactions between users nd helpers about software usage problems 0972

Issues in research on clinical computer applications for * health 01560

Spectral analysis of sinus arrhythmia: a measure of * effort 01737

Beyond heart rate in the cardiac psychophysiological assessment of *effort: the T-wave amplitude component of the electrocardiogram 01738

* gymnastics of sequential programming 01971

The user's * model of an information retrieval system: an experiment on a prototype online catalog 02099

Intelligent aids, * models, and the theory of machines 02171

The * rotation and perceived realism of computer-generated three-dimensional images 02213

Making the transition from print to electronic encyclopaedias: adapation of * models 02238

* models and software maintenance 02404

Further division of reintegration of * labour? CAD/CAP and work in design nd work preparation shops 03385

Assessment of * load for different strategies of man-computer dialogue by means of the heart rate power spectrum 03623

Performance in cognitive tasks and cardiovascular parameters as indicators of * load 03624

[MENU]

Influences of * load on reaction times in man-computer dialogues 03625
What should be computerized? Cognitive demands of * routine tasks and * load 03632
User-centered system design: design of * tasks 03646
Identification and prevention of work-related * and psycho-somatic disorders among two categories of VDU users 03744
* fatigue of VDU operators induced by monotonous and various tasks 03760
* models and failures in human-machine systems 03814
The role of * models in programming: from experiment to requirements for an interactive system 03827
Development of * models of an office system: a field study on an introductory course 03903
* models: towards a cognitive science of language, inference, and consciousness ● HCI-0063 †
* models and software maintenance HCI-0173 †
Semantic primitives or meaning postulates: * models or propositional representation? HCI-0339 †

MENU

User performance with command, *, and iconic interfaces 0414
Automatic * generation 0774
The effects of restricted syntax on *-based interaction 0775
Performance, preference, and visual scan patterns on a *-based system: implications for interface design 0855
The role of * titles as a navigational aid in hierarchical * 0888
Designing * display format to match input device format 0983
Item selection from *s: the influence of * organization, query interpretation, and programming experience on selection strategies 01011
The optimal number of * options per panel 01715
Optimizing the structure of database * indexes: a decision model of *search 01716

Alternative option selection methods in *-driven computer programs 01755
* organization and user expertise in information search tasks 01761
A * interface to formulate boolean logic-can it be done? 02034
A descriptive/prescriptive model for *-based interaction 02120
A comparison of * selection techniques: touch panel, mouse and keyboard 02122
Considerations of * structure and communication rate for the design of computer * displays 02124
* search: random or systematic? 02144
Adapting * layout to tasks 02182
Effects of breadth, depth and number responses on computer * search performance 02192
Toward a formal specification of *-based systems 02400
Transfer between * systems 02873
Le *: changing the user interface on a local area network 03128
MIKE: the * interaction kontrol environment HCI-0124 †
The depth/breadth trade-off in the design of *-driven user interfaces HCI-0135 †
A Multilevel *-driven user interface: Design and evaluation through simulation HCI-0170 †

MENUS

Making the right choices with * 0070
The role of menu titles as a navigational aid in hierarchical * 0888
Dynamic versus static *: an exploratory comparison 0997
Item selection from *: the influence of menu organization, query interpretation, and programming experience on selection strategies 01011
The impact of * and command-level feedback on learners' acquisition of data base language skills 01041
A notation for specifying * 01111
Some principles of perceptual and cognitive psychology applied to the design of help * 01200
Embedded *: selecting items in context 01320

Of mice and *: designing the user-friendly interface 01837
On meanings * for measurement: disentangling evaluative issues in system design 01997
Lean cuisine: a low fat notation for * 02062
An experiment to test user validation of requirements: data-flow diagrams vs task-oriented * 02131
An empirical comparison of pie vs. linear * 02871
Color-coding categories in * 02872
Keywords instead of hierarchical * 03912
A general user interface for creating and displaying tree-structures, hierarchies, decision trees, and nested * HCI-0136 †

MERGING

* acoustics and linguistics in speech understanding 04004

MERLIN

Relativized Arthur-* versus *-Arthur games 01912

MESHES

DIME: a programming environment for unstructured triangular * on a distributed-memory parallel processor 02909

MESSAGE

Techniques of user * design: developing a user * system to support cooperative work 0127
Diamond: a multimedia * system built on a distributed architecture (Reprint) 0380
Diamond: A multimedia * system built on a distributed architecture 0574
Attribute propagation by * passing 01100
Human factors in computer based * systems 01374
A formal specification of the QMS * system: the underlying abstract model 01406
Insights on the implementation of a computer-based * system 01917
Analysis of the performance of a genetic algorithm-based system for *classification in noisy environments 02156

* equivocality, media selection and manager performance: implications for information systems 02505
Cooperative work in the Andrew * system 02827
A study of group interaction over a computer-based * system 03257
Computer-based * services § 03319
Structured * passing on a shared-memory multiprocessor 03514
The 1984 Olympic * System: a test of behavioral principles of system design HCI-0125 †
A proposed solution to the problem of levels in error-* generation HCI-0126 †
A user agent for multiple computer-based * services HCI-0306 †

**MESSAGES**
The study of information: interdisciplinary * ● HCI-0036 †
Semistructured * are surprisingly useful for computer-supported coordination HCI-0290 †

**MESSAGING**
Voice * enhancing the user interface design based on field performance 0913
User friendly interface for * systems 03320

**MESSY**
A systems architecture for supporting senior managers' * tasks 01928

**META**
Evaluation of mental models and * models through interactions between users nd helpers about software usage problems 0972
Rule base management using * knowledge 01081
The effects of modes of information presentation on decision-making: a review and *-analysis 02358

**METACOMMUNICATION**
Representing and using * to control speakers' relationships in natural-language dialogue 02136
An approach to * in human-computer interaction 03592

**METADATA**
Integrating data and * to enhance the user interface 03280

**METAKNOWLEDGE**
Use of * in the verification of knowledge-based systems 02945

**METAORGANIZATION**
Tensor network theory and its application in computer modeling of the * of sensorimotor hierarchies of gaze 02753

**METAPHOR**
The * machine: a database method for creativity support 01670
The application of *, analogy, and conceptual models in computer systems 02070
*, computing systems, and active learning 02091
The travel * as design principle and training aid for navigating around complex systems 03195
The spatial * for user interfaces: experimental tests of reference by location versus name HCI-0268 †

**METAPHORIC**
Binary jargon: the * language of computing 01044

**METAPHORS**
Mental models and *: implications for the design of adaptive user-system interfaces 0539

**METASTABLE**
Short-term memory as a * state. III. Diffusion approximation 01611

**METEOROLOGICAL**
Applications of computer graphics to the visualization of * data 02819

**METHODOLOGIES**
* for intelligent systems § 03026
* for intelligent systems § 03633
Information systems design * and their compliance with cognitive ergonomy HCI-0097 †

**METRIC**
Grid analysis: continuing the search for a * of shape 02367
Recent results on the application of a *-space search algorithm (AESA) to multispeaker data 03997

**METRICS**
Experimental evaluation of program quality using external * HCI-0176 †

**MFDBS**
* 87 § 03943

**MGB**
Identification of * cells by Volterra kernels. III. A glance into the black box 01259

**MHD**
An object-oriented expert system for coal-fired * power plant fault monitoringand diagnosis 02973

**MICE**
Of * and menus: designing the user-friendly interface 01837

**MICRO**
User friendly * computer program for solving fractional and linear programming problems 01509
The effects of sources of applications programs on user satisfaction: an empirical study of *, mini & mainframe computers using an interactive artificial intelligence expert-system 01601
Using the *-computer to simplify database access: designing interfaces to complex files HCI-0275 †

**MICROBEAM**
X-ray * method for measurement of articulatory dynamics-techniques and results 02641

**MICROCODE**
A development environment for horizontal * programs 01079

**MICROCOMPUTER**
Supporting the * end user 0187
Interactivity in *-based instruction: its essential elements and how it can be enhanced 0275
Instructional designs for * courseware ● 0464
The role of social processes in children's * use 0471
The * as a symbolic medium 0583
Towards universality of access: interfacing physically disabled students to the Icon educational * 0821
Interactive * programs for linear and non-linear static analysis of frameworks 01165

[MICROCOMPUTING]

Communication barriers in *—based courses 01319
The design of a user friendly engineering economy analysis package for a * 01507
Interactive multiple objective linear programming system implemented on a * 01508
Biomechanical evaluation of lifting tasks: a *-based model 01524
Ergonomic job design in frequent manual lifting tasks: a *-based model 01532
* applications: an empirical look at usage 01949
*-based user interface 02044
The effect of * presentation and response medium on digit span 02090
* software. 2. Scientific and technical word processing on a personal computer: has the time come? 02266
An interactive system SDI on * 02272
Student evaluation of motivational and learning attributes of * soft 02274
A comparison of a * progressive state drill and flashcards for learning paired associates 02295
* availability to public library clients 02461
* hardware education at a Czechoslovakian Technical University 02488
A Unix distributed application support suitable for mini and *based systems 02489
Mainframe and *-based business graphics: end user computing comparisons and trends 02805
An evaluation and selection methodology of * training software: Implications for human resource managers and computer personnel 03002
An empirical study of user satisfaction with a *-based campus-wide 03137
The evolution of * laboratory services at the University of Notre Dame 03159
Contextual structure analysis of * manuals 03227

An innovative user interface for *-based computer-aided design 03865
User involvement with * software 04063
A dedicated * for handwritten interaction with a software tool: system prototyping HCI-0119 †
Speed of response using keyboard and screen-based * response media HCI-0192 †
Mainframe and *-based business graphics: What satisfies users? HCI-0216 †
The * as a classroom audio visual device: the concept, and prospects HCI-0223 †
An almost path-free very high-level interactive data manipulation language for m*based database system HCI-0261†

**MICROCOMPUTING**
* in motion analysis 02384

**MICROELECTRONICS**
The silent force of the screen. A research note on the impact of * on work autonomy among clerical workers in public administration 01437

**MICROFICHE**
Reading from *, a VDT, and the printed page: subjective fatigue and performance 01712

**MICROPROCESSOR**
Real-time interfacing: engineering aspects of * peripheral systems ● 0224
Graphbug - a * software debugging tool 02496

**MICROPROCESSORS**
Modelling 8-bit * for a general-purpose simulator 02499

**MICROPROGRAMS**
The design of an interactive compiler for optimizing * 01078

**MICROS**
Managers, * and mainframes: integrating systems for end-users ● 0455
Managers, * and mainframes: an introduction 0456
Advanced interactive cobol for *: a practical approach ● 0521
Advanced interactive COBOL for *: a practical approach ● 0522

Information retrieval using * 01225

**MICROSOFT**
History in the making: a report from *'s First International Conference on CD ROM 0279
* windows 2.0 program development ● 0446
Domesticating * windows 01309

**MICROSTRUCTURES**
Parallel distributed processing: explorations in the * of cognition; Vol. 2: Psychological and biological models ● 0629

**MICROTECHNOLOGY**
* and user friendly systems—the CONNECT dialogue executor 02382

**MICROWORLD**
Experimental data for the design of a *-based system for algebra 0543
Children's collaborative use of a computer * 02825

**MICROWORLDS**
Designing computer-based * 0742
Computer-based *—a definition to aid design HCI-0432 †

**MIDAS**
The * database system 02387
The * display system 02388
*: molecular interactive display and simulation 04061

**MIGRATION**
The * of expert systems into the production environment 0740

**MIKE**
*: the menu interaction kontrol environment HCI-0124 †

**MILITARY**
* systems 0138
Color computer graphics in * cockpits 0261

**MIMICKING**
A note on * additive reaction time models 02373

**MINDSET**
Managing the diffusion of end-user computing technologies: a fifties *with eighties tools 0459

**MINERALS**
MINID—a BASIC program to assist in the optical identification of * in thin section 01505

## MINI
The effects of sources of applications programs on user satisfaction: an empirical study of micro, * & mainframe computers using an interactive artificial intelligence expert-system 01601
A Unix distributed application support suitable for * and microcomputer based systems 02489

## MINIATURE
Comprehension and recall of * programs 02087

## MINID
*—a BASIC program to assist in the optical identification of minerals in thin section 01505

## MINIMALIST
* design for active users 0086

## MINIMIZATION
Model *—an alternative to circumscription 02263

## MINIMUM
On the * number of templates required for shift, rotation and size invariant pattern recognition 02531

## MINIS
A computing service using linked * 01674

## MINORITY
A user perspective on computer-assisted translation for * languages 01557

## MINOS
The multimedia object presentation manager of *: a symmetric approach 01083

## MINUS
Seven plus or * two central issues in human-computer interaction 0937
The magical number three—plus or * zero 01622

## MIRAGE
The * rapid interface prototyping system 03112

## MIRRORS
* of minds: patterns of experience in educational computing ● 0575
The */II simulator 03502

## MIS
Power, politics, and * implementation 0042
A human information processing model of the managerial mind: some *implications 0205
Validation of a Jungian instrument for * research 01022
An evaluation of a realistic approach to * 01027
The age of the end-user and the shift from corporate * to corporate DSS 01676
An exploratory contingency model of user participation and * use 01919
Cognitive process as a basis for * and DSS design 02476
Perspectives on the academic preparation of * professionals 03006

## MISCOMMUNICATION
Ill-formedness and * in person-machine dialogue 01957

## MISCONCEIVED
* misconceptions? 02881

## MISCONCEPTIONS
Recognizing and responding to plan-oriented * 01350
Reasoning on a highlighted user model to respond to * 01351
Misconceived * 02881

## MISINFORMED
User programmer and costs of the * user 02415

## MISORIENTATION
Spatial * exacerbated by collimated virtual flight display 01979

## MISPERCEPTIONS
Modeling managerial behavior: * of feedback in a dynamic decision making experiment 02483

## MISUSE
Legal liability for malfunction and * of expert systems 0939
The use and * of VDU'S 01375

## MJOLNER
The * envirnment: direct interaction with abstractions 03794

## MMI
'Remember to lock the door': * and the hacker 01910

## MODAL
The use of * default reasoning in information systems 02095

## MODALITIES
Codes and * in multiple resources: a success and a qualification 01793

## MODALITY
An empirical investigation of voice as an input * for computer programming HCI-0237 †
Speech-controlled text-editing: effects of input * and of command structure HCI-0397 †

## MODE
* errors: a user-centered analysis and some preventative measures using keying-contingent sound 02107
Coupled * theory for neural networks 02730
Natural language with discrete speech as a * for human-to-machine HCI-0355 †

## MODEL
A functional * of vision and space 0027
The keystroke-level * for user performance time with interactive systems 0055
The evaluation of online help systems: a conceptual * 0129
A human information processing * of the managerial mind: some MIS implications 0205
Develping decision support systems from a * of the DSS/user interface 0253
Computer interface engineering with *-based analysis ● 0337
Learning by chunking: a production system * of practice 0483
Self-modifying production system * of cognitive development 0486
Interactive video as a school resource: Rolls-Royce or * T Ford? 0513
Computer-aided * building 0544
On language and connectionism: analysis of a parallel distributed processing * of language acquisition 0590
* generation and modification for dynamic systems from geometric data 0604

[MODEL]

Interactive processes in speech perception: the TRACE * 0631
The programmable blackboard * of reading 0632
A distributed * of human learning and memory 0633
A fuzzy rule-based * of human problem solving 0656
Data * issues for object-oriented applications 0712
Constraint grammars–a new * for specifying graphical applications 0875
A cognitive * of database querying: a tool for novice instruction 0905
An input-output * of interactive systems 0926
A * of mental * construction 0931
In search of a user interface reference * 0944
Dialogue management reference * 0945
How would your favourite user * cope with these scenarios? 0999
Including a user interface management system (UIMS) in the performance relationship * 01000
Reference * for DBMS user facility 01086
Adaptive interface design: a symmetric * and a knowledge-based implementation 01091
A * and an implementation of a logic programming environment 01107
User interface support for the integration of software tools: an iconic *of interaction 01139
Data * issues for object-oriented applications 01157
A Computational * for interfaces 01163
A * of the neocortex 01164
What we know and what we need to know: the user * versus the user's *in human-computer interaction 01243
Muscle *s: what is gained and what is lost by varying * complexity 01251
Diffusion approximation of the neuronal * with synaptic reversal potentials 01254
Single sweep analysis of visual evoked potentials through a * of parametric identification 01261

Simulation of chaotic EEG patterns with a dynamic * of the olfactory system 01263
A scaling * for dichotomous branching processes 01264
A *-based monitor of human sleep stages 01269
A * of the motor servo: Incorporating nonlinear spindle receptor and muscle mechanical properties 01273
Physiology based simulation * of triangle shape recognition 01277
Self-organizing system obtaining communication ability primitive * for language generation 01279
ER * clustering as an aid for user communication and documentation in database design 01331
Competitive dynamics in a dual-route connectionist * of print-to-sound transformation 01341
Reasoning on a highlighted user * to respond to misconceptions 01351
VLSI implementation of a neural network * 01363
Dialogue cell resource * and basic dialogue cells 01400
A formal specification of the QMS message system: the underlying abstract * 01406
Initial work on a system-independent computer * of a 3D anthropomorphic dummy 01476
A similarity-based reasoning * for intelligent interfaces 01503
A structure for enhancing user participation in * development 01514
Biomechanical evaluation of lifting tasks: a microcomputer-based * 01524
Ergonomic job design in frequent manual lifting tasks: a microcomputer-based * 01532
The human immune system as an information systems security reference * 01547
* of the neuro-muscular recruitment example of the extensor digitorum communis muscle in man: I—identification of

KEYWORD INDEX

motoneurons and of muscular fibers 01595
A logical * of co-operative processes in cerebral dynamics 01615
Understanding and validating results in *-based decision support systems 01666
A natural language discourse * to explain linear programming *s and solutions 01671
Optimizing the structure of database menu indexes: a decision * of menu search 01716
A simultaneous regression * for double stimulation tasks 01726
A closed-loop causal * of workload based on a comparison of fuzzy and crisp measurement techniques 01746
A * for the fading of stabilized images in a visual system 01864
Application of a mathematical * of human decisionmaking for human-computer communication 01866
A discrete control * of operator function: A methodology for information dislay design 01874
A rule-based * for the human operator in a time-constrained competing-task environment 01877
Neural network * with rhythm-assimilation capacity 01881
A qualitative * of human interaction with complex dynamic systems 01891
An exploratory contingency * of user participation and MIS use 01919
The implementation of information systems for workers: a structural equation * 01948
Evaluation of the user interface in an information retrieval system: a * 02012
A practical approach to transforming extended ER diagrams into the relational * 02022
A semantic data * as the basis for an automated database design tool 02036
Action based * of information system 02037

# KEYWORD INDEX [MODEL]

Embedded user *-where next? 02059

The user's mental * of an information retrieval system: an experiment on a prototype online catalog 02099

A virtual protocol * for computer-human interaction 02106

An empirical comparison of *-based and explicit communication for dynamic human-computer task allocation 02109

A three-level human-computer interface * 02112

A descriptive/prescriptive * for menu-based interaction 02120

*ling operators in accident conditions: advances and perspectives on a cognitive * 02169

A * of fault diagnosis performance of expert marine engineers 02199

* minimization—an alternative to circumscription 02263

A natural language interface processor based on the hierarchical-tree structure * of relation tables 02315

Using a cognitive * of dialogue for reference retrieval 02317

A group * of form recognition under plane similarity transformations 02366

Expectation and variance of item resemblance distributions in a convolution-correction * of distributed memory 02369

The accumulator * of two-choice discrimination 02371

A probabilistic dominance measure for binary choices: analytic aspects of a multi-attribute random weights * 02372

A regression * to identify successful learner traits with CAI 02376

A cookbook for using the *-view controller user interface paradigm in Smalltalk-80 02390

A study of user interface aids for *-oriented decision support systems 02479

A * of the controller responses of the human temperature regulating system to changes in water temperature 02487

A * for assessing the performance of a local area network employing technical office protocol (TOP) as part of MAP/TOP network in a computer integrated manufacturing (CIM) research project, for the transmission of real time interactive speech 02491

A * for graphical interaction 02610

A LISP implementation of the * for 'communicating sequential processes' 02632

A computer * of peripheral auditory processing incorporating phase-locking, suppression and adaptation effects 02650

Speech motor control and stuttering: a computational * of adaptive sensory-motor processing 02655

Electronic communications and collaboration: the emerging * for computer aided communications in science and medicine 02678

Development and sensitivity analysis of adaptive predictor for human eye movement * 02681

A compact * of a power house boiler 02683

Bifurcation analysis of oscillating network * of pattern recognition in the rabbit olfactory bulb 02725

High order correlation * for associative memory 02729

A * for cortical function 02731

Hopfield * applied to vowel and consonant discrimination 02735

A dynamic * of olfactory discrimination 02737

A drive-reinforcement * of single neuron function: An alternative to the Hebbian neuronal * 02743

A neural network * for the mechanism of pattern information processing 02748

Firing response of a neural * with threshold modulation and neural dynamics 02761

A layered neural network * applied to the auditory system 02763

Precedent-based legal reasoning and knowledge acquisition in contract law: A process * 02776

User development of applications: a study of a * of success 02807

A display system for the Stellar Graphics Supercomputer * GS1000 02816

Adding browsing semantics to the hypertext * 02834

The data * is the heart of interface design 02875

A new conceptual * for interactive user recovery and command reuse facilities 02884

Providing natural language assistance in locating objects: a general * for information selection and generation 02951

The actem * for decision *ling in a scene management system 02954

Informational zooming: an interaction * for the graphical access to text knowledge bases 03073

A new * for user services: distributed support 03153

Refining early design decisions with a black-box * 03200

An editing * for generating graphical user interfaces 03289

An extended relational database * based on user views 03452

Knowledge representation for * libraries 03479

GMMS: global * management system: a conceptional design framework for *management systems for distributed decision support systems 03484

Reasoning in * management systems 03487

A cost * for estimating the costs of developing software in the Ada programming language 03539

MEISTER: a * enhanced intelligent and skillful teleoperational robot system 03562

Generic surface interpretation: observability * 03563

Concept for a * databased remote maintenance system 03565

A functional * of questions for natural language processing systems 03575

Psychosocial work environment and use of visual display terminals:8mfrom theoretical * to action 03742

A * for evaluating stress effects of work with display units 03756

821

[MODELING]

A * for an object management system for software engineering environments 03843
Concepts in user interfaces: a reference * for command and response languages § 03872
A cortical network * for early vision processing 03957
A systems * of cognition for improving human factors of computing environments 04058
Daydreaming and computation: a computer * of everyday creativity, learning nd emotions in the human stream of thought 04067
A neural * of human prehension 04072
Automatic contour definition on left ventriculograms by image evidence and a multiple template-based * 04073
Concepts in user interfaces: a reference * for command and response languages ● HCI-0032 †
A research * for studying the gender/power aspects of human-computer communication HCI-0193 †
Users and experts in the document retrieval system * HCI-0270 †
A generalized * management system for mathematical programming HCI-0302 †
A * for the interpretation of verbal predictions HCI-0316 †
A fuzzy rule-based * of human problem solving HCI-0359 †
Synthesis of print-quality cursive script based on a * of the human handwriting mechanism HCI-0402 †

**MODELING**

* of robot system dynamics for CAD based robot programming 0605
Looking at worksheet * through expert system eyes 0696
Computing needs in thunderstorm *: supercomputers and interactive graphics 0730
Cognition-sensitive design and user * for syntax-directed editors 0828
User * in UC, the UNIX consultant 0894
* of control and learning in a stepping motion 01250
* the user in natural language systems 01348
* the user's plans and goals 01349
Providing effective decision support: * users and their requirements 01668
Towards the development of human work-performance standards in futuristic man-machine systems: a fuzzy * approach 01692
* fault diagnosis as the activation and use of a frame system 01729
The role of practice in dual-task performance: toward workload * in a connectionist/control architecture 01790
* the Cognitive content of displays 01800
* of task-dependent characteristics of human operator dynamics during pursuit manual tracking 01859
Open-loop experiments for * the human eye movement system 01870
Capturing expertise: Some approaches to * command decisionmaking in combat analysis 01883
Graphic equivalence, graphic explanations, and embedded process * for enhanced user-system interaction 01888
Qualitative approximation methodology for * and simulation of large dynamic systems: Applications to a Marine power plant 01900
User * in intelligent information retrieval 01994
* rule-based systems by stochastic programmed production systems 02017
Manual control of an intrinsically unstable system and its * by fuzzy logic 02026
Design goals for sloppy * systems 02206
Mathematical * of fatigue in physically demanding jobs 02363
An interactive * program for DNA 02385
MOL3D, a modular and interactive program for molecular * and conformational analysis: I—basic modules 02389
Automated interactive simulation * system: AISIM 02399
* managerial behavior: misperceptions of feedback in a dynamic decision making experiment 02483
Tensor network theory and its application in computer * of the metaorganization of sensorimotor hierarchies of gaze 02753
Legal data *: The prohibited transaction exemption analyst 02779
Applications of qualitative * to knowledge-based risk assessment studies 02970
Measurement and * of Computer Systems § 03024
Supporting natural language database update by * real world actions 03179
Interactive 3-D * with personal computers 03296
3-D balance in legged locomotion: * and simulation for the one-legged case 03352
Trends in office * 03355
Issues in * supervisory control in flexible manufacturing systems 03363
Humane: A designer's assistant for * and evaluating function allocation options 03397
Lessons learned from * a secure multilevel relational database system 03580
* uncertainty in human perception 03825
Qualitative * of physical systems for knowledge based control 03834
Interactive solid * in hut design 03837
High performance interactive graphics: *, rendering and animating for IBM PCs and compatibles ● HCI-0071 †
Postscript: computers and the * of mind HCI-0348 †
An economical approach to * speech recognition accuracy HCI-0354 †
Computer-aided * and planning (CAMP) HCI-0415 †

**MODELLER**

Unified interactive geometric * for simulating highly complex environments 01472

# KEYWORD INDEX [MODELS]

**MODELLERS**
The CADME approach to the interface of solid * 03867

**MODELLING**
VP$^2$: the role of user * in correcting errors in second language learning 0222
VLSI for solid * 0232
Geometric * 0236
* novice programmer behaviour 0744
* novice programmer behaviour 0751
Approximate * of cognitive activity: towards an expert system design aid 0801
A multivariate solution for cyclic data, applied in * locomotor forces 01252
Approximate * of cognitive activity with an expert system: a theory-based strategy for developing an interactive design tool 01415
SML: a solid * language 01471
Functional * in the execution of actions 01485
* the human factors aspects of a computer-based text-graphics layout system 01518
CAD system GISK for interactive graphical * of planar mechanisms 01570
Usage of linguistic variable concept for human operator * 01694
* degrees of item interest for a general database query system 02083
* human expertise in knowledge engineering: some preliminary observations 02134
* operators in accident conditions: advances and perspectives on a cognitive model 02169
Human supervisor *: some new developments 02170
* blind users' interactions with an auditory computer interface 02237
* 8-bit microprocessors for a general-purpose simulator 02499
Hierarchical, modular discrete-event * in an object-oriented environment 02588
A practical approach to data * in spatial applications 02616
BNETD—A * tool to computer systems performance evaluation 02668
SATURN—a tool for * and performance evaluation of computer systems 02670
A general user * facility 02880
The actem model for decision * in a scene management system 02954
Task-related knowledge structures: analysis, * and application 03218
Application * in a user interface management system 03262
* generic user-interfaces with functional programs 03265
* and controlling user inference 03582
Intentional and operational aspects of decision behaviour and their * 03666
Report from the working group on "socialist experience with * and using systems" 03667
Low cost geometric * system for CAM 03866
* and control ● HCI-0068 †
Ada-based executable * of distributed systems HCI-0098 †
On models and * in human-computer co-operation HCI-0182 †
UMFE: a user * front-end subsystem HCI-0325 †

**MODELS**
Neural network * for optical computing ● 0032
Some observations on mental * 0057
Computational * of natural language processing ● 0095
Computer * of mind: computational approaches in theoretical psychology ● 0152
Adaptive general audience *: a research framework 0202
Mental * in human-computer interaction: research issues about what the user of software knows ● 0214
A critique and empirical investigation of the "One-Best-Way-*" in human-computer interaction 0317
On methods of analysis of mental * and the evaluation of interactive computer systems 0319
Priniciples from the psychology of thinking and mental * 0329
From * to modules: studies in cognitive science from the McGill workshops ● 0352
The optimal level of abstraction for * of cerebral representation of language processes: the state of the question 0356
Production system * of learning and development ● 0478
Mental * and metaphors: implications for the design of adaptive user-system interfaces 0539
The relation between linguistic structure and associative theories of language learning *: constructive critique of some connectionist learning * 0591
Parallel distributed processing: explorations in the microstructures of cognition; Vol. 2: Psychological and biological * ● 0629
Schemata and sequential thought processes in PDP * 0630
Neural and conceptual interpretation of PDP * 0638
Biologically plausible * of place recognition and goal location 0639
Mental * in cognitive science 0647
* of human problem solving: detection, diagnosis, and compensation for system failures 0653
Skills, rules, and knowledge; signals, signs, and symbols, and other distinctions in human performance * 0654
Conceptual design of decision support systems utilizing management science * 0658
Thinking: information processing, mathematical * and computer simulation ● 0667
Qualitative student * 0721
Programmable user * for predictive evaluation of interface designs 0800
* of user interactions with graphical interfaces: 1. statistical 0883

[MODELS]

Intelligent interfaces: user * and planners 0932
On user interface reference * 0946
Designing conceptual * of dialog: a case for dialog charts 0968
Evaluation of mental * and meta * through interactions between users nd helpers about software usage problems 0972
Report on the workshop on analytical * 01001
Reference *, window systems, and concurrency 01058
A survey of three dialogue * 01152
Human intelligence * and their implications for expert system structure and research 01242
Muscle *: what is gained and what is lost by varying model complexity 01251
Disjunctive * of boolean category learning 01262
Interpolation coding: A representation for numbers in neural * 01271
The relationship between user * and discourse * 01353
Implementing neural network * on parallel computers 01403
Exchange of solid *: current state and future trends 01475
A natural language discourse model to explain linear programming * and solutions 01671
Internal *, tracking strategies and dual-task performance 01751
* of procedural control for human performance simulation 01752
Review and evaluation of physiological cost prediction * for manual materials handling 01757
Near-real-time control of human figure * 01829
Significance testing of rules in rule-based * of human problem solving 01867
Electronic implementation of associative memory based on neural network * 01895
An empirical investigation as to the need for multicomponent decision * 01898
The application of metaphor, analogy, and conceptual * in computer systems 02070

Intelligent aids, mental *, and the theory of machines 02171
* of the decision maker in unforeseen accidents 02172
Analysis of competition-based spreading activation in connectionist * 02179
$DM^2$: an algorithm for diagnostic reasoning that combines analytical * and experiential knowledge 02190
The effect of different conceptual * using reasoning in a database query writing task 02201
A survey of formal tools and * for developing user interfaces 02207
Combining stochastic uncertainty and linguistic inexactness: theory and experimental evaluation of four fuzzy probability * 02218
Rough sets and dependency analysis among attributes in computer implementations of expert's inference * 02231
Making the transition from print to electronic encyclopaedias: adapation of mental * 02238
The effects of relational and entity-relationship data * on query performance of end users 02247
Research and evaluation * for the study of interactive video 02283
Cognitive * in information retrieval—an evaluative review 02298
Counting and timing * in psychophysics and the conjoint Weber's law 02368
Psychological * of deferred decision making 02370
A note on mimicking additive reaction time * 02373
Mental * and software maintenance 02404
Conceptual * of interacitve knowledge acquisition tools 02457
The role of computer graphics in validating simulation * 02486
Neural network * of learning and adaptation 02560
Higher pole correction in vocal tract * and terminal analogs 02657
Connectionist * and parallelism in high level vision 02700

Concepts in connectionist * 02724
Choosing between methods: analysing the user's decision space in terms of schemas and linear * 02879
Knowledge acquisition and conceptual *: a cognitive analysis of the interface 03214
Abstract, generic * of interactive systems 03219
Principles and interaction * for window managers 03264
Near-real-time control of human figure * 03295
* for design of computer integrated manufacturing systems 03378
Structured what if analysis in DSS * 03481
Composite * in symms 03485
Building interprocess communication * using Stile 03528
Interaction * and the principled design of interactive systems 03799
Mental * and failures in human-machine systems 03814
The role of mental * in programming: from experiment to requirements for an interactive system 03827
Development of mental * of an office system: a field study on an introductory course 03903
Relational * in natural and artificial vision 03953
Petri nets: applications and relationships to other * of concurrency § 03973
The use of explicit user * in text generation: tailoring to a user's level of expertise 04051
Mental *: towards a cognitive science of language, inference, and consciousness ● HCI-0063 †
Undo support * HCI-0144 †
Mental * and software maintenance HCI-0173 †
On * and modelling in human-computer co-operation HCI-0182 †
Representational frameworks and * for human-computer interfaces HCI-0188 †

Analysing the scope of cognitive * in human-computer interaction: a trade-off approach HCI-0245 †
On the applied use of human memory *: the memory extender personal filing system HCI-0271 †
Cognitive *, cognitive tasks, and information retrieval HCI-0331 †
Semantic primitives or meaning postulates: mental * or propositional representation? HCI-0339 †
Connectionist * and parallelism in high level vision HCI-0363 †
An experimental comparison of RGB, YIQ, LAB, HSV, and opponent color * HCI-0381 †

## MODERATING
* effects of age, education, and tenure on the job satisfaction-job performance relationship 03021

## MODERNIZATION
Human aspects of factory * 01513

## MODERNIZING
Transportable applications environment (TAE) plus experiences in "Object"-ively * a user interface environment 01126

## MODES
Sites, *, and trails: Telling the user of an interactive system where he is, what he can do, and how to get to places (excerpt) 0068
Learning * and subsequent use of computer-mediated communication systems 0912
* survey 0963
* survey results 0998
The effects of * of information presentation on decision-making: a review and meta-analysis 02358
Distinctive regions and *: a new theory of speech production 02659

## MODIFIABILITY
An empirical study of the effects of modularity on program * HCI-0155 †

## MODIFIABLE
GENIE: a * computer-based task for experiments in human-computer interaction HCI-0194 †

## MODIFYING
Self-* production system model of cognitive development 0486
Building a self-* user interface 01424
Pride-II physical layout program of * Forth for "non-believers" 02312

## MODULA
Automated construction of interactive learning programs in *-2 01500
EM2—a *-2 programming environment 02392

## MODULAR
A * user-oriented decision support for physical database design 01669
MOL3D, a * and interactive program for molecular modeling and conformational analysis: I—basic modules 02389
Hierarchical, * discrete-event modelling in an object-oriented environment 02588
A * window system for Unix 03929

## MODULARITY
Structured editor support for * and data abstraction 01105
An empirical study of the effects of * on program modifiability HCI-0155 †
* and lexical access HCI-0350 †

## MODULATION
Firing response of a neural model with threshold * and neural dynamics 02761

## MODULE
An evaluation of the effectiveness of the adaptive interface * (AIM) in matching dialogues to users 03212

## MODULES
From models to *: studies in cognitive science from the McGill workshops ● 0352
Efficacy of higher cognitive and factual questions in computer assisted instruction * 02278
MOL3D, a modular and interactive program for molecular modeling and conformational analysis: I—basic * 02389

## MODULO
A logic-functional approach to the execution of CCS specifications *behavioural equivalences 03874

## MOLECULAR
The lure of * computing 01833
MOL3D, a modular and interactive program for * modeling and conformational analysis: I—basic modules 02389
MIDAS: * interactive display and simulation 04061

## MOLES
Of * and men: the design of foot controls for workstations 0935

## MOL3D
*, a modular and interactive program for molecular modeling and conformational analysis: I—basic modules 02389

## MOMENT
Desktop publishing and user services; * in the evolution of user support documentation at UNH 03158

## MOMENTUM
Visual *: a concept to improve the cognitive coupling of person and computer HCI-0238 †

## MONDO
* media 02552

## MONEY
Building user interfaces before writing code saves time and * 02662

## MONITOR
A model-based * of human sleep stages 01269
Human factors design of a video * emulator and display (VMED) for visually impaired computer users 02379
A study on the safety operation of robots using * hold 03412

## MONITORING
User-interface design for a clinical neurophysiological intensive *system 0881
Knowledge base refinement by * abstract control knowledge 02160
The accuracy of cognitive * during computer-based instruction 02281

PISCES: an expert system for coal fired power plant * and diagnostics 02915
The development of an automated flight test management system for flight test planning and * 02928
Electronic * and the redundancy of control systems: The role of the supervisor 03000
* and performance measuring distributed systems during operation 03025
Plan recognition for intelligent * 03261
Human visual requirements for control and * of a space telerobot 03391
Human-machine interface in remote * and control of flexible manufacturing systems 03399
Acting-out and burn-out behaviours of operators * automated systems 03440
Vision * of VDU operators and relaxation of visual stress by means of laser speckle system 03738
* distributed systems HCI-0169 †

## MONITORINGAND
An object-oriented expert system for coal-fired MHD power plant fault * diagnosis 02973

## MONITORS
The effects of communication * on user satisfaction HCI-0221 †

## MONOPOLY
The effects of bargaining orientation and communication medium on negotiations in the bilateral * task: a comparison of decision room and computer conferencing communication media 0809

## MONOTONOUS
Mental fatigue of VDU operators induced by * and various tasks 03760
Videocoding - a highly * VDU work in a new technique for mail sorting 03762

## MONTE
The * Carlo processor: designing and implementing a language for *Carlo work 03317

## MOOD
An evaluation of * disturbances and somatic discomfort under slow computer-response time and incentive-pay conditions 03765

## MOOERS
The convergence of Moore's/*' laws 01996

## MOORE
The convergence of *'s/Mooers' laws 01996

## MORAL
The * cracker? 01546
* judgements in designing better systems 02064
* issues in information science 02321

## MORPHOLOGIC
* machines and conservative networks 01604

## MORPHOLOGICAL
* representation of speech knowledge for automatic speech recognition systems 03992

## MORPHOLOGY
An interaction between * and discourse 0355

## MORTAL
Seven * sins of systems work 03645

## MOSI
Lessons from the * project 01450

## MOTION
Visual analysis during * 0020
Computational techniques in * processing 0025
CAD Based verification and refinement of high level compliant * primitives 0600
Modeling of control and learning in a stepping * 01250
Contingent aftereffects and isoluminance: psychophysical evidence for separation of color, orientation, and * 01463
Effects of visual display and * system delays on operator performance and ueasiness in a driving simulator 01772
Interactive design of 3D computer-animated legged animal * 01828
On kineopsis and cimputation of structure and * 01839
Microcomputing in * analysis 02384
Estimating articulatory * from speech wave 02643
* correspondence and analog networks 02739
* interpolation by optimal control 02817
Virya—a * control editor for kinematic and dynamic animation 03294
Correspondence in apparent *: defining the heuristics 03308
*: representation and perception § 03321
How human perception deals with * 03322
The scope of research on *: sensations, perception, representation and generation 03323
* perception: second thoughts on the correspondence problem 03325
The perception of coherent * in two-dimensional patterns 03327
Real and apparent *: one mechanism or two? 03328
Coherent global * percepts from stochastic local * 03329
Determining the instantaneous axis of translation from optic flow generated by rbitrary sensot m* 03332
Adapting optical-flow to measure object * in reflectance and X-ray image sequences 03334
* and time-varying imagery 03336
Determining * parameters for scenes with translation and rotation 03338
Determining 3-D * parameters of a rigid body: a vector-geometrical approach 03339
A hybrid approach to structure-from-* 03340
* from continuous or discontinuous arrangements 03342
The cross-ratio and the perception of * and structure 03344
Selective attention to aspects of * configurations: common vs. relative * 03345
* analysis of grammatical processes in a visual-gestural language 03347
* graphics, description and control 03348

A multiple track animator system for * synchronization 03350
Unexpected * hazard exposures on a large robotic assembly 03409
Gribs—an approach to a realistic realtime simulation of human arm * 03432
The alternatives allowed by a rectangularity postulate, and a pragmatic approach to interpreting * 03550
Image segregation by *: cortical mechanisms and implementation in neural networks 03958

## MOTIONS
Coherent global motion percepts from stochastic local * 03329

## MOTIVATION
* analysis, abductive unification, and nonmonotonic equality 01211
* norms of knowledge engineers compared to those of software engineers 02349

## MOTIVATIONAL
Student evaluation of * and learning attributes of microcomputer soft 02274
Causes of * problems among AI managers 03004

## MOTIVATIONS
* and behaviors of software professionals 03003

## MOTIVATORS
* vs. de* in the IS environment 02433

## MOTONEURONS
Model of the neuro-muscular recruitment example of the extensor digitorum communis muscle in man: I—identification of * and of muscular fibers 01595

## MOTOR
A model of the * servo: Incorporating nonlinear spindle receptor and muscle mechanical properties 01273
Design of an integral computer-based wheelchair controller/linear synchronous * system 02378
Design and implementation of an interactive optimization system for network design in the * carrier industry 02528

Speech * control and stuttering: a computational model of adaptive sensory-* processing 02655
Topology conserving mappings for learning * tasks 02758
Spatial and temporal transformations in visuo-* coordination 03963
Neural networks for * program generation 03964
Innate and learned components in a simple visuo-* reflex 03965
Proprioceptive feedback for sensory-* control 04008

## MOTORS
Process control and people at General *' Delta Engine Plant 01905
Process control and people at General *' Delta engine plant 03431

## MOULDING
The impact of advanced manufacturing in work organization: The Portugese case of the plastic * industry 03374

## MOUSE
Evaluation of *, rate-controlled isometric joystick, step keys, and text keys, for text selection on a CRT 0064
Circling: a method of *-based selection without button presses 0847
More on the * 01642
An experimental comparison of a * and arrow-jump keys for an interactive encyclopedia 02098
A comparison of menu selection techniques: touch panel, * and keyboard 02122
Programming the * in Turbo Pascal 4.0 02393
Text representation and manipulation in a *-driven interface 03266
Touch screen, cursor keys and * interaction 03769

## MOVE
ISDN and the * to integrated communications—an introduction 01455

## MOVEMENT
The statutes and standards * 0049

Describing * control at two levels of abstraction 0403
Open-loop experiments for modeling the human eye * system 01870
A system for the representation of human body * from dance scores 02540
Development and sensitivity analysis of adaptive predictor for human eye * model 02681
Human aspects of QC circle * in Japanese manufacturing: Natures and problems 03450
The applicability of eye * analysis in the ergonomic evaluation of human-computer interaction 03766
Cursor * during text editing HCI-0113 †
Eye * analysis system using fundus images HCI-0243 †

## MOVEMENTS
Eye * in reading: perceptual and language processes ● 0609
The control of hand equilibrium trajectories in multi-joint arm * 01275
Intermittent illumination from visual display units and fluorescent lighting affects * of the eyes across text 01713
A new approach to cursor * in user interfaces of integrated programming environments 01974
Human response to unexpected robot * at selected slow speeds 03405
Extending Kohonen's self-organizing mapping algorithms to learn ballistic * 03967

## MOVING
Quantitative determination of orientational and directional components in the response of visual cortical cells to * stimuli 01268
The * target: future trends in networking 01282
Factors affecting the readability of * text on a computer display 01764
Reading self-paced * text on a computer display 01777

The representation and perception of geometric structure in * visual patterns 03326
Tracking three-dimensional * light displays 03337

**MRC**
Computing facilities in the * clinical research centre 02688

**MRP**
*/* II 0620

**MSC**
Professional education and subsequent careers in library/information work: a follow-up study of former students on the MA/* information studies course at the University of Sheffield 02336

**MSV**
Using IBM's ISPF dialog manager: under *, VM, and VSE ● 0304

**MUFFIN**
*: a user interface design experiment for a theorem proving assistant 04037

**MULTI**
*-media presentation in CAD systems 0007
Advanced databases *-media interface 0418
A *-processor workstation with a logic-enhanced distributed frame buffer 0496
The effects of structured, *-level documentation 0907
*-process structuring of user interface software 01066
*-thread input 01070
The control of hand equilibrium trajectories in *-joint arm movements 01275
An interactive outranking system for *-attribute decision making 01539
A *-purpose system for alpha-numeric input to computers via a reduced keyboard 02118
*-window displays for readers of lengthy texts 02142
A probabilistic dominance measure for binary choices: analytic aspects of a *-attribute random weights model 02372
A * media approach to the user interface 02693

Design of a *-media vehicle for social browsing 02822
*-Input fuzzy inference engine on a systolic array 02953
A conceptual dependency network approach to *-task assignments in man-machine (teleoperated) systems 03388
An investigation of performance, productivity, and rationality in *-criteria decision making 03463
Study of visual performance on a *-color VDU of color defective and normal Trichromatic subjects 03701
A design environment for computer-aided control system design via *-objective optimisation 03835
The effects of limited data in *-frequency reflection diffraction tomography 04020
Interactive fuzzy decision-making for *-objective nonlinear programming using reference membership intervals HCI-0295 †

**MULTICOMPUTER**
Experience with a functional layered * architecture for interactive processing 02402
* architectures for real-time perception 03341

**MULTICUE**
Display proximity in * information integration: the benefits of boxes 01763

**MULTIDIMENSIONAL**
A * approach to the measurement of human-computer performance 01410
* attribute analyhsis and pattern recognition for seismic interpretation 02530
The application of scene synthesis techniques to the display of * image data HCI-0371 †

**MULTIEXPERT**
Interactive learning: a * paradigm for acquiring new knowledge 0776

**MULTIFARIOUS**
MH: a * user agent 01428

**MULTILEVEL**
Intelligent interfaces for secure * database systems 02990

Lessons learned from modeling a secure * relational database system 03580
A * menu-driven user interface: Design and evaluation through simulation HCI-0170 †

**MULTILINGUAL**
* programming: Coordinating programs, user interfaces, on-line help nd documentation 02785
Vidura—an interactive * publishing system—specification & design 03186

**MULTILOOP**
Automation effects in a * manual control system 01865

**MULTIMEDIA**
Interactive * ● 0011
Investigations in * design documentation 0116
GENIE-M: A generator for * information environments 0268
Diamond: a * message system built on a distributed architecture (Reprint) 0380
An experiment in integrated * conferencing 0381
Diamond: A * message system built on a distributed architecture 0574
Teachers' adoption of * technologies for science and mathematics instruction 0577
The * object presentation manager of MINOS: a symmetric approach 01083
An object-oriented approach to * databases 01084
Virtual video editing in interactive * applications 01326
DVI—a digital * technology 01327
An architecture for a * teleconferencing system 02802
The rapport * conferencing system 03037
Browsing within time-driven * documents 03046
Design and performance considerations for an optical disk-based, *object server HCI-0265 †
An experimental * mail system HCI-0309 †

# KEYWORD INDEX [MUSCLE]

## MULTIMODAL
* detection and recognition performance of sonar operators 01709
* response planning: an adaptive rule based approach 02894

## MULTIPARADIGM
A * user interface for intelligent CAD systems 0716

## MULTIPLE
THESYS—implementation of a knowledge-based design system with *viewpoints 0010
A *, virtual-workspace interface to support user task switching 0813
A user interface for *-process, turnkey systems targeted for the novice user 0911
A natural language interface to a * databased office information system 01094
Rooms: the use of * virtual workspaces to reduce space contention in a window-based graphical user interface 01151
Managing * context-frames through GKS 01389
Interactive * objective linear programming system implemented on a microcomputer 01508
Codes and modalities in * resources: a success and a qualification 01793
* resources for processing and storage in short-term working memory 01794
Task-sharing within and between hemispheres: a *-resources approach 01795
Accidents at sea: * causes and impossible consequences 02168
Validation in a knowledge support system: construing and consistency with * experts 02203
Induction of categories: The problem of * equilibria 02360
Tools for management and support of * constraints in a writer's assistant 03251
A * track animator system for motion synchronization 03350
* representation document development (extende abstract) 03518

* inheritance and genericity for the integration of a database management system in an object-oriented approach 03844
Manipulation of embedded context using the * world mechanism 03921
Automatic contour definition on left ventriculograms by image evidence and a * template-based model 04073
General *-objective decision functions and linguistically quantified statements HCI-0110 †
Cognitive layouts of windows and * screens for user interfaces HCI-0122 †
PECAN: program development systems that support * views HCI-0145 †
A user agent for * computer-based message services HCI-0306 †

## MULTIPROCESSOR
A * system for real-time robotic control 02023
* Smalltalk: a case study of a *-based programming environment 03061
Structured message passing on a shared-memory * 03514
Real-time large vocabulary word recognition via diphone spotting and * implementation 03996

## MULTIRULE
Implementation of a *, multistage quality control program in a clinical laboratory computer system 02380

## MULTISOLUTION
A human-computer interactive design program for a * nonlinear problem 01168

## MULTISPEAKER
Recent results on the application of a metric-space search algorithm (AESA) to * data 03997

## MULTISTAGE
Implementation of a multirule, * quality control program in a clinical laboratory computer system 02380

## MULTITASKING
A * switchboard approach to user interface management 01053

The BCC180 * controller part 3: memory management and windowing 01295
Iconic shells for * workstations 02792

## MULTITERMINAL
The selection of a servicing discipline in a * conversational information retrieval system 01233

## MULTIUSER
WYSIWIS revised: early experiences with * interfaces 01158

## MULTIVARIATE
A * solution for cyclic data, applied in modelling locomotor forces 01252
Uncertainty analysis of human EEG spectra: A * information theoretical method for the analysis of brain activity 01270
A perceptual study of the Flury-Riedwyl faces for graphically displaying * data 02126
ProCEED: an expert system for * process control systems design 02935
* data representation and analysis by face pattern using facial expression characteristics HCI-0394 †

## MULTIVIEW
Information systems definition: the * approach ● HCI-0085 †

## MULTIWINDOW
The user interface in a hypertext, * program browser 02072

## MULTIWINDOWING
Textvision: elicitation and acquisition of conceptual knowledge by graphic representation and * 03902

## MUNICIPALITIES
Informatics and *: the Greek approach 01940

## MUSCLE
* models: what is gained and what is lost by varying model complexity 01251
A model of the motor servo: Incorporating nonlinear spindle receptor and *mechanical properties 01273

Model of the neuro-muscular recruitment example of the extensor digitorum communis * in man: I—identification of motoneurons and of muscular fibers 01595
Generation of * tension related to a demand of continuing attention 03710
Analogs of biological tissues for mechanoelectrical transduction: tactile sensors and *-like actuators 04014

**MUSCULAR**
Model of the neuro-* recruitment example of the extensor digitorum communis muscle in man: I—identification of motoneurons and of * fibers 01595

**MUSCULO**
VDUs and *-skeletal problems at the Australian National University. A case study 03709

**MUSCULOSKELETAL**
The impact of automation on * disorders 03437
Subject reports about * discomfort in VDU work as a complex phenomenon 03708

**MUSIC**
An interactive environment for object-oriented * composition and sound synthesis 01131
Systematic evaluation strategies for computer-based * instruction systems 02275
*—a language for typesetting * scores 02622
Computer-* interfaces: a survey HCI-0412 †

**MUSICAL**
The computer as * accompanist 0897

**NAIVE**
UNIX and the * user: children meet a grown-up operating system 0752
A new approach for introducing Prolog to * users 04029
* algorithm design techniques—a case study HCI-0360 †

**NAME**
Dialing a *: alphabetic entry through a telephone keypad 0973

The spatial metaphor for user interfaces: experimental tests of reference by location versus * HCI-0268 †

**NAMING**
The profile * service 01149
* errors and automatic error correction in human-computer interaction 03770

**NATIVE**
Toward * language software for information management HCI-0138 †

**NATURAL**
*-language interfaces 0069
Computational models of * language processing ● 0095
Knowledge representation and * language: extending the expressive power of proposition nodes 0096
Text processing with the START * language system 0100
* languages 0136
Considerations for the development of *-language interfaces to database management systems 0161
Studies in the evaluation of a domain-independent * language query system 0162
An interactive customization program for a * language database query system 0163
The semantics-based * language interface to relational databases 0164
Talking it over: the * language dialog system HAM-ANS 0165
* language processing: a survey 0181
A practical * language interface to databases 0199
Perceptual organization and the representation of * form 0302
Developing a * language interface to complex data 0393
Transportability and generality in a *-language interface system 0394
* computation: selected readings ● 0617
A * language interface for computer-aided design ● 0664
*-language interfaces 0693
*-language interfaces 0720

Synergistic use of direct manipulation and * language 0857
Conversational hypertext: information access through * language dialogues with computers 0867
A * language interface to a multiple databased office information system 01094
Understanding * languages 01172
How to choose * language software 01183
YANLI: a powerful * language front-end tool 01194
Choice of words in the generation process of a * language interface 01206
Impact of a restricted * language interface on ease of learning and productivity 01334
Summarizing * language database responses 01343
Modeling the user in * language systems 01348
* language querying of historical data bases 01354
GRAFLOG: understanding drawings through * language 01396
* language interface to the question-answering system for physicians 01478
Processor for man-machine *-language-like communication 01484
Evaluating user utterances in * language interfaces to databases 01486
The direct memory access paradigm and its applications to * language processing 01489
An industrial chemical hazards database with a * language interface: an application of artificial intelligence 01533
Artificial intelligence and * language systems 01541
A * language discourse model to explain linear programming models and solutions 01671
Providing quality responses with * language interfaces: the null value problem 01848
Interpretation of * language database queries using optimization methods 01861

A priori analysis of * language queries 02006
Querying the French *Yellow Pages*: * language access to the directory 02007
Prospects for knowledge-based customization of * languages query systems 02008
Temporal semantics and * language processing in a decision support system 02038
Shaping user input: a strategy for * language dialogue design 02067
Exploiting convergence to improve * language understanding 02071
* artificial languages: low level processes 02082
Is top-down *? Some experimental results from non-procedural languages 02123
Representing and using metacommunication to control speakers' relationships in *-language dialogue 02136
XTRA: a *-language access system to expert systems 02244
A * language interface processor based on the hierarchical-tree structure model of relation tables 02315
An approach to *-language semantics in logic programming 02342
A database primer on * language 02413
* language interface based on keyword extraction using AWK 02498
Can mathematics explain * intelligence? 02565
* language processing and the language-impaired 02570
* language and computers: a general survey of written text interpretation methods 02671
NLI-ESD: An expert * language interface to a statistical data bank 02712
PHRAN-SPAN: a * language interface for system specifications 02829
A computer training tool using Chinese * language 02948
SIMTALK: Pros and cons of * language for manufacturing simulation 02950

Providing * language assistance in locating objects: a general model for information selection and generation 02951
Logic programmable * language processor of a knowledge-base management system 02965
A knowledge representation for * language understanding 02987
Shifting to a higher gear in a * language system 03169
A temporal logic for reasoning about changing data bases in the context of * language question-answering 03176
The IRUS transportable * language database interface 03177
Supporting * language database update by modeling real world actions 03179
Identifying the knowledge requirements of an expert system's * language processing interface 03259
A processing system for program specifications in a * language 03537
A * language interface for expert systems: system architecture 03551
On one aspect of *-language based knowledge acquisition 03571
A rule-based system for fuzzy * language robot control 03574
A functional model of questions for * language processing systems 03575
User requirements in * language communication with database systems 03615
Some aspects of communication in the * language and user's involvement in software development 03670
* language communication with computers: some problems, perspectives, and new directions 03913
Generating * language responses appropriate to conversational situations—in the case of Japanese 03922
* Language at the Computer § 03947
Relational models in * and artificial vision 03953

Towards a * language interface for computer aided design 04049
Introduction to * language processing ● HCI-0065 †
Readings in * language processing ● HCI-0067 †
What non-programmers know about programming: * language procedure specification HCI-0211 †
HERCULES: database query using * language fragments HCI-0253 †
Using restricted * language for data retrieval: a plan for field evaluation HCI-0255 †
* language query processing in a temporal database HCI-0257 †
A * language information retrieval system with extentions towards fuzzy reasoning HCI-0281 †
Reasoning in * language for designing a data base HCI-0322 †
*-language interface for an instructable robot HCI-0324 †
A * language front end to databases with evaluative feedback HCI-0338 †
Knowledge-intensive * language generation HCI-0343 †
TEAM: an experiment in the design of transportable *-language interfaces HCI-0351 †
* language with discrete speech as a mode for human-to-machine HCI-0355 †
Customers' requirements for * language systems: results of an inquiry HCI-0426 †

**NATURALISTIC**
Justified advice: a semi-* study of advisory strategies 02887

**NATURAL LANGUAGE**
The flexibility of case grammar representations: a porting procedure for * interfaces 02255

**NATURES**
Human aspects of QC circle movement in Japanese manufacturing: * and problems 03450

**NAVAL**
AI development and the Office of * Research 0140

## NAVIGATION
An image processing language with ICON-assisted * HCI-0387 †

## NAVIGATIONAL
The role of menu titles as a * aid in hierarchical menus 0888
* aids and learning styles: structural optimal training for computer users 0970
How to tell people where to go: comparing * aids 02096
Pictures and category labels as * aids for catalog browsing 02877
Logic interface system on * database systems 03818

## NAVY
Transporting the linguistic string project system from a medical to a *domain HCI-0352 †

## NCA
The network control assistant (*), a real-time prototype expert system for network management 02930

## NCUBE
Interactive performance display and debugging using the * real-time graphicssystem 02907

## NEGLECTED
Interface design: a * issue in educational software 0826
Fragile knowledge and * strategies in novice programmers HCI-0177 †

## NEGOTIABLE
A flexible * interactive learning environment 03197

## NEGOTIATED
Negotiating IS: Observations on changes in structure from a * order perspective 03016

## NEGOTIATING
* IS: Observations on changes in structure from a negotiated order perspective 03016

## NEGOTIATIONS
The effects of bargaining orientation and communication medium on *in the bilateral monopoly task: a comparison of decision room and computer conferencing communication media 0809
On two roles decision support systems can play in * 01998

Computer-assisted *: a case history from the law of the sea * and speculation regarding future uses HCI-0443 †

## NEOCORTEX
A model of the * 01164

## NERVOUS
The central * system as a low and high level control system 04007

## NESTED
* structures of control: an intuitive view 01464
Algebras for * relations 01623
Q'Nial: a portable interpreter for the * interactive array language, Nial 02635
* window flow controls with packet fragmentation 04055
A general user interface for creating and displaying tree-structures, hierarchies, decision trees, and * menus HCI-0136 †

## NET
Live-* in education 01381
A self-optimizing, nonsymmetrical neural * for content addressable memory and pattern recognition 02562
Forgetting as a way to improve neural-* behavior 02759
VISION: VHDL induced schematic imaging on *-lists 02830
The PFG environment: parallel programming with petri * semantics 03527

## NETGRAPH
*: an object-oriented graphical toolset for risk assessment 02972

## NETS
An introduction to computing with neural * 0769
Catching knowledge in neural * 01171
Neural * for adaptive filtering and adaptive pattern recognition 01362
Extending Petri * for specifying man-machine dialogues 02183
Are there individual concepts? Proper names and individual concepts in SI-* 02233
Biological aspects of neural * 02311
Petri *: applications and relationships to other models of concurrency § 03973

Human-machine interaction and role/function/action-* 03974
* in office automation 03975

## NETWORK
Neural * models for optical computing ● 0032
Color graphic displays for * planning and design 0260
The NeWS book: an introduction to the */extensible window system ● 0358
Neural * architectures for artificial intelligence ● 0434
Information and the "Aging *" 0525
An integrated system for neural * simulations 0771
Twelve neural * cliches 01186
A self-organizing neural * sharing features of the mammalian visual system 01248
Perception and acceptance of a local area * and electronic mail 01284
Basins of attraction in a perceptron-like neural * 01340
VLSI implementation of a neural * model 01363
The ART of adaptive pattern recognition by a self-organizing neural * 01364
Self-organization in a perceptual * 01366
User-* interfaces 01384
Implementing neural * models on parallel computers 01403
Traffic study on primary rate ISDN user-* interface 01442
* generation using the Prufer code 01536
Neural * model with rhythm-assimilation capacity 01881
Electronic implementation of associative memory based on neural * models 01895
Effects of computer programming experience on * representations of abstract programming concepts 02204
Implementation of the Geac circulation system within the CLANN * 02458
A model for assessing the performance of a local area * employing technical office protocol (TOP) as part of

# KEYWORD INDEX [NETWORKS]

MAP/TOP * in a computer integrated manufacturing (CIM) research project, for the transmission of real time interactive speech 02491

Design and implementation of an interactive optimization system for *design in the motor carrier industry 02528

Pattern storage and associative memory in quasi-neural * 02537

Neural * models of learning and adaptation 02560

A teachable neural * based on an unorthodox neuron 02561

Machine learning using a higher order correlation * 02563

Bifurcation analysis of oscillating * model of pattern recognition in the rabbit olfactory bulb 02725

Influence of noise on the behavior of an autoassociative neural * 02727

Absolutely stable learning of recognition codes by a self-organizing neural * 02728

Neural * refinements and extensions 02732

Application of neural * algorithms and architectures to correlation/tracking and identification 02734

A comparison of neural * and matched filter processing for detecting lines in images 02738

Neurons with hysteresis form a * that can learn without any changes in synaptic connection strengths 02741

A neural * model for the mechanism of pattern information processing 02748

Tensor * theory and its application in computer modeling of the metaorganization of sensorimotor hierarchies of gaze 02753

Digial signal processor accelerators for neural * simulations 02754

Designing a neural * satisfying a given set of constraints 02755

A layered neural * model applied to the auditory system 02763

Sherlock—a system for diagnosing power distribution ring * faults 02916

The * control assistant (NCA), a real-time prototype expert system for * management 02930

The design of a traffic control expert system for long distance *contingencies 02952

Le Menu: changing the user interface on a local area * 03128

A suppport strategy for users of a campus-wide local area * 03157

The integration of the * and relational approaches in a DBMS 03283

A conceptual dependency * approach to multi-task assignments in man-machine (teleoperated) systems 03388

Man-computer interaction research (MACINTER-I): Proceedings of the first * § 03589

On the design of a graphical transition * editor 03830

Experiences with the development of a portable * operating system 03882

A cortical * model for early vision processing 03957

Exploring three possibilities in * design: spontaneous node activity, node plasticity and temporal coding 03962

Dynamical properties of a new type of neural * 03969

A communication system supporting large datagrams on a local area * HCI-0166 †

The complexity of some polynomial * consistency algorithms for constraint satisfaction problems HCI-0361 †

A neural * for visual pattern recognition HCI-0391 †

TEXTNET: a *-based approach to text handling HCI-0401 †

## NETWORKED

User behaviour in computer * groups 0473

Symbiotic software: development and usage issues on stand-alone and *systems 0474

## NETWORKING

The moving target: future trends in * 01282

## NETWORKS

Visual-cognitive neuronal * 0029

Government infostructures: a guide to the * of information resources and technologies at federal, state, and local levels ● 0523

Software for neural * 0770

Conference report: IEEE 1'st Int'l conference on neural * 0772

Neural * primer, part I 01178

Neural * primer, Part II 01181

Neural * primer, part III 01182

Integrating neural * with robots 01187

Neural * primer, part IV 01188

Twelve-product wrap-up: neural * 01189

Neural * primer, Part VII 01192

Neural * and NP-complete optimization problems; a performance study on the graph bisection problem 01339

Computing with structured neural * 01365

PC *: usage and graphics tutorials 01499

* without user observability 01545

Morphologic machines and conservative * 01604

Stochastic dynamics of neural * 01863

Hidden patterns in combined and adaptive knowledge * 02073

Study of combination of belief intevals in lattice-structured * 02223

High performance neural * 02313

Handprinted chinese character recognition via neural * 02529

Neural * for Computing § 02723

Coupled mode theory for neural * 02730

Optical analog of two-dimensional neural * and their application in recognition of radar targets 02733

Lyapunov function for parallel neural * 02736

Motion correspondence and analog * 02739

Memory * with asymmetric bonds 02740

A preliminary analysis of recursively generated * 02749

A simple selectionist learning rule for neural * 02756

VLSI architectures for implementation of neural * 02762

Local area *: sailing from the past to the present and into the future 03152
Generative transition *: a new communication control abstraction 03241
Management of distributed applications in large * 03515
* in office automation § 03637
A graphics interface for interactive simulation of packet-switched * 03869
Structured neural * in nature and in computer science 03950
Parallelism and redundancy in neural * 03952
Image segregation by motion: cortical mechanisms and implementation in neural * 03958
Computational * in early vision: from orientation selection to optical flow 03961
Neural * for motor program generation 03964
DEC * and architectures ● HCI-0003 †
Access to academic * ● HCI-0050 †
Computing with structured connectionist * HCI-0314 †
Learning in parallel *: simulating learning in a probabilistic system HCI-0332 †
Selective * and recognition automata HCI-0390 †
Using low-cost workstations to investigate computer * and distributed systems HCI-0437 †

**NEURAL**
* network models for optical computing ● 0032
* connections, mental computation ● 0229
* network architectures for artificial intelligence ● 0434
* and conceptual interpretation of PDP models 0638
State-dependent factors influencing * plasticity: a partial account of the 0640
An introduction to computing with * nets 0769
Software for * networks 0770
An integrated system for * network simulations 0771
Conference report: IEEE 1'st Int'l conference on * networks 0772
Catching knowledge in * nets 01171
* networks primer, part I 01178
* networks primer, Part II 01181
* networks primer, part III 01182
Twelve * network cliches 01186
Integrating * networks with robots 01187
* networks primer, part IV 01188
Twelve-product wrap-up: * networks 01189
* networks primer, Part VII 01192
A self-organizing * network sharing features of the mammalian visual system 01248
On the identification of * responses 01260
Interpolation coding: A representation for numbers in * models 01271
* networks and NP-complete optimization problems; a performance study on the graph bisection problem 01339
Basins of attraction in a perceptron-like * network 01340
* nets for adaptive filtering and adaptive pattern recognition 01362
VLSI implementation of a * network model 01363
The ART of adaptive pattern recognition by a self-organizing * network 01364
Computing with structured * networks 01365
* computing: ideas from the brain 01379
Implementing * network models on parallel computers 01403
Kinetic theory of "hot" * systems 01613
Stochastic dynamics of * networks 01863
* network model with rhythm-assimilation capacity 01881
Electronic implementation of associative memory based on * network models 01895
Arithmetic codes resembling * encoding 02021
Dynamics and architecture for * computation 02270
Biological aspects of * nets 02311
High performance * networks 02313
Handprinted chinese character recognition via * networks 02529
Pattern storage and associative memory in quasi-* network 02537
* network models of learning and adaptation 02560
A teachable * network based on an unorthodox neuron 02561
A self-optimizing, nonsymmetrical * net for content addressable memory and pattern recognition 02562
* Networks for Computing § 02723
Influence of noise on the behavior of an autoassociative * network 02727
Absolutely stable learning of recognition codes by a self-organizing *network 02728
Coupled mode theory for * networks 02730
* network refinements and extensions 02732
Optical analog of two-dimensional * networks and their application in recognition of radar targets 02733
Application of * network algorithms and architectures to correlation/tracking and identification 02734
Lyapunov function for parallel * networks 02736
A comparison of * network and matched filter processing for detecting lines in images 02738
Nonlinear dynamics of artificial * systems 02747
A * network model for the mechanism of pattern information processing 02748
A machine for * computation of acoustical patterns with application to real time speech recognition 02751
Digital signal processor accelerators for * network simulations 02754
Designing a * network satisfying a given set of constraints 02755
A simple selectionist learning rule for * networks 02756
Forgetting as a way to improve *-net behavior 02759
Firing response of a * model with threshold modulation and * dynamics 02761

VLSI architectures for implementation of * networks 02762
A layered * network model applied to the auditory system 02763
* computers § 03949
Structured * networks in nature and in computer science 03950
Conventional fault-tolerance and * computers 03951
Parallelism and redundancy in * networks 03952
Why cortices? * computation in the vertebrate visual system 03956
Image segregation by motion: cortical mechanisms and implementation in *networks 03958
* computers in vision: processing of high dimensional data 03960
* networks for motor program generation 03964
Limited interconnectivity in synthetic * systems 03968
Dynamical properties of a new type of * network 03969
A * model of human prehension 04072
A * network for visual pattern recognition HCI-0391 †

## NEURO

Model of the *-muscular recruitment example of the extensor digitorum communis muscle in man: I—identification of moto*ns and of muscular fibers 01595
From schema theory to computational (*-)linguistics HCI-0345 †

## NEUROCOMPUTERS

Tensor geometry: a language of brains & *. Generalized coordinates in neuroscience & robotics 03966

## NEUROCOMPUTING

*—neurons as microcomputers 01691
* 01836

## NEURON

Statistical inference on spontaneous *al discharge patterns. I. Single * 01247
A teachable neural network based on an unorthodox * 02561

A drive-reinforcement model of single * function: An alternative to the Hebbian *al model 02743
A comparison of algorithms for *-like cells 02752

## NEURONAL

Visual-cognitive * networks 0029
Statistical inference on spontaneous * discharge patterns. I. Single neuron 01247
Diffusion approximation of the * model with synaptic reversal potentials 01254
Characteristics of * systems in the visual cortex 01255
A drive-reinforcement model of single neuron function: An alternative to the Hebbian * model 02743
An iterative and interactive simulation method to reconstruct unknown inputs contributing to known outputs of * systems 04018

## NEURONS

* with hysteresis form a network that can learn without any changes in synaptic connection strengths 02741

## NEUROPHILOSOPHY

*: toward a unified science of the mind-brain ● 0219

## NEUROPHYSIOLOGICAL

User-interface design for a clinical * intensive monitoring system 0881

## NEUROSCIENCE

Tensor geometry: a language of brains & neurocomputers. Generalized coordinates in * & robotics 03966

## NEVEZH

Recognition of speaker-dependent continuous speech with Keal-* 04002

## NEWS

The * book: an introduction to the network/extensible window system ● 0358
Conceptual information extraction form financial * 03489

## NEWSPAPERS

Psychological aspects on blind peoples's reading of radio-distributed daily * 03700

## NEXUS

Artifact as theory-*: hermeneutics meets theory-based design 0798

## NIAL

Q'*: a portable interpreter for the nested interactive array language, * 02635

## NICK

Project *: meetings augmentation and analysis HCI-0156 †

## NLI

*-ESD: An expert natural language interface to a statistical data bank 02712
IR-* II: applying man-machine interaction and artificial intelligence conceptsto information retrieval 03070

## NLP

Perspectives in artificial intelligence vol. 2: machine translation, *, databases and computer-aided instruction ● 0198

## NODES

Knowledge representation and natural language: extending the expressive power of proposition * 0096

## NOISE

No effect of * on vigilance performance? 01724
Effect of pixel height, display height, and vertical resolution on the detection of a simple vertical line signal in visual * 01753
Generalization and * 02155
The effect of varying voice and * parameters on the perception of voicing in Dutch two-obstruent sequences 02653
The measurement of the signal-to-* ratio (SNR) in continuous speech 02654
Influence of * on the behavior of an autoassociative neural network 02727

## NOISY

Automated concept acquisition in * environments 01841
Analysis of the performance of a genetic algorithm-based system for message classification in * environments 02156

## NONDESTRUCTIVE
Signal processing and pattern recognition in * evaluation of materials § 04019

## NONEXPERT
Formatting space-related displays to optimize expert and * user performance 0927

## NONFACTORY
Occupational accidents to the hand: A comparison of factory and *injuries 03438

## NONINTEGRATION
Display formatting in information integration and * tasks 01750

## NONLINEAR
Limited freedom: linear reflections on * texts 0121
A human-computer interactive design program for a multisolution *problem 01168
A model of the motor servo: Incorporating * spindle receptor and muscle mechanical properties 01273
* dynamics of pattern formation and pattern recognition in the rabbit olfactory bulb 02558
Linearization of the dynamic transfer response of time invariant *systems—in connection with the parallel information processing in living organisms 02665
* dynamics of artificial neural systems 02747
* discriminant functions and associative memories 02757
Alkahest III: automatic analysis of periodic weakly * ODEs 03087
Interactive fuzzy decision-making for multi-objective * programming using reference membership intervals HCI-0295 †

## NONMONOTONIC
Motivation analysis, abductive unification, and * equality 01211

## NONPROGRAMMER
Programmer-* differences in specifying procedures to people and computers 02405
Programmer/* differences in specifying procedures to people and computers HCI-0174 †

## NONSYMMETRICAL
A self-optimizing, * neural net for content addressable memory and pattern recognition 02562

## NORDIC
Intelligent interfaces to * data bases 0738

## NORMAL
Comparison of color sensation in dichoptic and in * vision 01272
Non-first * form universal relations: an application to information retrieval systems 02039

## NORMALIZATION
Vowel * by frequency warped spectral matching 02649
Perceptual * of the vowels of a man and a child in various contexts 02656

## NORMATIVE
A critical view of factors affecting successful application of * and socio-technical systems development approaches 01914

## NORMS
Motivation * of knowledge engineers compared to those of software engineers 02349

## NORWAY
Video display terminals and birth defects. A study of pregnancy outcomes of employees of the Postal-Giro Center, Oslo, * 03691

## NOSE
Gas sensors: towards an artificial * 04015

## NOTEBOOK
An online interface within a hypertext system: project Jefferson's electronic * 02524

## NOTECARDS
* in a nutshell 0810
Reflections on *: seven issues for the next generation of hypermedia systems HCI-0293 †

## NOTION
A new * of encapsulation 01104

## NOTRE
The evolution of microcomputer laboratory services at the University of *Dame 03159

## NOVICE
A graded interface for */expert interaction 0270
What stories should we tell * PROLOG programmers? 0421
Modelling * programmer behaviour 0744
Modelling * programmer behaviour 0751
A cognitive model of database querying: a tool for * instruction 0905
A user interface for multiple-process, turnkey systems targeted for the *user 0911
Preferences for power in expert systems by * users 0971
The application of human factors to the needs of the * computer user 02079
Cognitive processing differences between * and expert computer programmers 02145
Fragile knowledge and neglected strategies in * programmers HCI-0177 †
Analyzing the high frequency bugs in * programs HCI-0178 †
A * user's interface to information retrieval systems HCI-0219 †
The relationship of problem-solving ability and course performance among *programmers HCI-0435 †

## NOVICES
Graphical vs. textual representation: an empirical study of *' program comprehension 0566
Practices of * and experts in critical inquiry 0585
* on the computer: a review of the literature 02129
Analogy and other sources of difficulty in *' very first text-editing 02148
KITTEN: knowledge initiation and transfer tools for experts and * 02159
Information-seeking strategies of * using a full-text electronic encyclopedia 02452
Fatal error in pass zero: how not to confuse * HCI-0164 †

KEYWORD INDEX [OBJECT]

**NP**
Neural networks and *-complete optimization problems; a performance study on the graph bisection problem 01339

**NTT**
Speech analysis and synthesis methods developed at ECL in *-From LPC to LSP- 02646

**NUCLEUS**
The software structure of extended * based on BTRON specification 03494

**NULL**
Providing quality responses with natural language interfaces: the * value problem 01848

**NULLING**
Vertical disparity * in random-dot stereograms 01256

**NUMBERING**
The man-machine interface aspect of an automatic classification *system in a computerized library system 02316

**NUMERALS**
A high accuracy algorithm for recognition of handwritten * 02532

**NUMERIC**
A multi-purpose system for alpha-* input to computers via a reduced keyboard 02118
Datastream: * data—all you can use at a fixed price 02525

**NUMERICAL**
Problem solving performance and display preference for information displays depicting * functions 0978
Automation, work organization and skills: the case of * control 01234
Interactive color graphical postprocessing as a unifying influence in *analysis research 01684
Building and understanding adaptive systems: a statistical/* approach to factory automation and brain research 01890
GPROC—an integrated system for the processing of * scientific data 02631

User services consulting supportr tools at the NASA * aerodynamic simula 03161

**NUTSHELL**
Notecards in a * 0810

**NYNEX**
* intelligent systems group 0814

**OA**
*: bridging the language gap 01376
The real cost of * 01647

**OAKDEC**
*, a program for studying the effects on users of a procedural expert system for database searching 02003

**OBJECT**
Using an *-oriented programming language to create audience-driven hypermedia environments 0101
*-oriented graphics 0234
Design and implementation of an *-oriented user interface management system 0412
*-oriented concepts, databases, and applications • 0475
Directions in *-oriented research 0477
* oriented programming in Concurrent Prolog 0677
Research directions in *-oriented programming • 0690
A substrate for *-oriented interface design 0691
Data model issues for *-oriented applications 0712
Some strategies of reuse in an *-oriented programming environment 0820
An *-oriented user interface management system 01055
An *-oriented construction and tool kit for human-computer communication 01061
The multimedia * presentation manager of MINOS: a symmetric approach 01083
An *-oriented approach to multimedia databases 01084
Use of *-oriented programming in a time series analysis system 01112
Teaching *-oriented programming with the KEE system 01113
An *-oriented framework for interactive data graphics 01115

Common LISP * system specification X3J13 Document 88-002R 01121
An interactive environment for *-oriented music composition and sound synthesis 01131
An *-oriented framework of pattern recognition systems 01133
Data model issues for *-oriented applications 01157
Tailoring * descriptions to a user's level of expertise 01352
A user-interface toolkit in *-oriented PostScript 01391
A first order theory of common sense * positioning 01563
Edmas: an *-oriented, locally distributed mail system 01857
An *-oriented approach to the design of a mail system for a heterogeneous environment 01944
An input/output primitive for *-oriented systems 01969
Support for tentative design: incorporating the screen image, as a graphical *, into PROLOG 02116
Hierarchical, modular discrete-event modelling in an *-oriented environment 02588
Direct manipulation of an * store 02608
CAD Data management using *-oriented paradigms 02958
NetGraph: an *-oriented graphical toolset for risk assessment 02972
An *-oriented expert system for coal-fired MHD power plant fault monitoringand diagnosis 02973
* oriented rapid prototyping with G2 02984
*-oriented programming systems, languages and applications § 03030
Mach and Matchmaker: kernel and language support for *-oriented distributed systems 03031
Impulse-86: a substrate for *-oriented interface design 03032
Experience with Flamingo: a distributed, *-oriented user interface system 03033
*-oriented programming systems, languages and applications § 03035

**837**

## [OBJECTIVE]

Adapting optical-flow to measure * motion in reflectance and X-ray image sequences 03334
A programming environment supporting reuse of *-oriented software 03509
Language level persistence for an *-oriented application programming platform 03522
*-oriented signal processing systems 03573
The construction of user interfaces and the * paradigm 03791
ECOOP '88 (European Conference on *-Oriented Programming) § 03793
Advances in *-oriented database systems § 03841
A distributed * server 03842
A model for an * management system for software engineering environments 03843
Multiple inheritance and genericity for the integration of a database management system in an *-oriented approach 03844
ROSE: An *-oriented database system for interactive computer graphics applications 03845
On the acquisition of * concepts from sensory data 03959
Real-time * measurement and classification § 03985
* lens: a "spreadsheet" for cooperative work HCI-0206 †
Design and performance considerations for an optical disk-based, multimedia * server HCI-0265 †

## OBJECTIVE
Interactive multiple * linear programming system implemented on a microcomputer 01508
Effects of computerization on job demands and stress: the correspondence of subjective and * data 03622
A design environment for computer-aided control system design via multi-* optimisation 03835
General multiple-* decision functions and linguistically quantified statements HCI-0110 †
Interactive fuzzy decision-making for multi-* nonlinear programming using reference membership intervals HCI-0295 †

## OBJECTS
An information system based on distributed * 01116
A user interface toolkit based on graphical * and constraints 01125
Diagramming * 01177
Graphic * 01190
New methods for matching 3-D * with single perspective views 01844
Features and * in visual processing 02577
Providing natural language assistance in locating *: a general model for information selection and generation 02951
Editing graphical * using procedural representations 04056
Recognizing unexpected *: a proposed approach HCI-0389 †

## OBLOG
*-2: A hybrid knowledge representation system for defeasible reasoning 02778

## OBSERVABILITY
Networks without user * 01545
Generic surface interpretation: * model 03563

## OBSOLETE
Are writers * in the computer industry? 0109

## OBSTACLE
Fuzzy control of a mobile robot for * avoidance 02025

## OBSTRUENT
The effect of varying voice and noise parameters on the perception of voicing in Dutch two-* sequences 02653

## OCCASIONAL
A method framework for the statistical package SPSS/PC+ to support *users 01202
Electronic publishing: The predicament of * users in the editorial proc 02446

## OCCUPATIONAL
Changes in electromyographic activity associated with * stress and poor performance in the workplace 01734
Effects of automation on * safety & health 03435
* accidents to the hand: A comparison of factory and nonfactory injuries 03438
An empirical study of * stress, attitudes and health among information systems personnel HCI-0451 †

## OCULAR
Visual impairment and subjective * symptomatology in VDT operators 03734

## ODES
Alkahest III: automatic analysis of periodic weakly nonlinear * 03087

## ODYSSEY
From database to hypertext via electronic publishing: an information * 0122

## OFFICE
Speech filing—An * system for principals 0037
Human factors challenges in creating a principal support * system—The speh filing system approach 0038
Issues and approaches to appraising technological change in the *: A consequentialist perspective 0043
The changing workplace: A guide to managing the people, organizational, and regulatory aspects of * technology (book excerpt) 0044
Human factors testing in the design of Xerox's 8010 "Star" * workstation 0090
AI development and the * of Naval Research 0140
Usability assessment for the *: methodological choices and their implications 0318
* information systems and computer science (Reprint) 0373
User interfaces for * systems 0756
The design requirements of * systems 0757
How faithfully should the electronic * simulate real one? 0958

# KEYWORD INDEX

[ONLINE]

Some design guidelines for an information center to support * information systems 01093
A natural language interface to a multiple databased * information system 01094
Understanding the *: A social-analytic perspective 01156
*-by-example: an integrated * system and database manager 01159
* automation—can it be justified? 01383
Employing usability engineering in the development of * products 01413
Presentation of a description language for * tasks 01434
Successful implementation of an * system 01438
Supporting end users in the * 01444
Power and credibility in * automation 01657
Your * is where you are 01703
Education and training in * technology 02330
Viewdata in the *—user-friendly page identification 02334
A model for assessing the performance of a local area network employing technical * protocol (TOP) as part of MAP/TOP network in a computer integrated manufacturing (CIM) research project, for the transmission of real time interactive speech 02491
* Information Systems § 03036
OTM: specifying * tasks 03039
Interactive retrieval * documents 03047
Design issues of an intelligent workstation for the * 03165
Advanced * systems: An empirical look at use and satisfaction 03172
Understanding the nature of the * for the design of third wave *systems 03248
Usability engineering in * product development 03258
* Systems § 03354
Trends in * modeling 03355
Architectural implications of * systems 03356
Human factors in * systems 03357

Organizational implications of * systems: toward a critical social action perspective 03358
Security of * systems 03359
Implementation of * systems 03360
POEM: An * system for international use 03457
Networks in * automation § 03637
The * between humanization and control 03651
Environmental stressors and perceived health symptoms among * workers 03680
Lighting the electronic * 03717
Work at video display terminals among * employees: visual ergonomics and lighting 03718
* automation and work organization: making use of the scope of choice 03746
* automation as an opportunity for an organizational check-up 03749
Development of mental models of an * system: a field study on an introductory course 03903
Nets in * automation 03975
A formal specification for a user interface for * automation 04053
* automation: a social and organizational perspective ● HCI-0048 †
A generator of direct manipulation * systems HCI-0250 †
Electronic calendars in the *: an assessment of user needs and current technology HCI-0287 †
* systems HCI-0291 †
The dimensions of accessibility to online information: implications for implementing * information systems HCI-0304 †
Strategies for encouraging successful adoption of * communication systems HCI-0307 †

## OFFICERS
No members, no *, no dues: A ten year history of the software psychology society 0943

## OFFICES
Methodological problems of field-research on workplaces in * 0249
The effect of VDU on the interior design of * 03714

## OIL
* and water? 01654
Process design of * and gas production facilities using expert systems 02933

## OLFACTORY
Simulation of chaotic EEG patterns with a dynamic model of the * system 01263
Nonlinear dynamics of pattern formation and pattern recognition in the rabbit * bulb 02558
Bifurcation analysis of oscillating network model of pattern recognition in the rabbit * bulb 02725
A dynamic model of * discrimination 02737

## OLYMPIC
The 1984 * Message System: a test of behavioral principles of system design HCI-0125 †

## ONLINE
Hypertext: a way of incorporating user feedback into * documentation 0102
* information, hypermedia, and the idea of literacy 0112
* information: what do people want? What do people need? 0113
Textual intervention, collaboration, and the * environment 0126
The evaluation of * help systems: a conceptual model 0129
Escher effects in * text 0130
The economics of * ● 0194
DOMAIN/DELPHI: retrieving documents * 0906
* use and end-users in media and advertising: an overview 01216
* searching: a five star review of research 01314
The linear file—restrictions on * information use: a searcher's perspective 01634
Evaluating the usability of the Glasgow * 01808
* text retrieval via browsing 01999
A comparative survey of the friendliness of * 'help' in interactive information 02010
* searching using speech as a man/machine interface 02013

User interaction with the authority structure of the * catalog: results of a survey 02049
Improved browsable displays for * subject access 02051
The user's mental model of an information retrieval system: an experiment on a prototype * catalog 02099
* library catalog systems: an analysis of user errors 02128
Comparison of manual and * searches of chemical abstracts 02265
End-user searching of CAS *. Results of a cooperative experiment between Imperial Chemical Industries and Chemical Abstracts Services 02269
Subject searching behaviour at the library catalogue and at the shelves: implications for * interactive catalogues 02302
Voice input/output interface for * searching: some design and human factor onsiderations 02335
The computer as mask: a problem of inadequate human interaction examined with particular regard to * public access catalogues 02337
An investigation of * searcher traits and their relationship to search outcomes 02447
The user at the * catalogue 02462
Effects of the adoption of an integrated * system on a technical services department 02463
How good an * searcher are you? Twenty questions about BIOSIS previews 02521
An * interface within a hypertext system: project Jefferson's electronic notebook 02524
OST— a training package for end-users of * systems 02568
* help systems: design and implementation issues (panel) 02902
A knowledge-based approach to * document retrieval system design 03027
Videotex and * services: competition or collateral 03557

Integrating CD-ROM with printed and * services: a silver platter end-user perspective 03558
* library catalogues as information retrieval systems: what can we learn from research? 04040
Assessing the usability of user interfaces: guidance and * help features 04065
* help systems: design and implementation ● HCI-0009 †
* information retrieval: concepts, principles, and techniques ● HCI-0046 †
* communities ● HCI-0051 †
Designing * information HCI-0152 †
Technical writers as computer scientists: the challenges of * documentation HCI-0153 †
Creating a style for * help HCI-0154 †
Observations of end-user * searching behavior over eleven years HCI-0235 †
An intelligent interface for * interaction HCI-0264 †
Testing bibliographic displays for * catalogs HCI-0285 †
The dimensions of accessibility to * information: implications for implementing office information systems HCI-0304 †

## ONTOLOGICAL
* analysis of document usage: an exploratory study 03467

## ONTOLOGY
Temporal * and temporal reference 01347
Creating the domain of discourse: * and inventory 02158

## OPAC
A comparative study of subject searching in an * among branch libraries of a university library system 02050

## OPERATE
Why users must co-* internationally on standardization 01457

## OPERATED
Exploratory evaluation of a planar foot-* cursor-positioning device 02858

## OPERATING
UNIX and the naive user: children meet a grown-up * system 0752
Using representation clauses as an * system interface 0764
A UNIX clone with source code for * systems courses 01095
Advanced interactive executive (AIX) * system overview 01815
Structure of a directory space: a case study with a UNIX * system 02138
Unix: tomorrow's * system? 02555
Project source file management under the UNIX * system 03168
Illumination requirements for * a space remote manipulator 03392
Procedures for participation in planning, developing and * information systems 03659
Using data flow specifications and interactive editing in the * system user interface 03800
Experiences with the development of a portable network * system 03882
Graph-theoretical tools and their use in a practical distributed *system design case 03886
A methodology for designing distributed, fault-tolerant, and reactive real-time * systems 04071
An * systems vade mecum: 2nd edition ● HCI-0025 †
The design of the UNIX * system ● HCI-0026 †
* system design. Vol. 1: the XINU approach (PC edition) ● HCI-0029 †

## OPERATIONAL
The quantification of * suitability 01359
Automatic information processing activities and * decision making: a case study of consequence 01950
Intentional and * aspects of decision behaviour and their modelling 03666

## OPERATIONS
Implementation issues for * research software 01537
A workstation assessor for crew *-WOSTAS 02093
An * advisor for an on-line computer banking system with graphics interface 02983

# KEYWORD INDEX [OPTIMISING]

Evaluating the meaningfulness of icon sets to represent command * 03277

**OPERATIVE**

A logical model of co-* processes in cerebral dynamics 01615

**OPERATOR**

Posture and VDU * satisfaction 0988

A smalltalk implementation of an intelligent *'s associate 01132

Smart help for * performance 01528

Usage of linguistic variable concept for human * modelling 01694

A psychophysiological assessment of * workload during simulated flight missions 01735

* effort and the measurement of heart-rate variability 01736

Effects of functionally or topographically presented process schemes on * performance 01749

* performance as a function of type of display: conventional versus perspective 01769

Effects of visual display and motion system delays on * performance and ueasiness in a driving simulator 01772

Aiding the * during novel fault diagnosis 01858

Modeling of task-dependent characteristics of human * dynamics during pursuit manual tracking 01859

A discrete control model of * function: A methodology for information dislay design 01874

A rule-based model for the human * in a time-constrained competing-task environment 01877

* assistant systems 02165

Automation—implications for knowledge retention as a function of *control responsibility 03207

Robot vs. human * for speed, precision and other aspects 03403

Some remarks on a measure of computer * workload: changes in pupil reflex 03626

Determinants of the VDU *'s well-being 03679

The effect of VDT symbol characteristics on * performance and visual comfort 03728

* work load: when is enough enough? HCI-0222 †

**OPERATORS**

Multimodal detection and recognition performance of sonar * 01709

Adapting expert systems to simulation training of process * 02056

How can computer-based visual displays aid * 02162

Modelling * in accident conditions: advances and perspectives on a cognitive model 02169

The mission * planning assistant 02674

Acting-out and burn-out behaviours of * monitoring automated systems 03440

Analysis of the competence of * confronting new technologies: some methodological problems and some results 03594

Task-load and endocrinological risk for pregnancy in women VDU * 03692

A Rosacea-like skin rash in VDU-* 03695

Sensitivity to light and visual strain in VDT *: basic data for the design of work stations 03732

Visual impairment and subjective ocular symptomatology in VDT * 03734

Vision monitoring of VDU * and relaxation of visual stress by means of laser speckle system 03738

Refraction in VDU *—a comparison with other professions 03740

Workers education and user participation in the development of protective policies for VDT * 03752

Mental fatigue of VDU * induced by monotonous and various tasks 03760

Process control software design: how will the * work? 03764

**OPPONENT**

An experimental comparison of RGB, YIQ, LAB, HSV, and * color models HCI-0381 †

**OPS5**

A dietary recommendation expert system using * 03498

**OPTIC**

Facts on * flow 01257

Determining the instantaneous axis of translation from * flow generated by rbitrary sensot motion 03332

**OPTICAL**

Neural network models for * computing ● 0032

MINID—a BASIC program to assist in the * identification of minerals in thin section 01505

* systems that imitate human memory 01576

* analog of two-dimensional neural networks and their application in recognition of radar targets 02733

* flow 03330

Adapting *-flow to measure object motion in reflectance and X-ray image sequences 03334

* information systems '86 § 03556

Work distance and * correction 03736

Computational networks in early vision: from orientation selection to *flow 03961

Practical applications of * disk image systems in document management 04041

Design and performance considerations for an * disk-based, multimedia object server HCI-0265 †

**OPTIMISATION**

Cognitive * of Videotex dialogues: a formal—empirical approach 0320

A design environment for computer-aided control system design via multi-objective * 03835

**OPTIMISING**

Training for * transfer between word processors HCI-0447 †

## OPTIMIZATION
Collective computation, content-addressable memory, and * problems 0004
Designing the "cockpit": the application of a human-centered design philosophy to make * systems accessible 01016
Neural networks and NP-complete * problems; a performance study on the graph bisection problem 01339
Interpretation of natural language database queries using * methods 01861
The emergence of Zipf's law: Spontaneous encoding * by users of a command language 01875
* of string length for spoken digit input with error correction 02185
Design and implementation of an interactive * system for network design in the motor carrier industry 02528
Some cognitive aspects of interface design in a two-variable * task HCI-0111 †

## OPTIMIZE
Formatting space-related displays to * expert and nonexpert user performance 0927

## OPTIMIZED
Improving the VDU workplace by introducing a physiologically *bright-background screen with dark characters: advantages and requirements 03721

## OPTIMIZING
The design of an interactive compiler for * microprograms 01078
* the structure of database menu indexes: a decision model of menu search 01716
* the touch tablet: the effects of control display gain and method of cursor control 01730
A self-*, nonsymmetrical neural net for content addressable memory and pattern recognition 02562
* the usability of computer-generated displays 03278

## OPTIMUM
Designing * CRT text blinking video image presentation 0795
* display arrangements for presenting visual reminders 03237
* stresses and strains represented by examples from shop practice 03441

## ORAL
Experimentation in the specification of an * dialogue 04005

## ORDERING
The effect of number * and orientation on marking speed and errors for mark-sensed labels 01717
Library—An electronic * system 01991

## ORDINALS
* and the hemispheres of the brain 01620

## ORGANIC
"Structure—reaction type" paradigm in the conventional methods of describing * reactions and the concept of imaginary transitions structures overcoming this paradigm 02268

## ORGANISATIONS
The supplier's role in the design of products for * 01412

## ORGANISMS
Linearization of the dynamic transfer response of time invariant nonlinear systems—in connection with the parallel information processing in living * 02665

## ORGANIZATION
Figure-ground * affects the early visual processing 0021
The psychology of work and *: current trends and issues ● 0239
Automation in public libraries: effects on the *, quality of working life, and quality of services 0246
The sequential * of spoken word recognition 0291
Perceptual * and the representation of natural form 0302
The variable impact of computer technologies on the * of work activities 0388

Item selection from menus: the influence of menu *, query interpretation, and programming experience on selection strategies 01011
Automation, work * and skills: the case of numerical control 01234
Self-* in a perceptual network 01366
Successful use of CADCAM—a combination of technology, *, and people 01569
The way you look determines what you see (or self-* in management and society) 01614
Cybernetics and * theory: a critical review 01617
Menu * and user expertise in information search tasks 01761
Perceptual * and curve partitioning 01838
Using perceptual * to extract 3-D structures 01842
GISMO: A visual problem-structuring and knowledge-* tool 01871
* and learnability in computer languages 02085
A theory of information structure. II. A theory of perceptual * 02362
Perception of * in a random stimulus 02706
A case study of CSCW in a dispersed * 02866
Instilling professionalism in a software development * 03019
The impact of advanced manufacturing in work *: The Portugese case of the plastic moulding industry 03374
Differential * impacts of the transition from stand-alone to integrated flexible production 03380
Computerized manufacturing technology and work * effects on labor relations and worker satisfaction 03443
Job * and allocation of functions between man and computer: I analysis and assessment 03628
Job * and allocation of functions between man and computer: II. job * 03629

# KEYWORD INDEX

[OVERVIEW]

The importance of work * by systems design 03648
Office automation and work *: making use of the scope of choice 03746
Corporate culture, technical documentation, and * diagnosis HCI-0151 †
Perception of * in a random stimulus HCI-0364 †

**ORGANIZATIONALLY**
Towards a framework for identifying *-compatible AMT 03372

**ORGANIZER**
A study of an advance * as a technique for teaching computer programming concepts 01042

**ORGNIZATIONAL**
Information technologies for the 1990's: an * impact perspective 01336

**ORGPLAN**
* an information-decisive aid system to resolving organizing problems 01573

**ORIENTATION**
The effects of bargaining * and communication medium on negotiations in the bilateral monopoly task: a comparison of decision room and computer conferencing communication media 0809
Bat brushes: on the uses of six position and * parameters in a paint program 0846
Contingent aftereffects and isoluminance: psychophysical evidence for separation of color, *, and motion 01463
The effect of number ordering and * on marking speed and errors for mark-sensed labels 01717
User * for the electronic encyclopedia 02605
Environment-centered and viewer-centered perception of surface * 02705
Visualization of process information in improving work * 03619
Computational networks in early vision: from * selection to optical flow 03961

Environment-centered and viewer-centered perception of surface * HCI-0392 †

**ORIENTATIONAL**
Quantitative determination of * and directional components in the response of visual cortical cells to moving stimuli 01268

**ORIENTEERING**
Travel around a learning support environment: rambling, * or touring? 02900

**ORIENTING**
The effects of * objectives and review on learning from interactive video 02287
The effects of *, processing, and practicing activities on learning from interactive video 02289

**ORTHODOX**
* dialectical interfaces 01423

**ORTHOPEDIC**
Automated design and analysis system for design of custom * implants 02931

**OSI**
An implementation of * protocols in SM-4 host computers 03638

**OSLO**
Video display terminals and birth defects. A study of pregnancy outcomes of employees of the Postal-Giro Center, *, Norway 03691

**OST**
*— a training package for end-users of online systems 02568

**OTM**
*: specifying office tasks 03039

**OUTCOME**
Measuring implementation *: beyond success and failure 01933
Pregnancy * and VDU-work in a cohort of insurance clerks 03690

**OUTCOMES**
An investigation of online searcher traits and their relationship to search * 02447
Video display terminals and birth defects. A study of pregnancy * of employees of the Postal-Giro Center, Oslo, Norway 03691

**OUTPUT**
Screen input/* programming techniques using Turbo Pascal • 0714
A case example of human factors in product definition: needs finding for a voice * workstation for the blind 0819
An input-* model of interactive systems 0926
An input/* primitive for object-oriented systems 01969
Voice input/* interface for online searching: some design and human factor onsiderations 02335
A parallel formant synthesizer for machine voice * HCI-0396 †

**OUTPUTS**
An iterative and interactive simulation method to reconstruct unknown inputs contributing to known * of neuronal systems 04018

**OUTRANKING**
An interactive * system for multi-attribute decision making 01539

**OVERCOME**
Using hypertext to * the knowledge base development bottleneck: a case study 02914

**OVERCOMING**
"Structure—reaction type" paradigm in the conventional methods of describing organic reactions and the concept of imaginary transitions structures * this paradigm 02268
* conceptual difficulties in physical science through computer-based Socratic dialogs 03877

**OVERLAPPING**
A comparison of tiled and * windows 0904
Combining * information 02477

**OVERLOAD**
Data entry task on VDU: underload or * 03761

**OVERVIEW**
Vision, brain, and cooperative computation: an * 0015
An * of system design for human interaction 0646

843

An * of T³-PBE 0784
Characteristics and functions of software environments: an * 01145
Online use and end-users in media and advertising: an * 01216
The programmer's apprentices: a research * 01368
OS/2 query manager * and prompted interface 01809
Advanced interactive executive (AIX) operating system * 01815
Readability formulas: An * 02301
An informal * of CUINFO (Cornell's computer-based bulletin board) 02783
An * of the C toolkit 03109
Reasoning about knowledge: an * 03167
The star user interface: an * 03171
* of research issues in robot safety 03417
Knowledge representation techniques in artificial intelligence: an * 03900
An * of local environment sensing in robotics applications 04012
Compact disc-interactive: a designer's * ● HCI-0078 †
An * of research and co-operation in advanced information technology HCI-0442 †

## OVERWHELMING

A powerful solution meets an * problem 02053

## OWNED

Sharing in a privately * workstation environment 04076

## OWNERS

The computer imperative among * of home computers: explanation by social factors HCI-0217 †

## PACED

Reading self-* moving text on a computer display 01777
The influence of personality on self-* instruction 02291

## PACKAGE

A method framework for the statistical * SPSS/PC+ to support occasional users 01202
The design of a user friendly engineering economy analysis * for a microcomputer 01507

The design of a user friendly interactive personal computer * for quality control charts, project management, and linear programming applications 01521
OST— a training * for end-users of online systems 02568
The design of a terminal independent * 02619
Tree doctor, a software * for graphical manipulation and animation of tree structures 03901

## PACKAGERS

Videotex information *: a field study aimed at tomorrow's videotex authoring interface 0962

## PACKAGES

A methodology for interactive evaluation of user reactions to software *:an empirical analysis of system performance, interaction, and run time 02080
Produciton and inventory management software * related to user reactions 02567

## PACKAGING

Enhancing search results by editing, analysis and * 02035

## PACKET

A graphics interface for interactive simulation of *-switched networks 03869
Nested window flow controls with * fragmentation 04055

## PACS

User interfaces for CD'ROM * 02466

## PAGE

From arcane ASCII to the printed * - computer basics 01148
The workstation: the interpress * and document description language 01356
Reading from microfiche, a VDT, and the printed *: subjective fatigue and performance 01712
Viewdata in the office—user-friendly * identification 02334
Interface abstractions for an *naplps* * creation system 03863

## PAGES

Querying the French *Yellow* *: natural language access to the directory 02007

## PAGINATION

Back to basics: Simple but high-quality text * systems 0271

## PAINLESS

* panes for Smalltalk windows 01118

## PAIRED

A comparison of a microcomputer progressive state drill and flashcards for learning * associates 02295

## PANACEA

Why desktop publishing is not a * 03131

## PANELS

Human factors and flat * challenge the CRT 01982

## PANES

Painless * for Smalltalk windows 01118

## PANTAPM

*: an integrated software development environment 03796

## PAPA

Organizational humanity and architecture: Duality and complementarity of *-logic and mama-logic in managerial conceptualizations of change 01609

## PARADIGM

Introduction: a new * for writing with and for the computer 0099
Interactive learning: a multiexpert * for acquiring new knowledge 0776
Planar maps: an interaction * for graphic design 0873
Helgon: extending the retrieval by reformulation * 0880
Graph attribution as a specification * 01138
A supervisory control * for real-time control of flexible manufacturing systems 01205
The direct memory access * and its applications to natural language processing 01489
A survey on systems informational * to the psychic 01606

The fuzzy * for knowledge representation in cerebral dynamics 01699
"Structure—reaction type" * in the conventional methods of describing organic reactions and the concept of imaginary transitions structures overcoming this * 02268
A cookbook for using the model-view controller user interface * in Smalltalk-80 02390
Encapsulators: a new software * in Smalltalk-80 03034
Human supervisory control in discrete manufacturing: Translating the * 03364
The construction of user interfaces and the object * 03791
Towards a new research * in information retrieval HCI-0273 †
Instructionless learning about a complex device: the * and observations HCI-0333 †

**PARADIGMS**
Readings in computer vision: issues, problems, principles, and * ● 0296
Emerging communications technology * 02320
CAD Data management using object-oriented * 02958

**PARADOXICAL**
The practice of the use of computers. A * encounter between different traditions of knowledge 0343

**PARALLEL**
Cortical connections and * processing: structure and function 0028
* computers for AI databases 0183
* computation and computers for artificial intelligence ● 0488
Application of the butterfly * processor in artificial intelligence 0489
On language and connectionism: analysis of a * distributed processing model of language acquisition 0590
* distributed processing: explorations in the microstructures of cognition; Vol. 2: Psychological and biological models ● 0629
Reflections on cognition and * distributed 0642
Nueral & massively * computers: the sixth generation ● 0702
Implementing neural network models on * computers 01403
Real-time failure detection on complex mechanical structures via * data processing 01561
Patterns of inductive reasoning in a * expert system 02219
Psychological concepts in a * system 02564
Linearization of the dynamic transfer response of time invariant nonlinear systems—in connection with the * information processing in living organisms 02665
Early vision: from computational structure to algorithms and * hardware 02703
Lyapunov function for * neural networks 02736
* structures in human and computer memory 02742
Programming a massively *, computation universal system: Static behavior 02746
DIME: a programming environment for unstructured triangular meshes on a distributed-memory * processor 02909
The PFG environment: * programming with petri net semantics 03527
Interactive scientific visualization and * display techniques 03542
* algorithms and architectures § 03819
* in sequence—towards the architecture of an elementary cortical processor 03820
Parcella '88: Fourth International Workshop on * Processing by Cellular Automata and Arrays § 03971
Learning in * networks: simulating learning in a probabilistic system HCI-0332 †
Early vision: from computational structure to algorithms and * hardware HCI-0365 †
A * formant synthesizer for machine voice output HCI-0396 †

**PARALLELISM**
Language, the mind, and psychophysical * 0357
Digital *, perpendicularity, and rectangles 01843
Connectionist models and * in high level vision 02700
Event-driven user interfaces based on quasi-* 03111
* and redundancy in neural networks 03952
Connectionist models and * in high level vision HCI-0363 †

**PARAMETER**
Interactive curve drawing by segmented Bezier approximation with a control * 02535
* estimation in array processing 04021

**PARAMETERS**
Visual * for color CRTs 0257
On the * of human visual performance: an investigation of the benefits of antialiasing 0799
Bat brushes: on the uses of six position and orientation * in a paint program 0846
The effect of varying voice and noise * on the perception of voicing in Dutch two-obstruent sequences 02653
Determining motion * for scenes with translation and rotation 03338
Determining 3-D motion * of a rigid body: a vector-geometrical approach 03339
Performance in cognitive tasks and cardiovascular * as indicators of mental load 03624
The use of prosodic * in automatic speech recognition 03988
Phonetic segmentation using psychoacoustic speech * 03991

**PARAMETRIC**
Single sweep analysis of visual evoked potentials through a model of *identification 01261
* Fourier image characterization toolkit 02798

**PARASIGHT**
Non-intrusive and interactive profiling in * 01123

## PARCEL
* sorting by speech recognition: human factors issues 03209

## PARCELLA
* '88: Fourth International Workshop on Parallel Processing by Cellular Automata and Arrays § 03971

## PARSER
A programmer-friendly LL(1) * generator 02626

## PARSING
Task-oriented * - a diagnostic method to be used adaptive systems 02896

## PARTICIPANTS
Information systems development success: Perspectives from project team * 02501

## PARTICIPATIVE
* design and requirements on planning, software engineering and education 03658
Experiences in * systems design 03665

## PARTICIPATORY
Community design and gaming/simulation: Comparison of communications techniques in * design sessions 02596

## PARTICLE
Facial * exposure in the VDU environment: the role of static electricity 03694

## PARTITIONING
Perceptual organization and curve * 01838
* of function in window systems 03931

## PASCAL
Programming the IBM User Interface: Using Turbo * ● 0286
Screen input/output programming techniques using Turbo * ● 0714
Turbo * windowing system 01306
Advanced diagnostics: a * interactive system 01958
Programming the mouse in Turbo * 4.0 02393
An external data structure tool for * 02495
Plan-based representations of * and fortran code 02897

## PASK
Learning styles in conversation—a practical application of *'s learning theory to human-computer interaction 03608

## PASSWORD
User-friendly * methods for computer-mediated information systems HCI-0167 †

## PATH
Psychological evaluation of * hypotheses in cognitive diagnosis 0537
Off-line programming and * generation for robot manipulators 0603
An almost *-free very high-level interactive data manipulation language for microcomputer-based database system HCI-0261 †
Interactive critical * analysis (ICPA)—microcomputer implementation of a project management and knowledge engineering tool HCI-0445 †

## PATHOLOGICAL
An acoustic of * voice and its application to the evaluation of laryngeal pathology 02644

## PATHOLOGY
An acoustic of pathological voice and its application to the evaluation of laryngeal * 02644
An interactionist's view of system * 03813

## PATHS
Empirical studies of programmers: the territory, *, and destination 02691

## PATIENT
* management systems: the early years 02852
EPVM: An expert *-ventilator manager for chemical warfare casualties 02956

## PATIENTS
An evaluation of auditory performances in * with Cochlear implants 02658

## PATTERN
Syntactic and structural * recognition ● 0292
Application of structural * recognition in histopathology 0295
An object-oriented framework of * recognition systems 01133
Visual * recognition in humans: I. Evidence for adaptive filtering 01274
Neural nets for adaptive filtering and adaptive * recognition 01362
The ART of adaptive * recognition by a self-organizing neural network 01364
Knowledge representation and use in * analysis 02030
Multidimensional attribute analyhsis and * recognition for seismic interpretation 02530
On the minimum number of templates required for shift, rotation and size invariant * recognition 02531
* storage and associative memory in quasi-neural network 02537
Nonlinear dynamics of * formation and * recognition in the rabbit olfactory bulb 02558
A self-optimizing, nonsymmetrical neural net for content addressable memory and * recognition 02562
Recognition of phonemes using time-spectrum * 02648
Bifurcation analysis of oscillating network model of * recognition in the rabbit olfactory bulb 02725
A neural network model for the mechanism of * information processing 02748
Mapping images to a hierarchical data structure—a way to knowledge-based * recognition 03954
Signal processing and * recognition in nondestructive evaluation of materials § 04019
* recognition: human and mechanical ● HCI-0072 †
A neural network for visual * recognition HCI-0391 †
Multivariate data representation and analysis by face * using facial expression characteristics HCI-0394 †

## PATTERNED
* systems design 01625

* systems design—HCI in commercial data processing 03193

## PATTERNS
Using * and plans in chess 0528
Mirrors of minds: * of experience in educational computing ● 0575
Performance, preference, and visual scan * on a menu-based system: implications for interface design 0855
Statistical inference on spontaneous neuronal discharge *. I. Single neuron 01247
Simulation of chaotic EEG * with a dynamic model of the olfactory system 01263
Effects of information-processing demands on physiological response * 01740
Hidden * in combined and adaptive knowledge networks 02073
Experience of programming beauty: some * of programming aesthetics 02184
* of inductive reasoning in a parallel expert system 02219
Citation * in the computer-based instruction literature 02290
A machine for neural computation of acoustical * with application to real time speech recognition 02751
The representation and perception of geometric structure in moving visual * 03326
The perception of coherent motion in two-dimensional * 03327
Usage * in an integrated voice and data communications system HCI-0311 †

## PBE
An overview of T$^3$-* 0784

## PC
Experiencing artificial intelligence: an interactive approach to the IBM * ● 0550
* networks: usage and graphics tutorials 01499
A *-interactives stereonet plotting program 01504
Magic *- the "UN-LANGUAGE" approach 01639
Managing the * revolution 01643
A * policy primer 01660

An incidence-matrix-driven panel system for the IBM * 01814
Graphics fundamentals for a *B-CAD * system 02494
The body in question: how to stay healthy at the * 02548
One hundred differential equations execute directly on the IBM * 02582
Interactive graphics in GPSS/* 02586
ACTES/Proceedings Symposium 1988 ACM SIGSMAll/* § 02787
* Version of a knowledge-based expert system with voice interface 02964
User interface in new * software 03771
Operating system design. Vol. 1: the XINU approach (* edition) ● HCI-0029 †

## PC+
A method framework for the statistical package SPSS/* to support occasional users 01202

## PCB
Graphics fundamentals for a *-CAD PC system 02494

## PCS
High performance interactive graphics: modeling, rendering and animating for IBM * and compatibles ● HCI-0071 †

## PCTE
Ecilpse—an APSE based on * 03181

## PDP
Schemata and sequential thought processes in * models 0630
Neural and conceptual interpretation of * models 0638

## PECAN
*: program development systems that support multiple views HCI-0145 †

## PEDAGOGICAL
* design for interactive video 0505
* development of computer-based learning material 03878

## PEGASYS
The * System: pictures as formal documentation of large programs HCI-0146 †

## PENCIL
Comparison of student performance in arithmetic exercises TOAM us paper-and-* testing 02249

## PENDANTS
Development of a human engineering design standard for robot teach * 03411

## PENSION
An expert system for screening employee * plans for the Internal Revenue Service 02773

## PEOPLES
Psychological aspects on blind *'s reading of radio-distributed daily newspapers 03700

## PEOPLEWARE
* 02557

## PERCEIVING
* and recovering structure from events 03346

## PERCEPTION
Textons, the fundamental elements in preattentive vision and * of textures 0297
Interactive processes in speech *: the TRACE model 0631
* and acceptance of a local area network and electronic mail 01284
An empirical investigation of DSS usage and the user's * of DSS training 01934
An experiment in graphical * 02125
The psychophysical function of binocular space * 02375
The effect of varying voice and noise parameters on the * of voicing in Dutch two-obstruent sequences 02653
* of transparency in man and machine 02697
Environment-centered and viewer-centered * of surface orientation 02705
* of organization in a random stimulus 02706
The * of system and the reduction of uncertainty 02850
Motion: representation and * § 03321
How human * deals with motion 03322

The scope of research on motion: sensations, *, representation and generation 03323
Motion *: second thoughts on the correspondence problem 03325
The representation and * of geometric structure in moving visual patterns 03326
The * of coherent motion in two-dimensional patterns 03327
Multicomputer architectures for real-time * 03341
* of rotation in depth: the psychophysical evidence 03343
The cross-ratio and the * of motion and structure 03344
Human * of the work envelope of an industrial robot 03410
The efficiency of letter * in function of color combinations: a study of video-screen colors 03616
Modeling uncertainty in human * 03825
* of organization in a random stimulus HCI-0364 †
* of transparency in man and machine HCI-0367 †
Environment-centered and viewer-centered * of surface orientation HCI-0392 †

## PERCEPTIONS

Job characteristic * of manual drafting and CADD: A field study of the effects of computerization on drafting & design personnel 01523
* of the information search process in libraries: a study of changes from high school through college 02002
User * of decision support system restrictiveness: an experiment 02353
The effects of task differences on the work satisfaction, job characteristics, nd role p*of programmer/analysts 02359
Student * of skill acquisition through cases and a general management simulation 02589
* of the CIS graduate's workstyle: undergraduate business students versus CIS faculty 02999
* of system effectiveness as viewed by executives, users, and information specialists 03469

User * of DSS restrictiveness: an experiment 03470
Programmer * of productivity and programming tools HCI-0099 †

## PERCEPTRON

Basins of attraction in a *-like neural network 01340

## PERCEPTS

Coherent global motion * from stochastic local motions 03329

## PERCEPTUAL

The diversity of * grouping 0022
* color spaces for computer graphics 0258
* organization and the representation of natural form 0302
Eye movements in reading: * and language processes ● 0609
Some principles of * and cognitive psychology applied to the design of help menus 01200
Self-organization in a * network 01366
* organization and curve partitioning 01838
Using * organization to extract 3-D structures 01842
* structure cueing in a simple command language 02086
A * study of the Flury-Riedwyl faces for graphically displaying multivariate data 02126
A theory of information structure. II. A theory of * organization 02362
* normalization of the vowels of a man and a child in various contexts 02656
Primary * units in word recognition 03994

## PERFORMANCE

The keystroke-level model for user * time with interactive systems 0055
How effective is interactive video in improving * and attitude? 0278
Toward high-* knowledge workers (Reprint) 0369
Short-term memory limits in human * 0398
User * with command, menu, and iconic interfaces 0414
Power windows: maximizing the speed and * of Windows 2.0 & Windows 386 ● 0423

Skills, rules, and knowledge; signals, signs, and symbols, and other distinctions in human * models 0654
Measures of human problem solving * in fault diagnosis tasks 0655
Response time and display rate in human * with computers 0760
On the parameters of human visual *: an investigation of the benefits of antialiasing 0799
*, preference, and visual scan patterns on a menu-based system: implications for interface design 0855
Voice messaging enhancing the user interface design based on field * 0913
Formatting space-related displays to optimize expert and nonexpert user * 0927
Problem solving * and display preference for information displays depicting numerical functions 0978
Including a user interface management system (UIMS) in the *relationship model 01000
A cognitively based methodology for evaluating human * in the computer-aided design task domain 01240
Neural networks and NP-complete optimization problems; a * study on the graph bisection problem 01339
A multidimensional approach to the measurement of human-computer * 01410
Computer literacy in secondary education: the * and engagement of girls 01495
Smart help for operator * 01528
Towards the development of human work-* standards in futuristic man-machine systems: a fuzzy modeling approach 01692
Multimodal detection and recognition * of sonar operators 01709
Reading from microfiche, a VDT, and the printed page: subjective fatigue and * 01712
An integrated display for vertical and translational flight: eight factors affecting pilot * 01714

No effect of noise on vigilance * 01724
The influence of visual workload history on visual * 01725
Changes in electromyographic activity associated with occupational stress and poor * in the workplace 01734
Improving visual * through volitional focus control 01744
Effects of functionally or topographically presented process schemes on operator * 01749
Internal models, tracking strategies and dual-task * 01751
Models of procedural control for human * simulation 01752
Slot versus insertion magnetic stripe readers: user * and preference 01756
The effects of panel arrangements and locus of attention on * 01759
Operator * as a function of type of display: conventional versus perspective 01769
Effects of visual display and motion system delays on operator * and ueasiness in a driving simulator 01772
Human * evaluation of digitizer pucks for computer input of spatial information 01774
Long workdays versus restdays: assessing fatigue and alertness with a portable * 01778
* measurement during simulated air-to-air combat 01787
Speech responses and dual-task *: better time-sharing or asymmetric transfer? 01789
The role of practice in dual-task *: toward workload modeling in a connectionist/control architecture 01790
Capacity equivalence curves: a double trade-off curve method for equating task * 01796
Ergonomic improvements boost AS/RS * 01904
Utilizing high technology: computer-aided-design and user * 01954
Effect of computer knowledge on user * over time 01975
A methodology for interactive evaluation of user reactions to software packages:an empirical analysis of system *, interaction, and run time 02080
On comprehending a computer manual: analysis of variables affecting * 02135
Analysis of the * of a genetic algorithm-based system for message classification in noisy environments 02156
Effects of breadth, depth and number responses on computer menu search * 02192
A model of fault diagnosis * of expert marine engineers 02199
Human * in relational algebra, tuple calculus, and domain calculus 02208
The effects of relational and entity-relationship data models on query * of end users 02247
Comparison of student * in arithmetic exercises TOAM us paper-and-pencial testing 02249
Compiling Forth for * 02309
High * neural networks 02313
The effect of presentation media on recipient * in text-based information systems 02350
A model for assessing the * of a local area network employing technical office protocol (TOP) as part of MAP/TOP network in a computer integrated manufacturing (CIM) research project, for the transmission of real time interactive speech 02491
Message equivocality, media selection and manager *: implications for information systems 02505
Comparison of video game and conventional test * 02594
Team cohesion effects on business game * 02597
* evaluation of simulators 02663
BNETD—A modelling tool to computer systems * evaluation 02668
The KOMPLEX * prediction tool 02669
SATURN—a tool for modelling and * evaluation of computer systems 02670
The measurement of the * of communications protocols from the user's viewpoint 02684
High-* polygon rendering 02814
Interactive * display and debugging using the NCUBE real-time graphicssystem 02907
Improving * of an electrical power expert system with genetic algorithms 02925
SPA: a systems for diagnosis of computer * problems 02969
Evaluating * appraisal systems for IS personnel 03011
An update measure of supervisor-rated job * for programmer/analysis 03012
Male/female programmer and systems analyst Job * 03020
Moderating effects of age, education, and tenure on the job satisfaction-job * relationship 03021
Monitoring and * measuring distributed systems during operation 03025
A review of human * and preferences with different input devices to computer systems 03231
Measuring the * of statisticians with statistical software 03314
100 Percent assured * for robotic assistive devices for handicapped and elderly persons 03414
* evaluation of three pressure mats as robot workstation safety sensors 03428
An investigation of *, productivity, and rationality in multi-criteria decision making 03463
jThe assessment of human/computer *: a case for connectivity 03535
* in cognitive tasks and cardiovascular parameters as indicators of mental load 03624
Study of visual * on a multi-color VDU of color defective and normal Trichromatic subjects 03701
Influence of age on * and health of VDU workers 03702
The effect of VDT symbol characteristics on operator * and visual comfort 03728

## [PERFORMANCES]

Human * engineering: using human factors/ergonomics to achieve computer system usability (2nd ed.) ● HCI-0042 †
* and computer-aided design ● HCI-0068 †
High * interactive graphics: modeling, rendering and animating for IBM PCs and compatibles ● HCI-0071 †
Some observations on user interface design and user * HCI-0117 †
An experimental evaluation of the impact of data display format on recall * HCI-0202 †
Reading and writing with computers: a framework for explaining differences in * HCI-0204 †
Design and * considerations for an optical disk-based, multimedia object server HCI-0265 †
A laboratory study of user characteristics and decision-making * in end-user computing HCI-0301 †
An approach to CAD system * evaluation HCI-0414 †
The relationship of problem-solving ability and course * among novice programmers HCI-0435 †

### PERFORMANCES
An evaluation of auditory * in patients with Cochlear implants 02658

### PERILS
* and pitfalls 01302

### PERIODIC
Alkahest III: automatic analysis of * weakly nonlinear ODEs 03087

### PERIPHERAL
Real-time interfacing: engineering aspects of microprocessor * systems ● 0224
A computer model of * auditory processing incorporating phase-locking, suppression and adaptation effects 02650

### PERMISSIONS
Privacy respecting * and rights 03583

### PERPENDICULARITY
Digital parallelism, *, and rectangles 01843

### PERSEUS
The * project: an interactive curriculum on classical greek civilization 01680

### PERSISTENCE
Data types and * ● 0033
Language level * for an object-oriented application programming platform 03522
Visual phenomena and their relation to top luminance, phosphor * time and contrast polarity 03729

### PERSON
Ill-formedness and miscommunication in *-machine dialogue 01957
Change and the systems * 02417
*-to-* communication in an applied research/service delivery setting 02445
Where * meets machine 02601
In search of the *: philosophical explorations in cognitive science ● HCI-0062 †
Visual momentum: a concept to improve the cognitive coupling of * and computer HCI-0238 †
Extended *-machine interface HCI-0344 †

### PERSONAL
A history of * workstations ● 0347
Distributed databases and distributed processing between * computers and mainframes 0458
Keyboarding for * computer use ● 0492
Cognition & * structure ● 0533
The development of a postmodern self: a computer-assisted comparative analysis of * documents ● 0732
The MAGNEX text editor for the Comodore Amiga * computer 0782
The memory extender * filing system 0930
Issuing each undergraduate student a * computer: living with it for three years 01028
The use of the IBM * computer in the man-machine interface to a nuclear research accelerator 01454
An investigation of data entry methods with a * computer 01490

The design of a user friendly interactive * computer package for quality control charts, project management, and linear programming applications 01521
Design of * information retrieval systems 02032
Measuring the effectiveness of * database structures 02246
* computer training software for adaptive control 02262
Microcomputer software. 2. Scientific and technical word processing on a * computer: has the time come? 02266
* transferable skills for the modern information professional: a discussion paper 02338
Quality control of * computing 02443
A * computer based graphic workstation 02493
What's new in * information managers 02556
Image processing with * computers 02581
Threat to privacy: the federal government's use of * information in the new communication environment 02680
ALIEN: a programming environment generator for * computers 02790
Medical informatics: a * view of sowing the seeds 02841
Health care information systems: a * historic review 02849
The history of * workstations § 03091
Toward a history of (*) workstations 03092
A * view of the * work station: some firsts in the Fifties 03093
* distributed computing: the Alto and Ethernet hardware 03095
* distributed computing: the Alto and Ethernet software 03096
Interactive 3-D modeling with * computers 03296
Device-independent graphics: with examples from IBM * computers ● HCI-0070 †
Andrew: a distributed * computing environment HCI-0091 †

On the applied use of human memory models: the memory extender * filing system HCI-0271 †

The user interface of a * calendar program HCI-0286 †

* computing for decision support HCI-0299 †

Interface design in computerized conferencing systems: a * view HCI-0305 †

**PERSONALITY**

Drama and * in user interface design 0830

* characteristics of junior high school students successful with computers 01592

The influence of * on self-paced instruction 02291

Chief executive * and corporate strategy and structure in small firms 02472

* traits of the worker within the :20man-machine" system at automated production 03593

**PERSONALIZED**

Towards an intelligent and * retrieval system 03028

Specification and generation of variable, * graphical interfaces HCI-0134 †

**PERSONALLY**

Managers who * use information technology frequently: a profile of some invisible computer personnel 03007

**PERSONNEL**

Job characteristic perceptions of manual drafting and CADD: A field study of the effects of computerization on drafting & design * 01523

Underlying dimensions of human problem solving and learning: implications for * selection, training tasks design and expert system 02225

Computer * research § 02803

Management of Information Systems * § 02996

An evaluation and selection methodology of microcomputer training software: Implications for human resource managers and computer * 03002

Managers who personally use information technology frequently: a profile of some invisible computer * 03007

Evaluating performance appraisal systems for IS * 03011

Repositioning the information systems management function: Implications for information systems * 03015

An investigation into the existence of subgroup concept in information systems * management 03022

Problems among managers of AI * 03460

An empirical study of occupational stress, attitudes and health among information systems * HCI-0451 †

**PERSONS**

User interface primitives to allow full functional use of computers by physically disabled * 0979

Computer work skills training for * with developmental disabilities 01559

100 Percent assured performance for robotic assistive devices for handicapped and elderly * 03414

Human factors considerations in the design of a VDU for visually impaired * 03698

**PESYS**

Developing and running expert systems with * 01690

**PETRI**

Extending * nets for specifying man-machine dialogues 02183

The PFG environment: parallel programming with * net semantics 03527

* nets: applications and relationships to other models of concurrency § 03973

**PFG**

The * environment: parallel programming with petri net semantics 03527

**PHARMACEUTICAL**

The foreign language barrier: a study among * research workers 02333

**PHASE**

The analysis * in development of knowledge based systems 0324

Impact of prototyping on user information satisfaction during the IS specification * 01955

A computer model of peripheral auditory processing incorporating *-locking, suppression and adaptation effects 02650

Speeded * discrimination: evidence for global to local processing 03307

**PHIGS**

*: a standard, dynamic, interactive graphics interface 01826

**PHILOSOPHICAL**

A * basis for decision aiding 0649

In search of the person: * explorations in cognitive science ● HCI-0062 †

**PHILOSOPHY**

Designing the "cockpit": the application of a human-centered design * to make optimization systems accessible 01016

Super consulting for supercomputer users: a * of user support 03145

**PHONE**

The design of *-based interfaces for consumers 0878

**PHONEME**

Composite * units for the speech synthesis of Japanese 02647

**PHONEMES**

Recognition of * using time-spectrum pattern 02648

**PHONETIC**

The "neural" * typewriter 01361

An acoustic-* oriented system for synthesizing Chinese 02661

* segmentation using psychoacoustic speech parameters 03991

An expert system for mapping acoustic cues into * features HCI-0328 †

The * basis for computer speech processing HCI-0358 †

**PHONETICS**

Acoustic *, auditory *, speaker sex and speech recognition: a thread 0288

**PHONOLOGY**

* and syntax: the relationship between sound and structure ● 0672

## PHOSPHOR
Visual phenomena and their relation to top luminance, * persistence time and contrast polarity 03729

## PHOSPHORS
Optimal colors, *, and illuminant characteristics of CRT displays: the lgorithmic approach 01710

## PHOTOGRAPHS
Using a top-down and bottom-up strategy to analyze high resolution aerial * of urban areas 02960

## PHOTOPIC
The effects of target wavelength on dynamic visual acuity under * and scotopic viewing 01762

## PHRAN
*-SPAN: a natural language interface for system specifications 02829

## PHYSICAL
The * environment 0045
A modular user-oriented decision support for * database design 01669
Fuzzy reasoning in pseudo-* logics 01695
Pride-II * layout program of modifying Forth for "non-believers" 02312
Some * factors at VDT work stations and ski problems 03693
Short- and long-term effects of extreme * inactivity. A review 03703
On the significance of * activity on sedentary work 03704
Qualitative modeling of * systems for knowledge based control 03834
Overcoming conceptual difficulties in * science through computer-based Socratic dialogs 03877

## PHYSICALLY
Towards universality of access: interfacing * disabled students to the Icon educational microcomputer 0821
User interface primitives to allow full functional use of computers by * disabled persons 0979
Mathematical modeling of fatigue in * demanding jobs 02363

New technology work aids for the * disabled 03273
Voice-input aids for the * disabled HCI-0089 †
Design of computer programs for the * handicapped HCI-0096 †

## PHYSICIANS
Natural language interface to the question-answering system for * 01478

## PHYSICS
Cognitive economy in * reasoning: implications for designing instructional materials 0542
Retinex: * and the theory of color vision 01574
On the * and mathematics of thought 03778
Integrating * and computer education in a single process 03879

## PHYSIOLOGICAL
A knowledge-based system for assessment of human * abilities in manual lifting tasks 01519
Effects of information-processing demands on * response patterns 01740
Review and evaluation of * cost prediction models for manual materials handling 01757
* principles for the effective use of color HCI-0378 †

## PHYSIOLOGICALLY
Improving the VDU workplace by introducing a * optimized bright-background screen with dark characters: advantages and requirements 03721

## PHYSIOLOGY
Certain aspects of the anatomy and * of the cerebral cortex 0636
* based simulation model of triangle shape recognition 01277
* and psychophysics in taste and smell 04009
The * and psychophysics of touch 04010

## PICT
*: an interactive graphical programming environment HCI-0143 †

## PICTOGRAPHIC
An investigation of * form in relation to mechanisms of knowledge acquisition 03824

## PICTORIAL
* representations of abstract concepts relating to human-computer interaction 0947
Comparison of speech and * displays in a cockpit environment 01731
* dialogue methods 02251
* knowledge bases 03201
A comparison of presentation and representation: linguistic and * 03898
* information systems in medicine § 03976
On the architecture for * information systems 03977
Software tools for the development of * information systems in medicine—the ISQL experience 03980
* interfaces to data bases HCI-0116 †
IDECAP: interactive * information system for demographic and environmental planning applications HCI-0411 †

## PICTURE
The elicitation of system knowledge by * probes 0921
CRT * vibration caused by low-frequency magnetic field and its reduction method 01987
Integrating text with non-text:a * is worth 1k words. Proceedings of the I § 04043

## PICTURES
Making drawings talk: * in minds and machines 01392
* and category labels as navigational aids for catalog browsing 02877
The PegaSys System: * as formal documentation of large programs HCI-0146 †

## PIE
An empirical comparison of * vs. linear menus 02871

## PIGEONHOLE
Computer literacy: the * principle 0789

## PILOT
An integrated display for vertical and translational flight: eight factors affecting * performance 01714

Perspective traffic display format and airline * traffic avoidance 01748

Applying a * system and prototyping approach to systems development and implementation 01915

## PIPELINED
An automatic wafer inspection system using * image processing techniques 01840

## PISCES
*: an expert system for coal fired power plant monitoring and diagnostics 02915

## PITMAN
On-line recognition of *'s hand-written shorthand—an evaluation of potential 02111

## PIXEL
*-planes 4: a summary 0495

Effect of * height, display height, and vertical resolution on the detection of a simple vertical line signal in visual noise 01753

## PIXIE
Enhancing *'s tutoring capabilities 02187

## PLANE
A group model of form recognition under * similarity transformations 02366

Alleys on an apparent frontoparallel * 02374

## PLANES
Pixel-* 4: a summary 0495

## PLANNER
Development of the wedding *—extensions to reach a young audience 01502

## PLANNERS
Intelligent interfaces: user models and * 0932

## PLANNING
Color graphic displays for network * and design 0260

Cognitive psychology of * ● 0435

ARIADNE: A knowledge-based interactive system for * and decision support 0661

Skilled financial *: the cost of translating ideas into action 0834

* for hospital information systems using the Lancaster Soft Systems methodology 01228

Some historical currents concerning the 'societal learning' approach to policy and * 01603

ARIADNE: a knowledge-based interactive system for * and decision support 01860

Adaptive user interfaces for * and decision aids in $C^3I$ systems 01887

Technology's impact on library interior * 02464

The mission operators * assistant 02674

A * system for a cognitive problem 02719

Explanation for an expert system that performs estate * 02767

* for advising 02886

Multimodal response *: an adaptive rule based approach 02894

SIMS: a uniform environment for * and performing user's tasks 02921

The development of an automated flight test management system for flight test * and monitoring 02928

An expert database for material and production * 02937

A mission * architecture for an autonomous vehicle 02939

* as feedback to designers 02978

* in the context of human-computer interaction 03213

GOMS meets STRIPS: the integration of * with skilled procedure execution in human-computer interaction 03243

Crisis * systems: tools for intelligent action 03404

Participative design and requirements on *, software engineering and education 03658

Procedures for participation in *, developing and operating information systems 03659

The interactive * work station: a graphics-based UNIX tool for application users and developers 03860

The learning and * of actions 04069

* and design of information systems ● HCI-0045 †

O-Plan: control in the open * architecture HCI-0362 †

IDECAP: interactive pictorial information system for demographic and environmental * applications HCI-0411 †

Computer-aided modeling and * (CAMP) HCI-0415 †

## PLANS
Using patterns and * in chess 0528

Modeling the user's * and goals 01349

An expert system for screening employee pension * for the Internal Revenue Service 02773

* and situated actions: the problem of human-machine communication ● HCI-0040 †

## PLANTING
* the seeds 02840

## PLASTIC
The impact of advanced manufacturing in work organization: The Portugese case ofthe * moulding industry 03374

## PLASTICITY
State-dependent factors influencing neural *: a partial account of the 0640

Exploring three possibilities in network design: spontaneous node activity, node * and temporal coding 03962

## PLATFORM
Language level persistence for an object-oriented application programming * 03522

## PLATTER
Integrating CD-ROM with printed and online services: a silver * end-user perspective 03558

## PLAUSIBLE
Biologically * models of place recognition and goal location 0639

## PLAYFUL
Making computer tasks at work more *: Implications for systems analysts and designers 03005

## PLEIADE
*: A system for interactive manipulation of structured documents 0265

## PLEXACT
*: an architecture & design of a knowledge-based system for information systems development 01020

## PLOSIVE
Speaker-independent automatic recognition of * sound in letters and digits 03993

## PLOTTING
A PC-interactives stereonet * program 01504

## PLUG
Interface concepts for *-compatible production management systems 01566

## PM
A drafted * glossary 0625

## PNEUMATIC
* manipulating system provided with active compliance function 03426

## POEM
*: An office system for international use 03457

## POGO
*: a declarative representation system for graphics 0476

## POINT
User-oriented suggestions for floating-* and complex-arithmetic Forth standard extensions 02306
The economic evaluation on implementation industrial robot from user * of view 03447
User participation from the * of view of the workers and trade union policy 03652

## POINTING
User technology: from * to pondering 0350
User technology—from * to pondering 03098

## POINTS
*: a theory of the structure of stories in memory 0392

## POLARISATION
The * approach to intelligent artifacts 02714

## POLARITY
Visual phenomena and their relation to top luminance, phosphor persistence time and contrast * 03729

## POLE
Higher * correction in vocal tract models and terminal analogs 02657

## POLITICAL
The Socio/* Environment 0040
The * economy of interactive video in British higher education 0512
Systems design and social responsibility: the * implications of "computer-supported cooperative work". A commentary 02516

## POLITICS
Power, *, and MIS implementation 0042
Information * 01656

## POLYGON
High-performance * rendering 02814

## POLYLINES
Image compression using * 02533

## POLYLITH
*: an environment to support management of tool interfaces 01096

## POLYNOMIAL
The complexity of some * network consistency algorithms for constraint satisfaction problems HCI-0361 †

## PONDERING
User technology: from pointing to * 0350
User technology—from pointing to * 03098

## POP
*-11: an AI programming language 0748
*-11 for everyone 0749

## PORTABILITY
* of syntax and semantics in DATALOG HCI-0340 †

## PORTABLE
The architecture of an inexpensive and * talking-tactile terminal to aid the visually handicapped 01452
Long workdays versus restdays: assessing fatigue and alertness with a *performance 01778
Emeraude * common tool environment 01970
An inexpensive and * talking-tactile terminal for the visually handicapped 02377
A * query language for small scale systems 02492
Q'Nial: a * interpreter for the nested interactive array language, Nial 02635
A * user interface for a scientific programming environment 03125
Experiences with the development of a * network operating system 03882

## PORTALS
Database *: a new application program interface 0707

## PORTFOLIO
*: kaleidoscopic visions 02551

## PORTING
The flexibility of case grammar representations: a * procedure for naturallanguage interfaces 02255

## PORTUGESE
The impact of advanced manufacturing in work organization: The * case of the plastic moulding industry 03374

## POSITIONING
* human factors in the user interface development chain 0835
A first order theory of common sense object * 01563
Exploratory evaluation of a planar foot-operated cursor-* device 02858

## POST
Visual accommodation and target detection in the vicinity of a window * 01802

## POSTAL
Video display terminals and birth defects. A study of pregnancy outcomes of employees of the *-Giro Center, Oslo, Norway 03691

## POSTER
CHI '88 * session papers and abstracts 0992

KEYWORD INDEX [PREDICTING]

Development and evaluation of direct manipulation lists (* session) 0993

**POSTFIX**

An experimental evaluation of prefix and * notation in command language sytax 02110

**POSTMODERN**

The development of a * self: a computer-assisted comparative analysis of personal documents ● 0732

**POSTPROCESSING**

Interactive color graphical * as a unifying influence in numerical analysis research 01684

**POSTSCRIPT**

A user-interface toolkit in object-oriented * 01391

*: computers and the modeling of mind HCI-0348 †

**POSTULATE**

The alternatives allowed by a rectangularity *, and a pragmatic approach to interpreting motion 03550

**POSTULATES**

Semantic primitives or meaning *: mental models or propositional representation? HCI-0339 †

**POSTURE**

* and VDU operator satisfaction 0988

**POSTURES**

Task compatibility of manipulator * 02258

**POTENTIALS**

Diffusion approximation of the neuronal model with synaptic reversal * 01254

Single sweep analysis of visual evoked * through a model of parametric identification 01261

The spatial allocation of visual attention as indexed by event-related brain * 01739

**POWER**

*, politics, and MIS implementation 0042

Knowledge representation and natural language: extending the expressive *of proposition nodes 0096

* windows: maximizing the speed and performance of Windows 2.0 & Windows 386 ● 0423

C/C++ for expert systems: "unleashes the * of a artificial intelligence" ● 0439

The AutoCAD productivity book: tapping the hidden * of AutoCAD: 2nd edition ● 0668

Preferences for * in expert systems by novice users 0971

Teachware for * engineering education 01203

* and credibility in office automation 01657

Qualitative approximation methodology for modeling and simulation of large dynamic systems: Applications to a Marine * plant 01900

Integrated communications and work efficiency: impacts on organizational structure and * 02031

* plant simulation using a distributed control system 02057

* plant simulation and reactor safety 02682

A compact model of a * house boiler 02683

PISCES: an expert system for coal fired * plant monitoring and diagnostics 02915

Sherlock—a system for diagnosing * distribution ring network faults 02916

Improving performance of an electrical * expert system with genetic algorithms 02925

A blackboard architecture for problem solving and machine learning in an expert system for * system voltage control 02926

Graphics-based qualitative simulation generator for * distribution systems 02946

An object-oriented expert system for coal-fired MHD * plant fault monitoring and diagnosis 02973

Assessment of mental load for different strategies of man-computer dialogue by means of the heart rate * spectrum 03623

The AutoCAD productivity book: tapping the hidden * of AutoCAD ● HCI-0076 †

A research model for studying the gender/* aspects of human-computer communication HCI-0193 †

**POWERMATH**

*—A system for the Macintosh 03083

**PRAGMATIC**

The rational, the * and the inquiry process: The social study of information- communication systems 0786

The alternatives allowed by a rectangularity postulate, and a *approach to interpreting motion 03550

How to improve * quality of information systems 03662

VDAFS—a * interface for the exchange of sculptured surface data HCI-0420 †

**PREATTENTIVE**

Textons, the fundamental elements in * vision and perception of textures 0297

* processing in vision 02709

* processing in vision HCI-0366 †

**PRECEDENT**

*-based legal reasoning and knowledge acquisition in contract law: A process model 02776

**PRECISION**

Estimating reliability with small samples: increased * with averaged correlations 01728

Robot vs. human operator for speed, * and other aspects 03403

Visual hyperacuity: representation and computation of high * position information HCI-0393 †

**PREDICAMENT**

Electronic publishing: The * of occasional users in the editorial proc 02446

**PREDICTING**

* the time to recall computer command abbreviations 0806

* end-user acceptance of microcomputers in the workplace 02147

855

## PREDICTION
Review and evaluation of physiological cost * models for manual materials handling 01757
* of the smallest channel in early human vision 01894
The KOMPLEX performance * tool 02669

## PREDICTIONS
A model for the interpretation of verbal * HCI-0316 †

## PREDICTIVE
Linear * coding of speech 0289
Programmable user models for * evaluation of interface designs 0800

## PREDICTOR
Self-efficacy expectations as a * of computer use: a look at early childhood administrators 01590
Development and sensitivity analysis of adaptive * for human eye movement model 02681

## PREDICTORS
Job histories as * of career success in management information systems 01021
A study of organizational effectiveness and its * 02471

## PREFERENCE
Performance, *, and visual scan patterns on a menu-based system: implications for interface design 0855
Problem solving performance and display * for information displays depicting numerical functions 0978
Slot versus insertion magnetic stripe readers: user performance and * 01756
A user * guided approach to conflict resolution in rule-based expert systems 01872

## PREFERENCES
* for power in expert systems by novice users 0971
Word processing techniques and user learning * 0984
Users' * among different techniques for displaying the evaluation of LISP functions in an interactive debugger 02863

A review of human performance and * with different input devices to computer systems 03231

## PREGNANCY
* and VDT work—an evaluation of the state of the art 03686
Birth defects, course of *, and work with VDUs: a Finnish case-referent study 03689
* outcome and VDU-work in a cohort of insurance clerks 03690
Video display terminals and birth defects. A study of * outcomes of employees of the Postal-Giro Center, Oslo, Norway 03691
Task-load and endocrinological risk for * in women VDU operators 03692

## PREHENSION
A neural model of human * 04072

## PREPOSITIONS
Various views on spatial * 01196

## PREREQUISITES
Social psychological * and consequences of new information technologies 03631

## PRESCHOOL
The effects of gender and age on * children's choice of the computer as a child-selected activity 02450

## PRESCRIBED
Automatic construction of surfaces with * shape 01474

## PRESCRIPTIVE
A descriptive/* model for menu-based interaction 02120

## PRESENTATIONS
Automating the design of graphical * of relational information 01150

## PRESENTED
Effects of functionally or topographically * process schemes on operator performance 01749

## PRESERVED
Libraries as programs * within compiler continuations 01102

## PRESSES
Circling: a method of mouse-based selection without button * 0847

## PRESSURE
Measurement of seat * distribution 01760

Performance evaluation of three * mats as robot workstation safety sensors 03428
Intraocular * during VDT work 03683

## PREVENTATIVE
Mode errors: a user-centered analysis and some * measures using keying-contingent sound 02107

## PREVENTING
* back strain 0047
AGV safety system designed for * hazardous human contact 03423

## PREVIEWS
How good an Online searcher are you? Twenty questions about BIOSIS * 02521

## PRICE
Datastream: numeric data—all you can use at a fixed * 02525

## PRIDE
*-II physical layout program of modifying Forth for "non-believers" 02312

## PRIMATE
The role of the * superior colliculus in sensorimotor integration 0017

## PRIMITIVE
Self-organizing system obtaining communication ability * model for language generation 01279
An input/output * for object-oriented systems 01969

## PRIMITIVES
CAD Based verification and refinement of high level compliant motion * 0600
User interface * to allow full functional use of computers by physically disabled persons 0979
Selection of image * for general-purpose visual processing 01467
Cognitive * 02214
Cortical representation of texture * 03306
How people comprehend unknown system structures: conceptual * in systems' surface representations 03828
Semantic * or meaning postulates: mental models or propositional representation? HCI-0339 †

# KEYWORD INDEX [PRODUCTION]

**PRINCIPALS**
Speech filing—An office system for * 0037

**PRINCIPLED**
Interaction models and the * design of interactive systems 03799

**PRINICIPLES**
* from the psychology of thinking and mental models 0329

**PRINT**
Competitive dynamics in a dual-route connectionist model of *-to-sound transformation 01341
Making the transition from * to electronic encyclopaedias: adapation of mental models 02238
Computer user manuals in *: Do they have a future? 02782
Synthesis of *-quality cursive script based on a model of the human handwriting mechanism HCI-0402 †

**PRINTED**
From arcane ASCII to the * page - computer basics 01148
Reading from microfiche, a VDT, and the * page: subjective fatigue and performance 01712
Computer aided concurrent design for * wiring boards 02981
Integrating CD-ROM with * and online services: a silver platter end-user perspective 03558

**PRINTER**
Trends in * technology 01624

**PRIVACY**
A tolerance for surveillance: American public opinion concerning * and civil liberties 0524
Threat to *: the federal government's use of personal information in the new communication environment 02680
* respecting permissions and rights 03583

**PRIVATE**
* copying, reproduction costs, and the supply of intellectual property 01988

**PRIVATELY**
Sharing in a * owned workstation environment 04076

**PROBABILISTIC**
A * dominance measure for binary choices: analytic aspects of a multi-attribute random weights model 02372
Learning in parallel networks: simulating learning in a * system HCI-0332 †

**PROBABILITIES**
Decision making with unreliable * 0652
Classifying sensory inspectors with heterogeneous inspection-error * 02396

**PROBABILITY**
Extension of conditional * and measures of belief and disbelief in a hypothesis based on uncertain evidence 01846
Combining stochastic uncertainty and linguistic inexactness: theory and experimental evaluation of four fuzzy * models 02218
Subjective * and information retrieval: a review of the psychological literature 02303

**PROBES**
The elicitation of system knowledge by picture * 0921

**PROCEED**
*: an expert system for multivariate process control systems design 02935

**PROCESSOR**
Learning to use a word *: by doing, by thinking, and by knowing 0060
Application of the butterfly parallel * in artificial intelligence 0189
A two-dimensional frame buffer * 0494
A multi-* workstation with a logic-enhanced distributed frame buffer 0496
Learning disabled students' difficulties in learning to use a word *: implications for design 0889
* for man-machine natural-language-like communication 01484

A natural language interface * based on the hierarchical-tree structure model of relation tables 02315
Digial signal * accelerators for neural network simulations 02754
DIME: a programming environment for unstructured triangular meshes on a distributed-memory parallel * 02909
Logic programmable natural language * of a knowledge-base management system 02965
Embedded training in AI technology through an expert system interface: an alarm * application 02991
The Monte Carlo *: designing and implementing a language for Monte Carlo work 03317
Parallel in sequence—towards the architecture of an elementary cortical * 03820
Control of sensory processing - a hypothesis on and simulation of the architecture of an elementary cortical * 03972
Learning to use a word *: by doing, by thinking, and by knowing HCI-0292 †
The mapping between grammar and * HCI-0346 †

**PROCESSORS**
Learning to use word *: problems and prospects 0059
Architectures of graphic * for interactive 2D graphics 01395
Testing and validation of IGES * HCI-0423 †
Training for optimising transfer between word * HCI-0447 †

**PRODUCER**
Interactive video—a *'s medium 0511

**PRODUCITON**
* and inventory management software packages related to user reactions 02567

**PRODUCTION**
Design and * of videodisc programming 0276
* system models of learning and development ● 0478
Learning, development, and * systems 0479

[PRODUCTIVITY]

Learning by chunking: a * system model of practice 0483
Composition of * 0485
Self-modifying * system model of cognitive development 0486
* systems, learning, and tutoring 0487
Fundamentals of engineering drawing: with an introduction to interactive computer graphics for design and *, (9th ed.) ● 0531
Computer-aided * management IFIP ● 0618
* management systems 0619
* control in car industry 0623
* control in the aircraft industry 0624
The migration of expert systems into the * environment 0740
People and organizations in software *: a review of the literature 01023
Interface concepts for plug-compatible * management systems 01566
A high level language-based computing enviornment to support * and execution of reliable programs 01855
Modeling rule-based systems by stochastic programmed * systems 02017
Using worker's survey to improve * 02566
Distinctive regions and modes: a new theory of speech * 02659
Process design of oil and gas * facilities using expert systems 02933
An expert database for material and * planning 02937
Design of distribution of * control functions between humans and artificially intelligent devices 03375
Differential organization impacts of the transition from stand-alone to integrated flexible * 03380
The evaluation of selected ergonomical factors by * automation growth 03429
An evaluation of * systems from the ergonomical viewpoint: a plea for an integral approach to design 03430

Accident analysis of blind * workers 03439
Personality traits of the worker within the :20man-machine" system at automated * 03593
Architectures for * systems: an inside look for those who study human-computer interaction 03906

PRODUCTIVITY

The AutoCAD * book: tapping the hidden power of AutoCAD: 2nd edition ● 0668
Increasing * with ISPF/APL2 0767
Impact of a restricted natural language interface on ease of learning and * 01334
Demanding higher * 01630
A theory of * in the creative process 01824
End-user computing environments—finding a balance between * and control 01927
Decision support systems for workers: a bridge to advancing * 01947
Effects of interface design upon user * 02891
The experimental validation of a programmer * measure 03013
Computers' impact on * and work life 03040
Health and * issues of CAD/CAM systems 03436
An investigation of performance, *, and rationality in multi-criteria decision making 03463
System design for human development and *: participation and beyond § 03640
Report from the working group on "goals and strategies of trade unions and other social groups in systems design for human development and *." 03657
Influence of individual characteristics and group cohesiveness on programmer * 04050
Effects of an immediate feedback tool on designer * and design usability 04052
The AutoCAD * book: tapping the hidden power of AutoCAD ● HCI-0076 †

Programmer perceptions of * and programming tools HCI-0099 †
Computerization, *, and quality of work-life HCI-0441 †

PROFESSIONAL

Designing the user interface: * development courses from the Univ. of Maryland ● 0688
* and expert systems: a meeting of minds 0790
End user—IS design * interaction—information exchange for firm profit or end user satisfaction? 01936
* education and subsequent careers in library/information work: a follow-up study of former students on the MA/MSc information studies course at the University of Sheffield 02336
Personal transferable skills for the modern information *: a discussion paper 02338

PROFESSIONALISM

Instilling * in a software development organization 03019

PROFESSIONALS

Human factors reference guide for electronics and computer * ● 0733
Human factors reference guide for electronics and computer * ● 0734
Behavioural and organisational factors involved in the turnover of high tech * 01024
Responsibility sharing between sophisticated users and * in structured prototyping 01978
The end user attack: Will the real computer * stand up and fight 02424
Motivations and behaviors of software * 03003
Perspectives on the academic preparation of MIS * 03006

PROFESSIONS

Refraction in VDU operators—a comparison with other * 03740

PROFILE

* of undergraduate software engineering courses: results from a survey 01035
The * naming service 01149

* data acquisition for the JCPDS-ICDD database s 01232
Managers who personally use information technology frequently: a * of some invisible computer personnel 03007

**PROFILING**
Non-intrusive and interactive * in parasight 01123

**PROFIT**
End user—IS design professional interaction—information exchange for firm * or end user satisfaction? 01936

**PROGAMMERS**
Experimental study of a two-dimensional language vs. FORTRAN for first-course * HCI-0171 †

**PROGRAMS**
Toward interactive design of correct * 0614
Inducing * in a direct-manipulation environment 0816
Separating the user interface from the functionality of application * 0948
A development environment for horizontal microcode * 01079
Libraries as * preserved within compiler continuations 01102
Transformational derivation of * using the focus system 01140
Interactive microcomputer * for linear and non-linear static analysis of frameworks 01165
Construction of interactive * in computer graphics 01398
Automated construction of interactive learning * in Modula-2 01500
Adolescents' chunking of computer * 01586
The effects of sources of applications * on user satisfaction: an empirical study of micro, mini & mainframe computers using an interactive artificial intelligence expert-system 01601
Alternative option selection methods in menu-driven computer * 01755

A high level language-based computing enviornment to support production and execution of reliable * 01855
Synchronizing the I/O behavior of functional * with feedback 02016
Comprehension and recall of miniature * 02087
Generating reversible * 02620
Generation of file processing * based on JSP 02639
Multilingual programming: Coordinating *, user interfaces, on-line help nd documentation 02785
Affect-chaining and dependency oriented flow analysis applied to queries of * 02789
Experience with a data base of * 03050
Modelling generic user-interfaces with functional * 03265
User *: a way to match computer systems and human cognition 03271
The influence of individual differences on the reading of computer * 03456
An environment for understanding * 03525
Introducing CAL: a practical guide to writing computer-assisted learning * ● HCI-0079 †
Design of computer * for the physically handicapped HCI-0096 †
A generalized user interface for applications * (II) HCI-0112 †
Showing * on a screen HCI-0141 †
A debugger for concurrent * HCI-0142 †
The PegaSys System: pictures as formal documentation of large * HCI-0146 †
Analyzing the high frequency bugs in novice * HCI-0178 †
Goal and plan knowledge representations: from stories to text editors and * HCI-0183 †
Effects of experience and comprehension on reading time and memory for computer * HCI-0197 †

**PROHIBITED**
Legal data modeling: The * transaction exemption analyst 02779

**PROJECTED**
* free fall trajectories. I. Theory and simulation 01265
* free fall trajectories. II. Human experiments 01266

**PROLOG**
What stories should we tell novice * programmers? 0421
Concurrent *: collected papers ● 0674
Object oriented programming in Concurrent * 0677
A grammar kit in * 0745
Implementation of a *-INGRES interface 01087
A * simulation for a Delphi-based problem solver 01141
Support for tentative design: incorporating the screen image, as a graphical object, into * 02116
A new approach for introducing * to naive users 04029

**PROLONGED**
The back during * sitting 03706

**PROMETHEUS**
Strategic management of technostress: The chaining of * HCI-0452 †

**PROMIS**
A history of the * technology: an effective human interface 0349
A history of the * technology: an effective human interface 03097

**PROMOD**
* at the age of 5 03802

**PROMOTING**
REPTIL-* dialog between humanoid and computer 02307

**PROMPTED**
OS/2 query manager overview and * interface 01809

**PROMPTING**
Adaptive command * in an on-line documentation 02121
*, feedback and error correction in the design of a scenario machine 02176
Evaluating RECONSIDER: a computer program for diagnostic * HCI-0410 †

## PROOF
Efforts of display format on
*-reading with VDUs 01246
## PROOFS
DYNABOARD: user animated
display of deductive * in
mathematics 02221
Automatizing geometric * and
constructions 03851
## PROPAEDEUTICS
* of decision-making: supporting
managerial learning and
innovation 01667
## PROPAGATING
An interactive approach to local
remeshing around a * crack
01685
## PROPAGATION
Attribute * by message passing
01100
Scaling relationships in back-*
learning 01338
Generalizing back * to computation
02726
## PROPERTIES
A model of the motor servo:
Incorporating nonlinear spindle
receptor and muscle mechanical *
01273
Representations of perceived
relations among the * and
variables of a complex system
01892
Proving * of interactive systems
03267
On global context dependencies and
their * (extended abstract) 03945
Dynamical * of a new type of neural
network 03969
## PROPOSITION
Knowledge representation and
natural language: extending the
expressive power of * nodes 0096
## PROPOSITIONAL
A * language for text representation
0097
Semantic primitives or meaning
postulates: mental models or
*representation? HCI-0339 †
## PROPRIOCEPTIVE
* feedback for sensory-motor
control 04008

## PROS
SIMTALK: * and cons of natural
language for manufacturing
simulation 02950
## PROSODIC
Changes in * features of speech due
to environmental factors 02651
The use of * parameters in
automatic speech recognition
03988
* features in German speech: stress
assignment by man and machine
03989
## PROSPECT
Computers for the people: HCI in *.
An introduction to the HCI '88
conference 03216
## PROSTHESES
Cognitive aids in process
environments: * or tools? 02161
## PROTECTING
* user interfaces through copyright:
the debate 0827
## PROTECTIVE
Workers education and user
participation in the development
of *policies for VDT operators
03752
## PROTEIN
Gripe: a graphical interface to a
knowledge based system which
reasons about * topology 03234
## PROTEUS
The * bibliography: Representation
and interactive display in
databases 01085
## PROTOCOLS
Directed dialogue *: verbal data for
user interface design 0866
What "question-asking *" can say
about the user interface 02130
Layered * for computer-human
dialogue. 1: principles 02195
Layered * for computer-human
dialogue. 11: some practical issues
02196
The measurement of the
performance of communications *
from the user's viewpoint 02684
Communications and architecture &
* § 02801
An implementation of OSI * in
SM-4 host computers 03638

## PROTOS
*: an examplar-based learning
apprentice 02210
## PROTOTYPE
The user's mental model of an
information retrieval system: an
experiment on a * online catalog
02099
The ISA expert system: a * system
for failure diagnosis on the space
station 02913
INQUEST: A * intelligence tool
02918
The network control assistant
(NCA), a real-time * expert system
for network management 02930
A * autonomous agent for crew and
equipment retrieval in space
02994
A * electronic encyclopedia
HCI-0278 †
## PROTOTYPER
Mac programming tools: * version
2.0 eases interface design 02394
## PROTOTYPES
* from standard user interface
management systems 01370
* for user training 02421
The construction of information
management system * in Ada
02613
## PROTOTYPIFICATION
A limitation theorem for the
differentiable * of shape 02365
## PROTOTYPING
Statemaster: A UIMS based on
statechart for * and target
implementation 0850
* techniques for different problem
contexts 0862
Rapid * and system development:
examination of an interface
toolkit for voice and telephony
applications 0918
RAPID: * control panel interfaces
01120
A graphical tool for the design and *
of distributed systems 01146
The use of * and simulation in the
development of large-scale
applications 01411
End-user *: sophisticated users
supporting system development
01636

# KEYWORD INDEX [PSYCHOLOGY]

A system for specification and rapid * of application command languages 01849

Applying a pilot system and * approach to systems development and implementation 01915

Impact of * on user information satisfaction during the IS specification phase 01955

Trillium: an interface design * tool 01965

Responsibility sharing between sophisticated users and professionals in structured * 01978

Dynamic reconfigurability for fast * of user interfaces 02609

Object oriented rapid * with G2 02984

The mirage rapid interface * system 03112

INTERA/P: a user interface * tool 03205

ECS - A technique for the formal specification and rapid * of human-computer interaction 03253

Rapid * of dialogue for human factors research: the EASIE approach 03254

Express—rapid * and product development via integrated knowledge-based executable specifications 03492

* user interfaces for applications depicted by graphs 03523

the role of user * in the system design process 03747

Storyboard *: a new approach to user requirements analysis ● HCI-0005 †

A dedicated microcomputer for handwritten interaction with a software tool: system * HCI-0119 †

Graphical * of graphical tools HCI-0375 †

## PROVIDED

Pneumatic manipulating system * with active compliance function 03426

## PROVISIONAL

A * evaluation of a new chord keyboard, the Velotype 03907

## PROVISIONS

Authorship * in AUGMENT (Reprint) 0370

## PROXIMITY

Display * in multicue information integration: the benefits of boxes 01763

## PRUFER

Network generation using the * code 01536

## PSG

The *—programming system generator 01098

Context-sensitive editing with * environments 03780

## PSI

Information science and the * phenomenon 01281

## PSYCHIC

The informational substrata of * illnesses 01600

A survey on systems informational paradigm to the * 01606

## PSYCHOACOUSTIC

Phonetic segmentation using * speech parameters 03991

## PSYCHOLINGUISTIC

Visual presentation of text: the process of reading from a *perspective 03895

## PSYCHOLOGICAL

The * study of programming 0053

* issues of human-computer interaction in the work place ● 0305

Social * aspects of computer-mediated communication (Reprint) 0384

* evaluation of path hypotheses in cognitive diagnosis 0537

Parallel distributed processing: explorations in the microstructures of cognition; Vol. 2: * and biological models ● 0629

The * costs of master computer 01655

The application of * scaling techniques to knowledge elicitation for knowledge-based systems 02139

An application of computerized fuzzy graphics rating scale to the *measurement of individual differences 02200

Subjective probability and information retrieval: a review of the *literature 02303

* models of deferred decision making 02370

* concepts in a parallel system 02564

* methods for assembling procedures in text management systems 03600

Machine adaption to * differences among users in instructive information exchanges with computers 03609

Design of programming languages under * aspects 03613

* principles for allocation of functions in man-robot system 03630

Social * prerequisites and consequences of new information technologies 03631

* aspects on blind peoples's reading of radio-distributed daily newspapers 03700

Artificial behavior: computer simulation of * processes ● HCI-0073 †

## PSYCHOLOGICALLY

* based techniques for improving learning within computerized tutorials 02277

## PSYCHOLOGISTS

Communication issues among * working with computers: a view from the top 02606

## PSYCHOLOGY

Software *: the need for an interdisciplinary program 0052

Computer models of mind: computational approaches in theoretical * ● 0152

Readings in cognitive science: a perspective from * & artificial intelligence ● 0223

The * of work and organization: current trends and issues ● 0239

Contexts and conflicts between ergonomics and industrial * 0240

Ergonomics and organizational consulting: accentuation or neglect of * 0242

Applying cognitive * to user-interface design ● 0325

[PSYCHOMETRIC]

The role of cognitive * in user-interface design 0327
Key areas of cognitive *: a historical perspective 0328
Priniciples from the * of thinking and mental models 0329
Principles from the * of memory: Part I-Working memory 0330
Principles from the * of memory: Part II-Episodic and semantic memory 0331
Principles from the * of skill acquisition 0332
Principles from the * of language 0333
Human Factors * ● 0397
Cognitive * of planning ● 0435
Computers, cognition, and development: issues for * and education ● 0643
The ergonomics * project at Inria 0844
Some principles of perceptual and cognitive * applied to the design of help menus 01200
How can cognitive * help solve an artificial intelligence problem? 01480
The contemporary * of thinking and expert systems 01487
The application of cognitive * to CAD 03239
* and the user interface: science is soft at the frontier 03297
GPS and the * of th Rubik cubist: a study in reasoning about actions 03311
Common and uncommon issues in artificial intelligence an * 03312
Necessary contributions of cognitive * to computer knowledge representation and manipulation systems 03598
Current research in the * of learning and teaching 03876
Artificial intelligence and cognitive *: a new look at human factors 03904
* and information technology HCI-0225 †
Relations between cognitive * and computer system design HCI-0244 †

## PSYCHOMETRIC
Use of * tools for knowledge acquistion: a case study 0323

A short-form measure of user information satisfaction: a *evaluation and notes on use 02351

## PSYCHONOMIC
Human-computer interaction: * aspects § 03887
Introduction: human-computer interaction: * aspects 03888

## PSYCHOPHYSICAL
Language, the mind, and * parallelism 0357
Contingent aftereffects and isoluminance: * evidence for separation of color, orientation, and motion 01463
The * function of binocular space perception 02375
Perception of rotation in depth: the * evidence 03343

## PSYCHOPHYSICS
Counting and timing models in * and the conjoint Weber's law 02368
Physiology and * in taste and smell 04009
The physiology and * of touch 04010

## PSYCHOPHYSIOLOGICAL
* investigation of stress induced by temporal factors in human-computer interaction 0311
A * assessment of operator workload during simulated flight missions 01735
Beyond heart rate in the cardiac * assessment of mental effort: the T-wave amplitude component of the electrocardiogram 01738

## PSYCHOSOCIAL
Human—computer interactions in the workplace: * aspects of VDT use 0306
* work environment and use of visual display terminals:8mfrom theoretical model to action 03742
VDT technology: * and stress concerns 03755

## PSYCHOSOMATIC
Fundamentals of * transduction 01594

## PSYCHOVISUAL
Thresholding for edge detection using human * phenomena 02538
* issues in the display of medical images 03978

## PUBLIC
Automation in * libraries: effects on the organization, quality of working life, and quality of services 0246
A decision support system for vehicle scheduling in * transport 0339
A tolerance for surveillance: American * opinion concerning privacy and civil liberties 0524
Attitudes toward unauthorized software copying: general * vs. business faculty member 01142
The silent force of the screen. A research note on the impact of microelectronics on work autonomy among clerical workers in * administration 01437
The computer as mask: a problem of inadequate human interaction examined with particular regard to online * access catalogues 02337
Microcomputer availability to * library clients 02461
Barriers to cooperative computerized circulation systems in * libraries 02573
Simulations and anxiety related to * speaking 02592
Communications technology and the * sector: understanding the process of adoption 02679
* Law 99-506, "Section 508" Electronic Equipment Accessibility for disabled workers 02893

## PUBLISHERS
Writers as total desktop *: developing a conceptual approach to training 0108

## PUBLISHING
From database to hypertext via electronic *: an information odyssey 0122
Desktop * 0238
Toward hypertext * 01075

# KEYWORD INDEX [QUESTION]

Electronic *: The predicament of occasional users in the editorial proc 02446
Why desktop * is not a panacea 03131
Desktop * and user services; moment in the evolution of user support documentation at UNH 03158
Vidura—an interactive multilingual * system—specification & design 03186
The ethics of automated * systems (a response to Dr. Brockmann) HCI-0170 †

## PUCKS
Human performance evaluation of digitizer * for computer input of spatial information 01774

## PUPIL
Some remarks on a measure of computer operator workload: changes in * reflex 03626

## PUPILS
*, computers and history teaching 0746

## PURGATORY
A change of mind or the story of Fuzzies in * 0961

## PURSUIT
Modeling of task-dependent characteristics of human operator dynamics during * manual tracking 01859

## PUSHDOWN
* automata for user interface management HCI-0382 †

## PYGMALION
* at the interface HCI-0349 †

## PYRAMID
Line connectivity algorithms for an asynchronous * computer 01468

## QC
Human aspects of * circle movement in Japanese manufacturing: Natures and problems 03450

## QMR
The background of INTERNIST I and * 02853

## QMS
A formal specification of the * message system: the underlying abstract model 01406

## QUALIFICATION
Reasoning about action II: the * problem 01213
Codes and modalities in multiple resources: a success and a * 01793

## QUALIFIED
* CAD work: an intensive case study 03763

## QUALIFIERS
Tense, *, and contexts 01346

## QUALITIES
* of a good forms designer 02412

## QUANTIFICATION
The * of operational suitability 01359
Computer * of delta activity in sleep EEG 01491

## QUANTITATIVE
* determination of orientational and directional components in the response of visual cortical cells to moving stimuli 01268
A * theory of human-computer interaction HCI-0198 †
Attitudes towards specific uses of the computers *, decision-making and record-keeping applications HCI-0234 †

## QUANTIZED
Computer, * time and human duration 01593

## QUERY
Studies in the evaluation of a domain-independent natural language * system 0162
An interactive customization program for a natural language database *system 0163
A framework for choosing a database * language 0761
Item selection from menus: the influence of menu organization, *interpretation, and programming experience on selection strategies 01011
OS/2 * manager overview and prompted interface 01809
Prospects for knowledge-based customization of natural languages * systems 02008
Modelling degrees of item interest for a general database * system 02083

Dealing with a database * language in a new situation 02119
Procedural and non-procedural * languages revisited: a comparison of relational algebra and relational calculus 02146
The effect of different conceptual models using reasoning in a database *writing task 02201
The effects of relational and entity-relationship data models on *performance of end users 02247
Equivalence of views by * capacity 02271
A portable * language for small scale systems 02492
Towards interactive * expansion 03067
Inference control via * restriction vs. data modification: a perspective 03581
Visual business graphics * interface 03840
Generalized *-by-rule: a heterogeneous database * language HCI-0252 †
HERCULES: database * using natural language fragments HCI-0253 †
* languages—a taxonomy HCI-0254 †
Natural language * processing in a temporal database HCI-0257 †

## QUERYING
A cognitive model of database *: a tool for novice instruction 0905
Natural language * of historical data bases 01354
* the French *Yellow Pages*: natural language access to the directory 02007
* external databases HCI-0233 †

## QUESTION
Using "word-knowledge" reasoning for * answering 0131
The optimal level of abstraction for models of cerebral representation of language processes: the state of the * 0356
A * of delivery—an outline classification of interactive video delivery systems 0510
The telephone in *: *s on communication 01436

Natural language interface to the *-answering system for physicians 01478

* asking when learning a text-editing system 02202

The body in *: how to stay healthy at the PC 02548

A temporal logic for reasoning about changing data bases in the context of natural language *-answering 03176

Anticipating false implicatures: cooperative responses in *-answer systems 03178

## QUILL
*: An extensible system for editing documents of mixed type 03517

## QWERTY
* and keyboard reform: the soft keyboard option HCI-0190 †

## RABBIT
Nonlinear dynamics of pattern formation and pattern recognition in the *olfactory bulb 02558

Bifurcation analysis of oscillating network model of pattern recognition in the * olfactory bulb 02725

What makes * run? HCI-0256 †

## RADAR
Optical analog of two-dimensional neural networks and their application in recognition of * targets 02733

Distributed database considerations in an expert system for * analysis 03175

## RADIATION
* detection by ear and by eye 01732

The dubious dangers of VDT * 01902

* emissions from VDUs 03684

Video display terminals—electromagnetic * and health 03687

## RADICAL
Barriers to plant transparency, barriers to plant rigidity—A sketch of the problems posed by the * changes in work forms in the machine-building industry 01562

## RADIO
Health hazards assessment of * frequency electromagnetic fields emitted by video display terminals 03685

Psychological aspects on blind peoples's reading of *-distributed daily newspapers 03700

## RADIOLOGICAL
The history of the use of computers in the interpretation of * images 02845

## RAMBLING
Travel around a learning support environment: *, orienteering or touring? 02900

## RANDOM
Vertical disparity nulling in *-dot stereograms 01256

Menu search: * or systematic? 02144

A probabilistic dominance measure for binary choices: analytic aspects of a multi-attribute * weights model 02372

Perception of organization in a * stimulus 02706

A display editor with * access and continuous control HCI-0140 †

Perception of organization in a * stimulus HCI-0364 †

## RANKING
Weighting, * and relevance feedback in a front-end system 02329

## RAPPORT
The * multimedia conferencing system 03037

## RASH
A Rosacea-like skin * in VDU-operators 03695

## RATED
An update measure of supervisor-* job performance for programmer/analysis 03012

## RATING
An application of computerized fuzzy graphics * scale to the psychological measurement of individual differences 02200

## RATIONAL
Deals among * agents 0170

The *, the pragmatic and the inquiry process: The social study of information-communication systems 0786

## RAY
X-* microbeam method for measurement of articulatory dynamics-techniques and results 02641

Adapting optical-flow to measure object motion in reflectance and X-* image sequences 03334

A simple, general method for * tracing bicubic surfaces 03853

## REACT
The human side of robotics: how workers * to a robot 0443

## REACTION
A note on mimicking additive * time models 02373

Influences of mental load on * times in man-computer dialogues 03625

## REACTIONS
Designing a quality voice: an analysis of listeners' * to synthetic voices 0914

A methodology for interactive evaluation of user * to software packages:an empirical analysis of system performance, interaction, and run time 02080

"Structure—reaction type" paradigm in the conventional methods of describing organic * and the concept of imaginary transitions structures overcoming this paradigm 02268

Produciton and inventory management software packages related to user * 02567

## REACTIVE
A methodology for designing distributed, fault-tolerant, and * real-time operating systems 04071

## REACTOR
Power plant simulation and * safety 02682

## READABILITY
Factors affecting the * of moving text on a computer display 01764

* formulas: An overview 02301

Enhancing program * and comprehensibility with tools for program visualization 03510

The influence of color on program * and comprehensibility HCI-0120 †

# KEYWORD INDEX [RECOGNISERS]

**READER**
Some remarks on videotex interaction. How to write for a new * 01433
*-controlled computerized presentation of text 01785
Development and validation of a *-based documentation measure 02236

**READERS**
How "friendly" is your writing for * around the world? 0110
Slot versus insertion magnetic stripe *: user performance and preference 01756
Multi-window displays for * of lengthy texts 02142

**REALISM**
* in synthetic speech 0066
The mental rotation and perceived * of computer-generated three-dimensional images 02213

**REALISTIC**
An evaluation of a * approach to MIS 01027
Gribs—an approach to a * realtime simulation of human arm motion 03432

**REALIZATION**
Visual programming—toward * of user-friendly programming environments 03493

**REALTIME**
Gribs—an approach to a realistic * simulation of human arm motion 03432

**REAPPRAISAL**
Cognitive issues in the process of software development: review and * 02222

**REASONING**
Using "word-knowledge" * for question answering 0131
Cognitive economy in physics *: implications for designing instructional materials 0542
Understanding Bayesian * via graphical displays 0884
* about action II: the qualification problem 01213
* on a highlighted user model to respond to misconceptions 01351
A similarity-based * model for intelligent interfaces 01503

Fuzzy * in pseudo-physical logics 01695
Rule-based * as Boolean transformations 01901
* with imprecise knowledge in expert systems 02018
On the applicability of maximum entropy to inexact * 02074
The use of modal default * in information systems 02095
Training by exploration: facilitating the transfer of procedural knowledge through analogical * 02103
Information and * in intelligent decision support systems 02173
$DM^2$: an algorithm for diagnostic * that combines analytical models and experiential knowledge 02190
The effect of different conceptual models using * in a database query writing task 02201
Patterns of inductive * in a parallel expert system 02219
AI/learn: an interactive videodisk system for teaching medical concepts and * 02381
A process specification of expert lawyer * 02768
Legal * in 3-D 02774
Precedent-based legal * and knowledge acquisition in contract law: A process model 02776
* about 'hard' cases in Talmudic law 02777
Oblog-2: A hybrid knowledge representation system for defeasible * 02778
Generic expert system shell for diagnostic * 02911
Approximate spatial * 02917
Towards * visualization in expert systems 02992
* about knowledge: an overview 03167
A temporal logic for * about changing data bases in the context of natural language question-answering 03176
GPS and the psychology of th Rubik cubist: a study in * about actions 03311
Representing and * about change 03353

Decision support for * about values 03486
* in model management systems 03487
The lexicon, grammatical categories and temporal * 03549
Theoretical aspects of * about knowledge § 03559
A support system for formal *: requirements and status 04035
An artificial intelligence approach to legal * • HCI-0061 †
Approaches to human *: an analytic framework HCI-0239 †
A natural language information retrieval system with extentions towards fuzzy * HCI-0281 †
* in natural language for designing a data base HCI-0322 †
Selecting a humanly understandable knowledge representation for * about knowledge HCI-0330 †

**RECALL**
Predicting the time to * computer command abbreviations 0806
The effect of adding symbols to written warning labels on user behavior and * 01788
Comprehension and * of miniature programs 02087
Information flow in a user interface: the effect of experience and context on the * of MacWrite screens 03228
An experimental evaluation of the impact of data display format on *performance HCI-0202 †

**RECEIVED**
An analysis of humanists' requests * by an information service for the humanities 02318

**RECEPTOR**
A model of the motor servo: Incorporating nonlinear spindle * and muscle mechanical properties 01273

**RECIPIENT**
The effect of presentation media on * performance in text-based information systems 02350

**RECLAMATION**
Tenuring policies for generation-based storage * 01124

**RECOGNISERS**
Interfacing standards for * 0178

## RECOGNITION

System design for speech * and generation 0065
Electronic speech *: techniques, technology, and applications ● 0174
The elements of speech * 0176
Human factors in speech * 0177
Acoustic phonetics, auditory phonetics, speaker sex and speech *: a thread 0288
The sequential organization of spoken word * 0291
Syntactic and structural pattern * ● 0292
Problems in * of drawings 0294
Application of structural pattern * in histopathology 0295
Rule-based detection of speech features for automatic speech * 0419
Biologically plausible models of place * and goal location 0639
Issues limiting the acceptance of user interfaces using gesture input and handwriting character * 0845
Speech * enhancement by lip information 0915
Interactive * of handprinted characters for computer input 0940
FINGER—Formalizing Interaction for Gesture * 01017
An object-oriented framework of pattern * systems 01133
Visual pattern * in humans: I. Evidence for adaptive filtering 01274
Physiology based simulation model of triangle shape * 01277
Neural nets for adaptive filtering and adaptive pattern * 01362
The ART of adaptive pattern * by a self-organizing neural network 01364
Improving speaker consistency in an automatic speech * framework 01448
Multimodal detection and * performance of sonar operators 01709
On-line * of Pitman's hand-written shorthand—an evaluation of potential 02111

A group model of form * under plane similarity transformations 02366
Handprinted chinese character * via neural networks 02529
Multidimensional attribute analyhsis and pattern * for seismic interpretation 02530
On the minimum number of templates required for shift, rotation and size invariant pattern * 02531
A high accuracy algorithm for * of handwritten numerals 02532
Effect of fuzzy membership on * of gray level images 02539
Nonlinear dynamics of pattern formation and pattern * in the rabbit olfactory bulb 02558
A self-optimizing, nonsymmetrical neural net for content addressable memory and pattern * 02562
Research on individuality features in speech waves and automatic speaker * techniques 02645
* of phonemes using time-spectrum pattern 02648
Bifurcation analysis of oscillating network model of pattern * in the rabbit olfactory bulb 02725
Absolutely stable learning of * codes by a self-organizing neural network 02728
Optical analog of two-dimensional neural networks and their application in * of radar targets 02733
A machine for neural computation of acoustical patterns with application to real time speech * 02751
An improved automatic lipreading system to enhance speech * 02859
Character * of cursive scripts 02961
Parcel sorting by speech *: human factors issues 03209
Plan * for intelligent monitoring 03261
Interactive error recovery expert system for robot with voice *subsystem 03420
A consideration of learning in speech * from the viewpoint of AI class-description learning 03533

Mapping images to a hierarchical data structure—a way to knowledge-based pattern * 03954
The use of prosodic parameters in automatic speech * 03988
* of speech using temporal decomposition 03990
Morphological representation of speech knowledge for automatic speech * systems 03992
Speaker-independent automatic * of plosive sound in letters and digits 03993
Primary perceptual units in word * 03994
Computer * of spoken letters and digits 03995
Real-time large vocabulary word * via diphone spotting and multiprocessor implementation 03996
* of speaker-dependent continuous speech with Keal-Nevezh 04002
Modification of Earley's algorithm for speech * 04003
Signal processing and pattern * in nondestructive evaluation of materials § 04019
Error detection and correction in a speech * system: a knowledge based system approach 04054
Pattern *: human and mechanical ● HCI-0072 †
An economical approach to modeling speech * accuracy HCI-0354 †
Selective networks and * automata HCI-0390 †
A neural network for visual pattern * HCI-0391 †

## RECOGNIZE

How to * interesting topics to provide cooperative answering 02043

## RECOGNIZERS

'Transparent' interfacing of speech * to microcomputers 02497
Dynamic spectral adaptation of automatic speech * to new speakers 03999

## RECOGNIZING

* and responding to plan-oriented misconceptions 01350
* unexpected objects: a proposed approach HCI-0389 †

## RECOLLECTIONS
* on the processing of biomedical signals 02846

## RECOMMENDATION
A dietary * expert system using OPS5 03498

## RECONFIGURABILITY
Dynamic * for fast prototyping of user interfaces 02609

## RECONSIDER
Evaluating *: a computer program for diagnostic prompting HCI-0410 †

## RECONSTRUCT
An iterative and interactive simulation method to * unknown inputs contributing to known outputs of neuronal systems 04018

## RECONSTRUCTIBLE
Boxer: a * computational medium HCI-0121 †

## RECONSTRUCTION
* and display of the retina 03310

## RECORD
Attitudes towards specific uses of the computers quantitative, decision-making and *-keeping applications HCI-0234 †

## RECORDING
Human-computer interface * 01414

## RECOVERING
Color constancy: a method for * surface spectral reflectance 0298
Perceiving * structure from events 03346

## RECRUITMENT
Model of the neuro-muscular * example of the extensor digitorum communis muscle in man: I—identification of motoneurons and of muscular fibers 01595

## RECTANGLES
Digital parallelism, perpendicularity, and * 01843
Star, maximal *, lattices: a new perspective on Q-analysis 02105

## RECTANGULARITY
The alternatives allowed by a * postulate, and a pragmatic approach to interpreting motion 03550

## RECURSION
Learning iteration * from examples 02215

## RECURSIVE
* complementarity in the cybernetics of education 01598

## RECURSIVELY
A preliminary analysis of * generated networks 02749

## REDUCING
* social context cues: electronic mail in organizational communication (Reprint) 0385
* social context cues: electronic mail in organizational communication 02473

## REDUCTION
CRT picture vibration caused by low-frequency magnetic field and its *method 01987
The perception of system and the * of uncertainty 02850

## REDUNDANCY
Electronic monitoring and the * of control systems: The role of the supervisor 03000
Parallelism and * in neural networks 03952

## REDUX
Videotex * 02545

## REENTRANT
An approach to a mathematics of phenomena: canonical aspects of * form eigenbehavior in the extended calculus of indications 01621

## REFERENCE
X Protocol * manual for version II: vol. 0 ● 0669
Human factors * guide for electronics and computer professionals ● 0733
Human factors * guide for electronics and computer professionals ● 0734
In search of a user interface * model 0944
Dialogue management * model 0945
On user interface * models 0946
* models, window systems, and concurrency 01058
* model for DBMS user facility 01086

* identification and * identification failures 01345
Temporal ontology and temporal * 01347
The human immune system as an information systems security * model 01547
Using a cognitive model of dialogue for * retrieval 02317
Lets "Deep-Six" our * manuals 02955
Concepts in user interfaces: a * model for command and response languages § 03872
The synthesizer generator * manual (3rd ed.) ● HCI-0024 †
Concepts in user interfaces: a * model for command and response languages ● HCI-0032 †
The spatial metaphor for user interfaces: experimental tests of * by location versus name HCI-0268 †
Interactive fuzzy decision-making for multi-objective nonlinear programming using * membership intervals HCI-0295 †

## REFERENTIAL
Extending a relational database with deferred * integrity checking andintelligent joins 01089

## REFINEMENT
Learning through incremental * of procedures 0482
CAD Based verification and * of high level compliant motion primitives 0600
Knowledge base * by monitoring abstract control knowledge 02160

## REFINING
* problem-solving knowledge in repertory grids using a consultation mechanism 02205
* early design decisions with a black-box model 03200

## REFLECTANCE
Color constancy: a method for recovering surface spectral * 0298
A method for computing spectral * 01267
Adapting optical-flow to measure object motion in * and X-ray image sequences 03334

## REFLECTION
The computer as a tool for learning through * 0535
The effects of limited data in multi-frequency * diffraction tomography 04020

## REFLEX
Some remarks on a measure of computer operator workload: changes in pupil * 03626
Innate and learned components in a simple visuo-motor * 03965

## REFORM
The human costs of manufacturing * 01706
QWERTY and keyboard *: the soft keyboard option HCI-0190 †

## REFORMULATION
Helgon: extending the retrieval by * paradigm 0880

## REFRACTION
* in VDU operators—a comparison with other professions 03740

## REFRACTIVE
VDU work, * errors and binocular vision 03739

## REFRESH
Influence of CRT * rates on accommodation aftereffects 03731

## REGIONS
A new algorithm for extracting the interior of bounded * based on chain coding 01469
Distinctive * and modes: a new theory of speech production 02659

## REGRESSION
A simultaneous * model for double stimulation tasks 01726
A * model to identify successful learner traits with CAI 02376

## REGULARIZATION
Computational vision and * theory 0301

## REGULATING
A self-* adaptive system 0829
A model of the controller responses of the human temperature * system to changes in water temperature 02487

## REGULATORY
The changing workplace: A guide to managing the people, organizational, and * aspects of office technology (book excerpt) 0044

## REIMANNIAN
Non-* approach to geometry of visual space: An application of affinely connected geometry to visual alleys and horopter 02364

## REINTEGRATION
Further division of * of mental labour? CAD/CAP and work in design nd work preparation shops 03385

## REJECTED
The case of the * applicants 02438

## RELATIONAL
The semantics-based natural language interface to * databases 0164
The INGRES papers: anatomy of a * database system ● 0706
System R: a * approach to database management 0709
Interfacing Ada and * databases 0762
Extending a * database with deferred referential integrity checking and intelligent joins 01089
Automating the design of graphical presentations of * information 01150
DATENBANK-DIALOG: a German language interface for * databases 01208
A practical approach to transforming extended ER diagrams into the *model 02022
Convexly combined fuzzy * equations and several aspects of their application to fuzzy information processing 02027
Procedural and non-procedural query languages revisited: a comparison of * algebra and * calculus 02146
Human performance in * algebra, tuple calculus, and domain calculus 02208
The effects of * and entity-relationship data models on query performance of end users 02247
Relative information capacity of simple * database schemata 02579
The integration of the network and * approaches in a DBMS 03283
Knowledge base enhancements to * databases 03285
An extended * database model based on user views 03452
Lessons learned from modeling a secure multilevel * database system 03580
Design tools for large * database systems 03946
* models in natural and artificial vision 03953
ARES: a * database with the capability of performing flexible interpretation of queries HCI-0248 †
Update and retrieval in a * database through a universal schema interface HCI-0260 †

## RELATIONSHIP
The effects of relational and entity-* data models on query performance of end users 02247

## RELATIVIZED
* Arthur-Merlin versus Merlin-Arthur games 01912

## RELAXATION
Vision monitoring of VDU operators and * of visual stress by means of laser speckle system 03738

## RELEVANCE
*: communication and cognition ● 0704
Weighting, ranking and * feedback in a front-end system 02329

## RELIABILITY
* in computing: the role of interval methods in scientific computing ● 0548
Knowledge-based system for task analysis and * enhancement 01516
An approach to human * on man-machine systems using error possibility 01702
Beware the * of slope scores for individuals 01727

Estimating * with small samples: increased precision with averaged correlations 01728
A representation of human * using fuzzy concepts 02024
On the representation and the impact of * on expert system weights 02211
Adaptive information systems control: A *-based approach 02345
An abstract description generator for the * analysis in the design of real time systems 02490
* and robustness of engineering software § 03451
Human * in information systems 03809
A computer assisted learning system for * engineering 04060

**RELIABLE**
A high level language-based computing enviornment to support production and execution of * programs 01855

**RELIEF**
Geomatic: a 3-D graphic * simulation system HCI-0395 †

**RELIGION**
The cybernetic principle: its transdisciplinarity to science and * and the challenging task 01596

**RELUCTANCE**
Reasons for computer utilization * by teachers with computer training 04059

**REMESHING**
An interactive approach to local * around a propagating crack 01685

**REMINDERS**
Optimum display arrangements for presenting visual * 03297

**REMOTE**
Computing advice at a distance: the '* advisory' concept 02617
Illumination requirements for operating a space * manipulator 03392
Human-machine interface in * monitoring and control of flexible manufacturing systems 03399
Concept for a model databased * maintenance system 03565

**RENDERING**
High-performance polygon * 02814
High performance interactive graphics: modeling, * and animating for IBM PCs and compatibles ● HCI-0071 †

**REPAIR**
DARN: Toward a community memory for diagnosis and * tasks 0428
Communication failure in dialogue and discourse: detection and * processes ● 0611

**REPERTOIRES**
How much is enough? A study of user command * 03240

**REPLACE**
Graphical search and * 02812

**REPLACED**
Will you be * by a knowledge base? 02055

**REPORTER**
Time-life, world * and the secretary: experiments with end-users 02325

**REPOSITIONING**
* the information systems management function: Implications for information systems personnel 03015

**REPRESENTATIONAL**
* frameworks and models for human-computer interfaces HCI-0188 †

**REPRESENTATIVES**
Selection systems for sales * 02408

**REPRESENTED**
Are machines as good as people in drawing conclusions from knowledge * in catalogues, data bases and expert systems? 0736
Optimum stresses and strains * by examples from shop practice 03441

**REPRESENTING**
* and using metacommunication to control speakers' relationships in natural-language dialogue 02136
* the structure of jobs in job analysis 02181
* and reasoning about change 03353

**REPRINT**
As we may think (* 0367

A conceptual framework for the augmentation of man's intellect (* 0368
Toward high-performance knowledge workers (* 0369
Authorship provisions in AUGMENT (* 0370
Interactive human communication (* 0371
Thinking ahead: what to expect from teleconferencing (* 0372
Office information systems and computer science (* 0373
Communication and management support in system development environments (* 0374
Callisto: an intelligent project management system (* 0375
Beyond the chalkboard: computer support for collaboration and problem solving in meetings (* 0376
Computer-based real-time conferencing systems (* 0377
Hypertext: an introduction and survey (* 0378
Data sharing in group work (* 0379
Diamond: a multimedia message system built on a distributed architecture (* 0380
Evolution of an organizational interface: the new business department at a large insurance firm (* 0382
A language/action perspective on the design of cooperative work (* 0383
Social psychological aspects of computer-mediated communication (* 0384
Reducing social context cues: electronic mail in organizational communication (* 0385
Cognitive science and organizational design: a case study of computer conferencing (* 0386
Relationships and tasks in scientific research collaborations (* 0387

**REPRODUCTION**
Private copying, * costs, and the supply of intellectual property 01988

**REPTIL**
*-promoting dialog between humanoid and computer 02307

## REQUEST
How to interface to advisory systems? Users * help with a very simple language 02888

## REQUESTS
An analysis of humanists' * received by an information service for the humanities 02318

## REQUISITE
Providing the * knowledge via software documentation 02898

## RESEARCHERS
Formative evaluation of pre-Logo programming environments: a collaborative effort of *, teachers, and children 02292

A supporting system for effective construction and sharing of scientific databases by general * HCI-0262 †

## RESEMBLANCE
Expectation and variance of item * distributions in a convolution-correction model of distributed memory 02369

## RESEMBLING
Arithmetic codes * neural encoding 02021

## RESISTANT
Designing keybindings to be easy to learn and * to forgetting even when the set of commands is large 02890

## RESOLVING
ORGPLAN an information-decisive aid system to * organizing problems 01573

## RESOURCE
Interactive video as a school *: Rolls-Royce or Model T Ford? 0513

Producing * discs—the Domesday project experience 0514

ICE: information center expert: a consultation system for * allocation 0781

* management scheme in distributed environments 01018

Technology adaptation: a typology for strategic human * management 01238

Dialogue cell * model and basic dialogue cells 01400

Key human * issues in IS in the 1990s: Views of IS executives versus human * executives 01939

An entity-relationship framework for information * management 01943

User-developers: the new software * 02052

Expert systems as human * management decision tools 02440

DORUS: an architecture for dynamic optimal * utilization systems 02979

An evaluation and selection methodology of microcomputer training software: Implications for human * managers and computer personnel 03002

A consultation system for information center * allocation 03100

Starting and maintaining a computing * center: lessons we've learned 03149

A scarce * in undergraduate software engineering courses: user interface design materials 04027

## RESOURCES
Cognitive * and the learning of human-computer dialogs 0209

Government infostructures: a guide to the networks of information * and technologies at federal, state, and local levels ● 0523

Conversational * for situated action 0861

Automaticity, *, and memory: theoretical controversies and practical implications 01792

Codes and modalities in multiple *: a success and a qualification 01793

Multiple * for processing and storage in short-term working memory 01794

Task-sharing within and between hemispheres: a multiple-* approach 01795

## RESPECTING
Privacy * permissions and rights 03583

## RESPONSES
Questions, answers, and *: interacting with knowledge base systems 0182

On the identification of neural * 01260

Summarizing natural language database * 01343

Speech * and dual-task performance: better time-sharing or asymmetric transfer? 01789

Providing quality * with natural language interfaces: the null value problem 01848

Effects of breadth, depth and number * on computer menu search performance 02192

A model of the controller * of the human temperature regulating system to changes in water temperature 02487

Anticipating false implicatures: cooperative * in question-answer systems 03178

Generating natural language * appropriate to conversational situations—in the case of Japanese 03922

## RESPONSIBILITY
System user/system implementer: a joint * for success 01535

* sharing between sophisticated users and professionals in structured prototyping 01978

Systems design and social *: the political implications of "computer-supported cooperative work". A commentary 02516

Automation—implications for knowledge retention as a function of operator control * 03207

Fault management, knowledge support, and * in man-machine systems 03812

## RESPONSIVE
Designing interactive, * instruction: a set of procedures 0274

The * system: a new challenge for AI 02920

## RESTDAYS
Long workdays versus *: assessing fatigue and alertness with a portable performance 01778

## RESTING
Is the * state of our eyes a favorable viewing distance for VDU-work? 03737

## RESTORING

* a sense of control during implementation: how user involvement leads to system acceptance 02509

## RESTRICTION

Inference control via query * vs. data modification: a perspective 03581

## RESTRICTIVENESS

User perceptions of decision support system *: an experiment 02353

User perceptions of DSS *: an experiment 03470

## RETENTION

A comparison of textual information * from CRT terminals and paper 0954

Automation—implications for knowledge * as a function of operator control responsibility 03207

## RETINA

Reconstruction and display of the * 03310

## RETINEX

*: physics and the theory of color vision 01574

## RETRAINING

* high school teachers to teach computer science—observations on the first course 01030

## RETRIEVAL

Hypertext and intelligent interfaces for text * 0115

Knowledge engineering: expert systems and information * ● 0735

A knowledge-based intermediary system for information * 0737

Helgon: extending the * by reformulation paradigm 0880

The study of user behavior on information * systems 01046

Comment on some recent comments on information * 01074

IRX: an information * system for experimentation and user applications 01076

An information * system for software components 01077

Information * using a hypertext-based help system 01155

Information * using micros 01225

The selection of a servicing discipline in a multiterminal conversational information * system 01233

A feature matching approach to the * of graphical information 01245

Coding image sequences for interactive * 01330

The value of information and computer-aided information seeking: problem formulation and application to fiction * 01989

A common interface for accessing document * systems and dbms for * of bibliographic data 01990

User modeling in intelligent information * 01994

Online text * via browsing 01999

All users of information * systems are not created equal: an exploration into individual differences 02011

Evaluation of the user interface in an information * system: a model 02012

Design of personal information * systems 02032

Non-first normal form universal relations: an application to information * systems 02039

The user's mental model of an information * system: an experiment on a prototype online catalog 02099

Theoretical training and problem detection in a computerized database *task 02239

Support for browsing in an intelligent text * system 02240

A graphical thesaurus-based information * system 02243

Cognitive models in information *—an evaluative review 02298

Interactive document display and its use in information * 02300

Subjective probability and information *: a review of the psychological literature 02303

A behavioral approach to information * system design 02304

Using a cognitive model of dialogue for reference * 02317

A connectionist approach to conceptual information * 02772

* systems for the information seeker: can the role of the intermediary be automated? 02864

A prototype autonomous agent for crew and equipment * in space 02994

A knowledge-based approach to online document * system design 03027

Towards an intelligent and personalized * system 03028

Employing voice back channels of facilitate audio document * 03045

Interactive * office documents 03047

Research & Development in Information * § 03062

How do the experts do it? The use of ethnographic methods as an aid to understanding the cognitive processing and * of large bodies of text 03063

On the nature and fuction of explanation in intelligent information * 03064

Information * using impression of documents as a clue 03065

Concept based * in classical IR systems 03066

* based on user behaviour 03068

Some measures and procedures for evaluation of the user interface in an information * system 03069

IR-NLI II: applying man-machine interaction and artificial intelligence conceptsto information * 03070

Integrated information * for law in a hypertext environment 03071

Research and development in information * § 03072

Why do some people have more difficulty learning to use an information * system than others? 03075

A * system for on-line English-Japanese dictionaries 03078

An advanced full-text * and analysis system 03079

Research and development in information * § 03287

Problems in the design of information * systems: user competence and information complexity 03602

Online library catalogues as information * systems: what can we learn from research? 04040
Intelligent interfaces for information * systems: architecture problems in the construction of expert systems for document * 04042
Information *: the future 04045
Online information *: concepts, principles, and techniques ● HCI-0046 †
A novice user's interface to information * systems HCI-0219 †
Using restricted natural language for data *: a plan for field evaluation HCI-0255 †
Update and * in a relational database through a universal schema interface HCI-0260 †
Users and experts in the document * system model HCI-0270 †
Architecture problems in the construction of expert systems for document * HCI-0272 †
Towards a new research paradigm in information * HCI-0273 †
A natural language information * system with extentions towards fuzzy reasoning HCI-0281 †
Cognitive models, cognitive tasks, and information * HCI-0331 †

**RETRIEVING**
DOMAIN/DELPHI: * documents online 0906

**RETROSPECTIVE**
UNIX Emacs: a * (lessons for flexible system design) 03114
Ten years of window systems—a * view 03926

**RETURNS**
History offers clues to the future: user control * 02517

**REVENUE**
An expert system for screening employee pension plans for the Internal *Service 02773

**REVERSAL**
Diffusion approximation of the neuronal model with synaptic * potentials 01254

**REVERSE**
* engineering the brain HCI-0368 †

**REVERSIBLE**
Generating * programs 02620

**RGB**
An experimental comparison of *, YIQ, LAB, HSV, and opponent color models HCI-0381 †

**RHYTHM**
A study of stability of electrocortical * generators 01258
Neural network model with *-assimilation capacity 01881

**RIEDWYL**
A perceptual study of the Flury-* faces for graphically displaying multivariate data 02126

**RIGHT**
Making the * choices with menus 0070
The user is always * 01966

**RIGIDITY**
Barriers to plant transparency, barriers to plant *—A sketch of the problems posed by the radical changes in work forms in the machine-building industry 01562

**RING**
The * machine 01483
Sherlock—a system for diagnosing power distribution * network faults 02916

**ROBOT**
Employment skills for the * age 0442
The human side of *ics: how workers react to a * 0443
Man is not a * 0445
* simulation and off-line programming—an integrated CAE-CAD approach 0599
Experiences with off-line * programming via standardized interfaces 0601
Off-line programming and path generation for * manipulators 0603
Modeling of * system dynamics for CAD based * programming 0605
Is man a * ● 0697
An interactive programming system for the IBM 7545 * 01517
Fuzzy control of a mobile * for obstacle avoidance 02025
Human nature and * nature 03401

* vs. human operator for speed, precision and other aspects 03403
Human response to unexpected * movements at selected slow speeds 03405
Human perception of the work envelope of an industrial * 03410
Development of a human engineering design standard for * teach pendants 03411
Overview of research issues in * safety 03417
Safety considerations in * design 03418
Interactive error recovery expert system for * with voice recognition subsystem 03420
Performance evaluation of three pressure mats as * workstation safety sensors 03428
The economic evaluation on implementation industrial * from user point of view 03447
MEISTER: a model enhanced intelligent and skillful teleoperational * system 03562
A rule-based system for fuzzy natural language * control 03574
Psychological principles for allocation of functions in man-* system 03630
Integration of * sensory systems 04016
* components and systems ● HCI-0068 †
Natural-language interface for an instructable * HCI-0324 †

**ROBOTIC**
A multiprocessor system for real-time * control 02023
Some recent documentation of * safety from Sweden 03407
Unexpected motion hazard exposures on a large * assembly 03409
Man-machine interfaces for mobile * systems 03413
100 Percent assured performance for * assistive devices for handicapped and elderly persons 03414
Standards requirements for mobile * systems 03415
Ergonomic evaluation of safety devices in * systems 03449
Evolution of a * excavator 03569

## ROBOTICS
A flexible and intelligent system for fast measurements in binary images for in-line * control 03986

## ROBOTICS
Education and training in * ● 0440
The human side of *: how workers react to a robot 0443
* and Material Flow ● 0558
U.S. Army field * focus and key technology issues 03402
Methods for field evaluation of safety in a * workplace 03408
CAD and * in architecture and construction § 03568
Tensor geometry: a language of brains & neurocomputers. Generalized coordinates in neuroscience & * 03966
An overview of local environment sensing in * applications 04012
Teleoperations and *: applications and technology ● HCI-0068 †

## ROBOTIZATION
"Automation, * in particular, is always economically desirable"—fact or fiction? 03448

## ROBUST
Integrated processing produces * understanding 01342

## ROBUSTNESS
Reliability and * of engineering software § 03451

## ROM
CD * joins the new media homesteaders 0281
The CD * handbook ● 0678
An historical perspective of CD * 0679
Designing a CD * information structure 0682
User interfaces for CD'* PACs 02466
Integrating CD-* with printed and online services: a silver platter end-user perspective 03558

## ROOMS
*: the use of multiple virtual workspaces to reduce space contention in a window-based graphical user interface 01151

## ROOT
Chinese character processing system based on character-* combination and graphic processing 03187

## ROOTS
Information science: its * and relation as viewed from the perspective of cognitive science HCI-0185 †

## ROSACEA
A *-like skin rash in VDU-operators 03695

## ROSE
*: An object-oriented database system for interactive computer graphics applications 03845

## ROTATION
The mental * and perceived realism of computer-generated three-dimensional images 02213
On the minimum number of templates required for shift, * and size invariant pattern recognition 02531
A study in interactive 3-D * using 2-D control devices 02813
Determining motion parameters for scenes with translation and * 03338
Perception of * in depth: the psychophysical evidence 03343

## ROUGH
* sets and dependency analysis among attributes in computer implementations of expert's inference models 02231

## ROUNDTABLE
A * discussion on women, computers and participation 03673

## ROUTE
Competitive dynamics in a dual-* connectionist model of print-to-sound transformation 01341

## ROUTINE
Computer text-editing: an information-processing analysis of a *cognitive skill 0056
What should be computerized? Cognitive demands of mental * tasks and mental load 03632

## ROUTING
One-layer * without component constraints HCI-0090 †

## RS
Ergonomic improvements boost AS/* performance 01904

## RUBIK
GPS and the psychology of th * cubist: a study in reasoning about actions 03311

## RULE
*-based detection of speech features for automatic speech recognition 0419
A fuzzy *-based model of human problem solving 0656
* base management using meta knowledge 01081
The role of stimulus-to-* consistency in learning rapid application of spatial * 01765
Significance testing of *s in *-based models of human problem solving 01867
A user preference guided approach to conflict resolution in *-based expert systems 01872
A *-based model for the human operator in a time-constrained competing-task environment 01877
*-based reasoning as Boolean transformations 01901
Modeling *-based systems by stochastic programmed production systems 02017
The influence of *-generated stress on computer-synthesized speech 02081
Issues in the verification of knowledge in *-based systems 02226
The efficacy of computer-assisted video instruction on * learning and attitudes 02286
A simple selectionist learning * for neural networks 02756
Multimodal response planning: an adaptive * based approach 02894
A *-based system for interactive proposal evaluation 02927
A *-based system for fuzzy natural language robot control 03574
Generalized query-by-*: a heterogeneous database query language HCI-0252 †
On the application of *-based techniques to the design of advice giving systems HCI-0315 †
A fuzzy *-based model of human problem solving HCI-0359 †

**RUN**
The *-time structure of UIMS-supported applications 01059
A methodology for interactive evaluation of user reactions to software packages:an empirical analysis of system performance, interaction, and * time 02080
What makes RABBIT * HCI-0256 †

**RUNNING**
Developing and * expert systems with PESYS 01690

**SAA**
Common user access—a consistent and usable human-computer interface for the * environments 01819
Designing * applications and user interfaces 01821

**SAFE**
VDTs: are they * 02549
SEE: a * editing environment; human-computer interaction for programmers 03225
A study of fail-* technology 03421
Construction and examples of sensor in * working system 03425

**SAFETY**
Power plant simulation and reactor * 02682
Some recent documentation of robotic * from Sweden 03407
Methods for field evaluation of * in a robotics workplace 03408
A study on the * operation of robots using monitor hold 03412
Critical issues in the * of software-dominant automated systems 03416
Overview of research issues in robot * 03417
* considerations in robot design 03418
A study on * evaluation index and industrial accident analysis from the viewpoint of the * confirmation type 03419
A study of intrinsic * asymmetrical actuator 03422
AGV * system designed for preventing hazardous human contact 03423

Experiences from the use of an intelligent * sensor with industrial robots 03427
Performance evaluation of three pressure mats as robot workstation *sensors 03428
Effects of automation on occupational * & health 03435
Ergonomic evaluation of * devices in robotic systems 03449

**SAILING**
Still * (and bailing): managing unexpected change in user support 03150
Local area networks: * from the past to the present and into the future 03152

**SALES**
Selection systems for * representatives 02408

**SAMPLES**
Estimating reliability with small *: increased precision with averaged correlations 01728

**SAMPLING**
Digital waveform * rate converter 01578

**SANDWICH**
Application of decision support system on * beams, verified by experiments 01572

**SASSAFRAS**
Supporting concurrency, communication, and synchronization in human-computer interaction—the * UIMS HCI-0102 †

**SATELLITE**
Principle of visual color coding applied to * images 03304

**SATISFACTION**
Posture and VDU operator * 0988
The effects of sources of applications programs on user *: an empirical study of micro, mini & mainframe computers using an interactive artificial intelligence expert-system 01601
Measuring user * 01677
User *: A vital management issue 01678

The influence of troubleshooting, education, and documentation on computer user * 01869
End user—IS design professional interaction—information exchange for firm profit or end user * 01936
Impact of prototyping on user information * during the IS specification phase 01955
A short-form measure of user information *: a psychometric evaluation and notes on use 02351
The effects of task differences on the work *, job characteristics, nd role perceptions of programmer/analysts 02359
TA: Can it improve worker * with organizational decision-making? 02414
The measurement of end-user computing * 02510
Development of an instrument measuring user * of the human-computer interface 02892
Moderating effects of age, education, and tenure on the job *-job performance relationship 03021
An empirical study of user * with a microcomputer-based campus-wide 03137
Advanced office systems: An empirical look at use and * 03172
Measuring user * 03230
Computerized manufacturing technology and work organization effects on labor relations and worker * 03443
The effects of communication monitors on user * HCI-0221 †
The complexity of some polynomial network consistency algorithms for constraint * problems HCI-0361 †
An empirical study of the impact of user involvement on system usage and information * HCI-0448 †

**SATISFIES**
Mainframe and microcomputer-based business graphics: What * users? HCI-0216 †

## SATISFYING
Designing a neural network * a given set of constraints 02755
## SATURN
*—a tool for modelling and performance evaluation of computer systems 02670
## SAUCI
*: a knowledge-based interface architecture 02895
## SAVES
Building user interfaces before writing code * time and money 02662
## SCALES
Colour coding * and computer graphics 03864
## SCALING
A * model for dichotomous branching processes 01264
* relationships in back-propagation learning 01338
The application of psychological * techniques to knowledge elicitation for knowledge-based systems 02139
## SCAN
Performance, preference, and visual * patterns on a menu-based system: implications for interface design 0855
## SCANDINAVIA
An assessment of the major computerised databases relating to disabled people in the UK and * 02326
## SCANNING
Statistical dependency in visual * 01719
## SCATTERPLOTS
Brushing * 02672
## SCENARIOS
How would your favourite user model cope with these * 0999
## SCENE
Task-oriented approach to interactive control of heavy-duty manipulators based on coarse * description ● 0546
Magnification effects with imaging displays depend on * content and viewing condition 01786

Autonomous * description with range imagery 02707
Hierarchical * structure representations to facilitate image understanding 02942
The actem model for decision modelling in a * management system 02954
The application of * synthesis techniques to the display of multidimensional image data HCI-0371 †
## SCHAUM
*'s outline of theories and problems of programming with advanced structured COBOL with file processing structured systems deveoplment and interactive cons ● 0555
## SCHEDULING
A decision support system for vehicle * in public transport 0339
Hierarchical * in an intelligent environmental control system 02976
Plant * expert system for batch processing 02977
An approach to knowledge elicitation in * FMS: Toward a hybrid intelligent system 03394
## SCHEMA
Representation of dynamic features in a conceptual * 01231
Update and retrieval in a relational database through a universal *interface HCI-0260 †
An expert system for conceptual * design: a machine learning approach HCI-0335 †
From * theory to computational (neuro-)linguistics HCI-0345 †
## SCHEMAS
* that integrate vision and touch for hand control 0026
Choosing between methods: analysing the user's decision space in terms of * and linear models 02879
## SCHEMATA
* and sequential thought processes in PDP models 0630
Relative information capacity of simple relational database * 02579

## SCHEMATIC
VISION: VHDL induced * imaging on net-lists 02830
## SCHEME
Resource management * in distributed environments 01018
## SCHEMES
Effects of functionally or topographically presented process * on operator performance 01749
On representation * for electronic promising 03488
## SCHOOL
Information technology and education: the changing * ● 0282
Interactive video as a * resource: Rolls-Royce or Model T Ford? 0513
Retraining high * teachers to teach computer science—observations on the first course 01030
Personality characteristics of junior high * students successful with computers 01592
Perceptions of the information search process in libraries: a study of changes from high * through college 02002
## SCIENCE
Computer support for organizations: toward an organizational * 0211
Improving human-computer interaction—a quest for cognitive * 0213
Neurophilosophy: toward a unified * of the mind-brain ● 0219
Readings in cognitive *: a perspective from psychology & artificial intelligence ● 0223
Color displays and color * 0255
From models to modules: studies in cognitive * from the McGill workshops ● 0352
Office information systems and computer * (Reprint) 0373
Cognitive * and organizational design: a case study of computer conferencing (Reprint) 0386
The computer and the mind: an introduction to cognitive * ● 0463
The new renaissance: art, * and universal machine 0530

[SCIENCES]

Teachers' adoption of multimedia technologies for * and mathematics instruction 0577
Computation and cognition: toward a foundation for cognitive * ● 0593
Mental models in cognitive * 0647
Conceptual design of decision support systems utilizing management *models 0658
Annual review of computer * vol. 1, 1986 ● 0719
The computational * revolution: technology, methodology, and sociology 0728
University of Colorado at Boulder, Institute of cognitive * 0811
Cumulating the * of HCI: from s-R compatibility to transcription typing 0831
Social * and system design: interdisciplinary collaborations 0833
Center for coordination *, MIT 0841
Cognitive * and machine intelligence laboratory, University of Michigan 0843
Retraining high school teachers to teach computer *—observations on the first course 01030
Dealing with disparate audiences in computer * courses using a project group within a traditional class 01031
A comparison of male and female computer * students' attitudes toward computers 01045
Information * and the PSI phenomenon 01281
A * of information for the information age 01285
The cybernetic principle: its transdisciplinarity to * and religion and the challenging task 01596
Expert systems in management * 01689
From vision * to HDTV: bridging the gap 01981
Moral issues in information * 02321
Electronic communications and collaboration: the emerging model for computer aided communications in * and medicine 02678

Advances in Cognitive * § 02720
Advances in cognitive * 02721
APL: The language of * and management 02799
Computer * education § 02809
History of the development of medical information systems at the Laboratory of Computer * at Massachusetts General Hospital 02842
Grasping reality through illusion—interactive graphics serving * 02857
Psychology and the user interface: * is soft at the frontier 03297
Computer * and statistics § 03313
Connectionism and cognitive * 03547
Overcoming conceptual difficulties in physical * through computer-based Socratic dialogs 03877
Graph-theoretic concepts in computer * § 03885
Structured neural networks in nature and in computer * 03950
Future Trends in Information * and Technology § 04039
Human factors of changing information * technology 04048
In search of the person: philosophical explorations in cognitive * ● HCI-0062 †
Mental models: towards a cognitive * of language, inference, and consciousness ● HCI-0063 †
Informatics (computer and information *): its ideology, methodology, and sociology HCI-0086 †
Information *: its roots and relation as viewed from the perspective of cognitive * HCI-0185 †
Cognitive engineering—cognitive * HCI-0200 †

**SCIENCES**
Computer assisted learning in the humanities and social * ● 0470
Aiding the human decisionmaker through the knowledge-based * 01880

**SCIENTIFIC**
Tacit knowledge, working life and * method 0345

KEYWORD INDEX

Relationships and tasks in * research collaborations (Reprint) 0387
Reliability in computing: the role of interval methods in * computing ● 0548
High-speed computing: * applications and algorithm design ● 0727
SMART: * database management and engineering analysis routines and tools 01166
Microcomputer software. 2. * and technical word processing on a personal computer: has the time come? 02266
GPROC—an integrated system for the processing of numerical * data 02631
The development of an intelligent user interface for NASA's * databases 02673
A portable user interface for a * programming environment 03125
Interactive * visualization and parallel display techniques 03542
Computer culture: the *, intellectual, and social impact of the computer § 03567
Some design principles for a mathematical knowledge representation system: a new approach to * calculation 03849
A supporting system for effective construction and sharing of *databases by general researchers HCI-0262 †

**SCIENTISTS**
Technical writers as computer *: the challenges of online documentation HCI-0153 †

**SCOPE**
The * of research on motion: sensations, perception, representation and generation 03323
Office automation and work organization: making use of the * of choice 03746
Analysing the * of cognitive models in human-computer interaction: a trade-off approach HCI-0245 †

**SCORES**
Beware the reliability of slope * for individuals 01727

A system for the representation of human body movement from dance * 02540

Music—a language for typesetting music * 02622

**SCOTOPIC**

The effects of target wavelength on dynamic visual acuity under photopic and * viewing 01762

**SCREENING**

An expert system for * employee pension plans for the Internal Revenue Service 02773

**SCREENS**

Presenting documents on workstation * 0267

Designing * for people to use easily 01531

Dynamic * and static paper 02786

Improving the accuracy of touch *: an experimental evaluation of three strategies 02860

Information flow in a user interface: the effect of experience and context on the recall of MacWrite * 03228

Touch-sensitive *: the technologies and their application HCI-0087 †

Reading text from computer * HCI-0088 †

Cognitive layouts of windows and multiple * for user interfaces HCI-0122 †

**SCRIPTING**

Eliminating the dichotomy between * and interaction 03299

**SCRIPTS**

Character recognition of cursive * 02961

**SCROLLING**

A comparison of hypertext, * and folding as mechanisms for program browsing 03235

**SCULPTURED**

VDAFS—a pragmatic interface for the exchange of * surface data HCI-0420 †

**SDI**

An interactive system * on microcomputer 02272

**SDL**

A set of tools supporting the software design based on * 03803

**SDSC**

Learning the ways: the enculturation of * users 03144

**SEARCHER**

The */information interface project—final report 02341

**SEARCH**

Design and test of a database for fiction, based on an analysis of children's * behavior 0451

* technology, Inc. 0872

In * of a user interface reference model 0944

Dialogue and the * for information 01223

Computer programming and generalized problem-solving skills: in * of direction 01585

In * of the perfect programmer 01648

Optimizing the structure of database menu indexes: a decision model of menu * 01716

On the selection and evaluation of visual display symbology: factors influencing * and identification times 01718

Menu organization and user expertise in information * tasks 01761

* success and expectations with a computer interface 01995

Perceptions of the information * process in libraries: a study of changes from high school through college 02002

Enhancing * results by editing, analysis and packaging 02035

The effects of entry arrangement in * times: a cross-generational study 02048

Menu *: random or systematic? 02144

Effects of breadth, depth and number responses on computer menu *performance 02192

Grid analysis: continuing the * for a metric of shape 02367

An investigation of online *er traits and their relationship to *outcomes 02447

An empirical formula for visual * 02526

Graphical * and replace 02812

A * for machine/human compatibility in manufacturing systems 03381

Experimental and theoretical analysis of visual * activities 03620

* strategies in internal and external memories 03911

Recent results on the application of a metric-space * algorithm (AESA) to multispeaker data 03997

Experimentation with an adaptive * strategy for solving a keyboard design/configuration problem 04070

In * of the person: philosophical explorations in cognitive science ● HCI-0062 †

On * in an incomplete database HCI-0214 †

In * of *ing skills HCI-0274 †

Knowledge-based * tactics for an intelligent intermediary system HCI-0277 †

**SEARCHED**

Writing to be *: A workshop on document creation principles 01073

**SEARCHER**

The linear file—restrictions on online information use: a *'s perspective 01634

A logic assistant for the database * 02001

An investigation of online * traits and their relationship to search outcomes 02447

How good an Online * are you? Twenty questions about BIOSIS previews 02521

**SEARCHES**

Comparison of manual and online * of chemical abstracts 02265

**SEARCHING**

Cost effectiveness of on-line * of chemical information: an industrial viewpoint 0195

Voice: technology * for communication needs 0808

End-user *—What are the implications? 01224

Online *: a five star review of research 01314

Assaying and isolating individual differences in * a hierarchical file system 01747

OAKDEC, a program for studying the effects on users of a procedural expert system for database * 02003
Online * using speech as a man/machine interface 02013
A comparative study of subject * in an OPAC among branch libraries of a university library system 02050
Accommodating individual differences in * a hierarchical file system 02212
End-user * of CAS ONLINE. Results of a cooperative experiment between Imperial Chemical Industries and Chemical Abstracts Services 02269
Subject * behaviour at the library catalogue and at the shelves: implications for online interactive catalogues 02302
Voice input/output interface for online *: some design and human factor onsiderations 02335
Observations of end-user online * behavior over eleven years HCI-0235 †
In search of * skills HCI-0274 †
Views on end-user * HCI-0283 †

## SEAT
Measurement of * pressure distribution 01760

## SECONDARY
Computer literacy in * education: the performance and engagement of girls 01495
Computer programming and general problem solving by * students 01587
The relationship of computer programming and mathematics in * students 01588
Simps: * ion mass image processing system 02267

## SECRETARY
Time-life, world reporter and the *: experiments with end-users 02325

## SECRETS
A case-based system for trade * law 02769

## SECTOR
A survey of information technology in the U.K. service * 01916

Communications technology and the public *: understanding the process of adoption 02679

## SECURE
Intelligent interfaces for * multilevel database systems 02990
Lessons learned from modeling a * multilevel relational database system 03580

## SECURITY
A human approach to the technological challenges in data * 01543
The human immune system as an information systems * reference model 01547
* of office systems 03359
Computer *: a global challenge § 03577
Database *: Status and Prospects § 03579
Role-based * in data base management systems 03584
Data * and confidentiality in Europe HCI-0450 †

## SEDENTARY
On the significance of physical activity on * work 03704

## SEEDS
Planting the * 02840
Medical informatics: a personal view of sowing the * 02841

## SEEKER
Retrieval systems for the information *: can the role of the intermediary be automated? 02864

## SEGMENTATION
* using contrast and homogeneity measures 02543
Image * based on color and texture gradient 03303
Selection and use of image features for * of boundary images 03305
Phonetic * using psychoacoustic speech parameters 03991

## SEGMENTED
Interactive curve drawing by * Bezier approximation with a control parameter 02535

## SEGREGATION
Image * by motion: cortical mechanisms and implementation in neural networks 03958

## SEGUE
*: support for distributed graphical interfaces 01369
*: Support for distributed graphical interfaces 03526

## SEISMIC
Multidimensional attribute analyhsis and pattern recognition for * interpretation 02530

## SELECT
Human foundations of advanced computing technology: the guide to the *literature 0001

## SELECTING
* a shell 01176
Embedded menus: * items in context 01320
* an Ada environment ● HCI-0015 †
* a humanly understandable knowledge representation for reasoning about knowledge HCI-0330 †

## SELECTION
Evaluation of mouse, rate-controlled isometric joystick, step keys, and text keys, for text * on a CRT 0064
Circling: a method of mouse-based * without button presses 0847
Fine tuning * semantics in a structure editor based programming environment: some experimental results 0975
Methodology for comparative * of interactive database interface types 01005
Item * from menus: the influence of menu organization, query interpretation, and programming experience on * strategies 01011
The * of a servicing discipline in a multiterminal conversational information retrieval system 01233
* of image primitives for general-purpose visual processing 01467
On the * and evaluation of visual display symbology: factors influencing search and identification times 01718
Alternative option * methods in menu-driven computer programs 01755

* devices for users of an electronic encyclopedia: an empirical comparison of four possibilities 02009
A comparison of menu * techniques: touch panel, mouse and keyboard 02122
An interactive environment for tool *, specification and composition 02141
Underlying dimensions of human problem solving and learning: implications for personnel *, training tasks design and expert system 02225
* systems for sales representatives 02408
End user software * 02434
Message equivocality, media * and manager performance: implications for information systems 02505
Providing natural language assistance in locating objects: a general model for information * and generation 02951
An evaluation and * methodology of microcomputer training software: Implications for human resource managers and computer personnel 03002
* and use of image features for segmentation of boundary images 03305
An expert system framework for forecasting method * 03468
Computational networks in early vision: from orientation * to optical flow 03961
Interactive computer program for the * of interference fits HCI-0406 †

**SELECTIONIST**

A simple * learning rule for neural networks 02756

**SELF**

*-modifying production system model of cognitive development 0486
The development of a postmodern *: a computer-assisted comparative analysis of personal documents ● 0732
A *-regulating adaptive system 0829

A *-organizing neural network sharing features of the mammalian visual system 01248
*-organizing system obtaining communication ability primitive model for language generation 01279
The ART of adaptive pattern recognition by a *-organizing neural network 01364
*-organization in a perceptual network 01366
Building a *-modifying user interface 01424
*-efficacy expectations as a predictor of computer use: a look at early childhood administrators 01590
*-authorization: A characteristic of some elements in certain *-organizing systems 01610
The way you look determines what you see (or *-organization in management and society) 01614
*-organizing systems and transformational-generative (TG) grammar 01619
Reading *-paced moving text on a computer display 01777
The influence of personality on *-paced instruction 02291
A *-optimizing, nonsymmetrical neural net for content addressable memory and pattern recognition 02562
Absolutely stable learning of recognition codes by a *-organizing neural network 02728
Representation of sensory information in *-organizing feature maps 02744
Design of an AI-Based *-sustaining habitats control system 02959
Increase organizational effectiveness: Support *-managed IS development teams 03014
Extending Kohonen's *-organizing mapping algorithms to learn ballistic movements 03967
The second *: computers and the human spirit ● HCI-0082 †

**SEMANTIC**

Principles from the psychology of memory: Part II-Episodic and * memory 0331
A * editor 01101

Implementing a * interpreter using conceptual graphs 01812
* feedback in the Higgens UIMS 01851
A * data model as the basis for an automated database design tool 02036
Structural aspects of *-directed clusters 02534
Using latent * analysis to improve access to textual information 02901
Goal-directed * tutor 02919
The * language episode understanding 03576
* primitives or meaning postulates: mental models or propositional representation? HCI-0339 †
Managing the * content of graphical data HCI-0374 †

**SEMANTICS**

* 0154
The *-based natural language interface to relational databases 0164
Fine tuning selection * in a structure editor based programming environment: some experimental results 0975
Temporal * and natural language processing in a decision support system 02038
An approach to natural-language * in logic programming 02342
Adding browsing * to the hypertext model 02834
The PFG environment: parallel programming with petri net * 03527
Who is user and who is affected: a proposal to better * 03647
Icon *—a formal approach to icon system design HCI-0161 †
Portability of syntax and * in DATALOG HCI-0340 †

**SEMINARS**

Advanced information technology in the new industrial society: the Kingston * ● 0225

**SEMIOTICS**

* and informatics: computers as media 0448

## SEMISTRUCTURED
* messages are surprisingly useful for computer-supported coordination HCI-0290 †

## SENIOR
A systems architecture for supporting * managers' messy tasks 01928

Computer decision support for * managers: encouraging exploration HCI-0298 †

## SENSATION
Comparison of color * in dichoptic and in normal vision 01272

## SENSATIONS
The scope of research on motion: *, perception, representation and generation 03323

## SENSED
The effect of number ordering and orientation on marking speed and errors for mark-* labels 01717

## SENSES
An experiment in computational discrimination of English word * 01813

## SENSING
An overview of local environment * in robotics applications 04012

Force and tactile * for robots 04013

## SENSITIVITY
Changes in contrast * function produced by VDT use 02189

Development and * analysis of adaptive predictor for human eye movement model 02681

* to light and visual strain in VDT operators: basic data for the design of work stations 03732

## SENSOR
Construction and examples of * in safe working system 03425

Experiences from the use of an intelligent safety * with industrial robots 03427

## SENSORIMOTOR
The role of the primate superior colliculus in * integration 0017

Tensor network theory and its application in computer modeling of the metaorganization of * hierarchies of gaze 02753

## SENSORIUM
Visual information processing: artificial intelligence and the * of sight 0300

## SENSORS
Performance evaluation of three pressure mats as robot workstation safety * 03428

* and sensory systems for advanced robots § 04006

Analogs of biological tissues for mechanoelectrical transduction: tactile * and muscle-like actuators 04014

Gas *: towards an artificial nose 04015

## SENSORY
CAD Based Programming for * Robots ● 0597

Classifying * inspectors with heterogeneous inspection-error probabilities 02396

Speech motor control and stuttering: a computational model of adaptive *-motor processing 02655

Representation of * information in self-organizing feature maps 02744

On the acquisition of object concepts from * data 03959

Control of * processing - a hypothesis on and simulation of the architecture of an elementary cortical processor 03972

Sensors and * systems for advanced robots § 04006

Proprioceptive feedback for *-motor control 04008

Integration of robot * systems 04016

## SENSOT
Determining the instantaneous axis of translation from optic flow generated by rbitrary s*motion 03332

## SENTENCE
Mechanisms of * processing: assigning roles to constituents 0635

Problems of machine translation system - effect of cultural differences on * structure 01687

## SENTENTIAL
Interactive communication of * structure and content: an alternative approach to man-machine communication 02220

What awareness isn't: a * view of implicit and explicit belief 03560

## SEPARATING
* the user interface from the functionality of application programs 0948

Expert systems and interactive video tutorials: * strategies from subject matter 02293

* content from form: A language for formatting on-line documentation and dialog 02781

## SEQUENCE
Parallel in *—towards the architecture of an elementary cortical processor 03820

## SEQUENCES
Coding image * for interactive retrieval 01330

The effect of varying voice and noise parameters on the perception of voicing in Dutch two-obstruent * 02653

Intelligible encoding of ASL image * at extremely low information rates 02708

Navigating integrated facilities: initiating and terminating interaction * 02876

Adapting optical-flow to measure object motion in reflectance and X-ray image * 03334

On the estimation of dense displacement vector fields from image * 03335

## SEQUENTIAL
The * organization of spoken word recognition 0291

Schemata and * thought processes in PDP models 0630

Mental gymnastics of * programming 01971

A LISP implementation of the model for 'communicating * processes' 02632

## SERIAL
Information transfer rate with * and simultaneous visual display formats 01770

# KEYWORD INDEX [SET]

A * interface for process control 02383

## SERIES
Use of object-oriented programming in a time * analysis system 01112
Apollo domain * 3000 01170
Experiences in use of SSADM: * of case studies. Part 1: first time users 01976
Experiences in use of SSADM: * of case studies. Part 2: experienced users 01977

## SERVER
A distributed object * 03842
Design and performance considerations for an optical disk-based, multimedia object * HCI-0265 †

## SERVERS
Automated document distribution using AI based workstations and knowledge based * 03466

## SERVICE
The profile naming * 01149
A computing * using linked minis 01674
Tennessee Eastman employee teamwork raises quality, customer * 01907
A survey of information technology in the U.K. * sector 01916
An analysis of humanists' requests received by an information * for the humanities 02318
Person-to-person communication in an applied research/* delivery setting 02445
* support levels: An organizational approach to end-user computing 02503
An expert system for screening employee pension plans for the Internal Revenue * 02773
Expert system applications in customer * 03101
Advisor—an electronic mail consulting * 03151

## SERVICES
Automation in public libraries: effects on the organization, quality of working life, and quality of * 0246
The evaluation of information *: a typology 0452

ACM SIGUCCS User * Conference XIV 01925
End-user searching of CAS ONLINE. Results of a cooperative experiment between Imperial Chemical Industries and Chemical Abstracts * 02269
Man—machine interaction by voice: developments in speech technology. Part 2: general applications and potential applications in libraries and information * 02332
The dimensions of perceived accessibility to information: Implications for the delivery if information systems and * 02448
Forecasting consumer adoption of information technology and *—lessons from home video forecasting 02451
User * § 03127
User * Conference § 03130
User *—a british perspective 03132
I didn't even know it was user * 03133
From user to client *; making the transition for supercomputing 03138
The evolution of user * 03139
Software engineering meets user *: a methodology for developing user 03141
A new model for user *: distributed support 03153
Hypermedia: a face lift for presentation research and development: a user * function 03154
Desktop publishing and user *; moment in the evolution of user support documentation at UNH 03158
The evolution of microcomputer laboratory * at the University of Notre Dame 03159
User * consulting supportr tools at the NASA numerical aerodynamic simula 03161
Organizational videotex: information * for the end user 03166
Computer-based message * § 03319
Videotex and online *: competition or collateral 03557

Integrating CD-ROM with printed and online *: a silver platter end-user perspective 03558
Equipment and workstation design for banking * 03712
Information technology and home-based *: improving the usability of teleshopping HCI-0226 †
A user agent for multiple computer-based message * HCI-0306 †

## SERVICING
The selection of a * discipline in a multiterminal conversational information retrieval system 01233

## SERVING
Grasping reality through illusion—interactive graphics * science 02857

## SERVO
A model of the motor *: Incorporating nonlinear spindle receptor and muscle mechanical properties 01273

## SESSIONS
Community design and gaming/simulation: Comparison of communications techniques in participatory design * 02596

## SET
Designing interactive, responsive instruction: a * of procedures 0274
The effects of * size on color matching using CRT displays 01711
Designing a neural network satisfying a given * of constraints 02755
A highly integrated tool * for program development support 02788
Designing keybindings to be easy to learn and resistant to forgetting even when the * of commands is large 02890
An intelligent tutoring system for basic * theory 02993
Towards the construction of a maximally-contrasting * of colours 03233
A * of tools supporting the software design based on SDL 03803

**SETS**
Authoring tools for complex document * 0120
Fuzzy * and decision analysis 0651
Rough * and dependency analysis among attributes in computer implementations of expert's inference models 02231
Evaluating the meaningfulness of icon * to represent command operations 03277
CNS-HLS mapping using fuzzy * HCI-0380 †

**SEX**
Acoustic phonetics, auditory phonetics, speaker * and speech recognition: a thread 0288
Computer anxiety: *, race and age 02133

**SHAPES**
Codon constraints on closed 2D * 02704

**SHAPING**
* user input: a strategy for natural language dialogue design 02067

**SHARED**
Collaboration in KMS, a * hypermedia system 0807
Knowledge-based tools to promote * goals and terminology between interface designers 01160
Structured message passing on a *-memory multiprocessor 03514

**SHARING**
Data * in group work (Reprint) 0379
The information lens: an intelligent system for information * in organizations 0891
A self-organizing neural network * features of the mammalian visual system 01248
Intelligent information-* systems 01322
Speech responses and dual-task performance: better time-* or asymmetric transfer? 01789
Task-* within and between hemispheres: a multiple-resources approach 01795
Responsibility * between sophisticated users and professionals in structured prototyping 01978
* in a privately owned workstation environment 04076

A supporting system for effective construction and * of scientific databases by general researchers HCI-0262 †

**SHEFFIELD**
Professional education and subsequent careers in library/information work: a follow-up study of former students on the MA/MSc information studies course at the University of * 02336

**SHELL**
Selecting a * 01176
A visual * interface to a database 02640
Generic expert system * for diagnostic reasoning 02911
Applications of an AI design * ENGINEOUS to advanced engineering products 02932
UNIX * programming ● HCI-0027 †

**SHELLS**
Iconic * for multitasking workstations 02792

**SHELVES**
Subject searching behaviour at the library catalogue and at the *: implications for online interactive catalogues 02302

**SHERLOCK**
*—a system for diagnosing power distribution ring network faults 02916

**SHIFT**
The age of the end-user and the * from corporate MIS to corporate DSS 01676
On the minimum number of templates required for *, rotation and size invariant pattern recognition 02531

**SHIFTING**
* to a higher gear in a natural language system 03169

**SHIRSHOV**
Some applications of a theorem of * to language theory HCI-0181 †

**SHOP**
Stress, coping, and worker well-being in computer-aided manufacturing: A field investigation of a CNC machine * 03373

Optimum stresses and strains represented by examples from * practice 03441

**SHOPS**
Further division of reintegration of mental labour? CAD/CAP and work in design nd work preparation s* 03385

**SHORTHAND**
On-line recognition of Pitman's hand-written *—an evaluation of potential 02111

**SHOWING**
The Mac interface: * its age 01311
* programs on a screen HCI-0141 †

**SHUCKING**
* Dp 01644

**SICK**
Do VDU's make you * 01219

**SIDES**
Attacking a complex distributed algorithm from different *: an experience wih complementary validation tools 01429

**SIGBDP**
The 1987 ACM *-SIGCPR Conference § 03099

**SIGCPR**
The 1987 ACM SIGBDP-* Conference § 03099

**SIGDOC**
ACM * '85 § 02780

**SIGHT**
Visual information processing: artificial intelligence and the sensorium of * 0300

**SIGMOD**
* International Conference on Management of Data § 03089

**SIGNAL**
Effect of pixel height, display height, and vertical resolution on the detection of a simple vertical line * in visual noise 01753
The measurement of the *-to-noise ratio (SNR) in continuous speech 02654
Digial * processor accelerators for neural network simulations 02754
Object-oriented * processing systems 03573
On the temporal stability of * detection processes 03617

KEYWORD INDEX [SIMULATION]

* processing and pattern recognition in nondestructive evaluation of materials § 04019

**SIGNALS**
Skills, rules, and knowledge; *, signs, and symbols, and other distinctions in human performance models 0654
Recollections on the processing of biomedical * 02846

**SIGNATURES**
Coupling visual and dynamic features to study handwritten * 03309

**SIGNIFICANCE**
* testing of rules in rule-based models of human problem solving 01867
On the * of physical activity on sedentary work 03704

**SIGNS**
Skills, rules, and knowledge; signals, *, and symbols, and other distinctions in human performance models 0654

**SIGSMALL**
ACTES/Proceedings Symposium 1988 ACM */PC § 02787

**SIGUCCS**
ACM * User Services Conference XIV 01925

**SILENT**
The * force of the screen. A research note on the impact of microelectronics on work autonomy among clerical workers in public administration 01437

**SIMONA**
The * project: the introduction of information processing in labour market administration 0248

**SIMPLIFY**
Methods improvement kit uses IE technique to * work 01909
Using the micro-computer to * database access: designing interfaces to complex files HCI-0275 †

**SIMPLIFYING**
* decision trees 02157

**SIMPS**
*: Secondary ion mass image processing system 02267

**SIMS**
*: a uniform environment for planning and performing user's tasks 02921

**SIMTALK**
*: Pros and cons of natural language for manufacturing simulation 02950

**SIMULA**
User services consulting supportr tools at the NASA numerical aerodynamic * 03161

**SIMULATE**
How faithfully should the electronic office * real one? 0958

**SIMULATED**
Learning by doing with * intelligent help 0132
Visual information pick-up in a * driving situation 0251
A psychophysiological assessment of operator workload during * flight missions 01735
Part-task training strategies in * carrier landing final-approach training 01741
Performance measurement during * air-to-air combat 01787
Analysis of user procedural compliance in controlling a * process 01879
Learning by doing with * intelligent help HCI-0229 †

**SIMULATING**
Life before the chips: * digital video interactive technology 01328
Unified interactive geometric modeller for * highly complex environments 01472
But what will the workers do? * what the workers do to us when we do what we do to them 02590
Learning in parallel networks: * learning in a probabilistic system HCI-0332 †

**SIMULATION**
Computer applications in water supply: vol. 1—systems analysis and * ● 0227
Robot * and off-line programming—an integrated CAE-CAD approach 0599
Off-line programming of robots using 3D graphical * system 0602

Thinking: information processing, mathematical models and computer * ● 0667
INSIST: Interactive * in Smalltalk 01119
A prolog * for a Delphi-based problem solver 01141
A man-machine interface for computer-aided and * of control systems 01237
* of chaotic EEG patterns with a dynamic model of the olfactory system 01263
Projected free fall trajectories. I. Theory and * 01265
Physiology based * model of triangle shape recognition 01277
Intelligent interactive video * of a code inspection 01329
The use of prototyping and * in the development of large-scale applications 01411
An interactive * description interpreter 01538
* of CNC controller features in graphics-based programming 01568
Models of procedural control for human performance * 01752
Spatial requirements for visual * of aircraft at real-world distances 01768
Two * studies investigating means of human-computer communication for dynamic task allocation 01882
Qualitative approximation methodology for modeling and * of large dynamic systems: Applications to a Marine power plant 01900
Adapting expert systems to * training of process operators 02056
Power plant * using a distributed control system 02057
Automated interactive * modeling system: AISIM 02399
The role of computer graphics in validating * models 02486
An expert manufacturing * system 02584
Visual interactive * - history, recent developments, and major issues 02585

[SIMULATIONS]

Student perceptions of skill acquisition through cases and a general management * 02589
Human and computer involvement in * 02593
The marble company: The design and implementation of a * board game 02595
Community design and gaming/*: Comparison of communications techniques in participatory design sessions 02596
Using * to study complex problem solving: a review of studies in the FRG 02598
Power plant * and reactor safety 02682
Getting graphics in gear: graphics and dynamics in driving * 02818
Graphics-based qualitative * generator for power distribution systems 02946
SIMTALK: Pros and cons of natural language for manufacturing * 02950
An advisory system for digital logic * 02986
Developing intelligent * language to support telerobotic workstation activities 02995
3-D balance in legged locomotion: modeling and * for the one-legged case 03352
Gribs—an approach to a realistic realtime * of human arm motion 03432
Proceedings of the 21st Annual * Symposium § 03499
Using distributed * for distributed application development 03500 * § 03501
Visual * 03503
HORSE: a * of the horizon supercomputer 03541
A graphics interface for interactive * of packet-switched networks 03869
Control of sensory processing - a hypothesis on and * of the architecture of an elementary cortical processor 03972
An iterative and interactive * method to reconstruct unknown inputs contributing to known outputs of neuronal systems 04018

MIDAS: molecular interactive display and * 04061
Artificial behavior: computer * of psychological processes ● HCI-0073 †
A Multilevel menu-driven user interface: Design and evaluation through * HCI-0170 †
Real time graphic * of visual effects of egomotion HCI-0379 †
Geomatic: a 3-D graphic relief * system HCI-0395 †

SIMULATIONS
An integrated system for neural network * 0771
* of behavior in competitive situations 02591
* and anxiety related to public speaking 02592
Digial signal processor accelerators for neural network * 02754

SIMULATOR
Maintenance training * fidelity and individual differences in transfer of training 01722
Effects of visual display and motion system delays on operator performance and ueasiness in a driving * 01772
* design and instructional features for air-to-ground attack: a transfer study 01804
Modelling 8-bit microprocessors for a general-purpose * 02499
An interactive * for the designing of woven fabric structures second place 02583
ATLANTIS—a software * for behavior analysis of protocol specificationsand their target implementations 02667
The MIRRORS/II * 03502

SIMULATORS
Performance evaluation of * 02663

SINKERS
Teaching users to fish: hooks, lines and * for reading computer documentat 03156

SINS
Seven mortal * of systems work 03645

SINUS
Spectral analysis of * arrhythmia: a measure of mental effort 01737

KEYWORD INDEX

SITES
*, modes, and trails: Telling the user of an interactive system where he is, what he can do, and how to get to places (excerpt) 0068

SITUATED
Conversational resources for * action 0861
Plans and * actions: the problem of human-machine communication ● HCI-0040 †

SKELETAL
VDUs and musculo-* problems at the Australian National University. A case study 03709

SKELETONIZATION
An investigation into the * approach of Hilditch HCI-0388 †

SKETCHED
Continuous processing of images through user * functional blocks 01399
Real-time processing of cursive writing and * graphics 03908

SKETCHER
*, an interactive, graphical Ada software tool—its development and use HCI-0100 †

SKETCHING
Part structure for 3-D * 03300

SKETCHPAD
* a man-machine graphical communication system 03103

SKI
Some physical factors at VDT work stations and * problems 03693

SKILLED
* financial planning: the cost of translating ideas into action 0834
GOMS meets STRIPS: the integration of planning with * procedure execution in human-computer interaction 03243

SKILLFUL
MEISTER: a model enhanced intelligent and * teleoperational robot system 03562

SKILLS
Consulting * for technical writers 0124

Employment * for the robot age 0442
From trigger video to videodisc: a case study in interpersonal * 0508
Logo and development of thinking * 0582
*, rules, and knowledge; signals, signs, and symbols, and other distinctions in human performance models 0654
The impact of menus and command-level feedback on learners' acquisition of data base language * 01041
Automation, work organization and *: the case of numerical control 01234
Computer work * training for persons with developmental disabilities 01559
Computer programming and generalized problem-solving *: in search of direction 01585
Acquisition of process control * 01878
Using interactive videotaped-based instruction to teach on-the-job social * to handicapped adolescents 02288
Personal transferable * for the modern information professional: a discussion paper 02338
Transferring * from training to the actual work situation: the role of task application knowledge, action styles and job decision latitude 02865
Information systems * requirements: 1980 & 1988 02997
Analysis and design * required by end-users in small organizations 03008
Programming in Basic or Logo: effect on critical thinking * 04062
In search of searching * HCI-0274 †

## SKIN
A Rosacea-like * rash in VDU-operators 03695
VDT work and the * 03696
* paroblems from VDT work-a summary 03697

## SKINS
New wine in old *, or, was all this ferment really necessary? 03140

## SLAVES
Algebra * and agents in a Logo-based mathematics curriculum 0517

## SLCSE
The Software Life Cycle Support Environment (*): a computer based framework for developing software systems HCI-0147 †

## SLEEP
A model-based monitor of human * stages 01269
Computer quantification of delta activity in * EEG 01491

## SLOPE
Beware the reliability of * scores for individuals 01727

## SLOPPY
Design goals for * modeling systems 02206

## SLOT
* versus insertion magnetic stripe readers: user performance and preference 01756

## SLOWER
Why reading was * from CRT displays than from paper 0797
Reading is * from CRT displays than from paper: attempts to isolate a single-variable explanation 01743

## SM
An implementation of OSI protocols in *-4 host computers 03638

## SMALL
The * computer assisted lecturing system 01043
Estimating reliability with * samples: increased precision with averaged correlations 01728
Local work station concepts in a * distributed system 02054
Chief executive personality and corporate strategy and structure in * firms 02472
A portable query language for * scale systems 02492
The LINC was early and * 02843
Analysis and design skills required by end-users in * organizations 03008
Toward the successful design and implementation of computer based management information systems in * companies 03256
Failure analysis of information systems in * manufacturing enterprises: the importance of the human interface 03815

## SMALLEST
Prediction of the * channel in early human vision 01894

## SMALLTALK
Painless panes for * windows 01118
INSIST: Interactive Simulation in * 01119
An integrated color *-80 system 01127
A * window system based on constraints 01128
Configuring stand-alone *-80 applications 01129
A * implementation of an intelligent operator's associate 01132
A cookbook for using the model-view controller user interface paradigm in *-80 02390
Encapsulators: a new software paradigm in *-80 03034
Multiprocessor *: a case study of a multiprocessor-based programming environment 03061

## SMART
*: Scientific database management and engineering analysis routines and tools 01166
* help for operator performance 01528
In the age of the * machine: the future of work and power ● HCI-0083 †

## SMARTGEN
*: the implementation of an expert system for the generation of digital logic diagnostic tests 02929

## SMARTSLIM
*: a DSS for controlling biases during problem formulation 0203

## SMELL
Physiology and psychophysics in taste and * 04009

## SML
*: a solid modelling language 01471

## SMOOTH
A travel consultation system: towards a * conversation in Japanese 03917

## SNAP
*-dragging 01052

## SNR
The measurement of the signal-to-noise ratio (*) in continuous speech 02654

## SOCIAL
The society of text: hypertext, hypermedia, and the * construction of information ● 0111
* psychological aspects of computer-mediated communication (Reprint) 0384
Reducing * context cues: electronic mail in organizational communication (Reprint) 0385
Generation as a * action 0389
Computer assisted learning in the humanities and * sciences :9B 0470
The role of * processes in children's microcomputer use 0471
The rational, the pragmatic and the inquiry process: The * study of information- communication systems 0786
* science and system design: interdisciplinary collaborations 0833
Understanding the office: A *-analytic perspective 01156
Keyboarding as a * form 01551
Using interactive videotaped-based instruction to teach on-the-job *skills to handicapped adolescents 02288
Reducing * context cues: electronic mail in organizational communication 02473
Systems design and * responsibility: the political implications of "computer-supported cooperative work". A commentary 02516
Design of a multi-media vehicle for * browsing 02822
* choice theory and distributed decision making 03044
Organizational implications of office systems: toward a critical * action perspective 03358
The * cybernetics of human interaction with automated systems 03442

Computer culture: the scientific, intellectual, and * impact of the computer § 03567
* psychological prerequisites and consequences of new information technologies 03631
Report from the working group on "goals and strategies of trade unions and other * groups in systems design for human development and productivity." 03657
On the detection of * effects in man-computer interaction—a contribution to systems design 03672
Office automation: a * and organizational perspective ● HCI-0048 †
The computer imperative among owners of home computers: explanation by *factors HCI-0217 †

## SOCIALIZATION
The effects of computer use in early childhood * 0793

## SOCIALIZING
* the intelligent tutor: bringing empathy to computer tutors 0541

## SOCIETY
The * of text: hypertext, hypermedia, and the social construction of information ● 0111
Advanced information technology in the new industrial *: the Kingston seminars ● 0225
The uneasy eighties: the transition to an information * 0792
No members, no officers, no dues: A ten year history of the software psychology * 0943
Two notes concerning the * theory of thinking 01479
The way you look determines what you see (or self-organization in management and * 01614
The real information *: present situation and some forecasts 02322

## SOCIO
The */Political Environment 0040
*-tech: what is it (and why should we care)? 0908

*-technical aspects of electronic mail implementation 01439
A critical view of factors affecting successful application of normative and *-technical systems development approaches 01914

## SOCIOLOGY
The computational science revolution: technology, methodology, and * 0728
Informatics (computer and information science): its ideology, methodology, and * HCI-0086 †

## SOCIOTECHNICAL
* design of advanced manufacturing systems 03370

## SOCRATIC
Overcoming conceptual difficulties in physical science through computer-based * dialogs 03877

## SOFT
The AT&T * touch-sensitive screen 01226
Planning for hospital information systems using the Lancaster * Systems methodology 01228
Student evaluation of motivational and learning attributes of microcomputer * 02274
Psychology and the user interface: science is * at the frontier 03297
The * side of *ware: a management approach to computer documentation ● HCI-0016 †
QWERTY and keyboard reform: the * keyboard option HCI-0190 †

## SOFTLIB
*—A documentation management system HCI-0149 †

## SOLID
VLSI for * modelling 0232
SML: a * modelling language 01471
Exchange of * models: current state and future trends 01475
Interactive * modeling in hut design 03837
The CADME approach to the interface of * modellers 03867

## SOLO
A very friendly software environment for * 0743

## SOMATIC

Identification and prevention of work-related mental and psycho-*disorders among two categories of VDU users 03744

An evaluation of mood disturbances and * discomfort under slow computer-response time and incentive-pay conditions 03765

## SONAR

Multimodal detection and recognition performance of * operators 01709

## SOPHISTICATION

A study of managerial computer users: the impact of user * on decision structure and attributes of decision-related information (end user) 04078

## SORTING

Parcel * by speech recognition: human factors issues 03209

## SOUND

Communicating with * 0067

Phonology and syntax: the relationship between * and structure ● 0672

An interactive environment for object-oriented music composition and *synthesis 01131

The look and feel . . . and * of the user interface 01315

Competitive dynamics in a dual-route connectionist model of print-to-*transformation 01341

Mode errors: a user-centered analysis and some preventative measures using keying-contingent * 02107

Speaker-independent automatic recognition of plosive * in letters and digits 03993

## SOURCE

A UNIX clone with * code for operating systems courses 01095

dBUG III offers * level solutions 01641

Project * file management under the UNIX operating system 03168

## SOURCES

A directory of * for interactive technologies 0941

The effects of * of applications programs on user satisfaction: an empirical study of micro, mini & mainframe computers using an interactive artificial intelligence expert-system 01601

Analogy and other * of difficulty in novices' very first text-editing 02148

* of Difficulty in troubleshooting automated manufacturing systems 03367

Investigating * of error in the management of crises: theoretical assumptions and a methodological approach 03807

## SOWING

Medical informatics: a personal view of * the seeds 02841

## SPA

*: a systems for diagnosis of computer performance problems 02969

## SPACE

A functional model of vision and * 0027

* 0134

NASA Johnson * Center, Human-Computer Interaction 0815

Formatting *-related displays to optimize expert and nonexpert user performance 0927

Information detective: a workstation for exploring three dimensional information * 01010

Rooms: the use of multiple virtual work*s to reduce * contention in a window-based graphical user interface 01151

Structure of a directory *: a case study with a UNIX operating system 02138

Non-Reimannian approach to geometry of visual *: An application of affinely connected geometry to visual alleys and horopter 02364

The psychophysical function of binocular * perception 02375

Choosing between methods: analysing the user's decision * in terms of schemas and linear models 02879

A prototype autonomous agent for crew and equipment retrieval in * 02994

Human factors in the Columbus * station 03250

Human visual requirements for control and monitoring of a * telerobot 03391

Illumination requirements for operating a * remote manipulator 03392

The * station information system and software support environment 03512

Recent results on the application of a metric-* search algorithm (AESA) to multispeaker data 03997

## SPACES

Perceptual color * for computer graphics 0258

## SPAN

The effect of microcomputer presentation and response medium on digit * 02090

PHRAN-*: a natural language interface for system specifications 02829

## SPATIAL

The interdependence of temporal and * information in early vision 0023

Various views on * prepositions 01196

The effect of perspective geometry on judged direction in * information instruments 01720

Visual fatigue and * frequency adaptation to video displays of text 01721

The * allocation of visual attention as indexed by event-related brain potentials 01739

The role of stimulus-to-rule consistency in learning rapid application of * rules 01765

* requirements for visual simulation of aircraft at real-world distances 01768

Human performance evaluation of digitizer pucks for computer input of *information 01774

[SPEAKER]

\* misorientation exacerbated by collimated virtual flight display 01979
ISIS: the interactive \* information system 02193
Joint \*/\*-frequency representation 02580
A practical approach to data modelling in \* applications 02616
Toward a theory of the perceived \* layout of scenes 02701
Approximate \* reasoning 02917
Temporal and \* stability in visual displays 03730
\* and temporal transformations in visuo-motor coordination 03963
The \* metaphor for user interfaces: experimental tests of reference by location versus name HCI-0268 †

**SPEAKER**
Acoustic phonetics, auditory phonetics, \* sex and speech recognition: a thread 0288
Improving \* consistency in an automatic speech recognition framework 01448
Research on individuality features in speech waves and automatic \*recognition techniques 02645
\*-independent automatic recognition of plosive sound in letters and digits 03993
Recognition of \*-dependent continuous speech with Keal-Nevezh 04002

**SPEAKERS**
Representing and using metacommunication to control \*' relationships in natural-language dialogue 02136
Dynamic spectral adaptation of automatic speech recognizers to new \* 03999

**SPEAKING**
Simulations and anxiety related to public \* 02592

**SPECIAL**
A study of Arab computer users: a \* case of a general HCI methodology 04031

**SPECIALISTS**
Collaboration of UIMS designers and human factors \* 01060

Perceptions of system effectiveness as viewed by executives, users, and information \* 03469

**SPECIALTIES**
The \* 01835

**SPECIF**
\*-X: a tool for CASE 03801

**SPECIFICATION**
Extending state transition diagrams for the \* of human-computer interaction 0080
A coherent \* method for the human interface to documentation systems 0269
Graphical \* of procedural knowledge for an expert system 0427
Graphical \* of user interfaces with behavior abstraction 0840
The formal \* of adaptive user interfaces using command language grammar 0925
Transformations on a formal \* of user-computer interfaces 01062
Common LISP object system \* X3J13 Document 88-002R 01121
Graph attribution as a \* paradigm 01138
Human factors in the IT \* process 01372
Experience with chisl, a configurable hierarchical interface \*language 01397
A formal \* of the QMS message system: the underlying abstract model 01406
Evaluation and intergration of \* languages 01430
Comments on "formal \* of user interfaces: a comparison and evaluation of four axiomatic approaches" 01847
A system for \* and rapid prototyping of application command languages 01849
A preliminary \* of an on-line expert help system 01930
Impact of prototyping on user information satisfaction during the IS \* phase 01955
Information requirements \* II: Brainstorming collective decision-making technique 02005

On methods for interface \* and design 02114
An interactive environment for tool selection, \* and composition 02141
Toward a formal \* of menu-based systems 02400
Towards the formal \* of a simple programming support environment 02607
A process \* of expert lawyer reasoning 02768
Some experiences in integrating \* of human computer interaction within a structured system development method 03222
ECS - A technique for the formal \* and rapid prototyping of human-computer interaction 03253
The interactive \* of human animation 03292
The software structure of extended nucleus based on BTRON \* 03494
Formal \* of user interfaces: two application studies 03772
\* of a tool for viewing program text 03884
Experimentation in the \* of an oral dialogue 04005
The VIP VDM \* language 04036
The use of VDM on the \* of Chinese characters 04038
A formal \* for a user interface for office automation 04053
A methodology, \* language, and automated support environment for com1uter-aided design systems 04068
A \* language for direct-manipulation user interfaces HCI-0123 †
\* and generation of variable, personalized graphical interfaces HCI-0134 †
An approach to user \* of interactive display interfaces HCI-0137 †
Extending state transition diagrams for the \* of human-computer interaction HCI-0191 †
What non-programmers know about programming: natural language procedure \* HCI-0211 †

* and verification of database dynamics HCI-0251 †

**SPECIFICATIONS**
PHRAN-SPAN: a natural language interface for system * 02829
Knowledge base applications with software engineering: a tool for requirements * 02924
The incorporation of early interface evaluation into command language grammar * 03191
Express—rapid prototyping and product development via integrated knowledge-based executable * 03492
A processing system for program * in a natural language 03537
Using data flow * and interactive editing in the operating system user interface 03800
A logic-functional approach to the execution of CCS * modulo behavioural equivalences 03874
ATLANTIS—a software simulator for behavior analysis of protocol * and their target implementations 02667

**SPECIFICS**
Human * fuzzy categories and counteraction in decision making problems 01696

**SPECIFYING**
Constraint grammars–a new model for * graphical applications 0875
A notation for * menus 01111
Extending Petri nets for * man-machine dialogues 02183
Programmer-nonprogrammer differences in * procedures to people and computers 02405
Conceptual documents: a mechanism for * active views in hypertext 02833
OTM: * office tasks 03039
EDGE - a graph based tool for * interaction 03106
Programmer/nonprogrammer differences in * procedures to people and computers HCI-0174 †

**SPECKLE**
Vision monitoring of VDU operators and relaxation of visual stress by means of laser s*system 03738

**SPECTRA**
Uncertainty analysis of human EEG *: A multivariate information theoretical method for the analysis of brain activity 01270

**SPECTRAL**
Color constancy: a method for recovering surface * reflectance 0298
A method for computing * reflectance 01267
* analysis of sinus arrhythmia: a measure of mental effort 01737
Vowel normalization by frequency warped * matching 02649
Dynamic * adaptation of automatic speech recognizers to new speakers 03999

**SPECTRUM**
Recognition of phonemes using time-* pattern 02648
Assessment of mental load for different strategies of man-computer dialogue by means of the heart rate power * 03623

**SPECULATING**
* on the future of mathematics 01210

**SPECULATION**
Computer-assisted negotiations: a case history from the law of the sea negotiations and * regarding future uses HCI-0443 †

**SPEECH**
* filing—An office system for principals 0037
System design for * recognition and generation 0065
Realism in synthetic * 0066
Electronic * recognition: techniques, technology, and applications ● 0174
The nature of * 0175
The elements of * recognition 0176
Human factors in * recognition 0177
Computer * processing ● 0287
Acoustic phonetics, auditory phonetics, speaker sex and * recognition: a thread 0288
Linear predictive coding of * 0289
Aspects of human * understanding 0290
Elements of a plan-based theory of * acts 0390
Fundamentals in computer understanding: * and vision ● 0416
Rule-based detection of * features for automatic * recognition 0419
Interactive processes in * perception: the TRACE model 0631
* & language based interaction with machines ● 0723
* and language-based interaction with machines: towards the conversational computer ● 0724
* and gestures for graphic image manipulation 0859
* recognition enhancement by lip information 0915
Improving speaker consistency in an automatic * recognition framework 01448
Real time * synthesis—development and employment 01482
Comparison of * and pictorial displays in a cockpit environment 01731
* responses and dual-task performance: better time-sharing or asymmetric transfer? 01789
Online searching using * as a man/machine interface 02013
The influence of rule-generated stress on computer-synthesized * 02081
The utility of * input in user-computer interfaces 02230
Man—machine interaction by voice: developments in * technology. Part I: The state-of-the-art 02331
Man—machine interaction by voice: developments in * technology. Part 2: general applications and potential applications in libraries and information services 02332

A model for assessing the performance of a local area network employing technical office protocol (TOP) as part of MAP/TOP network in a computer integrated manufacturing (CIM) research project, for the transmission of real time interactive * 02491
"Transparent" interfacing of * recognizers to microcomputers 02497
Estimating articulatory motion from * wave 02643
Research on individuality features in * waves and automatic speaker recognition techniques 02645
* analysis and synthesis methods developed at ECL in NTT-From LPC to LSP- 02646
Composite phoneme units for the * synthesis of Japanese 02647
Changes in prosodic features of * due to environmental factors 02651
The measurement of the signal-to-noise ratio (SNR) in continuous * 02654
* motor control and stuttering: a computational model of adaptive sensory-motor processing 02655
Distinctive regions and modes: a new theory of * production 02659
A machine for neural computation of acoustical patterns with application to real time * recognition 02751
An improved automatic lipreading system to enhance * recognition 02859
Human factors and the problems of evaluation in the design of * systems interfaces 03192
Parcel sorting by * recognition: human factors issues 03209
* and expression: a computer solution to face animation 03293
A consideration of learning in * recognition from the viewpoint of AI class-description learning 03533
The use of * in man-machine interaction 03910
Recent advances in * understanding and dialog systems § 03987

The use of prosodic parameters in automatic * recognition 03988
Prosodic features in German *: stress assignment by man and machine 03989
Recognition of * using temporal decomposition 03990
Phonetic segmentation using psychoacoustic * parameters 03991
Morphological representation of * knowledge for automatic *recognition systems 03992
An experimental environment for generating word hypotheses in continuous * 03998
Dynamic spectral adaptation of automatic * recognizers to new speakers 03999
On-line interpretation in * understanding and dialogue systems 04000
Knowledge based systems for * understanding 04001
Recognition of speaker-dependent continuous * with Keal-Nevezh 04002
Modification of Earley's algorithm for * recognition 04003
Merging acoustics and linguistics in * understanding 04004
Error detection and correction in a * recognition system: a knowledge based system approach 04054
Chip talk: projects in * synthesis • HCI-0002 †
An economical approach to modeling * recognition accuracy HCI-0354 †
Natural language with discrete * as a mode for human-to-machine HCI-0355 †
Tones of voice: the role of intonation in computer * understanding HCI-0356 †
Text processing by *: dialogue design and usability issues in the provision of a system for disabled users HCI-0357 †
The phonetic basis for computer * processing HCI-0358 †
*-controlled text-editing: effects of input modality and of command structure HCI-0397 †

**SPEEDED**
* phase discrimination: evidence for global to local processing 03307

**SPEEDS**
Visual control of displacement at slow * 01797
A comparison of children's reading comprehension and reading rates at three text presentation * on a CRT 02280
Human response to unexpected robot movements at selected slow * 03405

**SPEEDSERVO**
Visuomotor control by a combined position- and *. Theoretical considerations and experimental results in man 02666

**SPEH**
Human factors challenges in creating a principal support office system—The * filing system approach 0038

**SPINDLE**
A model of the motor servo: Incorporating nonlinear * receptor and muscle mechanical properties 01273

**SPIRIT**
Maintaining the * of excitement in growing companies 01025
The second self: computers and the human * • HCI-0082 †

**SPOTTING**
Real-time large vocabulary word recognition via diphone * and multiprocessor implementation 03996

**SPREADING**
Analysis of competition-based * activation in connectionist models 02179

**SPREADSHEET**
A * interface for logic programming 0822
Visual information chunking in * calculation 02232
A longitudinal study of * program use 02354
A longitudinal study of * program use 03482

## SPREADSHEETS
* with incremental queries as a user interface for logic programming 02515

## SPSS
A method framework for the statistical package */PC+ to support occasional users 01202

## SPYING
* on windows 01290

## SQL
Ada-embedded *: the options 0763

## SSADM
Experiences in use of *: series of case studies. Part 1: first time users 01976
Experiences in use of *: series of case studies. Part 2: experienced users 01977

## STABILITY
A study of * of electrocortical rhythm generators 01258
On the temporal * of signal detection processes 03617
Temporal and spatial * in visual displays 03730

## STABILIZED
A model for the fading of * images in a visual system 01864

## STABLE
Absolutely * learning of recognition codes by a self-organizing neural network 02728

## STANDARD
Guide to the Draft American National * for Human Factors Engineering of Visual Display Terminal Workstations 0048
The * factor 01003
Prototypes from * user interface management systems 01370
Guide to the draft American national * for human factors engineering of visual display terminal workstations 01549
The design of distributed transport systems as a major * interface in computer integrated manufacturing 01564
PHIGS: a *, dynamic, interactive graphics interface 01826

User-oriented suggestions for floating-point and complex-arithmetic Forth * extensions 02306
Development of a human engineering design * for robot teach pendants 03411
Participation in the development of software and the utilisation of *software 03663

## STANDARDISATION
A user view of virtual terminal * 01432

## STANDARDIZATION
Why users must co-operate internationally on * 01457
* aspects on software for CAD of control systems 01565

## STANDARDIZED
Experiences with off-line robot programming via * interfaces 0601

## STANDARDS
The statutes and * movement 0049
Interfacing * for recognisers 0178
The * factor 0938
The * factor 0952
The * factor 0965
The * factor 0986
The development of ergonomic * 0987
User system interaction * 01386
A map of the world of software-related *, guidelines, and recommended practices 01453
Computer graphics language bindings: programmer interface * 01473
* and system development 01629
Towards the development of human work-performance * in futuristic man-machine systems: a fuzzy modeling approach 01692
User interface management and graphics * 01964
* requirements for mobile robotic systems 03415
Graphical * HCI-0417 †
Experimental results do not support some ergonomic * for computer video terminal design HCI-0428 †

## STAR
Designing the * user interface 0089
Online searching: a five * review of research 01314

*, maximal rectangles, lattices: a new perspective on Q-analysis 02105
The * user interface: an overview 03171

## STARTS
The evaluation of project support environments for the * user guide 0173

## STATECHART
Statemaster: A UIMS based on * for prototyping and target implementation 0850

## STATEGIC
* imperatives in software engineering education 04024

## STATEMASTER
*: A UIMS based on statechart for prototyping and target implementation 0850

## STATISTICAL
* evaluation of behavioural data 0051
Environments for supporting * strategy 0322
Models of user interactions with graphical interfaces: 1. * 0883
A method framework for the * package SPSS/PC+ to support occasional users 01202
* inference on spontaneous neuronal discharge patterns. I. Single neuron 01247
* dependency in visual scanning 01719
Building and understanding adaptive systems: a */numerical approach to factory automation and brain research 01890
Inference control mechanism for * database frequency-imposed data distortions 02449
The accuracy of combining judgemental and * forecasts 02474
NLI-ESD: An expert natural language interface to a * data bank 02712
Measuring the performance of statisticians with * software 03314
Essential ingredients for a * workstation 03315
* software, graphics and future workstations for data analysis 03316

[STATISTICIANS]                                                                                   KEYWORD INDEX

Displaying *
information—ergonomic considerations 03893
**STATISTICIANS**
Measuring the performance of * with statistical software 03314
**STATISTICS**
Artificial intelligence and * ● 0321
Computer science and * § 03313
**STATUTES**
The * and standards movement 0049
**STAY**
The body in question: how to * healthy at the PC 02548
**STEEL**
* yields in Pa. 01649
**STELLAR**
A display system for the * Graphics Supercomputer Model GS1000 02816
**STEPPING**
Modeling of control and learning in a * motion 01250
**STEPS**
User-developed DSS: * toward quality control 0461
Three * of better documentation 03160
* toward making robots see 04011
**STEREO**
Static * vision depth distortions in teleoperation 03390
**STEREOGRAMS**
Vertical disparity nulling in random-dot * 01256
**STEREONET**
A PC-interactives * plotting program 01504
**STEREOTYPES**
Usability: * and traps 0104
**STILE**
Building interprocess communication models using * 03528
**STIMULATION**
A simultaneous regression model for double * tasks 01726
Information systems and the * of creativity 02327

**STIMULI**
Quantitative determination of orientational and directional components in the response of visual cortical cells to moving * 01268
**STIMULUS**
The role of *-to-rule consistency in learning rapid application of spatial rules 01765
Perception of organization in a random * 02706
Perception of organization in a random * HCI-0364 †
**STOCHASTIC**
* dynamics of neural networks 01863
Modeling rule-based systems by * programmed production systems 02017
Combining * uncertainty and linguistic inexactness: theory and experimental evaluation of four fuzzy probability models 02218
Coherent global motion percepts from * local motions 03329
**STORAGE**
Tenuring policies for generation-based * reclamation 01124
Multiple resources for processing and * in short-term working memory 01794
Pattern * and associative memory in quasi-neural network 02537
**STORE**
Direct manipulation of an object * 02608
Strongly typed user interfaces in an abstract data * 02618
A window-based graphics frame * architecture HCI-0369 †
**STORED**
Internal representation of externally * information 03601
**STORIES**
Points: a theory of the structure of * in memory 0392
What * should we tell novice PROLOG programmers? 0421
Goal and plan knowledge representations: from * to text editors and programs HCI-0183 †

**STORYBOARD**
* prototyping: a new approach to user requirements analysis ● HCI-0005 †
**STRAIGHT**
Getting * again 01658
**STRAIN**
Preventing back * 0047
Repetition * injury in Australian VDU users 03681
Sensitivity to light and visual * in VDT operators: basic data for the design of work stations 03732
**STRAINS**
Optimum stresses and * represented by examples from shop practice 03441
**STRAITJACKET**
STATUS with IQ—escaping from the Boolean * 02569
**STRATEGIC**
ISPF: the * dailog manager ● 0035
Technology adaptation: a typology for * human resource management 01238
* IRM plan: user involvement spells success 02432
A framework of composite information systems for * advantage 03465
* issues in knowledge engineering HCI-0317 †
* management of technostress: The chaining of Prometheus HCI-0452 †
**STRATEGIES**
* for research on information systems in organizations. A critical analysis of research purpose and time frame 0158
James D. Foley, Oct. 12: user interface * '88 ● 0303
Screen design * for computer-assisted instruction ● 0424
* for interactive design systems 0466
Thomas W. Malone, Oct. 5: user interface * '88 ● 0532
Donald A. Norman, Oct. 12: user interface * '88 ● 0560
User interface * '88 (Videotape) ● 0684
Ben Shneiderman, Oct. 5,12: user interface * '88 ● 0685

# KEYWORD INDEX [STRESS]

Some * of reuse in an object-oriented programming environment 0820

Item selection from menus: the influence of menu organization, query interpretation, and programming experience on selection * 01011

The FAA's Advanced Automation System: * for future air traffic control systems 01357

Part-task training * in simulated carrier landing final-approach training 01741

Internal models, tracking * and dual-task performance 01751

* for managing user developed systems 01923

The dual role of information centers: an assessment of end user computing management * 01942

Comparison of decision support * in expert consultation systems 02101

* in controlling a continuous process with long response latencies: needs for computer support to diagnosis 02217

Systematic evaluation * for computer-based music instruction systems 02275

Expert systems and interactive video tutorials: separating * from subject matter 02293

* for end-user computing: An integrative framework 02348

* for managing end user computing 02436

Information-seeking * of novices using a full-text electronic encyclopedia 02452

The effect of task demands and graphical format on information processing * 02482

Firm * for costly engineering learning 02485

Improving the accuracy of touch screens: an experimental evaluation of three * 02860

Justified advice: a semi-naturalistic study of advisory * 02887

Display * for program browsing 03545

Assessment of mental load for different * of man-computer dialogue by means of the heart rate power spectrum 03623

Report from the working group on "goals and * of trade unions and other social groups in systems design for human development and productivity." 03657

Management * and information failure 03806

Search * in internal and external memories 03911

Designing the user interface: * for effective human-computer interaction ● HCI-0006 †

An empirical investigation into problem decomposition * used in program design HCI-0103 †

Fragile knowledge and neglected * in novice programmers HCI-0177 †

* for encouraging successful adoption of office communication systems HCI-0307 †

## STRATEGY

Environments for supporting statistical * 0322

The problem of levels and automatic response generation in a "Let's Talk AboutIt" * 0410

Approximate modelling of cognitive activity with an expert system: a theory-based * for developing an interactive design tool 01415

Information systems * and end-user application development 01637

Effects of vehicle handling characteristics on driving * 01773

Shaping user input: a * for natural language dialogue design 02067

Negative knowledge towards a * for asking in logic programming 02115

The impact of information systems * on end user computing 02423

Chief executive personality and corporate * and structure in small firms 02472

A generic * for diagnostic assistance: the technician's assistant 02957

Using a top-down and bottom-up * to analyze high resolution aerial photographs of urban areas 02960

A suppport * for users of a campus-wide local area network 03157

Human-computer-software interaction (HCSI) * in the design of global intelligent computer integrated management (ICIM) systems 03396

Experimentation with an adaptive search * for solving a keyboard design/configuration problem 04070

## STRENGTHS

Neurons with hysteresis form a network that can learn without any changes in synaptic connection * 02741

## STRESS

Psychophysiological investigation of * induced by temporal factors in human-computer interaction 0311

The cybernetic mechanisms of * 01599

* 01651

High tech, high * 01652

Changes in electromyographic activity associated with occupational * and poor performance in the workplace 01734

The influence of rule-generated * on computer-synthesized speech 02081

*, coping, and worker well-being in computer-aided manufacturing: A field investigation of a CNC machine shop 03373

Effects of computerization on job demands and *: the correspondence of subjective and objective data 03622

Vision monitoring of VDU operators and relaxation of visual * by means of laser speckle system 03738

VDT technology: psychosocial and * concerns 03755

A model for evaluating * effects of work with display units 03756

Work content, * and health in computer-mediated work: a seven year follow-up study 03758

893

Prosodic features in German speech: * assignment by man and machine 03989

An empirical study of occupational *, attitudes and health among information systems personnel HCI-0451 †

**STRESSES**

Optimum * and strains represented by examples from shop practice 03441

**STRESSORS**

Environmental * and perceived health symptoms among office workers 03680

**STRICT**

Non-* languages-programming and implementation 01418

**STRIM**

Implementation of a VDA interface in the CAD system * 100 03983

**STRING**

A * correction method based on the context-dependent similarity 0293

Optimization of * length for spoken digit input with error correction 02185

The accuracy of approximate * matching algorithms 02279

Algorithms for approximate * matching HCI-0180 †

Transporting the linguistic * project system from a medical to a Navy domain HCI-0352 †

**STRIPE**

Slot versus insertion magnetic * readers: user performance and preference 01756

**STRUCTURAL**

Syntactic and * pattern recognition ● 0292

Application of * pattern recognition in histopathology 0295

Navigational aids and learning styles: * optimal training for computer users 0970

The implementation of information systems for workers: a * equation model 01948

* displays as learning aids 02188

* aspects of semantic-directed clusters 02534

A * approach to the maintenance of structure-oriented environments 03054

* visibility and program comprehension 03274

Human interface in * analysis software 03453

**STRUCTURE**

Cortical connections and parallel processing: * and function 0028

Computer assisted language learning: program * and principles ● 0196

Points: a theory of the * of stories in memory 0392

Human decision processes: Heuristics and task * 0401

Cognition & personal * ● 0533

The relation between linguistic * and associative theories of language learning models: constructive critique of some connectionist learning models 0591

Phonology and syntax: the relationship between sound and * ● 0672

Designing a CD ROM information * 0682

Fine tuning selection semantics in a * editor based programming environment: some experimental results 0975

The run-time * of UIMS-supported applications 01059

The * of Cedar 01109

Human intelligence models and their implications for expert system *and research 01242

Attention, intention, and the * of discourse 01344

Detecting * by symbolic constructions on tokens 01466

A * for enhancing user participation in model development 01514

Time, * and levels of consciousness 01608

Problems of machine translation system - effect of cultural differences on sentence * 01687

Optimizing the * of database menu indexes: a decision model of menu search 01716

On kineopsis and cimputation of * and motion 01839

Principles of information * common to six levels of the human cognitive system 02019

Integrated communications and work efficiency: impacts on organizational * and power 02031

User interaction with the authority * of the online catalog: results of a survey 02049

Perceptual * cueing in a simple command language 02086

Considerations of menu * and communication rate for the design of computer menu displays 02124

* of a directory space: a case study with a UNIX operating system 02138

Representing the * of jobs in job analysis 02181

Interactive communication of sentential * and content: an alternative approach to man-machine communication 02220

The * of command languages: an experiment on task-action grammar 02224

A natural language interface processor based on the hierarchical-tree *model of relation tables 02315

A theory of information *. I. General principles 02361

A theory of information *. II. A theory of perceptual organization 02362

Chief executive personality and corporate strategy and * in small firms 02472

An external data * tool for Pascal 02495

* of German syllable initial and final consonant clusters based on articulatory features 02652

Early vision: from computational * to algorithms and parallel hardware 02703

Innovation of decision support system-matplan based on * matrix supported by APL 02800

Hierarchical scene * representations to facilitate image understanding 02942

# KEYWORD INDEX [STRUCTURES]

Negotiating IS: Observations on changes in * from a negotiated order perspective 03016
A structural approach to the maintenance of *-oriented environments 03054
Contextual * analysis of microcomputer manuals 03227
A viewdata-* editor designed around a task/action mapping 03269
Part * for 3-D sketching 03300
The representation and perception of geometric * in moving visual patterns 03326
A hybrid approach to *-from-motion 03340
The cross-ratio and the perception of motion and * 03344
Perceiving and recovering * from events 03346
* and policy in computer integrated manufacturing systems: human factors implications 03371
The software * of extended nucleus based on BTRON specification 03494
The control * diagram: an automated graphical representation for software 03524
Effectiveness of training as a function of the teacher knowledge * 03604
Programming for interactive * analysis 03776
Mapping images to a hierarchical data *—a way to knowledge-based pattern recognition 03954
From surface form to the * of the interface - studies in human computer interaction at INRIA 03984
A study of managerial computer users: the impact of user sophistication on decision * and attributes of decision-related information (cnd user) 04078
Early vision: from computational * to algorithms and parallel hardware HCI-0365 †
Speech-controlled text-editing: effects of input modality and of command * HCI-0397 †
Visual * and the transmission of meaning HCI-0404 †

**STRUCTURED**
PLEIADE: A system for interactive manipulation of * documents 0265
Schaum's outline of theories and problems of programming with advanced * COBOL with file processing * systems deveolpment and interactive cons ● 0555
VAX-BASIC with * problem solving: 2nd edition ● 0725
The effects of *, multi-level documentation 0907
* editor support for modularity and data abstraction 01105
Computing with * neural networks 01365
A knowledge-based human-computer cooperative system for ill-*management domains 01873
Responsibility sharing between sophisticated users and professionals in * prototyping 01978
Study of combination of belief intevals in lattice-* networks 02223
State trees as * finite state machines for user interfaces 03107
Some experiences in integrating specification of human computer interaction within a * system development method 03222
* what if analysis in DSS models 03481
A box * methodology for solving business problems 03483
* message passing on a shared-memory multiprocessor 03514
Windows, viewports and * display files 03930
* neural networks in nature and in computer science 03950
A * approach to designing human-computer dialogues HCI-0106 †
Computing with * connectionist networks HCI-0314 †
A system for interactive viewing of * documents HCI-0400 †
Computer mediated work: the interplay between technology and * jobs HCI-0440 †

**STRUCTURES**
VDU—work and user—friendly human—computer interaction: analysis of dialogue * 0310
Coherent and chaotic * in 2D vortex dynamics: progress and problems 0729
Data-* students may prefer to learn algorithms using graphical methods 01032
Nested * of control: an intuitive view 01464
Real-time failure detection on complex mechanical * via parallel data processing 01561
Using perceptual organization to extract 3-D * 01842
Directed graph representations of association *: A systematic approach 01862
On matching programmers' chunks with program *: an empirical investigation 02150
Measuring the effectiveness of personal database * 02246
"Structure—reaction type" paradigm in the conventional methods of describing organic reactions and the concept of imaginary transitions * overcoming this paradigm 02268
An interactive simulator for the designing of woven fabric * second place 02583
GMB: a tool for manipulating and animating graph data * 02636
Order and disorder in knowledge * 02722
Parallel * in human and computer memory 02742
Task-related knowledge *: analysis, modelling and application 03218
Problem oriented design of interaction * 03614
Knowledge * for intelligent interaction 03636
Systems, processes, and * 03644
Establishing * of requirements for the application of automated information processing (AIP)—an approach for the development of computer-aided systems 03660
Effect of visual presentation of different dialogue * on human-computer interaction 03768

How people comprehend unknown system *: conceptual primitives in systems' surface representations 03828
Tree doctor, a software package for graphical manipulation and animation of tree * 03901
* task group 03941
Conceptual *: information processing in mind and machine ● HCI-0057 †
A general user interface for creating and displaying tree-*, hierarchies, decision trees, and nested menus HCI-0136 †

## STUDENT

Qualitative * models 0721
Issuing each undergraduate * a personal computer: living with it for three years 01028
Leadership style vs. succssus in * chief programmer teams 01029
*-oriented features of an interactive programming environment 01036
A scale for assessing * attitudes toward computers preliminary findings 01579
Comparison of * performance in arithmetic exercises TOAM us paper-and-pencil testing 02249
* evaluation of motivational and learning attributes of microcomputer soft 02274
Computers as composition tools: a case study of * attitudes 02296
* perceptions of skill acquisition through cases and a general management simulation 02589

## STUDENTS

Learning with interactive media: dynamic support for * and teachers 0519
Towards universality of access: interfacing physically disabled * to the Icon educational microcomputer 0821
Learning disabled *' difficulties in learning to use a word processor: implications for design 0889
Data-structures * may prefer to learn algorithms using graphical methods 01032

Interactive graphics: a tool for beginning programming * in discovering solutions to novel problems 01038
A comparison of male and female computer science *' attitudes toward computers 01045
Computer programming and general problem solving by secondary * 01587
The relationship of computer programming and mathematics in secondary * 01588
Personality characteristics of junior high school * successful with computers 01592
Computer analysis of *' procedural "bugs" in an arithmetic domain 02273
Professional education and subsequent careers in library/information work: a follow-up study of former * on the MA/MSc information studies course at the University of Sheffield 02336
Perceptions of the CIS graduate's workstyle: undergraduate business *versus CIS faculty 02999
A comparison of the effects of computer-assisted instruction, interactive video, and traditional instruction on third-grade * in art education 04064

## STUTTERING

Speech motor control and *: a computational model of adaptive sensory-motor processing 02655

## STYLE

Leadership * vs. succssus in student chief programmer teams 01029
Some effects of cognitive * on learning UNIX 02252
Effects of decision support training and cognitive * on decision process attributes 02346
The importance of individual differences in end-user training: The case for learning * 03009
The representation of user interface * 03221
When and how cognitive * impacts decision making 03474
Creating a * for online help HCI-0154 †

Resistance to computerization: an examination of the relationship between resistance and the cognitive * of the clinician HCI-0407 †

## STYLES

Navigational aids and learning *: structural optimal training for computer users 0970
Transferring skills from training to the actual work situation: the role of task application knowledge, action * and job decision latitude 02865
Learning * in conversation—a practical application of Pask's learning theory to human-computer interaction 03608

## SUBGOALING

Universal * and chunking: the automatic generation and learning of goal hierarchies ● 0497

## SUBGROUP

An investigation into the existence of * concept in information systems personnel management 03022

## SUBJECTS

Study of visual performance on a multi-color VDU of color defective and normal Trichromatic * 03701

## SUBLANGUAGE

Language, *, and the promise of machine translation 01554

## SUBSCRIBERSHIP

Understanding cable * as telecommunications behavior 02676

## SUBSTANCE

Optimal allocation of a work force in a toxic * environment 01534

## SUBSTRATA

The informational * of psychic illnesses 01600

## SUBSTRATE

A * for object-oriented interface design 0691
Impulse-86: a * for object-oriented interface design 03032

KEYWORD INDEX [SUPPORT]

**SUBSYSTEM**
Interactive error recovery expert system for robot with voice recognition * 03420
UMFE: a user modelling front-end * HCI-0325 †

**SUBTLE**
Are there * changes in vision after use of VDTs? 03733

**SUITABILITY**
The quantification of operational * 01359
Issues governing the * of programming languages for programming tasks 03224

**SUMMARIZING**
* natural language database responses 01343

**SUN**
Dbxtool: A window-based symbolic debugger for * workstations 02614

**SUNDEW**
*—a distributed and extensible window system 03927

**SUPERBOOK**
Formative design evaluation of * 01154

**SUPERCOMPUTER**
A display system for the Stellar Graphics * Model GS1000 02816
Super consulting for * users: a philosophy of user support 03145
* applications: helping users cope with tough programming problems 03147
HORSE: a simulation of the horizon * 03541
Design and implementation of a * frame buffer system 03543

**SUPERCOMPUTING**
From user to client services; making the transition for * 03138
*'88 § 03540

**SUPERIMPOSER**
A study on an error recovery expert system using a * and a digitizer in the advanced teleoperator system 03389

**SUPERVISORY**
A * control paradigm for real-time control of flexible manufacturing systems 01205

The use of measures of entropy in evaluating human * control of a manufacturing system 01897
Human * control in flexible manufacturing systems: Allocation of functions and system size 02456
Issues in modeling * control in flexible manufacturing systems 03363
Human * control in discrete manufacturing: Translating the paradigm 03364
Cognitive attributes: implications for display design in * control systems HCI-0242 †

**SUPPLIER**
The *'s role in the design of products for organisations 01412

**SUPPLY**
Computer applications in water *: vol. 1—systems analysis and simulation ● 0227
Private copying, reproduction costs, and the * of intellectual property 01988

**SUPPORT**
Human factors challenges in creating a principal * office system—The speh filing system approach 0038
Techniques of user message design: developing a user message system to *cooperative work 0127
Knowledge-based * of cooperative activities 0171
The evaluation of project * environments for the STARTS user guide 0173
Computer * for organizations: toward an organizational science 0211
Evaluation of expert systems for decision * 0244
Knowledge based management * systems ● 0252
Develping decision * systems from a model of the DSS/user interface 0253
A decision * system for vehicle scheduling in public transport 0339
Communication and management * in system development environments (Reprint) 0374

Beyond the chalkboard: computer * for collaboration and problem solving inmeetings (Reprint) 0376
Learning with interactive media: dynamic * for students and teachers 0519
Conceptual design of decision * systems utilizing management science models 0658
A conceptual architecture for generalized decision * system software 0659
Concept design of a program manager's decision * system 0660
ARIADNE: A knowledge-based interactive system for planning and decision * 0661
A multiple, virtual-workspace interface to * user task switching 0813
Computer-* cooperative work 0956
Designing real-time, decision * computer-human interaction 0982
CHI '88 Workshop on Real Time, decision * computer-human interaction 0991
UIMS * for direct manipulation interfaces 01065
Some design guidelines for an information center to * office information systems 01093
Polylith: an environment to * management of tool interfaces 01096
Structured editor * for modularity and data abstraction 01105
User interface * for the integration of software tools: an iconic model of interaction 01139
A method framework for the statistical package SPSS/PC+ to * occasional users 01202
Graphical data presentation for decision * systems 01229
Segue: * for distributed graphical interfaces 01369
The committee * system 01460
User facilities for engineering * stations 01512
Application of decision * system on sandwich beams, verified by experiments 01572
Designing a user manual to * an in-house database 01635

897

[SUPPORT]

Understanding and validating results in model-based decision * systems 01666
Providing effective decision *: modeling users and their requirements 01668
A modular user-oriented decision * for physical database design 01669
The metaphor machine: a database method for creativity * 01670
Human factors * for product development 01681
A high level language-based computing enviornment to * production and execution of reliable programs 01855
ARIADNE: a knowledge-based interactive system for planning and decision * 01860
Decision * systems for workers: a bridge to advancing productivity 01947
MAJIC—an integrated program * environment 01960
On two roles decision * systems can play in negotiations 01998
Temporal semantics and natural language processing in a decision * system 02038
Comparison of decision * strategies in expert consultation systems 02101
* for tentative design: incorporating the screen image, as a graphical object, into PROLOG 02116
Information and reasoning in intelligent decision * systems 02173
Validation in a knowledge * system: construing and consistency with multiple experts 02203
Strategies in controlling a continuous process with long response latencies: needs for computer * to diagnosis 02217
* for browsing in an intelligent text retrieval system 02240
Integration issues in knowledge * system 02253
Controlling bias in user assertions in expert decision * systems for problem formulation 02343
Effects of decision * training and cognitive style on decision process attributes 02346

User perceptions of decision * system restrictiveness: an experiment 02353
Current and future uses of the group decision * system technology: report on a recent empirical study 02355
A study of user interface aids for model-oriented decision * systems 02479
A Unix distributed application * suitable for mini and microcomputer based systems 02489
Service * levels: An organizational approach to end-user computing 02503
Dialogue management: * for dialogue independence 02512
Descriptive analysis for computer-based decision * 02527
Towards the formal specification of a simple programming * environment 02607
* for graphs of processes in a command interpreter 02633
The provision of terminal-based user * 02686
User interfaces for problem solving * 02695
A highly integrated tool set for program development * 02788
Innovation of decision * system-matplan based on structure matrix *ed by APL 02800
GDSS: a brief look at a new concept in decision * 02804
Travel around a learning * environment: rambling, orienteering or touring? 02900
Developing intelligent simulation language to * telerobotic workstation activities 02995
Increase organizational effectiveness: * self-managed IS development teams 03014
Mach and Matchmaker: kernel and language * for object-oriented distributed systems 03031
Dost: an environment to * automatic generation of user interfaces 03053
Super consulting for supercomputer users: a philosophy of user * 03145

KEYWORD INDEX

Still sailing (and bailing): managing unexpected change in user * 03150
A new model for user services: distributed * 03153
Desktop publishing and user services; moment in the evolution of user *documentation at UNH 03158
Tools for management and * of multiple constraints in a writer's assistant 03251
MacCadd - an enabling software method * tool 03252
Decision * using qualitative evidence 03398
Decision * and Knowledge Based Systems Track § 03461
On building future decision * systems 03472
Flexible user interface decision * systems 03473
Knowledge-based * of cooperative activities 03478
GMMS: global model management system: a conceptional design framework for model management systems for distributed decision * systems 03484
Decision * for reasoning about values 03486
Tool interfaces in integrated project * environments 03506
The space station information system and software * environment 03512
Segue: * for distributed graphical interfaces 03526
The integrity lock * environment 03578
Decision * systems: theory and application § 03788
Fault management, knowledge *, and responsibility in man-machine systems 03812
* environments for VDM 03832
A * system for formal reasoning: requirements and status 04035
A methodology, specification language, and automated * environment for com1uter-aided design systems 04068
Executive * systems: the emergence of top management computer use
● HCI-0049 †

# KEYWORD INDEX [SURVEY]

Undo * models HCI-0144 †
PECAN: program development systems that * multiple views HCI-0145 †
The Software Life Cycle * Environment (SLCSE): a computer based framework for developing software systems HCI-0147 †
Understanding the effectiveness of computer graphics for decision *: a cumulative experimental approach HCI-0215 †
A user oriented design process for user recovery and command reuse * HCI-0284 †
Change, attitude to change, and decision * system success HCI-0296 †
Communications design for Co-oP: a group decision * system HCI-0297 †
Computer decision * for senior managers: encouraging exploration HCI-0298 †
Personal computing for decision * HCI-0299 †
Impact of design methods on decision * systems success: an empirical assessment HCI-0303 †
Beyond the chalkboard: computer * for collaboration and problem solving in meetings HCI-0312 †
Experimental results do not * some ergonomic standards for computer video terminal design HCI-0428 †

## SUPPORTING
* collaboration in hypermedia: issues and experiences 0117
* the microcomputer end user 0187
Environments for * statistical strategy 0322
Tools for * cooperative work near and far: highlights from the CSCW conference 0879
A communication mechanism * actions 01441
* end users in the office 01444
End-user prototyping: sophisticated users * system development 01636
Propaedeutics of decision-making: * managerial learning and innovation 01667

A systems architecture for * senior managers' messy tasks 01928
* collaboration in Hypermedia: issues and experiences 02454
Linking mechanism * end-user computing 02806
* natural language database update by modeling real world actions 03179
A programming environment * reuse of object-oriented software 03509
* document development with concordia 03521
* flexible and efficient tool integration 03783
A set of tools * the software design based on SDL 03803
* concurrency, communication, and synchronization in human-computer interaction—the Sassafras UIMS HCI-0102 †
A communication system * large datagrams on a local area network HCI-0166 †
A note on the nature of creativity in engineering: implications for *system design HCI-0220 †
A * system for effective construction and sharing of scientific databases by general researchers HCI-0262 †

## SUPPORT
User services consulting * tools at the NASA numerical aerodynamic simula 03161
A * strategy for users of a campus-wide local area network 03157

## SUPPRESSION
A computer model of peripheral auditory processing incorporating phase-locking, * and adaptation effects 02650

## SURFACE
Color constancy: a method for recovering * spectral reflectance 0298
Environment-centered and viewer-centered perception of * orientation 02705
Generic * interpretation: observability model 03563

How people comprehend unknown system structures: conceptual primitives in systems' * representations 03828
From * form to the structure of the interface - studies in human computer interaction at INRIA 03984
Environment-centered and viewer-centered perception of * orientation HCI-0392 †
VDAFS—a pragmatic interface for the exchange of sculptured * data HCI-0420 †
Approximation methods used in the exchange of geometric information via the VDA/VDMA * interface HCI-0421 †

## SURFACES
An approach to learning control * by connectionist systems 0030
Automatic construction of * with prescribed shape 01474
Describing * 02699
A simple, general method for ray tracing bicubic * 03853

## SURPRISINGLY
Semistructured messages are * useful for computer-supported coordination HCI-0290 †

## SURROUNDINGS
Non-visual effects of visual * 03720

## SURVEILLANCE
A tolerance for *: American public opinion concerning privacy and civil liberties 0524

## SURVEY
Natural language processing: a * 0181
Hypertext: an introduction and * (Reprint) 0378
Dialog management in interactive systems: a comparative * 0949
Modes * 0963
Modes * results 0998
Profile of undergraduate software engineering courses: results from a * 01035
A * of three dialogue models 01152
Hypertext: an introduction and * 01360
A * on systems informational paradigm to the psychic 01606
A * of information technology in the U.K. service sector 01916

**899**

A comparative * of the friendliness of online 'help' in interactive information 02010
User interaction with the authority structure of the online catalog: results of a * 02049
A * of formal tools and models for developing user interfaces 02207
A * of general-purpose manipulation 02259
Using worker's * to improve production 02566
Natural language and computers: a general * of written text interpretation methods 02671
Charting the course of a user * that will rock the boat 03136
CIM and manufacturing industry in the north east of England: A * of some current issues 03377
Computer-music interfaces: a * HCI-0412 †

**SWEDEN**
Some recent documentation of robotic safety from * 03407

**SWEEP**
Single * analysis of visual evoked potentials through a model of parametric identification 01261

**SWITCHBOARD**
A multitasking * approach to user interface management 01053

**SWITCHED**
A graphics interface for interactive simulation of packet-* networks 03869

**SWITCHING**
A multiple, virtual-workspace interface to support user task * 0813

**SYLLABLE**
Structure of German * initial and final consonant clusters based on articulatory features 02652

**SYMBIOSIS**
Task analysis, systems analysis and design: * or synthesis? 02058
User-friendliness - from sugar to * 03774

**SYMBIOTIC**
* software: development and usage issues on stand-alone and networked systems 0474

* systems for complex problems 02922

**SYMBOL**
The effect of VDT * characteristics on operator performance and visual comfort 03728

**SYMBOLIC**
The microcomputer as a * medium 0583
Detecting structure by * constructions on tokens 01466
GI/S: A graphical user interface for * computation systems 02397
Dbxtool: A window-based * debugger for sun workstations 02614
Iris: design of a user interface program for * algebra 03081
Symsac '86—Proceedings of the 1986 symposium on * and algebraic manipulation § 03084
Iris: design of an user interface program for * algebra 03085

**SYMBOLOGY**
On the selection and evaluation of visual display *: factors influencing search and identification times 01718

**SYMBOLS**
Connections and * ● 0588
Skills, rules, and knowledge; signals, signs, and *, and other distinctions in human performance models 0654
The effect of adding * to written warning labels on user behavior and recall 01788

**SYMMETRIC**
The multimedia object presentation manager of MINOS: a * approach 01083
Adaptive interface design: a * model and a knowledge-based implementation 01091

**SYMMS**
Composite models in * 03485

**SYMPTOMATOLOGY**
Visual impairment and subjective ocular * in VDT operators 03734

**SYMPTOMS**
Environmental stressors and perceived health * among office workers 03680

**SYMSAC**
* '86 § 03080
* '86—Proceedings of the 1986 symposium on symbolic and algebraic manipulation § 03084

**SYNAPTIC**
Diffusion approximation of the neuronal model with * reversal potentials 01254
Neurons with hysteresis form a network that can learn without any changes in * connection strengths 02741

**SYNCHRONIZATION**
A multiple track animator system for motion * 03350
Supporting concurrency, communication, and * in human-computer interaction—the Sassafras UIMS HCI-0102 †

**SYNCHRONIZING**
* the I/O behavior of functional programs with feedback 02016

**SYNCHRONOUS**
Design of an integral computer-based wheelchair controller/linear *motor system 02378

**SYNERGISTIC**
* use of direct manipulation and natural language 0857

**SYNONYM**
A flexible * interface with application examples in CAL and help environments 01404

**SYNTACTIC**
* and structural pattern recognition ● 0292
The effects of * complexity on the human-computer interaction 01708
A practical method for LR and LL * error diagnosis and recovery HCI-0163 †

**SYNTAX**
Phonology and *: the relationship between sound and structure ● 0672
The effects of restricted * on menu-based interaction 0775
Cognition-sensitive design and user modeling for *-directed editors 0828

KEYWORD INDEX [TARGET]

On the usefulness of * directed editors 03781
Portability of * and semantics in DATALOG HCI-0340 †
The use of colour in language * analysis HCI-0385 †

**SYNTHESIS**
Computer aided application program * for industrial robots 0606
An interactive environment for object-oriented music composition and sound * 01131
Real time speech *—development and employment 01482
Task analysis, systems analysis and design: symbiosis or * 02058
A review and * of recent research in intelligent computer-assisted instruction 02108
Speech analysis and * methods developed at ECL in NTT-From LPC to LSP- 02646
Composite phoneme units for the speech * of Japanese 02647
Analogical program * from program components 03920
Chip talk: projects in speech * ● HCI-0002 †
The application of scene * techniques to the display of multidimensional image data HCI-0371 †
* of print-quality cursive script based on a model of the human handwriting mechanism HCI-0402 †

**SYNTHESIZED**
The influence of rule-generated stress on computer-* speech 02081

**SYNTHESIZER**
The * generator: a system for constructing language-based editors ● HCI-0024 †
A parallel formant * for machine voice output HCI-0396 †

**SYNTHESIZING**
An acoustic-phonetic oriented system for * Chinese 02661

**SYNTHETIC**
Realism in * speech 0066
A * visual environment with hand gesturing and voice input 0858

Designing a quality voice: an analysis of listeners' reactions to *voices 0914
Limited interconnectivity in * neural systems 03968

**SYSTEMIC**
* implications of leap and an improved two-part cursor 0848

**SYSTOLIC**
Multi-Input fuzzy inference engine on a * array 02953

**SYNTAX**
An experimental evaluation of prefix and postfix notation in command language * 02110

**TA**
*: Can it improve worker satisfaction with organizational decision-making? 02414

**TABLES**
A natural language interface processor based on the hierarchical-tree structure model of relation * 02315

**TABLET**
Issues and techniques in touch-sensitive * input 0063
Optimizing the touch *: the effects of control display gain and method of cursor control 01730

**TABLETOPS**
Guided tours and *: tools for communicating in a hypertext environment 01161
Guided tours and *: tools for communicating in a hypertext environment 02823

**TABULAR**
Effects of graphic boundaries in * displays: a human factors evaluation 01526
An experimental comparison of * and graphic data presentation HCI-0236 †

**TACIT**
* knowledge, working life and scientific method 0345

**TACTICAL**
Distributed * decisionmaking: conceptual framework and empirical results 01885

**TACTICS**
Knowledge-based search * for an intelligent intermediary system HCI-0277 †

**TACTILE**
The architecture of an inexpensive and portable talking-* terminal to aid the visually handicapped 01452
An inexpensive and portable talking-* terminal for the visually handicapped 02377
Force and * sensing for robots 04013
Analogs of biological tissues for mechanoelectrical transduction: *sensors and muscle-like actuators 04014

**TAE**
Transportable applications environment (*) plus experiences in "Object"-ively modernizing a user interface environment 01126

**TALKING**
* it over: the natural language dialog system HAM-ANS 0165
TNT: a * tutor 'n' trainer for teaching use of interactive computer systems 0895
The architecture of an inexpensive and portable *-tactile terminal to aid the visually handicapped 01452
* to computers: an empirical investigation 02186
An inexpensive and portable *-tactile terminal for the visually handicapped 02377

**TALMUDIC**
Reasoning about 'hard' cases in * law 02777

**TANGENCIES**
An interactive procedure for constructing line and circle * 01823

**TARGET**
Statemaster: A UIMS based on statechart for prototyping and *implementation 0850
The moving *: future trends in networking 01282
The effects of * wavelength on dynamic visual acuity under photopic and scotopic viewing 01762

901

# [TARGETED] KEYWORD INDEX

Visual accommodation and * detection in the vicinity of a window post 01802
ATLANTIS—a software simulator for behavior analysis of protocol specificationsand their * implementations 02667

## TARGETED
A user interface for multiple-process, turnkey systems * for the novice user 0911

## TARGETS
Optical analog of two-dimensional neural networks and their application in recognition of radar * 02733

## TASK
The limitations of * complexity through information technologies: results of a field study 0307
Human decision processes: Heuristics and * structure 0401
*-oriented approach to interactive control of heavy-duty manipulators based on coarse scene description ● 0546
* allocation between humans and robots in manufacturing 0559
The effects of type of knowledge upon human problem solving in a process control * 0657
The effects of bargaining orientation and communication medium on negotiations in the bilateral monopoly *: a comparison of decision room and computer conferencing communication media 0809
A multiple, virtual-workspace interface to support user * switching 0813
*-oriented representation of asynchronous user interfaces 0851
How are windows used? Some notes on creating an empirically-based windowing benchmark * 0903
A cognitively based methodology for evaluating human performance in the computer-aided design * domain 01240
Knowledge-based system for * analysis and reliability enhancement 01516

The cybernetic principle: its transdisciplinarity to science and religion and the challenging * 01596
Part-* training strategies in simulated carrier landing final-approach training 01741
Training consistent * components: application of automatic and controlled processing theory to industrial * training 01742
Hesitations in continuous tracking induced by a concurrent discrete * 01745
Internal models, tracking strategies and dual-* performance 01751
Speech responses and dual-* performance: better time-sharing or asymmetric transfer? 01789
The role of practice in dual-* performance: toward workload modeling in a connectionist/control architecture 01790
*-sharing within and between hemispheres: a multiple-resources approach 01795
Capacity equivalence curves: a double trade-off curve method for equating *performance 01796
Modeling of *-dependent characteristics of human operator dynamics during pursuit manual tracking 01859
Two simulation studies investigating means of human-computer communication for dynamic * allocation 01882
A framework for * cooperation within systems containing intelligent components 01884
* analysis, systems analysis and design: symbiosis or synthesis? 02058
An empirical comparison of model-based and explicit communication for dynamic human-computer * allocation 02109
An experiment to test user validation of requirements: data-flow diagrams vs *-oriented menus 02131
The effect of different conceptual models using reasoning in a database query writing * 02201

The structure of command languages: an experiment on *-action grammar 02224
An interface architecture to provide adaptive *-specific context for the user 02228
Theoretical training and problem detection in a computerized database retrieval * 02239
* compatibility of manipulator postures 02258
The effects of * differences on the work satisfaction, job characteristics, nd role perceptions of programmer/analysts 02359
The effect of * demands and graphical format on information processing strategies 02482
Transferring skills from training to the actual work situation: the role of * application knowledge, action styles and job decision latitude 02865
*-oriented parsing - a diagnostic method to be used adaptive systems 02896
*-related knowledge structures: analysis, modelling and application 03218
A viewdata-structure editor designed around a */action mapping 03269
A conceptual dependency network approach to multi-* assignments in man-machine (teleoperated) systems 03388
Coding of information in man-computer systems based on cognitive * analysis 03618
A methodology for dynamic * allocation in man-machine system 03635
*-load and endocrinological risk for pregnancy in women VDU operators 03692
* and the adjustment of ergonomic chairs 03711
Data entry * on VDU: underload or overload 03761
Application program interface * group 03940
Structures * group 03941
Some cognitive aspects of interface design in a two-variable optimization * HCI-0111 †

GENIE: a modifiable computer-based * for experiments in human-computer interaction HCI-0194 †

**TASKS**
Complete vs. incomplete working *—a concept and its verification 0241
Integrated software-design: a work-oriented approach to the humanization of computerized clerical * 0243
Relationships and * in scientific research collaborations (Reprint) 0387
DARN: Toward a community memory for diagnosis and repair * 0428
Measures of human problem solving performance in fault diagnosis * 0655
Learning and transfer of measurement * 0832
Comparison of elderly and younger users on keyboard and voice input computer-based composition * 0916
Presentation of a description language for office * 01434
A knowledge-based system for assessment of human physiological abilities in manual lifting * 01519
Biomechanical evaluation of lifting *: a microcomputer-based model 01524
Ergonomic job design in frequent manual lifting *: a microcomputer-based model 01532
A simultaneous regression model for double stimulation * 01726
Display formatting in information integration and nonintegration * 01750
Menu organization and user expertise in information search * 01761
Conceptualizing in assembly * 01776
Processing demands, effort, and individual differences in four different vigilance * 01801
A systems architecture for supporting senior managers' messy * 01928

Adapting menu layout to * 02182
Underlying dimensions of human problem solving and learning: implications for personnel selection, training * design and expert system 02225
Critical factors in the user environment: an experimental study of users, organizations and * 02507
Topology conserving mappings for learning motor * 02758
SIMS: a uniform environment for planning and performing user's * 02921
Making computer * at work more playful: Implications for systems analysts and designers 03005
OTM: specifying office * 03039
Issues governing the suitability of programming languages for programming * 03224
Understanding learning problems in computer aided * 03607
Performance in cognitive * and cardiovascular parameters as indicators of mental load 03624
What should be computerized? Cognitive demands of mental routine * and mental load 03632
User-centered system design: design of mental * 03646
Mental fatigue of VDU operators induced by monotonous and various * 03760
Cognitive models, cognitive *, and information retrieval HCI-0331 †

**TASTE**
Physiology and psychophysics in * and smell 04009

**TAXONOMY**
Interactive lesson designs: a * 0273
User cube: a * of end users 01335
A * of user-oriented functions 02104
A * for the study of human factors in management information systems HCI-0205 †
Query languages—a * HCI-0254 †

**TAYLORISM**
Human and computer aided manufacturing: The end of * 03379

**TDS**
History of the * medical information system 02851

**TEACH**
Retraining high school *ers to * computer science—observations on the first course 01030
Using interactive videotaped-based instruction to * on-the-job social skills to handicapped adolescents 02288
Development of a human engineering design standard for robot * pendants 03411

**TEACHABLE**
A * neural network based on an unorthodox neuron 02561

**TEACHER**
Effectiveness of training as a function of the * knowledge structure 03604

**TEACHWARE**
* for power engineering education 01203

**TEAM**
Adaptive coordination of a learning * 02475
Information systems development success: Perspectives from project *participants 02501
* cohesion effects on business game performance 02597
*: an experiment in the design of transportable natural-language interfaces HCI-0351 †

**TEAMS**
Leadership style vs. succssus in student chief programmer * 01029
Increase organizational effectiveness: Support self-managed IS development * 03014

**TEAMWORK**
Tennessee Eastman employee * raises quality, customer service 01907

**TEAR**
Growth and challenge VS wear and * of humans in computer mediated work 03757

**TECHNICIAN**
A generic strategy for diagnostic assistance: the *'s assistant 02957

## TECHNOACCEPTANCE
Implementing computer-mediated communication technologies: a *approach to critical mass utilization 01931

## TECHNOLOGICAL
Issues and approaches to appraising * change in the office: A consequentialist perspective 0043
* development and the integrated workstation 01313
A human approach to the * challenges in data security 01543
Human implications of * change 03369

## TECHNOLOGIES
Management, organizations and the new * 0145
Ergonomics and the new * 0147
On knowledge base management systems: integrating artificial intelligence and d atabase * ● 0180
The limitations of task complexity through information *: results of a field study 0307
The variable impact of computer * on the organization of work activities 0388
Managing the diffusion of end-user computing *: a fifties mindset with eighties tools 0459
Government infostructures: a guide to the networks of information resources and * at federal, state, and local levels ● 0523
Teachers' adoption of multimedia * for science and mathematics instruction 0577
A directory of sources for interactive * 0941
Cognitive *: The design of joint human-machine cognitive systems 01193
Information * for the 1990's: an orgnizational impact perspective 01336
Implementing computer-mediated communication *: a technoacceptance approach to critical mass utilization 01931
Analysis of the competence of operators confronting new *: some methodological problems and some results 03594
Designing learning processes for work activities in automated * 03605
Social psychological prerequisites and consequences of new information * 03631
Touch-sensitive screens: the * and their application HCI-0087 †
The next generation of interactive * HCI-0384 †

## TECHNOLOGY
Human foundations of advanced computing *: the guide to the select literature 0001
Information * and the experience of work 0041
The changing workplace: A guide to managing the people, organizational, and regulatory aspects of office * (book excerpt) 0044
* + design + research = information design 0107
Information * & people: designing for the future ● 0144
Attitudes to information * 0150
Electronic speech recognition: techniques, *, and applications ● 0174
Advanced information * in the new industrial society: the Kingston seminars ● 0225
The management of advanced information * 0226
Adopting interactive videodisc * for education 0272
Information * and education: the changing school ● 0282
Assessment of trends in the * and techniques of human-computer interaction 0335
A history of the promis *: an effective human interface 0349
User *: from pointing to pondering 0350
Coping with new *: the need for training 0441
Preparing for new * 0444
Information * and information use: towards a unified view of information and information * ● 0447
Critical issues in information processing management and *: vol. 6 ● 0594
Information * in the humanities: tools, techniques and applications ● 0595
The computational science revolution: *, methodology, and sociology 0728
Oxford Surveys in Information * ● 0753
The diffusion and impacts of information * in households 0754
Oxford surveys in information *; vol. 2, 1985 ● 0755
Voice: * searching for communication needs 0808
Search *, Inc. 0872
The effects of device * on the usability of advanced telephone functions 0876
Developing computer aided design * in China 0942
Report on the Collaborative * Developers' Workshop 0994
Introducing information *: experiences of a large industrial unit 01217
* adaptation: a typology for strategic human resource management 01238
DVI—a digital multimedia * 01327
Life before the chips: simulating digital video interactive * 01328
Successful use of CADCAM—a combination of *, organization, and people 01569
Trends in printer * 01624
How * brings blind people into the workplace 01705
A survey of information * in the U.K. service sector 01916
Utilizing high *: computer-aided-design and user performance 01954
Developing the * for intelligent maintenance advisors 02276
Improved design of graphic displays in thesauri—through * and ergonomics 02297
Emerging communications * paradigms 02320
Education and training in office * 02330
Man—machine interaction by voice: developments in speech *. Part I: The state-of-the-art 02331
Man—machine interaction by voice: developments in speech *. Part 2:

# KEYWORD INDEX [TELEROBOT]

general applications and potential applications in libraries and information services 02332

Current and future uses of the group decision support system *: report on a recent empirical study 02355

Forecasting consumer adoption of information * and services—lessons from home video forecasting 02451

Assessing the impacts of new * on library employees 02459

*'s impact on library interior planning 02464

Managerial influence in the implementation of new * 02481

LSP-automatic translation and information * 02513

Choreography for * and humans 02518

* and the author's labour 02574

Communications * and the public sector: understanding the process of adoption 02679

The application of expert systems * to case-based law 02771

GTEX—A group * expert system 02936

Embedded training in AI * through an expert system interface: an alarm processor application 02991

Managers who personally use information * frequently: a profile of some invisible computer personnel 03007

A history of the Promis *: an effective human interface 03097

User *—from pointing to pondering 03098

New * work aids for the physically disabled 03273

Theory and practice of software * § 03361

U.S. Army field robotics focus and key * issues 03402

A study of fail-safe * 03421

Computerized manufacturing * and work organization effects on labor relations and worker satisfaction 03443

Union acceptance of automation *: A case study 03444

The information * champion: aiding and abetting, care and feeding 03459

Exploring *: today and tomorrow § 03491

VDT *: psychosocial and stress concerns 03755

Challenges in the application of graphics * to the management of geographic information 03871

Future Trends in Information Science and * § 04039

Human factors of changing information science * 04048

Teleoperations and robotics: applications and * ● HCI-0068 †

* transfer: a new computer-based system HCI-0203 †

Psychology and information * HCI-0225 †

Information * and home-based services: improving the usability of teleshopping HCI-0226 †

Electronic calendars in the office: an assessment of user needs and current * HCI-0287 †

The development and use of information * in health care HCI-0408 †

Information * in the home: promises as yet unrealized HCI-0425 †

Computer mediated work: the interplay between * and structured jobs HCI-0440 †

An overview of research and co-operation in advanced information * HCI-0442 †

## TECHNOSTRESS

Strategic management of *: The chaining of Prometheus HCI-0452 †

## TELECOM

Design and evaluation of the AID adaptive front-end to * Gold 03260

## TELECOMMUNICATIONS

Understanding cable subscribership as * behavior 02676

## TELECOMMUTING

* the organizational and behavioral effects of working at home ● 0596

## TELECONFERENCING

Thinking ahead: what to expect from * (Reprint) 0372

An architecture for a multimedia * system 02802

## TELECOURSES

Interaction of CMC with video * for distance education 02677

## TELEMATIC

An interdisciplinary approach to human factors in * systems. A review of the problems and possible solutions by a COST-11 ter working group 01440

## TELEOPERATED

Human factor issues in * systems 03387

A conceptual dependency network approach to multi-task assignments in man-machine (*) systems 03388

## TELEOPERATION

Static stereo vision depth distortions in * 03390

## TELEOPERATIONAL

MEISTER: a model enhanced intelligent and skillful * robot system 03562

## TELEOPERATIONS

* and robotics: applications and technology ● HCI-0068 †

## TELEOPERATOR

Evaluating the impact of camera placement on * efficiency 02940

A study on an error recovery expert system using a superimposer and a digitizer in the advanced * system 03389

## TELEPHONE

The effects of device technology on the usability of advanced *functions 0876

Dialing a name: alphabetic entry through a * keypad 0973

The * in question: questions on communication 01436

## TELEPHONY

Rapid prototyping and system development: examination of an interface toolkit for voice and * applications 0918

## TELEROBOT

Human visual requirements for control and monitoring of a space * 03391

## TELEROBOTIC
Developing intelligent simulation language to support * workstation activities 02995

## TELESHOPPING
Information technology and home-based services: improving the usability of * HCI-0226 †

## TEMPERATURE
A model of the controller responses of the human * regulating system to changes in water * 02487

## TEMPLATE
Automatic contour definition on left ventriculograms by image evidence and multiple *-based model 04073

## TEMPLATES
Editing *: a user interface generation tool 01827
On the minimum number of * required for shift, rotation and size invariant pattern recognition 02531

## TEMPLES
A gestural representation of the pr ocess of composing Chinese * 03855

## TEMPORAL
The interdependence of * and spatial information in early vision 0023
Psychophysiological investigation of stress induced by * factors in human-computer interaction 0311
Animated graphical interfaces using * constraints 0909
* ontology and * reference 01347
* resolution: an insight into the video display terminal (VDT) "problem" 01754
* semantics and natural language processing in a decision support system 02038
Absolute dates and relative dates in an inferential system on *dependencies between events 02235
A * logic for reasoning about changing data bases in the context of natural language question-answering 03176

The lexicon, grammatical categories and * reasoning 03549
On the * stability of signal detection processes 03617
* and spatial stability in visual displays 03730
Exploring three possibilities in network design: spontaneous node activity, node plasticity and * coding 03962
Spatial and * transformations in visuo-motor coordination 03963
Recognition of speech using * decomposition 03990
Natural language query processing in a * database HCI-0257 †

## TENNESSEE
* Eastman employee teamwork raises quality, customer service 01907

## TENSES
On learning the past * of English verbs 0634

## TENSION
Experiences with the alternate reality kit: an example of the * between literalism and magic 0817
Generation of muscle * related to a demand of continuing attention 03710

## TENSOR
* network theory and its application in computer modeling of the metaorganization of sensorimotor hierarchies of gaze 02753
* geometry: a language of brains & neurocomputers. Generalized coordinates in neuroscience & robotics 03966

## TENURE
Moderating effects of age, education, and * on the job satisfaction-job performance relationship 03021

## TENURING
* policies for generation-based storage reclamation 01124

## TERM
Short-* memory limits in human performance 0398
Short-* memory as a metastable state.III. Diffusion approximation 01611

Multiple resources for processing and storage in short-* working memory 01794
Correlation of * usage and * indexing frequencies 02004
Short- and long-* effects of extreme physical inactivity. A review 03703
Development of a * association interface for browsing bibliographic data bases based on end users' word associations HCI-0266 †

## TERMINAL
Guide to the Draft American National Standard for Human Factors Engineering of Visual Display * Workstations 0048
The 'window' * 01405
A user view of virtual * standardisation 01432
The architecture of an inexpensive and portable talking-tactile * to aid the visually handicapped 01452
Guide to the draft American national standard for human factors engineering of visual display * workstations 01549
Temporal resolution: an insight into the video display * (VDT) "problem" 01754
An inexpensive and portable talking-tactile * for the visually handicapped 02377
The design of a * independent package 02619
Higher pole correction in vocal tract models and * analogs 02657
The provision of *-based user support 02686
Experimental results do not support some ergonomic standards for computer video * design HCI-0428 †

## TERMINALS
A comparison of textual information retention from CRT * and paper 0954
ISPBXs and * 01385
Visual * and user interfaces 01686
Health impact of work with visual display * 03678
Health hazards assessment of radio frequency electromagnetic fields emitted by video display * 03685

## KEYWORD INDEX [TEXT]

Video display *—electromagnetic radiation and health 03687
Video display * and birth defects. A study of pregnancy outcomes of employees of the Postal-Giro Center, Oslo, Norway 03691
Work at video display * among office employees: visual ergonomics and lighting 03718
Psychosocial work environment and use of visual display *:8mfrom theoretical model to action 03742

**TERMINATING**
Navigating integrated facilities: initiating and * interaction sequences 02876

**TERMINOLOGY**
Knowledge-based tools to promote shared goals and * between interface designers 01160

**TERMS**
Choosing between methods: analysing the user's decision space in * of schemas and linear models 02879

**TERRITORY**
Empirical studies of programmers: the *, paths, and destination 02691

**TEST**
Design and * of a database for fiction, based on an analysis of children's search behavior 0451
A * of a common elements theory of transfer 0901
Necessary functions of institutions for * and certification from the viewpoint of users in IT 01456
An experiment to * user validation of requirements: data-flow diagrams vs task-oriented menus 02131
Toward a theory of computer program bugs: an empirical * 02216
Comparison of video game and conventional * performance 02594
The development of an automated flight * management system for flight *planning and monitoring 02928
The 1984 Olympic Message System: a * of behavioral principles of system design HCI-0125 †

**TESTBED**
The design of a flexible distributed * for communication systems 03538

**TESTING**
Human factors * in the design of Xerox's 8010 "Star" office workstation 0090
Usability * in the real world 0917
Usability * in the real world 0951
Usability * in the real world 0953
Stimulating change through usability * 01006
Significance * of rules in rule-based models of human problem solving 01867
Comparison of student performance in arthimetic exercises TOAM us paper-and-pencil * 02249
* for usability 03163
Computer usability * & evaluation ● HCI-0014 †
* bibliographic displays for online catalogs HCI-0285 †
* and validation of IGES processors HCI-0423 †

**TESTS**
Beta * and end-user surveys: are they valid? 01631
SMARTGEN: the implementation of an expert system for the generation of digital logic diagnostic * 02929
The effects of program-dependent and program-independent deletions on software cloze * HCI-0175 †
The spatial metaphor for user interfaces: experimental * of reference by location versus name HCI-0268 †

**TEXT**
Computer *-editing: an information-processing analysis of a routine cognitive skill 0056
The evaluation of * editors: Methodology and empirical results 0058
Evaluation of mouse, rate-controlled isometric joystick, step keys, and *keys, for * selection on a CRT 0064
A propositional language for * representation 0097
*, con*, and hyper*: writing with and for the computer ● 0098

* processing with the START natural language system 0100
The society of *: hyper*, hypermedia, and the social construction of information ● 0111
Hyper* and intelligent interfaces for * retrieval 0115
Escher effects in online * 0130
Designer labyrinths: * mazes for language learners 0197
Back to basics: Simple but high-quality * pagination systems 0271
The MAGNEX * editor for the Comodore Amiga personal computer 0782
Designing optimum CRT * blinking video image presentation 0795
Transfer between * editors 0804
Learning and transfer for * and graphics editing with a direct manipulation interface 0900
Autocompletion in full * transaction entry: a method for humanized input 0934
Computer * access 01493
Modelling the human factors aspects of a computer-based *-graphics layout system 01518
The fuzzy logic of * understanding 01701
Intermittent illumination from visual display units and fluorescent lighting affects movements of the eyes across * 01713
Visual fatigue and spatial frequency adaptation to video displays of * 01721
Factors affecting the readability of moving * on a computer display 01764
Reading self-paced moving * on a computer display 01777
A human factors design investigation of a computerized layout system of *-graphic technical materials 01779
Reader-controlled computerized presentation of * 01785
Comprehensino aids for on-line reading of expository * 01798
Online * retrieval via browsing 01999

907

Analogy and other sources of difficulty in novices' very first *-editing 02148

The use of hand-drawn gestures for * editing 02151

Question asking when learning a *-editing system 02202

Support for browsing in an intelligent * retrieval system 02240

A comparison of children's reading comprehension and reading rates at three * presentation speeds on a CRT 02280

The effect of presentation media on recipient performance in *-based information systems 02350

Information-seeking strategies of novices using a full-* electronic encyclopedia 02452

Natural language and computers: a general survey of written * interpretation methods 02671

Understanding * with an accompanying diagram 02947

How do the experts do it? The use of ethnographic methods as an aid to understanding the cognitive processing and retrieval of large bodies of * 03063

Informational zooming: an interaction model for the graphical access to *knowledge bases 03073

An advanced full-* retrieval and analysis system 03079

A gesture based * editor 03232

* representation and manipulation in a mouse-driven interface 03266

Psychological methods for assembling procedures in * management systems 03600

Eye-head coordination and information uptake during * processing 03767

Plan-based * generation in an on-line help system 03817

Specification of a tool for viewing program * 03884

Visual presentation of *: the process of reading from a psycholinguistic perspective 03895

Integrating * with non-*:a picture is worth 1k words. Proceedings of the I § 04043

Integrating graphics and * in computer products 04044

The use of explicit user models in * generation: tailoring to a user's level of expertise 04051

Reading * from computer screens HCI-0088 †

Cursor movement during * editing HCI-0113 †

Goal and plan knowledge representations: from stories to * editors and programs HCI-0183 †

Reading continuous * from a one-line visual display HCI-0187 †

The evaluation of * editors: methodology and empirical results. HCI-0209 †

Computing * constituency: an algorithmic approach to the generation of *graphs HCI-0267 †

* processing by speech: dialogue design and usability issues in the provision of a system for disabled users HCI-0357 †

Speech-controlled *-editing: effects of input modality and of command structure HCI-0397 †

*NET: a network-based approach to * handling HCI-0401 †

## TEXT_10

Ada info: apologies to * 02395

## TEXTNET

*: a network-based approach to text handling HCI-0401 †

## TEXTONS

*, the fundamental elements in preattentive vision and perception of textures 0297

## TEXTS

Limited freedom: linear reflections on nonlinear * 0121

Help * vs. help mechanisms: A new mandate for documentation writers 01047

The fuzzy decodings of educative * 01700

Multi-window displays for readers of lengthy * 02142

Help * vs. help mechanisms: A new mandate for documentation writers 02784

The legibility of visual display * 03889

## TEXTUAL

* intervention, collaboration, and the online environment 0126

Graphical vs. * representation: an empirical study of novices' program comprehension 0566

A comparison of * information retention from CRT terminals and paper 0954

Using latent semantic analysis to improve access to * information 02901

Handling * information in a GDSS database: experience with the Arizona analyst information system 03475

## TEXTURE

Shape from * 01278

Image segmentation based on color and * gradient 03303

Cortical representation of * primitives 03306

## TEXTURES

Textons, the fundamental elements in preattentive vision and perception of * 0297

## TEXTVISION

*: elicitation and acquisition of conceptual knowledge by graphic representation and multiwindowing 03902

## TF30

Concept demonstration of the use of interactive fault diagnosis and isolation for * engines 02968

## TG

Self-organizing systems and transformational-generative (*) grammar 01619

## THEMATIC

How map designers can represent their ideas in * maps: effective user interfaces for * map design 03870

## THEORETIC

Graph-* concepts in computer science § 03885

## THEORETICAL

Computer models of mind: computational approaches in * psychology ● 0152

* issues in the investigation of words of internal report 0354

# KEYWORD INDEX [TOOLKIT]

Intelligent CAD systems I: * and methodological aspects ● 0715
Uncertainty analysis of human EEG spectra: A multivariate information * method for the analysis of brain activity 01270
Evolution of interactional human behavior with age: a */experimental pproach 01618
Automaticity, resources, and memory: * controversies and practical implications 01792
* training and problem detection in a computerized database retrieval task 02239
A * framework for interactivating linear video 02284
Visuomotor control by a combined position- and speedservo. *considerations and experimental results in man 02666
* aspects of reasoning about knowledge § 03559
Experimental and * analysis of visual search activities 03620
Participation, organizational choices and time-economy: some *questions 03650
Psychosocial work environment and use of visual display terminals:8mfrom * model to action 03742
Investigating sources of error in the management of crises: *assumptions and a methodological approach 03807
Graph-* tools and their use in a practical distributed operating system design case 03886

## THESAURI
Improved design of graphic displays in *—through technology and ergonomics 02297

## THESAURUS
A graphical *-based information retrieval system 02243
Knowledge based systems versus * : an architecture problem about expert systems design HCI-0323 †

## THESYS
*—implementation of a knowledge-based design system with multiple viewpoints 0010

## THIN
MINID—a BASIC program to assist in the optical identification of minerals in * section 01505

## THINK
Designing for usability: Key principles and what designers * 0078
As we may * (Reprint) 0367
Designing for usability: key principles and what designers * HCI-0231 †

## THOUGHTS
Motion perception: second * on the correspondence problem 03325
What do users ask? Some * on diagnostic advice HCI-0326 †

## THREAD
Acoustic phonetics, auditory phonetics, speaker sex and speech recognition: a * 0288
Multi-* input 01070

## THREAT
End-users: *, challenge or myth? 01221
* to privacy: the federal government's use of personal information in the new communication environment 02680
UIMSs: * or menace? 02889

## THRESHOLD
Firing response of a neural model with * modulation and neural dynamics 02761

## THRESHOLDING
* for edge detection using human psychovisual phenomena 02538

## THUNDERSTORM
Computing needs in * modeling: supercomputers and interactive graphics 0730

## TILED
A comparison of * and overlapping windows 0904

## TIMESHARING
From * to the sixth generation: the development of human-computer interaction. Part I 02097

## TIMETABLING
Interactive * in universities 01501

## TIMING
Counting and * models in psychophysics and the conjoint Weber's law 02368

## TINKERTOY
The * graphical programming environment 01850

## TIPS
Hypertext *: experiences in developing a hypertext tutorial 03236

## TITLES
The role of menu * as a navigational aid in hierarchical menus 0888

## TNT
*: a talking tutor 'n' trainer for teaching use of interactive computer systems 0895

## TOKENS
Detecting structure by symbolic constructions on * 01466

## TOLERANCE
A * for surveillance: American public opinion concerning privacy and civil liberties 0524
An interactive * system 02975
Conventional fault-* and neural computers 03951

## TOLERANT
Conceptual design of a human error * interface for complex engineering systems 01235
A methodology for designing distributed, fault-*, and reactive real-time operating systems 04071

## TOMOGRAPHY
The effects of limited data in multi-frequency reflection diffraction * 04020

## TONES
* of voice: the role of intonation in computer speech understanding HCI-0356 †

## TOOLBOX
A groupware * 01304

## TOOLKIT
Interactive * ● 0340
LIZA: an extensible groupware * 0805

Rapid prototyping and system development: examination of an interface *for voice and telephony applications 0918
A user interface * based on graphical objects and constraints 01125
A user-interface * in object-oriented PostScript 01391
Parametric Fourier image characterization * 02798
Experience of constructing a fault localisation expert system using an AI * 02923
An overview of the C * 03109
The architecture of a user interface * 03110
JACK: a * for manipulating articulated figures 03126

### TOOLSET
NetGraph: an object-oriented graphical * for risk assessment 02972

### TOP
End-user computing by * executives 0780
A * down method for interactive drawing 01401
Is *-down natural? Some experimental results from non-procedural languages 02123
A model for assessing the performance of a local area network employing technical office protocol (*) as part of MAP/* network in a computer integrated manufacturing (CIM) research project, for the transmission of real time interactive speech 02491
Communication issues among psychologists working with computers: a view from the * 02606
Using a *-down and bottom-up strategy to analyze high resolution aerial photographs of urban areas 02960
Visual phenomena and their relation to * luminance, phosphor persistence time and contrast polarity 03729
Executive support systems: the emergence of * management computer use ● HCI-0049 †

### TOPOGRAPHICALLY
Effects of functionally or * presented process schemes on operator performance 01749

### TOPOLOGY
* conserving mappings for learning motor tasks 02758
Gripe: a graphical interface to a knowledge based system which reasons about protein * 03234

### TOUCH
Schemas that integrate vision and * for hand control 0026
Issues and techniques in *-sensitive tablet input 0063
The AT&T soft *-sensitive screen 01226
Optimizing the * tablet: the effects of control display gain and method of cursor control 01730
A comparison of menu selection techniques: * panel, mouse and keyboard 02122
Improving the accuracy of * screens: an experimental evaluation of three strategies 02860
* screen, cursor keys and mouse interaction 03769
The physiology and psychophysics of * 04010
*-sensitive screens: the technologies and their application HCI-0087 †

### TOUCHSCREEN
* usage in plant computer systems: a case study 01530

### TOUR
The engineering information system: a guided * 02046
Programming languages: a grand * (2nd ed.) ● HCI-0018 †

### TOURING
Travel around a learning support environment: rambling, orienteering or * 02900

### TOURIST
The * artificial reality 0868

### TOURS
Guided * and tabletops: tools for communicating in a hypertext environment 01161
Guided * and tabletops: tools for communicating in a hypertext environment 02823

### TOXIC
Optimal allocation of a work force in a * substance environment 01534

### TRACE
A * of memory: an evolutionary perspective on the visual system 0019
Interactive processes in speech perception: the * model 0631

### TRACING
A simple, general method for ray * bicubic surfaces 03853

### TRACK
A multiple * animator system for motion synchronization 03350
Applications * § 03455
Decision Support and Knowledge Based Systems * § 03461
Software * § 03513

### TRACKING
Hesitations in continuous * induced by a concurrent discrete task 01745
Internal models, * strategies and dual-task performance 01751
Modeling of task-dependent characteristics of human operator dynamics during pursuit manual * 01859
Application of neural network algorithms and architectures to correlation/* and identification 02734
* three-dimensional moving light displays 03337

### TRADE
Capacity equivalence curves: a double *-off curve method for equating task performance 01796
A case-based system for * secrets law 02769
User participation from the point of view of the workers and * union policy 03652
Report from the working group on "goals and strategies of * unions and other social groups in systems design for human development and productivity." 03657
Teaching the tricks of the * 04023
The depth/breadth *-off in the design of menu-driven user interfaces HCI-0135 †

Analysing the scope of cognitive models in human-computer interaction: a *-off approach HCI-0245 †

**TRADITIONS**
The practice of the use of computers. A paradoxical encounter between different * of knowledge 0343

**TRAFFIC**
The FAA's Advanced Automation System: strategies for future air * control systems 01357
Engineering the man-machine interface for air * control 01358
* study on primary rate ISDN user-network interface 01442
Perspective * display format and airline pilot * avoidance 01748
The design of a * control expert system for long distance network contingencies 02952
Error auditing in air * control 03810

**TRAILS**
Sites, modes, and *: Telling the user of an interactive system where he is, what he can do, and how to get to places (excerpt) 0068

**TRAIN**
Putting on a show: using computer graphics to * end-users 02520

**TRAINER**
TNT: a talking tutor 'n' * for teaching use of interactive computer systems 0895

**TRAJECTORIES**
Projected free fall *. I. Theory and simulation 01265
Projected free fall *. II. Human experiments 01266
The control of hand equilibrium * in multi-joint arm movements 01275

**TRANSACTION**
Autocompletion in full text * entry: a method for humanized input 0934
Legal data modeling: The prohibited * exemption analyst 02779

**TRANSCRIPTION**
Cumulating the science of HCI: from s-R compatibility to * typing 0831

**TRANSDISCIPLINARITY**
The cybernetic principle: its * to science and religion and the challenging task 01596

**TRANSFER**
ETS—a system for the * of human expertise 0491
* between text editors 0804
Learning and * of measurement tasks 0832
* between word processing systems 0899
Learning and * for text and graphics editing with a direct manipulation interface 0900
A test of a common elements theory of * 0901
A * of skill between programming languages 01015
Maintenance training simulator fidelity and individual differences in *of training 01722
Information * rate with serial and simultaneous visual display formats 01770
Speech responses and dual-task performance: better time-sharing or asymmetric * 01789
Simulator design and instructional features for air-to-ground attack: a * study 01804
Training by exploration: facilitating the * of procedural knowledge through analogical reasoning 02103
KITTEN: knowledge initiation and * tools for experts and novices 02159
Linearization of the dynamic * response of time invariant nonlinear systems—in connection with the parallel information processing in living organisms 02665
* between menu systems 02873
* of learning in inference problems 03552
Expertise * for expert system design ● HCI-0059 †
Technology *: a new computer-based system HCI-0203 †
Expertise * and complex problems: using AQUINAS as a knowledge-acquisition workbench for knowledge-based systems HCI-0336 †

Interfaces and data * formats in computer graphics systems HCI-0419 †
Training for optimising * between word processors HCI-0447 †

**TRANSFERABLE**
Personal * skills for the modern information professional: a discussion paper 02338

**TRANSFERRING**
* skills from training to the actual work situation: the role of task application knowledge, action styles and job decision latitude 02865

**TRANSFORMATION**
Competitive dynamics in a dual-route connectionist model of print-to-sound * 01341

**TRANSFORMATIONAL**
* derivation of programs using the focus system 01140
Self-organizing systems and *-generative (TG) grammar 01619

**TRANSFORMATIONS**
* on a formal specification of user-computer interfaces 01062
Rule-based reasoning as Boolean * 01901
A group model of form recognition under plane similarity * 02366
Spatial and temporal * in visuo-motor coordination 03963

**TRANSFORMING**
A practical approach to * extended ER diagrams into the relational model 02022

**TRANSITION**
Extending state * diagrams for the specification of human-computer interaction 0080
The uneasy eighties: the * to an information society 0792
Making the * from print to electronic encyclopaedias: adapation of mental models 02238
APL in * § 02793
From user to client services; making the * for supercomputing 03138
Generative * networks: a new communication control abstraction 03241

Differential organization impacts of the * from stand-alone to integrated flexible production 03380
On the design of a graphical * network editor 03830
Extending state * diagrams for the specification of human-computer interaction HCI-0191 †

**TRANSITIONS**
"Structure—reaction type" paradigm in the conventional methods of describing organic reactions and the concept of imaginary *structures overcoming this paradigm 02268

**TRANSLATING**
Skilled financial planning: the cost of * ideas into action 0834
Human supervisory control in discrete manufacturing: * the paradigm 03364

**TRANSLATION**
Perspectives in artificial intelligence vol. 2: machine *, NLP, databases and computer-aided instruction ● 0198
Language, sublanguage, and the promise of machine * 01554
A user perspective on computer-assisted * for Minority languages 01557
A holography-based computer-aided * system-conceptual analysis 01607
Machine assisted * with a human face 01627
Problems of machine * system - effect of cultural differences on sentence structure 01687
LSP-automatic * and information technology 02513
Determining the instantaneous axis of * from optic flow generated by rbitrary sensot motion 03332
Determining motion parameters for scenes with * and rotation 03338
A framework of a mechanical * between Japanese and English by analogy principle HCI-0353 †

**TRANSLATIONAL**
An integrated display for vertical and * flight: eight factors affecting pilot performance 01714

**TRANSLATOR**
The engineering of a * workstation 01555

**TRANSLATORS**
Two-level data banks for * 01556

**TRANSMISSION**
A model for assessing the performance of a local area network employing technical office protocol (TOP) as part of MAP/TOP network in a computer integrated manufacturing (CIM) research project, for the * of real time interactive speech 02491
Visual structure and the * of meaning HCI-0404 †

**TRANSPARENCY**
Articulating the experience of *: an example of field research techniques 0977
Barriers to plant *, barriers to plant rigidity—A sketch of the problems posed by the radical changes in work forms in the machine-building industry 01562
Perception of * in man and machine 02697
* and system design 03655
Perception of * in man and machine HCI-0367 †

**TRANSPARENT**
* information systems through gateways, front ends, intermediaries, and interfaces HCI-0276 †

**TRANSPORT**
A decision support system for vehicle scheduling in public * 0339
The design of distributed * systems as a major standard interface in computer integrated manufacturing 01564

**TRANSPORTABILITY**
* and generality in a natural-language interface system 0394

**TRANSPORTABLE**
* applications environment (TAE) plus experiences in "Object"-ively modernizing a user interface environment 01126
Icecream, * software for creating friendly human interfaces 02615

The IRUS * natural language database interface 03177
ASK is * in half a dozen ways HCI-0279 †
TEAM: an experiment in the design of * natural-language interfaces HCI-0351 †

**TRANSPORTING**
* the linguistic string project system from a medical to a Navy domain HCI-0352 †

**TRAVEL**
* around a learning support environment: rambling, orienteering or touring? 02900
The * metaphor as design principle and training aid for navigating around complex systems 03195
A * consultation system: towards a smooth conversation in Japanese 03917

**TREE**
A natural language interface processor based on the hierarchical-* structure model of relation tables 02315
* doctor, a software package for graphical manipulation and animation of * structures 03901
A general user interface for creating and displaying *-structures, hierarchies, decision *s, and nested menus HCI-0136 †

**TREES**
Simplifying decision * 02157
State * as structured finite state machines for user interfaces 03107
A general user interface for creating and displaying tree-structures, hierarchies, decision *, and nested menus HCI-0136 †
Decision *: a contribution to automatic interpretation of GUHA results HCI-0329 †

**TREND**
Utilizing the * of end user development 02444
Factors influencing the detection of * deviations on VDTs 03894

**TRIANGLE**
Physiology based simulation model of * shape recognition 01277

# KEYWORD INDEX [TYPOGRAPHY]

**TRICHROMATIC**
Study of visual performance on a multi-color VDU of color defective and normal * subjects 03701

**TRICKS**
Teaching the * of the trade 04023

**TRIGGER**
From * video to videodisc: a case study in interpersonal skills 0508

**TRILLIUM**
The * user interface design environment 0082
The * user interface design environment 0919
*: an interface design prototyping tool 01965

**TRIP**
CHI '88 * report 0981
The 1988 CSCW: * report 01008

**TRON**
* Project 1987—Open-architecture computer systems § 03821

**TROUBLESHOOTING**
The influence of *, education, and documentation on computer user satisfaction 01869
Sources of Difficulty in * automated manufacturing systems 03367

**TRUST**
* between humans and machines, and the design of decision aids 02164

**TRUSTED**
Status of * DBMS interpretations 03585

**TRUTH**
* versus appropriateness: relating declarative to procedural knowledge 0484
Epistemic necessity, possibility, and *. Tools for dealing with imprecision and uncertainty in fuzzy knowledge-based systems 02075

**TUNING**
Fine * selection semantics in a structure editor based programming environment: some experimental results 0975

**TUPLE**
Human performance in relational algebra, * calculus, and domain calculus 02208

**TURBO**
Graphics programming in * C ● 0013
Programming the IBM User Interface: Using * Pascal ● 0286
Screen input/output programming techniques using * Pascal ● 0714
Advanced * C programming :9B 0726
* pascal windowing system 01306
* windows 01421
Programming the mouse in * Pascal 4.0 02393

**TURING**
The Universal * Machine § 03777

**TURNKEY**
A user interface for multiple-process, * systems targeted for the novice user 0911

**TURNOVER**
Behavioural and organisational factors involved in the * of high tech professionals 01024

**TUTOR**
Socializing the intelligent *: bringing empathy to computer * 0541
TNT: a talking * 'n' trainer for teaching use of interactive computer systems 0895
Development of a hand-held computerized vocabulary * 02468
Error analysis and * design 02469
A graphical programming language interface for an intelligent LISP * 02862
Goal-directed semantic * 02919
The LISP *: it approaches the effectiveness of a human * HCI-0431 †

**TUTORIAL**
Color, graphics, and animation in a computer-assisted learning * lesson 02294
Hypertext tips: experiences in developing a hypertext * 03236

**TUTORIALS**
On-line *: What kind of inference leads to the most effective learning? 0823
The effectiveness of a keystroke line in interactive * 0969
PC networks: usage and graphics * 01499

Psychologically based techniques for improving learning within computerized * 02277
Expert systems and interactive video *: separating strategies from subject matter 02293

**TUTORING**
Production systems, learning, and * 0487
Artificial intelligence and education; vol. 1: learning environments and * systems ● 0516
Learning Issues for Intelligent * Systems ● 0534
Learning issues for intelligent * systems ● 0545
Foundations of intelligent * systems ● 0592
Enhancing PIXIE's * capabilities 02187
Some considerations on intelligent * systems 02963
An intelligent * system for basic set theory 02993
Artificial intelligence and * systems: computational and cognitive approaches to the communication of knowledge ● HCI-0080 †
The automated * of introductory computer programming HCI-0438 †

**TUTORS**
Socializing the intelligent tutor: bringing empathy to computer * 0541

**TYPESETTING**
Music—a language for * music scores 02622

**TYPEWRITER**
The "neural" phonetic * 01361

**TYPING**
Cumulating the science of HCI: from s-R compatibility to transcription * 0831
A note on undetected * errors HCI-0399 †

**TYPISTS**
Comparison of well-being among non-machine interactive clerical workers and full-time and part-time VDT users and * 03745

**TYPOGRAPHY**
Document manipulation and * § 03182

Digital *: an introduction to type and composition for computer system design ● HCI-0074 †

### TYPOLOGY
The evaluation of information services: a * 0452
Technology adaptation: a * for strategic human resource management 01238

### UC
User modeling in *, the UNIX consultant 0894

### UCLA
The * Brain Research Institute data processing laboratory 02844

### UEASINESS
Effects of visual display and motion system delays on operator performance and * in a driving simulator 01772

### UIMS
Statemaster: A * based on statechart for prototyping and target implementation 0850
Including a user interface management system (*) in the performance relationship model 01000
The run-time structure of *-supported applications 01059
Collaboration of * designers and human factors specialists 01060
* support for direct manipulation interfaces 01065
Marcosby example in a graphical * 01831
Semantic feedback in the Higgens * 01851
Using active data in a * 03121
Design principles behind Chiron: a * for software environments 03511
The Higgens * and its efficient implementation of Undo 03861
Supporting concurrency, communication, and synchronization in human-computer interaction—the Sassafras * HCI-0102 †

### UIMSS
Gaining general acceptance for * 01067
*: threat or menace? 02889

### UK
An assessment of the major computerised databases relating to disabled people in the * and Scandinavia 02326

### UMFE
*: a user modelling front-end subsystem HCI-0325 †

### UNAUTHORIZED
Attitudes toward * software copying: general public vs. business faculty member 01142

### UNCERTAIN
Extension of conditional probability and measures of belief and disbelief in a hypothesis based on * evidence 01846
A hybrid approach to deductive * inference 02191

### UNCERTAINTY
* analysis of human EEG spectra: A multivariate information theoretical method for the analysis of brain activity 01270
Epistemic necessity, possibility, and truth. Tools for dealing with imprecision and * in fuzzy knowledge-based systems 02075
Combining stochastic * and linguistic inexactness: theory and experimental evaluation of four fuzzy probability models 02218
Man-machine procedures of decision making under * based on linear programming 02664
The perception of system and the reduction of * 02850
* in knowledge-based systems. International Conference on Information § 03822
Modeling * in human perception 03825
* and intelligent systems § 04030

### UNDERLOAD
Data entry task on VDU: * or overload 03761

### UNDERSTANDABLE
Selecting a humanly * knowledge representation for reasoning about knowledge HCI-0330 †

### UNDERSTANDING
* the elements of system design 0156

Computers and children's historical thinking and * 0283
Aspects of human speech * 0290
Fundamentals in computer *: speech and vision ● 0416
Doing, *, and learning in problem solving 0480
Image * 1985-86 ● 0615
* & using application software ● 0626
* Bayesian reasoning via graphical displays 0884
The enhancement of * through visual representations 0898
* the office: A social-analytic perspective 01156
* natural languages 01172
Integrated processing produces robust * 01342
GRAFLOG: * drawings through natural language 01396
* and validating results in model-based decision support systems 01666
The fuzzy logic of text * 01701
* and enhancing user acceptance of computer 01889
Building and * adaptive systems: a statistical/numerical approach to factory automation and brain research 01890
* and evaluating a computer graphics display 01984
Exploiting convergence to improve natural language * 02071
VIS: a virtual image system for image-* research 02629
* cable subscribership as telecommunications behavior 02676
Communications technology and the public sector: * the process of adoption 02679
Human image *: recent research and a theory 02698
Hierarchical scene structure representations to facilitate image * 02942
* text with an accompanying diagram 02947
A knowledge representation for natural language * 02987
How do the experts do it? The use of ethnographic methods as an aid to * the cognitive processing and

retrieval of large bodies of text 03063
Describing a product opportunity: a method of * the users' environment 03194
* the nature of the office for the design of third wave office systems 03248
An environment for * programs 03525
The semantic language episode * 03576
* learning problems in computer aided tasks 03607
Recent advances in speech * and dialog systems § 03987
On-line interpretation in speech * and dialogue systems 04000
Knowledge based systems for speech * 04001
Merging acoustics and linguistics in speech * 04004
* computers and cognition • HCI-0054 †
* the effectiveness of computer graphics for decision support: a cumulative experimental approach HCI-0215 †
Tones of voice: the role of intonation in computer speech * HCI-0356 †

## UNDERWATER
Simultaneous adaptation to size, distance, and curvature * 01803

## UNDETECTED
A note on * typing errors HCI-0399 †

## UNDO
The Higgens UIMS and its efficient implementation of * 03861
* support models HCI-0144 †

## UNEASY
The * eighties: the transition to an information society 0792

## UNFORESEEN
Models of the decision maker in * accidents 02172

## UNFRIENDLY
A user-* WELCOME 02603

## UNH
Desktop publishing and user services; moment in the evolution of user support documentation at * 03158

## UNIFICATION
Motivation analysis, abductive *, and nonmonotonic equality 01211
A * of software and hardware; a new tool for human thought 02314

## UNIFIED
Neurophilosophy: toward a * science of the mind-brain • 0219
Information technology and information use: towards a * view of information and information technology • 0447
Is the * keyboard better? 0768
* interactive geometric modeller for simulating highly complex environments 01472

## UNIFORM
SIMS: a * environment for planning and performing user's tasks 02921
Maintaining a * user interface for an Ada programming environment 04066

## UNIFORMS
*: an automatic forms facility 01628

## UNIONS
Report from the working group on "goals and strategies of trade * and other social groups in systems design for human development and productivity." 03657

## UNISON
Broderbund Software, Inc. v. * World, Inc. 648 F. Supp. 1127 (1986). 01477

## UNITED
Environments: Austria compared to the * States 01026

## UNIVERSAL
* subgoaling and chunking: the automatic generation and learning of goal hierarchies • 0497
The new renaissance: art, science and * machine 0530
Non-first normal form * relations: an application to information retrieval systems 02039
Programming a massively parallel, computation * system: Static behavior 02746
The * Turing Machine § 03777
Data manipulation languages for the * relation view DURST 03944

Update and retrieval in a relational database through a * schema interface HCI-0260 †

## UNIVERSALITY
Towards * of access: interfacing physically disabled students to the Icon educational microcomputer 0821

## UNIVERSITIES
Interactive timetabling in * 01501

## UNIX
* system V: release 3.0 Intel 80286/80386 computer version: system administrator's guide • 0031
* and the naive user: children meet a grown-up operating system 0752
User modeling in UC, the * consultant 0894
A * clone with source code for operating systems courses 01095
The economics of * workstations 01312
The Berkeley * consultant project 01355
Helping users use * 01529
WIMP interface for * 01973
An icon-driven end-user interface to * 02089
Structure of a directory space: a case study with a * operating system 02138
An attempt to incorporate expertise about users into an intelligent interface for * 02248
Some effects of cognitive style on learning * 02252
A * distributed application support suitable for mini and microcomputer based systems 02489
*: tomorrow's operating system? 02555
Dynamic compilation in the * environment 02621
fsh—a functional * command interpreter 02624
* Emacs: a retrospective (lessons for flexible system design) 03114
Project source file management under the * operating system 03168
The interactive planning work station: a graphics-based * tool for

application users and developers 03860
Introducing windows to *: user expectations 03924
A modular window system for * 03929
A window manager for bitmapped displays and * 03933
The design of the * operating system ● HCI-0026 †
* shell programming ● HCI-0027 †
4.2BSD and 4.3BSD as examples of the * system HCI-0165 †

## UNPREDICTABLE
'This is a very * machine': on computers and human cognition 0364

## UNRELIABLE
Decision making with * probabilities 0652

## UNSOLVABLE
* problems related to the view integration approach 03915

## UNSTABLE
Manual control of an intrinsically * system and its modeling by fuzzy logic 02026

## UNSTRUCTURED
DIME: a programming environment for * triangular meshes on a distributed-memory parallel processor 02909

## UPDAT
Information processing today, with applications and BASIC: * 87/88 ● 0570

## UPDATE
A library for incremental * of bitmap images 02836
An * measure of supervisor-rated job performance for programmer/analysis 03012
Supporting natural language database * by modeling real world actions 03179
* and retrieval in a relational database through a universal schema interface HCI-0260 †

## UPDATING
Causality and maximum entropy * 02076

## UPTAKE
Eye-head coordination and information * during text processing 03767

## URBAN
Using a top-down and bottom-up strategy to analyze high resolution aerial photographs of * areas 02960

## USABILITY
Designing for *: Key principles and what designers think 0078
*: stereotypes and traps 0104
* assessment for the office: methodological choices and their implications 0318
Evaluating * of human-computer interfaces: a practical method ● 0608
The effects of device technology on the * of advanced telephone functions 0876
* testing in the real world 0917
User-derived impact analysis as a tool for * engineering 0922
On designing for *: an application of four key principles 0923
* testing in the real world 0951
* testing in the real world 0953
Stimulating change through * testing 01006
Teaching user interface design based on * engineering 01007
Employing * engineering in the development of office products 01413
Evaluating the * of the Glasgow online 01808
AIX * enhancements and human factors 01817
Testing for * 03163
Can cognitive complexity theory (CCT) produce an adequate measure of system * 03229
People and computers: designing for * § 03244
People and computers: designing for * 03245
Ergonomics in design for * 03247
The role of iterative evaluation in designing systems for * 03255
* engineering in office product development 03258
Optimizing the * of computer-generated displays 03278
Effects of an immediate feedback tool on designer productivity and design * 04052
Assessing the * of user interfaces: guidance and online help features 04065
Computer * testing & evaluation ● HCI-0014 †
Human performance engineering: using human factors/ergonomics to achieve computer system * (2nd ed.) ● HCI-0042 :8E
Information technology and home-based services: improving the * of teleshopping HCI-0226 †
Designing for *: key principles and what designers think HCI-0231 †
Text processing by speech: dialogue design and * issues in the provision of a system for disabled users HCI-0357 †
A plan for evaluating * of software products HCI-0449 †

## UTILISATION
Participation in the development of software and the * of standard software 03663

## UTILITY
The * of speech input in user-computer interfaces 02230

## UTILIZATION
KIWI: knowledge-based user-friendly system for the * of information bases 0739
Implementing computer-mediated communication technologies: a technoacceptance approach to critical mass * 01931
DORUS: an architecture for dynamic optimal resource * systems 02979
Reasons for computer * reluctance by teachers with computer training 04059

## UW
Design and implementation of the * Illustrated compiler 03059

## VAGUELY
Responding to "HUH?": answering * articulated follow-up questions 0825

## VALID
Beta tests and end-user surveys: are they * 01631

## VALIDATING
Understanding and * results in model-based decision support systems 01666
The role of computer graphics in * simulation models 02486

## VALIDATION
* of a Jungian instrument for MIS research 01022
Electric and magnetic fields of the brain computed by way of a discrete systems analytical approach: Theory and * 01276
Attacking a complex distributed algorithm from different sides: an experience wih complementary * tools 01429
User * of information systems requirements: some empirical results 01852
An experiment to test user * of requirements: data-flow diagrams vs task-oriented menus 02131
* in a knowledge support system: construing and consistency with multiple experts 02203
Development and * of a reader-based documentation measure 02236
The quality of user documentation: an instrument * 02356
The experimental * of a programmer productivity measure 03013
Testing and * of IGES processors HCI-0423 †

## VARIABILITY
Operator effort and the measurement of heart-rate * 01736
* in brightness matching of colored lights 01767
Focusing * during visual work 03759

## VARIABLE
The * impact of computer technologies on the organization of work activities 0388
Usage of linguistic * concept for human operator modelling 01694
Reading is slower from CRT displays than from paper: attempts to isolate a single-* explanation 01743
Some cognitive aspects of interface design in a two-* optimization task HCI-0111 †

Specification and generation of *, personalized graphical interfaces HCI-0134 †

## VARIABLES
Representations of perceived relations among the properties and * of a complex system 01892
On comprehending a computer manual: analysis of * affecting performance 02135

## VARIANCE
Expectation and * of item resemblance distributions in a convolution-correction model of distributed memory 02369

## VARIATIONS
* in user involvement with educational software 01498
Programmer * in software debugging approaches 02250

## VARYING
Muscle models: what is gained and what is lost by * model complexity 01251
The effect of * voice and noise parameters on the perception of voicing in Dutch two-obstruent sequences 02653
Motion and time-* imagery 03336

## VAX
*-BASIC with structured problem solving: 2nd edition ● 0725

## VDA
Implementation of a * interface in the CAD system STRIM 100 03983
Approximation methods used in the exchange of geometric information via the */VDMA surface interface HCI-0421 †

## VDAFS
*—a pragmatic interface for the exchange of sculptured surface data HCI 0420 †
A tentative implementation of * HCI-0422 †

## VDM
* '87: *—a formal method at work § 03831
Support environments for * 03832
*—The Way Ahead § 04033
The VIP * specification language 04036
The use of * on the specification of Chinese characters 04038

## VDMA
Approximation methods used in the exchange of geometric information via the VDA/* surface interface HCI-0421 †

## VDT
Human factors issues in * use: Environmental and workstation design considerations 0046
Human limits and the * computer interface (excerpt) 0054
Human—computer interactions in the workplace: psychosocial aspects of * use 0306
Reading from microfiche, a *, and the printed page: subjective fatigue and performance 01712
Temporal resolution: an insight into the video display terminal (*) "problem" 01754
The dubious dangers of * radiation 01902
Changes in contrast sensitivity function produced by * use 02189
Intraocular pressure during * work 03683
Pregnancy and * work—an evaluation of the state of the art 03686
Some physical factors at * work stations and ski problems 03693
* work and the skin 03696
Skin paroblems from * work-a summary 03697
Preferred settings in * work: The Zürich Experience 03707
The effect of * symbol characteristics on operator performance and visual comfort 03728
Sensitivity to light and visual strain in * operators: basic data for the design of work stations 03732
Visual impairment and subjective ocular symptomatology in * operators 03734
Effects on visual accommodation and subjective visual discomfort from * work intensified through split screen technique 03735
Comparison of well-being among non-machine interactive clerical workers and full-time and

[VDTS]

part-time * users and typists 03745
Workers education and user participation in the development of protective policies for * operators 03752
Trends in U.S. user policies for * work 03753
Characterization of * work 03754
* technology: psychosocial and stress concerns 03755
Human factors issues in * use: environmental and workstation design considerations HCI-0210 †

VDTS
An experimental study of Chinese information displays on * 01784
The * are here: health hazard and all 02439
*: are they safe? 02549
* and health—fact or fancy? 03677
Are there subtle changes in vision after use of * 03733
Factors influencing the detection of trend deviations on * 03894

VDU
*—work and user—friendly human—computer interaction: analysis of dialogue structures 0310
Posture and * operator satisfaction 0988
Do *'s make you sick? 01219
The use and misuse of *'S 01375
Determinants of the * operator's well-being 03679
Repetition strain injury in Australian * users 03681
Eye Fatigue among * users and non-* users 03682
Pregnancy outcome and *-work in a cohort of insurance clerks 03690
Task-load and endocrinological risk for pregnancy in women * operators 03692
Facial particle exposure in the * environment: the role of static electricity 03694
A Rosacea-like skin rash in *-operators 03695
Human factors considerations in the design of a * for visually impaired persons 03698
*-work and dyslexia. a case report 03699

Study of visual performance on a multi-color * of color defective and normal Trichromatic subjects 03701
Influence of age on performance and health of * workers 03702
Subject reports about musculoskeletal discomfort in * work as a complex phenomenon 03708
The effect of * on the interior design of offices 03714
Recent results on the illumination of * and CAD workstations 03719
Improving the * workplace by introducing a physiologically optimized bright-background screen with dark characters: advantages and requirements 03721
Vision monitoring of * operators and relaxation of visual stress by means of laser speckle system 03738
* work, refractive errors and binocular vision 03739
Refraction in * operators—a comparison with other professions 03740
How identify organizational factors crucial of *-health? A context-oriented method approach 03741
Identification and prevention of work-related mental and psycho-somatic disorders among two categories of * users 03744
Analyzing and improving * working conditions: workers' education 03751
Mental fatigue of * operators induced by monotonous and various tasks 03760
Data entry task on *: underload or overload 03761
Videocoding - a highly monotonous * work in a new technique for mail sorting 03762

VECTOR
On the estimation of dense displacement * fields from image sequences 03335
Determining 3-D motion parameters of a rigid body: a *-geometrical approach 03339

KEYWORD INDEX

VEHICLE
A decision support system for * scheduling in public transport 0339
Effects of * handling characteristics on driving strategy 01773
Design of a multi-media * for social browsing 02822
A mission planning architecture for an autonomous * 02939

VEHICLES
A study of auditory warning alarms evaluation for automated guided * 03424

VELOCITY
Computing the * field along contours 03331

VELOTYPE
A provisional evaluation of a new chord keyboard, the * 03907

VENTILATOR
EPVM: An expert patient-* manager for chemical warfare casualties 02956

VENTRICULOGRAMS
Automatic contour definition on left * by image evidence and a multiple template-based model 04073

VENTURE
Report on German Joint * Tool Integration Projects 03495

VERBAL
Directed dialogue protocols: * data for user interface design 0866
A model for the interpretation of * predictions HCI-0316 †

VERBS
On learning the past tenses of English * 0634

VERIFICATION
Complete vs. incomplete working tasks—a concept and its * 0241
CAD Based * and refinement of high level compliant motion primitives 0600
Issues in the * of knowledge in rule-based systems 02226
Use of metaknowledge in the * of knowledge-based systems 02945
Specification and * of database dynamics HCI-0251 †

## VERIFIED
Algorithms for * inclusions—theory and practice 0549
Application of decision support system on sandwich beams, * by experiments 01572

## VERIFYING
* identity via keystroke characteristics 02178

## VERTEBRATE
Why cortices? Neural computation in the * visual system 03956

## VHDL
VISION: * induced schematic imaging on net-lists 02830

## VIBRATION
CRT picture * caused by low-frequency magnetic field and its reduction method 01987

## VICINITY
Visual accommodation and target detection in the * of a window post 01802

## VIDEO
How effective is interactive * in improving performance and attitude? 0278
Computer-assisted learning and interactive * 0504
Pedagogical design for interactive * 0505
From trigger * to *disc: a case study in interpersonal skills 0508
A question of delivery—an outline classification of interactive *delivery systems 0510
Interactive *—a producer's medium 0511
The political economy of interactive * in British higher education 0512
Interactive * as a school resource: Rolls-Royce or Model T Ford? 0513
Digital * interactive 0681
The disconnection: how to interface computers and * ● 0703
Designing optimum CRT text blinking * image presentation 0795
Digital * interactive 01308
The coming revolution in interactive digital * 01325
Virtual * editing in interactive multimedia applications 01326

Life before the chips: simulating digital * interactive technology 01328
Intelligent interactive * simulation of a code inspection 01329
Interactive * in language learning 01380
Some issues related to the design and development of an interactive * disc 01497
Computer assisted * analysis system 01683
Visual fatigue and spatial frequency adaptation to * displays of text 01721
Temporal resolution: an insight into the * display terminal (VDT) "problem" 01754
Are * displays a health hazard? 01980
Research and evaluation models for the study of interactive * 02283
A theoretical framework for interactivating linear * 02284
The efficacy of computer-assisted * instruction on rule learning and attitudes 02286
The effects of orienting objectives and review on learning from interactive * 02287
The effects of orienting, processing, and practicing activities on learning from interactive * 02289
Expert systems and interactive * tutorials: separating strategies from subject matter 02293
Human factors design of a * monitor emulator and display (VMED) for visuallyimpaired computer users 02379
Forecasting consumer adoption of information technology and services—lessons from home * forecasting 02451
Inactive * at work 02571
Comparison of * game and conventional test performance 02594
Interaction of CMC with * telecourses for distance education 02677
*: Data for studying human-computer interaction 02878
* browsing and system response time 03203

Flexible intelligent interactive-* 03238
The efficiency of letter perception in function of color combinations: a study of *-screen colors 03616
Health hazards assessment of radio frequency electromagnetic fields emitted by * display terminals 03685
* display terminals—electromagnetic radiation and health 03687
* display terminals and birth defects. A study of pregnancy outcomes of employees of the Postal-Giro Center, Oslo, Norway 03691
Work at * display terminals among office employees: visual ergonomics and lighting 03718
Colors in * displays 03725
A comparison of the effects of computer-assisted instruction, interactive *, and traditional instruction on third-grade students in art education 04064
Interactive *: vol. 1 ● HCI-0081 †
Experimental results do not support some ergonomic standards for computer *terminal design HCI-0428 †

## VIDEOCODING
* - a highly monotonous VDU work in a new technique for mail sorting 03762

## VIDEODISC
Adopting interactive * technology for education 0272
Design and production of * programming 0276
Design factors for successful *-based instruction 0277
Setting up an interactive * project 0502
From trigger video to *: a case study in interpersonal skills 0508
* and videotex: love-match or passing acquaintance? 0515
An interactive * drama: The case of Frank hall 02285

## VIDEODISCS
Interactive * control and computer-based training on the Apple Macintosh 02305

## VIDEODISK
AI/learn: an interactive * system for teaching medical concepts and reasoning 02381

## VIDEOTAPE
User interface strategies '88 (* ● 0684
Designing the user interface (* ● 0687

## VIDEOTAPED
Using interactive *-based instruction J*to teach on-the-job social skills to handicapped adolescents 02288

## VIDEOTEX
Cognitive optimisation of * dialogues: a formal—empirical approach 0320
Videodisc and *: love-match or passing acquaintance? 0515
* information packagers: a field study aimed at tomorrow's *authoring interface 0962
Some remarks on * interaction. How to write for a new reader 01433
* redux 02545
Organizational *: information services for the end user 03166
* and online services: competition or collateral 03557
*: anatomy of a failure HCI-0313 †

## VIDURA
*—an interactive multilingual publishing system—specification & design 03186

## VIEW
* management in distributed data base systems 0218
Information technology and information use: towards a unified * of information and information technology ● 0447
A folklore * of information 01222
A user * of virtual terminal standardisation 01432
Nested structures of control: an intuitive * 01464
A critical * of factors affecting successful application of normative and socio-technical systems development approaches 01914
One * of the future of industrial control 01921

Interacting with electronic mail can be a dream or a night: a user's point of * 02069
A cookbook for using the model-* controller user interface paradigm in Smalltalk-80 02390
Communication issues among psychologists working with computers: a * from the top 02606
Medical informatics: a personal * of sowing the seeds 02841
**A personal * of the personal work station: some firsts in the Fifties 03093**
The economic evaluation on implementation industrial robot from user point of * 03447
What awareness isn't: a sentential * of implicit and explicit belief 03560
User participation from the point of * of the workers and trade union policy 03652
An interactionist's * of system pathology 03813
Towards an integrated * of 3-D computer animation 03859
Unsolvable problems related to the * integration approach 03915
Ten years of window systems—a retrospective * 03926
Data manipulation languages for the universal relation * DURST 03944
Interface design in computerized conferencing systems: a personal * HCI-0305 †

## VIEWDATA
* in the office—user-friendly page identification 02334
A *-structure editor designed around a task/action mapping 03269

## VIEWER
Environment-centered and *-centered perception of surface orientation 02705
Environment-centered and *-centered perception of surface orientation HCI-0392 †

## VIEWPOINTS
THESYS—implementation of a knowledge-based design system with multiple * 0010

## VIEWPORTS
Windows, * and structured display files 03930

## VIGILANCE
Processing demands, training, and the * decrement 01723
No effect of noise on * performance? 01724
Processing demands, effort, and individual differences in four different * tasks 01801

## VILE
A VLSI interactive layout editor (* 02611

## VIP
The * VDM specification language 04036

## VIRTUAL
A multiple, *-workspace interface to support user task switching 0813
Rooms: the use of multiple * workspaces to reduce space contention in a window-based graphical user interface 01151
* video editing in interactive multimedia applications 01326
A user view of * terminal standardisation 01432
Spatial misorientation exacerbated by collimated * flight display 01979
A * protocol model for computer-human interaction 02106
VIS: a * image system for image-understanding research 02629
* graphics 02815
Collaborative learning in a * classroom: highlights of findings 02826

## VIRUS
The case of the "Gerbil *" that wasn't 01548

## VIRYA
*—a motion control editor for kinematic and dynamic animation 03294

## VIS
*: a virtual image system for image-understanding research 02629

# KEYWORD INDEX [VISUAL]

## VISIBILITY
Structural * and program comprehension 03274

## VISION
*, brain, and cooperative computation ● 0014
*, brain, and cooperative computation: an overview 0015
The interdependence of temporal and spatial information in early * 0023
Schemas that integrate * and touch for hand control 0026
A functional model of * and space 0027
Ergonomic * 0259
Readings in computer *: issues, problems, principles, and paradigms ● 0296
Textons, the fundamental elements in preattentive * and perception of textures 0297
Computational * and regularization theory 0301
Fundamentals in computer understanding: speech and * ● 0416
Towards computer * 0564
Computer aids for * and employment (CAVE) 0976
A * of education in user-centered system and interface design 0985
Comparison of color sensation in dichoptic and in normal * 01272
Retinex: physics and the theory of color * 01574
Prediction of the smallest channel in early human * 01894
From * science to HDTV: bridging the gap 01981
An outline of the primal sketch in human * 02541
An appropriate representation for early * 02542
Human and Machine * II § 02696
Connectionist models and parallelism in high level * 02700
Early *: from computational structure to algorithms and parallel hardware 02703
Preattentive processing in * 02709
*: VHDL induced schematic imaging on net-lists 02830
Graphics Interface '86/* Interface '86 § 03288
A knowledge-based approach to computer * systems 03302
Static stereo * depth distortions in teleoperation 03390
Are there subtle changes in * after use of VDTs? 03733
* monitoring of VDU operators and relaxation of visual stress by means of laser speckle system 03738
VDU work, refractive errors and binocular * 03739
Relational models in natural and artificial * 03953
A cortical network model for early * processing 03957
Neural computers in *: processing of high dimensional data 03960
Computational networks in early *: from orientation selection to optical flow 03961
Active *: integration of fixed and mobile cameras 04017
Connectionist models and parallelism in high level * HCI-0363 †
Early *: from computational structure to algorithms and parallel hardware HCI-0365 †
Preattentive processing in * HCI-0366 †

## VISIONS
Portfolio: kaleidoscopic * 02551
Generation of * in systems development: a supplement to the tool box 03661

## VISUAL
A trace of memory: an evolutionary perspective on the * system 0019
* analysis during motion 0020
Figure-ground organization affects the early * processing 0021
*-cognitive neuronal networks 0029
Guide to the Draft American National Standard for Human Factors Engineering of * Display Terminal Workstations 0048
* information pick-up in a simulated driving situation 0251
* parameters for color CRTs 0257
* information processing: artificial intelligence and the sensorium of sight 0300
* routines 0616
* programming ● 0694
On the parameters of human * performance: an investigation of the benefits of antialiasing 0799
Performance, preference, and * scan patterns on a menu-based system: implications for interface design 0855
A synthetic * environment with hand gesturing and voice input 0858
An experiment into the use of auditory cues to reduce * workload 0877
The enhancement of understanding through * representations 0898
* system browser 0995
Fabrik: a * programming environment 01130
A self-organizing neural network sharing features of the mammalian * system 01248
Representation of local geometry in the * system 01249
Characteristics of neuronal systems in the * cortex 01255
Single sweep analysis of * evoked potentials through a model of parametric identification 01261
Quantitative determination of orientational and directional components in the response of * cortical cells to moving stimuli 01268
* pattern recognition in humans: I. Evidence for adaptive filtering 01274
Selection of image primitives for general-purpose * processing 01467
Guide to the draft American national standard for human factors engineering of * display terminal workstations 01549
* terminals and user interfaces 01686
Intermittent illumination from * display units and fluorescent lighting affects movements of the eyes across text 01713
On the selection and evaluation of * display symbology: factors influencing search and identification times 01718
Statistical dependency in * scanning 01719

921

[VISUAL]

* fatigue and spatial frequency adaptation to video displays of text 01721
The influence of * workload history on * performance 01725
The spatial allocation of * attention as indexed by event-related brain potentials 01739
Improving * performance through volitional focus control 01744
Effect of pixel height, display height, and vertical resolution on the detection of a simple vertical line signal in * noise 01753
The effects of target wavelength on dynamic * acuity under photopic and scotopic viewing 01762
Spatial requirements for * simulation of aircraft at real-world distances 01768
Information transfer rate with serial and simultaneous * display formats 01770
Effects of * display and motion system delays on operator performance and ueasiness in a driving simulator 01772
* control of displacement at slow speeds 01797
* Displays: the highlighting Paradox 01799
* accommodation and target detection in the vicinity of a window post 01802
A model for the fading of stabilized images in a * system 01864
GISMO: A * problem-structuring and knowledge-organization tool 01871
A knowledge-based system with audio-* aids 02068
Preserving the integrity of the medium: a method of measuring * and auditory comprehension of electronic media 02084
How can computer-based * displays aid operators? 02162
* information chunking in spreadsheet calculation 02232
Critical review of * inspection 02260
Non-Reimannian approach to geometry of * space: An application of affinely connected geometry to * alleys and horopter 02364
An empirical formula for * search 02526

Features and objects in * processing 02577
* interactive simulation - history, recent developments, and major issues 02585
A * shell interface to a database 02640
Conman: a * programming language for interactive graphics 02811
* languages and human computer interaction 03202
Optimum display arrangements for presenting * reminders 03237
Interfacing image processing and computer graphics systems using an artificial * system 03301
Principle of * color coding applied to satellite images 03304
Coupling * and dynamic features to study handwritten signatures 03309
The representation and perception of geometric structure in moving *patterns 03326
Motion analysis of grammatical processes in a *-gestural language 03347
Human * requirements for control and monitoring of a space telerobot 03391
* programming—toward realization of user-friendly programming environments 03493
Building a * designer's environment 03496
Out of Flatland: towards 3-D * programming 03497
* simulation 03503
A * programming language designed for automatic programming 03529
Experimental and theoretical analysis of * search activities 03620
Subjective load in introducing * display units 03627
Health impact of work with * display terminals 03678
Study of * performance on a multi-color VDU of color defective and normal Trichromatic subjects 03701
Lighting for * display unit workplaces 03715
Work at video display terminals among office employees: * ergonomics and lighting 03718

Non-* effects of * surroundings 03720
Display image characteristics and * response 03722
Matching display characteristics to human * capacity 03723
Criteria for the subjective quality of * display units 03724
The effect of VDT symbol characteristics on operator performance and *comfort 03728
* phenomena and their relation to top luminance, phosphor persistence time and contrast polarity 03729
Temporal and spatial stability in * displays 03730
Sensitivity to light and * strain in VDT operators: basic data for the design of work stations 03732
* impairment and subjective ocular symptomatology in VDT operators 03734
Effects on * accommodation and subjective * discomfort from VDT work intensified through split screen technique 03735
Vision monitoring of VDU operators and relaxation of * stress by means of laser speckle system 03738
Psychosocial work environment and use of * display terminals:8mfrom theoretical model to action 03742
Focusing variability during * work 03759
Effect of * presentation of different dialogue structures on human-computer interaction 03768
On * interfaces and their conceptual analysis 03829
* business graphics query interface 03840
The legibility of * display texts 03889
The use of color in * displays 03890
* fatigue with work on * display units: the current state of knowledge 03891
* comfort as a criterion for designing display units 03892
* presentation of text: the process of reading from a psycholinguistic perspective 03895

Design principles for a front-end * systems 03955
Why cortices? Neural computation in the vertebrate * system 03956
Reading continuous text from a one-line * display HCI-0187 †
The microcomputer as a classroom audio * device: the concept, and prospects HCI-0223 †
* momentum: a concept to improve the cognitive coupling of person and computer HCI-0238 †
A * approach to browsing in a database environment HCI-0258 †
Real time graphic simulation of * effects of egomotion HCI-0379 †
A neural network for * pattern recognition HCI-0391 †
* hyperacuity: representation and computation of high precision position information HCI-0393 †
* structure and the transmission of meaning HCI-0404 †

## VISUALIZATION

Interactive data * 01986
Applications of computer graphics to the * of meteorological data 02819
Towards reasoning * in expert systems 02992
Enhancing program readability and comprehensibility with tools for program * 03510
Interactive scientific * and parallel display techniques 03542
* of process information in improving work orientation 03619
* in programming. 5th Interdisciplinary Workshop in Informatics and § 03826
Heuristic rules for * 03868
* in programming § 04032

## VISUALLY

Depth and detours: an essay on * guided behavior 0018
The architecture of an inexpensive and portable talking-tactile terminal to aid the * handicapped 01452
An inexpensive and portable talking-tactile terminal for the *handicapped 02377
The design of auditory interfaces for * disabled users 02869

Human factors considerations in the design of a VDU for * impaired persons 03698

## VISUALLY IMPAIRED

Human factors design of a video monitor emulator and display (VMED) for * computer users 02379

## VISUOMOTOR

Why * systems don't like negative feedback and how they avoid it 0016
* control by a combined position- and speedservo. Theoretical considerations and experimental results in man 02666
Spatial and temporal transformations in * coordination 03963
Innate and learned components in a simple * reflex 03965

## VITAL

User satisfaction: A * management issue 01678
The design and construction of a * database 02460

## VLSI

* for solid modelling 0232
* image processing ● 0563
* implementation of a neural network model 01363
A * interactive layout editor (VILE) 02611
* architectures for implementation of neural networks 02762
Display architecture for *-based graphics workstations 03786

## VM

Using IBM's ISPF dialog manager: under MSV, *, and VSE ● 0304
*/CMS: a user's guide ● HCI-0028 †

## VMED

Human factors design of a video monitor emulator and display (*) for visually impaired computer users 02379

## VOCABULARY

Development of a hand-held computerized * tutor 02468
Real-time large * word recognition via diphone spotting and multiprocessor implementation 03996
The * problem in human-system communication HCI-0224 †

## VOCAL

Higher pole correction in * tract models and terminal analogs 02657

## VOCALLY

Communication methods of the * disabled: a review 0783

## VOICE

* input applications in aerospace 0179
*: technology searching for communication needs 0808
A case example of human factors in product definition: needs finding for a * output workstation for the blind 0819
A synthetic visual environment with hand gesturing and * input 0858
* messaging enhancing the user interface design based on field performance 0913
Designing a quality *: an analysis of listeners' reactions to synthetic * 0914
Comparison of elderly and younger users on keyboard and * input computer-based composition tasks 0916
Rapid prototyping and system development: examination of an interface toolkit for * and telephony applications 0918
Man—machine interaction by *: developments in speech technology. Part I: The state-of-the-art 02331
Man—machine interaction by *: developments in speech technology. Part 2: general applications and potential applications in libraries and information services 02332
* input/output interface for online searching: some design and human factor onsiderations 02335
An acoustic of pathological * and its application to the evaluation of laryngeal pathology 02644
The effect of varying * and noise parameters on the perception of voicing in Dutch two-obstruent sequences 02653
PC Version of a knowledge-based expert system with * interface 02964

[VOICES]                                                        KEYWORD INDEX

Employing * back channels of facilitate audio document retrieval 03045

* versus keyboard: use of a comparative analysis of learning to identify skill requirements of input devices 03275

Interactive error recovery expert system for robot with * recognition subsystem 03420

*-input aids for the physically disabled HCI-0089 †

An empirical investigation of * as an input modality for computer programming HCI-0237 †

Usage patterns in an integrated * and data communications system HCI-0311 †

Tones of *: the role of intonation in computer speech understanding HCI-0356 †

A parallel formant synthesizer for machine * output HCI-0396 :8E

## VOICES

Designing a quality voice: an analysis of listeners' reactions to synthetic * 0914

## VOLITIONAL

Improving visual performance through * focus control 01744

## VOLTAGE

A blackboard architecture for problem solving and machine learning in an expert system for power system * control 02926

## VOLTERRA

Identification of MGB cells by * kernels. III. A glance into the black box 01259

## VORTEX

Coherent and chaotic structures in 2D * dynamics: progress and problems 0729

## VOWEL

* normalization by frequency warped spectral matching 02649

Hopfield model applied to * and consonant discrimination 02735

## VOWELS

Perceptual normalization of the * of a man and a child in various contexts 02656

## VSE

Using IBM's ISPF dialog manager: under MSV, VM, and * ● 0304

## VULNERABLE

Fallible humans and * systems: lessons learned from aviation 03808

## WADE

A workcell application design environment (* 0598

## WAFER

An automatic * inspection system using pipelined image processing techniques 01840

## WARFARE

EPVM: An expert patient-ventilator manager for chemical * casualties 02956

## WARNING

The effect of adding symbols to written * labels on user behavior and recall 01788

A study of auditory * alarms evaluation for automated guided vehicles 03424

## WARPED

Vowel normalization by frequency * spectral matching 02649

## WATER

Computer applications in * supply: vol. 1—systems analysis and simulation ● 0227

Oil and * 01654

A model of the controller responses of the human temperature regulating system to changes in * temperature 02487

## WAVE

Beyond heart rate in the cardiac psychophysiological assessment of mental effort: the T-* amplitude component of the electrocardiogram 01738

User interface wars: the next * 02544

Estimating articulatory motion from speech * 02643

Information in the air and in the * 03146

Understanding the nature of the office for the design of third * office systems 03248

## WAVEFORM

Digital * sampling rate converter 01578

## WAVELENGTH

The effects of target * on dynamic visual acuity under photopic and scotopic viewing 01762

## WAVES

Research on individuality features in speech * and automatic speaker recognition techniques 02645

## WAYS

Learning the *: the enculturation of SDSC users 03144

ASK is transportable in half a dozen * HCI-0279 †

## WEAKLY

Alkahest III: automatic analysis of periodic * nonlinear ODEs 03087

## WEAR

Growth and challenge VS * and tear of humans in computer mediated work 03757

## WEATHER

Computerization and skill in local * forecasting 0344

## WEDDING

Development of the * planner—extensions to reach a young audience 01502

## WEIGHTS

On the representation and the impact of reliability on expert system * 02211

A probabilistic dominance measure for binary choices: analytic aspects of a multi-attribute random * model 02372

## WELCOME

A user-unfriendly * 02603

## WELL

How * do we acknowledge intellectual debts? 02299

How * do you write user documentation? 02442

Stress, coping, and worker *-being in computer-aided manufacturing: A field investigation of a CNC machine shop 03373

Determinants of the VDU operator's *-being 03679

Comparison of *-being among non-machine interactive clerical workers and full-time and part-time VDT users and typists 03745

**WHEELCHAIR**
Design of an integral computer-based * controller/linear synchronous motor system 02378

**WHIM**
*, the window handler and input manager 01825

**WHITEBOARDS**
*: a graphical database tool HCI-0289 †

**WIH**
Attacking a complex distributed algorithm from different sides: an experience * complementary validation tools 01429

**WIMP**
* interface for Unix 01973

**WINDOWING**
How are windows used? Some notes on creating an empirically-based *benchmark task 0903
A simple * system, part 1: basic principles 01286
Comparison of * Systems 01293
The BCC180 multitasking controller part 3: memory management and * 01295
Turbo pascal * system 01306

**WINDOWLIKE**
* user interfaces link systems and applications 01388

**WINDOWS**
Power *: maximizing the speed and performance of * 2.0 & * 386 ● 0423
Microsoft * 2.0 program development ● 0446
How are * used? Some notes on creating an empirically-based windowing benchmark task 0903
A comparison of tiled and overlapping * 0904
The effect of * on man-machine interfaces 01048
Painless panes for Smalltalk * 01118
Spying on * 01290
* for BASIC 01292
Domesticating microsoft * 01309
Turbo * 01421

Building a great * system 02550
Extending knowledge-based systems through closely-coupled graphics and * 02985
Introducing * to Unix: user expectations 03924
*, viewports and structured display files 03930
Opening * ● HCI-0007 †
Introduction to * programming ● HCI-0013 †
Cognitive layouts of * and multiple screens for user interfaces HCI-0122 †
An aspect of aesthetics in human-computer communications: pretty * HCI-0213 †

**WINS**
XY-*: an integraded environment for developing graphical user interfaces 03118

**WIRING**
Computer aided concurrent design for printed * boards 02981

**WOMEN**
A roundtable discussion on *, computers and participation 03673
*, work and computerization: opportunities and disadvantages § 03674
System development in a *'s perspective 03675
Task-load and endocrinological risk for pregnancy in * VDU operators 03692

**WORD**
Learning to use * processors: problems and prospects 0059
Learning to use a * processor: by doing, by thinking, and by knowing 0060
The sequential organization of spoken * recognition 0291
Learning disabled students' difficulties in learning to use a * processor: implications for design 0889
Transfer between * processing systems 0899
* processing techniques and user learning preferences 0984

An experiment in computational discrimination of English * senses 01813
Microcomputer software. 2. Scientific and technical * processing on a personal computer: has the time come? 02266
The effect on reading speed of * divisions at the end of a line 03896
Primary perceptual units in * recognition 03994
Real-time large vocabulary * recognition via diphone spotting and multiprocessor implementation 03996
An experimental environment for generating * hypotheses in continuous speech 03998
Development of a term association interface for browsing bibliographic data bases based on end users' * associations HCI-0266 †
Learning to use a * processor: by doing, by thinking, and by knowing HCI-0292 †
Training for optimising transfer between * processors HCI-0447 †

**WORDS**
Theoretical issues in the investigation of * of internal report 0354
Choice of * in the generation process of a natural language interface 01206
Integrating text with non-text:a picture is worth 1k *. Proceedings of the I § 04043

**WORKBENCH**
A mixed-initiative * for knowledge acquisition 02154
The database designer's * HCI-0249 †
Expertise transfer and complex problems: using AQUINAS as a knowledge-acquisition * for knowledge-based systems HCI-0336 †

**WORKCELL**
A * application design environment (WADE) 0598

## WORKDAYS
Long * versus restdays: assessing fatigue and alertness with a portable performance 01778

## WORKER
TA: Can it improve * satisfaction with organizational decision-making? 02414

Using *'s survey to improve production 02566

Stress, coping, and * well-being in computer-aided manufacturing: A field investigation of a CNC machine shop 03373

Computerized manufacturing technology and work organization effects on labor relations and * satisfaction 03443

Personality traits of the * within the "man-machine" system at automated production 03593

## WORKERS
Toward high-performance knowledge * (Reprint) 0369

The human side of robotics: how * react to a robot 0443

The silent force of the screen. A research note on the impact of microelectronics on work autonomy among clerical * in public administration 01437

Decision support systems for *: a bridge to advancing productivity 01947

The implementation of information systems for *: a structural equation model 01948

The foreign language barrier: a study among pharmaceutical research * 02333

But what will the * do? simulating what the * do to us when we do what we do to them 02590

Public Law 99-506, "Section 508" Electronic Equipment Accessibility for disabled * 02893

Accident analysis of blind production * 03439

User participation from the point of view of the * and trade union policy 03652

Environmental stressors and perceived health symptoms among office * 03680

Influence of age on performance and health of VDU * 03702

Comparison of well-being among non-machine interactive clerical * and full-time and part-time VDT users and typists 03745

Analyzing and improving VDU working conditions: *' education 03751

* education and user participation in the development of protective policies for VDT operators 03752

## WORKFORCE
Use of an entire * as computer 03748

## WORKLOAD
Mental * 0400

An experiment into the use of auditory cues to reduce visual * 0877

The influence of visual * history on visual performance 01725

A psychophysiological assessment of operator * during simulated flight missions 01735

A closed-loop causal model of * based on a comparison of fuzzy and crisp measurement techniques 01746

The role of practice in dual-task performance: toward * modeling in a connectionist/control architecture 01790

Some remarks on a measure of computer operator *: changes in pupil reflex 03626

## WORKPLACE
The changing *: A guide to managing the people, organizational, and regulatory aspects of office technology (book excerpt) 0044

Human—computer interactions in the *: psychosocial aspects of VDT use 0306

Computerized design and analysis of sitting * 01506

How technology brings blind people into the * 01705

Changes in electromyographic activity associated with occupational stress and poor performance in the * 01734

Predicting end-user acceptance of microcomputers in the * 02147

Methods for field evaluation of safety in a robotics * 03408

Improving the VDU * by introducing a physiologically optimized bright-background screen with dark characters: advantages and requirements 03721

## WORKPLACES
Methodological problems of field-research on * in offices 0249

Lighting for visual display unit * 03715

## WORKSHEET
Looking at * modeling through expert system eyes 0696

## WORKSHOPS
From models to modules: studies in cognitive science from the McGill * ● 0352

## WORKSPACES
Rooms: the use of multiple virtual * to reduce space contention in a window-based graphical user interface 01151

## WORKSTATION
Human factors issues in VDT use: Environmental and * design considerations 0046

Human factors testing in the design of Xerox's 8010 "Star" office * 0090

Presenting documents on * screens 0267

A multi-processor * with a logic-enhanced distributed frame buffer 0496

CAD-based off-line programming applied to a cleaning and deburring * 0607

A case example of human factors in product definition: needs finding for a voice output * for the blind 0819

Information detective: a * for exploring three dimensional information space 01010

Requirements checklist for a system development * 01144

Technological development and the integrated * 01313

The *: the interpress page and document description language 01356
The engineering of a translator * 01555
A * assessor for crew operations-WOSTAS 02093
Studying depth cues in a three-dimensional computer graphics * 02117
A personal computer based graphic * 02493
A debugger for a graphical * 02623
The ANALYST—A * for analysis and design 02713
A hand biomechanics * 02820
Developing intelligent simulation language to support telerobotic *activities 02995
Design issues of an intelligent * for the office 03165
Essential ingredients for a statistical * 03315
Performance evaluation of three pressure mats as robot * safety sensors 03428
Equipment and * design for banking services 03712
Looking at * architectures from the viewpoint of interaction 03787
Sharing in a privately owned * environment 04076
Human factors issues in VDT use: environmental and * design considerations HCI-0210 †

**WORKSTATIONS**
Second IEEE Conference on Computer *: proceedings ● 0002
Product and process design in intelligent CAD * 0009
Guide to the Draft American National Standard for Human Factors Engineering of Visual Display Terminal * 0048
Interactive * ● 0216
* and publication systems ● 0264
A history of personal * ● 0347
Designing advanced * 0457
Of moles and men: the design of foot controls for * 0935
The economics of UNIX * 01312
Needs and perceived needs of electronic * by engineering project managers 01515
Guide to the draft American national standard for human factors engineering of visual display terminal * 01549
The emerging role of * in the library environment 02467
Dbxtool: A window-based symbolic debugger for sun * 02614
Iconic shells for multitasking * 02792
The history of personal * § 03091
Toward a history of (personal) * 03092
Statistical software, graphics and future * for data analysis 03316
Automated document distribution using AI based * and knowledge based servers 03466
Recent results on the illumination of VDU and CAD * 03719
Display architecture for VLSI-based graphics * 03786
Executive *: issues and requirements HCI-0288 †
The electronic classroom: * for teaching HCI-0436 †
Using low-cost * to investigate computer networks and distributed systems HCI-0437 †

**WORKSTYLE**
Perceptions of the CIS graduate's *: undergraduate business students versus CIS faculty 02999

**WORLDS**
Cognitive engineering in complex dynamic * ● 0436
Artificial * and real experience 0518
Cognitive engineering in complex dynamic * 02167

**WOSTAS**
A workstation assessor for crew operations-* 02093

**WOVEN**
An interactive simulator for the designing of * fabric structures second place 02583

**WRAP**
Twelve-product *-up: neural networks 01189

**WRITERS**
* as total desktop publishers: developing a conceptual approach to training 0108
Are * obsolete in the computer industry? 0109
Consulting skills for technical * 0124
Help texts vs. help mechanisms: A new mandate for documentation * 01047
Help texts vs. help mechanisms: A new mandate for documentation * 02784
Automatic identification of * 03909
Technical * as computer scientists: the challenges of online documentation HCI-0153 †

**WYSIWIS**
* revised: early experiences with multiuser interfaces 01158

**XEROX**
Human factors testing in the design of *'s 8010 "Star" office workstation 0090

**XINU**
Operating system design. Vol. 1: the * approach (PC edition) ● HCI-0029 †

**XLIB**
* programming manual for version 11: Vol. 1 ● 0561

**XTRA**
*: a natural-language access system to expert systems 02244

**XVISION**
*: a comprehensive software system for image processing research, education, and applications 03124

**X3J13**
Common LISP object system specification * Document 88-002R 01121

**YANLI**
*: a powerful natural language front-end tool 01194

**YIELDS**
Steel * in Pa. 01649

## YIQ

An experimental comparison of RGB, *, LAB, HSV, and opponent color models HCI-0381 †

## YOUNGER

Comparison of elderly and * users on keyboard and voice input computer-based composition tasks 0916

## ZERO

The magical number three—plus or minus * 01622

Fatal error in pass *: how not to confuse novices HCI-0164 †

## ZIPF

The emergence of *'s law: Spontaneous encoding optimization by users of a command language 01875

## ZOG

Experience with the * human-computer interface system HCI-0246 †

## ZOOMING

Informational *: an interaction model for the graphical access to text knowledge bases 03073

## 80386

UNIX system V: release 3.0 Intel 80286/* computer version: system administrator's guide ● 0031

# ACM COMPUTING REVIEWS CLASSIFICATION SYSTEM

## Introduction to the CR Classification System

### A DESCRIPTION OF THE CLASSIFICATION SCHEME

The classification scheme involves a numbered tree containing unnumbered subject descriptors.

#### The Tree and Subject Descriptors

1. The *tree* consists of eleven first level nodes:

   General Literature
   Hardware
   Computer Systems Organization
   Software
   Data
   Theory of Computation
   Mathematics of Computing
   Information Systems
   Computing Methodologies
   Computing Applications
   Computing Milieux

   and one or two more numbered levels under each of these. The set of children of all first and second level nodes begins with a node *General* and ends with a node *Miscellaneous*. The first level nodes in the new scheme have letter designations (A through K) with numerals used for the second and third levels. Thus, for example,

   | | |
   |---|---|
   | H.2 | DATABASE MANAGEMENT |
   | I.4 | IMAGE PROCESSING |
   | D.3.2 | Language Classifications |
   | K.6.1 | Project and People Management |

2. A set of *subject descriptors* is associated with most leaves of the tree (although seldom with the *General* and *Miscellaneous* leaves). These subject descriptors are essentially fourth level nodes (albeit unnumbered) intended to subdivide the subject area denoted by the leaves into subareas which

## ACM COMPUTING REVIEWS CLASSIFICATION SYSTEM

☐ will serve to group reviews usefully but
☐ may not have such permanent life in the discipline that they would always be wanted in the classification scheme; later developments could cause a subject descriptor to be deleted or subdivided.

While we expect the set of subject descriptors associated with each leaf to change slowly, we do expect them to change. Since the subject descriptor idea is a new approach for *CR*, an estimate of the rate at which the set of subject descriptors will change is pure speculation.

Note that a major update to the Classification System has been completed and will be published in the January 1991 issue of *Computing Reviews*. Those areas of the Classification System requiring the greatest change concerned the topics that are central to the growing HCI Community. Members of ACM's Special Interest Group on Computer Human Interaction provided their input and review to the update editor, Neal Coulter, of Florida Atlantic University.

An important, although frequently misunderstood concept is that of "implied subject descriptor." This merely means that names of languages or systems *can* be included under the proper numbered node, even though they are not listed in the actual tree. Thus, PASCAL is an implied subject descriptor under D.3.2 Language Classifications, VM is appropriate to show under the D.4.0 Operating Systems—General node, and PDP-11 could be listed under C.1.1 Single Data Stream Architectures. Reviews will be printed under the proper names whenever appropriate, and the implied subject descriptors will be listed with cross references to other reviews whenever they are relevant. In this volume, proper nouns can be found in the Proper Noun Index, beginning on page 249.

In actual classification usage, first level nodes (e.g., B. Hardware) are never used to classify material. The General node (which always has the digit 0) at the first or second level can serve two purposes: it is used for papers that include broad treatments of the topic covered by its parent node (i.e., the node immediately preceding it in the tree), or it may cover several topics related to some (but not necessarily all or even any other one) of its sibling nodes (e.g., K.7.0—General, in K.7 The Computing Profession can be used to classify a paper on "The Future of Programming" which treats programmers, their salaries, working environments, and responsibilities). The Miscellaneous node (always designated with the letter m to allow expansion of its preceding siblings) covers specific subjects (associated with its parent node) for which there are no other relevant numbered nodes.

# Top two levels of CR classification tree

In order for the reader to be able to grasp the essential structure and coverage of the classification scheme, we present first the top two levels of the tree (i.e., the third-level nodes and subject descriptors are omitted). Node designations in parentheses are cross-references to other nodes which cover similar or related material.

## A. General Literature
- A.0 GENERAL
- A.1 INTRODUCTORY AND SURVEY
- A.2 REFERENCE (e.g., dictionaries, encyclopedias, glossaries)
- A.m MISCELLANEOUS

## B. Hardware
- B.0 GENERAL
- B.1 CONTROL STRUCTURES AND MICROPROGRAMMING (D.3.2)
- B.2 ARITHMETIC AND LOGIC STRUCTURES
- B.3 MEMORY STRUCTURES
- B.4 INPUT/OUTPUT AND DATA COMMUNICATIONS
- B.5 REGISTER-TRANSFER-LEVEL IMPLEMENTATION
- B.6 LOGIC DESIGN
- B.7 INTEGRATED CIRCUITS
- B.m MISCELLANEOUS

## C. Computer Systems Organization
- C.0 GENERAL
- C.1 PROCESSOR ARCHITECTURES
- C.2 COMPUTER-COMMUNICATION NETWORKS
- C.3 SPECIAL-PURPOSE AND APPLICATION-BASED SYSTEMS (J.7)
- C.4 PERFORMANCE OF SYSTEMS
- C.5 COMPUTER SYSTEM IMPLEMENTATION
- C.m MISCELLANEOUS

## D. Software
- D.0 GENERAL
- D.1 PROGRAMMING TECHNIQUES (E)
- D.2 SOFTWARE ENGINEERING (K.6.3)
- D.3 PROGRAMMING LANGUAGES
- D.4 OPERATING SYSTEMS (C)
- D.m MISCELLANEOUS

## E. Data
- E.0 GENERAL
- E.1 DATA STRUCTURES
- E.2 DATA STORAGE REPRESENTATIONS
- E.3 DATA ENCRYPTION
- E.4 CODING AND INFORMATION THEORY (H.1.1)
- E.5 FILES (D.4.3, H.2)
- E.m MISCELLANEOUS

## F. Theory of Computation
- F.0 GENERAL
- F.1 COMPUTATION BY ABSTRACT DEVICES
- F.2 ANALYSIS OF ALGORITHMS AND PROBLEM COMPLEXITY (B.6-7, F.1.3)
- F.3 LOGICS AND MEANINGS OF PROGRAMS
- F.4 MATHEMATICAL LOGIC AND FORMAL LANGUAGES
- F.m MISCELLANEOUS

## G. Mathematics of Computing
- G.0 GENERAL
- G.1 NUMERICAL ANALYSIS
- G.2 DISCRETE MATHEMATICS
- G.3 PROBABILITY AND STATISTICS
- G.4 MATHEMATICAL SOFTWARE
- G.m MISCELLANEOUS

## H. Information Systems
- H.0 GENERAL
- H.1 MODELS AND PRINCIPLES
- H.2 DATABASE MANAGEMENT (E.5)
- H.3 INFORMATION STORAGE AND RETRIEVAL
- H.4 INFORMATION SYSTEMS APPLICATIONS
- H.m MISCELLANEOUS

ACM *COMPUTING REVIEWS* CLASSIFICATION SYSTEM

## I. Computing Methodologies

- I.0 GENERAL
- I.1 ALGEBRAIC MANIPULATION
- I.2 ARTIFICIAL INTELLIGENCE
- I.3 COMPUTER GRAPHICS
- I.4 IMAGE PROCESSING
- I.5 PATTERN RECOGNITION
- I.6 SIMULATION AND MODELING (G.3)
- I.7 TEXT PROCESSING (H.4)
- I.m MISCELLANEOUS

## J. Computer Applications

- J.0 GENERAL
- J.1 ADMINISTRATIVE DATA PROCESSING
- J.2 PHYSICAL SCIENCES AND ENGINEERING
- J.3 LIFE AND MEDICAL SCIENCES
- J.4 SOCIAL AND BEHAVIORAL SCIENCES
- J.5 ARTS AND HUMANITIES
- J.6 COMPUTER-AIDED ENGINEERING
- J.7 COMPUTERS IN OTHER SYSTEMS (C.3)
- J.m MISCELLANEOUS

## K. Computing Milieux

- K.0 GENERAL
- K.1 THE COMPUTER INDUSTRY
- K.2 HISTORY OF COMPUTING
- K.3 COMPUTERS AND EDUCATION
- K.4 COMPUTERS AND SOCIETY
- K.5 LEGAL ASPECTS OF COMPUTING
- K.6 MANAGEMENT OF COMPUTING AND INFORMATION SYSTEMS
- K.7 THE COMPUTING PROFESSION
- K.8 PERSONAL COMPUTING
- K.m MISCELLANEOUS

## ACM *COMPUTING REVIEWS* CLASSIFICATION SYSTEM

# THE FULL *COMPUTING REVIEWS* CLASSIFICATION SCHEME

## FULL TREE WITH SUBJECT DESCRIPTORS

Unnumbered items are *subject descriptors.* Node numbers in parentheses indicate a cross-reference to related material.

## A. General Literature

A.0 GENERAL

*Biographies/Autobiographies*
*Conference proceedings*

A.1 INTRODUCTORY AND SURVEY

A.2 REFERENCE (e.g., dictionaries, encyclopedias, glossaries)

A.m MISCELLANEOUS

## B. Hardware

B.0 GENERAL

B.1 CONTROL STRUCTURES AND MICROPROGRAMMING (D.3.2)

B.1.0 General

B.1.1 Control Design Styles

*Hardwired control*
*Microprogrammed logic arrays*
*Writable control store*

B.1.2 Control Structure Performance Analysis and Design Aids

*Automatic synthesis*
*Formal models*
*Simulation*

B.1.3 Control Structure Reliability, Testing and Fault-Tolerance

*Diagnostics*
*Error-checking*
*Redundant design*
*Test generation*

B.1.4 Microprogram Design Aids (D.2.2, D.2.4, D.3.2, D.3.4)

*Firmware engineering*
*Languages and compilers*
*Machine-independent microcode generation*
*Optimization*
*Verification*

B.1.5 Microcode Applications

*Direct data manipulation*
*Firmware support of operating systems/instruction sets*
*Instruction set interpretation*
*Peripheral control*
*Special-purpose*

B.1.m Miscellaneous

B.2 ARITHMETIC AND LOGIC STRUCTURES

B.2.0 General

B.2.1 Design Styles (C.1.1-2)

*Calculator*
*Parallel*
*Pipeline*

B.2.2 Performance Analysis and Design Aids

*Simulation*
*Verification*
*Worst-case analysis*

B.2.3 Reliability, Testing and Fault-Tolerance

*Diagnostics*
*Error-checking*
*Redundant design*
*Test generation*

B.2.m Miscellaneous

B.3 MEMORY STRUCTURES

B.3.0 General

B.3.1 Unassigned

B.3.2 Design Styles (D.4.2)

*Associative memories*
*Cache memories*
*Interleaved memories*
*Mass storage*
*Primary memory*
*Sequential-access memory*
*Shared memory*
*Virtual memory*

## ACM *COMPUTING REVIEWS* CLASSIFICATION SYSTEM

- B.3.3 Performance Analysis and Design Aids (C.4)

    *Formal models*
    *Simulation*
    *Worst-case analysis*

- B.3.4 Reliability, Testing and Fault-Tolerance

    *Diagnostics*
    *Error-checking*
    *Redundant design*
    *Test generation*

- B.3.m Miscellaneous

### B.4 INPUT/OUTPUT AND DATA COMMUNICATIONS

- B.4.0 General
- B.4.1 Data Communications Devices

    *Processors*
    *Receivers (e.g., voice, data, image)*
    *Transmitters*

- B.4.2 Input/Output Devices

    *Channels and controllers*
    *Data terminals and printers*
    *Image display*
    *Voice*

- B.4.3 Interconnections (subsystems)

    *Asynchronous/synchronous operation*
    *Fiber optics*
    *Interfaces*
    *Physical structures (e.g., backplanes, cables, chip carriers)*
    *Topology (e.g., bus, point-to-point)*

- B.4.4 Performance Analysis and Design Aids

    *Formal models*
    *Simulation*
    *Verification*
    *Worst-case analysis*

- B.4.5 Reliability, Testing and Fault-Tolerance

    *Built-in tests*
    *Diagnostics*
    *Error-checking*
    *Hardware reliability*
    *Redundant design*
    *Test generation*

- B.4.m Miscellaneous

### B.5 REGISTER-TRANSFER-LEVEL IMPLEMENTATION

- B.5.0 General
- B.5.1 Design

    *Arithmetic and logic units*
    *Control design*
    *Data-path design*
    *Memory design*
    *Styles (e.g., parallel, pipelined, special-purpose)*

- B.5.2 Design Aids

    *Automatic synthesis*
    *Hardware description languages*
    *Optimization*
    *Simulation*
    *Verification*

- B.5.3 Reliability and Testing

    *Built-in tests*
    *Error-checking*
    *Redundant design*
    *Test generation*
    *Testability*

- B.5.m Miscellaneous

### B.6 LOGIC DESIGN

- B.6.0 General
- B.6.1 Design Styles

    *Cellular arrays and automata*
    *Combinational logic*
    *Logic arrays*
    *Memory control and access*
    *Memory used as logic*
    *Parallel circuits*
    *Sequential circuits*

- B.6.2 Reliability and Testing

    *Built-in tests*
    *Error-checking*
    *Redundant design*
    *Test generation*
    *Testability*

- B.6.3 Design Aids

    *Automatic synthesis*
    *Hardware description languages*
    *Optimization*
    *Simulation*
    *Switching theory*
    *Verification*

- B.6.m Miscellaneous

B.7 INTEGRATED CIRCUITS

B.7.0 General

B.7.1 Types and Design Styles

*Advanced technologies*
*Algorithms implemented in hardware*
*Gate arrays*
*Input/Output circuits*
*Memory technologies*
*Microprocessors and microcomputers*
*Standard cells*
*VLSI (very large scale integration)*

B.7.2 Design Aids

*Graphics*
*Layout*
*Placement and routing*
*Simulation*
*Verification*

B.7.3 Reliability and Testing

*Built-in tests*
*Error-checking*
*Redundant design*
*Testability*
*Test generation*

B.7.m Miscellaneous

B.m MISCELLANEOUS

*Design management*

# C. Computer Systems Organization

C.0 GENERAL

*Hardware/software interfaces*
*Instruction set design*
*System architectures*
*Systems specification methodology*

C.1 PROCESSOR ARCHITECTURES

C.1.0 General

C.1.1 Single Data Stream Architectures

*Multiple-instruction-stream,*
*single-data-stream processors (MISD)*
*Pipeline processors*
*Single-instruction-stream,*
*single-data-stream processors (SISD)*
*Von Neumann architectures*

C.1.2 Multiple Data Stream Architectures (Multiprocessors)

*Array and vector processors*
*Associative processors*
*Interconnection architectures (e.g., common bus, multiport memory, crossbar switch)*
*Multiple-instruction-stream, multiple-data-stream processors (MIMD)*
*Parallel processors*
*Pipeline processors*
*Single-instruction-stream, multiple-data-stream processors (SIMD)*

C.1.3 Other Architecture Styles

*Adaptable architectures*
*Capability architectures*
*Cellular architecture*
*Data-flow architectures*
*High-level language architectures*
*Stack-oriented processors*

C.1.m Miscellaneous

*Analog computers*
*Hybrid systems*

C.2 COMPUTER-COMMUNICATION NETWORKS

C.2.0 General

*Data communications*
*Open System Interconnection reference model (OSI)*
*Security and protection*

C.2.1 Network Architecture and Design

*Centralized networks*
*Circuit switching networks*
*Distributed networks*
*Network communications*
*Network topology*
*Packet networks*
*Store and forward networks*

C.2.2 Network Protocols

*Protocol architecture*
*Protocol verification*

C.2.3 Network Operations

*Network management*
*Network monitoring*
*Public networks*

C.2.4 Distributed Systems

*Distributed applications*
*Distributed databases*
*Network operating systems*

ACM *COMPUTING REVIEWS* CLASSIFICATION SYSTEM

- C.2.5 Local Networks
    - Access schemes
    - Buses
    - Rings
- C.2.m Miscellaneous
- C.3 SPECIAL-PURPOSE AND APPLICATION-BASED SYSTEMS (J.7)
    - Microprocessor/microcomputer applications
    - Process control systems
    - Real-time systems
    - Signal processing systems
- C.4 PERFORMANCE OF SYSTEMS
    - Design studies
    - Measurement techniques
    - Modeling techniques
    - Performance attributes
    - Reliability, availability, and serviceability
- C.5 COMPUTER SYSTEM IMPLEMENTATION
    - C.5.0 General
    - C.5.1 Large and Medium ("Mainframe") Computers
        - Super (very large) computers
    - C.5.2 Minicomputers
    - C.5.3 Microcomputers
        - Microprocessors
    - C.5.4 VLSI Systems
    - C.5.m Miscellaneous
- C.m MISCELLANEOUS

# D. Software

- D.0 GENERAL
- D.1 PROGRAMMING TECHNIQUES (E)
    - D.1.0 General
    - D.1.1 Applicative (Functional) Programming
    - D.1.2 Automatic Programming (I.2.2)
    - D.1.3 Concurrent Programming
    - D.1.4 Sequential Programming
    - D.1.m Miscellaneous
- D.2 SOFTWARE ENGINEERING (K.6.3)
    - D.2.0 General (K.5.1)
        - Protection mechanisms
        - Standards
    - D.2.1 Requirements/Specifications (D.3.1)
        - Languages
        - Methodologies
        - Tools
    - D.2.2 Tools and Techniques
        - Decision tables
        - Flow charts
        - Modules and interfaces
        - Programmer workbench
        - Software libraries
        - Structured programming
        - Top-down programming
        - User interfaces
    - D.2.3 Coding
        - Pretty printers
        - Program editors
        - Reentrant code
        - Standards
    - D.2.4 Program Verification (F.3.1)
        - Assertion checkers
        - Correctness proofs
        - Reliability
        - Validation
    - D.2.5 Testing and Debugging
        - Debugging aids
        - Diagnostics
        - Dumps
        - Error handling and recovery
        - Monitors
        - Symbolic execution
        - Test data generators
        - Tracing
    - D.2.6 Programming Environments
        - Interactive
    - D.2.7 Distribution and Maintenance
        - Corrections
        - Documentation
        - Enhancement
        - Extensibility
        - Portability
        - Restructuring
        - Version control

### D.2.8 Metrics (D.4.8)

*Complexity measures*
*Performance measures*
*Software science*

### D.2.9 Management (K.6.3, K.6.4)

*Copyrights*
*Cost estimation*
*Life cycle*
*Productivity*
*Programming teams*
*Software configuration management*
*Software quality assurance (SQA)*

### D.2.10 Design

*Methodologies*
*Representation*

### D.2.m Miscellaneous

*Rapid prototyping*
*Reusable software*

## D.3 PROGRAMMING LANGUAGES

### D.3.0 General

*Standards*

### D.3.1 Formal Definitions and Theory (D.2.1, F.3.1-2, F.4.2-3)

*Semantics*
*Syntax*

### D.3.2 Language Classifications

*Applicative languages*
*Data-flow languages*
*Design languages*
*Extensible languages*
*Macro and assembly languages*
*Microprogramming languages*
*Nonprocedural languages*
*Specialized application languages*
*Very high-level languages*

### D.3.3 Language Constructs (E.2)

*Abstract data types*
*Concurrent programming structures*
*Control structures*
*Coroutines*
*Data types and structures*
*Input/Output*
*Modules, packages*
*Procedures, functions and subroutines*

### D.3.4 Processors

*Code generation*
*Compilers*
*Interpreters*
*Optimization*
*Parsing*
*Preprocessors*
*Run-time environments*
*Translator writing systems and compiler generators*

### D.3.m Miscellaneous

## D.4 OPERATING SYSTEMS (C)

### D.4.0 General

### D.4.1 Process Management

*Concurrency*
*Deadlocks*
*Multiprocessing/multiprogramming*
*Mutual exclusion*
*Scheduling*
*Synchronization*

### D.4.2 Storage Management

*Allocation/deallocation strategies*
*Distributed memories*
*Main memory*
*Secondary storage devices*
*Segmentation*
*Storage hierarchies*
*Swapping*
*Virtual memory*

### D.4.3 File Systems Management (E.5)

*Access methods*
*Directory structures*
*Distributed file systems*
*File organization*
*Maintenance*

### D.4.4 Communications Management (C.2)

*Buffering*
*Input/Output*
*Message sending*
*Network communication*
*Terminal management*

### D.4.5 Reliability

*Backup procedures*
*Checkpoint/restart*
*Fault-tolerance*
*Verification*

## ACM *COMPUTING REVIEWS* CLASSIFICATION SYSTEM

- **D.4.6 Security and Protection**
  - *Access controls*
  - *Authentication*
  - *Cryptographic controls*
  - *Information flow controls*
  - *Security kernels*
  - *Verification*

- **D.4.7 Organization and Design**
  - *Batch processing systems*
  - *Distributed systems*
  - *Hierarchical design*
  - *Interactive systems*
  - *Real-time systems*

- **D.4.8 Performance (C.4, D.2.8, I.6)**
  - *Measurements*
  - *Modeling and prediction*
  - *Monitors*
  - *Operational analysis*
  - *Queueing theory*
  - *Simulation*
  - *Stochastic analysis*

- **D.4.9 Systems Programs and Utilities**
  - *Command and control languages*
  - *Linkers*
  - *Loaders*

- **D.4.m Miscellaneous**

- **D.m MISCELLANEOUS**
  - *Software psychology*

# E. Data

- **E.0 GENERAL**

- **E.1 DATA STRUCTURES**
  - *Arrays*
  - *Graphs*
  - *Lists*
  - *Tables*
  - *Trees*

- **E.2 DATA STORAGE REPRESENTATIONS**
  - *Composite structures*
  - *Contiguous representations*
  - *Hash-table representations*
  - *Linked representations*
  - *Primitive data items*

- **E.3 DATA ENCRYPTION**
  - *Data encryption standard (DES)*
  - *Public key cryptosystems*

- **E.4 CODING AND INFORMATION THEORY (H.1.1)**
  - *Data compaction and compression*
  - *Formal models of communication*
  - *Nonsecret encoding schemes*

- **E.5 FILES (D.4.3, F.2.2, H.2)**
  - *Backup/recovery*
  - *Optimization*
  - *Organization/structure*
  - *Sorting/searching*

- **E.m MISCELLANEOUS**

# F. Theory of Computation

- **F.0 GENERAL**

- **F.1 COMPUTATION BY ABSTRACT DEVICES**
  - **F.1.0 General**
  - **F.1.1 Models of Computation (F.4.1)**
    - *Automata (e.g., finite, push-down, resource-bounded)*
    - *Bounded-action devices (e.g., Turing machines, random access machines)*
    - *Computability theory*
    - *Relations among models*
    - *Self-modifying machines*
    - *Unbounded-action devices (e.g., cellular automata, circuits, networks of machines)*
  - **F.1.2 Modes of Computation**
    - *Alternation and nondeterminism*
    - *Parallelism*
    - *Probabilistic computation*
    - *Relations among modes*
    - *Relativized computation*
  - **F.1.3 Complexity Classes (F.2)**
    - *Complexity hierarchies*
    - *Machine-independent complexity*
    - *Reducibility and completeness*
    - *Relations among complexity classes*
    - *Relations among complexity measures*
  - **F.1.m Miscellaneous**

## F.2 ANALYSIS OF ALGORITHMS AND PROBLEM COMPLEXITY (B.6-7, F.1.3)

### F.2.0 General

### F.2.1 Numerical Algorithms and Problems (G.1, G.4, I.1)

*Computation of transforms (e.g., fast Fourier transform)*
*Computations in finite fields*
*Computations on matrices*
*Computations on polynomials*
*Number-theoretic computations (e.g., factoring, primality testing)*

### F.2.2 Nonnumerical Algorithms and Problems (E.2-5, G.2, H.2-3)

*Complexity of proof procedures*
*Computations on discrete structures*
*Geometrical problems and computations*
*Pattern matching*
*Routing and layout*
*Sequencing and scheduling*
*Sorting and searching*

### F.2.3 Tradeoffs among Complexity Measures (F.1.3)

### F.2.m Miscellaneous

## F.3 LOGICS AND MEANINGS OF PROGRAMS

### F.3.0 General

### F.3.1 Specifying and Verifying and Reasoning about Programs (D.2.1, D.2.4, D.3.1, E.1)

*Assertions*
*Invariants*
*Logics of programs*
*Mechanical verification*
*Pre- and post-conditions*
*Specification techniques*

### F.3.2 Semantics of Programming Languages (D.3.1)

*Algebraic approaches to semantics*
*Denotational semantics*
*Operational semantics*

### F.3.3 Studies of Program Constructs (D.3.2-3)

*Control primitives*
*Functional constructs*
*Program and recursion schemes*
*Type structure*

### F.3.m Miscellaneous

## F.4 MATHEMATICAL LOGIC AND FORMAL LANGUAGES

### F.4.0 General

### F.4.1 Mathematical Logic (F.1.1, I.2.2-3)

*Computability theory*
*Computational logic*
*Lambda calculus and related systems*
*Logic programming*
*Mechanical theorem proving*
*Model theory*
*Proof theory*
*Recursive function theory*

### F.4.2 Grammars and Other Rewriting Systems (D.3.1)

*Decision problems*
*Grammar types (e.g., context-free, context-sensitive)*
*Parallel rewriting systems (e.g., developmental systems, L-systems)*
*Parsing*
*Thue systems*

### F.4.3 Formal Languages (D.3.1)

*Algebraic language theory*
*Classes defined by grammars or automata (e.g., context-free languages, regular sets, recursive sets)*
*Classes defined by resource-bounded automata*
*Decision problems*
*Operations on languages*

### F.4.m Miscellaneous

## F.m MISCELLANEOUS

# G. Mathematics of Computing

## G.0 GENERAL

## G.1 NUMERICAL ANALYSIS

### G.1.0 General

*Computer arithmetic*
*Condition (and ill-condition)*
*Error analysis*
*Numerical algorithms*
*Parallel algorithms*
*Stability (and instability)*

## ACM COMPUTING REVIEWS CLASSIFICATION SYSTEM

G.1.1 Interpolation

*Difference formulas*
*Extrapolation*
*Interpolation formulas*
*Smoothing*
*Spline and piecewise polynomial interpolation*

G.1.2 Approximation

*Chebyshev approximation and theory*
*Elementary function approximation*
*Least squares approximation*
*Linear approximation*
*Minimax approximation and algorithms*
*Nonlinear approximation*
*Rational approximation*
*Spline and piecewise polynomial approximation*

G.1.3 Numerical Linear Algebra

*Conditioning*
*Determinants*
*Eigenvalues*
*Error analysis*
*Linear systems (direct and iterative methods)*
*Matrix inversion*
*Pseudoinverses*
*Sparse and very large systems*

G.1.4 Quadrature and Numerical Differentiation

*Adaptive quadrature*
*Equal interval integration*
*Error analysis*
*Finite difference methods*
*Gaussian quadrature*
*Iterated methods*
*Multiple quadrature*

G.1.5 Roots of Nonlinear Equations

*Convergence*
*Error analysis*
*Iterative methods*
*Polynomials, methods for*
*Systems of equations*

G.1.6 Optimization

*Constrained optimization*
*Gradient methods*
*Integer programming*
*Least squares methods*
*Linear programming*
*Nonlinear programming*

G.1.7 Ordinary Differential Equations

*Boundary value problems*
*Convergence and stability*
*Error analysis*
*Initial value problems*
*Multistep methods*
*Single step methods*
*Stiff equations*

G.1.8 Partial Differential Equations

*Difference methods*
*Elliptic equations*
*Finite element methods*
*Hyperbolic equations*
*Method of lines*
*Parabolic equations*

G.1.9 Integral Equations

*Fredholm equations*
*Integro-differential equations*
*Volterra equations*

G.1.m Miscellaneous

G.2 DISCRETE MATHEMATICS

G.2.0 General

G.2.1 Combinatorics (F.2.2)

*Combinatorial algorithms*
*Counting problems*
*Generating functions*
*Permutations and combinations*
*Recurrences and difference equations*

G.2.2 Graph Theory (F.2.2)

*Graph algorithms*
*Network problems*
*Path and circuit problems*
*Trees*

G.2.m Miscellaneous

G.3 PROBABILITY AND STATISTICS

*Probabilistic algorithms (including Monte Carlo)*
*Random number generation*
*Statistical computing*
*Statistical software*

G.4 MATHEMATICAL SOFTWARE

*Algorithm analysis*
*Certification and testing*
*Efficiency*
*Portability*
*Reliability and robustness*
*Verification*

G.m MISCELLANEOUS

*Queueing theory*

# H. Information Systems

**H.0 GENERAL**

**H.1 MODELS AND PRINCIPLES**

   H.1.0 General

   H.1.1 Systems and Information Theory (E.4)
- *General systems theory*
- *Information theory*
- *Value of information*

   H.1.2 User/Machine Systems
- *Human factors*
- *Human information processing*

   H.1.m Miscellaneous

**H.2 DATABASE MANAGEMENT (E.5)**

   H.2.0 General
- *Security, integrity, and protection*

   H.2.1 Logical Design
- *Data models*
- *Normal forms*
- *Schema and subschema*

   H.2.2 Physical Design
- *Access methods*
- *Deadlock avoidance*
- *Recovery and restart*

   H.2.3 Languages
- *Data description languages (DDL)*
- *Data manipulation languages (DML)*
- *Query languages*
- *Report writers*

   H.2.4 Systems
- *Concurrency*
- *Distributed systems*
- *Query processing*
- *Transaction processing*

   H.2.5 Heterogeneous Databases
- *Data translation*
- *Program translation*

   H.2.6 Database Machines

   H.2.7 Database Administration
- *Data dictionary/directory*
- *Logging and recovery*

   H.2.8 Database Applications

   H.2.m Miscellaneous

**H.3 INFORMATION STORAGE AND RETRIEVAL**

   H.3.0 General

   H.3.1 Content Analysis and Indexing
- *Abstracting methods*
- *Dictionaries*
- *Indexing methods*
- *Linguistic processing*
- *Thesauruses*

   H.3.2 Information Storage
- *File organization*
- *Record classification*

   H.3.3 Information Search and Retrieval
- *Clustering*
- *Query formulation*
- *Retrieval models*
- *Search process*
- *Selection process*

   H.3.4 Systems and Software
- *Current awareness systems (selective dissemination of information-SDI)*
- *Information networks*
- *Question-answering (fact retrieval) systems*

   H.3.5 On-Line Information Services
- *Data bank sharing*

   H.3.6 Library Automation

   H.3.m Miscellaneous

**H.4 INFORMATION SYSTEMS APPLICATIONS**

   H.4.0 General

   H.4.1 Office Automation (I.7)
- *Equipment*
- *Word processing*

   H.4.2 Types of Systems
- *Decision support (e.g., MIS)*
- *Logistics*

   H.4.3 Communications Applications
- *Electronic mail*
- *Teleconferencing*
- *Videotex*

   H.4.m Miscellaneous

**H.m MISCELLANEOUS**

ACM *COMPUTING REVIEWS* CLASSIFICATION SYSTEM

# I. Computing Methodologies

## I.0 GENERAL

## I.1 ALGEBRAIC MANIPULATION

### I.1.0 General

### I.1.1 Expressions and Their Representation (E.1-2)

Representations (general and polynomial)
Simplification of expressions

### I.1.2 Algorithms (F.2.1-2)

Algebraic algorithms
Analysis of algorithms
Nonalgebraic algorithms

### I.1.3 Languages and Systems (D.3.2-3, F.2.2)

Evaluation strategies
Nonprocedural languages
Special-purpose algebraic systems
Special-purpose hardware
Substitution mechanisms

### I.1.4 Applications

### I.1.m Miscellaneous

## I.2 ARTIFICIAL INTELLIGENCE

### I.2.0 General

### I.2.1 Applications and Expert Systems (H.4, J)

Cartography
Games
Industrial automation
Law
Medicine and science
Natural language interfaces
Office automation

### I.2.2 Automatic Programming (D.1.2, F.3.1)

Automatic analysis of algorithms
Program modification
Program synthesis
Program transformation
Program verification

### I.2.3 Deduction and Theorem Proving

Answer/reason extraction
Deduction (e.g., natural, rule-based)
Logic programming
Mathematical induction
Metatheory
Nonmonotonic reasoning and belief revision
Resolution
Uncertainty, "fuzzy," and probabilistic reasoning

### I.2.4 Knowledge Representation Formalisms and Methods

Frames and scripts
Predicate logic
Relation systems
Representation languages
Representations (procedural and rule-based)
Semantic networks

### I.2.5 Programming Languages and Software (D.3.2)

Expert system tools and techniques

### I.2.6 Learning (K.3.2)

Analogies
Concept learning
Induction
Knowledge acquisition
Language acquisition
Parameter learning

### I.2.7 Natural Language Processing

Language generation
Language models
Language parsing and understanding
Machine translation
Speech recognition and understanding
Text analysis

### I.2.8 Problem Solving, Control Methods and Search (F.2.2)

Backtracking
Dynamic programming
Graph and tree search strategies
Heuristic methods
Plan execution, formation, generation

### I.2.9 Robotics

Manipulators
Propelling mechanisms
Sensors

## I.2.10 Vision and Scene Understanding (I.4.8, I.5)

*Architecture and control structures*
*Intensity, color, photometry and thresholding*
*Modeling and recovery of physical attributes*
*Motion*
*Perceptual reasoning*
*Representations, data structures and transforms*
*Shape*
*Texture*

## I.2.m Miscellaneous

## I.3 COMPUTER GRAPHICS

### I.3.0 General

### I.3.1 Hardware Architecture (B.4.2)

*Hardcopy devices*
*Input devices*
*Raster display devices*
*Storage devices*
*Vector display devices*

### I.3.2 Graphics Systems (C.2.1, C.2.4, C.3)

*Distributed/network graphics*
*Remote systems*
*Stand-alone systems*

### I.3.3 Picture/Image Generation

*Digitizing and scanning*
*Display algorithms*
*Viewing algorithms*

### I.3.4 Graphics Utilities

*Application packages*
*Graphics packages*
*Picture description languages*
*Software support*

### I.3.5 Computational Geometry and Object Modeling

*Curve, surface, solid, and object representations*
*Geometric algorithms, languages, and systems*
*Hierarchy and geometric transformations*
*Modeling packages*

### I.3.6 Methodology and Techniques

*Device independence*
*Ergonomics*
*Interaction techniques*
*Languages*

### I.3.7 Three-Dimensional Graphics and Realism

*Animation*
*Color, shading, shadowing, and texture*
*Visible line/surface algorithms*

### I.3.m Miscellaneous

## I.4 IMAGE PROCESSING

### I.4.0 General

*Image displays*
*Image processing software*

### I.4.1 Digitization

*Quantization*
*Sampling*
*Scanning*

### I.4.2 Compression (coding) (E.4)

*Approximate methods*
*Exact coding*

### I.4.3 Enhancement

*Filtering*
*Geometric correction*
*Grayscale manipulation*
*Registration*
*Sharpening and deblurring*
*Smoothing*

### I.4.4 Restoration

*Inverse filtering*
*Kalman filtering*
*Pseudoinverse restoration*
*Wiener filtering*

### I.4.5 Reconstruction

*Series expansion methods*
*Summation methods*
*Transform methods*

### I.4.6 Segmentation

*Edge and feature detection*
*Pixel classification*
*Region growing, partitioning*

### I.4.7 Feature Measurement

*Invariants*
*Moments*
*Projections*
*Size and shape*
*Texture*

## ACM COMPUTING REVIEWS CLASSIFICATION SYSTEM

- I.4.8 Scene Analysis
  - *Depth cues*
  - *Photometry*
  - *Range data*
  - *Stereo*
  - *Time-varying imagery*
- I.4.9 Applications
- I.4.m Miscellaneous

### I.5 PATTERN RECOGNITION

- I.5.0 General
- I.5.1 Models
  - *Deterministic*
  - *Fuzzy set*
  - *Geometric*
  - *Statistical*
  - *Structural*
- I.5.2 Design Methodology
  - *Classifier design and evaluation*
  - *Feature evaluation and selection*
  - *Pattern analysis*
- I.5.3 Clustering
  - *Algorithms*
  - *Similarity measures*
- I.5.4 Applications
  - *Computer vision*
  - *Signal processing*
  - *Text processing*
  - *Waveform analysis*
- I.5.5 Implementation (C.3)
  - *Interactive systems*
  - *Special architectures*
- I.5.m Miscellaneous

### I.6 SIMULATION AND MODELING (G.3)

- I.6.0 General
- I.6.1 Simulation Theory
  - *Model classification*
  - *Types of simulation (continuous and discrete)*
- I.6.2 Simulation Languages
- I.6.3 Applications
- I.6.4 Model Validation and Analysis
- I.6.m Miscellaneous

### I.7 TEXT PROCESSING (H.4)

- I.7.0 General
- I.7.1 Text Editing
  - *Languages*
  - *Spelling*
- I.7.2 Document Preparation
  - *Format and notation*
  - *Languages*
  - *Photocomposition*
- I.7.3 Index Generation
- I.7.m Miscellaneous

### I.m MISCELLANEOUS

## J. Computer Applications

### J.0 GENERAL

### J.1 ADMINISTRATIVE DATA PROCESSING
- *Business*
- *Education*
- *Financial (e.g., EFTS)*
- *Government*
- *Law*
- *Manufacturing*
- *Marketing*
- *Military*

### J.2 PHYSICAL SCIENCES AND ENGINEERING
- *Aerospace*
- *Astronomy*
- *Chemistry*
- *Earth and atmospheric sciences*
- *Electronics*
- *Engineering*
- *Mathematics and statistics*
- *Physics*

### J.3 LIFE AND MEDICAL SCIENCES
- *Biology*
- *Health*
- *Medical information systems*

### J.4 SOCIAL AND BEHAVIORAL SCIENCES
- *Economics*
- *Psychology*
- *Sociology*

### J.5 ARTS AND HUMANITIES
- *Arts, fine and performing*
- *Language translation*
- *Linguistics*
- *Literature*
- *Music*

## J.6 COMPUTER-AIDED ENGINEERING

>   *Computer-aided design (CAD)*
>   *Computer-aided manufacturing (CAM)*

## J.7 COMPUTERS IN OTHER SYSTEMS (C.3)

>   *Command and control*
>   *Consumer products*
>   *Industrial control*
>   *Military*
>   *Process control*
>   *Publishing*
>   *Real time*

## J.m MISCELLANEOUS

# K. Computing Milieux

## K.0 GENERAL

## K.1 THE COMPUTER INDUSTRY

>   *Markets*
>   *Standards*
>   *Statistics*
>   *Suppliers*

## K.2 HISTORY OF COMPUTING

>   *Hardware*
>   *People*
>   *Software*
>   *Systems*
>   *Theory*

## K.3 COMPUTERS AND EDUCATION

### K.3.0 General

### K.3.1 Computer Uses in Education

>   *Computer-assisted instruction (CAI)*
>   *Computer-managed instruction (CMI)*

### K.3.2 Computer and Information Science Education

>   *Computer science education*
>   *Curriculum*
>   *Information systems education*
>   *Self-assessment*

### K.3.m Miscellaneous

>   *Accreditation*
>   *Computer literacy*

## K.4 COMPUTERS AND SOCIETY

### K.4.0 General

### K.4.1 Public Policy Issues

>   *Privacy*
>   *Regulation*
>   *Transborder data flow*

### K.4.2 Social Issues

>   *Abuse and crime involving computers*
>   *Employment*

### K.4.3 Organizational Impacts

### K.4.m Miscellaneous

## K.5 LEGAL ASPECTS OF COMPUTING

### K.5.0 General

### K.5.1 Software Protection

>   *Copyrights*
>   *Patents*
>   *Proprietary rights*
>   *Trade secrets*

### K.5.2 Governmental Issues

>   *Regulation*
>   *Taxation*

### K.5.m Miscellaneous

>   *Contracts*
>   *Hardware patents*

## K.6 MANAGEMENT OF COMPUTING AND INFORMATION SYSTEMS

### K.6.0 General

>   *Economics*

### K.6.1 Project and People Management

>   *Life cycle*
>   *Management techniques (e.g., PERT/CPM)*
>   *Staffing*
>   *Systems analysis and design*
>   *Systems development*
>   *Training*

### K.6.2 Installation Management

>   *Benchmarks*
>   *Computer selection*
>   *Computing equipment management*
>   *Performance and usage measurement*
>   *Pricing and resource allocation*

### K.6.3 Software Management

>   *Software development*
>   *Software maintenance*
>   *Software selection*

### K.6.4 System Management (D.2.9)

>   *Centralization/decentralization*
>   *Management audit*
>   *Quality assurance*

### K.6.m Miscellaneous

>   *Insurance*
>   *Security*

## ACM *COMPUTING REVIEWS* CLASSIFICATION SYSTEM

K.7 THE COMPUTING PROFESSION
- K.7.0 General
- K.7.1 Occupations
- K.7.2 Organizations
- K.7.3 Testing, Certification, and Licensing
- K.7.m Miscellaneous
  - *Codes of good practice*
  - *Ethics*

K.8 PERSONAL COMPUTING
- *Games*

K.m MISCELLANEOUS

# CATEGORY INDEX

The ACM *Computing Reviews* Classification System involves a four-level tree that has three numbered levels and an unnumbered level of descriptors (normally appearing at the fourth level). This tree comprises the categories and subject descriptors. We suggest using the following steps in searching the Category Index. First, refer to the top two levels in the classification tree (listed on page 931) and find any of the second-level nodes that seem to be relevant. Next, using the first- and second-level nodes of the classification scheme, look at the third-level nodes and the subject descriptors under them. Identify any descriptors that apply.

In cases where so much more material is classified than is readily useful for compiling a reference or reading list, we have retained only those items that were also reviewed and suppressed the rest. For example, as one would expect in a bibliography on human computer interaction, almost fifty percent of the entries were classified under the subject descriptor *Human factors*. By retaining only the reviewed citations, a more manageable list of several hundred items is presented, rather than several thousand. You will find a note under any category or subject descriptor where the listing has been shortened.

In addition to the printed list of descriptors you may look up implicit subject descriptors, which are *proper nouns* (the names of languages and systems). The implicit subject descriptors are associated with numbered nodes. In this Category Index, implicit subject descriptors appear under the appropriate node with pointers to the Proper Noun Index, where they may be searched alphabetically.

Look under a General node (at any level) if your topic covers most of the concepts in an area. If you cannot find any other relevant node, try a Miscellaneous node.

Once you have found the appropriate categories, scan the titles under the category, and note the review or citation number. Complete information can be found about each item in the Review or Bibliography section.

[A. GENERAL LITERATURE]   CATEGORY INDEX

## A. GENERAL LITERATURE

### A.0 GENERAL

New applications of data bases. § 02710
AFIPS Conference Proceedings; vol. 55 1986 National Computer Conference. § 03162

*Biographies/Autobiographies*

A boy and his brain machine. 02575

**Alan Turing** *see* Proper Noun Index

*Conference proceedings*

A history of personal workstations. ● 0347
An historical perspective of CD ROM. 0679
Conference report: IEEE 1'st Int'l conference on neural networks. 0772
CSCW '86 Conference summary report. 0955
Computer-support cooperative work. 0956
Classification of dialog techniques. 0960
Interact '87. 0964
CHI '88 trip report. 0981
Report on the Collaborative Technology Developers' Workshop. 0994
CSCW'88: report on the conference & review of the proceedings. 01002
Language and artificial intelligence conference report. 01688
CHI '86 - human factors in computing systems. 01918
BCS human—computer interaction conference. 01922
ACM SIGUCCS User Services Conference XIV. 01925
LSP-automatic translation and information technology. 02513
Computer Board Forum. 02685
Computer science education. § 02809
Document manipulation and typography. § 03182
Applicable algebra, error-correcting codes, combinatorics and computer algebra. § 03846
MFDBS 87. § 03943

### A.1 INTRODUCTORY AND SURVEY

Vision, brain, and cooperative computation: an overview. 0015
Computers for managing information. ● 0141
Principles of data communication. ● 0547
Annual review of computer science vol. 1, 1986. ● 0719
Neural networks primer, part IV. 01188
A survey of general-purpose manipulation. 02259
Readability formulas: An overview. 02301

Empirical studies of programmers: the territory, paths, and destination. 02691
Computer culture: the scientific, intellectual, and social impact of the computer. § 03567
Fifth generation computers: concepts, implementations and uses. ● HCI-0001 †
The computer culture. § HCI-0084 †

### A.2 REFERENCE (e.g., dictionaries, encyclopedias, glossaries)

A drafted PM glossary. 0625
Human factors reference guide for electronics and computer professionals. ● 0733
Human factors in computer systems: some useful readings. 0957
An annotated bibliography on user interface design. 01004
Bibliography of software tools for user interface development. 01071
A taxonomy of user-oriented functions. 02104
Indexes and bibliography. ● HCI-0068 †
A prototype electronic encyclopedia. HCI-0278 †

### A.m MISCELLANEOUS

Informatics (computer and information science): its ideology, methodology, and sociology. HCI-0086 †

## B. HARDWARE

### B.0 GENERAL

Design Automation. § 02828

### B.1 CONTROL STRUCTURES AND MICROPROGRAMMING (D.3.2)

Annual review of computer science vol. 1, 1986. ● 0719

#### B.1.1 Control Design Styles

*Hardwired control*

Foundations for the Arcadia environment architecture. 01135

#### B.1.2 Control Structure Performance Analysis and Design Aids

*Simulation*

Control of sensory processing - a hypothesis on and simulation of the architecture of an elementary cortical processor. 03972

### B.1.4 Microprogram Design Aids (D.2.2, D.2.4, D.3.2, D.3.4)

*Firmware engineering*

Control of sensory processing - a hypothesis on and simulation of the architecture of an elementary cortical processor. 03972

### B.1.5 Microcode Applications

DVI—a digital multimedia technology. 01327

*Peripheral control*

Compact disc–interactive. 0680

## B.2 ARITHMETIC AND LOGIC STRUCTURES

### B.2.1 Design Styles (C.1.1-2)

*Parallel*

High-performance polygon rendering. 02814

*Pipeline*

High-performance polygon rendering. 02814

## B.3 MEMORY STRUCTURES

### B.3.2 Design Styles (D.4.2)

Interactive media: working methods and practical applications. ● 0501
Setting up an interactive videodisc project. 0502
Pedagogical design for interactive video. 0505
Conversation theory as a basis for instructional design. 0507
From trigger video to videodisc: a case study in interpersonal skills. 0508
The creation of an integrated IVD curriculum. 0509
A question of delivery—an outline classification of interactive video delivery systems. 0510
Interactive video—a producer's medium. 0511
The political economy of interactive video in British higher education. 0512
Interactive video as a school resource: Rolls-Royce or Model T Ford?. 0513
Producing resource discs—the Domesday project experience. 0514
Videodisc and videotex: love-match or passing acquaintance?. 0515
The look and feel . . . and sound of the user interface. 01315
Putting Texas on disc. 01316
DVI—a digital multimedia technology. 01327
Interactive video in language learning. 01380

Some issues related to the design and development of an interactive video disc. 01497
An interactive videodisc drama: The case of Frank hall. 02285
User interfaces for CD'ROM PACs. 02466
Directories, DOS, and hard disks: impact on the user. 02604
Optical information systems '86. § 03556
Videotex and online services: competition or collateral. 03557
Integrating CD-ROM with printed and online services: a silver platter end-user perspective. 03558

*Associative memories*

Collective computation, content-addressable memory, and optimization problems. 0004
Annual review of computer science vol. 1, 1986. ● 0719
Constructing an associative memory. 01289
VLSI implementation of a neural network model. 01363
Dynamics and architecture for neural computation. 02270
Parallel in sequence—towards the architecture of an elementary cortical processor. 03820
Control of sensory processing - a hypothesis on and simulation of the architecture of an elementary cortical processor. 03972

*Interleaved memories*

Designing a CD ROM information structure. 0682
Annual review of computer science vol. 1, 1986. ● 0719

*Mass storage*

Designing a CD ROM information structure. 0682
Artificial intelligence systems. 0683
The coming revolution in interactive digital video. 01325
Coding image sequences for interactive retrieval. 01330

*Shared memory*

Structured message passing on a shared-memory multiprocessor. 03514

*Virtual memory*

CHI '88 poster session papers and abstracts. 0992
Development and evaluation of direct manipulation lists (poster session). 0993

## B.4 INPUT/OUTPUT AND DATA COMMUNICATIONS

Annual review of computer science vol. 1, 1986. ● 0719

### B.4.0 General

People and computers IV. § 03215

### B.4.1 Data Communications Devices

Interacting with electronic mail can be a dream or a night: a user's point of view. 02069

*Processors*

Traffic study on primary rate ISDN user-network interface. 01442
A model for assessing the performance of a local area network employing technical office protocol (TOP) as part of MAP/TOP network in a computer integrated manufacturing (CIM) research project, for the transmission of real time interactive speech. 02491

*Receivers (e.g., voice, data, image)*

Electronic speech recognition: techniques, technology, and applications. • 0174
A model for assessing the performance of a local area network employing technical office protocol (TOP) as part of MAP/TOP network in a computer integrated manufacturing (CIM) research project, for the transmission of real time interactive speech. 02491
An architecture for a multimedia teleconferencing system. 02802

### B.4.2 Input/Output Devices

User computer interface guidelines research for keyboards and function keys. 0201
Authorship provisions in AUGMENT (Reprint). 0370
Keyboarding for personal computer use. • 0492
Principles of data communication. • 0547
Eye movements in reading: perceptual and language processes. • 0609
The CD ROM handbook. • 0678
An historical perspective of CD ROM. 0679
Compact disc–interactive. 0680
Digital video interactive. 0681
Is the unified keyboard better?. 0768
A study in two-handed input. 0933
Interactive recognition of handprinted characters for computer input. 0940
The use of the IBM personal computer in the man-machine interface to a nuclear research accelerator. 01454
Touchscreen usage in plant computer systems: a case study. 01530
Designing screens for people to use easily. 01531
Oil and water?. 01654
Interactive communication of sentential structure and content: an alternative approach to man-machine communication. 02220
An inexpensive and portable talking-tactile terminal for the visually handicapped. 02377
Human factors design of a video monitor emulator and display (VMED) for visuallyimpaired computer users. 02379
Development of a hand-held computerized vocabulary tutor. 02468
Exploratory evaluation of a planar foot-operated cursor-positioning device. 02858
Toward a history of (personal) workstations. 03092
A personal view of the personal work station: some firsts in the Fifties. 03093
The augmented knowledge workshop. 03094
User technology—from pointing to pondering. 03098
Sketchpad a man-machine graphical communication system. 03103
Document manipulation and typography. § 03182
Touch screen, cursor keys and mouse interaction. 03769
Human-computer interaction: psychonomic aspects. § 03887
Introduction: human-computer interaction: psychonomic aspects. 03888
Speed of response using keyboard and screen-based microcomputer response media. HCI-0192 †
Design and performance considerations for an optical disk-based, multimedia object server. HCI-0265 †
Executive workstations: issues and requirements. HCI-0288 †

*Channels and controllers*

A multiprocessor system for real-time robotic control. 02023
Fuzzy control of a mobile robot for obstacle avoidance. 02025
Manual control of an intrinsically unstable system and its modeling by fuzzy logic. 02026
Convexly combined fuzzy relational equations and several aspects of their application to fuzzy information processing. 02027
A design for a fuzzy logic controller. 02028
Generative transition networks: a new communication control abstraction. 03241
Advanced computing concepts and techniques in control engineering. § 03833
Qualitative modeling of physical systems for knowledge based control. 03834
A design environment for computer-aided control system design via multi-objective optimisation. 03835
Phonetic segmentation using psychoacoustic speech parameters. 03991
Computer recognition of spoken letters and digits. 03995

*Data terminals and printers*

There's more to interaction than meets the eye: Some issues in manual. 0062
Issues and techniques in touch-sensitive tablet input. 0063

## [B. HARDWARE]

Evaluation of mouse, rate-controlled isometric joystick, step keys, and text keys, for text selection on a CRT. 0064
Ergonomics and the new technologies. 0147
Color displays and color science. 0255
Human factors for color display systems: concepts, methods, and research. 0256
Visual parameters for color CRTs. 0257
Human factors reference guide for electronics and computer professionals. ● 0733
Human-computer interaction research at the university of Maryland. 0887
Computing for the blind user. 01287
The workstation: the interpress page and document description language. 01356
The use and misuse of VDU'S. 01375
ISPBXs and terminals. 01385
Guide to the draft American national standard for human factors engineering of visual display terminal workstations. 01549
Trends in printer technology. 01624
Visual terminals and user interfaces. 01686
Optimizing the touch tablet: the effects of control display gain and method of cursor control. 01730
An experimental study of Chinese information displays on VDTs. 01784
Reader-controlled computerized presentation of text. 01785
The dubious dangers of VDT radiation. 01902
Selection devices for users of an electronic encyclopedia: an empirical comparison of four possibilities. 02009
A multi-purpose system for alpha-numeric input to computers via a reduced keyboard. 02118
A comparison of menu selection techniques: touch panel, mouse and keyboard. 02122
Changes in contrast sensitivity function produced by VDT use. 02189
The VDTs are here: health hazard and all. 02439
VDTs: are they safe?. 02549
Technology and the author's labour. 02574
Vidura—an interactive multilingual publishing system—specification & design. 03186
A review of human performance and preferences with different input devices to computer systems. 03231
A gesture based text editor. 03232
Towards the construction of a maximally-contrasting set of colours. 03233
Optimum display arrangements for presenting visual reminders. 03237
Psychological aspects on blind peoples's reading of radio-distributed daily newspapers. 03700
The effect on reading speed of word divisions at the end of a line. 03896
A provisional evaluation of a new chord keyboard, the Velotype. 03907
Systems software tools. ● HCI-0030 †

Digital typography: an introduction to type and composition for computer system design. ● HCI-0074 †
Touch-sensitive screens: the technologies and their application. HCI-0087 †
Cognitive layouts of windows and multiple screens for user interfaces. HCI-0122 †
QWERTY and keyboard reform: the soft keyboard option. HCI-0190 †
Experimental results do not support some ergonomic standards for computer video terminal design. HCI-0428 †

*Image display*

Color displays and color science. 0255
Human factors for color display systems: concepts, methods, and research. 0256
Visual parameters for color CRTs. 0257
Perceptual color spaces for computer graphics. 0258
Ergonomic vision. 0259
Color graphic displays for network planning and design. 0260
Human factors of color displays. 0438
Manipulation of 3D imagery. 0557
The AT&T soft touch-sensitive screen. 01226
Efforts of display format on proof-reading with VDUs. 01246
The 'window' terminal. 01405
Reading from paper versus reading from screen. 01416
VDUs can ruin your health. 01446
Visual terminals and user interfaces. 01686
Reading from microfiche, a VDT, and the printed page: subjective fatigue and performance. 01712
Visual fatigue and spatial frequency adaptation to video displays of text. 01721
Optimizing the touch tablet: the effects of control display gain and method of cursor control. 01730
Reading is slower from CRT displays than from paper: attempts to isolate a single-variable explanation. 01743
Display formatting in information integration and nonintegration tasks. 01750
Effect of pixel height, display height, and vertical resolution on the detection of a simple vertical line signal in visual noise. 01753
Temporal resolution: an insight into the video display terminal (VDT) "problem". 01754
Display proximity in multicue information integration: the benefits of boxes. 01763
Factors affecting the readability of moving text on a computer display. 01764
An experimental study of Chinese information displays on VDTs. 01784
Reader-controlled computerized presentation of text. 01785
Magnification effects with imaging displays depend on scene content and viewing condition. 01786

[B. HARDWARE]                                                                         CATEGORY INDEX

An intelligent braille display device. 01832
A discrete control model of operator function: A methodology for information dislay design. 01874
Are video displays a health hazard?. 01980
From vision science to HDTV: bridging the gap. 01981
Human factors and flat panels challenge the CRT. 01982
CRTs—present and future. 01985
Interactive data visualization. 01986
CRT picture vibration caused by low-frequency magnetic field and its reduction method. 01987
How can computer-based visual displays aid operators?. 02162
Reading from screen versus paper: there is no difference. 02175
Towards the construction of a maximally-contrasting set of colours. 03233
Optimum display arrangements for presenting visual reminders. 03237
Flexible intelligent interactive-video. 03238
Work with display units 86. § 03676
VDTs and health—fact or fancy?. 03677
Health impact of work with visual display terminals. 03678
Determinants of the VDU operator's well-being. 03679
Environmental stressors and perceived health symptoms among office workers. 03680
Repetition strain injury in Australian VDU users. 03681
Eye Fatigue among VDU users and non-VDU users. 03682
Intraocular pressure during VDT work. 03683
Radiation emissions from VDUs. 03684
Health hazards assessment of radio frequency electromagnetic fields emitted by video display terminals. 03685
Pregnancy and VDT work—an evaluation of the state of the art. 03686
Video display terminals—electromagnetic radiation and health. 03687
Birth defect, spontaneous abortion and work with VDUs. 03688
Birth defects, course of pregnancy, and work with VDUs: a Finnish case-referent study. 03689
Pregnancy outcome and VDU-work in a cohort of insurance clerks. 03690
Video display terminals and birth defects. A study of pregnancy outcomes of employees of the Postal-Giro Center, Oslo, Norway. 03691
Task-load and endocrinological risk for pregnancy in women VDU operators. 03692
Some physical factors at VDT work stations and ski problems. 03693
Facial particle exposure in the VDU environment: the role of static electricity. 03694
A Rosacea-like skin rash in VDU-operators. 03695
VDT work and the skin. 03696
Skin paroblems from VDT work-a summary. 03697

Human factors considerations in the design of a VDU for visually impaired persons. 03698
VDU-work and dyslexia. a case report. 03699
Study of visual performance on a multi-color VDU of color defective and normal Trichromatic subjects. 03701
The effect of VDU on the interior design of offices. 03714
Lighting for visual display unit workplaces. 03715
Lighting the display or displaying the lighting. 03716
Lighting the electronic office. 03717
Improving the VDU workplace by introducing a physiologically optimized bright-background screen with dark characters: advantages and requirements. 03721
Display image characteristics and visual response. 03722
Matching display characteristics to human visual capacity. 03723
Criteria for the subjective quality of visual display units. 03724
Colors in video displays. 03725
A colour atlas for graphical displays. 03726
Colour on displays—boon or curse?. 03727
The effect of VDT symbol characteristics on operator performance and visual comfort. 03728
Visual phenomena and their relation to top luminance, phosphor persistence time and contrast polarity. 03729
Temporal and spatial stability in visual displays. 03730
Influence of CRT refresh rates on accommodation after-effects. 03731
Are there subtle changes in vision after use of VDTs?. 03733
Visual impairment and subjective ocular symptomatology in VDT operators. 03734
Effects on visual accommodation and subjective visual discomfort from VDT work intensified through split screen technique. 03735
Is the resting state of our eyes a favorable viewing distance for VDU-work?. 03737
Vision monitoring of VDU operators and relaxation of visual stress by means of a laser speckle system. 03738
VDU work, refractive errors and binocular vision. 03739
Refraction in VDU operators—a comparison with other professions. 03740
Psychosocial work environment and use of visual display terminals:8mfrom theoretical model to action. 03742
Comparison of well-being among non-machine interactive clerical workers and full-time and part-time VDT users and typists. 03745
the role of user prototyping in the system design process. 03747
Analyzing and improving VDU working conditions: workers' education. 03751
Characterization of VDT work. 03754
VDT technology: psychosocial and stress concerns. 03755
A model for evaluating stress effects of work with display units. 03756

The legibility of visual display texts. 03889
The use of color in visual displays. 03890
Visual fatigue with work on visual display units: the current state of knowledge. 03891
Visual comfort as a criterion for designing display units. 03892
Displaying statistical information—ergonomic considerations. 03893
Factors influencing the detection of trend deviations on VDTs. 03894
Visual presentation of text: the process of reading from a psycholinguistic perspective. 03895
The effect on reading speed of word divisions at the end of a line. 03896
Document processing. 03897
Reading text from computer screens. HCI-0088 †
A window-based graphics frame store architecture. HCI-0369 †
Image processing aspects of type. HCI-0403 †
Experimental results do not support some ergonomic standards for computer video terminal design. HCI-0428 †

### Voice

Electronic speech recognition: techniques, technology, and applications. ● 0174
Interfacing standards for recognisers. 0178
Voice messaging enhancing the user interface design based on field performance. 0913
Rapid prototyping and system development: examination of an interface toolkit for voice and telephony applications. 0918
The multimedia object presentation manager of MINOS: a symmetric approach. 01083
An object-oriented approach to multimedia databases. 01084
Computing for the blind user. 01287
The influence of rule-generated stress on computer-synthesized speech. 02081
Man—machine interaction by voice: developments in speech technology. Part I: The state-of-the-art. 02331
Man—machine interaction by voice: developments in speech technology. Part 2: general applications and potential applications in libraries and information services. 02332
An architecture for a multimedia teleconferencing system. 02802
The use of speech in man-machine interaction. 03910
The use of prosodic parameters in automatic speech recognition. 03988
An experimental environment for generating word hypotheses in continuous speech. 03998
Chip talk: projects in speech synthesis. ● HCI-0002 †
Voice-input aids for the physically disabled. HCI-0089 †
Natural language with discrete speech as a mode for human-to-machine. HCI-0355 †

### B.4.3 Interconnections (subsystems)

Authorship provisions in AUGMENT (Reprint). 0370
The CD ROM handbook. ● 0678

### Asynchronous/synchronous operation

Generative transition networks: a new communication control abstraction. 03241

### Interfaces

Human-computer interface design guidelines. ● 0184
The world of GEM. ● 0396
Compact disc–interactive. 0680
Digital video interactive. 0681
Traffic study on primary rate ISDN user-network interface. 01442
Iris: design of a user interface program for symbolic algebra. 03081
MathScribe: a user interface for computer algebra systems. 03082
PowerMath—A system for the Macintosh. 03083
Optimum display arrangements for presenting visual reminders. 03237
Flexible intelligent interactive-video. 03238

### Topology (e.g., bus, point-to-point)

A model for assessing the performance of a local area network employing technical office protocol (TOP) as part of MAP/TOP network in a computer integrated manufacturing (CIM) research project, for the transmission of real time interactive speech. 02491
Advanced computing concepts and techniques in control engineering. § 03833

### B.4.4 Performance Analysis and Design Aids

### Simulation

Fuzzy control of a mobile robot for obstacle avoidance. 02025
Manual control of an intrinsically unstable system and its modeling by fuzzy logic. 02026
Convexly combined fuzzy relational equations and several aspects of their application to fuzzy information processing. 02027

### B.4.5 Reliability, Testing, and Fault-Tolerance

Guide to the draft American national standard for human factors engineering of visual display terminal workstations. 01549
A review of human performance and preferences with different input devices to computer systems. 03231

[B. HARDWARE]  CATEGORY INDEX

*Error-checking*

Integration of graphical tools in a computer algebra system. 03847

## B.6 LOGIC DESIGN

### B.6.0 General

Twenty-five years of electronic design automation. § 03102

### B.6.1 Design Styles

An advisory system for digital logic simulation. 02986
Parcella '88: Fourth International Workshop on Parallel Processing by Cellular Automata and Arrays. § 03971

*Cellular arrays and automata*

Parcella '88: Fourth International Workshop on Parallel Processing by Cellular Automata and Arrays. § 03971

*Combinational logic*

Logic and programming. ● HCI-0068 †

### B.6.2 Reliability and Testing

Parcella '88: Fourth International Workshop on Parallel Processing by Cellular Automata and Arrays. § 03971

*Test generation*

SMARTGEN: the implementation of an expert system for the generation of digital logic diagnostic tests. 02929

### B.6.3 Design Aids

VISION: VHDL induced schematic imaging on net-lists. 02830

**DIF** *see* Proper Noun Index

*Simulation*

An advisory system for digital logic simulation. 02986

### B.6.m Miscellaneous

Reverse engineering the brain. HCI-0368 †

## B.7 INTEGRATED CIRCUITS

Chip talk: projects in speech synthesis. ● HCI-0002 †

### B.7.1 Types and Design Styles

A natural language interface for computer-aided design. ● 0664
Parcella '88: Fourth International Workshop on Parallel Processing by Cellular Automata and Arrays. § 03971

Force and tactile sensing for robots. 04013

*Advanced technologies*

VLSI implementation of a neural network model. 01363
A parallel formant synthesizer for machine voice output. HCI-0396 †

*Algorithms implemented in hardware*

Parallel algorithms and architectures. § 03819

*Memory technologies*

Digital video interactive. 0681
The 'window' terminal. 01405
An overview of research and co-operation in advanced information technology. HCI-0442 †

*Microprocessors and microcomputers*

Digital video interactive. 0681

*VLSI (very large scale integration)*

VLSI image processing. ● 0563
INSIST: Interactive Simulation in Smalltalk. 01119
Architectures of graphic processors for interactive 2D graphics. 01395
Advanced computing concepts and techniques in control engineering. § 03833
Limited interconnectivity in synthetic neural systems. 03968
Integration of robot sensory systems. 04016
One-layer routing without component constraints. HCI-0090 †
An overview of research and co-operation in advanced information technology. HCI-0442 †

### B.7.2 Design Aids

Twenty-five years of electronic design automation. § 03102

*Graphics*

Graphics fundamentals for a PCB-CAD PC system. 02494
Virtual graphics. 02815
A display system for the Stellar Graphics Supercomputer Model GS1000. 02816

*Layout*

A VLSI interactive layout editor (VILE). 02611
One-layer routing without component constraints. HCI-0090 †

*Simulation*

INSIST: Interactive Simulation in Smalltalk. 01119

### B.7.3 Reliability and Testing

An automatic wafer inspection system using pipelined image processing techniques. 01840

### B.7.m Miscellaneous

Reverse engineering the brain. HCI-0368 †

# C. COMPUTER SYSTEMS ORGANIZATION

## C.0 GENERAL

Implications of current design practice for the use of HCI techniques. 03217
Exploring technology: today and tomorrow. § 03491
Fifth generation computer architectures. § 03586
Neural computers. § 03949
Petri nets: applications and relationships to other models of concurrency. § 03973
Relations between cognitive psychology and computer system design. HCI-0244 †
Computer systems software: the programmer/machine interface. ● HCI-0361 †

**Andrew** see Proper Noun Index

**GEM** see Proper Noun Index

*Hardware/software interfaces*

Ergonomic features of interactive systems—the interdependency of software and hardware. 0312
Digital video interactive. 0681
Human computer interaction in the year 2000. 0924
Videotex information packagers: a field study aimed at tomorrow's videotex authoring interface. 0962
The automated solution of logic puzzles. 02015
A unification of software and hardware; a new tool for human thought. 02314
Interfaces for advanced computing. 02578
Concepts in user interfaces: a reference model for command and response languages. § 03872
LisaLearning. HCI-0092 †

*Instruction set design*

INSIST: Interactive Simulation in Smalltalk. 01119

*System architectures*

Intelligent interfaces to Nordic data bases. 0738
Abstract, generic models of interactive systems. 03219

Some experiences in integrating specification of human computer interaction within a structured system development method. 03222
Issues governing the suitability of programming languages for programming tasks. 03224
The integration of the network and relational approaches in a DBMS. 03283
Knowledge-based support of cooperative activities. 03478
TRON Project 1987—Open-architecture computer systems. § 03821
Knowledge based systems for speech understanding. 04001
Fifth generation computers: concepts, implementations and uses. ● HCI-0001 †
Andrew: a distributed personal computing environment. HCI-0091 †

*Systems specification methodology*

Experiences in use of SSADM: series of case studies. Part 1: first time users. 01976
An abstract description generator for the reliability analysis in the design of real time systems. 02490
ATLANTIS—a software simulator for behavior analysis of protocol specifications and their target implementations. 02667
Knowledge base applications with software engineering: a tool for requirements specifications. 02924
Abstract, generic models of interactive systems. 03219
Some experiences in integrating specification of human computer interaction within a structured system development method. 03222
Experimentation in the specification of an oral dialogue. 04005
Cognitive models, cognitive tasks, and information retrieval. HCI-0331 †

## C.1 PROCESSOR ARCHITECTURES

### C.1.0 General

The multimedia object presentation manager of MINOS: a symmetric approach. 01083
A science of information for the information age. 01285
An architecture for a multimedia teleconferencing system. 02802

### C.1.1 Single Data Stream Architectures

**VAM** see Proper Noun Index

**VAX** see Proper Noun Index

### C.1.2 Multiple Data Stream Architectures (Multiprocessors)

Parallel computers for AI databases. 0183

[C. COMPUTER SYSTEMS ORGANIZATION]

Implementing neural network models on parallel computers. 01403
SATURN—a tool for modelling and performance evaluation of computer systems. 02670
A dataflow-based APL for the hypercube. 02905
Hypercube Concurrent Computers and Applications; vol. 2. § 02908
Multiprocessor Smalltalk: a case study of a multiprocessor-based programming environment. 03061
Parcella '88: Fourth International Workshop on Parallel Processing by Cellular Automata and Arrays. § 03971

*Array and vector processors*

A display system for the Stellar Graphics Supercomputer Model GS1000. 02816

*Associative processors*

Pixel-planes 4: a summary. 0495
An architecture of a distributed window system and its FCP implementation. 0676

*Interconnection architectures (e.g., common bus, multiport memory, crosbar switch)*

A multiprocessor system for real-time robotic control. 02023
An interface architecture to provide adaptive task-specific context for the user. 02228
Monitoring and performance measuring distributed systems during operation. 03025
Advanced computing concepts and techniques in control engineering. § 03833
Limited interconnectivity in synthetic neural systems. 03968
Real-time large vocabulary word recognition via diphone spotting and multiprocessor implementation. 03996
Culture, cognitive, and connectionism: Towards an hermeneutic anthropology of mind. 04077

*Multiple-instruction-stream, multiple-data-stream processors (MIMD)*

An integrated system for neural network simulations. 0771
Line connectivity algorithms for an asynchronous pyramid computer. 01468
HORSE: a simulation of the horizon supercomputer. 03541

*Parallel processors*

A two-dimensional frame buffer processor. 0494
On language and connectionism: analysis of a parallel distributed processing model of language acquisition. 0590
Parallel distributed processing: explorations in the microstructures of cognition; Vol. 2: Psychological and biological models. ● 0629
Schemata and sequential thought processes in PDP models. 0630
Reflections on cognition and parallel distributed. 0642
Nueral & massively parallel computers: the sixth generation. ● 0702
High-performance polygon rendering. 02814
Hypercube Concurrent Computers and Applications. § 02904
Interactive performance display and debugging using the NCUBE real-time graphicssystem. 02907
Structured message passing on a shared-memory multiprocessor. 03514
Parallel algorithms and architectures. § 03819
Advanced computing concepts and techniques in control engineering. § 03833
Real-time large vocabulary word recognition via diphone spotting and multiprocessor implementation. 03996
The architecture of fifth generation inference computers. HCI-0093 †

*Pipeline processors*

A development environment for horizontal microcode programs. 01079
An automatic wafer inspection system using pipelined image processing techniques. 01840

**VAX** *see* Proper Noun Index

### C.1.3 Other Architecture Styles

Experience with a functional layered multicomputer architecture for interactive processing. 02402
Knowledge base enhancements to relational databases. 03285
Fifth generation computer architectures. § 03586
The architecture of fifth generation inference computers. HCI-0093 †
O-Plan: control in the open planning architecture. HCI-0362 †

*Cellular architecture*

Parallel in sequence—towards the architecture of an elementary cortical processor. 03820
Parcella '88: Fourth International Workshop on Parallel Processing by Cellular Automata and Arrays. § 03971
A window-based graphics frame store architecture. HCI-0369 †

*Data-flow architectures*

A development environment for horizontal microcode programs. 01079
Software development approach in FMS. 01567

An architecture for a business and information system. 01818

Nested window flow controls with packet fragmentation. 04055

The architecture of fifth generation inference computers. HCI-0093 †

**Soar** *see* Proper Noun Index

### C.1.m Miscellaneous

Neural computers in vision: processing of high dimensional data. 03960

Exploring three possibilities in network design: spontaneous node activity, node plasticity and temporal coding. 03962

Tensor geometry: a language of brains & neurocomputers. Generalized coordinates in neuroscience & robotics. 03966

Dynamical properties of a new type of neural network. 03969

Control of the immune response. 03970

### *Analog computers*

Early vision: from computational structure to algorithms and parallel hardware. HCI-0365 †

### *Hybrid systems*

A model for assessing the performance of a local area network employing technical office protocol (TOP) as part of MAP/TOP network in a computer integrated manufacturing (CIM) research project, for the transmission of real time interactive speech. 02491

Recent advances in speech understanding and dialog systems. § 03987

Speaker-independent automatic recognition of plosive sound in letters and digits. 03993

## C.2 COMPUTER-COMMUNICATION NETWORKS

### C.2.0 General

Functional environments for microcomputers in education. 0578

Session on the requirements of international user groups. 01431

An interdisciplinary approach to human factors in telematic systems. A review of the problems and possible solutions by a COST-11 ter working group. 01440

Document manipulation and typography. § 03182

Networks in office automation. § 03637

Advanced computing concepts and techniques in control engineering. § 03833

Applicable algebra, error-correcting codes, combinatorics and computer algebra. § 03846

The design of the UNIX operating system. ● HCI-0026 †

Access to academic networks. ● HCI-0050 †

Communications design for Co-oP: a group decision support system. HCI-0297 †

Expert systems—where do we go from here?. HCI-0318 †

An overview of research and co-operation in advanced information technology. HCI-0442 †

### *Data communications*

Intelligence and the man-machine interface. 0363

Principles of data communication. ● 0547

The diffusion and impacts of information technology in households. 0754

Learning modes and subsequent use of computer-mediated communication systems. 0912

Live-Net in education. 01381

A formal specification of the QMS message system: the underlying abstract model. 01406

The telephone in question: questions on communication. 01436

Traffic study on primary rate ISDN user-network interface. 01442

Traffic study on primary rate ISDN user-network interface. 01442

A computing service using linked minis. 01674

Common user access—a consistent and usable human-computer interface for the SAA environments. 01819

Enabling the user interface. 01820

Designing SAA applications and user interfaces. 01821

Emerging communications technology paradigms. 02320

SATURN—a tool for modelling and performance evaluation of computer systems. 02670

Understanding cable subscribership as telecommunications behavior. 02676

Interaction of CMC with video telecourses for distance education. 02677

Electronic communications and collaboration: the emerging model for computer aided communications in science and medicine. 02678

Communications technology and the public sector: understanding the process of adoption. 02679

The ISA expert system: a prototype system for failure diagnosis on the space station. 02913

Experience of constructing a fault localisation expert system using an AI toolkit. 02923

Tele-cybernetics: implications for the international marketplace. 03458

Automated document distribution using AI based workstations and knowledge based servers. 03466

The space station information system and software support environment. 03512

The design of a flexible distributed testbeb for communication systems. 03538

Personal computing for decision support. HCI-0299 †

[C. COMPUTER SYSTEMS ORGANIZATION]

Visual structure and the transmission of meaning. HCI-0404 †

**ISDN** *see* Proper Noun Index

*Open System Interconnection reference model (OSI)*

UNIX system V: release 3.0 Intel 80286/80386 computer version: system administrator's guide. ● 0031
Innovations in Internetworking. ● 0573
BNETD—A modelling tool to computer systems performance evaluation. 02668
DEC networks and architectures. ● HCI-0003 †

*Security and protection*

Computer crime. ● 0722
Networks without user observability. 01545
Computer security: a global challenge. § 03577

**C.2.1 Network Architecture and Design**

Color graphic displays for network planning and design. 0260
Principles of data communication. ● 0547
SATURN—a tool for modelling and performance evaluation of computer systems. 02670
Hypercube Concurrent Computers and Applications. § 02904
Interactive performance display and debugging using the NCUBE real-time graphicssystem. 02907
Measurement and Modeling of Computer Systems. § 03024
The history of personal workstations. § 03091
Toward a history of (personal) workstations. 03092
XVISION: a comprehensive software system for image processing research, education, and applications. 03124
DEC networks and architectures. ● HCI-0003 †
Andrew: a distributed personal computing environment. HCI-0091 †

*Centralized networks*

High-speed computing: scientific applications and algorithm design. ● 0727

*Circuit switching networks*

The design of a traffic control expert system for long distance network contingencies. 02952
Architectural implications of office systems. 03356

*Distributed networks*

A history of personal workstations. ● 0347
Innovations in Internetworking. ● 0573
The computational science revolution: technology, methodology, and sociology. 0728

A communication mechanism supporting actions. 01441
ATLANTIS—a software simulator for behavior analysis of protocol specificationsand their target implementations. 02667
Management of distributed applications in large networks. 03515
Advanced computing concepts and techniques in control engineering. § 03833
Experiences with Distributed Systems. § 03881
Experiences with the development of a portable network operating system. 03882

**Ethernet** *see* Proper Noun Index

*Network communications*

Toward high-performance knowledge workers (Reprint). 0369
Social psychological aspects of computer-mediated communication (Reprint). 0384
The design of a traffic control expert system for long distance network contingencies. 02952
An overview of the C toolkit. 03109
A communication system supporting large datagrams on a local area network. HCI-0166 †
A distributed interoffice mail system. HCI-0308 †

*Network topology*

Study of combination of belief intevals in lattice-structured networks. 02223
Control of sensory processing - a hypothesis on and simulation of the architecture of an elementary cortical processor. 03972

**OSI** *see* Proper Noun Index

*Packet networks*

Authorship provisions in AUGMENT (Reprint). 0370
Innovations in Internetworking. ● 0573
A model for assessing the performance of a local area network employing technical office protocol (TOP) as part of MAP/TOP network in a computer integrated manufacturing (CIM) research project, for the transmission of real time interactive speech. 02491
Architectural implications of office systems. 03356
The space station information system and software support environment. 03512
Nested window flow controls with packet fragmentation. 04055

*Store and forward networks*

A graphics interface for interactive simulation of packet-switched networks. 03869

## [C. COMPUTER SYSTEMS ORGANIZATION]

### C.2.2 Network Protocols

X Protocol reference manual for version II: vol. 0. ● 0669
A substrate for object-oriented interface design. 0691
On the interface between the high level languages and Chinese character information. 01451
ISDN and the move to integrated communications—an introduction. 01455
Why users must co-operate internationally on standardization. 01457
Layered protocols for computer-human dialogue. 1: principles. 02195
Layered protocols for computer-human dialogue. 11: some practical issues. 02196
A model for assessing the performance of a local area network employing technical office protocol (TOP) as part of MAP/TOP network in a computer integrated manufacturing (CIM) research project, for the transmission of real time interactive speech. 02491
ATLANTIS—a software simulator for behavior analysis of protocol specifications and their target implementations. 02667
The measurement of the performance of communications protocols from the user's viewpoint. 02684
Communications and architecture & protocols. § 02801
Iris: design of a user interface program for symbolic algebra. 03081
An overview of the C toolkit. 03109
An implementation of OSI protocols in SM-4 host computers. 03638
DEC networks and architectures. ● HCI-0003 †

#### Protocol architecture

Innovations in Internetworking. ● 0573
Communications and architecture & protocols. § 02801
The design of a flexible distributed testbeb for communication systems. 03538
Experiences with the development of a portable network operating system. 03882

#### Protocol verification

Attacking a complex distributed algorithm from different sides: an experience wih complementary validation tools. 01429

**TCP/IP** *see* Proper Noun Index

### C.2.3 Network Operations

What users want. 01443

#### Network management

Innovations in Internetworking. ● 0573
The network control assistant (NCA), a real-time prototype expert system for network management. 02930
Knowledge-based interface to manufacturing computer systems. 02966

#### Network monitoring

The effects of communication monitors on user satisfaction. HCI-0221 †

### C.2.4 Distributed Systems

On language and connectionism: analysis of a parallel distributed processing model of language acquisition. 0590
Resource management scheme in distributed environments. 01018
Monitoring and performance measuring distributed systems during operation. 03025
Personal distributed computing: the Alto and Ethernet software. 03096
Experiences with Distributed Systems. § 03881
Andrew: a distributed personal computing environment. HCI-0091 †
Using low-cost workstations to investigate computer networks and distributed systems. HCI-0437 †

#### Distributed applications

Distributed systems, Vol. II: distributed data base systems. ● 0217
Innovations in Internetworking. ● 0573
Diamond: A multimedia message system built on a distributed architecture. 0574
Parallel distributed processing: explorations in the microstructures of cognition; Vol. 2: Psychological and biological models. ● 0629
Schemata and sequential thought processes in PDP models. 0630
Reflections on cognition and parallel distributed. 0642
The profile naming service. 01149
A communication mechanism supporting actions. 01441
What users want. 01443
Edmas: an object-oriented, locally distributed mail system. 01857
Power plant simulation using a distributed control system. 02057
An overview of the C toolkit. 03109
Using distributed simulation for distributed application development. 03500
Management of distributed applications in large networks. 03515
Extending the DARTS software design method to distributed real time applications. 03516
Grand computer conferencing: What have we learned?. 03536
The design of a flexible distributed testbeb for communication systems. 03538
A programmable interface language for heterogeneous distributed systems. HCI-0094 †

[C. COMPUTER SYSTEMS ORGANIZATION]

Monitoring distributed systems. HCI-0169 †
An experimental multimedia mail system. HCI-0309 †

### Distributed databases

Beyond the chalkboard: computer support for collaboration and problem solving in meetings (Reprint). 0376
Computer-based real-time conferencing systems (Reprint). 0377
Diamond: a multimedia message system built on a distributed architecture (Reprint). 0380
The profile naming service. 01149

### Network operating systems

A communication mechanism supporting actions. 01441
Traffic study on primary rate ISDN user-network interface. 01442
A model for assessing the performance of a local area network employing technical office protocol (TOP) as part of MAP/TOP network in a computer integrated manufacturing (CIM) research project, for the transmission of real time interactive speech. 02491
BNETD—A modelling tool to computer systems performance evaluation. 02668
The KOMPLEX performance prediction tool. 02669
SATURN—a tool for modelling and performance evaluation of computer systems. 02670
Generative transition networks: a new communication control abstraction. 03241
Advanced computing concepts and techniques in control engineering. § 03833
A programmable interface language for heterogeneous distributed systems. HCI-0094 †

### C.2.5 Local Networks

An experiment in integrated multimedia conferencing. 0381
User behaviour in computer networked groups. 0473
Symbiotic software: development and usage issues on stand-alone and networked systems. 0474
Innovations in Internetworking. ● 0573
Innovations in Internetworking. ● 0573
Communication analysis in the company. 01435
Edmas: an object-oriented, locally distributed mail system. 01857
A model for assessing the performance of a local area network employing technical office protocol (TOP) as part of MAP/TOP network in a computer integrated manufacturing (CIM) research project, for the transmission of real time interactive speech. 02491
BNETD—A modelling tool to computer systems performance evaluation. 02668
SATURN—a tool for modelling and performance evaluation of computer systems. 02670
Personal distributed computing: the Alto and Ethernet hardware. 03095

Local area networks: sailing from the past to the present and into the future. 03152
A suppport strategy for users of a campus-wide local area network. 03157
Segue: Support for distributed graphical interfaces. 03526
Experiences with the development of a portable network operating system. 03882
Andrew: a distributed personal computing environment. HCI-0091 †
A communication system supporting large datagrams on a local area network. HCI-0166 †
gIBIS: a hypertext tool for exploratory policy discussion. HCI-0300 †

### Access schemes

Diamond: A multimedia message system built on a distributed architecture. 0574
Grand computer conferencing: What have we learned?. 03536
Access to academic networks. ● HCI-0050 †

### Rings

The ring machine. 01483

## C.3 SPECIAL-PURPOSE AND APPLICATION-BASED SYSTEMS (J.7)

Distributed Artificial Intelligence. ● 0168
Knowledge-based support of cooperative activities. 0171
Annual review of computer science vol. 1, 1986. ● 0719
Digital typography: an introduction to type and composition for computer system design. ● HCI-0074 †

### Microprocessor/Microcomputer applications

Managers, micros and mainframes: an introduction. 0456
An historical perspective of CD ROM. 0679
Computers : the user perspective. ● 0705
The diffusion and impacts of information technology in households. 0754
End-user searching—What are the implications?. 01224
Information retrieval using micros. 01225
Microcomputer applications: an empirical look at usage. 01949
Interactive video: vol. 1. ● HCI-0081 †
Design of computer programs for the physically handicapped. HCI-0096 †
A dedicated microcomputer for handwritten interaction with a software tool: system prototyping. HCI-0119 †

### Process control systems

Power plant simulation using a distributed control system. 02057

A model for assessing the performance of a local area network employing technical office protocol (TOP) as part of MAP/TOP network in a computer integrated manufacturing (CIM) research project, for the transmission of real time interactive speech. 02491
Advanced computing concepts and techniques in control engineering. § 03833

### Real-time systems

Real-time interfacing: engineering aspects of microprocessor peripheral systems. ● 0224
History in the making: a report from Microsoft's First International Conference on CD ROM. 0279
Anticipating compact disc-interactive (CD-I): ten guidelines for prospective authors. 0280
CD ROM joins the new media homesteaders. 0281
A multi-processor workstation with a logic-enhanced distributed frame buffer. 0496
Designing real-time, decision support computer-human interaction. 0982
An object-oriented approach to the design of a mail system for a heterogeneous environment. 01944
A multiprocessor system for real-time robotic control. 02023
An abstract description generator for the reliability analysis in the design of real time systems. 02490
A model for assessing the performance of a local area network employing technical office protocol (TOP) as part of MAP/TOP network in a computer integrated manufacturing (CIM) research project, for the transmission of real time interactive speech. 02491
ATLANTIS—a software simulator for behavior analysis of protocol specificationsand their target implementations. 02667
The myth of the infinitely fast machine. 03204
Abstract, generic models of interactive systems. 03219
Real-time object measurement and classification. § 03985

### Signal processing systems

Dynamics and architecture for neural computation. 02270
Recollections on the processing of biomedical signals. 02846
Advanced computing concepts and techniques in control engineering. § 03833
Factors influencing the detection of trend deviations on VDTs. 03894
Recent advances in speech understanding and dialog systems. § 03987
The use of prosodic parameters in automatic speech recognition. 03988
Prosodic features in German speech: stress assignment by man and machine. 03989
Phonetic segmentation using psychoacoustic speech parameters. 03991

Experimentation in the specification of an oral dialogue. 04005
The central nervous system as a low and high level control system. 04007
Proprioceptive feedback for sensory-motor control. 04008
Analogs of biological tissues for mechanoelectrical transduction: tactile sensors and muscle-like actuators. 04014
Integration of robot sensory systems. 04016
Signal processing and pattern recognition in nondestructive evaluation of materials. § 04019
The effects of limited data in multi-frequency reflection diffraction tomography. 04020
Parameter estimation in array processing. 04021

## C.4 PERFORMANCE OF SYSTEMS

Setting up an interactive videodisc project. 0502
Producing resource discs—the Domesday project experience. 0514
Annual review of computer science vol. 1, 1986. ● 0719
Instrumenting systems to measure components of interactive response times. 01230
VLSI implementation of a neural network model. 01363
Architectures of graphic processors for interactive 2D graphics. 01395
A user view of virtual terminal standardisation. 01432
Networks without user observability. 01545
CRTs—present and future. 01985
Experience with a functional layered multicomputer architecture for interactive processing. 02402
Datastream: numeric data—all you can use at a fixed price. 02525
Neural network models of learning and adaptation. 02560
Performance evaluation of simulators. 02663
Design Automation. § 02828
The myth of the infinitely fast machine. 03204
Advanced computing concepts and techniques in control engineering. § 03833
HutWindows: an improved architecture for a user interface management system. 03854
Conventional fault-tolerance and neural computers. 03951
Why cortices? Neural computation in the vertebrate visual system. 03956
Neural computers in vision: processing of high dimensional data. 03960
Neural networks for motor program generation. 03964
Limited interconnectivity in synthetic neural systems. 03968
Performance and computer-aided design. ● HCI-0068 †

### Design studies

The look and feel . . . and sound of the user interface. 01315

[C. COMPUTER SYSTEMS ORGANIZATION]

Initial work on a system-independent computer model of a 3D anthropomorphic dummy. 01476
The lure of molecular computing. 01833
Coping with human errors through system design: implications for ecological interface design. 02254
A model for assessing the performance of a local area network employing technical office protocol (TOP) as part of MAP/TOP network in a computer integrated manufacturing (CIM) research project, for the transmission of real time interactive speech. 02491
Implications of current design practice for the use of HCI techniques. 03217
User-driven adaptive behaviour, a comparative evaluation and an inductive analysis. 03226
Towards the construction of a maximally-contrasting set of colours. 03233
People and computers: designing for usability. 03245
A design environment for computer-aided control system design via multi-objective optimisation. 03835
Dynamical properties of a new type of neural network. 03969
Text processing by speech: dialogue design and usability issues in the provision of a system for disabled users. HCI-0357 †

### Measurement techniques

Performance measurement during simulated air-to-air combat. 01787
An abstract description generator for the reliability analysis in the design of real time systems. 02490
BNETD—A modelling tool to computer systems performance evaluation. 02668
The KOMPLEX performance prediction tool. 02669
Measurement and Modeling of Computer Systems. § 03024
Monitoring and performance measuring distributed systems during operation. 03025
Can cognitive complexity theory (CCT) produce an adequate measure of system usability?. 03229
Teleoperations and robotics: applications and technology. ● HCI-0068 †
A communication system supporting large datagrams on a local area network. HCI-0166 †

### Modeling techniques

Traffic study on primary rate ISDN user-network interface. 01442
Performance measurement during simulated air-to-air combat. 01787
The application of metaphor, analogy, and conceptual models in computer systems. 02070
Design goals for sloppy modeling systems. 02206
A model for assessing the performance of a local area network employing technical office protocol (TOP) as part of MAP/TOP network in a computer integrated manufacturing (CIM) research project, for the transmission of real time interactive speech. 02491
Modelling 8-bit microprocessors for a general-purpose simulator. 02499
BNETD—A modelling tool to computer systems performance evaluation. 02668
The KOMPLEX performance prediction tool. 02669
SATURN—a tool for modelling and performance evaluation of computer systems. 02670
Measurement and Modeling of Computer Systems. § 03024
Measuring user satisfaction. 03230
Using distributed simulation for distributed application development. 03500
Simulation. § 03501
Factors influencing the detection of trend deviations on VDTs. 03894
Nets in office automation. 03975
Computer recognition of spoken letters and digits. 03995

### Performance attributes

Understanding the elements of system design. 0156
Digital video interactive. 0681
The influence of rule-generated stress on computer-synthesized speech. 02081
A generic strategy for diagnostic assistance: the technician's assistant. 02957
Measurement and Modeling of Computer Systems. § 03024
Monitoring and performance measuring distributed systems during operation. 03025
Performance evaluation of three pressure mats as robot workstation safety sensors. 03428
A design environment for computer-aided control system design via multi-objective optimisation. 03835
What makes users happy?. HCI-0427 †

### Reliability, availability, and serviceability

An abstract description generator for the reliability analysis in the design of real time systems. 02490
ATLANTIS—a software simulator for behavior analysis of protocol specificationsand their target implementations. 02667
SPA: a systems for diagnosis of computer performance problems. 02969
Applications of qualitative modeling to knowledge-based risk assessment studies. 02970
A computer assisted learning system for reliability engineering. 04060
The effects of communication monitors on user satisfaction. HCI-0221 †
Training for optimising transfer between word processors. HCI-0447 †

## C.5 COMPUTER SYSTEM IMPLEMENTATION

### C.5.0 General

Service support levels: An organizational approach to end-user computing. 02503
TRON Project 1987—Open-architecture computer systems. § 03821
Advanced computing concepts and techniques in control engineering. § 03833

### C.5.1 Large and Medium ("Mainframe") Computers

IBM 3270 full screen interactive programming without CICS. 01040
An informal overview of CUINFO (Cornell's computer-based bulletin board). 02783

**CRAY-1** *see* Proper Noun Index

**CRAY X-MP** *see* Proper Noun Index

**IBM System/370** *see* Proper Noun Index

*Super (very large) computers*

High-speed computing: scientific applications and algorithm design. ● 0727
The computational science revolution: technology, methodology, and sociology. 0728
Coherent and chaotic structures in 2D vortex dynamics: progress and problems. 0729
Computing needs in thunderstorm modeling: supercomputers and interactive graphics. 0730
Supercomputers in the classroom. 01577
From user to client services; making the transition for supercomputing. 03138
Learning the ways: the enculturation of SDSC users. 03144
Super consulting for supercomputer users: a philosophy of user support. 03145
Information in the air and in the wave. 03146
Supercomputer applications: helping users cope with tough programming problems. 03147
Supercomputing '88. § 03540
HORSE: a simulation of the horizon supercomputer. 03541
Interactive scientific visualization and parallel display techniques. 03542
Design and implementation of a supercomputer frame buffer system. 03543
Parcella '88: Fourth International Workshop on Parallel Processing by Cellular Automata and Arrays. § 03971
An investigation of the effectiveness of communication between systems analysts and end users in the design of large computer systems. 04075

### C.5.2 Minicomputers

A history of the promis technology: an effective human interface. 0349

### C.5.3 Microcomputers

ISPF: the strategic dailog manager. ● 0035
Management, organizations and the new technologies. 0145
Interactive workstations. ● 0216
A history of personal workstations. ● 0347
Computer-supported cooperative work: a book of readings. ● 0366
Authoring systems for ICAI. 0469
Keyboarding for personal computer use. ● 0492
Advanced interactive COBOL for micros: a practical approach. ● 0522
The microcomputer as a symbolic medium. 0583
Pupils, computers and history teaching. 0746
A personal computer based graphic workstation. 02493
Graphics fundamentals for a PCB-CAD PC system. 02494
'Transparent' interfacing of speech recognizers to microcomputers. 02497
Affect-chaining and dependency oriented flow analysis applied to queries of programs. 02789
ALIEN: a programming environment generator for personal computers. 02790
A user interface for database creation use and maintenance. 02791
Iconic shells for multitasking workstations. 02792
PowerMath—A system for the Macintosh. 03083
The evolution of microcomputer laboratory services at the University of Notre Dame. 03159
Chinese character processing system based on character-root combination and gra phic processing. 03187
A biparty grammar as a tool for defining a man-machine dialogue. 03639
User involvement with microcomputer software. 04063

**Apple** *see* Proper Noun Index

**IBM PC** *see* Proper Noun Index

**Intel 80386** *see* Proper Noun Index

*Microprocessors*

Real-time interfacing: engineering aspects of microprocessor peripheral systems. ● 0224
Modelling 8-bit microprocessors for a general-purpose simulator. 02499
A compact model of a power house boiler. 02683
Operating system design. Vol. 1: the XINU approach (PC edition). ● HCI-0029 †

Motorola 68000 *see* Proper Noun Index

### C.5.4 VLSI Systems

VLSI for solid modelling. 0232
VLSI architectures for implementation of neural networks. 02762
Display architecture for VLSI-based graphics workstations. 03786
Knowledge representation techniques in artificial intelligence: an overview. 03900
Conventional fault-tolerance and neural computers. 03951
Neural computers in vision: processing of high dimensional data. 03960
Sensors and sensory systems for advanced robots. § 04006
Active vision: integration of fixed and mobile cameras. 04017
A window-based graphics frame store architecture. HCI-0369 †

### C.5.m Miscellaneous

High performance neural networks. 02313

### C.m MISCELLANEOUS

The FAIM-1 user interface—human engineering for the fifth generation. 03587
Structured neural networks in nature and in computer science. 03950
Conventional fault-tolerance and neural computers. 03951

# D. SOFTWARE

## D.0 GENERAL

Research directions in object-oriented programming. ● 0690
Evaluation of mental models and meta models through interactions between users and helpers about software usage problems. 0972
Profile of undergraduate software engineering courses: results from a survey. 01035
ACM SIGUCCS User Services Conference XIV. 01925
APL in transition. § 02793
Object-oriented programming systems, languages and applications. § 03030
People and computers III. § 03189
Exploring technology: today and tomorrow. § 03491
ECOOP '87. § 03790
ESEC '87. § 03795

Logic programming '86. § 03816

## D.1 PROGRAMMING TECHNIQUES (E.)

### D.1.0 General

The psychological study of programming. 0053
OS/2 programming: an introduction. ● 0670
Programming the Macintosh User Interface. ● 0698
VAX-BASIC with structured problem solving: 2nd edition. ● 0725
Advanced Turbo C programming. ● 0726
Intelligent help systems. 01959
Programmer perceptions of productivity and programming tools. HCI-0099 †

### D.1.1 Applicative (Functional) Programming

Functional databases, functional languages. 0034
Computer aided application program synthesis for industrial robots. 0606
Dialogues: a basis for constructing programming environments. 01097
A semantic editor. 01101
An environment for logic programming. 01106
A model and an implementation of a logic programming environment. 01107
Synchronizing the I/O behavior of functional programs with feedback. 02016
A foundation for programming environments. 03057

### D.1.2 Automatic Programming (I.2.2)

Creating highly-interactive and graphical user interfaces by demonstration. 0084
The programmer's apprentices: a research overview. 01368
Automated construction of interactive learning programs in Modula-2. 01500
A visual programming language designed for automatic programming. 03529
Analogical program synthesis from program components. 03920

### D.1.3 Concurrent Programming

Directions in object-oriented research. 0477
Non-intrusive and interactive profiling in parasight. 01123
A dataflow-based APL for the hypercube. 02905
DIME: a programming environment for unstructured triangular meshes on a distributed-memory parallel processor. 02909
A foundation for programming environments. 03057
Debugging concurrent processes: a case study. 03060
Design principles behind Chiron: a UIMS for software environments. 03511

CATEGORY INDEX [D. SOFTWARE]

The PFG environment: parallel programming with petri net semantics. 03527
A debugger for concurrent programs. HCI-0142 †
Monitoring distributed systems. HCI-0169 †

**CSP** *see* Proper Noun Index

### D.1.4 Sequential Programming

Mental gymnastics of sequential programming. 01971

### D.1.m Miscellaneous

Design of knowledge-based systems with a knowledge-based assistant. 01853
An input/output primitive for object-oriented systems. 01969
A Unix distributed application support suitable for mini and microcomputer based systems. 02489
Impulse-86: a substrate for object-oriented interface design. 03032
Encapsulators: a new software paradigm in Smalltalk-80. 03034
The construction of user interfaces and the object paradigm. 03791
Icon semantics—a formal approach to icon system design. HCI-0161 †

### D.2 SOFTWARE ENGINEERING (K.6.3)

Exploring artificial intelligence. ● 0692
A multiple, virtual-workspace interface to support user task switching. 0813
Some strategies of reuse in an object-oriented programming environment. 0820
A case study of user interface management system development and application. 0836
Graphical specification of user interfaces with behavior abstraction. 0840

### D.2.0 General (K.5.1)

Object-oriented concepts, databases, and applications. ● 0475
Directions in object-oriented research. 0477
Thomas W. Malone, Oct. 5: user interface strategies '88. ● 0592
Informing the design of software through context-based research. 0584
Readings in artificial intelligence and software engineering. ● 0612
Oxford surveys in information technology; vol. 2, 1985. ● 0755
A study of an advance organizer as a technique for teaching computer programming concepts. 01042
Characteristics and functions of software environments: an overview. 01145

Teaching software engineering at university. 01968
Cognitive systems engineering: new wine in new bottles. 02078
Measuring change in the programming process. 02242
Motivation norms of knowledge engineers compared to those of software engineers. 02349
A user interface for database creation use and maintenance. 02791
Software engineering meets user services: a methodology for developing user. 03141
Document manipulation and typography. § 03182
People and computers IV. § 03215
Theory and practice of software technology. § 03361
Simulation. § 03501
Software Engineering. § 03504
Software Track. § 03513
Advanced programming environments. § 03779
Visualization in programming. 5th Interdisciplinary Workshop in Informatics and. § 03826
Software Engineering Education. § 04022
The art of programming. HCI-0095 †
Design of computer programs for the physically handicapped. HCI-0096 †
Programmer/nonprogrammer differences in specifying procedures to people and computers. HCI-0174 †
The Japanese and software: is it a good match?. HCI-0429 †

*Protection mechanisms*

Configuring stand-alone smalltalk-80 applications. 01129

*Standards*

The standards factor. 0965
Goals and objectives for user interface software. 01056
Ergonomic guidelines for computerized user interfaces. 01449
Lessons from the MOSI project. 01450
A map of the world of software-related standards, guidelines, and recommended practices. 01453

### D.2.1 Requirements/Specifications (D.3.1)

A book on C. ● 0143
The evolution of interface requirements for expert systems. 0431
Transformations on a formal specification of user-computer interfaces. 01062
On formalisms. 01280
User interface design from a real time perspective. 01323
The programmer's apprentices: a research overview. 01368
Comments on "formal specification of user interfaces: a comparison and evaluation of four axiomatic approaches". 01847
The application of human factors to the needs of the novice computer user. 02079

## [D. SOFTWARE]

An interactive environment for tool selection, specification and composition. 02141
Cognitive issues in the process of software development: review and reappraisal. 02222
An abstract description generator for the reliability analysis in the design of real time systems. 02490
Knowledge base applications with software engineering: a tool for requirements specifications. 02924
Express—rapid prototyping and product development via integrated knowledge-based executable specifications. 03492
Supporting flexible and efficient tool integration. 03783
SPECIF-X: a tool for CASE. 03801
Software tools for the development of pictorial information systems in medicine—the ISQL experience. 03980
A formal specification for a user interface for office automation. 04053
User-centered requirements analysis. ● HCI-0004 †
Storyboard prototyping: a new approach to user requirements analysis. ● HCI-0005 †
Formally-based tools and techniques for human-computer dialogues. ● HCI-0021 †
Planning and design of information systems. ● HCI-0045 †
An approach to user specification of interactive display interfaces. HCI-0137 :8E
The PegaSys System: pictures as formal documentation of large programs. HCI-0146 †
Extending state transition diagrams for the specification of human-computer interaction. HCI-0191 †
Specification and verification of database dynamics. HCI-0251 †
Electronic calendars in the office: an assessment of user needs and current technology. HCI-0287 †

**ACT/1** *see* Proper Noun Index

### Languages

Intelligent interfaces to Nordic data bases. 0738
Resource management scheme in distributed environments. 01018
Evaluation and intergration of specification languages. 01430
ATLANTIS—a software simulator for behavior analysis of protocol specificationsand their target implementations. 02667
A processing system for program specifications in a natural language. 03537
IDL: past experience and new ideas. 03782
VDM—The Way Ahead. § 04033
The use of VDM on the specification of Chinese characters. 04038
User-oriented computer languages: analysis and design. ● HCI-0019 †

Ada-based executable modelling of distributed systems. HCI-0098 †
A specification language for direct-manipulation user interfaces. HCI-0123 †
Specification and generation of variable, personalized graphical interfaces. HCI-0134 †

**CCS** *see* Proper Noun Index

### Methodologies

The psychological study of programming. 0053
A coherent specification method for the human interface to documentation systems. 0269
Tools and methodology for user interface development. 01057
Constraint hierarchies. 01114
Towards the formal specification of a simple programming support environment. 02607
Abstract, generic models of interactive systems. 03219
The representation of user interface style. 03221
Some experiences in integrating specification of human computer interaction within a structured system development method. 03222
Generative transition networks: a new communication control abstraction. 03241
User requirements for expert system explanation: what, why and when?. 03242
A support system for formal reasoning: requirements and status. 04035
Information systems design methodologies and their compliance with cognitive ergonomy. HCI-0097 †
Ada-based executable modelling of distributed systems. HCI-0098 †
gIBIS: a hypertext tool for exploratory policy discussion. HCI-0300 †
Customers' requirements for natural language systems: results of an inquiry. HCI-0426 †

**PSL** *see* Proper Noun Index

### Tools

Tools and methodology for user interface development. 01057
Bibliography of software tools for user interface development. 01071
Emeraude portable common tool environment. 01970
INTERA/P: a user interface prototyping tool. 03205
MacCadd - an enabling software method support tool. 03252
The database designer's workbench. HCI-0249 †
gIBIS: a hypertext tool for exploratory policy discussion. HCI-0300 †

# CATEGORY INDEX

[D. SOFTWARE]

## D.2.2 Tools and Techniques

Software psychology: the need for an interdisciplinary program. 0052
The psychological study of programming. 0053
Authorship provisions in AUGMENT (Reprint). 0370
Cognitive impacts of the user interface. 0432
Hypertext hands-on!: an introduction to a new way of organizing and accessing information. ● 0686
The enhancement of understanding through visual representations. 0898
A transfer of skill between programming languages. 01015
The Mesa programming environment. 01108
Non-intrusive and interactive profiling in parasight. 01123
On interface requirements for expert systems. 01198
A FORTRAN input program generator. 01227
User interface design from a real time perspective. 01323
Non-strict languages-programming and implementation. 01418
Software development approach in FMS. 01567
Authoring considerations for hypertext. 01679
Software engineering for user interfaces. 01854
Interactive documentation. 02612
BNETD—A modelling tool to computer systems performance evaluation. 02668
SATURN—a tool for modelling and performance evaluation of computer systems. 02670
The provision of terminal-based user support. 02686
Planning as feedback to designers. 02978
A foundation for programming environments. 03057
Iris: design of a user interface program for symbolic algebra. 03081
MathScribe: a user interface for computer algebra systems. 03082
SEE: a safe editing environment; human-computer interaction for programmers. 03225
Report on German Joint Venture Tool Integration Projects. 03495
ECOOP '88 (European Conference on Object-Oriented Programming). § 03793
User-centered requirements analysis. ● HCI-0004 †
The synthesizer generator: a system for constructing language-based editors. ● HCI-0024 †
Systems software tools. ● HCI-0030 †
Programmer perceptions of productivity and programming tools. HCI-0099 †
SKETCHER, an interactive, graphical Ada software tool—its development and use. HCI-0100 †
Extended programming in the large in a software development environment. HCI-0101 †
The Software Life Cycle Support Environment (SLCSE): a computer based framework for developing software systems. HCI-0147 †
Human-computer interface development: concepts and systems for its management. HCI-0444 †

**DAISTS** *see* Proper Noun Index

### Decision tables

The migration of expert systems into the production environment. 0740
A general user interface for creating and displaying tree-structures, hierarchies, decision trees, and nested menus. HCI-0136 †

### Flow charts

Prototyping user interfaces for applications depicted by graphs. 03523
The control structure diagram: an automated graphical representation for software. 03524

**Glazier** *see* Proper Noun Index

**HIPO** *see* Proper Noun Index

**IRIS** *see* Proper Noun Index

**JSP** *see* Proper Noun Index

**Microsoft Windows** *see* Proper Noun Index

**MIKE** *see* Proper Noun Index

### Modules and interfaces

GENIE-M: A generator for multimedia information environments. 0268
A coherent specification method for the human interface to documentation systems. 0269
An experiment in integrated multimedia conferencing. 0381
Automating interfaces in a software system. ● 0701
Polylith: an environment to support management of tool interfaces. 01096
Automated construction of interactive learning programs in Modula-2. 01500
An interface architecture to provide adaptive task-specific context for the user. 02228
Graphics fundamentals for a PCB-CAD PC system. 02494
An external data structure tool for Pascal. 02495
A graphical programming language interface for an intelligent LISP tutor. 02862
Plan-based representations of pascal and fortran code. 02897
Tool interfaces in integrated project support environments. 03506
Extending the DARTS software design method to distributed real time applications. 03516

[D. SOFTWARE]    CATEGORY INDEX

The Mjølner environment: direct interaction with abstractions. 03794
Integration of graphical tools in a computer algebra system. 03847
Methodology of window management. § 03923
The VIP VDM specification language. 04036
Abstract data type development and implementation: an example. HCI-0162 †

### Programmer workbench

Transportable applications environment (TAE) plus experiences in "Object"-ively modernizing a user interface environment. 01126
The representation of user interface style. 03221
Programmer perceptions of productivity and programming tools. HCI-0099 †
Expertise transfer and complex problems: using AQUINAS as a knowledge-acquisition workbench for knowledge-based systems. HCI-0336 †

**Sassafras** *see* Proper Noun Index

### Software libraries

Graphics programming in Turbo C. ● 0013
The AutoCAD productivity book: tapping the hidden power of AutoCAD: 2nd edition. ● 0668
OS/2 programming: an introduction. ● 0670
Libraries as programs preserved within compiler continuations. 01102
Fabrik: a visual programming environment. 01130
A Computational model for interfaces. 01163
The programmer's apprentices: a research overview. 01368
JACK: a toolkit for manipulating articulated figures. 03126
Ada-components: libraries and tools. § 03180
Ecilpse—an APSE based on PCTE. 03181
The design and evaluation of an animated programming environment. 03220
A programming environment supporting reuse of object-oriented software. 03509
Graph-theoretical tools and their use in a practical distributed operating system design case. 03886
Software tools at the University: Why, What and How. 04026
Programmer perceptions of productivity and programming tools. HCI-0099 †

### Structured programming

Schaum's outline of theories and problems of programming with advanced structured COBOL with file processing structured systems deveolpment and interactive cons. ● 0555
Bringing graphic dialogues to APL. 0765

The design and evaluation of an animated programming environment. 03220
An empirical investigation into problem decomposition strategies used in program design. HCI-0103 †

### Top-down programming

A multiparadigm user interface for intelligent CAD systems. 0716
Is top-down natural? Some experimental results from non-procedural languages. 02123
A program development system for the casual programmer. 02808
The design and evaluation of an animated programming environment. 03220
Specification and generation of variable, personalized graphical interfaces. HCI-0134 †

### User interfaces

[*Unreviewed items have been suppressed from this listing.]
DEC networks and architectures. ● HCI-0003 †
Designing the user interface: strategies for effective human-computer interaction. ● HCI-0006 †
Opening Windows. ● HCI-0007 †
Creating user interfaces by demonstration. ● HCI-0008 †
Online help systems: design and implementation. ● HCI-0009 †
Designing user interfaces for software. ● HCI-0010 †
Human-computer interface design guidelines. ● HCI-0011 †
Software ergonomics: advances and applications. ● HCI-0012 †
Introduction to Windows programming. ● HCI-0013 †
Selecting an Ada environment. ● HCI-0015 †
User-oriented computer languages: analysis and design. ● HCI-0019 †
The AWK programming language. ● HCI-0020 †
Formally-based tools and techniques for human-computer dialogues. ● HCI-0021 †
An operating systems vade mecum: 2nd edition. ● HCI-0025 †
UNIX shell programming. ● HCI-0027 †
Authoring: a guide to the design of instructional software. ● HCI-0031 †
Concepts in user interfaces: a reference model for command and response languages. ● HCI-0032 †
Human factors and interactive computer systems. § HCI-0038 †
Readings on cognitive ergonomics - mind and computers. § HCI-0039 †
Human performance engineering: using human factors/ergonomics to achieve computer system usability (2nd ed.). ● HCI-0042 †
Human-computer interface design. HCI-0043 †
Introduction to natural language processing. ● HCI-0065 †

Cooperative interfaces to information systems. ● HCI-0066 †

Information systems definition: the Multiview approach. ● HCI-0085 †

LisaLearning. HCI-0092 †

A programmable interface language for heterogeneous distributed systems. HCI-0094 †

Design of computer programs for the physically handicapped. HCI-0096 †

Ada-based executable modelling of distributed systems. HCI-0098 †

SKETCHER, an interactive, graphical Ada software tool—its development and use. HCI-0100 †

Anatomy of a compact user interface development tool. HCI-0104 †

Holophrasted displays in an interactive environment. HCI-0105 †

A structured approach to designing human-computer dialogues. HCI-0106 †

Consistent user interface. HCI-0107 †

Active help systems. HCI-0108 †

The role of context and adaptation in user interfaces. HCI-0109 †

General multiple-objective decision functions and linguistically quantified statements. HCI-0110 †

Some cognitive aspects of interface design in a two-variable optimization task. HCI-0111 †

A generalized user interface for applications programs (II). HCI-0112 †

Cursor movement during text editing. HCI-0113 †

Abstractions for user interface design. HCI-0114 †

Experimental evaluation of dialogue types for data entry. HCI-0115 †

Pictorial interfaces to data bases. HCI-0116 †

Some observations on user interface design and user performance. HCI-0117 †

Efficient computer-user interface in electronic mail systems. HCI-0118 †

A dedicated microcomputer for handwritten interaction with a software tool: system prototyping. HCI-0119 †

The influence of color on program readability and comprehensibility. HCI-0120 †

Boxer: a reconstructible computational medium. HCI-0121 †

Cognitive layouts of windows and multiple screens for user interfaces. HCI-0122 †

A specification language for direct-manipulation user interfaces. HCI-0123 †

MIKE: the menu interaction kontrol environment. HCI-0124 †

The 1984 Olympic Message System: a test of behavioral principles of system design. HCI-0125 †

A proposed solution to the problem of levels in error-message generation. HCI-0126 †

Cost/benefit analysis for incorporating human factors in the software lifecycle. HCI-0127 †

Between man and machine. HCI-0128 †

The designer as user: building requirements for design tools from design practice. HCI-0129 †

Applying software engineering principles to the user application interface. HCI-0130 †

Composing user interfaces with InterViews. HCI-0131 †

Heuristics for designing enjoyable user interfaces: lessons from computer games. HCI-0132 †

Graphical user interfaces. HCI-0133 †

Specification and generation of variable, personalized graphical interfaces. HCI-0134 †

The depth/breadth trade-off in the design of menu-driven user interfaces. HCI-0135 †

A general user interface for creating and displaying tree-structures, hierarchies, decision trees, and nested menus. HCI-0136 †

An approach to user specification of interactive display interfaces. HCI-0137 †

Toward native language software for information management. HCI-0138 †

Experimental adaptive interface. HCI-0139 †

Showing programs on a screen. HCI-0141 †

A debugger for concurrent programs. HCI-0142 †

Undo support models. HCI-0144 †

PECAN: program development systems that support multiple views. HCI-0145 :8E

The PegaSys System: pictures as formal documentation of large programs. HCI-0146 †

The Software Life Cycle Support Environment (SLCSE): a computer based framework for developing software systems. HCI-0147 †

SOFTLIB—A documentation management system. HCI-0149 †

The future of "writing" for the computer industry. HCI-0150 †

Human factors in software engineering: a review of the literature. HCI-0157 †

Towards an integration between language and software development environment. HCI-0158 †

Computer-aided hierarchical diagrams. HCI-0160 †

Icon semantics—a formal approach to icon system design. HCI-0161 †

Abstract data type development and implementation: an example. HCI-0162 †

A practical method for LR and LL syntactic error diagnosis and recovery. HCI-0163 †

Fatal error in pass zero: how not to confuse novices. HCI-0164 †

A communication system supporting large datagrams on a local area network. HCI-0166 †

Monitoring distributed systems. HCI-0169 †

A Multilevel menu-driven user interface: Design and evaluation through simulation. HCI-0170 †

Experimental study of a two-dimensional language vs. FORTRAN for first-course progammers. HCI-0171 †

[D. SOFTWARE]                  CATEGORY INDEX

On models and modelling in human-computer co-operation. HCI-0182 †
The future of interactive systems and the emergence of direct manipulation. HCI-0186 †
Representational frameworks and models for human-computer interfaces. HCI-0188 †
Stages and levels in human-machine interaction. HCI-0189 †
QWERTY and keyboard reform: the soft keyboard option. HCI-0190 †
Extending state transition diagrams for the specification of human-computer interaction. HCI-0191 †
Speed of response using keyboard and screen-based microcomputer response media. HCI-0192 †
GENIE: a modifiable computer-based task for experiments in human-computer interaction. HCI-0194 †
Reading and writing with computers: a framework for explaining differences in performance. HCI-0204 †
Interacting with Computers. HCI-0207 †
Training wheels in a user interface.. HCI-0208 †
The evaluation of text editors: methodology and empirical results.. HCI-0209 †
An aspect of aesthetics in human-computer communications: pretty windows. HCI-0213 †
A novice user's interface to information retrieval systems. HCI-0219 †
Organizing for human factors. HCI-0230 †
Designing for usability: key principles and what designers think. HCI-0231 †
An experimental comparison of tabular and graphic data presentation. HCI-0236 †
An empirical investigation of voice as an input modality for computer programming. HCI-0237 †
Visual momentum: a concept to improve the cognitive coupling of person and computer. HCI-0238 †
Human cognition and human computer interaction. HCI-0241 †
Analysing the scope of cognitive models in human-computer interaction: a trade-off approach. HCI-0245 †
Experience with the ZOG human-computer interface system. HCI-0246 †
ARES: a relational database with the capability of performing flexible interpretation of queries. HCI-0248 †
The database designer's workbench. HCI-0249 †
Using restricted natural language for data retrieval: a plan for field evaluation. HCI-0255 †
What makes RABBIT run?. HCI-0256 †
A visual approach to browsing in a database environment. HCI-0258 †
Update and retrieval in a relational database through a universal schema interface. HCI-0260 †
An interactive database end user facility for the definition and manipulation of forms. HCI-0263 †
Development of a term association interface for browsing bibliographic data bases based on end users' word associations. HCI-0266 †

Architecture problems in the construction of expert systems for document retrieval. HCI-0272 †
Towards a new research paradigm in information retrieval. HCI-0273 †
Electronic calendars in the office: an assessment of user needs and current technology. HCI-0287 †
Office systems. HCI-0291 †
Learning to use a word processor: by doing, by thinking, and by knowing. HCI-0292 †
A generalized model management system for mathematical programming. HCI-0302 †
An experimental multimedia mail system. HCI-0309 †
Beyond the chalkboard: computer support for collaboration and problem solving in meetings. HCI-0312 †
Applications of AI in engineering. HCI-0321 †
UMFE: a user modelling front-end subsystem. HCI-0325 †
Selecting a humanly understandable knowledge representation for reasoning about knowledge. HCI-0330 †
Pygmalion at the interface. HCI-0349 †
Natural language with discrete speech as a mode for human-to-machine. HCI-0355 †
Computer systems software: the programmer/machine interface. ● HCI-0361 †
O-Plan: control in the open planning architecture. HCI-0362 †
Graphical prototyping of graphical tools. HCI-0375 †
Physiological principles for the effective use of color. HCI-0378 †
Pushdown automata for user interface management. HCI-0382 †
A performing medium for working group graphics. HCI-0383 †
An image processing language with ICON-assisted navigation. HCI-0387 †
A system for interactive viewing of structured documents. HCI-0400 †
Interactive computer program for the selection of interference fits. HCI-0406 †
The doctor's use of a computer in the consulting room: an analysis. HCI-0409 †
Customers' requirements for natural language systems: results of an inquiry. HCI-0426 †
The electronic classroom: workstations for teaching. HCI-0436 †
Interactive critical path analysis (ICPA)—microcomputer implementation of a project management and knowledge engineering tool. HCI-0445 †

**Windows** *see* Proper Noun Index

### D.2.3 Coding

Reading continuous text from a one-line visual display. HCI-0187 †

[D. SOFTWARE]

## Pretty printers

Programmer perceptions of productivity and programming tools. HCI-0099 †
Holophrasted displays in an interactive environment. HCI-0105 †

## Program editors

A substrate for object-oriented interface design. 0691
A substrate for object-oriented interface design. 0691
A system for example-based programming. 0818
Mathematical formula editor for CAI. 0885
Fine tuning selection semantics in a structure editor based programming environment: some experimental results. 0975
The PSG—programming system generator. 01098
A semantic editor. 01101
Libraries as programs preserved within compiler continuations. 01102
Relations and attributes. 01103
Structured editor support for modularity and data abstraction. 01105
An environment for logic programming. 01106
Embedded menus: selecting items in context. 01320
The adaptable user interface. 01337
A VLSI interactive layout editor (VILE). 02611
A program development system for the casual programmer. 02808
Implementing a user interface as a system of attributes. 03052
Knowledge-based editors for directed graphs. 03797
Using data flow specifications and interactive editing in the operating system user interface. 03800
On the design of a graphical transition network editor. 03830
The synthesizer generator: a system for constructing language-based editors. ● HCI-0024 †
The synthesizer generator reference manual (3rd ed.). ● HCI-0024 †
Programmer perceptions of productivity and programming tools. HCI-0099 †
A display editor with random access and continuous control. HCI-0140 †
Showing programs on a screen. HCI-0141 †
PECAN: program development systems that support multiple views. HCI-0145 †
An empirical investigation of voice as an input modality for computer programming. HCI-0237 †

## Standards

An environment for understanding programs. 03525

## D.2.4 Program Verification (F.3.1)

Algorithms for verified inclusions—theory and practice. 0549

Stimulating change through usability testing. 01006
Intelligent interactive video simulation of a code inspection. 01329
Issues in the verification of knowledge in rule-based systems. 02226

## Assertion checkers

Monitoring distributed systems. HCI-0169 †

## Correctness proofs

Goal-directed semantic tutor. 02919
Abstract, generic models of interactive systems. 03219
A logic-functional approach to the execution of CCS specifications modulo behavioural equivalences. 03874
A support system for formal reasoning: requirements and status. 04035
Muffin: a user interface design experiment for a theorem proving assistant. 04037
Specification and verification of database dynamics. HCI-0251 †

## Reliability

A high level language-based computing enviornment to support production and execution of reliable programs. 01855
Critical issues in the safety of software-dominant automated systems. 03416
Ada: first users—pleased; prospective users—still hesitant. HCI-0159 †

## Validation

CAD Based verification and refinement of high level compliant motion primitives. 0600
The CD ROM handbook. ● 0678
Compact disc–interactive. 0680
Development and validation of a reader-based documentation measure. 02236
ATLANTIS—a software simulator for behavior analysis of protocol specificationsand their target implementations. 02667

## D.2.5 Testing and Debugging

DARN: Toward a community memory for diagnosis and repair tasks. 0428
The Greenblatt chess program. 0527
Usability testing in the real world. 0917
Stimulating change through usability testing. 01006
A grammar-based approach to automatic generation of user-interface dialogues. 02868
Interactive performance display and debugging using the NCUBE real-time graphicssystem. 02907
HORSE: a simulation of the horizon supercomputer. 03541
Context-sensitive editing with PSG environments. 03780

On the usefulness of syntax directed editors. 03781
Computer usability testing & evaluation. ● HCI-0014 †
A general user interface for creating and displaying tree-structures, hierarchies, decision trees, and nested menus. HCI-0136 †
Monitoring distributed systems. HCI-0169 †
Analyzing the high frequency bugs in novice programs. HCI-0178 †
Goal and plan knowledge representations: from stories to text editors and programs. HCI-0183 †

**CBUG** *see* Proper Noun Index

### Debugging aids

Experiences with off-line robot programming via standardized interfaces. 0601
The Logix system user manual version 1.21. 0675
Non-intrusive and interactive profiling in parasight. 01123
Adaptive aiding for human/computer control. 01782
A high level language-based computing enviornment to support production and execution of reliable programs. 01855
Toward a theory of computer program bugs: an empirical test. 02216
Programmer variations in software debugging approaches. 02250
Graphbug - a microprocessor software debugging tool. 02496
Dbxtool: A window-based symbolic debugger for sun workstations. 02614
A debugger for a graphical workstation. 02623
JDB: an adaptable interface for debugging. 02628
Users' preferences among different techniques for displaying the evaluation of LISP functions in an interactive debugger. 02863
Goal-directed semantic tutor. 02919
Debugging concurrent processes: a case study. 03060
Display strategies for program browsing. 03545
Issues in the design of off-line programming systems. 03564
Teaching the tricks of the trade. 04023
Programmer perceptions of productivity and programming tools. HCI-0099 †
A proposed solution to the problem of levels in error-message generation. HCI-0126 †
A debugger for concurrent programs. HCI-0142 †

### Diagnostics

Advanced diagnostics: a PASCAL interactive system. 01958
A generic strategy for diagnostic assistance: the technician's assistant. 02957
Debugging concurrent processes: a case study. 03060

### Error handling and recovery

Designing for error. 0087
User errors in human—computer interaction. 0313
The problem of levels and automatic response generation in a "Let's Talk AboutIt" strategy. 0410
An interface architecture to provide adaptive task-specific context for the user. 02228
SIMS: a uniform environment for planning and performing user's tasks. 02921
A provisional evaluation of a new chord keyboard, the Velotype. 03907
A proposed solution to the problem of levels in error-message generation. HCI-0126 †
Undo support models. HCI-0144 †
A practical method for LR and LL syntactic error diagnosis and recovery. HCI-0163 †

### Monitors

Graphbug - a microprocessor software debugging tool. 02496

### Test data generators

Programmer perceptions of productivity and programming tools. HCI-0099 †

### D.2.6 Programming Environments

Software engineering environments. ● 0172
The evaluation of project support environments for the STARTS user guide. 0173
Artificial intelligence programming environments. ● 0420
What stories should we tell novice PROLOG programmers?. 0421
An historical perspective of CD ROM. 0679
A substrate for object-oriented interface design. 0691
Beginners need powerful systems. 0747
Response time and display rate in human performance with computers. 0760
Fabrik: a visual programming environment. 01130
Foundations for the Arcadia environment architecture. 01135
Characteristics and functions of software environments: an overview. 01145
The tinkertoy graphical programming environment. 01850
Design of knowledge-based systems with a knowledge-based assistant. 01853
MAJIC—an integrated program support environment. 01960
GRAPE programming environment. 01967
A new approach to cursor movements in user interfaces of integrated programming environments. 01974
The application of human factors to the needs of the novice computer user. 02079

## [D. SOFTWARE]

An interactive environment for tool selection, specification and composition. 02141
Pride-II physical layout program of modifying Forth for "non-believers". 02312
EM2—a Modula-2 programming environment. 02392
DRAT: A program for maintaining listings. 02401
Environments for Eurota. 02514
Towards the formal specification of a simple programming support environment. 02607
Direct manipulation of an object store. 02608
GMB: a tool for manipulating and animating graph data structures. 02636
The KOMPLEX performance prediction tool. 02669
ACTES/Proceedings Symposium 1988 ACM SIGSMAll/PC. § 02787
A highly integrated tool set for program development support. 02788
Practical Software Development Environments. § 03048
Experience with a data base of programs. 03050
XY-WINS: an integraded environment for developing graphical user interfaces. 03118
Building interfaces interactively. 03119
XVISION: a comprehensive software system for image processing research, education, and applications. 03124
A portable user interface for a scientific programming environment. 03125
JACK: a toolkit for manipulating articulated figures. 03126
An introduction to Gargoyle: an interactive illustration tool. 03185
Vidura—an interactive multilingual publishing system—specification & design. 03186
The design and evaluation of an animated programming environment. 03220
The representation of user interface style. 03221
SEE: a safe editing environment; human-computer interaction for programmers. 03225
Express—rapid prototyping and product development via integrated knowledge-based executable specifications. 03492
Building a visual designer's environment. 03496
Out of Flatland: towards 3-D visual programming. 03497
Using distributed simulation for distributed application development. 03500
Tool interfaces in integrated project support environments. 03506
A programming environment supporting reuse of object-oriented software. 03509
Design principles behind Chiron: a UIMS for software environments. 03511
Context-sensitive editing with PSG environments. 03780
Views for tools in integrated environments. 03784
The Mjølner environment: direct interaction with abstractions. 03794
PantaPM: an integrated software development environment. 03796

Support environments for VDM. 03832
Integration of graphical tools in a computer algebra system. 03847
Selecting an Ada environment. ● HCI-0015 †
Hypertext/hypermedia. ● HCI-0047 †
Programmer perceptions of productivity and programming tools. HCI-0099 †
SKETCHER, an interactive, graphical Ada software tool—its development and use. HCI-0100 †
Holophrasted displays in an interactive environment. HCI-0105 †
Boxer: a reconstructible computational medium. HCI-0121 †
PICT: an interactive graphical programming environment. HCI-0143 †
PICT: an interactive graphical programming environment. HCI-0143 †
Towards an integration between language and software development environment. HCI-0158 †
A practical method for LR and LL syntactic error diagnosis and recovery. HCI-0163 †
Monitoring distributed systems. HCI-0169 †
The electronic classroom: workstations for teaching. HCI-0436 †

**Ada** *see* Proper Noun Index

**Andrew** *see* Proper Noun Index

**BALSA** *see* Proper Noun Index

**CEDAR** *see* Proper Noun Index

**Eclipse** *see* Proper Noun Index

**GENIE** *see* Proper Noun Index

**HyperCard** *see* Proper Noun Index

*Interactive*

Interactive multimedia. ● 0011
Functional databases, functional languages. 0034
Text processing with the START natural language system. 0100
Using an object-oriented programming language to create audience-driven hypermedia environments. 0101
Hypertext: a way of incorporating user feedback into online documentation. 0102
The on-line environment and in-house training. 0106
Knowledge-based support of cooperative activities. 0171
A practical natural language interface to databases. 0199
A systems approach to extended GINAS applications. 0228
APL: a problem-oriented introduction. ● 0230

## [D. SOFTWARE]

PLEIADE: A system for interactive manipulation of structured documents. 0265
Adopting interactive videodisc technology for education. 0272
Interactive lesson designs: a taxonomy. 0273
Designing interactive, responsive instruction: a set of procedures. 0274
Interactivity in microcomputer-based instruction: its essential elements and how it can be enhanced. 0275
Design and production of videodisc programming. 0276
Design factors for successful videodisc-based instruction. 0277
How effective is interactive video in improving performance and attitude?. 0278
History in the making: a report from Microsoft's First International Conference on CD ROM. 0279
Anticipating compact disc-interactive (CD-I): ten guidelines for prospective authors. 0280
CD ROM joins the new media homesteaders. 0281
Computer-supported cooperative work: a book of readings. • 0366
As we may think (Reprint). 0367
Authorship provisions in AUGMENT (Reprint). 0370
Interactive human communication (Reprint). 0371
Communication and management support in system development environments (Reprint). 0374
Callisto: an intelligent project management system (Reprint). 0375
Instructional designs for microcomputer courseware. • 0464
An example-base environment for beginning programmers. 0520
Advanced interactive cobol for micros: a practical approach. • 0521
Advanced interactive COBOL for micros: a practical approach. • 0522
The Greenblatt chess program. 0527
Algorithms for verified inclusions—theory and practice. 0549
Experiencing artificial intelligence: an interactive approach to the IBM PC. • 0550
Experiencing artificial intelligence: an interactive approach for the APPLE. • 0551
Programming the OS/2 presentation manager. • 0587
An historical perspective of CD ROM. 0679
Compact disc–interactive. 0680
Designing the user interface (Videotape). • 0687
Designing the user interface: professional development courses from the Univ. of Maryland. • 0688
Designing the user interface: supplemental materials. • 0689
"Fill-in-Form" programming. 0710
Interactive learning: a multiexpert paradigm for acquiring new knowledge. 0776
Hypertext as a means for knowledge acquisition. 0777
A system for example-based programming. 0818

A spreadsheet interface for logic programming. 0822
Constraint grammars–a new model for specifying graphical applications. 0875
The Trillium user interface design environment. 0919
An interactive environment for dialogue development: its design, use and evaluation; or, is aide useful?. 0920
On designing for usability: an application of four key principles. 0923
Human factors in teaching. 0989
The design of an interactive compiler for optimizing microprograms. 01078
Polylith: an environment to support management of tool interfaces. 01096
Dialogues: a basis for constructing programming environments. 01097
The PSG—programming system generator. 01098
Maintained and constructor attributes. 01099
Attribute propagation by message passing. 01100
A semantic editor. 01101
Libraries as programs preserved within compiler continuations. 01102
Relations and attributes. 01103
A new notion of encapsulation. 01104
Structured editor support for modularity and data abstraction. 01105
An environment for logic programming. 01106
A model and an implementation of a logic programming environment. 01107
The Mesa programming environment. 01108
The structure of Cedar. 01109
Integration mechanisms in Cedar. 01110
Use of object-oriented programming in a time series analysis system. 01112
Teaching object-oriented programming with the KEE system. 01113
INSIST: Interactive Simulation in Smalltalk. 01119
Non-intrusive and interactive profiling in parasight. 01123
Tenuring policies for generation-based storage reclamation. 01124
Transportable applications environment (TAE) plus experiences in "Object"-ively modernizing a user interface environment. 01126
An interactive environment for object-oriented music composition and sound synthesis. 01131
Interactive blackbox debugging for concurrent languages. 01134
Centaur: the system. 01136
Interacting with an active, integrated environment. 01137
Graph attribution as a specification paradigm. 01138
Transformational derivation of programs using the focus system. 01140
Interactive microcomputer programs for linear and nonlinear static analysis of frameworks. 01165
SMART: Scientific database management and engineering analysis routines and tools. 01166
The coming revolution in interactive digital video. 01325

CATEGORY INDEX [D. SOFTWARE]

Virtual video editing in interactive multimedia applications. 01326
The programmer's apprentices: a research overview. 01368
Non-strict languages-programming and implementation. 01418
MINID—a BASIC program to assist in the optical identification of minerals in thin section. 01505
Interactive CAD/CAM in engineering industry. 01571
Application of decision support system on sandwich beams, verified by experiments. 01572
ORGPLAN an information-decisive aid system to resolving organizing problems. 01573
Authoring considerations for hypertext. 01679
The Perseus project: an interactive curriculum on classical greek civilization. 01680
Adaptive aiding for human/computer control. 01782
Hyperwelcome. 01805
Hypermedia as an interpretive act. 01806
Structuring knowledge bases for designers of learning materials. 01807
Evaluating the usability of the Glasgow online. 01808
Conceptual models of interacitve knowledge acquisition tools. 02457
An abstract description generator for the reliability analysis in the design of real time systems. 02490
An external data structure tool for Pascal. 02495
Design and implementation of an interactive optimization system for network design in the motor carrier industry. 02528
Q'Nial: a portable interpreter for the nested interactive array language, Nial. 02635
A session editor with incremental execution functions. 02637
Explanation for an expert system that performs estate planning. 02767
Affect-chaining and dependency oriented flow analysis applied to queries of programs. 02789
ALIEN: a programming environment generator for personal computers. 02790
Capturing the capture concepts: a case study in the design of computer-supported meeting environments. 02824
Children's collaborative use of a computer microworld. 02825
Collaborative learning in a virtual classroom: highlights of findings. 02826
Hypertext engineering: practical methods for creating a compact disk encyclopedia. 02832
Conceptual documents: a mechanism for specifying active views in hypertext. 02833
Adding browsing semantics to the hypertext model. 02834
The design of a document database. 02835
A dataflow-based APL for the hypercube. 02905
DIME: a programming environment for unstructured triangular meshes on a distributed-memory parallel processor. 02909
Integral-C—a practical environment for C programming. 03049
AWB-ADE: an application development environment for interactive, integrated systems. 03051
Implementing a user interface as a system of attributes. 03052
Dost: an environment to support automatic generation of user interfaces. 03053
A structural approach to the maintenance of structure-oriented environments. 03054
A methodology for evaluating environments. 03055
The kernel of a generic software development environment. 03056
A foundation for programming environments. 03057
Multiprocessor Smalltalk: a case study of a multiprocessor-based programming environment. 03061
Towards interactive query expansion. 03067
Illustrated description of an interactive knowledge based indexing system. 03076
Toward a history of (personal) workstations. 03092
State trees as structured finite state machines for user interfaces. 03107
Clue: a common lisp user interface environment. 03113
Interface usage measurements in a user interface management system. 03115
Building interfaces interactively. 03119
Captive...a new tool. 03129
Hypermedia, help and how-to. 03155
Abstraction and integration in IDE, an editing and formatting environment. 03184
Abstract, generic models of interactive systems. 03219
User-driven adaptive behaviour, a comparative evaluation and an inductive analysis. 03226
Generative transition networks: a new communication control abstraction. 03241
Visual programming—toward realization of user-friendly programming environments. 03493
HORSE: a simulation of the horizon supercomputer. 03541
Interactive scientific visualization and parallel display techniques. 03542
Design and implementation of a supercomputer frame buffer system. 03543
Interaction models and the principled design of interactive systems. 03799
A design environment for computer-aided control system design via multi-objective optimisation. 03835
A model for an object management system for software engineering environments. 03843
Architectures for production systems: an inside look for those who study human-computer interaction. 03906
The central nervous system as a low and high level control system. 04007

[D. SOFTWARE]

The B tool. 04034
INTERLISP: the language and its usage. • HCI-0022 †
The synthesizer generator: a system for constructing language-based editors. • HCI-0024 †
The synthesizer generator reference manual (3rd ed.). • HCI-0024 †
UNIX shell programming. • HCI-0027 †
Interactive video: vol. 1. • HCI-0081 †
Extended programming in the large in a software development environment. HCI-0101 †
Undo support models. HCI-0144 †
Designing online information. HCI-0152 †
Creating a style for online help. HCI-0154 †
Goal and plan knowledge representations: from stories to text editors and programs. HCI-0183 †
Specification and verification of database dynamics. HCI-0251 †
A research center for augmenting human intellect. HCI-0334 †
The next generation of interactive technologies. HCI-0384 †

**NeWS** *see* Proper Noun Index

**PECAN** *see* Proper Noun Index

**PegaSys** *see* Proper Noun Index

**SLCSE** *see* Proper Noun Index

**SODOS** *see* Proper Noun Index

### D.2.7 Distribution and Maintenance

Callisto: an intelligent project management system (Reprint). 0375
Intelligent interactive video simulation of a code inspection. 01329
An architectural approach to improved program maintainability. 02627
Report on German Joint Venture Tool Integration Projects. 03495
An environment for understanding programs. 03525
Conference on software maintenance–1985. § 03544
Context-sensitive editing with PSG environments. 03780
On the usefulness of syntax directed editors. 03781
An empirical study of the effects of modularity on program modifiability. HCI-0155 †
Processes in computer program comprehension. HCI-0172 †
Mental models and software maintenance. HCI-0173 †
Experimental evaluation of program quality using external metrics. HCI-0176 †

*Corrections*

ATLANTIS—a software simulator for behavior analysis of protocol specificationsand their target implementations. 02667
Supporting document development with concordia. 03521
Specification of a tool for viewing program text. 03884

*Documentation*

Text, context, and hypertext: writing with and for the computer. • 0098
Introduction: a new paradigm for writing with and for the computer. 0099
Using an object-oriented programming language to create audience-driven hypermedia environments. 0101
Hypertext: a way of incorporating user feedback into online documentation. 0102
Information development is part of product development—not an afterthought. 0103
Usability: stereotypes and traps. 0104
Investment in computer-product documentation: causes and effects. 0105
The on-line environment and in-house training. 0106
Are writers obsolete in the computer industry?. 0109
How "friendly" is your writing for readers around the world?. 0110
Investigations in multimedia design documentation. 0116
The effects of structured, multi-level documentation. 0907
Help texts vs. help mechanisms: A new mandate for documentation writers. 01047
Documentation for user-developed applications with high documentation requirements. 01049
A help system for command driven applications. 01050
Breaking the grip of user manuals. 01051
Guided tours and tabletops: tools for communicating in a hypertext environment. 01161
The quality of user documentation. 01924
An interface architecture to provide adaptive task-specific context for the user. 02228
Development and validation of a reader-based documentation measure. 02236
The quality of user documentation: an instrument validation. 02356
Application software documentation. 02418
How well do you write user documentation?. 02442
Interactive documentation. 02612
ACM SIGDOC '85. § 02780
Separating content from form: A language for formatting on-line documentation and dialog. 02781
Computer user manuals in print: Do they have a future?. 02782

# [D. SOFTWARE]

Multilingual programming: Coordinating programs, user interfaces, on-line help and documentation. 02785
Dynamic screens and static paper. 02786
Providing the requisite knowledge via software documentation. 02898
User Services. § 03127
User-driven adaptive behaviour, a comparative evaluation and an inductive analysis. 03226
Contextual structure analysis of microcomputer manuals. 03227
Information flow in a user interface: the effect of experience and context on the recall of MacWrite screens. 03228
The application of cognitive psychology to CAD. 03239
Enhancing program readability and comprehensibility with tools for program visualization. 03510
A hypertext system to manage software life cycle documents. 03519
Specification of a tool for viewing program text. 03884
Online help systems: design and implementation. ● HCI-0009 †
Designing user interfaces for software. ● HCI-0010 †
The soft side of software: a management approach to computer documentation. ● HCI-0016 †
How to write a really good user's manual. ● HCI-0017 †
LisaLearning. HCI-0092 †
Literate programming. HCI-0148 †
SOFTLIB—A documentation management system. HCI-0149 †
The future of "writing" for the computer industry. HCI-0150 †
Corporate culture, technical documentation, and organization diagnosis. HCI-0151 †
Designing online information. HCI-0152 †
Technical writers as computer scientists: the challenges of online documentation. HCI-0153 †
Creating a style for online help. HCI-0154 †
Monitoring distributed systems. HCI-0169 †
The ethics of automated publishing systems (a response to Dr. Brockmann). HCI-0170 †
CONTEXT: an on-line documentation system. HCI-0280 †

### Enhancement

Knowledge base enhancements to relational databases. 03285
Enhancing program readability and comprehensibility with tools for program visualization. 03510
Extended programming in the large in a software development environment. HCI-0101 †
Cognitive processes in program comprehension. HCI-0179 †

### Extensibility

Extended programming in the large in a software development environment. HCI-0101 †
ASK is transportable in half a dozen ways. HCI-0279 †

### Portability

Evaluating user utterances in natural language interfaces to databases. 01486
A portable query language for small scale systems. 02492
XVISION: a comprehensive software system for image processing research, education, and applications. 03124
A portable user interface for a scientific programming environment. 03125
Ecilpse—an APSE based on PCTE. 03181
Experiences with the development of a portable network operating system. 03882
ASK is transportable in half a dozen ways. HCI-0279 †

### D.2.8 Metrics (D.4.8)

A string correction method based on the context-dependent similarity. 0293
Response time and display rate in human performance with computers. 0760
Comprehension and recall of miniature programs. 02087
Measuring change in the programming process. 02242
SATURN—a tool for modelling and performance evaluation of computer systems. 02670
Programmer perceptions of productivity and programming tools. HCI-0099 †
Programmer/nonprogrammer differences in specifying procedures to people and computers. HCI-0174 †
The effects of program-dependent and program-independent deletions on software cloze tests. HCI-0175 †
Experimental evaluation of program quality using external metrics. HCI-0176 †
Fragile knowledge and neglected strategies in novice programmers. HCI-0177 †
Cognitive processes in program comprehension. HCI-0179 †
What non-programmers know about programming: natural language procedure specification. HCI-0211 †
The relationship of problem-solving ability and course performance among novice programmers. HCI-0435 †

### Complexity measures

Visual information chunking in spreadsheet calculation. 02232
Goal and plan knowledge representations: from stories to text editors and programs. HCI-0183 †
Analysing the scope of cognitive models in human-computer interaction: a trade-off approach. HCI-0245 †

[D. SOFTWARE]                                CATEGORY INDEX

### Performance measures

A methodology for interactive evaluation of user reactions to software packages:an empirical analysis of system performance, interaction, and run time. 02080
Development and validation of a reader-based documentation measure. 02236
ATLANTIS—a software simulator for behavior analysis of protocol specificationsand their target implementations. 02667
BNETD—A modelling tool to computer systems performance evaluation. 02668
The KOMPLEX performance prediction tool. 02669
The experimental validation of a programmer productivity measure. 03013
Interface usage measurements in a user interface management system. 03115
User-driven adaptive behaviour, a comparative evaluation and an inductive analysis. 03226
Contextual structure analysis of microcomputer manuals. 03227
Information flow in a user interface: the effect of experience and context on the recall of MacWrite screens. 03228
Can cognitive complexity theory (CCT) produce an adequate measure of system usability?. 03229
Measuring user satisfaction. 03230
Software engineering for distributed applications: the design project. 03508
Experimental evaluation of dialogue types for data entry. HCI-0115 †
The influence of color on program readability and comprehensibility. HCI-0120 †
An approach to CAD system performance evaluation. HCI-0414 †
Training for optimising transfer between word processors. HCI-0447 †

### Software science

Empirical studies of programmers. § 02690
Empirical studies of programmers: the territory, paths, and destination. 02691
Task-related knowledge structures: analysis, modelling and application. 03218
The design and evaluation of an animated programming environment. 03220
The representation of user interface style. 03221
Issues governing the suitability of programming languages for programming tasks. 03224
Information flow in a user interface: the effect of experience and context on the recall of MacWrite screens. 03228
An empirical study of the effects of modularity on program modifiability. HCI-0155 †
Mental models and software maintenance. HCI-0173 †

Analyzing the high frequency bugs in novice programs. HCI-0178 †
Cognitive processes in program comprehension. HCI-0179 †
Analysing the scope of cognitive models in human-computer interaction: a trade-off approach. HCI-0245 †

### D.2.9 Management (K.6.3)

Software psychology: the need for an interdisciplinary program. 0052
Callisto: an intelligent project management system (Reprint). 0375
Beacons an initial program comprehension. 01014
Establishing user-centered criteria for information systems: a software ergonomics perspective. 01920
The effect of user involvement on system success: a contingency approach. 02508
Display strategies for program browsing. 03545
The role of mental models in programming: from experiment to requirements for an interactive system. 03827
SOFTLIB—A documentation management system. HCI-0149 †
Project Nick: meetings augmentation and analysis. HCI-0156 †
Goal and plan knowledge representations: from stories to text editors and programs. HCI-0183 †
An approach to CAD system performance evaluation. HCI-0414 †
An empirical study of the impact of user involvement on system usage and information satisfaction. HCI-0448 †

### Cost estimation

A string correction method based on the context-dependent similarity. 0293
A cost model for estimating the costs of developing software in the Ada programming language. 03539

### Life cycle

Positioning human factors in the user interface development chain. 0835
Characteristics and functions of software environments: an overview. 01145
Knowledge base applications with software engineering: a tool for requirements specifications. 02924
The kernel of a generic software development environment. 03056
Describing a product opportunity: a method of understanding the users' environment. 03194
SEE: a safe editing environment; human-computer interaction for programmers. 03225
Software engineering for distributed applications: the design project. 03508
A hypertext system to manage software life cycle documents. 03519

The Software Life Cycle Support Environment (SLCSE): a computer based framework for developing software systems. HCI-0147 †
Towards an integration between language and software development environment. HCI-0158 †
Designing for usability: key principles and what designers think. HCI-0231 †

### Productivity

Usability: stereotypes and traps. 0104
Demanding higher productivity. 01630
A theory of productivity in the creative process. 01824
The implementation of information systems for workers: a structural equation model. 01948
Programmer variations in software debugging approaches. 02250
Visual programming—toward realization of user-friendly programming environments. 03493
Influence of individual characteristics and group cohesiveness on programmer productivity. 04050
The future of "writing" for the computer industry. HCI-0150 †
Designing online information. HCI-0152 †
An empirical study of the effects of modularity on program modifiability. HCI-0155 †
Ada: first users—pleased; prospective users—still hesitant. HCI-0159 †
The Japanese and software: is it a good match?. HCI-0429 †

### Programming teams

Techniques of user message design: developing a user message system to support cooperative work. 0127
Design factors for successful videodisc-based instruction. 0277
Authorship provisions in AUGMENT (Reprint). 0370
Leadership style vs. succssus in student chief programmer teams. 01029
Knowledge-based tools to promote shared goals and terminology between interface designers. 01160
A study of conflict in group design activities: implications for computer-supported cooperative work environments. 03477

### Software configuration management

Dynamic reconfigurability for fast prototyping of user interfaces. 02609
Experience with a data base of programs. 03050
Ecilpse—an APSE based on PCTE. 03181
The influence of individual differences on the reading of computer programs. 03456
Management of distributed applications in large networks. 03515

### Software quality assurance (SQA)

User interface support for the integration of software tools: an iconic model of interaction. 01139
Intelligent interactive video simulation of a code inspection. 01329
Computer usability testing & evaluation. ● HCI-0014 †
Experimental evaluation of program quality using external metrics. HCI-0176 †
Designing for usability: key principles and what designers think. HCI-0231 †
The Japanese and software: is it a good match?. HCI-0429 †

### D.2.10 Design

Computer assisted language learning: program structure and principles. ● 0196
Designing the user interface (Videotape). ● 0687
Emeraude portable common tool environment. 01970
Mental gymnastics of sequential programming. 01971
Environment-centered and viewer-centered perception of surface orientation. 02705
People and computers IV. § 03215
Software Track. § 03513
Human-computer interface design. HCI-0043 †
The designer as user: building requirements for design tools from design practice. HCI-0129 †
The PegaSys System: pictures as formal documentation of large programs. HCI-0146 †
Goal and plan knowledge representations: from stories to text editors and programs. HCI-0183 †

### Methodologies

Speech filing—An office system for principals. 0037
Human factors challenges in creating a principal support office system—The speh filing system approach. 0038
Software psychology: the need for an interdisciplinary program. 0052
The psychological study of programming. 0053
Developing interactive information systems with the user software engineering methodology. 0077
Methods for designing software to fit human needs and capabilities (excerpt). 0079
Extending state transition diagrams for the specification of human-computer interaction. 0080
Semantics. 0154
Communication and management support in system development environments (Reprint). 0374
Direct manipulation user interfaces for expert systems. 0429
Pixel-planes 4: a summary. 0495
Algebra slaves and agents in a Logo-based mathematics curriculum. 0517
A workcell application design environment (WADE). 0598

[D. SOFTWARE]

Robot simulation and off-line programming—an integrated CAE-CAD approach. 0599
CAD-based off-line programming applied to a cleaning and deburring workstation. 0607
Object oriented programming in Concurrent Prolog. 0677
The migration of expert systems into the production environment. 0740
A system for example-based programming. 0818
Some strategies of reuse in an object-oriented programming environment. 0820
CHI research at MCC. 0842
The enhancement of understanding through visual representations. 0898
The Trillium user interface design environment. 0919
Designing in the dark: logics that compete with the user. 0928
A study of an advance organizer as a technique for teaching computer programming concepts. 01042
The design of an interactive compiler for optimizing microprograms. 01078
Teaching object-oriented programming with the KEE system. 01113
Impact of a restricted natural language interface on ease of learning and productivity. 01334
The programmer's apprentices: a research overview. 01368
Development of the wedding planner—extensions to reach a young audience. 01502
Software development approach in FMS. 01567
Authoring considerations for hypertext. 01679
The role of human factors in expert systems design and acceptance. 01780
Adaptive aiding for human/computer control. 01782
Lean cuisine: a low fat notation for menus. 02062
Experience of programming beauty: some patterns of programming aesthetics. 02184
Cognitive issues in the process of software development: review and reappraisal. 02222
BNETD—A modelling tool to computer systems performance evaluation. 02668
SATURN—a tool for modelling and performance evaluation of computer systems. 02670
A program development system for the casual programmer. 02808
Video: Data for studying human-computer interaction. 02878
Integrating human factors and software development. 02882
How users repeat their actions on computers: principles for design of history mechanisms. 02885
Plan-based representations of pascal and fortran code. 02897
Providing the requisite knowledge via software documentation. 02898
Control of cognitive processes during software design: what tools are needed?. 02899
Knowledge base applications with software engineering: a tool for requirements specifications. 02924
A rule-based system for interactive proposal evaluation. 02927
Design and implementation of the UW Illustrated compiler. 03059
Task-related knowledge structures: analysis, modelling and application. 03218
Abstract, generic models of interactive systems. 03219
The design and evaluation of an animated programming environment. 03220
Some experiences in integrating specification of human computer interaction within a structured system development method. 03222
SEE: a safe editing environment; human-computer interaction for programmers. 03225
A study of conflict in group design activities: implications for computer-supported cooperative work environments. 03477
The MIRRORS/II simulator. 03502
Software Engineering. § 03504
Software Engineering. § 03507
Software engineering for distributed applications: the design project. 03508
Enhancing program readability and comprehensibility with tools for program visualization. 03510
Design principles behind Chiron: a UIMS for software environments. 03511
Extending the DARTS software design method to distributed real time applications. 03516
Extending the DARTS software design method to distributed real time applications. 03516
Prototyping user interfaces for applications depicted by graphs. 03523
Multiple inheritance and genericity for the integration of a database management system in an object-oriented approach. 03844
The central nervous system as a low and high level control system. 04007
Software Engineering Education. § 04022
Teaching the tricks of the trade. 04023
Undergraduate software engineering education. 04025
A scarce resource in undergraduate software engineering courses: user interface design materials. 04027
A study of Arab computer users: a special case of a general HCI methodology. 04031
Visualization in programming. § 04032
A support system for formal reasoning: requirements and status. 04035
A methodology for designing distributed, fault-tolerant, and reactive real-time operating systems. 04071
User-oriented computer languages: analysis and design. ● HCI-0019 †

Planning and design of information systems. ● HCI-0045 †
Ada-based executable modelling of distributed systems. HCI-0098 †
SKETCHER, an interactive, graphical Ada software tool—its development and use. HCI-0100 †
MIKE: the menu interaction kontrol environment. HCI-0124 †
Composing user interfaces with InterViews. HCI-0131 †
Analysing the scope of cognitive models in human-computer interaction: a trade-off approach. HCI-0245 †
A user oriented design process for user recovery and command reuse support. HCI-0284 †
Graphical prototyping of graphical tools. HCI-0375 †
Human-computer interface development: concepts and systems for its management. HCI-0444 †

### Representation

Experiences with off-line robot programming via standardized interfaces. 0601
The enhancement of understanding through visual representations. 0898
SATURN—a tool for modelling and performance evaluation of computer systems. 02670
Plan-based representations of pascal and fortran code. 02897
The representation of user interface style. 03221
Building interprocess communication models using Stile. 03528
VDM—The Way Ahead. § 04033
The use of VDM on the specification of Chinese characters. 04038
SKETCHER, an interactive, graphical Ada software tool—its development and use. HCI-0100 †

### D.2.m Miscellaneous

Integrated software-design: a work-oriented approach to the humanization of computerized clerical tasks. 0243
IRX: an information retrieval system for experimentation and user applications. 01076
An information retrieval system for software components. 01077
Clarify function!. 01122
...from the end user angle. 01378
Jeff Garbers and the ergonomics of software. 01420
Dialogue management: support for dialogue independence. 02512
Testing for usability. 03163
INTERA/P: a user interface prototyping tool. 03205
Structural visibility and program comprehension. 03274
Participation in the development of software and the utilisation of standard software. 03663
ProMod at the age of 5. 03802

The influence of color on program readability and comprehensibility. HCI-0120 †
Human factors in software engineering: a review of the literature. HCI-0157 †

### Rapid prototyping

Statemaster: A UIMS based on statechart for prototyping and target implementation. 0850
Prototyping techniques for different problem contexts. 0862
Rapid prototyping and system development: examination of an interface toolkit for voice and telephony applications. 0918
The Trillium user interface design environment. 0919
RAPID: Prototyping control panel interfaces. 01120
A graphical tool for the design and prototyping of distributed systems. 01146
Constraint-based tools for building user interfaces. 01153
Prototypes from standard user interface management systems. 01370
The role of human factors in expert systems design and acceptance. 01780
Comments on "formal specification of user interfaces: a comparison and evaluation of four axiomatic approaches". 01847
A system for specification and rapid prototyping of application command languages. 01849
Developing interactive information systems with the user software engineering methodology. 01856
Mac programming tools: prototyper version 2.0 eases interface design. 02394
Dynamic reconfigurability for fast prototyping of user interfaces. 02609
ATLANTIS—a software simulator for behavior analysis of protocol specificationsand their target implementations. 02667
The development of an automated flight test management system for flight test planning and monitoring. 02928
AWB-ADE: an application development environment for interactive, integrated systems. 03051
Why do some people have more difficulty learning to use an information retrieval system than others?. 03075
The mirage rapid interface prototyping system. 03112
XY-WINS: an integraded environment for developing graphical user interfaces. 03118
Rapid prototyping of dialogue for human factors research: the EASIE approach. 03254
Software engineering for distributed applications: the design project. 03508
Prototyping user interfaces for applications depicted by graphs. 03523
The control structure diagram: an automated graphical representation for software. 03524

Software tools at the University: Why, What and How. 04026
Storyboard prototyping: a new approach to user requirements analysis. ● HCI-0005 †
Expertise transfer for expert system design. ● HCI-0059 †
MIKE: the menu interaction kontrol environment. HCI-0124 †
The 1984 Olympic Message System: a test of behavioral principles of system design. HCI-0125 †
Expertise transfer and complex problems: using AQUINAS as a knowledge-acquisition workbench for knowledge-based systems. HCI-0336 †
Graphical prototyping of graphical tools. HCI-0375 †

*Reusable software*

A system for example-based programming. 0818
Object oriented rapid prototyping with G2. 02984
Composite models in symms. 03485
A programming environment supporting reuse of object-oriented software. 03509
Ada-based executable modelling of distributed systems. HCI-0098 †

## D.3 PROGRAMMING LANGUAGES

### D.3.0 General

Software psychology: the need for an interdisciplinary program. 0052
Information systems in management: 3rd edition. ● 0673
Organization and learnability in computer languages. 02085
Perceptual structure cueing in a simple command language. 02086
Document manipulation and typography. § 03182
Simulation. § 03501
Software Track. § 03513
VDM '87: VDM—a formal method at work. § 03831
ESOP 86. § 03883
Boxer: a reconstructible computational medium. HCI-0121 †

*Standards*

The standard factor. 01003
Common LISP object system specification X3J13 Document 88-002R. 01121
The case against user interface consistency. 01333
On the interface between the high level languages and Chinese character information. 01451
User-oriented suggestions for floating-point and complex-arithmetic Forth standard extensions. 02306
SEE: a safe editing environment; human-computer interaction for programmers. 03225

### D.3.1 Formal Definitions and Theory (D.2.1, F.3.1-2, F.4.2-3)

Connections and symbols. ● 0588
Connectionism and cognitive architecture: a critical analysis. 0589
On language and connectionism: analysis of a parallel distributed processing model of language acquisition. 0590
Modelling novice programmer behaviour. 0751
Maintained and constructor attributes. 01099
Evaluation and intergration of specification languages. 01430
Natural artificial languages: low level processes. 02082
The structure of command languages: an experiment on task-action grammar. 02224
A temporal logic for reasoning about changing data bases in the context of natural language question-answering. 03176
Generative transition networks: a new communication control abstraction. 03241

*Semantics*

Natural languages. 0136
Object oriented programming in Concurrent Prolog. 0677
A study of an advance organizer as a technique for teaching computer programming concepts. 01042
The PSG—programming system generator. 01098
Attribute propagation by message passing. 01100
A semantic editor. 01101
Centaur: the system. 01136
Structural aspects of semantic-directed clusters. 02534
Goal-directed semantic tutor. 02919
A structural approach to the maintenance of structure-oriented environments. 03054
A processing system for program specifications in a natural language. 03537
The semantic language episode understanding. 03576
A logic-functional approach to the execution of CCS specifications modulo behavioural equivalences. 03874
Natural language communication with computers: some problems, perspectives, and new directions. 03913
Data manipulation languages for the universal relation view DURST. 03944
On-line interpretation in speech understanding and dialogue systems. 04000
The VIP VDM specification language. 04036

*Syntax*

Natural languages. 0136
The impact of menus and command-level feedback on learners' acquisition of data base language skills. 01041
The PSG—programming system generator. 01098
Attribute propagation by message passing. 01100
Centaur: the system. 01136

[D. SOFTWARE]

An experimental evaluation of prefix and postfix notation in command language sytax. 02110
Toward a theory of computer program bugs: an empirical test. 02216
Patterns of inductive reasoning in a parallel expert system. 02219
Strongly typed user interfaces in an abstract data store. 02618
A structural approach to the maintenance of structure-oriented environments. 03054
Natural language communication with computers: some problems, perspectives, and new directions. 03913
The VIP VDM specification language. 04036

**VDM** *see* Proper Noun Index

### D.3.2 Language Classifications

Data types and persistence. • 0033
Object-oriented concepts, databases, and applications. • 0475
Directions in object-oriented research. 0477
A substrate for object-oriented interface design. 0691
Advanced Turbo C programming. • 0726
New horizons in educational computing. • 0741
A very friendly software environment for SOLO. 0743
POP-11: an AI programming language. 0748
POP-11 for everyone. 0749
New horizons in educational computing. • 0750
Designing with databases. 01425
Evaluation and intergration of specification languages. 01430
On the interface between the high level languages and Chinese character information. 01451
A high level language-based computing enviornment to support production and execution of reliable programs. 01855
An experimental evaluation of prefix and postfix notation in command language sytax. 02110
Experience of programming beauty: some patterns of programming aesthetics. 02184
Use of fourth generation languages: application development and documentation problems. 02435
Mach and Matchmaker: kernel and language support for object-oriented distributed systems. 03031
Impulse-86: a substrate for object-oriented interface design. 03032
Object-oriented programming systems, languages and applications. § 03035
Programming Language design and Implementation. § 03058
Issues governing the suitability of programming languages for programming tasks. 03224
The Monte Carlo processor: designing and implementing a language for Monte Carlo work. 03317
Intuitive representations and interaction languages: an exploratory experiment. 03611

Computer languages: everything you always wanted to know but no one can tell you. 03612
Design of programming languages under psychological aspects. 03613
IDL: past experience and new ideas. 03782
Supporting flexible and efficient tool integration. 03783
Fifth generation computers: concepts, implementations and uses. • HCI-0001 †
Programming languages: a grand tour (2nd ed.). • HCI-0018 †
User-oriented computer languages: analysis and design. • HCI-0019 †
The art of programming. HCI-0095 †
Towards an integration between language and software development environment. HCI-0158 †
Experimental study of a two-dimensional language vs. FORTRAN for first-course progammers. HCI-0171 †

**ACRONYM** *see* Proper Noun Index

**Ada** *see* Proper Noun Index

**ALGOL-60** *see* Proper Noun Index

**ALGOL-68** *see* Proper Noun Index

**ALGOL-W** *see* Proper Noun Index

**APL** *see* Proper Noun Index

**Apple** *see* Proper Noun Index

### Applicative languages

Non-strict languages-programming and implementation. 01418
Music—a language for typesetting music scores. 02622
Programming languages: a grand tour (2nd ed.). • HCI-0018 †
INTERLISP: the language and its usage. • HCI-0022 †
A programmable interface language for heterogeneous distributed systems. HCI-0094 †
A generalized model management system for mathematical programming. HCI-0302 †

**AWK** *see* Proper Noun Index

**BASIC** *see* Proper Noun Index

**C** *see* Proper Noun Index

**C++** *see* Proper Noun Index

**Cedar** *see* Proper Noun Index

**CLU** *see* Proper Noun Index

**COBOL** *see* Proper Noun Index

[D. SOFTWARE]                      CATEGORY INDEX

**Concurrent Pascal** *see* Proper Noun Index

**Concurrent Prolog** *see* Proper Noun Index

**CORAL** *see* Proper Noun Index

**CSP** *see* Proper Noun Index

**Daisy** *see* Proper Noun Index

*Data-flow languages*

Conman: a visual programming language for interactive graphics. 02811

**DIAG 2** *see* Proper Noun Index

**EUCLID** *see* Proper Noun Index

*Extensible languages*

Use of object-oriented programming in a time series analysis system. 01112
CLAM- an open system for graphical user interfaces. 01117
A portable query language for small scale systems. 02492
Abstraction and integration in IDE, an editing and formatting environment. 03184

**Flavors** *see* Proper Noun Index

**FORTH** *see* Proper Noun Index

**FORTRAN** *see* Proper Noun Index

**FORTRAN 77** *see* Proper Noun Index

**G** *see* Proper Noun Index

**ICON** *see* Proper Noun Index

**INTERLISP** *see* Proper Noun Index

**KLO** *see* Proper Noun Index

**LISP** *see* Proper Noun Index

**LOGO** *see* Proper Noun Index

*Macro and assembly languages*

Windows for BASIC. 01292
Marcosby example in a graphical UIMS. 01831
Music—a language for typesetting music scores. 02622
An environment for understanding programs. 03525

**Modula-2** *see* Proper Noun Index

**Nial** *see* Proper Noun Index

*Nonprocedural languages*

Constraint-based tools for building user interfaces. 01153
Is top-down natural? Some experimental results from non-procedural languages. 02123
Conman: a visual programming language for interactive graphics. 02811
A generalized model management system for mathematical programming. HCI-0302 †

**Pascal** *see* Proper Noun Index

**PDP-11 assembly language** *see* Proper Noun Index

**PORTAL** *see* Proper Noun Index

**PostScript** *see* Proper Noun Index

**Prolog** *see* Proper Noun Index

**SCHEME** *see* Proper Noun Index

**SDL** *see* Proper Noun Index

**SIMULA** *see* Proper Noun Index

**Smalltalk** *see* Proper Noun Index

**Smalltalk-80** *see* Proper Noun Index

*Specialized application languages*

Using an object-oriented programming language to create audience-driven hypermedia environments. 0101
Logic and programming. ● HCI-0068 †

**Turbo BASIC** *see* Proper Noun Index

**Turbo C** *see* Proper Noun Index

**Turbo Pascal** *see* Proper Noun Index

**VAL** *see* Proper Noun Index

*Very high-level languages*

Using an object-oriented programming language to create audience-driven hypermedia environments. 0101
A framework for choosing a database query language. 0761
Icon semantics—a formal approach to icon system design. HCI-0161 †

## D.3.3 Language Constructs (E.2)

Using an object-oriented programming language to create audience-driven hypermedia environments. 0101
A book on C. ● 0143
ECOOP '88 (European Conference on Object-Oriented Programming). § 03793
Programming languages: a grand tour (2nd ed.). ● HCI-0018 †
Literate programming. HCI-0148 †

### Abstract data types

An input-output model of interactive systems. 0926
Use of object-oriented programming in a time series analysis system. 01112
Teaching object-oriented programming with the KEE system. 01113
CLAM- an open system for graphical user interfaces. 01117
Effects of computer programming experience on network representations of abstract programming concepts. 02204
Patterns of inductive reasoning in a parallel expert system. 02219
Strongly typed user interfaces in an abstract data store. 02618
Abstraction and integration in IDE, an editing and formatting environment. 03184
Design principles behind Chiron: a UIMS for software environments. 03511
Tree doctor, a software package for graphical manipulation and animation of tree structures. 03901
Composing user interfaces with InterViews. HCI-0131 †
Abstract data type development and implementation: an example. HCI-0162 †
An expert system for conceptual schema design: a machine learning approach. HCI-0335 †

### Concurrent programming structures

Concurrent Prolog: collected papers. ● 0674
The Logix system user manual version 1.21. 0675
Object oriented programming in Concurrent Prolog. 0677
A substrate for object-oriented interface design. 0691
Interactive blackbox debugging for concurrent languages. 01134
Edmas: an object-oriented, locally distributed mail system. 01857
Debugging concurrent processes: a case study. 03060
Concurrency 88. § 03873
A logic-functional approach to the execution of CCS specifications modulo behavioural equivalences. 03874
An operating systems vade mecum: 2nd edition. ● HCI-0025 †

### Control structures

ATLANTIS—a software simulator for behavior analysis of protocol specificationsand their target implementations. 02667
SEE: a safe editing environment; human-computer interaction for programmers. 03225
How much is enough? A study of user command repertoires. 03240
Advanced computing concepts and techniques in control engineering. § 03833
A design environment for computer-aided control system design via multi-objective optimisation. 03835
What non-programmers know about programming: natural language procedure specification. HCI-0211 †

### Data types and structures

Data types and persistence. ● 0033
A change of mind or the story of Fuzzies in Purgatory. 0961
A new notion of encapsulation. 01104
Algebras for nested relations. 01623
MAJIC—an integrated program support environment. 01960
Knowledge-based editors for directed graphs. 03797

### Input/Output

Abstract interaction tools: a language for user interface management systems. 01162
Application screen management: an APL2 approach. 02794

### Modules, packages

Using representation clauses as an operating system interface. 0764
A new notion of encapsulation. 01104
The design of a user friendly interactive personal computer package for quality control charts, project management, and linear programming applications. 01521
An object-oriented approach to the design of a mail system for a heterogeneous environment. 01944
A methodology for interactive evaluation of user reactions to software packages:an empirical analysis of system performance, interaction, and run time. 02080
An interface architecture to provide adaptive task-specific context for the user. 02228
Music—a language for typesetting music scores. 02622
An evaluation of the effectiveness of the adaptive interface module (AIM) in matching dialogues to users. 03212
An empirical study of the effects of modularity on program modifiability. HCI-0155 †

[D. SOFTWARE]

### Procedures, functions, and subroutines

Learning iteration recursion from examples. 02215
Programming the mouse in Turbo Pascal 4.0. 02393

### D.3.4 Processors

A FORTRAN input program generator. 01227
The trouble with application generators. 01662
Programming Language design and Implementation. § 03058

**Clipper** *see* Proper Noun Index

### Code generation

MAJIC—an integrated program support environment. 01960
Generating reversible programs. 02620
A grammar-based approach to automatic generation of user-interface dialogues. 02868

### Compilers

The design of an interactive compiler for optimizing microprograms. 01078
The BCC180 multitasking controller part 3: memory management and windowing. 01295
Compiling Forth for performance. 02309
A stand-alone Forth system. 02310
Dynamic compilation in the Unix environment. 02621
A programmer-friendly LL(1) parser generator. 02626
A visual shell interface to a database. 02640
SATURN—a tool for modelling and performance evaluation of computer systems. 02670
g - A compact language for real-time graphics. 02906
Design and implementation of the UW Illustrated compiler. 03059
A rule-based system for fuzzy natural language robot control. 03574
A practical method for LR and LL syntactic error diagnosis and recovery. HCI-0163 †

### Interpreters

The problem of identification. 01088
Implementing a semantic interpreter using conceptual graphs. 01812
fsh—a functional UNIX command interpreter. 02624
Support for graphs of processes in a command interpreter. 02633
Q'Nial: a portable interpreter for the nested interactive array language, Nial. 02635
g - A compact language for real-time graphics. 02906

### Optimization

The design of an interactive compiler for optimizing microprograms. 01078
g - A compact language for real-time graphics. 02906

### Parsing

Office-by-example: an integrated office system and database manager. 01159
A programmer-friendly LL(1) parser generator. 02626
Design principles behind Chiron: a UIMS for software environments. 03511
The synthesizer generator: a system for constructing language-based editors. ● HCI-0024 †
A practical method for LR and LL syntactic error diagnosis and recovery. HCI-0163 †
The use of colour in language syntax analysis. HCI-0385 †
The use of colour in language syntax analysis. HCI-0385 †

### Preprocessors

Fatal error in pass zero: how not to confuse novices. HCI-0164 †

### Run-time environments

SATURN—a tool for modelling and performance evaluation of computer systems. 02670
A methodology, specification language, and automated support environment for com1uter-aided design systems. 04068
Holophrasted displays in an interactive environment. HCI-0105 †

### Translator writing systems and compiler generators

The PSG—programming system generator. 01098
Maintained and constructor attributes. 01099
A session editor with incremental execution functions. 02637
Affect-chaining and dependency oriented flow analysis applied to queries of programs. 02789
ALIEN: a programming environment generator for personal computers. 02790
The synthesizer generator: a system for constructing language-based editors. ● HCI-0024 †
The synthesizer generator reference manual (3rd ed.). ● HCI-0024 †

### D.3.m Miscellaneous

Program generation for Ada—a case study. 02634
Playing the language-games of design and use-on skill and participation. 03043
Cognitive aspects of learning and using a programming language. HCI-0439 †

## D.4 OPERATING SYSTEMS (C.)

### D.4.0 General

The CD ROM handbook. ● 0678
Information retrieval using micros. 01225

CATEGORY INDEX [D. SOFTWARE]

Advanced interactive executive (AIX) operating system overview. 01815
Advanced interactive executive program development environment. 01816
AIX usability enhancements and human factors. 01817
Hypercube Concurrent Computers and Applications. § 02904
A dataflow-based APL for the hypercube. 02905
A structural approach to the maintenance of structure-oriented environments. 03054
User-driven adaptive behaviour, a comparative evaluation and an inductive analysis. 03226
Software Track. § 03513
Petri nets: applications and relationships to other models of concurrency. § 03973
An operating systems vade mecum: 2nd edition. • HCI-0025 †
Personal computing for decision support. HCI-0299 †
Computer systems software: the programmer/machine interface. • HCI-0361 †

**DOS** *see* Proper Noun Index

**Mercury** *see* Proper Noun Index

**MS-DOS** *see* Proper Noun Index

**OS/2** *see* Proper Noun Index

**PICK** *see* Proper Noun Index

**UNIX** *see* Proper Noun Index

**UNIX System V** *see* Proper Noun Index

**VAX/VMS** *see* Proper Noun Index

**VICE** *see* Proper Noun Index

**VM/CMS** *see* Proper Noun Index

**XINU** *see* Proper Noun Index

### D.4.1 Process Management

An operating systems vade mecum: 2nd edition. • HCI-0025 †
The design of the UNIX operating system. • HCI-0026 †

*Concurrency*

Concurrent Prolog: collected papers. • 0674
The Logix system user manual version 1.21. 0675
Reference models, window systems, and concurrency. 01058
Multi-thread input. 01070
Office-by-example: an integrated office system and database manager. 01159

Patterns of inductive reasoning in a parallel expert system. 02219
The PFG environment: parallel programming with petri net semantics. 03527
Concurrency 88. § 03873
A logic-functional approach to the execution of CCS specifications modulo behavioural equivalences. 03874

*Deadlocks*

The economics of UNIX workstations. 01312
Edmas: an object-oriented, locally distributed mail system. 01857

*Multiprocessing/multiprogramming*

Knowledge-based support of cooperative activities. 0171
Application of the butterfly parallel processor in artificial intelligence. 0489
A user interface for multiple-process, turnkey systems targeted for the novice user. 0911
A multitasking switchboard approach to user interface management. 01053
The BCC180 multitasking controller part 3: memory management and windowing. 01295
Structured message passing on a shared-memory multiprocessor. 03514
Systems software tools. • HCI-0030 †

*Scheduling*

A communication mechanism supporting actions. 01441
A workstation assessor for crew operations-WOSTAS. 02093
Graph-theoretical tools and their use in a practical distributed operating system design case. 03886

*Synchronization*

Synchronizing the I/O behavior of functional programs with feedback. 02016

### D.4.2 Storage Management

Tenuring policies for generation-based storage reclamation. 01124
Search strategies in internal and external memories. 03911
An operating systems vade mecum: 2nd edition. • HCI-0025 †

*Distributed memories*

On language and connectionism: analysis of a parallel distributed processing model of language acquisition. 0590
DIME: a programming environment for unstructured triangular meshes on a distributed-memory parallel processor. 02909

[D. SOFTWARE] CATEGORY INDEX

### Secondary storage devices

An historical perspective of CD ROM. 0679
Digital video interactive. 0681
Designing a CD ROM information structure. 0682
Artificial intelligence systems. 0683
Design and performance considerations for an optical disk-based, multimedia object server. HCI-0265 †

### Segmentation

Visual information chunking in spreadsheet calculation. 02232

### Storage hierarchies

Refining problem-solving knowledge in repertory grids using a consultation mechanism. 02205
Visual information chunking in spreadsheet calculation. 02232

### Virtual memory

CHI '88 poster session papers and abstracts. 0992
Development and evaluation of direct manipulation lists (poster session). 0993
Rooms: the use of multiple virtual workspaces to reduce space contention in a window-based graphical user interface. 01151

### D.4.3 File Systems Management (E.5)

UNIX system V: release 3.0 Intel 80286/80386 computer version: system administrator's guide. ● 0031
Compact disc–interactive. 0680
Advanced Turbo C programming. ● 0726
Generation of file processing programs based on JSP. 02639
Project source file management under the UNIX operating system. 03168
An operating systems vade mecum: 2nd edition. ● HCI-0025 †
The design of the UNIX operating system. ● HCI-0026 †
Andrew: a distributed personal computing environment. HCI-0091 †

### Access methods

Designing a CD ROM information structure. 0682

### Directory structures

Structure of a directory space: a case study with a UNIX operating system. 02138
Tree doctor, a software package for graphical manipulation and animation of tree structures. 03901

### File organization

Guided tours and tabletops: tools for communicating in a hypertext environment. 01161

Tree doctor, a software package for graphical manipulation and animation of tree structures. 03901

### Maintenance

SEE: a safe editing environment; human-computer interaction for programmers. 03225

### D.4.4 Communications Management (C.2)

An operating systems vade mecum: 2nd edition. ● HCI-0025 †

### Buffering

A model for assessing the performance of a local area network employing technical office protocol (TOP) as part of MAP/TOP network in a computer integrated manufacturing (CIM) research project, for the transmission of real time interactive speech. 02491

### Input/Output

Speech responses and dual-task performance: better time-sharing or asymmetric transfer?. 01789
A user interface mangement system generator. 04074

### Message sending

Diamond: a multimedia message system built on a distributed architecture (Reprint). 0380
Human factors in computer based message systems. 01374
MH: a multifarious user agent. 01428
Distributed database considerations in an expert system for radar analysis. 03175
Computer-based message services. § 03319
A communication system supporting large datagrams on a local area network. HCI-0166 †
Architecture problems in the construction of expert systems for document retrieval. HCI-0272 †

### Network communication

Attacking a complex distributed algorithm from different sides: an experience wih complementary validation tools. 01429
A communication mechanism supporting actions. 01441
A communication system supporting large datagrams on a local area network. HCI-0166 †

### Terminal management

The design of a terminal independent package. 02619
The X window system. HCI-0370 †

### D.4.5 Reliability

A computer assisted learning system for reliability engineering. 04060

[D. SOFTWARE]

### Fault-tolerance

Experience of constructing a fault localisation expert system using an AI toolkit. 02923
A methodology for designing distributed, fault-tolerant, and reactive real-time operating systems. 04071

### Verification

Issues in the verification of knowledge in rule-based systems. 02226

### D.4.6 Security and Protection

A human approach to the technological challenges in data security. 01543
The hackers' comfort. 01544
'Remember to lock the door': MMI and the hacker. 01910
Computer security: a global challenge. § 03577
Automatic identification of writers. 03909

### Access controls

Access-control software. 01911
The integrity lock support environment. 03578
Database Security: Status and Prospects. § 03579
Lessons learned from modeling a secure multilevel relational database system. 03580
Inference control via query restriction vs. data modification: a perspective. 03581
Privacy respecting permissions and rights. 03583
Role-based security in data base management systems. 03584
Status of trusted DBMS interpretations. 03585
User-friendly password methods for computer-mediated information systems. HCI-0167 †

### Authentication

The integrity lock support environment. 03578
Database Security: Status and Prospects. § 03579
Role-based security in data base management systems. 03584
User-friendly password methods for computer-mediated information systems. HCI-0167 †

### Cryptographic controls

Database Security: Status and Prospects. § 03579
Privacy respecting permissions and rights. 03583

### Information flow controls

The integrity lock support environment. 03578
Modelling and controlling user inference. 03582
Nested window flow controls with packet fragmentation. 04055

### Verification

Verifying identity via keystroke characteristics. 02178
Database Security: Status and Prospects. § 03579

### D.4.7 Organization and Design

ISPF: the strategic dailog manager. ● 0035
A book on C. ● 0143
Adaptive general audience models: a research framework. 0202
Human-computer interaction: psychonomic aspects. § 03887
Methodology of window management. § 03923

### Batch processing systems

BNETD—A modelling tool to computer systems performance evaluation. 02668
The KOMPLEX performance prediction tool. 02669
The KOMPLEX performance prediction tool. 02669
Undo support models. HCI-0144 †

### Distributed systems

An experiment in integrated multimedia conferencing. 0381
Distributed databases and distributed processing between personal computers and mainframes. 0458
Connections and symbols. ● 0588
An architecture of a distributed window system and its FCP implementation. 0676
A graphical tool for the design and prototyping of distributed systems. 01146
Instrumenting systems to measure components of interactive response times. 01230
A communication mechanism supporting actions. 01441
Speech responses and dual-task performance: better time-sharing or asymmetric transfer?. 01789
A multiprocessor system for real-time robotic control. 02023
Computing advice at a distance: the 'remote advisory' concept. 02617
Mach and Matchmaker: kernel and language support for object-oriented distributed systems. 03031
Software engineering for distributed applications: the design project. 03508
Experiences with Distributed Systems. § 03881
Experiences with the development of a portable network operating system. 03882
Graph-theoretical tools and their use in a practical distributed operating system design case. 03886
A methodology for designing distributed, fault-tolerant, and reactive real-time operating systems. 04071
A programmable interface language for heterogeneous distributed systems. HCI-0094 †

[D. SOFTWARE]                                                    CATEGORY INDEX

### Hierarchical design

The KOMPLEX performance prediction tool. 02669
Tree doctor, a software package for graphical manipulation and animation of tree structures. 03901
An empirical investigation into problem decomposition strategies used in program design. HCI-0103 †

### Interactive systems

ISPF: the strategic dailog manager. ● 0035
Knowledge-based support of cooperative activities. 0171
Interactive workstations. ● 0216
Color graphic displays for network planning and design. 0260
On methods of analysis of mental models and the evaluation of interactive computer systems. 0319
Interactive media: working methods and practical applications. ● 0501
Setting up an interactive videodisc project. 0502
Lessons from computer-based learning. 0503
Computer-assisted learning and interactive video. 0504
Pedagogical design for interactive video. 0505
Why do instructional designers need conversation theory?. 0506
Conversation theory as a basis for instructional design. 0507
From trigger video to videodisc: a case study in interpersonal skills. 0508
The creation of an integrated IVD curriculum. 0509
A question of delivery—an outline classification of interactive video delivery systems. 0510
Interactive video—a producer's medium. 0511
The political economy of interactive video in British higher education. 0512
Interactive video as a school resource: Rolls-Royce or Model T Ford?. 0513
Producing resource discs—the Domesday project experience. 0514
Videodisc and videotex: love-match or passing acquaintance?. 0515
Schaum's outline of theories and problems of programming with advanced structured COBOL with file processing structured systems deveolpment and interactive cons. ● 0555
"Fill-in-Form" programming. 0710
Speech and language-based interaction with machines: towards the conversational computer. ● 0724
A knowledge-based intermediary system for information retrieval. 0737
POP-11 for everyone. 0749
Designing for designers: an analysis of design practice in the real world. 0839
Dialog management in interactive systems: a comparative survey. 0949
Modes survey. 0963
Interact '87. 0964

The effectiveness of a keystroke line in interactive tutorials. 0969
Student-oriented features of an interactive programming environment. 01036
A study of an advance organizer as a technique for teaching computer programming concepts. 01042
Instrumenting systems to measure components of interactive response times. 01230
Profile data acquisition for the JCPDS-ICDD database s. 01232
Coding image sequences for interactive retrieval. 01330
Interactive video in language learning. 01380
Live-Net in education. 01381
Attacking a complex distributed algorithm from different sides: an experience wih complementary validation tools. 01429
Some issues related to the design and development of an interactive video disc. 01497
Automated construction of interactive learning programs in Modula-2. 01500
Interactive timetabling in universities. 01501
An interactive programming system for the IBM 7545 robot. 01517
The design of a user friendly interactive personal computer package for quality control charts, project management, and linear programming applications. 01521
Network generation using the Prufer code. 01536
Interactive L systems with a fast local growth. 01673
A computing service using linked minis. 01674
Advanced interactive executive (AIX) operating system overview. 01815
Advanced interactive executive program development environment. 01816
The feature chart: A tool for communicating the analysis for a decision support system. 01913
Synchronizing the I/O behavior of functional programs with feedback. 02016
The engineering information system: a guided tour. 02046
A methodology for interactive evaluation of user reactions to software packages:an empirical analysis of system performance, interaction, and run time. 02080
On methods for interface specification and design. 02114
A descriptive/prescriptive model for menu-based interaction. 02120
Using computer knowledge in the design of interactive systems. 02137
ISIS: the interactive spatial information system. 02193
An interactive system SDI on microcomputer. 02272
An interactive videodisc drama: The case of Frank hall. 02285
Interactive document display and its use in information retrieval. 02300
AI/learn: an interactive videodisk system for teaching medical concepts and reasoning. 02381

[D. SOFTWARE]

Experience with a functional layered multicomputer architecture for interactive processing. 02402
Forecasting consumer adoption of information technology and services—lessons from home video forecasting. 02451
A model for assessing the performance of a local area network employing technical office protocol (TOP) as part of MAP/TOP network in a computer integrated manufacturing (CIM) research project, for the transmission of real time interactive speech. 02491
Videotex redux. 02545
Inactive video at work. 02571
One hundred differential equations execute directly on the IBM PC. 02582
Icecream, transportable software for creating friendly human interfaces. 02615
A debugger for a graphical workstation. 02623
fsh—a functional UNIX command interpreter. 02624
Support for graphs of processes in a command interpreter. 02633
BNETD—A modelling tool to computer systems performance evaluation. 02668
The KOMPLEX performance prediction tool. 02669
Power plant simulation and reactor safety. 02682
A compact model of a power house boiler. 02683
The rapport multimedia conferencing system. 03037
Browsing within time-driven multimedia documents. 03046
Interactive retrieval office documents. 03047
Formally-based techniques for dialogue design. 03190
A flexible negotiable interactive learning environment. 03197
Visual languages and human computer interaction. 03202
The myth of the infinitely fast machine. 03204
Some critical remarks on abstractions for adaptable dialogue managers. 03211
Planning in the context of human-computer interaction. 03213
Abstract, generic models of interactive systems. 03219
The design and evaluation of an animated programming environment. 03220
Some experiences in integrating specification of human computer interaction within a structured system development method. 03222
SEE: a safe editing environment; human-computer interaction for programmers. 03225
Generative transition networks: a new communication control abstraction. 03241
Ease of use - the ultimate deception. 03249
Modelling generic user-interfaces with functional programs. 03265
Proving properties of interactive systems. 03267
User programs: a way to match computer systems and human cognition. 03271
Investigations into a command and response language interface. 03531

Videotex and online services: competition or collateral. 03557
Programming for interactive structure analysis. 03776
Interaction models and the principled design of interactive systems. 03799
Plan-based text generation in an on-line help system. 03817
Concepts in user interfaces: a reference model for command and response languages. § 03872
Graph-theoretical tools and their use in a practical distributed operating system design case. 03886
Keywords instead of hierarchical menus. 03912
Natural language communication with computers: some problems, perspectives, and new directions. 03913
A methodology for designing distributed, fault-tolerant, and reactive real-time operating systems. 04071
Online help systems: design and implementation. ● HCI-0009 †
Human-computer interface design guidelines. ● HCI-0011 †
The design of the UNIX operating system. ● HCI-0026 †
VM/CMS: a user's guide. ● HCI-0028 †
Operating system design. Vol. 1: the XINU approach (PC edition). ● HCI-0029 †
Systems software tools. ● HCI-0030 †
Authoring: a guide to the design of instructional software. ● HCI-0031 †
Human factors and interactive computer systems. § HCI-0038 †
Compact disc-interactive: a designer's overview. ● HCI-0078 †
Holophrasted displays in an interactive environment. HCI-0105 †
4.2BSD and 4.3BSD as examples of the UNIX system. HCI-0165 †
Equal opportunity interactive systems. HCI-0168 †
Cognitive models, cognitive tasks, and information retrieval. HCI-0331 †

*Real-time systems*

The evaluation of project support environments for the STARTS user guide. 0173
Speech responses and dual-task performance: better time-sharing or asymmetric transfer?. 01789
A multiprocessor system for real-time robotic control 02023
A model for assessing the performance of a local area network employing technical office protocol (TOP) as part of MAP/TOP network in a computer integrated manufacturing (CIM) research project, for the transmission of real time interactive speech. 02491
A compact model of a power house boiler. 02683
Interactive performance display and debugging using the NCUBE real-time graphicssystem. 02907
The software structure of extended nucleus based on BTRON specification. 03494

[D. SOFTWARE]

TRON Project 1987—Open-architecture computer systems. § 03821
Real-time processing of cursive writing and sketched graphics. 03908
Real-time large vocabulary word recognition via diphone spotting and multiprocessor implementation. 03996
A methodology for designing distributed, fault-tolerant, and reactive real-time operating systems. 04071

### D.4.8 Performance (C.4, D.2.8, I.6)

IBM DOS 4.0: a bridge to OS/2. 02523
Measurement and Modeling of Computer Systems. § 03024
The software structure of extended nucleus based on BTRON specification. 03494

*Measurements*

Instrumenting systems to measure components of interactive response times. 01230
A methodology for interactive evaluation of user reactions to software packages:an empirical analysis of system performance, interaction, and run time. 02080
The experimental validation of a programmer productivity measure. 03013

*Modeling and prediction*

BNETD—A modelling tool to computer systems performance evaluation. 02668
The KOMPLEX performance prediction tool. 02669

*Monitors*

Likelihood alarm displays. 01783
Interactive performance display and debugging using the NCUBE real-time graphicssystem. 02907
Monitoring distributed systems. HCI-0169 †

*Operational analysis*

Likelihood alarm displays. 01783

*Queueing theory*

Traffic study on primary rate ISDN user-network interface. 01442
BNETD—A modelling tool to computer systems performance evaluation. 02668
The KOMPLEX performance prediction tool. 02669

*Simulation*

Attacking a complex distributed algorithm from different sides: an experience wih complementary validation tools. 01429

BNETD—A modelling tool to computer systems performance evaluation. 02668
The KOMPLEX performance prediction tool. 02669

### D.4.9 Systems Programs and Utilities

A systems approach to extended GINAS applications. 0228
Concurrent Prolog: collected papers. ● 0674

*Command and control languages*

Sites, modes, and trails: Telling the user of an interactive system where he is, what he can do, and how to get to places (excerpt). 0068
Design principles for human-computer interfaces. 0075
Authorship provisions in AUGMENT (Reprint). 0370
A knowledge-based intermediary system for information retrieval. 0737
Intelligent interfaces to Nordic data bases. 0738
Open fullscreen systems. 0766
Speech responses and dual-task performance: better time-sharing or asymmetric transfer?. 01789
A system for specification and rapid prototyping of application command languages. 01849
The emergence of Zipf's law: Spontaneous encoding optimization by users of a command language. 01875
GRAPE programming environment. 01967
An icon-driven end-user interface to UNIX. 02089
The structure of command languages: an experiment on task-action grammar. 02224
fsh—a functional UNIX command interpreter. 02624
GCI—a tool for developing interactive CAD user interfaces. 02625
Ergonomic considerations in the design of command languages. 02694
The incorporation of early interface evaluation into command language grammar specifications. 03191
The design and evaluation of an animated programming environment. 03220
How much is enough? A study of user command repertoires. 03240
A visual programming language designed for automatic programming. 03529
Investigations into a command and response language interface. 03531
Using data flow specifications and interactive editing in the operating system user interface. 03800
Opening Windows. ● HCI-0007 †
UNIX shell programming. ● HCI-0027 †
VM/CMS: a user's guide. ● HCI-0028 †
Concepts in user interfaces: a reference model for command and response languages. ● HCI-0032 †
A Multilevel menu-driven user interface: Design and evaluation through simulation. HCI-0170 †
Architecture problems in the construction of expert systems for document retrieval. HCI-0272 †

## D.m MISCELLANEOUS

Common user access—a consistent and usable human-computer interface for the SAA environments. 01819
Enabling the user interface. 01820
Designing SAA applications and user interfaces. 01821
Cognitive systems engineering: new wine in new bottles. 02078
Empirical studies of programmers. § 02690

### Software psychology

Cognitive resources and the learning of human-computer dialogs. 0209
Ergonomic features of interactive systems—the interdependency of software and hardware. 0312
A theory of control and complexity: implications for software design and integration of computer systems into the work place. 0315
Usability assessment for the office: methodological choices and their implications. 0318
Communication and management support in system development environments (Reprint). 0374
Callisto: an intelligent project management system (Reprint). 0375
Empirical studies of programmers: second workshop. • 0565
Graphical vs. textual representation: an empirical study of novices' program comprehension. 0566
Usability testing in the real world. 0953
Videotex information packagers: a field study aimed at tomorrow's videotex authoring interface. 0962
People and organizations in software production: a review of the literature. 01023
Environments: Austria compared to the United States. 01026
Computer programming and generalized problem-solving skills: in search of direction. 01585
Problem solving and software design. 01589
User validation of information systems requirements: some empirical results. 01852
Software engineering for user interfaces. 01854
Establishing user-centered criteria for information systems: a software ergonomics perspective. 01920
Effect of computer knowledge on user performance over time. 01975
On the interaction of man and EDP use as work activity. 02094
Modelling human expertise in knowledge engineering: some preliminary observations. 02134
Procedural and non-procedural query languages revisited: a comparison of relational algebra and relational calculus. 02146
Conditional statements, looping constructs, and program comprehension: an experiments study. 02177
Effects of computer programming experience on network representations of abstract programming concepts. 02204
The influence of programmers' cognitive complexity on program comprehension and modification. 02245
Cognitive processes in program comprehension. 02403
Mental models and software maintenance. 02404
Programmer-nonprogrammer differences in specifying procedures to people and computers. 02405
Development of a hand-held computerized vocabulary tutor. 02468
Empirical studies of programmers: the territory, paths, and destination. 02691
A plan for empirical studies of programmers. 02692
The influence of training on use of end-user software. 03042
Task-related knowledge structures: analysis, modelling and application. 03218
The design and evaluation of an animated programming environment. 03220
The representation of user interface style. 03221
Issues governing the suitability of programming languages for programming tasks. 03224
Information flow in a user interface: the effect of experience and context on the recall of MacWrite screens. 03228
Effects of an immediate feedback tool on designer productivity and design usability. 04052
Human factors in computer systems. • HCI-0037 †
Human factors and interactive computer systems. § HCI-0038 †
An empirical investigation into problem decomposition strategies used in program design. HCI-0103 †
A structured approach to designing human-computer dialogues. HCI-0106 †
Some cognitive aspects of interface design in a two-variable optimization task. HCI-0111 †
Cursor movement during text editing. HCI-0113 †
The designer as user: building requirements for design tools from design practice. HCI-0129 †
An empirical study of the effects of modularity on program modifiability. HCI-0155 †
User-friendly password methods for computer-mediated information systems. HCI-0167 †
Experimental study of a two-dimensional language vs. FORTRAN for first-course progammers. HCI-0171 †
Processes in computer program comprehension. HCI-0172 †
Mental models and software maintenance. HCI-0173 †
Programmer/nonprogrammer differences in specifying procedures to people and computers. HCI-0174 †
The effects of program-dependent and program-independent deletions on software cloze tests. HCI-0175 †
Experimental evaluation of program quality using external metrics. HCI-0176 †

Fragile knowledge and neglected strategies in novice programmers. HCI-0177 †
Analyzing the high frequency bugs in novice programs. HCI-0178 †
Cognitive processes in program comprehension. HCI-0179 †
Information science: its roots and relation as viewed from the perspective of cognitive science. HCI-0185 †
Representational frameworks and models for human-computer interfaces. HCI-0188 †
Cognitive analysis of people's use of software. HCI-0199 †
Technology transfer: a new computer-based system. HCI-0203 †
On search in an incomplete database. HCI-0214 †
The vocabulary problem in human-system communication. HCI-0224 †
Attitudes towards specific uses of the computers quantitative, decision-making and record-keeping applications. HCI-0234 †
An experimental comparison of tabular and graphic data presentation. HCI-0236 †
Visual momentum: a concept to improve the cognitive coupling of person and computer. HCI-0238 †

# E. DATA

## E.0 GENERAL

Data, expert knowledge and decisions. ● 0338
Computational Geometry and its Applications. § 03850
Graph-theoretic concepts in computer science. § 03885
Goal and plan knowledge representations: from stories to text editors and programs. HCI-0183 †

## E.1 DATA STRUCTURES

An introduction to data and activity analysis. ● 0610
Compact disc–interactive. 0680
Advanced Turbo C programming. ● 0726
Document manipulation and typography. § 03182
People and computers IV. § 03215
Issues governing the suitability of programming languages for programming tasks. 03224
Undo support models. HCI-0144 †

### Arrays

Hypertext in context. 0114
VAX-BASIC with structured problem solving: 2nd edition. ● 0725

Interactive graphics: a tool for beginning programming students in discovering solutions to novel problems. 01038
Multi-Input fuzzy inference engine on a systolic array. 02953
Structured message passing on a shared-memory multiprocessor. 03514

### Graphs

Annual review of computer science vol. 1, 1986. ● 0719
TEXTNET: a network-based approach to text handling. HCI-0401 †
Interactive critical path analysis (ICPA)—microcomputer implementation of a project management and knowledge engineering tool. HCI-0445 †

### Lists

DRAT: A program for maintaining listings. 02401

### Tables

Annual review of computer science vol. 1, 1986. ● 0719

### Trees

Annual review of computer science vol. 1, 1986. ● 0719
Relations and attributes. 01103
Visual information chunking in spreadsheet calculation. 02232
Strongly typed user interfaces in an abstract data store. 02618
Generic diagnostic knowledge acquisition tool. 02944
A structural approach to the maintenance of structure-oriented environments. 03054
Drag: a graph drawing system. 03183

## E.2 DATA STORAGE REPRESENTATIONS

The proteus bibliography: Representation and interactive display in databases. 01085
Office-by-example: an integrated office system and database manager. 01159
Document manipulation and typography. § 03182
People and computers IV. § 03215

### Composite structures

DYNABOARD: user animated display of deductive proofs in mathematics. 02221
Drag: a graph drawing system. 03183
Abstraction and integration in IDE, an editing and formatting environment. 03184
Visual structure and the transmission of meaning. HCI-0404 †

## Linked representations

Computer-supported cooperative work: a book of readings. ● 0366
Beyond the chalkboard: computer support for collaboration and problem solving inmeetings (Reprint). 0376
Hypertext: an introduction and survey (Reprint). 0378
Data sharing in group work (Reprint). 0379
Hypertext hands-on!: an introduction to a new way of organizing and accessing information. ● 0686
Effects of computer programming experience on network representations of abstract programming concepts. 02204
Visual information chunking in spreadsheet calculation. 02232
A comparison of hypertext, scrolling and folding as mechanisms for program browsing. 03235
Hypertext tips: experiences in developing a hypertext tutorial. 03236
Design tools for large relational database systems. 03946
TEXTNET: a network-based approach to text handling. HCI-0401 †

## Primitive data items

A comparison of hypertext, scrolling and folding as mechanisms for program browsing. 03235
Interfaces for CAD applications. HCI-0418 †

## E.3 DATA ENCRYPTION

Computer security: a global challenge. § 03577
Codes and cryptography. ● HCI-0033 †

## E.4 CODING AND INFORMATION THEORY (H.1.1)

Color computer graphics in military cockpits. 0261
Color and the instructional use of the computer. 0263
Arithmetic codes resembling neural encoding. 02021
Codes and cryptography. ● HCI-0033 †

## Data compaction and compression

Digital video interactive. 0681
Digital video interactive. 01308

## Formal models of communication

Rule-based detection of speech features for automatic speech recognition. 0419
Relevance: communication and cognition. ● 0704
Applicable algebra, error-correcting codes, combinatorics and computer algebra. § 03846

## Nonsecret encoding schemes

Intelligible encoding of ASL image sequences at extremely low information rates. 02708
Vidura—an interactive multilingual publishing system—specification & design. 03186
The use of speech in man-machine interaction. 03910
Visual structure and the transmission of meaning. HCI-0404 †

## E.5 FILES (D.4.3, H.2)

Compact disc–interactive. 0680
Andrew: a distributed personal computing environment. HCI-0091 †

## Organization/structure

Designing a CD ROM information structure. 0682
Effects of computer programming experience on network representations of abstract programming concepts. 02204
Visual information chunking in spreadsheet calculation. 02232

## Sorting/searching

End-user searching—What are the implications?. 01224
Information retrieval using micros. 01225
Design goals for sloppy modeling systems. 02206

# F. THEORY OF COMPUTATION

## F.0 GENERAL

International conference on database theory. § 03914

## F.1 COMPUTATION BY ABSTRACT DEVICES

Algorithms for verified inclusions—theory and practice. 0549

### F.1.0 General

Petri nets: applications and relationships to other models of concurrency. § 03973

### F.1.1 Models of Computation (F.4.1)

Neural connections, mental computation. ● 0229
Early vision: from computational structure to algorithms and parallel hardware. 02703

[F. THEORY OF COMPUTATION]

Hypercube Concurrent Computers and Applications; vol. 2. § 02908
Abstract, generic models of interactive systems. 03219
Brains, machines, and mathematics (2nd ed.). ● HCI-0034 †
Induction: processes of inference, learning, and discovery. ● HCI-0064 †

*Automata (e.g., finite, push-down, resource-bounded)*

A survey of three dialogue models. 01152
A FORTRAN input program generator. 01227
Adding browsing semantics to the hypertext model. 02834
State trees as structured finite state machines for user interfaces. 03107
Extensions to C for interface programming. 03108
On the physics and mathematics of thought. 03778
Experimentation in the specification of an oral dialogue. 04005
Pushdown automata for user interface management. HCI-0382 †

*Bounded-action devices (e.g., Turing machines, random access machines)*

Finance. 0135
The Universal Turing Machine. § 03777

*Relations among models*

Building interprocess communication models using Stile. 03528
Mental models: towards a cognitive science of language, inference, and consciousness. ● HCI-0063 †

*Unbounded-action devices (e.g., cellular automata, circuits, networks of machines)*

Connections and symbols. ● 0588
Connectionism and cognitive architecture: a critical analysis. 0589
The relation between linguistic structure and associative theories of language learning models: constructive critique of some connectionist learning models. 0591
An introduction to computing with neural nets. 0769
Software for neural networks. 0770
An integrated system for neural network simulations. 0771
Conference report: IEEE 1'st Int'l conference on neural networks. 0772
Representation of dynamic features in a conceptual schema. 01231
Scaling relationships in back-propagation learning. 01338
Neural networks and NP-complete optimization problems; a performance study on the graph bisection problem. 01339

Basins of attraction in a perceptron-like neural network. 01340
The ring machine. 01483
Morphologic machines and conservative networks. 01604
Neurocomputing. 01836
Extending Petri nets for specifying man-machine dialogues. 02183
Dynamics and architecture for neural computation. 02270
Lyapunov function for parallel neural networks. 02736
A drive-reinforcement model of single neuron function: An alternative to the Hebbian neuronal model. 02743
A preliminary analysis of recursively generated networks. 02749
A comparison of algorithms for neuron-like cells. 02752
Parcella '88: Fourth International Workshop on Parallel Processing by Cellular Automata and Arrays. § 03971
Control of sensory processing - a hypothesis on and simulation of the architecture of an elementary cortical processor. 03972
Human-machine interaction and role/function/action-nets. 03974
Nets in office automation. 03975
Culture, cognitive, and connectionism: Towards an hermeneutic anthropology of mind. 04077
A neural network for visual pattern recognition. HCI-0391 †

**F.1.2 Modes of Computation**

*Alternation and nondeterminism*

Abstract, generic models of interactive systems. 03219

*Parallelism*

Parallel computers for AI databases. 0183
Parallel computation and computers for artificial intelligence. ● 0488
Application of the butterfly parallel processor in artificial intelligence. 0489
Connections and symbols. ● 0588
Connectionism and cognitive architecture: a critical analysis. 0589
An introduction to computing with neural nets. 0769
Implementing neural network models on parallel computers. 01403
Real-time failure detection on complex mechanical structures via parallel data processing. 01561
Electronic implementation of associative memory based on neural network models. 01895
Psychological concepts in a parallel system. 02564
Parallel structures in human and computer memory. 02742
Programming a massively parallel, computation universal system: Static behavior. 02746
Digital signal processor accelerators for neural network simulations. 02754

CATEGORY INDEX                                    [F. THEORY OF COMPUTATION]

DIME: a programming environment for unstructured triangular meshes on a distributed-memory parallel processor. 02909
Event-driven user interfaces based on quasi-parallelism. 03111
Connectionism and cognitive science. 03547
Parallelism and redundancy in neural networks. 03952
Exploring three possibilities in network design: spontaneous node activity, node plasticity and temporal coding. 03962
Parcella '88: Fourth International Workshop on Parallel Processing by Cellular Automata and Arrays. § 03971
Mental models: towards a cognitive science of language, inference, and consciousness. ● HCI-0063 †
Connectionist models and parallelism in high level vision. HCI-0363 †

*Probabilistic computation*

A probabilistic dominance measure for binary choices: analytic aspects of a multi-attribute random weights model. 02372
Abstract, generic models of interactive systems. 03219

### F.1.3 Complexity Classes (F.2)

The Universal Turing Machine. § 03777

*Reducibility and completeness*

Automatizing geometric proofs and constructions. 03851

*Relations among complexity classes*

On the physics and mathematics of thought. 03778

## F.2 ANALYSIS OF ALGORITHMS AND PROBLEM COMPLEXITY (B.6-7, F.1.3)

### F.2.0 General

Symsac '86—Proceedings of the 1986 symposium on symbolic and algebraic manipulation. § 03084

### F.2.1 Numerical Algorithms and Problems (G.1, G.4, I.1)

Reliability in computing: the role of interval methods in scientific computing. ● 0548
Applicable algebra, error-correcting codes, combinatorics and computer algebra. § 03846

*Computations on matrices*

Algorithms for verified inclusions—theory and practice. 0549
CAD Based verification and refinement of high level compliant motion primitives. 0600
Rule-based reasoning as Boolean transformations. 01901

Hidden patterns in combined and adaptive knowledge networks. 02073

*Number-theoretic computations (e.g., factoring, primality testing)*

Arithmetic codes resembling neural encoding. 02021

### F.2.2 Nonnumerical Algorithms and Problems (E.2-4, G.2, H.2-3)

Complexity in information theory. ● 0003
Graph-theoretic concepts in computer science. § 03885
MFDBS 87. § 03943

*Complexity of proof procedures*

Annual review of computer science vol. 1, 1986. ● 0719

*Computations on discrete structures*

Reasoning about action II: the qualification problem. 01213
On the relation between default and autoepistemic logic. 01214
An approach to human reliability on man-machine systems using error possibility. 01702
A representation of human reliability using fuzzy concepts. 02024
Epistemic necessity, possibility, and truth. Tools for dealing with imprecision and uncertainty in fuzzy knowledge-based systems. 02075
On global context dependencies and their properties (extended abstract). 03945
Design tools for large relational database systems. 03946
The complexity of some polynomial network consistency algorithms for constraint satisfaction problems. HCI-0361 †

*Geometrical problems and computations*

VLSI for solid modelling. 0232
Representation of local geometry in the visual system. 01249
An interactive approach to local remeshing around a propagating crack. 01685
Simplicial differential geometric theory for language cortical dynamics. 01698
Digital parallelism, perpendicularity, and rectangles. 01843
Non-Reimannian approach to geometry of visual space: An application of affinely connected geometry to visual alleys and horopter. 02364
Grid analysis: continuing the search for a metric of shape. 02367
Computational Geometry and its Applications. § 03850
Automatizing geometric proofs and constructions. 03851

[F. THEORY OF COMPUTATION]

### Pattern matching

Tensor geometry: a language of brains & neurocomputers. Generalized coordinates in neuroscience & robotics. 03966
Recognition of speech using temporal decomposition. 03990

*Pattern matching*

Annual review of computer science vol. 1, 1986. ● 0719
Catching knowledge in neural nets. 01171
Architectures for production systems: an inside look for those who study human-computer interaction. 03906
Automatic identification of writers. 03909
Real-time large vocabulary word recognition via diphone spotting and multiprocessor implementation. 03996
Physiology and psychophysics in taste and smell. 04009
Analogical problem solving. ● HCI-0044 †
Algorithms for approximate string matching. HCI-0180 †

*Routing and layout*

The fuzzy approach to facilities layout problems. 01697
The design of a traffic control expert system for long distance network contingencies. 02952
One-layer routing without component constraints. HCI-0090 †

*Sequencing and scheduling*

A supervisory control paradigm for real-time control of flexible manufacturing systems. 01205
Symbiotic systems for complex problems. 02922
Plant scheduling expert system for batch processing. 02977
An approach to knowledge elicitation in scheduling FMS: Toward a hybrid intelligent system. 03394

## F.3  LOGICS AND MEANINGS OF PROGRAMS

### F.3.0  General

Document manipulation and typography. § 03182
VDM '87: VDM—a formal method at work. § 03831

### F.3.1  Specifying and Verifying and Reasoning about Programs (D.2.1, D.2.4, D.3.1, E.1)

Cognitive systems engineering: new wine in new bottles. 02078
Experience of programming beauty: some patterns of programming aesthetics. 02184
Issues governing the suitability of programming languages for programming tasks. 03224
Software Engineering. § 03504

*Invariants*

A string correction method based on the context-dependent similarity. 0293

*Logics of programs*

A deductive database based on Aristotelian logic. 02398
Legal reasoning in 3-D. 02774
Muffin: a user interface design experiment for a theorem proving assistant. 04037
Specification and verification of database dynamics. HCI-0251 †

*Mechanical verification*

Attacking a complex distributed algorithm from different sides: an experience wih complementary validation tools. 01429
Automatizing geometric proofs and constructions. 03851
The PegaSys System: pictures as formal documentation of large programs. HCI-0146 †

*Pre- and post-conditions*

Specification and verification of database dynamics. HCI-0251 †

*Specification techniques*

The programmer's apprentices: a research overview. 01368
A formal specification of the QMS message system: the underlying abstract model. 01406
Attacking a complex distributed algorithm from different sides: an experience wih complementary validation tools. 01429
Expert systems in law: out of the research laboratory and into the marketplace. 02765
Analogical program synthesis from program components. 03920
A formal specification for a user interface for office automation. 04053
A specification language for direct-manipulation user interfaces. HCI-0123 †
Specification and verification of database dynamics. HCI-0251 †

### F.3.2  Semantics of Programming Languages (D.3.1)

Tense, qualifiers, and contexts. 01346
Temporal ontology and temporal reference. 01347
MFDBS 87. § 03943

## Operational semantics

Adding browsing semantics to the hypertext model. 02834
Knowledge base enhancements to relational databases. 03285

### F.3.3 Studies of Program Constructs (D.3.2-3)

How people comprehend unknown system structures: conceptual primitives in systems' surface representations. 03828

## Control primitives

An input/output primitive for object-oriented systems. 01969
Cognitive primitives. 02214

## Functional constructs

Functional databases, functional languages. 0034
Clarify function!. 01122
Effects of computer programming experience on network representations of abstract programming concepts. 02204
An expert system for conceptual schema design: a machine learning approach. HCI-0335 †

## Program and recursion schemes

Learning iteration recursion from examples. 02215

## Type structure

Constraint hierarchies. 01114

# F.4 MATHEMATICAL LOGIC AND FORMAL LANGUAGES

## F.4.0 General

Document manipulation and typography. § 03182
ESOP 86. § 03883
MFDBS 87. § 03943
Readings in natural language processing. ● HCI-0067 †

### F.4.1 Mathematical Logic (F.1.1, I.2.2-3)

Neural connections, mental computation. ● 0229
The use of prosodic parameters in automatic speech recognition. 03988
Brains, machines, and mathematics (2nd ed.). ● HCI-0034 †
Icon semantics—a formal approach to icon system design. HCI-0161 †

## Computability theory

Advances in Cognitive Science. § 02720
The Universal Turing Machine. § 03777

## Computational logic

An approach to human reliability on man-machine systems using error possibility. 01702
Relativized Arthur-Merlin versus Merlin-Arthur games. 01912
Manual control of an intrinsically unstable system and its modeling by fuzzy logic. 02026
Convexly combined fuzzy relational equations and several aspects of their application to fuzzy information processing. 02027
Epistemic necessity, possibility, and truth. Tools for dealing with imprecision and uncertainty in fuzzy knowledge-based systems. 02075
Causality and maximum entropy updating. 02076
Study of combination of belief intevals in lattice-structured networks. 02223

## Logic programming

Concurrent Prolog: collected papers. ● 0674
The Logix system user manual version 1.21. 0675
A model and an implementation of a logic programming environment. 01107
Negative knowledge towards a strategy for asking in logic programming. 02115
Spreadsheets with incremental queries as a user interface for logic programming. 02515
Logic programmable natural language processor of a knowledge-base management system. 02965
Logic programming '86. § 03816
Logic programming '85. § 03916
Logic programming '87. § 03919
Third international conference on logic programming. § 04028

## Mechanical theorem proving

On-line interpretation in speech understanding and dialogue systems. 04000

## Model theory

On the applicability of maximum entropy to inexact reasoning. 02074
Instructionless learning about a complex device: the paradigm and observations. HCI-0333 †

**Prolog** *see* Proper Noun Index

## Proof theory

The B tool. 04034

## Recursive function theory

Learning iteration recursion from examples. 02215
Reasoning in model management systems. 03487

### F.4.2 Grammars and Other Rewriting Systems (D.3.1)

Graph attribution as a specification paradigm. 01138
The flexibility of case grammar representations: a porting procedure for naturallanguage interfaces. 02255
Task-related knowledge structures: analysis, modelling and application. 03218
The mapping between grammar and processor. HCI-0346 †

### Grammar types (e.g., context-free, context-sensitive)

Design of a graphics interface for computer-based biomedical applications. 01427
On methods for interface specification and design. 02114
The structure of command languages: an experiment on task-action grammar. 02224
Structural aspects of semantic-directed clusters. 02534
A grammar-based approach to automatic generation of user-interface dialogues. 02868
EDGE - a graph based tool for specifying interaction. 03106

### Parsing

Knowledge representation. 0137
Design of a graphics interface for computer-based biomedical applications. 01427
Implementing a semantic interpreter using conceptual graphs. 01812
An approach to natural-language semantics in logic programming. 02342
A grammar-based approach to automatic generation of user-interface dialogues. 02868
Mental models: towards a cognitive science of language, inference, and consciousness. ● HCI-0063 †
Pushdown automata for user interface management. HCI-0382 †

### F.4.3 Formal Languages (D.3.1)

Graph attribution as a specification paradigm. 01138
Natural artificial languages: low level processes. 02082
Software Engineering. § 03504
Some applications of a theorem of Shirshov to language theory. HCI-0181 †

### Algebraic language theory

A string correction method based on the context-dependent similarity. 0293
Automatizing geometric proofs and constructions. 03851

### Classes defined by grammars or automata (e.g., context-free languages, regular sets, recursive sets)

The problem of identification. 01088
Polylith: an environment to support management of tool interfaces. 01096
Dialogues: a basis for constructing programming environments. 01097
Modeling rule-based systems by stochastic programmed production systems. 02017
Extending Petri nets for specifying man-machine dialogues. 02183
A biparty grammar as a tool for defining a man-machine dialogue. 03639
Development of mental models of an office system: a field study on an introductory course. 03903
Natural language communication with computers: some problems, perspectives, and new directions. 03913
On-line interpretation in speech understanding and dialogue systems. 04000
Knowledge based systems for speech understanding. 04001
Modification of Earley's algorithm for speech recognition. 04003
Mental models: towards a cognitive science of language, inference, and consciousness. ● HCI-0063 †

### Decision problems

An analysis of human and computer decision-making capabilities. 01951

### F.4.m Miscellaneous

Once more, with meaning. 0967

### F.m MISCELLANEOUS

Conceptual structures: information processing in mind and machine. ● HCI-0057 †

# G. MATHEMATICS OF COMPUTING

## G.0 GENERAL

Learning about computers and learning about mathematics. 0208
Speculating on the future of mathematics. 01210
Ordinals and the hemispheres of the brain. 01620
Can mathematics explain natural intelligence?. 02565
Symsac '86—Proceedings of the 1986 symposium on symbolic and algebraic manipulation. § 03084

CATEGORY INDEX　　　　　　　　　　　　　　　　[G. MATHEMATICS OF COMPUTING]

Reliability and robustness of engineering software. § 03451

## G.1 NUMERICAL ANALYSIS

### G.1.0 General

Applied algebra, algorithmics and error-correcting codes. § 03848

*Computer arithmetic*

User-oriented suggestions for floating-point and complex-arithmetic Forth standard extensions. 02306
Some design principles for a mathematical knowledge representation system: a new approach to scientific calculation. 03849

*Parallel algorithms*

Parallel computation and computers for artificial intelligence. ● 0488
Getting graphics in gear: graphics and dynamics in driving simulation. 02818
Interactive performance display and debugging using the NCUBE real-time graphicssystem. 02907
Parallel algorithms and architectures. § 03819
Real-time large vocabulary word recognition via diphone spotting and multiprocessor implementation. 03996
Steps toward making robots see. 04011

*Stability (and instability)*

Parameter estimation in array processing. 04021

### G.1.1 Interpolation

Motion interpolation by optimal control. 02817
Recognition of speech using temporal decomposition. 03990

*Interpolation formulas*

Interpolation coding: A representation for numbers in neural models. 01271

### G.1.2 Approximation

Reliability in computing: the role of interval methods in scientific computing. ● 0548
Design and implementation of an interactive optimization system for network design in the motor carrier industry. 02528

*Least squares approximation*

Dynamic spectral adaptation of automatic speech recognizers to new speakers. 03999

*Linear approximation*

Automatic construction of surfaces with prescribed shape. 01474

*Minimax approximation and algorithms*

Connectionist models and parallelism in high level vision. 02700

*Nonlinear approximation*

Parameter estimation in array processing. 04021

### G.1.3 Numerical Linear Algebra

A man-machine interface for computer-aided and simulation of control systems. 01237
Applicable algebra, error-correcting codes, combinatorics and computer algebra. § 03846
Integration of graphical tools in a computer algebra system. 03847

*Matrix inversion*

Parametric Fourier image characterization toolkit. 02798

### G.1.4 Quadrature and Numerical Differentiation

A user-friendly interface to Kendrick's DUAL code. 01447

*Iterative methods*

Learning iteration recursion from examples. 02215

*Multiple quadrature*

A design environment for computer-aided control system design via multi-objective optimisation. 03835

### G.1.5 Roots of Nonlinear Equations

Applicable algebra, error-correcting codes, combinatorics and computer algebra. § 03846
An iterative and interactive simulation method to reconstruct unknown inputs contributing to known outputs of neuronal systems. 04018

*Iterative methods*

Learning iteration recursion from examples. 02215

### G.1.6 Optimization

Collective computation, content-addressable memory, and optimization problems. 0004
Reliability in computing: the role of interval methods in scientific computing. ● 0548

[G. MATHEMATICS OF COMPUTING]

Neural networks and NP-complete optimization problems; a performance study on the graph bisection problem. 01339
Application of decision support system on sandwich beams, verified by experiments. 01572
Computational Geometry and its Applications. § 03850

*Constrained optimization*

A design environment for computer-aided control system design via multi-objective optimisation. 03835
Early vision: from computational structure to algorithms and parallel hardware. HCI-0365 †

*Gradient methods*

Generalizing back propagation to computation. 02726

*Integer programming*

A generalized model management system for mathematical programming. HCI-0302 †

*Least squares methods*

Curve tailoring with interactive computer. 01209

*Linear programming*

A graphics interface for linear programming. 01332
A user-friendly interface to Kendrick's DUAL code. 01447
Automatic construction of surfaces with prescribed shape. 01474
Interactive timetabling in universities. 01501
Interactive multiple objective linear programming system implemented on a microcomputer. 01508
User friendly micro computer program for solving fractional and linear programming problems. 01509
A natural language discourse model to explain linear programming models and solutions. 01671
Design and implementation of an interactive optimization system for network design in the motor carrier industry. 02528
Man-machine procedures of decision making under uncertainty based on linear programming. 02664
Dynamic spectral adaptation of automatic speech recognizers to new speakers. 03999
A generalized model management system for mathematical programming. HCI-0302 †
Computer-aided modeling and planning (CAMP). HCI-0415 †

*Nonlinear programming*

Curve tailoring with interactive computer. 01209
A design environment for computer-aided control system design via multi-objective optimisation. 03835

CATEGORY INDEX

Interactive fuzzy decision-making for multi-objective nonlinear programming using reference membership intervals. HCI-0295 †
A generalized model management system for mathematical programming. HCI-0302 †

### G.1.7 Ordinary Differential Equations

Alkahest III: automatic analysis of periodic weakly nonlinear ODEs. 03087

### G.1.8 Partial Differential Equations

*Finite element methods*

Interactive color graphical postprocessing as a unifying influence in numerical analysis research. 01684
An interactive approach to local remeshing around a propagating crack. 01685
Automated design and analysis system for design of custom orthopedic implants. 02931
Product engineering in the CIM environment. 03376

### G.1.9 Integral Equations

Morphologic machines and conservative networks. 01604

*Integro-differential equations*

A design environment for computer-aided control system design via multi-objective optimisation. 03835

### G.1.m Miscellaneous

Digital waveform sampling rate converter. 01578

## G.2 DISCRETE MATHEMATICS

### G.2.1 Combinatorics (F.2.2)

Computational Geometry and its Applications. § 03850
Graph-theoretic concepts in computer science. § 03885

*Combinatorial algorithms*

Convexly combined fuzzy relational equations and several aspects of their application to fuzzy information processing. 02027
Study of combination of belief intevals in lattice-structured networks. 02223
Implementing imprecision in information systems. HCI-0259 †

*Permutations and combinations*

Study of combination of belief intevals in lattice-structured networks. 02223

1002

## G.2.2 Graph Theory (F.2.2)

A cognitive approach for graph drawing. 01616
Implementing a semantic interpreter using conceptual graphs. 01812
Directed graph representations of association structures: A systematic approach. 01862
User interface wars: the next wave. 02544
EDGE - a graph based tool for specifying interaction. 03106
Computational Geometry and its Applications. § 03850
Graph-theoretic concepts in computer science. § 03885
Conceptual structures: information processing in mind and machine. ● HCI-0057 †

### Graph algorithms

Application of structural pattern recognition in histopathology. 0295
Interactive timetabling in universities. 01501
Applications of computer graphics to the visualization of meteorological data. 02819
NetGraph: an object-oriented graphical toolset for risk assessment. 02972
Drag: a graph drawing system. 03183
Integration of graphical tools in a computer algebra system. 03847
Graph-theoretical tools and their use in a practical distributed operating system design case. 03886

### Network problems

An introduction to computing with neural nets. 0769
Software for neural networks. 0770
An integrated system for neural network simulations. 0771
Conference report: IEEE 1'st Int'l conference on neural networks. 0772
A graphical tool for the design and prototyping of distributed systems. 01146
Representation of dynamic features in a conceptual schema. 01231
Basins of attraction in a perceptron-like neural network. 01340
Network generation using the Prufer code. 01536
An incidence-matrix-driven panel system for the IBM PC. 01814
Analysis of competition-based spreading activation in connectionist models. 02179
Study of combination of belief intevals in lattice-structured networks. 02223
Dynamics and architecture for neural computation. 02270
Sherlock—a system for diagnosing power distribution ring network faults. 02916
The application of cognitive psychology to CAD. 03239

Spatial and temporal transformations in visuo-motor coordination. 03963

### Trees

Generalized fisheye views. 0893
Transformational derivation of programs using the focus system. 01140
Parametric Fourier image characterization toolkit. 02798

## G.2.m Miscellaneous

Neural networks and NP-complete optimization problems; a performance study on the graph bisection problem. 01339
Algebraic approach to the problem of addressation. 01488
Evaluating formatted alphanumeric displays. 01525
Morphologic machines and conservative networks. 01604
The magical number three—plus or minus zero. 01622
A fuzzy knowledge base of an expert system for analysis of manual lifting tasks. 01693
The fuzzy approach to facilities layout problems. 01697
Simplicial differential geometric theory for language cortical dynamics. 01698
The fuzzy decodings of educative texts. 01700
The fuzzy logic of text understanding. 01701
A closed-loop causal model of workload based on a comparison of fuzzy and crisp measurement techniques. 01746
Automated concept acquisition in noisy environments. 01841
Rule-based reasoning as Boolean transformations. 01901
Hidden patterns in combined and adaptive knowledge networks. 02073
Star, maximal rectangles, lattices: a new perspective on Q-analysis. 02105
Human supervisor modelling: some new developments. 02170
An application of computerized fuzzy graphics rating scale to the psychological measurement of individual differences. 02200
Rough sets and dependency analysis among attributes in computer implementations of expert's inference models. 02231
A group model of form recognition under plane similarity transformations. 02366
Alleys on an apparent frontoparallel plane. 02374
Modeling uncertainty in human perception. 03825
Computational networks in early vision: from orientation selection to optical flow. 03961
Limited interconnectivity in synthetic neural systems. 03968

[G. MATHEMATICS OF COMPUTING]    CATEGORY INDEX

## G.3  PROBABILITY AND STATISTICS

Artificial intelligence and statistics. ● 0321
Environments for supporting statistical strategy. 0322
Use of psychometric tools for knowledge acquistion: a case study. 0323
The analysis phase in development of knowledge based systems. 0324
A method framework for the statistical package SPSS/PC+ to support occasional users. 01202
Statistical inference on spontaneous neuronal discharge patterns. I. Single neuron. 01247
A study of stability of electrocortical rhythm generators. 01258
Uncertainty analysis of human EEG spectra: A multivariate information theoretical method for the analysis of brain activity. 01270
Modeling of task-dependent characteristics of human operator dynamics during pursuit manual tracking. 01859
ARIADNE: a knowledge-based interactive system for planning and decision support. 01860
A design for a fuzzy logic controller. 02028
A perceptual study of the Flury-Riedwyl faces for graphically displaying multivariate data. 02126
The application of psychological scaling techniques to knowledge elicitation for knowledge-based systems. 02139
Classifying sensory inspectors with heterogeneous inspection-error probabilities. 02396
The accuracy of combining judgemental and statistical forecasts. 02474
A study of user interface aids for model-oriented decision support systems. 02479
Memory networks with asymmetric bonds. 02740
Computer science and statistics. § 03313
Essential ingredients for a statistical workstation. 03315
Statistical software, graphics and future workstations for data analysis. 03316
The Monte Carlo processor: designing and implementing a language for Monte Carlo work. 03317
An iterative approach to improving data analysis in the classroom. 03318
Primary perceptual units in word recognition. 03994

### Probabilistic algorithms (including Monte Carlo)

Describing movement control at two levels of abstraction. 0403
Understanding Bayesian reasoning via graphical displays. 0884
An approach to human reliability on man-machine systems using error possibility. 01702
Modeling the Cognitive content of displays. 01800
Process control and people at General Motors' Delta Engine Plant. 01905
A fuzzy decision-making method and its application to a company choice problem. 02029
Study of combination of belief intevals in lattice-structured networks. 02223
An abstract description generator for the reliability analysis in the design of real time systems. 02490
Morphological representation of speech knowledge for automatic speech recognition systems. 03992
Speaker-independent automatic recognition of plosive sound in letters and digits. 03993

### Statistical computing

Linear predictive coding of speech. 0289
Describing movement control at two levels of abstraction. 0403
Use of object-oriented programming in a time series analysis system. 01112
The design of a user friendly engineering economy analysis package for a microcomputer. 01507
A theory of information structure. I. General principles. 02361
Inference control mechanism for statistical database frequency-imposed data distortions. 02449
Planning for advising. 02886
Justified advice: a semi-naturalistic study of advisory strategies. 02887
How to interface to advisory systems? Users request help with a very simple language. 02888
Measuring the performance of statisticians with statistical software. 03314
Implementation plan for the use of on-line fiber analysis in the textile industry. 03433
Acting-out and burn-out behaviours of operators monitoring automated systems. 03440
Visual comfort as a criterion for designing display units. 03892
Displaying statistical information—ergonomic considerations. 03893
Factors influencing the detection of trend deviations on VDTs. 03894
Morphological representation of speech knowledge for automatic speech recognition systems. 03992
Speaker-independent automatic recognition of plosive sound in letters and digits. 03993
Parameter estimation in array processing. 04021
The elements of graphing data. ● HCI-0035 †
Knowledge elicitation: dissociating conscious reflections from automatic processes. HCI-0337 †

## [G. MATHEMATICS OF COMPUTING]

### Statistical software

Visual comfort as a criterion for designing display units. 03892

Displaying statistical information—ergonomic considerations. 03893

## G.4 MATHEMATICAL SOFTWARE

A method framework for the statistical package SPSS/PC+ to support occasional users. 01202

Measuring the performance of statisticians with statistical software. 03314

Statistical software, graphics and future workstations for data analysis. 03316

An iterative approach to improving data analysis in the classroom. 03318

Applicable algebra, error-correcting codes, combinatorics and computer algebra. § 03846

**XMP** *see* Proper Noun Index

## G.m MISCELLANEOUS

Diffusion approximation of the neuronal model with synaptic reversal potentials. 01254

Identification of MGB cells by Volterra kernels. III. A glance into the black box. 01259

Projected free fall trajectories. I. Theory and simulation. 01265

Quantitative determination of orientational and directional components in the response of visual cortical cells to moving stimuli. 01268

A model-based monitor of human sleep stages. 01269

Neural nets for adaptive filtering and adaptive pattern recognition. 01362

Optimal allocation of a work force in a toxic substance environment. 01534

An interactive outranking system for multi-attribute decision making. 01539

Brain research: theory and experiment. 01575

An approach to a mathematics of phenomena: canonical aspects of reentrant form eigenbehavior in the extended calculus of indications. 01621

Neurocomputing—neurons as microcomputers. 01691

Counting, computing, and the representation of numbers. 01771

On the representation and the impact of reliability on expert system weights. 02211

Task compatibility of manipulator postures. 02258

Induction of categories: The problem of multiple equilibria. 02360

Mathematical modeling of fatigue in physically demanding jobs. 02363

A limitation theorem for the differentiable prototypification of shape. 02365

Counting and timing models in psychophysics and the conjoint Weber's law. 02368

Expectation and variance of item resemblance distributions in a convolution-correction model of distributed memory. 02369

Psychological models of deferred decision making. 02370

The accumulator model of two-choice discrimination. 02371

A probabilistic dominance measure for binary choices: analytic aspects of a multi-attribute random weights model. 02372

A note on mimicking additive reaction time models. 02373

The psychophysical function of binocular space perception. 02375

Combining overlapping information. 02477

Frames of mind in intertemporal choice. 02478

Firm strategies for costly engineering learning. 02485

An empirical formula for visual search. 02526

Joint spatial/spatial-frequency representation. 02580

Using simulation to study complex problem solving: a review of studies in the FRG. 02598

Linearization of the dynamic transfer response of time invariant nonlinear systems—in connection with the parallel information processing in living organisms. 02665

Influence of noise on the behavior of an autoassociative neural network. 02727

High order correlation model for associative memory. 02729

Coupled mode theory for neural networks. 02730

Neural network refinements and extensions. 02732

Application of neural network algorithms and architectures to correlation/tracking and identification. 02734

Hopfield model applied to vowel and consonant discrimination. 02735

Motion correspondence and analog networks. 02739

Differential Hebbian learning. 02745

Programming a massively parallel, computation universal system: Static behavior. 02746

A simple selectionist learning rule for neural networks. 02756

Nonlinear discriminant functions and associative memories. 02757

Forgetting as a way to improve neural-net behavior. 02759

### Queueing theory

The selection of a servicing discipline in a multiterminal conversational information retrieval system. 01233

## H. INFORMATION SYSTEMS

### H.0 GENERAL

Text, context, and hypertext: writing with and for the computer. ● 0098
Computers for managing information. ● 0141
Attitudes to information technology. 0150
Trends in information systems. ● 0498
Government infostructures: a guide to the networks of information resources and technologies at federal, state, and local levels. ● 0523
Information technology in the humanities: tools, techniques and applications. ● 0595
Oxford surveys in information technology; vol. 2, 1985. ● 0755
Competition and cooperation in information systems innovation. 01941
The dual role of information centers: an assessment of end user computing management strategies. 01942
The effects of display formats on information systems design. 02357
People and computers III. § 03189
Exploring technology: today and tomorrow. § 03491
System design for human development and productivity: participation and beyond. § 03640
Information systems: failure analysis. § 03804
International conference on database theory. § 03914

### H.1 MODELS AND PRINCIPLES

#### H.1.0 General

Text, context, and hypertext: writing with and for the computer. ● 0098
As we may think (Reprint). 0367
Oxford Surveys in Information Technology. ● 0753
Message equivocality, media selection and manager performance: implications for information systems. 02505
Applications Track. § 03455
Information systems definition: the Multiview approach. ● HCI-0085 †
Designing online information. HCI-0152 †
Project Nick: meetings augmentation and analysis. HCI-0156 †
On models and modelling in human-computer cooperation. HCI-0182 †
Goal and plan knowledge representations: from stories to text editors and programs. HCI-0183 †

#### H.1.1 Systems and Information Theory (E.4)

Critical issues in information systems research. ● 0153
Evolution of an organizational interface: the new business department at a large insurance firm (Reprint). 0382
Social psychological aspects of computer-mediated communication (Reprint). 0384
Reducing social context cues: electronic mail in organizational communication (Reprint). 0385
Cognitive science and organizational design: a case study of computer conferencing (Reprint). 0386
Relationships and tasks in scientific research collaborations (Reprint). 0387
The variable impact of computer technologies on the organization of work activities. 0388
Oxford Surveys in Information Technology. ● 0753
Principles of information. 01597
Cybernetics and organization theory: a critical review. 01617
Modelling degrees of item interest for a general database query system. 02083
Cognitive issues in the process of software development: review and reappraisal. 02222
Electronic information systems analysis. Present and future information systems use by academics involved in development studies. 02323
Trends in office modeling. 03355
Architectural implications of office systems. 03356
Human factors in office systems. 03357
Organizational implications of office systems: toward a critical social action perspective. 03358
The study of information: interdisciplinary messages. ● HCI-0036 †
Human information seeking and design of information systems.. HCI-0184 †
Information science: its roots and relation as viewed from the perspective of cognitive science. HCI-0185 †

*General systems theory*

Semantics. 0154
A conceptual framework for the augmentation of man's intellect (Reprint). 0368
Interface design and evaluation—Semiotic implications. 0409
The computer and the mind. ● 0462
Cognition & personal structure. ● 0533
Mental models in cognitive science. 0647
A philosophical basis for decision aiding. 0649
Fuzzy decision analysis. 0650
Fuzzy sets and decision analysis. 0651
Decision making with unreliable probabilities. 0652
Skills, rules, and knowledge; signals, signs, and symbols, and other distinctions in human performance models. 0654
Artificial intelligence & human learning: intelligent computer-aided instruction. ● 0671

CATEGORY INDEX [H. INFORMATION SYSTEMS]

Uncertainty analysis of human EEG spectra: A multivariate information theoretical method for the analysis of brain activity. 01270
Implementation issues for operations research software. 01537
Organizational humanity and architecture: Duality and complementarity of papa-logic and mama-logic in managerial conceptualizations of change. 01609
Self-authorization: A characteristic of some elements in certain self-organizing systems. 01610
Self-organizing systems and transformational-generative (TG) grammar. 01619
Building and understanding adaptive systems: a statistical/numerical approach to factory automation and brain research. 01890
A qualitative model of human interaction with complex dynamic systems. 01891
Qualitative approximation methodology for modeling and simulation of large dynamic systems: Applications to a Marine power plant. 01900
Towards a new theory of job design. 03368
The role of memory in intelligent information systems. 03462
A framework of composite information systems for strategic advantage. 03465
Composite models in symms. 03485
An interactionist's view of system pathology. 03813
How people comprehend unknown system structures: conceptual primitives in systems' surface representations. 03828
Qualitative modeling of physical systems for knowledge based control. 03834
A design environment for computer-aided control system design via multi-objective optimisation. 03835
The central nervous system as a low and high level control system. 04007
Proprioceptive feedback for sensory-motor control. 04008
Analysing the scope of cognitive models in human-computer interaction: a trade-off approach. HCI-0245 †

### Information theory

Complexity in information theory. ● 0003
Technology + design + research = information design. 0107
Semantics. 0154
Towards a framework for systems analysis practice. 0155
Understanding the elements of system design. 0156
Managerial expert systems and organizational change: some critical research issues. 0157
Strategies for research on information systems in organizations. A critical analysis of research purpose and time frame. 0158
The in-formation of information systems. 0159

The computer and the mind. ● 0462
Judgement and decision: theory and application. 0648
Relevance: communication and cognition. ● 0704
Annual review of computer science vol. 1, 1986. ● 0719
The diffusion and impacts of information technology in households. 0754
Cognitive user interface laboratory, GMD-IPSI. 0870
Introducing information technology: experiences of a large industrial unit. 01217
The concept of an information management system and its use within design studies. 01244
A science of information for the information age. 01285
Self-organization in a perceptual network. 01366
Reasoning with imprecise knowledge in expert systems. 02018
On the applicability of maximum entropy to inexact reasoning. 02074
Causality and maximum entropy updating. 02076
Experience of programming beauty: some patterns of programming aesthetics. 02184
Primary journals today and tomorrow. 02264
Notions and dynamics of information. 02319
The real information society: present situation and some forecasts. 02322
Research on information interaction and intelligent information provision mechanisms. 02328
A theory of information structure. I. General principles. 02361
A theory of information structure. II. A theory of perceptual organization. 02362
Linearization of the dynamic transfer response of time invariant nonlinear systems—in connection with the parallel information processing in living organisms. 02665
Advances in Cognitive Science. § 02720
Neural Networks for Computing. § 02723
Concepts in connectionist models. 02724
Generalizing back propagation to computation. 02726
Influence of noise on the behavior of an autoassociative neural network. 02727
Absolutely stable learning of recognition codes by a self-organizing neural network. 02728
High order correlation model for associative memory. 02729
Coupled mode theory for neural networks. 02730
Neural network refinements and extensions. 02732
Optical analog of two-dimensional neural networks and their application in recognition of radar targets. 02733
Application of neural network algorithms and architectures to correlation/tracking and identification. 02734
Lyapunov function for parallel neural networks. 02736
A comparison of neural network and matched filter processing for detecting lines in images. 02738
Motion correspondence and analog networks. 02739
Memory networks with asymmetric bonds. 02740

[H. INFORMATION SYSTEMS]

Neurons with hysteresis form a network that can learn without any changes in synaptic connection strengths. 02741

A drive-reinforcement model of single neuron function: An alternative to the Hebbian neuronal model. 02743

A preliminary analysis of recursively generated networks. 02749

Error correction and asymmetry in a binary memory matrix. 02750

A machine for neural computation of acoustical patterns with application to real time speech recognition. 02751

Tensor network theory and its application in computer modeling of the metaorganization of sensorimotor hierarchies of gaze. 02753

Digial signal processor accelerators for neural network simulations. 02754

Designing a neural network satisfying a given set of constraints. 02755

A simple selectionist learning rule for neural networks. 02756

Nonlinear discriminant functions and associative memories. 02757

Topology conserving mappings for learning motor tasks. 02758

Forgetting as a way to improve neural-net behavior. 02759

Higher-order Boltzmann machines. 02760

Firing response of a neural model with threshold modulation and neural dynamics. 02761

VLSI architectures for implementation of neural networks. 02762

A layered neural network model applied to the auditory system. 02763

User perceptions of DSS restrictiveness: an experiment. 03470

A box structured methodology for solving business problems. 03483

GMMS: global model management system: a conceptional design framework for model management systems for distributed decision support systems. 03484

Integration of graphical tools in a computer algebra system. 03847

The use of speech in man-machine interaction. 03910

Analogs of biological tissues for mechanoelectrical transduction: tactile sensors and muscle-like actuators. 04014

Some observations on user interface design and user performance. HCI-0117 †

### Value of information

Annual review of computer science vol. 1, 1986. ● 0719
The moral cracker?. 01546
The value of information and computer-aided information seeking: problem formulation and application to fiction retrieval. 01989

Refining problem-solving knowledge in repertory grids using a consultation mechanism. 02205

Person-to-person communication in an applied research/service delivery setting. 02445

### H.1.2 User/Machine Systems

[*Unreviewed items have been suppressed from this listing.]

Fifth generation computers: concepts, implementations and uses. ● HCI-0001 †

User-centered requirements analysis. ● HCI-0004 †

Storyboard prototyping: a new approach to user requirements analysis. ● HCI-0005 †

Online help systems: design and implementation. ● HCI-0009 †

Software ergonomics: advances and applications. ● HCI-0012 †

How to write a really good user's manual. ● HCI-0017 †

Formally-based tools and techniques for human-computer dialogues. ● HCI-0021 †

Codes and cryptography. ● HCI-0033 †

The study of information: interdisciplinary messages. ● HCI-0036 †

Human factors in computer systems. ● HCI-0037 †

Human factors and interactive computer systems. § HCI-0038 †

Readings on cognitive ergonomics - mind and computers. § HCI-0039 †

Plans and situated actions: the problem of human-machine communication. ● HCI-0040 †

Human-computer interaction: a design guide. ● HCI-0041 †

Human performance engineering: using human factors/ergonomics to achieve computer system usability (2nd ed.). ● HCI-0042 †

Human-computer interface design. HCI-0043 †

Planning and design of information systems. ● HCI-0045 †

Online information retrieval: concepts, principles, and techniques. ● HCI-0046 †

Online communities. ● HCI-0051 †

Artificial and human intelligence. § HCI-0052 †

Expertise transfer for expert system design. ● HCI-0059 †

Introduction to natural language processing. ● HCI-0065 †

Readings in natural language processing. ● HCI-0067 †

Digital typography: an introduction to type and composition for computer system design. ● HCI-0074 †

In the age of the smart machine: the future of work and power. ● HCI-0083 †

The computer culture. § HCI-0084 †

Informatics (computer and information science): its ideology, methodology, and sociology. HCI-0086 †

## [H. INFORMATION SYSTEMS]

Andrew: a distributed personal computing environment. HCI-0091 †
Anatomy of a compact user interface development tool. HCI-0104 †
A structured approach to designing human-computer dialogues. HCI-0106 †
Active help systems. HCI-0108 †
A generalized user interface for applications programs (II). HCI-0112 †
Cursor movement during text editing. HCI-0113 †
Abstractions for user interface design. HCI-0114 †
The 1984 Olympic Message System: a test of behavioral principles of system design. HCI-0125 †
Cost/benefit analysis for incorporating human factors in the software lifecycle. HCI-0127 †
Heuristics for designing enjoyable user interfaces: lessons from computer games. HCI-0132 †
Specification and generation of variable, personalized graphical interfaces. HCI-0134 †
The depth/breadth trade-off in the design of menu-driven user interfaces. HCI-0135 †
An approach to user specification of interactive display interfaces. HCI-0137 †
Experimental adaptive interface. HCI-0139 †
Project Nick: meetings augmentation and analysis. HCI-0156 †
Human factors in software engineering: a review of the literature. HCI-0157 †
Equal opportunity interactive systems. HCI-0168 †
A Multilevel menu-driven user interface: Design and evaluation through simulation. HCI-0170 †
Experimental study of a two-dimensional language vs. FORTRAN for first-course progammers. HCI-0171 †
Information science: its roots and relation as viewed from the perspective of cognitive science. HCI-0185 †
The future of interactive systems and the emergence of direct manipulation. HCI-0186 †
Reading continuous text from a one-line visual display. HCI-0187 †
Representational frameworks and models for human-computer interfaces. HCI-0188 †
Stages and levels in human-machine interaction. HCI-0189 †
QWERTY and keyboard reform: the soft keyboard option. HCI-0190 †
Extending state transition diagrams for the specification of human-computer interaction. HCI-0191 †
Speed of response using keyboard and screen-based microcomputer response media. HCI-0192 †
A research model for studying the gender/power aspects of human-computer communication. HCI-0193 †
GENIE: a modifiable computer-based task for experiments in human-computer interaction. HCI-0194 †
Taming and civilizing computers. HCI-0195 †
An experimental program investigating color-enhanced and graphical information presentation: an integration of the findings. HCI-0196 †
Effects of experience and comprehension on reading time and memory for computer programs. HCI-0197 †
A quantitative theory of human-computer interaction. HCI-0198 †
Cognitive analysis of people's use of software. HCI-0199 †
Cognitive engineering—cognitive science. HCI-0200 †
Behavioral experiments on handmarkings. HCI-0201 †
An experimental evaluation of the impact of data display format on recall performance. HCI-0202 †
Technology transfer: a new computer-based system. HCI-0203 †
Reading and writing with computers: a framework for explaining differences in performance. HCI-0204 †
A taxonomy for the study of human factors in management information systems. HCI-0205 †
Object lens: a "spreadsheet" for cooperative work. HCI-0206 †
Interacting with Computers. HCI-0207 †
Measuring the quality of linguistic forecasts. HCI-0247 †
Generalized query-by-rule: a heterogeneous database query language. HCI-0252 †
A visual approach to browsing in a database environment. HCI-0258 †
A supporting system for effective construction and sharing of scientific databases by general researchers. HCI-0262 †
An intelligent interface for online interaction. HCI-0264 †
Towards a new research paradigm in information retrieval. HCI-0273 †
Using the micro-computer to simplify database access: designing interfaces to complex files. HCI-0275 †
A prototype electronic encyclopedia. HCI-0278 †
CONTEXT: an on-line documentation system. HCI-0280 †
Reading and writing the electronic book. HCI-0282 †
Electronic calendars in the office: an assessment of user needs and current technology. HCI-0287 †
Executive workstations: issues and requirements. HCI-0288 †
Semistructured messages are surprisingly useful for computer-supported coordination. HCI-0290 †
The impact of DSS on organizational communication. HCI-0294 †
Interactive fuzzy decision-making for multi-objective non-linear programming using reference membership intervals. HCI-0295 †
Communications design for Co-oP: a group decision support system. HCI-0297 †
Computer decision support for senior managers: encouraging exploration. HCI-0298 †

[H. INFORMATION SYSTEMS]        CATEGORY INDEX

gIBIS: a hypertext tool for exploratory policy discussion. HCI-0300 †
The dimensions of accessibility to online information: implications for implementing office information systems. HCI-0304 †
A user agent for multiple computer-based message services. HCI-0306 †
Strategies for encouraging successful adoption of office communication systems. HCI-0307 †
Diversity in the use of electronic mail: a preliminary inquiry. HCI-0310 †
Usage patterns in an integrated voice and data communications system. HCI-0311 †
On the application of rule-based techniques to the design of advice giving systems. HCI-0315 †
UMFE: a user modelling front-end subsystem. HCI-0325 †
Decision trees: a contribution to automatic interpretation of GUHA results. HCI-0329 †
Selecting a humanly understandable knowledge representation for reasoning about knowledge. HCI-0330 †
Cognitive models, cognitive tasks, and information retrieval. HCI-0331 †
A research center for augmenting human intellect. HCI-0334 †
A natural language front end to databases with evaluative feedback. HCI-0338 †
Extended person-machine interface. HCI-0344 †
A framework for investigating language-mediated interaction with machines. HCI-0347 †
Pygmalion at the interface. HCI-0349 †
An economical approach to modeling speech recognition accuracy. HCI-0354 †
The phonetic basis for computer speech processing. HCI-0358 †
Computer systems software: the programmer/machine interface. ● HCI-0361 †
The application of scene synthesis techniques to the display of multidimensional image data. HCI-0371 †
Graphic design for computer graphics. HCI-0376 †
TEXTNET: a network-based approach to text handling. HCI-0401 †
The doctor's use of a computer in the consulting room: an analysis. HCI-0409 †
IDECAP: interactive pictorial information system for demographic and environmental planning applications. HCI-0411 †
An approach to CAD system performance evaluation. HCI-0414 †
Customers' requirements for natural language systems: results of an inquiry. HCI-0426 †
Paradox of the active user. HCI-0434 †
Computer mediated work: the interplay between technology and structured jobs. HCI-0440 †
Computerization, productivity, and quality of work-life. HCI-0441 †

Human-computer interface development: concepts and systems for its management. HCI-0444 †

*Human factors*

[*Unreviewed items have been suppressed from this listing.]
Designing the user interface: strategies for effective human-computer interaction. ● HCI-0006 †
Human-computer interface design guidelines. ● HCI-0011 †
Computer usability testing & evaluation. ● HCI-0014 †
The soft side of software: a management approach to computer documentation. ● HCI-0016 †
Human factors and interactive computer systems. § HCI-0038 †
Hypertext/hypermedia. ● HCI-0047 †
Office automation: a social and organizational perspective. ● HCI-0048 †
Executive support systems: the emergence of top management computer use. ● HCI-0049 †
Access to academic networks. ● HCI-0050 †
In search of the person: philosophical explorations in cognitive science. ● HCI-0062 †
The AutoCAD productivity book: tapping the hidden power of AutoCAD. ● HCI-0076 †
The second self: computers and the human spirit. ● HCI-0082 †
Information systems definition: the Multiview approach. ● HCI-0085 †
Touch-sensitive screens: the technologies and their application. HCI-0087 †
Reading text from computer screens. HCI-0088 †
Voice-input aids for the physically disabled. HCI-0089 †
Information systems design methodologies and their compliance with cognitive ergonomy. HCI-0097 †
Supporting concurrency, communication, and synchronization in human-computer interaction—the Sassafras UIMS. HCI-0102 †
Holophrasted displays in an interactive environment. HCI-0105 †
Consistent user interface. HCI-0107 †
The role of context and adaptation in user interfaces. HCI-0109 †
Some observations on user interface design and user performance. HCI-0117 †
A dedicated microcomputer for handwritten interaction with a software tool: system prototyping. HCI-0119 †
Boxer: a reconstructible computational medium. HCI-0121 †
Cognitive layouts of windows and multiple screens for user interfaces. HCI-0122 †
A specification language for direct-manipulation user interfaces. HCI-0123 †
MIKE: the menu interaction kontrol environment. HCI-0124 †

CATEGORY INDEX [H. INFORMATION SYSTEMS]

A proposed solution to the problem of levels in error-message generation. HCI-0126 †
Between man and machine. HCI-0128 †
Graphical user interfaces. HCI-0133 †
A general user interface for creating and displaying tree-structures, hierarchies, decision trees, and nested menus. HCI-0136 †
Toward native language software for information management. HCI-0138 †
A display editor with random access and continuous control. HCI-0140 †
Undo support models. HCI-0144 †
Literate programming. HCI-0148 †
The future of "writing" for the computer industry. HCI-0150 †
Corporate culture, technical documentation, and organization diagnosis. HCI-0151 †
Designing online information. HCI-0152 †
Technical writers as computer scientists: the challenges of online documentation. HCI-0153 †
Creating a style for online help. HCI-0154 †
An empirical study of the effects of modularity on program modifiability. HCI-0155 †
Ada: first users—pleased; prospective users—still hesitant. HCI-0159 †
Fatal error in pass zero: how not to confuse novices. HCI-0164 †
User-friendly password methods for computer-mediated information systems. HCI-0167 †
The ethics of automated publishing systems (a response to Dr. Brockmann). HCI-0170 †
On models and modelling in human-computer co-operation. HCI-0182 †
Reading and writing with computers: a framework for explaining differences in performance. HCI-0204 †
Training wheels in a user interface.. HCI-0208 †
The evaluation of text editors: methodology and empirical results.. HCI-0209 †
Human factors issues in VDT use: environmental and workstation design considerations. HCI-0210 †
What non-programmers know about programming: natural language procedure specification. HCI-0211 †
Man-machine interface issues in the construction and use of an expert system. HCI-0212 †
An aspect of aesthetics in human-computer communications: pretty windows. HCI-0213 †
On search in an incomplete database. HCI-0214 †
Understanding the effectiveness of computer graphics for decision support: a cumulative experimental approach. HCI-0215 †
Mainframe and microcomputer-based business graphics: What satisfies users?. HCI-0216 †
The computer imperative among owners of home computers: explanation by social factors. HCI-0217 †
On the purpose and analysis of EDP user systems. HCI-0218 †

A novice user's interface to information retrieval systems. HCI-0219 †
A note on the nature of creativity in engineering: implications for supporting system design. HCI-0220 †
The effects of communication monitors on user satisfaction. HCI-0221 †
Operator work load: when is enough enough?. HCI-0222 †
The microcomputer as a classroom audio visual device: the concept, and prospects. HCI-0223 †
The vocabulary problem in human-system communication. HCI-0224 †
Psychology and information technology. HCI-0225 †
Information technology and home-based services: improving the usability of teleshopping. HCI-0226 †
Expert systems as cognitive tools for human decision making. HCI-0227 †
Impact of system response time on state anxiety. HCI-0228 †
Learning by doing with simulated intelligent help. HCI-0229 †
Organizing for human factors. HCI-0230 †
Designing for usability: key principles and what designers think. HCI-0231 †
Computer anxiety in management: myth or reality?. HCI-0232 †
Querying external databases. HCI-0233 †
Attitudes towards specific uses of the computers quantitative, decision-making and record-keeping applications. HCI-0234 †
Observations of end-user online searching behavior over eleven years. HCI-0235 †
An experimental comparison of tabular and graphic data presentation. HCI-0236 †
An empirical investigation of voice as an input modality for computer programming. HCI-0237 †
Analysing the scope of cognitive models in human-computer interaction: a trade-off approach. HCI-0245 †
Experience with the ZOG human-computer interface system. HCI-0246 †
ARES: a relational database with the capability of performing flexible interpretation of queries. HCI-0248 †
Query languages—a taxonomy. HCI-0254 †
Using restricted natural language for data retrieval: a plan for field evaluation. HCI-0255 †
What makes RABBIT run?. HCI-0256 †
An almost path-free very high-level interactive data manipulation language for a microcomputer-based database system. HCI-0261 †
Design and performance considerations for an optical disk-based, multimedia object server. HCI-0265 †
Development of a term association interface for browsing bibliographic data bases based on end users' word associations. HCI-0266 †

[H. INFORMATION SYSTEMS]

The spatial metaphor for user interfaces: experimental tests of reference by location versus name. HCI-0268 †
Calibrating databases. HCI-0269 †
Users and experts in the document retrieval system model. HCI-0270 †
On the applied use of human memory models: the memory extender personal filing system. HCI-0271 †
Architecture problems in the construction of expert systems for document retrieval. HCI-0272 †
Transparent information systems through gateways, front ends, intermediaries, and interfaces. HCI-0276 †
Knowledge-based search tactics for an intelligent intermediary system. HCI-0277 †
Views on end-user searching. HCI-0283 †
A user oriented design process for user recovery and command reuse support. HCI-0284 †
Testing bibliographic displays for online catalogs. HCI-0285 †
The user interface of a personal calendar program. HCI-0286 †
Whiteboards: a graphical database tool. HCI-0289 †
Office systems. HCI-0291 †
Reflections on NoteCards: seven issues for the next generation of hypermedia systems. HCI-0293 †
Change, attitude to change, and decision support system success. HCI-0296 †
Personal computing for decision support. HCI-0299 †
A laboratory study of user characteristics and decision-making performance in end-user computing. HCI-0301 †
Impact of design methods on decision support systems success: an empirical assessment. HCI-0303 †
Interface design in computerized conferencing systems: a personal view. HCI-0305 †
A distributed interoffice mail system. HCI-0308 †
Beyond the chalkboard: computer support for collaboration and problem solving in meetings. HCI-0312 †
Videotex: anatomy of a failure. HCI-0313 †
Strategic issues in knowledge engineering. HCI-0317 †
Expert systems—where do we go from here?. HCI-0318 †
Expertise transfer and complex problems: using AQUINAS as a knowledge-acquisition workbench for knowledge-based systems. HCI-0336 †
Natural language with discrete speech as a mode for human-to-machine. HCI-0355 †
Tones of voice: the role of intonation in computer speech understanding. HCI-0356 †
Text processing by speech: dialogue design and usability issues in the provision of a system for disabled users. HCI-0357 †
The X window system. HCI-0370 †
Graphical prototyping of graphical tools. HCI-0375 †
The human factors of computer graphics interaction techniques. HCI-0377 †

Physiological principles for the effective use of color. HCI-0378 †
CNS-HLS mapping using fuzzy sets. HCI-0380 †
The use of colour in language syntax analysis. HCI-0385 †
Multivariate data representation and analysis by face pattern using facial expression characteristics. HCI-0394 †
Speech-controlled text-editing: effects of input modality and of command structure. HCI-0397 †
A note on undetected typing errors. HCI-0399 :8E
Document convergence in an interactive formatting system. HCI-0405 †
Resistance to computerization: an examination of the relationship between resistance and the cognitive style of the clinician. HCI-0407 †
The development and use of information technology in health care. HCI-0408 †
Computer-aided modeling and planning (CAMP). HCI-0415 †
Goals in the application of CAD interfaces. HCI-0416 †
Special Issue: The FAA's Advanced Automation Program. HCI-0424 †
Information technology in the home: promises as yet unrealized. HCI-0425 †
What makes users happy?. HCI-0427 †
Experimental results do not support some ergonomic standards for computer video terminal design. HCI-0428 †
The Japanese and software: is it a good match?. HCI-0429 †
Implications for education and training. HCI-0430 †
Adult learners: away with computerphobia. HCI-0433 †
The relationship of problem-solving ability and course performance among novice programmers. HCI-0435 †
Using low-cost workstations to investigate computer networks and distributed systems. HCI-0437 †
The automated tutoring of introductory computer programming. HCI-0438 †
An overview of research and co-operation in advanced information technology. HCI-0442 †
Computer-assisted negotiations: a case history from the law of the sea negotiations and speculation regarding future uses. HCI-0443 †
An empirical study of the impact of user involvement on system usage and information satisfaction. HCI-0448 †
A plan for evaluating usability of software products. HCI-0449 †
An empirical study of occupational stress, attitudes and health among information systems personnel. HCI-0451 †
Strategic management of technostress: The chaining of Prometheus. HCI-0452 †

[H. INFORMATION SYSTEMS]

## Human information processing

[*Unreviewed items have been suppressed from this listing.]

Chip talk: projects in speech synthesis. ● HCI-0002 †
Brains, machines, and mathematics (2nd ed.). ● HCI-0034 †
Analogical problem solving. ● HCI-0044 †
How we know. ● HCI-0053 †
Understanding computers and cognition. ● HCI-0054 †
Man-made minds: the promise of artificial intelligence. ● HCI-0055 †
Creative intelligences. ● HCI-0056 †
Conceptual structures: information processing in mind and machine. ● HCI-0057 †
A comprehensive guide to AI and expert systems. ● HCI-0058 †
An artificial intelligence approach to legal reasoning. ● HCI-0061 †
Mental models: towards a cognitive science of language, inference, and consciousness. ● HCI-0063 †
Induction: processes of inference, learning, and discovery. ● HCI-0064 †
Pattern recognition: human and mechanical. ● HCI-0072 †
Artificial behavior: computer simulation of psychological processes. ● HCI-0073 †
Introducing CAL: a practical guide to writing computer-assisted learning programs. ● HCI-0079 †
Artificial intelligence and tutoring systems: computational and cognitive approaches to the communication of knowledge. ● HCI-0080 †
Reading text from computer screens. HCI-0088 †
The art of programming. HCI-0095 †
Programmer perceptions of productivity and programming tools. HCI-0099 †
An empirical investigation into problem decomposition strategies used in program design. HCI-0103 †
Cognitive layouts of windows and multiple screens for user interfaces. HCI-0122 †
Processes in computer program comprehension. HCI-0172 †
Mental models and software maintenance. HCI-0173 †
Programmer/nonprogrammer differences in specifying procedures to people and computers. HCI-0174 †
The effects of program-dependent and program independent deletions on software cloze tests. HCI-0175 †
Experimental evaluation of program quality using external metrics. HCI-0176 †
Fragile knowledge and neglected strategies in novice programmers. HCI-0177 †
Analyzing the high frequency bugs in novice programs. HCI-0178 †
Cognitive processes in program comprehension. HCI-0179 †

On models and modelling in human-computer co-operation. HCI-0182 †
Goal and plan knowledge representations: from stories to text editors and programs. HCI-0183 †
Human information seeking and design of information systems.. HCI-0184 †
The vocabulary problem in human-system communication. HCI-0224 †
Visual momentum: a concept to improve the cognitive coupling of person and computer. HCI-0238 †
Approaches to human reasoning: an analytic framework. HCI-0239 †
The distributed processing of knowledge and belief in the human brain. HCI-0240 †
Human cognition and human computer interaction. HCI-0241 †
Cognitive attributes: implications for display design in supervisory control systems. HCI-0242 †
Eye movement analysis system using fundus images. HCI-0243 †
Relations between cognitive psychology and computer system design. HCI-0244 †
Analysing the scope of cognitive models in human-computer interaction: a trade-off approach. HCI-0245 †
Implementing imprecision in information systems. HCI-0259 †
Development of a term association interface for browsing bibliographic data bases based on end users' word associations. HCI-0266 †
In search of searching skills. HCI-0274 †
Learning to use a word processor: by doing, by thinking, and by knowing. HCI-0292 †
Beyond the chalkboard: computer support for collaboration and problem solving in meetings. HCI-0312 †
Computing with structured connectionist networks. HCI-0314 †
A model for the interpretation of verbal predictions. HCI-0316 †
Acquisition of control and domain knowledge by watching in a blackboard environment. HCI-0319 †
Knowledge and control for a mechanical design expert system. HCI-0320 †
What do users ask? Some thoughts on diagnostic advice. HCI-0326 †
Learning in parallel networks: simulating learning in a probabilistic system. HCI-0332 †
Instructionless learning about a complex device: the paradigm and observations. HCI-0333 †
An expert system for conceptual schema design: a machine learning approach. HCI-0335 †
Knowledge elicitation: dissociating conscious reflections from automatic processes. HCI-0337 †
Semantic primitives or meaning postulates: mental models or propositional representation?. HCI-0339 †

1013

Using focus to constrain language generation. HCI-0341 †

From schema theory to computational (neuro-)linguistics. HCI-0345 †

The mapping between grammar and processor. HCI-0346 †

Postscript: computers and the modeling of mind. HCI-0348 †

Modularity and lexical access. HCI-0350 †

Transporting the linguistic string project system from a medical to a Navy domain. HCI-0352 †

A framework of a mechanical translation between Japanese and English by analogy principle. HCI-0353 †

Text processing by speech: dialogue design and usability issues in the provision of a system for disabled users. HCI-0357 †

A fuzzy rule-based model of human problem solving. HCI-0359 †

Naive algorithm design techniques—a case study. HCI-0360 †

Connectionist models and parallelism in high level vision. HCI-0363 †

Perception of organization in a random stimulus. HCI-0364 †

Early vision: from computational structure to algorithms and parallel hardware. HCI-0365 †

Preattentive processing in vision. HCI-0366 †

Perception of transparency in man and machine. HCI-0367 †

Reverse engineering the brain. HCI-0368 †

Physiological principles for the effective use of color. HCI-0378 †

Real time graphic simulation of visual effects of egomotion. HCI-0379 †

A performing medium for working group graphics. HCI-0383 †

Color and the computer in cartography. HCI-0386 †

Recognizing unexpected objects: a proposed approach. HCI-0389 †

Selective networks and recognition automata. HCI-0390 †

A neural network for visual pattern recognition. HCI-0391 †

Environment-centered and viewer-centered perception of surface orientation. HCI-0392 †

Visual hyperacuity: representation and computation of high precision position information. HCI-0393 †

A parallel formant synthesizer for machine voice output. HCI-0396 †

Synthesis of print-quality cursive script based on a model of the human handwriting mechanism. HCI-0402 †

Image processing aspects of type. HCI-0403 †

Visual structure and the transmission of meaning. HCI-0404 †

Evaluating RECONSIDER: a computer program for diagnostic prompting. HCI-0410 †

The LISP tutor: it approaches the effectiveness of a human tutor. HCI-0431 †

Computer-based microworlds—a definition to aid design. HCI-0432 †

The automated tutoring of introductory computer programming. HCI-0438 †

Cognitive aspects of learning and using a programming language. HCI-0439 †

Open versus closed minds: the effect of dogmatism on an analyst's problem-solving behavior. HCI-0446 †

Training for optimising transfer between word processors. HCI-0447 †

**UIMS** *see* Proper Noun Index

**ZOG** *see* Proper Noun Index

### H.1.m Miscellaneous

Principles of information systems for management (2nd ed.). ● 0005

A folklore view of information. 01222

Measuring the quality of linguistic forecasts. HCI-0247 †

### H.2 DATABASE MANAGEMENT

The man-machine interface aspect of an automatic classification numbering system in a computerized library system. 02316

### H.2.0 General

Perspectives in artificial intelligence vol. 2: machine translation, NLP, databases and computer-aided instruction. ● 0198

Office information systems and computer science (Reprint). 0373

Expert systems: the user interface. ● 0425

Using a knowledge base to drive an expert system interface with a natural language component. 0430

Object-oriented concepts, databases, and applications. ● 0475

Hypertext hands-on!: an introduction to a new way of organizing and accessing information. ● 0686

Readings in database systems. ● 0708

New applications of data bases. § 02710

ACTES/Proceedings Symposium 1988 ACM SIGSMAll/PC. § 02787

The design of a document database. 02835

Research and development in information retrieval. § 03072

People and computers IV. § 03215

Proc. of the third British national conference on databases (BNCOD3). § 03279

Proceedings of the fourth British national conference on databases (BNCOD 4). § 03282

Proceedings of the Fifth British National Conference on Databases (BNCOD 5). § 03284

Methodological problems of designing dialogue-oriented components in information systems. 03595

Computational Geometry and its Applications. § 03850

Design and performance considerations for an optical disk-based, multimedia object server. HCI-0265 †

**ARES** *see* Proper Noun Index

**INGRES** *see* Proper Noun Index

*Security, integrity, and protection*

Computer crime. ● 0722

Office-by-example: an integrated office system and database manager. 01159

The hackers' comfort. 01544

The human immune system as an information systems security reference model. 01547

Design goals for sloppy modeling systems. 02206

Issues in the verification of knowledge in rule-based systems. 02226

Intelligent interfaces for secure multilevel database systems. 02990

Computer security: a global challenge. § 03577

The integrity lock support environment. 03578

Database Security: Status and Prospects. § 03579

Lessons learned from modeling a secure multilevel relational database system. 03580

Inference control via query restriction vs. data modification: a perspective. 03581

Modelling and controlling user inference. 03582

Privacy respecting permissions and rights. 03583

Role-based security in data base management systems. 03584

Status of trusted DBMS interpretations. 03585

Factors in the investigation of human error in accident causation. 03805

Management strategies and information failure. 03806

Investigating sources of error in the management of crises: theoretical assumptions and a methodological approach. 03807

Fallible humans and vulnerable systems: lessons learned from aviation. 03808

Human reliability in information systems. 03809

Error auditing in air traffic control. 03810

Failure analysis of information systems: reflections on the use of expert systems in information systems. 03811

Fault management, knowledge support, and responsibility in man-machine systems. 03812

An interactionist's view of system pathology. 03813

Mental models and failures in human-machine systems. 03814

Failure analysis of information systems in small manufacturing enterprises: the importance of the human interface. 03815

Specification and verification of database dynamics. HCI-0251 †

### H.2.1 Logical Design

Database portals: a new application program interface. 0707

System R: a relational approach to database management. 0709

The design requirements of office systems. 0757

The proteus bibliography: Representation and interactive display in databases. 01085

Office-by-example: an integrated office system and database manager. 01159

Responsibility sharing between sophisticated users and professionals in structured prototyping. 01978

Cognitive systems engineering: new wine in new bottles. 02078

Modelling degrees of item interest for a general database query system. 02083

The structure of command languages: an experiment on task-action grammar. 02224

A deductive database based on Aristotelian logic. 02398

SIGMOD International Conference on Management of Data. § 03089

Integrating data and metadata to enhance the user interface. 03280

An approach to interactive definition of database views. 03281

The integration of the network and relational approaches in a DBMS. 03283

Advances in object-oriented database systems. § 03841

Methodology of window management. § 03923

Active vision: integration of fixed and mobile cameras. 04017

Planning and design of information systems. ● HCI-0045 †

The database designer's workbench. HCI-0249 †

Update and retrieval in a relational database through a universal schema interface. HCI-0260 †

Using the micro-computer to simplify database access: designing interfaces to complex files. HCI-0275 †

Semistructured messages are surprisingly useful for computer-supported coordination. HCI-0290 †

An expert system for conceptual schema design: a machine learning approach. HCI-0335 †

Document convergence in an interactive formatting system. HCI-0405 †

[H. INFORMATION SYSTEMS]   CATEGORY INDEX

## Data models

The society of text: hypertext, hypermedia, and the social construction of information. ● 0111
Supporting collaboration in hypermedia: issues and experiences. 0117
From database to hypertext via electronic publishing: an information odyssey. 0122
Compact disc–interactive. 0680
Data model issues for object-oriented applications. 0712
Collaboration in KMS, a shared hypermedia system. 0807
The problem of identification. 01088
Extending a relational database with deferred referential integrity checking andintelligent joins. 01089
An object-oriented framework for interactive data graphics. 01115
Data model issues for object-oriented applications. 01157
Intelligent information-sharing systems. 01322
ER model clustering as an aid for user communication and documentation in database design. 01331
An alternative approach to the conceptual database design using fragments of nat. 01481
Evaluating user utterances in natural language interfaces to databases. 01486
Convexly combined fuzzy relational equations and several aspects of their application to fuzzy information processing. 02027
A semantic data model as the basis for an automated database design tool. 02036
Linkage versus integration for binding database and interactive graphics systems. 02040
Heuristic graph displayer for G-BASE. 02227
Absolute dates and relative dates in an inferential system on temporal dependencies between events. 02235
The effects of relational and entity-relationship data models on query performance of end users. 02247
A portable query language for small scale systems. 02492
Artificial Intelligence and Law. § 02764
Legal data modeling: The prohibited transaction exemption analyst. 02779
The data model is the heart of interface design. 02875
CAD Data management using object-oriented paradigms. 02958
Generating an individualized user interface. 03074
A design data manager. 03090
Using active data in a UIMS. 03121
User-driven adaptive behaviour, a comparative evaluation and an inductive analysis. 03226
Knowledge base enhancements to relational databases. 03285
Knowledge representation for model libraries. 03479
An environment for understanding programs. 03525
Lessons learned from modeling a secure multilevel relational database system. 03580
Inference control via query restriction vs. data modification: a perspective. 03581
Qualitative modeling of physical systems for knowledge based control. 03834
A model for an object management system for software engineering environments. 03843
ROSE: An object-oriented database system for interactive computer graphics applications. 03845
MFDBS 87. § 03943
Data manipulation languages for the universal relation view DURST. 03944
On global context dependencies and their properties (extended abstract). 03945
Design tools for large relational database systems. 03946
Pictorial interfaces to data bases. HCI-0116 †
Object lens: a "spreadsheet" for cooperative work. HCI-0206 †
A generator of direct manipulation office systems. HCI-0250 †
Specification and verification of database dynamics. HCI-0251 †
Generalized query-by-rule: a heterogeneous database query language. HCI-0252 †
Implementing imprecision in information systems. HCI-0259 †
An almost path-free very high-level interactive data manipulation language for a microcomputer-based database system. HCI-0261 †
Visual structure and the transmission of meaning. HCI-0404 †

**IDA** *see* Proper Noun Index

**Intermedia** *see* Proper Noun Index

## Schema and subschema

View management in distributed data base systems. 0218
Intelligent information-sharing systems. 01322
ER model clustering as an aid for user communication and documentation in database design. 01331
Evaluating user utterances in natural language interfaces to databases. 01486
A semantic data model as the basis for an automated database design tool. 02036
GISD: a graphical interactive system for conceptual database design. 02042
Heuristic graph displayer for G-BASE. 02227
Unsolvable problems related to the view integration approach. 03915
Data manipulation languages for the universal relation view DURST. 03944
Object lens: a "spreadsheet" for cooperative work. HCI-0206 †
A visual approach to browsing in a database environment. HCI-0258 †
Reasoning in natural language for designing a data base. HCI-0322 †

CATEGORY INDEX [H. INFORMATION SYSTEMS]

### H.2.2 Physical Design

Designing a CD ROM information structure. 0682
Office-by-example: an integrated office system and database manager. 01159
A modular user-oriented decision support for physical database design. 01669
Factors in the investigation of human error in accident causation. 03805
Advances in object-oriented database systems. § 03841
A supporting system for effective construction and sharing of scientific databases by general researchers. HCI-0262 †

### Access methods

Hypertext: an introduction and survey (Reprint). 0378
Data sharing in group work (Reprint). 0379
Designing a CD ROM information structure. 0682
A communication mechanism supporting actions. 01441
Algebraic approach to the problem of addressation. 01488
Informational zooming: an interaction model for the graphical access to text knowledge bases. 03073
Computer security: a global challenge. § 03577
The integrity lock support environment. 03578
Update and retrieval in a relational database through a universal schema interface. HCI-0260 †
CONTEXT: an on-line documentation system. HCI-0280 †

### Deadlock avoidance

Compact disc–interactive. 0680
Dialogue and the search for information. 01223

### Recovery and restart

dBUG III offers source level solutions. 01641
A new conceptual model for interactive user recovery and command reuse facilities. 02884

### H.2.3 Languages

Natural-language interfaces. 0693
Modelling degrees of item interest for a general database query system. 02083
SIGMOD International Conference on Management of Data. § 03089
The integration of the network and relational approaches in a DBMS. 03283
Database Security: Status and Prospects. § 03579
Advances in object-oriented database systems. § 03841
MFDBS 87. § 03943
Pictorial interfaces to data bases. HCI-0116 †
A visual approach to browsing in a database environment. HCI-0258 †

A user oriented design process for user recovery and command reuse support. HCI-0284 †
Computer-aided modeling and planning (CAMP). HCI-0415 †

**AWK** *see* Proper Noun Index

**CODIL** *see* Proper Noun Index

**DAPLEX** *see* Proper Noun Index

### Data description languages (DDL)

Desktop publishing. 0238
Intelligent information-sharing systems. 01322
The integration of the network and relational approaches in a DBMS. 03283
Object lens: a "spreadsheet" for cooperative work. HCI-0206 †
An almost path-free very high-level interactive data manipulation language for a microcomputer-based database system. HCI-0261 †
Semistructured messages are surprisingly useful for computer-supported coordination. HCI-0290 †

### Data manipulation languages (DML)

Principles of an icons-based language. 01080
The integration of the network and relational approaches in a DBMS. 03283
Privacy respecting permissions and rights. 03583
ROSE: An object-oriented database system for interactive computer graphics applications. 03845
Data manipulation languages for the universal relation view DURST. 03944
On global context dependencies and their properties (extended abstract). 03945
Generalized query-by-rule: a heterogeneous database query language. HCI-0252 †
Update and retrieval in a relational database through a universal schema interface. HCI-0260 †
An almost path-free very high-level interactive data manipulation language for a microcomputer-based database system. HCI-0261 †
ASK is transportable in half a dozen ways. HCI-0279 †

**dBASE III PLUS** *see* Proper Noun Index

**FIDO** *see* Proper Noun Index

**GQBR** *see* Proper Noun Index

**HERCULES** *see* Proper Noun Index

**MIDAS** *see* Proper Noun Index

**QUEL** *see* Proper Noun Index

[H. INFORMATION SYSTEMS]                                                                                               CATEGORY INDEX

## Query languages

Natural languages. 0136
The semantics-based natural language interface to relational databases. 0164
A knowledge-based intermediary system for information retrieval. 0737
A framework for choosing a database query language. 0761
Conversational hypertext: information access through natural language dialogues with computers. 0867
Office-by-example: an integrated office system and database manager. 01159
A common interface for accessing document retrieval systems and dbms for retrieval of bibliographic data. 01990
Dealing with a database query language in a new situation. 02119
Procedural and non-procedural query languages revisited: a comparison of relational algebra and relational calculus. 02146
The effect of different conceptual models using reasoning in a database query writing task. 02201
A portable query language for small scale systems. 02492
A visual shell interface to a database. 02640
Database maps. 03286
Privacy respecting permissions and rights. 03583
Interaction with IBS: an Icon-based system. 03838
Graphics interaction in databases. 03862
Querying external databases. HCI-0233 †
Generalized query-by-rule: a heterogeneous database query language. HCI-0252 †
HERCULES: database query using natural language fragments. HCI-0253 †
Query languages—a taxonomy. HCI-0254 †
Using restricted natural language for data retrieval: a plan for field evaluation. HCI-0255 †
What makes RABBIT run?. HCI-0256 †
Natural language query processing in a temporal database. HCI-0257 †
A visual approach to browsing in a database environment. HCI-0258 †
Implementing imprecision in information systems. HCI-0259 †
Update and retrieval in a relational database through a universal schema interface. HCI-0260 †
Architecture problems in the construction of expert systems for document retrieval. HCI-0272 †
A generalized model management system for mathematical programming. HCI-0302 †
A natural language front end to databases with evaluative feedback. HCI-0338 †

**Prolog** *see* Proper Noun Index

## Report writers

A generalized user interface for applications programs (II). HCI-0112 †
An approach to user specification of interactive display interfaces. HCI-0137 †

**SDL** *see* Proper Noun Index

**SQL** *see* Proper Noun Index

**VIADUCT** *see* Proper Noun Index

## H.2.4 Systems

Formflex: a user interface tool for forms definition and management. 0204
Advanced databases multi-media interface. 0418
The INGRES papers: anatomy of a relational database system. ● 0706
Readings in database systems. ● 0708
Rule base management using meta knowledge. 01081
Panel: user interfaces and database management systems. 01082
The multimedia object presentation manager of MINOS: a symmetric approach. 01083
An object-oriented approach to multimedia databases. 01084
Data model issues for object-oriented applications. 01157
Convexly combined fuzzy relational equations and several aspects of their application to fuzzy information processing. 02027
SIGMOD International Conference on Management of Data. § 03089
Expert database systems. § 03173
An interactive data dictionary facility for CAD/CAM data bases. 03174
A temporal logic for reasoning about changing data bases in the context of natural language question-answering. 03176
Anticipating false implicatures: cooperative responses in question-answer systems. 03178
Supporting natural language database update by modeling real world actions. 03179
Ecilpse—an APSE based on PCTE. 03181
SEE: a safe editing environment; human-computer interaction for programmers. 03225
User-driven adaptive behaviour, a comparative evaluation and an inductive analysis. 03226
Information flow in a user interface: the effect of experience and context on the recall of MacWrite screens. 03228
Database Security: Status and Prospects. § 03579
Advances in object-oriented database systems. § 03841
Experiences with Distributed Systems. § 03881
Generalized query-by-rule: a heterogeneous database query language. HCI-0252 †

A supporting system for effective construction and sharing of scientific databases by general researchers. HCI-0262 †

### Concurrency

Data sharing in group work (Reprint). 0379
Concurrency control in groupware systems. 01090
Concurrency in intelligent systems. 01169
The PFG environment: parallel programming with petri net semantics. 03527
Building interprocess communication models using Stile. 03528
Concurrency 88. § 03873
Specification and verification of database dynamics. HCI-0251 †

**DAVID** *see* Proper Noun Index

### Distributed systems

View management in distributed data base systems. 0218
A decision support system for vehicle scheduling in public transport. 0339
Callisto: an intelligent project management system (Reprint). 0375
Distributed databases and distributed processing between personal computers and mainframes. 0458
User interface. 0621
A graphical tool for the design and prototyping of distributed systems. 01146
The profile naming service. 01149
MH: a multifarious user agent. 01428
The ISA expert system: a prototype system for failure diagnosis on the space station. 02913
Monitoring and performance measuring distributed systems during operation. 03025
Distributed database considerations in an expert system for radar analysis. 03175
Trends in office modeling. 03355
POEM: An office system for international use. 03457
GMMS: global model management system: a conceptional design framework for model management systems for distributed decision support systems. 03484
FolioPub: A publication management system. 03520
Segue: Support for distributed graphical interfaces. 03526
PantaPM: an integrated software development environment. 03796
A distributed object server. 03842
Object lens: a "spreadsheet" for cooperative work. HCI-0206 †
Semistructured messages are surprisingly useful for computer-supported coordination. HCI-0290 †
Reflections on NoteCards: seven issues for the next generation of hypermedia systems. HCI-0293 †
Beyond the chalkboard: computer support for collaboration and problem solving in meetings. HCI-0312 †

### Query processing

Text processing with the START natural language system. 0100
An interactive customization program for a natural language database query system. 0163
Intelligent interfaces to Nordic data bases. 0738
A spreadsheet interface for logic programming. 0822
Conversational hypertext: information access through natural language dialogues with computers. 0867
Office-by-example: an integrated office system and database manager. 01159
OS/2 query manager overview and prompted interface. 01809
A priori analysis of natural language queries. 02006
Querying the French *Yellow Pages*: natural language access to the directory. 02007
Prospects for knowledge-based customization of natural languages query systems. 02008
The effect of different conceptual models using reasoning in a database query writing task. 02201
Interactive communication of sentential structure and content: an alternative approach to man-machine communication. 02220
A natural language interface processor based on the hierarchical-tree structure model of relation tables. 02315
Multimodal response planning: an adaptive rule based approach. 02894
INQUEST: A prototype intelligence tool. 02918
The IRUS transportable natural language database interface. 03177
Knowledge base enhancements to relational databases. 03285
A graphical entity-relationship database browser. 03532
Inference control via query restriction vs. data modification: a perspective. 03581
Natural language communication with computers: some problems, perspectives, and new directions. 03913
Data manipulation languages for the universal relation view DURST. 03944
Online library catalogues as information retrieval systems: what can we learn from research?. 04040
Readings in natural language processing. ● HCI-0067 †
ARES: a relational database with the capability of performing flexible interpretation of queries. HCI-0248 †
Implementing imprecision in information systems. HCI-0259 †
Update and retrieval in a relational database through a universal schema interface. HCI-0260 †
An interactive database end user facility for the definition and manipulation of forms. HCI-0263 †
Reflections on NoteCards: seven issues for the next generation of hypermedia systems. HCI-0293 †
A generalized model management system for mathematical programming. HCI-0302 †

[H. INFORMATION SYSTEMS]                                    CATEGORY INDEX

Acquisition of control and domain knowledge by watching in a blackboard environment. HCI-0319 †
Portability of syntax and semantics in DATALOG. HCI-0340 †
TEAM: an experiment in the design of transportable natural-language interfaces. HCI-0351 †

**ROSE** see Proper Noun Index

**System R** see Proper Noun Index

*Transaction processing*

Evolution of an organizational interface: the new business department at a large insurance firm (Reprint). 0382
Information retrieval using micros. 01225
A communication mechanism supporting actions. 01441
An architecture for a business and information system. 01818
Using hypertext to overcome the knowledge base development bottleneck: a case study. 02914
Patterned systems design—HCI in commercial data processing. 03193
Update and retrieval in a relational database through a universal schema interface. HCI-0260 †

**H.2.5 Heterogeneous Databases**

A knowledge-based intermediary system for information retrieval. 0737
Generalized query-by-rule: a heterogeneous database query language. HCI-0252 †
A supporting system for effective construction and sharing of scientific databases by general researchers. HCI-0262 †
Transparent information systems through gateways, front ends, intermediaries, and interfaces. HCI-0276 †

*Program translation*

Automated design and analysis system for design of custom orthopedic implants. 02931

**H.2.7 Database Administration**

Functional databases, functional languages. 0034
The database designer's workbench. HCI-0249 †

*Data dictionary/directory*

Querying the French *Yellow Pages*: natural language access to the directory. 02007
Directories, DOS, and hard disks: impact on the user. 02604

A supporting system for effective construction and sharing of scientific databases by general researchers. HCI-0262 †

*Logging and recovery*

A new conceptual model for interactive user recovery and command reuse facilities. 02884
SEE: a safe editing environment; human-computer interaction for programmers. 03225

**H.2.8 Database applications**

Data types and persistence. ● 0033
Text, context, and hypertext: writing with and for the computer. ● 0098
Using an object-oriented programming language to create audience-driven hypermedia environments. 0101
Hypertext: a way of incorporating user feedback into online documentation. 0102
Information development is part of product development—not an afterthought. 0103
Reflections on authoring, editing, and managing hypertext. 0119
Q & A simplified. ● 0167
Advanced information technology in the new industrial society: the Kingston seminars. ● 0225
The management of advanced information technology. 0226
Design and test of a database for fiction, based on an analysis of children's search behavior. 0451
Authoring systems for ICAI. 0469
Understanding & using application software. ● 0626
The CD ROM handbook. ● 0678
Artificial intelligence systems. 0683
A knowledge-based intermediary system for information retrieval. 0737
Intelligent interfaces to Nordic data bases. 0738
The migration of expert systems into the production environment. 0740
Assessment of an effort to integrate computer functions in an engineering design firm. 0779
Toward hypertext publishing. 01075
The problem of identification. 01088
Information retrieval using micros. 01225
Putting Texas on disc. 01316
A new algorithm for extracting the interior of bounded regions based on chain coding. 01469
Development of the wedding planner—extensions to reach a young audience. 01502
A comprehensive data base for the design of manual materials handling. 01510
An industrial chemical hazards database with a natural language interface: an application of artificial intelligence. 01533

ORGPLAN an information-decisive aid system to resolving organizing problems. 01573
Designing a user manual to support an in-house database. 01635
HutWindows: an improved architecture for a user interface management system. 01830
Marcosby example in a graphical UIMS. 01831
Linkage versus integration for binding database and interactive graphics systems. 02040
The electronic book Ebook3. 02234
The MIDAS database system. 02387
Linkage versus integration for binding database and interactive graphics systems. 02406
The development of an intelligent user interface for NASA's scientific databases. 02673
NLI-ESD: An expert natural language interface to a statistical data bank. 02712
Artificial Intelligence and Law. § 02764
Expert systems in law: out of the research laboratory and into the marketplace. 02765
A connectionist approach to conceptual information retrieval. 02772
Informational zooming: an interaction model for the graphical access to text knowledge bases. 03073
Architectural implications of office systems. 03356
Issues in modeling supervisory control in flexible manufacturing systems. 03363
Role-based security in data base management systems. 03584
Advances in object-oriented database systems. § 03841
Multiple inheritance and genericity for the integration of a database management system in an object-oriented approach. 03844
Textvision: elicitation and acquisition of conceptual knowledge by graphic representation and multiwindowing. 03902
Artificial intelligence and cognitive psychology: a new look at human factors. 03904

## H.2.m Miscellaneous

Considerations for the development of natural-language interfaces to database management systems. 0161
The semantics-based natural language interface to relational databases. 0164
On knowledge base management systems: integrating artificial intelligence and d atabase technologies. ● 0180
Parallel computers for AI databases. 0183
Participation–from Aristotle to today. 0499
Interfacing Ada and relational databases. 0762
Ada-embedded SQL: the options. 0763
Reference model for DBMS user facility. 01086
DATENBANK-DIALOG: a German language interface for relational databases. 01208
The selection of a servicing discipline in a multiterminal conversational information retrieval system. 01233
Technological development and the integrated workstation. 01313
Summarizing natural language database responses. 01343
Natural language querying of historical data bases. 01354
A graphical database interface. 01511
Organizational issues of end-user computing. 01638
Magic PC- the "UN-LANGUAGE" approach. 01639
dANALYST attempts to do it all. 01640
More on the mouse. 01642
The importance of good relations. 01645
A modular user-oriented decision support for physical database design. 01669
An architecture for a business and information system. 01818
Providing quality responses with natural language interfaces: the null value problem. 01848
Communicating with users during systems development. 01972
A practical approach to transforming extended ER diagrams into the relational model. 02022
Non-first normal form universal relations: an application to information retrieval systems. 02039
Creating categories for databases. 02149
ISIS: the interactive spatial information system. 02193
Toward intelligent dialogue with ISIS. 02198
Measuring the effectiveness of personal database structures. 02246
A database primer on natural language. 02413
Information systems development success: Perspectives from project team participants. 02501
Relative information capacity of simple relational database schemata. 02579
A practical approach to data modelling in spatial applications. 02616
The second generation intelligent user interface for the crustal dynamics data information system. 02675
Shifting to a higher gear in a natural language system. 03169
Research and development in information retrieval. § 03287
An extended relational database model based on user views. 03452
Logic interface system on navigational database systems. 03818
A new graphics user interface for accessing a database. 03839
Graphics interaction in databases. 03862
Challenges in the application of graphics technology to the management of geographic information. 03871
Unsolvable problems related to the view integration approach. 03915

[H. INFORMATION SYSTEMS]

Some observations on user interface design and user performance. HCI-0117 †
The database designer's workbench. HCI-0249 †

**dBase** *see* Proper Noun Index

## H.3 INFORMATION STORAGE AND RETRIEVAL

The value of information and computer-aided information seeking: problem formulation and application to fiction retrieval. 01989

### H.3.0 General

Cooperative interfaces to information systems. ● 0160
Authorship provisions in AUGMENT (Reprint). 0370
Data sharing in group work (Reprint). 0379
Designing a CD ROM information structure. 0682
Comment on some recent comments on information retrieval. 01074
Cognitive models in information retrieval—an evaluative review. 02298
New applications of data bases. § 02710
Research and development in information retrieval. § 03072
Research and development in information retrieval. § 03287
Analogical problem solving. ● HCI-0044 †
Cooperative interfaces to information systems. ● HCI-0066 †
Implementing imprecision in information systems. HCI-0259 †
An intelligent interface for online interaction. HCI-0264 †
Design and performance considerations for an optical disk-based, multimedia object server. HCI-0265 †

**QUILL** *see* Proper Noun Index

**SMART** *see* Proper Noun Index

### H.3.1 Content Analysis and Indexing

Data types and persistence. ● 0033
Artificial intelligence systems. 0683
A knowledge-based intermediary system for information retrieval. 0737
KIWI: knowledge-based user-friendly system for the utilization of information bases. 0739
Dialog management in interactive systems: a comparative survey. 0949
Problem solving performance and display preference for information displays depicting numerical functions. 0978
Designing menu display format to match input device format. 0983
Visual system browser. 0995
Seven experiences with contextual field research. 0996
A notation for specifying menus. 01111
Some principles of perceptual and cognitive psychology applied to the design of help menus. 01200
Intelligent information-sharing systems. 01322
The engineering of a translator workstation. 01555
The optimal number of menu options per panel. 01715
Optimizing the structure of database menu indexes: a decision model of menu search. 01716
Processes and problems in information consolidation. 01992
Considerations of menu structure and communication rate for the design of computer menu displays. 02124
Menu search: random or systematic?. 02144
Creating categories for databases. 02149
Adapting menu layout to tasks. 02182
A hybrid approach to deductive uncertain inference. 02191
Effects of breadth, depth and number responses on computer menu search performance. 02192
Support for browsing in an intelligent text retrieval system. 02240
How well do we acknowledge intellectual debts?. 02299
Readability formulas: An overview. 02301
A connectionist approach to conceptual information retrieval. 02772
Knowledge representation in "Default": An attempt to classify general types of knowledge used by legal experts. 02775
Optimal determination of user-oriented clusters. 03077
Video browsing and system response time. 03203
Integrating text with non-text:a picture is worth 1k words. Proceedings of the I. § 04043
Online information retrieval: concepts, principles, and techniques. ● HCI-0046 †
Object lens: a "spreadsheet" for cooperative work. HCI-0206 †
The vocabulary problem in human-system communication. HCI-0224 †
Design and performance considerations for an optical disk-based, multimedia object server. HCI-0265 †
Development of a term association interface for browsing bibliographic data bases based on end users' word associations. HCI-0266 †
Knowledge-based search tactics for an intelligent intermediary system. HCI-0277 †
Semistructured messages are surprisingly useful for computer-supported coordination. HCI-0290 †
TEXTNET: a network-based approach to text handling. HCI-0401 †
Visual structure and the transmission of meaning. HCI-0404 †

CATEGORY INDEX [H. INFORMATION SYSTEMS]

### Abstracting methods

The Drexel disk: an electronic "Guidebook". 03198
Computing text constituency: an algorithmic approach to the generation of text graphs. HCI-0267 †

### Dictionaries

Extending a relational database with deferred referential integrity checking and intelligent joins. 01089
Correlation of term usage and term indexing frequencies. 02004
Interactive communication of sentential structure and content: an alternative approach to man-machine communication. 02220
Multifunctional cursor for direct manipulation user interfaces. 02870
An interactive data dictionary facility for CAD/CAM data bases. 03174
An extended relational database model based on user views. 03452

### Indexing methods

As we may think (Reprint). 0367
Are machines as good as people in drawing conclusions from knowledge represented in catalogues, data bases and expert systems?. 0736
The memory extender personal filing system. 0930
A feature matching approach to the retrieval of graphical information. 01245
A modular user-oriented decision support for physical database design. 01669
Menu organization and user expertise in information search tasks. 01761
Indeterminacy in the subject access to documents. 01993
Correlation of term usage and term indexing frequencies. 02004
Improved browsable displays for online subject access. 02051
Using latent semantic analysis to improve access to textual information. 02901
Illustrated description of an interactive knowledge based indexing system. 03076
Keywords instead of hierarchical menus. 03912
Online library catalogues as information retrieval systems: what can we learn from research?. 04040
Intelligent interfaces for information retrieval systems: architecture problems in the construction of expert systems for document retrieval. 04042
Computing text constituency: an algorithmic approach to the generation of text graphs. HCI-0267 †
On the applied use of human memory models: the memory extender personal filing system. HCI-0271 †
Architecture problems in the construction of expert systems for document retrieval. HCI-0272 †

### Linguistic processing

Text processing with the START natural language system. 0100
Natural languages. 0136
On language and connectionism: analysis of a parallel distributed processing model of language acquisition. 0590
Dialogue and the search for information. 01223
Interactive communication of sentential structure and content: an alternative approach to man-machine communication. 02220
Development of a hand-held computerized vocabulary tutor. 02468
The effect on reading speed of word divisions at the end of a line. 03896
On-line interpretation in speech understanding and dialogue systems. 04000
Understanding computers and cognition. ● HCI-0054 †

### Thesauruses

A graphical thesaurus-based information retrieval system. 02243
Improved design of graphic displays in thesauri—through technology and ergonomics. 02297
Knowledge based systems versus thesaurus : an architecture problem about expert systems design. HCI-0323 †

## H.3.2 Information Storage

Information systems in management: 3rd edition. ● 0673
Compact disc–interactive. 0680
Artificial Intelligence and Law. § 02764
Online information retrieval: concepts, principles, and techniques. ● HCI-0046 †

### File organization

From database to hypertext via electronic publishing: an information odyssey. 0122
Hypertext: an introduction and survey (Reprint). 0378
Designing a CD ROM information structure. 0682
Are machines as good as people in drawing conclusions from knowledge represented in catalogues, data bases and expert systems?. 0736
The memory extender personal filing system. 0930
Assaying and isolating individual differences in searching a hierarchical file system. 01747
Accommodating individual differences in searching a hierarchical file system. 02212
Task-oriented parsing - a diagnostic method to be used adaptive systems. 02896
Handling textual information in a GDSS database: experience with the Arizona analyst information system. 03475

[H. INFORMATION SYSTEMS]                                                                                          CATEGORY INDEX

The spatial metaphor for user interfaces: experimental tests of reference by location versus name. HCI-0268 †
A distributed interoffice mail system. HCI-0308 †

### Record classification

Techniques of user message design: developing a user message system to support cooperative work. 0127
Are machines as good as people in drawing conclusions from knowledge represented in catalogues, data bases and expert systems?. 0736
Menu search: random or systematic?. 02144
On the applied use of human memory models: the memory extender personal filing system. HCI-0271 †

### H.3.3 Information Search and Retrieval

The society of text: hypertext, hypermedia, and the social construction of information. ● 0111
Online information: what do people want? What do people need?. 0113
Advanced databases multi-media interface. 0418
Hypertext hands-on!: an introduction to a new way of organizing and accessing information. ● 0686
Knowledge engineering: expert systems and information retrieval. ● 0735
The memory extender personal filing system. 0930
Writing to be searched: A workshop on document creation principles. 01073
Formative design evaluation of superbook. 01154
Information retrieval using a hypertext-based help system. 01155
End-user searching—What are the implications?. 01224
Algebraic approach to the problem of addressation. 01488
Comprehensino aids for on-line reading of expository text. 01798
A logic assistant for the database searcher. 02001
All users of information retrieval systems are not created equal: an exploration into individual differences. 02011
Evaluation of the user interface in an information retrieval system: a model. 02012
Tools for reading and browsing hypertext. 02014
Icon-based human-computer interaction. 02113
Making the transition from print to electronic encyclopaedias: adapation of mental models. 02238
Equivalence of views by query capacity. 02271
Subjective probability and information retrieval: a review of the psychological literature. 02303
A behavioral approach to information retrieval system design. 02304
Conceptual documents: a mechanism for specifying active views in hypertext. 02833
Browsing within time-driven multimedia documents. 03046
Research & Development in Information Retrieval. § 03062

How do the experts do it? The use of ethnographic methods as an aid to understanding the cognitive processing and retrieval of large bodies of text. 03063
On the nature and fuction of explanation in intelligent information retrieval. 03064
Some measures and procedures for evaluation of the user interface in an information retrieval system. 03069
IR-NLI II: applying man-machine interaction and artificial intelligence conceptsto information retrieval. 03070
Integrated information retrieval for law in a hypertext environment. 03071
Why do some people have more difficulty learning to use an information retrieval system than others?. 03075
A retrieval system for on-line English-Japanese dictionaries. 03078
An advanced full-text retrieval and analysis system. 03079
SIGMOD International Conference on Management of Data. § 03089
Video browsing and system response time. 03203
People and computers IV. § 03215
Information processing 86. § 03588
Internal representation of externally stored information. 03601
Problems in the design of information retrieval systems: user competence and information complexity. 03602
Computational Geometry and its Applications. § 03850
Human-computer interaction: psychonomic aspects. § 03887
MFDBS 87. § 03943
Future Trends in Information Science and Technology. § 04039
Information retrieval: the future. 04045
Interfaces and on-line reading. 04047
Online information retrieval: concepts, principles, and techniques. ● HCI-0046 †
Hypertext/hypermedia. ● HCI-0047 †
A novice user's interface to information retrieval systems. HCI-0219 †
Observations of end-user online searching behavior over eleven years. HCI-0235 †
The spatial metaphor for user interfaces: experimental tests of reference by location versus name. HCI-0268 †
A natural language information retrieval system with extentions towards fuzzy reasoning. HCI-0281 †
TEXTNET: a network-based approach to text handling. HCI-0401 †

### Clustering

Designing a CD ROM information structure. 0682
Optimal determination of user-oriented clusters. 03077
Structuring knowledge in a graph. 03899

### Query formulation

Studies in the evaluation of a domain-independent natural language query system. 0162

An interactive customization program for a natural language database query system. 0163
Intelligent interfaces to Nordic data bases. 0738
A framework for choosing a database query language. 0761
Performance, preference, and visual scan patterns on a menu-based system: implications for interface design. 0855
Conversational hypertext: information access through natural language dialogues with computers. 0867
Helgon: extending the retrieval by reformulation paradigm. 0880
A cognitive model of database querying: a tool for novice instruction. 0905
Dialing a name: alphabetic entry through a telephone keypad. 0973
Item selection from menus: the influence of menu organization, query interpretation, and programming experience on selection strategies. 01011
A feature matching approach to the retrieval of graphical information. 01245
Interpretation of natural language database queries using optimization methods. 01861
A common interface for accessing document retrieval systems and dbms for retrieval of bibliographic data. 01990
Dealing with a database query language in a new situation. 02119
The effect of different conceptual models using reasoning in a database query writing task. 02201
Retrieval systems for the information seeker: can the role of the intermediary be automated?. 02864
INQUEST: A prototype intelligence tool. 02918
Concept based retrieval in classical IR systems. 03066
Towards interactive query expansion. 03067
Keywords instead of hierarchical menus. 03912
Data manipulation languages for the universal relation view DURST. 03944
On global context dependencies and their properties (extended abstract). 03945
On-line interpretation in speech understanding and dialogue systems. 04000
Experimentation in the specification of an oral dialogue. 04005
Online library catalogues as information retrieval systems: what can we learn from research?. 04040
Intelligent interfaces for information retrieval systems: architecture problems in the construction of expert systems for document retrieval. 04042
On search in an incomplete database. HCI-0214 †
Querying external databases. HCI-0233 †
What makes RABBIT run?. HCI-0256 †
Development of a term association interface for browsing bibliographic data bases based on end users' word associations. HCI-0266 †
Calibrating databases. HCI-0269 †

*Retrieval models*

Hypertext in context. 0114
Hypertext and intelligent interfaces for text retrieval. 0115
Supporting collaboration in hypermedia: issues and experiences. 0117
Limited freedom: linear reflections on nonlinear texts. 0121
Hand-crafted hypertext-lessons from the ACM experiment. 0128
Hand-crafted hypertext-lessons from the ACM experiment. 0128
The evaluation of online help systems: a conceptual model. 0129
Using "word-knowledge" reasoning for question answering. 0131
KIWI: knowledge-based user-friendly system for the utilization of information bases. 0739
Conversational hypertext: information access through natural language dialogues with computers. 0867
Helgon: extending the retrieval by reformulation paradigm. 0880
IRX: an information retrieval system for experimentation and user applications. 01076
An information retrieval system for software components. 01077
Information retrieval using micros. 01225
Indeterminacy in the subject access to documents. 01993
Evaluation of the user interface in an information retrieval system: a model. 02012
Non-first normal form universal relations: an application to information retrieval systems. 02039
Design goals for sloppy modeling systems. 02206
Interactive communication of sentential structure and content: an alternative approach to man-machine communication. 02220
Theoretical training and problem detection in a computerized database retrieval task. 02239
Support for browsing in an intelligent text retrieval system. 02240
Interactive document display and its use in information retrieval. 02300
A behavioral approach to information retrieval system design. 02304
Using a cognitive model of dialogue for reference retrieval. 02317
Weighting, ranking and relevance feedback in a front-end system. 02329
STATUS with IQ—escaping from the Boolean straitjacket. 02569
Artificial Intelligence and Law. § 02764
A process specification of expert lawyer reasoning. 02768
A connectionist approach to conceptual information retrieval. 02772

[H. INFORMATION SYSTEMS] CATEGORY INDEX

Pictures and category labels as navigational aids for catalog browsing. 02877
Using latent semantic analysis to improve access to textual information. 02901
A knowledge-based approach to online document retrieval system design. 03027
Towards an intelligent and personalized retrieval system. 03028
Interactive retrieval office documents. 03047
Information retrieval using impression of documents as a clue. 03065
Retrieval based on user behaviour. 03068
Generating an individualized user interface. 03074
A comparison of hypertext, scrolling and folding as mechanisms for program browsing. 03235
Handling textual information in a GDSS database: experience with the Arizona analyst information system. 03475
Conceptual information extraction form financial news. 03489
Specification of a tool for viewing program text. 03884
Search strategies in internal and external memories. 03911
An experimental environment for generating word hypotheses in continuous speech. 03998
Experimentation in the specification of an oral dialogue. 04005
Online library catalogues as information retrieval systems: what can we learn from research?. 04040
Practical applications of optical disk image systems in document management. 04041
The depth/breadth trade-off in the design of menu-driven user interfaces. HCI-0135 †
Users and experts in the document retrieval system model. HCI-0270 †
On the applied use of human memory models: the memory extender personal filing system. HCI-0271 †
Architecture problems in the construction of expert systems for document retrieval. HCI-0272 †
Towards a new research paradigm in information retrieval. HCI-0273 †
In search of searching skills. HCI-0274 †
Cognitive models, cognitive tasks, and information retrieval. HCI-0331 †

*Search process*

Hypertext and intelligent interfaces for text retrieval. 0115
From database to hypertext via electronic publishing: an information odyssey. 0122
Intelligent interfaces to Nordic data bases. 0738
KIWI: knowledge-based user-friendly system for the utilization of information bases. 0739
The profile naming service. 01149
Dialogue and the search for information. 01223
End-user searching—What are the implications?. 01224
Online searching: a five star review of research. 01314
Embedded menus: selecting items in context. 01320
Menu organization and user expertise in information search tasks. 01761
Search success and expectations with a computer interface. 01995
Online text retrieval via browsing. 01999
Perceptions of the information search process in libraries: a study of changes from high school through college. 02002
OAKDEC, a program for studying the effects on users of a procedural expert system for database searching. 02003
Correlation of term usage and term indexing frequencies. 02004
Online searching using speech as a man/machine interface. 02013
Enhancing search results by editing, analysis and packaging. 02035
The effects of entry arrangement in search times: a cross-generational study. 02048
A comparative study of subject searching in an OPAC among branch libraries of a university library system. 02050
A hybrid approach to deductive uncertain inference. 02191
Effects of breadth, depth and number responses on computer menu search performance. 02192
Accommodating individual differences in searching a hierarchical file system. 02212
Comparison of manual and online searches of chemical abstracts. 02265
Subject searching behaviour at the library catalogue and at the shelves: implications for online interactive catalogues. 02302
Using a cognitive model of dialogue for reference retrieval. 02317
The seacher/information interface project—final report. 02341
An investigation of online searcher traits and their relationship to search outcomes. 02447
Information-seeking strategies of novices using a full-text electronic encyclopedia. 02452
How good an Online searcher are you? Twenty questions about BIOSIS previews. 02521
An online interface within a hypertext system: project Jefferson's electronic notebook. 02524
Datastream: numeric data—all you can use at a fixed price. 02525
Front end games. 02599
Travel around a learning support environment: rambling, orienteering or touring?. 02900
Structured what if analysis in DSS models. 03481
The legibility of visual display texts. 03889
Search strategies in internal and external memories. 03911

Keywords instead of hierarchical menus. 03912
Recent results on the application of a metric-space search algorithm (AESA) to multispeaker data. 03997
An experimental environment for generating word hypotheses in continuous speech. 03998
Modification of Earley's algorithm for speech recognition. 04003
Merging acoustics and linguistics in speech understanding. 04004
Development of a term association interface for browsing bibliographic data bases based on end users' word associations. HCI-0266 †
In search of searching skills. HCI-0274 †
Using the micro-computer to simplify database access: designing interfaces to complex files. HCI-0275 †
Transparent information systems through gateways, front ends, intermediaries, and interfaces. HCI-0276 †
Knowledge-based search tactics for an intelligent intermediary system. HCI-0277 †
Views on end-user searching. HCI-0283 †

### Selection process

Visual system browser. 0995
The profile naming service. 01149
Embedded menus: selecting items in context. 01320
Selection devices for users of an electronic encyclopedia: an empirical comparison of four possibilities. 02009
Search strategies in internal and external memories. 03911

## H.3.4 Systems and Software

The society of text: hypertext, hypermedia, and the social construction of information. ● 0111
The CD ROM handbook. ● 0678
Knowledge engineering: expert systems and information retrieval. ● 0735
Intelligent interfaces to Nordic data bases. 0738
Automating the design of graphical presentations of relational information. 01150
Intelligent information-sharing systems. 01322
All users of information retrieval systems are not created equal: an exploration into individual differences. 02011
The user interface in a hypertext, multiwindow program browser. 02072
Forecasting consumer adoption of information technology and services—lessons from home video forecasting. 02451
An online interface within a hypertext system: project Jefferson's electronic notebook. 02524
Datastream: numeric data—all you can use at a fixed price. 02525
Interactive retrieval office documents. 03047
People and computers IV. § 03215
A comparison of hypertext, scrolling and folding as mechanisms for program browsing. 03235

Hypertext tips: experiences in developing a hypertext tutorial. 03236
Flexible intelligent interactive-video. 03238
Querying external databases. HCI-0233 †
A supporting system for effective construction and sharing of scientific databases by general researchers. HCI-0262 †
Users and experts in the document retrieval system model. HCI-0270 †
A prototype electronic encyclopedia. HCI-0278 †
Reading and writing the electronic book. HCI-0282 †
Semistructured messages are surprisingly useful for computer-supported coordination. HCI-0290 †
TEXTNET: a network-based approach to text handling. HCI-0401 †

**ASK** *see* Proper Noun Index

### Information networks

Hypertext in context. 0114
Hypertext and intelligent interfaces for text retrieval. 0115
Supporting collaboration in hypermedia: issues and experiences. 0117
The missing link: why we're all doing hypertext wrong. 0118
Reflections on authoring, editing, and managing hypertext. 0119
Limited freedom: linear reflections on nonlinear texts. 0121
How to manage educational computing initiatives-lessons from the first five years of Project Athena at MIT. 0125
Textual intervention, collaboration, and the online environment. 0126
Hand-crafted hypertext-lessons from the ACM experiment. 0128
Computer-supported cooperative work: a book of readings. ● 0366
A knowledge-based intermediary system for information retrieval. 0737
The profile naming service. 01149
The profile naming service. 01149
End-user searching—What are the implications?. 01224
CONTEXT: an on-line documentation system. HCI-0280 †

**ORION** *see* Proper Noun Index

### Question-answering (fact retrieval) systems

Text, context, and hypertext: writing with and for the computer. ● 0098
Text processing with the START natural language system. 0100
Hypertext: a way of incorporating user feedback into online documentation. 0102

[H. INFORMATION SYSTEMS]

Artificial intelligence systems. 0683
KIWI: knowledge-based user-friendly system for the utilization of information bases. 0739
Dialog management in interactive systems: a comparative survey. 0949
The profile naming service. 01149
Profile data acquisition for the JCPDS-ICDD database s. 01232
Modeling the user in natural language systems. 01348
Modeling the user's plans and goals. 01349
Recognizing and responding to plan-oriented misconceptions. 01350
Reasoning on a highlighted user model to respond to misconceptions. 01351
Tailoring object descriptions to a user's level of expertise. 01352
The relationship between user models and discourse models. 01353
Natural language interface to the question-answering system for physicians. 01478
The feature chart: A tool for communicating the analysis for a decision support system. 01913
The engineering information system: a guided tour. 02046
A virtual protocol model for computer-human interaction. 02106
A descriptive/prescriptive model for menu-based interaction. 02120
Using computer knowledge in the design of interactive systems. 02137
ISIS: the interactive spatial information system. 02193
Toward intelligent dialogue with ISIS. 02198
Design goals for sloppy modeling systems. 02206
An interface architecture to provide adaptive task-specific context for the user. 02228
An interactive system SDI on microcomputer. 02272
Interactive document display and its use in information retrieval. 02300
Inactive video at work. 02571
Generating an individualized user interface. 03074
A temporal logic for reasoning about changing data bases in the context of natural language question-answering. 03176
Anticipating false implicatures: cooperative responses in question-answer systems. 03178
User requirements for expert system explanation: what, why and when?. 03242
Natural language communication with computers: some problems, perspectives, and new directions. 03913
An experimental environment for generating word hypotheses in continuous speech. 03998
On-line interpretation in speech understanding and dialogue systems. 04000
Knowledge based systems for speech understanding. 04001
Recognition of speaker-dependent continuous speech with Keal-Nevezh. 04002

CATEGORY INDEX

Experimentation in the specification of an oral dialogue. 04005
Online information retrieval: concepts, principles, and techniques. ● HCI-0046 †
Equal opportunity interactive systems. HCI-0168 †
On the purpose and analysis of EDP user systems. HCI-0218 †
Calibrating databases. HCI-0269 †
Architecture problems in the construction of expert systems for document retrieval. HCI-0272 †
Towards a new research paradigm in information retrieval. HCI-0273 †
A natural language information retrieval system with extentions towards fuzzy reasoning. HCI-0281 †
Expert systems—where do we go from here?. HCI-0318 †
Cognitive models, cognitive tasks, and information retrieval. HCI-0331 †
Portability of syntax and semantics in DATALOG. HCI-0340 †

**SuperBook** *see* Proper Noun Index

**Telesophy** *see* Proper Noun Index

### H.3.5 On-line Information Services

Online information, hypermedia, and the idea of literacy. 0112
Online information: what do people want? What do people need?. 0113
Hypertext in context. 0114
Hypertext and intelligent interfaces for text retrieval. 0115
The missing link: why we're all doing hypertext wrong. 0118
Reflections on authoring, editing, and managing hypertext. 0119
Authoring tools for complex document sets. 0120
Limited freedom: linear reflections on nonlinear texts. 0121
Textual intervention, collaboration, and the online environment. 0126
Techniques of user message design: developing a user message system to support cooperative work. 0127
The evaluation of online help systems: a conceptual model. 0129
Escher effects in online text. 0130
Using "word-knowledge" reasoning for question answering. 0131
Learning by doing with simulated intelligent help. 0132
Cooperative interfaces to information systems. ● 0160
The economics of online. ● 0194
Cost effectiveness of on-line searching of chemical information: an industrial viewpoint. 0195
The problem of levels and automatic response generation in a "Let's Talk AboutIt" strategy. 0410

# CATEGORY INDEX [H. INFORMATION SYSTEMS]

A knowledge-based intermediary system for information retrieval. 0737
Intelligent interfaces to Nordic data bases. 0738
Methodology for comparative selection of interactive database interface types. 01005
The study of user behavior on information retrieval systems. 01046
Introducing information technology: experiences of a large industrial unit. 01217
End-users: threat, challenge or myth?. 01221
End-user searching—What are the implications?. 01224
Online searching: a five star review of research. 01314
Beta tests and end-user surveys: are they valid?. 01631
Who's behind the help desk?. 01632
What the help desk needs from you. 01633
The linear file—restrictions on online information use: a searcher's perspective. 01634
Designing a user manual to support an in-house database. 01635
Evaluating the usability of the Glasgow online. 01808
Developing interactive information systems with the user software engineering methodology. 01856
A preliminary specification of an on-line expert help system. 01930
*Library*—An electronic ordering system. 01991
Online text retrieval via browsing. 01999
A comparative survey of the friendliness of online 'help' in interactive information. 02010
Evaluation of the user interface in an information retrieval system: a model. 02012
Online searching using speech as a man/machine interface. 02013
A menu interface to formulate boolean logic-can it be done?. 02034
User interaction with the authority structure of the online catalog: results of a survey. 02049
A comparative study of subject searching in an OPAC among branch libraries of a university library system. 02050
Improved browsable displays for online subject access. 02051
The user's mental model of an information retrieval system: an experiment on a prototype online catalog. 02099
Adaptive command prompting in an on-line documentation. 02121
Online library catalog systems: an analysis of user errors. 02128
Measuring the effectiveness of personal database structures. 02246
Comparison of manual and online searches of chemical abstracts. 02265
End-user searching of CAS ONLINE. Results of a cooperative experiment between Imperial Chemical Industries and Chemical Abstracts Services. 02269

Subject searching behaviour at the library catalogue and at the shelves: implications for online interactive catalogues. 02302
Time-life, world reporter and the secretary: experiments with end-users. 02325
Voice input/output interface for online searching: some design and human factor onsiderations. 02335
Professional education and subsequent careers in library/information work: a follow-up study of former students on the MA/MSc information studies course at the University of Sheffield. 02336
The computer as mask: a problem of inadequate human interaction examined with particular regard to online public access catalogues. 02337
Supporting collaboration in Hypermedia: issues and experiences. 02454
The user at the online catalogue. 02462
Effects of the adoption of an integrated online system on a technical services department. 02463
History offers clues to the future: user control returns. 02517
Choreography for technology and humans. 02518
End-users: Dreams or dollars. 02519
How good an Online searcher are you? Twenty questions about BIOSIS previews. 02521
An online interface within a hypertext system: project Jefferson's electronic notebook. 02524
OST— a training package for end-users of online systems. 02568
User orientation for the electronic encyclopedia. 02605
Developments in one-line information systems. 02687
A knowledge-based approach to online document retrieval system design. 03027
Informational zooming: an interaction model for the graphical access to text knowledge bases. 03073
A retrieval system for on-line English-Japanese dictionaries. 03078
Information in the air and in the wave. 03146
Ease of use - the ultimate deception. 03249
Modelling generic user-interfaces with functional programs. 03265
Proving properties of interactive systems. 03267
User programs: a way to match computer systems and human cognition. 03271
Videotex and online services: competition or collateral. 03557
Role-based security in data base management systems. 03584
Intelligent interfaces for information retrieval systems: architecture problems in the construction of expert systems for document retrieval. 04042
Online information retrieval: concepts, principles, and techniques. ● HCI-0046 †
Access to academic networks. ● HCI-0050 †
Querying external databases. HCI-0233 †
Observations of end-user online searching behavior over eleven years. HCI-0235 †

[H. INFORMATION SYSTEMS]   CATEGORY INDEX

Architecture problems in the construction of expert systems for document retrieval. HCI-0272 †
Using the micro-computer to simplify database access: designing interfaces to complex files. HCI-0275 †
Reading and writing the electronic book. HCI-0282 †
Views on end-user searching. HCI-0283 †
A user oriented design process for user recovery and command reuse support. HCI-0284 †
Testing bibliographic displays for online catalogs. HCI-0285 †
The dimensions of accessibility to online information: implications for implementing office information systems. HCI-0304 †
TEXTNET: a network-based approach to text handling. HCI-0401 †

### Data bank sharing

Computer-supported cooperative work: a book of readings. ● 0366
As we may think (Reprint). 0367
Beyond the chalkboard: computer support for collaboration and problem solving inmeetings (Reprint). 0376
Computer-based real-time conferencing systems (Reprint). 0377
Data sharing in group work (Reprint). 0379
The information lens: an intelligent system for information sharing in organizations. 0891
DOMAIN/DELPHI: retrieving documents online. 0906
On designing for usability: an application of four key principles. 0923
Starting end-users. 01215
Online use and end-users in media and advertising: an overview. 01216
The value of downloading for database users and database producers. 01218
Travel around a learning support environment: rambling, orienteering or touring?. 02900
Future Trends in Information Science and Technology. § 04039
Online library catalogues as information retrieval systems: what can we learn from research?. 04040
A supporting system for effective construction and sharing of scientific databases by general researchers. HCI-0262 †
Transparent information systems through gateways, front ends, intermediaries, and interfaces. HCI-0276 †
A performing medium for working group graphics. HCI-0383 †

### H.3.6 Library Automation

The economics of online. ● 0194
Automation in public libraries: effects on the organization, quality of working life, and quality of services. 0246
Semiotics and informatics: computers as media. 0448
Design and test of a database for fiction, based on an analysis of children's search behavior. 0451
Intelligent interfaces to Nordic data bases. 0738
Autocompletion in full text transaction entry: a method for humanized input. 0934
Starting end-users. 01215
End-users: threat, challenge or myth?. 01221
End-user searching—What are the implications?. 01224
*Library*—An electronic ordering system. 01991
Perceptions of the information search process in libraries: a study of changes from high school through college. 02002
Correlation of term usage and term indexing frequencies. 02004
Library processing systems and the man/machine interface. 02045
Investigating computer anxiety in an academic library. 02047
The effects of entry arrangement in search times: a cross-generational study. 02048
User interaction with the authority structure of the online catalog: results of a survey. 02049
A comparative study of subject searching in an OPAC among branch libraries of a university library system. 02050
Improved browsable displays for online subject access. 02051
Online library catalog systems: an analysis of user errors. 02128
Computer-assisted instruction in academic libraries. 02282
Subject searching behaviour at the library catalogue and at the shelves: implications for online interactive catalogues. 02302
The man-machine interface aspect of an automatic classification numbering system in a computerized library system. 02316
Professional education and subsequent careers in library/information work: a follow-up study of former students on the MA/MSc information studies course at the University of Sheffield. 02336
The computer as mask: a problem of inadequate human interaction examined with particular regard to online public access catalogues. 02337
Implementation of the Geac circulation system within the CLANN network. 02458
Assessing the impacts of new technology on library employees. 02459
The design and construction of a vital database. 02460
Microcomputer availability to public library clients. 02461
The user at the online catalogue. 02462
Effects of the adoption of an integrated online system on a technical services department. 02463
Technology's impact on library interior planning. 02464
Common sense and user interfaces: issues beyond the keyboard. 02465

CATEGORY INDEX [H. INFORMATION SYSTEMS]

User interfaces for CD'ROM PACs. 02466
The emerging role of workstations in the library environment. 02467
End-users: Dreams or dollars. 02519
Putting on a show: using computer graphics to train end-users. 02520
OST— a training package for end-users of online systems. 02568
STATUS with IQ—escaping from the Boolean straitjacket. 02569
Barriers to cooperative computerized circulation systems in public libraries. 02573
Front end games. 02599
Real librarians don't program...do they?. 02600
Where person meets machine. 02601
A user-unfriendly WELCOME. 02603
User orientation for the electronic encyclopedia. 02605
Some experiences in integrating specification of human computer interaction within a structured system development method. 03222
Future Trends in Information Science and Technology. § 04039
Online library catalogues as information retrieval systems: what can we learn from research?. 04040
A prototype electronic encyclopedia. HCI-0278 †
Testing bibliographic displays for online catalogs. HCI-0285 †

### H.3.m Miscellaneous

The moving target: future trends in networking. 01282
Multi-window displays for readers of lengthy texts. 02142
Knowledge elicitation using discourse analysis. 02152
Towards an intelligent and personalized retrieval system. 03028

## H.4 INFORMATION SYSTEMS APPLICATIONS

Effect of visual presentation of different dialogue structures on human-computer interaction. 03768

### H.4.0 General

Critical issues in information processing management and technology: vol. 6. ● 0594
An introduction to data and activity analysis. ● 0610
Information systems in management: 3rd edition. ● 0673
Hypertext hands-on!: an introduction to a new way of organizing and accessing information. ● 0686
The disconnection: how to interface computers and video. ● 0703
Oxford Surveys in Information Technology. ● 0753
The effects of device technology on the usability of advanced telephone functions. 0876
An experiment into the use of auditory cues to reduce visual workload. 0877

TNT: a talking tutor 'n' trainer for teaching use of interactive computer systems. 0895
How are windows used? Some notes on creating an empirically-based windowing benchmark task. 0903
Seven plus or minus two central issues in human-computer interaction. 0937
The 1988 CSCW: trip report. 01008
Interfaces for cooperative work: an eclectic look at CSCW '88. 01009
Information technologies for the 1990's: an orgnizational impact perspective. 01336
Restoring a sense of control during implementation: how user involvement leads to system acceptance. 02509
New applications of data bases. § 02710
Managers who personally use information technology frequently: a profile of some invisible computer personnel. 03007
Information processing 86. § 03588
In the age of the smart machine: the future of work and power. ● HCI-0083 †
The 1984 Olympic Message System: a test of behavioral principles of system design. HCI-0125 †
A taxonomy for the study of human factors in management information systems. HCI-0205 †

### H.4.1 Office Automation (I.7)

Second IEEE Conference on Computer Workstations: proceedings. ● 0002
Speech filing—An office system for principals. 0037
Human factors challenges in creating a principal support office system—The speh filing system approach. 0038
Issues and approaches to appraising technological change in the office: A consequentialist perspective. 0043
The statutes and standards movement. 0049
The missing link: why we're all doing hypertext wrong. 0118
Computers for managing information. ● 0141
Management, organizations and the new technologies. 0145
Psychological issues of human-computer interaction in the work place. ● 0305
Usability assessment for the office: methodological choices and their implications. 0318
Principles from the psychology of skill acquisition. 0332
Computer-supported cooperative work: a book of readings. ● 0366
Office information systems and computer science (Reprint). 0373
Data sharing in group work (Reprint). 0379
Evolution of an organizational interface: the new business department at a large insurance firm (Reprint). 0382
Reducing social context cues: electronic mail in organizational communication (Reprint). 0385

# [H. INFORMATION SYSTEMS]

Cognitive science and organizational design: a case study of computer conferencing (Reprint). 0386
User performance with command, menu, and iconic interfaces. 0414
Managers, micros and mainframes: integrating systems for end-users. ● 0455
Managers, micros and mainframes: an introduction. 0456
Managing the diffusion of end-user computing technologies: a fifties mindset with eighties tools. 0459
Company experiences with end-user computing. 0460
Information processing today, with applications. ● 0567
Information processing today, with applications. ● 0568
Information processing today, with applications and BASIC. ● 0569
Information processing today, with applications and BASIC: updat 87/88. ● 0570
Principles of information processing. ● 0571
Principles of information processing with applications and BASIC. ● 0572
Information systems in management: 3rd edition. ● 0673
Data model issues for object-oriented applications. 0712
Oxford Surveys in Information Technology. ● 0753
User interfaces for office systems. 0756
The design requirements of office systems. 0757
Transfer between text editors. 0804
Notecards in a nutshell. 0810
The interface is often not the problem. 0837
Learning and transfer for text and graphics editing with a direct manipulation interface. 0900
Learning modes and subsequent use of computer-mediated communication systems. 0912
How faithfully should the electronic office simulate real one?. 0958
The effectiveness of a keystroke line in interactive tutorials. 0969
Adaptive interface design: a symmetric model and a knowledge-based implementation. 01091
Efficiency vs. effectiveness. 01092
Some design guidelines for an information center to support office information systems. 01093
A natural language interface to a multiple databased office information system. 01094
Understanding the office: A social-analytic perspective. 01156
Data model issues for object-oriented applications. 01157
Office-by-example: an integrated office system and database manager. 01159
Intelligent information-sharing systems. 01322
Office automation—can it be justified?. 01383
Employing usability engineering in the development of office products. 01413
Human-computer interface recording. 01414
Presentation of a description language for office tasks. 01434
Communication analysis in the company. 01435

The silent force of the screen. A research note on the impact of microelectronics on work autonomy among clerical workers in public administration. 01437
Successful implementation of an office system. 01438
Supporting end users in the office. 01444
The committee support system. 01460
ORGPLAN an information-decisive aid system to resolving organizing problems. 01573
The real cost of OA. 01647
Power and credibility in office automation. 01657
Changes in electromyographic activity associated with occupational stress and poor performance in the workplace. 01734
Measuring implementation outcome: beyond success and failure. 01933
An object-oriented approach to the design of a mail system for a heterogeneous environment. 01944
Integrated communications and work efficiency: impacts on organizational structure and power. 02031
Education and training in office technology. 02330
The effect of presentation media on recipient performance in text-based information systems. 02350
A longitudinal study of spreadsheet program use. 02354
Components of user work stations. 02427
A model for assessing the performance of a local area network employing technical office protocol (TOP) as part of MAP/TOP network in a computer integrated manufacturing (CIM) research project, for the transmission of real time interactive speech. 02491
What's new in personal information managers. 02556
Office Information Systems. § 03036
The rapport multimedia conferencing system. 03037
OTM: specifying office tasks. 03039
Interactive retrieval office documents. 03047
Design issues of an intelligent workstation for the office. 03165
The star user interface: an overview. 03171
Advanced office systems: An empirical look at use and satisfaction. 03172
Designing electronic paper to fit user requirements. 03206
Understanding the nature of the office for the design of third wave office systems. 03248
Toward the successful design and implementation of computer based management information systems in small companies. 03256
Proceedings of the fourth British national conference on databases (BNCOD 4). § 03282
Office Systems. § 03354
Trends in office modeling. 03355
Architectural implications of office systems. 03356
Human factors in office systems. 03357
Organizational implications of office systems: toward a critical social action perspective. 03358
Security of office systems. 03359

# CATEGORY INDEX [H. INFORMATION SYSTEMS]

Implementation of office systems. 03360
Networks in office automation. § 03637
An implementation of OSI protocols in SM-4 host computers. 03638
A biparty grammar as a tool for defining a man-machine dialogue. 03639
Women, work and computerization: opportunities and disadvantages. § 03674
Work with display units 86. § 03676
VDU-work and dyslexia. a case report. 03699
Influence of age on performance and health of VDU workers. 03702
Short- and long-term effects of extreme physical inactivity. A review. 03703
On the significance of physical activity on sedentary work. 03704
Inactivity, night work, and fatigue. 03705
The back during prolonged sitting. 03706
Preferred settings in VDT work: The Zürich Experience. 03707
Subject reports about musculoskeletal discomfort in VDU work as a complex phenomenon. 03708
VDUs and musculo-skeletal problems at the Australian National University. A case study. 03709
Generation of muscle tension related to a demand of continuing attention. 03710
Task and the adjustment of ergonomic chairs. 03711
Equipment and workstation design for banking services. 03712
On the design of dealing desks. 03713
The effect of VDU on the interior design of offices. 03714
Lighting for visual display unit workplaces. 03715
Lighting the display or displaying the lighting. 03716
Lighting the electronic office. 03717
Work at video display terminals among office employees: visual ergonomics and lighting. 03718
Recent results on the illumination of VDU and CAD workstations. 03719
Non-visual effects of visual surroundings. 03720
Improving the VDU workplace by introducing a physiologically optimized bright-background screen with dark characters: advantages and requirements. 03721
Display image characteristics and visual response. 03722
Sensitivity to light and visual strain in VDT operators: basic data for the design of work stations. 03732
Are there subtle changes in vision after use of VDTs?. 03733
Visual impairment and subjective ocular symptomatology in VDT operators. 03734
Effects on visual accommodation and subjective visual discomfort from VDT work intensified through split screen technique. 03735
Work distance and optical correction. 03736
Is the resting state of our eyes a favorable viewing distance for VDU-work?. 03737

Vision monitoring of VDU operators and relaxation of visual stress by means of a laser speckle system. 03738
VDU work, refractive errors and binocular vision. 03739
Refraction in VDU operators—a comparison with other professions. 03740
How identify organizational factors crucial of VDU-health? A context-oriented method approach. 03741
Psychosocial work environment and use of visual display terminals:8mfrom theoretical model to action. 03742
On the user's opinion about systems design. 03743
Identification and prevention of work-related mental and psycho-somatic disorders among two categories of VDU users. 03744
Comparison of well-being among non-machine interactive clerical workers and full-time and part-time VDT users and typists. 03745
Office automation and work organization: making use of the scope of choice. 03746
the role of user prototyping in the system design process. 03747
Use of an entire workforce as computer. 03748
Office automation as an opportunity for an organizational check-up. 03749
Analyzing and improving VDU working conditions: workers' education. 03751
Workers education and user participation in the development of protective policies for VDT operators. 03752
Trends in U.S. user policies for VDT work. 03753
Characterization of VDT work. 03754
VDT technology: psychosocial and stress concerns. 03755
A model for evaluating stress effects of work with display units. 03756
Growth and challenge VS wear and tear of humans in computer mediated work. 03757
Work content, stress and health in computer-mediated work: a seven year follow-up study. 03758
Focusing variability during visual work. 03759
Mental fatigue of VDU operators induced by monotonous and various tasks. 03760
Data entry task on VDU: underload or overload. 03761
Videocoding - a highly monotonous VDU work in a new technique for mail sorting. 03762
An evaluation of mood disturbances and somatic discomfort under slow computer-response time and incentive-pay conditions. 03765
The applicability of eye movement analysis in the ergonomic evaluation of human-computer interaction. 03766
Eye-head coordination and information uptake during text processing. 03767
Touch screen, cursor keys and mouse interaction. 03769
Naming errors and automatic error correction in human-computer interaction. 03770
Visual fatigue with work on visual display units: the current state of knowledge. 03891
Nets in office automation. 03975

## [H. INFORMATION SYSTEMS]

Future Trends in Information Science and Technology. § 04039
Integrating text with non-text:a picture is worth 1k words. Proceedings of the I. § 04043
A formal specification for a user interface for office automation. 04053
Office automation: a social and organizational perspective. • HCI-0048 †
Online communities. • HCI-0051 †
Behavioral experiments on handmarkings. HCI-0201 †
The evaluation of text editors: methodology and empirical results.. HCI-0209 †
A generator of direct manipulation office systems. HCI-0250 †
The spatial metaphor for user interfaces: experimental tests of reference by location versus name. HCI-0268 †
A prototype electronic encyclopedia. HCI-0278 †
The user interface of a personal calendar program. HCI-0286 †
Electronic calendars in the office: an assessment of user needs and current technology. HCI-0287 †
Executive workstations: issues and requirements. HCI-0288 †
Whiteboards: a graphical database tool. HCI-0289 †
Semistructured messages are surprisingly useful for computer-supported coordination. HCI-0290 †
Office systems. HCI-0291 †
A user agent for multiple computer-based message services. HCI-0306 †
Usage patterns in an integrated voice and data communications system. HCI-0311 †
Computer mediated work: the interplay between technology and structured jobs. HCI-0440 †
Computerization, productivity, and quality of work-life. HCI-0441 †
An empirical study of occupational stress, attitudes and health among information systems personnel. HCI-0451 †

### Equipment

The changing workplace: A guide to managing the people, organizational, and regulatory aspects of office technology (book excerpt). 0044
The physical environment. 0045
Guide to the Draft American National Standard for Human Factors Engineering of Visual Display Terminal Workstations. 0048
Thinking ahead: what to expect from teleconferencing (Reprint). 0372
Interface design and evaluation—Semiotic implications. 0409
Human factors reference guide for electronics and computer professionals. • 0733
Of moles and men: the design of foot controls for workstations. 0935
The economics of UNIX workstations. 01312

Hypertext: an introduction and survey. 01360
Public Law 99-506, "Section 508" Electronic Equipment Accessibility for disabled workers. 02893
Managers who personally use information technology frequently: a profile of some invisible computer personnel. 03007
Systems for cooperative work and group decision making: status of use and problems in development. 03471
LisaLearning. HCI-0092 †
A distributed interoffice mail system. HCI-0308 †

**Lotus 1-2-3** *see* Proper Noun Index

### Word processing

Information technology and the experience of work. 0041
The changing workplace: A guide to managing the people, organizational, and regulatory aspects of office technology (book excerpt). 0044
Human factors issues in VDT use: Environmental and workstation design considerations. 0046
Preventing back strain. 0047
Learning to use word processors: problems and prospects. 0059
Learning to use a word processor: by doing, by thinking, and by knowing. 0060
Minimalist design for active users. 0086
From database to hypertext via electronic publishing: an information odyssey. 0122
Interface design and evaluation—Semiotic implications. 0409
Designing advanced workstations. 0457
Information systems in management: 3rd edition. • 0673
Misconception in human factors. 0758
A document layout system using automatic document architecture extraction. 0882
Learning disabled students' difficulties in learning to use a word processor: implications for design. 0889
Transfer between word processing systems. 0899
The effects of structured, multi-level documentation. 0907
Comparison of elderly and younger users on keyboard and voice input computer-based composition tasks. 0916
A model of mental model construction. 0931
Word processing techniques and user learning preferences. 0984
What we know and what we need to know: the user model versus the user's model in human-computer interaction. 01243
Prompting, feedback and error correction in the design of a scenario machine. 02176
A case study of CSCW in a dispersed organization. 02866
Transfer between menu systems. 02873
Electronic monitoring and the redundancy of control systems: The role of the supervisor. 03000

Automated document distribution using AI based workstations and knowledge based servers. 03466
Connections in context: The intermedia system. 03534
Development of mental models of an office system: a field study on an introductory course. 03903
Artificial intelligence and cognitive psychology: a new look at human factors. 03904
Real-time processing of cursive writing and sketched graphics. 03908
Practical applications of optical disk image systems in document management. 04041
Reading and writing with computers: a framework for explaining differences in performance. HCI-0204 †
Training wheels in a user interface.. HCI-0208 †
Learning to use a word processor: by doing, by thinking, and by knowing. HCI-0292 †
Editing by example. HCI-0398 †
A note on undetected typing errors. HCI-0399 †
Training for optimising transfer between word processors. HCI-0447 †

**WordPerfect** *see* Proper Noun Index

**WordStar** *see* Proper Noun Index

### H.4.2 Types of Systems

A human information processing model of the managerial mind: some MIS implications. 0205
WYSIWIS revised: early experiences with multiuser interfaces. 01158
Strategic IRM plan: user involvement spells success. 02432
What's new in personal information managers. 02556
Decision Support and Knowledge Based Systems Track. § 03461
Executive support systems: the emergence of top management computer use. ● HCI-0049 †
Compact disc-interactive: a designer's overview. ● HCI-0078 †
On the purpose and analysis of EDP user systems. HCI-0218 †
Reflections on NoteCards: seven issues for the next generation of hypermedia systems. HCI-0293 †

*Decision support (e.g., MIS)*

Principles of information systems for management (2nd ed.). ● 0005
Power, politics, and MIS implementation. 0042
Managerial expert systems and organizational change: some critical research issues. 0157
Strategies for research on information systems in organizations. A critical analysis of research purpose and time frame. 0158
Human factors in management information systems. ● 0200

SmartSLIM: a DSS for controlling biases during problem formulation. 0203
Evaluation of expert systems for decision support. 0244
Knowledge based management support systems. ● 0252
Develping decision support systems from a model of the DSS/user interface. 0253
Human decision processes: Heuristics and task structure. 0401
User-developed DSS: steps toward quality control. 0461
Expert judgment and expert systems. ● 0552
An overview of system design for human interaction. 0646
Judgement and decision: theory and application. 0648
A philosophical basis for decision aiding. 0649
Decision making with unreliable probabilities. 0652
Conceptual design of decision support systems utilizing management science models. 0658
A conceptual architecture for generalized decision support system software. 0659
Concept design of a program manager's decision support system. 0660
ARIADNE: A knowledge-based interactive system for planning and decision support. 0661
Information systems in management: 3rd edition. ● 0673
Looking at worksheet modeling through expert system eyes. 0696
End-user computing by top executives. 0780
ICE: information center expert: a consultation system for resource allocation. 0781
Designing real-time, decision support computer-human interaction. 0982
CHI '88 Workshop on Real Time, decision support computer-human interaction. 0991
Validation of a Jungian instrument for MIS research. 01022
An evaluation of a realistic approach to MIS. 01027
Introducing information technology: experiences of a large industrial unit. 01217
Graphical data presentation for decision support systems. 01229
On the design of man-machine systems: principles, practices and prospects. 01236
MADEMA: an approach to intelligent manufacturing systems. 01318
An interactive outranking system for multi-attribute decision making. 01539
The human immune system as an information systems security reference model. 01547
Application of decision support system on sandwich beams, verified by experiments. 01572
Information politics. 01656
Battling for new roles. 01664
A general purpose computer aid to judgemental forecasting: Rationale and procedure. 01665
Understanding and validating results in model-based decision support systems. 01666

[H. INFORMATION SYSTEMS]

Propaedeutics of decision-making: supporting managerial learning and innovation. 01667
Providing effective decision support: modeling users and their requirements. 01668
A modular user-oriented decision support for physical database design. 01669
The metaphor machine: a database method for creativity support. 01670
A framework for designing adaptive DSS Interfaces. 01672
The age of the end-user and the shift from corporate MIS to corporate DSS. 01676
Expert systems in management science. 01689
Usage of linguistic variable concept for human operator modelling. 01694
Human specifics fuzzy categories and counteraction in decision making problems. 01696
ARIADNE: a knowledge-based interactive system for planning and decision support. 01860
Directed graph representations of association structures: A systematic approach. 01862
Application of a mathematical model of human decision-making for human-computer communication. 01866
Aiding the human decisionmaker through the knowledge-based sciences. 01880
Capturing expertise: Some approaches to modeling command decisionmaking in combat analysis. 01883
Distributed tactical decisionmaking: conceptual framework and empirical results. 01885
Distributed decisionmaking with constrained decisionmakers: a case study. 01886
Adaptive user interfaces for planning and decision aids in $C^3I$ systems. 01887
Direct comparison of the relative efficiency on intuitive and analytical cognition. 01896
An empirical investigation as to the need for multicomponent decision models. 01898
Information systems engineering for distributed decisionmaking. 01899
The feature chart: A tool for communicating the analysis for a decision support system. 01913
An exploratory contingency model of user participation and MIS use. 01919
Encouraging user management participation in systems design. 01926
A systems architecture for supporting senior managers' messy tasks. 01928
An empirical investigation of DSS usage and the user's perception of DSS training. 01934
An object-oriented approach to the design of a mail system for a heterogeneous environment. 01944
Decision support systems for workers: a bridge to advancing productivity. 01947
The implementation of information systems for workers: a structural equation model. 01948

An analysis of human and computer decision-making capabilities. 01951
Information requirements specification II: Brainstorming collective decision-making technique. 02005
A fuzzy decision-making method and its application to a company choice problem. 02029
Temporal semantics and natural language processing in a decision support system. 02038
Comparison of decision support strategies in expert consultation systems. 02101
Human interaction with an "intelligent" machine. 02163
Trust between humans and machines, and the design of decision aids. 02164
Human supervisor modelling: some new developments. 02170
Models of the decision maker in unforeseen accidents. 02172
Information and reasoning in intelligent decision support systems. 02173
The MDR algorithm and its application to the generation of explanations for novel events. 02174
Subjective probability and information retrieval: a review of the psychological literature. 02303
Controlling bias in user assertions in expert decision support systems for problem formulation. 02343
Organizational factors affecting the success of end-user computing. 02344
Effects of decision support training and cognitive style on decision process attributes. 02346
User perceptions of decision support system restrictiveness: an experiment. 02353
A longitudinal study of spreadsheet program use. 02354
Current and future uses of the group decision support system technology: report on a recent empirical study. 02355
Structuring informal information. 02426
Cognitive process as a basis for MIS and DSS design. 02476
Combining overlapping information. 02477
A study of user interface aids for model-oriented decision support systems. 02479
Decision analysis: practice and promise. 02480
The effects of 3D imagery on managerial data interpretation. 02502
Service support levels: An organizational approach to end-user computing. 02503
Descriptive analysis for computer-based decision support. 02527
Expanding the domain of systems analysis. 02587
Computing advice at a distance: the 'remote advisory' concept. 02617
Man-machine procedures of decision making under uncertainty based on linear programming. 02664
Innovation of decision support system-matplan based on structure matrix supported by APL. 02800

GDSS: a brief look at a new concept in decision support. 02804
Health care information systems: a personal historic review. 02849
History of the TDS medical information system. 02851
Planning for advising. 02886
Justified advice: a semi-naturalistic study of advisory strategies. 02887
How to interface to advisory systems? Users request help with a very simple language. 02888
UIMSs: threat or menace?. 02889
Effects of interface design upon user productivity. 02891
The responsive system: a new challenge for AI. 02920
The actem model for decision modelling in a scene management system. 02954
Information systems skills requirements: 1980 & 1988. 02997
The systems analyst of the 1990's. 02998
Causes of motivational problems among AI managers. 03004
Perspectives on the academic preparation of MIS professionals. 03006
Managers who personally use information technology frequently: a profile of some invisible computer personnel. 03007
The importance of individual differences in end-user training: The case for learning style. 03009
Evaluating performance appraisal systems for IS personnel. 03011
An update measure of supervisor-rated job performance for programmer/analysis. 03012
Increase organizational effectiveness: Support self-managed IS development teams. 03014
Repositioning the information systems management function: Implications for information systems personnel. 03015
Negotiating IS: Observations on changes in structure from a negotiated order perspective. 03016
Social choice theory and distributed decision making. 03044
A consultation system for information center resource allocation. 03100
Issues in modeling supervisory control in flexible manufacturing systems. 03363
Decision support using qualitative evidence. 03398
Design of individual adaptive man-computer dialogues in the hybrid intelligence systems. 03400
The role of memory in intelligent information systems. 03462
An investigation of performance, productivity, and rationality in multi-criteria decision making. 03463
Crisis planning systems: tools for intelligent action. 03464
Ontological analysis of document usage: an exploratory study. 03467
An expert system framework for forecasting method selection. 03468

Perceptions of system effectiveness as viewed by executives, users, and information specialists. 03469
User perceptions of DSS restrictiveness: an experiment. 03470
Systems for cooperative work and group decision making: status of use and problems in development. 03471
On building future decision support systems. 03472
Flexible user interface decision support systems. 03473
Handling textual information in a GDSS database: experience with the Arizona analyst information system. 03475
The impact of "Messy" data on group decision making. 03476
Knowledge-based support of cooperative activities. 03478
An architecture for active DSS. 03480
Structured what if analysis in DSS models. 03481
A longitudinal study of spreadsheet program use. 03482
A box structured methodology for solving business problems. 03483
GMMS: global model management system: a conceptual design framework for model management systems for distributed decision support systems. 03484
Decision support for reasoning about values. 03486
Reasoning in model management systems. 03487
A financial investment assistant. 03490
Seven mortal sins of systems work. 03645
Decision support systems: theory and application. § 03788
Characteristics of a successful DSS user's needs vs. builder's needs. 03789
A study of managerial computer users: the impact of user sophistication on decision structure and attributes of decision-related information (end user). 04078
Executive support systems: the emergence of top management computer use. ● HCI-0049 †
Project Nick: meetings augmentation and analysis. HCI-0156 †
An experimental program investigating color-enhanced and graphical information presentation: an integration of the findings. HCI-0196 †
Understanding the effectiveness of computer graphics for decision support: a cumulative experimental approach. HCI-0215 †
Expert systems as cognitive tools for human decision making. HCI-0227 †
Executive workstations: issues and requirements. HCI-0288 †
The impact of DSS on organizational communication. HCI-0294 †
Interactive fuzzy decision-making for multi-objective nonlinear programming using reference membership intervals. HCI-0295 †
Change, attitude to change, and decision support system success. HCI-0296 †
Communications design for Co-oP: a group decision support system. HCI-0297 †

[H. INFORMATION SYSTEMS] CATEGORY INDEX

Computer decision support for senior managers: encouraging exploration. HCI-0298 †
Personal computing for decision support. HCI-0299 †
gIBIS: a hypertext tool for exploratory policy discussion. HCI-0300 †
A laboratory study of user characteristics and decision-making performance in end-user computing. HCI-0301 †
A generalized model management system for mathematical programming. HCI-0302 †
Impact of design methods on decision support systems success: an empirical assessment. HCI-0303 †
IDECAP: interactive pictorial information system for demographic and environmental planning applications. HCI-0411 †

*Logistics*

An expert system framework for forecasting method selection. 03468

### H.4.3 Communications Applications

Speech filing—An office system for principals. 0037
Human factors challenges in creating a principal support office system—The speh filing system approach. 0038
Expert systems and artificial intelligence. ● 0133
Computer-supported cooperative work: a book of readings. ● 0366
Toward high-performance knowledge workers (Reprint). 0369
Authorship provisions in AUGMENT (Reprint). 0370
Thinking ahead: what to expect from teleconferencing (Reprint). 0372
Beyond the chalkboard: computer support for collaboration and problem solving inmeetings (Reprint). 0376
Data sharing in group work (Reprint). 0379
An experiment in integrated multimedia conferencing. 0381
A language/action perspective on the design of cooperative work (Reprint). 0383
Social psychological aspects of computer-mediated communication (Reprint). 0384
Cognitive science and organizational design: a case study of computer conferencing (Reprint). 0386
Relationships and tasks in scientific research collaborations (Reprint). 0387
Relationships and tasks in scientific research collaborations (Reprint). 0387
Information processing today, with applications. ● 0567
Information processing today, with applications. ● 0568
Information processing today, with applications and BASIC. ● 0569
Information processing today, with applications and BASIC: updat 87/88. ● 0570
Principles of information processing. ● 0571

Principles of information processing with applications and BASIC. ● 0572
Digital video interactive. 0681
The effects of device technology on the usability of advanced telephone functions. 0876
The design of phone-based interfaces for consumers. 0878
Tools for supporting cooperative work near and far: highlights from the CSCW conference. 0879
Voice messaging enhancing the user interface design based on field performance. 0913
Rapid prototyping and system development: examination of an interface toolkit for voice and telephony applications. 0918
Computer-support cooperative work. 0956
Information detective: a workstation for exploring three dimensional information space. 01010
Perception and acceptance of a local area network and electronic mail. 01284
Intelligent information-sharing systems. 01322
Successful implementation of an office system. 01438
The committee support system. 01460
Implementing computer-mediated communication technologies: a technoacceptance approach to critical mass utilization. 01931
Design of personal information retrieval systems. 02032
Who's joking? The information system at play. 02066
Electronic publishing: The predicament of occasional users in the editorial proc. 02446
Mondo media. 02552
Understanding cable subscribership as telecommunications behavior. 02676
Interaction of CMC with video telecourses for distance education. 02677
Electronic communications and collaboration: the emerging model for computer aided communications in science and medicine. 02678
Communications technology and the public sector: understanding the process of adoption. 02679
An informal overview of CUINFO (Cornell's computer-based bulletin board). 02783
Computer-Supported Cooperative Work. § 02821
Design of a multi-media vehicle for social browsing. 02822
Guided tours and tabletops: tools for communicating in a hypertext environment. 02823
How can groups communicate when they use different languages?. 03038
Information in the air and in the wave. 03146
Flexible intelligent interactive-video. 03238
A study of group interaction over a computer-based message system. 03257
User friendly interface for messaging systems. 03320
Future Trends in Information Science and Technology. § 04039
Access to academic networks. ● HCI-0050 †

## [H. INFORMATION SYSTEMS]

Reading text from computer screens. HCI-0088 †
Toward native language software for information management. HCI-0138 †
Object lens: a "spreadsheet" for cooperative work. HCI-0206 †
Querying external databases. HCI-0233 †
Reading and writing the electronic book. HCI-0282 †
Semistructured messages are surprisingly useful for computer-supported coordination. HCI-0290 †
Communications design for Co-oP: a group decision support system. HCI-0297 †
The dimensions of accessibility to online information: implications for implementing office information systems. HCI-0304 †
Interface design in computerized conferencing systems: a personal view. HCI-0305 †
A user agent for multiple computer-based message services. HCI-0306 †
Strategies for encouraging successful adoption of office communication systems. HCI-0307 †
Videotex: anatomy of a failure. HCI-0313 †
Expert systems—where do we go from here?. HCI-0318 †

**EIES** *see* Proper Noun Index

### Electronic mail

Reducing social context cues: electronic mail in organizational communication (Reprint). 0385
User performance with command, menu, and iconic interfaces. 0414
Diamond: A multimedia message system built on a distributed architecture. 0574
How do experienced information lens users use rules?. 0854
Tools for supporting cooperative work near and far: highlights from the CSCW conference. 0879
The information lens: an intelligent system for information sharing in organizations. 0891
Learning modes and subsequent use of computer-mediated communication systems. 0912
The formal specification of adaptive user interfaces using command language grammar. 0925
Office-by-example: an integrated office system and database manager. 01159
An empirical investigation of two electronic mail systems. 01239
MH: a multifarious user agent. 01428
Socio-technical aspects of electronic mail implementation. 01439
Edmas: an object-oriented, locally distributed mail system. 01857
Insights on the implementation of a computer-based message system. 01917

An object-oriented approach to the design of a mail system for a heterogeneous environment. 01944
Interacting with electronic mail can be a dream or a night: a user's point of view. 02069
Talking to computers: an empirical investigation. 02186
The effect of presentation media on recipient performance in text-based information systems. 02350
Reducing social context cues: electronic mail in organizational communication. 02473
Dragonmail: an exercise in distributed computing. 02630
Cooperative work in the Andrew message system. 02827
A case study of CSCW in a dispersed organization. 02866
Groupware: interface design for meetings. 02883
The impact of electronic mail on managerial and organizational communications. 03041
Advisor—an electronic mail consulting service. 03151
Design and evaluation of the AID adaptive front-end to Telecom Gold. 03260
Computer-based message services. § 03319
POEM: An office system for international use. 03457
Automated document distribution using AI based workstations and knowledge based servers. 03466
Intelligent interfaces for information retrieval systems: architecture problems in the construction of expert systems for document retrieval. 04042
Efficient computer-user interface in electronic mail systems. HCI-0118 †
The 1984 Olympic Message System: a test of behavioral principles of system design. HCI-0125 †
A distributed interoffice mail system. HCI-0308 †
An experimental multimedia mail system. HCI-0309 †
Diversity in the use of electronic mail: a preliminary inquiry. HCI-0310 †
Usage patterns in an integrated voice and data communications system. HCI-0311 †

### Teleconferencing

Supporting collaboration in hypermedia: issues and experiences. 0117
Textual intervention, collaboration, and the online environment. 0126
Techniques of user message design: developing a user message system to support cooperative work. 0127
Computer-based real-time conferencing systems (Reprint). 0377
The effects of bargaining orientation and communication medium on negotiations in the bilateral monopoly task: a comparison of decision room and computer conferencing communication media. 0809
Tools for supporting cooperative work near and far: highlights from the CSCW conference. 0879
An architecture for a multimedia teleconferencing system. 02802
GDSS: a brief look at a new concept in decision support. 02804

[H. INFORMATION SYSTEMS]

Video: Data for studying human-computer interaction. 02878
Need of electronic tools in educational programmers and the impact in developing countries. 03023
The rapport multimedia conferencing system. 03037
Systems for cooperative work and group decision making: status of use and problems in development. 03471
Grand computer conferencing: What have we learned?. 03536
Online communities. ● HCI-0051 †
Beyond the chalkboard: computer support for collaboration and problem solving in meetings. HCI-0312 †

### Videotex

Cognitive optimisation of Videotex dialogues: a formal—empirical approach. 0320
Videodisc and videotex: love-match or passing acquaintance?. 0515
Videotex information packagers: a field study aimed at tomorrow's videotex authoring interface. 0962
The value of downloading for database users and database producers. 01218
MH: a multifarious user agent. 01428
Some remarks on videotex interaction. How to write for a new reader. 01433
Viewdata in the office—user-friendly page identification. 02334
The design and construction of a vital database. 02460
Organizational videotex: information services for the end user. 03166
A viewdata-structure editor designed around a task/action mapping. 03269
Videotex and online services: competition or collateral. 03557
Interface abstractions for an *naplps* page creation system. 03863
The legibility of visual display texts. 03889
Keywords instead of hierarchical menus. 03912
A comparison of the effects of computer-assisted instruction, interactive video, and traditional instruction on third-grade students in art education. 04064
Information technology and home-based services: improving the usability of teleshopping. HCI-0226 †
Videotex: anatomy of a failure. HCI-0313 †

### H.4.m Miscellaneous

Presenting documents on workstation screens. 0267
Toward hypertext publishing. 01075
WYSIWIS revised: early experiences with multiuser interfaces. 01158
Making the transition from print to electronic encyclopaedias: adapation of mental models. 02238

A cognitive study of the decision-making process in a business context: implications for design of expert systems. 02256
Can finding information be easy, fun and successful?. 02324
An assessment of the major computerised databases relating to disabled people in the UK and Scandinavia. 02326
Adaptive information systems control: A reliability-based approach. 02345
The impact of information systems strategy on end user computing. 02423
Managing end user computing when the only constant is change. 02425
Supporting collaboration in Hypermedia: issues and experiences. 02454
System development methods—a comparative investigation. 02504
Dialogue management: support for dialogue independence. 02512
Systems design and social responsibility: the political implications of "computer-supported cooperative work". A commentary. 02516
Computing facilities in the MRC clinical research centre. 02688
Research and development in information retrieval. § 03287
A note on the nature of creativity in engineering: implications for supporting system design. HCI-0220 †
Beyond the chalkboard: computer support for collaboration and problem solving in meetings. HCI-0312 †

**BSP** *see* Proper Noun Index

## H.m MISCELLANEOUS

Semiotics and informatics: computers as media. 0448
The evaluation of information services: a typology. 0452
PLEXACT: an architecture & design of a knowledge-based system for information systems development. 01020
Job histories as predictors of career success in management information systems. 01021
The information center approach for developing computer-based information systems. 01929
The convergence of Moore's/Mooers' laws. 01996
On meanings menus for measurement: disentangling evaluative issues in system design. 01997
On two roles decision support systems can play in negotiations. 01998
Will you be replaced by a knowledge base?. 02055
Comparison of decision support strategies in expert consultation systems. 02101
Moral issues in information science. 02321

User's complaints: Information system problems from the user's perspective. 02416
The dimensions of perceived accessibility to information: Implications for the delivery if information systems and services. 02448
Work design instead of system design. 03671

# I. COMPUTING METHODOLOGIES

Modeling the user's plans and goals. 01349

## I.1 ALGEBRAIC MANIPULATION

### I.1.0 General

Symsac '86. § 03080
Symsac '86—Proceedings of the 1986 symposium on symbolic and algebraic manipulation. § 03084
MFDBS 87. § 03943

### I.1.1 Expressions and Their Representation (E.1-2)

Applicable algebra, error-correcting codes, combinatorics and computer algebra. § 03846
Integration of graphical tools in a computer algebra system. 03847

*Representations (General and Polynomial)*

Tense, qualifiers, and contexts. 01346
Arithmetic codes resembling neural encoding. 02021
MathScribe: a user interface for computer algebra systems. 03082

*Simplification of expressions*

Design tools for large relational database systems. 03946

### I.1.2 Algorithms (F.2.1-2)

Reliability in computing: the role of interval methods in scientific computing. ● 0548
Annual review of computer science vol. 1, 1986. ● 0719
Data-structures students may prefer to learn algorithms using graphical methods. 01032
Industrial & Engineering Applications of Artificial Intelligence & Expert Systems: vol. II. § 02982
Applicable algebra, error-correcting codes, combinatorics and computer algebra. § 03846

*Algebraic algorithms*

User interfaces for office systems. 0756
Iris: design of a user interface program for symbolic algebra. 03081
Iris: design of an user interface program for symbolic algebra. 03085
Integration of graphical tools in a computer algebra system. 03847
Applied algebra, algorithmics and error-correcting codes. § 03848
Automatizing geometric proofs and constructions. 03851

*Analysis of algorithms*

The accuracy of approximate string matching algorithms. 02279

*Nonalgebraic algorithms*

Preferred settings in VDT work: The Zürich Experience. 03707
On the design of dealing desks. 03713
Teleoperations and robotics: applications and technology. ● HCI-0068 †

### I.1.3 Languages and Systems (D.3.2-3, F.2.2)

The effects of 3D imagery on managerial data interpretation. 02502
PowerMath—A system for the Macintosh. 03083
MathScribe: a user interface for computer algebra systems. 03086
Applicable algebra, error-correcting codes, combinatorics and computer algebra. § 03846
Icon semantics—a formal approach to icon system design. HCI-0161 †

**MACSYMA** *see* Proper Noun Index

**Maple** *see* Proper Noun Index

**REDUCE** *see* Proper Noun Index

*Special-purpose hardware*

MathScribe: a user interface for computer algebra systems. 03082

### I.1.4 Applications

The metaphor machine: a database method for creativity support. 01670

### I.1.m Miscellaneous

Construction of interactive programs in computer graphics. 01398
Two notes concerning the society theory of thinking. 01479
Human performance in relational algebra, tuple calculus, and domain calculus. 02208

## I.2 ARTIFICIAL INTELLIGENCE

Distributed Artificial Intelligence. ● 0168
Artificial intelligence and expert systems. ● 0665
Exploring artificial intelligence. ● 0692
Annual review of computer science vol. 1, 1986. ● 0719
Automating knowledge acquisition for aerial image interpretation. 01470

### I.2.0 General

The society of text: hypertext, hypermedia, and the social construction of information. ● 0111
Syntactic and structural pattern recognition. ● 0292
Artificial intelligence and statistics. ● 0321
Knowledge, skill and artificial intelligence. ● 0342
Intelligent machines for process control. 0362
'This is a very unpredictable machine': on computers and human cognition. 0364
A conceptual framework for the augmentation of man's intellect (Reprint). 0368
The computer and the mind: an introduction to cognitive science. ● 0463
Production system models of learning and development. ● 0478
Parallel computation and computers for artificial intelligence. ● 0488
Application of the butterfly parallel processor in artificial intelligence. 0489
Trends in information systems. ● 0498
Experiencing artificial intelligence: an interactive approach to the IBM PC. ● 0550
Experiencing artificial intelligence: an interactive approach for the APPLE. ● 0551
Critical issues in information processing management and technology: vol. 6. ● 0594
Readings in artificial intelligence and software engineering. ● 0612
Thinking: information processing, mathematical models and computer simulation. ● 0667
Oxford surveys in information technology; vol. 2, 1985. ● 0755
Idea for a mind. 0773
Preferences for power in expert systems by novice users. 0971
Apollo domain series 3000. 01170
Why artificial intelligence isn't (yet). 01175
The human factor in expert systems. 01179
Neural networks primer, part III. 01182
Cognitive technologies: The design of joint human-machine cognitive systems. 01193
The problem of extracting the knowledge of experts. 01195
What AI practitioners should know about the law, part 2. 01197
Knowledge and experience. 01207
Speculating on the future of mathematics. 01210
A folklore view of information. 01222
Advanced computers. 01387
Approximate modelling of cognitive activity with an expert system: a theory-based strategy for developing an interactive design tool. 01415
Two notes concerning the society theory of thinking. 01479
How can cognitive psychology help solve an artificial intelligence problem?. 01480
The contemporary psychology of thinking and expert systems. 01487
Questions, intelligence, and intelligent behavior. 01540
Questions, intelligence and intelligent behavior. 01542
The cybernetic principle: its transdisciplinarity to science and religion and the challenging task. 01596
The effects of sources of applications programs on user satisfaction: an empirical study of micro, mini & mainframe computers using an interactive artificial intelligence expert-system. 01601
Cybernetic consciousness. 01605
A survey on systems informational paradigm to the psychic. 01606
Putting expert systems to work. 01704
Cognitive factors in user/expert-system interaction. 01733
Building and understanding adaptive systems: a statistical/numerical approach to factory automation and brain research. 01890
Experience of programming beauty: some patterns of programming aesthetics. 02184
Introduction to expert systems. 02261
Mondo media. 02552
The immune system, adaptation, and machine learning. 02559
Computing advice at a distance: the 'remote advisory' concept. 02617
Expert systems & their applications. § 02711
The polarisation approach to intelligent artifacts. 02714
Expert systems & their applications. § 02715
Expert Systems & Their Applications. § 02717
History of Medical Informatics. § 02837
Methodologies for intelligent systems. § 03026
Common and uncommon issues in artificial intelligence an psychology. 03312
Advances in artificial intelligence. § 03546
Progress in artificial intelligence. § 03555
Theoretical aspects of reasoning about knowledge. § 03559
Computer culture: the scientific, intellectual, and social impact of the computer. § 03567
Fifth generation computer architectures. § 03586
Designing learning processes for work activities in automated technologies. 03605
Understanding learning problems in computer aided tasks. 03607
Methodologies for intelligent systems. § 03633

Decision support systems: theory and application. § 03788
Logic programming '86. § 03816
Computational Geometry and its Applications. § 03850
Uncertainty and intelligent systems. § 04030
Fifth generation computers: concepts, implementations and uses. ● HCI-0001 †
Brains, machines, and mathematics (2nd ed.). ● HCI-0034 †
Artificial and human intelligence. § HCI-0052 †
How we know. ● HCI-0053 †
Understanding computers and cognition. ● HCI-0054 †
Man-made minds: the promise of artificial intelligence. ● HCI-0055 †
Creative intelligences. ● HCI-0056 †
Conceptual structures: information processing in mind and machine. ● HCI-0057 †
Artificial intelligence and tutoring systems: computational and cognitive approaches to the communication of knowledge. ● HCI-0080 †
The computer culture. § HCI-0084 †
Goal and plan knowledge representations: from stories to text editors and programs. HCI-0183 †
Cognitive engineering—cognitive science. HCI-0200 †
Psychology and information technology. HCI-0225 †
Relations between cognitive psychology and computer system design. HCI-0244 †
Computing with structured connectionist networks. HCI-0314 †
Expert systems—where do we go from here?. HCI-0318 †

## I.2.1 Applications and Expert Systems (H.4, J.)

Intelligent CAD systems II: implementational issues. ● 0006
Product and process design in intelligent CAD workstations. 0009
THESYS—implementation of a knowledge-based design system with multiple viewpoints. 0010
A historical and intellectual perspective of the context of human computer interaction. 0039
Computer text-editing: an information-processing analysis of a routine cognitive skill. 0050
Text processing with the START natural language system. 0100
Expert systems and artificial intelligence. ● 0133
Space. 0134
Finance. 0135
Military systems. 0138
AI development and the Office of Naval Research. 0140
Critical issues in information systems research. ● 0153
Managerial expert systems and organizational change: some critical research issues. 0157

Questions, answers, and responses: interacting with knowledge base systems. 0182
Knowledge-based human-computer interfaces and software ergonomics. 0191
Knowledge-based systems and communication between computers and human beings. 0192
Perspectives in artificial intelligence vol. 2: machine translation, NLP, databases and computer-aided instruction. ● 0198
Artificial intelligence and its applications. ● 0221
Readings in cognitive science: a perspective from psychology & artificial intelligence. ● 0223
Advanced information technology in the new industrial society: the Kingston seminars. ● 0225
Evaluation of expert systems for decision support. 0244
Knowledge based management support systems. ● 0252
Environments for supporting statistical strategy. 0322
Use of psychometric tools for knowledge acquistion: a case study. 0323
The analysis phase in development of knowledge based systems. 0324
Data, expert knowledge and decisions. ● 0338
Computer-supported cooperative work: a book of readings. ● 0366
Callisto: an intelligent project management system (Reprint). 0375
Advances in human-computer interaction. ● 0407
Expert systems: the user interface. ● 0425
Introduction: designing interfaces for expert systems. 0426
DARN: Toward a community memory for diagnosis and repair tasks. 0428
Direct manipulation user interfaces for expert systems. 0429
The evolution of interface requirements for expert systems. 0431
Cognitive impacts of the user interface. 0432
Expert systems: the user interface. ● 0433
Cognitive engineering in complex dynamic worlds. ● 0436
C/C++ for expert systems: "unleashes the power of a artificial intelligence". ● 0439
Knowledge-based systems, artificial intelligence and human factors. 0449
Instructional designs for microcomputer courseware. ● 0464
Artificial intelligence and instruction: Applications and methods. ● 0468
Knowledge based problem solving. ● 0490
ETS—a system for the transfer of human expertise. 0491
Universal subgoaling and chunking: the automatic generation and learning of goal hierarchies. ● 0497
Artificial intelligence and education; vol. 1: learning environments and tutoring systems. ● 0516
Algebra slaves and agents in a Logo-based mathematics curriculum. 0517

[I. COMPUTING METHODOLOGIES]

Toward a theory of impasse-driven learning. 0536
Socializing the intelligent tutor: bringing empathy to computer tutors. 0541
Learning issues for intelligent tutoring systems. ● 0545
Expert judgment and expert systems. ● 0552
Expert systems and creativity. 0553
Foundations of intelligent tutoring systems. ● 0592
CAD Based Programming for Sensory Robots. ● 0597
An overview of system design for human interaction. 0646
Artificial intelligence and expert systems. ● 0665
Expert systems for commercial use. 0666
Artificial intelligence & human learning: intelligent computer-aided instruction. ● 0671
Artificial intelligence systems. 0683
Designing the user interface: supplemental materials. ● 0689
Expert systems for business. ● 0695
Building expert systems: cognitive emulation. ● 0700
Intelligent CAD systems I: theoretical and methodological aspects. ● 0715
A multiparadigm user interface for intelligent CAD systems. 0716
An integrated data description language for coding design knowledge. 0717
Knowledge engineering: expert systems and information retrieval. ● 0735
Are machines as good as people in drawing conclusions from knowledge represented in catalogues, data bases and expert systems?. 0736
KIWI: knowledge-based user-friendly system for the utilization of information bases. 0739
KIWI: knowledge-based user-friendly system for the utilization of information bases. 0739
The migration of expert systems into the production environment. 0740
Professional and expert systems: a meeting of minds. 0790
Approximate modelling of cognitive activity: towards an expert system design aid. 0801
University of Colorado at Boulder, Institute of cognitive science. 0811
NYNEX intelligent systems group. 0814
Graphic interfaces for knowledge-based system development. 0892
Learning and transfer for text and graphics editing with a direct manipulation interface. 0900
Intelligent interfaces: user models and planners. 0932
Legal liability for malfunction and misuse of expert systems. 0939
PLEXACT: an architecture & design of a knowledge-based system for information systems development. 01020
A smalltalk implementation of an intelligent operator's associate. 01132

A prolog simulation for a Delphi-based problem solver. 01141
Automating the design of graphical presentations of relational information. 01150
Cognitive technologies: The design of joint human-machine cognitive systems. 01193
On interface requirements for expert systems. 01198
Dialogue and the search for information. 01223
Human intelligence models and their implications for expert system structure and research. 01242
Computers on the brain, part 1. 01296
Error-free fractions. 01297
MADEMA: an approach to intelligent manufacturing systems. 01318
Interface design issues for advice-giving expert systems. 01321
Intelligent interactive video simulation of a code inspection. 01329
The Berkeley UNIX consultant project. 01355
The programmer's apprentices: a research overview. 01368
A flexible synonym interface with application examples in CAL and help environments. 01404
Artificial intelligence techniques in man–machine communication. 01459
The contemporary psychology of thinking and expert systems. 01487
Development of the wedding planner—extensions to reach a young audience. 01502
Knowledge-based system for task analysis and reliability enhancement. 01516
A knowledge-based system for assessment of human physiological abilities in manual lifting tasks. 01519
A brief review of developments in problem solving. 01581
Problem solving: a behavioral interpretation. 01582
The erotetic logic of problem-solving inquiry. 01583
Creative computer problem solving. 01584
Artificial intelligence in the man/machine interface. 01626
Expert systems in management science. 01689
Putting expert systems to work. 01704
The role of human factors in expert systems design and acceptance. 01780
Adaptive aiding for human/computer control. 01782
Likelihood alarm displays. 01783
Structuring knowledge bases for designers of learning materials. 01807
A knowledge-based human-computer cooperative system for ill-structured management domains. 01873
Information systems engineering for distributed decision-making. 01899
A preliminary specification of an on-line expert help system. 01930
Intelligent help systems. 01959

# [I. COMPUTING METHODOLOGIES]

OAKDEC, a program for studying the effects on users of a procedural expert system for database searching. 02003

A design for a fuzzy logic controller. 02028

Knowledge representation and use in pattern analysis. 02030

Will you be replaced by a knowledge base?. 02055

On the applicability of maximum entropy to inexact reasoning. 02074

Epistemic necessity, possibility, and truth. Tools for dealing with imprecision and uncertainty in fuzzy knowledge-based systems. 02075

Combining functions for certainty degrees in consulting systems. 02092

Modelling human expertise in knowledge engineering: some preliminary observations. 02134

Operator assistant systems. 02165

Information and reasoning in intelligent decision support systems. 02173

$DM^2$: an algorithm for diagnostic reasoning that combines analytical models and experiential knowledge. 02190

Evaluating the intelligence in dialogue systems. 02194

Surveying projects on intelligent dialogue. 02197

Effects of computer programming experience on network representations of abstract programming concepts. 02204

Refining problem-solving knowledge in repertory grids using a consultation mechanism. 02205

Design goals for sloppy modeling systems. 02206

On the representation and the impact of reliability on expert system weights. 02211

Patterns of inductive reasoning in a parallel expert system. 02219

Issues in the verification of knowledge in rule-based systems. 02226

Are there individual concepts? Proper names and individual concepts in SI-Nets. 02233

The electronic book Ebook3. 02234

Absolute dates and relative dates in an inferential system on temporal dependencies between events. 02235

Support for browsing in an intelligent text retrieval system. 02240

Expert systems and interactive video tutorials: separating strategies from subject matter. 02293

Color, graphics, and animation in a computer-assisted learning tutorial lesson. 02294

Controlling bias in user assertions in expert decision support systems for problem formulation. 02343

Motivation norms of knowledge engineers compared to those of software engineers. 02349

Expert systems as human resource management decision tools. 02440

An expert system for system design. 02441

A personal computer based graphic workstation. 02493

Mondo media. 02552

The second generation intelligent user interface for the crustal dynamics data information system. 02675

New applications of data bases. § 02710

A planning system for a cognitive problem. 02719

ACTES/Proceedings Symposium 1988 ACM SIGSMAll/PC. § 02787

Parametric Fourier image characterization toolkit. 02798

Medical informatics: a personal view of sowing the seeds. 02841

A knowledge-based user interface management system. 02867

SAUCI: a knowledge-based interface architecture. 02895

Industrial & Engineering Applications of Artificial Intelligence & Expert Systems. § 02910

The responsive system: a new challenge for AI. 02920

Improving performance of an electrical power expert system with genetic algorithms. 02925

The development of an automated flight test management system for flight test planning and monitoring. 02928

Industrial & Engineering Applications of Artificial Intelligence & Expert Systems. § 02941

Graphics-based qualitative simulation generator for power distribution systems. 02946

The design of a traffic control expert system for long distance network contingencies. 02952

Lets "Deep-Six" our reference manuals. 02955

Industrial & Engineering Applications of Artificial Intelligence & Expert Systems: vol. I. § 02967

SPA: a systems for diagnosis of computer performance problems. 02969

Hierarchical scheduling in an intelligent environmental control system. 02976

A process oriented approach to an intelligent design aid. 02980

Towards reasoning visualization in expert systems. 02992

Causes of motivational problems among AI managers. 03004

IR-NLI II: applying man-machine interaction and artificial intelligence conceptsto information retrieval. 03070

Research and development in information retrieval. § 03072

Illustrated description of an interactive knowledge based indexing system. 03076

The 1987 ACM SIGBDP-SIGCPR Conference. § 03099

A consultation system for information center resource allocation. 03100

Expert system applications in customer service. 03101

ACE: a color expert system for user interface design. 03117

Expert database systems. § 03173

An interactive data dictionary facility for CAD/CAM data bases. 03174

Distributed database considerations in an expert system for radar analysis. 03175

Expert systems 85. § 03188

[I. COMPUTING METHODOLOGIES]

Pictorial knowledge bases. 03201
User requirements for expert system explanation: what, why and when?. 03242
Using an expert system to convey HCI information. 03272
Interactive error recovery expert system for robot with voice recognition subsystem. 03420
Problems among managers of AI personnel. 03460
An expert system framework for forecasting method selection. 03468
Human-computer communication meets software engineering. 03505
A programming environment supporting reuse of object-oriented software. 03509
Artificial Intelligence and Information-Control systems of Robots-87. § 03570
On one aspect of natural-language based knowledge acquisition. 03571
Knowledge acquisition via a graphical interface. 03572
Object-oriented signal processing systems. 03573
Exploratory investigations in acquiring and using information in interactive problem solving. 03597
On the physics and mathematics of thought. 03778
Knowledge-based editors for directed graphs. 03797
Failure analysis of information systems: reflections on the use of expert systems in information systems. 03811
Fault management, knowledge support, and responsibility in man-machine systems. 03812
Mental models and failures in human-machine systems. 03814
Human-computer interaction: psychonomic aspects. § 03887
Introduction: human-computer interaction: psychonomic aspects. 03888
Tree doctor, a software package for graphical manipulation and animation of tree structures. 03901
Textvision: elicitation and acquisition of conceptual knowledge by graphic representation and multiwindowing. 03902
Textvision: elicitation and acquisition of conceptual knowledge by graphic representation and multiwindowing. 03902
Development of mental models of an office system: a field study on an introductory course. 03903
Artificial intelligence and cognitive psychology: a new look at human factors. 03904
Knowledge and expertise in expert systems. 03905
Architectures for production systems: an inside look for those who study human-computer interaction. 03906
Natural language communication with computers: some problems, perspectives, and new directions. 03913
KRIP: a knowledge representation system for laws relating to industrial property. 03918
Uncertainty and intelligent systems. § 04030
Experimentation with an adaptive search strategy for solving a keyboard design/configuration problem. 04070

A comprehensive guide to AI and expert systems. ● HCI-0058 †
Expertise transfer for expert system design. ● HCI-0059 †
Knowledge-based systems: implications for human-computer interfaces. ● HCI-0060 †
Decision and intelligence. ● HCI-0068 †
Artificial intelligence and tutoring systems: computational and cognitive approaches to the communication of knowledge. ● HCI-0080 †
The architecture of fifth generation inference computers. HCI-0093 †
Expert systems as cognitive tools for human decision making. HCI-0227 †
Learning by doing with simulated intelligent help. HCI-0229 †
Users and experts in the document retrieval system model. HCI-0270 †
Towards a new research paradigm in information retrieval. HCI-0273 †
On the application of rule-based techniques to the design of advice giving systems. HCI-0315 †
A model for the interpretation of verbal predictions. HCI-0316 †
Strategic issues in knowledge engineering. HCI-0317 †
Expert systems—where do we go from here?. HCI-0318 †
Acquisition of control and domain knowledge by watching in a blackboard environment. HCI-0319 †
Knowledge and control for a mechanical design expert system. HCI-0320 †
Cognitive models, cognitive tasks, and information retrieval. HCI-0331 †
Expertise transfer and complex problems: using AQUINAS as a knowledge-acquisition workbench for knowledge-based systems. HCI-0336 †
Knowledge elicitation: dissociating conscious reflections from automatic processes. HCI-0337 †
Implications for education and training. HCI-0430 †
The LISP tutor: it approaches the effectiveness of a human tutor. HCI-0431 †
An overview of research and co-operation in advanced information technology. HCI-0442 †
Interactive critical path analysis (ICPA)—microcomputer implementation of a project management and knowledge engineering tool. HCI-0445 †

**ACRONYM** *see* Proper Noun Index

**CAL** *see* Proper Noun Index

*Cartography*

Advances in computer graphics II. ● 0437
How to tell people where to go: comparing navigational aids. 02096

## CATEGORY INDEX — [I. COMPUTING METHODOLOGIES]

Beyond software ergonomics? Human control of automated systems. 03386
Human-machine interface in remote monitoring and control of flexible manufacturing systems. 03399
Experiences from the use of an intelligent safety sensor with industrial robots. 03427
Performance evaluation of three pressure mats as robot workstation safety sensors. 03428
Concept for a model databased remote maintenance system. 03565
How map designers can represent their ideas in thematic maps: effective user interfaces for thematic map design. 03870
Challenges in the application of graphics technology to the management of geographic information. 03871
Color and the computer in cartography. HCI-0386 †

**DSPL** *see* Proper Noun Index

**EMYCIN** *see* Proper Noun Index

**ESCORT** *see* Proper Noun Index

### Games

Computer chess compendium. ● 0526
The automated solution of logic puzzles. 02015
Breaking away. 02553
Comparison of video game and conventional test performance. 02594
Human-computer interaction in the game of Go. 03634

**GXMP** *see* Proper Noun Index

### Industrial automation

Natural languages. 0136
The management of advanced information technology. 0226
Complete vs. incomplete working tasks—a concept and its verification. 0241
Intelligent machines for process control. 0362
Attention. 0399
Adaptive control in human-machine systems. 0405
Man is not a robot. 0445
A workcell application design environment (WADE). 0598
Robot simulation and off-line programming—an integrated CAE-CAD approach. 0599
Experiences with off-line robot programming via standardized interfaces. 0601
Off-line programming and path generation for robot manipulators. 0603
Computer aided application program synthesis for industrial robots. 0606
CAD-based off-line programming applied to a cleaning and deburring workstation. 0607
Computer-aided production management IFIP. ● 0618
Production management systems. 0619
An expert system architecture for computer-aided control engineering. 0662
Automation, work organization and skills: the case of numerical control. 01234
Problems associated with the off-line programming of robots. 01241
Simulation of CNC controller features in graphics-based programming. 01568
Successful use of CADCAM—a combination of technology, organization, and people. 01569
CAD system GISK for interactive graphical modelling of planar mechanisms. 01570
Interactive CAD/CAM in engineering industry. 01571
Application of decision support system on sandwich beams, verified by experiments. 01572
ORGPLAN an information-decisive aid system to resolving organizing problems. 01573
A framework for task cooperation within systems containing intelligent components. 01884
Decision support systems for workers: a bridge to advancing productivity. 01947
Modelling human expertise in knowledge engineering: some preliminary observations. 02134
Strategies in controlling a continuous process with long response latencies: needs for computer support to diagnosis. 02217
Introduction to expert systems. 02261
A compact model of a power house boiler. 02683
Legal data modeling: The prohibited transaction exemption analyst. 02779
Using hypertext to overcome the knowledge base development bottleneck: a case study. 02914
PISCES: an expert system for coal fired power plant monitoring and diagnostics. 02915
The network control assistant (NCA), a real-time prototype expert system for network management. 02930
Automated design and analysis system for design of custom orthopedic implants. 02931
Applications of an AI design shell ENGINEOUS to advanced engineering products. 02932
Process control with the G2 real-time expert system. 02934
GTEX—A group technology expert system. 02936
An expert database for material and production planning. 02937
Generic diagnostic knowledge acquisition tool. 02944
Multi-Input fuzzy inference engine on a systolic array. 02953
Knowledge-based interface to manufacturing computer systems. 02966
Concept demonstration of the use of interactive fault diagnosis and isolation for TF30 engines. 02968
Applications of qualitative modeling to knowledge-based risk assessment studies. 02970
Artificial intelligence techniques applied to maintenance management. 02971

An object-oriented expert system for coal-fired MHD power plant fault monitoring and diagnosis. 02973
Jet engine technical advisor (JETA). 02974
An interactive tolerance system. 02975
Plant scheduling expert system for batch processing. 02977
Planning as feedback to designers. 02978
Embedded training in AI technology through an expert system interface: an alarm processor application. 02991
Developing intelligent simulation language to support telerobotic workstation activities. 02995
Automation—implications for knowledge retention as a function of operator control responsibility. 03207
Can cognitive complexity theory (CCT) produce an adequate measure of system usability?. 03229
The application of cognitive psychology to CAD. 03239
Ergonomics of Hybrid Automated Systems I. § 03362
Issues in modeling supervisory control in flexible manufacturing systems. 03363
Human supervisory control in discrete manufacturing: Translating the paradigm. 03364
The effects of the supervisor's knowledge in a complex automated system. 03366
Sources of Difficulty in troubleshooting automated manufacturing systems. 03367
Sociotechnical design of advanced manufacturing systems. 03370
Stress, coping, and worker well-being in computer-aided manufacturing: A field investigation of a CNC machine shop. 03373
The impact of advanced manufacturing in work organization: The Portugese case of the plastic moulding industry. 03374
Models for design of computer integrated manufacturing systems. 03378
Designing hybrid automated manufacturing systems: A European perspective. 03382
The man-machine integration. 03384
Further division of reintegration of mental labour? CAD/CAP and work in design and work preparation shops. 03385
Human factor issues in teleoperated systems. 03387
A conceptual dependency network approach to multitask assignments in man-machine (teleoperated) systems. 03388
A study on an error recovery expert system using a superimposer and a digitizer in the advanced teleoperator system. 03389
Illumination requirements for operating a space remote manipulator. 03392
Ergonomics of hybrid intelligence. 03393
Interactive aspects of knowledge representations. 03395
Human-computer-software interaction (HCSI) strategy in the design of global intelligent computer integrated management (ICIM) systems. 03396

Humane: A designer's assistant for modeling and evaluating function allocation options. 03397
Human nature and robot nature. 03401
Robot vs. human operator for speed, precision and other aspects. 03403
Ten fatal accidents due to robots in Japan. 03406
Some recent documentation of robotic safety from Sweden. 03407
Methods for field evaluation of safety in a robotics workplace. 03408
Unexpected motion hazard exposures on a large robotic assembly. 03409
Human perception of the work envelope of an industrial robot. 03410
Development of a human engineering design standard for robot teach pendants. 03411
A study on the safety operation of robots using monitor hold. 03412
Man-machine interfaces for mobile robotic systems. 03413
Standards requirements for mobile robotic systems. 03415
Critical issues in the safety of software-dominant automated systems. 03416
Overview of research issues in robot safety. 03417
Safety considerations in robot design. 03418
A study on safety evaluation index and industrial accident analysis from the viewpoint of the safety confirmation type. 03419
A study of fail-safe technology. 03421
A study of intrinsic safety asymmetrical actuator. 03422
A study of auditory warning alarms evaluation for automated guided vehicles. 03424
Pneumatic manipulating system provided with active compliance function. 03426
The evaluation of selected ergonomical factors by production automation growth. 03429
An evaluation of production systems from the ergonomic viewpoint: a plea for an integral approach to design. 03430
Process control and people at General Motors' Delta engine plant. 03431
Gribs—an approach to a realistic realtime simulation of human arm motion. 03432
Implementation plan for the use of on-line fiber analysis in the textile industry. 03433
Development of a continuous finishing line to improve working conditions. 03434
Effects of automation on occupational safety & health. 03435
Effects of automation on occupational safety & health. 03435
Health and productivity issues of CAD/CAM systems. 03436
The impact of automation on musculoskeletal disorders. 03437
Occupational accidents to the hand: A comparison of factory and nonfactory injuries. 03438

CATEGORY INDEX [I. COMPUTING METHODOLOGIES]

Accident analysis of blind production workers. 03439
Acting-out and burn-out behaviours of operators monitoring automated systems. 03440
Optimum stresses and strains represented by examples from shop practice. 03441
The social cybernetics of human interaction with automated systems. 03442
Union acceptance of automation technology: A case study. 03444
Human aspects of automated assembly lines. 03445
Human factors in automating manufacturing systems in India. 03446
The economic evaluation on implementation industrial robot from user point of view. 03447
"Automation, robotization in particular, is always economically desirable"—fact or fiction?. 03448
Ergonomic evaluation of safety devices in robotic systems. 03449
MEISTER: a model enhanced intelligent and skillful teleoperational robot system. 03562
Issues in the design of off-line programming systems. 03564
Concept for a model databased remote maintenance system. 03565
Evolution of a robotic excavator. 03569
Personality traits of the worker within the :20man-machine" system at automated production. 03593
Visualization of process information in improving work orientation. 03619
A methodology for dynamic task allocation in man-machine system. 03635
Advanced computing concepts and techniques in control engineering. § 03833
Qualitative modeling of physical systems for knowledge based control. 03834
Knowledge and control for a mechanical design expert system. HCI-0320 †
Applications of AI in engineering. HCI-0321 †

**JOBBES** see Proper Noun Index

*Law*

What AI practitioners should know about the law, part 2. 01197
Artificial Intelligence and Law. § 02764
Expert systems in law: out of the research laboratory and into the marketplace. 02765
Expert systems in law: The datalex project. 02766
Explanation for an expert system that performs estate planning. 02767
A process specification of expert lawyer reasoning. 02768
A case-based system for trade secrets law. 02769
Ashley,K. D.-But, see, accord: generating blue book citations in HYPO. 02770
The application of expert systems technology to case-based law. 02771

A connectionist approach to conceptual information retrieval. 02772
An expert system for screening employee pension plans for the Internal Revenue Service. 02773
Legal reasoning in 3-D. 02774
Knowledge representation in "Default": An attempt to classify general types of knowledge used by legal experts. 02775
Precedent-based legal reasoning and knowledge acquisition in contract law: A process model. 02776
Reasoning about 'hard' cases in Talmudic law. 02777
Human interfaces in a legal expert system. 03164
KRIP: a knowledge representation system for laws relating to industrial property. 03918
An artificial intelligence approach to legal reasoning. ● HCI-0061 †

*Medicine and science*

Application of structural pattern recognition in histopathology. 0295
The information lens: an intelligent system for information sharing in organizations. 0891
Natural language interface to the question-answering system for physicians. 01478
Adapting expert systems to simulation training of process operators. 02056
"Structure—reaction type" paradigm in the conventional methods of describing organic reactions and the concept of imaginary transitions structures overcoming this paradigm. 02268
The development of an intelligent user interface for NASA's scientific databases. 02673
The mission operators planning assistant. 02674
The HORSES project and its perspectives in knowledge engineering. 02716
How DENDRAL was conceived and born. 02839
The LINC was early and small. 02843
The history of the use of computers in the interpretation of radiological images. 02845
The perception of system and the reduction of uncertainty. 02850
The background of INTERNIST I and QMR. 02853
EPVM: An expert patient-ventilator manager for chemical warfare casualties. 02956
Design of an AI-Based self-sustaining habitats control system. 02959
Hierarchical scheduling in an intelligent environmental control system. 02976
Delphi: an intelligent interface for a dolphin communication laboratory. 02989
Gripe: a graphical interface to a knowledge based system which reasons about protein topology. 03234
A dietary recommendation expert system using OPS5. 03498
Structuring knowledge in a graph. 03899

Knowledge and expertise in expert systems. 03905
Medicine in the age of the computer. ● HCI-0075 †
A note on the nature of creativity in engineering: implications for supporting system design. HCI-0220 †
A natural language information retrieval system with extentions towards fuzzy reasoning. HCI-0281 †
Evaluating RECONSIDER: a computer program for diagnostic prompting. HCI-0410 †

**MYCIN** *see* Proper Noun Index

### Natural language interfaces

Natural-language interfaces. 0069
Knowledge representation and natural language: extending the expressive power of proposition nodes. 0096
A propositional language for text representation. 0097
Text, context, and hypertext: writing with and for the computer. ● 0098
Hypertext: a way of incorporating user feedback into online documentation. 0102
Using "word-knowledge" reasoning for question answering. 0131
Natural languages. 0136
Knowledge representation. 0137
Later years at IPTO. 0139
Considerations for the development of natural-language interfaces to database management systems. 0161
Studies in the evaluation of a domain-independent natural language query system. 0162
An interactive customization program for a natural language database query system. 0163
The semantics-based natural language interface to relational databases. 0164
Talking it over: the natural language dialog system HAM-ANS. 0165
An expert interface for effective man-machine interaction. 0166
Q & A simplified. ● 0167
Natural language processing: a survey. 0181
Computational linguistics. ● 0215
VP$^2$: the role of user modelling in correcting errors in second language le rning. 0222
Principles from the psychology of memory: Part II-Episodic and semantic memory. 0331
Design guidelines. 0334
Assessment of trends in the technology and techniques of human-computer interaction. 0335
Future directions. 0336
Computer interface engineering with model-based analysis. ● 0337
Intelligence and the man-machine interface. 0363
A language/action perspective on the design of cooperative work (Reprint). 0383
Developing a natural language interface to complex data. 0393

Transportability and generality in a natural-language interface system. 0394
GUS, a frame driven dialog system. 0395
Human factors and artificial intelligence. 0408
Interface design and evaluation—Semiotic implications. 0409
Rule-based detection of speech features for automatic speech recognition. 0419
Expert systems: the user interface. ● 0425
Using a knowledge base to drive an expert system interface with a natural language component. 0430
Application of the butterfly parallel processor in artificial intelligence. 0489
Lessons from computer-based learning. 0503
An example-base environment for beginning programmers. 0520
Information control problems in manufacturing. ● 0554
A natural language interface for computer-aided design. ● 0664
Natural-language interfaces. 0693
Looking at worksheet modeling through expert system eyes. 0696
Natural-language interfaces. 0720
Speech & language based interaction with machines. ● 0723
Working with Lotus HAL: a 1-2-3 user's guide. ● 0731
A knowledge-based intermediary system for information retrieval. 0737
Intelligent interfaces to Nordic data bases. 0738
A grammar kit in PROLOG. 0745
Beginners need powerful systems. 0747
Conversational resources for situated action. 0861
Rapid prototyping and system development: examination of an interface toolkit for voice and telephony applications. 0918
Dialogue management reference model. 0945
Writing to be searched: A workshop on document creation principles. 01073
Rule base management using meta knowledge. 01081
A natural language interface to a multiple databased office information system. 01094
Understanding natural languages. 01172
Mathematical building blocks. 01173
Designing a practical interface. 01174
How to choose natural language software. 01183
YANLI: a powerful natural language front-end tool. 01194
Choice of words in the generation process of a natural language interface. 01206
DATENBANK-DIALOG: a German language interface for relational databases. 01208
Information retrieval using micros. 01225
Integrated processing produces robust understanding. 01342
Summarizing natural language database responses. 01343

# CATEGORY INDEX [I. COMPUTING METHODOLOGIES]

Reference identification and reference identification failures. 01345
Tense, qualifiers, and contexts. 01346
Temporal ontology and temporal reference. 01347
Modeling the user in natural language systems. 01348
Modeling the user's plans and goals. 01349
Recognizing and responding to plan-oriented misconceptions. 01350
Reasoning on a highlighted user model to respond to misconceptions. 01351
Tailoring object descriptions to a user's level of expertise. 01352
The relationship between user models and discourse models. 01353
Natural language querying of historical data bases. 01354
The Berkeley UNIX consultant project. 01355
Natural language interface to the question-answering system for physicians. 01478
An alternative approach to the conceptual database design using fragments of nat. 01481
Processor for man-machine natural-language-like communication. 01484
Evaluating user utterances in natural language interfaces to databases. 01486
The direct memory access paradigm and its applications to natural language processing. 01489
A similarity-based reasoning model for intelligent interfaces. 01503
An industrial chemical hazards database with a natural language interface: an application of artificial intelligence. 01533
Artificial intelligence and natural language systems. 01541
Left-associative grammar: an informal outline. 01558
ORGPLAN an information-decisive aid system to resolving organizing problems. 01573
A natural language discourse model to explain linear programming models and solutions. 01671
Developing and running expert systems with PESYS. 01690
Alternative option selection methods in menu-driven computer programs. 01755
A theory for the representation of knowledge. 01811
Implementing a semantic interpreter using conceptual graphs. 01812
Providing quality responses with natural language interfaces: the null value problem. 01848
BCS human—computer interaction conference. 01922
Ill-formedness and miscommunication in person-machine dialogue. 01957
A common interface for accessing document retrieval systems and dbms for retrieval of bibliographic data. 01990
Querying the French *Yellow Pages*: natural language access to the directory. 02007
Prospects for knowledge-based customization of natural languages query systems. 02008
The automated solution of logic puzzles. 02015
Temporal semantics and natural language processing in a decision support system. 02038
Cooperative behaviour in the FIDO system. 02041
Shaping user input: a strategy for natural language dialogue design. 02067
Linguistic knowledge as expertise. 02077
The influence of rule-generated stress on computer-synthesized speech. 02081
Representing and using metacommunication to control speakers' relationships in natural-language dialogue. 02136
Talking to computers: an empirical investigation. 02186
Interactive communication of sentential structure and content: an alternative approach to man-machine communication. 02220
An interface architecture to provide adaptive task-specific context for the user. 02228
The utility of speech input in user-computer interfaces. 02230
Modelling blind users' interactions with an auditory computer interface. 02237
XTRA: a natural-language access system to expert systems. 02244
An attempt to incorporate expertise about users into an intelligent interface for Unix. 02248
Coping with human errors through system design: implications for ecological interface design. 02254
The flexibility of case grammar representations: a porting procedure for naturallanguage interfaces. 02255
"Structure—reaction type" paradigm in the conventional methods of describing organic reactions and the concept of imaginary transitions structures overcoming this paradigm. 02268
A natural language interface processor based on the hierarchical-tree structure model of relation tables. 02315
An approach to natural-language semantics in logic programming. 02342
A database primer on natural language. 02413
Natural language interface based on keyword extraction using AWK. 02498
STATUS with IQ—escaping from the Boolean straitjacket. 02569
Natural language processing and the language-impaired 02570
An expert manufacturing simulation system. 02584
Natural language and computers: a general survey of written text interpretation methods. 02671
NLI-ESD: An expert natural language interface to a statistical data bank. 02712
Order and disorder in knowledge structures. 02722
PHRAN-SPAN: a natural language interface for system specifications. 02829
An improved automatic lipreading system to enhance speech recognition. 02859

## [I. COMPUTING METHODOLOGIES]

How to interface to advisory systems? Users request help with a very simple language. 02888
A blackboard architecture for problem solving and machine learning in an expert system for power system voltage control. 02926
Automatic acquisition of domain and procedural knowledge. 02943
Understanding text with an accompanying diagram. 02947
A computer training tool using Chinese natural language. 02948
Interacting with expert systems. 02949
SIMTALK: Pros and cons of natural language for manufacturing simulation. 02950
Providing natural language assistance in locating objects: a general model for information selection and generation. 02951
Design of an AI-Based self-sustaining habitats control system. 02959
PC Version of a knowledge-based expert system with voice interface. 02964
Logic programmable natural language processor of a knowledge-base management system. 02965
Artificial intelligence techniques applied to maintenance management. 02971
Object oriented rapid prototyping with G2. 02984
A knowledge representation for natural language understanding. 02987
A dialog based interface to a design knowledge base that understands user design-intentions. 02988
Delphi: an intelligent interface for a dolphin communication laboratory. 02989
A prototype autonomous agent for crew and equipment retrieval in space. 02994
A knowledge-based approach to online document retrieval system design. 03027
Employing voice back channels of facilitate audio document retrieval. 03045
Shifting to a higher gear in a natural language system. 03169
A temporal logic for reasoning about changing data bases in the context of natural language question-answering. 03176
The IRUS transportable natural language database interface. 03177
Anticipating false implicatures: cooperative responses in question-answer systems. 03178
Supporting natural language database update by modeling real world actions. 03179
Human factors and the problems of evaluation in the design of speech systems interfaces. 03192
Expert systems—interface insight. 03210
People and computers IV. § 03215
Flexible intelligent interactive-video. 03238
Identifying the knowledge requirements of an expert system's natural language processing interface. 03259

The use of complexity theory in evaluating interfaces. 03270
Empirical evaluation of map interfaces. 03276
Evaluating the meaningfulness of icon sets to represent command operations. 03277
Animating human figures: perspectives and directions. 03291
Interactive error recovery expert system for robot with voice recognition subsystem. 03420
Conceptual information extraction form financial news. 03489
A processing system for program specifications in a natural language. 03537
A natural language interface for expert systems: system architecture. 03551
On one aspect of natural-language based knowledge acquisition. 03571
A rule-based system for fuzzy natural language robot control. 03574
A functional model of questions for natural language processing systems. 03575
The semantic language episode understanding. 03576
MACINTER—aim and goal. 03590
An approach to metacommunication in human-computer interaction. 03592
Machine adaption to psychological differences among users in instructive information exchanges with computers. 03609
On complexity of command-entry in man-computer dialogues. 03610
Intuitive representations and interaction languages: an exploratory experiment. 03611
User requirements in natural language communication with database systems. 03615
Some aspects of communication in the natural language and user's involvement in software development. 03670
A travel consultation system: towards a smooth conversation in Japanese. 03917
KRIP: a knowledge representation system for laws relating to industrial property. 03918
Analogical program synthesis from program components. 03920
Computational linguistics: issues and solutions. 03948
Issues in the design of human-computer interfaces. 03979
Phonetic segmentation using psychoacoustic speech parameters. 03991
Intelligent interfaces for information retrieval systems: architecture problems in the construction of expert systems for document retrieval. 04042
Towards a natural language interface for computer aided design. 04049
Error detection and correction in a speech recognition system: a knowledge based system approach. 04054
A computer assisted learning system for reliability engineering. 04060

CATEGORY INDEX [I. COMPUTING METHODOLOGIES]

Automatic contour definition on left ventriculograms by image evidence and a multiple template-based model. 04073
Knowledge-based systems: implications for human-computer interfaces. ● HCI-0060 †
Readings in natural language processing. ● HCI-0067 †
The architecture of fifth generation inference computers. HCI-0093 †
General multiple-objective decision functions and linguistically quantified statements. HCI-0110 †
The future of "writing" for the computer industry. HCI-0150 †
Man-machine interface issues in the construction and use of an expert system. HCI-0212 †
HERCULES: database query using natural language fragments. HCI-0253 †
Natural language query processing in a temporal database. HCI-0257 †
Development of a term association interface for browsing bibliographic data bases based on end users' word associations. HCI-0266 †
Computing text constituency: an algorithmic approach to the generation of text graphs. HCI-0267 †
Architecture problems in the construction of expert systems for document retrieval. HCI-0272 †
ASK is transportable in half a dozen ways. HCI-0279 †
A natural language information retrieval system with extentions towards fuzzy reasoning. HCI-0281 †
On the application of rule-based techniques to the design of advice giving systems. HCI-0315 †
Reasoning in natural language for designing a data base. HCI-0322 †
Knowledge based systems versus thesaurus : an architecture problem about expert systems design. HCI-0323 †
Natural-language interface for an instructable robot. HCI-0324 †
UMFE: a user modelling front-end subsystem. HCI-0325 †
What do users ask? Some thoughts on diagnostic advice. HCI-0326 †
KRITON: a knowledge-acquisition tool for expert systems. HCI-0327 †
An expert system for mapping acoustic cues into phonetic features. HCI-0328 †
An expert system for conceptual schema design: a machine learning approach. HCI-0335 †
Portability of syntax and semantics in DATALOG. HCI-0340 †
Language generation by computer. HCI-0342 †
Knowledge-intensive natural language generation. HCI-0343 †
Extended person-machine interface. HCI-0344 †
Pygmalion at the interface. HCI-0349 †
TEAM: an experiment in the design of transportable natural-language interfaces. HCI-0351 †

**NEOMYCIN** *see* Proper Noun Index

*Office automation*

Integrated software-design: a work-oriented approach to the humanization of computerized clerical tasks. 0243
Methodological problems of field-research on workplaces in offices. 0249
Principles from the psychology of skill acquisition. 0332
Design guidelines. 0334
Assessment of trends in the technology and techniques of human-computer interaction. 0335
Future directions. 0336
Office information systems and computer science (Reprint). 0373
Evolution of an organizational interface: the new business department at a large insurance firm (Reprint). 0382
Managers, micros and mainframes: an introduction. 0456
Designing advanced workstations. 0457
Managing the diffusion of end-user computing technologies: a fifties mindset with eighties tools. 0459
Company experiences with end-user computing. 0460
User interfaces for office systems. 0756
Educating the CBIS user: a case analysis. 0778
Assessment of an effort to integrate computer functions in an engineering design firm. 0779
Notecards in a nutshell. 0810
Cognition-sensitive design and user modeling for syntax-directed editors. 0828
How faithfully should the electronic office simulate real one?. 0958
Efficiency vs. effectiveness. 01092
Some design guidelines for an information center to support office information systems. 01093
A natural language interface to a multiple databased office information system. 01094
Knowledge-based tools to promote shared goals and terminology between interface designers. 01160
Intelligent information-sharing systems. 01322
OA: bridging the language gap. 01376
Office automation—can it be justified?. 01383
The silent force of the screen. A research note on the impact of microelectronics on work autonomy among clerical workers in public administration. 01437
Successful implementation of an office system. 01438
Supporting end users in the office. 01444
The real cost of OA. 01647
Power and credibility in office automation. 01657
Changes in electromyographic activity associated with occupational stress and poor performance in the workplace. 01734
Measuring implementation outcome: beyond success and failure. 01933
An entity-relationship framework for information resource management. 01943

## [I. COMPUTING METHODOLOGIES]

Integrated communications and work efficiency: impacts on organizational structure and power. 02031
Education and training in office technology. 02330
Components of user work stations. 02427
Multimodal response planning: an adaptive rule based approach. 02894
Lets "Deep-Six" our reference manuals. 02955
An operations advisor for an on-line computer banking system with graphics interface. 02983
Office Information Systems. § 03036
Design issues of an intelligent workstation for the office. 03165
The star user interface: an overview. 03171
Advanced office systems: An empirical look at use and satisfaction. 03172
Formal methods and the design of effective user interfaces. 03246
Understanding the nature of the office for the design of third wave office systems. 03248
Toward the successful design and implementation of computer based management information systems in small companies. 03256
Usability engineering in office product development. 03258
The role of memory in intelligent information systems. 03462
Automated document distribution using AI based workstations and knowledge based servers. 03466
Networks in office automation. § 03637
Work with display units 86. § 03676
VDU-work and dyslexia. a case report. 03699
Influence of age on performance and health of VDU workers. 03702
Short- and long-term effects of extreme physical inactivity. A review. 03703
On the significance of physical activity on sedentary work. 03704
Inactivity, night work, and fatigue. 03705
The back during prolonged sitting. 03706
Subject reports about musculoskeletal discomfort in VDU work as a complex phenomenon. 03708
VDUs and musculo-skeletal problems at the Australian National University. A case study. 03709
Generation of muscle tension related to a demand of continuing attention. 03710
Task and the adjustment of ergonomic chairs. 03711
Equipment and workstation design for banking services. 03712
The effect of VDU on the interior design of offices. 03714
Lighting for visual display unit workplaces. 03715
Lighting the electronic office. 03717
Work at video display terminals among office employees: visual ergonomics and lighting. 03718
Recent results on the illumination of VDU and CAD workstations. 03719

Non-visual effects of visual surroundings. 03720
Improving the VDU workplace by introducing a physiologically optimized bright-background screen with dark characters: advantages and requirements. 03721
Display image characteristics and visual response. 03722
Sensitivity to light and visual strain in VDT operators: basic data for the design of work stations. 03732
Are there subtle changes in vision after use of VDTs?. 03733
Visual impairment and subjective ocular symptomatology in VDT operators. 03734
Effects on visual accommodation and subjective visual discomfort from VDT work intensified through split screen technique. 03735
Work distance and optical correction. 03736
Is the resting state of our eyes a favorable viewing distance for VDU-work?. 03737
Vision monitoring of VDU operators and relaxation of visual stress by means of a laser speckle system. 03738
VDU work, refractive errors and binocular vision. 03739
Refraction in VDU operators—a comparison with other professions. 03740
How identify organizational factors crucial of VDU-health? A context-oriented method approach. 03741
Psychosocial work environment and use of visual display terminals—from theoretical model to action. 03742
On the user's opinion about systems design. 03743
Identification and prevention of work-related mental and psycho-somatic disorders among two categories of VDU users. 03744
Comparison of well-being among non-machine interactive clerical workers and full-time and part-time VDT users and typists. 03745
Office automation and work organization: making use of the scope of choice. 03746
the role of user prototyping in the system design process. 03747
Use of an entire workforce as computer. 03748
Office automation as an opportunity for an organizational check-up. 03749
Analyzing and improving VDU working conditions: workers' education. 03751
Workers education and user participation in the development of protective policies for VDT operators. 03752
Trends in U.S. user policies for VDT work. 03753
Characterization of VDT work. 03754
VDT technology: psychosocial and stress concerns. 03755
A model for evaluating stress effects of work with display units. 03756
Growth and challenge VS wear and tear of humans in computer mediated work. 03757
Work content, stress and health in computer-mediated work: a seven year follow-up study. 03758
Focusing variability during visual work. 03759
Mental fatigue of VDU operators induced by monotonous and various tasks. 03760

Data entry task on VDU: underload or overload. 03761
Videocoding - a highly monotonous VDU work in a new technique for mail sorting. 03762
An evaluation of mood disturbances and somatic discomfort under slow computer-response time and incentive-pay conditions. 03765
The applicability of eye movement analysis in the ergonomic evaluation of human-computer interaction. 03766
Eye-head coordination and information uptake during text processing. 03767
Effect of visual presentation of different dialogue structures on human-computer interaction. 03768
Touch screen, cursor keys and mouse interaction. 03769
Naming errors and automatic error correction in human-computer interaction. 03770
Nets in office automation. 03975
Experimentation with an adaptive search strategy for solving a keyboard design/configuration problem. 04070
Executive support systems: the emergence of top management computer use. ● HCI-0049 †
Semistructured messages are surprisingly useful for computer-supported coordination. HCI-0290 †

**PROUST** *see* Proper Noun Index

**UMFE** *see* Proper Noun Index

### I.2.2 Automatic Programming (D.1.2, F.3.1)

CAD Based Programming for Sensory Robots. ● 0597
An experiment in knowledge-based automatic programming. 0613
Toward interactive design of correct programs. 0614
Automatic menu generation. 0774
Applying a theory of graphical presentation to the graphic design of user interfaces. 03122
Using distributed simulation for distributed application development. 03500

*Automatic analysis of algorithms*

The programmer's apprentices: a research overview. 01368
A blackboard architecture for problem solving and machine learning in an expert system for power system voltage control. 02926

*Program modification*

An interface architecture to provide adaptive task-specific context for the user. 02228

*Program synthesis*

Creating highly-interactive and graphical user interfaces by demonstration. 0084

Computer aided application program synthesis for industrial robots. 0606
Creating highly-interactive and graphical user interfaces by demonstration. 01054
The programmer's apprentices: a research overview. 01368
Analogical program synthesis from program components. 03920
Expertise transfer for expert system design. ● HCI-0059 †
Editing by example. HCI-0398 †

*Program transformation*

The migration of expert systems into the production environment. 0740
A semantic editor. 01101
Transformational derivation of programs using the focus system. 01140
Dynamics and architecture for neural computation. 02270
ATLANTIS—a software simulator for behavior analysis of protocol specifications and their target implementations. 02667
Qualitative modeling of physical systems for knowledge based control. 03834

*Program verification*

Issues in the verification of knowledge in rule-based systems. 02226
Users' preferences among different techniques for displaying the evaluation of LISP functions in an interactive debugger. 02863

### I.2.3 Deduction and Theorem Proving

The computer and the mind: an introduction to cognitive science. ● 0463
Mental models in cognitive science. 0647
Building expert systems: cognitive emulation. ● 0700
Knowledge engineering: expert systems and information retrieval. ● 0735
New horizons in educational computing. ● 0741
Modeling the user in natural language systems. 01348
Cognitive systems engineering: new wine in new bottles. 02078
Combining functions for certainty degrees in consulting systems. 02092
The use of modal default reasoning in information systems. 02095
Simplifying decision trees. 02157
Refining problem-solving knowledge in repertory grids using a consultation mechanism. 02205
Cognitive issues in the process of software development: review and reappraisal. 02222
Issues in the verification of knowledge in rule-based systems. 02226

[I. COMPUTING METHODOLOGIES]

Rough sets and dependency analysis among attributes in computer implementations of expert's inference models. 02231
Notions and dynamics of information. 02319
A deductive database based on Aristotelian logic. 02398
Industrial & Engineering Applications of Artificial Intelligence & Expert Systems: vol. I. § 02967
A temporal logic for reasoning about changing data bases in the context of natural language question-answering. 03176
GPS and the psychology of th Rubik cubist: a study in reasoning about actions. 03311
The lexicon, grammatical categories and temporal reasoning. 03549
Knowing that and knowing what. 03554
Uncertainty and intelligent systems. § 04030
Induction: processes of inference, learning, and discovery. • HCI-0064 †
Decision and intelligence. • HCI-0068 †
Approaches to human reasoning: an analytic framework. HCI-0239 †
Implementing imprecision in information systems. HCI-0259 †
Decision trees: a contribution to automatic interpretation of GUHA results. HCI-0329 †
An overview of research and co-operation in advanced information technology. HCI-0442 †

*Answer/reason extraction*

Recognizing and responding to plan-oriented misconceptions. 01350
Reasoning on a highlighted user model to respond to misconceptions. 01351
Tailoring object descriptions to a user's level of expertise. 01352
Natural language interface to the question-answering system for physicians. 01478
User requirements for expert system explanation: what, why and when?. 03242
Structuring knowledge in a graph. 03899
Keywords instead of hierarchical menus. 03912
Natural language communication with computers: some problems, perspectives, and new directions. 03913
On the application of rule-based techniques to the design of advice giving systems. HCI-0315 †
UMFE: a user modelling front-end subsystem. HCI-0325 †
Extended person-machine interface. HCI-0344 †

*Deduction (e.g., natural, rule-based)*

Space. 0134
Finance. 0135
Connectionism and cognitive architecture: a critical analysis. 0589
Relevance: communication and cognition. • 0704

ICE: information center expert: a consultation system for resource allocation. 0781
Reasoning about action II: the qualification problem. 01213
On the relation between default and autoepistemic logic. 01214
Developing and running expert systems with PESYS. 01690
A theory for the representation of knowledge. 01811
Significance testing of rules in rule-based models of human problem solving. 01867
A user preference guided approach to conflict resolution in rule-based expert systems. 01872
A rule-based model for the human operator in a time-constrained competing-task environment. 01877
Modeling rule-based systems by stochastic programmed production systems. 02017
Reasoning with imprecise knowledge in expert systems. 02018
Design goals for sloppy modeling systems. 02206
DYNABOARD: user animated display of deductive proofs in mathematics. 02221
Absolute dates and relative dates in an inferential system on temporal dependencies between events. 02235
Artificial Intelligence and Law. § 02764
Expert systems in law: The datalex project. 02766
A process specification of expert lawyer reasoning. 02768
Ashley,K. D.-But, see, accord: generating blue book citations in HYPO. 02770
The application of expert systems technology to case-based law. 02771
An expert system for screening employee pension plans for the Internal Revenue Service. 02773
Precedent-based legal reasoning and knowledge acquisition in contract law: A process model. 02776
Expert diagnostic system. 02912
The ISA expert system: a prototype system for failure diagnosis on the space station. 02913
A blackboard architecture for problem solving and machine learning in an expert system for power system voltage control. 02926
Use of metaknowledge in the verification of knowledge-based systems. 02945
Use of metaknowledge in the verification of knowledge-based systems. 02945
Multi-Input fuzzy inference engine on a systolic array. 02953
The actem model for decision modelling in a scene management system. 02954
Some considerations on intelligent tutoring systems. 02963
On one aspect of natural-language based knowledge acquisition. 03571
The semantic language episode understanding. 03576
Design tools for large relational database systems. 03946

Mental models: towards a cognitive science of language, inference, and consciousness. ● HCI-0063 †
Towards a new research paradigm in information retrieval. HCI-0273 †
Instructionless learning about a complex device: the paradigm and observations. HCI-0333 †
A fuzzy rule-based model of human problem solving. HCI-0359 †

### Logic programming

A grammar kit in PROLOG. 0745
A spreadsheet interface for logic programming. 0822
A model and an implementation of a logic programming environment. 01107
Negative knowledge towards a strategy for asking in logic programming. 02115
Concept learning from examples and counter examples. 02229
Are there individual concepts? Proper names and individual concepts in SI-Nets. 02233
An approach to natural-language semantics in logic programming. 02342
Spreadsheets with incremental queries as a user interface for logic programming. 02515
Logic programmable natural language processor of a knowledge-base management system. 02965
Logic programming '85. § 03916
Logic programming '87. § 03919
Third international conference on logic programming. § 04028

### Mathematical induction

Flexible user interface decision support systems. 03473
Automatizing geometric proofs and constructions. 03851

### Metatheory

On the relation between default and autoepistemic logic. 01214
Artificial intelligence and cognitive psychology: a new look at human factors. 03904
Knowledge and expertise in expert systems. 03905

### Nonmonotonic reasoning and belief revision

Expert systems and creativity. 0553
On the relation between default and autoepistemic logic. 01214
Recognizing and responding to plan-oriented misconceptions. 01350
Reasoning on a highlighted user model to respond to misconceptions. 01351
The relationship between user models and discourse models. 01353
Study of combination of belief intevals in lattice-structured networks. 02223
Model minimization—an alternative to circumscription. 02263
The subjective ascription of belief to agents. 03553
What awareness isn't: a sentential view of implicit and explicit belief. 03560
On-line interpretation in speech understanding and dialogue systems. 04000
Mental models: towards a cognitive science of language, inference, and consciousness. ● HCI-0063 †

**Prolog** *see* Proper Noun Index

### Resolution

The programmer's apprentices: a research overview. 01368

### Uncertainty, "fuzzy," and probabilistic reasoning

Fuzzy sets and decision analysis. 0651
A fuzzy rule-based model of human problem solving. 0656
Fuzzy reasoning in pseudo-physical logics. 01695
Human specifics fuzzy categories and counteraction in decision making problems. 01696
The fuzzy paradigm for knowledge representation in cerebral dynamics. 01699
The fuzzy logic of text understanding. 01701
Extension of conditional probability and measures of belief and disbelief in a hypothesis based on uncertain evidence. 01846
A representation of human reliability using fuzzy concepts. 02024
Fuzzy control of a mobile robot for obstacle avoidance. 02025
Manual control of an intrinsically unstable system and its modeling by fuzzy logic. 02026
Convexly combined fuzzy relational equations and several aspects of their application to fuzzy information processing. 02027
A design for a fuzzy logic controller. 02028
A fuzzy decision-making method and its application to a company choice problem. 02029
Hidden patterns in combined and adaptive knowledge networks. 02073
On the applicability of maximum entropy to inexact reasoning. 02074
Epistemic necessity, possibility, and truth. Tools for dealing with imprecision and uncertainty in fuzzy knowledge-based systems. 02075
Causality and maximum entropy updating. 02076
Combining stochastic uncertainty and linguistic inexactness: theory and experimental evaluation of four fuzzy probability models. 02218
Patterns of inductive reasoning in a parallel expert system. 02219

[I. COMPUTING METHODOLOGIES]

Legal reasoning in 3-D. 02774
Oblog-2: A hybrid knowledge representation system for defeasible reasoning. 02778
The perception of system and the reduction of uncertainty. 02850
Approximate spatial reasoning. 02917
Multi-Input fuzzy inference engine on a systolic array. 02953
The impact of "Messy" data on group decision making. 03476
Uncertainty in knowledge-based systems. International Conference on Information. § 03822
Modeling uncertainty in human perception. 03825
Qualitative modeling of physical systems for knowledge based control. 03834
On global context dependencies and their properties (extended abstract). 03945
On-line interpretation in speech understanding and dialogue systems. 04000
Uncertainty and intelligent systems. § 04030
A study of Arab computer users: a special case of a general HCI methodology. 04031
Towards a new research paradigm in information retrieval. HCI-0273 †
Cognitive models, cognitive tasks, and information retrieval. HCI-0331 †
Expertise transfer and complex problems: using AQUINAS as a knowledge-acquisition workbench for knowledge-based systems. HCI-0336 †

**I.2.4 Knowledge Representation Formalisms and Methods**

Intelligent CAD systems II: implementational issues. ● 0006
Knowledge representation and natural language: extending the expressive power of proposition nodes. 0096
A propositional language for text representation. 0097
Introduction: a new paradigm for writing with and for the computer. 0099
Hypertext: a way of incorporating user feedback into online documentation. 0102
Talking it over: the natural language dialog system HAM-ANS. 0165
Mental models in human-computer interaction: research issues about what the user of software knows. ● 0214
$VP^2$: the role of user modelling in correcting errors in second language learning. 0222
The practice of the use of computers. A paradoxical encounter between different traditions of knowledge. 0343
Tacit knowledge, working life and scientific method. 0345
The optimal level of abstraction for models of cerebral representation of language processes: the state of the question. 0356

Expert systems: the user interface. ● 0425
DARN: Toward a community memory for diagnosis and repair tasks. 0428
Using a knowledge base to drive an expert system interface with a natural language component. 0430
C/C++ for expert systems: "unleashes the power of a artificial intelligence". ● 0439
Knowledge based problem solving. ● 0490
Trends in information systems. ● 0498
Artificial intelligence and education; vol. 1: learning environments and tutoring systems. ● 0516
Connections and symbols. ● 0588
An overview of system design for human interaction. 0646
Artificial intelligence systems. 0683
A substrate for object-oriented interface design. 0691
Building expert systems: cognitive emulation. ● 0700
Intelligent CAD systems I: theoretical and methodological aspects. ● 0715
Knowledge engineering: expert systems and information retrieval. ● 0735
Are machines as good as people in drawing conclusions from knowledge represented in catalogues, data bases and expert systems?. 0736
Guided tours and tabletops: tools for communicating in a hypertext environment. 01161
The Berkeley UNIX consultant project. 01355
The programmer's apprentices: a research overview. 01368
Cognitive engineering: human problem solving with tools. 01781
Structuring knowledge bases for designers of learning materials. 01807
Reasoning with imprecise knowledge in expert systems. 02018
A design for a fuzzy logic controller. 02028
How to recognize interesting topics to provide cooperative answering. 02043
A knowledge-based system with audio-visual aids. 02068
Combining functions for certainty degrees in consulting systems. 02092
The use of modal default reasoning in information systems. 02095
Generalization and noise. 02155
The structure of command languages: an experiment on task-action grammar. 02224
An approach to natural-language semantics in logic programming. 02342
A planning system for a cognitive problem. 02719
Artificial Intelligence and Law. § 02764
A connectionist approach to conceptual information retrieval. 02772
Knowledge representation in "Default": An attempt to classify general types of knowledge used by legal experts. 02775

CATEGORY INDEX [I. COMPUTING METHODOLOGIES]

Oblog-2: A hybrid knowledge representation system for defeasible reasoning. 02778
Industrial & Engineering Applications of Artificial Intelligence & Expert Systems. § 02910
Industrial & Engineering Applications of Artificial Intelligence & Expert Systems: vol. I. § 02967
Industrial & Engineering Applications of Artificial Intelligence & Expert Systems: vol. II. § 02982
Delphi: an intelligent interface for a dolphin communication laboratory. 02989
Logical foundations for knowledge representation in intelligent systems. 03029
Document manipulation and typography. § 03182
People and computers IV. § 03215
A gesture based text editor. 03232
Database maps. 03286
Decision Support and Knowledge Based Systems Track. § 03461
Knowledge structures for intelligent interaction. 03636
Visualization in programming. 5th Interdisciplinary Workshop in Informatics and. § 03826
Human-computer interaction: psychonomic aspects. § 03887
Introduction: human-computer interaction: psychonomic aspects. 03888
A comparison of presentation and representation: linguistic and pictorial. 03898
Tree doctor, a software package for graphical manipulation and animation of tree structures. 03901
MFDBS 87. § 03943
Recent advances in speech understanding and dialog systems. § 03987
Dynamic spectral adaptation of automatic speech recognizers to new speakers. 03999
Knowledge based systems for speech understanding. 04001
Uncertainty and intelligent systems. § 04030
Plans and situated actions: the problem of human-machine communication. ● HCI-0040 †
An artificial intelligence approach to legal reasoning. ● HCI-0061 †
In search of the person: philosophical explorations in cognitive science. ● HCI-0062 †
Induction: processes of inference, learning, and discovery. ● HCI-0064 †
Logic and programming. ● HCI-0068 †
Artificial intelligence and tutoring systems: computational and cognitive approaches to the communication of knowledge. ● HCI-0080 †
Goal and plan knowledge representations: from stories to text editors and programs. HCI-0183 †
The distributed processing of knowledge and belief in the human brain. HCI-0240 †
Natural language query processing in a temporal database. HCI-0257 †

Semistructured messages are surprisingly useful for computer-supported coordination. HCI-0290 †
A generalized model management system for mathematical programming. HCI-0302 †
Computing with structured connectionist networks. HCI-0314 †
Strategic issues in knowledge engineering. HCI-0317 †
Selecting a humanly understandable knowledge representation for reasoning about knowledge. HCI-0330 †
Cognitive models, cognitive tasks, and information retrieval. HCI-0331 †
Semantic primitives or meaning postulates: mental models or propositional representation?. HCI-0339 †
Knowledge-intensive natural language generation. HCI-0343 †
Selective networks and recognition automata. HCI-0390 †

*Frames and scripts*

Military systems. 0138
Algorithm animation. ● 0186
Various views on spatial prepositions. 01196
Reasoning about action II: the qualification problem. 01213
Intelligent information-sharing systems. 01322
Human language and computers. 01550
Knowledge representation and use in pattern analysis. 02030
Explanation for an expert system that performs estate planning. 02767
SIMS: a uniform environment for planning and performing user's tasks. 02921
Process design of oil and gas production facilities using expert systems. 02933
Automatic acquisition of domain and procedural knowledge. 02943
An intelligent tutoring system for basic set theory. 02993
Task-related knowledge structures: analysis, modelling and application. 03218
Knowledge acquisition via a graphical interface. 03572
The semantic language episode understanding. 03576
Knowledge representation techniques in artificial intelligence: an overview. 03900
Search strategies in internal and external memories. 03911
Keywords instead of hierarchical menus. 03912
Real-time large vocabulary word recognition via diphone spotting and multiprocessor implementation. 03996
Recent results on the application of a metric-space search algorithm (AESA) to multispeaker data. 03997
An experimental environment for generating word hypotheses in continuous speech. 03998
Merging acoustics and linguistics in speech understanding. 04004
Object lens: a "spreadsheet" for cooperative work. HCI-0206 †

[I. COMPUTING METHODOLOGIES]

An intelligent interface for online interaction. HCI-0264 †

Portability of syntax and semantics in DATALOG. HCI-0340 †

**KEE** *see* Proper Noun Index

**PECOS** *see* Proper Noun Index

*Predicate logic*

Studies in the evaluation of a domain-independent natural language query system. 0162

Reasoning about action II: the qualification problem. 01213

On the relation between default and autoepistemic logic. 01214

Epistemic necessity, possibility, and truth. Tools for dealing with imprecision and uncertainty in fuzzy knowledge-based systems. 02075

Causality and maximum entropy updating. 02076

Design goals for sloppy modeling systems. 02206

Toward a theory of computer program bugs: an empirical test. 02216

Qualitative modeling of physical systems for knowledge based control. 03834

Automatizing geometric proofs and constructions. 03851

Knowledge representation techniques in artificial intelligence: an overview. 03900

Data manipulation languages for the universal relation view DURST. 03944

On global context dependencies and their properties (extended abstract). 03945

Design tools for large relational database systems. 03946

On-line interpretation in speech understanding and dialogue systems. 04000

The central nervous system as a low and high level control system. 04007

Object lens: a "spreadsheet" for cooperative work. HCI-0206 †

*Relation systems*

Text processing with the START natural language system. 0100

The relation between linguistic structure and associative theories of language learning models: constructive critique of some connectionist learning models. 0591

The problem of identification. 01088

Evaluating user utterances in natural language interfaces to databases. 01486

Developing and running expert systems with PESYS. 01690

The automated solution of logic puzzles. 02015

Convexly combined fuzzy relational equations and several aspects of their application to fuzzy information processing. 02027

Causality and maximum entropy updating. 02076

Effects of computer programming experience on network representations of abstract programming concepts. 02204

Refining problem-solving knowledge in repertory grids using a consultation mechanism. 02205

Absolute dates and relative dates in an inferential system on temporal dependencies between events. 02235

Knowledge base enhancements to relational databases. 03285

Structuring knowledge in a graph. 03899

On global context dependencies and their properties (extended abstract). 03945

Design tools for large relational database systems. 03946

On-line interpretation in speech understanding and dialogue systems. 04000

Implementing imprecision in information systems. HCI-0259 †

*Representation languages*

A propositional language for text representation. 0097

Communication and management support in system development environments (Reprint). 0374

Connectionism and cognitive architecture: a critical analysis. 0589

Decision support for reasoning about values. 03486

A functional model of questions for natural language processing systems. 03575

Reasoning in natural language for designing a data base. HCI-0322 †

*Representations (procedural and rule-based)*

Multi-media presentation in CAD systems. 0007

Finance. 0135

Knowledge representation. 0137

Military systems. 0138

An expert interface for effective man-machine interaction. 0166

Cooperation without communication. 0169

Deals among rational agents. 0170

Callisto: an intelligent project management system (Reprint). 0375

Human factors and artificial intelligence. 0408

Design and implementation of an object-oriented user interface management system. 0412

Rule-based detection of speech features for automatic speech recognition. 0419

Direct manipulation user interfaces for expert systems. 0429

Universal subgoaling and chunking: the automatic generation and learning of goal hierarchies. ● 0497

An expert system architecture for computer-aided control engineering. 0662

The migration of expert systems into the production environment. 0740

CATEGORY INDEX [I. COMPUTING METHODOLOGIES]

Graphic interfaces for knowledge-based system development. 0892
Rule base management using meta knowledge. 01081
Adaptive interface design: a symmetric model and a knowledge-based implementation. 01091
What we know and what we need to know: the user model versus the user's model in human-computer interaction. 01243
Intelligent information-sharing systems. 01322
Reasoning on a highlighted user model to respond to misconceptions. 01351
The relationship between user models and discourse models. 01353
Automating knowledge acquisition for aerial image interpretation. 01470
A theory for the representation of knowledge. 01811
Automated concept acquisition in noisy environments. 01841
An entity-relationship framework for information resource management. 01943
Modeling rule-based systems by stochastic programmed production systems. 02017
Knowledge representation and use in pattern analysis. 02030
Causality and maximum entropy updating. 02076
Strategies in controlling a continuous process with long response latencies: needs for computer support to diagnosis. 02217
Patterns of inductive reasoning in a parallel expert system. 02219
Study of combination of belief intevals in lattice-structured networks. 02223
The structure of command languages: an experiment on task-action grammar. 02224
Issues in the verification of knowledge in rule-based systems. 02226
Structural aspects of semantic-directed clusters. 02534
Advances in Cognitive Science. § 02720
Advances in Cognitive Science. § 02720
Advances in cognitive science. 02721
Order and disorder in knowledge structures. 02722
Expert systems in law: The datalex project. 02766
Explanation for an expert system that performs estate planning. 02767
Multimodal response planning: an adaptive rule based approach. 02894
Task-oriented parsing - a diagnostic method to be used adaptive systems. 02896
Generic expert system shell for diagnostic reasoning. 02911
Expert diagnostic system. 02912
PISCES: an expert system for coal fired power plant monitoring and diagnostics. 02915
Sherlock—a system for diagnosing power distribution ring network faults. 02916
INQUEST: A prototype intelligence tool. 02918

SIMS: a uniform environment for planning and performing user's tasks. 02921
Symbiotic systems for complex problems. 02922
Experience of constructing a fault localisation expert system using an AI toolkit. 02923
A rule-based system for interactive proposal evaluation. 02927
Process design of oil and gas production facilities using expert systems. 02933
Process control with the G2 real-time expert system. 02934
A mission planning architecture for an autonomous vehicle. 02939
Automatic acquisition of domain and procedural knowledge. 02943
Generic diagnostic knowledge acquisition tool. 02944
The design of a traffic control expert system for long distance network contingencies. 02952
The actem model for decision modelling in a scene management system. 02954
A generic strategy for diagnostic assistance: the technician's assistant. 02957
Using a top-down and bottom-up strategy to analyze high resolution aerial photographs of urban areas. 02960
Using design expertise to develop an expert system. 02962
An object-oriented expert system for coal-fired MHD power plant fault monitoringand diagnosis. 02973
Jet engine technical advisor (JETA). 02974
Hierarchical scheduling in an intelligent environmental control system. 02976
Extending knowledge-based systems through closely-coupled graphics and windows. 02985
An advisory system for digital logic simulation. 02986
A knowledge representation for natural language understanding. 02987
A dialog based interface to a design knowledge base that understands user design-intentions. 02988
Task-related knowledge structures: analysis, modelling and application. 03218
A conceptual dependency network approach to multi-task assignments in man-machine (teleoperated) systems. 03388
A study on an error recovery expert system using a superimposer and a digitizer in the advanced teleoperator system. 03389
On building future decision support systems. 03472
Flexible user interface decision support systems. 03473
Knowledge-based support of cooperative activities. 03478
Knowledge representation for model libraries. 03479
On representation schemes for electronic promising. 03488
Artificial Intelligence and Information-Control systems of Robots-87. § 03570
Knowledge acquisition via a graphical interface. 03572

[I. COMPUTING METHODOLOGIES]

Qualitative modeling of physical systems for knowledge based control. 03834
Automatizing geometric proofs and constructions. 03851
Knowledge representation techniques in artificial intelligence: an overview. 03900
Artificial intelligence and cognitive psychology: a new look at human factors. 03904
Knowledge and expertise in expert systems. 03905
Architectures for production systems: an inside look for those who study human-computer interaction. 03906
Real-time processing of cursive writing and sketched graphics. 03908
Computational linguistics: issues and solutions. 03948
Morphological representation of speech knowledge for automatic speech recognition systems. 03992
On-line interpretation in speech understanding and dialogue systems. 04000
Mental models: towards a cognitive science of language, inference, and consciousness. ● HCI-0063 †
A quantitative theory of human-computer interaction. HCI-0198 †
Analysing the scope of cognitive models in human-computer interaction: a trade-off approach. HCI-0245 †
Applications of AI in engineering. HCI-0321 †
Knowledge elicitation: dissociating conscious reflections from automatic processes. HCI-0337 †
Modularity and lexical access. HCI-0350 †
The automated tutoring of introductory computer programming. HCI-0438 †

*Semantic networks*

Knowledge representation and natural language: extending the expressive power of proposition nodes. 0096
Supporting collaboration in hypermedia: issues and experiences. 0117
A practical natural language interface to databases. 0199
Hypertext: an introduction and survey (Reprint). 0378
KIWI: knowledge-based user-friendly system for the utilization of information bases. 0739
PLEXACT: an architecture & design of a knowledge-based system for information systems development. 01020
Rule base management using meta knowledge. 01081
Evaluating user utterances in natural language interfaces to databases. 01486
Modeling the Cognitive content of displays. 01800
Effects of computer programming experience on network representations of abstract programming concepts. 02204
Refining problem-solving knowledge in repertory grids using a consultation mechanism. 02205
Are there individual concepts? Proper names and individual concepts in SI-Nets. 02233
Structuring knowledge in a graph. 03899

Knowledge representation techniques in artificial intelligence: an overview. 03900
Textvision: elicitation and acquisition of conceptual knowledge by graphic representation and multiwindowing. 03902
Development of mental models of an office system: a field study on an introductory course. 03903
Knowledge and expertise in expert systems. 03905
Design tools for large relational database systems. 03946
An experimental environment for generating word hypotheses in continuous speech. 03998
Knowledge-based search tactics for an intelligent intermediary system. HCI-0277 †
An expert system for conceptual schema design: a machine learning approach. HCI-0335 †
Portability of syntax and semantics in DATALOG. HCI-0340 †

### I.2.5 Programming Languages and Software (D.3.2)

Communication and management support in system development environments (Reprint). 0374
Beyond the chalkboard: computer support for collaboration and problem solving inmeetings (Reprint). 0376
Artificial intelligence programming environments. ● 0420
Expert systems: the user interface. ● 0425
C/C++ for expert systems: "unleashes the power of a artificial intelligence". ● 0439
Connections and symbols. ● 0588
Connectionism and cognitive architecture: a critical analysis. 0589
Artificial intelligence systems. 0683
Knowledge engineering: expert systems and information retrieval. ● 0735
POP-11: an AI programming language. 0748
POP-11 for everyone. 0749
The Mesa programming environment. 01108
Natural artificial languages: low level processes. 02082
Industrial & Engineering Applications of Artificial Intelligence & Expert Systems. § 02910
Industrial & Engineering Applications of Artificial Intelligence & Expert Systems. § 02941
The semantic language episode understanding. 03576
Logic interface system on navigational database systems. 03818
Automatizing geometric proofs and constructions. 03851
Artificial intelligence and cognitive psychology: a new look at human factors. 03904
Third international conference on logic programming. § 04028
KRITON: a knowledge-acquisition tool for expert systems. HCI-0327 †
Expertise transfer and complex problems: using AQUINAS as a knowledge-acquisition workbench for knowledge-based systems. HCI-0336 †

# CATEGORY INDEX

[I. COMPUTING METHODOLOGIES]

**ADIPS** *see* Proper Noun Index

**Aquinas** *see* Proper Noun Index

*Expert system tools and techniques*

Space. 0134
Later years at IPTO. 0139
Computer-based real-time conferencing systems (Reprint). 0377
Hypertext: an introduction and survey (Reprint). 0378
Diamond: a multimedia message system built on a distributed architecture (Reprint). 0380
Pogo: a declarative representation system for graphics. 0476
Expert judgment and expert systems. ● 0552
Artificial intelligence and expert systems. ● 0665
KIWI: knowledge-based user-friendly system for the utilization of information bses. 0739
The migration of expert systems into the production environment. 0740
Hypertext as a means for knowledge acquisition. 0777
Modeling the user in natural language systems. 01348
Modeling the user's plans and goals. 01349
The p rogrammer's apprentices: a research overview. 01368
Cognitive engineering: human problem solving with tools. 01781
How to recognize interesting topics to provide cooperative answering. 02043
Underlying dimensions of human problem solving and learning: implications for personnel selection, training tasks design and expert system. 02225
Issues in the verification of knowledge in rule-based systems. 02226
Conceptual models of interacitve knowledge acquisition tools. 02457
Expert system tool evaluation. 02718
Generic expert system shell for diagnostic reasoning. 02911
Expert diagnostic system. 02912
INQUEST: A prototype intelligence tool. 02918
Experience of constructing a fault localisation expert system using an AI toolkit. 02923
ProCEED: an expert system for multivariate process control systems design. 02935
EPVM: An expert patient-ventilator manager for chemical warfare casualties. 02956
Using design expertise to develop an expert system. 02962
Some considerations on intelligent tutoring systems. 02963
Industrial & Engineering Applications of Artificial Intelligence & Expert Systems: vol. I. § 02967
NetGraph: an object-oriented graphical toolset for risk assessment. 02972

A rule-based system for fuzzy natural language robot control. 03574
Qualitative modeling of physical systems for knowledge based control. 03834
Tree doctor, a software package for graphical manipulation and animation of tree structures. 03901
Textvision: elicitation and acquisition of conceptual knowledge by graphic representation and multiwindowing. 03902
Development of mental models of an office system: a field study on an introductory course. 03903
Architectures for production systems: an inside look for those who study human-computer interaction. 03906
An experimental environment for generating word hypotheses in continuous speech. 03998
The central nervous system as a low and high level control system. 04007
Intelligent interfaces for information retrieval systems: architecture problems in the construction of expert systems for document retrieval. 04042
Architecture problems in the construction of expert systems for document retrieval. HCI-0272 †
Towards a new research paradigm in information retrieval. HCI-0273 †
Cognitive models, cognitive tasks, and information retrieval. HCI-0331 †
An expert system for conceptual schema design: a machine learning approach. HCI-0335 †
A performing medium for working group graphics. HCI-0383 †

**LISP** *see* Proper Noun Index

**LOGO** *see* Proper Noun Index

**PRISM** *see* Proper Noun Index

**Prolog** *see* Proper Noun Index

**XCON** *see* Proper Noun Index

### I.2.6  Learning (K.3.2)

Learning in man-computer interaction: a review of the literature. 0151
Computer assisted language learning: program structure and principles. ● 0196
Data, expert knowledge and decisions. ● 0338
Creativity, skill and human-centered systems. 0346
A conceptual framework for the augmentation of man's intellect (Reprint). 0368
Learning, development, and production systems. 0479
Learning through incremental refinement of procedures. 0482
Learning by chunking: a production system model of practice. 0483

[I. COMPUTING METHODOLOGIES]

Truth versus appropriateness: relating declarative to procedural knowledge. 0484
Composition of production. 0485
Self-modifying production system model of cognitive development. 0486
Production systems, learning, and tutoring. 0487
Universal subgoaling and chunking: the automatic generation and learning of goal hierarchies. ● 0497
An example-base environment for beginning programmers. 0520
Expert systems and creativity. 0553
Connections and symbols. ● 0588
Connectionism and cognitive architecture: a critical analysis. 0589
Computation and cognition: toward a foundation for cognitive science. ● 0593
Mental models in cognitive science. 0647
Relevance: communication and cognition. ● 0704
Are machines as good as people in drawing conclusions from knowledge represented in catalogues, data bases and expert systems?. 0736
A grammar kit in PROLOG. 0745
Concurrency in intelligent systems. 01169
Catching knowledge in neural nets. 01171
Neural nets for adaptive filtering and adaptive pattern recognition. 01362
The ART of adaptive pattern recognition by a self-organizing neural network. 01364
The memory channel machine: part of a proposed learning machine. 01602
GISMO: A visual problem-structuring and knowledge-organization tool. 01871
Metaphor, computing systems, and active learning. 02091
Knowledge elicitation using discourse analysis. 02152
Cognitive biases and corrective techniques: proposals for improving elicitation procedures for knowledge-based systems. 02153
Generalization and noise. 02155
KITTEN: knowledge initiation and transfer tools for experts and novices. 02159
Knowledge base refinement by monitoring abstract control knowledge. 02160
A deductive database based on Aristotelian logic. 02398
Inference control mechanism for statistical database frequency-imposed data distortions. 02449
Machine learning using a higher order correlation network. 02563
A comparison of algorithms for neuron-like cells. 02752
Higher-order Boltzmann machines. 02760
Industrial & Engineering Applications of Artificial Intelligence & Expert Systems. § 02941
Industrial & Engineering Applications of Artificial Intelligence & Expert Systems: vol. I. § 02967
Industrial & Engineering Applications of Artificial Intelligence & Expert Systems: vol. II. § 02982

Transfer of learning in inference problems. 03552
Characteristics of a successful DSS user's needs vs. builder's needs. 03789
Development of mental models of an office system: a field study on an introductory course. 03903
Exploring three possibilities in network design: spontaneous node activity, node plasticity and temporal coding. 03962
Recent advances in speech understanding and dialog systems. § 03987
Uncertainty and intelligent systems. § 04030
The learning and planning of actions. 04069
A neural model of human prehension. 04072
Culture, cognitive, and connectionism: Towards an hermeneutic anthropology of mind. 04077
Interaction with the environment. ● HCI-0068 †
Introducing CAL: a practical guide to writing computer-assisted learning programs. ● HCI-0079 †
Artificial intelligence and tutoring systems: computational and cognitive approaches to the communication of knowledge. ● HCI-0080 †
A quantitative theory of human-computer interaction. HCI-0198 †
Approaches to human reasoning: an analytic framework. HCI-0239 †
Computing with structured connectionist networks. HCI-0314 †
UMFE: a user modelling front-end subsystem. HCI-0325 †
Learning in parallel networks: simulating learning in a probabilistic system. HCI-0332 †
Instructionless learning about a complex device: the paradigm and observations. HCI-0333 †
A research center for augmenting human intellect. HCI-0334 †
An expert system for conceptual schema design: a machine learning approach. HCI-0335 †
A framework of a mechanical translation between Japanese and English by analogy principle. HCI-0353 †
Naive algorithm design techniques—a case study. HCI-0360 †
Implications for education and training. HCI-0430 †
The LISP tutor: it approaches the effectiveness of a human tutor. HCI-0431 †

*Analogies*

Introduction: a new paradigm for writing with and for the computer. 0099
The application of metaphor, analogy, and conceptual models in computer systems. 02070
Training by exploration: facilitating the transfer of procedural knowledge through analogical reasoning. 02103
Analogy and other sources of difficulty in novices' very first text-editing. 02148

CATEGORY INDEX                                    [I. COMPUTING METHODOLOGIES]

Control of sensory processing - a hypothesis on and simulation of the architecture of an elementary cortical processor. 03972
Analogical problem solving. ● HCI-0044 †

**Concept learning**

A general theory of discrimination learning. 0481
Effects of computer programming experience on network representations of abstract programming concepts. 02204
Concept learning from examples and counter examples. 02229
Advances in Cognitive Science. § 02720
Order and disorder in knowledge structures. 02722
Interacting with expert systems. 02949
Textvision: elicitation and acquisition of conceptual knowledge by graphic representation and multiwindowing. 03902
KRITON: a knowledge-acquisition tool for expert systems. HCI-0327 †

**Induction**

Military systems. 0138
Inducing programs in a direct-manipulation environment. 0816
On the applicability of maximum entropy to inexact reasoning. 02074
Patterns of inductive reasoning in a parallel expert system. 02219
The structure of command languages: an experiment on task-action grammar. 02224
Order and disorder in knowledge structures. 02722
Character recognition of cursive scripts. 02961
Intelligent interfaces for secure multilevel database systems. 02990
Manipulation of embedded context using the multiple world mechanism. 03921
Induction: processes of inference, learning, and discovery. ● HCI-0064 †

**Knowledge acquisition**

An expert interface for effective man-machine interaction. 0166
Knowledge based management support systems. ● 0252
Design and implementation of an object-oriented user interface management system. 0412
DARN: Toward a community memory for diagnosis and repair tasks. 0428
Using patterns and plans in chess. 0528
Enhancing incremental learning processes with knowledge-based systems. 0538
Mental models and metaphors: implications for the design of adaptive user-system interfaces. 0539
Improvement of the acquisition of knowledge by informing feedback. 0540

Cognitive economy in physics reasoning: implications for designing instructional materials. 0542
On language and connectionism: analysis of a parallel distributed processing model of language acquisition. 0590
A substrate for object-oriented interface design. 0691
Building expert systems: cognitive emulation. ● 0700
The migration of expert systems into the production environment. 0740
Modelling novice programmer behaviour. 0744
Interactive learning: a multiexpert paradigm for acquiring new knowledge. 0776
Hypertext as a means for knowledge acquisition. 0777
Key factors in knowledge acquisition. 01019
Modeling the user's plans and goals. 01349
The programmer's apprentices: a research overview. 01368
Interactive timetabling in universities. 01501
The role of human factors in expert systems design and acceptance. 01780
Structuring knowledge bases for designers of learning materials. 01807
Design of knowledge-based systems with a knowledge-based assistant. 01853
The application of psychological scaling techniques to knowledge elicitation for knowledge-based systems. 02139
A mixed-initiative workbench for knowledge acquisition. 02154
Analysis of the performance of a genetic algorithm-based system for message classification in noisy environments. 02156
Creating the domain of discourse: ontology and inventory. 02158
Refining problem-solving knowledge in repertory grids using a consultation mechanism. 02205
Design goals for sloppy modeling systems. 02206
Issues in the verification of knowledge in rule-based systems. 02226
Integration issues in knowledge support system. 02253
Dynamics and architecture for neural computation. 02270
Conceptual models of interacitve knowledge acquisition tools. 02457
Advances in Cognitive Science. § 02720
Advances in cognitive science. 02721
The ISA expert system: a prototype system for failure diagnosis on the space station. 02913
Improving performance of an electrical power expert system with genetic algorithms. 02925
SMARTGEN: the implementation of an expert system for the generation of digital logic diagnostic tests. 02929
Automatic acquisition of domain and procedural knowledge. 02943
Generic diagnostic knowledge acquisition tool. 02944
Using design expertise to develop an expert system. 02962

[I. COMPUTING METHODOLOGIES]

Knowledge-based interface to manufacturing computer systems. 02966
Concept demonstration of the use of interactive fault diagnosis and isolation for TF30 engines. 02968
Artificial intelligence techniques applied to maintenance management. 02971
NetGraph: an object-oriented graphical toolset for risk assessment. 02972
Plant scheduling expert system for batch processing. 02977
An operations advisor for an on-line computer banking system with graphics interface. 02983
GOMS meets STRIPS: the integration of planning with skilled procedure execution in human-computer interaction. 03243
A study on an error recovery expert system using a superimposer and a digitizer in the advanced teleoperator system. 03389
An approach to knowledge elicitation in scheduling FMS: Toward a hybrid intelligent system. 03394
The role of memory in intelligent information systems. 03462
On building future decision support systems. 03472
A dietary recommendation expert system using OPS5. 03498
On one aspect of natural-language based knowledge acquisition. 03571
Knowledge acquisition via a graphical interface. 03572
Computer assisted knowledge acquisition: towards a laboratory for protocol analysis of user dialogues. 03603
An investigation of pictographic form in relation to mechanisms of knowledge acquisition. 03824
Structuring knowledge in a graph. 03899
Textvision: elicitation and acquisition of conceptual knowledge by graphic representation and multiwindowing. 03902
Knowledge and expertise in expert systems. 03905
Speaker-independent automatic recognition of plosive sound in letters and digits. 03993
Computer recognition of spoken letters and digits. 03995
Recent results on the application of a metric-space search algorithm (AESA) to multispeaker data. 03997
Fundamental issues of knowledge acquisition: toward a human action perspective of knowledge systems. 04057
A computer assisted learning system for reliability engineering. 04060
Mental models: towards a cognitive science of language, inference, and consciousness. • HCI-0063 †
Strategic issues in knowledge engineering. HCI-0317 †
Acquisition of control and domain knowledge by watching in a blackboard environment. HCI-0319 †
KRITON: a knowledge-acquisition tool for expert systems. HCI-0327 †

Expertise transfer and complex problems: using AQUINAS as a knowledge-acquisition workbench for knowledge-based systems. HCI-0336 †
Knowledge elicitation: dissociating conscious reflections from automatic processes. HCI-0337 †

*Language acquisition*

Use of psychometric tools for knowledge acquistion: a case study. 0323
The acquisition of grammar. 0353
Theoretical issues in the investigation of words of internal report. 0354
The relation between linguistic structure and associative theories of language learning models: constructive critique of some connectionist learning models. 0591
Linguistic knowledge as expertise. 02077
Precedent-based legal reasoning and knowledge acquisition in contract law: A process model. 02776
Automatic acquisition of domain and procedural knowledge. 02943
Interacting with expert systems. 02949
EPVM: An expert patient-ventilator manager for chemical warfare casualties. 02956
The use of prosodic parameters in automatic speech recognition. 03988
Primary perceptual units in word recognition. 03994
From schema theory to computational (neuro-)linguistics. HCI-0345 †
The mapping between grammar and processor. HCI-0346 †

*Parameter learning*

The use of prosodic parameters in automatic speech recognition. 03988
Prosodic features in German speech: stress assignment by man and machine. 03989
Phonetic segmentation using psychoacoustic speech parameters. 03991
Speaker-independent automatic recognition of plosive sound in letters and digits. 03993
Real-time large vocabulary word recognition via diphone spotting and multiprocessor implementation. 03996
An experimental environment for generating word hypotheses in continuous speech. 03998
Dynamic spectral adaptation of automatic speech recognizers to new speakers. 03999
Recognition of speaker-dependent continuous speech with Keal-Nevezh. 04002
Selective networks and recognition automata. HCI-0390 †
A neural network for visual pattern recognition. HCI-0391 †

## I.2.7 Natural Language Processing

Natural-language interfaces. 0069
Knowledge representation and natural language: extending the expressive power of proposition nodes. 0096
Text, context, and hypertext: writing with and for the computer. ● 0098
Expert systems and artificial intelligence. ● 0133
Computer assisted language learning: program structure and principles. ● 0196
Perspectives in artificial intelligence vol. 2: machine translation, NLP, databases and computer-aided instruction. ● 0198
Computational linguistics. ● 0215
Computer speech processing. ● 0287
Principles from the psychology of language. 0333
From models to modules: studies in cognitive science from the McGill workshops. ● 0352
An interaction between morphology and discourse. 0355
Interactive human communication (Reprint). 0371
Generation as a social action. 0389
Elements of a plan-based theory of speech acts. 0390
Analyzing intention in utterances. 0391
Points: a theory of the structure of stories in memory. 0392
GUS, a frame driven dialog system. 0395
The computer and the mind: an introduction to cognitive science. ● 0463
Connections and symbols. ● 0588
The programmable blackboard model of reading. 0632
On learning the past tenses of English verbs. 0634
Relevance: communication and cognition. ● 0704
The effects of restricted syntax on menu-based interaction. 0775
Understanding natural languages. 01172
Mathematical building blocks. 01173
How to choose natural language software. 01183
Wall Street speaks English. 01184
Dialogue and the search for information. 01223
Competitive dynamics in a dual-route connectionist model of print-to-sound transformation. 01341
Reference identification and reference identification failures. 01345
Processor for man-machine natural-language-like communication. 01484
Evaluating user utterances in natural language interfaces to databases. 01486
Artificial intelligence and natural language systems. 01541
A first order theory of common sense object positioning. 01563
ORGPLAN an information-decisive aid system to resolving organizing problems. 01573
Providing effective decision support: modeling users and their requirements. 01668
An experiment in computational discrimination of English word senses. 01813
Temporal semantics and natural language processing in a decision support system. 02038
Linguistic knowledge as expertise. 02077
Representing and using metacommunication to control speakers' relationships in natural-language dialogue. 02136
Natural language and computers: a general survey of written text interpretation methods. 02671
Employing voice back channels of facilitate audio document retrieval. 03045
Research and development in information retrieval. § 03072
The IRUS transportable natural language database interface. 03177
Anticipating false implicatures: cooperative responses in question-answer systems. 03178
Supporting natural language database update by modeling real world actions. 03179
Natural Language at the Computer. § 03947
Recent advances in speech understanding and dialog systems. § 03987
Chip talk: projects in speech synthesis. ● HCI-0002 †
Understanding computers and cognition. ● HCI-0054 †
Introduction to natural language processing. ● HCI-0065 †
Cooperative interfaces to information systems. ● HCI-0066 †
Readings in natural language processing. ● HCI-0067 †
Artificial intelligence and tutoring systems: computational and cognitive approaches to the communication of knowledge. ● HCI-0080 †
The vocabulary problem in human-system communication. HCI-0224 †
Measuring the quality of linguistic forecasts. HCI-0247 †
Using restricted natural language for data retrieval: a plan for field evaluation. HCI-0255 †
ASK is transportable in half a dozen ways. HCI-0279 †
A natural language front end to databases with evaluative feedback. HCI-0338 †
Semantic primitives or meaning postulates: mental models or propositional representation?. HCI-0339 †
Computer-aided modeling and planning (CAMP). HCI-0415 †

**DATALOG** *see* Proper Noun Index

**HEARSAY-II** *see* Proper Noun Index

*Language generation*

Realism in synthetic speech. 0066
Communication methods of the vocally disabled: a review. 0783

Designing a quality voice: an analysis of listeners' reactions to synthetic voices. 0914
Choice of words in the generation process of a natural language interface. 01206
Self-organizing system obtaining communication ability primitive model for language generation. 01279
Linguistic knowledge as expertise. 02077
Voice input/output interface for online searching: some design and human factor onsiderations. 02335
Higher pole correction in vocal tract models and terminal analogs. 02657
Plan-based text generation in an on-line help system. 03817
Generating natural language responses appropriate to conversational situations—in the case of Japanese. 03922
The use of prosodic parameters in automatic speech recognition. 03988
Prosodic features in German speech: stress assignment by man and machine. 03989
Using focus to constrain language generation. HCI-0341 †
Language generation by computer. HCI-0342 †
Knowledge-intensive natural language generation. HCI-0343 †

### Language models

Computational models of natural language processing. ● 0095
The acquisition of grammar. 0353
Theoretical issues in the investigation of words of internal report. 0354
The optimal level of abstraction for models of cerebral representation of language processes: the state of the question. 0356
Language, the mind, and psychophysical parallelism. 0357
A language/action perspective on the design of cooperative work (Reprint). 0383
What stories should we tell novice PROLOG programmers?. 0421
On language and connectionism: analysis of a parallel distributed processing model of language acquisition. 0590
Designing a quality voice: an analysis of listeners' reactions to synthetic voices. 0914
Various views on spatial prepositions. 01196
The relationship between user models and discourse models. 01353
Human language and computers. 01550
Toward a theory of computer program bugs: an empirical test. 02216
Combining stochastic uncertainty and linguistic inexactness: theory and experimental evaluation of four fuzzy probability models. 02218

The structure of command languages: an experiment on task-action grammar. 02224
Manipulation of embedded context using the multiple world mechanism. 03921
Generating natural language responses appropriate to conversational situations—in the case of Japanese. 03922
Computer recognition of spoken letters and digits. 03995
Knowledge based systems for speech understanding. 04001
Merging acoustics and linguistics in speech understanding. 04004
A computer assisted learning system for reliability engineering. 04060
Portability of syntax and semantics in DATALOG. HCI-0340 †
Extended person-machine interface. HCI-0344 †
From schema theory to computational (neuro-)linguistics. HCI-0345 †
The mapping between grammar and processor. HCI-0346 †
A framework for investigating language-mediated interaction with machines. HCI-0347 †

### Language parsing and understanding

Text processing with the START natural language system. 0100
Using "word-knowledge" reasoning for question answering. 0131
Natural languages. 0136
Knowledge representation. 0137
A practical natural language interface to databases. 0199
A string correction method based on the context-dependent similarity. 0293
Theoretical issues in the investigation of words of internal report. 0354
Artificial intelligence techniques in language learning. ● 0500
Artificial intelligence systems. 0683
Natural-language interfaces. 0693
Designing conceptual models of dialog: a case for dialog charts. 0968
The direct memory access paradigm and its applications to natural language processing. 01489
Shaping user input: a strategy for natural language dialogue design. 02067
Exploiting convergence to improve natural language understanding. 02071
Interactive communication of sentential structure and content: an alternative approach to man-machine communication. 02220
Task-oriented parsing - a diagnostic method to be used adaptive systems. 02896
A computer training tool using Chinese natural language. 02948

Delphi: an intelligent interface for a dolphin communication laboratory. 02989
Conceptual information extraction form financial news. 03489
Enhancing program readability and comprehensibility with tools for program visualization. 03510
The lexicon, grammatical categories and temporal reasoning. 03549
On one aspect of natural-language based knowledge acquisition. 03571
A functional model of questions for natural language processing systems. 03575
Natural language communication with computers: some problems, perspectives, and new directions. 03913
A travel consultation system: towards a smooth conversation in Japanese. 03917
Computational linguistics: issues and solutions. 03948
The use of prosodic parameters in automatic speech recognition. 03988
On-line interpretation in speech understanding and dialogue systems. 04000
Recognition of speaker-dependent continuous speech with Keal-Nevezh. 04002
Modification of Earley's algorithm for speech recognition. 04003
Mental models: towards a cognitive science of language, inference, and consciousness. ● HCI-0063 †
A natural language information retrieval system with extentions towards fuzzy reasoning. HCI-0281 †
Natural-language interface for an instructable robot. HCI-0324 †
Portability of syntax and semantics in DATALOG. HCI-0340 †
Postscript: computers and the modeling of mind. HCI-0348 †
Pygmalion at the interface. HCI-0349 †
Modularity and lexical access. HCI-0350 †
TEAM: an experiment in the design of transportable natural-language interfaces. HCI-0351 †
Transporting the linguistic string project system from a medical to a Navy domain. HCI-0352 †

**LSP** *see* Proper Noun Index

### Machine translation

Language, sublanguage, and the promise of machine translation. 01554
The engineering of a translator workstation. 01555
Two-level data banks for translators. 01556
A user perspective on computer-assisted translation for Minority languages. 01557
A holography-based computer-aided translation system-conceptual analysis. 01607
Machine assisted translation with a human face. 01627
Problems of machine translation system - effect of cultural differences on sentence structure. 01687
Language and artificial intelligence conference report. 01688
Environments for Eurota. 02514
Interacting with expert systems. 02949
A framework of a mechanical translation between Japanese and English by analogy principle. HCI-0353 †

### Speech recognition and understanding

System design for speech recognition and generation. 0065
Conversing and computers. 0092
Electronic speech recognition: techniques, technology, and applications. ● 0174
The nature of speech. 0175
The elements of speech recognition. 0176
Human factors in speech recognition. 0177
Interfacing standards for recognisers. 0178
Voice input applications in aerospace. 0179
Computer speech processing. ● 0287
Acoustic phonetics, auditory phonetics, speaker sex and speech recognition: a thread. 0288
Linear predictive coding of speech. 0289
Aspects of human speech understanding. 0290
The sequential organization of spoken word recognition. 0291
Human factors and artificial intelligence. 0408
Fundamentals in computer understanding: speech and vision. ● 0416
Rule-based detection of speech features for automatic speech recognition. 0419
Interactive processes in speech perception: the TRACE model. 0631
Phonology and syntax: the relationship between sound and structure. ● 0672
Speech and language-based interaction with machines: towards the conversational computer. ● 0724
Voice: technology searching for communication needs. 0808
A case example of human factors in product definition: needs finding for a voice output workstation for the blind. 0819
A synthetic visual environment with hand gesturing and voice input. 0858
Speech and gestures for graphic image manipulation. 0859
The design of phone-based interfaces for consumers. 0878
Speech recognition enhancement by lip information. 0915
Comparison of elderly and younger users on keyboard and voice input computer-based composition tasks. 0916
The "neural" phonetic typewriter. 01361

## [I. COMPUTING METHODOLOGIES]

Improving speaker consistency in an automatic speech recognition framework. 01448
Artificial intelligence techniques in man–machine communication. 01459
The direct memory access paradigm and its applications to natural language processing. 01489
Online searching using speech as a man/machine interface. 02013
The influence of rule-generated stress on computer-synthesized speech. 02081
Optimization of string length for spoken digit input with error correction. 02185
Talking to computers: an empirical investigation. 02186
Man—machine interaction by voice: developments in speech technology. Part I: The state-of-the-art. 02331
Man—machine interaction by voice: developments in speech technology. Part 2: general applications and potential applications in libraries and information services. 02332
Voice input/output interface for online searching: some design and human factor onsiderations. 02335
'Transparent' interfacing of speech recognizers to microcomputers. 02497
X-ray microbeam method for measurement of articulatory dynamics-techniques and results. 02641
Influence of palate shape on lingual articulation. 02642
Estimating articulatory motion from speech wave. 02643
An acoustic of pathological voice and its application to the evaluation of laryngeal pathology. 02644
Research on individuality features in speech waves and automatic speaker recognition techniques. 02645
Speech analysis and synthesis methods developed at ECL in NTT-From LPC to LSP-. 02646
Composite phoneme units for the speech synthesis of Japanese. 02647
Recognition of phonemes using time-spectrum pattern. 02648
Vowel normalization by frequency warped spectral matching. 02649
A computer model of peripheral auditory processing incorporating phase-locking, suppression and adaptation effects. 02650
Changes in prosodic features of speech due to environmental factors. 02651
Structure of German syllable initial and final consonant clusters based on articulatory features. 02652
The effect of varying voice and noise parameters on the perception of voicing in Dutch two-obstruent sequences. 02653
An evaluation of auditory performances in patients with Cochlear implants. 02658
A machine for neural computation of acoustical patterns with application to real time speech recognition. 02751
An improved automatic lipreading system to enhance speech recognition. 02859
Understanding text with an accompanying diagram. 02947
PC Version of a knowledge-based expert system with voice interface. 02964
Logic programmable natural language processor of a knowledge-base management system. 02965
A knowledge representation for natural language understanding. 02987
Human factors and the problems of evaluation in the design of speech systems interfaces. 03192
Parcel sorting by speech recognition: human factors issues. 03209
Interactive error recovery expert system for robot with voice recognition subsystem. 03420
A consideration of learning in speech recognition from the viewpoint of AI class-description learning. 03533
Human-computer interaction: psychonomic aspects. § 03887
The use of speech in man-machine interaction. 03910
Recent advances in speech understanding and dialog systems. § 03987
The use of prosodic parameters in automatic speech recognition. 03988
Prosodic features in German speech: stress assignment by man and machine. 03989
Recognition of speech using temporal decomposition. 03990
Phonetic segmentation using psychoacoustic speech parameters. 03991
Morphological representation of speech knowledge for automatic speech recognition systems. 03992
Speaker-independent automatic recognition of plosive sound in letters and digits. 03993
Primary perceptual units in word recognition. 03994
Computer recognition of spoken letters and digits. 03995
Real-time large vocabulary word recognition via diphone spotting and multiprocessor implementation. 03996
Recent results on the application of a metric-space search algorithm (AESA) to multispeaker data. 03997
An experimental environment for generating word hypotheses in continuous speech. 03998
Dynamic spectral adaptation of automatic speech recognizers to new speakers. 03999
On-line interpretation in speech understanding and dialogue systems. 04000
Knowledge based systems for speech understanding. 04001
Recognition of speaker-dependent continuous speech with Keal-Nevezh. 04002
Modification of Earley's algorithm for speech recognition. 04003
Merging acoustics and linguistics in speech understanding. 04004
Experimentation in the specification of an oral dialogue. 04005
Error detection and correction in a speech recognition system: a knowledge based system approach. 04054
Voice-input aids for the physically disabled. HCI-0089 †

An empirical investigation of voice as an input modality for computer programming. HCI-0237 †
An expert system for mapping acoustic cues into phonetic features. HCI-0328 †
An economical approach to modeling speech recognition accuracy. HCI-0354 †
Natural language with discrete speech as a mode for human-to-machine. HCI-0355 †
Tones of voice: the role of intonation in computer speech understanding. HCI-0356 †
Text processing by speech: dialogue design and usability issues in the provision of a system for disabled users. HCI-0357 †
The phonetic basis for computer speech processing. HCI-0358 †
Speech-controlled text-editing: effects of input modality and of command structure. HCI-0397 †
An overview of research and co-operation in advanced information technology. HCI-0442 †

*Text analysis*

A propositional language for text representation. 0097
Text processing with the START natural language system. 0100
Theoretical issues in the investigation of words of internal report. 0354
Mechanisms of sentence processing: assigning roles to constituents. 0635
Artificial intelligence systems. 0683
Are machines as good as people in drawing conclusions from knowledge represented in catalogues, data bases and expert systems?. 0736
Tailoring object descriptions to a user's level of expertise. 01352
Retrieval systems for the information seeker: can the role of the intermediary be automated?. 02864
Understanding text with an accompanying diagram. 02947
Providing natural language assistance in locating objects: a general model for information selection and generation. 02951
On one aspect of natural-language based knowledge acquisition. 03571
Human-computer interaction: psychonomic aspects. § 03887
Visual presentation of text: the process of reading from a psycholinguistic perspective. 03895
The effect on reading speed of word divisions at the end of a line. 03896
A comparison of presentation and representation: linguistic and pictorial. 03898
Structuring knowledge in a graph. 03899
Computing text constituency: an algorithmic approach to the generation of text graphs. HCI-0267 †
Postscript: computers and the modeling of mind. HCI-0348 †

Modularity and lexical access. HCI-0350 †
Transporting the linguistic string project system from a medical to a Navy domain. HCI-0352 †
Visual structure and the transmission of meaning. HCI-0404 †

**I.2.8 Problem Solving, Control Methods, and Search (F.2.2)**

Data, expert knowledge and decisions. ● 0338
A conceptual framework for the augmentation of man's intellect (Reprint). 0368
What stories should we tell novice PROLOG programmers?. 0421
Cognitive impacts of the user interface. 0432
C/C++ for expert systems: "unleashes the power of a artificial intelligence". ● 0439
Knowledge based problem solving. ● 0490
Mental models and metaphors: implications for the design of adaptive user-system interfaces. 0539
Expert systems and creativity. 0553
Reasoning with imprecise knowledge in expert systems. 02018
A multiprocessor system for real-time robotic control. 02023
Fuzzy control of a mobile robot for obstacle avoidance. 02025
Simplifying decision trees. 02157
Concept learning from examples and counter examples. 02229
Absolute dates and relative dates in an inferential system on temporal dependencies between events. 02235
User interfaces for problem solving support. 02695
DORUS: an architecture for dynamic optimal resource utilization systems. 02979
Industrial & Engineering Applications of Artificial Intelligence & Expert Systems: vol. II. § 02982
GPS and the psychology of th Rubik cubist: a study in reasoning about actions. 03311
MFDBS 87. § 03943
The central nervous system as a low and high level control system. 04007
Experimentation with an adaptive search strategy for solving a keyboard design/configuration problem. 04070
Plans and situated actions: the problem of human-machine communication. ● HCI-0040 †
Analogical problem solving. ● HCI-0044 †
Interaction with the environment. ● HCI-0068 †
Decision and intelligence. ● HCI-0068 †
Artificial intelligence and tutoring systems: computational and cognitive approaches to the communication of knowledge. ● HCI-0080 †
Effects of experience and comprehension on reading time and memory for computer programs. HCI-0197 †

[I. COMPUTING METHODOLOGIES]

Development of a term association interface for browsing bibliographic data bases based on end users' word associations. HCI-0266 †
Architecture problems in the construction of expert systems for document retrieval. HCI-0272 †
Cognitive models, cognitive tasks, and information retrieval. HCI-0331 †
An expert system for conceptual schema design: a machine learning approach. HCI-0335 †
A fuzzy rule-based model of human problem solving. HCI-0359 †
Naive algorithm design techniques—a case study. HCI-0360 †

### Backtracking

MAJIC—an integrated program support environment. 01960
Refining problem-solving knowledge in repertory grids using a consultation mechanism. 02205
Patterns of inductive reasoning in a parallel expert system. 02219

### Dynamic programming

Communication and management support in system development environments (Reprint). 0374
Automating interfaces in a software system. ● 0701
Automated construction of interactive learning programs in Modula-2. 01500
Software development approach in FMS. 01567
Simulation of CNC controller features in graphics-based programming. 01568
Manual control of an intrinsically unstable system and its modeling by fuzzy logic. 02026
A design for a fuzzy logic controller. 02028
Refining problem-solving knowledge in repertory grids using a consultation mechanism. 02205
Design goals for sloppy modeling systems. 02206
The electronic book Ebook3. 02234
Dynamics and architecture for neural computation. 02270
Advanced computing concepts and techniques in control engineering. § 03833
Qualitative modeling of physical systems for knowledge based control. 03834
A design environment for computer-aided control system design via multi-objective optimisation. 03835
Real-time large vocabulary word recognition via diphone spotting and multiprocessor implementation. 03996
Recent results on the application of a metric-space search algorithm (AESA) to multispeaker data. 03997
Dynamic spectral adaptation of automatic speech recognizers to new speakers. 03999
On-line interpretation in speech understanding and dialogue systems. 04000
Recognition of speaker-dependent continuous speech with Keal-Nevezh. 04002

Modification of Earley's algorithm for speech recognition. 04003
Merging acoustics and linguistics in speech understanding. 04004
Sensors and sensory systems for advanced robots. § 04006
Proprioceptive feedback for sensory-motor control. 04008
An overview of local environment sensing in robotics applications. 04012
Force and tactile sensing for robots. 04013
Analogs of biological tissues for mechanoelectrical transduction: tactile sensors and muscle-like actuators. 04014
Specification and verification of database dynamics. HCI-0251 †

**GPSS** *see* Proper Noun Index

### Graph and tree search strategies

Strategies for interactive design systems. 0466
Universal subgoaling and chunking: the automatic generation and learning of goal hierarchies. ● 0497
Computer chess compendium. ● 0526
A feature matching approach to the retrieval of graphical information. 01245
A mission planning architecture for an autonomous vehicle. 02939
GOMS meets STRIPS: the integration of planning with skilled procedure execution in human-computer interaction. 03243
Textvision: elicitation and acquisition of conceptual knowledge by graphic representation and multiwindowing. 03902
Real-time large vocabulary word recognition via diphone spotting and multiprocessor implementation. 03996
An experimental environment for generating word hypotheses in continuous speech. 03998
On-line interpretation in speech understanding and dialogue systems. 04000
Knowledge based systems for speech understanding. 04001
Experimentation with an adaptive search strategy for solving a keyboard design/configuration problem. 04070
The depth/breadth trade-off in the design of menu-driven user interfaces. HCI-0135 †
The complexity of some polynomial network consistency algorithms for constraint satisfaction problems. HCI-0361 †

### Heuristic methods

Hypertext and intelligent interfaces for text retrieval. 0115
A heuristic program to solve geometric-analogy problems. 0299

Learning through incremental refinement of procedures. 0482

Universal subgoaling and chunking: the automatic generation and learning of goal hierarchies. ● 0497

Computer chess compendium. ● 0526

The Greenblatt chess program. 0527

Interactive timetabling in universities. 01501

Automated concept acquisition in noisy environments. 01841

Protos: an examplar-based learning apprentice. 02210

On the representation and the impact of reliability on expert system weights. 02211

INQUEST: A prototype intelligence tool. 02918

Symbiotic systems for complex problems. 02922

A blackboard architecture for problem solving and machine learning in an expert system for power system voltage control. 02926

SMARTGEN: the implementation of an expert system for the generation of digital logic diagnostic tests. 02929

Process design of oil and gas production facilities using expert systems. 02933

Process control with the G2 real-time expert system. 02934

GTEX—A group technology expert system. 02936

Applications of qualitative modeling to knowledge-based risk assessment studies. 02970

Reasoning in model management systems. 03487

Heuristic rules for visualization. 03868

Recent results on the application of a metric-space search algorithm (AESA) to multispeaker data. 03997

Acquisition of control and domain knowledge by watching in a blackboard environment. HCI-0319 †

Instructionless learning about a complex device: the paradigm and observations. HCI-0333 †

**O-plan** *see* Proper Noun Index

### Plan execution, formation, generation

Military systems. 0138

Callisto: an intelligent project management system (Reprint). 0375

Psychological evaluation of path hypotheses in cognitive diagnosis. 0537

Recognizing and responding to plan-oriented misconceptions. 01350

GOMS meets STRIPS: the integration of planning with skilled procedure execution in human-computer interaction. 03243

Morphological representation of speech knowledge for automatic speech recognition systems. 03992

The learning and planning of actions. 04069

A fuzzy rule-based model of human problem solving. HCI-0359 †

O-Plan: control in the open planning architecture. HCI-0362 †

### I.2.9 Robotics

Schemas that integrate vision and touch for hand control. 0026

Education and training in robotics. ● 0440

The human side of robotics: how workers react to a robot. 0443

Preparing for new technology. 0444

Man is not a robot. 0445

Robotics and Material Flow. ● 0558

Task allocation between humans and robots in manufacturing. 0559

CAD Based Programming for Sensory Robots. ● 0597

Experiences with off-line robot programming via standardized interfaces. 0601

Off-line programming of robots using 3D graphical simulation system. 0602

CAD-based off-line programming applied to a cleaning and deburring workstation. 0607

Is man a robot?. ● 0697

Integrating neural networks with robots. 01187

Problems associated with the off-line programming of robots. 01241

An interactive programming system for the IBM 7545 robot. 01517

A multiprocessor system for real-time robotic control. 02023

REPTIL-promoting dialog between humanoid and computer. 02307

Notions and dynamics of information. 02319

Approximate spatial reasoning. 02917

A mission planning architecture for an autonomous vehicle. 02939

Developing intelligent simulation language to support telerobotic workstation activities. 02995

The man-machine integration. 03384

Human factor issues in teleoperated systems. 03387

Some recent documentation of robotic safety from Sweden. 03407

Methods for field evaluation of safety in a robotics workplace. 03408

Unexpected motion hazard exposures on a large robotic assembly. 03409

Human perception of the work envelope of an industrial robot. 03410

Development of a human engineering design standard for robot teach pendants. 03411

A study on the safety operation of robots using monitor hold. 03412

Standards requirements for mobile robotic systems. 03415

Critical issues in the safety of software-dominant automated systems. 03416

A study on safety evaluation index and industrial accident analysis from the viewpoint of the safety confirmation type. 03419

[I. COMPUTING METHODOLOGIES]   CATEGORY INDEX

A study of auditory warning alarms evaluation for automated guided vehicles. 03424
Experiences from the use of an intelligent safety sensor with industrial robots. 03427
The impact of automation on musculoskeletal disorders. 03437
The social cybernetics of human interaction with automated systems. 03442
The economic evaluation on implementation industrial robot from user point of view. 03447
"Automation, robotization in particular, is always economically desirable"—fact or fiction?. 03448
Ergonomic evaluation of safety devices in robotic systems. 03449
CAD and robotics in architecture and construction. § 03568
Evolution of a robotic excavator. 03569
Artificial Intelligence and Information-Control systems of Robots-87. § 03570
A rule-based system for fuzzy natural language robot control. 03574
Psychological principles for allocation of functions in man-robot system. 03630
Towards an integrated view of 3-D computer animation. 03859
Neural networks for motor program generation. 03964
Tensor geometry: a language of brains & neurocomputers. Generalized coordinates in neuroscience & robotics. 03966
Extending Kohonen's self-organizing mapping algorithms to learn ballistic movements. 03967
A flexible and intelligent system for fast measurements in binary images for in-line robotic control. 03986
Prosodic features in German speech: stress assignment by man and machine. 03989
Sensors and sensory systems for advanced robots. § 04006
The central nervous system as a low and high level control system. 04007
Proprioceptive feedback for sensory-motor control. 04008
Steps toward making robots see. 04011
A neural model of human prehension. 04072
Teleoperations and robotics: applications and technology. ● HCI-0068 †
Interaction with the environment. ● HCI-0068 †
Teleoperations and robotics: evolution and development. ● HCI-0068 †
Robot components and systems. ● HCI-0068 †
Logic and programming. ● HCI-0068 †
Decision and intelligence. ● HCI-0068 †
Performance and computer-aided design. ● HCI-0068 †
Indexes and bibliography. ● HCI-0068 †
Natural-language interface for an instructable robot. HCI-0324 †

*Manipulators*

Space. 0134
Task-oriented approach to interactive control of heavy-duty manipulators based on coarse scene description. ● 0546
A workcell application design environment (WADE). 0598
Robot simulation and off-line programming—an integrated CAE-CAD approach. 0599
Off-line programming and path generation for robot manipulators. 0603
Modeling of robot system dynamics for CAD based robot programming. 0605
Computer aided application program synthesis for industrial robots. 0606
Mapping the manipulator workspace using interactive computer graphics. 02257
Task compatibility of manipulator postures. 02258
A survey of general-purpose manipulation. 02259
A comparison of the artistic aspects of various industrial robots. 02938
Evaluating the impact of camera placement on teleoperator efficiency. 02940
A prototype autonomous agent for crew and equipment retrieval in space. 02994
Ergonomics of Hybrid Automated Systems I. § 03362
A study on an error recovery expert system using a superimposer and a digitizer in the advanced teleoperator system. 03389
Human visual requirements for control and monitoring of a space telerobot. 03391
Illumination requirements for operating a space remote manipulator. 03392
Interactive aspects of knowledge representations. 03395
Human nature and robot nature. 03401
U.S. Army field robotics focus and key technology issues. 03402
Robot vs. human operator for speed, precision and other aspects. 03403
Human response to unexpected robot movements at selected slow speeds. 03405
Ten fatal accidents due to robots in Japan. 03406
Man-machine interfaces for mobile robotic systems. 03413
100 Percent assured performance for robotic assistive devices for handicapped and elderly persons. 03414
Safety considerations in robot design. 03418
Interactive error recovery expert system for robot with voice recognition subsystem. 03420
A study of fail-safe technology. 03421
A study of intrinsic safety asymmetrical actuator. 03422
AGV safety system designed for preventing hazardous human contact. 03423

Pneumatic manipulating system provided with active compliance function. 03426
Optimum stresses and strains represented by examples from shop practice. 03441
The fourth international symposium. § 03561
Issues in the design of off-line programming systems. 03564
The physiology and psychophysics of touch. 04010
An overview of local environment sensing in robotics applications. 04012
Force and tactile sensing for robots. 04013
Modelling and control. ● HCI-0068 †

### Propelling mechanisms

Fuzzy control of a mobile robot for obstacle avoidance. 02025
A comparison of the artistic aspects of various industrial robots. 02938
Ergonomics of Hybrid Automated Systems I. § 03362
Human response to unexpected robot movements at selected slow speeds. 03405
Man-machine interfaces for mobile robotic systems. 03413
Safety considerations in robot design. 03418
AGV safety system designed for preventing hazardous human contact. 03423

### Sensors

An extremum principle for shape from contour. 0024
Task-oriented approach to interactive control of heavy-duty manipulators based on coarse scene description. ● 0546
A workcell application design environment (WADE). 0598
CAD Based verification and refinement of high level compliant motion primitives. 0600
CAD Based verification and refinement of high level compliant motion primitives. 0600
Modeling of robot system dynamics for CAD based robot programming. 0605
A survey of general-purpose manipulation. 02259
Critical review of visual inspection. 02260
Recollections on the processing of biomedical signals. 02846
Health care information systems: a personal historic review. 02849
Patient management systems: the early years. 02852
Evaluating the impact of camera placement on teleoperator efficiency. 02940
A prototype autonomous agent for crew and equipment retrieval in space. 02994
Ergonomics of Hybrid Automated Systems I. § 03362
Human visual requirements for control and monitoring of a space telerobot. 03391
Human nature and robot nature. 03401

Robot vs. human operator for speed, precision and other aspects. 03403
Ten fatal accidents due to robots in Japan. 03406
A study on the safety operation of robots using monitor hold. 03412
Man-machine interfaces for mobile robotic systems. 03413
Overview of research issues in robot safety. 03417
Construction and examples of sensor in safe working system. 03425
Performance evaluation of three pressure mats as robot workstation safety sensors. 03428
The fourth international symposium. § 03561
MEISTER: a model enhanced intelligent and skillful teleoperational robot system. 03562
Generic surface interpretation: observability model. 03563
The use of prosodic parameters in automatic speech recognition. 03988
Dynamic spectral adaptation of automatic speech recognizers to new speakers. 03999
Sensors and sensory systems for advanced robots. § 04006
Physiology and psychophysics in taste and smell. 04009
The physiology and psychophysics of touch. 04010
An overview of local environment sensing in robotics applications. 04012
Force and tactile sensing for robots. 04013
Analogs of biological tissues for mechanoelectrical transduction: tactile sensors and muscle-like actuators. 04014
Gas sensors: towards an artificial nose. 04015
Integration of robot sensory systems. 04016
Active vision: integration of fixed and mobile cameras. 04017
An iterative and interactive simulation method to reconstruct unknown inputs contributing to known outputs of neuronal systems. 04018
Signal processing and pattern recognition in nondestructive evaluation of materials. § 04019
The effects of limited data in multi-frequency reflection diffraction tomography. 04020
Parameter estimation in array processing. 04021
Interaction with the environment. ● HCI-0068 †

### I.2.10 Vision and Scene Understanding (I.4.8, I.5)

Fundamentals in computer understanding: speech and vision. ● 0416
The computer and the mind: an introduction to cognitive science. ● 0463
Image understanding 1985-86. ● 0615
A new sense for depth of field. 01845
Human and Machine Vision II. § 02696

[I. COMPUTING METHODOLOGIES]    CATEGORY INDEX

Human image understanding: recent research and a theory. 02698
Toward a theory of the perceived spatial layout of scenes. 02701
Document manipulation and typography. § 03182
Sensors and sensory systems for advanced robots. § 04006
Interaction with the environment. ● HCI-0068 †
Connectionist models and parallelism in high level vision. HCI-0363 †
Perception of organization in a random stimulus. HCI-0364 †

### Architecture and control structures

A visual shell interface to a database. 02640
Issues in the design of off-line programming systems. 03564
Problem oriented design of interaction structures. 03614
Control of sensory processing - a hypothesis on and simulation of the architecture of an elementary cortical processor. 03972
Recognizing unexpected objects: a proposed approach. HCI-0389 †

### Intensity, color, photometry, and thresholding

Color displays and color science. 0255
Human factors for color display systems: concepts, methods, and research. 0256
Visual parameters for color CRTs. 0257
Perceptual color spaces for computer graphics. 0258
Color graphic displays for network planning and design. 0260
Perception of transparency in man and machine. 02697
Towards the construction of a maximally-contrasting set of colours. 03233
The legibility of visual display texts. 03889
The use of color in visual displays. 03890
Steps toward making robots see. 04011
An overview of local environment sensing in robotics applications. 04012
Perception of transparency in man and machine. HCI-0367 †
An experimental evaluation of computer graphics imagery. HCI-0373 †
Visual hyperacuity: representation and computation of high precision position information. HCI-0393 †
Image processing aspects of type. HCI-0403 †
Visual structure and the transmission of meaning. HCI-0404 †

### Modeling and recovery of physical attributes

Depth and detours: an essay on visually guided behavior. 0018
A functional model of vision and space. 0027

Visual-cognitive neuronal networks. 0029
Problems in recognition of drawings. 0294
Learning, development, and production systems. 0479
Doing, understanding, and learning in problem solving. 0480
A general theory of discrimination learning. 0481
Learning through incremental refinement of procedures. 0482
Learning by chunking: a production system model of practice. 0483
Self-modifying production system model of cognitive development. 0486
Production systems, learning, and tutoring. 0487
A model of the neocortex. 01164
How to talk to an expert. 01180
Neural networks primer, Part VII. 01192
A model of the motor servo: Incorporating nonlinear spindle receptor and muscle mechanical properties. 01273
The control of hand equilibrium trajectories in multi-joint arm movements. 01275
Competitive dynamics in a dual-route connectionist model of print-to-sound transformation. 01341
Real time speech synthesis—development and employment. 01482
Functional modelling in the execution of actions. 01485
Kinetic theory of "hot" neural systems. 01613
Models of procedural control for human performance simulation. 01752
Review and evaluation of physiological cost prediction models for manual materials handling. 01757
Spatial requirements for visual simulation of aircraft at real-world distances. 01768
Implementing computer-mediated communication technologies: a technoacceptance approach to critical mass utilization. 01931
Modelling operators in accident conditions: advances and perspectives on a cognitive model. 02169
Human supervisor modelling: some new developments. 02170
$DM^2$: an algorithm for diagnostic reasoning that combines analytical models and experiential knowledge. 02190
Psychological models of deferred decision making. 02370
The accumulator model of two-choice discrimination. 02371
A note on mimicking additive reaction time models. 02373
Modeling managerial behavior: misperceptions of feedback in a dynamic decision making experiment. 02483
A model of the controller responses of the human temperature regulating system to changes in water temperature. 02487
Multidimensional attribute analyhsis and pattern recognition for seismic interpretation. 02530

# [I. COMPUTING METHODOLOGIES]

Speech motor control and stuttering: a computational model of adaptive sensory-motor processing. 02655
Higher pole correction in vocal tract models and terminal analogs. 02657
Distinctive regions and modes: a new theory of speech production. 02659
Coproduction: evidence from EPG data. 02660
An acoustic-phonetic oriented system for synthesizing Chinese. 02661
Visuomotor control by a combined position- and speedservo. Theoretical considerations and experimental results in man. 02666
Power plant simulation and reactor safety. 02682
Perceiving and recovering structure from events. 03346
Modeling uncertainty in human perception. 03825
Spatial and temporal transformations in visuo-motor coordination. 03963
Extending Kohonen's self-organizing mapping algorithms to learn ballistic movements. 03967
Speaker-independent automatic recognition of plosive sound in letters and digits. 03993
The complexity of some polynomial network consistency algorithms for constraint satisfaction problems. HCI-0361 †
Early vision: from computational structure to algorithms and parallel hardware. HCI-0365 †
Preattentive processing in vision. HCI-0366 †
Perception of transparency in man and machine. HCI-0367 †

## Motion

Visual analysis during motion. 0020
Various views on spatial prepositions. 01196
Visual control of displacement at slow speeds. 01797
On kineopsis and cimputation of structure and motion. 01839
Microcomputing in motion analysis. 02384
Animating human figures: perspectives and directions. 03291
Virya—a motion control editor for kinematic and dynamic animation. 03294
Motion: representation and perception. § 03321
How human perception deals with motion. 03322
The scope of research on motion: sensations, perception, representation and generation. 03323
The fox and the forest: toward a type I/type II constraint for early optical flow. 03324
Motion perception: second thoughts on the correspondence problem. 03325
The representation and perception of geometric structure in moving visual patterns. 03326
The perception of coherent motion in two-dimensional patterns. 03327
Real and apparent motion: one mechanism or two?. 03328

Coherent global motion percepts from stochastic local motions. 03329
Optical flow. 03330
Computing the velocity field along contours. 03331
Determining the instantaneous axis of translation from optic flow generated by arbitrary sensot motion. 03332
Complex logarithmic mapping and the focus of expansion. 03333
Adapting optical-flow to measure object motion in reflectance and X-ray image sequences. 03334
On the estimation of dense displacement vector fields from image sequences. 03335
Motion and time-varying imagery. 03336
Tracking three-dimensional moving light displays. 03337
Determining motion parameters for scenes with translation and rotation. 03338
Determining 3-D motion parameters of a rigid body: a vector-geometrical approach. 03339
A hybrid approach to structure-from-motion. 03340
Multicomputer architectures for real-time perception. 03341
Motion from continuous or discontinuous arrangements. 03342
Perception of rotation in depth: the psychophysical evidence. 03343
The cross-ratio and the perception of motion and structure. 03344
Selective attention to aspects of motion configurations: common vs. relative motion. 03345
Perceiving and recovering structure from events. 03346
Motion analysis of grammatical processes in a visual-gestural language. 03347
Motion graphics, description and control. 03348
"Graphical marionette". 03349
A multiple track animator system for motion synchronization. 03350
Knowledge-based animation. 03351
3-D balance in legged locomotion: modeling and simulation for the one-legged case. 03352
Representing and reasoning about change. 03353
Image segregation by motion: cortical mechanisms and implementation in neural networks. 03958
Active vision: integration of fixed and mobile cameras. 04017
Early vision: from computational structure to algorithms and parallel hardware. HCI-0365 †

## Perceptual reasoning

Color displays and color science. 0255
Human factors for color display systems: concepts, methods, and research. 0256
Visual parameters for color CRTs. 0257
Perceptual color spaces for computer graphics. 0258
Eye movements in reading: perceptual and language processes. ● 0609

[I. COMPUTING METHODOLOGIES]

Various views on spatial prepositions. 01196
Fuzzy reasoning in pseudo-physical logics. 01695
The MDR algorithm and its application to the generation of explanations for novel events. 02174
DM$^2$: an algorithm for diagnostic reasoning that combines analytical models and experiential knowledge. 02190
Generative systems of analyzers. 02702
Early vision: from computational structure to algorithms and parallel hardware. 02703
Perception of organization in a random stimulus. 02706
Preattentive processing in vision. 02709
The lexicon, grammatical categories and temporal reasoning. 03549
Visual presentation of text: the process of reading from a psycholinguistic perspective. 03895
Phonetic segmentation using psychoacoustic speech parameters. 03991
Primary perceptual units in word recognition. 03994
Physiology and psychophysics in taste and smell. 04009
The physiology and psychophysics of touch. 04010
Steps toward making robots see. 04011
Gas sensors: towards an artificial nose. 04015
Active vision: integration of fixed and mobile cameras. 04017
Mental models: towards a cognitive science of language, inference, and consciousness. ● HCI-0063 †
Perception of transparency in man and machine. HCI-0367 †
Selective networks and recognition automata. HCI-0390 †
Visual structure and the transmission of meaning. HCI-0404 †

*Representations, data structures, and transforms*

Manipulation of 3D imagery. 0557
Model generation and modification for dynamic systems from geometric data. 0604
Drag: a graph drawing system. 03183
The representation and perception of geometric structure in moving visual patterns. 03326
The perception of coherent motion in two-dimensional patterns. 03327
Problem oriented design of interaction structures. 03614
The use of color in visual displays. 03890
Morphological representation of speech knowledge for automatic speech recognition systems. 03992
On-line interpretation in speech understanding and dialogue systems. 04000
Abstract data type development and implementation: an example. HCI-0162 †
Color and the computer in cartography. HCI-0386 †
Environment-centered and viewer-centered perception of surface orientation. HCI-0392 †

Visual hyperacuity: representation and computation of high precision position information. HCI-0393 †
Visual structure and the transmission of meaning. HCI-0404 †

*Shape*

An extremum principle for shape from contour. 0024
Manipulation of 3D imagery. 0557
Visual routines. 0616
Shape from texture. 01278
Generative systems of analyzers. 01461
A new algorithm for extracting the interior of bounded regions based on chain coding. 01469
A limitation theorem for the differentiable prototypification of shape. 02365
Grid analysis: continuing the search for a metric of shape. 02367
Describing surfaces. 02699
The use of color in visual displays. 03890
Steps toward making robots see. 04011
Integration of robot sensory systems. 04016
An investigation into the skeletonization approach of Hilditch. HCI-0388 †:6HTexture
Textons, the fundamental elements in preattentive vision and perception of textures. 0297
Shape from texture. 01278
Cortical representation of texture primitives. 03306
The physiology and psychophysics of touch. 04010
Force and tactile sensing for robots. 04013

**I.2.m Miscellaneous**

On knowledge base management systems: integrating artificial intelligence and database technologies. ● 0180
Questions, answers, and responses: interacting with knowledge base systems. 0182
Parallel computers for AI databases. 0183
From models to modules: studies in cognitive science from the McGill workshops. ● 0352
Parallel distributed processing: explorations in the microstructures of cognition; Vol. 2: Psychological and biological models. ● 0629
A very friendly software environment for SOLO. 0743
Modelling novice programmer behaviour. 0744
Selecting a shell. 01176
Neural networks primer, part I. 01178
Neural networks primer, Part II. 01181
Connectionism, cybernetics, and the cerebellum. 01185
Twelve neural network cliches. 01186
Neural networks primer, part IV. 01188
Twelve-product wrap-up: neural networks. 01189
Direct manipulation interfaces. 01191
Motivation analysis, abductive unification, and nonmonotonic equality. 01211

Towards a computational theory of cognitive maps. 01212
On the design of man-machine systems: principles, practices and prospects. 01236
Computing with structured neural networks. 01365
Neural computing: ideas from the brain. 01379
Computer, quantized time and human duration. 01593
A fuzzy knowledge base of an expert system for analysis of manual lifting tasks. 01693
Interfaces for knowledge-base builders' control knowledge and application-specific procedures. 01810
Human interaction with an "intelligent" machine. 02163
Validation in a knowledge support system: construing and consistency with multiple experts. 02203
Cognitive primitives. 02214
Integration issues in knowledge support system. 02253
A cognitive study of the decision-making process in a business context: implications for design of expert systems. 02256
Peopleware. 02557
A teachable neural network based on an unorthodox neuron. 02561
A self-optimizing, nonsymmetrical neural net for content addressable memory and pattern recognition. 02562
User-supported artificial intelligence. 02602
Reasoning about knowledge: an overview. 03167
Expert systems 85. § 03188
Research and development in information retrieval. § 03287
Connectionism and cognitive science. 03547
Intelligent machines: What chance?. 03548
Necessary contributions of cognitive psychology to computer knowledge representation and manipulation systems. 03598
Memory research and knowledge engineering. 03599
Some aspects of knowledge processing and participation. 03669
On the management of information imperfection in knowledge based systems. 03823
Why cortices? Neural computation in the vertebrate visual system. 03956
A neural model of human prehension. 04072
The study of information: interdisciplinary messages. ● HCI-0036 †
Approaches to human reasoning: an analytic framework. HCI-0239 †
A model for the interpretation of verbal predictions. HCI-0316 †
Reverse engineering the brain. HCI-0368 †

## I.3 COMPUTER GRAPHICS

Annual review of computer science vol. 1, 1986. ● 0719
Procedural elements for computer graphics. ● HCI-0069 †

### I.3.0 General

Towards a characterization of graphical interaction. 0074
The on-line environment and in-house training. 0106
Technology + design + research = information design. 0107
Readings in computer vision: issues, problems, principles, and paradigms. ● 0296
The world of GEM. ● 0396
Image understanding 1985-86. ● 0615
RAPID: Prototyping control panel interfaces. 01120
Dialogue cell resource model and basic dialogue cells. 01400
Optical systems that imitate human memory. 01576
Human and Machine Vision II. § 02696
Computer Graphics. § 02810
ACE: a color expert system for user interface design. 03117
XY-WINS: an integraded environment for developing graphical user interfaces. 03118
Applying a theory of graphical presentation to the graphic design of user interfaces. 03122
Document manipulation and typography. § 03182
Vidura—an interactive multilingual publishing system—specification & design. 03186
Chinese character processing system based on character-root combination and gra phic processing. 03187
Graphics Interface '86/Vision Interface '86. § 03288
Advances in computer graphics hardware I. § 03785
Advanced Computer Graphics. § 03836
Computer graphics 1987. § 03852
Product data interfaces in CAD/CAM applications: design, implementation and experiences. § 03981
Real-time object measurement and classification. § 03985
Editing graphical objects using procedural representations. 04056
Performance and computer-aided design. ● HCI-0068 †
Principles of interactive computer graphics (2nd ed.). ● HCI-0069 †
Computer graphics. ● HCI-0069 †
Fundamentals of interactive computer graphics. ● HCI-0069 †
Artificial behavior: computer simulation of psychological processes. ● HCI-0073 †
Creating a style for online help. HCI-0154 †
An experimental program investigating color-enhanced and graphical information presentation: an integration of the findings. HCI-0196 †
Understanding the effectiveness of computer graphics for decision support: a cumulative experimental approach. HCI-0215 †

### I.3.1 Hardware architecture (B.4.2)

The algorithmic approach in ergonomics: the case of optimal colours and ambients for display work. 0247

[I. COMPUTING METHODOLOGIES]    CATEGORY INDEX

A system for evaluating screen formats: Research and application. 0413
Human factors of color displays. 0438
DVI—a digital multimedia technology. 01327
Reading from paper versus reading from screen. 01416
Touchscreen usage in plant computer systems: a case study. 01530
Designing screens for people to use easily. 01531
The effects of set size on color matching using CRT displays. 01711
Reading from microfiche, a VDT, and the printed page: subjective fatigue and performance. 01712
Intermittent illumination from visual display units and fluorescent lighting affects movements of the eyes across text. 01713
Reading from CRT displays can be as fast as reading from paper. 01758
Operator performance as a function of type of display: conventional versus perspective. 01769
Human performance evaluation of digitizer pucks for computer input of spatial information. 01774
whim, the window handler and input manager. 01825
Human factors and flat panels challenge the CRT. 01982
CRTs—present and future. 01985
A powerful solution meets an overwhelming problem. 02053
Formatting alphanumeric crt displays. 02140
The VDTs are here: health hazard and all. 02439
Medical informatics: a personal view of sowing the seeds. 02841
Display strategies for program browsing. 03545
Work with display units 86. § 03676
VDTs and health—fact or fancy?. 03677
Health impact of work with visual display terminals. 03678
Determinants of the VDU operator's well-being. 03679
Environmental stressors and perceived health symptoms among office workers. 03680
Repetition strain injury in Australian VDU users. 03681
Eye Fatigue among VDU users and non-VDU users. 03682
Intraocular pressure during VDT work. 03683
Radiation emissions from VDUs. 03684
Health hazards assessment of radio frequency electromagnetic fields emitted by video display terminals. 03685
Pregnancy and VDT work—an evaluation of the state of the art. 03686
Video display terminals—electromagnetic radiation and health. 03687
Birth defect, spontaneous abortion and work with VDUs. 03688
Birth defects, course of pregnancy, and work with VDUs: a Finnish case-referent study. 03689
Pregnancy outcome and VDU-work in a cohort of insurance clerks. 03690

Video display terminals and birth defects. A study of pregnancy outcomes of employees of the Postal-Giro Center, Oslo, Norway. 03691
Task-load and endocrinological risk for pregnancy in women VDU operators. 03692
Some physical factors at VDT work stations and ski problems. 03693
Facial particle exposure in the VDU environment: the role of static electricity. 03694
A Rosacea-like skin rash in VDU-operators. 03695
VDT work and the skin. 03696
Skin paroblems from VDT work-a summary. 03697
Human factors considerations in the design of a VDU for visually impaired persons. 03698
Study of visual performance on a multi-color VDU of color defective and normal Trichromatic subjects. 03701
Lighting the display or displaying the lighting. 03716
Matching display characteristics to human visual capacity. 03723
Criteria for the subjective quality of visual display units. 03724
Colors in video displays. 03725
A colour atlas for graphical displays. 03726
Colour on displays—boon or curse?. 03727
The effect of VDT symbol characteristics on operator performance and visual comfort. 03728
Visual phenomena and their relation to top luminance, phosphor persistence time and contrast polarity. 03729
Temporal and spatial stability in visual displays. 03730
Influence of CRT refresh rates on accommodation after-effects. 03731
Display architecture for VLSI-based graphics workstations. 03786
Looking at workstation architectures from the viewpoint of interaction. 03787
Human-computer interaction: psychonomic aspects. § 03887
Introduction: human-computer interaction: psychonomic aspects. 03888
Real-time processing of cursive writing and sketched graphics. 03908
Design principles for a front-end visual systems. 03955

*Hardcopy devices*

Towards a characterization of graphical interaction. 0074
Computer graphics: A tool for the artist, designer and amateur. 0235
Desktop publishing. 0238
Color displays and color science. 0255
A cognitively based methodology for evaluating human performance in the computer-aided design task domain. 01240

CATEGORY INDEX                                    [I. COMPUTING METHODOLOGIES]

## Input devices

Conversing and computers. 0092
User interface management systems. 0233
Object-oriented graphics. 0234
User performance with command, menu, and iconic interfaces. 0414
Keyboarding for personal computer use. ● 0492
Bat brushes: on the uses of six position and orientation parameters in a paint program. 0846
Circling: a method of mouse-based selection without button presses. 0847
A study in two-handed input. 0933
Interactive recognition of handprinted characters for computer input. 0940
A directory of sources for interactive technologies. 0941
Apollo domain series 3000. 01170
Logical input devices and interaction. 01393
Improving the accuracy of touch screens: an experimental evaluation of three strategies. 02860
The design of auditory interfaces for visually disabled users. 02869
Color-coding categories in menus. 02872
Designing keybindings to be easy to learn and resistant to forgetting even when the set of commands is large. 02890
Software ergonomics: advances and applications. ● HCI-0012 †
Behavioral experiments on handmarkings. HCI-0201 †

## Raster display devices

Colour graphics—Blessing or Ballyhoo?. 0061
Making the right choices with menus. 0070
Window-based computer dialogues. 0071
User interface management systems. 0233
Color displays and color science. 0255
Human factors for color display systems: concepts, methods, and research. 0256
Visual parameters for color CRTs. 0257
Ergonomic vision. 0259
Color graphic displays for network planning and design. 0260
Color computer graphics in military cockpits. 0261
Color displays for medical imaging. 0262
Advances in computer graphics hardware II. ● 0493
A two-dimensional frame buffer processor. 0494
Pixel-planes 4: a summary. 0495
The use and misuse of VDU'S. 01375
Architectures of graphic processors for interactive 2D graphics. 01395
An experimental study of Chinese information displays on VDTs. 01784
Reader-controlled computerized presentation of text. 01785

Magnification effects with imaging displays depend on scene content and viewing condition. 01786
The dubious dangers of VDT radiation. 01902
Interactive document display and its use in information retrieval. 02300
VDTs: are they safe?. 02549
High-performance polygon rendering. 02814
Human-computer communication meets software engineering. 03505
Segue: Support for distributed graphical interfaces. 03526
Design and implementation of a supercomputer frame buffer system. 03543
Visual comfort as a criterion for designing display units. 03892
Displaying statistical information—ergonomic considerations. 03893
Methodology of window management. § 03923
A window-based graphics frame store architecture. HCI-0369 †
An experimental comparison of RGB, YIQ, LAB, HSV, and opponent color models. HCI-0381 †

## Storage devices

The CD ROM handbook. ● 0678
An historical perspective of CD ROM. 0679
Compact disc–interactive. 0680
Digital video interactive. 0681
Artificial intelligence systems. 0683
Practical applications of optical disk image systems in document management. 04041

## Vector display devices

User interface management systems. 0233
An improved automatic lipreading system to enhance speech recognition. 02859

## I.3.2 Graphics Systems (C.2.1, C.2.4, C.3)

Using an object-oriented programming language to create audience-driven hypermedia environments. 0101
Ergonomics and the new technologies. 0147
Pogo: a declarative representation system for graphics. 0476
An integrated color smalltalk-80 system. 01127
Embedded menus: selecting items in context. 01320
Graphics fundamentals for a PCB-CAD PC system. 02494
A debugger for a graphical workstation. 02623
Iconic shells for multitasking workstations. 02792
A library for incremental update of bitmap images. 02836
Creating user interfaces by demonstration. ● HCI-0008 †
Hypertext/hypermedia. ● HCI-0047 †
Compact disc-interactive: a designer's overview. ● HCI-0078 †

[I. COMPUTING METHODOLOGIES]  CATEGORY INDEX

The database designer's workbench. HCI-0249 †
Graphic design for computer graphics. HCI-0376 †
A performing medium for working group graphics. HCI-0383 †
Interactive critical path analysis (ICPA)—microcomputer implementation of a project management and knowledge engineering tool. HCI-0445 †

**CLAM** *see* Proper Noun Index

### Distributed/network graphics

An experiment in integrated multimedia conferencing. 0381
CLAM- an open system for graphical user interfaces. 01117
Managing multiple context-frames through GKS. 01389
A personal computer based graphic workstation. 02493
The X window system. HCI-0370 †

### Remote systems

Teleoperations and robotics: evolution and development. ● HCI-0068 †

### Stand-alone systems

Device-independent graphics: with examples from IBM personal computers. ● HCI-0070 †

### I.3.3 Picture/Image Generation

Color computer graphics in military cockpits. 0261
DVI—a digital multimedia technology. 01327
Computer Graphics. § 02810
The application of scene synthesis techniques to the display of multidimensional image data. HCI-0371 †
Geomatic: a 3-D graphic relief simulation system. HCI-0395 †

### Digitizing and scanning

Eye movements in reading: perceptual and language processes. ● 0609
Life before the chips: simulating digital video interactive technology. 01328
A hand biomechanics workstation. 02820

### Display algorithms

Geometric modelling. 0236
The user-computer interface in process control: a human factors engineering handbook. ● 0341
Advances in computer graphics hardware II. ● 0493
Progress in medical imaging. ● 0556
A cognitive approach for graph drawing. 01616
Optimal colors, phosphors, and illuminant characteristics of CRT displays: the algorithmic approach. 01710
Heuristic graph displayer for G-BASE. 02227

A personal computer based graphic workstation. 02493
Abstraction and integration in IDE, an editing and formatting environment. 03184
Selection and use of image features for segmentation of boundary images. 03305
Visual comfort as a criterion for designing display units. 03892
Displaying statistical information—ergonomic considerations. 03893
MIDAS: molecular interactive display and simulation. 04061
An aspect of aesthetics in human-computer communications: pretty windows. HCI-0213 †
Two-bit graphics. HCI-0372 †
An experimental evaluation of computer graphics imagery. HCI-0373 †

### Viewing algorithms

An experimental evaluation of computer graphics imagery. HCI-0373 †

### I.3.4 Graphics Utilities

Using an object-oriented programming language to create audience-driven hypermedia environments. 0101
Workstations and publication systems. ● 0264
Embedding graphics into documents by using a graphic-editor. 0266
A multitasking switchboard approach to user interface management. 01053
Computer graphics language bindings: programmer interface standards. 01473
Exchange of solid models: current state and future trends. 01475
Marcosby example in a graphical UIMS. 01831
Drag: a graph drawing system. 03183
Integration of graphical tools in a computer algebra system. 03847
Introducing windows to Unix: user expectations. 03924
Ten years of window systems—a retrospective view. 03926
SunDew—a distributed and extensible window system. 03927
Issues in window management design and implementation. 03928
A modular window system for Unix. 03929
Windows, viewports and structured display files. 03930
Partitioning of function in window systems. 03931
System aspects of low-cost bitmapped displays. 03932
Application program interface working group discussions. 03934
Application program interface working group final report. 03935
User interface working group discussions. 03936
User interface working group final report. 03937

CATEGORY INDEX [I. COMPUTING METHODOLOGIES]

Architecture working group discussions. 03938
Architecture working group final report. 03939
Application program interface task group. 03940
Structures task group. 03941
Future work. 03942
PICT: an interactive graphical programming environment. HCI-0143 †
Graphic design for computer graphics. HCI-0376 †
Testing and validation of IGES processors. HCI-0423 †

### Application packages

Direct manipulation: A step beyond programming languages. 0072
MacApp: An application framework. 0083
The problem of levels and automatic response generation in a "Let's Talk AboutIt" strategy. 0410
Microsoft windows 2.0 program development. ● 0446
User interface. 0621
Compact disc–interactive. 0680
A spreadsheet interface for logic programming. 0822
Skilled financial planning: the cost of translating ideas into action. 0834
How are windows used? Some notes on creating an empirically-based windowing benchmark task. 0903
A comparison of tiled and overlapping windows. 0904
Graphical data presentation for decision support systems. 01229
Claris CAD. 01310
Simulation of CNC controller features in graphics-based programming. 01568
Mainframe and microcomputer-based business graphics: end user computing comparisons and trends. 02805
Conman: a visual programming language for interactive graphics. 02811
Transferring skills from training to the actual work situation: the role of task application knowledge, action styles and job decision latitude. 02865
Dynamic construction of animated help from application context. 03123
A longitudinal study of spreadsheet program use. 03482
Quill: An extensible system for editing documents of mixed type. 03517
Language level persistence for an object-oriented application programming platform. 03522
Tree doctor, a software package for graphical manipulation and animation of tree structures. 03901
Methodology of window management. § 03923
The elements of graphing data. ● HCI-0035 †
Modern drafting: an introduction to CAD. ● HCI-0077 †
Composing user interfaces with InterViews. HCI-0131 †
Graphical prototyping of graphical tools. HCI-0375 †
A performing medium for working group graphics. HCI-0383 †
Geomatic: a 3-D graphic relief simulation system. HCI-0395 †

IDECAP: interactive pictorial information system for demographic and environmental planning applications. HCI-0411 †

### Graphics packages

Graphics programming in Turbo C. ● 0013
Object-oriented graphics. 0234
Computer graphics: A tool for the artist, designer and amateur. 0235
Planar maps: an interaction paradigm for graphic design. 0873
Learning and transfer for text and graphics editing with a direct manipulation interface. 0900
Animated graphical interfaces using temporal constraints. 0909
Defining constraints graphically. 0910
A user interface for multiple-process, turnkey systems targeted for the novice user. 0911
Videotex information packagers: a field study aimed at tomorrow's videotex authoring interface. 0962
Digital video interactive. 01308
GRAFLOG: understanding drawings through natural language. 01396
User-adaptive computer graphics. 02209
Graphics fundamentals for a PCB-CAD PC system. 02494
A model for graphical interaction. 02610
Parametric Fourier image characterization toolkit. 02798
Graphical search and replace. 02812
Multiple representation document development (extende abstract). 03518
FolioPub: A publication management system. 03520
Supporting document development with concordia. 03521
Tree doctor, a software package for graphical manipulation and animation of tree structures. 03901
Computer graphics. ● HCI-0069 †
Device-independent graphics: with examples from IBM personal computers. ● HCI-0070 †
The X window system. HCI-0370 †
Managing the semantic content of graphical data. HCI-0374 †
CNS-HLS mapping using fuzzy sets. HCI-0380 †

**GKS** *see* Proper Noun Index

**PHIGS** *see* Proper Noun Index

**PICT** *see* Proper Noun Index

### Picture description languages

Geometric modelling. 0236
Videotex information packagers: a field study aimed at tomorrow's videotex authoring interface. 0962

[I. COMPUTING METHODOLOGIES]

PICT: an interactive graphical programming environment. HCI-0143 †
Computer-aided hierarchical diagrams. HCI-0160 †

### Software support

Towards a comprehensive user interface management system. 0081
A graphics interface for linear programming. 01332
A user-interface toolkit in object-oriented PostScript. 01391
Editing templates: a user interface generation tool. 01827
Business graphics trends, two years later. 01945
Icons at the interface: their usefulness. 02065
Support for tentative design: incorporating the screen image, as a graphical object, into PROLOG. 02116
Graphics through the looking glass. 02391
Graphbug - a microprocessor software debugging tool. 02496
GMB: a tool for manipulating and animating graph data structures. 02636
The design and evaluation of an animated programming environment. 03220
Interaction with IBS: an Icon-based system. 03838
The elements of graphing data. ● HCI-0035 †
The X window system. HCI-0370 †
Two-bit graphics. HCI-0372 †
Graphical prototyping of graphical tools. HCI-0375 †
The electronic classroom: workstations for teaching. HCI-0436 †

### I.3.5 Computational Geometry and Object Modeling

Graphics programming in Turbo C. ● 0013
Fundamentals of engineering drawing: with an introduction to interactive computer graphics for design and production, (9th ed.). ● 0531
Manipulation of 3D imagery. 0557
CAD Based Programming for Sensory Robots. ● 0597
The multimedia object presentation manager of MINOS: a symmetric approach. 01083
An object-oriented approach to multimedia databases. 01084
What is the role of the intermediary in end-user training?. 02522
Computer Graphics. § 02810
Database maps. 03286
Computational Geometry and its Applications. § 03850
Low cost geometric modelling system for CAM. 03866
The CADME approach to the interface of solid modellers. 03867
Graph-theoretic concepts in computer science. § 03885
Editing graphical objects using procedural representations. 04056

### Curve, surface, solid, and object representations

Advances in Computer Graphics III. ● 0231
VLSI for solid modelling. 0232
Computer graphics: A tool for the artist, designer and amateur. 0235
Geometric modelling. 0236
CAD data exchange. 0237
Advances in computer graphics hardware II. ● 0493
Pixel-planes 4: a summary. 0495
A multi-processor workstation with a logic-enhanced distributed frame buffer. 0496
Off-line programming of robots using 3D graphical simulation system. 0602
Off-line programming and path generation for robot manipulators. 0603
Model generation and modification for dynamic systems from geometric data. 0604
Snap-dragging. 01052
Curve tailoring with interactive computer. 01209
A top down method for interactive drawing. 01401
Automatic construction of surfaces with prescribed shape. 01474
Exchange of solid models: current state and future trends. 01475
A PC-interactives stereonet plotting program. 01504
CAD system GISK for interactive graphical modelling of planar mechanisms. 01570
Counting, computing, and the representation of numbers. 01771
DYNABOARD: user animated display of deductive proofs in mathematics. 02221
Interactive curve drawing by segmented Bezier approximation with a control parameter. 02535
Portfolio: kaleidoscopic visions. 02551
Describing surfaces. 02699
Graphical search and replace. 02812
A study in interactive 3-D rotation using 2-D control devices. 02813
Getting graphics in gear: graphics and dynamics in driving simulation. 02818
Applications of computer graphics to the visualization of meteorological data. 02819
A hand biomechanics workstation. 02820
An introduction to Gargoyle: an interactive illustration tool. 03185
A gesture based text editor. 03232
Automatizing geometric proofs and constructions. 03851
High performance interactive graphics: modeling, rendering and animating for IBM PCs and compatibles. ● HCI-0071 †

CATEGORY INDEX [I. COMPUTING METHODOLOGIES]

## *Geometric algorithms, languages, and systems*

VLSI for solid modelling. 0232
A two-dimensional frame buffer processor. 0494
CAD-based off-line programming applied to a cleaning and deburring workstation. 0607
SML: a solid modelling language. 01471
Unified interactive geometric modeller for simulating highly complex environments. 01472
Automatic construction of surfaces with prescribed shape. 01474
A computer aided design system for artistic chinese fonts. 02455
An introduction to Gargoyle: an interactive illustration tool. 03185
Interactive solid modeling in hut design. 03837
Automatizing geometric proofs and constructions. 03851
A simple, general method for ray tracing bicubic surfaces. 03853
Geometric continuity with interpolating Bézier curves. 03857

## *Hierarchy and geometric transformations*

Device-independent graphics: with examples from IBM personal computers. ● HCI-0070 †

## *Modeling packages*

Geometric modelling. 0236
CAD data exchange. 0237
A workcell application design environment (WADE). 0598
Off-line programming of robots using 3D graphical simulation system. 0602
Off-line programming and path generation for robot manipulators. 0603
A top down method for interactive drawing. 01401
CAD system GISK for interactive graphical modelling of planar mechanisms. 01570
Interactive CAD/CAM in engineering industry. 01571
Grasping reality through illusion—interactive graphics serving science. 02857
Graphics-based qualitative simulation generator for power distribution systems. 02946
Interactive 3-D modeling with personal computers. 03296
MIDAS: molecular interactive display and simulation. 04061

## I.3.6 Methodology and Techniques

Creating highly-interactive and graphical user interfaces by demonstration. 0084
Design factors for successful videodisc-based instruction. 0277
CAD Based Programming for Sensory Robots. ● 0597
An integrated data description language for coding design knowledge. 0717
Office-by-example: an integrated office system and database manager. 01159
Abstract interaction tools: a language for user interface management systems. 01162
Of mice and menus: designing the user-friendly interface. 01837
Human-computer interaction: a design guide. ● HCI-0041 †
Computer graphics. ● HCI-0069 †
Icon semantics—a formal approach to icon system design. HCI-0161 †
Graphic design for computer graphics. HCI-0376 :8E
The human factors of computer graphics interaction techniques. HCI-0377 †

## *Device independence*

Online information, hypermedia, and the idea of literacy. 0112
Constraint grammars–a new model for specifying graphical applications. 0875
Interactive graphics: a tool for beginning programming students in discovering solutions to novel problems. 01038
Automating the design of graphical presentations of relational information. 01150
Logical input devices and interaction. 01393
Can cognitive complexity theory (CCT) produce an adequate measure of system usability?. 03229
Device-independent graphics: with examples from IBM personal computers. ● HCI-0070 †
The X window system. HCI-0370 †
Pushdown automata for user interface management. HCI-0382 †

## *Ergonomics*

The algorithmic approach in ergonomics: the case of optimal colours and ambients for display work. 0247
Color displays and color science. 0255
Human factors for color display systems: concepts, methods, and research. 0256
Visual parameters for color CRTs. 0257
Perceptual color spaces for computer graphics. 0258
Ergonomic vision. 0259
Color graphic displays for network planning and design. 0260
Color computer graphics in military cockpits. 0261
Color displays for medical imaging. 0262
A study in two-handed input. 0933
The development of ergonomic standards. 0987
Posture and VDU operator satisfaction. 0988

[I. COMPUTING METHODOLOGIES]     CATEGORY INDEX

Information detective: a workstation for exploring three dimensional information space. 01010
Item selection from menus: the influence of menu organization, query interpretation, and programming experience on selection strategies. 01011
Automating the design of graphical presentations of relational information. 01150
Rooms: the use of multiple virtual workspaces to reduce space contention in a window-based graphical user interface. 01151
Graphical interaction management. 01390
Making drawings talk: pictures in minds and machines. 01392
Contingent aftereffects and isoluminance: psychophysical evidence for separation of color, orientation, and motion. 01463
Nested structures of control: an intuitive view. 01464
Machines should not see as people do, but must know how people see. 01465
Selection of image primitives for general-purpose visual processing. 01467
Computer graphics language bindings: programmer interface standards. 01473
Effects of graphic boundaries in tabular displays: a human factors evaluation. 01526
Designing screens for people to use easily. 01531
Optimal colors, phosphors, and illuminant characteristics of CRT displays: the algorithmic approach. 01710
The effects of set size on color matching using CRT displays. 01711
Reading from microfiche, a VDT, and the printed page: subjective fatigue and performance. 01712
Intermittent illumination from visual display units and fluorescent lighting affects movements of the eyes across text. 01713
On the selection and evaluation of visual display symbology: factors influencing search and identification times. 01718
Reading from CRT displays can be as fast as reading from paper. 01758
An experimental study of Chinese information displays on VDTs. 01784
Reader-controlled computerized presentation of text. 01785
Magnification effects with imaging displays depend on scene content and viewing condition. 01786
Performance measurement during simulated air-to-air combat. 01787
Visual control of displacement at slow speeds. 01797
Visual Displays: the highlighting Paradox. 01799
User interface management and graphics standards. 01964
Display legibility guidelines: a design aid. 01983
Understanding and evaluating a computer graphics display. 01984

User-adaptive computer graphics. 02209
The effects of display formats on information systems design. 02357
The effects of modes of information presentation on decision-making: a review and meta-analysis. 02358
Graphics. 02554
Motion interpolation by optimal control. 02817
A gesture based text editor. 03232
Towards the construction of a maximally-contrasting set of colours. 03233
Automatic generation of graphical user interfaces. 03290
Psychology and the user interface: science is soft at the frontier. 03297
Eliminating the dichotomy between scripting and interaction. 03299
Part structure for 3-D sketching. 03300
The efficiency of letter perception in function of color combinations: a study of video-screen colors. 03616
Looking at workstation architectures from the viewpoint of interaction. 03787
A user interface design tool. 03798
A new graphics user interface for accessing a database. 03839
Visual business graphics query interface. 03840
The interactive planning work station: a graphics-based UNIX tool for application users and developers. 03860
The Higgens UIMS and its efficient implementation of Undo. 03861
Interface abstractions for an *naplps* page creation system. 03863
Colour coding scales and computer graphics. 03864
Human-computer interaction: psychonomic aspects. § 03887
Introduction: human-computer interaction: psychonomic aspects. 03888
The legibility of visual display texts. 03889
The use of color in visual displays. 03890
Visual fatigue with work on visual display units: the current state of knowledge. 03891
Visual comfort as a criterion for designing display units. 03892
Displaying statistical information—ergonomic considerations. 03893
Factors influencing the detection of trend deviations on VDTs. 03894
Visual presentation of text: the process of reading from a psycholinguistic perspective. 03895
The effect on reading speed of word divisions at the end of a line. 03896
Document processing. 03897
A comparison of presentation and representation: linguistic and pictorial. 03898
Tree doctor, a software package for graphical manipulation and animation of tree structures. 03901

# CATEGORY INDEX

[I. COMPUTING METHODOLOGIES]

Textvision: elicitation and acquisition of conceptual knowledge by graphic representation and multiwindowing. 03902
Real-time processing of cursive writing and sketched graphics. 03908
Introducing windows to Unix: user expectations. 03924
SunDew—a distributed and extensible window system. 03927
Issues in window management design and implementation. 03928
User interface working group discussions. 03936
User interface working group final report. 03937
Application program interface task group. 03940
Future work. 03942
A comparison of the effects of computer-assisted instruction, interactive video, and traditional instruction on third-grade students in art education. 04064
Experimentation with an adaptive search strategy for solving a keyboard design/configuration problem. 04070
The elements of graphing data. ● HCI-0035 †
Human performance engineering: using human factors/ergonomics to achieve computer system usability (2nd ed.). ● HCI-0042 †
Teleoperations and robotics: applications and technology. ● HCI-0068 †
Behavioral experiments on handmarkings. HCI-0201 †
Human factors issues in VDT use: environmental and workstation design considerations. HCI-0210 †
Cognitive attributes: implications for display design in supervisory control systems. HCI-0242 †
Testing bibliographic displays for online catalogs. HCI-0285 †
An experimental evaluation of computer graphics imagery. HCI-0373 †
The human factors of computer graphics interaction techniques. HCI-0377 †
Physiological principles for the effective use of color. HCI-0378 †
Real time graphic simulation of visual effects of egomotion. HCI-0379 †
CNS-HLS mapping using fuzzy sets. HCI-0380 †
An experimental comparison of RGB, YIQ, LAB, HSV, and opponent color models. HCI-0381 †
The use of colour in language syntax analysis. HCI-0385 †
Color and the computer in cartography. HCI-0386 †

## Interaction techniques

Second IEEE Conference on Computer Workstations: proceedings. ● 0002
Interactive 3D computer graphics. ● 0012
Graphics programming in Turbo C. ● 0013
Towards a comprehensive user interface management system. 0081
Investigations in multimedia design documentation. 0116
Supporting collaboration in hypermedia: issues and experiences. 0117
The missing link: why we're all doing hypertext wrong. 0118
Reflections on authoring, editing, and managing hypertext. 0119
Authoring tools for complex document sets. 0120
From database to hypertext via electronic publishing: an information odyssey. 0122
Techniques of user message design: developing a user message system to support cooperative work. 0127
Escher effects in online text. 0130
Learning by doing with simulated intelligent help. 0132
Space. 0134
Military systems. 0138
Advances in Computer Graphics III. ● 0231
VLSI for solid modelling. 0232
User interface management systems. 0233
Object-oriented graphics. 0234
Computer graphics: A tool for the artist, designer and amateur. 0235
Geometric modelling. 0236
CAD data exchange. 0237
Desktop publishing. 0238
Presenting documents on workstation screens. 0267
GENIE-M: A generator for multimedia information environments. 0268
A coherent specification method for the human interface to documentation systems. 0269
Application of structural pattern recognition in histopathology. 0295
Interactive Toolkit. ● 0340
Human factors and artificial intelligence. 0408
The gift of good design tools. 0411
Design and implementation of an object-oriented user interface management system. 0412
A system for evaluating screen formats: Research and application. 0413
User performance with command, menu, and iconic interfaces. 0414
Keyboarding for personal computer use. ● 0492
A two-dimensional frame buffer processor. 0494
Pixel-planes 4: a summary. 0495
A multi-processor workstation with a logic-enhanced distributed frame buffer. 0496
Algebra slaves and agents in a Logo-based mathematics curriculum. 0517
Fundamentals of engineering drawing: with an introduction to interactive computer graphics for design and production, (9th ed.). ● 0531
The computer as a tool for learning through reflection. 0535
Enhancing incremental learning processes with knowledge-based systems. 0538

## [I. COMPUTING METHODOLOGIES]

Computer-aided model building. 0544
Xlib programming manual for version 11: Vol. 1. • 0561
X window system user's guide for version 11: vol. 3. • 0562
Diamond: A multimedia message system built on a distributed architecture. 0574
A workcell application design environment (WADE). 0598
Robot simulation and off-line programming—an integrated CAE-CAD approach. 0599
CAD Based verification and refinement of high level compliant motion primitives. 0600
Experiences with off-line robot programming via standardized interfaces. 0601
Off-line programming of robots using 3D graphical simulation system. 0602
Off-line programming and path generation for robot manipulators. 0603
Model generation and modification for dynamic systems from geometric data. 0604
Modeling of robot system dynamics for CAD based robot programming. 0605
Computer aided application program synthesis for industrial robots. 0606
CAD-based off-line programming applied to a cleaning and deburring workstation. 0607
Production management systems. 0619
User interface. 0621
Systems analysis techniques. 0622
An architecture of a distributed window system and its FCP implementation. 0676
Object oriented programming in Concurrent Prolog. 0677
Digital video interactive. 0681
The disconnection: how to interface computers and video. • 0703
An integrated data description language for coding design knowledge. 0717
The computational science revolution: technology, methodology, and sociology. 0728
Coherent and chaotic structures in 2D vortex dynamics: progress and problems. 0729
Computing needs in thunderstorm modeling: supercomputers and interactive graphics. 0730
Bringing graphic dialogues to APL. 0765
Color in user interface design: functionally and aesthetics. 0803
LIZA: an extensible groupware toolkit. 0805
Collaboration in KMS, a shared hypermedia system. 0807
What is EuroParc?. 0812
NASA Johnson Space Center, Human-Computer Interaction. 0815
Inducing programs in a direct-manipulation environment. 0816
A spreadsheet interface for logic programming. 0822

How some advice fails. 0824
Skilled financial planning: the cost of translating ideas into action. 0834
A case study of user interface management system development and application. 0836
A high-level user interface management system. 0838
Graphical specification of user interfaces with behavior abstraction. 0840
CHI research at MCC. 0842
Bat brushes: on the uses of six position and orientation parameters in a paint program. 0846
Circling: a method of mouse-based selection without button presses. 0847
Systemic implications of leap and an improved two-part cursor. 0848
A programming language basis for user interface. 0849
Task-oriented representation of asynchronous user interfaces. 0851
Performance, preference, and visual scan patterns on a menu-based system: implications for interface design. 0855
Synergistic use of direct manipulation and natural language. 0857
A synthetic visual environment with hand gesturing and voice input. 0858
Speech and gestures for graphic image manipulation. 0859
Design rationale: the argument behind the artifact. 0860
The role of laboratory experiments in HCI: help, hindrance, or ho-hum?. 0863
Design environments for constructive and argumentative design. 0864
Generating highly interactive user interfaces. 0865
Planar maps: an interaction paradigm for graphic design. 0873
Encapsulating interactive behaviors. 0874
The effects of device technology on the usability of advanced telephone functions. 0876
An experiment into the use of auditory cues to reduce visual workload. 0877
Helgon: extending the retrieval by reformulation paradigm. 0880
User-interface design for a clinical neurophysiological intensive monitoring system. 0881
Models of user interactions with graphical interfaces: 1. statistical. 0883
Graphic interfaces for knowledge-based system development. 0892
Generalized fisheye views. 0893
TNT: a talking tutor 'n' trainer for teaching use of interactive computer systems. 0895
Learning and transfer for text and graphics editing with a direct manipulation interface. 0900
A test of a common elements theory of transfer. 0901
How are windows used? Some notes on creating an empirically-based windowing benchmark task. 0903

## CATEGORY INDEX [I. COMPUTING METHODOLOGIES]

DOMAIN/DELPHI: retrieving documents online. 0906
Animated graphical interfaces using temporal constraints. 0909
Defining constraints graphically. 0910
A study in two-handed input. 0933
Classification of dialog techniques. 0960
An empirical approach to the evaluation of icons. 01013
Designing the "cockpit": the application of a human-centered design philosophy to make optimization systems accessible. 01016
FINGER—Formalizing Interaction for Gesture Recognition. 01017
Application frameworks: experience with MacApp. 01039
IBM 3270 full screen interactive programming without CICS. 01040
The impact of menus and command-level feedback on learners' acquisition of data base language skills. 01041
Snap-dragging. 01052
Creating highly-interactive and graphical user interfaces by demonstration. 01054
An object-oriented user interface management system. 01055
Principles of traditional animation applied to 3D computer animation. 01072
A development environment for horizontal microcode programs. 01079
An object-oriented framework for interactive data graphics. 01115
Rooms: the use of multiple virtual workspaces to reduce space contention in a window-based graphical user interface. 01151
A survey of three dialogue models. 01152
Curve tailoring with interactive computer. 01209
A man-machine interface for computer-aided and simulation of control systems. 01237
A cognitively based methodology for evaluating human performance in the computer-aided design task domain. 01240
A feature matching approach to the retrieval of graphical information. 01245
Efforts of display format on proof-reading with VDUs. 01246
A simple windowing system, part 1: basic principles. 01286
Face to face with Open Look. 01305
Digital video interactive. 01308
Domesticating microsoft windows. 01309
Claris CAD. 01310
The Mac interface: showing its age. 01311
Bringing image processing into focus. 01317
Embedded menus: selecting items in context. 01320
Virtual video editing in interactive multimedia applications. 01326
DVI—a digital multimedia technology. 01327
Life before the chips: simulating digital video interactive technology. 01328
Intelligent interactive video simulation of a code inspection. 01329
A graphics interface for linear programming. 01332
The adaptable user interface. 01337
Segue: support for distributed graphical interfaces. 01369
Managing multiple context-frames through GKS. 01389
Graphical interaction management. 01390
A user-interface toolkit in object-oriented PostScript. 01391
Logical input devices and interaction. 01393
An editor for constructing graphics with $T_EX$. 01394
Architectures of graphic processors for interactive 2D graphics. 01395
GRAFLOG: understanding drawings through natural language. 01396
Experience with chisl, a configurable hierarchical interface specification language. 01397
Construction of interactive programs in computer graphics. 01398
A top down method for interactive drawing. 01401
The controller animation system. 01402
Design of a graphics interface for computer-based biomedical applications. 01427
A new algorithm for extracting the interior of bounded regions based on chain coding. 01469
Unified interactive geometric modeller for simulating highly complex environments. 01472
Automatic construction of surfaces with prescribed shape. 01474
Exchange of solid models: current state and future trends. 01475
Interactive graphic editor for analysis and enhancement of medical images. 01492
A PC-interactives stereonet plotting program. 01504
A graphical database interface. 01511
A graphics interface to an engineering economy program. 01520
Simulation of CNC controller features in graphics-based programming. 01568
Successful use of CADCAM—a combination of technology, organization, and people. 01569
CAD system GISK for interactive graphical modelling of planar mechanisms. 01570
Interactive CAD/CAM in engineering industry. 01571
Interactive color graphical postprocessing as a unifying influence in numerical analysis research. 01684
An interactive approach to local remeshing around a propagating crack. 01685
A graphics system architecture for interactive application-specific display functions. 01822
An interactive procedure for constructing line and circle tangencies. 01823
PHIGS: a standard, dynamic, interactive graphics interface. 01826
Editing templates: a user interface generation tool. 01827

## [I. COMPUTING METHODOLOGIES]

Interactive design of 3D computer-animated legged animal motion. 01828
Near-real-time control of human figure models. 01829
Marcosby example in a graphical UIMS. 01831
Using perceptual organization to extract 3-D structures. 01842
The tinkertoy graphical programming environment. 01850
Semantic feedback in the Higgens UIMS. 01851
Relativized Arthur-Merlin versus Merlin-Arthur games. 01912
Interactive data visualization. 01986
Tools for reading and browsing hypertext. 02014
Linkage versus integration for binding database and interactive graphics systems. 02040
GISD: a graphical interactive system for conceptual database design. 02042
A powerful solution meets an overwhelming problem. 02053
A knowledge-based system with audio-visual aids. 02068
User-adaptive computer graphics. 02209
Modelling blind users' interactions with an auditory computer interface. 02237
Mapping the manipulator workspace using interactive computer graphics. 02257
Interactive videodiscs control and computer-based training on the Apple Macintosh. 02305
An interactive modeling program for DNA. 02385
An interactive biomolecule graphics system. 02386
The MIDAS database system. 02387
The MIDAS display system. 02388
MOL3D, a modular and interactive program for molecular modeling and conformational analysis: I—basic modules. 02389
Graphics through the looking glass. 02391
Linkage versus integration for binding database and interactive graphics systems. 02406
The effect of task demands and graphical format on information processing strategies. 02482
A personal computer based graphic workstation. 02493
Graphics fundamentals for a PCB-CAD PC system. 02494
Interactive curve drawing by segmented Bezier approximation with a control parameter. 02535
Algorithm for interactive forming matrix data representation and estimation of its efficiency. 02536
User interface wars: the next wave. 02544
Building a great windows system. 02550
Graphics. 02554
Image processing with personal computers. 02581
An interactive simulator for the designing of woven fabric structures second place. 02583
Visual interactive simulation - history, recent developments, and major issues. 02585
Interactive graphics in GPSS/PC. 02586

A model for graphical interaction. 02610
A VLSI interactive layout editor (VILE). 02611
GPROC—an integrated system for the processing of numerical scientific data. 02631
Brushing scatterplots. 02672
Conman: a visual programming language for interactive graphics. 02811
Graphical search and replace. 02812
A study in interactive 3-D rotation using 2-D control devices. 02813
High-performance polygon rendering. 02814
Virtual graphics. 02815
A display system for the Stellar Graphics Supercomputer Model GS1000. 02816
Grasping reality through illusion—interactive graphics serving science. 02857
Exploratory evaluation of a planar foot-operated cursor-positioning device. 02858
Improving the accuracy of touch screens: an experimental evaluation of three strategies. 02860
Perspectives on algorithm animation. 02861
A graphical programming language interface for an intelligent LISP tutor. 02862
A grammar-based approach to automatic generation of user-interface dialogues. 02868
The design of auditory interfaces for visually disabled users. 02869
Multifunctional cursor for direct manipulation user interfaces. 02870
An empirical comparison of pie vs. linear menus. 02871
Color-coding categories in menus. 02872
Transfer between menu systems. 02873
Navigating integrated facilities: initiating and terminating interaction sequences. 02876
Pictures and category labels as navigational aids for catalog browsing. 02877
Choosing between methods: analysing the user's decision space in terms of schemas and linear models. 02879
Misconceived misconceptions?. 02881
Groupware: interface design for meetings. 02883
How users repeat their actions on computers: principles for design of history mechanisms. 02885
Planning for advising. 02886
Justified advice: a semi-naturalistic study of advisory strategies. 02887
UIMSs: threat or menace?. 02889
Designing keybindings to be easy to learn and resistant to forgetting even when the set of commands is large. 02890
Effects of interface design upon user productivity. 02891
Development of an instrument measuring user satisfaction of the human-computer interface. 02892

## CATEGORY INDEX

## [I. COMPUTING METHODOLOGIES]

Multimodal response planning: an adaptive rule based approach. 02894
SAUCI: a knowledge-based interface architecture. 02895
Travel around a learning support environment: rambling, orienteering or touring?. 02900
g - A compact language for real-time graphics. 02906
Interactive performance display and debugging using the NCUBE real-time graphicssystem. 02907
Using hypertext to overcome the knowledge base development bottleneck: a case study. 02914
Symbiotic systems for complex problems. 02922
Experience of constructing a fault localisation expert system using an AI toolkit. 02923
The network control assistant (NCA), a real-time prototype expert system for network management. 02930
Process design of oil and gas production facilities using expert systems. 02933
ProCEED: an expert system for multivariate process control systems design. 02935
An expert database for material and production planning. 02937
Evaluating the impact of camera placement on teleoperator efficiency. 02940
Graphics-based qualitative simulation generator for power distribution systems. 02946
Understanding text with an accompanying diagram. 02947
SIMTALK: Pros and cons of natural language for manufacturing simulation. 02950
The design of a traffic control expert system for long distance network contingencies. 02952
Jet engine technical advisor (JETA). 02974
An interactive tolerance system. 02975
Hierarchical scheduling in an intelligent environmental control system. 02976
Planning as feedback to designers. 02978
DORUS: an architecture for dynamic optimal resource utilization systems. 02979
A process oriented approach to an intelligent design aid. 02980
Computer aided concurrent design for printed wiring boards. 02981
An operations advisor for an on-line computer banking system with graphics interface. 02983
Extending knowledge-based systems through closely-coupled graphics and windows. 02985
An advisory system for digital logic simulation. 02986
Embedded training in AI technology through an expert system interface: an alarm processor application. 02991
Monitoring and performance measuring distributed systems during operation. 03025
Design and implementation of the UW Illustrated compiler. 03059
Debugging concurrent processes: a case study. 03060
Informational zooming: an interaction model for the graphical access to text knowledge bases. 03073
A design data manager. 03090
EDGE - a graph based tool for specifying interaction. 03106
Extensions to C for interface programming. 03108
An overview of the C toolkit. 03109
The architecture of a user interface toolkit. 03110
Designing the interface designer's interface. 03116
Building user interfaces by direct manipulation. 03120
GRASS3, a language for interactive graphics. 03170
An introduction to Gargoyle: an interactive illustration tool. 03185
Optimum display arrangements for presenting visual reminders. 03237
Database maps. 03286
An editing model for generating graphical user interfaces. 03289
Automatic generation of graphical user interfaces. 03290
The interactive specification of human animation. 03292
Virya—a motion control editor for kinematic and dynamic animation. 03294
Interactive 3-D modeling with personal computers. 03296
Psychology and the user interface: science is soft at the frontier. 03297
Eliminating the dichotomy between scripting and interaction. 03299
Part structure for 3-D sketching. 03300
Interfacing image processing and computer graphics systems using an artificial visual system. 03301
Coupling visual and dynamic features to study handwritten signatures. 03309
Issues in modeling supervisory control in flexible manufacturing systems. 03363
Sources of Difficulty in troubleshooting automated manufacturing systems. 03367
Individualizing the man-machine interface. 03404
Man-machine interfaces for mobile robotic systems. 03413
Safety considerations in robot design. 03418
Gribs—an approach to a realistic realtime simulation of human arm motion. 03432
Health and productivity issues of CAD/CAM systems. 03436
Acting-out and burn-out behaviours of operators monitoring automated systems. 03440
Quill: An extensible system for editing documents of mixed type. 03517
Multiple representation document development (extende abstract). 03518
A hypertext system to manage software life cycle documents. 03519
FolioPub: A publication management system. 03520
Supporting document development with concordia. 03521

## [I. COMPUTING METHODOLOGIES]

Language level persistence for an object-oriented application programming platform. 03522
Prototyping user interfaces for applications depicted by graphs. 03523
The control structure diagram: an automated graphical representation for software. 03524
Segue: Support for distributed graphical interfaces. 03526
The PFG environment: parallel programming with petri net semantics. 03527
Building interprocess communication models using Stile. 03528
A visual programming language designed for automatic programming. 03529
An efficient high-level man-machine interface. 03530
A graphical entity-relationship database browser. 03532
A consideration of learning in speech recognition from the viewpoint of AI class-description learning. 03533
jThe assessment of human/computer performance: a case for connectivity. 03535
The design of a flexible distributed testbeb for communication systems. 03538
A cost model for estimating the costs of developing software in the Ada programming language. 03539
Knowledge acquisition via a graphical interface. 03572
Object-oriented signal processing systems. 03573
Display architecture for VLSI-based graphics workstations. 03786
Looking at workstation architectures from the viewpoint of interaction. 03787
A set of tools supporting the software design based on SDL. 03803
Interactive solid modeling in hut design. 03837
Interaction with IBS: an Icon-based system. 03838
A new graphics user interface for accessing a database. 03839
Visual business graphics query interface. 03840
Multiple inheritance and genericity for the integration of a database management system in an object-oriented approach. 03844
ROSE: An object-oriented database system for interactive computer graphics applications. 03845
Automatizing geometric proofs and constructions. 03851
A simple, general method for ray tracing bicubic surfaces. 03853
HutWindows: an improved architecture for a user interface management system. 03854
A gestural representation of the process of composing Chinese temples. 03855
Geometric continuity with interpolating Bézier curves. 03857
ANIMENGINE: an engineering animation system. 03858
Towards an integrated view of 3-D computer animation. 03859
The interactive planning work station: a graphics-based UNIX tool for application users and developers. 03860
Graphics interaction in databases. 03862

A graphics interface for interactive simulation of packet-switched networks. 03869
Challenges in the application of graphics technology to the management of geographic information. 03871
Human-computer interaction: psychonomic aspects. § 03887
Introduction: human-computer interaction: psychonomic aspects. 03888
Tree doctor, a software package for graphical manipulation and animation of tree structures. 03901
Textvision: elicitation and acquisition of conceptual knowledge by graphic representation and multiwindowing. 03902
Real-time processing of cursive writing and sketched graphics. 03908
Introducing windows to Unix: user expectations. 03924
A comparison of some window managers. 03925
Ten years of window systems—a retrospective view. 03926
SunDew—a distributed and extensible window system. 03927
Issues in window management design and implementation. 03928
A modular window system for Unix. 03929
Windows, viewports and structured display files. 03930
Partitioning of function in window systems. 03931
System aspects of low-cost bitmapped displays. 03932
A window manager for bitmapped displays and Unix. 03933
Application program interface working group discussions. 03934
Application program interface working group final report. 03935
User interface working group discussions. 03936
User interface working group final report. 03937
Architecture working group discussions. 03938
Architecture working group final report. 03939
Application program interface task group. 03940
Structures task group. 03941
Future work. 03942
GKSGRAL—software and hardware realizations of the graphical kernel system. 03982
Implementation of a VDA interface in the CAD system STRIM 100. 03983
Online library catalogues as information retrieval systems: what can we learn from research?. 04040
Practical applications of optical disk image systems in document management. 04041
Editing graphical objects using procedural representations. 04056
MIDAS: molecular interactive display and simulation. 04061
A comparison of the effects of computer-assisted instruction, interactive video, and traditional instruction on third-grade students in art education. 04064

Assessing the usability of user interfaces: guidance and online help features. 04065
Human factors and interactive computer systems. § HCI-0038 †
Cooperative interfaces to information systems. ● HCI-0066 †
Principles of interactive computer graphics (2nd ed.). ● HCI-0069 †
Device-independent graphics: with examples from IBM personal computers. ● HCI-0070 †
High performance interactive graphics: modeling, rendering and animating for IBM PCs and compatibles. ● HCI-0071 †
The AutoCAD productivity book: tapping the hidden power of AutoCAD. ● HCI-0076 †
Modern drafting: an introduction to CAD. ● HCI-0077 †
Supporting concurrency, communication, and synchronization in human-computer interaction—the Sassafras UIMS. HCI-0102 †
Pictorial interfaces to data bases. HCI-0116 †
MIKE: the menu interaction kontrol environment. HCI-0124 †
Graphical user interfaces. HCI-0133 †
Specification and generation of variable, personalized graphical interfaces. HCI-0134 †
PICT: an interactive graphical programming environment. HCI-0143 †
Behavioral experiments on handmarkings. HCI-0201 †
A generator of direct manipulation office systems. HCI-0250 †
A distributed interoffice mail system. HCI-0308 †
A window-based graphics frame store architecture. HCI-0369 †
The X window system. HCI-0370 †
Two-bit graphics. HCI-0372 †
Managing the semantic content of graphical data. HCI-0374 †
The human factors of computer graphics interaction techniques. HCI-0377 †
An experimental comparison of RGB, YIQ, LAB, HSV, and opponent color models. HCI-0381 †
Pushdown automata for user interface management. HCI-0382 †
A performing medium for working group graphics. HCI-0383 †
The next generation of interactive technologies. HCI-0384 †
The use of colour in language syntax analysis. HCI-0385 †
An image processing language with ICON-assisted navigation. HCI-0387 †
Geomatic: a 3-D graphic relief simulation system. HCI-0395 †
Computer-music interfaces: a survey. HCI-0412 †

CAD/CAM: integration in the automobile industry. HCI-0413 †
Goals in the application of CAD interfaces. HCI-0416 †
Graphical standards. HCI-0417 †
Interfaces for CAD applications. HCI-0418 †
Interfaces and data transfer formats in computer graphics systems. HCI-0419 †
VDAFS—a pragmatic interface for the exchange of sculptured surface data. HCI-0420 †
Approximation methods used in the exchange of geometric information via the VDA/VDMA surface interface. HCI-0421 †
A tentative implementation of VDAFS. HCI-0422 †
Testing and validation of IGES processors. HCI-0423 †

### Languages

Toward a theory of impasse-driven learning. 0536
Xlib programming manual for version 11: Vol. 1. ● 0561
X window system user's guide for version 11: vol. 3. ● 0562
Constraint-based tools for building user interfaces. 01153
GRAFLOG: understanding drawings through natural language. 01396
Experience with chisl, a configurable hierarchical interface specification language. 01397
A new algorithm for extracting the interior of bounded regions based on chain coding. 01469
Computer graphics language bindings: programmer interface standards. 01473
An interface architecture to provide adaptive task-specific context for the user. 02228
Conman: a visual programming language for interactive graphics. 02811
A graphical programming language interface for an intelligent LISP tutor. 02862
Building interfaces interactively. 03119
GRASS3, a language for interactive graphics. 03170
Segue: Support for distributed graphical interfaces. 03526
Interaction with IBS: an Icon-based system. 03838
The use of VDM on the specification of Chinese characters. 04038
Device-independent graphics: with examples from IBM personal computers. ● HCI-0070 †
Supporting concurrency, communication, and synchronization in human-computer interaction—the Sassafras UIMS. HCI-0102 †
Specification and generation of variable, personalized graphical interfaces. HCI-0134 †
Specification and generation of variable, personalized graphical interfaces. HCI-0134 †
Designing online information. HCI-0152 †
CNS-HLS mapping using fuzzy sets. HCI-0380 †
The use of colour in language syntax analysis. HCI-0385 †

### I.3.7 Three-Dimensional Graphics and Realism

Interactive 3D computer graphics. ● 0012
Advances in computer graphics II. ● 0437
CAD Based Programming for Sensory Robots. ● 0597
The mental rotation and perceived realism of computer-generated three-dimensional images. 02213
Codon constraints on closed 2D shapes. 02704
Computer Graphics. § 02810
Part structure for 3-D sketching. 03300
Connections in context: The intermedia system. 03534
Computational Geometry and its Applications. § 03850
Editing graphical objects using procedural representations. 04056
High performance interactive graphics: modeling, rendering and animating for IBM PCs and compatibles. ● HCI-0071 †
Geomatic: a 3-D graphic relief simulation system. HCI-0395 †

### Animation

Algorithm animation. ● 0186
Modeling of robot system dynamics for CAD based robot programming. 0605
Animated graphical interfaces using temporal constraints. 0909
Principles of traditional animation applied to 3D computer animation. 01072
Constraint-based tools for building user interfaces. 01153
Exploring algorithms using Balsa-II. 01367
The controller animation system. 01402
Interactive design of 3D computer-animated legged animal motion. 01828
Near-real-time control of human figure models. 01829
DYNABOARD: user animated display of deductive proofs in mathematics. 02221
The electronic book Ebook3. 02234
A system for the representation of human body movement from dance scores. 02540
Visual interactive simulation - history, recent developments, and major issues. 02585
Motion interpolation by optimal control. 02817
Getting graphics in gear: graphics and dynamics in driving simulation. 02818
Grasping reality through illusion—interactive graphics serving science. 02857
Perspectives on algorithm animation. 02861
Dynamic construction of animated help from application context. 03123
The design and evaluation of an animated programming environment. 03220
Animating human figures: perspectives and directions. 03291
The interactive specification of human animation. 03292
Speech and expression: a computer solution to face animation. 03293
Virya—a motion control editor for kinematic and dynamic animation. 03294
Near-real-time control of human figure models. 03295
Motion graphics, description and control. 03348
"Graphical marionette". 03349
A multiple track animator system for motion synchronization. 03350
Knowledge-based animation. 03351
3-D balance in legged locomotion: modeling and simulation for the one-legged case. 03352
Gribs—an approach to a realistic realtime simulation of human arm motion. 03432
Enhancing program readability and comprehensibility with tools for program visualization. 03510
Design and implementation of a supercomputer frame buffer system. 03543
ANIMENGINE: an engineering animation system. 03858
Towards an integrated view of 3-D computer animation. 03859
Tree doctor, a software package for graphical manipulation and animation of tree structures. 03901

### Color, shading, shadowing, and texture

Color and the computer. ● 0254
Color displays and color science. 0255
Human factors for color display systems: concepts, methods, and research. 0256
Visual parameters for color CRTs. 0257
Perceptual color spaces for computer graphics. 0258
Ergonomic vision. 0259
Color graphic displays for network planning and design. 0260
Color computer graphics in military cockpits. 0261
Color displays for medical imaging. 0262
Color and the instructional use of the computer. 0263
Advances in computer graphics hardware II. ● 0493
A two-dimensional frame buffer processor. 0494
A multi-processor workstation with a logic-enhanced distributed frame buffer. 0496
User interface design for computer systems. ● 0628
Bat brushes: on the uses of six position and orientation parameters in a paint program. 0846
An experiment into the use of auditory cues to reduce visual workload. 0877
Interactive color graphical postprocessing as a unifying influence in numerical analysis research. 01684
Using color dimensions to display data dimensions. 01766
Variability in brightness matching of colored lights. 01767
A computer aided design system for artistic chinese fonts. 02455
Perception of transparency in man and machine. 02697

Graphical search and replace. 02812
High-performance polygon rendering. 02814
Getting graphics in gear: graphics and dynamics in driving simulation. 02818
Applications of computer graphics to the visualization of meteorological data. 02819
Applications of computer graphics to the visualization of meteorological data. 02819
A hand biomechanics workstation. 02820
Grasping reality through illusion—interactive graphics serving science. 02857
Towards the construction of a maximally-contrasting set of colours. 03233
Image segmentation based on color and texture gradient. 03303
Principle of visual color coding applied to satellite images. 03304
Cortical representation of texture primitives. 03306
The efficiency of letter perception in function of color combinations: a study of video-screen colors. 03616
Colors in video displays. 03725
A colour atlas for graphical displays. 03726
Colour coding scales and computer graphics. 03864
An experimental evaluation of computer graphics imagery. HCI-0373 †
Physiological principles for the effective use of color. HCI-0378 †
Color and the computer in cartography. HCI-0386 †

### Visible line/surface algorithms

Advances in Computer Graphics III. ● 0231
VLSI for solid modelling. 0232
Geometric modelling. 0236
CAD data exchange. 0237
Problems in recognition of drawings. 0294
Advances in computer graphics hardware II. ● 0493
A two-dimensional frame buffer processor. 0494
Manipulation of 3D imagery. 0557
Model generation and modification for dynamic systems from geometric data. 0604
Line connectivity algorithms for an asynchronous pyramid computer. 01468
Describing surfaces. 02699
Environment-centered and viewer-centered perception of surface orientation. 02705
Active vision: integration of fixed and mobile cameras. 04017

### I.3.m Miscellaneous

The 'window' terminal. 01405
Evaluating formatted alphanumeric displays. 01525
Display proximity in multicue information integration: the benefits of boxes. 01763

Factors affecting the readability of moving text on a computer display. 01764
Information transfer rate with serial and simultaneous visual display formats. 01770
Spatial misorientation exacerbated by collimated virtual flight display. 01979
Icon-based human-computer interaction. 02113
Icon-based human-computer interaction. 02113
Considerations of menu structure and communication rate for the design of computer menu displays. 02124
A graphical thesaurus-based information retrieval system. 02243
Brushing scatterplots. 02672
Visual languages and human computer interaction. 03202
Learning graphics programming by direct communication. 03298
Interfacing image processing and computer graphics systems using an artificial visual system. 03301
Speeded phase discrimination: evidence for global to local processing. 03307
Interaction with IBS: an Icon-based system. 03838
Heuristic rules for visualization. 03868
Mapping images to a hierarchical data structure—a way to knowledge-based pattern recognition. 03954
An experimental evaluation of the impact of data display format on recall performance. HCI-0202 †
Human factors issues in VDT use: environmental and workstation design considerations. HCI-0210 †
Mainframe and microcomputer-based business graphics: What satisfies users?. HCI-0216 †
The human factors of computer graphics interaction techniques. HCI-0377 †

## I.4 IMAGE PROCESSING

Annual review of computer science vol. 1, 1986. ● 0719

### I.4.0 General

Vision, brain, and cooperative computation: an overview. 0015
Readings in computer vision: issues, problems, principles, and paradigms. ● 0296
VLSI image processing. ● 0563
Image understanding 1985-86. ● 0615
Optical systems that imitate human memory. 01576
Multidimensional attribute analyhsis and pattern recognition for seismic interpretation. 02530
Human and Machine Vision II. § 02696
Medical informatics: a personal view of sowing the seeds. 02841
The history of the use of computers in the interpretation of radiological images. 02845
Industrial & Engineering Applications of Artificial Intelligence & Expert Systems. § 02941

[I. COMPUTING METHODOLOGIES]     CATEGORY INDEX

XVISION: a comprehensive software system for image processing research, education, and applications. 03124
Document manipulation and typography. § 03182
Vidura—an interactive multilingual publishing system—specification & design. 03186
Chinese character processing system based on character-root combination and gra phic processing. 03187
Graphics Interface '86/Vision Interface '86. § 03288
Visual simulation. 03503
Advances in computer graphics hardware I. § 03785
Computational Geometry and its Applications. § 03850
Computer graphics 1987. § 03852
Computer-generated images: the state of the art. § 03856
Control of sensory processing - a hypothesis on and simulation of the architecture of an elementary cortical processor. 03972
Real-time object measurement and classification. § 03985
Sensors and sensory systems for advanced robots. § 04006
Signal processing and pattern recognition in nondestructive evaluation of materials. § 04019
Compact disc-interactive: a designer's overview. ● HCI-0078 †
Visual structure and the transmission of meaning. HCI-0404 †

*Image displays*

Color displays and color science. 0255
Human factors for color display systems: concepts, methods, and research. 0256
Visual parameters for color CRTs. 0257
Perceptual color spaces for computer graphics. 0258
Ergonomic vision. 0259
Color graphic displays for network planning and design. 0260
Color computer graphics in military cockpits. 0261
Color displays for medical imaging. 0262
Presenting documents on workstation screens. 0267
Progress in medical imaging. ● 0556
Manipulation of 3D imagery. 0557
The computational science revolution: technology, methodology, and sociology. 0728
Designing optimum CRT text blinking video image presentation. 0795
Why reading was slower from CRT displays than from paper. 0797
Interactive graphic editor for analysis and enhancement of medical images. 01492
On the selection and evaluation of visual display symbology: factors influencing search and identification times. 01718
Display formatting in information integration and nonintegration tasks. 01750

Effect of pixel height, display height, and vertical resolution on the detection of a simple vertical line signal in visual noise. 01753
Temporal resolution: an insight into the video display terminal (VDT) "problem". 01754
Reading self-paced moving text on a computer display. 01777
An experimental study of Chinese information displays on VDTs. 01784
Reader-controlled computerized presentation of text. 01785
Magnification effects with imaging displays depend on scene content and viewing condition. 01786
A discrete control model of operator function: A methodology for information dislay design. 01874
Human factors and flat panels challenge the CRT. 01982
Display legibility guidelines: a design aid. 01983
Understanding and evaluating a computer graphics display. 01984
CRT picture vibration caused by low-frequency magnetic field and its reduction method. 01987
DYNABOARD: user animated display of deductive proofs in mathematics. 02221
Interactive scientific visualization and parallel display techniques. 03542
The legibility of visual display texts. 03889
The use of color in visual displays. 03890
Visual fatigue with work on visual display units: the current state of knowledge. 03891
Visual comfort as a criterion for designing display units. 03892
Displaying statistical information—ergonomic considerations. 03893
Factors influencing the detection of trend deviations on VDTs. 03894
Visual presentation of text: the process of reading from a psycholinguistic perspective. 03895
Cognitive attributes: implications for display design in supervisory control systems. HCI-0242 †
Testing bibliographic displays for online catalogs. HCI-0285 †
Two-bit graphics. HCI-0372 †
Color and the computer in cartography. HCI-0386 †

*Image processing software*

Progress in medical imaging. ● 0556
Office-by-example: an integrated office system and database manager. 01159
Active vision: integration of fixed and mobile cameras. 04017
An image processing language with ICON-assisted navigation. HCI-0387 †

CATEGORY INDEX [I. COMPUTING METHODOLOGIES]

IPL *see* Proper Noun Index

### I.4.1 Digitization

Problems in recognition of drawings. 0294
Life before the chips: simulating digital video interactive technology. 01328
Coding image sequences for interactive retrieval. 01330
Continuous processing of images through user sketched functional blocks. 01399

*Scanning*

Desktop publishing. 0238
Manipulation of 3D imagery. 0557
Connections in context: The intermedia system. 03534
An overview of local environment sensing in robotics applications. 04012
Practical applications of optical disk image systems in document management. 04041

### I.4.2 Compression (Coding) (E.4)

DVI—a digital multimedia technology. 01327
Life before the chips: simulating digital video interactive technology. 01328
Coding image sequences for interactive retrieval. 01330
Image compression using polylines. 02533

### I.4.3 Enhancement

Mapping images to a hierarchical data structure—a way to knowledge-based pattern recognition. 03954

*Filtering*

Progress in medical imaging. • 0556

*Geometric correction*

Steps toward making robots see. 04011

*Grayscale manipulation*

Problems in recognition of drawings. 0294
Image compression using polylines. 02533
Intelligible encoding of ASL image sequences at extremely low information rates. 02708
Image processing aspects of type. HCI-0403 †

*Sharpening and deblurring*

The use of color in visual displays. 03890

*Smoothing*

Motion interpolation by optimal control. 02817

### I.4.4 Restoration

An outline of the primal sketch in human vision. 02541

*Kalman filtering*

An expert system framework for forecasting method selection. 03468

### I.4.5 Reconstruction

Color displays for medical imaging. 0262
A hand biomechanics workstation. 02820
Reconstruction and display of the retina. 03310
An iterative and interactive simulation method to reconstruct unknown inputs contributing to known outputs of neuronal systems. 04018

*Transform methods*

Morphological representation of speech knowledge for automatic speech recognition systems. 03992
The effects of limited data in multi-frequency reflection diffraction tomography. 04020
Image processing aspects of type. HCI-0403 †

### I.4.6 Segmentation

Perceptual organization and curve partitioning. 01838
Using perceptual organization to extract 3-D structures. 01842
New methods for matching 3-D objects with single perspective views. 01844
Segmentation using contrast and homogeneity measures. 02543
Features and objects in visual processing. 02577
Image segmentation based on color and texture gradient. 03303
Selection and use of image features for segmentation of boundary images. 03305
Mapping images to a hierarchical data structure—a way to knowledge-based pattern recognition. 03954
Image segregation by motion: cortical mechanisms and implementation in neural networks. 03958
Computational networks in early vision: from orientation selection to optical flow. 03961
Phonetic segmentation using psychoacoustic speech parameters. 03991
Computer recognition of spoken letters and digits. 03995
Recognizing unexpected objects: a proposed approach. HCI-0389 †

*Edge and feature detection*

Application of structural pattern recognition in histopathology. 0295
Automating knowledge acquisition for aerial image interpretation. 01470
Thresholding for edge detection using human psychovisual phenomena. 02538
Human image understanding: recent research and a

[I. COMPUTING METHODOLOGIES]  CATEGORY INDEX

theory. 02698
Cortical representation of texture primitives. 03306
The use of prosodic parameters in automatic speech recognition. 03988
Recognition of speech using temporal decomposition. 03990
Speaker-independent automatic recognition of plosive sound in letters and digits. 03993
Primary perceptual units in word recognition. 03994
Real-time large vocabulary word recognition via diphone spotting and multiprocessor implementation. 03996
An experimental environment for generating word hypotheses in continuous speech. 03998
Dynamic spectral adaptation of automatic speech recognizers to new speakers. 03999
Recognition of speaker-dependent continuous speech with Keal-Nevezh. 04002
Modification of Earley's algorithm for speech recognition. 04003
Steps toward making robots see. 04011
Early vision: from computational structure to algorithms and parallel hardware. HCI-0365 †
Preattentive processing in vision. HCI-0366 †

### Pixel classification

Using a top-down and bottom-up strategy to analyze high resolution aerial photographs of urban areas. 02960

### Region growing, partitioning

Manipulation of 3D imagery. 0557
An interactive approach to local remeshing around a propagating crack. 01685

### I.4.7 Feature Measurement

Detecting structure by symbolic constructions on tokens. 01466
Using perceptual organization to extract 3-D structures. 01842
Generic surface interpretation: observability model. 03563
A flexible and intelligent system for fast measurements in binary images for in-line robotic control. 03986
Automatic contour definition on left ventriculograms by image evidence and a multiple template-based model. 04073

### Invariants

Dynamics and architecture for neural computation. 02270
On the minimum number of templates required for shift, rotation and size invariant pattern recognition. 02531
Active vision: integration of fixed and mobile cameras. 04017

### Moments

Force and tactile sensing for robots. 04013
Active vision: integration of fixed and mobile cameras. 04017

### Projections

Various views on spatial prepositions. 01196
CAD system GISK for interactive graphical modelling of planar mechanisms. 01570
Environment-centered and viewer-centered perception of surface orientation. 02705
The effects of limited data in multi-frequency reflection diffraction tomography. 04020

### Size and shape

An extremum principle for shape from contour. 0024
Manipulation of 3D imagery. 0557
Visual routines. 0616
Automatic construction of surfaces with prescribed shape. 01474
Magnification effects with imaging displays depend on scene content and viewing condition. 01786
Describing surfaces. 02699
Autonomous scene description with range imagery. 02707
An improved automatic lipreading system to enhance speech recognition. 02859
Hierarchical scene structure representations to facilitate image understanding. 02942
Steps toward making robots see. 04011
Integration of robot sensory systems. 04016
Active vision: integration of fixed and mobile cameras. 04017
An iterative and interactive simulation method to reconstruct unknown inputs contributing to known outputs of neuronal systems. 04018
An investigation into the skeletonization approach of Hilditch. HCI-0388 †

### Texture

Textons, the fundamental elements in preattentive vision and perception of textures. 0297
The physiology and psychophysics of touch. 04010
Force and tactile sensing for robots. 04013

### I.4.8 Scene Analysis

Visual routines. 0616
Detecting structure by symbolic constructions on tokens. 01466
Automating knowledge acquisition for aerial image interpretation. 01470
Using perceptual organization to extract 3-D structures. 01842

Spatial misorientation exacerbated by collimated virtual flight display. 01979
Microcomputing in motion analysis. 02384
Describing surfaces. 02699
Toward a theory of the perceived spatial layout of scenes. 02701
Using a top-down and bottom-up strategy to analyze high resolution aerial photographs of urban areas. 02960
The fourth international symposium. § 03561
On the acquisition of object concepts from sensory data. 03959
Connectionist models and parallelism in high level vision. HCI-0363 †
Preattentive processing in vision. HCI-0366 †

### Depth cues

Studying depth cues in a three-dimensional computer graphics workstation. 02117
Hierarchical scene structure representations to facilitate image understanding. 02942
Perception of rotation in depth: the psychophysical evidence. 03343
Static stereo vision depth distortions in teleoperation. 03390
The use of color in visual displays. 03890
Recent results on the application of a metric-space search algorithm (AESA) to multispeaker data. 03997
The physiology and psychophysics of touch. 04010

### Photometry

Towards the construction of a maximally-contrasting set of colours. 03233
An experimental evaluation of computer graphics imagery. HCI-0373 †
Visual hyperacuity: representation and computation of high precision position information. HCI-0393 †

### Range data

Autonomous scene description with range imagery. 02707

### Stereo

Static stereo vision depth distortions in teleoperation. 03390
The use of color in visual displays. 03890
Active vision: integration of fixed and mobile cameras. 04017

### Time-varying imagery

On kineopsis and cimputation of structure and motion. 01839
Motion and time-varying imagery. 03336
Image segregation by motion: cortical mechanisms and implementation in neural networks. 03958
The use of prosodic parameters in automatic speech recognition. 03988

Early vision: from computational structure to algorithms and parallel hardware. HCI-0365 †

### I.4.9 Applications

Graphic objects. 01190
Bringing image processing into focus. 01317
Virtual video editing in interactive multimedia applications. 01326
A graphics system architecture for interactive application-specific display functions. 01822
Graphic equivalence, graphic explanations, and embedded process modeling for enhanced user-system interaction. 01888
A perceptual study of the Flury-Riedwyl faces for graphically displaying multivariate data. 02126
The use of hand-drawn gestures for text editing. 02151
Pictorial dialogue methods. 02251
MOL3D, a modular and interactive program for molecular modeling and conformational analysis: I—basic modules. 02389
The role of computer graphics in validating simulation models. 02486
Putting on a show: using computer graphics to train end-users. 02520
A system for the representation of human body movement from dance scores. 02540
An interactive simulator for the designing of woven fabric structures second place. 02583
The mission operators planning assistant. 02674
The interactive specification of human animation. 03292
Visual business graphics query interface. 03840
A graphics interface for interactive simulation of packet-switched networks. 03869
How map designers can represent their ideas in thematic maps: effective user interfaces for thematic map design. 03870
Challenges in the application of graphics technology to the management of geographic information. 03871
Pictorial information systems in medicine. § 03976
On the architecture for pictorial information systems. 03977
Psychovisual issues in the display of medical images. 03978
Software tools for the development of pictorial information systems in medicine—the ISQL experience. 03980
Automatic contour definition on left ventriculograms by image evidence and a multiple template-based model. 04073
The next generation of interactive technologies. HCI-0384 †

### I.4.m Miscellaneous

Visual information processing: artificial intelligence and the sensorium of sight. 0300
Computational vision and regularization theory. 0301

[I. COMPUTING METHODOLOGIES]

Perceptual organization and the representation of natural form. 0302
Towards computer vision. 0564
On the parameters of human visual performance: an investigation of the benefits of antialiasing. 0799
Selection of image primitives for general-purpose visual processing. 01467
Algorithm for interactive forming matrix data representation and estimation of its efficiency. 02536
Image processing with personal computers. 02581
VIS: a virtual image system for image-understanding research. 02629
Learning graphics programming by direct communication. 03298
Principle of visual color coding applied to satellite images. 03304
Relational models in natural and artificial vision. 03953

## I.5 PATTERN RECOGNITION

Annual review of computer science vol. 1, 1986. ● 0719

### I.5.0 General

Syntactic and structural pattern recognition. ● 0292
Readings in computer vision: issues, problems, principles, and paradigms. ● 0296
Human and Machine Vision II. § 02696
Industrial & Engineering Applications of Artificial Intelligence & Expert Systems. § 02941
Research and development in information retrieval. § 03072
Computational Geometry and its Applications. § 03850
Real-time object measurement and classification. § 03985
Pattern recognition: human and mechanical. ● HCI-0072 †
Recognizing unexpected objects: a proposed approach. HCI-0389 †

### I.5.1 Models

Connectionist models and parallelism in high level vision. HCI-0363 †

*Fuzzy Set*

Fuzzy decision analysis. 0650
Fuzzy sets and decision analysis. 0651
Effect of fuzzy membership on recognition of gray level images. 02539
Approximate spatial reasoning. 02917
A mission planning architecture for an autonomous vehicle. 02939
The effects of the supervisor's knowledge in a complex automated system. 03366
Uncertainty and intelligent systems. § 04030

A fuzzy rule-based model of human problem solving. HCI-0359 †
CNS-HLS mapping using fuzzy sets. HCI-0380 †

*Geometric*

Manipulation of 3D imagery. 0557
New methods for matching 3-D objects with single perspective views. 01844

*Statistical*

Problems in recognition of drawings. 0294
Multidimensional attribute analyhsis and pattern recognition for seismic interpretation. 02530
Morphological representation of speech knowledge for automatic speech recognition systems. 03992
Morphological representation of speech knowledge for automatic speech recognition systems. 03992
Speaker-independent automatic recognition of plosive sound in letters and digits. 03993
Primary perceptual units in word recognition. 03994
Computer recognition of spoken letters and digits. 03995
Recent results on the application of a metric-space search algorithm (AESA) to multispeaker data. 03997
An experimental environment for generating word hypotheses in continuous speech. 03998
Dynamic spectral adaptation of automatic speech recognizers to new speakers. 03999
Knowledge based systems for speech understanding. 04001
Modification of Earley's algorithm for speech recognition. 04003
Merging acoustics and linguistics in speech understanding. 04004
Multivariate data representation and analysis by face pattern using facial expression characteristics. HCI-0394 †

*Structural*

Syntactic and structural pattern recognition. ● 0292
A string correction method based on the context-dependent similarity. 0293
Application of structural pattern recognition in histopathology. 0295
Using perceptual organization to extract 3-D structures. 01842
Structural aspects of semantic-directed clusters. 02534
A gesture based text editor. 03232
Architectures for production systems: an inside look for those who study human-computer interaction. 03906
Steps toward making robots see. 04011

### I.5.2 Design Methodology

Models of human problem solving: detection, diagnosis, and compensation for system failures. 0653

An automatic wafer inspection system using pipelined image processing techniques. 01840

Segmentation using contrast and homogeneity measures. 02543

A comparison of neural network and matched filter processing for detecting lines in images. 02738

A knowledge-based approach to computer vision systems. 03302

Morphological representation of speech knowledge for automatic speech recognition systems. 03992

Signal processing and pattern recognition in nondestructive evaluation of materials. § 04019

### Classifier design and evaluation

Profile data acquisition for the JCPDS-ICDD database s. 01232

VLSI implementation of a neural network model. 01363

Knowledge representation and use in pattern analysis. 02030

On the minimum number of templates required for shift, rotation and size invariant pattern recognition. 02531

Structural aspects of semantic-directed clusters. 02534

The immune system, adaptation, and machine learning. 02559

The use of prosodic parameters in automatic speech recognition. 03988

Prosodic features in German speech: stress assignment by man and machine. 03989

Recent results on the application of a metric-space search algorithm (AESA) to multispeaker data. 03997

Dynamic spectral adaptation of automatic speech recognizers to new speakers. 03999

Selective networks and recognition automata. HCI-0390 †

Multivariate data representation and analysis by face pattern using facial expression characteristics. HCI-0394 †

### Feature evaluation and selection

Using patterns and plans in chess. 0528

Graphical search and replace. 02812

Drag: a graph drawing system. 03183

Correspondence in apparent motion: defining the heuristics. 03308

Prosodic features in German speech: stress assignment by man and machine. 03989

Phonetic segmentation using psychoacoustic speech parameters. 03991

Speaker-independent automatic recognition of plosive sound in letters and digits. 03993

Primary perceptual units in word recognition. 03994

Computer recognition of spoken letters and digits. 03995

Real-time large vocabulary word recognition via diphone spotting and multiprocessor implementation. 03996

An experimental environment for generating word hypotheses in continuous speech. 03998

Dynamic spectral adaptation of automatic speech recognizers to new speakers. 03999

Recognition of speaker-dependent continuous speech with Keal-Nevezh. 04002

Modification of Earley's algorithm for speech recognition. 04003

The physiology and psychophysics of touch. 04010

Steps toward making robots see. 04011

### Pattern analysis

Problems in recognition of drawings. 0294

Application of structural pattern recognition in histopathology. 0295

Color constancy: a method for recovering surface spectral reflectance. 0298

Knowledge representation and use in pattern analysis. 02030

Dynamics and architecture for neural computation. 02270

A high accuracy algorithm for recognition of handwritten numerals. 02532

An outline of the primal sketch in human vision. 02541

Nonlinear dynamics of pattern formation and pattern recognition in the rabbit olfactory bulb. 02558

Character recognition of cursive scripts. 02961

A gesture based text editor. 03232

A consideration of learning in speech recognition from the viewpoint of AI class-description learning. 03533

Human-computer interaction: psychonomic aspects. § 03887

Automatic identification of writers. 03909

The use of speech in man-machine interaction. 03910

Search strategies in internal and external memories. 03911

The use of prosodic parameters in automatic speech recognition. 03988

Prosodic features in German speech: stress assignment by man and machine. 03989

Recognition of speech using temporal decomposition. 03990

Phonetic segmentation using psychoacoustic speech parameters. 03991

Speaker-independent automatic recognition of plosive sound in letters and digits. 03993

Primary perceptual units in word recognition. 03994

Computer recognition of spoken letters and digits. 03995

Real-time large vocabulary word recognition via diphone spotting and multiprocessor implementation. 03996

On-line interpretation in speech understanding and dialogue systems. 04000

Knowledge based systems for speech understanding. 04001

Recognition of speaker-dependent continuous speech with Keal-Nevezh. 04002

[I. COMPUTING METHODOLOGIES]  CATEGORY INDEX

Merging acoustics and linguistics in speech understanding. 04004
A neural network for visual pattern recognition. HCI-0391 †

### I.5.3 Clustering

Refining problem-solving knowledge in repertory grids using a consultation mechanism. 02205
Multidimensional attribute analyhsis and pattern recognition for seismic interpretation. 02530
Structural aspects of semantic-directed clusters. 02534

#### Algorithms

A string correction method based on the context-dependent similarity. 0293

#### Similarity measures

A string correction method based on the context-dependent similarity. 0293
Reasoning on a highlighted user model to respond to misconceptions. 01351
Primary perceptual units in word recognition. 03994
Recent results on the application of a metric-space search algorithm (AESA) to multispeaker data. 03997

### I.5.4 Applications

Vision, brain, and cooperative computation. ● 0014
Human image understanding: recent research and a theory. 02698
Graphical search and replace. 02812

#### Computer vision

Vision, brain, and cooperative computation: an overview. 0015
An extremum principle for shape from contour. 0024
Computational techniques in motion processing. 0025
Schemas that integrate vision and touch for hand control. 0026
A functional model of vision and space. 0027
Visual-cognitive neuronal networks. 0029
A heuristic program to solve geometric-analogy problems. 0299
Task-oriented approach to interactive control of heavy-duty manipulators based on coarse scene description. ● 0546
Progress in medical imaging. ● 0556
Manipulation of 3D imagery. 0557
Towards computer vision. 0564
A workcell application design environment (WADE). 0598
Off-line programming and path generation for robot manipulators. 0603
Visual routines. 0616

Issues limiting the acceptance of user interfaces using gesture input and handwriting character recognition. 0845
Various views on spatial prepositions. 01196
Neural nets for adaptive filtering and adaptive pattern recognition. 01362
The ART of adaptive pattern recognition by a self-organizing neural network. 01364
Anything you can do, I can do better (no you can't). 01462
Real-time failure detection on complex mechanical structures via parallel data processing. 01561
An interactive approach to local remeshing around a propagating crack. 01685
An automatic wafer inspection system using pipelined image processing techniques. 01840
New methods for matching 3-D objects with single perspective views. 01844
Fuzzy control of a mobile robot for obstacle avoidance. 02025
On-line recognition of Pitman's hand-written shorthand—an evaluation of potential. 02111
Critical review of visual inspection. 02260
Handprinted chinese character recognition via neural networks. 02529
A high accuracy algorithm for recognition of handwritten numerals. 02532
Effect of fuzzy membership on recognition of gray level images. 02539
An appropriate representation for early vision. 02542
VIS: a virtual image system for image-understanding research. 02629
Human and Machine Vision II. § 02696
Perception of transparency in man and machine. 02697
Connectionist models and parallelism in high level vision. 02700
Hierarchical scene structure representations to facilitate image understanding. 02942
Using a top-down and bottom-up strategy to analyze high resolution aerial photographs of urban areas. 02960
Graphics Interface '86/Vision Interface '86. § 03288
A knowledge-based approach to computer vision systems. 03302
Correspondence in apparent motion: defining the heuristics. 03308
Coupling visual and dynamic features to study handwritten signatures. 03309
Static stereo vision depth distortions in teleoperation. 03390
Interactive aspects of knowledge representations. 03395
U.S. Army field robotics focus and key technology issues. 03402
Visual simulation. 03503
The alternatives allowed by a rectangularity postulate, and a pragmatic approach to interpreting motion. 03550

CATEGORY INDEX [I. COMPUTING METHODOLOGIES]

The fourth international symposium. § 03561
Generic surface interpretation: observability model. 03563
Concept for a model databased remote maintenance system. 03565
Automatic identification of writers. 03909
A cortical network model for early vision processing. 03957
On the acquisition of object concepts from sensory data. 03959
Computational networks in early vision: from orientation selection to optical flow. 03961
A flexible and intelligent system for fast measurements in binary images for in-line robotic control. 03986
Steps toward making robots see. 04011
An overview of local environment sensing in robotics applications. 04012
Force and tactile sensing for robots. 04013
Signal processing and pattern recognition in nondestructive evaluation of materials. § 04019
The effects of limited data in multi-frequency reflection diffraction tomography. 04020
Parameter estimation in array processing. 04021
Interaction with the environment. ● HCI-0068 †
A dedicated microcomputer for handwritten interaction with a software tool: system prototyping. HCI-0119 †
Connectionist models and parallelism in high level vision. HCI-0363 †
Early vision: from computational structure to algorithms and parallel hardware. HCI-0365 †
An investigation into the skeletonization approach of Hilditch. HCI-0388 †
Recognizing unexpected objects: a proposed approach. HCI-0389 †
A neural network for visual pattern recognition. HCI-0391 †
Environment-centered and viewer-centered perception of surface orientation. HCI-0392 †
Visual hyperacuity: representation and computation of high precision position information. HCI-0393 †
Visual hyperacuity: representation and computation of high precision position information. HCI-0393 †
An overview of research and co-operation in advanced information technology. HCI-0442 †

*Signal processing*

The elements of speech recognition. 0176
Computer speech processing. ● 0287
Progress in medical imaging. ● 0556
Models of human problem solving: detection, diagnosis, and compensation for system failures. 0653
Neural nets for adaptive filtering and adaptive pattern recognition. 01362
Application of decision support system on sandwich beams, verified by experiments. 01572

Processing demands, training, and the vigilance decrement. 01723
Perceptual organization and curve partitioning. 01838
Knowledge representation and use in pattern analysis. 02030
Dynamics and architecture for neural computation. 02270
Joint spatial/spatial-frequency representation. 02580
X-ray microbeam method for measurement of articulatory dynamics-techniques and results. 02641
Influence of palate shape on lingual articulation. 02642
An acoustic of pathological voice and its application to the evaluation of laryngeal pathology. 02644
Research on individuality features in speech waves and automatic speaker recognition techniques. 02645
Speech analysis and synthesis methods developed at ECL in NTT-From LPC to LSP-. 02646
Composite phoneme units for the speech synthesis of Japanese. 02647
Recognition of phonemes using time-spectrum pattern. 02648
Vowel normalization by frequency warped spectral matching. 02649
The measurement of the signal-to-noise ratio (SNR) in continuous speech. 02654
Interfacing image processing and computer graphics systems using an artificial visual system. 03301
Object-oriented signal processing systems. 03573
On the temporal stability of signal detection processes. 03617
The use of speech in man-machine interaction. 03910
Recent advances in speech understanding and dialog systems. § 03987
The use of prosodic parameters in automatic speech recognition. 03988
Prosodic features in German speech: stress assignment by man and machine. 03989
Phonetic segmentation using psychoacoustic speech parameters. 03991
Morphological representation of speech knowledge for automatic recognition systems. 03992
Speaker-independent automatic recognition of plosive sound in letters and digits. 03993
Primary perceptual units in word recognition. 03994
Computer recognition of spoken letters and digits. 03995
Real-time large vocabulary word recognition via diphone spotting and multiprocessor implementation. 03996
Recent results on the application of a metric-space search algorithm (AESA) to multispeaker data. 03997
An experimental environment for generating word hypotheses in continuous speech. 03998
On-line interpretation in speech understanding and dialogue systems. 04000
Knowledge based systems for speech understanding. 04001
Modification of Earley's algorithm for speech recognition. 04003

Merging acoustics and linguistics in speech understanding. 04004
Experimentation in the specification of an oral dialogue. 04005
The physiology and psychophysics of touch. 04010
Force and tactile sensing for robots. 04013
Analogs of biological tissues for mechanoelectrical transduction: tactile sensors and muscle-like actuators. 04014
Gas sensors: towards an artificial nose. 04015
Signal processing and pattern recognition in nondestructive evaluation of materials. § 04019
The effects of limited data in multi-frequency reflection diffraction tomography. 04020
Parameter estimation in array processing. 04021
The phonetic basis for computer speech processing. HCI-0358 †
A parallel formant synthesizer for machine voice output. HCI-0396 †
Image processing aspects of type. HCI-0403 †

*Text processing*

The multimedia object presentation manager of MINOS: a symmetric approach. 01083
An object-oriented approach to multimedia databases. 01084
A feature matching approach to the retrieval of graphical information. 01245
The influence of rule-generated stress on computer-synthesized speech. 02081
The legibility of visual display texts. 03889
The use of color in visual displays. 03890
Editing by example. HCI-0398 †

*Waveform analysis*

Computer speech processing. ● 0287
Linear predictive coding of speech. 0289
Progress in medical imaging. ● 0556
Digital waveform sampling rate converter. 01578
Multidimensional attribute analyhsis and pattern recognition for seismic interpretation. 02530
The use of color in visual displays. 03890
The use of speech in man-machine interaction. 03910
The use of prosodic parameters in automatic speech recognition. 03988
Prosodic features in German speech: stress assignment by man and machine. 03989
Phonetic segmentation using psychoacoustic speech parameters. 03991
Morphological representation of speech knowledge for automatic speech recognition systems. 03992
Speaker-independent automatic recognition of plosive sound in letters and digits. 03993
Primary perceptual units in word recognition. 03994
Computer recognition of spoken letters and digits. 03995
Real-time large vocabulary word recognition via diphone spotting and multiprocessor implementation. 03996
Recent results on the application of a metric-space search algorithm (AESA) to multispeaker data. 03997
An experimental environment for generating word hypotheses in continuous speech. 03998
Dynamic spectral adaptation of automatic speech recognizers to new speakers. 03999
On-line interpretation in speech understanding and dialogue systems. 04000
Knowledge based systems for speech understanding. 04001
Modification of Earley's algorithm for speech recognition. 04003
Experimentation in the specification of an oral dialogue. 04005
Signal processing and pattern recognition in nondestructive evaluation of materials. § 04019
The effects of limited data in multi-frequency reflection diffraction tomography. 04020
Parameter estimation in array processing. 04021
A parallel formant synthesizer for machine voice output. HCI-0396 †
Image processing aspects of type. HCI-0403 †

## I.5.5 Implementation (C.3)

A dedicated microcomputer for handwritten interaction with a software tool: system prototyping. HCI-0119 †

*Interactive systems*

Designer labyrinths: text mazes for language learners. 0197
Using patterns and plans in chess. 0528
Manipulation of 3D imagery. 0557
Models of human problem solving: detection, diagnosis, and compensation for system failures. 0653
Skills, rules, and knowledge; signals, signs, and symbols, and other distinctions in human performance models. 0654
POP-11: an AI programming language. 0748
An object-oriented framework of pattern recognition systems. 01133
An automatic wafer inspection system using pipelined image processing techniques. 01840
Multidimensional attribute analyhsis and pattern recognition for seismic interpretation. 02530
A consideration of learning in speech recognition from the viewpoint of AI class-description learning. 03533
Real-time processing of cursive writing and sketched graphics. 03908
The use of speech in man-machine interaction. 03910
The use of prosodic parameters in automatic speech recognition. 03988
Real-time large vocabulary word recognition via diphone spotting and multiprocessor implementation. 03996

An experimental environment for generating word hypotheses in continuous speech. 03998
Dynamic spectral adaptation of automatic speech recognizers to new speakers. 03999
On-line interpretation in speech understanding and dialogue systems. 04000
Knowledge based systems for speech understanding. 04001
Recognition of speaker-dependent continuous speech with Keal-Nevezh. 04002
Merging acoustics and linguistics in speech understanding. 04004
An iterative and interactive simulation method to reconstruct unknown inputs contributing to known outputs of neuronal systems. 04018
The effects of limited data in multi-frequency reflection diffraction tomography. 04020
Parameter estimation in array processing. 04021
Multivariate data representation and analysis by face pattern using facial expression characteristics. HCI-0394 †
Editing by example. HCI-0398 †

*Special architectures*

Connectionist models and parallelism in high level vision. HCI-0363 †
Recognizing unexpected objects: a proposed approach. HCI-0389 †

### I.5.m Miscellaneous

Visual information processing: artificial intelligence and the sensorium of sight. 0300
Pattern storage and associative memory in quasi-neural network. 02537
A self-optimizing, nonsymmetrical neural net for content addressable memory and pattern recognition. 02562
Bifurcation analysis of oscillating network model of pattern recognition in the rabbit olfactory bulb. 02725
Nonlinear dynamics of artificial neural systems. 02747
Designing a neural network satisfying a given set of constraints. 02755
Relational models in natural and artificial vision. 03953

## I.6 SIMULATION AND MODELING (G.3)

Develping decision support systems from a model of the DSS/user interface. 0253
Annual review of computer science vol. 1, 1986. ● 0719

### I.6.0 General

Computer-aided model building. 0544
Mental models in cognitive science. 0647
A very friendly software environment for SOLO. 0743
Human intelligence models and their implications for expert system structure and research. 01242
What we know and what we need to know: the user model versus the user's model in human-computer interaction. 01243
A model for the fading of stabilized images in a visual system. 01864
Advances in Cognitive Science. § 02720
Advances in cognitive science. 02721
Proceedings of the 21st Annual Simulation Symposium. § 03499
Simulation. § 03501
HORSE: a simulation of the horizon supercomputer. 03541
The computer as an integral part of the laboratory. 03880
Graph-theoretic concepts in computer science. § 03885

### I.6.1 Simulation Theory

Life before the chips: simulating digital video interactive technology. 01328

*Types of simulation (continuous and discrete)*

An expert manufacturing simulation system. 02584
Visual interactive simulation - history, recent developments, and major issues. 02585
Interactive graphics in GPSS/PC. 02586

### I.6.2 Simulation Languages

One hundred differential equations execute directly on the IBM PC. 02582
ATLANTIS—a software simulator for behavior analysis of protocol specificationsand their target implementations. 02667
SIMTALK: Pros and cons of natural language for manufacturing simulation. 02950
Computer-aided modeling and planning (CAMP). HCI-0415 †

**GPSS** *see* Proper Noun Index

### I.6.3 Applications

Neural network models for optical computing. ● 0032
Computer models of mind: computational approaches in theoretical psychology. ● 0152
$VP^2$: the role of user modelling in correcting errors in second language learning. 0222
Visual information pick-up in a simulated driving situation. 0251
Linear predictive coding of speech. 0289
The acquisition of grammar. 0353
Describing movement control at two levels of abstraction. 0403

Neural network architectures for artificial intelligence. • 0434
Authoring systems for ICAI. 0469
Computer-aided model building. 0544
Robot simulation and off-line programming—an integrated CAE-CAD approach. 0599
Schemata and sequential thought processes in PDP models. 0630
Interactive processes in speech perception: the TRACE model. 0631
The programmable blackboard model of reading. 0632
A distributed model of human learning and memory. 0633
On learning the past tenses of English verbs. 0634
Mechanisms of sentence processing: assigning roles to constituents. 0635
Biologically plausible models of place recognition and goal location. 0639
A fuzzy rule-based model of human problem solving. 0656
The effects of type of knowledge upon human problem solving in a process control task. 0657
Thinking: information processing, mathematical models and computer simulation. • 0667
High-speed computing: scientific applications and algorithm design. • 0727
Coherent and chaotic structures in 2D vortex dynamics: progress and problems. 0729
Computing needs in thunderstorm modeling: supercomputers and interactive graphics. 0730
Pupils, computers and history teaching. 0746
Modelling novice programmer behaviour. 0751
Programmable user models for predictive evaluation of interface designs. 0800
Conversational resources for situated action. 0861
A cognitive model of database querying: a tool for novice instruction. 0905
Defining constraints graphically. 0910
A prolog simulation for a Delphi-based problem solver. 01141
Interactive microcomputer programs for linear and non-linear static analysis of frameworks. 01165
How to talk to an expert. 01180
A self-organizing neural network sharing features of the mammalian visual system. 01248
Modeling of control and learning in a stepping motion. 01250
Muscle models: what is gained and what is lost by varying model complexity. 01251
Diffusion approximation of the neuronal model with synaptic reversal potentials. 01254
Characteristics of neuronal systems in the visual cortex. 01255
Simulation of chaotic EEG patterns with a dynamic model of the olfactory system. 01263
Projected free fall trajectories. I. Theory and simulation. 01265
A model-based monitor of human sleep stages. 01269
Uncertainty analysis of human EEG spectra: A multivariate information theoretical method for the analysis of brain activity. 01270
A model of the motor servo: Incorporating nonlinear spindle receptor and muscle mechanical properties. 01273
The control of hand equilibrium trajectories in multi-joint arm movements. 01275
Physiology based simulation model of triangle shape recognition. 01277
Self-organizing system obtaining communication ability primitive model for language generation. 01279
Computing with structured neural networks. 01365
The architecture of an inexpensive and portable talking-tactile terminal to aid the visually handicapped. 01452
A structure for enhancing user participation in model development. 01514
Ergonomic job design in frequent manual lifting tasks: a microcomputer-based model. 01532
The design of distributed transport systems as a major standard interface in computer integrated manufacturing. 01564
Short-term memory as a metastable state.III. Diffusion approximation. 01611
Maintenance training simulator fidelity and individual differences in transfer of training. 01722
Spatial requirements for visual simulation of aircraft at real-world distances. 01768
Performance measurement during simulated air-to-air combat. 01787
Two simulation studies investigating means of human-computer communication for dynamic task allocation. 01882
Capturing expertise: Some approaches to modeling command decisionmaking in combat analysis. 01883
Qualitative approximation methodology for modeling and simulation of large dynamic systems: Applications to a Marine power plant. 01900
User modeling in intelligent information retrieval. 01994
Arithmetic codes resembling neural encoding. 02021
Power plant simulation using a distributed control system. 02057
Modelling human expertise in knowledge engineering: some preliminary observations. 02134
A model of fault diagnosis performance of expert marine engineers. 02199
Strategies in controlling a continuous process with long response latencies: needs for computer support to diagnosis. 02217
A regression model to identify successful learner traits with CAI. 02376
An interactive modeling program for DNA. 02385
Frames of mind in intertemporal choice. 02478

A model of the controller responses of the human temperature regulating system to changes in water temperature. 02487

Design and implementation of an interactive optimization system for network design in the motor carrier industry. 02528

Nonlinear dynamics of pattern formation and pattern recognition in the rabbit olfactory bulb. 02558

A self-optimizing, nonsymmetrical neural net for content addressable memory and pattern recognition. 02562

Psychological concepts in a parallel system. 02564

An interactive simulator for the designing of woven fabric structures second place. 02583

An expert manufacturing simulation system. 02584

Hierarchical, modular discrete-event modelling in an object-oriented environment. 02588

Simulations of behavior in competitive situations. 02591

Simulations and anxiety related to public speaking. 02592

Human and computer involvement in simulation. 02593

The marble company: The design and implementation of a simulation board game. 02595

Team cohesion effects on business game performance. 02597

A computer model of peripheral auditory processing incorporating phase-locking, suppression and adaptation effects. 02650

Speech motor control and stuttering: a computational model of adaptive sensory-motor processing. 02655

Higher pole correction in vocal tract models and terminal analogs. 02657

ATLANTIS—a software simulator for behavior analysis of protocol specificationsand their target implementations. 02667

BNETD—A modelling tool to computer systems performance evaluation. 02668

The KOMPLEX performance prediction tool. 02669

SATURN—a tool for modelling and performance evaluation of computer systems. 02670

Power plant simulation and reactor safety. 02682

A compact model of a power house boiler. 02683

Motion interpolation by optimal control. 02817

Getting graphics in gear: graphics and dynamics in driving simulation. 02818

Grasping reality through illusion—interactive graphics serving science. 02857

A general user modelling facility. 02880

Experience of constructing a fault localisation expert system using an AI toolkit. 02923

The development of an automated flight test management system for flight test planning and monitoring. 02928

Graphics-based qualitative simulation generator for power distribution systems. 02946

SIMTALK: Pros and cons of natural language for manufacturing simulation. 02950

A knowledge-based approach to online document retrieval system design. 03027

GOMS meets STRIPS: the integration of planning with skilled procedure execution in human-computer interaction. 03243

Virya—a motion control editor for kinematic and dynamic animation. 03294

Humane: A designer's assistant for modeling and evaluating function allocation options. 03397

The MIRRORS/II simulator. 03502

Visual simulation. 03503

Cognitive ergonomics: an approach for the design of user-oriented interactive systems. 03591

Intentional and operational aspects of decision behaviour and their modelling. 03666

Architectures for production systems: an inside look for those who study human-computer interaction. 03906

Real-time processing of cursive writing and sketched graphics. 03908

Spatial and temporal transformations in visuo-motor coordination. 03963

Proprioceptive feedback for sensory-motor control. 04008

The physiology and psychophysics of touch. 04010

MIDAS: molecular interactive display and simulation. 04061

A neural model of human prehension. 04072

Readings on cognitive ergonomics - mind and computers. § HCI-0039 †

Artificial behavior: computer simulation of psychological processes. ● HCI-0073 †

Analysing the scope of cognitive models in human-computer interaction: a trade-off approach. HCI-0245 †

Applications of AI in engineering. HCI-0321 †

Real time graphic simulation of visual effects of egomotion. HCI-0379 †

Geomatic: a 3-D graphic relief simulation system. HCI-0395 †

A parallel formant synthesizer for machine voice output. HCI-0396 †

### I.6.4 Model Validation and Analysis

On language and connectionism: analysis of a parallel distributed processing model of language acquisition. 0590

The relation between linguistic structure and associative theories of language learning models: constructive critique of some connectionist learning models. 0591

Models of user interactions with graphical interfaces: 1. statistical. 0883

Physiology based simulation model of triangle shape recognition. 01277

Open-loop experiments for modeling the human eye movement system. 01870

[I. COMPUTING METHODOLOGIES]

The role of computer graphics in validating simulation models. 02486
Hierarchical, modular discrete-event modelling in an object-oriented environment. 02588
Team cohesion effects on business game performance. 02597
Performance evaluation of simulators. 02663
ATLANTIS—a software simulator for behavior analysis of protocol specificationsand their target implementations. 02667
BNETD—A modelling tool to computer systems performance evaluation. 02668
The KOMPLEX performance prediction tool. 02669
SATURN—a tool for modelling and performance evaluation of computer systems. 02670
Use of metaknowledge in the verification of knowledge-based systems. 02945
Dynamic spectral adaptation of automatic speech recognizers to new speakers. 03999
A fuzzy rule-based model of human problem solving. HCI-0359†

### I.6.m Miscellaneous

Modelling novice programmer behaviour. 0744
Experiences with the alternate reality kit: an example of the tension between literalism and magic. 0817
Real time speech synthesis—development and employment. 01482
An interactive simulation description interpreter. 01538
Understanding and validating results in model-based decision support systems. 01666
Towards the development of human work-performance standards in futuristic man-machine systems: a fuzzy modeling approach. 01692
Usage of linguistic variable concept for human operator modelling. 01694
Fuzzy reasoning in pseudo-physical logics. 01695
A psychophysiological assessment of operator workload during simulated flight missions. 01735
Part-task training strategies in simulated carrier landing final-approach training. 01741
Effects of visual display and motion system delays on operator performance and ueasiness in a driving simulator. 01772
Automated interactive simulation modeling system: AI-SIM. 02399
One hundred differential equations execute directly on the IBM PC. 02582
Community design and gaming/simulation: Comparison of communications techniques in participatory design sessions. 02596
Using simulation to study complex problem solving: a review of studies in the FRG. 02598
Development and sensitivity analysis of adaptive predictor for human eye movement model. 02681

A neural network model for the mechanism of pattern information processing. 02748
Report from the working group on "socialist experience with modelling and using systems". 03667
Towards an integrated view of 3-D computer animation. 03859
A graphics interface for interactive simulation of packet-switched networks. 03869

## I.7 TEXT PROCESSING (H.4)

### I.7.0 General

Text, context, and hypertext: writing with and for the computer. ● 0098
Writers as total desktop publishers: developing a conceptual approach to training. 0108
Are writers obsolete in the computer industry?. 0109
Online information: what do people want? What do people need?. 0113
Hypertext and intelligent interfaces for text retrieval. 0115
Investigations in multimedia design documentation. 0116
Reflections on authoring, editing, and managing hypertext. 0119
Authoring tools for complex document sets. 0120
From database to hypertext via electronic publishing: an information odyssey. 0122
Trends in the emerging profession of technical communciation. 0123
Consulting skills for technical writers. 0124
Textual intervention, collaboration, and the online environment. 0126
Escher effects in online text. 0130
Desktop publishing. 0238
PLEIADE: A system for interactive manipulation of structured documents. 0265
Presenting documents on workstation screens. 0267
Computer-supported cooperative work: a book of readings. ● 0366
Authorship provisions in AUGMENT (Reprint). 0370
Diamond: a multimedia message system built on a distributed architecture (Reprint). 0380
An experiment in integrated multimedia conferencing. 0381
Systemic implications of leap and an improved two-part cursor. 0848
Human-computer interaction lab, University of Maryland. 0871
A document layout system using automatic document architecture extraction. 0882
Information retrieval using micros. 01225
Efforts of display format on proof-reading with VDUs. 01246
Efforts of display format on proof-reading with VDUs. 01246

## [I. COMPUTING METHODOLOGIES]

An experiment in computational discrimination of English word senses. 01813
The electronic book Ebook3. 02234
Interactive documentation. 02612
Research and development in information retrieval. § 03072
Informational zooming: an interaction model for the graphical access to text knowledge bases. 03073
Document manipulation and typography. § 03182
SEE: a safe editing environment; human-computer interaction for programmers. 03225
Information flow in a user interface: the effect of experience and context on the recall of MacWrite screens. 03228
A comparison of hypertext, scrolling and folding as mechanisms for program browsing. 03235
Optimum display arrangements for presenting visual reminders. 03237
Multiple representation document development (extende abstract). 03518
The effect on reading speed of word divisions at the end of a line. 03896
Document processing. 03897
Artificial intelligence and cognitive psychology: a new look at human factors. 03904
Real-time processing of cursive writing and sketched graphics. 03908
Computational linguistics: issues and solutions. 03948
Practical applications of optical disk image systems in document management. 04041
Integrating text with non-text:a picture is worth 1k words. Proceedings of the I. § 04043
The use of explicit user models in text generation: tailoring to a user's level of expertise. 04051
The ethics of automated publishing systems (a response to Dr. Brockmann). HCI-0170 †

### I.7.1  Text Editing

The evaluation of text editors: Methodology and empirical results. 0058
The adventure of getting to know a computer. 0088
The on-line environment and in-house training. 0106
Limited freedom: linear reflections on nonlinear texts. 0121
Using "word-knowledge" reasoning for question answering. 0131
Cognitive resources and the learning of human-computer dialogs. 0209
Desktop publishing. 0238
Workstations and publication systems. • 0264
A string correction method based on the context-dependent similarity. 0293
User technology: from pointing to pondering. 0350
Hypertext: an introduction and survey (Reprint). 0378
Data sharing in group work (Reprint). 0379

The MAGNEX text editor for the Comodore Amiga personal computer. 0782
Artifact as theory-nexus: hermeneutics meets theory-based design. 0798
Systemic implications of leap and an improved two-part cursor. 0848
The PSG—programming system generator. 01098
Maintained and constructor attributes. 01099
The user interface in a hypertext, multiwindow program browser. 02072
Analogy and other sources of difficulty in novices' very first text-editing. 02148
The use of hand-drawn gestures for text editing. 02151
How users repeat their actions on computers: principles for design of history mechanisms. 02885
UIMSs: threat or menace?. 02889
User technology—from pointing to pondering. 03098
Document manipulation and typography. § 03182
Abstraction and integration in IDE, an editing and formatting environment. 03184
Vidura—an interactive multilingual publishing system—specification & design. 03186
Chinese character processing system based on character-root combination and gra phic processing. 03187
Handling textual information in a GDSS database: experience with the Arizona analyst information system. 03475
Conceptual information extraction form financial news. 03489
Quill: An extensible system for editing documents of mixed type. 03517
Multiple representation document development (extende abstract). 03518
Supporting document development with concordia. 03521
Language level persistence for an object-oriented application programming platform. 03522
Connections in context: The intermedia system. 03534
On the usefulness of syntax directed editors. 03781
Development of mental models of an office system: a field study on an introductory course. 03903
The use of explicit user models in text generation: tailoring to a user's level of expertise. 04051
Cursor movement during text editing. HCI-0113 †
A display editor with random access and continuous control. HCI-0140 †
Goal and plan knowledge representations: from stories to text editors and programs. HCI-0183 †
Reading continuous text from a one-line visual display. HCI-0187 †
A quantitative theory of human-computer interaction. HCI-0198 †
Behavioral experiments on handmarkings. HCI-0201 †
Technology transfer: a new computer-based system. HCI-0203 †

[I. COMPUTING METHODOLOGIES]

Reading and writing with computers: a framework for explaining differences in performance. HCI-0204 †
A user oriented design process for user recovery and command reuse support. HCI-0284 †
A performing medium for working group graphics. HCI-0383 †
Speech-controlled text-editing: effects of input modality and of command structure. HCI-0397 †
Editing by example. HCI-0398 †

*Languages*

Retrieval systems for the information seeker: can the role of the intermediary be automated?. 02864
Using latent semantic analysis to improve access to textual information. 02901
Understanding text with an accompanying diagram. 02947
A computer training tool using Chinese natural language. 02948
A gesture based text editor. 03232
Document processing. 03897
Tree doctor, a software package for graphical manipulation and animation of tree structures. 03901
Textvision: elicitation and acquisition of conceptual knowledge by graphic representation and multiwindowing. 03902
Literate programming. HCI-0148 †
The evaluation of text editors: methodology and empirical results.. HCI-0209 †
Text processing by speech: dialogue design and usability issues in the provision of a system for disabled users. HCI-0357 †
Editing by example. HCI-0398 †

*Spelling*

Naming errors and automatic error correction in human-computer interaction. 03770
A note on undetected typing errors. HCI-0399 †

**TeX** *see* Proper Noun Index

**I.7.2  Document Preparation**

**troff** *see* Proper Noun Index

**I.7.1  Text Editing**

**WEB** *see* Proper Noun Index

**I.7.2  Document Preparation**

Authoring tools for complex document sets. 0120
Trends in the emerging profession of technical communication. 0123
Embedding graphics into documents by using a graphic-editor. 0266

GENIE-M: A generator for multimedia information environments. 0268
Back to basics: Simple but high-quality text pagination systems. 0271
A conceptual framework for the augmentation of man's intellect (Reprint). 0368
DOMAIN/DELPHI: retrieving documents online. 0906
Technology and the author's labour. 02574
Music—a language for typesetting music scores. 02622
Document Processing Systems. § 02831
The design of a document database. 02835
A library for incremental update of bitmap images. 02836
Document manipulation and typography. § 03182
Drag: a graph drawing system. 03183
Abstraction and integration in IDE, an editing and formatting environment. 03184
An introduction to Gargoyle: an interactive illustration tool. 03185
Vidura—an interactive multilingual publishing system—specification & design. 03186
Chinese character processing system based on character-root combination and gra phic processing. 03187
Hypertext tips: experiences in developing a hypertext tutorial. 03236
POEM: An office system for international use. 03457
Automated document distribution using AI based workstations and knowledge based servers. 03466
A hypertext system to manage software life cycle documents. 03519
FolioPub: A publication management system. 03520
Psychological methods for assembling procedures in text management systems. 03600
Digital typography: an introduction to type and composition for computer system design. ● HCI-0074 †
SOFTLIB—A documentation management system. HCI-0149 †
A system for interactive viewing of structured documents. HCI-0400 †
TEXTNET: a network-based approach to text handling. HCI-0401 †
Synthesis of print-quality cursive script based on a model of the human handwriting mechanism. HCI-0402 †
Image processing aspects of type. HCI-0403 †
Visual structure and the transmission of meaning. HCI-0404 †
Document convergence in an interactive formatting system. HCI-0405 †

*Format and notation*

From database to hypertext via electronic publishing: an information odyssey. 0122

CATEGORY INDEX [I. COMPUTING METHODOLOGIES]

Desktop publishing. 0238
Diamond: A multimedia message system built on a distributed architecture. 0574
A document layout system using automatic document architecture extraction. 0882
Videotex information packagers: a field study aimed at tomorrow's videotex authoring interface. 0962
Efforts of display format on proof-reading with VDUs. 01246
Reader-controlled computerized presentation of text. 01785
Music—a language for typesetting music scores. 02622
Quill: An extensible system for editing documents of mixed type. 03517
Multiple representation document development (extende abstract). 03518
Supporting document development with concordia. 03521
Language level persistence for an object-oriented application programming platform. 03522
Practical applications of optical disk image systems in document management. 04041
An experimental comparison of tabular and graphic data presentation. HCI-0236 †
Semistructured messages are surprisingly useful for computer-supported coordination. HCI-0290 †
An experimental multimedia mail system. HCI-0309 †
A system for interactive viewing of structured documents. HCI-0400 †
Document convergence in an interactive formatting system. HCI-0405 †

### *Languages*

Office-by-example: an integrated office system and database manager. 01159
The workstation: the interpress page and document description language. 01356
Supporting document development with concordia. 03521
The evaluation of text editors: methodology and empirical results.. HCI-0209 †

### *Photocomposition*

Videotex information packagers: a field study aimed at tomorrow's videotex authoring interface. 0962
Supporting document development with concordia. 03521
Document processing. 03897

**TeX** *see* Proper Noun Index

**TEXTNET** *see* Proper Noun Index

### I.7.3  Index Generation

Practical applications of optical disk image systems in document management. 04041

### I.7.m  Miscellaneous

Transfer between text editors. 0804
Cognition-sensitive design and user modeling for syntax-directed editors. 0828
A comparison of textual information retention from CRT terminals and paper. 0954
Modelling the human factors aspects of a computer-based text-graphics layout system. 01518
Trends in printer technology. 01624
Reading self-paced moving text on a computer display. 01777
A human factors design investigation of a computerized layout system of text-graphic technical materials. 01779
Structural displays as learning aids. 02188
Question asking when learning a text-editing system. 02202
Microcomputer software. 2. Scientific and technical word processing on a personal computer: has the time come?. 02266
Designing electronic paper to fit user requirements. 03206
Formal methods and the design of effective user interfaces. 03246
Tools for management and support of multiple constraints in a writer's assistant. 03251
Principles and interaction models for window managers. 03264
Text representation and manipulation in a mouse-driven interface. 03266
A viewdata-structure editor designed around a task/action mapping. 03269
Effectiveness of training as a function of the teacher knowledge structure. 03604
The efficiency of letter perception in function of color combinations: a study of video-screen colors. 03616
Eye-head coordination and information uptake during text processing. 03767
Integrating graphics and text in computer products. 04044
Holophrasted displays in an interactive environment. HCI-0105 †
Reading and writing the electronic book. HCI-0282 †
Reflections on NoteCards: seven issues for the next generation of hypermedia systems. HCI-0293 †
Training for optimising transfer between word processors. HCI-0447 †

# J. COMPUTER APPLICATIONS

## J.0 GENERAL

Computer-supported cooperative work: a book of readings. ● 0366
As we may think (Reprint). 0367
Ideas and information: managing in a high-tech world. ● 0586
Understanding & using application software. ● 0626
The CD ROM handbook. ● 0678
The multimedia object presentation manager of MINOS: a symmetric approach. 01083
An object-oriented approach to multimedia databases. 01084
Information technologies for the 1990's: an orgnizational impact perspective. 01336
Putting expert systems to work. 01704
People and computers IV. § 03215
Exploring technology: today and tomorrow. § 03491
Interacting with Computers. HCI-0207 †

## J.1 ADMINISTRATIVE DATA PROCESSING

Human factors in management information systems. ● 0200
Computer support for organizations: toward an organizational science. 0211
Beyond the chalkboard: computer support for collaboration and problem solving inmeetings (Reprint). 0376
Information processing 86. § 03588

### Business

Speech filing—An office system for principals. 0037
Human factors challenges in creating a principal support office system—The speh filing system approach. 0038
Usability: stereotypes and traps. 0104
Investment in computer-product documentation: causes and effects. 0105
Computers for managing information. ● 0141
Practical experience in designing software ergonomic projects for large application systems. 0190
Formflex: a user interface tool for forms definition and management. 0204
Knowledge based management support systems. ● 0252
Evolution of an organizational interface: the new business department at a large insurance firm (Reprint). 0382
Cognitive science and organizational design: a case study of computer conferencing (Reprint). 0386
Expert systems for business. ● 0695
Educating the CBIS user: a case analysis. 0778
End-user computing by top executives. 0780
The problem of identification. 01088
Online use and end-users in media and advertising: an overview. 01216
Modelling the human factors aspects of a computer-based text-graphics layout system. 01518
The effects of a computerized information system on a hospital. 01553
Organizational humanity and architecture: Duality and complementarity of papa-logic and mama-logic in managerial conceptualizations of change. 01609
Cybernetics and organization theory: a critical review. 01617
Uniforms: an automatic forms facility. 01628
Standards and system development. 01629
The age of the end-user and the shift from corporate MIS to corporate DSS. 01676
How technology brings blind people into the workplace. 01705
How executives can shape their company's information systems. 01707
An architecture for a business and information system. 01818
Insights on the implementation of a computer-based message system. 01917
Private copying, reproduction costs, and the supply of intellectual property. 01988
Representing the structure of jobs in job analysis. 02181
Organizational factors affecting the success of end-user computing. 02344
Classifying sensory inspectors with heterogeneous inspection-error probabilities. 02396
Selection systems for sales representatives. 02408
Education requirements for the entry level business systems analyst. 02409
The human connection in systems design. 02410
Documentation in a user work station environment. 02429
Expert systems as human resource management decision tools. 02440
A study of organizational effectiveness and its predictors. 02471
Chief executive personality and corporate strategy and structure in small firms. 02472
The accuracy of combining judgemental and statistical forecasts. 02474
Adaptive coordination of a learning team. 02475
Managerial influence in the implementation of new technology. 02481
The effect of task demands and graphical format on information processing strategies. 02482
Modeling managerial behavior: misperceptions of feedback in a dynamic decision making experiment. 02483
Forgetting and the learning curve: a laboratory study. 02484
Breaking away. 02553

What's new in personal information managers. 02556
Student perceptions of skill acquisition through cases and a general management simulation. 02589
But what will the workers do? simulating what the workers do to us when we do what we do to them. 02590
Team cohesion effects on business game performance. 02597
An expert system for screening employee pension plans for the Internal Revenue Service. 02773
APL: The language of science and management. 02799
User development of applications: a study of a model of success. 02807
Computer-supported cooperative work: breakthroughs for user acceptance. 02874
The systems analyst of the 1990's. 02998
Motivations and behaviors of software professionals. 03003
Managers who personally use information technology frequently: a profile of some invisible computer personnel. 03007
The 1987 ACM SIGBDP-SIGCPR Conference. § 03099
A consultation system for information center resource allocation. 03100
Expert system applications in customer service. 03101
Applications Track. § 03455
Tele-cybernetics: implications for the international marketplace. 03458
The information technology champion: aiding and abetting, care and feeding. 03459
Automated document distribution using AI based workstations and knowledge based servers. 03466
Perceptions of system effectiveness as viewed by executives, users, and information specialists. 03469
A box structured methodology for solving business problems. 03483
GMMS: global model management system: a conceptional design framework for model management systems for distributed decision support systems. 03484
On representation schemes for electronic promising. 03488
Report from the working group on "experience with participation: application in administration and health care". 03668
Visual business graphics query interface. 03840
Stategic imperatives in software engineering education. 04024
Executive support systems: the emergence of top management computer use. • HCI-0049 †
Applying software engineering principles to the user application interface. HCI-0130 †
Mainframe and microcomputer-based business graphics: What satisfies users?. HCI-0216 †
A laboratory study of user characteristics and decision-making performance in end-user computing. HCI-0301 †

### Education

Designing computer-based microworlds. 0742
Issuing each undergraduate student a personal computer: living with it for three years. 01028
Retraining high school teachers to teach computer science—observations on the first course. 01030
Dealing with disparate audiences in computer science courses using a project group within a traditional class. 01031
Putting Texas on disc. 01316
Interactive timetabling in universities. 01501
Recursive complementarity in the cybernetics of education. 01598
A study of organizational effectiveness and its predictors. 02471
An online interface within a hypertext system: project Jefferson's electronic notebook. 02524
Student perceptions of skill acquisition through cases and a general management simulation. 02589
Developments in one-line information systems. 02687
The Drexel disk: an electronic "Guidebook". 03198

### Financial (e.g., EFTS)

Expert systems and artificial intelligence. • 0133
Finance. 0135
An historical perspective of CD ROM. 0679
Skilled financial planning: the cost of translating ideas into action. 0834
Wall Street speaks English. 01184
Lets "Deep-Six" our reference manuals. 02955
An operations advisor for an on-line computer banking system with graphics interface. 02983
Conceptual information extraction form financial news. 03489
A financial investment assistant. 03490
Equipment and workstation design for banking services. 03712
On the design of dealing desks. 03713

### Government

Government infostructures: a guide to the networks of information resources and technologies at federal, state, and local levels. • 0523
A tolerance for surveillance: American public opinion concerning privacy and civil liberties. 0524
Information and the "Aging Network". 0525
Putting Texas on disc. 01316
The FAA's Advanced Automation System: strategies for future air traffic control systems. 01357
Engineering the man-machine interface for air traffic control. 01358
The quantification of operational suitability. 01359
The system understands. 01659

[J. COMPUTER APPLICATIONS]

Informatics and municipalities: the Greek approach. 01940
System design for local authorities: participation based on "information contracts". 03656

*Law*

Integrated information retrieval for law in a hypertext environment. 03071
Human interfaces in a legal expert system. 03164
KRIP: a knowledge representation system for laws relating to industrial property. 03918

*Manufacturing*

Coping with new technology: the need for training. 0441
Employment skills for the robot age. 0442
Man is not a robot. 0445
Information control problems in manufacturing. ● 0554
Computer-aided production management IFIP. ● 0618
Production management systems. 0619
User interface. 0621
Systems analysis techniques. 0622
Production control in car industry. 0623
Production control in the aircraft industry. 0624
A drafted PM glossary. 0625
A supervisory control paradigm for real-time control of flexible manufacturing systems. 01205
MADEMA: an approach to intelligent manufacturing systems. 01318
Human aspects of factory modernization. 01513
A structure for enhancing user participation in model development. 01514
Human-computer interaction in manufacturing. 01522
Smart help for operator performance. 01528
Ergonomic job design in frequent manual lifting tasks: a microcomputer-based model. 01532
Optimal allocation of a work force in a toxic substance environment. 01534
System user/system implementer: a joint responsibility for success. 01535
Barriers to plant transparency, barriers to plant rigidity—A sketch of the problems posed by the radical changes in work forms in the machine-building industry. 01562
The design of distributed transport systems as a major standard interface in computer integrated manufacturing. 01564
Interface concepts for plug-compatible production management systems. 01566
Successful use of CADCAM—a combination of technology, organization, and people. 01569
ORGPLAN an information-decisive aid system to resolving organizing problems. 01573
The human costs of manufacturing reform. 01706
The use of measures of entropy in evaluating human supervisory control of a manufacturing system. 01897

Ergonomic improvements boost AS/RS performance. 01904
Tennessee Eastman employee teamwork raises quality, customer service. 01907
Firm strategies for costly engineering learning. 02485
Service support levels: An organizational approach to end-user computing. 02503
Using worker's survey to improve production. 02566
Produciton and inventory management software packages related to user reactions. 02567
An expert manufacturing simulation system. 02584
Using hypertext to overcome the knowledge base development bottleneck: a case study. 02914
Human-computer-software interaction (HCSI) strategy in the design of global intelligent computer integrated management (ICIM) systems. 03396
An expert system framework for forecasting method selection. 03468
Failure analysis of information systems in small manufacturing enterprises: the importance of the human interface. 03815
Approximation methods used in the exchange of geometric information via the VDA/VDMA surface interface. HCI-0421 †
A tentative implementation of VDAFS. HCI-0422 †

*Marketing*

Data, expert knowledge and decisions. ● 0338
Automatic information processing activities and operational decision making: a case study of consequence. 01950

*Military*

An examination of the research evidence for computer-based instruction. 0415
Design of a control room for the air force logistics command (AFLC) command, control, and communication and intelligence ($C^3I$) system. 01612
Capturing expertise: Some approaches to modeling command decisionmaking in combat analysis. 01883
Adaptive user interfaces for planning and decision aids in $C^3I$ systems. 01887
Graphic equivalence, graphic explanations, and embedded process modeling for enhanced user-system interaction. 01888
Developing the technology for intelligent maintenance advisors. 02276
INQUEST: A prototype intelligence tool. 02918
Lessons learned from modeling a secure multilevel relational database system. 03580
Status of trusted DBMS interpretations. 03585

**MRP** *see* Proper Noun Index

**PROMIS** *see* Proper Noun Index

## J.2 PHYSICAL SCIENCES AND ENGINEERING

Relationships and tasks in scientific research collaborations (Reprint). 0387
Teachers' adoption of multimedia technologies for science and mathematics instruction. 0577
A science of information for the information age. 01285
GPROC—an integrated system for the processing of numerical scientific data. 02631
Electronic communications and collaboration: the emerging model for computer aided communications in science and medicine. 02678
Applications Track. § 03455
Interactive scientific visualization and parallel display techniques. 03542
Crystallographic Computing 4. § 03775
The computer as an integral part of the laboratory. 03880
A supporting system for effective construction and sharing of scientific databases by general researchers. HCI-0262 †

### Aerospace

Collective computation, content-addressable memory, and optimization problems. 0004
Text processing with the START natural language system. 0100
Expert systems and artificial intelligence. ● 0133
Space. 0134
Voice input applications in aerospace. 0179
Production control in the aircraft industry. 0624
NASA Johnson Space Center, Human-Computer Interaction. 0815
Formatting space-related displays to optimize expert and nonexpert user performance. 0927
The FAA's Advanced Automation System: strategies for future air traffic control systems. 01357
Engineering the man-machine interface for air traffic control. 01358
The quantification of operational suitability. 01359
Design of a control room for the air force logistics command (AFLC) command, control, and communication and intelligence ($C^3I$) system. 01612
An integrated display for vertical and translational flight: eight factors affecting pilot performance. 01714
Comparison of speech and pictorial displays in a cockpit environment. 01731
A psychophysiological assessment of operator workload during simulated flight missions. 01735
Perspective traffic display format and airline pilot traffic avoidance. 01748
Simulator design and instructional features for air-to-ground attack: a transfer study. 01804
The development of an intelligent user interface for NASA's scientific databases. 02673
The mission operators planning assistant. 02674
The second generation intelligent user interface for the crustal dynamics data information system. 02675
The HORSES project and its perspectives in knowledge engineering. 02716
APL: The language of science and management. 02799
The ISA expert system: a prototype system for failure diagnosis on the space station. 02913
The development of an automated flight test management system for flight test planning and monitoring. 02928
Evaluating the impact of camera placement on teleoperator efficiency. 02940
Concept demonstration of the use of interactive fault diagnosis and isolation for TF30 engines. 02968
Jet engine technical advisor (JETA). 02974
DORUS: an architecture for dynamic optimal resource utilization systems. 02979
A prototype autonomous agent for crew and equipment retrieval in space. 02994
Human factors in the Columbus space station. 03250
Human visual requirements for control and monitoring of a space telerobot. 03391
Illumination requirements for operating a space remote manipulator. 03392
Visual simulation. 03503
The space station information system and software support environment. 03512
Fallible humans and vulnerable systems: lessons learned from aviation. 03808
Error auditing in air traffic control. 03810

### Astronomy

The mission operators planning assistant. 02674
Computer science and statistics. § 03313

### Chemistry

Cost effectiveness of on-line searching of chemical information: an industrial viewpoint. 0195
High-speed computing: scientific applications and algorithm design. ● 0727
An industrial chemical hazards database with a natural language interface: an application of artificial intelligence. 01593
Primary journals today and tomorrow. 02264
Comparison of manual and online searches of chemical abstracts. 02265
Microcomputer software. 2. Scientific and technical word processing on a personal computer: has the time come?. 02266
Simps: Secondary ion mass image processing system. 02267
"Structure—reaction type" paradigm in the conventional methods of describing organic reactions and the

concept of imaginary transitions structures overcoming this paradigm. 02268
End-user searching of CAS ONLINE. Results of a cooperative experiment between Imperial Chemical Industries and Chemical Abstracts Services. 02269
An interactive modeling program for DNA. 02385
An interactive biomolecule graphics system. 02386
The MIDAS database system. 02387
The MIDAS display system. 02388
MOL3D, a modular and interactive program for molecular modeling and conformational analysis: I—basic modules. 02389

### Earth and atmospheric sciences

Computerization and skill in local weather forecasting. 0344
High-speed computing: scientific applications and algorithm design. ● 0727
The computational science revolution: technology, methodology, and sociology. 0728
Computing needs in thunderstorm modeling: supercomputers and interactive graphics. 0730
A PC-interactives stereonet plotting program. 01504
MINID—a BASIC program to assist in the optical identification of minerals in thin section. 01505
Multidimensional attribute analyhsis and pattern recognition for seismic interpretation. 02530
Portfolio: kaleidoscopic visions. 02551
Applications of computer graphics to the visualization of meteorological data. 02819
Design of an AI-Based self-sustaining habitats control system. 02959
Hierarchical scheduling in an intelligent environmental control system. 02976
A note on the nature of creativity in engineering: implications for supporting system design. HCI-0220 †
Geomatic: a 3-D graphic relief simulation system. HCI-0395 †
IDECAP: interactive pictorial information system for demographic and environmental planning applications. HCI-0411 †

### Electronics

Electronic speech recognition: techniques, technology, and applications. ● 0174
Human factors reference guide for electronics and computer professionals. ● 0734
Managers' reading habits in the electronics industry. 02339
Generic expert system shell for diagnostic reasoning. 02911
Expert diagnostic system. 02912
Improving performance of an electrical power expert system with genetic algorithms. 02925

### Engineering

Computer applications in water supply: vol. 1—systems analysis and simulation. ● 0227
Fundamentals of engineering drawing: with an introduction to interactive computer graphics for design and production, (9th ed.). ● 0531
High-speed computing: scientific applications and algorithm design. ● 0727
Assessment of an effort to integrate computer functions in an engineering design firm. 0779
Interactive microcomputer programs for linear and non-linear static analysis of frameworks. 01165
SMART: Scientific database management and engineering analysis routines and tools. 01166
A user-friendly program of human judgments in engineering decision analysis. 01167
A human-computer interactive design program for a multisolution nonlinear problem. 01168
Teachware for power engineering education. 01203
Automation, work organization and skills: the case of numerical control. 01234
Computerized design and analysis of sitting workplace. 01506
The design of a user friendly engineering economy analysis package for a microcomputer. 01507
Interactive multiple objective linear programming system implemented on a microcomputer. 01508
User friendly micro computer program for solving fractional and linear programming problems. 01509
A comprehensive data base for the design of manual materials handling. 01510
A graphical database interface. 01511
User facilities for engineering support stations. 01512
Human aspects of factory modernization. 01513
A structure for enhancing user participation in model development. 01514
Needs and perceived needs of electronic workstations by engineering project managers. 01515
Knowledge-based system for task analysis and reliability enhancement. 01516
A knowledge-based system for assessment of human physiological abilities in manual lifting tasks. 01519
A graphics interface to an engineering economy program. 01520
Job characteristic perceptions of manual drafting and CADD: A field study of the effects of computerization on drafting & design personnel. 01523
Biomechanical evaluation of lifting tasks: a microcomputer-based model. 01524
Assessing the impact of human factors on data processing inspection errors. 01527
Ergonomic job design in frequent manual lifting tasks: a microcomputer-based model. 01532
An industrial chemical hazards database with a natural

language interface: an application of artificial intelligence. 01533
Optimal allocation of a work force in a toxic substance environment. 01534
System user/system implementer: a joint responsibility for success. 01535
Real-time failure detection on complex mechanical structures via parallel data processing. 01561
CAD system GISK for interactive graphical modelling of planar mechanisms. 01570
Interactive CAD/CAM in engineering industry. 01571
Application of decision support system on sandwich beams, verified by experiments. 01572
An interactive approach to local remeshing around a propagating crack. 01685
Methods improvement kit uses IE technique to simplify work. 01909
Study of combination of belief intevals in lattice-structured networks. 02223
The ECLIPSE user interface. 02638
Power plant simulation and reactor safety. 02682
Hypertext engineering: practical methods for creating a compact disk encyclopedia. 02832
Transferring skills from training to the actual work situation: the role of task application knowledge, action styles and job decision latitude. 02865
Process design of oil and gas production facilities using expert systems. 02933
NetGraph: an object-oriented graphical toolset for risk assessment. 02972
Object oriented rapid prototyping with G2. 02984
Reliability and robustness of engineering software. § 03451
Human interface in structural analysis software. 03453
CAD and robotics in architecture and construction. § 03568
Evolution of a robotic excavator. 03569
Force and tactile sensing for robots. 04013
Signal processing and pattern recognition in nondestructive evaluation of materials. § 04019
Applications of AI in engineering. HCI-0321 †
Interactive computer program for the selection of interference fits. HCI-0406 †

### Mathematics and statistics

Environments for supporting statistical strategy. 0322
Use of psychometric tools for knowledge acquistion: a case study. 0323
The analysis phase in development of knowledge based systems. 0324
Experimental data for the design of a microworld-based system for algebra. 0543
Conceptual design of decision support systems utilizing management science models. 0658
Mathematical formula editor for CAI. 0885
A Computational model for interfaces. 01163
Effects of computer programming experience on network representations of abstract programming concepts. 02204
Comparison of student performance in artihmetic exercises TOAM us paper-and-pencial testing. 02249
Some considerations on intelligent tutoring systems. 02963
Essential ingredients for a statistical workstation. 03315
Statistical software, graphics and future workstations for data analysis. 03316
An iterative approach to improving data analysis in the classroom. 03318
Applicable algebra, error-correcting codes, combinatorics and computer algebra. § 03846
Integration of graphical tools in a computer algebra system. 03847

### Physics

Cognitive economy in physics reasoning: implications for designing instructional materials. 0542
Progress in medical imaging. ● 0556
High-speed computing: scientific applications and algorithm design. ● 0727
Coherent and chaotic structures in 2D vortex dynamics: progress and problems. 0729
Profile data acquisition for the JCPDS-ICDD database s. 01232
Retinex: physics and the theory of color vision. 01574
Optical systems that imitate human memory. 01576
Supercomputers in the classroom. 01577
Digital waveform sampling rate converter. 01578
Medical informatics: a personal view of sowing the seeds. 02841
The history of the use of computers in the interpretation of radiological images. 02845
Understanding text with an accompanying diagram. 02947
Overcoming conceptual difficulties in physical science through computer-based Socratic dialogs. 03877
Integrating physics and computer education in a single process. 03879

## J.3  LIFE AND MEDICAL SCIENCES

Vision, brain, and cooperative computation. ● 0014
Relationships and tasks in scientific research collaborations (Reprint). 0387
Professional and expert systems: a meeting of minds. 0790
An investigation of data entry methods with a personal computer. 01490
The fuzzy decodings of educative texts. 01700
A regression model to identify successful learner traits with CAI. 02376
AI/learn: an interactive videodisk system for teaching medical concepts and reasoning. 02381
Electronic communications and collaboration: the emerg-

ing model for computer aided communications in science and medicine. 02678
History of Medical Informatics. § 02837
Perspectives over forty years. 02847
Crystallographic Computing 4. § 03775
Pictorial information systems in medicine. § 03976
Medicine in the age of the computer. ● HCI-0075 †
Voice-input aids for the physically disabled. HCI-0089 †
Resistance to computerization: an examination of the relationship between resistance and the cognitive style of the clinician. HCI-0407 †

### Biology

Vision, brain, and cooperative computation: an overview. 0015
Why visuomotor systems don't like negative feedback and how they avoid it. 0016
The role of the primate superior colliculus in sensorimotor integration. 0017
Depth and detours: an essay on visually guided behavior. 0018
A trace of memory: an evolutionary perspective on the visual system. 0019
Visual analysis during motion. 0020
Figure-ground organization affects the early visual processing. 0021
The diversity of perceptual grouping. 0022
The interdependence of temporal and spatial information in early vision. 0023
A functional model of vision and space. 0027
Visual-cognitive neuronal networks. 0029
A model of the neocortex. 01164
Statistical inference on spontaneous neuronal discharge patterns. I. Single neuron. 01247
A self-organizing neural network sharing features of the mammalian visual system. 01248
Representation of local geometry in the visual system. 01249
Modeling of control and learning in a stepping motion. 01250
Muscle models: what is gained and what is lost by varying model complexity. 01251
A multivariate solution for cyclic data, applied in modelling locomotor forces. 01252
Information compression in biological systems. 01253
Diffusion approximation of the neuronal model with synaptic reversal potentials. 01254
Characteristics of neuronal systems in the visual cortex. 01255
Vertical disparity nulling in random-dot stereograms. 01256
Facts on optic flow. 01257
A study of stability of electrocortical rhythm generators. 01258
Identification of MGB cells by Volterra kernels. III. A glance into the black box. 01259
On the identification of neural responses. 01260
Single sweep analysis of visual evoked potentials through a model of parametric identification. 01261
Disjunctive models of boolean category learning. 01262
Simulation of chaotic EEG patterns with a dynamic model of the olfactory system. 01263
A scaling model for dichotomous branching processes. 01264
Projected free fall trajectories. I. Theory and simulation. 01265
Projected free fall trajectories. II. Human experiments. 01266
A method for computing spectral reflectance. 01267
Quantitative determination of orientational and directional components in the response of visual cortical cells to moving stimuli. 01268
Interpolation coding: A representation for numbers in neural models. 01271
The control of hand equilibrium trajectories in multi-joint arm movements. 01275
Electric and magnetic fields of the brain computed by way of a discrete systems analytical approach: Theory and validation. 01276
Physiology based simulation model of triangle shape recognition. 01277
Shape from texture. 01278
Self-organizing system obtaining communication ability primitive model for language generation. 01279
Stochastic dynamics of neural networks. 01863
On the applicability of maximum entropy to inexact reasoning. 02074
An interactive modeling program for DNA. 02385
An interactive biomolecule graphics system. 02386
Nonlinear dynamics of pattern formation and pattern recognition in the rabbit olfactory bulb. 02558
The immune system, adaptation, and machine learning. 02559
A teachable neural network based on an unorthodox neuron. 02561
A self-optimizing, nonsymmetrical neural net for content addressable memory and pattern recognition. 02562
Advances in Cognitive Science. § 02720
Advances in cognitive science. 02721
Bifurcation analysis of oscillating network model of pattern recognition in the rabbit olfactory bulb. 02725
A model for cortical function. 02731
A dynamic model of olfactory discrimination. 02737
A hand biomechanics workstation. 02820
How DENDRAL was conceived and born. 02839
Medical informatics: a personal view of sowing the seeds. 02841
The LINC was early and small. 02843
The UCLA Brain Research Institute data processing laboratory. 02844
The history of the use of computers in the interpretation of radiological images. 02845

Recollections on the processing of biomedical signals. 02846

Design of an AI-Based self-sustaining habitats control system. 02959

Gripe: a graphical interface to a knowledge based system which reasons about protein topology. 03234

Hypertext tips: experiences in developing a hypertext tutorial. 03236

Parallel in sequence—towards the architecture of an elementary cortical processor. 03820

Control of the immune response. 03970

On the purpose and analysis of EDP user systems. HCI-0218 †

Connectionist models and parallelism in high level vision. HCI-0363 †

Reverse engineering the brain. HCI-0368 †

## Health

The disabled. 0148

Color displays for medical imaging. 0262

Application of structural pattern recognition in histopathology. 0295

A language/action perspective on the design of cooperative work (Reprint). 0383

Manipulation of 3D imagery. 0557

Communication methods of the vocally disabled: a review. 0783

An overview of $T^3$-PBE. 0784

A user interface for deaf-blind people (preliminary report). 0794

A case example of human factors in product definition: needs finding for a voice output workstation for the blind. 0819

Towards universality of access: interfacing physically disabled students to the Icon educational microcomputer. 0821

User-interface design for a clinical neurophysiological intensive monitoring system. 0881

An authoring system for the creation of interfaces for disabled users. 0974

Computer aids for vision and employment (CAVE). 0976

User interface primitives to allow full functional use of computers by physically disabled persons. 0979

Do VDU's make you sick?. 1219

Are you sitting comfortably?. 01220

A model-based monitor of human sleep stages. 01269

Uncertainty analysis of human EEG spectra: A multivariate information theoretical method for the analysis of brain activity. 01270

Comparison of color sensation in dichoptic and in normal vision. 01272

A model of the motor servo: Incorporating nonlinear spindle receptor and muscle mechanical properties. 01273

Computing for the blind user. 01287

Computers on the brain, part 1. 01296

Error-free fractions. 01297

Computers on the brain, part 2. 01298

The use and misuse of VDU'S. 01375

Design of a graphics interface for computer-based biomedical applications. 01427

Helping the disabled. 01445

The architecture of an inexpensive and portable talking-tactile terminal to aid the visually handicapped. 01452

Computer quantification of delta activity in sleep EEG. 01491

Interactive graphic editor for analysis and enhancement of medical images. 01492

Optimal allocation of a work force in a toxic substance environment. 01534

Computer work skills training for persons with developmental disabilities. 01559

Issues in research on clinical computer applications for mental health. 01560

Fundamentals of psychosomatic transduction. 01594

Model of the neuro-muscular recruitment example of the extensor digitorum communis muscle in man: I—identification of motoneurons and of muscular fibers. 01595

The cybernetic mechanisms of stress. 01599

An approach to a mathematics of phenomena: canonical aspects of reentrant form eigenbehavior in the extended calculus of indications. 01621

Dp and the disabled. 01646

How technology brings blind people into the workplace. 01705

An intelligent braille display device. 01832

Neural network model with rhythm-assimilation capacity. 01881

The dubious dangers of VDT radiation. 01902

Biological aspects of neural nets. 02311

An assessment of the major computerised databases relating to disabled people in the UK and Scandinavia. 02326

An inexpensive and portable talking-tactile terminal for the visually handicapped. 02377

Design of an integral computer-based wheelchair controller/linear synchronous motor system. 02378

A model of the controller responses of the human temperature regulating system to changes in water temperature. 02487

Headstart—a lifeline for the disabled. 02500

The body in question: how to stay healthy at the PC. 02548

VDTs: are they safe?. 02549

An evaluation of auditory performances in patients with Cochlear implants. 02658

Development and sensitivity analysis of adaptive predictor for human eye movement model. 02681

Neurons with hysteresis form a network that can learn

[J. COMPUTER APPLICATIONS]   CATEGORY INDEX

without any changes in synaptic connection strengths. 02741
A hand biomechanics workstation. 02820
In praise of computing. 02838
Planting the seeds. 02840
The LINC was early and small. 02843
The UCLA Brain Research Institute data processing laboratory. 02844
The history of the use of computers in the interpretation of radiological images. 02845
Recollections on the processing of biomedical signals. 02846
Patient management systems: the early years. 02852
The background of INTERNIST I and QMR. 02853
EPVM: An expert patient-ventilator manager for chemical warfare casualties. 02956
New technology work aids for the physically disabled. 03273
100 Percent assured performance for robotic assistive devices for handicapped and elderly persons. 03414
Standards requirements for mobile robotic systems. 03415
Overview of research issues in robot safety. 03417
Safety considerations in robot design. 03418
Human factors considerations in the design of a VDU for visually impaired persons. 03698
On the architecture for pictorial information systems. 03977
Psychovisual issues in the display of medical images. 03978
Software tools for the development of pictorial information systems in medicine—the ISQL experience. 03980
Signal processing and pattern recognition in nondestructive evaluation of materials. § 04019
The effects of limited data in multi-frequency reflection diffraction tomography. 04020
Eye movement analysis system using fundus images. HCI-0243 †
The development and use of information technology in health care. HCI-0408 †
Evaluating RECONSIDER: a computer program for diagnostic prompting. HCI-0410 †

**Medical information systems**

A history of the promis technology: an effective human interface. 0349
Graphical specification of procedural knowledge for an expert system. 0427
Progress in medical imaging. ● 0556
User-interface design for a clinical neurophysiological intensive monitoring system. 0881
Understanding Bayesian reasoning via graphical displays. 0884
Principles of an icons-based language. 01080
Planning for hospital information systems using the Lancaster Soft Systems methodology. 01228

Visual pattern recognition in humans: I. Evidence for adaptive filtering. 01274
The effects of a computerized information system on a hospital. 01553
Issues in research on clinical computer applications for mental health. 01560
An error correcting protocol for medical expert systems. 02143
An interactive videodisc drama: The case of Frank hall. 02285
The foreign language barrier: a study among pharmaceutical research workers. 02333
Implementation of a multirule, multistage quality control program in a clinical laboratory computer system. 02380
Person-to-person communication in an applied research/service delivery setting. 02445
Computing facilities in the MRC clinical research centre. 02688
In praise of computing. 02838
Medical informatics: a personal view of sowing the seeds. 02841
History of the development of medical information systems at the Laboratory of Computer Science at Massachusetts General Hospital. 02842
An historical perspective on clinical laboratory information systems. 02848
Health care information systems: a personal historic review. 02849
The perception of system and the reduction of uncertainty. 02850
History of the TDS medical information system. 02851
Patient management systems: the early years. 02852
Illustrated description of an interactive knowledge based indexing system. 03076
A history of the Promis technology: an effective human interface. 03097
Hypertext tips: experiences in developing a hypertext tutorial. 03236
Applications Track. § 03455
A dietary recommendation expert system using OPS5. 03498
Report from the working group on "experience with participation: application in administration and health care". 03668
Software tools for the development of pictorial information systems in medicine—the ISQL experience. 03980
Automatic contour definition on left ventriculograms by image evidence and a multiple template-based model. 04073
On the purpose and analysis of EDP user systems. HCI-0218 †
Observations of end-user online searching behavior over eleven years. HCI-0235 †
Architecture problems in the construction of expert systems for document retrieval. HCI-0272 †

The doctor's use of a computer in the consulting room: an analysis. HCI-0409 †

**RECONSIDER** *see* Proper Noun Index

## J.4 SOCIAL AND BEHAVIORAL SCIENCES

Relationships and tasks in scientific research collaborations (Reprint). 0387
Social science and system design: interdisciplinary collaborations. 0833
Development of the wedding planner—extensions to reach a young audience. 01502
Issues in research on clinical computer applications for mental health. 01560
The fuzzy logic of text understanding. 01701
Computer culture: the scientific, intellectual, and social impact of the computer. § 03567
Intentional and operational aspects of decision behaviour and their modelling. 03666
Strategies for encouraging successful adoption of office communication systems. HCI-0307 †
Computer-assisted negotiations: a case history from the law of the sea negotiations and speculation regarding future uses. HCI-0443 †

### Economics

A user-friendly interface to Kendrick's DUAL code. 01447
A graphics interface to an engineering economy program. 01520
The dual role of information centers: an assessment of end user computing management strategies. 01942
Private copying, reproduction costs, and the supply of intellectual property. 01988

**IDECAP** *see* Proper Noun Index

### Psychology

Knowledge representation and natural language: extending the expressive power of proposition nodes. 0096
Learning in man-computer interaction: a review of the literature. 0151
Computer models of mind: computational approaches in theoretical psychology. ● 0152
Interfacing thought: cognitive aspects of human-computer interaction. ● 0207
Learning about computers and learning about mathematics. 0208
Effect of practice on knowledge and use of basic Lisp. 0210
Computer support for organizations: toward an organizational science. 0211
HCI, what is it and what research is needed?. 0212

Improving human-computer interaction—a quest for cognitive science. 0213
Contexts and conflicts between ergonomics and industrial psychology. 0240
Ergonomics and organizational consulting: accentuation or neglect of psychology. 0242
Psychological issues of human-computer interaction in the work place. ● 0305
A critique and empirical investigation of the "One-Best-Way-Models" in human-computer interaction. 0317
On methods of analysis of mental models and the evaluation of interactive computer systems. 0319
Applying cognitive psychology to user-interface design. ● 0325
Introduction. 0326
Future directions. 0336
Cognitive psychology of planning. ● 0435
Cognitive engineering in complex dynamic worlds. ● 0436
Computation and cognition: toward a foundation for cognitive science. ● 0593
Modelling novice programmer behaviour. 0744
Information science and the PSI phenomenon. 01281
Competitive dynamics in a dual-route connectionist model of print-to-sound transformation. 01341
Fundamentals of psychosomatic transduction. 01594
The informational substrata of psychic illnesses. 01600
The fuzzy decodings of educative texts. 01700
The effect of adding symbols to written warning labels on user behavior and recall. 01788
The effect of microcomputer presentation and response medium on digit span. 02090
An application of computerized fuzzy graphics rating scale to the psychological measurement of individual differences. 02200
The influence of personality on self-paced instruction. 02291
Induction of categories: The problem of multiple equilibria. 02360
A theory of information structure. I. General principles. 02361
A theory of information structure. II. A theory of perceptual organization. 02362
Mathematical modeling of fatigue in physically demanding jobs. 02363
Non-Reimannian approach to geometry of visual space: An application of affinely connected geometry to visual alleys and horopter. 02364
A limitation theorem for the differentiable prototypification of shape. 02365
A group model of form recognition under plane similarity transformations. 02366
Counting and timing models in psychophysics and the conjoint Weber's law. 02368

[J. COMPUTER APPLICATIONS]

Expectation and variance of item resemblance distributions in a convolution-correction model of distributed memory. 02369
Psychological models of deferred decision making. 02370
The accumulator model of two-choice discrimination. 02371
A probabilistic dominance measure for binary choices: analytic aspects of a multi-attribute random weights model. 02372
A note on mimicking additive reaction time models. 02373
Alleys on an apparent frontoparallel plane. 02374
The psychophysical function of binocular space perception. 02375
Communication issues among psychologists working with computers: a view from the top. 02606
MACINTER—aim and goal. 03590
Personality traits of the worker within the :20man-machine" system at automated production. 03593
Necessary contributions of cognitive psychology to computer knowledge representation and manipulation systems. 03598
Memory research and knowledge engineering. 03599
Artificial behavior: computer simulation of psychological processes. ● HCI-0073 †
Information science: its roots and relation as viewed from the perspective of cognitive science. HCI-0185 †
Psychology and information technology. HCI-0225 †
Approaches to human reasoning: an analytic framework. HCI-0239 †
Semantic primitives or meaning postulates: mental models or propositional representation?. HCI-0339 †
Language generation by computer. HCI-0342 †
The mapping between grammar and processor. HCI-0346 †
Multivariate data representation and analysis by face pattern using facial expression characteristics. HCI-0394 †
The automated tutoring of introductory computer programming. HCI-0438 †

### Sociology

The rational, the pragmatic and the inquiry process: The social study of information- communication systems. 0786
The effects of computer use in early childhood socialization. 0793
Computer work skills training for persons with developmental disabilities. 01559
Self-authorization: A characteristic of some elements in certain self-organizing systems. 01610
Captive...a new tool. 03129
The social cybernetics of human interaction with automated systems. 03442
In the age of the smart machine: the future of work and power. ● HCI-0083 †

## J.5  ARTS AND HUMANITIES

Computational models of natural language processing. ● 0095
Computer assisted language learning: program structure and principles. ● 0196
The practice of the use of computers. A paradoxical encounter between different traditions of knowledge. 0343
Computer assisted learning in the humanities and social sciences. ● 0470
The role of social processes in children's microcomputer use. 0471
Evaluation of a program on "distance". 0472
Symbiotic software: development and usage issues on stand-alone and networked systems. 0474
Learning with interactive media: dynamic support for students and teachers. 0519
Information technology in the humanities: tools, techniques and applications. ● 0595
The Perseus project: an interactive curriculum on classical greek civilization. 01680
An analysis of humanists' requests received by an information service for the humanities. 02318
Music—a language for typesetting music scores. 02622

### Arts, fine and performing

Computer graphics: A tool for the artist, designer and amateur. 0235
The computer revolution and the arts. ● 0529
The new renaissance: art, science and universal machine. 0530
Principles of traditional animation applied to 3D computer animation. 01072
A system for the representation of human body movement from dance scores. 02540
A human-computer interface for control system design. 03208
Can cognitive complexity theory (CCT) produce an adequate measure of system usability?. 03229
A comparison of the effects of computer-assisted instruction, interactive video, and traditional instruction on third-grade students in art education. 04064

### Language translation

Interactive video in language learning. 01380
Two-level data banks for translators. 01556
A user perspective on computer-assisted translation for Minority languages. 01557
Machine assisted translation with a human face. 01627
LSP-automatic translation and information technology. 02513
A framework of a mechanical translation between Japanese and English by analogy principle. HCI-0353 †

## Linguistics

Knowledge representation and natural language: extending the expressive power of proposition nodes. 0096
Natural languages. 0136
Knowledge representation. 0137
Semantics. 0154
Talking it over: the natural language dialog system HAM-ANS. 0165
Electronic speech recognition: techniques, technology, and applications. ● 0174
The nature of speech. 0175
Computational linguistics. ● 0215
Understanding natural languages. 01172
Mathematical building blocks. 01173
Lexical organisation from three different angles. 01199
Attention, intention, and the structure of discourse. 01344
Natural language querying of historical data bases. 01354
Interactive video in language learning. 01380
Human language and computers. 01550
Language, sublanguage, and the promise of machine translation. 01554
Left-associative grammar: an informal outline. 01558
An experiment in computational discrimination of English word senses. 01813
Expanatory dialogues. 02063
LSP-automatic translation and information technology. 02513
The measurement of the signal-to-noise ratio (SNR) in continuous speech. 02654
Perceptual normalization of the vowels of a man and a child in various contexts. 02656
Coproduction: evidence from EPG data. 02660
An acoustic-phonetic oriented system for synthesizing Chinese. 02661
Using latent semantic analysis to improve access to textual information. 02901
Character recognition of cursive scripts. 02961
Motion analysis of grammatical processes in a visual-gestural language. 03347
Decision support using qualitative evidence. 03398
A functional model of questions for natural language processing systems. 03575
Natural Language at the Computer. § 03947
Computational linguistics: issues and solutions. 03948
The use of VDM on the specification of Chinese characters. 04038
Mental models: towards a cognitive science of language, inference, and consciousness. ● HCI-0063 †
Semantic primitives or meaning postulates: mental models or propositional representation?. HCI-0339 †
Language generation by computer. HCI-0342 †
The mapping between grammar and processor. HCI-0346 †
A framework for investigating language-mediated interaction with machines. HCI-0347 †

## Literature

Writers as total desktop publishers: developing a conceptual approach to training. 0108
On one aspect of natural-language based knowledge acquisition. 03571

## Music

The computer as musical accompanist. 0897
An interactive environment for object-oriented music composition and sound synthesis. 01131
Systematic evaluation strategies for computer-based music instruction systems. 02275
Music—a language for typesetting music scores. 02622
Computer-music interfaces: a survey. HCI-0412 †

## J.6 COMPUTER-AIDED ENGINEERING

Information development is part of product development—not an afterthought. 0103
Advanced information technology in the new industrial society: the Kingston seminars. ● 0225
The management of advanced information technology. 0226
Creativity, skill and human-centered systems. 0346
Coping with new technology: the need for training. 0441
Approximate modelling of cognitive activity: towards an expert system design aid. 0801
Designing for designers: an analysis of design practice in the real world. 0839
On the design of man-machine systems: principles, practices and prospects. 01236
MADEMA: an approach to intelligent manufacturing systems. 01318
Computer graphics language bindings: programmer interface standards. 01473
Exchange of solid models: current state and future trends. 01475
User facilities for engineering support stations. 01512
Job characteristic perceptions of manual drafting and CADD: A field study of the effects of computerization on drafting & design personnel. 01523
Evaluating formatted alphanumeric displays. 01525
Touchscreen usage in plant computer systems: a case study. 01530
Simulation of CNC controller features in graphics-based programming. 01568
Successful use of CADCAM—a combination of technology, organization, and people. 01569
Interactive CAD/CAM in engineering industry. 01571
Application of decision support system on sandwich beams, verified by experiments. 01572

ORGPLAN an information-decisive aid system to resolving organizing problems. 01573
The specialties. 01835
Interactive data visualization. 01986
The user designer/developer and the user work station. 02431
An expert system for system design. 02441
New applications of data bases. § 02710
The ANALYST—A workstation for analysis and design. 02713
Reliability and robustness of engineering software. § 03451
Transparency and system design. 03655
Recent results on the illumination of VDU and CAD workstations. 03719
Qualified CAD work: an intensive case study. 03763
SPECIF-X: a tool for CASE. 03801
ProMod at the age of 5. 03802
Advanced computing concepts and techniques in control engineering. § 03833
Computer graphics 1987. § 03852
A gestural representation of the process of composing Chinese temples. 03855
Low cost geometric modelling system for CAM. 03866
The CADME approach to the interface of solid modellers. 03867
Product data interfaces in CAD/CAM applications: design, implementation and experiences. § 03981
A note on the nature of creativity in engineering: implications for supporting system design. HCI-0220 †
Geomatic: a 3-D graphic relief simulation system. HCI-0395 †
CAD/CAM: integration in the automobile industry. HCI-0413 †

**AutoCAD** *see* Proper Noun Index

### Computer-aided design (CAD)

Intelligent CAD systems II: implementational issues. • 0006
Multi-media presentation in CAD systems. 0007
A definitive programming approach to the implementation of CAD software. 0008
Product and process design in intelligent CAD workstations. 0009
THESYS—implementation of a knowledge-based design system with multiple viewpoints. 0010
A historical and intellectual perspective of the context of human computer interaction. 0039
Geometric modelling. 0236
CAD data exchange. 0237
Color graphic displays for network planning and design. 0260
Advances in computer graphics II. • 0437
Principles of computer-aided design: computability of design. • 0465
Strategies for interactive design systems. 0466
Designing with constraints. 0467
A multi-processor workstation with a logic-enhanced distributed frame buffer. 0496
Fundamentals of engineering drawing: with an introduction to interactive computer graphics for design and production, (9th ed.). • 0531
CAD Based Programming for Sensory Robots. • 0597
A workcell application design environment (WADE). 0598
Robot simulation and off-line programming—an integrated CAE-CAD approach. 0599
CAD Based verification and refinement of high level compliant motion primitives. 0600
Experiences with off-line robot programming via standardized interfaces. 0601
Off-line programming of robots using 3D graphical simulation system. 0602
Modeling of robot system dynamics for CAD based robot programming. 0605
Computer aided application program synthesis for industrial robots. 0606
CAD-based off-line programming applied to a cleaning and deburring workstation. 0607
Computer-aided production management IFIP. • 0618
Production control in car industry. 0623
An overview of system design for human interaction. 0646
An expert system architecture for computer-aided control engineering. 0662
Computer-aided engineering (CAE) for system analysis. 0663
A natural language interface for computer-aided design. • 0664
Intelligent CAD systems I: theoretical and methodological aspects. • 0715
A multiparadigm user interface for intelligent CAD systems. 0716
An integrated data description language for coding design knowledge. 0717
A synthetic visual environment with hand gesturing and voice input. 0858
A user interface for multiple-process, turnkey systems targeted for the novice user. 0911
Developing computer aided design technology in China. 0942
Designing the "cockpit": the application of a human-centered design philosophy to make optimization systems accessible. 01016
RAPID: Prototyping control panel interfaces. 01120
A human-computer interactive design program for a multisolution nonlinear problem. 01168
A man-machine interface for computer-aided and simulation of control systems. 01237

A cognitively based methodology for evaluating human performance in the computer-aided design task domain. 01240

Claris CAD. 01310

Making drawings talk: pictures in minds and machines. 01392

A new algorithm for extracting the interior of bounded regions based on chain coding. 01469

Unified interactive geometric modeller for simulating highly complex environments. 01472

Automatic construction of surfaces with prescribed shape. 01474

Initial work on a system-independent computer model of a 3D anthropomorphic dummy. 01476

Computerized design and analysis of sitting workplace. 01506

Standardization aspects on software for CAD of control systems. 01565

CAD system GISK for interactive graphical modelling of planar mechanisms. 01570

A human factors design investigation of a computerized layout system of text-graphic technical materials. 01779

An interactive procedure for constructing line and circle tangencies. 01823

An automatic wafer inspection system using pipelined image processing techniques. 01840

Utilizing high technology: computer-aided-design and user performance. 01954

A workstation assessor for crew operations-WOSTAS. 02093

Support for tentative design: incorporating the screen image, as a graphical object, into PROLOG. 02116

Pride-II physical layout program of modifying Forth for "non-believers". 02312

A computer aided design system for artistic chinese fonts. 02455

Graphics fundamentals for a PCB-CAD PC system. 02494

An interactive simulator for the designing of woven fabric structures second place. 02583

GCI—a tool for developing interactive CAD user interfaces. 02625

A study in interactive 3-D rotation using 2-D control devices. 02813

Getting graphics in gear: graphics and dynamics in driving simulation. 02818

A hand biomechanics workstation. 02820

Design Automation. § 02828

PHRAN-SPAN: a natural language interface for system specifications. 02829

VISION: VHDL induced schematic imaging on net-lists. 02830

Automated design and analysis system for design of custom orthopedic implants. 02931

Applications of an AI design shell ENGINEOUS to advanced engineering products. 02932

Process design of oil and gas production facilities using expert systems. 02933

ProCEED: an expert system for multivariate process control systems design. 02935

GTEX—A group technology expert system. 02936

CAD Data management using object-oriented paradigms. 02958

Using design expertise to develop an expert system. 02962

Industrial & Engineering Applications of Artificial Intelligence & Expert Systems: vol. I. § 02967

An interactive tolerance system. 02975

Planning as feedback to designers. 02978

A process oriented approach to an intelligent design aid. 02980

Computer aided concurrent design for printed wiring boards. 02981

Industrial & Engineering Applications of Artificial Intelligence & Expert Systems: vol. II. § 02982

A dialog based interface to a design knowledge base that understands user design-intentions. 02988

Incorporating the human factor in color CAD systems. 03104

An interactive data dictionary facility for CAD/CAM data bases. 03174

Contextual structure analysis of microcomputer manuals. 03227

Can cognitive complexity theory (CCT) produce an adequate measure of system usability?. 03229

The application of cognitive psychology to CAD. 03239

Ergonomics of Hybrid Automated Systems I. § 03362

Product engineering in the CIM environment. 03376

Further division of reintegration of mental labour? CAD/CAP and work in design and work preparation shops. 03385

Further division of reintegration of mental labour? CAD/CAP and work in design and work preparation shops. 03385

Interactive aspects of knowledge representations. 03395

Gribs—an approach to a realistic realtime simulation of human arm motion. 03432

Health and productivity issues of CAD/CAM systems. 03436

Report on German Joint Venture Tool Integration Projects. 03495

CAD and robotics in architecture and construction. § 03568

A design environment for computer-aided control system design via multi-objective optimisation. 03835

Advanced Computer Graphics. § 03836

Interactive solid modeling in hut design. 03837

Multiple inheritance and genericity for the integration of a database management system in an object-oriented approach. 03844

ROSE: An object-oriented database system for interactive computer graphics applications. 03845

An innovative user interface for microcomputer-based computer-aided design. 03865
Implementation of a VDA interface in the CAD system STRIM 100. 03983
Towards a natural language interface for computer aided design. 04049
A methodology, specification language, and automated support environment for comluter-aided design systems. 04068
Teleoperations and robotics: applications and technology. ● HCI-0068 †
Logic and programming. ● HCI-0068 †
Performance and computer-aided design. ● HCI-0068 †
Computer graphics. ● HCI-0069 †
High performance interactive graphics: modeling, rendering and animating for IBM PCs and compatibles. ● HCI-0071 †
The AutoCAD productivity book: tapping the hidden power of AutoCAD. ● HCI-0076 †
Modern drafting: an introduction to CAD. ● HCI-0077 †
A dedicated microcomputer for handwritten interaction with a software tool: system prototyping. HCI-0119 †
Computer-aided hierarchical diagrams. HCI-0160 †
Knowledge and control for a mechanical design expert system. HCI-0320 †
Reasoning in natural language for designing a data base. HCI-0322 †
An approach to CAD system performance evaluation. HCI-0414 †
Computer-aided modeling and planning (CAMP). HCI-0415 †
Goals in the application of CAD interfaces. HCI-0416 †
Graphical standards. HCI-0417 †
Interfaces for CAD applications. HCI-0418 †
Interfaces and data transfer formats in computer graphics systems. HCI-0419 †

### Computer-aided manufacturing (CAM)

Managing factory automation. 0146
CAD data exchange. 0237
Robotics and Material Flow. ● 0558
Task allocation between humans and robots in manufacturing. 0559
Robot simulation and off-line programming—an integrated CAE-CAD approach. 0599
Computer-aided production management IFIP. ● 0618
Production management systems. 0619
MRP/MRP II. 0620
Systems analysis techniques. 0622
Production control in car industry. 0623
Production control in the aircraft industry. 0624
A drafted PM glossary. 0625
A supervisory control paradigm for real-time control of flexible manufacturing systems. 01205

The design of a user friendly interactive personal computer package for quality control charts, project management, and linear programming applications. 01521
Human-computer interaction in manufacturing. 01522
Smart help for operator performance. 01528
The design of distributed transport systems as a major standard interface in computer integrated manufacturing. 01564
Interface concepts for plug-compatible production management systems. 01566
Software development approach in FMS. 01567
Ergonomic improvements boost AS/RS performance. 01904
Barriers to factory automation. 01906
Human supervisory control in flexible manufacturing systems: Allocation of functions and system size. 02456
Using worker's survey to improve production. 02566
The ISA expert system: a prototype system for failure diagnosis on the space station. 02913
Using hypertext to overcome the knowledge base development bottleneck: a case study. 02914
Knowledge-based interface to manufacturing computer systems. 02966
Industrial & Engineering Applications of Artificial Intelligence & Expert Systems: vol. I. § 02967
Planning as feedback to designers. 02978
Computer aided concurrent design for printed wiring boards. 02981
Industrial & Engineering Applications of Artificial Intelligence & Expert Systems: vol. II. § 02982
An interactive data dictionary facility for CAD/CAM data bases. 03174
Ergonomics of Hybrid Automated Systems I. § 03362
Issues in modeling supervisory control in flexible manufacturing systems. 03363
Human supervisory control in discrete manufacturing: Translating the paradigm. 03364
Custos IPSE: Towards a theory of the supervisor. 03365
Sources of Difficulty in troubleshooting automated manufacturing systems. 03367
Human implications of technological change. 03369
Sociotechnical design of advanced manufacturing systems. 03370
Structure and policy in computer integrated manufacturing systems: human factors implications. 03371
Towards a framework for identifying organizationally-compatible AMT. 03372
Stress, coping, and worker well-being in computer-aided manufacturing: A field investigation of a CNC machine shop. 03373
The impact of advanced manufacturing in work organization: The Portuguese case of the plastic moulding industry. 03374
Design of distribution of production control functions between humans and artificially intelligent devices. 03375

Product engineering in the CIM environment. 03376
CIM and manufacturing industry in the north east of England: A survey of some current issues. 03377
Models for design of computer integrated manufacturing systems. 03378
Human and computer aided manufacturing: The end of taylorism?. 03379
Differential organization impacts of the transition from stand-alone to integrated flexible production. 03380
A search for machine/human compatibility in manufacturing systems. 03381
A search for machine/human compatibility in manufacturing systems. 03381
Designing hybrid automated manufacturing systems: A European perspective. 03382
Macro-ergonomics and the computer-integrated enterprise. 03383
Further division of reintegration of mental labour? CAD/CAP and work in design and work preparation shops. 03385
Human factor issues in teleoperated systems. 03387
Static stereo vision depth distortions in teleoperation. 03390
Ergonomics of hybrid intelligence. 03393
Interactive aspects of knowledge representations. 03395
Human-computer-software interaction (HCSI) strategy in the design of global intelligent computer integrated management (ICIM) systems. 03396
Human-machine interface in remote monitoring and control of flexible manufacturing systems. 03399
Ten fatal accidents due to robots in Japan. 03406
Some recent documentation of robotic safety from Sweden. 03407
Methods for field evaluation of safety in a robotics workplace. 03408
Critical issues in the safety of software-dominant automated systems. 03416
A study of intrinsic safety asymmetrical actuator. 03422
AGV safety system designed for preventing hazardous human contact. 03423
Experiences from the use of an intelligent safety sensor with industrial robots. 03427
Performance evaluation of three pressure mats as robot workstation safety sensors. 03428
The evaluation of selected ergonomical factors by production automation growth. 03429
An evaluation of production systems from the ergonomic viewpoint: a plea for an integral approach to design. 03430
Process control and people at General Motors' Delta engine plant. 03431
Health and productivity issues of CAD/CAM systems. 03436
The social cybernetics of human interaction with automated systems. 03442

Computerized manufacturing technology and work organization effects on labor relations and worker satisfaction. 03443
Union acceptance of automation technology: A case study. 03444
Human aspects of automated assembly lines. 03445
Human factors in automating manufacturing systems in India. 03446
"Automation, robotization in particular, is always economically desirable"—fact or fiction?. 03448
Women, work and computerization: opportunities and disadvantages. § 03674
Failure analysis of information systems in small manufacturing enterprises: the importance of the human interface. 03815
Multiple inheritance and genericity for the integration of a database management system in an object-oriented approach. 03844
Sensors and sensory systems for advanced robots. § 04006
An overview of local environment sensing in robotics applications. 04012
Logic and programming. ● HCI-0068 †
VDAFS—a pragmatic interface for the exchange of sculptured surface data. HCI-0420 †
Approximation methods used in the exchange of geometric information via the VDA/VDMA surface interface. HCI-0421 †
A tentative implementation of VDAFS. HCI-0422 †
Testing and validation of IGES processors. HCI-0423 †

MAP/TOP *see* Proper Noun Index

## J.7 COMPUTERS IN OTHER SYSTEMS (C.3)

As we may think (Reprint). 0367
Coping with new technology: the need for training. 0441
Conceptual design of a human error tolerant interface for complex engineering systems. 01235
The design of a user friendly interactive personal computer package for quality control charts, project management, and linear programming applications. 01521
Assessing the impact of human factors on data processing inspection errors. 01527
Radiation detection by ear and by eye. 01732
Conceptualizing in assembly tasks. 01776
One view of the future of industrial control. 01921
Power plant simulation using a distributed control system. 02057
Embedded user model-where next?. 02059
Human supervisory control in flexible manufacturing systems: Allocation of functions and system size. 02456
Psychological principles for allocation of functions in man-robot system. 03630

Sensors and sensory systems for advanced robots. § 04006

**Command and control**

The Trillium user interface design environment. 0082
Space. 0134
Military systems. 0138
A workcell application design environment (WADE). 0598
An expert system architecture for computer-aided control engineering. 0662
Computer-aided engineering (CAE) for system analysis. 0663
RAPID: Prototyping control panel interfaces. 01120
Automation, work organization and skills: the case of numerical control. 01234
The FAA's Advanced Automation System: strategies for future air traffic control systems. 01357
Engineering the man-machine interface for air traffic control. 01358
The quantification of operational suitability. 01359
An interactive programming system for the IBM 7545 robot. 01517
Smart help for operator performance. 01528
Standardization aspects on software for CAD of control systems. 01565
Simulation of CNC controller features in graphics-based programming. 01568
Effects of functionally or topographically presented process schemes on operator performance. 01749
The role of practice in dual-task performance: toward workload modeling in a connectionist/control architecture. 01790
Aiding the operator during novel fault diagnosis. 01858
Modeling of task-dependent characteristics of human operator dynamics during pursuit manual tracking. 01859
Automation effects in a multiloop manual control system. 01865
Acquisition of process control skills. 01878
Analysis of user procedural compliance in controlling a simulated process. 01879
A framework for task cooperation within systems containing intelligent components. 01884
The use of measures of entropy in evaluating human supervisory control of a manufacturing system. 01897
Personal computer training software for adaptive control. 02262
Design of an integral computer-based wheelchair controller/linear synchronous motor system. 02378
Using hypertext to overcome the knowledge base development bottleneck: a case study. 02914
Sherlock—a system for diagnosing power distribution ring network faults. 02916

A blackboard architecture for problem solving and machine learning in an expert system for power system voltage control. 02926
Design of an AI-Based self-sustaining habitats control system. 02959
Using design expertise to develop an expert system. 02962
Knowledge-based interface to manufacturing computer systems. 02966
Knowledge-based interface to manufacturing computer systems. 02966
Hierarchical scheduling in an intelligent environmental control system. 02976
Embedded training in AI technology through an expert system interface: an alarm processor application. 02991
Electronic monitoring and the redundancy of control systems: The role of the supervisor. 03000
A human-computer interface for control system design. 03208
Issues in modeling supervisory control in flexible manufacturing systems. 03363
Custos IPSE: Towards a theory of the supervisor. 03365
The effects of the supervisor's knowledge in a complex automated system. 03366
Design of distribution of production control functions between humans and artificially intelligent devices. 03375
Human factor issues in teleoperated systems. 03387
Design of individual adaptive man-computer dialogues in the hybrid intelligence systems. 03400
Safety considerations in robot design. 03418
A study of fail-safe technology. 03421
Construction and examples of sensor in safe working system. 03425
The evaluation of selected ergonomical factors by production automation growth. 03429
Building interprocess communication models using Stile. 03528
Concept for a model databased remote maintenance system. 03565
Nested window flow controls with packet fragmentation. 04055
Modelling and control. ● HCI-0068 †
Teleoperations and robotics: evolution and development. ● HCI-0068 †
Cognitive attributes: implications for display design in supervisory control systems. HCI-0242 †
Special Issue: The FAA's Advanced Automation Program. HCI-0424 †

**Consumer products**

Effects of vehicle handling characteristics on driving strategy. 01773
Design of an integral computer-based wheelchair controller/linear synchronous motor system. 02378

Expert system applications in customer service. 03101
Compact disc-interactive: a designer's overview. ● HCI-0078 †
CAD/CAM: integration in the automobile industry. HCI-0413 †
Approximation methods used in the exchange of geometric information via the VDA/VDMA surface interface. HCI-0421 †
A tentative implementation of VDAFS. HCI-0422 †
Information technology in the home: promises as yet unrealized. HCI-0425 †

**DARPA** *see* Proper Noun Index

### Industrial control

Information technology and the experience of work. 0041
CAD-based off-line programming applied to a cleaning and deburring workstation. 0607
Computer-aided production management IFIP. ● 0618
Production management systems. 0619
Production control in car industry. 0623
ORGPLAN an information-decisive aid system to resolving organizing problems. 01573
Strategies in controlling a continuous process with long response latencies: needs for computer support to diagnosis. 02217
Design and implementation of an interactive optimization system for network design in the motor carrier industry. 02528
A compact model of a power house boiler. 02683
Applications of qualitative modeling to knowledge-based risk assessment studies. 02970
An interactive tolerance system. 02975
Planning as feedback to designers. 02978
Ergonomics of Hybrid Automated Systems I. § 03362
Issues in modeling supervisory control in flexible manufacturing systems. 03363
Product engineering in the CIM environment. 03376
CIM and manufacturing industry in the north east of England: A survey of some current issues. 03377
Models for design of computer integrated manufacturing systems. 03378
CAD and robotics in architecture and construction. § 03568
Evolution of a robotic excavator. 03569
Advanced computing concepts and techniques in control engineering. § 03833
An overview of local environment sensing in robotics applications. 04012
Force and tactile sensing for robots. 04013

### Military

Expert systems and artificial intelligence. ● 0133
Space. 0134
Military systems. 0138
Later years at IPTO. 0139
AI development and the Office of Naval Research. 0140
Color computer graphics in military cockpits. 0261
Off-line programming and path generation for robot manipulators. 0603
Concept design of a program manager's decision support system. 0660
Performance measurement during simulated air-to-air combat. 01787
U.S. Army field robotics focus and key technology issues. 03402

### Process control

Information technology and the experience of work. 0041
The user-computer interface in process control: a human factors engineering handbook. ● 0341
Intelligent machines for process control. 0362
Production control in car industry. 0623
Measures of human problem solving performance in fault diagnosis tasks. 0655
The effects of type of knowledge upon human problem solving in a process control task. 0657
Abstract interaction tools: a language for user interface management systems. 01162
Automation, work organization and skills: the case of numerical control. 01234
Software development approach in FMS. 01567
Simulation of CNC controller features in graphics-based programming. 01568
Process control and people at General Motors' Delta Engine Plant. 01905
Local work station concepts in a small distributed system. 02054
Adapting expert systems to simulation training of process operators. 02056
Strategies in controlling a continuous process with long response latencies: needs for computer support to diagnosis. 02217
Personal computer training software for adaptive control. 02262
A serial interface for process control. 02383
Parametric Fourier image characterization toolkit. 02798
PISCES: an expert system for coal fired power plant monitoring and diagnostics. 02915
Process control with the G2 real-time expert system. 02934
ProCEED: an expert system for multivariate process control systems design. 02935
Multi-Input fuzzy inference engine on a systolic array. 02953
Industrial & Engineering Applications of Artificial Intelligence & Expert Systems: vol. I. § 02967
Applications of qualitative modeling to knowledge-based risk assessment studies. 02970

An object-oriented expert system for coal-fired MHD power plant fault monitoringand diagnosis. 02973
Ergonomics of Hybrid Automated Systems I. § 03362
Human supervisory control in discrete manufacturing: Translating the paradigm. 03364
Sources of Difficulty in troubleshooting automated manufacturing systems. 03367
Sociotechnical design of advanced manufacturing systems. 03370
Stress, coping, and worker well-being in computer-aided manufacturing: A field investigation of a CNC machine shop. 03373
Process control and people at General Motors' Delta engine plant. 03431
Implementation plan for the use of on-line fiber analysis in the textile industry. 03433
Acting-out and burn-out behaviours of operators monitoring automated systems. 03440
Human aspects of automated assembly lines. 03445
Building interprocess communication models using Stile. 03528
jThe assessment of human/computer performance: a case for connectivity. 03535
Visualization of process information in improving work orientation. 03619
Process control software design: how will the operators work?. 03764
Advanced computing concepts and techniques in control engineering. § 03833
Qualitative modeling of physical systems for knowledge based control. 03834
A design environment for computer-aided control system design via multi-objective optimisation. 03835
Factors influencing the detection of trend deviations on VDTs. 03894

*Publishing*

Text, context, and hypertext: writing with and for the computer. ● 0098
Technology + design + research = information design. 0107
Writers as total desktop publishers: developing a conceptual approach to training. 0108
Hypertext and intelligent interfaces for text retrieval. 0115
From database to hypertext via electronic publishing: an information odyssey. 0122
Desktop publishing. 0238
Workstations and publication systems. ● 0264
Presenting documents on workstation screens. 0267
GENIE-M: A generator for multimedia information environments. 0268
The CD ROM handbook. ● 0678
Toward hypertext publishing. 01075
Efforts of display format on proof-reading with VDUs. 01246

Trends in printer technology. 01624
Why desktop publishing is not a panacea. 03131
Desktop publishing and user services; moment in the evolution of user support documentation at UNH. 03158
Document manipulation and typography. § 03182
Vidura—an interactive multilingual publishing system—specification & design. 03186
Quill: An extensible system for editing documents of mixed type. 03517
Multiple representation document development (extende abstract). 03518
FolioPub: A publication management system. 03520
Language level persistence for an object-oriented application programming platform. 03522
Psychological aspects on blind peoples's reading of radio-distributed daily newspapers. 03700
Digital typography: an introduction to type and composition for computer system design. ● HCI-0074 †
The ethics of automated publishing systems (a response to Dr. Brockmann). HCI-0170 †

*Real time*

Finance. 0135
CHI '88 Workshop on Real Time, decision support computer-human interaction. 0991
Concurrency control in groupware systems. 01090
Abstract interaction tools: a language for user interface management systems. 01162
Real-time failure detection on complex mechanical structures via parallel data processing. 01561
Getting graphics in gear: graphics and dynamics in driving simulation. 02818
An overview of local environment sensing in robotics applications. 04012

## J.m MISCELLANEOUS

A cognitive approach for graph drawing. 01616
Generating reversible programs. 02620
What do users ask? Some thoughts on diagnostic advice. HCI-0326 †

# K. COMPUTING MILIEUX

## K.0 GENERAL

Hyperwelcome. 01805
People and computers IV. § 03215
Interacting with Computers. HCI-0207 †

## K.1 THE COMPUTER INDUSTRY

Investment in computer-product documentation: causes and effects. 0105

Advanced information technology in the new industrial society: the Kingston seminars. ● 0225
Information technology and information use: towards a unified view of information and information technology. ● 0447
The CD ROM handbook. ● 0678
Gossip as creativity. 02576
Expert systems in law: out of the research laboratory and into the marketplace. 02765
Attitudes towards specific uses of the computers quantitative, decision-making and record-keeping applications. HCI-0234 †

### Markets

The management of advanced information technology. 0226
A survey of information technology in the U.K. service sector. 01916
Forecasting consumer adoption of information technology and services—lessons from home video forecasting. 02451
Videotex: anatomy of a failure. HCI-0313 †
Customers' requirements for natural language systems: results of an inquiry. HCI-0426 †
What makes users happy?. HCI-0427 †
An overview of research and co-operation in advanced information technology. HCI-0442 †

### Standards

Interfacing standards for recognisers. 0178
An historical perspective of CD ROM. 0679
Innovation in user interface development: obstacles and opportunities. 0852
The standards factor. 0938
The standards factor. 0952
The standards factor. 0965
Goals and objectives for user interface software. 01056
Reference model for DBMS user facility. 01086
User-network interfaces. 01384
A user view of virtual terminal standardisation. 01432
Ergonomic guidelines for computerized user interfaces. 01449
Lessons from the MOSI project. 01450
A map of the world of software-related standards, guidelines, and recommended practices. 01453
ISDN and the move to integrated communications—an introduction. 01455
Necessary functions of institutions for test and certification from the viewpoint of users in IT. 01456
Why users must co-operate internationally on standardization. 01457
User investigation into practical systems. 01458
The committee support system. 01460
Computer graphics language bindings: programmer interface standards. 01473

Guide to the draft American national standard for human factors engineering of visual display terminal workstations. 01549
The inept and the computer revolution: some clues from other innovations. 01552
Interface concepts for plug-compatible production management systems. 01566
Patterned systems design. 01625
Standards and system development. 01629
PHIGS: a standard, dynamic, interactive graphics interface. 01826
User interface management and graphics standards. 01964
A virtual protocol model for computer-human interaction. 02106
A model for graphical interaction. 02610
The measurement of the performance of communications protocols from the user's viewpoint. 02684
Computer assisted knowledge acquisition: towards a laboratory for protocol analysis of user dialogues. 03603
Interface abstractions for an *naplps* page creation system. 03863
Future work. 03942
Product data interfaces in CAD/CAM applications: design, implementation and experiences. § 03981
GKSGRAL—software and hardware realizations of the graphical kernel system. 03982
Graphical standards. HCI-0417 †
Interfaces for CAD applications. HCI-0418 †
Interfaces and data transfer formats in computer graphics systems. HCI-0419 †
Testing and validation of IGES processors. HCI-0423 :8E
Experimental results do not support some ergonomic standards for computer video terminal design. HCI-0428 †

### Statistics

Twelve-product wrap-up: neural networks. 01189
Intelligent software agents. 01303
Office automation—can it be justified?. 01383

### Suppliers

Are writers obsolete in the computer industry?. 0109
The management of advanced information technology. 0226
An historical perspective of CD ROM. 0679
How to choose natural language software. 01183
Twelve-product wrap-up: neural networks. 01189
Intelligent software agents. 01303
A groupware toolbox. 01304
Steel yields in Pa.. 01649
Putting expert systems to work. 01704
Competition and cooperation in information systems innovation. 01941
CRTs—present and future. 01985

KIDS. 02547
The effects of communication monitors on user satisfaction. HCI-0221 †
Transparent information systems through gateways, front ends, intermediaries, and interfaces. HCI-0276 †
Views on end-user searching. HCI-0283 †
The Japanese and software: is it a good match?. HCI-0429 †
An overview of research and co-operation in advanced information technology. HCI-0442 †

## K.2 HISTORY OF COMPUTING

History of Medical Informatics. § 02837
How DENDRAL was conceived and born. 02839
The history of personal workstations. § 03091
Toward a history of (personal) workstations. 03092
A personal view of the personal work station: some firsts in the Fifties. 03093
A history of the Promis technology: an effective human interface. 03097
User technology—from pointing to pondering. 03098
Man-made minds: the promise of artificial intelligence. ● HCI-0055 †
4.2BSD and 4.3BSD as examples of the UNIX system. HCI-0165 †
Information science: its roots and relation as viewed from the perspective of cognitive science. HCI-0185 †

**ASCII** *see* Proper Noun Index

### Hardware

A historical and intellectual perspective of the context of human computer interaction. 0039
Designing the star user interface. 0089
A history of personal workstations. ● 0347
An historical perspective of CD ROM. 0679
The diffusion and impacts of information technology in households. 0754
Medical informatics: a personal view of sowing the seeds. 02841
The LINC was early and small. 02843
The history of the use of computers in the interpretation of radiological images. 02845
The augmented knowledge workshop. 03094
Personal distributed computing: the Alto and Ethernet hardware. 03095
Document processing. 03897

**IBM** *see* Proper Noun Index

### People

Later years at IPTO. 0139
AI development and the Office of Naval Research. 0140
A history of personal workstations. ● 0347
An historical perspective of CD ROM. 0679

The diffusion and impacts of information technology in households. 0754
What users want. 01443
A boy and his brain machine. 02575
The Universal Turing Machine. § 03777

### Software

A historical and intellectual perspective of the context of human computer interaction. 0039
Computer chess compendium. ● 0526
Personal distributed computing: the Alto and Ethernet software. 03096
Document processing. 03897
Artificial intelligence and cognitive psychology: a new look at human factors. 03904
Programming languages: a grand tour (2nd ed.). ● HCI-0018 †
Ada: first users—pleased; prospective users—still hesitant. HCI-0159 †

### Systems

A historical and intellectual perspective of the context of human computer interaction. 0039
The missing link: why we're all doing hypertext wrong. 0118
Later years at IPTO. 0139
Key areas of cognitive psychology: a historical perspective. 0328
A history of personal workstations. ● 0347
Some reflections on early history. 0348
As we may think (Reprint). 0367
Hypertext: an introduction and survey (Reprint). 0378
Pupils, computers and history teaching. 0746
History, state and future of user interface management systems. 0966
A computing service using linked minis. 01674
From timesharing to the sixth generation: the development of human-computer interaction. Part I. 02097
In praise of computing. 02838
Planting the seeds. 02840
The UCLA Brain Research Institute data processing laboratory. 02844
The history of the use of computers in the interpretation of radiological images. 02845
Recollections on the processing of biomedical signals. 02846
Perspectives over forty years. 02847
An historical perspective on clinical laboratory information systems. 02848
Health care information systems: a personal historic review. 02849
The perception of system and the reduction of uncertainty. 02850
History of the TDS medical information system. 02851
Patient management systems: the early years. 02852

Humane: A designer's assistant for modeling and evaluating function allocation options. 03397
Ten years of window systems—a retrospective view. 03926
Fifth generation computers: concepts, implementations and uses. ● HCI-0001 †
An overview of research and co-operation in advanced information technology. HCI-0442 †

*Theory*

VLSI for solid modelling. 0232
Humane: A designer's assistant for modeling and evaluating function allocation options. 03397
The Universal Turing Machine. § 03777

**Alan Turing** *see* Proper Noun Index

**UNIVAC** *see* Proper Noun Index

**UNIX** *see* Proper Noun Index

## K.3  COMPUTERS AND EDUCATION

History of the development of medical information systems at the Laboratory of Computer Science at Massachusetts General Hospital. 02842

### K.3.0  General

How to manage educational computing initiatives-lessons from the first five years of Project Athena at MIT. 0125
Computers and children's historical thinking and understanding. 0283
Logic for learning. 0284
Learning environment criteria. 0285
An examination of the research evidence for computer-based instruction. 0415
Artificial intelligence and education; vol. 1: learning environments and tutoring systems. ● 0516
Artificial worlds and real experience. 0518
Learning with interactive media: dynamic support for students and teachers. 0519
Learning Issues for Intelligent Tutoring Systems. ● 0534
The computer as a tool for learning through reflection. 0535
Toward a theory of impasse-driven learning. 0536
Psychological evaluation of path hypotheses in cognitive diagnosis. 0537
Socializing the intelligent tutor: bringing empathy to computer tutors. 0541
Experimental data for the design of a microworld-based system for algebra. 0543
Mirrors of minds: patterns of experience in educational computing. ● 0575
The interpretation of Logo in practice. 0576
Functional environments for microcomputers in education. 0578

Practices of novices and experts in critical inquiry. 0585
The development of a postmodern self: a computer-assisted comparative analysis of personal documents. ● 0732
The diffusion and impacts of information technology in households. 0754
Staying afloat—a collective enterprise. 01147
Recursive complementarity in the cybernetics of education. 01598
Computer science education. § 02809
Video: Data for studying human-computer interaction. 02878
Need of electronic tools in educational programmers and the impact in developing countries. 03023
User services—a british perspective. 03132
From user to client services; making the transition for supercomputing. 03138
New wine in old skins, or, was all this ferment really necessary?. 03140
The many faces of faculty computing assistance. 03143
Learning the ways: the enculturation of SDSC users. 03144
How to build a help desk that floats. 03148
Starting and maintaining a computing resource center: lessons we've learned. 03149
The evolution of microcomputer laboratory services at the University of Notre Dame. 03159
Three steps of better documentation. 03160
Connections in context: The intermedia system. 03534
Reasons for computer utilization reluctance by teachers with computer training. 04059
User involvement with microcomputer software. 04063
Boxer: a reconstructible computational medium. HCI-0121 †
Implications for education and training. HCI-0430 †

### K.3.1  Computer Uses in Education

How to manage educational computing initiatives-lessons from the first five years of Project Athena at MIT. 0125
Perspectives in artificial intelligence vol. 2: machine translation, NLP, databases and computer-aided instruction. ● 0198
Interactive media: working methods and practical applications. ● 0501
Setting up an interactive videodisc project. 0502
Lessons from computer-based learning. 0503
Pedagogical design for interactive video. 0505
Why do instructional designers need conversation theory?. 0506
Conversation theory as a basis for instructional design. 0507
From trigger video to videodisc: a case study in interpersonal skills. 0508
The creation of an integrated IVD curriculum. 0509
A question of delivery—an outline classification of interactive video delivery systems. 0510

Interactive video—a producer's medium. 0511
The political economy of interactive video in British higher education. 0512
Interactive video as a school resource: Rolls-Royce or Model T Ford?. 0513
Producing resource discs—the Domesday project experience. 0514
Videodisc and videotex: love-match or passing acquaintance?. 0515
New horizons in educational computing. • 0750
UNIX and the naive user: children meet a grown-up operating system. 0752
Interface design: a neglected issue in educational software. 0826
Learning from a plan-based interface. 01496
Variations in user involvement with educational software. 01498
Development of the wedding planner—extensions to reach a young audience. 01502
A scale for assessing student attitudes toward computers preliminary findings. 01579
A brief review of developments in problem solving. 01581
Problem solving: a behavioral interpretation. 01582
The erotetic logic of problem-solving inquiry. 01583
Creative computer problem solving. 01584
Computer programming and generalized problem-solving skills: in search of direction. 01585
Automaticity, resources, and memory: theoretical controversies and practical implications. 01792
Preserving the integrity of the medium: a method of measuring visual and auditory comprehension of electronic media. 02084
Psychologically based techniques for improving learning within computerized tutorials. 02277
Research and evaluation models for the study of interactive video. 02283
A theoretical framework for interactivating linear video. 02284
The efficacy of computer-assisted video instruction on rule learning and attitudes. 02286
The effects of orienting objectives and review on learning from interactive video. 02287
Using interactive videotaped-based instruction to teach on-the-job social skills to handicapped adolescents. 02288
The effects of orienting, processing, and practicing activities on learning from interactive video. 02289
Citation patterns in the computer-based instruction literature. 02290
The effects of gender and age on preschool children's choice of the computer as a child-selected activity. 02450
Error analysis and tutor design. 02469
Inactive video at work. 02571

Industrial & Engineering Applications of Artificial Intelligence & Expert Systems: vol. II. § 02982
Designing computer-based learning materials. § 03875
Current research in the psychology of learning and teaching. 03876
Pedagogical development of computer-based learning material. 03878
Integrating physics and computer education in a single process. 03879
The computer as an integral part of the laboratory. 03880
Introducing CAL: a practical guide to writing computer-assisted learning programs. • HCI-0079 †
Andrew: a distributed personal computing environment. HCI-0091 †

*Computer-assisted instruction (CAI)*

The on-line environment and in-house training. 0106
Writers as total desktop publishers: developing a conceptual approach to training. 0108
Textual intervention, collaboration, and the online environment. 0126
The computer in the classroom: a force for change?. 0149
Computer assisted language learning: program structure and principles. • 0196
$VP^2$: the role of user modelling in correcting errors in second language learning. 0222
Color and the instructional use of the computer. 0263
Adopting interactive videodisc technology for education. 0272
How effective is interactive video in improving performance and attitude?. 0278
Interactive Toolkit. • 0340
Human computer interaction. 0404
An examination of the research evidence for computer-based instruction. 0415
Screen design strategies for computer-assisted instruction. • 0424
Instructional designs for microcomputer courseware. • 0464
Artificial intelligence and instruction: Applications and methods. • 0468
Authoring systems for ICAI. 0469
Computer assisted learning in the humanities and social sciences. • 0470
The role of social processes in children's microcomputer use. 0471
Evaluation of a program on "distance". 0472
User behaviour in computer networked groups. 0473
Symbiotic software: development and usage issues on stand-alone and networked systems. 0474
Artificial intelligence techniques in language learning. • 0500
Computer-assisted learning and interactive video. 0504

# CATEGORY INDEX [K. COMPUTING MILIEUX]

Artificial intelligence and education; vol. 1: learning environments and tutoring systems. ●0516
Algebra slaves and agents in a Logo-based mathematics curriculum. 0517
Artificial worlds and real experience. 0518
Learning with interactive media: dynamic support for students and teachers. 0519
An example-base environment for beginning programmers. 0520
Learning Issues for Intelligent Tutoring Systems. ●0534
The computer as a tool for learning through reflection. 0535
Toward a theory of impasse-driven learning. 0536
Psychological evaluation of path hypotheses in cognitive diagnosis. 0537
Mental models and metaphors: implications for the design of adaptive user-system interfaces. 0539
Improvement of the acquisition of knowledge by informing feedback. 0540
Socializing the intelligent tutor: bringing empathy to computer tutors. 0541
Cognitive economy in physics reasoning: implications for designing instructional materials. 0542
Experimental data for the design of a microworld-based system for algebra. 0543
Computer-aided model building. 0544
Learning issues for intelligent tutoring systems. ●0545
Mirrors of minds: patterns of experience in educational computing. ●0575
Teachers' adoption of multimedia technologies for science and mathematics instruction. 0577
Informing the design of software through context-based research. 0584
Foundations of intelligent tutoring systems. ●0592
Information technology in the humanities: tools, techniques and applications. ●0595
Computers, cognition, and development: issues for psychology and education. ●0643
Artificial intelligence & human learning: intelligent computer-aided instruction. ●0671
The three c's: children, computers, and communication. ●0713
Qualitative student models. 0721
New horizons in educational computing. ●0741
Designing computer-based microworlds. 0742
A very friendly software environment for SOLO. 0743
Pupils, computers and history teaching. 0746
POP-11 for everyone. 0749
Improving human/computer interactions. 0759
Artifact as theory-nexus: hermeneutics meets theory-based design. 0798
NYNEX intelligent systems group. 0814
On-line tutorials: What kind of inference leads to the most effective learning?. 0823
Responding to "HUH?": answering vaguely articulated follow-up questions. 0825

Mathematical formula editor for CAI. 0885
TNT: a talking tutor 'n' trainer for teaching use of interactive computer systems. 0895
Human factors in teaching. 0989
Interactive graphics: a tool for beginning programming students in discovering solutions to novel problems. 01038
The impact of menus and command-level feedback on learners' acquisition of data base language skills. 01041
The small computer assisted lecturing system. 01043
Teachware for power engineering education. 01203
Communication barriers in microcomputer—based courses. 01319
DVI—a digital multimedia technology. 01327
Intelligent interactive video simulation of a code inspection. 01329
Live-Net in education. 01381
A flexible synonym interface with application examples in CAL and help environments. 01404
Human factors in CAI design. 01494
Some issues related to the design and development of an interactive video disc. 01497
PC networks: usage and graphics tutorials. 01499
Automated construction of interactive learning programs in Modula-2. 01500
The effects of microcomputers on children's attention to reading. 01580
Computer programming and general problem solving by secondary students. 01587
The relationship of computer programming and mathematics in secondary students. 01588
Assessing gender bias in computer software. 01591
Personality characteristics of junior high school students successful with computers. 01592
The Perseus project: an interactive curriculum on classical greek civilization. 01680
Reader-controlled computerized presentation of text. 01785
Hypermedia as an interpretive act. 01806
A methodology for interactive evaluation of user reactions to software packages:an empirical analysis of system performance, interaction, and run time. 02080
Training by exploration: facilitating the transfer of procedural knowledge through analogical reasoning. 02103
A review and synthesis of recent research in intelligent computer-assisted instruction. 02108
Enhancing PIXIE's tutoring capabilities. 02187
Protos: an examplar-based learning apprentice. 02210
DYNABOARD: user animated display of deductive proofs in mathematics. 02221
Comparison of student performance in arithmetic exercises TOAM us paper-and-pencil testing. 02249
Pictorial dialogue methods. 02251
Computer analysis of students' procedural "bugs" in an arithmetic domain. 02273

Student evaluation of motivational and learning attributes of microcomputer soft. 02274

Systematic evaluation strategies for computer-based music instruction systems. 02275

Developing the technology for intelligent maintenance advisors. 02276

Efficacy of higher cognitive and factual questions in computer assisted instruction modules. 02278

The accuracy of approximate string matching algorithms. 02279

A comparison of children's reading comprehension and reading rates at three text presentation speeds on a CRT. 02280

The accuracy of cognitive monitoring during computer-based instruction. 02281

Computer-assisted instruction in academic libraries. 02282

The influence of personality on self-paced instruction. 02291

Formative evaluation of pre-Logo programming environments: a collaborative effort of researchers, teachers, and children. 02292

Expert systems and interactive video tutorials: separating strategies from subject matter. 02293

Color, graphics, and animation in a computer-assisted learning tutorial lesson. 02294

A comparison of a microcomputer progressive state drill and flashcards for learning paired associates. 02295

Computers as composition tools: a case study of student attitudes. 02296

A regression model to identify successful learner traits with CAI. 02376

AI/learn: an interactive videodisk system for teaching medical concepts and reasoning. 02381

Development of a hand-held computerized vocabulary tutor. 02468

Natural language interface based on keyword extraction using AWK. 02498

KIDS. 02547

Natural language processing and the language-impaired. 02570

Expert systems in law: The datalex project. 02766

Children's collaborative use of a computer microworld. 02825

Collaborative learning in a virtual classroom: highlights of findings. 02826

Travel around a learning support environment: rambling, orienteering or touring?. 02900

Graphics-based qualitative simulation generator for power distribution systems. 02946

A computer training tool using Chinese natural language. 02948

Some considerations on intelligent tutoring systems. 02963

An advisory system for digital logic simulation. 02986

Need of electronic tools in educational programmers and the impact in developing countries. 03023

The travel metaphor as design principle and training aid for navigating around complex systems. 03195

A flexible negotiable interactive learning environment. 03197

Contextual structure analysis of microcomputer manuals. 03227

Hypertext tips: experiences in developing a hypertext tutorial. 03236

Flexible intelligent interactive-video. 03238

Human implications of technological change. 03369

Overcoming conceptual difficulties in physical science through computer-based Socratic dialogs. 03877

Textvision: elicitation and acquisition of conceptual knowledge by graphic representation and multiwindowing. 03902

Development of mental models of an office system: a field study on an introductory course. 03903

A computer assisted learning system for reliability engineering. 04060

A comparison of the effects of computer-assisted instruction, interactive video, and traditional instruction on third-grade students in art education. 04064

Authoring: a guide to the design of instructional software. ● HCI-0031 †

Introducing CAL: a practical guide to writing computer-assisted learning programs. ● HCI-0079 †

Artificial intelligence and tutoring systems: computational and cognitive approaches to the communication of knowledge. ● HCI-0080 †

Interactive video: vol. 1. ● HCI-0081 †

The microcomputer as a classroom audio visual device: the concept, and prospects. HCI-0223 †

The LISP tutor: it approaches the effectiveness of a human tutor. HCI-0431 †

Computer-based microworlds—a definition to aid design. HCI-0432 †

The automated tutoring of introductory computer programming. HCI-0438 †

*Computer-managed instruction (CMI)*

Designer labyrinths: text mazes for language learners. 0197

An examination of the research evidence for computer-based instruction. 0415

Learning with interactive media: dynamic support for students and teachers. 0519

Learning Issues for Intelligent Tutoring Systems. ● 0534

The computer as a tool for learning through reflection. 0535

Enhancing incremental learning processes with knowledge-based systems. 0538

Foundations of intelligent tutoring systems. ● 0592

Interactive timetabling in universities. 01501

An intelligent tutoring system for basic set theory. 02993

**CATEGORY INDEX** [K. COMPUTING MILIEUX]

**GREATERP** *see* Proper Noun Index

### K.3.2 Computer and Information Science Education

Psychological issues of human-computer interaction in the work place. ● 0305
The practice of the use of computers. A paradoxical encounter between different traditions of knowledge. 0343
Education and training in robotics. ● 0440
Information technology and information use: towards a unified view of information and information technology. ● 0447
Mirrors of minds: patterns of experience in educational computing. ● 0575
Mapping the cognitive demands of learning to program. 0579
Integrated human and computer intelligence. 0580
Foundations of intelligent tutoring systems. ● 0592
Teaching user interface design based on usability engineering. 01007
Issuing each undergraduate student a personal computer: living with it for three years. 01028
Leadership style vs. succssus in student chief programmer teams. 01029
Retraining high school teachers to teach computer science—observations on the first course. 01030
Dealing with disparate audiences in computer science courses using a project group within a traditional class. 01031
A historical perspective for teaching. 01033
Let's motivate!. 01034
Profile of undergraduate software engineering courses: results from a survey. 01035
Student-oriented features of an interactive programming environment. 01036
A comparison of male and female computer science students' attitudes toward computers. 01045
Computer text access. 01493
Education requirements for the entry level business systems analyst. 02409
User Services. § 03127
Captive...a new tool. 03129
CAREing for users at Syracuse University. 03134
Women, work and computerization: opportunities and disadvantages. § 03674
Future Trends in Information Science and Technology. § 04039
Adult learners: away with computerphobia. HCI-0433 †
Paradox of the active user. HCI-0434 †

*Computer science education*

An example-base environment for beginning programmers. 0520

New horizons in educational computing. ● 0741
Designing computer-based microworlds. 0742
University of Colorado at Boulder, Institute of cognitive science. 0811
Developing computer aided design technology in China. 0942
A vision of education in user-centered system and interface design. 0985
Integrating software engineering into an intermediate programming class. 01037
Interactive graphics: a tool for beginning programming students in discovering solutions to novel problems. 01038
Application frameworks: experience with MacApp. 01039
IBM 3270 full screen interactive programming without CICS. 01040
The impact of menus and command-level feedback on learners' acquisition of data base language skills. 01041
A study of an advance organizer as a technique for teaching computer programming concepts. 01042
Teaching object-oriented programming with the KEE system. 01113
Metaphor, computing systems, and active learning. 02091
Conditional statements, looping constructs, and program comprehension: an experiments study. 02177
Learning iteration recursion from examples. 02215
Microcomputer hardware education at a Czechoslovakian Technical University. 02488
Learning in British Airways-A case of putting people first. 02572
Where have all the girls gone?. 02689
A computer training tool using Chinese natural language. 02948
Perceptions of the CIS graduate's workstyle: undergraduate business students versus CIS faculty. 02999
Instilling professionalism in a software development organization. 03019
The influence of individual differences on the reading of computer programs. 03456
Integrating physics and computer education in a single process. 03879
Software Engineering Education. § 04022
Teaching the tricks of the trade. 04023
Stategic imperatives in software engineering education. 04024
Undergraduate software engineering education. 04025
Software tools at the University: Why, What and How. 04026
A scarce resource in undergraduate software engineering courses: user interface design materials. 04027
The influence of color on program readability and comprehensibility. HCI-0120 †
Fragile knowledge and neglected strategies in novice programmers. HCI-0177 †
Analyzing the high frequency bugs in novice programs. HCI-0178 †

The relationship of problem-solving ability and course performance among novice programmers. HCI-0435 †
The electronic classroom: workstations for teaching. HCI-0436 †
Using low-cost workstations to investigate computer networks and distributed systems. HCI-0437 †
The automated tutoring of introductory computer programming. HCI-0438 †

### Curriculum

Towards a framework for systems analysis practice. 0155
Teachers' adoption of multimedia technologies for science and mathematics instruction. 0577
Graphic invention for user interfaces: an experimental course in user-interface design. 0950
Fine tuning selection semantics in a structure editor based programming environment: some experimental results. 0975
Word processing techniques and user learning preferences. 0984
A vision of education in user-centered system and interface design. 0985
An evaluation of a realistic approach to MIS. 01027
Data-structures students may prefer to learn algorithms using graphical methods. 01032
Integrating software engineering into an intermediate programming class. 01037
A UNIX clone with source code for operating systems courses. 01095
The many faces of HMI. 01382
Adolescents' chunking of computer programs. 01586
Computer programming and general problem solving by secondary students. 01587
Teaching software engineering at university. 01968
Question asking when learning a text-editing system. 02202
REPTIL-promoting dialog between humanoid and computer. 02307
Problems, problems, problems.... 02407
Microcomputer hardware education at a Czechoslovakian Technical University. 02488
Why do some people have more difficulty learning to use an information retrieval system than others?. 03075
Human factors in systems design: a case study. 03196
Learning graphics programming by direct communication. 03298
Software Engineering Education. § 04022
Undergraduate software engineering education. 04025
A scarce resource in undergraduate software engineering courses: user interface design materials. 04027
Using low-cost workstations to investigate computer networks and distributed systems. HCI-0437 †

### Information systems education

Information technology and education: the changing school. ● 0282
University of Colorado at Boulder, Institute of cognitive science. 0811
Perspectives on the academic preparation of MIS professionals. 03006
An empirical study of user satisfaction with a microcomputer-based campus-wide. 03137
Computer anxiety in management: myth or reality?. HCI-0232 †
A laboratory study of user characteristics and decision-making performance in end-user computing. HCI-0301 †
Implications for education and training. HCI-0430 †

### Self-assessment

Binary jargon: the metaphoric language of computing. 01044

### K.3.m Miscellaneous

Learning in man-computer interaction: a review of the literature. 0151
Computer culture: the scientific, intellectual, and social impact of the computer. § 03567
The relationship of problem-solving ability and course performance among novice programmers. HCI-0435 †
Cognitive aspects of learning and using a programming language. HCI-0439 †

### Computer literacy

Preparing new generations for the information age. 0453
Mirrors of minds: patterns of experience in educational computing. ● 0575
New horizons in educational computing. ● 0741
Beginners need powerful systems. 0747
UNIX and the naive user: children meet a grown-up operating system. 0752
Computer literacy: the pigeonhole principle. 0789
The effects of computer use in early childhood socialization. 0793
Computer literacy in secondary education: the performance and engagement of girls. 01495
Supercomputers in the classroom. 01577
Computer programming and generalized problem-solving skills: in search of direction. 01585
Computer programming and general problem solving by secondary students. 01587
The relationship of computer programming and mathematics in secondary students. 01588
Self-efficacy expectations as a predictor of computer use: a look at early childhood administrators. 01590
Personality characteristics of junior high school students successful with computers. 01592

CATEGORY INDEX                                            [K. COMPUTING MILIEUX]

Which way to computer literacy, programming or applications experience?. 02127
Computer anxiety: sex, race and age. 02133
Training end users: an exploratory study. 02506
The art of programming. HCI-0095 †
The computer imperative among owners of home computers: explanation by social factors. HCI-0217 †
Adult learners: away with computerphobia. HCI-0433 †

## K.4  COMPUTERS AND SOCIETY

Resistance to computerization: an examination of the relationship between resistance and the cognitive style of the clinician. HCI-0407 †

### K.4.0  General

Human foundations of advanced computing technology: the guide to the select literature. 0001
Issues and approaches to appraising technological change in the office: A consequentialist perspective. 0043
Text, context, and hypertext: writing with and for the computer. ● 0098
Introduction: a new paradigm for writing with and for the computer. 0099
Technology + design + research = information design. 0107
Attitudes to information technology. 0150
Man-computer interfaces: an introduction to software design and implementation. ● 0220
Artificial worlds and real experience. 0518
Cognition & personal structure. ● 0533
Ideas and information: managing in a high-tech world. ● 0586
The development of a postmodern self: a computer-assisted comparative analysis of personal documents. ● 0732
Oxford surveys in information technology; vol. 2, 1985. ● 0755
The interactionist perspective on computer implementation. 0785
The rational, the pragmatic and the inquiry process: The social study of information- communication systems. 0786
Applying the human relations perspective to the study of new media. 0787
The uneasy eighties: the transition to an information society. 0792
Understanding the office: A social-analytic perspective. 01156
Technology adaptation: a typology for strategic human resource management. 01238
Hypermedia as an interpretive act. 01806
Understanding and enhancing user acceptance of computer. 01889
The real information society: present situation and some forecasts. 02322

Computer culture: the scientific, intellectual, and social impact of the computer. § 03567
New horizons for the information profession: meeting the challenge of change. § 04046
The second self: computers and the human spirit. ● HCI-0082 †
The computer culture. § HCI-0084 †
Special Issue: The FAA's Advanced Automation Program. HCI-0424 †

### K.4.1  Public Policy Issues

The Socio/Political Environment. 0040
Information technology and information use: towards a unified view of information and information technology. ● 0447
A tolerance for surveillance: American public opinion concerning privacy and civil liberties. 0524
Tele-cybernetics: implications for the international marketplace. 03458
Transparent information systems through gateways, front ends, intermediaries, and interfaces. HCI-0276 †

**Alvey Report** *see* Proper Noun Index

**ESPRIT** *see* Proper Noun Index

*Privacy*

Threat to privacy: the federal government's use of personal information in the new communication environment. 02680
Developing awareness of computer ethics. 03010
Privacy respecting permissions and rights. 03583

*Regulation*

The effect of adding symbols to written warning labels on user behavior and recall. 01788

*Transborder data flow*

Data security and confidentiality in Europe. HCI-0450 †

### K.4.2  Social Issues

The Socio/Political Environment. 0040
How "friendly" is your writing for readers around the world?. 0110
Online information, hypermedia, and the idea of literacy. 0112
Managerial expert systems and organizational change: some critical research issues. 0157
The in-formation of information systems. 0159
Readings in cognitive science: a perspective from psychology & artificial intelligence. ● 0223
Advanced information technology in the new industrial society: the Kingston seminars. ● 0225
User interface management systems. 0233

1139

[K. COMPUTING MILIEUX]

Computerization versus computer aided mental. 0308
The chances of individualization in human-computer interaction and its consequences. 0309
Knowledge, skill and artificial intelligence. • 0342
Creativity, skill and human-centered systems. 0346
Computer-supported cooperative work: a book of readings. • 0366
As we may think (Reprint). 0367
Office information systems and computer science (Reprint). 0373
Social psychological aspects of computer-mediated communication (Reprint). 0384
The variable impact of computer technologies on the organization of work activities. 0388
Artificial worlds and real experience. 0518
Mirrors of minds: patterns of experience in educational computing. • 0575
Telecommuting the organizational and behavioral effects of working at home. • 0596
The diffusion and impacts of information technology in households. 0754
University of Colorado at Boulder, Institute of cognitive science. 0811
Keyboarding as a social form. 01551
Competition and cooperation in information systems innovation. 01941
Mondo media. 02552
Making computer tasks at work more playful: Implications for systems analysts and designers. 03005
Moderating effects of age, education, and tenure on the job satisfaction-job performance relationship. 03021
Need of electronic tools in educational programmers and the impact in developing countries. 03023
Organizational implications of office systems: toward a critical social action perspective. 03358
Ergonomics of Hybrid Automated Systems I. § 03362
Human supervisory control in discrete manufacturing: Translating the paradigm. 03364
Towards a new theory of job design. 03368
Human implications of technological change. 03369
Stress, coping, and worker well-being in computer-aided manufacturing: A field investigation of a CNC machine shop. 03373
The impact of advanced manufacturing in work organization: The Portugese case of the plastic moulding industry. 03374
Product engineering in the CIM environment. 03376
Human and computer aided manufacturing: The end of taylorism?. 03379
Differential organization impacts of the transition from stand-alone to integrated flexible production. 03380
Designing hybrid automated manufacturing systems: A European perspective. 03382
Macro-ergonomics and the computer-integrated enterprise. 03383
The man-machine integration. 03384

Further division of reintegration of mental labour? CAD/CAP and work in design and work preparation shops. 03385
Beyond software ergonomics? Human control of automated systems. 03386
Robot vs. human operator for speed, precision and other aspects. 03403
Individualizing the man-machine interface. 03404
Ten fatal accidents due to robots in Japan. 03406
Some recent documentation of robotic safety from Sweden. 03407
Effects of automation on occupational safety & health. 03435
Acting-out and burn-out behaviours of operators monitoring automated systems. 03440
Optimum stresses and strains represented by examples from shop practice. 03441
The social cybernetics of human interaction with automated systems. 03442
The social cybernetics of human interaction with automated systems. 03442
Human aspects of QC circle movement in Japanese manufacturing: Natures and problems. 03450
Tele-cybernetics: implications for the international marketplace. 03458
Sharing in a privately owned workstation environment. 04076
The second self: computers and the human spirit. • HCI-0082 †
In the age of the smart machine: the future of work and power. • HCI-0083 †
Design of computer programs for the physically handicapped. HCI-0096 †
Taming and civilizing computers. HCI-0195 †
The computer imperative among owners of home computers: explanation by social factors. HCI-0217 †
Adult learners: away with computerphobia. HCI-0433 †
Computer-assisted negotiations: a case history from the law of the sea negotiations and speculation regarding future uses. HCI-0443 †

*Abuse and crime involving computers*

Attitudes toward unauthorized software copying: general public vs. business faculty member. 01142
The moral cracker?. 01546
'Remember to lock the door': MMI and the hacker. 01910
Security of office systems. 03359

*Employment*

Issues and approaches to appraising technological change in the office: A consequentialist perspective. 0043
The changing workplace: A guide to managing the people, organizational, and regulatory aspects of office technology (book excerpt). 0044

Making computers accessible to disabled people. 0094
The on-line environment and in-house training. 0106
The management of advanced information technology. 0226
The psychology of work and organization: current trends and issues. ● 0239
Psychological issues of human-computer interaction in the work place. ● 0305
Human—computer interactions in the workplace: psychosocial aspects of VDT use. 0306
The limitations of task complexity through information technologies: results of a field study. 0307
Toward high-performance knowledge workers (Reprint). 0369
Employment skills for the robot age. 0442
Preparing for new technology. 0444
Computer ethics: an antidote to despair. 0791
Technology adaptation: a typology for strategic human resource management. 01238
Human aspects of factory modernization. 01513
The inept and the computer revolution: some clues from other innovations. 01552
The effects of a computerized information system on a hospital. 01553
Barriers to plant transparency, barriers to plant rigidity—A sketch of the problems posed by the radical changes in work forms in the machine-building industry. 01562
Steel yields in Pa.. 01649
Will you be replaced by a knowledge base?. 02055
Cognitive issues in the process of software development: review and reappraisal. 02222
Are information systems people different? An investigation of how they are and should be managed. 02511
Public Law 99-506, "Section 508" Electronic Equipment Accessibility for disabled workers. 02893
Recent trends in information systems law. 03017
New technology work aids for the physically disabled. 03273
Computerized manufacturing technology and work organization effects on labor relations and worker satisfaction. 03443
Union acceptance of automation technology: A case study. 03444
Human aspects of automated assembly lines. 03445
Human factors in automating manufacturing systems in India. 03446
The economic evaluation on implementation industrial robot from user point of view. 03447
"Automation, robotization in particular, is always economically desirable"—fact or fiction?. 03448
Women, work and computerization: opportunities and disadvantages. § 03674
Office automation: a social and organizational perspective. ● HCI-0048 †

The development and use of information technology in health care. HCI-0408 †
The Japanese and software: is it a good match?. HCI-0429 †
Computer mediated work: the interplay between technology and structured jobs. HCI-0440 †
Computerization, productivity, and quality of work-life. HCI-0441 †
An empirical study of occupational stress, attitudes and health among information systems personnel. HCI-0451 †

### K.4.3 Organizational Impacts

The Socio/Political Environment. 0040
Power, politics, and MIS implementation. 0042
Issues and approaches to appraising technological change in the office: A consequentialist perspective. 0043
The physical environment. 0045
The physical environment. 0045
Human factors issues in VDT use: Environmental and workstation design considerations. 0046
Preventing back strain. 0047
The statutes and standards movement. 0049
Information development is part of product development—not an afterthought. 0103
Online information: what do people want? What do people need?. 0113
How to manage educational computing initiatives-lessons from the first five years of Project Athena at MIT. 0125
Management, organizations and the new technologies. 0145
Managing factory automation. 0146
Critical issues in information systems research. ● 0153
Semantics. 0154
Towards a framework for systems analysis practice. 0155
Managerial expert systems and organizational change: some critical research issues. 0157
Strategies for research on information systems in organizations. A critical analysis of research purpose and time frame. 0158
Advanced information technology in the new industrial society: the Kingston seminars. ● 0225
The management of advanced information technology. 0226
The psychology of work and organization: current trends and issues. ● 0239
Contexts and conflicts between ergonomics and industrial psychology. 0240
Ergonomics and organizational consulting: accentuation or neglect of psychology. 0242
Automation in public libraries: effects on the organization, quality of working life, and quality of services. 0246
The SIMONA project: the introduction of information processing in labour market administration. 0248

[K. COMPUTING MILIEUX]

Methodological problems of field-research on workplaces in offices. 0249
The impact of changes in work ethics upon organizational life. 0250
Psychological issues of human-computer interaction in the work place. ● 0305
Human—computer interactions in the workplace: psychosocial aspects of VDT use. 0306
Computer-supported cooperative work: a book of readings. ● 0366
As we may think (Reprint). 0367
Social psychological aspects of computer-mediated communication (Reprint). 0384
The variable impact of computer technologies on the organization of work activities. 0388
Human factors and artificial intelligence. 0408
The human side of robotics: how workers react to a robot. 0443
Managers, micros and mainframes: integrating systems for end-users. ● 0455
Thomas W. Malone, Oct. 5: user interface strategies '88. ● 0532
Ideas and information: managing in a high-tech world. ● 0586
Telecommuting the organizational and behavioral effects of working at home. ● 0596
The CD ROM handbook. ● 0678
The three c's: children, computers, and communication. ● 0713
Center for coordination science, MIT. 0841
Innovation in user interface development: obstacles and opportunities. 0852
User interface design in large corporations: coordination and communication across disciplines. 0853
Human-computer interaction lab, University of Maryland. 0871
Socio-tech: what is it (and why should we care)?. 0908
The 1988 CSCW: trip report. 01008
Information detective: a workstation for exploring three dimensional information space. 01010
Speculating on the future of mathematics. 01210
A folklore view of information. 01222
Technology adaptation: a typology for strategic human resource management. 01238
An empirical investigation of two electronic mail systems. 01239
Problems associated with the off-line programming of robots. 01241
User cube: a taxonomy of end users. 01335
Information technologies for the 1990's: an orgnizational impact perspective. 01336
Job characteristic perceptions of manual drafting and CADD: A field study of the effects of computerization on drafting & design personnel. 01523
The effects of a computerized information system on a hospital. 01553

Software development approach in FMS. 01567
The human costs of manufacturing reform. 01706
Cognitive engineering: human problem solving with tools. 01781
Barriers to factory automation. 01906
A survey of information technology in the U.K. service sector. 01916
Competition and cooperation in information systems innovation. 01941
Examining the duality role of I.S. executives: a study of I.S. issues. 01953
Who's joking? The information system at play. 02066
Predicting end-user acceptance of microcomputers in the workplace. 02147
Managerial influence in the implementation of new technology. 02481
Critical factors in the user environment: an experimental study of users, organizations and tasks. 02507
Are information systems people different? An investigation of how they are and should be managed. 02511
Systems design and social responsibility: the political implications of "computer-supported cooperative work". A commentary. 02516
Mondo media. 02552
In praise of computing. 02838
Need of electronic tools in educational programmers and the impact in developing countries. 03023
Computers' impact on productivity and work life. 03040
Organizational implications of office systems: toward a critical social action perspective. 03358
Implementation of office systems. 03360
Ergonomics of Hybrid Automated Systems I. § 03362
Human supervisory control in discrete manufacturing: Translating the paradigm. 03364
Towards a new theory of job design. 03368
Human implications of technological change. 03369
Structure and policy in computer integrated manufacturing systems: human factors implications. 03371
Stress, coping, and worker well-being in computer-aided manufacturing: A field investigation of a CNC machine shop. 03373
The impact of advanced manufacturing in work organization: The Portuguese case ofthe plastic moulding industry. 03374
Product engineering in the CIM environment. 03376
CIM and manufacturing industry in the north east of England: A survey of some current issues. 03377
Human and computer aided manufacturing: The end of taylorism?. 03379
Differential organization impacts of the transition from stand-alone to integrated flexible production. 03380
Designing hybrid automated manufacturing systems: A European perspective. 03382
Macro-ergonomics and the computer-integrated enterprise. 03383

Further division of reintegration of mental labour? CAD/CAP and work in design and work preparation shops. 03385
Beyond software ergonomics? Human control of automated systems. 03386
Robot vs. human operator for speed, precision and other aspects. 03403
Effects of automation on occupational safety & health. 03435
Computerized manufacturing technology and work organization effects on labor relations and worker satisfaction. 03443
Union acceptance of automation technology: A case study. 03444
Human aspects of automated assembly lines. 03445
Human factors in automating manufacturing systems in India. 03446
The economic evaluation on implementation industrial robot from user point of view. 03447
Human aspects of QC circle movement in Japanese manufacturing: Natures and problems. 03450
The role of memory in intelligent information systems. 03462
An investigation of performance, productivity, and rationality in multi-criteria decision making. 03463
Crisis planning systems: tools for intelligent action. 03464
Role-based security in data base management systems. 03584
Participation, organizational choices and time-economy: some theoretical questions. 03650
The office between humanization and control. 03651
User participation from the point of view of the workers and trade union policy. 03652
Report from the working group on "goals and strategies of trade unions and other social groups in systems design for human development and productivity.". 03657
Establishing structures of requirements for the application of automated information processing (AIP)—an approach for the development of computer-aided systems. 03660
System development in a women's perspective. 03675
Use of an entire workforce as computer. 03748
Automation and work culture. 03750
A study of managerial computer users: the impact of user sophistication on decision structure and attributes of decision-related information (end user). 04078
Office automation: a social and organizational perspective. ● HCI-0048 †
Executive support systems: the emergence of top management computer use. ● HCI-0049 †
Online communities. ● HCI-0051 †
The computer culture. § HCI-0084 †
The future of "writing" for the computer industry. HCI-0150 †
Corporate culture, technical documentation, and organization diagnosis. HCI-0151 †
Designing online information. HCI-0152 †
A note on the nature of creativity in engineering: implications for supporting system design. HCI-0220 †
Computer anxiety in management: myth or reality?. HCI-0232 †
The impact of DSS on organizational communication. HCI-0294 †
Strategies for encouraging successful adoption of office communication systems. HCI-0307 †
Diversity in the use of electronic mail: a preliminary inquiry. HCI-0310 †
Expert systems—where do we go from here?. HCI-0318 †
Computer mediated work: the interplay between technology and structured jobs. HCI-0440 †
An overview of research and co-operation in advanced information technology. HCI-0442 †

**K.4.m Miscellaneous**

Supporting the microcomputer end user. 0187
Participation–from Aristotle to today. 0499
The effects of computer use in early childhood socialization. 0793
VDUs can ruin your health. 01446
The cybernetic principle: its transdisciplinarity to science and religion and the challenging task. 01596
Informatics and municipalities: the Greek approach. 01940
Investigating computer anxiety in an academic library. 02047
Reading, culture and modern mass media. 02340
Forecasting consumer adoption of information technology and services—lessons from home video forecasting. 02451
But what will the workers do? simulating what the workers do to us when we do what we do to them. 02590
Communications technology and the public sector: understanding the process of adoption. 02679
Fifth generation computers: concepts, implementations and uses. ● HCI-0001 †
Man-made minds: the promise of artificial intelligence. ● HCI-0055 †
Attitudes towards specific uses of the computers quantitative, decision-making and record-keeping applications. HCI-0234 †

# K.5 LEGAL ASPECTS OF COMPUTING

**K.5.0 General**

Computer ethics: an antidote to despair. 0791
Legal liability for malfunction and misuse of expert systems. 0939

[K. COMPUTING MILIEUX]

What AI practitioners should know about the law, part 2. 01197
Developing awareness of computer ethics. 03010

### K.5.1 Software Protection

Attitudes toward unauthorized software copying: general public vs. business faculty member. 01142

*Copyrights*

Protecting user interfaces through copyright: the debate. 0827
Why the look and feel of software user interfaces should not be protected by copyright law. 01324
Broderbund Software, Inc. v. Unison World, Inc. 648 F. Supp. 1127 (1986).. 01477

*Patents*

Protecting user interfaces through copyright: the debate. 0827

### K.5.2 Governmental Issues

An expert system for screening employee pension plans for the Internal Revenue Service. 02773
Organizational implications of office systems: toward a critical social action perspective. 03358

*Regulation*

Public Law 99-506, "Section 508" Electronic Equipment Accessibility for disabled workers. 02893
Developing awareness of computer ethics. 03010
Recent trends in information systems law. 03017
Towards a framework for identifying organizationally-compatible AMT. 03372

### K.5.m Miscellaneous

Computer-assisted negotiations: a case history from the law of the sea negotiations and speculation regarding future uses. HCI-0443 †

*Contracts*

Humans, computers, and contracts. 03223

## K.6 MANAGEMENT OF COMPUTING AND INFORMATION SYSTEMS

### K.6.0 General

Text, context, and hypertext: writing with and for the computer. ● 0098
Hypertext: a way of incorporating user feedback into online documentation. 0102
Advanced information technology in the new industrial society: the Kingston seminars. ● 0225

The CD ROM handbook. ● 0678
Oxford Surveys in Information Technology. ● 0753
Successful use of CADCAM—a combination of technology, organization, and people. 01569
Your office is where you are. 01703
An investigation of the effects of age, size, and hardware option on the critical success factors applicable to information centers. 02352
The measurement of end-user computing satisfaction. 02510
Computer personnel research. § 02803
The two cultures in computing. 03018
In the age of the smart machine: the future of work and power. ● HCI-0083 †
Operator work load: when is enough enough?. HCI-0222 †
Impact of system response time on state anxiety. HCI-0228 †

*Economics*

How to manage educational computing initiatives-lessons from the first five years of Project Athena at MIT. 0125
The management of advanced information technology. 0226
Steel yields in Pa.. 01649
The dual role of information centers: an assessment of end user computing management strategies. 01942
Need of electronic tools in educational programmers and the impact in developing countries. 03023
Humans, computers, and contracts. 03223
Human aspects of QC circle movement in Japanese manufacturing: Natures and problems. 03450

### K.6.1 Project and People Management

Human foundations of advanced computing technology: the guide to the select literature. 0001
The changing workplace: A guide to managing the people, organizational, and regulatory aspects of office technology (book excerpt). 0044
Investment in computer-product documentation: causes and effects. 0105
The on-line environment and in-house training. 0106
Authoring tools for complex document sets. 0120
Management, organizations and the new technologies. 0145
The management of advanced information technology. 0226
Human—computer interactions in the workplace: psychosocial aspects of VDT use. 0306
The limitations of task complexity through information technologies: results of a field study. 0307
Relationships and tasks in scientific research collaborations (Reprint). 0387
Managers, micros and mainframes: integrating systems for end-users. ● 0455

Thomas W. Malone, Oct. 5: user interface strategies '88. ● 0532
Critical issues in information processing management and technology: vol. 6. ● 0594
User interface strategies '88 (Videotape). ● 0684
Human factors reference guide for electronics and computer professionals. ● 0733
Oxford Surveys in Information Technology. ● 0753
Color in user interface design: functionally and aesthetics. 0803
Supporting end users in the office. 01444
Implementation issues for operations research software. 01537
The psychological costs of master computer. 01655
Battling for new roles. 01664
Definitional distinctions and implications for managing end user computing. 01946
Decision support systems for workers: a bridge to advancing productivity. 01947
Automatic information processing activities and operational decision making: a case study of consequence. 01950
A powerful solution meets an overwhelming problem. 02053
The application of human factors to the needs of the novice computer user. 02079
Organizational factors affecting the success of end-user computing. 02344
Information systems development success: Perspectives from project team participants. 02501
Mainframe and microcomputer-based business graphics: end user computing comparisons and trends. 02805
Computer-Supported Cooperative Work. § 02821
Human Factors in Computing Systems. § 02856
Human Factors in Computing Systems. § 02903
The 1987 ACM SIGBDP-SIGCPR Conference. § 03099
User Services Conference. § 03130
Supercomputer applications: helping users cope with tough programming problems. 03147
Still sailing (and bailing): managing unexpected change in user support. 03150
A new model for user services: distributed support. 03153
Teaching users to fish: hooks, lines and sinkers for reading computer documentat. 03156
User services consulting supportr tools at the NASA numerical aerodynamic simula. 03161
People and computers: designing for usability. § 03244
Human factors in office systems. 03357
Security of office systems. 03359
Implementation of office systems. 03360
Applications Track. § 03455
Decision Support and Knowledge Based Systems Track. § 03461
User or development of information systems: Which is more fundamental?. 03654

The central nervous system as a low and high level control system. 04007
Sharing in a privately owned workstation environment. 04076
User-centered requirements analysis. ● HCI-0004 †
How to write a really good user's manual. ● HCI-0017 †
Planning and design of information systems. ● HCI-0045 †
Interactive video: vol. 1. ● HCI-0081 †
Corporate culture, technical documentation, and organization diagnosis. HCI-0151 †
Human-computer interface development: concepts and systems for its management. HCI-0444 †
Strategic management of technostress: The chaining of Prometheus. HCI-0452 †

**Life cycle**

Prototyping techniques for different problem contexts. 0862
An exploratory contingency model of user participation and MIS use. 01919
Information requirements specification II: Brainstorming collective decision-making technique. 02005
Task analysis, systems analysis and design: symbiosis or synthesis?. 02058
Importance of the human factor in the information system life cycle. 02422
The kernel of a generic software development environment. 03056
Information systems definition: the Multiview approach. ● HCI-0085 †
A dedicated microcomputer for handwritten interaction with a software tool: system prototyping. HCI-0119 †
Cost/benefit analysis for incorporating human factors in the software lifecycle. HCI-0127 †

**Management techniques (e.g., PERT/CPM)**

The physical environment. 0045
Callisto: an intelligent project management system (Reprint). 0375
Cognitive science and organizational design: a case study of computer conferencing (Reprint). 0386
Conceptual design of decision support systems utilizing management science models. 0658
Managing the design of user-computer interfaces. 0936
Maintaining the spirit of excitement in growing companies. 01025
Successful implementation of an office system. 01438
Development of the wedding planner—extensions to reach a young audience. 01502
Successful use of CADCAM—a combination of technology, organization, and people. 01569
Some historical currents concerning the 'societal learning' approach to policy and planning. 01603
Managing the PC revolution. 01643

The real cost of OA. 01647
Users are people too. 01653
Power and credibility in office automation. 01657
A PC policy primer. 01660
User satisfaction: A vital management issue. 01678
Your office is where you are. 01703
The IE's future role in improving knowledge. 01903
Tennessee Eastman employee teamwork raises quality, customer service. 01907
Dow Chemical makes continuous improvement part of everyone's job. 01908
Methods improvement kit uses IE technique to simplify work. 01909
Strategies for managing user developed systems. 01923
End-user computing environments—finding a balance between productivity and control. 01927
A systems architecture for supporting senior managers' messy tasks. 01928
Managing information systems for effectiveness and humanity: applying research of organizational behavior. 01932
The management of the end-user environment: an empirical investigation. 01937
Key human resource issues in IS in the 1990s: Views of IS executives versus human resource executives. 01939
Competition and cooperation in information systems innovation. 01941
The dual role of information centers: an assessment of end user computing management strategies. 01942
Expansion and control of end-user computing. 02347
Strategies for end-user computing: An integrative framework. 02348
Selection systems for sales representatives. 02408
Qualities of a good forms designer. 02412
TA: Can it improve worker satisfaction with organizational decision-making?. 02414
User programmer and costs of the misinformed user. 02415
The impact of information systems strategy on end user computing. 02423
The end user attack: Will the real computer professionals stand up and fight. 02424
Managing end user computing when the only constant is change. 02425
Structuring informal information. 02426
Managing the work station environment. 02430
Strategic IRM plan: user involvement spells success. 02432
Motivators vs. demotivators in the IS environment. 02433
Strategies for managing end user computing. 02436
A practical guide to the first time user/systems developer. 02437
Service support levels: An organizational approach to end-user computing. 02503
Message equivocality, media selection and manager performance: implications for information systems. 02505

Critical factors in the user environment: an experimental study of users, organizations and tasks. 02507
The effect of user involvement on system success: a contingency approach. 02508
Restoring a sense of control during implementation: how user involvement leads to system acceptance. 02509
Linking mechanism supporting end-user computing. 02806
Choosing between methods: analysing the user's decision space in terms of schemas and linear models. 02879
Integrating human factors and software development. 02882
Planning for advising. 02886
Justified advice: a semi-naturalistic study of advisory strategies. 02887
Managers who personally use information technology frequently: a profile of some invisible computer personnel. 03007
Analysis and design skills required by end-users in small organizations. 03008
Evaluating performance appraisal systems for IS personnel. 03011
An update measure of supervisor-rated job performance for programmer/analysis. 03012
Increase organizational effectiveness: Support self-managed IS development teams. 03014
Repositioning the information systems management function: Implications for information systems personnel. 03015
Negotiating IS: Observations on changes in structure from a negotiated order perspective. 03016
An investigation into the existence of subgroup concept in information systems personnel management. 03022
Measuring the performance of statisticians with statistical software. 03314
Essential ingredients for a statistical workstation. 03315
Statistical software, graphics and future workstations for data analysis. 03316
The information technology champion: aiding and abetting, care and feeding. 03459
Crisis planning systems: tools for intelligent action. 03464
An investigation of the effectiveness of communication between systems analysts and end users in the design of large computer systems. 04075
The soft side of software: a management approach to computer documentation. • HCI-0016 †
Interactive critical path analysis (ICPA)—microcomputer implementation of a project management and knowledge engineering tool. HCI-0445 †

**Multiview** *see* Proper Noun Index

**Staffing**

Human limits and the VDT computer interface (excerpt). 0054

# CATEGORY INDEX

[K. COMPUTING MILIEUX]

The keystroke-level model for user performance time with interactive systems. 0055
The psychology of work and organization: current trends and issues. • 0239
An examination of the research evidence for computer-based instruction. 0415
Behavioural and organisational factors involved in the turnover of high tech professionals. 01024
Environments: Austria compared to the United States. 01026
Requirements checklist for a system development workstation. 01144
Dp and the disabled. 01646
In search of the perfect programmer. 01648
Managing information systems for effectiveness and humanity: applying research of organizational behavior. 01932
Utilizing high technology: computer-aided-design and user performance. 01954
The effects of task differences on the work satisfaction, job characteristics, and role perceptions of programmer/analysts. 02359
TA: Can it improve worker satisfaction with organizational decision-making?. 02414
Are information systems people different? An investigation of how they are and should be managed. 02511
Integrating human factors and software development. 02882
Management of Information Systems Personnel. § 02996
Information systems skills requirements: 1980 & 1988. 02997
The systems analyst of the 1990's. 02998
Perceptions of the CIS graduate's workstyle: undergraduate business students versus CIS faculty. 02999
Electronic monitoring and the redundancy of control systems: The role of the supervisor. 03000
Motivations and behaviors of software professionals. 03003
Causes of motivational problems among AI managers. 03004
Making computer tasks at work more playful: Implications for systems analysts and designers. 03005
Managers who personally use information technology frequently: a profile of some invisible computer personnel. 03007
Analysis and design skills required by end users in small organizations. 03008
The importance of individual differences in end-user training: The case for learning style. 03009
Evaluating performance appraisal systems for IS personnel. 03011
The experimental validation of a programmer productivity measure. 03013
Increase organizational effectiveness: Support self-managed IS development teams. 03014

Repositioning the information systems management function: Implications for information systems personnel. 03015
Recent trends in information systems law. 03017
Instilling professionalism in a software development organization. 03019
Male/female programmer and systems analyst Job performance. 03020
Moderating effects of age, education, and tenure on the job satisfaction-job performance relationship. 03021
An investigation into the existence of subgroup concept in information systems personnel management. 03022
The influence of individual differences on the reading of computer programs. 03456
Tele-cybernetics: implications for the international marketplace. 03458
Problems among managers of AI personnel. 03460
An empirical study of occupational stress, attitudes and health among information systems personnel. HCI-0451 †

### Systems analysis and design

Power, politics, and MIS implementation. 0042
How and when to collect behavioural data. 0050
Statistical evaluation of behavioural data. 0051
Human limits and the VDT computer interface (excerpt). 0054
The keystroke-level model for user performance time with interactive systems. 0055
Computer text-editing: an information-processing analysis of a routine cognitive skill. 0056
System design for speech recognition and generation. 0065
Design principles for human-computer interfaces. 0075
The human factor: Designing computer systems for people. 0076
Designing for usability: Key principles and what designers think. 0078
Designing for error. 0087
Human factors testing in the design of Xerox's 8010 "Star" office workstation. 0090
Usability: stereotypes and traps. 0104
Technology + design + research = information design. 0107
Are writers obsolete in the computer industry?. 0109
Reflections on authoring, editing, and managing hypertext. 0119
Consulting skills for technical writers. 0124
Escher effects in online text. 0130
Military systems. 0138
Critical issues in information systems research. • 0153
Towards a framework for systems analysis practice. 0155
Understanding the elements of system design. 0156
Managerial expert systems and organizational change: some critical research issues. 0157
The in-formation of information systems. 0159

1147

[K. COMPUTING MILIEUX]  CATEGORY INDEX

Man-computer interfaces: an introduction to software design and implementation. • 0220
Computerization versus computer aided mental. 0308
Callisto: an intelligent project management system (Reprint). 0375
The variable impact of computer technologies on the organization of work activities. 0388
Attention. 0399
Interface design and evaluation—Semiotic implications. 0409
User systems analysis: a user oriented approach to computer systems analysis, design, and implementation. • 0454
An introduction to data and activity analysis. • 0610
Systems analysis techniques. 0622
System design for human interaction. • 0644
System design for human interaction. • 0645
An overview of system design for human interaction. 0646
Judgement and decision: theory and application. 0648
Conceptual design of decision support systems utilizing management science models. 0658
A conceptual architecture for generalized decision support system software. 0659
Concept design of a program manager's decision support system. 0660
Computer-aided engineering (CAE) for system analysis. 0663
Artificial intelligence & human learning: intelligent computer-aided instruction. • 0671
Generalization, consistency, and control. 0796
Artifact as theory-nexus: hermeneutics meets theory-based design. 0798
Programmable user models for predictive evaluation of interface designs. 0800
Experience with contextual field research. 0802
LIZA: an extensible groupware toolkit. 0805
University of Colorado at Boulder, Institute of cognitive science. 0811
What is EuroParc?. 0812
NASA Johnson Space Center, Human-Computer Interaction. 0815
How some advice fails. 0824
Drama and personality in user interface design. 0830
Learning and transfer of measurement tasks. 0832
Statemaster: A UIMS based on statechart for prototyping and target implementation. 0850
A synthetic visual environment with hand gesturing and voice input. 0858
Design rationale: the argument behind the artifact. 0860
Design environments for constructive and argumentative design. 0864
Generating highly interactive user interfaces. 0865
Directed dialogue protocols: verbal data for user interface design. 0866
The tourist artificial reality. 0868

Socio-tech: what is it (and why should we care)?. 0908
User-derived impact analysis as a tool for usability engineering. 0922
On designing for usability: an application of four key principles. 0923
A formal interface design methodology based on user knowledge. 0929
Intelligent interfaces: user models and planners. 0932
Seven plus or minus two central issues in human-computer interaction. 0937
Modes survey. 0963
Designing real-time, decision support computer-human interaction. 0982
IRX: an information retrieval system for experimentation and user applications. 01076
An information retrieval system for software components. 01077
Some design guidelines for an information center to support office information systems. 01093
The concept of an information management system and its use within design studies. 01244
Working together. 01300
Where the action is. 01301
Perils and pitfalls. 01302
Intelligent software agents. 01303
A groupware toolbox. 01304
The supplier's role in the design of products for organisations. 01412
Approximate modelling of cognitive activity with an expert system: a theory-based strategy for developing an interactive design tool. 01415
Communication analysis in the company. 01435
The magical number three—plus or minus zero. 01622
Patterned systems design. 01625
End-user prototyping: sophisticated users supporting system development. 01636
The designing mind. 01661
How executives can shape their company's information systems. 01707
Adaptive aiding for human/computer control. 01782
Applying a pilot system and prototyping approach to systems development and implementation. 01915
Encouraging user management participation in systems design. 01926
Differences in analyst's attitudes towards information systems development: evidence and implications. 01935
End user—IS design professional interaction—information exchange for firm profit or end user satisfaction?. 01936
Information systems user–designer communication problems. 01938
Informatics and municipalities: the Greek approach. 01940
Competition and cooperation in information systems innovation. 01941

# CATEGORY INDEX [K. COMPUTING MILIEUX]

The implementation of information systems for workers: a structural equation model. 01948
Impact of prototyping on user information satisfaction during the IS specification phase. 01955
Experiences in use of SSADM: series of case studies. Part 1: first time users. 01976
Experiences in use of SSADM: series of case studies. Part 2: experienced users. 01977
The convergence of Moore's/Mooers' laws. 01996
On meanings menus for measurement: disentangling evaluative issues in system design. 01997
On two roles decision support systems can play in negotiations. 01998
The contribution of cognitive engineering to the effective design and use of information systems. 02033
Moral judgements in designing better systems. 02064
Cognitive systems engineering: new wine in new bottles. 02078
A survey of formal tools and models for developing user interfaces. 02207
Cognitive primitives. 02214
Toward a formal specification of menu-based systems. 02400
Education requirements for the entry level business systems analyst. 02409
Human factors principles. 02419
Designing systems for change. 02420
Prototypes for user training. 02421
The user designer/developer and the user work station. 02431
An expert system for system design. 02441
The design and evaluation of a front-end user interface for energy researchers. 02453
Peopleware. 02557
Expanding the domain of systems analysis. 02587
ATLANTIS—a software simulator for behavior analysis of protocol specificationsand their target implementations. 02667
User development of applications: a study of a model of success. 02807
Capturing the capture concepts: a case study in the design of computer-supported meeting environments. 02824
How users repeat their actions on computers: principles for design of history mechanisms. 02885
Designing keybindings to be easy to learn and resistant to forgetting even when the set of commands is large. 02890
Multimodal response planning: an adaptive rule based approach. 02894
SAUCI: a knowledge-based interface architecture. 02895
Control of cognitive processes during software design: what tools are needed?. 02899
ProCEED: an expert system for multivariate process control systems design. 02935

An expert database for material and production planning. 02937
A generic strategy for diagnostic assistance: the technician's assistant. 02957
Knowledge-based interface to manufacturing computer systems. 02966
DORUS: an architecture for dynamic optimal resource utilization systems. 02979
The systems analyst of the 1990's. 02998
Making computer tasks at work more playful: Implications for systems analysts and designers. 03005
Male/female programmer and systems analyst Job performance. 03020
Patterned systems design—HCI in commercial data processing. 03193
Human factors in systems design: a case study. 03196
A flexible negotiable interactive learning environment. 03197
Preliminary analysis for design. 03199
Refining early design decisions with a black-box model. 03200
Knowledge acquisition and conceptual models: a cognitive analysis of the interface. 03214
Implications of current design practice for the use of HCI techniques. 03217
Task-related knowledge structures: analysis, modelling and application. 03218
People and computers: designing for usability. § 03244
Ergonomics in design for usability. 03247
MacCadd - an enabling software method support tool. 03252
The role of iterative evaluation in designing systems for usability. 03255
Proving properties of interactive systems. 03267
Towards a new theory of job design. 03368
Sociotechnical design of advanced manufacturing systems. 03370
Structure and policy in computer integrated manufacturing systems: human factors implications. 03371
Towards a framework for identifying organizationally-compatible AMT. 03372
Design of distribution of production control functions between humans and artificially intelligent devices. 03375
Beyond software ergonomics? Human control of automated systems. 03386
Human factor issues in teleoperated systems. 03387
A conceptual dependency network approach to multi-task assignments in man-machine (teleoperated) systems. 03388
Illumination requirements for operating a space remote manipulator. 03392
Ergonomics of hybrid intelligence. 03393
An approach to knowledge elicitation in scheduling FMS: Toward a hybrid intelligent system. 03394

Humane: A designer's assistant for modeling and evaluating function allocation options. 03397
Human-machine interface in remote monitoring and control of flexible manufacturing systems. 03399
Unexpected motion hazard exposures on a large robotic assembly. 03409
An evaluation of production systems from the ergonomic viewpoint: a plea for an integral approach to design. 03430
Development of a continuous finishing line to improve working conditions. 03434
Human-computer interaction. § 03454
A framework of composite information systems for strategic advantage. 03465
Perceptions of system effectiveness as viewed by executives, users, and information specialists. 03469
User perceptions of DSS restrictiveness: an experiment. 03470
Systems for cooperative work and group decision making: status of use and problems in development. 03471
When and how cognitive style impacts decision making. 03474
An architecture for active DSS. 03480
Structured what if analysis in DSS models. 03481
Integrative participation—a challenge to the development of informatics. 03641
The design of information processing systems in relation to users. 03642
Systems, processes, and structures. 03644
User-centered system design: design of mental tasks. 03646
Who is user and who is affected: a proposal to better semantics. 03647
The importance of work organization by systems design. 03648
Contrastive analysis of the relationship of man and computer as a basis of system design. 03649
Different perspectives: What are they and how can they be used?. 03653
Transparency and system design. 03655
System design for local authorities: participation based on "information contracts". 03656
Participative design and requirements on planning, software engineering and education. 03658
How to improve pragmatic quality of information systems. 03662
Report from the working group on "methods and tools in system design for, with and by the users". 03664
Experiences in participative systems design. 03665
Work design instead of system design. 03671
On the detection of social effects in man-computer interaction—a contribution to systems design. 03672
A roundtable discussion on women, computers and participation. 03673
Women, work and computerization: opportunities and disadvantages. § 03674

Qualitative modeling of physical systems for knowledge based control. 03834
A distributed object server. 03842
An investigation of the effectiveness of communication between systems analysts and end users in the design of large computer systems. 04075
Storyboard prototyping: a new approach to user requirements analysis. ● HCI-0005 †
Information systems definition: the Multiview approach. ● HCI-0085 †
Information systems design methodologies and their compliance with cognitive ergonomy. HCI-0097 †
A taxonomy for the study of human factors in management information systems. HCI-0205 †
Executive workstations: issues and requirements. HCI-0288 †
Computer decision support for senior managers: encouraging exploration. HCI-0298 †
Impact of design methods on decision support systems success: an empirical assessment. HCI-0303 †
Cognitive models, cognitive tasks, and information retrieval. HCI-0331 †
An approach to CAD system performance evaluation. HCI-0414 †
Computer mediated work: the interplay between technology and structured jobs. HCI-0440 †
Open versus closed minds: the effect of dogmatism on an analyst's problem-solving behavior. HCI-0446 †

*Systems development*

Information development is part of product development—not an afterthought. 0103
Technology + design + research = information design. 0107
How to manage educational computing initiatives-lessons from the first five years of Project Athena at MIT. 0125
Techniques of user message design: developing a user message system to support cooperative work. 0127
Critical issues in information systems research. ● 0153
Towards a framework for systems analysis practice. 0155
Strategies for research on information systems in organizations. A critical analysis of research purpose and time frame. 0158
Authorship provisions in AUGMENT (Reprint). 0370
Thinking ahead: what to expect from teleconferencing (Reprint). 0372
Communication and management support in system development environments (Reprint). 0374
Callisto: an intelligent project management system (Reprint). 0375
Human factors and artificial intelligence. 0408
Schaum's outline of theories and problems of programming with advanced structured COBOL with file processing structured systems deveolpment and interactive cons. ● 0555
Production management systems. 0619

The migration of expert systems into the production environment. 0740
ICE: information center expert: a consultation system for resource allocation. 0781
Action research on systems development: case study of changing actor roles. 0788
Prototyping techniques for different problem contexts. 0862
Design environments for constructive and argumentative design. 0864
Rapid prototyping and system development: examination of an interface toolkit for voice and telephony applications. 0918
An interactive environment for dialogue development: its design, use and evaluation; or, is aide useful?. 0920
User-derived impact analysis as a tool for usability engineering. 0922
Requirements checklist for a system development workstation. 01144
Selecting a shell. 01176
A cognitively based methodology for evaluating human performance in the computer-aided design task domain. 01240
Life before the chips: simulating digital video interactive technology. 01328
Intelligent interactive video simulation of a code inspection. 01329
Information systems and user resistance: theory and practice. 01409
The use of prototyping and simulation in the development of large-scale applications. 01411
End-user prototyping: sophisticated users supporting system development. 01636
Information systems strategy and end-user application development. 01637
Propaedeutics of decision-making: supporting managerial learning and innovation. 01667
Evaluating the usability of the Glasgow online. 01808
The feature chart: A tool for communicating the analysis for a decision support system. 01913
A critical view of factors affecting successful application of normative and socio-technical systems development approaches. 01914
An exploratory contingency model of user participation and MIS use. 01919
Differences in analyst's attitudes towards information systems development: evidence and implications. 01935
Successful application of communication techniques to improve the systems development process. 01952
Methodology for end user computing in development administration. 01956
Communicating with users during systems development. 01972
Responsibility sharing between sophisticated users and professionals in structured prototyping. 01978
The convergence of Moore's/Mooers' laws. 01996

Importance of the human factor in the information system life cycle. 02422
A practical guide to the first time user/systems developer. 02437
Utilizing the trend of end user development. 02444
Restoring a sense of control during implementation: how user involvement leads to system acceptance. 02509
Innovation of decision support system-matplan based on structure matrix supported by APL. 02800
GDSS: a brief look at a new concept in decision support. 02804
User development of applications: a study of a model of success. 02807
A knowledge-based user interface management system. 02867
The data model is the heart of interface design. 02875
The ISA expert system: a prototype system for failure diagnosis on the space station. 02913
Knowledge base applications with software engineering: a tool for requirements specifications. 02924
The development of an automated flight test management system for flight test planning and monitoring. 02928
Automated design and analysis system for design of custom orthopedic implants. 02931
Process design of oil and gas production facilities using expert systems. 02933
Automatic acquisition of domain and procedural knowledge. 02943
Using design expertise to develop an expert system. 02962
Adequate documentation of user-developed applications: a new challenge for end-user computing management. 03001
Adequate documentation of user-developed applications: a new challenge for end-user computing management. 03001
The experimental validation of a programmer productivity measure. 03013
Implications of current design practice for the use of HCI techniques. 03217
Some experiences in integrating specification of human computer interaction within a structured system development method. 03222
Human-machine interface in remote monitoring and control of flexible manufacturing systems. 03399
Ontological analysis of document usage: an exploratory study. 03467
Perceptions of system effectiveness as viewed by executives, users, and information specialists. 03469
Systems for cooperative work and group decision making: status of use and problems in development. 03471
The impact of "Messy" data on group decision making. 03476
An architecture for active DSS. 03480

[K. COMPUTING MILIEUX]

Software engineering for distributed applications: the design project. 03508
The space station information system and software support environment. 03512
An efficient high-level man-machine interface. 03530
Seven mortal sins of systems work. 03645
Participative design and requirements on planning, software engineering and education. 03658
Procedures for participation in planning, developing and operating information systems. 03659
Establishing structures of requirements for the application of automated information processing (AIP)—an approach for the development of computer-aided systems. 03660
Generation of visions in systems development: a supplement to the tool box. 03661
System development in a women's perspective. 03675
An investigation of the effectiveness of communication between systems analysts and end users in the design of large computer systems. 04075
Information systems definition: the Multiview approach. ● HCI-0085 †
Computer decision support for senior managers: encouraging exploration. HCI-0298 †
An empirical study of the impact of user involvement on system usage and information satisfaction. HCI-0448 †

### Training

Software psychology: the need for an interdisciplinary program. 0052
Manual Dexterity: A user-oriented approach to creating computer documentation. 0085
Minimalist design for active users. 0086
The adventure of getting to know a computer. 0088
Ingredients of intelligent user interfaces. 0093
The on-line environment and in-house training. 0106
Are writers obsolete in the computer industry?. 0109
Textual intervention, collaboration, and the online environment. 0126
The evaluation of online help systems: a conceptual model. 0129
Learning by doing with simulated intelligent help. 0132
Towards a framework for systems analysis practice. 0155
Supporting the microcomputer end user. 0187
The management of advanced information technology. 0226
Five gambits for the advisory interface dilemma. 0314
Computer-supported cooperative work: a book of readings. ● 0366
Toward high-performance knowledge workers (Reprint). 0369
Education and training in robotics. ● 0440
Educating the CBIS user: a case analysis. 0778
On-line tutorials: What kind of inference leads to the most effective learning?. 0823
How some advice fails. 0824

Responding to "HUH?": answering vaguely articulated follow-up questions. 0825
Learning and transfer of measurement tasks. 0832
Advising roles of a computer consultant. 0896
Transfer between word processing systems. 0899
Learning modes and subsequent use of computer-mediated communication systems. 0912
The elicitation of system knowledge by picture probes. 0921
Navigational aids and learning styles: structural optimal training for computer users. 0970
What we know and what we need to know: the user model versus the user's model in human-computer interaction. 01243
OA: bridging the language gap. 01376
The real cost of OA. 01647
Grow your own programmers. 01663
Training consistent task components: application of automatic and controlled processing theory to industrial task training. 01742
Automaticity, resources, and memory: theoretical controversies and practical implications. 01792
An empirical investigation of DSS usage and the user's perception of DSS training. 01934
Effect of computer knowledge on user performance over time. 01975
A powerful solution meets an overwhelming problem. 02053
Adapting expert systems to simulation training of process operators. 02056
The application of human factors to the needs of the novice computer user. 02079
On comprehending a computer manual: analysis of variables affecting performance. 02135
Prompting, feedback and error correction in the design of a scenario machine. 02176
Effects of computer programming experience on network representations of abstract programming concepts. 02204
Theoretical training and problem detection in a computerized database retrieval task. 02239
Personal computer training software for adaptive control. 02262
Education and training in office technology. 02330
Effects of decision support training and cognitive style on decision process attributes. 02346
Prototypes for user training. 02421
System development methods—a comparative investigation. 02504
Training end users: an exploratory study. 02506
Putting on a show: using computer graphics to train end-users. 02520
Help texts vs. help mechanisms: A new mandate for documentation writers. 02784

CATEGORY INDEX [K. COMPUTING MILIEUX]

Transferring skills from training to the actual work situation: the role of task application knowledge, action styles and job decision latitude. 02865
A case study of CSCW in a dispersed organization. 02866
Navigating integrated facilities: initiating and terminating interaction sequences. 02876
Video: Data for studying human-computer interaction. 02878
Designing keybindings to be easy to learn and resistant to forgetting even when the set of commands is large. 02890
Effects of interface design upon user productivity. 02891
Development of an instrument measuring user satisfaction of the human-computer interface. 02892
Online help systems: design and implementation issues (panel). 02902
Knowledge-based interface to manufacturing computer systems. 02966
An evaluation and selection methodology of microcomputer training software: Implications for human resource managers and computer personnel. 03002
Motivations and behaviors of software professionals. 03003
Analysis and design skills required by end-users in small organizations. 03008
The importance of individual differences in end-user training: The case for learning style. 03009
Repositioning the information systems management function: Implications for information systems personnel. 03015
Instilling professionalism in a software development organization. 03019
The influence of training on use of end-user software. 03042
Establishing a computing assistance centre. 03142
Humans, computers, and contracts. 03223
The effects of the supervisor's knowledge in a complex automated system. 03366
CIM and manufacturing industry in the north east of England: A survey of some current issues. 03377
Development of mental models of an office system: a field study on an introductory course. 03903
Artificial intelligence and cognitive psychology: a new look at human factors. 03904
A provisional evaluation of a new chord keyboard, the Vclotype. 03907
Software tools at the University: Why, What and How. 04026
Online help systems: design and implementation. ● HCI-0009 †
Authoring: a guide to the design of instructional software. ● HCI-0031 †
The AutoCAD productivity book: tapping the hidden power of AutoCAD. ● HCI-0076 †
LisaLearning. HCI-0092 †

Computer anxiety in management: myth or reality?. HCI-0232 †
Implications for education and training. HCI-0430 †
Training for optimising transfer between word processors. HCI-0447 †

### K.6.2 Installation Management

The changing workplace: A guide to managing the people, organizational, and regulatory aspects of office technology (book excerpt). 0044
Adaptive information systems control: A reliability-based approach. 02345
Linking mechanism supporting end-user computing. 02806
A personal view of the personal work station: some firsts in the Fifties. 03093
Humans, computers, and contracts. 03223
The evaluation of text editors: methodology and empirical results.. HCI-0209 †

*Benchmarks*

The pick of the crop. 01675

*Computer selection*

Designing the star user interface. 0089
Human factors testing in the design of Xerox's 8010 "Star" office workstation. 0090
Color in user interface design: functionally and aesthetics. 0803
Mainframe and microcomputer-based business graphics: end user computing comparisons and trends. 02805
Public Law 99-506, "Section 508" Electronic Equipment Accessibility for disabled workers. 02893

*Computing equipment management*

The physical environment. 0045
Human factors issues in VDT use: Environmental and workstation design considerations. 0046
Preventing back strain. 0047
Guide to the Draft American National Standard for Human Factors Engineering of Visual Display Terminal Workstations. 0048
The statutes and standards movement. 0049
Human limits and the VDT computer interface (excerpt). 0054
The keystroke-level model for user performance time with interactive systems. 0055
Computer text-editing: an information-processing analysis of a routine cognitive skill. 0056
Computer text-editing: an information-processing analysis of a routine cognitive skill. 0056
Learning to use word processors: problems and prospects. 0059

[K. COMPUTING MILIEUX]

Learning to use a word processor: by doing, by thinking, and by knowing. 0060
How to manage educational computing initiatives-lessons from the first five years of Project Athena at MIT. 0125
Of moles and men: the design of foot controls for workstations. 0935
Speech responses and dual-task performance: better time-sharing or asymmetric transfer?. 01789
Public Law 99-506, "Section 508" Electronic Equipment Accessibility for disabled workers. 02893
An evaluation and selection methodology of microcomputer training software: Implications for human resource managers and computer personnel. 03002

### Performance and usage measurement

Information technology and the experience of work. 0041
How and when to collect behavioural data. 0050
Statistical evaluation of behavioural data. 0051
Human limits and the VDT computer interface (excerpt). 0054
The keystroke-level model for user performance time with interactive systems. 0055
The evaluation of text editors: Methodology and empirical results. 0058
Issues and techniques in touch-sensitive tablet input. 0063
Evaluation of mouse, rate-controlled isometric joystick, step keys, and text keys, for text selection on a CRT. 0064
A system for evaluating screen formats: Research and application. 0413
User performance with command, menu, and iconic interfaces. 0414
On designing for usability: an application of four key principles. 0923
Instrumenting systems to measure components of interactive response times. 01230
A multidimensional approach to the measurement of human-computer performance. 01410
Measuring user satisfaction. 01677
User satisfaction: A vital management issue. 01678
End-user computing environments—finding a balance between productivity and control. 01927
Measuring implementation outcome: beyond success and failure. 01933
The dual role of information centers: an assessment of end user computing management strategies. 01942
Business graphics trends, two years later. 01945
Microcomputer applications: an empirical look at usage. 01949
On meanings menus for measurement: disentangling evaluative issues in system design. 01997
On two roles decision support systems can play in negotiations. 01998

The effects of task differences on the work satisfaction, job characteristics, and role perceptions of programmer/analysts. 02359
Choosing between methods: analysing the user's decision space in terms of schemas and linear models. 02879
Development of an instrument measuring user satisfaction of the human-computer interface. 02892
SPA: a systems for diagnosis of computer performance problems. 02969
Making computer tasks at work more playful: Implications for systems analysts and designers. 03005
Evaluating performance appraisal systems for IS personnel. 03011
An update measure of supervisor-rated job performance for programmer/analysis. 03012
The experimental validation of a programmer productivity measure. 03013
Instilling professionalism in a software development organization. 03019
Crisis planning systems: tools for intelligent action. 03464
Perceptions of system effectiveness as viewed by executives, users, and information specialists. 03469
A longitudinal study of spreadsheet program use. 03482
Strategies for encouraging successful adoption of office communication systems. HCI-0307 †

### Pricing and resource allocation

Investment in computer-product documentation: causes and effects. 0105
Callisto: an intelligent project management system (Reprint). 0375
An examination of the research evidence for computer-based instruction. 0415
Speech responses and dual-task performance: better time-sharing or asymmetric transfer?. 01789
Negotiating IS: Observations on changes in structure from a negotiated order perspective. 03016
Instilling professionalism in a software development organization. 03019

### K.6.3 Software Management

Critical issues in information processing management and technology: vol. 6. ● 0594
Conceptual design of decision support systems utilizing management science models. 0658
A conceptual architecture for generalized decision support system software. 0659
Annual review of computer science vol. 1, 1986. ● 0719
Interface design: a neglected issue in educational software. 0826
People and organizations in software production: a review of the literature. 01023
Human factors for design and evaluation of software. 01283
Assessing gender bias in computer software. 01591

# CATEGORY INDEX [K. COMPUTING MILIEUX]

User-developers: the new software resource. 02052
On matching programmers' chunks with program structures: an empirical investigation. 02150
Extending knowledge-based systems through closely-coupled graphics and windows. 02985
Motivations and behaviors of software professionals. 03003
The importance of individual differences in end-user training: The case for learning style. 03009
An update measure of supervisor-rated job performance for programmer/analysis. 03012
Testing for usability. 03163
MacCadd - an enabling software method support tool. 03252
A framework of composite information systems for strategic advantage. 03465
Software Engineering. § 03504
Advanced programming environments. § 03779
ESEC '87. § 03795
ProMod at the age of 5. 03802
Computer usability testing & evaluation. ● HCI-0014 †
A dedicated microcomputer for handwritten interaction with a software tool: system prototyping. HCI-0119 †
Cost/benefit analysis for incorporating human factors in the software lifecycle. HCI-0127 †
A plan for evaluating usability of software products. HCI-0449 †

## *Software development*

Methods for designing software to fit human needs and capabilities (excerpt). 0079
Extending state transition diagrams for the specification of human-computer interaction. 0080
MacApp: An application framework. 0083
Are writers obsolete in the computer industry?. 0109
How to manage educational computing initiatives-lessons from the first five years of Project Athena at MIT. 0125
Man-computer interfaces: an introduction to software design and implementation. ● 0220
The variable impact of computer technologies on the organization of work activities. 0388
The gift of good design tools. 0411
Symbiotic software: development and usage issues on stand-alone and networked systems. 0474
Algebra slaves and agents in a Logo-based mathematics curriculum. 0517
Evaluating usability of human-computer interfaces: a practical method. ● 0608
Concept design of a program manager's decision support system. 0660
Concurrent Prolog: collected papers. ● 0674
Developing effective user documentation: a human factors approach. ● 0699
A system for example-based programming. 0818
Some strategies of reuse in an object-oriented programming environment. 0820

Cognitive science and machine intelligence laboratory, University of Michigan. 0843
Innovation in user interface development: obstacles and opportunities. 0852
User interface design in large corporations: coordination and communication across disciplines. 0853
Human-computer interaction department, Hewlett-Packard Laboratories. 0869
Usability testing in the real world. 0917
Application frameworks: experience with MacApp. 01039
A study of an advance organizer as a technique for teaching computer programming concepts. 01042
The Mesa programming environment. 01108
Applying direct manipulation concepts. 01143
Individual and organizational factors and the design of IPSEs. 01408
Broderbund Software, Inc. v. Unison World, Inc. 648 F. Supp. 1127 (1986).. 01477
Software development approach in FMS. 01567
Human factors support for product development. 01681
Task analysis, systems analysis and design: symbiosis or synthesis?. 02058
Effects of computer programming experience on network representations of abstract programming concepts. 02204
Building a great windows system. 02550
A program development system for the casual programmer. 02808
Hypertext engineering: practical methods for creating a compact disk encyclopedia. 02832
Integrating human factors and software development. 02882
Plan-based representations of pascal and fortran code. 02897
Providing the requisite knowledge via software documentation. 02898
Control of cognitive processes during software design: what tools are needed?. 02899
Sherlock—a system for diagnosing power distribution ring network faults. 02916
Knowledge base applications with software engineering: a tool for requirements specifications. 02924
The two cultures in computing. 03018
Instilling professionalism in a software development organization. 03019
Integral-C—a practical environment for C programming. 03049
Experience with a data base of programs. 03050
AWB-ADE: an application development environment for interactive, integrated systems. 03051
Implementing a user interface as a system of attributes. 03052
Dost: an environment to support automatic generation of user interfaces. 03053
A structural approach to the maintenance of structure-oriented environments. 03054

[K. COMPUTING MILIEUX]

A methodology for evaluating environments. 03055
The kernel of a generic software development environment. 03056
A foundation for programming environments. 03057
Describing a product opportunity: a method of understanding the users' environment. 03194
Task-related knowledge structures: analysis, modelling and application. 03218
SEE: a safe editing environment; human-computer interaction for programmers. 03225
ECS - A technique for the formal specification and rapid prototyping of human-computer interaction. 03253
Further division of reintegration of mental labour? CAD/CAP and work in design and work preparation shops. 03385
Beyond software ergonomics? Human control of automated systems. 03386
Overview of research issues in robot safety. 03417
A study of conflict in group design activities: implications for computer-supported cooperative work environments. 03477
Software Engineering. § 03507
Software engineering for distributed applications: the design project. 03508
The space station information system and software support environment. 03512
Extending the DARTS software design method to distributed real time applications. 03516
A hypertext system to manage software life cycle documents. 03519
Prototyping user interfaces for applications depicted by graphs. 03523
The control structure diagram: an automated graphical representation for software. 03524
The PFG environment: parallel programming with petri net semantics. 03527
A processing system for program specifications in a natural language. 03537
A cost model for estimating the costs of developing software in the Ada programming language. 03539
Issues in the design of off-line programming systems. 03564
Methods for designing software to fit human needs and capabilities. § 03566
Participation in the development of software and the utilisation of standard software. 03663
Some aspects of communication in the natural language and user's involvement in software development. 03670
Views for tools in integrated environments. 03784
PantaPM: an integrated software development environment. 03796
Some design principles for a mathematical knowledge representation system: a new approach to scientific calculation. 03849
Architectures for production systems: an inside look for those who study human-computer interaction. 03906

Software Engineering Education. § 04022
Stategic imperatives in software engineering education. 04024
Software tools at the University: Why, What and How. 04026
A scarce resource in undergraduate software engineering courses: user interface design materials. 04027
A study of Arab computer users: a special case of a general HCI methodology. 04031
Visualization in programming. § 04032
VDM—The Way Ahead. § 04033
A support system for formal reasoning: requirements and status. 04035
User-centered requirements analysis. ● HCI-0004 †
Extended programming in the large in a software development environment. HCI-0101 †
An empirical study of the impact of user involvement on system usage and information satisfaction. HCI-0448 †

*Software maintenance*

The information center approach for developing computer-based information systems. 01929
A methodology for interactive evaluation of user reactions to software packages:an empirical analysis of system performance, interaction, and run time. 02080
Mental models and software maintenance. 02404
An architectural approach to improved program maintainability. 02627
Providing the requisite knowledge via software documentation. 02898
A mission planning architecture for an autonomous vehicle. 02939
Management of distributed applications in large networks. 03515
An environment for understanding programs. 03525
Conference on software maintenance–1985. § 03544
Display strategies for program browsing. 03545
Stategic imperatives in software engineering education. 04024

*Software selection*

Integrating software engineering into an intermediate programming class. 01037
How to choose natural language software. 01183
Student evaluation of motivational and learning attributes of microcomputer soft. 02274
End user software selection. 02434
Produciton and inventory management software packages related to user reactions. 02567
Mainframe and microcomputer-based business graphics: end user computing comparisons and trends. 02805
Public Law 99-506, "Section 508" Electronic Equipment Accessibility for disabled workers. 02893
An evaluation and selection methodology of microcomputer training software: Implications for human resource managers and computer personnel. 03002

Enhancing program readability and comprehensibility with tools for program visualization. 03510
A plan for evaluating usability of software products. HCI-0449 †

### K.6.4 System Management

Technology + design + research = information design. 0107
Oxford Surveys in Information Technology. ● 0753
The dual role of information centers: an assessment of end user computing management strategies. 01942
The measurement of end-user computing satisfaction. 02510
Linking mechanism supporting end-user computing. 02806
The ISA expert system: a prototype system for failure diagnosis on the space station. 02913
Repositioning the information systems management function: Implications for information systems personnel. 03015
The information technology champion: aiding and abetting, care and feeding. 03459

*Centralization/decentralization*

Cognitive science and organizational design: a case study of computer conferencing (Reprint). 0386
User cube: a taxonomy of end users. 01335
Management of distributed applications in large networks. 03515

*Management audit*

Negotiating IS: Observations on changes in structure from a negotiated order perspective. 03016

*Quality assurance*

Investment in computer-product documentation: causes and effects. 0105
SPA: a systems for diagnosis of computer performance problems. 02969

### K.6.m Miscellaneous

Human factors reference guide for electronics and computer professionals. ● 0734
An overview of $T^3$-PBE. 0784
Friendly or frivolous?. 01650
Interaction ergonomics, control and separation: open problems in user interface management. 01962
Trillium: an interface design prototyping tool. 01965
A new approach to cursor movements in user interfaces of integrated programming environments. 01974
An experiment to test user validation of requirements: data-flow diagrams vs task-oriented menus. 02131
Beacons in computer program comprehension. 02132
Some aspects of user-oriented dialogue design. 03643

The soft side of software: a management approach to computer documentation. ● HCI-0016 †

*Security*

Computer crime. ● 0722
A human approach to the technological challenges in data security. 01543
The case of the "Gerbil Virus" that wasn't. 01548
Quality control of personal computing. 02443
Developing awareness of computer ethics. 03010
Computer security: a global challenge. § 03577
Database Security: Status and Prospects. § 03579
Data security and confidentiality in Europe. HCI-0450 †

## K.7 THE COMPUTING PROFESSION

### K.7.0 General

Online information, hypermedia, and the idea of literacy. 0112
Trends in the emerging profession of technical communciation. 0123
The psychology of work and organization: current trends and issues. ● 0239
User interface design for computer systems. ● 0628
Generalization, consistency, and control. 0796
Experience with contextual field research. 0802
What is EuroParc?. 0812
User interface design in large corporations: coordination and communication across disciplines. 0853
Representing the structure of jobs in job analysis. 02181
Transferring skills from training to the actual work situation: the role of task application knowledge, action styles and job decision latitude. 02865
The two cultures in computing. 03018
New horizons for the information profession: meeting the challenge of change. § 04046

### K.7.1 Occupations

Trends in the emerging profession of technical communciation. 0123
Consulting skills for technical writers. 0124
Key factors in knowledge acquisition. 01019
Job histories as predictors of career success in management information systems. 01021
Behavioural and organisational factors involved in the turnover of high tech professionals. 01024
Maintaining the spirit of excitement in growing companies. 01025
Environments: Austria compared to the United States. 01026
Information management—the realities. 01377
Shucking Dp. 01644
In search of the perfect programmer. 01648
Stress. 01651

[K. COMPUTING MILIEUX] CATEGORY INDEX

High tech, high stress?. 01652
Users are people too. 01653
Getting straight again. 01658
The designing mind. 01661
Grow your own programmers. 01663
Battling for new roles. 01664
Informatics and municipalities: the Greek approach. 01940
Professional education and subsequent careers in library/information work: a follow-up study of former students on the MA/MSc information studies course at the University of Sheffield. 02336
Personal transferable skills for the modern information professional: a discussion paper. 02338
Motivation norms of knowledge engineers compared to those of software engineers. 02349
Education requirements for the entry level business systems analyst. 02409
Qualities of a good forms designer. 02412
Change and the systems person. 02417
Motivators vs. demotivators in the IS environment. 02433
The case of the rejected applicants. 02438
Are information systems people different? An investigation of how they are and should be managed. 02511
Management of Information Systems Personnel. § 02996
Information systems skills requirements: 1980 & 1988. 02997
The systems analyst of the 1990's. 02998
Perceptions of the CIS graduate's workstyle: undergraduate business students versus CIS faculty. 02999
Electronic monitoring and the redundancy of control systems: The role of the supervisor. 03000
Adequate documentation of user-developed applications: a new challenge for end-user computing management. 03001
Motivations and behaviors of software professionals. 03003
Causes of motivational problems among AI managers. 03004
Making computer tasks at work more playful: Implications for systems analysts and designers. 03005
Perspectives on the academic preparation of MIS professionals. 03006
Repositioning the information systems management function: Implications for information systems personnel. 03015
The two cultures in computing. 03018
Instilling professionalism in a software development organization. 03019
Moderating effects of age, education, and tenure on the job satisfaction-job performance relationship. 03021
The evolution of user services. 03139
Software engineering meets user services: a methodology for developing user. 03141
Applications Track. § 03455
Problems among managers of AI personnel. 03460

A roundtable discussion on women, computers and participation. 03673
The Japanese and software: is it a good match?. HCI-0429 †

### K.7.2 Organizations

An historical perspective of CD ROM. 0679
Computer Board Forum. 02685
Instilling professionalism in a software development organization. 03019
Problems among managers of AI personnel. 03460

**ACM** *see* Proper Noun Index

### K.7.3 Testing, Certification, and Licensing

Necessary functions of institutions for test and certification from the viewpoint of users in IT. 01456

### K.7.m Miscellaneous

Getting straight again. 01658
An empirical study of occupational stress, attitudes and health among information systems personnel. HCI-0451 †
Strategic management of technostress: The chaining of Prometheus. HCI-0452 †

*Ethics*

Computer ethics: an antidote to despair. 0791
Moral judgements in designing better systems. 02064
Moral issues in information science. 02321
Developing awareness of computer ethics. 03010
Intelligent machines: What chance?. 03548
The ethics of automated publishing systems (a response to Dr. Brockmann). HCI-0170 †

### K.8 PERSONAL COMPUTING

Learning by doing with simulated intelligent help. 0132
The microcomputer as a symbolic medium. 0583
Informing the design of software through context-based research. 0584
An historical perspective of CD ROM. 0679
The three c's: children, computers, and communication. ● 0713
Advanced Turbo C programming. ● 0726
The diffusion and impacts of information technology in households. 0754
Issuing each undergraduate student a personal computer: living with it for three years. 01028
A simple windowing system, part 1: basic principles. 01286
Computing for the blind user. 01287
Constructing an associative memory. 01289
Comparison of Windowing Systems. 01293
A groupware toolbox. 01304

1158

CATEGORY INDEX [K. COMPUTING MILIEUX]

Digital video interactive. 01308
HIC: the human interface column. 01422
An investigation of data entry methods with a personal computer. 01490
PC networks: usage and graphics tutorials. 01499
Managing the PC revolution. 01643
A PC policy primer. 01660
Instrumentation. 01834
Microcomputer applications: an empirical look at usage. 01949
Local work station concepts in a small distributed system. 02054
Personal computer training software for adaptive control. 02262
Quality control of personal computing. 02443
Development of a hand-held computerized vocabulary tutor. 02468
User interface wars: the next wave. 02544
Videotex redux. 02545
NEXT. 02546
KIDS. 02547
The body in question: how to stay healthy at the PC. 02548
Image processing with personal computers. 02581
Directories, DOS, and hard disks: impact on the user. 02604
Managers who personally use information technology frequently: a profile of some invisible computer personnel. 03007
PowerMath—A system for the Macintosh. 03083
An empirical study of user satisfaction with a microcomputer-based campus-wide. 03137
Advisor—an electronic mail consulting service. 03151
Interactive 3-D modeling with personal computers. 03296
User interface in new PC software. 03771
User involvement with microcomputer software. 04063
Opening Windows. ● HCI-0007 †
Andrew: a distributed personal computing environment. HCI-0091 †
Design of computer programs for the physically handicapped. HCI-0096 †
The computer imperative among owners of home computers: explanation by social factors. HCI-0217 †
Personal computing for decision support. HCI-0299 †
A user agent for multiple computer-based message services. HCI-0306 †

**Apple** *see* Proper Noun Index

**Commodore** *see* Proper Noun Index

*Games*

Functional environments for microcomputers in education. 0578
Comparison of video game and conventional test performance. 02594

**IBM PC** *see* Proper Noun Index

**Macintosh** *see* Proper Noun Index

# Proper Noun Subject Index

The Proper Noun Subject Index presents an alphabetical listing of the names of languages and systems that have appeared as significant subjects in the literature on Human-Computer Interaction. Titles are posted under each proper noun with their HCI review numbers or bibiographic numbers for full source and citation look-up. Proper nouns are part of the ACM *Computing Reviews* Classification Scheme even though they are not published in the official tree due to their number and unevenness of importance.

**MS-DOS**
Power windows: maximizing the speed and performance of Windows 2.0 & Windows 386. ● 0423

**OS/2 General**
Programming the OS/2 presentation manager. ● 0587
OS/2 programming: an introduction. ● 0670
OS/2 query manager overview and prompted interface. 01809

**dBase**
dBUG III offers source level solutions. 01641

**dBASE III PLUS**
Programming the dBASE III Plus user interface. ● 0627
The impact of menus and command-level feedback on learners' acquisition of data base language skills. 01041

**troff**
Document processing. 03897

**Ada**
Maintaining a uniform user interface for an Ada programming environment. 04066
Interfacing Ada and relational databases. 0762
Ada-embedded SQL: the options. 0763
Using representation clauses as an operating system interface. 0764
ADDS-a dialogue development system for the Ada programming language. 02102
Ada info: apologies to TEXT_10. 02395
The construction of information management system prototypes in Ada. 02613
Program generation for Ada—a case study. 02634
Ada-components: libraries and tools. § 03180
Ecilpse—an APSE based on PCTE. 03181
Design principles behind Chiron: a UIMS for software environments. 03511
A cost model for estimating the costs of developing software in the Ada programming language. 03539
Selecting an Ada environment. ● HCI-0015 †
Programming languages: a grand tour (2nd ed.). ● HCI-0018 †
Ada-based executable modelling of distributed systems. HCI-0098 †
SKETCHER, an interactive, graphical Ada software tool—its development and use. HCI-0100 †
Ada: first users—pleased; prospective users—still hesitant. HCI-0159 †

**Alan Turing**
The Universal Turing Machine. § 03777
On the physics and mathematics of thought. 03778
The Universal Turing Machine. § 03777
On the physics and mathematics of thought. 03778

**Alvey Report**
The management of advanced information technology. 0226
GOMS meets STRIPS: the integration of planning with skilled procedure execution in human-computer interaction. 03243
An overview of research and co-operation in advanced information technology. HCI-0442 †

### Andrew
Andrew: a distributed personal computing environment. HCI-0091 †
Reading and writing with computers: a framework for explaining differences in performance. HCI-0204 †

### Apple
Designing the star user interface. 0089
Experiencing artificial intelligence: an interactive approach for the APPLE. ● 0551
Programming the Macintosh User Interface. ● 0698
The representation of user interface style. 03221
Information flow in a user interface: the effect of experience and context on the recall of MacWrite screens. 03228
LisaLearning. HCI-0092 †
Programming the Macintosh User Interface. ● 0698
Computer graphics: A tool for the artist, designer and amateur. 0235
Desktop publishing. 0238
Experiencing artificial intelligence: an interactive approach for the APPLE. ● 0551
Programming the Macintosh User Interface. ● 0698
A programming language basis for user interface. 0849
Task-oriented representation of asynchronous user interfaces. 0851
"My user interface is the best because...". 0856
Application frameworks: experience with MacApp. 01039
The Mac interface: showing its age. 01311
Oil and water?. 01654
WIMP interface for Unix. 01973
Interactive videodiscs control and computer-based training on the Apple Macintosh. 02305
Hyperbiorhythms. 02470
Headstart—a lifeline for the disabled. 02500

### Aquinas
Refining problem-solving knowledge in repertory grids using a consultation mechanism. 02205

### AutoCAD
The AutoCAD productivity book: tapping the hidden power of AutoCAD: 2nd edition. ● 0668

### ACM
Hand-crafted hypertext-lessons from the ACM experiment. 0128

### ACRONYM
Help texts vs. help mechanisms: A new mandate for documentation writers. 02784
Help texts vs. help mechanisms: A new mandate for documentation writers. 01047

### ACT/1
The gift of good design tools. 0411

### ADIPS
Real-time processing of cursive writing and sketched graphics. 03908

### ALGOL-W
Programming languages: a grand tour (2nd ed.). ● HCI-0018 †

### ALGOL-60
Programming languages: a grand tour (2nd ed.). ● HCI-0018 †

### ALGOL-68
Programming languages: a grand tour (2nd ed.). ● HCI-0018 †

### APL
APL: a problem-oriented introduction. ● 0230
Bringing graphic dialogues to APL. 0765
Open fullscreen systems. 0766
Increasing productivity with ISPF/APL2. 0767
Is the unified keyboard better?. 0768
APL in transition. § 02793
Application screen management: an APL2 approach. 02794
Screen management in the "real world". 02795
Design of a new user interface for APL. 02796
APL88. § 02797
APL: The language of science and management. 02799
Innovation of decision support system-matplan based on structure matrix supported by APL. 02800
A dataflow-based APL for the hypercube. 02905
Programming languages: a grand tour (2nd ed.). ● HCI-0018 †

### ARES
ARES: a relational database with the capability of performing flexible interpretation of queries. HCI-0248 †

### ASCII
From arcane ASCII to the printed page - computer basics. 01148

### ASK
ASK is transportable in half a dozen ways. HCI-0279 †

### AWK
The AWK programming language. ● HCI-0020 †

Natural language interface based on keyword extraction using AWK. 02498

## BALSA
Algorithm animation. ● 0186
Exploring algorithms using Balsa-II. 01367

## BASIC
Information processing today, with applications. ● 0568
Information processing today, with applications and BASIC. ● 0569
Information processing today, with applications and BASIC: updat 87/88. ● 0570
Principles of information processing with applications and BASIC. ● 0572
Windows for BASIC. 01292
The BCC180 multitasking controller part 3: memory management and windowing. 01295
MINID—a BASIC program to assist in the optical identification of minerals in thin section. 01505
Programming in Basic or Logo: effect on critical thinking skills. 04062
Fragile knowledge and neglected strategies in novice programmers. HCI-0177 †

## BSP
Mondo media. 02552

## C
A book on C. ● 0143
User interfaces in C: programmer's guide to state-of-the-art interfaces. ● 0351
C/C++ for expert systems: "unleashes the power of a artificial intelligence". ● 0439
Xlib programming manual for version 11: Vol. 1. ● 0561
OS/2 programming: an introduction. ● 0670
The Logix system user manual version 1.21. 0675
Advanced Turbo C programming. ● 0726
A C Interface. 01294
g - A compact language for real-time graphics. 02906
Artificial intelligence techniques applied to maintenance management. 02971
An interactive tolerance system. 02975
Integral-C—a practical environment for C programming. 03049
Extensions to C for interface programming. 03108
Enhancing program readability and comprehensibility with tools for program visualization. 03510
A distributed object server. 03842
Experiences with the development of a portable network operating system. 03882
Programming languages: a grand tour (2nd ed.). ● HCI-0018 †
Systems software tools. ● HCI-0030 †
A debugger for concurrent programs. HCI-0142 †

## C++
C/C++ for expert systems: "unleashes the power of a artificial intelligence". ● 0439
Statemaster: A UIMS based on statechart for prototyping and target implementation. 0850

## Cedar
An introduction to Gargoyle: an interactive illustration tool. 03185

## Clipper
More on the mouse. 01642

## Commodore
There's more to interaction than meets the eye: Some issues in manual. 0062
Issues and techniques in touch-sensitive tablet input. 0063
Direct manipulation: A step beyond programming languages. 0072
The MAGNEX text editor for the Comodore Amiga personal computer. 0782

## Concurrent Pascal
Programming languages: a grand tour (2nd ed.). ● HCI-0018 †

## Concurrent Prolog
Concurrent Prolog: collected papers. ● 0674
The Logix system user manual version 1.21. 0675
An architecture of a distributed window system and its FCP implementation. 0676
Object oriented programming in Concurrent Prolog. 0677

## CAL
OTM: specifying office tasks. 03039

## CBUG
A debugger for concurrent programs. HCI-0142 †

## CCS
A logic-functional approach to the execution of CCS specifications modulo behavioural equivalences. 03874

## CEDAR
The structure of Cedar. 01109
Integration mechanisms in Cedar. 01110
Whiteboards: a graphical database tool. HCI-0289 †

## CLAM
CLAM- an open system for graphical user interfaces. 01117

## CLU
Programming languages: a grand tour (2nd ed.). ● HCI-0018 †

## COBOL
Advanced interactive cobol for micros: a practical approach. ● 0521
Advanced interactive COBOL for micros: a practical approach. ● 0522
Schaum's outline of theories and problems of programming with advanced structured COBOL with file processing structured systems deveolpment and interactive cons. ● 0555
IBM 3270 full screen interactive programming without CICS. 01040
MAJIC—an integrated program support environment. 01960
Experimental evaluation of program quality using external metrics. HCI-0176 †

## CODIL
The use of colour in language syntax analysis. HCI-0385 †

## CORAL
A user interface toolkit based on graphical objects and constraints. 01125

## CRAY X-MP
High-speed computing: scientific applications and algorithm design. ● 0727
The computational science revolution: technology, methodology, and sociology. 0728

## CRAY-1
The computational science revolution: technology, methodology, and sociology. 0728
Coherent and chaotic structures in 2D vortex dynamics: progress and problems. 0729

## CSP
A LISP implementation of the model for 'communicating sequential processes'. 02632
Formally-based techniques for dialogue design. 03190
Formally-based tools and techniques for human-computer dialogues. ● HCI-0021 †

## Daisy
Dialogues: a basis for constructing programming environments. 01097

## DAISTS
Building a great windows system. 02550

## DAPLEX
A practical approach to data modelling in spatial applications. 02616

## DARPA
Later years at IPTO. 0139
AI development and the Office of Naval Research. 0140

## DATALOG
Portability of syntax and semantics in DATALOG. HCI-0340 †

## DAVID
An interactive database end user facility for the definition and manipulation of forms. HCI-0263 †

## DIAG 2
Computer-aided hierarchical diagrams. HCI-0160 †

## DIF
A hypertext system to manage software life cycle documents. 03519

## DOS
The AutoCAD productivity book: tapping the hidden power of AutoCAD: 2nd edition. ● 0668
Enhanced console driver. 01288
DOS 4.0. 01299
IBM DOS 4.0: a bridge to OS/2. 02523
Building a great windows system. 02550
Directories, DOS, and hard disks: impact on the user. 02604

## DSPL
Knowledge and control for a mechanical design expert system. HCI-0320 †

## Eclipse
The ECLIPSE user interface. 02638
Ecilpse—an APSE based on PCTE. 03181
Graphical prototyping of graphical tools. HCI-0375 †

## Ethernet
Personal distributed computing: the Alto and Ethernet hardware. 03095
Personal distributed computing: the Alto and Ethernet software. 03096
The space station information system and software support environment. 03512

## EIES
Analysis and design skills required by end-users in small organizations. 03008

Interface design in computerized conferencing systems: a personal view. HCI-0305 †

## EMYCIN
The migration of expert systems into the production environment. 0740

## ESCORT
An operations advisor for an on-line computer banking system with graphics interface. 02983

## ESPRIT
Advanced information technology in the new industrial society: the Kingston seminars. ● 0225
KIWI: knowledge-based user-friendly system for the utilization of information bases. 0739
Measuring user satisfaction. 03230
An overview of research and co-operation in advanced information technology. HCI-0442 †

## EUCLID
Programming languages: a grand tour (2nd ed.). ● HCI-0018 †

## Flavors
Use of object-oriented programming in a time series analysis system. 01112

## FIDO
Cooperative behaviour in the FIDO system. 02041

## FORTH
User-oriented suggestions for floating-point and complex-arithmetic Forth standard extensions. 02306
A single-board Forth computer with versatile analog I/O circuitry. 02308
Compiling Forth for performance. 02309
A stand-alone Forth system. 02310
Pride-II physical layout program of modifying Forth for "non-believers". 02312

## FORTRAN
A FORTRAN input program generator. 01227
Initial work on a system-independent computer model of a 3D anthropomorphic dummy. 01476
Interactive documentation. 02612
Plan-based representations of pascal and fortran code. 02897
ProCEED: an expert system for multivariate process control systems design. 02935
Programming languages: a grand tour (2nd ed.). ● HCI-0018 †
Experimental study of a two-dimensional language vs. FORTRAN for first-course progammers. HCI-0171 †

## FORTRAN 77
SMART: Scientific database management and engineering analysis routines and tools. 01166

## G
g - A compact language for real-time graphics. 02906

## Glazier
Painless panes for Smalltalk windows. 01118

## GEM
The world of GEM. ● 0396

## GENIE
GENIE: a modifiable computer-based task for experiments in human-computer interaction. HCI-0194 †

## GKS
Object-oriented graphics. 0234
Logical input devices and interaction. 01393
Interactive CAD/CAM in engineering industry. 01571
A personal computer based graphic workstation. 02493
A model for graphical interaction. 02610
Integration of graphical tools in a computer algebra system. 03847
GKSGRAL—software and hardware realizations of the graphical kernel system. 03982
Device-independent graphics: with examples from IBM personal computers. ● HCI-0070 †
Graphical standards. HCI-0417 †

## GPSS
Interactive graphics in GPSS/PC. 02586
Interactive graphics in GPSS/PC. 02586

## GQBR
Generalized query-by-rule: a heterogeneous database query language. HCI-0252 †

## GREATERP
The LISP tutor: it approaches the effectiveness of a human tutor. HCI-0431 †

## GXMP
A generalized model management system for mathematical programming. HCI-0302 †

## HyperCard
Hand-crafted hypertext-lessons from the ACM experiment. 0128
Artifact as theory-nexus: hermeneutics meets theory-based design. 0798

### HEARSAY-II
Computer recognition of spoken letters and digits. 03995
Merging acoustics and linguistics in speech understanding. 04004

### HERCULES
HERCULES: database query using natural language fragments. HCI-0253 †

### HIPO
A generator of direct manipulation office systems. HCI-0250 †

### Intel 80386
UNIX system V: release 3.0 Intel 80286/80386 computer version: system administrator's guide. ● 0031
Building a great windows system. 02550

### Intermedia
Connections in context: The intermedia system. 03534

### IBM
AI development and the Office of Naval Research. 0140

### IBM PC
Experiencing artificial intelligence: an interactive approach to the IBM PC. ● 0550
Systems software tools. ● HCI-0030 †
Training for optimising transfer between word processors. HCI-0447 †
How to manage educational computing initiatives-lessons from the first five years of Project Athena at MIT. 0125
Programming the IBM User Interface: Using Turbo Pascal. ● 0286
Experiencing artificial intelligence: an interactive approach to the IBM PC. ● 0550
Modeling of robot system dynamics for CAD based robot programming. 0605
An experiment into the use of auditory cues to reduce visual workload. 0877
Designing a quality voice: an analysis of listeners' reactions to synthetic voices. 0914
Domesticating microsoft windows. 01309
The use of the IBM personal computer in the man-machine interface to a nuclear research accelerator. 01454
An incidence-matrix-driven panel system for the IBM PC. 01814
Advanced interactive executive (AIX) operating system overview. 01815
Advanced interactive executive program development environment. 01816
AIX usability enhancements and human factors. 01817
Portfolio: kaleidoscopic visions. 02551
Parametric Fourier image characterization toolkit. 02798
INQUEST: A prototype intelligence tool. 02918
The network control assistant (NCA), a real-time prototype expert system for network management. 02930
High performance interactive graphics: modeling, rendering and animating for IBM PCs and compatibles. ● HCI-0071 †

### IBM System/370
An environment for understanding programs. 03525

### ICON
Principles of an icons-based language. 01080

### IDA
An object-oriented framework for interactive data graphics. 01115

### IDECAP
IDECAP: interactive pictorial information system for demographic and environmental planning applications. HCI-0411 †

### INGRES
The INGRES papers: anatomy of a relational database system. ● 0706
Implementation of a Prolog-INGRES interface. 01087
Data manipulation languages for the universal relation view DURST. 03944

### INTERLISP
INTERLISP: the language and its usage. ● HCI-0022 †

### IPL
An image processing language with ICON-assisted navigation. HCI-0387 †

### IRIS
Conman: a visual programming language for interactive graphics. 02811

### ISDN
User-network interfaces. 01384
ISPBXs and terminals. 01385
Traffic study on primary rate ISDN user-network interface. 01442
ISDN and the move to integrated communications—an introduction. 01455

### JOBBES
Acquisition of control and domain knowledge by watching in a blackboard environment. HCI-0319 †

## JSP
Generation of file processing programs based on JSP. 02639

## KEE
Teaching object-oriented programming with the KEE system. 01113

## KLO
The architecture of fifth generation inference computers. HCI-0093 †

## Lotus 1-2-3
Working with Lotus HAL: a 1-2-3 user's guide. ● 0731
Protecting user interfaces through copyright: the debate. 0827
Impact of a restricted natural language interface on ease of learning and productivity. 01334

## LISP
Effect of practice on knowledge and use of basic Lisp. 0210
Object-oriented graphics. 0234
Enhancing incremental learning processes with knowledge-based systems. 0538
The AutoCAD productivity book: tapping the hidden power of AutoCAD: 2nd edition. ● 0668
Helgon: extending the retrieval by reformulation paradigm. 0880
Teaching object-oriented programming with the KEE system. 01113
Common LISP object system specification X3J13 Document 88-002R. 01121
Centaur: the system. 01136
Graphic objects. 01190
A LISP implementation of the model for 'communicating sequential processes'. 02632
A graphical programming language interface for an intelligent LISP tutor. 02862
Users' preferences among different techniques for displaying the evaluation of LISP functions in an interactive debugger. 02863
Clue: a common lisp user interface environment. 03113
On building future decision support systems. 03472
A financial investment assistant. 03490
Object-oriented signal processing systems. 03573
Programming languages: a grand tour (2nd ed.). ● HCI-0018 †
LISPcraft. ● HCI-0023 †
The LISP tutor: it approaches the effectiveness of a human tutor. HCI-0431 †
Users' preferences among different techniques for displaying the evaluation of LISP functions in an interactive debugger. 02863
Generic expert system shell for diagnostic reasoning. 02911
A blackboard architecture for problem solving and machine learning in an expert system for power system voltage control. 02926
Automated design and analysis system for design of custom orthopedic implants. 02931
Applications of an AI design shell ENGINEOUS to advanced engineering products. 02932
ProCEED: an expert system for multivariate process control systems design. 02935
On building future decision support systems. 03472
A financial investment assistant. 03490
Object-oriented signal processing systems. 03573
Knowledge representation techniques in artificial intelligence: an overview. 03900
The LISP tutor: it approaches the effectiveness of a human tutor. HCI-0431 †

## LOGO
Algebra slaves and agents in a Logo-based mathematics curriculum. 0517
An example-base environment for beginning programmers. 0520
Improvement of the acquisition of knowledge by informing feedback. 0540
Mirrors of minds: patterns of experience in educational computing. ● 0575
The interpretation of Logo in practice. 0576
Functional environments for microcomputers in education. 0578
Mapping the cognitive demands of learning to program. 0579
Integrated human and computer intelligence. 0580
Logo and development of thinking skills. 0582
Formative evaluation of pre-Logo programming environments: a collaborative effort of researchers, teachers, and children. 02292
Modification of Earley's algorithm for speech recognition. 04003
Programming in Basic or Logo: effect on critical thinking skills. 04062
Formative evaluation of pre-Logo programming environments: a collaborative effort of researchers, teachers, and children. 02292

## LSP
Transporting the linguistic string project system from a medical to a Navy domain. HCI-0352 †

## Macintosh
Mac programming tools: prototyper version 2.0 eases interface design. 02394

## Maple
Iris: design of a user interface program for symbolic algebra. 03081

Iris: design of an user interface program for symbolic algebra. 03085

**Mercury**
IBM DOS 4.0: a bridge to OS/2. 02523

**Microsoft Windows**
Power windows: maximizing the speed and performance of Windows 2.0 & Windows 386. ● 0423
Domesticating microsoft windows. 01309
Opening Windows. ● HCI-0007 †

**Modula-2**
Automated construction of interactive learning programs in Modula-2. 01500
EM2—a Modula-2 programming environment. 02392
Programming languages: a grand tour (2nd ed.). ● HCI-0018 †

**Motorola 68000**
Monitoring and performance measuring distributed systems during operation. 03025

**Multiview**
Information systems definition: the Multiview approach. ● HCI-0085 †

**MACSYMA**
GI/S: A graphical user interface for symbolic computation systems. 02397

**MAP/TOP**
A model for assessing the performance of a local area network employing technical office protocol (TOP) as part of MAP/TOP network in a computer integrated manufacturing (CIM) research project, for the transmission of real time interactive speech. 02491

**MIDAS**
The MIDAS database system. 02387
The MIDAS display system. 02388
MIDAS: molecular interactive display and simulation. 04061

**MIKE**
MIKE: the menu interaction kontrol environment. HCI-0124 †

**MRP**
MRP/MRP II. 0620

**MYCIN**
Extension of conditional probability and measures of belief and disbelief in a hypothesis based on uncertain evidence. 01846

Computational linguistics: issues and solutions. 03948

**NeWS**
The NeWS book: an introduction to the network/extensible window system. ● 0358

**Nial**
Q'Nial: a portable interpreter for the nested interactive array language, Nial. 02635

**NEOMYCIN**
Knowledge and expertise in expert systems. 03905

**O-plan**
O-Plan: control in the open planning architecture. HCI-0362 †

**ORION**
Data model issues for object-oriented applications. 0712

**OSI**
Technological development and the integrated workstation. 01313
User-network interfaces. 01384
User investigation into practical systems. 01458
An implementation of OSI protocols in SM-4 host computers. 03638

**Pascal**
Design and implementation of an object-oriented user interface management system. 0412
Screen input/output programming techniques using Turbo Pascal. ● 0714
A programming language basis for user interface. 0849
Application frameworks: experience with MacApp. 01039
Turbo windows. 01421
Programming the mouse in Turbo Pascal 4.0. 02393
An external data structure tool for Pascal. 02495
Generating reversible programs. 02620
Plan-based representations of pascal and fortran code. 02897
Goal-directed semantic tutor. 02919
The influence of individual differences on the reading of computer programs. 03456
Specification of a tool for viewing program text. 03884
Programming languages: a grand tour (2nd ed.). ● HCI-0018 †

**PegaSys**
The PegaSys System: pictures as formal documentation of large programs. HCI-0146 †

**PostScript**
The NeWS book: an introduction to the network/extensible window system. ● 0358

## Prolog

Improvement of the acquisition of knowledge by informing feedback. 0540
Concurrent Prolog: collected papers. ● 0674
A grammar kit in PROLOG. 0745
A spreadsheet interface for logic programming. 0822
Implementation of a Prolog-INGRES interface. 01087
An environment for logic programming. 01106
How to recognize interesting topics to provide cooperative answering. 02043
Dynamic compilation in the Unix environment. 02621
The network control assistant (NCA), a real-time prototype expert system for network management. 02930
Character recognition of cursive scripts. 02961
Logic programmable natural language processor of a knowledge-base management system. 02965
Computer aided concurrent design for printed wiring boards. 02981
Logic programming '87. § 03919
The architecture of fifth generation inference computers. HCI-0093 †
An environment for logic programming. 01106
An environment for logic programming. 01106
An environment for logic programming. 01106
Logic programmable natural language processor of a knowledge-base management system. 02965
What stories should we tell novice PROLOG programmers?. 0421
Programming the dBASE III Plus user interface. ● 0627
Automatic menu generation. 0774
An environment for logic programming. 01106
Task-oriented parsing - a diagnostic method to be used adaptive systems. 02896
Sherlock—a system for diagnosing power distribution ring network faults. 02916
The network control assistant (NCA), a real-time prototype expert system for network management. 02930
Character recognition of cursive scripts. 02961
Gripe: a graphical interface to a knowledge based system which reasons about protein topology. 03234
Knowledge representation techniques in artificial intelligence: an overview. 03900
A new approach for introducing Prolog to naive users. 04029

## PDP-11 assembly language

Support for tentative design: incorporating the screen image, as a graphical object, into PROLOG. 02116

## PECAN

PECAN: program development systems that support multiple views. HCI-0145 †

## PECOS

An experiment in knowledge-based automatic programming. 0613

## PHIGS

PHIGS: a standard, dynamic, interactive graphics interface. 01826

## PICK

The pick of the crop. 01675

## PICT

PICT: an interactive graphical programming environment. HCI-0143 †

## PRISM

A general theory of discrimination learning. 0481
Negative knowledge towards a strategy for asking in logic programming. 02115

## PROMIS

A history of the Promis technology: an effective human interface. 03097

## PROUST

Enhancing incremental learning processes with knowledge-based systems. 0538

## PSL

The construction of information management system prototypes in Ada. 02613

## QUEL

The INGRES papers: anatomy of a relational database system. ● 0706

## QUILL

Quill: An extensible system for editing documents of mixed type. 03517
Language level persistence for an object-oriented application programming platform. 03522

## RECONSIDER

Evaluating RECONSIDER: a computer program for diagnostic prompting. HCI-0410 †

## REDUCE

Dialogue in REDUCE: experience and development. 03088

## ROSE

ROSE: An object-oriented database system for interactive computer graphics applications. 03845

## Sassafras

Supporting concurrency, communication, and synchronization in human-computer interaction—the Sassafras UIMS. HCI-0102 †

PROPER NOUN SUBJECT INDEX [UIMS]

**Smalltalk**
Animated graphical interfaces using temporal constraints. 0909
A smalltalk window system based on constraints. 01128
A smalltalk implementation of an intelligent operator's associate. 01132
Sherlock—a system for diagnosing power distribution ring network faults. 02916
Multiprocessor Smalltalk: a case study of a multiprocessor-based programming environment. 03061
A graphical entity-relationship database browser. 03532
A distributed object server. 03842

**Smalltalk-80**
Object-oriented graphics. 0234
An information system based on distributed objects. 01116
Painless panes for Smalltalk windows. 01118
INSIST: Interactive Simulation in Smalltalk. 01119
An integrated color smalltalk-80 system. 01127
Configuring stand-alone smalltalk-80 applications. 01129
An interactive environment for object-oriented music composition and sound synthesis. 01131
An object-oriented framework of pattern recognition systems. 01133
Diagramming objects. 01177
A knowledge-based system with audio-visual aids. 02068
A cookbook for using the model-view controller user interface paradigm in Smalltalk-80. 02390
Graphics through the looking glass. 02391
Encapsulators: a new software paradigm in Smalltalk-80. 03034
Multiprocessor Smalltalk: a case study of a multiprocessor-based programming environment. 03061

**Soar**
Universal subgoaling and chunking: the automatic generation and learning of goal hierarchies. ● 0497

**SuperBook**
Formative design evaluation of superbook. 01154

**System R**
System R: a relational approach to database management. 0709

**SCHEME**
A semantic editor. 01101

**SDL**
A set of tools supporting the software design based on SDL. 03803
A set of tools supporting the software design based on SDL. 03803

**SIMULA**
Event-driven user interfaces based on quasi-parallelism. 03111
The design of a flexible distributed testbeb for communication systems. 03538

**SLCSE**
The Software Life Cycle Support Environment (SLCSE): a computer based framework for developing software systems. HCI-0147 †

**SMART**
SMART: Scientific database management and engineering analysis routines and tools. 01166

**SODOS**
RAPID: Prototyping control panel interfaces. 01120

**SQL**
An interactive customization program for a natural language database query system. 0163
Ada-embedded SQL: the options. 0763
OS/2 query manager overview and prompted interface. 01809

**Telesophy**
An information system based on distributed objects. 01116

**TeX**
An editor for constructing graphics with $T_EX$. 01394
Document processing. 03897
An editor for constructing graphics with $T_EX$. 01394

**Turbo BASIC**
Building a self-modifying user interface. 01424

**Turbo C**
Graphics programming in Turbo C. ● 0013

**Turbo Pascal**
Programming the IBM User Interface: Using Turbo Pascal. ● 0286

**TCP/IP**
A distributed object server. 03842

**TEXTNET**
TEXTNET: a network-based approach to text handling. HCI-0401 †

**UIMS**
User interface management systems. 0233

Design and implementation of an object-oriented user interface management system. 0412
Creating user interfaces by demonstration. ● HCI-0008 †
Supporting concurrency, communication, and synchronization in human-computer interaction—the Sassafras UIMS. HCI-0102 †

**UMFE**
UMFE: a user modelling front-end subsystem. HCI-0325 †

**UNIVAC**
AI development and the Office of Naval Research. 0140

**UNIX**
A book on C. ● 0143
UNIX and the naive user: children meet a grown-up operating system. 0752
Using representation clauses as an operating system interface. 0764
User modeling in UC, the UNIX consultant. 0894
A UNIX clone with source code for operating systems courses. 01095
Face to face with Open Look. 01305
The Berkeley UNIX consultant project. 01355
MH: a multifarious user agent. 01428
Helping users use UNIX. 01529
The pick of the crop. 01675
WIMP interface for Unix. 01973
An icon-driven end-user interface to UNIX. 02089
Structure of a directory space: a case study with a UNIX operating system. 02138
An attempt to incorporate expertise about users into an intelligent interface for Unix. 02248
Some effects of cognitive style on learning UNIX. 02252
A Unix distributed application support suitable for mini and microcomputer based systems. 02489
Natural language interface based on keyword extraction using AWK. 02498
Unix: tomorrow's operating system?. 02555
Dbxtool: A window-based symbolic debugger for sun workstations. 02614
Dynamic compilation in the Unix environment. 02621
fsh—a functional UNIX command interpreter. 02624
Support for graphs of processes in a command interpreter. 02633
How users repeat their actions on computers: principles for design of history mechanisms. 02885
SAUCI: a knowledge-based interface architecture. 02895
Task-oriented parsing - a diagnostic method to be used adaptive systems. 02896
UNIX Emacs: a retrospective (lessons for flexible system design). 03114
SEE: a safe editing environment; human-computer interaction for programmers. 03225
Investigations into a command and response language interface. 03531
The interactive planning work station: a graphics-based UNIX tool for application users and developers. 03860
Introducing windows to Unix: user expectations. 03924
A modular window system for Unix. 03929
A window manager for bitmapped displays and Unix. 03933
The design of the UNIX operating system. ● HCI-0026 †
UNIX shell programming. ● HCI-0027 †
4.2BSD and 4.3BSD as examples of the UNIX system. HCI-0165 †
A communication system supporting large datagrams on a local area network. HCI-0166 †
The Japanese and software: is it a good match?. HCI-0429 †
Integrating software engineering into an intermediate programming class. 01037

**UNIX System V**
UNIX system V: release 3.0 Intel 80286/80386 computer version: system administrator's guide. ● 0031
An external data structure tool for Pascal. 02495

**VAL**
Problems associated with the off-line programming of robots. 01241

**VAM**
The space station information system and software support environment. 03512

**VAX**
VAX-BASIC with structured problem solving: 2nd edition. ● 0725
VAX-BASIC with structured problem solving: 2nd edition. ● 0725

**VAX/VMS**
Expert diagnostic system. 02912
SPA: a systems for diagnosis of computer performance problems. 02969

**VDM**
Support environments for VDM. 03832
VDM—The Way Ahead. § 04033
A support system for formal reasoning: requirements and status. 04035
The VIP VDM specification language. 04036
Muffin: a user interface design experiment for a theorem proving assistant. 04037
The use of VDM on the specification of Chinese characters. 04038

**VIADUCT**
An almost path-free very high-level interactive data manipulation language for a microcomputer-based database system. HCI-0261 †

**VICE**
Andrew: a distributed personal computing environment. HCI-0091 †

**VM/CMS**
VM/CMS: a user's guide. ● HCI-0028 †

**Windows**
Introduction to Windows programming. ● HCI-0013 †

**WordPerfect**
Training for optimising transfer between word processors. HCI-0447 †

**WordStar**
Training for optimising transfer between word processors. HCI-0447 †

**WEB**
Literate programming. HCI-0148 †

**XCON**
Managerial expert systems and organizational change: some critical research issues. 0157

**XINU**
Operating system design. Vol. 1: the XINU approach (PC edition). ● HCI-0029 †

**XMP**
A generalized model management system for mathematical programming. HCI-0302 †

**ZOG**
Collaboration in KMS, a shared hypermedia system. 0807
Representation of dynamic features in a conceptual schema. 01231
Relative information capacity of simple relational database schemata. 02579
The data model is the heart of interface design. 02875
A comparison of hypertext, scrolling and folding as mechanisms for program browsing. 03235
Experience with the ZOG human-computer interface system. HCI-0246 †

# Reviewer Index

**Abrahams, P. W.**
Showing programs on a screen.   Meyer, B.; Nerson, J.; and Ko, S. H.   HCI-0141
Undo support models.   Yang, Y.   HCI-0144

**Abramson, G. W.**
Access to academic networks.   Holligan, P. J. ●   HCI-0050

**Aiken, R. M.**
Taming and civilizing computers.   Chapanis, A.   HCI-0195

**Albeanu, G.**
A neural network for visual pattern recognition.   Fukushima, K.   HCI-0391

**Amarel, S.**
The complexity of some polynomial network consistency algorithms for constraint satisfaction problems.   Mackworth, A. K.; and Freuder, E. C.   HCI-0361

**Andrianoff, S. K.**
VM/CMS: a user's guide.   Chase, P. ●   HCI-0028

**Apte, C. V.**
O-Plan: control in the open planning architecture.   Currie, K.; and Tate, A.   HCI-0362

**Aron, J. D.**
Beyond the chalkboard: computer support for collaboration and problem solving in meetings.   Stefik, M.; Foster, G.; Bobrow, D. G.; Kahn, K.; Lanning, S.; and Suchman, L.   HCI-0312

**Artz, J. M.**
Executive support systems: the emergence of top management computer use.   Rockart, J. F.; and De Long, D. W. ●   HCI-0049
How we know.   Shafto, M. (Ed.) ●   HCI-0053
Understanding computers and cognition.   Winograd, T.; and Flores, F. (Eds.) ●   HCI-0054
HERCULES: database query using natural language fragments.   Cuff, R. N.   HCI-0253
Computer decision support for senior managers: encouraging exploration.   Smithin, T.; and Eden, C.   HCI-0298

**Attanasio, C. R.**
ARES: a relational database with the capability of performing flexible interpretation of queries.   Ichikawa, T.; and Hirakawa, M.   HCI-0248

**Babilonia, J. E.**
Using low-cost workstations to investigate computer networks and distributed systems.   Sherman, M.; and Marks, A.   HCI-0437

**Bagert, D. J.**
The electronic classroom: workstations for teaching.   van Dam, A.   HCI-0436

**Baker, F. T.**
Designing for usability: key principles and what designers think.   Gould, J. D.; and Lewis, C.   HCI-0231

**Barfield, W.**
Cognitive processes in program comprehension.   Letovsky, S.   HCI-0179
Human factors issues in VDT use: environmental and workstation design considerations.   Smith, M. J.   HCI-0210
Resistance to computerization: an examination of the relationship between resistance and the cognitive style of the clinician.   Mandell, S. F.   HCI-0407

**Barnard, D. T.**
The second self: computers and the human spirit.   Turkle, S. ●   HCI-0082

**Barnard, P.**
Understanding the effectiveness of computer graphics for decision support: a cumulative experimental approach.   Dickson, G. W.; DeSanctis, G.; and McBride, D. J.   HCI-0215

**Barzescu, G. C.**
VDAFS—a pragmatic interface for the exchange of sculptured surface data.   Renz, W.   HCI-0420
Approximation methods used in the exchange of geometric information via the VDA/VDMA surface interface.   Nowacki, H.; and Dannenberg, L.   HCI-0421
A tentative implementation of VDAFS.   Hopert, D.; and Weissbarth, T.   HCI-0422

**Bash, C. W.**
A general user interface for creating and displaying tree-structures, hierarchies, decision trees, and nested menus.   Reitman-Olson, J. S.; Whitten, W. B.; and Gruenenfelder, T. M.   HCI-0136
The database designer's workbench.   Cobb, R. E.; Fry, J. P.; and Teorey, T. J.   HCI-0249

**Bassler, R. A.**
Computer-assisted negotiations: a case history from the law of the sea negotiations and speculation regarding future uses. Straus, D. B. HCI-0443

**Begg, V. S.**
Analogical problem solving. Keane, M. T. ● HCI-0044
Effects of experience and comprehension on reading time and memory for computer programs. Schmidt, A. L. HCI-0197

**Bennett, J. L.**
Creating user interfaces by demonstration. Myers, B. A. ● HCI-0008
Designing user interfaces for software. Dumas, J. S. ● HCI-0010
Supporting concurrency, communication, and synchronization in human-computer interaction—the Sassafras UIMS. Hill, R. D. HCI-0102
A generalized user interface for applications programs (II). Bass, L. J. HCI-0112
Boxer: a reconstructible computational medium. diSessa, A. A.; and Abelson, H. HCI-0121
Representational frameworks and models for human-computer interfaces. Rohr, G.; and Tauber, M. J. HCI-0188
GENIE: a modifiable computer-based task for experiments in human-computer interaction. Lindquist, T. E.; Fainter, R. G.; and Hakkinen, M. T. HCI-0194
A laboratory study of user characteristics and decision-making performance in end-user computing. Kasper, G. M.; and Cerveny, R. P. HCI-0301
Open versus closed minds: the effect of dogmatism on an analyst's problem-solving behavior. Paddock, C. E.; and Swanson, N. E. HCI-0446

**Bettinger, R. J.**
A Multilevel menu-driven user interface: Design and evaluation through simulation. Savage, R. E.; and Habinek, J. K. HCI-0170
The evaluation of text editors: methodology and empirical results. Roberts, T. L.; and Moran, T. P. HCI-0209

**Bishop, M. A.**
An operating systems vade mecum: 2nd edition. Finkel, R. A. ● HCI-0025
A proposed solution to the problem of levels in error-message generation. Efe, K. HCI-0126

**Blostein, D.**
Image processing aspects of type. Morris, R. A. HCI-0403
Visual structure and the transmission of meaning. Southall, R. HCI-0404

**Boehm-Davis, D. A.**
Behavioral experiments on handmarkings. Gould, J. D.; and Salaun, J. HCI-0201

**Booth, A. D.**
Informatics (computer and information science): its ideology, methodology, and sociology. Gorn, S. (Ed.) HCI-0086
Touch-sensitive screens: the technologies and their application. Pickering, J. A. HCI-0087

**Booth, K. H. V.**
Computing text constituency: an algorithmic approach to the generation of text graphs. Hahn, U.; and Reimer, U. HCI-0267
Portability of syntax and semantics in DATALOG. Hafner, C. D.; and Godden, K. HCI-0340

**Borko, H.**
Reading and writing the electronic book. Yankelovich, N.; Meyrowitz, N.; and van Dam, A. HCI-0282
Testing bibliographic displays for online catalogs. Crawford, W. HCI-0285
Computerization, productivity, and quality of work-life. Kraut, R. E.; Dumais, S. T.; and Koch, S. HCI-0441

**Boswell, G. T.**
The architecture of fifth generation inference computers. Hertzberger, L. O. HCI-0093
Customers' requirements for natural language systems: results of an inquiry. Morik, K. HCI-0426

**Bovet, D. P.**
Authoring: a guide to the design of instructional software. Kearsley, G. ● HCI-0031

**Brown, H.**
How to write a really good user's manual. Katzin, E. ● HCI-0017

**Brown, M. R.**
Whiteboards: a graphical database tool. Donahue, J.; and Widom, J. HCI-0289

**Bulow, K.**
Geomatic: a 3-D graphic relief simulation system. Laurent, D.; and Motet, S. HCI-0395

**Burkhart, H.**
Concepts in user interfaces: a reference model for command and response languages. Beech, D. (Ed.) ● HCI-0032

**Burton, H. D.**
A prototype electronic encyclopedia. Weyer, S. A.; and Borning, A. H. HCI-0278

**Cannon, R. L.**
The application of scene synthesis techniques to the display of multidimensional image data. Robertson, P. K.; and O'Callaghan, J. F. HCI-0371

**Carey, T.**
Designing the user interface: strategies for effective human-computer interaction. Shneiderman, B. ● HCI-0006
Online help systems: design and implementation. Kearsley, G. ● HCI-0009
Abstractions for user interface design. Coutaz, J. HCI-0114
The depth/breadth trade-off in the design of menu-driven user interfaces. Kiger, J. I. HCI-0135
An empirical study of occupational stress, attitudes and health among information systems personnel. Ivancevich, J. M.; Napier, H. A.; and Wetherbe, J. C. HCI-0451

**Carlson, G.**
Eye movement analysis system using fundus images. Kawai, H.; Tamura, S.; Kani, K.; and Kariya, K. HCI-0243

**Caruso, G. A.**
The future of "writing" for the computer industry. Haselkorn, M. P. HCI-0150
User-friendly password methods for computer-mediated information systems. Barton, B. F.; and Barton, M. S. HCI-0167

**Chavez, E. R.**
Man-made minds: the promise of artificial intelligence. Waldrop, M. M. ● HCI-0055

**Chokhani, S.**
UNIX shell programming. Arthur, L. J. ● HCI-0027
Readings in natural language processing. Grosz, B. J.; Sparck-Jones, K.; and Webber, B. L. (Eds.) ● HCI-0067
A novice user's interface to information retrieval systems. Crawford, R. G.; and Becker, H. S. HCI-0219
The spatial metaphor for user interfaces: experimental tests of reference by location versus name. Jones, W. P.; and Dumais, S. T. HCI-0268

**Chrz, T.**
Cooperative interfaces to information systems. Bolc, L.; and Jarke, M. (Eds.) ● HCI-0066

**Cohen, B. F.**
Attitudes towards specific uses of the computers quantitative, decision-making and record-keeping applications. Kerber, K. W. HCI-0234

**Cohill, A. M.**
The soft side of software: a management approach to computer documentation. Foehr, T.; and Cross, T. B. ● HCI-0016
Consistent user interface. Otte, F. H. HCI-0107

Active help systems. Fischer, G.; Lemke, A.; and Schwab, T. HCI-0108
Heuristics for designing enjoyable user interfaces: lessons from computer games. Malone, T. W. HCI-0132
An approach to user specification of interactive display interfaces. Bass, L. J. HCI-0137
Experimental adaptive interface. Mason, M. V.; and Thomas, R. C. HCI-0139
Mental models and software maintenance. Littman, D. C.; Pinto, J.; Letovsky, S.; and Soloway, E. HCI-0173
CONTEXT: an on-line documentation system. Ragan, R. R. HCI-0280
Office systems. Christie, B.; and Gardiner, M. M. HCI-0291

**Cosma, M.**
Interfaces and data transfer formats in computer graphics systems. Encarnação, J. HCI-0419

**Coulter, N. S.**
An empirical investigation into problem decomposition strategies used in program design. Ratcliff, B.; and Siddiqi, J. I. HCI-0103
A quantitative theory of human-computer interaction. Polson, P. G. HCI-0198
Experience with the ZOG human-computer interface system. McCracken, D. L.; and Akscyn, R. M. HCI-0246

**Crawford, C. R.**
Goals in the application of CAD interfaces. Vöge, E. HCI-0416

**Crawford, R. G.**
Architecture problems in the construction of expert systems for document retrieval. Sparck Jones, K. HCI-0272
Towards a new research paradigm in information retrieval. Ingwersen, P. HCI-0273
Cognitive models, cognitive tasks, and information retrieval. Hollnagel, E. HCI-0331

**Cremers, A. B.**
Operating system design. Vol. 1: the XINU approach (PC edition). Comer, D.; and Fossum, T. V. ● HCI-0029

**Crowe, W. R.**
Information technology in the home: promises as yet unrealized. Frude, N. HCI-0425

**Cupak, J. J.**
User-centered requirements analysis. Martin, C. F. ● HCI-0004
The ethics of automated publishing systems (a response to Dr. Brockmann). James, G. HCI-0170

**Curtis, B.**
Cognitive analysis of people's use of software.  Olson, J. R.  HCI-0199

**Dain, J. A.**
The synthesizer generator: a system for constructing language-based editors.  Reps, T. W.; and Teitelbaum, T. •  HCI-0024
The synthesizer generator reference manual (3rd ed.).  Reps, T. W.; and Teitelbaum, T. •  HCI-0024

**Damerau, F. J.**
Semistructured messages are surprisingly useful for computer-supported coordination.  Malone, T. W.; Grant, K. R.; Lai, K.; Rao, R.; and Rosenblitt, D.  HCI-0290

**Davenport, J. H.**
LISPcraft.  Wilensky, R. •  HCI-0023

**Davis, G. B.**
Human information seeking and design of information systems.  Rouse, W. B.; and Rouse, S. H.  HCI-0184

**Davis, T. M.**
Stages and levels in human-machine interaction.  Norman, D. A.  HCI-0189
Man-machine interface issues in the construction and use of an expert system.  Kidd, A. L.; and Cooper, M. B.  HCI-0212
Mainframe and microcomputer-based business graphics: What satisfies users?  Lehman, J.; Van Wetering, J.; and Vogel, D.  HCI-0216

**Dearholt, D. W.**
Brains, machines, and mathematics (2nd ed.).  Arbib, M. A. •  HCI-0034

**Dreifus, H. N.**
Readings on cognitive ergonomics - mind and computers.  van der Veer, G. C.; Tauber, M. J.; Green, T. R.; and Gorny, P. (Eds.) §  HCI-0039

**Duncan, K. A.**
Evaluating RECONSIDER: a computer program for diagnostic prompting.  Nelson, S. J.; Blois, M. S.; Tuttle, M. S.; Erlbaum, M.; Harrison, P.; Kim, H.; Winkelmann, B.; and Yamashita, D.  HCI-0410

**Dykman, C. A.**
The art of programming.  Hall, W.  HCI-0095

**Egan, L. G.**
SOFTLIB—A documentation management system.  Sommerville, I.; Welland, R.; Bennett, I.; and Thompson, R.  HCI-0149

**Elliott, R. W.**
In search of searching skills.  Fairhall, D.  HCI-0274

**Ellis, C. A.**
Electronic calendars in the office: an assessment of user needs and current technology.  Kincaid, C. M.; Dupont, P. B.; and Kaye, A. R.  HCI-0287

**Evans, M. A.**
Perception of transparency in man and machine.  Beck, J.  HCI-0367

**Fawcett, W. H.**
The AutoCAD productivity book: tapping the hidden power of AutoCAD.  Schaefer, A. T.; and Brittain, J. L. •  HCI-0076
Modern drafting: an introduction to CAD.  Bethune, J. D.; and Kee, B. A. •  HCI-0077
Knowledge and control for a mechanical design expert system.  Brown, D. C.; and Chandrasekaran, B.  HCI-0320

**Fedorowicz, J.**
Operator work load: when is enough enough?  LeMay, M.; and Hird, E.  HCI-0222
Impact of system response time on state anxiety.  Guynes, J. L.  HCI-0228
Query languages—a taxonomy.  Vassiliou, Y.; and Jarke, M.  HCI-0254
The doctor's use of a computer in the consulting room: an analysis.  Brownbridge, G.; Fitter, M.; and Sime, M.  HCI-0409

**Fendrich, J. W.**
Selecting an Ada environment.  Lyons, T. G.; and Nissen, J. C. •  HCI-0015

**Fenton, R. G.**
CAD/CAM: integration in the automobile industry.  Wilfert, H. G.; and Seeland, H.  HCI-0413

**Ferguson, L.**
A plan for evaluating usability of software products.  Kopp, E. F.; and Timmer, H. J.  HCI-0449

**Feustel, E. A.**
Opening Windows.  O'Brien, B. •  HCI-0007

**Firschein, O.**
Connectionist models and parallelism in high level vision.  Feldman, J. A.  HCI-0363

**Fischer, H.**
Ada-based executable modelling of distributed systems.  Bruno, G.; and Balsamo, A.  HCI-0098
SKETCHER, an interactive, graphical Ada software tool—its development and use.  Brintzenhoff, A. L.  HCI-0100

**Fowler, S. L.**
Corporate culture, technical documentation, and organization diagnosis.  Levine, L. B.  HCI-0151

**Fox, C.**
Human-computer interface design guidelines.  Brown, C. M. •  HCI-0011
Hypertext/hypermedia.  Jonassen, D. H. •  HCI-0047

**Frakes, W. B.**
User-oriented computer languages: analysis and design.  Klerer, M. •  HCI-0019

Specification and generation of variable, personalized graphical interfaces. Bournique, R.; and Treu, S. HCI-0134

Pygmalion at the interface. Slator, B. M.; Anderson, M. P.; and Conley, W. HCI-0349

**Fulda, J. S.**
Goal and plan knowledge representations: from stories to text editors and programs. Black, J. B.; Kay, D. S.; and Soloway, E. M. HCI-0183

Expert systems as cognitive tools for human decision making. Schmalhofer, F. HCI-0227

Expert systems—where do we go from here? Taylor, J. HCI-0318

Knowledge elicitation: dissociating conscious reflections from automatic processes. Stevenson, R. J.; Manktelow, K. I.; and Howard, M. J. HCI-0337

Cognitive aspects of learning and using a programming language. Mayer, R. E. HCI-0439

**Gabrieli, H. S.**
Computer usability testing & evaluation. Spencer, R. H. ● HCI-0014

Special Issue: The FAA's Advanced Automation Program. Mulder, M. C. (Ed.) HCI-0424

**Gagliardo, E.**
Computer-music interfaces: a survey. Pennycook, B. W. HCI-0412

**Garbacea, I.**
Visual hyperacuity: representation and computation of high precision position information. Krotkov, E. P. HCI-0393

**Garrett, R. L.**
Strategic issues in knowledge engineering. Chignell, M. H.; and Peterson, J. G. HCI-0317

**Gebhardt, F.**
Online information retrieval: concepts, principles, and techniques. Harter, S. P. ● HCI-0046

An interactive database end user facility for the definition and manipulation of forms. Laender, A. H.F.; and Stocker, P. M. HCI-0263

**Geissman, J. R.**
IDECAP: interactive pictorial information system for demographic and environmental planning applications. van den Bos, J.; van Naelten, M.; and Teunissen, W. HCI-0411

**Geller, D. P.**
Information systems design methodologies and their compliance with cognitive ergonomy. Traünmuller, R. HCI-0097

**Ghezzi, C.**
Ada: first users—pleased; prospective users—still hesitant. Myers, W. HCI-0159

**Gini, M. L.**
Modelling and control. Coiffet, P. ● HCI-0068

Interaction with the environment. Coiffet, P. ● HCI-0068

Teleoperations and robotics: evolution and development. Vertut, J.; and Coiffet, P. ● HCI-0068

Teleoperations and robotics: applications and technology. Vertut, J.; and Coiffet, P. ● HCI-0068

Robot components and systems. L'Hote, F.; Kauffmann, J.; André, P.; and Taillard, J. ● HCI-0068

Logic and programming. Parent, M.; and Laurgeau, C. ● HCI-0068

Decision and intelligence. Aleksander, I.; Farreny, H.; and Ghallab, M. ● HCI-0068

Performance and computer-aided design. Liégeois, A. ● HCI-0068

Indexes and bibliography. Coiffet, P. ● HCI-0068

**Giuse, D. A.**
INTERLISP: the language and its usage. Kaisler, S. H. ● HCI-0022

Composing user interfaces with InterViews. Linton, M. A.; Vissides, J. M.; and Calder, P. R. HCI-0131

**Goldberg, M.**
Document convergence in an interactive formatting system. Chamberlin, D. D. HCI-0405

**Golshani, F.**
Natural language query processing in a temporal database. De, S.; Pan, S.; and Whinston, A. B. HCI-0257

**Gordon, M. L.**
Anatomy of a compact user interface development tool. Stott, J. W.; and Kottemann, J. E. HCI-0104

Some observations on user interface design and user performance. Newman, A.; and Sethi, J. HCI-0117

An empirical study of the effects of modularity on program modifiability. Korson, T. D.; and Vaishnavi, V. K. HCI-0155

**Gorsline, G. W.**
Experimental study of a two-dimensional language vs. FORTRAN for first-course progammers. Klerer, M. HCI-0171

**Graesser, A.**
LisaLearning. Carroll, J. M.; and Mazur, S. A. HCI-0092

**Grecu, E.**
Reading text from computer screens. Mills, C. B.; and Weldon, L. J. HCI-0088

**Grimson, J. B.**
A visual approach to browsing in a database environment. Larson, J. A. HCI-0258

Using the micro-computer to simplify database access: designing interfaces to complex files.   Pratt, G. E.C.   HCI-0275

**Grunbaum, W. F.**
An artificial intelligence approach to legal reasoning.   Gardner, A. v.d.L. ●   HCI-0061

**Guthrie, G. R.**
Two-bit graphics.   Salesin, D.; and Barzel, R.   HCI-0372

**Haddad, D. C.**
Impact of design methods on decision support systems success: an empirical assessment.   Mahmood, M. A.; and Medewitz, J. N.   HCI-0303

The relationship of problem-solving ability and course performance among novice programmers.   Nowaczyk, R. H.   HCI-0435

**Hammer, J. M.**
A structured approach to designing human-computer dialogues.   Benbasat, I.; and Wand, Y.   HCI-0106

Training wheels in a user interface.   Carroll, J. M.; and Carrithers, C.   HCI-0208

Selecting a humanly understandable knowledge representation for reasoning about knowledge.   Maida, A. S.   HCI-0330

An empirical study of the impact of user involvement on system usage and information satisfaction.   Baroudi, J. J.; Olson, M. H.; and Ives, B.   HCI-0448

**Hammerton, J. C.**
The computer imperative among owners of home computers: explanation by social factors.   McQuarrie, E. F.   HCI-0217

Strategies for encouraging successful adoption of office communication systems.   Ehrlich, S. F.   HCI-0307

Graphical standards.   Enderle, G.   HCI-0417

**Hankley, W. J.**
Software ergonomics: advances and applications.   Bullinger, H. (Ath.) Gunzenhäuser, R. (Ed.) ●   HCI-0012

Graphical user interfaces   Herot, C. F.   HCI-0133

**Hansen, W. J.**
TEXTNET: a network-based approach to text handling.   Trigg, R. H.; and Weiser, M.   HCI-0401

**Harris, D. R.**
Information science: its roots and relation as viewed from the perspective of cognitive science.   Pylyshyn, Z. W.   HCI-0185

Organizing for human factors.   Thomas, J. C.   HCI-0230

A model for the interpretation of verbal predictions.   Zimmer, A. C.   HCI-0316

**Harris, M. C.**
Querying external databases.   Lockhovsky, F. H.; and Tsichritzis, D. C.   HCI-0233

**Harrison, M. A.**
Some applications of a theorem of Shirshov to language theory.   Restivo, A.; and Reutenauer, C.   HCI-0181

**Harrison, W. A.**
Experimental evaluation of program quality using external metrics.   Harold, F. G.   HCI-0176

**Henderson, T. C.**
Multivariate data representation and analysis by face pattern using facial expression characteristics.   Honda, N.; and Sugimoto, F.   HCI-0394

**Herberts, L. G.**
The influence of color on program readability and comprehensibility.   Rambally, G. K.   HCI-0120

**Herbison-Evans, D.**
Procedural elements for computer graphics.   Rogers, D. F. ●   HCI-0069

Fundamentals of interactive computer graphics.   Foley, J. D.; and Van Dam, A. ●   HCI-0069

Principles of interactive computer graphics (2nd ed.).   Sproull, R. F. (Ath.) Newman, W. M. (Ed.) ●   HCI-0069

Computer graphics.   Hearn, D.; and Baker, M. P. ●   HCI-0069

**Hirschfelder, J. J.**
Information systems definition: the Multiview approach.   Wood-Harper, A. T.; Antill, L.; and Avison, D. E. ●   HCI-0085

Some cognitive aspects of interface design in a two-variable optimization task.   Bridger, R. S.; and Long, J.   HCI-0111

Human cognition and human computer interaction.   Schneider, W.; Lind, M.; Allard, R.; and Sandblad, B.   HCI-0241

**Hirst, G. J.**
Digital typography: an introduction to type and composition for computer system design.   Rubinstein, R. ●   HCI-0074

An empirical investigation of voice as an input modality for computer programming.   Leggett, J.; and Williams, G.   HCI-0237

Extended person-machine interface.   Reichman-Adar, R.   HCI-0344

Text processing by speech: dialogue design and usability issues in the provision of a system for disabled users.   Hewitt, J.; and Furner, S.   HCI-0357

A note on undetected typing errors.   Peterson, J. L.   HCI-0399

**Hoffer, E. P.**
Medicine in the age of the computer.  Flynn, G. J. ● HCI-0075

**Hoffman, W. S.**
A specification language for direct-manipulation user interfaces.  Jacob, R. J.K.  HCI-0123
Designing online information.  Rubens, P.; and Krull, R.  HCI-0152
Technical writers as computer scientists: the challenges of online documentation.  Shirk, H. N.  HCI-0153
Creating a style for online help.  Price, J.  HCI-0154
Fatal error in pass zero: how not to confuse novices.  du Boulay, B.; and Matthew, I.  HCI-0164

**Hofkin, R. J.**
Andrew: a distributed personal computing environment.  Morris, J. H.; Satyanarayanan, M.; Conner, M. H.; Howard, J. H.; Rosenthal, D. S.; and Smith, F. D.  HCI-0091

**Holt, C. M.**
Formally-based tools and techniques for human-computer dialogues.  Alexander, H. ● HCI-0021

**Holzmann, G. J.**
A communication system supporting large datagrams on a local area network.  Linton, A.; and Panzieri, F.  HCI-0166
The X window system.  Scheifler, R. W.; and Gettys, J.  HCI-0370

**Houston, S. R.**
The impact of DSS on organizational communication.  Sanders, G. L.; Courtney, J. F.; and Loy, S. L.  HCI-0294
Change, attitude to change, and decision support system success.  Barki, H.; and Huff, S. L.  HCI-0296

**Howard, G. S.**
Adult learners: away with computerphobia.  Kneller, G. R.  HCI-0433

**Huang, T. C.**
Computer-aided modeling and planning (CAMP).  Sagie, I.  HCI-0415

**Huber, A. R.**
Design and performance considerations for an optical disk-based, multimedia object server.  Christodoulakis, S.; and Faloutsos, C.  HCI-0265

**Hudson, P.**
An experimental evaluation of the impact of data display format on recall performance.  Schmell, R. W.; and Umanath, N. S.  HCI-0202

**James, E. B.**
The distributed processing of knowledge and belief in the human brain.  Lavorel, P. M.  HCI-0240
UMFE: a user modelling front-end subsystem.  Sleeman, D.  HCI-0325

Naive algorithm design techniques—a case study.  Kant, E.; and Newell, A.  HCI-0360
Computer-based microworlds—a definition to aid design.  Squires, D.; and Dougall, A.  HCI-0432

**Javey, S.**
The PegaSys System: pictures as formal documentation of large programs.  Moriconi, M.; and Hare, D. F.  HCI-0146

**Jeffries, R.**
Cognitive layouts of windows and multiple screens for user interfaces.  Norman, K. L.; Weldon, L. J.; and Shneiderman, B.  HCI-0122
The automated tutoring of introductory computer programming.  Anderson, J. R.; and Skwarecki, E.  HCI-0438

**Jenkins, G. K.**
Personal computing for decision support.  Lee, D. T.  HCI-0299
Videotex: anatomy of a failure.  Noll, A. M.  HCI-0313

**Jungert, E.**
Icon semantics—a formal approach to icon system design.  Chang, S.  HCI-0161

**Kallman, E. A.**
Computer anxiety in management: myth or reality?  Howard, G. S.; and Smith, R. D.  HCI-0232

**Kandel, A.**
Pattern recognition: human and mechanical.  Watanabe, S. ●  HCI-0072

**Kaufman, A.**
An image processing language with ICON-assisted navigation.  Chang, S.; Jungert, E.; Levialdi, S.; Tortora, G.; and Ichikawa, T.  HCI-0387

**Kaujalgi, V. B.**
Human-computer interface design.  Sutcliffe, A.  HCI-0043
On models and modelling in human-computer co-operation.  Oberquelle, H.  HCI-0182

**Kelly, M. D.**
Early vision: from computational structure to algorithms and parallel hardware.  Poggio, T.  HCI-0365

**Kiper, J. D.**
The designer as user: building requirements for design tools from design practice.  Rosson, M. B.; Kellogg, W.; and Maass, S.  HCI-0129
The Software Life Cycle Support Environment (SLCSE): a computer based framework for developing software systems.  Strelich, T.  HCI-0147

**Kirkman, D. A.**
Communications design for Co-oP: a group decision support system.  Bui, T. X.; and Jarke, M.  HCI-0297

**Klaczak, J. J. A.**
Systems software tools. Biggerstaff, T. J. ● HCI-0030

A user agent for multiple computer-based message services. Kaye, A. R.; and McDowell, R. HCI-0306

**Kornfeld, J. R.**
An experimental comparison of tabular and graphic data presentation. Powers, M.; Lashley, C.; Sanchez, P.; and Shneiderman, B. HCI-0236

An economical approach to modeling speech recognition accuracy. Spine, T. M.; Williges, B. H.; and Maynard, J. F. HCI-0354

A fuzzy rule-based model of human problem solving. Hunt, R. M.; and Rouse, W. B. HCI-0359

Speech-controlled text-editing: effects of input modality and of command structure. Morrison, D. L.; Green, T. R.; Shaw, A. C.; and Payne, S. J. HCI-0397

**Kraft, D. H.**
A natural language information retrieval system with extentions towards fuzzy reasoning. Bolc, L.; Kowalski, A.; Kozlowska, M.; and Strzalkowski, T. HCI-0281

**Kurtz, T. E.**
Fragile knowledge and neglected strategies in novice programmers. Perkins, D. N.; and Martin, F. HCI-0177

**Kyle, J. W.**
DEC networks and architectures. Malamud, C. ● HCI-0003

**Lai, W. S.**
The effects of communication monitors on user satisfaction. Rushinek, A.; and Rushinek, S. F. HCI-0221

**Lamb, D. A.**
Storyboard prototyping: a new approach to user requirements analysis. Andriole, S. J. ● HCI-0005

**Lambert, R. W.**
Voice input aids for the physically disabled. Damper, R. I. HCI-0089

**Land, F.**
Project Nick: meetings augmentation and analysis. Cook, P.; Ellis, C.; Graf, M.; Rein, G.; and Smith, T. HCI-0156

Interface design in computerized conferencing systems: a personal view. Turoff, M. HCI-0305

**Lebowitz, M.**
Acquisition of control and domain knowledge by watching in a blackboard environment. Boyle, C. D. HCI-0319

**Lecarme, O. L. M.**
Literate programming. Knuth, D. E. HCI-0148

**Lee, W. T.**
A generator of direct manipulation office systems. Hudson, S. E.; and King, R. HCI-0250

**Leiss, E. L.**
Codes and cryptography. Welsh, D. ● HCI-0033

**Levine, J. R.**
Compact disc-interactive: a designer's overview. Philips International, I. (Ed.) ● HCI-0078

Toward native language software for information management. Santaella, E. M.; and Slamecka, V. HCI-0138

**Lister, R. P.**
Expertise transfer and complex problems: using AQUINAS as a knowledge-acquisition workbench for knowledge-based systems. Boose, J. H.; and Bradshaw, J. M. HCI-0336

**Logan, G. M.**
The second self: computers and the human spirit. Turkle, S. ● HCI-0082

**Lorentz, R. J.**
Algorithms for approximate string matching. Ukkonen, E. HCI-0180

**Lowe, T. C.**
Information technology and home-based services: improving the usability of teleshopping. Long, J. HCI-0226

On the applied use of human memory models: the memory extender personal filing system. Jones, W. P. HCI-0271

What makes users happy? Rushinek, A.; and Rushinek, S. F. HCI-0427

**Mahmood, M. A.**
A research center for augmenting human intellect. Engelbart, D. C.; and English, W. K. HCI-0334

**Major, J. H.**
Reading continuous text from a one-line visual display. Monk, A. F. HCI-0187

A framework for investigating language-mediated interaction with machines. Zoeppritz, M. HCI-0347

**Marcus, R. S.**
The vocabulary problem in human-system communication. Furnas, G. W.; Landauer, T. K.; Gomez, L. M.; and Dumais, S. T. HCI-0224

The use of colour in language syntax analysis. Reynolds, C. F. HCI-0385

**Martin, D.**
Ada-based executable modelling of distributed systems. Bruno, G.; and Balsamo, A. HCI-0098

SKETCHER, an interactive, graphical Ada software tool—its development and use. Brintzenhoff, A. L. HCI-0100

**Mayforth, G. R.**
A display editor with random access and continuous control.  Hammer, J. M.  HCI-0140
Paradox of the active user.  Carroll, J. M.; and Rosson, M. B.  HCI-0434

**McGee, W. C.**
An almost path-free very high-level interactive data manipulation language for a microcomputer-based database system.  Schach, S. R.; and Wood, P. T.  HCI-0261

**McInnis, L. M.**
4.2BSD and 4.3BSD as examples of the UNIX system.  Quarterman, J. S.; Silberschatz, A.; and Peterson, J. L.  HCI-0165
Speed of response using keyboard and screen-based microcomputer response media.  Beaumont, J. G.  HCI-0192

**McKenney, J. L.**
An overview of research and co-operation in advanced information technology.  Oakley, B.  HCI-0442

**McQuilken, D. R.**
An experimental program investigating color-enhanced and graphical information presentation: an integration of the findings.  Benbasat, I.; Dexter, A. S.; and Todd, P.  HCI-0196

**Meads, J. A.**
Pictorial interfaces to data bases.  Barker, P. G.; and Najah, M.  HCI-0116
What non-programmers know about programming: natural language procedure specification.  Galotti, K. M.; and Gangon, W. F.  HCI-0211

**Menon, A. K.**
Tones of voice: the role of intonation in computer speech understanding.  Longuet-Higgins, C.  HCI-0356

**Meyer, J. M.M.**
High performance interactive graphics: modeling, rendering and animating for IBM PCs and compatibles.  Adams, L. •  HCI-0071
A note on the nature of creativity in engineering: implications for supporting system design.  Rouse, W. B.  HCI-0220

**Mihalo, W. E.**
Introducing CAL: a practical guide to writing computer-assisted learning programs.  Hudson, K. •  HCI-0079
The microcomputer as a classroom audio visual device: the concept, and prospects.  Hativa, N.  HCI-0223

**Miller, D. M.**
Training for optimising transfer between word processors.  Pollock, C.  HCI-0447

**Mirsepassi, T. J.**
Interactive computer program for the selection of interference fits.  Lagodimos, A. G.; and Scarr, A. J.  HCI-0406

**Mirzaian, A.**
One-layer routing without component constraints.  Lloyd, E. L.; and Ravi, S. S.  HCI-0090

**Mitchell, D. B.**
Design of computer programs for the physically handicapped.  Perkins, J.; and Isaacs, R. I.  HCI-0096

**Modell, M. E.**
Generalized query-by-rule: a heterogeneous database query language.  Patnaik, L. M.; and Chowdhary, D. M.  HCI-0252
ASK is transportable in half a dozen ways.  Thompson, B. H.; and Thompson, F. B.  HCI-0279
Computer mediated work: the interplay between technology and structured jobs.  Turner, J. A.  HCI-0440

**Moeller, R. R.**
Learning to use a word processor: by doing, by thinking, and by knowing.  Carroll, J. M.; and Mack, R. L.  HCI-0292

**Moisa, T.**
A programmable interface language for heterogeneous distributed systems.  Falcone, J. R.  HCI-0094

**Monmonier, M. S.**
Color and the computer in cartography.  Olson, J. M.  HCI-0386

**Moore, J. W.**
MIKE: the menu interaction kontrol environment.  Olsen, D. R.  HCI-0124

**Mowshowitz, A.**
Data security and confidentiality in Europe.  Chamoux, J. P.  HCI-0450

**Murphy, M. G.**
Applying software engineering principles to the user application interface.  Sena, J. A.; and Smith, L. M.  HCI-0130
A practical method for LR and LL syntactic error diagnosis and recovery.  Burke, M. G.; and Fisher, G. A.  HCI-0163

**Nadeau, L.**
Designing the user interface: strategies for effective human-computer interaction.  Shneiderman, B. •  HCI-0006

**Naumann, J. D.**
Cost/benefit analysis for incorporating human factors in the software lifecycle.  Mantei, M. M.; and Teorey, T. J.  HCI-0127

# REVIEWER INDEX

**Naur, P.**
In search of the person: philosophical explorations in cognitive science.   Arbib, M. A. ●   HCI-0062
Processes in computer program comprehension.   Weidenbeck, S.   HCI-0172
What do users ask? Some thoughts on diagnostic advice.   Kidd, A. L.   HCI-0326

**Newpeck, F. F.**
The dimensions of accessibility to online information: implications for implementing office information systems.   Culnan, M. J.   HCI-0304

**Nicolescu, R.**
Abstract data type development and implementation: an example.   Ford, R.; and Miller, K.   HCI-0162

**Nirenburg, S.**
Reasoning in natural language for designing a data base.   Colombetti, M.; Guida, G.; Pernici, B.; and Somalvico, M.   HCI-0322

**Novatchev, D. D.**
Holophrasted displays in an interactive environment.   Smith, S. R.; Barnard, D. T.; and Macleod, I. A.   HCI-0105

**O'Connor, B. W.**
Between man and machine.   Tello, E. R.   HCI-0128
Analyzing the high frequency bugs in novice programs.   Spohrer, J. G.; and Soloway, E.   HCI-0178

**O'Rourke, J.**
Environment-centered and viewer-centered perception of surface orientation.   Sedgwick, H. A.; and Levy, S.   HCI-0392

**Obermeier, K. K.**
Knowledge-intensive natural language generation.   Jacobs, P. S.   HCI-0343
Modularity and lexical access.   Seidenberg, M. S.; and Tanenhaus, M. K.   HCI-0350

**Oh, Y. H.**
Chip talk: projects in speech synthesis.   Prochnow, D. ●   HCI-0002
A parallel formant synthesizer for machine voice output.   Holmes, J. N.   HCI-0396

**Oniga, T.**
On the application of rule-based techniques to the design of advice giving systems.   Jackson, P.; and Lefrere, P.   HCI-0315
Natural-language interface for an instructable robot.   Maas, R. E.; and Suppes, P.   HCI-0324
A natural language front end to databases with evaluative feedback.   Boguraev, B. K.; and Sparck Jones, K.   HCI-0338

**Ourusoff, N.**
Fifth generation computers: concepts, implementations and uses.   Bishop, P. ●   HCI-0001

**Pasieka, G. E.**
An expert system for mapping acoustic cues into phonetic features.   De Mori, R.; Giordana, A.; Laface, P.; and Saitta, L.   HCI-0328

**Paton, K. A.**
An investigation into the skeletonization approach of Hilditch.   Naccache, N. J.; and Shinghal, R.   HCI-0388

**Patton, P. C.**
Computing with structured connectionist networks.   Feldman, J. A.; Fanty, M. A.; Goddard, N. H.; and Lynne, K. J.   HCI-0314

**Payne, A. J.**
Selective networks and recognition automata.   Reeke, G. N.; and Edelman, G. M.   HCI-0390

**Perreault, L.**
Knowledge-based systems: implications for human-computer interfaces.   Cleal, D. M.; and Heaton, N. O. ●   HCI-0060

**Petry, F. E.**
General multiple-objective decision functions and linguistically quantified statements.   Yager, R. R.   HCI-0110
Measuring the quality of linguistic forecasts.   Yager, R. R.   HCI-0247

**Podolsky, J. L.**
Office automation: a social and organizational perspective.   Hirschheim, R. A. ●   HCI-0048
A taxonomy for the study of human factors in management information systems.   Beard, J. W.; and Peterson, T. O.   HCI-0205
Object lens: a "spreadsheet" for cooperative work.   Lai, K.; Malone, T. W.; and Yu, K.   HCI-0206

**Popescu, C.**
A performing medium for working group graphics.   Lakin, F.   HCI-0383

**Powell, A. J.**
The Japanese and software: is it a good match?   Belady, L. A.   HCI-0429

**Powers, V. M.**
Reverse engineering the brain.   Stevens, J. K.   HCI-0368

**Price, K. E.**
Recognizing unexpected objects: a proposed approach.   Rosenfeld, A.   HCI-0389

**Rathja, R. C.**
Interfaces for CAD applications.   Pasemann, K.   HCI-0418

**Rey, W. J.J.**
A dedicated microcomputer for handwritten interaction with a software tool: system prototyping.   Plamondon, R.; and Baron, R.   HCI-0119

**Ricart, G.**
Computer systems software: the programmer/machine interface.   Ellzey, R. S. ●   HCI-0361

**Riel, A. J.**
Language generation by computer.   Hovy, E. H.; and Schank, R. C.   HCI-0342

**Riesbeck, C. K.**
Conceptual structures: information processing in mind and machine.   Sowa, J. F. ●   HCI-0057
KRITON: a knowledge-acquisition tool for expert systems.   Diederich, J.; Ruhmann, I.; and May, M.   HCI-0327

**Ritschdorff, J. T.**
Artificial intelligence and tutoring systems: computational and cognitive approaches to the communication of knowledge.   Wenger, E. ●   HCI-0080

**Rogers, J. L.**
Interactive video: vol. 1.   Educational Technology Publica ●   HCI-0081

**Rolph, R. N.**
The human factors of computer graphics interaction techniques.   Foley, J. D.; Wallace, V. L.; and Chan, P.   HCI-0377

**Ronse, C.**
CNS-HLS mapping using fuzzy sets.   Farhoosh, H.; and Schrack, G.   HCI-0380

**Root, R. W.**
Human-computer interaction: a design guide.   Jones, M. S. ●   HCI-0041

**Rose, J. N.**
Psychology and information technology.   Howarth, I.   HCI-0225
Visual momentum: a concept to improve the cognitive coupling of person and computer.   Woods, D. D.   HCI-0238
Cognitive attributes: implications for display design in supervisory control systems.   Murphy, E. D.; and Mitchell, C. M.   HCI-0242
Analysing the scope of cognitive models in human-computer interaction: a trade-off approach.   Simon, T.   HCI-0245
Instructionless learning about a complex device: the paradigm and observations.   Shrager, J.; and Klahr, D.   HCI-0333
Semantic primitives or meaning postulates: mental models or propositional representation?   Johnson-Laird, P. N.   HCI-0339
Perception of organization in a random stimulus.   Smith, B. J.   HCI-0364

**Sabella, P. E.**
An experimental evaluation of computer graphics imagery.   Meyer, G. W.; Rushmeier, H. E.; Cohen, M. F.; Greenberg, D. P.; and Torrance, K. E.   HCI-0373
An experimental comparison of RGB, YIQ, LAB, HSV, and opponent color models.   Schwarz, M. W.; Cowan, W. B.; and Beatty, J. C.   HCI-0381

**Salton, G.**
Using focus to constrain language generation.   McKeown, K. R.   HCI-0341

**Salwin, A. E.**
Programmer/nonprogrammer differences in specifying procedures to people and computers.   Onorato, L. A.; and Schvaneveldt, R. W.   HCI-0174
Natural language with discrete speech as a mode for human-to-machine.   Biermann, A. W.; Rodman, R. D.; Rubin, D. C.; and Heidlage, J. F.   HCI-0355

**Sammet, J. E.**
Programming languages: a grand tour (2nd ed.).   Horowitz, E. (Ed.) ●   HCI-0018

**Sampson, J. R.**
Learning in parallel networks: simulating learning in a probabilistic system.   Hinton, G. E.   HCI-0332

**Sauvain, R. W.**
Online communities.   Hiltz, S. R. ●   HCI-0051
Using restricted natural language for data retrieval: a plan for field evaluation.   Turner, J. A.; Jarke, M.; Stohr, E. A.; Vassiliou, Y.; and White, N.   HCI-0255
The user interface of a personal calendar program.   Greif, I.   HCI-0286

**Sava-Segal, E.**
Update and retrieval in a relational database through a universal schema interface.   Brosda, V.; and Vossen, G.   HCI-0260
TEAM: an experiment in the design of transportable natural-language interfaces.   Grosz, B. J.; Appelt, D. E.; Martin, P. A.; and Pereira, F. C.N.   HCI-0351

**Sawyer, R. K.**
PECAN: program development systems that support multiple views.   Reiss, S. P.   HCI-0145

**Scacchi, W.**
Reflections on NoteCards: seven issues for the next generation of hypermedia systems.   Halasz, F. G.   HCI-0293

**Schneider, H. J.**
Editing by example.   Nix, R. P.   HCI-0398

**Shaw, M. C.**
Cursor movement during text editing.   Gould, J. D.; Lewis, C.; and Barnes, V.   HCI-0113

**Shaw, S. S.**
Cursor movement during text editing. Gould, J. D.; Lewis, C.; and Barnes, V. HCI-0113

**Shipman, F. S.**
Applications of AI in engineering. Faught, W. S. HCI-0321

**Shneiderman, B.**
A research model for studying the gender/power aspects of human-computer communication. Fulton, M. A. HCI-0193

What makes RABBIT run? Williams, M. D. HCI-0256

gIBIS: a hypertext tool for exploratory policy discussion. Conklin, J.; and Begeman, M. L. HCI-0300

**Slade, M. S.**
From schema theory to computational (neuro-)linguistics. Arbib, M. A. HCI-0345

Transporting the linguistic string project system from a medical to a Navy domain. Marsh, E.; and Friedman, C. HCI-0352

The LISP tutor: it approaches the effectiveness of a human tutor. Anderson, J. R.; and Reiser, B. J. HCI-0431

**Smith, H.**
The depth/breadth trade-off in the design of menu-driven user interfaces. Kiger, J. I. HCI-0135

**Smith, H. R.**
Postscript: computers and the modeling of mind. Hockenos, W. HCI-0348

A framework of a mechanical translation between Japanese and English by analogy principle. Nagao, M. HCI-0353

**Smith, L. B.**
PICT: an interactive graphical programming environment. Gilnert, E. P.; and Tanimoto, S. L. HCI-0143

Managing the semantic content of graphical data. Broyaye, P.; Pudet, T.; and Vicard, J. HCI-0374

Graphical prototyping of graphical tools. England, D. HCI-0375

Testing and validation of IGES processors. Grabowski, H.; and Glatz, R. HCI-0423

**Smithson, S. C.**
An intelligent interface for online interaction. Vickery, A. HCI-0264

**Smyth, W. F.**
A generalized model management system for mathematical programming. Dolk, D. R. HCI-0302

**Snodgrass, R. T.**
Monitoring distributed systems. Joyce, J.; Lomow, G.; Slind, K.; and Unger, B. HCI-0169

**Snyder, M.**
Strategic management of technostress: The chaining of Prometheus. Caro, D. H.; and Sethi, A. S. HCI-0452

**Soergel, D.**
Observations of end-user online searching behavior over eleven years. Sewell, W.; and Teitelbaum, S. HCI-0235

**Spohrer, J. C.**
Plans and situated actions: the problem of human-machine communication. Suchman, L. A. ● HCI-0040

Creative intelligences. Gregory, R. L.; and Marstrand, P. K. (Eds.) ● HCI-0056

Expertise transfer for expert system design. Boose, J. H. ● HCI-0059

The effects of program-dependent and program-independent deletions on software cloze tests. Thomas, M.; and Zweben, S. HCI-0175

Reading and writing with computers: a framework for explaining differences in performance. Hansen, W. J.; and Haas, C. HCI-0204

**Stavely, A. M.**
The AWK programming language. Aho, A. V.; Kernighan, B. W.; and Weinberger, P. J. ● HCI-0020

**Stetter, F.**
Towards an integration between language and software development environment. Montanari, U. HCI-0158

**Stevens, A. P.**
Implications for education and training. Humphries, C. HCI-0430

**Stout, R. L.**
Cognitive engineering—cognitive science. Norman, D. A. HCI-0200

Interactive fuzzy decision-making for multi-objective nonlinear programming using reference membership intervals. Sakawa, M.; and Yano, H. HCI-0295

The development and use of information technology in health care. Fritter, M. J. HCI-0408

**Studebaker, D. A.**
Views on end-user searching. Ojala, M. HCI-0283

**Swanson, L. C.**
Development of a term association interface for browsing bibliographic data bases based on end users' word associations. Pejtersen, A. M.; Olsen, S. E.; and Zunde, P. HCI-0266

Calibrating databases. Fischhoff, B.; and MacGregor, D. HCI-0269

Knowledge-based search tactics for an intelligent intermediary system. Smith, P. J.; Shute, S. J.; Galdes, B.; and Chignell, M. H. HCI-0277

**Swigger, K. M.**
Technology transfer: a new computer-based system. Foss, D. J.; and DeRidder, M. HCI-0203

On the purpose and analysis of EDP user systems. Pilgrim, J. HCI-0218

Relations between cognitive psychology and computer system design. Landauer, T. K. HCI-0244

The next generation of interactive technologies. Frenkel, K. A. HCI-0384

Human-computer interface development: concepts and systems for its management. Hartson, H. R.; and Hix, D. HCI-0444

**Taggart, W. M.**
Approaches to human reasoning: an analytic framework. Sternberg, R. J.; and Lasaga, M. I. HCI-0239

**Tanimoto, S. L.**
Pushdown automata for user interface management. Olsen, D. R. HCI-0382

**Tarka, M. P.**
Human performance engineering: using human factors/ergonomics to achieve computer system usability (2nd ed.). Bailey, R. W. ● HCI-0042

The 1984 Olympic Message System: a test of behavioral principles of system design. Gould, J. D.; Boies, S. J.; Levy, S.; Richards, J. T.; and Schoonard, J. HCI-0125

Human factors in software engineering: a review of the literature. Laughery, K. R.; and Laughery, K. R. HCI-0157

Equal opportunity interactive systems. Runciman, C.; and Thimbleby, H. HCI-0168

The future of interactive systems and the emergence of direct manipulation. Shneiderman, B. HCI-0186

Extending state transition diagrams for the specification of human-computer interaction. Wasserman, A. I. HCI-0191

Learning by doing with simulated intelligent help. Carroll, J.; and Aaronson, A. HCI-0229

**Tarr, S. C.**
Efficient computer-user interface in electronic mail systems. Akin, O.; and Rao, D. R. HCI-0118

A distributed interoffice mail system. Sakata, S.; and Ueda, T. HCI-0308

**Tepandi, J.**
Implementing imprecision in information systems. Zemankova, M.; and Kandel, A. HCI-0259

**Teplitzky, P. H.**
Planning and design of information systems. Blokdijk, A.; and Blokdijk, P. ● HCI-0045

Interactive critical path analysis (ICPA)—microcomputer implementation of a project management and knowledge engineering tool. Barber, T. J.; Marshall, G.; and Boardman, J. T. HCI-0445

**Thalheim, B.**
Specification and verification of database dynamics. Fiadeiro, J.; and Sernadas, A. HCI-0251

**Tharp, A. L.**
The role of context and adaptation in user interfaces. Croft, W. B. HCI-0109

On search in an incomplete database. Linde, L.; and Waern, Y. HCI-0214

**Thisted, R. A.**
The elements of graphing data. Cleveland, W. S. ● HCI-0035

Physiological principles for the effective use of color. Murch, G. M. HCI-0378

**Tomayko, J. E.**
Introduction to Windows programming. Quedens, G.; and Beason, P. S. ● HCI-0013

**Treu, D. S.**
QWERTY and keyboard reform: the soft keyboard option. Cumming, G. HCI-0190

An aspect of aesthetics in human-computer communications: pretty windows. Gait, J. HCI-0213

**Tufts, R. J.**
Transparent information systems through gateways, front ends, intermediaries, and interfaces. Williams, M. E. HCI-0276

A user oriented design process for user recovery and command reuse support. Yang, Y. HCI-0284

**Unger, E. A.B.**
Executive workstations: issues and requirements. Power, D. J.; and Hevner, A. R. HCI-0288

**Utting, I.**
Synthesis of print-quality cursive script based on a model of the human handwriting mechanism. Dooijes, E. H. HCI-0402

**Van Cleef, R. E.**
The design of the UNIX operating system. Bach, M. J. ● HCI-0026

**Van den Bos, J.**
Device-independent graphics: with examples from IBM personal computers. Sproull, R. F.; Sutherland, W. R.; and Ullner, M. K. ● HCI-0070

A window-based graphics frame store architecture. Westmore, R. J. HCI-0369

Real time graphic simulation of visual effects of egomotion. Peruch, P.; Cavallo, V.; Deutsch, C.; and Pailhous, J. HCI-0379

Experimental results do not support some ergonomic standards for computer video terminal design. Abernethy, C. N.; and Akagi, K. HCI-0428

**Vanker, A. D.**
A comprehensive guide to AI and expert systems. Levine, R. I.; Drang, D. E.; and Edelson, B. ● HCI-0058

**Vaskevitch, D.**
An experimental multimedia mail system. Postel, J. B.; Finn, G. G.; Katz, A. R.; and Reynolds, J. K. HCI-0309

**Vondracek, P.**
A supporting system for effective construction and sharing of scientific databases by general researchers. Amano, K.; and Mochida, A. HCI-0262

**Wallach, M. J.**
Users and experts in the document retrieval system model. Danilowicz, C. HCI-0270

**Warburton, R. D.H.**
A debugger for concurrent programs. Gait, J. HCI-0142

**Ward, N. G.**
Induction: processes of inference, learning, and discovery. Holland, J. H.; Holyoak, K. J.; Nisbett, R. E.; and Thagard, P. R. ● HCI-0064

**Weiss, D. M.**
Experimental evaluation of dialogue types for data entry. Eklundh, K. S.; Marmolin, H.; and Hedin, C. HCI-0115

**Weiss, E. A.**
In the age of the smart machine: the future of work and power. Zuboff, S. ● HCI-0083

**Weiss, L. P.**
Usage patterns in an integrated voice and data communications system. Nicholson, R. T. HCI-0311

**Wexelblat, A. D.**
Diversity in the use of electronic mail: a preliminary inquiry. Mackay, W. E. HCI-0310

**White, G. M.**
Introduction to natural language processing. Harris, M. D. ● HCI-0065

**Whitelaw, M. W.**
Extended programming in the large in a software development environment. Lewerentz, C. HCI-0101

**Wilkerson, R. W.**
Decision trees: a contribution to automatic interpretation of GUHA results. Renc, Z.; and Setíkovská, L. HCI-0329

**Willee, G.**
The mapping between grammar and processor. Frazier, L. HCI-0346

**Witten, I. H.**
Knowledge based systems versus thesaurus: an architecture problem about expert systems design. Defude, B. HCI-0323

The phonetic basis for computer speech processing. Ladefoged, P. HCI-0358

**Wolfe, C. A.**
A system for interactive viewing of structured documents. Witten, I. H.; and Bramwell, B. HCI-0400

**Zelkowitz, M. V.**
Programmer perceptions of productivity and programming tools. Hanson, S. J.; and Rosinski, R. R. HCI-0099

**Zlatuska, J.**
Mental models: towards a cognitive science of language, inference, and consciousness. Johnson-Laird, P. N. ● HCI-0063

**Zobrist, A. L.**
Preattentive processing in vision. Treisman, A. HCI-0366

**Zobrist, G. W.**
Artificial behavior: computer simulation of psychological processes. Steinhauer, G. D. ● HCI-0073

Computer-aided hierarchical diagrams. Brown, A. D. HCI-0160

Graphic design for computer graphics. Marcus, A. HCI-0376

An approach to CAD system performance evaluation. Strelnikov, Y. N.; Pulkkis, G.; and Dmitrevich, G. D. HCI-0414

# Periodicals Cited

Addresses of the journal publishers and International Standard Serial Numbers (ISSN) are provided to facilitate obtaining copies of articles or subscriptions. The abbreviations of journal titles used in citations conform to the following international standards: ISO 4, *Documentation—International code for the abbreviation of titles and periodicals* and ISO 833, *Documentation—International list of periodical title word abbreviations* (both published by the International Organization for Standardization, in Geneva), as well as the current supplement: *International list of periodical title word abbreviations—supplement 1971–1976* published by the International Center for Registration of Serials, in Paris.

*Abacus*
Ceased publication
Springer-Verlag New York, Inc.
175 Fifth Avenue
New York, NY 10010
 ISSN 0724-6722

*ACM Computing Surveys*
**ACM Comput. Surv.**
ACM Press
11 West 42nd St.
New York, NY 10036
 ISSN 0360-0300

*ACM SIGADA Ada Letters*
**Ada Lett.**
ACM Press
11 West 42nd St.
New York, NY 10036

*ACM SIGAPL APL Quote Quad*
**APL Quote Quad**
ACM Press
11 West 42nd St.
New York, NY 10036
 ISSN 0163-6006

*ACM SIGARCH Computer Architecture News*
**Comput. Archit. News.**
ACM Press
11 West 42nd St.
New York, NY 10036

*ACM SIGART Newsletter*
**SIGART Newsl.**
ACM Press
11 West 42nd St.
New York, NY 10036

*ACM SIGBDP Data Base*
**Data Base**
ACM Press
11 West 42nd St.
New York, NY 10036

*ACM SIGCAPH Newsletter*
**SIGCAPH Newsl.**
ACM Press
11 West 42nd St.
New York, NY 10036

*ACM SIGCAS Computers and Society*
**SIGCAS Comput. Soc.**
ACM Press
11 West 42nd St.
New York, NY 10036

*ACM SIGCHI Bulletin*
**SIGCHI Bull.**
ACM Press
11 West 42nd St.
New York, NY 10036

*ACM SIGCOMM Computer Communication Review*
**Comput. Commun. Rev.**
ACM Press
11 West 42nd St.
New York, NY 10036

*ACM SIGCPR Computer Personnel*
**Comput. Pers.**
ACM Press
11 West 42nd St.
New York, NY 10036

*ACM SIGCSE Bulletin*
**SIGCSE Bull.**
ACM Press
11 West 42nd St.
New York, NY 10036

*ACM SIGCUE Outlook*
**Outlook**
ACM Press
11 West 42nd St.
New York, NY 10036

JOURNALS [ACTA INFORMATICA]

*ACM SIGDOC Asterisk\**
**Asterisk\***
ACM Press
11 West 42nd St.
New York, NY 10036

*ACM SIGGRAPH Computer Graphics*
**Comput. Graph.**
ACM Press
11 West 42nd St.
New York, NY 10036

*ACM SIGIR Forum*
**SIGIR Forum**
ACM Press
11 West 42nd St.
New York, NY 10036

*ACM SIGMICRO Newsletter*
**SIGMICRO Newsl.**
ACM Press
11 West 42nd St.
New York, NY 10036

*ACM SIGMOD Record*
**SIGMOD Rec.**
ACM Press
11 West 42nd St.
New York, NY 10036

*ACM SIGOIS Bulletin*
**SIGOIS Bull.**
ACM Press
11 West 42nd St.
New York, NY 10036

*ACM SIGOPS Operating Systems Review*
**Oper. Syst. Rev.**
ACM Press
11 West 42nd St.
New York, NY 10036

*ACM SIGPLAN Notices*
**SIGPLAN Notices**
ACM Press
11 West 42nd St.
New York, NY 10036

*ACM SIGSIM Simulation Digest*
*Formerly SIMULETTER*
**Simul. Dig.**
ACM Press
11 West 42nd St.
New York, NY 10036

*ACM SIGSMALL/PC Notes*
**SIGSMALL/PC Notes**
ACM Press
11 West 42nd St.
New York, NY 10036

*ACM SIGSOFT Software Engineering Notes*
**Softw. Eng. Notes**
ACM Press
11 West 42nd St.
New York, NY 10036

*ACM SIGUCCS Newsletter*
**SIGUCCS Newsl.**
ACM Press
11 West 42nd St.
New York, NY 10036

*ACM SIGUCCS Newsletter*
**ACM SIGUCCS Newsl.**
ACM Press
11 West 42nd St.
New York, NY 10036

*ACM Transactions on Computer Systems*
**ACM Trans. Comput. Syst.**
ACM Press
11 West 42nd St.
New York, NY 10036
ISSN 0734-2071

*ACM Transactions on Database Systems*
**ACM Trans. Database Syst.**
ACM Press
11 West 42nd St.
New York, NY 10036
ISSN 0362-5915

*ACM Transactions on Graphics*
**ACM Trans. Graph.**
ACM Press
11 West 42nd St.
New York, NY 10036
ISSN 0730-0301

*ACM Transactions on Information Systems*
*Formerly ACM Transactions on Office Information Systems*
**ACM Trans. Inf. Syst.**
ACM Press
11 West 42nd St.
New York, NY 10036
ISSN 0734-2047

*ACM Transactions on Mathematical Software*
**ACM Trans. Math. Softw.**
ACM Press
11 West 42nd St.
New York, NY 10036
ISSN 0098-3500

*ACM Transactions on Programming Languages and Systems*
**ACM Trans. Program. Lang. Syst.**
ACM Press
11 West 42nd St.
New York, NY 10036
ISSN 0164-0925

*Acta Informatica*
**Acta Inf.**
Springer-Verlag New York, Inc.
175 Fifth Avenue
New York, NY 10010
ISSN 0001-5903

*Advances in Applied Mathematics*
**Adv. Appl. Math.**
Academic Press, Inc.
1250 Sixth Ave
San Diego, CA 92101
ISSN 0196-8858

*Advances in Engineering Software*
**Adv. Eng. Softw.**
C.M.L. Publications
Ashurst Lodge
Ashurst, Hants., SO4 2AA
UK
   ISSN 0141-1187

*AI Expert*
CL Publications, Inc.
131 Townsend St.
San Francisco, CA 94107
   ISSN 0888-3758

*AI Magazine*
**AI Mag.**
Amer. Assn. for Artificial Intelligence
445 Burgess Drive
Menlo Park, CA 94025
   ISSN 0738-4602

*ALLC Journal*
**ALLC J.**
Literary and Linguistic Computing Centre
Sidgwick Site
Cambridge CB3 9DA
UK
   ISSN 0143-3385

*Angewandte Informatik*
**Angew. Inf.**
Friedrich Vieweg & Sohn Gmbh
Burgplatz 1
P.O. Box 185
D 33 Braunschweig
W. Germany
   ISSN 0013-5704

*Annals of Operations Research*
**Ann. Oper. Res.**
J. C. Baltzer AG
Scientific Publishing Co.
Wettsteinplatz 10
CH-4058 Basel
Switzerland
   ISSN 0254-5330

*Applied Artificial Intelligence*
**Appl. Artif. Intell.**
Hemisphere Publishing Corp.
1025 Vermont Ave. NW
Washington, DC 20005
   ISSN 0883-9514

*Applied Mathematics Letters*
**Appl. Math. Lett.**
Pergamon Press, Inc.
Maxwell House
Fairview Park
Elmsford, NY 10523
   ISSN 0893-9659

*Artificial Intelligence*
**Artif. Intell.**
Elsevier North-Holland, Inc.
52 Vanderbilt Ave.
New York, NY 10017
   ISSN 0004-3702

*ASLIB Proceedings*
**ASLIB Proc.**
ASLIB
26-27 Boswell Street
London WC1N 3JZ
UK
   ISSN 0001-253X

*AT&T Technical Journal*
**AT&T Tech. J.**
AT&T Bell Laboratories, Inc.
Room 1K424
101 JFK Parkway
Short Hills, NJ 07078
   ISSN 8576-2324

*Australian Computer Journal*
**Aust. Comput. J.**
Australian Computer Society, Inc.
G.P.O. Box 4944
Sydney, NSW 2001
Australia
   ISSN 0004-8917

*Australian Computer Science Communications*
**Aust. J. Phys.**
Commonwealth Scientific and Industrial
Research Organization
314 Albert St.
East Melbourne, Victoria 3002
Australia
   ISSN 0004-9506

*Automatic Control and Computer Sciences*
**Autom. Control Comput. Sci.**
Allerton Press, Inc.
150 Fifth Ave.
New York, NY 10011
   ISSN 0146-4116

*Automatica (Journal of IFAC)*
Pergamon Press, Inc.
Maxwell House
Fairview Park
Elmsford, NY 10523
   ISSN 0005-1098

*Behaviour & Information Technology*
**Behav. Inf. Tech.**
Taylor & Francis, Ltd.
10-14 Macklin Street
London WC2B 5NF
UK
   ISSN 0144-929X

*Biological Cybernetics*
**Biol. Cybern.**
Springer-Verlag New York, Inc.
175 Fifth Avenue
New York, NY 10010
   ISSN 0340-1200

*BIT*
Data A/S
Kronprinsensgade 14
DK-1114 Copenhagen K.
Denmark
   ISSN 0006-3835

## JOURNALS [COMPUTER LANGUAGES]

*Bulletin of the American Society for Information Science*
**Bull. Am. Soc. Inf. Sci.**
ASIS
1155 16th St. NW
Washington, DC 20036
ISSN 0095-4403

*BYTE*
McGraw-Hill, Inc.
One Phoenix Mill Lane
Peterborough, NH 03458
ISSN 0360-5280

*CAD/CAM Digest*
**CAD/CAM Dig.**
Productivity International Inc.
P.O. Box 8100
Dallas, TX 75205
ISSN 0263-6190

*Canadian Journal of Information Science*
**Can. J. Inf. Sci.**
Canadian Assoc. for Information Science
C P 6174
Station J
Ottawa, Ontario K2A 1T2
Canada

*CD-ROM Review*
**CD-ROM Rev.**
CW Communications/Peterborough Inc.
80 Elm Street
Peterborough, NH 03458

*CIM Review*
**CIM Rev.**
Auerbach Publishers, Inc.
6560 N. Park Drive
Pennsauken, NJ 08109
ISSN 0748-0474

*Collegiate Microcomputer*
**Collegiate Microcomput.**
Rose-Hulman Institute of Technology
Terre Haute, IN 47803
ISSN 0731-4213

*Communications of the ACM*
**Commun. ACM**
ACM Press
11 West 42nd St.
New York, NY 10036
ISSN 0001-0782

*Complex Systems*
**Complex Syst.**
Complex Systems Publications, Inc.
P.O. Box 6149
Champaign, IL 61821-8149
ISSN 0891-2513

*Computational Linguistics*
**Comput. Linguist.**
Assoc. for Computational Linguistics
c/o Dr. D. E. Walker, ACL Sec./Treasurer
Bell Communications Research
445 South St., MRE 2A379
Morristown, NJ 07960-1961
ISSN 0362-613X

*Computer*
IEEE Press
345 E. 47th St.
New York, NY 10017
ISSN 0018-9162
ISSN 0010-4469

*Computer Bulletin*
**Comput. Bull.**
British Computer Society
Attn: Journals Publicity Manager
13 Mansfield Street
London W2M 0BP
UK
ISSN 0010-4531

*Computer Communications*
**Comput. Commun.**
Butterworth Scientific Ltd.
P. O. Box 63
Westbury House, Bury St.
Guildford, Surrey GU2 5BH
UK
ISSN 0140-3664

*Computer Design*
**Comput. Des.**
PennWell Publishing Company
119 Russell Street
Littleton, MA 01460
ISSN 0010-4566

*Computer Graphics Forum*
**Comput. Graph. Forum**
Elsevier North-Holland, Inc.
52 Vanderbilt Ave.
New York, NY 10017
ISSN 0167-7055

*Computer Journal*
**Comput. J.**
British Computer Society
Attn: Journals Publicity Manager
13 Mansfield Street
London W2M 0BP
UK
ISSN 0010-4620

*Computer Language*
**Comput. Lang. (San Francisco, CA)**
CL Publications, Inc.
131 Townsend St.
San Francisco, CA 94107
ISSN 0096-0551

*Computer Languages*
**Comput. Lang. (Elmsford, NY)**
Pergamon Press, Inc.
Maxwell House
Fairview Park
Elmsford, NY 10523
ISSN 0096-0551

*Computer Networks and ISDN Systems*
**Comput. Networks ISDN Syst.**
Int. Council for Computer Communication
P. O. Box 9745
Washington, D.C. 20016
ISSN 0376-5075

*Computer Newsletter*
**Comput. Newsl.**
British Computer Society
Attn: Journals Publicity Manager
13 Mansfield Street
London W2M 0BP
UK
ISSN 0266-4631

*Computer Science in Economics and Management*
**Comput. Sci. Econ. Manage.**
Kluwer Academic Publishers
101 Philip Dr.
Norwell, MA 02061
ISSN 0921-2736

*Computer Speech and Language*
**Comput. Speech Lang.**
Academic Press Inc. (London)
24-28 Oval Road
London NW1 7DX
UK
ISSN 0885-2308

*Computer Standards and Interfaces*
**Comput. Stand. Interfaces**
Elsevier Sequoia S. A.
P. O. Box 851
1001 Lausanne 1
Switzerland
ISSN 0920-5489

*Computer Vision, Graphics, and Image Processing*
**Comput. Vision Graph. Image Process.**
Academic Press, Inc.
1250 Sixth Ave
San Diego, CA 92101
ISSN 0734-189X

*Computer-Aided Design*
**Comput. Aided Des.**
Butterworth Scientific Ltd.
P. O. Box 63
Westbury House, Bury St.
Guildford, Surrey GU2 5BH
UK
ISSN 0010-4485

*Computer/Law Journal*
**Comput./Law J.**
Center for Computer/Law
1112 Ocean Drive, Suite 101
Manhattan Beach, CA 90266
ISSN 0164-8756

*Computers and Artificial Intelligence*
**Comput. Artif. Intell.**
Slovak Academy of Science
Veda Publishing House
Bratislava 814 30
Czechoslovakia

*Computers and Biomedical Research*
**Comput. Biomed. Res.**
Academic Press, Inc.
1250 Sixth Ave
San Diego, CA 92101
ISSN 0010-4809

*Computers and Education*
**Comput. Educ. (Elmsford, NY)**
Pergamon Press, Inc.
Maxwell House
Fairview Park
Elmsford, NY 10523
ISSN 0360-1315

*Computers and Electrical Engineering*
**Comput. Electr. Eng.**
Pergamon Press, Inc.
Maxwell House
Fairview Park
Elmsford, NY 10523
ISSN 0045-7906

*Computers and Geosciences*
**Comput. Geosci.**
Pergamon Press, Inc.
Maxwell House
Fairview Park
Elmsford, NY 10523
ISSN 0098-3004

*Computers and Industrial Engineering*
**Comput. Ind. Eng.**
Pergamon Press, Inc.
Maxwell House
Fairview Park
Elmsford, NY 10523
ISSN 0360-8352

*Computers and Operations Research*
**Comput. Oper. Res.**
Pergamon Press, Inc.
Maxwell House
Fairview Park
Elmsford, NY 10523
ISSN 0305-0548

*Computers and People*
**Comput. People**
Berkeley Enterprises Inc.
815 Washington St.
Newtonville, MA 02160
ISSN 0361-1442

*Computers and Security*
**Comput. Secur.**
North-Holland Publishing Co.
P.O. Box 211
1000AE Amsterdam
The Netherlands
ISSN 0167-4048

*Computers and Standards*
**Comput. Stand.**
North-Holland Publishing Co.
P.O. Box 211
1000AE Amsterdam
The Netherlands
ISSN 0167-8051

JOURNALS

*Computers and the Humanities*
**Comput. Hum.**
Paradigm Press
P.O. Box 1057
Osprey, FL 33559-1057
  ISSN 0010-4817

*Computers and the Social Sciences*
**Comput. Soc. Sci.**
Paradigm Press
P.O. Box 1057
Osprey, FL 33559-1057
  ISSN 0748-9269

*Computers and Translation*
**Comput. Transl.**
Paradigm Press
P.O. Box 1057
Osprey, FL 33559-1057
  ISSN 0084-0709

*Computers in Human Services*
**Comput. Hum. Serv.**
Haworth Press
75 Griswold Street
Binghamton, NY 13904
  ISSN 0740-445X

*Computers in Industry*
**Comput. Ind.**
North-Holland Publishing Co.
P.O. Box 211
1000AE Amsterdam
The Netherlands
  ISSN 0166-3615

*Computers in Physics*
**Comput. Phys.**
American Institute of Physics
335 E. 45 St.
New York, NY 10017
  ISSN 0894-1866

*Computers in the Schools*
**Comput. Sch.**
Haworth Press, Inc.
28 East 22nd Street
New York, NY 10010
  ISSN 0738-0569

*Cybernetica*
Plenum Publishing Corp.
Internat. Assoc. for Cybernetics
Place Andre Rijkmans
Namur
Belium
  ISSN 0011-4227

*Cybernetics and Systems*
**Cybern. Syst.**
Hemisphere Publishing Corp.
1025 Vermont Ave. NW
Washington, DC 20005
  ISSN 0196-9722

*Data & Knowledge Engineering*
**Data Knowl. Eng.**
Elsevier North-Holland, Inc.
52 Vanderbilt Ave.
New York, NY 10017
  ISSN 0169-023X

*Data Engineering*
**Data Eng.**
IEEE Computer Society
1730 Massachusetts Ave. NW
Washington, DC 20036-1903

*Data Processing*
**Data Process.**
Butterworth Scientific Ltd.
P. O. Box 63
Westbury House, Bury St.
Guildford, Surrey GU2 5BH
UK
  ISSN 0011-684X

*Database*
Online
11 Tannery Lane
Weston, CT 06883
  ISSN 0162-4105

*DataBased Advisor*
**DataBased Advis.**
Data Based Solutions
1975 5th Avenue, Suite 105
San Diego, CA 92101
  ISSN 0740-5200

*Datamation*
Technical Publishing Co.
875 Third Ave.
New York, NY 10023
  ISSN 0011-6963

*Decision Support Systems*
**Decis. Support Syst.**
Elsevier North-Holland, Inc.
52 Vanderbilt Ave.
New York, NY 10017
  ISSN 0167-9236

*Discrete Applied Mathematics*
**Discrete Appl. Math.**
North-Holland Publishing Co.
P.O. Box 211
1000AE Amsterdam
The Netherlands
  ISSN 0166-218X

*EDP Performance Review*
**EDP Perform. Rev.**
Applied Computer Research
P.O Box 9280
Phoenix, AZ 85068
  ISSN 0091-7206

*Educational Technology*
**Educ. Technol.**
Educational Technology Publications
720 Palisade Ave.
Englewood Cliffs, NJ 07632
  ISSN 0013-1962

*Electrical Communication*
**Electr. Commun.**
IT&T Corp.
190 Strand
London WC2R IDU
UK

*Finite Elements in Analysis and Design*
**Finite Elem. Anal. Des.**
North-Holland Publishing Co.
P.O. Box 211
1000AE Amsterdam
The Netherlands
   ISSN 0168-874X

*Future Generations Computer Systems*
**Future Gener. Comput. Syst.**
Elsevier North-Holland, Inc.
52 Vanderbilt Ave.
New York, NY 10017
   ISSN 0167-739X

*Fuzzy Sets and Systems*
**Fuzzy Sets Syst.**
Elsevier North-Holland, Inc.
52 Vanderbilt Ave.
New York, NY 10017
   ISSN 0165-0114

*Harvard Business Review*
**Harvard Bus. Rev.**
Harvard Univ. Grad. Sch. of Bus. Admin.
Subscription Service Dept.
P.O. Box 9730
Greenwich, CT 06835
   ISSN 0017-8012

*Human Factors*
**Hum. Factors**
Human Factors Society, Inc.
P.O. Box 1369
Santa Monica, CA 90406
   ISSN 0018-7208

*Hypermedia*
Taylor Graham Publishers
500 Chesham House
150 Regent St.
London W1R 5FA
UK
   ISSN 0955-8543

*IBM Journal of Research and Development*
**IBM J. Res. Dev.**
IBM Corp.
Armonk, NY 10504
   ISSN 0018-8646

*IBM Systems Journal*
**IBM Syst. J.**
IBM Corp.
Armonk, NY 10504
   ISSN 0018-8670

*IEEE Computer Graphics and Applications*
**IEEE Comput. Graph. Appl.**
IEEE Press
345 E. 47th St.
New York, NY 10017
   ISSN 0272-1716

*IEEE Micro*
IEEE Press
345 E. 47th St.
New York, NY 10017
   ISSN 0272-1732

*IEEE Spectrum*
IEEE Press
345 E. 47th St.
New York, NY 10017
   ISSN 0018-9235

*IEEE Transactions on Pattern Analysis and Machine Intelligence*
**IEEE Trans. Pattern Anal. Mach. Intell.**
IEEE Computer Society
1730 Massachusetts Ave. NW
Washington, DC 20036-1903
   ISSN 0162-8828

*IEEE Transactions on Software Engineering*
**IEEE Trans. Softw. Eng.**
IEEE Press
345 E. 47th St.
New York, NY 10017
   ISSN 0098-5589

*IEEE Transactions on Systems, Man and Cybernetics*
**IEEE Trans. Syst. Man Cybern.**
IEEE Press
345 E. 47th St.
New York, NY 10017
   ISSN 0018-9472

*IMC Journal*
**IMC J.**
Int. Information Management Congress
P. O. Box 34404
Bethesda, MD 20817-0404
   ISSN 0019-0012

*Industrial Engineering*
**Ind. Eng.**
American Inst. of Industrial Engineers
25 Technology Park/Atlanta
Norcross, GA 30071
   ISSN 0019-8234

*Information Age*
**Inf. Age**
Butterworth Scientific Ltd.
P. O. Box 63
Westbury House, Bury St.
Guildford, Surrey GU2 5BH
UK
   ISSN 0261-4103

*Information and Computation*
**Inf. Comput.**
Academic Press, Inc.
P.O. Box 52650
Duluth, MN 55806-0208
   ISSN 0890-5401

*Information and Management*
**Inf. Manage.**
North-Holland Publishing Co.
P.O. Box 211
1000AE Amsterdam
The Netherlands
   ISSN 0378-7206

*Information and Software Technology*
**Inf. Softw. Technol.**
Butterworth Scientific Ltd.
P. O. Box 63
Westbury House, Bury St.
Guildford, Surrey GU2 5BH
UK
    ISSN 0950-5849

*Information Display*
MetaData Inc.
310 East 44th Street
New York, NY 10017
    ISSN 0362-0972

*Information Economics and Policy*
**Inf. Econ. Policy**
Elsevier North-Holland, Inc.
52 Vanderbilt Ave.
New York, NY 10017
    ISSN 6167-6245

*Information Processing and Management*
**Inf. Process. Manage.**
Pergamon Press, Inc.
Maxwell House
Fairview Park
Elmsford, NY 10523
    ISSN 0306-4573

*Information Processing Letters*
**Inf. Process. Lett.**
Elsevier North-Holland, Inc.
52 Vanderbilt Ave.
New York, NY 10017:2QISSN
    0020-0190

*Information Sciences*
**Inf. Sci. (New York)**
Elsevier North-Holland, Inc.
52 Vanderbilt Ave.
New York, NY 10017
    ISSN 0020-0255

*Information Services and Use*
**Inf. Serv. Use**
Elsevier Sci. Pub. B. V.
Sara Burgerhartstraat 25
P.O. Box 211
AE Amsterdam, 1000
The Netherlands
    ISSN 0167-5265

*Information Systems*
**Inf. Syst.**
Pergamon Press, Inc.
Maxwell House
Fairview Park
Elmsford, NY 10523
    ISSN 0306-4379

*Information Technology and Libraries*
**Inf. Technol. Libr.**
American Library Association
50 E. Huron
Chicago, IL 60611
    ISSN 0730-9295

*Information Technology Research Development Applications*
**Inf. Tech. Res. Dev. Appl.**
Butterworth Publishers
80 Montvale Ave.
Stoneham, MA 02180

*Infosystems*
Hitchcock Publishing Company
Geneva Rd.
Wheaton, IL 60187
    ISSN 0364-5533

*Instruction Delivery Systems*
**Instr. Deliv. Syst.**
Communicative Technology Corporation
50 Culpeper Street
Warrenton, VA 22186
    ISSN 0892-4872

*InTech*
Instrument Society of America
67 Alexander Drive
P.O. Box 12277
Research Triangle Park, NC 27709
    ISSN 0192-303X

*Interacting with computers: the interdisciplinary journal of human-computer interaction*
**Interact. Comput.**
Butterworth & Co., Ltd.
Westbury Subscription Services
P.O. Box 101
Sevenoaks
Kent TN15 8PL
UK
    ISSN 0953-5438

*International Journal of Approximate Reasoning*
**Int. J. Approx. Reasoning**
North-Holland Publishing Co.
P.O. Box 211
1000AE Amsterdam
The Netherlands
    ISSN 0888-613X

*International Journal of Expert Systems*
**Int. J. Expert Syst.**
Jai Press, Inc.
55 Old Post Road, No. 2
P. O. Box 1678
Greenwich, CT 06836-1678
    ISSN 0894-9077

*International Journal of Man-Machine Studies*
**Int. J. Man-Mach. Stud.**
Academic Press, Inc.
P.O. Box 52650
Duluth, MN 55806-0208
    ISSN 0020-7373

*International Journal of Pattern Recognition and Artificial Intelligence*
**Int. J. Pattern Recogn. Artif. Intell.**
World Scientific Publishing Co., Inc.
687 Hartwell St.
Teaneck, NJ 07666
    ISSN 0218-0014

*International Journal of Robotics Research*
**Int. J. Rob. Res.**
MIT Press
55 Hayward St.
Cambridge, MA 02142
ISSN 0278-3649

*Journal a*
**J. a**
Koninklijke Vlaamse Ingenieursvereniging
Jan van Rijswijcklaan 58
B-2000 Antwerp
Belgium
ISSN 0771-1107

*Journal of Automated Reasoning*
**J. Autom. Reasoning**
D. Reidel Publishing Co., Inc.
160 Old Derby Street
Hingham, MA 02043
ISSN 0168-7433

*Journal of Chemical Information & Computer Sciences*
**J. Chem. Inf. Comput. Sci.**
American Chemical Society
P. O. Box 3337
Columbus, OH 43210
ISSN 0095-2338

*Journal of Complexity*
**J. Complexity**
Academic Press, Inc.
1250 Sixth Ave
San Diego, CA 92101:2QISSN 0885-064X

*Journal of Computer and System Sciences*
**J. Comput. Syst. Sci.**
Academic Press, Inc.
1250 Sixth Ave
San Diego, CA 92101
ISSN 0022-0000

*Journal of Computer Science and Technology*
**J. Comput. Sci. Technol.**
Allerton Press, Inc.
150 Fifth Ave.
New York, NY 10011
ISSN 1000-9000

*Journal of Computer-Based Instruction*
**J. Comput.-Based Instruct.**
Assoc. Dev. Computer-based Instr. Sys.
Miller Hall 409
Western Washington University
Bellingham, WA 98225
ISSN 0098-597X

*Journal of Documentation*
**J. Doc.**
ASLIB
26-27 Boswell Street
London WC1N 3JZ
UK
ISSN 0022-0418

*Journal of FORTH Application and Research*
**J. FORTH Appl. Res.**
Institute for Applied FORTH Research
70 Elmwood Avenue
Rochester, NY 14611
ISSN 0738-2022

*Journal of Information Processing*
**J. Inf. Process.**
Information Processing Society of Japan
Kikai-Shinko Kaikan
3-5-8 Shiba-koen
Minato-ku, Tokyo 105
Japan
ISSN 0387-6101

*Journal of Information Science: Principles & Practice*
**J. Inf. Sci. Princ. Pract.**
Elsevier North-Holland, Inc.
52 Vanderbilt Ave.
New York, NY 10017
ISSN 0165-5515

*Journal of Logic Programming*
**J. Logic Program.**
Elsevier North-Holland, Inc.
52 Vanderbilt Ave.
New York, NY 10017
ISSN 0743-1066

*Journal of Management Information Systems*
**J. Manage. Inf. Syst.**
M. E. Sharpe, Inc.
80 Business Park Drive
Armonk, NY 10504
ISSN 0742-1222

*Journal of Mathematical Psychology*
**J. Math. Psychol.**
Academic Press, Inc.
1250 Sixth Ave
San Diego, CA 92101
ISSN 0022-2496

*Journal of Medical Systems*
**J. Med. Syst.**
Plenum Publishing Corp.
233 Spring St.
New York, NY 10013
ISSN 0148-5598

*Journal of Microcomputer Applications*
**J. Microcomput. Appl.**
Academic Press Inc. (London)
24-28 Oval Road
London NW1 7DX
UK
ISSN 0745-7138

*Journal of Object-Oriented Programming*
**J. Object-Oriented Program.**
SIGS Publications, Inc.
310 Madison Avenue
Suite 503
New York, NY 10017
ISSN 0896-8434

*Journal of Pascal, Ada & Modula-2*
**J. Pascal Ada Modula-2**
West Publishing Co.
50 W. Kellogg Blvd.
St. Paul, MN 55102
    ISSN 0735-1232

*Journal of Quality Technology*
**J. Qual. Technol.**
American Society for Quality Control
161 W. Wisconsin Ave.
Milwaukee, WI 53203
    ISSN 0022-4065

*Journal of Symbolic Computation*
**J. Symbolic Comput.**
Academic Press Inc. (London)
24-28 Oval Road
London NW1 7DX
UK
    ISSN 0747-7171

*Journal of Systems and Software*
**J. Syst. Softw.**
Elsevier North-Holland, Inc.
52 Vanderbilt Ave.
New York, NY 10017
    ISSN 0164-1212

*Journal of Systems Management*
**J. Syst. Manage.**
Association for Systems Management
24587 Bagley Rd.
Cleveland, OH 44138
    ISSN 0022-4839

*Journal of the American Society for Information Science*
**J. Am. Soc. Inf. Sci.**
ASIS
1155 16th St. NW
Washington, DC 20036:2QISSN 0002-8231

*Journal of the Chinese Institute of Engineers*
**J. Chin. Inst. Eng.**
Chinese Institute of Engineers
1, 4th Fl., 2nd Sec.
Jen-Ai Road
Taipei
Taiwan
    ISSN 0253-3839

*Knowledge Acquisition*
**Knowl. Acquis.**
Academic Press Inc. (London)
24-28 Oval Road
London NW1 7DX
UK
    ISSN 1042-8143

*LASIE: Bulletin of LASIE Australia Company Ltd.*
**LASIE Bull.**
LASIE
c/o Mr. B. Pedersen
Executive Secretary
P.O. Box 602
Lane Cove, NSW 2066
Australia

*Library Hi Tech*
**Libr. Hi Tech**
Pierian Press, Inc.
P.O. Box 1808
Ann Arbor, MI 48106
    ISSN 0737-8831

*Machine-Mediated Learning*
**Mach.-Mediat. Learn.**
Crane, Russak & Co., Inc.
3 E. 44th St.
New York, NY 10017
    ISSN 0732-6718

*Macintosh Hands On*
MicroSPARC, Inc.
52 Domino Drive
Concord, MA 01742
    ISSN 1041-2611

*Management Science*
**Manage. Sci.**
Institute of Management Sciences
146 Westminster St.
Providence, RI 02903
    ISSN 0025-1909

*Mathematics and Computers in Simulation*
**Math. Comput. Simul.**
Elsevier North-Holland, Inc.
52 Vanderbilt Ave.
New York, NY 10017
    ISSN 0378-4754

*Microprocessing & Microprogramming*
**Microprocess. Microprogram.**
Elsevier North-Holland, Inc.
52 Vanderbilt Ave.
New York, NY 10017
    ISSN 0165-6074

*Microprocessors & Microsystems*
**Microprocess. Microsyst.**
Butterworth Scientific Ltd.
P. O. Box 63
Westbury House, Bury St.
Guildford, Surrey GU2 5BH
UK
    ISSN 0141-9331

*Mini-Micro Software*
**Mini-Micro Softw.**
A. P. Publications Ltd.
322 St. John St.
London EC1V 4HQ
UK
    ISSN 0038-0652

*Mini-Micro Systems*
**Mini-Micro Syst.**
Cahners Publishing Company
275 Washington St.
Newton, MA 02158
    ISSN 0364-9342

*MIS Quarterly*
**MIS Q.**
Society for Mgt. Inf. & Inf. Res. Cent.
University of Minnesota
269 19th Avenue So.
Minneapolis, MN 55455
    ISSN 0276-7783

*MUG Quarterly*
**MUG Q**
MUMPS Users' Group
4321 Hartwick Rd., Suite 100
College Park, MD 20740
   ISSN 0193-0885

*Pattern Recognition*
**Pattern Recogn.**
Pergamon Press, Inc.
Maxwell House
Fairview Park
Elmsford, NY 10523
   ISSN 0031-3203

*Pattern Recognition Letters*
**Pattern Recogn. Lett.**
Elsevier North-Holland, Inc.
52 Vanderbilt Ave.
New York, NY 10017
   ISSN 0167-8655

*PC/Computing*
**PC/Comput.**
Ziff-Davis Publishing Co.
1 Park Ave.
New York, NY 10016
   ISSN 0899-1847

*Personal Computing*
**Pers. Comput.**
Benwill Publishing Corp.
167 Corey Rd.
Brookline, MA 02146
   ISSN 0192-5490

*Perspectives on Technology*
**Perspec. Technol.**
Metropolitan Life
1 Madison Ave.
New York, NY 10010-3690

*Physica D*
Elsevier North-Holland, Inc.
52 Vanderbilt Ave.
New York, NY 10017
   ISSN 0167-2789

*Production and Inventory Management*
**Prod. Inventory Manage.**
Am. Prod. and Invent. Control Soc., Inc.
500 West Annandale Road
Falls Church, VA 22046
   ISSN 0032-9843

*Program*
ASLIB
26–27 Boswell St.
London WC1N 3JZ
UK
   ISSN 0033-0337

*Programmed Learning and Educational Technology*
**Program. Learn. Educ. Technol.**
Kogan Page Ltd.
120 Pentonville Rd.
London M1 9JN
UK

*Resource Sharing and Information Networks*
**Resour. Shar. Inf. Networks**
Haworth Press, Inc.
28 East 22nd Street
New York, NY 10010
   ISSN 0737-7797

*Scholarly Publishing*
**Sch. Publ.**
University of Toronto Press
33 E. Tupper Street
Buffalo, NY 14203
   ISSN 0036-634X

*Science Digest*
**Sci. Dig.**
Hearst Corporation
959 Eighth Avenue
New York, N.Y. 10019
   ISSN 0036-8296

*Science of Computer Programming*
**Sci. Comput. Program.**
Elsevier North-Holland, Inc.
52 Vanderbilt Ave.
New York, NY 10017
   ISSN 0167-6423

*Scientific American*
**Sci. Am.**
Scientific American, Inc.
415 Madison Ave.
New York, NY 10017
   ISSN 0036-8733

*SIAM Journal on Control and Optimization*
**SIAM J. Control Optim.**
Soc. for Industrial and Applied Math.
3600 University City Science Center
Philadelphia, PA 19104-7999
   ISSN 0363-0129

*Signal Processing*
**Signal Process.**
North-Holland Publishing Co.
P.O. Box 211
1000AE Amsterdam
The Netherlands
   ISSN 0165-1684

*Simulation*
Society for Computer Simulation
P.O. Box 17900
San Diego, CA 92117-7900
   ISSN 0037-5497

*Simulation and Games*
**Simul. Games**
Sage Publications, Inc.
275 S. Beverly Drive
Beverly Hills, CA 90212
   ISSN 0037-5500

*Small Computers in Libraries*
**Small Comput. Libr.**
Meckler Publishing
11 Ferry Lane West
Westport, CT 06880
   ISSN 0275-6722

## JOURNALS

*Social Science Computer Review*
**Soc. Sci. Comput. Rev.**
Duke University Press
Box 6697, College Sta.
Durham, NC 27708
   ISSN 0894-4393

*Software Engineering Journal*
**Softw. Eng. J.**
Institution of Electrical Engineers
P.O. Box 8
Southgate House
Stevenage, Herts. SG1 1HQ
UK
   ISSN 0268-6961

*Software-Practice & Experience*
**Softw. Pract. Exper.**
John Wiley & Sons, Inc.
605 Third Avenue
New York, NY 10016
   ISSN 0038-6644

*Speech Communication*
**Speech Commun.**
Elsevier North-Holland, Inc.
52 Vanderbilt Ave.
New York, NY 10017
   ISSN 0167-6393

*System Development*
**Syst. Dev.**
Applied Computer Research
P.O Box 9280
Phoenix, AZ 85068
   ISSN 0275-6617

*Systems Analysis Modeling Simulation*
**Syst. Anal. Model. Simul.**
Akademie-Verlag
Leipziger Str. 3-4
DDR-108 Berlin
East Germany
   ISSN 0232-9298

*Technique et Science Informatiques*
**Tech. Sci. Inf.**
Assn. Francaise pour Cybern. Econ. Tech.
Dunod Gauthier Villars B.
93104 Montreuil Cedex
France
   ISSN 0752-4072

*Technometrics*
Amer. Soc. Qual. Contr. Amer. Stat. Assn
P. O. Box 587
Benjamin Franklin Sta.
Washington, DC 20044
   ISSN 0040-1706

*Telematics and Informatics*
**Telem. Inf.**
Pergamon Press, Inc.
Maxwell House
Fairview Park
Elmsford, NY 10523
   ISSN 0736-5853

*Transactions of the Society for Computer Simulation*
**Trans. Soc. Comput. Simul.**
Society for Computer Simulation
P.O. Box 17900
San Diego, CA 92117-7900
   ISSN 0740-6797

*University Computing*
**Univ. Comput.**
Blackwell Scientific Publications, Ltd.
5 Alfred St.
Oxford
UK
   ISSN 0265-4385